Standard Catalog of® WORLD PAPER MONEY

11th Edition

General Issues • 1368-1960

Volume Two

Edited by
George S. Cuhaj

Numismatic Cataloging Supervisor
Randy Thern

Data Entry Coordinat
Lori Anderson & Cari Ul

Book Designer
Sally Olson

Special Consultants

Colin R. Bruce II, Guido Crapanzano, Flemming Lyngbeck Hansen, Tony Pisciotta, Lawrence Pope, Neil Shafer, Mark Tomasko

Cover Illustrations Provided By:

Mel & Jeremy Steinberg

Based on the original work of Albert Pick

Published by

700 East State Street • Iola, WI 54990-0001
715-445-2214 • 888-457-2873
www.krausebooks.com

Our toll-free number to place an order or obtain a free catalog is (800) 258-0929.

Library of Congress Catalog Number: 1538-2001

ISBN 13: 978-0-89689-356-6
ISBN 10: 10-0-89689-412-6

Designed by:
Sally Olson

Edited by:
George Cuhaj

Printed in the United States of America

Table of Contents

Advertiser's Index

ACKNOWLEDGEMENTS

The contributions to this catalog have been many and varied, and to recognize them all would be a volume in itself. Accordingly, we wish to acknowledge these collectors, scholars and dealers in the world paper money field, both past and present, for their specific contributions to this work through the submission of notes for illustration, improved descriptive information and market valuations.

Alex Abezgauz
James Adams
Esko Ahlroth
Jan Alexandersson
Walter D. Allan
Milan Alusic
Carl A. Anderson
Jorge E. Arbelaez
Donald Arnone
Emad Ateya
Norman Athy
David August
Keith Austin
Cem Barlok
William L. S. Barrett
Adriaan C. F. Beck
Michel Becuwe
Milt Blackburn
Ed Bohannon
Joseph E. Boling
Angus E. Bruce
Colin R. Bruce II
Mahdi Bseiso
Weldon D. Burson
Lance K. Campbell
David Carlson
Larry Casey
Robert Clark
Arthur D. Cohen
George Conrad
Scott E. Cordry
Guido Crapanzano
Ray Czahor
Jehangir B. Dalal
Howard A. Daniel III
Anthony L. della Volpe
Michel Dufour
Louis Di Lauro
Arnoldo Efron
Wilhelm Eglseer
Esko Ekman
Theo F. A. van Elmpt
Ricardo Faillace
Jack G. Fischer
Guvendik Fisekcioglu
Luis H. Flores
Edward Feltcorn
W. A. Frick
Brian Giese
Illan Glasner
Lee Gordon
Rajni Gupta
Ray Hackett
Edmond Hakimian
Murray Hanewich
Allan Hauck
Flemming Lynbeck Hansen
Len Harsel
James A. Haxby
William G. Henderson
Gene Hessler
Anton Holt
Armen Hovsepian
Louis Hudson
Mikhail Istomin
Kishore Jhunjhunwalla
Alex Kaglyan
Olaf Kiener
Josef Klaus
Tristan Kolm
David C. Kranz
Chester L. Krause
Michael Kvasnica
Samson Kim Chiu Lai
Michael Lang
David Leong
Claire Lobel
Rudi Lotter
L. K. Loimaranta
Alan Luedeking
Stu Lumsden
Dennis Lutz
Ma Tak Wo
Martan MacDevitt
Rolf Marklin
Ranko Mandic
Ian A. Marshall
John T. Martin
Arthur C. Matz
Ali Mehilba
Donald Medcalf
Lazar Mishev
Michael Morris
Arthur H. Morowitz
Richard Murdoch
Tanju Mutlu
Colin Narbeth
Son Zuan Nguyen
Andrew Oberbillig
Geoffrey P. Oldham
Julian Papenfus
Frank Passic
Antonio E. Pedraza
Juan Pena
Albert Pick
A.A.C. de Albergaria Pinheiro
Tony Pisciotta
Laurence Pope
Rick Ponterio
Miguel A. Pratt-Myans
Michel Prieur
Richard Puls
Yahya J. Qureshi
Nazir Rahemtulla
Kavan Ratnatunga
Beate Rauch
Andrew Rekay
John Rishel
Alistair Robb
Manuel Rodriguez C.
Rudolph Richter
William M. Rosenblum
Michel Saade
Alan Sadd
Karl Saethre
Milton Arguedas Salas
Wolfgang Schuster
Michael Schone
Hartmut Schoenawa
Carlton "Fred" Schwan
Alan Sealey
Timothy R.G. Sear
David Seelye
Christian Selvais
Joel Shafer
Neil Shafer
Brian A. Silsbee
Ladislav Sin
Evzen Sknouril
Arlie Slabaugh
Larry Smulczenski
Gary Snover
Mauricio Soto
Daryl Spelbring
Lee Shin Song
Jimmie C. Steelman
Jeremy Steinberg
Mel Steinberg
Tim Steiner
Zeljko Stojanovic
Roger B. Stolberg
Mark Strumph
Alim A. Sumana
Peter Symes
Imre Szatmari
Ricardo de Leon Tallavas
Steven Tan
Reiny Tetting
Alphons Thoele
Mark Tomasko
Anthony Tumonis
Jan Vandersande
Michael Vort-Ronald
Ludek Vostal
Pam West
Stewart Westdal
Trevor Wilkin
Heinz Wirz
Yu Chien Hua
Joseph Zaffern
Christof Zellweger

INSTITUTIONS AND SOCIETIES:

American Numismatic Association
American Numismatic Society
International Bank Note Society
Smithsonian Institutio

Introduction

Welcome to this eleventh edition of the *Standard Catalog of World Paper Money, General Issues – 1368 to 1960.* The scope of this volume is world paper money from the earliest known Chinese notes (1368) to issues circulating in 1960, though some later issues appear to complete a series or offer the reader material one would hope to find within this work. The general 1960 cut-off was done to better keep pace with the ever increasing 'modern' listings and keep current in major price fluctuations by splitting off issues since 1961 into their own annual volume – the *Standard Catalog of World Paper Money, Modern Issues – 1961 to present.*

For the ease of identification, notes are listed under their historic country name and/or the name as it appears on the banknote. Notes of a particular bank are listed in date order and then grouped in ascending denomination order. In the cases of countries where more than one issuing authority is in effect at a single time, follow the bank headings in the listings and it will become apparent if that country's listing is by date or alphabetical by issuing authority. In the cases where a country has changed from a kingdom to a republic all the banknotes of the kingdom's era would be listed before that of the republic's.

A review of paper money collecting

Paper money collecting is undoubtedly nearly as old as paper money itself, this segment of the numismatic hobby did not begin to reach a popularity approaching that of coin collecting until the later half of the 1970's. While coins and paper money are alike in that both served as legal obligations to facilitate commerce, long-time paper money enthusiasts know the similarity ends there.

Coins were historically guaranteed by the intrinsic value of their metallic content – at least until recent years when virtually all circulating coins have become little more than legal tender tokens, containing little or no precious metal – while paper money possesses a value only when it is accepted for debts or converted into bullion or precious metals. With many note issues, this conversion privilege was limited and ultimately negated by the imposition of redemption cut-off dates.

Such conditions made collecting of bank notes a risky business, particularly with notes possessing a high face value. This is why in most instances, except where issued were withdrawn shortly after release or became virtually worthless due to hyper-inflation, early high denomination notes are extremely difficult to locate, especially in choice to uncirculated grades of preservations.

The development of widespread collector interest in paper money of most nations were long inhibited by a near total absence of adequate documentary literature. No more than four decades ago collectors could refer to only a few catalogs and dealer price lists of limited scope, most of which were incomplete and difficult to acquire, or they could build their own knowledge through personal collecting pursuits and contact with fellow collectors.

The early catalogs authored by Albert Pick chronicled issues of Europe and the Americas and were assembled as stepping stones to the ultimate objective which became reality with publication of the first *Standard Catalog of World Paper Money* in 1975. That work provided collectors with near complete listings and up-to-date valuations of all recorded government note issues of the 20th century, incorporating Pick's previously unpublished manuscripts on Africa, Asia and Oceania, plus other earlier issues.

This completely revised and updated eleventh edition presents a substantial extension of the cataloging effort initiated in 1975 and revised in succeeding editions. As the most comprehensive world paper money reference ever assembled, it fully documents the many and varied legal tender paper currency issued circulated by nearly 300 past and current governments of the world from 1368 to 1960.

Falling within the scope of this General Issues volume are all legal tender issues circulated under the auspices of recognized national governments and their banking agents, including notes which enjoyed wide circulating in their respective countries. Exceptions are the multitudinous notes of the German states and cities, especially those of the World War I and postwar period to 1923, and the vast category of Chinese local issues and similar limited-circulation issues of other countries.

An Invitation

Users of this catalog may find a helpful adjunct is the Bank Note Reporter, the only monthly newspaper devoted exclusively to North American and world paper money. Each issue presents up-to-date news, feature articles and information – including appearances of the World Paper Money Update on the latest world paper money releases and discoveries. Listings in these presentations are all keyed to the standard Catalog numbering system utilized in this catalog. Purchasers of this catalog are invited to subscribe to the *Bank Note Reporter.* Requests for a sample copy should be addressed to Bank Note Reporter, 700 East State Street, Iola, WI 54990-0001

Soon To Be Available On The Web

Visit www.numismaster.com for additional information.

Country Index

Denomination Index

Adopengo ... Hungary
Afghani ... Afghanistan
Aksha ... Tannu-Tuva
Angolar ... Angola
Anna ... Burma
Anna ... India
Ariary ... Madagascar
At ... Lao
Att ... Thailand
Avos ... Macao
Avos ... Timor
Baht ... Thailand
Balboa ... Panama
Bani ... Romania
Belga ... Belgium
Bolivares ... Venezuela
Boliviano ... Bolivia
B-Pengo ... Hungary
Cac ... Viet Nam
Cash ... China
Cash ... Taiwan
Cent ... British North Borneo
Cent ... Burma
Cent ... Canada
Cent ... Ceylon
Cent ... China
Cent ... Taiwan
Cent ... Fiji
Cent ... French Indo-China
Cent ... Hong Kong
Cent ... Liberia
Cent ... Malaya
Cent ... Mauritius
Cent ... Netherlands Indies
Cent ... Newfoundland
Cent ... Poland
Cent ... Sarawak
Cent ... Seychelles
Cent ... Suriname
Cent ... Texas
Cent ... United States
Cent ... Yugoslavia
Centai ... Lithuania
Centas ... Lithuania
Centavo ... Angola
Centavo ... Argentina
Centavo ... Bolivia
Centavo ... Cape Verde
Centavo ... Chile
Centavo ... Colombia
Centavo ... Cuba
Centavo ... Dominican Republic
Centavo ... Honduras
Centavo ... Mexico
Centavo ... Mozambique
Centavo ... Nicaragua
Centavo ... Paraguay
Centavo ... Philippines
Centavo ... Portugal
Centavo ... Portuguese Guinea
Centavo ... Saint Thomas and Prince
Centavos Fuertes ... Dominican Republic
Centen ... Suriname
Centesimi ... Italy
Centesimo ... Chile
Centesimo ... Paraguay
Centesimo ... Uruguay
Centime ... Algeria
Centime ... Cameroun
Centime ... France
Centime ... French Equatorial Africa
Centime ... French Oceania
Centime ... Germany
Centime ... Guadeloupe
Centime ... French Guinea
Centime ... Haiti
Centime ... Ivory Coast
Centime ... Luxembourg
Centime ... Monaco
Centime ... Morocco
Centime ... New Caledonia
Centime ... Reunion
Centime ... Tahiti
Centime ... Tunisia
Centimo ... Costa Rica
Centimo ... Spain
Centims ... Andorra
Centu ... Lithuania
Chang ... Thailand
Chelne ... Gibraltar
Chervonets ... Ukraine
Chervonetsa ... Ukraine
Chervonetz ... Japan
Chervonetz ... Russia
Chervonetz ... Tannu-Tuva
Chervonetza ... Tannu-Tuva
Chervontsa ... Russia
Chervontsev ... Russia
Chiao ... China
Choh ... China
Chon ... North Korea
Chon ... South Korea
Colon ... Costa Rica
Colon ... El Salvador
Condor ... Chile
Conto de Rei ... Brazil
Copper Coin ... China
Coppers ... China
Cordoba ... Nicaragua
Cruzeiro ... Brazil
Customs Gold Unit ... China
Daler Kopparmynt ... Sweden
Daler Silvermynt ... Sweden
Dalere ... Danish West Indies
Deutsche Mark ... Germany (DDR)
Deutsche Mark ... Germany (FDR)
Dinar ... Iraq
Dinar ... Jordan
Dinar ... Serbia
Dinar ... Yugoslavia
Dinara ... Serbia
Dinara ... Yugoslavia
Dinara Srebru ... Serbia
Dinara Zlatu ... Serbia
Dirham ... Morocco
Dollar ... Barbados
Dollar ... British Caribbean Territories
Dollar ... British Guiana
Dollar ... British Honduras
Dollar ... British North Borneo
Dollar ... Canada
Dollar ... China
Dollar ... Taiwan
Dollar ... Confederate States of America
Dollar ... Cuba
Dollar ... Danish West Indies
Dollar ... Ethiopia
Dollar ... Fiji
Dollar ... French Indo-China
Dollar ... Germany
Dollar ... Hawaii
Dollar ... Hong Kong
Dollar ... Kiau Chau
Dollar ... Liberia
Dollar ... Malaya
Dollar ... Malaya & British Borneo
Dollar ... Mauritius
Dollar ... Mongola
Dollar ... Newfoundland
Dollar ... Poland
Dollar ... Puerto Rico
Dollar ... Sarawak
Dollar ... Texas
Dollar ... Thailand
Dollar ... Trinidad and Tobago
Dollar ... United States
Dong ... French Indo-China
Dong ... Viet Nam
Dong ... South Viet Nam
Drachma ... Greece
Drachmai ... Greece
Ducat ... Moldova
Ducati ... Moldova
Ecu ... France
Escalin ... Haiti
Escudo ... Angola
Escudo ... Cape Verde
Escudo ... Mozambique
Escudo ... Portugal
Escudo ... Portuguese Guinea
Escudo ... Portuguese India
Escudo ... Saint Thomas and Prince
Escudo ... Timor
Fen ... China
Filler ... Hungary
Fils ... Jordan
Florin ... Belgium
Florin ... East Africa
Florin ... Suriname
Forint ... Croatia
Forint ... Hungary
Franc ... Algeria
Franc ... Congo Free State
Franc ... Belgian Congo
Franc ... Belgium
Franc ... Cameroun
Franc ... Comoros
Franc ... Dahomey
Franc ... Danish West Indies
Franc ... French Somaliland
Franc ... France
Franc ... French Equatorial Africa
Franc ... French Guiana
Franc ... French Oceania
Franc ... French Sudan
Franc ... French West Africa
Franc ... Germany
Franc ... Guadeloupe
Franc ... Guernsey
Franc ... French Guinea
Franc ... Guinea
Franc ... Ivory Coast
Franc ... Libya
Franc ... Luxembourg
Franc ... Madagascar
Franc ... Martinique
Franc ... Monaco
Franc ... New Caledonia
Franc ... New Hebrides
Franc ... Reunion
Franc ... Saint Pierre and Miquelon
Franc ... Senegal
Franc ... Switzerland
Franc ... Tahiti
Franc ... Tunisia
Franc ... Upper Sengal
Franc ... West African States
Franchi ... Switzerland
Franco ... Tangier
Francs ... Morocco
Frang ... Luxembourg
Franga ... Albania
Frank ... Luxembourg
Frank ... Switzerland
Franka Ari ... Albania

Denomination	Country
Pound	Gilbert and Ellice Islands
Pound	United Kingdom
Pound	England
Pound	Guernsey
Pound	Hejaz
Pound	Ireland
Pound	Northern Ireland
Pound	Isle of Man
Pound	Israel
Pound	Jamaica
Pound	Jersey
Pound	Libya
Pound	Mauritius
Pound	New Zealand
Pound	Nigeria
Pound	Oceania
Pound	Palestine
Pound	Rhodesia and Nyasaland
Pound	Scotland
Pound	Solomon Island
Pound	South Africa
Pound	Southwest Africa
Pound	Southern Rhodesia
Pound	Syria
Pound	Tonga
Pound	Turkey
Pound	Turks & Caicos Islands
Pound	Western Samoa
Pounds Scots	Scotland
Pruta	Israel
Quetzal	Guatemala
Real	Colombia
Real	Paraguay
Real	Puerto Rico
Real	Venezuela
Real de Inca	Peru
Reichsmark	Austria
Reichsmark	Germany
Reichspfennig	Germany
Reis	Angola
Reis	Azores
Reis	Brazil
Reis	Cape Verde
Reis	Madeira Islands
Reis	Mozambique
Reis	Portugal
Reis	Saint Thomas and Prince
Rentenmark	Germany
Rial	Iran
Rials	Morocco
Riel	Cambodia
Riel	French Indo-China
Riffan	Morocco
Rigsbankdaler	Denmark
Rigsbankdaler	Greenland
Rigsbankdaler	Norway
Rigsbank-skilling	Norway
Rigsdaler	Danish West Indies
Rigsdaler	Denmark
Rigsdaler	Greenland
Rigsdaler	Iceland
Rigsdaler	Norway
Rigsdaler Courant	Denmark
Rigsdaler Specie	Denmark
Riksdaler	Finland
Riksdaler	Sweden
Riksdaler Specie	Sweden
Rix Dollar	Ceylon
Rix Dollar	South Africa
Rixdaler Banco Specie	Denmark
Rixdaler Croner	Norway
Riyal	Saudi Arabia
Riyal	Tunisia
Roepiah	Netherlands Indies
Roupie	French India
Rubel	Germany
Rubel	Poland
Ruble	Armenia
Ruble	Azerbaijan
Ruble	Finland
Ruble	Georgia
Ruble	Japan
Ruble	Russia
Ruble	Tannu-Tuva
Ruble	Ukraine
Ruble	Uzbekistan
Rubli	Latvia
Rupee	Afghanistan
Rupee	Burma
Rupee	Ceylon
Rupee	East Africa
Rupee	India
Rupee	Maldives
Rupee	Mauritius
Rupee	Nepal
Rupee	Pakistan
Rupee	Seychelles
Rupee	Zanzibar
Rupia	Italian Somaliland
Rupia	Portuguese India
Rupiah	Indonesia
Rupie	German East Africa
Rupien	German East Africa
Satang	Thailand
Schillingar	Sweden
Schillingar Banco	Sweden
Schillingar Specie	Sweden
Schilling	Austria
Schillinge	Austria
Sen	Taiwan
Sen	French Indo-China
Sen	Indonesia
Sen	Japan
Sen	Korea
Shahi	Iran
Shahiv	Ukraine
Shilling	Australia
Shilling	Bahamas
Shilling	Bermuda
Shilling	British West Africa
Shilling	Cook Islands
Shilling	Cyprus
Shilling	Falkland Islands
Shilling	Fiji
Shilling	Ghana
Shilling	Gibraltar
Shilling	Gilbert and Ellice Islands
Shilling	United Kingdom
Shilling	England
Shilling	Grenada
Shilling	Guernsey
Shilling	Ireland
Shilling	Northern Ireland
Shilling	Jamaica
Shilling	Jersey
Shilling	Leeward Islands
Shilling	Mauritius
Shilling	New Zealand
Shilling	Nigeria
Shilling	Oceania
Shilling	Rhodesia and Nyasaland
Shilling	Saint Lucia
Shilling	Scotland
Shilling	Solomon Island
Shilling	South Africa
Shilling	Southwest Africa
Shilling	Southern Rhodesia
Shilling	Tonga
Shilling	Turkey
Shilling	Turks & Caicos Islands
Shilling	Western Samoa
Silver Yuan	China
Skilling	Denmark
Skilling	Faroes
Skilling	Greenland
Skilling	Norway
Skilling Specie	Finland
Skilling Specie	Norway
Skillingar Riksgalds Mynt	Denmark
Sol	Peru
Soles de Oro	Peru
Sols	Isles of France & Bourbon
Sols	TournoisIsles of France & Bourbon
Somali	Italian Somaliland
Sou	France
Sovereign	Australia
Speciedaler	Norway
Srang	Tibet
Sucres	Ecuador
Tael	China
Tael	Japan
Tael	Kiau Chau
Talar	Poland
Tam	Tibet
Tam Srang	Tibet
Tamlung	Thailand
Tanga	Portuguese India
Tengas	Uzbekistan
Thaler	Ethiopia
Thaler	Luxembourg
Tiao	China
Tical	Thailand
Toman	Iran
Tugrik	Mongola
Won	Korea
Won	North Korea
Won	South Korea
Xu	Viet Nam
Yang	Korea
Yen	Taiwan
Yen	French Indo-China
Yen	Japan
Yen	Korea
Yuan	China
Yuan	Taiwan
Yuan	Hong Kong
Zlote	Poland
Zloty	Poland
Zlotych	Poland

Issurer and Bank Index

HOW TO USE THIS CATALOG

Catalog listings consist of all regular and provisional notes attaining wide circulation in their respective countries for the period covered. Notes have been listed under the historical country name. Thus Dahomey is not under Benin, and so on, as had been the case in some past catalogs. Where catalog numbers have changed, and you may find some renumbering in this edition, the old catalog numbers appear in parentheses directly below the new number. The listings continue to be grouped by issue range rather than by denomination, and a slight change in the listing format should make the bank name, issue dates as well as catalog numbers and denominations easier to locate. These changes have been made to make the catalog as easy to use as possible for you.

The editors and publisher make no claim to absolute completeness, just as they acknowledge that some errors and pricing inequities will appear. Correspondence is invited with interested persons who have notes previously unlisted or who have information to enhance the presentation of existing listings in succeeding editions of this catalog.

Catalog Format

Listings proceed generally according to the following sequence: country, geographic or political, chronology, bank name and sometimes alphabetically or by date of first note issue. Release within the bank, most often in date order, but sometimes by printer first.

Catalog number — The basic reference number at the beginning of each listing for each note. For this Modern Issues volume the regular listings require no prefix letters except when 'A' or 'B' appear within the catalog number. (Military and Regional prefixes are explained later in this section.)

Denomination — the value as shown on the note, in western numerals. When denominations are only spelled out, consult the numerics chart.

Date — the actual issue date as printed on the note in day-month-year order. Where more than one date appears on a note, only the latest is used. Where the note has no date, the designation ND is used, followed by a year date in parentheses when it is known. If a note is dated by the law or decree of authorization, the date appears with an L or D and is italicized.

Descriptions of the note are broken up into one or more items as follows:

Color — the main color(s) of the face, and the underprint are given first. If the colors of the back are different, then they follow the face design description.

Design — The identification and location of the main design elements if known. Back design elements identified if known.

If design elements and or signatures are the same for an issue group then they are printed only once at the heading of the issue, and apply for the group that follows.

Printer — often a local printer has the name shown in full. Abbreviations are used for the most prolific printers. Refer to the list of printer abbreviations elsewhere in this introduction. In these listings the use of the term "imprint" refers to the logo or the printer's name as usually appearing in the bottom frame or below in the margin of the note.

Valuations — are generally given under the grade headings of Good, Fine and Extremely Fine for early notes; and Very Good, Very Fine and Uncirculated for the later issues. Listings that do not follow these two patterns are clearly indicated. UNC followed by a value is used usually for specimens and proofs when lower grade headings are used for a particular series of issued notes.

Catalog prefix or suffix letters

A catalog number preceded by a capital 'A' indicated the incorporation of an earlier listing as required by type or date; a capital letter following the catalog number usually shows the addition of a later issue. Both may indicate newly discovered lower or higher denominations to a series. Listings of notes for regional circulation are distinguished from regular national issues with the prefix letter 'R'; military issues use a 'M' prefix; foreign exchange certificates are assigned a 'FX' prefix. Varieties, specific date or signature listings are shown with small letters 'a' following a number within their respective entries. Some standard variety letters include: 'p' for proof notes, 'r' for remainder notes, 's' for specimen notes and 'x' for errors.

Denominations

The denomination as indicated on many notes issued by a string of countries stretching from eastern Asia, through western Asia and on across northern Africa, often appears only in unfamiliar non-Western numeral styles. With the listings that follow, denominations are always indicated in Western numerals.

A comprehensive chart keying Western numerals to their non-Western counterparts is included elsewhere in this introduction as an aid to the identification of note types. This compilation features not only the basic numeral systems such as Arabic, Japanese and Indian, but also the more restricted systems such as Burmese, Ethiopian, Siamese, Tibetan, Hebrew, Mongolian and Korean. Additionally, the list includes other localized variations that have been applied to some paper money issues.

In consulting the numeral systems chart to determine the denomination of a note, one should remember that the actual numerals styles employed in any given area, or at a particular

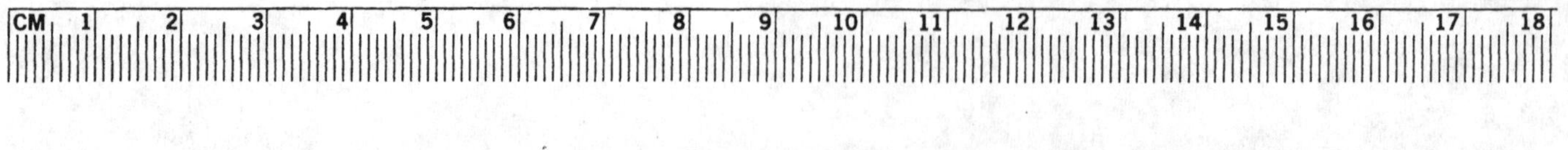

time, may vary significantly from these basic representations. Such variations can be deceptive to the untrained eye, just as variations from Western numeral styles can prove deceptive to individuals not acquainted with the particular style employed.

Dates and Date Listing Policy

In previous editions of this work it was the goal to provide a sampling of the many date varieties that were believed to exist. In recent times, as particular dates (and usually signature combinations) were known to be scarcer, that particular series was expanded to include listings of individual dates. At times this idea has been fully incorporated, but with some series it is not practicable, especially when just about every day in a given month could have been an issue date for the notes.

Accordingly, where it seems justifiable that date spans can be realistically filled with individual dates, this has been done. In order to accommodate the many new dates, the idea of providing variety letters to break them up into narrower spans of years has been used. If it appears that there are too many dates for a series, with no major differences in value, then a general inclusive date span is used (beginning and ending) and individual dates within this span are not shown.

For those notes showing only a general date span, the only important dates become those that expand the range of years, months or days earlier or later. But even they would have no impact on the values shown.

Because a specific date is not listed does not necessarily mean it is rare. It may be just that it has not been reported. Those date varieties known to be scarcer are cataloged separately. Newly reported dates in a wide variety of listings are constantly being reported. This indicates that research into the whole area is very active, and a steady flow of new dates is fully expected upon publication of this edition.

Abbreviations

Certain abbreviations have been adopted for words occurring frequently in note descriptions. Following is a list of these:

#	-	number (catalog or serial)
bldg.	-	building
ctr.	-	center
dk.	-	dark
FV	-	face value
Gen.	-	General
govt.	-	government
Kg.	-	king
l.	-	left
lg.	-	large
lt.	-	light
m/c	-	multicolored
ND	-	no date
ovpt.	-	overprint
portr.	-	portrait
Qn.	-	queen
r.	-	right
sign.	-	signature or signatures
sm.	-	small
unpt.	-	underprint (background printing)
wmk.	-	watermark
w/	-	with
w/o	-	without

Valuations

Valuations are given for most notes in three grades. Earlie issues are usually valued in the grade headings of Good, Fin and Extremely Fine; later issues take the grade headings o Very Good, Very Fine and Uncirculated. While it is true tha some early notes cannot be valued in Extremely Fine and som later notes have no premium value in Very Good, it is felt tha this coverage provides the best uniformity of value data to th collecting community. There are exceptional cases wher headings are adjusted for either single notes or a series tha really needs special treatment.

Valuations are determined generally from a consensus o individuals submitting prices for evaluation. Some notes hav NO values; this does not necessarily mean they are expensiv or even rare, but it shows that no pricing information wa forthcoming. A number of notes have a 'Rare' designation, an no values. Such notes are generally not available on the mar ket, and when they do appear the price is a matter betwee buyer and seller. No book can provide guidance in thes instances except to indicate rarity.

Valuations used in this book are based on the IBNS gradin standards and are stated in U.S. dollars. They serve only as aid in evaluating paper money since actual market condition throughout the worldwide collector community are constantl changing. In addition, particularly choice examples of man issues listed often bring higher premiums than values listed Users should remember that a catalog such as this is only guide to values.

FV (for Face Value) is used as a value designation on nev issues as well as older but still redeemable legal tender notes i lower conditions. FV may appear in one or both condition col umns before Uncirculated, depending on the relative age an availability of the note in question.

Collection care

The proper preservation of a collection should be of paramount importance to all in the hobby - dealers, collectors and scholars. Only a person who has housed notes in a manner giving pleasure to him or herself and others will keep alive the pleasure of collecting for future generations. The same applies to the way of housing as to the choice of the collecting specialty: it is chiefly a question of what most pleases the individual collector.

Arrangement and sorting of a collection is most certainly a basic requirement. Storing the notes in safe paper envelopes and filing boxes should, perhaps, be considered only when building a new section of a collection, for accommodating varieties or for reasons of saving space when the collection has grown quickly.

Many paper money collections are probably housed in some form of plastic-pocketed album, which are today manufactured in many different sizes and styles to accommodate many types of world paper money. Because the number of bank note collectors has grown continually over the past thirty-five years, some specialty manufacturers of albums have developed a paper money selection. The notes, housed in clear plastic pockets, individually or in groups, can be viewed and exchanged without difficulty. These albums are not cheap, but the notes displayed in this manner do make a lasting impression on the viewer.

A word of concern: certain types of plastic and all vinyl used for housing notes may cause notes to become brittle over time, or cause an irreversible and harmful transfer of oils from the vinyl onto the bank notes.

The high demand for quality that stamp collectors make on their products cannot be transferred to the paper money collecting fraternity. A postage stamp is intended for a single use, then is relegated to a collection. With paper money, it is nearly impossible to acquire uncirculated specimens from a number of countries because of export laws or internal bank procedures. Bends from excessive counting, or even staple holes, are commonplace. Once acquiring a circulated note, the collector must endeavor to maintain its state of preservation.

The fact that there is a classification and value difference between notes with greater use or even damage is a matter of course. It is part of the opinion and personal taste of the individual collector to decide what is considered worthy of collecting and what to pay for such items.

For the purposed of strengthening and mending torn paper money, under no circumstances should one use plain cellophane tape or a similar material. These tapes warp easily, with sealing marks forming at the edges, and the tape frequently discolors. Only with the greatest of difficulty (and often not at all) can these tapes be removed, and damage to the note or the printing is almost unavoidable. The best material for mending tears is an archival tape recommended for the treatment and repair of documents.

There are collectors who, with great skill, remove unsightly spots, repair badly damaged notes, replace missing pieces and otherwise restore or clean a note. There is a question of morality by tampering with a note to improve its condition, either by repairing, starching, ironing, pressing or other methods to possibly deceive a potential future buyer. Such a question must, in the final analysis, be left to the individual collector.

IBNS GRADING STANDARDS FOR WORLD PAPER MONEY

The following introduction and Grading Guide is the result of work prepared under the guidance of the Grading Committee of the International Bank Note Society (IBNS). It has been adopted as the official grading standards of that society.

Introduction

Grading is the most controversial component of paper money collecting today. Small differences in grade can mean significant Vdifferences in value. The process of grading is so subjective and dependent on external influences such as lighting, that even a very experienced individual may well grade the same note differently on separate occasions.

To facilitate communication between sellers and buyers, it is essential that grading terms and their meanings be as standardized and as widely used as possible. This standardization should reflect common usage as much as practicable. One difficulty with grading is that even the actual grades themselves are not used everywhere by everyone. For example, in Europe the grade 'About Uncirculated' (AU) is not in general use, yet in North America it is widespread. The European term 'Good VF' may roughly correspond to what individuals in North America call 'Extremely Fine' (EF).

The grades and definitions as set forth below cannot reconcile all the various systems and grading terminology variants. Rather, the attempt is made here to try and diminish the controversy with some common-sense grades and definitions that aim to give more precise meaning to the grading language of paper money.

How to look at a banknote

In order to ascertain the grade of a note, it is essential to examine it out of a holder and under a good light. Move the note around so that light bounces off of it at different angles. Try holding the note obliquely, so the note is even with your eye as you look up at the light. Hard-to-see folds or slight creases will show up under such examination. Some individuals also lightly feel along the surface of the note to detect creasing.

Cleaning, Washing, Pressing of Banknotes

a) Cleaning, washing or pressing paper money is generally harmful and reduces both the grade and the value of a note. At the very least, a washed or pressed note may lose its original sheen and its surface may become lifeless and dull. The defects a note had, such as folds and creases, may not necessarily be completely eliminated and their telltale marks can be detected under a good light. Carelessly washed notes may also have white streaks where the folds or creases were (or still are).

b) Processing of a note which started out as Extremely Fine will automatically reduce it at least one full grade.

Unnatural Defects

Glue, tape or pencil marks may sometimes be successfuly removed. While such removal will leave a cleaned surface, it will improve the overall appearance of the note without concealing any of its defects. Under such circumstances, the grade of that note may also be improved.

The words “pinholes”, “staple holes”, “trimmed”, “graffiti”, “writing on face”, “tape marks” etc. should always be added to the description of a note. It is realized that certain countries routinely staple their notes together in groups before issue. In such cases, the description can include a comment such as “usual staple holes” or something similar. After all, not everyone knows that certain notes cannot be found otherwise.

The major point of this section is that one cannot lower the overall grade of a note with defects simply because of the defects. The value will reflect the lowered worth of a defective note, but the description must always include the specific defects.

GRADING
Definitions of Terms

UNCIRCULATED: A perfectly preserved note, never mishandled by the issuing authority, a bank teller, the public or a collector.
Paper is clean and firm, without discoloration. Corners are sharp and square without any evidence of rounding. (Rounded corners are often a tell-tale sign of a cleaned or “doctored” note.)

NOTE: Some note issues are most often available with slight evidence of very light counting folds which do not “break” the paper. Also, French-printed notes usually have a slight ripple in the paper. Many collectors and dealers refer to such notes as AU-UNC.

ABOUT UNCIRCULATED: A virtually perfect note, with some minor handling. May show very slight evidence of bank counting folds at a corner or one light fold through the center, but not both. An AU note canot be creased, a crease being a hard fold which has usually “broken” the surface of the note.
Paper is clean and bright with original sheen. Corners are not rounded.

NOTE: Europeans will refer to an About Uncirculated or AU note as “EF-Unc” or as just “EF”. The Extremely Fine note described below will often be referred to as “GVF” or “Good Very Fine”.

EXTREMELY FINE: A very attractive note, with light handling. May have a maximum of three light folds or one strong crease.
Paper is clean and firm, without discoloration. Corners are sharp and square without any evidence of rounding. (Rounded corners are often a tell-tale sign of a cleaned or “doctored” note.)

VERY FINE: An attractive note, but with more evidence of handling and wear. May have several folds both vertically and horizontally.
Paper may have minimal dirt, or possible color smudging. Paper itself is still relatively crisp and not floppy.
There are no tears into the border area, although the edges do show slight wear. Corners also show wear but not full rounding.

FINE: A note that shows consideralble circulation, with many folds, creases and wrinkling.
Paper is not excessively dirty but may have some softness.
Edges may show much handling, with minor tears in the border area. Tears may not extend into the design. There will be no center hole because of excessive folding.
Colors are clear but not very bright. A staple hole or two would would not be considered unusual wear in a Fine note. Overall appearance is still on the desirable side.

VERY GOOD: A well used note, abused but still intact.
Corners may have much wear and rounding, tiny nicks, tears may extend into the design, some discoloration may be prsent, staining may have occurred, and a small hole may sometimes be seen at center from excessive folding.
Staple and pinholes are usually present, and the note itself is quite limp but NO pieces of the note can be missing. A note in VG condition may still have an overall not unattractive appearance.

GOOD: A well worn and heavily used note. Normal damage from prolonged circulation will include strong multiple folds and creases, stains, pinholes and/or staple holes, dirt, discoloration, edge tears, center hole, rounded corners and an overall unattractive appearance. No large pieces of the note may be missing. Graffiti is commonly seen on notes in G condition.

FAIR: A totally limp, dirty and very well used note. Larger pieces may be half torn off or missing besides the defects mentioned under the Good category. Tears will be larger, obscured portions of the note will be bigger.

POOR: A “rag” with severe damage because of wear, staining, pieces missing, graffiti, larger holes. May have tape holding pieces of the note together. Trimming may have taken place to remove rough edges. A Poor note is desiralble only as a “filler” or when such a note is the only one known of that particular issue.

A word on crimps to otherwise uncirculated notes.
Due to inclusion of wide security foils, crimps appear at the top and bottom edge during production or counting. Thus notes which are uncirculated have a crimp. Examples without these crimps are beginning to command a premium.

Foreign Exchange Table

The latest foreign exchange fixed rates below apply to trade with banks in the country of origin. The left column shows the number of units per U.S. dollar at the official rate. The right column shows the number of units per dollar at the free market rate.

Country	Official #/$	Market #/$
Afghanistan (New Afghani)	43	–
Albania (Lek)	120	–
Algeria (Dinar)	77.5	–
Andorra uses Euro	.88	–
Angola (Readjust Kwanza)	81	–
Anguilla uses E.C.Dollar	2.67	–
Antigua uses E.C.Dollar	2.67	–
Argentina (Peso)	2.93	–
Armenia (Dram)	560	–
Aruba (Florin)	1.79	–
Australia (Dollar)	1.533	–
Austria (Euro)	.88	–
Azerbaijan (Manat)	4,950	–
Bahamas (Dollar)	1.00	–
Bahrain Is.(Dinar)	.377	–
Bangladesh (Taka)	58	–
Barbados (Dollar)	1.99	–
Belarus (Ruble)	2,100	–
Belgium (Euro)	.88	–
Belize (Dollar)	1.97	–
Benin uses CFA Franc West	580	–
Bermuda (Dollar)	.98	–
Bhutan (Ngultrum)	47.6	–
Bolivia (Boliviano)	7.70	–
Bosnia-Herzegovina (Deutschmark)	1.72	–
Botswana (Pula)	4.88	–
British Virgin Islands uses U.S.Dollar	1.00	–
Brazil (Real)	2.99	–
Brunei (Dollar)	1.75	–
Bulgaria (Lev)	1.73	–
Burkina Faso uses CFA Fr.West	580	–
Burma (Kyat)	6.2	–
Burundi (Franc)	1,050	–
Cambodia (Riel)	3,835	–
Cameron uses CFA Franc Central	580	–
Canada (Dollar)	1.391	–
Cape Verde (Escudo)	110	–
Cayman Is.(Dollar)	0.82	–
Central African Rep.	580	–
CFA Franc Central	580	–
CFA Franc West	580	–
CFP Franc	102.2	–
Chad uses CFA Franc Central	580	–
Chile (Peso)	700	–
China, P.R. (Renminbi Yuan)	8.278	–
Colombia (Peso)	2,875	–
Comoros (Franc)	455	–
Congo uses CFA Franc Central	580	–
Congo-Dem.Rep. (Congolese Franc)	575	–
Cook Islands (Dollar)	1.73	–
Costa Rica (Colon)	405	–
Croatia (Kuna)	6.7	–
Cuba (Peso)	1.00	22
Cyprus (Pound)	.52	–
Czech Republic (Koruna)	28.4	–
Denmark (Danish Krone)	6.58	–
Djibouti (Franc)	175	–
Dominica uses E.C.Dollar	2.67	–
Dominican Republic (Peso)	32.5	–
East Caribbean (Dollar)	2.67	–
Ecuador uses U.S. Dollar	1.00	–
Egypt (Pound)	6.13	–
El Salvador uses U.S. Dollar	1.00	–
Equatorial Guinea uses CFA Franc Central	580	–
Eritrea (Nafka)	9.6	–
Estonia (Kroon)	13.8	–
Ethiopia (Birr)	8.58	–

Country	#/$	#/$
Euro	.88	–
Falkland Is. (Pound)	.627	–
Faroe Islands (Krona)	6.58	–
Fiji Islands (Dollar)	1.85	–
Finland (Euro)	.88	–
France (Euro)	.88	–
French Polynesia uses CFP Franc	102.2	–
Gabon (CFA Franc)	580	–
Gambia (Dalasi)	28.9	–
Georgia (Lari)	2.15	–
Germany (Euro)	.88	–
Ghana (Cedi)	8,450	–
Gibraltar (Pound)	.627	–
Greece (Euro)	.88	–
Greenland uses Danish Krone	6.58	–
Grenada uses E.C.Dollar	2.67	–
Guatemala (Quetzal)	7.92	–
Guernsey (Pound Sterling)	.624	–
Guinea Bissau (CFA Franc)	580	–
Guinea Conakry (Franc)	2,000	–
Guyana (Dollar)	180	–
Haiti (Gourde)	38	–
Honduras (Lempira)	17.4	–
Hong Kong (Dollar)	7.8	–
Hungary (Forint)	230	–
Iceland (Krona)	78.4	–
India (Rupee)	46	–
Indonesia (Rupiah)	8,560	–
Iran (Rial)	8,235	–
Iraq (Dinar)	.312	1,300
Ireland (Euro)	.88	–
Isle of Man (Pound Sterling)	.624	–
Israel (New Sheqalim)	4.4	–
Italy (Euro)	.88	–
Ivory Coast uses CFA Franc West	580	–
Jamaica (Dollar)	58	–
Japan (Yen)	119	–
Jersey (Pound Sterling)	.624	–
Jordan (Dinar)	.71	–
Kazakhstan (Tenge)	150	–
Kenya (Shilling)	75	–
Kiribati uses Australian Dollar	1.533	–
Korea-PDR (Won)	2.2	300
Korea-Rep. (Won)	1,180	–
Kuwait (Dinar)	.3	–
Kyrgyzstan (Som)	44.5	–
Laos (Kip)	7,600	–
Latvia (Lat)	.572	–
Lebanon (Pound)	1,510	–
Lesotho (Maloti)	7.25	–
Liberia (Dollar) "JJ"	1.00	20.00
"Liberty"	–	40.00
Libya (Dinar)	1.22	–
Liechtenstein uses Swiss Franc	1.36	–
Lithuania (Litas)	3.05	–
Luxembourg (Euro)	.88	–
Macao (Pataca)	8.03	–
Macedonia (New Denar)	52.4	–
Madagascar (Franc)	5,950	–
Malawi (Kwacha)	99	–
Malaysia (Ringgit)	3.8	–
Maldives (Rufiya)	12.8	–
Mali uses CFA Franc West	580	–
Malta (Lira)	.38	–
Marshall Islands uses U.S.Dollar	1.00	–
Mauritania (Ouguiya)	265	–
Mauritius (Rupee)	29	–
Mexico (Peso)	10.7	–
Moldova (Leu)	14	–
Monaco uses Euro	.88	–
Mongolia (Tugrik)	1,125	–
Montenegro uses Yugo New Dinar	58	–
Montserrat uses E.C.Dollar	2.67	–
Morocco (Dirham)	9.58	–
Mozambique (Metical)	23,550	–
Myanmar (Burma) (Kyat)	6.2	–
Namibia (Rand)	7.24	–
Nauru uses Australian Dollar	1.533	–
Nepal (Rupee)	74.6	–

Country	#/$	#/$
Netherlands (Euro)	.88	
Netherlands Antilles (Gulden)	1.78	
New Caledonia uses CFP Franc	102.2	
New Zealand (Dollar)	1.721	
Nicaragua (Cordoba Oro)	15.1	
Niger uses CFA Franc West	580	
Nigeria (Naira)	130	
Northern Ireland (Pound Sterling)	.624	
Norway (Krone)	7.23	
Oman (Rial)	.385	
Pakistan (Rupee)	57.5	
Palau uses U.S.Dollar	1.00	
Panama (Balboa) uses U.S.Dollar	1.00	
Papua New Guinea (Kina)	3.41	
Paraguay (Guarani)	6,275	
Peru (Nuevo Sol)	3.48	
Philippines (Peso)	54.7	
Poland (Zloty)	3.9	
Portugal (Euro)	.88	
Qatar (Riyal)	3.64	
Romania (Leu)	33,000	
Russia (New Ruble)	30.4	
Rwanda (Franc)	525	
St.Helena (Pound)	.627	
St.Kitts uses E.C.Dollar	2.67	
St.Lucia uses E.C.Dollar	2.67	
St.Vincent uses E.C.Dollar	2.67	
San Marino uses Euro	.88	
Sao Tome e Principe (Dobra)	8,700	
Saudi Arabia (Riyal)	3.75	
Scotland (Pound Sterling)	.624	
Senegal uses CFA Franc West	580	
Seychelles (Rupee)	5.18	6.
Sierra Leone (Leone)	2,350	2,60
Singapore (Dollar)	1.76	
Slovakia (Sk. Koruna)	37	
Slovenia (Tolar)	205	
Solomon Is.(Dollar)	7.52	
Somalia (Shilling)	2,620	
Somaliland (Somali Shilling)	1,800	4,0
South Africa (Rand)	7.39	
Spain (Euro)	.88	
Sri Lanka (Rupee)	97	
Sudan (Dinar)	260	3
Surinam (Guilder)	2,515	
Swaziland (Lilangeni)	7.25	
Sweden (Krona)	8.14	
Switzerland (Franc)	1.36	
Syria (Pound)	46	
Taiwan (NT Dollar)	34.5	
Tajikistan (Somoni)	3.08	
Tanzania (Shilling)	1,045	
Thailand (Baht)	41.9	
Togo uses CFAFranc West	580	
Tonga (Paíanga)	2.15	
Transdniestra (Ruble)	6.51	
Trinidad & Tobago (Dollar)	6.14	
Tunisia (Dinar)	1.28	
Turkey (Lira)	1,410,000	
Turkmenistan (Manat)	5,150	
Turks &Caicos uses U.S.Dollar	1.00	
Tuvalu uses Australian Dollar	1.533	
Uganda (Shilling)	2,000	
Ukraine (Hryvnia)	5.33	
United Arab Emirates (Dirham)	3.673	
United Kingdom (Pound Sterling)	.624	
Uruguay (Peso Uruguayo)	28.2	
Uzbekistan (Som)	970	
Vanuatu (Vatu)	122	
Vatican City uses Euro	.88	
Venezuela (Bolivar)	1,600	
Vietnam (Dong)	15,500	
Western Samoa (Tala)	3.0	
Yemen (Rial)	178	
Yugoslavia (Novih Dinar)	58	
Zambia (Kwacha)	4,750	
Zimbabwe (Dollar)	825	3,0

Dating

Determining the date of issue of a note is a basic consideration of attribution. As the reading of dates is subject not only to the vagaries of numeric styling, but to variations in dating roots caused by the observation of differing religious eras or regal periods from country to country, making this determination can sometimes be quite difficult. Most countries outside the North African and Oriental spheres rely on Western date numerals and the Christian (AD) reckoning, although in a few instances note dating has been tied to the year of a reign or government.

Countries of the Arabic sphere generally date their issues to the Muslim calendar that commenced on July 16, 622 AD when the prophet Mohammed fled from Mecca to Medina. As this calendar is reckoned by the lunar year of 354, its is about three percent (precisely 3.3 percent) shorter than the Christian year. A conversion formula requires you to subtract that percent from the AH date, and then add 621 to gain the AD date.

A degree of confusion arises here because the Muslim calendar is not always based on the lunar year (AH). Afghanistan and Iran (Persia) used a calendar based on a solar year (SH) introduced around 1920. These dates can be converted to AD by simply adding 621. In 1976, Iran implemented a solar calendar based on the founding of the Iranian monarchy in 559 BC. The first year observed on this new system was 2535(MS) which commenced on March 20, 1976.

Several different eras of reckoning, including the Christian (AD) and Muslim (AH), have been used to date paper money of the Indian subcontinent. The two basic systems are the Vikrama Samvat (VS) era that dates from October 18, 58 BC,. and the Saka (SE) era, the origin of which is reckoned from March 3, 78 AD. Dating according to both eras appears on notes of several native states and countries of the area.

Thailand (Siam) has observed three different eras for dating. The most predominant is the Buddhist (BE) era originating in 543 BC. Next is the Bangkok or Ratanakosind-sok (RS) era dating from 1781 AD (and consisting of only 3 numerals), followed by the Chula-Sakarat (CS) era dating from 638 AD, with the latter also observed in Burma.

Other calendars include that of the Ethiopian (EE) era that commenced 7 years, 8 months after AD dating, and that of the Hebrew nation beginning on October 7, 3761 BC. Korea claims a dating from 2333 BC which is acknowledged on some note issues.

The following table indicates the years dating from the various eras that correspond to 2007 by Christian (AD) calendar reckoning. It must be remembered that there are overlaps between the eras in some instances:

Christian Era (AD)	—	2007
Mohammedan era (AH)	—	AH1428
Solar year (SH)	—	SH1386
Monarchic Solar era (MS)	—	MS2566
Vikrama Samvat era (VS)	—	SE2064
Saka era (SE)	—	Saka 1929
Buddhist era (BE)	—	BE2550
Bangkok era (RS)	—	RS226
Chula-Sakarat era (CS)	—	CS1369
Ethiopian era (EE)	—	EE1999
Jewish era	—	5767
Korean era	—	4340

Paper money of Oriental origin - principally Japan, Korea, China, Turkestan and Tibet - generally date to the year of the government, dynastic, regnal or cyclical eras, with the dates indicated in Oriental characters usually reading from right to left. In recent years some dating has been according to the Christian calendar and in Western numerals reading from left to right.

More detailed guides to the application of the less prevalent dating systems than those described, and others of strictly local nature, along with the numeral designations employed, are presented in conjunction with the appropriate listings.

Some notes carry dating according to both the locally observed and Christian eras. This is particularly true in the Arabic sphere, where the Muslim date may be indicated in Arabic numerals and the Christian date in Western numerals.

In general the date actually shown on a given paper money issue is indicated in some manner. Notes issued by special Law or Decree will have L or D preceding the date. Dates listed within parentheses may differ from the date appearing on the note; they have been documented by other means. Undated notes are listed with ND, followed by a year only when the year of actual issue is known.

Timing differentials between the 354-day Muslim and the 365-day Christian year cause situations whereby notes bearing dates of both eras have two date combinations that may overlap from one or the other calendar system.

China — Republic 9th year, 1st month, 15th day (15.1.1920), read r. to l.

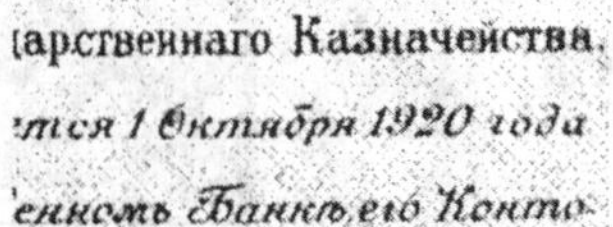

Russia — 1 October 1920

Thailand (Siam) — 1 December 2456

Korea — 4288 (1955)

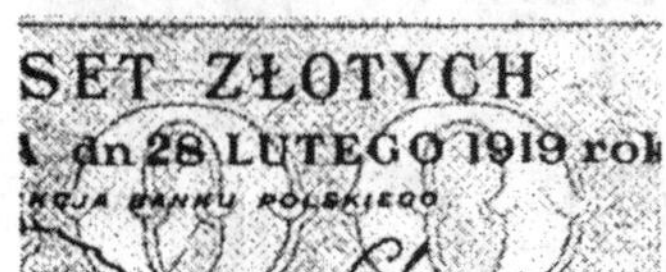

Poland — 28 February 1919

Afghanistan — Solar Year 1356

Israel — 1973, 5733

Indonesia — 1 January 1950

Egypt — 1967 December 2

Greece — 5 March 1943

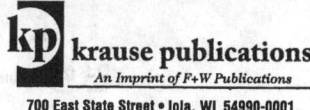

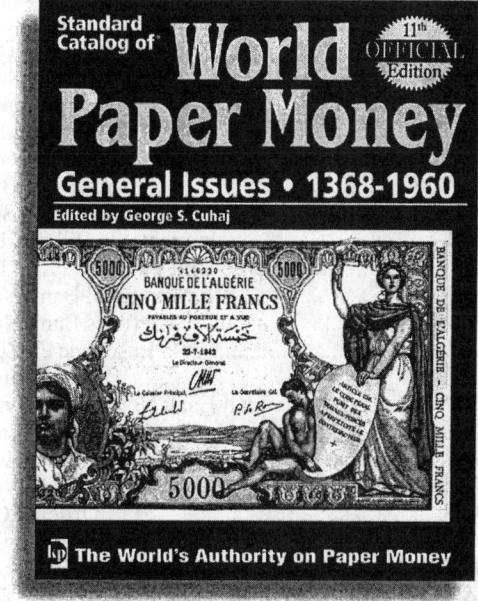

BANK NOTE PRINTERS

Printers' names, abbreviations or monograms will usually appear as part of the frame design or below it on face and/or back. In some instances the engraver's name may also appear in a similar location on a note. The following abbreviations identify printers for many of the notes listed in this volume:

ABNC .... American Bank Note Company (USA)
BABN(C) .... British American Bank Note Co., Ltd. (Canada)
B&S .... Bouligny & Schmidt (Mexico)
BDDK .... Bunddesdruckerei (Germany)
BEPP .... Bureau of Engraving & Printing, Peking (China)
BF .... Banque de France (France)
BFL .... Barclay & Fry Ltd. (England)
BWC .... Bradbury, Wilkinson & Co. (England)
CABB .... Compania Americana de Billetes de Banco (ABNC)
CBC .... Columbian Banknote Co. (US)
CBNC .... Canadian Bank Note Company (Canada)
CC .... Ciccone Calcografica S.A. (Italy)
CCBB .... Compania Columbiana de Billetes de Banco (CBC)
CdM- .... Casa da Moeda (Brazil)
CdM- .... Casa de Moneda (Argentina, Chile, etc.)
CHB .... Chung Hua Book Co. (China)
CMN .... Casa de Moneda de la Nacion (Argentina)
CMPA .... Commercial Press (China)
CNBB .... Compania Nacional de Billetes de Banco (NBNC)
CONB .... Continental Bank Note Company (US)
CPF .... Central Printing Factory (China)
CSABB .... Compania Sud/Americana de Billetes de Banco .... (Argentina)
CS&E .... Charles Skipper & East (England)
DLR .... De La Rue (England)
DTB .... Dah Tung Book Co., and Ta Tung Printing (China)
E&C .... Evans & Cogswell (CSA)
EAW .... E.A. Wright (US)
FLBN .... Franklin-Lee Bank Note Company (US)
FNMT .... Fabrica Nacional de Moneda y Timbre (Spain)
G&D .... Giesecke & Devrient (Germany)
HBNC .... Hamilton Bank Note Compay (USA)
HKB .... Hong Kong Banknote (Hong Kong)
HKP .... Hong Kong Printing Press (Hong Kong)
H&L .... Hoyer & Ludwig, Richmond, Virginia (CSA)
HLBNC .... Homer Lee Bank Note Co. (US)
H&S .... Harrison & Sons Ltd. (England)
IBB .... Imprenta de Billetes-Bogota (Colombia)
IBSFB .... Imprenta de Billetes-Santa Fe de Bogota (Colombia)
IBNC .... International Bank Note Company (US)
JBNC .... Jeffries Bank Note Company (US)
JEZ .... Joh. Enschede en Zonen (Netherlands)
K&B .... Keatinge & Ball (CSA)
KBNC .... Kendall Bank Note Company, New York (USA)
LN .... Litografia Nacional (Colombia)
NAL .... Nissen & Arnold (England)
NBNC .... National Bank Note Company (US)
OCV .... Officina Carte-Valori (Italy)
ODBI .... Officina Della Banca D'Italia (Italy)
OFZ .... Orell Füssli, Zurich (Switzerland)
P&B .... Perkins & Bacon (England)
PBC .... Perkins, Bacon & Co. (England)
PB&P .... Perkins, Bacon & Petch (England)
SBNC .... Security Banknote Company (US)
TDLR .... Thomas De La Rue (England)
UPC .... Union Printing Co. (China)
UPP .... Union Publishers & Printers Fed. Inc. (China)
USBNC .... United States Banknote Corp. (US)
WDBN .... Western District Banknote Fed. Inc.
W&S .... Waterlow & Sons Ltd. (England)
WPCo .... Watson Printing Co. (China)
WWS .... W.W. Sprague & Co. Ltd. (England)

SPECIMEN NOTES

To familiarize private banks, central banks, law enforcement agencies and treasuries around the world with newly issued currency, many nations provide them with special "Specimen" examples of their notes. Specimens are actual bank notes, complete with dummy or all zero serial numbers and signatures and bearing the overprinted and/or perforated word "SPECIMEN" in the language of the country of origin itself or where the notes were printed.

Some countries have made specimen notes available for sale to collectors. These include Cuba, Czechoslovakia, Poland and Slovakia after World War II and a special set of four denominations of Jamaica notes bearing red matched star serial numbers. Also, in 1978, the Franklin Mint made available to collectors specimen notes from 15 nations, bearing matching serial numbers and a Maltese cross device used as a prefix. Several other countries have also participated in making specimen notes available to collectors at times.

Aside from these collectors issues, specimen notes may sometimes command higher prices than regular issue notes of the same type, even though there are far fewer collectors of specimens. In some cases, notably older issues in high denominations, specimens may be the only form of such notes available to collectors today. Specimen notes are not legal tender or redeemable, thus have no real "face value" which also is indicated on some examples.

The most unusual forms of specimens were produced by Waterlow and Sons. They printed special off colored notes for salesman's sample books adding the word SPECIMEN and their seal. These salesman's samples are not included in catalog listings. In most cases they are less valuable than true color specimens but may command a premium in more popularly collected countries.

Some examples of how the word "SPECIMEN" is represented in other languages or on notes of other countries follow:

AMOSTRA: Brazil
CAMPIONE: Italy
CONTOH: Malaysia
ÈKSEMPLAAR: South Africa
ESPÉCIME: Portugal and Colonies
ESPECIMEN: Various Spanish-speaking nations
GIAY MAU: Vietnam
MINTA: Hungary
MODELO: Brazil
MODEL: Albania
MUSTER: Austria, Germany
MUESTRA: Various Spanish-speaking nations
NUMUNEDIR GECMEZ: Turkey
ORNEKTIR GECMEZ: Turkey
ОБРАЗЕЦ or **ОБРАЗЕЦЪ:** Bulgaria, Russia, U.S.S.R.
PARAUGS: Latvia
PROFTRYK: Sweden
UZORAK: Croatia
WZOR: Poland
ЗАГВАР: Mongolia

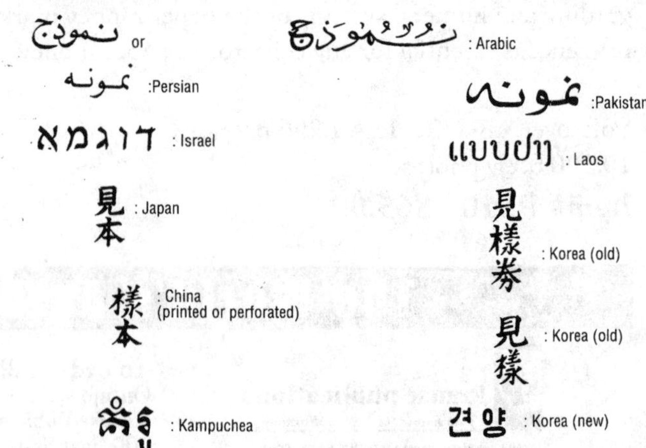

	January	February	March	April	May	June	July	August	September	October	November	December
Albanian	Kallnuer	Fruer	Mars	Prill	Maj	Qershuer	Korrik	Gusht	Shtatuer	Tetuer	Nanduer	Dhetuer
Czech	Leden	Únor	Brezen	Duben	Kveten	Cerven	Cervenec	Srpen	Zári	Ríjen	Listopad	Prosinec
Danish	Januar	Februari	Maart	April	Maj	Juni	Juli	August	September	Oktober	November	December
Dutch	Januari	Februari	Maart	April	Mei	Juni	Juli	Augustus	September	Oktober	November	December
Estonian	Jaanuar	Veebruar	Marts	Aprill	Mai	Juuni	Juuli	August	September	Oktoober	November	Detsember
French	Janvier	Fevrier	Mars	Avril	Mai	Juin	Jillet	Août	Septembre	Octobre	Novembre	Decembre
Finnish	Tammikuu	Helmikuu	Maaliskuu	Huhtikuu	Toukokuu	Kesakuu	Heinakuu	Elokuu	Syyskuu	Lokakuu	Marraskuu	Joulukuu
German	Januar	Februar	Marz	April	Mai	Juni	Juli	August	September	Oktober	November	Dezember
Hungarian	Januar	Februar	Marcius	Aprilis	Majus	Junius	Julius	Augusztus	Szeptember	Oktober	November	December
Indonesian	Djanuari	Februari	Maret	April	Mai	Djuni	Djuli	Augustus	September	Oktober	Nopember	Desember
Italian	Gennaio	Fabbraio	Marzo	Aprile	Maggio	Giugno	Luglio	Agosto	Settembre	Ottobre	Novembre	Dicembre
Lithuanian	Sausis	Vasaris	Kovas	Balandis	Geguzis	Birzelis	Liepos	Rugpiutis	Rugsejis	Spalis	Lapkritis	Gruodis
Norwegian	Januar	Februar	Mars	April	Mai	Juni	Juli	August	September	Oktober	November	Desember
Polish	Styczen	Luty	Marzec	Kwiecien	Maj	Cerwiec	Lipiec	Sierpien	Wrzesien	Pazdziernik	Listopad	Grudzien
Portuguese	Janerio	Fevereiro	Marco	Abril	Maio	Junho	Julho	Agosto	Setembro	Outubro	Novembro	Dezembro
Romanian	Ianuarie	Februarie	Martie	Aprilie	Mai	Iunie	Iulie	August	Septembrie	Octombrie	Noiembrie	Decembrie
Croatian	Sijecanj	Veljaca	Ozujak	Travanj	Svibanj	Lipanj	Srpanj	Kolovoz	Rujan	Listopad	Studeni	Prosinac
Spanish	Enero	Febrero	Marzo	Abril	Mayo	Junio	Julio	Agosto	Septiembre	Octubre	Noviembre	Diciembre
Swedish	Januari	Februari	Mars	April	Maj	Juni	Juli	Augusti	September	Oktober	November	December
Turkish	Ocak	Subat	Mart	Nisan	Mayis	Haziran	Temmuz	Agusto	Eylul	Ekim	Kasim	Aralik
Arabic-New (condensed)	يناير	فبراير	مارس	ابريل	مايو	يونيو	يوليو	أغسطس	سبتمبر	أكتوبر	نوفمبر	ديسمبر
(extended)	يناير	فبراير	مارس	ابريل	مايو	يونيه	يوليه	اغسطس	سبتمبر	اكتوبر	نوفمبر	ديسمبر
Persian (Solar)	فروردين	ارديبهشت	خرداد	تير	مرداد	شهريور	مهر	آبان	آذر	دى	بهمن	اسفند
(Lunar)	محرم	صفر	ربيع الاول	ربيع الثانى	جمادى الاول	جمادى الثانى	رجب	شعبان	رمضان	شوال	ذيقعده	ذوالحجه
Chinese	正月	二月	三月	四月	五月	六月	七月	八月	九月	十月	十一月	十二月
Japanese	一月	二月	三月	四月	五月	六月	七月	八月	九月	十月	十一月	十二月
Greek	Ιανοναριοδ	Φεβροναριοδ	Μαρτιοδ	Απιλιοδ	Μαιοδ	Ιουνιοδ	Ιουλιοδ	Αυγουατοδ	Εεπτεμβπιοδ	Οκτωβπιοδ	Νοεμπιοσ	Δεκεμβριος
Russian	ЯНВАРЬ	ФЕВРАЛЬ	МАРТ	АПРЕЛЬ	МАИ	ИЮНЬ	ИЮЛЬ	АВГУСТ	СЕПТЯБРЬ	ОКТЯБРЬ	НОЯБРЬ	ДЕКАБРЬ
Serbian	Јануар	Фебруар	Март	Април	Мај	Јун	Јул	Август	Септембар	Октобар	Новембар	Децембар
Ukranian	Січень	Лютий	Березень	Квітень	Травень	Червень	Липень	Серпень	Вересень	Жовтень	Листопад	Грудень
Yiddish	יאַנואַר	פֿעברואַר	מערץ	אַפּריל	מײַ	יוני	יולי	אויגוסט	סעפּטעמבער	אָקטאָבער	נאָוועמבער	דעצעמבער
Hebrew (Israeli)	ינואר	פברואר	מרץ	אפריל	מאי	יוני	יולי	אוגוסט	ספטמבר	אוקטובר	נובמבר	דצמבר

Note: Word spellings and configurations as represented on actual notes may vary significantly from those shown on this chart.

A GUIDE TO INTERNATIONAL NUMERICS

	ENGLISH	CZECH	DANISH	DUTCH	ESPERANTO	FRENCH
1/4	one-quarter	jeden-ctvrt	én kvart	een-kwart	unu-kvar'ono	un-quart
1/2	one-half	jeden-polovieni or pul	én halve	een-half	unu-du'one	un-demi
1	one	jeden	én	een	unu	un
2	two	dve	to	twee	du	deux
3	three	tri	trre	drie	tri	trois
4	four	ctyri	fire	vier	kvar	quatre
5	five	pet	fem	vijf	kvin	cinq
6	six	sest	seks	zes	ses	six
7	seven	sedm	syv	zeven	sep	sept
8	eight	osm	otte	acht	ok	huit
9	nine	devet	ni	negen	nau	neuf
10	ten	deset	ti	tien	dek	dix
12	twelve	dvanáct	tolv	twaalf	dek du	douze
15	fifteen	patnáct	femten	vijftien	dek kvin	quinze
20	twenty	dvacet	tyve	twintig	du'dek	vingt
24	twenty-four	dvacet-ctyri	fireog tyve	twintig-vier	du'dek kvar	vingt-quatre
25	twenty-five	dvacet-pet	fem og tyve	twintig-vijf	du'dek kvin	vingt-cinq
30	thirty	tricet	tredive	dertig	tri'dek	trente
40	forty	ctyricet	fyrre	veertig	kvar'dek	quarante
50	fifty	padesát	halytreds	vijftig	kvin'dek	cinquante
60	sixty	sedesát	tres	zestig	ses'dek	soixante
70	seventy	sedmdesát	halvfjerds	zeventig	sep'dek	soixante dix
80	eighty	osemdesát	firs	tachtig	ok'dek	quatre-vingt
90	ninety	devadesát	halvfjerds	negentig	nau'dek	quatre-vingt-dix
100	one hundred	jedno sto	et hundrede	een-honderd	unu-cento	un-cent
1000	thousand	tisíc	tusind	duizend	mil	mille

	GERMAN	HUNGARIAN	INDONESIAN	ITALIAN	NORWEGIAN	POLISH
1/4	ein viertel	egy-negyed	satu-suku	uno-guarto	en-fjeerdedel	jeden-c weirc
1/2	einhalb	egy-fél	satu-setengah	uno-mezzo	en-halv	jeden-polowa
1	ein	egy	satu	uno	en	jeden
2	zwei	kettö	dud	due	to	dwa
3	drei	három	tiga	tre	tre	trzy
4	vier	négy	empot	quattro	fire	cztery
5	fünf	öt	lima	cinque	fem	piec'
6	sechs	hat	enam	sei	seks	szes'c'
7	sieben	hét	tudjuh	'sette	sju	siedem
8	acht	nyolc	delapan	otto	atte	osiem
9	neun	kilenc	sembilan	nove	ni	dziewiec'
10	zehn	tí z	sepuluh	dieci	ti	dziesiec'
12	zwölf	tizenketto	duabelas	dodici	tolv	dwanas' cie
15	fünfzehn	tizenöt	lima belas	quindici	femten	pietnas'cie
20	zwanzig	húsz	dua pulah	venti	tjue or tyve	dwadzies'cia
24	vierundzwanzig	húsz-négy	dua pulah-empot	venti-quattro	tjue-fire or tyve-fire	dwadzies'cia-cztery
25	fünfundzwanzig	húsz-öt	dua-pulah-lima	venti-cinque	tjue-fem or tyve-fem	dwadzies'cia-piec
30	dreissig	harminc	tigapulah	trenta	tredve	trydzies'ci
40	vierzig	negyven	empat pulah	quaranta	forti	czterdries'ci
50	fünfzig	otven	lima pulah	cinquanta	femti	piec'dziesiat
60	sechzig	hatvan	enam pulah	sessanta	seksti	szes'c'dziesiat
70	siebzig	hetven	tudjuh pulu	settanta	sytti	siedemdziesiat
80	achtzig	nyolvan	delapan puluh	ottonta	atti	osiemdziesiat
90	neunzig	kilencven	sembilan puluh	novanta	nitty	dziewiec'dziesiat
100	ein hundert	egy-száz	satu-seratus	uno-cento	en-hundre	jeden-sto
1000	tausend	ezer	seribu	mille	tusen	tysiac

	PORTUGUESE	ROMANIAN	SERBO-CROATIAN	SPANISH	SWEDEN	TURKISH
1/4	um-quarto	un-sfert	jedan-ceturtina	un-cuarto	en-fjärdedel	bir-ceyrek
1/2	un-meio	o-jumatate	jedan-polovina	un-medio	en-hälft	bir-yarim
1	um	un	jedan	uno	en	bir
2	dois	doi	dva	dos	tva	iki
3	trés	trei	tri	tres	tre	üc
4	quatro	patru	cetiri	cuatro	fyra	dört
5	cinco	cinci	pet	cinco	fem	bes
6	seis	sase	sest	seis	sex	alti
7	sete	sapte	sedam	siete	sju	yedi
8	oito	opt	osam	ocho	atta	sekiz
9	nove	noua	devet	nueve	io	dokuz
10	dez	zece	deset	diez	tio	on
12	doze	doisprezece	dvanaest	doce	tolv	on iki
15	quinze	cincisprezece	petnaest	quince	femton	on bes
20	vinte	douazeci	dvadset	veinte	tjugu	yirmi
24	vinte-quatro	douazeci-patru	dvadesel-citiri	veinticuatro	tjugu-fyra	yirmi-dört
25	vinte-cinco	douazeci-cinci	dvadeset-pet	veinticinco	tjugu-fem	yirmi-bes
30	trinta	treizeci	trideset	treinta	trettio	otuz
40	quarenta	patruzeci	cetrdeset	cuarenta	fyrtio	kirk
50	cinqüenta	cincizeci	padeset	cincuenta	femtio	elli
60	sessenta	saizeci	sezdeset	sesenta	sextio	altmis
70	setenta	saptezeci	sedamdeset	setenta	sjuttio	yetmis
80	oitenta	optzeci	osamdeset	ochenta	attio	seksen
90	noventa	novazeci	devedeset	noventa	nittio	doksan
100	un-cem	o-suta	jedan-sto	cien	en-hundra	bir-yüz
1000	mil	mie	hiljada	mil	tusen	bin

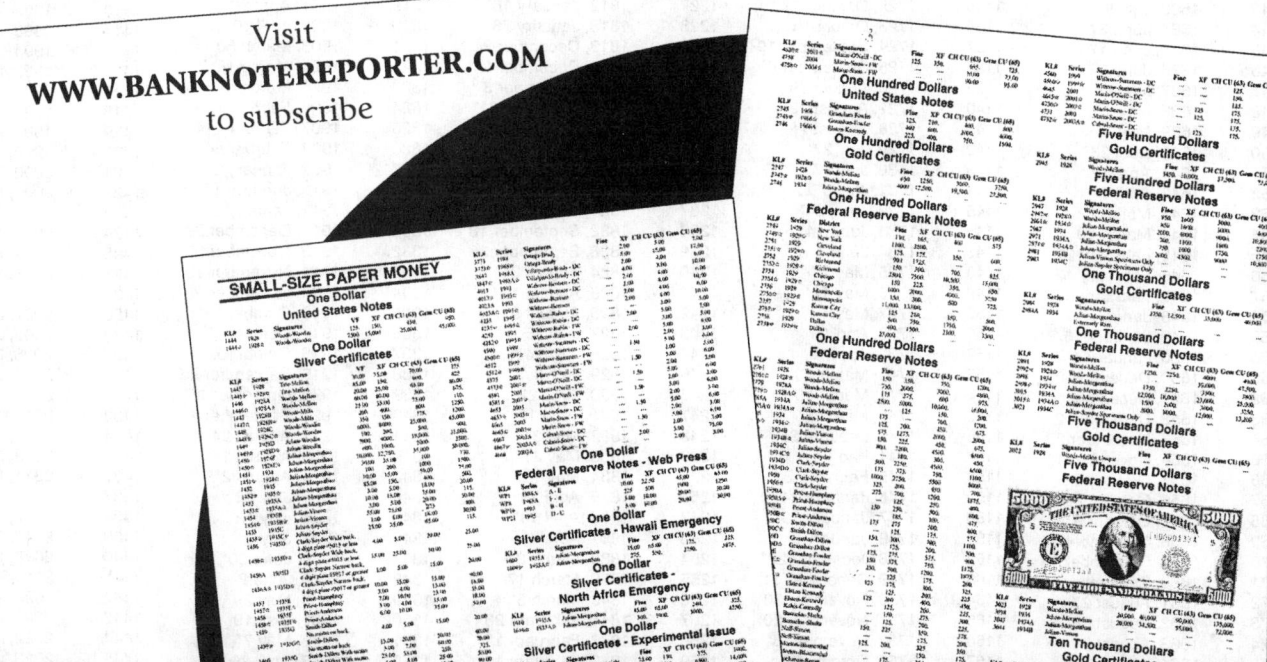

HEJIRA DATE CONVERSION CHART

HEJIRA (Hijira, Hegira), the name of the Muslim era (A.H. = Anno Hegirae) dates back to the Christian year 622 when Mohammed "fled" from Mecca, escaping to Medina to avoid persecution from the Koreish tribemen. Based on a lunar year the Muslim year is 11 days shorter.

*=Leap Year (Christian Calendar)

AH Hejira	AD Christian Date
1010	1601, July 2
1011	1602, June 21
1012	1603, June 11
1013	1604, May 30
1014	1605, May 19
1015	1606, May 19
1016	1607, May 9
1017	1608, April 28
1018	1609, April 6
1017	1608, April 28
1018	1609, April 6
1019	1610, March 26
1020	1611, March 16
1021	1612, March 4
1022	1613, February 21
1023	1614, February 11
1024	1615, January 31
1025	1616, January 20
1026	1617, January 9
1027	1617, December 29
1028	1618, December 19
1029	1619, December 8
1030	1620, November 26
1031	1621, November 16
1032	1622, November 5
1033	1623, October 25
1034	1624, October 14
1035	1625, October 3
1036	1626, September 22
1037	1627, Septembe 12
1038	1628, August 31
1039	1629, August 21
1040	1630, July 10
1041	1631, July 30
1042	1632, July 19
1043	1633, July 8
1044	1634, June 27
1045	1635, June 17
1046	1636, June 5
1047	1637, May 26
1048	1638, May 15
1049	1639, May 4
1050	1640, April 23
1051	1641, April 12
1052	1642, April 1
1053	1643, March 22
1054	1644, March 10
1055	1645, February 27
1056	1646, February 17
1057	1647, February 6
1058	1648, January 27
1059	1649, January 15
1060	1650, January 4
1061	1650, December 25
1062	1651, December 14
1063	1652, December 2
1064	1653, November 22
1065	1654, November 11
1066	1655, October 31
1067	1656, October 20
1068	1657, October 9
1069	1658, September 29
1070	1659, September 18
1071	1660, September 6
1072	1661, August 27
1073	1662, August 16
1074	1663, August 5
1075	1664, July 25
1076	1665, July 14
1077	1666, July 4
1078	1667, June 23
1079	1668, June 11
1080	1669, June 1
1081	1670, May 21
1082	1671, May 10
1083	1672, April 29
1084	1673, April 18
1085	1674, April 7
1086	1675, March 28
1087	1676, March 16*
1088	1677, March 6
1089	1678, February 23
1090	1679, February 12
1091	1680, February 2*
1092	1681, January 21
1093	1682, January 10
1094	1682, December 31
1095	1683, December 20
1096	1684, December 8*
1097	1685, November 28
1098	1686, November 17
1099	1687, November 7
1100	1688, October 26*
1101	1689, October 15
1102	1690, October 5
1103	1691, September 24
1104	1692,September 12*
1105	1693, September 2
1106	1694, August 22
1107	1695, August 12
1108	1696, July 31*
1109	1697, July 20
1110	1698, July 10
1111	1699, June 29
1112	1700, June 18
1113	1701, June 8
1114	1702, May 28
1115	1703, May 17
1116	1704, May 6*
1117	1705, April 25
1118	1706, April 15
1119	1707, April 4
1120	1708, March 23*
1121	1709, March 13
1122	1710, March 2
1123	1711, February 19
1124	1712, Feburary 9*
1125	1713, January 28
1126	1714, January 17
1127	1715, January 7
1128	1715, December 27
1129	1716,December 16*
1130	1717, December 5
1131	1718, November 24
1132	1719, November 14
1133	1720, November 2*
1134	1721, October 22
1135	1722, October 12
1136	1723, October 1
1137	1724, September 19
1138	1725, September 9
1139	1726, August 29
1140	1727, August 19
1141	1728, August 7*
1142	1729, July 27
1143	1730, July 17
1144	1731, July 6
1145	1732, June 24*
1146	1733, June 14
1147	1734, June 3
1148	1735, May 24
1149	1736, May 12*
1150	1737, May 1
1151	1738, April 21
1152	1739, April 10
1153	1740, March 29*
1154	1741, March 19
1155	1742, March 8
1156	1743, Febuary 25
1157	1744, February 15*
1158	1745, February 3
1159	1746, January 24
1160	1747, January 13
1161	1748, January 2
1162	1748,December 22*
1163	1749, December 11
1164	1750, November 30
1165	1751, November 20
1166	1752, November 8*
1167	1753, October 29
1168	1754, October 18
1169	1755, October 7
1170	1756,September 26*
1171	1757, September 15
1172	1758, September 4
1173	1759, August 25
1174	1760, August 13*
1175	1761, August 2
1176	1762, July 23
1177	1763, July 12
1178	1764, July 1*
1179	1765, June 20
1180	1766, June 9
1181	1767, May 30
1182	1768, May 18*
1183	1769, May 7
1184	1770, April 27
1185	1771, April 16
1186	1772, April 4*
1187	1773, March 25
1188	1774, March 14
1189	1775, March 4
1190	1776, February 21*
1191	1777, February 91
1192	1778, January 30
1193	1779, January 19
1194	1780, January 8*
1195	1780,December 28*
1196	1781, December 17
1197	1782, December 7
1198	1783, November 26
1199	1784,November 14*
1200	1785, November 4
1201	1786, October 24
1202	1787, October 13
1203	1788, October 2*
1204	1789, September 21
1205	1790, September 10
1206	1791, August 31
1207	1792, August 19*
1208	1793, August 9
1209	1794, July 29
1210	1795, July 18
1211	1796, July 7*
1212	1797, June 26
1213	1798, June 15
1214	1799, June 5
1215	1800, May 25
1216	1801, May 14
1217	1802, May 4
1218	1803, April 23
1219	1804, April 12*
1220	1805, April 1
1221	1806, March 21
1222	1807, March 11
1223	1808, February 28*
1224	1809, February 16
1225	1810, Febauary 6
1226	1811, January 26
1227	1812, January 16*
1228	1813, Janaury 26
1229	1813, December 24
1230	1814, December 14
1231	1815, December 3
1232	1816,November 21*
1233	1817, November 11
1234	1818, October 31
1235	1819, October 20
1236	1820, October 9*
1237	1821, September 28
1238	1822, September 18
1239	1823, September 18
1240	1824, August 26*
1241	1825, August 16
1242	1826, August 5
1243	1827, July 25
1244	1828, July 14*
1245	1829, July 3
1246	1830, June 22
1247	1831, June 12
1248	1832, May 31*
1249	1833, May 21
1250	1834, May 10
1251	1835, April 29
1252	1836, April 18*
1253	1837, April 7
1254	1838, March 27
1255	1839, March 17
1256	1840, March 5*
1257	1841, February 23
1258	1842, February 12
1259	1843, February 1
1260	1844, January 22*
1261	1845, January 10
1262	1845, December 30
1263	1846, December 20
1264	1847, December 9
1265	1848,November 27*
1266	1849, November 17
1267	1850, November 6
1268	1851, October 27
1269	1852, October 15*
1270	1853, October 4
1271	1854, September 24
1272	1855, September 13
1273	1856, September 1*
1274	1857, August 22
1275	1858, August 11
1276	1859, July 31
1277	1860, July 20*
1278	1861, July 9
1279	1862, June 29
1280	1863, June 18
1281	1864, June 6*
1282	1865, May 27
1283	1866, May 16
1284	1867, May 5
1285	1868, April 24*
1286	1869, April 13
1287	1870, April 3
1288	1871, March 23
1289	1872, March 11*
1290	1873, March 1
1291	1874, February 18
1292	1875, Febuary 7
1293	1876, January 28*
1294	1877, January 16
1295	1878, January 5
1296	1878, December 26
1297	1879, December 15
1298	1880, December 4*
1299	1881, November 23
1300	1882, November 12
1301	1883, November 2
1302	1884, October 21*
1303	1885, October 10
1304	1886, September 30
1305	1887, September 19
1306	1888, September 7*
1307	1889, August 28
1308	1890, August 17
1309	1891, August 7
1310	1892, July 26*
1311	1893, July 15
1312	1894, July 5
1313	1895, June 24
1314	1896, June 12*
1315	1897, June 2
1316	1898, May 22
1317	1899, May 12
1318	1900, May 1
1319	1901, April 20
1320	1902, april 10
1321	1903, March 30
1322	1904, March 18*
1323	1905, March 8
1324	1906, February 25
1325	1907, February 14
1326	1908, February 4*
1327	1909, January 23
1328	1910, January 13
1329	1911, January 2
1330	1911, December 22
1332	1913, November 30
1333	1914, November 19
1334	1915, November 9
1335	1916, October 28*
1336	1917, October 17
1337	1918, October 7
1338	1919, September 26
1339	1920,September 15*
1340	1921, September 4
1341	1922, August 24
1342	1923, August 14
1343	1924, August 2*
1344	1925, July 22
1345	1926, July 12
1346	1927, July 1
1347	1928, June 20*
1348	1929, June 9
1349	1930, May 29
1350	1931, May 19
1351	1932, May 7*
1352	1933, April 26
1353	1934, April 16
1354	1935, April 5
1355	1936, March 24*
1356	1937, March 14
1357	1938, March 3
1358	1939, February 21
1359	1940, February 10*
1360	1941, January 29
1361	1942, January 19
1362	1943, January 8
1363	1943, December 28
1364	1944,December 17*
1365	1945, December 6
1366	1946, November 25
1367	1947, November 15
1368	1948, November 3*
1369	1949, October 24
1370	1950, October 13
1371	1951, October 2
1372	1952,September 21*
1373	1953, September 10
1374	1954, August 30
1375	1955, August 20
1376	1956, August 8*
1377	1957, July 29
1378	1958, July 18
1379	1959, July 7
1380	1960, June 25*
1381	1961, June 14
1382	1962, June 4
1383	1963, May 25
1384	1964, May 13*
1385	1965, May 2
1386	1966, April 22
1387	1967, April 11
1388	1968, March 31*
1389	1969, march 20
1390	1970, March 9
1391	1971, February 27
1392	1972, February 16*
1393	1973, February 4
1394	1974, January 25
1395	1975, January 14
1396	1976, January 3*
1397	1976,December 23*
1398	1977, December 12
1399	1978, December 2
1400	1979, November 21
1401	1980, November 9*
1402	1981, October 30
1403	1982, October 19
1404	1984, October 8
1405	1984,September 27*
1406	1985, September 16
1407	1986, September 6
1409	1987, August 26
1409	1988, August 14*
1410	1989, August 3
1411	1990, July 24
1412	1991, July 13
1413	1992, July 2*
1414	1993, June 21
1415	1994, June 10
1416	1995, May 31
1417	1996, May 19*
1418	1997, May 9
1419	1998, April 28
1420	1999, April 17
1421	2000, April 6*
1422	2001, March 26
1423	2002, March 15
1424	2003, March 5
1425	2004, February 22*
1426	2005, February 10
1427	2006, January 31
1428	2007, January 20
1429	2008, January 10*
1430	2008, December 29
1431	2009, December 18
1432	2010, December 8
1433	2011,November 27*
1434	2012, November 15
1435	2013, November 5
1436	2014, October 25
1437	2015, October 15*
1438	2016, October 3
1439	2017, September 22
1440	2018, September 12
1441	2019,September 11*
1442	2020, August 20
1443	2021, August 10
1444	2022, July 30
1445	2023, July 19*
1446	2024, July 8
1447	2025, June 27
1448	2026, June 17
1449	2027, June 6*
1450	2028, May 25

STANDARD INTERNATIONAL GRADING TERMINOLOGY AND ABBREVIATIONS

U.S. and ENGLISH SPEAKING LANDS	UNCIRCULATED	EXTREMELY FINE	VERY FINE	FINE	VERY GOOD	GOOD	POOR
Abbreviation	UNC	EF or XF	VF	FF	VG	G	PR
BRAZIL	(1) DW	(3) S	(5) MBC	(7) BC	(8)	(9) R	UTGeG
DENMARK	O	01	1+	1	1÷	2	3
FINLAND	0	01	1+	1	1?	2	3
FRANCE	NEUF	SUP	TTB or TB	TB or TB	B	TBC	BC
GERMANY	KFR	II / VZGL	III / SS	IV / S	V / S.g.E.	VI / G.e.	G.e.s.
ITALY	FdS	SPL	BB	MB	B	M	—
JAPAN	未使用	極美品	美品	並品	—	—	—
NETHERLANDS	FDC	Pr.	Z.F.	Fr.	Z.g.	G	—
NORWAY	0	01	1+	1	1÷	2	3
PORTUGAL	Novo	Soberbo	Muito bo	—			
SPAIN	Lujo	SC, IC or EBC	MBC	BC	—	RC	MC
SWEDEN	0	01	1+	1	1?	2	—

BRAZIL

FE — Flor de Estampa
S — Soberba
MBC — Muito Bem Conservada
BC — Bem Conservada
R — Regular
UTGeG — Um Tanto Gasto e Gasto

DENMARK

O — Uncirkuleret
01 — Meget Paent Eksemplar
1+ — Paent Eksemplar
1 — Acceptabelt Eksemplar
1 —Noget Slidt Eksemplar
2 — Darlight Eksemplar
3 — Meget Darlight Eskemplar

FINLAND

00 — Kiitolyonti
0 — Lyontiveres
01 — Erittain Hyva
1+ — Hyva
1? — Keikko
3 — Huono

FRANCE

NEUF — New
SUP — Superbe
TTB — Tres Tres Beau
TB — Tres Beau
B — Beau
TBC — Tres Bien Conserve
BC — Bien Conserve

GERMANY

VZGL — Vorzüglich
SS — Sehr schön
S — Schön
S.g.E. — Sehr gut erhalten
G.e. — Gut erhalten
G.e.S. — Gering erhalten
Schlect

ITALY

Fds — Fior di Stampa
SPL — Splendid
BB — Bellissimo
MB — Molto Bello
B — Bello
M — Mediocre

JAPAN

未使用 — Mishiyo
極美品 — Goku Bihin
美品 — Bihin
並品 — Futuhin

NETHERLANDS

Pr. — Prachtig
Z.F. — Zeer Fraai
Fr. — Fraai
Z.g. — Zeer Goed
G — Good

NORWAY

0 — Usirkuleret eks
01 — Meget pent eks
1+ — Pent eks
1 — Fullgodt eks
1- — Ikke Fullgodt eks
2 — Darlig eks

ROMANIA

NC — Necirculata (UNC)
FF — Foarte Frumoasa (VF)
F — Frumoasa (F)
FBC — Foarte Bine Conservata (VG)
BC — Bine Conservata (G)
M — Mediocru Conservata (POOR)
Schlecht
— Goed

SPAIN

EBC — Extraordinariamente Bien Conservada
SC — Sin Circular
IC — Incirculante
MBC — Muy Bien Conservada
BC — Bien Conservada
RC — Regular Conservada
MC — Mala Conservada

SWEDEN

0 — Ocirkulerat
01 — Mycket Vackert
1+ — Vackert
1 — Fullgott
1? — Ej Fullgott
2 — Dalight

STANDARD INTERNATIONAL NUMERAL SYSTEMS

WESTERN	0	½	1	2	3	4	5	6	7	8	9	10	50	100	500	1000
ROMAN			I	II	III	IV	V	VI	VII	VIII	IX	X	L	C	D	M
ARABIC-TURKISH	٠	١/٢	١	٢	٣	٤	٥	٦	٧	٨	٩	١٠	٥٠	١٠٠	٥٠٠	١٠٠٠
MALAY-PERSIAN	۰	۱/۲	۱	۲	۳	۴	۵	٦ or ۶	۷	۸	۹	۱۰	۵۰	۱۰۰	۵۰۰	۱۰۰۰
EASTERN ARABIC	۰	۱/۲	۱	۲	۳	۴	۵	۶	۷	۸	۹	۱۰	۵۰	۱۰۰	۵۰۰	۱۰۰۰
HYDERABAD ARABIC	۰	۱/۲	۱	۲	۳	۴	۵	۶	۷	۸	۹	۱۰	۵۰	۱۰۰	۵۰۰	۱۰۰۰
INDIAN (Sanskrit)	०	१/२	१	२	३	४	५	६	७	८	९	१०	५०	१००	५००	१०००
ASSAMESE	০	১/২	১	২	৩	৪	৫	৬	৭	৮	৯	১০	৫০	১০০	৫০০	১০০০
BENGALI	০	১/২	১	২	৩	৪	৫	৬	৭	৮	৯	১০	৫০	১০০	৫০০	১০০০
GUJARATI	૦	૧/૨	૧	૨	૩	૪	૫	૬	૭	૮	૯	૧૦	૫૦	૧૦૦	૫૦૦	૧૦૦૦
KUTCH	०	१/२	१	२	३	४	५	६	७	८	९	१०	५०	१००	५००	१०००
DEVAVNAGRI	०	९/२	९	२	३	४	५	६ or ६	७	८	९ or ९	९०	५०	९००	५००	९०००
NEPALESE	०	१/२	१	२	३	४	५	६	७	८	९	१०	५०	१००	५००	१०००
TIBETAN	༠	༡/༢	༡	༢	༣	༤	༥	༦	༧	༨	༩	༡༠	༥༠	༡༠༠	༥༠༠	༡༠༠༠
MONGOLIAN	᠐	᠑/᠒	᠑	᠒	᠓	᠔	᠕	᠖	᠗	᠘	᠙	᠑᠐	᠕᠐	᠑᠐᠐	᠕᠐᠐	᠑᠐᠐᠐
BURMESE	၀	၁/၂	၁	၂	၃	၄	၅	၆	၇	၈	၉	၁၀	၅၀	၁၀၀	၅၀၀	၁၀၀၀
THAI-LAO	๐	๑/๒	๑	๒	๓	๔	๕	๖	๗	๘	๙	๑๐	๕๐	๑๐๐	๕๐๐	๑๐๐๐
JAVANESE	꧐		꧑	꧒	꧓	꧔	꧕	꧖	꧗	꧘	꧙	꧑꧐	꧕꧐	꧑꧐꧐	꧕꧐꧐	꧑꧐꧐꧐
ORDINARY CHINESE JAPANESE-KOREAN	零	半	一	二	三	四	五	六	七	八	九	十	十五	百	百五	千
OFFICIAL CHINESE			壹	貳	叁	肆	伍	陸	柒	捌	玖	拾	拾伍	佰	佰伍	仟
COMMERCIAL CHINESE			〡	〢	〣	〤	〥	〦	〧	〨	〩	十	〥十	〡百	〥百	〡千
KOREAN		반	일	이	삼	사	오	육	칠	팔	구	십	오십	백	오백	천
GEORGIAN			ა	ბ	გ	დ	ე	ვ	ზ	ჱ	თ	ი	ნ	რ	ფ	ჩ
			11 [illegible]	20 კ	30 ლ	40 მ	50 ნ	60 ჲ	70 ო	80 პ	90 ჟ	100 რ	200 ს, 300 ტ	400 უ	600 ქ, 700 ღ	800 ყ
ETHIOPIAN	◆		፩	፪	፫	፬	፭	፮	፯	፰	፱	፲	፶	፻	፭፻	፲፻
				20 ፳	30 ፴	40 ፵		60 ፷	70 ፸	80 ፹	90 ፺					
HEBREW			א	ב	ג	ד	ה	ו	ז	ח	ט	י	נ	ק	תק	
				20 כ	30 ל	40 מ		60 ס	70 ע	80 פ	90 צ		200 ר, 300 ש	400 ת	600 תר, 700 תש	800 תת
GREEK			Α	Β	Γ	Δ	Ε	ΣΤ	Ζ	Η	Θ	Ι	Ν	Ρ	Φ	Α
				20 Κ	30 Λ	40 Μ	60 Ξ	70 Ο	80 Π		200 Σ	300 Τ	400 Υ	600 Χ	700 Ψ	800 Ω

The Islamic Republic of Afghanistan, which occupies a mountainous region of Southwest Asia, has an area of 251,773 sq. mi. (652,090 sq. km.) and a population of 25.59 million. Presently about a fifth of the total population reside mostly in Pakistan in exile as refugees. Capital: Kabul. It is bordered by Iran, Pakistan, Tajikistan, Turkmenistan, Uzbekistan and Peoples Republic of China's Sinkiang Province. Agriculture and herding are the principal industries; textile mills and cement factories are recent additions to the industrial sector. Cotton, wool, fruits, nuts, sheepskin coats and hand-woven carpets are exported but foreign trade has been sporadic since 1979.

Because of its strategic position astride the ancient land route to India, Afghanistan - formerly known as Aryana and Khorasan - was conquered by Darius I, Alexander the Great, various Scythian tribes, the Arabs, the Turks, Genghis Khan, Tamerlane, the Mughals, the Persians, and in more recent times by Great Britain.

It was a powerful empire under the Kushans, Hephthalites, Ghaznavids and Ghorids. The name Afghanistan, *Land of the Afghans,* came into use in the eighteenth and nineteenth centuries to describe the realm of the Afghan kings. Previously this mountainous region was the easternmost frontier of the Iranian world, with strong cultural influences from the Turks and Mongols to the north and India to the south.

The first Afghan king, Ahmad Shah Abdali, founder of the Durrani dynasty, established his rule at Qandahar in 1747. He conquered large territories in India and eastern Iran, which were lost by his grandson Zaman Shah. A new family, the Barakzays, drove the Durrani king out of Kabul in 1819, but the Durranis were not eliminated completely until 1858. Further conflicts among the Barakzays prevented full unity until the reign of 'Abd al-Rahman in 1880. In 1929 a commoner, Baccha-i-Saqao, *Son of the Water-Carrier,* drove King Amanullah from the throne and ruled as Habibullah Ghazi for less than a year before he was defeated by Muhammad Nadir Shah. The last king, Muhammad Zahir Shah, became a constitutional, though still autocratic, monarch in 1964. In 1973 a *coup d'etat* displaced him and created the Republic of Afghanistan. A subsequent military *coup* established the pro-Soviet Khalq Democratic Republic of Afghanistan under Nur Muhammad Taraqi in 1978. Mounting resistance and violence led to the Soviet invasion of late 1979 and the installation of Babrak Kamal as prime minister. A brutal civil war ensued, even after Soviet forces withdrew in 1989 and Kamal's government was defeated in 1992. An unstable coalition of former *Mujahideen* (Freedom Fighters) factions attempted to govern for several years but were gradually overcome by the Taliban, a Muslim fundamentalist force supported from Pakistan. On Sept. 26, 1996 Taliban forces captured Kabul and set up a government under Mohammed Rabbani. Afghanistan was declared a complete Islamic state under Sharia law.

In the Fall of 2001 the continuing revolution came to a head and by December the Taliban government was overthrown with the assistance of the U.S. military and a grand council endorsed the Transitional Authority, which continues to govern the country and is preparing for elections to take place in late 2004.

RULERS:

Amanullah, SH1298-1307/1919-1929AD
Habibullah Ghazi (rebel, known as Baccha-i-Saqao) SH1347-1348/1929AD
Muhammad Nadir Shah, SH1310-1312/1929-1933AD
Muhammad Zahir Shah, SH1312-1352/1933-1973AD

MONETARY SYSTEM:

1 Rupee = 100 Paise to 1925
1 Rupees = 10 Afghani, 1925-
1 Afghani = 100 Pul
1 Amani = 20 Afghani

KINGDOM - PRE-REBELLION

TREASURY

1919-20 ISSUES

#1-5 are encountered w/ and w/o counterfoils at l. Add 20% to market valuations indicated for unissued examples of these notes complete w/counterfoil.

		VG	VF	UNC
1	**1 Rupee** SH1298-99. Green. Uniface. Arms of Kg. Amanullah at r. ctr. Seal on back.			
	a. SH1298 (1919). Red serial #.	4.00	17.50	60.00
	b. SH1299 (1920). Red, black or blue serial #.	2.00	8.00	35.00

		Good	Fine	XF
1A	**1 Rupee** SH1299 (1920). Brown. Arms of Kg. Amanullah at r. ctr. W/o serial #. Back w/o seal Color trial (?). 2 known.	100.	300.	—

		VG	VF	UNC
2	**5 Rupees** ND; SH1298-99. Black on brownish pink unpt. Arms at top ctr. Date on design at l. and r. ctr. Uniface. Back green, purple and tan. Seal.			
	a. SH1298 (1919).	5.00	20.00	65.00
	b. SH1299 (1920).	3.00	10.00	40.00
3	***Deleted.***	—	—	—

		VG	VF	UNC
4	**50 Rupees** SH1298 (1919). Black on green unpt. Arms at top ctr. Uniface.	7.50	30.00	120.

		VG	VF	UNC
5	**100 Rupees** SH1299 (1920). Green and gray. Arms at top ctr. Uniface.	5.00	25.00	90.00

1926-28 ISSUES

#6 and #8-10 back w/French text, w/o additional handstamps. For similar notes w/handstamps see #11-13.

		VG	VF	UNC
6	**5 Afghanis** ND. Lt. brown and gray on pink and lt. green unpt. Arms at top ctr. Back greenish gray.	3.00	8.50	45.00

		VG	VF	UNC
7	**5 Afghanis** SH1305 (1926). Dk. red. Denomination in upper corners.			
	a. Back green, purple and tan.	20.00	60.00	160.
	b. Face green, purple and tan. Back lilac. Toughra at ctr.	20.00	85.00	250.
	c. Uniface. Back lilac.	12.00	30.00	100.
	d. Uniface. Back blue. Rare..			

		VG	VF	UNC
8	**10 Afghanis** ND. Brown w/tan border. Back green; French text at l. on back.	1.00	5.00	25.00

		VG	VF	UNC
9	**10 Afghanis** SH1307 (1928). Black and orange w/green border. Back brown; French text at l. on back. W/ or w/o serial #.			
	a. W/o wmk.	4.00	15.00	60.00
	b. Wmk: Small squares.	3.00	12.50	40.00

		VG	VF	UNC
10	**50 Afghanis** SH1307 (1928). Green, and red w/lt. brown unpt. French text at l., Persian at r. W/ and w/o serial #. Back green.			
	a. W/o wmk.	3.00	8.00	30.00
	b. Wmk: Small squares. Lt. and dk. green varieties.	4.00	17.50	60.00

1928 Rebellion

Baccha I Saqao

1928 Afghani Issue

#11-13 face w/1 validation handstamp and 3 different handstamps on back, one having the date SH1307 (1928).

		Good	Fine	XF
11	**5 Afghanis** SH1307 (1928). Lt. brown and gray on pink and lt. green unpt. National emblem at top ctr. and handstamps. Back greenish gray. Handstamps on #6.	5.00	17.50	90.00

		Good	Fine	XF
12	**10 Afghanis** SH1307 (1928). Brown w/tan border. Handstamps. Back green; French text at l., Persian at r. Handstamps on #8.	4.00	10.00	45.00
13	**50 Afghanis** SH1307 (1928). Green and red w/lt. brown unpt. W/ and w/o serial # and handstamps. Back green. Lt. and dk. green varieties. Handstamps on #10.	3.00	8.00	45.00

1928 Rupee Issue

		Good	Fine	XF
14	**1 Rupee** ND (1928-29). Green on yellow unpt. French text at l. Uniface.			
	a. W/o additional handstamps.	10.00	30.00	75.00
	b. W/additional handstamps similar to #11-13.	13.00	40.00	100.

Kingdom - Post Rebellion

Ministry of Finance

1936 Issues

#15-20 dated SH1315 (1936) w/face in Pashtu and back in Farsi languages. Block letters and serial #.

#15-20A printer: OF-Z.

		Good	Fine	XF
15	**2 Afghanis** SH1315 (1936). Blue and m/c. Emblem at top ctr. Independence Monument at ctr. on back	4.00	12.00	45.00

		Good	Fine	XF
16	**5 Afghanis** SH1315 (1936). Lilac and m/c. Emblem at l, monument a r. Printer: OFZ.	10.00	35.00	90.00
16A	**5 Afghanis** SH1315 (1936). Green and m/c. Emblem at l, monument at r. Like #16.	10.00	35.00	90.00
17	**10 Afghanis** SH1315 (1936). Dk. brown and m/c. Arms at l, monument at r. Printer: OFZ.	15.00	55.00	120.
18	**20 Afghanis** SH1315 (1936). Red-brown and m/c. Arms at l, monument at r. Printer: OFZ.	35.00	90.00	250.

		Good	Fine	XF
19	**50 Afghanis** SH1315 (1936). Blue and m/c. Arms at l., monument at r. Printer: OFZ.	50.00	175.	500.
20	**100 Afghanis** SH1315 (1936). Violet and m/c. Arms at l., monument at r. Printer: OFZ.	75.00	250.	750.

Note: #16-20 w/block letters only. Unc. set $400.00.

ND Issue

#16B, 16C, 17A-20. No date. Face in Farsi and back in Pashtu. Like #16-20. red serial #.

		VG	VF	UNC
16B	**5 Afghanis** ND. Green and m/c. Emblem at l, Independence monument at r. Printer: OFZ.	10.00	35.00	90.00
16C	**5 Afghanis** ND. Green and m/c. Like #16B.	50.00	225.	—
17A	**10 Afghanis** ND. Dk. brown and m/c. Arms at l, monument at r. Printer: OFZ.	10.00	40.00	100.
18A	**20 Afghanis** ND. Red-brown and m/c. Arms at l., monument at r. Printer: OFZ.	20.00	60.00	200.
19A	**50 Afghanis** ND. Blue and m/c. Arms at l., monument at r. Printer: OFZ.	25.00	100.	300.

		VG	VF	UNC
20A	**100 Afghanis** ND. Violet and m/c. Arms at l., monument at r. Printer: OFZ.	40.00	200.	500.

Bank of Afghanistan

1939 Issue

#21-27A Kg. Muhammad Zahir (first portrait). W/o imprint.

		VG	VF	UNC
21	**2 Afghanis** SH1318 (1939). Brown and m/c. Portr. Kg. Muhammad Zahir at l. Colossal Buddha statue at Bamiyan (destroyed by the Taliban) on back.	1.00	3.00	10.00

		VG	VF	UNC
22	**5 Afghanis** SH1318 (1939). Green and m/c. Kg. Muhammad Zahir.	1.00	3.00	10.00
23	**10 Afghanis** SH1318; 1325. Dk. red. Kg. Muhammad Zahir. a. SH1318 (1939).	3.50	7.50	20.00
24	**20 Afghanis** SH1318; 1325. Violet and m/c. Kg. Muhammad Zahir. a. SH1318 (1939).	80.00	350.	—

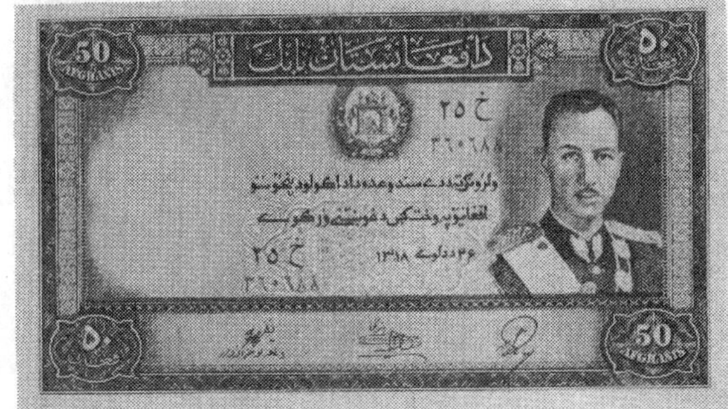

		VG	VF	UNC
25	**50 Afghanis** SH1318; 1325. Blue and m/c. Kg. Muhammad Zahir. a. SH1318 (1939).	7.50	15.00	45.00
26	**100 Afghanis** SH1318; 1325. Dk. green and m/c. Kg. Muhammad Zahir. a. SH1318 (1939).	10.00	25.00	65.00
27	**500 Afghanis** SH1318 (1939). Lilac and m/c. Kg. Muhammad Zahir.	50.00	150.	600.
27A	**1000 Afghanis** SH1318 (1939). Brown, green and m/c. Kg. Muhammad Zahir.	60.00	275.	800.

1948-51 Issues

#28-36 Kg. Muhammad Zahir (second portrait). W/o imprint. Sign. varieties.

		VG	VF	UNC
28	**2 Afghanis** SH1327 (1948). Black, blue and m/c. Kg. Muhammad Zahir. Back black, fortress.	.75	2.00	8.00

		VG	VF	UNC
29	**5 Afghanis** SH1327 (1948). Green and m/c. Kg. Muhammad Zahir. Back green.	.75	2.00	8.00
30	**10 Afghanis** SH1327-36. Greenish brown m/c. Kg. Muhammad Zahir.			
	a. SH1327 (1948).	3.00	10.00	30.00
	b. SH1330 (1951).	2.00	6.00	20.00
	c. SH1333 (1954).	2.00	12.00	35.00
	d. SH1336 (1957).	1.25	4.00	15.00
30A	**10 Afghanis** SH1327 (1948). Brown and m/c. Kg. Muhammad Zahir.	2.00	5.00	12.50

		VG	VF	UNC
31	**20 Afghanis** SH1327-36. Blue and m/c. Kg. Muhammad Zahir.			
	a. SH1327 (1948).	2.50	10.00	35.00
	b. SH1330 (1951).	2.50	15.00	45.00
	c. SH1333 (1954).	2.50	10.00	30.00
	d. SH1336 (1957).	2.00	6.00	27.50
32	**50 Afghanis** SH1327 (1948). Green and m/c. Kg. Muhammad Zahir.	4.00	10.00	30.00

		VG	VF	UNC
33	**50 Afghanis** Kg. Muhammad Zahir. SH 1330-36. Brown and m/c.			
	a. SH1330 (1951).	5.00	15.00	40.00
	b. SH1333 (1954).	6.00	20.00	50.00
	c. SH1336 (1957).	5.00	15.00	35.00

		VG	VF	UNC
34	**100 Afghanis** SH1327-36. Purple and m/c. Kg. Muhammad Zahir. Tomb of Kg. Habibullah in Jalalabad on back.			
	a. SH1327 (1948).	5.00	15.00	90.00
	b. SH1330 (1951).	4.00	15.00	75.00
	c. SH1333 (1954).	4.00	30.00	120.
	d. SH1336 (1957).	3.00	10.00	55.00
35	**500 Afghanis** SH1327; 1336. Blue and green. Kg. Muhammad Zahir.			
	a. SH1327 (1948).	20.00	70.00	275.
	b. SH1333 (1954).	20.00	80.00	300.
	c. SH1336 (1957).	20.00	50.00	200.

		VG	VF	UNC
36	**1000 Afghanis** SH1327 (1948). Brown. Kg. Muhammad Zahir.	35.00	100.	350.

The Republic of Albania, a Balkan republic bounded by the rump Yugoslav state of Montenegro and Serbia, Macedonia, Greece and the Adriatic Sea, has an area of 11,100 sq. mi. (28,748 sq. km.) and a population of 3.5 million. Capital: Tirana. The country is mostly agricultural, although recent progress has been made in the manufacturing and mining sectors. Petroleum, chrome, iron, copper, cotton textiles, tobacco and wood products are exported.

Since it had been part of the Greek and Roman Empires, little is known of the early history of Albania. After the disintegration of the Roman Empire, Albania was overrun by Goths, Byzantines, Venetians and Turks. Skanderbeg, the national hero, resisted the Turks and established an independent Albania in 1443, but in 1468 the country again fell to the Turks and remained part of the Ottoman Empire for more than 400 years.

Independence was re-established by revolt in 1912, and the present borders established in 1913 by a conference of European powers which, in 1914, placed Prince William of Wied on the throne; popular discontent forced his abdication within months. In 1920, following World War I occupancy by several nations, a republic was set up. Ahmet Zogu seized the presidency in 1925, and in 1928 proclaimed himself king with the title of Zog I. King Zog fled when Italy occupied Albania in 1939 and enthroned King Victor Emanuel of Italy. Upon the surrender of Italy to the Allies in 1943, German troops occupied the country. They withdrew in 1944, and communist partisans seized power, naming Gen. Enver Hoxha provisional president. In 1946, following a victory by the communist front in the 1945 elections, a new constitution modeled on that of the USSR was adopted. In accordance with the constitution of Dec. 28, 1976, the official name of Albania was changed from the People's Republic of Albania to the People's Socialist Republic of Albania. A general strike by trade unions in 1991 forced the communist government to resign. A new government was elected in March 1992. In 1997 Albania had a major financial crisis which caused civil disturbances and the fall of the administration.

RULERS:

Ahmet Zogu-King Zog 1, 1928-1939
Vittorio Emanuele III (Italy), 1939-1943.

MONETARY SYSTEM:

1 Lek = 100 Qindar Leku
1 Franga (Franka) Ari = 1 Lek = 100 Qindar Ari to 1946

NOTE: Certain listings encompassing issues circulated by various bank and regional authorities are contained in Vol. 1.

KINGDOM

BANKA KOMBËTARE E SHQIPNIS

BANCA NAZIONALE D'ALBANIA

1925-26 ISSUES

		Good	Fine	XF
1	**5 Lek / 1 Frank AR** ND (1925). Brown and green on m/c unpt. Eagle on shield at lower ctr. Back brown on m/c unpt. Printer: Richter & Co, Naples.			
	a. Issued note.	—	Rare	—

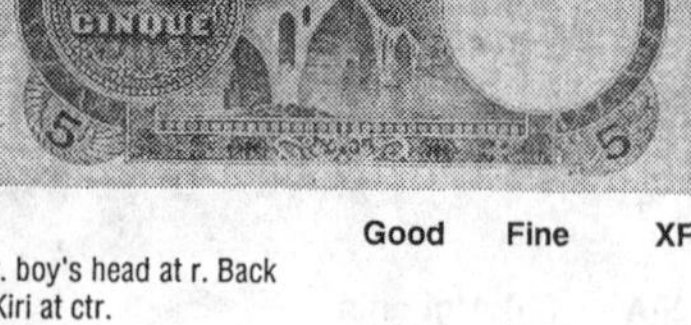

		Good	Fine	XF
2	**5 Franka Ari** ND (1926). Dk. green on m/c unpt. Portr. boy's head at r. Back purple and m/c; Vizirs Bridge over river Kiri at ctr.			
	a. Sign. Alberti. Series A-L.	20.00	60.00	150.
	s. Specimen.			100.

		Good	Fine	XF
3	**20 Franka Ari** ND (1926). Dk. blue on m/c unpt. Portr. youth's head at l. Back red-brown; Drin Bridge and country landscape near Skutari at ctr.			
	a. Issued note.	5.00	25.00	100.
	s. Specimen.	—	Unc	100.

		Good	Fine	XF
4	**100 Franka Ari** ND (1926). Lilac on m/c unpt. Gomsiqe Bridge near Puka at ctr., portr. Kg. A. Zogu at r. Back blue-green and lilac; landscape w/river Drin near Skutari.			
	a. Issued note.	300.	1000.	2500.
	s. Specimen.	—	Unc	225.

ITALIAN OCCUPATION - 1939-42

BANKA KOMBËTARE E SHQIPNIS

BANCA NAZIONALE D'ALBANIA

1939 ND PROVISIONAL ISSUE

		Good	Fine	XF
5	**100 Franka Ari** ND (1939). Lilac on m/c unpt. Lg. black double headed eagle ovpt. on #4 at r. on face.	200.	700.	1350.

Note: many of these notes have been chemically washed.

1939 ND ISSUE

		VG	VF	UNC
6	**5 Franga** ND (1939). Olive-green and blue. Back blue on m/c unpt.; double headed eagle at l. ctr. Wmk: Head of Victor Emanuel III.			
	a. Issued note.	2.50	10.00	75.00
	s. Specimen.			150.

		Good	Fine	XF
7	**20 Franga** ND (1939). Green on olive-green unpt. Seated Roma at bottom ctr., wolf w/Romulus and Remus at r. Back red-brown and m/c; double headed eagle at ctr. Wmk: Victor Emanuel III at l. Skanderbeg at r. Printer: ODBI.	3.00	12.50	50.00

1940 ND ISSUE

		Good	Fine	XF
8	**100 Franga** ND (1940). Lilac-brown on m/c unpt. Peasant woman seated on sheaves w/sickle, green double headed eagle in ctr. Back red-brown and lilac. Printer: ODBI.	7.50	40.00	125.

		VG	VF	UNC
9	**2 Lek** ND (1940). Lilac-blue on orange-brown unpt. Male head at r., crowned arms at l. ctr. Crowned double-headed eagle at l. on back.	5.00	20.00	75.00

		VG	VF	UNC
10	**5 Lek** ND (1940). Blue and black on yellow unpt. Double-headed eagle at bottom ctr. crowned arms at l., Italia at r. and as wmk. Back dk. brown on yellow unpt. Crowned arms at l., female bust at r. Printer: ODBI.	4.00	20.00	65.00

		VG	VF	UNC
11	**10 Lek** ND (1940). Red and black on brown unpt. Double-headed eagle at bottom ctr. Back blue on yellow unpt.; crowned arms at l., Italia at r. Back dk. blue on yellow unpt. Crowned arms at l., female bust at r. Wmk: Victor Emanuel III. Printer: ODBI.	4.00	10.00	35.00

PEOPLES REPUBLIC

BANKA E SHTETIT SHQIPTAR

1945 PROVISIONAL ISSUE

#12-14 new bank name and double headed eagle in rectangular ovpt. on earlier issues of the Banka Kombëtare e Shqipnis.

Note: Ovpt. on #10 and 11 exist; however these are currently considered unofficial.

		Good	Fine	XF
12	**20 Franka Ari**			
	ND (1945). Dk. blue on m/c unpt. Portr. youth's head at l. Ovpt. on #3.			
	a. Prefix A-E.	12.50	75.00	—
	b. Prefix F-J.	5.00	30.00	200.

		Good	Fine	XF
13	**20 Franga**			
	ND (1945). Blue and brown on green unpt. Reclining Roma at bottom ctr., wolf w/Romulus and Remus at r. Ovpt. on #7.	12.50	60.00	150.

		Good	Fine	XF
14	**100 Franga**			
	ND (1945). Lilac-brown. Peasant woman seated on sheaves w/sickle and sheaves at r. Ovpt. on #8.	15.00	70.00	225.

Note: The note previously listed as #15 could not be confirmed as existing.

1945 ISSUE

#16-18A Skanderbeg at l. Arms (eagle) at l. on back.

		VG	VF	UNC
15	**5 Franga**			
	1.5.1945. Green, blue and brown on blue unpt. Back green on m/c unpt.	1.50	5.00	15.00

		VG	VF	UNC
16	**20 Franga**			
	1.5.1945. Dk. blue and brown on m/c unpt. Back dk. blue on m/c unpt.	1.50	5.00	20.00

		VG	VF	UNC
17	**100 Franga**			
	1.5.1945. Brown and green on m/c unpt. Back brown on m/c unpt.	3.00	10.00	25.00

		VG	VF	UNC
18	**500 Franga**			
	1.5.1945. Brown and dk. blue on m/c unpt. Back brown on m/c unpt.	20.00	60.00	160.

Note: The note formerly listed as #18 could not be confirmed as existing.

1947 ISSUE

#19-23 arms (eagle) at l., soldier w/rifle at r.

		VG	VF	UNC
19	**10 Lekë**			
	1947. Brown on m/c unpt. Soldier w/rifle at r.	1.00	4.00	10.00

		VG	VF	UNC
20	**50 Lekë** 1947. Dk. brown on green unpt. Soldier w/rifle at r.	1.50	6.00	20.00

		VG	VF	UNC
21	**100 Lekë** 1947. Violet on m/c unpt. Soldier w/rifle at r.	4.00	15.00	60.00

		VG	VF	UNC
22	**500 Lekë** 1947. Brown on m/c unpt. Arms at l., soldier w/rifle at r.	7.50	32.50	80.00

		VG	VF	UNC
23	**1000 Lekë** 1947. Dk. brown on m/c unpt. Soldier w/rifle at r.	8.00	40.00	175.

1949 ISSUE

		VG	VF	UNC
24	**10 Lekë** 1949. Red and dk. blue on green unpt. Arms at ctr. Back red on green unpt.; arms at r.	1.00	4.00	10.00
25	**50 Lekë** 1949. Dk. blue on green and m/c unpt. Skanderbeg at r. Back dk. blue on green unpt., soldier's head at r.	1.50	5.00	12.50

		VG	VF	UNC
26	**100 Lekë** 1949. Green on m/c unpt. Soldier at l., arms at upper ctr. r.	2.50	7.00	15.00
27	**500 Lekë** 1949. Brown-violet on m/c unpt. Hay harvest scene w/tractor, Peasant woman w/sheaf of wheat at l., arms at r. on back.	3.50	10.00	27.50

		VG	VF	UNC
27A	**1000 Lekë** 1949. Dk brown on m/c unpt. Portr. Skanderbeg at l., oil well derricks at r. Arms at l., miner w/jackhammer at r. on back.	4.50	15.00	65.00

1957 ISSUE

#28-32 like #24-27A. wmk: *BSHSH* within outlines, repeated.

		VG	VF	UNC
28	**10 Lekë** 1957. Red, blue and green. Arms at ctr. Watermark: BSHSH with outlines, repeated.			
	a. Issued note.	.25	.75	2.00
	s. Specimen ovpt: *MODEL.*	—	—	5.00

		VG	VF	UNC
29	**50 Lekë** 1957. Violet on green unpt. Watermark: BSHSH with outlines, repeated. Skanderbeg at r. Arms ctr., soldier at r. on back.			
	a. Issued note.	.35	1.25	4.00
	s. Specimen ovpt: *MODEL.*	—	—	5.00

30	100 Lekë	VG	VF	UNC
	1957. Green. Soldier at l., arms at upper r. ctr. Watermark: BSHSH with outlines, repeated.			
	a. Issued note.	.50	1.75	5.00
	s. Specimen ovpt: *MODEL.*	—	—	6.00

31	500 Lekë	VG	VF	UNC
	1957. Brown-violet. Harvest scene at ctr., Skanderbeg at r. Watermark: BSHSH with outlines, repeated. Peasant woman w/sheaf of wheat at l., arms at r. on back.			
	a. Issued note.	1.00	3.00	10.00
	s. Specimen ovpt: *MODEL.*	—	—	7.50

32	1000 Lekë	VG	VF	UNC
	1957. Violet on m/c unpt. Portr. Skanderbeg at l., oil well derricks at r. Arms at l., miner w/jackhammer at r. Watermark: BSHSH with outlines, repeated.			
	a. Issued note.	1.25	4.00	12.50
	s. Specimen ovpt: *MODEL.*	—	—	8.00

FOREIGN EXCHANGE CERTIFICATES

BANKA E SHTETIT SHQIPTAR

1950 ISSUE

FX1	5 Lek			
	July 1950. Black on orange unpt. Back orange.	—	—	—

1953 ISSUE

		VG	VF	UNC
FX4	**1 Lek** 1953. Brown and red on m/c unpt. Arms at r. Back brown-orange and purple on yellow unpt.; bank seal at ctr.	—	—	3.00
FX5	**5 Lek** 1953. Green and red on m/c unpt. Arms at r. Back green and purple on m/c unpt.; bank seal at ctr.	—	—	3.50
FX6	**10 Lek** 1953. Purple and red on m/c unpt. Arms at r. Back purple on m/c unpt.; bank seal at ctr.	—	—	4.00

		VG	VF	UNC
FX7	**50 Lek** 1953. Black and red on yellow unpt. Arms at r. Back green on orange and yellow unpt.; bank seal at ctr.	—	—	5.00
FX8	**100 Lek** 1953. Brown, purple and red on yellow unpt. Arms at r. Back purple on red and yellow unpt.; bank seal at ctr.	—	—	7.50
FX9	**500 Lek** 1953. Grayish green and red on m/c unpt. Arms at r. Back red on yellow unpt.; bank seal at ctr.	—	—	10.00

Note: A hoard of about 70-80 sets of FX4-FX9 came on the market in the late 1990s.

1956 ISSUE

FX10	1/2 Lek	VG	VF	UNC
	1956. Gray on red-orange unpt. Arms at r. Back pale purple and m/c; bank seal at ctr.	30.00	90.00	175.

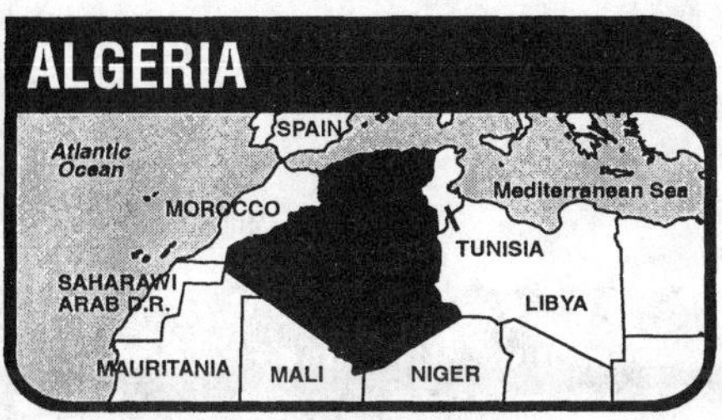

The Democratic and Popular Republic of Algeria, a North African country fronting on the Mediterranean Sea between Tunisia and Morocco, has an area of 919,595 sq. mi. (2,381,741 sq. km.) and a population of 28.6 million. Capital: Algiers (Alger). Most of the country's working population is engaged in agriculture although a recent industrial diversification, financed by oil revenues, is making steady progress. Wines, fruits, iron and zinc ores, phosphates, tobacco products, liquified natural gas, and petroleum are exported.

Algiers, the capital and chief seaport of Algeria, was the site of Phoenician and Roman settlements before the present Moslem city was founded about 950. Nominally part of the sultanate of Tlemcen, Algiers had a large measure of independence under the amirs of its own. In 1492 the Jews and Moors who had been expelled from Spain settled in Algiers and enjoyed an increasing influence until the imposition of Turkish control in 1518. For the following three centuries Algiers was the headquarters of the notorious Barbary pirates. The French took Algiers in 1830, and after a long and wearisome war completed the conquest of Algeria and annexed it to France, 1848. Following the armistice signed by France and Nazi Germany on June 22, 1940, Algeria fell under Vichy Government control until liberated by the Allied invasion forces under the command of Gen. Dwight D. Eisenhower on Nov. 8, 1942. The inability to obtain equal rights with Frenchmen led to an organized revolt which began on Nov. 1, 1954 and lasted until a ceasefire was signed on July 1, 1962. Independence was proclaimed on July 5, 1962, following a self-determination referendum.

RULERS:

French

MONETARY SYSTEM:

1 Franc = 100 Centimes to 1960
1 Nouveau Franc = 100 Old Francs, 1959-64
1 Dinar = 100 Centimes, 1964-

French Administration

Banque de l'Algérie

Alger (Algiers)

1852 Issue

#1-4 held in reserve.

#5 and 6 allegorical male w/ship's rudder and mast w/sail at l., allegorical male w/trident and anchor at r., ancient galleys at upper l. and r.

#	Denomination	Good	Fine	XF
3	**100 Francs** ca. 1852-60. Black. "France" greeting Arab between 2 reclining women at bottom ctr. Proof.	—	—	—
5	**500 Francs** ca. 1852-60. Black. Allegorical male w/ship's rudder and mast w/sail at l., allegorical male w/trident and anchor at r., ancient galleys at upper l. and r. "France" greeting Arab between 2 reclining women at bottom ctr. Proof.	—	—	—
6	**1000 Francs** 16.10.1870. Blue. Allegorical male w/ship's rudder and mast w/sail at l., allegorical male w/trident and anchor at r., ancient galleys at upper l. and r. Medallic caduceus between 2 reclining women at bottom ctr.	—	—	—

1861 Issue

#7-9 held in reserve.

#10 and 11 allegorical male w/ship's rudder and mast w/sail at l., allegorical male w/trident and anchor at r., caduceus between 2 cornucopiae at top ctr.

#	Denomination	Good	Fine	XF
10	**100 Francs** ca. 1861-68. Blue. Allegorical male w/ship's rudder and mast w/sail at l., allegorical male w/trident and anchor at r., caduceus between 2 cornucopiae at top ctr. Ancient galley between 2 reclining women at bottom ctr. Proof.	—	—	—
11	**500 Francs** ca. 1861-68. Blue. Allegorical male w/ship's rudder and mast w/sail at l., allegorical male w/trident and anchor at r., caduceus between 2 cornucopiae at top ctr. Frame for date w/*ALGER* between 2 reclining women at bottom ctr.			
	a. Issued note w/o ovpt.	—	—	—
	b. Ovpt: *Succ. d'Oran.* 26.7.1865.	—	—	—
	c. Ovpt: *Succ de Bone.* 14.4.1868.	—	—	—
	d. Ovpt: *Succ de Constantine.* 4.10.1870; 16.11.1870.	—	—	—

Alger (Algiers)

1868-77 Issue

#12 held in reserve.

Note: For 1000 Francs on 100 Francs 1892, ovpt: *BANQUE DE L'ALGÉRIE* on remainders of Banque de France type (#65b), see Tunisia #31.

#	Denomination	Good	Fine	XF
13	**5 Francs** 31.5.1873. Blue. Mercury at l., peasant at r.	375.	—	—

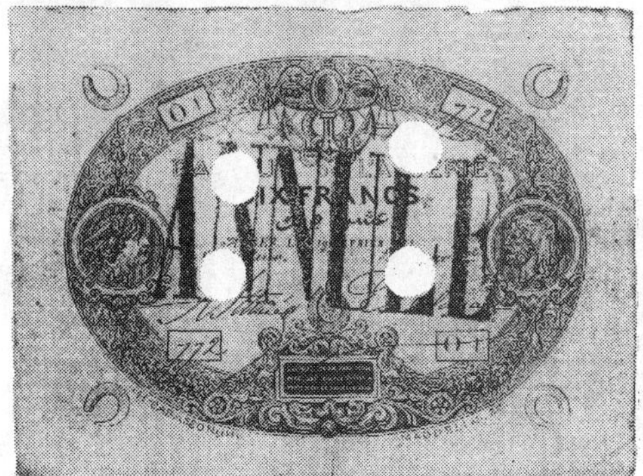

#	Denomination	Good	Fine	XF
14	**10 Francs** 10.2.1871; 15.5.1871; 20.11.1871. Blue. Head at l. and r. Rare.	—	—	—

#	Denomination	Good	Fine	XF
15	**20 Francs** 1873; 22.10.1874; 2.8.1877; 24.8.1887; 27.10.1892. Blue. Mercury at l., Hercules at r.	500.	1000.	2000.
16	**25 Francs** 15.10.1870; 15.10.1872. Blue. Standing figure at l. and r., head at lower ctr. Rare.	—	—	—

		Good	Fine	XF
17	**50 Francs** 1873; 21.6.1877. Blue. Cherubs at lower l. and r., woman's head at bottom ctr. 4 medallic heads on oval band design on back.	500.	1000.	2000.

		Good	Fine	XF
18	**100 Francs** 1874; 1883; 1887; 1892; 1903. Blue. Boy w/oar and hammer at l., boy w/shovel and sickle at r., woman's head between snakes at bottom ctr.	500.	1200.	2500.
19	**500 Francs** 1874; 1903. Blue. Fortuna at l., Mercury at r. Two boys seated at bottom. Rare.	—	—	—
20	**1000 Francs** 1875; 1903. Blue. Woman w/oar at l., blacksmith at r., Two boys w/lion at bottom. Rare.	—	—	—

NOTICE

Readers with unlisted dates, signature varieties, etc. are invited to submit photocopies or, high resolution (300 dpi, 100% size) scans of their notes to: Standard Catalog of World Paper Money, 700 East State St. Iola, WI 54990-0001, or E-Mail: george.cuhaj@fwpubs.com.

Bone

1868-77 Issue

#21-24 held in reserve.

#25 and 27 ovpt: *BONE* and *SUCCURSALE DE BONE.*

		Good	Fine	XF
25	**50 Francs** 14.4.1868. Blue. Rare.	—	—	—

		Good	Fine	XF
27	**100 Francs** 9.8.1877. Blue. Boy w/oar and hammer at l., boy w/shovel and sickle at r., woman's head between snakes at bottom ctr. Punched hole cancelled, ovpt: *ANNULÉ*. Rare.	—	—	—

Constantine

1868-77 Issue

#28-33, 35-37, 39 held in reserve.

#34, 38 and 40 ovpt: *SUCCURSALE DE CONSTANTINE.*

		Good	Fine	XF
34	**50 Francs** 20.9.1870. Blue. Rare.	—	—	—

		Good	Fine	XF
38	**500 Francs** 4.10.1870; 16.11.1870. Blue. Allegorical male w/ship's rudder and mast w/sail at l., allegorical male w/trident and anchor at r., caduceus between 2 cornucopiae at top ctr., frame for date w/*ALGER* between 2 reclining women at bottom ctr. Punched hole cancelled, ovpt: *ANNULÉ*. Rare.	—	—	—

		Good	Fine	XF
40	**1000 Francs** 18.5.1869. Blue. Rare.	—	—	—

ORAN

1861 ISSUE

#41-44, 47-48, 50 held in reserve.

#45, 46 and 49 ovpt: *SUCCURSALE D'ORAN.*

		Good	Fine	XF
45	**50 Francs** 26.7.1864; 26.10.1864. Blue. Rare.	—	—	—

		Good	Fine	XF
46	**100 Francs** 26.10.1861; 8.4.1864. Black. Allegorical male w/ship's rudder and mast w/sail at l., allegorical male w/trident and anchor at r., caduceus between 2 cornucopiae at top ctr., "France" greeting Arab between 2 reclining women at bottom ctr. Punched hole cancelled, ovpt: *ANNULÉ*. Rare.	—	—	—

		Good	Fine	XF
49	**1000 Francs** 11.8.1868. Blue. Allegorical male w/ship's rudder and mast w/sail at l., allegorical male w/trident and anchor at r., ancient galleys at upper l. and r., medallic caduceus between 2 reclining women at ctr. Punched hold cancelled, ovpt: *ANNULÉ*. Rare.	—	—	—

W/O BRANCH

1903-12 ISSUE

#50-70 held in reserve for Philippeville and Tlemcen branches, from which no notes are currently known.

#71-76 like #13, 15, 17-20 but w/o *ALGER* or any branch name ovpt.

		Good	Fine	XF
71	**5 Francs** 1909-25. Blue. Mercury seated at l., peasant seated at r. Facing lion's head at top, medallic head of Mercury at l. and Alexander the Great at r. on back.			
	a. 15.12.1909; 4.7.1911; 12.6.1912; 17.7.1914; 23.11.1914; 2.3.1915.	20.00	80.00	275.
	b. 1.8.1916-17.3.1925.	15.00	60.00	235.

		Good	Fine	XF
72	**20 Francs** July 1903; May 1910. Blue. Mercury at l., Hercules at r.	250.	500.	—

		Good	Fine	XF
73	**50 Francs** 21.3.1903; 2.3.1904; 15-29.4.1910. Blue. Cherubs at lower l. and r., woman's head at bottom ctr. 4 medallic heads on oval band design on back.	100.	300.	600.
74	**100 Francs** 6.3.1907; 18.9.1911; 6.10.1911; 9.10.1911. Blue. Boy w/oar and hammer at l., boy w/shovel and sickle at r., woman's head between snakes at bottom ctr.	65.00	175.	500.

		Good	Fine	XF
75	**500 Francs** 1903-24. Blue. Fortuna at l., Mercury at r., 2 boys seated at bottom.			
	a. 1903; 15.5.1909.	125.	350.	900.
	b. 28.11.1918; 3.12.1918; 24.1.1924; 22.2.1924; 25.2.1924.	75.00	200.	650.
	s. Specimen. 33.5.3091 (sic).	—	Unc	750.

		Good	Fine	XF
76	**1000 Francs** 1903-24. Blue. Woman w/oar at l., blacksmith at r., 2 boys w/lion at bottom.			
	a. 1903; 1909.	300.	600.	1500.
	b. 16.11.1918; 25.11.1918; 28.11.1918; 5.1.1924; 8.2.1924; 25.3.1924; 16.4.1924; 7.5.1924.	100.	250.	650.

ALGER (ALGIERS)

1913-26 ISSUES

77	5 Francs	VG	VF	UNC
	1924-41. Red-orange, blue and m/c. Girl w/kerchief at r. Back blue and m/c; veiled woman w/fruist at ctr. r., whart scene behind. Wmk: draped head of woman.			
	a. Serial # at upper ctr. 1924-15.1.1941.	.50	5.00	30.00
	b. W/o serial #. 24.1.1941-25.9.1941.	.25	2.00	22.50

78	20 Francs	VG	VF	UNC
	1914-42. Dull purple on blue unpt. Portr. young woman at lower r. 2 youths w/plants on back. Wmk: Arabic seal top l., draped head of woman bottom r. 166 x 105mm. 4 sign.			
	a. 9.2.1914-1921.	50.00	250.	—
	b. 17.6.1924-31.5.1932.	2.00	35.00	150.
	c. 1933-13.3.1942.	1.00	6.00	70.00

79	50 Francs	Good	Fine	XF
	1.8.1913; 11.9.1913; 17.9.1913. Violet. Mosque at r., aerial view of city of Algiers at bottom ctr. Child picking fruit from tree, woman seated at ctr. on back. Wmk: Draped head of woman at l., Arabic seal at r.	300.	700.	—

80	50 Francs	VG	VF	UNC
	28.5.1920-1938. Green. Like #79. 3 sign. varieties.			
	a. Issued note.	50.00	100.	300.
	s. Specimen. 1.2.9124 (sic).	—	Unc	225.

81	100 Francs	VG	VF	UNC
	1921-38. Purple and brown on blue unpt. 2 boys at l., Arab w/camel at r.			
	a. 3.1.1921; 22.9.1921;	60.00	200.	—
	b. 1.5.1928-20.10.1938.	30.00	100.	250.

82 **500 Francs**

	VG	VF	UNC
28.6.1926; 2.8.1926; 20.9.1938; 21.9.1938; 25.2.1942. Green and blue-violet on m/c unpt. Girl's head at l., woman w/torch and youth at r. Seated and standing figures w/pictures and landscape in background on back.	40.00	275.	—

83 **1000 Francs**

	VG	VF	UNC
28.6.1926-21.9.1939. Brown-violet. Woman w/sword and child at l. Algerian woman w/child at r. "France" seated w/arm on shoulder of seated Arab woman at upper ctr. on back.			
a. Issued note.	100.	425.	—
s. Specimen. ND.	—	Unc	650.

1938-39 Issue

84 **50 Francs**

	VG	VF	UNC
2.9.1938-19.8.1942. M/c. Veiled woman and man w/red fez at r. City w/ruins of amphitheatre in background on back. Wmk: Woman's head.	1.00	10.00	60.00

85 **100 Francs**

	VG	VF	UNC
3.7.1939-5.3.1942. M/c. Algerian w/turban at l. Plowing w/oxen at ctr. on back. Wmk: Woman's head.	1.50	20.00	90.00

Vichy Government

Banque de l'Algérie

1941 Issue

86 **1000 Francs**

	Good	Fine	XF
17.8.1942; 7.10.1942; 6.11.1942. M/c. French colonial family and field work. Wmk: Woman's head.	15.00	75.00	275.

Note: For #86 w/ovpt.: *TRESOR*, see France #112.

1942 Issue

87 **50 Francs**

	VG	VF	UNC
27.7.1942-3.4.1945. M/c. Like #84. Veiled woman and man w/red fez at r. City w/ruins of amphitheatre in background on back. Wmk. wording: *BANQUE DE L'ALGÉRIE.*	1.25	10.00	65.00

88 **100 Francs**

	VG	VF	UNC
27.3.1942-23.7.1945. M/c. Like #85. Algerian w/turban at l. Plowing w/oxen at ctr. on back. Wmk. wording: *BANQUE DE L'ALGÉRIE.*	1.00	12.50	75.00

89 **1000 Francs**

	Good	Fine	XF
17.8.1942; 7.10.1942; 6.11.1942. M/c. French colonial family and field work. Wmk. wording: *BANQUE DE L'ALGÉRIE.* Like #86.	15.00	75.00	275.

90 **5000 Francs** VG VF UNC
1942. Blue and pink. Young Algerian woman at l., woman w/torch and shield at r. 2 women w/jugs at ctr. on back. Wmk: Ornamental design and head.

	VG	VF	UNC
a. 2.1.1942; 23.1.1942; 20.2.1942; 9.4.1942; 18.5.1942; 22.6.1942; 17.8.1942; 22.8.1942.	200.	500.	—
s. Specimen. 9.4.1942; 26.6.1942.	—	—	650.

Note: For #90 w/ovpt.: *TRESOR*, see France #113.

ALLIED OCCUPATION

BANQUE DE L'ALGÉRIE

1942-43 ISSUE

		VG	VF	UNC
91	**5 Francs** 16.11.1942. Green. Facing woman at r. on back.	.25	1.50	6.50

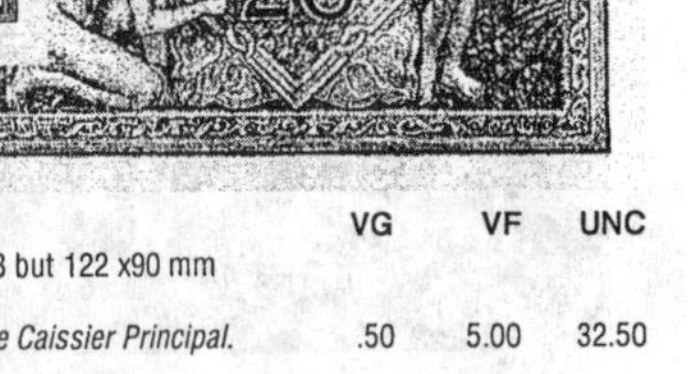

92 **20 Francs**
1942-45. Purple on blue unpt. Similar to #78 but 122 x90 mm w/wmk. wording: *BANQUE de l'ALGÉRIE.*

	VG	VF	UNC
a. Sign. titles: *L'Inspecteur Général* and *Le Caissier Principal.* 11.11.1942-30.5.1944.	.50	5.00	32.50
b. Sign. titles: *Le Caissier Principal* and *Le Secrétaire Général.* 29.11.1944; 2.2.1945; 3.4.1945; 7.5.1945.	.50	6.00	35.00

92A **20 Francs**
17.3.1943. Dk. green w/red and black text. Specimen perforated *SPECIMEN.*

		Good	Fine	XF
93	**500 Francs** 29.3.1943-23.12.1943. Blue and green. 2 boys at l., Bedouin w/camel at r.	10.00	75.00	225.

Note: For #93 w/ovpt: *TRESOR* see France #111.

1944-45 ISSUE

94 **5 Francs**
1944. Red, blue and m/c. Girl w/kerchief at r. Similar to #77 but smaller size.

	VG	VF	UNC
a. Sign. titles: *L'Inspecteur Gal.* and *Le Caissier Pal.* 8.2.1944.	.25	1.00	7.00
b. Sign. titles: *Secret. Gen.* and *Caissier Principal.* 2.10.1944.	.25	1.00	6.50

		Good	Fine	XF
95	**500 Francs** 15.9.1944. Violet. 2 boys at l., Bedouin w/camel at l. Wmk. wording: *BANQUE DE L'ALGÉRIE* repeated. Like #93.	10.00	75.00	225.
96	**1000 Francs** 23.3.1945; 23.5.1945; 23.3.1949. M/c. Woman at l., sailing ship at r. Farmers at l., woman w/Liberty at r. on back.	500.	1500.	—

FRENCH ADMINISTRATION - POST WWII

REGION ECONOMIQUE D'ALGÉRIE

1944 FIRST ISSUE

Law 31.1.1944

#97-99 fig trees at ctr., palm tree at l. and r., 8 coat-of-arms in border on back.

This series was exchangeable until 1.3.1949.

97 **50 Centimes**
L.1944. Red.

	VG	VF	UNC
a. Series letter: C; C1-C4.	.35	1.50	7.50
b. Series letter: F; F1.	.75	3.00	15.00

		VG	VF	UNC
98	**1 Franc** L.1944. Blue to dk blue.			
	a. Series letter: B; B1-B4.	.35	1.50	7.50
	b. Series letter: E; E1.	.75	3.00	15.00

		VG	VF	UNC
99	**2 Francs** L.1944. Dk. green to olive-black.			
	a. Series letter: A; A1-A3.	.50	2.00	10.00
	b. Series letter: D; D1; D2.	1.00	4.00	20.00

1944 Second Issue

#98-102 like #97-99. Fig trees at ctr., palm tree at l. and r. Ovpt: *2e T.* at l., series letter at r. 8 coat-of-arms in border on back.

		VG	VF	UNC
100	**50 Centimes** L.1944. Orange to red.	.40	1.75	8.50

		VG	VF	UNC
101	**1 Franc** L.1944. Blue to dk blue.	.40	1.75	8.50
102	**2 Francs** L.1944. Dk. green.	.50	2.25	11.50

Banque de l'Algérie

1946-48 Issue

		VG	VF	UNC
103	**20 Francs** 4.6.1948. Green. Ornamental design.	1.00	7.50	50.00
104	**1000 Francs** 9.12.1946; 7.2.1947; 18.9.1947; 4.11.1947; 18.11.1947. Brown and yellow. Isis at r.	40.00	150.	350.
105	**5000 Francs** 4.11.1946; 7.10.1949. M/c. Pythian Apollo at l.	40.00	150.	350.

Banque de l'Algérie et de la Tunisie

1949-55 Issue

		VG	VF	UNC
106	**500 Francs** 3.1.1950-8.8.1956. Green and m/c. Ram at ctr., Bacchus at r.	20.00	85.00	275.

		VG	VF	UNC
107	**1000 Francs** 1949-58. Brown and yellow. Isis at r. Like #104.			
	a. 13.10.1949; 22.11.1949; 8.3.1950; 6.7.1950; 20.9.1950; 14.12.1950.	17.50	85.00	250.
	b. 17.4.1953-24.4.1958.	15.00	75.00	225.
108	**5000 Francs** 25.11.1949; 2.2.1950; 15.5.1951. M/c. Pythian Apollo at l., penal code blacked out at bottom ctr. Like #105.	25.00	100.	300.
109	**5000 Francs** 1949-56. M/c. Pythian Apollo at l., penal code shows at bottom ctr. Like #108.			
	a. 7.10.1949; 8.11.1949; 3.5.1950; 20.7.1950; 25.7.1950; 31.7.1950; 15.5.1951; 3.10.1951; 6.11.1951; 12.11.1951.	25.00	100.	300.
	b. 11.2.1952; 20.3.1953; 12.5.1953; 22.6.1953; 1.9.1953; 12.5.1955; 21.6.1955; 1.12.1955; 11.12.1955; 4.1.1956.	25.00	85.00	250.

		VG	VF	UNC
110	**10,000 Francs** 31.1.1955-9.10.1957. Blue and m/c. Audouin's gulls w/city of Algiers in background.	25.00	125.	350.

1960 Provisional Issue

Nouveau franc ovpt. on notes dated 1956-1958.

		VG	VF	UNC
111	**5 NF on 500 Francs** 29.10.1956; 2.11.1956; 13.11.1956. Green and m/c. Ovpt. on #106.	75.00	250.	600.
112	**10 NF on 1000 Francs** 13.5.1958; 27.5.1958; 22.7.1958; 23.7.1958. Brown and yellow. Ovpt. on #107.	75.00	250.	600.

		VG	VF	UNC
113	**50 NF on 5000 Francs** 1.3.1956; 27.2.1956. M/c. Ovpt. on #109.	150.	400.	—

		VG	VF	UNC
114	**100 NF on 10,000 Francs** 22.1.1958-14.3.1958. Blue and m/c. Ovpt. on #110.	150.	400.	—

		VG	VF	UNC
115	**100 Francs** ND. M/c. Like #116. (Not issued).	—	—	1500.

		VG	VF	UNC
116	**500 Francs** 8.2.1956; 17.5.1956. M/c. Head at r. (Not issued).			
	a. Fully printed note.	—	—	1500.
	s. Specimen.	—	—	—

		VG	VF	UNC
117	**500 Francs** 2.1.1958-22.4.1958. Blue-green and m/c. Griffon vulture and Tawny Eagle perched on rock. Native objects and sheep on back.	15.00	75.00	250.
117A	**1000 Francs** ND. M/c. Rare.	—	—	—
117B	**5000 Francs** ND. M/c. Rare.	—	—	—

BANQUE DE L'ALGÉRIE (RESUMED)

1959 ISSUE

		VG	VF	UNC
118	**5 Nouveaux Francs** 1959. Green and m/c. Ram at bottom ctr., Bacchus at r. Like #106.			
	a. 31.7.1959; 18.12.1959.	12.50	75.00	300.
	s. Specimen. 31.7.1959.	—	—	160.

		VG	VF	UNC
119	**10 Nouveaux Francs** 1959-61. Brown and yellow. Isis at r. Like #104.			
	a. 31.7.1959-2.6.1961.	12.50	85.00	325.
	s. Specimen. 31.7.1959.	—	—	165.

		VG	VF	UNC
120	**50 Nouveaux Francs**			
	1959. M/c. Pythian Apollo at l. Like #109.			
	a. 31.7.1959; 18.12.1959.	32.50	165.	500.
	s. Specimen. 31.7.1959.	—	—	375.
121	**100 Nouveaux Francs**			
	1959-61. Blue and m/c. Seagulls w/city of Algiers in background. Like #110.			
	a. 31.7.1959; 18.12.1959.	60.00	200.	550.
	b. 3.6.1960; 25.11.1960; 10.2.1961; 29.9.1961.	20.00	100.	375.
	s. Specimen. 31.7.1959.	—	—	175.

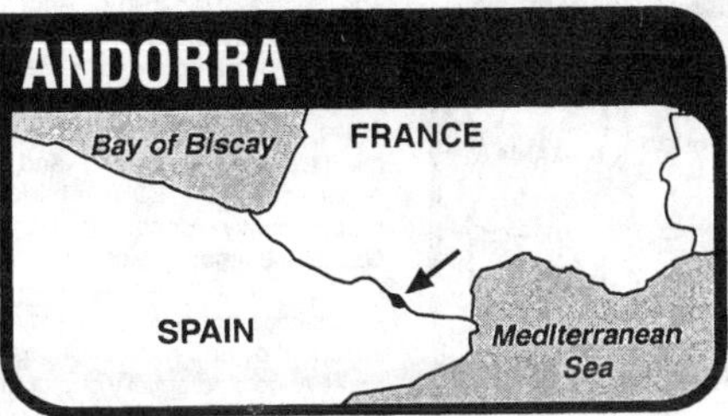

Andorra (Principal d' Andorra), previously an autonomous co-principality that became a sovereign nation with a constitution in May 1993. It is situated on the southern slopes of the Pyreness Mountains between France and Spain, has an area of 175 sq. mi. (453 sq. km.) and a population of 80,000. Capital: Andorra la Vella. Tourism is the chief source of income. Timber, cattle and derivatives, and furniture are exported.

According to tradition, the independence of Andorra derives from a charter Charlemagne granted the people of Andorra in 806 in recognition of their help in battling the Moors. An agreement between the Court of Foix (France) and the Bishop of Seo de Urgel (Spanish) in 1278 to recognize each other as Co-Princes of Andorra gave the state what has been its politcal form and territoral extent continously to the present day. Over the years, the title on the French side passed to the Kings of Navarre, then to the Kings of France, and is now held by the President of France. In 1806, Napoleon declared Andorra a republic, but today it is referred to as a principality.

During the Spanish Civil War, there was an issue of emergency money in the Catalan language.

MONETARY SYSTEM:

1 Pesseta (Catalan) = 100 Centims

1936 Spanish Civil War

Consell General de les Valls d'Andorra

Decret No. 112 - 1936 First Issue

#1-9 arms at top ctr.

		VG	VF	UNC
1	**1 Pesseta** 19.12.1936. Blue.	150.	450.	1250.
2	**2 Pessetes** 19.12.1936. Blue.	175.	550.	1500.

		VG	VF	UNC
3	**5 Pessetes** 19.12.1936. Blue.	200.	650.	1800.
4	**10 Pessetes** 19.12.1936. Blue.	300.	850.	2500.

1936 Second Issue

		VG	VF	UNC
5	**50 Centims** 19.12.1936. Brown.	35.00	100.	350.
6	**1 Pesseta** 19.12.1936. Brown.	35.00	100.	350.
7	**2 Pessetes** 19.12.1936. Brown.	125.	375.	1000.
8	**5 Pessetes** 19.12.1936. Brown.	175.	550.	1500.

		VG	VF	UNC
9	**10 Pessetes** 19.12.1936. Brown.	225.	700.	2000.

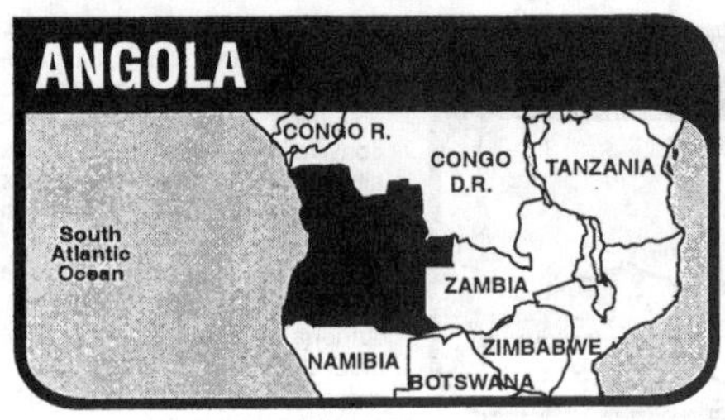

The Peoples Republic of Angola, a country on the west coast of southern Africa bounded by Zaïre, Zambia and Namibia (South-West Africa), has an area of 481,354 sq. mi. (1,246,700 sq. km.) and a population of 12.78 million, predominantly Bantu in origin. Capital: Luanda. Most of the people are engaged in subsistence agriculture. However, important oil and mineral deposits make Angola potentially one of the richest countries in Africa. Iron and diamonds are exported.

Angola was discovered by Portuguese navigator Diogo Cao in 1482. Portuguese settlers arrived in 1491, and established Angola as a major slaving center which sent about 3 million slaves to the New World.

A revolt against Portuguese rule, characterized by guerrilla warfare, began in 1961 and continued until 1974, when a new regime in Portugal offered independence. The independence movement was actively supported by three groups, the National Front, d in Zaïre, the Soviet-backed Popular Movement, and the moderate National Union. Independence was proclaimed on Nov. 11, 1975.

RULERS:

Portuguese

MONETARY SYSTEM:

1 Milreis = 1000 Reis = 20 Macutas to 1911
100 Centavos - 1 Escudo, 1911
1 Escudo = 1 Milreis
1 Escudo = 100 Centavos, 1954-77
1 Kwanza = 100 Lwei, 1977-95
1 Kwanza Reajustado = 1,000 "old" Kwanzas, 1995-

SIGNATURE VARIETIES

STEAMSHIP SEALS

Type I	Type II	Type III
LOANDA	LISBOA	C,C,A

C,C,A = Colonias, Commercio, Agricultura.

PORTUGUESE ADMINISTRATION

JUNTA DA FAZENDA PUBLICA DA PROVINCIA D'ANGOLA

1861 ISSUE

#1-4 Various date and sign. varieties.

		Good	Fine	XF
1	**1000 Reis** Arms at top ctr., legend ends: ...*D'ANGOLA*. 1.7.1861; 13.9.1867. Black.	—	—	—
2	**2000 Reis** 1.7.1861. Red. Arms at top ctr., legend ends: ...*D'ANGOLA*.	—	—	—
3	**5000 Reis** 1861. Black. Arms at top ctr., legend ends: ...*D'ANGOLA*.	—	—	—
4	**20,000 Reis** 1861. Black. Arms at top ctr., legend ends: ...*D'ANGOLA*.	—	—	—

1877-84 ISSUE

#5-9 Various date and sign. varieties.

		Good	Fine	XF
5	**1000 Reis** 1.10.1884. Black on gray unpt. Arms at top ctr., legend ends: ...*DE ANGOLA*.	—	—	—
6	**2000 Reis** Arms at top ctr., legend ends: ...*DE ANGOLA*.	—	—	—
7	**5000 Reis** Arms at top ctr., legend ends: ...*DE ANGOLA*. Black.	—	—	—
8	**10,000 Reis** Arms at top ctr., legend ends: ...*DE ANGOLA*. Black.	—	—	—

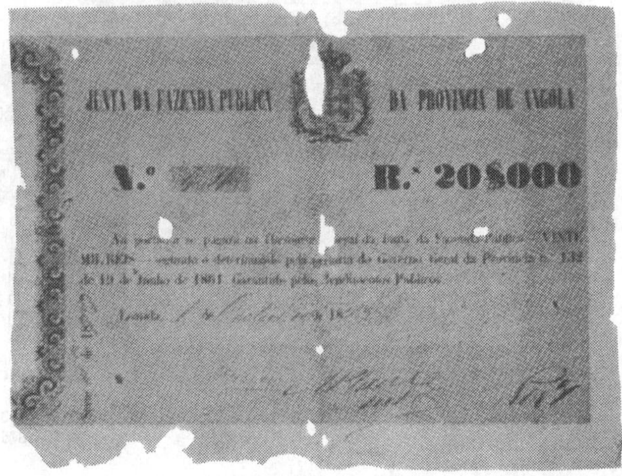

		Good	Fine	XF
9	**20,000 Reis** 1.10.1877. Black on blue unpt. Arms at top ctr., legend ends: ...*DE ANGOLA*.	—	—	—

BANCO NACIONAL ULTRAMARINO

1865 ISSUE

#10-12 Various date and sign varieties.

		Good	Fine	XF
10	**5000 Reis** 1865. Black. Sailing ship at top ctr. *Succursal* (Branch) *em LOANDA*	—	—	—

		Good	Fine	XF
11	**10,000 Reis** 7.7.1865. Black. Sailing ship at top ctr. *Succursal* (Branch) *em LOANDA*	—	—	—
12	**20,000 Reis** 1865. Black. Sailing ship at top ctr. *Succursal* (Branch) *em LOANDA*	—	—	—

1876-77 ISSUE

#13-15 Various date and sign. varieties.

		Good	Fine	XF
13	**1000 Reis** 1876. Black. Sailing ship at top ctr.	—	—	—

		Good	Fine	XF
14	**2000 Reis** 1.6.1877. Black. Sailing ship at top ctr.	—	—	—
15	**2500 Reis** 1876. Black. Sailing ship at top ctr.	—	—	—

1878-90 Issue

#16-20 Various date and sign. varieties.

		Good	Fine	XF
16	**1000 Reis** 1878-90. Black. Sailing ship at top ctr.	—	—	—

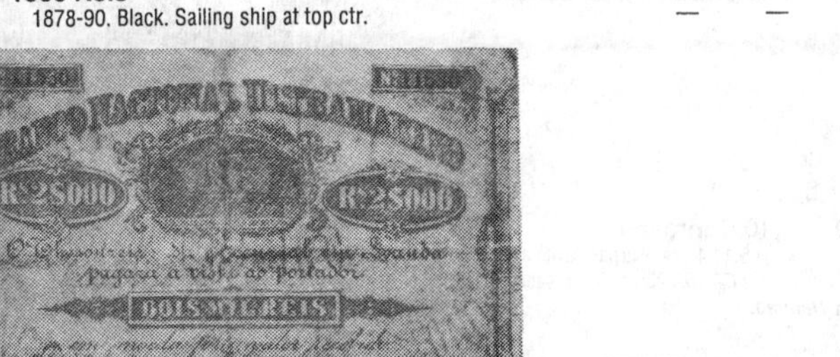

		Good	Fine	XF
17	**2000 Reis** 21.3.1888. Green. Sailing ship at top ctr.	—	—	—

		Good	Fine	XF
18	**5000 Reis** 1878-90. Sailing ship at top ctr.			
	a. Issued note.	—	—	—
	b. W/2 oval handstamps: *Cobre 1896.* (-old date 30.6.1880).	—	—	—
19	**10,000 Reis** 1878-90. Sailing ship at top ctr.	—	—	—
20	**20,000 Reis** 28.1.1890. Gray-green. Sailing ship at top ctr. Similar to #14.	—	—	—

1892 Emergency Issue

Issued because of small change shortages. Redeemed in 1905.

#20A-20C crowned arms at upper ctr.

		Good	Fine	XF
20A	**100 Reis** 1892; 1893; 1895. Black on red-brown unpt.	150.	450.	—
20B	**200 Reis** 1892; 1893; 1895. Red on green unpt.	—	—	—
20C	**500 Reis** 1892; 1893; 1895. Blue on ivory unpt.	—	—	—

1897-1905 Issue

#21-24 various date and sign. varieties.

		Good	Fine	XF
21	**1000 Reis** 2.1.1897. Green. Man w/bow and arrow at l., ship at top ctr.	—	—	—

		Good	Fine	XF
22	**2500 Reis** 20.2.1905. Gray-blue. Sailing ship at l., landscape at ctr.	—	—	—

		Good	Fine	XF
23	**5000 Reis** 2.1.1897. Purple. Woman seated, sailing ship at ctr r.	—	—	—

		Good	Fine	XF
24	**10,000 Reis** 20.2.1905. Lilac. Woman seated at l., sailing ship at ctr., Mercury at r.	—	—	—

1909 Provisional Issue

		Good	Fine	XF
25	**2500 Reis** 1.3.1909. Red ovpt: *Pagavel na Filial de Loanda* on St. Thomas and Prince #8a.	—	—	—
26	**5 Mil Reis** 1.3.1909.	—	—	—

1909 Regular Issues

#27-38 ovpt: *LOANDA*. Printer: BWC.

Note: For provisional 2500 Reis see #25, for provisional 5 Mil Reis see #26.

		Good	Fine	XF
27	**1000 Reis** 1.3.1909. Green and yellow unpt. Steamship seal Type I.	150.	450.	—
28	**1000 Reis** 1.3.1909. Green and yellow unpt. Steamship seal Type III.	150.	450.	—

#29-38 portr. Vasco da Gama at l., arms at upper ctr. steamship seal below. Seated allegorical woman looking out at ships on back.

		Good	Fine	XF
29	**2500 Reis** 1.3.1909. Black on m/c unpt. Portr. Vasco da Gama at l. Seated allegorical woman looking out at ships. Steamship seal Type I. Sailing ships at r.	175.	550.	—
30	**2500 Reis** 1.3.1909. Black on m/c unpt. Portr. Vasco da Gama at l. Seated allegorical woman looking out at ships. Steamship seal Type III.	200.	550.	—
31	**5 Mil Reis** 1.3.1909. Black on m/c unpt. Steamship seal Type I. Vasco da Gama at l. Seated allegorical woman looking out at sailing ships at ctr. Printer: BWC. Sailing ships at r.	200.	700.	—
32	**5 Mil Reis** 1.3.1909. Black on m/c. Portr. Vasco da Gama at l. Seated allegorical woman looking out at ships. Steamship seal Type III.	200.	700.	—
33	**10 Mil Reis** 1.3.1909. Black on m/c unpt. Portr. Vasco da Gama at l. Seated allegorical woman looking out at ships. Steamship seal Type I. Sailing ships at r.	200.	800.	—
34	**10 Mil Reis** 1.3.1909. Black on m/c unpt. Portr. Vasco da Gama at l. Seated allegorical woman looking out at ships. Steamship seal Type III.	200.	800.	—

		Good	Fine	XF
35	**20 Mil Reis** 1.3.1909. Black on m/c unpt. Portr. Vasco da Gama at l. Seated allegorical woman looking out at ships. Steamship seal Type I. Harbor scene at r.	225.	950.	—
36	**20 Mil Reis** 1.3.1909. Black on m/c unpt. Portr. Vasco da Gama at l. Seated allegorical woman looking out at ships. Steamship seal Type III.	225.	950.	—
37	**50 Mil Reis** 1.3.1909. Black-green on m/c unpt. Portr. Vasco da Gama at l. Seated allegorical woman looking out at ships. Steamship seal Type I. Harbor scene at r.	300.	1250.	—
38	**50 Mil Reis** 1.3.1909. Black-green on m/c unpt. Portr. Vasco da Gama at l. Seated allegorical woman looking out at ships. Steamship seal Type III.	300.	1250.	—

1914 Issues

#39-46 arms at r., steamship seal at lower ctr. Seated allegorical woman looking out at ships on back. Printer: BWC.

		Good	Fine	XF
39	**10 Centavos** 5.11.1914. Purple. Arms at r. Printer: BWC. Steamship seal Type II.			
	a. Black ovpt: *LOANDA* 28mm long; letters w/serifs.	7.00	50.00	175.
	b. Green ovpt: *LOANDA* 23mm long; sans-serif letters.	7.00		

		Good	Fine	X
40	**10 Centavos** 5.11.1914. Purple. Arms at r. Steamship seal Type III. Green ovpt: *LOANDA* 23mm long; sans-serif letters.	7.00	40.00	10

#41 *Deleted.*

		Good	Fine	X
42	**20 Centavos** 5.11.1914. Blue. Arms at r. BWC.Steamship seal Type II.			
	a. Black ovpt: *LOANDA* 28mm long; letters w/serifs.	7.50	50.00	17
	b. Red ovpt: *LOANDA* 23mm long; sans-serif letters.	7.50	40.00	10

		Good	Fine	X
43	**20 Centavos** 5.11.1914. Blue. Red ovpt: *LOANDA* 23mm long; sans-serif letters.Steamship seal Type III.	5.00	40.00	10

#44 *Deleted.*

		Good	Fine	X
45	**50 Centavos** 5.11.1914. Green. Arms at r. Printer: BWC. Black ovpt: *LOANDA* 28mm long; letters w/serifs.Steamship seal Type II.	7.50	40.00	11

		Good	Fine	X
46	**50 Centavos** 5.11.1914. Green. Arms at r. BWC.Steamship seal Type III.			
	a. Blue ovpt: *LOANDA* 28mm long; letters w/serifs.	10.00	50.00	12
	b. Red ovpt: *LOANDA* 23mm long; sans-serif letters.	7.50	35.00	95.0

1914 Provisional Issues

#47 and 48 printer: BWC.

		Good	Fine	X
47	**50 Centavos** 5.11.1914. Green. Arms at r. Printer: BWC.	40.00	350.	—
48	**50 Centavos** 5.11.1914. Green. Arms at r. Steamship seal Type II w/ovpt: *LOANDA* over *S. THOME* on St. Thomas and Prince #18. BWC.	55.00	400.	—

1918 ISSUE

#49-50 design of steamship seal Type II at ctr. on back.

		Good	Fine	XF
49	**5 Centavos** 19.4.1918. Gray-green on yellow unpt. Design similar to Steamship seal Type II at r.	10.00	40.00	175.
50	**20 Centavos** 19.4.1918. Brown on yellow-orange unpt. Pillar at l. and r., seated woman at r.	50.00	350.	—

1920 ISSUE

#51-53 ovpt: *ANGOLA*.

		Good	Fine	XF
51	**10 Centavos** 1.1.1920. Red. Ship at l. and r.	40.00	250.	—
52	**20 Centavos** 1.1.1920. Green. Angels at l. and r.	60.00	350.	—
53	**50 Centavos** 1.1.1920. Blue. Mercury at l., allegory at r. Back brown; ship at ctr.	60.00	350.	—
54	**50 Escudos** 1.1.1920. Blue on lt. green unpt. Arms at upper ctr. Back brown on gold unpt.; lake and trees at ctr.	—	—	—

Note: #54 is known as the "Porto Issue" as the notes were printed there.

1921 ISSUE

#55-61 portr. Francisco de Oliveira Chamico at l., arms at bottom ctr., steamship seal at r. Back like #27-38.

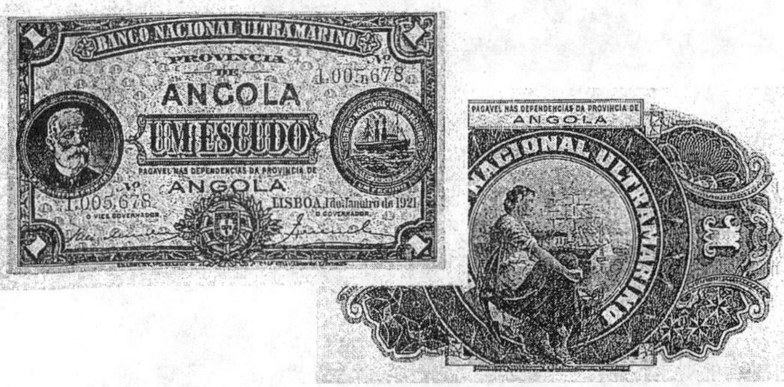

		Good	Fine	XF
55	**1 Escudo** 1.1.1921. Green. Portr. Francisco de Oliveira Chamico at l., steamship at r. Seated allegorical woman looking out at ships. Printer: BWC Steamship seal Type III.	10.00	50.00	175.
56	**2.50 Escudos** 1.1.1921. Blue. Portr. Francisco de Oliveira Chamico at l., steamship at r. Seated allegorical woman looking out at ships. Printer: TDLR. Steamship seal Type III.	20.00	125.	400.
57	**5 Escudos** 1.1.1921. Dk. green. Portr. Francisco de Oliveira Chamico at l., steamship at r. Seated allegorical woman looking out at ships. Printer: BWC. Steamship seal Type III.	20.00	125.	400.
58	**10 Escudos** 1.1.1921. Brown. Portr. Francisco de Oliveira Chamico at l., steamship at r. Seated allegorical woman looking out at ships. Printer: BWC. Steamship seal Type III.	45.00	225.	575.

		Good	Fine	XF
59	**20 Escudos** 1.1.1921. Blue. Portr. Francisco de Oliveira Chamico at l., steamship at r. Seated allegorical woman looking out at ships. Printer: BWC. Steamship seal Type III.	50.00	250.	650.
60	**50 Escudos** 1.1.1921. Lt. Brown. Portr. Francisco de Oliveira Chamico at l., steamship at r. Seated allegorical woman looking out at ships. Printer: BWC Steamship seal Type II.	175.	675.	—
61	**100 Escudos** 1.1.1921. Green. Portr. Francisco de Oliveira Chamico at l., steamship at r. Seated allegorical woman looking out at ships. Printer: BWC Steamship seal Type III.	250.	850.	—

REPUBLICA PORTUGUESA - ANGOLA

1921 ISSUE

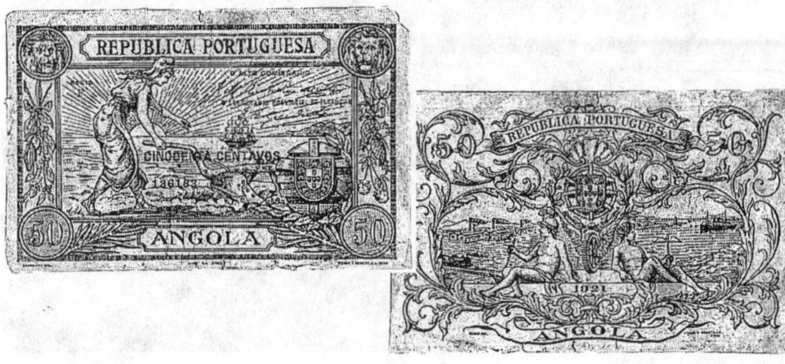

		VG	VF	UNC
62	**50 Centavos** 1921. Gray on lt. brown unpt. Woman plowing at l. ctr., arms at lower r. Allegories of Industry at l., Navigation at r., arms at ctr. on back.	5.00	40.00	125.

1923 ISSUE

		VG	VF	UNC
63	**50 Centavos** 1923. Brown w/red text at ctr. Dock scene at l., woman seated holding wreath at r. Explorers at shoreline on back.	4.00	15.00	100.

PROVINCIA DE ANGOLA - JUNTA DA MOEDA

DECREE NO. 12.124 OF 14.8.1926

#64-66 sign. varieties. Printer: TDLR.

		Good	Fine	XF
64	**1 Angolar** D.1926. Green. Portr. Diogo Cao at lower l., plants at r. Waterbuck head at ctr. on back.	6.00	40.00	135.

		Good	Fine	XF
65	**2 1/2 Angolares** D.1926. Purple. Portr. Paulo Dias de Novaes at lower l., palms at r. Black rhinoceros at ctr. on back.	10.00	95.00	275.

		Good	Fine	XF
66	**5 Angolares** D.1926. Red-brown. Portr. Paulo Dias de Novaes at l., palms at r. Elephant at ctr., on back.	40.00	225.	500.

		Good	Fine	XF
67	**10 Angolares** D.1926. Blue. 2 people weaving and spinning at l. ctr., bridge and mountain at r. Lion at ctr. on back.	60.00	325.	725.

PROVINCIA DE ANGOLA - GOVERNO GERAL DE ANGOLA

DECREE NO. 31.942 OF 28.3.1942

#68 and 69 printer: TDLR.

		Good	Fine	XF
68	**1 Angolar** D.1942. Green. Portr. Diogo Cao at lower l. Waterbuck head at ctr. on back. Like #64.	4.00	25.00	110.

		Good	Fine	XF
69	**2 1/2 Angolares** D.1942. Purple. Portr. Paulo Dias de Novaes at lower l. Rhinoceros at ctr. on back. Like #65. TDLR.	7.50	35.00	130.

COMMEMORATIVE ISSUE

DECREE NO. 37.086 OF 6.10.1948

300th Anniversary Restoration of Angola to Portuguese Rule 1648-1948

		VG	VF	UNC
70	**1 Angolar** D.1948. Green. Landing boat, seamen and sailing ships at l. ctr. Waterbuck head at ctr. on back.	15.00	75.00	225.

		VG	VF	UNC
71	**2 1/2 Angolares** D.1948. Purple. Bombardment of fortress. Rhinoceros at ctr. on back.	20.00	100.	300.

BANCO DE ANGOLA

1927 ISSUE

#72-76 portr. Salvador Correia at ctr. (#72-74A) or at l. (#75-76). Sign. title varieties. Printer: TDLR.

		Good	Fine	XF
72	**20 Angolares** 1.6.1927. Red on blue unpt. Jungle river. Hippo at ctr. on back.	80.00	325.	850
73	**20 Angolares** 1.6.1927. Dk. brown on green unpt. Like #72. Jungle river. Hippo at ctr. on back.	70.00	300.	825
74	**50 Angolares** 1.6.1927. Purple on rose unpt. Waterfall. Leopard on back.	125.	575.	1250
74A	**50 Angolares** 1.6.1927. Purple on green unpt. Like #74. Waterfall. Back brown-violet; leopard.	125.	575.	1250

		Good	Fine	XF
75	**100 Angolares** 1.6.1927. Green on blue unpt. Flamingos. Crocodile on back.	200.	1000.	

		Good	Fine	XF
76	**500 Angolares** 1.6.1927. Blue on green unpt. Shoreline with palm trees. Eagle on back.			
	a. Issued note.	—	—	
	s. Specimen.	—	—	

944-46 Issue

		VG	VF	UNC
7	**5 Angolares** 1.1.1947. Brown on yellow unpt. 3 men at l., Portr. Gen. Carmona at r. Back green; 2 women at l., small monument at r. Printer: W&S.	8.00	50.00	200.

		VG	VF	UNC
8	**10 Angolares** D.14.8.1946 (1.6.1947). Dk. blue and dk. brown. Portr. Padre A. Barroso at r., children at l. Back dk. blue; *Treaty of Simalambuco 1885.*	12.50	100.	300.

9-82 printer: TDLR.

		Good	Fine	XF
	20 Angolares 1.12.1944. Lilac. Man standing at l., portr. Correia at r., fortress at ctr. Back w/*Reconquest of Luanda 1648.*	17.50	110.	275.
	50 Angolares 1.10.1944. Green. Portr. Pereira at r. Back w/*Founding of Benguela 1617.*	40.00	225.	500.
	100 Angolares 2.12.1946. Blue. Portr. Sousa Coutinho at r., arms at lower ctr. European explorers and Africans on back.	75.00	275.	625.
	1000 Angolares 1.6.1944. Carmine, blue and m/c. Portr. Joao II at r. Back purple; return of Diogo Cao, 1489.			
	a. Issued note.	—	—	—
	s. Specimen.			

51-52 Issue

		Good	Fine	XF
	20 Angolares 1.3.1951. Lilac. Like #79. Portr. Correia at r., fortress at ctr. Back w/*Reconquest of Luanda 1648.* Printer: TDLR.	12.50	100.	300.
	50 Angolares 1.3.1951. Green. Like #80. Portr. Pereira at r. *Founding of Benguela 1617* on back.	30.00	200.	450.
	100 Angolares 1.3.1951. Red-brown and deep blue. Like #81. Portr. Sousa Coutinho at r. European explorers and Africans on back.	50.00	250.	575.

		Good	Fine	XF
86	**1000 Angolares** 1.3.1952. Carmine. Portr. Joao II at r. Purple. *Return of Diogo Cao, 1489.* Printer: TDLR			
	a. Issued note.	—	—	—
	s. Specimen.			

1956 Issue

Escudo System

#87-91 sign. varieties. Printer: TDLR.

		VG	VF	UNC
87	**20 Escudos** 15.8.1956. Lilac on m/c. Portr. Porto at r., dock at l. Back red-brown; gazelle running.	1.50	4.00	20.00

		VG	VF	UNC
88	**50 Escudos** 15.8.1956. Green on m/c. Portr. H. de Carvalho at r., airport at l. Wildebeest herd at waterhole on back.			
	a. Issued note.	2.00	9.00	50.00
	s. Specimen.	—	—	—

		VG	VF	UNC
89	**100 Escudos** 15.8.1956. Blue on m/c unpt. Portr. S. Pinto at r., Salazar Bridge at l. Printer: TDLR. Back purple; elephants at waterhole.			
	a. Issued note.	3.00	20.00	150.
	s. Specimen.	—	—	—

90	500 Escudos	VG	VF	UNC
	Printer: TDLR. 15.8.1956. Orange on blue unpt. Portr. R. Ivens at l., Port of Luanda at ctr. Back purple, 2 rhinoceros at ctr.	12.50	100.	400.

91	1000 Escudos	VG	VF	UNC
	Printer: TDLR. 15.8.1956. Brown on m/c unpt. Portr. B. Capelo at r., dam at l. ctr. Back black; sable herd at ctr.	22.50	150.	500.

The Argentine Republic, located in South America, has an area of 1,068,301 sq. mi. (2,766,889 sq. km.) and a population of 37.03 million. Capital: Buenos Aires. Its varied topography ranges from the subtropical lowlands of the north to the towering Andean Mountains in the west and the windswept Patagonian steppe in the south. The rolling, fertile pampas of central Argentina are ideal for agriculture and grazing, and support most of the republic's population. Meat packing, flour milling, textiles, sugar refining and dairy products are the principal industries. Oil is found in Patagonia, but most of the mineral requirements must be imported.

Argentina was discovered in 1516 by the Spanish navigator Juan de Solis. A permanent Spanish colony was established at Buenos Aires in 1580, but the colony developed slowly. When Napoleon conquered Spain, the Argentines set up their own government in the name of the Spanish king on May 25, 1810. Independence was formally declared on July 9, 1816.

REPLACEMENT NOTES:

#260d onward: *R* prefix before serial #. Note: The listings encompassing issues circulated by various bank and regional authorities are contained in Volume 1.

L. 1883 FIRST ISSUE

#1-4 printer: R. Lange, Buenos Aires. Sign. varieties.

1	5 Centavos	Good	Fine	XF
	1.1.1884. Black on gray unpt. Nicolás Avellaneda at l., arms at upper r. ctr. Green. Printer: R. Lange. Buenos Aires.	7.50	22.50	75.00

2	10 Centavos	Good	Fine	XF
	1.1.1884. Black on pink and yellow unpt. Arms at lower l., portr. Domingo Sarmiento at r. Brown. Liberty head at l. Printer: R. Lange. Buenos Aires.	12.50	37.50	125.

3	20 Centavos	Good	Fine	XF
	1.1.1884. Black on green unpt. Portr. Bartolomé Mitre at upper ctr., arms below. Orange. Printer: R. Lange. Buenos Aires.	3.00	15.00	60.00

3a	20 Centavos	Good	Fine	XF
	1.1.1884. Black on blue unpt. Arms at l., Mitre at ctr. Blue. Arms at ctr.	15.00	60.00	150.

4 **50 Centavos**

	Good	Fine	XF
1.1.1884. Black on grayish-brown unpt. Portr. Josto Jose Urquiza at ctr., arms below. Brown. Woman at ctr.	15.00	60.00	150.

REPUBLIC

BANCO NACIONAL

.. 1883 SECOND ISSUE - NOTES DATED 1884

5-8 printer: ABNC. 3 sign. varieties.

5 Centavos

	Good	Fine	XF
1.1.1884. Black on brown and yellow unpt unpt. Portr. Avellaneda at l., arms at r. Back brown; helmeted Athena at ctr.	3.00	12.50	25.00

10 Centavos

	Good	Fine	XF
1.1.1884. Black on green unpt. Portr. Sarmiento at l., arms at r. 2 serial # varieties. Back green; gaucho on horseback at ctr.	3.00	12.50	25.00

20 Centavos

	Good	Fine	XF
1.1.1884. Arms at l., portr. Mitre at r.			
a. Black on lt. reddish-brown unpt. 2 serial # varieties. Back brown; steer's head at ctr.	5.00	15.00	26.00
b. Black w/o unpt. Series P.	—	—	—

50 Centavos

	Good	Fine	XF
1.1.1884. Black on brown unpt. Arms at lower l., portr. Urquiza at r. Back red-brown; 3 girls at ctr.	10.00	25.00	75.00

. 1890 ISSUE - NOTES DATED 1891

/ No. 2707 del 21 de Agosto de 1890

)9-212A Printer: CSABB, Buenos Aires.

209 **5 Centavos**

	Good	Fine	XF
1.11.1891. Black on blue unpt. Arms at l., Avellaneda at r. Back gray to blue-green; helmeted Athena at ctr. 5 sign. varieties. Large and small serial # varieties.	3.00	10.00	20.00

210 **10 Centavos**

	Good	Fine	XF
1.11.1891. Black on brown unpt. Arms at l., portr. Domingo Sarmiento at r. Back brown; gaucho on horseback at ctr. 5 sign. varieties.	3.00	10.00	22.50

211 **20 Centavos**

	Good	Fine	XF
1.11.1891. Black on green unpt. Portr. Bartolomé Mitre at l., arms at r. Back green; steer's head at ctr.			
a. Sign. titles: *Inspector.../Presidente...*	10.00	25.00	75.00
b. Sign. titles: *Sindico/Presidente...* 4 sign varieties.	3.00	10.00	20.00

212 **50 Centavos**

	Good	Fine	XF
1.1.1891. Lt. ochre and black. Justo Jose Urquiza at l., arms at r. *CINCUENTA* unpt. Back brown; 3 girls at ctr. Signature titles as 211a.	25.00	45.00	175.

212A **50 Centavos**

	Good	Fine	XF
1.11.1891. Lt. ochre and black. Urquiza at l., arms at r. *50* in unpt. Back brown; 3 girls at ctr. Like #212 but unpt.: *50*. 3 sign. varieties. Sign. titles as 211b.	5.00	25.00	60.00

BANCO DE LA NACIÓN ARGENTINA

L. 1891 ISSUE - NOTES DATED 1892

Ley No. 2822 del 29 Septembre de 1891

#213-216 printer: CSABB, Buenos Aires. 3 sign. varieties.

		Good	Fine	XF
213	**5 Centavos** 1.5.1892. Black on blue unpt. Similar to #209. Arms at l., Avellaneda at r. Back gray to blue-green; helmeted Athena at ctr.	5.00	25.00	60.00

		Good	Fine	XF
214	**10 Centavos** 1.5.1892. Black on brown unpt. Similar to #210. Arms at l., portr. Sarmiento at r. Back brown; gaucho on horseback at ctr.	5.00	25.00	60.00

		Good	Fine	XF
215	**20 Centavos** 1.5.1892. Black on green unpt. Similar to #211. Portr. Mitre at l., arms at r. Back green; steer's head at ctr.	5.00	25.00	60.00

		Good	Fine	XF
216	**50 Centavos** 1.5.1892. Lt. ochre and black. Similar to #212A. Urquiza at l., arms at r. *50* in unpt. Back brown; 3 girls at ctr.	7.50	30.00	75.00

1895 FIRST ISSUE

Ley No. 3062 del 8 de Enero de 1894

#218-227 printer: CSABB, Buenos Aires.

		Good	Fine	XF
218	**1 Peso** 1.1.1895. Black on green and brown. Portr. Adm. Brown at l., arms at ctr., woman w/lyre at r. Back green; arms at ctr. Rectangular *Ley 20.9.1897* ovpt. on face. 2 sign. varieties.			
	a. Issued note.	6.00	20.00	75.00
	b. Remainder perforated: *SIN VALOR.*	—	Unc	75.00

		Good	Fine	XF
219	**2 Pesos** 1.1.1895. Black on lt. brown and green unpt. Child w/flag at l., Portr. Alvear at r. Brown. Arms of the 14 provinces around large numeral at ctr. Printer: CSABB, Buenos Aires. 1 sign. variety.			
	a. Issued note.	100.	400.	—
	b. Remainder perforated: *SIN VALOR.*	—	Unc	325.
	p. Face and back proofs perforated like b.	—	Unc	350.

		Good	Fine	XF
220	**5 Pesos** 1.1.1895. Black on pink and green unpt. Dragon at l., arms at upper ctr., portr. V. Sarsfield at r. Back slate blue; sailing ships at ctr. 3 sign. varieties.			
	a. Issued note.	50.00	200.	—
	b. Remainder perforated: *SIN VALOR.*	—	Unc	175.

		Good	Fine	XF
221	**10 Pesos** 1.1.1895. Black on yellow-brown unpt. Woman and monument at l., arms at upper ctr., portr. N. Laprida at r. Back brown; ornamental design. 3 sign. varieties.			
	a. Issued note.	100.	400.	—
	b. Remainder perforated: *SIN VALOR.*	—	Unc	350.

		Good	Fine	XF
222	**20 Pesos** 1.1.1895. Black on lt. green and lt. orange unpt. Seated woman writing at l., arms at upper ctr., portr. Arenales at r. Back green; Liberty w/cap at ctr. 2 sign. varieties.			
	a. Issued note.	150.	650.	—
	b. Remainder perforated: *SIN VALOR.*	—	Unc	400.

		Good	Fine	XF
23	**50 Pesos** 1.1.1895. Black on red unpt. Ship at l., protr. Pueyrredon at r., arms at ctr. Ship at ctr. Printer: CSABB, Buenos Aires. 2 sign. varieties.			
	a. Issued note.	—	—	—
	b. Remainder perforated: *SIN VALOR.*	—	Unc	500.

		Good	Fine	XF
24	**100 Pesos** 1.1.1895. Blac on red and celeste unpt. Portr. Moreno and child at l. arms at ctr. Printer: CSABB, Buenos Aires. 2 sign. varieties.			
	a. Issued note.	500.	1000.	1500.
	b. Remainder perforated: *SIN VALOR.* Rare..	—	—	—

		Good	Fine	XF
25	**200 Pesos** 1.1.1895. Black on red and celeste unpt. Portr. Rivadavia at r., reclining female w/sheep at l., arms at upper ctr. Allegorical woman on back. Printer: CSABB, Buenos Aires. 2 sign. varieties.			
	a. Issued note.	700.	1000.	1500.
	b. Remainder perforated: *SIN VALOR.* Rare..	—	—	—

		Good	Fine	XF
226	**500 Pesos** 1.1.1895. Black on red and celeste unpt. Portr. Belgrano and engel w/globe at l., arms at upper ctr. Printer: CSABB, Buenos Aires. 2 sign. varieties.			
	a. Issued note. Rare..	—	—	—
	b. Remainder perforated: *SIN VALOR.* Rare..	—	—	—

		Good	Fine	XF
227	**1000 Pesos** 1.1.1895. Black on red unpt. Portr. San Martin at r., seated wman and child at l., arms at upper ctr. Printer: CSABB, Buenos Aires. 2 sign. varieties.			
	a. Issued note. Rare..	—	—	—
	b. Remainder perforated: *SIN VALOR.* Rare..	—	—	—

1895 SECOND ISSUE

Ley No. 2707 del 21 de Agosto de 1890

#228-230 printer: BWC.

		Good	Fine	XF
228	**10 Centavos** 19.7.1895. Black on red unpt. Arms at l., portr. Sarmiento at r. Back red; Liberty at ctr.	3.00	12.50	35.00

		Good	Fine	XF
229	**20 Centavos** 19.7.1895. Black on green unpt. Portr. Mitre at l., arms at r. Back green; helmeted woman at ctr.	5.00	25.00	50.00

		Good	Fine	XF
230	**50 Centavos** 19.7.1895. Black on brown unpt. Arms at l., portr. Urquiza at r. Back brown; Columbus at ctr. 3 sign. varieties.	5.00	25.00	75.00

CAJA DE CONVERSION

1899 ISSUE

Ley de 20 de Septiembre de 1897

WATERMARK VARIETIES		
Wmk. A:	Wmk. B:	Wmk. C:
PE of PESO	PE of PESO	Pe of PESO

#231-233 woman seated w/torch (Progreso motif) at l.,

		Good	Fine	XF
231	**50 Centavos** ND (1899-1900). Gray-blue. W/o unpt. Woman seated w/torch (Progreso motif) at l., 7 digit red serial # w/special code prefix and suffix.	40.00	125.	300.
232	**1 Peso** ND (1900). Gray-blue-pink. W/o unpt. Woman seated w/torch (Progreso motif) at l., 7 digit red serial # w/special code prefix and suffix.	45.00	150.	350.
233	**100 Pesos** ND (1899). Blue and green. W/o unpt. Woman seated w/torch (Progreso motif) at l., 7 digit red serial # w/special code prefix and suffix.	200.	600.	—

1900-01 ISSUE

#234-241 Liberty (Progreso) w/torch at l., 7 digit red serial # w/prefix letter and special code suffix.

		Good	Fine	XF
234	**50 Centavos** ND (1900). Gray-blue. Liberty (Progreso) w/torch at l., 7 digit red serial # w/prefix letter and special code suffix. Letter A.	60.00	175.	350.

		Good	Fine	XF
235	**1 Peso** ND (1900-03). Gray-blue. Liberty (Progreso) w/torch at l., 7 digit red serial # w/prefix letter and special code suffix. Letter B.	60.00	175.	350.
236	**5 Pesos** ND (1900-03). Blue, yellow and pink. Liberty (Progreso) w/torch at l., 7 digit red serial # w/prefix letter and special code suffix. Letter C.	60.00	175.	350.
237	**10 Pesos** ND (1900-03). Blue and gray. Liberty (Progreso) w/torch at l., 7 digit red serial # w/prefix letter and special code suffix. Letter D.	70.00	200.	450.
238	**50 Pesos** ND (1900-03). Pinkish-blue and gray. Liberty (Progreso) w/torch at l., 7 digit red serial # w/prefix letter and special code suffix. Letter E.	100.	250.	550.
239	**100 Pesos** ND (1900-03). Liberty (Progreso) w/torch at l., 7 digit red serial # w/prefix letter and special code suffix. 200 x 107 mm. Letter H.	200.	600.	—
240	**500 Pesos** ND (1900-01). Blue and yellow. Liberty (Progreso) w/torch at l., 7 digit red serial # w/prefix letter and special code suffix. Letter H. Rare.	—	—	—
241	**1000 Pesos** ND (1901). Pinkish-blue and violet. Liberty (Progreso) w/torch at l., 7 digit red serial # w/prefix letter and special code suffix. Letter P. Rare.	—	—	—

1903-05 ISSUE

#236A-241A reduced size.

		Good	Fine	XF
236A	**5 Pesos** ND (1903-07). 144 x 72mm. 3 sign. varieties. Letter C.	60.00	175.	350.
237A	**10 Pesos** ND (1903-07). 158 x 77mm. 3 sign. varieties. Letter D.	60.00	175.	350.
238A	**50 Pesos** ND (1903-06). 173 x 83mm. 3 sign. varieties. Letter E.	70.00	200.	450.
239A	**100 Pesos** ND (1903-06). 180 x 88mm. 2 sign. varieties. Letter H.	100.	250.	550.
240A	**500 Pesos** ND (1905). Letter N. Rare.	—	—	—
241A	**1000 Pesos** ND (1905-08). Letter P. Rare.	—	—	—

1906-07 ISSUE

#235B-239B w/7-digit red serial # w/special code prefix and suffix letter.

		Good	Fine	XF
235B	**1 Peso** ND (1906-08). 130 x 65mm. 2 sign. varieties. Letters A-D.	50.00	175.	350.
236B	**5 Pesos** ND (1907-08). 144 x 71mm. 2 sign. varieties. Letters A-D.	60.00	175.	350.
237B	**10 Pesos** ND (1907-08). 158 x 77mm. 2 sign. varieties. Letters A-C.	60.00	175.	350.
238B	**50 Pesos** ND (1906-08). 2 sign. varieties. Letters A-B.	—	—	—
239B	**100 Pesos** ND (1906-08). 2 sign. varieties. Letters A-B.	—	—	—

1908-23 ISSUES

#242-249 Liberty (Progreso) w/torch at l., w/*RA* monogram at upper l. 8-digit serial #. Major wmk. varieties. Many sign. varieties.

		VG	VF	UNC
242	**50 Centavos** ND (1918-21). Dk. blue on aqua, lilac and lt .green unpt. Liberty (Progreso) w/torch. Printed *RA* monogram and *50 CENTAVOS* in lt. green. 1 sign. variety.	1.50	5.00	15.00
242A	**50 Centavos** ND (1922-26). Dk. blue on lt. blue-green unpt. Liberty (Progreso) w/torch. Like #242 but wmk: *RA* monogram and *50 CENTAVOS.* 2 sign. varieties.	.75	2.25	7.50
243	**1 Peso** ND (1908-35). Blue on pink paper. Liberty (Progreso) w/torch. Back green. 130 x 65mm. Wmk: *RA* monogram.			
	a. Wmk: A. ND (1908-25). Series A-C. 7 sign. varieties.	2.00	10.00	40.00
	b. Wmk: B. ND (1925-32). Series D-E. 3 sign. varieties.	1.50	6.00	15.00
	c. Wmk: C. ND (1932-35). Series F. 2 sign. varieties.	1.00	3.00	7.00

		VG	VF	UNC
244	**5 Pesos** ND (1908-35). Blue. Liberty (Progreso) w/torch. Back dk. red.			
	a. Wmk: A. ND (1908-25). Series A. 7 sign. varieties.	5.00	20.00	60.00
	b. Wmk: B. ND (1925-32). Series B. 3 sign. varieties.	5.00	15.00	35.00
	c. Wmk: C. ND (1933-35). Series C.	2.00	7.50	30.00

		VG	VF	UNC
245	**10 Pesos**			
	ND (1908-35). Blue. Liberty (Progreso) w/torch. Back green.			
	a. Wmk: A. ND (1908-25). Series A. 7 sign. varieties.	5.00	15.00	35.00
	b. Wmk: B. ND (1925-32). Series B. 3 sign. varieties.	5.00	15.00	35.00
	c. Wmk: C w/Gen. San Martin at upper l. ND (1933-35). Series C. 2 sign. varieties.	2.00	5.00	15.00
246	**50 Pesos**			
	ND (1908-35). Blue. Liberty (Progreso) w/torch.			
	a. Wmk: A. ND (1908-25). Series A. 7 sign. varieties.	20.00	75.00	150.
	b. Wmk: B. ND (1925-32). Series B . 2 sign. varieties.	15.00	60.00	140.
	c. Wmk: C w/Gen. San Martin at upper l. ND (1934-35). Series C.	15.00	50.00	125.

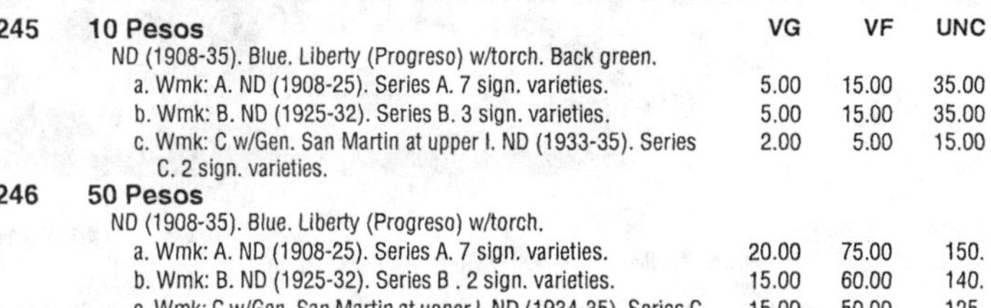

		VG	VF	UNC
247	**100 Pesos**			
	ND (1908-32). Blue on aqua unpt. Liberty (Progreso) w/torch. Back olive. 180 x 88mm.			
	a. Wmk: A. ND (1908-25). Series A. 5 sign. varieties.	50.00	125.	250.
	b. Wmk: B. ND (1926-32). Series B. 2 sign. varieties.	15.00	40.00	90.00
248	**500 Pesos**			
	ND (1909-35). Blue on blue paper. Liberty (Progreso) w/torch. Back brownish-purple. 188 x 93mm.			
	a. Wmk: A. ND (1909-24). Series A. 4 sign. varieties.	125.	300.	750.
	b. Wmk: B. ND (1929-30). Series B.	60.00	150.	375.
	c. Wmk: C w/Gen. San Martin at upper l. ND (1935). Series C.	40.00	100.	225.
249	**1000 Pesos**			
	ND (1910-34). Blue on aqua unpt. Liberty (Progreso) w/torch. Back red. 196 x 98mm.			
	a. Wmk: A. ND (1910-27). Series A. 3 sign. varieties.	125.	250.	600.
	b. Wmk: B. ND (1929). Series B.	125.	250.	600.
	c. Wmk: C. w/Gen. San Martin at upper l. ND (1934). Series C.	60.00	125.	350.

BANCO CENTRAL

ART. 36 - LEY 12.155 (FIRST ISSUE)

		VG	VF	UNC
249A	**1 Peso**			
	ND. Dp. brown-orange. Head of Republica at ctr. Uniface face proof w/o sign., serial # or wmk.	—	—	15.00

		VG	VF	UNC
249B	**5 Pesos**			
	ND. Blue-black. Head of Republica at r. Uniface face proof w/o sign., serial # or wmk.	—	—	15.00

ART. 36 - LEY 12.155 (SECOND ISSUE)

#250-252 Liberty (Progreso) w/torch at l. Many sign. varieties. Notes have Banco Central designation just above signs. at bottom.

		VG	VF	UNC
250	**50 Centavos**			
	ND (1942-48). Blue. Liberty (Progreso) w/torch at l. 4 sign. varieties. 2 wmk. varieties.			
	a. Sign. titles: C in black. Serie C, D.	1.00	3.50	7.50
	b. Sign. titles: C in blue. Serie D.	1.50	4.50	12.50
	c. Sign. titles: E in blue. Serie D.	1.50	4.50	12.50
251	**1 Peso**			
	ND (1935). Blue on pink paper. Liberty (Progreso) w/torch at l. 6 sign. varieties.			
	a. Sign. titles: C in blue. Serie I.	.75	2.25	6.00
	b. *SUB* added in black to sign. titles C in blue. Serie I-J.	1.25	3.00	7.50
	c. Sign. titles: E in black. Serie J-K.	1.25	3.00	7.50
	d. Sign. titles: C in black. Serie G-I.	1.00	3.00	7.50
252	**5 Pesos**			
	ND (1935). Blue. Liberty (Progreso) w/torch at l. 4 sign. varieties.			
	a. Sign. titles: C in blue. Serie D.	2.00	5.00	15.00
	b. Sign. titles: E in black. Serie D.	3.75	15.00	30.00
	c. Sign. titles: C in black. Serie E.	2.00	5.00	15.00

1935 - LEY NO. 12.155 DE 28 DE MARZO DE 1935

#253-255 lg. heading: *El Banco Central.* Liberty (Progreso) w/torch at l. Wmk: San Martin. Sign. titles: C.

		VG	VF	UNC
253	**10 Pesos**			
	L.1935 (1936-46). Blue. Large heading *El Banco Central.* Liberty (Progreso) w/torch at l. Green. Watermark: San Martin. 2 sign. varieties. Serie D.			
	a. Issued note.	6.00	17.50	50.00
	s. Specimen. Ovpt.: *MUESTRA.*	—	—	225.
254	**50 Pesos**			
	L.1935 (1936-43). Blue. Large heading *El Banco Central.* Liberty (Progreso) w/torch at l. Watermark: San Martin. Serie D.	11.50	35.00	100.

		VG	VF	UNC
255	**100 Pesos**			
	L.1935 (1936-43). Blue on green unpt. Large heading *El Banco Central.* Liberty (Progreso) w/torch at l. Gray. Watermark: San Martin. Serie C.	10.00	30.00	80.00

1948 - LEY NO. 12.962 DEL 27 DE MARZO DE 1947

#256-258 Liberty (Progreso) w/torch at l. Printer: CMN.

		VG	VF	UNC
256	**50 Centavos**			
	L.1947 (1948-50). Blue. Liberty (Progreso) w/torch at l. 2 sign. varieties. Serie E.	.35	1.00	3.00

		VG	VF	UNC
257	**1 Peso**			
	L.1947 (1948-51). Blue on pink paper. Liberty (Progreso) w/torch at l. Back green. 2 sign. varieties. Serie L-N.	.50	1.50	4.00

258 5 Pesos
L.1947 (1949-51). Blue. Liberty (Progreso) w/torch at l. Back lt. red. Serie F. | .65 | 1.85 | 5.00

1950 - Ley No. 12.962 del 27 de Marzo de 1947

		VG	VF	UNC
259	**50 Centavos**			
	L.1947 (1950-51). Brown. Head of Republica at l. Back green; open book of constitution at ctr.			
	a. *Garrasi* at lower r., letter A. (1950).	.25	1.00	3.00
	b. W/o *Garrasi* at lower r., letter A. (1951).	.25	1.00	3.00

Note: For 50 centavos type of #259 w/letter B see #261.

1952 Commemorative Issue

#260, Declaration of Economic Independence (#263 regular issue) w/dates: *1816-1947*.

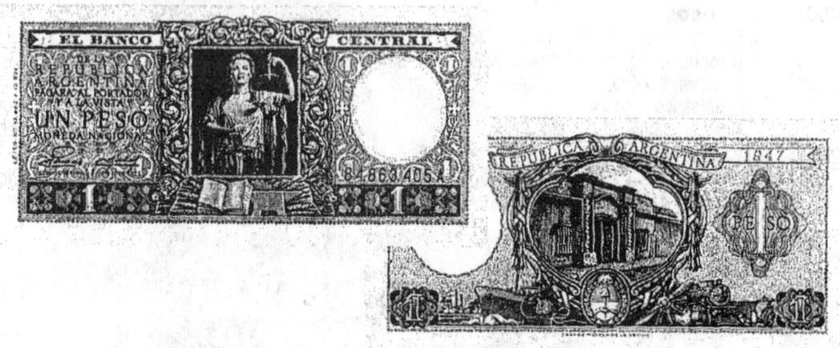

		VG	VF	UNC
260	**1 Peso**			
	ND (1952-55). Brown, violet and blue. Justice holding sword and scale at ctr. Bldg. at ctr., *"1816-1947"* at top on back.			
	a. Sign. Bosio-Gomez Morales. Serie A.	.50	3.50	10.00
	b. Sign. Palarea-Revestido. Serie A-C.	.25	1.00	3.00

1951 - Leyes Nos. 12.962 y 13.571

#261-264 Liberty (Progreso) w/torch at l. Sign. varieties. Printer: CMN.

		VG	VF	UNC
261	**50 Centavos**			
	ND (1951-56). Brown. Like #259. Head of Republica at l. Letter B. 2 sign. varieties.	.25	1.00	3.00
262	**1 Peso**			
	ND (1951-52). Blue on pink paper. Liberty (Progreso) w/torch at l. Back green. Serie Ñ.	.35	1.50	4.00

		VG	VF	UNC
263	**1 Peso**			
	ND (1956). Brown, violet and blue. Justice holding sword and scale at ctr. Like #260 but w/o *1816-1947* on back. 2 sign. varieties. Serie C-D.			
	a. Wmk: *1* w/o dk. line in upper part.	.25	1.00	3.00
	b. Wmk: *1* w/dk. line in upper part.	.25	1.00	3.00

		VG	VF	UNC
264	**5 Pesos**			
	ND (1951-59). Blue. Liberty (Progreso) w/torch at l. Back lt. red. 6 sign. varieties. Serie G-H.			
	a. Wmk: A, red serial #.	.50	2.00	6.00
	b. Wmk: B, red serial #.	.50	2.00	6.00
	c. Wmk: C, red serial #.	.50	2.00	6.00
	d. Wmk: C, black serial #. Serie H.	.35	1.50	6.00
	x. Error w/*Leyes Nos. 19.962 y 13.571*. Serie H.	1.00	4.00	12.50

1943 - Ley No. 12.155 de 28 de Marzo de 1935

#265-269 Portr. Gen. San Martin in uniform at r. Sign. varieties.

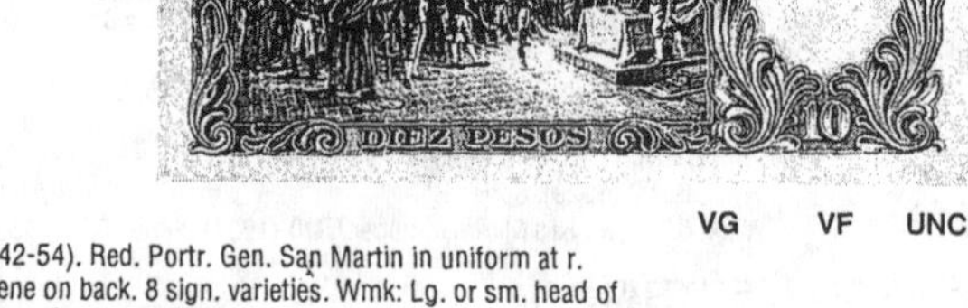

		VG	VF	UNC
265	**10 Pesos**			
	L.1935 (1942-54). Red. Portr. Gen. San Martin in uniform at r. Meeting scene on back. 8 sign. varieties. Wmk: Lg. or sm. head of Gen. Belgrano. Serie A-C.			
	a. Red sign. w/sign titles C.	2.50	12.50	40.00
	b. Black sign. w/sign. titles C.	.60	1.75	5.00
	c. Red sign. w/sign. titles E.	2.00	8.00	25.00

		VG	VF	UNC
266	**50 Pesos**			
	L.1935 (1942-54). Green. Portr. Gen. San Martin in uniform at r. Army in mountains on back. 6 sign. varieties. Serie A. Sign. titles: C.			
	a. Green sign.	4.00	25.00	60.00
	b. Black sign.	1.75	7.00	20.00
	c. Red serial #.	15.00	35.00	70.00
267	**100 Pesos**			
	L.1935 (1943-57). Brown. Portr. Gen. San Martin in uniform at r. Spanish and Indians on back. 7 sign. varieties. Serie A.			
	a. Brown sign. w/sign. titles E.	3.50	20.00	50.00
	s. Black sign. w/sign. titles C.	1.75	7.00	20.00

NOTICE

Readers with unlisted dates, signature varieties, etc. are invited to submit photocopies or, high resolution (300 dpi, 100% size) scans of their notes to: Standard Catalog of World Paper Money, 700 East State St. Iola, WI 54990-0001, or E-Mail: george.cuhaj@fwpubs.com.

		VG	VF	UNC
267A	**100 Pesos**			
	L.1935. Purple and violet on pale green and orange unpt. Portr. Gen. San Martin in uniform at r. Uniface face proof w/o sign., serial # or wmk.	—	—	15.00

		VG	VF	UNC
268	**500 Pesos**			
	L.1935. (1944-54). Blue. Portr. Gen. San Martin in uniform at r. Banco Central on back. 5 sign. varieties. Serie A.			
	a. Blue sign. w/sign. titles E.	12.50	60.00	150.
	b. Black sign. w/sign. titles C.	6.25	25.00	60.00
268A	**500 Pesos**			
	L.1935. Dp. blue on pale green unpt. Portr. Gen. San Martin in uniform at r. Banco Central on back. Proof w/o sign., serial # or wmk.	—	—	15.00

		VG	VF	UNC
269	**1000 Pesos**			
	L.1935. (1944-55). Purple. Portr. Gen. San Martin in uniform at r. Sailing ship on back. 5 sign. varieties. Serie A.			
	a. Purple sign. w/sign. titles E.	12.50	60.00	150.
	b. Black sign. w/sign. titles C.	4.50	17.50	55.00

1954-57 ND Issue

Leyes Nos. 12.962 y 13.571. #270-274 Portr. Gen. Jose San Martin in uniform at r. Sign. varieties.

		VG	VF	UNC
270	**10 Pesos**			
	ND (1954-63). Red. Portr. Gen. San Martin in uniform at r. Meeting scene on back 10 sign. varieties. Serie D-G.			
	a. Sign. titles: C.	.40	1.25	4.00
	b. Sign. titles: D.	.40	1.25	4.00
	c. Sign. titles: E.	.25	1.00	3.00
271	**50 Pesos**			
	ND (1955-68). Green. Portr. Gen. San Martin in uniform at r. 3 serial # varieties. Series B-C w/gray unpt. Series D w/o unpt. Army in mountains on back. 13 sign. varieties in red or black.			
	a. Sign. titles: C.	.50	2.00	6.00
	b. Sign. titles: D.	.20	1.25	20.00
	c. Sign. titles: E.	.60	2.25	7.00
	d. Litho printing on back. Sign. titles: E. Serie C, D.	.25	1.00	3.00
272	**100 Pesos**			
	ND (1957-67). Brown. Portr. Gen. San Martin in uniform at r. Spanish and Indians on back. 10 sign. varieties. 2 serial # varieties. Serie B-D w/gray unpt. Serie D w/o unpt.			
	a. Sign. titles: C.	.50	2.00	6.00
	b. Sign. titles: D.	1.25	5.00	15.00
	c. Sign. titles: E.	.50	2.00	6.00
273	**500 Pesos**			
	ND (1954-64). Blue. Portr. Gen. San Martin in uniform at r. Banco Central on back. 6 sign. varieties. 3 serial # varieties in red or black. Serie B.			
	a. Sign. titles: C.	2.50	10.00	30.00
	b. Sign. titles: E.	3.25	13.50	40.00
274	**1000 Pesos**			
	ND (1955-65). Purple. Portr. Gen. San Martin in uniform at r. Sailing ship on back. 9 sign. varieties. 3 serial # varieties in red or black. Serie B, C.			
	a. Sign. titles: C.	1.25	5.00	15.00
	b. Sign. titles: D.	1.25	5.00	15.00
	c. Sign. titles: E.	1.00	4.00	12.00

1960-69 ND Issue

W/o Ley- Moneda Nacional

#275-277, 279-280 Portr. Gen. José de San Martín in uniform at r. Sign. varieties.

Notes begin with *SERIE A* unless noted.

		VG	VF	UNC
275	**5 Pesos**			
	ND (1960-62). Brown on yellow unpt. People gathering before bldg. on back. Printer: CMN. 3 sign. varieties. Serie A.			
	a. Sign. titles: D.	.30	1.50	6.00
	b. Sign. titles: C.	.75	3.00	12.50
	c. Sign. titles: E.	.40	1.75	5.50

		VG	VF	UNC
279	**1000 Pesos**			
	ND (1966-69). Purple. Portr. young Gen J. de San Martín in uniform at r. Sailing ship on back. Serie C, D. 3 sign. varieties.			
	a. Sign. titles: E.	1.00	3.75	15.00
	b. Sign. titles: C.	.75	3.25	10.00

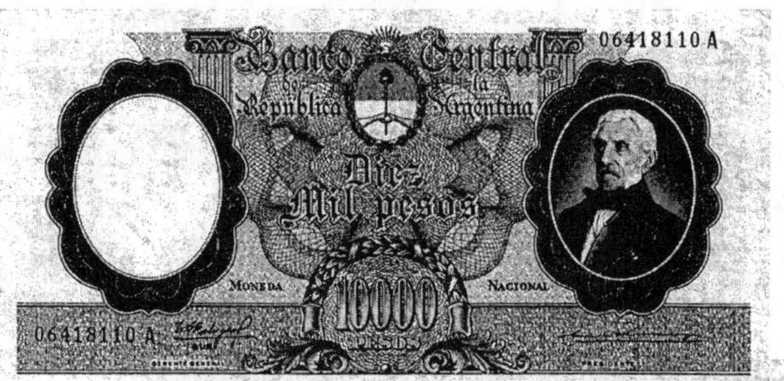

		VG	VF	UNC
281	**10,000 Pesos** ND (1961-69). Deep red on blue and yellow unpt. Portr. elderly Gen J. de San Martín not in uniform at r. Armies in the field on back. Serie A, B. 5 sign. varieties.			
	a. Sign. titles: E. Serie A, B.	4.50	15.00	50.00
	b. Sign. titles: C. Serie B.	2.50	12.50	35.00
	s. As a. Specimen.	—	—	200.

The Republic of Armenia (formerly the Armenian S.S.R.) is bounded to the north by Georgia, to the east by Azerbaijan and to the south and west by Turkey and Iran. It has an area of 11,490 sq. mi. (29,800 sq. km) and a population of 3.7 million. Capital: Yerevan. Agriculture including cotton, vineyards and orchards, hydroelectricity, chemicals - primarily synthetic rubber and fertilizers, and vast mineral deposits of copper, zinc and aluminum and production of steel and paper are major industries.

The earliest history of Armenia records continuous struggles with Babylonia and later Assyria. In the sixth century B.C. it was called Armina. Later under under the Persian empire it was a vassal state. Conquered by Macedonia, it later defeated the Seleucids and thus Greater Armenia was founded under the Artaxis dynasty. Christianity was established in 303 A.D. which led to religious wars with the Persians and Romans who then divided it into two zones of influence. The Arabs succeeded the Sassanids. In 862 A.D. Ashot V was recognized as the "prince of princes" and established a throne recognized by Baghdad and Constantinople in 886 A.D. The Seljuks overran the whole country and united with Kurdistan whic eventually ran the new government. From 1240 A.D. onward the Mongols occupied almost all of western Asia until their downfall in 1375 A.D. when various Kurdish, Armenian and Turkoman independent principalities arose. After the defeat of the Persians in 1516 A.D. the Ottoman Turks gradually took control with Kurdish tribes settling within Armenian lands. In 1605 A.D, the Persians relocated thousands of Armenians as far as India to develop colonies. Persia and the Ottoman Turks were again at war, with the Ottomans once again prevailing. The Ottomans later gave absolute civil authority to a Christian bishop allowing the Armenians free enjoyment of their religion and traditions.

Russia occupied Armenia in 1801 until the Russo-Turkish war of 1878. British intervention excluded either side from remaining although the Armenian remained more loyal to the Ottoman Turks. In 1894 the Ottoman Turks sent in an expeditionary force of Kurds fearing a revolutionary movement. Large massacres were followed by retaliations, an amnesty was proclaimed which continued to 1916, when Armenia was occupied by Russian forces. From 1917-1918 the Georgians, Armenians and Azerbaijanis formed the short-lived Transcaucasian Federal Republic which split into three independent republics on May 26, 1918. Communism developed and in Sept. 1920 the Turks attacked the Armenian Republic; the Russians soon followed suit, routing the Turks. On Nov. 29, 1920 Armenia was proclaimed a Soviet Socialist Republic. On March 12, 1922, Armenia, Georgia and Azerbaijan were combined to form the Transcaucasian Soviet Federated Socialist republic, which on Dec. 30, 1922, became a part of U.S.S.R. On Dec. 5, 1936, the Transcaucasian federation was dissolved and Armenia became a constituent republic of the U.S.S.R.

A new constitution was adopted in April 1978. Elections took place on May 20, 1990. The Supreme Soviet adopted a declaration of sovereignty in Aug. 1991, voting to unite Armenia with Nagorno-Karabakh. This newly constituted Republic of Armenia became independent by popular vote in Sept. 1991. It joined the CIS in Dec.1991.

Fighting between Christians in Armenia and Muslim forces of Azerbaijan escalated in 1992 and continued through early 1994. Each country claimed the Nagorno-Karabakh, an Armenian ethnic enclave in Azerbaijan. A temporary cease-fire was announced in May 1994.

MONETARY SYSTEM:

1 Ruble = 100 Kopeks
1 Dram = 100 Lumma

Note: For later issues of the Armenian Socialist Soviet Republic refer to Volume 1, Russia-Transcaucasia, and for current issues of the new Republic refer to Volume 3.

AUTONOMOUS REPUBLIC

ГОСУДАРСТВЕННАГО БАНКА ЭРИВАНСКОЕ ОТД ЛЕНIЕ

GOVERNMENT BANK, YEREVAN BRANCH

1919 FIRST ISSUE

#1-29 date on face: АВГУСТЬ (August) 1919. Many color shades.

#1-18 w/date 15 НОЯБРЯ (November) 1919 on back.

#1-13 w/o Armenian text at upper l. and r.

		Good	Fine	XF
1	**5 Rubles** 1919. Black on blue unpt.	3.00	10.00	30.00
2	**10 Rubles** 1919. Black on pink unpt.			
	a. Issued note.	2.50	8.00	25.00
	x. Misprint w/text inverted.	4.50	14.00	40.00
3	**25 Rubles** 1919. Dk. gray. Value numerals in middle and 4 corners.			
	a. Issued note.	10.00	30.00	85.00
	x. Error printed in brown.	22.50	65.00	175.
4	**50 Rubles** 1919. Green. Value numerals in middle and 4 corners.	17.50	50.00	150.

		Good	Fine	XF
5	**100 Rubles** 1919. Green. Plain value numerals in black.	5.00	17.50	50.00
6	**250 Rubles** 1919. Orange. Like #5.	5.00	17.50	50.00
7	**500 Rubles** 1919. Blue. Like #5.	5.00	17.50	50.00
8	**1000 Rubles** 1919. Lilac. Like #5.	5.00	17.50	50.00

1919 Second Issue

#9-13 w/ornamental numerals of value.

		Good	Fine	XF
9	**50 Rubles** 1919. Green. Ornamental value numerals.	4.00	12.50	40.00
10	**100 Rubles** 1919. Lt. green. Like #9.			
	a. Issued note.	4.00	12.00	40.00
	x. Error printed in yellow.	7.00	25.00	70.00

		Good	Fine	XF
11	**250 Rubles** 1919. Lt. brown. Like #9.	4.00	15.00	40.00
12	**500 Rubles** 1919. Blue. Like #9.	4.00	15.00	40.00
13	**1000 Rubles** 1919. Lilac. Like #9.	7.50	25.00	70.00

1920 First Issue

#14-18 w/Armenian text at upper l. and r.

		Good	Fine	XF
14	**5 Rubles** 1919 (1920). Gray-blue.			
	a. Issued note.	2.25	7.50	20.00
	x. Misprint w/text: ГОЧУДАРЧТВЕНАГО.	2.25	7.50	20.00
	y. Misprint w/text on back.	5.00	17.50	50.00

		Good	Fine	XF
15	**10 Rubles** 1919 (1920). Pink-brown.			
	a. Issued note.	2.25	7.50	20.00
	x. Misprint w/text: ГОЧУДАРЧТВЕНАГО.	3.00	10.00	25.00
	y. Misprint w/unpt. inverted.	3.00	10.00	25.00
	z. Misprint w/text: ДЕЕЧЯТЬ.	4.50	15.00	30.00
16	**25 Rubles** 1919 (1920). Brown.			
	a. Issued note.	2.25	7.50	20.00
	x. Misprint w/text: ГОЧУДАРЧТВЕНАГО.	3.00	10.00	25.00
	y. Misprint w/text: ДВАДЦАШЬ.	4.00	12.50	35.00
17	**50 Rubles** 1919 (1920). Black on turquoise unpt.			
	a. Issued note.	2.25	7.50	20.00
	x. Misprint w/text on back.	3.00	10.00	25.00
	y. Misprint w/text on back inverted.	3.00	10.00	25.00
	z. Misprint w/text: ГОЧУДАРЧТВЕНАГО.	2.25	7.50	20.00
18	**100 Rubles** 1919 (1920). Black on yellow-green unpt.			
	a. Issued note.	2.25	7.50	20.00
	x. Misprint w/text on back.	2.25	7.50	20.00
	y. Misprint w/text on back inverted.	4.00	12.50	35.00
	z. Misprint w/text: МИНЧТЕРЧТВОМЪ.	4.00	12.50	35.00

1920 Second Issue

#19-29 w/date 15 ЯНВАРЯ (January) 1920 on back.

		Good	Fine	XF
19	**25 Rubles** 1919 (1920). Gray-brown. Sign. stamped on back.			
	a. Issued note.	4.00	15.00	40.00
	x. Misprint w/text on back.	6.50	25.00	60.00
	y. Misprint w/text on back inverted.	6.50	25.00	60.00
20	**25 Rubles** 1919 (1920). Brown. Sign. on back in facsimile print.			
	a. Issued note.	4.00	15.00	35.00
	x. Misprint w/text on back.	4.00	15.00	35.00
	y. Misprint w/unpt. inverted.	4.00	15.00	35.00

		Good	Fine	XF
21	**50 Rubles** 1919 (1920). Green-blue.	4.00	15.00	40.00
22	**100 Rubles** 1919 (1920). Lt. green.	3.00	10.00	30.00
23	**250 Rubles** 1919 (1920). Pink. Sign. stamped on back.			
	a. Issued note.	3.00	10.00	30.00
	x. Misprint w/text: ПЯТЬДЕЧТЯЪ.	4.00	15.00	40.00
	y. Misprint w/text on back inverted.	3.00	10.00	30.00
24	**250 Rubles** 1919 (1920). Yellow-brown. Numerals of value in black. Sign. on back in facsimile print.	4.50	15.00	45.00
25	**250 Rubles** 1919 (1920). Yellow-brown. Like #24 but numerals of value in lt. blue.	7.50	25.00	70.00

		Good	Fine	XF
26	**500 Rubles** 1919 (1920). Lt. blue to gray-blue.			
	a. Issued note.	4.00	15.00	40.00
	x. Misprint w/unpt. inverted.	6.50	25.00	60.00
27	**1000 Rubles** 1919 (1920). Black.			
	a. Lt. violet unpt.	3.00	10.00	30.00
	b. Orange-brown unpt.	3.00	10.00	30.00
	c. Pink unpt. White paper.	3.00	10.00	30.00
	d. Pink unpt. Wmk. buff paper.	3.00	10.00	30.00
	x. Misprint w/text on back.	3.00	10.00	30.00
	y. Misprint w/unpt. inverted.	3.00	10.00	30.00

		Good	Fine	XF
28	**5000 Rubles** 1919 (1920). Black.			
	a. Gray unpt.	4.50	15.00	45.00
	b. Lt. purple unpt. White paper.	6.50	25.00	60.00
	c. Lt. purple unpt. Wmk. buff paper.	4.50	15.00	45.00
	x. Misprint w/unpt. inverted.	8.00	25.00	70.00
29	**10,000 Rubles** 1919 (1920). Green. Sign. stamped on back.			
	a. Issued note.	3.00	10.00	30.00
	x. Misprint w/numerals of value reversed.	6.50	25.00	60.00
	y. Misprint w/text on back.	6.50	25.00	60.00
	z. Misprint w/margin text from top to bottom at l.	4.50	15.00	45.00

1920 THIRD ISSUE

#30-32 printer: W&S.

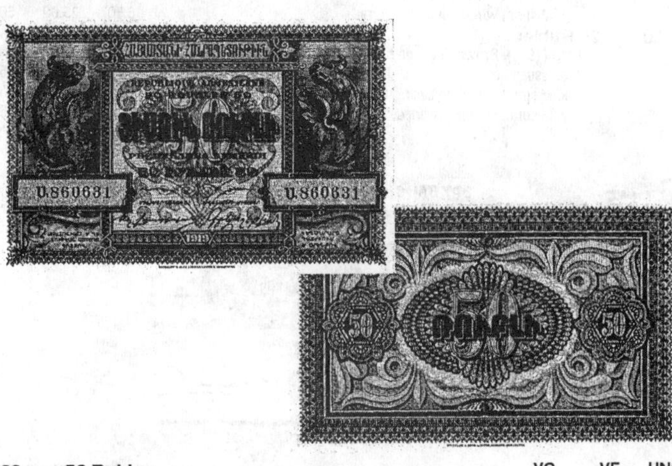

		VG	VF	UNC
30	**50 Rubles** 1919 (1920). Brown on orange unpt. Facing dragons at l. and r.	4.00	12.50	30.00

		VG	VF	UNC
31	**100 Rubles** 1919 (1920). Green on orange and yellow unpt. Landscape w/mountains. Eagle at ctr. on back.	5.00	15.00	35.00

		VG	VF	UNC
32	**250 Rubles** 1919 (1920). Violet on green and yellow unpt. woman spinning at l. on back.	6.00	20.00	60.00

The Commonwealth of Austral the smallest continent and large island in the world, is locat south of Indonesia between t Indian and Pacific oceans. It h an area of 2,967,909 sq. r (7,686,849 sq. km.) and population of 18.84 millic Capital: Canberra. Due to its ea and sustained isolation, Austra is the habitat of such curious a unique fauna as the kangarc koala, platypus, wombat a barking lizard. The contine possesses extensive mine deposits, the most important which are gold, coal, silv nickel, uranium, lead and zir Livestock raising, mining a manufacturing are the princip industries. Chief exports a wool, meat, wheat, iron ore, cc and nonferrous metals.

The first caucasians to s Australia probably we Portuguese and Spani navigators of the late 16 century. In 1770, Captain Jam Cook explored the east coast and annexed it for Great Britain. The Colony of New South Wal was founded by Captain Arthur Phillip on Jan. 26, 1788, a date now celebrated as Australia Da Dates of creation of six colonies that now comprise the states of the Australian Commonwea are: New South Wales, 1823; Tasmania, 1825; Western Australia, 1838; South Australia, 184 Victoria, 1851; Queensland, 1859. A constitution providing for federation of the colonies w approved by the British Parliament in 1900; the Commonwealth of Australia came into being 1901. Australia passed the Statute of Westminster Adoption Act on Oct. 9, 1942, which officia established Australia's complete autonomy in external and internal affairs, thereby formalizing situation that had existed for years.

During WWII Australia was the primary supply and staging area for Allied forces in the Sou Pacific Theatre.

Australia is a member of the Commonwealth of Nations. Elizabeth II is Head of State Queen of Australia.

RULERS:

MONETARY SYSTEM:

- 1 Shilling = 12 Pence
- 1 Pound = 20 Shillings = 2 Dollars
- 1 Pound = 20 Shillings; to 1966
- 1 Dollar = 100 Cents, 1966-

COMMONWEALTH

AUSTRALIAN BANK OF COMMERCE (SUPERSCRIBED)

1910 SUPERSCRIBED ISSUE

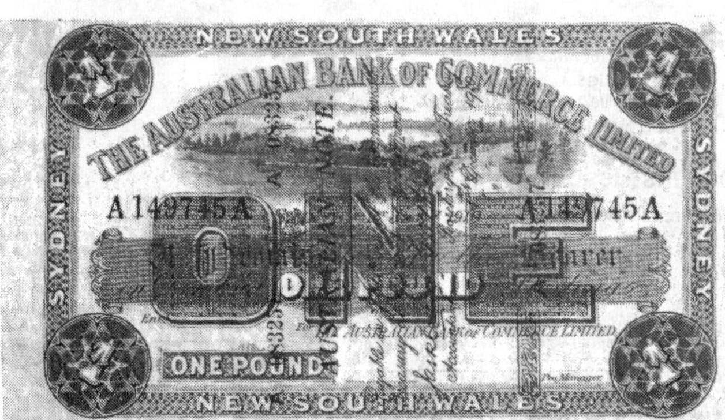

		Good	Fine	X
A72	**1 Pound** ND (1910).	8000.	23,000.	60,0C
A73	**5 Pounds** ND (1910).	—	—	
A74	**10 Pounds** ND (1910).	—	—	
A75	**50 Pounds** ND (1910).	—	—	

BANK OF ADELAIDE (SUPERSCRIBED)

1910 SUPERSCRIBED ISSUE

		Good	Fine	X
A76	**1 Pound** ND (1910).	6000.	20,000.	50,0C
A77	**5 Pounds** ND (1910).	10,000.	30,000.	75,0C
A78	**10 Pounds** ND (1910).	—	—	
A79	**20 Pounds** ND (1910).	—	—	
A80	**50 Pounds** ND (1910).	—	—	

		Good	Fine	XF
A81	**1 Pound**			
	ND (1910).			
	a. Adelaide.	—	—	—
	b. Hobart.	6000.	20,000.	55,000.
	c. Melbourne.	—	—	—
	d. Perth.	7000.	22,000.	60,000.
	e. Sydney.	7000.	22,000.	60,000.

BANK OF AUSTRALASIA (SUPERSCRIBED)

1910 SUPERSCRIBED ISSUE

		Good	Fine	XF
A82	**5 Pounds**			
	ND (1910).			
	a. Hobart.	—	—	—
	b. Perth.	—	—	—
A83	**10 Pounds**			
	ND (1910).			
	a. Adelaide.	—	—	—
	b. Brisbane.	20,000.	60,000.	110,000.
	c. Hobart.	—	—	—
	d. Melbourne.	—	—	—
	e. Perth.	20,000.	60,000.	110,000.
	f. Sydney.	—	—	—
A84	**50 Pounds**			
	ND (1910).			
	a. Adelaide.	—	—	—
	b. Hobart.	—	—	—
	c. Melbourne.	—	—	—
	d. Sydney.	—	—	—
A85	**100 Pounds**			
	ND (1910).			
	a. Melbourne.	—	—	—

BANK OF NEW SOUTH WALES (SUPERSCRIBED)

1910 SUPERSCRIBED ISSUE

		Good	Fine	XF
A86	**1 Pound**			
	ND (1910).			
	a. Melbourne.	12,000.	40,000.	85,000.
	b. Sydney.	10,000.	30,000.	75,000.
	c. No domicile.	—	—	—
A87	**5 Pounds**			
	ND (1910).			
	a. Sydney.	—	—	—
A88	**10 Pounds**			
	ND (1910).			
	a. Adelaide.	—	—	—
	b. Melbourne.	—	—	—
	c. Sydney.	—	—	—
	d. No domicile.	25,000.	70,000.	125,000.
A89	**20 Pounds**			
	ND (1910).			
	a. Adelaide.	—	—	—
	b. Melbourne.	—	—	—
	c. Perth.	—	—	—
	d. Sydney.	—	—	—
A90	**50 Pounds**			
	ND (1910).			
	a. Adelaide.	—	—	—
	b. Melbourne.	—	—	—
	c. Sydney.	—	—	—
A91	**100 Pounds**			
	ND (1910).			
	a. Adelaide.	—	—	—
	b. Melbourne.	—	—	—
	c. Sydney.	—	—	—

BANK OF VICTORIA (SUPERSCRIBED)

1910 SUPERSCRIBED ISSUE

		Good	Fine	XF
A92	**1 Pound**			
	ND (1910).	6000.	20,000.	50,000.
A93	**5 Pounds**			
	ND (1910).	—	—	—
A94	**10 Pounds**			
	ND (1910).			
	a. Adelaide.	—	—	—
	b. Melbourne.	25,000.	70,000.	125,000.
	c. Perth.	—	—	—
	d. Sydney.	—	—	—
A95	**20 Pounds**			
	ND (1910).	—	—	—
A96	**50 Pounds**			
	ND (1910).	—	—	—

CITY BANK OF SYDNEY (SUPERSCRIBED)

1910 SUPERSCRIBED ISSUE

		Good	Fine	XF
A97	**1 Pound**			
	ND (1910).	12,000.	40,000.	85,000.
A98	**5 Pounds**	Good	Fine	XF
	ND (1910).	—	—	—
A99	**10 Pounds**			
	ND (1910).	—	—	—
A100	**20 Pounds**			
	ND (1910).	—	—	—
A101	**50 Pounds**			
	ND (1910).	—	—	—

COMMERCIAL BANK OF AUSTRALIA (SUPERSCRIBED)

1910 SUPERSCRIBED ISSUE

		Good	Fine	XF
A102	**1 Pound**			
	ND (1910).			
	a. Melbourne.	—	—	—
	b. Perth.	13,000.	42,000.	90,000.
A103	**5 Pounds**			
	ND (1910).			
	a. Hobart.	—	—	—

COMMERCIAL BANK OF TASMANIA (SUPERSCRIBED)

1910 SUPERSCRIBED ISSUE

		Good	Fine	XF
A104	**1 Pound**			
	ND (1910).			
	a. Hobart.	10,000.	35,000.	80,000.
	b. Launceston.	12,000.	38,000.	85,000.
A105	**5 Pounds**			
	ND (1910).			
	a. Launceston.	—	—	—
A106	**10 Pounds**			
	ND (1910).			
	a. Hobart.	—	—	—
A107	**20 Pounds**			
	ND (1910).	—	—	—

Commercial Banking Company of Sydney (Superscribed)

1910 Superscribed Issue

		Good	Fine	XF
A108	**1 Pound** ND (1910).	5000.	15,000.	45,000.
A109	**5 Pounds** ND (1910).	—	—	—
A110	**10 Pounds** ND (1910).	—	—	—

English, Scottish & Australian Bank (Superscribed)

1910 Superscribed Issue

		Good	Fine	XF
A111	**1 Pound** ND (1910).			
	a. Adelaide.	—	—	—
	b. Melbourne.	8000.	23,000.	60,000.
	c. Sydney.	—	—	—
A112	**5 Pounds** ND (1910).			
	a. Adelaide.	—	—	—
	b. Melbourne.	—	—	—
	c. Sydney.	—	—	—
A113	**10 Pounds** ND (1910).			
	a. Adelaide.	—	—	—
	b. Melbourne.	—	—	—

		Good	Fine	XF
A114	**20 Pounds** ND (1910).			
	a. Adelaide.	—	—	—
	b. Melbourne.	—	—	—
A115	**50 Pounds** ND (1910).			
	a. Adelaide.	—	—	—
	b. Melbourne.	—	—	—
	c. Sydney.	—	—	—

London Bank of Australia (Superscribed)

1910 Superscribed Issue

		Good	Fine	XF
A116	**1 Pound** ND (1910).			
	a. Adelaide.	—	—	—
	b. Melbourne.	3000.	9000.	35,000.
A117	**5 Pounds** ND (1910).	—	—	—
A118	**10 Pounds** ND (1910).			
	a. Adelaide.	—	—	—
	b. Melbourne.	—	—	—
	c. Sydney.	—	—	—
A119	**50 Pounds** ND (1910).			
	a. Adelaide.	—	—	—
	b. Melbourne.	—	—	—
	c. Sydney.	—	—	—
A120	**100 Pounds** ND (1910).			
	a. Adelaide.	—	—	—
	b. Melbourne.	—	—	—
	c. Sydney.	—	—	—

National Bank of Australasia (Superscribed)

1910 Superscribed Issue

		Good	Fine	XF
A121	**1 Pound** ND (1910).			
	a. Adelaide.	—	—	—
	b. Melbourne.	3000.	9000.	35,000.
	c. Perth.	6000.	15,000.	50,000.
	d. Sydney.	—	—	—
A122	**5 Pounds** ND (1910).			
	a. Adelaide.	—	—	—
	b. Melbourne.	8000.	25,000.	50,000.
	c. Perth.	—	—	—
	d. Sydney.	—	—	—
A123	**10 Pounds** ND (1910).			
	a. Adelaide.	20,000.	60,000.	110,000.
	b. Melbourne.	—	—	—
	c. Perth.	23,000.	65,000.	120,000.
A124	**20 Pounds** ND (1910).			
	a. Adelaide.	—	—	—
	b. Melbourne.	35,000.	85,000.	220,000.
	c. Perth.	—	—	—
A125	**50 Pounds** ND (1910).			
	a. Adelaide.	—	—	—
	b. Melbourne.	—	—	—
	c. Sydney.	—	—	—

		Good	Fine	XF
A126	**100 Pounds** ND (1910).			
	a. Ovpt. on Melbourne.	—	—	—
	b. Ovpt. on Perth.	—	—	—

QUEENSLAND GOVERNMENT (SUPERSCRIBED)

1910 SUPERSCRIBED ISSUE

		Good	Fine	XF
A127	**1 Pound** ND (1910).	—	—	—
A128	**5 Pounds** ND (1910).	—	—	—

ROYAL BANK OF AUSTRALIA (SUPERSCRIBED)

1910 SUPERSCRIBED ISSUE

		Good	Fine	XF
A129	**1 Pound** ND (1910).			
	a. Melbourne.	15,000.	45,000.	85,000.
	b. Sydney.	12,000.	40,000.	80,000.

UNION BANK OF AUSTRALIA (SUPERSCRIBED)

1910 SUPERSCRIBED ISSUE

		Good	Fine	XF
A130	**1 Pound** ND (1910).			
	a. Adelaide.	10,000.	30,000.	75,000.
	b. Melbourne.	800.	25,000.	60,000.
	c. Perth.	10,000.	30,000.	75,000.
A131	**5 Pounds** ND (1910).			
	a. Adelaide.	—	—	—
	b. Hobart.	—	—	—
	c. Melbourne.	—	—	—
	d. Perth.	—	—	—
	e. Sydney.	—	—	—
A132	**10 Pounds** ND (1910).			
	a. Adelaide.	—	—	—
	b. Hobart.	—	—	—
	c. Perth.	—	—	—
	d. Sydney.	—	—	—
A133	**20 Pounds** ND (1910).			
	a. Adelaide.	—	—	—
	b. Hobart.	—	—	—
	c. Melbourne.	35,000.	85,000.	220,000.
	d. Perth.	—	—	—
	e. Sydney.	—	—	—
A134	**50 Pounds** ND (1910).			
	a. Adelaide.	—	—	—
	b. Melbourne.	—	—	—

WESTERN AUSTRALIAN BANK (SUPERSCRIBED)

1910 SUPERSCRIBED ISSUE

		Good	Fine	XF
A135	**1 Pound** ND (1910).	12,000.	40,000.	85,000.
A136	**5 Pounds** ND (1910).	—	—	—
A137	**10 Pounds** ND (1910).	—	—	—

COMMONWEALTH OF AUSTRALIA, TREASURY NOTES

1913 FIRST ISSUE

Note:#1B: Because of the shortage of currency created by WWI, old plates from the English, Scottish & Australian Bank Ltd. were used for a special printing of 1,300,000 notes.

		Good	Fine	XF
1	**5 Shillings** ND (ca. 1916). Black on green unpt. Portr. Kg. George V at l. Back green.			
	a. Sign. C. J. Cerutty and J. R. Collins. (Not issued).	—	—	—
	s1. Specimen w/o sign.	—	—	—
	s2. W/violet handstamp: *Specimen*. Sign. C. J. Cerutty and J. R. Collins. (Not issued).	—	—	—

		Good	Fine	XF
1A	**10 Shillings** ND (1913). Dk. blue on m/c unpt. Arms at l. Red serial #. Goulburn Weir (Victoria) at ctr on back. Sign. J. R. Collins and G. T. Allen.	10,000.	25,000.	75,000.
1B	**1 Pound** ND (1914-15 -old date 1.9.1894). Pale blue and pink. Allegorical woman w/anchor standing at l., arms at r. A reprint of the English, Scottish & Australian Bank Limited superscribed: *AUSTRALIAN NOTE* w/text. Sign. J. R. Collins and G. T. Allen.			
	a. Serial # prefix and suffix *A*. Rare.	12,000.	28,000.	80,000.
	b. Serial # prefix and suffix *B*.	12,000.	28,000.	80,000.

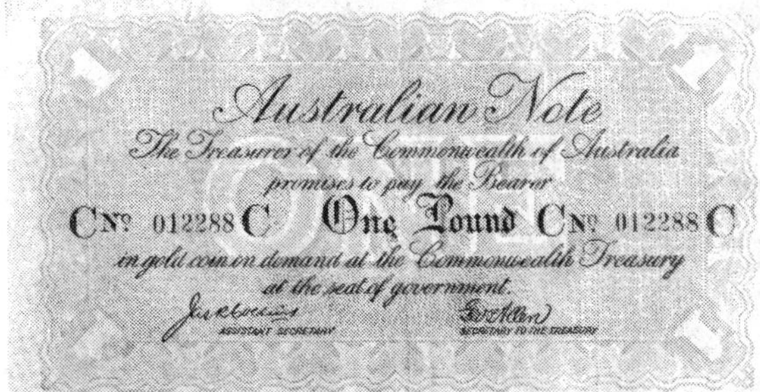

		Good	Fine	XF
2	**1 Pound** ND (1913-14). Black text on blue, orange and m/c unpt. *Australian Note* at top. Sign. J. R. Collins and G. T. Allen.			
	a. W/*No.* by serial #.	8000.	18,000.	75,000.
	b. W/o *No.* by serial #.	8000.	18,000.	75,000.
2A	**1000 Pounds** ND (1914-24). Lt. blue. Arms at bottom ctr. Flock of Merino sheep (Bungaree, S.A.) at ctr.			
	a. Sign. J. R. Collins and G. T.	—	—	—
	b. Sign. J. Kell and J. R.	—	—	—

Note: #2A was issued primarily for interbank transactions only, but a few were released to the public.

1913 SECOND ISSUE

		Good	Fine	XF
3	**10 Shillings** ND (1913-18). Dk. blue on m/c unpt. Arms at l. Goulburn Weir (Victoria) at ctr. on back. Black serial #. Ovpt: *HALF SOVEREIGN* in borders.			
	a. Sign. J. R. Collins and G. T. Allen (1914). Five serial # varieties.	3000.	6000.	40,000.
	b. Sign. C. J. Cerutty and J. R. Collins (1918). Seriffed serial #.	2500.	5500.	38,000.

		Good	Fine	XF
4	**1 Pound** ND (1913-18). Dk. blue on m/c unpt. Crowned arms at ctr. Gold mine workers at ctr. on back.			
	a. Sign. J. R. Collins and G. T. Allen (1914). Red serial #	5000.	15,000.	60,000.
	d. Sign. C. J. Cerutty and J. R. Collins (1918).	400.	2000.	8000.
4A	**5 Pounds** ND (1913). Dk. blue on m/c unpt. Arms at l. River landscape (Hawkesbury) at ctr. w/o mosaic unpt. of 5's on back.	10,000.	30,000.	80,000.

		Good	Fine	XF
5	**5 Pounds** ND (1913-18). Dk. blue on m/c unpt. Arms at l. River landscape (Hawkesbury) at ctr. w/mosaic unpt of 5's.			
	a. Sign. J. R. Collins and G. T. varieties.	450.	1650.	4500.
	b. Sign. C. J. Cerutty and J. R. Collins (1918).	250.	800.	2400.

		Good	Fine	XF
6	**10 Pounds** ND (1913-18). Dk. blue on m/c unpt. Arms at bottom ctr. Horse drawn wagons loaded w/sacks of grain (Narwonah, N.S.W.) at ctr. on back.			
	a. Sign. J. R. Collins and G. T.	4000.	10,000.	—
	b. Sign. C. J. Cerutty and J. R. Collins (1918). 2 serial # varieties.	2000.	6000.	12,500.

		Good	Fine	XF
9	**100 Pounds** ND (1914-18). Blue on m/c unpt. Arms at l. Upper Yarra River (Victoria) at l. ctr., Leura Falls (N.S.W.) at ctr. r. on back.			
	a. Sign. J. R. Collins and G. T.	6000.	13,500.	—
	b. Sign. C. J. Cerutty and J. R. Collins (1918).	3500.	10,000.	20,000.

		Good	Fine	XF
7	**20 Pounds** ND (1914-18). Dk. blue on m/c unpt. Arms at l. Lumberjacks cutting a tree (Bruny Isle, Tasmania) at ctr. on back.			
	a. Sign. J. R. Collins and G. T.	3500.	8000.	19,000.
	b. Sign. C. J. Cerutty and J. R. Collins (1918).	3000.	6500.	15,500.
8	**50 Pounds** ND (1914-18). Blue on m/c unpt. Arms at top ctr. Flock of Merino sheep (Bungaree, S. A.) at ctr. on back.			
	a. Sign. J. R. Collins and G. T.	—	—	—
	b. Sign. C. J. Cerutty and J. R. Collins (1918).	1700.	5000.	13,500.

COMMONWEALTH BANK OF AUSTRALIA

1923-25 ISSUE

		VG	VF	UNC
10	**1/2 Sovereign** ND (1923). Dk. brown and brown on m/c unpt. Portr. Kg. George V at r., arms at l. Sign. title: *CHAIRMAN OF DIRECTORS NOTE ISSUE DEPT./COMMONWEALTH BANK OF AUSTRALIA* below l. sign. Goulburn Weir (Victoria) at ctr on back. Sign. D. Miller and J. R. Collins.	350.	1200.	4000.

		VG	VF	UNC
11	**1 Pound** ND (1923). Dk. olive-green on m/c unpt. Portr. Kg. George V at r., arms at l. w/title: *CHAIRMAN OF DIRECTORS NOTE ISSUE DEPT./COMMONWEALTH BANK OF AUSTRALIA* below l. sign. Capt. Cook's Landing at Botany Bay at ctr. on back. Sign. D. Miller and J. R. Collins. Printer: T. S. Harrison.			
	a. Serial # prefix H; J; K.	1000.	2500.	6000.
	b. Fractional serial # prefix.	250.	700.	2500.
12	**1 Pound** ND (1923). Dk. olive-green on m/c unpt. Portr. Kg. George V at r., arms at l. w/title: *CHAIRMAN OF DIRECTORS NOTE ISSUE DEPT./COMMONWEALTH BANK OF AUSTRALIA* below l. sign. W/o imprint. Capt. Cook's landing at Botany Bay at ctr. on back. Sign. D. Miller and J. R. Collins. Like #11 but w/o printer's name.			
	a. Serial # prefix J; K.	3000.	6500.	—
	b. Fractional serial # prefix.	200.	600.	1700.

13 5 Pounds

ND (1924-27). Deep blue on m/c unpt. Portr. Kg. George V at r., arms at l. w/title: *CHAIRMAN OF DIRECTORS NOTE ISSUE DEPT./COMMONWEALTH BANK OF AUSTRALIA* below l. sign. River landscape (Hawkesbury) at ctr. on back.

	VG	VF	UNC
a. J. Kell and J. R. Collins (1924).	350.	1250.	3500.
b. J. Kell and J. Heathershaw (1927).	500.	1750.	4500.
c. Sign. E. C. Riddle and J. Heathershaw (1927).	3000.	7500.	—

14 10 Pounds

	VG	VF	UNC
ND (1925). Dp. red on m/c unpt. Portr. Kg. George V at r., arms at l. at r. w/title: *CHAIRMAN OF DIRECTORS NOTE ISSUE DEPT./COMMONWEALTH BANK OF AUSTRALIA* below l. sign. Horse drawn wagons loaded w/sacks of grain at lower ctr. on back. Proof w/o sign.	—	Unc	10,000.

1926-27 ISSUE

#15-19 portr. Kg. George V at r., arms at l. w/title: *GOVERNOR/COMMONWEALTH BANK OF AUSTRALIA* below lower l. sign.

15 1/2 Sovereign

ND (1926-33). Dk. brown and brown on m/c unpt. Portr. Kg. George V at r., arms at l. w/title: *GOVERNOR / COMMONWEALTH BANK OF AUSTRALIA* below lower l. sign. Goulburn Weir (Victoria) at ctr. on back. Like #10.

	VG	VF	UNC
a. J. Kell and J. R. Collins (1926).	225.	800.	2400.
b. J. Kell and J. Heathershaw (1927).	350.	950.	3500.
c. Sign. E. C. Riddle and J. Heathershaw (1927).	125.	400.	1400.
d. Sign. E. C. Riddle and H. J. Sheehan (1933).	325.	900.	2400.

16 1 Pound

ND (1926-32). Dk. olive-green on m/c unpt. W/o imprint. Portr. Kg. George V at r., arms at l. w/title: *GOVERNOR / COMMONWEALTH BANK OF AUSTRALIA* below lower l. sign. Capt. Cook's landing at Botany Bay at ctr. on back. Like #12.

	VG	VF	UNC
a. J. Kell and J. R. Collins (1926).	120.	350.	1700.
b. J. Kell and J. Heathershaw (1927).	100.	325.	2000.
c. Sign. E. C. Riddle and J. Heathershaw (1927).	30.00	100.	500.
d. Sign. E. C. Riddle and H. J. Sheehan (1932).	65.00	300.	1800.

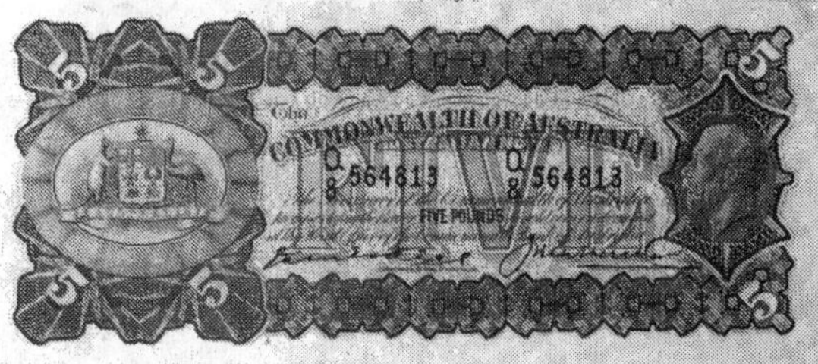

17 5 Pounds

ND (1927-32). Dp. blue on m/c unpt. Portr. Kg. George V at r., arms at l. w/title: *GOVERNOR / COMMONWEALTH BANK OF AUSTRALIA* below lower l. sign. River landscape (Hawkesbury) at ctr. at back. Like #13.

	VG	VF	UNC
a. J. Kell and J. Heathershaw (1927).	650.	2200.	6000.
b. Sign. E. C. Riddle and J. Heathershaw (1928).	200.	750.	3000.
c. Sign. E. C. Riddle and H. J. Sheehan (1932).	400.	1000.	4500.

18 10 Pounds

ND (1925-33). Dp. red on m/c unpt. Portr. Kg. George V at r., arms at l. w/title: *GOVERNOR / COMMONWEALTH BANK OF AUSTRALIA* below lower l. sign. Horse drawn wagons loaded w/sacks of grain (Narwonah, N.S.W.) at ctr. at back. Like #14.

	VG	VF	UNC
a. J. Kell and J. R. Collins (1925).	1750.	4500.	12,000.
b. Sign. E. C. Riddle and J. Heathershaw (1925).	650.	2000.	6500.
c. Sign. E. C. Riddle and H. J. Sheehan (1933).	3000.	8000.	18,500.

1933-34 ISSUES

#19-24 Sign. E. C. Riddle and H. J. Sheehan. Wmk: Edward (VIII), Prince of Wales.

19 10 Shillings

	VG	VF	UNC
ND (1933). Brown on m/c unpt. Portr. Kg. George V at r. Allegorical manufacturers at ctr., lg. *1/2* at l. on back.	200.	750.	4000.

20 10 Shillings

	VG	VF	UNC
ND (1934). Brown on m/c unpt. Red ovpt: *TEN SHILLINGS* in margins on #19.	100.	350.	1500.

21 10 Shillings

	VG	VF	UNC
ND (1936-39). Orange on m/c unpt. Reduced size from #19 and #20. Allegorical manufacturers at ctr., lg. *10/-* at l. on back.	85.00	250.	800.

		VG	VF	UNC
22	**1 Pound**			
	ND (1933-38). Dk. green on m/c unpt. Portr. Kg. George V at r. Shepherds w/sheep at ctr., lg. *L1* at l. on back.			
	a. Issued note.	30.00	70.00	375.
	s. Specimen.	—	—	—

		VG	VF	UNC
23	**5 Pounds**			
	ND (1933-39). Dp. Blue on m/c unpt. Portr. Kg. George V at l. Dock workers w/sacks, bales and barrels at upper l. on back.	150.	450.	1600.

		VG	VF	UNC
24	**10 Pounds**			
	ND (1934-39). Dp. red on m/c unpt. Portr. Kg. George V at ctr. Group symbolizing agriculture at upper r. on back.	175.	600.	1800.

1938-40 ISSUE

#25-28B wmk: Captain Cook.

Note: #28A and 28B were intended for interbank use during WWII only. All but a few specimens were destroyed in 1958.

		VG	VF	UNC
24A	**5 Shillings**			
	ND (1946). Black on red-brown unpt. Portr. Kg. George VI at ctr. Back red-brown; Australian crown coin design at ctr. Sign. H. T. Armitage and S. G. McFarlane. (Not issued).	—	—	—

		VG	VF	UNC
25	**10 Shillings**			
	ND (1939-52). Orange on m/c unpt. Portr. Kg. George VI at r. Allegorical manufacturers at ctr., lg *10/* at l. on back. Like #21.			
25	**10 Shillings**			
	a. Orange sign. H. J. Sheehan and S. G. McFarlane (1939).	3.00	25.00	250.
	b. Black sign. H. T. Armitage and S. G. McFarlane (1942).	2.50	15.00	100.
	c. Black sign. H. C. Coombs and G. P. N. Watt (1949).	3.50	20.00	200.
	d. Black sign. H. C. Coombs and R. Wilson (1952).	3.50	20.00	200.

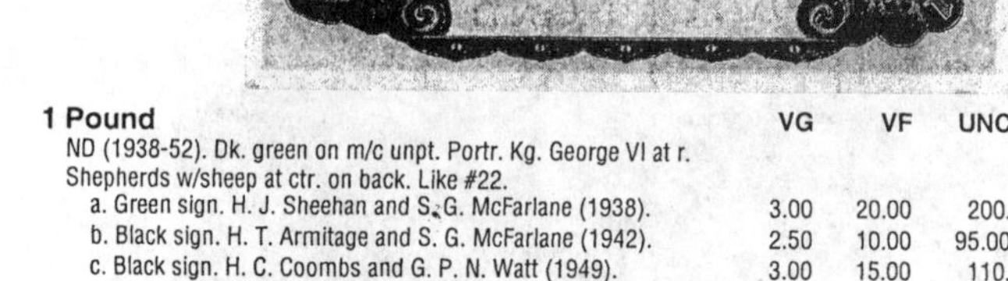

		VG	VF	UNC
26	**1 Pound**			
	ND (1938-52). Dk. green on m/c unpt. Portr. Kg. George VI at r. Shepherds w/sheep at ctr. on back. Like #22.			
	a. Green sign. H. J. Sheehan and S. G. McFarlane (1938).	3.00	20.00	200.
	b. Black sign. H. T. Armitage and S. G. McFarlane (1942).	2.50	10.00	95.00
	c. Black sign. H. C. Coombs and G. P. N. Watt (1949).	3.00	15.00	110.
	d. Black sign. H. C. Coombs and R. Wilson (1952).	4.00	14.00	95.00

		VG	VF	UNC
27	**5 Pounds**			
	ND (1939-52). Dp. blue on m/c unpt. Portr. Kg. George VI at l. Workers w/sacks, bales and barrels at upper l. on back. Like #23.			
	a. Blue sign. H. J. Sheehan and S. G. McFarlane (1939).	20.00	55.00	700.
	b. Black sign. H. T. Armitage and S. G. McFarlane (1941).	15.00	40.00	300.
	c. Black sign. H. C. Coombs and G. P. N. Watt (1949).	15.00	45.00	400.
	d. Black sign. H. C. Coombs and R. Wilson (1952).	12.00	35.00	300.

#		VG	VF	UNC
28	**10 Pounds** ND (1940-52). Dp. red on m/c unpt. Portr. Kg. George VI at bottom ctr. Group symbolizing agriculture at upper r. on back. Like #24.			
	a. Red sign. H. J. Sheehan and S. G. McFarlane (1940).	45.00	250.	1750.
	b. Black sign. H. T. Armitage and S. G. McFarlane (1942).	30.00	90.00	500.
	c. Black sign. H. C. Coombs and G. P. N. Watt (1949).	30.00	100.	600.
	d. Black sign. H. C. Coombs and R. Wilson (1952).	50.00	300.	1500.
28A	**50 Pounds** ND (1939). Purple on m/c unpt. Portr. Kg. George VI. Specimen.	—	—	—

#		VG	VF	UNC
28B	**100 Pounds** ND (1939). Brown on m/c unpt. Portr. Kg. George VI. Sign: H. J. Sheehan and S. G. McFarlane. Specimen.	—	—	—

1953-54 Issue

#29-32 sign. H. C. Coombs and R. Wilson. w/title: *GOVERNOR/COMMONWEALTH BANK OF AUSTRALIA* below lower l. sign. Wmk: Captain Cook.

#		VG	VF	UNC
29	**10 Shillings** ND (1954-60). Dk. brown on m/c unpt. Arms at lower l. portr. M. Flinders at r. Parliament in Canberra at l. ctr. on back.	2.00	6.00	40.00

#		VG	VF	UNC
30	**1 Pound** ND (1953-60). Dk. green on m/c unpt. Arms at upper ctr., medallic portr. Qn. Elizabeth II at r. Facing medallic portr. C. Sturt and H. Hume on back.	2.00	6.00	45.00
31	**5 Pounds** ND (1954-59). Blue on m/c unpt. Arms at upper l., portr. Sir J. Franklin at r. Sheep and agricultural products between bull and cow's head on back.			
	a. Issued note.	8.00	20.00	100.
	s. Specimen.	—	—	—
32	**10 Pounds** ND (1954-59). Red and black on m/c unpt. Portr. Gov. Phillip at l., arms at upper ctr. Symbols of science and industry at ctr., allegorical woman kneeling w/compass at r. on back.			
	a. Issued note.	20.00	40.00	250.
	s. Specimen.	—	—	—

Commonwealth of Australia

Reserve Bank

1960-61 ND Issue

#33-36 like #29-32. Sign. H. C. Coombs w/title: *GOVERNOR/RESERVE BANK of AUSTRALIA* below lower l. sign. R. Wilson. Wmk: Capt. James Cook. Replacement notes: Serial # suffix *.

#		VG	VF	UNC
35	**5 Pounds** ND (1960-65). Black on blue unpt. Arms at upper l., portr. Sir John Franklin at r. Back blue; cattle, sheep and agricultural products across ctr. Like #31.			
	a. Issued note.	20.00	45.00	400.
	r. Serial # suffix *, replacement.	750.	7500.	30,000.
	s. Specimen.	1250.	8500.	35,000.

		VG	VF	UNC
36	**10 Pounds** ND (1960-65). Black on red unpt. Arms at top ctr., portr. Gov. Arthur Philip at l. Symbols of science and industry on back. Like #32.			
	a. Issued note.	40.00	100.	1200.
	s. Specimen.	1500.	9000.	38,000.

The Republic of Austri (Oesterreich), a parliamenta democracy located mountainous central Europe, ha an area of 32,374 sq. mi. (83,84 sq. km.) and a population of 8. million. Capital: Vienna. Austria primarily an industrial countr Machinery, iron and steel, textile yarns and timber are exported.

The territories later to be know as Austria were overrun in pr Roman times by various tribe including the Celts. Upon the fa of the Roman Empire, th country became a margravate of Charlemagne's Empire. Premysl 2 Otakar, King of Bohemi gained possession in 1252, only to lose the territory to Rudolf of Habsburg in 1276. Thereafte until World War I, the story of Austria was that of the ruling Habsburgs, Holy Roman emperors fro 1438-1806. From 1815-1867 it was a member of the *Deutsche Bund* (German Union).

During World War I, the Austro-Hungarian Empire was one of the Central Powers wi Germany, Bulgaria and Turkey. At the end of the war, the empire was dissolved and Austr established as an independent republic. In March 1938, Austria was incorporated into Germany Third Reich. Allied forces of both East and West liberated Austria in April 1945, and subsequent divided it into four zones of military occupation. On May 15, 1955, the four powers formal recognized Austria as a sovereign independent democratic state.

RULERS:

Maria Theresa, 1740-1780
Joseph II, jointly with his Mother, 1765-1780 alone, 1780-1790
Leopold II, 1790-1792
Franz II (I), 1792-1835 (as Franz II, 1792-1806) (as Franz I, 1806-1835)
Ferdinand I, 1835-1848
Franz Joseph, 1848-1916
Karl I, 1916-1918

MONETARY SYSTEM:

1 Gulden = 60 Kreuzer, 1754-1857
1 Gulden = (Florin) = 100 Kreuzer, 1857-1892
1 Krone = 100 Heller, 1892-1924
1 Schilling = 100 Groschen, 1924-1938, 1945-2002
1 Euro = 100 Cents, 2002-

KINGDOM

Note on "Formulare": Corresponding to the following listings through the 1840's the existed so-called "Formulare" w/o seal, sign. or serial # destined to be displayed in various bankir houses. These are included in many collections. Market value of "Formulare" is shown in ea respective section.

WIENER STADT BANCO

1759 ISSUE

Zettel **= Note.**

Note: Market value for "Formulare" #A1 and #A2 is $500.00.

#A11, 50 Gulden

#A23, 10 Gulden

		Good	Fine
A1	**10 Gulden** 1.11.1759. Black. Unique.	—	—
A2	**25 Gulden** 1.11.1759. Black. Unique.	—	—

1762 ISSUE

Note: Market value for "Formulare" #A3-A7 is $350.00.

		Good	Fine
A3	**5 Gulden** 1.7.1762. Black.	—	—

		Good	Fine	XF
A4	**10 Gulden** 1.7.1762. Black, value red.	—	—	—
A5	**25 Gulden** 1.7.1762. Black, value ochre.	—	—	—
A6	**50 Gulden** 1.7.1762. Black, value green.	—	—	—
A7	**100 Gulden** 1.7.1762. Red, value green.	—	—	—

1771 ISSUE

#A8-A14 size 85x170mm. Note: Market value for "Formulare" #A8-A14 is $325.00.

		Good	Fine	XF
A8	**5 Gulden** 1.7.1771. Black.	—	—	—
A9	**10 Gulden** 1.7.1771. Black.	—	—	—
A10	**25 Gulden** 1.7.1771. Black.	—	—	—
A11	**50 Gulden** 1.7.1771. Black.	—	—	—
A12	**100 Gulden** 1.7.1771. Black.	—	—	—
A13	**500 Gulden** 1.7.1771. Black.	—	—	—
A14	**1000 Gulden** 1.7.1771. Black.	—	—	—

1784 ISSUE

#A15-A21 wmk: *WIENER STADT / BANCO ZETTEL*. Note: Market value for "Formulare" #A15-A21 is $225.00.

		Good	Fine	XF
A15	**5 Gulden** 1.11.1784. Black.	—	—	—
A16	**10 Gulden** 1.11.1784. Black.	—	—	—
A17	**25 Gulden** 1.11.1784. Black.	—	—	—
A18	**50 Gulden** 1.11.1784. Black.	—	—	—
A19	**100 Gulden** 1.11.1784. Black.	—	—	—
A20	**500 Gulden** 1.11.1784. Black.	—	—	—
A21	**1000 Gulden** 1.11.1784. Black.	—	—	—

1796 ISSUE

#A22-A28 wmk: *WIENER STADT / BANCO ZETTEL*.

		Good	Fine	XF
A22	**5 Gulden** 1.8.1796. Black.			
	a. Issued note.	100.	325.	650.
	s. Formulare.	—	—	—
A23	**10 Gulden** 1.8.1796. Black.	150.	400.	800.
A24	**25 Gulden** 1.8.1796. Black.	—	—	—
A25	**50 Gulden** 1.8.1796. Black.	—	—	—
A26	**100 Gulden** 1.8.1796. Black.	—	—	—
A27	**500 Gulden** 1.8.1796. Black.	—	—	—
A28	**1000 Gulden** 1.8.1796. Black.	—	—	—

1800 ISSUE

#A29-A37 wmk: Value as Arabic and Roman Numeral.

Note: #A31-A37 exist as forgeries printed in France during the reign of Napoleon (often on blue paper). These are valued about the same as originals.

Note: Market value for "Formulare" #A33-A35 is $75.00.

		Good	Fine	XF
A29	**1 Gulden** 1.1.1800. Black.	4.00	15.00	40.00
A30	**2 Gulden** 1.1.1800. Black.	5.00	17.50	45.00

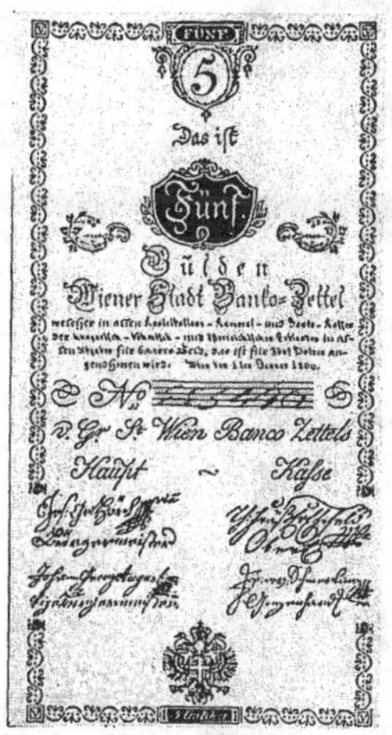

		Good	Fine	XF
A31	**5 Gulden** 1.1.1800. Black.	6.00	20.00	60.00

		Good	Fine	XF
A32	**10 Gulden** 1.1.1800. Black.	8.50	25.00	75.00

		Good	Fine	XF
A33	**25 Gulden** 1.1.1800. Black.	17.50	40.00	100.
A34	**50 Gulden** 1.1.1800. Black.	50.00	200.	—
A35	**100 Gulden** 1.1.1800. Black.	37.50	150.	—
A36	**500 Gulden** 1.1.1800. Black.	1000.	3000.	—
A37	**1000 Gulden** 1.1.1800. Black.	800.	2500.	—

1806 ISSUE

Note: Market value for "Formulare" #A38-A43 is $60.00.

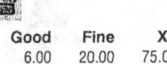

		Good	Fine	XF
A38	**5 Gulden** 1.6.1806. Black.	6.00	20.00	75.00

		Good	Fine	XF
A39	**10 Gulden** 1.6.1806. Black.	8.50	25.00	90.00

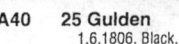

		Good	Fine	XF
A40	**25 Gulden** 1.6.1806. Black.	30.00	100.	400.

		Good	Fine	XF
A41	**50 Gulden** 1.6.1806. Black and brown.	35.00	200.	500.

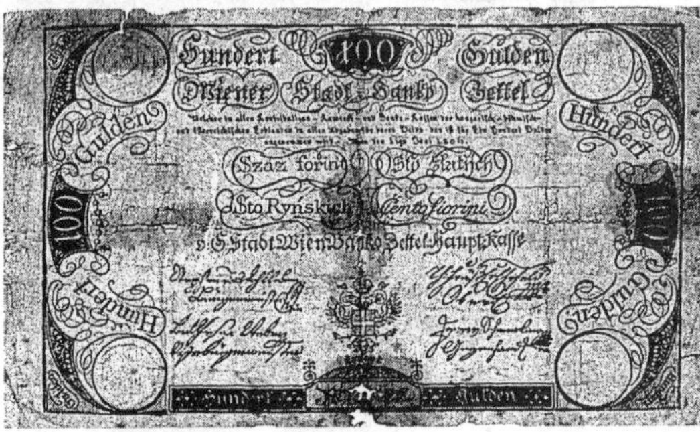

		Good	Fine	XF
A42	**100 Gulden** 1.6.1806. Black and red.	50.00	200.	—
A43	**500 Gulden** 1.6.1806. Black and red. Rare	—	—	—

PRIVILEGIRTE VEREINIGTE EINLÖSUNGS UND TILGUNGS DEPUTATION

1811 ISSUE

Einlösungs - Scheine **= Demand Notes**

Note: Market value for "Formulare" #A44-A49 is $60.00.

		Good	Fine	XF
A44	**1 Gulden** 1.3.1811. Black.	12.00	25.00	100.
A45	**2 Gulden** 1.3.1811. Black.	100.	200.	450.
A46	**5 Gulden** 1.3.1811. Black.	120.	400.	—

		Good	Fine	XF
A47	**10 Gulden** 1.3.1811. Black.	200.	500.	—
A48	**20 Gulden** 1.3.1811. Black. Rare	—	—	—
A49	**100 Gulden** 1.3.1811. Black. Rare	—	—	—

1813 ISSUE

Anticipations - Scheine (Anticipation Notes)

Note: Market value for "Formulare" #A50-A53 is $60.00.

		Good	Fine	XF
A50	**2 Gulden** 16.4.1813. Black.	15.00	30.00	150.
A51	**5 Gulden** 16.4.1813. Black.	100.	200.	—
A52	**10 Gulden** 16.4.1813. Black. Rare	—	—	—
A53	**20 Gulden** 16.4.1813. Black.	500.	1000.	—

OESTERREICHISCHE NATIONAL ZETTEL BANK

1816 ISSUE

Note: Market value for "Formulare" #A54-A60 is $60.00.

		Good	Fine	XF
A54	**5 Gulden** 1.7.1816. Black.	75.00	225.	450.
A55	**10 Gulden** 1.7.1816. Black.	200.	450.	1000.
A56	**25 Gulden** 1.7.1816. Black.	—	—	—
A57	**50 Gulden** 1.7.1816. Black.	—	—	—
A58	**100 Gulden** 1.7.1816. Black.	—	—	—
A59	**500 Gulden** 1.7.1816. Black.	—	—	—
A60	**1000 Gulden** 1.7.1816. Black.	—	—	—

PRIVILEGIRTE OESTERREICHISCHE NATIONAL-BANK

1825 ISSUE

#A61-A66 wmk: value and ornaments.

Note: Market value for "Formulare" #A61-A67 is $30.00.

		Good	Fine	XF
A61	**5 Gulden** 23.6.1825. Black and red.	100.	250.	—
A62	**10 Gulden** 23.6.1825. Black and red.	200.	—	—
A63	**25 Gulden** 23.6.1825. Black and red.	—	—	—

		Good	Fine	XF
A64	**50 Gulden** 23.6.1825. Black and red.	—	—	—
A65	**100 Gulden** 23.6.1825. Black and red.	—	—	—
A66	**500 Gulden** 23.6.1825. Black and red.	—	—	—

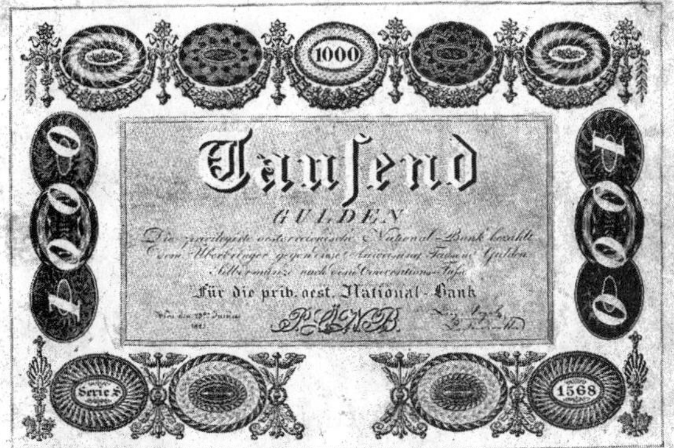

		Good	Fine	XF
A67	**1000 Gulden** 23.6.1825. Black.	—	—	—

1833-34 ISSUE

#A68-A69 wmk: Bank name and value.

		Good	Fine	XF
A68	**5 Gulden** 9.12.1833. Black.	200.	—	—
A69	**10 Gulden** 8.12.1834. Black.	200.	—	—

1841 ISSUE

#A70-A74 wmk: PÖNB and value.

Note: Market value for "Formulare" #A70-A74 is $150.00.

		Good	Fine	XF
A70	**5 Gulden** 1.1.1841. Black. Profile of Austria at top ctr., arms between cherubs below.	25.00	120.	—
A71	**10 Gulden** 1.1.1841. Black. Austria at top ctr.	150.	350.	—

		Good	Fine	XF
A72	**50 Gulden** 1.1.1841. Black. Eleven female heads (Pomona) at top ctr.	—	—	—
A73	**100 Gulden** 1.1.1841. Black. Eleven female heads (Pomona) at top ctr.	—	—	—

A74	**1000 Gulden** 1.1.1841. Black. Eleven female heads (Pomona) at top ctr., 2 heads of Austria facing below, allegorical woman standing at l. and r.	—	—	—

1847 Issue

#A75-A78 wmk: value and ornaments.

		Good	Fine	XF
A75	**5 Gulden** 1.1.1847. Black. Atlas and Minerva at l., Austria at r.	30.00	125.	—
A76	**10 Gulden** 1.1.1847. Black. Atlas and Minerva at l., Austria at r.	35.00	150.	—

A77	**100 Gulden** 1.1.1847. Black. Austria at l., Atlas and Minerva at r., crowned shield at top ctr., arms below. Rare	—	—	—
A78	**1000 Gulden** 1.1.1847. Black. Austria at lower l. and r., Atlas and Minerva at l. and r. Rare	—	—	—

1848-54 Issue

		Good	Fine	XF
A81	**1 Gulden** 1.7.1848. Black. Austria at top ctr., arms below at bottom	10.00	20.00	80.00

		Good	Fine	XF
A82	**2 Gulden** 1.7.1848. Black. Atlas and Minerva at l., Austria at r., arms at bottom ctr.	15.00	50.00	200.
A83	**10 Gulden** 1.7.1854. Black. Austria at l., Atlas and Minerva at r.	125.	400.	—

1858 Issue

		Good	Fine	XF
A84	**1 Gulden** 1.1.1858. Black and red. Austria at top ctr., arms at bottom.	5.00	10.00	40.00
A85	**10 Gulden** 1.1.1858. Black and red. Man w/genius on pedestal at l. and r., Austria w/lion below.	100.	300.	—

A86	**100 Gulden** 1.3.1858. Black and red. Austria at l., arms between 2 cherubs at top ctr., god of the river Danube at r. Rare	—	—	—
A87	**1000 Gulden** 1.3.1858. Black and red. Woman symbolizing power at l., w/symbol of abundance. Rare	—	—	—

1859-63 Issue

		Good	Fine	XF
A88	**5 Gulden** 1.5.1859. Black and red. Austria at top ctr., Imperial eagle at bottom	12.50	40.00	250.
A89	**10 Gulden** 15.1.1863. Black and red. Shepherd, miner and peasant.	65.00	150.	350.

		Good	Fine	XF
A90	**100 Gulden** 15.1.1863. Black and green. 2 cherubs w/coins at l., supported arms at bottom ctr., 2 cherubs w/sword, book and purse at r.	150.	600.	—

1848 ISSUE

		Good	Fine	XF
A79	**1 Gulden** 1.5.1848. Black and green. Uniface.	25.00	60.00	200.
A80	**2 Gulden** 1.5.1848. Black. Uniface.	30.00	120.	300.

K.K. HAUPTMÜNZAMT

MÜNZSCHEINE

1849 ISSUE

		Good	Fine	XF
A91	**6 Kreuzer** 1.7.1849. Black on green unpt. Arms at ctr.	2.00	8.00	25.00
A92	**10 Kreuzer** 1.7.1849. Black. Arms at ctr.			
	a. Rose unpt.	2.00	7.50	20.00
	b. Lt. blue unpt.	2.00	7.50	20.00

1860 ISSUE

		Good	Fine	XF
A93	**10 Kreuzer** 1.11.1860. Black on lt. brown unpt. of waves.			
	a. Plain edges.	1.50	5.00	15.00
	b. Serrated edges. White wmk. paper.	1.50	5.00	15.00

		Good	Fine	XF
A94	**10 Kreuzer** 1.11.1860. Black on lt. brown unpt. Back green; *Oest.* at bottom l., *Wahr.* at r. 87 x 39mm.	2.00	6.00	25.00

		Good	Fine	XF
A95	**10 Kreuzer** 1.11.1860. Black on green unpt. *10* at bottom l. and	2.00	6.00	25.00

K.U.K. STAATS-CENTRAL-CASSA

CASSA-ANWEISUNGEN

1848 ISSUE

Note: Market value for "Formulare" #A96-A101 ranges from $500. to $750.

		Good	Fine	XF
A96	**30 Gulden** 1.9.1848.	—	—	—
A97	**60 Gulden** 1.9.1848.	—	—	—
A98	**90 Gulden** 1.9.1848.	—	—	—
A99	**300 Gulden** 1.9.1848.	—	—	—
A100	**600 Gulden** 1.9.1848.	—	—	—
A101	**900 Gulden** 1.9.1848.	—	—	—

1849 FIRST ISSUE

Note: Market value for "Formulare" #A102-A107 ranges from $50. to $100.

		Good	Fine	XF
A102	**10 Gulden** 1.1.1849.	—	—	—

		Good	Fine	XF
A103	**25 Gulden** 1.1.1849.	—	—	—
A104	**50 Gulden** 1.1.1849.	—	—	—
A105	**100 Gulden** 1.1.1849.	—	—	—
A106	**500 Gulden** 1.1.1849.	—	—	—
A107	**1000 Gulden** 1.1.1849.	—	—	—

1849 THIRD ISSUE

		Good	Fine	XF
A115	**30 Gulden** 1.3.1849.	—	—	—
A116	**60 Gulden** 1.3.1849.	—	—	—
A117	**90 Gulden** 1.3.1849.	—	—	—
A118	**300 Gulden** 1.3.1849.	—	—	—
A119	**600 Gulden** 1.3.1849.	—	—	—
A120	**900 Gulden** 1.3.1849.	—	—	—

1850 ISSUE

		Good	Fine	XF
A128	**50 Gulden** 1.1.1850.	—	—	—
A129	**100 Gulden** 1.1.1850.	—	—	—
A130	**500 Gulden** 1.1.1850.	—	—	—
A131	**1000 Gulden** 1.1.1850.	—	—	—

1849 SECOND ISSUE

		Good	Fine	XF
A108	**5 Gulden** 1.3.1849.	200.	400.	1000.

		Good	Fine	XF
A109	10 Gulden 1.3.1849.	—	—	—
A110	25 Gulden 1.3.1849.	—	—	—
A111	50 Gulden 1.3.1849.	—	—	—
A112	100 Gulden 1.3.1849.	—	—	—
A113	500 Gulden 1.3.1849.	—	—	—
A114	1000 Gulden 1.3.1849.	—	—	—

1849 Fourth Issue

		Good	Fine	XF
A121	5 Gulden 1.7.1849.	—	—	—
A122	10 Gulden 1.7.1849.	—	—	—
A123	25 Gulden 1.7.1849.	—	—	—
A124	50 Gulden 1.7.1849.	—	—	—
A125	100 Gulden 1.7.1849.	—	—	—
A126	500 Gulden 1.7.1849.	—	—	—
A127	1000 Gulden 1.7.1849.	—	—	—

K.K. Staats-Central-Casse

Reichs-Schatzscheine

1850 Issue

#A132-A134 wmk: KKCK and ornament.

Note: Market value for "Formulare" #A132-A134 is $100.00.

		Good	Fine	XF
A132	100 Gulden 1.1.1850. Black. 2 women, miner and farmers.	—	—	—
A133	500 Gulden 1.1.1850. Black.	—	—	—
A134	1000 Gulden 1.1.1850. Black. Husband and wife w/dog, scientist, merchant.	—	—	—

1851 Issue

#A135-A137 wmk: KKCK and wreath or ornament.

Note: Market value for "Formulare" #A135-A137 is $15.00.

		Good	Fine	XF
A135	5 Gulden 1.1.1851. Black. Bearded man w/club at l., helmeted woman at r., arms at bottom ctr.	20.00	120.	400.
A136	10 Gulden 1.1.1851. Black. Floating woman at l., floating warrior at r.	50.00	200.	—

		Good	Fine	XF
A137	50 Gulden 1.1.1851. Black. Scene of plowing w/Emperor Joseph II, aide and O. Trnka, farmer from Slavikovice (Moravia) at lower ctr.	200.	800.	—
A138	100 Gulden 1.1.1851.	—	—	—

		Good	Fine	XF
A139	500 Gulden 1.1.1851.	—	—	—
A140	1000 Gulden 1.1.1851.	—	—	—

1852 Issue

		Good	Fine	XF
A141	100 Gulden 1.1.1852.	—	—	—
A142	500 Gulden 1.1.1852.	—	—	—
A143	1000 Gulden 1.1.1852.	—	—	—

1853 First Issue

Note: Market value for "Formulare" #A144-A146 is $100.00.

		Good	Fine	XF
A144	100 Gulden 1.1.1853.	—	—	—
A145	500 Gulden 1.1.1853.	—	—	—
A146	1000 Gulden 1.1.1853.	—	—	—

1853 Second Issue

NOTE: Market value for "Formulare" #A147-A149 is $100.00.

		Good	Fine	XF
A147	100 Gulden 8.10.1853.	—	—	—
A148	500 Gulden 8.10.1853.	—	—	—
A149	1000 Gulden 8.10.1853.	—	—	—

K.K. Staats-Central-Casse

1866 Issue

#A150-A151 wmk: STN.

		Good	Fine	XF
A150	1 Gulden 7.7.1866. Black on green unpt. Woman seated holding gear at lower l., Mercury seated at r. Back gray; 10 coats-of-arms in border.	3.00	15.00	35.00

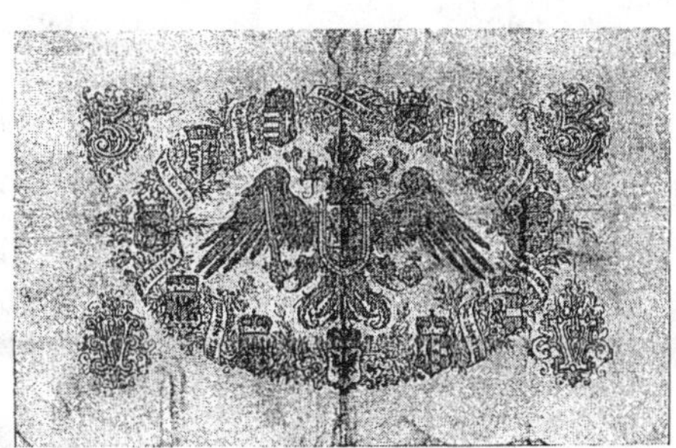

		Good	Fine	XF
A151	**5 Gulden** 1866-67. Black on pink unpt. Woman w/lyre at upper l., elderly man seated at upper r. Back brown. Eagle.			
	a. 7.7.1866-18.1.1867. Black serial (block) #.	25.00	80.00	250.
	b. Red serial (block) #.	10.00	30.00	150.

		Good	Fine	XF
A152	**50 Gulden** 25.8.1866. Black on green-blue unpt. Warrior w/lion at l., woman w/dragon and book at r. Back olive and brown. 2 men.	75.00	375.	—

K.K. REICHS-CENTRAL-CASSA

1881-84 ISSUE

#A153-A156 medallic head of Emperor Franz Joseph at upper ctr. German text on face, back with Hungarian text.

		Good	Fine	XF
A153	**1 Gulden** 1.1.1882. Blue on gray-brown unpt.	2.25	7.50	25.00

		Good	Fine	XF
A154	**5 Gulden** 1.1.1881. Green on gray-brown unpt. Woman w/book at l., woman in armor at r.	10.00	40.00	100.

		Good	Fine	XF
A155	**50 Gulden** 1.1.1884. Blue on gray-brown unpt. 2 boys at l. and at r.	500.	1250.	—

1888 ISSUE

		Good	Fine	XF
A156	**1 Gulden** 1.7.1888. Blue. Medallion portr. Franz Joseph I top, kneeling angel at bottom r. Reversed image at top on back, kneeling angel at bottom l. German text on face, Hungarian text on back.	5.00	15.00	50.00

OESTERREICHISCH-UNGARISCHE BANK

AUSTRO-HUNGARIAN BANK

1880 ISSUE

Note: The face description refers to the side of the note w/German text. Hungarian text is on back.

		Good	Fine	XF
1	**10 Gulden** 1.5.1880. Blue and brown. Women at l. and r.	15.00	50.00	250.

		Good	Fine	XF
2	**100 Gulden** 1.5.1880. Blue and brown. Boy w/sheaf and sickle at l., boy w/book at r.	400.	800.	—
3	**1000 Gulden** 1.5.1880. Blue and orange. Child at l. and r. Rare	—	—	—

1900-02 Issue

		Good	Fine	XF
4	**10 Kronen** 31.3.1900. Lilac and gray. Young angel at l. and r.	20.00	70.00	200.

		Good	Fine	XF
5	**20 Kronen** 31.3.1900. Red and green unpt. Cherub w/portr. woman over arms at l.	15.00	50.00	250.

		Good	Fine	XF
6	**50 Kronen** 2.1.1902. Blue on rose unpt. Seated woman at l. and at r., arms at upper ctr.	8.00	30.00	120.

		Good	Fine	XF
7	**100 Kronen** 2.1.1902. Green on rose unpt. Seated woman w/child at l., blacksmith stands at anvil at r.	70.00	200.	1000.

		Good	Fine	X
8	**1000 Kronen** 2.1.1902. Blue. Woman at r.			
	a. Gray-green unpt.	1.00	4.00	12.0
	b. Rose unpt. Later issue from Series #1440 onward.	.50	2.00	6.0

1904-12 Issue

		Good	Fine	X
9	**10 Kronen** 2.1.1904. Purple on red, dk. blue and dk. green unpt. Portr. Princess Rohan at r.	1.50	6.00	20.0

		Good	Fine	X
10	**20 Kronen** 2.1.1907. Blue on red-brown and green unpt. Arms at upper l., Austria at upper ctr., portr. woman at r.	6.00	15.00	50.(
11	**100 Kronen** 2.1.1910. Blue. Woman w/flowers at r.	50.00	150.	40

		Good	Fine	XF
12	100 Kronen 2.1.1912. Green on red and blue unpt. Facing portr. woman at r. Profile portr. of woman at upper r. on back.	.50	2.00	6.00

1913-14 Issue

		VG	VF	UNC
13	20 Kronen 2.1.1913. Blue on green and red unpt. Portr. woman at upper l., arms at upper r. Arms at upper l., portr. woman at upper r. on back.	.25	2.00	8.00
14	20 Kronen 2.1.1913. Blue on green and red unpt. Like #13 but w/*II AUFLAGE* (2nd issue) at l. border. Wmk: XX XX.	.25	2.00	8.00
15	50 Kronen 2.1.1914. Blue and green. Woman at ctr. Wmk: tile pattern.	.50	3.00	10.00

1914-15 Issue

		VG	VF	UNC
16	1 Krone 5.8.1914. Woman at ctr. Proof. Rare	—	—	—

		VG	VF	UNC
17	2 Kronen 5.8.1914. Blue on green and red unpt. Portr. girl at upper ctr. Back brown-orange on green unpt.			
	a. Thin paper, series A or B. 2 serial # varieties.	2.00	8.00	20.00
	b. Heavier paper, series C.	.25	.75	2.00
18	5 Kronen 5.8.1914. Red and green. Woman in relief at r. Proof. Rare	—	—	—

		VG	VF	UNC
19	10 Kronen 2.1.1915. Blue and green. Arms at upper l., portr. boy at bottom ctr. Arms at upper l., portr. young man at upper r. on back.	.25	.75	3.50

1916-18 Issue

		VG	VF	UNC
20	1 Krone 1.12.1916. Red. Woman's head at upper l. and r. Helmeted warrior's bust at ctr. on back. Block #1000-1700.	.10	.20	.40

		VG	VF	UNC
21	2 Kronen 1.3.1917. Red on gray unpt. Woman at l. and r. Block #1000-1600 and Block #A1000-1100. 2 serial # varieties.	.15	.25	1.50

Note: For #20 and #21 w/block # over 7000 see Hungary #10 and #11.

		VG	VF	UNC
22	5 Kronen 1.10.1918. Woman at l. and r. Proof. Rare	—	—	—
23	25 Kronen 27.10.1918. Blue on gray-brown unpt. Girl at l. Up to block #2000.	10.00	25.00	100.

Note: For #23 w/block # over 3000 see Hungary #12 and #13.

		VG	VF	UNC
24	200 Kronen 27.10.1918. Green on pink unpt. Girl at l. Series B.	30.00	70.00	200.

Note: For #24 Series A see Hungary #14-16.

		VG	VF	UNC
25	**10,000 Kronen** 2.11.1918. Purple. Woman at r.	15.00	60.00	150.

KRIEGSDARLEHENSKASSE KASSENSCHEIN

WAR STATE LOAN BANK

1914 ISSUE

#26-28 arms at l., 3 allegorical figures standing at r. Black text on back.

		VG	VF	UNC
26	**250 Kronen** 26.9.1914. Red and green on lt. red unpt. Arms at l., 3 allegorical figures standing at r.	75.00	250.	500.

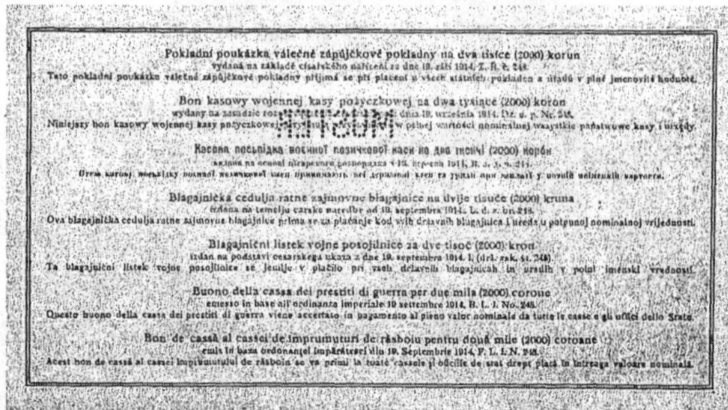

		VG	VF	UNC
27	**2000 Kronen** 26.9.1914. Green and brown on lt. green unpt. Arms at l., 3 allegorical figures standing at r.	75.00	250.	500.

		VG	VF	UNC
28	**10,000 Kronen** 26.9.1914. Lilac and dk. blue on lt. lilac unpt. Arms at l., 3 allegorical figures standing at r.	75.00	250.	500.

REPUBLIC - PRE WWII

OESTERREICHISCH-UNGARISCHEN BANK KASSENSCHEIN

1918-19 ISSUE

		Good	Fine	XF
29	**1000 Kronen** 28.10.1918. Green. Uniface.	200.	400.	1000.
30	**1000 Kronen** 30.10.1918. Green. Uniface. Like #29.	200.	400.	1000.
31	**5000 Kronen** 25.10.1918.	200.	400.	1000.
32	**5000 Kronen** 5.2.1919. Olive. Back printed.	200.	400.	1000.
33	**10,000 Kronen** 26.10.1918. Back printed.	200.	400.	1000.
34	**10,000 Kronen** 4.11.1918. Back printed.	200.	400.	1000.
35	**100,000 Kronen** 3.10.1918. Violet and brown. Back printed.	200.	400.	1000.
36	**1,000,000 Kronen** 18.11.1918. Red-brown. Uniface.	300.	600.	1500.

1921 ISSUE

Note: For Treasury notes of various Hungarian branch offices, see Hungary #4-9.

		Good	Fine	XF
37	**1000 Kronen** 23.12.1921. Green.	200.	400.	1000.

		Good	Fine	XF
38	**5000 Kronen** 23.12.1921. Olive.	200.	400.	1000.
39	**10,000 Kronen** 23.12.1921. Blue.	200.	400.	1000.
40	**100,000 Kronen** 23.12.1921. Violet.	200.	400.	1000.

1920 Issue

#41-45 ovpt: *Ausgegeben nach dem 4. Oktober 1920* (issued after October 4, 1920) on Oesterreichisch-Ungarische Bank issues.

		Good	Fine	XF
41	**1 Krone** 4.10.1920. Green ovpt. on #20.	10.00	25.00	60.00
42	**2 Kronen** 4.10.1920. Green ovpt. on #21.			
	a. Ovpt. on German side.	10.00	25.00	60.00
	b. Ovpt. on Hungarian side.	18.00	25.00	100.

		Good	Fine	XF
43	**10 Kronen** 4.10.1920. Red ovpt. on #19.	7.00	17.50	70.00
44	**20 Kronen** 4.10.1920. Red ovpt. on #13.	9.00	22.50	90.00
45	**20 Kronen** 4.10.1920. Red ovpt. on #14.	7.00	17.50	70.00
46	**50 Kronen** 4.10.1920. Red ovpt. on #15.	7.00	17.50	70.00
47	**100 Kronen** 4.10.1920. Red ovpt. on #12.	7.00	17.50	70.00

		Good	Fine	XF
48	**1000 Kronen** 4.10.1920 (-old date 2.1.1902). Red ovpt. on #8.	8.00	20.00	50.00

1919 Issue

49-66 ovpt: *DEUTSCHÖSTERREICH* on Oesterreichisch-Ungarische Bank issues.

		VG	VF	UNC
49	**1 Krone** ND (1919 -old date 1.12.1916). Green ovpt. on #20.	.10	.25	1.00

NOTICE

Readers with unlisted dates, signature varieties, etc. are invited to submit photocopies or, high resolution (300 dpi, 100% size) scans of their notes to: Standard Catalog of World Paper Money, 700 East State St. Iola, WI 54990-0001, or E-Mail: george.cuhaj@fwpubs.com.

		VG	VF	UNC
50	**2 Kronen** ND (1919 -old date 1.3.1917). Green ovpt. on #21.	.15	.25	1.00
51	**10 Kronen** ND (1919 -old date 2.1.1915). Orange ovpt. on #19.			
	a. Issued note.	.15	.25	1.00
	b. W/handstamp: *NOTE ECHT, STEMPEL FALSCH* (note genuine, ovpt. forged). Reported not confirmed	—	—	—

		VG	VF	UNC
52	**20 Kronen** ND (1919 -old date 2.1.1913). Red ovpt. on #13.	.20	.60	3.00

		VG	VF	UNC
53	**20 Kronen** ND (1919 -old date 2.1.1913). Red ovpt. on #14.			
	a. Issued note.	.15	.35	2.00
	b. W/handstamp: *NOTE ECHT, STEMPEL FALSCH* (note genuine, ovpt. forged.)	10.00	20.00	35.00

		VG	VF	UNC
54	**50 Kronen** ND (1919 -old date 2.1.1914). Red ovpt. on #15.			
	a. Issued note.	.15	.50	3.00
	b. W/handstamp: *NOTE ECHT, STEMPEL FALSCH* (note genuine, ovpt. forged.)	30.00	60.00	200.

		VG	VF	UNC
55	**100 Kronen**			
	ND (1919 -old date 2.1.1912). Back in Hungarian. Red ovpt. on #12.			
	a. Issued note.	.15	.50	3.00
	b. W/handstamp: *NOTE ECHT, STEMPEL FALSCH* (note genuine, ovpt. forged.)	30.00	60.00	200.
	c. W/handstamp: *NOTE ECHT, STEMPEL NICHT KONSTATIERBAR* (note genuine, ovpt. cannot be verified.)	35.00	75.00	250.

		VG	VF	UNC
56	**100 Kronen**			
	ND (1919 -old date 2.1.1912). Green. Like # 12 and #55, but German text on back. Red ovpt.	.25	2.00	5.00
57	**1000 Kronen**			
	ND (1919 -old date 2.1.1902). Hungarian text on back. Red ovpt. on #8b.			
	a. Issued note.	.25	.50	2.00
	b. W/handstamp: *NOTE ECHT, STEMPEL FALSCH* (note genuine, ovpt. forged.)	20.00	60.00	200.
	c. W/handstamp: *NOTE ECHT, STEMPEL NICHT KONSTATIERBAR* (note genuine, ovpt. cannot be verified). Reported not confirmed	—	—	—

		VG	VF	UNC
58	**1000 Kronen**			
	ND (1919 -old date 2.1.1902). Blue. Red ovpt. on #57, w/additional black ovpt: *ECHT / OESTERREICHISCH-UNGARISCHE BANK / HAUPTANSTALT WIEN.*	15.00	30.00	75.00

		VG	VF	UNC
59	**1000 Kronen**			
	ND (1919 -old date 2.1.1902). Blue. Like #8 and #57 but w/German text on back and red ovpt.	1.00	3.00	20.00

		VG	VF	UNC
60	**1000 Kronen**			
	ND (1919 -old date 2.1.1902). Blue. Like #8 and #57 but w/ornaments, portr. woman at upper l. and r. on back. Red ovpt.	.50	2.00	6.00
61	**1000 Kronen**			
	ND (1919 -old date 2.1.1902). Blue. Like #60 but w/additional red ovpt: *II AUFLAGE* (2nd issue).	.50	2.00	6.00

NOTICE

Readers with unlisted dates, signature varieties, etc.
are invited to submit photocopies or,
high resolution (300 dpi, 100% size) scans of their notes to:
Standard Catalog of World Paper Money,
700 East State St. Iola, WI 54990-0001,
or E-Mail: george.cuhaj@fwpubs.com.

		VG	VF	UNC
62	**10,000 Kronen** ND (1919 -old date 2.11.1918). Purple. Woman at r. Hungarian text on back. Red ovpt. on #25.			
	a. Issued note.	50.00	150.	350.
	b. W/handstamp *NOTE ECHT, STEMPEL FALSCH* (note genuine, ovpt. forged).	60.00	200.	450.
63	**10,000 Kronen** ND (1919 -old date 2.11.1918). Purple. Red ovpt. on #62. W/additional black ovpt: *ECHT. ÖSTERR - UNGAR. BANK HAUPTANSTALT WIEN.*	50.00	150.	350.
64	**10,000 Kronen** ND (1919 -old date 2.11.1918). Purple. Like #25 and #62. German text on back. Red ovpt.	2.00	8.00	20.00

		VG	VF	UNC
65	**10,000 Kronen** ND (1919 -old date 2.11.1918). Purple. Like #25 and #62 w/red ovpt. Ornaments, portr. woman at upper l. and r. on back.	2.00	8.00	20.00
66	**10,000 Kronen** ND (1919 -old date 2.11.1918). Purple. Like #65, but *II AUFLAGE* (2nd issue) in left margin. Ornaments and portr. woman at upper l. and r. on back.	.50	1.00	5.50

AUSTRIAN GOVERNMENT

1922 FIRST ISSUE

		VG	VF	UNC
73	**1 Krone** 2.1.1922. Red. Uniface.	.10	.15	.40

		VG	VF	UNC
74	**2 Kronen** 2.1.1922. Red. Woman at upper r. Uniface.	.10	.15	.40

		VG	VF	UNC
75	**10 Kronen** 2.1.1922. Blue-violet. Child at r.	.10	.20	.75

		VG	VF	UNC
76	**20 Kronen** 2.1.1922. Purple. Bearded man at r.	.10	.20	.75

		VG	VF	UNC
77	**100 Kronen** 2.1.1922. Green. Princess Rohan at r.	.10	.20	1.00

		VG	VF	UNC
78	**1000 Kronen** 2.1.1922. Blue. Woman at r.	.10	.25	2.00

		VG	VF	UNC
79	**5000 Kronen** 2.1.1922. Green and red-brown. Portr. woman at r.	1.00	5.00	20.00

		VG	VF	UNC
80	**50,000 Kronen** 2.1.1922. Red-brown and green. Portr. woman at r. 2 serial # varieties.	5.00	25.00	70.00

		VG	VF	UNC
81	**100,000 Kronen** 2.1.1922. Blue and green. Portr. woman in floral frame at r.	15.00	60.00	200.

1922 SECOND ISSUE

82	**100,000 Kronen** 11.9.1922. Purple.	—	—	—
83	**5,000,000 Kronen** 11.9.1922. Green.	—	—	—

1922 THIRD ISSUE

		VG	VF	UNC
84	**500,000 Kronen** 20.9.1922. Brown-lilac. Portr. woman w/3 children at r.	25.00	175.	450.

OESTERREICHISCHE NATIONALBANK

AUSTRIAN NATIONAL BANK

1924 FIRST ISSUE

		VG	VF	UNC
85	**10,000 Kronen** 2.1.1924. Purple and green. Girl at upper r.	.75	5.00	25.00
86	**1,000,000 Kronen** 1.7.1924. Woman at r.	—	—	—

1924 REFORM ISSUE

		VG	VF	UNC
87	**1 Schilling on 10,000 Kronen** 2.1.1924. Red ovpt: *Ein Schilling* at ctr. and *II Auflage* in lower margin on #85.	.60	4.00	20.00

1925 ISSUE

		Good	Fine	XF
88	**5 Schillinge** 2.1.1925. Green. Arms at upper l., portr. youth (by painter E. Zwiauer) at upper r.	12.50	40.00	150.
89	**10 Schillinge** 2.1.1925. Brown-violet. Man at r.	15.00	50.00	175.

		Good	Fine	XF
90	**20 Schillinge** 2.1.1925. Green. Arms at upper l., portr. woman at upper r.	17.50	100.	300.
91	**100 Schillinge** 2.1.1925. Blue and m/c. Woman at r.	75.00	250.	750.

		Good	Fine	XF
92	**1000 Schillinge** 2.1.1925. Blue on green and red-brown unpt. Portr. woman at r.	250.	800.	—

1927-30 ISSUE

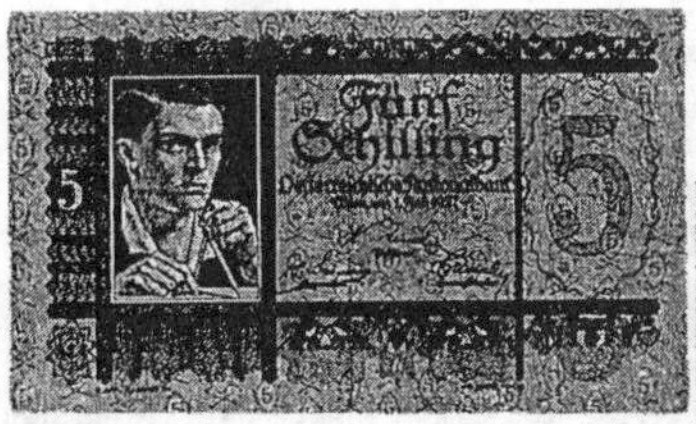

		Good	Fine	XF
93	**5 Schilling** 1.7.1927. Blue on green unpt. Portr. Prof. Dr. H. Brücke w/compasses at l. Terraced iron ore mining near Eisenerz (Steirmark) at top l. ctr. on back.	2.00	15.00	50.00

		Good	Fine	XF
94	**10 Schilling** 3.1.1927. Blue on green and red unpt. Mercury at top. Allegorical woman (Harvest) and Dürnstein Castle at bottom on back.	3.00	20.00	85.00

		Good	Fine	XF
95	**20 Schilling** 2.1.1928. Green. Girl at l., farmer at r. Farmer in field on back.	5.00	25.00	100.

		Good	Fine	XF
96	**50 Schilling** 2.1.1929. Blue on brown-olive. Woman at l., man at r.	40.00	175.	500.
97	**100 Schilling** 3.1.1927. Violet and green. Allegorical female (Sciences) at r. Science Academy in Vienna on back.	15.00	40.00	150.

		Good	Fine	XF
98	**1000 Schilling** 2.1.1930. Blue-violet on green unpt. Woman w/statue of Athena at upper r. Salzburg in mountains on back. Wmk: Women's head.			
	a. Issued note.	350.	1500.	—
	s. Specimen.	—	Unc	1500.

1933-36 ISSUE

		VG	VF	UNC
99	**10 Schilling** 2.1.1933. Blue. Woman in national costume at top. Arms above Grossglockner Mountain at top on back.			
	a. Numerals of value in 4 corners on diagonal lines.	4.00	15.00	80.00
	b. Numerals of value in 4 corners on diagonal and vertical lines.	4.00	15.00	80.00

		VG	VF	UNC
100	**50 Schilling** 2.1.1935. Blue-violet on green unpt. Hubert Sterrer as youth at r. Village of Maria Wörth and Lake Wörth *(Wörthersee)* on back.	40.00	250.	1000.

101	**100 Schilling** 2.1.1936. Dk. green on m/c unpt. Woman w/Edelweiss at r. (Not issued).	—	Unc	1000.

Note: During 1938-45 the following German notes were in circulation: #171, 173, 174, 179-186, 188-190.

ALLIED OCCUPATION - WWII

ALLIIERTE MILITÄRBEHÖRDE

ALLIED MILITARY AUTHORITY

1944 ISSUE

#102-111 issued from 1944 through 29.5.1945. Wmk: "a" printed by Forbes Lithograph Corp. for U.S.B.E.P. and wmk: "b" in England.

		VG	VF	UNC
102	**50 Groschen** 1944. Red-brown.			
	a. Printer: Forbes Lithograph Corp. Wmk: *MILITARY AUTHORITY.* Wmk. barely visible and w/o wavy lines.	10.00	25.00	45.00
	b. Printed in England. Wmk: Wavy lines.	.20	.50	4.00

		VG	VF	UNC
103	**1 Schilling** 1944. Blue on green unpt.			
	a. Printer: Forbes Lithograph Corp. Wmk: *MILITARY AUTHORITY.* Wmk. barely visible and w/o wavy lines.	.75	2.00	8.00
	b. Printed in England. Wmk: Wavy lines.	.40	1.00	4.00

		VG	VF	UNC
104	**2 Schilling** 1944. Blue and black.			
	a. Printer: Forbes Lithograph Corp. Wmk: *MILITARY AUTHORITY.* Wmk. barely visible and w/o wavy lines.	.75	2.00	10.00
	b. Printed in England. Wmk: Wavy lines.	.40	1.00	4.00

		VG	VF	UNC
105	**5 Schilling** 1944. Lilac.	.40	1.00	7.50

		VG	VF	UNC
106	**10 Schilling** 1944. Green.	.40	1.00	7.50

		VG	VF	UNC
107	**20 Schilling** 1944. Blue on violet unpt.	1.25	3.00	10.00
108	**25 Schilling** 1944. Brown on lilac unpt.			
	a. Issued note.	50.00	85.00	200.
	r. Replacement w/small "x" to r. of serial #.	—	—	—

		VG	VF	UNC
109	**50 Schilling** 1944. Brown on lt. orange unpt.	2.00	5.00	15.00

		VG	VF	UNC
10	**100 Schilling** 1944. Green on m/c unpt.			
	a. Serial # prefix fraction w/o line.	2.00	5.00	15.00
	b. Serial # prefix fraction w/line.	3.00	7.50	20.00
11	**1000 Schilling** 1944. Blue on green and m/c unpt.	50.00	175.	650.

RUSSIAN OCCUPATION - WWII

REPUBLIK ÖSTERREICH

1945 ISSUE

Issued (20.12.1945) during the Russian occupation.

12	**50 Reichspfennig** ND. Brown on orange unpt. Specimen stamped and perforated: *MUSTER.*	—	Unc	700.

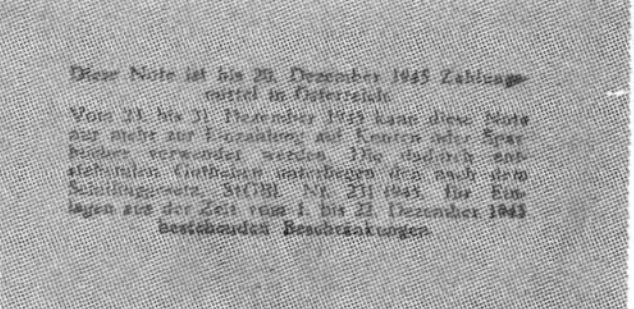

		VG	VF	UNC
13	**1 Reichsmark** ND. Green.			
	a. Space below *1* at l. and *Reichs-/mark* 2mm.	3.00	8.00	30.00
	b. Space below *1* at l. and *Reichs-/mark* 3mm.	3.00	8.00	30.00

REPUBLIC

OESTERREICHISCHE NATIONALBANK

AUSTRIAN NATIONAL BANK

1945 ISSUES

		VG	VF	UNC
114	**10 Schilling** 29.5.1945. Blue-violet on brown unpt. Similar to #99. Woman in national costume. Arms above Grossglockner Mountain at top on back. 2 serial # varieties.	.50	2.00	12.50

		VG	VF	UNC
115	**10 Schilling** 29.5.1945. Blue-violet. Like #114, but *ZWEITE AUSGABE* (2nd issue) in lower design. 2 serial # varieties.	3.00	15.00	35.00

		VG	VF	UNC
116	**20 Schilling** 29.5.1945. Blue-green on brown unpt. Similar to #95. Girl at l., farmer at r. Farmer in field on back. Many color variations. 2 serial # varieties.	1.00	2.50	15.00

		VG	VF	UNC
117	**50 Schilling** 29.5.1945. Dk. green on brown unpt. Similar to #100. Hubert Sterrer as youth at r. Many color varieties. Bldg. and lake scene on back.	3.00	15.00	50.00

		VG	VF	UNC
118	**100 Schilling** 29.5.1945. Blue-violet on gray unpt. Woman (allegory of the sciences) at r. Academy of Sciences in Vienna at ctr. on back. Many color varieties.	.50	4.00	15.00

		Good	Fine	XF
119	**100 Schilling** 29.5.1945. Blue-violet on gray unpt. Like #118, but w/*ZWEITE AUSGABE* (2nd issue) vertically at r. Many color varieties.	40.00	100.	350.

		Good	Fine	XF
120	**1000 Schilling** 29.5.1945. Green. Similar to #98. Woman w/figure of Athena at upper r. Salzburg in mountains on back.			
	a. Issued note.	100.	250.	—
	s. Specimen.	—	Unc	500.

1945-47 ISSUES

		VG	VF	UNC
121	**5 Schilling** 4.9.1945. Blue or violet on gray-green unpt. Similar to #93. Portr. Prof. Dr. H. Brücke w/compass at l. Terraced iron mining near Eisenerz (Steirmark) at top l. ctr. on back. Many color varieties.	1.00	3.00	20.00

		VG	VF	UNC
122	**10 Schilling** 2.2.1946. Brown and m/c. Portr. woman at upper r. Mint tower in Solbad Hall (Tirol) at top ctr. on back.	1.50	15.00	100.

		VG	VF	UN
123	**20 Schilling** 2.2.1946. Brown and m/c. Woman at ctr. St. Stephen's church in Vienna at ctr. on back.	2.50	20.00	11

		VG	VF	UNC
124	**100 Schilling** 2.1.1947. Dk. green on violet, blue and m/c unpt. Portr. woman in national costume at r. Back lilac and green; mountain scene.	12.50	30.00	200

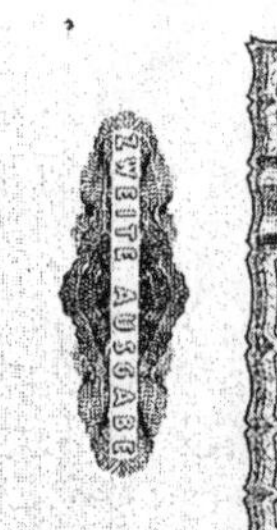

		VG	VF	UNC
125	**1000 Schilling** 1.9.1947. Dk. brown on gray green unpt. Woman w/figure of Athena at upper r., w/*ZWEITE AUSGABE* vertically at l. (2nd issue). Salzburg in mountains on back.	100.	400.	900.

1949-54 ISSUES

		VG	VF	UNC
126	**5 Schilling** 1951. Violet on gray-green. Like #121, but w/*AUSGABE 1951* in l. margin.	5.00	20.00	80.00

		VG	VF	UNC
127	**10 Schilling** 2.1.1950. Purple. Bldgs. at lower l. ctr., horseman of the Spanish Royal Riding School at r. Back brown; Belvedere Castle in Vienna at l. ctr.	1.00	4.00	50.00
128	**10 Schilling** 2.1.1950. Purple. Like #127 but w/ovpt: *2 AUFLAGE* (2nd issue) at upper r. on back.	2.00	8.00	70.00

		VG	VF	UNC
129	**20 Schilling** 2.1.1950. Brown on red and blue unpt. Portr. Joseph Haydn at r. Tower at l., cherub playing kettledrum at ctr. on back.			
	a. *OESTERREICHISCHE* in unpt.	2.00	10.00	80.00
	b. Error in bank name *OESTERREICHISCEE* in unpt. (Error visible in second or third line at bottom of unpt. at bottom).	15.00	30.00	100.

		VG	VF	UNC
130	**50 Schilling** 2.1.1951. Lilac and violet on m/c unpt. Portr. J. Prandtauer at r. Woman at l., cloister at. Melk at ctr., urn at r. on back.	4.00	15.00	80.00
131	**100 Schilling** 3.1.1949. Dk. green on lilac and purple unpt. Cherub at lower l., woman's head at upper r. Back olive green and purple; mermaid at l. ctr., Vienna in background.	7.00	15.00	85.00

		VG	VF	UNC
132	**100 Schilling** 3.1.1949. Dk. green on lilac and purple unpt. Like #131 but w/ovpt: *2 AUFLAGE* (2nd issue) at lower l.	7.00	15.00	85.00

		VG	VF	UNC
133	**100 Schilling** 2.1.1954. Green on m/c unpt. F. Grillparzer at r. Castle Dürnstein on back.			
	a. Issued note.	7.00	15.00	70.00
	s. Specimen.	—	Unc	50.00

		VG	VF	UNC
134	**500 Schilling** 2.1.1953. Dk. brown on blue and red unpt. Prof. Wagner-Jauregg at r. University of Vienna on back.			
	a. Issued note.	40.00	85.00	200.
	s. Specimen.	—	Unc	50.00

		VG	VF	UNC
135	**1000 Schilling** 2.1.1954. Blue on m/c unpt. A. Bruckner at r. Bruckner organ at St. Florian on back.			
	a. Issued note.	75.00	175.	450.
	s. Specimen.	—	Unc	50.00

1956-65 Issues

		VG	VF	UNC
136	**20 Schilling** 2.7.1956. Brown on red-brown and m/c unpt. Carl Auer Freiherr von Welsbach at r., arms at l. Village Maria Rain, church and Karawanken mountains on back.			
	a. Issued note.	.75	7.50	15.00
	s. Specimen.	—	Unc	50.00

		VG	VF	UNC
138	**100 Schilling** 1.7.1960 (1961). Dk. green on m/c unpt. Violin and music at lower l., Johann Strauss at r., arms at l. Schönbrunn Castle on back.			
	a. Issued note.	3.00	10.00	40.00
	s. Specimen.	—	Unc	50.00
140	**1000 Schilling** 2.1.1961 (1962). Dk. blue on m/c unpt. Viktor Kaplan at r. Dam and Persenburg Castle, arms at r. on back. 148 x 75mm.			
	a. Issued note. Rare.	—	—	—
	s. Specimen.	—	Unc	800.

Note: #140 was in use for only 11 weeks.

		VG	VF	UNC
141	**1000 Schilling** 2.1.1961 (1962). Dk. blue on m/c unpt. Like #140 but w/blue lined unpt. up to margin. 158 x 85mm.			
	a. Issued note.	35.00	90.00	185.
	s. Specimen. Ovpt. and perforated: *Muster.*	—	Unc	1500.

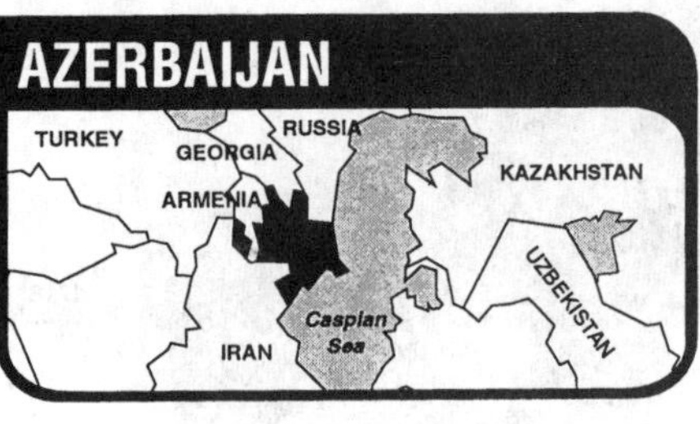

The Republic of Azerbaijan includes the Nakhichevan Autonomous Republic and Nagorno-Karabakh Autonomous Region (which was abolished in 1991). Situated in the eastern area of Transcaucasia, it is bordered in the west by Armenia, in the north by Georgia and the Russian Federation of Dagestan, to the east by the Caspian Sea and to the south by Iran. It has an area of 33,430 sq. mi. (86,600 sq. km.) and a population of 7.83 million. Capital: Baku. The area is rich in mineral deposits of aluminum, copper, iron, lead, salt and zinc, with oil as its leading industry. Agriculture and livestock follow in importance.

In ancient times home of Scythian tribes and known under the Romans as Albania and to the Arabs as Arran, the country of Azerbaijan formed at the time of its invasion by Seljuk Turks a prosperous state under Persian suzerainty. From the 16th century the country was a theatre of fighting and political rivalry between Turkey, Persia and later Russia. Baku was first annexed to Russia by Czar Peter I in 1723. After the Russian retreat in 1735, the whole of Azerbaijan north of the Aras River became a khanate under Persian control until 1813 when annexed by Czar Alexander I into the Russian empire.

Until the Russian Revolution of 1905 there was no political life in Azerbaijan. A Mussavat (Equality) party was formed in 1911. After the Russian Revolution of March 1917, the party started a campaign for independence, but Baku, the capital, with its mixed population, constituted an alien enclave in the country. While a national Azerbaijani government was established at Gandzha (Elizavetpol), a Communist-controlled council assumed power at Baku. The Gandzha government joined first, on Sept. 20, 1917, a Transcaucasian federal republic, but on May 28, 1918, proclaimed the independence of Azerbaijan. On June 4, 1918, at Batum, a peace treaty was signed with Turkey and a Turko-Azerbaijani force started an offensive against Baku, but it was occupied on Aug. 17, 1918 by 1,400 British troops coming by sea from Anzali, Persia. On Sept. 14 the British evacuated Baku, returning to Anzali, and three days later the Azerbaijan government, headed by Fath Ali Khan Khoysky, established itself at Baku.

After the collapse of the Ottoman empire the British returned to Baku, at first ignoring the Azerbaijan government. A general election with universal suffrage for the Azerbaijan constituent assembly took place on Dec. 7, 1918 and out of 120 members there were 84 Mussavat supporters; Ali Marden Topchibashev was elected speaker, and Nasib Usubekov formed a new government. On Jan. 15, 1920, the Allied powers recognized Azerbaijan de facto but on April 27 of the same year the Red army invaded the country and a Soviet Republic of Azerbaijan was proclaimed the next day.

The Azerbaijan Communist party held its first congress at Baku in Feb. 1920. From 1921 to 1925 its first secretary was a Russian, S.M. Kirov, who directed a mass deportation to Siberia of about 120,000 Azerbaijani "nationalist deviationists," among them the country's first two premiers. Later it became a member of the Transcaucasian Federation joining the U.S.S.R. on Dec. 30, 1922. It became a self-constituent republic in 1936.

In 1990 it adopted a declaration of republican sovereignty, and in Aug. 1991 declared itself formally independent; this was approved by a vote of referendum in Jan. 1992.

The Armed forces of Azerbaijan and the Armenian separatists of the Armenian ethnic enclave of Nagurno-Karabakh supported in all spheres by Armenia fought over the control of the enclave in 1992-94. A cease-fire was declared in May 1994 with Azerbaijan actually losing control over the territory. A Treaty of Friendship and Cooperation w/Russia was signed on 3 July 1997.

Autonomous Republic

Independent from May 26, 1918 to April 30, 1920, when it was conquered by Bolshevik forces.

Azerbaijan Republic

АЗЕРБАИДЖАНСКАЯ РЕСПУБЛИКА

1919 First Issue

Ruble system Many variations of color, paper and serial # are known.

		VG	VF	UNC
1	**25 Rubles** 1919. Lilac and brown.	1.50	5.00	15.00

		VG	VF	UNC
2	**50 Rubles** 1919. Blue-green and brown.	1.75	6.00	18.00

1919 SECOND ISSUE

		VG	VF	UNC
5	**100 Rubles** 1919. Brown. Similar to #9 except Persian instead of Russian title on face, different Russian title on back.	1.75	6.00	18.00

		VG	VF	UNC
6	**250 Rubles** 1919. Lilac, brown and green.			
	a. Issued note.	2.00	6.50	20.00
	p. Green, brown and rose. Proof.	—	Unc	120.

1920 FIRST ISSUE

Issuer's name in Arabic and French: Republique d'Azerbaidjan.

Note: For note issues as a Socialist Soviet Republic, 1920-23, refer to Volume 1 - Russia/Transcaucasia. The latter series of #7 fall, by rights, in the time of the Soviet Republic of Azerbaijan.

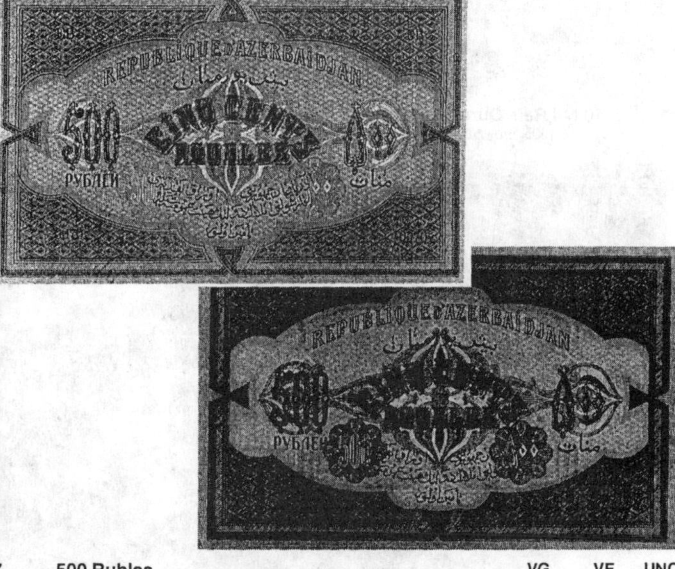

		VG	VF	UNC
7	**500 Rubles** 1920. Dk. brown and dull gray-green on lilac and m/c unpt. Series I-LV.	2.25	7.50	22.50

1920 SECOND ISSUE

		VG	VF	UNC
8	**1 Ruble** 1920. Unfinished proof print.	—	Unc	70.00

AZERBAIJAN GOVERNMENT

АЄЕРБАИДЖАНСКОЕ ПРАВИТЕЛЬСТВО

1919 ISSUE

		VG	VF	UNC
9	**100 Rubles** 1919. Brown. Similar to #5 except Russian replaces Persian title on face, different Russian title on back.			
	a. W/o series on back.	2.25	7.50	22.50
	b. W/СЕРІЯ (ВТОРАЯ) series on back.	2.25	7.50	22.50

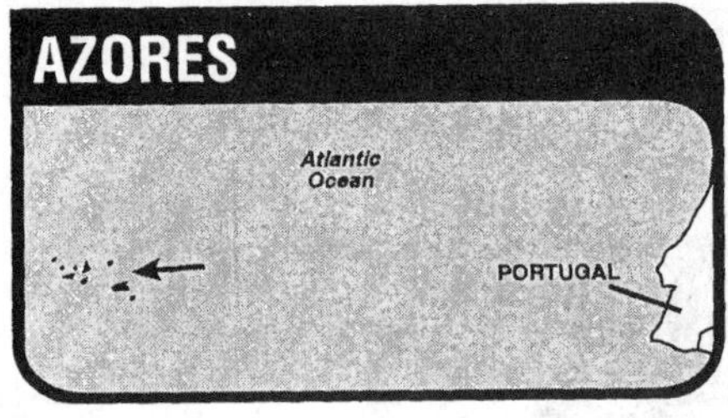

The Azores, an archipelago of nine islands of volcanic origin, are located in the Atlantic Ocean 740 miles (1,190 km.) west of Cape de Roca, Portugal. They are under the administration of Portugal, and have an area of 902 sq. mi. (2,336 sq. km.) and a population of 252,000. Principal city: Ponta Delgada. The natives are mainly of Portuguese descent and earn their livelihood by fishing, wine making, basket weaving, and the growing of fruit, grains and sugar cane. Pineapples are the chief item of export. The climate is particularly temperate, making the islands a favorite winter resort.

The Azores were discovered about 1427 by the Portuguese navigator Diago de Silves. Portugal secured the islands in the 15th century and established the first settlement, on Santa Maria, about 1432. From 1580 to 1640 the Azores were subject to Spain.

Angra on Terceira Island became the capital of the captaincy-general of the Azores in 1766 and it was here in 1826 that the constitutionalists set up a pro-Pedro government in opposition to King Miguel in Lisbon. The whole Portuguese fleet attacked Terceira Island and was repelled at Praia, after which Azoreans, Brazilians and British mercenaries defeated Miguel in Portugal. Maria de Gloria, Pedro's daughter, was proclaimed queen of Portugal on Terceira Island in 1828.

A U.S. naval was established at Ponta Delgada in 1917.

After World War II, the islands acquired a renewed importance as a refueling stop for transatlantic air transport. The United States maintains defense s in the Azores as part of the collective security program of NATO.

Since 1976 the Azores are an Autonomous Region with a regional government and parliament.

RULERS:

Portuguese

MONETARY SYSTEM:

1 Milreis = 1000 Reis to 1910
1 Escudo = 100 Centavos 1910-

PORTUGUESE ADMINISTRATION

BANCO DE PORTUGAL

1876-85 ISSUE

#1-3 ovpt: *S. MIGUEL*. Hand dated.

#		Good	Fine	XF
1	**5 Mil Reis** 1.12.1885. Blue. Standing figure at l. and r., arms at lower ctr. Arms at ctr. on back. Red ovpt.: *PAGAVEL NA AGENCIA DE S. MIGUEL EM MOEDA INSULANA PRATA* on face at lower ctr., on back in each corner.	—	—	—
2	**10 Mil Reis** 28.1.1878. Blue. Ovpt. on Portugal #58. Rare	—	—	—
3	**20 Mil Reis** 30.8.1876. Blue and brown. Portr. of Kg. w/crown above at upper ctr. Back lt. brown. Rare	—	—	—

1895 ISSUE

#4-7 w/inscription: *Pagavel nos Agencias dos Acôres.*

#		Good	Fine	XF
4	**5 Mil Reis** 1.10.1895. Lt. blue. Allegorical figure of "Patria" at l. arms at upper ctr. Arms at ctr. on back.	—	—	—
5	**10 Mil Reis** 1.10.1895. Lt. brown. Allegorical figure of Agriculture at l., Commerce at r. Standing figure at l. and r. on back. Rare	—	—	—
6	**20 Mil Reis** 1.10.1895. Orange. Allegorical figure of Industry at l., Commerce at r. Back blue on dk. orange unpt. Rare	—	—	—
7	**50 Mil Reis** 1.10.1895. Red. Allegorical figure of Industry at l., Commerce at r., arms at lower ctr. Back red and blue; arms at ctr. Rare	—	—	—

1905-10 ISSUES

#8-14 ovpt: *MOEDA INSULANA*, w/ or w/o lg. *AÇÔRES* diagonally on face in red between bars of *AÇÔRES* one or more times on face and back. Regular issue Portuguese types and designs are used, though colors may vary. Notes payable in silver (prata) or gold (ouro). This issue circulated until 1932.

#		Good	Fine	XF
8	**2 1/2 Mil Reis Prata** 30.6.1906; 30.7.1909. Black on orange, blue and olive unpt. Ovpt. on Portugal #107.			
	a. Face w/o diagonal ovpt. 2 Sign. varieties.	75.00	225.	850.
	b. Face w/red diagonal ovpt: *ACORES*.	75.00	225.	850.

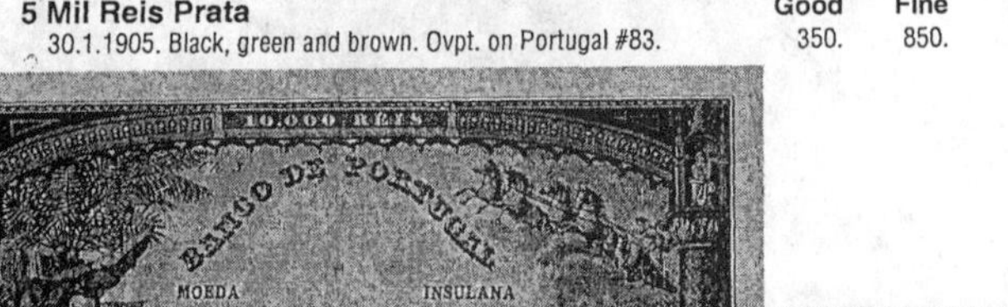

#		Good	Fine	XF
9	**5 Mil Reis Prata** 30.1.1905. Black, green and brown. Ovpt. on Portugal #83.	350.	850.	-

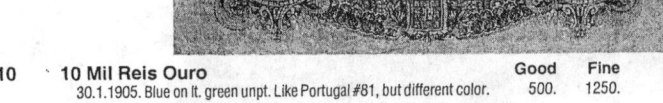

#		Good	Fine	XF
10	**10 Mil Reis Ouro** 30.1.1905. Blue on lt. green unpt. Like Portugal #81, but different color.	500.	1250.	-

#		Good	Fine	XF
11	**10 Mil Reis Ouro** 30.1.1905. Brown and yellow. Ovpt. on Portugal #81.	500.	1250.	-

#		Good	Fine	XF
12	**10 Mil Reis Ouro** 30.9.1910. Green on lt. tan unpt. Ovpt. on design type of Portugal #108.	500.	1250.	

		Good	Fine	XF
13	**20 Mil Reis Ouro** 30.1.1905. Brown and lt. red. Ovpt. on Portugal #82.	450.	1100.	—

14	**50 Mil Reis Ouro** 30.1.1905. Blue on red unpt. Ovpt. on design type of Portugal #85. Rare	—	—	—

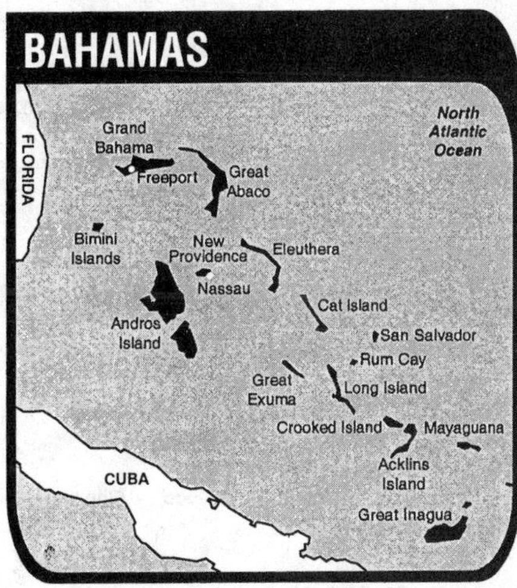

The Commonwealth of The Bahamas is an archipelago of about 3,000 islands, cays and rocks located in the Atlantic Ocean east of Florida and north of Cuba. The total land area of the 800-mile (1.287 km.) long chain of islands is 5,380 sq. mi. (13,935 sq. km.). They have a population of 302,000. Capital: Nassau. The Bahamas imports most of their food and manufactured products and exports cement, refined oil, pulpwood and lobsters. Tourism is the principal industry.

The Bahamas were discovered by Columbus in October, 1492, but Spain made no attempt to settle them. British influence began in 1626 when Charles I granted them to the lord proprietors of Carolina. They continued under British proprietors until 1717, when the civil and military governments were surrendered to the King and the islands designated a British Crown Colony. The Bahamas obtained complete internal self-government under the constitution of Jan. 7, 1964. Full independence was achieved on July 10, 1973. The Bahamas is a member of the Commonwealth of Nations. Elizabeth II is Head of State, as Queen of Bahamas.

RULERS:

MONETARY SYSTEM:

1 Shilling = 12 Pence
1 Pound = 20 Shillings to 1966
1 Dollar = 100 Cents 1966-

BRITISH ADMINISTRATION

BANK OF NASSAU

ND ISSUE (CA. 1870'S)

#A1-A4A printer: CS&E.

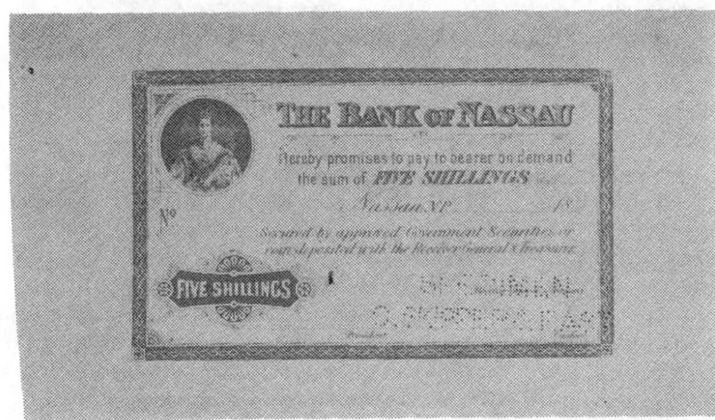

		Good	Fine	XF
A1	**5 Shillings** 18xx. Red. Portr. Qn. Victoria at upper l. Specimen. Printer: CS&E.	—	—	600.

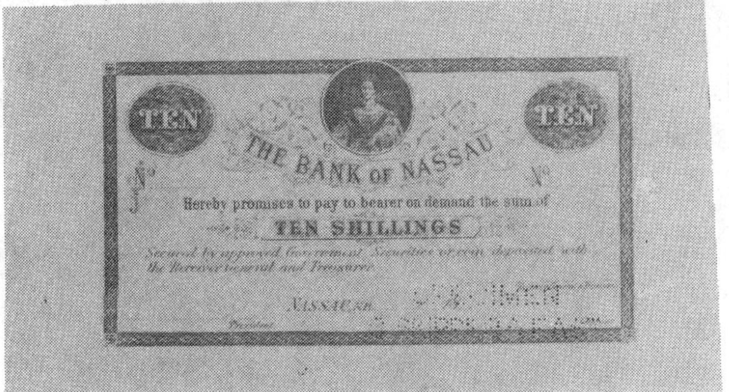

		Good	Fine	XF
A2	**10 Shillings** 18xx. Red. Qn. Victoria at top ctr. Specimen. Printer: CS&E.	—	—	600.
A3	**10 Shillings** 18xx. Blue. Specimen. Printer: CS&E.	—	—	600.
A4	**10 Shillings** 18xx. Brown. Printer: CS&E.	—	—	600.
A4A	**1 Pound** 18xx. Lt. orange. Qn. Victoria at ctr. Specimen. Printer: CS&E.	—	—	600.

1897 ISSUE

#A4B-A7 ship seal at l., portr. man at r. Uniface.

		Good	Fine	XF
A4B	**5 Shillings** 18xx. Black. Ship seal at l., portr. man at l.	—	—	600.

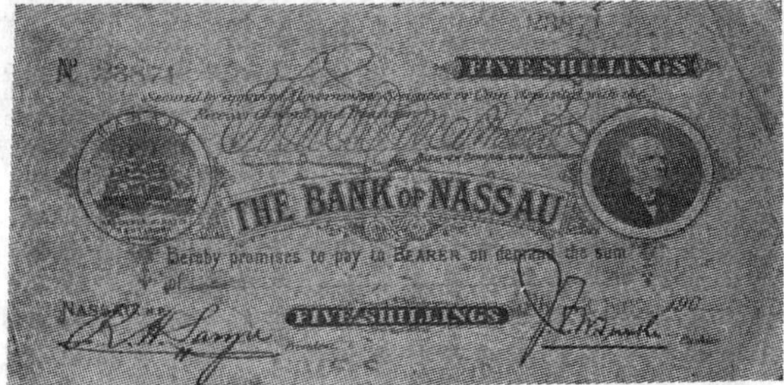

		Good	Fine	XF
A5	**5 Shillings** 28.1.1897; 3.4.1902. Blue. Ship seal at l., portr. man at r.	425.	1500.	—

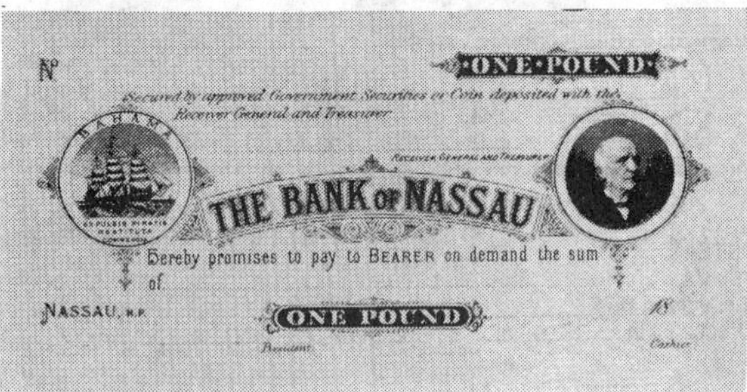

		Good	Fine	XF
A7	**1 Pound** 190x. Blue. Ship seal at l., portr. man at r.	—	—	—

1906 ISSUE

#A8-A8B ship seal at l., portr. man at r.

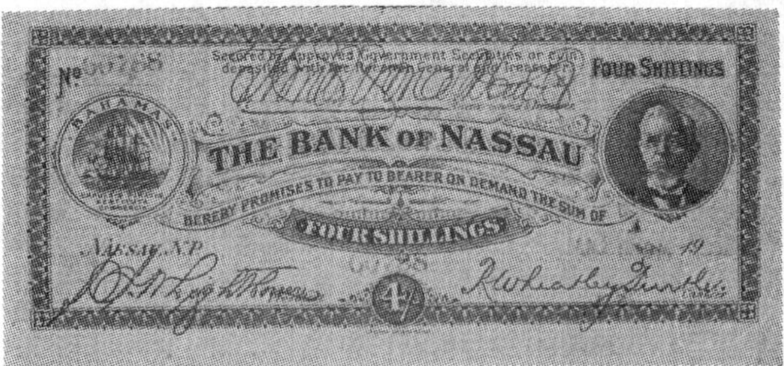

		Good	Fine	XF
A8	**4 Shillings** 11.5.1906; 22.10.1910; 19.3.1913; 16.4.1913; 21.1.1916. Green. Arms at l., man at r. Printer: CS&E.	375.	1000.	—

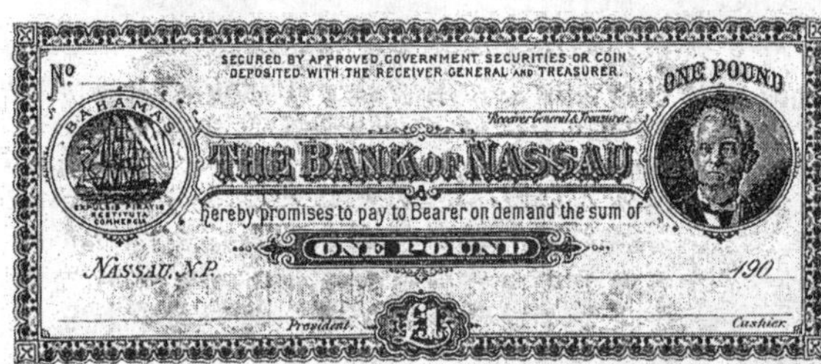

		Good	Fine	XF
A8A	**1 Pound** 190x. Black. Ship seal at l., portr. man at r. Back red-brown. Unsigned remainder.	—	—	—

		Good	Fine	XF
A8B	**1 Pound** 190x. Dp. green. Ship seal at l., portr. man at r. Proof.	—	—	—

PUBLIC TREASURY/NASSAU

1868 ISSUE

#A9, handwritten dates 1868-1869. Various date and sign. varieties.

		Good	Fine	XF
A9	**1 Pound** 4.11.1868. Circular Public Treasury seal at upper l. Rare.	—	—	—

BAHAMAS GOVERNMENT

1869 ISSUE

#A10 and A11 circular Public Treasury seal at upper l. Printer: Major and Knapp.

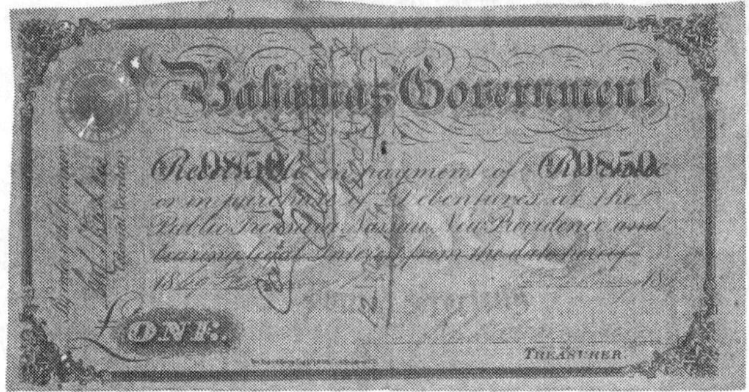

		Good	Fine	XF
A10	**1 Pound** 1.2.1869. Black on lt. blue unpt. Printer: Major and Knapp. Rare.	—	—	—

		Good	Fine	XF
A11	**5 Pounds** 2.1.1869; 1.2.1869. Black on red-violet unpt. Printer: Major and Knapp. Rare.	—	—	—

1919 CURRENCY NOTE ACT

#2-4 donkey cart at l., ship seal at ctr., bushes at r. Printer: CBNC (w/o imprint).

		Good	Fine	XF
1	**4 Shillings** L.1919. Ship seal at r. Gov't bldg. on back. Rare	—	—	—

		Good	Fine	XF
2	**4 Shillings** L.1919. Black on green unpt. Donkey cart at l., ship seal at ctr., bushes at r. Printer: CBNC. Back green.			
	a. No serial # prefix. H. E. W. Grant at l.	125.	350.	1250.
	b. Serial # prefix *A*. A. C. Burns at l.	100.	275.	950.
3	**10 Shillings** L.1919. Black on red unpt. Donkey cart at l., ship seal at ctr., bushes at r. Printer: CBNC. Back red.			
	a. No serial # prefix. H. E. W. Grant at l.	250.	1000.	—
	b. Serial # prefix *A*. A. C. Burns at l.	250.	1000.	—
4	**1 Pound** L.1919. Black on gray unpt. Donkey cart at l., ship seal at ctr., bushes at r. Printer: CBNC. Back black.			
	a. No serial # prefix. H. E. W. Grant at l.	225.	850.	3000.
	b. Serial # prefix *A*. A. C. Burns at l.	225.	800.	2500.

1919 CURRENCY NOTE ACT (1930)

#5-7 ship seal at l., Kg. George V at r. Printer: W&S. Sign. varieties.

		Good	Fine	XF
5	**4 Shillings** L.1919 (1930). Green. Ship seal at l., Kg. George V at r. Printer: W&S.	75.00	225.	850.

		Good	Fine	XF
6	**10 Shillings** L.1919 (1930). Red. Ship seal at l., Kg. George V at r. Printer: W&S.	275.	950.	—

		Good	Fine	XF
7	**1 Pound** L.1919 (1930). Black. Ship seal at l., Kg. George V at r. Printer: W&S.	125.	400.	1000.

1936 CURRENCY NOTE ACT

#9-11 ship seal at l., Portr. Kg. George VI at r. Wmk: Columbus. Printer: TDLR.

		VG	VF	UNC
9	**4 Shillings** L.1936. Green. Ship seal at l., Kg. George VI at r. Printer: TDLR.			
	a. Sign. J. H. Jarrett w/sign. title: *COLONIAL SECRETARY COMMISSIONER OF CURRENCY* at l.	20.00	85.00	500.
	b. W. L. Heape at l.	15.00	60.00	425.
	c. D. G. Stewart at l., sign. Walter K. Moore at r.	20.00	75.00	425.
	d. D. G. Stewart at l., sign. Basil Burnside at r.	20.00	85.00	475.
	e. *COMMISSIONER OF CURRENCY* at l.	8.00	40.00	350.

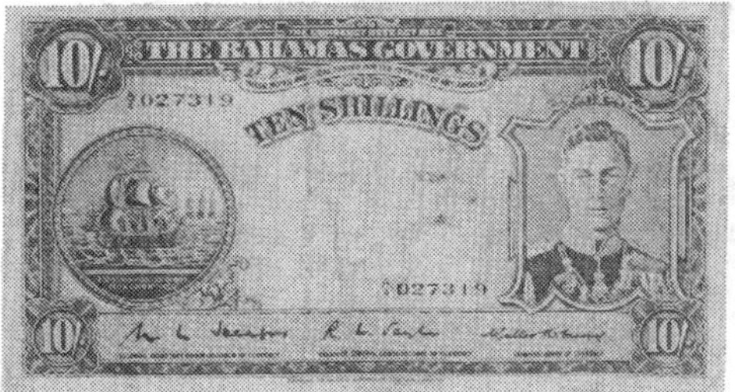

		VG	VF	UNC
10	**10 Shillings** L.1936. Red. Ship seal at l., portr. Kg. George VI at r. Printer: TDLR.			
	a. Sign. J. H. Jarrett w/sign. title: *COLONIAL SECRETARY COMMISSIONER OF CURRENCY* at l.	40.00	250.	900.
	b. W. L. Heape at l.	30.00	225.	900.
	c. D. G. Stewart at l., sign. Walter K. Moore at r.	30.00	225.	800.
	d. *COMMISSIONER OF CURRENCY* at l.	20.00	85.00	700.

		VG	VF	UNC
11	**1 Pound** L.1936. Black. Ship seal at l., Kg. George VI at r. Printer: TDLR.			
	a. Sign. J. H. Jarrett w/sign. title: *COLONIAL SECRETARY COMMISSIONER OF CURRENCY* at l.	50.00	225.	950.
	b. W. L. Heape at l.	45.00	200.	900.
	c. D. G. Stewart at l., sign. Walter K. Moore at r.	60.00	225.	900.
	d. D. G. Stewart at l., sign. Basil Burnside at r.	45.00	175.	850.
	e. *COMMISSIONER OF CURRENCY* at l.	35.00	150.	750.
12	**5 Pounds** L.1936. Blue-violet on m/c unpt. Ship seal at l., Kg. George VI at r. Printer: TDLR.			
	a. Sign. D. J. Stewart w/sign. title: *COLONIAL SECRETARY COMMISSIONER OF CURRENCY* at l.	400.	1100.	—
	b. *COMMISSIONER OF CURRENCY* at l.	90.00	300.	900.

COMMONWEALTH

GOVERNMENT OF THE BAHAMAS

1953 ISSUE

#13-15 ship seal at l., portr Qn. Elizabeth II at r. Printer: TDLR.

13	4 Shillings	VG	VF	UNC
	ND (1953). Green.			
	a. Ctr. sign. H. R. Latreille, sign. Basil Burnside at r.	1.50	15.00	100.
	b. Ctr. sign. W. H. Sweeting, sign. Basil Burnside at r.	1.00	10.00	80.00
	c. Ctr. sign. W. H. Sweeting, sign. Chas. P. Bethel at r.	1.00	12.50	95.00
	d. Ctr. sign. W. H. Sweeting, sign. George W. K. Roberts at r.	1.00	7.50	60.00

14	10 Shillings	VG	VF	UNC
	ND (1953). Red.			
	a. Ctr. sign. H. R. Latreille, sign. Basil Burnside at r.	4.00	25.00	275.
	b. Ctr. sign. W. H. Sweeting, sign. Basil Burnside at r.	4.00	17.50	200.
	c. Ctr. sign. W. H. Sweeting, sign. Chas. P. Bethel at r.	4.00	20.00	225.
	d. Ctr. sign. W. H. Sweeting, sign. George W. K. Roberts at r.	2.00	15.00	150.

15	1 Pound	VG	VF	UNC
	ND (1953). Black.			
	a. Ctr. sign. H. R. Latreille, sign. Basil Burnside at r.	5.00	27.50	450.
	b. Ctr. sign. W. H. Sweeting, sign. Basil Burnside at r.	5.00	22.50	350.
	c. Ctr. sign. W. H. Sweeting, sign. Chas. P. Bethel at r.	5.00	28.50	350.
	d. Ctr. sign. W. H. Sweeting, sign. George W. K. Roberts at r.	3.00	17.50	200.

16	5 Pounds	VG	VF	UNC
	ND (1953). Blue.			
	a. Ctr. sign. H. R. Latreille, sign. Basil Burnside at r. Rare	—	—	—
	b. Ctr. sign. W. H. Sweeting, sign. Basil Burnside at r.	40.00	350.	1500.
	c. Ctr. sign. W. H. Sweeting, sign. Chas. P. Bethel at r.	50.00	375.	1500.
	d. Ctr. sign. W. H. Sweeting, sign. George W. K. Roberts at r.	37.50	300.	1350.

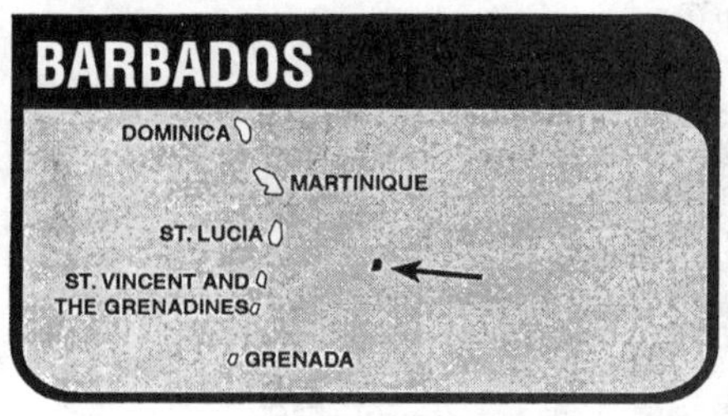

Barbados, an independent state within the British Commonwealth, is located in the Windward Islands of the West Indies east of St. Vincent. The coral island has an area of 166 sq. mi. (431 sq. km) and a population of 269,000. Capital: Bridgetown. The economy is d on sugar and tourism. Sugar, petroleum products, molasses and rum are exported.

Barbados was named by the Portuguese who achieved the first landing on the island in 1563. British sailors landed at the site of present-day Holetown in 1624. Barbados was under uninterrupted British control from the time of the first British settlement in 1627 until it obtained independence on Nov. 30, 1966. It is a member of the Commonwealth of Nations. Elizabeth II is Head of State, as Queen of Barbados.

Barbados was included in the issues of the British Caribbean Territories - Eastern Group and later the East Caribbean Currency Authority until 1973.

RULERS:

British

MONETARY SYSTEM:

1 Dollar = 100 Cents, 1950-
1 British West Indies Dollar = 4 Shillings - 2 Pence
5 British West Indies Dollars = 1 Pound - 10 Pence
1 Dollar = 100 Cents, 1950-
1 British West Indies Dollar = 4 Shillings - 2 Pence
5 British West Indies Dollars = 1 Pound - 10 Pence

BRITISH ADMINISTRATION

GOVERNMENT OF BARBADOS

1915 ISSUE

1	1 Pound	Good	Fine	XF
	1915-17. (28,000 issued).	—	—	—

1938-43 ISSUE

#2-6 Neptune on seahorse cart at l., portr. Kg. George VI at r. Date and sign. varieties. Wmk: 2 horse heads. Printer: BWC.

2	1 Dollar	VG	VF	UNC
	1938-49. Green, brown-violet and m/c. Portr. Kg. George VI at r. Printer: BWC.			
	a. 3.1.1938.	20.00	85.00	600.
	b. 1.9.1939; 1.12.1939; 1.6.1943.	15.00	80.00	550.
	c. 1.1.1949.	30.00	100.	600.
3	2 Dollars			
	1938-49. Brown and green. Portr. Kg. George VI at r. Printer: BWC.			
	a. 3.1.1938.	40.00	150.	700.
	b. 1.9.1939; 1.12.1939; 1.6.1943.	35.00	125.	650.
	c. 1.1.1949.	50.00	200.	700.

4	5 Dollars	Good	Fine	XF
	1939-43. Purple and blue. Portr. Kg. George VI at r. Printer: BWC.			
	a. 1.9.1939; 1.12.1939.	50.00	200.	650.
	b. 1.6.1943.	40.00	125.	550.

#		Good	Fine	XF
5	**20 Dollars** 1.6.1943. Pink and green. Portr. Kg. George VI at r. Printer: BWC.			
	a. Issued note.	500.	600.	—
	s. Specimen.	—	Unc	1350.

#		Good	Fine	XF
6	**100 Dollars** 1.6.1943. Brown and black. Portr. Kg. George VI at r. Printer: BWC. (One verified).			
	a. Issued note. Rare.	—	—	—
	s. Specimen.			

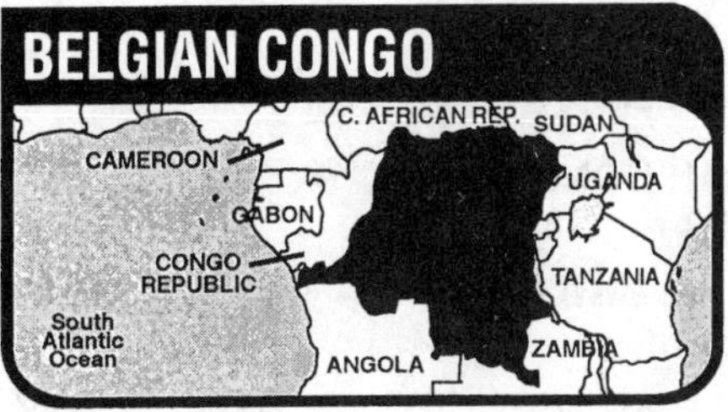

Belgian Congo (now the Congo Democratic Republic), located in the south-central part of Africa, has an area of 905,378 sq. mi. (2,344,920 sq. km.) and a population of 13.6 million. Capital: Kinshasa. The mineral-rich country produces copper, tin, diamonds, gold, zinc, cobalt and uranium.

In ancient times the territory comprising the Belgium Congo was occupied by Negrito peoples (Pygmies) pushed into the mountains by Bantu and Nilotic invaders. The interior was first explored by the American correspondent Henry Stanley, who was subsequently commissioned by King Leopold II of Belgium to conclude development treaties with the local chiefs. The Berlin conference of 1885 awarded the area to Leopold, who administered and exploited it as his private property until it was annexed to Belgium in 1907. Belgium received the mandate for the German territories of Ruanda-Urundi as a result of the international treaties after WWI. During WWII Belgian Congolese troops fought on the side of the Allies, notably in Ethiopia. Following the eruption of bloody independence riots in 1959, Belgium granted the Belgian Congo independence as the Republic of the Congo on June 30, 1960.

RULERS:

Leopold II, 1885-1907
Belgium, 1907-1960

MONETARY SYSTEM:

1 Franc = 100 Centimes to 1967

CONGO FREE STATE

ETAT INDEPENDANT DU CONGO

INDEPENDENT STATE OF THE CONGO

1896 ISSUE

#1 and 2 also circulated in Belgium in 1914. Issued in Bruxelles. Printer: W&S.

#		Good	Fine	XF
1	**10 Francs** Printer: W&S. 7.2.1896. Black on yellow and green unpt. Child holding cornucopia at ctr. Woman's head at l. on back.			
	a. Issued note.	1800.	2500.	3000.
	b. As a. Punched hole cancelled.	300.	500.	750.
	r. Remainder w/o date or sign.	—	—	—

#		Good	Fine	XF
2	**100 Francs** Printer: W&S. 7.2.1896. Black on yellow and brown unpt. Woman seated holding caduceus at l. ctr., lion at upper r. Portr. woman at ctr. on back.			
	a. Issued note.	2500.	3250.	4000.
	b. As a. Punched hole cancelled.	600.	900.	1000.
	r. Remainder w/o date or sign.	—	—	—

BELGIAN CONGO

BANQUE DU CONGO BELGE

BANK OF THE BELGIAN CONGO

1914 ISSUE

#3-4C Various date and sign. varieties. Printer: W&S.

#3A Deleted

		Good	Fine	XF
3	**1 Franc** 9.10.1914; 9.1.1920; 2.6.1920. Black on red unpt. Woman seated w/sheaf of grain and wheel at l. *ELISABETHVILLE.* Printer: W&S.	75.00	175.	250.

		Good	Fine	XF
3B	**1 Franc** 15.10.1914; 15.1.1920; 26.6.1920. Black on red unpt. Woman seated w/sheaf of grain and wheel at l. *MATADI.* Printer: W&S.	60.00	150.	250.

#4-4C woman seated w/child by beehive at l. Elephant and hippo at ctr.l on back.

		Good	Fine	XF
4	**5 Francs** Printer: W&S. 9.10.1914; 19.3.1919; 2.3.1920; 2.6.1920; 2.4.1921; 2.4.1924. Black on pale blue unpt. Woman seated w/child at l. *ELIZABETHVILLE.* Elephant and hippo at ctr. on back.	75.00	200.	300.
4A	**5 Francs** 26.10.1914; 19.3.1919; 3.3.1920; 3.6.1920; 3.4.1921; 3.4.1924. Black on pale blue unpt. Woman seated w/child at l. *KINSHASA.* Elephant and hippo at ctr. on back. Like #4.	75.00	200.	300.

		Good	Fine	XF
4B	**5 Francs** 15.10.1914; 26.3.1920; 26.4.1921. Black on pale blue unpt. Woman seated w/child by beehive at l. *MATADI.* Like #4.	75.00	200.	300.
4C	**5 Francs** 30.10.1914; 4.3.1920; 4.4.1921. Black on pale blue unpt. Woman seated w/child at l. *STANLEYVILLE.* Like #4. W&S.	75.00	200.	300.

1912-37 ISSUE

#8-12 wmk: Elephant's head. Printer: BNB (w/o imprint).

		Good	Fine	XF
8	**5 Francs** 1924-30. Red, brown and green. Huts, palm trees at l. Watermark: Wmk: Elephant's head.Wmk: Elephant's head. Printer: BNB (w/o imprint). River steamboat on back.			
	a. *ELISABETHVILLE.* 2.12.1924; 2.7.1926.	75.00	150.	400.
	b. Ovpt: *LEOPOLDVILLE.* 3.12.1924; 3.7.1926.	75.00	150.	400.
	c. *MATADI.* 26.12.1924; 26.7.1926.	75.00	150.	400.
	d. Ovpt: *STANLEYVILLE.* 4.12.1924; 4.7.1926.	75.00	150.	400.
	e. W/o office ovpt. 21.1.1929; 4.4.1930.	25.00	75.00	250.

		Good	Fine	XF
9	**10 Francs** Watermark: Wmk: Elephant's head.Wmk: Elephant's head. Printer: BNB (w/o imprint). 10.9.1937. Brown. Market scene. Water bucks, trees at ctr. r. on back.	50.00	75.00	150

		Good	Fine	XF
10	**20 Francs** Watermark: Wmk: Elephant's head.Wmk: Elephant's head. Printer: BNB (w/o imprint). 1912-37. Green. Portr. Ceres at upper l., woman kneeling w/hammer and anvil, woman reclining w/elephant tusk at l. Waterfront village and canoe on back.			
	a. *ELISABETHVILLE.* 10.9.1912; 2.5.1914; 2.3.1920; 2.11.1920; 2.10.1925; 2.7.1926; 2.7.1927.	400.	650.	950
	b. *KINSHASA.* 10.9.1912; 3.5.1914; 3.3.1917; 3.3.1920; 3.11.1920; 2.2.1922.	400.	800.	1250.
	c. *LEOPOLDVILLE.* 3.10.1925; 3.7.1926; 3.7.1927.	400.	650.	1250
	d. *MATADI.* 10.9.1912; 26.4.1914; 26.3.1920; 26.11.1920;26.10.1925; 26.7.1926; 26.6.1927.	400.	650.	1250
	e. *STANLEYVILLE.* 10.9.1912; 4.5.1914; 4.3.1920; 4.11.1920; 4.10.1925; 4.7.1926; 4.7.1927.	400.	650.	1250.
	f. W/o office ovpt. 1.2.1929; 15.9.1937.	75.00	200.	350

		Good	Fine	XF
11	**100 Francs** 1912-29. Blue. Watermark: Wmk: Elephant's head.Wmk: Elephant's head. Printer: BNB (w/o imprint). Woman standing holding portr. Ceres, young boy seated on rock w/elephant tusks and produce below at l., woman kneeling w/fabric at r. Woman and child at l., fisherman w/canoe paddle and fishing net on back.			
	a. *ELISABETHVILLE.* 2.2.1914; 2.3.1920; 2.11.1920; 2.7.1926; 2.7.1927.	250.	750.	1500.
	b. *KINSHASA.* 10.9.1912; 3.2.1914; 3.3.1917; 3.11.1920.	300.	850.	1500.
	c. *LEOPOLDVILLE.* 3.7.1926; 3.7.1927.	250.	750.	1500.
	d. *MATADI.* 10.9.1912; 26.2.1914; 26.3.1917; 26.3.1920; 26.11.1920; 26.7.1926; 26.6.1927.	250.	750.	1500.
	e. *STANLEYVILLE.* 10.9.1912; 4.3.1912; 4.3.1917; 4.3.1920; 4.7.1926; 4.11.1920.	250.	750.	1500.
	f. W/o office ovpt. 1.2.1929.	125.	350.	700.

No.	Description	Good	Fine	XF
12	**1000 Francs** Watermark: Wmk: Elephant's head.Wmk: Elephant's head. Printer: BNB (w/o imprint). 1920. Brown. 2 men and child at l. w/ head of Ceres. Seated woman w/lyre at l. on back			
	a. *ELISABETHVILLE*. 2.11.1920. Reported not confirmed	—	—	—
	b. *KINSHASA*. 3.11.1920.	750.	1500.	3750.
	c. *LEOPOLDVILLE*. 1926/27. Reported not confirmed	—	—	—
	d. *MATADI*. 26.11.1920.	750.	1500.	3750.
	e. *STANLEYVILLE*. 4.11.1920.	1875.	3500.	—

1941-50 Issue

No.	Description	Good	Fine	XF
13	**5 Francs** 10.6.1942. Red on green unpt. Woman seated w/child by beehive at l. Elephant and hippo at ctr. on back. Ovpt:*DEUXIEME EMISSION-1942*. Printer: W&S. W/o wmk.	25.00	100.	300.

No.	Description	Good	Fine	XF
13A	**5 Francs** 1943-47. Blue-gray on orange unpt. Woman seated w/child by beehive at l. Elephant and hippo at ctr. on back. Like #13.			
	a. 10.1.1943. *TROISIEME EMISSION-1943.*	10.00	50.00	125.
	b. 10.8.1943. *QUATRIEME EMISSION-1943.*	10.00	50.00	125.
	c. 10.3.1944. *CINQUIEME EMISSION-1944.*	10.00	50.00	125.
	d. 10.4.1947. *SIXIEME EMISSION-1947.*	10.00	50.00	125.
13B	**5 Francs** 18.5.1949; 7.9.1951; 15.2.1952. Blue-gray on orange unpt. Woman seated w/child by beehive at l. Elephant and hippo at ctr. on back. W/o *EMISSION* ovpt. Like #13.	7.50	20.00	60.00
14	**10 Francs** 10.12.1941. Green on blue and pink unpt. Dancing Watusi at l. Soldiers on parade at r. on back. Wmk: Giraffe's head. Printer: W&S.	25.00	75.00	225.
14B	**10 Francs** 10.7.1942. Brown on green and pink unpt. Dancing Watusi at l. Soldiers on parade at r. Watermark: Giraffe's head.Giraffe's head. Printer: W&S. Like #14. Ovpt:*DEUXIEME EMISSION-1942*.			
	a. Issued note.	30.00	100.	275.
	s. Specimen.	—	—	—

No.	Description	Good	Fine	XF
14C	**10 Francs** 10.2.1943. Violet on pink unpt. Dancing Watusi at l. Soldiers on parade at r. Watermark: Hornless antelope.Hornless antelope. Printer: W&S. Like #14. Ovpt:*TROISIEME EMISSION-1943.*	30.00	125.	300.
14D	**10 Francs** 10.6.1944. Gray-blue on pink unpt. Dancing Watusi at l. Soldiers on parade at r. Watermark: Hornless antelope.Hornless antelope. Printer: W&S. Like #14. Ovpt:*QUATRIEME EMISSION-1944.*	10.00	30.00	150.
14E	**10 Francs** 11.11.1948; 15.8.1949; 14.3.1952; 12.5.1952. Gray-blue on pink unpt. Dancing Watusi at l. Soldiers on parade at r. Watermark: Hornless antelope.Hornless antelope. Printer: W&S. Like #14. W/o *EMISSION*. ovpt.	7.50	30.00	125.

#15-15H pirogue w/7 oarsmen at l. ctr. Working elephant at ctr. r. on back. Wmk: Elephant's head. Printer: TDLR.

No.	Description	Good	Fine	XF
15	**20 Francs** 10.9.1940. Blue. Longboat w/7 oarsmen at l ctr. Working elephant at ctr r. on back. ovpt. Wmk: Elephant's head. Printer: TDLR. W/o *EMISSION*.	25.00	100.	300.
15A	**20 Francs** 10.3.1942. Violet. Like #15.	25.00	100.	300.
15B	**20 Francs** 10.12.1942. Orange. Like #15.	25.00	100.	300.
15C	**20 Francs** 10.3.1943. Orange. Like #15.	25.00	100.	300.
15D	**20 Francs** 10.5.1944. Orange. Like #15.	25.00	100.	300.
15E	**20 Francs** 10.4.1946. Blue. Like #15. W/o *EMISSION*. ovpt.	15.00	65.00	225.
15F	**20 Francs** 10.8.1948. Blue. Longboat w/7 oarsmen at l. ctr. Working elephant ctr. r. Watermark: Elephant's head.Elephant's head. Printer: TDLR. Like #15. *SEPTIEME EMISSION-1948.*	7.50	30.00	150.
15G	**20 Francs** 18.5.1949. Blue. Longboat w/7 oarsmen at l. ctr. Working elephant at ctr. r. Watermark: Elephant's head.Elephant's head. Printer: TDLR. Like #15. *HUITIEME EMISSION-1949.*	7.50	30.00	150.
15H	**20 Francs** 11.4.1950. Blue. Like #15. *NEUVIEME EMISSION-1950.*	7.50	30.00	150.

No.	Description	Good	Fine	XF
16	**50 Francs** ND (1941-42); 1943-52. Black on m/c unpt. Woman at r. Leopard at ctr. on back. Printer: ABNC. W/o wmk.			
	a. Serial # repeated 5 times. W/o *EMISSION* ovpt. Series: A; B.	50.00	150.	450.
	b. Serial # repeated 4 times. Ovpt: *EMISSION-1943.* Series C.	40.00	120.	450.
	c. Ovpt: *EMISSION 1945.* Series D.	40.00	120.	450.
	d. Ovpt: *EMISSION 1946.* Series E.	40.00	120.	450.
	e. Ovpt: *EMISSION 1947.* Series F.	40.00	120.	450.
	f. Ovpt: *EMISSION-1948.* Series G; H.	40.00	120.	450.
	g. Ovpt: *EMISSION 1949.* Series I; J; K; L.	40.00	100.	250.
	h. Ovpt: *EMISISON 1950.* Series M; N; O; P.	40.00	100.	250.
	i. Ovpt: *EMISSION 1951.* Series Q; R; S; T.	40.00	100.	250.
	j. Ovpt: *EMISSION 1952.* Series U; V.	40.00	100.	200.
	s. Like a, g, i, j. Specimen. Punch hole cancelled.			

		Good	Fine	XF
17	**100 Francs** 1944-51. Blue and green. 2 Elephants, palm trees at ctr. Man, 3 oxen at ctr. r. on back. Wmk: Zebra's head. Printer: W&S.			
	a. W/o *EMISSION.* ovpt. 10.5.1944.	50.00	135.	400.
	b. *DEUXIEME EMISSION-1944.* 10.6.1944.	60.00	150.	350.
	c. W/o *EMISSION.* ovpt. 11.3.1946; 10.4.1947.	40.00	100.	350.
	d. W/o *EMISSION.* ovpt. 16.7.1949; 14.9.1949; 13.3.1951; 7.9.1951.	40.00	100.	350.

		Good	Fine	XF
18	**500 Francs** ND (1929). Black on m/c unpt. Portr. woman at upper ctr. Elephants bathing at ctr. on back. W/o *EMISSION.* ovpt. Series 1. Serial # repeated 5 times. Printer: ABNC.	500.	1500.	3000.
18A	**500 Francs** ND (1941); 1943; 1945. Brown, yellow and blue. Woman at upper ctr. Elephants bathing at centre on back. Printer: ABNC. Like #18.			
	a. Series 2. Serial # repeated 5 times. W/o *EMISSION*, ovpt. ND (1941).	500.	1500.	2500.
	b. Series 3. Ovpt: *EMISSION 1943.* Serial # repeated 4 times.	750.	1500.	—
	c. Series 4. *EMISSION 1945.* Serial # repeated 4 times.	400.	1250.	—
	s. As a, b. Specimen. Punch hole cancelled.	—	—	—

		Good	Fine	XF
19	**1000 Francs** 1944-47. Brown-black, yellow and blue. 3 Warega fisherman at l. 2 musicians at l. and ctr., portr. youth at r. on back. Wmk: Leopard's head. Printer: W&S.			
	a. 10.5.1944.	600.	1500.	3000.
	b. 11.2.1946; 10.4.1947.	225.	600.	1500.
19A	**5000 Francs** 7.8.1950. Red-brown on m/c unpt. Portr. female at l. Three men in canoe at ctr. on back. Wmk: lion hd. Printer: W&S. Specimen.	—	Unc	4500.

20	**10,000 Francs** 10.3.1942. Black and green. Uniface. Watermark: Wmk: BCB/BBC and a 5 pointed star. Printer: W&S.	—	—	—

Note: #20 is believed to have been used in interbank and realestate transactions.

BANQUE CENTRALE DU CONGO BELGE ET DU RUANDA-URUNDI

1952 ISSUE

#21-29 various date and sign. varieties.

		VG	VF	UNC
21	**5 Francs** 1.10.1952-15.9.1953. Blue-gray on orange unpt. Woman seated w/child by beehive at l. Elephant and hippo at ctr. on back. Printer: W&S. Similar to #13. W/o wmk.	10.00	20.00	85.00

22 10 Francs — VG 15.00 | VF 50.00 | UNC 225.

1.7.1952-31.8.1952. Gray-blue on pink unpt. Dancing Watusi at l. Soldiers on parade at r. on back. Wmk: Giraffe's head. Printer: W&S. Similar to #14.

23 20 Francs — VG 20.00 | VF 100. | UNC 400.

1.7.1952-1.9.1952. Blue. Pirogue w/7 oarsmen at l. ctr. Working elephant at ctr. r. on back. Wmk: Elephant's head. Printer: TDLR. Similar to #15.

24 50 Francs

15.7.1952-15.12.1952. M/c. Woman at r. Leopard at ctr. on back. Printer: ABNC. Similar to #16. W/o wmk.

	VG	VF	UNC
a. Issued note.	50.00	200.	500.
s. Specimen. Punch hole cancelled.	—	—	—

25 100 Francs

1952-54. Blue and green. 2 elephants, palm trees at ctr. Native, 3 oxen at ctr. r. on back. Wmk: Zebra's head. Printer: W&S. Similar to #17.

	VG	VF	UNC
a. 1.7.1952-15.11.1953.	30.00	150.	450.
b. 15.12.1954.	30.00	150.	450.

1953 ISSUE

26 20 Francs — VG 10.00 | VF 75.00 | UNC 300.

15.12.1953-15.4.1954. Olive green on yellow unpt. Woman at l., waterfall in background at ctr. Qn. Astrid laboratory in Leopoldville at ctr., man w/spear at r. on back. Wmk: Elephant's head. Printer: TDLR.

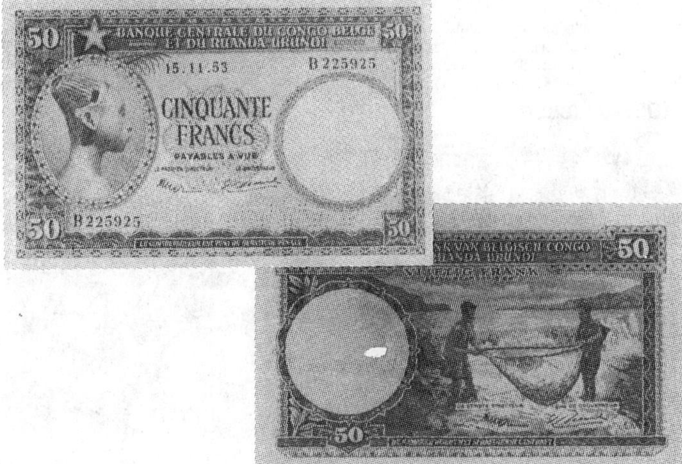

27 50 Francs

1953-1955. Green on m/c unpt. Portr. woman at l. 2 fisherwomen w/net at ctr r. on back. Wmk: Leopard's head. Printer: BWC.

	VG	VF	UNC
a. 15.11.1953-15.4.1954.	20.00	125.	450.
b. 1.1.1955-1.3.1955.	15.00	100.	400.

28 500 Francs

15.3.1953-1.1.1955. Purple on orange unpt. Portr. girl at l. Okapi at ctr. on back. Wmk: Lion's head. Printer: BWC.

	Good	Fine	XF
a. 15.3.1953; 15.4.1953.	125.	350.	1000.
b. 1.1.1955.	125.	350.	1000.

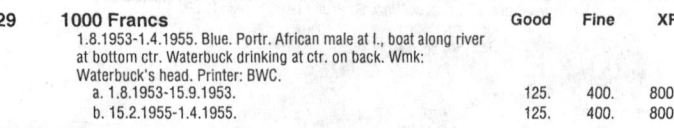

29	1000 Francs	Good	Fine	XF
	1.8.1953-1.4.1955. Blue. Portr. African male at l., boat along river at bottom ctr. Waterbuck drinking at ctr. on back. Wmk: Waterbuck's head. Printer: BWC.			
	a. 1.8.1953-15.9.1953.	125.	400.	800.
	b. 15.2.1955-1.4.1955.	125.	400.	800.

1955-58 Issue

30	10 Francs	VG	VF	UNC
	1955-59. Gray-blue on blue and orange unpt. Soldier at l. Antelope at r. on back Wmk: Giraffe's head. Printer: W&S.			
	a. Sign. titles: *LE PREMIER-DIRECTEUR* and *LE GOUVERNEUR.* 15.1.1955-1.6.1955.	2.00	7.50	35.00
	b. Sign. titles: *UN DIRECTEUR* and *LE GOUVERNEUR.* 15.7.1956-1.12.1959.	2.00	7.50	50.00

31	20 Francs	VG	VF	UNC
	1.12.1956-1.12.1959. Green on m/c unpt. Young boy at l., reservoir in background at ctr. River landscape at ctr., young girl at r. on back. Wmk: Elephant's head. Printer: TDLR.	3.00	10.00	40.00

32	50 Francs	VG	VF	UNC
	1.3.1957-1.10.1959. Red on m/c unpt. Workers at modern weaving machinery at ctr. r. Huts, weaving by hand at l. on back. Wmk: Leopard's head. Printer: BWC (w/o imprint).	4.00	15.00	60.00

33	100 Francs	VG	VF	UNC
	1955-60. Green on m/c unpt. Portr. Kg. Leopold II at l. Basket weavers at ctr. on back. Printer: BNB (w/o imprint).			
	a. Sign. titles: *LE GOUVERNEUR* and *LE PREMIER-DIRECTEUR.* Wmk: Elephant's head. 15.1.1955-1.10.1956.	4.00	15.00	60.00
	b. Sign. titles: *LE GOUVERNEUR* and *UN DIRECTEUR.* Wmk: Elephant's head. 1.10.1956-1.4.1960.	4.00	15.00	60.00
	c. Like b. 1.9.1960. W/o wmk.	4.00	15.00	60.00

34	500 Francs	VG	VF	UNC
	1.9.1957-1.7.1959. Brown-violet on m/c unpt. Ships dockside at Leo-Kinshasa wharf at ctr. Africans transporting fruit in pirogue at ctr. on back. Wmk: Lion's head. Printer: TDLR.	20.00	150.	450.

		VG	VF	UNC
35	**1000 Francs** 15.7.1958-1.9.1959. Dp. blue on m/c unpt. Portr. Kg. Baudouin at l., aerial view of Leopoldville at lower ctr. Huts at r. on back. Wmk: Waterbuck's head. Printer: BWC (w/o imprint).	15.00	75.00	350.

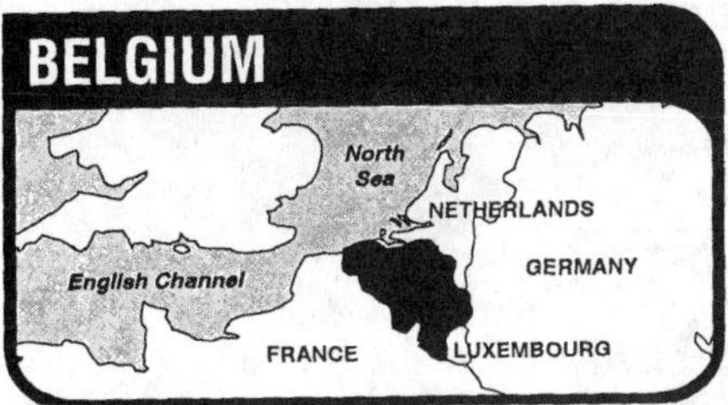

The Kingdom of Belgium, a constitutional monarchy in northwest Europe, has an area of 11,779 sq. mi. (30,513 sq. km.) and a population of 10.26 million, chiefly Dutch-speaking Flemish and French-speaking Walloons. Capital: Brussels. Agriculture, dairy farming, and the processing of raw materials for re-export are the principal industries. "Beurs voor Diamant" in Antwerp is the world's largest diamond trading center. Iron and steel, machinery, motor vehicles, chemicals, textile yarns and fabrics comprise the principal exports.

The Celtic tribe called "Belgae," from which Belgium derived its name, was described by Caesar as the most courageous of all the tribes of Gaul. The Belgae eventually capitulated to Rome and the area remained for centuries as a part of the Roman Empire known as Belgica.

As Rome began its decline, Frankish tribes migrated westward and established the Merovingian, and subsequently, the Carolingian empires. At the death of Charlemagne, Europe was divided among his three sons Karl, Lothar and Ludwig. The eastern part of today's Belgium lay in the Duchy of Lower Lorraine while much of the western parts eventually became the County of Flanders. After further divisions, the area was absorbed into the Duchy of Burgundy from whence it passed into Hapsburg control when Marie of Burgundy married Maximilian of Austria. Phillip I (the Fair), son of Maximilian and Marie, then added Spain to the Hapsburg empire by marrying Johanna, daughter of Ferdinand and Isabella. Charles and Ferdinand, sons of Phillip and Johanna, began the separate Spanish and Austrian lines of the Hapsburg family. The Burgundian lands, along with the northern provinces which make up present day Netherlands, became the Spanish Netherlands. The northern provinces successfully rebelled and broke away from Hapsburg rule in the late 16th century and early 17th century. The southern provinces along with the Duchy of Luxembourg remained under the influence of Spain until the year 1700 when Charles II, last of the Spanish Hapsburg line, died without leaving an heir and the Spanish crown went to the Bourbon family of France. The Spanish Netherlands then reverted to the control of the Austrian line of Hapsburgs and became the Austrian Netherlands. The Austrian Netherlands along with the Bishopric of Liege fell to the French Republic in 1794.

At the Congress of Vienna in 1815 the area was united with the Netherlands but in 1830 independence was gained and the constitutional monarchy of Belgium was established. A large part of the Duchy of Luxembourg was incorporated into Belgium and the first king was Leopold I of Saxe-Coburg-Gotha. It was invaded by the German army in Aug. 1914 and the German forces carried on a devastating occupation of most of the territory until the Armistice. Belgium joined the League of Nations. On May 10, 1940 it was invaded again by Nazi German armies. The Belgian and Allied forces were quickly overwhelmed and were evacuated through Dunkirk. Allied troops reached Belgium again in Sept. 1944. Prince Charles, Count of Flanders assumed King Leopold's responsibilities until his liberation by the U.S. army in Austria on May 8, 1945. From 1920-1940 and since 1944 Eupen-Malmedy went from Germany to Belgium.

RULERS:

Leopold I, 1831-1865
Leopold II, 1865-1909
Albert I, 1909-34
Leopold III, 1934-51
Baudouin I, 1952-93
Albert II, 1993-

MONETARY SYSTEM:

1 Franc = 100 Centimes to 2001
1 Belga = 5 Francs
1 Euro = 100 Cents, 2002-

KINGDOM - 1810-1914

SOCIETÉ DE COMMERCE DE BRUXELLES

CA 1810 ISSUE

#1, 2, 4, 7 are held in reserve.

		Good	Fine	XF
3	**100 Francs** ND. Black. Uniface.	—	—	—
5	**1000 Francs** ND. Black. Uniface. Rare.	—	—	—
6	**1000 Francs** ND. Blue. Uniface. Reported not confirmed.	—	—	—

NOTICE

Readers with unlisted dates, signature varieties, etc. are invited to submit photocopies or, high resolution (300 dpi, 100% size) scans of their notes to: Standard Catalog of World Paper Money, 700 East State St. Iola, WI 54990-0001, or E-Mail: george.cuhaj@fwpubs.com.

Société Générale pour Favoriser l'Industrie Nationale

1822-26 Issues

Various dates from 1826. Sign. varieties.

		Good	Fine	XF
8	**1/2 Florin** 1.10.1826. Uniface. Rare.	—	—	—
9	**1 Florin** Reported not confirmed.	—	—	—
10	**2 Florins** Reported not confirmed.	—	—	—
11	**3 Florins** Rare.	—	—	—
12	**5 Florins** Reported not confirmed.	—	—	—
13	**10 Florins** Uniface. Rare.	—	—	—
14	**25 Florins** Rare.	—	—	—
15	**50 Florins** Rare.	—	—	—
16	**100 Florins** Rare.	—	—	—
17	**250 Florins** Rare.	—	—	—
18	**500 Florins** Rare.	—	—	—
19	**1000 Florins** 1822-30. Uniface. Rare.	—	—	—

1837-48 Issue

		Good	Fine	XF
20	**5 Francs** ND (1848). Uniface.	1500.	2500.	4000.
21	**20 Francs** ND (1848). Uniface. Rare.	—	—	—
22	**50 Francs** 6.2.1837. Uniface. Rare.	—	—	—
23	**100 Francs** 6.2.1837. Uniface. Rare.	—	—	—
24	**500 Francs** 6.2.1837. Uniface. Rare.	—	—	—
25	**1000 Francs** 6.2.1837. Uniface. Rare.	—	—	—

Banque de Belgique

1835 Issue

		Good	Fine	XF
26	**5 Francs** ND (1835). Uniface. Rare.	—	—	—

Note: Denominations of 20, 50, 100, and 1000 Francs are also reported. #27-31 not assigned.

Banque de Flandre

Ghent

1841 Issue

		Good	Fine	XF
32	**100 Francs** ND (1841). Uniface. Rare.	—	—	—

		Good	Fine	XF
33	**250 Francs** ND (1841). Uniface. Rare.	—	—	—

Note: Denominations of 25 and 1000 Francs are also reported.

Banque Liègeoise et Caisse d'Épargnes

Liège

1835 Issue

		Good	Fine	XF
34	**5 Francs** ND (1835). Yellow. Rare.	—	—	—
35	**10 Francs** ND (1835). Yellow. Rare.	—	—	—
36	**25 Francs** ND (1835). Green. Rare.	—	—	—
37	**50 Francs** ND (1835). Green. Rare.	—	—	—

Note: Denominations of 100, 200, 500 and 100 Francs are also reported. #38-40 not assigned.

Banque Nationale de Belgique

1851-56 Issues

		Good	Fine	XF
41	**20 Francs** L.5.5.1850. Black. Ceres reclining at lower l., Neptune at lower r. 16 sign. varieties. Rare.	—	—	—

		Good	Fine	XF
42	**20 Francs** L.5.5.1850. (ca.1851-62). Blue on green unpt. Ceres reclining at lower l., Neptune at lower r. 7 sign. varieites.	1250.	2500.	—
43	**50 Francs** 2.1.1851-4.10.1851. Rose. Cherubs in corners. Back: pink.	1500.	3250.	—

		Good	Fine	XF
44	**50 Francs** 1.6.1852. Blue. Cherubs in 4 corners. Rare.	—	—	—
45	**50 Francs** ca.1851-2.1.1862. Blue on green unpt. Cherubs in 4 corners. 5 sign. varieties.	2000.	4000.	—
46	**100 Francs** 2.1.1851-1.6.1852. Cherubs in 4 corners. Rare.	—	—	—
47	**100 Francs** 2.1.1856. Blue. Woman seated w/2 lions at bottom ctr. Rare.	—	—	—
48	**500 Francs** 2.1.1851. Blue. Cherubs in 4 corners. Rare.	—	—	—
49	**500 Francs** 1.6.1852. Black. 2 allegorical figures at l. (Industry and Trade) and at r. (Liberty and Justice). 3 sign. varieties. Rare.	—	—	—
50	**500 Francs** 1.6.1852. Blue. 2 allegorical figures at l. (Industry and Trade) and at r. (Liberty and Justice). 3 sign. varieties. Rare.	—	—	—

		Good	Fine	XF
51	**1000 Francs** 2.1.1851-1.6.1852. Black. Cherubs in 4 corners. Rare.	—	—	—
52	**1000 Francs** 22.8.1853. Blue. Cherubs in 4 corners. 4 sign. varieties. Rare.	—	—	—

1869-73 ISSUE

		Good	Fine	XF
53	**20 Francs** 25.1.1869-29.6.1878. Blue. 2 allegorical figures (Agriculture and Cattle Breeding). 4 sign. varieties.	1500.	3000.	—

		Good	Fine	XF
54	**50 Francs** 3.4.1871-6.7.1871. Blue. Woman and 2 children at l., child w/crown of laurel leaves at r. Children leaning on cornucopia. Rare.	—	—	—
55	**100 Francs** 4.3.1869-14.8.1882. Blue. Seated man at l., woman w/sceptre at r. 2 allegorical figures (Security) at l., (Progress) at r. on back. 5 sign varieties. Rare.	—	—	—
56	**500 Francs** 9.5.1873-25.9.1886. Blue on pink unpt. Allegorical figures at l. (Science) and at r. (Art). Rare.	—	—	—
57	**1000 Francs** 31.5.1870-2.2.1884. Blue. Neptune at l., and Amphitrite at r. 4 sign. varieties. Rare.	—	—	—

1875 ISSUE

58	**50 Francs** 19.7.1875-30.6.1879. Blue on gray unpt. Woman and 2 children at l., group of children in background. Red serial #. Rare.

1879; 1881 ISSUE

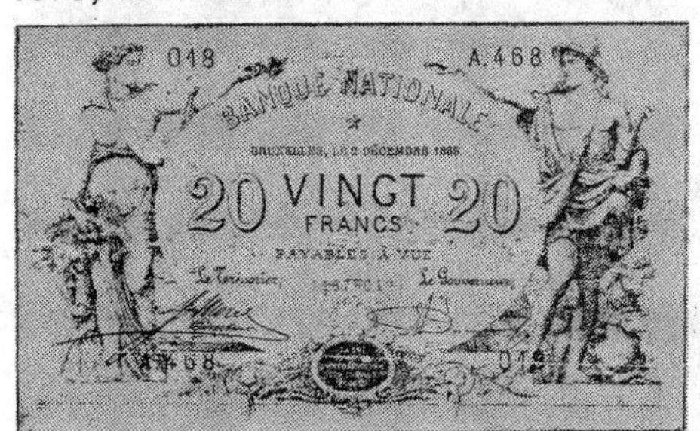

		Good	Fine	XF
59	**20 Francs** 8.8.1879-17.10.1892. Blue on gray unpt. 2 allegorical figures (Agriculture and Cattle Breeding). W/o counterfoil. 5 sign. varieties.	400.	1000.	1800.

		Good	Fine	XF
60	**50 Francs** 3.1.1881-23.9.1887. Blue. Women and 2 children at l., modifications in engraving. W/o counterfoil.	1000.	2000.	—

1883-96 ISSUE

		Good	Fine	XF
61	**20 Francs** 13.12.1892-29.6.1896. Blue on brown unpt. Allegorical figures at l. (Agriculture and Trade) and at r. (Industry).	500.	750.	1250.

NOTICE

Readers with unlisted dates, signature varieties, etc. are invited to submit photocopies or, high resolution (300 dpi, 100% size) scans of their notes to: Standard Catalog of World Paper Money, 700 East State St. Iola, WI 54990-0001, or E-Mail: george.cuhaj@fwpubs.com.

		Good	Fine	XF
62	**20 Francs** 30.7.1896-30.12.1909. Dk. red and green. Minerva w/lion at l. Back brown; arms of 30 towns. 3 sign. varieties.	75.00	225.	400.

		VG	VF	UNC
63	**50 Francs** 26.9.1887-30.12.1908. Blue and black. Medallic female head and children. 5 sign. varieties.	750.	1750.	—

		VG	VF	UNC
64	**100 Francs** 5.6.1883-31.7.1905. Blue on lt. brown unpt. Seated man at l., woman w/sceptre at r. Modifications in engraving and w/o counterfoil. 2 allegorical figures (Security) at l., (Progress) at r. on back. Wmk: Minerva. 6 sign. varieties.	600.	1250.	—

		VG	VF	UNC
65	**500 Francs** 1.1.1887-11.3.1908. Blue and red on gray unpt. Bank name and denomination in red surrounded by women and small angels. 3 sign. varieties.	1250.	2250.	—

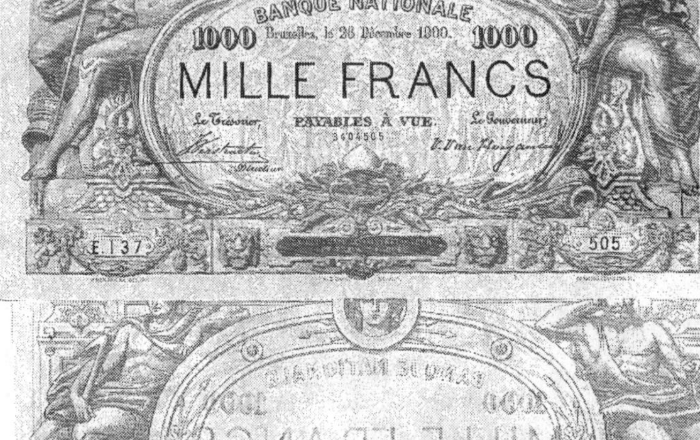

		VG	VF	UNC
66	**1000 Francs** 3.1.1884-30.4.1908. Blue and m/c. Like #73 but slight design changes. 4 sign. varieties.	1875.	3000.	450

1905-10 ISSUES

		VG	VF	UNC
67	**20 Francs** 3.1.1910-19.7.1920. Red and green. Minerva w/lion at l. Black serial #. Back brown; arms of 30 towns. 3 sign. varieties.	5.00	20.00	50.0

68 50 Francs

1909-26. Dk. green on lt. green and blue unpt. Seated woman (Agriculture) at l. and (Law) at r. Several figures (Intelligence and Industry) on back.

	VG	VF	UNC
a. 1.5.1909-5.2.1914. W/embossed arabesque design on border. 2 sign. varieties.	20.00	75.00	225.
b. 1919-1.10.1926. W/o embossed arabesque design on border. 3 sign. varieties.	10.00	30.00	80.00

69 100 Francs

	VG	VF	UNC
31.7.1905-7.3.1906. Blue and brown. Seated man at l., woman w/sceptre at r. W/brown denomination. 2 allegorical figures (Security) at l., (Progress) at r. on back. Like #64.	400.	1000.	—

70 100 Francs

	VG	VF	UNC
15.3.1906-21.12.1908. Brown and black. Quadrigas driven by Ceres at l. and Neptune at r. Back green; women (Sowing) at l. and (Harvesting) at r.	250.	500.	1000.

71 100 Francs

	VG	VF	UNC
12.1.1909-1914. Black and brown on pink and pale green unpt. Quadrigas driven by Ceres at l. and Neptune at r. Back green; women (Sowing) at l. and (Harvesting) at r. Medallion and white edges below and r. embossed arabesque. Wmk: Minerva. Similar to #70. 2 sign. varieties.	15.00	30.00	75.00

72 500 Francs

1910-25. Blue and green on gray unpt. Bank name and denomination (only in Francs) in green surrounded by women and small angels. Similar to #65. 4 sign. varieties.

	VG	VF	UNC
a. 13.10.1910-1914. W/embossed arabesque design on border. 2 sign. varieties.	300.	750.	—
b. 25.1.1919-31.7.1925. W/o embossed arabesque design on border. 3 sign. varieties.	35.00	100.	300.

73 1000 Francs

	VG	VF	UNC
3.7.1909-24.1.1921. Green. 3 sign. varieties.	500.	1500.	—

1914; 1919 Issues

		VG	VF	UNC
74	**5 Francs** 1914; 1919. Brown and orange. Allegorical figures at l. and r. 3 allegorical figures on back.			
	a. 1.7.1914.	10.00	40.00	150.
	b. 25.1.1919. Wmk: *BNB.*	10.00	40.00	150.
75	**5 Francs** 1914-21. Green and brown. Allegorical figures at l. and r. Like #74.			
	a. 1.7.1914.	10.00	30.00	100.
	b. 27.12.1918-3.1.1921. Wmk: *BNB.*	10.00	30.00	100.

		VG	VF	UNC
76	**20 Francs** 1.9.1914. Red and green. Minerva w/lion at l. Red serial #, date below. Back brown; arms of 30 towns. Like #67.	300.	750.	1400.

		VG	VF	UNC
77	**50 Francs** 1.8.1914. Green. W/embossed arabesque design on border. Red serial #. Like #68.	800.	1500.	2500.
78	**100 Francs** 1914-16.10.1920. Black and brown. Quadrigas driven by Ceres at l. and Neptune at r. Back green; women (Sowing) at l. and (Harvesting) at r. Medallion and white edges below. Wmk: Minerva. Like #71 but w/o embossed arabesque. 2 sign varieties.	2.50	10.00	30.00
79	**100 Francs** 12.9.1914-1.10.1914. Black and brown. Like #78 but w/red serial #. Wmk: Minerva.	1500.	3500.	—

		VG	VF	UNC
80	**1000 Francs** 17.1.1919-31.3.1919. Brownish-yellow and black. Like #73 but w/o edge printing.	150.	400.	1250.

1914 Comptes Courants Issue

		VG	VF	UNC
81	**1 Franc** 27.8.1914. Blue on gray unpt.	10.00	30.00	75.00
82	**2 Francs** 27.8.1914. Brown on gray unpt.	20.00	50.00	125

#83-85 portr. Kg. Leopold I at l.

		VG	VF	UNC
83	**20 Francs** 27.8.1914. Blue and brown. Kg. Leopold I at l.	400.	750.	1750.

		VG	VF	UNC
84	**100 Francs** 27.8.1914. Blue on gray unpt. Kg. Leopold I at l.	1200.	3000.	—

		VG	VF	UNC
85	**1000 Francs** 27.8.1914. Wine red. Kg. Leopold I at l. Rare.	—	—	—

GERMAN OCCUPATION - WWI

SOCIÉTÉ GÉNÉRALE DE BELGIQUE

1915 ISSUE

#86-88, 90 portr. Qn. Louise-Marie at l.

Notes issued by the bank during the German occupation and after the war carry various printing dates during 1915-18.

		VG	VF	UNC
86	**1 Franc** 1915-1918. Portr. Qn. Louise-Marie at l.			
	a. 1.3.1915-31.1.1916. Violet on pink unpt.	2.00	8.00	25.00
	b. 1.2.1916-29.10.1918. Mauve on pink unpt.	2.00	8.00	25.00

		VG	VF	UNC
87	**2 Francs** 1.4.1915-25.5.1918. Reddish brown on lt. green unpt. Portr. Qn. Louise-Marie at l.	10.00	50.00	80.00

		VG	VF	UNC
88	**5 Francs** 2.1.1915-14.7.1918. Green on gray unpt. Portr. Qn. Louise-Marie at l. Blue and green.	40.00	100.	300.

		VG	VF	UNC
89	**20 Francs** 1.2.1915-11.10.1918. Blue on pink unpt. Portr. P. P. Rubens at l.	75.00	250.	750.

		VG	VF	UNC
90	**100 Francs** 26.12.1914-2.9.1918. Brown and green on pink and green unpt. Portr. Qn. Louise-Marie at l.	325.	650.	1500.

		VG	VF	UNC
91	**1000 Francs** 18.9.1915-26.10.1918. Brown and green on lt. green unpt. Portr. P. P. Rubens at l.	5000.	10,000.	—

KINGDOM - 1920-44

BANQUE NATIONALE DE BELGIQUE

1920-22 ISSUE

#92-96 denominations in Francs only. Various date and sign. varieties. Conjoined portr. Kg. Albert and Qn. Elisabeth at l.

		VG	VF	UNC
92	**1 Franc** 1.3.1920-8.6.1922. Blue on gray unpt. Portr. Kg. Albert and Qn. Elisabeth at l. Arms at upper corners and ctr. on back	1.00	7.50	15.00
93	**5 Francs** 1.4.1922-25.6.1926. Blue on lt. brown unpt. Portr. Kg. Albert and Qn. Elisabeth at l. Seated man looking at factory scene on back. 2 sign. varieties.	1.50	8.00	25.00

		VG	VF	UNC
94	**20 Francs** 1.6.1921-10.4.1926. Brown on lt. blue and brown unpt. Portr. Kg. Albert and Qn. Elisabeth at l. City view w/lg. bldgs. at ctr. r. on back. 2 sign varieties.	20.00	60.00	150.

		VG	VF	UNC
95	**100 Francs** 1.4.1921-2.6.1927. Lilac-brown. Portr. Kg. Albert and Qn. Elisabeth at l. Man w/tools at r. on back. 3 sign varieties.	5.00	15.00	30.00
96	**1000 Francs** 15.6.1922-28.10.1927. Blue on pink unpt. Portr. Kg. Albert and Qn. Elisabeth at l. 3 sign varieties.	30.00	75.00	175.

1926 ISSUE

#97-98 like #93-94 but *TRÉSORERIE-THESAURIE* ovpt. on face.

		VG	VF	UNC
97	**5 Francs** 14.6.1926-10.5.1931. Blue on lt. brown unpt. Portr. Kg. Albert and Qn. Elisabeth at l. Seated man looking at factory scene. 2 sign. varieties.	1.00	6.00	20.00

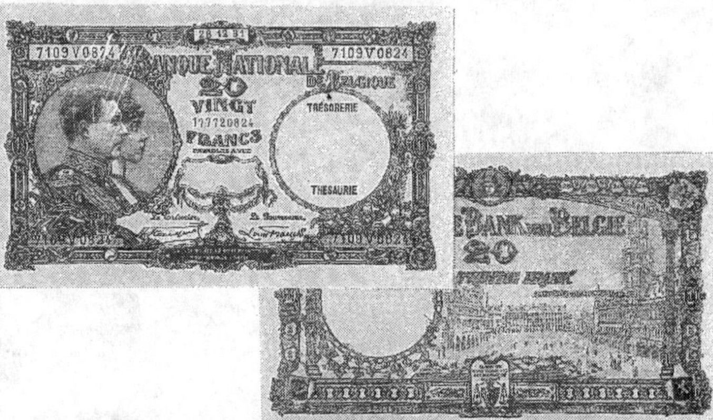

		VG	VF	UNC
98	**20 Francs** 14.4.1926-27.1.1940. Brown on lt. blue and yellow-green unpt. Portr. Kg. Albert and Qn. Elisabeth at l. 3 sign. varieties.	4.00	15.00	30.00

1927-29 ISSUES

#99-107 denominations in Francs and Belgas. Various date (from 1927) and sign. varieties.

99	50 Francs-10 Belgas	VG	VF	UNC
	1.3.1927; 23.3.1927. Green. Like #68b but w/o embossed arabesque design on border. 3 sign. varieties.	100.	300.	500.

00	50 Francs-10 Belgas	VG	VF	UNC
	1.9.1927-6.1.1928. Brown on yellow unpt. Peasant woman w/sheaf and 2 horses at l. ctr. Allegorical figure holding sailing ship and large cornucopia.	100.	300.	500.
01	**50 Francs-10 Belgas**			
	1.10.1928-20.4.1935. Green on yellow unpt. Peasant woman w/sheaf and 2 horses at l. ctr. Allegorical figure holding sailing ship and lg. cornucopia. Like #100.	5.00	15.00	30.00

te: For #101 w/*TRÉSORERIE* ovpt. see #106.

2	100 Francs-20 Belgas	VG	VF	UNC
	1.7.1927-2.8.1932. Blue-black on ochre and pale blue unpt. Portraits of Kg. Albert and Qn. Elizabeth at l. Wmk: Kg. Leopold I. Similar to #95.	3.00	10.00	20.00

103	500 Francs-100 Belgas	VG	VF	UNC
	3.1.1927-16.11.1936. Blue and green. Bank name and denomination surrounded by women and small angels. Sign. on face only. 2 sign. varieties.	3.00	20.00	50.00

104	1000 Francs-200 Belgas	VG	VF	UNC
	2.4.1928-28.11.1939. Green on m/c unpt. Portr. Kg. Albert and Qn. Elisabeth at l. Sign. on face only. 3 sign. varieties.	2.00	15.00	40.00

		VG	VF	UNC
105	**10,000 Francs-2000 Belgas** 22.11.1929-28.8.1942. Blue on pink unpt. Quadrigas driven by Ceres at l., and Neptune at r., lion at ctr. 2 allegorical figures on back. 3 sign. varieties.	100.	300.	600.

1933; 1935 ISSUE

		VG	VF	UNC
106	**50 Francs-10 Belgas** 20.4.1935-28.4.1947. Dk. green on blackish green on lt. green and orange unpt. Peasant woman w/sheaf and 2 horses at l. ctr. Allegorical figure holding sailing ship and large cornucopia on back. Like #100 but ovpt: *TRÉSORERIE* on face and *THESAURIE* on back. 6 sign. varieties.	.50	3.00	10.00

		VG	VF	UNC
107	**100 Francs-20 Belgas** 1.5.1933-15.9.1943. Gray on lt. brown unpt. Portr. Qn. Elisabeth at l., woman w/crown and fruit at ctr., portr. Kg. Albert at r. French text on back. Allegorical figures at ctr. on back. Wmk: Kg. Leopold I. 4 sign. varieties.	.50	2.00	9.00

1938 ISSUE

		VG	VF	UNC
108	**5 Francs** 1.3.1938-11.5.1938. Blue on lt. brown unpt. Portr. Kg. Albert and Qn. Elisabeth at l. Seated man looking at factory scene. Like #93 but ovpt: *TRÉSORERIE - THESAURIE* on face. 2 sign. varieties.			
	a. Issued note.	1.00	3.00	10.0
	x. Error date: 4.5.1988.	2.00	10.00	25.0

		VG	VF	UNC
109	**500 Francs-100 Belgas** 3.2.1938-4.10.1943. Blue and green. Bank name and denomination surrounded by women and small angels. Like # 103 but sign on both sides. 2 sign. varieties.	2.00	12.50	27.5

1939 ISSUE

		VG	VF	UNC
110	**1000 Francs-200 Belgas** 12.12.1939-26.10.1944. Green. Portr. Kg. Albert and Qn. Elisabeth at l. Like #104 but sign. on both sides. 2 sign. varieties.	2.00	10.00	20.00

1940 ISSUE

		VG	VF	UNC
111	**20 Francs** 27.1.1940-13.6.1947. Brown on lt. blue and brown unpt. Portr. Kg. Albert and Qn. Elisabeth at l. Like #94 but w/ovpt: *TRÉSORERIE* on face and *THESAURIE* on back. Date at top ctr. 4 sign. varieties.	1.00	7.50	20.00

1941 ISSUE

		VG	VF	UNC
112	**100 Francs-20 Belgas** 17.1.1941-10.9.1943. Gray on lt. brown unpt. Portr. Qn. Elisabeth at l., woman w/crown and fruit at ctr., portr. Kg. Albert at r. Like #107 but w/Flemish text on face.	.50	1.50	9.00

1944 ISSUE

		VG	VF	UNC
113	**100 Francs-20 Belgas** 20.9.1944-4.11.1944. Orange. Portr. Qn. Elisabeth at l., woman w/crown and fruit at ctr., portr. Kg. Albert at r. Like #107 but w/French text on face.	10.00	30.00	75.00
114	**100 Francs-20 Belgas** 20.9.1944-4.11.1944. Orange. Portr. Qn. Elisabeth at l., woman w/crown and fruit at ctr., portr. Kg. Albert at r. Like #112 but w/Flemish text on face.	10.00	35.00	100.
115	**1000 Francs-200 Belgas** 20.9.1944-26.10.1944. Red. Portr. Kg. Albert and Qn. Elisabeth at l. Sign. on both sides. Like #110.	400.	750.	1500.

1948 ISSUE

		VG	VF	UNC
116	**20 Francs** 1.9.1948. Brown. Portr. Kg. Albert and Qn. Elisabeth at l., wings at top ctr. Date at top l. 4 sign. varieties.	1.00	8.00	20.00

GERMAN OCCUPATION - WWII

BANQUE D'EMISSION A BRUXELLES

CA 1941 ISSUE

		VG	VF	UNC
117	**50 Francs** ND. Gray-blue on yellow unpt. Reported not confirmed.	—	—	—
118	**100 Francs** ND. Green. Reported not confirmed.	—	—	—
119	**100 Francs** ND. Brown. Reported not confirmed.	—	—	—

		VG	VF	UNC
120	**10,000 Francs** ND. Blue. Farm woman w/sickle and plants at ctr. 5 standing allegorical female figures under tree on back. (Not issued). Rare.	—	—	—

KINGDOM IN EXILE - 1943

BANQUE NATIONALE DE BELGIQUE

1943-45 ISSUE

#121 and 122 printer: TDLR (w/o imprint).

		VG	VF	UNC
121	**5 Francs-1 Belga** 1.2.1943 (1944). Red on pink and lt. blue unpt.	.25	2.00	7.50

		VG	VF	UNC
122	**10 Francs-2 Belgas** 1.2.1943 (1944). Green on lt. green and lt. pink unpt.	.25	2.00	7.50

#123-125 printer: BWC (w/o imprint).

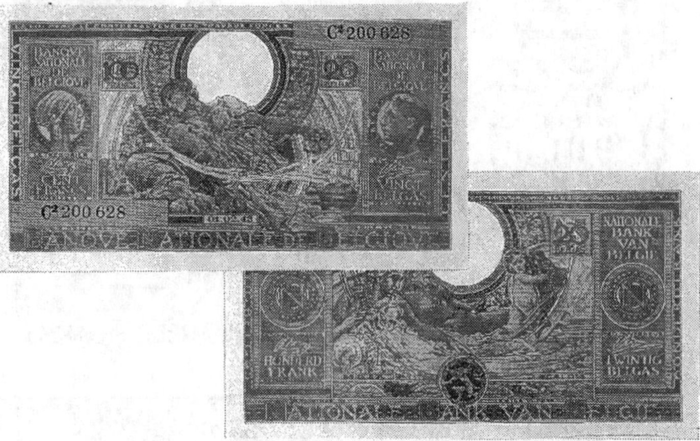

		VG	VF	UNC
123	**100 Francs-20 Belgas** 1.2.1943 (1944). Red and green. Qn. Elisabeth at l., woman w/crown and fruit at ctr. Kg. Albert at r. Like #107 but smaller size.	FV	10.00	30.00

		VG	VF	UNC
124	**500 Francs-100 Belgas** 1.2.1943 (1944). Blue, pink and m/c. Reclining figure on back. Like #123 but different value and color.	FV	100.	250.
125	**1000 Francs-200 Belgas** 1.2.1943 (1944). Brown and violet. Qn. Elisabeth at l., woman w/crown and fruit at ctr. Kg. Albert at r. Reclining figure on back. Like #123 but different value and color.	100.	350.	750.

KINGDOM - 1944-PRESENT

BANQUE NATIONALE DE BELGIQUE

NATIONALE BANK VAN BELGIE

1944-45 ISSUE

		VG	VF	UNC
126	**100 Francs** 3.11.1945-31.12.1950. Brown, pink and yellow. Portr. Leopold I at l. and as wmk. Justice Palace, Brussels at ctr. Mounted troops at ctr. r. on back. 2 sign. varieties.	3.00	15.00	35.00

		VG	VF	UNC
127	**500 Francs** 7.11.1944-1.4.1947. Brown and yellow. Portr. Kg. Leopold II wearing a military cap at l., Antwerp Cathedral at ctr. Congo landscape and boat on back. 2 sign. varieties.	25.00	85.00	250.

		VG	VF	UNC
128	**1000 Francs** 16.10.1944-1.7.1948. Blue. Portr. Kg. Albert I wearing steel helmet at l., monument at ctr. City view of Veurne on back. 3 sign. varieties.	20.00	75.00	200.

1950-52 ISSUE

29	100 Francs	VG	VF	UNC
	1952-59. Black on brown and m/c unpt. Portr. Kg. Leopold I at l. Bldg. at ctr., portr. Fr. Orban on back.			
	a. Sign. Frère-Pirsoul. 1.8.1952-4.12.1952.	FV	10.00	40.00
	b. Sign. Frère-Vincent. 10.9.1953-30.6.1957.	FV	6.50	30.00
	c. Sign. Ansiaux-Vincent. 1.7.1957-26.2.1959.	FV	5.00	25.00
	s. As a. Specimen.	—	—	—

30	500 Francs	VG	VF	UNC
	1.4.1952-29.5.1958. Brown and yellow. Portr. Kg. Leopold II at l. 4 heads (painting by P. P. Rubens) on back. 3 sign. varieties.			
	a. Issued note.	FV	60.00	175.
	s. Specimen.	—	—	—

1	1000 Francs	VG	VF	UNC
	2.1.1950-28.7.1958. Blue and m/c. Portr. Kg. Albert at l. Geeraert and lock scene on back. 3 sign. varieties.			
	a. Issued note.	FV	50.00	125.
	s. Specimen.	—	—	—

NOTICE

Readers with unlisted dates, signature varieties, etc. are invited to submit photocopies or, high resolution (300 dpi, 100% size) scans of their notes to: Standard Catalog of World Paper Money, 700 East State St. Iola, WI 54990-0001, or E-Mail: george.cuhaj@fwpubs.com.

ROYAUME DE BELGIQUE - TRÉSORERIE

KONINKRIJK BELGIE - THESAURIE

1948; 1950 ISSUE

132	20 Francs	VG	VF	UNC
	1950; 1956. Lilac, violet and blue. Portr. R. de Lassus at ctr. Portr. P. de Monte at ctr. on back. Wmk: Kg. Leopold I.			
	a. Sign. Van Heureck 1.7.1950.	.25	1.25	6.00
	b. Sign. Williot 3.4.1956.	.25	.50	4.00

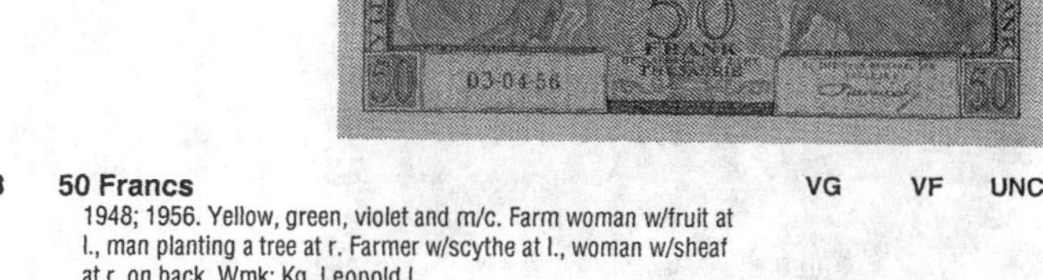

133	50 Francs	VG	VF	UNC
	1948; 1956. Yellow, green, violet and m/c. Farm woman w/fruit at l., man planting a tree at r. Farmer w/scythe at l., woman w/sheaf at r. on back. Wmk: Kg. Leopold I.			
	a. Sign. Van Heureck 1.6.1948.	.50	1.50	7.00
	b. Sign. Williot 3.4.1956.	.25	1.00	4.00

MILITARY OCCUPATION OF GERMANY

ARMÉE BELGE - BELGISCH LEGER

MILITARY PAYMENT CERTIFICATES

#M1-M8 issued under the authority of the Ministry of Defense for Belgian troops stationed in Germany after World War II.

M1	1 Franc	Good	Fine	XF
	1.8.1946. Green and blue.			
	a. Serial # prefix *A*.	3.00	10.00	30.00
	b. Serial # prefix *B*.	20.00	50.00	100.
	s. Specimen.	—	Unc	150.
M2	**2 Francs**			
	1.8.1946. Green and violet.			
	a. Issued note.	3.00	30.00	80.00
	s. Specimen.			

		Good	Fine	XF
M3	**5 Francs**			
	1.8.1946. Green and red.			
	a. Serial # prefix *A*.	3.00	32.50	85.00
	b. Serial # prefix *B*.	50.00	100.	200.
	s. Specimen.	—	Unc	150.

		Good	Fine	XF
M4	**10 Francs**			
	1.8.1946. Brown and blue.			
	a. Issued note.	10.00	50.00	130.
	s. Specimen.	—	Unc	150.

		Good	Fine	XF
M5	**20 Francs**			
	1.8.1946. Brown and green			
	a. Issued note.	15.00	65.00	200.
	s. Specimen.	—	Unc	150.
M6	**50 Francs**			
	1.8.1946. Brown and red.			
	a. Issued note.	30.00	125.	325.
	s. Specimen.	—	Unc	300.

		Good	Fine	XF
M7	**100 Francs**			
	1.8.1946. Gray-blue and violet.			
	a. Issued note.	100.	400.	700.
	s. Specimen.	—	Unc	500.

		Good	Fine	XF
M8	**500 Francs**			
	1.8.1946. Gray-blue and green.			
	a. Issued note.	500.	1250.	—
	s. Specimen.	—	Unc	1500.

The Parliamentary British Colo[ny] of Bermuda, situated in th[e] western Atlantic Ocean 660 mile[s] (1,062 km.) east of North Carolin[a] has an area of 20.6 sq. mi. (53 s[q.] km.) and a population of 60,10[0]. Capital: Hamilton. Concentrate[d] essences, beauty preparation[s] and cut flowers are exported. Mo[st] Bermudians derive their livelihoo[d] from tourism.

Bermuda was discovered b[y] Juan de Bermudez, a Spanis[h] navigator, in 1503. Briti[sh] influence dates from 1609 whe[n] a group of Virginia-bound British colonists under the command of Sir George Somers w[as] shipwrecked on the islands for 10 months. The islands were settled in 1612 by 60 British colonis[ts] from the Virginia Colony and became a crown colony in 1684. Internal autonomy was obtained [by] the constitution of June 8, 1968.

In February, 1970, Bermuda converted from its former currency, the British pound, to [a] decimal currency, termed a dollar, On July 31, 1972, Bermuda severed its monetary link with t[he] British pound and pegged its dollar to be the same value as the U.S. dollar.

RULERS:

MONETARY SYSTEM:

1 Shilling = 12 Pence
1 Pound = 20 Shillings, to 1970
1 Dollar = 100 Cents, 1970-

BRITISH ADMINISTRATION

BERMUDA GOVERNMENT

1914 ISSUE

		Good	Fine
1	**1 Pound**		
	2.12.1914. Black on green unpt. Arms at l. Back green. Printer: ABNC.	750.	2000.

1920-27 ISSUE

		Good	Fine
2	**2 Shillings 6 Pence**		
	1.8.1920. Brown. Portr. Kg. George V at ctr. Sailing ship at ctr. on back. (Not issued). Rare.	—	—

		Good	Fine
3	**5 Shillings**		
	1920; 1935. Brown and green. Portr. Kg. George V at ctr. Back purple; sailing ship at ctr. Printer: TDLR.		
	a. Sign. title: *RECEIVER GENERAL*. 1.8.1920.	350.	850.
	b. Sign. title: *COLONIAL TREASURER*. ND (1935).	325.	800.

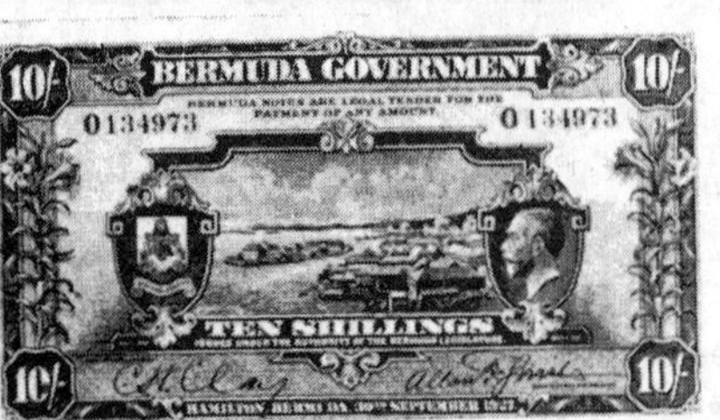

		Good	Fine
4	**10 Shillings**		
	30.9.1927. Red on m/c unpt. Arms at l., harbor at St. George at ctr., portr. Kg. George V at r. Royal crest at ctr. on back. Printer: W&S.	300.	750.

5	1 Pound	VG	VF	UNC
	30.9.1927. Blue on m/c unpt. Arms at l., view of Hamilton at ctr., Kg. George V at r. Printer: W&S.	300.	650.	2500.

1937-41 ISSUES

#6-10 portr. Kg. George VI at upper ctr. Royal crest on back. Printer: BWC.

6	1 Shilling	VG	VF	UNC
	1.3.1939. Portr. Kg. George VI. Royal crest. Printer: BWC. M/c. Specimen only.	—	—	—
7	2 Shillings 6 Pence			
	1.3.1939. Portr. Kg. George VI. Royal crest. Printer: BWC. M/c. Specimen only.	—	—	—

8	5 Shillings	VG	VF	UNC
	12.5.1937. Brown on m/c unpt. Portr. Kg. George VI. Date in bottom ctr. frame under picture of Hamilton harbor.			
	a. Single letter prefix.	15.00	90.00	500.
	b. Fractional style letter-number prefix.	7.50	40.00	325.

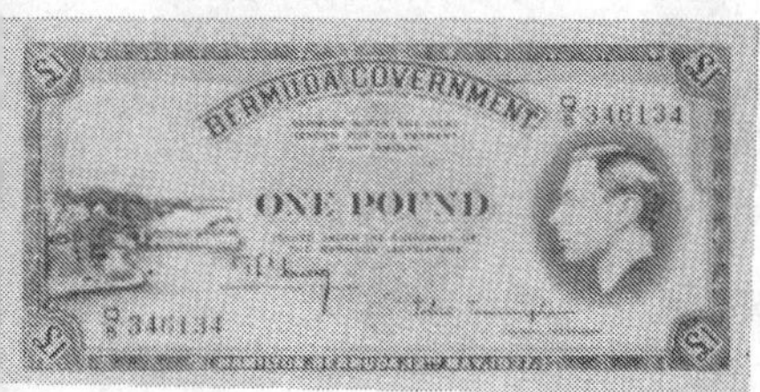

9	10 Shillings	VG	VF	UNC
	12.5.1937. Green on m/c unpt. Portr. Kg. George VI. Date in bottom ctr. frame under picture of Gate's Fort in St. George. Royal crest. Printer: BWC.	275.	850.	—
10	10 Shillings			
	12.5.1937. Red on m/c unpt. Portr. Kg. George VI. Date in bottom ctr. frame under picture of Gate's Fort in St. George. Like #9. Royal crest. Printer: BWC.			
	a. Single letter prefix.	35.00	225.	900.
	b. Fractional style letter-number prefix.	20.00	150.	650.

11	1 Pound	VG	VF	UNC
	12.5.1937. Blue on m/c unpt. Portr. Kg. George VI. Bridge at l. Royal crest. Printer: BWC.			
	a. Single letter prefix.	30.00	175.	—
	b. Fractional style letter-number prefix.	20.00	150.	650.

#11-13 portr. Kg. george VI at r.

12	5 Pounds	VG	VF	UNC
	1.8.1941. Brown on m/c unpt. Portr. Kg. George VI. Ship entering Hamilton harbor at l. Royal crest. Printer: BWC. Back brown, pink and green.	450.	1500.	—
13	5 Pounds			
	1.8.1941. Orange on m/c unpt. Portr. Kg. George VI. Ship entering Hamilton harbor at l. Royal crest. Printer: BWC. Like #12.	350.	1150.	—

1943 ISSUE

13A	10 Shillings	VG	VF	UNC
	1.4.1943. Portr. Kg. George VI at ctr. Like #15. Specimen.	—	—	—

1947 ISSUE

#14 and 15 portr. Kg. George VI at upper ctr. Royal crest on back. Printer: BWC.

14	5 Shillings	VG	VF	UNC
	17.2.1947. Brown on m/c unpt. Portr. Kg. George VI, date at l. Similar to #8. Royal Crest Printer: BWC.	10.00	75.00	400.
15	10 Shillings			
	17.2.1947. Red on m/c unpt. Portr. Kg. George VI. Date at l., Gate's Fort in St. George at bottom ctr. Similar to #9. Date at l. Royal crest Printer: BWC.	25.00	200.	750.

16	1 Pound	VG	VF	UNC
	17.2.1947. Blue on m/c unpt. Portr. Kg. George VI in profile at r., bridge at l., date at ctr. above *ONE POUND*. Similar to #11. Royal crest Printer: BWC.	20.00	150.	700.

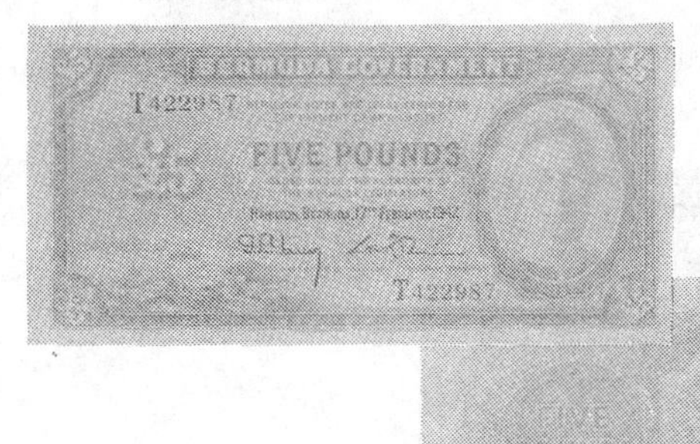

17	5 Pounds	VG	VF	UNC
	17.2.1947. Lt. orange on m/c unpt. Portr. Kg. George VI, facing at r., ship entering Hamilton Harbor at l. Similar to #13. Royal crest Printer: BWC. Back lt. orange and green.	100.	450.	1500.

1952 ISSUE

Royal crest on back. Printer: BWC.

18	5 Shillings	VG	VF	UNC
	1952; 1957. Brown on m/c unpt. Portr. Qn. Elizabeth II at upper ctr. Hamilton Harbor in frame at bottom ctr.			
	a. 20.10.1952.	10.00	35.00	135.
	b. 1.5.1957.	8.00	30.00	100.
	s. As b. Specimen.	—	—	—

1952-66 ISSUE

#18-22 arms at ctr. on back. Printer: BWC.

19 10 Shillings
1952-66. Red on m/c unpt. Portr. Qn. Elizabeth II at upper ctr. Gate's Fort in St. George in frame at bottom ctr.

	VG	VF	UNC
a. 20.10.1952.	25.00	70.00	350.
b. 1.5.1957.	15.00	40.00	175.
c. 1.10.1966.	18.00	60.00	250.
s. As b. Specimen.	—	—	—

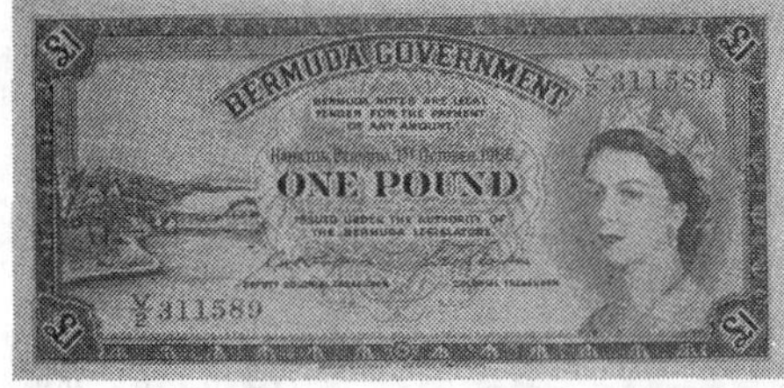

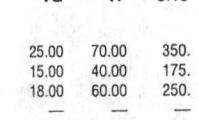

20 1 Pound
1952-66. Blue on m/c unpt. Qn. Elizabeth II at r. Bridge at l.

	VG	VF	UNC
a. 20.10.1952.	30.00	90.00	450.
b. 1.5.1957. W/o security strip.	25.00	70.00	375.
c. 1.5.1957. W/security strip.	22.50	70.00	350.
d. 1.10.1966.	20.00	60.00	275.
s. As d. Specimen.	—	—	—

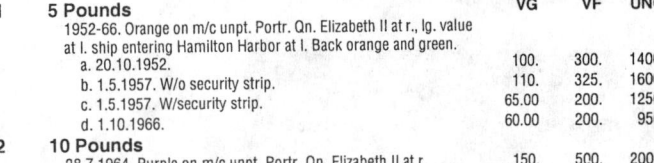

21 5 Pounds
1952-66. Orange on m/c unpt. Portr. Qn. Elizabeth II at r., lg. value at l. ship entering Hamilton Harbor at l. Back orange and green.

	VG	VF	UNC
a. 20.10.1952.	100.	300.	1400.
b. 1.5.1957. W/o security strip.	110.	325.	1600.
c. 1.5.1957. W/security strip.	65.00	200.	1250.
d. 1.10.1966.	60.00	200.	950.

22 10 Pounds
28.7.1964. Purple on m/c unpt. Portr. Qn. Elizabeth II at r.

	VG	VF	UNC
	150.	500.	2000.

BOHEMIA & MORAVIA

Bohemia, a province in northwest Czechoslovakia, was combined with the majority of Moravia in central Czechoslovakia (excluding parts of north and south Moravia which were joined with Silesia in 1938) to form a German protectorate in March 1939. Toward the end of 1945, the protectorate was dissolved and Bohemia and Moravia once again became part of Czechoslovakia.

MONETARY SYSTEM:
1 Koruna = 100 Haleru

German Occupation - WWII

Protektorat Böhmen und Mähren

Protectorate of Bohemia and Moravia

1939 Provisional Issue

#1, 2 are state notes w/circular handstamp (usually blurred printing w/larger letters) or machine (usually finer printing w/smaller letters) ovpt: ***Protektorat Böhmen und Mähren, Protektorat Cechy a Morava.***

1 1 Koruna
ND (1939). Blue. Liberty wearing cap at r. Back red and blue; arms at l. Ovpt. on Czechoslovakia #27.

	VG	VF	UNC
a. Handstamp: *Böhmen und Mähren...*	1.50	6.00	17.50
b. Machine ovpt: *Böhmen und Mähren...*	2.00	7.50	20.00
s. Perforated: *SPECIMEN.*			

2 5 Korun
ND (1939). Lilac and violet. Portr. J. Jungmann at r. Back violet; woman at l. Ovpt. on Czechoslovakia #28.

	VG	VF	UNC
a. Handstamp: *Böhmen und Mähren...*	2.50	10.00	30.0
b. Machine ovpt: *Böhmen und Mähren...*	5.00	25.00	60.0
s. Perforated: *SPECIMEN.*			

1940 Issues

3 1 Koruna
ND (1940). Brown on blue unpt. Girl at r. Back red and blue; arms at l.

	VG	VF	UNC
a. Issued note.	.25	1.00	5.0
s. Perforated: *SPECIMEN.*	—	.25	1.0

4 5 Korun
ND (1940). Green on blue and brown unpt. Woman at r. Back violet; woman at l.

	VG	VF	UNC
a. Issued note.	.50	2.50	7.5
s. Perforated: *SPECIMEN.*	—	.75	3.0

		VG	VF	UNC
5	**50 Korun**			
	12.9.1940. Dk. brown on gray unpt. Woman at r. Back green; arms at l.			
	a. Issued note.	2.00	6.00	20.00
	p. Print proof of woman.	—	—	10.00
	s. Perforated: *SPECIMEN.*	—	1.50	5.00

		VG	VF	UNC
6	**100 Korun**			
	20.8.1940. Blue. View of Castle and Charles Bridge in Prague. Back red ctr. w/blue and maroon lettering. W/o *II AUFLAGE* at l.			
	a. Issued note.	.50	3.50	12.50
	s. Perforated: *NEPLATNÉ* or *SPECIMEN.*	—	1.00	6.00

		VG	VF	UNC
7	**100 Korun**			
	20.8.1940. Blue. View of Castle and Charles Bridge in Prague. Like #6 but blue ctr. and lettering on back. Back blue ctr. w/blue lettering. *II. AUFLAGE* (2nd issue) at l. margin.			
	a. Issued note.	.25	2.50	10.00
	b. Issued note series Gb.	—	—	10.00
	s. Perforated: *SPECIMEN.*	—	1.00	6.00

1942-44 ISSUE

		VG	VF	UNC
8	**10 Korun**			
	8.7.1942. Brown on lt. orange unpt. Portr. girl at r. 2 serial # varieties. Arms at ctr. r. in unpt. on back.			
	a. Issued note.	.25	1.50	8.00
	b. Issued note series Nb.	—	—	25.00
	s. Perforated: *NEPLATNÉ* or *SPECIMEN.*	—	1.00	3.00

		VG	VF	UNC
9	**20 Korun**			
	24.1.1944. Green on lt. green unpt. Fruit across ctr., portr. boy at r. 3 serial # varieties. Arms at ctr. in unpt. on back.			
	a. Issued note.	.50	2.50	9.00
	s. Perforated: *SPECIMEN.*	—	1.00	3.00

		VG	VF	UNC
10	**50 Korun**			
	25.9.1944. Brownish gray. Wreath at ctr. portr. woman at r. Arms at ctr. in unpt. on back.			
	a. Issued note.	.50	4.00	20.00
	s. Perforated: *NEPLATNÉ* or *SPECIMEN.*	—	2.00	7.50

NATIONALBANK FÜR BÖHMEN UND MÄHREN

NATIONAL BANK FOR BOHEMIA AND MORAVIA

1942-44 ISSUES

		VG	VF	UNC
11	**500 Korun**			
	24.2.1942. Dk. brown on m/c unpt. Portr. P. Brandl at r. Back olive and m/c. W/o *II. AUFLAGE - II VYDANI.*.			
	a. Issued note.	3.00	10.00	40.00
	s. Perforated: *SPECIMEN.*	—	2.50	10.00

		VG	VF	UNC
12	**500 Korun** 24.2.1942. Dk. brown on m/c unpt. Portr. P. Brandl at r. Back olive and m/c. *II. AUFLAGE - II. VYDANI.* (2nd issue) at l. margin.			
	a. Issued note.	1.50	5.00	25.00
	p. Print proofs of L. Brandl.	—	—	10.00
	s. Perforated: *SPECIMEN.*	—	1.50	7.50

		VG	VF	UNC
13	**1000 Korun** 24.10.1942. Dk. green on green and brown unpt. Portr. P. Parler at r. W/o *II. AUFLAGE* on back.			
	a. Issued note.	4.00	15.00	45.00
	s. Perforated: *SPECIMEN.*	—	3.00	15.00
14	**1000 Korun** 24.10.1942. Dk. green. Portr. P. Parler at r. Like #13. Blue and brown guilloche on back. *II AUFLAGE - II VYDANI* (2nd issue) at l. margin.			
	a. Issued note.	2.00	7.50	25.00
	s. Perforated: *NEPLATNÉ* or *SPECIMEN.*	—	1.50	7.50
15	**1000 Korun** 24.10.1942. Dk. green. Portr. P. Parler at r. M/c guilloche on back. *II AUFLAGE-II VYDANI* Like #13. (2nd issue) at l. margin.			
	a. Issued note.	2.00	7.50	40.00
	p. Print proofs of P. Farler	—	—	10.00
	s. Perforated: *SPECIMEN.*	—	1.50	7.50
16	**5000 Korun** 25.10.1943 (-old date 6.7.1920). Brown-violet. Red ovpt: *NATIONALBANK FUR BÖHMEN UND MÄHREN* on Czechoslovakia #19. Perforated: *SPECIMEN.*	—	15.00	60.00

		VG	VF	UNC
17	**5000 Korun** 24.2.1944. Gray. Portr. St. Weyels Las l at r. Back brown and m/c.			
	a. Issued note.	8.00	30.00	80.00
	p. Print proofs of St. Wenesslar.	—	—	10.00
	s. Perforated: *SPECIMEN.*	—	5.00	12.50

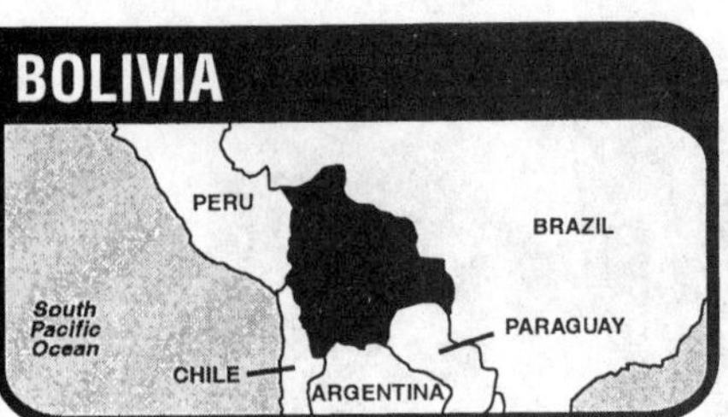

The Republic of Bolivia, a landlocked country in wes central South America, has a area of 424,165 sq. m (1,098,581 sq. km.) and population of 8.33 million Capitals: La Paz (administrative) Sucre (constitutional). Mining i the principal industry and tin th most important metal. Minerals petroleum, natural gas, cotto and coffee are exported.

The Incas, who ruled one of th world's greatest dynasties incorporated the area that is no western Bolivia into their empire about 1200AD. Their control was maintained until the Spaniard arrived in 1535 and reduced the predominantly Indian population to slavery. When Napoleo occupied Madrid in 1808 and placed his brother Joseph on the Spanish throne, a fervor c revolutionary activity quickened in Bolivia, culminating with the 1809 proclamation c independence. Sixteen years of struggle ensued before the republic, named for the famed liberatc General Simón Bolívar, was established on August 6, 1825. Since then, Bolivia has had more tha 60 revolutions, 70 presidents and 11 constitutions.

RULERS:

Spanish to 1825

MONETARY SYSTEM:

1 Boliviano = 100 (Centavos) to 1965
1 Bolivar = 100 Centavos, 1945-1962

SPECIMEN NOTES:

All *SPECIMEN, MUESTRA, MUESTRA SIN VALOR* and *ESPECIMEN* notes always hav serial #'s of zero.

REPUBLIC

TESORERIA DE LA REPÚBLICA DE BOLIVIA

1902 ISSUE

#91-95 intended for circulation in the northwest during the Acre territory conflict with Brazil. Printer: ABNC.

		VG	VF	UN
91	**50 Centavos** 29.11.1902. Black on green unpt. Shield w/flags and eagle at ctr. Printer: ABNC. Back green. Series E-J.	1.50	5.00	25.0

		VG	VF	UN
92	**1 Boliviano** 29.11.1902. Black on brown and olive unpt. Shield w/flags and eagle at l., tropical vegetation at r. Printer: ABNC. Back brown. Series F-I; K.	2.00	5.00	25.0

		VG	VF	UN
93	**5 Bolivianos** 29.11.1902. Black on pale blue unpt. Shield w/flags and eagle at l., tree on hill at r. Printer: ABNC. Back dk. blue.			
	p. W/o series. Proof.	—	—	
	r. Unsigned remainder.	—	—	
94	**10 Bolivianos** 29.11.1902. Black on orange unpt. Shield w/flags and eagle at l., tropical vegetation at r. Printer: ABNC. Back orange; woman's head at ctr.			
	p. W/o series. Proof.	—	—	
	r. Unsigned remainder.	—	—	
95	**20 Bolivianos** 29.11.1902. Black on olive unpt. Tropical trees at. l., man tapping tree at r. Printer: ABNC. Back olive. woman's head at ctr.			
	p. W/o series. Proof.	—	—	
	r. Unsigned remainder.	—	—	

Note: Beware of notes with forged signs.

BANCO DE LA NACIÓN BOLIVIANA

ND 1911 PROVISIONAL ISSUE

New bank name ovpt. in red on earlier issues of the Banco Bolivia y Londres. Old date 1.2.1909.

		Good	Fine	XF
96	**1 Boliviano** ND (1911). Series A.	75.00	400.	—
97	**5 Bolivianos** ND (1911).	—	—	—
98	**10 Bolivianos** ND (1911).	—	—	—
99	**20 Bolivianos** ND (1911).	—	—	—
100	**50 Bolivianos** ND (1911).	—	—	—
101	**100 Bolivianos** ND (1911).	—	—	—

1911 REGULAR ISSUE

#102,103 and 105-111 arms at ctr. on back. Sign. varieties. Printer: ABNC.

		Good	Fine	XF
102	**1 Boliviano** 11.5.1911. Black w/brown, green and purple guilloches at sides. Mercury at ctr. Arms at ctr. Back green.			
	a. Black series letters from A-Z and AA-ZZ. (AB-AL have large letters, AM-AZ small letters).	1.00	3.00	10.00
	b. Red series A1-Z2.	1.00	3.00	10.00

		Good	Fine	XF
103	**1 Boliviano** 11.5.1911. Black on green and m/c unpt. Different guilloches at sides. Mercury at ctr. Arms at ctr. Similar to #102. Back green. Red series A1-J1.	1.00	3.00	10.00

		Good	Fine	XF
104	**1 Boliviano** 11.5.1911. Frame similar to #102 but w/o vignette. At ctr., large wmk. (head of Mercury). Back dp. green. Printer: CPM. Series A1-Z1.	30.00	125.	275.

		Good	Fine	XF
105	**5 Bolivianos** 11.5.1911. Black w/ m/c guilloche. Mercury seated at l. Arms at ctr. Printer: ABNC. Back blue-gray.			
	a. Black series A-Z, AA-JJ, KK-PP.	1.00	4.00	15.00
	b. Red series QQ-ZZ, A1-D1.	1.00	4.00	15.00

		Good	Fine	XF
106	**5 Bolivianos** 11.5.1911. Black on tan and blue unpt. w/different guilloche. Mercury seated at l. Arms at ctr. Printer: ABNC. Back blue-gray. Similar to #105. Red series A-E.	1.00	4.00	15.00

		Good	Fine	XF
107	**10 Bolivianos** 11.5.1911. Black on m/c guilloches. Mercury seated at r. Arms at ctr. Printer: ABNC. Back dp. brown.			
	a. Black series A-K.	1.00	5.00	15.00
	b. Red series L-P.	1.00	5.00	15.00

		Good	Fine	XF
108	**20 Bolivianos** 11.5.1911. Black on m/c guilloches. Mercury seated at ctr. Printer: ABNC. Back orange; error *VEINTE PESOS* as entire border text.			
	a. Issued note. Series A.	275.	—	—
	p. Back proof.			
109	**20 Bolivianos** 11.5.1911. Black on m/c guilloches. Mercury seated at ctr. Printer: ABNC. Like #108. Back orange; corrected inscription *VEINTE BOLIVIANOS* in frame. 184 x 89mm.			
	a. Black series A; B.	5.00	20.00	60.00
	b. Red series C; D.	5.00	20.00	60.00

#109A deleted, now 109b.

		Good	Fine	XF
109B	**20 Bolivianos** 11.5.1911. Black on m/c guilloches. Mercury seated at ctr. Printer: ABNC. Similar to #109 but different guilloches. Red series A. Back orange, corrected inscription *VEINTE BOLIVIANOS* in frame. 184 x 89mm.	5.00	20.00	60.00

		Good	Fine	XF
110	**50 Bolivianos** 11.5.1911. Black on m/c guilloches. Mercury seated at l. Arms at ctr. Printer: ABNC. Back olive. Black series A.	20.00	70.00	150.
111	**100 Bolivianos** 11.5.1911. Black on m/c guilloches. Mercury seated at ctr. Arms at ctr. Printer: ABNC. Black series A.	12.00	40.00	110.

BANCO CENTRAL DE BOLIVIA

1929 PROVISIONAL ISSUE

New bank name ovpt. (1928) on earlier series of El Banco de la Nación Boliviana. Old date 11.5.1911. Sign. varieties.

		Good	Fine	XF
112	**1 Boliviano** ND (1929). Blue or black ovpt: *BANCO CENTRAL DE BOLIVIA* on #103. Red series from K1-Z4.	.20	1.00	4.00

		Good	Fine	XF
113	**5 Bolivianos** ND (1929). Blue ovpt: *BANCO CENTRAL DE BOLIVIA* on #106. Red series F-U.	.30	1.50	10.00

		Good	Fine	XF
114	**10 Bolivianos** ND (1929). Blue ovpt: *BANCO CENTRAL DE BOLIVIA.* on face of #107 but w/different gullioche. Back brown-orange. Red series A-H.	.60	3.00	15.00

		Good	Fine	XF
115	**20 Bolivianos** ND (1929). Blue ovpt: *BANCO CENTRAL DE BOLIVIA* on #109. Red series B-D.	4.00	12.00	60.00

		Good	Fine	XF
116	**50 Bolivianos** ND (1929). Blue ovpt: *BANCO CENTRAL DE BOLIVIA.* on #110 but w/different guilloche. Red series A.	4.00	12.00	60.00

		Good	Fine	XF
117	**100 Bolivianos** ND (1929). Red-violet ovpt: *BANCO CENTRAL DE BOLIVIA.* Red series A.	8.00	20.00	80.00

NOTICE

Readers with unlisted dates, signature varieties, etc.
are invited to submit photocopies or,
high resolution (300 dpi, 100% size) scans of their notes to:
Standard Catalog of World Paper Money,
700 East State St. Iola, WI 54990-0001,
or E-Mail: george.cuhaj@fwpubs.com.

LAW OF 20.7.1928 FIRST ISSUE

#118-127 arms on back. Printer: ABNC.

#118 and 120-122 portr. S. Bolívar at l., view of Potosíand mountain at r. ctr. Many sign. varieties.

		VG	VF	UNC
118	**1 Boliviano** L.1928. Dp. brown on green, orange and rose unpt. Portr. S. Bolívar at l., view of Potosí and mountain at r. ctr. Printer: ABNC. Back dp. blue. Series A-Z; A1-A6.			
	a. Issued note.	.20	1.00	5.00
	s. Specimen. Red ovpt.: *SPECIMEN* twice on face. W/o sign. Series J5. Punched hole cancelled.	—	—	50.00

		VG	VF	UNC
119	**1 Boliviano** L.1928. Dp. brown. Portr. S. Bolívar at ctr. Printer: ABNC. Back dp. blue. Series A-Z1.			
	a. Issued note.	.20	1.00	4.00
	s. Specimen. Red ovpt: *SPECIMEN* on face twice. W/o series; series A.	—	—	50.00

		VG	VF	UNC
120	**5 Bolivianos** L.1928. Dp. green on blue, brown and rose unpt. Portr. S. Bolívar at l., view of Potosí and mountain at r. Printer: ABNC. Back dp. blue. Series A-Z; A1-Z10.			
	a. Issued note.	.40	2.00	7.50
	s. Specimen. Red ovpt.: *SPECIMEN* twice on face. W/o sign. Series H7; U3. Punched hole cancelled.	—	—	50.00

		VG	VF	UNC
121	**10 Bolivianos** L.1928. Dp. blue on rose, green and lilac unpt. Portr. S. Bolívar at l., view of Potosí and mountain at r. Arms. Printer: ABNC. Back red. Series A-V4.			
	a. Issued note.	.60	3.00	12.50
	s. Specimen. Red ovpt.: *SPECIMEN* twice on face. W/o sign. Series B4. Punched hole cancelled.	—	—	50.00

		VG	VF	UNC
122	**20 Bolivianos** L.1928. Brown on m/c unpt. Portr. S. Bolívar at l., view of Potosí and mountain at r. Arms. Printer: ABNC. Back green. Series A-Z3.			
	a. Issued note.	.80	4.00	17.50
	s. Specimen. Blue ovpt.: *SPECIMEN* twice on face. W/o sign. Series R. Punched hole cancelled.	—	—	50.00

#123-127 portr. Bolivar at l., view of La Paz at ctr., portr. Sucre at r.

		VG	VF	UNC
123	**50 Bolivianos** L.1928. Purple on green, lilac and yellow unpt. Portr. S. Bolívar at l., view of La Paz at ctr., portr. of A.J. de Sucre at r. Arms. Printer: ABNC. Back red. Series A-G.	3.00	15.00	50.00

		VG	VF	UNC
124	**50 Bolivianos** L.1928. Purple on green, lilac and yellow unpt. Portr. S. Bolívar at l., view of La Paz at ctr., Portr. of A.J. de Sucre at r. Arms. Printer: ABNC. Like #123, but back orange. Series H-Z.	2.00	10.00	35.00

		VG	VF	UNC
125	**100 Bolivianos** L.1928. Blue-black on rose, ochre and green. Portr. S. Bolívar at l., view of La Paz at ctr., portr. of A.J. de Sucre at r. Arms. Printer: ABNC. Back dp. brown. Series A-M.	1.75	9.00	37.50

Note: The rose unpt. on #125 fades easily; no premium for notes w/o rose unpt.

126 500 Bolivianos — VG / VF / UNC

L.1928. Olive-green on m/c unpt. Portr. S. Bolívar at l., view of La Paz at ctr., portr. of A.J. de Sucre at r. Arms. Printer: ABNC. Back purple.

	VG	VF	UNC
a. Series A. Hand signed.	60.00	200.	—
b. Series A, B. Printed sign.	4.00	20.00	75.00

127 1000 Bolivianos

L.1928. Red on green, orange and lilac unpt. Portr. S. Bolívar at l., view of La Paz at ctr., portr. A.J. de Sucre at r. Arms. Printer: ABNC. Back dp. blue-gray. Series A.

	VG	VF	UNC
a. Hand sign.	60.00	200.	—
b. Printed sign.	15.00	75.00	175.

Law of 20.7.1928 Second Issue

#128-135 arms on back. Printer: W&S.

#128-130 portr. of S. Bolívar at ctr. Sign. varieties.

128 1 Boliviano

L.1928. Brown. Portr. S. Bolívar at ctr. Arms. Printer: W&S. Back dp. blue.

	VG	VF	UNC
a. W/o *EMISION.* ovpt. Series A-D14.	.10	.50	1.50
b. *EMISION 1951.* Series E14-Q14.	.50	3.00	10.00
c. *EMISION 1952.* Series Q14-R16.	.05	.25	.75

129 5 Bolivianos

	VG	VF	UNC
L.1928. Grayish green. Portr. S. Bolívar at ctr. Arms. Printer: W&S. Back olive. Series A-R6.	.10	.50	3.00

130 10 Bolivianos

	VG	VF	UNC
L.1928. Dp. blue on green and yellow unpt. Portr. S. Bolívar at ctr. Arms. Printer: W&S. Back red. Series A-T3.	.25	1.25	6.00

131 20 Bolivianos

	VG	VF	UNC
L.1928. Brown on green, lilac and orange unpt. View of Potosí at l. ctr., portr. S. Bolívar at r. Arms. Printer: W&S. Back dp. green. Series A L6.	.25	1.50	7.50

#131-133 view of Potosí at l. ctr., portr. S. Bolívar at r. Sign. varieties.

132 50 Bolivianos

	VG	VF	UNC
L.1928. Purple on green, lilac and yellow unpt. View of Potosí at l. ctr., portr. S. Bolívar at r. Arms. Printer: W&S. Back orange. Series A-H3.	.50	2.00	15.0

133 100 Bolivianos

	VG	VF	UNC
L.1928. Dk. gray on orange, lilac and rose unpt. View of Potosí at l. ctr., portr. S. Bolívar at r. Arms. Printer: W&S. Back dp. brown. Series A-E2.	2.00	10.00	30.0

#134-135 view of La Paz at l. ctr. Sign. varieties.

134 500 Bolivianos

	VG	VF	UNC
L.1928. Olive-green on rose and pale yellow-green unpt. View of La Paz at l. ctr., Portr. S. Bolívar at r. Arms. Printer: W&S. Back purple. Series A-G.	3.00	15.00	45.0

135 1000 Bolivianos

	VG	VF	UNC
L.1928. Rose on yellow, green and lt. blue unpt. View of La Paz at l. ctr. Arms. Printer: W&S. Back gray. Series A-D.	5.00	25.00	75.0

Decree of 16.3.1942

#136-137 back black on pink, yellow and green unpt., w/arms at ctr. Sign varieties. Series A. Printer: W&S

136 5000 Bolivianos

	VG	VF	UNC
D.1942. Red-brown and m/c. Miner at ctr. Black on pink, yellow and green unpt. w/arms at ctr. Printer: W&S. Back dp. greenish gray.	30.00	85.00	225

		VG	VF	UNC
137	**10,000 Bolivianos** D.1942. Dp. blue and m/c. Puerta del Sol at ctr. Black on pink, yellow and green unpt. w/arms at ctr. Printer: W&S. Back dp. greenish gray.	30.00	85.00	225.

LAW OF 20.12.1945

#138-146 Sign. varieties. Printer TDLR.

		VG	VF	UNC
138	**5 Bolivianos** L.1945. Brown on green and sky blue unpt. Portr. S. Bolívar at r., arms at l. Printer: TDLR. Back brown; arms at ctr.			
	a. W/o *EMISION* ovpt. Series A-Q.	.20	.40	1.00
	b. *EMISION 1951* in 1 or 2 lines. Series C; D.	.50	2.00	6.00
	c. *EMISION 1952*. Series D.	.25	.75	2.25
	d. Remainder w/o ovpt. or sign. Series K; C1.	—	—	1.50

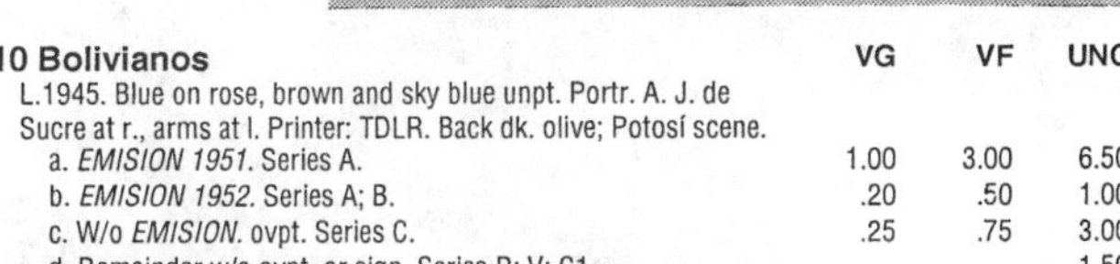

		VG	VF	UNC
139	**10 Bolivianos** L.1945. Blue on rose, brown and sky blue unpt. Portr. A. J. de Sucre at r., arms at l. Printer: TDLR. Back dk. olive; Potosí scene.			
	a. *EMISION 1951*. Series A.	1.00	3.00	6.50
	b. *EMISION 1952*. Series A; B.	.20	.50	1.00
	c. W/o *EMISION*. ovpt. Series C.	.25	.75	3.00
	d. Remainder w/o ovpt. or sign. Series R; V; C1.	—	—	1.50

		VG	VF	UNC
140	**20 Bolivianos** L.1945. Brown and m/c. Portr. S. Bolívar at r., arms at l. Printer: TDLR. Back dp. red; obv. and rev. of 1862 coin and Potosí Mint. Series A-Q.			
	a. Issued note.	.20	.40	1.50
	r. Remainder w/o sign. Series B1.	—	—	—

		VG	VF	UNC
141	**50 Bolivianos** L.1945. Purple on green and sky blue unpt. Printer: TDLR. Portr. A. J. de Sucre at r., arms at l. Back green; cows at water hole. Series A-Z; A1-K1.	.25	.75	2.50

		VG	VF	UNC
142	**100 Bolivianos** L.1945. Black and m/c. Portr. S. Bolívar at r., arms at l. Printer: TDLR. Back purple; farmers. Series A-W.	.75	3.00	10.00

		VG	VF	UNC
143	**500 Bolivianos** L.1945. Green on red, lilac and yellow unpt. Portr. A. J. de Sucre at r., arms at l. Printer: TDLR. Back orange; oil well. Series A-C.	1.25	5.00	15.00

		VG	VF	UNC
144	**1000 Bolivianos** L.1945. Red on m/c unpt. Portr. S. Bolívar at r., arms at l. Printer: TDLR. Back black; miners at ctr. Series A-C.	1.75	8.50	25.00

		VG	VF	UNC
145	**5000 Bolivianos** L.1945. Brown and m/c. Portr. A. J. de Sucre at r., arms at l. Printer: TDLR. Back blue; Puerta del Sol and llama at l. Series A.	5.00	17.50	55.00

		VG	VF	UNC
146	**10,000 Bolivianos** L.1945. Blue and m/c. Portr. S. Bolívar at r., arms at l., flags at ctr. Printer: TDLR. Back green; Independence proclamation at l. ctr. Series A.	6.00	25.00	75.00

LAW OF 20.12.1945 SECOND ISSUE

#147-151 altered design or reduced size. Arms at l. Sign. varieties. Printer: TDLR.

		VG	VF	UNC
147	**100 Bolivianos** L.1945. Black and m/c. Portr. G. Villarroel at r. Printer: TDLR. Back purple; oil refinery. Series A-Z; A1-T1.	.15	.40	1.50

		VG	VF	UNC
148	**500 Bolivianos** L.1945. Green on red, blue and orange unpt. Portr. Busch at r. Printer: TDLR. Back orange; miners. Series A-Z; A1-D1.	.50	1.50	7.50

		VG	VF	UNC
149	**1000 Bolivianos** L.1945. Red on green, rose and blue unpt. Portr. Murillo at r. Printer: TDLR. Back black; man w/native horn at ctr. Series A-Z; A1-C1.	.50	1.50	7.50

		VG	VF	UNC
150	**5000 Bolivianos** L.1945. Brown and m/c. Portr. A. J. de Sucre at r. Printer: TDLR. Back blue. Puerta del Sol at ctr. Series AP.	2.00	8.50	25.00

		VG	VF	UNC
151	**10,000 Bolivianos** L.1945. Blue and m/c. Flags at ctr., portr. S. Bolívar at r. Printer: TDLR. Back green; Independence proclamation at ctr. Series A-Z; A1-C2.	2.00	8.50	25.00

The Federative Republic of Brazil, which comprises half the continent of South America, is the only Latin American country deriving its culture and language from Portugal. It has an area of 3,286,470 sq. mi. (8,511,965 sq. km.) and a population of 169.2 million. Capital: Brasília. The economy of Brazil is as varied and complex as any in the developing world. Agriculture is a mainstay of the economy, although but 4 percent of the area is under cultivation. Known mineral resources are almost unlimited in variety and size of reserves. A large, relatively sophisticated industry ranges from basic steel and chemical production to finished consumer goods. Coffee, cotton, iron ore and cocoa are the chief exports.

Brazil was discovered and claimed for Portugal by Admiral Pedro Alvares Cabral in 1500. Portugal established a settlement in 1532 and proclaimed the area a royal colony in 1549. During the Napoleonic Wars, Dom João VI established the seat of Portuguese government in Rio de Janeiro. When he returned to Portugal, his son Dom Pedro I declared Brazil's independence on Sept. 7, 1822, and became emperor of Brazil. The Empire of Brazil was maintained until 1889 when a republic was established. The Federative Republic was established in 1946 by terms of a constitution drawn up by a constituent assembly. Following a coup in 1964, the armed forces retained overall control under dictatorship until a civilian government was restored on March 15, 1985. The current constitution was adopted in 1988.

Portuguese Administration

Administracão Geral dos Diamantes

Royal Diamond Administration

1771-92 Colonial Issue

Drafts issued by the Administration to pay successful diamond prospectors. Values of the drafts were filled in by hand for amounts of gold paid for the diamonds. Drafts were exchangeable into coins and circulated at full face value as paper currency.

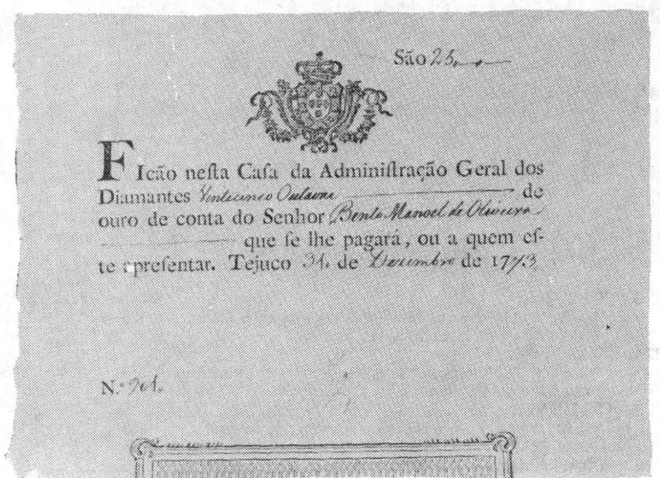
São 25

Ficão nesta Casa da Administração Geral dos Diamantes Vinte cinco Oitavas de ouro de conta do Senhor Bento Manoel de Oliveira que se lhe pagará, ou a quem este apresentar. Tejuco 31 de Dezembro de 1773

N.º 701

		Good	Fine	XF
A101	**VARIOUS AMOUNTS** 1771-1792. Stubs from draft forms printed in Lisbon.	25.00	60.00	150.

Imperio do Brasil

Trocos de Cobre

Copper Exchange Notes

Lei de 3 de Outobro de 1833

Notes issued throughout all provincial offices in exchange for debased copper coinage. Names of individual provinces were handwritten on each piece issued. All denominations were reportedly issued by all 18 provinces, though some in small amounts. Almost all were issued in Ceará Province. Values shown are for the most available of each denomination.

#A151-A157 arms at l. Uniface. Printed in Rio de Janeiro. Many notes are found w/paper damaged by tannic acid in the early ink used for official handwritten signatures.

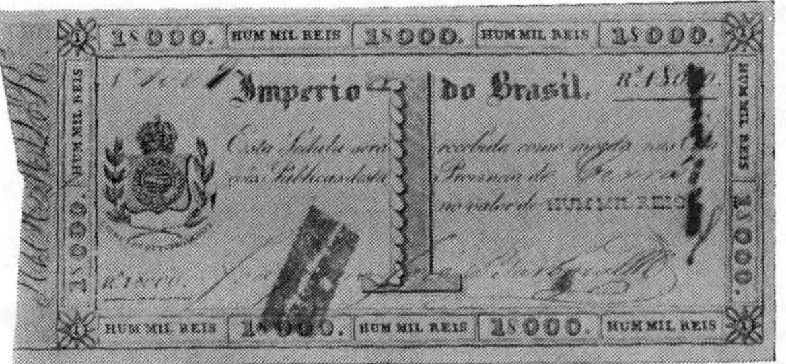

		Good	Fine	XF
A151	**1 Mil Reis** ND. Black. Arms at l.			
	a. 1 sign.	10.00	30.00	160.
	b. 2 sign.	10.00	25.00	130.
A152	**2 Mil Reis** ND. Black. Arms at l.			
	a. 1 sign.	10.00	30.00	160.
	b. 2 sign.	10.00	25.00	130.
A153	**5 Mil Reis** ND. Black. Arms at l.			
	a. 1 sign.	10.00	30.00	160.
	b. 2 sign.	10.00	25.00	130.
A154	**10 Mil Reis** ND. Lt. green. Arms at l.			
	a. 1 sign.	12.50	40.00	190.
	b. 2 sign.	12.50	30.00	160.
A155	**20 Mil Reis** ND. Lt. green. Arms at l.			
	a. 1 sign.	15.00	50.00	200.
	b. 2 sign.	12.50	40.00	160.

		Good	Fine	XF
A156	**50 Mil Reis** ND. Dk. green. Arms at l.			
	a. 1 sign.	15.00	60.00	225.
	b. 2 sign.	15.00	50.00	175.
A157	**100 Mil Reis** ND. Olive. Arms at l.			
	a. 1 sign.	25.00	75.00	250.
	b. 2 sign.	25.00	60.00	200.

No Thesouro Nacional

National Treasury

Decreto de 1 Junho de 1833 (1835-36) Estampa 1

#A201-A209 black. Arms crowned at l., decreto at r. Vignettes at upper ctr. Uniface. Printer: PB&P.

		Good	Fine	XF
A201	**1 Mil Reis** D. 1833. Black. Arms crowned at l., decreto at r., Agriculture view at upper ctr. Printer: BP&P.	40.00	100.	225.
A202	**2 Mil Reis** D. 1833. Black. Crowned at l., decreto at r., The Arts at upper ctr. Printer: BP&P.	70.00	175.	375.
A203	**5 Mil Reis** D. 1833. Black. Crowned at l., decreto at r., Commerce at upper ctr. Printer: BP&P.	140.	375.	700.
A204	**10 Mil Reis** D. 1833. Black. Crowned at l., decreto at r., Portr. Dom Pedro II at ctr. Printer: BP&P.	150.	350.	750.
A205	**20 Mil Reis** D. 1833. Black. Crowned at l., decreto at r., 2 seated figures (Justice) w/date of Brazilian Independence at upper ctr. Printer: BP&P.	200.	450.	1000.

		Good	Fine	XF
A206	**50 Mil Reis** D. 1833. Black. Crowned at l., decreto at r., Allegory of the discovery of Brazil at upper ctr. Printer: BP&P.	200.	450.	1000.
A207	**100 Mil Reis** D. 1833. Black. Crowned at l., decreto at r., Scene at Recife at upper ctr. Printer: BP&P.	900.	1750.	3000.
A208	**200 Mil Reis** D. 1833. Black. Crowned at l., decreto at r., View of Bahia at upper ctr. Printer: BP&P.	900.	1800.	3250.
A209	**500 Mil Reis** D. 1833. Black. Crowned at l., decreto at r., View of Rio de Janeiro at upper ctr. Printer: BP&P.	1750.	3500.	7500.

Decreto de 1 Junho de 1833 (1830-44) Estampa 2

#A210-A218 Decreto at l., arms at r. Uniface. Printer: PB&P.

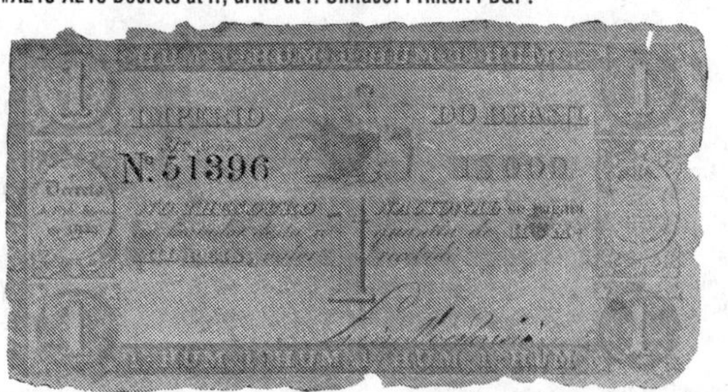

		Good	Fine	XF
A210	**1 Mil Reis** D. 1833. Orange on yellow paper. Decree at l., arms at r., Commerce at upper ctr. Printer: PB&P. Like #A203.	160.	375.	700.
A211	**2 Mil Reis** D. 1833. Orange. Decree at l., arms at r., Agriculture view at upper ctr. Printer: PB&P. Like #A201.	60.00	140.	300.
A212	**5 Mil Reis** D. 1833. Orange. Decree at l., arms at r., The arts at upper ctr. Printer: PB&P. Like #A202.	200.	425.	850.
A213	**10 Mil Reis** D. 1833. Blue and sepia. Decree at l., arms at r., Allegory of the discovery of Brazil at upper ctr. Printer: PB&P. Like #A206.	150.	350.	750.

		Good	Fine	XF
A214	**20 Mil Reis** D. 1833. Blue and sepia. Decree at l., arms at r., Dom Pedro II at ctr. Printer: PB&P. Like #A204.	175.	350.	750.
A215	**50 Mil Reis** D. 1833. Blue and sepia. Decree at l., arms at r., 2 seated figures (Justice) w/date of independence of Brazil at upper ctr. Printer: PB&P. Like #A205.	160.	375.	800.
A216	**100 Mil Reis** D. 1833. Green. Decree at l., arms at r., View of Rio de Janeiro at upper ctr. Printer: PB&P. Like #A209.	650.	1300.	2500.
A217	**200 Mil Reis** D. 1833. Green. Decree at l., arms at r., Scene of Recife at upper ctr. Printer: PB&P. Like #A207.	1000.	2000.	3500.
A218	**500 Mil Reis** D. 1833. Green. Decree at l., arms at r., View of Bahia at upper ctr. Printer: PB&P. Like #A208.	1600.	3250.	6500.

Decreto de 1 Junho de 1833 (1843-60) Estampa 3

#A219-A227 Uniface.

#A219-A220 printer: PBC.

		Good	Fine	XF
A219	**1 Mil Reis** D. 1833. Black on blue unpt. Commerce at upper ctr. Printer: PBC.	35.00	95.00	180.

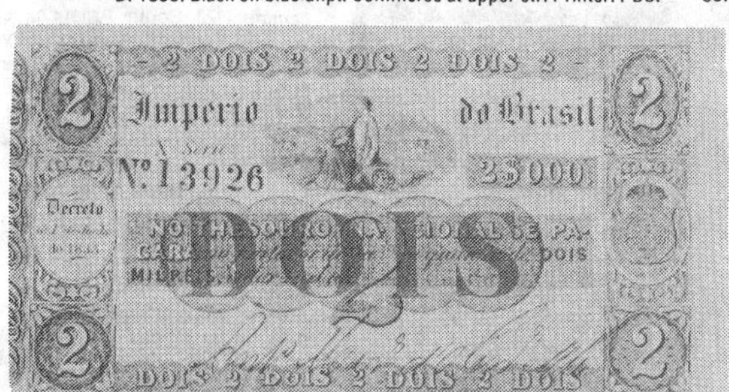

		Good	Fine	XF
A220	**2 Mil Reis** D. 1833. Black on green unpt. Agriculture view at upper ctr. Printer: PBC.	40.00	90.00	200.

W/o Decreto ca. 1850

#A221-A227 printer: PB&P.

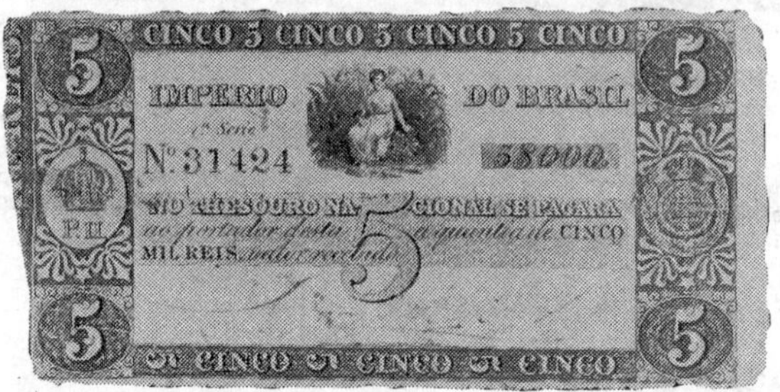

		Good	Fine	XF
A221	**5 Mil Reis** ND. Black. Royal emblem w/crown at l., agriculture view at upper ctr., arms at r. Printer: PB&P.	90.00	200.	425.
A222	**10 Mil Reis** ND. Orange. Royal crest at l., 2 seated figures (Justice) w/date of independence at upper ctr., arms at r. Printer: PB&P.	150.	350.	700.

		Good	Fine	XF
A223	**20 Mil Reis** ND. Printer: PB&P. Blue on yellow paper. Royal crest at l., allegory of the discovery of Brazil at upper ctr., arms at r.	125.	250.	500.
A224	**50 Mil Reis** ND. Printer: PB&P. Black on red unpt. Royal crest at l., portr. Dom Pedro II at upper ctr., arms at r.	275.	750.	1600.
A225	**100 Mil Reis** ND. Black. Arms at l., view of Bahia at upper ctr., royal crest at r. Printer: PB&P.	1250.	2500.	5000.
A226	**200 Mil Reis** ND. Black. Arms at l., view of Rio de Janeiro at upper ctr., royal crest at r. Printer: PB&P.	750.	1650.	2600.
A227	**500 Mil Reis** ND. Black on orange paper. Arms at l., scene of Recife at upper ctr., royal crest at r. Printer: PB&P.	1600.	3250.	7500.

Estampa 4, 1852-67

#A228-A236 w/o date. Uniface.

		Good	Fine	XF
A228	**1 Mil Reis** ND. Black on blue unpt. Portr. Dom Pedro II at l., Justice, Agriculture and Commerce seated at upper ctr., crowned arms at r. Printer: PBC.	40.00	100.	225.
A229	**2 Mil Reis** ND. Black on green unpt. Justice and Truth at upper ctr. Printer: PBC.	42.50	100.	210.
A230	**5 Mil Reis** ND. Black. Arms at l., 2 seated figures (Justice) w/date of independence at upper ctr., royal emblem w/crown at r. Printer: PB&P.	85.00	190.	375.
A231	**10 Mil Reis** ND. Black on brown unpt. Agriculture w/Brazilian arms at upper ctr. Printer: PBC. Note: Most examples of #A231 are counterfeits. Unpt. wording on these forgeries ends in *REIS* at r. instead of *MIL* as on genuine notes. Forgeries have irregular imprint lettering.			
	a. Issued note.	75.00	160.	325.
	x. Counterfeit.			
A232	**20 Mil Reis** ND. Black. Peace, Agriculture and Science at upper ctr. Printer: PB&P.	175.	350.	750.
A233	**50 Mil Reis** ND. Black on blue unpt. upper ctr. W/ or w/o Agriculture and Commerece at *ESTAMPA 4a* on note. Printer: PBC.			
	a. Issued note.	160.	350.	750.

		Good	Fine	XF
A234	**100 Mil Reis** ND. Black on purple unpt. Allegrical figures at l. and r., allegory of the discovery of Brazil at upper ctr. Printer: PBC.	300.	700.	1500.

		Good	Fine	XF
A235	**200 Mil Reis** ND. Black on purple unpt. Dom Pedro II at upper l. and lower r., arms at lower l. and upper r., 2 seated figures (Justice) w/date of independence at upper ctr., and w/o date on column. Printer: PBC.	500.	1000.	2000.
A236	**500 Mil Reis** ND. Black on green unpt. Allegorical figures at l. and r., Agriculture, Art and Commerce at ctr. Printer: PBC.	1000.	2750.	4350.

ESTAMPA 5, 1860-68

#A237-S239 w/o date. Uniface. Printer: PBC.

		Good	Fine	XF
A237	**5 Mil Reis** ND. Black on brown unpt. Arms at l., Justice and Commerece w/arms at ctr., Portr. Dom Pedro II at r. Printer: PBC.	65.00	140.	275.
A238	**10 Mil Reis** ND. Black on purple unpt. Allegorical figures l. and r., portr. Dom Pedro II at upper ctr., arms w/cherubs at lower ctr. Printer: PBC.	180.	375.	750.

		Good	Fine	XF
A239	**20 Mil Reis** ND. Black on green unpt. Portr. Dom Pedro II at l., Commerce at ctr., arms at r.			
	a. W/o *ESTAMPA*. Series 1-8.	90.00	180.	375.
	b. W/*ESTAMPA 5a*. Series 9-10.	85.00	175.	375.

ESTAMPA 6, 1866-70

#A240-A241 w/o date. Uniface. Printer: PBC.

		Good	Fine	XF
A240	**5 Mil Reis** ND. Black on brown unpt. Commerece, Art and Science w/medallic portr. of Dom Pedro II at ctr. Printer: PBC.	135.	300.	550.

		VG	VF	UNC
A241	**20 Mil Reis** ND. Black on green unpt. Allegorical figures at l. and r., Rio de Janeiro harbor at ctr. Printer: PBC.			

ESTAMPA 1, 1874

		Good	Fine	XF
A242	**500 Reis** ND (21.12.1874). Black on orange unpt. Arms at l., Portr. Dom Pedro II at ctr., seated woman at r. Back orange. Printer: ABNC.	80.00	185.	375.

ESTAMPA 2, 1880

		Good	Fine	XF
A243	**500 Reis** ND (1.9.1880). Black on orange-brown unpt. Woman reclining at l., portr. Dom Pedro II at ctr., woman sitting at r. Back orange-brown. Printer: ABNC.			
	a. 1 serial #, 1880.	40.00	110.	220.
	b. 2 serial #, 1885.	45.00	115.	230.

ESTAMPA 5, 1870-78

#A244-A249 printer: ABNC.

		Good	Fine	XF
A244	**1 Mil Reis** ND (1870). Printer: ABNC. Black on blue unpt. Portr. Dom Pedro II at l., boat, tree and steam train at ctr., arms at r. Back blue.	50.00	210.	375.

		Good	Fine	XF
A245	**2 Mil Reis** ND (1870). Printer: ABNC. Black on green unpt. Portr. Dom Pedro II at l., arms at ctr., trees at r. Back green.	15.00	120.	250.

		Good	Fine	XF
A246	**50 Mil Reis** ND (1874-1885). Black on lt. green and brown unpt. Dom Pedro II at l., abundance at ctr., arms at r. Printer: ABNC. Back brown.	35.00	375.	750.
A247	**100 Mil Reis** ND (1877). Black on red and green unpt. Arms at l., Dom Pedro II at ctr., woman at r. Back orange, arms at ctr.			
	a. Single serial #.	60.00	450.	900.
	b. 2 serial #.	60.00	475.	950.

		Good	Fine	XF
A248	**200 Mil Reis** ND (1874). Black on red and blue unpt. Tree at l., Dom Pedro II at ctr., arms at r. Printer: ABNC. Back green and black, seated woman at l. and r.	175.	850.	1750.
A249	**500 Mil Reis** ND (ca.1885). Black on orange and blue unpt. Arms at l., portr. Dom Pedro II at ctr., woman at r. Printer: ABNC. Back brown and black, portr. Dom Pedro II at l., arms at r.	1250.	2500.	5000.

ESTAMPA 6, 1869-82

#A250-A254 printer: ABNC.

		Good	Fine	XF
A250	**1 Mil Reis** ND (1879). Black on green unpt. Arms at l., portr. Dom Pedro II at ctr., seated woman at r. Printer: ABNC. Back green.			
	a. 1 serial #, 1879.	60.00	160.	340.
	b. 2 serial #, 1885.	60.00	160.	340.

		Good	Fine	XF
A251	**2 Mil Reis** ND (1882). Black on blue unpt. Cherub w/ arms at l. ("Bachus"), Dom Pedro II at r. ctr. Printer: ABNC. Back blue.	10.00	125.	275.

		Good	Fine	XF
A252	**10 Mil Reis** ND (1869). Printer: ABNC. Black on green unpt. Portr. Dom Pedro II at l., 2 seated women w/arms at ctr., tree at r. Back green.	22.50	210.	550.
A252A	**20 Mil Reis** ND (ca.1868). Black on orange unpt. Allegorical woman w/industrial elements at l., Portr. Dom Pedro II at ctr., arms at r. Printer: ABNC. Back orange. Proof.	—	—	—

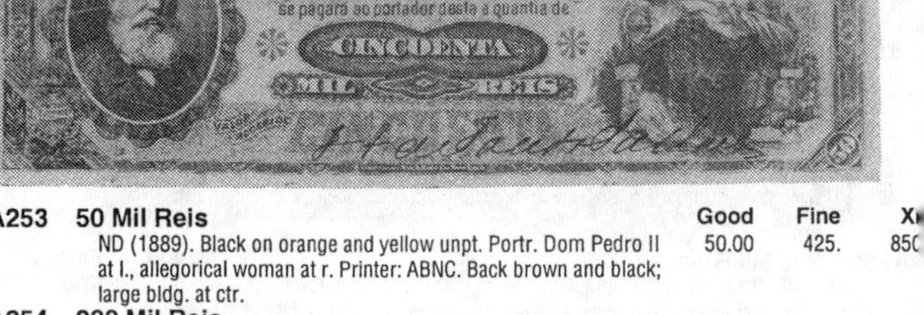

		Good	Fine	XF
A253	**50 Mil Reis** ND (1889). Black on orange and yellow unpt. Portr. Dom Pedro II at l., allegorical woman at r. Printer: ABNC. Back brown and black; large bldg. at ctr.	50.00	425.	850.
A254	**200 Mil Reis** ND (1889). Black on blue and yellow unpt. Shoreline scene at l., Dom Pedro II at ctr., arms at r. Printer: ABNC. Back black and orange; scene of the first Mass held in Brazil at ctr.	600.	1200.	2500.

ESTAMPA 7, 1869-83

#A255-A259 pritner: ABNC.

		Good	Fine	XF
A255	**1 Mil Reis** ND. Black on green unpt. Bldg. and arms at l., portr. Dom Pedro II at r. Printer: ABNC. Back black and green, equestrian statue of D. Pedro I.	10.00	150.	300.

A256 2 Mil Reis — Good 10.00 | Fine 150. | XF 300.
ND. Black on brown unpt. Portr. Dom Pedro II at l., arms at r. Printer: ABNC. Back brown; arms at l.

A257 5 Mil Reis — Good 20.00 | Fine 125. | XF 275.
ND (1869). Black on brown unpt. Printer: ABNC. Truth at l., arms at ctr., portr. Dom Pedro II at r. W. or w/o *ESTAMPA 7* (1874) on note. Back brown.

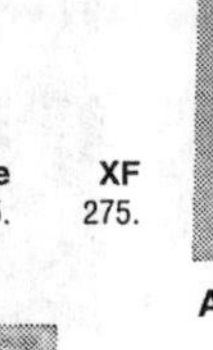

A258 10 Mil Reis
ND (1883). Black on orange and green unpt. Justice w/arms at l., portr. Dom Pedro II at ctr., 2 rams at r. Printer: ABNC. Back green; arms at ctr.

	Good	Fine	XF
a. 1 serial #, 1883.	35.00	300.	600.
b. 2 serial #, 1886.	40.00	300.	600.

A259 20 Mil Reis — Good 40.00 | Fine 360. | XF 750.
ND. Black on gold and green unpt. Portr. Dom Pedro II at l., woman leaning on column w/arms at ctr., seated woman at r. Printer: ABNC. Back brown; arms at ctr.

ESTAMPA 8, CA. 1885

#A260-A263 printer: ABNC.

A260 2 Mil Reis — Good 17.50 | Fine 150. | XF 300.
ND. Black on brown unpt. Portr. Dom Pedro II at l., church at r. Printer: ABNC. Back blue and black; street scene and Rio de Janeiro Post Office.

A261 5 Mil Reis — Good 22.50 | Fine 175. | XF 400.
ND. Black on purple, orange and blue unpt. Woman w/wheat at l., portr. Dom Pedro II at ctr., man w/sheep at r. Printer: ABNC. Back brown; arms at ctr. 1 or 2 serial #.

A262 10 Mil Reis — Good 40.00 | Fine 250. | XF 500.
ND. Black on green and orange unpt. Portr. Dom Pedro II at l., arms at ctr., standing woman at r. ("Fortuna"). Printer: ABNC. Back green; arms at ctr.

A263 20 Mil Reis — Good 40.00 | Fine 250. | XF 500.
ND. Black on orange and green unpt. 2 women w/arms in column at l., portr. Dom Pedro II at r. Printer: ABNC. Back brown; arms at l.

ESTAMPA 9, 1888

A264 5 Mil Reis — Good 17.50 | Fine 165. | XF 375.
ND (6.1888). Black on orange and blue unpt. Portr. Dom Pedro II at l., cherub at ctr., Art at r. Back brown; arms at ctr. Printer: ABNC.

REPUBLICA DOS ESTADOS UNIDOS DO BRASIL

THESOURO NACIONAL

1891-1931 ISSUE

#1-93 w/o date; some individual notes are designated by Estampas...(*E* = printings).

1 500 Reis
E. 3A (1893). Black on yellow unpt. Woman w/sheep at l., woman at r. Printer: ABNC

	Good	Fine	XF
a. 1 handwritten sign. Serie 1-20; 151-160.	7.50	40.00	85.00
b. 2 printed sign. Serie 21-150.	7.50	45.00	100.

2 500 Reis — Good 12.50 | Fine 110. | XF 225.
W/o *Estampa* (1901). Violet on ochre unpt. Liberty at l. Back blue-gray; Arms at ctr. Printer: BWC.

3 1 Mil Reis
E. 7A (1891). Black on green unpt. Imperial Museum at l., child holding caduceus at r. Back green. Printer: ABNC.

	Good	Fine	XF
a. Back frame 63mm high. 1 handwritten sign. W/serie letter.	4.00	30.00	85.00
b. Back frame 65mm high. 2 printed sign. W/serie letter.	5.00	75.00	150.

4 1 Mil Reis — Good 9.00 | Fine 75.00 | XF 200.
W/o *Estampa E.8A* (1902). Blue on ochre unpt. Liberty at top ctr. Printer: BWC.

#		Good	Fine	XF
5	**1 Mil Reis** E. 9A (1917). Black on orange unpt. Imperial Museum at l., child holding caduceus at r. Back orange. Printer: ABNC. Like #3.	6.00	40.00	100.
6	**1 Mil Reis** E. 10A (1919). Blue on m/c unpt. Padre D. A. Feijo at ctr. Back green. Printer: ABNC.	5.00	30.00	85.00

#		Good	Fine	XF
7	**1 Mil Reis** E. 11A (1920). Blue on pink unpt. Portr. D. Campista at ctr. Printer: CdM (w/o imprint).	5.00	35.00	90.00
8	**1 Mil Reis** E. 12A (1921). Blue on olive unpt. Portr. D. Campista at ctr. Printer: CdM.	4.00	12.50	35.00
9	**1 Mil Reis** E. 13A (1923). Brown on ochre unpt. Portr. D. Campista at ctr. Printer: CdM.	5.00	12.50	35.00
10	**2 Mil Reis** E. 8A (1890). Black on ochre unpt. Woman seated w/child at l., bldg. and church at r. Printer: ABNC.			
	a. Small background lettering at top: *IMPERIO DO BRASIL DOIS MIL REIS*. Series 11-45.	5.00	75.00	300.
	b. Small background lettering at top, only *DOIS MIL REIS*. Series 46-140.	5.00	75.00	300.
	c. W/o series letter. Series 28.	5.00	60.00	250.
11	**2 Mil Reis** E. 9A (1900). Black on lilac and violet unpt. Woman at r. ("Zella"). Woman w/spear at ctr. on back. Printer: ABNC.	10.00	75.00	225.

#		Good	Fine	XF
12	**2 Mil Reis** W/o *Estampa E.10A* (1902). Green on ochre unpt. Liberty at lower r. Printer: BWC.	15.00	100.	300.

#		Good	Fine	XF
13	**2 Mil Reis** E. 11A (1918). Black on red-brown and green unpt. Like #11. Back orange. Printer: ABNC.	8.00	40.00	150.
14	**2 Mil Reis** E. 12A (1919). Blue on m/c unpt. Marques de Olinda, P. de Araujo Lima at ctr. Printer: ABNC.	10.00	60.00	200.
15	**2 Mil Reis** E. 13A (1920). Blue on ochre unpt. Portr. J. Murtinho at ctr. Printer: CdM (w/o imprint).	10.00	60.00	200.
16	**2 Mil Reis** E. 14A (1921). Blue on olive unpt. Portr. J. Murtinho at l. Printer: CdM (w/o imprint).	6.00	25.00	100.
17	**2 Mil Reis** E. 15A (1923). Brown on yellow unpt. Portr. J. Murtinho at ctr. Printer: CdM.	6.00	25.00	75.00

#		Good	Fine	XF
18	**5 Mil Reis** E. 9A (1890). Black on pink and blue unpt. Man at l., woman seated at r. ("Arts"). Back brown. Printer: ABNC. Letters A-E.	10.00	75.00	300.
19	**5 Mil Reis** E. 10A (1903). Brown on ochre unpt. Woman seated w/flowers and fruits. Designer: Georges Duval Inv. et del. Letter A-F.	10.00	75.00	300.
20	**5 Mil Reis** E. 11A (1907). Sepia. Woman seated w/flowers and fruits. Like #19 but w/o designer's name. Printer: CdM.	25.00	250.	750.
21	**5 Mil Reis** E. 12A (1908). Sepia on ochre unpt. Woman seated w/flowers and fruits. Like #19 and 20, w/o designer's name. Printer: George Duval and CdM.	20.00	250.	750.

#		Good	Fine	XF
22	**5 Mil Reis** E. 13A (1909). Black on m/c unpt. Woman seated w/laurel wreath and statuette at l. Printer: ABNC.	10.00	75.00	300.
23	**5 Mil Reis** E. 14A (1912). Black on m/c unpt. Woman seated at r. Printer: ABNC. (Not issued).	125.	1000.	2250.

#		Good	Fine	XF
24	**5 Mil Reis** E. 14A (1913). Black on m/c unpt. Portr. B. do rio Branco (foreign minister) at ctr. Portr. ABNC.	7.50	50.00	150.
25	**5 Mil Reis** E. 15A (1918). Black on claret unpt. Wmk. at l. Back wine red. Printer: CPM.	17.50	85.00	325.
26	**5 Mil Reis** E. 16A (1920). Green on lt. green. Pres. F. de Paula Rodrigues Alves at ctr. Printer: CdM.	10.00	75.00	250.
27	**5 Mil Reis** E. 17A (1922). Brown on green unpt. Pres. F. de Paula Rodrigues Alves at ctr. Like #26. Printer: CdM.	10.00	75.00	250.
28	**5 Mil Reis** E. 18A (1923). Sepia on yellow unpt. Portr. Pres. F. de Paula Rodrigues Alves at ctr. Printer: CdM.	7.50	100.	225.

#		Good	Fine	XF
29	**5 Mil Reis** E. 19A (1925). Blue on m/c unpt. Back reddish-brown; 3 allegorical figures at ctr. B. do Rio Branco (foreign minister) at ctr. Printer: ABNC.			

No.	Description	Good	Fine	XF
29	**5 Mil Reis**			
	a. *BRAZIL*. 1 handwritten sign.	2.50	10.00	65.00
	b. *BRASIL; Estampa* and serial # together.	2.00	8.00	45.00
	c. *BRASIL; Estampa* and serial # separated.	2.00	8.00	45.00

No.	Description	Good	Fine	XF
30	**10 Mil Reis** E. 8A (1892). Black on m/c unpt. Girl w/distaff at l., woman w/wheel at r. ("Fortuna"). Back green. Printer: ABNC. Letters A-D.	25.00	125.	450.
31	**10 Mil Reis** E. 9A (1903). Carmine on yellow unpt. Woman w/boy at r. Letters A-D. Printer George Duval.	25.00	450.	900.
32	**10 Mil Reis** E. 10A (1907). Brown on ochre unpt. Woman w/boy at r. Printer: Like #31. Printer: CdM.	20.00	450.	900.
33	**10 Mil Reis** E. 11A (1907). Black on red-brown, green and orange unpt. Woman holding law book w/lion at l. Back green; Caixa de Amortizacao at ctr. Printer: ABNC.	20.00	150.	325.
34	**10 Mil Reis** E. 12A (1912). Black on m/c unpt. Woman w/eagle at l. Back purple. Printer: ABNC.	15.00	150.	325.
35	**10 Mil Reis** E. 13A (1914). Pink and brown unpt. Printer: CPM.	15.00	160.	325.
36	**10 Mil Reis** E. 14A (1918). Blue on m/c unpt. Portr. F. de Campos Salles at ctr. Printer: ABNC.	15.00	100.	275.
37	**10 Mil Reis** E. 15A (1923). Ochre unpt. Woman w/plants at ctr. Printer: CdM.	15.00	200.	550.
38	**10 Mil Reis** E. 16A (1924). Green. S. Alves Barroso Jr. at ctr. Printer: CdM.	15.00	200.	450.

No.	Description	Good	Fine	XF
39	**10 Mil Reis** E. 17A (1925). Blue on m/c unpt. Portr. Pres. Manuel Ferraz de Campos Salles at ctr. Printer: ABNC.			
	a. *BRAZIL*. 1 handwritten sign.	2.50	15.00	65.00
	b. *BRAZIL*. 2 printed sign.	5.00	100.	200.
	c. *BRASIL; Estampa* and serial # separated, handwritten signature.	2.00	12.50	45.00
	d. *BRASIL; Estampa* and serial # together, handwritten signature.	2.00	12.50	45.00
40	**20 Mil Reis** E. 8A (1892). Black on orange unpt. 2 women w/cupid at l., women repeating at r. Printer: ABNC.	20.00	200.	500.
41	**20 Mil Reis** W/o *Estampa* (1900). Violet on ochre unpt. Woman w/boy at l., woman at r. Back pale blue; arms. Printer: BWC.			
	a. W/*NOVEMBRE*.	17.50	250.	500.
	b. W/*NOVEMBRO*.	17.50	125.	275.
42	**20 Mil Reis** E. 10A (1905). Brown on ochre unpt. Boy seated at l., and at r., woman in circle at lower l. Back pale blue, arms. Printer George Duval.	15.00	250.	800.
43	**20 Mil Reis** E. 11A (1907). Brown on ochre unpt. Boy seated at l., and at r., woman in circle at lower l. Like #42. Back pale blue, arms. Printer: CdM and George Duval.	15.00	250.	650.

No.	Description	Good	Fine	XF
44	**20 Mil Reis** E. 12A (1909). Black on m/c unpt. Woman seated w/branch at ctr. Printer: ABNC.	15.00	200.	500.

No.	Description	Good	Fine	XF
45	**20 Mil Reis** E. 13A (1912). Black on m/c unpt. Woman reclining at ctr. Printer: ABNC.	15.00	85.00	300.
46	**20 Mil Reis** E. 14A (1919). Blue on m/c unpt. 1st Pres. M. Manuel Deodoro do Fonseca at ctr. Printer: ABNC.	12.50	75.00	275.
47	**20 Mil Reis** E. 15A (1923). Brown on yellow unpt. Woman w/child at ctr. Printer: CdM.	25.00	300.	900.

No.	Description	Good	Fine	XF
48	**20 Mil Reis** E. 16A (1931). Blue on m/c unpt. 1st Pres. Manuel Deodoro do Fonseca at ctr. Back orange; allegorical woman at ctr. Printer: ABNC.			
	a. *BRAZIL*. 1 handwritten sign.	3.00	45.00	100.
	b. *BRAZIL*. 2 printed sign.	3.00	75.00	225.
	c. *BRASIL; Estampa* and serial # separated, handwritten signature.	3.00	20.00	45.00
	d. *BRASIL; Estampa* and serial # together, handwritten signature.	3.00	20.00	115.

No.	Description	Good	Fine	XF
49	**50 Mil Reis** E. 7A (1893). Yellow unpt. Woman seated w/2 children at l., woman standing with flag at r. Back brown and black, First Mass in Brazil at ctr. Printer: ABNC. Letters A-D.	20.00	250.	600.
50	**50 Mil Reis** W/o *Estampa E.8A*. (1900). Violet on ochre unpt. Woman seated at l., woman at ctr. Printer: BWC.			
	a. W/*NOVEMBRE*.	20.00	250.	750.
	b. W/ *NOVEMBRO*.	20.00	250.	750.
51	**50 Mil Reis** E. 9A (1906). Brown on green unpt. Boy at l. and at r., woman in circle l. of ctr. Printer: George Duval	20.00	600.	1750.
52	**50 Mil Reis** E. 10A (1908). Sepia-green and red-brown. Boy at l. and at r., woman in circle l. of ctr. Like #51. Printer: CdM and George Duval.	20.00	700.	1600.
53	**50 Mil Reis** E. 11A (1908). Black on m/c unpt. Steamboat w/sails. Back olive; city view, river, mountains at ctr. Printer: ABNC and George Duval.	20.00	700.	1300.

No.	Description	Good	Fine	XF
54	**50 Mil Reis** E. 12A (1912). Black on m/c unpt. Youth seated at r. Printer: ABNC.	17.50	250.	550.

No.		Good	Fine	XF
55	**50 Mil Reis** E. 13A (1915). Black on ochre unpt. Printer: CPM.			
	a. 1 handwritten sign.	15.00	100.	325.
	b. 2 printed sign.	15.00	80.00	325.
56	**50 Mil Reis** E. 14A (1916). Black and m/c. Woman seated w/sword and flag at l., woman w/wreath at r. Printer: ABNC.	15.00	80.00	325.
57	**50 Mil Reis** E. 15A (1923). Blue on yellow-green. Woman seated w/scarf at ctr. Printer: CdM.	25.00	1750.	3750.

No.		Good	Fine	XF
58	**50 Mil Reis** E. 16A (1925). Blue on m/c unpt. Pres. A da Silva Bernardes at ctr. Printer: ABNC.	10.00	50.00	225.
59	**50 Mil Reis** E. 17A (1936). Violet. Portr. J. Xavier da Silveira, Jr. at l. Printer: W&S.	7.50	25.00	125.
60	**100 Mil Reis** E. 6A (1892). Black on m/c unpt. Street scene w/ bldgs. at l., ship at r., woman at ctr. Printer: ABNC. Letters A-D.	30.00	200.	600.
61	**100 Mil Reis** E. 7A (1897). Black on m/c unpt. Woman seated w/Cupid at r. Printer: ABNC.	30.00	150.	600.
62	**100 Mil Reis** W/o *Estampa* (1901). Blue on ochre unpt. Woman w/sickle and Cupid at l. Printer: BWC. Letters A-D.	35.00	250.	900.
62A	**100 Mil Reis** W/o *Estampa E.8A* (1901). Blue and pink on tan paper. Liberty w/ stars at l. Back brown. Printer: BWC.	35.00	500.	1100.

No.		Good	Fine	XF
63	**100 Mil Reis** E. 9A (1904). Blue on yellow unpt. Woman seated w/2 children reading at ctr. Printer: George Duval.	35.00	400.	1050.
64	**100 Mil Reis** E. 10A (1907). Carmine on ochre unpt. Woman in circle at lower l.	30.00	400.	900.
65	**100 Mil Reis** E. 11A (1909). Black on m/c unpt. Woman seated w/child at l. Printer: ABNC.	30.00	400.	900.
66	**100 Mil Reis** E. 12A (1912). Black on m/c unpt. Woman seated w/wreath at l. Printer: ABNC.	25.00	250.	700.
67	**100 Mil Reis** E. 13A (1915). Green unpt. Printer: CPM.	25.00	200.	550.

NOTICE

Readers with unlisted dates, signature varieties, etc. are invited to submit photocopies or, high resolution (300 dpi, 100% size) scans of their notes to: Standard Catalog of World Paper Money, 700 East State St. Iola, WI 54990-0001, or E-Mail: george.cuhaj@fwpubs.com.

No.		Good	Fine	XF
68	**100 Mil Reis** E. 14A (1919). Blue on m/c unpt. Portr. A. Augusto Moreira Pena at ctr. Printer: ABNC.	25.00	150.	55
69	**100 Mil Reis** E. 15A (1924). Sepia on ochre unpt. Portr. R. Barbosa at ctr. Printer: CdM.	25.00	550.	125

No.		Good	Fine	XF
70	**100 Mil Reis** E. 16A (1925). Blue on m/c unpt. Portr. A. Augusto Moreira Pena at ctr. Printer: ABNC.			
	a. *BRAZIL.* 1 handwritten sign.	7.50	75.00	225
	b. *BRAZIL.* 2 printed sign.	7.50	100.	375
	c. *BRASIL; Estampa* and serial # together, handwritten signature.	6.00	75.00	225
	d. *BRASIL; Estampa* and serial # separated, handwritten signature.	6.00	75.00	225

No.		Good	Fine	XF
71	**100 Mil Reis** E. 17A (1936). Dk. blue on m/c unpt. Portr. A. Santos Dumont at r. Printer: W&S.	7.50	50.00	200
72	**200 Mil Reis** E. 7A (1892). Black on m/c unpt. Woman seated at l. and at r., helmsman at ctr. Printer: ABNC. Letters A-C.	45.00	750.	1600
73	**200 Mil Reis** E. 8A (1897). Black on bicolored unpt. Woman w/child at r. Printer: ABNC. Letters A-D.	45.00	675.	1300.
74	**200 Mil Reis** W/o *Estampa E.9A.* (1901). Violet on ochre unpt. Woman seated w/child at l., woman at ctr. Printer: BWC.	45.00	750.	1500.

No.		Good	Fine	XF
75	**200 Mil Reis** E. 10A (1905). Blue on yellow unpt. Ship and coastline at ctr., flanked by 2 women. Printer: George Duval and Emile Grosbie.	45.00	600.	1200.
76	**200 Mil Reis** E. 11A (1908). black on m/c unpt. Woman and child reading at ctr. Printer: ABNC.	45.00	350.	800.
77	**200 Mil Reis** E. 12A (1911). Black on m/c unpt. 2 women seated at r. Printer: ABNC.	45.00	400.	900.

		Good	Fine	XF
78	**200 Mil Reis** E. 13A (1916). Black on ochre unpt. Bldg. on back. Plate modifications on back. Printer: CPM			
	a. 1 handwritten sign.	45.00	400.	1000.
	b. 2 printed sign.	45.00	500.	1100.
79	**200 Mil Reis** E. 14A (1919). Blue on m/c unpt. Portr. P. Jose de Moraes e Barros at ctr. Printer: ABNC.	45.00	275.	500.
80	**200 Mil Reis** E. 15A (1922). Sepia on ochre unpt. Woman seated at ctr. Printer: CdM.	45.00	600.	1450.

		Good	Fine	XF
81	**200 Mil Reis** E. 16A (1925). Blue on m/c unpt. Portr. P. Jose de Moraes e Barros at ctr. Back brown; bldg. at ctr. Printer: ABNC.			
	a. *BRAZIL.* 1 handwritten sign.	7.50	150.	325.
	b. *BRASIL; Estampa* and serial # together.	6.00	125.	300.
	c. *BRASIL; Estampa* and serial # separated.	6.00	125.	300.

		Good	Fine	XF
82	**200 Mil Reis** E. 17A (1936). Red-brown on m/c unpt. J. Saldanha Marinho at r. Printer: W&S.	7.50	75.00	200.
83	**500 Mil Reis** E. 6A (1897). Black on m/c unpt. Woman seated at ctr. flanked by women in circles. Printer: ABNC. Letters A-C.	100.	1200.	2400.
84	**500 Mil Reis** W/o *Estampa E.7A* (1901). Green on ochre unpt. Woman w/distaff at l., woman at r. Printer: BWC.	100.	1200.	2400.
85	**500 Mil Reis** E. 8A (1904). Red. Woman w/child at l. and r.	100.	1350.	2750.
86	**500 Mil Reis** E. 9A (1908). Black on m/c unpt. Woman w/trumpet and sword at l., woman w/wreath and palm branch at r. Printer: ABNC.	100.	1250.	2750.

		Good	Fine	XF
87	**500 Mil Reis** E. 10A (1911). Black m/c unpt. Woman w/wreath at ctr. flanked by Cupids. Printer: ABNC.	50.00	225.	450.
88	**500 Mil Reis** E. 11A (1917). Black on m/c unpt. Bldg. on back. Printer: CPM.	100.	1150.	2350.
89	**500 Mil Reis** E. 12A (1919). Blue on m/c unpt. Portr. J. Bonifacio de Andrade e Silva at ctr. Printer: ABNC.	50.00	325.	1000.
90	**500 Mil Reis** E. 13A (1924). Red. Man seated at ctr. w/train in background. Printer: CdM.	125.	1500.	3000.

NOTICE

Readers with unlisted dates, signature varieties, etc. are invited to submit photocopies or, high resolution (300 dpi, 100% size) scans of their notes to: Standard Catalog of World Paper Money, 700 East State St. Iola, WI 54990-0001, or E-Mail: george.cuhaj@fwpubs.com.

		Good	Fine	XF
91	**500 Mil Reis** E. 14A (1925). Blue on m/c unpt. J. Bonifacio de Andrade e Silva at ctr. Like #89. Printer: ABNC.			
	a. *BRAZIL.* 1 Handwritten sign.	35.00	250.	750.
	b. *BRAZIL.* 2 Printed sign.	40.00	300.	850.

		Good	Fine	XF
92	**500 Mil Reis** E. 15A (1931). Blue on m/c unpt. M. Peixoto at ctr. Printer: ABNC.			
	a. *BRAZIL.* 1 handwritten sign.	10.00	50.00	350.
	b. *BRAZIL.* 2 printed sign.	10.00	50.00	250.
	c. *BRASIL; Estampa* and serial # together. Handwritten signature.	7.50	30.00	225.
	d. *BRASIL; Estampa* and serial # separated. Handwritten signature.	7.50	30.00	225.
93	**1000 Mil Reis** E. 1A (1921). Blue on yellow unpt. Woman seated w/sword and Mercury symbol at l. Printer: CdM.	125.	1500.	3250.

CAIXA DE CONVERSÃO

1906, ESTAMPA 1

#94-98 printer: W&S.

		Good	Fine	XF
94	**10 Mil Reis** 6.12.1906. Brown. Woman w/shield at l., Portr. A. Pena at ctr. Bank bldg. at ctr. on back.	7.50	25.00	75.00

Note: #94 is very often encountered as a lithographic counterfeit.

		Good	Fine	XF
95	**20 Mil Reis** 6.12.1906. Blue. Portr. A. Pena at l., bank bldg. at r. Steam train at ctr. on back.	12.50	30.00	60.00
96	**50 Mil Reis** 6.12.1906. Brown and pink. Portr. A. Pena at l., bank bldg. at ctr. 3 allegorical women at ctr. on back.	22.50	100.	200.
97	**100 Mil Reis** 6.12.1906. Green and yellow. Portr. A. Pena at ctr., bank bldg. at r. Trees at ctr. on back. Letters A-C.	30.00	150.	300.

		Good	Fine	XF
98	**200 Mil Reis** 6.12.1906. Black, yellow and red. Portr. A. Pena at r., bank bldg. at ctr. Allegorical women w/cows, sheaves and farm implements on back. Letters A-D.	35.00	200.	400.

1906, Estampa 1A

#99-100 printer: JEZ.

		Good	Fine	XF
99	**500 Mil Reis** 6.12.1906. Green. Man standing at l., Portr. A. Pena at r. Bank at lower ctr. on back. Printer: JEZ.	60.00	350.	750.
100	**1 Conto De Reis = 1000 Mil Reis** 6.12.1906. Brown. Winged allegorical male at l., Portr. A. Pena at r. Bank at lower ctr. on back Printer: JEZ.	325.	1500.	3000.

1910, Estampa 2

#101-102 printer: CPM.

		Good	Fine	XF
101	**10 Mil Reis** 31.12.1910. *E. 2.* Blue. Printer: CPM.	25.00	200.	600.
102	**50 Mil Reis** 31.12.1910. *E. 2A.* Brown. Bldg. at ctr. Back purple. Printer: CPM.	35.00	350.	700.

Provisional Issue

Black *NA CAIXA DE CONVERSAO* on modified plates or ovpt. on Thesauro Nacional notes.

		Good	Fine	XF
102A	**10 Mil Reis** E. 1A. L. 1906. Carmine on yellow unpt. Woman w/boy at r. New text and modified plate of #31.	35.00	600.	1300.
102C	**20 Mil Reis** E. 1A. L. 1906. Brown on ochre unpt. Boy seated at l. and at r., woman in circle at lower l. New text and modified plate of #42.	35.00	650.	1350.
102E	**100 Mil Reis** E. 10A. L. 1906. Ovpt. on #64.	35.00	800.	1600.
102F	**500 Mil Reis** E. 8A. L. 1906. Ovpt. on #85.	100.	1500.	3250.

Caixa de Estabilizacao, Valor Recebido em Ouro

Estampa 1A

#103-109 black on m/c guilloche. Woman at ctr. ("Reverie"). 6 sign. varieties. Printer: ABNC.

		Good	Fine	XF
103	**10 Mil Reis** 18.12.1926. Black on m/c guilloche. Woman at ctr. Printer: ABNC. Back dk. brown; coastal scenery.	10.00	80.00	200.
104	**20 Mil Reis** 18.12.1926. Black on m/c guilloche. Woman at ctr. Printer: ABNC. Back red, city and trees at ctr.	12.50	90.00	250.

		Good	Fine	XF
105	**50 Mil Reis** 18.12.1926. Black on m/c guilloche. Woman at ctr. Printer: ABNC. Back orange, cavalry charge at ctr.	30.00	200.	550.
106	**100 Mil Reis** 18.12.1926. Black on m/c guilloche. Woman at ctr. Printer: ABNC. Back green, Bank at ctr.	60.00	275.	850.
107	**200 Mil Reis** 18.12.1926. Black on m/c guilloche. Woman at ctr. Printer: ABNC. Back blue-black, cavalry and infantry battle scene at ctr.	60.00	300.	950.
108	**500 Mil Reis** 18.12.1926. Black on m/c guilloche. Woman at ctr. Printer: ABNC. Back blue, naval battle at ctr.	110.	750.	2000.
109	**1 Conto De Reis = 1000 Mil Reis** 18.12.1926. Black on m/c guilloche. Woman at ctr. Printer: ABNC. Back purple, mission scene.	160.	1000.	3000.

1926 Issue

#109A-109F Black *A CAIXA DE ESTABILISACAO...* ovpt. within rectangular frame on Thesouro Nacional notes. 2 printed sign. at lower part of note.

		Good	Fine	XF
109A	**10 Mil Reis** E. 17A. Series 10. Ovpt. on #39.	10.00	65.00	200.
109B	**20 Mil Reis** E. 16A. Series 10. Ovpt. on #48.	10.00	75.00	225.

		Good	Fine	XF
109C	**50 Mil Reis** E. 16A. Series 9, 10. Ovpt. on #58.	10.00	65.00	200.
109D	**100 Mil Reis** E. 16A. Series 10. Ovpt. on #70.	17.50	125.	300.
109E	**200 Mil Reis** E. 16A. Series 10. Ovpt. on #81.	15.00	100.	275.
109F	**500 Mil Reis** E. 14A. Series 5. Ovpt. on # 91.	100.	1250.	2250.

Banco do Brasil

Lei N. 4635 a de 8 de Janeriode 1923

#110B-123 printer: ABNC.

#110B-113, 115, 117 w/1 hand sign. All others w/2 printed sign.

#110B-113 arms on back.

		Good	Fine	XF
110B	**1 Mil Reis** L. 1923. E. 1A. Black on green unpt. Portr. C. Salles at ctr. Series #1-278. Printer: ABNC. Back green on pink unpt.; arms at ctr.	1.00	4.00	8.00

Note: #110B w/series #279-500 were issued in 1944 as Cruzeiro notes. See #131A.

		Good	Fine	XF
111	**2 Mil Reis** L. 1923. E. 1A. Black on m/c unpt. Portr. P. de Moraes at r. Arms. Printer: ABNC.	2.50	7.50	15.00

		Good	Fine	XF
112	**5 Mil Reis** L. 1923. E. 1A. Black on yellow-green unpt. Portr. B. do Rio Branco at l. Printer: ABNC. Back red and m/c; arms at ctr.	2.50	15.00	60.00
113	**5 Mil Reis** L. 1923. E. 2A. Black on yellow-green unpt. Portr. B. do Rio Branco at l. Printer: ABNC. Face like #112 but w/different guilloche. Back blue.	2.50	15.00	75.00

		Good	Fine	XF
114	**10 Mil Reis** L. 1923. E. 1A. Black on m/c unpt. Portr. S. Vidal at ctr. Printer: ABNC. Back orange; bldg. at ctr.	5.00	25.00	125.

		Good	Fine	XF
115	**10 Mil Reis** L. 1923. E. 2A. Black on m/c unpt. Portr. R. Alves at ctr. Printer: ABNC. Back dk. brown; bldg. at ctr.	7.50	35.00	150.

		Good	Fine	XF
116	**20 Mil Reis** L. 1923. E. 1A. Black on m/c unpt. Portr. A. Bernardes at r. Printer: ABNC. Back blue; Monroe Palace at ctr.	10.00	50.00	175.
117	**20 Mil Reis** L. 1923. E. 2A. Black on m/c unpt. Portr. A. Bernardes at r. Printer: ABNC. Like #116. Back brown; bldg. at ctr.	7.50	45.00	160.

		Good	Fine	XF
118	**50 Mil Reis** L. 1923. E. 1A. Black on m/c unpt. Portr. D. da Fonseca at l. Printer: ABNC. Back brown; canal at ctr.	25.00	150.	450.

		Good	Fine	XF
119	**50 Mil Reis** L. 1923. E. 2A. Black on m/c unpt. Portr. M. de Olinda at l. Back red; canal at ctr.	25.00	150.	450.

		Good	Fine	XF
120	**100 Mil Reis** L. 1923. E. 1A. Black on m/c unpt. Portr. R. Feijo at ctr. Back green; shoreline at r.	35.00	275.	650.
121	**200 Mil Reis** L. 1923. E. 1A. Black on m/c unpt. Portr. Dom Pedro II at r. Printer: ABNC. Back black; city and shoreline mountains behind at ctr.	35.00	275.	650.
122	**500 Mil Reis** L. 1923. E. 1A. Blue on yellow unpt. Man seated w/locomotive in background. Back brown. Printer: CdM.	100.	750.	1500.

		Good	Fine	XF
122A	**500 Mil Reis** L. 1923. E. 1A. Black on m/c impt. Portr. J. Bonifacio at l. Printer: ABNC. Back dp. orange; city and trees at ctr. Specimen.			
123	**1000 Mil Reis = 1 Conto de Reis** L. 1923. E. 1A. Black on m/c unpt. Portr. Dom Pedro I at ctr. Printer: ABNC. Back purple; cavalry charge at ctr.	100.	750.	1500.

#124 Deleted. See #131A.

1923 Provisional Issue

		Good	Fine	XF
110	**500 Mil Reis** 8.1.1923. Blue on yellow unpt. Man seated w/train in background. Back brown. Printer: CdM.	100.	1700.	3500.
110A	**1000 Mil Reis = 1 Conto de Reis** E. 1A. ND. Carmine. Diagonal ovpt: *NO BANCO DO BRASIL DE ACORDO...* on #93.	100.	2000.	4000.

1942 Casa da Moeda ProvisionalIssue

#125-131 are 5-500 Mil Reis notes ovpt: *CASA DA MOEDA* and new Cruzeiro denominations in a blue rosette.

		Good	Fine	XF
125	**5 Cruzeiros on 5 Mil Reis** ND (1942). Dk. blue on m/c unpt. Ovpt. on #29b.	2.50	12.50	50.00
126	**10 Cruzeiros on 10 Mil Reis** ND (1942). Dk. blue on m/c unpt. Ovpt. on #39c.	4.00	25.00	85.00

		Good	Fine	XF
127	**20 Cruzeiros on 20 Mil Reis** ND (1942). Dk. blue on m/c unpt. Ovpt. on #48c.	6.00	35.00	150.

		Good	Fine	XF
128	**50 Cruzeiros on 50 Mil Reis** ND (1942). Violet on m/c unpt. Ovpt. on #59.	125.	1400.	2750.

		Good	Fine	XF
129	**100 Cruzeiros on 100 Mil Reis** ND (1942). Dk. blue on m/c unpt. Ovpt. on #70c.	20.00	100.	400.
130	**200 Cruzeiros on 200 Mil Reis** ND (1942). Dk. blue on m/c unpt.			
	a. Ovpt. on #81b.	37.50	750.	2250.
	b. Ovpt. on #81c.	37.50	750.	2250.
130A	**200 Cruzeiros on 200 Mil Reis** ND (1942). Red-brown on m/c unpt. Ovpt. on #82. Unique	—	—	—
131	**500 Cruzeiros on 500 Mil Reis** ND (1942). Dk. blue on m/c unpt.			
	a. Ovpt. on 92c.	25.00	400.	850.
	b. Ovpt. on 92d.	20.00	150.	400.

1944 EMERGENCY ISSUE

#131A, 1 Mil Reis of Banco do Brasil w/o ovpt. issued as 1 Cruzeiro.

		Good	Fine	XF
131A	**1 Mil Reis (Cruzeiro)** ND (1944). Black on green unpt. Portr. C. Salles at ctr. Arms on back. Like #110B but series #279-500.	.50	2.00	6.00

TESOURO NACIONAL, VALOR RECEBIDO

1943-44, W/O ESTAMPA (1A)

#132-141 blue on m/c guilloches, hand-signed across face of note. Printer: ABNC.

		VG	VF	UNC
132	**1 Cruzeiro** ND (1944). Blue on m/c guilloches. Portr. Marqués de Tamandare at ctr. Printer: ABNC. Back blue; naval school at ctr. Series: #1-1000.	.15	.50	3.00
133	**2 Cruzeiros** Blue on m/c guilloches. Printer: ABNC. ND (1944). Portr. Duque de Caxias at ctr. Back gold; military school at ctr. Series: #1-500.	.20	.75	4.00
134	**5 Cruzeiros** ND (1943). Blue on m/c guilloches. Portr. Barão do Rio Branco at ctr. Printer: ABNC. Back brown; *Amazonia* scene. Series: #1-500.	1.25	7.50	25.00

		VG	VF	UNC
135	**10 Cruzeiros** ND (1943). Blue on m/c guilloches. Portr. Getulio Vargas at ctr. Printer: ABNC. Back green; allegorical man w/industrial implements at ctr. Series: #1-330.	1.25	7.50	25.00

		VG	VF	UNC
136	**20 Cruzeiros** Blue on m/c guilloches. Printer: ABNC. ND (1943). Portr. Deodoro da Fonseca at ctr. Back red; allegory of the Republic at ctr. Series: #1-460.	1.25	7.50	25.00
137	**50 Cruzeiros** ND (1943). Blue on m/c guilloches. Portr. Princesa Isabel at ctr. Printer: ABNC. Back purple; allegory of Law at ctr. Series: #1-320.	2.50	10.00	45.00
138	**100 Cruzeiros** ND (1943). Blue on m/c guilloches. Dom Pedro II at ctr. Printer: ABNC. Back red-brown; allegory of National Culture. Series: #1-235.	2.50	12.50	75.00

		VG	VF	UNC
139	**200 Cruzeiros** ND (1943). Blue on m/c guilloches. Portr. D. Pedro I at ctr. Printer: ABNC. Back olive-green; battle scene. Series: #1-320.	4.00	15.00	100.
140	**500 Cruzeiros** ND (1943). Blue on m/c guilloches. Portr. Joao VI at ctr. Printer: ABNC. Back blue-black; maritime allegory w/ships at ctr. Series #1-160.	10.00	100.	375.
141	**1000 Cruzeiros** ND (1943). Blue on m/c guilloches. Portr. Pedro Alvares Cabral at ctr. Printer: ABNC. Back orange; first Mass scene at ctr. Series: #1-230.	7.50	50.00	200.

1949-50, ESTAMPA 2A

#142-149 hand-signed acros face of note. Like #134-141. Printer: TDLR.

		VG	VF	UNC
142	**5 Cruzeiros** ND (1950). Brown on m/c unpt. Portr. B. do Rio Branco at ctr. Printer: TDLR. Back brown; *Amazonia* scene. Series: #1-500.	.50	2.00	10.00
143	**10 Cruzeiros** ND (1950). Green on m/c unpt. Portr. G.Vargas at ctr. Printer: TDLR. Back green; allegorical man w/industrial implements at ctr. Series: #1-435.	.50	2.50	12.50
144	**20 Cruzeiros** ND (1950). Red-brown on m/c unpt. Portr. D. da Fonseca at ctr. Printer: TDLR. Back red; allegory of the Republic at ctr. Series: #1-370.	1.25	5.00	25.00

#	Denomination	VG	VF	UNC
145	**50 Cruzeiros** ND (1949). Purple on m/c unpt. Portr. Princesa Isabel at ctr. Printer: TDLR. Back purple; allegory of Law at ctr. Series: #1-115.	4.50	20.00	135.
146	**100 Cruzeiros** ND (1949). Red on m/c unpt. Portr. D. Pedro II at ctr. Printer: TDLR. Back red-brown, allegory of National Culture. Series #1-115.	6.00	50.00	175.
147	**200 Cruzeiros** ND (1949). Green. Portr. D. Pedro I at ctr. Printer: TDLR. Back olive-green; battle scene. Series: #1-30.	37.50	300.	900.
148	**500 Cruzeiros** ND (1949). Dk. green. Portr. D. Joao VI at ctr. Printer: TDLR. Back blue-black; maritime allegory w/ships at ctr. Series: #1-120.	12.50	100.	300.

#	Denomination	VG	VF	UNC
149	**1000 Cruzeiros** ND (1949). Orange. Portr. P. Alvares Cabral at ctr. Printer: TDLR. Back orange; first Mass scene at ctr. Series: #1-90.	17.50	250.	900.

SIGNATURE VARIETIES

1	CLAUDIONOR S. LEMOS, 1953 HORACIO LAFER	2	CLAUDIONOR S. LEMOS, 1954 OSWALDO ARANHA
3	CLAUDIONOR S. LEMOS, 1955 JOSE M. WHITAKER	4	CLAUDIONOR S. LEMOS, 1955-56 EUGENIO GUDIN
5	CLAUDIONOR S. LEMOS, 1956 JOSE MARIA ALKIMIN	6	CLAUDIONOR S. LEMOS. 1958 LUCAS LOPES
7	AFFONSO ALMINO, 1959 LUCAS LOPES		

1953-59 W/O ESTAMPA 1A

#150-156 blue on m/c guilloches, 2 printed sign. Printer: ABNC.

#	Denomination	VG	VF	UNC
150	**1 Cruzeiro** ND (1954-58). Blue on m/c guilloches. Portr. M. de Tamandare at ctr. Back blue; naval school at ctr. Like #132.			
	a. Sign. 2. Series #1001-1800.	.05	.20	1.00
	b. Sign. 3. Series #1801-2700.	.05	.20	1.00
	c. Sign. 5. Series #2701-3450.	.05	.20	1.00
	d. Sign. 6. Series #3451-3690.	.05	.20	1.00

#	Denomination	VG	VF	UNC
151	**2 Cruzeiros** ND (1954-58). Blue on m/c guilloches. Portr. D. de Caxias at ctr. Back gold; military school at ctr. Like #133.			
	a. Sign. 2. Series #501-900.	.05	.20	1.00
	b. Sign. 6. Series #901-1135.	.05	.20	1.00

#	Denomination	VG	VF	UNC
152	**50 Cruzeiros** ND (1956-59). Blue on m/c guilloches. Portr. Princesa Isabel at ctr. Back purple; allegory of Law at ctr. Like #137.			
	a. Sign. 5. Series #321-470.	1.00	4.00	20.00
	b. Sign. 6. Series #471-620.	1.00	4.00	20.00
	c. Sign. 7. Series #621-720.	1.00	5.00	25.00
153	**100 Cruzeiros** ND (1955-59). Blue on m/c guilloches. Portr. D. Pedro II at ctr. Back red-brown; allegory of National Culture. Like #138.			
	a. Sign. 3. Series #236-435.	1.00	5.00	22.50
	b. Sign. 5. Series #436-535.	1.00	5.00	25.00
	c. Sign. 6. Series #536-660.	1.00	5.00	22.50
	d. Sign. 7. Series #661-760.	1.50	7.00	35.00

#	Denomination	VG	VF	UNC
154	**200 Cruzeiros** ND (1955-59). Blue on m/c guilloches. Portr. D. Pedro I at ctr. Back olive-green; battle scene at ctr. Like #139.			
	a. Sign. 3. Series #321-520.	1.25	6.00	30.00
	b. Sign. 6. Series #521-620.	2.00	10.00	50.00
	c. Sign. 7. Series #621-670.	7.00	35.00	175.
155	**500 Cruzeiros** ND (1953). Blue on m/c guilloches. Portr. D. Joao VI at ctr. Back blue-black; maritime allegory w/ships at ctr. Like #140. Sign. 1. Series #161-260.	9.00	45.00	225.
156	**1000 Cruzeiros** ND (1953-59). Blue on m/c guilloches. Portr. P. Alvares Cabral at ctr. Back orange; scene of first mass at ctr. Like #141.			
	a. Sign. 1. Series #231-330.	9.00	45.00	225.
	b. Sign. 3. Series #331-630.	2.00	12.50	65.00
	c. Sign. 4. Series #631-930.	2.00	12.50	55.00
	d. Sign. 6. Series #931-1000.	3.00	15.00	75.00
	e. Sign. 7. Series #1081-1330.	2.50	12.50	60.00

1953-60 ESTAMPA 2A

#157-165 2 printed sign. Printer: TDLR.

#	Denomination	VG	VF	UNC
157	**2 Cruzeiros** ND (1955). Turquoise on m/c unpt. Portr. D. de Caxias at ctr. Military school at ctr. Back ochre. Like #133. Sign. 3. Series #1-230.	.05	.20	1.00
157A	**2 Cruzeiros** ND (1956-58). Turquoise on m/c unpt. Like #157 but back orange.			
	a. Sign. 3. Series #231-600.	.05	.20	1.00
	b. Sign. 5. Series #601-900.	.05	.20	1.00
	c. Sign. 6. Series #901-1045.	.05	.20	1.50

158	5 Cruzeiros	VG	VF	UNC
	ND (1953-59). Brown on m/c unpt. Portr. B. do Rio Branco at ctr. Back brown; *Amazonia* scene.			
	a. Sign. 1. Series #501-1000.	.10	.50	3.00
	b. Sign. 2. Series #1001-1300.	.10	.50	3.00
	c. Sign. 5. Series #1301-1800.	.10	.50	2.50
	d. Sign. 6. Series #1801-2050.	.10	.50	3.00
	e. Sign. 7. Series #2051-2301	.10	.50	2.50

159	10 Cruzeiros	VG	VF	UNC
	ND (1953-60). Green on m/c unpt. Portr. G. Vargas at ctr. Back green; allegorical man w/industrial implements at ctr. Like #135.			
	a. Sign. 1. Series #436-735.	.10	.50	2.50
	b. Sign. 2. Series #736-1235.	.10	.40	2.00
	c. Sign. 5. Series #1236-1435.	.10	.40	2.00
	d. Sign. 6. Series #1436-1685.	.10	.40	2.00
	e. Sign. 7. Series #1686-1885.	.10	.50	2.50
	f. Sign. 8. Series #1886-2355.	.05	.20	1.00

160	20 Cruzeiros	VG	VF	UNC
	ND (1955-61). Red-brown on m/c unpt. Portr. D. da Fonseca at ctr. Back red; allegory of the Republic at ctr. Like #136.			
	a. Sign. 3. Series #371-870.	.10	.50	3.00
	b. Sign. 6. Series #871-1175.	.15	.75	4.00
	c. Sign. 7. Series #1176-1225.	.50	4.00	20.00
	d. Sign. 8. Series #1226-1575.	.10	.50	3.00
161	50 Cruzeiros			
	ND (1954-61). Purple on m/c unpt. Portr. Princesa Isabel at ctr. Like #137.			
	a. Sign. 2. Series #116-215.	2.00	10.00	50.00
	b. Sign. 3. Series #216-415.	.25	1.50	7.50
	c. Sign. 8. Series #416-585.	.25	1.50	7.50
162	100 Cruzeiros			
	ND (1960). Red on m/c unpt. Portr. D. Pedro II at ctr. Back red-brown; allegory of National Culture. Sign. 8. Series #116-215. Like #138.	1.50	2.50	12.50
163	200 Cruzeiros			
	ND (1960). Olive on m/c unpt. Portr. D. Pedro I at ctr. Back olive-green; battle scene at ctr. Sign. 8. Series #31-110. Like #139.	3.00	7.50	20.00

164	500 Cruzeiros	VG	VF	UNC
	ND (1955-60). Dk. olive on m/c unpt. Portr. D. Joao VI at ctr. Back blue-black; maritime allegory w/ships at ctr. Like #140.			
	a. 3. #121-420.	1.50	6.50	32.50
	b. 4. #421-720.	1.00	5.00	25.00
	c. 6. #721-770.	3.50	17.50	85.00
	d. 8. #771-1300.	1.00	5.00	15.00

165	1000 Cruzeiros	VG	VF	UNC
	ND (1960). Orange on m/c unpt. Portr. P. Alvares Cabral at ctr. Scene of first mass at ctr. Sign. 8. Series #91-790.	.50	2.50	12.50

Note: for similar issues but w/*VALOR LEGAL* inscription, see listing in Volume 3.

The British Caribbean Territories (Eastern Group), a currency board formed in 1950, comprised the British West Indies territories of Trinidad and Tobago; Barbados; the Leeward Islands of Anguilla, Saba, St. Christopher, Nevis and Antigua; the Windward Islands of St. Lucia, Dominica, St. Vincent and Grenada; British Guiana and the British Virgin Islands.

As time progressed, the members of this Eastern Group varied.

For later issues see East Caribbean States listings in Volume 3, Modern issues.

RULERS:
British

MONETARY SYSTEM:
1 Dollar = 100 Cents

BRITISH ADMINISTRATION

BRITISH CARIBBEAN TERRITORIES, EASTERN GROUP

1950-51 ISSUE

#1-6 map at lower l., portr. Kg. George VI at r. Arms of the various territories on back. Sign. varieties. Printer: BWC.

		VG	VF	UNC
1	**1 Dollar** 28.11.1950; 1.9.1951. Red on m/c unpt.	3.50	50.00	275.
2	**2 Dollars** 28.11.1950; 1.9.1951. Blue on m/c unpt.	15.00	125.	650.

		VG	VF	UNC
3	**5 Dollars** 28.11.1950; 1.9.1951. Green on m/c unpt.	12.50	100.	600.
4	**10 Dollars** 28.11.1950; 1.9.1951. Lt. brown on m/c unpt.	35.00	250.	—
5	**20 Dollars** 28.11.1950; 1.9.1951. Purple on m/c unpt.	50.00	350.	—

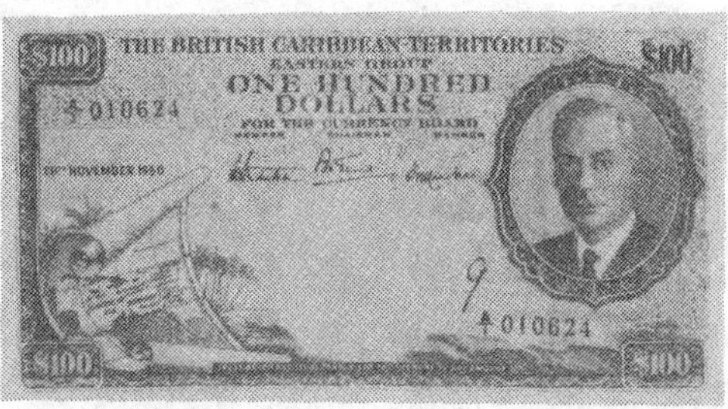

		VG	VF	UNC
6	**100 Dollars** 28.11.1950. Black on m/c unpt.	350.	1250.	—

1953 ISSUE

#7-12 map at lower l., portr. Qn. Elizabeth II at r. Arms in all 4 corners on back. Printer: BWC.

		VG	VF	UNC
7	**1 Dollar** 1953-64. Red on m/c unpt.			
	a. Wmk: Sailing ship. 5.1.1953.	15.00	75.00	325.
	b. Wmk: Qn. Elizabeth II. 1.3.1954-2.1.1957.	8.00	30.00	225.
	c. 2.1.1958-2.1.1964.	7.00	25.00	185.
8	**2 Dollars** 1953-64. Blue on m/c unpt.			
	a. Wmk: Sailing ship. 5.1.1953.	30.00	225.	850.
	b. Wmk: Qn. Elizabeth II. 1.3.1954-1.7.1960.	20.00	85.00	650.
	c. 2.1.1961-2.1.1964.	18.00	75.00	550.

		VG	VF	UNC
9	**5 Dollars** 1953-64. Green on m/c unpt.			
	a. Wmk: Sailing ship. 5.1.1953.	35.00	275.	1100.
	b. Wmk: Qn. Elizabeth II. 3.1.1955-2.1.1959.	25.00	100.	925.
	c. 2.1.1961-2.1.1964.	22.50	90.00	850.
10	**10 Dollars** 1953-64. Brown on m/c unpt.			
	a. Wmk: Sailing ship. 5.1.1953.	60.00	400.	—
	b. Wmk: Qn. Elizabeth II. 3.1.1955-2.1.1959.	40.00	250.	1750.
	c. 2.1.1961; 2.1.1962; 2.1.1964.	37.50	200.	1500.

		VG	VF	UNC
11	**20 Dollars** 1953-64. Purple on m/c unpt.			
	a. Wmk: Sailing ship. 5.1.1953.	90.00	600.	—
	b. Wmk: Qn. Elizabeth II. 2.1.1957-2.1.1964.	45.00	300.	—
12	**100 Dollars** 1953-63. Black on m/c unpt.			
	a. Wmk: Sailing ship. 5.1.1953.	500.	2000.	—
	b. Wmk: Qn. Elizabeth II. 1.3.1954; 2.1.1957; 2.1.1963.	300.	1350.	—
	s. As b. Specimen.	—	—	2500.

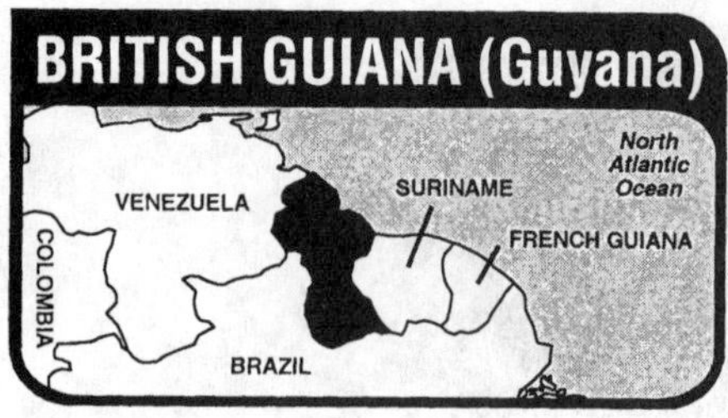

The Cooperative Republic of Guyana, (formerly British Guiana) an independent member of the British Commonwealth situated on the northeast coast of South America, has an area of 83,000 sq. mi. (214,969 sq. km.) and a population of 779,000. Capital: Georgetown. The economy is basically agrarian. Sugar, rice and bauxite are exported.

The original area of Guyana, which included present-day Surinam, French Guiana, and parts of Brazil and Venezuela, was sighted by Columbus in 1498. The first European settlement was made late in the 16th century by the Dutch. For the next 150 years, possession alternated between the Dutch and the British, with a short interval of French control. The British exercised de facto control after 1796, although the area, which included the Dutch colonies of Essequebo, Demerary and Berbice, was not ceded to them by the Dutch until 1814. From 1803 to 1831, Essequebo and Demerary were administered separately from Berbice. The three colonies were united in the British Crown Colony of British Guiana in 1831. British Guiana won internal self-government in 1952 and full independence, under the traditional name of Guyana, on May 26, 1966.

Notes of the British Caribbean Currency Board circulated from 1950-1965. For later issues see Guyana, Volume 3, Modern Issues.

RULERS:

British to 1966

MONETARY SYSTEM:

1 Joe = 22 Guilders to 1836
1 Dollar = 4 Shillings 2 Pence, 1837-1965

DEMERARY AND ESSEQUEBO

COLONIES OF DEMERARY AND ESSEQUEBO

1830S FIRST ISSUE

#A1-A4, ornate *D-E* at upper ctr. (Not issued.)

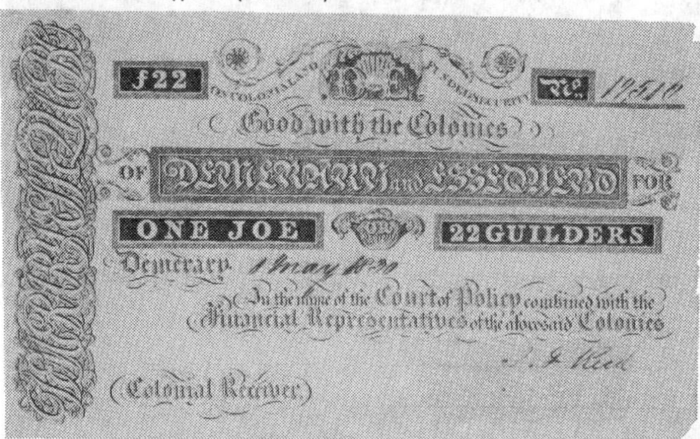

		Good	Fine	XF
A1	**1 Joe or 22 Guilders** 1.5.1830. Black.	—	200.	485.
A4	**10 Joes or 220 Guilders** ND (ca. 1830s). Reddish brown.	—	—	650.

1830S SECOND ISSUE

#B1-B4 black. Woman w/anchor at upper l. W/or w/o counterfoil. (Not issued.)

		Good	Fine	XF
B1	**1 Joe of 22 Guilders** ND (1830s).	—	200.	600.
B2	**2 Joes of 22 Guilders Each** ND (1830s).	—	—	—
B3	**3 Joes of 22 Guilders Each** ND (1830s).	—	300.	700.
B4	**10 Joes of 22 Guilders Each** ND (1830s).	—	300.	700.

BRITISH ADMINISTRATION

GOVERNMENT OF BRITISH GUIANA

1916-20 ISSUES

Various date and sign. varieties.

		Good	Fine	XF
1	**1 Dollar** 1.8.1916; 2.1.1918. red-brown. Sailing ship at l. 118 x 63mm.	200.	650.	—

		Good	Fine	XF
1A	**1 Dollar** 1.1.1920; 1.10.1924. Red-brown. Like #1. Sailing ship at l. Tan or gray paper. 150 x 85mm. Printer: TDLR.	150.	550.	—
2	**2 Dollars** 1.8.1916; 2.1.1918. Blue. Sailing ship at upper ctr. Ship at ctr. on back. 115 x 73mm. Printer: TDLR.	300.	1000.	—

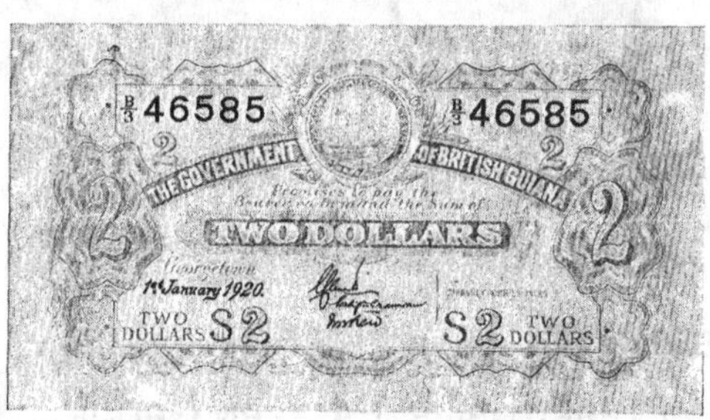

		Good	Fine	XF
2A	**2 Dollars** 1.1.1920; 1.10.1924. Blue. Like #2, but larger format. Sailing ship at upper ctr. 150 x 85mm. Printer: TDLR.	225.	800.	—

#3-5 Deleted.

1929 ISSUE

#6-7 Toucan at l., Kaieteur Falls at ctr., sailing ship seal at r. Portr. Kg. George V at ctr. on back. Larger size notes. Printer: W&S.

		Good	Fine	XF
6	**1 Dollar** 1.1.1929; 1.1.1936. Red.	85.00	375.	—
7	**2 Dollars** 1.1.1929; 1.1.1936. Green.	300.	1000.	—

#8-11 Deleted.

1937-42 ISSUE

#12-17 Like #6-7. Toucan at l., Kaieteur Falls at ctr., sailing ship seal at r. Portr. Kg. George VI at ctr. on back. Reduced size notes. Printer: W&S.

		Good	Fine	XF
12	**1 Dollar** 1937-42. Red. Kg. in 3/4 facing portr. on back.			
	a. 1.6.1937.	15.00	45.00	175.
	b. 1.10.1938.	10.00	30.00	135.
	c. 1.1.1942.	5.00	20.00	125.

		Good	Fine	XF
13	**2 Dollars**			
	1937-42. Green. Like #12. Kg. in 3/4 facing portr. on back.			
	a. 1.6.1937.	20.00	125.	550.
	b. 1.10.1938.	20.00	100.	475.
	c. 1.1.1942.	20.00	85.00	425.

		Good	Fine	XF
14	**5 Dollars**			
	1938; 1942. Olive. Like #12. Kg. in 3/4 facing portr. on back.			
	a. 1.10.1938.	20.00	80.00	400.
	b. 1.1.1942.	15.00	70.00	350.
15	**10 Dollars**			
	1.1.1942. Blue. Facing portr. on back.	200.	800.	—
16	**20 Dollars**			
	1.1.1942. Violet. Like #15. Facing portr. on back.	—	—	—
17	**100 Dollars**			
	Like #12. Yellow. Like #15. Facing portr. on back. Rare.	—	—	—

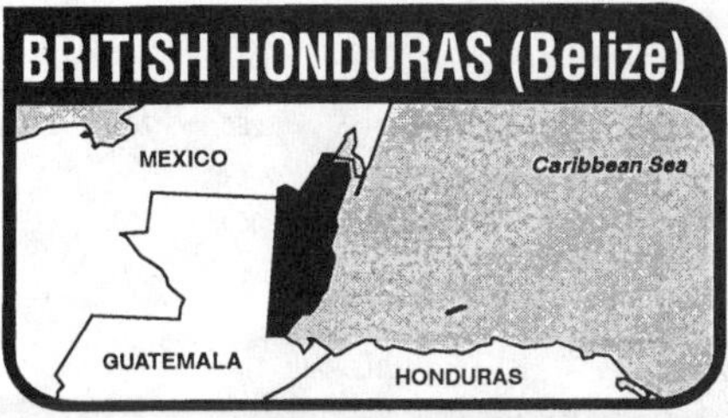

The former British colony of British Honduras is now Belize, a self-governing dependency of the United Kingdom situated in Central America south of Mexico and east and north of Guatemala, has an area of 8,867 sq. mi. (22,965 sq. km.) and a population of 209,000. Capital: Belmopan. Sugar, citrus fruits, chicle and hard woods are exported.

The area, site of the ancient Mayan civilization, was sighted by Columbus in 1502, and settled by shipwrecked English seamen in 1638. British buccaneers settled the former capital of Belize in the 17th century. Britain claimed administrative right over the area after the emancipation of Central America from Spain, and declared it a colony subordinate to Jamaica in 1862. It established as the separate Crown Colony of British Honduras in 1884. The anti-British People's United Party, which attained power in 1954, won a constitution, effective in 1964 which established self-government under a British appointed governor. British Honduras became Belize on June 1, 1973, following the passage of a surprise bill by the Peoples United Party, but the constitutional relationship with Britain remained unchanged.

In Dec. 1975, the U.N. General Assembly adopted a resolution supporting the right of the people of Belize to self-determination, and asking Britain and Guatemala to renew their negotiations on the future of Belize. Belize obtained independence on Sept. 21, 1981.

RULERS:

British

MONETARY SYSTEM:

1 Dollar = 100 Cents

BRITISH HONDURAS

GOVERNMENT OF BRITISH HONDURAS

1894 ISSUE

Note: Usually encountered w/various circular city handstamps on back.

		Good	Fine	XF
1	**1 Dollar**			
	17.10.1894. Blue. Uniface. Usually encountered w/various circular (postal?) city handstamps. Perforated at l. Rare.	—	—	—
2	**2 Dollars**			
	1894. Rare.	—	—	—
3	**5 Dollars**			
	1894. Rare.	—	—	—
4	**10 Dollars**			
	1894. Rare.	—	—	—
5	**50 Dollars**			
	1894. Rare.	—	—	—
6	**100 Dollars**			
	1894. Rare.	—	—	—

1895 ISSUES

#7-12 arms at top ctr. Printer: TDLR (w/o imprint).

		Good	Fine	XF
7	**1 Dollar**			
	1.1.1895. Blue and red. Perforated at l. Arms at top ctr. Back blue.	725.	1750.	—
8	**1 Dollar**			
	1.1.1895. Gray and dk. rd. Straight edge at l. Arms at top ctr. Back gray.	500.	1500.	—
9	**1 Dollar**			
	1.5.1912; 1.3.1920. Arms at top ctr.	550.	1500.	—

		Good	Fine	XF
10	**2 Dollars**			
	1895-1912. Brown and blue. Arms at top ctr. Back brown.			
	a. 1.1.1895. Perforated l. edge. Rare..	—	—	—
	b. 23.2.1904; 1.5.1912. Straight l. edge.	600.	1500.	—
12	**50 Dollars**			
	1.1.1895. Gray-blue and red. Specimen. Rare.	—	—	—

1924 ISSUES

#14-19 arms at top ctr. Printer: TDLR.

		Good	Fine	XF
14	**1 Dollar** 1.5.1924; 1.10.1928. Blue on brown and green unpt. Arms at top ctr. Printer: TDLR. Back blue.	250.	700.	2000.
15	**2 Dollars** 1.5.1924; 1.10.1928. Brown on green unpt. Arms at top ctr. Printer: TDLR.	350.	900.	—

		Good	Fine	XF
16	**5 Dollars** 1.5.1924; 1.10.1928. Green on brown unpt. Arms at top ctr. Printer: TDLR.	600.	1500.	—

		Good	Fine	XF
17	**10 Dollars** 1.5.1924; 1.10.1928. Purple on green and yellow unpt. Arms at top ctr. Printer: TDLR. Back purple. Rare.	—	—	—
18	**50 Dollars** 1.5.1924; 1.10.1928. Arms at top ctr. Printer: TDLR. Rare.	—	—	—
19	**100 Dollars** 1.5.1924; 1.10.1928. Arms at top ctr. Printer: TDLR. Rare.	—	—	—

1939 ISSUE

#20-23 arms at l., portr. Kg.George VI at r.

		VG	VF	UNC
20	**1 Dollar** 2.10.1939; 15.4.1942. Blue on m/c unpt. Arms at l., portr. of Kg. George VI at r.	35.00	250.	1250.
21	**2 Dollars** 2.10.1939; 15.4.1942. Brown on m/c unpt. Arms at l., portr. of Kg. Geor ge VI at r.	60.00	450.	1750.
22	**5 Dollars** 2.10.1939; 15.4.1942. Purple on m/c unpt. Arms at l., portr. of Kg. Geor ge VI at r.	70.00	600.	—
23	**10 Dollars** 2.10.1939; 15.4.1942. Dk. olive-brown on m/c unpt. Arms at l., portr. of Kg. George VI at r.	150.	650.	—

1947 ISSUE

#24-27 arms at l., portr. Kg. George VI at r.

		VG	VF	UNC
24	**1 Dollar** 1947-52. Green on m/c unpt. Arms at l., portr. of Kg. George VI at r.			
	a. 30.1.1947.	35.00	275.	1250.
	b. 1.11.1949; 1.2.1952.	25.00	225.	1150.
25	**2 Dollars** 1947-52. Purple on m/c unpt. Arms at l., portr. of Kg. George VI at r.			
	a. 30.1.1947.	50.00	425.	1450.
	b. 1.11.1949; 1.2.1952.	50.00	375.	1350.
26	**5 Dollars** 1947-52. Red on m/c unpt. Arms at l., portr. of Kg. George VI at r.			
	a. 30.1.1947.	40.00	250.	800.
	b. 1.11.1949; 1.2.1952.	30.00	185.	700.
27	**10 Dollars** 1947-51. Black on m/c unpt. Arms at l., portr. of Kg. George VI at r.			
	a. 30.1.1947.	75.00	275.	—
	b. 1.11.1949.	75.00	275.	—
	c. 1.6.1951.	35.00	175.	800.

1952-53 ISSUE

#28-32 arms at l., portr. Qn. Elizabeth II at r.

		VG	VF	UNC
28	**1 Dollar** 1953-73. Green on m/c unpt.			
	a. 15.4.1953-1.10.1958.	6.00	30.00	225
	b. 1.1.1961-1.5.1969.	5.00	15.00	100.
	c. 1.6.1970-1.1.1973.	5.00	10.00	90.00
	s. As a, b, c. Specimen.	—	—	75.00

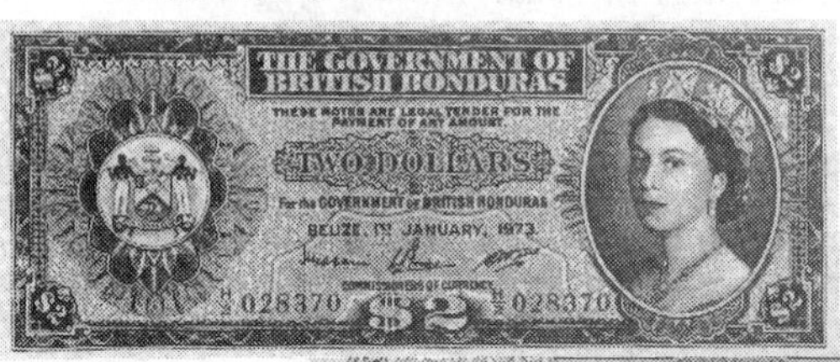

		VG	VF	UNC
29	**2 Dollars** 1953-73. Purple on m/c unpt.			
	a. 15.4.1953-1.10.1958.	10.00	65.00	550
	b. 1.10.1960-1.5.1965.	7.50	30.00	225
	c. 1.1.1971-1.1.1973.	5.00	20.00	175
	s. As a, b, c. Specimen.	—	—	50.00

		VG	VF	UNC
30	**5 Dollars** 1953-73. Red on m/c unpt.			
	a. 15.4.1953-1.10.1958.	15.00	85.00	700
	b. 1.3.1960-1.5.1965.	10.00	45.00	450
	c. 1.1.1970-1.1.1973.	10.00	35.00	275
	s. As a, c. Specimen.	—	—	75.0

		VG	VF	UNC
31	**10 Dollars**			
	1958-73. Black on m/c unpt.			
	a. 1.10.1958-1.11.1961.	35.00	200.	—
	b. 1.4.1964-1.5.1969.	20.00	100.	900.
	c. 1.1.1971-1.1.1973.	15.00	75.00	700.
	s. As a, c. Specimen.	—	—	150.
32	**20 Dollars**			
	1952-73. Brown on m/c unpt.			
	a. 1.12.1952-1.10.1958.	50.00	285.	—
	b. 1.3.1960-1.5.1969.	37.50	200.	1650.
	c. 1.1.1970-1.1.1973.	30.00	175.	1500.
	s. As a, c. Specimen.	—	—	200.

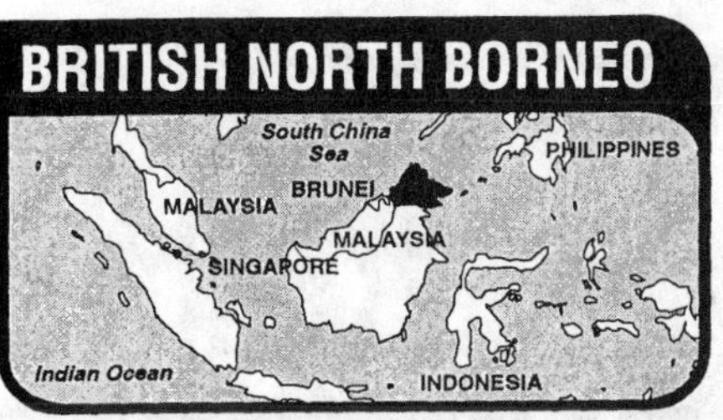

British North Borneo, a former British protectorate and crown colony, occupies the northern tip of the island of Borneo. The island of Labuan, which lies 6 miles off the northwest coast of the island of Borneo, was incorporated with British North Borneo in 1946.

The Portuguese and Spanish established trading relations with Borneo early in the 16th century. Their monopoly was broken by the Dutch and British at the beginning of the 17th century. British North Borneo was administered by the North Borneo Company from 1877 to 1942, and later came under British military control, finally to become a British protectorate. Japan quickly eliminated the British and Dutch forces on Borneo and occupied the entire island during World War II. The island was retaken in 1945, and in July 1946, British North Borneo was made a crown colony. Britain relinquished its sovereignty over the colony in 1963. At that time it joined the Malaysian federation under the name of Sabah.

RULERS:

Japan, 1942-1945
British, 1945-1963

MONETARY SYSTEM:

1 Dollar = 100 Cents

BRITISH ADMINISTRATION

BRITISH NORTH BORNEO COMPANY

1886-96 ISSUE

#1-8 date and sign. varieties. Dates partially or completely handwritten or handstamped on partially printed dates, i.e., 18xx, 189x, etc. Printer: Blades, East & Blades Ltd., London.

		Good	Fine	XF
1	**25 Cents** 11.6.1895; 19.8.1895. Brown. Arms at l. Uniface. Printer: Blades, East & Blades Ltd., London.	175.	600.	—
2	**50 Cents** 20.8.1895. Green. Uniface. Printer: Blades, East & Blades Ltd., London.	200.	650.	—

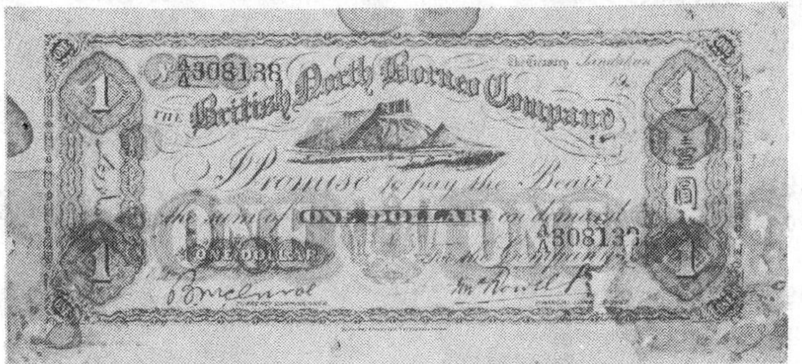

		Good	Fine	XF
3	**1 Dollar** 21.3.1886-8.10.1920. Black on red unpt. Mount Kinabalu at upper ctr. Printer: Blades, East & Blades Ltd., London. Back green. 192 x 89mm.	125.	400.	—
3A	**1 Dollar** 26.2.1920. Black on red unpt. Like #3. 200 x 90mm.	200.	—	—

		Good	Fine	XF
4	**5 Dollars**			
	189x-1926. Black on green unpt. Arms at upper ctr. Back red. Printer: Blades, East & Blades Ltd., London.			
	a. 14.5.189x; 1.10.1901.	300.	800.	—
	b. 10.1914; 14.1.1920; 26.2.1920; 1.12.1922; 7.8.1926.	185.	550.	—

		Good	Fine	XF
5	**10 Dollars** 1896-1926. Black on brown unpt. Mount Kinabalu at upper ctr., arms at l. Printer: Blades, East & Blades Ltd., London. Black blue. 215 x 115mm.			
	a. 3.3.1896; 11.8.1904; 3.1.1905; 25.10.1909; 1.7.1911.	400.	1000.	—
	b. 13.3.1920; 5.3.1921.	275.	700.	—
	c. 1.12.1922; 1.12.1926.	225.	600.	—

1900; 1901 ISSUE

		Good	Fine	XF
7	**25 Cents** 1900-20. Dp. red-brown. Arms at l. Uniface. Printer: Blades, East & Blades Ltd., London.			
	a. 17.10.1900; 1.10.1902; 24.1.1903; 26.11.1903; 5.10.1907.	135.	500.	—
	b. 1.1.1912; 13.10.1913; 3.11.1920.	100.	400.	—
8	**50 Cents** 11.2.1901; 26.11.1902; 9.5.1910. Green. Arms at l. Uniface. 167 x 50mm. Blades, East & Blades Ltd., London.	150.	650.	—

1910 ISSUE

		Good	Fine	XF
10	**50 Cents** 9.5.1910; 1.7.1911. Dp. brown. Arms at l. Uniface. Printer: Blades, East & Blades Ltd., London.	150.	600.	—

1916-1922 ISSUES

#19-23 Mt. Kinabalu at upper ctr.

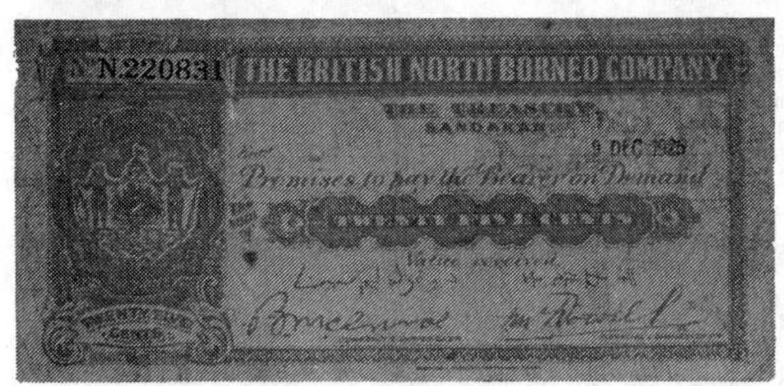

		Good	Fine	XF
12	**25 Cents** 1917-25. Red. Arms at l. Uniface.			
	a. 11.8.1917; 26.3.1919; 9.9.1920. Handstamped dates.	150.	600.	—
	b. 1.3.1921. Printed date.	80.00	250.	800.
	c. 9.12.1925. Handstamped date.	100.	400.	—
13	**50 Cents** 8.11.1916. Black. Arms at l. Uniface. Printer: Blades, East & Blades Ltd., London.	150.	600.	—

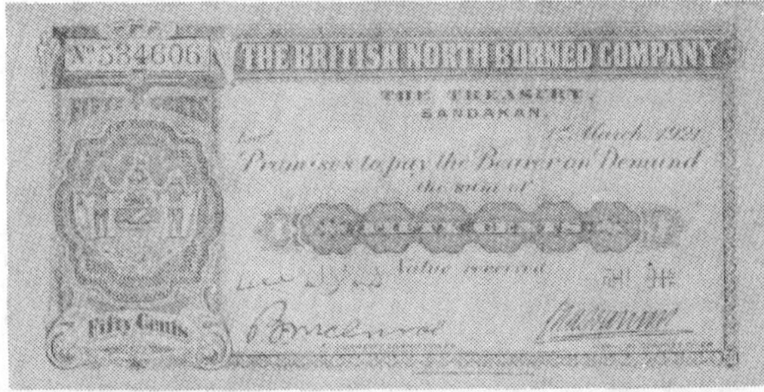

		Good	Fine	XF
14	**50 Cents** 1918-29. Green. Arms at l. Printed or handstamped date.			
	a. 12.6.1918; 26.6.1918; 23.4.1919; 25.2.1920.	150.	600.	—
	b. 1.3.1921; 1.6.1929.	80.00	250.	800.

		Good	Fine	XF
15	**1 Dollar** 30.7.1919; 2.1.1922; 2.5.1922. Black on red unpt. Mount Kinabalu at upper ctr. Printer: Blades, East & Blades Ltd., London. Back green. 184 x 82mm.	100.	300.	650.

		Good	Fine	XF
17	**25 Dollars** Printer: Blades, East & Blades Ltd., London. 1.12.1922-1.1.1927. Black on green unpt. Mount Kinabalu at upper ctr. Back brown. 200 x 123mm.	325.	1000.	—

1927 ISSUES

		Good	Fine	XF
19	**1 Dollar** 1.1.1927. Black on dk. green unpt. Mount Kinabalu at upper ctr. Back gray. 205 x 93mm.	175.	550.	—

		Good	Fine	XF
20	**1 Dollar** 29.7.1927; 1.1.1930. Black on dk. green unpt. Mount Kinabalu at upper ctr. Back gray. 135 x 77mm.	75.00	200.	550.
22	**10 Dollars** 1.1.1927. Black on red-brown unpt. Mount Kinabalu at upper ctr. Back blue-green. 205 x 93mm.	250.	650.	—
23	**25 Dollars** 1.1.1927; 1.7.1929. Black on green. Arms at ctr. Back brown. 201 x 126mm.	325.	1000.	—

1930 ISSUE

		Good	Fine	XF
25	**50 Cents** 1.1.1930. Green. Arms at l. Back green. 129 x 75mm.	55.00	140.	400.

1936; 1938 ISSUE

		Good	Fine	XF
27	**50 Cents** 1.1.1938. Olive-green. Arms at l., w/o *No.* at upper l.	45.00	125.	400.

28	1 Dollar	Good	Fine	XF
	1.1.1936. Black on red unpt. Mount Kinabalu at upper ctr. Printer: Blades, East & Blades Ltd., London. Back black. 123 x 67mm.	22.50	50.00	200.

940 ISSUE

29-32 arms at ctr.

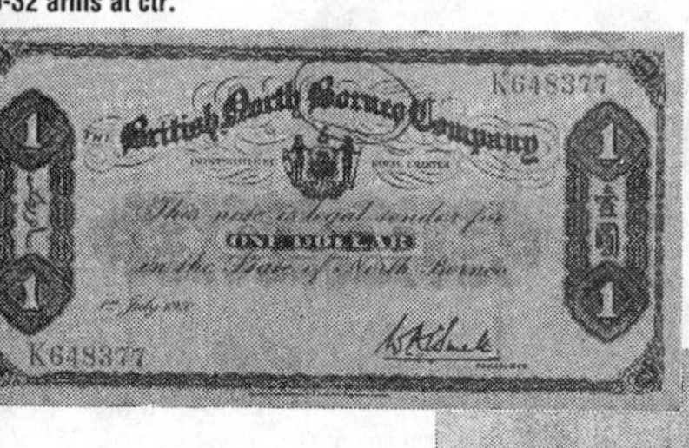

9	1 Dollar	Good	Fine	XF
	1.7.1940. Black on red unpt. Arms at ctr.	25.00	65.00	250.

0	5 Dollars	Good	Fine	XF
	1.1.1940. Black on dk. green unpt. Arms at ctr. Back red. 145 x 76mm.	100.	300.	—
1	10 Dollars			
	1.7.1940. Black on brown unpt. Arms at ctr.	—	—	—
2	25 Dollars			
	1.7.1940. Black on green unpt. Arms at ctr.	—	—	—

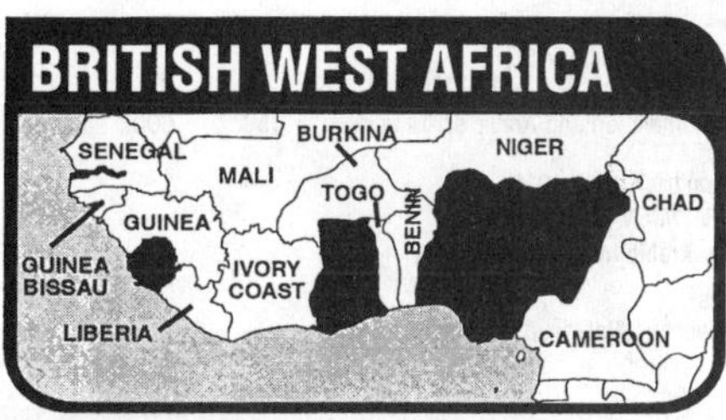

British West Africa was an administrative grouping of the four former British West Africa colonies of Gambia, Sierra Leone, Nigeria and Gold Coast (now Ghana). All are now independent republics and members of the British Commonwealth of Nations. These four colonies were supplied with a common currency by the West African Currency Board from 1907 through 1962.

Also see Gambia, Ghana, Nigeria and Sierra Leone for related currency and for individual statistics and history.

RULERS:

British to 1952

MONETARY SYSTEM:

1 Shilling = 12 Pence
1 Pound = 20 Shillings

BRITISH ADMINISTRATION

WEST AFRICAN CURRENCY BOARD

1916-20 ISSUE

#2-5 various date and sign. varieties.

1	1 Shilling	Good	Fine	XF
	30.11.1918. Black. Salmon paper. Coin w/palm tree at lower ctr. Uniface.			
	a. Issued note.	15.00	85.00	350.
	s. Specimen.	—	Unc	350.

#2-6 palm tree at ctr. Printer: W&S.

2	2 Shillings	Good	Fine	XF
	1916-18. Blue-gray. Palm tree at ctr. Printer: W&S.			
	a. 30.6.1916. Uniface.	125.	500.	—
	b. 30.3.1918. Arabic script on back.	65.00	200.	500.
3	5 Shillings			
	1.3.1920. Red-brown. (Not issued). Reported not confirmed.	—	—	—
4	10 Shillings			
	1916-18. Green. W/*10* at l. and r.			
	a. 31.3.1916. Uniface.	—	—	—
	b. 30.3.1918. Arabic script on back.	125.	500.	—
	s. Specimen. Arabic script on back. 31.3.1916.	—	—	—

		Good	Fine	XF
5	**20 Shillings** 1916-18. Black. Red *20* at l. and r. Printer: W&S.			
	a. 31.3.1916. Uniface.	—	—	—
	b. 30.3.1918. Back black, Denomination and Arabic script in black on back.	150.	600.	—
	s1. Specimen. Arabic script on back. 31.3.1916.	—	—	—
	s2. Specimen perforated: *SPECIMEN*. 30.3.1918.	—	—	1,000

Note: Color trials exist for #4a and 5a but w/Arabic inscription on back.

6	**100 Shillings = 5 Pounds** 1.3.1919. Black. Palm tree at lower ctr. (Not issued). Printer: W&S. Rare.	—	—	—

1928 ISSUE

#7 and 8 palm tree at ctr. Printer: W&S.

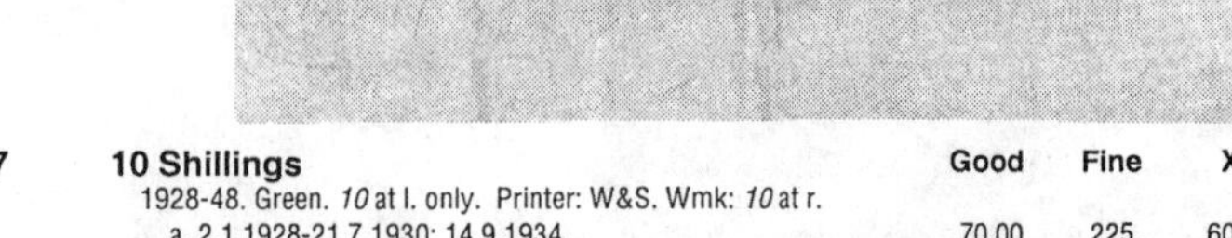

		Good	Fine	XF
7	**10 Shillings** 1928-48. Green. *10* at l. only. Printer: W&S. Wmk: *10* at r.			
	a. 2.1.1928-21.7.1930; 14.9.1934.	70.00	225.	600.
	b. 4.1.1937-24.12.1948.	10.00	45.00	250.

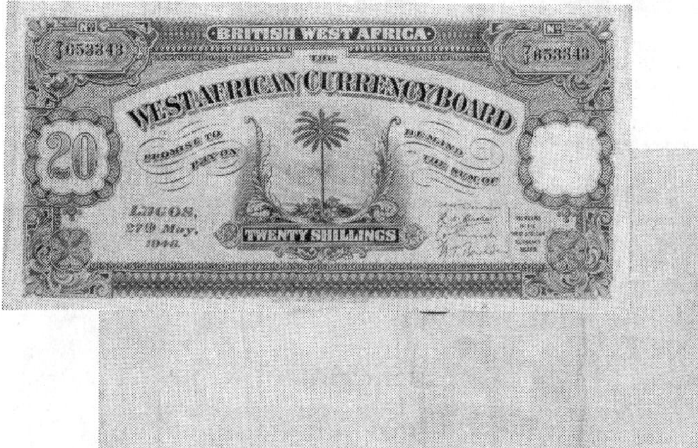

		Good	Fine	XF
8	**20 Shillings** 1928-51. Black and red on lt. green and pink unpt. *20* at l. only. Denomination and Arabic script in black. Printer: W&S. Wmk: *20* at r.			
	a. 2.1.1928-21.7.1930; 14.9.1934.	50.00	200.	450.
	b. 4.1.1937-2.7.1951.	7.50	25.00	160.

1953-54 ISSUE

#9-11 river scene w/palm trees at l. Printer: W&S.

		VG	VF	UNC
9	**10 Shillings** 31.3.1953-4.2.1958. Black and green. River scene w/palm trees at l. Field workers on back.			
	a. Issued note.	12.50	45.00	250.
	s. Specimen.	—	—	150.

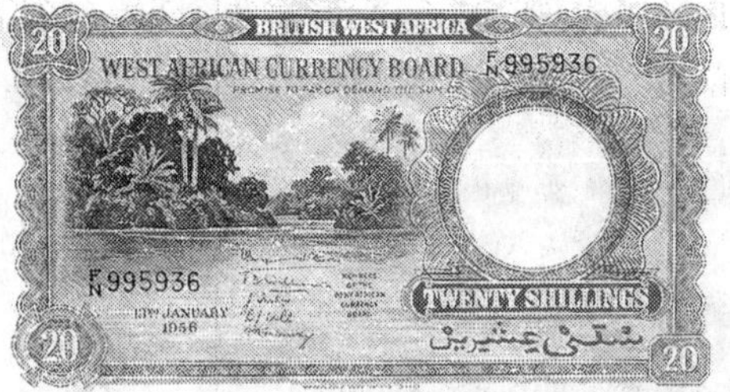

		VG	VF	UNC
10	**20 Shillings** 31.3.1953-20.1.1957. Black and red. River scene w/palm trees at l. Harvesting on back.			
	a. Issued note.	10.00	35.00	225.
	s. Specimen.	—	—	200.

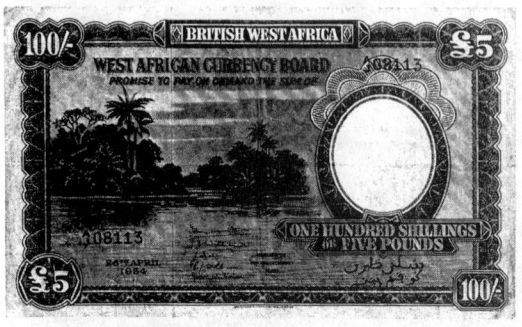

		Good	Fine	XF
11	**100 Shillings = 5 Pounds** 1953-54. Blue. River scene w/palm trees at l. Man harvesting on back.			
	a. 31.3.1953.	35.00	150.	550.
	b. 26.4.1954.	35.00	150.	525.
	s. Specimen.	—	—	350.

		VG	VF	UNC
11A	**1000 Pounds** 26.4.1954. Black. Uniface. Specimen.	—	—	5,000

The Republic of Bulgaria (formerly the Peoples Republic of Bulgaria), a Balkan country on the Black Sea in southeastern Europe, has an area of 42,855 sq. mi. (110,993 sq. km.) and a population of 8.31 million. Capital: Sofia. Agriculture remains a key component of the economy but industrialization, particularly he- avy industry, has been emphasized since the late 1940's. Machinery, tobacco and cigarettes, wines and spirits, clothing and metals are the chief exports.

The area now occupied by Bulgaria was conquered by the Bulgars, an Asiatic tribe, in the 7th century. Bulgarian kingdoms continued to exist on the peninsula until it came under Turkish rule in 1395. In 1878, after nearly 500 years of Turkish rule, Bulgaria was made a principality under Turkish suzerainty. Union seven years later with Eastern Rumelia created a Balkan state with borders approximating those of present-day Bulgaria. A Bulgarian kingdom fully independent of Turkey was proclaimed Sept. 22, 1908.

During WWI Bulgaria had been aligned with Germany. After the Armistice certain land concessions were granted to Greece and Romania. In 1934 King Boris III suspended all political parties and established a dictatorial monarchy. In 1938 the military began rearming through the aid of the Anglo-French loan. As WWII developed Bulgaria again supported the Germans but Boris protected its Jewish community. Boris died mysteriously in 1943 and Simeon II became king at the age of six. The country was then ruled by a pro-Nazi regency until it was invaded by Soviet forces in 1944. The monarchy was abolished and Simeon was ousted by plebiscite in 1946, and Bulgaria became a People's Republic in the Soviet pattern. Following demonstrations and a general strike, the communist government resigned in Nov. 1990. A new government was elected in Oct. 1991.

Thrace, a name applied at various periods to areas of different extent, is a territory divided at present between Greece, Turkey and Bulgaria. Bulgaria's claim came as a result of the end of the first Balkan War of 1912, at which time it took control of most of Thrace.

The second Balkan War altered this status but the whole area remained in turmoil until after the end of World War I. At that point, Greece had taken most of Thrace, but the Allies believed Bulgaria needed an economic outlet to the Aegean Sea. Article 48 of the Treaty of Neuilly declared that Bulgaria had the right of transit over its former Thracian territory to the various ports assigned to Greece. Nothing worked out as planned, and the area was again reapportioned in 1923.

RULERS:

Alexander I, 1879-1886
Ferdinand I, as Prince, 1887-1908
Ferdinand I, as King, 1908-1918
Boris III, 1918-1943
Simeon II, 1943-1946

MONETARY SYSTEM:

1 Lev LHV = 100 Stotinki STOTINKI until 1999

KINGDOM

БЪЛГАРСКАТА НАРОДНА БАНКА

BULGARIAN NATIONAL BANK

1885-87 GOLD ISSUE

#A1-A3 printer: ЗПГБ St. Petersburg, Russia. Sign. varieties.

#A1 and A2 arms at upper l.

		Good	Fine	XF
A1	**20 Leva Zlato** 1.8.1885. Lt. ochre.	200.	575.	—
A2	**50 Leva Zlato** 1.8.1885. Lt. green.	300.	750.	—

		Good	Fine	XF
A3	**100 Leva Zlato** 1887. Blue-gray and ochre. Arms at l., woman seated w/child at r. Back blue, pale blue and ochre; floral spray at ctr.	300.	1000.	—

1890 ND GOLD ISSUE

#A4 and A5 printer: BWC. Sign. varieties.

		Good	Fine	XF
A4	**5 Leva Zlato** ND (1890). Black on brown unpt. Arms at l. Back dk. brown; farmer plowing with 2 horses at ctr. Like #A6.	100.	500.	—

		Good	Fine	XF
A5	**10 Leva Zlato** ND (1890). Black on blue and ochre unpt. Farm girl carrying roses at l., arms at r. Back blue; shepherd tending flock of sheep at ctr. Like #A7.	150.	650.	—

1899 ND SILVER ISSUE

#A6 and A7 printer: BWC.

		Good	Fine	XF
A6	**5 Leva Srebro** ND (1899). Black on brown unpt. Like #A4. Arms at l. Back dk. brown; farmer plowing w/2 horses.	100.	500.	—
A7	**10 Leva Srebro** ND (1899). Black on blue and ochre unpt. Like #A5. Farm girl carrying roses at l., arms at r. Back blue; shepherd tending flock of sheep at ctr.	100.	500.	—

		Good	Fine	XF
A8	**50 Leva Srebro** ND (1899 -old date 1.8.1885). Lt. green. Arms at upper l. *ZLATO* crossed out. Ovpt: *SREBRO* on #A2.	250.	900.	—

1904-09 ND Silver Issue

#1-6 by Orlov. Denomination in *LEVA SREBRO* w/o wmk., various sign. varieties. Printed in St. Petersburg, Russia (w/o imprint). Vertical format.

		Good	Fine	XF
1	**5 Leva Srebro** ND (1904). Black on red, gray-green and m/c unpt. Arms w/o inscription at ctr. on back.			
	a. Issued note.	6.50	25.00	90.00
	s. Specimen.	—	Unc	125.

		Good	Fine	XF
2	**5 Leva Srebro** ND (1909). Black on green, lilac and m/c unpt. Arms w/ЦАРСТВО БЪЛГАРИЯ on back.			
	a. 2 serial #.	4.00	20.00	75.00
	b. 4 serial #.	4.00	20.00	75.00
	s. Specimen.	—	Unc	110.

		Good	Fine	XF
3	**10 Leva Srebro** ND (1904). Dk. green on m/c unpt. Arms at upper ctr. on back.			
	a. 2 serial #.	4.00	20.00	75.00
	b. 4 serial #.	4.00	20.00	75.00
	s. Specimen.	—	Unc	110.
4	**50 Leva Srebro** ND (1904). M/c. Arms at ctr. on back.			
	a. Issued note.	20.00	80.00	275.
	s. Specimen.	—	Unc	300.
5	**100 Leva Srebro** ND (1904). M/c. Arms at upper ctr. on back.			
	a. Issued note.	40.00	135.	500.
	s. Specimen.	—	Unc	525.
6	**500 Leva Srebro** ND (1907). M/c. Arms at upper ctr. on back.			
	a. Issued note.	250.	500.	1400.
	s. Specimen.	—	Unc	1850.

Note: #3-6 also exist w/various Serbian handstamps. These are valued at 25-50% more.

1904 ND Provisional Gold Issue

		Good	Fine	XF
7	**5 Leva Zlato** ND (1907). Black on red, gray-green and m/c unpt. Like #1 but w/СРЕБРО crossed out. Arms at ctr. Ovpt: ЗЛАТО at l. and r.	15.00	75.00	250.
8	**10 Leva Zlato** ND (1907). Dk. green on m/c. Like #3 but w/СРЕБРО crossed out. Arms at ctr. Ovpt: ЗЛАТО at l. and r.	17.50	75.00	250.

Note: #7 and 8 also exist w/various Serbian handstamps. They are valued at 25-50% more.

1904-07 ND Gold Issue

#9-12 by Orlov. Arms at upper ctr., denomination in *LEVA ZLATO*, w/o wmk., sign varieties. Horizontal format. Printed in St. Petersburg, Russia (w/o imprint).

		Good	Fine	XF
9	**20 Leva Zlato** ND (1904). Black text and arms, edge pink, frame red and blue. Arms at upper ctr.			
	a. Black sign.	3.00	15.00	60.00
	b. Blue sign.	3.00	15.00	60.00
	s. Specimen.	—	Unc	200.
10	**50 Leva Zlato** ND (1907). Black text and arms, edge pink, frame blue and green. Arms at upper ctr.			
	a. Issued note.	10.00	40.00	150.
	s. Specimen.	—	Unc	275.
11	**100 Leva Zlato** ND (1906). Black text and arms, edge pink, frame lt. blue. Arms at upper ctr. Arms at l. ctr. on back.			
	a. Issued note.	30.00	100.	300.
	s. Specimen.	—	Unc	400.

		Good	Fine	XF
12	**500 Leva Zlato** ND (1907). Black text and arms, edge green, frame pink and green. Arms at upper ctr.			

	Good	Fine	XF
a. Issued note.	125.	300.	750.
s. Specimen.	—	Unc	1000.

ote: #9-12 also exist w/various Serbian handstamps. They are valued at 25-50% more.

916 КАСОВ БОНЪ (CASHIER'S BOND) ISSUE

3	1000 Leva Zlatni	Good	Fine	XF
	10.5.1916. Lt. blue-green. Bulgarian printing. Watermark: Wmk: Cross and curl pattern.Wmk: Cross and curl pattern.			
	a. Issued note.	150.	400.	800.
	s. Specimen.	—	Unc	1000.

te: #13 exists w/various Serbian handstamps. These are valued at 25-50% more.

916 ND SILVER ISSUE

4-20 printer: RDK (w/o imprint). Wmk: Cross and curl pattern.

4	1 Lev Srebro	Good	Fine	XF
	ND (1916). Black on green and blue unpt. Cross and curl pattern. Back blue on lilac unpt.			
	a. Issued note.	.25	2.00	8.50
	s. Specimen.	—	Unc	30.00

5	2 Leva Srebro	Good	Fine	XF
	ND (1916). Black on green and pink unpt. Back red on tan unpt.			
	a. Issued note.	.50	4.00	12.50
	s. Specimen.	—	Unc	35.00

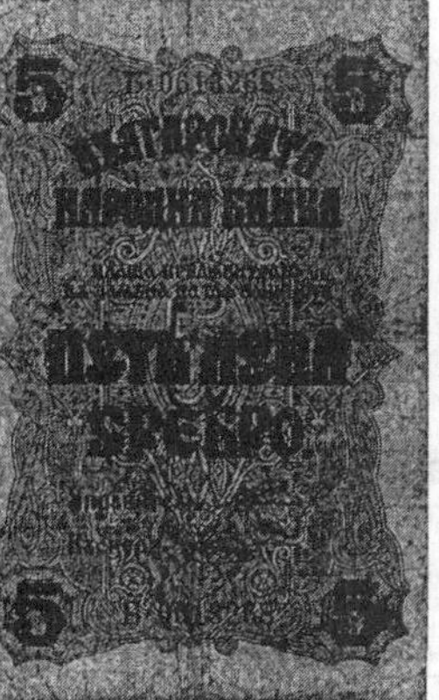

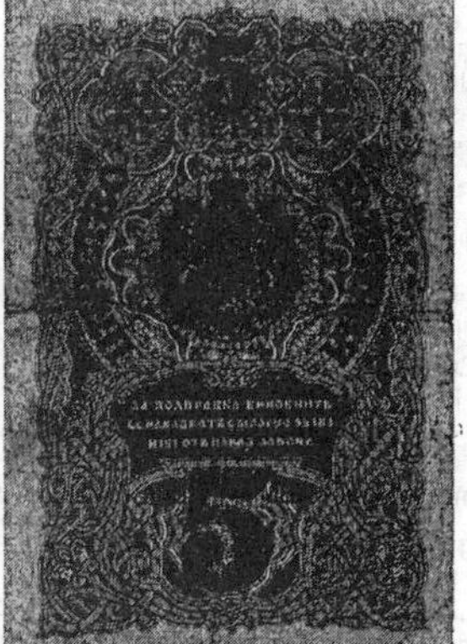

6	5 Leva Srebro	Good	Fine	XF
	ND (1916). Black on blue and gray unpt. Arms at upper ctr. on back Off-white paper.			
	a. Issued note.	.75	6.00	25.00
	s. Specimen.	—	Unc	40.00

17	10 Leva Srebro	Good	Fine	XF
	ND (1916). Black text, edge blue-green, ornament red and lilac. Back dk. brown on green unpt.; arms at upper ctr.			
	a. Issued note.	1.00	7.00	35.00
	s. Specimen.	—	Unc	45.00

Note: #14-17 exist w/various Serbian handstamps. These are valued at 25-50% more.

1916 ND GOLD ISSUE

#18-20 arms at upper ctr. Wmk: Cross and curl pattern. Printer: RDK (w/o imprint). Horizontal format.

18	20 Leva Zlato	Good	Fine	XF
	ND (1916). Black on green unpt. Arms at upper ctr.			
	a. Issued note.	4.00	22.50	65.00
	s. Specimen.	—	Unc	75.00
19	50 Leva Zlato			
	ND (1916). Black on orange-brown unpt. Arms at upper ctr. Back brown and blue; arms at ctr.			
	a. Issued note.	10.00	35.00	150.
	s. Specimen.	—	Unc	165.

20	100 Leva Zlato	Good	Fine	XF
	ND (1916). Black text and arms, edge green, ornament blue, lilac and violet. Arms at upper ctr.			
	a. W/o series. Serial # w/o prefix letter.	4.00	20.00	80.00
	b. Serial # w/prefix letter.	2.00	18.00	70.00
	c. As b, w/ СЕРИЯ А (Series A) at upper l. and lower r.	70.00	200.	550.
	s. As a. Specimen.	—	Unc	110.

Note: #18-20 exist w/various Serbian handstamps. These are valued at 25-50% more.

1917 ND ISSUE

#21-25 printer: G&D, Leipzig. Wmk: БНБ (BNB).

21	5 Leva Srebrni	Good	Fine	XF
	ND (1917). Black on olive and lilac unpt. Arms at top ctr. Back lilac on green unpt.; crown at ctr.			
	a. Issued note.	.50	3.00	17.50
	s. Specimen.	—	Unc	50.00

22	10 Leva Zlatni	Good	Fine	XF
	ND (1917; 1922). Black on lt. green and pink unpt. Arms at top ctr. Back green on pink unpt.			
	a. Arms w/supporters w/o flags. (1917).	.75	4.00	22.50
	b. Arms w/supporters w/o flags. serial # (1922).	5.00	25.00	75.00
	s1. As a. Specimen.	—	Unc	65.00
	s2. As b. Specimen.	—	Unc	110.

23	20 Leva Zlatni	Good	Fine	XF
	ND (1917). Brown on lt. blue-green and pink unpt. Arms at top ctr. Initials (BNB) in unpt. at ctr. Back lilac on green unpt.			
	a. Issued note.	1.00	5.00	45.00
	s. Specimen.	—	Unc	75.00

24	50 Leva Zlatni	Good	Fine	X
	ND (1917). Brown on blue, green and salmon unpt. Arms at upper l. Back brown on green unpt.			
	a. Serial # begins w/*No.*	3.00	15.00	65.0
	b. Serial # begins w/prefix letter.	2.00	12.50	60.0
	s. Specimen.	—	Unc	90.0

25	100 Leva Zlatni	Good	Fine	X
	ND (1917). Green, ochre, purple and pink. Portr. woman w/sheaf at l.			
	a. Issued note.	12.50	45.00	20
	s. Specimen.	—	Unc	22

Note: #21-25 also exist w/various Serbian handstamps. They are valued at 25-50% more.

1918 Treasury Bond Issue

26	1000 Leva Zlatni	Good	Fine	
	ND (1918). Blue-green and tan. Arms at l. Printer: Gebr. Parcus, Munich.			
	a. Issued note.	8.00	40.00	1
	s. Specimen.	—	Unc	2

1919 Treasury Bond Issue

#27 and 28 red diagonal ovpt. on invalidated state treasury bill issue of 1918.

		Good	Fine
27	500 Leva Zlatni 1919. Rare.	—	—
28	5000 Leva Zlatni 1919. Rare.	—	—

1919 ND Provisional Treasury Bond Issue

#29 red diagonal ovpt. on invalidated state treasury bill issue of 1918.

29	10,000 Leva Zlatni 1919. Rare.	—	—

NOTICE

Readers with unlisted dates, signature varieties, etc. are invited to sub mit photocopies or, high resolution (300 dpi, 100% size) scans of thei notes to: Standard Catalog of World Paper Money, 700 East State St Iola, WI 54990-0001, or E-Mail: george.cuhaj@fwpubs.com.

1920 ND Silver Issue

#30 and 31 printer: W&S.

		Good	Fine	XF
30	**1 Lev Srebro** ND (1920). Dk. green and brown. Arms at l., woman at r. Back brown; old Bank bldg. at ctr.			
	a. Issued note.	.25	2.00	12.50
	s. Specimen.	—	Unc	25.00

		Good	Fine	XF
31	**2 Leva Srebro** ND (1920). Dk. brown and yellow. Woman at l., arms at r. Back lt. green; National Assembly bldg. at ctr.			
	a. Issued note.	.50	3.00	17.50
	s. Specimen.	—	Unc	30.00

1920 ND Treasury Bond Issue

		Good	Fine	XF
32	**500 Leva Zlato** ND (1920). Black on green and ochre. Portr. Kg. Boris III at l., woman at r. Arms at ctr. on back.			
	a. Issued note.	—	Unc	1250.
	s. Specimen.	—	Unc	1100.

		Good	Fine	XF
33	**1000 Leva Zlatni** ND (1920). Blue-green and tan. Like #26. Arms at l. Like #26. Printer: BWC.			
	a. Issued note.	8.00	40.00	175.
	s. Specimen.	—	Unc	200.

1922 Issue

#34-40 arms at ctr. Printer: ABNC.

		Good	Fine	XF
34	**5 Leva** 1922. Brown on lt. orange and green unpt. Back brown and green; beehives at ctr.			
	a. Issued note.	.75	4.50	30.00
	s. Specimen. Ovpt: ОБРАЗЕЦЪ.	—	Unc	40.00

		Good	Fine	XF
35	**10 Leva** 1922. Purple on orange and green unpt. Back purple and brown; farm woman w/turkey at ctr.			
	a. Issued note.	1.00	6.00	50.00
	s. Specimen. Ovpt: ОБРАЗЕЦЪ.	—	Unc	55.00
36	**20 Leva** 1922. Green on blue, lt. green and orange unpt. Back orange and olive-gray; farm women working at ctr.			
	a. Issued note.	3.00	15.00	85.00
	s. Specimen. Ovpt: ОБРАЗЕЦЪ.	—	Unc	100.
37	**50 Leva** 1922. Green and m/c. Back green; boy shepherd w/flute at ctr.			
	a. Issued note.	5.00	25.00	150.
	s. Specimen. Ovpt: ОБРАЗЕЦЪ.	—	Unc	125.

		Good	Fine	XF
38	**100 Leva** 1922. Brown and m/c. Back brown; man plowing w/oxen at ctr.			
	a. Issued note.	10.00	45.00	200.
	s. Specimen. Ovpt: ОБРАЗЕЦЪ.	—	Unc	200.
39	**500 Leva** 1922. Blue and m/c. Arms at ctr. Back blue; harbor scene.			
	a. Issued note.	25.00	90.00	300.
	s. Specimen. Ovpt: ОБРАЗЕЦЪ.	—	Unc	250.
40	**1000 Leva** 1922. Red-brown, green and pink. Back brown; picking cotton at ctr.			
	a. Issued note.	40.00	175.	550.
	s. Specimen. Ovpt: ОБРАЗЕЦЪ.	—	Unc	500.

1924 Issue

		Good	Fine	XF
41	**5000 Leva** 1924. Green, brown-violet and m/c. Arms at l., portr. Kg. Boris III at r. Man at l. on back.			
	a. Issued note.	75.00	250.	600.
	s. Specimen ovpt: ОБРАЗЕЦЪ.	—	Unc	1200.

1924 ND Provisional Treasury Bond Issue

		Good	Fine	XF
42	**1000 Leva Zlatni** ND (1924). Blue-green and tan. Arms at l. Red Cyrillic ovpt: *"This note is only valid within the kingdom"* w/additional red series and serial # at upper l. on #26.	35.00	150.	400.

		Good	Fine	XF
43	**1000 Leva Zlatni** ND (1924). Blue-green and tan. Arms at l. Red Cyrillic ovpt: *"This note is only valid within the kingdom"* w/additional red series letter and serial # at upper l. on #33.	35.00	150.	400.

1925 ISSUE

#45-49 portr. Kg. Boris III at r. Printer: BWC.

		VG	VF	UNC
45	**50 Leva** 1925. Brown on m/c unpt. Portr. Kg. Boris III at r., Arms at l. Printer: BWC. Back blue; farm women working at ctr.			
	a. Issued note.	3.00	17.50	60.00
	s. Specimen.	—	—	65.00

		VG	VF	UNC
46	**100 Leva** 1925. ~~Dk. blue on~~ m/c unpt. Portr. Kg. Boris III at r., Arms at l. Printer: BWC. Back dk. green; people gathered in front of house at ctr.			
	a. Issued note.	4.50	20.00	75.00
	s. Specimen.	—	—	75.00
47	**500 Leva** 1925. Dk. green on m/c unpt. Portr. Kg. Boris III at r. Printer: BWC. Man w/oxen on back.			
	a. Issued note.	12.50	85.00	250.
	s. Specimen.	—	—	265.
48	**1000 Leva** 1925. Brown on m/c unpt. Portr. Kg. Boris III at r. Printer: BWC. Allegorical figure on back.			
	a. Issued note.	20.00	100.	350.
	s. Specimen.	—	—	375.
49	**5000 Leva** 1925. Purple on m/c unpt. Portr. Kg. Boris III at r., Arms at l. Printer: BWC. Aleksandr Nevski Cathedral, Sofia, on back.			
	a. Issued note.	55.00	225.	550.
	s. Specimen.	—	—	500.

1928 ND ISSUE

		VG	VF	UNC
49A	**20 Leva** ND (1928). Ochre and brown. Portr. Kg. Boris III at ctr. Salt-cellars on back.			
	a. Issued note.	7.00	40.00	165.
	s. Specimen.	—	—	175.

1929 ISSUE

#50-54 portr. Kg. Boris III at r. Printer: TDLR.

		VG	VF	UNC
50	**200 Leva** 1929. Black on olive and lt. blue unpt. Kg. Boris III at r., Arms at bottom ctr. Printer: TDLR. Back green; old man at ctr. Wmk: Rampant lion.			
	a. Issued note.	1.50	10.00	45.00
	s. Specimen.	—	—	55.00

#51-55 arms at l.

		VG	VF	UNC
51	**250 Leva** 1929. Black and purple on peach unpt. Kg. Boris III at r., arms at l. Printer: TDLR. Back purple; aerial view of Tirnovo at ctr.			
	a. Issued note.	3.00	15.00	70.00
	s. Specimen.	—	—	85.00
52	**500 Leva** 1929. Blue and m/c. Kg. Boris III at r., Arms at l. Printer: TDLR. River canyon on back.			
	a. Issued note.	9.00	50.00	150.
	s. Specimen.	—	—	150.
53	**1000 Leva** 1929. Red-brown on lt. green and tan unpt. Kg. Boris III at r., arms at l. Printer: TDLR. Mountain lake on back.			
	a. Issued note.	25.00	125.	350.
	s. Specimen.	—	—	350.
54	**5000 Leva** 1929. Brown and brown-violet. Kg. Boris III at r., arms at l. Printer: TDLR. Monastery on back.			
	a. Issued note.	90.00	225.	500.
	s. Specimen.	—	—	500.

1938 Issue

#55-57 portr. Kg. Boris III at l. Printer: G&D.

		VG	VF	UNC
55	**500 Leva** 1938. Lilac, brown and green. Arms at r. Sheaf of wheat at r. on back. Wmk: Woman's head.			
	a. Issued note.	8.00	45.00	135.
	s. Specimen.	—	—	110.
56	**1000 Leva** 1938. Lilac, brown and green. Printer: G&D. Flowers on back. Wmk: Child's head.			
	a. Issued note.	12.50	80.00	275.
	s. Specimen.	—	—	225.
57	**5000 Leva** 1938. Green. New bank bldg. on back.			
	a. Issued note.	65.00	200.	600.
	s. Specimen.	—	—	450.

1940 Issue

#58 and 59 portr. Kg. Boris III at r., arms at l. Printer: RDK.

		VG	VF	UNC
58	**500 Leva** 1940. Blue on green unpt. Arms at l. Boat at dockside on back.			
	a. Issued note.	1.50	15.00	75.00
	s. Specimen.	—	—	85.00

		VG	VF	UNC
59	**1000 Leva** 1940. Red and brown. Man plowing w/oxen on back.			
	a. Issued note.	3.00	30.00	100.
	s. Specimen.	—	—	120.

NOTICE

Readers with unlisted dates, signature varieties, etc. are invited to submit photocopies or, high resolution (300 dpi, 100% size) scans of their notes to: Standard Catalog of World Paper Money, 700 East State St. Iola, WI 54990-0001, or E-Mail: george.cuhaj@fwpubs.com.

1942 Issue

#60-62 portr. Kg. Boris III at l. Wmk: БНБ (BNB). Printer: G&D.

		VG	VF	UNC
60	**500 Leva** 1942. Black and blue on green and brown unpt. Woman at r. on back.			
	a. Issued note.	.75	7.00	30.00
	s. Specimen.	—	—	45.00

		VG	VF	UNC
61	**1000 Leva** 1942. Lt. and dk. brown on orange and blue unpt. Monastery at r. on back.			
	a. Issued note.	1.00	12.50	45.00
	s. Specimen.	—	—	65.00
62	**5000 Leva** 1942. Brown and m/c. National Assembly bldg. on back.			
	a. Issued note.	4.00	40.00	150.
	s. Specimen.	—	—	200.

1943 Issue

		VG	VF	UNC
63	**20 Leva** 1943. Blue-black on lt. red unpt. Year date in lower r. margin. Back brown; arms at l.			
	a. Issued note.	.50	2.50	35.00
	s. Specimen perforated: *MUSTER*.	—	—	60.00

#64-66 portr. young Kg. Simeon II at l., arms at r. #64-67A printer: RDK.

64	200 Leva	VG	VF	UNC
	1943. Brown and black. View of Tirnovo on back.			
	a. Issued note.	1.50	7.50	30.00
	s. Specimen perforated: *MUSTER*.	—	—	60.00

65	250 Leva	VG	VF	UNC
	1943. Green and brown. Man w/oxen on back.			
	a. Issued note.	1.50	7.50	30.00
	s. Specimen perforated: *MUSTER*.	—	—	60.00

66	500 Leva	VG	VF	UNC
	1943. Blue on brown unpt. Back blue and brown; boy shepherd w/flute.			
	a. Issued note.	1.00	6.00	25.00
	s. Specimen perforated: *MUSTER*.	—	—	50.00

67	1000 Leva	VG	VF	UNC
	1943. Red and dk. brown on purple unpt. Portr. Kg. Simeon II at r., arms at l. Nevski Cathedral on back.			
	a. W/normal serial #. (Not issued).	—	—	150
	s. Specimen perforated: *MUSTER*.	—	—	150

67A	5000 Leva			
	1943. Brown and red. Portr. Kg. Simeon II at r., arms at l. Back orange and green; rose harvest scene. Specimen perforated: *MUSTER*.	—	Unc	1850

STATE TREASURY

1942 ISSUE

#67B-67F arms at r. (Not issued).

		Good	Fine	XF
67B	**1000 Leva** 25.3.1942. Arms at r.			
67C	**5000 Leva** 15.12.1942. Red on blue and pink unpt. Arms at r. Back red on green and brown unpt.			
67D	**10,000 Leva** 15.12.1942. Brown on blue and pink unpt. Arms at r.			
67E	**20,000 Leva** 5.12.1942. Gray on green and purple unpt. Arms at r.			
67F	**50,000 Leva** 5.12.1942. Blue on green and purple unpt. Arms at r.			

1943 ISSUES

#67G-67J arms at r.

Note: Reportedly used as currency during and after WWII.

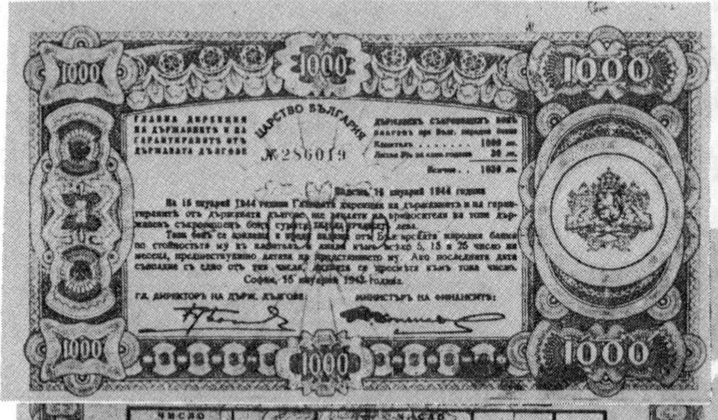

		VG	VF	UNC
67G	**1000 Leva** 15.1.1943. Orange on lt. blue and ochre unpt. Arms at r. Back orange on green unpt.	25.00	50.00	100.
67H	**1000 Leva** 25.1.1943. Green on lt. blue and orange unpt. Arms at r. Back green on grayish green and ochre unpt.	25.00	50.00	100.
67I	**1000 Leva** 15.6.1943. Brownish orange on m/c unpt. Arms at r. Back blue on orange and blue unpt.	50.00	100.	200.
67J	**5000 Leva** 15.6.1943. Green on m/c unpt. Arms at r. Back blue on orange and blue unpt. (Not issued).	100.	300.	500.

1944 ISSUE

67K-67N arms at r.

Note: Reportedly used as currency during and after WWII.

		VG	VF	UNC
67K	**1000 Leva** 15.1.1944. Blue on green and purple unpt. Arms at r.	25.00	50.00	100.
67L	**1000 Leva** 5.7.1944. Lt. brown on green and ochre unpt. Arms at r.	25.00	50.00	100.
67M	**1000 Leva** 15.11.1944. Ochre on pink and yellow. Arms at r. Back dk. brown on lt. blue and ochre unpt.	20.00	40.00	80.00
67N	**5000 Leva** 15.11.1944. Brown on gray and lt. brown. Arms at r. Back orange on lt. blue and ochre unpt.	20.00	40.00	80.00

1944-45 ISSUE

67O and 67P arms at upper ctr.

Note: Reportedly used as currency during and after WWII.

		VG	VF	UNC
67O	**1000 Leva** 5.3.1945. Brown on lt. brown and lt. blue unpt. Arms at upper ctr. Back green on lt. brown unpt.	15.00	25.00	40.00

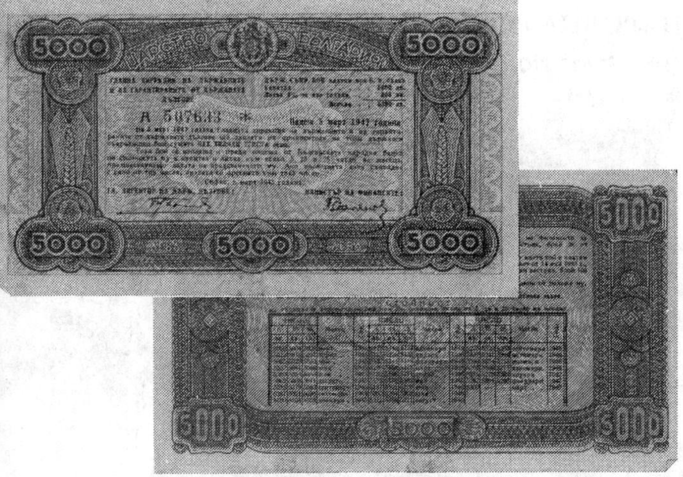

		VG	VF	UNC
67P	**5000 Leva** 5.3.1945. Purple on yellow and gray unpt. Arms at upper ctr. Back ochre on lt. brown and yellow unpt.	20.00	35.00	60.00

1946 ISSUE

67Q and 67R modified arms at upper ctr.

Note: Reportedly used as currency after WWII.

		VG	VF	UNC
67Q	**1000 Leva** 5.11.1946. Dk. blue on lt. blue and pink unpt.	15.00	25.00	40.00
67R	**5000 Leva** 5.11.1946. Red on lt. green and pink unpt.	20.00	35.00	60.00

RUSSIAN ADMINISTRATION

БЪЛГАРСКАТА НАРОДНА БАНКА

BULGARIAN NATIONAL BANK

1944-45 ISSUE

		VG	VF	UNC
68	**20 Leva** 1944. Brown. Year date in lower right margin. Arms at ctr. on back.			
	a. Red serial # w/star. Salmon unpt.	1.00	4.00	25.00
	b. Brown serial # w/o star. Lt. orange unpt.	.75	3.00	15.00
	s. Specimen.	—	—	20.00

69-73 Russian printing.

		VG	VF	UNC
69	**200 Leva** 1945. Dk. brown on green and tan unpt. Arms at ctr.			
	a. Issued note.	3.00	12.00	55.00
	s. Specimen.	—	—	45.00

		VG	VF	UNC
70	**250 Leva** 1945. Green on lt. brown unpt. Arms at upper ctr.			
	a. Issued note.	3.00	12.00	55.00
	s. Specimen.	—	—	45.00

		VG	VF	UNC
71	**500 Leva** 1945. Blue on m/c unpt. Arms at l. Back brown on blue and orange unpt.			
	a. Issued note.	2.50	9.00	45.00
	s. Specimen.	—	—	40.00

		VG	VF	UNC
72	**1000 Leva** 1945. Brown on lt. blue and salmon unpt. Arms at l. Back wine on m/c unpt.			
	a. Issued note.	4.00	15.00	65.00
	s. Specimen.	—	—	55.00
73	**5000 Leva** 1945. Brown on m/c unpt. Arms at upper ctr.			
	a. Issued note.	6.00	30.00	115.
	s. Specimen.	—	—	100.

NOTICE

Readers with unlisted dates, signature varieties, etc. are invited to submit photocopies or, high resolution (300 dpi, 100% size) scans of their notes to: Standard Catalog of World Paper Money, 700 East State St. Iola, WI 54990-0001, or E-Mail: george.cuhaj@fwpubs.com.

PEOPLES REPUBLIC

БЪЛГАРСКА НАРОДНА БАНКА

BULGARIAN NATIONAL BANK

1947-48 ISSUES

		VG	VF	UNC
74	**20 Leva** 1947. Dk. gray on pale blue unpt. Year after imprint in lower margin. Bank bldg. at ctr. on back. Like #79.			
	a. Issued note.	.50	2.00	10.00
	s. Specimen.	—	—	15.00

Note: For similar design note but dated 1950 see #79. #75-78 arms w/*9.IX.1944* at l.

		VG	VF	UNC
75	**200 Leva** 1948. Brown. Year date w/printer's name in lower margin. Miner on back.			
	a. Issued note.	2.00	6.00	20.00
	s. Specimen.	—	—	30.00

		VG	VF	UNC
76	**250 Leva** 1948. Green on lt. brown unpt. Steam passenger train at ctr. on back.			
	a. Issued note.	2.50	12.50	40.00
	s. Specimen.	—	—	55.00

		VG	VF	UNC
77	**500 Leva** 1948. Blue-black on brown unpt. Tobacco harvesting on back.			
	a. Issued note.	2.00	6.00	20.00
	s. Specimen.	—	—	30.00

		VG	VF	UNC
78	**1000 Leva** 1948. Brown on blue unpt. Soldier at r. Tractor and factory scene at lower ctr. on back.			
	a. Normal serial #. (Not issued).	—	—	50.0
	s. Specimen.	—	—	75.0

БЪЛГАРСКА НАРОДНА БАНКА

BULGARIAN NATIONAL BANK

1950 ISSUE

		VG	VF	UNC
79	**20 Leva** 1950. Brown on lt. tan unpt. Bank bldg. at ctr. on back. Like #74.	1.00	4.00	15.0

Note: For similar note but dated 1947 see #74.

НАРОДНА РЕПУБЛИКА БЪЛГАРИЯ

1951 STATE NOTE ISSUE

#80-82 upright hands holding hammer and sickle on back. Wmk: БНБ (BNB) w/hammer and sickle.

		VG	VF	UN
80	**1 Lev** 1951. Brown on pale olive-green and orange unpt. Arms at l. Upright hands holding hammer and sickle. Watermark: BNB (BNB)BNB (BNB)			
	a. Issued note.	.20	.80	2.
	s. Specimen.	—	—	6.

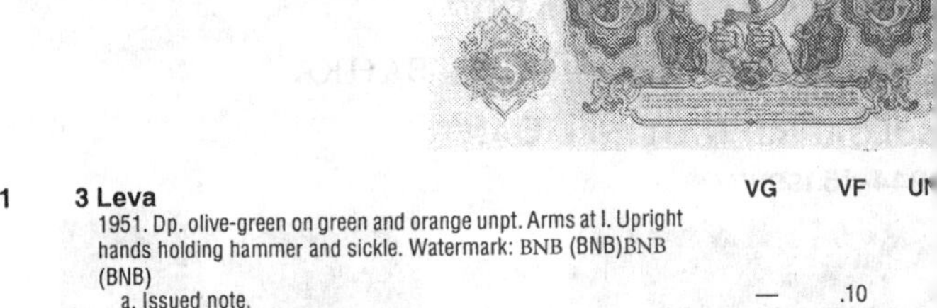

		VG	VF	UI
81	**3 Leva** 1951. Dp. olive-green on green and orange unpt. Arms at l. Upright hands holding hammer and sickle. Watermark: BNB (BNB)BNB (BNB)			
	a. Issued note.	—	.10	
	s. Specimen.	—	—	6

		VG	VF	UI
82	**5 Leva** 1951. Blue and green. Arms at l. ctr. Upright hands holding hammer and sickle. Watermark: BNB (BNB)BNB (BNB)			
	a. Issued note.	—	.10	
	s. Specimen.	—	—	6

1951 ISSUE

#83-87A portr G. Dimitrov at l., arms at r. on back.

#83-85 wmk: БНБ (BNB) w/hammer and sickle.

		VG	VF	UNC
83	**10 Leva** 1951. Red-brown on m/c unpt. Farm tractor at r. G. Dimitrov at l. Watermark: BNB (BNB) w/hammer and sickle.BNB (BNB) w/hammer and sickle.			
	a. Issued note.	—	.10	.25
	s. Specimen.	—	—	6.50

		VG	VF	UNC
84	**25 Leva** 1951. Gray blue on m/c unpt. Railroad construction at ctr. G. Dimitrov at l. Watermark: BNB (BNB) w/hammer and sickle.BNB (BNB) w/hammer and sickle.			
	a. Issued note.	—	.10	.25
	s. Specimen.	—	—	6.50

		VG	VF	UNC
85	**50 Leva** 1951. Brown on m/c unpt. Peasant woman w/baskets of roses at ctr. G. Dimitrov at l. Watermark: BNB BNB) w/hammer and sickle.BNB BNB) w/hammer and sickle.			
	a. Issued note.	—	.10	.25
	s. Specimen.	—	—	6.50

#86-87A wmk: Hammer and sickle.

		VG	VF	UNC
86	**100 Leva** 1951. Green and blue on m/c unpt. Woman picking grapes in vineyard. G. Dimitrov at l. Watermark: Wmk: BNB (BNB). Hammer and sickle.Wmk: BNB (BNB). Hammer and sickle.			
	a. Issued note.	—	.10	.25
	s. Specimen.	—	—	6.50

		VG	VF	UNC
87	**200 Leva** 1951. Gray-blue and black on m/c unpt. Farmers harvesting tobacco at ctr. G. Dimitrov at l. Watermark: Wmk: BNB (BNB). Hammer and sickle.Wmk: BNB (BNB). Hammer and sickle.			
	a. Issued note.	—	.10	.25
	s. Specimen.	—	—	6.50
87A	**500 Leva** 1951. Purple and m/c. G. Dimitrov at l. Watermark: Hammer and sickle.Hammer and sickle.			
	a. W/normal serial #. (Not issued).	—	—	60.00
	s. Specimen.	—	—	150.

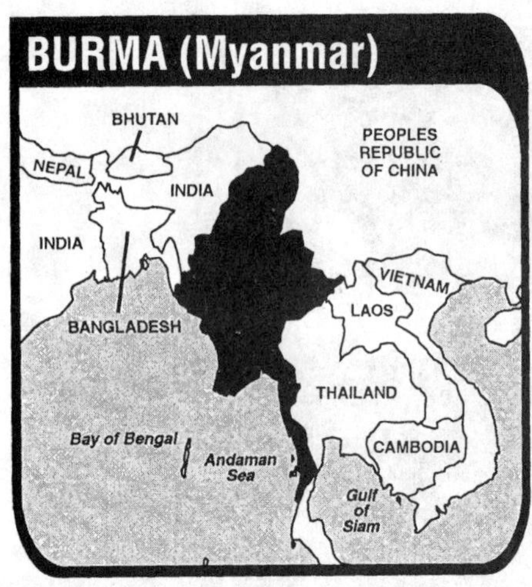

The Socialist Republic of the Union of Burma (now called Myanmar), a country of Southeast Asia fronting on the Bay of Bengal and the Andaman Sea, has an area of 261,228 sq. mi. (676,577 sq. km.) and a population of 49.34 million. Capital: Rangoon. Myanmar is an agricultural country heavily dependent on its leading product (rice) which embodies two-thirds of the cultivated area and accounts for 40 percent of the value of exports. Petroleum, lead, tin, silver, zinc, nickel, cobalt and precious stones are exported.

The first European to reach Burma, about 1435, was Nicolo Di Conti, a merchant of Venice. During the beginning of the reign of Bodawpaya (1782-1819AD) the kingdom comprised most of the same area as it does today including Arakan which was taken over in 1784-85. The British East India Company, while unsuccessful in its 1612 effort to establish posts along the Bay of Bengal, was enabled by the Anglo-Burmese Wars of 1824-86 to expand to the whole of Burma and to secure its annexation to British India. In 1937, Burma was separated from India, becoming a separate British colony with limited self-government. The Japanese occupied Burma in 1942, and on Aug. 1, 1943 Burma became an "independent and sovereign state" under Dr. Ba Maw who was appointed the Adipadi (head of state). This puppet state later collapsed with the surrender of Japanese forces. Burma became an independent nation outside the British Commonwealth on Jan. 4, 1948, the constitution of 1948 providing for a parliamentary democracy and the nationalization of certain industries. However, political and economic problems persisted, and on March 2, 1962, Gen. Ne Win took over the government, suspended the constitution, installed himself as chief of state, and pursued a socialistic program with nationalization of nearly all industry and trade. On Jan. 4, 1974, a new constitution adopted by referendum established Burma as a "socialist republic" under one-party rule. The country name was changed formally to the Union of Myanmar in 1989.

For later issues refer to Myanmar.

RULERS:

British to 1948
Japanese, 1942-45

MONETARY SYSTEM:

1 Rupee (Kyat) = 10 Mu = 16 Annas (Pe) to 1942, 1945-52
1 Rupee = 100 Cents, 1942-43
1 Kyat = 100 Pya, 1943-45, 1952-89

BRITISH ADMINISTRATION

GOVERNMENT OF INDIA

RANGOON

1897-1915 ISSUE

#A1-A3 Colonial type, w/4 language panels. Uniface. Ovpt: *RANGOON*.

Note: For similar notes from other branch offices see India.

		Good	Fine	XF
A1	**5 Rupees** 1904-05. Black on green unpt.			
	a. Sign. F. Atkinson. 1.6.1904.	75.00	350.	—
	b. Sign. H. J. Brereton. 19.5.1905.	75.00	350.	—

NOTICE

Readers with unlisted dates, signature varieties, etc. are invited to submit photocopies or, high resolution (300 dpi, 100% size) scans of their notes to: Standard Catalog of World Paper Money, 700 East State St. Iola, WI 54990-0001, or E-Mail: george.cuhaj@fwpubs.com.

		Good	Fine	XF
A2	**10 Rupees** 1897-1907. Black on green unpt.			
	a. Sign. R. E. Hamilton. 3.4.1897.	150.	500.	—
	b. Sign. M. F. Gauntlett. 16.8.1907; 6.9.1907.	100.	400.	—
A3	**100 Rupees** 1915-22. Black on green unpt.			
	a. Sign. M. M. S. Gubbay. 27.11.1915; 30.11.1915. Rare.	—	—	—
	b. Sign. H. Denning. 18.8.1922. Rare.	—	—	—

1911-14 ISSUE

#A4 and A5 Colonial type, w/8 language panels. Uniface. Ovpt: *R* at lower l. and r.

		Good	Fine	XF
A4	**5 Rupees** 21.9.1914. Black on red unpt. Sign. M. M. S. Gubbay.	60.00	300.	750.

		Good	Fine	XF
A5	**10 Rupees** 1911-18. Black on red unpt.			
	a. Sign. R. W. Gillan. 7.7.1911-30.11.1912.	30.00	200.	550.
	b. Sign. H. F. Howard. 2.1.1915.	30.00	200.	550.
	c. Sign. M. M. S. Gubbay. 28.3.1916-20.11.1918.	30.00	200.	550.

1927 ND PROVISIONAL ISSUE

#A7 and A8 portr. Kg. George V at r. and as wmk. Ovpt: *RANGOON* in lg. or sm. letters.

		Good	Fine	XF
A7	**50 Rupees** ND (1927). Lilac and brown. Portr. Kg. George V at r. and as wmk. Ovpt. on India #9. Sign. J. B. Taylor.	150.	600.	—

		Good	Fine	XF
A8	**100 Rupees** ND (1927-37). Violet and green. Portr. Kg. George V at r. and as wmk. Ovpt. on India #10.			
	a. Sign. H. Denning. Ovpt: *RANGOON* in sm. black letters. Series S.	100.	400.	—
	b. Sign. H. Denning. Ovpt: *RANGOON* in sm. green letters. Series S.	100.	400.	—
	c. Sign. H. Denning. Ovpt: *RANGOON* in lg. green letters. Series S. Reported not confirmed	—	—	—
	d. Sign. J. B. Taylor. Ovpt: *RANGOON* in lg. green letters. Series S.	100.	400.	—
	e. Sign. J. B. Taylor. Ovpt: *RANGOON* in lg. green letters. Series T.	100.	400.	—
	f. Sign. J. W. Kelly. Ovpt: *RANGOON* in sm. green letters. Series T.	100.	400.	—

1917 ND Provisional Issue

		Good	Fine	XF
A6	**2 Rupees 8 Annas** ND (1917). Black on green and red-brown unpt. Portr. Kg. George V in octagonal frame at upper l. Ovpt: *R1* on India #2.	—	—	—

Reserve Bank of India

Burma

1937 ND Provisional Issue

#1-3 portr. Kg. George V at r. and as wmk. Ovpt: *LEGAL TENDER IN BURMA ONLY*.

		Good	Fine	XF
1	**5 Rupees** ND (1937). Brown-violet on tan unpt. Ovpt. on India #15. Sign. J. W. Kelly.			
	a. Red ovpt. in margins.	35.00	100.	300.
	b. Black ovpt. on face at ctr. and on back at bottom.	35.00	100.	300.

		Good	Fine	XF
2	**10 Rupees** ND (1937). Dk. blue. Ovpt. on India #16. Sign. J. W. Kelly.			
	a. Red ovpt. in margins.	30.00	80.00	225.
	b. Black ovpt. near ctr. on face and back.	30.00	80.00	225.

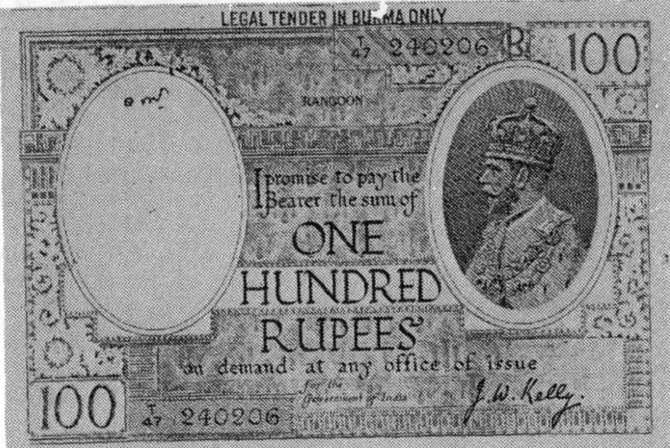

		Good	Fine	XF
3	**100 Rupees** ND (1937). Ovpt. on Burma #A8f on face and back in margins. Sign. J. W. Kelly. Rare.	—	—	—

1938-39 ND Issue

#4-8 portr. Kg. George VI and as wmk.

		Good	Fine	XF
4	**5 Rupees** ND (1938). Violet and green. Portr. Kg. George VI at r. and as wmk., peacock at ctr. Elephant on back.	1.00	5.00	25.00

		Good	Fine	XF
5	**10 Rupees** ND (1938). Green and m/c. Portr. Kg. George VI at r. and as wmk., ox plow and cart at ctr. Dhow on back.	2.00	10.00	40.00

		Good	Fine	XF
6	**100 Rupees** ND (1939). Blue and m/c. Portr. Kg. George VI at r. and as wmk., peacock at ctr. Elephant w/logs on back.	50.00	250.	750.

		Good	Fine	XF
7	**1000 Rupees** ND (1939). Brown and m/c. Portr. Kg. George VI at ctr. and as wmk. Tiger on back.	200.	850.	—
8	**10,000 Rupees** ND (1939). Green and m/c. Portr. Kg. George VI at ctr. and as wmk. Waterfalls on back. Rare.	—	—	—

JAPANESE OCCUPATION - WWII

JAPANESE GOVERNMENT

1942-44 ND ISSUE

#9-17 w/B prefix or B/ in block letters.

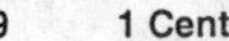

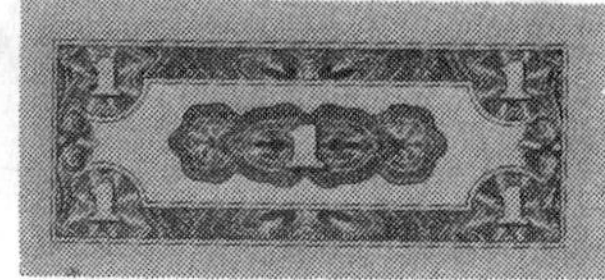

		VG	VF	UNC
9	**1 Cent**			
	ND (1942). Red and lt. blue. Back red.			
	a. Block letters: BA-BP; BR-BZ.	.10	.20	.60
	b. Fractional block letters: B/AA-B/EX.	.10	.25	.75
	s. Specimen ovpt: *Mihon.*	—	—	80.00

		VG	VF	UNC
10	**5 Cents**			
	ND (1942). Violet and lt. green. Back violet.			
	a. Block letters: BA-BV.	.15	.35	1.00
	b. Fractional block letters: B/AB-B/BX.	.05	.15	.50
	s. Specimen ovpt: *Mihon.*	—	—	80.00
11	**10 Cents**			
	ND (1942). Brown and tan. Back brown.			
	a. Block letters: BA-BZ.	.15	.35	1.00
	b. Fractional block letters: B/AA-B/AR.	.25	1.00	4.00
	s. Specimen ovpt: *Mihon.*	—	—	80.00
12	**1/4 Rupee**			
	ND (1942). Blue and tan. Back blue.			
	a. Block letters: BA-BV.	.15	.35	1.00
	s. Specimen ovpt: *Mihon.*	—	—	100.

#13-17 Ananda Temple in Pagan at r.

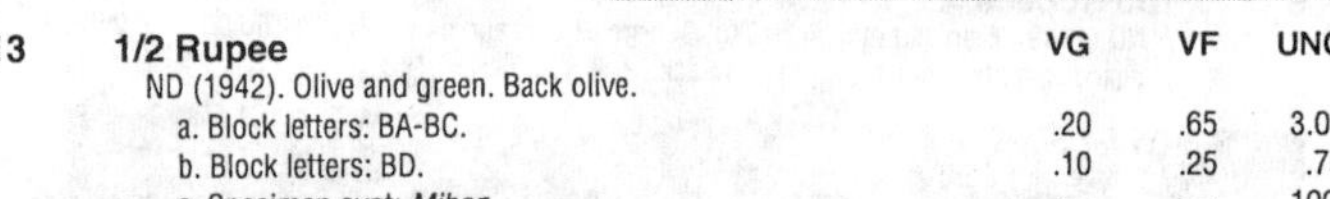

		VG	VF	UNC
13	**1/2 Rupee**			
	ND (1942). Olive and green. Back olive.			
	a. Block letters: BA-BC.	.20	.65	3.00
	b. Block letters: BD.	.10	.25	.75
	s. Specimen ovpt: *Mihon.*	—	—	100.

		VG	VF	UNC
14	**1 Rupee**			
	ND (1942). Green and pink. Back green.			
	a. Block letters: BA-BD closely spaced. Off-white paper.	.25	.75	4.00
	b. Block letters: BD spaced farther apart.	.10	.25	.75
	s. Specimen ovpt: *Mihon.*	—	—	110.

		VG	VF	UN
15	**5 Rupees**			
	ND (1942-44). Violet and yellow. Back violet.			
	a. Block letters: BA.	1.00	2.50	8.0
	b. Block letters: BB.	.10	.25	1.0
	s. Specimen ovpt: *Mihon.*	—	—	12

		VG	VF	UN
16	**10 Rupees**			
	ND (1942-44). Dull red and lt. green. Back dull red.			
	a. Wmk. Block letters: BA. 8mm wide.	.20	.65	3.
	b. W/o wmk. Block letters: BA. 6.5mm wide. Silk threads.	.15	.50	2.
	s. Specimen ovpt: *Mihon.*	—	—	13

		VG	VF	UN
17	**100 Rupees**			
	ND (1944). Dk. green and gray-violet. Back dk. green.			
	a. Wmk. Block letters: BA. 7.5mm wide.	.50	1.00	4.
	b. W/o wmk. Block letters: BA. 6.5mm wide. Silk threads.	.10	.40	1.
	s. Specimen ovpt: *Mihon.*	—	—	14

STATE OF BURMA

BURMA STATE BANK

1944 ND ISSUE

#18-21 peacock at l., scene in Mandalay at r. on back. Wmk: Three Burmese characters.

		VG	VF	UN
18	**1 Kyat**			
	ND (1944). Blue, pink and violet. Back blue.			
	a. Block #3; 17; 21; 22; 26; 29.	—	275.	45
	s1. Red ovpt: *Specimen* in script. Block #21.	—	—	45
	s2. Red Japanese characters. Ovpt: *Mihon* (Specimen) on face only.	—	—	50

		VG	VF	UNC
19	**5 Kyats** ND (1944). Red, purple and gray-green. Back red, yellow and gray. Specimens only. Japanese characters *Mihon* (Specimen) ovpt. on face. Ovpt: *Specimen* in script on back. Block #0.	—	—	1000.
20	**10 Kyats** ND (1944). Green, orange and violet. Back green, pink and blue.			
	a. Block #0, 1, 23.	—	350.	600.
	s. Ovpt: *Specimen* in script on face and back. Block #0.	—	—	600.

		VG	VF	UNC
21	**100 Kyats** ND (1944). Orange, blue and lt. green. Back orange, pink and lt. blue.			
	a. Block #1.	—	175.	350.
	s1. Red ovpt: *Specimen* on face and back. Block #1.	—	—	300.
	s2. Red Japanese characters. Ovpt: *Mihon* (Specimen) on face only. Block #1.	—	—	400.

1945 ND ISSUE

#22, printed in Rangoon on unwmk. paper.

		VG	VF	UNC
22	**100 Kyats** ND (1945). Dk. blue on green unpt. Stylized peacock at lower l., portr. Ba Maw at upper r. Back blue; stylized peacock at bottom ctr. Like #21.			
	a. Serial # in open box directly below ctr.	—	35.00	125.
	b. W/o serial #.	—	—	70.00
	c. Sheet of 4.	—	—	—

MILITARY

MILITARY ADMINISTRATION OF BURMA

1943 ND PROVISIONAL ISSUE

#23 and 24 prepared in booklet form. Specimens.

		VG	VF	UNC
23	**4 Annas** ND (1943). Green. Portr. Kg. George VI at r.	—	—	—

		VG	VF	UNC
24	**8 Annas** ND (1943). Purple. Portr. Kg. George VI at ctr.	—	—	—

1945 ND ISSUE

#25-29 ovpt: *MILITARY ADMINISTRATION OF BURMA. LEGAL TENDER IN BURMA ONLY* on India notes.

		VG	VF	UNC
25	**1 Rupee** ND (1945 - old date 1940). Blue-gray on m/c unpt. Red ovpt. on India #25. Coin w/Kg. George VI at upper r. Coin w/date at upper l. on back. Wmk: Kg. George VI.			
	a. W/o lg. *A* after black serial #.	.50	3.00	15.00
	b. Lg. *A* after green serial #.	.25	1.00	6.00
	s. As a. Specimen.	—	—	100.

#26-29 portr. Kg. George VI at r. and as wmk.

		VG	VF	UNC
26	**5 Rupees** ND (1945). Brown and green. Dk. blue ovpt. on India #18.			
	a. Sign. J. B. Taylor.	.75	3.00	20.00
	b. Sign. C. D. Deshmukh.	.50	2.00	15.00
	s. As a. Specimen.	—	—	120.

		VG	VF	UNC
27	**10 Rupees** ND (1945). Blue-violet on olive unpt. Ovpt. on India #19. Specimen.	—	—	300.

		VG	VF	UNC
28	**10 Rupees** ND (1945). Violet on m/c unpt. Red ovpt. on India #24. Sign. C. D. Deshmukh.	1.50	5.00	25.00

		VG	VF	UNC
29	**100 Rupees** ND (1945). Dk. green on lilac unpt. Red ovpt. on India #20.			
	a. Sign. J. B. Taylor.	30.00	100.	325.
	b. Sign. C. D. Deshmukh.	25.00	75.00	250.
	s. As a. Specimen.	—	—	175.

STATE OF BURMA - POST WWII

BURMA CURRENCY BOARD

1947 ND PROVISIONAL ISSUE

#30-33 ovpt: *BURMA CURRENCY BOARD, LEGAL TENDER IN BURMA ONLY* on India notes.

		VG	VF	UNC
30	**1 Rupee** ND (1947 - old date 1940). Blue-gray on m/c unpt. Red ovpt. on India #25c. Coin w/Kg. George VI at upper r.	.75	2.00	12.50
31	**5 Rupees** ND (1947). Brown and green. Dk. blue ovpt. on India #18.	2.50	10.00	30.00

		VG	VF	UNC
32	**10 Rupees** ND (1947). Blue-violet on olive unpt. Red ovpt. on India #24.	2.50	10.00	30.00

		VG	VF	UNC
33	**100 Rupees** ND (1947). Dk. green on lilac unpt. Red ovpt. on India #20.	30.00	125.	300.

GOVERNMENT OF BURMA

1948 ND ISSUE

#34 and 35 wmk: Peacock. Printer: TDLR.

		VG	VF	UNC
34	**1 Rupee** ND (1948). Gray, lt. green and pink. Peacock at r. Back gray; dhows at ctr.	1.00	4.00	20.00

		VG	VF	UNC
35	**5 Rupees** ND (1948). Brown and m/c. Chinze statue at r. Back brown; woman and spinning wheel.	4.00	20.00	100.

GOVERNMENT OF THE UNION OF BURMA

1948-50 ND ISSUE

		VG	VF	UNC
36	**10 Rupees** ND (1949). Blue and m/c. Peacock at r. Back blue; elephant lifting log at ctr.	2.00	7.50	30.00
37	**100 Rupees** 1.1.1948 (1950). Green. Peacock at ctr., head of mythical animal at r. Worker w/oxen on back.	10.00	35.00	125.

UNION BANK OF BURMA

1953 ND RUPEE ISSUE

#38-41 wmk: Peacock.

		VG	VF	UNC
38	**1 Rupee** ND (1953). Gray, lt. green and pink. Similar to #34. Back gray.	.25	.75	3.00

		VG	VF	UNC
39	**5 Rupees** ND (1953). Brown and m/c. Similar to #35. Back brown.	2.50	7.50	25.00
40	**10 Rupees** ND (1953). Blue and m/c. Similar to #36. Back blue.	2.50	7.50	25.00

		VG	VF	UNC
41	**100 Rupees** ND (1953). Green on pink unpt. Similar to #37. Back green.	5.00	15.00	50.00

1953 ND ISSUE

#42-45 wmk: Peacock.

		VG	VF	UNC
42	**1 Kyat** ND (1953). Gray, lt. green and pink. Like #38. Back gray.	.25	.50	3.00
43	**5 Kyats** ND (1953). Brown and m/c. Like #39. Back brown.	.50	2.00	8.50

		VG	VF	UNC
44	**10 Kyats** ND (1953). Blue and m/c. Like #40. Back blue.	.75	2.50	12.50
45	**100 Kyats** ND (1953). Green on lt. pink unpt. Like #41. Back green.	1.00	5.00	35.00

1958 ND Issue

#46-51 Gen. Aung San w/hat at r. and as wmk.

		VG	VF	UNC
46	**1 Kyat** ND (1958). Black, green and pink. Back similar to #42.			
	a. Issued note.	.15	.30	1.50
	s. Specimen.	—	—	25.00

		VG	VF	UNC
47	**5 Kyats** ND (1958). Brown and m/c. Back similar to #43.			
	a. Issued note.	.25	.75	3.50
	s. Specimen.	—	—	25.00
48	**10 Kyats** ND (1958). Blue and m/c. Back similar to #44.			
	a. Issued note.	.50	1.50	4.00
	s. Specimen.	—	—	25.00

		VG	VF	UNC
49	**20 Kyats** ND (1958). Purple and m/c. Field workers on back. 2 serial # varieties.			
	a. Issued note.	.50	2.00	9.00
	s. Specimen.	—	—	25.00
50	**50 Kyats** ND (1958). Lt. brown and m/c. Mandalay Temple on back.			
	a. Issued note.	.50	1.50	5.00
	s. Specimen.	—	—	25.00

		VG	VF	UNC
51	**100 Kyats** ND (1958). Green and m/c. Back similar to #45.			
	a. Issued note.	.50	1.50	5.00
	s. Specimen.	—	—	25.00

Note: For later issues see Myanmar.

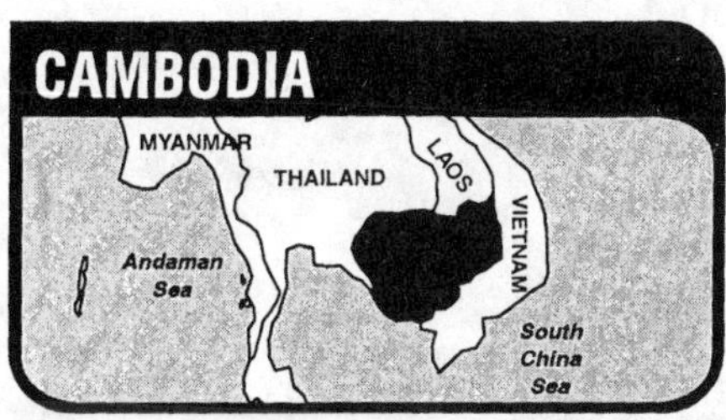

Cambodia, formerly known as Democratic Kampuchea and the Khmer Republic, a land of paddy fields and forest-clad hills located on the Indo-Chinese peninsula fronting on the Gulf of Thailand, has an area of 69,898 sq. mi. (181,035 sq. km.) and a population of 9.86 million. Capital: Phnom Penh. Agriculture is the basis of the economy, with rice the chief crop. Native industries include cattle breeding, weaving and rice milling. Rubber, cattle, corn, and timber are exported.

The region was the nucleus of the Khmer empire which flourished from the 5th to the 12th century and attained an excellence in art and architecture still evident in the magnificent ruins at Angkor. The Khmer empire once ruled over much of Southeast Asia, but began to decline in the 13th century as the Thai and Vietnamese invaded the region and attached its territories. At the request of the Cambodian king, a French protectorate attached to Cochin-China was established over the country in 1863, saving it from dissolution, and in 1885, Cambodia was included in the French Union of Indo-China. France established a constitutional monarchy for Cambodia within the French Union in 1949. The 1954 Geneva Convention resulted in full independence for the Kingdom of Cambodia. King Sihanouk abdicated to his father and won the office of Prime Minister.

Prince Sihanouk was toppled by a bloodless coup led by Lon Nol in March of 1970. Sihanouk moved to Peking to head a government-in-exile. On Oct. 9, 1970, Cambodia became the Khmer Republic, and Lon Nol its President. The government of Lon Nol was in turn toppled, April 17, 1975, by the Khmer Rouge insurgents who took control of the government and renamed the country Democratic Kampuchea.

The Khmer Rouge completely eliminated the economy and created a state without money, exchange or barter. Everyone worked for the state and was taken care of by the state. The Vietnamese supported People's Republic of Kampuchea was installed in accordance with the constitution of January 5, 1976. The name of the country was changed from Democratic Cambodia to Democratic Kampuchea, afterwards reverting to Cambodia.

In the early 1990's the UN supervised a ceasefire and in 1992 Norodom Sihanouk returned as Chief of State. He was crowned king in 1993, and in 2004 abdicated in favor of one of his sons.

RULERS:

Norodom Sihanouk, 1941-1955
Norodom Suramarit, 1955-1960
Norodom Sihanouk (as Chief of State), 1960-1970

MONETARY SYSTEM:

1 Riel = 100 Sen

SIGNATURE CHART

	Governor	Chief Inspector	Advisor	Date
1				28.10.1955
2				1956
3				1956
4				Late 1961
5				Mid 1962
6				1963
7				1965
8				1968
9				1968
10				1969
11				1970
12				1972
13				1972

CAMBODIA - KINGDOM

BANQUE NATIONALE DU CAMBODGE

1955-56 ND ISSUE

		VG	VF	UNC
1	**1 Riel**			
	ND (1955). Blue. Figure "Kinnari" w/raised arms at l. Back blue and brown; royal houseboat at l. Back similar to Fr. Indochina #94. Wmk: Elephant. Sign. 1. Printer: TDLR (w/o imprint).			
	a. Issued note.	5.00	50.00	175.
	s. TDLR Specimen (red oval).			

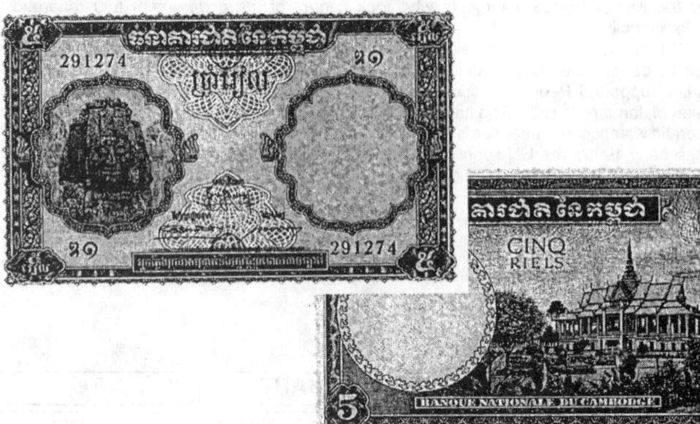

		VG	VF	UNC
2	**5 Riels**			
	ND (1955). Purple. Sculpture (Bayon head) at l. Royal palace entrance at Chanchhaya at r. on back. Wmk: Buddha. Sign. 1. Printer: BWC (w/o imprint).	2.00	10.00	55.00

		VG	VF	UNC
3	**10 Riels**			
	ND (1955). Brown. Temple of Banteal Srei at r. Back brown and green; central market at Phnom-Penh. Wmk: Buddha. Sign. 1. Printer: TDLR (w/o imprint).			
	a. Issued note.	2.00	10.00	60.00
	s. Specimen.	—	—	—
	s2. Specimen TDLR (red oval).			

		VG	VF	UN
3A	**50 Riels**			
	ND (1956). M/c. Cambodian w/bamboo water vessels at l. Stupas at Botoum-Waddei on back. Wmk: Buddha. Sign. 1. Printer: BdF (w/o imprint).			
	a. Issued note.	35.00	150.	60
	s. Specimen.	—	—	200

1956; 1958 ND SECOND ISSUE

		VG	VF	UN
4	**1 Riel**			
	ND (1956-75). Grayish green on m/c unpt. Boats dockside in port of Phnom-Penh. Royal palace throne room on back. Printer: BWC (w/o imprint).			
	a. Sign. 1; 2.	.50	3.00	15.
	b. Sign. 6; 7; 8; 10; 11.	.15	.25	3.
	c. Sign. 12.	.10	.15	1.
	s. Specimen. Sign. 1. Perforated and printed: *SPECIMEN.*	—	—	15

		VG	VF	UN
5	**20 Riels**			
	ND (1956-75). Brown on m/c unpt. Combine harvester at r. Phnom Penh pagoda on back. Wmk: Buddha. Printer: BWC (w/o imprint).			
	a. Sign. 3.	.25	1.00	10.
	b. Sign. 6.	.25	.75	4.
	c. Sign. 7; 8; 10.	.20	.50	2.
	d. Sign. 12.	.10	.25	1.

#6 not assigned.

		VG	VF	UN
7	**50 Riels**			
	ND (1956-75). Blue and orange. Fishermen fishing from boats w/lg. nets in Lake Tonle Sap at l. and r. Back blue and brown; Angkor Wat. Wmk: Buddha. Printer: TDLR (w/o imprint).			
	a. Western numeral in plate block designator. Sign. 3.	.50	3.00	20.
	b. Cambodian numeral in plate block designator. 5-digit serial #. Sign. 7; 10.	.25	1.00	3.
	c. As b. Sign. 12.	.25	.50	1.
	d. Cambodian serial # 6-digits. Sign. 12.	.10	.20	1.
	s. As c. Specimen.	—	—	1
	s2. As a. Specimen.	—	—	1

		VG	VF	UNC
8	**100 Riels**			
	ND (1957-75). Brown and green on m/c unpt. Statue of Lokecvara at l. Long boat on back. Wmk: Buddha.			
	a. Imprint: *Giesecke & Devrient AG, Munchen.* Sign. 3.	.50	3.00	20.00
	b. As a. Sign. 7; 8; 11.	.50	1.00	4.00
	c. Imprint: *Giesecke & Devrient-Munchen.* Sign. 12; 13.	.20	.50	2.00
	s. Specimen. As a. Sign. 3. Perforated *Specimen. Uniface printings.*	—	—	200.

		VG	VF	UNC
9	**500 Riels**			
	ND (1958-70). Green and brown on m/c unpt. Sculpture of 2 royal women dancers - *Devatas* at l. 2 royal dancers in ceremonial costumes on back. Wmk: Buddha. Printer: G&D.			
	a. Sign. 3.	3.00	20.00	75.00
	b. Sign. 6.	2.00	17.50	55.00
	c. Sign. 9.	1.00	3.00	12.50
	s. Specimen. Sign 3.			

Note: This banknote was withdrawn in March 1970 because of counterfeiting.

1962-63 ND THIRD ISSUE

		VG	VF	UNC
10	**5 Riels**			
	ND (1962-75). Red on m/c unpt. Bayon stone 4 faces of Avalokitesvara at l. Royal Palace Entrance - Chanchhaya at r. on back. Wmk: Buddha. Printer: BWC (w/o imprint).			
	a. Sign. 4; 6.	.50	3.00	20.00
	b. Sign. 7; 8; 11.	.20	.50	4.00
	c. Sign. 12.	.10	.25	1.00
	s. Specimen. Sign. 4, 8. Perforated *SPECIMEN.*	—	—	200.

		VG	VF	UNC
11	**10 Riels**			
	ND (1962-75). Red-brown on m/c unpt. Temple of Banteay Srei at r. Central Market bldg. at Phnom-Penh at l. on back. Wmk: Buddha. Printer: TDLR (w/o imprint).			
	a. Sign. 5; 6.	.50	3.00	20.00
	b. Sign. 7; 8; 11.	.20	.50	3.00
	c. Sign. 12. 5 digit serial #.	.10	.25	1.00
	d. As c. 6 digit serial #.	.20	.50	2.00
	s. Specimen. Sign. 6, 8.	—	—	125.
	s2. TDLR Specimen. Sign 6.			125.

		VG	VF	UNC
12	**100 Riels**			
	ND (1963-72). Blue-black, dk. green and dk. brown on m/c unpt. Sun rising behind Temple of Preah Vihear at l. Back blue, green and brown; aerial view of the Temple of Preah Vihear. Wmk: Buddha. Printer: G&D.			
	a. Sign. 6.	.50	3.00	20.00
	b. Sign. 13. (Not issued).	.10	.20	1.00
	s. Specimen. Sign. 6.	—	—	200.

		VG	VF	UNC
13	**100 Riels**			
	ND (1956-1972). Blue on lt. blue unpt. 2 oxen at r. 3 ceremonial women on back.			
	a. Printer: ABNC w/ imprint on lower margins, face and back. Sign. 3.	3.00	20.00	100.
	b. W/o imprint on either side. Sign. 12.	.10	.25	2.00
	p. Uniface proofs.	FV	FV	75.00
	s. As a. Specimen. Sign. 3.	—	—	200.

		VG	VF	UNC
14	**500 Riels**			
	ND (1958-1970). M/c. Farmer plowing w/2 water buffalo. Pagoda at r., doorway of Preah Vihear at l. on back. Wmk: Buddha. Printer: BdF (w/o imprint).			
	a. Sign. 3.	.50	4.00	30.00
	b. Sign. 5; 7.	.50	2.00	10.00
	c. Sign. 9.	.50	1.50	9.00
	d. Sign. 12.	.15	1.00	5.00
	x1. Lithograph counterfeit; wmk. barely visible. Sign. 3; 5.	20.00	50.00	100.
	x2. As x1. Sign 7; 9.	15.00	45.00	80.00
	x3. As x1. Sign. 12.	7.50	22.50	55.00

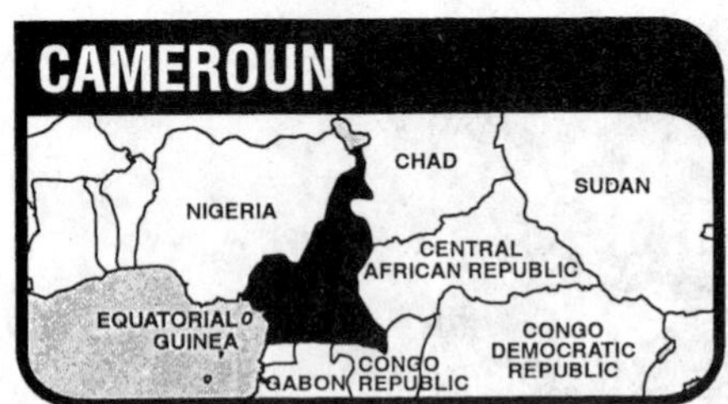

The United Republic of Cameroun, located in west-central Africa on the Gulf of Guinea, has an area of 185,568 sq. mi. (475,440 sq. km.) and a population of 15.13 million. Capital: Yaounde. About 90 percent of the labor force is employed on the land; cash crops account for 80 percent of the country's export revenue. Cocoa, coffee, aluminum, cotton, rubber and timber are exported.

European contact with what is now the United Republic of Cameroun began in the 16th century with the voyage of Portuguese navigator Fernando Po. The following three centuries saw continuous activity by Spanish, Dutch and British traders and missionaries. The land was spared colonial rule until 1884, when treaties with tribal chiefs brought German domination. After Germany's defeat in WWI, the League of Nations in 1919 divided the Cameroons between Great Britain and France, with the larger eastern area going to France. The French and British mandates were converted into United Nations trusteeships in 1946. French Cameroon became the independent Cameroun Republic on Jan. 1, 1960. The federation of East (French) and West (British) Cameroun was established in 1961 when the southern part of British Cameroun voted for reunification with the Cameroun Republic, and the northern part for union with Nigeria. On Nov. 1, 1995 the Republic of Cameroun joined the Commonwealth. Issues continue under Central African States.

MONETARY SYSTEM:

1 Franc = 100 Centimes

SIGNATURE VARIETIES:

Refer to introduction of Central African States.

GERMAN KAMERUN

RULERS:

German to 1914

MONETARY SYSTEM:

1 Mark = 100 Pfennig Note: German Reichsbanknoten and Reichskassenscheine circulated freely until 1914.

KAISERLICHES GOUVERNEMENT

TREASURY NOTES

DUALA

1914 SCHATZSCHEINE

		Good	Fine	XF
1	**5 Mark**			
	12.8.1914. Black on blue unpt.			
	a. Issued note.	75.00	300.	—
	b. Cancelled.	60.00	250.	500.

Note: 10 and 20 Mark notes may possibly have been printed; they were not issued. Later they were destroyed with no surviving examples.

		Good	Fine	XF
2	**50 Mark**			
	12.8.1914. Gray-brown cardboard.			
	a. Lt. brown eagle; 2 varieties of eagles.	25.00	100.	275.
	b. Red-brown eagle.	25.00	100.	275.
	c. Cancelled.	20.00	80.00	225.

		Good	Fine	XF
3	**100 Mark**			
	12.8.1914. Gray-brown cardboard.			
	a. Blue eagle.	25.00	100.	300.
	b. Green-blue eagle.	20.00	60.00	275.
	c. Cancelled.	20.00	80.00	225.

FRENCH MANDATE POST WWI

1922 TERRITOIRE DU CAMEROUN

1922 ISSUE

#4 and 5 *TC* monogram at top ctr., palm fronds at l. and r. on back.

		VG	VF	UNC
4	**50 Centimes**			
	ND (1922). Red.	75.00	225.	600.
5	**1 Franc**			
	ND (1922). Brown and pink.	90.00	325.	750.

Canada is located to the north of the United States, and spans the full breadth of the northern portion of North America from Atlantic to Pacific oceans, except for the State of Alaska. It has a total area of 3,850,000 sq. mi. (9,970,610 sq. km.) and a population of 30.68 million. Capital: Ottawa.

Jacques Cartier, a French explorer, took possession of Canada for France in 1534, and for more than a century the history of Canada was that of a French colony. Samuel de Champlain helped to establish the first permanent colony in North America, in 1604 at Port Royal, Acadia - now Annapolis Royal, Nova Scotia. Four years later he founded the settlement of Quebec.

The British settled along the coast to the south while the French, motivated by a grand design, pushed into the interior. France's plan for a great American empire was to occupy the Mississippi heartland of the country, and from there to press in upon the narrow strip of English coastal settlements from the rear. Inevitably, armed conflict erupted between the French and the British; consequently, Britain acquired Hudson Bay, Newfoundland and Nova Scotia from the French in 1713. British control of the rest of New France was secured in 1763, largely because of James Wolfe's great victory over Montcalm near Quebec in 1759.

During the American Revolution, Canada became a refuge for great numbers of American Royalists, most of whom settled in Ontario, thereby creating an English majority west of the Ottawa River. The ethnic imbalance contravened the effectiveness of the prevailing French type of government, and in 1791 the Constitutional act was passed by the British parliament, dividing Canada at the Ottawa River into two parts, each with its own government: Upper Canada, chiefly English and consisting of the southern section of what is now Ontario; and Lower Canada, chiefly French and consisting principally of the southern section of Quebec. Subsequent revolt by dissidents in both sections caused the British government to pass the Union act, July 23, 1840, which united Lower and Upper Canada (as Canada East and Canada West) to form the Province of Canada, with one council and one assembly in which the two sections had equal numbers.

The union of the two provinces did not encourage political stability; the equal strength of the French and British made the task of government all but impossible. A further change was made with the passage of the British North American act, which took effect on July 1, 1867, and established Canada as the first federal union in the British Empire. Four provinces entered the union at first: Upper Canada as Ontario, Lower Canada as Quebec, Nova Scotia and New Brunswick. The Hudson's Bay Company's territories were acquired in 1869 out of which were formed the provinces of Manitoba, Saskatchewan and Alberta. British Columbia joined in 1871 and Prince Edward Island in 1873. Canada took over the Arctic Archipelago in 1895. In 1949 Newfoundland came into the confederation. Canada is a member of the Commonwealth. Elizabeth II is Head of State as Queen of Canada.

RULERS:

French 1534-1763
British 1763-

MONETARY SYSTEM:

French:
- 12 Deniers = 1 Sou (sols)
- 20 Sous or Sols = 1 Livre Coloniale
- 1 Liard = 3 Deniers
- 1 Ecu = 6 Livres
- 1 Louis D'or = 4 Ecus

English:
- 4 Farthings = 1 Penny
- 12 Pence = 1 Shilling
- 20 Shillings = 1 Pound

Canadian Decimal Currency
- 100 Cents = 1 Dollar

Note: Certain listings encompassing issues circulated by provincial, state and commercial banking authorities are contained in Volume 1.

REPLACEMENT NOTES:

#66-70A and 74b, asterisk in front of fractional prefix letters.
#76, 78-81, triple letter prefix ending in X (AAX, BAX, etc.).
Exceptions: #82, no asterisk but serial number starts with 510 or 516;
#83, serial number starts with 31 (instead of 30).
#84-90, as #76 and 78-81.

PROVINCE OF CANADA

PROVINCE OF CANADA

1866 ISSUE

#1-7A black on lt. green unpt. Province of Canada notes w/additional ovpt.

#		Good	Fine	XF
1	**1 Dollar** 1.10.1866. Portr. Samuel de Champlain at lower l., arms at top ctr., flanked by farmer at l., and sailor at r., J. Cartier at lower r.			
	a. Ovpt. *PAYABLE AT MONTREAL.*	375.	1400.	3250.
	b. Ovpt. *PAYABLE AT TORONTO.*	500.	1600.	3500.
	c. Ovpt. *PAYABLE AT ST. JOHN.*	1500.	4500.	—

#		Good	Fine	XF
2	**2 Dollars** 1.10.1866. Indian woman at lower l., Britannia at top ctr. flanked by a woman w/ agricultural produce at l. and woman playing harp at r., sailor and lion at lower r.			
	a. Ovpt: *PAYABLE AT MONTREAL.*	750.	2500.	5500.
	b. Ovpt: *PAYABLE AT TORONTO.*	1000.	2750.	—
	c. Ovpt: *PAYABLE AT ST. JOHN.*	2000.	5000.	—

#		Good	Fine	XF
3	**5 Dollars** 1.10.1866. Qn. Victoria at l., arms w/lion and woman seated at top ctr., sailing ship at lower r.			
	a. Ovpt: *PAYABLE AT MONTREAL.*	1500.	6000.	—
	b. Ovpt: *PAYABLE AT TORONTO.*	2500.	9000.	—
	c. Ovpt: *PAYABLE AT HALIFAX.*	2500.	9000.	—
	d. Ovpt: *PAYABLE AT ST. JOHN.*	2500.	9000.	—
4	**10 Dollars** 1.10.1866. Columbus and explorers at l., lion at ctr., beaver at r.			
	a. Ovpt: *PAYABLE AT MONTREAL.*	5000.	11,000.	—
	b. Ovpt: *PAYABLE AT TORONTO.* Face proof.	—	Unc	1000.
	c. Ovpt: *PAYABLE AT ST. JOHN.* Reported not confirmed.	—	—	—
5	**20 Dollars** 1.10.1866. Portr. Princess of Wales at l., beaver repairing dam at ctr., Prince Consort Albert at r.			
	a. Ovpt: *PAYABLE AT MONTREAL.* Rare..	—	—	—
	b. Ovpt: *PAYABLE AT TORONTO.* Reported not confirmed.	—	—	—
	c. Ovpt: *PAYABLE AT ST. JOHN.* Reported not confirmed.	—	—	—
6	**50 Dollars** 1.10.1866. Mercury w/map of British America, harbor w/ships and train in background.			
	a. *PAYABLE AT MONTREAL.* Face proof. Rare..	—	—	—
	b. *PAYABLE AT TORONTO.* Face proof.	—	Unc	1000.
	c. Ovpt: *PAYABLE AT ST. JOHN.* Reported not confirmed.	—	—	—
7	**100 Dollars** 1.10.1866. Qn. Victoria at ctr.			
	a. *PAYABLE AT MONTREAL.* Face proof.	—	Unc	1000.
	b. *PAYABLE AT TORONTO.* Face proof.	—	Unc	1000.
7A	**500 Dollars** 1.10.1866. Provincial arms of Canada flanked by woman w/lion at l. and agricultural produce at r.			
	a. *PAYABLE AT MONTREAL.* Face proof.	—	Unc	1000.
	b. *PAYABLE AT TORONTO.* Face proof.	—	Unc	1000.

DOMINION

DOMINION OF CANADA

FRACTIONAL ISSUES

#8-11 are commonly referred to as "shinplasters."

		VG	VF	UNC
8	**25 Cents** 1.3.1870. Black on green unpt. Britannia w/spear at ctr. Printer: BABNC.			
	a. W/o plate letter.	17.50	65.00	600.
	b. Plate letter *A* below date.	200.	600.	1800.
	c. Plate letter *B* below date.	25.00	100.	850.

		VG	VF	UNC
9	**25 Cents** 2.1.1900. Black on lt. brown unpt. Britannia seated w/shield and trident at r., sailing ship in background. Printer: ABNC.			
	a. Sign. Courtney.	6.00	17.50	225.
	b. Sign. Boville.	5.00	15.00	200.
	c. Sign. Saunders.	5.00	17.50	250.

#10-11 printer: CBNC.

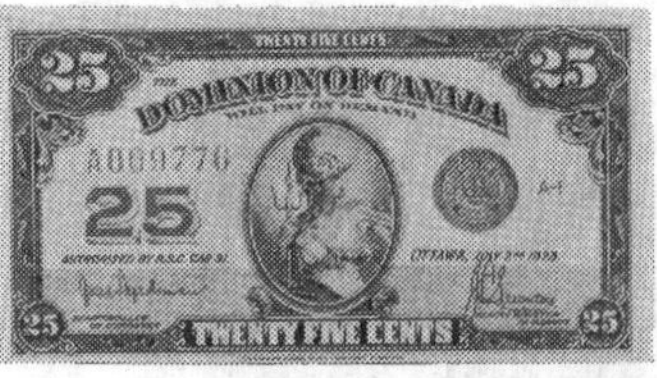

		VG	VF	UNC
10	**25 Cents** 2.7.1923. Black on brown unpt. Britannia w/trident at ctr. w/text *AUTHORIZED BY R.S.C. CAP. 31.* across lower l. and r. Sign. Hyndman-Saunders. Printer: CBNC.	12.50	35.00	225.

		VG	VF	UNC
11	**25 Cents** 2.7.1923. Like #10 w/o text *AUTHORIZED BY...* but w/letters A-E, H, or J-L at l. of large *25.* Printer: CBNC.			
	a. Sign. Hyndman-Saunders.	12.50	35.00	225.
	b. Sign. McCavour-Saunders.	5.00	15.00	130.
	c. Sign. Campbell-Clark.	5.00	15.00	130.

1870 ISSUE

#12-16A printer: BABNC.

		Good	Fine	XF
12	**1 Dollar** 1.7.1870. Black on green unpt. Portr. J. Cartier at upper l., reclining woman w/child and globe at ctr.			
	a. *PAYABLE AT MONTREAL* on back.	225.	1000.	3000
	b. *PAYABLE AT TORONTO* on back.	225.	1000.	3000
	c. Ovpt: *MANITOBA* on face. *PAYABLE AT TORONTO* on back.	3000.	5500.	—
	d. *PAYABLE AT HALIFAX* on back.	1200.	3750.	—
	e. *PAYABLE AT ST. JOHN* on back.	1200.	3750.	—
	f. *PAYABLE AT VICTORIA* on back.	3000.	11,000.	—
	g. Ovpt: *MANITOBA* on face. *PAYABLE AT MONTREAL* on back. Rare..	—	—	—

		Good	Fine	XF
13	**2 Dollars** 1.7.1870. Black on green unpt. Portr. Gen. de Montcalm at lower r., seated Indian chief overlooking steam train at ctr., portr. Gen. J. Wolfe at lower l.			
	a. *PAYABLE AT MONTREAL* on back.	1100.	3000.	9000
	b. *PAYABLE AT TORONTO* on back.	1100.	3000.	9000
	c. Ovpt: *MANITOBA* on face. *PAYABLE AT TORONTO* on back.	3000.	—	—
	d. *PAYABLE AT HALIFAX* on back.	1900.	5500.	—
	e. *PAYABLE AT ST. JOHN* on back.	2000.	7500.	—
	f. *PAYABLE AT VICTORIA* on back. Reported not confirmed.	—	—	—
	g. Ovpt: *MANITOBA* on face. *PAYABLE AT MONTREAL* on back. , Unknown	—	—	—

1871 ISSUE

#14 and 15 face and back proofs are known. All are rare.

		Good	Fine	XF
14	**500 Dollars** 1.7.1871. Black on green unpt. Portr. young Qn. Victoria at ctr.			
	a. *PAYABLE AT MONTREAL.*	—	—	—
	b. *PAYABLE AT TORONTO.*	—	—	—
	c. *PAYABLE AT HALIFAX.*	—	—	—
	d. *PAYABLE AT ST. JOHN.*	—	—	—
	e. *PAYABLE AT VICTORIA.*	—	—	—
	f. *PAYABLE AT WINNIPEG.*	—	—	—
	g. *PAYABLE AT CHARLOTTETOWN.*	—	—	—
	h. *PAYABLE AT OTTAWA* ovpt.	—	—	—
15	**1000 Dollars** 1.7.1871. Black on green unpt. Canadian arms at ctr. flanked by woman w/lion at l., agricultural produce at r.			
	a. *PAYABLE AT MONTREAL.*	—	—	—
	b. *PAYABLE AT TORONTO.*	—	—	—
	c. *PAYABLE AT HALIFAX.*	—	—	—
	d. *PAYABLE AT ST. JOHN.*	—	—	—
	e. *PAYABLE AT VICTORIA.*	—	—	—
	f. *PAYABLE AT WINNIPEG.*	—	—	—
	g. *PAYABLE AT CHARLOTTETOWN.*	—	—	—
	h. *PAYABLE AT OTTAWA* ovpt.	—	—	—

1872 ISSUE

#16 and 16A face and back proofs are known. All are rare.

		Good	Fine	XF
16	**50 Dollars** 1.3.1872. Black on green unpt. Mercury w/map of British America at ctr., harbor w/ships and train in background.			
	a. *PAYABLE AT MONTREAL.*	—	—	—
	b. *PAYABLE AT TORONTO.*	—	—	—
	c. *PAYABLE AT OTTAWA.*	—	—	—
16A	**100 Dollars** 1.3.1872. Parliament bldg. at ctr.			
	a. *PAYABLE AT MONTREAL.*	—	—	—
	b. *PAYABLE AT TORONTO.*	—	—	—
	c. *PAYABLE AT OTTAWA.*	—	—	—

1878 ISSUE

#17-21 printer: BABNC.

		Good	Fine	XF
17	**1 Dollar** 1.6.1878. Black on green unpt. Portr. Countess of Dufferin at ctr. Scalloped borders, corners w/o numeral.			
	a. *PAYABLE AT MONTREAL* on back.	125.	500.	125
	b. *PAYABLE AT TORONTO* on back.	125.	500.	125
	c. *PAYABLE AT HALIFAX* on back.	500.	1500.	450
	d. *PAYABLE AT ST. JOHN* on back.	500.	1500.	450

18 **1 Dollar** | Good | Fine | XF

1.6.1878. Like #17 but w/ *1* in a circle at corners; also lettered border.

	Good	Fine	XF
a. W/o series letter; Series A-C. *PAYABLE AT MONTREAL* on back.	70.00	250.	140.
b. W/o series letter; Series A. *PAYABLE AT TORONTO* on back.	75.00	275.	1500.
c. *PAYABLE AT HALIFAX* on back.	550.	2250.	—
d. *PAYABLE AT ST. JOHN* on back.	550.	2250.	—

19 **2 Dollars**

1.6.1878. Black on green unpt. Portr. Earl of Dufferin (Gov. Gen.) at ctr.

	Good	Fine	XF
a. *PAYABLE AT MONTREAL* on back.	650.	2750.	8000.
b. *PAYABLE AT TORONTO* on back.	650.	3000.	9000.
c. *PAYABLE AT HALIFAX* on back.	1000.	3750.	11,500.
d. *PAYABLE AT ST. JOHN* on back.	1250.	4250.	—

1882 ISSUE

20 **4 Dollars**

	Good	Fine	XF
1.5.1882. Black on green unpt. Portr. Duke of Argyll (Gov. Gen. Marquis of Lorne) at ctr.	325.	1700.	4500.

1887 ISSUE

21 **2 Dollars**

2.7.1887. Black and green. Portr. Marchioness and Marquis of Lansdowne (Gov. Gen.) at lower l. and lower r.

	Good	Fine	XF
a. W/o series letter.	200.	1500.	2500.
b. Series Letter *A*.	500.	1800.	4500.

1896 BANK LEGAL ISSUE

#21A-21C used in bank transactions only. Printer: BABNC.

21A **500 Dollars**

2.7.1896. Black on peach unpt. Genius at lower l., Portr. Marquis of Lorne at ctr., Parliament bldg. tower at lower r. Back blue; seal of Canada at ctr.

	VG	VF	UNC
a. Issued note, cancelled.	—	5000.	—
p1. Face proof.	—	—	3000.
p2. Back proof.	—	—	500.
s. Specimen.	—	—	4000.

21B **1000 Dollars**

2.7.1896. Black. Portr. Qn. Victoria at l. Back deep brown; seal of Canada at ctr.

	VG	VF	UNC
a. Issued note, cancelled.	—	6500.	—
p1. Face proof.	—	—	3000.
p2. Back proof.	—	—	500.
s. Specimen.	—	—	4000.

21C **5000 Dollars**

2.7.1896. Black on yellow-orange unpt. Portr. J. A. MacDonald at l. Back red-brown; seal of Canada at top ctr.

	VG	VF	UNC
a. Issued note, cancelled.	—	6500.	—
p1. Face proof.	—	—	3000.
p2. Back proof.	—	—	500.
s. Specimen.	—	—	4000.

1897-1900 ISSUE

#22-25 printer: ABNC-Ottawa.

22 **1 Dollar**

	VG	VF	UNC
2.7.1897. Black on green unpt. Portr. Countess and Earl of Aberdeen (Gov. Gen.) at l. and r., lumberjacks at ctr. Back green; Parliament bldg. at ctr.	350.	1750.	7000.

#23 deleted.

24 **1 Dollar**

	VG	VF	UNC
31.3.1898. Like #22 but *ONE's* at l. and r. edge on back curved inward. Sign. Courtney. Series A-D.	110.	600.	2250.

24A **1 Dollar**

31.3.1898. Like #24 but *ONE's* at l. and r. edge on back curved outward.

	VG	VF	UNC
a. Sign. Courtney. Series D-K.	85.00	650.	1800.
b. Sign. Boville. Series L-S.	75.00	600.	1600.

24B **2 Dollars**

	VG	VF	UNC
2.7.1897. Black on green unpt. Portr. Edward, Prince of Wales, at l., boat w/fisherman at ctr. Back red-brown; farmers threshing wheat at ctr. Sign. Courtney.	1250.	3000.	—

24C **2 Dollars**

2.7.1897. Like #24B but dk. brown back.

	VG	VF	UNC
a. Sign. Courtney. W/o Series or w/Series A-C.	125.	750.	3000.
b. Sign. Boville. Series D-L.	110.	600.	2750.

25 **4 Dollars**

	VG	VF	UNC
2.7.1900. Black on green unpt. Portr. Countess and Earl of Minto (Gov. Gen.) at l. and r., ship in locks at Sault Ste. Marie (error: view of U.S. side of locks) at ctr. Back green; Parliament bldg. and library at l. ctr.	425.	2000.	7250.

1901 BANK LEGAL ISSUE

#25A-25B used in bank transactions only. Printer: ABNC-Ottawa.

25A **1000 Dollars**

2.1.1901. Black on green unpt. Portr. Lord E. Roberts at l. Back green.

	VG	VF	UNC
a. Issued note, cancelled.	—	3500.	—
p1. Face proof.	—	—	3000.
p2. Back proof.	—	—	500.
s. Specimen.	—	—	4000.

25B	5000 Dollars	VG	VF	UNC
	2.1.1901. Yellow-brown. Portr. Qn. Victoria at l. Back brown.			
	a. Issued note, cancelled.	—	3500.	—
	p1. Face proof.	—	—	3000.
	p2. Back proof.	—	—	500.
	s. Specimen.	—	—	4000.

1902 Issues

#26-26A printer: ABNC-Ottawa.

26	4 Dollars	VG	VF	UNC
	2.1.1902. Similar to #25 but vignette at ctr. changed to show ship in Canadian side of locks at Sault Ste. Marie, w/4's on top, *Four* on bottom.	800.	2500.	8500.

26A	4 Dollars	VG	VF	UNC
	2.1.1902. Like #26 but w/*FOUR* twice on top, 4's on bottom.	450.	1750.	6000.

1911 Issue

#27-32 printer: ABNC-Ottawa.

27	1 Dollar	VG	VF	UNC
	3.1.1911. Black on green unpt. Portr. Earl (Gov. Gen.) and Countess of Grey at ctr. Back green; Parliament bldg. at ctr.			
	a. Green line above sign. Series A-L.	50.00	200.	1250.
	b. Black line above sign. Series L-Y.	50.00	200.	1250.
28	**500 Dollars**			
	3.1.1911. Black on green unpt. Portr. young Qn. Mary at ctr. Back green.			
	a. Issued note. Rare..	—	—	—
	s. Specimen.	—	—	1500.

29	1000 Dollars	VG	VF	UNC
	3.1.1911. Black on blue unpt. Portr. Kg. George V at ctr. Back blue.			
	a. Issued note.	Rare		
	s. Specimen.	—	—	1250.

1912-14 Issue

30	2 Dollars	VG	VF	UNC
	2.1.1914. Black on lt. brown and olive unpt. Portr. Duke and Duchess of Connaught at l. and r. Back olive-green; 9 provincial shields around Royal arms at ctr.			
	a. Text: *WILL PAY...* curved above ctr. *2*. Sign. Boville at r.	60.00	300.	1400.
	b. Text: *WILL PAY...* straight above ctr. *2*. Sign. Boville at r.	75.00	325.	1500.
	c. W/o seal over r. *TWO*. Sign. Saunders at r.	75.00	325.	1500.
	d. Black seal over r. *TWO*. Sign. Hyndman-Saunders.	125.	450.	2250.
	e. Black seal, w/o *TWO* at r. Sign. Hyndman-Saunders.	125.	450.	2250.

31	5 Dollars	VG	VF	UNC
	1.5.1912. Black on blue unpt. Steam passenger train *Ocean Limited* in Nova Scotia at ctr. Back blue.			
	a. W/o seal over *FIVE* at r. Sign. Boville at r.	300.	750.	3000.
	b. W/o seal over *FIVE* at r. Sign. Boville at r. B after sheet no.	400.	1000.	3500.
	c. W/o seal over *FIVE* at r. Sign. Boville at r. B before sheet no.	225.	500.	1750.
	d. Blue seal over *FIVE* at r. Sign. Hyndman-Boville.	250.	700.	2500.
	e. Blue seal over *FIVE* at r. Sign. Hyndman-Saunders.	300.	750.	3000.
	f. Blue seal only at r. Sign. Hyndman-Saunders.	225.	500.	1750.
	g. Like d. Sign. McCavour-Saunders. Rare..	—	—	—

1917 Issue

32	1 Dollar	VG	VF	UNC
	17.3.1917. Black on green unpt. Portr. Princess Patricia Ramsey (Princess of Connaught) at ctr. W/o seal over r. *ONE*. Back green; Parliament bldg. at ctr.			
	a. W/o *ABNCo.* imprint. Sign. Boville at r.	35.00	125.	850.
	b. W/*ABNCo.* imprint. Sign. Boville at r.	35.00	125.	850.
	c. W/*ABNCo.* imprint. Sign. Saunders at r.	30.00	100.	750.
	d. Black seal over right *ONE*. Sign. Hyndman-Saunders.	35.00	125.	850.
	e. W/o *ONE* at r. Sign. Hyndman-Saunders.	35.00	125.	850.

1918 Bank Legal Issues

#32A-32B used in bank transactions only. Printer: ABNC.

32A 5000 Dollars

2.1.1918. Black on brown unpt. Portr. Qn. Victoria at l. Back yellow-brown.

	VG	VF	UNC
a. Issued note: Cancelled.	—	4000.	—
p1. Face proof.	—	—	3000.
p2. Back proof.	—	—	500.
s. Specimen.	—	—	4000.

32B 50,000 Dollars

2.1.1918. Black on olive-green unpt. Portr. Kg. George V and Qn. Mary at ctr. Back deep olive-green.

	VG	VF	UNC
a. Issued note: Cancelled.	—	6000.	—
p1. Face proof.	—	—	4000.
p2. Back proof.	—	—	800.
s. Specimen.	—	—	4500.

1923-25 Regular Issues

#33-34 printer: CBNC.

33 1 Dollar

2.7.1923. Black on green unpt. Portr. Kg. George V at ctr.; seal at r. Back green; Library of Parliament at ctr.

	VG	VF	UNC
a. Black seal. Sign. Hyndman-Saunders. Group 1.	35.00	100.	625.
b. Red seal. Sign. McCavour-Saunders. Group 1.	35.00	100.	625.
c. Blue seal. Sign. McCavour-Saunders. Group 1.	30.00	90.00	650.
d. Green seal. Sign. McCavour-Saunders. Group 1.	30.00	90.00	600.
e. Bronze seal. Sign. McCavour-Saunders. Group 1.	30.00	90.00	600.
f. Black seal. Sign. McCavour-Saunders. Group 2.	30.00	90.00	550.
g. Red seal. Sign. McCavour-Saunders. Group 2.	25.00	75.00	500.
h. Blue seal. Sign. McCavour-Saunders. Group 2A.	25.00	80.00	550.
i. Bronze seal. Sign. McCavour-Saunders. Group 2B.	25.00	75.00	350.
j. Green seal. Sign. McCavour-Saunders. Group 2C.	25.00	80.00	375.
k. Purple seal. Sign. McCavour-Saunders. Group 1.	125.	400.	1600.
l. Purple seal. Sign. Campbell-Sellar. Group 1.	200.	700.	2250.
m. Black seal. Sign. McCavour-Saunders. Group 3.	225.	750.	2400.
n. Black seal. Sign. Campbell-Sellar. Group 3.	20.00	65.00	300.
o. Black seal. Sign. Campbell-Clark. Group 4E.	17.50	45.00	175.
p. Black seal. Sign. Campbell-Clark. Group 4F.	40.00	100.	450.

Note: The Group # for 2, 3 and 4 is found to the right of the seal.

33A 1 Dollar

	VG	VF	UNC
2.7.1923. Like #33g. Serial # 1000001-1078500 on special Howard Smith Paper Co. stock.	350.	1000.	—

34 2 Dollars

23.6.1923. Black on olive unpt. Portr. Edward, Prince of Wales at ctr. Back olive-green; arms of Canada at ctr.

	VG	VF	UNC
a. Black seal. Sign. Hyndman-Saunders. Group 1.	50.00	150.	750.
b. Red seal. Sign. McCavour-Saunders. Group 1.	50.00	140.	650.
c. Blue seal. Sign. McCavour-Saunders. Group 1.	50.00	150.	800.
d. Green seal. Sign. McCavour-Saunders. Group 1.	60.00	150.	750.
e. Bronze seal. Sign. McCavour-Saunders. Group 1.	50.00	150.	700.
f. Black seal. Sign. McCavour-Saunders. Group 2.	50.00	150.	700.
g. Red seal. Sign. McCavour-Saunders. Group 2.	50.00	135.	650.
h. Blue seal. Sign. McCavour-Saunders. Group 2.	60.00	170.	700.
i. Blue seal. Sign. Campbell-Seller. Group 2.	55.00	160.	600.
j. Black seal. Sign. Campbell-Sellar. Group 3.	40.00	150.	650.
k. Black seal. Sign. Campbell-Clark. Group 3.	50.00	150.	650.
l. Black seal. Sign. Campbell-Clark. Group 4.	45.00	135.	650.

Note: The Group # is found to the right of the seal.

1924 Bank Legal Issue

#34A-34C used in bank transactions only. Printer: CBNC.

34A 1000 Dollars

2.1.1924. Black on green unpt. Portr. Lord E. Roberts at l. Back green.

	VG	VF	UNC
a. Issued note: Cancelled.	—	5000.	—
p1. Face proof.	—	—	3000.
p2. Back proof.	—	—	500.
s. Specimen.	—	—	3500.

34B 5000 Dollars

2.1.1924. Black on brown unpt. Portr. Qn. Victoria at l. Back yellow-brown.

	VG	VF	UNC
a. Issued note: Cancelled.	—	5000.	—
p1. Face proof.	—	—	3000.
p2. Back proof.	—	—	500.
s. Specimen.	—	—	3500.

34C 50,000 Dollars

2.1.1924. Black on olive-green unpt. Portr. Kg. George V and Qn. Mary at ctr. Back olive-green.

	VG	VF	UNC
a. Issued note: Cancelled.	—	6000.	—
p1. Face proof.	—	—	4000.
p2. Back proof.	—	—	500.
s. Specimen.	—	—	4500.

1924-25 Regular Issue

#35-37 printer: CBNC.

35 5 Dollars

	VG	VF	UNC
26.5.1924. Black on blue unpt. Portr. Qn. Mary at ctr. Back blue; east view of Parliament bldgs. at ctr.	1200.	2500.	7000.

36 500 Dollars

2.1.1925. Black on blue unpt. Portr. Kg. George V at ctr.

	VG	VF	UNC
a. Issued note. Rare..	—	—	—
s. Specimen.	—	—	2500.

#		VG	VF	UNC
37	**1000 Dollars** 2.1.1925. Black and orange. Portr. Qn. Mary at ctr.			
	a. Issued note. Rare..	—	—	—
	s. Specimen.	—	—	2500.

Banque du Canada / Bank of Canada

1935 Issues

#38-57 separate series in English and in French. Allegorical figures on back.

#38-39 printer: CBNC.

#		VG	VF	UNC
38	**1 Dollar** 1935. Black on green unpt. Portr. Kg. George V at l. English text. Back green; Agriculture seated at ctr. Series A; B.	15.00	50.00	240.
39	**1 Dollar** 1935. Like #38 but French text. Series F.	25.00	80.00	400.

#		VG	VF	UNC
40	**2 Dollars** 1935. Black on blue unpt. Portr. Qn. Mary at l. English text. Back blue; Mercury standing w/various modes of transportation at ctr.; Series A.	30.00	90.00	550.

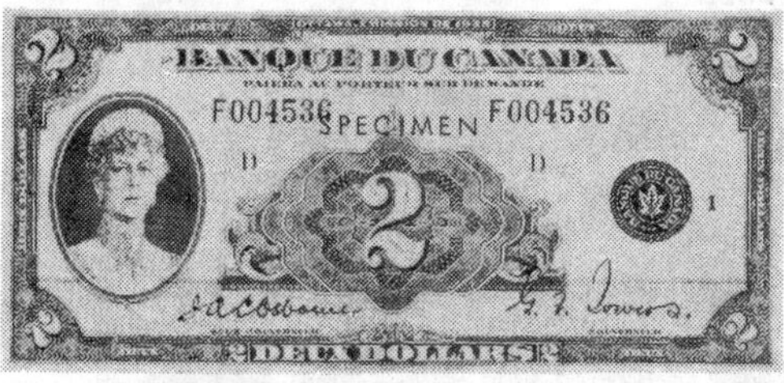

#		VG	VF	UNC
41	**2 Dollars** 1935. Like #40 but French text. Series F.	55.00	275.	2000.
42	**5 Dollars** 1935. Black on orange unpt. Portr. Edward, Prince of Wales at l. Back orange; Electric Power seated at ctr. English text. Series A.	45.00	150.	900.

#		VG	VF	UNC
43	**5 Dollars** 1935. Like #42 but French text. Series F.	55.00	320.	1500.

#		VG	VF	UNC
44	**10 Dollars** 1935. Black on purple unpt. Portr. Princess Mary at l. English text. Back purple; Harvest seated at ctr. Series A.	45.00	150.	850.
45	**10 Dollars** 1935. Like #44 but French text. Series F.	65.00	225.	1400.

#		VG	VF	UNC
46	**20 Dollars** 1935. Black on rose unpt. Portr. Princess Elizabeth at l. English text. Back rose; Agriculture w/farmer at ctr. Printer: CBNC. Series A.			
	a. Large seal.	225.	1000.	5500.
	b. Small seal.	175.	750.	4250.
47	**20 Dollars** 1935. Like #46 but French text. Series F.	300.	1400.	6250.

1935 Commemorative Issue

#48 and 49, Silver Jubilee of Accession of George V. Printer: CBNC.

#		VG	VF	UNC
48	**25 Dollars** 6.5.1935. Black on purple unpt. Portr. Kg. George V and Qn. Mary at ctr. English text. Back purple; Windsor Castle at ctr. Series A.	700.	1600.	4250.

#		VG	VF	UNC
49	**25 Dollars** 6.5.1935. Like #48 but French text. Series F.	900.	2100.	5750.

1935 Regular Issues

#50-57 printer: CBNC.

#		VG	VF	UNC
50	**50 Dollars** 1935. Black on brown unpt. Portr. Prince George, Duke of York (later Kg. George VI) at l. English text. Back brown; allegorical figure w/modern inventions at ctr. Series A.	400.	1150.	5000.
51	**50 Dollars** 1935. Like #50 but French text. Series F.	650.	1750.	6000.

#		VG	VF	UNC
52	**100 Dollars** 1935. Black on dk. brown unpt. Portr. Prince Henry, Duke of Gloucester at l. English text. Back dk. brown; Commerce seated w/youth standing at ctr. Series A.	350.	800.	3250.

#	Denomination / Description	VG	VF	UNC
53	**100 Dollars** 1935. Like #52 but French text. Series F.	625.	2100.	5750.
54	**500 Dollars** 1935. Black on brown unpt. Portr. Sir John A. MacDonald at l. English text. Back brown; Fertility reclining at ctr. Series A.	7000.	—	—
55	**500 Dollars** 1935. Like #54 but French text. Series F. Rare.	—	—	—
56	**1000 Dollars** 1935. Black on olive green unpt. Portr. Sir Wilfred Laurier at l. English text. Back olive-green; Security w/shield kneeling w/child at ctr. Series A.	850.	1300.	2500.
57	**1000 Dollars** 1935. Like #56 but French text. Series F.	1500.	3200.	6500.

1937 Issue

#58-65 bilingual notes. Allegorical figures on back like #38-47, 50-57.

#58-63 portr. Kg. George VI at ctr.

#	Denomination / Description	VG	VF	UNC
58	**1 Dollar** 2.1.1937. Black on green unpt. Back green. Printer: CBNC.			
	a. Sign. Osborne-Towers. Narrow (9mm) sign. panels.	6.00	17.50	115.
	b. Sign. Gordon-Towers. Narrow (9mm) sign. panels. Prefix H/A.	45.00	175.	475.
	c. Sign. Gordon-Towers. as b1. Prefix J/A.	120.	400.	900.
	d. Sign. Gordon-Towers. Wide (11mm) sign. panels. Prefix K/A-O/M.	3.00	8.00	30.00
	e. Sign. Coyne-Towers.	3.00	8.00	30.00
	#59-61 printer: BABNC.			
59	**2 Dollars** 2.1.1937. Black on red-brown unpt. Back red-brown. Printer: BABNC.			
	a. Sign. Osborne-Towers.	12.50	50.00	260.
	b. Sign. Gordon-Towers.	7.50	15.00	80.00
	c. Sign. Coyne-Towers.	7.50	15.00	80.00
60	**5 Dollars** 2.1.1937. Black on blue unpt. Back blue. Printer: BACNC.			
	a. Sign. Osborne-Towers.	40.00	120.	1100.
	b. Sign. Gordon-Towers.	7.50	15.00	80.00
	c. Sign. Coyne-Towers.	7.50	15.00	80.00
61	**10 Dollars** 2.1.1937. Black on purple unpt. Back purple. Printer: BABNC.			
	a. Sign. Osborne-Towers.	25.00	75.00	650.
	b. Sign. Gordon-Towers.	9.00	15.00	75.00
	c. Sign. Coyne-Towers.	9.00	15.00	75.00
	#62-65 printer: CBNC.			
62	**20 Dollars** 2.1.1937. Black on olive-green unpt. Back olive-green. Printer: CBNC.			
	a. Sign. Osborne-Towers.	30.00	100.	825.
	b. Sign. Gordon-Towers.	15.00	25.00	85.00
	c. Sign. Coyne-Towers.	15.00	25.00	85.00
63	**50 Dollars** 2.1.1937. Black on orange unpt. Back orange. Printer: CBNC.			
	a. Sign. Osborne-Towers	200.	650.	3750.
	b. Sign. Gordon-Towers.	45.00	65.00	400.
	c. Sign. Coyne-Towers.	45.00	65.00	400.

#	Denomination / Description	VG	VF	UNC
64	**100 Dollars** 2.1.1937. Black on brown unpt. Portr. Sir John A. MacDonald at ctr. Back brown. Printer: CBNC.			
	a. Sign. Osborne-Towers.	140.	250.	1300.
	b. Sign. Gordon-Towers.	70.00	120.	400.
	c. Sign. Coyne-Towers.	70.00	120.	400.
65	**1000 Dollars** 2.1.1937. Black on rose unpt. Portr. Sir Wilfred Laurier at ctr. Back rose. Sign. Osborne-Towers. Printer: CBNC.	900.	1150.	2500.

REPLACEMENT NOTES:

#66-70A and 74b, asterisk in front of fractional prefix letters. #76, 78-81, triple letter prefix ending in X (AAX, BAX, etc.). Exceptions: #82, no asterisk but serial number starts with 510 or 516; #83, serial number starts with 31 (instead of 30).

#84-90, as #76 and 78-81.

1954 'Devil's Face Hairdo' Issue

Devil's Face Hairdo

Modified Hairdo

#	Denomination / Description	VG	VF	UNC
66	**1 Dollar** 1954. Black on green unpt. "Devil's face" in Queen's hairdo. Back green; western prairie scene. Printer: CBNC.			
	a. Sign. Coyne-Towers.	4.50	9.00	45.00
	b. Sign. Beattie-Coyne.	3.50	6.00	37.50
	#67-69 printer: BABNC.			
67	**2 Dollars** 1954. Black on red-brown unpt. "Devil's face" in Queen's hairdo. Back red-brown; Quebec scenery. Printer: BABNC.			
	a. Sign. Coyne-Towers.	6.00	15.00	110.
	b. Sign. Beattie-Coyne.	4.50	10.00	75.00

#	Denomination / Description	VG	VF	UNC
68	**5 Dollars** 1954. Black on blue unpt. "Devil's face" in Queen's hairdo. Back blue; Otter Falls along the Alaska Highway. Printer: BABNC.			
	a. Sign. Coyne-Towers.	9.00	22.50	110.
	b. Sign. Beattie-Coyne.	8.00	17.50	90.00
69	**10 Dollars** 1954. Black on purple unpt. "Devil's face" in Queen's hairdo. Back purple; Mt. Burgess, British Columbia. Printer: BABNC.			
	a. Sign. Coyne-Towers.	10.00	20.00	90.00
	b. Sign. Beattie-Coyne.	9.00	17.50	85.00
	#70-73 printer: CBNC.			
70	**20 Dollars** 1954. Black on olive green unpt. "Devil's face" in Queen's hairdo. Back olive-green; Laurentian Hills in winter. Printer: CBNC.			
	a. Sign. Coyne-Towers.	15.00	30.00	140.
	b. Sign. Beattie-Coyne.	15.00	30.00	140.
71	**50 Dollars** 1954. Black on orange unpt. "Devil's face" in Queen's hairdo. Back orange; Atlantic coastline in Nova Scotia. Printer: CBNC.			
	a. Sign. Coyne-Towers.	35.00	60.00	250.
	b. Sign. Beattie-Coyne.	35.00	65.00	325.
72	**100 Dollars** 1954. Black on brown unpt. "Devil's face" in Queen's hairdo. Back brown; Okanagan Lake, British Columbia. Printer: CBNC.			
	a. Sign. Coyne-Towers.	75.00	110.	250.
	b. Sign. Beattie-Coyne.	75.00	110.	325.
73	**1000 Dollars** 1954. Black on rose unpt. "Devil's face" in Queen's hairdo. Back rose; central Canadian landscape. Sign. Coyne-Towers. Printer: CBNC.	1000.	1450.	3750.

1954 Modified Hair Style Issue

No.	Description	VG	VF	UNC
74	**1 Dollar**			
	1954 (1955-72). Black on green unpt. Like #66 but Queen's hair in modified style. Back green; western prairie scene. Printer: CBNC.			
	a. Sign. Beattie-Coyne. (1955-61).	1.00	2.50	15.00
	b. Sign. Beattie-Rasminsky. (1961-72).	1.00	2.00	12.50
75	**1 Dollar**			
	1954 (1955-74). Like #74. Printer: BABNC.			
	a. Sign. Beattie-Coyne. (1955-61).	1.00	2.50	20.00
	b. Sign. Beattie-Rasminsky. (1961-72).	1.00	1.50	7.50
	c. Sign. Bouey-Rasminsky. (1972-73).	1.00	1.50	8.50
	d. Sign. Lawson-Bouey. (1973-74).	1.00	1.50	7.50

No.	Description	VG	VF	UNC
76	**2 Dollars**			
	1954 (1955-75). Black on red-brown unpt. Like #67 but Queen's hair in modified style. Back red-brown. Quebec scenery. Printer: BABNC.			
	a. Sign. Beattie-Coyne. (1955-61).	1.75	4.00	30.00
	b. Sign. Beattie-Rasminsky. (1961-72).	1.75	3.00	20.00
	c. Sign. Bouey-Rasminsky. (1972-73).	1.75	3.00	15.00
	d. Sign. Lawson-Bouey. (1973-75).	1.75	3.00	15.00
77	**5 Dollars**			
	1954 (1955-72). Black on blue unpt. Like #68 but Queen's hair in modified style. Back blue; river in the north country. Printer: CBNC.			
	a. Sign. Beattie-Coyne. (1955-61).	5.00	10.00	65.00
	b. Sign. Beattie-Rasminsky. (1961-72).	4.50	7.50	35.00
	c. Sign. Bouey-Rasminsky. (1972).	4.50	7.50	30.00
78	**5 Dollars**			
	1954 (1955-61). Like #77. Sign. Beattie-Coyne. Printer: BABNC.	4.50	10.00	65.00

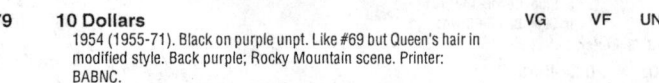

No.	Description	VG	VF	UNC
79	**10 Dollars**			
	1954 (1955-71). Black on purple unpt. Like #69 but Queen's hair in modified style. Back purple; Rocky Mountain scene. Printer: BABNC.			
	a. Sign. Beattie-Coyne. (1955-61).	9.00	12.50	55.00
	b. Sign. Beattie-Rasminsky. (1961-71).	9.00	12.50	45.00

No.	Description	VG	VF	UNC
80	**20 Dollars**			
	1954 (1955-70) Black on olive olive-green unpt. Like #70 but Queen's hair in modified style. Back olive green; Laurentian hills in winter. Printer: CBNC.			
	a. Sign. Beattie-Coyne. (1955-61).	17.50	25.00	100.
	b. Sign. Beattie-Rasminsky. (1961-70).	FV	20.00	65.00

No.	Description	VG	VF	UNC
81	**50 Dollars**			
	1954 (1955-75). Black on orange unpt. Like #71 but Queen's hair in modified style. Back orange; Atlantic coastline. Printer: CBNC.			
	a. Sign. Beattie-Coyne. (1955-61).	FV	50.00	175
	b. Sign. Beattie-Rasminsky. (1961-72).	FV	50.00	150
	c. Sign. Lawson-Bouey. (1973-75).	FV	65.00	20

No.	Description	VG	VF	UNC
82	**100 Dollars**			
	1954 (1955-76). Black on brown unpt. Queen's hair in modified style. Back brown; mountain lake. Printer: CBNC.			
	a. Sign. Beattie-Coyne. (1955-61).	FV	100.	275
	b. Sign. Beattie-Rasminsky. (1961-72).	FV	100.	225
	c. Sign. Lawson-Bouey. (1973-76).	FV	100.	25

No.	Description	VG	VF	UNC
83	**1000 Dollars**			
	1954 (1955-87). Black on rose unpt. Like #73 but Queen's hair in modified style. Back rose; central Canadian landscape.			
	a. Sign. Beattie-Coyne. (1955-61).	800.	1250.	2500
	b. Sign. Beattie-Rasminsky. (1961-72).	FV	950.	1750
	c. Sign. Bouey-Rasminsky. (1972).	FV	950.	1700
	d. Sign. Lawson-Bouey. (1973-84).	FV	FV	1250
	e. Sign. Thiessen-Crow. (1987).	FV	1000.	1500

1967 Commemorative Issue

#84, Centennial of Canadian Confederation

No.	Description	VG	VF	UNC
84	**1 Dollar**			
	1967. Black on green unpt. Qn. Elizabeth II at r. Back green; First Parliament Building. Sign. Beattie-Rasminsky.			
	a. Centennial dates: *1867-1967* replaces serial #.	1.00	1.50	3.50
	b. Regular serial #'s.	1.00	1.50	5.00

CAPE VERDE

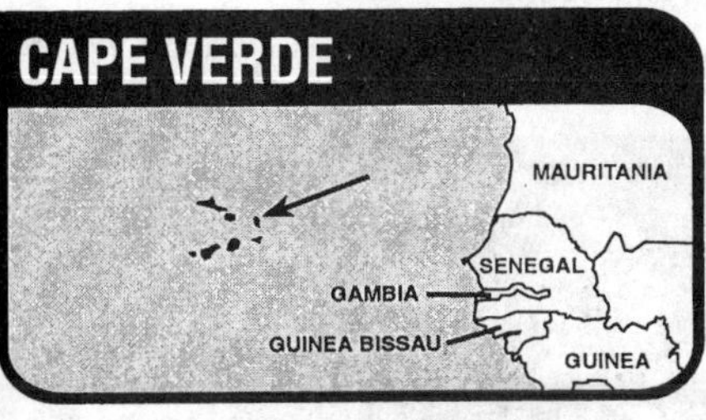

The Republic of Cape Verde, is located in the Atlantic Ocean, about 370 miles (595 km.) west of Dakar, Senegal off the coast of Africa. The 14-island republic has an area of 1,557 sq. mi. (4,033 sq. km.) and a population of 437,000. Capital: Praia. The refueling of ships and aircraft is the chief economic function of the country. Fishing is important and agriculture is widely practiced, but the Cape Verdes are not self-sufficient in food. Fish products, salt, bananas, coffee, peanuts and shellfish are exported.

The date of discovery of the islands is uncertain. Possibly they were visited by Venetian Captain Alvise Cadamosto in 1456. Portuguese navigator Diogo Gomes claimed them for Portugal in May of 1460. Settlement began two years later. The early importance and wealth of the islands, which caused them to be attacked by Sir Francis Drake and the Dutch, resulted from the monopoly of the Guinea slave trade granted the inhabitants in 1466. Poverty and famine occasioned by frequent periods of severe drought have marked the history of the country since abolition of the slave trade in 1876.

After 500 years of Portuguese rule, the Cape Verdes became independent on July 5, 1975.

RULERS:

Portuguese to 1975

MONETARY SYSTEM:

1 Mil Reis = 1000 Reis
1 Escudo = 100 Centavos, 1911-

STEAMSHIP SEALS:

Type I
S. THIAGO

Type II
LISBOA

Type III
C, C&A

C, C&A = Colonias, Commercio, Agricultura.

PORTUGUESE ADMINISTRATION

BANCO NACIONAL ULTRAMARINO

S. THIAGO DE CABO VERDE

1897 ISSUE

#1-3 *Agencia de S. Thiago de Cabo Verde.*

#		Good	Fine	XF
1	**1 Mil Reis** 2.1.1897. Brown. Man standing w/bow and arrow at l., embossed steamship seal at lower r.	—	—	—
2	**2 1/2 Mil Reis** 2.1.1897. Blue. Woman standing next to embossed steamship seal at lower r.	—	—	—
3	**5 Mil Reis** 2.1.1897. Bush at l., embossed steamship seal at lower r.	—	—	—

S. THIAGO

1909 ISSUE

#		Good	Fine	XF
4	**1000 Reis** 1.3.1909. Black on green and yellow unpt. Steamship seal at r. *S. Thiago.* ovpt. Printer: BWC.			
	a. Steamship seal Type I.	75.00	175.	500.
	b. Steamship seal Type III.	65.00	150.	450.

#5-9 portr. Vasco da Gama at l. Seated allegorical woman looking out at sailing ships on back. Ovpt: *S. Thiago.* Printer: BWC.

#		Good	Fine	XF
5	**2500 Reis** 1.3.1909. Black on m/c unpt. Sailing ships at r.			
	a. Steamship seal Type I.	90.00	275.	675.
	b. Steamship seal Type III.	85.00	250.	650.
6	**5 Mil Reis** 1.3.1909. Black on m/c unpt. Sailing ships at r.			
	a. Steamship seal Type I.	110.	350.	900.
	b. Steamship seal Type III.	100.	300.	800.

Note: For #6b w/rectangular ovpt: *PAGAVEL... GUINÉ* see Portuguese Guinea #5F.

#		Good	Fine	XF
7	**10 Mil Reis** 1.3.1909. Black on m/c unpt. Sailing ship at l. and r.			
	a. Steamship seal Type I.	160.	500.	—
	b. Steamship seal Type III.	150.	400.	—
8	**20 Mil Reis** 1.3.1909. Black on m/c unpt. Vasco da Gama embarking at r., palm fronds at lower l. and r.			
	a. Steamship seal Type I.	185.	650.	—
	b. Steamship seal Type III.	175.	550.	—
9	**50 Mil Reis** 1.3.1909. Black on m/c unpt. Palm trees at l., Vasco da Gama embarking at r.			
	a. Steamship seal Type I.	265.	1000.	—
	b. Steamship seal Type III.	250.	850.	—

1914 PROVISIONAL ISSUE

#		Good	Fine	XF
9A	**10 Centavos** 5.11.1914. Purple. Arms at r., steamship seal Type II at bottom ctr. Ovpt: *PAGAVEL EM S. TIAGO* on Port. Guinea #6.	100.	450.	—

1914 REGULAR ISSUES

#10-17 Arms at r., steamship seal at lower ctr. Allegorical woman looking out at sailing ships at ctr. on back. Red ovpt: *S. Tiago.* Printer: BWC.

#		Good	Fine	XF
10	**4 Centavos** 5.11.1914. Blue-green on m/c unpt. Steamship seal Type III.	12.50	70.00	275.
11	**5 Centavos** 5.11.1914. Rose on m/c unpt. Steamship seal Type I.	12.50	70.00	275.
11A	**5 Centavos** 5.11.1914. Rose on m/c unpt. Steamship seal Type III.	12.50	70.00	275.

#		Good	Fine	XF
11B	**5 Centavos** 5.11.1914. Bluish purple on m/c unpt. Steamship seal Type III.	10.00	35.00	175.
12	**10 Centavos** 5.11.1914. Purple on m/c unpt. Steamship seal Type I.	12.50	70.00	275.
12A	**10 Centavos** 5.11.1914. Purple on m/c unpt. Steamship seal Type II.	6.00	50.00	200.
13	**10 Centavos** 5.11.1914. Purple on m/c unpt. Steamship seal Type III.	10.00	35.00	175.
14	**20 Centavos** 5.11.1914. Blue on m/c unpt. Steamship seal Type II.	15.00	80.00	300.
15	**20 Centavos** 5.11.1914. Blue on m/c unpt. Steamship seal Type III.	10.00	35.00	175.

#		Good	Fine	XF
16	**50 Centavos** 5.11.1914. Green on m/c unpt. Steamship seal Type II.	15.00	80.00	300.
17	**50 Centavos** 5.11.1914. Green on m/c unpt. Steamship seal Type III.	15.00	80.00	300.

1920 ND Porto Issue

		Good	Fine	XF
18	**10 Centavos** 1.1.1920. Red. Sailing ship at l. and r.	75.00	300.	—
19	**50 Centavos** 1.1.1920. Blue. Mercury at l., ships at lower l., farmer and allegory at r. Back brown; sailing ship at ctr.	100.	500.	—
19A	**50 Centavos** 1.1.1920. Dk. blue. Arms at top ctr. Rare.	—	—	—

1921 Provisional Issue

#20-22A arms at r., steamship seal at lower ctr. Allegorical woman looking out at sailing ships at ctr. on back. Black ovpt: *CABO VERDE*. Various sign. varieties. Printer: BWC.

		Good	Fine	XF
20	**10 Centavos** ND (1921 - old date 5.11.1914). Purple on m/c unpt. Ovpt. on Mozambique #59.	8.00	30.00	165.
21	**20 Centavos** ND (1921 - old date 5.11.1914). Blue on m/c unpt. Ovpt. on Mozambique #60.	25.00	100.	350.
22	**50 Centavos** ND (1921 - old date 5.11.1914). Green on m/c unpt. Ovpt. on Mozambique #61.	30.00	125.	475.
22A	**50 Centavos** ND (1921 - old date 1.1.1921). Green on m/c unpt. Ovpt. on Portuguese Guinea #11. Rare.	—	—	—

1922 ND First Provisional Issue

#23-28 ovpt: *Emissao Chamico* in rectangular frame.

		Good	Fine	XF
23	**1000 Reis** ND (1922 - old date 1.3.1909). Black on green and yellow unpt. Ovpt. on #4b.	250.	1000.	—

#24-28 black on m/c unpt.

		Good	Fine	XF
24	**2500 Reis** ND (1922 - old date 1.3.1909). Ovpt. on #5. Rare.	—	—	—
26	**10 Mil Reis** ND (1922 - old date 1.3.1909). Ovpt. on #7. Rare.	—	—	—
27	**20 Mil Reis** ND (1922 - old date 1.3.1909). Ovpt. on #8. Rare.	—	—	—
28	**50 Mil Reis** ND (1922 - old date 1.3.1909). Ovpt. on #9. Rare.	—	—	—

1922 ND Second Provisional Issue

#29-31 portr. Francisco de Oliveira Chamico at l., steamship seal at r., arms at bottom ctr. Ovpt: *CABO VERDE* on notes of Portuguese Guinea.

		Good	Fine	XF
29	**20 Escudos** ND (1922 - old date 1.1.1921). Dk. blue on m/c unpt. Ovpt. on Port. Guinea #16.	250.	1000.	—
30	**50 Escudos** ND (1922 - old date 1.1.1921). Blue on m/c unpt. Ovpt. on Port. Guinea #17. Rare.	—	—	—
31	**100 Escudos** ND (1922 - old date 1.1.1921). Brown on m/c unpt. Ovpt. on Port. Guinea #18. Rare.	—	—	—

Cabo Verde

1921 Issue

#32-38 portr. Francisco de Oliveira Chamico at l., steamship seal at r., arms at bottom ctr. Allegorical woman looking out at sailing ships at ctr. on back. Printer: BWC.

		Good	Fine	XF
32	**1 Escudo** 1.1.1921. Green on m/c unpt.	6.00	35.00	125.
33	**5 Escudos** 1.1.1921. Green on m/c unpt. Ovpt. on #32.	35.00	200.	700.

		Good	Fine	XF
34	**5 Escudos**			
	1.1.1921. Black on m/c unpt.	15.00	100.	500.
35	**10 Escudos**			
	1.1.1921. Brown on m/c unpt.	20.00	150.	—
36	**20 Escudos**			
	1.1.1921. Dk. blue on m/c unpt.	50.00	325.	—
37	**50 Escudos**			
	1.1.1921. Red on m/c unpt.	—	—	—
38	**100 Escudos**			
	1.1.1921. Purple on m/c unpt.	—	—	—

1941 ISSUE

39 and 40 portr. Francisco de Oliveira Chamico at l., steamship seal at r., arms at bottom ctr. Allegorical woman looking out at sailing ships at ctr. on back.

		Good	Fine	XF
39	**50 Escudos**			
	1.8.1941. Red on m/c unpt.	—	—	—

		Good	Fine	XF
40	**1000 Escudos**			
	1.8.1941. Purple on m/c unpt.			
	a. Issued note.	—	—	—
	s. Specimen: punched hole cancelled.	—	—	—

1945 ISSUE

41-46 portr. Bartolomeu Dias at r., steamship seal at l., arms at upper ctr. Allegorical woman looking out at sailing ships at ctr. on back. Printer: BWC.

		VG	VF	UNC
41	**5 Escudos**			
	16.11.1945. Olive-brown.	8.00	40.00	125.
42	**10 Escudos**			
	16.11.1945. Purple.	10.00	85.00	250.

		VG	VF	UNC
43	**20 Escudos**			
	16.11.1945. Green.	20.00	250.	—
44	**50 Escudos**			
	16.11.1945. Blue.	35.00	350.	—
45	**100 Escudos**			
	16.11.1945. Red.	50.00	500.	—
46	**500 Escudos**			
	16.11.1945. Brown and violet.			

1958 ISSUE

Decreto Lei 39221

47-50 portr. Serpa Pinto at r., sailing ship seal at l. Allegorical woman looking out at sailing ships at ctr. on back. Sign. titles: *O-ADMINISTRADOR* and *VICE- GOVERNADOR*. Printer: BWC.

		VG	VF	UNC
47	**20 Escudos**			
	16.6.1958. Green on m/c unpt.			
	a. Issued note.	1.00	7.50	40.00
	s. Specimen.	—	—	50.00
	ct. Color trial. Blue on m/c unpt.	—	—	175.
48	**50 Escudos**			
	16.6.1958. Blue on m/c unpt.			
	a. Issued note.	4.00	35.00	175.
	s. Specimen.	—	—	50.00
	ct. Color trial. Green on m/c unpt.	—	—	300.

		VG	VF	UNC
49	**100 Escudos**			
	16.6.1958. Red on m/c unpt.			
	a. Issued note.	2.00	15.00	50.00
	s. Specimen.	—	—	50.00
	ct. Color trial. Brown on m/c unpt.	—	—	175.
50	**500 Escudos**			
	16.6.1958. Brown-violet on m/c unpt.			
	a. Issued note.	12.50	50.00	200.
	s. Specimen.	—	—	50.00
	ct. Color trial. Red on m/c unpt.	—	—	350.

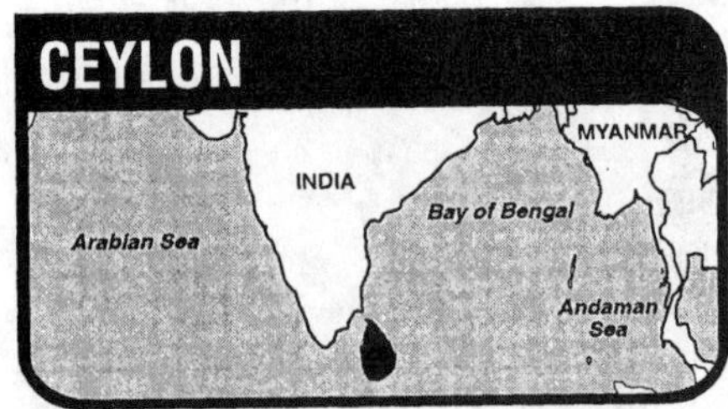

Ceylon (later to become the Democratic Socialist Republic of Sri Lanka), situated in the Indian Ocean 18 miles (29 km.) southeast of India, has an area of 25,332 sq. mi. (65,610 sq. km.) and a population of 18.82 million. Capital: Colombo. The economy is chiefly agricultural. Tea, coconut products and rubber are exported.

The earliest known inhabitants of Ceylon, the Veddahs, were subjugated by the Sinhalese from northern India in the 6th century BC. Sinhalese rule was maintained until 1498, after which the island was controlled by China for 30 years. The Portuguese came to Ceylon in 1505 and maintained control of the coastal area for 150 years. They were supplanted by the Dutch in 1658, who were in turn supplanted by the British who seized the Dutch colonies in 1796, and made them a Crown Colony in 1802. In 1815, the British conquered the independent Kingdom of Kandy in the central part of the island. Constitutional changes in 1931 and 1946 granted the Ceylonese a measure of autonomy and a parliamentary form of government. Ceylon became a self-governing dominion of the British Commonwealth on February 4, 1948. On May 22, 1972, the Ceylonese adopted a new constitution which declared Ceylon to be the Republic of Sri Lanka - "Resplendent Island." Sri Lanka is a member of the Commonwealth of Nations. The president is Chief of State. The prime minister is Head of Government.

For later issues, see Sri Lanka.

RULERS:

Dutch to 1796
British, 1796-1972

MONETARY SYSTEM:

1 Rix Dollar = 48 Stivers
1 Rupee = 100 Cents

Note: Certain listings encompassing issues circulated by various bank and regional authorities are contained in Volume 1.

BRITISH ADMINISTRATION

GENERAL TREASURY

1870s ISSUE

#1, 2 and 6 held in reserve.

#3-5 Britannia seated at ctr. w/lion and shield, elephant and palm trees in background. Printer: PB&P. (Not issued).

		Good	Fine	XF
3	**1 Pound**			
	18xx. Like #4.			
	r. Unsigned remainder.	—	—	350.
	s. Ovpt: *SPECIMEN.*	—	—	475.

		Good	Fine	XF
4	**2 Pounds**			
	18xx. Colombo.			
	r. Unsigned remainder.	—	—	400.
	s. Ovpt: *SPECIMEN.*	—	—	525.

		Good	Fine	XF
5	**5 Pounds**			
	18xx. Like #4.			
	r. Unsigned remainder.	—	—	400.
	s. Ovpt: *SPECIMEN.*	—	—	600.

GOVERNMENT

1809-26 ISSUE

#7 and 8 Britannia seated w/shield and trident at upper l. Uniface.

		Good	Fine	X
7	**2 Rix Dollars**			
	1.11.1826.	—	—	-

		Good	Fine
8	**5 Rix Dollars**		
	1.1.1809; x.2.1809.	—	—

1885-99 ISSUE

#9, 10, 13 and 14 held in reserve.

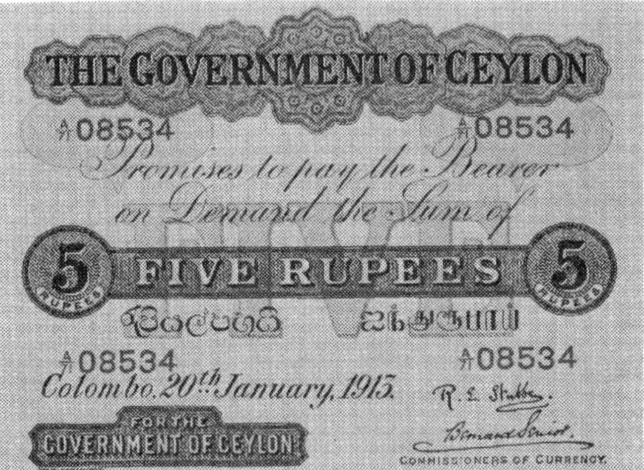

		Good	Fine	
11	**5 Rupees**			
	1885-1925. Black on green unpt. Uniface. 173 x 130mm.			
	a. 1885-1.11.1909.	175.	375.	8
	b. 2.1.1913-8.12.1919.	75.00	165.	4
	c. 1.9.1922; 1.9.1923; 1.10.1924; 1.10.1925.	50.00	150.	4

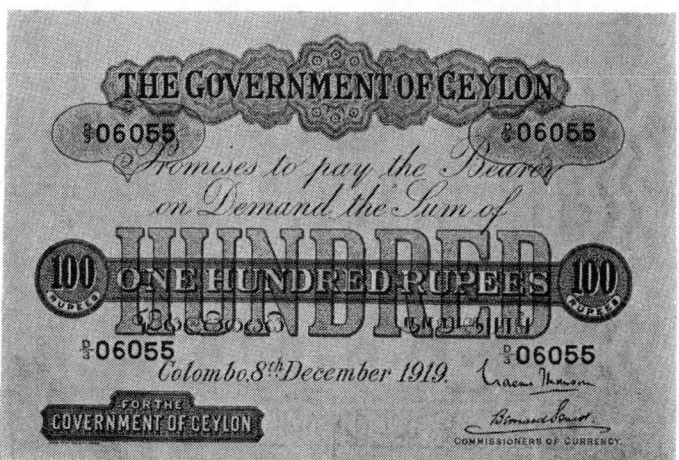

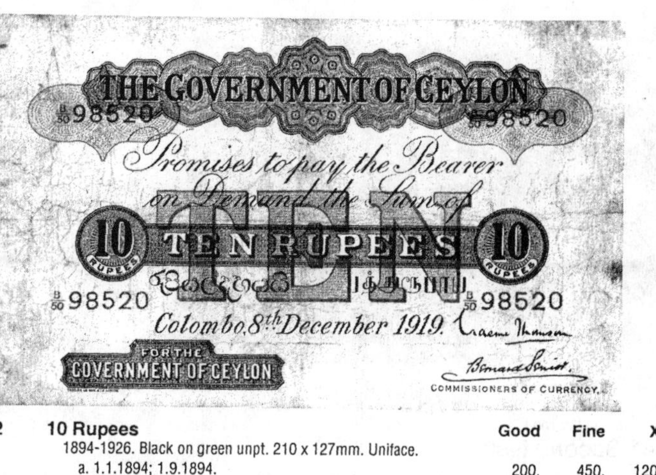

		Good	Fine	XF
12	**10 Rupees**			
	1894-1926. Black on green unpt. 210 x 127mm. Uniface.			
	a. 1.1.1894; 1.9.1894.	200.	450.	1200.
	b. 18.5.1908.	160.	350.	1000.
	c. 1.4.1914-1.6.1926.	75.00	225.	650.
15	**1000 Rupees**	Good	Fine	XF
	1.8.1899; 1.4.1915. 234 x 145mm. Uniface. Rare.	—	—	—

1914-19 Issues

16-29 w/o pictorial design, different dates, Colombo. Sign. varieties. Printer: TDLR.

		Good	Fine	XF
16	**1 Rupee**			
	1917-39. Blue on green, gray and lilac unpt. Back blue. Perforated or straight edge at l.			
	a. 1.5.1917-1.10.1924.	3.50	12.50	45.00
	b. 1.10.1925-2.10.1939.	2.50	8.00	30.00
17	**2 Rupees**			
	1.3.1917. Reddish brown on green and ochre unpt. *2* in circle at l. and r. Uniface.	20.00	120.	450.

		Good	Fine	XF
18	**2 Rupees**			
	10.11.1917; 23.3.1918; 1.10.1921. Black on green unpt. Uniface.	10.00	50.00	200.

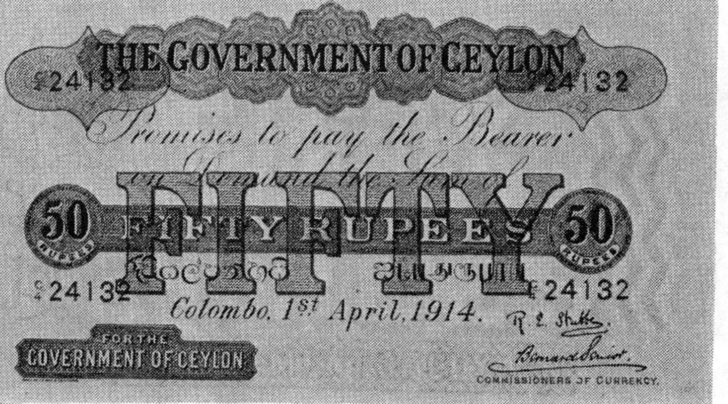

		Good	Fine	XF
19	**50 Rupees**			
	1.4.1914. Black on green unpt. 233 x 125mm. Uniface.	200.	450.	—

		Good	Fine	XF
20	**100 Rupees**			
	8.12.1919. Black on green unpt. 216 x 145mm. Uniface.	350.	900.	—

1926-32 Issues

		Good	Fine	XF
21	**2 Rupees**			
	1925-39. Black on green and lilac unpt. Back green; palm trees and elephant in central vignette. Perforated or straight edge at l.			
	a. Red serial #, yellow unpt. 1.10.1925; 1.6.1926; 1.9.1928; 1.7.1929.	5.00	30.00	100.
	b. Green serial #, dk. green unpt. 10.9.1930-2.10.1939.	3.00	15.00	65.00

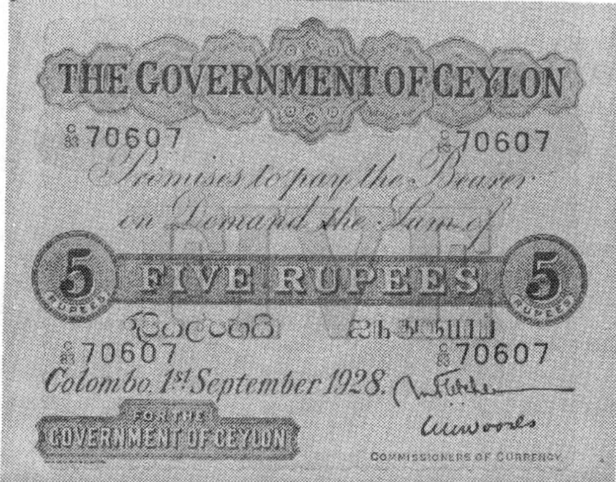

		Good	Fine	XF
22	**5 Rupees**			
	1.12.1925; 1.6.1926; 1.9.1927; 1.9.1928. Black on green and orange unpt. Back like #21. 170 x 130mm.	60.00	125.	375.

		Good	Fine	XF
23	**5 Rupees**			
	1.7.1929-2.10.1939. Black on green, orange and lilac unpt. Back like #21. Perforated or straight edge at l. 136 x 88mm.	10.00	30.00	125.

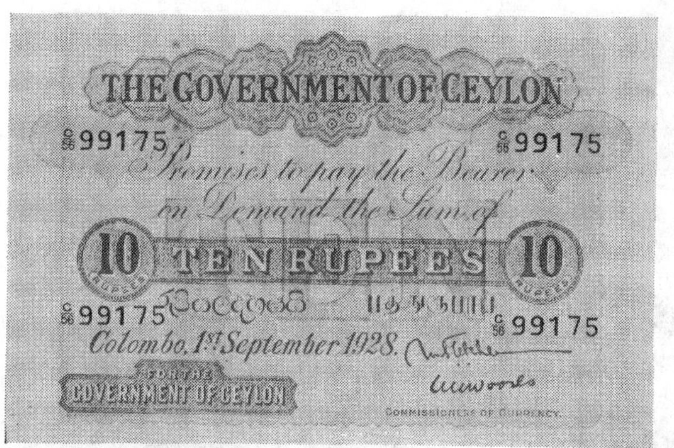

		Good	Fine	XF
24	**10 Rupees** 6.1.1927; 1.9.1928. Black on dull red and yellow-green unpt. Back dull red. Like #21. 198 x 127mm.	70.00	200.	550.

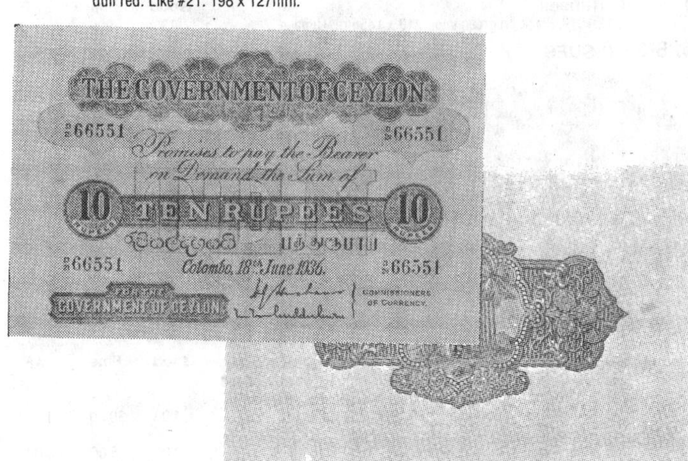

		Good	Fine	XF
25	**10 Rupees** 1.7.1929-2.10.1939. Gray on violet and yellow-green unpt. Back brown. 152 x 102mm.	9.00	45.00	175.
26	**50 Rupees** 1922-39. Similar to #25 but reduced size.	60.00	250.	850.
27	**100 Rupees** 1926-39. Similar to #20 but reduced size.	125.	450.	—
28	**500 Rupees** 1.6.1926. 233 x 145mm. Rare.	—	—	—
29	**1000 Rupees** 1.7.1929. Similar to #28 but reduced size. Rare.	—	—	—

1941 First Issue

#30-33 portr. Kg. George VI at l., text at upper ctr. begins *PROMISES TO PAY...* Title on face begins *THE GOVERNMENT...* Wmk: Chinze. Printed in India.

		VG	VF	UNC
30	**1 Rupee** 1.2.1941. Olive, lilac and blue. Elephant head on back. Perforated or straight l. edge.	5.00	15.00	50.00

		VG	VF	UNC
31	**2 Rupees** 1.2.1941. Violet on brown, blue and green unpt. Sigiriya Rock on back.	10.00	30.00	125.
32	**5 Rupees** 1.2.1941. Brown on lilac and blue unpt. Thuparama Dagoba on back.	15.00	60.00	200.

		VG	VF	UNC
33	**10 Rupees** 1.2.1941. Blue and m/c. Back blue on brown and tan unpt.; Temple of the Tooth.	25.00	100.	325.

1941 Second Issue

#34-39 portr. Kg. George VI at l. Text begins: *THIS NOTE IS LEGAL TENDER...* Printed in India.

		VG	VF	UNC
34	**1 Rupee** 20.12.1941-1.3.1949. Olive, lilac and blue. Similar to #30. Perforated or straight edge at l.	2.50	10.00	30.00

		VG	VF	UNC
35	**2 Rupees** 20.12.1941-1.3.1949. Violet and brown on blue and green unpt. Similar to #31. Perforated or straight edge at l.	4.00	15.00	50.00

		VG	VF	UNC
36	**5 Rupees** 20.12.1941-1.3.1949. Lilac and brown on green and blue unpt. Similar to #32. Perforated or straight edge at l.	7.50	45.00	120.

		VG	VF	UNC
6A	**10 Rupees** 20.12.1941-7.5.1946. Blue and m/c. Similar to #33.	10.00	50.00	175.

		VG	VF	UNC
7	**50 Rupees** 1941-45. Purple on green, blue and brown unpt. Back brown; farmer plowing w/water buffalo in rice paddy field.			
	a. Issued note. 4.8.1943; 12.7.1944; 24.6.1945.	100.	425.	—
	s. Specimen. 1.9.1941.	—	—	850.
8	**100 Rupees** 1941-45. Green on brown and red unpt. Back green and brown; Laxapana Waterfall.			
	a. Issued note. 4.8.1943; 24.6.1945.	100.	300.	850.
	s. Specimen. 1.9.1941.	—	—	525.

		VG	VF	UNC
	1000 Rupees 1.9.1941. Sailboat and costal scene on back. Specimen.	—	—	3000.
A	**10,000 Rupees** 15.10.1947. Green on m/c unpt. Kandy Lake scene on back. Specimen.	—	—	25,000.

ended for use with inter-bank transactions only.

1942 First Issue

		VG	VF	UNC
40	**25 Cents** 1.1.1942. Black text on green unpt. Uniface.	15.00	55.00	125.

		VG	VF	UNC
41	**50 Cents** 1.1.1942. Black text on red unpt. Uniface. Like #40.	35.00	100.	250.

1942 Second Issue

#43-46 text begins: *THIS NOTE IS LEGAL TENDER...* Printed in India.

		VG	VF	UNC
42	**5 Cents** 1.6.1942. Blue-gray. 2 and 3 cent postal card impressions w/portr. Kg. George VI. Uniface. (Sometimes rouletted down ctr. for ease of separation.)			
	a. W/o roulettes down ctr.	12.50	30.00	100.
	b. Rouletted 7 (7 dashes per 20mm) down ctr.	15.00	50.00	175.

		VG	VF	UNC
43	**10 Cents** 1942-43. Blue and m/c. Portr. Kg. George VI at ctr. Serial # on back. Uniface.			
	a. 1.2.1942; 14.7.1942.	2.50	12.00	20.00
	b. 23.12.1943.	2.50	15.00	20.00

		VG	VF	UNC
44	**25 Cents** 1942-49. Brown and m/c. Portr. Kg. George VI at ctr. Serial # on back. Uniface.			
	a. 1.2.1942; 14.7.1942.	2.00	12.50	25.00
	b. 7.5.1946; 1.3.1947; 1.6.1948; 1.12.1949.	2.50	15.00	25.00

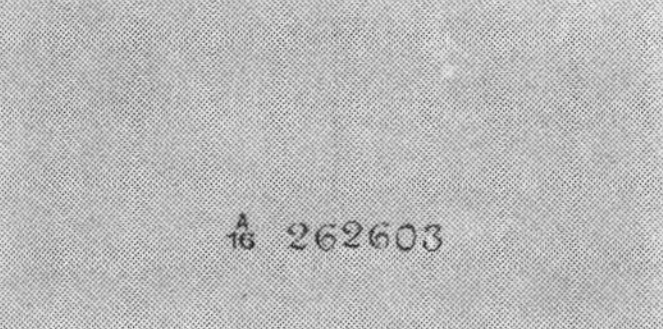

		VG	VF	UNC
45	**50 Cents** 1942-49. Lilac and m/c. Kg. George VI at l. Serial # on back. Uniface.			
	a. 1.2.1942; 14.7.1942; 7.5.1946; 1.6.1948.	3.00	20.00	50.00
	b. 1.12.1949.	5.00	20.00	60.00

CENTRAL BANK OF CEYLON

1951 ISSUE

#47 and 48 portr. Kg. George VI at l. Wmk: Chinze. Printer: BWC.

		VG	VF	UNC
47	**1 Rupee** 20.1.1951. Blue on orange and green unpt. Ornate stairway on back.	2.50	15.00	70.00

		VG	VF	UNC
48	**10 Rupees** 20.1.1951. Green on violet, brown and blue unpt. Ceremonial figures on back.	10.00	60.00	350.

1952 ISSUE

#49-55 portr. Qn. Elizabeth II at l. Wmk: Chinze. Printer: BWC.

		VG	VF	UNC
49	**1 Rupee** 3.6.1952; 16.10.1954. Similar to #47.	2.50	15.00	60.00

		VG	VF	UNC
50	**2 Rupees** 3.6.1952; 16.10.1954. Brown and lilac on blue and green unpt. Pavilion on back.	4.00	25.00	125.

		VG	VF	UNC
51	**5 Rupees** 3.6.1952. Purple on blue, green and orange unpt. Standing figure on back.	25.00	100.	500.
52	**50 Rupees** 3.6.1952; 12.5.1954. Blue, purple and m/c. Back blue and m/c; ornate stairway.	30.00	100.	—

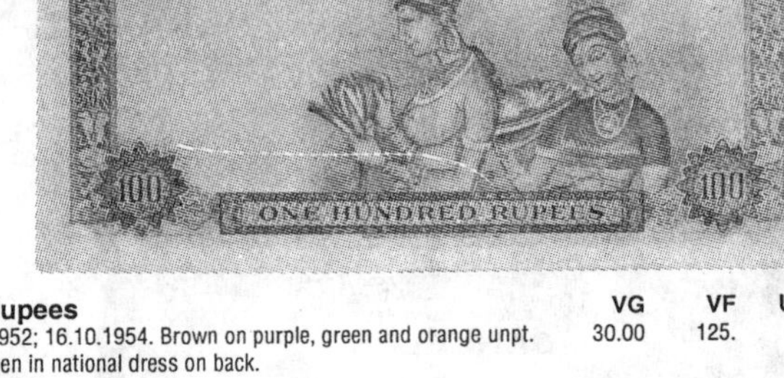

		VG	VF	UNC
53	**100 Rupees** 3.6.1952; 16.10.1954. Brown on purple, green and orange unpt. Women in national dress on back.	30.00	125.	85

1953-54 ISSUE

		VG	VF	UN
54	**5 Rupees** 16.10.1954. Orange on aqua, green and brown unpt. Like #51.	10.00	35.00	27
55	**10 Rupees** 1.7.1953; 16.10.1954. Similar to #48.	10.00	45.00	3C

STATE

CENTRAL BANK OF CEYLON

1956 ISSUE

#56-61 arms of Ceylon at l. W/o bank name in English. Various date and sign. varieties. Wmk: Chin Printer: BWC.

		VG	VF	UI
56	**1 Rupee** 1956-63. Blue on orange, green and brown unpt. Ornate stairway on back.			
	a. W/o security strip. 30.7.1956.	1.00	5.00	25.
	b. W/o security strip. 31.5.1957; 9.4.1958; 7.11.1958; 11.9.1959.	.75	2.00	10
	c. W/security strip. 18.8.1960; 29.1.1962; 5.6.1963.	.50	1.50	7.

		VG	VF	UI
57	**2 Rupees** 1956-62. Brown and lilac on blue and green unpt. Pavilion on back.			
	a. W/o security strip. 30.7.1956-11.9.1959.	2.00	6.00	30
	b. Security strip. 18.8.1960; 29.1.1962.	2.00	6.00	22

		VG	VF	UNC
58	**5 Rupees** 1956-62. Orange on aqua, green and brown unpt. Standing figure on back.			
	a. W/o security strip. 30.7.1956; 31.5.1957; 10.6.1958; 1.7.1959.	3.00	9.00	70.00
	b. Security strip. 18.8.1960; 29.1.1962.	2.50	6.00	45.00

		VG	VF	UNC
59	**10 Rupees** 1956-63. Green on violet, brown and blue unpt. Ceremonial figures on back.			
	a. W/o security strip. 30.7.1956; 7.11.1958; 11.9.1959.	3.00	8.00	50.00
	b. Security strip. 18.8.1960; 7.4.1961; 5.6.1963.	2.00	7.00	45.00

		VG	VF	UNC
60	**50 Rupees** 30.7.1956; 7.11.1958; 11.9.1959. Blue and violet on m/c unpt. Ornate stairway on back.	22.50	60.00	250.
61	**100 Rupees** 24.10.1956. Brown on m/c unpt. 2 women in national dress on back.	25.00	100.	450.

Note: For later issues see Ceylon and Sri Lanka listings in Volume 3, Modern Issues.

The Republic of Chile, a ribbonlike country on the Pacific coast of southern South America, has an area of 292,258 sq. mi. (756,945 sq. km.) and a population of 15.21 million. Capital: Santiago. Historically, the economic of Chile has been the rich mineral deposits of its northern provinces. Copper, of which Chile has about 25 percent of the world's reserves, has accounted for more than 75 per cent of Chile's export earnings in recent years. Other important exports are iron ore, iodine, fruit and nitrate of soda.

Diego de Almargo was the first Spaniard to attempt to wrest Chile from the Incas and Araucanian tribes, 1536. He failed, and was followed by Pedro de Valdivia, a favorite of Pizarro, who founded Santiago in 1541. When the Napoleonic Wars involved Spain, leaving the constituent parts of the Spanish Empire to their own devices, Chilean patriots formed a national government and proclaimed the country's independence, Sept. 18, 1810. Independence, however, was not secured until Feb. 12, 1818, after a bitter struggle led by Generals Bernardo O'Higgins and José de San Martín.

In 1925, the constitution was ratified to strengthen the Executive branch at the expense of the Legislature.

MONETARY SYSTEM:

1 Peso = 100 Centavos
1 Condor = 100 Centavos
1 Peso = 100 Centavos
1 Condor = 10 Pesos to 1960
1 Escudo = 100 Centesimos, 1960-75
1 Peso = 100 "old" Escudos, 1975-

REPLACEMENT NOTES:

#109, 111-112, R next to serial # on earlier notes, R next to small series # on later notes.

Note: Certain listings encompassing issues circulated by provincial, state and commercial banking authorities are contained in Volume 1.

VALIDATION HANDSTAMPS:

The Regional and Republic issues are found w/ or w/o various combinations of round validation handstamps.

Type I: *DIRECCION DEL TESORO-SANTIAGO* around National Arms (lg. and sm. size).

Type II: *DIRECCION DE CONTABILIDAD-SANTIAGO* around plumed shield on open book.

Type III: *SUPERINTENDENCIA DE LA CASA DE MONEDA* around screwpress/SANTIAGO.

Type IV: *CONTADURIA MAYOR* around plumed shield on open book.

REPUBLIC

REPÚBLICA DE CHILE

1880-81 ISSUE

#1-8 w/text: *convertible en oro o plata* (convertible in gold or silver). Text w/law date 10.4.1879 at r. on back. Printer: ABNC.

		Good	Fine	XF
1	**1 Peso** 5.4.1881. Black on orange unpt. 2 women seated at l., one holding a caduceus, bldg. at ctr. r., portr. Prat at lower r. Back green. Handstamps Type III and IV.	120.	400.	—

		Good	Fine	XF
2	**2 Pesos** 3.5.1880-19.2.1881. Black on green unpt. Man in uniform at upper l., village landscape at ctr. r., national arms at lower r. Back brown. Handstamps Type III and IV.	120.	400.	—

		Good	Fine	XF
3	**5 Pesos** 13.6.1880-12.11.1881. Black on brown unpt. Village landscape at upper l., plumed shield at ctr. r., portr. Gen. R. Freire at lower r. Back red-orange. Handstamps Type III and IV.	150.	450.	—
4	**10 Pesos** 4.1.1881-12.11.1881. Black on pink unpt. Towered bridge at upper l., portr. Pres. J. J. Perez at r. Back red-brown. 185 x 80mm. Handstamps Type III and IV.	200.	550.	—
5	**20 Pesos** ND (ca.1879). Black on brown unpt. Flower girl at l., man at l. ctr., bldg. at r., *VEINTE PESOS* w/o fringe along bottom margin. Back dk. brown. Specimen or proof.	—	—	—
6	**50 Pesos** ND (ca.1879). Black on blue unpt. Man in uniform l., bldg. at ctr., national arms at lower r., w/1 plate letter at upper l. and upper r. Back orange. Specimen or proof.	—	—	—
7	**100 Pesos** 4.1.1881; 26.1.1881; 12.11.1881. Black on orange unpt. Portr. B. O'Higgins at lower l., monument at ctr., 2 women seated w/shield at r., w/o double border. Back blue; text w/o border. 183 x 78mm. Handstamps Type III and IV.	250.	650.	—
8	**1000 Pesos** 12.11.1881. Black on olive unpt. Monument at l., national arms at ctr. r., man at lower r., w/o double border. Back red-brown; text w/o border. Handstamps Type III and IV.	—	—	—

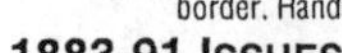

1883-91 Issues

#9-10 fractional currency issue. Printer: ABNC.

		Good	Fine	XF
9	**20 Centavos** ND (1891). Black on brown unpt. Portr. Liberty at upper l. Back green; arms at ctr. (Not issued).	15.00	40.00	85.00

		Good	Fine	XF
10	**50 Centavos** 10.6.1891. Black on green unpt. Portr. Liberty at top ctr. 2 date style varieties. Back brown; arms at ctr.			
	a. Handstamp Type I.	5.00	25.00	75.00
	r. Remainder w/o date, sign. or handstamp.	—	—	30.00

#11-14 convertible in gold or silver. Text w/law date 10.4.1879 at r. on back. Printer: ABNC.

		Good	Fine	XF
11	**1 Peso** 1883-98. Black on red-orange unpt. Similar to #1 but w/arms at l. and 1's in corners. Back green. Reduced size.			
	a. Handstamps Type III and IV. 17.2.1883.	20.00	75.00	160.
	b. Handstamps Type I and II. 17.5.1884-1.5.1895.	15.00	55.00	120.

		Good	Fine	XF
12	**2 Pesos** 17.11.1885-1.5.1895. Black on green unpt. Similar to #2 but reduced size. Back brown. Handstamps Type I and II.	30.00	100.	250.
13	**100 Pesos** ca.1880-90. Black on orange unpt. Similar to #7 but w/double border on face, single plate letter. Back blue.			
	p. Proof.	—	—	—
	s. Specimen.	—	—	—
14	**1000 Pesos** 18.8.1891. Black on olive unpt. Similar to #8 but w/double border on face, single plate letter. Back dk. red.	—	—	—

1898-1920 Issues

#15-28 convertible in gold only.

		Good	Fine	XF
15	**1 Peso** 1898-1919. Black on re-orange unpt. Similar to #11 but further reduced in size. Back dk. green. Printer: ABNC.			
	a. Handstamps Type I and III. 17.11.1898-7.6.1911.	2.00	10.00	35.00
	b. Handstamps Type I and II. 8.11.1911-13.8.1919.	1.00	5.00	20.00

#16-28 denomination numeral at r. on back.

		Good	Fine	XF
16	**2 Pesos** 17.11.1898-22.2.1912. Black on green unpt. Similar to #12 but further reduced in size. Handstamps Type I and II. Printer: ABNC.	5.00	25.00	60.00

		Good	Fine	XF
17	**2 Pesos** 22.2.1912-26.3.1919. Black on green unpt. Like #16. Handstamps Type I and II. Printer: W&S.	5.00	25.00	60.00

18	5 Pesos	Good	Fine	XF
	1899-1918. Black on brown unpt. Similar to #3. Back red-orange. Printer: W&S.			
	a. Handstamps Type I and III. 3.4.1899-25.4.1906.	25.00	100.	325.
	b. Handstamps Type I and II. 21.7.1916-20.6.1918.	12.50	50.00	150.

19	5 Pesos	Good	Fine	XF
	1906-16. Black on brown unpt. Similar to #18 but w/modified guilloches around *5's*, and other plate changes. Printer: ABNC.			
	a. Handstamps Type I and III. 23.5.1906-18.10.1910.	10.00	40.00	125.
	b. Handstamps Type I and II. 31.1.1911-21.7.1916.	8.00	35.00	100.

20	10 Pesos	Good	Fine	XF
	19.11.1899-6.6.1905. Black on red-brown unpt. Similar to #4. Handstamps Type I and III. Printer: W&S.	40.00	150.	350.

21	10 Pesos	Good	Fine	XF
	1905-18. Black on pink unpt. Similar to #20 but w/modified guilloches and other plate changes. Printer: ABNC.			
	a. Handstamps Type I and III. 28.9.1905-23.11.1910.	30.00	125.	275.
	b. Handstamps Type I and II. 7.6.1911-20.6.1918.	20.00	60.00	150.

22	20 Pesos	Good	Fine	XF
	1906-14. Black on brown unpt. Similar to #5 but w/fringe around *VEINTE PESOS* along bottom margin. Back dk. brown. Printer: ABNC.			
	a. Handstamps Type I and III. 31.3.1906-21.6.1910.	30.00	125.	300.
	b. Handstamps Type I and II. 13.5.1912-1.8.1914.	20.00	60.00	150.

23	20 Pesos	Good	Fine	XF
	1900-04. Black on red unpt. Similar to #22. Printer: W&S.			
	a. Handstamps Type I and III. 6.12.1900; 31.8.1903; 27.10.1904.	30.00	125.	300.
	b. Handstamps Type I and II. 18.11.1903; 30.4.1904.	30.00	125.	300.

24	50 Pesos	Good	Fine	XF
	1899-1914. Black on blue unpt. Similar to #6. Back orange. Printer: ABNC.			
	a. Handstamps Type I and III. 16.12.1899; 30.12.1904; 4.3.1905.	50.00	150.	450.
	b. Handstamps Type I and II. 18.7.1912, 25.9.1912, 31.10, 1912, 1.8.1914, 18.7.1912-1.8.1914.	45.00	125.	350.

25	100 Pesos	Good	Fine	XF
	1920. Black on blue and gold unpt. Similar to #13 but w/o *plata*, w/double plate letter. Back green. Printer: ABNC.			
	a. Handstamps Type I and III.	100.	350.	—
	b. Handstamps Type I and II. 29.3.1920.	80.00	300.	—

NOTICE

Readers with unlisted dates, signature varieties, etc. are invited to submit photocopies or, high resolution (300 dpi, 100% size) scans of their notes to: Standard Catalog of World Paper Money, 700 East State St. Iola, WI 54990-0001, or E-Mail: george.cuhaj@fwpubs.com.

26	100 Pesos	Good	Fine	XF
	1906-16. Black on blue and red unpt. B. O'Higgins at l., monument at r. Back orange. Printer: ABNC.			
	a. Handstamps Type I and III. 23.5.1906.	90.00	325.	—
	b. Handstamps Type I and II. 4.3.1912; 31.3.1913; 22.12.1916.	75.00	250.	—

27	500 Pesos	Good	Fine	XF
	14.5.1912; 12.8.1912; 15.5.1917. Black on green and yellow unpt. Man at l. ctr., bldg. at r. Handstamps Type I and II. Back orange. Printer: ABNC.	300.	700.	—
27a	1000 Pesos			
	12.11.1881. Monument at l., arms at ctr. r., men at lower r. Back red-brown; text at r. and w/o border. 185 x 80mm. Printer: ABNC.	—	—	—
28a	1000 Pesos			
	12.8.1912. Similar to #14 but w/o *plata*, w/double plate letter. Back dk. red. Printer: ABNC.	350.	1000.	—

1898 Provisional Issue on Banco de José Bunster

Lei 1054 de 31 de Julio de 1898.

Date 14.9.1898 on face of most notes.

29	1 Peso	Good	Fine	XF
	17.8.1898. Black on yellow unpt. Ovpt. on #S131. Rare.	—	—	—

1898 Provisional Issue on Banco Comercial de Chile

30	1 Peso	Good	Fine	XF
	17.8.1898. Black on yellow and pink unpt. Ovpt. on #S151. Rare.	—	—	—

31	2 Pesos	Good	Fine	XF
	17.8.1898. Black on green and pink unpt. Ovpt. on #S152. Rare.	—	—	—

32	10 Pesos	Good	Fine	XF
	17.8.1898 (- old date 8.6.1893). Black on green and rose unpt. Ovpt. on #S160. Rare.	—	—	—
33	20 Pesos			
	1.8.1898 (-old date 8.6.1893). Ovpt. on #S161. Rare.	—	—	—

1898 Provisional Issue on Banco de Concepción

34	1 Peso	Good	Fine	XF
	14.9.1898. Black on green and m/c unpt. Ovpt. on #S176.	300.	750.	—

1898 Provisional Issue on Banco de Curicó

35	5 Pesos	Good	Fine	XF
	14.9.1898. Black on green and peach unpt. Ovpt. on #S218. Rare.	—	—	—

		Good	Fine	XF
36	**20 Pesos** 18.8.1898; 14.9.1898. Black on blue and yellow unpt. Ovpt. on #S220. Rare.	—	—	—

1898 Provisional Issue on Banco de Escobar Ossa y Ca

Spurious Issue.

		Good	Fine	XF
37	**5 Pesos** 14.9.1898. Black on blue unpt. Ovpt. on #S253. Rare.	—	—	—

		Good	Fine	XF
38	**10 Pesos** 14.9.1898. Black on brown unpt. Ovpt. on #S254. Rare.	—	—	—
39	**20 Pesos** 14.9.1898. Black on rose-pink unpt. Ovpt. on #S255. Rare.	—	—	—

1898 Provisional Issue on Banco de D. Matte y Ca

		Good	Fine	XF
40	**10 Pesos** 1.8.1898. Black on yellow and green unpt. Ovpt. on #S278. Rare.	—	—	—

1898 Provisional Issue on Banco de Matte, Mac-Clure y Ca

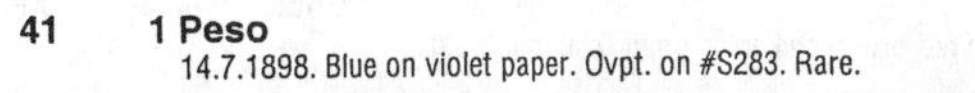

		Good	Fine	XF
41	**1 Peso** 14.7.1898. Blue on violet paper. Ovpt. on #S283. Rare.	—	—	—

1898 Provisional Issue on Banco de Melipilla

		Good	Fine	XF
42	**5 Pesos** 1.8.1898. Black on tan unpt. Ovpt. on #S297. Rare.	—	—	—

1898 Provisional Issue on Banco de Mobiliario

		Good	Fine	XF
43	**1 Peso** 17.8.1898. Black on green and gold unpt. Ovpt. on #S306. Rare.	—	—	—

		Good	Fine	XF
44	**10 Pesos** 14.9.1898. Black. Ovpt. on #S308. Rare.	—	—	—

1898 Provisional Issue on Banco Nacional de Chile, Valparaiso

		Good	Fine	XF
45	**1 Peso** 17.8.1898. Black on green and peach unpt. Ovpt. on #S331.	300.	700.	—

		Good	Fine	XF
46	**2 Pesos** 17.8.1898. Black on red-brown and green unpt. Ovpt. on #S332. Rare.	—	—	—
47	**5 Pesos** 31.7.1898. Black on green and orange unpt. Ovpt. on #S333. Rare.	—	—	—
48	**10 Pesos** 17.8.1898. Black on green and brown unpt. Ovpt. on #S334. Rare.	—	—	—
49	**500 Pesos** 17.8.1898. Black on green and yellow unpt. Ovpt. on #S338. Rare.	—	—	—

1898 Provisional Issue on Banco San Fernando

		Good	Fine	XF
50	**5 Pesos** 16.5.1899. Black on green unpt. Ovpt. on #S397. Rare.	—	—	—

Note: Some authorities believe that all notes from this bank appearing to have been issued are in reality fraudulently dated and signed.

1898 Provisional Issue on Banco de Santiago

		Good	Fine	XF
51	**1 Peso** 14.9.1898. (- old date 25.2.1896). Black on brown unpt. Ovpt. on #S411.	60.00	275.	—

Note: Regular commercial bank issues of #29-51 including other denominations w/o ovpt: *EMISION FISCAL* are listed in Volume 1.

1898 Provisional Issue on República de Chile

		Good	Fine	XF
52	**1 Peso** 17.8.1898; 26.9.1898. Ovpt. on #11.	60.00	275.	—

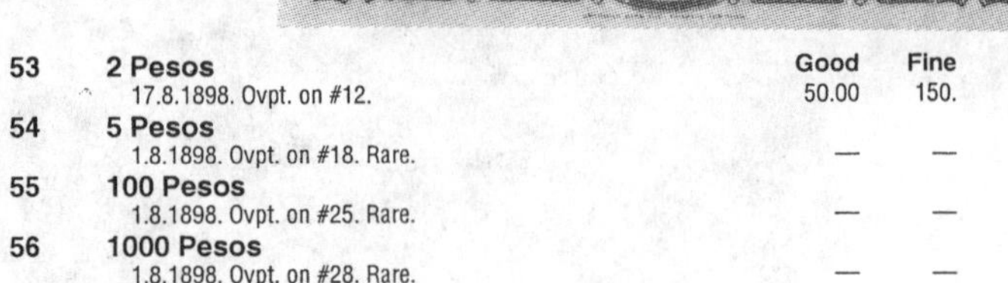

		Good	Fine	XF
53	**2 Pesos** 17.8.1898. Ovpt. on #12.	50.00	150.	—
54	**5 Pesos** 1.8.1898. Ovpt. on #18. Rare.	—	—	—
55	**100 Pesos** 1.8.1898. Ovpt. on #25. Rare.	—	—	—
56	**1000 Pesos** 1.8.1898. Ovpt. on #28. Rare.	—	—	—

1918-25 Regular Issues

#57-66 w/handstamps Type I and II.

		Good	Fine	XF
57	**2 Pesos** ND. Black on blue and lt. brown unpt. Heading in 1 line. Condor at r. Back dk. olive; seated woman w/shield at ctr. (Not issued).	—	—	—

		Good	Fine	XF
58	**2 Pesos** 19.10.1920-30.1.1922. Blue on green and red unpt. Woman seated w/shield at r. Back brown on red unpt. Red serial #.	2.50	7.50	45.00
59	**2 Pesos** 1922-25. Blue on yellow unpt. Similar to #58. Back brown w/o unpt.			
	a. Brown serial #. 5.5.1922.	2.50	7.50	45.00
	b. Blue serial #. 20.12.1922-22.9.1925.	2.00	6.00	30.00

		Good	Fine	XF
60	**5 Pesos** 14.8.1918-2.1.1922. Blue. Woman seated w/shield at l., value at r. Red serial #. Allegorical figures at l. and r. on back.	4.00	20.00	60.00
61	**5 Pesos** 16.8.1922-22.9.1925. Blue on yellow unpt. Like #60. Date in 1 or 2 lines. Blue serial #. 2 sign. varieties.	2.50	10.00	45.00

		Good	Fine	XF
62	**10 Pesos** 11.12.1918-2.1.1922. Brown on pink unpt. Condor at l., woman seated w/shield at ctr.	7.50	30.00	80.00
63	**10 Pesos** 31.7.1922-22.9.1925. Brown in green unpt. Like #62. 2 sign. varieties.	4.00	20.00	65.00
64	**20 Pesos** 1919-24. Green on rose unpt. Condor at l., woman seated w/shield at r.			
	a. Red serial #. Series A. 24.6.1919-10.6.1920.	20.00	60.00	200.
	b. Blue serial #. Series B. 25.2.1924.	20.00	60.00	200.

		Good	Fine	XF
65	**50 Pesos** 4.5.1917-17.6.1923. Blue-green. Woman seated w/shield at l., ships at r. Back blue.	30.00	100.	350.
66	**100 Pesos** 1917-24. Blue on lt. blue paper. Woman seated w/shield at l., 3 women reclining at r. Back brown; woman and globe at ctr.			
	a. Red unpt. and serial #. Date placement higher or lower. 19.9.1917-30.6.1921.	45.00	225.	600.
	b. Blue unpt. and serial #. 17.7.1923-31.10.1924.	40.00	200.	500.
66A	**500 Pesos** ND (ca. 1919). Dk. blue on purple unpt. Seated figure at l., woman seated w/shield at r. Allegorical figures of Agriculture at l., Music at r. on back. Specimen.	—	—	—
66B	**1000 Pesos** 4.3.1921. Dk. brown on purple and yellow unpt. Seated woman at l., seated woman w/shield at r. Seated woman at l. and r. on back.	450.	950.	—

VALE DEL TESORO

1921-24 ISSUES

#67-70 special issue backed by saltpeter instead of gold.

		Good	Fine	XF
67	**50 Pesos** 1921; 1924. Lt. blue. Woman reclining at l. Handstamps Type I and II.			
	a. Series B. 7.9.1921. White paper.	150.	400.	—
	b. Series C. 2.12.1924. Blue paper. Wmk. diff. from a.	150.	400.	—
68	**100 Pesos** 1921; 1924. Brown and ochre. Woman at l.			
	a. Series B. Face ochre, back gold. Ochre paper. 7.9.1921.	150.	400.	—
	b. Series C. Dk. brown on lt. brown paper. 2.12.1924. Wmk. diff. from a.	150.	400.	—
69	**500 Pesos** 25.4.1921; 2.12.1924. Black on lilac unpt. Seated woman at l. Rare.	—	—	—
70	**1000 Pesos** 4.3.1921; 2.12.1924. Seated allegorical figure at l. and r. Rare.	—	—	—

BANCO CENTRAL DE CHILE

1925 FIRST PROVISIONAL ISSUE

#71-81 ovpt: new bank name, value in Condores, *BILLETE PROVISIONAL* and bank validation stamp on República de Chile notes.

		Good	Fine	XF
71	**5 Pesos = 1/2 Condor** 10.12.1925. Blue on yellow unpt. Woman seated w/shield at l. Ovpt. on #61.	2.50	10.00	35.00
72	**5 Pesos = 1/2 Condor** 10.12.1925. Dk. blue on lt. blue and yellow unpt. Woman seated w/shield at l. Back blue; condor at ctr., allegorical figure at r.	2.50	10.00	35.00
73	**10 Pesos = 1 Condor** 10.12.1925. Brown. Woman seated w/shield at l. Back blue-green.	3.00	12.50	50.00

		Good	Fine	XF
74	**10 Pesos = 1 Condor** 10.12.1925. Brown on green unpt. Condor at l., seated woman w/shield at ctr. Ovpt. on #63.	3.00	12.50	50.00
75	**100 Pesos = 10 Condores** 10.12.1925. Black on blue unpt. Woman seated w/shield at l., 3 women reclining at r. Blue paper. Ovpt. on #66b.	45.00	150.	350.

		Good	Fine	XF
76	**500 Pesos = 50 Condores** 10.12.1925. Brown on orange unpt. Woman reclining at l., woman seated w/shield at r. Back blue.	80.00	250.	650.
77	**1000 Pesos = 100 Condores** 10.12.1925. Dk. brown on violet and yellow unpt. Woman seated w/horns at l., woman seated w/shield at r. Back violet.	—	—	—

1925 SECOND PROVISIONAL ISSUE

#78-81 printed bank name.

		Good	Fine	XF
78	**50 Pesos** 10.12.1925. Blue. Similar to #67. Back green. Series D.	—	—	—
79	**100 Pesos** 10.12.1925. Brown. Similar to #68. Back brown. Series D.	—	—	—
80	**500 Pesos** 10.12.1925. Similar to #76. Rare.	—	—	—
81	**1000 Pesos** 10.12.1925. Similar to #77. Rare.	—	—	—

1927-29 BILLETE PROVISIONAL ISSUE

Values in Pesos and Condores.

#82-87 various dates and sign. varieties. W/lg. or sm. serial # varieties. Wmk: BANCO CENTRAL DE CHILE.

		Good	Fine	XF
82	**5 Pesos = 1/2 Condor** 18.4.1927-2.6.1930. Black on green unpt. Blue paper. Back brown. Series B-E.	1.50	7.50	25.00

		Good	Fine	XF
83	**10 Pesos = 1 Condor** 1927-30. Black on salmon unpt. Yellow paper. Back dk. blue. Series B-C.			
	a. Printer's name in margin. 18.4.1927.	2.00	10.00	30.00
	b. Printer's name in frame. 14.5.1928-2.6.1930.	1.50	7.50	25.00

84	50 Pesos = 5 Condores	Good	Fine	XF
	1927-30. Black on brown unpt. Pink paper. Condor at upper l. Back brown. Series E-K.			
	a. Printer's name in margin. 28.3.1927.	10.00	25.00	75.00
	b. Printer's name in frame. 14.5.1928-2.6.1930.	5.00	20.00	50.00

		Good	Fine	XF
85	**100 Pesos = 10 Condores** 28.3.1927-2.6.1930. Black on lt. blue and red-brown unpt. Back dk. green. Series E-H.	10.00	25.00	75.00
86	**500 Pesos = 50 Condores** 29.1.1929. Green on purple unpt. Condor at upper l. Back red-orange. Series D.	50.00	150.	300.

		Good	Fine	XF
87	**1000 Pesos = 100 Condores** 29.1.1929. Blue on pink and purple unpt. Andean condor at upper l. Back dk. purple.	90.00	200.	500.

1932 Billete Provisional Issue

88	1 Peso = 1/10 Condor	VG	VF	UNC
	1932-33. Black frame, blue ctr. w/wide diagonal pink stripe. Back green. 120 x 60mm.			
	a. Tan paper. 12.9.1932.	1.00	4.00	15.00
	b. Peach paper. 7.3.1933.	1.00	4.00	15.00

1942-43 Billete Provisional Issues

		VG	VF	UNC
89	**1 Peso = 1/10 Condor** 11.2.1942. Like #82 but blue frame. Pink paper. 124 x 62mm.	1.00	3.00	10.00

90	1 Peso = 1/10 Condor	VG	VF	UNC
	3.3.1943. Blue on yellow unpt. 88 x 50mm.			
	a. Back lt. orange; w/A-A.	.50	2.00	5.00
	b. Back purple; w/B-B.	.50	2.00	5.00
	c. Back green; w/C-C.	.50	2.00	5.00
	d. Back red-orange; w/D-D.	.50	2.00	5.00
	e. Back blue; w/E-E. (Not issued). Rare..	—	—	—

1931-42 Issues

#91-101 w/o name under portr. Values given in Pesos and Condores. Various date and sign. varieties.

91	5 Pesos = 1/2 Condor	VG	VF	UNC
	1932-42. Blue on lt. orange unpt. Portr. B. O'Higgins at r.			
	a. 26.9.1932.	6.00	15.00	30.00
	b. 17.6.1933.	3.00	7.00	15.00
	c. 3.7.1935-8.7.1942.	1.00	3.00	10.00

92	10 Pesos = 1 Condor	VG	VF	UNC
	1931-42. Red-brown on lt. yellow unpt. Portr. Bulnes at r. Back brown.			
	a. Month in letters. 9.2.1931.	2.50	10.00	30.00
	b. Month in Roman numerals. 29.9.1932.	2.00	8.00	25.00
	c. 7.6.1933; 22.11.1933.	1.00	6.00	20.00
	d. 31.12.1934-8.7.1942.	1.00	3.00	10.00

93	20 Pesos = 2 Condores	VG	VF	UNC
	1939-47. Portr. Capt. Valdivia at ctr. Statue in park w/trees and bldg. at ctr. on back.			
	a. Purple-brown. Back vignette lilac. 22.11.1939.	1.50	5.00	15.00
	b. Brown. Back vignette brown. 2.4.1947; 24.12.1947.	1.00	4.00	12.50

94	50 Pesos = 5 Condores	VG	VF	UNC
	1932-42. Green. Portr. Pinto at r. Back green on lt. gold unpt. German-style lettering and numerals at corners and l. ctr.			
	a. 22.8.1932.	3.00	15.00	40.00
	b. 22.11.1933.	2.50	12.00	30.00
	c. 3.7.1935-8.7.1942.	1.00	8.00	20.00

		VG	VF	UNC
95	**100 Pesos = 10 Condores** 7.6.1933-10.3.1937. Red. Portr. Prat at r. Face w/white unpt.	3.00	20.00	50.00
96	**100 Pesos = 10 Condores** 19.4.1939-20.1.1943. Face w/red unpt. Different plate from #95.	2.00	10.00	35.00

		VG	VF	UNC
97	**500 Pesos = 50 Condores** 7.6.1933; 3.7.1935; 1.4.1936. Black on yellow unpt. Portr Montt at ctr. Back black on brown unpt.; explorer on horseback at l.	6.00	40.00	90.00
98	**500 Pesos = 50 Condores** 8.7.1942; 18.8.1943. Red-brown. Portr. Montt at ctr. Back grayish-purple; Spaniards at l.	5.00	30.00	70.00

		VG	VF	UNC
99	**1000 Pesos = 100 Condores** 7.6.1933-18.8.1943. Brown on green unpt. Portr. Blanco at r. Back brown; Spaniards at ctr.	25.00	60.00	175.

		VG	VF	UNC
100	**5000 Pesos = 500 Condores** 1.2.1932. Brown on yellow unpt. Portr. M. A. Tocornal at ctr. Lg. *5000* on back.	75.00	250.	550.
101	**10,000 Pesos = 1000 Condores** 1.2.1932. Blue on m/c unpt. Portr. M. Balmaceda at ctr. Lg. *10,000* on back.	400.	1000.	—

1940-45 Issue

#102-109 dated notes. Name under portr. Various date and sign. varieties.

		VG	VF	UNC
102	**5 Pesos = 1/2 Condor** 19.4.1944; 3.7.1946; 30.4.1947. Blue. Like #91.	.50	2.00	6.00

		VG	VF	UNC
103	**10 Pesos = 1 Condor** 18.8.1943-20.11.1946. Red-brown. Like #92.	1.00	3.00	10.00
104	**50 Pesos = 5 Condores** 19.1.1944-1.10.1947. Green. Like #94.	1.50	4.00	15.00

		VG	VF	UNC
105	**100 Pesos = 10 Condores** 1943-48. Red. Like #96. a. W/o security thread. 29.5.1943-28.5.1947. b. W/security thread. 24.11.1948.	 1.50 1.50	 4.00 4.00	 15.00 15.00
106	**500 Pesos = 50 Condores** 28.2.1945. Orange-brown. Similar to #98. Back dk. brown.	6.00	20.00	60.00

		VG	VF	UNC
107	**1000 Pesos = 100 Condores** 28.2.1945; 1.10.1947. Brown on green unpt. Like #99. Back brown.	6.00	20.00	65.00
108	**5000 Pesos = 500 Condores** 2.10.1940. Blue. Portr. M. A. Tocornal at ctr. Battle scene on back.	25.00	80.00	225.

		VG	VF	UNC
109	**10,000 Pesos = 1000 Condores** 2.10.1940. Violet on brown unpt. Portr. M. Balmaceda at ctr. Military horseman on back.	40.00	125.	350.

1947-48 ND Issue

#110-118 name under portr. but w/o date. Sign. varieties, also sm. or lg. size sign. W/or w/o security thread. Wmk: D. Diego Portales in jacket. Printer: Talleres de Especies Valoradas, Santiago, Chile.

		VG	VF	UNC
110	**5 Pesos = 1/2 Condor** ND (1947-58). Blue. Like #91. Back blue, or blue on pink unpt. 2 sign. varieties.	.15	.50	2.00

111 10 Pesos = 1 Condor

ND (1947-58). Red-brown. Like #92. Back red-brown or dk. brown. 2 block # varieties. 2 sign. varieties.

VG	VF	UNC
.15	.50	2.00

112 50 Pesos = 5 Condores

ND (1947-58). Green. Like #94. 2 sign. varieties.

VG	VF	UNC
.25	1.25	5.00

113 100 Pesos = 10 Condores

ND (1947-56). Red. Similar to #95. Sm. black seal at ctr. on back. 2 sign. varieties.

VG	VF	UNC
.50	2.00	8.00

114 100 Pesos = 10 Condores

ND (1947-58). Red. Face like #113. Different design w/lg. red seal at bottom on back. 2 serial # varieties.

VG	VF	UNC
.50	1.50	7.50

115 500 Pesos = 50 Condores

ND (1947-59). Blue. Portr. Montt at ctr. Explorer on horseback on back. 4 sign. varieties.

VG	VF	UNC
1.00	3.50	15.00

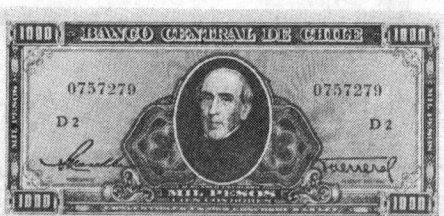

116 1000 Pesos = 100 Condores

ND (1947-59). Dk. brown. Portr. Encalada at ctr. Founding of Santiago on back. 3 sign. varieties.

VG	VF	UNC
2.00	6.00	20.00

117 5000 Pesos = 500 Condores

ND (1947-59). Brown-violet. Portr. M. A. Tocornal at ctr. Smaller size than #100. Battle of Rancagua on back.

	VG	VF	UNC
a. Larger size, printed portion 169mm horizontally.	3.00	10.00	30.00
b. Smaller size, printed portion 166mm.	3.00	10.00	30.00

118 10,000 Pesos = 1000 Condores

ND (1947-59). Violet. Portr. M. Balmaceda at ctr. Soldiers meeting on back. Dual wmk: Man at l., words *DIEZ varieties. MIL* at r. 3 sign.

VG	VF	UNC
3.00	15.00	50.00

1958 ND Issue

#119-123 w/o date. Name under portr. Sign. varieties, lg. size sign. Printer: CdM-Chile.

119 5 Pesos = 1/2 Condor

ND (1958-59). Blue. Like #91. 2 sign. varieties.

VG	VF	UNC
.10	.25	1.00

120 10 Pesos = 1 Condor

ND (1958-59). Red-brown. Like #92. 2 sign. varieties.

VG	VF	UNC
.10	.25	1.00

121 50 Pesos = 5 Condores
ND (1958-59). Green. Face like #94. Green seal at bottom ctr. on back. 2 sign. varieties.

	VG	VF	UNC
a. Imprint length 23mm.	.25	.50	2.00
b. Imprint length 26mm.	.25	.50	2.00

122 100 Pesos = 10 Condores
ND (1958-59). Red. Like #114. 3 sign. varieties.

VG	VF	UNC
.25	.50	3.00

123 50,000 Pesos = 5000 Condores
ND (1958-59). Dk. green. Portr. Alessandri at ctr. 2 sign. varieties.

VG	VF	UNC
25.00	50.00	150.

1960 ND Provisional Issue

1 Escudo = 1000 Pesos (= 100 Centesimos)

#124-133 Escudo denominations in red as part of new plates overprinted in wmk. area on back. Wmk: D. Diego Portales. Sign. titles: *PRESIDENTE* and *GERENTE GENERAL*. Sign. varieties. Printer: CdM-Chile.

124 1/2 Centesimo on 5 Pesos
ND (1960-61). Blue. Portr. Bernard O'Higgins at l. Ovpt. on #119. Rare.

VG	VF	UNC
—	—	—

125 1 Centesimo on 10 Pesos
ND (1960-61). Red-brown. Portr. Manuel Bulnes at l. Series F. Ovpt. on #120.

VG	VF	UNC
1.00	2.50	12.50

126 5 Centesimos on 50 Pesos
ND (1960-61). Green. Portr. Anibal Pinto at l. Series C. Ovpt. on #121. 3 sign. varieties.

	VG	VF	UNC
a. Imprint on face 25mm wide.	.25	1.00	2.50
b. Imprint on face 22mm wide.	.10	.20	2.00
s. Specimen.	—	—	12.50

127 10 Centesimos on 100 Pesos
ND (1960-61). Red. Portr. Arturo Prat at l. Ovpt. on #122. 3 sign. varieties. Light and dark back varietes. Series C-K.

	VG	VF	UNC
a. Issued note.	.25	1.00	2.50
s. Specimen.	—	—	12.50

128 50 Centesimos on 500 Pesos
ND (1960-61). Blue. Portr. Manuel Montt at r. Ovpt. on #115. Series A.

VG	VF	UNC
.50	2.50	15.00

		VG	VF	UNC
129	**1 Escudo on 1000 Pesos** ND (1960-61). Dk. brown. Portr. Manuel Blanco Encalada at l. Ovpt. on #116. Series A.	.50	2.00	12.50
130	**5 Escudos on 5000 Pesos** ND (1960-61). Brown-violet. Portr. Manuel Antonio Tocornal at l. Ovpt. on #117. 2 sign. varieties. Series J.	1.00	5.00	25.00
131	**10 Escudos on 10,000 Pesos** ND (1960-61). Purple on lt. blue unpt. Portr. Jose Manuel Balmaceda at l. Ovpt. on #118. Dual wmk: Head at l., words *DIEZ MIL* at r. Series F.	2.00	10.00	40.00
132	**10 Escudos on 10,000 Pesos** ND (1960-61). Red-brown. Portr. Jose Manuel Balmaceda at l. Similar to #131 but w/o wmk. at r. Series F.	2.00	15.00	55.00
133	**50 Escudos on 50,000 Pesos** ND (1960-61). Blue-green Portr. Arturo Alessandri at l. and brown on m/c unpt. Ovpt. on #123. Series A.	4.50	25.00	75.00

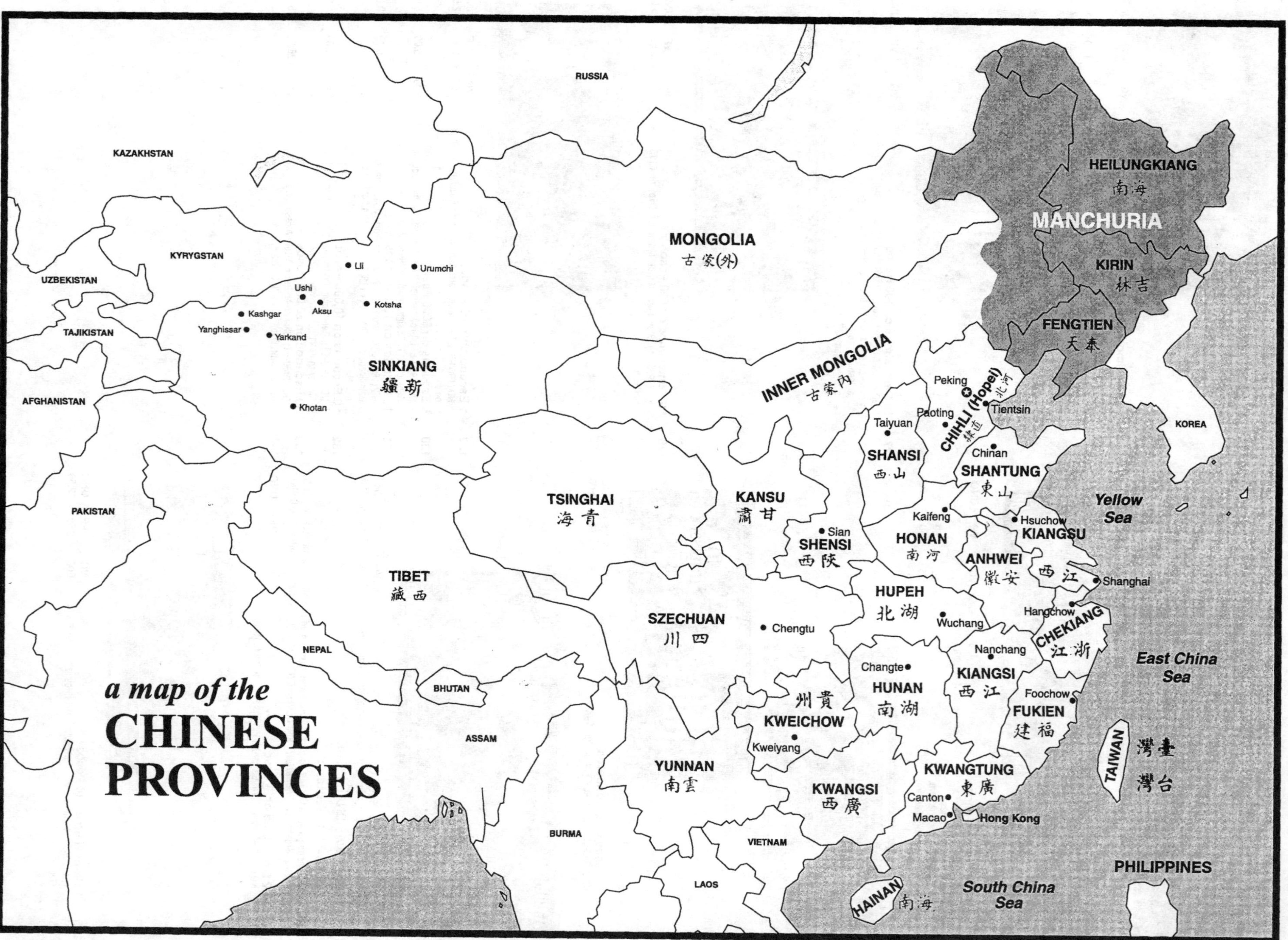
RUSSIA
KAZAKHSTAN
MONGOLIA
KYRYGSTAN
UZBEKISTAN
TAJIKISTAN
Urumchi
Ili
Ushi
Aksu
Kotsha
Kashgar
Yanghissar
Yarkand
SINKIANG
AFGHANISTAN
Khotan
HEILUNGKIANG
MANCHURIA
KIRIN
FENGTIEN
INNER MONGOLIA
Peking
CHIHLI (Hopei)
Tientsin
Paoting
Taiyuan
SHANSI
KOREA
Chinan
SHANTUNG
Yellow Sea
PAKISTAN
TSINGHAI
KANSU
Kaifeng
Hsuchow
KIANGSU
Sian
SHENSI
HONAN
ANHWEI
Shanghai
TIBET
HUPEH
Hangchow
CHEKIANG
SZECHUAN
Chengtu
Wuchang
Nanchang
East China Sea
NEPAL
Changte
HUNAN
KIANGSI
BHUTAN
Foochow
FUKIEN
KWEICHOW
Kweiyang
TAIWAN
ASSAM
YUNNAN
KWANGTUNG
KWANGSI
Canton
Macao
Hong Kong
BURMA
VIETNAM
LAOS
PHILIPPINES
HAINAN
South China Sea
a map of the
CHINESE
PROVINCES

EMPIRE

China's ancient civilization began in the Huang Ho basin about 1500 BC. The warring feudal states comprising early China were first united under Emperor Ch'in Shih Huang Ti (246-210 BC) who gave China its name and first central government. Subsequent dynasties alternated brilliant cultural achievements with internal disorder until the Empire was brought down by the revolution of 1911, and the Republic of China installed in its place. Chinese culture attained a pre-eminence in art, literature and philosophy, but a traditional backwardness in industry and administration ill prepared China for the demands of 19th century Western expansionism which exposed it to military and political humiliations, and mandated a drastic revision of political practice in order to secure an accommodation with the modern world.

The Republic of 1911 barely survived the stress of World War I, and was subsequently all but shattered by the rise of nationalism and the emergence of the Chinese Communist movement. Moscow, which practiced a policy of cooperation between Communists and other parties in movements for national liberation, sought to establish an entente between the Chinese Communist Party and the Kuomintang (National People's Party) of Dr. Sun Yat-sen. The ensuing cooperation was based on little more than the hope each had of using the other.

An increasingly uneasy association between the Kuomintang and the Chinese Communist Party developed and continued until April 12, 1927, when Chiang Kai-shek, Dr. Sun Yat-sen's political heir, instituted a bloody purge to stamp out the Communists within the Kuomintang and the government and virtually paralyzed their ranks throughout China. Some time after the mid-1927 purges, the Chinese Communist Party turned to armed force to resist Chiang Kai-shek and during the period of 1930-34 acquired control over large parts of Kiangsi, Fukien, Hunan and Hupeh. The Nationalist Nanking government responded with a series of campaigns against the soviet power bases and, by October of 1934, succeeded in driving the remnants of the Communist army to a refuge in Shensi Province.

Subsequently, the Communists under the leadership of Mao Tse-tung defeated the Nationalists and on September 21, 1949 formally established the People's Republic.

EMPERORS

Reign title: Hsien Feng	咸豐	文宗	WEN TSUNG 1851-1861
1st Reign title: Ch'i-hsiang	祺祥	穆宗	MU TSUNG 1861
2nd Reign title: T'ung Chih	同治		1862-1875
Reign title: Kuang Hsu	光緒	德宗	TE TSUNG 1875-1908
(Hsun Ti) Reign title: Hsuan T'ung	宣統	宣統帝 遜帝	HSUAN T'UNG TI 1908-1911
Proposed Reign title: Hung Hsien	洪憲		YUAN SHIH-KAI Dec. 15, 1915- March 21, 1916

MONETARY SYSTEMS

1 Tael = 800-1600 Cash*

***NOTE: In theory, 1000 cash were equal to a tael of silver, but in actuality the rate varied from time to time and from place to place.**

Dollar System

1 Cent (fen, hsien) = 10 Cash (wen)
1 Chiao (hao) = 10 Cents
1 Dollar (yuan) = 100 Cents

Tael System

1 Fen (candareen) = 10 Li
1 Ch'ien (mace) = 10 Fen
1 Liang (tael) = 10 Ch'ien (mace)

NOTE: Many listings encompassing issues circulated by provincial, military, including early Communist, larger commercial and foreign banking authorities are contained in *Standard Catalog of World Paper Money, Specialized Issues*, Vol. 1 by Krause Publications.

ARRANGEMENT

Imperial .... #AA2-AA3, AA10, A1-A83J
Republican .... #A84-A138, 1-643
Peoples Republic .... #800-876
Taiwan .... #900-970
Taiwan - Offshore Islands .... #R102-R143
Japanese Puppet .... #J1-J146
Japanese Military .... #M1-M30
Russian Military .... #M30A-M36

ISSUER IDENTIFICATION

Ming Dynasty, 1368-1644
#AA2-AA3, AA10
Ta Ming T'ung Hsing Pao Ch'ao

大清銀行
Ch'ing Dynasty, 1644-1911
#A1-A8
Ta Ch'ing Pao Ch'ao

戶部官票
Board of Revenue
#A9-A13
Hu Pu Kuan P'iao

交通銀行
General Bank of Communications
#A13A-A19E
Chiao T'ung Yin Hang

財政部印刷局
Bureau of Engraving and Printing
#A20-A23
Ts'ai Cheng Pu Yin Shua Chü

戶部銀行
Hu Pu Bank, Peking
#A24-A35
Hu Pu Yin Hang
兌換銀票
Tui Huan Yin P'iao
北京戶部銀行
Pei Ching Hu Pu Yin Hang

中國通商銀行
Imperial Bank of China
#A36-A55A
Chung Kuo T'ung Shang Yin Hang

北洋鐵軌官路總局
Imperial Chinese Railways
#A56-A61
Pei Yang T'ieh Kuei Kuan Lu Tsung Chü

Ningpo Commercial Bank, Limited
#A61A-A61D
Shang Hai Szu Ming Yin Hang

大清銀行
Ta Ch'ing Government Bank
#A62-A82
Ta Ch'ing Yin Hang

Ta Ch'ing Government Bank, Shansi
#A83-A83J
Shan Hsi Ta Ch'ing Yin Hang
大清戶部銀行
Ta Ch'ing Hu Pu Yin Hang

四省農民銀行
Agricultural Bank of the Four Provinces
#A84-A91E
Szu Sheng Nung Min Yin Hang
豫鄂皖贛四省農民銀行
Yü O Huan Kan Szu Sheng Nung Min Yin Hang

中國農工銀行
Agricultural and Industrial Bank of China
#A92-A112
Chung Kuo Nung Kung Yin Hang

農商銀行
Bank of Agriculture and Commerce
#A113-A120
Nung Shang Yin Hang

中國絲茶銀行
China Silk and Tea Industrial Bank
#A120A-A120C
Chung Kuo Szu Ch'a Yin Hang

中南銀行
China and South Sea Bank
#A121-A133
Chung Nan Yin Hang

中國通商銀行
Commercial Bank of China
#A133A-A138, 1-15
Chung Kuo T'ung Shang Yin Hang

中國銀行
Bank of China, КИТАЙСКІЙ БАНКЪ
#16-100
Chung Kuo Yin Hang

Chung Kuo Yin Hang Tui Huan Ch'uan

交通銀行
Bank of Communications, БАНКЪ ПЧТИ СООЩЕНІЯ
#102-166
Chiao T'ung Yin Hang

中央銀行
Central Bank of China (National)
#167-170
Chung Yan Yin Hang

Central Bank of China (Quasi-national)
#171-192
Chung Yan Yin Hang

Central Bank of China (National - Cont.)
#193-450T
Chung Yun Yin Hang

中國農民銀行
Farmers Bank of China
#451-484
Chung Kuo Nung Min Yin Hang

蒙疆銀行
Great Northwestern Bank
#485-490
Men Tsang Yin Hang

勸業銀行
Industrial Development Bank of China
#491-500
Ch'üan Yeh Yin Hang

中國墾業銀行
Land Bank of China, Limited
#501-506
Chung Kuo K'en Yeh Yin Hang

中華國家銀行
National Bank of China, Nanking
#507-510
Chung Hua Kuo Chia Yin Hang

中華民國銀行
National Bank of China, Canton
#511-516
Chung Hua Kuo Min Yin Hang

浙江興業銀行
The National Commercial Bank, Limited
#516A-519C
Che Chiang Hsing Yeh Yin Hang

中國實業銀行
National Industrial Bank of China
#520-534
Chung Kuo Shih Yeh Yin Hang

四明銀行
Ningpo Commercial Bank
#539-550
Szu Ming Yin Hang

Tah Chung Bank
#551-565
行銀中大
Ta Chung Yin Hang

Bank of Territorial Development,
ТЕРРИТОРІАЛЬНО ПРОМЫШЛЕННЫЙ БАНКЪ В'БКИТАБ
#566-585B
行銀邊殖
Chih Pien Yin Hang

Ministry of Communications - Peking-Hankow Railway
#585C-594
券付支路鐵漢京部通交
Chiao T'ung Pu Ching Han T'ieh Lu Chih Fu Ch'üan

Military Exchange Bureau
#595
局兌滙需軍部政財
Ts'ai Cheng Pu Chün Hsu Hui Tui Chü

Market Stabilization Currency Bureau
#597-622
局錢官市平部政財
Ts'ai Cheng Pu P'ing Shih Kuan Ch'ien Chü

Ministry of Finance - Special Circulating Notes
#623-625
券通流別特部政財
Ts'ai Cheng Pu T'e Pieh Liu T'ung Ch'üan

Ministry of Finance - Fixed Term Treasury Notes
#626-637
券庫國利有期定部政財
Ts'ai Cheng Pu Ting Ch'i Yu Li Kuo K'u Ch'üan

Ministry of Finance - Short Term Exchange Notes
#638-640
券換兌利有期短部政財
Ts'ai Cheng Pu Tuan Ch'i Yu Li Tui Huan Ch'üan

Ministry of Finance - Circulating Notes
#641-643
券通流利有部政財
Ts'ai Cheng Pu Yu Li Liu T'ung Ch'üan

Peoples Bank of China
#800-858A
中國人民銀行
Chung Kuo Jen Min Yin Hang / Zhong Guo Ren Min Yin Hang

#859-876
行銀民人國中
Chung Kuo Jen Min Yin Hang

T'ai-nan Kuan Yin P'iao
#900-906
票銀官南臺
Tai Nan Kuan Yin P'iao

Hu Li T'ai Nan Fu Cheng Tang Chung

Bank of Taiwan - Japanese Influence
#907-913
T'ai Wan Yin Hang

Bank of Taiwan - Taiwan Government General
#914-920
Bank of Taiwan Limited - Taiwan Bank
#921-934
Tai Wan Yin Hang Ch'üan

Bank of Taiwan - Chinese Administration
#935-970
行銀灣臺
T'ai Wan Yin Hang

Bank of Taiwan
#R102-R108, R113-R116, R119-R121, R140-R143
行銀灣臺
T'ai Wan Yin Hang

Central Reserve Bank of China
#J1-J44
行銀備儲央中
Chung Yang Ch'u Pei Yin Hang

Federal Reserve Bank of China
#J45-J92
行銀備準合聯國中
Chung Kuo Lien Ho Chun Pei Yin Hang

Hua Hsing Commercial Bank
#J93-J100
行銀業商興華
Hua Hsing Shang Yeh Yin Hang

Mengchiang Bank
#J101-J112
行銀疆蒙
Meng Chiang Yin Hang

Chi Tung Bank
#J113-J117
行銀東冀
Chi Tung Yin Hang

Chanan Bank
#J118-J119
行銀南察
Ch'a Nan Yin Hang

Central Bank of Manchukuo
#J120-J146
行銀央中洲滿
Man Chou Chung Yang Yin Hang

Japanese Imperial Government, Military
#M1-M30
府政國帝本日大
Ta Jih Pen Ti Kuo Cheng Fu

South China Expeditionary Army
M30A
Soviet Red Army Headquarters
#M31-M36
蘇聯紅軍司令部
Su Lien Hung Chün Szu Ling Pu

EMPIRE DATING

The mathematical discrepancy in this is accounted for by the fact that the first year is includ in the elapsed time.

Most struck Chinese banknotes are dated by year within a given period, such as the regior eras or the republican periods. A 1907 issue, for example, would be dated in the 33rd year of t Kuang Hsu era (1875 + 33 - 1 = 1907).

CYCLICAL DATING

Another method of dating is a 60-year, repeating cycle, outlined in the table below. The da is shown by the combination of two characters, the first from the top row and the second from t column at left, in this catalog, when a cyclical date is used, the abbreviation CD appears befo the AD date.

	庚	辛	壬	癸	甲	乙	丙	丁	戊	己
戌	1850 1910		1862 1922		1874 1934		1886 1946		1838 1898	
亥		1851 1911		1863 1923		1875 1935		1887 1947		1839 1899
子	1840 1900		1852 1912		1864 1924		1876 1936		1888 1948	
丑		1841 1901		1853 1913		1865 1925		1877 1937		1889 1949
寅	1830 1890		1842 1902		1854 1914		1866 1926		1878 1938	
卯		1831 1891		1843 1903		1855 1915		1867 1927		1879 1939
辰	1880 1940		1832 1892		1844 1904		1856 1916		1868 1928	
巳		1881 1941		1833 1893		1845 1905		1857 1917		1869 1929
午	1870 1930		1882 1942		1834 1894		1846 1906		1858 1918	
未		1871 1931		1883 1943		1835 1895		1847 1907		1859 1919
申	1860 1920		1872 1932		1884 1944		1836 1896		1848 1908	
酉		1861 1921		1873 1933		1885 1945		1837 1897		1849 1909

This chart has been adopted from *Chinese Banknotes* by Ward Smith and Brian Matravers. Calligraphy b Marian C. Smith.

REPUBLIC DATING

A modern note of 1926 issue is dated in the 15th year of the Republic (1912 + 15 - 1 = 1926 The mathematical discrepancy again is accounted for by the fact that the first year is included i the elapsed time.

Years of the Republic

Year		AD	Year		AD	Year		AD	Year		AD
1	一	= 1912	11	一十	= 1922	21	一十二	= 1932	31	一十三	= 1942
2	二	= 1913	12	二十	= 1923	22	二十二	= 1933	32	二十三	= 1943
3	三	= 1914	13	三十	= 1924	23	三十二	= 1934	33	三十三	= 1944
4	四	= 1915	14	四十	= 1925	24	四十二	= 1935	34	四十三	= 1945
5	五	= 1916	15	五十	= 1926	25	五十二	= 1936	35	五十三	= 1946
6	六	= 1917	16	六十	= 1927	26	六十二	= 1937	36	六十三	= 1947
7	七	= 1918	17	七十	= 1928	27	七十二	= 1938	37	七十三	= 1948
8	八	= 1919	18	八十	= 1929	28	八十二	= 1939	38	八十三	= 1949
9	九	= 1920	19	九十	= 1930	29	九十二	= 1940	39	九十三	= 1950
10	十	= 1921	20	十二	= 1931	30	十三	= 1941	40	十四	= 1951

NOTE: Chinese dates are normally read from right to left, except for the modern issues of the Peoples Republic of China from 1953 where the Western date is read from left to right.

NOTICE

Readers with unlisted dates, signature varieties, etc. are invited to submit photocopies of their notes to: Standard Catalog of World Paper Money, 700 East State St. Iola, WI 54990-0001, fax: 1-715-445-4087, or E-Mail: thernr@krause.com.

MONETARY UNITS

Dollar Amounts		
Dollar (*Yuan*)	元 or 員	圓 or 圜
Half Dollar (*Pan Yuan*)	圓半	
50¢ (*Chiao/Hao*)	角伍	毫伍
10¢ (*Chiao/Hao*)	角壹	毫壹
1¢ (*Fen/Hsien*)	分壹	仙壹

Tael Amounts	
Tael (*Liang*)	兩
Half Tael (*Pan Liang*)	兩半
5 Mace (*Wu Ch'ien*)	錢伍
1 Mace (*1 Ch'ien*)	錢壹
Ku Ping (*Tael*)*	平庫

Copper and Cash Coin Amounts			
Copper (*Mei*)	枚	String (*Tiao*)	吊
Cash (*Wen*)	文	String (*Tiao*)	弔
String (*Kuan*)	貫	String (*Ch'uan*)	串

Common Prefixes			
Copper (*T'ung*)	銅	"Small money"	洋小
Silver (*Yin*)	銀	"Big money"	洋大
Gold (*Chin*)	金	"Big money"	洋英

These tables have been adopted from *CHINESE BANKNOTES* by Ward Smith and Brian Matravers. Calligraphy in special instances by Marian C. Smith.

NUMERICAL CHARACTERS

A. CONVENTIONAL

B. FORMAL

C. COMMERCIAL

No.	A	B	C
1	一 正 元	壹 弌	〡
2	二	弍 貳	〢
3	三	弎 叁	〣
4	四	肆	〤
5	五	伍	〥
6	六	陸	〦
7	七	柒	〧
8	八	捌	〨
9	九	玖	〩

No.	A	B	C
10	十	拾 什	十
20	十二 廿	拾貳 念	〢十
25	五十二 五廿	伍拾貳	〢十〥
30	十三 卅	拾叁	〣十
100	百一	佰壹	〡百
1,000	千一	仟壹	〡千
10,000	萬一	萬壹	〡万
100,000	萬十 億一	萬拾 億壹	十万
1,000,000	萬百一	萬佰壹	〡百万

REPUBLIC ISSUES

PORTRAIT ABBREVIATIONS

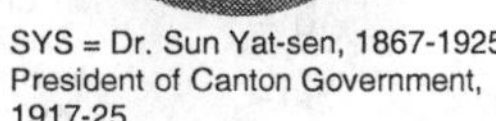

SYS = Dr. Sun Yat-sen, 1867-1925
President of Canton Government, 1917-25

CKS = Chiang Kai-shek 1886-1975
President in Nanking, 1927-31
Head of Formosa Government, Taiwan, 1949-1975

NOTE: Because of the frequency of the above appearing in the following listings, their initials are used only in reference to their portraits.

OVERPRINTS

The various city or regional overprints are easily noted, being normally two or three Chinese characters usually in two or more places on a note and sometimes found in English on the other side of the note.

Various single Chinese control characters were applied, and appear in two or more places on a note. Sometimes western numerals were utilized and appear in circles, or outlined squares, etc.

The most frequently encountered overprint in the Three Eastern Provinces and Manchurian series is a four Chinese character overprint in a 21mm square outline. This *Official Controller's Seal* overprint supervised the amount of issue of certain banks and guaranteed the notes.

In certain cases we find available an original printers' specimen, an issued note, an issued note with the official overprint along with a "local" specimen of a circulated note bearing normal serial numbers. The purpose of this overprint at present eludes the authors at this writing.

S/M # is in reference to *CHINESE BANKNOTES* by Ward D. Smith and Brian Matravers.

MING DYNASTY, 1368-1644

大明通行寶鈔

Ta Ming T'ung Hsing Pao Ch'ao

The Ming Dynasty was characterized by a tapering off in note production and circulation, terminating in the complete suspension of official issues, probably in about 1450. The *Chüan Pu T'ung Chih* specifically refers to some 60 isues in three out of the four earliest reigns, covering the period from 1368 to 1426. This is almost certainly an understatement of the probable volume, although it is a larger total than in any other known source and, of course, few of the notes themselves have survived. The conspicuous exception is the 1-kuan note of the *Hung Wu* era (1368-99), listed below as #AA10 *(S/M #T36-20)*. In addition to this note below, issues reported for the *Hung Wu* reign include 100, 200, 300, 400 and 500 cash denominations and for the *Yung Lo* reign (1403-25), a tael series in 26 denominations from 1 through 20, plus 25, 30, 35, 40, 45 and 50 taels, none of which have surfaced.

1368-75 CIRCULATING NOTE ISSUE

NOTE: Other issues and denominatins have been reported, but not confirmed.

NOTE: S/M#s are in reference to *Chinese Banknotes*, by Ward D. Smith and Brian Matravers.

		Good	Fine	XF
AA2	**20 Cash** 1375. Black w/red seal handstamps. 2 strings of 10 cash coins at upper ctr. Blue-gray mulberry paper. 270 x 165mm. *(S/M #T36-2)*. Rare.	—	—	—

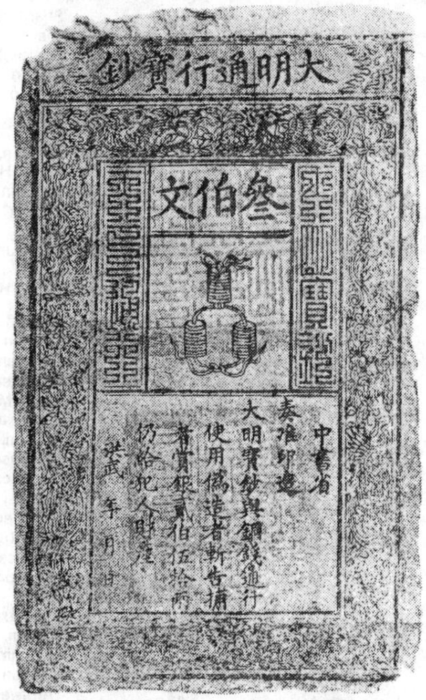

		Good	Fine	XF
AA3	**300 Cash** 1368-99. Black w/red seal handstamps. 3 strings of cash coins at upper ctr. Blue-gray mulberry paper. 110 x 193mm. *(S/M #T36-3)*.	—	—	—

PLACE NAMES

The following list is designed for users unfamiliar with written Chinese who wish to check place names appearing on notes, usually as overprints. For this reason, the arrangement is based on the number of strokes in the first character, normally found at the right or top. This is a selected list. Some obscure locations have been omitted.

English names are a mixture of popular names or variants thereon, which appear on notes, and Wade-Giles romanizations for places which lack well established English names.

Chinese place names tend to be simple descriptive terms relating to a geographical feature, e.g., "north of the lake" (Hupel), "southern capital" (Nanking) or "on the sea" (Shanghai". Most provincial names show this characteristic. In the latter case, many are paired, which has the disadvantage to the western eye and ear of making them look and sound much the same. Hunan-Hupei, Hunan-Hopei, Kwangtung-Kwangsi, Kiangsu-Kiangsi (plus Kiangnan on older notes) and Shantung-Shansi are not difficult to confuse. The most serious problem, however, is Shansi-Shensi. Here, the last characters are the same rather than the first but the first characters, i nounced correctly, differ only in tone. Even the meanings are close. Shansi, literally, is "mour west," while Shensi is "mountain passes west," although the first character in this instance often used in this meaning. The difference in English spelling is generally accepted conve Chinese find no difficulty in keeping the two separated because the tonal difference is suffici the spoken language and written forms for the first characters are totally dissimilar.

Westerners who might be tempted to consider these or other problems in terminology as r ing from mysterious oriental mental processes should first appraise their own place names, are rarely as logical or as simple. Inconsistent spellings of place names in romanization to primarily western rather than Chinese errors. If confusion does arise, the reasons are com and in any event, no satisfactory solution has yet been found.

Kiukiang, Kiangsi	江九
Pa Pu, Kwangsi	步八
Szechuan (alt)	川
Ch'uan Sha, Kiangsi	沙川
Ch'uan K'ang, Szechuan	康川
Shansi	西山
Shantung	東山
Shanhaikuan Chihli/Hopei	關海山
Shanghai, Kiangsu	海上
Shang Jao, Kiangsi	饒上
Ta T'ung Shansi	同大
Ta Cheng Chihli/Hopei	城大
Ta Ch'en Fukien	陳大
Dairen, Liaoning	連大
Honan (alt)	州中
China (alt)	華中
China	國中
Newchwang Liaoning	莊牛
Niu T'ou Chihli/Hopei	頭牛
T'ai Ku Shansi	谷太
T'ai Yuan, Shansi	原太
Tientsin, Chihli/Hopei	津天
Wen An, Chihli/Hope	安文
Wu Ch'ang, Kirin	常五
Cheng yang, Honan	陽正
Tibet	藏西
Hsien Yu, Fukien	遊仙
Kansu	肅甘
Paotow, Suiyuan	頭包
Peiping, Chihli/Hopei	平北
Peking, Chihli/Hopei	京北
Pakhoi, Kwangtung	海北
Shih I, Chihli/Hopei	邑石
Shihkiachwang, Chihli/Hopei	莊家石
Szechuan	川四
T'ai T'ou Chihli/Hopei	頭台
Taiwan (alt)	灣台
Yung Ch'ing, Chihli/Hopei	清永
Yung Ning, Chihli/Hopei	寧永
Anhwei	徽安
Chengtu, Szechuan	都成
Kirin	林吉
Chi Hsien, Chihli/Hopei	縣吉
Kiangsi	西江
Kiangnan	南江
Kiangsu	蘇江
Sian, Shensi	安西
Sikang	康西
Ili, Sinkiang	犂伊
Swatow, Kwangtung	頭汕
Tulunnoerh, Chahar	倫多
Ch'ih Feng, Jehol	峯赤
Hsin Tien, Chihli/Hopei	店辛
Li Chia K'ou, Kwangsi	口家李
Sha P'ing, Shansi	坪沙
Kiangsu (al (literary)	吳
Changsha, Hunan	沙長
Changchun, Kirin	春長
Ch'ang Cheng (Great Wall)	城長
Ch'ang Li, Chihli/Hopei	黎昌
Chihli	隸直
Quemoy (Kinmen) Fukien	門金
Peking/Peiping, Chihli/Hopei	京兆
Tsingtao, Shantung	島青
Chinghai (or Tsinghai)	海青
Fengtien	天奉
Feng Hsin, Kiangsi	新奉
Fou Cheng, Chihli/Hopei	城阜
Hangchow, Chekiang	州杭
Hopei	北河
Honan	南河
Ho Chien, Chihli/Hopei	間河
Hulun, Heilungkiang	倫呼
Kunming, Yunnan	明昆
Manchuria	省三東
Manchuria (alt.)	九北東
Wu Ning, Szechuan	寧武
Wu Han, Hupei	漢武
Yenan Shensi	安延
Chekiang	江浙
Chien Ch'ang, Kiangsi	昌建
Chien Yang, Kiangsu	陽建
Chungking, Szechuan	慶重
Harbin, Heilungkiang	賓爾哈
Hsin An, Chihli/Hopei	安信
Kuling, Kiangsi	嶺牯
Liuchow, Kwangsi	州柳
Nan Chiang, Szechuan	江南
Nanchang, Kiangsi	昌南
Nanking, Kiangsu	京南
Nan Kuan Chen, Chihli/Hopei	鎮關南
Nan Hsiung, Kwangtung	雄南
Nanning, Kwangsi	(甯)寧南
Paoting, Chihli/Hopei	定保
T'ai An, Shantung	安泰
Tihua, Sinkiang	化廸
Weihaiwei, Shantung	衛海威
Shansi (literary)	(晉)晋
Chin Tz'u Shansi	祠晋
Shensi (Literary)	秦
Chinwangtao, Shantung	島皇秦
Haikow Kwangtung	口海
Hailar, Heilungkiang	爾拉海
Hainan, Kwangtung	南海
Hong Kong	港香
Hsuchow, Kiangsu	州徐
Kwangsi (literary)	桂
Kweilin, Kwangsi	林桂
Urga, Mongolia	倫庫
Matsu, Fukien	祖馬
Ma T'ou Chen Shantung	鎮頭馬
Hupei (literary)	鄂
P'u T'ien Fukien	田莆
Shensi	西陝
Tongshan, Chihli/Hopei	山唐
T'ao Yuan Hunan	源桃
Chefoo, Shantung	台烟
Kalgan, Chihli/Hopei	口家張
Ch'ang Te, Hunan	德常
Tsingkiangpu, Kiangsu	浦江清
Ch'ung Ming, Kiangsu	明崇
Huai Hai, Kiangsu	海淮
Kuo Hsien, Shansi	縣崞
Liao Cheng, Shantung	城聊
Pi'ng Hsien, Kiangsi	縣萍
Pukow, Kiangsu	口浦
Mukden, Liaoning	京盛
Su Hsien, Anhwei	縣宿
Ts'ao Ts'un, Shantung	村曹
T'ung Cheng, Hopei	城通
Wuchow, Kwangsi	州梧
Yeh Hsien, Shantung	縣掖
Chi Ning, Chahar	寧集
Chingtechen, Kiangsi	鎮德景
Hei Ho, Heilungkiang	河黑
Heilungkiang	江龍黑
Hunan (literary)	湘
Hupei	北湖
Hunan	南湖
Anhwei (literary)	皖
Kaifeng, Honan	封開
Kweichow	州貴
Kweiyang, Kwangsi	陽貴
Lung Ch'ang Szechuan	昌隆
Ningpo, Chekiang	波寧
Sheng Fang Chihli/Hopei	芳勝
Wusih, Kiangsu	錫無
Yu Tz'u, Shansi	次榆
Kwangtung/ Kwangsi (lit)	粵
Yunnan	南雲
Fu An, Fukien	安福
Foochow, Fukien	州福
Fu I, Fukien	邑福
Fukien	建福
Fu Ch'ing, Fukien	清福
Amoy, Fukien	門廈
Sinkiang	疆新
Jui Ch'ang Kiangsi	昌瑞
Fukien (literary)	閩
P'eng Lai, Shantung	萊蓬
Po Hai, Chihli/Hopei	海渤
Suiyuan	遠綏
Tan Hsien, Shantung	縣單
Yangchow, Kiangsu	州揚
Chefoo (alt) Shantung	台煙
Chahar	爾哈察
Chao Hsien, Chihli/Hopei	縣趙
Chia Ting, Kiangsu	定嘉
Hankow, Hupei	口漢
Ningpo (alt) Chekiang	波寧
Ninghsia	夏寧
Pinkiang, Heilungkiang	江濱
Shou Kuang, Shantung	光壽
Tainan, Taiwan	南臺
Taiwan (alt)	灣臺
Yunnan	滇
Chengchow, Honan	州鄭
Jehol	河熱
Kuang An Chen Chihli/Hopei	鎮安廣
Kwangsi	西廣
Canton, Kwangtung	州廣
Kwangtung	東廣
Manchukuo	國洲滿
Manchouli, Heilungkiang	里洲滿
Shantung (literary)	魯
Hopei (literary)	冀
Kweichow (literary)	黔
Chui Tzu Shan, Jehol	山字錐
Liaoning (al	東遼
Liaoning	寧遼
Lungkow, Shantung	口龍
Lungchow, Kwangsi	州龍
Mongolia	古蒙
Meng Chiang (Mongolia)	疆蒙
Honan (literary)	豫
Macao	門澳
Chinan (Tsinan) Shantung	南濟
Yingkow, Liaoning	口營
Chenkiang, Kiangsu	江鎮
Fengchen, Suiyuan	鎮豐
Li Chiang Chihli/Hopei	港鯉
Kuantung, Liaoning	東關
Lanchow, Kansu	州蘭
Kansu (literary)	隴
Kiangsu (literary)	蘇
Soochow, Kiangsu	州蘇
Su Ch'ao Chen Honan	鎮橋蘇
Hsien Hsien Chihli/Hopei	縣獻
Lu Hsien Szechuan	縣瀘
Pa Hsien Chihli / Hopei	縣霸
Li Hsien Chihli / Hopei	縣蠡
Kiangsi (literary)	贛
Watlam, Kwangsi	林鬱
Yungtsun	遵永

The above chart listings are taken from "CHINESE BANKNOTES" by Ward D. Smith and Brian Matravers (published 1970).

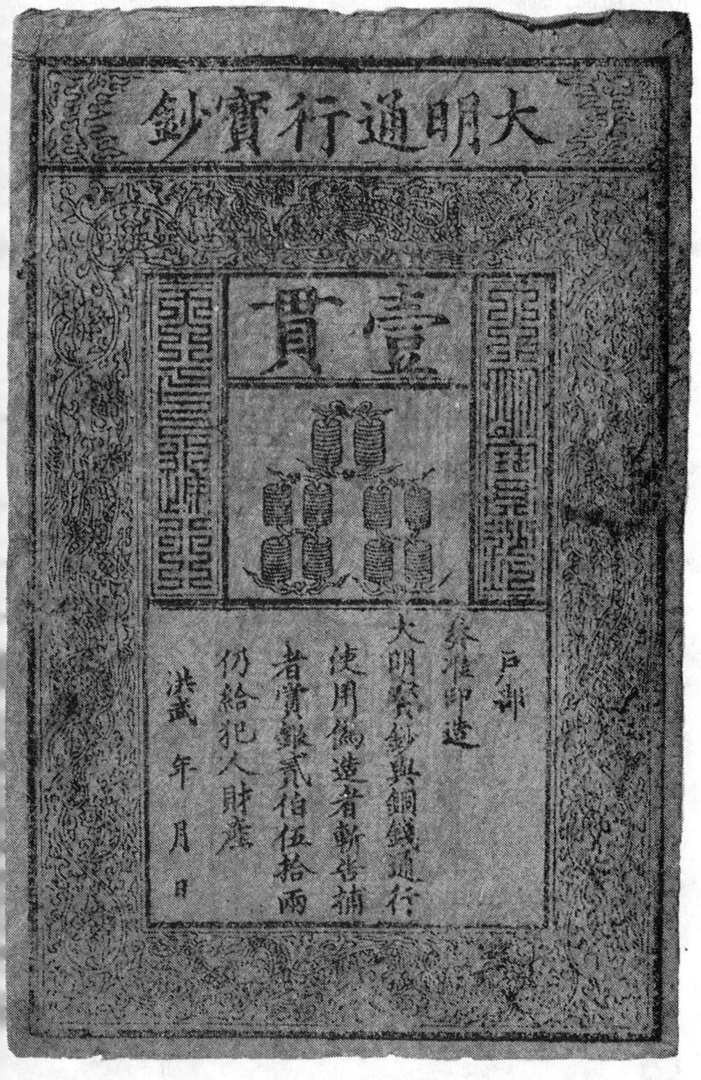

		Good	Fine	XF
AA10	**1 Kuan** 1368-99. Black w/2 red square seal hand-stamps 10 strings of cash coins at ctr., Back w/1 red and 1 black square seal ovpt. Deep gray mulberry paper. Uniface. 209 x 320mm. *(S/M #T36-20).*	250.	750.	1750.

Note: Other issues and denominations have been reported but not confirmed. Note: S/M #s are in reference to *Chinese Banknotes*, by Ward D. Smith and Brian Matravers.

CH'ING DYNASTY, 1644-1911

鈔寶清大
Ta Ch'ing Pao Ch'ao

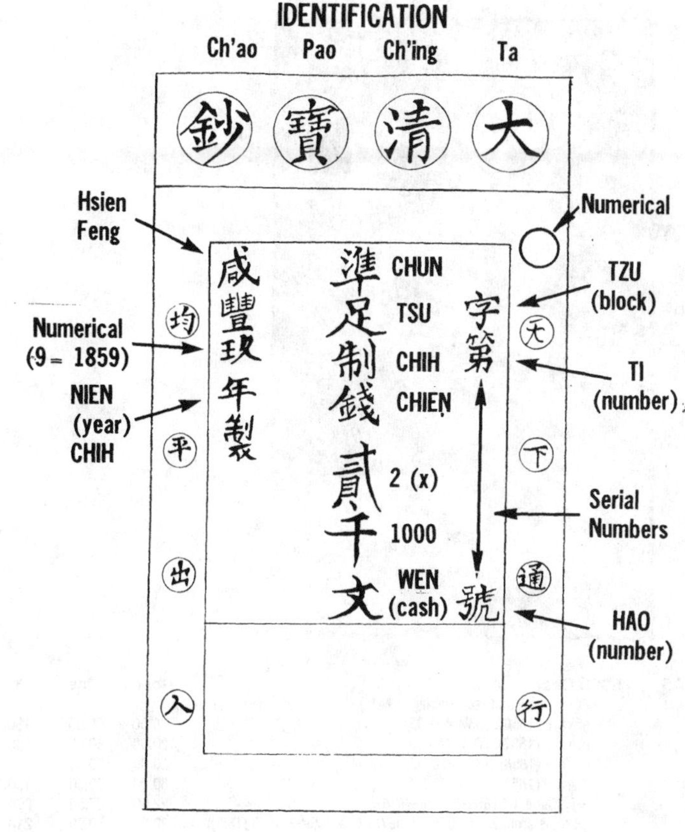

1853 ISSUE

IDENTIFICATION Top: *Ta Ch'ing Pao Ch'ao* = Ch'ing Dynasty note.

Right Side: *T'ien Hsia T'ung Hsing* = Circulates everywhere (i.e. under the heavens).

Left side: *Chun P'ing Ch'u Ju* = (Pay) equally when paying or receiving. (In other words, payable at face value; no discounts for buyers or sellers.)

Center right: *Tzu* identifies the block character as *Ti . . . Hoa* = serial number less than the block numerical character.

Center: *Chun Tsu Chih Ch'ien Erh Ch'ien Wen* = Equivalent to 2000 cash (payable in) standard (or regulated) coins. Or plain legal tender. (Getting into just what constituted Chih ch'ien in 1859 would be more than slightly complex.)

Center at left: *Hsien Feng*

		Good	Fine	XF
A1	**500 Cash** 1853-58. Blue and red.			
	a. Yr. 3 (1853). *(S/M #T6-1).*	15.00	40.00	120.
	b. Yr. 4 (1854). *(S/M #T6-10).*	15.00	40.00	120.
	c. Yr. 5 (1855). *(S/M #T6-20).*	15.00	40.00	120.
	d. Yr. 6 (1856). *(S/M #T6-30).*	15.00	40.00	120.
	e. Yr. 7 (1857). *(S/M #T6-40).*	15.00	40.00	120.
	f. Yr. 8 (1858). *(S/M#T6-).*	15.00	40.00	120.
	g. Reissue. CD1861-64. *(S/M#T6-).*	15.00	45.00	135.
A2	**1000 Cash** 1853-58. Blue and red. Similar to #A1.			
	a. Yr. 3 (1853). *(S/M #T6-2).*	15.00	40.00	120.
	b. Yr. 4 (1854). *(S/M #T6-11).*	15.00	40.00	120.
	c. Yr. 5 (1855). *(S/M #T6-21).*	15.00	40.00	120.
	d. Yr. 6 (1856). *(S/M #T6-31).*	15.00	40.00	120.
	e. Yr. 7 (1857). *(S/M #T6-41).*	15.00	40.00	120.
	f. Yr. 8 (1858). *(S/M #T6-50).*	15.00	40.00	120.
	g. Reissue. CD 1861-64 *S/M#T6-).*	15.00	45.00	135.
A3	**1500 Cash** 1854. Blue and red. Similar to #A1.			
	a. Yr.4 (1854). *(S/M #T6-12).*	30.00	90.00	250.
	b. Reissue. CD1861-64. *(S/M #T6-).* Reported not confirmed.	—	—	—
A4	**2000 Cash** 1853-59. Blue and red. Similar to #A1.			
	a. Yr. 3 (1853). *(S/M #T6-4).*	17.50	50.00	150.
	b. Yr. 4 (1854). *(S/M #T6-13).*	17.50	50.00	150.
	c. Yr. 5 (1855). *(S/M #T6-22).*	17.50	50.00	150.
	d. Yr. 6 (1856). *(S/M #T6-32).*	17.50	50.00	150.
	e. Yr. 7 (1857). *(S/M #T6-42).*	17.50	50.00	150.
	f. Yr. 8 (1858). *(S/M #T6-51).*	17.50	50.00	150.
	g. Yr. 9 (1859). *(S/M #T6-60).*	17.50	50.00	150.
	h. Reissue. CD1861-64. *(S/M#T6-).*	17.50	55.00	165.

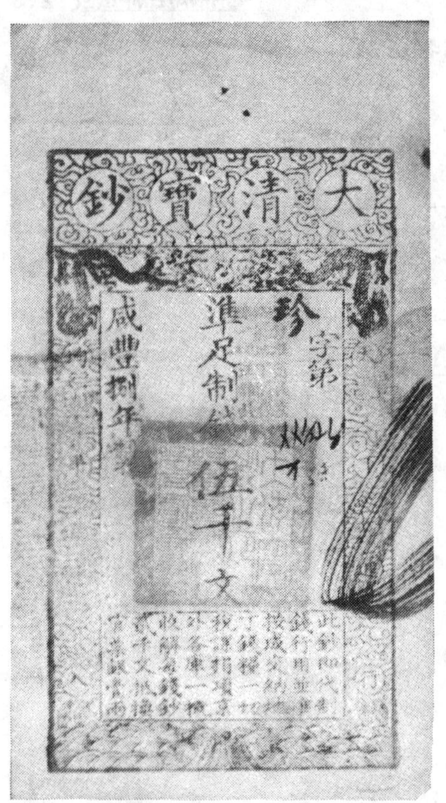

		Good	Fine	XF
A5	**5000 Cash**			
	1856-59. Blue and red. Similar to #A1.			
	a. Yr. 6 (1856). *(S/M #T6-33).*	20.00	60.00	180.
	b. Yr. 7 (1857). *(S/M #T6-43).*	20.00	60.00	180.
	c. Yr. 8 (1858). *(S/M #T6-52).*	20.00	60.00	180.
	d. Yr. 9 (1859). *(S/M#T6-).*	80.00	60.00	180.
	e. Reissue. CD1861-64. *(S/M#T6-).*	22.50	67.50	200.
	f. Handstamp: Kiangsu Province (21 Characters). Yr. 8 (1858). *(S/M#T6-).*	22.50	70.00	210.

		Good	Fine	XF
A6	**10,000 Cash**			
	1857-59. Blue and red. Similar to #A1.			
	a. Yr. 7 (1857). *(S/M #T6-44).*	30.00	90.00	275.
	b. Yr. 8 (1858). *(S/M #T6-53).*	30.00	90.00	275.
	c. Yr. 9 (1859). *(S/M#T6-).*	30.00	90.00	275.
	d. Reissue. CD1861-64. *(S/M#T6-).*	32.50	100.	300.
	e. Handstamp: Kiangsu Province (21 Characters). Yr. 8 (1858). *(S/M#T6-).*	32.50	100.	300.

		Good	Fine	XF
A7	**50,000 Cash**			
	1857-59. Blue and red. Similar to #A1.			
	a. Yr. 7 (1857). *(S/M #T6-45).*	90.00	275.	800
	b. Yr. 8 (1858). *(S/M #T6-54).*	90.00	275.	800
	c. Yr. 9 (1859). *(S/M#T6-).*	90.00	275.	800
A8	**100,000 Cash**			
	1857-59. Blue and red. Similar to #A1.			
	a. Yr. 7 (1857). *(S/M #T6-46).*	110.	350.	1000
	b. Yr. 8 (1858). *(S/M #T6-55).*	110.	350.	1000
	c. Yr. 9 (1859). *(S/M#T6-).*	110.	350.	1000
	d. Reissue. CD1861-64. *(S/M#T6-).*	125.	400.	1150
	e. Handstamp: Kiangsu Province (21 characters). Yr. 8 (1858). *(S/M#T6-).*	125.	400.	1150

BOARD OF REVENUE

HU PU KUAN P'IAO

1853-57 ISSUE

#A9-A13 uniface except for occasional endorsements on back.

		Good	Fine	XF
A9	**1 Tael**			
	1853-56. Blue and red.			
	a. Yr. 3 (1853). *(S/M #H176-1).*	30.00	90.00	275
	b. Yr. 4 (1854). *(S/M #H176-100).*	30.00	90.00	275
	c. Yr. 5 (1855). *(S/M #H176-20).*	30.00	90.00	275
	d. Yr. 6 (1856). *(S/M #H176-30).*	30.00	90.00	275
	e. Reissue. CD1861-64. *(S/M#H176-).*	32.50	100.	300
A10	**3 Taels**			
	1853-58. Blue and red. Similar to #A9.			
	a. Yr. 3 (1853). *(S/M #H176-2).*	40.00	120.	360
	b. Yr. 4 (1854). *(S/M #H176-11).*	40.00	120.	360
	c. Yr. 5 (1855). *(S/M #H176-21).*	40.00	120.	360
	d. Yr. 6 (1856). *(S/M #H176-31).*	40.00	120.	360.
	e. Yr. 7 (1857). *(S/M #H176-40).*	40.00	120.	360.
	f. Yr. 8 (1858). *(S/M#H176-).*	40.00	120.	360.
	g. Reissue. CD1861-64. *(S/M#H176-).*	47.50	140.	420
A11	**5 Taels**			
	1853-57. Blue and red. Similar to #A9.			
	a. Yr. 3 (1853). *(S/M #H176-3).*	50.00	150.	450
	b. Yr. 4 (1854). *(S/M #H176-12).*	50.00	150.	450.
	c. Yr. 5 (1855). *(S/M #H176-22).*	50.00	150.	450
	d. Yr. 6 (1856). *(S/M #H176-32).*	50.00	150.	450.
	e. Yr. 7 (1857). *(S/M #H176-41).*	50.00	150.	450.
	f. Reissue. CD1861-64. *(S/M#H176-).*	52.50	160.	480.

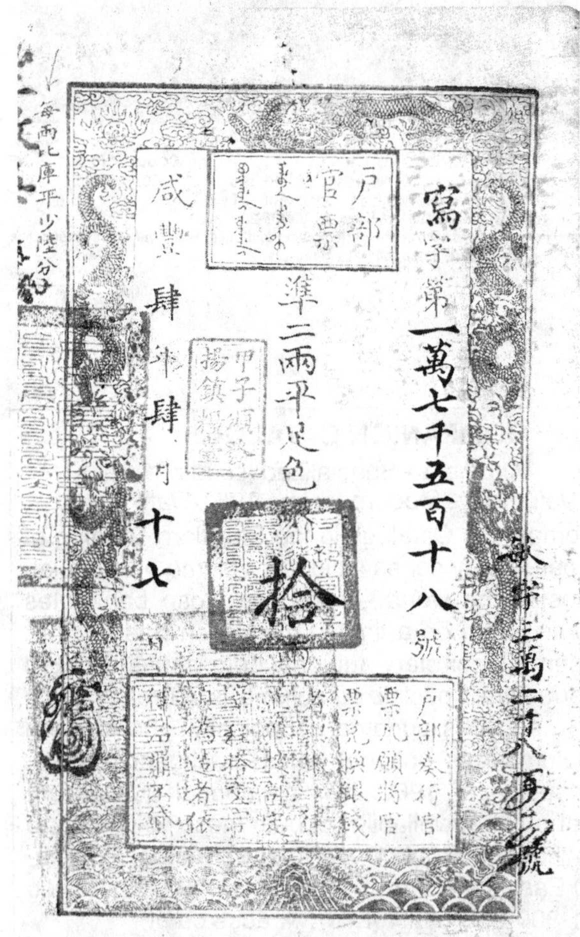

		Good	Fine	XF
A12	**10 Taels** 1853-56. Blue and red. Similar to #A9.			
	a. Yr. 3 (1853). *(S/M #H176-4).*	65.00	225.	625.
	b. Yr. 4 (1854). *(S/M #H176-13).*	65.00	225.	625.
	c. Yr. 5 (1855). *(S/M #H176-23).*	65.00	225.	625.
	d. Yr. 6 (1856). *(S/M #H176-33).*	65.00	225.	625.
	e. Reissue. CD1861-64. *(S/M#H176-).*	60.00	200.	600.
A13	**50 Taels** 1853-56. Blue and red. Similar to #A9.			
	a. Yr. 3 (1853). *(S/M #H176-5).*	135.	400.	1250.
	b. Yr. 4 (1854). *(S/M #H176-14).*	135.	400.	1250.
	c. Yr. 5 (1855). *(S/M #H176-24).*	135.	400.	1250.
	d. Yr. 6 (1856). *(S/M #H176-34).*	135.	400.	1250.
	e. Reissue. CD1861-64.	150.	450.	1350.

GENERAL BANK OF COMMUNICATIONS 行銀通交

Chiao T'ung Yin Hang

W/O BRANCH

1909 GENERAL ISSUE

		Good	Fine	XF
A13A	**10 Cents** 1909. *(S/M #C126-).* Reported not confirmed.	—	—	—

CANTON BRANCH 州廣

1909 ISSUE

#A14-A19E. Printer: CMPA.

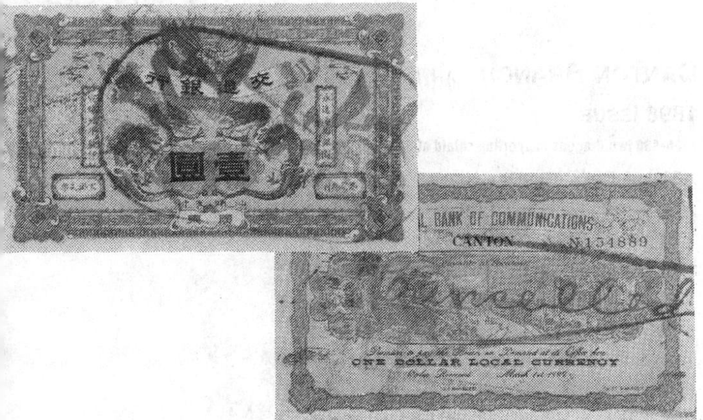

		Good	Fine	XF
A14	**1 Dollar** 1.3.1909. Brown w/black text on yellow unpt. Two dragons facing value at ctr. Ship dockside, steam passenger train at ctr. on back. Red ovpt. *Payable at Swatow* on back. *(S/M #C126-1a).*			
	a. Issued note.	200.	750.	1400.
	b. Cancelled w/perforated Chinese characters.	—	100.	300.
	c. Hand cancelled.	—	80.00	250.

#A15-A16 two dragons facing value at ctr., ship, station and train below.

		Good	Fine	XF
A15	**5 Dollars** 1.3.1909. Green and m/c. Back red and green. *(S/M #C126-).*			
	a. Issued note.	250.	1000.	2200.
	b. Cancelled w/perforated Chinese characters.	—	100.	300.
A16	**10 Dollars** 1.3.1909. Blue and red. *(S/M #C126-4).*			
	a. Issued note.	300.	1250.	2750.
	b. Cancelled w/perforated Chinese characters.	—	100.	500.

HANKOW BRANCH 口漢

1909 ISSUE

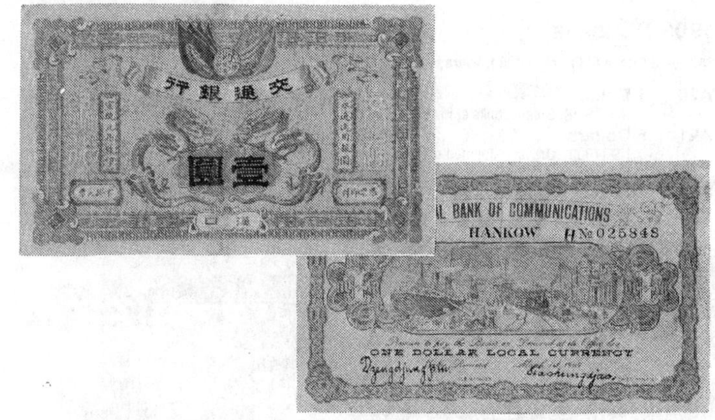

		Good	Fine	XF
A16A	**1 Dollar** 1.3.1909. Brown w/black text on yellow unpt. Like #A14. *(S/M #C126-)*	—	—	—
A16B	**5 Dollars** 1.3.1909. Green and m/c. Like #A15. Back red and green. *(S/M #C126-).*	—	—	—
A16C	**5 Dollars** 1.3.1909. Green and red. Like #A15. Back blue and red. *(S/M #C126-).* Reported not confirmed	—	—	—
A16D	**10 Dollars** 1.3.1909. Blue, orange and green. Like #A16. Back brown on blue unpt. *(S/M #C126-).*	—	—	—

SHANGHAI BRANCH 海上

1909 ISSUE

		Good	Fine	XF
A17	**1 Dollar** 1.3.1909. Brown and yellow. Like #A14. Back green. *(S/M #C126-1b).*			
	a. Issued note.	300.	900.	2400.
	b. Cancelled w/perforated Chinese characters.	—	200.	600.

KAIFENG BRANCH 封開

1909 ISSUE

		Good	Fine	XF
A17C	**5 Dollars** 1.3.1909. Green and red. Like #A15. Back blue and red. *(S/M #C126-).* Reported not confirmed	—	—	—
A17D	**10 Dollars** 1.3.1909. Blue, yellow and green. Back brown. Unsigned remainder. *(S/M #C126-).*	—	—	—

SHANGHAI BRANCH 海上

1909 ISSUE

		Good	Fine	XF
A18	**5 Dollars** 1.3.1909. Green and red. Like #A15. Back blue and red. *(S/M #C126-3).*			
	a. Issued note.	400.	1000.	3500.
	b. Cancelled w/perforated Chinese characters.	—	300.	1350.

SWATOW BRANCH 頭汕

1909 ISSUE

		Good	Fine	XF
A18A	**1 Dollar** 1.3.1909. Brown and yellow. Like #A14. Back green. *(S/M #C126-).* Reported not confirmed.	—	—	—

SHANGHAI BRANCH 海上

1909 ISSUE

		Good	Fine	XF
A19	**10 Dollars** 1.3.1909. Blue and green. Like #A16. Back brown and green. *(S/M #C126-5).*			
	a. Issued note.	600.	1800.	5000.
	b. Cancelled w/perforated Chinese characters.	—	200.	1250.

WUSIH BRANCH 錫無

1909 ISSUE

		Good	Fine	XF
A19B	**5 Dollars** 1.3.1909. Green and m/c. Like #A15. Back red and green. *(S/M #C126-).*	—	—	—
A19C	**5 Dollars** 1.3.1909. Green and red. Like #A15. Back blue and red. *(S/M #C126-).*	—	—	—

YINGKOW BRANCH 口營

1909 ISSUE

		Good	Fine	XF
A19E	**1 Dollar** 1.3.1909. Brown and yellow. Like #A14. Back green. *(S/M #C126-).*	—	—	—

BUREAU OF ENGRAVING AND PRINTING

財政部印刷局

Ts'ai Cheng Pu Yin Shua Chü

1909 ND ISSUE

#A20-A23 Prince Chün, regent at l. w/dragon at upper ctr.

		VG	VF	UNC
A20	**1 Dollar** ND (1909). Green. Junks at lower r. *(S/M #T190-1).* Proof.	—	—	1000.
A21	**5 Dollars** ND (1909). Orange. Mounted patrol at lower r. *(S/M #T190-2).* Proof.	—	—	2000.
A22	**10 Dollars** ND (1909). Blue. Great Wall at lower r. *(S/M #T190-3).* Proof.	—	—	3000.

		VG	VF	UNC
A23	**100 Dollars** ND (1909). Purple. Farm workers at lower r. *(S/M T190-4).* Proof.	—	—	4000.

HU PU BANK, PEKING

户部銀行

Hu Pu Yin Hang

兌換銀票

Tui Huan Yin P'iao

北京户部銀行

Pei Ching Hu Pu Yin Hang

1905 DOLLAR ISSUE

		VG	VF	UNC
A24	**1 Dollar** 12.11.yr. 31 (1905). Black text, orange on green unpt. 2 facing dragons at upper l. and r. Uniface. *(S/M #H177-1).*			

1909 TAEL ISSUE

		VG	VF	UNC
A25	**1 Tael** c. 1909. Orange and brown. Specimen. *(S/M #H177-10).*			
A26	**2 Taels** ca. 1909. Orange and brown. Specimen. *(S/M #H177-11).*			
A27	**3 Taels** ca. 1909. Orange and brown. Specimen. *(S/M #H177-1).*			
A28	**4 Taels** ca. 1909. Orange and brown. Specimen. *(S/M #H177-13).*			
A29	**5 Taels** ca. 1909. Orange and brown. Specimen. *(S/M #H177-14).*			
A30	**6 Taels** ca. 1909. Green and brown. Specimen. *(S/M #H177-15).*			
A31	**8 Taels** ca. 1909. Green and brown. Specimen. *(S/M #H177-16).*			
A32	**10 Taels** ca. 1909. Green and brown. Specimen. *(S/M #H177-17).*			
A33	**50 Taels** ca. 1909. Gray and blue. Specimen. *(S/M #H177-20).*			
A34	**100 Taels** 1909. Green on lt. blue unpt. *(S/M #H177-21).*			
A35	**500 Taels** ca. 1909. Green on lt. green unpt. *(S/M #H177-22).*			
	r. Remainder.			
	s. Specimen.			

IMPERIAL BANK OF CHINA

中國通商銀行

Chung Kuo T'ung Shang Yin Hang

CANTON BRANCH 廣州

1898 ISSUE

#A36-A38 two dragons supporting shield at upper ctr. Printer: BFL.

		VG	VF	UNC
A36	**1 Dollar** 22.1.1898. *(S/M #C293-10b).*			
	a. Issued note.	400.	2000.	—
	r. Remainder perforated: *CANCELLED.*	—	—	1000.

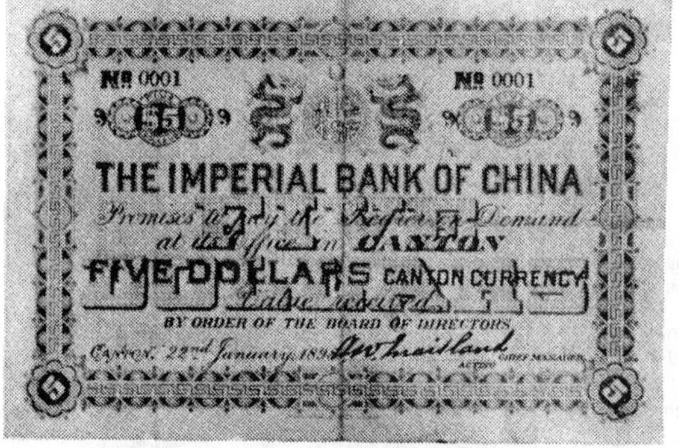

		VG	VF	UNC
A37	**5 Dollars** 22.1.1898. *(S/M #C293-11b).*			
	a. Issued note.	1200.	4500.	—
	r. Remainder perforated: *CANCELLED.*	—	—	1200.
A38	**10 Dollars** 22.1.1898. *(S/M #C293-12b).*			
	a. Issued note.	—	—	—
	r. Remainder perforated: *CANCELLED.*	—	—	1500.

PEKING BRANCH 北京

1898 ISSUE

#A39-A44 similar to #A36-A38. Printer: BFL.

		VG	VF	UNC
A39	**5 Mace** 14.11.1898. Dk. blue, brown and red on orange unpt. *(S/M #C293-1b).*			
	a. Issued note.	150.	350.	—
	r. Remainder perforated: *CANCELLED.*	—	—	250.

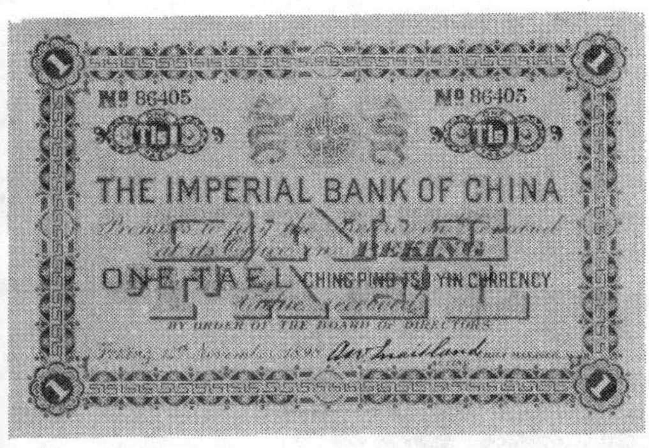

		VG	VF	UNC
A40	**1 Tael**			
	14.11.1898. *(S/M #C293-2b).*			
	a. Issued note.	250.	600.	1200.
	r. Remainder perforated: *CANCELLED.*	—	—	675.
A41	**5 Taels**			
	14.11.1898. *(S/M #C293-3b).*			
	a. Issued note.	600.	1800.	—
	r. Remainder perforated: *CANCELLED.*	—	—	800.
A42	**10 Taels**			
	14.11.1898. *(S/M #C293-4b).*			
	a. Issued note.	600.	1800.	—
	r. Remainder perforated: *CANCELLED.*	—	—	900.
A43	**50 Taels**			
	14.11.1898. *(S/M #C293-5b).*			
	a. Issued note. Reported not confirmed.	—	—	—
	r. Remainder perforated: *CANCELLED.*	—	—	1500.
A44	**100 Taels**			
	14.11.1898. *(S/M #C293-6b).*			
	a. Issued note. Reported not confirmed.	—	—	—
	r. Remainder perforated: *CANCELLED.*	—	—	3000.

SHANGHAI BRANCH 海上

1898 TAEL ISSUE

#A45-A55A similar to #A36-A38. Printer: BFL.

		VG	VF	UNC
A45	**1/2 Tael**			
	22.1.1898. *(S/M #C293-1a).*			
	a. Issued note.	250.	750.	—
	r. Remainder perforated: *CANCELLED.*	—	—	450.
A46	**1 Tael**			
	22.1.1898. Purple, brown and red on yellow unpt. *(S/M #C293-2a).*			
	a. Issued note.	450.	1100.	—
	r. Remainder perforated: *CANCELLED.*	—	—	500.
A47	**5 Taels**			
	22.1.1898. *(S/M #C293-3a).*			
	a. Issued note.	550.	1600.	—
	r. Remainder perforated: *CANCELLED.*	—	—	600.
A48	**10 Taels**			
	22.1.1898. *(S/M #C293-4a).*			
	a. Issued note.	700.	2200.	—
	r. Remainder perforated: *CANCELLED.*	—	—	950.
A49	**50 Taels**			
	22.1.1898. *(S/M #C293-5a).*			
	a. Issued note. Reported not confirmed.	—	—	—
	r. Remainder perforated: *CANCELLED.*	—	—	2000.

		VG	VF	UNC
A50	**100 Taels**			
	22.1.1898. Purple, brown and red on yellow unpt. *(S/M #C293-6a).*			
	a. Issued note.	1200.	4000.	—
	r. Remainder perforated: *CANCELLED.*	—	—	2200.

1898 DOLLAR ISSUE

		VG	VF	UNC
A51	**1 Dollar**			
	22.1.1898. *(S/M #C293-10a).*			
	a. Issued note.	300.	900.	—
	r. Remainder perforated: *CANCELLED.*	—	—	500.
A52	**5 Dollars**			
	22.1.1898. *(S/M #C293-11a).*			
	a. Issued note.	600.	1500.	—
	r. Remainder perforated: *CANCELLED.*	—	—	600.
A53	**10 Dollars**			
	22.1.1898. *(S/M #C293-12a).*			
	a. Issued note.	700.	2000.	—
	r. Remainder perforated: *CANCELLED.*	—	—	900.

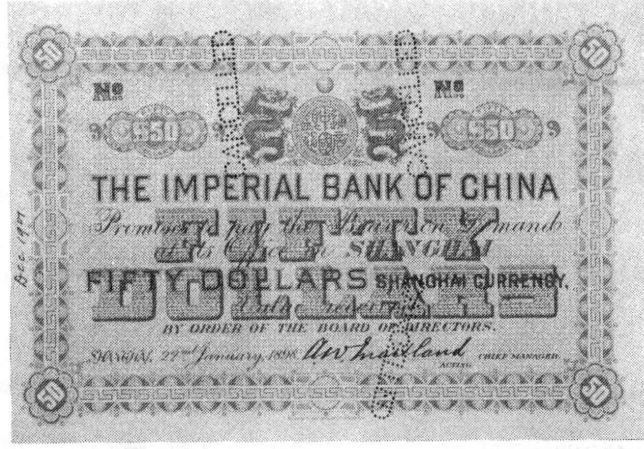

		VG	VF	UNC
A54	**50 Dollars**			
	22.1.1898. Red and brown on orange unpt. *(S/M #C293-).*			
	a. Issued note.	300.	3500.	—
	r. Remainder perforated: *CANCELLED.*	—	—	2000.
A54A	**100 Dollars**			
	22.1.1898. Red on yellow unpt. *(S/M #C293-).*			
	a. Issued note.	350.	4000.	—
	r. Remainder perforated: *CANCELLED.*	—	—	2200.

Note: See also #A133.

1904 ISSUE

A55B *Deleted.* See #A55Ac.

Note: For similar issues w/Worthy see Commercial Bank of China, #A133A-A138, #1-15.

		VG	VF	UNC
A55	**5 Dollars**			
	16.2.1904. Black on m/c unpt. Confucius standing at lower r. *(S/M #C293-20).*			
	a. Sm. sign. Printer: BWC.	600.	1500.	6000.
	b. Lg. sign. W/o imprint.	600.	1500.	6000.
	r. Remainder perforated: *CANCELLED.*	—	—	1200.

NOTICE

Readers with unlisted dates, signature varieties, etc. are invited to submit photocopies or, high resolution (300 dpi, 100% size) scans of their notes to: Standard Catalog of World Paper Money, 700 East State St. Iola, WI 54990-0001, or E-Mail: george.cuhaj@fwpubs.com.

		VG	VF	UNC
A55A	**10 Dollars**			
	16.2.1904. Black on m/c unpt. Similar to #A55. *(S/M #C293-21).*			
	a. Sm. sign. Printer: BWC.	1000.	4500.	—
	b. Lg. sign. W/o imprint.	1000.	4500.	—
	r. Remainder perforated: *CANCELLED.*	—	—	1500.

IMPERIAL CHINESE RAILWAYS 局總路官軌鐵洋北

Pei Yang T'ieh Kuei Kuan Lu Tsung Chü

PEIYANG BRANCH 洋北

1895 ISSUE

#A56, handwritten dates exist over printed date. Printer: BFL.

		Good	Fine	XF
A56	**1 Dollar**			
	22.4.1895. Blue on orange unpt. Train passing through fortress at ctr. Back red; boat, shoreline w/mountains in background. *(S/M #P34-1).*			
	a. Issued note.	120.	350.	750.
	r. Unsigned remainder.	—	—	—

#A57-A58 *Deleted.*

SHANGHAI BRANCH 海上

1899 ISSUE

#A59-A61 train passing through fortress at ctr. W/o sign.

		Good	Fine	XF
A59	**1 Dollar**			
	2.1.1899. Blue on orange unpt. Back red. *(S/M #S13-1).*	25.00	100.	300.
A60	**5 Dollars**			
	2.1.1899. Blue on orange unpt. *(S/M #S13-2).*	180.	450.	1000.
A61	**10 Dollars**			
	2.1.1899. *(S/M #S13-3).*			
	a. Issued note.	220.	700.	1400.
	r. Remainder perforated: *CANCELLED.*	—	Unc	650.

NINGPO COMMERCIAL BANK, LIMITED 行銀明四海上

Shang Hai Szu Ming Yin Hang

1909 ISSUE

#A61A-A61D dragons at upper ctr. on face and back. Chinese printer: TSPC.

		Good	Fine	XF
A61A	**1 Dollar**			
	22.1.1909. Gray. *SHANGHAI. (S/M #S107-1).*			
	a. Issued note.	110.	375.	900
	b. *HK* monogram (Hankow)/*SHANGHAI.*	150.	450.	1000
	c. *NP* (Ningpo)/*SHANGHAI.*	185.	525.	1200
	d. *SH* monogram *SHANGHAI.*	185.	525.	1500
A61B	**2 Dollars**			
	22.1.1909. Green and yellow. *SHANGHAI. (S/M #S107-2).*			
	a. Issued note.	150.	450.	1350
	r. Part printed remainder.			
A61C	**5 Dollars**			
	22.1.1909. Black and yellow. *SHANGHAI. (S/M #S107-3).*	400.	850.	2500
A61D	**10 Dollars**			
	22.1.1909. Black and brown. *SHANGHAI. (S/M #S107-4).*	600.	1200.	3000

Note: For later issues see #539-550.

TA CH'ING GOVERNMENT BANK 行銀清大

Ta Ch'ing Yin Han

CHINANFU BRANCH 福南濟 行銀部戸清大

Ta Ch'ing Hu Pu Yin Han

1906 ISSUE

#A62A-A75A supported arms at upper ctr. on back. Printer: CMPA.

		Good	Fine	X
A62	**1 Dollar**			
	1.9.1906. Green and lilac. *(S/M #T10-).*	300.	900.	–

FENGTIEN BRANCH 天奉

1907 ISSUE

		Good	Fine	X
A62A	**50 Cents**			
	1907. Purple and blue. Back red. *(S/M #T10-).*	400.	1200.	-

FOOCHOW BRANCH 州福

1906 PROVISIONAL ISSUE

A62B 1 Dollar VG VF UNC
1.9.1906. Violet ovpt: 12 Chinese characters across top on #A71D. *(S/M #T10-).* 350. 1000. —

HANGCHOW BRANCH 州杭

1906 ISSUE

A63 1 Dollar VG VF UNC
1.9.1906. Ovpt. on #A62. *(S/M #T10-1b).* — — —

HANKOW BRANCH 口漢

1906 ISSUE

A63A 1 Dollar VG VF UNC
1.9.1906. Supported arms at upper ctr. on back. *(S/M #T10-).* 90.00 300. —

A64 5 Dollars
1.9.1906. Blue and orange. Crossed flags at ctr. *(S/M #T10-2a).* 125. 400. —

A65 10 Dollars VG VF UNC
1.9.1906. Lilac and yellow. Crossed flags at top ctr. *(S/M #T10-3a).*
a. Issued note. 125. 450. —
r. Unsigned remainder. — — 300.

1907 ISSUE

A66 1 Dollar VG VF UNC
1.6.1907. Green and lilac. *(S/M #T10-10a).*
a. Issued note. 60.00 200. —
r. Unsigned remainder. — — 120.

HUNAN BRANCH 南湖

1906-07 ISSUE

A66A 1 Dollar VG VF UNC
1.9.1906. Ovpt. on #A63A. *(S/M #T10-).* — — —

A67 5 Dollars
1.6.1907. Blue and orange. Crossed flags at ctr. *(S/M #T10-11).* — — —

A68 10 Dollars
1.6.1907. Lilac and yellow. Crossed flags at top ctr. *(S/M #T10-12).* — — —

KAIFONG BRANCH 封開

1906 PROVISIONAL ISSUE

A69 1 Dollar VG VF UNC
1.9.1906. Ovpt. on #A72. *(S/M #T10-1c).*
a. Issued note. Rare. — — —
r. Unsigned remainder. — — 350.

A70 5 Dollars VG VF UNC
1.9.1906. Ovpt. on #A73. *(S/M #T10-2c).*
a. Issued note. — — —
r. Unsigned remainder. — 120. 350.

A71 10 Dollars
1.9.1906. Ovpt. on #A74. *(S/M #T10-3c).*
a. Issued note. — — —
r. Unsigned remainder. — 150. 450.

KALGAN BRANCH 口家張

1906 ISSUE

A71A 1 Dollar VG VF UNC
1.9.1906. Dk. green and lilac on yellow unpt. Back blue on brown unpt. *(S/M #T10-).* — — —

KWANGCHOW (CANTON) BRANCH 州廣

1908 ISSUE

A71B 1 Dollar VG VF UNC
1.3.1908. Dk. green and lilac on yellow unpt. Back blue on brown unpt. *(S/M #T10-).* 200. 450. 1250.

A71C 10 Dollars
1.3.1908. Brown and yellow. Crossed flags at top ctr. *(S/M #T10-).* — — —

PEKING BRANCH 京北

1906 ISSUE

A71D 1 Dollar VG VF UNC
1.9.1906. Supported arms at upper ctr. on back. *(S/M #T10).* — — —

SHANGHAI BRANCH 上港

1906 ISSUE

A71H 5 Dollars VG VF UNC
1.9.1906. Red-violet on green unpt. Similar to #A75A but 9 seal characters in frame at bottom ctr. *(S/M #T10-).* — — —

TIENTSIN BRANCH 津天

1906 ISSUE

A72 1 Dollar VG VF UNC
1.9.1906. Green and lilac. *(S/M #T10-1a).* — — —

A73 5 Dollars
1.9.1906. Blue and orange. Crossed flags at ctr. *(S/M #T10-2a).*
a. Issued note. — — —
r. Unsigned remainder. — — 300.

A74 10 Dollars
1.9.1906. Lilac and yellow. Crossed flags at ctr. *(S/M #T10-3a).* — — —

URGA BRANCH 倫庫

1908 ISSUE

		VG	VF	UNC
A75	**1 Dollar** 1.3.1908. Green and lilac. *(S/M #T10-20).*	—	—	—

		VG	VF	UNC
A75A	**5 Dollars** 1.3.1908. Blue and orange. *(S/M #T10-).*	—	—	—
A75B	**10 Dollars** 1.3.1908. *(S/M #T10-).*	—	—	—

WUHU BRANCH

1906 PROVISIONAL ISSUE

		VG	VF	UNC
A75E	**1 Dollar** 1.9.1906. Ovpt. on #A72. *(S/M #T10-).*	—	—	—

YINGKOW BRANCH 口營

1906 ISSUE

		VG	VF	UNC
A75J	**1 Dollar** 1.6.1906. Specimen. Uniface pair. *(S/M #T10-).*	—	—	—
A75K	**5 Dollars** 1.6.1906. Specimen. Uniface pair. *(S/M #T10-).*	—	—	—
A75L	**10 Dollars** 1.6.1906. Specimen. Uniface pair. *(S/M #T10-).*	—	—	—

YUNNAN BRANCH 南雲

1906 PROVISIONAL ISSUE

		VG	VF	UNC
A75P	**1 Dollar** 1.9.1906. Ovpt. on #A71B. *(S/M #T10-).*	—	—	—

W/O BRANCH

1909 GENERAL ISSUE

#A76-A78 black text. Portr. Li Hung Chan at l. W/o office of issue or sign. Printer: ABNC (Not issued).

Note: See also Bank of China provisional issue #16-18.

		VG	VF	UNC
A76	**1 Dollar** 1.10.1909. Olive-brown on red-orange unpt. Hillside village, railraod at r. Waterfront park at ctr. on back. *(S/M #T10-30).*	125.	350.	1000.

		VG	VF	UNC
A77	**5 Dollars** 1.10.1909. Brown on blue and m/c unpt. Gazebo at r. Hillside pagoda, village at ctr. on back. *(S/M #T10-31).*	300.	800.	2000
A78	**10 Dollars** 1.10.1909. Teahouse at r. Great Wall at ctr. on back. *(S/M #T10-32).*	350.	900.	2200

		VG	VF	UNC
A78A	**50 Dollars** 1.10.1909. Fortified city gates at r. Pagodas atop monastery at ctr. r. on back. *(S/M #T10-33).*	225.	1150.	2500
A78B	**100 Dollars** 1.10.1909. Temple of Heaven at r. Teahouse w/gazebos at ctr. on back. *(S/M #T10-34).*	600.	1800.	—

Note: See also Bank of China provisional issue, #16-18.

SHANGHAI BRANCH 倫庫

1907 ISSUE

		VG	VF	UNC
A71J	**1 Dollar** 1.9.1907. *(S/M #T10-).*	—	—	—

URGA BRANCH 倫庫

1907 ISSUE

		VG	VF	UNC
A74A	**1 Dollar** 1.6.1907. *(S/M #T10-).*	—	—	—
A74C	**10 Dollars** 1.6.1907. *(S/M #T10-).*	—	—	—

W/O BRANCH

1910 ND ISSUE

#A79-A82 portr. Prince Chun at l., dragon at upper ctr. W/o date, sign. or serial #.

Note: Crudely printed, but deceptive, souvenir copies exist.

		VG	VF	UNC
A79	**1 Dollar** ND (1910). Green. Junks at lower r. *(S/M #T10-40).* (Not issued).	125.	450.	1500
A80	**5 Dollars** ND (1910). Red. Mounted patrol at lower r. *(S/M #T10-41).* (Not issued).	400.	850.	2500

		VG	VF	UNC
A81	**10 Dollars** ND (1910). Black. Great Wall at lower r. *(S/M #T10-42).*			
	a. Issued note.	1200.	3000.	—
	r. Unsigned remainder w/o seal stamps on back.	—	—	1600.

		VG	VF	UNC
A82	**100 Dollars** ND (1910). Dk. green. Field workers at lower r. *(S/M #T10-43).* (Not issued).	—	—	—

TA CH'ING GOVERNMENT BANK, SHANSI

陝西大清銀行

Shan Hsi Ta Ch'ing Yin Hang

1911 ISSUE

#A83, A83A, A83H and A83J; facing dragons w/crossed flags at top ctr. Unissued remainders w/ or w/o counterfoils.

		VG	VF	UNC
A83	**1 Tael** ca.1911. Purple on lt. green unpt. Remainder. *(S/M #T10-50).*	—	—	450.
A83A	**3 Taels** ca.1911. Remainder. *(S/M #T10-51).*	—	—	550.

		VG	VF	UNC
A83H	**100 Taels** ca.1909. Purple on lt. green unpt. Remainder. *(S/M #T10-54).*	—	—	850.
A83J	**1000 Taels** ca.1911. Brown-orange on pale olive-green unpt. Remainder. *(S/M #T10-60).*	—	—	1200.

Note: Beware of remainders missing red validation seal stampings over the denomination which were "created" in recent times for collectors.

REPUBLIC

AGRICULTURAL BANK OF THE FOUR PROVINCES

四省農民銀行

Szu Sheng Nung Min Yin Hang

豫鄂皖贛四省農民銀行

Yü O Huan Kan Szu Sheng Nung Min Yin Hang

1933 ISSUE

		Good	Fine	XF
A84	**10 Cents** ND (1933). Red. Farmer at ctr. Printer: TYPC. *(S/M #S110-1).*			
	a. Issued note.	10.00	40.00	125.
	s. Specimen.			
A84A	**20 Cents** 1933. Purple and yellow. Back red and green. Printer: TYPC. *(S/M #S110-).*	—	Unc	200.
	a. Issued note.	—	—	—
	s. Specimen.	—	Unc	150.
A84B	**20 Cents** 1933. Purple. Back green and yellow. *(S/M #S110-).*	—	—	—

		Good	Fine	XF
A85	**20 Cents** 1933. Green and purple. Farmers carrying baskets at r. Printer: CCCA. *(S/M #S110-2).*			
	a. Issued note.	7.50	35.00	100.
	r. Remainder w/o sign. or serial #.	—	Unc	50.00
	s. Specimen.	—	Unc	75.00

		Good	Fine	XF
A86	**50 Cents** ND (1933). Blue. Farmer plowing w/ox at ctr. Farm workers at r. on back. Printer: CCCA. *(S/M #S110-3).*			
	a. Issued note.	20.00	50.00	150.
	r. Remainder w/o sign. or serial #.	—	Unc	75.00

		Good	Fine	XF
A87	**1 Dollar** 1933. Brown on yellow unpt. Farm workers at l. and r. Back blue and green; farm workers at ctr. Printer: TYPC. *(S/M #S110-10).*			
	a. Issued note.	40.00	100.	300.
	b. Ovpt: *SIAN.*	50.00	120.	400.
	s. As a. Specimen.	—	Unc	125.

1933 Provisional Issue

#A88-A90 joint issue w/Hupeh Provincial Bank. New issuer ovpt. on notes of Hupeh Provincial Bank.

		VG	VF	UNC
A88	**1 Dollar** ND (1933 - old date 1929). Violet on m/c unpt. Pagoda at r. Ovpt. on #S2104. *(S/M #S110-20).*	50.00	225.	—
A89	**5 Dollars** ND (1933 - old date 1929). Green on m/c unpt. Pagoda at ctr. Ovpt. on #S2105. *(S/M #S110-21).*	60.00	275.	—
A90	**10 Silver Yüan** ND (1933 - old date 1929). Red on m/c unpt. Pagoda at l. Ovpt. on #S2106. *(S/M #S110-22).*	60.00	325.	—

1934 Issue

		VG	VF	UNC
A91A	**10 Cents** 1934. Orange and blue. Back purple and orange. Printer: TYPC. *(S/M #S110-).*	—	—	—
A91B	**20 Cents** 1934. Purple and yellow. Back red and green. Printer: TYPC. *(S/M #S110-).*	—	—	—

		Good	Fine	XF
A91E	**1 Dollar** 1.5.1934. Red. Farm workers at upper l. Back green; ox at ctr. Chinese printer: TYPC.			
	a. *Foochow. (S/M #S110-30a).*	20.00	80.00	250.
	b. *HANG CHOW. (S/M #S110-30b).*	30.00	90.00	350.
	c. Control ovpt: *Yu.*	20.00	80.00	225.
	s. As a, b. Specimen.	—	Unc	150.

Agricultural and Industrial Bank of China

中國農工銀行

Chung Kuo Nung Kung Yin Hang

1927 Dollar Issues

#A92-A108 Printer: BEPP (Peiping or Peking).

		Good	Fine	XF
A92	**10 Cents** 1.2.1927. Purple. Bridge over water at ctr.			
	a. *Peking. (S/M #C287-1a).*	6.00	15.00	50.00
	b. *Tientsin. (S/M #C287-1c).*	7.50	22.50	65.00
A93	**10 Cents** 1.2.1927. Purple. Like #A92 but printer: BEP-Peking.			
	a. *Peking. (S/M #C287-2).*	8.50	25.00	70.00
	b. *Tientsin (S/M #C287-1b).*	10.00	30.00	95.00

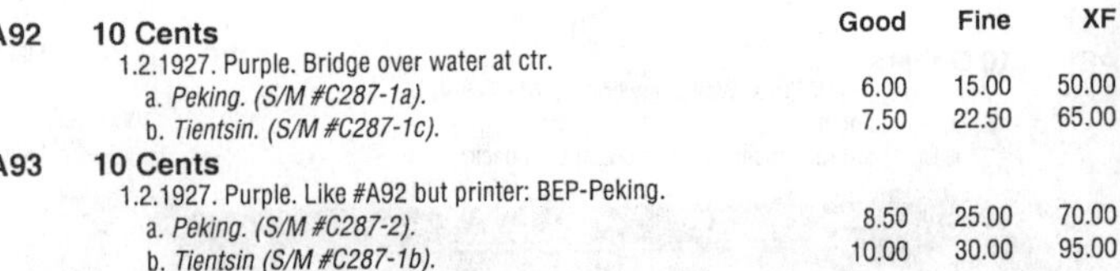

		Good	Fine	XF
A94	**20 Cents** 1.2.1927. Green. Bridge over water at ctr.			
	a. *Peking. (S/M #C287-3a).*	4.50	15.00	55.00
	b. *Tientsin. (S/M #C287-3c).*	7.50	22.50	65.00
A94A	**20 Cents** 1.2.1927. Green. Like P#A94 but printer: BEP-Peiping.			
	a. *Peking. (S/M #C287-).*	4.50	15.00	55.00
	b. *Tientsin. (S/M #C287-3b).*	7.50	22.50	65.00
	s. As a, specimen.	—	Unc	75.00

		Good	Fine	XF
A94B	**50 Cents** 1.2.1927. Orange. Bridge over water at ctr. Back orange. Peking. *(S/M #C287-).*	20.00	70.00	200.

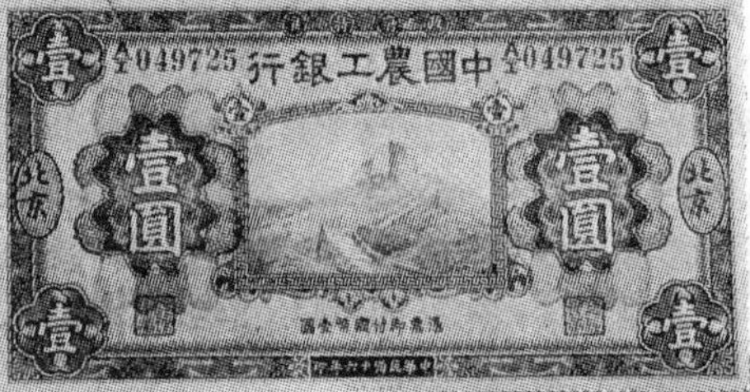

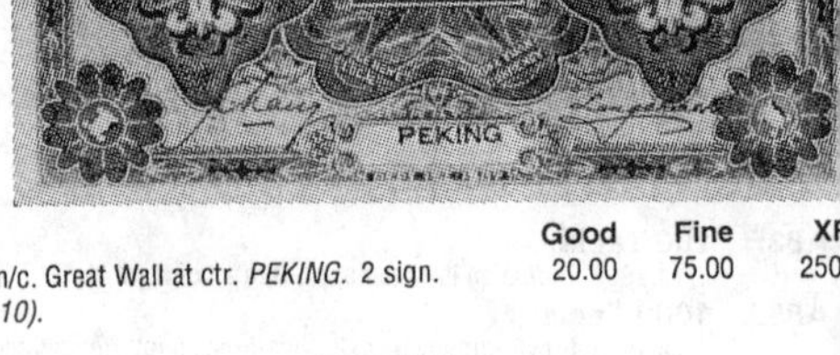

		Good	Fine	XF
A95	**1 Dollar** 1.9.1927. Brown and m/c. Great Wall at ctr. *PEKING.* 2 sign. varieties. *(S/M #C287-10).*	20.00	75.00	250
A98	**5 Dollars** 1.9.1927. Red-orange on m/c unpt. Like #A99. *PEKING. (S/M #C287-13).*			
	a. Issued note.	30.00	125.	400
	s. 2 part specimen.	—	Unc	160

		Good	Fine	XF
A99	**5 Dollars**			
	1.9.1927. Red and m/c. Sailing ships at ctr.			
	a. *HANKOW. (S/M #C287-14a).*	37.50	100.	375.
	b. *HANKOW, PAYABLE AT CHANGSHA* ovpt. *(S/M #C287-14b).*	37.50	125.	450.
	s. As b. Specimen.	—	Unc	170.
A100	**5 Dollars**			
	1.9.1927. Orange and m/c. *TIENTSIN. (S/M #C287-15).*	40.00	130.	375.

		Good	Fine	XF
A101	**5 Dollars**			
	1.9.1927. Green and m/c. Like #A99. *SHANGHAI. (S/M #C287-16).*			
	a. Issued note.	40.00	130.	550.
	s. Specimen.	—	Unc	170.

A102 Deleted.

		Good	Fine	XF
A105	**10 Dollars**			
	1.9.1927. Green and m/c. Like #A104.			
	a. *SHANGHAI. (S/M #C287-22a).*	50.00	150.	600.
	b. *TIENTSIN. (S/M #C287-22b).*	40.00	120.	550.
	s. As b. Specimen.	—	Unc	180.
A106	**10 Dollars**			
	1.9.1927. Brown and m/c. Like #A104. *SHANGHAI. (S/M #C287-23).*	17.50	40.00	200.

1932 ISSUE

A109-A111 Sign. varieties. Printer: ABNC.

		Good	Fine	XF
A107	**10 Cents**			
	1.1.1932. Brown and red. Bridge over water at ctr. *HANKOW. (S/M #C287-31).*	10.00	30.00	120.
A108	**20 Cents**			
	1.1.1932. Yellow. *HANKOW. (S/M #C287-31).*	12.50	22.50	150.

		Good	Fine	XF
A109	**1 Dollar**			
	1932. Red and m/c. Farmer plowing w/water buffalo at ctr. *SHANGHAI. (S/M #C287-40).*			
	a. Issued note.	12.50	37.50	135.
	b. W/various numerical ovpt.	15.00	37.50	150.

		Good	Fine	XF
A110	**5 Yüan**			
	1932. Green and m/c. Farmer plowing w/water buffalo at l.			
	a. *HANKOW.* W/various numerical ovpt.: 11; 21; 22. *(S/M #C287-41a).*	30.00	60.00	375.
	b. *SHANGHAI.* W/various numerical ovpt.: 11-43, etc. *(S/M #C287-41b).*	15.00	50.00	250.
	c. *PEIPING. (S/M #C287-41c).*	15.00	50.00	250.
	d. *HANKOW.* Ovpt: *PAYABLE AT CHANGSHA. (S/M #C287-41d).*	30.00	60.00	375.
	s. As b. 2 part specimen.	—	—	160.
	s1. Specimen w/o place name.	—	—	140.

		Good	Fine	XF
A111	**10 Yüan**			
	1932. Purple and m/c. Farmer plowing w/water buffalo at r.			
	a. *HANKOW.* W/various numerical ovpt: 3; 4; 7, etc. *(S/M #C287-42a).*	50.00	150.	500.
	b. *SHANGHAI.* W/various numerical ovpt.: 33; 40; 43 etc. *(S/M #C287-42b).*	40.00	135.	400.

1934 ISSUE

		Good	Fine	XF
A112	**1 Yüan**			
	1934. Red and m/c. Farmer plowing w/water buffalo at ctr. Printer: W&S.			
	a. *SHANGHAI. (S/M #C287-50a).*	12.50	35.00	165.
	b. *PEIPING. (S/M #C287-50b).*	12.50	35.00	165.
	c. W/o place name. *(S/M #C287-50c).*	12.50	25.00	125.
	d. *TIENTSIN (S/M #C287-50d).*	12.50	35.00	150.
	s1. As a 2 part specimen.	—	—	140.
	s2. As b 2 part specimen.	—	—	140.

1927 YUAN ISSUES

		Good	Fine	XF
A96	**1 Yüan**			
	1.9.1927. Green and m/c. Like #A95.			
	a. *HANKOW. (S/M #C287-11a).*	40.00	90.00	250.
	b. *HANKOW, PAYABLE AT CHANGSHA* ovpt. *(S/M #C287-11b).*	40.00	130.	500.
	s. 2 part specimen.	—	Unc	160.
A97	**1 Yüan**			
	1.9.1927. Red and m/c. Like #A95. *SHANGHAI. (S/M #C287-12).*	17.50	65.00	400.
A103	**10 Yüan**			
	1927. *PEKING. (S/M #C287-20).* Reported not confirmed.	—	—	—
A104	**10 Yüan**			
	1.9.1927. Purple and m/c. Farm workers at ctr.			
	a. *HANKOW. (S/M #C287-21a).*	50.00	150.	600.
	b. *HANKOW, PAYABLE AT CHANGSHA* ovpt. *(S/M #C287-21b).*	55.00	150.	700.
	s. As a, b. Specimen.	—	Unc	200.

BANK OF AGRICULTURE AND COMMERCE

行銀商農

Nung Shang Yin Hang

1921 ISSUE

For former #A112A-A112C see A114A or A117C, D.

#A113-A117D printer: Wu Foong Industrial Development Co. Ltd., Peking.

		Good	Fine	XF
A113	**1 Yüan**			
	Yr.11 (1921). Red-brown and blue. Harvesting grain.			
	a. *SHANGHAI.* Specimen. *(S/M #N23-1).*	—	—	—
	b. *PEKING.* Specimen. *(S/M #N23-).*	—	—	—
	c. *HANKOW. (S/M #N23-).*	100.	600.	—

		Good	Fine	XF
A114	**5 Yüan**			
	Yr. 11 (1921). Gray and m/c. Similar to #A113.			
	a. *SHANGHAI.* Specimen. *(S/M #N23-).*	—	—	—
	b. *PEKING. (S/M #N23-).* Reported not confirmed.	—	—	—
A114A	**5 Yüan**			
	ND. (1921) Lilac. Similar to #A117C. Specimen. *(S/M #N23-).*	—	Unc	400
A115	**10 Yüan**			
	Yr. 11 (1921).			
	a. *SHANGHAI. (S/M #N23-3).*	75.00	225.	750
	b. *PEKING. (S/M #N23-).*	—	—	—
	s. As a. Specimen.			
A116	**50 Yüan**			
	Yr. 11 (1921). *SHANGHAI. (S/M #N23-).* Reported not confirmed.	—	—	—
A117	**100 Yüan**			
	Yr. 11 (1921). *SHANGHAI. Specimen. (S/M #N23-).*	—	Unc	1500

1922 DOLLAR ISSUE

#A117A and A117B printer: BEPP.

		Good	Fine	XF
A117A	**1 Dollar**			
	1.5.1922. Red and blue. *(S/M #N23-).*			
	a. Issued note.	—	—	—
	s. 2 part specimen, Shanghai, red and yellow, back red.	—	—	—

		Good	Fine	XF
A117B	**5 Dollars**			
	1.5.1922. Green and yellow. River scene at center.			
	a. *SHANGHAI. (S/M #N23-).*	75.00	225.	750
	b. *HANKOW. (S/M #N23-).*	55.00	150.	550

1922 YUAN ISSUE

		VG	VF	UNC
A117C	**1 Yüan**			
	1922. Red. Agricultural workers. *(S/M #N23-).*			
	s1. Specimen.	—	—	300
	s2. Specimen perforated: *UNGÜLTIG.*	—	—	300
A117D	**5 Yüan**			
	1922. Dk. brown and violet. Similar to #A117C. Specimen. *(S/M #N23-).*	—	—	300

1926 ISSUE

#A118-A120 pagoda on hilltop, shoreline at ctr. Printer: ABNC.

		Good	Fine	XF
A118	**1 Yüan**			
	1.12.1926. Brown and m/c. *SHANGHAI. (S/M #N23-10).*			
	a. Issued note.	50.00	135.	350
	s. Specimen. Uniface face and back.	—	Unc	300
A119	**5 Yüan**			
	1.12.1926. Green and m/c.			
	a. *SHANGHAI.* W/various numerical ovpt: 3; 6; 10; 21. *(S/M #N23-11a).*	25.00	65.00	175
	b. *CHANGSHA. (S/M #N23-11b).*	25.00	75.00	200.
	c. *HANKOW. (S/M #N23-11c).*	25.00	65.00	175.
	s. As a. Specimen. Uniface face and back.	—	—	250
	s1. As c. Specimen. Uniface face and back.	—	—	250
	s2. Peking. Specimen. Uniface face and back.	—	—	250.

		Good	Fine	XF
A120	10 Yüan 1.12.1926. Purple and blue. *SHANGHAI. (S/M #N23-12).*			
	a. Issued note.	35.00	100.	450.
	s. Specimen. Uniface face and back.	—	—	300.
	s1. Hanken. Specimen uniface face and back.	—	Unc	300.

China Silk and Tea Industrial Bank

中國絲茶銀行

Chung Kuo Szu Ch'a Yin Hang

1925 Issue

#A120A-A120C harvesting tea at ctr. Weaving at ctr. on back. Printer: BEPP.

		Good	Fine	XF
A120A	1 Dollar 15.8.1925. Blue on m/c unpt.			
	a. *PEKING. (S/M #C292-1a).*	25.00	75.00	250.
	b. *TIENTSIN. (S/M #C292-1b).*	25.00	75.00	250.
	c. *CHENGCHOW / PEKING. (S/M #C292-1c).*	25.00	75.00	250.

		Good	Fine	XF
A120B	5 Dollars 15.8.1925. Orange on m/c unpt.			
	a. *PEKING. (S/M #C292-2a).*	30.00	100.	350.
	b. *TIENTSIN. (S/M #C292-2b).*	25.00	75.00	250.
	c. *CHENGCHOW / PEKING. (S/M #C292-2c).*	30.00	100.	350.
A120C	10 Dollars 15.8.1925. Green on m/c unpt.			
	a. *PEKING. (S/M #C292-3a).*	75.00	225.	900.
	b. *TIENTSIN. (S/M #C292-3b).*	75.00	225.	900.
	c. *CHENGCHOW / PEKING. (S/M #C292-3c).*	60.00	180.	750.

China and South Sea Bank, Limited

中南銀行

Chung Nan Yin Hang

Established 1921. Though bearing only the China and South Sea Bank's name, all these notes were backed and circulated by a coalition of four major Shanghai banks, of which the issuer was one. These notes achieved wide circulation and acceptance.

1921 Issue

#A122-A123A common w/various letter and numerical control ovpt: *SK; SK-b; SK-P; SS, etc.* Printer: ABNC.

		Good	Fine	XF
A121	1 Yüan 1.10.1921. Blue on m/c unpt. Monument at ctr. Sign. varieties.			
	a. *SHANGHAI.* Title: *CHAIRMAN* below sign. on back. *(S/M #C295-1a).*	17.50	50.00	175.
	b. *SHANGHAI.* W/o title: *CHAIRMAN* below sign. on back. *(S/M #C295-1a).*	20.00	60.00	195.
	c. *HANKOW.* Title: *CHAIRMAN* below sign. on back. *(S/M #295-1b).*	25.00	75.00	250.
	d. *TIENTSIN. (S/M #C295-1c).*	25.00	75.00	290.
	e. *AMOY.*	25.00	75.00	290.
A122	5 Yüan 1.10.1921. Purple on m/c unpt. Monument at l. Title: *CHAIRMAN* below sign. on back. *SHANGHAI. (S/M #C295-2).*	25.00	75.00	250.
A123	10 Yüan 1.10.1921. Black and m/c. Monument at r.			
	a. *SHANGHAI. (S/M #C295-3a).*	40.00	125.	500.
	b. *TIENTSIN. (S/M #C295-3b).*	40.00	125.	500.
	c. *HANKOW. (S/M #C295-3c).*	60.00	150.	600.
A123A	50 Yüan 1.10.1921. *SHANGHAI.* Monument at ctr. *(S/M #C295-4).*	—	—	—
A123B	100 Yüan 1.10.1921. Monument at l. Proof.	—	—	—

1924 Issue

#A124 and A125 common w/letter control ovpt: *SK* or *SY*. Printer: ABNC.

		Good	Fine	XF
A124	5 Yüan 1924. Purple and m/c. Like #A122.			
	a. *SHANGHAI. (S/M #C295-10a).*	22.50	60.00	225.
	b. *TIENTSIN. (S/M #C295-10b).*	22.50	60.00	225.
	c. *HANKOW. (S/M #C295-10c).*	22.50	75.00	250.
	d. *AMOY. (S/M #C295-10d).*	25.00	75.00	250.
A125	10 Yüan 1924. Black and m/c. Like #A123.			
	a. *SHANGHAI. (S/M #C295-11a).*	25.00	75.00	225.
	b. *TIENTSIN. (S/M #C295-11b).*	25.00	90.00	250.
	c. *HANKOW. (S/M #C295-11c).*	25.00	90.00	250.
	d. *AMOY. (S/M #C295-11d).*	37.50	125.	375.

1927 Issue

		Good	Fine	XF
A126	**1 Yüan**			
	1927. Purple and m/c. 3 women's busts over dollar coin at ctr. 2 women's busts over Yuan Shih Kai dollar coin on back. Printer: W&S.			
	a. *SHANGHAI.* W/various control ovpt. *(S/M #C295-20a).*	45.00	180.	625.
	b. *TIENTSIN. (S/M #C295-20b).*	75.00	200.	750.
A127	**5 Yüan**			
	1927. Red and m/c. Similar to #A124. Printer: ABNC. Also various numerical, letter or Chinese character control ovpt.			
	a. *HANKOW. (S/M #C295-21b).*	60.00	180.	700.
	b. *SHANGHAI. (S/M #C295-21a).*	60.00	180.	600.
A128	**5 Yüan**			
	1927. Purple and m/c. Similar to #A129. *SHANGHAI.* Also w/various letter or Chinese character control ovpt. Printer: ABNC. *(S/M #C295-22).*	60.00	180.	675.

		Good	Fine	XF
A129	**10 Yüan**			
	1927. Brown and red. 2 women's busts at l. and r. Back brown and blue, 3 women's busts at l., ctr. and r. 2 sign. varieties. Printer: W&S. *SHANGHAI.* Also various letter or Chinese character control ovpt. *(S/M #C295-23).*	100.	300.	1000.
A130	**50 Yüan**			
	1927. Purple. Printer: ABNC. *(S/M #C295-24).* Reported not confirmed.	—	—	—
A131	**100 Yüan**			
	1927. Red. Printer: ABNC. *(S/M #C295-25).* Reported not confirmed.	—	—	—

1931-32 ISSUE

		Good	Fine	XF
A132	**1 Yüan**			
	1931. Blue and m/c. Monument at l. Printer: W&S.			
	a. *SHANGHAI. (S/M*	17.50	35.00	140.
	b. *TIENTSIN. (S/M #C295-30b).*	22.50	60.00	175.

		Good	Fine	XF
A133	**5 Yüan**			
	Jan. 1932. Purple and m/c. Control letter ovpt: *HK. SHANGHAI.* Printer: TDLR. *(S/M #C295-40).*	25.00	100.	350.

COMMERCIAL BANK OF CHINA

中國通商銀行

Chung Kuo T'ung Shang Yin Hang

1913 PROVISIONAL TAEL ISSUE

#A133A-A133B ovpt: *COMMERCIAL/IMPERIAL.*

		Good	Fine	XF
A133A	**1 Tael**			
	ND. (1913-old date 22.1.1898). Red ovpt. on #A46. *(S/M #C293-).*	250.	1000.	2500.

1913 PROVISIONAL DOLLAR ISSUE

		Good	Fine	XF
A133B	**5 Dollars**			
	ND (1913-old date 16.2.1904). Black and m/c. Ovpt. on #A55. *(S/M #C293-).*	300.	1250.	3000.

		Good	Fine	XF
A133C	**10 Dollars**			
	ND (1913-old date 16.2.1904). Ovpt. on #A55B. *(S/M #C293-).*	350.	1400.	3500.

920 SHANGHAI TAEL ISSUE 海上

A134-A138 "Confucius" standing at ctr. Medallion supported by 2 lions on back. Printer: ABNC.

		Good	Fine	XF
134	**1 Tael**			
	15.1.1920. Blue on m/c unpt. Back brown. *(S/M #C293-30).*			
	a. Issued note.	27.50	40.00	275.
	p. Proof.	—	Unc	200.
	s. Specimen.	—	Unc	125.
135	**5 Taels**			
	15.1.1920. Yellow-orange on m/c unpt. Back purple. *(S/M #C293-31).*			
	a. Issued note.	100.	250.	1100.
	p. Proof.	—	Unc	200.
	s. Specimen.	—	Unc	200.

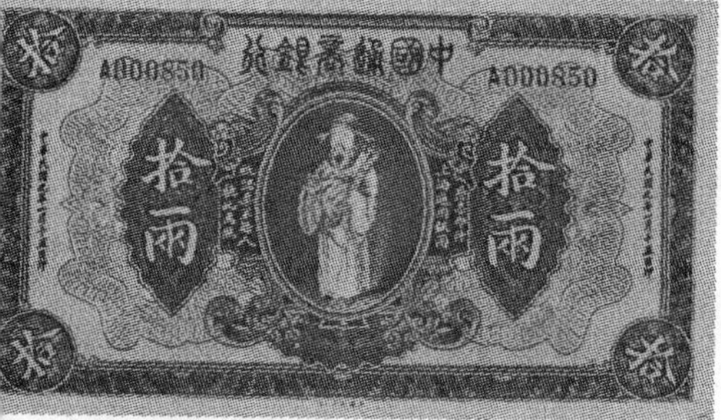

		Good	Fine	XF
136	**10 Taels**			
	15.1.1920. Purple on m/c unpt. Back brown. *(S/M #C293-32).*			
	a. Issued note.	150.	400.	1200.
	p. Proof.	—	Unc	300.
	s. Specimen.	—	Unc	250.
137	**50 Taels**			
	15.1.1920. *(S/M #C293-33).* Reported not confirmed.	—	—	—
138	**100 Taels**			
	15.1.1920. *(S/M #C293-34).* Reported not confirmed.	—	—	—

920 DOLLAR ISSUES

8 "Worthy" standing at ctr. Medallion supported by 2 lions on back. Printer: ABNC.

		Good	Fine	XF
	1 Dollar			
	15.1.1920. Black and m/c. *(S/M #C293-40).*			
	a. Issued note.	17.50	60.00	180.
	p. Proof.			
	s. Specimen.			
	1 Dollar			
	15.1.1920. Blue and m/c. *(S/M #C293-41).*			
	a. Issued note.	15.00	50.00	150.
	b. W/character ovpt: *Yuan.*	12.50	40.00	125.
	p. Proof.	—	Unc	150.
	s. Specimen.	—	Unc	125.

		Good	Fine	XF
3	**5 Dollars**			
	15.1.1920. Purple and m/c. *(S/M #C293-42).*			
	a. Issued note.	20.00	75.00	200.
	b. W/character ovpt: *Yuan.*	15.00	50.00	150.
	s. Specimen.	—	Unc	150.

		Good	Fine	XF
4	**5 Dollars**			
	15.1.1920. Yellow and m/c. *(S/M #C293-43).*	25.00	80.00	280.
4A	**5 Dollars**			
	15.1.1920. Brown and m/c. *(S/M #293-).*			
	a. Issued note.	75.00	250.	750.
	p. Proof.	—	Unc	350.
	s. Specimen.	—	Unc	250.

		Good	Fine	XF
5	**10 Dollars**			
	15.1.1920. Yellow and m/c. *(S/M #C293-44).*			
	a. Issued note.	40.00	120.	400.
	b. W/character ovpt.	17.50	50.00	175.
	p. Proof.	—	Unc	200.
	s. Specimen.	—	Unc	175.
6	**10 Dollars**			
	15.1.1920. Red and m/c. *(S/M #C293-45).*			
	a. Issued note.	22.50	65.00	225.
	b. W/character ovpt.	20.00	60.00	200.
	p. Proof.	—	Unc	200.
	s. Specimen.	—	Unc	175.
7	**50 Dollars**			
	15.1.1920. Blue and m/c. *(S/M #C293-46).*			
	a. Issued note.	400.	1200.	—
	p. Proof.	—	Unc	250.
	s. Specimen.	—	Unc	225.

		Good	Fine	XF
8	**100 Dollars** 15.1.1920. Olive-green and m/c. Back purple. *(S/M #C293-47).*			
	a. Issued note.	500.	2000.	—
	p. Proof.	—	Unc	600.
	s. Specimen.	—	Unc	550.

1926 SHANGHAI ISSUE 海上

#9-10 harbor scene at l., Confucius standing at r. Medallion supported by 2 lions on back. Printer: W&S.

		Good	Fine	XF
9	**5 Dollars** Jan. 1926. Green and m/c. *(S/M #C293-50).*	20.00	60.00	225.
10	**10 Dollars** Jan. 1926. Brown and m/c. *(S/M #C293-51).*	30.00	100.	300.

1929 NATIONAL CURRENCY ISSUE

#11-13 medallion supported by lions at top ctr., Confucius standing at r. Medallion supported by 2 lions on back. W/o printer.

		Good	Fine	XF
11	**1 Dollar** Jan. 1929. Black and green.			
	a. *SHANGHAI. (S/M #C292-60a).*	17.50	60.00	180.
	b. *SHANGHAI/AMOY. (S/M #C293-60b).*	17.50	60.00	180.
	c. *HANKOW. (S/M #C293-60c).*	25.00	90.00	250.
	d. *AMOY. (S/M #C293-60d).*	30.00	125.	300.

1929 SHANGHAI CURRENCY ISSUE

		Good	Fine	X
12	**1 Dollar** Jan. 1929. Black and yellow. Similar to #13. *SHANGHAI. (S/M #C293-61).*	17.50	60.00	20

		Good	Fine	X
13	**1 Dollar** Jan. 1929. Blue and m/c. Back blue and yellow. *SHANGHAI. (S/M #C293-62).*	17.50	60.00	20
13A	**1 Dollar** 1929. Purple. *(S/M #C293-63).*	17.50	60.00	20

1932 ISSUE

#14-15 w/ and w/o various Chinese character control ovpt. Printer: W&S.

		Good	Fine	
14	**5 Dollars** June 1932. Purple and m/c. Similar to #9.			
	a. *SHANGHAI. (S/M #C293-70a).*	15.00	50.00	1
	b. *AMOY. (S/M #C293-70b).*	25.00	80.00	2
15	**10 Dollars** June 1932. Red and m/c. Similar to #10. *SHANGHAI. (S/M #C293-71).*	20.00	60.00	2

BANK OF CHINA

КИТАЙСКIЙ БАНКЪ

行銀國

Chung Kuo Yin H

1912 PROVISIONAL ISSUE

#16-18 ovpt. new issuer name on Ta Ching Government Bank notes. Sign. varieties.

		Good	Fine	
16	**1 Dollar** ND (1912 - old date 1.10.1909). Ovpt. on #A76.			
	a. Ovpt: *Chung Kuo* at l. and *Yin Hang* at r. Dated yr. 1. *(S/M #C294-1a).*	225.	1000.	2
	b. *HANKOW. (S/M #C294-1b).*	300.	1350.	3
	c. *HONAN. (S/M #C294-1c).*	300.	1350.	3
	d. *PEKING. (S/M #C294-1d).*	250.	1150.	2
	e. *SHANTUNG. (S/M #C294-1e).*	300.	1350.	3
	f. *SHANTUNG/CHIHLI. (S/M #C294-1f).*	325.	1500.	3

	Good	Fine	XF
g. *TIENTSIN* ovpt. in red on #16a. *(S/M #C294-1g).*	300.	1350.	3000.
h. *SHANGHAI. (S/M #C294-1h).*	325.	1500.	3300.
i. *MANCHURIA (S/M #C294-1i).*	375.	1800.	3750.
j. *CHIHLI (S/M #C294-1j).*	350.	1500.	3300.

17 5 Dollars

ND (1912 - old date 1.10.1909). Ovpt. on #A77.

	Good	Fine	XF
a. Ovpt: *Chung Kuo* at l. and *Yin Hang* at r. *(S/M #C294-2a).*	300.	1100.	3000.
b. *HANKOW. (S/M (S/M #C294-2b).*	375.	1500.	3600.
c. *HONAN. (S/M #C294-2c).*	375.	1500.	3600.
d. *PEKING. (S/M #C294-2d).*	300.	1100.	3000.
e. *SHANTUNG. (S/M #C294-2e).*	375.	1500.	3600.
f. *SHANTUNG/CHIHLI. (S/M #C294-2f).).*	600.	1800.	4000.
g. *TIENTSIN. (S/M #C294-2g).*	300.	1100.	3000.
h. *TIENTSIN/PEKING. (S/M #C294-2h).*	600.	1800.	4000.
i. *SHANGHAI. (S/M #C294-2i).*	375.	1500.	3600.
j. *MANCHURIA. (S/M #C294-2j).*	375.	1500.	3600.

18 10 Dollars

ND (1912 - old date 1.10.1909). Ovpt. on #A78.

	Good	Fine	XF
a. Ovpt: *Chung Kuo* at l. *Yin Hang* at r. (S/M #C294-3a).	600.	2250.	4000.
b. *HANKOW. (S/M #C294-3b).*	750.	2250.	4500.
c. *HONAN. (S/M #C294-3c).*	750.	2250.	4500.
d. *PEKING. (S/M #C294-3d).*	600.	1900.	4250.
e. *SHANTUNG. (S/M #C294-3e).*	4500.	2250.	4500.
f. *SHANTUNG/CHIHLI. (S/M #C294-3f).*	425.	1800.	4250.
g. *TIENTSIN. (S/M #C294-3g).*	425.	1800.	4250.

#19-24 *Deleted.*

1912 ISSUES

#25-27 portr. Emperor Huang-ti at l., rural vignettes similar to #A76-A78 at r. Printer: ABNC.

25 1 Dollar

1.6.1912. Dk. green on m/c. unpt.

	Good	Fine	XF
a. *ANHWEI. (S/M #C294-30a).*	40.00	200.	500.
b. *CANTON. (S/M #C294-30b).*	20.00	60.00	200.
c. *CHEFOO. (S/M #C294-30c).*	70.00	300.	800.
d. *CHEHKIANG. (S/M #C294-30d).*	50.00	250.	750.
e. *FUHKIEN* (Fukien). *(S/M #C294-30e).*	50.00	250.	750.
f. *HANKOW. (S/M #C294-30f).*	40.00	200.	500.
g. *HONAN. (S/M #C294-30g).*	50.00	225.	600.
h. *KIANGSI. (S/M #C294-30h).*	40.00	200.	500.
i. *KIANGSU. (S/M #C294-30i).*	40.00	200.	500.
j. *KUEISUI. (S/M #C294-30j).*	50.00	175.	550.
l. *MANCHURIA. (S/M #C294-30l).*	50.00	125.	450.
m. *MUKDEN. (S/M #C294-30m).*	30.00	100.	300.
n. *SHANSI. (S/M #C294-30n).*	50.00	250.	750.
o. *SHANTUNG. (S/M #C294-30o).*	50.00	250.	750.
p. *Szechuen* in Chinese characters in oval frames at l. and r. edge on face. Lg. *SZECHUEN* below date at bottom ctr. on back. *(S/M #C294-30p).*	50.00	200.	450.
q. *One Dollar* in Chinese characters in oval frames at l. and r. edge on face. *One Dollar* / sm. *SZECHUEN* below date at bottom ctr. on back. *(S/M #C294-30p).*	50.00	200.	450.
r. *THREE EASTERN PROVINCES. (S/M #C294-30q).*	75.00	250.	750.
s. *YUNNAN. (S/M #C294-30r).*	12.50	35.00	125.
t. *SHANGHAI. (S/M #C294-30s).*	40.00	100.	450.
u. *TIENTSIN. (S/M #C294-30t).*	50.00	200.	450.
v. КАЛГАНЪ (Kalgan). *(S/M #C294-30u).*	50.00	250.	750.
w. *PEKING. (S/M #C294-30w).*	50.00	200.	550.
k1. *KWANGTUNG.* Ovpt: *N.B. Payable in subsidiary (silver) coins... on back. (S/M #C294-30k).*	25.00	75.00	250.
k2. *KWEICHOW.*	150.	400.	—

26 5 Dollars

1.6.1912. Black on m/c. unpt.

	Good	Fine	XF
a. *ANHWEI. (S/M #C294-31a).*	65.00	200.	650.
b. *CANTON. (S/M #C294-31b).*	20.00	75.00	200.
c. *CHEFOO. (S/M #C294-31c).*	100.	400.	1000.
d. *CHEHKIANG. (S/M #C294-31d).*	85.00	350.	900.
e. *FUHKIEN* (Fukien). *(S/M #C294-31e).*	85.00	350.	900.
f. *HANKOW. (S/M #C294-31f).*	75.00	300.	750.
g. *HONAN. (S/M #C294-31g).*	85.00	400.	900.
h. *KIANGSI. (S/M #C294-31h).*	60.00	250.	600.
i. *KIANGSU. (S/M #C294-31i).*	50.00	200.	600.
j. *KUEISUI. (S/M #C294-31j).*	125.	650.	1200.
k. *KWANGTUNG.* Ovpt. *N.B. Payable in subsidiary (silver) coins....* on back. *(S/M #C294-31k).*	25.00	75.00	250.
l. *MANCHURIA. (S/M #C294-31l).*	50.00	150.	450.
m. *MUKDEN. (S/M #C294-31m).*	50.00	175.	500.
n. *SHANSI. (S/M #C294-31n).*	65.00	250.	650.
o. *SHANTUNG. (S/M #C294-31o).*	50.00	175.	500.
p. *SZECHUAN. (S/M #C294-31p).*	50.00	200.	600.
q. *THREE EASTERN PROVINCES. (S/M #C294-31q).*	100.	450.	1000.
r. *YUNNAN. (S/M #C294-31r).*	20.00	60.00	175.
s. *KWEICHOW. (S/M #C294-).*	75.00	350.	700.
t. W/o place name. Specimen. *(S/M #C294-).*	—	Unc	250.
u. *SHANGHAI.*	50.00	250.	—
v. *TIENTSIN.*	50.00	250.	—

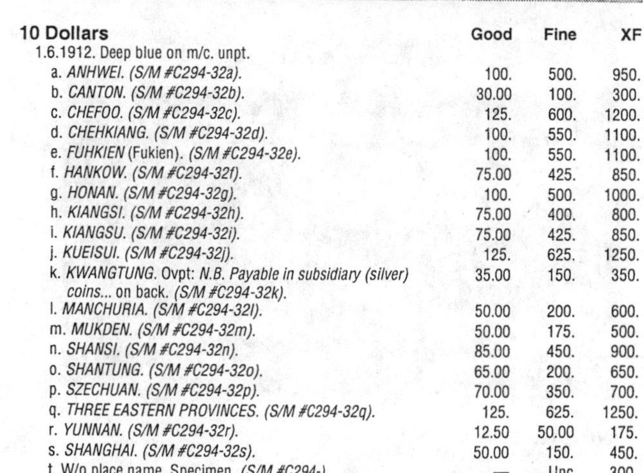

27 10 Dollars

1.6.1912. Deep blue on m/c. unpt.

	Good	Fine	XF
a. *ANHWEI. (S/M #C294-32a).*	100.	500.	950.
b. *CANTON. (S/M #C294-32b).*	30.00	100.	300.
c. *CHEFOO. (S/M #C294-32c).*	125.	600.	1200.
d. *CHEHKIANG. (S/M #C294-32d).*	100.	550.	1100.
e. *FUHKIEN* (Fukien). *(S/M #C294-32e).*	100.	550.	1100.
f. *HANKOW. (S/M #C294-32f).*	75.00	425.	850.
g. *HONAN. (S/M #C294-32g).*	100.	500.	1000.
h. *KIANGSI. (S/M #C294-32h).*	75.00	400.	800.
i. *KIANGSU. (S/M #C294-32i).*	75.00	425.	850.
j. *KUEISUI. (S/M #C294-32j).*	125.	625.	1250.
k. *KWANGTUNG.* Ovpt: *N.B. Payable in subsidiary (silver) coins...* on back. *(S/M #C294-32k).*	35.00	150.	350.
l. *MANCHURIA. (S/M #C294-32l).*	50.00	200.	600.
m. *MUKDEN. (S/M #C294-32m).*	50.00	175.	500.
n. *SHANSI. (S/M #C294-32n).*	85.00	450.	900.
o. *SHANTUNG. (S/M #C294-32o).*	65.00	200.	650.
p. *SZECHUAN. (S/M #C294-32p).*	70.00	350.	700.
q. *THREE EASTERN PROVINCES. (S/M #C294-32q).*	125.	625.	1250.
r. *YUNNAN. (S/M #C294-32r).*	12.50	50.00	175.
s. *SHANGHAI. (S/M #C294-32s).*	50.00	150.	450.
t. W/o place name. Specimen. *(S/M #C294-).*	—	Unc	300.

1913 PROVISIONAL ISSUE

#29 and 29A ovpt. new bank name on notes of the Provincial Bank of Kwangtung Province.

#28 *Deleted.*

		Good	Fine	XF
29	**5 Dollars** ND (-old date 1.1.1913). Dk. green on m/c unpt. Ovpt. on #S2398. *(S/M #C294-41).*	60.00	200.	600.
29A	**10 Dollars** ND (-old date 1.1.1913). Ovpt. on #S2399. *(S/M #C294-42).*	100.	350.	1000.

1913 REGULAR ISSUE

#30-32B portr. Huang Ti (Yellow Emperor) at l., rural vignettes at r. Printer: ABNC.

		Good	Fine	XF
30	**1 Dollar** 1.6.1913. Olive and red. Similar to #25.			
	a. *CANTON. (S/M #C294-42a).*	25.00	100.	220.
	b. *FUKIEN. (S/M #C294-42b).*	75.00	350.	750.
	c. *SHANTUNG. (S/M #C294-42c).*	17.50	75.00	180.
	d. *SHANSI. (S/M #C294-42d).*	85.00	425.	850.
	e. W/o place name. (S/M #C294-42).	20.00	100.	200.
31	**5 Dollars** 1.6.1913. Black and brown on blue and m/c unpt. Similar to #26.			
	a. *CANTON. (S/M #C294-43a).*	125.	450.	1350.
	b. *FUKIEN. (S/M #C294-43b).*	150.	600.	1800.
	c. *SHANTUNG. (S/M #C294-43c).*	150.	675.	1950.
32	**10 Dollars** 1.6.1913. Similar to #27.			
	a. *CANTON. (S/M #C294-44a).*	150.	525.	1650.
	b. *FUKIEN. (S/M #C294-44b).*	150.	600.	1800.
	c. *SHANTUNG. (S/M #C294-44c).*	200.	675.	1950.

32A	**50 Dollars** 1.6.1913. Purple on m/c unpt. Lg. bldg. at r. *PEKING.* Specimen perforated w/Chinese characters. *(S/M #C294-45a).*	—	Unc	2000.

32B	**100 Dollars** 1.6.1913. Dk. olive-green on m/c unpt. Temple of Heaven at r. *PEKING.* Specimen perforated w/Chinese characters. *(S/M #C294-46a).*	—	Unc	2000.

1914 PROVISIONAL ISSUE

		Good	Fine	XF
32C	**1 Dollar** 1914 (-old date-1.10.1909). Olive-brown on red-orange unpt. Ovpt. on #A76. *CHIHLI. (S/M #C294-46).*	—	—	—

1914 "YUAN SHIH-KAI" ISSUE

#33-35B black on m/c unpt. Portr. Yuan Shih-kai at ctr. Unsigned remainders w/ or w/o perforated "cancelled" in Chinese characters. Printer: ABNC.

		VG	VF	UNC
33	**1 Yüan** 4.10.1914. Back black. *(S/M #294-50).*	—	400.	1000.
34	**5 Yüan** 4.10.1914. Back brown. *(S/M #294-51).*	—	500.	1200.
35	**10 Yüan** 4.10.1914. Back brown. *(S/M #294-52).*	—	650.	1500

		VG	VF	UN
35A	**50 Yüan** 4.10.1914. Back brown. *(S/M #294-53).*	—	—	—
35B	**100 Yüan** 4.10.1914. Back dk. olive-green. *(S/M #C294-54).*	—	—	—

1914 "SMALL CHANGE" ISSUE

#36 and 37 Great Wall at ctr. Printer: BEPP.

		VG	VF	UNC
36	**20 Cents** 1.12.1914.			
	a. Black on green unpt. Back red. *MANCHURIA.*	30.00	75.00	250.
	b. As a, but back brown.	—	—	—
	c. Back orange.Black on green unpt. *MANCHURIA. (S/M #C294-60).* 2 sign. varieties.	15.00	50.00	150.

		VG	VF	UNC
37	**50 Cents** 1.12.1914. Brown on red unpt. *MANCHURIA. (S/M #C294-61).*	35.00	175.	350.

1915 "HUANG TI" ISSUE

#37A-37C *Deleted.* See #37D-37F.

#37D-37F portr. Emperor Huang Ti at l. Proofs w/o sign. or office of issue. Printer: ABNC.

		VG	VF	UNC
37D	**1 Dollar** 1.7.1915. Green. Back blue and red. Proof. *(S/M #C294-62).*	—	—	500.
37E	**5 Dollars** 1.7.1915. Black. Back blue, red and brown. Proof. *(S/M #C294-63).*	—	—	600.
37F	**10 Dollars** 1.7.1915. Blue. Back blue, red and brown. Proof. *(S/M #C294-64).*	—	—	700.

1917 "TSAO KUAN" ISSUE

37J-37N Tsao Kuan at l. or r. Proofs w/o sign. or office of issue. Printer: ABNC.

		VG	VF	UNC
37J	**1 Dollar** 1.5.1917. Black on blue, red and purple unpt. Back brown. Proof. *(S/M #C294-65).*	—	—	1200.
37K	**5 Dollars** 1.5.1917. Black on blue, red and green unpt. Back dk. green. Proof. *(S/M #C294-66).*	—	—	1700.
37L	**10 Dollars** 1.5.1917. Black on red, blue and ochre unpt. Back red-orange. Proof. *(S/M #C294-67).*	—	—	2200.

		VG	VF	UNC
37M	**50 Dollars** 1.5.1917. Black on olive-green, red and blue unpt. Back: olive-green. Proof. *(S/M # #C294-68).*	—	—	3000.
37N	**100 Dollars** 1.5.1917. Black on blue, brown and green unpt. Back: blue. Proof. *(S/M #C294-69).*	—	—	3750.

1917 "TIENTSIN" ISSUE

#38-40 gateways at l. or r. Printer: ABNC.

		VG	VF	UNC
38	**1 Dollar** Yr. 6//1.5.1917. Black on brown, purple and green unpt. Back blue-gray. *TIENTSIN.* Proof. *(S/M #C294-80).*	—	—	450.
39	**5 Dollars** Yr. 6//1.5.1917. Blue-black on red, blue and brown unpt. *TIENTSIN.* Proof. *(S/M #C294-81).*	—	—	450.
40	**10 Silver Yüan** Yr. 6//1.5.1917. Black on blue, purple and green unpt. Back deep green. *TIENTSIN.* Proof. *(S/M #C294-82).*	—	—	500.

Note: For similar notes dated yr. 7/1.5.1917 see #54A and 54C. #40A *Deleted.* See #54.

1917 "SMALL CHANGE" ISSUES

#41-45 printer: BEPP.

45A and 45B *Deleted.* See #58 and 59.

		Good	Fine	XF
41	**5 Cents** 1.10.1917. Brown. *HARBIN. (S/M #C294-70).*	7.50	25.00	75.00

		Good	Fine	XF
42	**10 Cents = 1 Chiao** 1.10.1917. Green. Temple at l. *Harbin. (S/M #C294-71).*			
	a. *HARBIN. (S/M #C294-71).*	17.50	45.00	185.
	b. *MANCHURIA. (S/M #C294-).*	12.50	30.00	125.
	r. Remainder, w/o serial #, sign. or place name. *(S/M #C294-).*			

		Good	Fine	XF
43	**10 Cents = 1 Chiao** 1.10.1917. Bridge at ctr.			
	b. *HARBIN.* Orange. Exchange clause blocked out on face and back. Ovpt. new exchange clause in Chinese at l. and r. on back. *(S/M #C294-72b).*	30.00	100.	360.
	c. КАЛГАНЪ *Kalgan* in Chinese at l. and r. Brown. *(S/M #C294-72c).*	12.50	50.00	150.
	d. *KIANGSI. (S/M #C294-72d).*	30.00	90.00	300.
	e. *KUEISUI.* Green. *(S/M #C294-72e).*	75.00	300.	750.
	f. *MANCHURIA.* Orange. *(S/M #C294-72f).*	20.00	75.00	200.
	g. *PAOTING.* Green. *(S/M #C294-72g).*	75.00	300.	750.
	h. *SHANSI.* Brown. *(S/M #C294-72h).*	20.00	60.00	300.
	i. *SHANGTUNG.* Purple. Back green. *(S/M #C294-72i).*	20.00	60.00	300.
	j. *TSINGKIANGPU.* Red. *(S/M #C294-72j).*	75.00	300.	750.
	k. *TSINGTAO.* Brown. *(S/M #C294-72k).*	30.00	120.	300.
	l. *TSINGTAO/SHANTUNG. (S/M #C294-72l).*	37.50	150.	375.
	m. Калганъ. *KALGAN* in Manchu at l., Chinese at r. on face. Green. Back purple; Russian text. *(S/M #C294-72m).*	25.00	100.	250.
	r. Remainder, w/o serial #, sign. or place name. Green. Back purple. *(S/M #C294-72a).*	—	Unc	150.

		Good	Fine	XF
44	**20 Cents = 2 Chiao**			
	1.10.1917. Pagoda on hill at shoreline at ctr.			
	b. *HARBIN.* Violet. Exchange clause blocked out on face and back. Ovpt. new exchange clause in Chinese at l. and r. on back. *(S/M #C294-73b).*	25.00	75.00	250.
	c. КАЛГАНЪ (Kalgan). Black. Back dk. brown. *(S/M #C294-73c).*	35.00	150.	350.
	d. *KIANGSI.* Red. *(S/M #C294-73d).*	50.00	200.	500.
	e. *KUEISUI.* Brown. *(S/M #C294-73e).*	65.00	300.	750.
	f. *MANCHURIA.* *(S/M #C294-73f).*	35.00	175.	350.
	g. *PAOTING.* Orange. *(S/M #C294-73g).*	75.00	300.	750.
	h. *SHANSI.* Green. *(S/M #C294-73h).*	50.00	200.	550.
	i. *SHANGTUNG.* *(S/M #C294-73i).*	50.00	250.	550.
	j. *TSINGKIANGPU.* *(S/M #C294-73j).*	75.00	375.	900.
	k. *TSINGTAO.* Orange. *(S/M #C294-73k).*	50.00	250.	600.
	l. *TSINGTAO/SHANTUNG.* *(S/M #C294-73l).*	60.00	250.	600.
	r. Remainder w/o serial #, sign. or place name. Green. Back violet. *(S/M #C294-73a).*	—	Unc	150.
45	**50 Cents = 5 Chiao**			
	1.10.1917. Various colors. Bridge w/bldg. in background at ctr.			
	b. *HARBIN.* Exchange clause blocked out on face and back. Ovpt. new exchange clause in Chinese at l. and r. on back. *(S/M #C294-74b).*	10.00	30.00	125.
	c. КАЛГАНЪ (Kalgan). *(S/M #C294-74c).*	75.00	300.	750.
	d. *KIANGSI.* *(S/M #C294-74d).*	60.00	240.	600.
	e. *KUEISUI.* *(S/M #C294-74e).*	60.00	240.	600.
	f. *MANCHURIA.* *(S/M #C294-74f).*	45.00	175.	450.
	g. *PAOTING.* *(S/M #C294-74g).*	90.00	375.	900.
	h. *SHANSI.* *(S/M #C294-74h).*	90.00	375.	900.
	i. *SHANTUNG.* *(S/M #C294-74i).*	75.00	350.	850.
	j. *TSINGKIANGPU.* *(S/M #C294-74j).*	90.00	375.	900.
	k. *TSINGTAO.* *(S/M #C294-74k).*	90.00	375.	900.
	l. *TSINGTAO/SHANTUNG.* *(S/M #C294-74l).*	75.00	325.	700.
	r. Remainder w/o serial #, sign. or place name. *(S/M #C294-74a).*	—	Unc	150.

1918 ND ISSUE

		Good	Fine	XF
46	**5 Fen** ND (1918). Blue on red unpt. Chinese printer. *HARBIN.* *#C294-90).*	15.00	45.00	175.
46A	**5 Fen** ND (1918). Blue and red. Printer: BEPP. *HARBIN.* *(S/M #C294-91).*	15.00	45.00	175.

1918 ISSUES

#48-54C sign. varieties. Also w/various Chinese character or western numeral or letter control ovpts: *D; HS; TF, etc.* Printer: ABNC.

		Good	Fine	XF
47	**2 Tiao = 98 Copper Coins**			
	Sept. 1918. Gray-green and orange. Back red. Remainder w/o sign. or serial #. *SHANTUNG.* *(S/M #C294-).*			
	a. Issued note.			
48	**10 Cents = 1 Chiao**			
	Sept. 1918. Black and m/c. Temple of Heaven at r. W/bank name also in Russian on back.			
	a. *HARBIN.* *(S/M #C294-93a).*	3.50	15.00	55.0
	b. *SHANGHAI/HARBIN.* 2 sign. varieties. *(S/M #C294-93b).*	3.50	17.50	50.0
	c. As a. but w/red official 4-Chinese character ovpt. *(S/M #C294-93c).*	5.00	20.00	60.0
	s. As a. Specimen.			

		Good	Fine	XF
49	**20 Cents = 2 Chiao**			
	Sept. 1918. Black and m/c. Temple of Heaven at l. W/bank name also in Russian on back.			
	a. *HARBIN.* *(S/M #C294-94a).*	5.00	20.00	60.0
	b. *SHANGHAI/HARBIN.* *(S/M #C294-94b).*	4.00	20.00	55.0
	c. As a. but red official 4-Chinese character ovpt. *(S/M #C294-94c).*	5.00	20.00	60.0
	s. As a. Specimen.	—	Unc	10
50	**50 Cents = 5 Chiao**			
	Sept. 1918. Green and m/c. Temple of Heaven at l. w/bank name also in Russian on back.			
	a. *HARBIN.* *(S/M #C294-95a).*	25.00	100.	27
	b. *SHANGHAI/HARBIN.* *(S/M #C294-95b).*	10.00	50.00	12

		Good	Fine	XF
51A	**1 Dollar**			
	Sept. 1918. Back orange; similar to #51 but w/bank name also in Russian text. *HARBIN.* *(S/M #C294-100f).*			
	a. Issued note.	100.	400.	100
	s. Specimen.	—	Unc	40

		Good	Fine	XF
51B	**1 Dollar** Sept. 1918. Orange on m/c unpt. 2 bldgs. at r. Back: olive-green. Printer: ABNC. *Shanghai.* Proof. *(S/M #C294-100.5).*	—	Unc	45

51 **1 Dollar or Yüan**	Good	Fine	XF
Sept. 1918. Temple of Heaven at ctr. Color, sign. and serial # varieties.			
a. *AMOY-FUKIEN.* Green on m/c unpt. Back green. *(S/M #C294-100d).*	5.00	17.50	50.00
b. *ANHWEI.* Back red-orange. *(S/M #C294-100a).*	40.00	200.	400.
c. *CHEFOO-SHANTUNG.* Orange. *(S/M #C294-100-).*	40.00	200.	400.
d. *CHEKIANG.* Orange on m/c unpt. Back dk. green. *(S/M #C294-100q).*	40.00	200.	400.
e. *CHENGTU-SZECHUAN.* Back orange. *(S/M #C294-100q).*	65.00	325.	650.
f. *FUKIEN.* Green. *(S/M #C294-100c).*	15.00	75.00	150.
g. *HANKOW.* Green. Back orange. *(S/M #C294-100e).*	35.00	175.	350.
h. *KALGAN.* Green. *(S/M #C294-100g).*	15.00	75.00	150.
i. *KIANGSI.* Orange on m/c unpt. Back orange. *(S/M #C294-100h).*	35.00	175.	350.
j. *KIANGSU.* Brown. Back brown. *(S/M (S/M #C294-100i).*	35.00	175.	350.
k. *PEKING.* Blue-black. Back black. *(S/M (S/M #C294-100j).*	30.00	150.	300.
l. *SHANGHAI/PEKING.* Blue-black. Back blue-black. *(S/M #C294-100k).*	22.50	100.	220.
m. *SHANGHAI.* Brown. Back blue. 3 sign varieties. *(S/M #C294-100k).*	4.00	12.50	35.00
n. *SHANSI.* Back purple. *(S/M #C294-100m).*	55.00	275.	550.
o. *SHANTUNG.* Orange on m/c unpt. Back orange. *(S/M #C294-100n).*	17.50	90.00	180.
p. *SZECHUAN.* Back red-orange. *(S/M #C294-100p).*	70.00	350.	700.
q. *TIENTSIN.* Brown. 2 sign. varieties. *(S/M #C294-100r).*	5.00	15.00	30.00
r. *TIENTSIN/KALGAN.* Green. Back green. *(S/M #C294-100s).*	12.50	60.00	120.
s. *TIENTSIN/PEKING.* Blue-black. *(S/M #C294-100-).*	20.00	100.	200.
t. *TSINGTAO.* Back Orange. *(S/M #C294-100-).*	45.00	225.	450.
u. *TSINGTAO/SHANTUNG.* Orange. (S/M #C294-100-).	40.00	200.	400.
v. *KIUKIANG.* *(S/M #C294-100-).*	70.00	350.	700.
w. *SHANTUNG WEIHAIWEI.* *(S/M #C294-100-).*	45.00	225.	450.
s1. *KIATING/SZECHUAN.* Orange. Specimen. *(S/M #C294-).*	—	Unc	200.

2A **5 Dollars**			
Sept. 1918. Back brown; similar to #52 but w/bank name also in Russian text. *HARBIN.* *(S/M #C294-101f).*			
a. Issued note.	200.	550.	1200.
s. Specimen.	—	Unc	250.

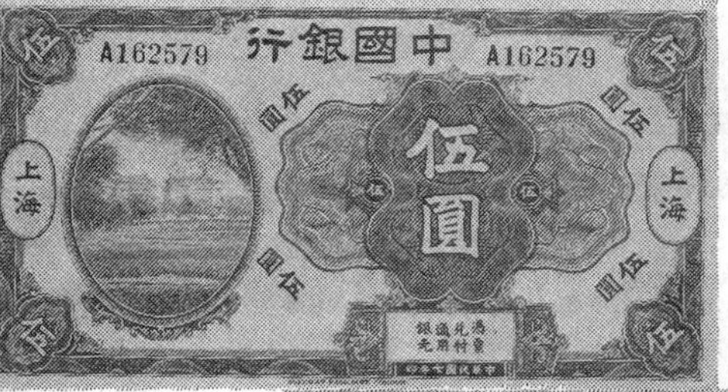

2B **5 Dollars**	Good	Fine	XF
Sept. 1918. Green on m/c unpt. 2 bldgs. at l. Back brown. *SHANGHAI.* *(S/M #C294-101.5).*			
a. Issued note.	75.00	400.	800.
s. Specimen.	—	Unc	300.

2 **5 Dollars or Yüan**	Good	Fine	XF
Sept. 1918. Houses w/Peking pagoda at ctr. Color, sign. and serial # varieties. Local or National Currency.			
a. *AMOY-FUKIEN.* Purple. *(S/M #C294-101d).*	5.00	17.50	50.00
b. *ANHWEI.* Blue-black. Back olive-green. *(S/M #C294-101a).*	450.	225.	450.
c. *CHEKIANG.* Green. Back blue. *(S/M #C294-101b).*	40.00	200.	400.
d. *CHENGTU-SZECHUAN.* Back green. *(S/M #C294-101q).*	60.00	300.	600.
e. *FUKIEN.* Purple. Back purple. Sign. varieties. *(S/M #C294-101c).*	15.00	75.00	150.
f. *HANKOW.* Back brown. *(S/M #C294-101e).*	50.00	250.	500.
g. *KALGAN.* Back purple. *(S/M #C294-101g).*	60.00	300.	600.
h. *KIANGSI.* Back gray-brown. *(S/M #C294-101h).*	45.00	225.	450.
i. *KIANGSU.* Brown. Back red-orange. *(S/M #C294-101i).*	40.00	200.	400.
j. *PEKING.* Brown. *(S/M #C294-101j).*	45.00	225.	450.
k. *SHANGHAI.* Dk. blue. Sign. varieties. *(S/M #C294-101k).*	17.50	75.00	175.
l. *SHANGHAI/PEKING.* Brown. *(S/M #C294-101l).*	30.00	150.	300.
m. *SHANSI.* Back orange. *(S/M #C294-101m).*	50.00	250.	500.
n. *SHANTUNG.* Green. Back dk. green. *(S/M #C294-101n).*	42.50	200.	425.
o. *SZECHUAN.* Back green. *(S/M #C94-101p).*	65.00	325.	650.
p. *TIENTSIN.* Back orange. Sign. varieities. *(S/M #C294-101r).*	10.00	40.00	110.
q. *TIENTSIN/KALGAN.* *(S/M #C294-101s).*	17.50	60.00	175.
r. *TIENTSIN/PEKING.* Brown. *(S/M #C294-101-).*	15.00	45.00	150.
s. *TSINGTAO/SHANTUNG.* Green. *(S/M #C294-100o).*	25.00	100.	250.

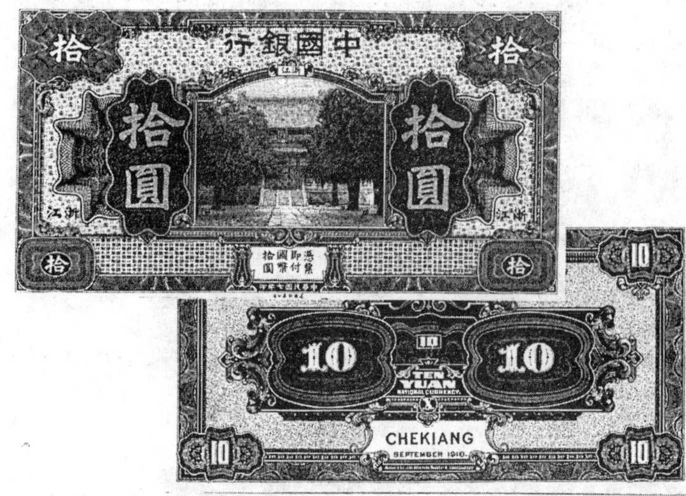

53 **10 Dollars**	Good	Fine	XF
Sept. 1918. Various colors. Temple behind trees at ctr. Sign. varieties.			
a. *AMOY-FUKIEN.* Orange. *(S/M #C294-102d).*	5.00	17.50	50.00
b. *ANHWEI.* Back green. *(S/M #C294-102a).*	60.00	300.	600.
c. *CHEFOO-SHANTUNG.* Brown. *(S/M #C294-102-).*	45.00	225.	450.
d. *CHEKIANG.* Orange. Back red-brown. *(S/M #C294-102b)*	50.00	250.	500.
e. *CHENGTU-SZECHUAN.* Back brown. *(S/M #C294-102q).*	75.00	375.	750.
f. *FUKIEN.* Orange. Back red-orange. Sign. varieties. *(S/M #C294-102c).*	5.00	25.00	60.00
g. *HANKOW.* Dk. green. Back purple. *(S/M #C294-102e).*	55.00	250.	550.
h. *KALGAN.* Back orange. *(S/M #C294-102g).*	65.00	325.	650.
i. *KIANGSI.* Back blue. *(S/M #C294-102h).*	50.00	250.	500.
j. *KIANGSU.* Back blue-gray. *(S/M #C294-102i).*	45.00	225.	450.
k. *PEKING.* Green. *(S/M #C294-102j).*	60.00	300.	600.
l. *SHANGHAI/PEKING.* Back orange. *(S/M #C294-102l).*	60.00	300.	600.
m. *SHANGHAI.* Back red-orange. Sign. varieties. *(S/M #C294-102k).*	55.00	275.	550.
n. *SHANTUNG.* Brown. Back brown. *(S/M #C294-102n).*	20.00	100.	200.
o. *SZECHUAN.* Back red-brown. *(S/M #C294-102p).*	75.00	400.	800.
p. *TIENTSIN.* Green. Sign. varieties. *(S/M #C294-102r).*	10.00	45.00	90.00
q. *TIENTSIN/KALGAN.* *(S/M #C294-102s).*	20.00	100.	200.
r. *TIENTSIN/PEKING.* Green. *(S/M #C294-102-).*	20.00	100.	200.
s. *TSINGTAU/SHANTUNG.* Brown. *(S/M #C294-102o).*	55.00	275.	550.
t. *WEIHAWAI-SHANTUNG.* *(S/M #C294-).*	65.00	325.	650.
u. *SHANSI.* Back green. *(S/M #C294-102m).*	75.00	400.	800.

53A **10 Dollars**			
Sept. 1918. Back blue; similar to #53 but w/bank name also in Russian text. *HARBIN.* *(S/M #C294-102f).*			
a. Issued note.	150.	750.	1500.
s. Specimen.	—	Unc	600.

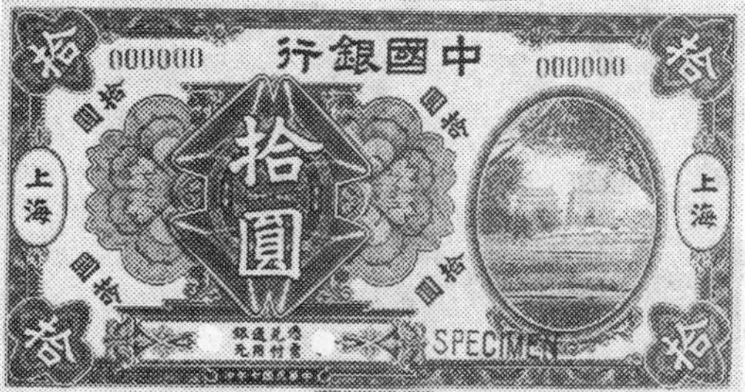

53B **10 Dollars**	Good	Fine	XF
Sept. 1918. Brown on m/c unpt. 2 bldgs. at r. *SHANGHAI.* Specimen. *(S/M #C294-102.3).*	—	Unc	350.

54 **50 Dollars**	Good	Fine	XF
Sept. 1918. Purple on m/c unpt. 2 bldgs. at l. *SHANGHAI.* Proof. *(S/M #C294-102.4).*	—	Unc	600.

		Good	Fine	XF
54A	**50 Dollars** Yr. 7//1.5.1917. Black on brown, green and purple unpt. Gateways at l. Back green. *TIENTSIN.* Proof. *(S/M #C294-102.5).*	—	Unc	750.

Note: Often confusing as the face is dated yr. 7 while the back is dated 1st May 1917. For similar notes dated Yr. 6 1.5.1917, see #38-40.

54B	**100 Dollars** Sept. 1918. Olive-green on m/c unpt. Back olive-green. *SHANGHAI.* Proof. *(S/M #C294-102.5).*	—	Unc	800.

		Good	Fine	XF
54C	**100 Dollars** Yr. 7 1.5.1917. Black on m/c unpt. Gateways at r. Back purple. *TIENTSIN. (S/M #C294-103).*	300.	800.	1600.

1919 ISSUE

#56-61 Printer: BEPP.

		Good	Fine	XF
56	**10 Copper Coins** March 1919. Brown. Temple and trees at shoreline at l. Back blue and red. *Kiukiang. (S/M #C294-110).*	30.00	150.	300.
57	**50 Copper Coins** March 1919. Violet.			
	a. *Kiukiang. (S/M #C294-111a).*	35.00	175.	350.
	b. *Kalgan. (S/M #C294-111b).*	20.00	100.	200.

		Good	Fine	XF
58	**1 Yüan** May 1919. Dk. blue-black. Pavilion in park at ctr. Back brown on lt. blue unpt. *HARBIN, MANCHURIA. (S/M #C294-120).*			
	a. Issued note.	17.50	80.00	160.
	r. Remainder, w/o serial #, sign. seals, w/ or w/o place name.	—	Unc	100.

		Good	Fine	XF
59	**5 Yüan** May 1919. Orange. Pavilion in park at ctr. Back purple on lt. yellow unpt. *HARBIN, MANCHURIA. (S/M #C294-121).*			
	a. Issued note.	20.00	75.00	225
	r. Remainder, w/o serial #, sign. seals or place name.	—	Unc	100
60	**10 Yüan** May 1919. Dk. brown. Back brown on lt. green unpt. *HARBIN, MANCHURIA. (S/M #C294-122).*			
	a. Issued note.	30.00	150.	300
	r. Remainder, w/o serial #, sign. seals or place name.	—	Unc	100

1920 ISSUE

		Good	Fine	XF
61	**100 Copper Coins** 1920. Orange. *Kiukiang. (S/M #C294-130).* Reported not confirmed	—	—	—

1924 ISSUE

		Good	Fine	XF
62	**10 Yüan** 1924. Purple. Houses and pagoda at shoreline at ctr. 3 sign. varieties. Back brown. Printer: ABNC. *Shanghai. (S/M #C294-140).*	15.00	50.00	15

1925 ISSUES

#62A-65 printer: W&S.

		Good	Fine	X
62A	**10 Cents** 1925. Brown. *Chenkiang. (S/M #C294-150).* Reported not confirmed	—	—	—

		VG	VF	UN
63	**10 Cents** 1.7.1925. Brown. Pagoda by house at water's edge. Back blue. 7 sign. varieties. *SHANGHAI. (S/M #C294-151).*	2.00	10.00	20.
64	**20 Cents** 1.7.1925. Dk. blue on olive. Monument of Bull w/bridge in background at top. Back brown. 4 sign. varieties. *SHANGHAI. (S/M #C294-152).*			
	a. Issued note.	3.00	9.00	27.
	s. Specimen.	7.50	35.00	70.
65	**50 Cents** 1.7.1925. Orange. Stag and man w/beard at top. Back green. *SHANGHAI. (S/M #C294-153).*			
	a. Issued note.	7.50	35.00	70.
	s. Specimen.	8.00	40.00	80.

1925 Provisional Issue

#65A-65C *Fengtien-MUKDEN, MANCHURIA* office. Printer: ABNC.

65A	**1 Dollar** 1.7.1925. Green on m/c unpt. Temple of Heaven at ctr. Back olive-green. Proof. *(S/M #C294-154).*	—	Unc	650.

65B	**5 Dollars** 1.7.1925. Orange on m/c unpt. Temple and Peking pagoda at ctr. Back orange. Proof. *(S/M #C294-155).*	—	Unc	800.

65C	**10 Silver Yüan** 1.7.1925. Blue on m/c unpt. Temple in woods at ctr. Back blue. Proof. *(S/M #C294-156).*	—	Unc	1000.

#65E-65F ovpt: *Liaoning* on face; *Promises to pay... Silver dollars...* on back.

1925 ND Provisional Issue

#65E and 65F ovpt: *Liaoning* on face; *Promises to pay... Silver dollars...* on back.

		VG	VF	UNC
65E	**5 Dollars** ND (old date - 1.7.1925). Ovpt. on #65Ba. Specimen. *(S/M #C294-158).*	—	—	650.

		VG	VF	UNC
65F	**10 Silver Yüan** ND (old date - 1.7.1925). Ovpt. on #65Ca. Specimen. *(S/M C294-159).*	—	—	800.

1926 Issue

		Good	Fine	XF
66	**5 Yüan** 1926. Black on m/c unpt. Temple and Peking Pagoda on hilltop at ctr. Back green on m/c unpt; bank at ctr. *SHANGHAI.* Printer: ABNC. Also various letter, numeral and Chinese character control ovpt.			
	a. Black sign. (3 varieties). *(S/M #C294-160a).*	7.50	25.00	75.00
	b. Red Sign. (5 varieties). *(S/M #C294-160b/i).*	5.00	20.00	60.00

1930 Issue

#67-69 printer: ABNC.

		Good	Fine	XF
67	**1 Dollar** Oct. 1930. Dk. green on red and m/c unpt. Temple of Heaven at ctr. *AMOY. (S/M #C294-170).*	4.00	20.00	60.00
68	**5 Dollars** Oct. 1930. Purple on m/c unpt. Temple and Peking Pagoda at ctr. *AMOY.* 2 sign. varieties. *(S/M #C294-171).*	4.00	15.00	40.00

		Good	Fine	XF
69	**10 Silver Yüan** Oct. 1930. Orange on m/c unpt. Temple behind trees at ctr. *AMOY.* 2 sign varieties. *(S/M #C294-172).*	4.00	20.00	40.00

1931 Issue

		VG	VF	UNC
70	**5 Yüan** Jan. 1931. Orange and black. Temple of Heaven at l., landscape, mountains at r. Bank on back. *TIENTSIN.* Printer: TDLR. *(S/M #C294-180).*			
	a. Serial # face only.	6.00	30.00	60.00
	b. Serial # face and back.	1.00	4.00	15.00

1934 Issue

#71-73 printer: TDLR.

		VG	VF	UNC
71	**1 Yüan** Feb. 1934. Yellow-brown. Colonnade, animal figures at ctr. Long stairway on back. *SHANTUNG. (S/M #C294-190).*			
	a. Issued note.	3.00	15.00	30.00
	s. Specimen as above, 2 part.	—	—	150.

		VG	VF	UNC
71A	**1 Yüan** 1934. Red and brown. Farmer plowing w/oxen. *TIENTSIN. (S/M #C294-191).*	100.	500.	1000.
72	**5 Yüan** Feb. 1934. Green. Portico behind trees at ctr. House in rocks on back.			
	a. *SHANTUNG. (S/M #C294-192a).*	7.50	35.00	70.00
	b. *TSINGTAU/SHANTUNG. (S/M #C294-192b).*	22.50	110.	220.
	c. *CHEFOO/SHANTUNG. (S/M #C294-192c).*	45.00	225.	450.
	d. *WEI HAI WEI/SHANTUNG. (S/M #C294-192d).*	45.00	225.	450.
	s. As a, 2 part specimen.	—	—	150.
72A	**5 Yüan** 1934. *TIENTSIN. (S/M #C294-193).*	10.00	50.00	100.
73	**10 Yüan** Oct. 1934. Dk. green. Shepherd, sheep at ctr. Great Wall on back, pavilion at r. *TIENTSIN. (S/M #C294-194).*			
	a. Issued note.	5.00	15.00	45.00
	s. Two part specimen.	—	—	150.

1935 First Issue

		VG	VF	UNC
74	**1 Yüan** 1935. Dk. brown. Temple of Heaven at ctr. Back blue; junk 1 Yuan coin at ctr. Printer: W&S. *SHANGHAI.* W/o ovpt. *(S/M #C294-200).*			
	a. Issued note.	1.50	5.00	17.50
	b. Ovpt: *TN* on face.	2.00	7.50	25.00
	c. Ovpt: *TN* on face and back.	2.00	7.50	25.00

		VG	VF	UNC
75	**10 Yüan** Jan. 1935. Brown. Temple behind trees at ctr. *SHANTUNG.* Printer: TDLR. *(S/M #C294-204).*	7.50	20.00	75.00

1935 Second Issue

#76 and #77 printer: TDLR.

Note: The "Bottle Pagoda" structure was erected in Peking as a complimentary gesture towards Tibet.

		VG	VF	UNC
76	**1 Yüan** March 1935. Brown. Farmer plowing w/horse at l., irrigation system at r. Junk 1 Yuan coin at ctr. on back. *TIENTSIN. (S/M #C294-201).*	1.25	5.00	15.00

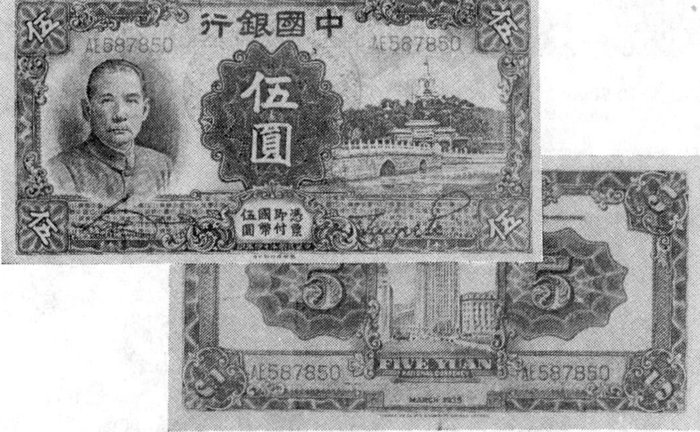

		VG	VF	UNC
77	**5 Yüan** March 1935. Black on m/c unpt. SYS at l., bridge to Bottle Pagoda at r. Back: deep green on pale yellow orange unpt. w/bank bldg. at ctr.			
	a. *SHANGHAI. (S/M #C294-202).*	2.00	5.00	20.00
	b. W/o *SHANGHAI. (S/M #C294-203).*	1.00	2.50	15.00

1936 Issue

		VG	VF	UNC
78	**1 Yüan** May 1936. Green on m/c unpt. SYS at l. Back blue; junk 1-Yuan coin at ctr. Printer: TDLR. *(S/M #C294-210).*	.75	3.25	10.00

1937 ISSUE

#79-81 printer: TDLR.

		VG	VF	UNC
79	**1 Yüan** 1937. Blue. SYS at l. Skyscraper at r. on back. *(S/M #C294-220).*	.50	1.50	6.00

		VG	VF	UNC
80	**5 Yüan** 1937. Violet on m/c unpt. SYS at l. Skyscraper at ctr. on back. *(S/M #C294-221).*	.25	.50	3.00
81	**10 Yüan** 1937. Green on m/c unpt. SYS at l. Skyscraper at r. on back. *(S/M #C294-222).*	.25	.50	3.00

1939 ISSUE

#81A-81C portr. Liao Chung-kai at l. Bank bldg. at r. on back. Printer: ABNC.

		VG	VF	UNC
81A	**1 Yüan** 1939. Purple on m/c unpt. *(S/M #C294-223).*			
	p. Proof.	—	—	400.
	r. Unsigned remainder.	75.00	375.	750.

		VG	VF	UNC
81B	**5 Yüan** 1939. Brown and m/c. Proof. *(S/M #C294-224).*	—	—	600.
81C	**10 Yüan** 1939. Black and m/c. Back blue-gray. Proof. *(S/M #C294-225).*	—	—	900.

1940 ISSUE

#84-88 portr. SYS at l., Temple of Heaven at r. on back. Printer: ABNC.

Note: #85 w/ovpt: *SHENSI PROVINCE* and *CHUNGKING* have been determined to be modern fantasies.

Note: #88 ovpt: *SHENSI PROVINCE* is believed to be a modern fantasy.

		VG	VF	UNC
82	**10 Cents** ND (1940). Red. Temple of Heaven at r. Back brown and green. Chinese printer: TTBC. *(S/M #C294-230).*	.50	1.50	7.00

		VG	VF	UNC
83	**20 Cents** ND (1940). Blue. Great Wall at l. Back green and brown-violet. Chinese printer: TTBC. *(S/M #C294-231).*	.50	1.50	7.00

		VG	VF	UNC
84	**5 Yüan** 1940. Blue on m/c unpt. *(S/M #C294-240).*	.25	1.50	3.00
85	**10 Yüan** 1940. Red on m/c unpt.			
	a. Serial # on face. *(S/M #C294-241a).*	.25	2.00	6.00
	b. Serial # on face and back. *(S/M #C294-241b).*	.25	1.50	3.00

Note: #85 w/ovpt: *SHENSI PROVINCE* and *CHUNGKING* have been determined to be modern fantasies.

		VG	VF	UNC
86	**25 Yüan** 1940. Green on m/c unpt. *(S/M #C294-242).*	5.00	20.00	60.00
87	**50 Yüan** 1940. Brown on m/c unpt.			
	a. Serial # on face. *(S/M #C294-243c).*	5.00	15.00	50.00
	b. Serial # on face and on back. *(S/M #C294-243d).*	5.00	15.00	50.00
	c. Serial # and *CHUNGKING* on face. *CHUNGKING* on back. *(S/M #C294-243b).*	1.50	4.00	20.00
	d. Serial # and *CHUNGKING* on face. Serial # and *CHUNGKING* on back. *(S/M #C294-243b).*	1.50	4.00	20.00

		VG	VF	UNC
88	**100 Yüan** 1940. Purple on m/c unpt.			
	a. Serial # on face and back. *(S/M #C294-244d).*	2.50	12.50	25.00
	b. Serial # and *Chungking* at l. and r. on face. *CHUNGKING* on back. *(S/M #C294-244a).*	1.25	6.00	12.00
	c. Serial # and *Chungking* at l. and r. on face. Serial # and *CHUNGKING* on back. *(S/M #C294-244b).*	1.00	5.00	10.00

Note: #88 ovpt: *SHENSI PROVINCE* is believed to be a modern fantasy.

1941 ISSUE

		VG	VF	UNC
89	**10 Cents** 1941. Green. Temple of Heaven at top. Vertical format. *(S/M #C294-250).*			
	a. Issued note.	20.00	100.	200.
	s. Specimen.	—	—	75.00
90	**20 Cents** 1941. Red on yellow and pink unpt. Temple of Heaven at top. Vertical format. *(S/M #C294-251).*			
	a. Issued note.	15.00	75.00	150.
	s. Specimen.	—	—	75.00

#91 and 92 printer: ABNC.

		VG	VF	UNC
91	**1 Yüan**			
	1941. Blue on m/c unpt. SYS at top. Celestial Temple at bottom on back. *(S/M #C294-260).*			
	a. Issued note.	25.00	125.	250.
	s. Specimen.	—	—	120.
92	**5 Yüan**			
	1941. Red on m/c unpt. Like #91. *(S/M #C294-261).*			
	a. Issued note.	25.00	125.	250.
	s. Specimen.	—	—	120.

		VG	VF	UNC
93	**5 Yüan**			
	1941. Blue on m/c unpt. Temple at r. Gateway at r. on back. Printer: CMPA. *(S/M #C294-262).*	7.50	20.00	75.00

Note: For #93 w/ovpt: *HONG KONG GOVERNMENT* see Hong Kong #7.

		VG	VF	UNC
94	**10 Yüan**			
	1941. Purple on m/c unpt. Similar to #91. Printer: ABNC. *(S/M #C294-264).*			
	a. Issued note.	30.00	150.	300.
	s. Specimen.	—	—	120.
95	**10 Yüan**			
	1941. Red on m/c unpt. SYS at ctr. Chinese printer: DTBC. *(S/M #C294-263).*	5.00	25.00	50.00

#96 and 97 printer: ABNC.

		VG	VF	UNC
96	**100 Yüan**			
	1941. Similar to #91. *(S/M #C294-265).*			
	a. Issued note.	40.00	150.	400.
	s. Specimen.	—	—	175.
97	**500 Yüan**			
	1941. Brown on m/c unpt. Similar to #91. *(S/M #C294-266).*			
	a. Issued note.	40.00	150.	450.
	s. Specimen.	—	—	185.

1942 ISSUE

		VG	VF	UNC
98	**50 Yüan**			
	1942. Green and m/c. Steam passenger train at l. Chinese printer: TTBC. *(S/M #C294-270).*	12.50	60.00	120.

#99 and 100 printer: ABNC.

		VG	VF	UN
99	**500 Yüan**			
	1942. Olive-green and m/c. SYS at l. *(S/M #C294-271).*	15.00	50.00	15
100	**1000 Yüan**			
	1942. Green and m/c. Like #99. *(S/M #C294-272).*			
	a. Issued note.	40.00	200.	40
	s. Specimen.	—	—	16

BANK OF COMMUNICATIONS

БАНКЪ ПУТИ СООБШЕНІЯ

行銀通交

Chiao T'ung Yin Ha

1912 ISSUE

#102-109 sailing ships dockside by depot and train at bottom ctr.

		Good	Fine	X
102	**50 Cents**			
	1912. *YINGKOW. (S/M #C126-10).*	100.	500.	100

		Good	Fine	X
103	**100 Cents**			
	1912. *(S/M #C126-).*			
	a. *MUKDEN. (S/M #C126-11).*	100.	500.	100
	b. *CHANGCHUN. (S/M #C126-).*	125.	625.	125
	c. *YINGKOW. (S/M #C126-).*	100.	—	-
104	**1 Dollar**			
	1912. Green and yellow. Back blue and red.			
	a. *PEKING. (S/M #C126-20a).*	200.	600.	180
	b. *SHANGHAI. (S/M #C126-20b).*	200.	600.	180
	c. *TSINAN (S/M #C126-20c).*	—	—	-
	d. *HONAN.* Perforated and ovpt: *SPECIMEN. (S/M #C126-).*	—	Unc	60
105	**1 Dollar**			
	1.9.1912. Green and m/c. Back blue and green. Specimen. *(S/M #C126-21).*			

		Good	Fine	XF
106	**500 Cents** 1.9.1912. Purple and blue on yellow unpt. *Mukden* handstamp. *(S/M #C126-215).*	—	—	—

		Good	Fine	XF
107	**5 Dollars** 1.9.1912. Blue and m/c. Back brown and green.			
	a. *CHANGCHUN.* Cancelled remainder. *(S/M #C126-24a).*	—	—	1300.
	b. *HONAN.* Perforated and ovpt. *SPECIMEN. (S/M # C126-24b).*	—	Unc	1300.
	c. *PEKING. (S/M #C126-23).*	200.	700.	2000.
	d. *YINGKOW.* Specimen. *(S/M #C126-22).*	—	Unc	1400.
	e. W/o place name. Specimen. *(S/M #C126-24c).*	—	Unc	500.
107A	**1000 Cents** 1.9.1912. Green w/black text. *FENGTIEN. (S/M #C126-).*	—	—	—

		Good	Fine	XF
108	**10 Dollars** 1.9.1912. Blue. Crossed flags at top ctr., steam passenger train below. Back brown.			
	a. *HONAN.* Perforated and ovpt: *SPECIMEN. (S/M #C126-25a).*	—	Unc	1800.
	b. *KALGAN. (S/M #C126-25b)*	—	—	—
	c. *TIENTSIN. (S/M #C126-25c).*	250.	800.	2400.
	d. W/o place name. Specimen. *(S/M #C126-25d).*	—	Unc	1300.
109	**100 Dollars** 1.9.1912. *(S/M #C126-26).*	400.	1000.	2500.

1913 Issue

#110-111C printer: ABNC. Specimens were also prepared from notes w/normal serial numbers.

		Good	Fine	XF
110	**1 Dollar** 1.7.1913. Red-orange on m/c unpt. Electric direct current generator at ctr. Sailing ship at ctr. on back.			
	a. *CHANGCHUN.* Chinese ovpt. on face. English ovpt: *N.B. Payable in subsidiary (silver) coins....* on back. *(S/M #C126-31d).*	150.	600.	1250.
	b. *CHUNGKING.* Specimen. *(S/M #C126-31d).*	—	Unc	1250.
	c. *HUNAN. (S/M #C126-31a).*	150.	600.	1250.
	d. *Fengtien//MUKDEN.* Chinese ovpt. on face. English ovpt: *N.B. This note is exchangeable...* on back. *(S/M #C126-).*	175.	800.	1650.
	e. *PUKOW. (S/M #C126-31e).*	150.	800.	1650.
	f. *TIENTSIN. (S/M #C126-30a).*	125.	600.	1250.
	g. *TSITSIHAR.* Chinese ovpt. on face. English ovpt.: *N.B. Payable in subsidiary (silver) coins....* on back. Specimen. *(S/M #C126-31f).*	—	Unc	250.
	h. *YOCHOW/KALGAN.* Specimen. *(S/M #C126-31f).*	—	Unc	200.
	i. *PEKING (S/M #C126-31g).*	125.	350.	950.
	j. *WUSIH.* Specimen. *(S/M #C126-30b).*	—	Unc	200.
	k. *CHEFOO. (S/M #C126-31h).*	—	—	—
	l. *LUNGKOW/CHEFOO. (S/M #C126-30i).*	150.	700.	1400.
	m. *HANKOW. (S/M #C126-30m).*	150.	700.	1400.
	n. *TSINAN.*	—	—	—

		Good	Fine	XF
111	**5 Dollars** 1.7.1913. Green on m/c unpt. Steam passenger train in ravine at l. Back green; steam passenger train at ctr.			
	a. *CHANGCHUN.* Chinese ovpt. on face. English ovpt: *N.B. Payable in subsidiary (silver) coins...* on back. Specimen. *(S/M #C126-32b).*	—	Unc	550.
	b. *CHUNGKING.* Specimen. *(S/M #C126-32c).*	—	Unc	550.
	c. *HUNAN.* Specimen *(S/M #C126-32a).*	—	Unc	550.
	d. *TIENTSIN.* Specimen. *(S/M #C126-32d).*	—	Unc	550.
	e. *CHEFOO.* Specimen. *(S/M #C126-32e).*	—	Unc	550.
	f. *HANKOW.* Specimen. *(S/M #C126-32f).*	—	Unc	550.
	g. *HONAN.* Specimen. *(S/M #C126-32g).*	—	Unc	550.
	h. *KALGAN.* Specimen. *(S/M #C126-32h)*	—	Unc	550.
	i. *Fengtien//MUKDEN.* Chinese ovpt. on face. English ovpt: *N.B. This note is exchangeable...* on back. Specimen. *(S/M #C126-32i).*	—	Unc	550.
	l. *TSITSIHAR.* Chinese ovpt. on face. English ovpt: *N.B. Payable in subsidiary (silver) coins...* on back. Specimen. *(S/M #C126-326).*	—	Unc	600.
	m. *YOCHOW.* Specimen. *(S/M #C126-32m).*	—	Unc	600.
	n. *SHANGHAI. (S/M #C126-32n).*	150.	400.	1200.
	j1. *PEKING.* Issued note.	150.	400.	1200.
	j2. *PEKING.* Specimen. *(S/M #C126-32j).*	—	Unc	400.
	k1. *PUKOW.* Specimen. *(S/M #C126-32k).*	—	Unc	600.
	k2. <Y>TSINAN.	150.	750.	1500.

		Good	Fine	XF
111A	**10 Dollars**			
	1.7.1913. Purple and m/c. Steam passenger train in ravine at l. Back green; steam passenger train at ctr.			
	a. *HUNAN. (S/M #C126-40a).*	175.	900.	1800.
	b. *CHANGCHUN.* Chinese ovpt. on face. English ovpt: *N.B. Payable in subsidiary (silver) coins...* on back. *(S/M #C126-40b).*	—	Unc	600.
	c. *ANHUI.* Specimen. *(S/M #C126-40c).*	—	Unc	600.
	d. *LUNGKOW/CHEFOO. (S/M #C126-40d).*	—	Unc	700.
	e. *CHUNGKING.* Specimen. *(S/M #126-40e).*	—	Unc	600.
	f. *Fengtien//MUKDEN.* Chinese on face. English ovpt: *N.B. this note is exchangeable...* on back. *(S/M #C126-40f).*	—	Unc	600.
	g. *HANKOW.* Specimen. *(S/M #C126-40g).*	—	Unc	600.
	h. *KALGAN.* Specimen. *(S/M #C126-40h).*	—	Unc	600.
	i. *TIENTSIN.* Specimen. *(S/M #C126-40i).*	—	Unc	600.
	j. *TSITSIHAR.* Chinese ovpt. on face. English ovpt: *N.B. Payable in subsidiary (silver) coins...* on back. Specimen. *(S/M #C126-40j).*	—	Unc	750.
	k. *WUSIH.* Specimen. *(S/M #C126-40k).*	—	Unc	700.

		Good	Fine	XF
111B	**50 Dollars**			
	1.7.1913. Blue and m/c. Steam passenger train at ctr. Back blue; w/Maritime Customs bldg., street car at ctr.			
	a. *CHANGCHUN.* Chinese ovpt. on face. English ovpt: *N.B. Payable in subsidiary (silver) coins...* on back. Specimen. *(S/M #C126-40.5a).*	—	Unc	1250.
	b. *LUNGKOW/CHEFOO.* Specimen. *(S/M #C126-40.5b).*	—	Unc	1250.
	c. *KALGAN.* Specimen. *(S/M #C126-40.5c).*	—	Unc	1250.
	d. *FENGTIEN.* Specimen. *(S/M #C126-40.5d).*	—	Unc	1250.
	e. *HSUCHOW. (S/M #C126-40.5e).*	—	—	—
	f. *SHANTUNG.* Brown and m/c.	—	—	—
	g. *PEKING.*	—	—	—

		Good	Fine	XF
111C	**100 Dollars**			
	1.7.1913. Blue and m/c. Ship at dockside, steam train at ctr. Back: blue w/sailing ships at ctr.			
	a. *CHANGCHUN.* Chinese ovpt. on face. English ovpt: *N.B. Payable in subsidiary (silver) coins...* on back. *(S/M #C126-41b).*	—	Unc	1250.
	b. *Fengtien/MUKDEN.* Chinese ovpt. on face. English ovpt: *N.B. This note is exchangeable...* on back. Specimen. *(S/M #C126-41d).*	—	Unc	1250.
	c. *HANKOW.* Specimen. *(S/M #C126-41d).*	—	Unc	1250.
	d. *HUNAN.* Specimen. *(S/M #C126-41a).*	—	Unc	1250.
	e. *KIANGSU. (S/M #C126-41e).*	—	—	—
	f. *TSINAN.*	—	—	—

1914 ISSUE

#112-115 printer: BEPP.

Note: The original issues have Chinese script signatures while the more common reissues have red Chinese sign. seals on face. All have handwritten English sign. (i.e. *S.M. Tong - T.S. Wong*) on back. Various Western control letter, numeral or Chinese characters are encountered on earlier issues, but rarely on the WWII reissues. In addition, earlier issues w/various banking commercial and private handstamps are encountered and command a small premium.

		Good	Fine	XF
112	**5 Fen**			
	ND (1914). Green and m/c.			
	a. *HARBIN.* Specimen. *(S/M #C126-50a).*	—	Unc	110.
	b. *KALGAN. (S/M #C126-50b).*	25.00	100.	275.
	c. *TAIHEIHO. (S/M #C126-50c).*	30.00	100.	325.
	d. *TULUNNOERH. (S/M #C126-50d)*	30.00	100.	325.
	e. W/o place name. Specimen. *(S/M #C126-50).*	—	Unc	75.00

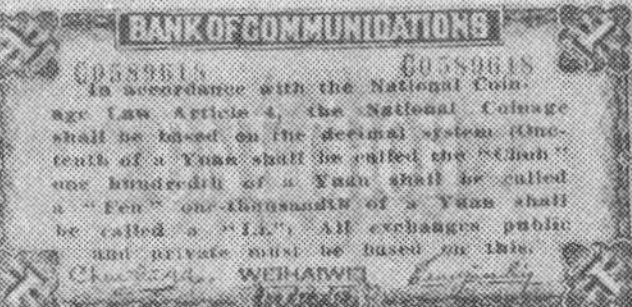

		Good	Fine	XF
113	**1 Choh (Chiao)**			
	ND (1914). Black and red-brown on lt. green unpt.			
	a. *HARBIN. (S/M #C126-51d).*	15.00	45.00	135.
	b. *KALGAN. (S/M #C126-51e).*	15.00	45.00	150.
	c. *SHIHKIACHWANG. (S/M #C126-51a).*	17.50	75.00	200.
	d. *TSINGTAU. (S/M #C126-51b).*	15.00	75.00	150.
	e. *TULUNNOERH. (S/M #C126-51c).*	17.50	75.00	200.
	f. *WEIHAIWEI. (S/M #C126-f).*	15.00	45.00	150.
	g. *WEIHAIWEI/HARBIN. (S/M #C126-51g).*	10.00	25.00	100.
	h. W/o place name. Specimen. *(S/M #C126-51).*	—	Unc	100.
114	**2 Choh (Chiao)**			
	ND (1914). Blue-black and blue-gray on pink unpt. Similar to #113.			
	a. *HARBIN.* Specimen. *(S/M #C126-52c).*	—	Unc	100.
	b. *KALGAN. (S/M #C126-52a).*	10.00	30.00	90.00
	c. *TAIHEIHO. (S/M #C126-52d).*	20.00	100.	200.
	d. *TSINGTAU. (S/M #C126-52e).*	17.50	75.00	175.
	e. *TULUNNOERH. (S/M #C126-52f).*	17.50	75.00	175.
	f. *WEIHAIWEI/HARBIN. (S/M #C126-52b).*	10.00	35.00	100.
	g. *PAOTOW. (S/M #C126-52g).*	20.00	100.	200.
	h. *WEIHAIWEI. (S/M #C126-52h).*	15.00	75.00	150.
	i. W/o place name. Specimen. *(S/M #C126-52).*	—	Unc	120.
115	**5 Choh (Chiao)**			
	ND (1914). Brown. Similar to #113.			
	a. *HARBIN.* Specimen. *(S/M #C126-53a).*	—	Unc	125.
	b. *KALGAN. (S/M #C126-54b).*	25.00	90.00	250.
	c. *TSINGTAU. (S/M #C126-54c).*	25.00	90.00	250.
	d. *WEIHAIWEI. (S/M #C126-54d).*	25.00	90.00	250.
	e. W/o place name. Specimen. *(S/M #C126-54).*	—	Unc	125.

#116-120 printer: ABNC.

116 1 Yüan

1.10.1914. Steam passenger train in ravine at ctr. Sailing ship on back. Also w/various ovpt.

	Good	Fine	XF
a. *AMOY. (S/M #C126-60).*	35.00	175.	350.
b. *CHANGCHUN. (S/M #C126-63).*	60.00	300.	600.
c. *CHEFOO.* Dk. brown and m/c. *(S/M #C126-61).*	45.00	225.	450.
d. *CHEKIANG. (S/M #C126-62).*	65.00	375.	650.
e. *CHUNGKING.* Violet and m/c. *(S/M #C126-64).*	4.50	22.50	45.00
f. *HANKOW.* Brown and m/c. *(S/M #C126-65).*	45.00	225.	450.
g. *HONAN. (S/M #C126-66).*	50.00	250.	500.
h. *KALGAN.* Orange and m/c. *(S/M #C126-67).*	85.00	425.	850.
i. *KIANGSU. (S/M #C126-70).*	65.00	325.	650.
k. *KIUKIANG.* Dk. brown and m/c. *(S/M #C126-71).*	70.00	350.	700.
l. *PUKOW.* Dk. brown and m/c. *(S/M #C126-72).*	80.00	400.	800.
m. *SHANGHAI.* Purple and m/c. *(S/M #C126-73).*	.60	3.00	6.00
n. *SHANGHAI.* Dk. brown and m/c. 2 sign. varieties. *(S/M #C126-74).*	45.00	225.	450.
o. *SHANGHAI.* Blue and m/c. *(S/M #C126-75).*	7.50	40.00	80.00
p. *SHANTUNG. (S/M #C126-76).*	4.00	20.00	40.00
q. *SIAN.* Violet and m/c. *(S/M #C126-77).*	45.00	225.	450.
s. *TSINGTAO.* Dk. brown and m/c. *(S/M #C126-79).*	60.00	300.	600.
t. *SHANGHAI.* Violet and m/c. Red control letter *P* at l. and r. *(S/M #C126-73a).*	4.00	20.00	40.00
u. *TULUNNOERH.* Brown and m/c. Mongol text at l. and r. *(S/M #C126-79.6).*	—	—	—
v. W/o place name. Specimen. *(S/M #C126-).*	—	Unc	50.00
r1. *TIENTSIN.* Purple and m/c. *(S/M #C126-78).*	1.50	7.50	15.00
r2. *TIENTSIN.* Brown and m/c.	45.00	225.	450.

117 5 Yüan

1.10.1914. Steam passenger train at ctr. Post Office at ctr. on back. Also w/various ovpt.

	Good	Fine	XF
a. *AMOY.* Dk. brown and m/c. *(S/M #C126-80).*	12.50	60.00	120.
b. *CHANGCHUN. (S/M #C126-84).*	20.00	100.	200.
c. *CHEFOO. (S/M #C126-82).*	45.00	225.	450.
d. *CHEKIANG. (S/M #C126-83).*	50.00	250.	500.
e. *CHUNGKING.* Dk. brown and m/c. *(S/M #C126-85).*	3.50	17.50	35.00
f. *FOOCHOW/AMOY.* Dk. brown and m/c. *(S/M #C126-81).*	35.00	175.	350.
g. *HANKOW. (S/M #C126-86).*	45.00	225.	450.
h. *HONAN.* Blue-black and m/c. *(S/M #C126-87).*	50.00	250.	500.
i. *KALGAN.* Green on m/c unpt. *(S/M #C126-88).*	65.00	325.	650.
k. *KIANGSU. (S/M #C126-90).*	50.00	250.	500.
l. *KIUKIANG.* Blue and m/c. *(S/M #C126-91).*	65.00	325.	650.
m. *PUKOW. (S/M #C126-92).*	90.00	450.	900.
n. *SHANGHAI.* Dk. brown and m/c. *Shanghai* ovpt. in black w/red sign. seals. *(S/M #C126-93a).*	—	Unc	3.00
o. *SHANGHAI.* Dk. brown and m/c. *Shanghai* ovpt. and script sign. in blue-black. *(S/M #C126-93).*	5.00	25.00	50.00
p. *SHANTUNG.* Dk. brown and m/c. *(S/M #C126-).*	3.00	15.00	30.00
q. *SHANTUNG.* Blue-black and m/c. *(S/M #C126-94).*	12.50	60.00	120.
r. *SIAN.* Orange and m/c. *(S/M #C126-95).*	25.00	125.	250.
s. *TIENTSIN.* Red and m/c. *(S/M #C126-96).*	5.00	25.00	50.00
t. *TIENTSIN.* Dk. brown and m/c. *(S/M #C126-99).*	2.50	12.50	25.00
u. *TSINGTAU.* Dk. blue and m/c. *(S/M #C126-97).*	50.00	250.	500.
v. *TULUNNOERH.* Mongol text at l. and r. *(S/M #C126-98).*	—	—	—
w. *SHANGHAI.* Blue and m/c. *(S/M #C126-).*	20.00	100.	200.
x. *SHANGHAI.* Dk. brown and m/c. Red control letter *P* at l. and r. *(S/M #C126-93b).*	—	—	3.00
y. *SHANGHAI.* Black and m/c. *(S/M #C126-).*	55.00	275.	550.

118 10 Yüan

1.10.1914. Maritime Customs bldg., streetcar at ctr. Ship at dockside, steam passenger train at ctr. on back. Also w/various ovpt.

	Good	Fine	XF
a. *AMOY.* Blue and m/c. *(S/M #C126-100).*	55.00	275.	550.
b. *AMOY.* Red and m/c. *(S/M #C126-101).*	20.00	100.	200.
c. *CHANGCHUN. (S/M #C126-104).*	25.00	125.	250.
d. *CHEFOO. (S/M #C126-102).*	55.00	275.	550.
e. *CHEKIANG. (S/M #C126-103).*	55.00	275.	550.
f. *CHUNGKING.* Red and m/c. *(S/M #C126-105).*	2.50	12.50	25.00
g. *HANKOW. (S/M #C126-106).*	60.00	300.	600.
h. *HONAN. (S/M #C126-107).*	65.00	325.	650.
i. *KALGAN.* Orange and m/c. *(S/M #C126-110).*	90.00	450.	900.
j. *KALGAN.* Green and m/c. *(S/M #C126-111).*	80.00	400.	800.
k. *KANSU. (S/M #C126-109).*	55.00	275.	550.
l. *KIUKIANG.* Green and m/c. *(S/M #C126-112).*	60.00	300.	600.
m. *PUKOW. (S/M #C126-113).*	90.00	450.	900.
n. *SHANGHAI.* Green and m/c. *(S/M #C126-114).*	75.00	375.	750.
o. *SHANGHAI.* Red and m/c. *Shanghai* and sign. in blue-black. *(S/M #C126-115).*	—	Unc	25.00
p. *SHANGHAI.* Red and m/c. *Shanghai* in black w/red sign. seals. *(S/M #C126-115a).*	—	Unc	3.00
q. *SHANGHAI.* Red and m/c. *Shanghai* in blue-black w/red sign. seals. *(S/M #C126-115b).*	—	Unc	200
r. *SHANTUNG.* Red and m/c. *(S/M #C126-116).*	2.50	12.50	25.00
s. *SIAN. (S/M #C126-117).*	50.00	250.	500.
t. *TIENTSIN.* Purple and *(S/M #C126-120).*	2.50	12.50	25.00
u. *SHANGHAI.* Red and m/c. *Shanghai* in black w/red sign. seals and red control letter *P* at l. and r. *(S/M #C126-115a).*	—	Unc	25.00
v. *NANKING.* Green and m/c. Ovpt: *SPECIMEN* on issued note.	—	—	—

Note: #118q w/ovpt: *KANSU PROVINCE / SHANGHAI* is a modern fabrication.

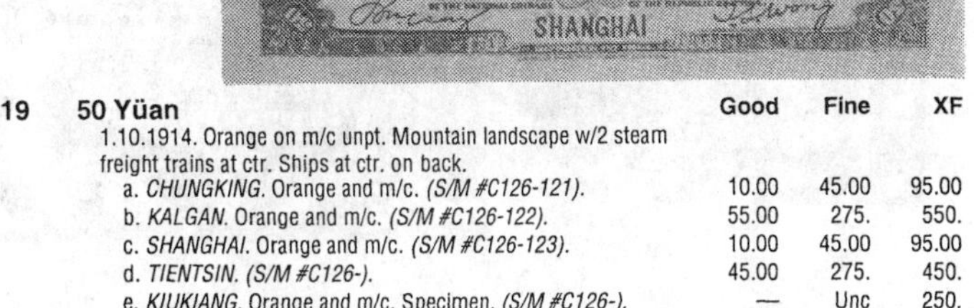

119 50 Yüan

1.10.1914. Orange on m/c unpt. Mountain landscape w/2 steam freight trains at ctr. Ships at ctr. on back.

	Good	Fine	XF
a. *CHUNGKING.* Orange and m/c. *(S/M #C126-121).*	10.00	45.00	95.00
b. *KALGAN.* Orange and m/c. *(S/M #C126-122).*	55.00	275.	550.
c. *SHANGHAI.* Orange and m/c. *(S/M #C126-123).*	10.00	45.00	95.00
d. *TIENTSIN. (S/M #C126-).*	45.00	275.	450.
e. *KIUKIANG.* Orange and m/c. Specimen. *(S/M #C126-).*	—	Unc	250.
f. *PEKING.* Orange and m/c. Specimen. *(S/M #C126-).*	15.00	75.00	150.

		Good	Fine	XF
120	**100 Yüan** 1.10.1914. Purple and m/c. Steam passenger train crossing bridge at ctr. Steam passenger train at ctr. on back.			
	a. *CHUNGKING. (S/M #C126-124).*	6.00	30.00	60.00
	b. *KALGAN. (S/M #C126-125).*	50.00	250.	500.
	c. *SHANGHAI. (S/M #C126-126).*	4.50	22.50	45.00
	d. *TIENTSIN. (S/M #C126-).*	17.50	85.00	175.
	e. *KIUKIANG.* Specimen. *(S/M #C126-).*	—	Unc	300.
	f. *PEKING.* Ovpt: Specimen on issued note. *(S/M #C126-).*	12.50	60.00	120.

1915 ISSUE

#121-122B printer: ABNC.

		Good	Fine	XF
121	**50 Cents** 1.1.1915. Black. Ship at l.			
	a. *CHANGCHUN. (S/M #C126-).*	60.00	250.	750.
	b. *CHANGCHUN/YINGKOW.*	75.00	300.	900.

		Good	Fine	XF
122	**100 Cents** 1.1.1915. Black. Steam locomotive at r.			
	a. *CHANGCHUN (S/M #C126-).*	50.00	225.	750.
	b. *CHANGCHUN/YINGKOW.*	60.00	175.	600.

		Good	Fine	XF
122A	**500 Cents** 1.1.1915. Gray. Steam passenger train in mountain pass at l.			
	a. *YINGKOW.*	75.00	225.	900.
	s. *YINGKOW.* Specimen. *(S/M #C126-).*	—	Unc	250.

		Good	Fine	X
122B	**1000 Cents** 1.1.1915. Gray. Steam passenger train at r. *(S/M #C126-).*			
	a. *YINGKOW.*	115.	375.	115
	s. As a. Specimen.	—	Unc	30

1917 ISSUE

		Good	Fine	X
123	**10 Cents** 1.8.1917. Orange. *CHANGCHUN. (S/M #C126-).*	45.00	115.	45

		Good	Fine	X
124	**20 Cents** 1.8.1917. Black. River view at ctr. *CHANGCHUN. (S/M #C126-).*	50.00	225.	50

124A	**50 Cents** 1.8.1917. Green. Steam passenger train at ctr. Back green. *MUKDEN.* Specimen. *(S/M #C126-).*	—	Unc	25

1919 ISSUE

#125-127 printer: BEPP.

		Good	Fine	X
125	**1 Yüan** 1.7.1919. Blue. Village near mountain at ctr. Back brown and green. *HARBIN.* 2 sign. varieties. *(S/M #C126-131).*			
	a. Issued note.	45.00	150.	45
	r. Remainder w/o serial # or place name.	—	Unc	12

		Good	Fine	X
126	**5 Yüan** 1.7.1919. Green. Bridge across brook. Back brown and green.			
	a. *HARBIN. (S/M #C126-132).*	75.00	200.	6
	b. *TAHEIHO.* Specimen. *(S/M #C126-).*	—	Unc	2
	r. Remainder w/o place name. *(S/M #C126-).*	—	Unc	1

		Good	Fine	XF
127	**10 Yüan** 1.7.1919. Pagoda near mountain. Back: brown and orange.			
	a. *HARBIN.* Cancelled. *(S/M #C126-133).*	75.00	200.	600.
	b. *TAHEIHO.* Specimen. *(S/M #C126-).*	—	Unc	250.

1920 Harbin Issue

#128-130B similar to #116-120 but w/bank name, office of issue and denomination also in Russian text. Printer: ABNC.

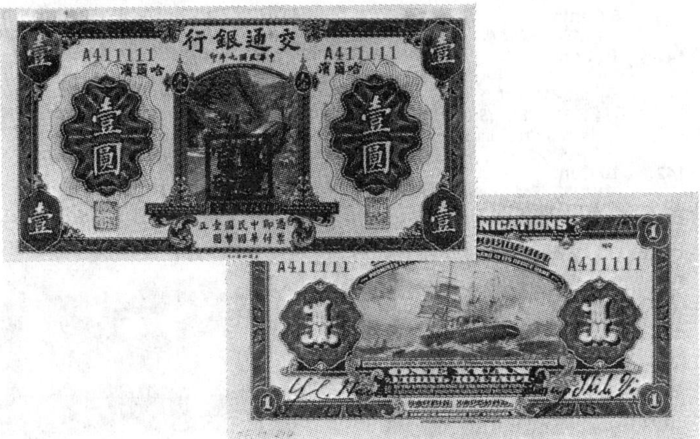

		VG	VF	UNC
128	**1 Yüan** 1.12.1920. Black. Similar to #116. Red official 4-Chinese character ovpt. on face. 2 sign. varieties. *HARBIN. (S/M #C126-140).*			
	a. Issued note.	75.00	250.	700.
	s. Specimen.	—	—	300.

		VG	VF	UNC
129	**5 Yüan** 1.12.1920. Similar to #117. Red official 4-Chinese character ovpt. on face. *HARBIN. (S/M #C126-141).*			
	a. Issued note.	75.00	250.	800.
	s. Specimen.	—	—	350.
130	**10 Yüan** 1.12.1920. Similar to #118. Red official 4-Chinese character ovpt. on face. *HARBIN. (S/M #C126-142).*			
	a. Issued note.	200.	500.	1000.
	s. Specimen.	—	—	400.

NOTICE

Readers with unlisted dates, signature varieties, etc. are invited to submit photocopies or, high resolution (300 dpi, 100% size) scans of their notes to: Standard Catalog of World Paper Money, 700 East State St. Iola, WI 54990-0001, or E-Mail: george.cuhaj@fwpubs.com.

		VG	VF	UNC
130A	**50 Yüan** 1.12.1920. Similar to #119. *HARBIN.* Proof. *(S/M #C126-143).*	—	—	550.

		VG	VF	UNC
130B	**100 Yüan** 1.12.1920. Similar to #120. *HARBIN.* Proof. *(S/M #C126-144).*	—	—	700.

1923 Issue

#131-133 printer: ABNC.

		VG	VF	UNC
131	**1 Dollar** 1.1.1923. Orange and m/c. Electric direct current generator at ctr. Sailing ship on back. *FENGTIEN PROVINCE.* Specimen. *(S/M #C126-150).*	—	—	300.

		VG	VF	UNC
132	**5 Dollars** 1.1.1923. Green and m/c. Steam passenger train at ctr. Steam passenger train at ctr. on back. *FENGTIEN PROVINCE.* Specimen. *(S/M #C126-151).*	—	—	300.
133	**10 Dollars** 1.1.1923. Purple and m/c. Steam passenger train at ctr. Back purple; bank bldg. at ctr. *FENGTIEN PROVINCE. (S/M #C126-152).*	75.00	350.	750.

1924 ISSUE

#134-137 printer: W&S.

		Good	Fine	XF
134	**1 Yüan** 1.7.1924. Brown. Steam passenger train at ctr. Bank bldg. at ctr. on back. *SHANGHAI. (S/M #C126-160).*			
	a. Issued note.	80.00	200.	450.
	s. Specimen.	—	Unc	250.

		Good	Fine	XF
135	**5 Yüan** 1.7.1924. Black-brown. Steam passenger train at ctr. Bank bldg. at ctr. on back.			
	a. *KIUKIANG. (S/M #C126-).*	55.00	250.	550.
	b. *SHANGHAI. (S/M #C126-161).*	40.00	200.	400.
	s. No place name.	—	Unc	250.

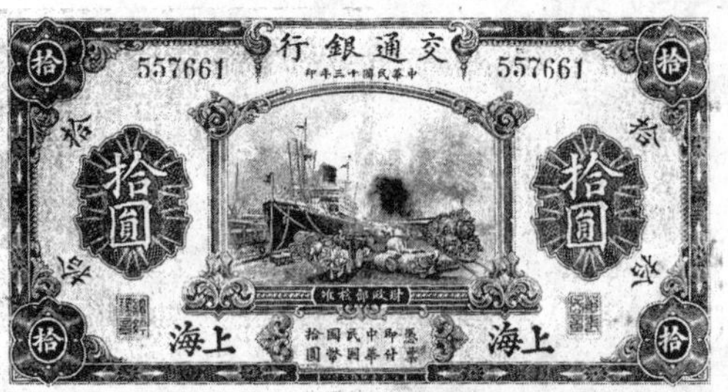

		Good	Fine	XF
136	**10 Yüan** 1.7.1924. Green. Ship dockside. Steam passenger train at ctr. Back green; bank bldg. at ctr. *SHANGHAI. (S/M #C126-162).*	60.00	300.	600.

		Good	Fine	XF
137	**20 Yüan** 1.7.1924. Blue. Ship, airplane, steam locomotive and truck at ctr.			
	a. *SHANGHAI. (S/M #C126-).*	150.	700.	1400.
	s. W/o place name. Specimen. *(S/M #C126-163).*	—	Unc	700.

Note: #137 is reported to commemorate the 20th anniversary of the General Bank of Communications.

1925 ISSUE

#138-140 printer: BEPP.

		Good	Fine	XF
138	**10 Cents** 1.7.1925. Green. Steamship at ctr.			
	a. *HARBIN. (S/M #C126-170a).*	12.50	60.00	120.
	b. *SHANGHAI. (S/M #C126-).*	7.50	40.00	80.00
	c. *TSINGTAU. (S/M #C126-170b).*	10.00	50.00	100.
	d. *WEIHAIWEI. (S/M #C126-170c).*	7.50	40.00	80.00
	e. *SHIH-KIA CHUANG. (S/M #C126-).*	15.00	75.00	150.
	s. Specimen, 2 part.			

		Good	Fine	XF
139	**20 Cents** 1.7.1925. Orange. Steam passenger train at ctr.			
	a. *HARBIN. (S/M #C126-171b).*	17.50	50.00	175.
	b. *SHANGHAI. (S/M #C126-171a).*	5.00	15.00	45.00
	c. *TSINGTAU. (S/M #C126-).*	7.50	25.00	75.00
	d. *WEIHAIWEI. (S/M #C126-).*	7.50	25.00	75.00

1927 FIRST ISSUES

#141-143 printer: W&S.

		Good	Fine	XF
140	**5 Cents** 1.1.1927. *HARBIN. (S/M #C126-180).*	25.00	125.	250.
141	**10 Cents** 1.1.1927. Blue. Similar to #143. Back lilac-brown.			
	a. *SHANGHAI. (S/M #C126-181a).*	6.00	30.00	60.00
	b. *TSINGTAU. (S/M #C126-181b).*	7.50	35.00	75.00
	s. W/o place name. Specimen uniface face and back. *(S/M #C126-181-).*	—	Unc	50.00
142	**10 Cents** 1.1.1927. Red. Similar to #143. Back violet-black. *TSINGTAU. (S/M #C126-182).*			
	a. Issued note.	6.00	30.00	60.00
	s. 2 part specimen.	—	Unc	50.00

		Good	Fine	XF
143	**20 Cents** 1.1.1927. Red-brown. Steamship l., steam locomotive at r. Back blue.			
	a. *KALGAN. (S/M #C126-183a).*	6.50	35.00	65.00
	b. *SHANGHAI* in black. *(S/M #C126-183b).*	12.50	60.00	120.
	c. *SHIHKIACHWANG. (S/M #C126-183c).*	20.00	100.	200.
	d. *TSINAN. (S/M #C126-183d).*	10.00	50.00	100.
	e. *TSINGTAU. (S/M #C126-183e).*	7.50	40.00	80.00
	f. *SHANGHAI* in blue. Specimen. Uniface face and back. *(S/M #C126-183b-a).*	—	Unc	80.00
	s. 2 part specimen.	—	Unc	60.00
144	**50 Cents** 1.1.1927. *HARBIN. (S/M #C126-184).*	15.00	45.00	150.

1927 SECOND ISSUES

#145-147C printer: ABNC.

		Good	Fine	XF
145	**1 Yüan** 1.11.1927. Purple and m/c. Steam passenger train in ravine at ctr. *FENGTIEN. (S/M #C126-190).*			
	a. Issued note.	30.00	150.	300.
	s. Specimen.	—	Unc	150.

		Good	Fine	XF
145A	**1 Yüan** 1.11.1927. Similar to #145 but different colors and guilloches. *SHANGHAI.*			
	a. Purple and m/c. *(S/M #C126-191).*	20.00	100.	200.
	b. Brown and m/c. *(S/M #C126-192).*	20.00	100.	200.
	c. Blue and m/c. 2 English sign. on back. *(S/M #C126-193).*	7.50	35.00	75.00
	d. Like c. 2 Chinese sign. on back.	7.50	25.00	75.00

145B	1 Yüan	Good	Fine	XF
	1.11.1927. Yellow-orange and m/c. Similar to #145 but different guilloches.			
	a. *SHANTUNG. (S/M #C126-194).*	7.50	30.00	75.00
	b. *CHEFOO/SHANTUNG.* Black Chinese sign. on face and back. *(S/M #C126-195).*	10.00	40.00	100.
	c. *CHEFOO/SHANTUNG.* Red sign. seals. Black English sign. on back. *(S/M #C126-195).*	10.00	40.00	100.
	d. *LUNGKOW/SHANTUNG. (S/M #C126-196).*	10.00	40.00	100.
	e. *TSINAN/SHANTUNG. (S/M #C126-197).*	10.00	40.00	100.
	f. *TSINGTAU/SHANTUNG. (S/M #C126-198).* 2 sign.	10.00	40.00	100.
	g. *WEIHAIWEI/SHANTUNG. (S/M #C126-199).* 2 sign.	12.50	60.00	125.
	s. As a, specimen.	—	Unc	50.00

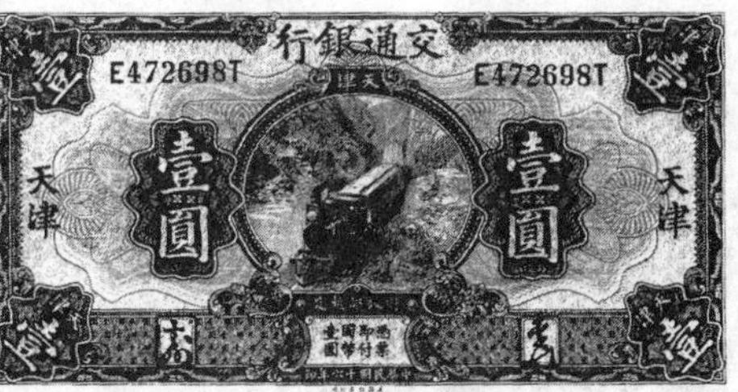

45C	1 Yüan	Good	Fine	XF
	1.11.1927. Green and m/c. Similar to #145 but different guilloches. *TIENTSIN. (S/M #C126-200).*	7.50	20.00	75.00
46	5 Yüan			
	1.11.1927. Brown and m/c. Steam passenger train at ctr. *FENGTIEN. (S/M #C126-201).*			
	a. Issued note.	30.00	150.	300.
	s. Specimen.	—	Unc	200.
46A	5 Yüan			
	1.11.1927. Green and m/c. Similar to #146 but different guilloches. *HANKOW. (S/M #C126-202).).*	22.50	110.	220.
46B	5 Yüan			
	1.11.1927. Olive-brown and m/c. Similar to #146 but different guilloches. *SHANGHAI. (S/M #C126-203).*	6.00	30.00	60.00

46C	5 Yüan	Good	Fine	XF
	1.11.1927. Purple and m/c. Similar to #146 but different guilloches.			
	a. *SHANTUNG.* English sign. *(S/M #C126-204).*	10.00	40.00	100.
	b. *CHEFOO/SHANTUNG. (S/M #C126-210).*	10.00	40.00	100.
	c. *LUNGKOW/SHANTUNG. (S/M #C126-211).*	10.00	40.00	100.
	d. *TSINAN/SHANTUNG. (S/M #C126-212).*	10.00	40.00	100.
	e. *TSINGTAU/SHANTUNG. (S/M #C126-213).*	10.00	40.00	100.
	f. *WEIHAIWEI/SHANTUNG. (S/M #C126-).*	10.00	40.00	100.
	g. *SHANTUNG.* Chinese sign. *(S/M #C126-).*	10.00	40.00	100.
	s. As a, specimen.	—	Unc	60.00
46D	5 Yüan			
	1.11.1927. Orange and m/c. Similar to #146 but different guilloches. *TIENTSIN. (S/M #C126-214).*	8.00	35.00	80.00
47	10 Yüan			
	1.11.1927. Similar to #A147A but blue and different guilloches. *FENGTIEN. (S/M #C126-220).*			
	a. Issued note.	40.00	200.	400.
	s. Specimen.	—	Unc	250.

NOTICE

Readers with unlisted dates, signature varieties, etc. are invited to submit photocopies or, high resolution (300 dpi, 100% size) scans of their notes to: Standard Catalog of World Paper Money, 700 East State St. Iola, WI 54990-0001, or E-Mail: george.cuhaj@fwpubs.com.

147A	10 Yüan	Good	Fine	XF
	1.11.1927. Red and m/c. Maritime Customs bldg., street car at ctr. *SHANGHAI. (S/M #C126-221).*	7.50	25.00	75.00

147B	10 Yüan	Good	Fine	XF
	1.11.1927. Green and m/c. Similar to #147 but different guilloches.			
	a. *SHANTUNG.* English sign. *(S/M #C126-222).*	7.50	22.50	60.00
	b. *CHEFOO/SHANTUNG. (S/M #C126-223).*	7.50	30.00	75.00
	c. *LUNGKOW/SHANTUNG. (S/M #C126-224).*	7.50	30.00	75.00
	d. *TSINAN/SHANTUNG. (S/M #C126-225).*	7.50	30.00	75.00
	e. *TSINGTAU/SHANTUNG. (S/M #C126-226).*	7.50	22.50	60.00
	f. *WEIHAIWEI/SHANTUNG. (S/M #C126-).*	15.00	50.00	125.
	g. *SHANTUNG.* Chinese sign. *(S/M #C126-).*	7.50	22.50	60.00
	s. As a, specimen.	—	Unc	70.00
147C	10 Yüan			
	1.11.1927. Brown and m/c. Similar to #147 but different guilloches.			
	a. *TIENTSIN. (S/M #C126-227).*	20.00	50.00	200.
	b. *HANKOW. (S/M #C126-).* Olive green.	25.00	75.00	250.
	s. As a, 2 part specimen.	—	Unc	150.

1931 ISSUE

148	1 Yüan	VG	VF	UNC
	1.1.1931. Red. Steam passenger train at ctr. Back red; houses and pagoda at ctr. Printer: TDLR. *SHANGHAI. (S/M #C126-230).*			
	a. English sign. and red sign. seals printed separately at lower l. and r.	—	—	—
	b. Red sign. seals printed separately at lower l. and r.	2.50	7.50	30.00
	c. Red sign. seals engraved in frame design at lower l. and r.	.50	2.00	6.00
	s. Specimen without seals on front.	—	—	150.
	s2. Specimen with seals on front.	—	—	150.

1935 FIRST PROVISIONAL ISSUE

New issuer ovpt. of 9-Chinese characters and/or English on National Industrial Bank of China notes.

149	1 Yüan	VG	VF	UNC
	ND (1935-old date 1931). Purple and m/c. Ovpt. on #531c. *(S/M #C126-231).*	35.00	150.	350.

		VG	VF	UNC
150	**5 Yüan** ND (1935-old date 1931). Red and m/c. Black Chinese ovpt. on 532a. *(S/M #C126-232).*	22.50	100.	220.

		VG	VF	UNC
151	**10 Yüan** ND (1935-old date 1931). Green and m/c. Black Chinese ovpt. on #533. *(S/M #C126-233).*	17.50	75.00	160.

1935 SECOND PROVISIONAL ISSUE

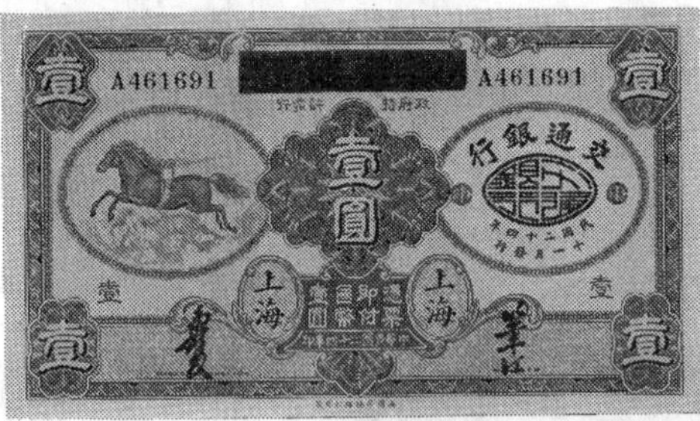

		VG	VF	UNC
152	**1 Yüan** Nov. 1935 (-old date 1935). Red and m/c. Red Chinese ovpt. Black English ovpt. on back on #534. *(S/M #C126-240).*	17.50	90.00	180.

1935 REGULAR ISSUE

#153-155 pagoda on hill, shoreline at ctr. on back. Printer: TDLR.

		VG	VF	UNC
153	**1 Yüan** 1935. Purple on green unpt. Steam locomotive at ctr. *(S/M #C126-241).*	.50	2.00	10.00

		VG	VF	UN
154	**5 Yüan** 1935. Dk. green on pink unpt. Junks at ctr. *(S/M #C126-242).*			
	a. Issued note.	.10	.50	3.0
	r. Remainder w/o red sign. seals on face at lower l. and r.	5.00	10.00	25.0

		VG	VF	UN
155	**10 Yüan** 1935. Red on yellow-orange unpt. High voltage electric towers at r. Back red. *(S/M #C126-243).*	.25	.50	3.

1941 ISSUES

#156-162 Nationalist issues w/*CHUNGKING* while those w/o any place name were issued in Japanese co trolled areas.

		VG	VF	UN
156	**5 Yüan** 1941. Brown and m/c. Steam passenger train at ctr. Back brown; bank at ctr. Printer: ABNC. *(S/M #C126-252).*	2.00	7.50	25.

		VG	VF	UI
157	**5 Yüan** 1941. Brown and m/c. Ship at ctr. Printer: CMPA. *(S/M #C126-251).*			
	a. Issued note.	.50	1.50	6
	s. 2 part specimen.	—	—	1

		VG	VF	UNC
158	**10 Yüan** 1941. Red and m/c. Bldg. w/clock tower at ctr. Back red; dockside scene at ctr. Printer: ABNC. *(S/M #C126-253).*	2.00	7.50	18.00

		VG	VF	UNC
159	**10 Yüan** 1941. Brown and m/c. Steam passenger train at ctr. Chinese printer: Dah Tung Book. *(S/M #C126-254).*			
	a. Serial # face and back.	.75	3.50	7.50
	b. Serial # on face only.	.75	3.50	7.50
	c. W/o serial # or sign. seals.	.75	3.50	7.50
	d. Mismatched serial #.	2.50	7.50	20.00
	e. Cancellation handstamp, serial # on face and back.	.75	3.50	7.50
	f. Cancellation handstamp, w/o serial # or sign. seals.	.75	3.50	7.50
	g. Cancellation handstamp and mismatched serial #.	4.00	10.00	2.50
	h. Serial # on back only.	.75	3.50	7.50
	s. Specimen.	—	—	100.

#160-163 printer: ABNC.

		VG	VF	UNC
160	**25 Yüan** 1941. Green and m/c. Electric direct current generator, Zeppelin and plane at ctr. Back green; airplane at ctr. *(S/M #C126-260).*	15.00	37.50	150.

		VG	VF	UNC
161	**50 Yüan** 1941. Brown and m/c. 2 railroad trains in a mountain pass. Back brown; ships at ctr.			
	a. *CHUNGKING. (S/M (S/M #C126-261b).*	3.50	15.00	35.00
	b. W/o place name. *(S/M #C126-261a).*	3.00	15.00	30.00

		VG	VF	UNC
162	**100 Yüan** 1941. Purple and m/c. Steam passenger train on bridge at ctr. Back purple; steam train at ctr.			
	a. *CHUNGKING. (S/M #C126-262b).*	3.00	15.00	30.00
	b. W/o place name. *(S/M #C126-262a).*	2.00	10.00	20.00

		VG	VF	UNC
163	**500 Yüan** 1941. Blue on m/c unpt. Ship at dockside at ctr. Back blue; steam passenger train, high voltage electrical towers across landscape. *(S/M #C126-263).*			
	a. Issued note.	55.00	225.	550.
	s. Specimen.	—	—	350.

1942 ISSUE

#164-165 issued under Japanese control. Chinese printer: Ta Tung (Dah Tung) Printing.

		VG	VF	UNC
164	**50 Yüan** 1942. Steam passenger train at l. *(S/M #C126-270).*			
	a. Purple.	15.00	30.00	150.
	b. Brown-violet.	10.00	20.00	100.

		VG	VF	UNC
165	**100 Yüan** 1942. Brown. Steam train at l., ships at r. Large value *100* on back. *(S/M #C126-271).*	7.50	35.00	75.00

1949 Circulating Cashier's Checks Issue

#165A-165D steam passenger train at upper ctr. on back.

165A	**500 Yüan** ND (1949). Lt. brown on lt. green. Specimen. *(S/M #C126-).*	—	Unc	90.00

		Good	Fine	XF
165B	**1000 Yüan** ND (1949). Green. *(S/M #C126-).*			
	a. Issued note.	20.00	100.	200.
	s. Specimen.	—	Unc	90.00
165C	**2000 Yüan** ND (1949). Red. *(S/M #C126-).*			
	a. Issued note.	20.00	100.	200.
	s. Specimen.	—	Unc	90.00
165D	**5000 Yüan** ND (1949). Purple. Specimen. *(S/M #C126-).*	—	Unc	90.00

		Good	Fine	XF
166	**1000 Gold Yüan** ND (1949). Green. Printer: CPF. *(S/M #C126-280).*	12.50	45.00	125.

Central Bank of China (National)

中央銀行

Chung Yan Yin Hang

1928 (ND) Coin Note Issue

		VG	VF	UNC
167	**10 Coppers** ND. (1928) Violet and green unpt. Pagoda at l. W/o ovpt.			
	a. Black ovpt: *SHENSI.*	7.50	30.00	70.00
	b. Red Chinese ovpt: *5 Fen* (5 Cents) (Legal tender for circulation in Szechuan Province).	5.00	12.50	25.00
	c. Similar to #167b but w/additional black Chinese ovpt: *5 Fen.*	12.50	45.00	125.

		VG	VF	UNC
168	**20 Coppers** ND. (1928) Dk. blue on red unpt. Pagoda at r.			
	a. Black ovpt: *SHENSI.*	12.50	45.00	125.
	b. Red ovpt: *1 CHIAO* (10 Cents). Similar to #167b.	3.50	15.00	35.00
	c. Similar to #168b but w/additional Chinese ovpt: *1 Chiao* over *20 Coppers.*	5.00	15.00	45.00

		VG	VF	UNC
169	**50 Coppers** ND. (1928) Lilac-brown on lt. brown. Pagoda at r.			
	a. Black ovpt: *SHENSI.*	15.00	75.00	150.
	b. Red ovpt: *2 CHIAO 5 FEN* (25 Cents). Similar to #167b and #168b.	6.00	25.00	60.00

1920 Provisional Issue

		Good	Fine	XF
170	**5 Dollars** ND (1928-old date 1.9.1920). Red and m/c. Ovpt. on #541.			
	a. English ovpt. 80mm. on back.	25.00	125.	250.
	b. English ovpt. 83mm. on back.	25.00	125.	250.

NOTICE

Readers with unlisted dates, signature varieties, etc. are invited to submit photocopies or, high resolution (300 dpi, 100% size) scans of their notes to: Standard Catalog of World Paper Money, 700 East State St. Iola, WI 54990-0001, or E-Mail: george.cuhaj@fwpubs.com.

CENTRAL BANK OF CHINA (QUASI-NATIONAL)

中央銀行

Chung Yan Yin Hang

1923 ISSUE

#171-179B portr. SYS at ctr. Printer: ABNC.

		Good	Fine	XF
171	**1 Dollar**			
	1923. Green and m/c. Back blue. English sign.			
	a. English sign.	2.00	10.00	20.00
	b. Chinese sign.	2.00	7.50	20.00
	c. Ovpt: *HUNAN, KIANGSI & KWANGSI* on back. English sign.	22.50	100.	240.
	d. Red ovpt: 4-Chinese characters in circles at corners, (Kwangchow) on face. English sign.	30.00	150.	320.
	e. Ovpt: *Swatow* at l. and r. SWATOW at lower ctr. w/Swatow diagonally at l. and r. on back. English sign.	3.00	10.00	30.00
	f. SWATOW. W/circular violet Central Bank handstamp.	3.50	17.50	35.00
	g. Red ovpt: *HUPEH, HUNAN, & KWANGSI* on back.	20.00	100.	200.
	h. Ovpt: *Kwangtung* above portr.	4.50	22.50	45.00
	i. Large oval branch office handstamp: *HUNAN, KIANGSI & KWANGSI* also w/Chinese characters on face.	—	—	—
	s. Specimen.	—	Unc	90.00
171A	**1 Dollar**			
	1923. Dk. green and m/c. Back brown.			
	a. *Haikow* at l. and r. *HAI KOW* at lower l. and r. on back. Specimen.	—	Unc	220.
	b. *Kongmoon* at l. and r. *KONG MOON* at lower l. and r. on back. Specimen.	—	Unc	220.
	c. *Meiluck* at l. and r. *MEI LUCK* at lower l. and r. on back. Specimen.	—	Unc	220.
	d. *Pakhoi* at l. and r. *PAK HOI* at lower l. and r. on back. Specimen.	—	Unc	220.
	e. *Suichow* at l. and r. *SUI CHOW* at lower l. and r. on back. Specimen.	—	Unc	220.
	f. *Swatow* at l. and r. *SWATOW* at lower l. and r. on back. Specimen.	—	Unc	220.

		Good	Fine	XF
172	**1 Dollar**			
	1923. Yellow-orange and m/c. Similar to #171. Back black.			
	a. English sign.	6.00	25.00	60.00
	b. Chinese sign.	5.50	25.00	55.00
	c. Ovpt: *Kwangtung* at l. and r. of portr.	6.00	25.00	60.00
	d. 4-Chinese character ovpt: *Kwang-Chung-Tsung-Hang* for Kwangchow head office. Chinese sign.	40.00	200.	400.
	e. Ovpt: *Kwangchow* and *Kwangtung*.	20.00	100.	200.
	s. Specimen.	—	Unc	135.
173	**5 Dollars**			
	1923. Brown and m/c. SYS at ctr. Back blue.			
	a. English sign.	7.50	30.00	70.00
	b. Chinese sign.	7.50	30.00	70.00
	c. Ovpt: *HUNAN, KIANGSI & KWANGSI* on back. English sign.	45.00	200.	450.
	d. 4 character Chinese ovpt: *Kwang-Chung-Tsung-Hang* for Kwang-chow head office in circles in corners. English sign.	30.00	150.	300.
	e. Red ovpt: *HUPEH, HUNAN & KIANGSI* on back.	40.00	200.	400.
	f. Lg. oval branch office handstamp: *HUNAN, KIANGSI, & KWANGSI* also w/Chinese characters on face.	—	—	—
	g. Ovpt: *PAKHOI*.	25.00	125.	250.
	h. *PAKHOI*. English sign.	25.00	125.	250.
	s. Specimen.	—	Unc	120.

		Good	Fine	XF
174	**5 Dollars**			
	1923. Red. Similar to #173. Back yellow.			
	a. Chinese and English sign.	37.50	175.	500.
	b. Ovpt: *Kwangtung* above portr. Chinese and English sign.	37.50	175.	500.
	c. Ovpt: *Kwangtung* above portr. English sign.	37.50	175.	500.
	d. 4 character Chinese ovpt: *Kwang-Chung-Tsung-Hang* for Kwanchow head office.	50.00	275.	600.
	s. Specimen.	—	Unc	180.
175	**5 Dollars**			
	1923. Green and m/c. Similar to #174. Back red.			
	a. *Haikow* at l. and r. *KAI KOW* on back. Specimen.	—	Unc	275.
	b. *Kongmoon* at l. and r. *KONG MOON* at l. and r. on back. Specimen.	—	Unc	275.
	c. *Meiluck* at l. and r. *MEI LUCK* at l. and r. on back. Specimen.	—	Unc	275.
	d. *Pakhoi* at l. and r. *PAK HOI* at l. and r. on back. Specimen.	—	Unc	275.
	e. *Suichow* at l. and r. *SUI CHOW* at l. and r. on back. Specimen.	—	Unc	275.
	f. *Swatow* at l. and r. *SWATOW* at l. and r. on back. Specimen.	—	Unc	275.

		Good	Fine	XF
176	**10 Dollars**			
	1923. Brown on m/c unpt. SYS at ctr. Back olive. Printed area is either 157 x 78mm or 152 x 76mm.			
	a. Ovpt: *Kwangtung* in Chinese on face (single black characters at upper l. and r. ctr.), English sign. 152 x	1.00	7.50	15.00
	b. As a. Chinese and English sign. 152 x 76mm.	2.00	10.00	20.00
	c. As a., 157 x 78mm.	1.00	7.50	15.00
	d. As b. 157 x 78mm.	1.00	7.50	15.00
	e. W/o ovpt: *Kwangtung* on face. Chinese sign. 157 x 78mm.	1.00	6.00	12.00
	s. Specimen.	—	Unc	120.
176A	**10 Dollars**			
	1923. Pink and m/c. Similar to #176. Back orange.			
	a. *Haikow* at l. and r. *HAI KOW* on back. Specimen.	—	Unc	375.
	b. *Kongmoon* at l. and r. *KONG MOON* at l. and r. on back. Specimen.	—	Unc	375.
	c. *Meiluck* at l. and r. *MEI LUCK* at l. and r. on back. Specimen.	—	Unc	375.
	d. *Suichow* at l. and r. *SUI CHOW* at l. and r. on back. Specimen.	—	Unc	375.
	e. *Pakhoi* at l. and r. *Pak Hoi* at l. and r. on back. Specimen.	—	Unc	375.
	f. *Swatow* at l. and r. *SWATOW* at l. and r. on back. Specimen.	—	Unc	375.

HUPEH, HUNAN & KIANGSI

		Good	Fine	XF
177	**10 Dollars**			
	1923. Green and m/c. Similar to #176 but w/*10* in large outlined Chinese characters. Back blue.			
	a. Red ovpt: *HUPEH, HUNAN & KIANGSI* and *TEN STANDARD DOLLARS* on back.	45.00	225.	600.
	b. Blue 4 character Chinese ovpt: *Kwang-Chung-Tsung-Hang* for Kwangchow head office in circles.	45.00	225.	600.
	c. Lg. oval branch office handstamp: *HUNAN, KIANGSI, & KWANGSI* also w/Chinese characters on face.	—	—	—
	s. Specimen.	—	Unc	150.
178	**50 Dollars**			
	1923. Orange and m/c. Back dk. blue.			
	a. English sign.	45.00	225.	600.
	b. *SWATOW.* W/circular violet *Central Bank* handstamp on face.	45.00	225.	600.
	c. Ovpt: *The Central Bank of China - SWATOW* on face and back.	75.00	375.	1000.
	s. Specimen.	—	Unc	550.
178A	**50 Dollars**			
	1923. Green and m/c. Back black.			
	a. *Kongmoon* at l. and r. *KONG MOON* at l. and r. on back. Specimen.	—	Unc	450.
	b. *Suichow* at l. and r. *SUI CHOW* at l. and r. on back. Specimen.	—	Unc	450.
	c. *Swatow* at l. and r. *SWA TOW* at l. and r. on back. Specimen.	—	Unc	600.
178B	**50 Dollars**			
	1923. Blue and m/c. Back violet. Specimen.	—	Unc	675.
179	**100 Dollars**			
	1923. Brown. Back blue.			
	a. Issued note.	75.00	375.	1000.
	b. Ovpt: *HUNAN, KIANGSI & KWANGSI* on back.	75.00	375.	1000.
	s. Specimen.	—	Unc	600.
179A	**100 Dollars**			
	1923. Green and m/c. Back red. Specimen.	—	Unc	600.

CENTRAL BANK OF CHINA (QUASI-NATIONAL)

Chung Yan Yin Hang

1923 COMMEMORATIVE ISSUE

#180 and 180A death of Sun Yat Sen.

		VG	VF	UNC
180	**5 Dollars**			
	1923. Brown and m/c. Back blue. Black ovpt. on #173.	125.	400.	1000.
180A	**10 Dollars**			
	1923. Green and m/c. Back blue. Black commemorative ovpt. on #177.	150.	500.	1350.

1926 PROVISIONAL ISSUE

		Good	Fine	XF
181	**1 Dollar**			
	ND (1926). Orange and m/c. Ovpt. on Bank of Kiangsi #S1097.	37.50	125.	300.

180 *Deleted.* See #205B. 181 *Deleted.* See #205C.

1926 ISSUE

#182-184B printer: ABNC.

		Good	Fine	XF
182	**1 Dollar**			
	1926. Blue on m/c unpt. Portr. SYS at l. Back brown.			
	a. *CHUNGKING* and *ONE YUAN LOCAL CURRENCY...* ovpt. on back.	25.00	125.	250.
	b. *FUKIEN.*	12.50	60.00	120.
	c. *HANKOW.*	30.00	150.	300.

		Good	Fine	XF
183	**5 Dollars**			
	1926. Orange on m/c unpt. Portr. SYS at r. Back dk. green.			
	a. *CHUNGKING.* Green ovpt. *FIVE YUAN LOCAL CURRENCY...* on back.	50.00	150.	500.
	b. *FUKIEN.*	20.00	100.	300.
	c. *HANKOW* w/control letters *TH.*	37.50	175.	550.
	d. *HOIKOW.*	37.50	175.	550.
	e. *SHANGHAI.*	37.50	175.	550.
184	**10 Dollars**			
	1926. Red on m/c unpt. Portr. SYS at ctr. Back blue.			
	a. *CHUNGKING. TEN YUAN LOCAL CURRENCY...* ovpt.	25.00	150.	500.
	b. *FUKIEN.*	30.00	125.	350.
	s. Specimen.	—	Unc	180.
184A	**50 Dollars**			
	1926. Black and m/c. Portr. SYS. Back orange.			
	a. *HANKOW.*	37.50	200.	750.
	b. *SHANGHAI.*	37.50	200.	750.
	s. Specimen w/o office of issue.	—	Unc	450.
184B	**100 Dollars**			
	1926.			
	p. Proof.	—	Unc	450.
	s. Specimen.	—	Unc	550.

1926 MILITARY ISSUE

		Good	Fine	XF
185	**1 Dollar**			
	1926. Lilac-brown. Sailing ship at l., steamer at r. Back purple; w/large red handstamp.			
	a. Red serial #.	30.00	150.	350.
	b. Blue serial #.	30.00	150.	350.
	c. Cancelled w/Chinese handstamp.	25.00	125.	275.

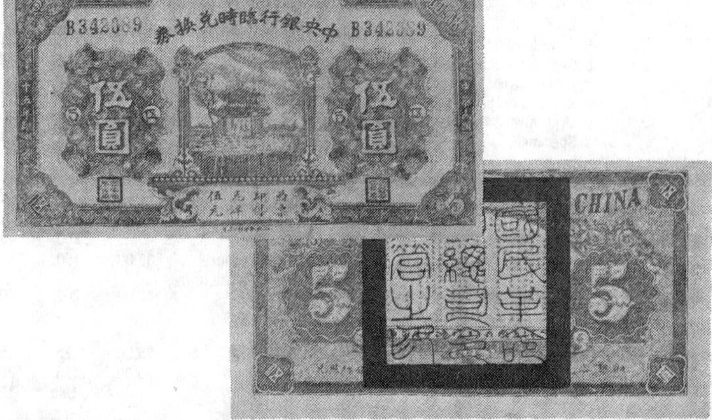

		Good	Fine	XF
186	**5 Dollars**			
	1926. Gray-green. Temple at ctr. Back black; w/lg. red handstamp.			
	a. Issued note.	25.00	125.	400.
	b. Cancelled w/Chinese handstamp.	25.00	125.	400.

		Good	Fine	XF
187	**10 Dollars**			
	1926. Brown. Ship at ctr. Back violet; w/lg. red handstamp.			
	a. Issued note.	30.00	150.	500.
	b. Cancelled w/Chinese handstamp.	30.00	150.	500.

1927 ISSUE

#188 *Deleted.* See #193.

#190 *Deleted.* See #194.

		Good	Fine	XF
189	**1 Chiao = 10 Cents**			
	1927. Green. Temple of Heaven. Printer: CHB.	45.00	175.	550.
191	**2 Chiao = 20 Cents**			
	1927. Red. Temple of Heaven. Printer: CHB.	45.00	175.	550.

		Good	Fine	XF
192	**5 Chiao = 50 Cents**			
	1927. Orange. Temple of Heaven at ctr. Printer: CHB.	30.00	125.	400.

CENTRAL BANK OF CHINA (NATIONAL-CONTINUED)

中央銀行

Chung Yuan Yin Hang.

SIGNATURE/TITLE VARIETIES

1	GENERAL MANAGER	MANAGER
2	ASST. MANAGER	GENERAL MANAGER
3	ASST. MANAGER	GENERAL MANAGER
4	ASST. MANAGER	GENERAL MANAGER
5	ASST. MANAGER	GENERAL MANAGER

SIGNATURE/TITLE VARIETIES

6	ASST. GENERAL MANAGER	GENERAL MANAGER
7	ASST. GENERAL MANAGER	GENERAL MANAGER
8	ASST. GENERAL MANAGER	GENERAL MANAGER
9	ASST. GENERAL MANAGER	GENERAL MANAGER
10	GENERAL MANAGER	GOVERNOR
11	GENERAL MANAGER	GOVERNOR
12	ASST. GENERAL MANAGER	GENERAL MANAGER

1924 ISSUE

#193 and 194 printer: ABNC.

		VG	VF	UNC
193	**1 Chiao = 10 Cents**			
	ND (1924). Black on m/c unpt. Back brown and purple; pagoda at l.			
	a. Sign. 1.	1.00	5.00	15.00
	b. Sign. 5.	1.00	5.00	15.00
	s. As a. Specimen.	—	—	50.00

		VG	VF	UNC
194	**2 Chiao = 20 Cents**			
	ND (1924). Black on m/c unpt. Pagoda at r. Back green and lilac.			
	a. Sign. 1.	2.50	10.00	25.00
	b. Sign. 2.	2.50	10.00	25.00
	c. Sign. 5.	4.00	15.00	40.00
	s. Specimen.	—	—	50.00

NOTICE

Readers with unlisted dates, signature varieties, etc. are invited to submit photocopies or, high resolution (300 dpi, 100% size) scans of their notes to: Standard Catalog of World Paper Money, 700 East State St. Iola, WI 54990-0001, or E-Mail: george.cuhaj@fwpubs.com.

1928 ISSUE

#195-200A printer: ABNC.

#195-196 also/various control ovpt: symbols, numerals and Chinese characters.

		VG	VF	UNC
195	**1 Dollar**			
	1928. Green. Back brown; portr. SYS at l. Serial # on face and back. *SHANGHAI.*			
	a. Sign. 2.	10.00	50.00	—
	b. Sign. 3.	10.00	50.00	—
	c. Sign. 5.	.50	2.00	10.00
196	**5 Dollars**			
	1928. Olive and m/c. Back red; portr. SYS at r. Serial # on face and back. Black sign. *SHANGHAI.*			
	a. Sign. 2.	20.00	75.00	300.
	b. Sign. 3.	20.00	75.00	300.
	c. Sign. 5.	20.00	75.00	300.
	d. Sign. 8.	20.00	75.00	300.

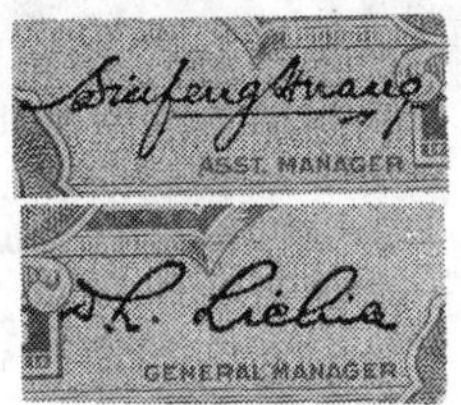

Small black sign.

Large black sign.

		VG	VF	UNC
197	**10 Dollars**			
	1928. Dk. blue and m/c. Back green; portr. SYS at ctr. *SHANGHAI.*			
	a. Sign. 2.	1.75	6.00	20.00
	b. Sign. 3.	1.25	4.50	15.00
	c. Sign. 4.	1.75	6.00	20.00
	d. Sign. 5a. Small black sign.	.40	1.00	3.50
	e. Sign. 5b. Large black sign.	.75	1.25	4.50
	f. Sign. 7 in black. Serial # on face and back.	.75	1.75	6.00
	g. As f. Serial # on face only.	.40	1.00	3.50
	h. Sign. 7 in green as part of plate.	.40	.75	2.50
198	**50 Dollars**			
	1928. Orange and m/c. Back blue-gray; portr. SYS at ctr. *SHANGHAI.*			
	a. Sign. 5.	.75	3.00	9.00
	b. Sign. 5. Ovpt: *CHUNGKING/SHANGHAI.*	1.50	5.00	15.00
	c. Sign. 6.	2.50	7.50	30.00
	d. Sign. 7 in blue.	2.25	10.00	37.50
	e. Sign. 7 in black. Serial # on face and back.	1.25	4.50	17.50
	f. As e. Serial # on face only.	1.50	6.00	25.00
	g. As e. Sign. thinner, as part of plate.	1.25	6.00	17.50

Note: #198a-g, 199a-g w/various control ovpt. are considered spurious.

		VG	VF	UN
199	**100 Dollars**			
	1928. Olive and m/c. Back purple; portr. SYS at ctr. *SHANGHAI.*			
	a. Sign. 5. Serial # on face and back.	1.50	6.00	22.5
	b. As a. Serial # on face only.	1.50	6.00	22.5
	c. As a. Ovpt: *CHUNGKING/SHANGHAI.*	1.50	6.00	22.5
	d. Sign. 6.	1.50	5.00	17.5
	e. Sign. 7. Black.	1.50	6.00	22.5
	f. Sign. 7. Purple as part of plate.	1.50	5.00	17.5

Note: #198a-g, 199a-g w/various control ovpt. are considered spurious.

1930 ISSUE

		VG	VF	UN
200	**5 Dollars**			
	1930. Dk. green and m/c. SYS at ctr. Back green; temple at ctr. *SHANGHAI.* Also w/various control ovpt. Printer: ABNC.			
	a. Sign. 2.	2.50	7.50	25.
	b. Sign. 3.	1.75	6.00	20.
	c. Sign. 4.	2.50	7.50	25.
	d. Sign. 5.	1.00	2.50	6.
	e. Sign. 7 in black. Serial # on face and back.	1.00	2.50	6.
	f. Sign. 7 in green as part of plate. Serial # on back only.	.75	1.75	5.
	s1. Specimen	—	—	1
	s2. As b, 2 part specimen	—	—	90.
	s3. As f, specimen	—	—	1

201 Deleted. See #205A.

1931 ISSUE

#201 *Deleted.* See #205A.

#202-205A printer: CHB.

		VG	VF	U
202	**10 Cents = 1 Chiao**			
	ND (1931). Green. Temple behind trees at l. Back blue and green.	.15	.40	1

		VG	VF	UNC
203	**20 Cents = 2 Chiao** ND (1931). Blue. Chu-Shui-Bridge at r. Back aqua, brown and purple.	.25	.75	2.50

		VG	VF	UNC
204	**25 Cents** ND (1931). Lilac. P'ai-lou (commemorative archway) at l. Back blue.	2.50	12.50	35.00

		VG	VF	UNC
205	**50 Cents** ND (1931). Purple. Temple of Confucius at l. Back brown and blue. Paper and 3 serial # varieties.	3.00	15.00	40.00

1934 Provisional Issue

		VG	VF	UNC
205A	**1 Dollar** ND (-old date 1934). Ovpt. on #A112.			
	a. *SHANGHAI.*	30.00	100.	275.
	b. *TIENTSIN.*	30.00	100.	275.
	c. *PEIPING.*	30.00	100.	275.
	d. W/o place name.	17.50	60.00	175.

1935 Regular Issue

#205B-205C portr. SYS at upper ctr. on back. *SZECHUEN.*

		VG	VF	UNC
205B	**10 Cents** ND (1935). Dk. blue. Back violet.	35.00	150.	425.
205C	**20 Cents** ND (1935). Brown. Back green.	40.00	175.	500.

#206-208 *CHUNGKING.*

		VG	VF	UNC
206	**1 Yüan** 1935. Orange on yellow and lt. blue unpt. Ships at ctr. Back green. Printer: CHB.	65.00	300.	650.
207	**5 Yüan** 1935. Red on pink unpt. M/c guilloche at ctr. Portr. SYS at l. Back dk. blue. Printer: BEPP.	50.00	250.	550.

		VG	VF	UNC
208	**10 Yüan** 1935. Green on lt. green and brown unpt. Portr. SYS at l. Back purple. Printer: BEPP.	40.00	175.	425.

1936 "CHB" Issues

#209-211 printer: CHB.

		VG	VF	UNC
209	**1 Yüan** 1936. Orange on m/c unpt. Wan Ku Chang Ch'un monument at r. Back brown. 2 sign. varieties.	25.00	125.	275.

		VG	VF	UNC
210	**1 Yüan** 1936. Orange and black. Similar to #209 but monument in black at r. Back dk. brown. 135 x 65mm. Sign. 5.	3.00	12.50	30.00
211	**1 Yüan** 1936. Orange on m/c unpt. Vessel at l., SYS at r. Back dk. brown. Confucius meeting Lao Tzu; men w/2 horse-drawn carts.			
	a. Sign. 10.	.25	1.25	4.50
	b. Sign. 11.	.50	4.00	12.50

1936 "TDLR" Issues

#212-214 printer (except #212A): TDLR.

#215 *Deleted.*

		VG	VF	UNC
212	**1 Yüan**			
	1936. Orange and black on m/c unpt. SYS at l. and as wmk. Back brown; gateway and temple behind trees at ctr.			
	a. Sign. 5.	.25	.75	3.00
	b. Sign. 8.	.50	1.75	6.00
	c. Sign. 9.	.25	.75	3.00

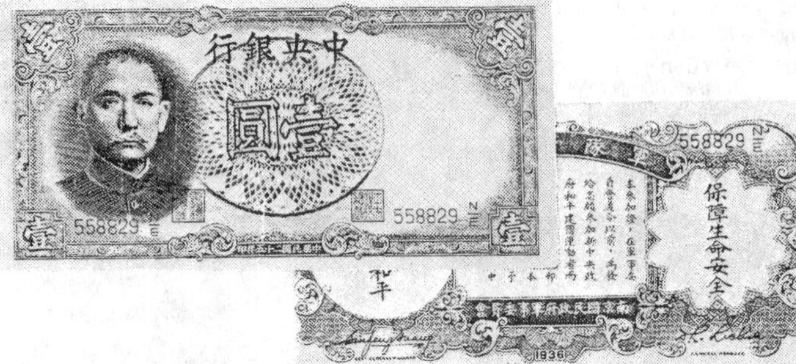

		VG	VF	UNC
212A	**1 Yüan**			
	ND (-old date 1936). Lithograph face like #213. Chinese text on back. (pass for Nanking Military Government).	150.	250.	—

		VG	VF	UNC
213	**5 Yüan**			
	1936. Dk. green and black on m/c unpt. SYS at l. and as wmk. Back olive-green; gateway and temple behind trees at ctr.			
	a. Sign. 5.	.10	.75	1.50
	b. Sign. 8.	.40	2.00	6.00
	c. Sign. 9.	.20	.75	3.00

		VG	VF	UNC
214	**10 Yüan**			
	1936. Dk. blue and black on m/c unpt. SYS at l. and as wmk. Back dk. green, gateway and temple behind trees at ctr.			
	a. Sign. 5.	.15	.75	3.00
	b. Sign. 8.	.50	2.75	8.00
	c. Sign. 9.	.25	1.25	4.50

1936 "W&S" Issue

#216-221 printer: W&S.

		VG	VF	UNC
216	**1 Yüan**			
	1936. Orange. SYS at l. Back brown; temple (Palace of China in Peking). 2 serial # varieties.			
	a. Sign. 5.	.10	.75	3.00
	b. Sign. 7.	.15	1.25	4.50
	c. Sign. 8.	.15	1.25	4.50
	d. Sign. 9.	.15	1.25	4.50
	e. Ovpt: Tibetan characters on face and back. Sign. 5; 7-9.	75.00	—	—
	s1. Specimen (2 part).	—	—	110.
	s2. Specimen - 2 part, as a.	—	—	110.

Note: The Tibetan ovpt. occurs on #216e, 217d, 218f, 219c and 220c, although the authenticity of the last two ovpt. is questionable. There are also many examples of the 1 to 10 year notes, 216e, 217d and 218f when the overprints have been later additions. Great care must be excercised to establish authenticity.

		VG	VF	UNC
217	**5 Yüan**			
	1936. Green on m/c unpt. SYS at l. Back green; Palace of China in Peking. 2 serial # varieties.			
	a. Sign. 5.	.10	.75	3.00
	b. Sign. 8.	.25	2.00	6.00
	c. Sign. 9.	.15	.75	3.00
	d. Ovpt: Tibetan characters on face and back. Sign. 5.	30.00	75.00	—

		VG	VF	UNC
218	**10 Yüan**			
	1936. Dk. blue and black on m/c unpt. SYS at l. and as wmk. Back blue-green; Palace of China in Peking at r.			
	a. Sign. 5.	.10	.45	1.50
	b. Sign. 6.	.10	.45	1.50
	c. Sign. 7.	.25	2.00	6.00
	d. Sign. 8 (heavier or lighter print).	.10	.45	1.50
	e. Sign. 9.	.25	2.00	4.50
	f. Ovpt: Tibetan characters on face and back. Sign. 5; 7.	20.00	50.00	—
219	**50 Yüan**			
	1936. Dk. blue and brown on m/c unpt. SYS at l. and as wmk. Back red; Palace of China in Peking at ctr.			
	a. Issued note. Sign. 11 in red.	.50	2.50	6.00
	b. Ovpt: *Chungking* in Chinese at l. and r. and in English at upper ctr. on back. Sign. 10 in black.	25.00	—	—
	c. Ovpt: Tibetan characters on face and back.	—	—	—

Note: #219 b-c are controversial.

Large sign.

Small sign.

20	100 Yüan	VG	VF	UNC
	1936. Olive-green and dk. brown on m/c unpt. SYS at l. and as wmk. Back purple; Palace of China in Peking at ctr.			
	a. Issued note. Sign. 11 in purple.	1.00	5.00	30.00
	b. Ovpt: *Chungking* in Chinese at l. and r. and in English at upper ctr. on back. Sign. 10 in black.	25.00	—	—
	c. Ovpt: Tibetan characters on face and back. Sign. 11 in black.	60.00	—	—

21	500 Yüan	VG	VF	UNC
	1936. Red-brown. SYS at l. Back blue; Palace of China in Peking at ctr.			
	a. Issued note. Sign. 11.	30.00	150.	350.
	s. Specimen.	—	—	150.

937 ISSUE

22 and 223 printer: CHB.

22	5 Yüan	VG	VF	UNC
	1937. Green on m/c unpt. Antique bronze tripod at l., portr. SYS at r. Back dk. olive-green; like #211.	8.00	35.00	80.00
23	10 Yüan			
	1937. Blue and green. SYS at l., vessel at r. Back blue-green; like #211.			
	a. Issued note.	15.00	75.00	160.
	b. W/o sign.	10.00	40.00	90.00

939 ISSUES

24	1 Fen = 1 Cent	VG	VF	UNC
	1939. Red. Pagoda at l. Coin at r. on back.			
	a. Printer: Union Publishers & Printers.	.10	.50	1.50
	b. Printer: Union Printing Co.	.75	3.50	8.00

225	5 Fen = 5 Cents	VG	VF	UNC
	1939. Green. Pagoda at l. Coin at ctr. on back.			
	a. Printer: Union Publishers & Printers.	.20	.75	2.00
	b. Printer: Union Printing Co.	1.00	3.50	15.00

225A	5 Fen = 5 Cents	VG	VF	UNC
	1939. Green. Face like #225 but back w/date 1936 and Chinese text (pass for the Nanking Military Government).	—	125.	250.

1940 ISSUE

#226-229 printer: CHB.

226	1 Chiao = 10 Cents	VG	VF	UNC
	1940. Green. Portr. SYS at r.	.15	.40	1.50
227	2 Chiao = 20 Cents			
	1940. Blue. Portr. SYS at r. Like #226.			
	a. Issued note.	.15	.40	1.50
	r. Remainder w/o sign.	—	—	—
228	10 Yüan			
	1940. Blue-gray. Portr. SYS at r. Back gray-green.	.30	.75	3.00

229	50 Yüan	VG	VF	UNC
	1940. Orange. Portr. SYS at r. Back blue. *CHUNG-KING.*			
	a. Sign. 5.	5.00	12.50	50.00
	b. Sign. 8.	4.00	10.00	40.00

1941 ISSUES

230	2 Yüan	VG	VF	UNC
	1941. Purple on lt. orange and blue unpt. SYS at r. Back blue. Printer: CHB.	.75	3.00	8.00

231	2 Yüan	VG	VF	UNC
	1941. Blue and m/c. SYS at l. Back blue; temple behind trees at ctr. 3 serial # varieties. Printer: TDLR.	1.50	5.00	15.00

232	2 Yüan	VG	VF	UNC
	1941. Blue and m/c. SYS at l. Back blue; pagoda near mountain slope (Wang He Lou). Printer: TDLR.	8.00	25.00	75.00
233	5 Yüan			
	1941. Green. SYS at l. Back olive. Similar to #237. Printer: W&S.	5.50	15.00	50.00

		VG	VF	UNC
234	**5 Yüan**			
	1941. Green on m/c unpt. Portr. SYS at lower r. Back green. 2 serial # varieties. Printer: CHB.			
	a. Issued note.	.75	2.00	9.00
	b. Ovpt: *Chungking* in Chinese at l. and r. on face. *CHUNGKING* in English on back.	3.00	10.00	37.50

		VG	VF	UNC
235	**5 Yüan**			
	1941. Lilac-brown. SYS at l. Back lilac-brown; pagoda near mountain slope (Wang He Lou). 2 serial # varieties. Printer: TDLR.	.25	1.00	4.00

		VG	VF	UNC
236	**5 Yüan**			
	1941. Dk. brown. SYS at l. Back dk. brown; temple behind trees at ctr. 3 serial # varieties. Printer: TDLR.	1.00	3.00	10.00
237	**10 Yüan**			
	1941. Dk. blue. SYS at l. Back green-blue. Printer: W&S.			
	a. Sign. 5.	1.25	4.50	12.50
	b. Sign. 6.	.40	1.50	6.00
	c. Sign. 7.	.40	1.50	6.00
	d. Sign. 8.	1.00	4.50	12.50
	e. Sign. 9.	.40	1.50	6.00

		VG	VF	UNC
238	**10 Yüan**			
	1941. Blue. P'ai-Lou Gate at l. Back dk. green. 2 serial # varieties. Chinese printer.			
	a. Sign. 7.	3.50	10.00	35.00
	b. Sign. 9.	2.50	10.00	25.00

#239-240 printer: SBNC.

		VG	VF	UNC
239	**10 Yüan**			
	1941. Blue. SYS at l. Back green.			
	a. Sign. 7 in black.	.40	2.50	6.00
	b. Sign. 12 in green as part of plate.	2.25	10.00	25.00
	s. 2 part specimen.	—	Unc	25.00

		VG	VF	UN
240	**20 Yüan**			
	1941. Red and m/c. Portr. SYS at l. Back brown.			
	a. Sign. 7 in black. Blue serial # and sign. seals.	1.00	5.00	20.
	b. As a but w/red serial # and sign. seals.	.75	4.00	15.
	c. Sign. 12 in brown as part of plate.	.50	2.00	10.
	s. 2 part specimen.	—	Unc	80.

#241 Deleted.

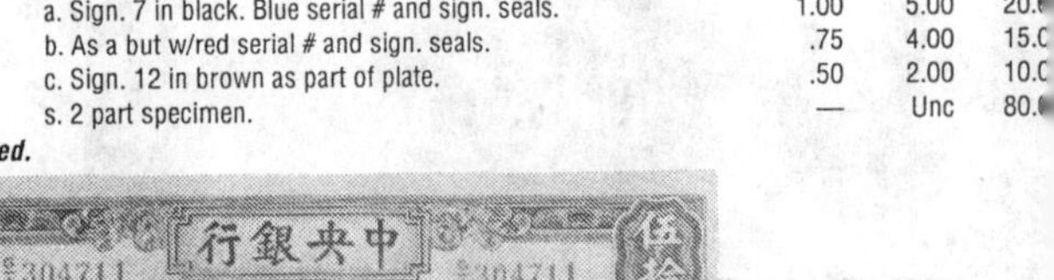

		VG	VF	UN
242	**50 Yüan**			
	1941. Green. P'ai-Lou Gate at r. Back brown. 2 serial # varieties.			
	a. Chinese printer 8 characters.	7.50	17.50	60.
	b. Chinese printer 7 characters.	17.50	40.00	12
	c. Chinese printer 6 characters.	17.50	40.00	12

		VG	VF	UN
243	**100 Yüan**			
	1941. Greenish gray on m/c unpt. Portr. SYS at l. Back purple. Printer: SBNC.			
	a. Issued note.	.10	.50	2.
	b. W/o serial #.	3.00	10.00	25.
	s. 2 part specimen.			80.

1942 ISSUES

#244 and 245 printer: TDLR.

		VG	VF	UN
244	**5 Yüan**			
	1942. Green. SYS at l. Airplane on back.			
	a. Sign. 6.	1.50	6.00	22
	b. Sign. 7.	1.50	6.00	22
	s. 2 part specimen.			

		VG	VF	UNC
245	**10 Yüan** 1942. Blue. Portr. SYS at l. Military trumpeter near Great Wall on back.			
	a. Sign. 5.	1.50	5.00	17.50
	b. Sign. 6.	.75	2.25	8.00
	c. Sign. 7.	.75	3.00	10.00
	d. Ovpt: *Chungking*. Sign. 7.	15.00	50.00	150.
246	**10 Yüan** 1942. Blue. SYS at l. Back w/o vignette. Printer: Dah Tung Book Company.	3.00	8.00	30.00

		VG	VF	UNC
247	**10 Yüan** 1942. Brown. P'ai-lou Gate at r. Back yellow-brown. 2 serial # and 2 paper varieties. Chinese printer.	7.50	30.00	70.00
248	**20 Yüan** 1942. Brown. P'ai-lou Gate at r. Back red. Chinese printer.	7.50	35.00	80.00

		VG	VF	UNC
249	**100 Yüan** 1942. Red. Victory Gate at ctr. Back blue.			
	a. Chinese printer 8 characters. Sign. 7.	4.50	12.50	50.00
	b. As a. Sign. 9.	3.00	7.50	25.00
	c. Chinese printer 7 characters. Sign. 7.	4.50	15.00	60.00
250	**100 Yüan** 1942. Red. SYS at r. Back green. Chinese printer.	7.50	35.00	80.00

#251-253 printer: TDLR.

		VG	VF	UNC
251	**500 Yüan** 1942. Red on gold unpt. SYS at l. Back red; ship at ctr.	.50	2.00	8.00
252	**1000 Yüan** 1942. Lilac on lt. green unpt. SYS at l. Great Wall at ctr. on back.	.50	2.00	8.00

		VG	VF	UNC
253	**2000 Yüan** 1942. Red on lt. green unpt. SYS at l. Back red; pagoda at shoreline.	.75	2.50	6.00

1943 Issue

		VG	VF	UNC
254	**100 Yüan** 1943. Green-black. Victory Gate at l. Chinese printer.	5.00	30.00	65.00

1944 Issues

#255-256 printer: TDLR.

		VG	VF	UNC
255	**50 Yüan** 1944. Deep purple on m/c unpt. SYS at l. and as wmk.	1.00	4.00	12.50
256	**100 Yüan** 1944. Dk. brown on m/c unpt. SYS at l. and as wmk.	.75	3.00	10.00

		VG	VF	UNC
257	**100 Yüan** 1944. Green on red unpt. SYS at l. Back brown; SYS memorial at r. Printer: W&S.	75.00	350.	800.

		VG	VF	UNC
258	**100 Yüan** 1944. Gray on lt. blue and pale orange unpt. P'ai-lou gateway at ctr. 150 x 64mm. Chinese printer.	7.50	30.00	75.00
259	**100 Yüan** 1944. Blue. P'ai-lou gateway at l. 151 x 77mm. Chinese printer.	7.50	30.00	75.00
260	**100 Yüan** 1944. Black on lt. gray and pale violet unpt. P'ai-lou gateway at l. 165 x 65mm. Chinese printer.	7.50	30.00	75.00
260A	**100 Yüan** 1944. Dk. gray on pale green unpt. Portr. SYS at r. Chinese printer 6 characters.	2.50	12.50	25.00

		VG	VF	UNC
261	**100 Yüan** 1944. Dk. brown. P'ai-lou gateway at ctr. 165 x 63mm. Chinese printer 8 characters.	5.00	20.00	55.00
262	**200 Yüan** 1944. Dk. green. Portr. SYS at lower l. Back brown. Chinese printer 6 characters.	5.00	25.00	60.00

263 **400 Yüan** — VG 10.00, VF 50.00, UNC 125.
1944. Green. Portr. SYS at lower l. Back brown. Chinese printer 6 characters.

264 **500 Yüan** — VG .75, VF 2.50, UNC 15.00
1944. Red. SYS at l. and as wmk. Printer: TDLR.

265 **500 Yüan** — VG 3.00, VF 12.50, UNC 30.00
1944. Red-brown. on pale orange and lt. yellow-green unpt. SYS at l. and as wmk. Printer: W&S.

266 **500 Yüan** — VG 10.00, VF 40.00, UNC 90.00
1944. Black on yellow-green and tan unpt. P'ai-lou gateway at l., portr. SYS at r. 179 x 76mm. Chinese printer 8 characters.

267 **500 Yüan** — VG 1.50, VF 7.50, UNC 15.00
1944. Dk. brown on pale orange and lt. olive-green unpt. Portr. SYS at l. Back blue. 2 serial # varieties. Printer: BABNC.

268 **1000 Yüan**
1944. Dp. brown on purple and m/c unpt. Portr. SYS at l. P'ai-lou gateway at r. Back blackish brown. Chinese printer 8 characters.

	VG	VF	UNC
a. Issued note.	2.00	10.00	20.00
b. W/2 red Chinese handstamps: "Army Command Northeast" and *Tung Pei* on face.	30.00	150.	300.

269 **1000 Yüan** — VG 12.00, VF 35.00, UNC 80.00
1944. Blue-gray. Portr. SYS at lower r. Chinese printer 6 characters.

Note: Also see special issues for Manchuria #375-379.

1945 ISSUES

269A **5 Yüan** — VG —, VF —, UNC —
1945. Green on red unpt. Portr. SYS at lower l. Back green. Vietnam. *(S/M #C300-)*.

269B **5 Yüan** — VG —, VF —, UNC —
1945. Blue. SYS at l. Back green. Taiwan. *(S/M #C300-219)*.

270 **10 Yüan** — VG .50, VF 2.50, UNC 6.0
1945. Green on pale green unpt. Portr. SYS at lower l. Chinese printer.

271 **10 Yüan** — VG —, VF —, UNC —
1945. Orange. SYS at l. Naval battle on back. Taiwan. (Not issued).

272 **10 Yüan** — VG —, VF —
1945. Burgundy. Portr. SYS at lower l. Vietnam.

273 **50 Yüan** — VG .50, VF 2.50, UNC 6.0
1945. Red on pale red unpt. Portr. SYS at l. Chinese printer.

Note: #273 w/5 character ovpt. for Vietnam is believed to be a modern fabrication.

274 **50 Yüan** — VG 40.00, VF 200., UNC 45
1945. Olive. SYS at l. Printer: CPF. Sinkiang.

275 **50 Yüan** — VG —, VF —, UNC —
1945. Red. SYS at l. Back blue; mirror printing of naval battle. Taiwan. (Not issued).

276 **50 Yüan** — VG —, VF —
1945. Blue. Portr. SYS at lower l. Vietnam. Rare

277 **50 Yüan** — VG 20.00, VF 100., UNC 2
1945. Green. Victory Gate.

		VG	VF	UNC
277A	**100 Yüan** 1945. Blue-gray. Portr. SYS at lower l. Sinkiang. Printer: CPF.	75.00	350.	750.
277B	**100 Yüan** 1945. Taiwan.	—	—	—

		VG	VF	UNC
278	**100 Yüan** 1945. Blue on pale blue unpt. Portr. SYS at lower l. Chinese printer.	1.75	7.50	18.00
279	**200 Yüan** 1945. Gray-blue. SYS at l. Chinese printer.	4.00	17.50	40.00

		VG	VF	UNC
280	**400 Yüan** 1945. Lilac. Portr. SYS at lower l. Chinese printer.	5.00	17.50	100.
281	**400 Yüan** 1945. Dk. blue-black on lt. blue-green and pink unpt. SYS at l. in unpt. Back: blue.	20.00	100.	220.

		VG	VF	UNC
282	**500 Yüan** 1945. Blackish green on lt. blue unpt. Portr. SYS at lower l. Chinese printer 8 characters.	2.50	7.50	25.00

		VG	VF	UNC
283	**500 Yüan** 1945. Black w/lt. blue national sunbursts in unpt. at l. and r. Portr. SYS at ctr. Back lt. olive-green. Chinese printer 8 characters.			
	a. Issued note.	1.00	2.50	10.00
	b. 2 Chinese handstamps: "Army Command Northeast" and *Tung Pei* on face.	12.50	75.00	150.
284	**500 Yüan** 1945. Green. SYS at l. Chinese printer 5 characters.	2.00	7.50	22.50

		VG	VF	UNC
285	**500 Yüan** 1945. Brown on lilac unpt. P'ai-lou Gate at r. Chinese printer 7 characters.	10.00	50.00	110.
286	**500 Yüan** 1945. Red. Chinese printer 8 characters.	10.00	50.00	120.

		VG	VF	UNC
287	**1000 Yüan** 1945. Red-orange on lilac unpt. Portr. SYS at lower l. Chinese printer 8 characters.	3.50	15.00	35.00

		VG	VF	UNC
288	**1000 Yüan** 1945. Brown-violet on pink unpt. Portr. SYS at lower l. Chinese printer 8 characters.	2.50	12.50	30.00

No.	Denomination / Description	VG	VF	UNC
289	**1000 Yüan** 1945. Brown. Portr. SYS at ctr. Chinese printer 8 characters.	1.00	4.00	12.00
290	**1000 Yüan** 1945. Purple. SYS at ctr. National sunburst at l. and r. on back. Printer: SBNC.	.40	1.75	4.00
291	**1000 Yüan** 1945. Black. SYS at r. Gray paper. Chinese printer 7 characters.	2.50	10.00	25.00

291A Deleted. See #290. 291B Deleted. See #294.

No.	Denomination / Description	VG	VF	UNC
292	**1000 Yüan** 1945. Brown on lilac unpt. SYS at l. Chinese printer 5 characters.	2.50	10.00	25.00
293	**1000 Yüan** 1945. Blue-gray on pale blue and lilac unpt. SYS at l. Chinese printer 5 characters.	2.50	10.00	25.00
294	**1000 Yüan** 1945. Brown on red-brown unpt. SYS at l. Chinese printer 10 characters.	1.50	7.50	15.00
295	**1000 Yüan** 1945. Dk. blue on pale blue and lilac unpt. Chinese printer 5 characters.	2.50	12.50	25.00
296	**1000 Yüan** 1945. Red on pink unpt. P'ai-lou Gate at ctr. Back blue. Chinese printer 7 characters.	10.00	50.00	100.
297	**1000 Yüan** 1945. Green. SYS at l. Back dk. blue. Chinese printer 6 characters.	3.50	15.00	35.00

No.	Denomination / Description	VG	VF	UNC
298	**1000 Yüan** 1945. Blue. Portr. SYS at lower l. Chinese sign. in thick or thin characters. Chinese printer 6 characters. White to gray paper.	2.50	12.50	25.00

No.	Denomination / Description	VG	VF	UNC
299	**2000 Yüan** 1945. Green. Great Wall at r. Back brown. Chinese printer 7 characters.	20.00	100.	220.
300	**2000 Yüan** 1945. Brown-violet. SYS at r. Chinese printer 5 characters.	2.50	10.00	25.00
301	**2000 Yüan** 1945. Violet. SYS at l. Chinese printer 5 character.			
	a. Issued note.	2.00	10.00	30.00
	b. W/2 Chinese handstamps: "Army Command Northeast" and *Tung Pei* on face.	25.00	100.	250.
302	**2000 Yüan** 1945. Green. SYS at l. Back: black. Chinese printer 6 characters.	7.50	35.00	80.00

No.	Denomination / Description	VG	VF	UNC
303	**2500 Yüan** 1945. Blue-lt. blue. Portr. SYS at l. Back dk. olive-green. 3 serial # varieties. Chinese printer 7 characters.	5.00	30.00	65.00
304	**2500 Yüan** 1945. Blue on green unpt. SYS at l. Back blue. Chinese printer 6 characters.	12.50	60.00	140.

No.	Denomination / Description	VG	VF	UNC
305	**5000 Yüan** 1945. Blue-black on m/c unpt. Portr. SYS at l. P'ai-lou Gate at r. Chinese printer 5 characters.	2.50	10.00	35.00
306	**5000 Yüan** 1945. Brown. SYS at l. 2 Chinese sign. varieties. 2 serial # varieties. Chinese printer 6 characters.	2.00	8.00	30.00

1946 Issue

No.	Denomination / Description	VG	VF	UNC
307	**2000 Yüan** 1946. Purple on gold unpt. SYS at l. Back dull red; SYS Mausoleum at ctr. r. Printer: W&S.	2.00	6.00	20.00

1947 Issues

No.	Denomination / Description	VG	VF	UNC
308	**2000 Yüan** 1947. Green on pale green and pink unpt. Portr. SYS at lower l. P'ai-lou Gate at r. Back black. Chinese printer 8 characters.	5.00	30.00	60.00
309	**5000 Yüan** 1947. Dk. blue on lt. green unpt. SYS at l. Back green. Chinese printer 8 characters.	1.50	6.50	20.00
310	**5000 Yüan** 1947. Purple. SYS at l. Printer: TDLR.	1.25	5.00	15.00
311	**5000 Yüan** 1947. Dk. lilac on gold unpt. SYS at l. Back lilac; SYS Mausoleum at ctr.	1.50	7.50	17.50

No.	Denomination / Description	VG	VF	UNC
312	**5000 Yüan** 1947. Blue on green unpt. Portr. SYS at lower l. Like #309. Back green. Chinese printer 5 characters.	1.50	7.50	15.00
313	**5000 Yüan** 1947. Green on lt. violet unpt. SYS at ctr. Back green. Chinese printer 6 characters.	1.50	7.50	15.00
314	**10,000 Yüan** 1947. Brown. SYS at l., mountains and river at r. Back blue. Chinese printer 8 characters.	.75	5.00	10.00

No.	Denomination / Description	VG	VF	UNC
315	**10,000 Yüan** 1947. Olive on m/c unpt. Portr. SYS at l., mountains and river at r. Back olive-green. 159 x 75mm. Chinese printer 8 characters.	7.50	40.00	90.00

#316 *Deleted.* See #320c.

		VG	VF	UNC
317	**10,000 Yüan** 1947. Red on pale blue and lt. green unpt. Portr. SYS at ctr. Back dull red. Printer: TDLR.	1.50	4.00	12.50
318	**10,000 Yüan** 1947. Gray-blue. SYS at l. 164 x 74mm. Chinese printer 8 characters.	1.50	6.00	20.00
319	**10,000 Yüan** 1947. Red-brown. SYS at ctr. Back gray-black. Printer: SBNC.	.75	2.50	7.50
	s. 2 part specimen.	—	—	70.00

		VG	VF	UNC
320	**10,000 Yüan** 1947. Blue-violet. Portr. SYS at lower l. Back blue-violet.			
	a. Chinese printer 5 characters. 2 paper and serial # varieties.	1.25	5.00	17.50
	b. Chinese printer 6 characters.	1.25	5.00	17.50
	c. Chinese printer 8 characters.	1.25	5.00	17.50
321	**10,000 Yüan** 1947. Dk. brown on m/c unpt. SYS at l. Back dk. lilac. Chinese printer 6 characters.	5.00	25.00	50.00

		VG	VF	UNC
322	**10,000 Yüan** 1947. Lilac. Portr. SYS at lower l. Back brown. 162 x 74mm. Chinese printer 8 characters.	5.00	25.00	50.00
322A	**50,000 Yüan** 1947. Brown on green unpt. SYS at r. Small house at ctr. on back. Printer: HBNC. (Not issued).	—	—	—

1930 Shanghai Customs Gold Units Issues

#323-374 portr. SYS at top ctr. Bank bldg. at l. ctr. on back. Vertical format except for #333 and #334 which are horizontal.

Note: This issue was primarily intended to facilitate customs payments, but during and after World War II the notes were used for general circulation. The 1930 issue was printed into the 1940s.

#323-331 w/m/c guilloche. Sign. varieties. Printer: ABNC.

		VG	VF	UNC
323	**10 Cents** 1930. Purple.			
	a. Sign. 4.	5.00	30.00	60.00
	b. Sign. 5.	2.50	7.50	25.00

		VG	VF	UNC
324	**20 Cents** 1930. Green.			
	a. Sign. 4.	5.00	25.00	50.00
	b. Sign. 5.	3.00	15.00	30.00
325	**1 Customs Gold Unit** 1930. Brown.			
	a. Sign. 4.	4.50	17.50	75.00
	b. Sign. 5.	638.	12.50	35.00
	c. Sign. 7 in black. Sign. title: *ASSISTANT MANAGER* at r. Serial # on face and back.	4.50	17.50	75.00
	d. Sign. 7 in brown as part of plate. Sign. title: *ASST. GENERAL MANAGER* at r. Serial # on back only.	.60	3.00	12.50
326	**5 Customs Gold Units** 1930. Black.			
	a. Sign. 4.	3.50	15.00	60.00
	b. Sign. 5.	3.00	9.00	35.00
	c. Sign. 7. Sign title: *ASSISTANT MANAGER* at r. Serial # on face and on back.	3.00	9.00	35.00
	d. Sign. 7 in plate. Sign. title: *ASST. GENERAL MANAGER* at r. Serial # on back only.	.30	1.00	2.50
327	**10 Customs Gold Units** 1930. Olive-gray.			
	a. Sign. 4.	4.50	17.50	75.00
	b. Sign. 5.	2.00	7.50	17.50
	c. Sign. 7 in black. Sign. title: *ASSISTANTT. MANAGER* at r. Serial # on face and on back.	2.00	7.50	17.50
	d. Sign. 7 in plate. Sign. title: *ASST. GENERAL MANAGER* at r. Serial # on back only.	.35	1.50	4.00
	s. Specimen as c.	—	—	150.

		VG	VF	UNC
328	**20 Customs Gold Units** 1930. Dk. green.	.35	1.50	4.00
329	**50 Customs Gold Units** 1930. Purple.	.35	1.50	4.00

		VG	VF	UNC
330	**100 Customs Gold Units** 1930. Red.			
	a. Issued note.	.50	2.50	6.00
	b. W/2 red Chinese handstamps: "Army Command Northeast" and *Tung Pei*.	—	—	—
331	**250 Customs Gold Units** 1930. Brown.	1.25	5.00	25.00

1930 (1947) Customs Gold Units Issues

		VG	VF	UNC
332	**500 Customs Gold Units** 1930 (1947). Blue. Printer: ABNC.	.75	4.00	10.00

Note: #332, though dated 1930, was issued after WW II.

1947 Customs Gold Units Issue

#333-334 horizontal format; m/c guilloche.

		VG	VF	UNC
333	**100 Customs Gold Units** 1947. Violet. Back blue. Specimen.	—	—	250.

		VG	VF	UNC
334	**500 Customs Gold Units** 1947. Blue on m/c unpt. Back brown. Horizontal format.	4.00	15.00	30.00

335

336

		VG	VF	UNC
335	**500 Customs Gold Units** 1947. Blue. *SHANGHAI*. Printer: ABNC.	.75	3.50	10.00
336	**500 Customs Gold Units** 1947. Lt. green. Printer: SBNC.	.75	4.00	10.00

#337 *Deleted*. See #339c.

338

339

		VG	VF	UNC
338	**1000 Customs Gold Units** 1947. Olive. Olive guilloche. Printer: CHB.	.50	3.50	7.00
339	**1000 Customs Gold Units** 1947. Gray. Brown and lilac guilloche.			
	a. Chinese printer 8 characters. Serial # 2mm tall.	.50	3.50	7.00
	b. Chinese printer 6 characters. Serial # 3mm tall.	.50	3.50	7.00
	c. Chinese printer 5 characters. 2 serial # varieties.	.75	3.00	9.00

		VG	VF	UNC
340	**2000 Customs Gold Units** 1947. Orange. Printer: ABNC.	.75	4.00	10.00
341	**2000 Customs Gold Units** 1947. Lt. olive-brown. Printer: SBNC.	.50	3.00	8.00

#341A *Deleted*. See #342c.

		VG	VF	UNC
342	**2000 Customs Gold Units** 1947. Green.			
	a. Chinese printer 5 characters.	.75	3.00	10.00
	b. Chinese printer 6 characters.	.75	3.00	10.00
	c. Chinese printer 9 characters.	.75	3.00	10.00

343

344

		VG	VF	UNC
343	**2000 Customs Gold Units** 1947. Dk. brown. Printer: CHB.	.75	3.00	10.00
344	**2000 Customs Gold Units** 1947. Blue-violet. Printer: TDLR.	.50	2.50	8.00

345

347

		VG	VF	UNC
345	**2500 Customs Gold Units** 1947. Olive. Printer: CHB.	3.00	15.00	30.00

		VG	VF	UNC
346	**2500 Customs Gold Units** 1947. Violet. Printer 5 characters. Reported not confirmed.	—	—	—
347	**5000 Customs Gold Units** 1947. Brown. Printer: TDLR.	2.50	7.50	25.00
348	**5000 Customs Gold Units** 1947. Green. Printer: TDLR. Reported not confirmed	—	—	—
349	**5000 Customs Gold Units** 1947. Blue. Printer: SBNC.	2.00	7.50	20.00

		VG	VF	UNC
350	**5000 Customs Gold Units** 1947. Green. Chinese printer 5 characters.	1.00	4.00	15.00
351	**5000 Customs Gold Units** 1947. Red. Chinese printer 5 characters.			
	a. Issued note.	1.00	3.00	10.00
	p. Proof.	—	—	225.

		VG	VF	UNC
352	**5000 Customs Gold Units** 1947. Brown on gold unpt. Back black. Chinese printer 5 characters. Lg. or sm. serial #.	1.00	4.00	15.00

353

354

		VG	VF	UNC
353	**5000 Customs Gold Units** 1947. Brown. Back slate blue. Printer: CHB.	.75	3.00	10.00
354	**10,000 Customs Gold Units** 1947. Blue. Printer: TDLR.	.75	3.00	10.00
355	**10,000 Customs Gold Units** 1947. Printer: SBNC. Reported not confirmed.	—	—	—

#356 not assigned.

1948 CUSTOMS GOLD UNITS ISSUES

357

358

		VG	VF	UNC
357	**2000 Customs Gold Units** 1948. Orange. Chinese printer 5 characters.	.50	2.50	10.00
358	**2500 Customs Gold Units** 1948. Lilac-brown. Chinese printer 5 characters. Large or small serial #.	1.75	7.50	17.50

359

360

		VG	VF	UNC
359	**5000 Customs Gold Units** 1948. Purple. Printer: ABNC.	2.50	7.50	30.0
360	**5000 Customs Gold Units** 1948. Blue. Printer: SBNC.	1.50	6.00	15.0

361

362

		VG	VF	UNC
361	**5000 Customs Gold Units** 1948. Purple. Chinese printer 5 characters. Large or small serial # and 2 paper varieties.	1.00	3.00	10.0
362	**5000 Customs Gold Units** 1948. Blue. Printer: CHB.	1.00	3.00	10.0
363	**10,000 Customs Gold Units** 1948. Blue. Printer: SBNC.	1.25	6.00	15.0
364	**10,000 Customs Gold Units** 1948. Blue. Chinese printer 5 characters. 2 serial # varieties.	1.00	3.00	10.0
364A	**10,000 Customs Gold Units** 1948. Printer: W&S.	—	—	—
365	**25,000 Customs Gold Units** 1948. Brown. Printer: ABNC.	6.00	27.50	60.0

366

370

		VG	VF	UNC
366	**25,000 Customs Gold Units** 1948. Green. Chinese printer 5 characters. Large or small serial #.	1.50	6.00	15.00
367	**25,000 Customs Gold Units** 1948. Lilac-brown. Printer: CHB.	5.00	15.00	45.00
368	**50,000 Customs Gold Units** 1948. Red. Printer: CHB.			
	a. Issued note.	50.00	175.	550.
	s. Specimen.	—	—	130.
369	**50,000 Customs Gold Units** 1948. Pink. Similar to #368 but different guilloche. Specimen. Printer: CHB.	—	—	130.
369A	**50,000 Customs Gold Units** 1948. Purple. Printer: SBNC. (Not issued).	—	—	—
370	**50,000 Customs Gold Units** 1948. Red. Chinese printer 5 characters. 2 serial # varieties. 64 x 154mm.	2.00	7.50	20.00
371	**50,000 Customs Gold Units** 1948. Orange. Chinese printer 5 characters. 70 x 162mm.			
	a. Issued note.	2.50	12.50	30.00
	p. Proof.	—	—	200.
372	**50,000 Customs Gold Units** 1948. Deep purple on lt. blue unpt. Chinese printer 5 characters.	2.50	17.50	40.00

373

374

		VG	VF	UNC
373	**50,000 Customs Gold Units** 1948. Brown-violet. Chinese printer 5 characters.	3.75	15.00	60.00
374	**250,000 Customs Gold Units** 1948. Red and m/c.	20.00	100.	220.

1945-48 "9 NORTHEASTERN PROVINCES" BRANCH ISSUES

Issued at a rate of 20 to 1 current yuan.

#375-386 city gate at l. Under the bank title are 7 Chinese characters which translates "note for circulation in the northeast 9 provinces."

東北九省流通券

Tung Pei Chiu Sheng Liu T'ung Ch'üan

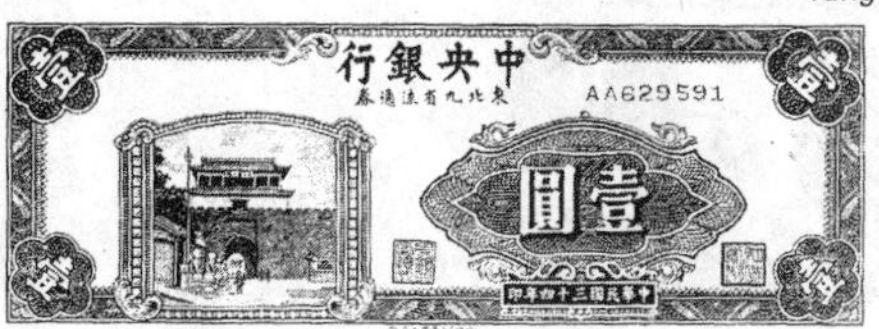

		VG	VF	UNC
375	**1 Yüan** 1945. Brown on pink unpt. *(S/M #C303-1).*	6.00	25.00	60.00
376	**5 Yüan** 1945. Orange. *(S/M #C303-2).*	5.00	17.50	40.00
376A	**5 Yüan** 1945. Red. Peking printer. *(SM #C303-2.5).*	—	600.	1000.
377	**10 Yüan** 1945. Blue on purple unpt. Back blue. *(S/M #C303-3).*	2.50	10.00	40.00
378	**50 Yüan** 1945. Purple on green unpt. *(S/M #C303-4).*	5.00	12.50	50.00
379	**100 Yüan** 1945. Olive-green on lt. tan unpt. Back dk. olive-green. 2 serial # varieties. *(S/M #C303-5).*	.50	2.50	6.00

		VG	VF	UNC
380	**500 Yüan** 1946; 1947. Dk. green on lilac unpt. Back dk. green.			
	a. Shanghai printer. *(S/M #C303-10).* (1946).	.50	2.50	6.00
	b. Peking printer. *(S/M #C303-21).* (1947).	1.25	5.00	12.50

#380A *Deleted.* See #380b. #381 Great Wall on back.

		VG	VF	UNC
381	**500 Yüan** 1947. Dk. brown on orange unpt. *(S/M #C303-20).*	.75	3.00	7.00
382	**1000 Yüan** 1947. Blue-black on pink unpt.			
	a. Chinese printer 5 characters. *(S/M #C303-22).*	5.00	12.50	35.00
	b. Chinese printer 8 characters. *(S/M #C303-23).*	.50	1.75	6.00
	c. As b but w/o underprint.	2.00	5.00	12.50
383	**2000 Yüan** 1947. Brown. *(S/M #C303-24).*	1.00	3.00	10.00
384	**2000 Yüan** 1948. Brown-violet on m/c unpt. *(S/M #C303-30).*	.25	2.00	4.00

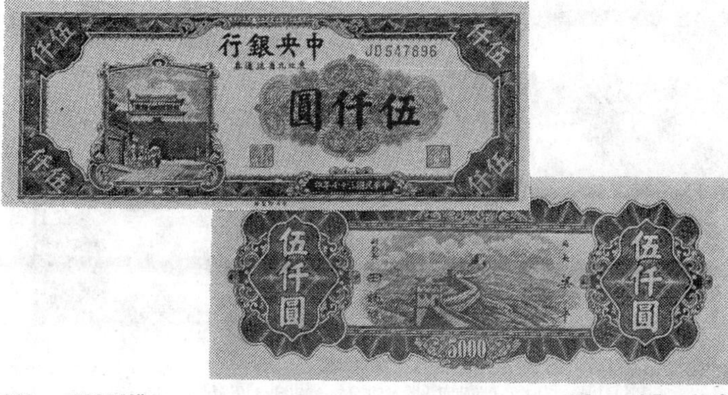

		VG	VF	UNC
385	**5000 Yüan** 1948. Dk. blue-black on red and tan guilloche. 2 serial # varieties. *(S/M #C303-31a).*	.50	2.25	5.00
385A	**5000 Yüan** 1948. Greenish blue-black on brown and olive-green guilloche. *(S/M #C303-31b).*	1.00	5.00	12.50
386	**10,000 Yüan** 1948. Brown on m/c unpt. Back: brown. *(S/M #C303-32).*	.50	2.00	5.00

1948 (1945 DATED) GOLD *CHIN YUAN* ISSUE

This system was introduced in August 1948, to replace the previous currency at an exchange rate of GY$1 for $3,000,000 in the old currency.

#387-394 *Fa Pi* currency withheld because of high inflation and later issued as gold yuan. Printer: ABNC.

		VG	VF	UNC
387	**1 Yüan** 1945. (1948). Blue on m/c unpt. CKS at ctr. *(S/M #C302-1).*	.50	2.75	6.00

		VG	VF	UNC
388	**5 Yüan** 1945 (1948). Olive-green on m/c unpt. Lin Sun at l. 3 sign. varieties. *(S/M #C302-2).*	.50	2.75	6.00
389	**5 Yüan** 1945 (1948). Blue. SYS at ctr. National sunbursts at l. and r. Junks at ctr. on back. Printer: SBNC. Specimen. *(S/M #C302-3).*	—	—	150.
389A	**5 Yüan** 1945. Like #389 but black. Green back. Wide margin. Specimen.	—	—	—

		VG	VF	UNC
390	**10 Yüan** 1945 (1948). Brown on m/c unpt. CKS at r. Bridge at l. on back. 3 sign. varieties. *(S/M #C302-4).*	1.00	5.00	12.00

		VG	VF	UNC
391	**20 Yüan** 1945 (1948). Green. Lin Sun at ctr.	1.75	7.50	17.50
392	**50 Yüan** 1945 (1948). Black on m/c unpt. SYS at ctr. 2 sign. varieties. *(S/M #C302-6).*	.50	1.50	8.00

		VG	VF	UNC
393	**50 Yüan** 1945 (1948). Black on m/c unpt. CKS at ctr. 3 sign. varieties. *(S/M #C302-7)*	.50	2.00	10.00
394	**100 Yüan** 1945 (1948). Red on m/c unpt. Lin Sun at l. CKS at r. 2 sign. varieties. *(S/M #C302-8).*	1.00	4.00	15.00

1948 (1946 DATED) GOLD *CHIN YUAN* ISSUE

Portr. CKS at r. Printer: TDLR.

		VG	VF	UNC
395	**10 Cents** 1946. Brown. Shoreline village, pagoda at ctr. on back. *(S/M #C302-10).*	.40	2.00	4.00
395A	**20 Cents** 1946. Black. Back green; sampans at anchor. Specimen.	—	—	40.00
396	**20 Cents** 1946. Orange. Sampans at anchor on back. *(S/M #C302-11).*	.50	2.75	6.00

1948 GOLD *CHIN YUAN* ISSUE

		VG	VF	UNC
396A	**10 Cents** 1948. CKS at ctr. Printer: CPF. (Not issued).	—	—	—

		VG	VF	UNC
397	**50 Cents** 1948. Brown on yellow unpt. CKS at r. Printer: CPF. *(S/M #C302-20).*	.50	2.75	6.00
398	**50 Cents** 1948. Violet. CKS at r. Printer: SBNC. *(S/M #C302-21).*	12.50	40.00	120.

		VG	VF	UNC
399	**10 Yüan** 1948. Green on m/c unpt. CKS at r. Printer: CPF. *(S/M #C302-30).*	.50	2.75	6.00
400	**20 Yüan** 1948. Brown on m/c unpt. CKS at r. Printer: CHB. *(S/M #C302-32).*	2.50	7.50	20.00
401	**20 Yüan** 1948. Red on m/c unpt. CKS at r. Printer: CPF. *(S/M #C302-31).*	.75	4.00	9.00

		VG	VF	UNC
402	**50 Yüan** 1948. Deep red on gold and lt. blue unpt. CKS at ctr. Printer: CHB. *(S/M #C302-41).*	1.00	3.50	12.50
403	**50 Yüan** 1948. Violet on m/c unpt. CKS at r. Printer: CPF. *(S/M #C302-40).*	.50	2.00	6.00

		VG	VF	UNC
404	**50 Yüan** 1948. Black on m/c unpt. CKS at ctr. Yangtze Ganges at ctr. on back. Printer: TDLR. *(S/M #C302-42).*	35.00	125.	350.
405	**50 Yüan** 1948. Red. CKS at r. Printer: SBNC. *(S/M #C302-43).*	10.00	30.00	90.00
406	**100 Yüan** 1948. Green. CKS at ctr. Printer: CHB. *(S/M #C302-45).*	1.50	7.50	16.00
407	**100 Yüan** 1948. Dk. blue on m/c unpt. CKS at r. Printer: CPF. *(S/M #C302-44).*	1.00	3.00	9.00

1949 GOLD *CHIN YUAN* ISSUES

		VG	VF	UNC
408	**100 Yüan** 1949. Orange on m/c unpt. CKS at r. Printer: CPF. *(S/M #C302-50).*	1.00	3.00	9.00

		VG	VF	UNC
409	**500 Yüan** 1949. Dk. green on m/c unpt. CKS at r. Printer: CPF. *(S/M #C302-51).*	1.50	7.50	16.00
410	**500 Yüan** 1949. Violet on m/c unpt. CKS at r. Printer: CHB. *(S/M #C302-52).*	2.50	5.00	15.00
411	**1000 Yüan** 1949. Brown. CKS at r. Back red; temple at r. Printer: CHB. *(S/M #C302-55).*	2.50	5.00	15.00

		VG	VF	UNC
412	**1000 Yüan** 1949. Blue-gray on m/c unpt. CKS at r.			
	a. Printer: CPF. *(S/M #C302-54a).*	1.25	3.00	10.00
	b. Printer: CPF1. *(S/M #C302-54b).*	1.25	3.50	12.00
	c. Printer: CPF2. *(S/M #C302-54c).*	1.25	3.50	12.00
	d. Printer: CPF3. *(S/M #C302-54d).*	1.25	3.50	12.00
	e. Printer: CPF4. *(S/M #C302-54e).*	1.25	3.50	12.00
413	**1000 Yüan** 1949. Brown. CKS at r. Printer: CPF. *(S/M #C302-55).*	.75	4.00	8.00
414	**5000 Yüan** 1949. Red. CKS at r. Back red; w/bridge. Printer: CHB. *(S/M #C302-57).*	.50	2.75	6.00

		VG	VF	UNC
415	**5000 Yüan** 1949. Red on m/c unpt. CKS at r. Back red; w/bank at l.			
	a. Printer: CPF. *(S/M #C302-56a).*	.75	4.00	8.00
	b. Printer: CPF3. *(S/M #C302-56b).*	1.50	7.50	16.00
416	**10,000 Yüan** 1949. Blue on m/c unpt. CKS at r. Back blue; w/bridge. Printer: CHB. *(S/M #C302-61).*	1.25	7.00	14.00

#	Denomination	VG	VF	UNC
417	**10,000 Yüan** 1949. Blue on m/c unpt. CKS at r. Back blue; bank at l.			
	a. Printer: CPF. *(S/M #C302-60a).*	1.00	4.00	10.00
	b. Printer: CPF1. *(S/M #C302-60b).*	1.50	6.00	20.00
	c. Printer: CPF2. *(S/M #C302-60c).*	1.50	6.00	20.00
418	**50,000 Yüan** 1949. Red-orange on m/c unpt. CKS at r. Printer: CPF. *(S/M #C302-62).*	1.25	7.00	14.00

#	Denomination	VG	VF	UNC
419	**50,000 Yüan** 1949. Brown and m/c. CKS at r. Similar to $418 but w/different guilloche.			
	a. Printer: CPF. *(S/M #C302-63a).*	1.25	5.00	12.00
	b. Printer: CPF1. *(S/M #C302-63b).*	1.25	6.00	18.00
	c. Printer: CPF2. *(S/M #C302-63c).*	1.25	5.00	15.00
	p. Proof.	—	—	60.00
420	**50,000 Yüan** 1949. Red. CKS at ctr. Printer: TDLR. *(S/M #C302-64).*	12.50	45.00	150.
421	**100,000 Yüan** 1949. Lilac. CKS at r. Printer: CHB. *(S/M #C302-71).*	1.25	3.00	10.00

#	Denomination	VG	VF	UNC
422	**100,000 Yüan** 1949. Grayish green. CKS at r.			
	a. Printer: CPF. *(S/M # #C302-72a).*	.75	2.00	8.00
	b. Printer: CPF1. *(S/M #C302-72b).*	1.50	6.00	17.50
	c. Printer: CPF2. *(S/M #C302-72c).*	1.50	6.00	20.00
	d. Printer: CPF3. *(S/M #C302-72d).*	1.50	6.00	20.00
	e. Printer: CPF4. *(S/M #C302-72e).*	1.50	6.00	20.00
	f. Printer: CPF-Taipei. *(S/M #C302-72f).*	20.00	85.00	200.
423	**500,000 Yüan** 1949. Greenish black on m/c unpt. Temple at ctr. on back. Printer: CHB. *(S/M #C302-73).*	2.00	5.00	15.00

#	Denomination	VG	VF	UNC
424	**500,000 Yüan** 1949. Lilac-brown on m/c unpt. Back lilac; bank at ctr.			
	a. Printer: CPF. *(S/M #C302-72a).*	2.00	5.00	15.00
	b. Printer: CPF1. *(S/M #C302-72b).*	2.00	7.00	20.00
	c. Printer: CPF2.*(S/M #C302-72c).*	2.00	7.00	25.00
	d. Printer: CPF3. *(S/M #C302-72d).*	2.00	7.00	25.00
	e. Printer: CPF4. *(S/M # #C302-72e).*	2.00	7.00	25.00
	f. Printer: CPF-Taipei. *(S/M #C302-72f).*	12.50	45.00	225.
425	**500,000 Yüan** 1949. Green. CKS at r. Printer: SBNC. *(S/M #C302-74).*	15.00	45.00	125.
426	**1,000,000 Yüan** 1949. Brown and blue. CKS at r. Back brown. Printer: CHB. *(S/M #C302-75).*	6.00	18.00	60.00

#	Denomination	VG	VF	UNC
427	**5,000,000 Yüan** 1949. Red and blue. CKS at r. Back red. Printer: CHB. *(S/M #C302-77).*	50.00	175.	500.

1949 Silver *Yin Yuan* Issue

#	Denomination	VG	VF	UNC
428	**1 Cent** 1949. Green. CKS at ctr. Vertical format. Printer: CPF-Chungking. *(S/M #C304-1).*	5.00	30.00	65.00
429	**5 Cents** 1949. Red. CKS at ctr. Vertical format. Printer: CPF-Chungking. *(S/M #C304-2).*	17.50	90.00	180.
430	**5 Cents** 1949. Green. SYS at r. Temple of Heaven on back. Printer: CPF-Taipei. *(S/M #C304-3).*	15.00	80.00	160.

#	Denomination	VG	VF	UNC
431	**5 Cents** 1949. Red-violet. Pier at ctr. *Tsingtao. (S/M #C304-4).*	15.00	75.00	150.
432	**10 Cents** 1949. Blue on red unpt. CKS at ctr. Vertical format. Printer: CPF-Chungking. I>(S/M #C304-5).	15.00	80.00	160.

#	Denomination	VG	VF	UNC
433	**10 Cents** 1949. Purple. SYS at r. Printer: CHB. *(S/M #C304-6).*	.75	4.00	8.00
434	**10 Cents** 1949. Gray-green. Pier at ctr. *Tsingtao. (S/M #C304-7).*	17.50	90.00	180.
435	**20 Cents** 1949. Orange. CKS at ctr. Vertical format. Printer: CPF-Chungking. *(S/M #C304-10).*	17.50	90.00	190.
436	**20 Cents** 1949. Green. SYS at r. Printer: CHB. *(S/M #C304-11).*	1.00	4.00	10.00

NOTICE

Readers with unlisted dates, signature varieties, etc. are invited to submit photocopies or, high resolution (300 dpi, 100% size) scans of their notes to: Standard Catalog of World Paper Money, 700 East State St. Iola, WI 54990-0001, or E-Mail: george.cuhaj@fwpubs.com.

		VG	VF	UNC
437	**50 Cents** 1949. Lilac. CKS at ctr. Vertical format. Printer: CPF-Chungking. *(S/M #C304-12).*	15.00	75.00	150.
438	**50 Cents** 1949. Brown. SYS at r. Printer: CPF-Taipei. *(S/M #C304-13).*	10.00	30.00	100.
438A	**50 Cents** 1949. Yellow-green. *Tsingtao. (S/M #C304-14).* Reported not confirmed.	—	—	—

#439-448 printer: CHB. #439-447 Silver 'junk' 1-Yuan coin at ctr. on back.

		VG	VF	UNC
439	**1 Dollar** 1949. Blue on m/c unpt. Portr. SYS at r. Printer: CHB. *(S/M #C304-20).*	2.00	7.50	201.

		VG	VF	UNC
440	**1 Dollar** 1949. Lilac-brown. SYS at r. *CHUNGKING.* Printer: CHB. *(S/M #C304-22).*	1.50	4.00	8.00

		VG	VF	UNC
441	**1 Dollar** 1949. Black-blue. SYS at r. *CANTON.* Printer: CHB. *(S/M #C304-21).*	1.50	5.00	20.00
442	**5 Dollars** 1949. SYS at r. Printer: CHB. *(S/M #C304-23).*	2.50	10.00	30.00
443	**5 Dollars** 1949. Dk. brown on m/c unpt. SYS at r. *CHUNGKING.* Printer: CHB. *(S/M #C304-25).*	1.00	4.00	10.00
444	**5 Dollars** 1949. Brown and red. SYS at r. *CANTON.* Printer: CHB. *(S/M #C304-24).*			
	a. Issued note.	1.00	2.50	8.00
	b. Sign. on back.	17.50	60.00	—

		VG	VF	UNC
445	**10 Dollars** 1949. Red. SYS at r. Printer: CHB. *(S/M #C304-30).*	3.00	10.00	30.00
446	**10 Dollars** 1949. Pink. SYS at r. *CHUNGKING.* Printer: CHB. *(S/M #C304-32).*	5.00	20.00	60.00
447	**10 Dollars** 1949. Black on m/c unpt. SYS at r. Printer: CHB. *(S/M #C304-31).*			
	a. *CHUNGKING.*	.50	3.00	7.00
	b. *CANTON.*	1.50	4.00	12.50
448	**100 Dollars** 1949. Green. SYS at r. *CHUNGKING.* Printer: CHB. Specimen. *(S/M #C304-33).*	—	—	90.00

CENTRAL BANK OF CHINA (BRANCHES - NATIONAL RESUMED)

GENERAL ISSUE - SHANGHAI CHECKS BRANCH

1949 GENERAL GOLD *CHIN YUAN* ISSUE

Circulating Bearer Cashier's Checks.

		Good	Fine	XF
449	**50,000 Yüan** 1949. Green on blue unpt. *(S/M #C302-).*	12.50	50.00	150.
449A	**100,000 Yüan** 1949. Red on pink unpt. *(S/M #C302-).*	12.50	50.00	150.

GENERAL ISSUE - SHANGHAI CHECKS BRANCH

1949 GENERAL GOLD *CHIN YUAN* ISSUE

Circulating Bearer Cashier's Checks.

		Good	Fine	XF
449B	**300,000 Yüan** 1949. Green. *(S/M #C302-).*	12.50	50.00	150.
449C	**500,000 Yüan** 28.4.1949. Blue on pink unpt. *(S/M #C302-).*	12.50	50.00	150.
449D	**1,000,000 Yüan** 1949. Violet on green unpt. *(S/M #C302-).*	12.50	50.00	150.

		Good	Fine	XF
449E	**5,000,000 Yüan** 7.5.1949. Brown on yellow unpt. *(S/M #C302-93).*	12.50	50.00	150.
449F	**10,000,000 Yüan** 1949. (Not issued). *(S/M #C302-).*			

CHANGCHUNG BRANCH

1948 FIRST ISSUE

		Good	Fine	XF
449G	**100,000 Yüan** 1948. Green on violet unpt. *(S/M #C302-).*	12.50	50.00	150.
449GE	**200,000 Yüan** 1948. *(S/M #C302-).*	12.50	50.00	150.
449GF	**500,000 Yüan** 1948. *(S/M #C302-).*	12.50	50.00	150.
449GG	**1,000,000 Yüan** 1948. *(S/M #C302-).*	12.50	50.00	150.
449GH	**2,000,000 Yüan** 1948. *(S/M #C302-).*	12.50	50.00	150.

		Good	Fine	XF
449H	**10,000,000 Yüan** 1948. *(S/M #C302-).*	12.50	50.00	150.
449HH	**15,000,000 Yüan** 1948. *(S/M #C302-).*	12.50	50.00	150.
449I	**30,000,000 Yüan = 50 Gold Yüan** 1948. Gray on blue unpt. *(S/M #C302-).*	12.50	50.00	150.
449J	**50,000,000 Yüan** 1948. Gray on blue unpt. *(S/M #C302-).*	125.	50.00	150.

#449K

#449M

		Good	Fine	XF
449K	**60,000,000 Yüan = 10 Gold Yüan** 1948. Purple on lilac unpt. *(S/M #C302-95).*	6.00	17.50	50.00
449L	**120,000,000 Yüan** 1948. Blue on gray unpt. *(S/M #C302-).*	7.50	20.00	60.00
449M	**180,000,000 Yüan** 1948. Purple on brown unpt. *(S/M #C302-).*	7.50	20.00	60.00

1948 Second Issue

		Good	Fine	XF
449N	**5,000,000 Yüan** 24.8.1948. *(S/M #C302-).*	7.50	25.00	100.
449O	**50,000,000 Yüan** 1948. *(S/M #C302-).*	7.50	25.00	85.00

1948 Provisional Issue

		Good	Fine	XF
449P	**4,500,000 Yüan** 1948. Ovpt. on #449N. *(S/M #C302-).*	7.50	25.00	100.
449Q	**30,000,000 Yüan = 50 Gold Yüan** 1948. Ovpt. on #449O. *(S/M #C302-).*	7.50	25.00	100.

Chengtu Branch 春長

1949 Gold *Chin Yuan* First Issue

		Good	Fine	XF
449Z	**5000 Yüan** 7.4.1949-18.4.1949. Brown on yellow unpt., black text. *(S/M #C302-).*			
	a. Issued note.	9.00	27.50	110.
	b. Remainder w/counterfoil.	6.00	17.50	75.00

Chengtu Branch

1949 Gold *Chin Yuan* Second Issue

#449Y

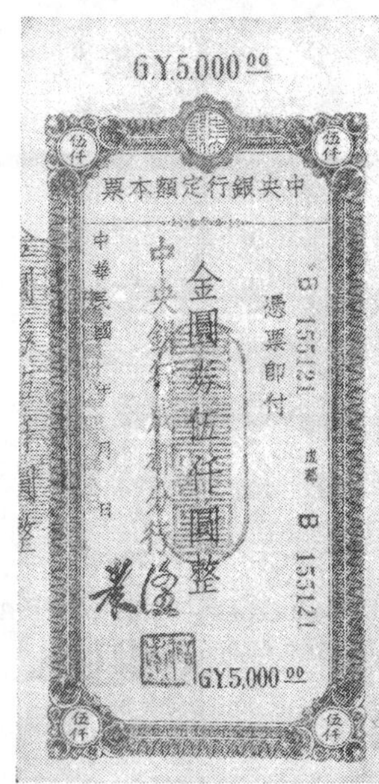

#449Z

		Good	Fine	XF
449Y	**2000 Yüan** 30.3.1949-13.4.1949. Violet-brown on lt. blue unpt., black text. *(S/M #C302-).*	9.00	27.50	110.

1949 Gold *Chin Yuan* Second Issue

		Good	Fine	XF
449AA	**10,000 Yüan** 25.4.1949-28.4.1949. Red-violet on lt. green unpt. *(S/M #C302-).*	10.00	27.50	115.

1949 Gold *Chin Yuan* Second Issue

		Good	Fine	XF
449R	**10,000,000 Yüan** 1949. *(S/M #C302-).*	10.00	30.00	120.

Chungking Branch 慶重

1949 Gold *Chin Yuan* Issue

#499U

#449V

		Good	Fine	XF
449S	**50,000 Yüan** 1949. Brown. *(S/M #C302-).*	12.50	45.00	120.
449T	**500,000 Yüan** 1949. Red. *(S/M #C302-).*	12.50	45.00	120.
449U	**1,000,000 Yüan** 14.6.1949. Red on yellow unpt. *(S/M #C302-91).*	12.50	45.00	120.
449V	**5,000,000 Yüan** 1.6.1949. Green. *(S/M #C302-92).*	12.50	45.00	120.
449W	**5,000,000 Yüan** 1949. Purple on yellow unpt. *(S/M #C302-94).*	7.50	25.00	100.

		Good	Fine	XF
449X	**10,000,000 Yüan** 14.6.1949. Red on lt. blue unpt. *(S/M #C302-)*.	7.50	25.00	100.

FOOCHOW BRANCH 福州

1949 GOLD *CHIN YUAN* FIRST ISSUE

		Good	Fine	XF
449AF	**50,000 Yüan** 1.9.1949. Bank title in seal script w/flower bud outline in all 4 corners. *(S/M #C302-)*.	7.50	25.00	100.

FOOCHOW BRANCH

1949 GOLD *CHIN YUAN* SECOND ISSUE

#450A *Deleted*.

450

450 B

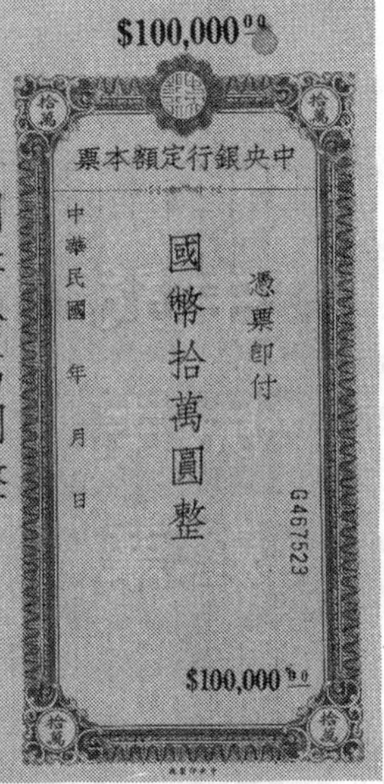

450 G

		Good	Fine	XF
450	**1000 Yüan** April 1949. Purple. *(S/M #C302-80)*.	7.50	25.00	100.
450A Deleted.				
450B	**20,000 Yüan** April 1949. Red-brown. *(S/M #C302-)*.	7.50	25.00	100.
450BB	**50,000 Yüan** April 1949. *(S/M #C302-)*.	7.50	25.00	100.

1949 NATIONAL *KUO PI YUAN* ISSUE

#450C-450G printer: CPF.

		Good	Fine	XF
450C	**20,000 Yüan** ND (1949). Red. (Not issued). *(S/M #C302-)*.	—	—	—
450D	**30,000 Yüan** ND (1949). Green. (Not issued). *(S/M #C302-)*.	—	—	—
450E	**40,000 Yüan** ND (1949). Lt. blue. (Not issued). *(S/M #C302-)*.	—	—	—
450F	**50,000 Yüan** ND (1949). Dk. blue. (Not issued). *(S/M #C302-)*.	—	—	—
450G	**100,000 Yüan** ND (1949). Brown on yellow unpt. (Not issued). *(S/M #C302-)*.	—	—	—

1949 GOLD *CHIN YUAN* PROVISIONAL ISSUE

#450H

#450J

		Good	Fine	XF
450H	**20,000 Yüan** 25.4.1949. Ovpt. on #450C. *(S/M #C302-81)*.	9.00	25.00	90.00
450I	**30,000 Yüan** 25.4.1949. Ovpt. on #450D. *(S/M #C302-82)*.	9.00	25.00	90.00
450J	**40,000 Yüan** 25.4.1949. Ovpt. on #450E. *(S/M #C302-83)*.	9.00	25.00	90.00
450K	**50,000 Yüan** 25.4.1949. Ovpt. on #450F. *(S/M #C302-84)*.	9.00	25.00	90.00
450L	**100,000 Yüan** 25.4.1949. Ovpt. on #450G. *(S/M #C302-85)*.	9.00	25.00	90.00

1949 GOLD *CHIN YUAN* FOURTH ISSUE

#450M, 450N SYS at upper ctr.

#450M

#450N

		Good	Fine	XF
450M	**100,000 Yüan** April 1949. Brown on lt. blue unpt. *(S/M #C302-)*.	7.50	25.00	95.00
450N	**500,000 Yüan** April 1949. Blue on yellow unpt. *(S/M #C302-90)*.	7.50	25.00	95.00

KUNMING BRANCH 昆明

1945-47 ISSUE

		Good	Fine	XF
450O	**100,000 Yüan** 1945. Violet on yellow unpt. *(S/M #C302-)*.	10.00	27.50	110.
450P	**300,000 Yüan** 1947. Green on brown unpt. *(S/M #C302-)*.	10.00	27.50	110.

MUKDEN, MANCHURIA BRANCH 京盛

1948 NORTHWEST *YUAN* ISSUE

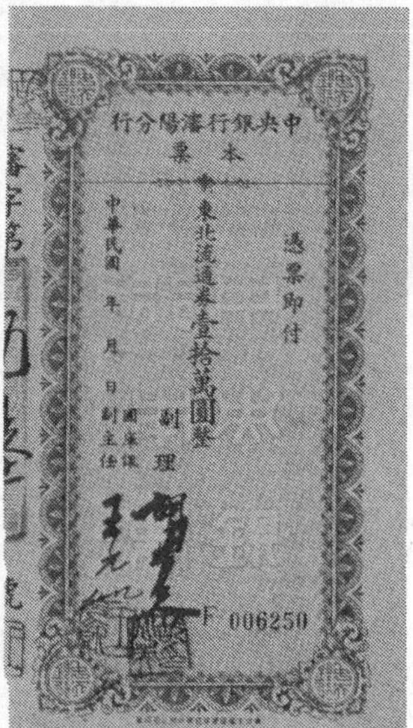

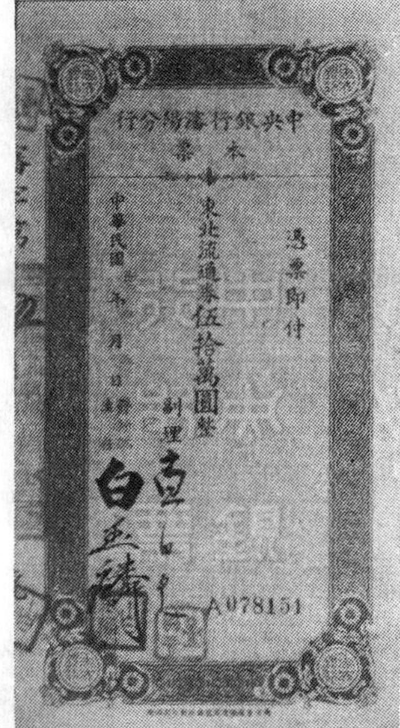

		Good	Fine	XF
450Q	**100,000 Yüan** 1948. Dk. brown on lt. gray unpt., black text. *(S/M #C303-).*	9.50	30.00	120.
450R	**500,000 Yüan** 1948. Blue on yellow-orange unpt. black text. *(S/M #C303-).*	9.50	30.00	120.
450S	**5,000,000 Yüan** 2.4.1948. *(S/M #C30-).*	9.50	30.00	120.

YIBIN BRANCH

1944 NATIONAL *KUO PI YUAN* ISSUE

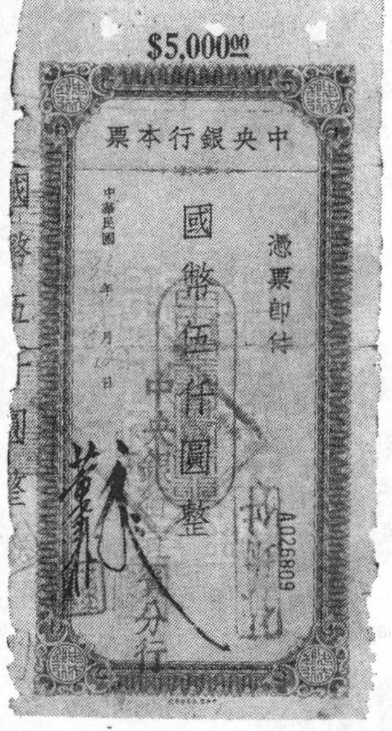

		Good	Fine	XF
450T	**5000 Yüan** 12.9.1944. Brown-violet on lt. blue unpt., black text. *(S/M #C302-).*	12.00	35.00	145.

FARMERS BANK OF CHINA

中國農民銀行

Chung Kuo Nung Min Yin Hang

1934 ISSUE

#451-456 Chinese printer: TYPC. Sign. varieties.

		Good	Fine	XF
451	**1 Chiao = 10 Cents** ND. (1934) Red. Farm laborer at ctr. Back green. Vertical format. *(S/M #C290-1).*	7.50	25.00	70.00
452	**2 Chiao = 20 Cents** ND. (1934) Red. *(S/M #C290-2).*	9.00	25.00	90.00

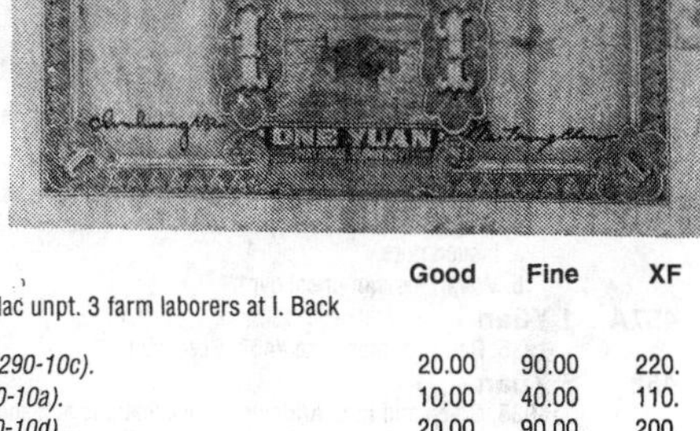

		Good	Fine	XF
453	**1 Yüan** 1934. Red on lt. green and lilac unpt. 3 farm laborers at l. Back green; farmer plowing w/ox.			
	a. *CHENGCHOW. (S/M #C290-10c).*	20.00	90.00	220.
	b. *FOOCHOW. (S/M #C290-10a).*	10.00	40.00	110.
	c. *LANCHOW. (S/M #C290-10d).*	20.00	90.00	200.
	d. W/o place name. *(S/M #C290-10b).*	10.00	40.00	110.
	e. *CHANGSHA. (S/M #C290-10e).*	20.00	90.00	200.
	f. *HANKOW. (S/M #C290-10f).*	20.00	90.00	220.
	g. *KWEIYANG. (S/M #C290-10g).*	20.00	90.00	220.
	h. *SIAN. (S/M #C290-10h).*	17.50	75.00	180.
	s. 2 part specimen as d.			
453A	**1 Yüan** 1934. Similar to #453 but face dk. blue. Back brown. Chinese ovpt: *Shanghai* on face. *(S/M #C290-).*	15.00	90.00	200.

1935 FIRST ISSUE

		VG	VF	UNC
454	**20 Cents = 2 Chiao** Feb. 1935. Red. Farmer plowing w/ox at top. Back green. 2 sign. varieties. *(S/M #C290-20).*	10.00	45.00	110.

1935 SECOND ISSUE

#457-460 printer: TDLR.

		VG	VF	UNC
455	**10 Cents = 1 Chiao** 1.3.1935. Red. Farmer in irrigation system at top. Back green. 2 sign. varieties. *(S/M #C290-21).*			
	a. Issued note.	3.00	15.00	30.00
	s. 2 part specimen.	—	—	90.00
456	**20 Cents = 2 Chiao** 1.4.1935. Black and red. Farmer plowing w/ox at top. Back orange. 2 sign. varieties. *(S/M #C290-22).*	5.00	25.00	50.00

		VG	VF	UNC
457	**1 Yüan** 1.4.1935. Red on green and m/c unpt. Farming scenes at l. and r. Back red; house at ctr., sheep at r. 2 sign. varieties. *(S/M #C290-30).*			
	a. Issued note.	2.00	10.00	20.00
	b. W/various numerical ovpt.	2.25	10.00	30.00
457A	**1 Yüan** 1935. Red w/o unpt. Like #457. Specimen.	—	—	150.
458	**5 Yüan** 1935. Green and m/c. Agricultural occupations at l. and r. Back green; temple at ctr., ox at r. 2 sign. varieties. *(S/M #C290-31).*			
	a. Issued note.	2.50	12.50	25.00
	b. W/various numerical ovpt.	5.00	17.50	50.00
	s. 2 part specimen.			

		VG	VF	UNC
459	**10 Yüan** 1935. Purple and m/c. Agricultural occupations at l. and r. Pagoda at ctr., horse at r. on back. 3 sign. varieties. *(S/M #C290-32).* -			
	a. Issued note.	2.50	10.00	20.00
	b. W/various numerical ovpt.	5.00	17.50	50.00

1936 ISSUE

		VG	VF	UNC
460	**50 Cents** 1936. Blue. Agricultural occupations at l. and r. Hillside pagoda at ctr., goat head at r. on back. *(S/M #C290-40).*	1.25	6.00	12.50

1937 ISSUE

#461-465 Chinese printer: TYPC.

		VG	VF	UNC
461	**10 Cents** 1937. Blue. Landscape. Back brown, green and purple. 2 serial # varieites. *(S/M #C290-50).*	.50	2.00	6.00
461A	**10 Cents** 1937. Blue. Face like #461 but back w/Chinese text (pass for the Nanking Military Government).	60.00	180.	—

		VG	VF	UNC
462	**20 Cents** 1937. Green. Agricultural scene. Back green, brown and blue. 2 serial # varieties. *(S/M #C290-51).*	1.00	5.00	10.00

1940 REGULAR ISSUE

		VG	VF	UNC
463	**1 Yüan** 1940. Red. Workers at lower r. Back brown, blue and green. *(S/M #C290-60).*	1.00	5.00	10.00

		VG	VF	UNC
464	**10 Yüan** 1940. Red. Farmer working in irrigation system. Back blue, lilac and brown. 2 serial # varieites. *(S/M #C290-65).*	1.50	5.00	15.00

		VG	VF	UNC
465	**20 Yüan** 1940. Blue. Worker by houses along river. 2 serial # varieties. *(S/M #C290-70).*	4.50	20.00	45.00

1940 First Provisional Issue

#466-468 new issuer name ovpt. on notes of the Hupeh Provincial Bank.

		Good	Fine	XF
466	**1 Yüan** ND (1940 - old date 1929). Purple and m/c. Ovpt. on #S2104. *(S/M #C290-62).*	40.00	200.	400.

		Good	Fine	XF
467	**5 Yüan** ND (1940 - old date 1929). Green and m/c. Ovpt. on #S2105.			
	a. *HANKOW. (S/M #C290-63b).*	30.00	150.	320.
	b. *HUPEH. (S/M #C290-63c).*	40.00	200.	400.
	c. *SHANTUNG. (S/M #C290-63d).*	40.00	200.	400.
	d. W/o place name. *(S/M #C290-63a).*	30.00	125.	350.

		Good	Fine	XF
468	**10 Yüan** ND (1940 - old date 1929). Red and m/c. Ovpt. on #S2106. *(S/M #C290-66).*	40.00	200.	400.

1940 Second Provisional Issue

#469, new issuer name ovpt. on notes of the Provincial Bank of Kwangtung Province. It is considered spurious by some authorities.

		Good	Fine	XF
469	**1 Yüan** ND (1940 - old date 1.1.1918). Blue and m/c. Ovpt. on #S2401b. *(S/M #C290-61).*	—	—	—

1940 Third Provisional Issue

#470 and 471 new issuer name ovpt. on notes of the Szechuan Provincial Bank.

		Good	Fine	XF
470	**5 Yüan** ND (1940 - old date 1.7.1937). Green and m/c. Ovpt. on #S2823. *(S/M #C290-64).*	17.50	85.00	180.
471	**10 Yüan** ND (1940 - old date 1.7.1937). Purple and m/c. Ovpt. on #S2824. *(S/M #C290-67).*	20.00	100.	220.

1940 Fourth Provisional "Reconstruction" Issue

#472 and 473 new issuer m/c name ovpt. on notes of the Szechuan Provincial Government.

		Good	Fine	XF
472	**50 Yüan** ND (1940 - old date 1937). Blue and green. Ovpt. on #S2816. *Chungking. (S/M #C290-71).*	35.00	150.	500.

		Good	Fine	XF
473	**100 Yüan** ND (1940 - old date 1937). Orange and yellow. Ovpt. on #S2817. *Chungking. (S/M #C290-72).*	50.00	300.	600.

1941 Issue

#474 and 475 printer: TDLR.

		VG	VF	UNC
474	1 Yüan 1941. Brown on m/c unpt. SYS at l. House at ctr., sheep at r. on back. 3 serial # varieties. *(S/M #C290-80).*	.50	2.50	7.50

		VG	VF	UNC
475	5 Yüan 1941. Blue on m/c unpt. SYS at l. Temple at ctr., ox at r. on back. 3 serial # varieties. *(S/M #C290-81).*	.75	3.50	12.50

#476-478 boats near bridge at ctr. Bridge at ctr. on back. Printer: ABNC.

		VG	VF	UNC
476	50 Yüan 1941. Brown on green and m/c unpt. *(S/M #C290-82b).*			
	a. Issued note. Reported not confirmed	—	—	—
	b. Ovpt: *Chungking (S/M #C290-82a).*	2.50	5.00	15.00
	s. As b, 2 part specimen.	—	—	—
477	100 Yüan 1941. Purple on green and m/c unpt. *(S/M #C290-83b).*			
	a. Serial # on face only.	2.50	5.00	15.00
	b. Ovpt: *Chungking.* Serial # on face and back. *(S/M #C290-83a).*	2.00	4.00	14.00

		VG	VF	UNC
478	500 Yüan 1941. Green on brown and m/c unpt. Similar to #476. *(S/M #C290-84b).*			
	a. Issued note.	10.00	35.00	110.
	b. Black ovpt. *Chungking.* Specimen *(S/M #C290-84a).*	—	—	150.

1942 Issue

		VG	VF	UNC
479	50 Yüan 1942. Brown. Steam passenger train at l. Chinese printer: TTBC. *(S/M #C290-90).*	10.00	40.00	100.

		VG	VF	UNC
480	100 Yüan 1942. Green. Landscape and agricultural scene at r. Chinese printer: TYPC. *(S/M #C290-91).*	7.50	25.00	90.00

1943 Issue

#480A-482 agricultural scenes at l. and r. Ovpt: 7 characters below bank title. Printer: CTPA.

		Good	Fine	XF
480A	5 Yüan 1.10.1943. *(S/M #C290-97).*	25.00	50.00	150.
480B	10 Yüan 1.10.1943. Purple. Uniface. *(S/M #C290-98).*	17.50	35.00	120.

		Good	Fine	XF
481	**50 Yüan** 1.10.1943. Red. Like #480A. Back blue. *(S/M #C290-100).*	12.50	35.00	180.
482	**100 Yüan** 1.10.1943. Brown. Like #480A. *(S/M, #C290-101).*	12.50	45.00	175.

1945 Circulating Cashiers Check Issue

		Good	Fine	XF
483	**500 Yüan** 1945. Orange. Chinese printer: YAWY. *(S/M #C290-110).*	7.50	40.00	100.

		Good	Fine	XF
484	**1000 Yüan** 1945. Purple. Chinese printer: YAWY. *Shang Jao. (S/M #C290-111).*	7.50	40.00	100.

Great Northwestern Bank

行銀藏蒙

Men Tsang Yin Hang

1924 Issue

		Good	Fine	XF
485	**10 Cents** 1924. Red. *TIENTSIN. (S/M #M14-1).*	30.00	100.	500.

		Good	Fine	XF
486	**20 Cents** 1924. Dk. brown. *TIENTSIN. (S/M #M14-2).*	40.00	125.	700.
487	**50 Cents** 1924. *TIENTSIN. (S/M #M14-3).* Reported not confirmed.	—	—	—
488	**1 Dollar** 1924. *(S/M #M14-10).* Reported not confirmed.	—	—	—
489	**5 Dollars** 1924. *(S/M #M14-11).* Reported not confirmed.	—	—	—
490	**10 Silver Yüan** 1924. *(S/M #M14-12).* Reported not confirmed.	—	—	—

Industrial Development Bank of China

行銀業勸

Ch'uan Yeh Yin Hang

1921 Issues

		Good	Fine	XF
491	**1 Yüan** 1.2.1921. Red and m/c. Village gateway, bldg. at ctr. Printer: ABNC.			
	a. *PEKING. (S/M #C245-1a).*	12.50	55.00	220.
	b. *CHENGCHOW. (S/M #C245-1b).*	10.00	42.50	175.
	p. Proof.	—	Unc	130.
	r. Remainder w/o place name. *(S/M #C245-1c).*	—	Unc	120.
	s. Specimen.	—	Unc	80.00
492	**1 Yüan** 1921. Green and black. Bldg. at ctr. Printer: BEPP.			
	a. *PEKING. (S/M #C245-2a).*	30.00	175.	350.
	b. Remainder w/o place name. *(S/M #C245-2b).*	—	Unc	90.00

		Good	Fine	XF
493	**5 Yüan** 1.2.1921. Dk. blue and m/v. Village gateway, bldg. at ctr. Also w/various control letter ovpts. Printer: ABNC.			
	a. *PEKING. (S/M #C245-3a).*	20.00	60.00	250.
	b. *CHENGCHOW. (S/M #C245-3b).*	15.00	50.00	225.
	p. Proof.	—	Unc	120.
	s. Specimen.	—	Unc	65.00
494	**5 Yüan** 1.5.1921. Black and m/c. Back: brown. Printer: BEPP.			
	a. *PEKING. (S/M #C245-4a).*	15.00	60.00	300.
	b. *NANKING. (S/M #C245-4b).*	40.00	175.	400.
	c. *TIENTSIN. (S/M #C245-4c).*	25.00	145.	300.

		Good	Fine	XF
495	**10 Yüan**			
	1.2.1921. Dk. green and m/c. Village gateway, bldg. at ctr. Printer: ABNC.			
	a. *PEKING. (S/M #C245-5b).*	25.00	150.	320.
	p. Proof.	—	Unc	110.
	r. Remainder w/o place name. *(S/M #C245-5b).*	—	Unc	150.
	s. Specimen.	—	Unc	90.00

		Good	Fine	XF
496	**10 Yüan**			
	1.7.1921. Green and m/c. Back: brown. Printer: BEPP. *PEKING. (S/M #C245-6).*	25.00	150.	320.
496A	**50 Yüan**			
	1.2.1921. Orange on red and green unpt. Village gateway at ctr. Back: orange. *(S/M #C245-7).*			
	p. Proof w/o office of issue.	—	Unc	660.
	s. Specimen w/o office of issue.	—	Unc	500.
496B	**100 Yüan**			
	1.2.1921. Lt. blue on orange and olive-green unpt. Village gateway at ctr. Back: blue. *PEKING. (S/M #C245-8).*			
	a. Issued note. Reported not confirmed.	—	—	—
	p. Proof w/o office of issue.	—	Unc	1100.
	s. Specimen w/o office of issue.	—	Unc	825.

1927 ISSUE

#497 and 498 w/ovpt: *King Ching Tung Chun* at top on back. Printer: BEPP.

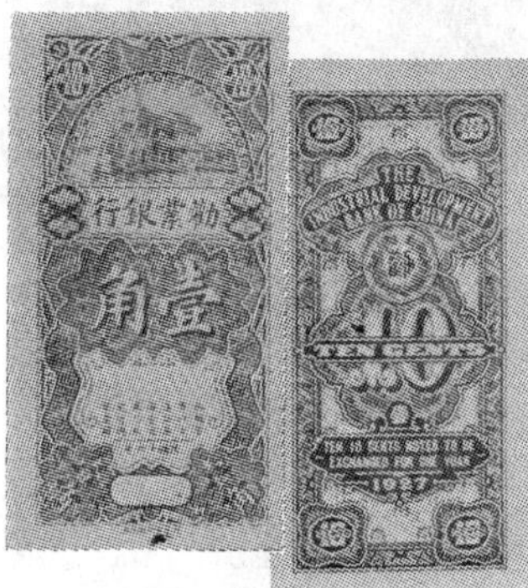

		Good	Fine	XF
497	**10 Cents**			
	1927. Dk. green. Waterfront palace at top ctr.			
	a. *TIENTSIN. (S/M #C245-10a).*	15.00	80.00	200.
	r. Remainder, w/o place name *(S/M #C245-10b).*	—	Unc	60.00
498	**20 Cents**			
	1927. Orange. Hillside pagoda at top ctr.			
	a. *TIENTSIN/PEKING. (S/M #C245-11a).*	20.00	50.00	125.
	r. Remainder, w/o place name. *(SM #C245-11b).*	—	Unc	50.00

1928 ISSUE

#499-500 fortress city at l. Temple of Heaven at ctr. on back. Printer: BEPP.

		Good	Fine	XF
499	**10 Cents**			
	1.9.1928. Red. *PEIPING. (S/M #C245-20a).*			
	a. Issued note.	10.00	20.00	100.
	r. Remainder, w/o place name.	—	Unc	40.00
499A	**10 Cents**			
	1.9.1928. Brown. *TIENTSIN. (S/M #C245-20b).*			
	a. Issued note.	10.00	40.00	120.
	r. Remainder, w/o place name.	—	Unc	60.00

		Good	Fine	XF
500	**20 Cents**			
	1.9.1928. Purple.			
	a. *PEIPING. (S/M #C245-21a).*	17.50	90.00	180
	b. *TIENTSIN. (S/M #C245-21b).*	14.00	70.00	140
	r. Remainder w/o place name. *(S/M #C245-21c).*	—	Unc	90.0

LAND BANK OF CHINA, LIMITED

行銀業墾國中

Chung Kuo K'en Yeh Yin Han

1926 ISSUE

#501-506 cliffs at l., shoreline temple at ctr. r. Shoreline at l. on back. Also w/various numerical, lette and Chinese character control ovpt. Printer: W&S.

		Good	Fine	X
501	**1 Dollar**			
	1.6.1926. Brown and m/c.			
	a. *SHANGHAI. (S/M #C285-1a).*	35.00	175.	35
	b. *TIENTSIN. (S/M #C285-1b).*	50.00	250.	50

		Good	Fine	X
502	**5 Dollars**			
	1.6.1926. Purple and green.			
	a. *SHANGHAI. (S/M #C285-2a).*	30.00	120.	5
	b. *TIENTSIN. (S/M #C285-2b).*	25.00	150.	7
503	**10 Dollars**			
	1.6.1926. Green and m/c.			
	a. *SHANGHAI. (S/M #C285-3a).*	35.00	150.	6
	b. *TIENTSIN. (S/M #C285-3b).*	50.00	200.	8

1931 Issue

		Good	Fine	XF
504	**1 Dollar** 1.6.1931. Red and green. *SHANGHAI. (S/M #C285-10).*	17.50	40.00	150.
505	**5 Dollars** 1.6.1931. Green and red. *SHANGHAI. (S/M #C285-11).*	25.00	50.00	175.
506	**10 Dollars** 1.6.1931. Yellow. *SHANGHAI. (S/M #C285-12).*	35.00	90.00	300.

National Bank of China - Nanking

中華國家銀行

Chung Hua Kuo Chia Yin Hang

1930 Issue

#507-510 Temple of Heaven at ctr. PEKING. Printer: BEPP.

		VG	VF	UNC
507	**20 Cents** 1930. Specimen. *(S/M #C260-1).*	—	—	700.

		VG	VF	UNC
508	**1 Dollar** 1930. Brown. Specimen. *(S/M #C260-10).*	—	—	600.

		VG	VF	UNC
509	**5 Dollars** 1930. Deep olive-green. Specimen. *(S/M #C260-11).*	—	—	600.
510	**10 Dollars** 1930. Orange. Specimen. *(S/M #C260-12).*	—	—	600.

National Bank of China - Canton

1921 Issue

#511-516 SYS at ctr. w/palm trees at l. and r. 3 men and a farmer w/an ox at ctr. on back.

		Good	Fine	XF
511	**10 Cents** 1921. Blue and black on pink unpt. Back brown. *(S/M #C261-1).*	75.00	225.	1000.
512	**20 Cents** 1921. *(S/M #C261-2).* Reported not confirmed.	—	—	—
513	**50 Cents** 1921. *(S/M #C261-3).* Reported not confirmed.	—	—	—
514	**1 Dollar** 1921. Blue and black on pink unpt. Back brown. *(S/M #C261-10).*	200.	800.	2400.
515	**5 Dollars** 1921. Green and black on pink unpt. Back brown on blue unpt. *(S/M #C261-11).*	150.	700.	2000.

		Good	Fine	XF
516	**10 Dollars** 1921. Red and black on yellow unpt. Back blue on yellow unpt. *(S/M #C261-12).*	375.	900.	3000.

The National Commercial Bank, Limited

中華國民銀行

Che Chiang Hsing Yeh Yin Hang

Law 4.7.1907

		Good	Fine	XF
516A	**1 Dollar** ND. Mandarin at l. Rooster at r. on back.			
	a. *HUPEH. (S/M #C22-).*	150.	600.	1750.
	b. *SHANGHAI. (S/M #C22-).*	200.	750.	2200.

		Good	Fine	XF
516B	**5 Dollars** ND. Orange. Mandarin at r. *(S/M #C22-).*			
	a. *HUPEH. (S/M #C22-).*	200.	750.	2000.
	b. *SHANGHAI. (S/M #C22-).*	250.	900.	2500.

		Good	Fine	XF
516C	**10 Dollars** ND. Brown. Mandarin at l. Rooster at r. on back. *SHANGHAI.* Specimen. *(S/M #C22-).*	300.	900.	2750.

1923 ISSUE

#517-519 printer: ABNC.

		Good	Fine	XF
517	**1 Dollar** 1.10.1923. Black and m/c. Mandarin at r. Rooster on back. Also w/various control letter ovpts.			
	a. *SHANGHAI. (S/M #C22-1a).*	22.50	75.00	225.
	b. *TIENTSIN. (S/M #C22-1b).*	22.50	75.00	225.
	c. *HUPEH. (S/M #C22-1c).*	30.00	110.	300.
	s. 2 part specimen as a.			

		Good	Fine	XF
518	**5 Dollars** 1.10.1923. Red and m/c. Mandarin at ctr. Rooster at r. on back. Also w/various control letter and Chinese character ovpts.			
	a. *SHANGHAI.* W/o sign. on face *(S/M #C22-2a).*	30.00	150.	300.
	b. *SHANGHAI.* Sign. on face. *(S/M #C22-2b).*	30.00	150.	300.
	c. *TIENTSIN. (S/M #C22-2c).*	35.00	175.	350.
	d. *NANKING. (S/M #C22-2d).*	45.00	225.	450.
	e. *HUPEH. (S/M #C22-2e).*	35.00	175.	350.

		Good	Fine	XF
519	**10 Dollars** 1.10.1923. Green and m/c. Old man at ctr. Rooster at l. on back.			
	a. *HUPEH. (S/M #C22-3c).*	55.00	225.	550.
	b. *SHANGHAI. (S/M #C22-3a).*	40.00	200.	400.
	c. *TIENTSIN. (S/M #C22-3b).*	50.00	250.	500.
519C	**10 Dollars** 1.10.1929. Fortress at l. *SHANGHAI.* Specimen. *(S/M #C22-).*	—	Unc	225.

NATIONAL INDUSTRIAL BANK OF CHINA

中國實業銀行

Chung Kuo Shih Yeh Yin Hang

1922 ISSUE

#520-524 landscape at l. Landscape at ctr. on back. Printer: BEPP.

		Good	Fine	XF
520	**1 Yüan** 1.6.1922.			
	a. *HANKOW. (S/M #C291-).*	45.00	180.	—
	b. *PEKING.* Specimen. *(S/M #C291-).*	—	Unc	200.
	c. *SHANGHAI.* Specimen. *(S/M #C291-).*	—	Unc	200.
	d. *TIENTSIN. (S/M #C291-).*	45.00	180.	—
521	**5 Yüan** 1.6.1922.			
	a. *HANKOW.* Specimen. *(S/M #C291-).*	—	Unc	300.
	b. *PEKING.* Specimen. *(S/M #C291-).*	—	Unc	300.
	c. *SHANGHAI.* 2 part specimen Shanghai.	—	Unc	300.
522	**10 Yüan** 1.6.1922.			
	a. *PEKING. (S/M #C291-1).*	40.00	200.	400.
	s1. W/o place name. Specimen. *(S/M #C291-).*			
	s2. 2 part specimen Shanghai.	—	—	—
523	**50 Yüan** 1.6.1922.			
	a. *PEKING.* Specimen. *(S/M #C291-).*	—	—	—
	s1. W/o place name. Specimen. *(S/M #C291-).*	—	—	—
	s2. 2 part specimen Shanghai.	—	—	—

		Good	Fine	XF
524	**100 Yüan** 1.6.1922.			
	a. *PEKING.* Specimen. *(S/M #C291-).*	—	—	—
	b. 2 part specimen Shanghai.	—	—	—
	s1. W/o place name. Specimen. *(S/M #C291-).*	—	—	—

1924 ISSUES

#525-530 Great Wall at ctr. on back. Sign. varieties. Also w/various numerical, letter and Chinese character ovpt. Printer: ABNC.

		Good	Fine	XF
525	**1 Yüan**			
	1924. Violet on m/c unpt. Running horse at upper l.			
	a. *SHANGHAI. (S/M #C291-1c).*	10.00	45.00	150.
	b. *TSINGTAO. (S/M #C291-1a).*	15.00	50.00	200.
	c. *WEIHAIWEI. (S/M #C291-1b).*	25.00	90.00	350.
	d. *PEKING. (S/M #C291-1e).*	15.00	50.00	200.
	e. *TIENTSIN (S/M #C291-1d).*	15.00	50.00	200.
	f. *SHANTUNG. (S/M #C291-1f).*	30.00	90.00	300.
526	**5 Yüan**			
	1924. Red and m/c. Running horse at ctr.			
	a. *HANKOW. (S/M #C291-2b).*	40.00	200.	400.
	b. *SHANGHAI. (S/M #C291-2a).*	20.00	85.00	190.
	c. *TIENTSIN. (S/M #C291-2c).*	22.50	60.00	225.
	d. *TSINGTAO. (S/M #C291-2d).*	37.50	125.	400.
	e. *PEKING. (S/M #C291-2e).*	30.00	100.	350.
	f. *WEIHAIWEI. (S/M #C291-2f).*	50.00	250.	500.

		Good	Fine	XF
527	**10 Yüan**			
	1924. Green and m/c. Running horse at r.			
	a. *SHANGHAI. (S/M #C291-3a).*	30.00	150.	300.
	b. *TIENTSIN. (S/M #C291-3b).*	40.00	150.	400.
	c. *PEKING. (S/M #C291-3c).*	40.00	150.	400.
	d. *SHANTUNG. (S/M #C291-3d).*	60.00	300.	600.
528	**50 Yüan**			
	1924. Orange. Running horse at ctr.			
	a. *PEKING. (S/M #C291-4a).*	75.00	400.	800.
	b. *SHANTUNG. (S/M #C291-4b).*	75.00	400.	800.
	c. *SHANGHAI. (S/M #C291-4c).*	—	Unc	600.
	s. Specimen. *(S/M #C291-4).*	—	Unc	400.

		Good	Fine	XF
529	**100 Yüan**			
	1924. Blue and m/c. Running horse at ctr.			
	a. *PEKING. (S/M #C291-5b).*	100.	500.	1000.
	b. *SHANGHAI. (S/M #C291-5a).*	120.	600.	1200.
	s. Specimen. *(S/M #C291-5).*	—	Unc	450.
530	**100 Yüan**			
	1924. Red. Specimen. *(S/M #C291-6).*	—	Unc	500.

1931 Issue

#531-533 Running horse at ctr. Bank bldg. at ctr. on back. Sign. varieties. Also w/various numerical, letter and Chinese characters ovtp. Printer: ABNC.

		Good	Fine	XF
531	**1 Yüan**			
	1931. Purple and m/c. 2 sign. varieties.			
	a. *FUKIEN. (S/M #C291-).*	25.00	125.	250.
	b. *Shanghai* on face; *SHANGHAI* on back. *(S/M #C291-10a).*	17.50	90.00	180.
	c. *Shanghai* on face only. *(S/M #C291-10b).*	15.00	70.00	140.
	d. *SHANTUNG. (S/M #C291-10c).*	35.00	175.	350.
	e. *TSINGTAO. (S/M #C291-10d).*	30.00	150.	300.
	f. *TIETSION.*	20.00	60.00	350.
	r. Remainder, w/o place name. *(S/M #C291-10).*	—	Unc	120.

		Good	Fine	XF
532	**5 Yüan**			
	1931. Red and m/c.			
	a. *SHANGHAI.* 2 sign. varieties. *(S/M #C291-11a).*	20.00	110.	220.
	b. *TIENTSIN. (S/M #C291-11b).*	27.50	140.	280.
	c. *FUKIEN. (S/M #C291-11c).*	40.00	200.	400.
	d. *FOOCHOW/FUKIEN. (S/M #C291-11d).*	40.00	200.	400.
	e. *AMOY/FUKIEN.*	50.00	150.	400.
	r. Remainder, w/o place name. *(S/M #C291-11).*			
533	**10 Yüan**			
	1931. Green and m/c.			
	a. *SHANGHAI. (S/M #C291-12).*	15.00	45.00	180.
	b. *TSINGTAO.*	17.50	75.00	250.

1935 Issue

		Good	Fine	XF
534	**1 Yüan**			
	1935. Red. Printer: W&S. *Shanghai. (S/M #C291-20).*	20.00	100.	200.

NINGPO COMMERCIAL AND SAVINGS BANK LIMITED
NINGPO COMMERCIAL BANK LIMITED
NINGPO COMMERCIAL BANK

四明銀行

Szu Ming Yin Hang

1920 ISSUES

#540-544 also w/various Chinese character ovpt. Printer: ABNC.

ovpt. see #170.

		Good	Fine	XF
539	**1 Dollar** 1920. Blue and m/c. *Shanghai. (S/M #S107-10).*			
	a. Issued note.	40.00	200.	400.
	b. Ovpt: *SH.*	40.00	200.	400.
540	**1 Dollar** 1.9.1920. Blue. Back orange. *Shanghai. (S/M #S107-11).*			
	a. Issued note.	40.00	200.	450.
	b. Ovpt: *SH.*	40.00	200.	450.

		Good	Fine	XF
541	**5 Dollars** 1.9.1920. Red and m/c. Bank at ctr. Floral pot at ctr on back. *SHANGHAI. (S/M #S107-12).*			
	a. Issued note.	20.00	100.	200.
	b. Ovpt: *NP.*	25.00	100.	250.
	c. Ovpt: *SH.*	25.00	100.	250.
	d. Ovpt: *Y.*	25.00	100.	250.

Note: For #541 w/additional *CENTRAL BANK* ovpt. see #170.

		Good	Fine	XF
542	**10 Dollars** 1.9.1920. Green. *SHANGHAI. (S/M #S107-13).*	40.00	150.	400.
543	**50 Dollars** 1.9.1920. Red and m/c. *SHANGHAI. (S/M #S107-14).*	75.00	350.	800.
544	**100 Dollars** 1.9.1920. Blue and m/c. *SHANGHAI. (S/M #S107-15).*	100.	400.	1100.

1921 ISSUE

		Good	Fine	XF
545	**1 Dollar** 1.11.1921. Red. Bank at ctr. Printer: BEPP. *SHANGHAI. (S/M #S107-20).*			
	a. Issued note.	35.00	125.	350.
	s. Specimen.			

NOTICE

Readers with unlisted dates, signature varieties, etc. are invited to submit photocopies or, high resolution (300 dpi, 100% size) scans of their notes to: Standard Catalog of World Paper Money, 700 East State St. Iola, WI 54990-0001, or E-Mail: george.cuhaj@fwpubs.com.

1925 ISSUES

#546-548B printer: G&D.

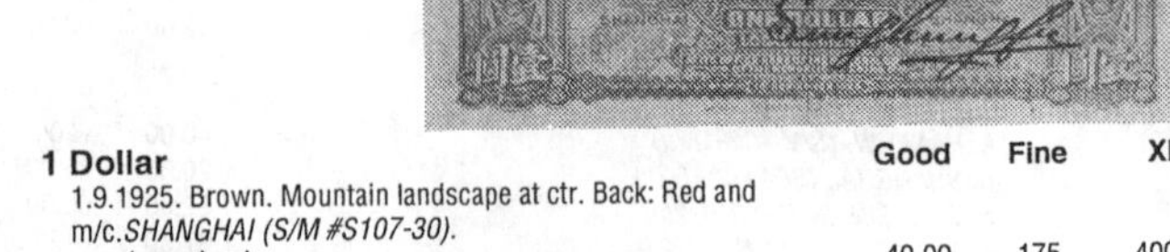

		Good	Fine	XF
546	**1 Dollar** 1.9.1925. Brown. Mountain landscape at ctr. Back: Red and m/c.*SHANGHAI (S/M #S107-30).*			
	a. Issued note.	40.00	175.	400.

		Good	Fine	XF
546A	**1 Dollar** 1.9.1925. Red on black unpt. Bank at ctr. Back red; similar to #546. *SHANGHAI (S/M #S107-).*	40.00	175.	400
547	**5 Dollars** 1.9.1925. Green. Mountain landscape at ctr. *SHANGHAI (S/M #S107-31).*	40.00	175.	450

Deceptive forgeries of this exist.

		Good	Fine	XF
547A	**5 Dollars** 1.9.1925. Green on m/c unpt. Back orange; bank at ctr. Specimen. *(S/M #S107-).*	—	Unc	180

		Good	Fine	XF
548	**10 Dollars** 1.9.1925. Black and red. Mountain landscape at ctr. *SHANGHAI. (S/M #S107-32).*	40.00	175.	425
548A	**10 Dollars** 1.9.1925. Black and red. Bank at ctr. *(S/M #S107-33).*	60.00	300.	600

		Good	Fine	XF
548B	**100 Dollars** 1.9.1925. Violet and m/c. Mountain landscape. Back similar to #541. *SHANGHAI (S/M #S107-35).*	75.00	375.	750.

1932-34 Issue

#549 and 550 printer: W&S.

Note: Mismatched dates on face and back.

		Good	Fine	XF
549	**1 Dollar** Jan. yr. 21 (1932) 11.1.1933. Red-brown. Mountain landscape at l. Back green. *SHANGHAI.*			
	a. Green serial #. *(S/M #S107-40a).*	7.50	30.00	120.
	b. Blue serial #. *(S/M #S107-40b).*	7.50	30.00	120.
	c. W/o serial # on face. *(S/M #S107-40c).*	7.50	30.00	120.

Note: Mismatched dates on face and back.

		Good	Fine	XF
550	**10 Dollars** January 1934. Red. Mountain landscape at l. *SHANGHAI. (S/M #S107-50).*	20.00	100.	200.

Tah Chung Bank

行銀中大

Ta Chung Yin Hang

1921 First Issue

#551-556 landscape at l., Great Wall at r. Printer: BEPP.

		VG	VF	UNC
551	**10 Cents** 1921. Green.			
	a. *HANKOW.* Specimen. *(S/M #T12-1b).*	—	—	150.
	b. *TIENTSIN. (S/M #T12-1a).*	15.00	45.00	160.
	c. *TSINGTAU.* Specimen. *(S/M #T12-1c).*	—	—	150.
552	**20 Cents** 1921. Orange.			
	a. *HANKOW.* Specimen. *(S/M #T12-2b).*	—	—	150.
	b. *TIENTSIN. (S/M #T12-2a).*	15.00	50.00	180.
	c. *TSINGTAU.* Specimen. *(S/M #T12-2c).*	—	—	150.
553	**50 Cents** 1921. Purple.			
	a. *HANKOW.* Specimen. *(S/M #T12-3b).*	—	—	150.
	b. *TIENTSIN.* Specimen. *(S/M #T12-3a).*	—	—	150.
	c. *TSINGTAU.* Specimen. *(S/M #T12-3c).*	—	—	150.

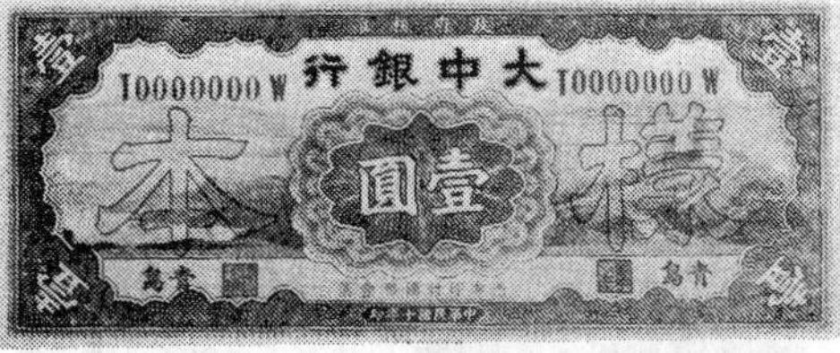

		VG	VF	UNC
554	**1 Yüan** 15.7.1921. Green and black.			
	a. *HANKOW.* Specimen. *(S/M #T12-10a).*	—	—	160.
	b. *TSINGTAU.* Specimen. *(S/M #T12-10b).*	—	—	160.
	c. *TIENTSIN. (S/M #T12-10c).*	15.00	40.00	220.
555	**5 Yüan** 15.7.1921. Orange and black.			
	a. *HANKOW.* Specimen. *(S/M #T12-11a).*	—	—	170.
	b. *TSINGTAU.* Specimen. *(S/M #T12-11b).*	—	—	170.
556	**10 Yüan** 15.7.1921. Purple and black.			
	a. *HANKOW.* Specimen. *(S/M #T12-12a).*	—	—	180.
	b. *TSINGTAU.* Specimen. *(S/M #T12-12b).*	—	—	180.
	c. *TIENTSIN. (S/M #T12-).*	30.00	150.	300.
	d. *CHUNGKING. (S/M #T12-).*	40.00	200.	400.

1921 Second Issue

#557 and 557A printer: BEPP.

		VG	VF	UNC
557	**1 Dollar** 1.1.1921. Brown. Landscape at ctr. *CHUNGKING.* Specimen. *(S/M #T12-).*	—	—	280.

		VG	VF	UNC
557A	**10 Dollars** 1.1.1921. Green and m/c. Landscape at ctr.			
	a. *PEKING.* Specimen. *(S/M #T12-13a).*	—	—	350.
	b. *CHUNGKING. (S/M #T12-13b).*	—	—	—

1932 Issue

		VG	VF	UNC
558	**10 Cents** 1932. Brown. Bell at ctr. *Tientsin. (S/M #T12-20).*	22.50	100.	220.

		VG	VF	UNC
559	**20 Cents** 1932. Green. Bell at ctr. *Tientsin. (S/M #T12-21).*	22.50	100.	220.
560	**50 Cents** 1932. *(S/M #T12-22).*	25.00	125.	280.

		VG	VF	UNC
561	**1 Yüan** 1.9.1932. Green. Back black; dollar coin at ctr. *SHANGHAI.* Specimen. *(S/M #T12-30).*	—	—	300.

		VG	VF	UNC
562	**5 Yüan** 1.9.1932. Black on m/c unpt. Bell at ctr. Back black; five 1-Yuan coins. *SHANGHAI.* Specimen. *(S/M #T12-31).*	—	—	350.
563	**10 Yüan** 1.9.1932. *SHANGHAI. (S/M #T12-32).*	—	—	400.

1938 ISSUE

#564-565 *PEKING.* Printer: BEPP.

		VG	VF	UNC
564	**1 Yüan** 15.1.1938. Green and black. Landscape at l., Great Wall at r. *(S/M #T12-40).*	20.00	75.00	200.
565	**5 Yüan** 15.1.1938. Orange and black. *(S/M #T12-41).*	20.00	100.	220.

BANK OF TERRITORIAL DEVELOPMENT

ТЕРРИТОРІАЛЬНО ПРОМЫШЛЕННЫЙ БАНКЪ В'Ъ КИТАЪ

行銀邊殖

Chih Pien Yin Har

1914 ISSUE

#566-572 printer: BEPP. Changchun issues w/ovpt: *N.B. Payable in subsidiary (silver) coins at par... on bac*

		Good	Fine	X
566	**1 Dollar** 1.12.1914. Green and black. Workers and camels along road at ctr.			
	a. *CHANGCHUN.* W/ovpt: *N.B. Payable by Ten Coins to The Dollar,* on back. *(S/M #C165-1a).*	10.00	60.00	180
	b. *CHANGCHUN/CHEKIANG. (S/M #C165-2a).*	10.00	60.00	180
	c. *CHANGCHUN/DOLONOR. (S/M #C165-2b).*	22.50	90.00	225
	d. *CHANGCHUN/HANKOW. (S/M #C165-2c).*	10.00	60.00	180
	e. CHANGCHUN/KIANGSU. (S/M #C165- 2d).	10.00	60.00	180
	f. *CHANGCHUN/SHANGHAI. (S/M #C165-2e).*	5.00	17.50	75.0
	g. *CHANGCHUN/TIENTSIN. (S/M #C165-2f).*	5.00	17.50	75.0
	h. *CHEKIANG. (S/M #C165-1b).*	5.00	60.00	180
	i. *HARBIN. (S/M #C165-1c).*	25.00	110.	300
	j. *KIANGSU. (S/M #C165-1d).*	10.00	60.00	180
	k. *KIRIN. (S/M #C165-1e).*	10.00	60.00	180
	l. *Fengtien//MOUKDEN. (S/M #C165-1f).*	10.00	60.00	180
	m. *Fengtien/ /MOUKDEN/CHANGCHUN. (S/M #C165-3a).*	10.00	60.00	180
	n. *Fengtien//MOUKDEN/YUNNAN. (S/M #C165-3b).*	10.00	60.00	180
	o. *SHANGHAI. (S/M #C165-1g).*	5.00	17.50	75.0
	p. *TIENTSIN. (S/M #C165-1h).*	5.00	17.50	75.0
	q. *CHANGCHUN/MUKDEN. (S/M #C165-).*	10.00	45.00	180
	r. Remainder, w/o place name or sign. *(S/M #C165-1i).*	5.00	15.00	50.0

		Good	Fine	X
567	**5 Dollars** 1.12.1914. Purple on yellow unpt. Hut along shoreline, ships at ctr.			
	a. *CHANGCHUN. (S/M #C165-4a).*	10.00	37.50	135
	b. *CHANGCHUN/CHEKIANG. (S/M #C165-5a).*	10.00	37.50	135
	c. *CHANGCHUN/HANKOW. (S/M #C165-5b).*	10.00	37.50	135
	d. *CHANGCHUN/HARBIN. (S/M #C165-5c).*	15.00	60.00	180
	e. *CHANGCHUN/KIANGSU. (S/M #C165-5d).*	10.00	37.50	135
	f. *CHANGCHUN/SHANGHAI. (S/M #C165-5e).*	10.00	37.50	135
	g. *DOLONOR. (S/M #C165-4b).*	30.00	135.	350
	h. *HARBIN. (S/M #C165-4c).*	30.00	135.	350
	i. *MANCHURIA.* w/ *N.B. payable in silver...* and *To be converted into silver dollars...* on back. *(S/M #C165-4d).*	15.00	60.00	180

	Good	Fine	XF
k. *Fengtien-MOUKDEN. (S/M #C165-4e).*	10.00	30.00	135.
l. *Fengtien-MOUKDEN/SHANGHAI. (S/M #C165-6a).*	10.00	30.00	135.
m. *Fengtien-MOUKDEN/YUNNAN. (S/M #C165-6b).*	10.00	30.00	135.
n. *SHANGHAI. (S/M #C165-4f).*	10.00	30.00	135.
o. *TIENTSIN. (S/M #C165-4g).*	10.00	30.00	135.
p. *CHEKIANG. (S/M #C165-).*	10.00	30.00	135.
q. *KIANGSI. (S/M #C165-).*	10.00	30.00	135.
r. *KIANGSU. (S/M #C165-).*	10.00	30.00	135.
s. *YUNNAN. (S/M #C165-).*	10.00	30.00	135.
t. Remainder, w/o place name or sign. *(S/M #C165-).*	7.50	22.50	90.00

568 10 Dollars	Good	Fine	XF
1.12.1914. Yellow and red. Roadbuilding at ctr.			
a. *CHANGCHUN. (S/M #C165-7a).*	15.00	60.00	180.
b. *CHANGCHUN/HANKOW. (S/M #C165-8a).*	15.00	60.00	180.
c. *CHANGCHUN/KIANGSU. (S/M #C165-8b).*	15.00	60.00	180.
d. *DOLONOR. (S/M #C165-7b).*	30.00	120.	360.
e. *KIANGSU. (S/M #C165-7c).*	15.00	60.00	180.
f. *KIRIN. (S/M #C165-7d).*	15.00	60.00	180.
g. *MANCHURIA. (S/M #C165-7e).*	22.50	75.00	225.
h. *SHANGHAI. (S/M #C165-7f).*	10.00	60.00	180.
i. *TIENTSIN. (S/M #C165-7g).*	10.00	60.00	180.
j. *CHANGCHUN/KALGAN. (S/M #C165-).*	10.00	60.00	180.
k. *CHANGCHUN/Fengtien/ /MOUKDEN. (S/M #C165-).*	10.00	60.00	180.
l. *CHANGCHUN/SHANGHAI.*	10.00	60.00	180.
m. *CHANGCHUN/TIENTSIN. (S/M #C165-).*	10.00	60.00	180.
r. Remainder, w/o place name or sign. *(S/M #C165-7h).*	7.50	30.00	120.

1915 ISSUE

#573-575 Russian text on back. Printer: CMN.

	Good	Fine	XF
569 5 Cents 1915. Red. *(S/M #C165-10).*	15.00	37.50	180.
570 10 Cents 1915. Purple. *(S/M #C165-11).*	15.00	37.50	180.

	Good	Fine	XF
571 20 Cents 1.11.1915. Green. Farm workers at l. *MANCHURIA. (S/M #C165-12).*	7.50	20.00	80.00

	Good	Fine	XF
572 50 Cents 1.11.1915. Black. Landscape at l. *MANCHURIA. (S/M #C165-13).*	15.00	60.00	150.
573 1 Dollar 1915. Green. *(S/M #C165-20).* Reported not confirmed	—	—	—

574 5 Dollars
1915. Brown and black on pink unpt. Similar to #575. *Urga.* Remainder w/o sign. *(S/M #C165-21).* — Unc 300.

575 10 Dollars
1915. Blue. *Urga.* Remainder w/o sign. *(S/M #C165-22).* — Unc 800.

1916 ISSUE

#576 and 577 w/# fields.

	VG	VF	UNC
576 100 Coppers 1916. Red and yellow. Remainder w/o place name, serial # or sign. *(S/M #C165-30).*			220.

577 200 Coppers
1916. Dk. green. Remainder w/o place name, serial # or sign. *(S/M #C165-31).* — Unc 300.

		VG	VF	UNC
578	**10 Cents**			
	1.11.1916. Purple. Cows at l.			
	a. *CHANGCHUN. (S/M #C165-40b).*	7.50	40.00	130.
	b. *MANCHURIA. (S/M #C165-40a).*	15.00	75.00	180.
	r. Remainder w/o serial #. *(S/M #C165-40).*	—	—	60.00
579	**20 Cents**			
	1916. *(S/M #C165-41).* Reported not confirmed	—	—	—

		VG	VF	UNC
580	**40 Cents**			
	1.11.1916. Black and red. Houses along shoreline at l. Back brown. *CHANGCHUN. (S/M #C165-42).*	20.00	100.	250.
581	**50 Cents**			
	1916. Black. *MANCHURIA.* Printer: BEPP. *(S/M #C165-43).*	25.00	125.	280.

#582-585 printer: ABNC.

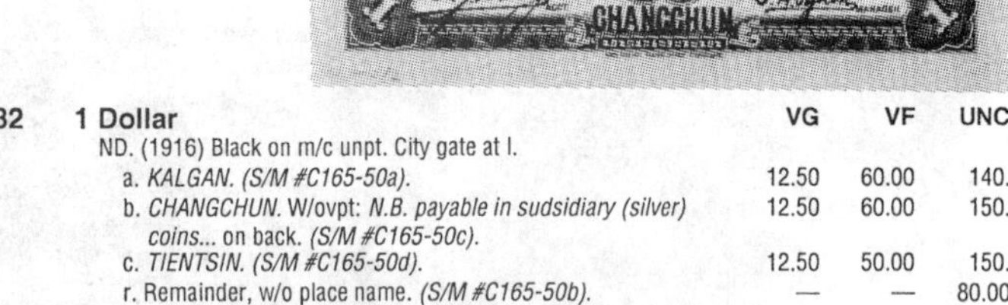

		VG	VF	UNC
582	**1 Dollar**			
	ND. (1916) Black on m/c unpt. City gate at l.			
	a. *KALGAN. (S/M #C165-50a).*	12.50	60.00	140.
	b. *CHANGCHUN.* W/ovpt: *N.B. payable in sudsidiary (silver) coins...* on back. *(S/M #C165-50c).*	12.50	60.00	150.
	c. *TIENTSIN. (S/M #C165-50d).*	12.50	50.00	150.
	r. Remainder, w/o place name. *(S/M #C165-50b).*	—	—	80.00

		VG	VF	UNC
583	**5 Dollars**			
	ND. (1916) Black on m/c unpt. Bldg. at shoreline at r.			
	a. *KALGAN. (S/M #C165-51b).*	15.00	75.00	180.
	b. *TIENTSIN. (S/M #C165-51a).*	15.00	75.00	180.
	c. *ANHWEI. (S/M #C165-51c).*	25.00	125.	300.
	d. *CHANGCHUN.* W/ovpt: *N.B. payable in subsidiary (silver) coins...* on back. *(S/M #C165-51).*	12.50	75.00	150.
	r. Remainder, w/o place name. *(S/M #C165-51).*	—	—	95.00

		VG	VF	UNC
584	**10 Dollars**			
	ND. (1916) Black on m/c unpt. Bldg. at l.			
	a. *SHANGHAI. (S/M #C165-52b).*	15.00	100.	200.
	b. *TIENTSIN. (S/M #C165-52a).*	15.00	100.	200.
	r. Remainder w/o place name. *(S/M #C165-52).*	—	—	120.
585	**50 Dollars**			
	ND. (1916) Black on m/c unpt. Bldg. r. Remainder w/o place name. *(S/M #C165-53).*	—	—	300.

1918 ISSUE

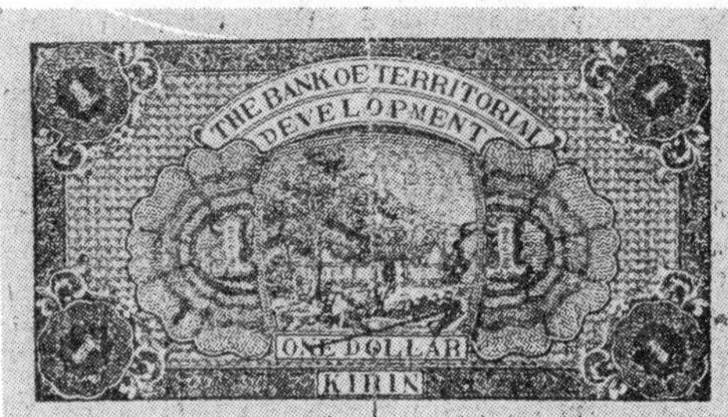

		VG	VF	UNC
585A	**1 Dollar**			
	1918. Green and black. Temple at l., rural bldgs. at r. Back green; rural bldgs. at ctr. *KIRIN. (S/M #C165-61).*	50.00	200.	500.

		VG	VF	UNC
585B	**5 Dollars**			
	1918. Lilac and green. Temple at l. *Kirin. (S/M #C165-).*	75.00	250.	750.

MINISTRY OF COMMUNICATIONS - PEKING-HANKOW RAILWAY

交通部京漢鐵路支付券

Chiao T'ung Pu Ching Han T'ieh Lu Chih Fu Ch'üan

6 MONTH SERIES 第十六期

		VG	VF	UNC
585C	10 Dollars Feb. 1922. Blue and red. *(S/M #C125-2c).*	1.25	4.00	12.50

24 MONTH SERIES 第二十四期

		VG	VF	UNC
586	5 Dollars Feb. 1922. Purple and red. *(S/M #C125-1a).*	1.25	4.00	12.50
587	10 Dollars Feb. 1922. Blue and red. *(S/M #C125-2a).*	1.25	4.00	12.50
588	50 Dollars Feb. 1922. Green and red. *(S/M #C125-3a).*	10.00	25.00	100.

25 MONTH SERIES 第二十五期

		VG	VF	UNC
588B	10 Dollars Feb. 1921. Blue and red. *(S/M #C125-2d).*	1.00	3.00	10.00

32 MONTH SERIES 第三十二期

		VG	VF	UNC
589	5 Dollars Feb. 1922. Purple and red. *(S/M #C125-1b).*	1.00	3.00	10.00
590	10 Dollars Feb. 1922. Blue and red. *(S/M #C125-2b).*	1.25	4.00	12.00
591	50 Dollars Feb. 1922. Green and red. *(S/M #C125-3b).*	10.00	40.00	100.

36 MONTH SERIES 第三十六期

		VG	VF	UNC
592	5 Dollars Feb. 1922. Purple and red. *(S/M #C125-1e).*	1.25	4.00	12.00
593	10 Dollars Feb. 1922. Blue and red. *(S/M #C125-2e).*	1.25	4.00	12.00
594	50 Dollars Feb. 1922. Green and red. *(S/M #C125-3e).*	10.00	40.00	100.

MILITARY EXCHANGE BUREAU

財政部軍需滙兌局

Ts'ai Cheng Pu Chün Hsü Hui Tui Chü

1927 ISSUE

		VG	VF	UNC
595	1 Yüan 1927. Black and m/c. Junks at upper l., ships at upper r. Back green; Great Wall at ctr. *(S/M #T181-1).*	50.00	200.	500.

MARKET STABILIZATION CURRENCY BUREAU

財政部平市官錢局

Ts'ai Cheng Pu P'ing Shih Kuan Ch'ien Chü

1910's (ND) ISSUE

#597 and 598 Temple of Heaven at ctr.

		VG	VF	UNC
597	20 Coppers ND. Brown. Back: green. *Peking. (S/M #T183-).*	—	—	—

		VG	VF	UNC
598	50 Coppers ND. (1910) Brown and blue. Back blue. *Honan.* Printer: BEPP. *(S/M #T183-).*	250.	600.	—
598A	100 Coppers ND (1910). Similar to #598.	—	—	—

1915 ISSUE

#599-603 have hillside pagoda at l.; Temple of Heaven at r.

		VG	VF	UNC
599	10 Coppers 1915. Black, blue and yellow.			
	a. *Ching Chao* (Peking). *(S/M #T183-1a).*	7.50	18.00	75.00
	b. *Ching Chao/Three Eastern Provinces. (S/M #T183-1c).*	9.00	25.00	90.00
	c. *Tientsin/Chihli. (S/M #T183-1b).*	9.00	25.00	90.00
	d. *Kiangsi. (S/M #T183-1d).*	6.00	17.50	60.00

		VG	VF	UNC
600	20 Coppers 1915. Black, purple and blue.			
	a. *Ching Chao. (S/M #T183-2a).*	9.00	30.00	95.00
	b. *Ching Chao/Chihli. (S/M #T183-2d).*	8.00	25.00	85.00
	c. *Ching Chao/Honan. (S/M #T183-2f).*	8.00	25.00	85.00
	d. *Ching Chao/Kiangsi. (S/M #T183-2c).*	8.00	25.00	85.00

	VG	VF	UNC
e. *Ching Chao/Shantung. (S/M #T183-2e).*	8.00	25.00	85.00
f. *Ching Chao/Three Eastern Provinces. (S/M #T183-2g).*	8.00	25.00	85.00
g. *Tientsin/Chihli. (S/M #T183-2b).*	8.00	25.00	85.00

601 40 Coppers
1915. Black, brown and green.

	VG	VF	UNC
a. *Chihli. (S/M #T183-3b).*	8.00	25.00	85.00
b. *Ching Chao. (S/M #T183-3a).*	7.50	18.00	75.00
c. *Ching Chao/Anhwei. (S/M #T183-3d).*	8.00	25.00	85.00
d. *Ching Chao/Chihli. (S/M #T183-3e).*	8.00	25.00	85.00
e. *Ching Chao/Honan. (S/M #T183-3f).*	8.00	25.00	85.00
f. *Ching Chao/Kiangsi. (S/M #T183-3g).*	8.00	25.00	85.00
g. *Ching Chao/Shantung. (S/M #T183-3h).*	8.00	25.00	85.00
h. *Kiangsu. (S/M #T183-3c).*	8.00	25.00	85.00
i. *Ching Chao/Peking. (S/M #T183-3i).*	8.00	25.00	85.00
j. *Shantung. (S/M #T183-3).*	8.00	25.00	85.00

602 50 Coppers
1915. Black, red and green.

	VG	VF	UNC
a. *Chihli. (S/M #T183-4b).*	6.00	18.00	75.00
b. *Ching Chao. (S/M #T183-4a).*	4.00	12.00	40.00
c. *Ching Chao/Heilungkiang. (S/M #T183-4f).*	6.00	15.00	55.00
d. *Ching Chao/Honan. (S/M #T183-4g).*	6.00	15.00	55.00
e. *Ching Chao/Kiangsi. (S/M #T183-4h).*	6.00	15.00	55.00
f. *Ching Chao/Kiangsu. (S/M #T183-4i).*	6.00	15.00	55.00
g. *Honan. (S/M #T183-4c).*	6.00	15.00	55.00
h. *Kiangsu. (S/M #T183-4d).*	6.00	15.00	55.00
i. *Kiangsu/Heilungkiang. (S/M #T183-4j).*	6.00	15.00	55.00
j. *Shantung. (S/M #T183-4e).*	6.00	15.00	55.00
k. *Peking. (S/M #T183-4k).*	6.00	15.00	55.00
l. *KIANGSI/HONAN. (S/M #T183-41).*	6.00	18.00	60.00
r. Remainder, w/o place name. *(S/M T183-4).*	6.00	15.00	55.00

603 100 Coppers
1915. Black, green and orange.

	VG	VF	UNC
a. *Anhwei. (S/M #T183-5b).*	6.00	18.00	90.00
b. *Chihli. (S/M #T183-5c).*	6.00	18.00	85.00
c. *Ching Chao. (S/M #T183-5a).*	6.00	18.00	85.00
d. *Ching Chao/Heilungkiang. (S/M #T183-5h).*	6.00	18.00	85.00
e. *Honan. (S/M #T183-5d).*	6.00	18.00	85.00
f. *Kiangsi. (S/M #T183-5d).*	6.00	18.00	85.00
g. *Shansi. (S/M #T183-5f).*	6.00	18.00	85.00
h. *Shantung. (S/M #T183-5g).*	6.00	18.00	85.00
i. *Peking. (S/M #T183-5i).*	6.00	18.00	85.00

1919 First Issue

		VG	VF	UNC
603A	**10 Coppers** Jan. 1919. Blue on green unpt. *Ching Chao. (S/M #T183-).*	7.50	35.00	75.00
603B	**20 Coppers** Jan. 1919. Blue-green on orange unpt. *Tientsin. (S/M #T183-).*	8.00	35.00	80.00

1919 Second Issues

604 10 Coppers
1919. Black and dk. blue-violet on lt. orange unpt. Back ochre and gray. Printer: BEPP.

	VG	VF	UNC
a. *Ching Chao. (S/M #T183-10a).*	7.50	25.00	100
b. *Ching Chao/Yen T'ai. (S/M #T183-10b).*	12.50	37.50	145
c. *Ching Chao/Peking. (S/M #T183-10c).*	12.50	37.50	145
d. *ChiNan. (S/M #T183-10d).*	12.50	37.50	14

1919 Third Issues

604A 10 Coppers
1919. Like #604 but back red-brown and lt. green.

	VG	VF	UN
a. *Chefoo, Shantung. (S/M #T183-).*	12.50	37.50	14
b. *Peking/? (S/M #T183-).*	12.50	37.50	14

605 20 Coppers
1919. Black, purple and blue. Printer: BEPP.

	VG	VF	UN
a. *Ching Chao. (S/M #T183-11a).*	10.00	25.00	10
b. *Ching Chao/Yen T'ai. (S/M #T183-11b).*	10.00	30.00	12
c. *Ching Chao/Peking. (S/M #T183-11c).*	10.00	30.00	12
d. *ChiNan. (S/M #T183-11d).*	15.00	60.00	18

1920 Issue

606 20 Coppers
1920. Black, blue and m/c. Printer: ABNC.

	VG	VF	UN
a. *Chihli. (S/M #T183-20b).*	9.00	25.00	1
b. *Ching Chao. (S/M #T183-20a).*	9.00	25.00	1

1921 First Issues

607 10 Coppers
1921. Black, blue and orange. Back w/o English.

	VG	VF	UN
a. *Chihli. (S/M #T183-30b).*	4.00	12.50	50
b. *Ching Chao. (S/M #T183-30a).*	4.00	12.50	50
c. *Peking. (S/M #T183-30c).*	4.00	12.50	50

		VG	VF	UN
607A	**10 Coppers** 1921. Similar to #607, but w/*10 COPPER COINS* on back. *Ching Chao. (S/M #T183-).*	5.00	18.00	50

608 20 Coppers
1921. Black, purple and blue.

	VG	VF	UN
a. *Ching Chao. (S/M #T183-31a).*	5.00	18.00	50
b. *Ching Chao/Chihli. (S/M #T183-31b).*	5.00	18.00	50

1922 Issues

		VG	VF	U
609	**10 Coppers** 1922. Black, blue and yellow. Printer: BEPP. *Ching Chao. (S/M #T183-40).*	6.00	18.00	55

610 20 Coppers
1922. Black, purple and blue. Printer: BEPP. 120 x 72mm.

	VG	VF	U
a. *Ching Chao. (S/M #T183-41a).*	5.00	12.50	4
b. *Ching Chao/Kiangsu. (S/M #T183-41b).*	5.00	12.50	4
c. *Shantung. (S/M #T183-41c).*	5.00	12.50	4

		VG	VF	UNC
611	**20 Coppers** 1922. Black, purple and blue. 139 x 82mm. *Ching Chao. (S/M #T183-42).*	4.00	12.50	40.00

1923 Issue

		VG	VF	UNC
612	**10 Coppers** 1923. Black, blue and yellow. 112 x 60mm.			
	a. *Ching Chao. (S/M #T183-50a).*	2.00	7.50	15.00
	b. *Shantung. (S/M #T183-50b).*	2.50	10.00	25.00
	c. *Tientsin. (S/M #T183-50c).*	2.50	10.00	25.00
613	**10 Coppers** 1923. Black, blue and yellow. 110 x 55mm. *Ching Chao. (S/M #T183-51).*	3.00	12.50	30.00

		VG	VF	UNC
614	**20 Coppers** 1923. Black, purple and blue.			
	a. *Ching Chao. (S/M #T183-52a).*	2.50	7.50	20.00
	b. *SHANTUNG. (S/M #T183-52b).*	5.00	17.50	50.00
615	**40 Coppers** 1923. Black, brown and green. *Ching Chao. (S/M #T183-53).*	4.50	15.00	45.00

1923 Second Issues

#616-622 printer: BEPP.

		VG	VF	UNC
616	**10 Cents** 1.6.1923. Blue. Palace at ctr. Back maroon.			
	a. *Peking. (S/M #T183-60b).*	1.25	5.00	15.00
	r. Remainder, w/o place name. *(S/M #T183-60a).*	1.00	2.50	12.50
617	**20 Cents** 1.6.1923. Purple. Similar to #531. Back orange.			
	a. *Peking. (S/M #T183-61b).*	1.25	5.00	15.00
	r. Remainder, w/o place name. *(S/M #T183-61a).*	1.00	2.50	12.50
618	**50 Cents** 1.6.1923. Green. Similar to #531. Back dk. brown.			
	a. *Kalgan. (S/M #T183-62c).*	4.50	12.50	45.00
	b. *Peking. (S/M #T183-62b).*	4.50	12.50	45.00
	r. Remainder, w/o place name. *(S/M #T183-62a).*	2.00	5.00	18.00
619	**1 Yüan** ND. (1923) Brown. Shrine at ctr. Remainder, w/o place name. *(S/M #T183-70).*	—	Unc	100.
620	**5 Yüan** ND. (1923) Purple. *(S/M #T183-71).*	10.00	40.00	120.
621	**10 Yüan** ND. (1923) *(S/M #T183-72).* Reported not confirmed.	—	—	—
622	**100 Yüan** ND. (1923) *(S/M #T183-73).* Reported not confirmed.	—	—	—

Special Circulating Notes

財政部特別流通券

Ts'ai Cheng Pu T'e Pieh Liu T'ung Ch'üan

#623-625 various dates 1923-24 w/an elongated purple hand stamped seal diagonally. This indicates that they were once presented for payment and then affixed to a separate document providing for redemption on a monthly installment basis through 1926. The full sheet has 39 stamp-sized coupons for the holder to clip and turn in. Peking: Printer: BEPP.

1923 Issue

		VG	VF	UNC
623	**1 Yüan** 1923. Blue. Arched bridge over stream at ctr. *(S/M #T184-1).*	2.00	7.50	20.00
624	**5 Yüan** 1923. Brown. Arched bridge over stream at ctr. *(S/M #T184-2).*	2.50	10.00	25.00
625	**10 Yüan** 1923. Red. Temple at ctr. *(S/M #T184-3).*	5.00	12.50	45.00

Fixed Term, Interest-bearing Treasury Notes

財政部定期有利國庫券

Ts'ai Cheng Pu Ting Ch'i Yu Li Kuo K'u Ch'üan

1919-20 Issue

#626-628 original date October 1919, vertically at lower r. and reissue date vertically at lower l. Printer: BEPP.

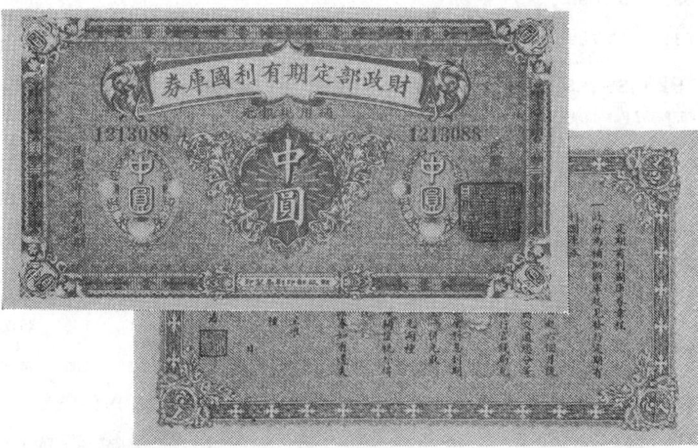

		VG	VF	UNC
626	**1/2 Yüan** 1919-20. Blue.			
	a. Aug., Oct., Dec. 1919. *(S/M #T185-1a).*	1.50	3.00	18.00
	b. April 1920. *(S/M #T185-1b).*	1.50	3.00	18.00
	c. June 1920. *(S/M #T185-1c).*	1.50	3.00	18.00
	r. Remainder, w/o date. *(S/M #T185-1d).*			15.00

		VG	VF	UNC
627	**1 Yüan** 1919-20. Orange.			
	a. Aug. 1919. *(S/M #T185-10a).*	1.50	3.00	18.00
	b. April 1920. *(S/M #T185-10b).*	1.50	3.00	18.00
	c. June 1920. *(S/M #T185-10c).*	1.50	3.00	18.00
	r. Remainder, w/o date. *(S/M #T185-10d).*	—	—	15.00

		VG	VF	UNC
628	**5 Yüan**			
	1919-20. Green.			
	a. Aug., Oct., Dec. 1919. *(S/M #T185-11a).*	2.00	4.50	22.50
	b. Feb., April, June, July 1920. *(S/M #T185-11b).*	2.00	4.50	22.50
	c. Aug., Oct. 1920. *(S/M #T185-11c).*	2.00	4.50	22.50
	r. Remainder, w/o date. *(S/M #T185-11d).*	—	—	15.00

1922 ISSUE

#629-631 Peking. Printer: BEPP.

		VG	VF	UNC
629	**1 Yüan**			
	1922. Brown. Back red. *(S/M #T185-20).*	2.00	6.00	22.50
630	**5 Yüan**			
	1922. Purple. Back red. *(S/M #T185-21).*	3.00	12.50	37.50
631	**10 Yüan**			
	1922. Green. Back red. *(S/M #T185-22).*	4.50	15.00	45.00

1923 ISSUES

#632-637 Peking. Printer: BEPP.

		VG	VF	UNC
632	**1 Yüan**			
	Feb. 1923. Red. Back blue. *(S/M #T185-30).*	2.00	6.00	22.50
633	**1 Yüan**			
	June 1923. Blue. Back green. *(S/M #T185-31).*	2.00	6.00	22.50
634	**5 Yüan**			
	Feb. 1923. Blue. *(S/M #T185-32).*	4.00	10.00	37.50
635	**5 Yüan**			
	June 1923. Brown. Back green. *(S/M #T185-33).*	4.00	10.00	37.50
636	**10 Yüan**			
	Feb. 1923. Purple. Back blue. *(S/M #T185-34).*	4.50	15.00	45.00
637	**10 Yüan**			
	June 1923. Red. Back green. *(S/M #T185-35).*	4.50	15.00	4.50

SHORT TERM, INTEREST-BEARING EXCHANGE NOTES

財政部短期有利兌換券

Ts'ai Cheng Pu Tuan Ch'i Yu Li Tui Huan Ch'üan

1922 ISSUE

		VG	VF	UNC
638	**1 Yüan**			
	1922. Brown. Temple at ctr. *(S/M #T186-1).*	2.25	6.00	22.50

		VG	VF	UNC
639	**5 Yüan**			
	1922. Purple. *(S/M #T186-2).*	3.00	12.50	30.00
640	**10 Yüan**			
	1922. Green. *(S/M #T186-3).*	3.00	10.00	30.00

INTEREST-BEARING, CIRCULATING NOTES

財政部有利流通券

Ts'ai Cheng Pu Yu Li Liu T'ung Ch'üan

1923 ISSUE

		VG	VF	UNC
641	**1 Yüan**			
	1.2.1923. Red. Pagoda on hill shoreline at ctr. *(S/M #T187-1).*			
	a. Issued note.	2.00	4.00	18.00
	b. Ovpt: 2 vertical columns 20 Chinese characters at l. on back.	3.00	9.00	25.00
	c. Punched hole cancelled.			12.50

		VG	VF	UNC
642	**5 Yüan**			
	1.2.1923. Blue. Arched bridge over stream at ctr. *(S/M #T187-2).*	2.50	5.00	20.00

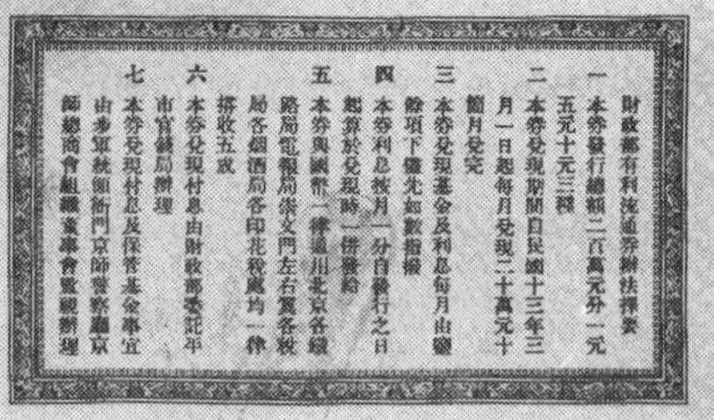

		VG	VF	UNC
643	**10 Yüan**			
	1.2.1923. Purple. House, bridge at ctr. *(S/M #T187-3).*	2.00	6.00	22.50

PEOPLES REPUBLIC OF CHINA

The Peoples Republic of China, located in eastern Asia, has an area of 3,696,100 sq. mi. (9,572,900 sq. km.), including Manchuria and Tibet, and a population of 1.14 billion. Capital: Beijing (Peking). The economy is based on agriculture, mining and manufacturing. Textiles, clothing, metal ores, tea and rice are exported.

In the fall of 1911, the middle business class of China and Chinese students educated in Western universities started a general uprising against the Manchu Dynasty which forced the abdication on Feb. 12, 1912, of the boy emperor Hsuan T'ung (Pu-yi), thus bringing to an end the Manchu Dynasty that had ruled China since 1644. Five days later, China formally became a republic with physician and revolutionist Dr. Sun Yat-sen as first provisional president.

Dr. Sun and his supporters founded a new party called the Kuomintang, and planned a Chinese republic based upon the Three Principles of Nationalism, Democracy and People's Livelihood. They failed, however, to win control over all of China, and Dr. Sun resigned the presidency in favor of Yuan Shih Kai, the most powerful of the Chinese Army generals. Yuan ignored the constitution of the New Republic and tried to make himself emperor.

After the death of Yuan in 1917, Dr. Sun Yat-sen and the Kuomintang established a republic in Canton. It also failed to achieve the unification of China, and in 1923 Dr. Sun entered into an agreement with the Soviet Union known as the Canton-Moscow Entente. The Kuomintang agreed to admit Chinese communists to the party. The Soviet Union agreed to furnish military advisers to train the army of the Canton Republic. Dr. Sun died in 1925 and was succeeded by one of his supporters, General Chiang Kai-shek.

Chiang Kai-shek launched a vigorous campaign to educate the Chinese and modernize their industries and agriculture. Under his command, the armies of the Kuomintang captured Nanking (1927) and Peking (1928). In 1928, Chiang was made president of the Chinese Republic. His government was recognized by most of the great powers, but he soon began to exercise dictatorial powers. Prodded by the conservative members of the Kuomintang, he initiated a break between these members and the Chinese Communists which, once again, prevented the unification of China.

Persuaded that China would fare better under the leadership of its businessmen in alliance with the capitalist countries than under the guidance of the Chinese Communists in alliance with the Soviet Union, Chiang expelled all Communists from the Kuomintang, sent the Russian advisers home, and hired German generals to train his army.

The Communists responded by setting up a government and raising an army that during the period of 1930-34 acquired control over large parts of Kiangsi, Fukien, Hunan, Hupeh and other provinces. These early Communist centers issued local currency in the form of some copper and silver coins and many varieties of notes printed mostly on paper and a few issues on cloth. A lack of minting facilities limited the issue of coins. Low mintage and the demonetization of silver in China in 1935 have elevated the surviving coinage specimens to the status of highly valued numismatic rarities. The issues of notes, the majority of which bore revolutionary slogans and often cartoon-like vignettes have also suffered a high attrition rate and certain issues command appreciable premiums in today's market.

When his army was sufficiently trained and equipped, Chiang Kai-shek led several military expeditions against the Communist Chinese which, while unable to subdue them, dislodged them south of the Yangtze, forcing them to undertake in 1935 a celebrated "Long March" of 6,000 miles (9,654 km.) from Hunan northwest to a refuge in Shensi province just south of Inner Mongolia from which Chiang was unable to displace them.

The Japanese menace had now assumed warlike proportions. Chiang rejected a Japanese offer of cooperation against the Communists, but agreed to suppress the movement himself. His generals, however, persuaded him to negotiate a truce with the Communists to permit united action against the greater menace of Japanese aggression. Under the terms of the truce, Communists were again admitted to the Kuomintang. They, in turn, promised to dissolve the Soviet Republic of China and to cease issuing their own currency.

The war with Japan all but extinguished the appeal of the Kuomintang, appreciably increased the power of the Communists, and divided China into three parts. The east coast and its principal cities - Peking, Tientsin, Nanking, Shanghai and Canton - were in Japanese-controlled, puppet-ruled states. The Communists controlled the countryside in the north where they were the de facto rulers of 100 million peasants. Chiang and the Kuomintang were driven toward the west, from where they returned with their prestige seriously damaged by their wartime performance.

At the end of World War II, the United States tried to bring the Chinese factions together in a coalition government. American mediation failed, and within weeks the civil war resumed.

By the fall of 1947, most of northeast China was under Communist control. During the following year, the war turned wholly in favor of the Communists. The Kuomintang armies in the north-east surrendered, two provincial capitals in the north were captured, a large Kuomintang army in the Huai river basin surrendered. Four Communist armies converged upon the demoralized Kuomintang forces. The Communists crossed the Yangtse in April 1949. Nanking, the Nationalist capital, fell. The civil war on the mainland was virtually over.

Chiang Kai-shek relinquished the presidency to Li Tsung-jen, his deputy, and after moving to Canton, to Chungking and Chengtu, retreated from the mainland to Taiwan (Formosa) where he resumed the presidency.

The Communist Peoples Republic of China was proclaimed on September 21, 1949. Thereafter relations between the Peoples Republic and the Soviet union steadily deteriorated. China emerged as an independent center of Communist power in 1958.

During and following World War II, the Chinese Communists again established banks at the various Communist centers to issue local currency. Prominent among Communist regional banks were the Bank of Central China, Bank of Peihai, and Bank of Shansi, Chahar and Hopeh.

The complexity of regional banks with their widely varying exchange rates was replaced in December 1948 by the Peoples Bank of China. Beneficial effects of the centralization were not immediately apparent. The pace of inflation was unslowed and regional note-issuing agencies continued to operate in remote areas for more than a year. Upon the defeat of the Kuomintang and the establishment of the Peoples Republic of China, the Communist government issued a new form of currency, the "Peoples Currency", as a replacement for all other notes in an effort to inject a stabilizing influence into the disorganized economy. Peoples Currency, Foreign Exchange Certificates and certain local or emergency issues are the only forms of paper money permitted to circulate by the Communist government.

TITLES:

Issuer's name reads from r. to l. until 1951 and from then on it reads from l. to r.

DATING:

The new Peoples Republic carried on with the years of the old Republic into 1949. Then they converted to western dating reading r. to l. in Chinese into 1951 when it was then reversed to be read from l. to r.

MONETARY SYSTEM:

1 Yüan = 10 Chiao
1 Chiao = 10 Fen

PEOPLES BANK OF CHINA

行銀民人國中

Chung Kuo Jen Min Yin Hang

Zhong Guo Ren Min Yin Hang

1948 ISSUES

		VG	VF	UNC
800	**1 Yüan** 1948. Blue and lt. red. 2 workers at l. Back brown. *(S/M #C282-1).*	2.50	7.50	25.00

		VG	VF	UNC
801	**5 Yüan** 1948. Dk. blue. Junks at l. Back green. *(S/M #C282-3).*	3.00	10.00	30.00

		VG	VF	UNC
802	**5 Yüan** 1948. Green. Sheep at l. *(S/M #C282-2).*	2.50	10.00	30.00

		VG	VF	UNC
803	**10 Yüan** 1948. Blue-green and black on lt. green unpt. Farm laborers at l., coal mine at r. Back lt. blue. *(S/M #C282-4).*	5.00	20.00	40.00

		VG	VF	UNC
804	**20 Yüan** 1948. Brown. Chinese w/donkeys at l., steam passenger trains at r. Back dk. red. *(S/M #C282-5).*	10.00	60.00	150.

		VG	VF	UNC
805	**50 Yüan** 1948. Red-brown and black on lt. green unpt. Donkey operated well at l., coal mine at r. Back tan on ochre unpt. *(S/M #C282-6).*	10.00	150.	400.

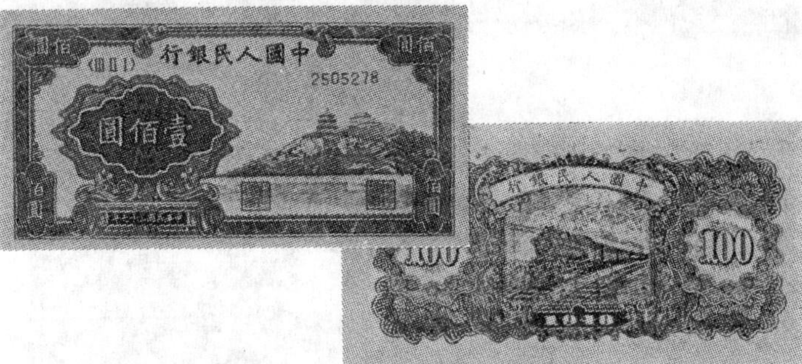

		VG	VF	UNC
806	**100 Yüan** 1948. Dk. green. Hillside pagoda, shoreline at r. Steam passenger train at ctr. on back. *(S/M #C282-11).*	12.50	60.00	140.

		VG	VF	UNC
807	**100 Yüan** 1948. Brown-violet w/olive green guilloche at ctr. Factory at l., steam passenger trains at r. Back brown on gold unpt. *(S/M #C282-10).*			
	a. Blue unpt. on face.	10.00	55.00	300.
	b. W/o unpt. on face.	10.00	55.00	300.

		VG	VF	UNC
808	**100 Yüan** Black and brownish red. Farm couple plowing w/ox at l., factory at r. Back lt. orange-brown. *(S/M #C282-9).*	10.00	65.00	150.

#809 not assigned.

		VG	VF	UNC
810	**1000 Yüan** 1948. Gray-violet. Farmer plowing w/horses at l. Back brown; Temple of Heaven at ctr. 2 serial # varieties. *(S/M #C282-14).*	15.00	75.00	200.

1949 ND PROVISIONAL ISSUE

		VG	VF	UNC
811	**150 Yüan** ND (-old date 1949). Ovpt: *150 Yuan* on #821.	30.00	150.	350.

1949 ISSUES

		VG	VF	UNC
812	**1 Yüan** 1949. Dk. purple on lt. blue unpt. Factory at l. Back dk. purple. *(S/M #C282-20).*	2.50	12.50	25.00

		VG	VF	UNC
813	**5 Yüan** 1949. Brown on lt. yellow unpt. 2 women weaving at l. Back brown. *(S/M #C282-21).*	2.50	12.50	25.00

		VG	VF	UNC
813A	**5 Yüan** 1949. Red. Vertical format. *Kiangsi. (S/M #C282-22).*	45.00	225.	450

		VG	VF	UNC
814	**5 Yüan** 1949. Lt. blue. Plow at l., man w/donkey cart at ctr., steer at r. Back purple. *(S/M #C282-).*	40.00	150.	45

		VG	VF	UNC
814A	**5 Yüan** 1949. Blue. Factory at l. Back: brown w/hydro-electric plant at ctr. Specimen. *(S/M #C282-).*	—	—	120
814B	**5 Yüan** 1949. Purple. Sawing wood, planting rice, steam passenger train at l. W/o serial #. *(S/M #C282-).*	—	—	

		VG	VF	UNC
815	**10 Yüan**			
	1949. Red and black. Workers at l., farmer plowing w/ox at r. 2 serial # varieties. Back brown. *(S/M #C282-25).*	2.50	12.50	25.00

		VG	VF	UNC
816	**10 Yüan**			
	1949. Gray-blue on green unpt. Farmer and worker at l. *(S/M #C282-23).*	2.50	12.50	25.00

		VG	VF	UNC
817	**10 Yüan**			
	1949. Brown on yellow and olive-green unpt. Steam passenger train in front of factory at l. Back olive-green. *(S/M #C282-24).*			
	a. Issued note.	17.50	90.00	180.
	s. Specimen.	—	—	—
818	**10 Yüan**			
	1949. Vertical format. *Kiangsi. (S/M #C282-26).*	—	—	400.
818A	**10 Yüan**			
	1949. Purple and yellow. Truck by factory at l., ox drawn irrigation system at r. W/o serial #. *(S/M #C282-).*	—	—	—
818B	**10 Yüan**			
	1949. Blue and brown. Like #818A. W/o serial #. *(S/M #C282-).*	—	—	—

		VG	VF	UNC
819	**20 Yüan**			
	1949. Lilac-brown. Pagoda at shoreline in foreground at l. Back black. *(S/M #C282-31).*	17.50	85.00	190.
820	**20 Yüan**			
	1949. Blue. Similar to #819. Back black. *(S/M #C282-30).*	10.00	50.00	100.

		VG	VF	UNC
821	**20 Yüan**			
	1949. Green w/brown and black guilloche. Factory, bridge and steam passenger train at l. Back green. *(S/M #C282-32).*	3.50	17.50	35.00

Note: For issues w/5 Chinese character ovpt. at r. see 150 Yuan, #836A.

		VG	VF	UNC
822	**20 Yüan**			
	1949. Violet on lt. ochre unpt. Junks at l., coal mine at r. Back tan. *(S/M #C282-27).*	30.00	125.	300.
823	**20 Yüan**			
	1949. Blue on lt. blue unpt. Agricultural occupations. *(S/M #C282-).*	20.00	90.00	200.
824	**20 Yüan**			
	1949. Bluish purple on lt. green unpt. 2 workers pushing ore car at ctr. Back olive-green. *(S/M #C282-33).*	4.50	20.00	45.00

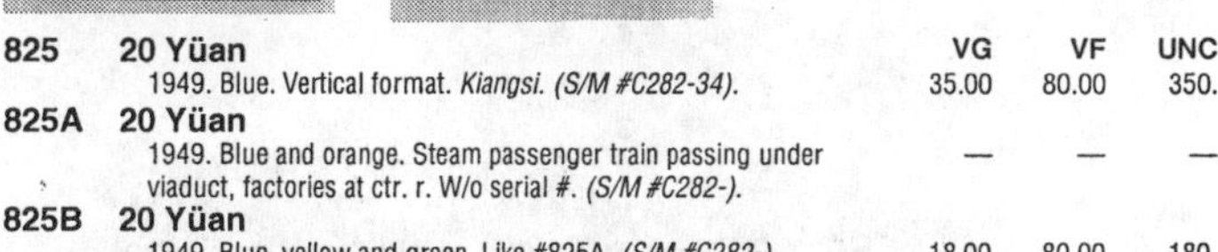

		VG	VF	UNC
825	**20 Yüan**			
	1949. Blue. Vertical format. *Kiangsi. (S/M #C282-34).*	35.00	80.00	350.
825A	**20 Yüan**			
	1949. Blue and orange. Steam passenger train passing under viaduct, factories at ctr. r. W/o serial #. *(S/M #C282-).*	—	—	—
825B	**20 Yüan**			
	1949. Blue, yellow and green. Like #825A. *(S/M #C282-).*	18.00	80.00	180.

		VG	VF	UNC
826	**50 Yüan**			
	1949. Dk. blue w/purple guilloche at ctr. Steam passenger train at l., bridge at r. Back red. *(S/M #C282-41).*	35.00	175.	350.
827	**50 Yüan**			
	1949. Red w/orange guilloche at ctr. Similar to #826. Back blue. *(S/M #C282-41).*	75.00	325.	750.

		VG	VF	UNC
828	**50 Yüan**			
	1949. Gray-olive w/brown guilloche at l. Steam roller at r. Back reddish brown. *(S/M #C282-37).*	25.00	125.	250.

		VG	VF	UNC
829	**50 Yüan** 1949. Dk. blue and black on lt. gold unpt. Steam passenger train at ctr. 2 serial # varieties. Back brown. *(S/M #C282-35).*	4.00	20.00	40.00

		VG	VF	UNC
830	**50 Yüan** 1949. Red-brown. Farmer and laborer at ctr. 2 serial # varieties. *(S/M #C282-36).*	4.00	15.00	90.00

		VG	VF	UNC
831	**100 Yüan** 1949. Red on orange unpt. Brown and red guilloche. Ship dockside at r. Back red on orange unpt. *(S/M #C282-43).*	3.00	15.00	30.00

		VG	VF	UNC
832	**100 Yüan** 1949. Dk. brown and black on blue unpt. Bridge and Peking pagoda at l., shrine at r. 3 serial # varieties. Back like #833. *(S/M #C282-44).*	10.00	45.00	100.
833	**100 Yüan** 1949. Brown and black on orange unpt. Similar to #832. Back purple on blue unpt. *(S/M #C282-45).*			
	a. Red sign. seals 20mm apart.	10.00	45.00	100.
	b. Red sign. seals 42mm apart.	10.00	45.00	100.

		VG	VF	UN
834	**100 Yüan** 1949. Red on purple unpt. Factories at l. and r. Back brown. *(S/M #C282-42).*	2.00	15.00	15

		VG	VF	UN
835	**100 Yüan** 1949. Brown on green unpt. Sampans at l. *(S/M #C282-).*	125.	550.	125

		VG	VF	U
836	**100 Yüan** 1949. Brown and black on lt. gold unpt. Donkey train w/factories behind at l. ctr., peasants hoeing at r. Back blue-green. *(S/M #C282-46).*	3.00	15.00	30

		VG	VF	U
837	**200 Yüan** 1949. Lilac-brown w/green guilloche at l. Pagoda near shoreline at r. 2 serial # varieties. Back dk. brown on lt. olive unpt. *(S/M #C282-51).*	10.00	50.00	1

		VG	VF	U
838	**200 Yüan** 1949. Purple on green unpt. Great Wall at r. Back purple. *(S/M #C282-47).*	7.50	35.00	7
838A	**200 Yüan** 1949. Like #838 but blue-gray on green unpt. Back brown. *(S/M #C282-47.5).*	4.00	20.00	4

		VG	VF	UNC
839	**200 Yüan** 1949. Blue-green. Harvesting at l. *(S/M #C282-52).*	50.00	175.	550.

		VG	VF	UNC
840	**200 Yüan** 1949. Brown w/blue and black guilloche on orange unpt. Steel plant at l. White or tan paper. Back brown on orange unpt. *(S/M #C282-53).*	7.00	35.00	70.00

		VG	VF	UNC
841	**200 Yüan** 1949. Blue on lt. orange unpt. House at l. behind bronze cow, bridge at r. Back red-brown. *(S/M #C282-50).*	25.00	125.	250.

		VG	VF	UNC
842	**500 Yüan** 1949. Reddish-brown. Peasant walking at l., small bridge at r. Back aqua. *(S/M #C282-56).*	22.50	110.	220.

		VG	VF	UNC
843	**500 Yüan** 1949. Brown and black. Steam shovel at r. Back dk. brown. *(S/M #C282-55).*	10.00	50.00	100.

		VG	VF	UNC
844	**500 Yüan** 1949. Dk. brown on lilac and lt. blue unpt. City gate at ctr. Back dk. brown on lt. blue unpt. *(S/M #C282-57).*	27.50	140.	280.

		VG	VF	UNC
845	**500 Yüan** 1949. Violet and black on brown and lt. blue unpt. Farmer plowing w/mule at ctr. Back brown. *(S/M #C282-).*	40.00	200.	400.

		VG	VF	UNC
846	**500 Yüan** 1949. Green on lt. green and red unpt. Tractor plowing at l. Back green on tan unpt. *(S/M #C282-54).*	5.00	15.00	75.00

		VG	VF	UNC
847	**1000 Yüan** 1949. Black w/ m/c guilloche at l. Town view and bridge at r. Back purple. *(S/M #C282-61).*	2.50	7.50	30.00

		VG	VF	UNC
848	**1000 Yüan** 1949. Blue-black. Tractors at l. and at r. Farmer at ctr. on back. *(S/M #C282-63).*	12.50	60.00	225.

		VG	VF	UNC
849	**1000 Yüan** 1949. Dk. green and brown on lt. blue unpt. Harvesting scene w/donkey cart at r. Back dk. green. *(S/M #C282-60).*	5.00	12.50	60.00

		VG	VF	UNC
850	**1000 Yüan** 1949. Lilac-brown on gray and brown unpt. Factory at l. w/man pushing ore hopper in foreground, farmer plowing w/2 donkeys at r. Back lilac-brown; ship dockside at ctr. *(S/M #C282-62).*	10.00	50.00	200.

		VG	VF	UNC
851	**5000 Yüan** 1949. Dk. gray-green on lt. green and blue unpt. Tractor tilling at ctr. *(S/M #C282-65).*	7.50	40.00	160.

		VG	VF	UNC
852	**5000 Yüan** 1949. Black-green. 3 tractors at l., factory at r. Back black on tan and blue unpt. *(S/M #C282-64).*	7.50	35.00	90.00

		VG	VF	UNC
853	**10,000 Yüan** 1949. Dk. brown and yellow on lt. brown unpt. Farmers plowing w/horses at ctr. Back lilac; boy w/farm animals at ctr. *(S/M #C282-67).*	4.00	10.00	45.00

		VG	VF	UNC
854	**10,000 Yüan** 1949. Green on m/c unpt. Warship at ctr. Back brown. *(S/M #C282-66).*	5.00	25.00	50.00

1950 Issue

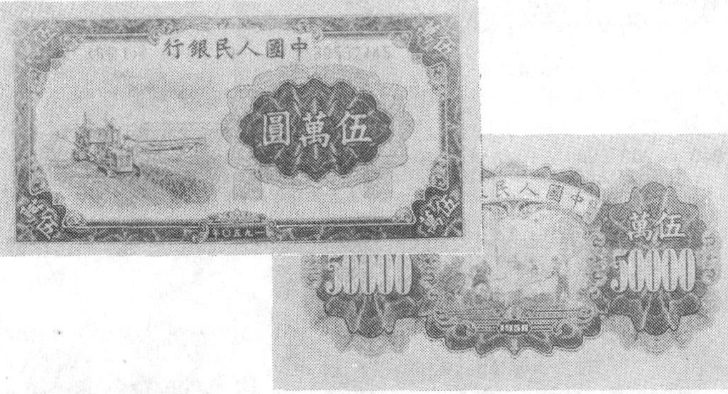

		VG	VF	UN
855	**50,000 Yüan** 1950. Dk. green. Combine harvester at l. Back dk. brown-violet; foundry workers at ctr. *(S/M #C282-).*	300.	750.	-

		VG	VF	UN
856	**50,000 Yüan** 1950. Blue on lt. green unpt. Bldg. at r. *(S/M #C282-).*	100.	850.	20

1951 Issue

Note: Specimen books of #857-859 were "liberated" from the Peoples Bank. They usually have glue sta on back at l. and r. edges.

		VG	VF	U
857	**500 Yüan** 1951. Violet. City gate, Arabic legends w/*Sinkiang* on back. *(S/M #C282-70).*			
	a. Issued note.	500.	2250.	5
	s. Specimen.	—	—	1

857A 1000 Yüan

1951. Horses grazing by tents. Arabic legends w/*Singkiang* on back. *(S/M #C282-).*

	VG	VF	UNC
a. Issued note.	300.	1500.	3000.
s. Specimen.	—	—	1000.

857B 5000 Yüan

1951. Blue-green and black. Tents and camel at r. Back dk. blue. *(S/M #C282-).*

	VG	VF	UNC
a. Issued note.	1000.	3500.	—
b. Specimen.	—	—	1000.

57C 5000 Yüan

1951. Purple and black on yellow unpt. Sheep grazing at r. Back green; Arabic legends w/*Sinkiang at ctr. (S/M #C282-).*

	VG	VF	UNC
a. Issued note.	250.	1200.	2500.
s. Specimen.	—	—	950.

58 10,000 Yüan

1951. Red-brown on purple. Camel caravan. Arabic legends w/*Sinkiang* on back. *(S/M #C282-).*

	VG	VF	UNC
a. Issued note.	350.	1500.	3500.
s. Specimen.	—	—	1000.

858A 10,000 Yüan

1951. Brown-violet on black unpt. Herdsman w/horses at l. ctr. Back brown. *(S/M #C282-).*

	VG	VF	UNC
a. Issued note.	2000.	8000.	—
s. Specimen.	—	—	1200.

1953 First Issue

859 5000 Yüan

1953. Brown-violet on m/c unpt. Steam passenger train crossing bridge at l. ctr. Back red-brown, green and blue. *(S/M #C282-).*

	VG	VF	UNC
a. Issued note.	40.00	200.	400.
s. Specimen.	—	—	150.

1953 Second Issue

#860-870 arms at ctr. on back.

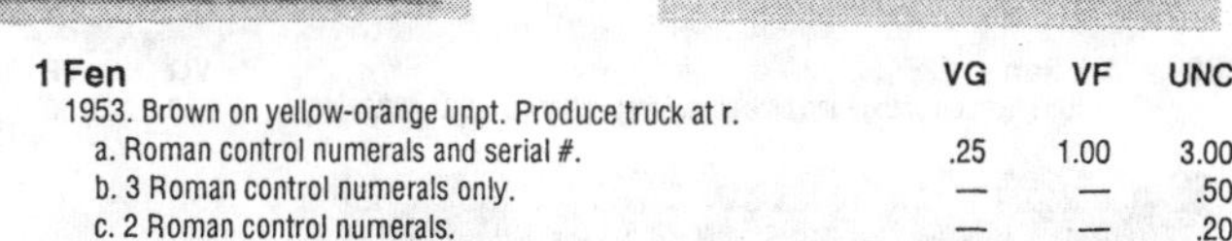

860 1 Fen

1953. Brown on yellow-orange unpt. Produce truck at r.

	VG	VF	UNC
a. Roman control numerals and serial #.	.25	1.00	3.00
b. 3 Roman control numerals only.	—	—	.50
c. 2 Roman control numerals.	—	—	.20

861 2 Fen

1953. Dk. blue on lt. blue unpt. Airplane at r.

	VG	VF	UNC
a. Roman control numerals and serial #.	.25	1.25	4.00
b. Roman control numerals only.	FV	.20	.50

862 5 Fen

1953. Dk. green on green unpt. Cargo ship at r.

	VG	VF	UNC
a. Roman control numerals and serial #.	1.50	7.00	18.00
b. Roman control numerals only.	—	.20	.50

863 1 Jiao — VG | VF | UNC
1953. Brown-violet. Farm tractor at l. *(S/M #C283-4).* — 1.50 | 6.00 | 15.00

864 2 Jiao — VG | VF | UNC
1953. Black on dk. green and m/c unpt. Steam passenger train at l. Back black on green and lt. tan unpt. *(S/M #C283-5).* — 4.00 | 20.00 | 40.00

865 5 Jiao — VG | VF | UNC
1953. Violet on lilac and lt. blue unpt. Dam at l. Back brown on lilac and gold unpt. *(S/M #C283-6).* — .50 | 2.00 | 4.00

866 1 Yüan — VG | VF | UNC
1953. Red on orange and pink unpt. Great Hall at ctr. *(S/M #C283-10).* — 4.50 | 20.00 | 45.00

867 2 Yüan — VG | VF | UNC
1953. Blue on lt. tan unpt. Pagoda near rock at ctr. *(S/M #C283-10).* — 5.50 | 25.00 | 55.00

868 3 Yüan — VG | VF | UNC
1953. Green and black on lt. orange unpt. Old bridge at ctr. *(S/M #C283-12).* — 25.00 | 150. | 250.

869 5 Yüan — VG | VF | UNC
1953. Red-brown on lt. lilac unpt. Demonstrators at ctr. Back red-brown on blue and yellow unpt. *(S/M #C283-13).* — 12.50 | 80.00 | 225

870 10 Yüan — VG | VF | UNC
1953. Gray-black. Farm couple at ctr. *(S/M #C283-14).* — 450. | 1000. | 2500.

1956 ISSUE

871 1 Yüan — VG | VF | UNC
1956. Black on lt. orange and blue unpt. Similar to #866. *(S/M #C283-40).* — 2.50 | 12.50 | 35.00

872 5 Yüan
1956. Dk. brown and m/c. Similar to #869. *(S/M #C283-43).* — 2.50 | 15.00 | 40.00

1960 ISSUE

#873-876 arms at r. on back.

873 1 Jiao — VG | VF | UNC
1960. Red-brown. Workers at ctr. Wmk: Stars. *(S/M #C284-1).* — 25.00 | 60.00 | 100.

874 1 Yüan — VG | VF | UNC
1960. Red-brown and red-violet on m/c unpt. Woman driving tractor at ctr. *(S/M #C284-).*

	VG	VF	UNC
a. Wmk: Lg. star and 4 small stars.	.75	3.00	22.50
b. Wmk: Stars and ancient *Pu* (pants) coins.	1.25	5.00	60.00
c. Serial # prefix: 2 Roman numerals.	.75	2.00	30.00

		VG	VF	UNC
875	**2 Yüan**			
	1960. Black and green on m/c unpt. Machinist working at lathe at ctr.			
	a. Wmk: Lg. star and 4 small stars. Serial # prefix: 2 or 3 Roman numerals.	1.00	5.00	40.00
	b. Wmk: Stars and ancient *Pu* (pants) coins. *(S/M #C284-106).*	1.00	3.00	25.00

		VG	VF	UNC
876	**5 Yüan**			
	1960. Brown and black on m/c unpt. Foundry worker at ctr. Wmk: Lg. star and 4 small stars. *(S/M #C284-11).*			
	a. Serial # prefix: 3 Roman numerals.	3.00	12.50	30.00
	b. Serial # prefix: 2 Roman numerals.	7.00	25.00	70.00

REPUBLIC OF CHINA - TAIWAN

The Republic of China, comprising Taiwan (an island located 90 miles (145 km.) off the southeastern coast of mainland China), the offshore islands of Quemoy and Matsu and nearby islets of the Pescadores chain, has an area of 14,000 sq. mi. (35,981 sq. km.) and a population of 20.2 million. Capital: Taipei. During the past decade, manufacturing has replaced agriculture in importance. Fruits, vegetables, plywood, textile yarns and fabrics and clothing are exported.

Chinese migration to Taiwan began as early as the sixth century. The Dutch established a base on the island in 1624 and held it until 1661, when they were driven out by supporters of the Ming dynasty who used it as a base for their unsuccessful attempt to displace the ruling of Manchu dynasty of mainland China. After being occupied by Manchu forces in 1683, Taiwan remained under the suzerainty of China until its cession to Japan in 1895. It was returned to China following World War II. On December 8, 1949, Taiwan became the last remnant of Sun Yatsen's Republic of China when Chiang Kai-shek moved his army and government from mainland China to the island following his defeat by the Communist forces of Mao Tse-tung.

RULERS:

Japanese, 1895-1945

MONETARY SYSTEM:

Chinese:
1 Chiao = 10 Fen (Cents)
1 Yuan (Dollar) = 10 Chiao
Japanese:
1 Yen = 100 Sen

Note: S/M # in reference to *CHINESE BANKNOTES* by Ward D. Smith and Brian Matravers.

T'AI-NAN KUAN YIN P'IAO

T'AI-NAN OFFICIAL SILVER NOTES

票銀官南臺
Tai Nan Kuan Yin P'iao

忠堂正府南臺理護
Hu Li T'ai Nan Fu Cheng Tang Chung

1895 FIRST ISSUE

#1900-1902 are dated in the 21st year of the reign of Kuang Hsu and are in the Chinese lunar calendar. Add approximately 7 weeks for western dates. Uniface with occasional endorsements on back.

		Good	Fine	XF
1900	**1 Dollar**			
	June Yr. 21 (1895). Blue. Red seal. *(S/M #T63-1).*			
	a. Issued note.	120.	325.	875.
	b. Reissue w/2 additional smaller vertical chinese character ovpt. *(S/M #T63-1-).*	100.	300.	800.

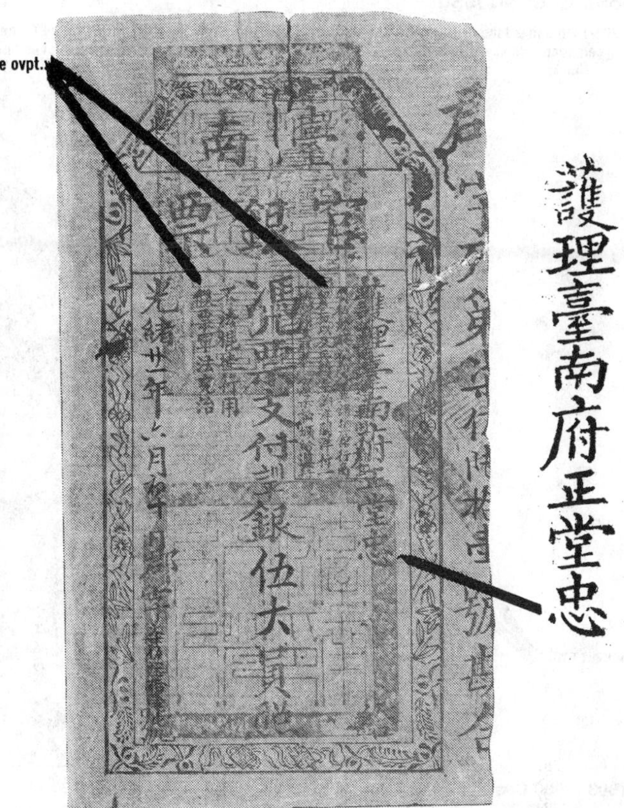

		Good	Fine	XF
1901	**5 Dollars**			
	June Yr. 21 (1895). Blue. Red seal. *(S/M #T63-2).*			
	a. Issued note.	120.	325.	875.
	b. Reissue w/2 additional smaller vertical Chinese character ovpt. *(S/M #T63-2-).*	100.	300.	800.

		Good	Fine	XF
1902	**10 Dollars**			
	June Yr. 21 (1895). Blue. Red seal. *(S/M #T63-3).*			
	a. Issued note.	125.	350.	1000.
	b. Reissue w/2 additional smaller vertical Chinese character ovpt. *(S/M #T63-3-).*	110.	325.	850.

1895 SECOND ISSUE

#1903-1906 dated June or August in the 21st year of the reign of Kuang Hsu and are in the Chinese lunar calendar. Add approximately 7 weeks for western dates. Uniface except for occasional endorsements on back.

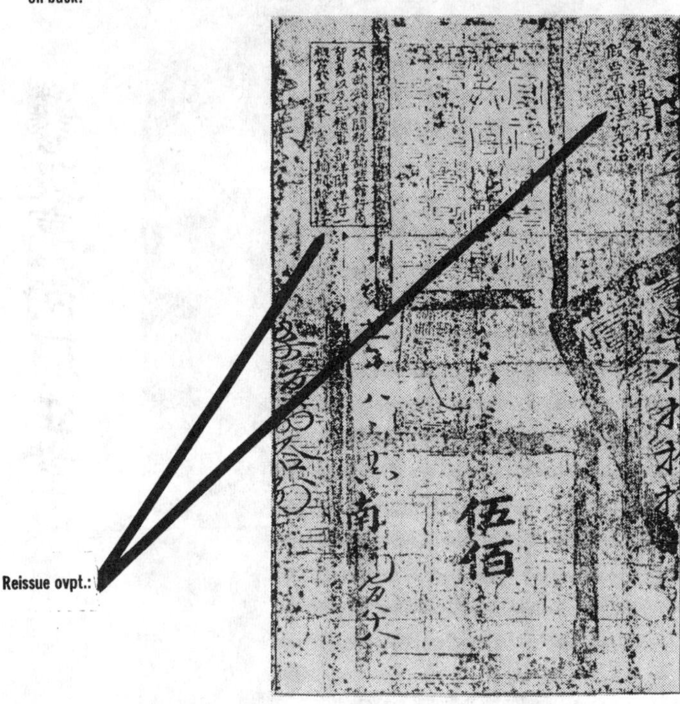

1903	500 Cash	Good	Fine	XF
	Aug. Yr. 21 (1895). Green. Red seals.			
	a. 131 x 237mm. *(S/M #T63-10).*	125.	350.	1000.
	b. 128 x 246mm. *(S/M #T63-11).*	110.	325.	850.
	c. Reissue w/2 additional smaller vertical Chinese character ovpt. *(S/M #T63-).*	100.	300.	800.

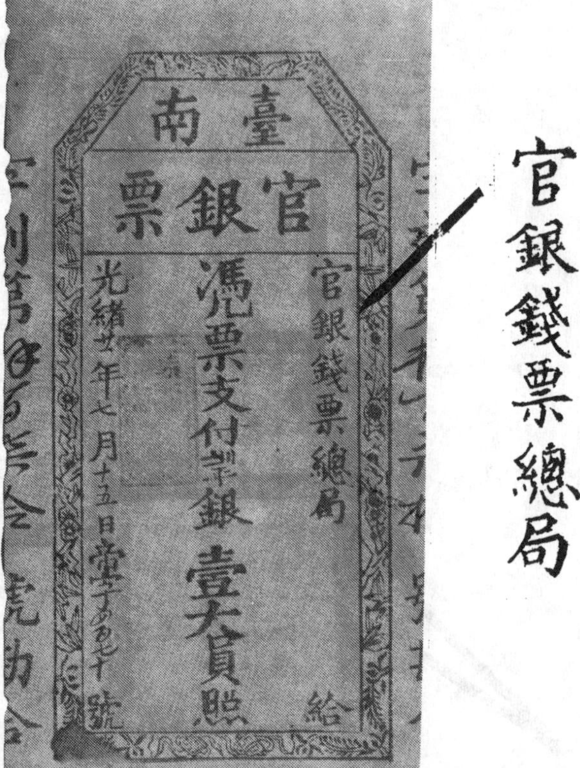

1904	1 Dollar	Good	Fine	XF
	June/July Yr. 21 (1895). Blue. Red handstamped seals.			
	a. Thick paper. *(S/M #T63-20b).*	100.	300.	800.
	b. Thin paper. *(S/M #T63-20a).*	90.00	275.	750.
	c. Reissue w/2 additional smaller vertical Chinese character ovpt. *(S/M #T63-20-).*	85.00	250.	700.

Reissue ovpt.:

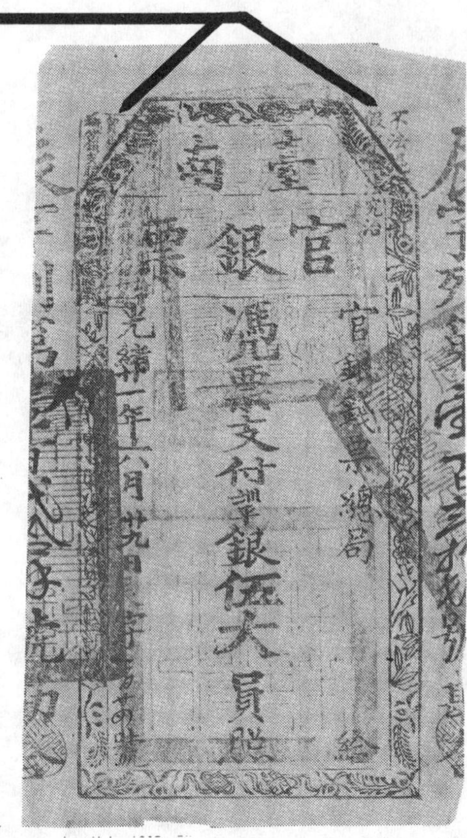

1905	5 Dollars	Good	Fine	XF
	June/July Yr. 21 (1895). Blue. Red handstamped seals.			
	a. Thick paper. *(S/M #T63-21b).*	120.	300.	800
	b. Thin paper. *(S/M #T63-21a).*	120.	300.	800
	c. Reissue w/2 additional smaller vertical Chinese character ovpt. *(S/M #T63-21-).*	100.	250.	750
1906	**10 Dollars**			
	June/July Yr. 21 (1895.) Blue. 2 red handstamped seals.			
	a. Thick paper. *(S/M #T63-22b).*	140.	350.	900
	b. Thin paper. *(S/M #T63-22a).*	140.	350.	900
	c. Reissue w/2 additional smaller vertical Chinese character ovpt. *(S/M #T63-22-).*	100.	250.	750

JAPANESE INFLUENCE

BANK OF TAIWAN

行銀灣臺

T'ai Wan Yin Han

1899-1901 ND SILVER NOTE ISSUE

#1907-1910 vertical format w/2 facing Onagadori cockerels at upper ctr. 2 facing dragons below. W/text *THE BANK OF TAIWAN Promises to pay the bearer on demand... Yen in Silver* on back.

1907	1 Yen	Good	Fine	XF
	ND (1899). Black on lt. green unpt. Back ochre. *(S/M #T70-1).*	1200.	1600.	3750
1908	**5 Yen**			
	ND (1899). Black on brown-orange unpt. Back gray-violet. *(S/M #T70-2).*	2500.	5000.	—
1909	**10 Yen**			
	ND (1901). Black on gray-violet unpt. Back green. *(S/M #T70-3).*	—	—	—
1910	**50 Yen**			
	ND (1900). Black on lt. orange unpt. Back blue-gray. Specimen. *(S/M #T70-4).*	—	—	—

1904-1906 ND Gold Note Issue

#1911-1913 vertical format w/2 Onagadori cockerels at upper ctr. 2 facing dragons below. W/text: *THE BANK OF TAIWAN Promises to pay the bearer on demand ... Yen in Gold* on back.

		Good	Fine	XF
1911	**1 Yen** ND (1904). Black on yellow-orange unpt. Back purple. *(S/M #70-10).*	20.00	100.	200.
1912	**5 Yen** ND (1904). Black on blue unpt. Back ochre. *(S/M #T70-11).*	120.	450.	1000.

		Good	Fine	XF
1913	**10 Yen** ND (1906). Black on pale gray unpt. Back green. *(S/M #T70-12).*	200.	700.	1500.

Taiwan Government General

1917 Emergency Postage Stamp Subsidiary Coinage

Japanese postage stamps (Type Tazawa) pasted on special forms called *Tokubetsu Yubin Kitte Daishi* (Special Postage Stamp Cards).

#1914-1917 black text and circle on back.

		Good	Fine	XF
1914	**5 Sen** ND (1917). Purple adhesive stamp on blue form. *(S/M #T70-).*	300.	500.	700.

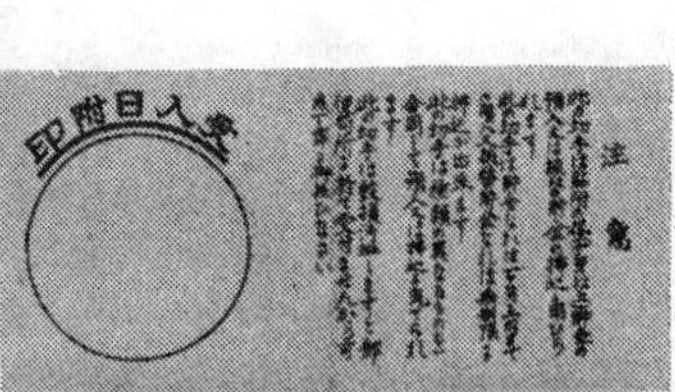

		Good	Fine	XF
1915	**10 Sen** ND (1917). Blue adhesive stamp on pink form. *(S/M #T70-).*	300.	500.	700.
1916	**20 Sen** ND (1917). Purple adhesive stamp on green form. *(S/M #T70-).*	300.	500.	700.

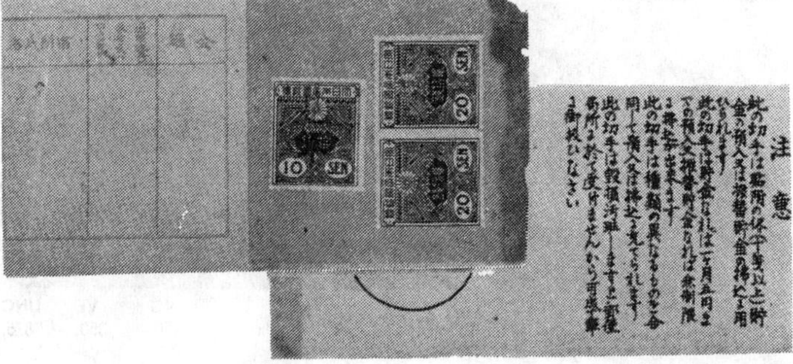

		Good	Fine	XF
1917	**50 Sen** ND (1917). Two *20 Sen* plus one *10 Sen* adhesive stamps on orange form. *(S/M #T70-).*	500.	700.	900.

1918 Emergency Postage Stamp Subsidiary Coinage Issue

#1918-1920 only black circle on back.

		Good	Fine	XF
1918	**1 Sen** ND (1918). Orange adhesive stamp on orange form. *(S/M #T70-1).*	300.	500.	700.

		Good	Fine	XF
1919	**3 Sen** ND (1918). Red adhesive stamp on purple form.*(S/M #T70-).*	300.	500.	700.

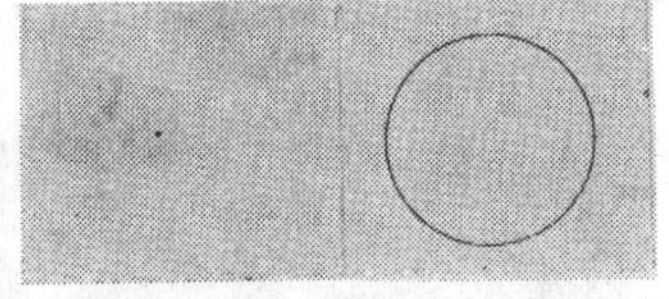

		Good	Fine	XF
1920	**5 Sen** ND (1918). Purple adhesive stamp on red form. *(S/M #T70-).*	300.	500.	700.

Bank of Taiwan Limited - Taiwan Bank

臺灣銀行券

Tai Wan Yin Hang Ch'uan

1914-16 ND Issue

#1921-1932 various seascapes of a lighthouse point on back.

#1921-28, 1930, 1931 and 1933 engraved.

		VG	VF	UNC
1921	**1 Yen** ND (1915). Blue on lilac and lt. green unpt. Temple and stairs at r. Back dk. green on ochre unpt. *(S/M #T70-20).*	12.50	40.00	125.

		VG	VF	UNC
1922	**5 Yen** ND (1914). Gray on ochre and pink unpt. Temple and stairs at r. Back lt. violet-brown on lt. green unpt. *(S/M #T70-21).*	150.	325.	750.

		VG	VF	UNC
1923	**10 Yen** ND (1916). Black on tan unpt. Temple and stairs at r. Back dk. purple and pale green. *(S/M #T70-22).*	150.	350.	875.

1921 ISSUE

		VG	VF	UNC
1924	**50 Yen** 1921. Black on ochre and lt. brown unpt. Temple and stairs at r. Back black and pale violet. *(S/M #T70-23).*	400.	1000.	3000.

1932-37 ND ISSUE

		VG	VF	UNC
1925	**1 Yen** ND (1933; 1944). Black on gray, ochre and olive-green unpt. Temple and stairs at l. Back dull greenish black on ochre unpt.			
	a. Serial # and block # (1933). *(S/M #T70-30).*	1.00	4.00	15.00
	b. Block # only (1944). *(S/M #T70-40).*	1.00	5.00	17.50
	s1. As a. Specimen.	—	—	175.
	s2. As b. Specimen.	—	—	425.

		VG	VF	UNC
1926	**5 Yen** ND (1934). Black on pink and green unpt. Pillared portico at l. Shrine and stairs in background. Back dk. brown, olive-green and violet; Japanese characters *5 YEN* at r. *(S/M #T70-31).*			
	a. Issued note.	6.00	40.00	140.
	s1. Specimen.	—	—	400.
	s2. Specimen w/normal serial #.	—	—	150.

		VG	VF	UNC
1927	**10 Yen** ND (1932). Black on dk. green, gray and ochre unpt. Lanterns on road to Taiwan Jinja. Back dk. blue-gray on ochre unpt.; *10 YEN* at lower ctr. *(S/M #T70-32).*			
	a. Issued note.	6.00	40.00	140.
	s1. Specimen.	—	—	400.
	s2. Specimen w/normal serial #.	—	—	150.

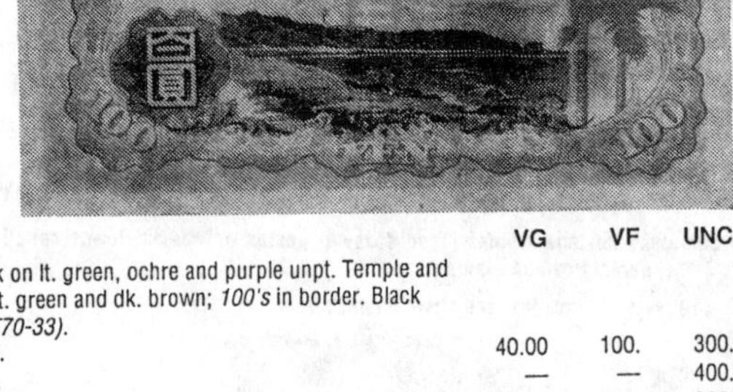

		VG	VF	UNC
1928	**100 Yen** ND (1937). Black on lt. green, ochre and purple unpt. Temple and stairs at l. Back lt. green and dk. brown; *100's* in border. Black serial #. *(S/M #T70-33).*			
	a. Issued note.	40.00	100.	300.
	s1. Specimen.	—	—	400.
	s2. Specimen w/normal serial #.	—	—	200.

1944 ND ISSUE

		VG	VF	UNC
1929	**5 Yen** ND (1944). Like #1926 but green, purple and brown unpt. Back lt. brown on green unpt.; golden kite over *5* at r. *(S/M #T70-42).*			
	a. Issued note.	10.00	60.00	150.
	s1. Specimen.	—	—	400.
	s2. Specimen w/normal serial #.	—	—	150.

		VG	VF	UNC
1930	**10 Yen** ND (1944-45). Face like #1927 but lt. green and lilac unpt. Back dk. blue-gray on lt. lilac unpt.; golden kite at r., palm trees at ctr. r., *10's* in border.			
	a. Black serial # and block # (1944). *(S/M #T70-).*	10.00	60.00	150.
	b. Red block # only (1945). *(S/M #T70-43).*	10.00	60.00	150.
	s1. Specimen. Wmk: Bank of Taiwan logos. *(S/M #T70-).*	—	—	175.
	s2. As a. Specimen	—	—	400.
	s3. As a. Specimen w/normal serial #.	—	—	150.
	s4. As b. Specimen.	—	—	150.

1945 ND ISSUE

		VG	VF	UNC
1931	**10 Yen** ND (1945). Face like #1927 but olive unpt. w/green at ctr. (color shade varieties). Crude paper. Back dk. blue-green w/o lilac unpt. Red block # only. *(S/M #T70-45).*			
	a. Issued note.	12.50	60.00	175.
	s. Specimen.	—		175.
1932	**100 Yen** ND (1945). Face like #1928 but black on lt. blue and blue-violet to gray unpt. Back purple to grayish purple w/golden kite at lower l., *100* at bottom ctr. Crude paper.			
	a. W/o wmk. Block #1-2. *(S/M #T70-46b).*	15.00	100.	300.
	b. Wmk.: Bank of Taiwan logos. Block #2-7. *(S/M #T70-46b).*	10.00	60.00	150.
	s1. As a. Specimen	—	—	175.
	s2. As b. Specimen.	—	—	175.

		VG	VF	UNC
1933	**1000 Yen** ND (1945). Ovpt. on Japan #45. Red seal of the Bank of Taiwan and vertical characters; *Tai Wan Yin Hang* at ctr. on back. *(S/M #T70-).*			
	a. Issued note.	1250.	2400.	4250.
	s. Specimen.	—	—	2500.

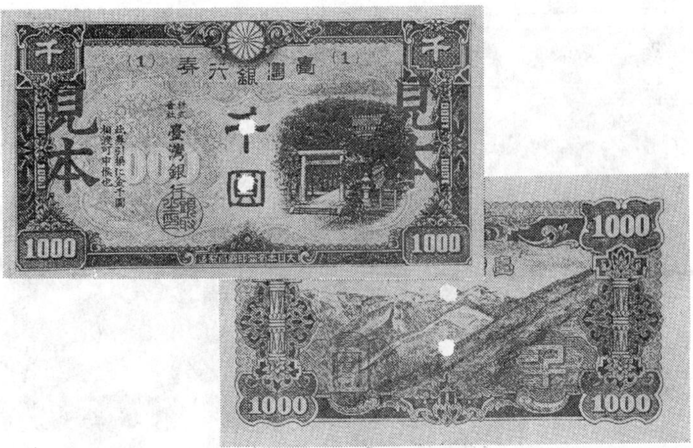

		VG	VF	UNC
1934	**1000 Yen** ND (1945). Black on yellow-green and gray unpt. Shrine at r. Back black on tan unpt., mountain range. Specimen. *(S/M #T70-47).* Rare.	—	—	—

TAIWAN - CHINESE ADMINISTRATION

BANK OF TAIWAN

台灣銀行
T'ai Wan Yin Hang

PRINTERS, 1946-

CPF: 中央印製廠
(Central Printing Factory)

CPFT: 中央印製廠台北廠
(Central Printing Factory, Taipei)

FPFT: 第一印刷廠
(First Printing Factory)

PFBT: 臺灣銀行印刷所
(Printing Factory of Taiwan Bank)

1946 ISSUE

#1935-1944 bank bldg. at l., portr. SYS at ctr. Naval battle scene at ctr. on back.

#1935-1940 printer: CPF.

		VG	VF	UNC
1935	**1 Yüan** 1946. Blue. *(S/M #T72-1).*	1.50	6.00	15.00
1936	**5 Yüan** 1946. Red. *(S/M #T72-2).*	1.75	7.50	17.50
1937	**10 Yüan** 1946. Gray. *(S/M #T72-3).*	1.75	7.50	17.50
1938	**50 Yüan** 1946. Brown. *(S/M #T72-4).*	25.00	125.	250.

		VG	VF	UNC
1939	**100 Yüan** 1946. Green. *(S/M #T72-5).*	2.25	7.50	22.50
1940	**500 Yüan** 1946. Red. 2 serial # varieties. *(S/M #T72-6).*	3.50	20.00	50.00

1947-49 Issues

		VG	VF	UNC
1941	**100 Yüan** 1947. Green. Like #1939 but bank bldg. w/o car, w/flag at top of front of bldg. Naval battle scene in circular ornament on back. Chinese printer: FPFT. *(S/M #T72-10).*	3.00	6.00	30.00
1942	**1000 Yüan** 1948. Blue. Like #1939 w/car in front of bldg., flag over l. side of bldg. Naval battle scene in oval ornament on back. Printer: CPF. *(S/M #T72-20).*	3.00	15.00	50.00
1943	**1000 Yüan** 1948. Blue. Like #1942 but bank bldg. w/o car at l., w/flag on top of front of bldg. Naval battle scene in circular ornament on back. Chinese printer: FPFT. *(S/M #T72-21).*	7.50	35.00	80.00

		VG	VF	UNC
1944	**10,000 Yüan** 1948. Dk. green. Chinese printer: FPFT. *(S/M #T72-23).*	100.	100.	200.

		VG	VF	UNC
1945	**10,000 Yüan** 1949. Red and green. Portr. SYS at l. Bank bldg. on back. Printer: CPF. *(S/M #T72-30).*	4.00	20.00	40.00
1945A	**100,000 Yüan** 1949. SYS at ctr. Printer: FPFT. *(S/M #T72-).* (Not issued.)	—	—	—

1949 Issues

#1946 and 1947 bank bldg. at upper ctr. Taiwan outlined on back. Printer: CPF.

#1946

#1947

		VG	VF	UNC
1946	**1 Cent** 1949. Blue. *(S/M #T73-1).*	1.50	4.00	10.00
1947	**5 Cents** 1949. Brown. *(S/M #T73-2).*	1.50	4.50	15.00

#1948-1957 portr. SYS at upper ctr. Bank at upper ctr. on back.

#1948

#1949

		VG	VF	UNC
1948	**10 Cents** 1949. Green. Printer: CPF. *(S/M #T73-3).*	9.00	45.00	90.00
1949	**50 Cents** 1949. Orange. Printer: CPF. *(S/M #T73-4).*			
	a. Serial # w/2 letter prefix.	.50	1.00	5.00
	b. Serial # w/1 letter prefix and suffix.	.10	.50	3.00

#1950

#1951

		VG	VF	UNC
1950	**1 Yüan** 1949. Brown-violet. Bank in circular frame at top on back. Printer: FPFT. 2 serial # varieties. *(S/M #T73-11).*	9.00	45.00	90.00
1951	**1 Yüan** 1949. Red. Printer: CPF. *(S/M #T73-10).*	30.00	140.	280.

#1952-1954 Chinese printer: FPFT.

#1952

#1953

		VG	VF	UNC
1952	**5 Yüan** 1949. Green. Back lt. orange; *1949* above lower frame. *(S/M #T73-13).* Rare	—	—	—

		VG	VF	UNC
1953	**5 Yüan** 1949. Red w/red and purple guilloche. *1949* within lower frame on back. *(S/M #T73-12).*	17.50	90.00	180.

#1954 #1955

		VG	VF	UNC
1954	**10 Yüan** 1949. Blue on lt. blue unpt. Back brown; *1949* above lower frame. *(S/M #T73-15).*	50.00	140.	800.

#1955-1957 printer: CPF.

1955	**10 Yüan** 1949. Blue-black on lt. green and pink unpt. Portr. SYS in simple oval frame at top. Back blue-black; *1949* in lower ornamental frame. *(S/M #T73-14).*	12.50	60.00	120.

#1956

#1957

		VG	VF	UNC
1956	**100 Yüan** 1949. Brown-violet w/blue and pink guilloche. *(S/M #T73-17).*	150.	700.	2000.
1957	**100 Yüan** 1949. Brown-violet w/brown-violet guilloche. *(S/M #T73-16).*	125.	700.	1600.

1948-49 CIRCULATING BANK CASHIER'S CHECK ISSUE

#1958-1961 uniface w/occasional Chinese endorsements on back, vertical format w/bank at upper ctr. Chinese printer: FPFT.

5000 Yuan

10,000 Yuan

100,000 Yuan

		Good	Fine	XF
1958	**5000 Yüan** (1948). Orange. *(S/M #T72-22).*	18.00	75.00	180.
1959	**10,000 Yüan** (1948). Blue. *(S/M #T72-24).*	18.00	75.00	180.
1960	**100,000 Yüan** (1949). Red. *(S/M #T72-31).*	15.00	60.00	165.
1961	**1,000,000 Yüan** (1949). Brown. *(S/M #T72-32).*	22.50	90.00	220.

1950 ISSUE

1962	**10 Yüan** 1950. M/c. Similar to #R105. Specimen. *(S/M #T73-).*	—	Unc	150.

1954 ISSUE

#1964-1969 Chinese printer: PFBT.

		VG	VF	UNC
1963	**1 Cent** 1954. Blue. Bank. Printer: CPF. *(S/M #T73-20).*	.50	2.50	6.00
1964	**1 Yüan** 1954. Blue. *(S/M #T73-31).*	1.50	4.00	15.00

#1965

#1967

		VG	VF	UNC
1965	**1 Yüan** 1954. Deep green on lt. blue-green unpt. *(S/M #T73-30).*	1.75	5.00	25.00
1966	**1 Yüan** 1954. Deep green on lt. green unpt. Back dull olive-green on lt. green unpt. (litho). *(S/M #T73-31).*	1.75	10.00	35.00
1967	**10 Yüan** 1954. Blue. *(S/M #T73-32).*	1.75	10.00	35.00

1955 ISSUE

		VG	VF	UNC
1968	**5 Yüan** 1955. Red w/red and blue guilloche. *(S/M #T73-40).*	1.75	10.00	35.00

1960 ISSUE

		VG	VF	UNC
1969	**10 Yüan** 1960. Blue on m/c unpt. SYS at l., bridge at r. *(S/M#T73-50).*	1.25	5.00	18.00

		VG	VF	UNC
1970	**10 Yüan** 1960. Red on yellow and lt. green unpt. Like #1969 but w/o printer. *(S/M #T73-51).*	1.25	3.00	9.00

OFF-SHORE ISLAND CURRENCY

BANK OF TAIWAN

臺灣銀行

T'ai Wan Yin Hang

KINMEN (QUEMOY) BRANCH

1949-51 (1963; 1967) ISSUE

#R101-R109 portr. SYS at upper ctr. Vertical format.

		VG	VF	UNC
R101	**1 Yüan** 1949 (1963). Green on m/c unpt. Printer: CPF.	.25	2.00	10.00
R102	**1 Yüan** 1949 (1952). Green. Printer: FPFT. *(S/M #T74-2).*	7.50	40.00	150.

		VG	VF	UNC
R102A	**1 Yüan** 1949. Reddish brown on lt. orange unpt. Back blue; lg. red outlined character ovpt: *Chin Men.* Buff paper. *(S/M #T74-3)*	150.	400.	1000.
R102B	**5 Yüan** 1949. Dk. green on lt. blue and m/c unpt. Back dk. green on lt. green unpt.; lg. red outlined character ovpt: *Chin Men. (S/M #T74-4).*	250.	650.	1200.

1950-51 ISSUES

		VG	VF	UNC
R103	**10 Cents** 1950 (1952). Blue.			
	a. Ovpt. at bottom of face. *(S/M #T74-10a).*	7.50	30.00	150.
	b. Ovpt. at middle and bottom of face. *(S/M #T74-10b).*	6.00	25.00	125.
R104	**50 Cents** 1950 (1952). Brown. Ovpt: *Chin Men* at lower l. and r. on face. Printer: CPF. *(S/M #T74-11).*			
	a. Ovpt: *Chin* at r., *Men* at l. on back.	8.00	50.00	175.
	b. Ovpt: *Chin Men* at l. and r. on back.	7.50	45.00	160.
R105	**10 Yüan** 1950 (1952). Blue on m/c unpt. Printer: FPFT. *(S/M #T74-21).*	7.50	20.00	75.00
R106	**10 Yüan** 1950 (1963). Blue. Printer: CPF.	.50	1.50	18.00

		VG	VF	UNC
R107	**50 Yüan** 1951 (1967). Green. Printer: FPFT.	3.00	20.00	120.

1955-72 ISSUES

		VG	VF	UNC
R108	**5 Yüan** 1955 (1956). Violet. Printer: PFBT. *(S/M #T74-40).*	3.00	20.00	150
R109	**5 Yüan** 1966. Violet-brown. Printer: CPF.	.75	3.00	20.00

		VG	VF	UNC
R110	**10 Yüan** 1969 (1975). Red on m/c unpt. Red ovpt. on #1979a.	1.00	2.00	10.00

		VG	VF	UNC
R111	**50 Yüan** 1969 (1970). Dk. blue on m/c unpt. SYS at r.	2.00	3.50	25.00

		VG	VF	UNC
R112	**100 Yüan** 1972 (1975). Green ovpt. on #1983.	4.00	7.50	40.00

1976; 1981 Issue

		VG	VF	UNC
R112A	**10 Yüan** 1976. Ovpt. on #1984.	.25	.75	10.00
R112B	**100 Yüan** 1981. Ovpt. on #1988.	5.00	8.00	30.00
R112C	**1000 Yüan** 1981. Ovpt. on #1988.	35.00	50.00	200.

Matsu Branch

Notes of the Bank of Taiwan and later notes of the Republic of China/Bank of Taiwan w/ovpt: 祖馬

用通區地祖馬限

Hsien Ma Tsu Ti Ch'u T'ung Yung

1950-51 Dated (1964; 1967) Issue

#R113-R115 horizontal format.

#R117 and 118 portr. SYS at upper ctr. Vertical format.

		VG	VF	UNC
R113	**10 Cents** 1950. Specimen. *(S/M #T75-).*			150.
R114	**50 Cents** 1950. Green. Specimen. *(S/M #T75-).*			150.
R115	**1 Yüan** 1950. Red.			
	a. W/ imprint. Specimen. *(S/M #T75-).*			150.
	b. W/o imprint. Specimen. *(S/M #T75-).*			150.

		VG	VF	UNC
R116	**10 Yüan** 1950 (1959). Blue. Printer: FPFT. *(S/M #T75-1).*	7.50	22.50	150.
R117	**10 Yüan** 1950 (1964). Blue on m/c unpt. Printer: CPF.	1.00	3.00	25.00

		VG	VF	UNC
R118	**50 Yüan** 1951 (1967). Green on m/c unpt. Printer: FPDT.	3.00	8.00	80.00

Matsu Branch

1969; 1972 Issue

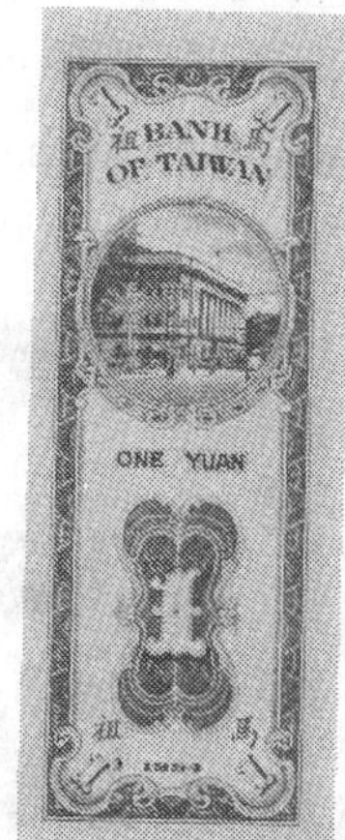

		VG	VF	UNC
R119	**1 Yüan** 1954 (1959). Brown. Printer: PFBT. *(S/M #T75-20).*	.25	1.00	5.00
R120	**1 Yüan** 1954. Brown. Printer: CPF. *(S/M #T75-).*	.25	1.00	5.00

		VG	VF	UNC
R121	**5 Yüan** 1955 (1959). Dk. green. Printer: PFBT. *(S/M #T75-30).*	.75	3.00	15.00

		VG	VF	UNC
R122	**10 Yüan** 1969 (1975). Red on m/c unpt. Ovpt. on #1979a. Printer: CPF.	.50	1.00	10.00

		VG	VF	UNC
R123	**50 Yüan** 1969 (1970). Violet on m/c unpt. Printer: CPF.	2.00	4.00	30.00
R124	**100 Yüan** 1972 (1975). Dk. green, lt. green and orange on m/c unpt. Green ovpt. on #1983. Printer: CPF.	4.00	10.00	80.00

1976; 1981 ISSUE

		VG	VF	UNC
R125	**10 Yüan** 1976. Red on m/c unpt. Ovpt. on #1984.	.40	1.00	8.00
R126	**500 Yüan** 1981. Brown and red-brown on m/c unpt. Ovpt. on #1987.	FV	20.00	80.00
R127	**1000 Yüan** 1981. Blue-black on m/c unpt. Ovpt. on #1988.	FV	37.50	200.

TACHEN BRANCH 陳大

1949 ISSUES

#R140-R143 vertical format w/SYS at upper ctr.

		VG	VF	UNC
R140	**1 Yüan** 1949 (1953). Green. Printer: FPFT. *(S/M #T76-1).*	60.00	160.	500.

TACHEN BRANCH

1950 ISSUE

#R141

#R142

		VG	VF	UNC
R141	**10 Cents** 1950 (1953). Red. Printer: CPF. *(S/M #T76-10).*	110.	325.	750.
R142	**50 Cents** 1950 (1953). Green. Printer: CPF. *(S/M #T76-11).*	110.	325.	750.

		VG	VF	UNC
R143	**10 Yüan** 1950 (1953). Blue. Printer: FPFT. *(S/M #T76-20).*	90.00	300.	1200.

JAPANESE PUPPET BANKS

Japan's attempt to assert political and economic control over East Asia, an expansionist program called "Asia for the Asiatics," and later the "Co-Prosperity Sphere for East Asia," was motivated by economic conditions and the military tradition of the Japanese people. Living space, food, and raw materials were urgently needed. To secure them and also markets for their manufactured goods, the Japanese thought they had to establish control over the markets and resources of East Asia. They planned: (1) to add nearby islands to the islands of Japan, (2) to obtain possession of Korea, (3) to absorb the Malay Peninsula, Indo-China, Thailand, the Philippines, and the numerous Southwest Pacific islands into the Empire of Japan, and (4) to assert at least economic control over China.

By the eve of World War I, the Japanese had succeeded in occupying the Bonin Islands (1874), annexing Formosa and the Pescadores Islands (1895), annexing the Liaotung peninsula and the southern half of Sakhalin island (Russo-Japanese War), and annexing Korea (1910).

During World War I, Japan managed to gain economic control over Manchuria and Inner Mongolia, and to take the Shantung Peninsula from Germany. Further territorial expansion was achieved by the Paris Peace Settlement (1919) which mandated to Japan all of the Caroline, Marshall, and Mariana islands except Guam. The Japanese were, however, forced to give the Shantung Peninsula back to China.

Japan's military thrust against mainland China began in earnest on Sept. 18, 1931, when with a contrived incident for an excuse, the Japanese army seized the strategic centers in Manchuria and set up (1932) the puppet nation of Manchukuo with Henry Pu-Yi, ex-emperor of China, as emperor under the protection and control of the Japanese army. Not content with the seizure of Manchuria, the Japanese army then invaded the Chinese province of Jehol and annexed it to Manchukuo (1933). In 1934, Japan proclaimed Manchukuo an independent nation and the Japanese army penetrated into Inner Mongolia and some of China's northern provinces, and established a garrison near Peiping. Although determined to resist the invasion of their country, the Chinese were able to do little more than initiate a boycott of Japanese goods.

War between the two powers quickened in July 1937, when Japanese and Chinese troops clashed at the Marco Polo Bridge near Peiping, an incident Japanese leaders used as an excuse to launch a full-fledged invasion of China without a declaration of war. Peiping and Tientsin were taken in a month. Shanghai fell in Nov. 1937. Nanking fell in Dec. 1937 and was established as a puppet state under a Chinese president. Canton fell in 1938.

Though badly mauled and weakened by repeated Japanese blows, the Chinese continued to fight, and to meet defeat, while Japanese armies overran large sections of Eastern China and occupied the essential seaports. Trading space for time, Chiang Kai-shek kept his army intact and moved his capital from Nanking to Chungking behind the mountains in western China. Factory machinery, schools and colleges were moved to the west. With the aid of the Flying Tigers, a volunteer force of American aviators commanded by General Claire Chennault, and military supplies from the United States and Great Britain moved slowly over the dangerous Burma Road, the Chinese continued to resist the hated invader. The war came to a stalemate. The Japanese made no attempt to take Chungking. The Chinese could not drive the Japanese armies from the provinces they had conquered.

The defeat of Japan was brought about by the decision of the Japanese government to execute their plan to drive the United States, France, Great Britain, and the Netherlands out of the East, a plan initiated by an air attack on U.S. military installations at Pearl Harbor, Hawaii. Japan's dream of dominance in East Asia began to fade with the defeat of a powerful Japanese fleet at the Battle of Midway (June 3, 1942), and flickered out at Hiroshima and Nagasaki in Aug. 1945 in the wake of "a rain of ruin from the air, the like of which had never been seen on this earth." Upon the defeat of Japan by the Allies, control of the China-Japanese puppet states reverted to Chinese factions.

During the existence of the China-Japanese puppet states, Japanese occupation authorities issued currency through Japanese puppet banks, the most important of which were the Central Reserve Bank of China, Federal Reserve Bank of China, Hua-Hsing Commercial Bank, and Chi Tung Bank.

Operations of the Central Reserve Bank of China, the state bank of the puppet Republic of China government at Nanking, began sometime in 1940, although the official inauguration date is Jan. 1, 1941. To encourage public acceptance, the notes of this puppet bank carried, where size permitted, the portrait of Sun Yat-sen, Chinese nationalist revolutionary leader and founder of the Chinese republic, on the face, and his mausoleum on the back. The number of notes issued by the Central Reserve Bank of China exceeds the total number issued by all other Japanese puppet banks in China.

An interesting feature of the issues of the Central Reserve Bank of China is the presence of clandestine propaganda messages engraved on some of the plates by patriotic Chinese engravers. The 50-cent notes of 1940 carry a concealed propaganda message in Chinese. The initials "U S A C" and the date 1945 ("U.S. Army Coming, 1945") appear on the 1944 200-yuan note. Two varieties of the 1940 10-yuan note include in the face border design devices resembling bisected turtles, an animal held in low esteem in China.

A small number of notes issued by the Central Reserve Bank of China carry overprints, the exact purpose of which is unclear, with the exception of those which indicate a circulation area. Others are thought to be codes referring to branch offices or Japanese military units.

The Federal Reserve Bank of China, located in Peiping, was the puppet financial agency of the Japanese in northeast China. This puppet bank issued both coins and currency, but in modest amounts. The first series of notes has a curious precedent. The original plates were prepared by two American engravers who journeyed to China in 1909 to advise officials of the Bureau of Engraving and Printing, Peking (BEPP) on engraving techniques of the Western World. The Chinese gentleman appearing on the 1-yuan notes of 1938 is said to be making an obscene gesture to indicate Chinese displeasure with the presence of the Japanese.

The Hua Hsing Commercial Bank was a financial agency created and established by the government of Japan and its puppet authorities in Nanking. Notes and coins were issued until sometime in 1941, with the quantities restricted by Chinese aversion to accepting them.

The Chi Tung Bank was the banking institution of the "East Hopei Autonomous Government" established by the Japanese in 1938 to undermine the political position of China in the northwest provinces. It issued both coins and notes between 1937 and 1939 with a restraint uncharacteristic of the puppet banks of the China-Japanese puppet states. The issues were replaced in 1940 by those of the Federal Reserve Bank of China.

CENTRAL RESERVE BANK OF CHINA

中央儲備銀行

Chung Yang Ch'u Pei Yin Hang

1940 ISSUE

J1 1 Fen = 1 Cent
1940. Red on lt. brown unpt.

	VG	VF	UNC
a. Imprint and serial #.	1.50	8.00	20.00
b. W/o imprint, w/block letters and #.	.50	2.00	5.00
s1. As a. Specimen w/blue ovpt: *Yang Pen. Specimen* on back. Uniface pair.	—	—	60.00
s2. As b. Specimen w/ovpt: *Yang Pen. Specimen* on back.	—	—	60.00

J2 5 Fen = 5 Cents
1940. Green on pale green unpt.

	VG	VF	UNC
a. Imprint and serial #.	1.00	4.00	10.00
b. W/o imprint, w/block letters and #.	.25	1.50	4.00
s1. As a. Specimen w/red ovpt: *Yang Pen. Specimen* on back. Uniface pair.	—	—	60.00
s2. As b. Specimen w/red ovpt: *Yang Pen. Specimen* on back.	—	—	60.00

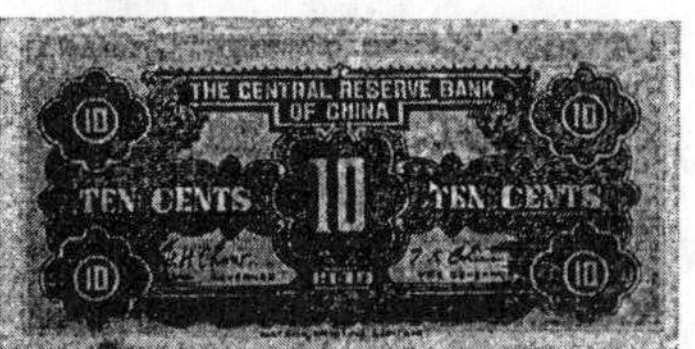

J3 10 Cents = 1 Chiao
1940. Green. Back m/c.

	VG	VF	UNC
a. Issued note.	.25	1.50	5.00
s1. Specimen w/red ovpt: *Yang Pen. Specimen* on back. Uniface pair.	—	—	60.00
s2. Specimen w/red ovpt: *Yang Pen. Specimen* on back.	—	—	60.00

J4 20 Cents = 2 Chiao
1940. Blue. Back m/c.

	VG	VF	UNC
a. Issued note.	.25	1.25	6.00
s1. Specimen w/red ovpt: *Yang Pen. Specimen* on back. Uniface pair.	—	—	60.00
s2. Specimen w/red ovpt: *Yang Pen. Specimen* on back.	—	—	60.00

J5 50 Cents = 5 Chiao
1940. (1941). Red-brown. Back m/c.

	VG	VF	UNC
a. Issued note.	.50	2.50	10.00
s. Specimen w/blue ovpt: *Yang Pen.* Red *Specimen* on back.	—	—	60.00

J6 50 Cents = 5 Chiao
1940. Orange. Back m/c.

	VG	VF	UNC
	1.00	4.00	12.50

J7 50 Cents = 5 Chiao
1940. Purple. Back m/c.

	VG	VF	UNC
a. Issued note.	.50	2.00	10.00
s1. Specimen w/red ovpt: *Yang Pen. Specimen* on back. Uniface pair.	—	—	60.00
s2. Specimen w/red ovpt: *Yang Pen. Specimen* on back.	—	—	50.00

J8 1 Yüan
1940. Green on yellow unpt. Portr. SYS at l., mausoleum of SYS at ctr. Back green w/black sign. 150 x 78mm.

	VG	VF	UNC
a. Issued note.	.50	2.50	8.00
b. Red ovpt: *HSING* twice on face and back.	3.00	8.00	20.00
c. Control ovpt: *I (Yi)* twice on face and back.	15.00	40.00	100.
s. Specimen w/red ovpt: *Yang Pen. Specimen* on back.	—	—	125.

J9 1 Yüan
1940. Purple on lt. blue unpt. Like #J8. Back Purple on pink and yellow-green unpt.

	VG	VF	UNC
a. Black sign. on back 151 x 79mm. (1.5.1942).	2.00	5.00	15.00
b. Purple sign. Serial # format: LL123456L. 151 x 79mm.	1.00	3.00	10.00
c. Purple sign. Serial # format: L/L 123456L. 146 x 78mm.	1.00	3.00	8.00
s1. As a. Specimen w/red ovpt: *Yang Pen. Specimen* on back.	—	—	125.
s2. As b. Specimen w/red ovpt: *Yang Pen. Specimen* on back.	—	—	125.

		VG	VF	UNC
J10	**5 Yüan** 1940. Red. Portr. SYS at ctr. Back red; mausoleum at ctr.			
	a. Face w/ yellow and blue-green unpt. Serial # on face and back. Black sign. (6.1.1941).	5.00	15.00	45.00
	b. As a. Black control ovpt. on face and back.	10.00	35.00	100.
	c. Face w/pink and blue unpt. Serial # on face only. Black sign. (19.12.1941).	1.50	4.00	10.00
	d. As c. Black control ovpt. on face and back.	3.00	10.00	30.00
	e. As c. Red sign.	.25	1.50	4.00
	f. As e. Red ovpt: *Wuhan* over seals on face.	3.00	10.00	30.00
	g. As e. Black ovpt: *Kwangtung* horizontally on lower corners of face.	3.00	10.00	30.00
	h. W/o serial #; black sign.	—	—	75.00
	s1. As a. Specimen.	—	—	125.
	s2. As c. Specimen w/blue ovpt: *Yang Pen. Specimen* on back.	—	—	125.
	s3. As c. Specimen w/red ovpt: *Mi-hon.*	—	—	125.

J11	**5 Yüan** 1940. Red w/repeated gold Chinese 4 character unpt. Proof.	—	Unc	300.

		VG	VF	UNC
J12	**10 Yüan** 1940. Blue on blue-green and lt. brown unpt. Similar to #J10. Back blue.			
	a. Bright blue face and back. Serial # on face and back. Black sign. (6.1.1941).	12.50	37.50	150.
	b. As a. Red control ovpt. on face and back.	37.50	150.	—
	c. Dk. blue face and back. Serial # on face only, black sign.	1.00	4.00	10.00
	d. As c. Red control ovpt. on face and back.	5.00	20.00	60.00
	e. As c. Black ovpt: *Kwangtung* vertically at l. and r.	2.50	7.50	25.00
	f. As e. Smaller blue ovpt: *Kwangtung.*	2.50	7.50	25.00
	g. As c. Lt. blue ovpt: *Wuhan* over red seals on face.	2.50	7.50	25.00
	h. Color similar to c. Serial # on face only, blue sign. (19.12.1941).	.50	1.50	4.00
	i. As h. Ovpt: *Wuhan* over sign. seals at lower l. and r. (as g.).	2.50	7.50	25.00
	j. As h. Ovpt: *Wuhan* vertically at sides on face.	2.50	7.50	25.00
	k. As h. Black ovpt: *Kwangtung* at l. and r. (as e.).	2.50	7.50	25.00
	l. As h. Blue ovpt: *Kwangtung* at l. and r. in different style of type.	2.50	7.50	25.00
	s1. As a. Specimen w/red ovpt: *Yang Pen. Specimen* on back.	—	—	150.
	s2. As c. Specimen w/red ovpt: *Yang Pen. Specimen* on back.	—	—	125.
	s3. As c. Specimen w/red ovpt: *Mi-hon.* Regular serial #.	—	—	100.
	s4. As h. Specimen w/red ovpt: *Yang Pen. Specimen* on back.	—	—	125.
	s5. As h. Specimen w/red ovpt: *Mi-hon.* Regular serial #.	—	—	100.

Note: Many are of the opinion that ovpt: *Wuhan* and *Kwangtung* on #J10 are fantasies.

1942 ISSUE

***#J13 Deleted.* See #J12.**

		VG	VF	UNC
J14	**100 Yüan** 1942. Dk. green on m/c unpt. Portr. SYS at ctr. SYS Mausoleum at ctr. on back.			
	a. Blue sign.	1.50	6.00	15.00
	b. Black sign. (17.6.1942).	10.00	32.50	100.
	s. As b. Specimen w/red ovpt: *Yang Pen. Specimen* on back.	—	—	150.

		VG	VF	UNC
J15	**500 Yüan** 1942. Brown on m/c unpt. Portr. SYS at l. SYS Mausoleum at r. on back. *Kwangtung* at lower l. and r.			
	a. Wmk: *500 Yuan.*	3.00	10.00	45.00
	b. W/o wmk.	3.00	10.00	25.00
	s. Specimen w/red ovpt: *Yang Pen. Specimen* on back. W/o *Kwangtung.*	—	—	150.

1943 ISSUES

		VG	VF	UNC
J16	**10 Cents = 1 Chiao** 1943. Green. SYS Mausoleum at ctr. W/o imprint, w/block #.			
	a. Issued note.	1.00	3.50	8.00
	s. Specimen w/red ovpt: *Yang Pen.* Uniface pair.	—	—	60.00
J17	**20 Cents = 2 Chiao** 1943. Blue. SYS Mausoleum at ctr. W/o imprint, w/block #.			
	a. Issued note.	1.00	4.00	9.00
	s. Specimen w/red ovpt: *Yang Pen.* Uniface pair.	—	—	60.00

		VG	VF	UNC
J18	**50 Cents = 5 Chiao** 1943. Red-brown. SYS Mausoleum at ctr.			
	a. W/o imprint, w/block #.	1.00	3.50	8.00
	b. W/o imprint, w/block letter and #.	1.25	4.00	12.00
	s. As a. Specimen w/blue ovpt: *Yang Pen.* Uniface pair.	—	—	75.00

J19 1 Yüan

1943. Green on lt. blue unpt. Portr. SYS at ctr. SYS Mausoleum at ctr. on back.

	VG	VF	UNC
a. Issued note.	1.00	3.50	8.00
s. Specimen w/red ovpt: *Yang Pen.*	—	—	125.

J20 10 Yüan

1943. Brown on m/c unpt. Portr. SYS at l. SYS Mausoleum at ctr. on back.

	VG	VF	UNC
a. Issued note.	2.00	8.00	20.00
b. Ovpt: *Kwangtung.* vertically at l. and r.	3.00	10.00	35.00
s. As a. Specimen w/red ovpt: *Yang Pen.*	—	—	125.

#J21-J28 portr. SYS at ctr. SYS Mausoleum at ctr. on back.

J21 100 Yüan

1943. Dk. olive-green on m/c unpt. Back lt. green-dk. green. W/serial #.

	VG	VF	UNC
a. Issued note.	1.00	3.50	8.00
b. Red ovpt: *Wuhan.*	3.00	10.00	30.00

#J22 *Deleted.* See #J21.

J23 100 Yüan

1943 (1944). Blue on m/c unpt. Back green; w/block letters.

	VG	VF	UNC
a. Wmk: Clouds.	.50	2.00	6.00
b. W/o wmk.	.50	2.00	6.00
s. Specimen w/ovpt: *Yang Pen.*	—	—	125.

***Wuhan* ovpt.**

J24 500 Yüan

1943 (1944). Brown on m/c unpt. 180 x 96mm. Block letters.

	VG	VF	UNC
a. Wmk: *500* in Chinese characters.	3.25	10.00	30.00
b. W/o wmk.	1.00	4.00	12.50
c. Red ovpt: *Kwangtung.*	2.50	7.50	25.00
d. Red ovpt: *Wuhan* vertically at l. and r.	2.50	7.50	25.00
s1. Specimen w/red ovpt: *Yang Pen. Specimen* on back.	—	—	125.
s2. Specimen w/red ovpt: *Mi-hon.*	—	—	125.
s3. As d. Specimen w/red ovpt: *Yang Pen. Specimen* on back.	—	—	125.

J24A 500 Yüan

1943 (1944). Dk. brown on m/c unpt. Back dk. brown. Serial #. 187 x 95mm.

	VG	VF	UNC
a. Issued note.	5.00	17.50	50.00
s. Specimen w/red ovpt: *Yang Pen. Specimen* on back.	—	—	125.

J25 500 Yüan

1943 (1944). Deep purple-brownish purple on m/c unpt. 187 x 95mm. Serial #. Guilloche in the unpt. Back violet, lithographed.

	VG	VF	UNC
a. Wmk: *500* in Chinese characters.	4.50	20.00	45.00
b. Wmk: Cloud forms.	3.50	15.00	35.00
c. W/o wmk.	2.50	12.00	25.00
s1. Specimen w/red ovpt: *Yang Pen. Specimen* on back.	—	—	125.
s2. Specimen w/red ovpt: *Mi-hon.*	—	—	125.

J26 500 Yüan

1943 (1944). Pale purple on pink unpt. Like #J25 but w/o guilloche in the unpt. Back w/plate varieties. Wmk: cloud form.

	VG	VF	UNC
a. Issued note.	3.00	12.50	30.00
s. Specimen w/red ovpt: *Yang Pen. Specimen* on back.	—	—	140.

J27 500 Yüan

1943 (1945). Brown on lt. brown unpt. Brown guilloche. Block letters. 169 x 84mm.

	VG	VF	UNC
a. Issued note.	2.50	12.00	25.00
s. Specimen w/red ovpt: *Yang Pen. Specimen* on back.	—	—	125.

J28 500 Yüan

1943. Brown on lilac. M/c guilloche. Block letters. 169 x 84mm.

	VG	VF	UNC
a. Wmk: Cloud forms.	2.50	12.00	25.00
b. W/o wmk.	2.00	8.00	20.00
s. Specimen w/red ovpt: *Yang Pen. Specimen* on back.	—	—	125.

1944 ISSUES

#J29-J39 portr. SYS at ctr. SYS Mausoleum at ctr. on back. Wmk: Cloud forms may be vertical or horizontal.

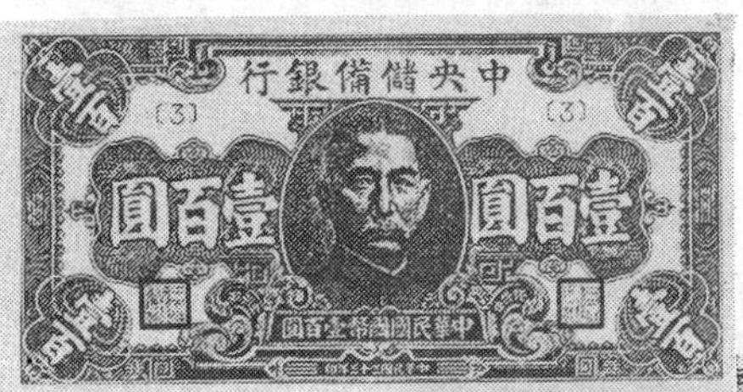

J29 100 Yüan

1944 (1945). Blue on pale green unpt. Back blue. Wmk: Cloud forms.

	VG	VF	UNC
a. Issued note.	3.00	15.00	40.00
s. Specimen w/red ovpt: *Yang Pen. Specimen* on back.	—	—	125.

		VG	VF	UNC
J30	**200 Yüan** 1944. Red-brown on pink unpt. Back red-brown.			
	a. Issued note.	1.50	7.50	15.00
	s. Specimen w/ovpt: *Yang Pen. Specimen* on back.	—	—	125.

Note: #J30 has letters *USAC* hidden in frame design.

		VG	VF	UNC
J31	**1000 Yüan** 1944 (1945). Dk. blue on m/c unpt. Back deep blue-gray on m/c unpt. Serial #. 185 x 94mm.			
	a. Issued note.	3.00	12.50	40.00
	s. Specimen w/red ovpt: *Yang Pen. Specimen* on back.	—	—	125.

		VG	VF	UNC
J32	**1000 Yüan** 1944 (1945). Deep gray-blue on m/c unpt. Block letters. 185 x 94mm.			
	a. Wmk: Cloud forms.	1.25	6.00	12.50
	b. W/o wmk.	1.00	4.00	9.00
	c. Red ovpt: *Wuhan.*	3.00	10.00	35.00
	s. Specimen w/red ovpt: *Yang Pen. Specimen* on back.	—	—	125.
J33	**1000 Yüan** 1944 (1945). Deep gray-blue on ochre unpt. Block letters. 169 x 84mm.			
	a. Issued note.	1.50	6.00	14.00
	s. Specimen w/red ovpt: *Yang Pen. Specimen* on back.	—	—	125.
J34	**1000 Yüan** 1944 (1945). Gray. Block letters. 163 x 65mm.			
	a. Issued note.	5.00	20.00	80.00
	s. Specimen w/red ovpt: *Yang Pen. Specimen* on back.	—	—	125.

		VG	VF	UNC
J35	**1000 Yüan** 1944 (1945). Green on lt. blue unpt. Back green. Block #. 149 x 79mm.			
	a. Issued note.	5.00	25.00	90.00
	s1. Specimen w/red ovpt: *Yang Pen. Specimen* on back.	—	—	125.
	s2. As s1. W/o *Specimen* on back.	—	—	100.
	s3. Specimen w/red ovpt: *Mi-hon.*	—	—	100.
J36	**10,000 Yüan** 1944 (1945). Dk. brown on pink unpt. Serial #. 184 x 94mm.			
	a. Wmk: Cloud forms.	8.00	25.00	110.
	s. Specimen w/red ovpt: *Yang Pen. Specimen* on back.	—	—	125.

		VG	VF	UNC
J37	**10,000 Yüan** 1944 (1945). Dk. green on tan or pale yellow-brown unpt. Serial #. 184 x 94mm. Backs w/vignette varieties.			
	a. Back w/pink sky in ctr.	4.00	20.00	80.00
	b. Back w/green sky in ctr.	7.50	25.00	90.00
	s1. Specimen w/red ovpt: *Yang Pen. Specimen* on back.	—	—	195.
	s2. Specimen w/red ovpt: *Mi-hon.*	—	—	225.
J38	**10,000 Yüan** 1944 (1945). Green on pale yellow-brown unpt. Block letters. 170 x 83mm.			
	a. Issued note.	4.00	17.50	75.00
	s. Specimen w/red ovpt: *Yang Pen. Specimen* on back.	—	—	195.

		VG	VF	UNC
J39	**10,000 Yüan** 1944 (1945). Green on pale yellow-brown unpt. Block letters. 166 x 65mm.			
	a. Issued note.	8.00	30.00	100.
	s. Specimen w/red ovpt: *Yang Pen. Specimen* on back.	—	—	250.

1945 ISSUES

#J40-J44 portr. SYS at ctr. SYS Mausoleum at ctr. on back.

		VG	VF	UNC
J40	**5000 Yüan** 1945. Gray-green on pale green unpt. Back gray-green. Serial #. 166 x 90mm.			
	a. Printer: CRBCPW.	2.50	10.00	30.00
	b. W/o imprint.	5.00	17.50	50.00
	s. As a. Specimen w/red ovpt: *Yang Pen. Specimen* on back.	—	—	125.

		VG	VF	UNC
J41	**5000 Yüan** 1945. Dk. gray-green on pale green unpt. Like #J40. Block letters. 170 x 84mm.			
	a. Issued note.	5.00	10.00	55.00
	s. Specimen w/red ovpt: *Yang Pen. Specimen* on back.	—	—	125.

	J42 5000 Yüan	VG	VF	UNC
	1945. Black. Back dk. gray. Block letters. 166 x 65mm.			
	a. Issued note.	10.00	50.00	110.
	s. Specimen w/red ovpt: *Yang Pen. Specimen* on back.	—	—	140.

	J43 100,000 Yüan	VG	VF	UNC
	1945. Red-violet on pale green unpt. Serial #. 185 x 95mm.			
	a. Issued note.	75.00	250.	950.
	s. Specimen w/ovpt: *Mi-hon.*	—	—	300.

	J44 100,000 Yüan	VG	VF	UNC
	1945. Purple on yellow-brown unpt. 168 x 64mm.			
	a. Block letters.	125.	350.	1100.
	r. Remainder w/o block letters or sign. seals. Back purple to red-violet.	50.00	150.	450.

FEDERAL RESERVE BANK OF CHINA

中國聯合準備銀行

Chung Kuo Lien Ho Chun Pei Yin Hang

1938 FIRST ISSUE

#J45-J47 17 arch bridge at summer palace at ctr.

	J45 1/2 Fen	VG	VF	UNC
	1938. Lt. blue on yellow unpt. *(S/M #C286-1).*			
	a. Issued note.	3.50	10.00	35.00
	s. Specimen w/ovpt: *Yang Pen. Specimen* on back. Uniface pair.	—	—	60.00

	J46 1 Fen	VG	VF	UNC
	1938. Lt. brown on pale green unpt. *(S/M #C286-2).*			
	a. Issued note.	1.50	7.00	15.00
	s. Specimen w/ovpt: *Yang Pen. Specimen* on back. Uniface pair.	—	—	75.00

	J47 5 Fen	VG	VF	UNC
	1938; 1939. Red on pink unpt.			
	a. 1938. *(S/M #C286-3).*	1.00	4.00	10.00
	b. 1939. *(S/M #C286-30).*	.50	2.00	5.00
	s. As a. Specimen w/red ovpt: *Yang Pen* on face. Blue ovpt. on back. Uniface pair.	—	—	60.00

	J48 10 Fen = 1 Chiao	VG	VF	UNC
	1938; 1940. Red-brown on pink unpt. Tower of summer palace at r.			
	a. 1938. *(S/M #C286-4).*	.50	2.00	5.00
	b. 1940. *(S/M #C286-31).*	1.00	4.00	10.00
	s. As a. Specimen w/red ovpt: *Yang Pen* on face and back. Uniface pair.	—	—	75.00

	J49 20 Fen = 2 Chiao	VG	VF	UNC
	1938; 1940. Blue on pale blue unpt. Temple of Heaven at r.			
	a. 1938. *(S/M #C286-5).*	.75	2.50	8.00
	b. 1940. *(S/M #C286-32).*	1.00	3.25	10.00
	s. As a. Specimen w/red ovpt: *Yang Pen* on face and back. Uniface pair.	—	—	70.00

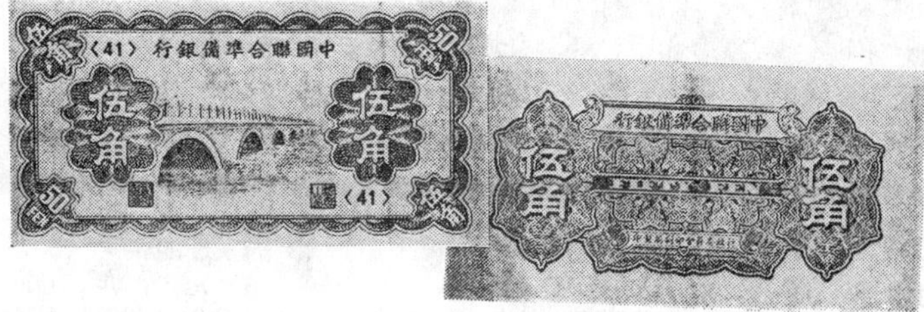

	J50 50 Fen = 5 Chiao	VG	VF	UNC
	ND (1938). Orange on pale green unpt. Marco Polo bridge at ctr. *(S/M #C286-60).*			
	a. Issued note.	3.50	10.00	35.00
	s. Specimen w/ovpt: *Yang Pen. Specimen* on back.	—	—	120.

1938 SECOND ISSUE

#J51-J54 printer: BEPP.

	J51 10 Cents = 1 Chiao	VG	VF	UNC
	1938. Brown-violet. Dragon at r. *(S/M #C286-5).*			
	a. Issued note.	10.00	30.00	90.00
	s. Specimen w/red ovpt: *Yang Pen. Specimen* on back. Uniface pair.	—	—	100.

	J52 20 Cents = 2 Chiao	VG	VF	UNC
	1938. Green. Dragon at r. *(S/M #C286-7).*			
	a. Issued note.	12.50	45.00	135.
	s. Specimen w/ovpt: *Yang Pen. Specimen* on back. Uniface pair.	—	—	110.

	J53 50 Cents = 5 Chiao	VG	VF	UNC
	1938. Orange. Dragon at r. *(S/M #C286-8).*			
	a. Issued note.	15.00	60.00	175.
	s. Specimen w/ovpt: *Yang Pen. Specimen* on back. Uniface pair.	—	—	100.

	J54 1 Dollar	VG	VF	UNC
	1938. Green. Portr. Confucius at l., junks at lower ctr. r., dragon above. 183 x 93mm. *(S/M #C286-10).*			
	a. Issued note.	10.00	50.00	120.
	s. Specimen w/ovpt: *Yang Pen. Specimen* on back.	—	—	200.

		VG	VF	UNC
J55	**1 Dollar** 1938. Green. Like #J54 but poor printing. *(S/M #C286-11).*	15.00	60.00	180.

Note: Doubtful whether war printing or forgery.

		VG	VF	UNC
J58	**100 Dollars** 1938. Purple. Portr. Huang Ti at l., farm laborer at lower r., dragon above. 190 x 107mm. *(S/M #C286-20).*			
	a. Issued note.	200.	700.	2000.
	s. Specimen w/ovpt: *Yang Pen. Specimen* on back.	—	—	600.

		VG	VF	UNC
J56	**5 Dollars** 1938. Orange. Portr. Yüeh Fei at l., horseback patrol at lower r., dragon above. 184 x 97mm. *(S/M #C286-13).*			
	a. Issued note.	85.00	250.	750.
	s. Specimen w/ovpt: *Yang Pen. Specimen* on back.	—	—	350.

		VG	VF	UNC
J57	**10 Dollars** 1938. Blue. Portr. Kuan-yü at l., Great Wall at lower r., dragon above. 190 x 102mm. *(S/M #C286-15).*			
	a. Issued note.	85.00	250.	750.
	s. Specimen w/ovpt: *Yang Pen. Specimen* on back.	—	—	350.

NOTICE

Readers with unlisted dates, signature varieties, etc. are invited to submit photocopies or, high resolution (300 dpi, 100% size) scans of their notes to: Standard Catalog of World Paper Money, 700 East State St. Iola, WI 54990-0001, or E-Mail: george.cuhaj@fwpubs.com.

		VG	VF	UNC
J59	**100 Yüan** 1938 (1944). Brown. Face like #J63. Plain pattern on back. Outer frame of back has color varieties. *(S/M #C286-22).*	6.50	30.00	65.00

1938 (1939) Issue

#J60 *Deleted.*

		VG	VF	UNC
J61	**1 Yüan** 1938 (1939). Yellow-green. Boats at ctr., dragon above, portr. Confucius at r. Pagoda at ctr. on back. 148 x 72mm. *(S/M #C286-12).*			
	a. Issued note.	2.50	7.50	25.00
	s. Specimen w/red ovpt: *Yang Pen. Specimen* on back. Uniface pair.	—	—	125.
J62	**5 Yüan** 1938 (1939). Orange. Horseback patrol at ctr., dragon above, portr. Yüeh Fei at r. Engraved. m155 x 76mm. *(S/M #C286-14).*			
	a. Issued note.	3.50	17.50	35.00
	s. Specimen w/red ovpt: *Yang Pen. Specimen* on back. Uniface pair.	—	—	125.
	x. Lithograph counterfeit. Block #4.	—	—	25.00
J63	**10 Yüan** 1938 (1939). Blue. Great Wall at ctr., dragon above, portr. Kuan-yü at r. Paper w/many or few fibers. 164 x 83mm. *(S/M #C286-16).*			
	a. Issued note.	6.50	30.00	65.00
	s. Specimen w/red ovpt: *Yang Pen. Specimen* on back. Uniface pair.	—	—	125.
J64	**100 Yüan** 1938 (1939). Purple. Ships along shoreline at l., farm laborers at r. ctr., w/dragon above, portr. Huang Ti at r. Pagoda at ctr. on back. 178 x 95mm. *(S/M #C286-21).*			
	a. Issued note.	35.00	175.	350.
	s. Specimen w/red ovpt: *Yang Pen. Specimen* on back. Uniface pair.	—	—	150.

#J65 *Deleted.* See #J47. #J66 *Deleted.* See #J48.

1944 Issue

#J67 *Deleted.* See #J49.

		VG	VF	UNC
J68	**50 Fen = 5 Chiao** 1944. Violet on ochre and violet unpt. Temple of the clouds at l. *(S/M #C286-40).*			
	a. Issued note.	1.00	3.00	10.00
	s. Specimen perforated: *Yang Pen.* Uniface pair.	—	—	75.00

		VG	VF	UNC
J69	**1 Yüan** 1944. Dk. gray on dk. olive-green or olive-brown (shades) unpt. Partial view of temple, Confucius at r. 125 x 65mm. *(S/M #C286-50).*			
	a. Issued note.	1.25	4.00	10.00
	s. Specimen perforated: *Yang Pen.* Uniface pair.	—	—	75.00

1941 ND ISSUE

***#J70 Deleted.* See #J50.**

***#J71 Deleted.* See #J73.**

		VG	VF	UNC
J72	**1 Yüan** ND (1941). Gray-green on green and pink ovpt. Partial view of temple at l., Confucius at r. 146 x 70mm. *(S/M #C286-70).*			
	a. Issued note.	.75	2.50	8.00
	s. Specimen w/red ovpt. and perforated: *Yang Pen. Specimen* on back.	—	—	100.

		VG	VF	UNC
J73	**5 Yüan** ND (1941). Orange on m/c unpt. Temple at l., Yüeh Fei at r. *(S/M #C286-71).*			
	a. Icsued note.	2.50	7.50	25.00
	s. Specimen w/ovpt. and perforated: *Yang Pen. Specimen* on back. Uniface pair.	—	—	100.

		VG	VF	UNC
J74	**10 Yüan** ND (1941). Blue on m/c unpt. Wu Ying Hall at l., man w/cap at r. *(S/M #C286-74).*			
	a. Issued note.	2.50	8.00	22.50
	s. Specimen w/red ovpt. and perforated: *Yang Pen. Specimen* on back.	—	—	120.

		VG	VF	UNC
J75	**100 Yüan** ND (1941). Brown on green and purple unpt. House w/stairs at l., Huang Ti at r. 174 x 93mm. Chinese printer. *(S/M #C286-84).*			
	a. Issued note.	8.00	30.00	85.00
	s. Specimen w/red ovpt. and perforated: *Yang Pen. Specimen* on back.	—	—	175.

1943 ND ISSUE

		VG	VF	UNC
J76	**10 Yüan** ND (1943). Dk. blue-gray on green and brown unpt. Kuan Yü at l. Jade Peak Pagoda at r. 160 x 85mm. *S/M #C286-73).*			
	a. Issued note.	4.00	17.50	40.00
	s. Specimen perforated: *Yang Pen.* Uniface pair.	—	—	140.

		VG	VF	UNC
J77	**100 Yüan** ND (1943). Brown on m/c unpt. Huang Ti at l. temple near mountainside at r. 176 x 95mm *(S/M #C286-83).*			
	a. Issued note.	4.00	15.00	40.00
	s. Specimen w/ovpt. and perforated *Yang Pen. Yang Pen on back. Uniface pair.*	—	—	125.

J78	500 Yüan	VG	VF	UNC
	ND (1943). Brownish black on pale green and olive unpt. Temple of Heaven at l. Confucius at r. Onagadori cocks unpt. at l. and at r. of vertical denomination at ctr. *500* once on back. Block letters and serial #. 179 x 98mm. *(S/M #C286-90).*			
	a. Back frame brown. Imprint 26mm.	8.00	25.00	75.00
	b. Back frame brown. Imprint 29mm.	4.00	15.00	40.00
	s. Back frame red-brown. Imprint 24mm. Specimen perforated: *Yang Pen.* Uniface pair.	—	—	125.

1944 ND ISSUE

J79	5 Yüan	VG	VF	UNC
	ND (1944). Brown on yellow unpt. Small house at l., Yüeh Fei w/book at r. *(S/M #C286-72).*			
	a. Black on yellow unpt. Seal 8mm high at l. Wmk: Clouds and *FRB* logo.	1.75	5.00	15.00
	b. Wmk: *FRB* logo.	1.75	5.00	15.00
	c. Dk. brown on lt. brown unpt. Seal 7mm high at l. W/o wmk.	2.50	7.50	22.50
	s. Specimen perforated: *Yang Pen.* Uniface pair.	—	—	125.

J80	10 Yüan	VG	VF	UNC
	ND (1944). Blue on lt. brown unpt. Kuan-yü at l., wall of house w/tree and rock at r. w/*10 YUAN* at bottom ctr. on back. 158 x 78mm. *(S/M #C286-75).*			
	a. Issued note.	1.75	5.00	15.00
	s1. Specimen w/red ovpt: *Yang Pen. Yang Pen* on back. Uniface pair.	—	—	125.
	s2. Specimen perforated: *Yang Pen.* Uniface pair.	—	—	125.

J81	10 Yüan	VG	VF	UNC
	ND (1944). Purple on m/c unpt. Man w/mustache at r. *(S/M #C286-80).*			
	a. Issued note.	2.50	12.50	35.00
	s. Specimen w/red ovpt. and perforated: *Yang Pen.*	—	—	125.

J82	10 Yüan	VG	VF	UNC
	ND (1944). Blue on m/c unpt. Similar to #J81. *(S/M #C286-81).*			
	a. Issued note.	4.00	12.50	35.00
	s1. Specimen w/red ovpt. and perforated: *Yang Pen.*	—	—	125.
	s2. Specimen w/red ovpt: *Mi-hon.*	—	—	100.

J83	100 Yüan	VG	VF	UNC
	ND (1944). Dk. brown on green-blue and violet. House w/stairs at l., Huang Ti at r. Back brown and violet. 178 x 95mm. W/o imprint. *(S/M #C286-85).*			
	a. Issued note.	6.00	17.50	55.00
	b. Horizontal quadrille paper.	6.00	17.50	55.00
	s1. Specimen w/red ovpt. and perforated: *Yang Pen.*	—	—	150.
	s2. Specimen w/red ovpt: *Mi-hon.*	—	—	150.

J84	500 Yüan	VG	VF	UNC
	ND (1944). Dk. green on tan and purple unpt. Temple of Heaven at l., Confucius at r. Unpt. w/Onagadori cock above guilloche at ctr. Back brown on yellow-brown unpt; *500* five times. 181 x 99mm. *(S/M #C286-91).*			
	a. Horizontal quadrille paper.	15.00	45.00	140.
	b. Non-quadrille paper.	15.00	45.00	140.
	s1. Specimen w/red ovpt. and perforated: *Yang Pen.* Uniface pair.	—	—	125.
	s2. Specimen w/red ovpt: *Mi-hon.*	—	—	150

J84A	500 Yüan	VG	VF	UNC
	ND (1944). Like #J89 but litho. Back brown on yellow unpt. Block #1. Specimen w/red ovpt: *Mi-hon.*	—	—	150

1945 ND ISSUE

J85	1 Yüan	VG	VF	UNC
	ND (1945). Dk. brown on lt. orange-brown unpt. Bridge and pavilion at l., numeral at r. 123 x 63mm. (Not issued). *(S/M #C286-65).*			
	a. Block #.	—	200.	500
	s. Specimen perforated: *Yang Pen.* Uniface pair.	—	—	500

		VG	VF	UNC
J86	**10 Yüan** ND (1945). Violet on lt. brown unpt. Kuan-yü at l., wall of house w/tree and rock at r. W/o *10 YUAN* on back. 143 x 72mm.			
	a. Chinese printer (11 characters). *(S/M #C286-77).*	1.75	5.00	15.00
	b. Chinese printer (14 characters). *(S/M #C286-76).*	1.75	5.00	15.00
	s. As b. Specimen perforated: *Yang Pen.*	—	—	125.

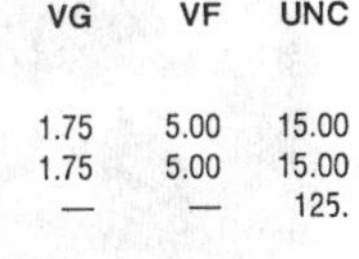

		VG	VF	UNC
J87	**50 Yüan** ND (1945). Violet-brown. Man w/beard at l. *(S/M #C286-82).*			
	a. Wmk. *FRB* logo and clouds. Block #1.	10.00	50.00	110.
	b. W/o wmk. Block #2.	10.00	25.00	100.
	s. As a. Specimen perforated: *Yang Pen.* Uniface pair.	—	—	150.

		VG	VF	UNC
J88	**100 Yüan** ND (1945). Brown to red-brown. Imperial Resting Quarters near mountainside at at l., Huang Ti at r. Back red-brown. 170 x 90mm. *S/M #C286-86).*			
	a. Issued note.	1.50	7.00	15.00
	s. Specimen perforated: *Yang Pen.* Uniface pair.	—	—	125.
J88A	**100 Yüan** ND (1945). Gray and red-brown. Like #J88. Back brown. Block #16.	4.00	15.00	50.00

		VG	VF	UNC
J89	**500 Yüan** ND (1945). Blue on lt. blue-green and yellow-brown unpt. Temple of Heaven at l. Wmk: *FRB* logo and clouds. 185 x 83mm. *(S/M #C286-92).*			
	a. Issued note.	2.50	12.50	80.00
	s. Specimen perforated: *Yang Pen.* Uniface pair.	—	—	150.

		VG	VF	UNC
J90	**500 Yüan** ND (1945). Blue-gray on orange-yellow to salmon unpt. Like #J87 but reduced size 168 x 78mm. *(S/M #C286-93).*	2.00	10.00	20.00

		VG	VF	UNC
J91	**1000 Yüan** ND (1945). Dk. green. Great Wall at ctr. r. Ch'ien Men fortress at ctr. on back. *(S/M #C286-94).*			
	a. Engraved, w/serial # and block #1-3. Wmk: *1* in oval, ovals horizontal.	3.50	17.50	35.00
	b. Engraved, w/serial # and block #1-3. Wmk: *1* in oval, ovals vertical.	3.50	17.50	35.00
	c. Wmk: *FRB* logo repeated.	5.00	15.00	50.00
	r. Remainder, w/o serial #, block #, or sign. seals.	—	—	35.00
	s. As b. Specimen perforated: *Yang Pen.* Uniface pair.	—	—	150.

		VG	VF	UNC
J92	**5000 Yüan** ND (1945). Brown. State stone barge at l. (Empress Dowager's summer palace, *I Ho Yuan*). Wmk: *FRB* logo. *(S/M #C286-95).*			
	a. Issued note.	40.00	200.	450.
	r. Remainder w/o serial # or block #.	—	100.	250.

Note: The "State Barge" is a marble boat in the Empress dowager's summer palace *(I Ho Yuan)*, a most unseaworthy craft.

Hua-Hsing Commercial Bank

華興商業銀行

Hua Hsing Shang Yeh Yin Hang

1938 Issues

		VG	VF	UNC
J93	**10 Cents = 1 Chiao** 1938. Green on pink and lt. blue unpt. Junks at l. *S/M #H184-1).*			
	a. Issued note.	80.00	225.	550.
	s. Specimen w/ovpt: *Yang Pen. Specimen* on back.	—	—	550.

		VG	VF	UNC
J94	**20 Cents = 2 Chiao** 1938. Brown. Pagoda at ctr. Back lt. blue. *(S/M #H184.2).*			
	a. Issued note.	55.00	175.	450.
	s. Specimen w/ovpt: *Yang Pen. Specimen* on back.	—	—	400.

J95 Deleted.

		VG	VF	UNC
J96	**1 Yüan** 1938. Green on yellow and gray unpt. Trees along roadway at l. ctr. *(S/M #H184-10).*			
	a. Issued note.	150.	400.	1000.
	s. Specimen w/ovpt: *Yang Pen. Specimen* on back.	—	—	500.
J97	**5 Yüan** ND (1938). Blue on m/c unpt. Liu Ho Pagoda at l., Yüeh Fei at r. *(S/M #184H-11).*			
	a. Issued note. Rare.	—	—	—
	s. Specimen w/ovpt: *Yang Pen. Specimen* on back.	—	—	1250.

		VG	VF	UNC
J98	**5 Yüan** 1938. Dk. green and black on ochre and gray. House, arch, bridge, and pagoda at ctr. *(S/M #H184-12).*			
	a. Black ovpt. Sign of bank president Ch'en Chin Tao on back.	—	—	450.
	s. Specimen w/ovpt: *Yang Pen* on face and back.	—	—	400.
J99	**10 Yüan** ND (1938). Black on m/c unpt. Ta Ch'eng Tien bldg. at l. Confucius at r. *(S/M #H184-13).*			
	a. Issued note. (Sea salvaged).	1250.	—	—
	s. Specimen w/ovpt: *Yang Pen* on face and back.	—	—	1500.

		VG	VF	UNC
J100	**10 Yüan** 1938. Brown-orange and black on ochre and lt. green unpt. Temple at ctr. *(S/M #H184-14).*			
	a. Issued note.	150.	350.	600.
	r. Remainder w/o sign.	—	—	450.
	s. Specimen w/ovpt: *Yang Pen* on face and back.	—	—	450.

MENGCHIANG BANK

行銀疆蒙

Meng Chiang Yin Hang

1938-45 ND ISSUES

		VG	VF	UNC
J101	**5 Fen** ND (1940). Gray. Herd of sheep at ctr. Back brown-orange. *(S/M #M11-1).*			
	a. Issued note.	1.00	2.50	10.00
	s. Specimen w/ovpt: *Yang Pen.* on face and back.	—	—	60.00

		VG	VF	UNC
J101A	**1 Chiao** ND (1940). Brown and black on lt. blue unpt. Herd of camels at ctr. Back blue-gray. *(S/M #M11-2).*			
	a. Issued note.	1.50	5.00	17.50
	s. Specimen w/red ovpt: *Yang Pen* on face and back.	—	—	60.00

		VG	VF	UNC
J102	**5 Chiao** ND (1944). Black on yellow-brown unpt. Temple courtyard. Back green. *(S/M #M11-4).*			
	a. Issued note.	40.00	125.	375.
	s. Specimen w/red-orange ovpt: *Mi-hon.*	—	—	200.

		VG	VF	UNC
J103	**5 Chiao = 50 Fen** ND (1940). Dk. purple and black on green and pale blue unpt. Herd of camels at ctr. Back blue-gray. *(S/M #M11-3).*			
	a. Issued note.	3.00	15.00	45.00
	s. Specimen w/red ovpt: *Yang Pen* on face and back.	—	—	60.00

		VG	VF	UNC
J104	**1 Yüan** ND. Dk. green on ochre unpt. Great Wall at l. ctr. Back blue. *(S/M #M11-10).*	1.00	3.00	10.00

		VG	VF	UNC
J105	**1 Yüan** ND (1938). Dk. green and black on ochre and m/c unpt. Herd of sheep at ctr. Back blue-gray. *(S/M #M11-11).*			
	a. Issued note.	4.00	12.50	50.00
	s. Specimen w/red ovpt: *Yang Pen* on face and back. Toppan Printing Co. imprint. Uniface pair.	—	—	150

		VG	VF	UNC
J106	**5 Yüan**			
	ND (1938). Orange-brown and black w/violet guilloche. Pagoda at l., fortress at r. Back tan; rural bldg. at ctr. *(S/M #M11-12).*			
	a. Issued note.	2.50	7.50	25.00
	s. Specimen w/red ovpt: *Yang Pen* on face and back. Toppan Printing Co. imprint. Uniface pair.	—	—	150.

		VG	VF	UNC
J107	**5 Yüan**			
	ND (1944). Purple on pale purple and orange unpt. Lama monastery at l. ctr. Back dk. blue. Specimen. *(S/M #M11-13).* Rare	—	—	—

		VG	VF	UNC
J108	**10 Yüan**			
	ND (1944). Dk. blue-gray on yellow unpt. Camel at l., men on horseback, w/oxen and horses at ctr. Back lt. blue w/Buddhas at ctr.			
	a. Wmk: Bank logo. Serial # and block #. *(S/M #M11-15).*	15.00	50.00	150.
	b. W/o wmk. Serial # and block #. *(S/M #M11-).*	5.00	17.50	60.00
	c. Block # only. *(S/M #M11-).*	8.00	25.00	75.00
J108A	**10 Yüan**			
	ND (1944). Brown and black on ochre unpt. Like #J108. Back dk. red. *(S/M #M11-).*			
	r. Remainder. Block # only.	8.00	25.00	75.00
	s. Specimen w/red-orange ovpt:	—	—	125.

		VG	VF	UNC
J109	**10 Yüan**			
	ND (1938). Dk. brown. Sheep at ctr. Back blue. *(S/M #M11-14).*			
	a. Issued note.	5.00	25.00	75.00
	s. Specimen w/red ovpt: *Yang Pen* on face and back. Toppan Printing Co. imprint. Uniface pair.	—	—	150.

		VG	VF	UNC
J110	**100 Yüan**			
	ND (1945). Dk. green on lt. brown unpt. Herdsman w/goats. *(S/M #M11-22).*			
	a. Issued note.	3.00	10.00	30.00
	s. Specimen w/red-orange ovpt: *Mi-hon.*	—	—	125.

		VG	VF	UNC
J111	**100 Yüan**			
	ND (1945). Black on yellow-green unpt. Lama monastary. *(S/M #M11-21).*	5.00	15.00	40.00

		VG	VF	UNC
J112	**100 Yüan**			
	ND (1938). Purple and black on olive-geen and m/c unpt. Pavilion at l., camel at r. *(S/M #M11-21).*			
	a. Issued note.	4.00	12.50	55.00
	s. Specimen w/red ovpt: *Yang Pen* on face and back. Toppan Printing Co. imprint. Uniface pair.	—	—	150.

CHI TUNG BANK

行銀東冀

Chi Tung Yin Hang

1937 ISSUE

		VG	VF	UNC
J113	**5 Chiao = 50 Fen**			
	ND (1937). Dk. green on lt. blue and pink unpt. Gateway at l. ctr. Back pale green. *(S/M #C84-1).*			
	a. Issued note.	275.	700.	1750.
	s1. Specimen w/ovpt: *Yang Pen.* and *SPECIMEN.*	—	—	750.
	s2. As a. Specimen w/ovpt: *Yang Pen* and *Specimen* on face and back, perforated serial #.	—	—	700.

		VG	VF	UNC
J114	**1 Yüan** ND (1937). Orange on lt. green and ochre unpt. Great Wall at r. Back tan. *(S/M #C284-2).*			
	a. Issued note.	275.	700.	1750.
	s1. Specimen (English).	—	—	750.
	s2. As a. Specimen w/ovpt: *Yang Pen* and *Specimen* on face and back, perforated serial #.	—	—	700.

		VG	VF	UNC
J115	**5 Yüan** ND (1937). Purple on m/c unpt. Tower at Tunghsien at r. *(S/M #C84-3).*			
	s1. Specimen (English).	—	—	1500.
	s2. Specimen w/ovpt: *Yang Pen* and *Specimen* on face and back, perforated serial #.	—	—	1400.

		VG	VF	UNC
J116	**10 Yüan** ND (1937). Black on m/c unpt. Temple at r. Back ochre. *(S/M #C84-4).*			
	s1. Specimen (English).	—	—	2500.
	s2. Specimen w/ovpt: *Yang Pen* and *Specimen* on face and back. Perforated serial #.	—	—	2400.

		VG	VF	UNC
J117	**100 Yüan** ND (1937). Dk. blue on m/c unpt. Bldg. at r. Back blue. *(S/M #C84-5).*			
	s1. Specimen (English).	—	—	4000.
	s2. Specimen w/ovpt: *Yang Pen* and *Specimen* on face and back. Perforated serial #.	—	—	4000.

CHANAN BANK

行銀南察

Ch'a Nan Yin Hang

PROVISIONAL ISSUE

#J118-J119 ovpt. on notes of the Central Bank of Manchukuo. This is the second ovpt. w/*Ch'a Nan Yin Hang* in Chinese vertically at l. and r. on face. First ovpt. is for Central Bank of Manchukuo. Chanan Bank notes have the face ovpt. for CBM line out, but w/o any new ovpt. on back leaving the CBM ovpt.

		VG	VF	UNC
J118	**1 Yüan** ND (1937- old date 1929). Black and m/c. Ovpt. on #J120. *(S/M #C4-1).*			
	a. Double line through red ovpt. below pavilion.	300.	600.	2000.
	b. Single line through red ovpt. below pavilion.	300.	600.	2000.
	s. Specimen w/red handstamp: *Yang Pen.* Punched hole cancelled.	—	—	600.

		VG	VF	UNC
J119	**10 Yüan** ND (1937- old date 1929). Green and m/c. Ovpt. on #J122. *(S/M #C4-3).*			
	a. Issued note.	1500.	2500.	—
	s. Specimen w/red handstamp: *Yang Pen.* Punched hole cancelled.	—	—	2500.

MANCHUKUO

Under the lax central government of the Republic of China, Manchuria attained a relatively large measure of automony. This occurred in 1917, under the leadership of Marshal Chang Tso-lin and his son, Chang Hsueh-liang. Following the Japanese occupation, the State of Manchukuo was established on February 18, 1932, with the annexation of the Chinese Province of Jehol. Under japanese auspices, Manchukuo was ruled by Pu Yi, the last emperor of the Manchu (Ching) Dynasty. In 1934, Manchukuo was decla

RULERS:

Ta Tung, Years 1-3, 1932-1934
Kang Teh, Years 1-12, 1934-1945

MONETARY SYSTEM:

1 Yuan = 10 Chiao = 100 Fen

CENTRAL BANK OF MANCHUKUO

行銀央中洲滿

Man Chou Chung Yang Yin Hang

PROVISIONAL ISSUE

#J120-J122 ovpt. new bank name on notes of the Provincial Bank of the Three Eastern Provinces. Dated first year of Ta Tung (1932).

Note: For #J120 and J122 w/additional vertical Chinese ovpt: *Cha Nan Yin Hang,* see Chanan Bank #J118 and #J119.

		VG	VF	UNC
J120	**1 Yüan** 1932 (-old date Nov. 1929). Black and m/c. ovpt. on #S2962a. *(S/M #M2-1).*			
	a. Issued note.	400.	1000.	3000.
	s1. Specimen w/ovpt: *Yang Pen* and *Specimen. Specimen* on back. Uniface pair.	—	—	1000.
	s2. As a. Specimen w/ovpt: *Yang Pen* and *Specimen.* Punched hole cancelled.	—	—	800.

		VG	VF	UNC
J121	**5 Yüan**			
	1932 (- old date Nov. 1929). Brown and m/c. ovpt. on #S2963a. Specimen w/ovpt: *Yang Pen* and *Specimen* on back. Uniface pair. *(S/M #M2-)*.	—	—	1200.
J122	**10 Yüan**			
	1932 (- old date Nov. 1929). Green and m/c. ovpt. on #S2964a. *(S/M #M2-2)*.			
	a. Issued note.	1200.	3000.	—
	s1. Specimen w/ovpt: *Yang Pen* and *Specimen*. *Specimen* on back. Uniface pair.	—	—	1000.
	s2. As a. Specimen w/ovpt: *Yang Pen*. Punched hole cancelled.	—	—	800.

#J123 *Deleted.*

1932 Issue

		VG	VF	UNC
J124	**5 Chiao = 50 Fen**			
	ND (1932). Dk. blue on ochre unpt. Back pale green. *(S/M #M2-10)*.			
	a. Issued note.	50.00	175.	500.
	s. Specimen w/ovpt: *Yang Pen* and *Specimen* on face and back. Uniface pair.	—	—	450.

1932-33 ND Issue

#J125-J128 m/c flag at l., bldg. at r.

		VG	VF	UNC
J125	**1 Yüan**			
	ND (1932). Blue on yellow yellow unpt. *(S/M #M2-20)*.			
	a. Issued note.	25.00	125.	280.
	s. Specimen w/ovpt: *Yang Pen* and *Specimen* on face and back. Uniface pair.	—	—	250.

		VG	VF	UNC
J126	**5 Yüan**			
	ND (1933). Dk. brown on tan unpt. *(S/M #M2-21)*.			
	a. Issued note.	100.	300.	650.
	s. Specimen w/ovpt: *Yang Pen* and *Specimen* on face and back. Punched hole cancelled. Uniface pair.	—	—	300.
J127	**10 Yüan**			
	ND (1932). Blue on orange unpt. *(S/M #M2-22)*.			
	a. Issued note.	100.	350.	700.
	s. Specimen w/ovpt: *Yang Pen* and *Specimen* on face and back. Uniface pair.	—	—	350.

		VG	VF	UNC
J128	**100 Yüan**			
	ND (1933). Blue on yellow-orange unpt. *(S/M #M2-23)*.			
	a. Issued note.	150.	350.	600.
	s. Specimen w/ovpt: *Yang Pen* and *Specimen* on face and back. Uniface pair.	—	—	400.

1935-38 ND Issue

		VG	VF	UNC
J129	**5 Chiao = 50 Fen**			
	ND (1935). Brown on green and lilac unpt. Ch'ien Lung at r. Back brown and olive. *(S/M #M2-30)*.			
	a. Issued note.	3.00	8.00	40.00
	s. Specimen w/ovpt: *Yang Pen* and *Specimen* on face and back. Uniface pair.	—	—	75.00

		VG	VF	UNC
J130	**1 Yüan**			
	ND (1937). Black on green and yellow unpt. at ctr. T'ien Ming at r. Back green. *(S/M #M2-40)*.			
	a. 6-digit serial #.	3.00	10.00	30.00
	b. 7-digit serial #.	2.00	5.00	12.50
	s. Specimen w/ovpt: *Yang Pen* and *Specimen* on face and back. Uniface pair.	—	—	60.00

		VG	VF	UNC
J131	**5 Yüan**			
	ND (1938). Black on brown unpt. at ctr. Man w/beard wearing feather crown at r. Back brown. *(S/M #M2-41).*			
	a. 6-digit serial #.	15.00	50.00	150.
	b. 7-digit serial #.	8.00	25.00	75.00
	s. Specimen w/ovpt: *Yang Pen* and *Specimen* on face and back. Punched hole cancelled. Uniface pair.	—	—	60.00

		VG	VF	UNC
J132	**10 Yüan**			
	ND (1937). Black on brown unpt. at ctr. Emperor Ch'ien Lung at r. Back purple. *(S/M #M2-42).*			
	a. 6-digit serial #.	7.50	20.00	50.00
	b. 7-digit serial #.	3.00	8.00	25.00
	s. Specimen w/ovpt: *Yang Pen* and *Specimen* on face and back. Uniface pair.	—	—	60.00

		VG	VF	UNC
J133	**100 Yüan**			
	ND (1938). Black on green unpt. at ctr. Confucius at r., Ta Ch'eng Tien bldg. at l. Back blue; w/sheep. *(S/M #M2-43).*			
	a. 6-digit serial #.	30.00	100.	200.
	b. 7-digit serial #.	6.00	15.00	35.00
	s. Specimen w/ovpt: *Yang Pen* and *Specimen* on face and back. Uniface pair.	—	—	60.00

1944 ND ISSUE

#J135-J138 w/block # and serial #. New back designs.

		VG	VF	UNC
J134	**5 Chiao = 50 Fen**			
	ND (1944). Blue-green on pale blue unpt. Ta Ch'eng Tien bldg. at l. ctr. Back brown. *(S/M #M2-50).*	10.00	35.00	90.00

		VG	VF	UNC
J135	**1 Yüan**			
	ND (1944). Face like #J130 but violet unpt. at ctr. Back violet.			
	a. Block # and serial #. *(S/M #M2-60).*	1.50	6.00	12.50
	b. Block # only. *(S/M #M2-80).*	2.00	7.50	20.00
	s1. As a. Specimen w/ovpt: *Yang Pen. Specimen* on back. Uniface pair.	—	—	60.00
	s2. As b. Specimen w/ovpt: *Yang Pen.*	—	—	75.00

		VG	VF	UNC
J136	**5 Yüan**			
	ND (1944). Face like #J131 but orange unpt. at ctr. Back green.			
	a. Block # and serial #. *(S/M #M2-61).*	2.50	7.50	20.00
	s. Block # only. Specimen w/ovpt: *Yang Pen. (S/M #M2-81).*	—	—	175.

		VG	VF	UNC
J137	**10 Yüan**			
	ND (1944). Face like #J132 but green unpt. at ctr. Back blue.			
	a. Block # and serial #. Wmk: *MANCHU CENTRAL BANK. (S/M #M2-62).*	1.50	7.00	17.50
	b. Revalidation *10 Yuan* adhesive stamp on face. See #M35.	—	—	—
	c. Block # only. Wmk. as a. *(S/M #M2-82).*	2.00	7.50	20.00
	d. Revalidation *10 Yuan* adhesive stamp on face. See #M35.	—	—	—
	e. Block # only. Wmk: Chinese character: *Man* in clouds repeated.	2.50	12.50	30.00
	s1. As a. Specimen w/ovpt: *Yang Pen. Specimen* on back. Uniface pair.	—	—	90.00
	s2. As e. Specimen w/ovpt: *Yang Pen.*	—	—	60.00

		VG	VF	UNC
J138	**100 Yüan**			
	ND (1944). Face like #J133 but w/blue unpt. at ctr. Back brown w/men and donkey carts by storage silos at ctr. *(S/M #M2-63).*			
	a. Wmk: *MANCHU CENTRAL BANK.*	5.00	15.00	55.0
	b. Wmk: Chinese character: *Man* in clouds repeated.	4.00	10.00	35.0
	s1. As a. Specimen w/ovpt: *Yang Pen. Specimen* on back. Block #1. Uniface pair.	—	—	60.0
	s2. As b. Specimen w/ovpt: *Yang Pen.*	—	—	75.0

1941-45 Issue

#J139-J141; J145-J146 w/o serial #, only block letters.

		VG	VF	UNC
J139	**5 Fen** ND (1945). Blue-green. Back orange; tower at ctr. *(S/M #M2-70).*	17.50	60.00	165.

		VG	VF	UNC
J140	**10 Fen = 1 Chiao** ND (1944). Yellow-orange unpt. Back green; house at ctr. on back. *(S/M #M2-71).*	1.00	3.00	8.00

		VG	VF	UNC
J141	**5 Chiao = 50 Fen** ND (1941). Green on pink and orange unpt. Ch'ien Lung at r. Back blue. *(S/M #M2-72).*			
	a. Issued note.	1.00	3.00	8.00
	s. Specimen w/ovpt: *Yang Pen* and *Specimen.* Uniface pair.	—	—	75.00

#J142-J144 *Deleted.* See #J135b, J136s, J137c.

		VG	VF	UNC
J145	**100 Yüan** ND (1945). Like #J138 but w/only 1 serial #. Local printer. *(S/M #M2-83).*	350.	1000.	—

		VG	VF	UNC
J146	**1000 Yüan** ND (1944). Dk. brown and violet. Confucius at r., Ta Ch'eng Tien bldg. at l. Back green and brown; bank bldg. at ctr. *(S/M #M2-84).*	300.	900.	2700.

Japanese Military - WWII

Note: See also Japan #M7-M12.

Japanese Imperial Government

大日本帝國政府

Ta Jih Pen Ti Kuo Cheng Fu

1937 Issue

#M1-M5 2 facing Onagadori cockerels at upper ctr., 2 facing dragons below. Showa yr. 12.

		VG	VF	UNC
M1	**10 Sen** Yr. 12 (1937). Black on blue unpt. *(S/M #T27-20).*			
	a. Issued note.	18.00	90.00	180.
	s. Specimen w/red ovpt: *Mi-hon. Specimen* on back.	—	—	250.
M2	**50 Sen** Yr. 12 (1937). Black on yellow unpt. *(S/M #T27-22).*			
	a. Issued note.	40.00	200.	400.
	s. Specimen w/red ovpt: *Mi-hon. Specimen* on back.	—	—	300.

		VG	VF	UNC
M3	**1 Yen** Yr. 12 (1937). Black on lt. lilac unpt. *(S/M #T27-30).*			
	a. Issued note.	50.00	255.	550.
	s. Specimen w/red ovpt: *Mi-hon. Specimen* on back.	—	—	400.
M4	**5 Yen** Yr. 12 (1937). Black on pink unpt. *(S/M #T27-31).*			
	a. Issued note.	400.	750.	2250.
	s. Specimen w/red ovpt: *Mi-hon. Specimen* on back.	—	—	2000.
M5	**10 Yen** Yr. 12 (1937). Black on lt. green unpt. *(S/M #T27-32).*			
	a. Issued note.	800.	2000.	3500.
	s. Specimen w/red ovpt: *Mi-hon. Specimen* on back.	—	—	2500.

1939-40 ND Issues

TITLES:

Line A: 大日本帝國政府

Line B: 大日本帝國政府 軍用手票

A: *Ta Jih Pen Ti Kuo Cheng Fu.*

B: *Ta Jih Pen Ti Kuo Cheng Fu Chung Yung Shou Piao.*

Note: Forgeries exist of #M10. Forgeries exist on #M21 on plain white paper.

Note: For similar notes in different color printings see French Indochina #M1-M7.

		VG	VF	UNC
M6	**2 1/2 Rin** ND (1940). Black on brown unpt. Vertical note. Title A. *(S/M #T30-1).*	180.	450.	900.

		VG	VF	UNC
M7	**1 Sen** ND (1939). Brown on blue-gray unpt. Dragon at r. Title A. *(S/M #T30-2).*			
	a. Issued note.	.50	2.50	5.00
	s. Specimen w/ovpt: *Mi-hon.*	—	—	100.
M8	**1 Sen** ND (1939). Brown on blue-gray unpt. Dragon at r. Title B. *(S/M #T31-1).*	.50	1.75	5.00
M9	**5 Sen** ND (1940). Blue and brown on pink unpt. Dragon at r. Title A. *(S/M #T30-3).*			
	a. Issued note.	.25	1.00	3.00
	s. Specimen w/ovpt: *Mi-hon.*	—	—	120.

M10 5 Sen

	VG	VF	UNC
ND (1939). Blue and brown on pink ovpt. Dragon at r. Title B. *(S/M #T31-2).*	1.00	4.00	10.00

M11 10 Sen

	VG	VF	UNC
ND (1940). Black on yellow-orange and violet unpt. Dragon at r. Title A. *(S/M #T30-4).*			
a. Issued note.	.50	2.00	6.00
s. Specimen w/ovpt: *Mi-hon.*	—	—	100.

M12 10 Sen

	VG	VF	UNC
ND (1938). Black on yellow-orange and violet unpt. Dragon at r. Title B. *(S/M #T31-3).*	4.50	12.50	40.00

M13 50 Sen

	VG	VF	UNC
ND (1940). Black on green and pink unpt. Dragon at l. Title A. *(S/M #T30-5).*	.25	1.50	5.00

M14 50 Sen

	VG	VF	UNC
ND (1938). Black on green and pink unpt. Dragon at l. Title B. *(S/M #T31-4).*	.50	1.50	5.00

M15 1 Yen

	VG	VF	UNC
ND (1940). Black on pink and yellow unpt. Onagadori cock at l. Title A. *(S/M #T30-10).*			
a. Issued note.	1.00	3.25	10.00
s. Specimen w/ovpt: *Mi-hon.*	—	—	100.

M16 1 Yen

	VG	VF	UNC
ND (1939). Black on pink and yellow unpt. Onagadori cock at l. Title B. *(S/M #T31-10).*	10.00	40.00	200.

M17 5 Yen

	VG	VF	UNC
ND (1940). Black on blue and yellow unpt. Onagadori cock at l. and r. Title A. *(S/M #T30-11).*			
a. Issued note.	.50	2.00	6.00
r. Remainder w/o serial #, block # or seal.	—	12.50	40.00
s. Specimen w/ovpt: *Mi-hon.*	—	—	100.

M18 5 Yen

	VG	VF	UNC
ND (1939). Black on blue and yellow unpt. Onagadori cock at l. and r. Title B. *(S?M #T31-11).*			
a. Issued note.	2.00	6.50	20.00
r. Remainder w/o seal.	—	12.50	40.00

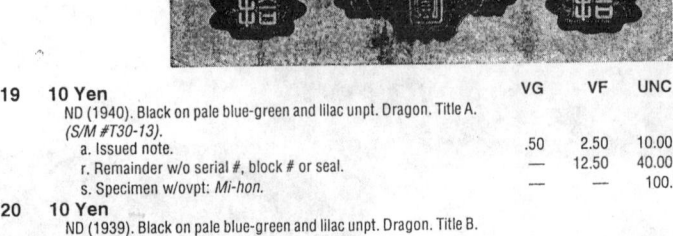

M19 10 Yen

	VG	VF	UNC
ND (1940). Black on pale blue-green and lilac unpt. Dragon. Title A. *(S/M #T30-13).*			
a. Issued note.	.50	2.50	10.00
r. Remainder w/o serial #, block # or seal.	—	12.50	40.00
s. Specimen w/ovpt: *Mi-hon.*	—	—	100.

M20 10 Yen

	VG	VF	UNC
ND (1939). Black on pale blue-green and lilac unpt. Dragon. Title B. *(S/M #T31-12).*			
a. Issued note.	4.50	12.50	40.00
r. Remainder w/o serial # or block #.	—	12.50	40.00

1945 ND Issue

M21 100 Yen

	VG	VF	UNC
ND (1945). Black on yellow-green unpt. Onagadori cock at l. and r. Title A. Back green. *(S/M #T30-14).*			
a. Issued note.	1.00	5.00	15.00
s. Specimen w/ovpt: *Mi-hon.*	—	—	100

Military Note

軍用手票

Chun Yung Shou P'i

1938 ND Issues

M22 1 Yen

	VG	VF	UNC
ND (1938). Lt. brown. Ovpt: 4 Japanese characters across ctr., 11 characters below, 8 characters (Bank of Japan) blocked out at top. Ovpt: red. *(S/M #J11-1).*			
a. Issued note.	7.50	25.00	75.00
b. W/handstamp: Type II.	10.00	35.00	—

M23	1 Yen	VG	VF	UNC
	ND (1938). Lt. brown. Ovpt: 4 Japanese characters across ctr. *(S/M #T32-1).*			
	a. Issued note.	1.50	4.50	25.00
	b. W/handstamp: Type II.	4.00	10.00	—
	s. Specimen.			600.

M24	5 Yen	VG	VF	UNC
	ND (1938). Green and brown unpt. Hooded man at r. Ovpt: 4 Japanese characters across ctr., 11 characters below, 7 characters (Bank of Japan Convertible Note) blocked out at top. *(S/M #J11-2).*			
	a. Issued note.	3.00	15.00	30.00
	b. W/handstamp: Type II.	10.00	35.00	—

M25	5 Yen	VG	VF	UNC
	ND (1938; 1944). Green and brown unpt. Ovpt: 4 Japanese characters across ctr.			
	a. Wmk: Plum flowers (1938). *(S/M #T32-2).*	.50	1.50	15.00
	b. Wmk: 2 birds (1944). *(S/M #32-3).*	.50	1.50	15.00

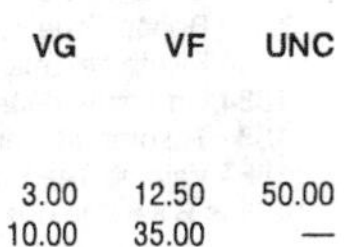

M26	10 Yen	VG	VF	UNC
	ND (1938). Green unpt. Ovpt: 4 Japanese characters across ctr., 11 characters below, 7 characters (Bank of Japan Convertible Note) blocked out at top. *(S/M #J11-3).*			
	a. Issued note.	3.00	12.50	50.00
	b. W/handstamp: Type II.	10.00	35.00	—

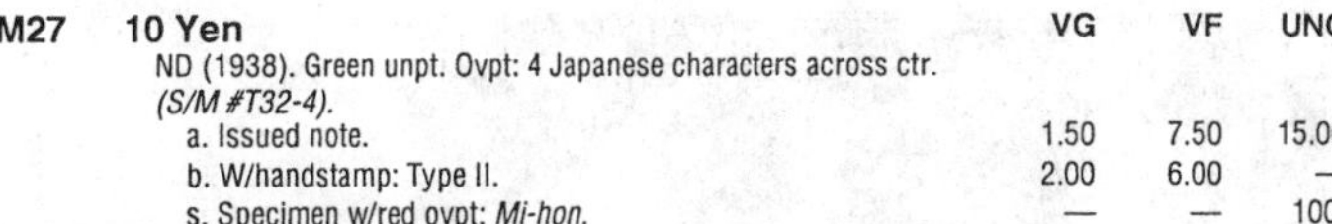

M27	10 Yen	VG	VF	UNC
	ND (1938). Green unpt. Ovpt: 4 Japanese characters across ctr. *(S/M #T32-4).*			
	a. Issued note.	1.50	7.50	15.00
	b. W/handstamp: Type II.	2.00	6.00	—
	s. Specimen w/red ovpt: *Mi-hon.*	—	—	100.

1945 ND Hong Kong Issues

		VG	VF	UNC
M28	100 Yen ND (1945). Black on lt. blue and brown unpt. Ovpt: 4 Japanese characters across ctr., 7 characters below, 5 characters at top and 4 vertical characters at l. blocked out. *(S/M #J11-4).*	2.00	10.00	20.00
M29	100 Yen ND (1945). Black on green and violet unpt. Like #M28. Ovpt: 4 Japanese characters across ctr. and seal at l. *(S/M #T32-5).*	1.00	6.00	12.50
M30	100 Yen ND (1945). Red-brown on green unpt. Similar to #M29. Ovpt: 4 Japanese characters at ctr. Back orange. *(S/M #T32-6).*	.40	2.00	5.00

South China Expeditionary Army

1944 Issue

M30A	1000 Yen	VG	VF	UNC
	Yr. 33 (1944). Red, blue and black on yellow-green unpt. Back purple on yellow unpt. *(S/M #T32-7).*	4500.	1000.	—

Russian Military - WWII

Soviet Red Army Headquarters

蘇聯紅軍司令部

Su Lien Hung Chun Szu Ling Pu

1945 Issue

		VG	VF	UNC
M31	1 Yüan 1945. Blue on green unpt. *(S/M #S82-1a).*	5.00	17.50	60.00
M32	5 Yüan 1945. Brown on green unpt. *(S/M #S82-2a).*	5.00	17.50	60.00

NOTICE

Readers with unlisted dates, signature varieties, etc. are invited to submit photocopies or, high resolution (300 dpi, 100% size) scans of their notes to: Standard Catalog of World Paper Money, 700 East State St. Iola, WI 54990-0001, or E-Mail: george.cuhaj@fwpubs.com.

M33 **10 Yüan** 1945. Red on lilac unpt. *(S/M #S82-3a).*

M34 **100 Yüan** 1945. Blue on pink unpt. *(S/M #S82-4a).*

		VG	VF	UNC
M33	10 Yüan 1945. Red on lilac unpt. *(S/M #S82-3a).*	2.00	5.00	25.00
M34	100 Yüan 1945. Blue on pink unpt. *(S/M #S82-4a).*	3.00	10.00	40.00

1945 ND Revalidated Issue

Note: The 10 Yuan adhesive stamp is also known affixed to Manchukuo 10 Yuan notes. Refer to Manchukuo listings.

		VG	VF	UNC
M35	10 Yüan ND (1946 - old date 1945). Brown revalidation *10 Yuan* adhesive stamp on #M33. *(S/M #S82-3b).*	3.00	12.50	50.00

		VG	VF	UNC
M36	100 Yüan ND (1946 - old date 1945). Green revalidation *100 Yuan* adhesive stamp on #M34. *(S/M #S82-4b).*	3.00	12.50	60.00

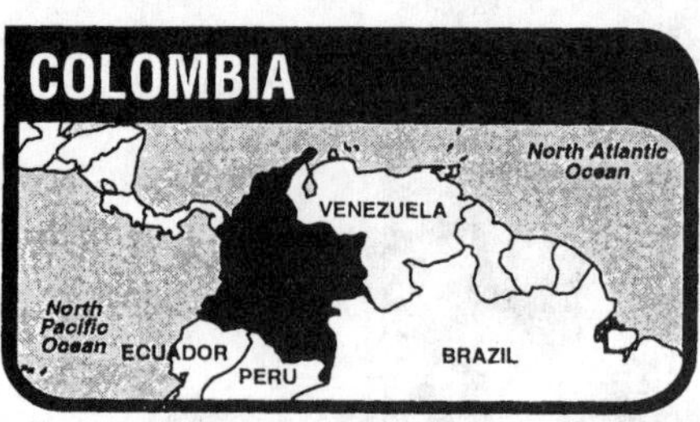

The Republic of Colombia, located in the northwestern corner of South America, has an area of 439,737 sq. mi. (1,138,914 sq. km.) and a population of 42.3 million. Capital: Bogotá. The economy is primarily agricultural with a mild rich coffee the chief crop. Colombia has the world's largest platinum deposits and important reserves of coal, iron ore, petroleum and limestone; precious metals and emeralds are also mined. Coffee, crude oil, bananas, sugar, coal and flowers are exported.

The northern coast of present Colombia was one of the first parts of the American continent to be visited by Spanish navigators, and the site, at Darien in Panama, of the first permanent European settlement on the American mainland in 1510. New Granada, as Colombia was known until 1861, stemmed from the settlement of Santa Maria in 1525. New Granada was established as a Spanish Colony in 1549. Independence was declared in 1810, and secured in 1824. In 1819, Simón Bolívar united Colombia, Venezuela, Panama and Ecuador as the Republic of Greater Colombia. Venezuela withdrew from the Republic in 1829; Ecuador in 1830; and Panama in 1903.

MONETARY SYSTEM:

1 Real = 1 Decimo = 10 Centavos, 1870's
1 Peso = 10 Decimos = 10 Reales, 1880's
1 Peso = 100 Centavos 1993

ARRANGEMENT

Listings for Colombia are divided into four major sections. The first contains regional or state issues issued from 1857 to 1885. The second lists all bank issues for the period 1869 to 1923. The third section consists of various government-sponsored issues from 1880 to 1919 and includes the revolution issue of 1900 under General Urribe. The fourth lists regional or state issues from 1898 to 1919.

The civil war period of 1899-1902 and the years of monetary chaos following are reflected in the many local printings and special overprint issues of the time. It is the plethora of such notes that caused the division of listings into the various sections as outlined above and as detailed below:

Section V

Regular Issues, 1819-1900

República de Colombia

1819 Issue .... #1-4
1820s Issue .... #5-7

Tesorería Jeneral de los Estados Unidos de Nueva Granada

1860s Issue .... #59-66

Tesorería Jeneral de los Estados Unidos de Colombia

1860s Issue .... #67

Estados Unidos de Colombia

1863 Treasury Issue .... #71-78
1869 Issue .... #80
1876 Issue .... #81

Banco Nacional de los Estados Unidos de Colombia

ND Issue .... #122-123
1881 First Issue .... #134-138
1881 Second Issue .... #141-146
1882 Issue .... #153
1885 Issue .... #161-165; 170-171

Banco Nacional de Colombia

1885 Issue .... #181-182
1886 Issue .... #186
1887 Issue .... #189-190

Banco Nacional de la República de Colombia

1886 Issue .... #191-195
1888 Issue .... #211-218
1893 Issue .... #221-228
1895 Issue .... #234-241
1899 Civil War Issues .... #251-260
1900 Civil War Issues .... #262-282

Section VI

Treasury and Special Administrative Issues, 1864-1889

Estados Unidos de Colombia

1864 Bono Flotante al 3 por 100 Anual Issue .... #283-283D
1878 Vale Por Indemnificación de Estranjeros Issue .... #284-284C
1880 Libranza Contra las Aduanas Issue .... #285
1883 Bonos Especiales de 4% Issue .... #286-286B
1884 Billete de Tesorería Issue .... #287
1884 Libranzas de la Empresa de la Ferrería de la Pradera Issue .... #288-288D
1884 Tesorería General de la Union Issue .... #289-289D
1884 Vale de Tesorería al Portador Issue .... #290-290D
1880s Billete de dos Unidades .... #290E

República de Colombia

1886 Administración General de las Salinas Maritimas Issue .... #291
1888 Libranza Contra Las Oficinas de Espendio de Sal Marina .... #291A
1888 Libranza Contra las Aduanas de la Costa Atlántica Issue .... #292
1889 Bono Colombiano Issue .... #293-293C

Section VII

Civil War and Special Administrative Issues, 1899-1922

República de Colombia

1895 Vale por Exacciones en la Guerra de 1895 Issue .... #294-294E
1900 Tesorería del Gobierno Provisional Issue .... #295 -295C
1905 Deuda Exterior Consolidada Issue .... #296
1905 Pagaré del Tesoro Issue .... #297-297D
1906-07 Vale por Exacciones en la Guerra de 1899 Issue .... #298-298G
1907 Vale de Tesorería Sin Interés Issue .... #299-299A

Section VIII

Regular Issues 1904-1960

República de Colombia 1904-22

República de Colombia 1938-53

Banco de la República

NOTE: Certain listings encompassing issues circulated by various bank and regional authorities are contained in Vol. 1.

REPUBLIC

SECTION V

REGULAR ISSUES 1819-1900

REPÚBLICA DE COLOMBIA

1819 ISSUE

#1-4 uniface. Printer: Peter Maverick, New York, U.S.A.

		Good	Fine	XF
1	**6 1/4 Centavos = Medio Real** ND (ca.1819). Black. Pineapple at upper ctr.	40.00	100.	300.
2	**12 1/2 Centavos = 1 Real** ND (ca.1819). Black. Similar to #1.	40.00	100.	300.

		Good	Fine	XF
3	**25 Centavos = 2 Reales** ND (ca.1819). Black. Loaded burro at upper ctr.	40.00	100.	300.
4	**50 Centavos = 4 Reales** ND (ca.1819). Black. Similar to #3.	40.00	100.	—

1820s ISSUE

#5-8 *BOLIVAR* above arms at ctr. Uniface. Printer: Peter Maverick, New York, U.S.A. (From cut up 4-subject sheets of unissued remainders.)

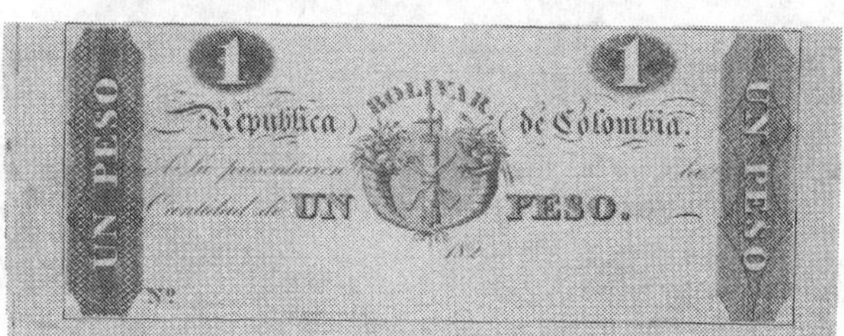

		VG	VF	UNC
5	**1 Peso** 182x. Black.			200.
6	**2 Pesos** 182x. Black.			200.
7	**3 Pesos** 182x. Black.			200.

		VG	VF	UNC
8	**5 Pesos** 182x. Black.			200.

#9-58 not assigned.

TESORERÍA JENERAL DE LOS ESTADOS UNIDOS DE NUEVA GRANADA

1860s ISSUE

#59-66 printer: Lit. Ayala.

		Good	Fine	XF
59	**20 Centavos = 2 Reales** (ca.1860)	40.00	125.	300.

#60 not assigned.

		Good	Fine	XF
61	**1 Peso = 10 Reales** 186x. Pink unpt. Steamship at upper l. and r.	60.00	200.	400.

		Good	Fine	XF
62	**2 Pesos = 20 Reales** Dec. 1862. Yellow unpt. Steamship at upper l. and r.	75.00	225.	550.

		Good	Fine	XF
63	**3 Pesos = 30 Reales** 186x. Implements.	80.00	250.	600.
64	**10 Pesos = 100 Reales** 186x. Implements.	90.00	275.	650.
65	**20 Pesos = 200 Reales** 186x. Implements.	110.	300.	750.
66	**100 Pesos = 1000 Reales** 1.3.1861. Blue unpt. Implements. Rare.	—	—	—

TESORERÍA JENERAL DE LOS ESTADOS UNIDOS DE COLOMBIA

1860s ISSUE

		Good	Fine	XF
67	**25 Centavos = 2 1/2 Reales** ND (ca. 1860s). Black. Standing allegorical woman w/cornucopia at ctr.	—	—	—

ESTADOS UNIDOS DE COLOMBIA

1863 TREASURY ISSUE

		Good	Fine	XF
71	**5 Centavos** ND. Blue. Farm tools at ctr.	80.00	200.	500.
72	**10 Centavos** ND. Blue. Horse.	80.00	200.	500.
73	**20 Centavos** ND. Black. Seated woman w/shield at ctr. Printer sign. on back.	80.00	200.	500.

#74-78 printer: ABNC.

		Good	Fine	XF
74	**1 Peso** 2.1.1863. Black on brown unpt. Portr. man at lower l., bldg. at upper l. ctr., arms at lower r.	65.00	175.	500.

		Good	Fine	XF
75	**2 Pesos** 2.1.1863. Black on red unpt. Arms at lower l., horse and rider at top ctr., portr. Bolívar at lower r. Series A-C.	90.00	250.	700.

		Good	Fine	XF
76	**5 Pesos** 2.1.1863. Black on green unpt. Portr. man at lower l., standing woman at ctr., arms at r.	100.	300.	750.
77	**10 Pesos** 2.1.1863. Black on green unpt. Arms at l., steamboat at r. ctr., portr. man at lower r.	125.	350.	900.
78	**20 Pesos** 2.1.1863. Black on yellow unpt. Arms at l., man w/mule cart at ctr., portr. Caldas at r. Rare.	—	—	—

#79 Deleted.

1869 Issue

		Good	Fine	XF
80	**3 Pesos** 28.8.1869. Rare.	—	—	—

1876 Issue

		Good	Fine	XF
81	**5 Centavos** 24.11.1876. Black. Tobacco, beehive, plow and shovel at ctr. Printed sign. and dk. red oval stamping on back. Printer: Ayala i Medrano.	80.00	200.	500.

#82-121 not assigned.

Banco Nacional de los Estados Unidos de Colombia

ND Issue

		Good	Fine	XF
122	**20 Centavos** ND. Black on blue unpt. Portr. R. Nuñez at upper ctr. Back red-brown. Series Y. Printer: Chaix.	30.00	75.00	200.
123	**20 Centavos** ND. Black on blue unpt. Like #122. Printer: Litografia de Villaveces, Bogotá.	—	—	—

#124-133 not assigned.

1881 First Issue

#134, 135 and 138 Liberty seated at l., arms at top ctr. r. Printer: Lit D. Paredes, Bogotá. Partially printed date.

		Good	Fine	XF
134	**1 Peso** 1.3.1881. Blue. Series A.	100.	250.	600.
135	**5 Pesos** 1.3.1881. Black and red. Stamping and handwritten sign. on plain back.	100.	250.	600.
138	**20 Pesos** 1.3.1881. Date partially handwritten. Rare.	—	—	—

#139-140 not assigned.

1881 Second Issue

#141-146 printer: ABNC.

		Good	Fine	XF
141	**1 Peso** 1.3.1881. Black on brown unpt. Portr. helmeted Athena at lower l., portr. S. Bolívar at upper ctr., arms at lower r. Back brown. Series A. a. Issued note	100.	250.	600.
142	**5 Pesos** 1.3.1881. Black on green unpt. Woman at l., man in uniform at ctr., arms at r. Back green. a. Issued note.	100.	250.	600

		Good	Fine	XF
143	**10 Pesos** 1.3.1881. Black on orange unpt. Arms at lower l., steam locomotive at ctr., portr. Caldas at r. Back red.	125.	300.	750

		Good	Fine	XF
144	**20 Pesos** 1.3.1881. Black on blue unpt. Arms at l., unloading bales at ctr., Portr. Nariño at r. Back blue.	150.	360.	90
145	**50 Pesos** 1.3.1881. Black on brown unpt. Arms at l., globe w/ship and train at ctr., portr. Torres at r. Back brown.	300.	750.	
146	**100 Pesos** 1.3.1881. Black on brown-orange unpt. Miners at lower l., allegorical woman flanking shield at ctr., portr. Santander at lower r. Back brown-orange.	375.	950.	

#147-152 held in reserve.

1882 ISSUE

		Good	Fine	XF
153	**50 Centavos** 1.3.1882. Orange and black. Arms at ctr. Purple stamping on back.	35.00	90.00	225.

#154-160 not assigned.

1885 ISSUE

#161-165 printer: Lit. D. Paredes.

		Good	Fine	XF
161	**10 Centavos** 1885. Black on orange-gold unpt. Arms at upper ctr. Printed sign. and stamping on back. Series Z.			
	a. 15.3.1885.	7.50	20.00	60.00
	b. 5.8.1885.	7.50	20.00	60.00

		Good	Fine	XF
162	**20 Centavos** 15.3.1885. Black on aqua unpt. Similar to #161. Printed sign. and stamping on back. Series Y.	7.50	20.00	60.00

#163 not assigned.

		Good	Fine	XF
164	**1 Peso** 6.10.1885. Black on green unpt. Arms at upper ctr. Sign. and stamping on back. Series A.	7.50	20.00	60.00
165	**1 Peso** 6.10.1885. Black on pink unpt. Like #164.	7.50	20.00	60.00

#155-169 not assigned.

		Good	Fine	XF
170	**50 Pesos** 22.7.1885. Condor.	—	—	—
171	**100 Pesos** 3.3.1885. Black on orange unpt. Woman.	—	—	—

#172-180 not assigned.

BANCO NACIONAL DE COLOMBIA

1885 ISSUE

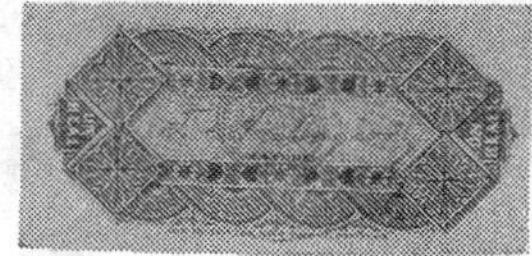

		Good	Fine	XF
81	**10 Centavos = 1 Real** 5.8.1885. Black on green unpt. Arms at l. Back green; printed sign. across. Red seal at ctr. Series C-I; K; M; O. Printer: HLBNC.	2.50	10.00	25.00
82	**10 Centavos = 1 Real** 5.8.1885. Like #181, but blue seal on face and back. Series F; K; O; Q; T; Printer: CABB (ABNC).	2.50	10.00	25.00

83-185 not assigned.

886 ISSUE

		Good	Fine	XF
86	**20 Centavos** ND (1886). Black on orange unpt. Man at l. Back blue; stamped date in oval *21.11.1886*. Printer: Villaveces, Bogotá.	8.00	25.00	50.00

7-188 not assigned.

887 ISSUE

		Good	Fine	XF
39*	**20 Centavos = 2 Reales** 1.1.1887. Black on gold unpt. Portr. man at lower l., arms at lower r. Back brown. Series B; D; E; H; I-N. Printer: HLBNC.	5.00	20.00	50.00
0	**50 Centavos** 1.5.1887. Printer: Villaveces, Bogotá.	—	—	—

NOTICE

Readers with unlisted dates, signature varieties, etc. are invited to submit photocopies or, high resolution (300 dpi, 100% size) scans of their notes to: Standard Catalog of World Paper Money, 700 East State St. Iola, WI 54990-0001, or E-Mail: george.cuhaj@fwpubs.com.

BANCO NACIONAL DE LA REPÚBLICA DE COLOMBIA

1886 ISSUE

#191-195 printer: HLBNC.

		Good	Fine	XF
191	**50 Centavos** 1.9.1886. Green. Justice at upper l., shield at lower r. Series 1.	7.50	30.00	110.

		Good	Fine	XF
192	**1 Peso** 1.9.1886. Green. Helmeted woman at upper l., arms at upper r. Back green. Series 2A.			
	a. Issued note.	6.00	25.00	100.
193	**1 Peso** 1.9.1886. Like #192. Back blue.	7.50	30.00	110.

		Good	Fine	XF
194	**5 Pesos** 1.9.1886. Green on orange unpt. Shield at lower l., helmeted Minerva at upper ctr. Series 2A.	27.50	120.	425.

		Good	Fine	XF
195	**10 Pesos** 1.9.1886. Brown. Reclining allegorical seated figures w/arms at ctr. Back blue. Series 2A.	35.00	150.	500.

#196-210 not assigned.

1888 ISSUE

#211, 214-218 circular red bank seal on back. Printer: ABNC.

		Good	Fine	XF
211	**10 Centavos = 1 Real** 1.3.1888. Black on yellow unpt. Arms at lower l. Back green; printed sign. At least 11 Greek and English series letters.	3.00	15.00	45.00

#212-213 not assigned.

		Good	Fine	XF
214	**1 Peso** 1.3.1888. Black on orange and yellow unpt. Arms at l., portr. S. Bolívar at r. Back brown. At least 15 Greek and English series letters.	4.50	20.00	55.00

		Good	Fine	XF
215	**5 Pesos** 1.3.1888. Black on orange and yellow unpt. Arms at l., allegorical woman w/bale seated at l. ctr., portr. S. Bolívar at r. Back brown. Series A.	8.00	32.50	150.
216	**10 Pesos** 1.3.1888. Black on brown and yellow unpt. Standing allegorical woman and pedestal of Liberty at l., portr. S. Bolívar at ctr., arms at r. Back brown. Series A.	12.50	50.00	200.

		Good	Fine	XF
217	**50 Pesos** 1.3.1888. Black on blue and yellow unpt. Portr. S. Bolívar at l., arms at ctr., seated allegorical woman at lower r. Back blue. Series A.	22.00	90.00	400.

		Good	Fine	XF
218	**100 Pesos** 1.3.1888. Black on green and yellow unpt. Arms at l., cherub at ctr., portr. S. Bolívar at r. Back orange. Series A.	37.50	150.	550.

1893 Issue

#221, 224, 227-228 printer: ABNC.

#222, 223, 225, 226, 229-233 held in reserve.

		Good	Fine	XF
221	**10 Centavos = 1 Real** 2.1.1893. Like #211. At least 16 Greek and English series letters.	1.00	4.00	12.00

		Good	Fine	XF
224	**1 Peso** 2.1.1893. Like #214. At least 13 Greek and English series letters.	2.50	10.00	35.00
227	**50 Pesos** 2.1.1893. Like #217. Series A.	17.50	70.00	300.
228	**100 Pesos** 2.1.1893. Like #218.	30.00	125.	450.

1895 Issue

#234-236, 238-239 printer: ABNC.

		Good	Fine	XF
234	**1 Peso** 4.3.1895. Like #214. At least 21 Greek and English series letters.	1.50	6.00	30.00

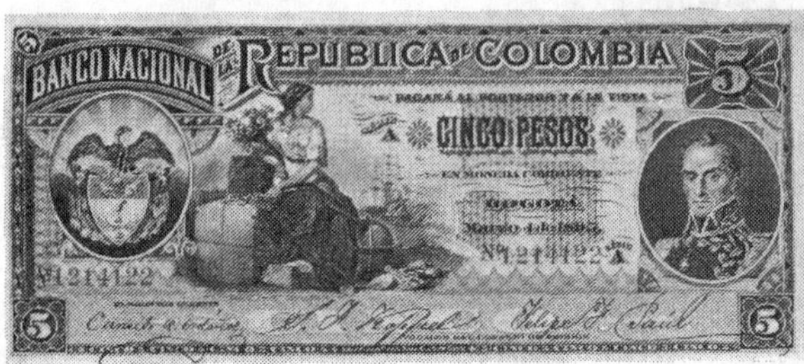

		Good	Fine	XF
235	**5 Pesos** 4.3.1895. Like #215. Series A.	5.50	22.50	135
236	**10 Pesos** 4.3.1895. Like #216. Series A.	7.50	30.00	175
237	**25 Pesos** 4.3.1895. Black on orange and green unpt. Dog at l., Liberty at lower r. Back brown. Series 1. Printer: FLBN.	32.50	150.	450

		Good	Fine	XF
238	**50 Pesos** 4.3.1895. Like #217. Series A.	15.00	75.00	325
239	**100 Pesos** 4.3.1895. Like #218. Series A.	32.50	135.	450

#240 not assigned.

241 **1000 Pesos**

	Good	Fine	XF
4.3.1895. Black on pink and blue unpt. Woman at l. Woman w/head covered on red back. Printer: FLBN.	—	725.	2000.

#242-250 held in reserve.

1899 Civil War Issues

Notes of 1899 and 1900 show great variance in printing quality, color shades, types of paper used. There was also a considerable amount of forgery of these notes.

251 **2 Pesos**

	Good	Fine	XF
28.10.1899. Black on pink unpt. Liberty facing l. at l. Back blue. Series A-C; G; K; M; N.			
a. Issued note.	2.00	10.00	42.00
b. Punched hole cancelled.	2.00	8.00	35.00

252 **2 Pesos**

	Good	Fine	XF
28.10.1899. Black on pink unpt. Liberty facing r. at l. *SEGUNDA EDICION* at lower l. Back blue. Series A-L. Printer: LN.	2.00	15.00	50.00

253 **5 Pesos**

	Good	Fine	XF
29.10.1899. Black on blue unpt. Arms and allegorical seated figures at ctr. Back slate green. Series B; D; E; F. Imprint: Otto Schroeder.	5.00	25.00	72.00

254 **5 Pesos**

	Good	Fine	XF
29.10.1899. Face like #253 w/Schroeder imprint. *SEGUNDA EDICION* at lower r. on back, along with LN imprint. Series A; D.	4.00	20.00	60.00

255 **5 Pesos**

	Good	Fine	XF
29.10.1899. Like #253, but *2A EMISION* at lower ctr. and LN imprint at lower r. on face. Back green. Series A; B; E.	4.00	20.00	80.00

256 **5 Pesos**

	Good	Fine	XF
29.10.1899. Like #255, but *3A EMISION* at lower ctr. on face. Series A-C; E; F.	4.50	22.00	85.00

#257-259, 261 held in reserve.

260 **100 Pesos**

	Good	Fine	XF
29.10.1899. Black on orange-tan unpt. Portr. S. Bolívar at l., Spaniards landing at ctr., arms at r. Back brown; arms at ctr. Series A. Imprint: Otto Schroeder.	40.00	125.	425.

1900 Civil War Issues

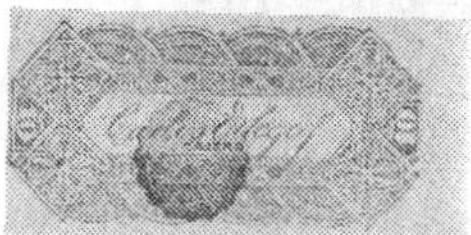

262 **10 Centavos**

	VG	VF	UNC
2.1.1900. Black on green unpt. Arms at l. Back green. Plain edge. Series A. Imprint: Villaveces, Bogotá.			
a. Serial # across lower ctr.	1.00	4.50	20.00
b. W/o serial #.	1.00	4.50	20.00
c. Numeral 2 for day in date missing. Perforated edge.	—	—	—
d. W/o serial #. Perforated edge.	—	—	—

263 **10 Centavos**

	VG	VF	UNC
30.9.1900. Blue on orange unpt. Arms at upper l. Back orange. Series A-C; E-F; H-J; L-M; O-P at l. or r. on back. Printer: LN.	1.00	5.00	22.00

264 **20 Centavos**

	VG	VF	UNC
25.3.1900. Black on lt. blue-gray unpt. Arms at l. Back blue to deep blue. At least 13 series letters.	1.00	4.50	20.00

265 **20 Centavos**

	VG	VF	UNC
30.9.1900. Black on wine or lilac unpt. Arms at lower l. Back green or shades of purple or violet, arms at ctr. At least 17 series letters. Printer: LN.	.75	3.00	15.00

265A **20 Centavos**

	VG	VF	UNC
30.9.1900. Black w/o unpt. Like #265 but back dark blue.	2.50	10.00	35.00

266 **50 Centavos**

	Good	Fine	XF
20.7.1900. Black on blue unpt. Arms at upper r. Back brown (shades); inverted position. Series B; E. Imprint: Otto Schroeder (both sides of note).	2.25	10.00	40.00

267 **50 Centavos**

	Good	Fine	XF
20.7.1900. Similar to #266 but *2A EMISION* at lower l. and no Schroeder imprint at lower r. Back has Schroeder imprint at bottom and is not inverted. Series F.	2.25	10.00	40.00

268 **50 Centavos**

	Good	Fine	XF
20.7.1900. Blue or green unpt. Like #267. Back has *2A EMISION* at bottom margin, and no Schroeder imprint. Series B-P; V. (Series H; L have inverted backs).	1.75	7.50	30.00

269 **1 Peso**

	Good	Fine	XF
25.4.1900. Black on lt. red unpt. Arms at ctr. Back black. Series B; E; G; I; O; P. Printer: Lit. D. Paredes.	3.00	15.00	50.00

		Good	Fine	XF
270	**1 Peso** 30.9.1900. Black on lt. red unpt. Man at l. Back blue; arms at ctr. At least 12 series letters. Printer: LN.	1.75	7.50	35.00

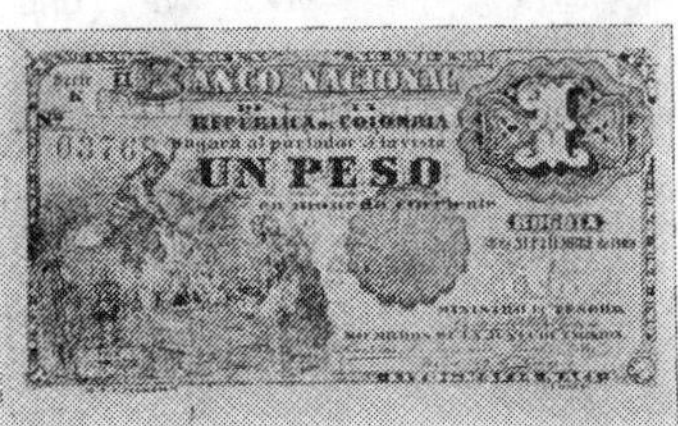

		Good	Fine	XF
271	**1 Peso** 30.9.1900. Black on red-orange unpt. Man and woman watering horses at l., blue bank seal at r. ctr. *2A EMISION* at lower l. margin. Back brown or violet; *2A EMISION* at lower ctr. in margin. Series A; H; I; K; N. Printer: LN.	3.00	12.50	50.00
273	**5 Pesos** 30.9.1900. *2A EMISION*. Reported not confirmed.	—	—	—
274	**10 Pesos** 30.9.1900. Black on orange-brown unpt. Miners at l., arms at ctr. Printer: LN.			
	a. No imprint at lower r. Back purple. Series A; B; I.	7.50	30.00	90.00
	b. Like a., but back blue. Series A; B.	8.00	32.00	100.
	c. Imprint at lower r. Back purple. Series H; M.	6.50	27.50	80.00
	d. Like a.; back inverted and blue. Series M.	6.50	27.50	80.00

		Good	Fine	XF
275	**10 Pesos** 30.9.1900. Like #274 but *2A EMISION* at lower ctr. Back blue; name *LEHNER* at l., LN imprint at bottom r. Series A; N; O.	6.50	27.50	85.00

		Good	Fine	XF
276	**20 Pesos** 30.9.1900. Black. Arms at ctr., farmer at r. Back brown; mules and boys on mountain trail at ctr. Printer: LN.			
	a. Blue unpt. Series B.	7.50	30.00	95.00
	b. Green unpt. Series A; C; F; M; O; P; Q.	6.50	27.50	85.00

		Good	Fine	XF
278	**50 Pesos** 15.2.1900. Black on green unpt. Arms at upper l., sailing ship and steam passenger train at upper ctr., portr. man at upper r. Back red; arms at ctr. Imprint: Otto Schroeder.			
	a. Series A; C.	17.50	70.00	250.
	b. Perforated *B de B (Banco de Bogotá)* at ctr. Series B.	17.50	70.00	250.

		Good	Fine	XF
279	**50 Pesos** 30.9.1900. Black on dull orange unpt. Woman and trough at lower l., arms at upper ctr., portr. S. Bolívar at lower r. Back pinkish orange; woman at ctr. Series A; C; D. Printer: LN.	17.50	70.00	250.
280	**50 Pesos** 30.9.1900. Blue on dull orange unpt. Like #279. Back orange. Series A-D. Printer: LN.	17.50	70.00	250.

		Good	Fine	XF
281	**100 Pesos** 30.9.1900. Black on orange unpt. Man at lower l., condor at upper ctr., arms at lower r. *SEGUNDA EDICION* at lower ctr. Back blue and pinkish violet; funeral of Atahualpa scene at ctr. Series A; C; F. Printer: LN.	25.00	100.	400.
282	**500 Pesos** 28.2.1900. Brown. Arms at upper l. Back black text, large blue eagle at ctr., 4 hand sign. below. Series A.	800.	1250.	2000.

SECTION VI

TREASURY AND SPECIAL ADMINISTRATIVE ISSUES 1864-1889

ESTADOS UNIDOS DE COLOMBIA

1864-69 *BONO FLOTANTE AL 3 POR 100 ANUAL* ISSUE

(3% Annual Bonds)

#283-283D arms at upper ctr.

		Good	Fine	XF
283	**10 Pesos** 16.8.1864. Black on lt. orange unpt.	—	—	—

		Good	Fine	XF
283D	**1000 Pesos** 13.2.1869. Black on lt. blue unpt.	—	—	—

1878 *LEI 57 DE 1878 VALE POR INDEMNIZACION DE ESTRANJEROS* ISSUE

#284-284C printer: Paredes.

		Good	Fine	XF
284	**10 Pesos** 18xx.	—	—	—
284A	**50 Pesos** 18xx.	—	—	—

		Good	Fine	XF
284B	**100 Pesos** 18xx. Black on orange unpt. Allegorical woman reclining at upper ctr. Unsigned remainder.	—	—	—
284C	**500 Pesos** 187x. Black on green unpt. Train at upper ctr. Unsigned remainder.	—	—	—

1880 *LIBRANZA CONTRA LAS ADUANAS* ISSUE

Bill of Exchange Against Customs
Issued at Bogotá.

		Good	Fine	XF
285	**100 Pesos** 11.1880.	—	—	—

1883 *BONOS ESPECIALES DE 4%* ISSUE

#286-286B arms at ctr.

		Good	Fine	XF
286	**10 Pesos** 1.12.1883. Black on blue unpt.	—	—	—
286B	**1000 Pesos** 1.12.1883. Black on red unpt.	—	—	—

1884 *BILLETE DE TESORERÍA* ISSUE

		Good	Fine	XF
287	**10 Pesos** 1884. Arms ar upper ctr.	—	—	—
287A	**10 Pesos** 188x. Black on pink and blue unpt. Arms at upper l. Printer: Villa Veces, Bogota.	—	—	—

1884 *LIBRANZAS DE LA EMPRESA DE LA FERRERÍA DE LA PRADERA* ISSUE

#288-288D printer: Paredes.

		Good	Fine	XF
288	**5 Pesos** 1884.	—	—	—
288A	**10 Pesos** 1884.	—	—	—
288B	**50 Pesos** 1884.	—	—	—
288C	**100 Pesos** 1884.	—	—	—
288D	**500 Pesos** 1884.	—	—	—

1884 *TESORERÍA GENERAL DE LA UNION* ISSUE

#289-289D arms at upper l.

		Good	Fine	XF
289	**5 Pesos** 188x. Green and black.	—	—	—

		Good	Fine	XF
289D	**500 Pesos** 1884. Brown and black.	—	—	—

1884 *VALE DE TESORERÍA AL PORTADOR* ISSUE

Articulo 12, Ley 53 de 1884

#290-290D interest-bearing notes. Arms at upper l. Printer: Paredes.

		Good	Fine	XF
290	**5 Pesos** 188x. Black on green unpt. Unsigned remainder.	—	—	—

		Good	Fine	XF
290D	**100 Pesos** 188x. Black on orange unpt. Unsigned remainder.	—	—	—

REPÚBLICA DE COLOMBIA

1880s *BILLETE DE DOS UNIDADES* ISSUE

		Good	Fine	XF
290E	**50 Pesos** 188_. Black and green. Dog's head at upper l., arms in unpt. at ctr. Back black on green unpt. Printer: Villaveces, Bogota.	—	—	—

1886 *Administración General de las Salinas Maritimas* Issue

		Good	Fine	XF
291	**50 Pesos** 1886. Brown on gold unpt. Woman at lower r. Unsigned remainder.	—	—	—

1888 *Libranza Contra las Oficinas de Espendio de Sal Marino* Issue

		Good	Fine	XF
291A	**10 Pesos** April, 1888. Black on lt. brown unpt. Portr. man at l. Back blue. Printer: Villaveces, Bogota.	—	—	—

1888 *Libranza Contra las Aduanas de la Costa Atlántica* Issue

		Good	Fine	XF
292	**500 Pesos** 1.11.1888. Train at ctr. Printer: Paredes.	—	—	—

1889 *Bono Colombiano* Issue

(S#) Indicate notes previously found in the Standard Catalog of World Paper Money - Specialized Issues Vol.I, 7th Editi on.

#293-293C printer: Villaveces, Bogotá.

		Good	Fine	XF
293	**5 Pesos** 11.6.1889. Black on blue unpt. Steam passenger train at upper r. Back blue.	—	—	—

		Good	Fine	XF
293A	**10 Pesos** 20.3.1889. Black on pink unpt. Dog head at upper r.	—	—	—

		Good	Fine	XF
293B	**50 Pesos** 18xx. Black. Romping horses at upper r. Unsigned remainder.	—	—	—

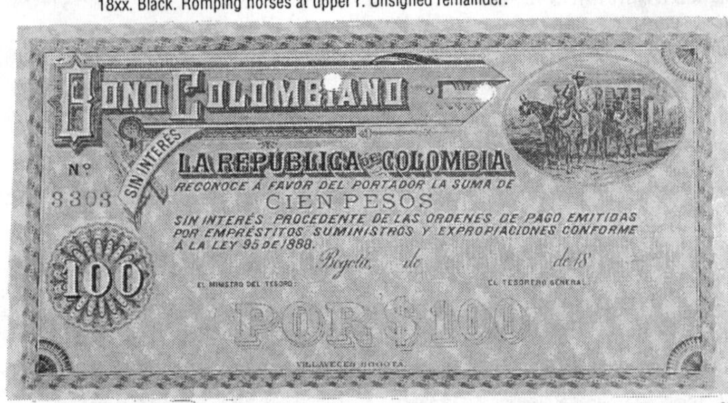

		Good	Fine	XF
293C	**100 Pesos** 18xx. Black. Horses w/rider and wagon at upper r. Unsigned remainder.	—	—	—

Section VII

Civil War and Special Administrative Issues 1899-1922

República de Colombia

Vale por Exacciones en la Guerra de 1895 Issue

Property Expropriation Voucher

		Good	Fine	XF
294	**5 Pesos** L. 1896. Black on green unpt. Waterfalls at l. Unsigned remainder.	—	—	—

		Good	Fine	XF
294A	**10 Pesos** 6.6.1907. Black on green unpt. Agriculture w/cherubs at l.	—	—	—

		Good	Fine	XF
294B	**50 Pesos** L.1896. Black on gray unpt. Justice seated at lower l. Unsigned remainder.	—	—	—
294C	**100 Pesos** 9.5.1906. Black on lt. orange unpt. Standing woman w/sheaf at l.	—	—	—
294E	**1000 Pesos** 21.3.1899. Similar to #298. Printer: Paredes.	—	—	—

1900 *Tesorería del Gobierno* Provisional Issue

Notes of the "Thousand Day War" issued by Liberal forces under Gen. Uribe at Ocaña.

		Good	Fine	XF
295	**20 Centavos** ND (1900). Black on red unpt. Arms at r. Printed sign. on back.	—	—	—

#295A-295C black. Heavy white lined paper.

		Good	Fine	XF
295A	**1 Peso** 15.6.1900. Justice standing at l. Footbridge over river at l. on back.	75.00	175.	275.

		Good	Fine	XF
295B	**5 Pesos** 15.6.1900. Soldier w/flag and cannon at l. ctr. Steamship *Peralonso* at l. on back.	100.	150.	250.
295C	**10 Pesos** 15.6.1900. Face and back like #295B.	100.	175.	300.

1905 *Deuda Exterior Consolidada* Issue

		Good	Fine	XF
296	**100 Pesos** 1905. Black on orange unpt. Seated figure w/globe at upper l. Unsigned remainder.	—	—	—

1905 *Pagaré del Tesoro* Issue

		Good	Fine	XF
297	**25 Centavos** 1.5.1905. Green on orange unpt. of arms at ctr.	—	—	—

		Good	Fine	XF
297A	**50 Centavos** 1.5.1905. Black on orange unpt. of arms at ctr.	—	—	—
297B	**1 Peso** 1.5.1905. Black on purple unpt. Arms at upper l. and in unpt. Back orange.	—	—	—

		Good	Fine	XF
297D	**25 Pesos** 1.2.1905. Black on lt. red unpt. of arms at ctr. Dog's head at upper l. Back blue. Printer: Lit. Nacional.	—	—	—

1906-07 *Vale por Exacciones en la Guerra de 1899* Issue

Issued as payment for property forcibly taken by the military during the revolution of 1899-1902. Each voucher states that no interest will be paid on the principal.

#298-298G w/2 allegorical women w/fasces at l., arms at lower r. Imprint (Paredes) blocked out at bottom on back. Some w/cancellation on back.

		Good	Fine	XF
298	**5 Pesos** 1.5.1907. Black. Peach paper.	—	—	—

		Good	Fine	XF
298A	**10 Pesos** 6.6.1907. Black. Peach paper.	—	—	—
298B	**50 Pesos** 18xx.	—	—	—
298C	**100 Pesos** 6.5.1906.	—	—	—

		Good	Fine	XF
298D	**500 Pesos** 1.5.1907. Black on gold unpt. Back lt. blue.	—	—	—
298E	**1000 Pesos** 1.5.1907. Back brown.	—	—	—
298F	**5000 Pesos** 25.7.1907.	—	—	—

		Good	Fine	XF
298G	**10,000 Pesos** 1.5.1907. Black on gold unpt. Back green. Rare.	—	—	—

1907 *Vale de Tesorería Sin Interés* Issue

#299-299A arms at lower l. Printer: Lit. Nacional.

		Good	Fine	XF
299	**1 Peso** April, 1907. Purple on green unpt.	—	—	—
299A	**5 Pesos** April, 1907. Purple on blue-green unpt.	—	—	—

1908 *Vale Especial por Primos de Exportación* Issue

#300-300D arms at upper ctr. Printer: Lit. Nacional.

		Good	Fine	XF
300	**1 Peso** 2.6.1908. Blue on green unpt.	—	—	—
300B	**10 Pesos** 2.6.1908. Black on lt. red unpt.	—	—	—
300C	**50 Pesos** 2.6.1908. Blue on green unpt.	—	—	—
300D	**100 Pesos** 2.5.1908. Black on lt. orange unpt.	—	—	—

190x *Ministerio del Tesoro - Tesorería General de la Republica* Issue

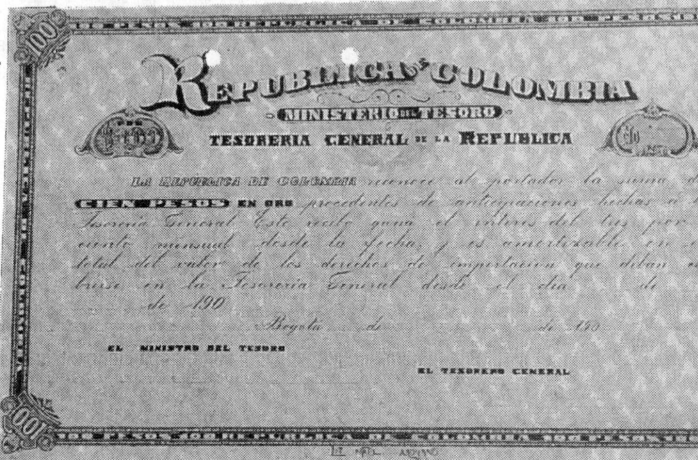

		Good	Fine	XF
301	**100 Pesos** 190x. Black on lt. blue-green unpt. Unsigned remainder.	—	—	—

1914-18 *Bono Colombiano* Issue

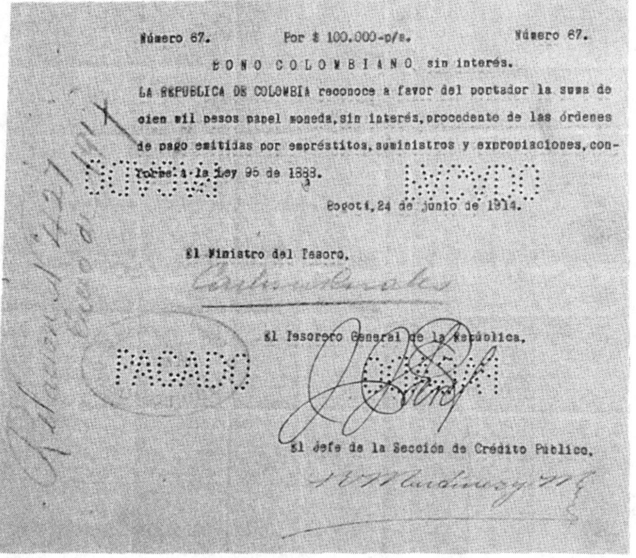
Número 67. Por $ 100.000-p/m. Número 67.

BONO COLOMBIANO sin interés.

LA REPUBLICA DE COLOMBIA reconoce a favor del portador la suma de cien mil pesos papel moneda, sin interés, procedente de las órdenes de pago emitidas por empréstitos, suministros y expropiaciones, conforme a la Ley 95 de 1883.

Bogotá, 24 de junio de 1914.

El Ministro del Tesoro,

El Tesorero General de la República,

El Jefe de la Sección de Crédito Público.

		Good	Fine	XF
302	**10 Pesos** L. 1918. Black and red. Arms at upper l., allegorical woman at lower r.	—	—	—
303	**100,000 Pesos** 24.6.1914. Typed text in blue. *PAGADO* punched hole cancellation 4 times.	—	—	—

1917 *VALE DE TESORERÍA* ISSUE

#304-304D arms at l.

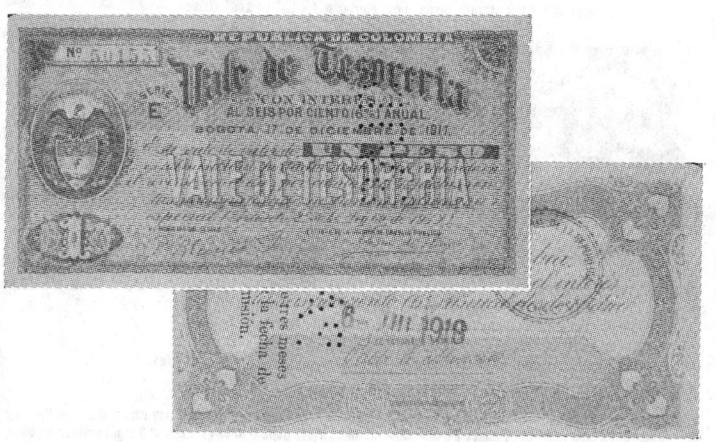

		Good	Fine	XF
304	**1 Peso** 17.12.1917. Black on red-orange unpt. Arms at l. Back blue; red vertical ovpt. at l., handstamped date: *6 JUL 1918* at ctr. Imprint (Paredes) blocked out. Perforated: *PAID.*	30.00	85.00	150.
304A	**5 Pesos** 17.12.1917. Black on orange unpt.	—	—	—
304B	**10 Pesos** 17.12.1917. Black on green unpt.	—	—	—
304C	**50 Pesos** 17.12.1917. Black on violet unpt.	—	—	—
304D	**100 Pesos** 17.12.1917. Black.	—	—	—

1921-22 *VALE DEL TESORO* ISSUE

		Good	Fine	XF
305	**1 Peso**	—	—	

#305A and 305B printer: Lit. Nacional.

		Good	Fine	XF
305A	**5 Pesos** 31.12.1921. Eagle.	—	—	—

		Good	Fine	XF
305B	**20 Pesos** 8.5.1922; 17.7.1922 (stamped on back). Black on red unpt. Eagle at upper l., arms at lower ctr. Back brown text.	20.00	70.00	150.

NOTICE

Readers with unlisted dates, signature varieties, etc.
are invited to submit photocopies or,
high resolution (300 dpi, 100% size) scans of their notes to:
Standard Catalog of World Paper Money,
700 East State St. Iola, WI 54990-0001,
or E-Mail: george.cuhaj@fwpubs.com.

SECTION VIII

REGULAR ISSUES, 1904-1960

REPÚBLICA DE COLOMBIA

1904 ISSUE

#309-315 printer: W&S.

		Good	Fine	XF
309	**1 Peso** April 1904. Black on gold unpt. Arms at l., Cordoba at ctr. Back purple; plantation scene.	2.50	15.00	65.00

		Good	Fine	XF
310	**2 Pesos** April 1904. Black on blue unpt. Arms at l., sheep at ctr. Back brown; portr. Rigaurte at ctr.	3.00	20.00	85.00

		Good	Fine	XF
311	**5 Pesos** April 1904. Black on green unpt. Arms at upper l., church at ctr. Back dk. red; portr. Torres at ctr.	5.00	30.00	100.
312	**10 Pesos** April 1904. Black on red unpt. Portr. Gen. A. Nariño at l., arms at r. Back brown; standing helmeted woman at l., riverboats at ctr.	7.50	50.00	150.

		Good	Fine	XF
313	**25 Pesos** April 1904. Black on orange unpt. Portr. Caldas at l., arms at r. Back green; observatory at ctr.	10.00	75.00	225.
314	**50 Pesos** April 1904. Black on green unpt. Portr. Gen. Santander at l., arms and cherubs at ctr., plantation scene at r. Back red-brown; standing Liberty and eagle at l., bridge scene at ctr.	22.50	100.	300.

		Good	Fine	XF
315	**100 Pesos** April 1904. Black on red unpt. Standing S. Bolivar at l., arms at ctr. Back orange; Plaza de Bolivar at ctr.	17.50	70.00	250.

1908 Issue

		Good	Fine	XF
316	**1000 Pesos** March 1908. Black on green unpt. Portr. S. Bolívar at ctr. between seated allegorical woman at l., Mercury at r. Printer: W&S. Rare.	—	—	—

1910 *Junta de Conversion* Issue

#317-318 printer: ABNC.

		Good	Fine	XF
317	**50 Pesos** Aug. 1910. Black on olive unpt. Arms at l., portr. S. Bolívar at r. Back olive; printed sign. across ctr. Series A; B; C; D..	8.00	50.00	150.

		Good	Fine	XF
318	**100 Pesos** Aug. 1910. Black on orange and yellow unpt. Arms at l., portr. S. Bolívar at ctr. r. Back brown; like #316. Series A.	20.00	100.	300.

1915 Pesos Oro Issue

#321-324 printer: ABNC.

		Good	Fine	XF
321	**1 Peso Oro** 20.7.1915. Black on green and m/c unpt. Portr. S. Bolívar at l. Back green; arms at ctr. Series A-J.	8.00	40.00	225.

		Good	Fine	XF
322	**2 Pesos Oro** 20.7.1915. Black on blue and m/c unpt. Portr. Gen. A. Nariño at ctr. Back blue; arms at ctr. Series A-E.	20.00	100.	400.

		Good	Fine	XF
323	**5 Pesos Oro** 20.7.1915. Black on orange and m/c unpt. Portr. Córdoba at l. ctr., condor at r. Back orange; arms at ctr. Series A-F.	10.00	50.00	300.

		Good	Fine	XF
324	**10 Pesos Oro** 20.7.1915. Black on green, purple and orange unpt. Portr. Gen. Santander at l., large dollar sign. at ctr., arms at r. Back lt. orange; national capitol, 3 printed sign. beneath. Series A-D.	18.00	125.	400.

#323 Series F and #324 Series D were actually issued by the Banco de la República.

1919 *Cédula de Tesorería* Provisional Issue

#325-327 ovpt. on Banco Central notes #S366-369. The entire bank name and portr. are blacked out on the face and bank name is partially obscured at bottom on back. Black ovpt: 6 lines of text and 3 sign. w/titles on back.

		Good	Fine	XF
325	**1 Peso** 1.4.1919; 1.6.1919. Ovpt. on #S366 or S367.	35.00	100.	250.
326	**5 Pesos** 1.4.1919. Ovpt. on #S368.	—	—	—
327	**10 Pesos** 1.4.1919. Ovpt. on #S369.	—	—	—

1922 *Bono del Tesoro* Treasury Bond Provisional Issue

#331-332 Junta de Conversion issue authorized by Law 6 and Decree #166 of 1922, and Public Notice #206 of 8.2.1922.

		VG	VF	UNC
331	**1 Peso Oro** 1922 (-old date 20.7.1915). Red ovpt. *BONO DEL TESORO* across face. Red ovpt. lg. heading at top w/10-line text in square at ctr. on back of #321. Series J.	50.00	175.	—
332	**5 Pesos Oro** 1922 (- old date 20.7.1915). Ovpt. on face and back of #323 as above.	100.	300.	—

1938 Pesos Oro Issue

#341-342 printer: ABNC.

		VG	VF	UNC
341	**5 Pesos Oro** 22.3.1938. Black on m/c unpt. Córdoba at ctr. Back red; arms at ctr. Series A.	7.50	30.00	120.

		VG	VF	UNC
342	**10 Pesos Oro** 22.3.1938. Black on m/c unpt. Portr. Gen. Santander at l., bust S. Bolívar at r. Back lt. orange; arms at ctr. Series B.	10.00	50.00	140.

Note: Since the Banco de la República could not issue notes without gold backing after 1923, the Treasury issued the 5 and 10 Pesos dated 1938 and the 1/2 Pesos of 1948 and 1953. These notes were signed by the Minister of Finance, the Treasurer and the Comptroller, and were designed to contravene the law concerning issuance of notes w/o gold backing. The notes were needed because of the worldwide depression of the 1930's. In reality these notes are emergency issues that eventually became legal tender within the Banco de la República system.

1948-53 Pesos Oro Issue

#	Denomination / Description	VG	VF	UNC
345	**1/2 Peso Oro**			
	1948; 1953. Brown on m/c unpt. Portr. Gen. A. Nariño at ctr. Back brown; arms at ctr. Series C. Printer: ABNC.			
	a. Prefix letter A; B. 16.1.1948.	1.00	4.00	50.00
	b. Prefix letter C. 18.2.1953.	1.00	4.00	50.00

Banco de la República

REPLACEMENT NOTES:

Earlier issues, small R just below and between signatures. Larger R used later. Some TDLR printings have R preceding serial number. Later Colombian-printed notes use circled asterisk usually close to sign. or a star at r. of upper serial #.

1923 *Certificados Sobre Consignación de Oro*

Gold Certificates Provisional Issue

#351-354 Gold Certificates. New bank name ovpt. on back: *BANCO DE LA REPÚBLICA / BILLETE PROVISIONAL* on Casa de Moneda de Medellín #S1026-S1029 (Volume 1). Printer: ABNC.

#	Denomination / Description	VG	VF	UNC
351	**2 1/2 Pesos**			
	ND (- old date 1.5.1920). Black on green and m/c unpt. Back green. Blue ovpt. on #S1026. Rare.	—	—	—
352	**5 Pesos**			
	ND (- old date 15.9.1919). Black on brown and m/c unpt. Back brown. Ovpt. on #S1027. Rare.	—	—	—
353	**10 Pesos**			
	ND. Black on orange and m/c unpt. Back orange. Ovpt. on #S1028. Rare.	—	—	—
354	**20 Pesos**			
	ND. Black on blue and m/c unpt. Back blue. Ovpt. on #S1029. Rare.	—	—	—

#355-360 not assigned.

1923 Pesos Oro Issue

#361-367 bank name below upper frame in Gothic lettering. Backs w/Liberty head at ctr., printed sign. below. Printer: ABNC.

#	Denomination / Description	VG	VF	UNC
361	**1 Peso Oro**			
	20.7.1923. Blue on m/c unpt. Portr. Caldas at ctr. Back red-brown. Series A.	20.00	100.	450.

#	Denomination / Description	VG	VF	UNC
362	**2 Pesos Oro**			
	20.7.1923. Green on m/c unpt. Portr. C. Torres at ctr. Back dk. brown. Series B.	45.00	150.	750.
363	**5 Pesos Oro**			
	20.7.1923. Brown on m/c unpt. Portr. Córdoba at l. Back green. Series C.	45.00	150.	800.
364	**10 Pesos Oro**			
	20.7.1923. Black on m/c unpt. Portr. Gen. A. Nariño at r. Back red. Series D.			
	a. Issued note.	42.50	140.	800.
	p1. Face proof. W/o series or serial #. Punched hole cancelled.	—	—	175.
	p2. Back proof. Punched hole cancelled.	—	—	100.
365	**50 Pesos Oro**			
	20.7.1923. Dk. brown on m/c unpt. Portr. A. J. de Sucre at l. Back orange. Series E.	150.	600.	—
366	**100 Pesos Oro**			
	20.7.1923. Purple on m/c unpt. Portr. Gen. Santander at ctr. Back red-brown. Series F.	125.	500.	—
367	**500 Pesos Oro**			
	20.7.1923. Olive green on m/c unpt. Portr. S. Bolívar at r. Back orange. Series G. Rare.	—	—	—

1926-28 Issue

#371-375A w/bank name as part of upper frame in standard lettering. Back design and sign. like #361-367. Printer: ABNC.

#	Denomination / Description	VG	VF	UNC
371	**1 Peso Oro**			
	1.1.1926. Orange on m/c unpt. Portr. S. Bolívar at ctr. Back blue. Series H.	9.00	37.50	225.
372	**2 Pesos Oro**			
	1.1.1926. Olive on m/c unpt. Portr. C. Torres at ctr. Back purple. Series I.	30.00	125.	600.

#	Denomination / Description	VG	VF	UNC
373	**5 Pesos Oro**			
	1926; 1928. Blue on m/c unpt. Portr. Córdoba at l. Back brown.			
	a. Series J. 1.1.1926.	25.00	100.	500.
	b. Series M. 1.1.1928.	3.50	17.50	125.
	p1. As a. Face proof. W/o series or serial #.	—	—	175.
	p2. As a. Back proof.	—	—	100.
374	**10 Pesos Oro**			
	1926; 1928. Purple on m/c unpt. Portr. Gen. A. Nariño at r. Back green.			
	a. Series K. 1.1.1926.	30.00	100.	575.
	b. Series N. 1.1.1928.	10.00	35.00	250.
	p1. As a. Face proof. W/o series or serial #.	—	—	175.
	p2. Back proof.	—	—	100.
375	**50 Pesos Oro**			
	1926; 1928. Green on m/c unpt. Portr. A.J. de Sucre at l. Back blue-black.			
	a. Series L. 1.1.1926.	50.00	200.	700.
	b. Series P. 20.7.1928.	30.00	110.	525.
	p1. As a. Face proof. W/o series or serial #.	—	—	175.
	p2. Back proof.	—	—	100.
375A	**100 Pesos Oro**			
	20.7.1928. Brown on m/c unpt. Portr. Gen. Santander at ctr. Back red. Series Q.			
	a. Issued note.	50.00	300.	850.
	p1. Face proof. W/o series or serial #.	—	—	175.
	p2. Back proof.	—	—	100.

1927 Issue

#376-378 wmk. area at r. Backs w/various branches of the Banco de la República and printed sign. below. Printer: TDLR.

		VG	VF	UNC
376	**5 Pesos Oro** 20.7.1927. Green on m/c unpt. Portr. Córdoba and seated allegorical woman at l. Older bank at Bogotá on back. Series M.	10.00	50.00	225.
377	**10 Pesos Oro** 20.7.1927. Blue on m/c unpt. Portr. Gen. A. Nariño and Mercury at l. Bank at Medellin on back. Series N.	20.00	125.	475.

		VG	VF	UNC
378	**20 Pesos Oro** 20.7.1927. Violet on m/c unpt. Portr. Caldas and allegorical woman at l. Older bank at Barranquilla on back. Series O.	25.00	125.	475.

1929 Issue

		VG	VF	UNC
380	**1 Peso Oro** 1929-54. Blue on m/c unpt. Portr. Gen. Santander and standing allegorical male at l., bust of S. Bolívar at r. Back blue; Liberty at ctr. Printer: ABNC.			
	a. Series R in red. 20.7.1929.	.75	3.50	25.00
	b. Sign. and series like a. 20.7.1940.	.25	2.00	20.00
	c. Series R in red. 20.7.1942; 20.7.1943.	.25	1.50	15.00
	d. Series R in blue. 20.7.1944; 1.1.1945.	.25	2.00	18.00
	e. Series R in blue. 20.7.1946; 7.8.1947 (prefixes A-F).	.25	2.00	18.00
	f. Series HH. 1.1.1950.	.25	1.00	7.00
	g. Series HH. 1.1.1954.	.25	1.00	7.00
	s. As e. Specimen.	—	—	—

1931 ND *Certificados de Plata*

Silver Certificates Provisional Issue

		VG	VF	UNC
381	**5 Pesos** ND (1931- old date 20.7.1915). Black ovpt: *CERTIFICADO DE PLATA* on back of #323.	75.00	200.	650.

1932 Issue

#382-383 printer: ABNC.

		VG	VF	UNC
382	**1 Peso** 1.1.1932. Green on m/c unpt. Portr. Gen. Santander at ctr. Liberty at ctr. on back. Prefix A.	6.50	40.00	225.

		VG	VF	UNC
383	**5 Pesos** 1.1.1932. Blue on m/c unpt. Portr. Gen. A. Nariño at ctr. Back red; like #382. Prefix B.			
	a. Issued note.	25.00	200.	600.
	p1. Face proof. W/o serial #.	—	—	175.
	p2. Back proof.	—	—	100.

1935 Peso Oro Issue

		VG	VF	UNC
384	**1/2 Peso Oro** 20.7.1935. Brown on m/c unpt. Bust of Caldas at l. ctr., bust of S. Bolívar at r. Liberty at ctr. on back. Series S. Printer: ABNC.	20.00	125.	475.

1938 Pesos Oro Commemorative Issue

#385, 400th Anniversary - Founding of Bogotá 1538-1938

		VG	VF	UNC
385	**1 Peso Oro** 6.8.1938. Blue on m/c unpt. Portr. G. Ximenez de Quesada in medallion supported w/2 allegorical angels at ctr. Back brown; scene of founding of Bogotá at ctr. Series T. Printer: ABNC.			
	a. Issued note.	15.00	50.00	375.
	p1. Face proof. W/o series or serial #.	—	—	175.
	p2. Back proof.	—	—	125.

1940 Issue

		VG	VF	UNC
386	**5 Pesos Oro** 1940-50. Like #373, but w/o title: *CAJERO* and sign. on back.			
	a. Series M in red. 20.7.1940.	1.00	6.00	40.00
	b. Series M in red. 20.7.1942; 20.7.1943.	.50	3.00	35.00
	c. Series M in blue. 20.7.1944; 1.1.1945; 20.7.1946; 7.8.1947.	.50	3.00	35.00
	d. Series M. 12.10.1949.	.25	1.50	22.50
	e. Series FF. 1.1.1950.	.25	1.50	22.50
	p1. As b. 20.7.1942. Face proof. W/o series or serial #.	—	—	175.
	p2. Back proof.	—	—	100.
	s. As c. Specimen.	—	—	—

1941 *Certificados de Plata* Silver Certificates Issue

		VG	VF	UNC
387	**1 Peso** 1.1.1941. Green on m/c unpt. Portr. Gen. Santander at l. Liberty at ctr. on back. Prefix B.	7.00	25.00	200.

		VG	VF	UNC
388	**5 Pesos** 1.1.1941. Black on m/c unpt. Portr. Gen. A. Nariño at l. Back blue; like #387. Prefix C.			
	a. Issued note.	4.00	15.00	100.
	p1. Face proof. W/o series #, punched hole cancelled.	—	—	175.
	p2. Back proof.	—	—	75.00

1941 Pesos Oro Issue

#389 backed by gold (pesos oro).

		VG	VF	UNC
389	**10 Pesos Oro** 1941-63. Purple on m/c unpt. Portr. Gen. A. Nariño at lower r. W/o title: *CAJERO* and sign. on back.			
	a. Series N in red. 20.7.1941.	1.50	8.00	50.00
	b. Series N. 20.7.1943; 20.7.1944; 7.8.1947.	1.00	5.00	30.00
	c. Series N. 1.1.1945.	1.25	7.50	40.00
	d. Series N. 12.10.1949.	.75	3.00	18.00
	e. Series EE. 1.1.1950.	.25	.75	7.50
	f. Series EE. 2.1.1963.	.25	.75	7.50
	s. As b. Specimen.	—	—	—

1942 Pesos Oro Issue

#390-391 printer: ABNC.

		VG	VF	UNC
390	**2 Pesos** 1942-55. Like #372, but w/o title: *CAJERO* and sign. on back.			
	a. Series I in red. 20.7.1942; 20.7.1943.	.50	4.00	35.00
	b. Series I in olive. 20.7.1944; 1.1.1945; 7.8.1947.	.50	3.00	30.00
	c. Series GG. 1.1.1950.	.50	2.50	25.00
	d. Series GG. 1.1.1955.	.25	1.00	8.00
	p1. As a. 20.7.1942. Face proof. W/o series or serial #.	—	—	175.
	p2. Back proof.	—	—	100.
	s. As b. Specimen.	—	—	—

		VG	VF	UNC
391	**500 Pesos** 1942-53. Like #367, but w/o title: *CAJERO* and sign. on back.			
	a. Series G in red. 20.7.1942.	50.00	225.	850.
	b. Series G in olive. 20.7.1944; 1.1.1945; 7.8.1947 (prefix A).	40.00	100.	385.
	c. Series AA. 1.1.1950.	15.00	60.00	325.
	d. Series AA. 1.1.1951; 1.1.1953.	10.00	30.00	90.00
	p1. As a. Face proof. W/o series or serial #. Punch hole cancelled.	—	—	150.
	p2. As d. 1.1.1951. Face proof. W/o serial #. Punch hole cancelled.	—	—	150.
	p3. As d. 1.1.1953. Face proof. W/o serial #. Punch hole cancelled.	—	—	150.

Note: For 500 Pesos dated 1964, see #408 in Volume 3, Modern Issues.

1943 Pesos Oro Issue

		VG	VF	UNC
392	**20 Pesos Oro** 1943-63. Purple and m/c. Bust of Francisco José de Caldas at l., bust of Simon Bolívar at r. Liberty at ctr. on back. Printer: ABNC.			
	a. Series U in red. 20.7.1943.	20.00	200.	500.
	b. Series U in purple. 20.7.1944; 1.1.1945.	10.00	60.00	200.
	c. Series U. Prefix A. 7.8.1947.	3.00	15.00	80.00
	d. Series DD. 1.1.1950; 1.1.1951.	1.50	7.50	50.00
	e. Series DD. 2.1.1963.	1.50	7.50	50.00
	s. Specimen.	—	—	65.00

Banco de la República

1943 Issue

#392 printer: ABNC.

#393-394 printer: ABNC.

		VG	VF	UNC
393	**50 Pesos Oro** 1944-58. Green on m/c unpt. Like #375, but w/o title: *CAJERO* and sign. on back.			
	a. Series P. 20.7.1944; 1.1.1945.	6.00	20.00	110.
	b. Series P. Prefix A. 7.8.1947.	1.00	5.00	60.00
	c. Series CC. 1.1.1950; 1.1.1951.	1.00	4.00	30.00
	d. Series CC. 1.1.1953.	1.00	4.00	30.00
	e. Series CC. 1.1.1958.	1.00	3.00	25.00
	p1. As a. 20.7.1944. Face proof. W/o series or serial #.	—	—	150.
	p2. As c. 1.1.1951. Face proof. W/o serial #. Punched hole cancelled.	—	—	150.
	p3. As d. 1.1.1953. Face proof. W/o serial #. Punched hole cancelled.	—	—	150.
	s. Specimen.	—	—	—

		VG	VF	UNC
394	**100 Pesos Oro** 1944-57. Like #375A, but w/o *CAJERO* title and sign. on back.			
	a. Series Q. 20.7.1944; 1.1.1945; 7.8.1947. Prefix A.	6.00	40.00	135.
	b. Series BB. 1.1.1950.	5.00	25.00	125.
	c. Series BB. 1.1.1951.	2.00	12.50	60.00
	d. Series BB. 1.1.1953; 20.7.1957.	1.50	6.00	35.00
	p1. As a. 20.7.1944. Face proof. W/o series or serial #.	—	—	150.
	p2. As c. Face proof. W/o serial #. Punch hole cancelled.	—	—	150.
	p3. As d. 1.1.1953. Face proof. W/o serial #. Punched hole cancelled.	—	—	150.
	p4. As d. 20.7.1957. Face proof. W/o serial #. Punched hole cancelled.	—	—	150.
	s. Specimen.	—	—	—

1946 ND Provisional Issue

As a result of a scarcity of coins in circulation, the Banco de la República took certain quantities of *R* series 1 Peso notes dated 1942 and 1943, sliced them in halves and ovpt. each half as a Half Peso. The 1942 dated notes are Serial #57 000 001 - 58 000 000 (Group 1), while the 1943 dated notes are Serial # 70 000 001 - 70 250 000 (Group 2).

		VG	VF	UNC
397	**1/2 Peso** ND (1946-old dates 20.7.1942 and 20.7.1943). Halves of *R* series of #380c ovpt. in black squares as Half Peso on face, words *MEDIO PESO* within square on back.			
	a. Printer's name: *LITOGRAFIA COLOMBIA, S.A. - BOGOTA* as part of black ovpt. on face of l. half. ND. Group 1.	75.00	250.	600.
	b. Ovpt. as a. on face of r. half (old date 20.7.1942). Group 1.	75.00	250.	600.

	VG	VF	UNC
c. W/o local printer's name as part of black ovpt. on l. half of face. ND. Group 1.	75.00	250.	600.
d. As c, on r. half (old date 20.7.1942). Group 1.	75.00	250.	600.
e. As c, but Group 2.	75.00	300.	700.
f. As d, but old date 20.7.1943. Group 2.	100.	350.	700.

1953 Pesos Oro Issue

398 1 Peso Oro

	VG	VF	UNC
7.8.1953. Blue on m/c unpt. Standing S. Bólivar statue at l., bridge of Boyaca at ctr., portr. Gen. Santander at r. Liberty at ctr. on back. Series A. Printer: W&S.	.25	.75	4.50

#399-401 printer: TDLR.

399 5 Pesos Oro

	VG	VF	UNC
1.1.1953. Green on m/c unpt. Similar to #376, but numeral in guilloche instead of wmk. at r. Long view of older bank bldg. at Bogotá on back. Series M.			
a. Issued note.	.25	2.50	17.50
s. Specimen. W/red TDLR oval stamp and *SPECIMEN.*	—	—	200.

1953 Pesos Oro Issue

#400-401 printer: TDLR.

400 10 Pesos Oro

	VG	VF	UNC
1953-61. Blue on m/c unpt. Similar to #377, but palm trees at r. instead of wmk. Portr. General Antonio Nariño w/Mercury alongside at l. Bank bldg. at Cali on back. Series N.			
a. 1.1.1953.	1.00	7.50	35.00
b. 1.1.1958; 1.1.1960.	1.00	7.50	35.00
c. 2.1.1961.	1.00	7.50	35.00
s. Specimen. W/red TDLR and *SPECIMEN* ovpt. Punched hole cancelled.	—	—	100.

401 20 Pesos Oro

	VG	VF	UNC
1953-65. Red-brown on m/c unpt. Similar to #378, but Liberty in circle at r. instead of wmk. Portr. Francisco José de Caldas and allegory at l. Newer bank bldg. at Barranquilla on back. Series O.			
a. 1.1.1953.	1.00	7.50	35.00
b. 1.1.1960.	1.00	7.50	35.00
c. 2.1.1961; 2.1.1965.	1.00	6.00	30.00
s1. Specimen. W/ red TDLR ovpt. and *SPECIMEN.* Punched hole cancelled.	—	—	100.
s2. Specimen. Red ovpt: *SPECIMEN.* Punched hole cancelled.	—	—	65.00

1958 Pesos Oro Issue

#402-403 printer: ABNC.

402 50 Pesos Oro

	VG	VF	UNC
1958-67. Lt. brown on m/c unpt. Portr. Antonio José de Sucre at lower l. Back olive-green; Liberty at ctr. Series Z.			
a. 20.7.1958; 7.8.1960.	1.00	10.00	60.00
b. 1.1.1964; 12.10.1967.	1.00	8.00	50.00
s1. Specimen.	—	—	135.
s2. Specimen. Red ovpt: *SPECIMEN.* Punched hole cancelled.	—	—	135.

403 100 Pesos Oro

	VG	VF	UNC
1958-67. Gray on m/c unpt. Portr. Gen. Francisco de Paula Santander at r. Back green; like #402. Series Y.			
a. 7.8.1958.	1.00	8.00	60.00
b. 1.1.1960; 1.1.1964.	1.00	6.00	40.00
c. 20.7.1965; 20.7.1967.	1.00	6.00	40.00
p1. Face proof. W/o date, signatures, series or serial #. Punched hole cancelled.	—	—	150.
s. Specimen.	—	—	75.00

1959-60 Pesos Oro Issue

Printer: Imprenta de Billets - Bogota.

404 1 Peso Oro

	VG	VF	UNC
1959-77. Blue on m/c unpt. Portr. Simón Bolívar at l., portr. General Francisco de Paula Santander at r. Liberty head and condor w/waterfall and mountain at ctr. on back.			
a. Security thread. 12.10.1959.	.25	2.50	10.00
b. Security thread. 2.1.1961; 7.8.1962; 2.1.1963; 12.10.1963; 2.1.1964; 12.10.1964.	.20	2.00	7.50
c. As b. 20.7.1966.	1.25	10.00	40.00
d. W/o security thread. 20.7.1966; 20.7.1967; 1.2.1968; 2.1.1969.	.15	1.25	5.00
e. W/o security thread. 1.5.1970; 12.10.1970; 7.8.1971; 20.7.1972; 7.8.1973; 7.8.1974.	.10	.50	3.00
f. As e. 1.1.1977.	.75	5.00	30.00
s1. Specimen.	—	—	50.00
s2. Specimen. Red ovpt: *ESPECIMEN.*	—	—	50.00

1959-60 Pesos Oro Issue

#402-403 printer: ABNC.

405 5 Pesos Oro

	VG	VF	UNC
20.7.1960. Green on m/c unpt. Face like #399. Portr. José María Córdoba and seated allegory at l. Tall view of new bank bldg. at Bogotá on back. Series M. Printer: TDLR.	1.00	3.00	12.50

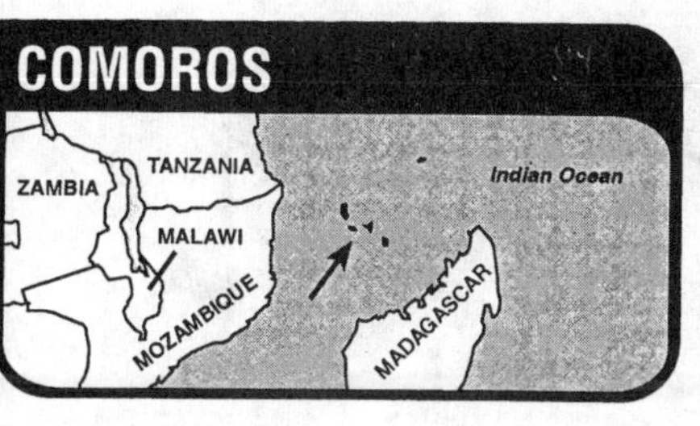

The Federal Islamic Republic of the Comoros, a volcanic archipelago located in the Mozambique Channel of the Indian Ocean 300 miles (483 km.) northwest of Madagascar, has an area of 838 sq. mi. (1,797 sq. km.) and a population of 714,000. Capital: Moroni. The economy of the islands is d on agriculture. There are practically no mineral resources. Vanilla, essence for perfumes, copra and sisal are exported.

Ancient Phoenician traders were probably the first visitors to the Comoros Islands, but the first detailed knowledge of the area was gathered by Arab sailors. Arab dominion and culture were firmly established when the Portuguese, Dutch and French arrived in the 16th century. In 1843 a Malagasy ruler ceded the island of Mayotte to France; the other three principal islands of the archipelago - Anjouan, Moheli and Grand Comore - came under French protection in 1886. The islands were joined administratively with Madagascar in 1912. The Comoros became partially autonomous, with the status of a French overseas territory in 1946 and achieved complete internal autonomy in 1961. On Dec. 31, 1975, after 133 years of French association, the Comoros Islands became the independent Republic of the Comoros.

Mayotte retained the option of determining its future ties and in 1976 voted to remain French. Its present status is that of a French Territorial Collectivity. Euro coinage and currency circulates there.

RULERS:
French

MONETARY SYSTEM:
1 Franc = 100 Centimes

French Administration

Government of the Comoros

1920 ND Emergency Postage Stamp Issue

#A1-1C small adhesive postage stamps of Madagascar depicting Navigation and Commerce, Scott #32, 43, 44, and 46; Moheli, Scott #12 affixed to rectangular pressboard w/animals printed on the back (similar to the Madagascar stamps, Scott #A7).

#1

#1A

		Good	Fine	XF
A1	**0.05 Franc** ND (1920). Green adhesive stamp. Blue legend at bottom *MADAGASCAR ET DEPENDANCES.* Dog on back. Reported not confirmed.	—	—	—
1	**0.50 Franc** ND (1920). Pink adhesive stamp. Blue legend at bottom *MADAGASCAR ET DEPENDANCES.* Dog on back.	350.	750.	—
1A	**0.50 Franc** ND (1920). Brown adhesive stamp. Red legend at bottom *MOHELI.* Dog on back.	350.	750.	—
1B	**0.50 Franc** ND (1920). Dk. pink adhesive stamp. Blue legend at bottom *MADAGASCAR ET DEPENDANCES.* Zebu on back.	—	—	—
1C	**1 Franc** ND (1920). Green adhesive stamp. Red legend at bottom *MADAGASCAR ET DEPENDANCES.* Dog on back.	—	—	—

Republic

Banque de Madagascar et des Comores

1960 ND Provisional Issue

#2-6 additional red ovpt: *COMORES.*

		VG	VF	UNC
2	**50 Francs** ND (1960-63). Brown and m/c. Woman w/hat at r. Man on back. Ovpt. on Madagascar #45.			
	a. Sign. titles: *LE CONTROLEUR GAL.* and *LE DIRECTEUR GAL.* ND (1960).	—	—	—
	b. Sign. titles: *LE DIRECTEUR GAL. ADJOINT* and *LE PRESIDENT DIRECTEUR GAL.* ND (1963). 2 sign varieties.	5.00	25.00	100.
	s. Specimen.	—	—	—

		VG	VF	UNC
3	**100 Francs** ND (1960-63). M/c. Woman at r., palace of the Qn. of Tananariva in background. Woman, boats and animals on back. Ovpt. on Madagascar #46.			
	a. Sign. titles: *LE CONTROLEUR GAL.* and *LE DIRECTEUR GAL.* ND (1960).	8.00	45.00	150.
	b. Sign. titles: *LE DIRECTEUR GAL. ADJOINT* and *LE PRESIDENT DIRECTEUR GAL.* ND (1963).	3.00	15.00	55.00
	s. Specimen.	—	—	—

#4-6 dated through 1952 have titles "a", those dated 1955 or ND have titles "b".

		VG	VF	UNC
4	**500 Francs** ND (1960-63). M/c. Man w/fruit at ctr. Ovpt. on Madagascar #47.			
	a. Sign. titles: *LE CONTROLEUR GAL* and *LE DIRECTEUR GAL.* - old date 30.6.1950; 9.10.1952 (1960).	25.00	150.	450.
	b. Sign. titles: *LE DIRECTEUR GAL. ADJOINT* and *LE PRESIDENT DIRECTEUR GAL.* ND (1963).	12.50	100.	350.
5	**1000 Francs** ND (1960-63). M/c. Woman and man at l. ctr. Ox cart on back. Ovpt. on Madagascar #48.			
	a. Sign. titles: *LE CONTROLEUR GAL.* and *LE DIRECTEUR GAL.* - old date 1950-52; 9.10.1952 (1960).	35.00	200.	550.
	b. Sign. titles: *LE DIRECTEUR GAL. ADJOINT* and *LE PRESIDENT DIRECTEUR GAL.* ND (1963).	20.00	125.	400.

		VG	VF	UNC
6	**5000 Francs** ND (1960-63). M/c. Portr. Gallieni at upper l., young woman at r. Huts at l., woman w/baby at r. on back. Ovpt. on Madagascar #49.			
	a. Sign. titles: *LE CONTROLEUR GAL.* and *LE DIRECTEUR GAL.* - old date 30.6.1950 (1960).	150.	425.	925.
	b. Sign. titles: *LE DIRECTEUR GAL. ADJOINT* and *LE PRESIDENT DIRECTEUR GAL.* ND (1963).	100.	325.	800.
	c. Sign. titles: *LE DIRECTEUR GÉNÉRAL* and *LE PRÉSIDENT DIRECTEUR GAL.*	125.	350.	800.

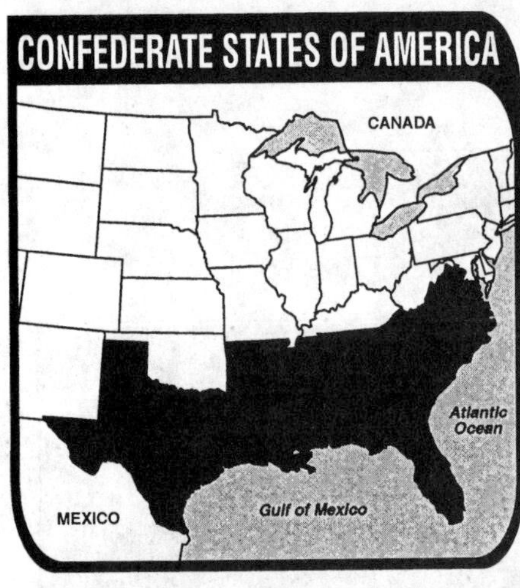

The Confederate States of America (1861-1865) was a federal republic constituted by the 11 Southern states which seceded from the United States after the election of Abraham Lincoln as President. In the order of their secession, the 11 members of the Confederate States of America were South Carolina, Mississippi, Florida, Alabama, Georgia, Louisiana, Texas, Arkansas, North Carolina, Virginia and Tennessee.

The seceded states had left the Union separately and were in effect separate nations, each too small to withstand economic pressures or attack by the Union Army. On Feb. 4, 1861, delegations from South Carolina, Mississippi, Florida, Alabama, Georgia, and Louisiana - Texas arrived later - met in Montgomery, Alabama to organize a Southern nation dedicated to states' rights and the protection of slavery. A provisional government was formed and Jefferson Davis was elected President. The secession crisis precipitated the Civil War - officially known as the War of the Rebellion and, in the South, as the War Between the States - which ended in Union victory and the collapse of the Confederate States of America. The secession states were eventually readmitted to the Union.

To finance the war, both the Confederacy and its constituent states issued paper currency, the redemption of which is specifically forbidden by Section 4 of the 14th Amendment to the U.S. Constitution. WATERMARKS "NY" "TEN" "FIVE" "CSA" in Block letters "CSA" in Script letters "J. WHATMAN 1862" "HODGKINSON & CO. WOOKEY HOLE MILL" "CSA" in block letters with wavy borderline.

MONETARY SYSTEM

1 Dollar = 100 Cents

Note: ***SL#*** **in the listings refer to** ***Confederate States Paper Money, 9th Edition*** **by Arlie R. Slabaugh.**

CONFEDERATE STATES

CONFEDERATE STATES OF AMERICA

MONTGOMERY, ALABAMA

1861 ISSUE

#1-4 Handwritten dates of May-June, 1861. Interest Bearing Notes. Printer: NBNC.

		Good	Fine	XF
1	**50 Dollars** 5.6.1861. Green and black. Blacks hoeing cotton at ctr. Plate letter A. 1,606 issued. *(SL #1).*	2500.	9000.	16,000.

		Good	Fine	XF
2	**100 Dollars** 5.6.1861. Green and black. Columbia at l., steam train depot scene at ctr. Plate letter A. 1,606 issued. *(SL #1).*	2500.	9000.	16,000.

		Good	Fine	XF
3	**500 Dollars** 5.6.1861. Green and black. Steam passenger train crossing viaduct, cattle below. Plate letter A. 607 issued. *(SL #3).*	5000.	14,500.	25,000.

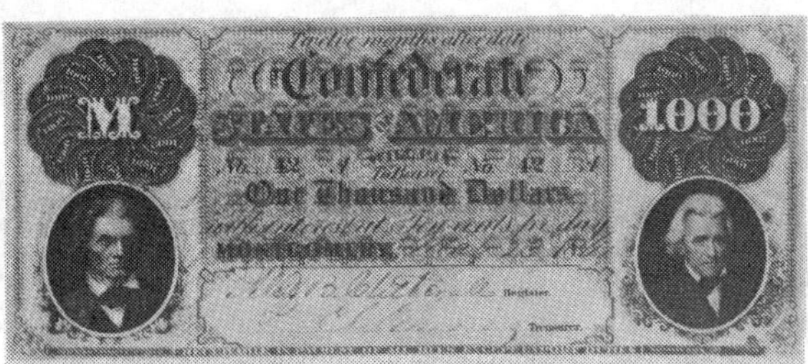

		Good	Fine	XF
4	**1000 Dollars** 5.6.1861. Green and black. Portr. Calhoun at lower l., Jackson at lower r. Plate letter A. 607 issued. *(SL #4).*	5000.	14,500.	25,000.

RICHMOND, VIRGINIA

1861 (FIRST) ISSUE, AUG.-SEPT.

#5-6 usually have handwritten dates of Aug.-Sept. 1861. Printer: Southern BNC. Interest Bearing Notes.

		Good	Fine	XF
5	**50 Dollars** 8.9.1861. Green and black. Justice at l., Pallas and Ceres seated on cotton bale at ctr., Portr. Washington at r. Plate letter B. *(SL #5).* 5,798 issued.	250.	700.	1200.

		Good	Fine	XF
6	**100 Dollars** 8.9.1861. Green and black. Justice at lower l., steam passenger train at ctr., Minerva at r. Plate letter B. *(SL #6).* 5,798 issued.	250.	850.	1350.

1861 (SECOND) ISSUE, JULY

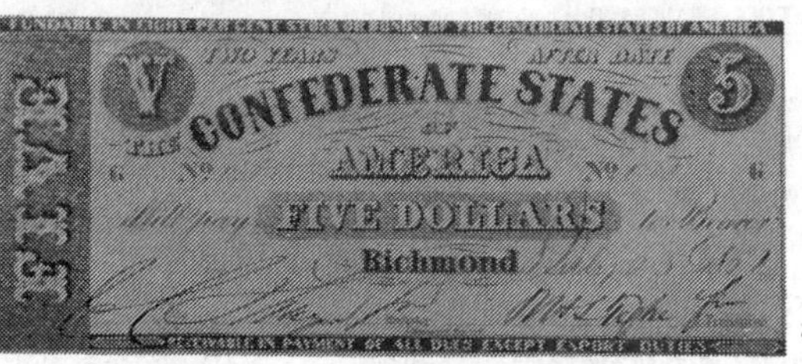

		Good	Fine	XF
7	**5 Dollars** 25.7.1861. *FIVE* at l. and *Confederate States of America* in blue. Plate letters F-I. Back blue. Printer: J. Manouvrier. *(SL #7).*	350.	1250.	7000.

		Good	Fine	XF
8	**5 Dollars** 25.7.1861. Sailor at lower l., Liberty seated above *5* w/eagle at ctr. Plate letters B; Bb. Printer: H & L. *(SL #8).*	500.	2500.	—

9 10 Dollars
25.7.1861. Woman at lower l., Liberty seated above shield w/flag and eagle at ctr. Plate letters A; B; C. Printer: H & L. *(SL #9).*

Good	Fine	XF
100.	300.	1500.

10 20 Dollars
25.7.1861. Sailing ship at ctr. Plate letters B, C; Cc; Ccc; D. Printer: H & L. *(SL #10).*

Good	Fine	XF
50.00	95.00	250.

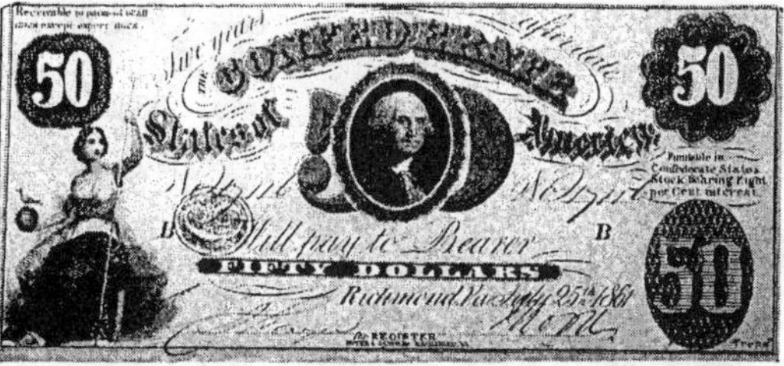

11 50 Dollars
25.7.1861. Tellus at l., portr. Washington at ctr. Plate letters B; Bb; C. Printer: H & L. *(SL #11).*

Good	Fine	XF
50.00	150.	250.

12 100 Dollars
25.7.1861. Portr. Washington at l., Ceres and Proserpine in flight at ctr. Plate letters B; C. Printer: H & L. *(SL #12).*

Good	Fine	XF
250.	800.	1800.

1861 (Third) Issue, Sept.

Note: #13 was incorrectly dated for an 1862 Issue.

13 2 Dollars
2.9.1861. Portr. Benjamin at upper l., personification of the South striking down the Union w/a sword at top ctr. Series 1-10. Printer: B. Duncan (S.C.). *(SC #26).*

Good	Fine	XF
165.	500.	3200.

14 5 Dollars
2.9.1861. Black and red on red fibre paper. Minerva at l., Commerce, Agriculture, Justice, Liberty and Industry at upper ctr., Washington statue at r. Plate letters A; B; C. Printer: Southern BNC. *(SL #22).*

Good	Fine	XF
100.	425.	1000.

15 5 Dollars
2.9.1861. Black and orange. Boy at lower l., blacksmith w/hammer, steam passenger train at lower r. Plate letters A; AA. Printer: Leggett, Keatinge & Ball. *(SL #31).*

Good	Fine	XF
150.	650.	2000.

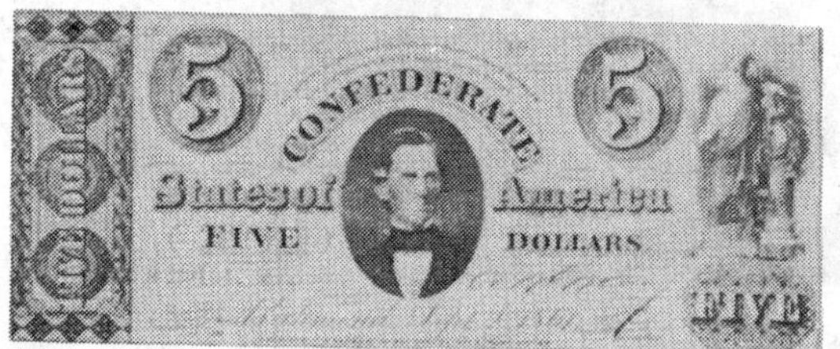

16 5 Dollars
2.9.1861. Black w/blue-green or yellow-green ornamentation. Portr. C. G. Memminger at ctr., Minerva at r. above Roman numeral V. *(SL #32).*

	Good	Fine	XF
a. Printer: Leggett, Keatinge & Ball.	100.	285.	550.
b. Printer: K & B(V.).	100.	285.	550.

17 5 Dollars
2.9.1861. Black. C. G. Memminger at ctr., Minerva at r. *(SL #33).*

	Good	Fine	XF
a. Printer: K & B (V.).	50.00	150.	300.
b. W/o imprint.	50.00	150.	300.

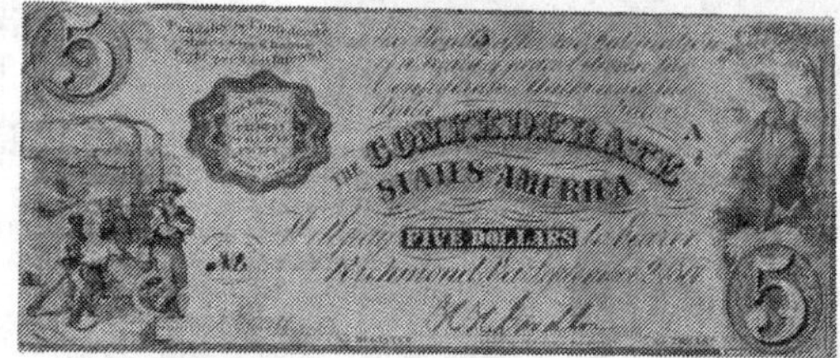

18 5 Dollars
1.9.1861. Loading cotton at dockside at lower l., Indian Princess at r. Printer H & L. *(SL #14).*

Good	Fine	XF
4500.	10,000.	—

19 5 Dollars
2.9.1861. Sailor at lower l., Ceres seated on a bale of cotton at top ctr. Serial #9A-16A. W/o series, also *SECOND* and *THIRD SERIES.* *(SL #19).*

	Good	Fine	XF
a. Printer: H & L.	25.00	50.00	135.
b. Printer: J. T. Paterson.	20.00	40.00	100.
c. Printer: J. T. Paterson & C.	20.00	40.00	100.

		Good	Fine	XF
20	**5 Dollars** 2.9.1861. Portr. C. G. Memminger at lower l., sailor reclining by cotton bales at upper ctr., Justice standing w/Ceres kneeling at r. *(SL #27).*			
	a. Plate letters A-H. Printer: B. Duncan (V.).	30.00	75.00	350.
	b. *SECOND SERIES*, serial #1-8. Printer: B. Duncan (S.C.)	30.00	75.00	350.

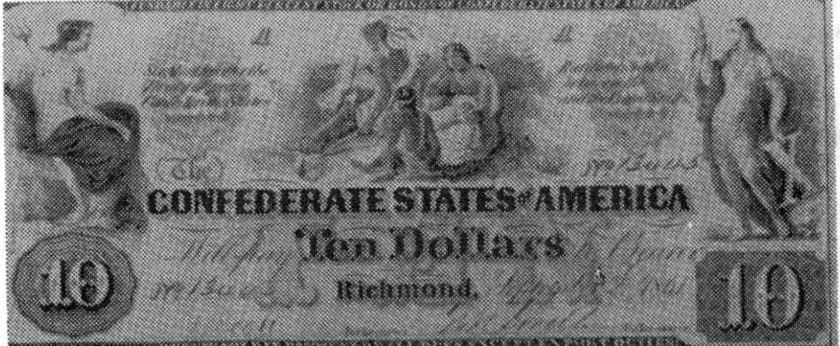

		Good	Fine	XF
21	**10 Dollars** 2.9.1861. Black and red. Thetis at upper l., Indian family at top ctr., Indian maiden at upper r. Plate letters A; B; C. Printer: Southern BNC. *(SL #23).*	125.	550.	1500.

		Good	Fine	XF
22	**10 Dollars** 2.9.1861. Black and orange-red. Portr. J. E. Ward at lower l., horse cart loaded w/cotton at ctr., man carrying sugar cane at lower r. Plate letters, A, A1. Printer: Leggett, Keatinge & Ball. *(SL #34).*	450.	1000.	2500.

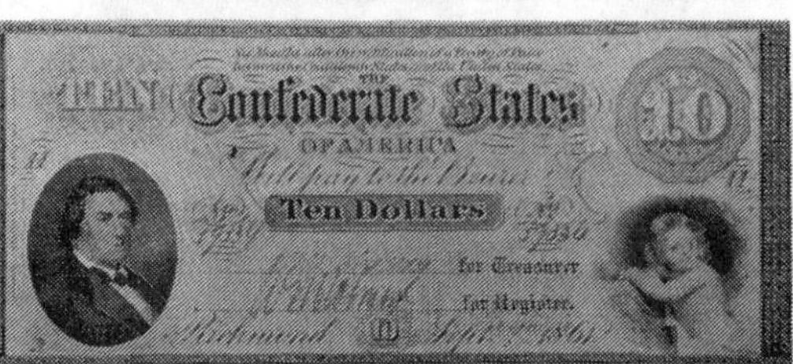

		Good	Fine	XF
23	**10 Dollars** 2.9.1861. Black and orange-red. Portr. R. M. T. Hunter at lower l., child at lower r. Plate letters: H-K. *(SL #35).*			
	a. Printer: Leggett, Keatinge & Ball.	50.00	200.	500.
	b. Printer: K & B.	50.00	200.	500.

		Good	Fine	XF
24	**10 Dollars** 2.9.1861. Portr. R. M. T. Hunter at lower l., Hope w/anchor at lower ctr., portr. C. G. Memminger at lower r. Plate letters W-Z. Printer: K & B. *(SL #36).*	40.00	125.	325.

		Good	Fine	XF
25	**10 Dollars** 2.9.1861. Red or orange. *X - X* protector in unpt. Like #24. Plate letters W-Z. Printer: K & B. *(SL #37).*	35.00	85.00	265.

		Good	Fine	XF
26	**10 Dollars** 2.9.1861. Liberty seated by shield and eagle at upper l., train at r. Printer: H & L (litho). *(SL #15).*			
	a. Plate letter Ab.	3000.	10,000.	30,000.
	b. Plate letters A9-A16. Rare.	—	—	—

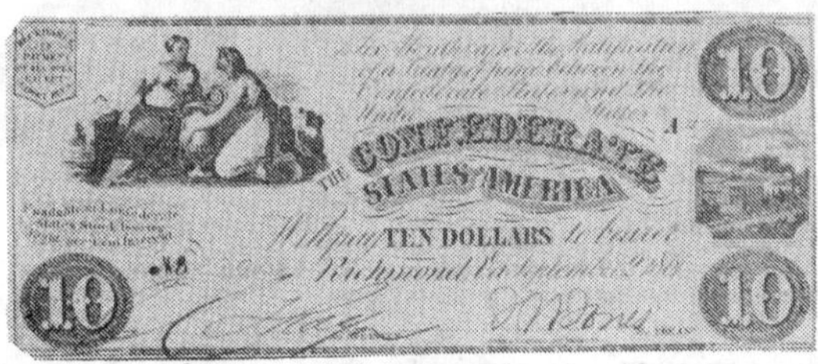

		Good	Fine	XF
27	**10 Dollars** 2.9.1861. Ceres and Commerce seated by an urn at upper l., train at r. Plate letters A9-A16. *(SL #20).*			
	a. Printer: J. T. Paterson.	20.00	60.00	250.
	b. Printer: H & L.	20.00	65.00	265.

		Good	Fine	XF
28	**10 Dollars** 2.9.1861. Black picking cotton at top ctr. Plate letters A-H. Printer: B. Duncan (V.). *(SL #28).*	100.	325.	900.

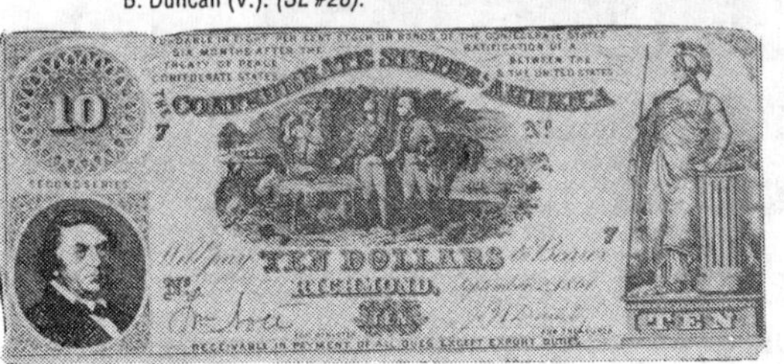

		Good	Fine	XF
29	**10 Dollars** 2.9.1861. Portr. R. M. T. Hunter at l., Gen. F. Marion's "Sweet Potato Dinner" scene at ctr., Minerva standing at r. *FIRST - FOURTH SERIES. (SL #29).*			
	a. Printer: B. Duncan (S.C.).	25.00	55.00	195.
	b. W/o imprint.	25.00	55.00	195.

		Good	Fine	XF
30	**20 Dollars** 2.9.1861. Black w/green ornamentation. Liberty at l., Ceres seated between Commerce and Navigation at upper r. ctr. Serial letter A. Printer: H & L. *(SL #16).*	125.	600.	1350.

31 **20 Dollars**

	Good	Fine	XF
2.9.1861. Sailor leaning on capstan at lower l., sailing ship at upper ctr. *(SL #21).*			
a. Printer: H & L.	20.00	30.00	50.00
b. Printer: J. T. Paterson.	20.00	40.00	80.00

32 **20 Dollars**

	Good	Fine	XF
2.9.1861. Minerva reclining w/shield at lower l., Navigation kneeling at top ctr., blacksmith by anvil at lower r. Plate letter A. Printer: Southern BNC. *(SL #24).*	500.	2000.	3500.

33 **20 Dollars**

	Good	Fine	XF
2.9.1861. Portr. Vice-Pres. A. H. Stevens at l., Industry seated between Cupid and beehive at ctr., Navigation at r. Plate #1-10. *FIRST-THIRD SERIES.* Printer: B. Duncan (V or SC). *(SL #30).*	25.00	50.00	85.00

34 **20 Dollars**

	Good	Fine	XF
2.9.1861. Portr. A. H. Stephens at ctr. between industrial and agricultural goods. Plate letters W-Z. Printer: K & B. (S.C.) *(SL #38).*	125.	300.	775.

35 **50 Dollars**

	Good	Fine	XF
2.9.1861. 2 sailors at lower lower l., Moneta seated with chest at upper ctr. Various serial letters and #'s. Printer: H & L. *(SL #17).*	35.00	75.00	150.

36 **50 Dollars**

	Good	Fine	XF
2.9.1861. Hope w/anchor at lower l., steam passenger train at top ctr., Justice at r. Plate letter A. Printer: Southern BNC. *(SL #25).*	1000.	2850.	5000.

37 **50 Dollars**

	Good	Fine	XF
2.9.1861. Black and green. Portr. Pres. J. Davis at ctr. W/o series, also *SECOND SERIES.*Plate letters WA-ZA. Printer: K & B (V.). *(SL #39).*	50.00	125.	525.

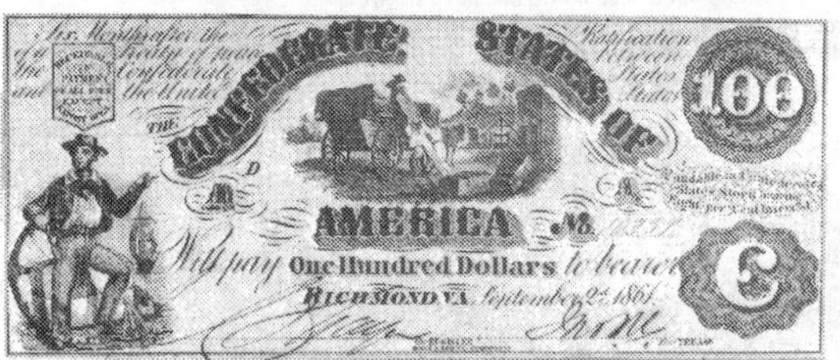

38 **100 Dollars**

	Good	Fine	XF
2.9.1861. Sailor w/anchor at lower l., slaves loading cotton on wagon at upper ctr. Various serial letters and #'s. Printer: H & L. *(SL #18).*	45.00	85.00	150.

1862 (FOURTH) ISSUE, JUNE

39 **1 Dollar**

	Good	Fine	XF
2.6.1862. Liberty standing at l., steam powered sailing ships at top ctr. r., portr. L. H. Pickens at lower r., *FIRST-THIRD SERIES.* Printer: B. Duncan (S.C.). *(SL #43).*	45.00	85.00	150.

40 **1 Dollar**

	Good	Fine	XF
2.6.1862. Like #39 but w/green *1* and *ONE* protector unpt. *FIRST, SECOND SERIES.* Printer: B. DUNCAN (S.C.). *(SL #44).*	25.00	50.00	135.

41 **2 Dollars**

	Good	Fine	XF
2.6.1862. Portr. J. Benjamin at upper l., personification of the South striking down the Union w/a sword at top ctr. *FIRST-THIRD SERIES.* Printer: B. Duncan (S.C.). *(SL #45).*	25.00	50.00	135.

42 **2 Dollars**

	Good	Fine	XF
2.6.1862. Like #41 but w/green *2* and *TWO* protector unpt. *SECOND SERIES.* Printer: B. Duncan. (S.C.). *(SL #46).*	35.00	125.	800.

		Good	Fine	XF
43	**100 Dollars** 1862. Milkmaid at lower l., steam passenger train at top ctr. w/straight steam blowing out of locomotive boiler. W/ or w/o various interest paid markings on back. *(SL #40).*			
	a. Plate letters A, Ab-Ah. Printer: H & L. 5.5.1862-5.9.1862.	20.00	50.00	110.
	b. Plate letters Aa-Ah. Printer: J. T. Paterson. 8.4.1862; May, 1862.	15.00	50.00	80.00

		Good	Fine	XF
44	**100 Dollars** 1862-63. Like #43 but w/diffused steam blowing out of locomotive boiler. Plate letters Aa-Ah. W/ or w/o various interest paid markings on back. Printer: J. T. Paterson & C. *(SL #41).*	20.00	50.00	75.00

		Good	Fine	XF
45	**100 Dollars** 26.8.1862. Red-orange *HUNDRED* ovpt. Portr. Calhoun at lower l., blacks hoeing cotton at top ctr., Columbia at r. W/ or w/o various interest paid markings on back. Printer: K & B (S.C.). *(SL #42).*	25.00	60.00	90.00

		Good	Fine	XF
46	**10 Dollars** 2.9.1862. Ceres reclining on cotton bales at top ctr. w/sailing ship in background, Portr. R. M. T. Hunter at lower r. Printer: H. & L. (w/o imprint). *(SL #47).*			
	a. Terms of redemption read: *Six Months after...*	30.00	70.00	215.
	b. Error: terms of redemption read: *Six Month after...*	30.00	70.00	215.

#47-48 printer: K & B. (S.C.). (Not regularly issued.)

		Good	Fine	XF
47	**10 Dollars** 2.9.1862. Ceres holding sheaf of wheat at top ctr., portr. R. M. T. Hunter at lower r. *(SL #48).*	2200.	4200.	—

		Good	Fine	XF
48	**20 Dollars** 2.9.1862. Liberty seated w/shield on bale of cotton top ctr., portr. R. M. T. Hunter at lower r. *(SL #49).*	2000.	4000.	—

Note: #46-48 should probably have been dated 1861.

1862 (FIFTH) ISSUE, DEC.

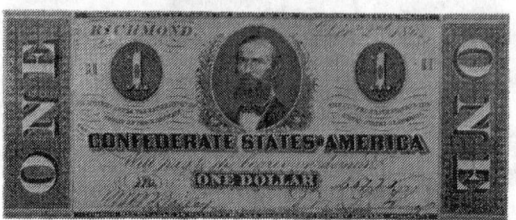

		VG	VF	UNC
49	**1 Dollar** 2.12.1862. Portr. C. C. Clay at top ctr. *(SL #50).*			
	a. *FIRST* or *SECOND* SERIES Printer: K & B. (S.C.).	40.00	125.	325.
	b. W/o Series. Printer: B. Duncan.	40.00	125.	325.

		VG	VF	UNC
50	**2 Dollars** 2.12.1862. J.P. Benjamin at r. *(SL #51).*			
	a. *FIRST* or *SECOND SERIES.* Printer: K & B (S.C.).	50.00	100.	250.
	b. W/o series. Printer: J. T. Paterson & C.	50.00	100.	250.

		VG	VF	UNC
51	**5 Dollars** 2.12.1862. Capital at Richmond, Va. at top ctr., portr. C. G. Memminger at lower r. Ornate blue back. *(SL #52).*			
	a. *FIRST* or *SECOND SERIES,* w/o imprint.	25.00	40.00	100.
	b. *FIRST* or *SECOND SERIES.* Printer: J. T. Paterson & C.	25.00	40.00	100.
	c. *FIRST-THIRD SERIES, Lithog'd by* J. T. Paterson & C.	25.00	40.00	100.
	d. *SECOND SERIES.* Printer: E & C.	25.00	40.00	100.
	e. *SECOND SERIES, Ptd. by* Evans & Cogswell and *Lithog'd by* J. T. Paterson & C.	25.00	40.00	100.
	f. *SECOND SERIES, Ptd. by* E & C. and J. T. Paterson & C.	25.00	40.00	100.

		VG	VF	UNC
52	**10 Dollars** 2.12.1862. Capital at Columbia, S.C., at top ctr., portr. R. M. T. Hunter at lower r. Ornate blue back. *(SL #53).*			
	a. W/o series. Printer: B. Duncan, K & B (S.C.).	25.00	50.00	110.
	b. *SECOND, THIRD* or *FOURTH SERIES,* Printer: B. Duncan.	25.00	50.00	110.
	c. W/o series, also *THIRD SERIES* Printer: E & C.	25.00	50.00	110.
	d. *THIRD* or *FOURTH SERIES.* Printer: E & C, B. Duncan.	25.00	50.00	110.

53 20 Dollars

2.12.1862. Capital at Nashville, Tenn. at top ctr., portr. A. H. Stephens at lower r. Ornate blue back. *(SL #54).*

	VG	VF	UNC
a. *FIRST SERIES. Printed by* J. T. Paterson & C.	50.00	110.	450.
b. *FIRST SERIES.* Printer: J. T. Paterson & C.	50.00	110.	450.
c. *FIRST SERIES.* w/o imprint.	50.00	110.	450.
d. *FIRST SERIES.* Printer: B. Duncan.	50.00	110.	450.
e. *FIRST SERIES. Printed by* Duncan.	50.00	110.	450.

54 50 Dollars

2.12.1862. Portr. Pres. J. Davis at ctr. Ornate green back. Engravers' names above or below *FUNDABLE...* at l. *(SL #55).*

	VG	VF	UNC
a. Printer: K & B (V).	110.	195.	1000.
b. Printer: K & B (S.C.).	110.	195.	1000.

55 100 Dollars

	VG	VF	UNC
2.12.1862. 2 soldiers at lower l., portr. L. H. Pickens at ctr., portr. G. W. Randolph at lower r. W/o series; also *SECOND SERIES* Printer: K & B (S.C.). *(SL #56).*	150.	295.	550.

1863 (SIXTH) ISSUE, APRIL

56 50 Cents

	VG	VF	UNC
6.4.1863. Black on pink paper. Portr. Pres. J. Davis at top ctr. Printed sign. *FIRST* or *SECOND SERIES.* Printer: Archer & Daly. *(SL #57).*	15.00	25.00	50.00

57 1 Dollar

6.4.1863. Portr. C. C. Clay at top ctr. *(SL #58).*

	VG	VF	UNC
a. *FIRST* or *SECOND SERIES.* Printer: K & B. (S.C.).	35.00	75.00	150.
b. W/o series, also *SECOND SERIES.* Printer: E & C. (litho).	35.00	75.00	150.

58 2 Dollars

6.4.1863. Pink paper. Portr. J. P. Benjamin at r. *(SL #59).*

	VG	VF	UNC
a. *FIRST* or *SECOND SERIES.* Printer: K & B (S.C.).	45.00	145.	325.
b. W/o series, also *SECOND SERIES.* Printer: E & C (litho) and K & B. (S.C.).	45.00	145.	325.

59 5 Dollars

6.4.1863. Capital at Richmond, Va. at top ctr., portr. C. G. Memminger at lower r. Date ovpt. from April, 1863 - Feb. 1864. Ornate blue back. *(SL #60).*

	VG	VF	UNC
a. *SECOND-THIRD SERIES.* Printer: K & B. (S.C.).	20.00	35.00	85.00
b. *FIRST-THIRD SERIES.* Printer: K & B and J. T. Paterson & C.	20.00	35.00	85.00
c. W/o series, *THIRD SERIES.* Printer: K & B, E & C.	20.00	35.00	85.00
d. W/o series, *FIRST SERIES.* Printer: K & B, J. T. Paterson & C., E & C.	20.00	35.00	85.00

60 10 Dollars

6.4.1863. Capital at Columbia, S.C. at top ctr., portr. R. M. T. Hunter at lower r. Date ovpt. from April,1863 - Feb. 1864. Ornate blue back. *(SL #61).*

	VG	VF	UNC
a. W/o series, *FIRST* and *FIFTH SERIES.* Printer: K & B (S.C.), E & C.	20.00	40.00	115.
b. *FIRST, SECOND, FIFTH SERIES.* Printer: K & B, B. Duncan.	20.00	40.00	115.
c. *SECOND SERIES.* Printer: K & B, J. T. Paterson & C.	40.00	85.00	175.

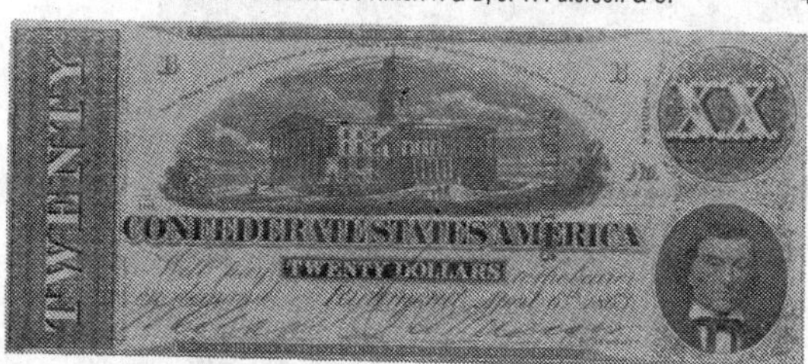

61 20 Dollars

6.4.1863. Capital at Nashville, Tenn. at top ctr., portr. A. H. Stephens at lower r. Date ovpt. from April - Oct. 1863. Ornate blue back. *(SL #62).*

	VG	VF	UNC
a. *FIRST SERIES.* Printer: K & B. (S.C.).	30.00	50.00	175.
b. W/o series, *FIRST-THIRD SERIES.* Printer: K & B, E & C.	30.00	50.00	175.
c. *FIRST SERIES.* Printer: K & B, J. T. Paterson & C.	30.00	50.00	175.

62 50 Dollars

	VG	VF	UNC
6.4.1863. Portr. Pres. J. Davis at ctr. Date ovpt. from April, 1863 - Feb., 1864. Ornate green back. Plate letters WA-ZA. W/o series, also *FIRST SERIES.* Imprint above or below *FUNDABLE...* at l. *(SL #63).*			

	VG	VF	UNC
a. Printer: K & B (Va.).	55.00	125.	200.
b. Printer: K & B (S.C.).	55.00	125.	200.

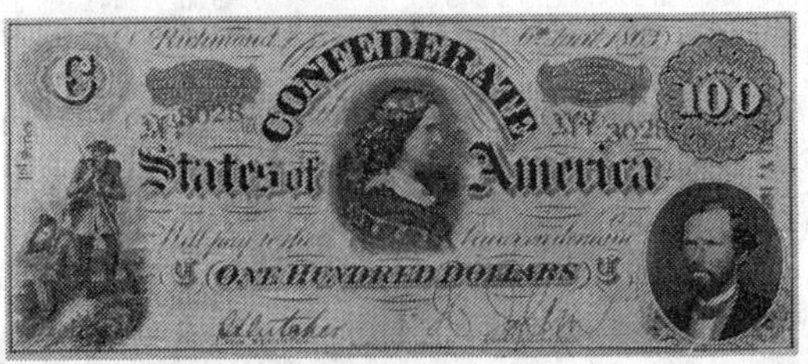

	VG	VF	UNC
63 100 Dollars 6.4.1863. 2 soldiers at l. Portr. L. H. Pickens at ctr., portr. G. W. Randolph at lower r. Date ovpt. from May, 1863 - Jan., 1864. W/o series, also *FIRST SERIES.* Printer: K & B (S.C.). *(SL #64).*	70.00	175.	300.

1864 (SEVENTH) ISSUE, FEB.

	VG	VF	UNC
64 50 Cents 17.2.1864. Pink paper. Portr. Pres. J. Davis at top ctr. Printed sign. Printer: Archer & Halpin. *(SL #65).*			
a. *FIRST SERIES.*	15.00	25.00	50.00
b. *SECOND SERIES.*	15.00	25.00	50.00

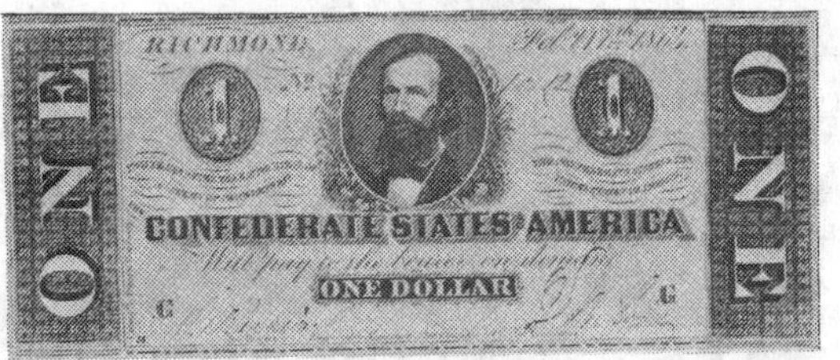

	VG	VF	UNC
65 1 Dollar 17.2.1864. Red unpt. Portr. C. C. Clay at top ctr. *(SL #66).*			
a. *ENGRAVED BY* K & B. (S.C.).	45.00	75.00	150.
b. *ENGRAVED & PRINTED BY* K & B. (S.C.).	45.00	75.00	150.
c. *ENGRAVED BY* K & B (S.C.) & *LITHOG'D BY* E & C.	45.00	75.00	150.

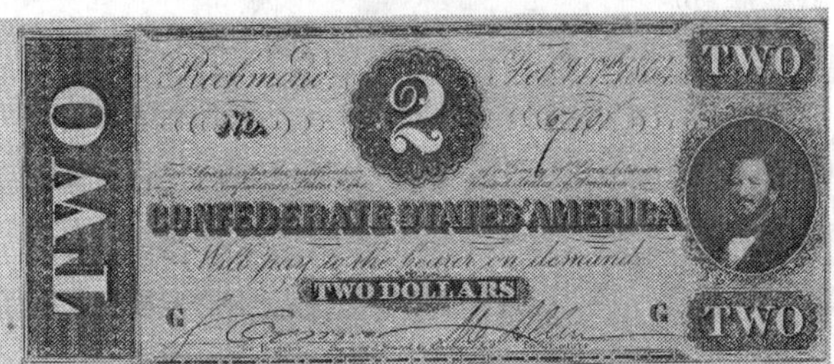

	VG	VF	UNC
66 2 Dollars 17.2.1864. Red unpt. Portr. J. P. Benjamin at r. *(SL #67).*			
a. *ENGRAVED BY* K & B. (S.C.).	35.00	50.00	100.
b. *ENGRAVED & PRINTED BY* K & B. (S.C.).	35.00	50.00	100.
c. *ENGRAVED BY* K & B. (S.C.) *LITHOG'D BY* E & C.	35.00	50.00	100.

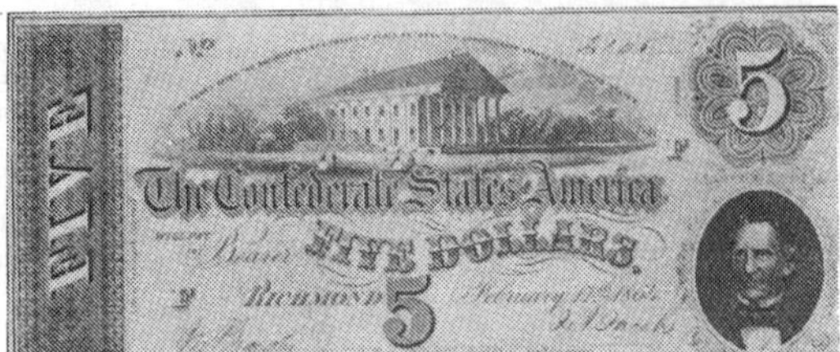

	VG	VF	UNC
67 5 Dollars 17.2.1864. Red unpt. Capital at Richmond, Va. at top ctr., portr. C. G. Memminger at lower r. Blue *FIVE* on back. W/o series, also *SERIES 1-7.* Printer: K & B. (S.C.). *(SL #68).*	20.00	35.00	50.00

	VG	VF	UNC
68 10 Dollars 17.2.1864. Red unpt. Artillery horseman pulling cannon at upper ctr. Portr. R. M. T. Hunter at lower r. Blue *TEN* on back. W/o series, also *FIRST-TENTH SERIES.* Printer: K & B. (S.C.). *(SL #69).*	15.00	25.00	45.00
69 20 Dollars 17.2.1864. Red unpt. Capital at Nashville, Tenn. at top ctr., portr. A. H. Stephens at lower r. Date ovpt. from April - Oct., 1863. Blue *TWENTY* on back. W/o series, also *SERIES 1-5,* also *VI-XI.* Printer: K & B (S.C.). *(SL #70).*	25.00	40.00	60.0
70 50 Dollars 17.2.1864. Red unpt. Portr. Pres. J. Davis at ctr. Blue *FIFTY* on back. W/o series, also *FIRST - FOURTH SERIES. (SL #71).*	40.00	60.00	12

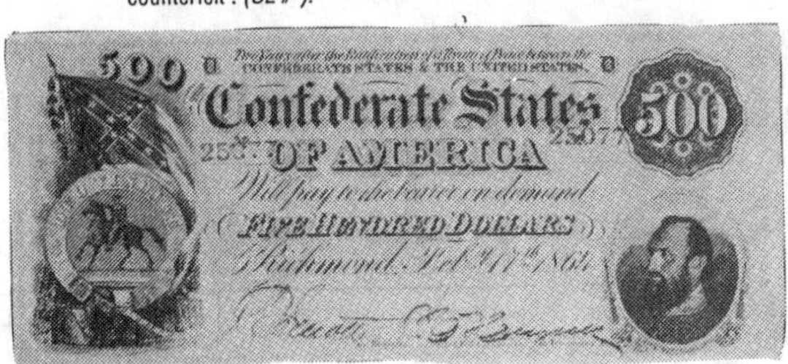

	VG	VF	UNC
71 100 Dollars 17.2.1864. Red unpt. 2 soldiers at l. Portr. L. H. Pickens at ctr., portr. G. W. Randolph at lower r. Blue *HUNDRED* on back. W/o series, also *SERIES I, II. (SL #72).*	45.00	80.00	15
72 100 Dollars 17.2.1864. Like #71 but reduced size. Plate letter D. "Havana counterfeit". *(SL #-).*	30.00	55.00	11
73 500 Dollars 17.2.1864. Red unpt. Confederate seal w/equestrian statue of G. Washington below Confederate flag at l., portr. Gen. T. J. "Stonewall" Jackson at lower r. *(SL #73).*	275.	425.	65

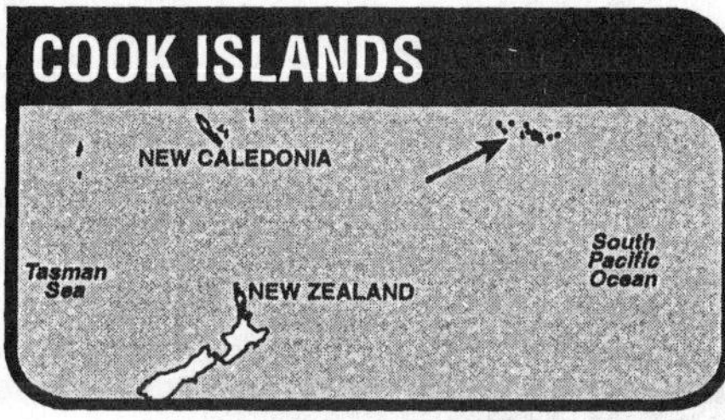

Cook Islands, a political dependency of New Zealand consisting of 15 islands located in the South Pacific Ocean about 2,000 miles (3,218 km.) northeast of New Zealand, has an area of 93 sq. mi. (234 sq. km.) and a population of 20,000. Capital: Avarua. The United States claims the islands of Danger, Manahiki, Penrhyn and Rakahanga atolls. Citrus, canned fruits and juices, copra, clothing, jewelry and mother-of-pearl shell are exported.

The islands were first sighted by Spanish navigator Alvaro de Mendada in 1595. Portuguese navigator Pedro Fernandes de Quieros landed on Rakahanga in 1606. English navigator Capt. James Cook sailed to the islands on three occasions: 1773, 1774 and 1777. He named them Hervey Islands, in honor of Augustus John Hervey, a lord of the Admiralty. The islands were declared a British protectorate in 1888, and were annexed to New Zealand in 1901. They were granted internal self-government in 1965. New Zealand provides an annual subsidy and retains responsibility for defense and foreign affairs.

As a territory of New Zealand, the Cook Islands are considered to be within the Commonwealth of Nations.

Note: In June 1995 the Government of the Cook Islands began redeeming all 10, 20 and 50 dollar notes in exchange for New Zealand currency while most coins originally intended for circulation along with their 3 dollar notes will remain in use.

RULERS:

New Zealand

MONETARY SYSTEM:

1 Shilling = 12 Pence
1 Pound = 20 Shillings, to 1967
1 Dollar = 100 Cents, 1967-

NEW ZEALAND ADMINISTRATION

GOVERNMENT OF THE COOK ISLANDS

1894 ISSUE

#1-2 crossed flags of Cook Islands at top ctr.

		Good	Fine	XF
1	**2 Shillings** 7.8.1894. Blue on pink unpt. (Not issued).	—	—	3000.

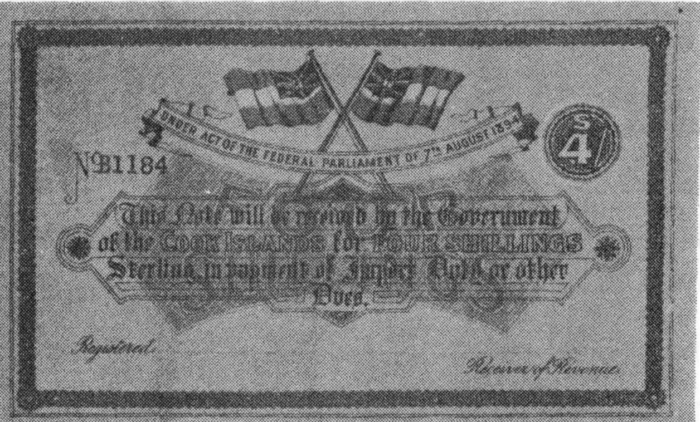

		Good	Fine	XF
2	**4 Shillings** 7.8.1894. Blue on green and orange unpt. (Not issued).	—	—	3000.

COSTA RICA

NICARAGUA
Caribbean Sea
North Pacific Ocean
PANAMA

The Republic of Costa Rica, located in southern Central America between Nicaragua and Panama, has an area of 19,575 sq. mi. (50,700 sq. km.) and a population of 3.8 million. Capital: San Jose. Agriculture predominates; coffee, bananas, beef and sugar contribute heavily to the country's export earnings.

Costa Rica was discovered by Christopher Columbus in 1502, during his last voyage to the new world, and was a colony of Spain from 1522 until independence in 1821. Columbus named the territory Nueva Cartago; the name Costa Rica wasn't generally employed until 1540. Bartholomew Columbus attempted to found the first settlement but was driven off by Indian attacks and the country wasn't pacified until 1530. Costa Rica was absorbed for two years (1821-23) into the Mexican Empire of Agustin de Iturbide. From 1823 to 1848 it was a constituent state of the Central American Republic (q.v.). It was established as a republic in 1848.

Constitution revisions followed in 1871 and 1948. In the early 1990's, Costa Rica was beset with economic problems.

MONETARY SYSTEM:

1 Peso = 100 Centavos to 1896
1 Colon = 100 Centimos

REPUBLIC

REPÚBLICA DE COSTA RICA

1865-71 ISSUE

#101-105 uniface. Printer: BWC.

Note: A number of issues earlier than 1865 are reported but not confirmed.

		Good	Fine	XF
101	**1 Peso** 2.1.1865. Black on green unpt. Arms at l., Mercury w/bales at r.			
	a. W/o circular stampings on back.	150.	550.	—
	b. Circular stampings on back: *EMISION DE GUERRA...* w/arms at ctr. embossed at l. *SECRETARIA DE HACIENDA Y COMERCIO...* stamped w/arms at ctr. r.	125.	500.	—

		Good	Fine	XF
102	**2 Pesos** 27.3.1871. Black on brown unpt. Arms at l., portr. young woman at r.			
	a. W/o circular stampings on back.	—	—	—
	b. W/stampings as #101b above on back.	300.	1200.	—

		Good	Fine	XF
103	**5 Pesos** 2.1.1865. Black on reddish tan unpt. Arms at l., sailing boat at r. W/o stampings on back. Rare.	—	—	—
103A	**5 Pesos** 2.1.1865 (1883). Similar to #103 but Gen. Prospero Fernandez vignette at r. Rare.	—	—	—
104	**10 Pesos** 2.1.1865. Black on green unpt. Arms at l., vignette at r. Rare.	—	—	—
104A	**10 Pesos** 2.1.1865 (1883). Similar to #104 but Gen. Prospero Fernandez vignette at r. Rare.	—	—	—
105	**25 Pesos** 2.1.1865. Black on blue unpt. Arms at l., oxen and cart at r. Rare.	—	—	—
106	**50 Pesos** 2.1.1865. Black on orange unpt. Arms at l., standing woman w/fruit basket at r. Rare.	—	—	—
107	**50 Pesos** 2.1.1865. Black on olive unpt. Arms at l., bldg. at r. Rare.	—	—	—

1877 ISSUE

		Good	Fine	XF
111	**1 Peso** 4.4.1877. Black and red. Arms at lower ctr. Uniface. Rare.	—	—	—

1880'S ISSUE

#120-124 printer: ABNC.

		Good	Fine	XF
120	**5 Pesos** 5.5.1884-1.5.1885. Black on red-orange unpt. Standing woman at l., arms at lower ctr., Raphael's Angel at r. Back red-orange.			
	a. Issued note. Rare.	—	—	—
	s. Specimen.			

		Good	Fine	XF
121	**10 Pesos** 4.5.1884-1.5.1885. Black on green unpt. Seated woman w/globe at l., arms at ctr., seated woman w/plants at r.			
	a. Circular black cancellation stamp: *JEFATURA DE SECCION DEL SELLO NACIONAL 26 DIC 89*, and hand sign. Back green; flowers. Rare.	—	—	—
	b. Punch holed cancelled. Rare.	—	—	—
	p. W/o circular black stamp or handsign proof.			

		Good	Fine	XF
122	**25 Pesos** 20.3.1885-9.10.1885. Black on orange unpt. Arms at l., Prospect Pt., Niagara Falls and Canadian Horseshoe Falls at ctr., Prospero Hernandes at r. Back brown.			
	a. Issued note, text like #121a. Rare.	—	—	—
	p1. Brown unpt. Uniface proof.			
	p2. Blue unpt. Uniface proof.			

		Good	Fine	XF
123	**50 Pesos** 20.3.1885-14.11.1888. Black on green unpt. Bldg. at l., Prospero Hernandes at ctr., arms at lower r.			
	a. Circular black cancellation hand stamp and hand sign. on face like #121. Back olive. Rare.	—	—	—
	b. Punch holed cancelled. Rare.	—	—	—
	p. W/o stamping. Proof.			
124	**100 Pesos** 20.3.1885-14.11.1888. Black on lt. orange unpt. Bldg. at at l., Prospero Hernandes at ctr., arms at r. Back orange-brown.			
	a. Issued note. Rare.	—	—	—
	s. Specimen.	—	—	450.

1897 GOLD CERTIFICATE ISSUE

#131-135 arms at ctr. on back. Printer: ABNC.

		Good	Fine	XF
131	**5 Colones** 1.1.1897. Black on yellow and green unpt. Portr. C. Columbus at ctr. Back blue-green. Series A. Proof. Rare.	—	—	—

		Good	Fine	XF
132	**10 Colones** 1.1.1897. Black on green and yellow unpt. Portr. C. Columbus at ctr. Back green. Series B. Proof. Rare.	—	—	—
133	**25 Colones** 1.1.1897. Black on blue and yellow unpt. Portr. C. Columbus at ctr. Back blue. Series C. Proof. Rare.	—	—	—
134	**50 Colones** 1.1.1897. Black on orange and yellow unpt. Portr. C. Columbus at l., seated Agriculture at ctr. Back orange. Series D. Proof. Rare.	—	—	—

		Good	Fine	XF
135	**100 Colones** 1.1.1897. Black on brown and yellow unpt. Portr. C. Columbus at l., allegorical woman w/globe and lute at ctr. Back brown. Series E. Proof. Rare.	—	—	—

1902-10 Silver Certificate Issue

A. Payable in 25 and 50 Centimos coins. Printer: ABNC.

		Good	Fine	XF
141	**1 Colón** 1.11.1902; 5.11.1902; 1.10.1903. (filled in by hand). Black on green and yellow unpt., uniface. Portr. C. Columbus at l., arms w/flags at r. Black circular stamping of arms at ctr. on plain back.			
	a. Issued note.	75.00	350.	—
	s. Specimen.	—	—	—

		Good	Fine	XF
142	**1 Colón** 1.10.1905; 1.7.1906; 1.11.1906. Like #141. Back dk. green w/black circular stamping of arms at l.			
	a. Issued note.	15.00	80.00	275.
	s. Specimen.	—	—	—

		Good	Fine	XF
143	**1 Colón** 23.5.1910; 10.11.1910; 1.12.1912; 1.10.1914. Like #142 but arms w/o flags. Black stamping of arms w/o circle at r. on back.			
	a. Issued note.	6.00	70.00	250.
	s. Specimen.	—	—	—

		Good	Fine	XF
144	**2 Colones** 1.11.1902; 5.11.1902; 1.10.1903; 1.10.1905. Black on yellow and orange unpt. Face like #141. Black circular stamping of arms on plain back.			
	a. Issued note.	100.	400.	—
	s. Specimen.	—	—	—
145	**2 Colones** 1.10.1905; 1.7.1906. Black on yellow and orange unpt. Like #142. Back red-orange.	25.00	100.	350.

		Good	Fine	XF
146	**2 Colones** 1.11.1910; 1.12.1912; 1.10.1914. Like #143.			
	a. Issued note.	15.00	80.00	275.
	s. Specimen.	—	—	—

1917 Silver Certificate Issue

B. Notes backed by coined silver. Printer: ABNC.

		Good	Fine	XF
147	**50 Centimos** 11.10.1917-21.11.1921. Black on olive unpt. Portr. C. Columbus at ctr. Back olive-brown, w/arms. Black stamped arms at r.			
	a. Issued note.	5.00	25.00	75.00
	s. Specimen.	—	—	—

		Good	Fine	XF
148	**1 Colón** 22.9.1917; 11.10.1917; 24.10.1917; 5.6.1918; 3.7.1918. Similar to #143 but w/diff. text below heading and diff. sign. titles.	7.50	35.00	150.

		Good	Fine	XF
149	**2 Colones** 2.2.1917; 22.9.1917; 5.11.1917. Similar to #146 but w/changes as #148.			
	a. Issued note.	50.00	250.	—
	s. Specimen.	—	—	—

		Good	Fine	XF
150	**50 Colones** ND (1917). Black on brown and m/c unpt. Portr. C. Columbus at ctr. Back brown; arms at ctr. Proof.	—	—	—

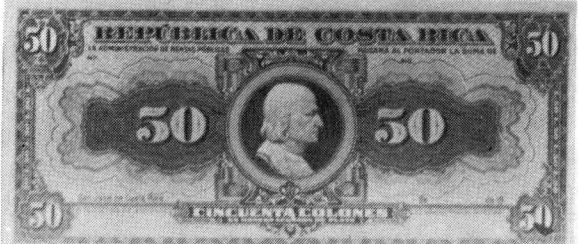

150A	100 Colones	Good	Fine	XF
	ND (1917). Black on blue and m/c unpt. Similar to #150. Back blue; arms at ctr. Specimen.	—	—	—

1918-20 Provisional Issues

151	2 Colones	Good	Fine	XF
	19.6.1918-22.12.1919. Red ovpt: *LEY NO. 3 BILLETE DE PLATA 23 JUNIO 1917* on face of #146. Red sign. and date.	15.00	70.00	150.

152	2 Colones	Good	Fine	XF
	11.8.1920. Black ovpt: *Aunque la leyenda...... 1917* on back of #146 in 5 lines. Black sign. and date.	15.00	70.00	150.

Banco Internacional de Costa Rica

Series A

156	25 Centimos	Good	Fine	XF
	9.10.1918-25.7.1919. Dk. green. Portr. Liberty at l.			
	a. Issued note.	3.00	20.00	75.00
	s. Specimen.	—	—	—

157	50 Centimos	Good	Fine	XF
	18.1.1918-24.10.1921. Black on brown unpt. Portr. woman at ctr. Back brown.			
	a. Issued note.	4.00	20.00	85.00
	s. Specimen.	—	—	—

158	1 Colón	Good	Fine	XF
	1918-35. Black on m/c unpt. Seated woman at ctr. Back blue; Liberty head.			
	a. 18.1.1918; 9.10.1918; 21.10.1918.	6.00	25.00	75.00
	b. 17.11.1922; 18.4.1923.	5.00	20.00	65.00
	c. 27.9.1929; 12.4.1935-9.10.1935.	4.00	17.50	60.00
	s. Specimen.	—	—	—

159	2 Colones	Good	Fine	XF
	1918-31. Black on m/c unpt. Reclining Liberty w/lion and book at ctr. Back olive; Liberty head.			
	a. 16.1.1918; 28.6.1919.	25.00	75.00	250.
	b. 24.5.1923-8.7.1931.	20.00	60.00	225.
	s. Specimen.	—	—	—

#160-164 sign. title ovpt. at l.: *EL SECRETARIO DE HACIENDA.*

160	5 Colones	Good	Fine	XF
	1.11.1914. Black. Indian girl w/pineapple basket at l., banana tree at r. Back orange; lg. V5.			
	a. Issued note.	35.00	115.	550.
	s. Specimen.	—	—	—

161	10 Colones	Good	Fine	XF
	1.11.1914. Black. 5 coffee bean pickers at ctr. Back brown.			
	a. Issued note.	45.00	225.	650.
	s. Specimen.	—	—	—

162	20 Colones	Good	Fine	XF
	1.11.1914. Black. Draped woman w/ship's wheel at r. Back olive-green. Like #169B.			
	a. Issued note. Rare.	—	—	—
	s. Specimen.	—	—	—

Note: For years only counterfeits (as the note illustrated) for #162 were known. A genuine piece is confirmed and is rare.

		Good	Fine	XF
163	**50 Colones** 1.11.1914. Black. Woman playing mandolin at ctr. Back blue-black.			
	a. Issued note. Rare.	—	—	—
	b. Specimen.	—	—	—
	s. Specimen.	—	—	—

		Good	Fine	XF
164	**100 Colones** 1.11.1914. Black. Seated female ("Study") at l. Back green.			
	a. Issued note.	75.00	200.	650.
	s. Specimen.	—	—	—

SERIES B - PROVISIONAL ISSUE (1935)

		Good	Fine	XF
65	**50 Centimos** 12.4.1935. Like #147. Red ovpt: *BANCO INTERNACIONAL DE COSTA RICA/AUNQUE LA LEYENDA... 1935* on back in 7 lines. 2 red sign. below. Sign. titles: *EL SECRETARIO DE HACIENDA* and *EL DIRECTOR DEL BANCO* ovpt. on face.	5.00	27.50	75.00

ote: #165A has been renumbered to #169B.

SERIES B 1916-35 ISSUES

		Good	Fine	XF
66	**1 Colón** 9.10.1935. Green on m/c unpt. Like #158. Back brown. Printer: ABNC.			
	a. Issued note.	5.00	30.00	100.
	s. Specimen.	—	—	—

		Good	Fine	XF
67	**2 Colones** 10.12.1931-31.10.1936. Brown on red, blue and green unpt. Portr. Mona Lisa at ctr. Back black; ox-cart. Printer: W&S.	25.00	200.	600.

68-170 printer: ABNC.

		Good	Fine	XF
68	**5 Colones** 1.12.1916. Black on m/c unpt. Portr. Pres. A. Gonzalez Flores at ctr. Back blue-gray.			
	a. Issued note.	60.00	375.	—
	s. Specimen.	—	—	—

		Good	Fine	XF
169	**10 Colones** 1.12.1916; 9.10.1918. Black on m/c unpt. Portr. W. J. Field Spencer, first director of the Banco, at ctr. Back orange.			
	a. Issued note.	70.00	400.	—
	s. Specimen.	—	—	—

		Good	Fine	XF
169A	**20 Colones** 1.12.1916. Deep blue on m/c unpt. Liberty seated w/sword and shield at ctr. French Marianne at ctr. on back. Series B. Printer: ABNC.			
	a. Issued note w/date. Rare.	—	—	—
	s. Black on blue unpt. Back green. ND. Specimen.	—	—	—
169B	**20 Colones** 21.10.1918. Black. Draped woman w/ship's wheel at r. Like #162. Rare.	—	—	—
170A	**50 Colones** 1.3.1916. Black. Seated woman playing mandolin at ctr. Like #163.			
	a. W/o punch cancellation. Rare.	—	—	—
	b. Punch hole cancelled. Rare.	—	—	—
170B	**100 Colones** 17.3.1916. Like #164. Rare.	—	—	—

1918-19 PROVISIONAL ISSUE

#171 and 172 black ovpt: *Acuerdo No. 225/de 9 de Octubre de 1918.*

		Good	Fine	XF
171	**5 Colones** 9.10.1918 (- old date 1.12.1916). Ovpt. at ctr. on back of #168.	45.00	300.	—
172	**10 Colones** 9.10.1918 (- old date 1.12.1916). Ovpt. at ctr. on back of #169.	45.00	300.	—

SERIES C

#173-178 printer: ABNC.

		Good	Fine	XF
173	**50 Centimos** 21.6.1935; 21.7.1935; 1.8.1935. Blue on tan unpt. Like #157. Back green.			
	a. Issued note.	5.00	20.00	75.00
	s. Specimen.	—	—	—

174	5 Colones	Good	Fine	XF
	1919-30. Dk. blue on m/c unpt. Indian girl w/pineapple basket at l., banana tree at r. Like #160. Back dk. brown.			
	a. 4.1.1919; 28.6.1919.	17.50	75.00	450.
	b. 17.7.1925-22.12.1930.	12.50	60.00	350.

175	10 Colones	Good	Fine	XF
	1919-32. Blue on m/c unpt. Like #161. Back olive-brown.			
	a. Date at lower r. 4.1.1919.	25.00	100.	500.
	b. Date at lower ctr. 13.9.1927-20.1.1932.	20.00	75.00	450.
	s. Specimen.	—	—	—

176	20 Colones	Good	Fine	XF
	1919-36. Dk. blue on m/c unpt. People cutting sugar cane at ctr. Back orange.			
	a. 4.1.1919-24.3.1924.	25.00	200.	600.
	b. Sign. title: *EL SUBDIRECTOR* ovpt. at r. 31.7.1933.	22.50	150.	500.
	c. W/o sign. title changes. 17.4.1928-3.7.1936.	20.00	140.	450.
	s. Specimen.	—	—	—

177	50 Colones	Good	Fine	XF
	1919-32. Dk. blue on m/c unpt. Woman playing mandolin at ctr. Like #163. Back green.			
	a. 4.1.1919-23.6.1927.	40.00	250.	650.
	b. 8.4.1929-5.11.1932.	30.00	200.	550.
	s. Specimen.	—	—	—

178	100 Colones	Good	Fine	XF
	1919-32. Dk. blue on m/c ovpt. Seated female ("Study") at l. Like #164. Back blue-black.			
	a. 4.1.1919-23.6.1927.	35.00	225.	600.
	b. 22.4.1930-11.2.1932.	30.00	150.	500.
	s. Specimen.	—	—	—
	x. Error date: 14.12.2931.	60.00	275.	650.

SERIES D PROVISIONAL ISSUE

179	10 Colones	Good	Fine	XF
	7.11.1931. Olive and blue on pink unpt. 3 workers on horseback at ctr. Red ovpt: *Certificado de Plata... 1931* in 3 lines on face. Red date and sign. Back brown; portr. Columbus at ctr. Lg. red ovpt: *CERTIFICADO DE PLATA* across ctr. Printer: TDLR.	90.00	375.	850

1931-33 SERIES D

180	5 Colones	Good	Fine	XF
	1931-36. Red-orange and blue on tan unpt. 3 coffee bean workers at r. Back tan; monument. Printer: TDLR.			
	a. 8.7.1931-31.10.1936.	10.00	85.00	350
	b. Sign. title: *EL SUBDIRECTOR* ovpt. at r. 27.8.1936.	10.00	85.00	350

181	10 Colones	Good	Fine	XF
	20.1.1932; 3.12.1935-17.12.1936. Like #179 but w/o ovpt. Black date and sign.	20.00	125.	450

182	100 Colones	Good	Fine	XF
	1933-35. Blue on m/c unpt. Woman standing w/basket of vegetables at l. Back red-brown; lg. bldg. Printer: W&S.			
	a. Sign. title: *EL SUBDIRECTOR* ovpt. at r. 2.6.1933-4.9.1933.	20.00	125.	450
	b. W/o sign. title changes. 17.1.1933; 30.10.1934; 26.3.1935.	20.00	125.	450

1933 SERIES E

		Good	Fine	XF
183	**50 Colones**			
	1933. Dk. green on m/c unpt. Woman standing at l. Back dk. blue; monument at ctr. Printer: W&S.			
	a. Sign. title: *EL SUBDIRECTOR* ovpt. at r. 31.7.1933.	22.50	175.	550.
	b. W/o sign. title changes. 17.1.1933; 24.11.1933.	22.50	175.	550.

CAJA DE CONVERSION

1924-25 ISSUE

#184-189 series A. Printer: ABNC.

		Good	Fine	XF
184	**2 Colones**			
	18.7.1924-5.2.1929. Dk. blue on m/c unpt. Allegorical woman standing w/model airplane by woman seated at r. Back brown.			
	a. Issued note.	15.00	75.00	300.
	s. Specimen.	—	—	—

		Good	Fine	XF
185	**5 Colones**			
	4.11.1925-12.12.1928. Dk. blue on m/c unpt. Woman seated at r. Back purple.			
	a. Issued note.	20.00	200.	—
	s. Specimen.	—	—	—

		Good	Fine	XF
186	**10 Colones**			
	15.7.1924; 6.1.1925; 27.12.1927. Dk. Blue on m/c unpt. Woman holding steam locomotive and woman seated at l. Back orange.			
	a. Issued note.	40.00	350.	—
	s. Specimen.	—	—	—

		Good	Fine	XF
187	**20 Colones**			
	15.7.1924-12.4.1928. Dk. blue m/c unpt. Seated woman holding book and wreath at r. Back lt. brown.			
	a. Issued note.	70.00	450.	—
	s. Specimen.	—	—	—

		Good	Fine	XF
188	**50 Colones**			
	15.7.1924-10.1.1927. Dk. blue on m/c unpt. Helmeted woman seated holding sword and palm branch at l. Back black.			
	a. Issued note. Rare.	—	—	—
	s. Specimen.	—	—	—

		Good	Fine	XF
189	**100 Colones**			
	24.12.1924-21.10.1927. Dk. blue on m/c unpt. Seated woman holding branch at r. Back green.			
	a. Issued note. Rare.	—	—	—
	s. Specimen.	—	—	—

Note: The 2, 5 and 10 Colones of Series B were used w/provisional ovpts. of the Banco Nacional, as were some of #184 and #187.

1929 ISSUE

#189A-189B printer: TDLR.

		Good	Fine	XF
189A	**5 Colones**			
	5.2.1929. Purple. Workers loading bananas on train. Like #198 but w/o ovpt. Rare.	—	—	—
189B	**10 Colones**			
	5.2.1929. Orange on yellow unpt. Workers in field drying coffee beans. Like #199 but w/o ovpt. Rare.	—	—	—

BANCO NACIONAL DE COSTA RICA

1937-43 PROVISIONAL ISSUE, OVPT. TYPE A, W/O LEY

#190-194 ovpt: *BANCO NACIONAL DE COSTA RICA/DEPARTAMENTO EMISOR* on face of Banco Internacional notes w/sign. titles changed.

		Good	Fine	XF
190	**1 Colón**			
	23.6.1943. Red ovpt. on #166. Series C/B. Red date and sign.	5.00	15.00	85.00

		Good	Fine	XF
191	**10 Colones** 10.3.1937. Black ovpt on #181.	15.00	85.00	450.
192	**20 Colones** 1937-38. Black ovpt. on #176.			
	a. Sign. titles: *PRESIDENTE* and *GERENTE*. 10.3.1937; 7.7.1937; 2.3.1938.	25.00	200.	425.
	b. Sign title: *VICEPRESIDENTE* at l. 22.6.1938.	25.00	200.	425.

		Good	Fine	XF
193	**50 Colones** 8.4.1941; 4.2.1942. Red ovpt. on #183. Red date and sign.	25.00	250.	550.

		Good	Fine	XF
194	**100 Colones** 1937-42. Red ovpt. on #182. Red date and sign.			
	a. Sign title: *GERENTE* at r. 3.11.1937; 29.3.1939; 30.10.1940; 4.2.1942.	15.00	100.	350.
	b. Sign title: *SUB-GERENTE* at r. 9.7.1941.	15.00	100.	350.

1937-38 Provisional Issue, Ovpt. Type B, Ley No. 16 de 5 de Noviembre de 1936

#195 black ovpt: *BANCO NACIONAL DE COSTA RICA/DEPARTAMENTO EMISOR* at top on back only of Banco Internacional - Caja de Conversion Series B notes. Added lines of ovpt. text through ctr.

		Good	Fine	XF
195	**2 Colones** 1937-38. Red-orange and purple on gold unpt. Portr. Columbus at l. Back blue; plantation workers. Series C/B. Printer: TDLR.			
	a. 4 lines of ovpt. added. Sign. titles: *PRESIDENTE* and GERENTE 4.1.1937-3.11.1937.	5.00	30.00	90.00
	b. Sign. titles: *VICE PRESIDENTE* at l. 22.6.1938.	5.00	30.00	90.00
	c. 5 lines of ovpt. added. Sign. title: *PRESIDENTE* at l. 2.3.1938.	5.00	30.00	90.00

1939-40 Provisional Issue, Ovpt. Type C, Ley No. 16 de 5 de Noviembre de 1936

#196 and 197 ovpt: *BANCO NACIONAL DE COSTA RICA/DEPARTAMENTO EMISOR* and text on face only of Banco Internacional - Caja de Conversion notes.

		Good	Fine	XF
196	**2 Colones** 15.2.1939. Black ovpt. on #195. Issue date at end of ovpt text. Series C/B.	5.00	30.00	90.00

		Good	Fine	XF
197	**2 Colones** 1940. Red ovpt. on #184. Series D/A.			
	a. 7.2.1940.	10.00	35.00	100.
	b. 9.5.1940.	5.00	12.50	70.00

1937-39 Provisional Issue, Ovpt. Type D, Ley No. 16 de 5 de Noviembre de 1936

#198-200 ovpt: *BANCO NACIONAL DE COSTA RICA/DEPARTMENTO EMISOR* on face and back of Banco Internacional - Caja de Conversion notes. Added lines of ovpt. text on back.

		Good	Fine	XF
198	**5 Colones** 1937-38. Purple. Workers loading train w/bananas at l., mountain view at r. Arms on back. Black ovpt. on #189A. Series E/B. Printer: TDLR.			
	a. Sign. title: *PRESIDENTE* at l. 10.3.1937-2.3.1938.	20.00	125.	400.
	b. Sign. title: *VICE PRESIDENTE* at l. 22.6.1938.	20.00	125.	400.

		Good	Fine	XF
199	**10 Colones** 11.8.1937; 3.11.1937; 2.3.1938. Orange on yellow unpt. Workers in field drying coffee beans at l. ctr. Back orange; lg. bldg. Black ovpt. on #189B. Series E/B. Printer: TDLR.	25.00	200.	450.

		Good	Fine	XF
200	**20 Colones** 1.2.1939. Red ovpt. on #187. Red date and sign. Series D/A.	30.00	250.	550.

1941 Series E

#201-202 printer: W&S.

		VG	VF	UNC
201	**2 Colones** 1941-45. Brown on m/c unpt. Portr. Juan V. de Coronado at ctr. Back brown; rescue scene w/Coronado at ctr.			
	a. W/o sign. title changes. 5.2.1941; 4.2.1942; 20.1.1943-16.2.1944.	2.00	7.50	35.00
	b. Sign. title: *SUB-GERENTE* ovpt. at r. 18.6.1941; 12.11.1941; 15.7.1942.	2.00	7.50	35.00
	c. Sign. title: *VICE-PRESIDENTE* ovpt. at l. 10.12.1942; 18.11.1942.	2.00	7.50	35.00
	d. Both sign. titles ovpt. 28.2.1945.	2.00	7.50	35.00

		VG	VF	UNC
202	**20 Colones** 1941-44. Red on m/c unpt. Portr. Juan de Cavallon at ctr. Back red; church at Orosi.			
	a. Sign. title: *SUB-GERENTE* ovpt. at r. 10.9.1941; 21.7.1943.	20.00	175.	500.
	b. Sign. title: *VICE-PRESIDENTE* ovpt. at l. 12.11.1942.	20.00	175.	500.
	c. W/o sign. title changes: 5.2.1941; 17.3.1942; 12.1.1944.	20.00	175.	500.

1939-46 Series F

		VG	VF	UNC
203	**2 Colones** 1946-49. Red on m/c unpt. Portr. Joaquin B. Calvo at ctr. Back dk. brown; plaza in San José. Printer: ABNC.			
	a. Both sign. titles ovpt. 18.9.1946; 13.11.1946; 14.12.1949.	1.00	5.00	25.00
	b. Sign. title: *SUB-GERENTE* ovpt. at r. 23.4.1947-13.8.1947; 7.12.1949.	1.00	5.00	25.00
	c. Sign. title: *VICE-PRESIDENTE* ovpt. at l. 28.1.1948.	1.00	5.00	25.00
	s. Specimen.			

		VG	VF	UNC
204	**5 Colones** 5.7.1939-28.10.1942. Green on m/c unpt. Portr. Juan Mora Fernandez at ctr. Back green; ruins in Cartago. Printer: W&S.	5.00	35.00	150.

		VG	VF	UNC
205	**10 Colones** 1939-41. Blue on m/c unpt. Portr. Florencio del Castillo at ctr. Back blue; Cacique Indian at ctr. Printer: W&S.			
	a. W/o sign. title changes. 8.9.1939-26.3.1941.	10.00	75.00	350.
	b. Sign. title: *SUB-GERENTE* ovpt. at r. 10.9.1941.	10.00	75.00	350.

		VG	VF	UNC
206	**20 Colones** 1945-48. Olive on m/c unpt. Portr. Gregorio J. Ramirez at r. Back orange; view of Poas Volcano at ctr. Printer: ABNC.			
	a. Both sign. titles ovpt. 28.2.1945.	15.00	175.	550.
	b. Sign. title: *SUB-GERENTE* ovpt. at r. 23.4.1947.	15.00	175.	550.
	c. W/o sign. title changes. 3.3.1948.	15.00	175.	550.
	d. Sign. title: *VICE PRESIDENTE*. 4.6.1947.	15.00	175.	550.
	s. Specimen.			

		VG	VF	UNC
207	**50 Colones** 1942. Black on green and gold unpt. Portr. C. Columbus at ctr. Back black; scene of Columbus at Cariari in 1502. Printer: W&S.			
	a. W/o sign. title changes. 9.9.1942.	15.00	150.	500.
	b. Sign. title: *VICE-PRESIDENTE* at l. 1.12.1942.	15.00	150.	500.

208	100 Colones	VG	VF	UNC
	3.6.1942; 19.8.1942; 26.8.1942. Olive on m/c unpt. Vaso Policromo artifact at ctr. Back olive; ceremonial altar. Printer: W&S.	25.00	175.	600.

1942-44 SERIES G

#209-212 printer: ABNC.

209	5 Colones	VG	VF	UNC
	1943-49. Brown on m/c unpt. Portr. B. Carillo at r. Back green; bridge at ctr.			
	a. W/o sign. title changes. 3.3.1943; 28.1.1948; 3.3.1948.	1.50	7.50	40.00
	b. Both sign. titles ovpt. 28.2.1945; 14.12.1949.	1.50	7.50	40.00
	c. Sign. title: *SUB-GERENTE* ovpt. at r. 16.10.1946; 13.8.1947; 31.8.1949; 30.11.1949; 14.12.1949.	1.50	7.50	40.00
	s. Specimen.			

210	10 Colones	VG	VF	UNC
	1942-49. Lt. orange on m/c unpt. Portr. Manuel J. Carazo at l. Back blue; large sailing ship at ctr.			
	a. W/o sign. title changes. 28.10.1942-12.1.1944; 28.1.1948-3.3.1948.	5.00	40.00	200.
	b. Sign. title: *SUB-GERENTE* ovpt. at r. 16.10.1946; 13.8.1947-10.12.1947; 31.8.1949; 30.11.1949.	5.00	40.00	200.
	c. Both sign. titles ovpt. 14.12.1949.	5.00	40.00	200.
	s. Specimen.			

211	50 Colones	VG	VF	UNC
	1944-48. Grayish green on m/c unpt. Portr. Manuel G. Escalante at l. Back black; church in Heredia at ctr.			
	a. Both sign. titles ovpt. 24.5.1944; 7.6.1944.	10.00	70.00	300
	b. Sign. title: *VICE-PRESIDENTE* ovpt. at l. 4.6.1947.	10.00	70.00	300
	c. W/o sign. title changes. 3.3.1948.	10.00	70.00	300
	s. Specimen.			

212	100 Colones	VG	VF	UNC
	1943-49. Green on m/c unpt. Portr. Dr. José M. Castro Madriz at l. Back olive; old University of Santo Tomas.			
	a. Sign. title: *SUB-GERENTE* ovpt. at r. 21.7.1943; 21.12.1949.	15.00	120.	400
	b. W/o sign. title changes. 10.10.1943; 20.10.1943; 16.2.1944; 22.10.1947; 3.3.1948.	15.00	120.	400
	c. Sign. title: *VICE PRESIDENTE.* 17.3.1943.	15.00	120.	400
	s. Specimen.	—	—	—

BANCO CENTRAL DE COSTA RICA

1950-67 PROVISIONAL ISSUE

Ovpt: *BANCO CENTRAL DE COSTA RICA/SERIE PROVISIONAL* on Banco Nacional notes.

215	5 Colones	VG	VF	UNC
	1950-51. Blue ovpt.on #209. Series G.			
	a. W/o sign. title changes. 20.7.1950; 5.10.1950; 6.12.1950.	3.00	35.00	175
	b. *POR* (for) added to l. of sign. title at l. 8.8.1951.	3.00	35.00	175
	c. Sign. title: *VICE-PRESIDENTE* ovpt. at l. 5.9.1951.	1.00	6.00	30.00
216	**10 Colones**			
	1950-51. Blue ovpt. on #210. Series G.			
	a. W/o sign. title changes. 3.4.1950; 8.8.1951.	10.00	60.00	300
	b. *SUB-GERENTE* sign. ovpt. at r. 20.0.1950.	10.00	60.00	300
217	**20 Colones**			
	3.4.1950; 8.11.1950; 7.3.1951. Blue ovpt. on #206. Series F.	6.00	30.00	375
218	**50 Colones**			
	1950-53. Blue ovpt. on #211. Series G.			
	a. W/o sign. title changes. 3.4.1950-5.3.1952.	8.00	45.00	400
	b. *POR* (for) added to left of sign. title on l. 10.10.1951; 5.12.1951; 25.3.1953.	8.00	45.00	400
219	**100 Colones**			
	1952-55. Blue ovpt. on #212. Series G.			
	a. W/o sign. title changes. 23.4.1952; 28.10.1953; 16.6.1954.	15.00	120.	425
	b. Sign. title: *SUB-GERENTE* ovpt. at r. 2.3.1955.	15.00	120.	425

Note: For 2 Colones 1967 ovpt. for Banco Central, see #235 in Vol. 3.

1951; 1952 ISSUE - SERIES A

220	5 Colones	VG	VF	UNC
	1951-58. Green on m/c unpt. Portr. B. Carillo at r. Back green; coffee worker. Printer: ABNC.			
	a. *POR* (for) added to l. of sign. title at r. 20.11.1952.	3.00	15.00	50.00
	b. W/o sign. title changes. 2.7.1952-6.8.1958.	3.00	15.00	50.00
	c. Sign. title: *SUB-GERENTE* ovpt. at r. 11.7.1956.	3.00	15.00	50.00
	d. *POR* added to l. of sign. title at l. 12.9.1951; 26.5.1954.	3.00	15.00	50.00
	s. Specimen.			

#221-223 printer: W&S.

		VG	VF	UNC
221	**10 Colones**			
	1951-62. Blue on m/c unpt. Portr. A. Echeverria at ctr. Back blue; ox-cart at ctr.			
	a. *POR* added to l. of sign .title at l. 24.10.1951; 8.11.1951; 19.11.1951; 5.12.1951; 29.10.1952.	6.00	25.00	100.
	b. *POR* added to both sign. titles. 28.11.1951.	6.00	25.00	100.
	c. W/o *POR* title changes. 2.7.1952; 28.10.1953-27.6.1962.	6.00	25.00	100.
	d. *POR* added to l. of sign. title at r. 20.11.1952.	6.00	25.00	100.

		VG	VF	UNC
222	**20 Colones**			
	1952-64. Red on m/c unpt. Portr. C. Picado at ctr. Back red; university bldg. at ctr.			
	a. Date at l. ctr., w/o sign. title changes. 26.2.1952; 11.6.1952; 11.8.1954; 14.10.1955; 13.2.1957; 10.12.62.	15.00	50.00	185.
	b. Sign. title: *SUB-GERENTE* ovpt. at r. 20.4.1955.	15.00	50.00	175.
	c. Date at lower l. 7.11.1957-9.9.1964.	15.00	50.00	175.
	d. *POR* added at l. of sign. title at l. 25.3.1953; 25.2.1954.	15.00	50.00	175.

		VG	VF	UNC
223	**50 Colones**			
	1952-64. Olive on m/c unpt. Portr. R. F. Guardia at ctr. Back olive; National Library at ctr.			
	a. 10.6.1952-25.11.1959.	15.00	50.00	225.
	b. 14.9.1960-9.9.1964.	15.00	45.00	200.

		VG	VF	UNC
224	**100 Colones**			
	1952-60. Black on m/c unpt. Portr. J. R. Mora at ctr. Back black; statue of J. Santamaría at ctr.			
	a. W/o sign. title changes: 11.6.1952-29.4.1960.	15.00	35.00	200.
	b. Sign. title: *SUB-GERENTE* ovpt. at r. 27.3.1957.	15.00	35.00	200.

#225-226 printer: ABNC.

		VG	VF	UNC
225	**500 Colones**			
	1951-77. Purple on m/c unpt. Portr. M. M. Gutiérrez at r. Back purple; National Theater at ctr.			
	a. 10.10.1951-6.5.1969.	60.00	300.	850.
	b. 7.4.1970-26.4.1977.	50.00	250.	650.
	s. Specimen.	—	—	650.

		VG	VF	UNC
226	**1000 Colones**			
	1952-74. Red on m/c unpt. Portr. J. Pena at l. Back red; Central and National Bank at ctr.			
	a. 11.6.1952-6.10.1959.	125.	500.	1350.
	b. 25.4.1962-6.5.1969.	100.	350.	850.
	c. 7.4.1970-12.6.1974.	60.00	150.	400.
	s. Specimen.	—	—	550.

1958 Issue

		VG	VF	UNC
227	**5 Colones**			
	29.10.1958-8.11.1962. Green on m/c unpt. Portr. B. Carrillo at ctr. Back green; coffee worker at ctr. Series B. Printer: W&S.	3.50	15.00	50.00

NOTICE

Readers with unlisted dates, signature varieties, etc. are invited to submit photocopies or, high resolution (300 dpi, 100% size) scans of their notes to: Standard Catalog of World Paper Money, 700 East State St. Iola, WI 54990-0001, or E-Mail: george.cuhaj@fwpubs.com.

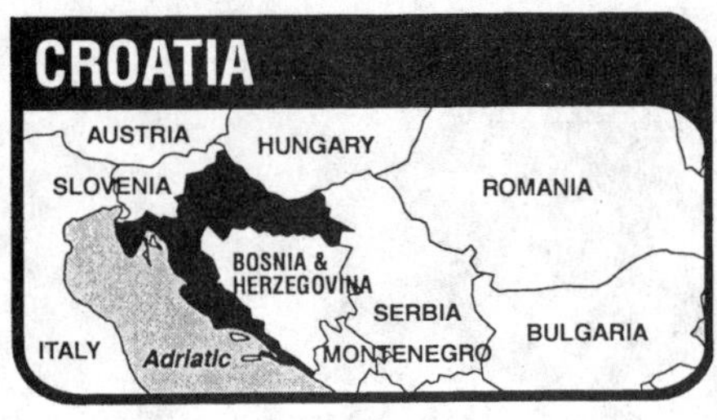

The Republic of Croatia (Hrvatska), formerly a federal republic of the Socialist Federal Republic of Yugoslavia, has an area of 21,829 sq. mi. (56,538 sq. km.) and a population of 4.48 million. Capital: Zagreb.

Countless archeological sites witness the rich history of the area dating from Greek and Roman times, continuing uninterruptedly through the Middle Ages until today. An Independent state under the first Count Borna (about 800 AD), Croatia was proclaimed a kingdom under Tomislav in 925. In 1102 the country joined the personal union with Hungary, and by 1527 all Croatian lands were included in the Habsburg kingdom, staying in the union until 1918, when Croatia became part of the Yugoslav kingdom together with Slovenia and Serbia. In the past, Croats played a leading role in the wars against the Turks, the Antemuralis Christianitatis, and were renown soldiers in the Napoleonic army. From 1941 to 1945 Croatia was an independent military puppet state; from 1945 to 1991 it was part of the Socialist state of Yugoslavia. Croatia proclaimed its independence from Yugoslavia on Oct. 8, 1991.

Local Serbian forces supported by the Yugoslav Federal Army had developed a military stronghold and proclaimed an independent "SRPSKE KRAJINA" state in the area around Knin, located in southern Croatia. In August 1995 Croat forces overran this political-military enclave.

RULERS:

Austrian, 1527-1918
Yugoslavian, 1918-1941

MONETARY SYSTEM:

1 Dinar = 100 Para 1918-1941, 1945-
1 Kuna = 100 Banica 1941-1945
1 Kuna = 100 Lipa, 1994-
1 Dinar = 100 Para

Note: Certain listings encompassing issues circulated by various bank and regional authorities are contained in Volume 1.

REVOLUTION OF 1848

CROATIA-SLAVONIA-DALMATIA

1848 ASSIGNAT ISSUE

#A1-A3 arms at upper ctr. Hand sign. of Count Jelacic, governor of the triple kingdom.

		Good	Fine	XF
A1	**25 Forint** 5.5.1848. Grayish blue. (Not issued). Rare.	—	—	—
A2	**100 Forint** 5.5.1848. (Not issued). Reported not confirmed.	—	—	—
A3	**1000 Forint** 5.5.1848. Olive green. (Not issued). Rare.	—	—	—

Note: In 1850 all but 8 pieces were apparently burned. 240 x 170mm.

KINGDOM, WWII AXIS INFLUENCE

NEZAVISNA DRZAVA HRVATSKA

INDEPENDENT STATE OF CROATIA

GOVERNMENT NOTES

1941 ISSUE

#1-5 printer: G&D.

		VG	VF	UNC
1	**50 Kuna** 26.5.1941. Red-brown. Arms at upper l.	1.00	5.00	20.00

		VG	VF	UNC
2	**100 Kuna** 26.5.1941. Blue-gray. Arms at l.	.75	3.00	12.50
3	**500 Kuna** 26.5.1941. Green. Corn sheaves at r. ctr. Arms in unpt. at l. on face, and at l. on back.	4.00	12.50	50.00

		VG	VF	UNC
4	**1000 Kuna** 26.5.1941. Brown. Croatian farmer's wife at l. Arms in unpt. at ctr. Low mountain range across ctr. on back.	.75	3.00	12.50

1941 SECOND ISSUE

		VG	VF	UNC
5	**10 Kuna** 30.8.1941. Olive and brown. Arms at lower r.	.75	3.50	15.00

1942 ISSUE

		VG	VF	UNC
6	**50 Banica** 25.9.1942. Blue and lt. brown. Vertical format. Arms at upper ctr. on back.	.75	3.00	12.50
7	**1 Kuna** 25.9.1942. Dk. blue and brown. Arms at r.	.50	2.00	10.00

		VG	VF	UNC
8	**2 Kune** 25.9.1942. Dk. brown and red-brown. Arms at r.	.50	2.00	10.00

1944 ISSUE

		VG	VF	UNC
9	**20 Kuna** 15.1.1944. Brown on tan unpt. Arms at r. (Not issued).	—	15.00	50.00
10	**50 Kuna** 15.1.1944. Black on green and lt. orange unpt. Arms at r. (Not issued).			
	a. W/o serial #.	—	Unc	200.
	b. W/normal serial #.	—	Unc	500.

HRVATSKA DRZAVNA BANKA

CROATIAN STATE BANK

1943 ISSUE

#11-13 printer: G&D.

		VG	VF	UNC
11	**100 Kuna** 1.9.1943. Dk. blue and brown. Round design of birds and flowers at r. Mother and child in Croatian dress at ctr. on back.	2.00	7.50	25.00
11A	**500 Kuna** 1.9.1943. Lilac and violet. (Not issued).			
	a. Normal serial #.	—	300.	850.
	s. Specimen.	—	—	600.

		VG	VF	UNC
12	**1000 Kuna** 1.9.1943. Dk. brown on yellow and green unpt. Frieze at ctr. Two Croatian women on back.	.50	1.50	6.00
13	**5000 Kuna** 1.9.1943. Red-brown, blue and brown. Hexagonal receptacle at r. Croatian couple on back.	.75	2.25	8.00

		VG	VF	UNC
14	**5000 Kuna** 15.7.1943. Brown on violet and green unpt. Woman in national costume at l. Back blue on lilac, brown and lt. green unpt.	2.00	6.50	22.50

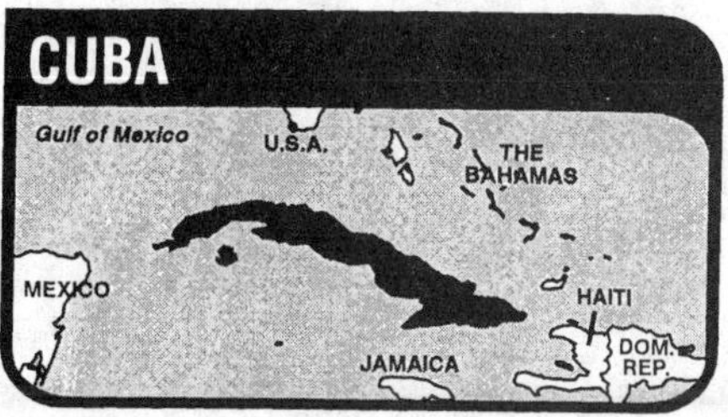

The Republic of Cuba, situated at the northern edge of the Caribbean Sea about 90 miles (145 km.) south of Florida, has an area of 44,218 sq. mi. (114,524 sq. km.) and a population of 11.2 million. Capital: Havana. The Cuban economy is d on the cultivation and refining of sugar, which provides 80 percent of export earnings.

Discovered by Columbus in 1492 and settled by Diego Velasquez in the early 1500s, Cuba remained a Spanish possession until 1898, except for a brief British occupancy in 1762-63. Cuban attempts to gain freedom were crushed, even while Spain was granting independence to its other American possessions. Ten years of warfare, 1868-78, between Spanish troops and Cuban rebels exacted guarantees of right which were never implemented. The final revolt, begun in 1895, evoked American sympathy, and with the aid of U.S. troops independence was proclaimed on May 20, 1902. Fulgencio Batista seized the government in 1952 and established a dictatorship. Opposition to Batista, led by Fidel Castro, drove him into exile on Jan. 1, 1959. A communist-type, 25-member collective leadership headed by Castro was inaugurated in March 1962.

RULERS:

Spanish

MONETARY SYSTEM:

1 Peso = 100 Centavos

1 Peso Convertible = 1 U.S.A. Dollar, 1995-

SPANISH ADMINISTRATION

EL BANCO ESPAÑOL DE LA HABANA

HABANA

1857 ISSUE

#A1-4 allegorical woman seated w/Indian, lion and symbols of commerce at top ctr. Various date and sign. varieties.

		Good	Fine	XF
A1	**50 Pesos** 18xx. Rare.	—	—	—
1	**100 Pesos** 1857-59. Black on blue paper. Rare.	—	—	—
2	**300 Pesos** 1857-59. Black. Rare.	—	—	—

		Good	Fine	XF
3	**500 Pesos** 1.2.1857-59. Black on pink paper. Rare.	—	—	—
4	**1000 Pesos** 1857-59. Black. Rare.	—	—	—

1867 Issue

#5-10 allegorical woman seated w/Indian, lion and symbols of commerce at top ctr. Various date and sign. combinations.

		Good	Fine	XF
5	**25 Pesos** 1867-68. Black on green unpt. Rare.	—	—	—
6	**50 Pesos** 1867-68. Black on tan unpt. Green paper. Rare.	—	—	—
7	**100 Pesos** 1867-68. Black on green unpt. Yellow paper. Rare.	—	—	—

		Good	Fine	XF
8	**300 Pesos** 13.7.1867-69. Black on tan unpt. Lt. purple paper. Rare.	—	—	—
9	**500 Pesos** 1867-68. Black on green unpt. Red paper. Rare.	—	—	—

		Good	Fine	XF
10	**1000 Pesos** 26.8.1867-68. Black on green unpt. White paper. Rare.	—	—	—

1869 Issue

#11-18 seated allegorical figure at upper ctr. Various date and sign. combinations. Printer: NBNC.

		Good	Fine	XF
11	**5 Pesos** 1869-79. Rust and black. Rare.	—	—	—
12	**10 Pesos** 1869-79. Rust and black. Rare.	—	—	—
13	**25 Pesos** 1869-79. Blue and black. Rare.	—	—	—
14	**50 Pesos** 1869-79. Yellow and black. Rare.	—	—	—

		Good	Fine	XF
15	**100 Pesos** 1869-79. Red and black. Rare.	—	—	—
16	**300 Pesos** 1869-79. Brown and black. Rare.	—	—	—
17	**500 Pesos** 1869-79. Tan and black. Rare.	—	—	—

		Good	Fine	XF
18	**1000 Pesos** 1869-79. Green and black. Rare.	—	—	—

1872 First Issue

#19-26 various date and sign. combinations. Uniface. Printer: BWC (w/o imprint).

		Good	Fine	XF
19	**5 Pesos** 1872-87. Black on pink and green unpt. Woman at upper ctr.	600.	2000.	—

		Good	Fine	XF
20	**10 Pesos** 1872-92. Woman by a beehive at upper ctr.	600.	2000.	—

		Good	Fine	XF
21	**25 Pesos** 1872-91. Mercury holding a caduceus at upper ctr.	1000.	3250.	—

		Good	Fine	XF
22	**50 Pesos** 1872-90. Youth carrying a bundle of sugar cane at upper ctr.	1200.	3750.	—
23	**100 Pesos** 1872-87. Black on lt. purple and green unpt. Woman at upper ctr.	—	—	—
24	**300 Pesos** 1872-87. Reported not confirmed.	—	—	—
25	**500 Pesos** 1872-87. Reported not confirmed.	—	—	—

		Good	Fine	XF
26	**1000 Pesos** 1872-87. Portr. Qn. Isabella I of Castile at upper ctr. Rare.	—	—	—

1872 Second Issue

#27 and 28 various date and sign. varieties. Columbus in sight of land on back. Printer: CNBB.

		Good	Fine	XF
27	**1 Peso** 1872-83. Black. Vignette like #11-18. Back black and green.			
	a. 15.6.1872.	30.00	125.	400.
	b. 1.7.1872.	30.00	125.	400.
	c. 15.5.1876.	30.00	125.	400.
	d. 31.5.1879.	30.00	125.	400.
	e. 6.8.1883.	30.00	125.	400.

		Good	Fine	XF
28	**3 Pesos** 1872-83. Black. Vignette like #11-18. Back black and deep orange.			
	a. 15.6.1872.	60.00	300.	1000.
	b. 1.7.1872.	60.00	300.	1000.
	c. 1.12.1877.	60.00	300.	1000.
	d. 7.3.1879. Reported not confirmed.	—	—	—
	e. 31.5.1879.	60.00	300.	1000.
	f. 6.8.1883.	60.00	300.	1000.

1872 Third Issue

#29-31 crowned shields at l. #29-32 allegorical figure seated on back. Printer: NBNC.

		Good	Fine	XF
29	**5 Centavos** 1872-83. Black on lt. tan or yellow paper. Back green.			
	a. 1.7.1872.	2.50	10.00	35.00
	b. ABNC monogram. 15.5.1876.	1.75	7.50	25.00
	c. W/o imprint. 15.5.1876.	—	—	—
	d. 6.8.1883.	1.75	7.50	25.00

		Good	Fine	XF
30	**10 Centavos** 1872-83. Black on lt. tan paper. Back brown.			
	a. 1.7.1872.	3.00	12.00	40.00
	b. Imprint. 15.5.1876.	2.50	10.00	35.00
	c. W/o imprint. 15.5.1876.	2.50	10.00	35.00
	d. 6.8.1883.	2.50	10.00	35.00

		Good	Fine	XF
31	**25 Centavos** 1872-76. Black. Back orange.			
	a. 1.7.1872.	6.00	25.00	85.00
	b. 15.5.1876. Reported not confirmed.	—	—	—

		Good	Fine	XF
32	**50 Centavos** 1872-76. Black. Crowned shield at l. ctr. Back orange.			
	a. 1.7.1872.	8.00	30.00	125.
	b. 15.5.1876.	6.00	25.00	100.

1889 Issue

		Good	Fine	XF
33	**50 Centavos** 28.10.1889. Black on tan paper. Spaniard and Indian at r. Back orange; Noble Havana fountain at ctr. Printer: ABNC.			
	a. W/ counterfoil.	35.00	125.	350.
	b. W/o counterfoil.	10.00	40.00	150.

Cardenas

1860's Issue

		Good	Fine	XF
33A	**10 Pesos** 186x. Rare.	—	—	—
33B	**25 Pesos** 186x. Rare.	—	—	—
33C	**50 Pesos** 186x. Rare.	—	—	—
33D	**100 Pesos** 186x. Rare.	—	—	—
33E	**300 Pesos** 186x. Rare.	—	—	—
33F	**500 Pesos** 186x. Rare.	—	—	—
33G	**1000 Pesos** 186x. Rare.	—	—	—

Matanzas

1860's Issue

#34-38 similar to #11-15. Printer: NBNC.

		Good	Fine	XF
34	**5 Pesos** 186x. Reported not confirmed.	—	—	—

		Good	Fine	XF
35	**10 Pesos** 186x. Lt. blue. Rare.	—	—	—
36	**25 Pesos** 186x. Reported not confirmed.	—	—	—

		Good	Fine	XF
37	**50 Pesos** 186x.			
	a. Issued note. Rare.	—	—	—
	b. Punched hole cancelled. Rare.	—	—	—
38	**100 Pesos** 186x. Reported not confirmed.	—	—	—

Sagua La Grande

1860's Issue

#38A-38G similar to #12-17. Printer: NBNC.

		Good	Fine	XF
38A	**10 Pesos** 186x. Rare.	—	—	—
38B	**25 Pesos** 186x. Rare.	—	—	—
38C	**50 Pesos** 186x. Rare.	—	—	—
38D	**100 Pesos** 186x. Red and black. Rare.	—	—	—
38E	**300 Pesos** 186x. Rare.	—	—	—
38F	**500 Pesos** 186x. Brown and black. Rare.	—	—	—
38G	**1000 Pesos** 186x. Rare.	—	—	—

Bonos del Tesoro

1865 Issue

		Good	Fine	XF
38J	**500 Pesos** 24.9.1865. Black. Arms in unpt. at ctr. Interest-bearing note payable to bearer. Punched hole cancellation at l.	—	—	—

1866 Provisional Issue

#38K and 38L Dominican Republic 1848 issue ovpt. on back for use in Cuba, 1866. Printer: Durand, Baldwin & Co., New York.

		Good	Fine	XF
38K	**20 Pesos** 1866 (- old date 1848). Black on lt. red unpt. Ovpt. on 1 Peso Dominican Republic #6 for use in Cuba.	—	—	—
38L	**50 Pesos** 1866 (- old date 1848). Brown. Ovpt. on 2 Pesos Dominican Republic #7 for use in Cuba.	—	—	—

BILLETE DEL TESORO

1874 ISSUE

#38M and 39N arms in unpt. at ctr.

		Good	Fine	XF
38M	**100 Pesos** 30.6.1874. Black. Interest-bearing note payable to bearer.	—	—	—
38N	**500 Pesos** 30.6.1874. Black. Similar to #38M.	—	—	—

EL TESORO DE LA ISLA DE CUBA

1891 TREASURY NOTE ISSUE

#39-44 almost always found w/o sign. Values are for such notes. Printer: BWC.

		Good	Fine	XF
39	**5 Pesos** 12.8.1891. Black on blue and orange unpt. Winged woman w/trumpet by woman w/book at l.	35.00	100.	250.

		Good	Fine	XF
40	**10 Pesos** 12.8.1891. Black on blue-green unpt. Mercury w/shield at r.	50.00	125.	325.

		Good	Fine	XF
41	**20 Pesos** 12.8.1891. Black on purple and green unpt. Woman seated w/shield at l.	52.50	135.	350.

		Good	Fine	XF
42	**50 Pesos** 12.8.1891. Black on purple and orange unpt. Mercury and youth seated at l.	65.00	175.	450.

		Good	Fine	XF
43	**100 Pesos** 12.8.1891. Black on purple and orange unpt. Young boy seated w/lamb at l., young girl seated at r.	75.00	200.	550.

		Good	Fine	XF
44	**200 Pesos** 12.8.1891. Black on brown and red unpt. Justice standing at l., young farm couple at r.	120.	350.	950.

BANCO ESPAÑOL DE LA ISLA DE CUBA

1896 ISSUE

#45-49 printer: ABNC.

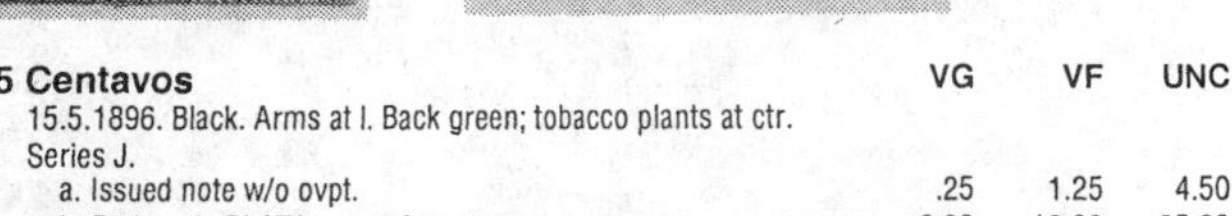

		VG	VF	UNC
45	**5 Centavos** 15.5.1896. Black. Arms at l. Back green; tobacco plants at ctr. Series J.			
	a. Issued note w/o ovpt.	.25	1.25	4.50
	b. Red ovpt: *PLATA* across face on a.	2.00	10.00	35.00

		VG	VF	UNC
46	**50 Centavos** 15.5.1896. Black. Arms at r. Back deep orange; tobacco plants at ctr. Series H.			
	a. Issued note w/o ovpt.	.50	3.00	9.00
	b. Red ovpt: *PLATA* across face on a.	2.50	15.00	45.00

		VG	VF	UNC
47	**1 Peso** 15.5.1896. Black. Arms at ctr. Back blue; Qn. Regent María Cristina at ctr. Series G.			
	a. Issued note w/o ovpt.	1.00	5.00	15.00
	b. Red ovpt: *PLATA* across face on a.	2.50	15.00	45.00

48	5 Pesos	VG	VF	UNC
	1896-97. Black on orange and gold unpt. Woman seated w/bales at ctr. Back brown; arms at ctr.			
	a. Issued note w/o ovpt. 15.5.1896.	.75	3.50	12.50
	b. Ovpt: PLATA in red on back of a. 15.5.1896.	.75	3.50	12.50
	c. W/o ovpt. 15.2.1897.	.75	3.50	12.50

49	10 Pesos	VG	VF	UNC
	15.5.1896. Black on green unpt. Ox cart at top ctr. Back green; arms at ctr.			
	a. Handwritten or hand stamped partially printed date, w/o ovpt.	1.00	5.00	17.50
	b. Handwritten date and month, handstamped sign.	75.00	200.	—
	c. Printed date, w/o ovpt.	1.00	4.00	12.50
	d. Printed date, ovpt: red *PLATA* on back of c.	1.00	5.00	15.00

#50-51B printer: BWC (w/o imprint).

50	50 Pesos	VG	VF	UNC
	15.5.1896. Black on red and green unpt. Allegorical woman at l.			
	a. Issued note w/o ovpt.	27.50	65.00	175.
	b. Ovpt: red PLATA on back of a.	20.00	50.00	150.
51	**100 Pesos**			
	15.5.1896. Black on orange and green unpt. Woman and cow at l. Back orange and green.	75.00	200.	750.
51A	**500 Pesos**			
	15.5.1896. Black on orange and blue unpt. Winged woman and spear at l. Columbus at ctr. on back.	—	—	—

51B	1000 Pesos	VG	VF	UNC
	15.5.1896. Black on brown and gray unpt. Justice w/scales at l. Back blue and brown. Rare.	—	—	—

1897 Issue

#52-53 printer: ABNC.

Note: For 5 Pesos dated 1897, see #48c.

52	10 Centavos	VG	VF	UNC
	15.2.1897. Black. Arms at r. Back brown; ship at ctr. Series K.	.25	1.50	7.50

53	20 Centavos	VG	VF	UNC
	15.2.1897. Black. Arms at ctr. Back gray; harvesting sugar cane at ctr. Series I.	.25	1.50	7.50

1868-76 Revolution

La Republica de Cuba

1869 Issue

#54-58 uniface.

54	50 Centavos	Good	Fine	XF
	1869. Black on gray unpt. Flag at ctr.	6.00	15.00	50.00

#55-60 day and month handwritten on some notes.

55	1 Peso	Good	Fine	XF
	1869. Black. Arms at upper l.			
	a. W/o sign. Red seal.	8.00	25.00	65.00
	b. As a. W/o red seal.	10.00	35.00	90.00
	c. Signed note, sign. stamped.	35.00	125.	275.

#56-58 draped shield at l.

		Good	Fine	XF
56	**5 Pesos**			
	1869. Black.			
	a. W/o sign.	12.50	37.50	125.
	b. Hand sign.	25.00	75.00	225.
	c. Stamped sign.	25.00	75.00	225.

		Good	Fine	XF
57	**10 Pesos**			
	1869. Black. Like #56.			
	a. W/o sign.	60.00	175.	550.
	b. Hand sign. of Céspedes.	125.	500.	1000.
58	**50 Pesos**			
	1869. Black. Like #56. Rare.	—	—	—

		Good	Fine	XF
59	**500 Pesos**			
	8.9.1869. Black. Angel at l., 3 women seated at r., eagle at lower ctr.	500.	1500.	—

		Good	Fine	XF
60	**1000 Pesos**			
	6.9.1869. Red and brown. Like #59.	250.	950.	1850.

JUNTA CENTRAL REPUBLICANA DE CUBA Y PUERTO RICO

1869 ISSUE

#61-64 issued by a military revolutionist group located in New York City. Uniface.

		Good	Fine	XF
61	**1 Peso**			
	17.8.1869. Black.	10.00	50.00	150.

		Good	Fine	XF
62	**5 Pesos**			
	17.8.1869. Blue. Like #61.	60.00	250.	650.
63	**10 Pesos**			
	17.8.1869. Green. Like #61.	450.	1500.	—
64	**20 Pesos**			
	17.8.1869. Red. Like #61. Rare.	—	—	—

REPUBLIC

BANCO NACIONAL DE CUBA

NATIONAL BANK OF CUBA

1905 FIRST ISSUE

Peso system

#65-68 back green; fortress at ctr. (Not issued). Printer: ABNC.

		VG	VF	UNC
65	**1 Peso**			
	ND (1905). Black. Portr. D. Méndez Capote at ctr. Rare.	—	—	—

		VG	VF	UNC
66	**2 Pesos**			
	ND (1905). Black. Portr. M. Gomez at r. Rare.	—	—	—

NOTICE

Readers with unlisted dates, signature varieties, etc. are invited to submit photocopies or, high resolution (300 dpi, 100% size) scans of their notes to: Standard Catalog of World Paper Money, 700 East State St. Iola, WI 54990-0001, or E-Mail: george.cuhaj@fwpubs.com.

#67-68 text on face: ***EN ORO DEL CUÑO ESPAÑOL PAGARA AL PORTADOR A LA PRESENTACION.***

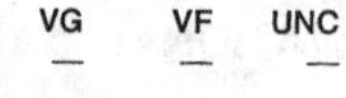

		VG	VF	UNC
67	**5 Pesos** ND (1905). Black. Portr. J. Montes at l. Rare.	—	—	—

		VG	VF	UNC
68	**10 Pesos** ND (1905). Black. Portr. T. Estrada Palma at ctr. Rare.	—	—	—

1905 Second Issue

#68A-68B text on face: ***ORO, O SU EQUIVALENTE EN MONEDA DE LOS E.U. DE AMERICA, PAGARA AL PORTADOR A LA VISTA.*** **Printer: ABNC.**

		VG	VF	UNC
68A	**1 Dollar** ND (ca.1905). Black. Similar to #65. Proof.	—	—	—
68B	**2 Dollars** ND (ca.1905). Black. Similar to #66. Proof.	—	—	—
68C	**5 Dollars** ND (ca.1905). Black. Similar to #67. Proof.	—	—	—
68D	**10 Dollars** ND (ca.1905). Black. Similar to #68. Proof.	—	—	—

República de Cuba

Certificados de Plata (Silver Certificates)

#69-73 and 75-76A arms at ctr. on back.

#69-74 printer: BEP, United States.

		Good	Fine	XF
69	**1 Peso** 1934-49. Black on blue unpt. Port. J. Martí at ctr. Back blue.			
	a. 1934.	4.00	20.00	75.00
	b. 1936.	4.00	32.50	125.
	c. 1936A.	4.00	25.00	90.00
	d. 1938.	4.00	18.00	70.00
	e. 1943.	4.00	18.00	70.00
	f. 1945.	4.00	18.00	70.00
	g. 1948.	4.00	18.00	70.00
	h. 1949.	4.00	22.50	85.00

		Good	Fine	XF
70	**5 Pesos** 1934-49. Black on orange unpt. Portr. M. M. Gomez at ctr. Back blue.			
	a. 1934.	15.00	45.00	175.
	b. 1936.	15.00	45.00	175.
	c. 1936A.	15.00	45.00	175.
	d. 1938.	15.00	40.00	160.
	e. 1943.	15.00	45.00	165.
	f. 1945.	15.00	40.00	160.
	g. 1948.	15.00	40.00	160.
	h. 1949.	15.00	45.00	175.

		Good	Fine	XF
71	**10 Pesos** 1934-48. Black on brown unpt. Portr. C. Manuel de Céspedes at ctr. Back brown.			
	a. 1934.	25.00	82.50	300.
	b. 1936.	25.00	82.50	300.
	c. 1936A.	25.00	82.50	300.
	d. 1938.	25.00	80.00	300.
	e. 1943.	25.00	82.50	300.
	f. 1945.	25.00	80.00	300.
	g. 1948.	25.00	80.00	300.

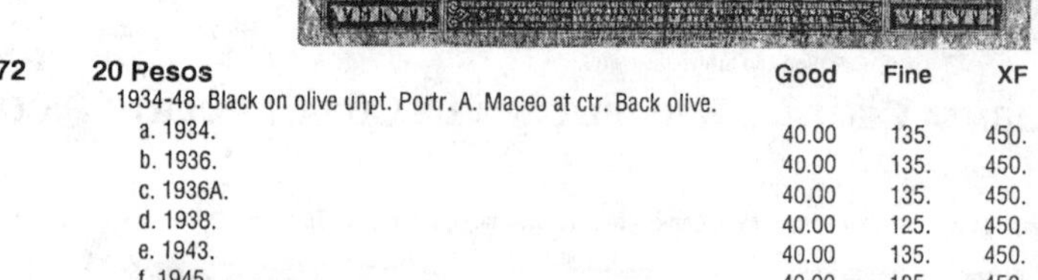

		Good	Fine	XF
72	**20 Pesos** 1934-48. Black on olive unpt. Portr. A. Maceo at ctr. Back olive.			
	a. 1934.	40.00	135.	450.
	b. 1936.	40.00	135.	450.
	c. 1936A.	40.00	135.	450.
	d. 1938.	40.00	125.	450.
	e. 1943.	40.00	135.	450.
	f. 1945.	40.00	125.	450.
	g. 1948.	40.00	125.	450.

		Good	Fine	XF
73	**50 Pesos** 1934-48. Black on lt. orange unpt. Portr. Calixto García Iñíguez ctr. Back lt. orange.			
	a. 1934.	100.	300.	900.
	b. 1936.	100.	300.	900.
	c. 1936A.	100.	300.	900.
	d. 1938.	100.	300.	900.
	e. 1943.	100.	300.	900.
	f. 1948.	100.	300.	900.

		Good	Fine	XF
74	**100 Pesos**			
	1936-48. Black on purple unpt. Portr. F. Aguilera at ctr. Back purple; capitol at l., cathedral at r.			
	a. 1936.	125.	400.	1250.
	b. 1938.	125.	400.	1250.
	c. 1943.	125.	400.	1250.
	d. 1945.	125.	400.	1250.
	e. 1948.	125.	400.	1250.

#75-76A printer: ABNC.

75	**500 Pesos**			
	1944. Black on red and violet unpt. Portr. S. Betancourt at ctr. Back red. Specimen.			

		Good	Fine	XF
75A	**500 Pesos**			
	1947. Similar to #75, but w/*LEY NO. 5 DE 2 DE MAYO DE 1942* beneath l. sign. title.			
	a. Issued note. Rare.	—	—	—
	s. Specimen.	—	—	—
76	**1000 Pesos**			
	1944; 1945. Black on dk. green unpt. Portr. T. E. Palma at ctr. Back green.			
	a. Issued note. 1944.	1650.	3350.	—
	b. Issued note. 1945.	750.	1500.	3750.
	s. Specimen. 1944; 1945.	—	—	1500.
76A	**1000 Pesos**			
	1947. Similar to #76, but w/*LEY NO. 5 DE 2 DE MAYO DE 1942* beneath l. sign. title.			
	a. Issued note.	1250.	2500.	6000.
	s. Specimen.	—	—	—

BANCO NACIONAL DE CUBA (RESUMED)

1949-50 ISSUE

#77-85 portr. at ctr. Arms. at ctr. on back. \ Printer: ABNC.

		VG	VF	UNC
77	**1 Peso**			
	1949; 1960. Black on blue unpt. Portr. J. Martí at ctr. Back blue.			
	a. Red serial #. 1949.	.50	4.00	20.00
	b. Black serial #. 1960.	.75	4.50	22.50
	s1. As a. Specimen ovpt: *MUESTRA.*	—	—	160.
	s2. As b. Specimen ovpt: *MUESTRA.*	—	—	150.

		VG	VF	UNC
78	**5 Pesos**			
	1949-50. Black on orange unpt. Portr. M. Gómez at ctr. Back orange.			
	a. 1949.	2.00	10.00	50.00
	b. 1950.	2.00	12.00	55.00
	s1. As a. Specimen ovpt: *MUESTRA.*	—	—	160.
	s2. As b. Specimen ovpt: *MUESTRA.*	—	—	150.

		VG	VF	UNC
79	**10 Pesos**			
	1949; 1960. Black on brown unpt. Portr. C. de Céspedes at ctr. Back brown.			
	a. Red serial #. 1949.	.50	4.00	20.00
	b. Black serial #. 1960.	.50	4.00	20.00
	s1. As a. Specimen ovpt: *MUESTRA.*	—	—	160.
	s2. As b. Specimen ovpt: *MUESTRA.*	—	—	100.

		VG	VF	UNC
80	**20 Pesos**			
	1949-60. Black on olive unpt. Portr. A. Maceo at ctr. Back olive.			
	a. Red serial #. 1949.	.75	5.00	22.50
	b. Red serial #. 1958.	.50	4.00	20.00
	c. Black serial #. 1960.	.50	4.00	20.00
	s1. As a. Specimen ovpt: *MUESTRA.*	—	—	150.
	s2. As b. Specimen ovpt: *MUESTRA.*	—	—	150.
	s3. As c. Specimen ovpt: *MUESTRA.*	—	—	125.

		VG	VF	UNC
81	**50 Pesos**			
	1950-60. Black on yellow unpt. Portr. Calixto García Iñiguez ctr. Back yellow-orange.			
	a. Red serial #. 1950.	1.00	6.00	30.00
	b. Red serial #. 1958.	1.00	6.00	30.00
	c. Black serial #. 1960.	2.00	10.00	55.00
	s1. As a. Specimen ovpt: *MUESTRA.*	—	—	160.
	s2. As b. Specimen ovpt: *MUESTRA.*	—	—	160.
	s3. As c. Specimen ovpt: *MUESTRA.*	—	—	150.

		VG	VF	UNC
82	**100 Pesos**			
	1950-58. Black on purple unpt. Portr. F. Aguilera at ctr. Red serial #. Back purple.			
	a. 1950.	2.00	10.00	55.00
	b. 1954.	1.00	6.00	30.00
	c. 1958.	2.00	10.00	55.00
	s1. As a. Specimen ovpt: *MUESTRA.*	—	—	160.
	s2. As b. Specimen ovpt: *MUESTRA.*	—	—	160.
	s3. As c. Specimen ovpt: *MUESTRA.*	—	—	150.

NOTICE

Readers with unlisted dates, signature varieties, etc. are invited to submit photocopies or, high resolution (300 dpi, 100% size) scans of their notes to: Standard Catalog of World Paper Money, 700 East State St. Iola, WI 54990-0001, or E-Mail: george.cuhaj@fwpubs.com.

		VG	VF	UNC
83	**500 Pesos** 1950. Black on red unpt. Portr. S. Cisneros Betancourt at ctr. Back red.	15.00	50.00	200.

		VG	VF	UNC
84	**1000 Pesos** 1950. Black on dk. green unpt. Portr. T. Estrada Palma at ctr. Back green.	5.00	20.00	75.00

		VG	VF	UNC
85	**10,000 Pesos** 1950. Black on olive unpt. Portr. I. Agramonte at ctr. Back olive.			
	a. Issued note (2 known). Rare.	—	—	—
	p. Proofs, face and back.	—	—	850.
	s. Specimen.	—	—	3000.

1953 Commemorative Issue

#86, Centennial Birth of José Martí

		VG	VF	UNC
86	**1 Peso** 1953. Black on blue unpt. Portr. J. Martí at lower l. *MANIFIESTO DE MONTECRISTI 1895* at ctr. Back blue; map of Cuba over arms at ctr., commemorative dates at l. Printer: ABNC.			
	a. Issued note.	10.00	45.00	150.
	s. Specimen.	—	—	160.

1956 Issue

#87-88 printer: TDLR.

Replacement notes #87 and 88: Small crosslet design in place of prefix letter.

		VG	VF	UNC
87	**1 Peso** 1956-58. Black on blue unpt. Monument at ctr., portr. J. Martí at r. Back blue; farm scene at l., arms at ctr., factory at r.			
	a. 1956.	.75	5.00	25.00
	b. 1957.	.75	4.00	20.00
	c. 1958.	.75	4.00	20.00
	s1. As a. Specimen perforated: *SPECIMEN.*	—	—	160.
	s2. As b. Specimen perforated: *SPECIMEN.*	—	—	160.

		VG	VF	UNC
88	**10 Pesos** 1956-60. Black on brown unpt. Ruins of the Demajagua Sugar Mill, portr. C. de Céspedes at r. Back brown; cows at l., arms at ctr., milk bottling factory at r.			
	a. 1956.	.50	4.00	30.00
	b. 1958.	.50	4.00	20.00
	c. 1960.	.50	3.00	15.00
	s1. As a. Specimen perforated: *SPECIMEN.*	—	—	160.
	s2. As b. Specimen perforated: *SPECIMEN.*	—	—	160.
	s3. As c. Specimen perforated: *SPECIMEN.*	—	—	150.

1958-60 Issues

Replacement notes #90-91: Small crosslet design in place of prefix letter.

		VG	VF	UNC
90	**1 Peso** 1959. Black on blue unpt. J. Martí addressing assembly at ctr., portr. J. Martí at r. Back blue; farm scene at l., arms at ctr., factory at r. Printer: TDLR.			
	a. Issued note.	.75	4.00	20.00
	s. Specimen perforated: *SPECIMEN.*	—	—	250.
91	**5 Pesos** 1958-60. Black on green unpt. Riders on horseback at ctr., Portr. M. Gómez at r. Back green; plantation at l., arms at ctr., cigar factory at r. Printer: TDLR.			
	a. 1958.	1.00	5.00	25.00
	b. 1959. (Not issued).	—	—	—
	c. 1960.	1.00	5.00	25.00
	s1. As a. Specimen perforated: *SPECIMEN.*	—	—	160.
	s2. As c. Specimen perforated: *SPECIMEN.*	—	—	150.

		VG	VF	UNC
92	**5 Pesos** 1960. Black on green unpt. Portr. M. Gómez at ctr. Arms at ctr. on green back. Printer: ABNC.			
	a. Issued note.	.75	4.00	20.00
	s. Specimen perforated: *SPECIMEN.*	—	—	150.
93	**100 Pesos** 1959-60. Black on orange unpt. Portr. F. Aguilera at ctr. Black serial #. Arms at ctr. on orange back. Printer: ABNC.			
	a. 1959.	.50	3.00	15.00
	s1. As a. Specimen perforated: *SPECIMEN.*	—	—	160.
	s2. Specimen perforated: *SPECIMEN.* 1960.	—	—	250.

Note: Several examples of #93s2 in "issued" form (w/serial #) are verified.

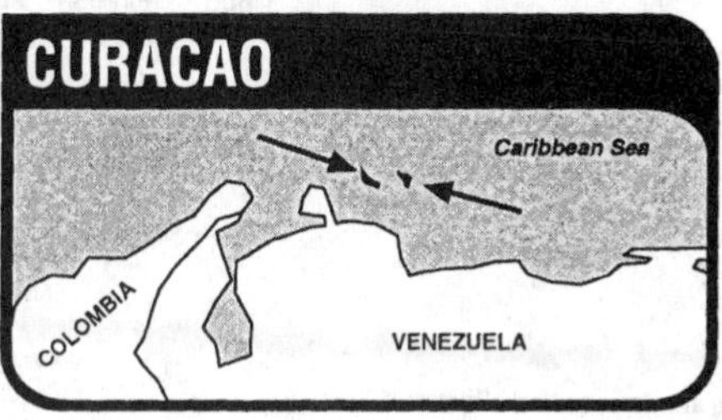

The island of Curaçao, the largest of the Netherlands Antilles, is an autonomous part of the Kingdom of the Netherlands located in the Caribbean Sea 40 miles off the coast of Venezuela. It has an area of 173 sq. mi. (472 sq. km.) and a population of 150,000. Capital: Willemstad. The chief industries are the refining of crude oil imported from Venezuela and Colombia, and tourism. Petroleum products, salt, phosphates and cattle are exported.

Curaçao was discovered by Spanish navigator Alonso de Ojeda in 1499 and was settled by Spain in 1527. The Dutch West India Company took the island from Spain in 1634 and administered it until 1787, when it was surrendered to the crown. The Dutch held it thereafter except for two periods during the Napoleonic Wars, 1800-1803 and 1807-1816, when it was occupied by the British. During World War II, Curaçao refined 60 percent of the oil used by the Allies; the refineries were protected by U.S. forces after Germany invaded the Netherlands in 1940.

RULERS:
Durch:

MONETARY SYSTEM:
1 Gulden = 100 Cents

DUTCH ADMINISTRATION

CURAÇAOSCHE BANK

1855 ISSUE

#A11-A14 locally printed. Ornate border, value at lower ctr.

		Good	Fine	XF
A11	**5 Gulden** 1855. Black. Rare.	—	—	—
A12	**10 Gulden** 1855. Black. Rare.	—	—	—
A13	**25 Gulden** 1855. Black. Rare.	—	—	—

		Good	Fine	XF
A14	**50 Gulden** 1855. Black. Rare.	—	—	—

1879 ISSUE

#A31-A34 black. Ornate border. Printer: JEZ.

		Good	Fine	XF
A31	**5 Gulden** 1879. Black on orange unpt. Rare.	—	—	—
A32	**10 Gulden** 1879. Black on green unpt. Rare.	—	—	—

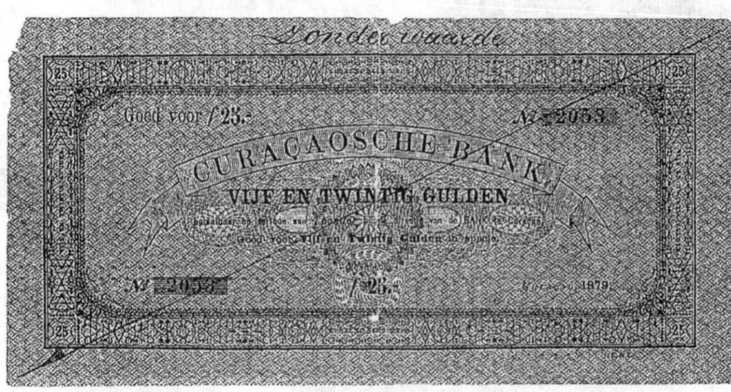

		Good	Fine	XF
A33	**25 Gulden** 1879. Black on red-brown unpt. Rare.	—	—	—

		Good	Fine	XF
A34	**50 Gulden** 1879. Black on blue unpt. Rare.	—	—	—

1892 ISSUE

#A51-A54 uniface. Handsigned on back. Printer: HBNC.

		Good	Fine	XF
A51	**25 Centen** 1892. Black on green unpt. Rare.	—	—	—
A52	**50 Centen** 1892. Black on blue unpt. Rare.	—	—	—
A53	**1 Gulden** 1892. Black on yellow unpt. Rare.	—	—	—
A54	**2 1/2 Gulden** 1892. Black on red unpt. Rare.	—	—	—

1900s ISSUE

		Good	Fine	XF
1	**5 Gulden** Ca. 1900.	—	—	—
2	**10 Gulden** Ca. 1900. Rare.	—	—	—
3	**25 Gulden** Ca. 1900. Rare.	—	—	—
4	**50 Gulden** Ca. 1900. Rare.	—	—	—
5	**100 Gulden** Ca. 1900. Rare.	—	—	—
6	**250 Gulden** Ca. 1900. Rare.	—	—	—
7	**500 Gulden** Ca. 1900. Rare.	—	—	—

1918; 1920 ISSUE

		Good	Fine	XF
7A	**1 Gulden** ND; 1918. Black on yellow unpt.	100.	475.	—

		Good	Fine	XF
7B	**2 1/2 Gulden** ND (ca.1918). Black on red unpt.	—	—	—

		Good	Fine	XF
7C	**2 1/2 Gulden** 1.7.1918; 1920. Red and yellow.			
	a. Issued note.	200.	750.	—
	r. Unsigned remainder.	—	125.	250.

		Good	Fine	XF
7E	**5 Gulden** 1918; 1920. Rare.	—	—	—

1920 ISSUE

		Good	Fine	XF
7F	**1 Gulden** 1920. Black on yellow unpt.	—	—	—
7G	**10 Gulden** 1920. Like #7E. Rare.	—	—	—

1925 ISSUE

		Good	Fine	XF
8	**5 Gulden** 1925. Purple. City view at lower ctr.	300.	1250.	—
9	**10 Gulden** 1925. Like #8. Rare.	—	—	—
11	**50 Gulden** 1925. Rare.	—	—	—
12	**100 Gulden** 1925. Rare.	—	—	—
13	**250 Gulden** 1925. Rare.	—	—	—
14	**500 Gulden** 1925. Rare.	—	—	—

1930 ISSUE

#15-21 woman seated w/scroll and flag at l. Arms on back. Printer: JEZ.

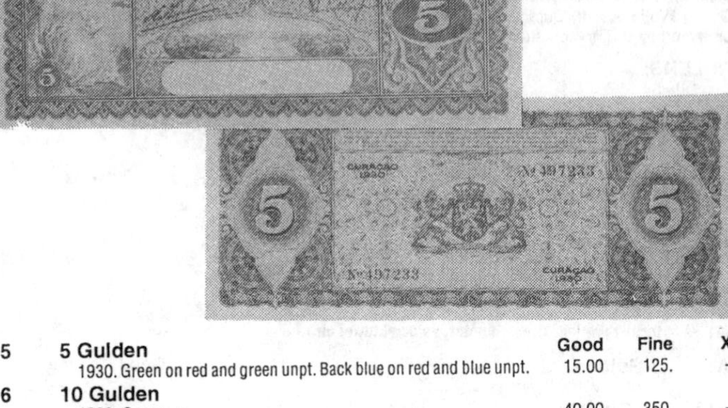

		Good	Fine	XF
15	**5 Gulden** 1930. Green on red and green unpt. Back blue on red and blue unpt.	15.00	125.	—
16	**10 Gulden** 1930. Green.	40.00	350.	—
17	**25 Gulden** 1930. Green.	—	—	—
18	**50 Gulden** 1930. Green. Back brown.	—	—	—
19	**100 Gulden** 1930. Green.	—	—	—
20	**250 Gulden** 1930. Green. Back olive-green.	—	—	—
21	**500 Gulden** 1930. Green. Back red.	—	—	—

1939 ISSUE

#22-24 printer: JEZ.

		Good	Fine	XF
22	**5 Gulden** 1939. Green. Coastline city at ctr. Back blue.	5.00	40.00	200.

		Good	Fine	XF
23	**10 Gulden** 1939. Green. Ships dockside at ctr.	12.50	100.	—
24	**25 Gulden** 1939.	40.00	350.	—

1943 ISSUE

#25-27 similar to #22-24 but w/printing in wmk. area at lower ctr. Printer: ABNC (w/o imprint).

		Good	Fine	XF
25	**5 Gulden** 1943. Green. Coastline city at ctr. Back blue and m/c.	10.00	60.00	25
26	**10 Gulden** 1943. Green. Ships dockside at ctr. Back green and m/c.	15.00	80.00	37
27	**25 Gulden** 1943. Green. View of city at ctr. Back black and m/c.	35.00	150.	50

#28 *Deleted.*

1948 ISSUE

#29-32 arms at ctr. on back. Printer: JEZ.

		Good	Fine	XF
29	**5 Gulden** 1948. Green. Bldg. on the waterfront at ctr. Back blue.	7.50	50.00	250.
30	**10 Gulden** 1948. Green. Bldg. w/tower at ctr.	12.50	75.00	350.
31	**50 Gulden** 1948. Green. Bldg. w/flag at ctr. Back olive-brown.	40.00	250.	—
32	**100 Gulden** 1948. Green. View of city at ctr. Back purple.	60.00	325.	—

CURACAO MUNTBILJETTEN

CURRENCY NOTES

1942 ISSUE

#35-36 printer: ABNC.

		VG	VF	UNC
35	**1 Gulden** 1942; 1947. Red. Mercury seated between ships at ctr. Arms at ctr. on back. a. 1942. 2 sign. var.	2.50	20.00	100.
	b. 1947.	3.00	25.00	135.

		VG	VF	UNC
36	**2 1/2 Gulden** 1942. Blue. Ship at dockside at ctr. Back like #35.	5.00	30.00	225.

CURAÇAOSCHE BANK (RESUMED)

1954 ISSUE

#38-44 woman seated w/scroll and flag at l. Title: *NEDERLANDSE ANTILLEN* over crowned supported arms at ctr. on back. Printer: JEZ.

		VG	VF	UNC
38	**5 Gulden** 25.11.1954. Blue. View of Curacao at ctr.	6.00	35.00	200.

		VG	VF	UNC
39	**10 Gulden** 25.11.1954. Green. Beach in Aruba at ctr.	10.00	50.00	250.
40	**25 Gulden** 25.11.1954. Black-gray. View of Bonaire at ctr.	15.00	75.00	300.
41	**50 Gulden** 25.11.1954. Red-brown. Coastline city of St. Maarten at ctr.	50.00	250.	—
42	**100 Gulden** 25.11.1954. Violet. Monument in St. Eustatius at ctr.	75.00	350.	—

		VG	VF	UNC
43	**250 Gulden** 25.11.1954. Olive. Boats on the beach in Saba at ctr.	—	—	—
44	**500 Gulden** 25.11.1954. Red. Oil refinery in Curacao at ctr.	—	—	—

1958 ISSUE

		VG	VF	UNC
45	**5 Gulden** 1958. Blue. Like #38.	8.00	25.00	125.
46	**10 Gulden** 1958. Green. Like #39.	10.00	40.00	150.

		VG	VF	UNC
47	**25 Gulden** 1958. Black-gray. Like #40.	17.50	75.00	300.
48	**50 Gulden** 1958. Brown. Like #41.	35.00	175.	—
49	**100 Gulden** 1958. Violet. Like #42.	70.00	325.	—
50	**250 Gulden** 1958. Olive. Like #43.	—	—	—

1960 ISSUE

		VG	VF	UNC
51	**5 Gulden** 1960. Blue. Like #38.	7.00	20.00	100.
52	**10 Gulden** 1960. Green. Like #39.	10.00	25.00	120.
53	**25 Gulden** 1960. Black-gray. Like #40.	15.00	60.00	250.
54	**50 Gulden** 1960. Brown. Like #41.	35.00	175.	—

		VG	VF	UNC
55	**100 Gulden** 1960. Violet. Like #42.	70.00	325.	—

Note: For later issues see Netherlands Antilles in Vol. 3.

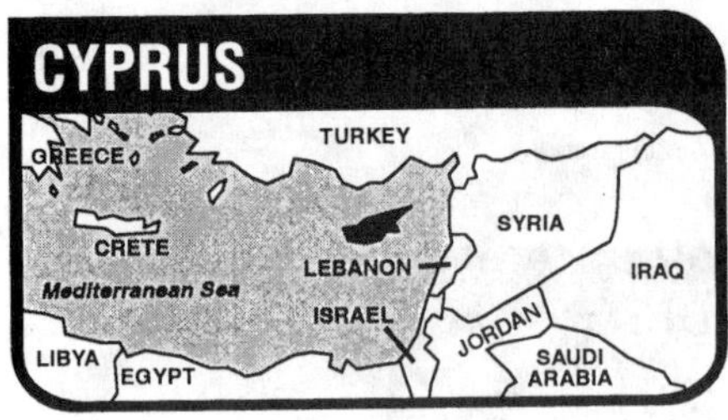

The Republic of Cyprus, a member of the European Commonwealth and Council, lies in the eastern Mediterranean Sea 44 miles (71 km.) south of Turkey and 60 miles (97 km.) west of Syria. It is the third largest island in the Mediterranean Sea, having an area if 3,572 sq. mi. (9,251 sq. km.) and a population of 757,000. Capital: Nicosia. Agriculture and mining are the chief industries. Asbestos, copper, citrus fruit, iron pyrites and potatoes are exported.

The importance of Cyprus dates from the Bronze Age when it was desired as a principal souce of copper (from which the island derived its name) and as a strategic trading center. Its role as an international marketplace made it a prime disseminator of the then prevalent cultures, a role that still influences the civilization of Western man. Because of its fortuitous position and influential role, Cyprus was conquered by a succession of empires; the Assyrian, Egyptian, Persian, Macedonian, Ptolemaic, Roman and Byzantine. It was taken from Isaac Comnenus by Richard the Lion-Hearted in 1191, sold to the Knights Templars, conquered by Venice and Turkey, and made a crown colony of Britain in 1925. Finally on Aug. 16, 1960, it became an independent republic.

In 1964, the ethnic Turks, who favor partition of Cyprus into separate Greek and Turkish states, withdrew from active participation in the government. Turkish forces invaded Cyprus in 1974 and gained control of 40 percent of the island. In 1975, Turkish Cypriots proclaimed their own Federated state in northern Cyprus. The UN held numerous discussions from 1985-92, without any results towards unification.

The president is Chief of State and Head of Government.

RULERS:

British

MONETARY SYSTEM:

1 Shilling = 9 Piastres
1 Pound = 20 Shillings to 1963
1 Shilling = 50 Mils
1 Pound = 1000 Mils, 1963-83
1 Pound = 100 Cents, 1983-

BRITISH ADMINISTRATION

GOVERNMENT OF CYPRUS

1914 FIRST ISSUE

		Good	Fine	XF
1	**1 Pound** 10.9.1914. Black. Arms at ctr.	—	—	—

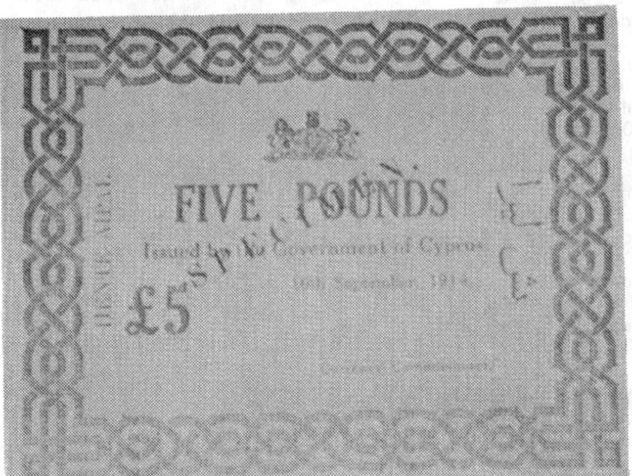

		Good	Fine	XF
2	**5 Pounds** 10.9.1914. Red. Arms at upper ctr. Rare.	—	—	—

1914 SECOND ISSUE

		Good	Fine	XF
3	**5 Shillings** 30.10.1914; 6.11.1914. Blue. Portr. Kg. George V at l. Rare.	—	—	—
4	**10 Shillings** 30.10.1914; 6.11.1914. Green. Portr. Kg. George V at l. Uniface. Rare.	—	—	—
5	**1 Pound** 30.10.1914; 6.11.1914. Black. Portr. Kg. George V at ctr. Rare.	—	—	—
6	**5 Pounds** 30.10.1914; 6.11.1914; 1.9.1916. Red-brown. Portr. Kg. George V at ctr. Rare.	—	—	—

1917 ISSUE

		Good	Fine	XF
7	**5 Shillings** 1.12.1917; 1.3.1918. Brown on blue and gray unpt. Portr. Kg. George V at ctr.	250.	1000.	—

		Good	Fine	XF
8	**10 Shillings** 30.6.1917; 1.3.1918; 1.4.1922. Blue. Portr. Kg. George at top ctr. Uniface.	300.	1250.	—

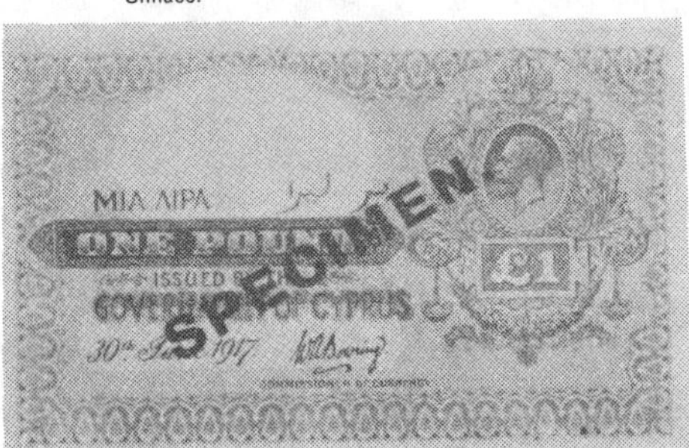

		Good	Fine	XF
9	**1 Pound** 1917-28. Purple on blue and green unpt. Portr. Kg. George V at r. Uniface.			
	a. Date at l. 30.6.1917-1.7.1925.	250.	1000.	—
	b. Date at ctr. 1.4.1926; 1.5.1926; 1.7.1927; 1.10.1928.	250.	1000.	—

		Good	Fine	XF
10	**10 Pounds** 30.6.1917; 1.9.1919. Red. Portr. Kg. George V at r. Rare.	—	—	—

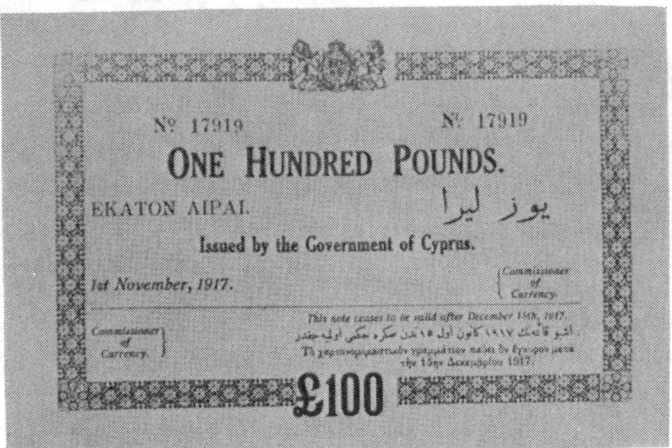

		Good	Fine	XF
11	**100 Pounds** 1.11.1917. Arms in upper frame at ctr. (Not issued). Rare.	—	—	—

1919 EMERGENCY ISSUE

		Good	Fine	XF
12	**1 Shilling** ND (12.11.1919).			
	a. Printed on 1/3 cut piece of #7 (- old date 1918). Rare.	—	—	—
	p. Printer's proof of ovpt. text for back of #7. 38 x 64mm. 1.11.1919. Rare.	—	—	—
13	**2 Shillings** 1.11.1919. Printer's proof. 42 x 78mm. Rare.	—	—	—

1920; 1926 ISSUE

#14-16 printer: TDLR.

		Good	Fine	XF
14	**1 Shilling** 1.3.1920. Dk. green. Portr. Kg. George V at r. Back blue.	200.	800.	—

15 **2 Shillings** — Good 300. · Fine 1250. · XF —
1.3.1920. Dk. red on blue unpt., green border. Portr. Kg. George V at ctr. Back green.

6 **5 Pounds** — Good — · Fine — · XF —
1.8.1926; 1.11.1927. Green. Portr. Kg. George V at r. Uniface.

930; 1933 ISSUE

7-19 w/text: ***GOVERNMENT OF CYPRUS*** **and arms on back.**

7 **10 Shillings** — Good 150. · Fine 600. · XF 2000.
1.8.1933; 1.9.1934; 2.1.1936. Gray and violet. Portr. Kg. George V at top ctr. Back violet.

8 **1 Pound** — Good 125. · Fine 500. · XF 1250.
2.1.1930; 1.9.1934; 3.9.1935; 2.1.1936. Gray-violet and brown. Portr. Kg. George V at upper r.

5 Pounds — Good 300. · Fine 1000. · XF —
2.1.1930; 2.1.1936. Green. Portr. Kg. George V at r.

937-39 ISSUE

-25 various date and sign. varieties.

1 Shilling — VG 10.00 · VF 45.00 · UNC 100.
3.1.1939-25.8.1947. Brown and green. Portr. Kg. George VI at ctr. Back red, green and blue.

2 Shillings — VG 20.00 · VF 100. · UNC 450.
3.1.1939-25.8.1947. Green and violet. Similar to #20. Back purple and violet.

22 **5 Shillings** — VG 15.00 · VF 75.00 · UNC 350.
3.1.1939-1.11.1950. Brown-violet and blue. Portr. Kg. George VI at ctr. Values in Greek and Arabic characters. Back red and purple.

#23-25 printer: TDLR.

23 **10 Shillings** — VG 35.00 · VF 125. · UNC 600.
12.5.1937-1.11.1950. Maroon on pink and olive unpt. Portr. Kg. George VI at top ctr. Values in Greek and Arabic characters.

24 **1 Pound** — VG 25.00 · VF 100. · UNC 400.
12.5.1937-30.9.1951. Brown on green unpt. Portr. Kg. George VI at upper r. Back brown.

25 **5 Pounds** — VG 100. · VF 500. · UNC 1500.
1.9.1938-30.9.1951. Green. Portr. Kg. George VI at upper r. Values in Greek and Arabic characters.

1943 PROVISIONAL ISSUE

Note: Previously listed variety #26b (ex #23b), back w/ovpt: *3* at lower l. and upper r. corners only; also lg. *3* at ctr., is now believed to be altered from #26.

26 **3 Piastres on 1 Shilling** — VG 75.00 · VF 200. · UNC 550.
ND (1943 - old date 30.8.1941). Brown and green. Ovpt. on #20: *THREE PIASTRES* in English and Greek, *3* in all 4 corners on face; lg. *3* at ctr., sm. *3* in all four corners on back.

27 **3 Piastres** — VG 50.00 · VF 125. · UNC 350.
1.3.1943. Brown on green. Ovpt: *THREE PIASTRES* in English and Greek on 2/5 cut of #20.

1943 REGULAR ISSUE

		VG	VF	UNC
28	**3 Piastres**			
	1943-44. Blue. Portr. Kg. George VI at ctr.			
	a. 18.6.1943; 6.4.1944.	2.00	10.00	40.00
	b. 15.9.1944; 25.9.1944. (Not issued).	—	—	—

1952-53 Issues

		VG	VF	UNC
29	**5 Shillings**			
	1.2.1952. Brown-violet and blue. Portr. Kg. George VI at ctr. Similar to #22 but values in Greek and modern Turkish characters.	25.00	125.	425.

		VG	VF	UNC
30	**5 Shillings**			
	1.9.1952. Brown-violet and blue. Portr. Qn. Elizabeth II at ctr.	20.00	100.	475.

		VG	VF	UNC
31	**10 Shillings**			
	1.9.1953; 31.7.1954. Maroon on pink and olive unpt. Portr. Kg. George VI at top ctr. Similar to #23 but values in Greek and modern Turkish characters.	50.00	175.	700.
32	**5 Pounds**			
	1.11.1953. Green. Portr. Kg. George VI at upper r. Similar to #25 but values in Greek and modern Turkish characters.	125.	600.	1750.

1955 Issue

#33-36 portr. Qn. Elizabeth II at r., map at lower r. Various date and sign. varieties. Arms at r. on back.

		VG	VF	UNC
33	**250 Mils**			
	1.6.1955; 1.2.1956; 1.3.1957; 1.3.1960. Blue on m/c unpt.			
	a. Issued note.	10.00	75.00	400.
	s. Specimen.	—	—	75.00

		VG	VF	UNC
34	**500 Mils**			
	1.6.1955; 1.2.1956; 1.3.1957. Green on m/c unpt.			
	a. Issued note.	30.00	200.	750.
	s. Specimen.	—	—	75.00

		VG	VF	UNC
35	**1 Pound**			
	1.6.1955; 1.2.1956; 1.3.1957. Brown on m/c unpt.			
	a. Issued note.	12.50	100.	450.
	s. Specimen.	—	—	75.00

		VG	VF	UNC
36	**5 Pounds**			
	1.6.1955; 1.2.1956; 1.3.1957; 15.3.1958; 1.3.1960. Green on m/c unpt.			
	a. Issued note.	25.00	150.	600.
	s. Specimen.	—	—	75.00

The Republic of Czechoslovakia, located in central Europe, had an area of 49,365 sq. mi. (127,859 sq. km.). Capital: Prague (Praha). Industrial production in the cities and agriculture and livestock in the rural areas were the chief occupations.

The Czech lands to the west were united with the Slovak to form the Czechoslovak Republic on October 28, 1918 upon the dissolution of the Austrian-Hungarian Empire. Tomas G. Masaryk was the first president. In the 1930s Hitlet provoked Czechoslovakia's German minority in the Sudetenland to agitate for autonomy. The territory was broken up for the benefit of Germany, Poland and Hungary by the Munich agreement signed by the United Kingdom, France, Germany and Italy on September 29, 1938. On March 15, 1939, Germany invaded Czechoslovakia and incorporated the Czech lands into the Third Reich as the "Protectorate of Bohemia and Moravia." eastern Slovakia, was constituted as a republic under Nazi infulence. A government-in-exile was set up in London in 1940. The Soviet and American forces liberated the area by May 1945. After World War II the physical integrity and independence of Czechoslovakia was re-established, while bringing it within the Russian sphere of influence. On February 23-25, 1948, the Communists seized control of the government in a *coup d'etat*, and adopted a constitution making the country a "people's republic." A new constitution adopted June 11, 1960, converted the country into a "socialist republic." Communist infulence increased steadily while pressure for liberalization culminated in the overthrow of the Stalinist leader Antonçin Novotny and his associates in January, 1968. The Communist Party then introduced far reaching reforms which received warnings from Moscow, followed by occupation of Warsaw Pact forces on August 21, 1968 resulting in stationing of Soviet troops. Student demonstrations for reform began in Prague on November 17, 1989. The Federal Assembly abolished the Communist Party's sole right to govern. In December, 1989, communism was overthrown. In January, 1990 the Czech and Slovak Federal Republic (CSFR) was formed. The movement for a democratic Slovakia was apparent in the June 1992 elections with the Slovak National Council adopting a declaration of sovereignty. The CSFR was disolved on December 31, 1992, and both new republics came into being on January 1, 1993.

See the Czech Republic and Slovakia sections for additional listings.

MONETARY SYSTEM:

1 Koruna = 100 Haleru

SPECIMEN NOTES:

Large quantities of specimens were made available to collectors. Notes issued after 1945 are distinguished by a perforation consisting of three small holes or a letter S (for Solvakia). Since the difference in value between issued notes and specimen notes is frequently very great, both types of notes are valued. Earlier issues recalled from circulation were perforated: *SPECIMEN* or *NEPLATNE* or with a letter *S* for collectors. Caution should be exercised while examining notes as examples of perforated notes having the holes filled in are known.

NOTE AVAILABILITY:

The Czech National Bank in 1997 made available to collectors uncirculated examples of #78-98, as a full set or in issue groups. As the notes were demonetized they had no cancellation holes nor were overprinted. They have regular serial #'s.

REPUBLIC

REPUBLIKA CESKOSLOVENSKÁ

1919 PROVISIONAL ISSUE

		Good	Fine	XF
1	**10 Korun** 1919 (- old date 2.1.1915). Blue imperforate 10 Haleru adhesive stamp on Austria #19. Large state emblem on stamp.			
	a. Imperforate stamp.	3.00	10.00	25.00
	b. Perforated stamp.	10.00	30.00	65.00
	x. Cancelled stamp (false).	5.00	15.00	30.00
	z. Hole stamp (imperforated).			

		Good	Fine	XF
2	**20 Korun** 1919 (- old date 2.1.1913). Red perforated 20 Haleru adhesive stamp on Austria #13. Small state emblem on stamp.	2.50	7.50	15.00

		Good	Fine	XF
2A	**20 Korun** 1919 (- old date 2.1.1913). Red 20 Haleru adhesive stamp on Austria #14.	8.00	20.00	40.00

		Good	Fine	XF
3	**50 Korun** 1919 (- old date 2.1.1914). Brown perforated 50 Haleru adhesive stamp on Austria #15. Stamp with small state emblem.	3.00	10.00	20.00

		Good	Fine	XF
4	**100 Korun** 1919 (- old date 2.1.1912). Orange-brown imperforate 1 Koruna adhesive stamp on Austria #12. Large state emblem on stamp.			
	a. Stamp w/straight edge.	3.00	8.00	17.50
	b. Stamp w/perforations.	10.00	35.00	75.00

		Good	Fine	XF
5	**1000 Korun** 1919 (- old date 2.1.1902). Reddish black 10K(orun) stamplike printed ovpt. on Austria #8. Frantisek Palacky on stamp.	7.50	17.50	40.00

Note: Some notes have an additional hand "cancellation" stamp, indicating in many cases that the adhesive stamp is forged. It reads: *BANK.UR.MIN.FIN / PRAHA.* (Banking Office of the Ministry of Finance, Prague).

1919 ISSUE

		Good	Fine	XF
6	**1 Koruna** 15.4.1919. Blue. Arms at ctr. on red back.			
	a. Issued note.	.50	2.00	5.00
	s. Specimen.	—	—	10.00
	x. Error date: 5.4.1919 (Series 014).	50.00	125.	300.

		Good	Fine	XF
7	**5 Korun** 15.4.1919. Red and black. woman at l. and r. Back blue on brown unpt. Red text.			
	a. Issued note.	3.00	12.50	35.00
	s. Specimen.	—	6.00	15.00

		Good	Fine	XF
8	**10 Korun** 15.4.1919. Purple on brown unpt. Helmeted Husite solder at lower l. and lower r. Back purple and tan; girl at l. and r. Series H, O.			
	a. Issued note.	8.00	35.00	95.00
	s. Specimen.	—	20.00	40.00

		Good	Fine	XF
9	**20 Korun** 15.4.1919. Blue and brown. 4 women's heads. Back red w/green text; head at l. and r. Series P, U.			
	a. Issued note.	10.00	40.00	150.
	s. Specimen.	—	12.50	30.00
	x. Error: back w/o green printed legend.	—	—	—

		Good	Fine	XF
10	**50 Korun** 15.4.1919. Brown and dk. red on lt. brown and green unpt. Woman at l. and r. Arms at ctr. on back.			
	a. Issued note.	20.00	80.00	300.
	s. Specimen.	—	25.00	55.00

		Good	Fine	XF
11	**100 Korun** 15.4.1919. Blue and violet. 4 arms across lower ctr. Woman at l. and r. of falcon on back.			
	a. Issued note.	25.00	125.	400
	s. Specimen.	5.00	20.00	50.0

		Good	Fine	XF
12	**500 Korun** 15.4.1919. Red and brown. Seated figures at ctr. Arms at upper l. and woman at upper r. above falcons on back.			
	a. Issued note. Rare.	—	—	—
	s. Specimen.	800.	1500.	—
	x. Counterfeit.	80.00	200.	400

Note: 60,000 pieces of #12 were counterfeited by Meczarosz in Graz, Austria shortly after it was released for circulation. Most of the pieces seen in collections today are counterfeits. These are distinguished easily by a printed imitation of the watermark and the lack of the hacek accent mark (resembling a small latter "v") over the letter "c" of the text "C.187," on the line of text that crosses the top the back. Genuine notes are seldom encountered. Most forgeries are Series: 020, 021, 022 and 023.

		Good	Fine	XF
13	**1000 Korun** 15.4.1919. Blue on m/c unpt. Allegorical figure w/globe at r. Standing women at l. on back. Printer: ABNC (w/o imprint).			
	a. Issued note. Series D.	80.00	250.	600
	s1. Perforated: *SPECIMEN.*	40.00	125.	300
	s2. Brown. Special uniface print by ABNC of "archive series" for collectors.	—	Unc	20.0
14	**5000 Korun** 15.4.1919. Red. Woman at r. Like Austria #8.			
	a. Issued note. Reported not confirmed.	—	—	—
	s. Perforated: *NEPLATNÉ* (invalid). Rare.	—	—	—

1920-23 ISSUE

		Good	Fine	XF
15	**5 Korun** 28.9. 1921. Blue and red-brown. Portr. J. A. Komensky at l. Arms at ctr. on back.	2.50	10.00	45.00

		Good	Fine	XF
16	**50 Korun** 12.7.1922. Brown, red and blue. Arms at upper l., woman's head at lower r. Farmer w/Trencin castle in background on purple back.	35.00	125.	400.

#17-19 printer: ABNC (w/o imprint).

		Good	Fine	XF
17	**100 Korun** 14.1.1920. Green on m/c unpt. Arms at l. ctr., Pagan priestess at r. Woman in Czech costume of Kyjov at l., Slovak costume of Piestany at r. View of Hradcany and Charles bridge across Valta River at ctr. on back.			
	a. Issued note.	20.00	80.00	180.
	s. Perforated: *SPECIMEN.*	—	30.00	70.00
18	**500 Korun** 6.10.1923. Brown. Arms at l., WWI Czech Legionnaire at r. Lion, Liberty head and child on back.			
	a. Issued note.	150.	500.	1500.
	s. Perforated: *SPECIMEN.*	—	350.	700.

NOTICE

Readers with unlisted dates, signature varieties, etc. are invited to submit photocopies or, high resolution (300 dpi, 100% size) scans of their notes to: Standard Catalog of World Paper Money, 700 East State St. Iola, WI 54990-0001, or E-Mail: george.cuhaj@fwpubs.com.

		Good	Fine	XF
19	**5000 Korun** 6.7.1920. Brown-violet on m/c unpt. River Elbe w/Rip mountain at l. ctr., girl in costume of Tabor at r. Back purple on green unpt.; standing allegorical woman at ctr.			
	a. Issued note.	45.00	200.	500.
	s. Perforated: *SPECIMEN.* Series B; C.	—	8.00	20.00

Note: Some of #19 are ovpt. for Bohemia-Moravia (see #16 under that heading).

NARODNI (A) BANKA CESKOSLOVENSKÁ

CZECHOSLOVAK NATIONAL BANK

1926-34 ISSUES

#22-26 printer: TB, Prague.

		VG	VF	UNC
20	**10 Korun** 2.1.1927. Dk. purple on lilac unpt. Like #8.			
	a. Issued note.	2.50	7.50	27.50
	s. Perforated: *SPECIMEN* or *NEPLATNÉ.*	—	2.50	12.50

		VG	VF	UNC
21	**20 Korun** 1.10.1926. Blue-violet, brown and red. Portr. Dr. Alois Rasin at l., arms at r. Back dk. blue on brown unpt.; portr. Dr. A. Rasin at r.			
	a. Issued note.	2.00	6.00	15.00
	s. Perforated: *SPECIMEN.*	—	1.25	5.00

22	50 Korun	VG	VF	UNC
	1.10.1929. Red-violet on brown unpt. Girl at upper l., ornate arms at ctr. Farmer, wife and tools of industry and agriculture on back.			
	a. Issued note.	5.00	10.00	30.00
	s. Perforated: *SPECIMEN.*	—	1.50	10.00

23	100 Korun	VG	VF	UNC
	10.1.1931. Dk. green on m/c unpt. Boy w/falcon at l., arms at ctr., Liberty at r. Allegorical figures at l., portr. Pres. T. Masaryk at r. on back.			
	a. Issued note.	5.00	10.00	30.00
	p. Black proofs. Uniface pair.	—	—	45.00
	s. Perforated: *SPECIMEN.*	—	—	10.00

24	500 Korun	VG	VF	UNC
	2.5.1929. Red on m/c unpt. Like #18. Printer: ABNC (w/o imprint).			
	a. Issued note.	7.00	20.00	125.
	s. Perforated: *SPECIMEN.* Series D; G.	—	2.00	15.00

NOTICE

Readers with unlisted dates, signature varieties, etc. are invited to submit photocopies or, high resolution (300 dpi, 100% size) scans of their notes to: Standard Catalog of World Paper Money, 700 East State St. Iola, WI 54990-0001, or E-Mail: george.cuhaj@fwpubs.com.

25	1000 Korun	VG	VF	UNC
	8.4.1932. Like #13. Printer: ABNC (w/o imprint).			
	a. Issued note. Series A.	12.00	50.00	250.
	s. Perforated: *SPECIMEN.*	—	4.00	20.00

26	1000 Korun	VG	VF	UNC
	25.5.1934. Blue on lt. blue and green unpt. Woman w/book and 2 children at l. Back dk. brown and m/c; portr. F. Palacky at r.			
	a. Issued note.	6.00	20.00	80.00
	s. Perforated: *SPECIMEN.*	—	2.00	15.00

REPUBLIKA CESKOSLOVENSKÁ(RESUMED)

REPUBLIC OF CZECHOSLOVAKIA

1938 ND ISSUE

#27 and 28 were prepared for use by the mobilized Czech army in 1938, but were not released. After the Nazis occupied Czechoslovakia, these notes were ovpt. for the new Bohemia and Moravia Protectorate (refer to those listings #1 and 2). Printer: TB, Prague.

27	1 Koruna	VG	VF	UNC
	ND (1938). Blue. Lettering in unpt. in l. circle, Liberty wearing cap at r. circle. Arms at l., *RADA* (series) in white rectangle and 5 lines of text on back. (Not issued).			
	a. Issued note.	8.00	20.00	55.00
	s. Perforated: *SPECIMEN.*	—	1.50	10.00

Note: For similar design issue see #58.

28	5 Korun	VG	VF	UNC
	ND (1938). Lilac and purple. Portr. J. Jungmann at r. Woman's head at l. on back. (Not issued).			
	a. Issued note.	20.00	60.00	180.
	s. Perforated: *SPECIMEN.*	—	2.00	15.00

#29-43 are now listed under Bohemia and Moravia as #3-17. #3-17.

1944-45 ISSUE

#45-50 w/o pictorial design. Printer: Goznak, Moscow.

45	1 Koruna	VG	VF	UNC
	1944. Red-brown on brown unpt.			
	a. Issued note.	.50	1.50	3.00
	s. Perforated: *SPECIMEN.*	—	1.00	2.00

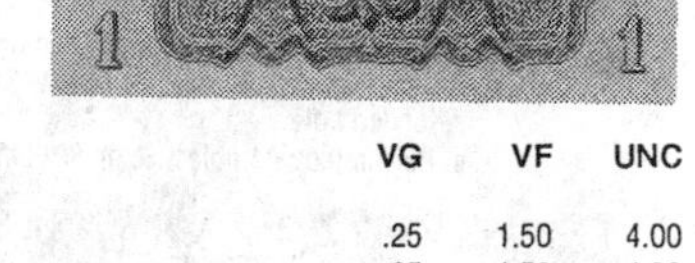

46	5 Korun	VG	VF	UNC
	1944. Dk. blue on lt. blue unpt.			
	a. Unpt. horizontal wavy lines.	.25	1.50	4.00
	b. Unpt. vertical wavy lines.	.25	1.50	4.00
	s. Perforated: *SPECIMEN* (a or b).	—	1.50	4.00

47	20 Korun	VG	VF	UNC
	1944. Blue-black on tan unpt. 2 serial # varieties.			
	a. Issued note.	1.00	2.50	6.00
	s. Perforated: *SPECIMEN* or *NEPLATNÉ.*	—	1.50	3.00

48	100 Korun	VG	VF	UNC
	1944. Green on lt. green unpt. 2 serial # varieties.			
	a. Issued note.	1.50	5.00	12.50
	s. Perforated: *SPECIMEN.*	—	1.50	4.00

49	500 Korun	VG	VF	UNC
	1944. Red on lt. brown unpt.			
	a. Issued note.	5.00	15.00	50.00
	s. Perforated: *SPECIMEN* or *NEPLATNÉ.*	—	1.50	4.00
50	1000 Korun			
	1944. Dk. blue on green unpt.			
	a. Issued note.	4.00	25.00	75.00
	s. Perforated: *SPECIMEN.*	—	1.50	4.00

50A	2000 Korun	VG	VF	UNC
	1945. Blue and black on green unpt. Arms w/produce at r. Back brown on lt. green and lt. orange unpt.			
	a. Issued note.	100.	450.	1000.
	s. Perforated: *SPECIMEN.*	—	1.50	6.00

1945 ND PROVISIONAL ISSUES

#51-57 issues of Slovakia and Republic w/Czechoslovak revalidation adhesive stamps portraying Pres. T. G. Masaryk (w/or w/o cap) affixed.

51	100 Korun	VG	VF	UNC
	ND (1945 - old date 7.10.1940). Yellow *K* adhesive stamp on Slovakia #10.			
	a. Issued note.	2.00	8.00	30.00
	s. Perforated: *SPECIMEN.*	—	1.00	3.00

52	100 Korun	VG	VF	UNC
	ND (1945 - old date 7.10.1940). Yellow *K* adhesive stamp on Slovakia #11. *II. Emisia* at l. margin on back.			
	a. Issued note.	2.00	8.00	35.00
	s. Perforated: *SPECIMEN.*	—	1.00	3.00

		VG	VF	UNC
53	**100 Korun** ND (1945 - old date 1944). Blue *E* adhesive stamp w/black ovpt: *100* on #48. 2 serial # varieties.			
	a. Issued note.	2.00	6.00	15.00
	s. Perforated: *SPECIMEN.*	—	1.00	3.00

		VG	VF	UNC
54	**500 Korun** ND (1945 - old date 12.7.1941). Orange *B* adhesive stamp on Slovakia #12.			
	a. Issued note.	6.00	25.00	60.00
	s. Perforated: *SPECIMEN.*	—	2.00	6.00

		VG	VF	UNC
55	**500 Korun** ND (1945 - old date 1944). Blue *E* adhesive stamp w/red ovpt: *500* on #49.			
	a. Issued note.	4.00	15.00	40.00
	s. Perforated: *SPECIMEN.*	—	1.50	4.00

		VG	VF	UNC
56	**1000 Korun** ND (1945 - old date 25.11.1940). Red *Y* adhesive stamp on Slovakia #13.			
	a. Issued note.	10.00	35.00	80.00
	s. Perforated: *SPECIMEN.*	—	3.00	8.00
57	**1000 Korun** ND (1945 - old date 1944). Blue *E* adhesive stamp w/red ovpt: *1000* on #50.			
	a. Issued note.	5.00	20.00	60.00
	s. Perforated: *SPECIMEN.*	—	1.50	4.00

Note: Originally the above issues were considered to be worth more with the adhesive stamps affixed as noted but quantities of unused adhesive stamps have made their way into today's market.

1945-46 ND Issue

		VG	VF	UNC
58	**1 Koruna** ND (1946). Blue. Similar to #27 but w/o unpt. in l. circle on face. Different unpt. design, w/o *RADA* (series), and 4 lines of text on back. (Not issued.)			
	a. W/o perforation holes.	.25	1.50	6.00
	s. Perforated w/3 holes.	—	—	3.00

		VG	VF	UNC
59	**5 Korun** ND (1945). Red on yellow unpt. Arms at ctr. on back. Printer: TDLR.			
	a. Issued note.	.25	.50	3.00
	s. Perforated w/3 holes, *S*, or *SPECIMEN.*	—	1.00	2.00

		VG	VF	UNC
60	**10 Korun** ND (1945). Green on pink and green unpt. Printer: TDLR.			
	a. Issued note.	.25	1.00	3.00
	s. Perforated w/3 holes, *S*, or *SPECIMEN.*	—	1.00	2.00

		VG	VF	UNC
61	**20 Korun** ND (1945). Blue on yellow and green unpt. Portr. K. Havlicek at l. Arms at lower ctr. on back. Printer: W&S.			
	a. Issued note.	.25	1.00	4.00
	s. Perforated w/3 holes, *S*, or *SPECIMEN.*	—	.50	1.50

		VG	VF	UNC
62	**50 Korun** ND (1945). Purple on lt. green unpt. Portr. Gen. M. Stefanik at l. Ornate arms at ctr. on back. Printer: W&S.			
	a. Issued note.	.25	1.50	6.0
	s. Perforated w/3 holes, *S*, or *SPECIMEN.*	—	.75	2.5

63 100 Korun
ND (1945). Black-green on orange and green unpt. Portr. Pres. T. Masaryk at l. Hradcany at ctr. on back. Printer: BWC.

	VG	VF	UNC
a. Issued note.	.50	2.00	7.50
s. Perforated w/3 holes, *S*, or *SPECIMEN*.	—	1.00	3.00

64 500 Korun
ND (1945). Brown on orange and m/c unpt. Portr. J. Kollar at l. w/black serial # and *MINISTER FINANCI* sign. and title. Lake Strbske pleso and High Tatra mountains on back. Wmk: Youth's head. Printer: BWC.

	VG	VF	UNC
a. Issued note.	3.00	15.00	50.00
s. Perforated w/3 holes, *S*, or *SPECIMEN*.	—	2.50	12.00

65 1000 Korun
ND (1945). Black on m/c unpt. Portr. Kg. J. Z. Podebrad at l. Karlstejn Castle at ctr. on back. Printer: BWC.

	VG	VF	UNC
a. Issued note.	.50	3.00	15.00
s. Perforated w/3 holes, *S*, or *SPECIMEN*.	—	1.75	6.00

1945-48 Dated Issue

#66-67 printer: TB, Prague.

66 50 Korun
3.7.1948. Deep blue on gray unpt. Gen. Stefanik at r. 3 serial # varieties. Back green; scene of Banska village and Bystrica mountains.

	VG	VF	UNC
a. Issued note.	.50	3.00	12.00
s. Perforated w/3 holes, *S*, or *SPECIMEN*.	—	1.00	3.00

67 100 Korun
16.5.1945. Gray-brown on blue and peach unpt. Liberty wearing cap at r. 3 serial # varieties. Back blue on red and blue unpt.

	VG	VF	UNC
a. Issued note.	.50	2.50	8.00
s. Perforated w/3 holes, *S*, or *SPECIMEN*.	—	.75	2.00

1949-50 Issue

#68-71 printer: TB, Prague.

68 5 Korun
25.1.1949. Red on lt. brown unpt. Similar to #59.

	VG	VF	UNC
a. Issued note.	.25	1.50	4.00
s. Perforated w/3 holes or *SPECIMEN*.	—	.75	2.00

69 10 Korun
4.4.1950. Green. Similar to #60.

	VG	VF	UNC
a. Issued note.	.25	1.00	3.00
s. Perforated w/3 holes, *S*, or *SPECIMEN*.	—	.75	1.50

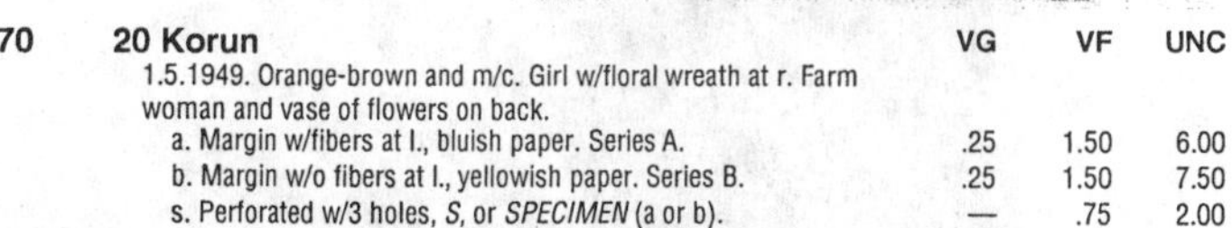

70 20 Korun
1.5.1949. Orange-brown and m/c. Girl w/floral wreath at r. Farm woman and vase of flowers on back.

	VG	VF	UNC
a. Margin w/fibers at l., bluish paper. Series A.	.25	1.50	6.00
b. Margin w/o fibers at l., yellowish paper. Series B.	.25	1.50	7.50
s. Perforated w/3 holes, *S*, or *SPECIMEN* (a or b).	—	.75	2.00

		VG	VF	UNC
71	**50 Korun**			
	29.8.1950. Dk. brown on tan unpt. Miner at r. Back green.			
	a. Margin w/fibers at l., bluish paper. Series A.	.50	2.00	7.50
	b. Margin w/o fibers at l., yellowish paper. Series B.	.50	2.00	7.50
	s. Perforated w/3 holes, *S*, or *SPECIMEN* (a or b).	—	1.00	2.50

1953 Issue

		VG	VF	UNC
72	**10 Korun**			
	25.2.1953. Brown. (Not issued).	—	—	—

		VG	VF	UNC
72A	**20 Korun**			
	25.2.1953. Blue. (Not issued).	—	—	400.

Narodni (a) Banka Ceskoslovenská (Resumed)

1945-46 Issue

#73-74 printer: TB, Prague.

		VG	VF	UNC
73	**500 Korun**			
	12.3.1946. Brown on orange and m/c unpt. Similar to #64, but w/orange serial # and 3 sign. w/o title.			
	a. Issued note.	1.00	3.00	12.00
	s. Perforated w/3 holes, *S*, or *SPECIMEN*.	—	1.50	5.00

		VG	VF	UNC
74	**1000 Korun**			
	16.5.1945. Dk. grayish brown on gray unpt. Girl at r. Back blue, red-orange and m/c; arms at ctr. r.			
	a. Wmk: Dk. "X" repeated between lt. colored lines. Paper yellowish and dense.	1.00	4.00	15.00
	b. Wmk. like a. Paper bluish and transparent.	1.00	4.00	15.00
	c. Wmk: Squarish pattern w/o "X" at center. Paper yellowish and dense.	1.00	4.00	15.00
	d. Wmk. like c. Paper bluish and transparent.	1.00	4.00	15.00
	s. Perforated: w/3 holes, *S*, *S-S*, or *SPECIMEN* (a, b, c, or d).	—	2.50	7.50

		VG	VF	UNC
75	**5000 Korun**			
	1.11.1945. Black on brownish gray unpt. B. Smetana at r. Back green; National Theater in Prague at ctr., wreath at r.			
	a. Issued note.	1.50	4.00	20.00
	s. Perforated w/3 holes, *S*, or *SPECIMEN*.	—	2.50	8.00

Státní Banka Ceskoslovenská

Czechoslovak State Bank

1951 Issue

#76-77 printer: STC, Prague.

		VG	VF	UNC
76	**100 Korun**			
	24.10.1951. Brown. Woman at r. Arms w/lion on m/c back. (Not issued).	—	—	300.

		VG	VF	UNC
77	**1000 Korun**			
	9.5.1951. Brown. Like #74. (Not issued).	—	—	500.

NOTICE

Readers with unlisted dates, signature varieties, etc. are invited to submit photocopies or, high resolution (300 dpi, 100% size) scans of their notes to: Standard Catalog of World Paper Money, 700 East State St. Iola, WI 54990-0001, or E-Mail: george.cuhaj@fwpubs.com.

PEOPLES REPUBLIC

STÁTOVKY REPUBLIKY CESKOSLOVENSKÉ

STATE NOTES OF THE REPUBLIC OF CZECHOSLOVAKIA

1953 ISSUE

#78-82 w/o pictorial design on face, arms at ctr. on back. #78-80 were printed by either Gosnak, Moscow (Russian serial #) or TB, Praha (Western serial #). Replacement notes: *Z* prefix.

		VG	VF	UNC
78	**1 Koruna** 1953. Brown on tan unpt.			
	a. Series prefix A, B, C, D, Z. Printer: Gosnak, Moscow.	.25	1.00	4.00
	b. Other series prefixes. Printer: TB, Prague.	.20	.50	2.00
	s. Perforated: *SPECIMEN.*	—	.50	2.00

		VG	VF	UNC
79	**3 Koruny** 1953. Blue on lt. blue unpt.			
	a. Series prefix: A, B, C, Z.	.50	2.00	8.00
	b. Other series prefixes.	.25	1.00	4.00
	s. Perforated w/1 hole or *SPECIMEN.*	—	.50	2.00

		VG	VF	UNC
80	**5 Korun** 1953. Olive on lt. green unpt. 2 serial # varieties.			
	a. Series prefix A, B, C, Z.	1.00	3.50	12.50
	b. Other series prefixes.	.50	1.50	6.00
	s. Perforated: *SPECIMEN.*	—	.50	2.00

SOCIALIST REPUBLIC

STÁTNÍ BANKA CESKOSLOVENSKÁ

CZECHOSLOVAK STATE BANK

1953 ISSUE

Printer: either Gosnak, Moscow (Russian series prefix) or TB, Prague. Replacement notes: *Z* prefix.

		VG	VF	UNC
81	**10 Korun** 1953. Brown on lt. green and orange unpt. Arms at l. on back.			
	a. Series prefix A, B, C, Z.	.50	2.00	8.00
	b. Other series prefixes.	.25	1.00	4.00
	s. Perforated w/3 holes.	—	—	2.00

		VG	VF	UNC
84	**25 Korun** 1953. Blue on lt. blue unpt. Equestrian statue of J. Zizka at l. Scene of Tabor on back.			
	a. Series prefix A, B, C, Z.	6.00	15.00	35.00
	b. Other series prefixes.	.75	4.00	12.50
	s. Perforated w/3 holes.	—	—	6.00

		VG	VF	UNC
85	**50 Korun** 1953. Green on lt. green unpt. Statue of partisan w/Russian soldier at l. Back blue and olive; scene of Banska Bystricka at ctr.			
	a. Series prefix A, B.	1.00	6.00	22.50
	b. Other series prefixes.	.50	3.00	12.00
	s. Perforated w/3 holes.	—	—	5.00
86	**100 Korun** 1953. Brown on tan and pink unpt. Worker and farmer at l. Scene of Prague on back.			
	a. Series prefix A, B, C, D.	1.00	5.00	20.00
	b. Other series prefixes.	.50	2.50	10.00
	s. Perforated w/3 holes.	—	—	5.00

1958 ISSUE

		VG	VF	UNC
87	**25 Korun** 1958. Blue-black on lt. blue unpt. Arms at l. ctr., portr. Jan Zizka at r. Tábor town square on back. Printer: TB, Prague.			
	a. Issued note.	2.00	8.00	20.00
	s. Perforated w/1 hole or *SPECIMEN.*	—	—	6.00

NOTICE

Readers with unlisted dates, signature varieties, etc. are invited to submit photocopies or, high resolution (300 dpi, 100% size) scans of their notes to: Standard Catalog of World Paper Money, 700 East State St. Iola, WI 54990-0001, or E-Mail: george.cuhaj@fwpubs.com.

1960-64 Issue

#88-98 printer: STC-Prague.

#88-91 Printed by wet photogravure or dry photogravure (wet printing has smaller image).

		VG	VF	UNC
88	**10 Korun**			
	1960. Brown on m/c unpt. 2 girls w/flowers at r. Orava Dam on back.			
	a. Series prefix: H; F (wet printing).	2.00	8.00	15.00
	b. Series prefixes: E, J, L, M, S, X (dry printing)	.10	.75	3.00
	s. Specimen.	—	—	—

Foreign Exchange Certificates

Podniku Zahranicniho Obchodu Tuzex

1957-58 Issue

		VG	VF	UNC
FX1	**0.50 Koruna** 1958. Rare.	—	—	—
FX2	**1 Koruna** 1957. Rare.	—	—	—
FX3	**5 Korun** 1957. Rare.	—	—	—
FX4	**10 Korun** 1957. Rare.	—	—	—
FX5	**20 Korun** 1957. Rare.	—	—	—
FX6	**50 Korun** 1957. Rare.	—	—	—
FX7	**71.5 Korun** 1957. Rare.	—	—	—
FX8	**100 Korun** 1957. Rare.	—	—	—

1959 Issue

		VG	VF	UNC
FX9	**0.50 Koruna** 1959. Rare.	—	—	—
FX10	**1 Koruna** 1959. Rare.	—	—	—
FX11	**5 Korun** 1959. Rare.	—	—	—
FX12	**10 Korun** 1959. Rare.	—	—	—
FX13	**20 Korun** 1959. Rare.	—	—	—
FX14	**50 Korun** 1959. Rare.	—	—	—
FX15	**71.5 Korun** 1959. Rare.	—	—	—
FX16	**100 Korun** 1959. Rare.	—	—	—

1960 Issue

		VG	VF	UNC
FX17	**0.50 Koruna** 1960.	5.00	15.00	50.00
FX18	**1 Koruna** 1960.	7.50	20.00	60.00
FX19	**5 Korun** 1960. Rare.	—	—	—
FX20	**10 Korun** 1960. Rare.	—	—	—
FX21	**20 Korun** 1960. Rare.	—	—	—
FX22	**50 Korun** 1960. Rare.	—	—	—
FX23	**71.5 Korun** 1960. Rare.	—	—	—
FX24	**100 Korun** 1960. Rare.	—	—	—

DAHOMEY

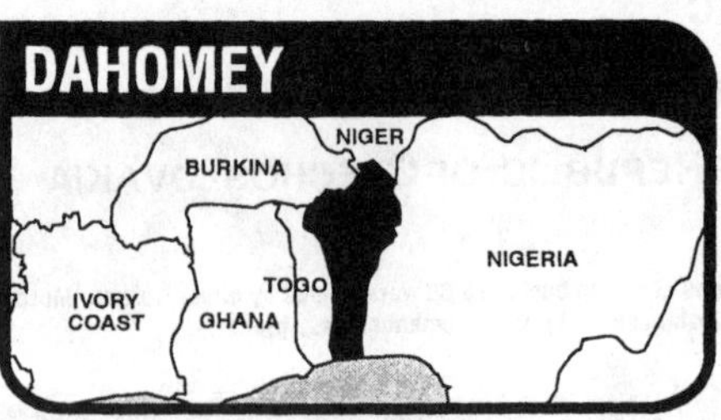

The Peoples Republic of Benin (former French colony that became the Republic of Dahomey), located on the south side of the West African bulge between Togo and Nigeria, has an area of 43,484 sq. mi. (112,622 sq. km.) and and a population of 6.22 million. Capital: Porto-Novo. The principal industry of Benin, one of the poorest countries of West Africa, is the processing of palm oil products. Palm kernel oil, peanuts, cotton and coffee are exported.

Porto-Novo, on the Bight of Benin, was founded as a trading post by the Portuguese in the 17th century. At that time, Benin was composed of an aggregation of mutually suspicious tribes, the majority of which were tributary to the powerful northern Kingdom of Abomey. In 1863, the King of Porto-Novo petitioned France for protection from Abomey. The French subjugated other militant tribes as well, and in 1892 organized the area as a protectorate of France; in 1904 it was incorporated into French West Africa as the Territory of Dahomey. After the establishment of the Fifth French Republic, the Territory of Dahomey became an autonomous state within the French community. On Aug. 1, 1960, it became the fully independent Republic of Dahomey. In 1974, the republic began a transition to a socialist society with Marxism-Leninism as its revolutionary philosophy. On Nov. 30, 1975, the name of the Republic of Dahomey was changed to the Peoples Republic of Benin.

Benin is a member of the "Union Monetaire Ouest-Africaine" with other west African states. Also see French West Africa, West African States.

RULERS:
French

MONETARY SYSTEM:
1 Franc = 100 Centimes

French Administration

Gouvernement Général de l'A.O.F. (Afrique Occidentale Francaise)

Colonie du Dahomey

1917 Emergency Issue

#1-2 Décret du 11.2.1917. French coin design at l. and r.

		Good	Fine	XF
1	**0.50 Franc**			
	D.1917. Orange and black. Coins at l. and r. Black text on back.			
	a. Wmk: Bees.	27.50	60.00	175.
	b. Wmk: Laurel leaves.	27.50	60.00	175.

		Good	Fine	XF
2	**1 Franc**			
	Coins at l. and r. *D.1917.* Black on orange and yellow unpt.			
	a. Wmk: Bees.	27.50	60.00	175.
	b. Wmk: Laurel leaves.	30.00	65.00	200.

DANISH WEST INDIES

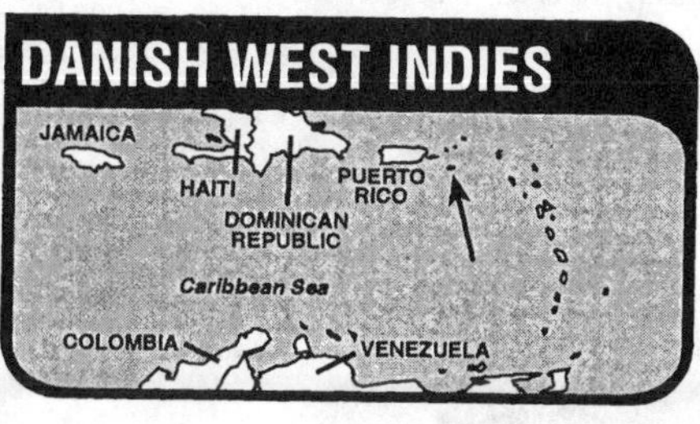

The Danish West Indies (now the organized unincorporated territory of the Virgin Islands of the United States) consists of the islands of St. Thomas, St. John, St. Croix, and 62 islets located in the Caribbean Sea 40 miles (64 km.) east of Puerto Rico. The islands have a combined area of 133 sq. mi (344 sq. km.) and a population of 110,000. Capital: Charlotte Amalie. Tourism is the principal industry. Watch movements, costume jewelry, pharmaceuticals and rum are exported.

The Virgin Islands were discovered by Columbus in 1493, during his second voyage to America. During the 17th century the islands, actually the peaks of a submerged mountain range, were held at various times by Spain, Holland, England, France and Denmark, and during the same period were favorite resorts of the buccaneers operating in the Caribbean and the coastal waters of eastern North America. Control of the 100-island chain finally passed to Denmark and England. The Danish islands were purchased by the United States in 1917 for $25 million, mainly because they command the Anegada Passage into the Caribbean Sea, a strategic point on the defense perimeter of the Panama Canal.

Currency of the United States of America is now in circulation.

RULERS:
Danish

MONETARY SYSTEM:
25 West Indies Rigsdaler Courant = 20 Danish Rigsdaler Courant
1 Franc = 20 Cents
1 Daler = 5 Francs
1 Dollar = 100 Cents

DANISH ADMINISTRATION

TREASURY

ST. CROIX

1784-85 PROVISIONAL ISSUE

#A1 reissue of 1775 Danish State notes.

		Good	Fine	XF
.1	**6 1/4 Rigsdaler** 4.9.1784; 2.3.1785 (- old date 1775). Black on white paper. Printed on back of Denmark 5 Rigsdaler #A29a.	—	—	—

ote: For similar revalued Danish notes refer to Faeroe Islands and Iceland listings.

788 ISSUE

.2-A74 various hand sign. across bottom. Black text. Uniface.

		Good	Fine	XF
2	**20 Rigsdaler** 1788. Rare.	—	—	—
3	**50 Rigsdaler** 1788. Rare.	—	—	—
4	**100 Rigsdaler** 1788. Rare.	—	—	—

799 ISSUE

		Good	Fine	XF
11	**20 Rigsdaler** 1799. Rare.	—	—	—
12	**50 Rigsdaler** 1799. Rare.	—	—	—
13	**100 Rigsdaler** 1799. Rare.	—	—	—

1806 ISSUE

		Good	Fine	XF
A21	**5 Rigsdaler** 1806. Rare.	—	—	—
A22	**10 Rigsdaler** 1806. Rare.	—	—	—
A23	**50 Rigsdaler** 1806. Rare.	—	—	—
A24	**100 Rigsdaler** 1806. Rare.	—	—	—

1814-15 ISSUE

		Good	Fine	XF
A31	**5 Rigsdaler** 1814-15. Rare.	—	—	—
A32	**10 Rigsdaler** 1814-15. Rare.	—	—	—
A33	**50 Rigsdaler** 1814-15. Rare.	—	—	—
A34	**100 Rigsdaler** 1814-15. Rare.	—	—	—

1822 ISSUE

		Good	Fine	XF
A41	**5 Rigsdaler** 1822. Rare.	—	—	—
A42	**10 Rigsdaler** 1822. Rare.	—	—	—
A43	**50 Rigsdaler** 1822. Rare.	—	—	—
A44	**100 Rigsdaler** 1822. Rare.	—	—	—

1829 ISSUE

		Good	Fine	XF
A51	**5 Rigsdaler** 1829. Rare.	—	—	—
A52	**10 Rigsdaler** 1829. Rare.	—	—	—
A53	**50 Rigsdaler** 1829. Rare.	—	—	—
A54	**100 Rigsdaler** 1829. Rare.	—	—	—

1836 ISSUE

		Good	Fine	XF
A61	**5 Rigsdaler** 1836. Rare.	—	—	—
A62	**10 Rigsdaler** 1836. Rare.	—	—	—
A63	**50 Rigsdaler** 1836. Rare.	—	—	—
A64	**100 Rigsdaler** 1836. Rare.	—	—	—

1842 ISSUE

#A71-A74 w/text in Gothic lettering. Black denomination line across top.

		Good	Fine	XF
A71	**5 Rigsdaler** 1842. Rare.	—	—	—
A72	**10 Rigsdaler** 1842. Rare.	—	—	—
A73	**50 Rigsdaler** 1842. Rare.	—	—	—
A74	**100 Rigsdaler** 1842. Rare.	—	—	—

STATE TREASURY

LAW OF 4.4.1849

#1-6 various dates and sign. varieties w/denominations in *VESTINDISKE DALERE* (West Indies dollars).

Note: Issued examples required 7 sign.

		Good	Fine	XF
1	**2 Dalere** L. 1849. Pink paper. Portr. Mercury in frame at l., portr. Zeus at r., arms at lower ctr.	200.	500.	1250.
2	**3 Dalere** L. 1849. Pink paper. Like #1.	300.	700.	—
3	**5 Dalere** L. 1849. Lt. violet paper. Like #1.	300.	700.	—
4	**10 Dalere** L. 1849 (1900). 1.6.1901 (hand dated). Lt. blue paper. Like #1. Back black w/white printing.	150.	450.	1000.

		Good	Fine	XF
5	**50 Dalere** L. 1849. Lt. blue paper. Like #1. Rare.	—	—	—
6	**100 Dalere** L. 1849. Like #1. Rare.	—	—	—

Laws of 4.4.1849 and 1860

		Good	Fine	XF
7	**2 Dalere** L. 1860. Like #1.	200.	500.	1250.

Laws of 4.4.1849 and 1898

		Good	Fine	XF
8	**2 Dalere** L. 1898. Brown paper. Like #1.			
	a. Issued note w/7 sign. 1.8.1899.	125.	250.	700.
	r. Remainder w/3 sign.	25.00	50.00	125.

Bank of St. Thomas

1837 Issue

#9-12 printer: New England Bank Note Co., Boston.

		Good	Fine	XF
9	**5 Dollars** 1837. Harbor scene at ctr., allegorical figures at l. and r. Rare.	—	—	—
10	**10 Dollars** 1837. Similar to #9. Rare.	—	—	—
11	**100 Dollars** 1837. Columbus and steamship at l., landing of Columbus at ctr., allegorical figures at r. Rare.	—	—	—
12	**500 Dollars** 1837. 4 women seated on globe, allegorical figures at l. and r. Rare.	—	—	—

Note: Reprints of #11 and #12 were inserted in a reference volume on Danish money by J. Wilcke. These are valued at $400.-$500. each.

1860 Issue

		Good	Fine	XF
13	**5 Dollars** 1860. Blue and red. Bank arms at top ctr. Denomination: *$5* on back. Printer: ABNC. Rare.	—	—	—

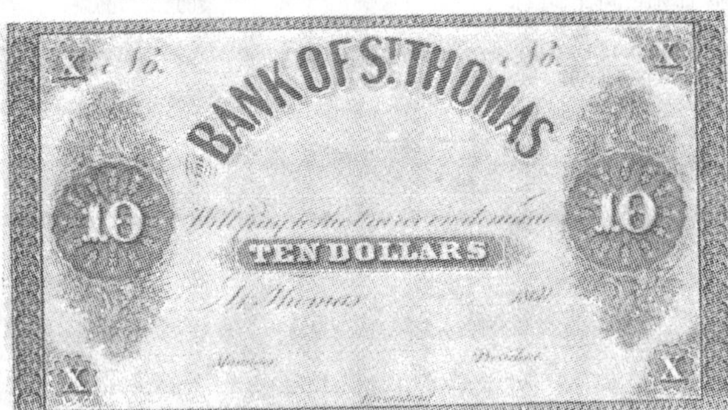

		Good	Fine	XF
14	**10 Dollars** 1860. Black. Uniface. Rare.	—	—	—
14A	**10 Dollars** 1860. Orange. Uniface. Rare.	—	—	—
14B	**100 Dollars** 1860. Brown. Bank arms at upper ctr. Uniface. Rare.	—	—	—

1889 Issue

#15-16 bank arms at l. Uniface.

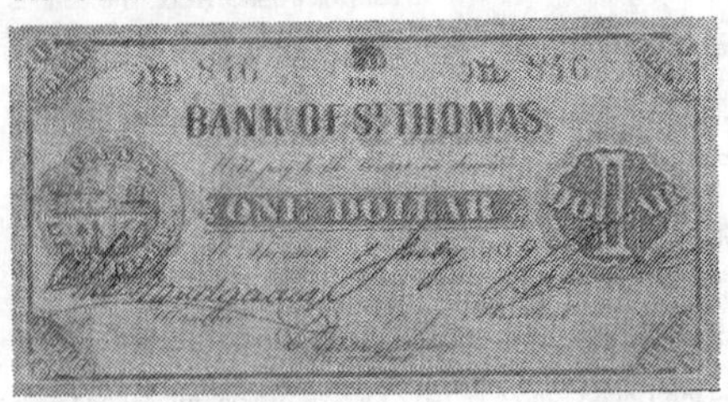

		Good	Fine	XF
15	**1 Dollar** 1.7.1889. Lt. green.			
	a. Issued note. Rare.	—	—	—
	r. Unsigned remainder. 188x. Rare.	—	—	—
16	**2 Dollars** 1889.			
	a. Issued note. Rare.	—	—	—
	r. Unsigned remainder. 188x. Rare.	—	—	—

Dansk-Vestindiske Nationalbank

National Bank of the Danish West Indies

1905 Issue

#17-20 printer: BWC.

		Good	Fine	XF
17	**5 Francs** 1905. Green and gray. Portr. Kg. Christian IX at lower l., palm tree at r. Village on back.	150.	350.	1250.

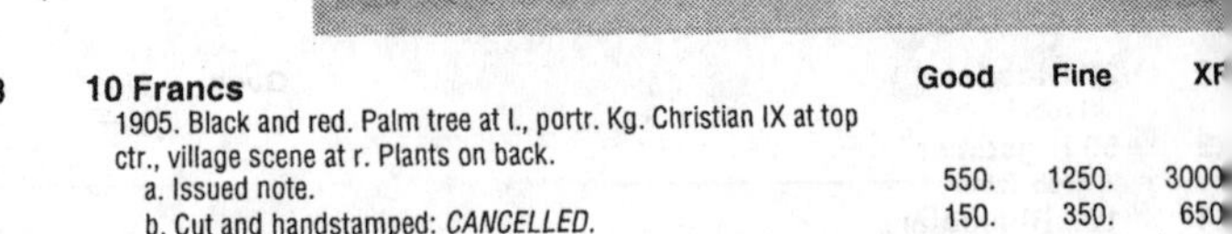

		Good	Fine	XF
18	**10 Francs** 1905. Black and red. Palm tree at l., portr. Kg. Christian IX at top ctr., village scene at r. Plants on back.			
	a. Issued note.	550.	1250.	3000.
	b. Cut and handstamped: *CANCELLED*.	150.	350.	650.

NOTICE

Readers with unlisted dates, signature varieties, etc. are invited to submit photocopies or, high resolution (300 dpi, 100% size) scans of their notes to: Standard Catalog of World Paper Money, 700 East State St. Iola, WI 54990-0001, or E-Mail: george.cuhaj@fwpubs.com.

19	20 Francs	Good	Fine	XF
	1905. Red and lt. green. Palm tree at l., portr. Kg. Christian IX at ctr., harbor scene at r. Several local scenes at l. and ctr. on back.			
	a. Issued note. Rare.	—	—	—
	b. Cut and handstamped: *CANCELLED.*	200.	450.	1250.

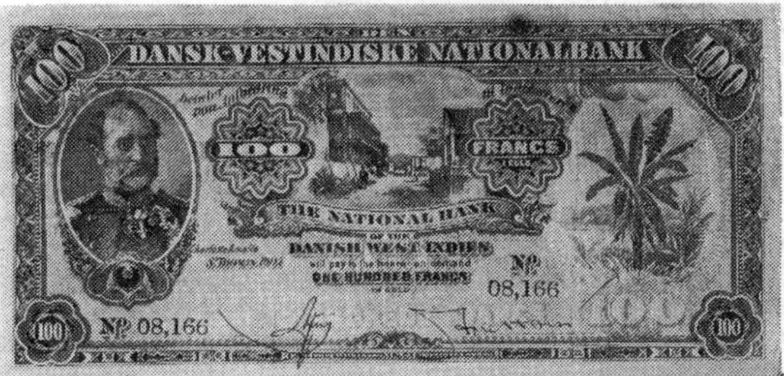

20	100 Francs	Good	Fine	XF
	1905. Gray and black. Portr. Kg. Christian IX at l., street scene at upper ctr., palm tree at r. Town scene at ctr. on back.			
	a. Issued note. Rare.	—	—	—
	b. Cut and handstamped: *CANCELLED.*	1000.	2500.	—

Danzig (Gdansk), the capital of Gdansk province, north-central Poland, is situated at the mouth of the Vistula River on the Baltic Sea. Danzig was first mentioned in 997 as belonging to Poland. It began its development as a trade center in 1260, upon the attainment of municipal autonomy. In 1308, the city was seized by the Teutonic Knights who held it until it was regained by Poland in 1466. It reached its peak during the Renaissance, becoming the most prosperous port on the Baltic.

Danzig's decline began during the Swedish wars of the 17th century. In 1772 it was seized by Prussia and in 1793 was incorporated as part of Prussia. Napoleon granted it the status of a free city in 1807, which it didn't want because it had a German majority, and later was relegated to the province of West Prussia.

From 1919 to 1939, Danzig again had the status of a free city. It was given to Poland in March 1945, following the defeat of the Axis powers. Polish currency is now in circulation.

MONETARY SYSTEM:

1 Mark = 100 Pfennige
1 MO (Million) = 1,000,000
1 MD (Milliarde) = 1,000,000,000 to 1923
1 Gulden = 100 Pfennig, 1923-1937

Note: Certain listings encompassing issues circulated by various bank and regional authorities are contained in Volume 1 under German States.

Note: Issues w/*UNGÜLTIG* marking are worth less than the values shown.

DANZIG

CITY COUNCIL

1914 EMERGENCY ISSUE

Note: #1-12 were issued by the city before its free city status began in 1919.

1	50 Pfennig	VG	VF	UNC
	10.8.1914. Violet.			
	a. Wmk: Scales.	20.00	80.00	350.
	b. Wmk: Wavy lines.	20.00	70.00	325.
	c. Wmk: Spades.	20.00	70.00	325.

2	1 Mark	VG	VF	UNC
	10.8.1914. Brown.			
	a. Wmk: Wavy lines.	20.00	90.00	375.
	b. Wmk: Spades.	20.00	90.00	375.
3	2 Mark			
	10.8.1914. Pink.	25.00	100.	450.
4	3 Mark			
	10.8.1914. Green.			
	a. Wmk: Spades.	25.00	125.	500.
	b. Wmk: Crosses in squares.	30.00	150.	600.

1916 ISSUE

5	10 Pfennig	VG	VF	UNC
	9.12.1916. Black on blue unpt.	2.00	7.00	25.00

6	50 Pfennig	VG	VF	UNC
	9.12.1916. Black on orange unpt.	2.00	7.00	25.00

1918 First Issue

		VG	VF	UNC
7	**5 Mark** 12.10.1918. Black on green unpt.			
	a. Wmk: Drops.	25.00	60.00	175.
	b. W/o wmk.	18.00	45.00	150.
8	**20 Mark** 12.10.1918. Black on brown unpt.			
	a. Wmk: Drops.	30.00	70.00	200.
	b. Wmk: Spades.	25.00	50.00	175.
	c. Wmk: Crosses in squares.	35.00	85.00	250.
	d. W/o wmk.	18.00	45.00	160.

1918 Second Issue

		VG	VF	UNC
9	**50 Pfennig** 1.11.1918. Brown. City Hall. 2 stylized lions and arms on back.	3.50	10.00	35.00

		VG	VF	UNC
10	**20 Mark** 15.11.1918. Black on lilac-brown unpt. Hanseatic galleon at l. Town view, 2 stylized lions and arms on back.	15.00	50.00	185.

1919 Issue

		VG	VF	UNC
11	**50 Pfennig** 15.4.1919. Brown and violet. Town view on back.	1.50	5.00	12.00
12	**50 Pfennig** 15.4.1919. Dk. green and olive-green. Like #11.	1.50	6.00	17.50

Senate of the Municipality - Free City 1919

Post-WWI Inflation Issues

1922 Issue

		VG	VF	UNC
13	**100 Mark** 31.10.1922. Green on gray unpt. St. Mary's Church at ctr. Bldg. at l. and r. on back.	10.00	25.00	100.

		VG	VF	UNC
14	**500 Mark** 31.10.1922. Blue. Arms at l., tall church at r. Krantor on back.	12.00	45.00	200.

		VG	VF	UNC
15	**1000 Mark** 31.10.1922. Olive-green and dk. brown. Arms at l., Hanseatic galleon at r. Town view on back.	12.00	45.00	200.

1923 First Issue

		VG	VF	UNC
16	**1000 Mark** 15.3.1923. Dk. green. Similar to #15.	12.00	45.00	200.

		VG	VF	UNC
17	**10,000 Mark** 20.3.1923. Dk. blue on lt. brown unpt. Town view at l. and r. Large bldg. on back.	12.00	50.00	200.

		VG	VF	UNC
18	**10,000 Mark** 26.6.1923. Dk. brown and blue. Portr. Danzig merchant at l. (painting by Hans Holbein the younger), ship at r. City view at l. and r. on back.	7.50	25.00	100.
19	**50,000 Mark** 20.3.1923. Lt. green on pale yellow unpt. St. Mary's Church at l. Arms at l., bldgs. at ctr. on back.	10.00	40.00	185.

		VG	VF	UNC
20	**50,000 Mark** 20.3.1923. Dk. brown. Like #19.	10.00	40.00	185.

1923 PROVISIONAL ISSUE

		VG	VF	UNC
21	**1 Million on 50,000 Mark** 8.8.1923 (- old date 20.3.1923). Red ovpt. on #20.	12.00	50.00	200.

		VG	VF	UNC
22	**1 Million on 50,000 Mark** 8.8.1923 (- old date 20.3.1923). Dk. blue ovpt. on #20.	12.00	50.00	225.

		VG	VF	UNC
23	**5 Millionen on 50,000 Mark** 15.10.1923 (- old date 20.3.1923). Green ovpt. on #20.	12.00	50.00	250.

1923 INFLATION ISSUES

		VG	VF	UNC
24	**1 Million Mark** 8.8.1923. Lilac and green. Arms at l., Chodowiecki at r. Ornate gateway on back.			
	a. 5-digit serial #.	8.00	25.00	100.
	b. 6-digit serial #.	10.00	35.00	150.

		VG	VF	UNC
25	**10 Millionen Mark** 31.8.1923. Green. Portr. J. Hevelius at upper l., arms at r. Margin printing upright. City view across back.			
	a. Lg. *A* at lower r. corner.	8.00	25.00	100.
	b. W/o *A* at lower r. corner.	10.00	30.00	125.
26	**10 Millionen Mark** 31.8.1923. Green. Like #25, but margin printing inverted.	9.00	25.00	150.

		VG	VF	UNC
27	**100 Millionen Mark** 22.9.1923. Black on lt. orange unpt. Uniface.			
	a. Wmk: Triangles.	10.00	30.00	180.
	b. Wmk: Tear drops.	10.00	35.00	200.

		VG	VF	UNC
28	**500 Millionen Mark** 26.9.1923. Dk. brown on violet unpt. Portr. Schopenhauer at top ctr. City view on back.			
	a. Upright lt. blue margin inscription.	10.00	30.00	180.
	b. Upright lt. yellow margin inscription.	10.00	30.00	180.
29	**500 Millionen Mark** 26.9.1923. Dk. brown on violet unpt. Like #28.			
	a. Inverted lt. blue margin inscription.	10.00	30.00	175.
	b. Inverted lt. yellow margin inscription.	10.00	30.00	185.
30	**5 Milliarden Mark** 11.10.1923. Black on blue unpt., uniface.	12.00	40.00	185.
31	**10 Milliarden Mark** 11.10.1923. Black on brown unpt.			
	a. Wmk: Interlaced lines.	10.00	37.50	185.
	b. Wmk: Tear drops.	10.00	40.00	190.

DANZIGER ZENTRALKASSE

DANZIG CENTRAL FINANCE DEPARTMENT

1923 FIRST GULDEN ISSUE, OCT.

#32-37 uniface.

		VG	VF	UNC
32	**1 Pfennig** 22.10.1923. Dk. blue on lt. brown unpt.	6.00	15.00	60.00
33	**2 Pfennige** 22.10.1923. Dk. green on orange unpt.	8.00	30.00	135.
34	**5 Pfennige** 22.10.1923. Black on green unpt. Like #35.			
	a. Wmk: Interlaced lines.	10.00	25.00	90.00
	b. Wmk: Octagons.	15.00	40.00	100.
35	**10 Pfennige** 22.10.1923. Dk. red on blue unpt.			
	a. Wmk: Interlaced lines.	10.00	30.00	150.
	b. Wmk: Hanseatic galleon.	12.00	45.00	175.
36	**25 Pfennige** 22.10.1923. Black on lilac-brown unpt.	12.00	45.00	200.
37	**50 Pfennige** 22.10.1923. Black on gray unpt. 2 serial # varieties.	20.00	50.00	225.
38	**1 Gulden** 22.10.1923. Black on green unpt.			
	a. Wmk: Interlaced lines.	25.00	65.00	275.
	b. Wmk: Hanseatic galleon.	45.00	90.00	325.
39	**2 Gulden** 22.10.1923. Lilac-brown. Hanseatic galleon at ctr. 2 serial # varieties.	60.00	150.	425.
40	**5 Gulden** 22.10.1923. Black on lt. brown and gray-green unpt. Hanseatic galleon at ctr.			
	a. Wmk: Interlaced lines.	80.00	225.	700.
	b. Wmk: Hanseatic galleon.	100.	275.	850.
41	**10 Gulden** 22.10.1923. Black on reddish brown unpt. Hanseatic galleon at l.	100.	375.	1150.
42	**25 Gulden** 22.10.1923. Black on olive unpt. Hanseatic galleon at l.	200.	575.	1600.

1923 SECOND GULDEN ISSUE, NOV.

#43-47 like #32-37. Uniface.

		VG	VF	UNC
43	**1 Pfennig** 1.11.1923. Dk. blue on lt. brown unpt.	35.00	70.00	200.
43A	**2 Pfennige** 1.11.1923. Dk. green on orange unpt.	100.	175.	500
44	**5 Pfennige** 1.11.1923. Black on green unpt.	45.00	110.	350.
45	**10 Pfennige** 1.11.1923. Dk. red on blue unpt.	60.00	140.	425
46	**25 Pfennige** 1.11.1923. Black on lilac-brown unpt.	70.00	140.	400
47	**50 Pfennige** 1.11.1923. Black on gray unpt.	70.00	140.	400
48	**1 Gulden** 1.11.1923. Black on green unpt.	100.	170.	500
49	**2 Gulden** 1.11.1923. Lilac-brown. Hanseatic galleon at ctr.	120.	250.	600
50	**5 Gulden** 1.11.1923. Black on lt. brown & gray-green unpt. Hanseatic galleon at ctr. in unpt.	200.	350.	900
51	**50 Gulden** 1.11.1923. Black on reddish brown unpt. Hanseatic galleon at ctr.	300.	500.	–
52	**100 Gulden** 1.11.1923. Black on olive unpt. Hanseatic galleon at ctr.	300.	600.	–

BANK VON DANZIG

BANK OF DANZIG

1924 ISSUE

#53-57 arms at l.

		VG	VF	UNC
53	**10 Gulden** 10.2.1924. Brown. *Artushof* (Artus' courtyard) at ctr.	150.	400.	110
54	**25 Gulden** 10.2.1924. St. Mary's Church at ctr.	250.	700.	–
55	**100 Gulden** 10.2.1924. Blue. River Mottlau dock scene at ctr.	300.	950.	–
56	**500 Gulden** 10.2.1924. Green. *Zeughaus* (the arsenal) at ctr.	50.00	140.	57

		VG	VF	UNC
57	**1000 Gulden** 10.2.1924. Red-orange on blue unpt. City Hall at ctr.	50.00	175.	650.

1928-30 Issue

		VG	VF	UNC
58	**10 Gulden** 1.7.1930. Brown, *Artushof* (Artus' courtyard) at ctr.	45.00	140.	600.
59	**25 Gulden** 1.10.1928. Dk. green. St. Mary's Church at ctr.	125.	475.	1500.

1931-32 Issue

		VG	VF	UNC
60	**20 Gulden** 2.1.1932. Lilac-brown. *Stockturm* (local tower) at ctr. 2 serial # varieties. Neptune at r. on back.	20.00	75.00	300.
61	**25 Gulden** 2.1.1931. Dk. green. St. Mary's Church at ctr.	65.00	225.	800.

		VG	VF	UNC
62	**100 Gulden** 1.8.1931. Blue. River Mottlau dock scene at ctr. Allegorical man at r. on back.	30.00	110.	350.

1937-38 Issue

		VG	VF	UNC
63	**20 Gulden** 1.11.1937. Dk. green. *Artushof*(Artus' courtyard) at ctr. 2 serial # varieties. Back like #62.	20.00	60.00	275.
64	**20 Gulden** 2.1.1938. Like #64, but blue-green and orange face. Back lilac-rose and green. Specimen. Rare.	—	—	—
65	**50 Gulden** 5.2.1937. Brown. The *Vorlaubenhaus* (building) at ctr. Allegorical man at r. on back.	25.00	90.00	325.

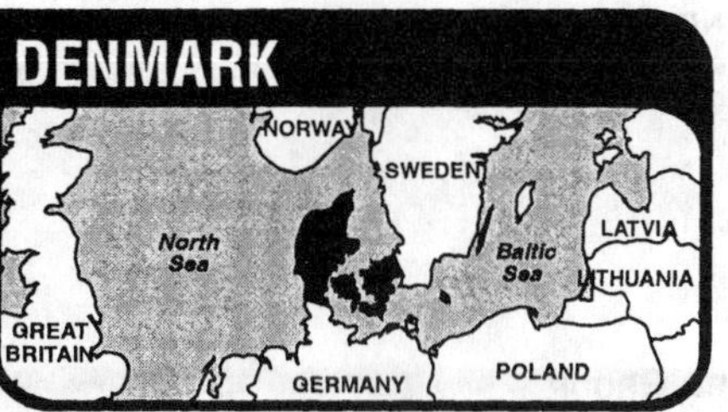

The Kingdom of Denmark, a constitutional monarchy located at the mouth of the Baltic Sea, has an area of 16,639 sq. mi. (43,070 sq. km.) and a population of 5.2 million. Capital: Copenhagen. Most of the country is arable. Agriculture, which used to employ the majority of the people, is now conducted by large farms served by cooperatives. The largest industries are food processing, iron and metal, and shipping. Machinery, meats (chiefly bacon), dairy products and chemicals are exported.

Denmark, a great power during the Viking period of the 9th-11th centuries, conducted raids on western Europe and England, and in the 11th century united England, Denmark and Norway under the rule of King Canute. Despite a struggle between the crown and the nobility (13th-14th centuries) which forced the king to grant a written constitution, Queen Margrethe (1353-1412) succeeded in uniting Denmark, Norway, Sweden, Finland and Greenland under the Danish crown, placing all Nordic countries under the rule of Denmark. Sweden and Finland were lost in 1523, and an unwise alliance with Napoleon caused the loss of Norway to Sweden in 1814. In the following years a liberal movement was fostered, which succeeded in making Denmark a constitutional monarchy in 1849.

The present decimal system of currency was introduced in 1874. As a result of a referendum held Sept. 28, 2000, the currency of the European Monetary Union, the Euro, will not be introduced in Denmark in the forseeable future.

RULERS:

Frederik IV, 1699-1730
Christian VI, 1730-1746
Frederik V, 1746-1766
Christian VII, 1766-1808
Frederik VI, 1808-1839
Christian VIII, 1839-1848
Frederik VII, 1848-1863
Christian IX, 1863-1906
Frederik VIII, 1906-1912
Christian X, 1912-1947
Frederik IX, 1947-1972
Margrethe II, 1972-
Christian IX, 1863-1906
Frederik VIII, 1906-1912
Christian X, 1912-1947
Frederik IX, 1947-1972
Margrethe II, 1972-
Frederik IX, 1947-1972
Margrethe II, 1972-

MONETARY SYSTEM:

1 Rigsdaler dansk Courant = 96 Skilling Courant = 6 Mark; at the same time, 1 Rigsdaler Species = 120 Skilling Courant, 1713-1813
1 Rigsbankdaler = 96 Rigsbankskilling (= 1/2 Rigsdaler Species), 1813-54
1 Daler Rigsmønt = 96 Skilling Rigsmønt (= 1 Rigsbankdaler), 1854-74
1 Krone = 100 Øre
1 Krone (1/2 Rigsdaler) = 100 Øre 1874-

Kingdom

Treasury

Decree of 8.4.1713 - "Authorized Notes"

#A1-A6 have crowned double monogram F4 printed at top l., handwritten denomination, 6 hand sign.

		Good	Fine	XF
A1	**1 Rigsdaler** 1713.	—	1000.	—
A2	**5 Rigsdaler** 1713. Rare.	—	—	—
A3	**10 Rigsdaler** 1713. Unknown.	—	—	—
A4	**25 Rigsdaler** 1713. Unknown.	—	—	—
A5	**50 Rigsdaler** 1713. Unknown.	—	—	—
A6	**100 Rigsdaler** 1713. Unknown.	—	—	—

DECREE OF 8.4.1713 - 2ND GROUP

#A7-A9 similar to A1-A6 but w/printed denominations, 6 hand sign.

		Good	Fine	XF
A7	**1 Rigsdaler** 1713. Unknown.	—	—	—
A8	**5 Rigsdaler** 1713. Unique.	—	—	—
A9	**10 Rigsdaler** 1713. Unknown.	—	—	—
A9A	**100 Rigsdaler** 1713.	—	—	—

DECREE OF 8.4.1713 - 3RD GROUP

#A10-A13 similar to A7-A9 but w/only 5 hand sign. Denominations in Mark and Rigsdaler.

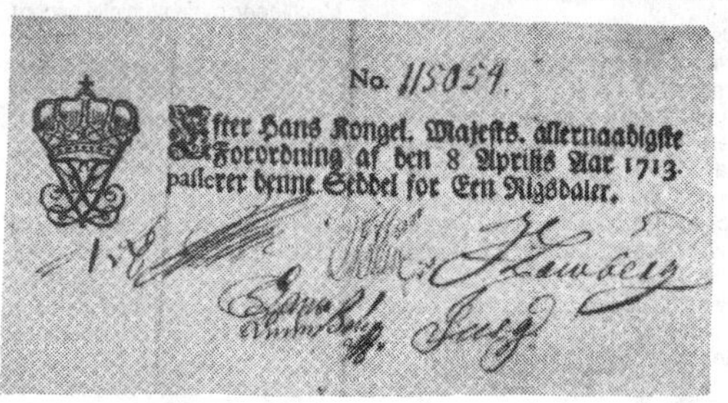

		Good	Fine	XF
A10	**1 (Een) Mark** 1713.	1800.	—	—
A11	**2 (Toe) Mark** 1713.			
	a. Issued note.	2500.	—	—
	r. Remainder.	2000.	—	—
A12	**3 Mark** 1713.			
	a. Value expressed as: *Tree Mark.*	2400.	—	—
	b. Value expressed as: *Tre Mark.*	2500.	—	—
	r. Remainder.	250.	700.	—

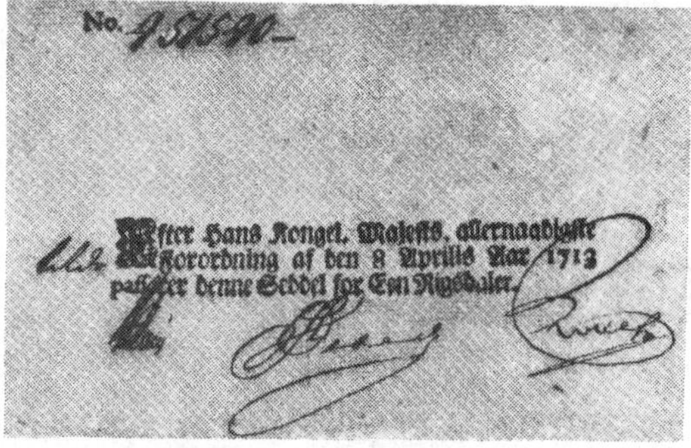

		Good	Fine	XF
A13	**1 (Een) Rigsdaler** 1713.			
	a. Issued note.	1600.	—	—
	r. Remainder.	—	125.	500.

DECREE OF 8.4.1713 - 4TH GROUP

#A14-A17 w/o monogram; impressed stamp w/imperial arms, 3 hand sign.

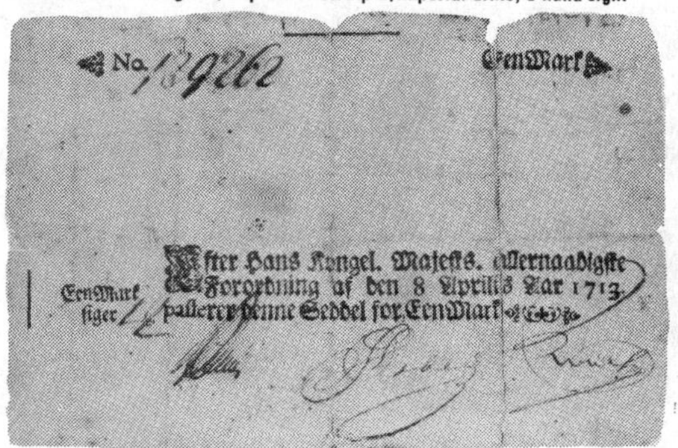

		Good	Fine	XF
A14	**1 (Een) Mark** 1713.	1000.	1600.	—
A15	**2 (Toe) Mark** 1713.	1200.	2000.	—
A16	**3 (Tree) Mark** 1713.	1500.	2500.	—

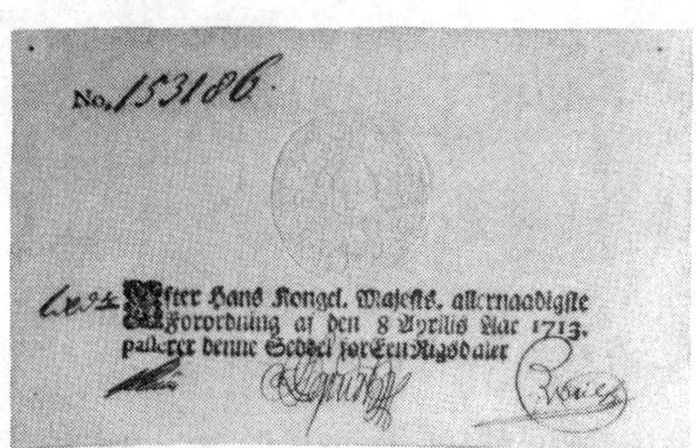

		Good	Fine	XF
A17	**1 (Een) Rigsdaler** 1713.	600.	1800.	6750.

Note: In a June, 1999 auction, #A17 brought $6,750 in XF.

KIÖBENHAVNSKE ASSIGNATION-, VEXEL- OG LAANE-BANQUE

COPENHAGEN NOTES, EXCHANGE AND MORTGAGE BANK

COPENHAGEN

1737 ISSUE

#A18-A23 have ornate column at l., handwritten denomination.

		Good	Fine	XF
A18	**10 Rigsdaler** 1737-1740.			
	a. *Rixdaler* in lines 2 and 6. 1737; 1740.	—	—	—
	b. *Rdl* in lines 2 and 6. , Unknown.	—	—	—
A19	**20 Rigsdaler** 1737.	—	—	—
A20	**30 Rigsdaler** 1737. Unknown.	—	—	—
A21	**40 Rigsdaler** 1737; 1740. Unknown.	—	—	—
A22	**50 Rigsdaler** 1737; 1740.	—	—	—
A23	**100 Rigsdaler** 1737; 1739; 1740. Unknown.	—	—	—

1748-1762 ISSUE

#A24-A27 printed denomination, design at l. in 3 styles. #A24-A25 3 hand sign.; #A26-A27 5 hand sign.

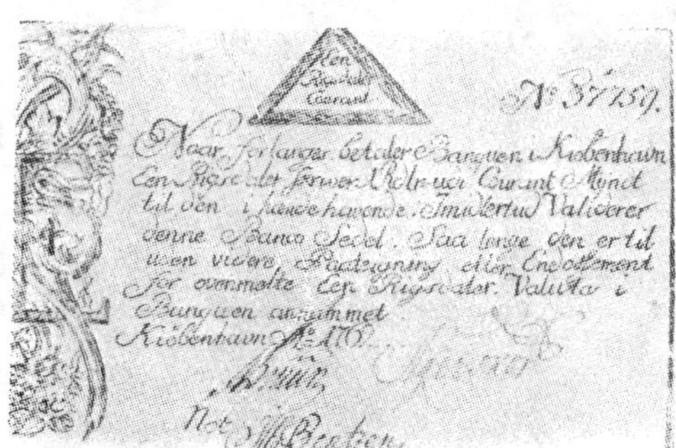

		Good	Fine	XF
A24	**1 Rigsdaler Courant** 1762-92. Black.			
	a. 1762-63 (only 1762 and 1763 known). No wmk.	800.	1700.	—
	b. 1766-67 (only 1766 known). Wmk.: crowned monogram *F5* w/letters A-F, *C7* w/impressed stamp.	—	—	—
	c. 1769-92. Wmk: crowned monogram w/impressed stamp *C7.*	75.00	175.	375.

		Good	Fine	XF
A25	**10 Rigsdaler Courant** 1748-88. Black.			
	a. 1748-63. Wmk: crowned monogram *F5* w/impressed stamp *F5.* No examples known.	3000.	6000.	—

NOTICE

Readers with unlisted dates, signature varieties, etc. are invited to submit photocopies or, high resolution (300 dpi, 100% size) scans of their notes to: Standard Catalog of World Paper Money, 700 East State St. Iola, WI 54990-0001, or E-Mail: george.cuhaj@fwpubs.com.

		Good	Fine	XF
	b. 1768-80. Wmk: crowned monogram *F5* w/impressed stamp *C7*.	800.	2400.	—
	c. 1772-88. Wmk: crowned monogram *C7* and impressed stamp *C7*.	800.	2400.	—

A26 50 Rigsdaler Courant
1748-87. Black.

	Good	Fine	XF
a. 1748-61. Wmk. and impressed stamp w/*F5*. Only 1748 date known.	—	—	—
b. 1770-87. Wmk. and impressed stamp w/*C7*. ,Unknown.	—	—	—

A27 100 Rigsdaler Courant
1748-88. Black.

	Good	Fine	XF
a. 1748-61. Wmk. and impressed stamp w/*F5*. ,Unknown	—	—	—
b. 1768. Wmk.: *F5*, impressed stamp *C7*. ,20934, Unknown.	—	—	—
c. 1772-88 (only 1773; 1782 known). Wmk. and impressed stamp w/*C7*.	—	3000.	—

1775-88 Issue

#A28-32 similar to previous issue. Anti-counterfeiting text added vertically at r. White paper (#A29a) or blue paper (#A28, A29b, A30-32).

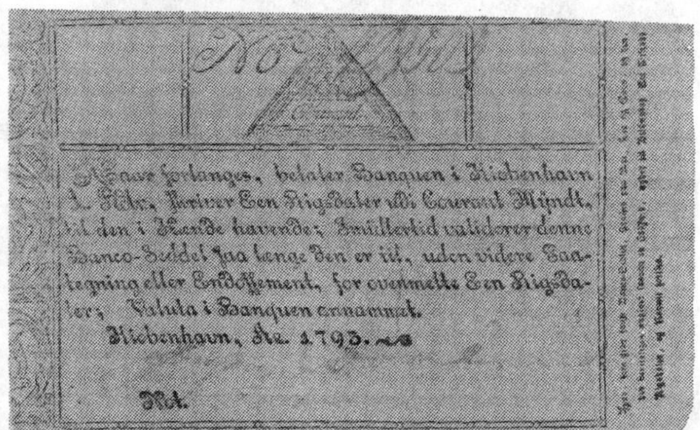

		Good	Fine	XF
A28	**1 Rigsdaler Courant** 1788-1808. Issued until 1813.	30.00	100.	500.

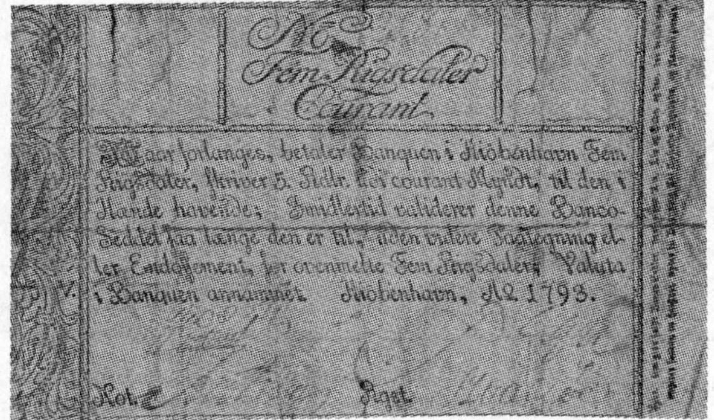

		Good	Fine	XF
A29	**5 Rigsdaler Courant** 1775-1800.			
	a. White paper. 1775-91. Issued until 1793.	125.	500.	1500.
	b. Blue paper. 1786-1800. Issued until 1813.	75.00	200.	800.

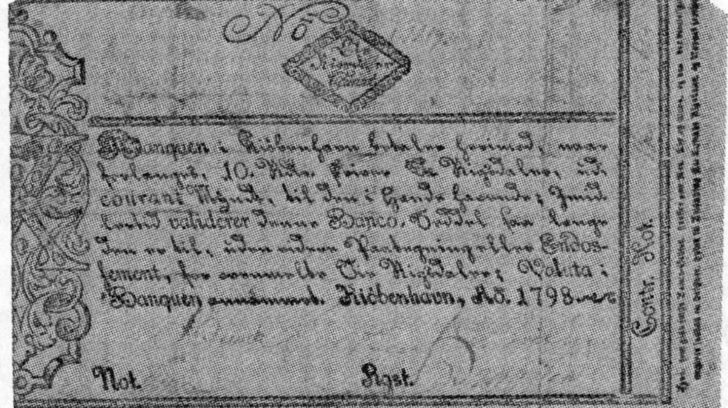

		Good	Fine	XF
A30	**10 Rigsdaler Courant** 1778-98. Issued until 1813.	800.	1800.	—
A31	**50 Rigsdaler Courant** 1785-94. Issued until 1812.	2250.	5000.	—

NOTICE

Readers with unlisted dates, signature varieties, etc. are invited to submit photocopies or, high resolution (300 dpi, 100% size) scans of their notes to: Standard Catalog of World Paper Money, 700 East State St. Iola, WI 54990-0001, or E-Mail: george.cuhaj@fwpubs.com.

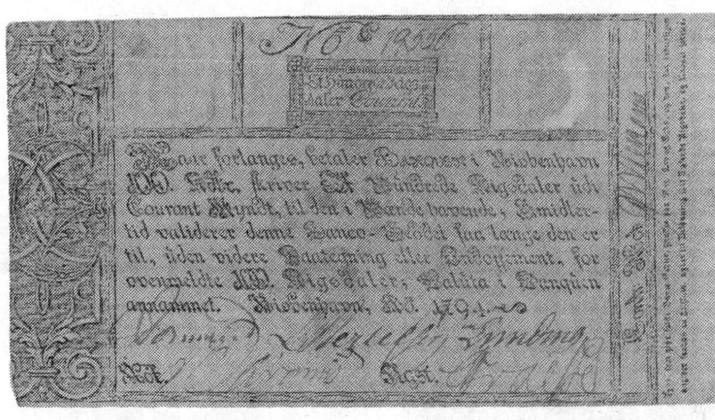

		Good	Fine	XF
A32	**100 Rigsdaler Courant** 1785-98. Issued until 1813.	2600.	—	—

Danske og Norske Species Banke i Kiöbenhavn

Danish-Norwegian Specie Bank in Copenhagen

1791-98 Issue

#A33-A37 in denominations of *Rigsdaler Specie*.

		Good	Fine	XF
A33	**8 Rigsdaler Specie** 1791; 1797.	—	—	—
A34	**20 Rigsdaler Specie** 1791.	—	—	—
A35	**40 Rigsdaler Specie** 1792-96. Unknown.	—	—	—
A36	**80 Rigsdaler Specie** 1791-97. Only a *formular* of 1791 and a regular issue of 1796 are known.	—	—	—
A37	**4 Rigsdaler Specie** 1798-1800. Only 1798 is known.	—	4000.	—

Drafts on the Revenue of the Treasury - Compensation Fund

Decree of 8.4.1808

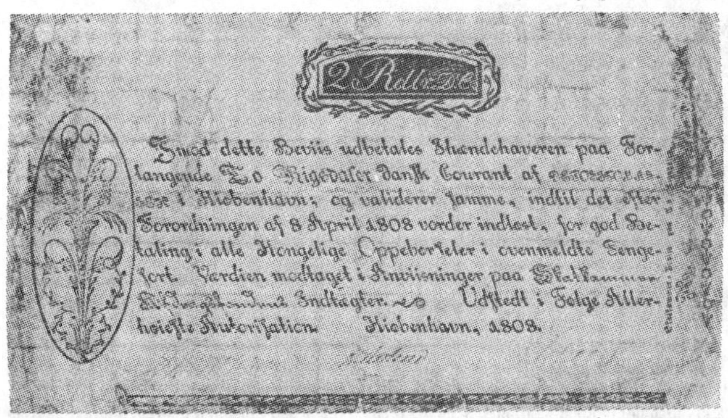

		Good	Fine	XF
A38	**2 Rigsdaler D.C.** D.1808.	500.	1000.	—

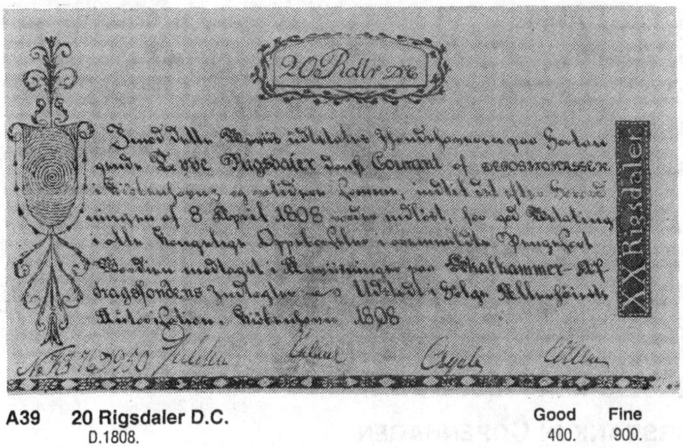

		Good	Fine	XF
A39	**20 Rigsdaler D.C.** D.1808.	400.	900.	—

DECREES OF 28.8.1809 AND 6.6.1810

#A40-A42 small change notes.

		Good	Fine	XF
A40	**8 Skilling** D.1809. Blue paper.	30.00	80.00	250.
A41	**12 Skilling** D.1809. Blue paper.	30.00	85.00	285.

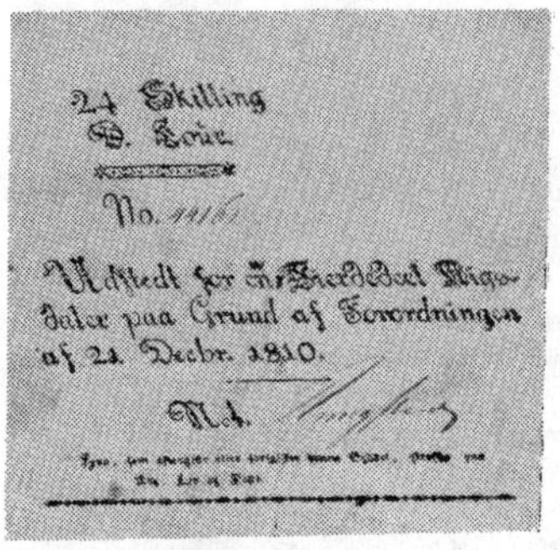

		Good	Fine	XF
A42	**24 Skilling** D.1810. White paper.	35.00	100.	350.

Notes of the "Committee for the Advantage of Commerce" of the Wholesalers' Society of 1799 (100, 400 and 800 Rigsdaler interest-bearing at 3 3/4%), 1806 (100 and 500 Rigsdaler Courant interest-bearing at 5%) and 1814 (5, 25 and 100 Rigsbankdaler interest-bearing at 3.55%), though issued with government sanction, cannot be included as true government issues.

ROYAL BANK

1813 DRAFTS

		Good	Fine	XF
A43	**100 Rigsbankdaler** 6.2.1813. Unknown.	—	—	—
A44	**250 Rigsbankdaler** 6.2.1813.	—	—	—
A45	**500 Rigsbankdaler** 6.2.1813. Unknown.	—	—	—

DANISH STATE

DRAFTS - ROYAL DECREE OF 30.9.1813

		Good	Fine	XF
A46	**100 Rigsbankdaler** 1813. Unknown.	—	—	—
A47	**200 Rigsbankdaler** 1813. Unknown.	—	—	—

RIGSBANKEN I KIØBENHAVN

RIGSBANK IN COPENHAGEN

1813 ISSUE

#A48-A52 uniface.

		Good	Fine	XF
A48	**1 Rigsbankdaler** 1813-15.	200.	500.	—
A49	**5 Rigsbankdaler** 1813-14.	300.	1250.	2500.
A50	**10 Rigsbankdaler** 1814.	600.	1600.	—

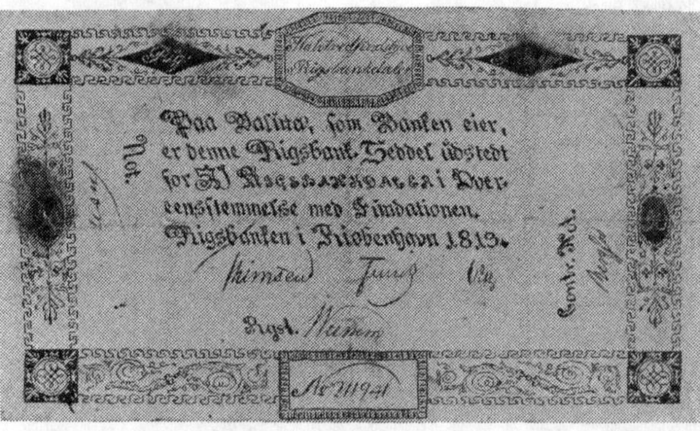

		Good	Fine	XF
A51	**50 Rigsbankdaler** 1813.	1600.	3800.	—
A52	**100 Rigsbankdaler** 1813.	1800.	4500.	—

NATIONALBANKEN I KIØBENHAVN

NATIONAL BANK IN COPENHAGEN

1819 ISSUE

#A53-A57 uniface.

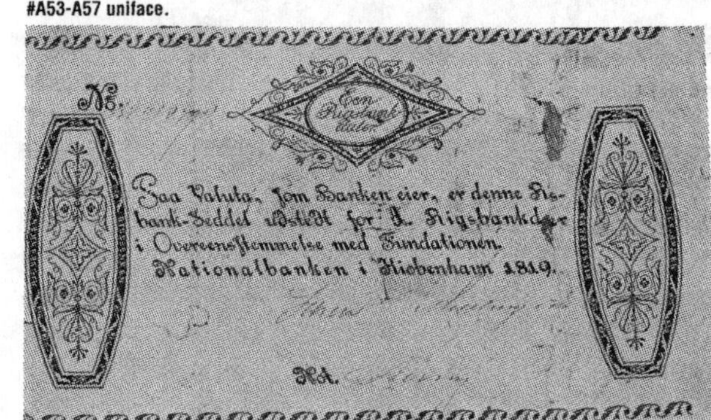

		Good	Fine	XF
A53	**1 Rigsbankdaler** 1819.	20.00	100.	400.
A54	**5 Rigsbankdaler** 1819.	250.	800.	—
A55	**10 Rigsbankdaler** 1819.	325.	2000.	—
A56	**50 Rigsbankdaler** 1819.	1500.	3500.	—

		Good	Fine	XF
A57	**100 Rigsbankdaler** 1819.	1800.	4000.	—

1834-51 Issue

No.	Description	Good	Fine	XF
A58	**5 Rigsbankdaler** 1835.	100.	400.	—
A59	**20 Rigsbankdaler** 1851.			
	a. Hand serial #, impressed stamps, back w/3 hand sign.	6000.	10,000.	—
	b. Printed serial #, no impressed stamps, no sign. on back (issued 1872).	—	—	—
A60	**50 Rigsbankdaler** 1834.			
	a. Plain back, impressed stamps, 5 hand sign.	—	—	—
	b. Brown back, impressed stamps, 5 hand sign. (issued 1850).	—	—	—
	c. Like b. but no impressed stamp, 2 hand sign. (issued 1870)., Unknown.	—	—	—
A61	**100 Rigsbankdaler** 1845.	—	—	—

1860-74 Issue

No.	Description	Good	Fine	XF
A62	**5 Rigsdaler** 1863-74.			
	a. Wmk. w/o wavy lines, impressed stamp, hand serial #. 1863.	500.	1500.	5000.
	b. Wmk. has wavy lines, no impressed stamp, printed serial #. 1872-74.	750.	2500.	—
A63	**10 Rigsdaler** 1860-74.			
	a. Impressed stamp, hand serial #, back w/3 hand sign. 1860.	650.	2500.	—
	b. No impressed stamp, printed serial #, no sign. 1872-74.	—	—	—
A64	**50 Rigsdaler** 1873-74.	—	—	—
A65	**100 Rigsdaler** 1870-74.	—	—	—

Interest-bearing Credit Notes 1848-70

Various Decrees and Laws

No.	Description	Good	Fine	XF
A66	**5 Rigsbankdaler** D.1848.	300.	400.	—
A67	**5 Rigsbankdaler** L.1850.	300.	400.	—

Law of 27.1.1851

No.	Description	Good	Fine	XF
A68	**5 Rigsbankdaler** L.1851.	300.	400.	—
A69	**50 Rigsbankdaler** L.1851. Unknown.	—	—	—
A70	**100 Rigsbankdaler** L.1851. Unknown.	—	—	—

Law of 26.8.1864

No.	Description	Good	Fine	XF
A71	**20 Rigsdaler** L.1864.	—	—	—
A72	**50 Rigsdaler** L.1864.	—	—	—
A73	**100 Rigsdaler** L.1864.	—	—	—

Law of 27.3.1866

No.	Description	Good	Fine	XF
A74	**20 Rigsdaler** L.1866.	—	—	—
A75	**50 Rigsdaler** L.1866.	—	—	—
A76	**100 Rigsdaler** L.1866.	—	—	—
A77	**500 Rigsdaler** L.1866.	—	—	—

Law of 1.8.1870

No.	Description	Good	Fine	XF
A78	**50 Rigsdaler** L.1870.	—	—	—
A79	**100 Rigsdaler** L.1870.	—	—	—
A80	**500 Rigsdaler** L.1870.	—	—	—

1875-1903 Issue

No.	Description	Good	Fine	XF
A81	**10 Kroner** 1875-90. Arms at upper ctr.	400.	800.	2250.
A82	**50 Kroner** 1875-81. Ornate panels at sides.	—	—	—
A83	**100 Kroner** 1875-87. Head at l. and r., ornate oval design between.	—	—	—

No.	Description	Good	Fine	XF
A84	**500 Kroner** 1875; 1889; 1903; 1907. Head of Mercury at l. and Ceres at r., arms at bottom ctr.			
	a. Issued note. Rare.		11,000.	
	b. Handstamped: *MAKULATUR* (waste paper) w/2 punched holes.	750.	3000.	—

1898-1904 Issue

No.	Description	Good	Fine	XF
1	**5 Kroner** 1899-1902. Blue. Ornamental design of *5s* and *FEM KRONER*. Serial # at bottom l. and r.	225.	575.	1500.
2	**10 Kroner** 1891-1903. Black on brown unpt. Shield at l., ten 1 krone coins along bottom on back.	140.	350.	850.
3	**50 Kroner** 1883-1902. Violet. Woman seated at l. Cancelled note. Handstamped: *MAKULATUR*.	500.	2000.	—
4	**100 Kroner** 1888-1902. Green. Woman standing w/scrolls at ctr. Cancelled note. Handstamped: >I>MAKULATUR.			
	a. Issued note.	600.	4000.	—
	b. Handstamped: *MAKULATUR.*	600.	5000.	—

1904-11 Issue

No.	Description	Good	Fine	XF
6	**5 Kroner** 1904-10. Blue. Similar to #1 but different wmk. of wavy lines. Serial # at top l. and r.			
	a. 1904 Prefix A.	—	—	—
	b. 1905 Prefix A.	275.	400.	—
	c. 1906 Prefix A.	250.	375.	1100.
	d. 1907 Prefix A.	250.	375.	1100.
	e. 1908 Prefix A.	200.	350.	900.
	f. 1908 Prefix B.	150.	250.	
	g. 1909 Prefix B.	150.	250.	750.
	h. 1910 Prefix B.	150.	250.	750.
	i. 1910 Prefix C.	140.	240.	700.

		Good	Fine	XF
7	**10 Kroner** 1904-11. Black on brown unpt. Like #2 but different wmk. of wavy lines.			
	a. 1904 Prefix A.	350.	500.	—
	b. 1905 Prefix A.	—	—	—
	c. 1906 Prefix A.	250.	350.	1000.
	d. 1906 Prefix B.	250.	350.	1000.
	e. 1907 Prefix B.	250.	350.	1000.
	f. 1908 Prefix C.	200.	275.	900.
	g. 1909 Prefix C.	200.	275.	700.
	h. 1909 Prefix D.	180.	275.	700.
	i. 1910 Prefix D.	150.	250.	600.
	j. 1910 Prefix E.	130.	200.	600.
	k. 1911 Prefix E.	130.	200.	600.
	l. 1911 Prefix F.	130.	200.	600.

		Good	Fine	XF
8	**50 Kroner** 1904-10. Brown. Like #3 but different wmk. of wavy lines.			
	a. Issued note.	3000.	10,000.	—
	b. Cancelled note.	800.	3500.	—

		Good	Fine	XF
9	**100 Kroner** 1905-1910. Green. Like #4 but different wmk. of wavy lines. Cancelled note.	—	8000.	—

1914-16 Issues

#10-15 w/o pictorial design. Arms on back.

		VG	VF	UNC
10	**1 Krone** 1914. Black on red paper. Arms in shield w/fish at lower l. for Iceland on back.			
	a. 6-digit serial #. Large digits.	4.00	25.00	75.00
	b. 7-digit serial #. Smaller digits.	3.50	22.50	70.00

		VG	VF	UNC
11	**1 Krone** 1914. Black on red paper. Arms in shield w/falcon at lower l. for Iceland on back. Face like 10b.	3.00	20.00	65.00

		VG	VF	UNC
12	**1 Krone** 1916; 1918; 1920; 1921. Blue on blue-green unpt.			
	a. 1916. W/o prefix letter.	1.50	4.00	12.50
	b. 1916. Prefix letter A-C.	1.00	3.00	12.00
	c. 1918. Prefix letter C.	15.00	50.00	—
	d. 1918. Prefix letter D-M.	1.00	3.25	10.00
	e. 1920. Prefix letter N-S.	1.00	3.25	10.00
	f. 1921. Prefix letter T-Ø.	1.00	3.00	8.50
	g. 1921. Prefix letter 2A-2N.	1.00	3.00	8.50
	h. 1921. Prefix letter 2O.	1.00	3.00	8.00

Statsbevis

State Treasury Notes

1914 Issue

5% interest bearing notes that passed as legal tender.

		Good	Fine	XF
16	**10 Kroner** 1.10.1914.			
	a. Series 1. 5 digit number.	100.	250.	—
	b. Series 2. 6 digit number.	100.	300.	—
17	**50 Kroner** 1.10.1914.	—	—	—
18	**100 Kroner** 1.10.1914.	—	—	—
19	**500 Kroner** 1.10.1914.	—	—	—

Nationalbanken i Kjøbenhavn

National Bank, Copenhagen

1910-31 Issue

Wmk: Dk. numerals of the notes' denominations.

#20-24 first sign. always V. Lange. Second sign. changes.

		VG	VF	UNC
20	**5 Kroner** 1912-29. Dark blue. landscape with stone-age burial site in ctr., surrounded by ornamentation of chrysanthemum flowers. Arms within birch branches on back.			
	a. 1912.	100.	300.	1000.
	b. 1915. Prefix A.	50.00	200.	650.
	c. 1917. Prefix A.	100.	300.	900.

		VG	VF	UNC
20	d. 1917. Prefix B.	40.00	150.	550.
	e. 1918. Prefix B.	27.50	120.	500.
	f. 1918. Prefix C.	30.00	140.	525.
	g. 1920. Prefix C.	20.00	90.00	350.
	h. 1920. Prefix D.	27.50	120.	400.
	i. 1922. Prefix D.	20.00	90.00	350.
	j. 1922. Prefix E.	20.00	100.	375.
	k. 1924. Prefix E.	20.00	90.00	350.
	l. 1924. Prefix F.	20.00	90.00	350.
	m. 1926. Prefix F.	20.00	90.00	350.
	n. 1926. Prefix G.	90.00	275.	1100.
	o. 1928. Prefix G.	15.00	70.00	250.
	p. 1929. Prefix G.	20.00	100.	375.
	q. 1929. Prefix H.	15.00	70.00	250.

		VG	VF	UNC
21	**10 Kroner** 1913-28. Brown. Lettering and denomination surrounded by ornamentation of seaweed. Mercury head, surrounded by three lions on back.			
	a. 1913.	20.00	100.	500.
	b. 1913. Prefix A.	20.00	100.	400.
	c. 1915. Prefix A.	50.00	200.	750.
	d. 1915. Prefix B.	20.00	100.	375.
	e. 1915. Prefix C.	20.00	100.	375.
	f. 1917. Prefix C.	22.00	120.	450.
	g. 1917. Prefix D.	22.00	70.00	350.
	h. 1919. Prefix E.	21.00	70.00	325.
	i. 1919. Prefix F.	20.00	90.00	350.
	j. 1920. Prefix F.	20.00	90.00	325.
	k. 1920. Prefix G.	20.00	85.00	325.
	l. 1921. Prefix G.	20.00	85.00	325.
	m. 1921. Prefix H.	20.00	90.00	375.
	n. 1922. Prefix H.	20.00	80.00	300.
	o. 1922. Prefix I.	20.00	80.00	300.
	p. 1923. Prefix I.	20.00	80.00	300.
	q. 1923. Prefix J.	20.00	85.00	325.
	r. 1924. Prefix J.	20.00	85.00	300.
	s. 1924. Prefix K.	20.00	85.00	335.
	t. 1925. Prefix K.	20.00	70.00	300.
	u. 1925. Prefix L.	20.00	70.00	300.
	v. 1925. Prefix M.	20.00	85.00	325.
	w. 1927. Prefix M.	20.00	70.00	300.
	x. 1927. Prefix N.	16.00	66.00	200.
	y. 1927. Prefix O.	100.	200.	800.
	z. 1928. Prefix O.	16.00	50.00	200.
	aa. 1928. Prefix P.	16.00	50.00	200.
	ab. 1928. Prefix Q.	20.00	70.00	300.
22	**50 Kroner** 1911-28. Blue-green. Three fishermen in boat pulling in a net, surrounded by ornamentation of hops. Arms surrounded by oak branches to l., and beach to r. on back.			
	a. 1911.	1500.	4500.	—
	b. 1914.	750.	2000.	—
	c. 1919.	500.	1500.	—
	d. 1923.	525.	1650.	—
	e. 1925.	275.	1100.	—
	f. 1926.	325.	1800.	—
	g. 1928.	1000.	2000.	—
	h. 1928. Prefix A.	325.	1300.	—
23	**100 Kroner** 1910-28. Brown-yellow. Lettering and denomination surrounded by ornamentation of dolphins. Arms surround by sea-weed, held by two mer-men in waves on back.			
	a. 1910.	1200.	3000.	—
	b. 1912.	1200.	3000.	—
	c. 1914.	1000.	2800.	—
	d. 1917.	600.	—	—
	e. 1920.	600.	1500.	—
	f. 1922.	120.	400.	—
	g. 1924.	—	—	—
	h. 1924. Prefix A.	70.00	200.	—
	i. 1926. Prefix A.	70.00	200.	—
	j. 1928. Prefix A.	70.00	200.	—
24	**500 Kroner** 1910-25. Gray-blue. Farmer plowing field with two horses surrounded by ornamentation of leaves. Arms surrounded by branches of oak at l. and beech at r. on back.			
	a. 1910.	—	—	—
	b. 1919.	—	—	—
	c. 1921.	650.	2000.	—
	d. 1925.	650.	2000.	—

1930-31 Issue

Text: *NATIONALBANKENS SEDLER INDLOSES MED GULD EFTER GAELDENDE LOV.* Wmk: Lt. numerals of value.

#25-29 first sign. V. Lange to 31.3.1935. Svendsen from 1.4.1935. Second sign. changes.

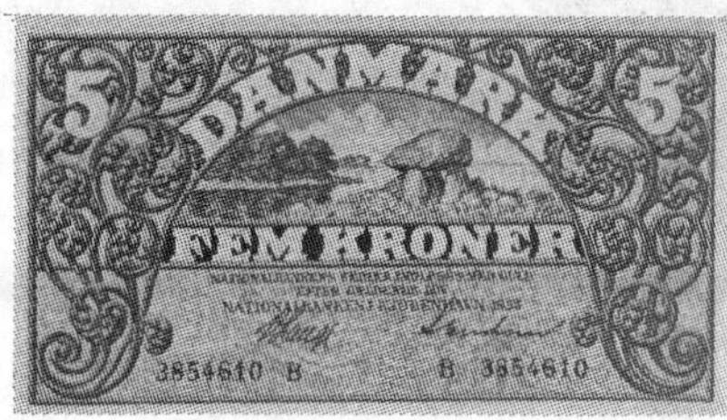

		VG	VF	UNC
25	**5 Kroner** 1931-36. Blue-green. Like #20.			
	a. 1931.	17.50	60.00	200.
	b. 1931. Prefix A.	30.00	100.	340.
	c. 1933. Prefix A.	20.00	80.00	260.
	d. 1933. Prefix B.	22.50	80.00	275.
	e. 1935. Prefix B.	22.50	80.00	275.
	f. 1935. Prefix C. First sign. A. Lange.	17.50	60.00	200.
	g. 1935. Prefix C. First sign. Svendsen.	17.50	60.00	200.
	h. 1935. Prefix D.	30.00	100.	350.
	i. 1936. Prefix D.	20.00	80.00	250.
26	**10 Kroner** 1930-36. Brown. Like #21.			
	a. 1930.	5.00	20.00	125.
	b. 1930. Prefix A.	5.00	20.00	125.
	c. 1932. Prefix B.	5.00	25.00	140.
	d. 1932. Prefix C.	5.00	25.00	145.
	e. 1933. Prefix C.	20.00	60.00	300.
	f. 1933. Prefix D.	5.00	22.50	140.
	g. 1933. Prefix E.	10.00	50.00	250.
	h. 1934. Prefix E.	5.00	25.00	150.
	i. 1934. Prefix F.	5.00	20.00	125.
	j. 1934. Prefix G.	7.50	37.50	200.
	k. 1935. Preifx G.	6.00	25.00	150.
	l. 1935. Prefix H.	5.00	22.50	125.
	m. 1936. Prefix H.	10.00	50.00	250.
	n. 1936. Prefix I.	5.00	22.50	140.
27	**50 Kroner** 1930-36. Blue-green. Like #22.			
	a. 1930.	35.00	175.	700.
	b. 1933.	40.00	200.	850.
	c. 1935.	37.50	175.	800.
	d. 1936.	50.00	250.	1000.
28	**100 Kroner** 1930-36. Brown. Like #23.			
	a. 1930.	25.00	80.00	210.
	b. 1932.	25.00	100.	240.
	c. 1935.	35.00	135.	270.
	d. 1936.	37.50	150.	270.

		VG	VF	UNC
29	**500 Kroner** 1931. Gray-blue. Like #24.	300.	1100.	—

Danmarks Nationalbank

1937-38 Issue

#30-34 like #20-29 but w/new bank name; first sign. Svendsen. Second sign. changes (17 different).

		VG	VF	UNC
30	**5 Kroner** 1937-43. Blue-green. Like #20 and #25.			
	a. 1937. Prefix E.	4.00	9.50	100.
	b. 1939. Prefix E.	5.00	10.00	120.
	c. 1939. Prefix F.	4.00	10.00	100.
	d. 1940. Prefix F.	4.00	10.00	60.00
	e. 1940. Prefix G.	4.00	10.00	40.00
	f. 1942. Prefix G.	5.00	10.00	50.00
	g. 1942. Prefix H.	4.00	7.50	35.00
	h. 1942. Prefix J.	4.00	7.50	35.00
	i. 1943. Prefix J.	6.00	15.00	45.00
	j. 1943. Prefix J. Sign. Svendson/Lund.	2.00	5.00	30.00
	k. 1943. Prefix K.	6.00	15.00	55.00

31	10 Kroner	VG	VF	UNC
	1937-43. Brown. Like #21 and #26.			
	a. 1937. Prefix K.	3.00	6.50	100.
	b. 1937. Prefix L.	3.00	6.50	100.
	c. 1937. Prefix M.	3.00	6.50	100.
	d. 1937. Prefix N.	30.00	75.00	400.
	e. 1939. Prefix N.	4.00	7.50	70.00
	f. 1939. Prefix O.	3.00	6.50	40.00
	g. 1939. Prefix P.	3.00	6.50	30.00
	h. 1939. Prefix Q.	8.00	20.00	80.00
	i. 1941. Prefix Q.	4.00	7.50	30.00
	j. 1941. Prefix R.	4.00	8.00	35.00
	k. 1942. Prefix R.	4.00	8.00	35.00
	l. 1942. Prefix S.	3.00	6.50	30.00
	m. 1942. Prefix T.	30.00	75.00	350.
	n. 1943. Prefix T.	4.00	7.50	30.00
	o. 1943. Prefix U.	3.00	6.50	30.00
	p. 1943. Prefix V.	4.00	7.50	27.50
	q. 1943. Prefix X.			

32	50 Kroner	VG	VF	UNC
	1938-42. Blue-green. Like #22 and #27.			
	a. 1938. Prefix C.	25.00	75.00	225.
	b. 1939. Prefix C.	15.00	50.00	175.
	c. 1941. Prefix C.	15.00	50.00	175.
	d. 1942. Prefix C.	12.50	37.50	135.

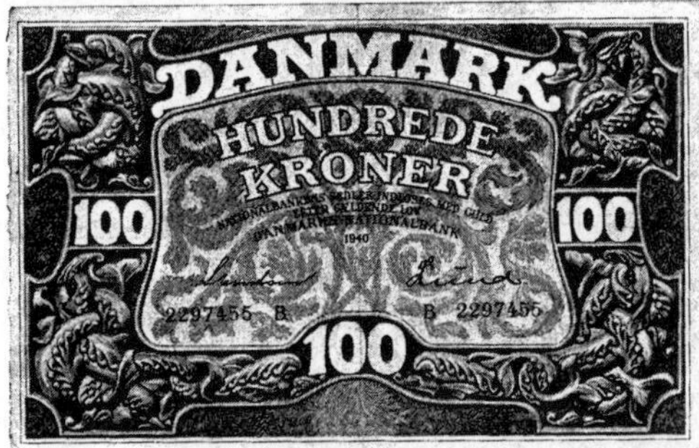

33	100 Kroner	VG	VF	UNC
	1938-43. Brown-yellow. Like #23 and #28.			
	a. 1938. Prefix B.	17.50	50.00	—
	b. 1940. Prefix B.	12.50	32.50	—
	c. 1941. Prefix B.	15.00	40.00	—
	d. 1943. Prefix B.	12.50	32.50	175.
34	500 Kroner			
	1938-41. Gray-blue. Like #24 and #29.			
	a. 1939. Prefix A.	200.	575.	—
	b. 1941. Prefix A.	200.	575.	—
	s. Specimen.	—	—	1100.

Note: For issues w/ovpt:...*FAERO. AMT, JUNI 1940.* See Faeroe Islands listings.

NOTICE

Readers with unlisted dates, signature varieties, etc. are invited to submit photocopies or, high resolution (300 dpi, 100% size) scans of their notes to: Standard Catalog of World Paper Money, 700 East State St. Iola, WI 54990-0001, or E-Mail: george.cuhaj@fwpubs.com.

1944-46 Issue

#35-41 first sign. Svendsen for #35, 36, 37a, 38, 39 - 1944-45. Halberg for #35, 37a, 37b, 38, 40, 1945-49. Riim for #35, 37b, 38, 40, 41 - 1948-62.

35	5 Kroner	VG	VF	UNC
	1944-50. Blue. *KRO 5 NER.* Arms on back.			
	a. 1944. Prefix AA-AP. Engraved.	25.00	100.	450.
	b. 1945. Prefix BA-BH.	7.50	32.50	160.
	c. 1946. Prefix BH-BO.	10.00	40.00	200.
	d. 1947. Prefix BO-BV.	6.50	27.50	125.
	e. 1948. Prefix BX-CH.	6.50	27.50	125.
	f. 1949. Prefix CH-DB.	6.50	27.50	125.
	g. 1950. Prefix DC-DAE.	5.00	25.00	100.
	s. Specimen.	—	—	—

36	10 Kroner	VG	VF	UNC
	1944. Brown. *10 TI KRONER 10.* Arms on back. Prefix AA-CM.			
	a. Issued note. Prefix AB-CM.	4.00	15.00	60.00
	s. Specimen.	—	—	450.

37	10 Kroner	VG	VF	UNC
	1945-48. Dk. green. Face like #31. Arms on back.			
	a. Hand-made paper, wmk: Floral ornaments at l. and r. 1945. Prefix A. Left sign: Svendsen.	27.50	100.	425.
	b. 1945. Prefix A. Left sign. Halbeig.	30.00	100.	425.
	c. 1945. Prefix B-D.	25.00	90.00	375.
	d. Wmk: Wavy lines and crowns. 1947. Prefix E-H.	15.00	40.00	150.
	e. 1948. Prefix H-O.	15.00	40.00	150.
	f. 1948. Prefix O-U. Left sigh. Riim.	15.00	40.00	150.
	s. As c-e. Specimen.	—	—	450.

38	50 Kroner	VG	VF	UNC
	1944-54. Purple. Fishermen in boat pulling in net. Face like #32. Arms at ctr. on back.			

38		VG	VF	UNC
	a. 1944. Prefix F. Left sign: Svendsen.	75.00	225.	750.
	b. 1945. Prefix F. Left sign: Svendsen.	60.00	220.	725.
	c. 1945. Prefix F. Left sign: Halberg	80.00	230.	750.
	d. 1948. Prefix F-K. Left sign: Halberg.	60.00	175.	700.
	e. 1948. Prefix K. Left sign: Riim.	80.00	230.	750.
	f. 1951. Prefix K, M. Left sign: Riim.	60.00	175.	700.
	g. 1953. Prefix M. Left sign: Riim.	70.00	200.	725.
	h. 1954. Prefix M-N. Left sign: Riim.	60.00	175.	700.
	s. Specimen. Left sign: Riim.	—	—	800.

39 100 Kroner

1944-60. Green. Face like #33. Arms only on back.

	VG	VF	UNC
a. 1944.	30.00	90.00	350.
b. 1946. Prefix E. Left sign. Svendsen.	25.00	75.00	325.
c. 1946. Prefix E-H. Left sign. Halberg.	20.00	60.00	300.
d. 1948. Prefix H. Left sign. Riim.	20.00	60.00	300.
e. 1948. Prefix K.	20.00	70.00	300.
f. 1951. Prefix K.	25.00	75.00	325.
g. 1953. Prefix K-N.	20.00	60.00	300.
h. 1955. Prefix N.	25.00	70.00	300.
i. 1955. Prefix O.	50.00	200.	—
j. 1956. Prefix O.	25.00	70.00	300.
k. 1957. Prefix O, R.	20.00	70.00	275.
l. 1958. Prefix R, S.	20.00	60.00	275.
m. 1959. Prefix S.	20.00	40.00	285.
n. 1960. Prefix T.	20.00	40.00	285.

#40 *Deleted*. Merged into #39.

41 500 Kroner

1944-62. Orange. Farmer w/horses at ctr. Arms on back.

	VG	VF	UNC
a. 1944. Prefix D. Left sign: Svendsen.	120.	225.	950.
b. 1945. Prefix D. Left sign: Halberg.	120.	225.	850.
c. 1948. Prefix D. Left sign: Halberg.	110.	200.	650.
d. 1948. Left sign: Riim.	110.	200.	675.
e. 1951. Prefix D. Left sign: Riim.	110.	225.	725.
f. 1952. Prefix D.	120.	225.	775.
g. 1953. Prefix D.	120.	225.	725.
h. 1954. Prefix D.	110.	200.	675.
i. 1956. Prefix D.	110.	200.	675.
j. 1959. Prefix D.	110.	200.	675.
k. 1961. Prefix D.	110.	200.	725.
l. 1962. Prefix D.	120.	200.	725.

1950 (1952)-63 ISSUE

Law of 7.4.1936

#42-47 first sign. changes. Usually there are 3 sign. combinations per prefix A0, A1, A2 etc. Second sign. Riim, (19)51-68 for #42, 43, 44a-f, (19)51-68 for #42, 43, 44a-f, 45a-b, 46a-b, 47. Valeur for (19)69 for #44g-h, 45c and 46b. The prefixes mentioned in the listings refer to the first two characters of the left serial #. The middle two digits indicate the date, and the last two characters indicate the sheet position of the note. Replacement Notes: #42-47, Serial # suffix: *OJ* (for whole sheet replacements) or *OK* (for single note replacements).

42 5 Kroner

(19)50; (19)52; (19)54-60. Blue-green. Portr. Bertil Thorvaldsen at l., 3 Graces at r. Kalundborg city view w/5 spire church at ctr. on back. Wmk: *5* repeated.

	VG	VF	UNC
a. 5 in the wmk. 11mm high. W/o dot after *7* in law date. (19)52. Prefix A0; A1.	9.00	45.00	150.
b. As a. (19)52. Prefix A2.	10.00	55.00	155.
c. As a., but w/dot after 7 in law date. (19)52. Prefix A2.	7.00	35.00	110.
d. As c. (19)52. Prefix A3.	11.00	60.00	160.
e. As c. (19)54-55. Prefix A3-A9.	5.00	20.00	70.00
f. 5 in the wmk. 13mm high.	4.25	16.00	35.00
g. As f. (19)55. Prefix B1.	6.00	25.00	80.00
h. As f. (19)56. Prefix B1-B3.	4.00	15.00	32.50
i. As f. (19)56. Prefix B4.	6.00	25.00	80.00
j. As f. (19)57. Prefix B4-B6.	3.75	12.50	30.00
k. As f. (19)58-59. Prefix B7-B9, C0-C1.	3.50	8.00	25.00
l. As f. (19)59. Prefix C3.	30.00	100.	250.
m. As f. (19)60. Prefix C3-C4.	3.00	7.50	22.50
r1. As a. Replacement note. (19)50. Suffix OK.	50.00	175.	300.
r2. As e. Replacement note. (19)50. Suffix OJ.	6.50	25.00	85.00
r3. As e. Replacement note. (19)50. Suffix OK.	35.00	135.	235.
r4. As f, g, h, j. Replacement note. (19)50. Suffix OJ.	5.00	20.00	45.00
r5. As k. Replacement note. (19)50. Suffix OJ.	4.50	12.50	35.00
r6. As m. Replacement note. (19)60. Suffix OJ.	4.00	9.00	27.50
s. Specimen.	—	—	275.

43 10 Kroner

(19)50-52. Black and olive-brown. Portr. Hans Christian Andersen at l., white storks in nest at r. Green landscape of Egeskov Mølle Fyn at ctr. on back. Wmk: *5* repeated. 125 x 65mm.

	VG	VF	UNC
a. (19)51. Prefix A0; A3; A4.	22.50	55.00	160.
b. (19)52. Prefix A1; A2; A5-B0.	17.50	45.00	120.
c. (19)52. Prefix B1.	22.50	55.00	160.
r. (19)50. Replacement note. Suffix OK.	125.	300.	—

44 10 Kroner

(19)50; (19)54-74. Black and brown. Similar to #43, but text line added in upper and lower frame. Portr. Hans Christian Andersen at l. Black landscape at ctr. on back. 125 x 71mm.

	VG	VF	UNC
a. Top and bottom line in frame begins w/*10*. Wmk: *10* repeated, 11mm high. (19)54. Prefix C0-C1.	9.00	30.00	100.
b. Like a but wmk. 13mm high. (19)54-55. Prefix C1-D5.	6.00	17.50	50.00
c. As b. (19)55. Prefix D6.	9.00	32.50	120.
d. As b. (19)56. Prefix D6.	6.00	17.50	50.00
e. As a. (19)56. Prefix D6-D8.	9.00	30.00	100.
f. As b. (19)56-57. Prefix D8-E4.	5.50	15.00	45.00
g. Top and bottom line in frame begins w/*TI*. (19)57. Prefix E4.	10.00	40.00	140.
h. As g. (19)57. Prefix E5-E6.	5.50	14.00	32.50
i. As g. (19)57. Prefix E7.	9.00	32.50	120.
j. As g. (19)58. Prefix E7-F3.	5.25	12.50	25.00
k. As g. (19)58-59. Prefix F4.	6.00	15.00	30.00
l. As g. (19)59-60. Prefix F5-G3.	5.00	12.50	22.50
m. As g. (19)61. Prefix G4-H6.	4.50	10.00	18.00
n. As g. (19)64-67. Prefix H7-K9.	4.00	6.50	12.00
o. As g. (19)68. Prefix A0-A3.	3.75	5.50	10.00
p. As g. (19)68. Second sign. Riim. Prefix A4.	4.50	9.00	17.00
q. As g. (19)69. Second sign. Valeur. Prefix A4.	4.50	9.00	17.00
r. As q. (19)69. Prefix A5-A8.	3.50	8.00	15.00
r1. As c or e. Replacement note. (19)50. Suffix OJ.	10.00	40.00	120.
r2. As b, d or f. Replacement note. (19)50. Suffix OJ.	7.50	25.00	70.00
r3. As j, k or l.Replacement note. (19)50; (19)60. Suffix OJ.	6.00	20.00	50.00
r4. As m-r, t. Replacement note. (19)61-74. Suffix OJ.	4.50	10.00	22.50
r5. As u. Replacement note. (19)71. Suffix OJ.	12.00	50.00	160.
r6. As v or x. Replacement note. (19)72-74. Suffix OJ.	3.00	4.75	7.50
r7. As y. Replacement note. (19)74. Suffix OJ.	3.50	5.00	8.50
r8. As b. (19)50. Replacement note. Suffix OK.	50.00	250.	—
r9. As n. Replacement note. (19)62-67. Suffix OK.	12.00	50.00	
r10. As t. Replacement note. (19)70-71. Suffix OK.	8.00	35.00	100.
r11. As t or v. Replacement note. (19)71-73. Suffix OK.	6.00	20.00	50.00
r12. As u. Replacement note. (19)71-73. Suffix OK.	12.00	50.00	160.

		VG	VF	UNC
44	r13. As x. Replacement note. (19)74. Suffix OK.	8.00	35.00	100.
	s. As q. (19)69. Prefix A9.	15.00	50.00	150.
	s1. Specimen.	—	—	250.
	t. As q. (19)70-71. Prefix A9-B9.	3.00	7.00	12.00
	u. As q. (19)71. Prefix C0.	15.00	50.00	150.
	v. As q. (19)72-73. Prefix C0-C9.	3.00	6.50	11.00
	w. As q. (19)74. prefix C9.	15.00	50.00	150.
	x. As q. (19)74. Prefix D0-D5.	3.00	9.00	10.00
	y. As q. (19)74. Prefix D6.	3.00	4.00	12.00
45	**50 Kroner** (19)50; (19)56-70. Blue on green unpt. Portr. Ole Rømer at l., Round Tower in Copenhagen at r. Back blue; Stone Age burial site Dolmen of Stenvad, Djursland at ctr.			
	a. Handmade paper. Wmk: Crowns and *50* (19)56-58.	22.50	65.00	225.
	b. Machine made paper. Wmk: Rhombuses and 50. (19)61/1962; (19)62; (19)63.	15.00	30.00	75.00
	c. As b. (19)66, (19)70.	12.00	22.50	55.00
	r1. As a. Replacement note. (19)50. Suffix OJ.	17.50	50.00	160.
	r2. As a. 1960. Replacement note. (19)60. Suffix OJ. Prefix A2, A3.	16.00	45.00	140.
	r3. As a. Replacement note. (19)50. Suffix OK.	40.00	120.	325.
	r4. As b. Replacement note. Suffix OJ.	15.00	35.00	80.00
	r5. As c. Replacement note. Suffix OJ.	12.00	22.50	55.00
	r6. As c. Replacement note. Suffix OK.	30.00	70.00	200.
46	**100 Kroner** (19)61-70. Red-brown on red-yellow unpt. Portr. Hans Christian Ørsted at l., compass card at r. Back brown; Kronborg castle in Elsinore.			
	a. Handmade paper. Wmk: Close wavy lines and compass. (19)61. Prefix A0.	30.00	75.00	275.
	b. Machine made paper. Wmk: *100.* (19)61. Prefix A2, A3; (19)62; (19)65; (19)70.	20.00	30.00	90.00
	r1. As a. Replacement note. Suffix OJ.	22.50	40.00	175.
	r2. As a. Replacement note. Suffix OK.	45.00	110.	325.
	r3. As b. Replacement note. Suffix OJ.	20.00	27.50	70.00
	r4. As b. Replacement note. Suffix OK.	35.00	100.	150.
47	**500 Kroner** 1963-67. Green. Portr. C. D. F. Reventlow at l., farmer plowing at r. Roskilde city view on back.			
	a. 1963.	100.	175.	500.
	b. 1965.	100.	200.	600.
	c. 1967.	90.00	150.	400.
	r1. As a. Replacement note. Suffix OJ.	100.	200.	550.
	r2. As b. Replacement note. Suffix OJ.	120.	225.	650.
	r3. As c. Replacement note. Suffix OJ.	75.00	150.	425.
	s. Specimen.	—	—	1000.

MILITARY

KGL. DANSKA FÄLT-COMMISARIATET, 1809

ROYAL DANISH COMMISSION

1809 ISSUE

#M1A-M4A printed w/Danish and Swedish values, printed for planned occupation of south Sweden. (Not issued).

Note: Trial printings exist for 12 Skillingar; 1, 6, 20 and 24 Riksdaler Riksgald.

		Good	Fine	XF
M1A	**8 Skillingar Riksgalds-Mynt** 1809.	—	—	—
M2A	**16 Skillingar Riksgalds-Mynt** 1809.	—	—	—
M3A	**2 Rixdaler Banco Specie** 1809.	—	—	—
M4A	**20 Rixdaler Banco Specie** 1809.	—	—	—

ALLIEREDE OVERKOMMANDO TIL BRUG I DANMARK

ALLIED COMMAND IN DENMARK, WWII

1945 ISSUE

		VG	VF	UNC
M1	**25 Øre** ND (1945). Brown and lilac.	10.00	25.00	70.00
M2	**1 Krone** ND (1945). Blue and lilac.	3.50	10.00	20.00

		VG	VF	UNC
M3	**5 Kroner** ND (1945). Green.	12.50	35.00	100.
M4	**10 Kroner** ND (1945). Dk. brown and blue.	12.50	35.00	100.
M5	**50 Kroner** ND (1945). Violet.	60.00	400.	800.
M6	**100 Kroner** ND (1945). Green-blue. Specimens only.			
	a. Issued note.	—	—	6000.
	s. Specimen.	—	—	5000.

DANSKE KRIGSMINISTERIUM, DEN DANSKE BRIGADE

ROYAL DANISH MINISTRY OF WAR,

POST LIBERATION WWII

1947-58 ISSUE

#M7-M12 issued for the troops first stationed in Germany, and later in other parts of the world.

		VG	VF	UNC
M7	**5 Øre** ND (1947-58). Blue. Arms at l.	2.50	7.50	20.00
M8	**10 Øre** ND (1947-58). Brown. Like #M7.	2.25	6.00	17.50
M9	**25 Øre** ND (1947-58). Blue. Like #M7.	4.00	8.00	22.50
M10	**1 Krone** ND (1947-58). Brown. Like #M12 .	5.00	10.00	25.00
M11	**5 Kroner** ND (1947-58). Blue. Like #M12.	35.00	110.	250.

		VG	VF	UNC
M12	**10 Kroner** ND (1947-58). Brown.	75.00	175.	400.

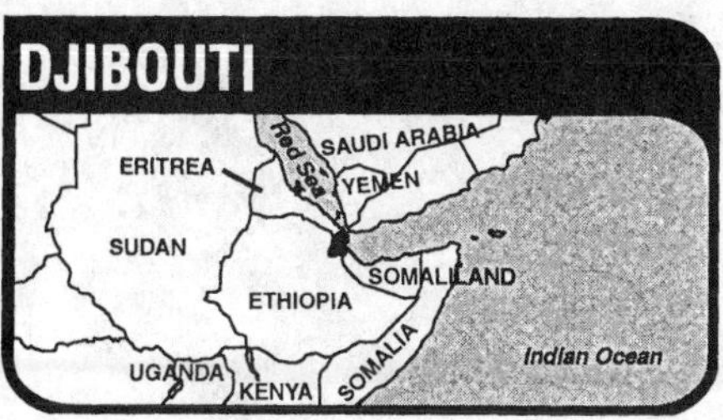

French Somaliland (later to become the French Overseas Territory of Afars and Issas, and then independent Dijbouti) was located in northeast Africa at the Bab el-Mandeb Strait connecting the Suez Canal and the Red Sea with the Gulf of Aden and the Indian Ocean. It had an area of 8,494 sq. mi. (22,000 sq. km.). Capital: Djibouti.

French interest in the area began in 1839 with concessions obtained by a French naval lieutenant from the provincial sultans. French Somaliland was made a protectorate in 1884 and its boundaries were delimited by the Franco-British and Ethiopian accords of 1887 and 1897. It became a colony in 1896 and a territory within the French Union in 1946. In 1958, it voted to join the new French Community as an overseas territory, and reaffirmed that choice by a referendum in March 1967. Its name was changed from French Somaliland to the French Territory of Afars and Issas on July 5, 1967.

On June 27, 1977 French Afars and Issas became Africa's 49th independent state as the republic of Djibouti.

RULERS:

French to 1977

MONETARY SYSTEM:

1 Franc = 100 Centimes

FRENCH SOMALILAND

BANQUE DE L'INDO-CHINE

DJIBOUTI

DECRETS DES 21.1.1875, 20.2.1888, 16.5.1900 ET 3.4.1901

#1-3 Various dates (until 1921) and sign. varieties.

		Good	Fine	XF
1	**5 Francs** 1913; 1919. Blue. Oriental woman seated below FRANCE seated holding caduceus at l.			
	a. Issued note. 14.3.1913; 26.8.1919.	250.	850.	—
	b. Cancelled note handstamped: *ANNULÉ*. 26.8.1919.	100.	400.	—

		Good	Fine	XF
2	**20 Francs** 1.5.1910; 4.5.1910. Blue. Neptune reclining holding trident at lower left.			
	a. Issued note.	375.	1650.	—
	b. Cancelled note handstamped: *ANNULÉ*.	125.	700.	—

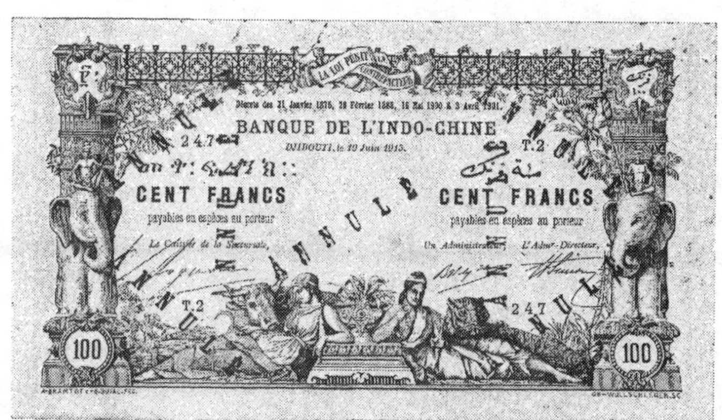

		Good	Fine	XF
3	**100 Francs** 1909; 1915. Elephant columns at l. and r., 2 women reclining with ox and tiger at bottom.			
	a. 1.5.1909. Sign. titles: *UN ADMINISTRATEUR* and *LE DIRECTEUR*. Rare.	—	—	—
	b. 10.6.1915. Sign. titles: *UN ADMINISTRATEUR* and *L'ADM-DIRECTEUR*.	375.	1800.	—
	c. Cancelled note handstamped: *ANNULÉ*.	125.	650.	—

1920 PROVISIONAL ISSUE

		Good	Fine	XF
4	**100 Francs** 2.1.1920 (-old date 10.3.1914). Like #5. Red ovpt. on Tahiti #3.			
	a. Issued note.	50.00	125.	350.
	b. Cancelled note handstamped: *ANNULÉ*.	20.00	65.00	135.

1920-23 REGULAR ISSUE

#4A-5 w/o decrets.

		Good	Fine	XF
4A	**5 Francs** 1.8.1923. Like #1.			
	a. Issued note.	200.	800.	—
	s. Perforated: *SPECIMEN*.	—	Unc.	200.
4B	**20 Francs** 3.1.1921. Like #2.	325.	1250.	—

		Good	Fine	XF
5	**100 Francs** 2.1.1920. Brown. Like #3.	35.00	85.00	250.

1928-38 ISSUES

#6-10 issued ca. 1926-38.

		Good	Fine	XF
6	**5 Francs** ND. Blue and red on lt. gold unpt. Woman wearing helmet at l.			
	a. Sign. titles: *UN ADMINISTRATEUR* and *LE DIRECTEUR*.	2.00	7.00	37.50
	b. Sign. titles: *LE PRÉSIDENT* and *LE DIRECTEUR GÉNÉRAL*.	2.00	7.00	37.50

		Good	Fine	XF
7	**20 Francs** ND. Lilac-brown and dk. lilac on lt. green unpt. Dk. blue text. Woman at r. Peacock at l. ctr. on back.			
	a. Run # through 18.	3.00	12.50	70.00
	b. Similar coloring but much lighter lilac and more visible lt. green unpt. Run #19-20 only.	4.00	15.00	85.00
7A	**20 Francs** ND. Blue and lt. lilac on lt. gold unpt. Like #7. Heavier green on back. Run #21-23.	4.00	15.00	85.00
7B	**20 Francs** ND. Like #7 but legend in black, and circle at bottom ctr. is red w/white numeral. Red *20 Fr* on back. Different from #7 or 7A. Specimen.	—	Unc	750.

		Good	Fine	XF
8	**100 Francs** ND. M/c. Woman w/head in laurel wreath holding small figure of Athena at ctr.	8.00	20.00	90.00
8A	**100 Francs** ND. M/c. Like #8 but w/circle at bottom r. is red w/white numeral. Specimen.	—	Unc	900.

		Good	Fine	XF
9	**500 Francs** 1927; 1938. Woman w/coat of arms and branch at l., ships in background.			
	a. Sign. titles: *UN ADMINISTRATEUR* and *LE DIRECTEUR*. 20.7.1927.	17.50	55.00	200.
	b. Sign. titles: *LE PRÉSIDENT* and *LE DIRECTEUR GÉNÉRAL*. 8.3.1938.	15.00	50.00	185.

		Good	Fine	XF
10	**1000 Francs** ND (1938). M/c. Market scene at l. and in background, woman sitting at r. Sign. titles: *LE PRÉSIDENT and LE DIRECTEUR GÉNÉRAL*.	20.00	50.00	250.
10A	**1000 Francs** ND (1938). Like #10 but bank title and denomination *1000* w/red background on face and back. Sign. titles: *LE PRÉSIDENT* and *LE DIRECTEUR GÉNÉRAL ADJOINT*. Perforated: *SPECIMEN*. Rare.	—	—	—

1943 Provisional Issues

		Good	Fine	XF
11	**5 Francs** ND (1943). Ovpt: Double cross of Lorraine and head of antelope on #6.	40.00	150.	350
12	**20 Francs** ND (1943). Ovpt: Double cross of Lorraine and head of antelope on #7A. Rare.	—	—	—

		Good	Fine	XF
12A	**20 Francs** ND (18.2.1943). Blue and red. Ovpt: *COTE FRANCAISE DES SOMALIS. B.I.C. DJIBOUTI* in rectangle on #7.	75.00	175.	55
13	**100 Francs** ND (1943). Ovpt: Double cross of Lorraine and head of antelope on #8.	100.	250.	65
13A	**100 Francs** ND (18.2.1943). Ovpt: *COTE FRANCAISE...* on #8.	100.	250.	65
13B	**500 Francs** ND (1943). Ovpt: Double cross of Lorraine and head of antelope on #9.	—	—	—
13C	**500 Francs** ND (18.2.1943). Ovpt: *COTE FRANCAISE...* on #9.	—	—	—
13D	**1000 Francs** ND (1943). Ovpt: Double cross of Lorraine and head of antelope on #10.	—	—	—
13E	**1000 Francs** ND (18.2.1943). Ovpt: *COTE FRANCAISE...* on #10.	—	—	—

Note: Dangerous counterfeits of #12 and 13A have appeared in the market recently. All genuine ovpt: B.I.C. notes can be verified by the alphabets appearing on them by refering to *Les billets de la Banque de l'Indochine* by Kolsky and Muszynski.

1945 Issue

#14-18 printer: Government Printer Palestine.

		Good	Fine	XF
14	**5 Francs** ND (19.2.1945). Lt. brown. Boat at ctr. on back.	10.00	70.00	275.

		Good	Fine	XF
15	**20 Francs** ND (19.2.1945). Red on yellow unpt. Bldg. on back.	15.00	100.	350.
16	**100 Francs** ND (19.2.1945). Green. Palms on back.	40.00	250.	—
17	**500 Francs** ND (19.2.1945). Purple and m/c. Swords and spears on back.	125.	850.	—

		Good	Fine	XF
18	**1000 Francs** ND (19.2.1945). Green, yellow and blue. Fish at ctr. on back.	200.	1200.	—

1946 Issue

		Good	Fine	XF
19	**10 Francs** ND (1946). M/c. Youth at l. Camel caravan on back. Wmk: Winged head of Mercury	10.00	50.00	200.

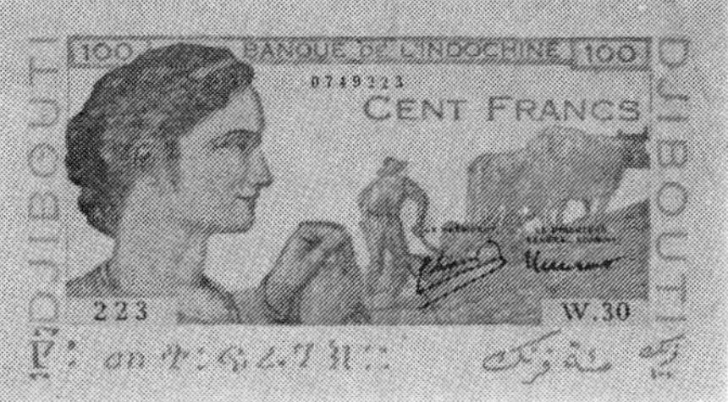

		Good	Fine	XF
19A	**100 Francs** ND (1946). M/c. Woman at l., farmer plowing w/oxen at r.	15.00	90.00	275.
20	**1000 Francs** ND (1946). M/c. Woman holding jug at l. ctr. on face and back.	40.00	175.	600.

Chambre de Commerce, Djibouti

1919 Emergency Issue

		Good	Fine	XF
21	**5 Centimes** ND (1919). Green cardboard; w/ or w/o perforations at l.	20.00	50.00	200.
22	**10 Centimes** ND (1919). Lt. brown cardboard; w/ or w/o perforations at l.	20.00	50.00	200.
23	**50 Centimes** 30.11.1919. Violet. 3 sign. varieties.	25.00	75.00	250.

		Good	Fine	XF
24	**1 Franc** 30.11.1919. Brown. 3 sign. varieties.	30.00	90.00	300.

Trésor Public, Côte Française des Somalis

1952 Issue

		VG	VF	UNC
25	**50 Francs** ND (1952). Lt. brown and m/c. Boat anchored at r. Camels on back.	1.00	8.00	45.00

		VG	VF	UNC
26	**100 Francs** ND (1952). M/c. Stylized corals. Trunk of palm tree on back.	2.00	25.00	100.
27	**500 Francs** ND (1952). Ochre and m/c. Ships at l. ctr. Jumping gazelle on back.	10.00	80.00	350.

		VG	VF	UNC
28	**1000 Francs** ND (1952). M/c. Like #20.	25.00	120.	450.

		VG	VF	UNC
29	**5000 Francs** ND (1952). M/c. Aerial view of harbor at Djibouti at ctr.	75.00	275.	800.

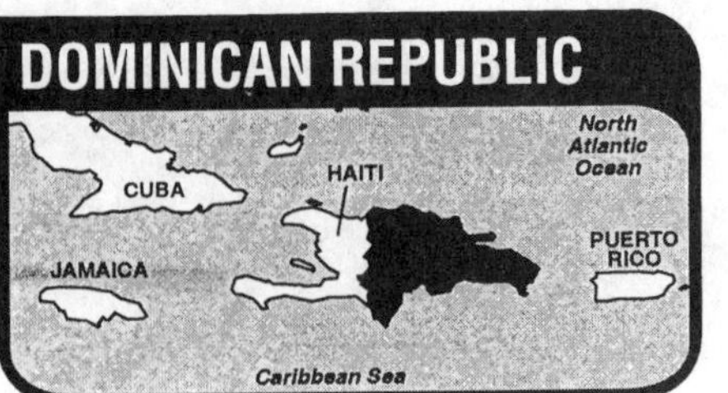

The Dominican Republic, occupying the eastern two-thirds of the island of Hispañiola, has an area of 18,816 sq. mi. (48,734 sq. km.) and a population of 8.49 million. Capital: Santo Domingo. The agricultural economy produces sugar, coffee, tobacco and cocoa.

Columbus discovered Hispaniola in 1492, and named it *La Isla Espanola* - "the Spanish Island." Santo Domingo, the oldest white settlement in the Western Hemisphere, was the from which Spain conducted its exploration of the New World. Later, French buccaneers settled the western third of Hispaniola, which in 1697 was ceded to France by Spain, and in 1804 became the Republic of Haiti - "mountainous country." At this time, the Spanish called their part of Hispaniola Santo Domingo, and the French called their part Saint-Domingue. In 1822, the Haitians conquered the entire island and held it until 1844, when Juan Pablo Duarte, the national hero of the Dominican Republic, drove them out of eastern Hispaniola and established an independent Dominican Republic. The republic returned voluntarily to Spanish dominion - after being rejected by France, Britain and the United States - from 1861 to 1865, when independence was restored.

Dictatorships and democratic rule was interspersced and from 1916 to 1924 it was occupied by the U.S. from 1930 to 1961, Rafael Trujillo was dictator. In the 1994 elections, a reform government gained power.

MONETARY SYSTEM:

1 Peso Oro = 100 Centavos Oro

SPECIMEN NOTES:

In 1998 the Banco Central once again began selling various specimens over the counter to the public. Current market valuations are being reflected, subject to change.

REPLACEMENT NOTES:

#53-61: Z prefix and suffix (TDLR printings).
#117-124: Z prefix and suffix (TDLR printings).

Spanish Administration

República Dominicana

1848 Provisional Issue

#6 and 7 ovpt:...*del decreto Congreso Nacional de 19 de Mayo de 1853...* on blank back. Printer: Durand, Baldwin & Co. N.Y.

		Good	Fine	XF
6	**20 Pesos on 1 Peso = 40 Centavos** 1848. Black. Like #A7.	50.00	175.	—

		Good	Fine	XF
7	**40 Pesos on 2 Pesos = 80 Centavos** 1848. Brown. Farm boy raking at l., arms at top ctr.	50.00	225.	—

Note: #6 and 7 are most often encountered with punched hole cancellations. Uncancelled notes are worth 30% more. #8 not assigned.

DECRETO 23.7.1849 REGULAR ISSUE

		Good	Fine	XF
9	**1 Peso** D.1849. Black. Arms at upper ctr.	150.	400.	—
10	**2 Pesos** D.1849. Black.	150.	400.	—
11	**5 Pesos** D.1849. Black.	175.	450.	—

#12 and 13 not assigned.

DECRETO 19.5.1853

		Good	Fine	XF
14	**1 Peso** D.1853. Arms at upper ctr.	150.	400.	—

		Good	Fine	XF
15	**2 Pesos** D.1853. Black. Arms at upper ctr.	150.	400.	—

#17 not assigned.

DECRETO 16.8.1858

		Good	Fine	XF
6	**5 Pesos** ND (1858). Black. Arms at upper ctr.	—	—	—

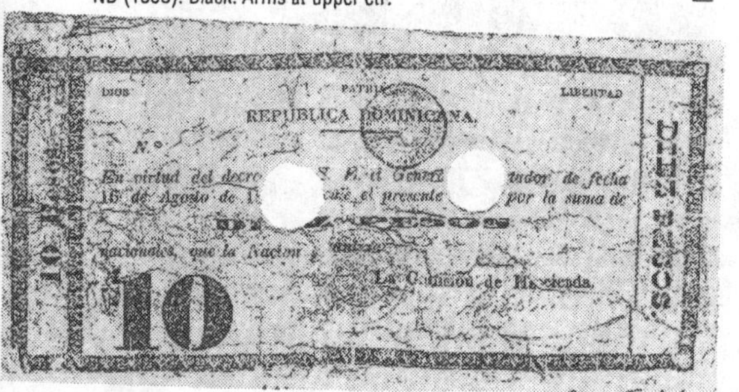

		Good	Fine	XF
8	**10 Pesos** D.1858. Black.	—	—	—
9	**50 Pesos** D.1858. Black.	—	—	—

860 ISSUE

		Good	Fine	XF
0	**50 Pesos** 17.5.1860; 28.12.1860. Black. 2 circular handstamps on face.	—	—	—

864 ISSUE

		Good	Fine	XF
1	**10 Pesos** 20.9.1864. Black on brown paper. Issued at Santiago de los Caballeros.	—	—	—
2	**20 Pesos** 1864. Black on white paper.	—	—	—

3 not assigned.

COMISIÓN DE HACIENDA

DECRETO 12 JULIO 1865

#25 and 27 held in reserve.

		Good	Fine	XF
24	**50 Pesos** D.1865.	—	—	—

		Good	Fine	XF
26	**200 Pesos** D.1865. 2 circular handstamps on face. Series J.	—	—	—

JUNTA DE CREDITO

DECRETO 23 OCTOBRE 1865

#30 held in reserve.

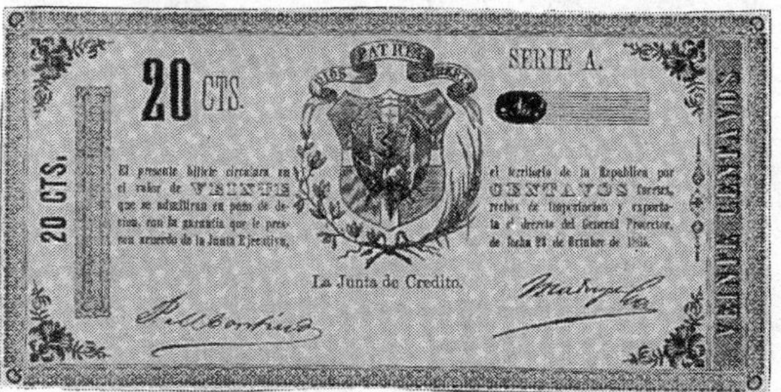

		Good	Fine	XF
28	**10 Centavos Fuertes** D.1865. Arms in rectangular frame at upper ctr., oval handstamp below. Series C.	—	—	—

		Good	Fine	XF
29	**20 Centavos Fuertes** D.1865. Black. Arms at upper ctr. Uniface.	—	—	—

#30 not assigned.

DECRETO 12 MARZO 1866

		Good	Fine	XF
31	**40 Centavos Fuertes** D.1866. Design in vertical guilloche at l., lg. arms at upper ctr. r., oval handstamp below. Uniface. Series B.	—	—	—

#32 not assigned.

DECRETO 29 JULIO 1866

		Good	Fine	XF
33	**5 Centavos Fuertes** ND. Arms at top ctr. Uniface.	85.00	200.	350.

		Good	Fine	XF
34	**10 Centavos Fuertes** D.1866. Black. Arms at top ctr., circular handstamp below. Uniface. Series D; E.	—	—	—
35	**10 Centavos Fuertes** 29.7.1866. Black. Arms at top ctr. Uniface.	50.00	200.	—

		Good	Fine	XF
36	**20 Centavos Fuertes** ND. Lg. arms at ctr. r., circular handstamp below to r. Series B. Uniface.	75.00	225.	—

#37 not assigned.

DECRETO 26 MARZO 1867

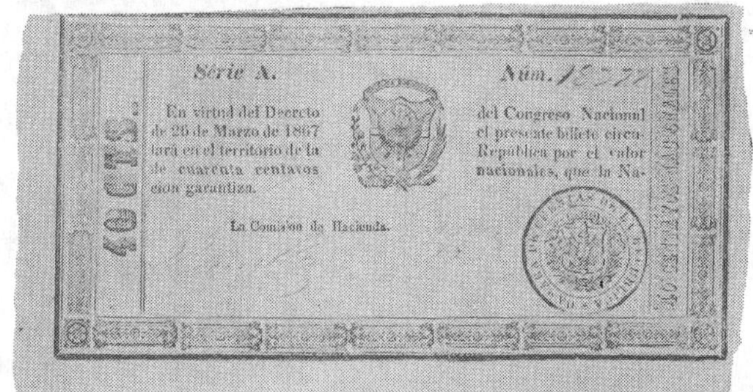

		Good	Fine	XF
38	**40 Centavos** D.1867. Sm. arms at top ctr., handstamp below to r. Uniface. Series A; B.	75.00	225.	—
39	**1 Peso** ND.	75.00	225.	—
40	**2 Pesos** 1867.	75.00	225.	—
42	**5 Pesos** 1867.	75.00	225.	—
43	**10 Pesos** D.1867.	75.00	225.	—

#44 not assigned.

DECRETO 30.9.1867

		Good	Fine	XF
45	**20 Pesos** D.1867. Black.	—	—	—

#46 not assigned.

INTENDENCIA DE SANTO DOMINGO

1860'S ISSUE

Issued during the period Spain considered Santo Domingo as a Spanish territory, March 3, 1861 to July 11, 1865.

#47-51 w/red handstamped oval seal: *MINISTERIO LA GUERRA Y...* around crowned Spanish arms.

		Good	Fine	XF
47	**1/2 Peso Fuerte** 1.5.1862. Blue. Series A.	250.	550.	—

		Good	Fine	XF
48	**2 Pesos Fuertes** 1.5.1862. Green. Series B.	250.	550.	—
49	**5 Pesos Fuertes** ca.1862. Series C.	300.	650.	—
50	**15 Pesos Fuertes** ca.1862. Series D.	400.	900.	—
51	**25 Pesos Fuertes** ca.1862. Series E.	600.	1350.	—

TREASURY

RESTORATION OF 16.8.1863

		Good	Fine	XF
55	**1 Peso Fuerte** 1870. Red. Allegorical figure of the Republic at l., arms at upper ctr. Uniface.	—	—	—

REPUBLICA DOMINICANA

BANCO CENTRAL DE LA REPÚBLICA DOMINICANA

1947 ND ISSUE

#59-67 face black w/orange seal w/text over seal: *CIUDAD TRUJILLO/DISTRITO DE SANTO DOMINGO/REPUBLICA DOMINICANA.* Unless otherwise stated, all notes have Indian (Liberty) head and national arms on back. Sign. and title varieties. Printer: ABNC.

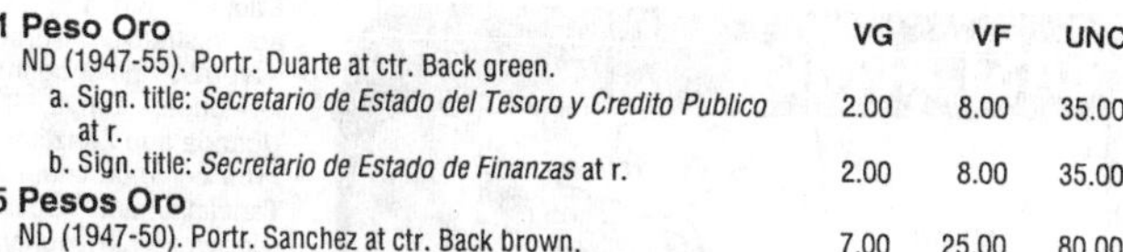

		VG	VF	UNC
60	**1 Peso Oro** ND (1947-55). Portr. Duarte at ctr. Back green.			
	a. Sign. title: *Secretario de Estado del Tesoro y Credito Publico* at r.	2.00	8.00	35.00
	b. Sign. title: *Secretario de Estado de Finanzas* at r.	2.00	8.00	35.00
61	**5 Pesos Oro** ND (1947-50). Portr. Sanchez at ctr. Back brown.	7.00	25.00	80.00

		VG	VF	UNC
62	**10 Pesos Oro** ND (1947-50). Portr. Mella at ctr. Back orange.	15.00	40.00	150.

		VG	VF	UNC
3	**20 Pesos Oro** ND (1947-50). *Puerta del Conde* (Gate) at ctr. Back blue.	30.00	150.	375.

		VG	VF	UNC
4	**50 Pesos Oro** ND (1947-50). Tomb of Columbus at ctr. Back green.	60.00	200.	450.
5	**100 Pesos Oro** ND (1947-50). Woman w/coffeepot and cup at ctr. Back green.	120.	300.	650.

		VG	VF	UNC
	500 Pesos Oro ND (1947-50). *Obelisco de Ciudad Trujillo* (Tower) at ctr. Back green.	—	—	—

NOTICE

Readers with unlisted dates, signature varieties, etc. are invited to sub-mit photocopies or, high resolution (300 dpi, 100% size) scans of their notes to: Standard Catalog of World Paper Money, 700 East State St. lola, WI 54990-0001, or E-Mail: george.cuhaj@fwpubs.com.

		VG	VF	UNC
67	**1000 Pesos Oro** ND (1947-50). *Basilica Menor de Santa Maria* at ctr. Back green.	—	—	—

1952 ND ISSUE

#68-70 printer: TDLR.

		VG	VF	UNC
68	**5 Pesos Oro** ND (1952). Similar to #61.	8.00	30.00	100.

		VG	VF	UNC
69	**10 Pesos Oro** ND (1952). Similar to #62 but many major differences.	20.00	50.00	185.

		VG	VF	UNC
70	**20 Pesos Oro** ND (1952). Portr. Trujillo at ctr. Trujillo's Peace Monument at ctr. between Indian head and arms on turquoise back.	50.00	175.	425.

1956 ND ISSUE

#71-78 face black w/orange seal. Text over seal: *CIUDAD TRUJILLO / DISTRITO NACIONAL / REPUBLICA DOMINICANA.* Sign. varieties. Printer: ABNC.

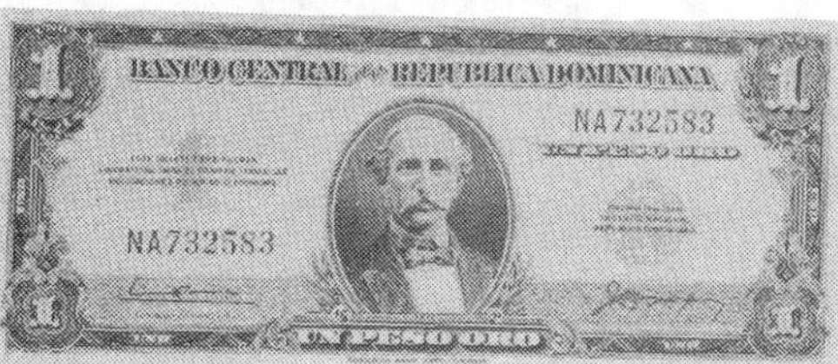

		VG	VF	UNC
71	**1 Peso Oro** ND (1957-61). Like #60. Printer: ABNC.	1.50	6.00	27.50

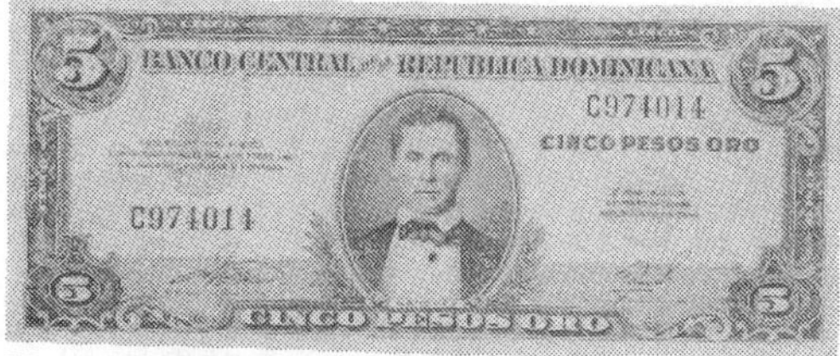

		VG	VF	UNC
72	**5 Pesos Oro** ND (1956-58). Similar to #61. Printer: ABNC.	3.50	15.00	55.00
73	**10 Pesos Oro** ND (1956-58). Similar to #62. Printer: ABNC.	8.00	25.00	95.00

		VG	VF	UNC
74	**20 Pesos Oro** ND (1956-58). Similar to #63. Printer: ABNC.	20.00	50.00	155.
75	**50 Pesos Oro** ND (1956-58). Like #64. Printer: ABNC.	60.00	140.	275.
76	**100 Pesos Oro** ND (1956-58). Like #65. Printer: ABNC.	40.00	100.	250.
77	**500 Pesos Oro** ND (1956-58). Like #66. Printer: ABNC.	—	—	—
78	**1000 Pesos Oro** ND (1956-58). Like #67. Printer: ABNC.	—	—	—

1956 ND COMMEMORATIVE ISSUE

		VG	VF	UNC
79	**20 Pesos Oro** ND (1956). Black. Portr. Trujillo at ctr., red ovpt: *AÑO DEL BENEFACTOR DE LA PATRIA* at upper l. Printer: ABNC.			
	a. Issued note. Rare.	—	—	—
	s. Specimen.	—	—	850.

1958 ND ISSUE

#80-84 similar to previous issue. Printer W&S (except for #83).

		VG	VF	UNC
80	**1 Peso Oro** ND (1958-59). Similar to #71. Printer: W&S.	2.00	8.00	35.00
81	**5 Pesos Oro** ND (1959). Similar to #72. Printer: W&S.	5.00	25.00	85.00
82	**10 Pesos Oro** ND (1959). Similar to #73. Printer: W&S.	10.00	32.50	110.
83	**20 Pesos Oro** ND (ca.1958). Like #79 but w/o commemorative text on face. Printer: ABNC.	—	—	—
84	**100 Pesos Oro** ND (1959). Like #76. Printer: W&S.	25.00	90.00	200.

Note: For fractional notes ND (1961) and ABNC issue similar to #80-84 but printed in red, ND (1962-63) see Volume 3.

East Africa was an administrative grouping of several neighboring British territories: Kenya, Tanganyika, Uganda and Zanzibar.

The common interest of Kenya, Tanzania and Uganda invited cooperation in economic matters and consideration of political union. The territorial governors, organized as the East Africa High Commission, met periodically to administer such common activities as taxation, industrial development and education. The authority of the Commission did not infringe upon the constitution and internal autonomy of the individual colonies. The common monetary system circulated for the territories by the East African Currency Board and was also used in British Somaliland and the Aden Protectorate subsequent to the independence of India (1947) whose currency had previously circulated in these two territories.

Also see British Somaliland, Zanzibar, Kenya, Uganda and Tanzania. Also see Somaliland Republic, Kenya, Uganda and Tanzania.

RULERS:
British

MONETARY SYSTEM:
1 Rupee = 100 Cents to 1920
1 Florin = 100 Cents, 1920-1921
1 Shilling = 100 Cents

BRITISH ADMINISTRATION

GOVERNMENT OF THE EAST AFRICA PROTECTORATE

MOMBASA ISSUE

1905 ISSUE

#1A-6A printer: TDLR.

		Good	Fine	XF
1A	**5 Rupees** 1.9.1905. Black on green unpt.	450.	1000.	—
1B	**10 Rupees** 1.9.1905. Black on yellow unpt.	550.	2000.	—
1C	**20 Rupees** 1.9.1905. Black on red unpt.	1250.	3000.	—

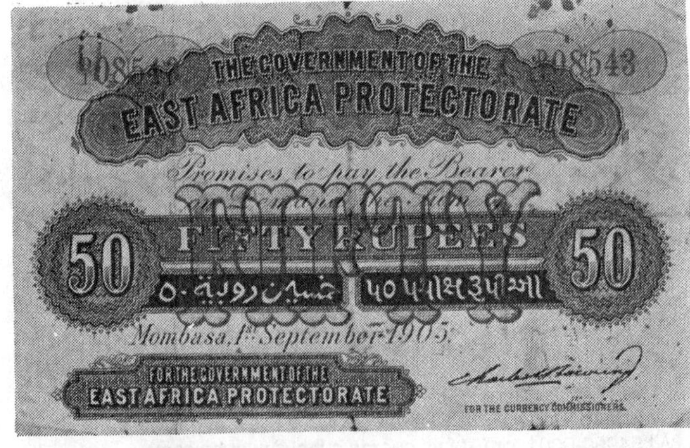

		Good	Fine
1D	**50 Rupees** 1.9.1905. Black on purple unpt. Rare.	—	—

		Good	Fine	XF
1E	**100 Rupees** 1.9.1905. Black on reddish brown unpt. Rare.	—	—	—
1F	**500 Rupees** 1.9.1905. Rare.	—	—	—

1912-16 ISSUE

#1-6 like previous issue but printed in brown. Various date and sign. varieties. Printer: TDLR.

		Good	Fine	XF
2	**5 Rupees** 1.5.1916; 1.12.1918.	275.	700.	1750.
2A	**10 Rupees** 1.7.1912; 15.1.1914; 1.5.1916; 1.12.1918.	350.	1200.	2250.
3	**20 Rupees** 1.7.1912; 1.5.1916; 1.12.1918.	800.	2000.	—
4	**50 Rupees** 1.7.1912.	1000.	2250.	—
5	**100 Rupees** 1.7.1912. Rare.	—	—	—
6	**500 Rupees** 1.7.1912; 1.5.1916. Rare.	—	—	—

EAST AFRICAN CURRENCY BOARD

1920 FIRST ISSUE

		Good	Fine	XF
7	**1 Rupee** 7.4.1920. Olive-brown and red. Portr. Kg. George V at r. Back blue; hippo at ctr. Printer: TDLR.	75.00	300.	900.

1920 SECOND ISSUE

		Good	Fine	XF
8	**1 Florin** 1.5.1920. Olive-brown and red. Similar to #7. Portr. Kg. George V at r. Back blue; hippo at ctr. on back.	35.00	125.	450.
9	**5 Florins** 1.5.1920. Blue and green. Portr. Kg. George V at r. Hippo at ctr. on back. Like #8.	400.	1000.	2500.

#10-12B portr. Kg. george V at top ctr. Printer: BWC.

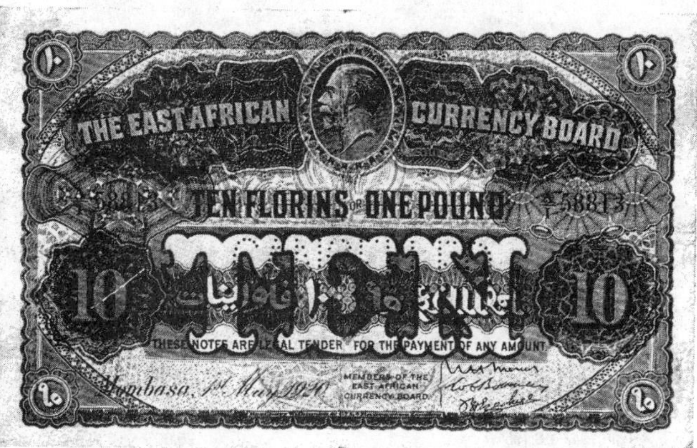

		Good	Fine	XF
10	**10 Florins = 1 Pound** 1.5.1920. Blue and orange. Rare.	—	—	—
11	**20 Florins = 2 Pounds** 1.5.1920. Rare.	—	—	—
12	**50 Florins = 5 Pounds** 1.5.1920. Rare.	—	—	—
12A	**100 Florins = 10 Pounds** 1.5.1920. Rare.	—	—	—
12B	**500 Florins = 50 Pounds** 1.5.1920. Rare.	—	—	—

1921 ISSUE

#13-19 portr. Kg. George V at upper or lower r. Lion at ctr. on back. Printer: TDLR.

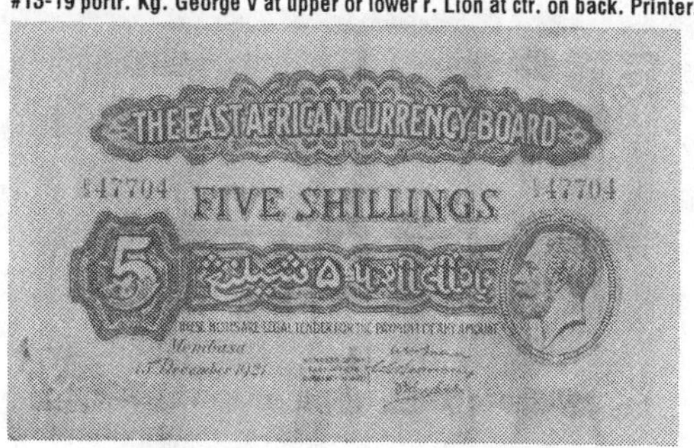

		Good	Fine	XF
13	**5 Shillings** 15.12.1921. Blue-black on brown and orange unpt.	60.00	200.	600.
14	**10 Shillings** 15.12.1921. Blue-black on green and pink unpt.	80.00	300.	950.
15	**20 Shillings = 1 Pound** 15.12.1921. Blue-black on yellow and orange unpt.	150.	550.	1500.

		Good	Fine	XF
16	**100 Shillings = 5 Pounds** 15.12.1921. Blue-black on lilac unpt.	300.	950.	—

		Good	Fine	XF
17	**200 Shillings = 10 Pounds** 15.12.1921. Blue-black on gray-blue unpt.	900.	2500.	—
18	**1000 Shillings = 50 Pounds** 15.12.1921. Blue-black on lt. brown unpt. Rare.	—	—	—
19	**10,000 Shillings = 500 Pounds** 15.12.1921. Blue-black on blue unpt. Rare.	—	—	—

NAIROBI ISSUE

1933 ISSUE

#20-26 portr. Kg. George V at upper or lower r. Printer: TDLR.

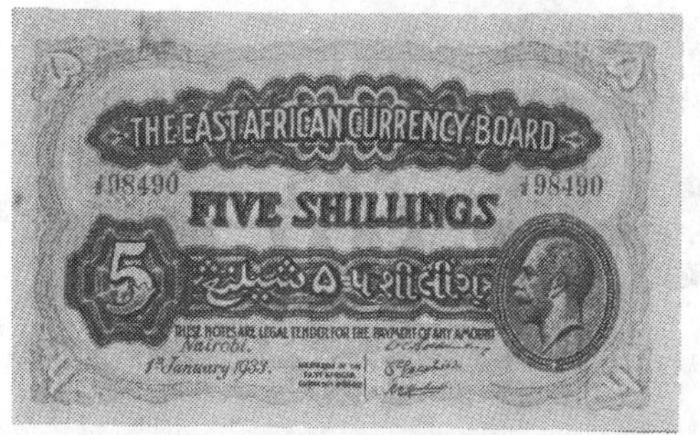

		Good	Fine	XF
20	**5 Shillings** 1.1.1933. Blue-black on brown and orange unpt. Back orange-brown; lion at ctr.	25.00	100.	400.

		Good	Fine	XF
21	**10 Shillings** 1.1.1933. Blue-black on green and pink unpt. Back green; lion at ctr.	40.00	160.	700.

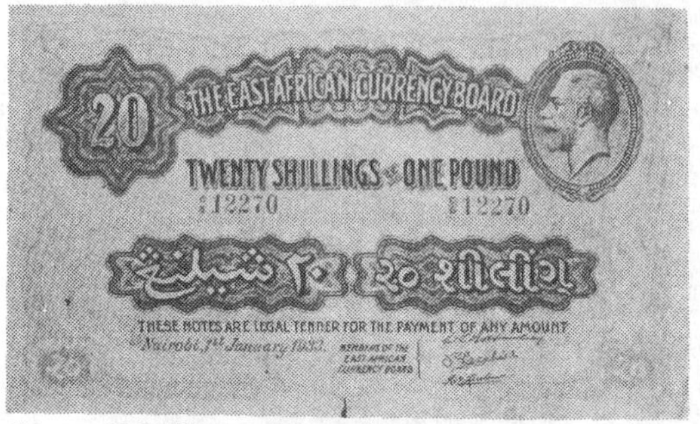

		Good	Fine	XF
22	**20 Shillings = 1 Pound** 1.1.1933. Blue-black on yellow and orange unpt. Back brown; lion at ctr.	85.00	300.	900.
23	**100 Shillings = 5 Pounds** 1.1.1933. Blue-black on green and lilac unpt. Back red-brown; lion at ctr.	200.	475.	1750.
24	**200 Shillings = 10 Pounds** 1.1.1933. Blue-black on gray-blue unpt. Rare.	—	—	—
25	**1000 Shillings = 50 Pounds** 1.1.1933. Blue-black on lt. brown unpt. Rare.	—	—	—
26	**10,000 Shillings = 500 Pounds** 1.1.1933. Blue-black on blue unpt. Rare.	—	—	—

1938-52 Issue

#27-32 like previous issue. Portr. Kg. George VI at upper or lower l. Various date, sign. and serial # varieties.

		VG	VF	UNC
27	**1 Shilling** 1.1.1943. Blue-black on purple unpt. Back purple; lion at ctr.	2.00	17.50	75.00

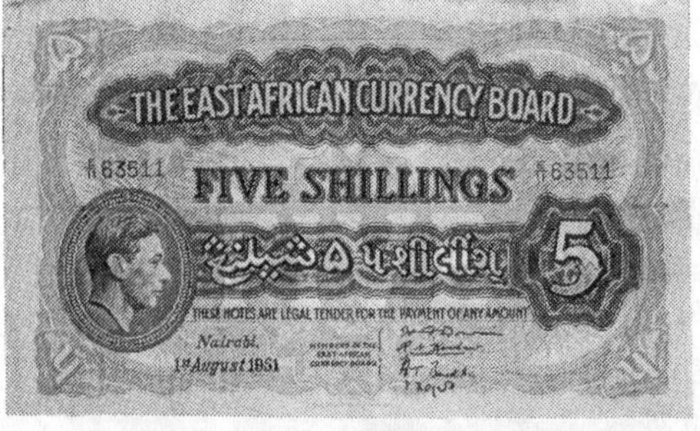

		VG	VF	UNC
28	**5 Shillings** 1938-52. Blue-black on brown unpt. Printer: TDLR.			
	a. 3 sign. 1.1.1938-42.	7.00	50.00	225.
	b. 4 sign. 1943-1.1.1952.	6.00	40.00	175.
28A	**5 Shillings** 1.8.1942. Like #28 but w/India style serial #. W/o imprint.	40.00	200.	—
29	**10 Shillings** 1938-52. Dk. blue on green and pink unpt. Printer: TDLR.			
	a. 3 sign. 1.1.1938-42.	9.00	60.00	275.
	b. 4 sign. 1943-1.1.1952.	8.00	50.00	210.

		VG	VF	UNC
29A	**10 Shillings** 1.8.1942. Like #29 but w/India style serial #. W/o imprint.	40.00	250.	—

		VG	VF	UNC
30	**20 Shillings = 1 Pound** 1938-52. Blue-black on yellow and orange unpt. Printer: TDLR.			
	a. 3 sign. 1.1.1938-42.	15.00	90.00	500.
	b. 4 sign. 1943-1.1.1952.	8.00	50.00	300.

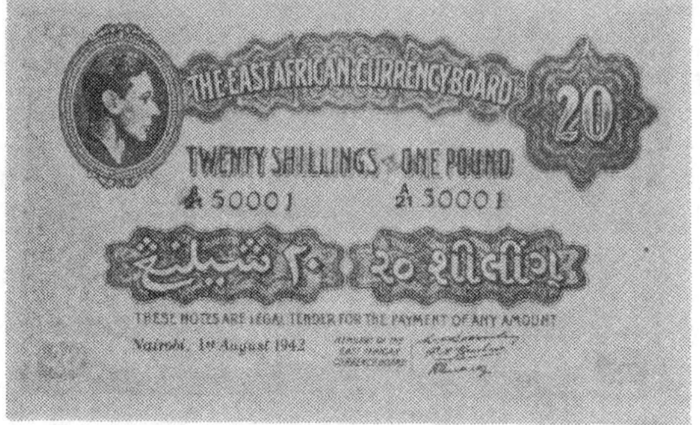

		VG	VF	UNC
30A	**20 Shillings = 1 Pound** 1.8.1942. Like #30 but w/India style serial #. W/o imprint.	75.00	400.	2500.

		VG	VF	UNC
31	**100 Shillings = 5 Pounds** 1938-51. Blue-black on green and lilac unpt. Printer: TDLR.			
	a. 3 sign. 1.1.1938-42.	80.00	450.	950.
	b. 4 sign. 1943-1.8.1951.	75.00	350.	800.
31B	**1000 Shillings = 50 Pounds** 2.1.1939. Blue-black on pale orange and lt. blue unpt. Back lt. brown. Specimen. Rare.	—	—	—

		VG	VF	UNC
31c	**100 Shillings = 5 Pounds** 1.8.1942. Blue-black on green and lilac unpt. Like #31 but w/India style serial #. W/o imprint. Specimen.	—	—	—
32	**10,000 Shillings = 500 Pounds** 1.1.1947; 1.8.1951. Blue-black on blue unpt. Printer: TDLR.			
	a. Issued note.	—	—	—

1939 Issue

#26A-26C portr Kg. George VI at upper or lower l. Backs like #20-22.

		Good	Fine	XF
26A	**5 Shillings** 1.6.1939. Blue-black on brown unpt.			
	a. Printer: TDLR. Serial # somewhat larger than later issues.	35.00	75.00	250.
	b. W/o imprint. Serial # same size as later issues.	30.00	70.00	200.
26b	**10 Shillings** 1.6.1939. Blue-black on green and pink unpt. W/o BWC imprint.	35.00	90.00	300.
26c	**20 Shillings = 1 Pound** 1.6.1939. Blue-black on yellow and orange unpt. W/o BWC imprint.	30.00	90.00	300.

1953 Issue

#33-36 portr. Qn. Elizabeth II at upper or lower r. Backs like #28-31. Various date and sign. varieties. Printer: TDLR.

		VG	VF	UNC
3	**5 Shillings** 31.3.1953-1.10.1957. Blue-black on lt. brown unpt.	4.00	40.00	350.
4	**10 Shillings** 31.3.1953-1.10.1957. Blue-black on green and pink unpt.	10.00	120.	650.

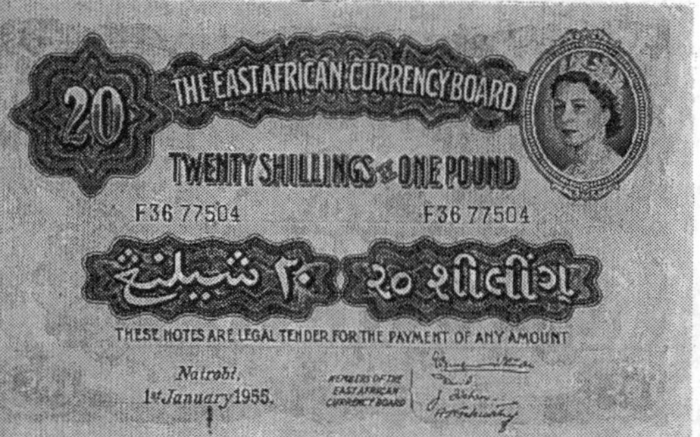

		VG	VF	UNC
	20 Shillings = 1 Pound 31.3.1953-1.2.1956. Blue-black on yellow and orange unpt.	7.00	50.00	325.

		VG	VF	UNC
36	**100 Shillings = 5 Pounds** 31.3.1953-1.2.1956. Blue-black on green and lilac unpt.	50.00	225.	1000.

East African Currency Board, Nairobi

W/o Office of Issue, N.D.

#37-40 portr. Qn. Elizabeth II at upper l. 4 sign. at lower r. Printer: TDLR.

		VG	VF	UNC
37	**5 Shillings** ND (1958-60). Brown on m/c unpt.	2.50	20.00	175.
38	**10 Shillings** ND (1958-60). Green on m/c unpt.	2.50	25.00	200.

		VG	VF	UNC
39	**20 Shillings** ND (1958-60). Blue on m/c unpt.	3.00	35.00	300.

		VG	VF	UNC
40	**100 Shillings** ND (1958-60). Red on m/c unpt.	20.00	200.	900.

1961 ND Issue

#41-44 portr. Qn. Elizabeth II at upper l. w/3 sign. at l. and 4 at r. Printer: TDLR.

		VG	VF	UNC
41	**5 Shillings** ND (1961-63). Brown on lt. red unpt.			
	a. Top l. sign: E. B. David. (1961).	5.00	20.00	250.
	b. Top l. sign: A. L. Adu. (1962-63).	3.50	15.00	200.

NOTICE

Readers with unlisted dates, signature varieties, etc. are invited to submit photocopies or, high resolution (300 dpi, 100% size) scans of their notes to: Standard Catalog of World Paper Money, 700 East State St. Iola, WI 54990-0001, or E-Mail: george.cuhaj@fwpubs.com.

		VG	VF	UNC
42	**10 Shillings**			
	ND (1961-63). Green on m/c unpt.			
	a. Top l. sign: E. B. David. (1961).	9.00	25.00	350.
	b. Top l. sign: A. L. Adu. (1962-63).	6.00	20.00	300.
43	**20 Shillings**			
	ND (1961-63). Blue on lt. pink unpt.			
	a. Top l. sign: E. B. David. (1961).	10.00	75.00	500.
	b. Top l. sign: A. L. Adu. (1962-63).	7.00	45.00	325.

		VG	VF	UNC
44	**100 Shillings**			
	ND (1961-63). Red on m/c unpt.			
	a. Top l. sign: E. B. David. (1961).	25.00	125.	950.
	b. Top l. sign: A. L. Adu. (1962-63).	20.00	90.00	700.

1964 ND Issue

#45-48 wmk: Rhinoceros, wmk. area at l., sailboat at l. ctr. Various plants on back.

		VG	VF	UNC
45	**5 Shillings**			
	ND (1964). Brown on m/c unpt.	3.00	12.50	90.00

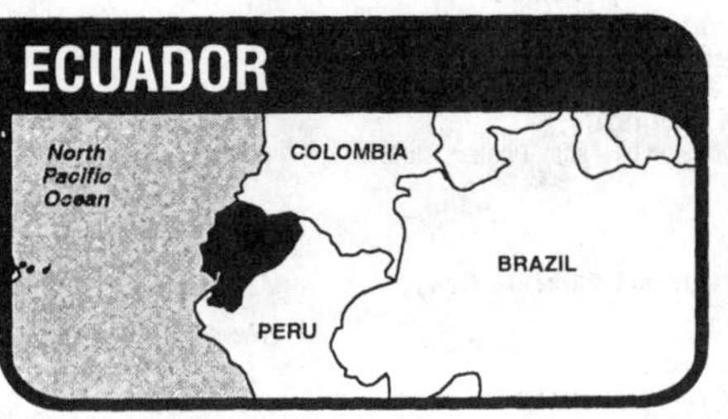

The Republic of Ecuador, located astride the equator on the Pacific coast of South America, has an area of 109,484 sq. mi. (283,561 sq. km.) and a population of 12.65 million. Capital: Quito. Agriculture is the mainstay of the economy but there are appreciable deposits of minerals and petroleum. It is the world's largest exporter of bananas and balsa wood. Coffee, cacao and shrimp are also valuable exports.

Ecuador was first sighted, 1526, by Bartolome Ruiz. Conquest was undertaken by Sebastian de Benalcazar who founded Quito in 1534. Ecuador was part of the province, later Vice-royalty, of Peru until 1739 when it became part of the Vice-royalty of New Granada. After two failed attempts to attain independence in 1810 and 1812, it successfully declared its independence in October 1820, and won final victory over Spanish forces May 24, 1822. Incorporated into the Gran Colombia confederacy, it loosened its ties in 1830 and regained full independence in 1835.

MONETARY SYSTEM:

1 Peso = 8 Reales
1 Peso = 100 Centavos
1 Sucre = 10 Decimos = 100 Centavos
1 Condor = 25 Sucres
1 USA Dollar = 25,000 Sucres (March 2001)

Government

La Caja Central de Emisión y Amortización

1926-27 Issue

		Good	Fine	XF
21	**1 Sucre**			
	30.11.1926. Ovpt. on #S221A.	150.	500.	—
31	**2 Sucres**			
	30.11.1926; 19.1.1927. Ovpt. on #S272.	150.	500.	—
41	**5 Sucres**			
	19.1.1927. Ovpt. on #S103.	150.	500.	—
51	**5 Sucres**			
	30.11.1926. Ovpt. on #S133.	150.	500.	—
61	**10 Sucres**			
	30.11.1926; 19.1.1927. Ovpt. on #S274.	150.	500.	—
71	**50 Sucres**			
	6.4.1927; 1.6.1927. Ovpt. on #S136.	—	—	—
72	**1000 Sucres**			
	6.4.1927. Ovpt. on #S164.	—	—	—

Republic

Banco Central del Ecuador

1928 Issue

#84-88 black on m/c unpt., w/text: *CAPITAL AUTORIZADO 10,000,000 SUCRES.* 2 sign.; sign. title ovpt: *TESORERO/GERENTE* at r. on #84b and 85b. Arms on back. Printer: ABNC.

		Good	Fine	XF
84	**5 Sucres**			
	1928-38. Woman seated ("Agriculture") at ctr. Back red.			
	a. 14.1.1928; 6.11.1928; 9.11.1932; 21.12.1933; 7.11.1935; 5.10.1937.	7.50	30.00	100.
	b. Sign. title ovpt: *Delegado de la Superintendencia de Bancos* across ctr. 27.10.1938.	7.50	30.00	100.

		Good	Fine	XF
85	**10 Sucres**			
	1928-38. Woman w/basket at ctr. Steam locomotive at l., ox-carts at r. in background. Back blue.			
	a. 30.5.1928; 6.11.1928; 9.11.1932; 21.12.1933; 7.11.1935; 5.10.1937.	10.00	65.00	150.
	b. Sign. title ovpt: *Delegado de la Superintendencia de Bancos* across ctr. 27.10.1938.	15.00	75.00	175.

86	20 Sucres	Good	Fine	XF
	30.5.1928; 6.11.1928; 9.11.1932; 21.12.1933; 7.11.1935; 12.2.1937. Woman seated w/symbols of commerce and industry at ctr. Back brown.	25.00	100.	250.

87	50 Sucres	Good	Fine	XF
	30.5.1928; 6.11.1928; 9.11.1932; 21.12.1933; 8.8.1934; 1.10.1936. Ship at l., woman seated w/globe and anvil at ctr., train at r. Back green.	30.00	125.	300.
88	**100 Sucres**			
	30.5.1928; 6.11.1928; 9.11.1932; 21.12.1933; 8.8.1934; 1.10.1936. Woman seated w/globe at ctr. Back purple.	50.00	200.	450.

#89 and 90 not assigned.

1939-44 Issue

#91-97 slight modifications from previous issue, w/text: *CAPITAL AUTORIZADO 20,000,000 SUCRES*. 3 sign.; various sign. title ovpts. Printer: ABNC.

91	5 Sucres	VG	VF	UNC
	1940-49. Similar to #84.			
	a. Printed sign. title: *TESORERO DE RESERVA* at r. 12.3.1940-28.11.1941.	4.50	20.00	70.00
	b. Sign. title ovpt: *GERENTE GENERAL* at r. 3.2.1945-1.4.1947.	4.00	17.50	60.00
	c. Like b., but sign. title printed. 21.10.1947-21.6.1949.	3.00	15.00	50.00
	s1. Specimen. Blue ovpt.: *SPECIMEN* twice on face. ND, Series FD (3.2.1945). Punched hole cancelled.	—	—	100.
	s2. As c. Specimen. Pin hole perforated: *SPECIMEN A.B.N. Co.* in two lines on face. ND. W/o series or serial #. Punched hole cancelled.	—	—	100.
	s3. As s2 but perforated on back.	—	—	50.00

92	10 Sucres	VG	VF	UNC
	1939-49. Similar to #85.			
	a. Sign. title ovpt: *PRESIDENTE* at l. Date at r. 17.10.1939-6.6.1944.	5.00	25.00	100.
	b. Printed sign. titles. 6.2.1942; 4.6.1943; 30.6.1947; 21.6.1949; 30.6.1949.	4.50	20.00	90.00
	c. Sign. title ovpt: *PRESIDENTE* at l., *GERENTE GENERAL* at r. Date at l. 5.10.1944; 19.12.1944; 23.1.1945.	4.00	15.00	80.00
	d. Sign title ovpt: *GERENTE GENERAL* at r. 22.8.1945; 7.11.1945; 8.2.1946; 25.7.1946; 22.11.1948; 21.6.1949.	3.00	12.50	75.00

93	20 Sucres	VG	VF	UNC
	1939-49. Similar to #86.			
	a. Date at upper r. ctr. 17.10.1939.	8.00	35.00	160.
	b. Printed sign. titles. Date at lower r. 5.7.1940-27.3.1944.	8.00	35.00	160.
	c. Sign. title ovpt: *PRESIDENTE* at l. Date at lower r. 5.7.1940-27.3.1944.	6.00	25.00	125.
	d. Sign. title ovpt: *PRESIDENTE* at l., *GERENTE GENERAL* at r. 25.10.1944.	6.00	25.00	125.
	e. Sign title ovpt: *GERENTE GENERAL* at r. Date at upper r. 21.9.1945; 26.12.1945; 12.7.1947; 22.11.1948; 17.3.1949.	5.00	20.00	110.
	f. Printed sign. titles w/*GERENTE GENERAL* at r. 24.3.1949; 6.5.1949.	5.00	20.00	110.

94	50 Sucres	VG	VF	UNC
	1939-1949. Similar to #87.			
	a. 17.10.1939-3.12.1943.	25.00	110.	325.
	b. Sign. title ovpt: *GERENTE GENERAL* at r. 16.10.1946; 12.7.1947; 22.11.1948; 27.1.1949.	20.00	100.	300.

95	100 Sucres	VG	VF	UNC
	1939-49. Similar to #88.			
	a. 17.10.1939-19.11.1943.	30.00	125.	300.
	b. 31.7.1944; 7.9.1944.	25.00	85.00	250.
	c. 7.11.1945-1.27.1949.	20.00	60.00	150.

1944-67 Issue

#96 and 97 black on m/c unpt. Printer: ABNC.

96	500 Sucres	VG	VF	UNC
	1944-66. Mercury seated at ctr. Back deep orange.			
	a. Sign. title ovpt: *PRESIDENTE* at l. 12.5.1944; 27.6.1944.	175.	400.	—
	b. Sign. title ovpt: *GERENTE GENERAL* at l., *VOCAL* at r. 31.7.1944; 7.9.1944.	150.	375.	—
	c. Sign. title ovpt: *GERENTE GENERAL* at r. 12.1.1945-12.7.1947.	125.	300.	—
	d. As c. 21.4.1961-17.11.1966.	125.	300.	—
	s. Specimen. ND.	—	—	400.

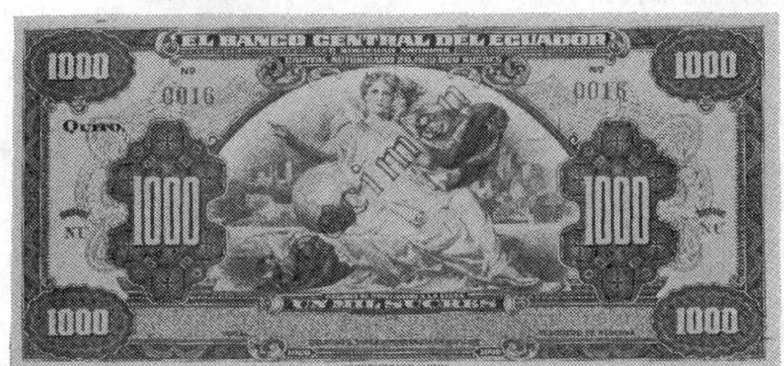

97	1000 Sucres	VG	VF	UNC
	1944-67. Woman reclining ("Telephone Service") at ctr. Back greenish gray.			
	a. Sign. title ovpt: *PRESIDENTE* at l. 12.5.1944; 27.6.1944.	300.	650.	—
	b. Sign. title ovpt: *GERENTE GENERAL* at l., *VOCAL* at r. 31.7.1944; 7.9.1944.	275.	550.	—
	c. Sign. title ovpt: *PRESIDENTE* at l., *GERENTE GENERAL* at r. 12.1.1945.	250.	500.	—
	d. Sign. title ovpt: *GERENTE GENERAL* at r. 16.10.1945; 12.7.1947.	225.	450.	—
	e. As d. 21.4.1961; 27.2.1962; 4.3.1964; 23.7.1964; 17.11.1966; 6.4.1967.	150.	350.	—
	s. Specimen. ND.	—	—	400.

Note: The following reduced size notes are listed by printer.

1950 Issue .... (1950-59) #98-99 printer: W&S.
1950-71 Issue .... (1950-74) #100-107 printer: ABNC.
1975-80 Issue .... (1975-83) #108-112 printer: ABNC.
1957-71 Issue .... (1957-82) #113-118 printer: TDLR.

1950 Issue - Reduced Size Notes

#98-99 arms at ctr. on back. Printer: W&S.

		VG	VF	UNC
98	**5 Sucres** 1950-55. Black on green unpt. Portr. Antonio Jose de Sucre at ctr. Date at l. or r. Back red.			
	a. 11.5.1950-13.7.1953.	2.25	15.00	75.00
	b. Sign. title ovpt: *SUBGERENTE GENERAL* at l. 21.9.1953.	4.50	20.00	85.00
	c. 31.5.1954-28.11.1955.	2.00	12.50	55.00
99	**50 Sucres** 1950-59. Black on green unpt. National monument at ctr. w/ bldgs. in background. Back green.			
	a. 11.5.1950; 26.7.1950; 13.10.1950; 3.4.1951; 26.9.1951.	7.50	50.00	150.
	b. Sign. title ovpt: *SUBGERENTE GENERAL* at l. 3.9.1952; 8.10.1954; 24.9.1957.	7.50	50.00	150.
	c. 10.12.1953; 19.6.1956; 25.11.1957; 25.11.1958; 8.4.1959.	6.00	40.00	125.
	s1. Specimen. Black ovpt.: *ESPÉCIMEN* on both sides. ND, w/0000 serial #, unsigned.	—	—	175.
	s2. Specimen. Red ovpt.: *MUESTRA* twice on both sides. ND, w/o serial # or signs. Punched hole cancelled.	—	—	175.

1950-71 Issue

#100-107 black on m/c unpt. Several date varieties, sign. title ovpts. and serial # styles. Arms on back 31mm. wide, w/o flagpole stems below. Printer: ABNC.

		VG	VF	UNC
100	**5 Sucres** 1956-73. Portr. Antonio Jose de Sucre at ctr. Back red.			
	a. 19.6.1956; 28.8.1956; 2.4.1957; 19.6.1957; 19.6.1957.	1.00	5.00	40.00
	b. Sign. title ovpt: *SUBGERENTE GENERAL*. 24.9.1957; 2.1.1958.	.75	5.00	40.00
	c. 2.2.1958; 1.1.1966.	.50	2.50	20.00
	d. 27.2.1970; 3.9.1973. Serial # varieties.	.25	1.50	3.50
101	**10 Sucres** 1950-1955. Portr. Sebastian de Benalcazar at ctr. Plain background. Back blue.			
	a. 14.1.1950-28.11.1955.	2.00	8.00	45.00
	b. 21.9.1953; 16.3.1954; 3.10.1955. Ovpt: *SUB GERENTE GENERAL*.	2.00	10.00	50.00
	s. Specimen.	—	—	100.

		VG	VF	UNC
101A	**10 Sucres** 1956-74. Like #101 but different guilloches and ornate background.			
	a. 15.6.1956-27.4.1966.	1.00	7.50	35.00
	b. 24.5.1968-2.1.1974.	.50	3.00	15.00
	s. Specimen.	—	—	100.

Note: #101A with date of 24.12.1957 has ovpt: *SUB GERENTE GENERAL*.

		VG	VF	UNC
102	**20 Sucres** 28.2.1950-28.7.1960. Church facade at ctr. Back brown.	2.50	15.00	50.00

		VG	VF	UNC
103	**20 Sucres** 1962-73. Like #102. Church facade at ctr., different guilloches and darker unpt. on face.			
	a. 12.12.1962-4.10.1967.	2.00	5.00	25.00
	b. 24.5.1968-3.9.1973.	1.00	3.00	15.00
	s. Specimen. ND.	—	—	125.

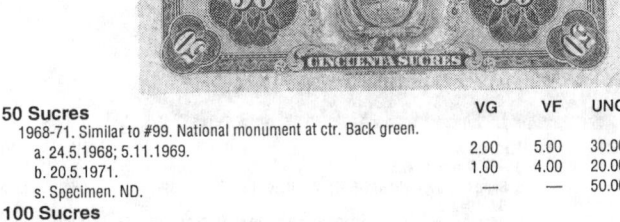

		VG	VF	UNC
104	**50 Sucres** 1968-71. Similar to #99. National monument at ctr. Back green.			
	a. 24.5.1968; 5.11.1969.	2.00	5.00	30.00
	b. 20.5.1971.	1.00	4.00	20.00
	s. Specimen. ND.	—	—	50.00
104A	**100 Sucres** 1952-57. Portr. Simon Bolivar at ctr. Back purple.			
	a. 3.9.1952-19.6.1957.	15.00	75.00	220.
	b. Sign. title: *SUBGERENTE*. 3.9.1952; 10.12.1953.	15.00	75.00	220.
105	**100 Sucres** 27.4.1966-7.7.1970. Like #104A, but different guilloches. Back purple.	5.00	10.00	50.00

		VG	VF	UNC
107	**1000 Sucres** 30.5.1969-20.9.1973. Banco Central bldg. at ctr. Back olive-gray.			
	a. Issued note.	20.00	85.00	250
	s. Specimen. ND.	—	—	75.0

NOTICE

Readers with unlisted dates, signature varieties, etc. are invited to submit photocopies or, high resolution (300 dpi, 100% size) scans of their notes to: Standard Catalog of World Paper Money, 700 East State St. Iola, WI 54990-0001, or E-Mail: george.cuhaj@fwpubs.com.

1975-80 ISSUE

#108-112 black on m/c unpt. Face designs like previous issue. New rendition of arms 29mm. wide w/flag-pole stems below on back. Printer: ABNC.

		VG	VF	UNC
108	**5 Sucres** 1975-83. Like #100. Portr. Antonio Jose de Sucre at ctr. Back red w/new rendition of arms.			
	a. 14.3.1975; 29.4.1977.	.25	1.50	7.50
	b. 20.8.1982; 20.4.1983.	.25	1.00	4.00

		VG	VF	UNC
109	**10 Sucres** 14.3.1975; 10.8.1976; 29.4.1977; 24.5.1978. Like #101A. Portr. Sebastian de Benalcazar at ctr. Back blue w/new rendition of arms.	.25	2.00	10.00

		VG	VF	UNC
110	**20 Sucres** 10.8.1976. Like #103. Church façade at ctr. Back brown w/new rendition of arms.	.25	2.50	15.00

1957-71 ISSUE

#113-118 black on m/c unpt. Similar to previous issues. Several sign. title ovpt. varieties. Security thread intermittent through 1969. Printer: TDLR.

		VG	VF	UNC
113	**5 Sucres** 1958-88. Similar to #108. Back red.			
	a. 2.1.1958-7.11.1962.	.75	4.00	15.00
	b. 23.5.1963-27.2.1970.	.50	1.00	10.00
	c. 25.7.1979-24.5.1980.	.25	.50	5.00
	d. 22.11.1988.	.10	.25	2.00
	s. Specimen. ND; 24.5.1968; 24.5.1980.	—	—	50.00
116	**50 Sucres** 1957-82. Similar to #111.			
	a. 2.4.1957; 7.7.1959.	2.50	15.00	60.00
	b. 7.11.1962; 29.10.1963; 29.1.1965; 6.8.1965.	1.00	8.00	35.00
	c. 1.1.1966; 27.4.1966; 17.11.1966.	1.00	4.00	25.00
	d. 4.10.1967; 30.5.1969; 17.7.1974.	.75	2.00	15.00
	e. 24.5.1980; 20.8.1982.	.50	1.25	10.00
	s. Specimen. ND; 1.1.1966.	—	—	20.00

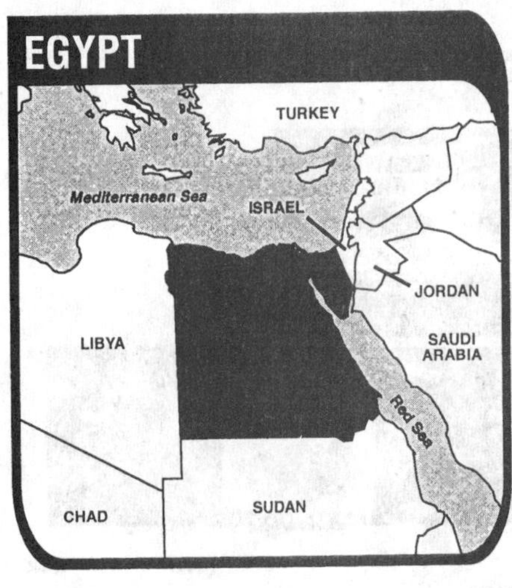

The Arab Republic of Egypt, located on the northeastern corner of Africa, has an area of 386,650 sq. mi. (1,000,000 sq. km.) and a population of 68.12 million. Capital: Cairo. Although Egypt is an almost rainless expanse of desert, its economy is predominantly agricultural. Cotton, rice and petroleum are exported.

Egyptian history dates back to about 4000 B.C. when the empire was established by uniting the upper and lower kingdoms. Following its "Golden Age" (16th to 13th centuries B.C.), Egypt was conquered by Persia (525 B.C.) and Alexander the Great (332 B.C.). The Ptolemies ruled until the suicide of Cleopatra (30 B.C.) when Egypt became a Roman colony. Arab caliphs ruled Egypt from 641 to 1517, when the Turks took it for their Ottoman Empire. Turkish rule, interrupted by the occupation of Napoleon (1798-1801), became increasingly casual, permitting Great Britain to inject its influence by purchasing shares in the Suez Canal. British troops occupied Egypt in 1882, becoming the de facto rulers. On Dec. 14, 1914, Egypt was made a protectorate of Britain. British occupation ended on Feb. 28, 1922, when Egypt became a sovereign, independent kingdom. The monarchy was abolished and a republic proclaimed on June 18, 1952.

On Feb. 1, 1958, Egypt and Syria formed the United Arab Republic. Yemen joined on March 8 in an association known as the United Arab States. Syria withdrew from the United Arab Republic on Sept. 29, 1961, and on Dec. 26 Egypt dissolved its ties with Yemen in the United Arab States. On Sept. 2, 1971, Egypt shed the name United Arab Republic in favor of the Arab Republic of Egypt.

RULERS:

OTTOMAN
- Abdul Mejid, AH1255-1277, 1839-1861AD
- Abdul Aziz, AH1277-1293, 1861-1876AD
- Abdul Hamid II, AH1293-1327, 1876-1909AD
- Abdul Hamid II, AH1293-1327, 1876-1909AD

EGYPTIAN
- Muhammad V, AH1327-1332, 1909-1914AD
- Hussein Kamil, AH1334-1336, 1915-1917AD
- Fuad I (Sultan), AH1336-1341, 1917-1922AD
- Fuad I (King), AH1341-1355, 1922-1936AD
- Farouk I, AH1355-1372, 1936-1952AD

MONETARY SYSTEM:
- 1 Piastre = 10 Ochr-El-Guerches
- 1 Piastre = 10 Ochr-El-Guerches
- 1 Pound = 100 Piastres, to 1916
- 1 Pound = 100 Piastres, to 1916
- 1 Piastre (Guerche) = 10 Milliemes
- 1 Pound (Junayh) = 100 Piastres, 1916-
- 1 Pound = 100 Piastres

OTTOMAN ADMINISTRATION

NATIONAL BANK OF EGYPT

DECREE OF 25.6.1898

		VG	VF	UNC
1	**50 Piastres** 1.1.1899. Black on green and pink unpt. Sphinx at ctr. Back green.			
	a. Sign. Palmer.	1500.	5000.	—
	b. Sign. Rowlatt.	1250.	4000.	—
	s. Specimen.			

		VG	VF	UNC
2	**1 Pound** 5.1.1899. Black on red and orange unpt. 2 camels at ctr. Back orange. Printer: BWC.			
	a. Sign. Palmer.	2000.	5000.	—
	b. Sign. Rowlatt.	1500.	4000.	—
	s. Specimen.	—	—	4000.

		VG	VF	UNC
3	**5 Pounds** 10.1.1899. Yellow, green and rose. Pyramids and palms at l. Specimen. Rare.	—	—	3000.

		VG	VF	UNC
4	**10 Pounds** 13.1.1899. Rose and lt. blue. Philae Temple w/2 sailboats at l. Specimen. Rare.	—	—	3000.
5	**50 Pounds** 15.1.1899 (21.3.1904). Blue, yellow and rose. Philae Temple at l. Specimen. Rare.	—	—	3500.

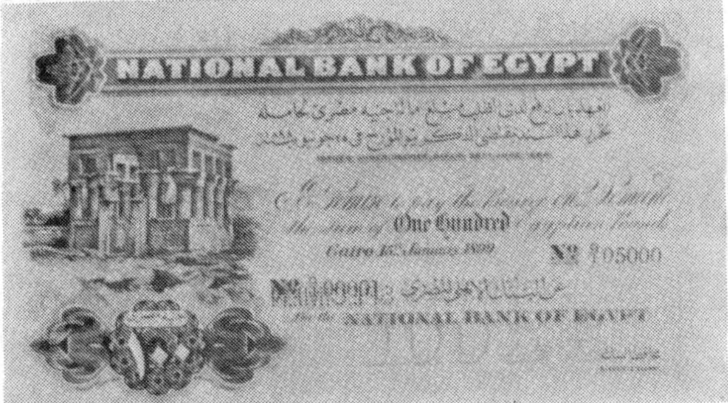

		VG	VF	UNC
6	**100 Pounds** 15.1.1899; 17.7.1906. Black on green and m/c unpt. Philae Temple at l. Back olive green. Specimen. Rare.	—	—	3500.

1912 ISSUE

		VG	VF	UNC
8	**10 Pounds** 1.1.1912. Like #4, but rose and dk. blue. Specimen. Rare.	—	Unc	2500.

1913-17 ISSUE

		VG	VF	UNC
10	**25 Piastres** 1917-51. Deep purple on m/c unpt. Banks of the Nile at ctr. Back dk. blue on pale orange and lt. gray unpt. Printer: BWC.			
	a. Sign. Rowlatt. 5.8.1917-18.6.1918.	50.00	200.	600.
	b. Sign. Cook. 6.6.1940; 7.6.1940.	20.00	75.00	300.
	c. Sign. Nixon. 18.12.1940-1946.	1.50	8.50	45.00
	d. Sign. Leith-Ross. 5.12.46; 1.12.1947-7.7.1950.	1.50	8.50	50.00
	e. Sign. Saad (Arabic). 15.5.1951-21.5.1951.	1.75	8.50	50.00
	f. As e, but w/Arabic serial #. 22.5.1951-23.5.1951.	1.75	8.50	50.00

		VG	VF	UNC
11	**50 Piastres** 1.8.1914-12.12.1920. Brown. Sphinx at l.	150.	500.	—

		VG	VF	UNC
2	**1 Pound** 1914-24. Blue on pink and lt. green unpt. Ruins at l. Back green.			
	a. Sign. Rowlatt. 21.9.1914-20.	70.00	250.	600.
	b. Sign. Hornsby. 1923-20.1.1924.	75.00	275.	650.

		VG	VF	UNC
3	**5 Pounds** 1.9.1913-11.11.1919. Pink and black. Small sailing ship at l.	225.	700.	—

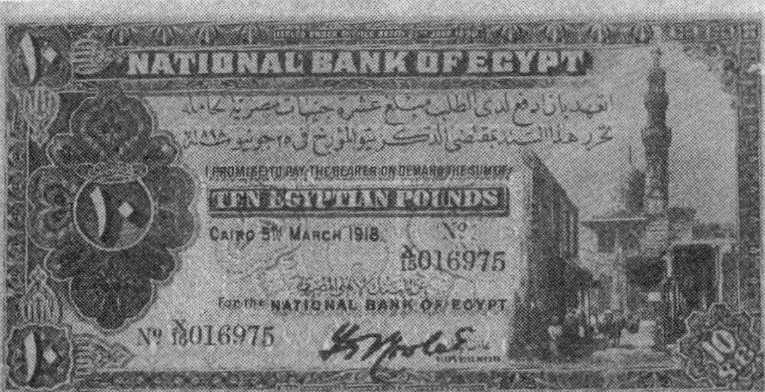

		VG	VF	UNC
14	**10 Pounds** 2.9.1913-30.5.1920. Brown and m/c. Mosque of Sultan Qala'un and street in Cairo. Printer: BWC.	150.	500.	—

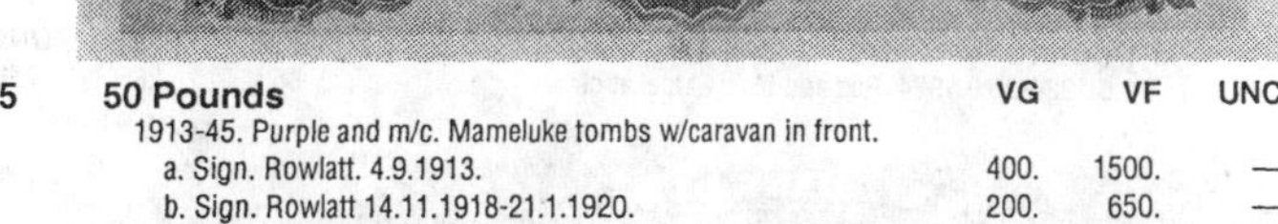

		VG	VF	UNC
15	**50 Pounds** 1913-45. Purple and m/c. Mameluke tombs w/caravan in front.			
	a. Sign. Rowlatt. 4.9.1913.	400.	1500.	—
	b. Sign. Rowlatt 14.11.1918-21.1.1920.	200.	650.	—
	c. Sign. Nixon. 6.2.1942-2.5.1945.	75.00	225.	750.

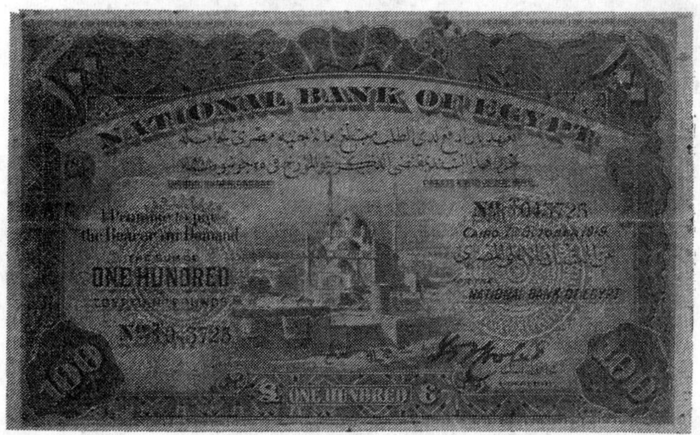

		VG	VF	UNC
16	**100 Pounds** 5.9.1913; 7.10.1919. Green. Citadel and mosque of Mohammed Ali at ctr. Rare.	—	—	—

1921 ISSUE

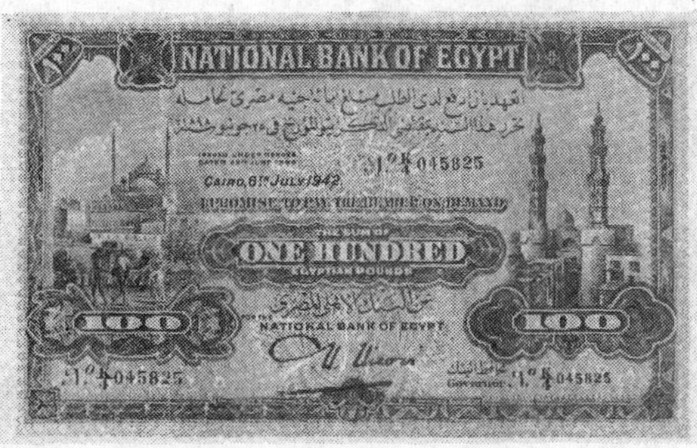

		VG	VF	UNC
17	**100 Pounds** 1921-45. Brown, red and green. Citadel of Cairo at l. Mosque at r. Small sailing boat and island of Philae on back.			
	a. Sign. Hornsby. 1.3.1921.	6000.	10,000.	—
	b. Sign. Hornsby. 1.9.1921.	700.	2000.	—
	c. Sign. Cook. 4.6.1936.	75.00	400.	—
	d. Sign. Nixon. 1942-45.	50.00	225.	800.

1924 ISSUE

		VG	VF	UNC
18	**1 Pound** 1.6.1924-20.9.1924. Red and blue. Camel at ctr.	85.00	285.	750.

		VG	VF	UNC
19	**5 Pounds** 1924-45. Green and purple. Bank at ctr. Back blue and red on green and orange unpt.; palms and bldg. at ctr.			
	a. Sign. Hornsby. 1.8.1924-13.1.1929.	50.00	250.	650.
	b. Sign. Cook. 1930-40.	15.00	45.00	250.
	c. Sign. Nixon. 1940-45.	12.50	35.00	150.

1926 ISSUE

		VG	VF	UNC
20	**1 Pound** 1.7.1926-10.1.1930. Green and dk. blue. Fellah at r. Back purple.	35.00	125.	475.

1930-35 ISSUE

		VG	VF	UNC
21	**50 Piastres** 1935-51. Green and m/c. Tutankhamen at l. Back blue; crescent and stars at l. Wmk: Scarab.			
	a. Sign. Cook. 7.5.1935-40.	10.00	40.00	150
	b. Lg. sign. Nixon. 1940-43.	2.00	10.00	50.0
	c. Sm. sign. Nixon. 1945-47.	2.00	10.00	50.0
	d. Sign. Leith-Ross. 1948-50.	2.00	10.00	50.0
	e. Sign. Saad (Arabic). 17.5.1951; 18.5.1951.	2.00	12.50	55.0

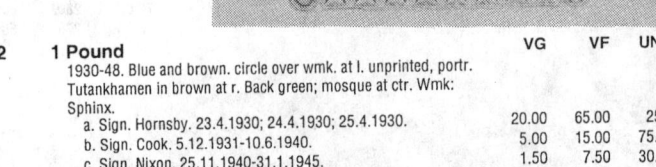

		VG	VF	UN
22	**1 Pound** 1930-48. Blue and brown. circle over wmk. at l. unprinted, portr. Tutankhamen in brown at r. Back green; mosque at ctr. Wmk: Sphinx.			
	a. Sign. Hornsby. 23.4.1930; 24.4.1930; 25.4.1930.	20.00	65.00	25
	b. Sign. Cook. 5.12.1931-10.6.1940.	5.00	15.00	75.
	c. Sign. Nixon. 25.11.1940-31.1.1945.	1.50	7.50	30.
	d. Sign. Leith-Ross. 26.5.1948-10.6.1948.	2.00	8.50	40.

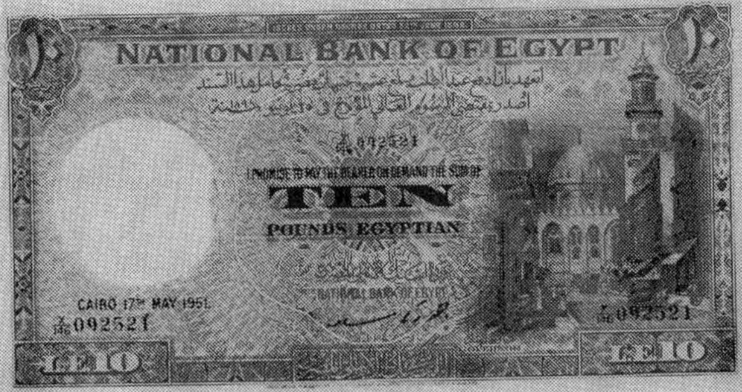

		VG	VF	U
23	**10 Pounds** 1931-51. Brown, yellow-green and m/c. Mosque of Sultan Qala'un and street in Cairo at r. Back blue; farm scene and trees. Printer: BWC.			
	a. Sign. Cook. 3.3.1931-1940.	25.00	65.00	4
	b. Sign. Nixon. 1940-47.	15.00	50.00	2
	c. Sign. Leith-Ross. 1948-50.	15.00	50.00	2
	d. Sign. Saad (Arabic). 24.5.1951.	15.00	55.00	2

1946-50 Issue

#24-27 portr. Kg. Farouk at r.

		VG	VF	UNC
24	**1 Pound**			
	1950-52. Blue and lilac.			
	a. European and Arabic serial #. 1.7.1950-13.7.1950.	3.50	22.50	90.00
	b. Arabic serial #. 15.5.1951-22.5.1951.	3.50	22.50	90.00
	c. Like b. W/o imprint. 8.5.1952-10.5.1952.	3.50	22.50	90.00

		VG	VF	UNC
25	**5 Pounds**			
	1946-51. Blue-green, violet and brown. Citadel of Cairo at l.			
	a. Sign. Leith-Ross. 1.5.1946-1950.	10.00	45.00	250.
	b. Sign. Saad (Arabic). 6.6.1951.	12.00	50.00	275.

		VG	VF	UNC
26	**50 Pounds**			
	1949-51. Green and brown. Ruins at lower l. ctr. City scene on back.			
	a. Sign. Leith-Ross. 1.11.1949-1950.	25.00	125.	700.
	b. Sign. Saad (Arabic). 16.5.1951.	25.00	125.	700.

		VG	VF	UNC
27	**100 Pounds**			
	1948-51. Lt. violet and green. Minaret at l. Mosque on back.			
	a. Sign. Leith-Ross. 1.7.1948-50.	35.00	200.	850.
	b. Sign. Saad (Arabic). 16.5.1951.	30.00	175.	850.

1952 Issue

#28-34 Tutankhamen at r.

		VG	VF	UNC
28	**25 Piastres**			
	8.5.1952-14.12.1957. Green. Mosque on back.	1.00	5.00	15.00
29	**50 Piastres**			
	8.5.1952-3.8.1960. Brown on m/c unpt. Ruins on back. Wmk: Sphinx.	1.00	5.00	15.00
30	**1 Pound**			
	12.5.1952-23.8.1960. Blue and lilac. Circle over wmk. at l. w/unpt. Back blue; ruins. Wmk: Sphinx.	1.00	5.00	15.00

		VG	VF	UNC
31	**5 Pounds**			
	8.5.1952-11.8.1960. Dk. green, gray-blue and brown. Mosque at l. Back green; allegorical figures. Wmk: Flower.	5.00	12.00	25.00

		VG	VF	UNC
32	**10 Pounds**			
	1.11.1952-31.5.1960. Red and lilac. Ruins on back. Wmk: Sphinx.	7.50	20.00	40.00
33	**50 Pounds**			
	29.10.1952; 30.10.1952. Green and brown. City scene on back, like #26.	20.00	100.	550.

		VG	VF	UNC
34	**100 Pounds** 29.10.1952; 30.10.1952. Violet and green. Minaret at l. Mosque on back, like #27.	20.00	125.	650.

EGYPTIAN GOVERNMENT

1916-17 ISSUE

		VG	VF	UNC
158	**5 Piastres** 27.5.1917. Blue on green and tan unpt. Back olive-green; ruins at ctr. (Not issued).	—	—	500.
159	**10 Piastres** ND (ca. 1917). Green and black. Specimen.	—	—	—

		VG	VF	UNC
160	**10 Piastres** 1916-17. Green on tan and lt. green unpt. Back blue; Colossi of Memnon at ctr. Printer: TDLR.			
	a. 17.7.1916.	75.00	300.	750.
	b. 27.5.1917.	25.00	75.00	250.

1918 ISSUE

		VG	VF	UNC
161	**5 Piastres** 1.5.1918-10.6.1918. Purple on green and orange unpt. Back green; ruins at ctr. Printer: Survey of Egypt.	100.	300.	800.

		VG	VF	UNC
162	**5 Piastres** 1.6.1918. Lilac-brown on green unpt. Caravan at lower ctr. Back blue. Printer: BWC.	25.00	75.00	300.

162A	**5 Piastres** 22.5.1920. Yellow-brown on m/c unpt. Back: Blue and pink. Sign. Fekry. Specimen, punch hole cancelled.	—	Unc	3500.

LAW 50/1940 ND ISSUES

#163-168 sign. varieties.

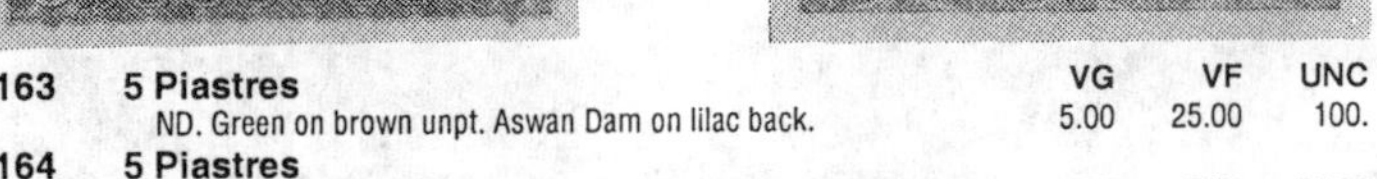

		VG	VF	UNC
163	**5 Piastres** ND. Green on brown unpt. Aswan Dam on lilac back.	5.00	25.00	100.
164	**5 Piastres** ND. Brown on yellow unpt. Mosque of Emir Khairbak at l. Back gray.	.75	7.50	50.00

		VG	VF	UNC
165	**5 Piastres** ND. Brown on yellow unpt. Portr. Kg. Farouk at l. Back gray-blue; like #164.			
	a. Sign. title: *MINISTER OF FINANCE* on back.	.75	8.00	60.00
	b. Sign. title: *MINISTER OF FINANCE AND ECONOMY* on back.	.75	10.00	80.00

		VG	VF	UNC
166	**10 Piastres** ND. Brown on lilac unpt. Nile scene w/Citadel on blue back.			
	a. W/o wmk. Arabic serial #.	3.00	20.00	200.
	b. Wmk: Geometric shape. Arabic serial #.	2.25	15.00	150.
	c. Wmk: Geometric shape. Arabic and Western serial #'s.	3.00	20.00	200.

		VG	VF	UNC
167	**10 Piastres** ND. Blue on green unpt. Temple of Philae at ctr. Color shading varieties. Back green on lt. orange unpt. Placement of series letter varies.			
	a. Single letter to l. of sign.	.75	7.50	50.00
	b. Letter and number above sign.	.75	7.50	50.00

		VG	VF	UNC
168	**10 Piastres** ND. Blue on green unpt. Portr. Kg. Farouk at r. Back green on lt. orange unpt.			
	a. Sign. title: *MINISTER OF FINANCE* on back.	.75	6.00	60.00
	b. Sign. title: *MINISTER OF FINANCE AND ECONOMY* on back.	1.50	8.00	80.00

EGYPTIAN ROYAL GOVERNMENT

Listings from #169-178 present notes of similar design but with significant differences. Face and back designs are designated with numbers for ease of identification, and to trace the progression of printings more easily.

Face A1: *EGYPTIAN ROYAL GOVERNMENT* in Arabic. (Regency of Farouk's son, Ahmed Fuad II).

Back 1A: as following issue.

1952 REVOLUTIONARY PROVISIONAL ISSUE

		VG	VF	UNC
169	**5 Piastres** ND. (1952). Similar to #170 but different heading at top. Rare.			
	s. Specimen.	—	—	1500.

		VG	VF	UNC
169A	**10 Piastres** ND. (1952). Similar to #171 but different heading at top. Dhow at riverbank at ctr. Rare.			
	s. Specimen.	—	—	1500.

EGYPTIAN STATE

Face 1: *EGYPTIAN STATE CURRENCY NOTE* in Arabic.

Back 1A: *EGYPTIAN CURRENCY NOTE* in English. Sign. title: *MINISTER OF FINANCE AND ECONOMY*. Imprint: Survey of Egypt.

1952 ND ISSUE

		VG	VF	UNC
170	**5 Piastres** ND. (1952). Lilac on gray-olive unpt. Portr. Qn. Nefertiti at r. Ovpt. pattern on Kg. Farouk wmk. at l. Back brown.	25.00	100.	250.

		VG	VF	UNC
171	**10 Piastres** ND (1952). Gray-blue on brown unpt. Group of people and flag w/3 stars and crescent at r. Ovpt. pattern on Farouk wmk. at l. Back black and red.	125.	400.	750.

EGYPTIAN REPUBLIC

Face 2: *EGYPTIAN REPUBLIC CURRENCY NOTE* in Arabic.

Back 1A: Like previous issue *(EGYPTIAN CURRENCY NOTE)* and sign. as above).

1952 PROVISIONAL ISSUE

		VG	VF	UNC
172	**5 Piastres** ND (1952). Similar to #170 w/ovpt. pattern on Farouk wmk. at l.	50.00	150.	300.

1952 REGULAR ISSUE

		VG	VF	UNC
174	**5 Piastres** ND (1952-58). Lilac. Like #172 but w/o pattern ovpt. on wmk. area.			
	a. Wmk: Pyramids. 3 sign. varieties.	1.00	5.00	25.00
	b. Wmk: Crown and letters (paper from #165 and #168).	1.00	5.00	35.00

		VG	VF	UNC
175	**10 Piastres** ND (1952-58). Gray-blue to black. Similar to #171 but w/o ovpt. pattern on wmk. area.			
	a. Wmk: Pyramids. 3 sign. varieties.	1.00	5.00	35.00
	b. Wmk: Crown and letters (paper as on #174b).	1.00	6.00	35.00

UNITED ARAB REPUBLIC

ARAB REPUBLIC OF EGYPT

Face 3: ***UNITED ARAB REPUBLIC-EGYPTIAN REGION*** **in Arabic (main heading plus small lines of Arabic text underneath).**

Back 1B: ***EGYPTIAN CURRENCY NOTE*** **in English. Sign. title changed to :** ***MINISTER OF TREASURY.*** **Imprint: Survey of Egypt.**

1958-71 ND ISSUE

		VG	VF	UNC
176	**5 Piastres** ND. Red-lilac to violet. Similar to #174.			
	a. Wmk: Pyramids.	1.50	5.00	40.00
	b. Wmk: Eagles. 2 sign. varieties.	1.50	5.00	20.00
	c. Wmk: *U A R* letters in Arabic and English. Lilac or dk. purple.	.25	2.00	10.00

		VG	VF	UNC
177	**10 Piastres** ND. Blue-black to black. Similar to #175 but flag w/2 stars and w/o crescent.			
	a. Wmk: Pyramids. 2 sign. varieties.	1.50	5.00	40.00
	b. Wmk: Eagles.	1.50	5.00	30.00
	c. Wmk: *U A R* letters in Arabic and English.	.25	1.50	20.00
178	**10 Piastres** ND. "Mule" note combining Face 3 w/back 1A.	40.00	150.	400.

ITALIAN OCCUPATION - WW II

CASSA MEDITERRANEA DI CREDITO PER L'EGITTO

1942 ND ISSUE

NOTE: Only one complete specimen set is known. For similar notes w/*PER IL SVDAN* refer to Sudan #M1-M8; for similar notes w/*CASSA MEDITERRANEA...LA GRECIA* refer to Greece #M1-M9.

		VG	VF	UNC
M1	**5 Piastre** ND (1942). Purple on blue. Bust of Apollo at r. Stylized grain at l. on back.			
	a. Issued note. Rare.	—	—	—
	s. Specimen.	—	—	2500.
MA1	**1 Piastra** ND (1942). Red on pink unpt. Specimen. Rare.	—	—	—
M2	**10 Piastre** ND (1942). Red-orange. Bust of Apollo at r. Stylized ancient galley prows at l. on back.			
	a. Issued note. Rare.	—	—	—
	s. Specimen.	—	—	2500.

		VG	VF	UNC
M3	**50 Piastre** ND (1942). Red-orange. Portr. Emperor Octavian at l.			
	a. Issued note. Rare.	—	—	—
	s. Specimen.	—	—	2500.
M4	**1 Lira** ND (1942). Dull purple and dk. brown on ochre unpt. Portr. Emperor Octavian at l.			
	a. Issued note. Rare.	—	—	—
	s. Specimen.	—	—	2500

		VG	VF	UNC
M5	**5 Lire** ND (1942). Dk. brown and purple on ochre unpt. Portr. Emperor Octavian at l.			
	a. Issued note. Rare.	—	—	—
	s. Specimen.	—	—	2500
M6	**10 Lire** ND (1942). Violet and purple. Face like #M5. Specimen.	—	—	2500

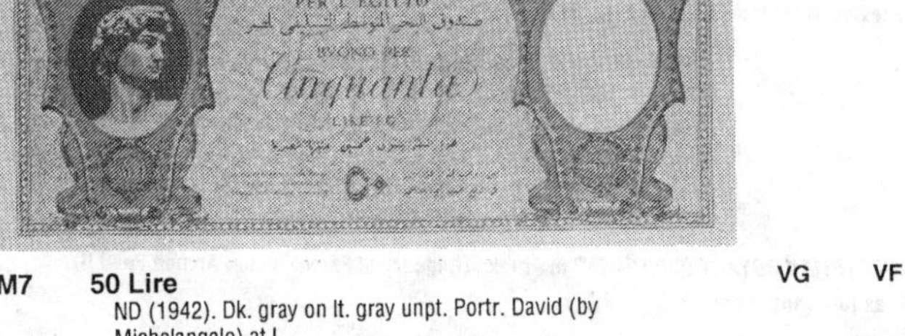

		VG	VF	UNC
M7	**50 Lire** ND (1942). Dk. gray on lt. gray unpt. Portr. David (by Michelangelo) at l.			
	a. Issued note. Rare.	—	—	—
	s. Specimen.	—	—	250
M8	**100 Lire** ND (1942). Portr. David (by Michelangelo) at l.			
	a. Issued note. Rare.	—	—	—
	s. Specimen.	—	—	250

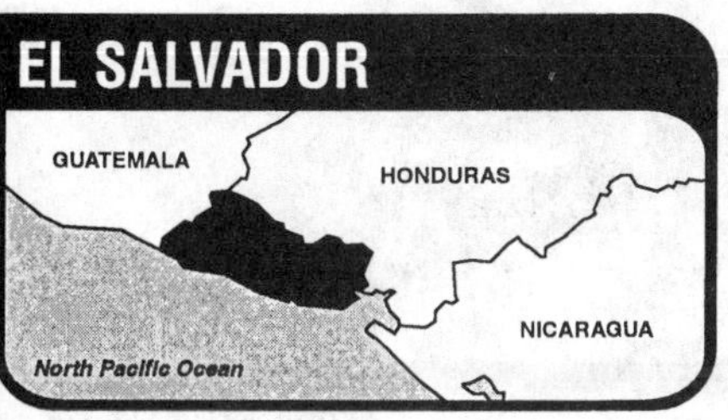

The Republic of El Salvador, a Central American country bordered by Guatemala, Honduras and the Pacific Ocean, has an area of 8,260 sq. mi. (21,041 sq. km.) and a population of 6.32 million. Capital: San Salvador. This most intensely cultivated country of Latin America produces coffee (the major crop), sugar and balsam for export. Gold, silver and other metals are largely unexploited.

The first Spanish attempt to subjugate the area was undertaken in 1523 by Pedro de Alvarado, Cortes' lieutenant. He was forced to retreat by superior Indian forces, but returned in 1525 and succeeded in bringing the region under control of the captaincy general of Guatemala, where it remained until 1821. In 1821, El Salvador and the other Central American provinces declared their independence from Spain. In 1823, the Federal Republic of Central America was formed by the five Central American States. When this federation was dissolved in 1829, El Salvador became an independent republic.

A twelve-year civil war was ended in 1992 with the signing of a UN sponsored Peace Accord. Free elections, with full participation of all political parties, were held in 1994 and 1997. Armando Calderón-Sol was elected as president in 1994 for a 5-year term.

On January 1, 2001, a monetary reform established the U.S. dollar as the accounting unit for all financial transactions, and fixed the exchange rate as 8.75 colones per dollar. In addition, the Central Reserve Bank has indicated that it will cease issuing coins and notes.

MONETARY SYSTEM:

1 Peso = 100 Centavos to 1919
1 Colón = 100 Centavos 1919-

DATING SYSTEM:

Dates listed for notes are those found on the face, regardless of the ovpt. issue dates on back which were applied practically on a daily basis as notes were needed for circulation.

REPUBLIC

GOBIERNO DEL SALVADOR

GOVERNMENT OF EL SALVADOR

1877 ISSUE

#1-8 arms at upper ctr. on face, arms at ctr. on back. 180 x 82mm. Printer: NBNC.

#		VG	VF	UNC
1	**1 Peso** 1.4.1877. Blue and black. Back brown.			
	a. Issued note.	—	—	300.
	s. Specimen.	—	—	300.
2	**2 Pesos** 1.4.1877. Brown and black. Back blue. Specimen.	—	—	300.
3	**5 Pesos** 1.4.1877. Green and black. Back orange. Specimen.	—	—	300.
4	**10 Pesos** 1.4.1877. Orange and black. Back green. Specimen.	—	—	300.
5	**25 Pesos** 1.4.1877. Orange-brown and black. Back blue. Specimen.	—	—	400.
6	**50 Pesos** 1.4.1877. Red-orange and black. Back brown. Specimen.	—	—	400.
7	**100 Pesos** 1.4.1877. Blue and black. Back red-orange. Specimen.	—	—	500.
8	**500 Pesos** 1.4.1877. Gold and black. Back orange-brown. Specimen.	—	—	500.

DEUDA INTERIOR DEL PAIS

Circulating Interior Debt Notes

#9-15 similar in color and design to #1-8.

#9-18 larger size, 215 x 127mm. Printer: NBNC.

#		VG	VF	UNC
9	**1 Peso** 1.4.1877. Blue and black. Back brown.			
	a. Issued note.	—	—	—
	s. Specimen.	—	—	300.
10	**2 Pesos** 1.4.1877. Brown and black. Back blue. Specimen.	—	—	300.
11	**5 Pesos** 1.4.1877. Green and black. Back green. Specimen.	—	—	300.
12	**10 Pesos** 1.4.1877. Orange and black. Back blue. Specimen.	—	—	300.
13	**25 Pesos** 1.4.1877. Orange-brown and black. Back blue. Specimen.	—	—	—
14	**50 Pesos** 1.4.1877. Red-orange and black. Back brown.			
	a. Issued note.	—	—	—
	s. Specimen.	—	—	—
15	**100 Pesos** 1.4.1877. Blue and black. Back red-orange. Specimen.	—	—	—
16	**200 Pesos** 1.4.1877. Black on brown unpt. Back deep red. Specimen.	—	—	—
17	**500 Pesos** 1.4.1877. Gold and black. Back orange-brown. Specimen.	—	—	—
18	**1000 Pesos** 1.4.1877. Black on deep red unpt. Back yellow. Specimen.	—	—	—

DEUDA PUBLICA DEL SALVADOR

Circulating Public Debt Notes. Ca. 1880

#		VG	VF	UNC
35	**25 Pesos** 18xx. Brown and black. Mercury l., arms at upper ctr. Printer: BWC. Specimen.	—	—	—

BANCO CENTRAL DE RESERVA DE EL SALVADOR

VALIDATION OVERPRINTS

The Government decreed that after 1907 all issued banknotes should have a validation stamp with the text: *TOMADO RAZON* accompanied by the official seal and sign. Varieties of sign. and numerous dates may exist for some issues. Later issues have only the seal, sign. and date after San Salvador. The dates listed throughout are only those found on the face of the note.

TRIBUNAL DE CUENTAS

Sergio Castellanos	1907-1910

TRIBUNAL SUPERIOR DE CUENTAS

Sergio Castellanos	1910-1916	Alb. Galindo	1924-1927
Jose E. Suay	1917-1918	D. Rosales Sol	1928-1929
Luis Valle M.	1919	C.V. Martinez	1939

JUNTA DE VIGILANCIA DE BANCOS Y S.A.

V.C. Barriere	1935-1944	B. Glower V.	1952
C. Valmore M.	1940	M. Ant. Ramirez	1954-1958

V.M. Valdes	1946-1948	Antonio Serrano L.	1956-1958
M.E. Hinds	1949	Pedro A. Delgado	1959
Jorge Sol	1950-1953	R. Rubino	1961

CORTE DE CUENTAS

M.E. Hinds	1940-1943

SUPERINTENDENCIA DE BANCOS Y OTRAS INSTITUCIONES FINANCIERAS

Juan S. Quinteros	1962-1975	Marco T. Guandique	1977-Feb. 1981
Jose A. Mendoza	1968-1975	Rafael T. Carbonell	1981-
Jorge A. Dowson	1975-1977	Raul Nolasco	1981-

NOTE: Certain listings encompassing issues circulated by various bank and regional authorities are contained in Volume 1.

1934 ISSUE

#75-80 allegorical woman reclining w/fruits and branch at ctr. Portr. C. Columbus at ctr. on back. Printer: ABNC.

		VG	VF	UNC
75	**1 Colón** 31.8.1934; 4.9.1941; 14.1.1943. Black on pale blue and m/c unpt. Back orange.	7.50	25.00	125.

		VG	VF	UNC
76	**2 Colones** 31.8.1934-14.5.1952. Black on m/c unpt. Back red-brown.	12.50	40.00	150.

		VG	VF	UNC
77	**5 Colones** 31.8.1934. Black on m/c unpt. Back green.	15.00	50.00	175.

		VG	VF	UNC
78	**10 Colones** 31.8.1934. Black on m/c unpt. Back dk. brown.	25.00	75.00	225.

		VG	VF	UNC
79	**25 Colones** 31.8.1934; 14.2.1951; 17.3.1954. Black on m/c unpt. Back deep blue.	30.00	85.00	275.

		VG	VF	UNC
80	**100 Colones** 31.8.1934; 9.2.1937. Brown and green unpt. Back dull olive-green.	30.00	100.	325.

1938 ISSUE

#81 and 82 portr. C. Columbus at ctr. on back. Printer: W&S.

		VG	VF	UNC
81	**1 Colón** 10.5.1938. Black on m/c unpt. Woman w/basket of fruit on her head at l. Back orange.	6.00	20.00	100.

		VG	VF	UNC
82	**5 Colones** 10.5.1938-17.3.1954. Black on m/c unpt. Similar to #81. Woman w/basket of fruit on her head at l. Back green.	10.00	35.00	150.

1942-44 ISSUE

#83-86 portr. C. Columbus at ctr. on back. Printer: ABNC.

		VG	VF	UNC
83	**1 Colón** 26.9.1944-14.5.1952. Black on pale blue and m/c unpt. Farmer plowing w/oxen at ctr. Back orange.	3.00	12.50	60.00

		VG	VF	UNC
84	**5 Colones** 11.8.1942-14.5.1952. Black on m/c unpt. Delgado addressing crowd at ctr. Back green.	7.50	25.00	150.

		VG	VF	UNC
85	**10 Colones** 14.3.1943-14.5.1952. Black on m/c unpt. Portr. M.J. Arce at l. Back brown.	10.00	50.00	200.
86	**100 Colones** 1942-54. Black on m/c unpt. Independence monument at ctr. Back olive-green.			
	a. Brown and green unpt. 11.8.1942-31.1.1951.	25.00	75.00	250.
	b. Green unpt. 17.3.1954.	25.00	75.00	250.

1950; 1954 ISSUE

#87-88 printer: W&S.

		VG	VF	UNC
87	**1 Colón** 10.1.1950; 6.11.1952; 17.3.1954. Black on m/c unpt. Coffee bush at l., Lake Coatepeque at r. Back orange.	5.00	12.50	40.00

		VG	VF	UNC
88	**10 Colones** 17.3.1954. Black on dull purple and m/c unpt. M.J. Arce at upper ctr. Back dk. brown. Series ZA.	12.50	50.00	200.

#89 Deleted, see #86b.

1955 ISSUE

#90-92 portr. C. Columbus at ctr. on back. Printer: W&S.

		VG	VF	UNC
90	**1 Colón** 1955-60. Black on m/c unpt. Coffee bush at lower l., bank at r. Back orange.			
	a. Paper w/o metal thread. 13.4.1955.	2.50	5.00	20.00
	b. Paper w/metal thread. 15.2.1956-17.8.1960.	1.00	2.50	15.00

		VG	VF	UNC
91	**2 Colones** 1955-58. Black on m/c unpt. Coffee bush at l. w/field workers in background. Back red-brown.			
	a. Plain paper w/o security thread. 13.4.1955.	5.00	12.00	50.00
	b. Paper w/metal thread. Wmk: *BANCO CENTRAL*. 27.8.1958.	3.00	10.00	45.00

		VG	VF	UNC
92	**5 Colones** 1955-59. Black on m/c unpt. Woman w/basket of fruit on her head. Back green.			
	a. Plain paper w/o security thread. 13.4.1955.	4.00	15.00	65.00
	b. Paper w/metal thread. Wmk: *BANCO CENTRAL*. 25.1.1957-25.11.1959.	4.00	15.00	65.00

1957-58 ISSUE

#93-98 portr. C. Columbus at ctr. on back. Printer: ABNC.

		VG	VF	UNC
93	**1 Colón** 4.9.1957. Black on pink and pale green unpt. *SAN SALVADOR* at lower l., farmer plowing w/oxen at ctr. Red serial # and series letters. Back orange.	3.00	8.00	25.00

		VG	VF	UNC
94	**2 Colones** 9.11.1960. Black on m/c unpt. Allegorical woman reclining w/fruits and branch at ctr. Like #76 but reduced size.	4.00	15.00	65.00

		VG	VF	UNC
95	**5 Colones** 15.2.1956; 9.11.1960. Black on m/c unpt. *SAN SALVADOR* at lower l., Delgado addressing crowd at ctr. Red serial # at upper l. and r. Back green.	4.00	10.00	45.00

		VG	VF	UNC
96	**10 Colones** 4.9.1957. Black on m/c unpt. Portr. M.J. Arce at l. Back brown.	7.50	30.00	100.

		VG	VF	UNC
97	**25 Colones** 29.12.1958; 9.11.1960. Black on m/c unpt. Reservoir in frame at ctr. Back blue.	8.00	30.00	100.

		VG	VF	UNC
98	**100 Colones** 29.12.1958; 9.11.1960. Black on m/c unpt. *SAN SALVADOR* at lower l., Independence monument at ctr. Serial # at upper l. and upper r. Back olive.	25.00	90.00	300.

1959 ISSUE

		VG	VF	UNC
99	**10 Colones** 25.11.1959. Black on pale green and m/c unpt. Portr. M.J. Arce at upper ctr. Reduced size, 67 x 156mm. Back slate gray; portr. C. Columbus at ctr. Printer: W&S.	4.00	20.00	80.00

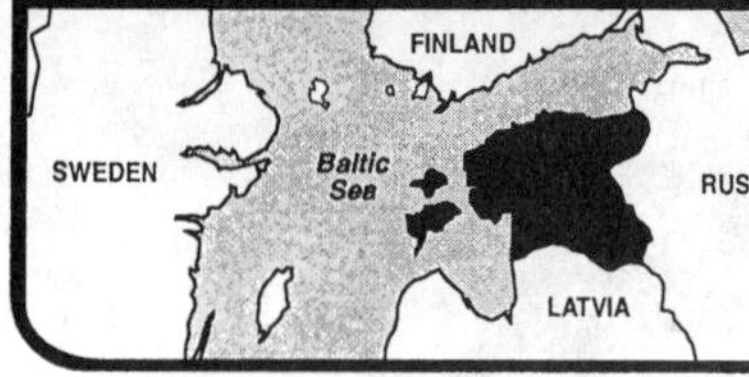

The Republic of Estonia (formerly the Estonian Soviet Socialist Republic of the U.S.S.R.) is the northernmost of the three Baltic states in eastern Europe. It has an area of 17,413 sq. mi. (45,100 sq. km.) and a population of 1.42 million. Capital: Tallinn. Agriculture and dairy farming are the principal industries. Butter, eggs, bacon, timber are exported.

This small and ancient Baltic state has enjoyed but two decades of independence since the 13th century. After having been conquered by the Danes, the Livonian Knights, the Teutonic Knights of Germany, the Swedes, the Poles and the Russians. Estonia declared itself an independent republic on Nov. 15, 1917, The peace treaty was signed Feb. 2, 1920. Shortly after the start of World War II, it was again occupied by Russia and incorporated as the 16th state of the U.S.S.R. Germany occupied Estonia from 1941 to 1944, after which it was retaken by Russia.

On August 20, 1991, the Parliament of the Estonian S.S.R. voted to reassert the republic's independence.

MONETARY SYSTEM

1 Mark = 100 Penni to 1928
1 Kroon = 100 Senti

In 1919 the notes of the Russian Northwest Army (Gen. Yudenich) also circulated in Estonia; in other areas the notes of the Special Corps of the North Army under Gen. Rodzianko. German reichsmark circulated between 1941-1944.

REPUBLIC

TALLINNA ARVEKOJA MAKSUTÄHT

PAYMENT NOTES OF THE CLEARING HOUSE OF TALLINN

1919 FIRST ISSUE

		Good	Fine	XF
A1	**50 Ost. Marka** 1919-22. Green. Rare.	—	—	—

1919 SECOND ISSUE

		Good	Fine	XF
A2	**50 Marka** 1919. Blue.			
	a. W/o issued branch stamp.	250.	450.	900.
	b. W/issued branch stamp.	200.	400.	800.
A3	**100 Marka** 1919. Brown.	350.	700.	1350.

1920 ISSUE

		Good	Fine	XF
A4	**5000 Marka** 192x (1920-23). Green. Rare.	—	—	—
A5	**10,000 Marka** 192x (1920-23). Green and brown. Rare.	—	—	—
A6	**25,000 Marka** 192x (1920-23). Green and brown. Rare.	—	—	—

EESTI WABARIIGI 5% WÕLAKOHUSTUS

REPUBLIC DEBT OBLIGATIONS OF 5% INTEREST

1919 SERIES A ISSUES

		Good	Fine	XF
1	**50 Marka** 1.5.1919. Gray. Uniface.	30.00	150.	—
1A	**50 Marka** 1.5.1919. Gray. Printed on both sides.	50.00	175.	—
2	**100 Marka** 1.5.1919. Gray. Uniface.	75.00	225.	—
2A	**100 Marka** 1.5.1919. Gray. Printed on both sides.	60.00	200.	—
3	**200 Marka** 1.5.1919. Gray. Uniface.	90.00	350.	—
3A	**200 Marka** 1.5.1919. Gray. Printed on both sides.	80.00	300.	—
4	**500 Marka** 1.5.1919. Uniface.	100.	375.	—
5	**500 Marka** 1.5.1919. Gray. Printed on both sides.	110.	400.	—
6	**1000 Marka** 1.5.1919. Gray. Uniface.	400.	850.	—
6A	**5000 Marka** 1.5.1919. Gray. Uniface. Rare.	—	—	—
6B	**10,000 Marka** 1.5.1919. Gray. Uniface. Rare.	—	—	—

1919 SERIES B ISSUES

		Good	Fine	XF
7	**50 Marka** 1.6.1919. Yellow-brown. Uniface.	30.00	150.	—
8	**50 Marka** 1.6.1919. Yellow-brown. Printed on both sides.	25.00	100.	—

		Good	Fine	XF
9	**100 Marka** 1.6.1919. Yellow-brown. Uniface.	60.00	200.	—
9A	**100 Marka** 1.6.1919. Yellow-brown. Printed on both sides.	50.00	175.	—
10	**200 Marka** 1.6.1919. Yellow. Uniface.	100.	375.	—

		Good	Fine	XF
11	**200 Marka** 1.6.1919. Yellow-brown. Printed on both sides.	110.	400.	—
12	**500 Marka** 1.6.1919. Yellow-brown. Uniface.	200.	600.	—
12A	**500 Marka** 1.6.1919. Yellow-brown. Printed on both sides. Rare.	—	—	—
13	**1000 Marka** 1.6.1919. Yellow-brown. Uniface.	350.	850.	—
13A	**1000 Marka** 1.6.1919. Yellow-brown. Printed on both sides. Rare.	—	—	—
13B	**5000 Marka** 1.6.1919. Yellow-brown. Uniface. Rare.	—	—	—
13C	**10,000 Marka** 1.6.1919. Yellow-brown. Uniface. Rare.	—	—	—

1919 Series D Issues

		Good	Fine	XF
14	**50 Marka** 1.7.1919. Green. Uniface.	25.00	100.	—
14A	**100 Marka** 1.7.1919. Green. Printed on both sides.	20.00	80.00	—
15	**100 Marka** 1.7.1919. Green. Uniface.	75.00	225.	—
15A	**100 Marka** 1.7.1919. Green. Printed on both sides.	50.00	175.	—
16	**200 Marka** 1.7.1919. Green. Uniface.	80.00	300.	—
17	**200 Marka** 1.7.1919. Green. Printed on both sides.	95.00	350.	—
18	**500 Marka** 1.7.1919. Green. Uniface.	150.	500.	—
19	**500 Marka** 1.7.1919. Green. Printed on both sides.	175.	550.	—
20	**1000 Marka** 1.7.1919. Green. Uniface.	350.	850.	—
20A	**1000 Marka** 1.7.1919. Green. Printed on both sides. Rare.	—	—	—
20B	**5000 Marka** 1.7.1919. Green. Uniface. Rare.	—	—	—
20C	**10,000 Marka** 1.7.1919. Green. Uniface. Rare.	—	—	—

1919 W/o Series First Issue

		Good	Fine	XF
21	**50 Marka** 1.11.1919. Gray.	25.00	100.	—
22	**100 Marka** 1.11.1919. Yellow-brown.	45.00	160.	—
23	**200 Marka** 1.11.1919. Orange.	75.00	275.	—
24	**500 Marka** 1.11.1919. Green.	200.	600.	—

1919 W/o Series Second Issue

		Good	Fine	XF
25	**50 Marka** 1.12.1919. Gray.	30.00	150.	—
26	**100 Marka** 1.12.1919. Yellow-brown.	50.00	175.	—
27	**200 Marka** 1.12.1919. Orange.	80.00	300.	—
28	**500 Marka** 1.12.1919. Green.	350.	800.	—

1920 First Issue

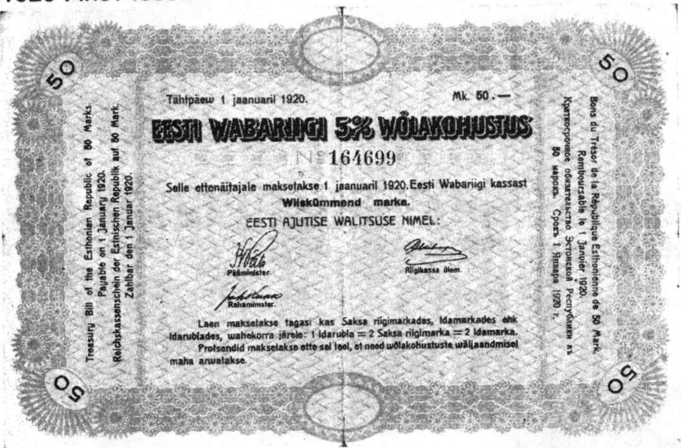

		Good	Fine	XF
29	**50 Marka** 1.1.1920. Gray.	20.00	80.00	—
30	**50 Marka** 1.1.1920. Blue.	17.50	75.00	—
31	**100 Marka** 1.1.1920. Gray.	45.00	160.	—
32	**100 Marka** 1.1.1920. Yellow-brown.	40.00	150.	—

#33 deleted.

		Good	Fine	XF
34	**500 Marka** 1.1.1920. Gray.	—	—	—
35	**500 Marka** 1.1.1920. Green.	—	—	—

#36 and 37, deleted.

1920 Second Issue

		Good	Fine	XF
38	**200 Marka** 1.5.1920. Gray.	—	—	—
38A	**200 Marka** 1.5.1920. Orange.	80.00	275.	—

Eesti Vabariigi 6%-line Kassa-veksel

Promissory Notes of the Treasury of the Republic of Estonia

1920 Series A

Issue of 4.5% interest.

		Good	Fine	XF
38B	**1000 Marka** 1.7.1920. Lilac.	400.	900.	—
38C	**5000 Marka** 1.7.1920. Blue-gray.	700.	1500.	—
38D	**10,000 Marka** 1.7.1920. Blue.	900.	2000.	—
38E	**25,000 Marka** 1.7.1920. Pink. Rare.	—	—	—
38F	**100,000 Marka** 1.7.1920. Yellow. Rare.	—	—	—

1920 Series B

Issue of 5% Interest.

		Good	Fine	XF
38G	**1000 Marka** 1.9.1920. Lilac.	400.	900.	—
38H	**5000 Marka** 1.9.1920. Blue-gray.	700.	1500.	—
38I	**10,000 Marka** 1.9.1920. Blue. Rare.	—	—	—
38J	**25,000 Marka** 1.9.1920. Pink. Rare.	—	—	—
38K	**100,000 Marka** 1.9.1920. Yellow. Rare.	—	—	—

1920 Series D

Issue of 5.5% Interest.

		Good	Fine	XF
38L	**1000 Marka** 1.12.1920. Lilac.	400.	900.	—
38M	**5000 Marka** 1.12.1920. Blue-gray.	700.	1500.	—
38N	**10,000 Marka** 1.12.1920. Blue.	900.	2000.	—
38O	**25,000 Marka** 1.12.1920. Pink. Rare.	—	—	—
38P	**100,000 Marka** 1.12.1920. Yellow. Rare.	—	—	—

1921 Series E

Issue of 6% Interest.

		Good	Fine	XF
38Q	**1000 Marka** 1.2.1921. Black.	400.	900.	—
38R	**5000 Marka** 1.2.1921. Blue-gray.	700.	1500.	—
38S	**10,000 Marka** 1.2.1921. Blue.	900.	2000.	—
38T	**25,000 Marka** 1.2.1921. Pink. Rare.	—	—	—
38U	**100,000 Marka** 1.2.1921. Yellow. Rare.	—	—	—

Note: #38A-38U are reported to exist in Specimen form also.

Eesti Vabariigi Kassatäht

Republic of Estonia Treasury Notes

1919-1920 Issue

		VG	VF	UNC
39	**5 Penni** ND (1919). Green. Owl in tree at ctr.			
	a. Issued note.	1.00	2.00	5.00
	s. Specimen.	20.00	50.00	115.

		VG	VF	UNC
40	**10 Penni** ND (1919). Ship at ctr.			
	a. Gray. Printer: Bergmann, Tartu.	5.00	10.00	25.00
	b. Brown. Printer: Riigi Trkikoda, Tallinn.	1.00	2.50	6.00
	s. Specimen.	20.00	50.00	115.

		VG	VF	UNC
41	**20 Penni** ND (1919). Yellow. Windmill at ctr.			
	a. Issued note.	1.00	2.50	7.50
	s. Specimen.	10.00	25.00	50.00

NOTICE

Readers with unlisted dates, signature varieties, etc. are invited to submit photocopies or, high resolution (300 dpi, 100% size) scans of their notes to: Standard Catalog of World Paper Money, 700 East State St. Iola, WI 54990-0001, or E-Mail: george.cuhaj@fwpubs.com.

		VG	VF	UNC
42	**50 Penni** 1919. Blue. Ornamental design at ctr.			
	a. Issued note.	1.50	4.00	12.50
	p. Proof. Black ovpt on white paper.	—	125.	250.
	s. Specimen.	—	—	125.

		VG	VF	UNC
43	**1 Mark** 1919. Brown on gold unpt. Sheaves of wheat and sickles at ctr.			
	a. Issued note.	1.50	5.00	15.00
	p1. Proof. Black ovpt. on white paper.	—	75.00	150.
	p2. Proof. Green ovpt. on yellow paper.	—	75.00	150.
	s. Specimen.	25.00	60.00	125.

Note: #42 and 43 also exist w/ovpt: *POHJAN POJAT RYKMENTIN...* See #M1 and M3.

		VG	VF	UNC
44	**3 Marka** 1919. Green on olive unpt. Agricultural symbols at ctr.			
	a. Issued note.	2.50	7.50	25.00
	s. Specimen.	25.00	60.00	125.

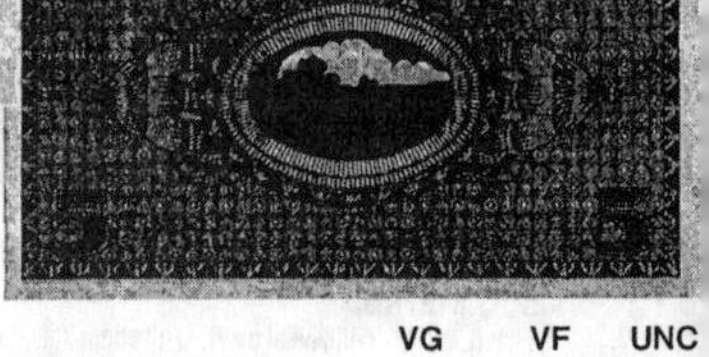

		VG	VF	UNC
45	**5 Marka** 1919. Blue and lt. brown. Farmer plowing at ctr. Field scene on back. Thin or thick paper.			
	a. Issued note.	3.00	10.00	35.00
	s. Specimen.	10.00	25.00	50.00

		VG	VF	UNC
46	**10 Marka** 1919. Brown. Shepherd blowing a horn while standing between a cow and some sheep. Man w/horse between cornucopiae on back.			
	a. *KÜMME MARKA* in blue border on back. Wmk: lt. horizontal lines (blue).	5.00	15.00	50.00
	b. *KÜMME MARKA* w/blue border. Wmk: Lt. vertical lines.	5.00	15.00	50.00
	c. *KÜMME MARKA* w/o border. Wmk: Lt. horizontal lines.	5.00	15.00	50.00
	d. *KÜMME MARKA* w/o border. Wmk: Lt. vertical lines.	5.00	15.00	50.00
	s. Specimen.	15.00	35.00	75.00

		VG	VF	UNC
47	**25 Marka**			
	1919. Blackish purple and brown. Tree at l. and r., harvesting potatoes at ctr. Fishermen w/boats and nets on back.			
	a. Wmk: Horizontal wavy lines.	7.50	30.00	100.
	b. Wmk: Vertical wavy lines.	7.50	30.00	100.
	s. Specimen.	15.00	35.00	75.00

		VG	VF	UNC
48	**100 Marka**			
	1919. Brown on tan unpt. Woman at spinning wheel at ctr. Man at l., woman at r.			
	a. Wmk: Horizontal wavy lines.	10.00	30.00	90.00
	b. *SEERIA II.*	10.00	30.00	90.00
	c. *SEERIA III.*	10.00	30.00	90.00
	d. Wmk: Vertical lines.	10.00	30.00	90.00
	s. Specimen.	20.00	40.00	90.00
49	**500 Marka**			
	ND (1920-21). Bluish green and violet. Back black on olive unpt. Lt. green eagle and shield at ctr.			
	a. Wmk: *500.* (1920).	20.00	75.00	200.
	b. *SEERIA II.* (1920).	20.00	75.00	200.
	c. *SEERIA III.* (1920).	17.50	60.00	175.
	d. *SEERIA A.* Wmk: *EV.* (1920)	15.00	55.00	150.
	e. *SEERIA B.* (1920).	12.50	45.00	135.
	f. *SEERIA D.* (1921).	12.50	45.00	135.
	s. Specimen.	35.00	75.00	150.

		VG	VF	UNC
50	**1000 Marka**			
	ND (1920-21). Green and brown. *Birth of Liberty* on back. Wmk: *EV.*			
	a. W/o series prefix letters. (1920).	125.	400.	1100.
	b. *SEERIA A.* Wmk: *EV.* (1921).	125.	400.	1100.
	c. *SEERIA B.* (1921).	125.	400.	1100.
	s. Specimen.	90.00	350.	700.

1923 Issue

		VG	VF	UNC
51	**100 Marka**			
	1923. Green and brown. Bank at ctr. Wmk: *EV.*			
	a. W/o series.	12.50	50.00	150.
	b. *SEERIA A.* (1927).	12.50	50.00	150.
	s. Specimen.	35.00	75.00	150.

		VG	VF	UNC
52	**500 Marka**			
	1923. Gray-blue and brown. Toompea Castle at ctr. Wmk: Rhombic patterns.			
	a. Issued note.	70.00	200.	500.
	s. Specimen.	70.00	200.	500.

Eesti Vabariigi Vahetustäht

Republic of Estonia Exchange Note

1922 Issue

		VG	VF	UNC
53	**10 Marka**			
	1922. Blackish green on red-brown unpt. Back red-brown and brown.			
	a. W/o serial # prefix letters. Wmk: *EV.*	3.00	10.00	30.00
	b. Series A. Wmk: Squares (1924).	4.00	12.50	40.00
	s. Specimen.	15.00	35.00	75.00
54	**25 Marka**			
	1922. Brown on olive and lilac unpt. Back lilac on gray unpt.			
	a. W/o serial # prefix letters. Wmk: Horizontal wavy lines.	12.50	50.00	150.
	b. Series A. Different sign. (1926).	10.00	40.00	125.
	c. Series A. Wmk: Vertical wavy lines. (1926).	10.00	40.00	125.
	s. Specimen.	20.00	40.00	85.00

Eesti Pangatäht

Estonian Banknote

1919-1921 Issue

#		VG	VF	UNC
55	**50 Marka**			
	1919. Brown on olive unpt. Globe at ctr. on back.			
	a. Wmk: Horizontal lt. lines.	10.00	30.00	100.
	b. Wmk: Vertical lt. lines.	10.00	30.00	100.
	s. Specimen.	30.00	65.00	135.

#		VG	VF	UNC
56	**100 Marka**			
	1921. Brown. 2 blacksmiths at ctr. Monogram at ctr. on back.			
	a. Wmk: Horizontal lt. lines.	20.00	65.00	175.
	b. Wmk: Vertical lt. lines.	20.00	65.00	175.
	s. Specimen.	40.00		185.
57	**500 Marka**			
	1921. Lt. green and gray. Ornamental design. Wmk: *EV*.			
	a. Issued note.	175.	500.	1500.
	s. Specimen.	150.	400.	900.

1922-1923 ISSUE

#		VG	VF	UNC
58	**100 Marka**			
	1922. Black on lilac, brown and green unpt. Galleon on back. Wmk: Lt. and dk. keys.			
	a. Issued note. Serial letter A; B; D or E.	50.00	165.	450.
	s. Specimen.	40.00	100.	250.

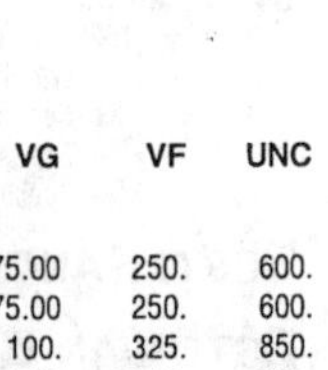

#		VG	VF	UNC
59	**1000 Marka**			
	ND (1922). Black on lilac and green unpt. Port view of the city of Tallinn (Reval) on back. Wmk: Lt. and dk. keys.			
	a. W/o serial letter.	75.00	250.	600.
	b. Serial letter A in black.	75.00	250.	600.
	c. Serial letter B in red.	100.	325.	850.
	d. Serial letter B in black.	100.	325.	850.
	e. Serial letter D in blue.	75.00	250.	600.
	f. Serial letters Aa (1927).	70.00	200.	475.
	s. Specimen.	60.00	175.	425.

#		VG	VF	UNC
60	**5000 Marka**			
	1923. Blue, brown and green. Arms at ctr. r. Bank at l. ctr. on back. Wmk: *5000, EV*.			
	a. Issued note.	1000.	2250.	—
	s. Specimen.	—	1200.	2250.

EESTI VABARIIGI KASSATÄHT (RESUMED)

1928 PROVISIONAL ISSUE

#		VG	VF	UNC
61	**1 Kroon on 100 Marka**			
	ND. (1928-old date 1923). Red ovpt. on #51.			
	a. Issued note.	12.50	50.00	150.
	s. Specimen.	10.00	40.00	125.

EESTI PANK

BANK OF ESTONIA

1928-35 ISSUE

#62-65 arms at upper l. on back.

#		VG	VF	UNC
62	**5 Krooni**			
	1929. Red-brown. Fisherman holding oar at l. Back red-brown and m/c. Wmk: *5* between wavy lines.			
	a. Issued note.	3.00	10.00	35.00
	s. Specimen.	10.00	20.00	45.00

#		VG	VF	UNC
63	**10 Krooni**			
	1928. Blue. Woman in national costume carrying sheaf of wheat and sickle at l. 2 sign. Back blue and m/c. Wmk: *10* between wavy lines.			
	a. Issued note.	2.00	8.50	25.00
	s. Specimen.	10.00	20.00	45.00

		VG	VF	UNC
64	**20 Krooni** 1932. Green and brown. Shepherd blowing horn at l. Back m/c on gray-green unpt. Wmk: *20* between zigzag lines.			
	a. Issued note.	1.50	6.50	20.00
	s. Specimen.	8.50	17.50	40.00
65	**50 Krooni** 1929. Brown. Coastline of Rannamoisa at l. Wmk: *Eesti Pank* and *L*.			
	a. Issued note.	5.00	12.50	35.00
	s. Specimen.	10.00	30.00	70.00

		VG	VF	UNC
66	**100 Krooni** 1935. Blue. Blacksmith working at an anvil at l. Wmk: *100* surrounded by oak leaves and acorns.			
	a. Issued note.	10.00	35.00	125.
	s. Specimen.	10.00	25.00	60.00

1937 Issue

		VG	VF	UNC
67	**10 Krooni** 1937. Blue. Like #63, but 3 sign. Woman in national costume carrying sheaf of wheat and sickle at l. Back blue and m/c. Series A.			
	a. Issued note.	2.00	7.50	20.00
	s. Specimen.	8.00	17.50	40.00

1940 Issue

		VG	VF	UNC
68	**10 Krooni** 1940. Blue. Like #67. Series B. (Not issued).			
	a. Finished printing.	—	150.	350.
	p1. Back printing only. Wide or narrow margins. Full color print.	—	50.00	125.
	p2. Back printing only. Wide or narrow margins. Two color print.	—	65.00	150.
	s. Specimen.	—	150.	400.

Military - WW I

Finnish Regiment - Sons of the North

1919 ND Issues

M1-M3 ovpt: ***Pohjan Pojat Rykmentin Rahaston hoitaja.***

		VG	VF	UNC
M1	**50 Penni** ND (1919-old date 1919). Ovpt. on #42.	—	—	—
M2	**1 Markka** ND (1919-old date 1916). Ovpt. on Finland #19.	—	—	—
M3	**1 Marka** ND (1919-old date 1919). Ovpt on #43.	—	—	—

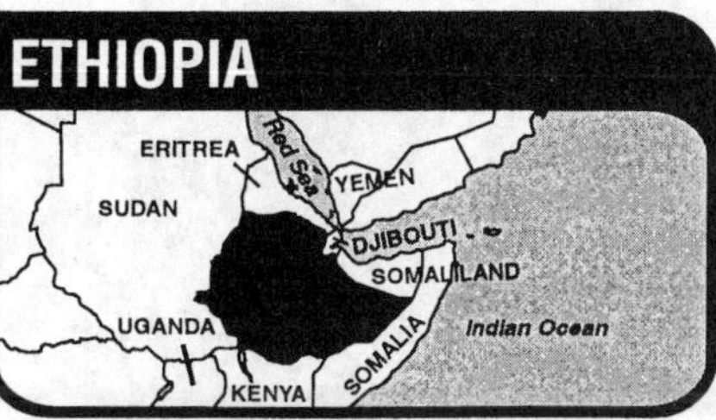

The Federal Republic of Ethiopia (formerly the Peoples Democratic Republic and the Empire of Ethiopia) is located in east-central Africa. The country has an area of 424,214 sq. mi. (1.099,900 sq. km.) and a population of 66.18 million people who are divided among 40 tribes that speak some 270 languages and dialects. Capital: Addis Ababa. The economy is predominantly agricultural and pastoral. Gold and platinum are mined and petroleum fields are being developed. Coffee, oilseeds, hides and cereals are exported.

Legend claims that Menelik I, the son born to Solomon, King of Israel, by the Queen of Sheba, settled in Axum in northern Ethiopia to establish the dynasty which then reigned - with only brief interruptions - until 1974. Modern Ethiopian history began with the reign of Emperor Menelik II (1889-1913) under whose guidance the country emerged from medieval isolation. Ethiopia was invaded by fascist Italy in 1935, and together with Italian Somaliland and Eritrea became part of Italian East Africa until liberated by British and Ethiopian troops in 1941. Haile Selassie I, 225th consecutive Solomonic ruler, was deposed by a military committee on Sept. 12, 1974. In July 1976, Ethiopia's military provisional government referred to the country as Socialist Ethiopia. After establishing a new regime in 1991, Ethiopia became a federated state.

Eritrea, a former Ethiopian province fronting on the Red Sea, was an Italian colony from 1890 until its incorporation into Italian East Africa in 1936. It was under British military administration from 1941 to Sept. 15, 1952, when the United Nations designated it an autonomous unit within the federation of Ethiopia and Eritrea. On Nov. 14, 1962, it was fully integrated with Ethiopia. On May 24, 1993, Eritrea became an independent nation.

RULERS:

Menelik II, 1889-1913
Lij Yasu, 1913-1916
Zauditu, Empress, 1916-1930
Haile Selassie I, 1930-1936, 1941-1974

MONETARY SYSTEM:

1 Thaler = 16 Gersh (Piastres) to 1930
1 Thaler = 100 Matonas, 1931-1935
1 Birr (Dollar) = 100 Santeems (Cents), since 1944

Empire

Bank of Abyssinia

1915 Issue

		Good	Fine	XF
1	**5 Thalers** 1915-1.6.1929. Greater Kudu at ctr.			
	a. Issued note.	—	—	—
	s. Specimen.	—	—	1250.

		Good	Fine	XF
2	**10 Thalers** 1915-1.6.1929. Leopard at ctr.			
	a. Issued note. Rare.	—	—	—
	s. Specimen.	—	—	1500.
3	**50 Thalers** 1915-1.6.1929. Lion at ctr.			
	a. Issued note. Rare.	—	—	—
	s. Specimen.	—	—	2000.

		Good	Fine	XF
4	**100 Thalers**			
	1915-1.6.1929. Elephant at r.			
	a. Issued note. Rare.	—	—	—
	s. Specimen.	—	—	2750.

		Good	Fine	XF
5	**500 Thalers**			
	1915-1.6.1929. Warrior standing at l.			
	a. Issued note. Rare.	—	—	—
	s. Specimen.	—	—	3500.

BANK OF ETHIOPIA

1932-33 ISSUE

#6-11 printer: BWC.

		Good	Fine	XF
6	**2 Thalers** 1.6.1933. Dk. blue on green and m/c unpt. Jugate busts of Emperor Haile Selassie and Empress at ctr.	10.00	50.00	150.

#7-11 designs like #1-5.

		Good	Fine	XF
7	**5 Thalers** 1.5.1932; 29.4.1933. Purple on m/c unpt. Greater Kudu head at ctr., bank bldg. at l., arms at r.	15.00	75.00	325.

		Good	Fine	XF
8	**10 Thalers** 1.5.1932; 29.4.1933; 31.5.1935. Blue-green on m/c unpt. Leopard at ctr., arms at l., bank bldg. at r.	20.00	100.	350

		Good	Fine	XF
9	**50 Thalers** 1.5.1932; 29.4.1933. Blue-green on m/c unpt. Lion at ctr., bank bldg. at upper l., arms at upper r.	40.00	125.	40[illegible]

		Good	Fine	XF
10	**100 Thalers** 1.5.1932; 29.4.1933. Blue on m/c unpt. Elephant at r., bank bldg. at l., arms at upper l. ctr.	50.00	175.	55[illegible]

		Good	Fine	XF
11	**500 Thalers** 1.5.1932; 29.4.1933. Purple on m/c unpt. Warrior standing at l., arms at top ctr., bank bldg. at r.	250.	500.	15[illegible]

STATE BANK OF ETHIOPIA

1945 ISSUE

#12-17 Emperor Haile Selassie at l. Arms at ctr. on back. Printer: SBNC. The notes were originally issued on 23.7.1945, the emperor's birthday.

12	1 Dollar	VG	VF	UNC
	ND (1945). Black on orange unpt. Farmer plowing w/oxen at ctr. Back green.			
	a. Sign. 1.	4.00	25.00	100.
	b. Sign. 2.	3.00	17.50	65.00
	c. Sign. 3.	3.00	12.50	45.00

13	5 Dollars	VG	VF	UNC
	ND (1945). Black and lilac on orange unpt. Acacia tree with beehives at ctr. r. Back orange.			
	a. Sign. 1.	7.50	50.00	275.
	b. Sign. 2.	5.00	40.00	175.
	c. Sign. 3.	3.50	30.00	125.

14	10 Dollars	VG	VF	UNC
	ND (1945). Black on orange and blue unpt. St. George's Square w/equestrian monument to Menelik II w/domed bldg. in background at ctr. Back red.			
	a. Sign. 1.	25.00	100.	375.
	b. Sign. 2.	15.00	80.00	250.
	c. Sign. 3.	10.00	50.00	175.

15	50 Dollars	VG	VF	UNC
	ND (1945). Black on green and yellow unpt. Parliament bldg. at ctr.			
	a. Sign. 1.	40.00	200.	750.
	b. Sign. 2.	30.00	150.	550.
	c. Sign. 3.	25.00	125.	350.

16	100 Dollars	VG	VF	UNC
	ND (1945). Black on green unpt. Imperial Palace of Haile Selassie I (now a university) at ctr.			
	a. Sign. 1.	75.00	350.	950.
	b. Sign. 2.	50.00	250.	750.
	c. Sign. 3.	35.00	175.	450.

17	500 Dollars	VG	VF	UNC
	ND (1945). Black on yellow and olive unpt. Holy Trinity Church in Addis Ababa at ctr.			
	a. Sign. 1.	300.	700.	1500.
	b. Sign. 2.	225.	500.	1100.
	c. Sign. 3.	150.	350.	750.

The Faroes, a self-governing community within the kingdom of Denmark, are situated in the North Atlantic between Iceland and the Shetland Islands. The 17 inhabited islets and reefs have an area of 540 sq. mi. (1,399 sq. km.) and a population of 43,678. Capital: Thorshavn. The principal industries are fishing and grazing. Fish and fish products are exported.

While it is thought that Irish hermits lived on the islands in the 7th and 8th centuries, the present inhabitants are descended from the 6th century Norse settlers. The Faroes became a Norwegian fief in 1035 and became Danish in 1380 when Norway and Denmark were united. They have ever since remained in Danish possession and were granted self-government (except for an appointed governor-general) with their own legislature, executive and flag in 1948.

The islands were occupied by British troops during World War II, while the Germans occupied Denmark.

RULERS:
Danish

MONETARY SYSTEM:
1 Króne = 100 Øre

Danish Administration

Government

1809-12 Emergency Issue

#A3-A9 handwritten on oval card stock or paper. Uniface. Thorshavn.

A1, A2 and A10 Held in reserve.

		Good	Fine	XF
A3	**3 Skilling** 1809.	—	—	—
A4	**4 Skilling** 1809.	—	—	—
A5	**5 Skilling** 1812.	—	—	—
A6	**6 Skilling** 1809.	—	—	—
A9	**5 Mark** 1810.	—	—	—

1815 Provisional Issue

#A11 reissue of Danish Rigsbanken i København notes dated 1814.

		Good	Fine	XF
A11	**1 Rigsbankdaler** 15.4.1815 (-old date 1814). Printed on back of Denmark #A48.	—	—	—

Note: For similar provisional issues refer to Danish West Indies and Iceland listings.

Færø Amt

1940 WWII Provisional Issue

#1-6 red ovpt: *KUN GYLDIG PAA FAERØERNE, FAERØ AMT, JUNI 1940* w/sign. of *Hilbert* on Danish notes.

		Good	Fine	XF
1	**5 Kroner** June 1940. Blue-green. Printed sign.	125.	350.	900.

		VG	VF	UNC
2	**10 Kroner** June 1940. Brown. Handwritten sign. and ovpt. on Denmark #31. Serial #M9627001-9627500.	40.00	100.	280.

Note: #2 is rarely seen below XF.

		VG	VF	UNC
3	**10 Kroner** June 1940. Brown. Printed sign.	40.00	150.	500.
4	**50 Kroner** June 1940. Blue. Printed sign.	2000.	4000.	7000.
5	**100 Kroner** June 1940. Brown. Printed sign.	2250.	5000.	—
6	**500 Kroner** June 1940. Gray-blue. Printed sign. Rare.	—	—	—

Note: Various types of Danish notes are known w/ovpt. since new or older notes in circulation were also ovpt.

Faerøerne

1940 First Emergency Issue

		Good	Fine	XF
7	**10 Kroner** 1.10.1940. a. Brown. b. Olive.	 150. 175.	 450. 500.	 1000. 1100.
8	**100 Kroner** 1.10.1940. Red-brown. Ram's head at upper r.	600.	1800.	4000.

1940 Second Emergency Issue

		VG	VF	UNC
9	**1 Krone** Nov. 1940. Blue on lilac and lt. red unpt. Like #10.	4.50	20.00	80.00

		VG	VF	UNC
10	**5 Kroner** Nov. 1940. Green and blue-green.	30.00	225.	900.
11	**10 Kroner** Nov. 1940. Brown on lilac and green unpt. Like #10.	25.00	180.	700.
12	**100 Kroner** Nov. 1940. Green and brown. Like #10.	400.	1400.	—

Føroyar

1951-54 Issue

Law of 12.4.1949

		VG	VF	UNC
13	**5 Krónur** L.1949 (1951-60). Black on green unpt. Coin w/ram at l. Fishermen w/boat on green back. a. Sign. C. A. Vagn-Hansen and Kr. Djurhuus. b. Sign. N. Elkaer-Hansen and Kr. Djurhuus.	 20.00 20.00	 80.00 75.00	 275. 225.

		VG	VF	UNC
14	**10 Krónur** L.1949 (1954). Black on orange unpt. Shield w/ram at l. Rural scene on orange back. a. Sign. C. A. Vagn-Hansen and Kr. Djurhuus. Wmk: *10.* 10.5mm. b. As a but w/13mm wmk. c. Sign. M. Wahl and P. M. Dam. Wmk: *10.* 13mm. d. Sign. M. Wahl and A. P. Dam.	 15.00 10.00 2.50 2.00	 30.00 25.00 7.50 4.00	 80.00 60.00 20.00 8.00

#		VG	VF	UNC
15	**100 Krónur** L.1949 (1952-63). Blue-green. Porpoises on back. Irregular margins at l. and r. (straight margins are trimmed).			
	a. Sign. C. A. Vagn-Hansen and Kr. Djurhuus.	35.00	100.	175.
	b. Sign. N. Elkaer-Hansen and Kr. Djurhuus.	35.00	100.	175.
	c. Sign. M. Wahl and P. M. Dam.	32.50	90.00	160.

FALKLAND ISLANDS

CHILE
ARGENTINA
South Atlantic Ocean
SOUTH GEORGIA ISLAND (U.K.)

The Colony of the Falkland Islands and Dependencies, a British colony located in the South Atlantic about 500 miles northeast of Cape Horn, has an area of 4,700 sq. mi. (12,173 sq. km.) and a population of 2,564. East Falkland, West Falkland, South Georgia, and South Sandwich are the largest of the 200 islands. Capital: Port Stanley. Fishing and sheep are the industry. Wool, whale oil, and seal oil are exported.

The Falklands were discovered by British navigator John Davis (Davys) in 1592, and named by Capt. John Strong - for Viscount Falkland, treasurer of the British navy - in 1690. French navigator Louis De Bougainville established the first settlement, at Port Louis, in 1764. The following year Capt. John Byron claimed the islands for Britain and left a small party at Saunders Island. Spain later forced the French and British to abandon their settlements but did not implement its claim to the islands. In 1829 the Republic of Buenos Aires, which claimed to have inherited the Spanish rights, sent Louis Vernet to develop a colony on the islands. In 1831 he seized three American sailing vessels, whereupon the men of the corvette *U.S.S. Lexington,* destroyed his settlement and proclaimed the Falklands to be "free of all governance." Britain, which had never renounced its claim, re-established its settlement in 1833.

The Islands were important in the days of sail and steam shipping as a location to re-stock fresh food and fuel, and make repairs after trips around Cape Horn. Argentine forces In 1990 the Argentine congrees declared the Falklands and other islands in the region part of the province of Tierra del Fuego. occupied the islands in April 1982, and after a short military campaign Britain regained control in June.

RULERS:

British

MONETARY SYSTEM:

1 Shilling = 12 Pence
1 Pound = 20 Shillings to 1966
1 Pound = 100 Pence, 1966-

BRITISH ADMINISTRATION

GOVERNMENT

1899-1905 ISSUE

#A1-A4 uniface. Printer: TDLR.

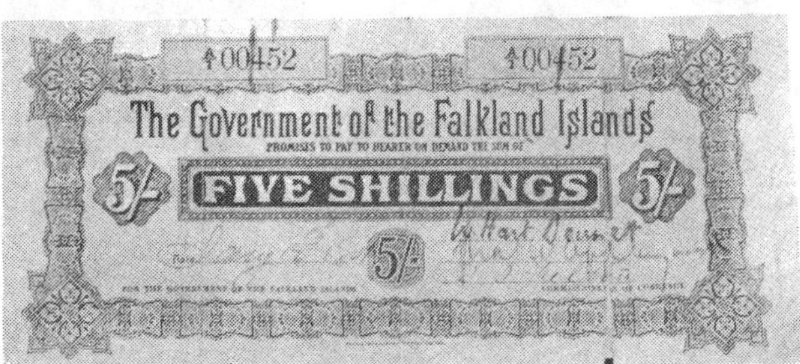

#		Good	Fine	XF
A1	**5 Shillings** 12.1.1901; 15.1.1901. Green on pink unpt.	—	—	—
A1A	**5 Shillings** 1.2.1905; 12.10.1908; 27.11.1916. Brown on pink unpt. Like #A1.	1000.	2750.	—
A2	**10 Shillings** Like #A1. Reported not confirmed.	—	—	—

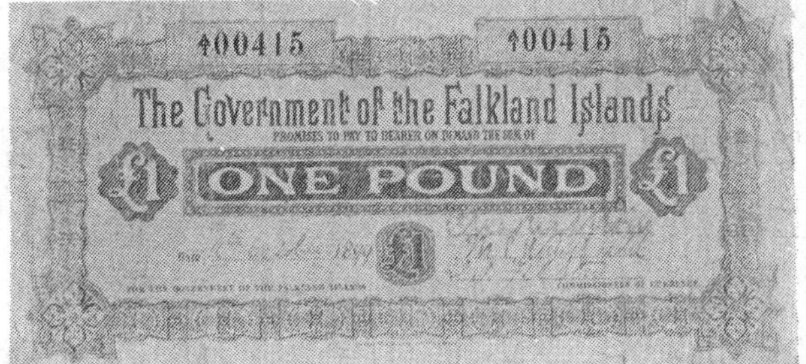

#		Good	Fine	XF
A3	**1 Pound** 16.10.1899; 28.8.1915. Blue on pink unpt.	1750.	4000.	—
A4	**5 Pounds** ND. Red on gray unpt. Color trial. Like #A3. Rare.	—	—	—

NOTICE

Readers with unlisted dates, signature varieties, etc. are invited to submit photocopies or, high resolution (300 dpi, 100% size) scans of their notes to: Standard Catalog of World Paper Money, 700 East State St. Iola, WI 54990-0001, or E-Mail: george.cuhaj@fwpubs.com.

1921 ISSUE

#1-3 portr. Kg. George V at r. Printer: TDLR.

		Good	Fine	XF
1	**10 Shillings** 1921-32. Brown on gray unpt.			
	a. 2 sign. 1.2.1921; 10.1.1927.	550.	2000.	—
	b. 1 sign. 10.2.1932.	400.	1500.	—

		Good	Fine	XF
2	**1 Pound** 1921-32. Blue on green unpt.			
	a. 2 sign. 1.2.1921; 10.1.1927.	800.	2500.	—
	b. 1 sign. 10.2.1932.	600.	1500.	—
3	**5 Pounds** 1.2.1921; 10.2.1932. Red on green unpt. Rare.	—	—	—

1938-51 ISSUE

#4-6 portr. Kg. George VI at r. Printer: TDLR.

		VG	VF	UNC
4	**10 Shillings** 19.5.1938. Brown on gray unpt.	12.50	70.00	200.

		VG	VF	UNC
5	**1 Pound** 19.5.1938. Blue on green and lilac unpt.	15.00	100.	425.

		VG	VF	UNC
6	**5 Pounds** 20.2.1951. Red on green, blue and lt. tan unpt.	65.00	250.	900

1960-67 ISSUE

#7-9 portr. Qn. Elizabeth II at r. Printer: TDLR.

		VG	VF	UNC
7	**10 Shillings** 10.4.1960. Brown on gray unpt.			
	a. Issued note.	15.00	65.00	450
	s. Specimen.	—	—	—

		VG	VF	UNC
9	**5 Pounds** 1960; 1975. Red on green unpt.			
	a. Sign: L. Gleadell: 10.4.1960.	20.00	60.00	300
	b. Sign: H. T. Rowlands: 30.1.1975.	17.50	50.00	250
	s. Specimen. As a-b.	—	—	—

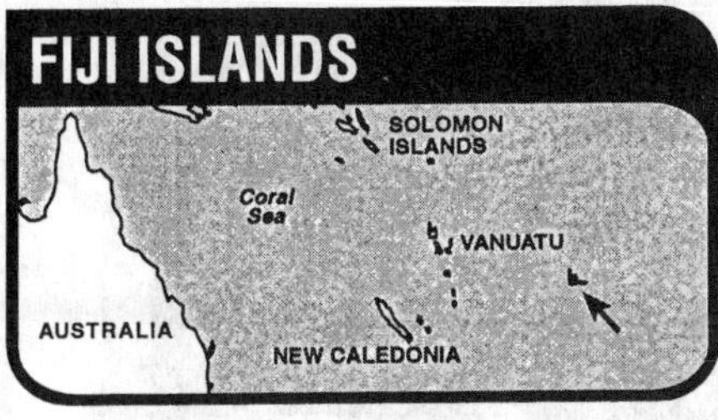

The republic of Fiji is an independent member of the British Commonwealth. It consists of about 320 islands located in the southwestern Pacific 1,100 miles (1,770 km.) north of New Zealand. The islands have a combined area of 7,056 sq. mi. (18,274 sq. km.) and a population of 848,000. Capital: Suva, on the island of Viti Levu. Fiji's economy is d on agriculture and mining. Sugar, coconut products, manganese and gold are exported.

The first European to sign Fiji was the Dutch navigator Abel Tasman in 1643. The island was visited by British naval captain James Cook in 1774. The first complete survey of the island was conducted by the United States in 1840. Settlement by missionaries from Tonga and traders attracted by the sandalwood trade began in 1835. Following a lengthy period of intertribal warfare, the islands were unconditionally and voluntarily ceded to Great Britain in 1874 by King Cakobau. The trading center was Levuka on the island of Ovalau which was also the capital under the British from 1874-82. Fiji became an independent nation on Oct 10, 1970, the 96th anniversary of the cession of the islands to Queen Victoria.

RULERS:

Thakombau (Cakobau), until 1874
British, 1874-

NOTICE:
Fiji has been renumbered

MONETARY SYSTEM:

1 Shilling = 12 Pence
1 Pound = 20 Shillings to 1969
1 Dollar = 100 Cents, 1969-

KINGDOM

C.R. - CAKOBAU REX

1871 TREASURY NOTE ISSUE

#1-3 C.R. top ctr. Handwritten dates and serial #. Handsigned. Uniface. Printer: Gazette Office, Levuka, Ovalau, Fiji.

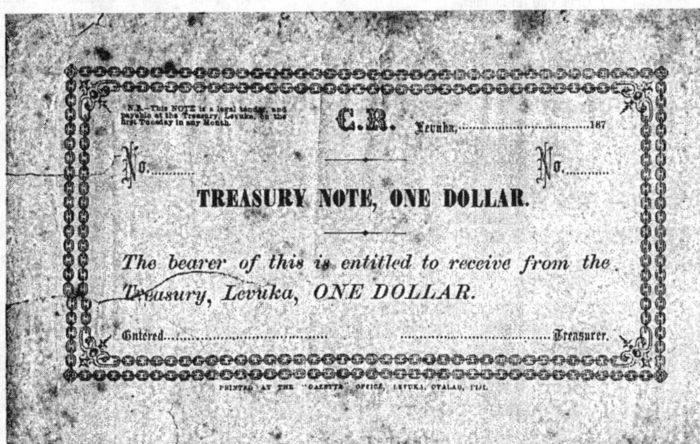

#		Good	Fine	XF
1	**1 Dollar**			
	ca.1871. Black on buff paper; double chain border.			
	a. Sign: S.C. Burt.	1250.	2000.	5000.
	b. Sign: F.W. Hennings.	1000.	1500.	3000.
	r. Unissued remainder.	750.	1000.	2500.

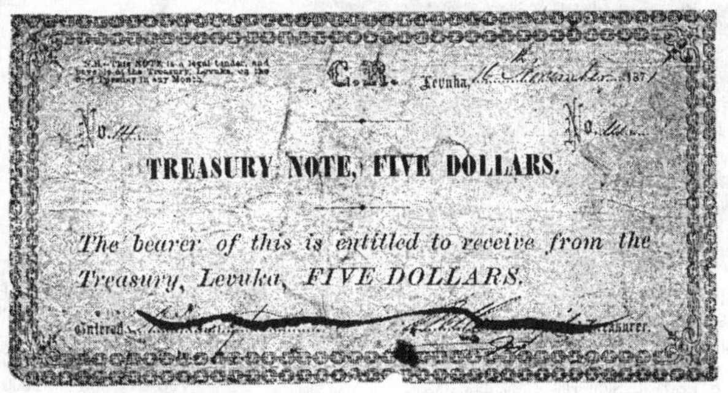

#		Good	Fine	XF
2	**5 Dollars**			
	16.11.1871. Lt. brown.			
	a. Issued note.	—	—	—
	r. Remainder.	—	—	—
3	**10 Dollars**			
	ca.1871.	—	—	—

1871 GOVERNMENT DEBENTURES

Public Loans Act 1871

#4-6 Arms at top ctr., handwritten dates, handsigned. Value ovpt. twice in brown vertical on face. Uniface. Printer: Gazette Office, Levuka, Ovalau, Fiji.

#		Good	Fine	XF
4	**5 Dollars**			
	1.1.1872. Black.			
	a. Sign. F.W. Hennings.	150.	450.	1000.
	b. Sign. Smith or Clarkson.	185.	650.	1200.
	c. "FIVE" altered to "TEN" by hand.	500.	1000.	2000.
	r. Unissued remainder.	125.	475.	750.
5	**10 Dollars**	Good	Fine	XF
	1.1.1872.			
	a. Value handwritten.	140.	400.	—
	b. Value printed.	140.	400.	—

1872-73 VAKACAVACAVA FRACTIONAL TAX NOTES

#7-13 C.R. top ctr., handwritten dates and serial #. Handsigned (Turaga ni Lavo). Uniface. Printer: Gazette Office, Levuka, Ovalau.

Spurious signatures exist - e.g. "Page."

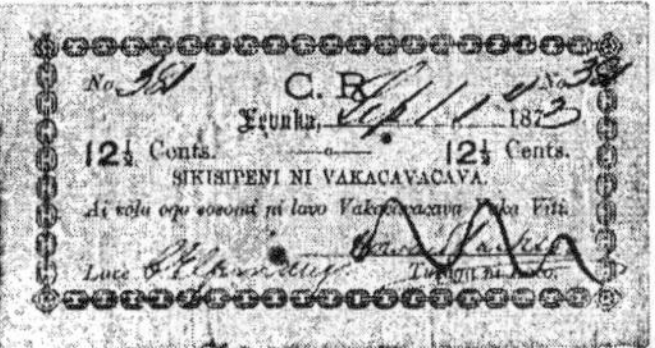

#		Good	Fine	XF
7	**12 1/2 Cents**			
	1873. Blue. Single chain border.			
	a. Issued note. 1.9.1873.	85.00	200.	425.
	b. Pen cancelled. 13.10.1873.	70.00	175.	325.
8	**25 Cents**			
	ca. 1873. Black on dk. blue paper. Single chain border.	—	—	—

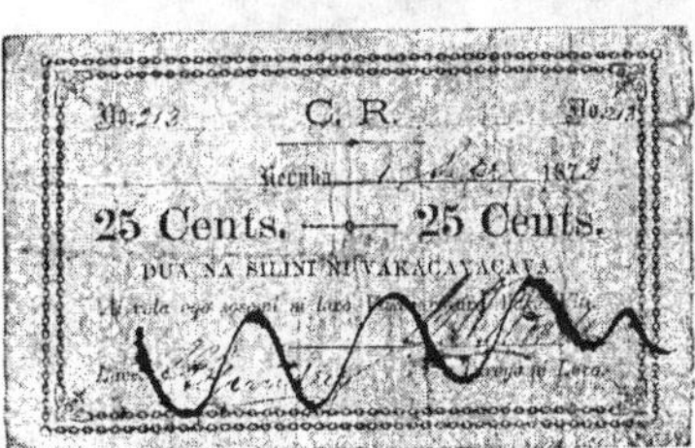

#		Good	Fine	XF
9	**25 Cents**			
	1.9.1873. Red. Double chain border.	60.00	150.	300.
10	**50 Cents**			
	5.1.1872. Black. Single chain border.	120.	250.	500.

#		Good	Fine	XF
11	**50 Cents**			
	1.9.1873. Green. Double chain border.	60.00	150.	300.

#		Good	Fine	XF
12	**100 Cents**			
	1.4.1872. Brown. Single chain border.	70.00	175.	325.
13	**100 Cents**			
	ca. 1873. Double chain border.	—	—	—

1872 Treasury Note Issue

#14-18 C.R. monogram at top ctr.; arms below, handwritten dates and serial #., handsigned (Treasurer). Printer: S.T. Leigh & Co., Sidney.

Spurious signatures exist - e.g."Page."

		Good	Fine	XF
14	**1 Dollar** 10.2.1872; 11.11.1872; 11.1.1873; 11.2.1873; 1.9.1873. Black. Handstamped: *CANCELLED.*	90.00	225.	475.

		Good	Fine	XF
15	**5 Dollars** 20.2.1872; 4.4.1872; 12.6.1873; 16.11.1873. Pale purple.			
	a. Handstamped: *CANCELLED.*	100.	250.	500.

		Good	Fine	XF
16	**10 Dollars** 1.3.1872-1.6.1872; 17.3.1873. Brown.			
	a. Handstamped: *CANCELLED.*	90.00	225.	475.
17	**25 Dollars** 23.3.1872; 5.4.1872; 15.7.1872; 11.11.1872; 12.6.1873. Blue.			
	a. Pen cancelled through sign., w/ or w/o handstamps: *CANCELLED.*	120.	350.	650.

		Good	Fine	XF
18	**50 Dollars** 1.4.1872; 15.7.1872; 11.3.1873; 12.6.1873. Red.			
	a. Pen cancelled through sign., w/ or w/o handstamps: *CANCELLED.*	90.00	225.	475.
	r. Remainder w/sign.	90.00	225.	475.

Fiji Banking & Commercial Company

1873 Issue

		Good	Fine	XF
19	**5 Shillings** Green and black.			
	a. Issued note. Rare.	—	—	—
	r. Unissued remainder.	—	850.	1650.
20	**10 Shillings** Green and black.			
	a. Issued note. Rare.	—	—	—
	r. Unissued remainder.	—	—	—
21	**1 Pound** Black.			
	a. Issued note. Rare.	—	—	—
	r. Unissued remainder.	—	500.	1600.
22	**5 Pounds** Blue and black.			
	a. Issued note. Rare.	—	—	—
	r. Unissued remainder.	—	—	1750.
23	**10 Pounds** Maroon and black.			
	a. Issued note. Rare.	—	—	—
	r. Unissued remainder.	—	500.	1900.

Ad-Interim Administration

1874 Certificate of Indebtedness

		Good	Fine	XF
24	**1 Dollar** Grey.			
	a. Class I: Currency of four months.	125.	200.	—
	b. Class II: Currency of six months.	150.	300.	700.
	c. Uncancelled issue.	250.	500.	950.
	r. Unissued remainder.	175.	400.	800.

British Administration

Government

1917-26 Issue

#25-30 arms at top ctr. Uniface. Printer: TDLR.

		Good	Fine	XF
25	**5 Shillings** 1.9.1920-8.12.1933. Black and green on brown unpt. Arms at upper ctr. Uniface.			
	a. 1.1.1920. Sign. Rankine, Brabant, Marks.	250.	900.	3000.
	b. 1.8.1920. Sign. Fell, Brabant, Marks.	250.	900.	3000.
	c. 1.9.1920. Sign. Fell, Brabant, Marks.	200.	800.	2750.
	d. 4.2.1923.	250.	850.	3000.
	e. 5.12.1925. Sign. Stewart, Rushton, Marks.	175.	800.	2750.
	f. 4.2.1928. Sign. McOwan, Harcourt, Marks.	175.	800.	2750.
	g. 1.7.1929. Sign. Rushton, Harcourt, Marks.	175.	800.	2750.
	h. 31.10.1932. Sign. Seymour, Chamberlain, Hayward.	150.	800.	2500.
	i. 9.11.1933.	150.	750.	2500.
	j. 8.12.1933. Sign. Seymour, Chamberlain, Boyd.	150.	750.	2500.
	r. Unissued remainder.	400.	900.	3500.
	s. Specimen. Various dates.	500.	1100.	4000.

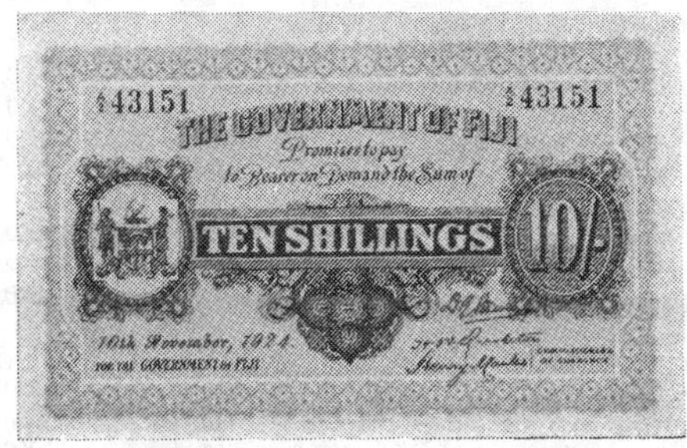

		Good	Fine	XF
26	**10 Shillings**			
	1918-32. Black and blue on green unpt. Arms at l. Uniface.			
	a. 29.10.1918. Sign. Rushton, Rankine, Marks.	750.	3000.	—
	b. 1.1.1920. Sign. Rankine, Brabant, Marks.	750.	3000.	—
	c. 1.8.1920. Sign. Fell, Brabant, Marks.	750.	3000.	—
	d. 10.11.1924. Sign. Stewart, Rushton, Marks.	750.	3000.	—
	e. 5.12.1925. Sign. Stewart, Rushton, Marks.	750.	5000.	3000.
	f. 1.1.1926. Sign. Stewart, Ruchton, Marks.	750.	3000.	—
	g. 4.2.1928. Sign. McOwan, Harcourt, Marks.	750.	3000.	—
	h. 14.7.1932. Sign. Seymour, Craig, Boyd.	750.	3000.	—
	i. 23.9.1932.	900.	4000.	—
	j. 8.12.1933. Sign. Seymour, Chamberlain, Boyd.	750.	3000.	—
	r. Unsigned remainder.	1000.	7500.	10,000.
	s. Specimen. Various dates.	700.	5000.	7000.

		Good	Fine	XF
27	**1 Pound**			
	1.3.1917; 5.12.1925; 21.1.1930. Black and green on pink unpt. Uniface.			
	a. 1.3.1917. Sign. Huston, Montgomerie, Marks.	450.	1750.	
	b. 5.12.1925. Sign. Stewart, Rushton, Marks.	450.	1750.	5000.
	c. 21.1.1930. Sign. Seymour, March, Marks.	450.	1750.	5000.
	r. Unsigned remainder.	750.	2000.	7000.
	s. Specimen. Various dates.	650.	1900.	6000.
28	**5 Pounds**			
	1.3.1917; 20.8.1926; 4.2.1928. Black and mulberry on orange unpt.			
	a. 1.3.1917. Sign. Hutson, Montgomerie, Marks.	650.	—	—
	b. 20.8.1926. Sign. McOwan, Rushton, Marks.	650.	—	—
	c. 4.2.1928. Sign. McOwan, Harcourt, Marks.	650.	—	—
	r. Unsigned reaminder.	1000.	—	—
	s. Specimen.	900.	1750.	

		Good	Fine	XF
29	**10 Pounds**			
	1.3.1917; 5.12.1925; 20.8.1926; 4.2.1928. Black and blue on grey unpt.			
	a. 1.3.1917. Sign. Hutson, Montgomerie, Marks.	950.	—	—
	b. 5.12.1925. Sign. Stewart, Rushton, Marks.	950.	—	—
	c. 20.8.1926. Sign. McOwan, Rushton, Marks.	950.	—	—
	d. 4.2.1928. Sign. McOwan, Harcourt, Marks.	950.	—	—
	r. Unissued remainder.	1400.	—	—
	s. Specimen. Various dates.	1200.	2750.	8500.
30	**20 Pounds**			
	1.3.1917; 20.8.1926.			
	a. 1.3.1917.	1300.	—	—
	b. 20.8.1926.	1300.	—	—
	r. Unissued remainder.	1750.	—	—
	s. Specimen. Various dates.	1500.	3500.	10,000.

1934 Issue

#31-36 portr. Kg. George V at r., arms at top ctr. Printer: BWC.

		Good	Fine	XF
31	**5 Shillings**			
	1.1.1934; 1.6.1934; 1.3.1935. Dk. blue and brown.			
	a. 1.1.1934. Sign. Seymour, Chamberlain, Boyd.	200.	700.	1500.
	b. 1.6.1934. Sign. Wright, Craig, Boyd.	200.	700.	1500.
	c. 1.3.1935. Sign. Wright, Craig, Boyd.	200.	700.	1500.
	s. Specimen. Various dates.	450.	900.	1900.
	cs. Commercial (false color) specimen.	300.	800.	1600.
32	**10 Shillings**			
	1.1.1934; 1.6.1934; 1.3.1935. Dk. brown and blue.			
	a. 1.1.1934. Sign. Seymour, Chamberlain, Boyd.	750.	2000.	5500.
	b. 1.6.1934. Sign. Weight, Craig, Boyd.	750.	2000.	5500.
	c. 1.3.1935. Sign. Wright, Craig, Boyd.	750.	2000.	5500.
	s. Specimen. Various dates.	—	—	—
	cs. Commemrical (false color) specimen.	—	—	—
33	**1 Pound**			
	1.1.1934; 1.6.1934; 1.3.1935. Green and red.			
	a. 1.1.1934. Sign. Seymour, Chamberlain, Boyd.	600.	1250.	3500.
	b. 1.6.1934. Sign. Wright, Craig, Boyd.	600.	1250.	3500.
	c. 1.3.1935. Sign. Wright, Craig, Boyd.	600.	1250.	3500.
	s. Specimen. Various dates.	—	—	—
	cs. Commercial (false color) specimen.	—	—	—
34	**5 Pounds**			
	13.9.1934; 1.3.1935. Pink, red and green.			
	a. 13.9.1934. Sign. Wright, Craig, Boyd.	900.	2000.	6500.
	b. 1.3.1935. Sign. Wright, Craig, Boyd.	900.	2000.	6500.
	s. Specimen. Various dates.	1100.	3000.	7500.
	cs. Commercial (false color) specimen.	—	—	—
35	**10 Pounds**			
	1.1.1934; 12.7.1934; 13.9.1934; 1.3.1935. Black and blue on grey unpt.			
	a. 1.1.1934. Sign. Seymour, Chamberlain, Boyd.	1100.	3000.	7500.
	b. 12.7.1934. Sign. Wright, Craig, Boyd.	1100.	3000.	7500.
	c. 13.9.1934. Sign. Wright, Craig, Boyd.	1100.	3000.	7500.
	d. 1.3.1935. Sign. Wright, Craig, Boyd.	1100.	3000.	7500.
	s. Specimen.	—	—	—
	cs. Commercial (false color) specimen.	—	—	—

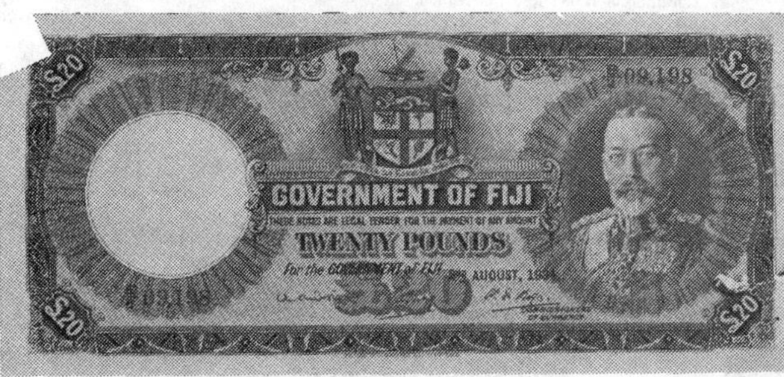

		Good	Fine	XF
36	**20 Pounds**			
	12.7.1934; 3.8.1934; 2.9.1934. Black on purple unpt.			
	a. 12.7.1934. Sign. Wright, Craig, Boyd.	1500.	5000.	10,000.
	b. 3.8.1934. Sign. Wright, Craig, Boyd.	1500.	5000.	10,000.
	c. 2.9.1934. Sign. Wright, Craig, Boyd.	1500.	5000.	10,000.
	s. Specimen. Various dates.	—	—	—
	cs. Commercial (false color) specimen.	—	—	—

1937-42 Issue

#37-43 portr. Kg. George VI at r., facing front or 3/4 l. Printer: BWC.

		VG	VF	UNC
37	**5 Shillings**			
	1937-51. Dk. blue and brown. Portr. Kg. George VI facing l. at r.			
	a. 1.3.1937. Sign. Barton, Craig, Savage.	20.00	175.	950.
	b. 1.3.1938. Sign. Barton, Craig, Savage.	20.00	175.	950.
	c. 1.10.1940. Sign. Robertson, Hayward, Ackland.	20.00	160.	900.
	d. 1.1.1941. Sign. Robertson, Hayward, Banting.	20.00	150.	900.
	e. 1.1.1942. Sign. Robertson, Hayward, Banting.	20.00	150.	900.
	f. 1.7.1943. Sign. Robertson, Banting, Allen.	20.00	140.	900.
	g. 1.1.1946. Sign. Robertson, Banting, Hayward.	20.00	130.	850.
	h. 1.9.1948. Sign. Taylor, Banting, Smith.	20.00	130.	800.
	i. 1.8.1949. Sign. Taylor, Banting, Smith.	20.00	125.	800.
	j. 1.7.1950. Sign. Taylor, Banting, Smith.	20.00	125.	800.
	k. 1.6.1951. Sign. Taylor, Donovan, Smith.	15.00	160.	950.
	s. Specimen. Various dates.	—	—	1100.
	cs. Commercial (false color) specimen.	—	—	750.

38 10 Shillings
1937-51. Dk. brown and blue. Portr. Kg. George VI facing l. at r.

	VG	VF	UNC
a. 1.3.1937. Sign. Barton, Craig, Savage.	30.00	275.	1400.
b. 1.3.1938. Sign. Barton, Craig, Savage.	30.00	275.	1200.
c. 1.10.1940. Sign. Robertson, Hayward, Ackland.	30.00	250.	1100.
d. 1.1.1941. Sign. Robertson, Hayward, Banting.	30.00	250.	1100.
e. 1.1.1942. Sign. Robertson, Hayward, Banting.	30.00	250.	1100.
f. 1.7.1943. Sign. Robertson, Banting, Allen.	30.00	250.	1100.
g. 1.1.1946. Sign. Robertson, Banting, Hayward.	30.00	225.	1050.
h. 1.9.1948. Sign. Taylor, Banting, Smith.	25.00	225.	1000.
i. 1.8.1949. Sign. Taylor, Banting, Smith.	25.00	225.	1000.
j. 1.7.1950. Sign. Taylor, Banting, Smith.	25.00	225.	1000.
k. 1.7.1950. Sign. Taylor, Donovan, Smith.	20.00	185.	950.
s. Specimen. Various dates.	—	—	1250.
cs. Commercial (false color) specimen.	—	—	900.

39 1 Pound
1937-40. Green and red. Portr. Kg. George VI facing l. at r.

	VG	VF	UNC
a. 1.3.1937. Sign. Barton, Craig, Savage.	35.00	475.	1300.
b. 1.3.1938. Sign. Barton, Craig, Savage.	35.00	475.	1200.
c. 1.7.1940. Sign. Robertson, Hayward, Ackland.	35.00	450.	1100.
s. Specimen. Various dates.	—	—	1350.
cs. Commercial (false color) specimen.	—	—	1000.

40 1 Pound
1941-51. Black and green on red unpt. Portr. Kg. George VI facing l. at r.

	VG	VF	UNC
a. 1.1.1941. Sign. Robertson, Hayward, Banting.	35.00	425.	950.
b. 1.1.1946. Sign. Robertson, Banting, Hayward.	35.00	425.	925.
c. 1.9.1948. Sign. Taylor, Banting, Smith.	35.00	400.	950.
d. 1.8.1949. Sign. Taylor, Banting, Smith.	35.00	400.	900.
e. 1.7.1950. Sign. Taylor, Banting, Smith.	30.00	375.	900.
f. 1.6.1951. Sign. Taylor, Donovan, Smith.	25.00	350.	850.
s. Specimen. Various dates.	—	—	1400.
cs. Commercial (false color) specimens.	—	—	1000.

41 5 Pounds
1941-51. Black adn purple on green unpt. Portr. Kg. George VI facing l. at r.

	VG	VF	UNC
a. 1.1.1941. Sign. Robertson, Hayward, Banting.	175.	1000.	1500.
b. 1.7.1943. Sign. Robertson, Banting, Allen.	175.	1000.	1500.
c. 1.1.1946. Sign. Robertson, Banting, Hayward.	150.	975.	1250.
d. 1.8.1949. Sign. Taylor, Banting, Hayward.	125.	900.	1250.
e. 1.7.1950. Sign. Taylor, Banting, Smith.	125.	900.	1200.
f. 1.6.1951. Sign. Taylor, Donovan, Smith.	110.	850.	1100.
s. Specimen. Various dates.	—	—	1950.
cs. Commercial (false color) specimen.	—	—	1000.

42 10 Pounds
1942-51. Black on blue and grey unpt. Portr. Kg. George VI facing front at r.

	VG	VF	UNC
a. 1.1.1942. Sign. Robertson, Hayward, Banting.	350.	1750.	2000.
b. 1.7.1943. Sign. Robertson, Banting, Allen.	350.	1750.	2000.
c. 1.1.1946. Sign. Robertson, Banting, Hayward.	300.	1450.	1850.
d. 1.8.1949. Sign. Taylor, Banting, Smith.	250.	1300.	1800.
e. 1.7.1950. Sign. Taylor, Banting, Smith.	250.	1300.	1800.
f. 1.6.1951. Sign. Taylor, Donovan, Smith.	225.	1200.	1600.
s. Specimen. Various dates.	—	—	3000.
cs. Commercial (false color) specimen.	—	—	1800.

43 20 Pounds
1937-51. Black on purple unpt.

	VG	VF	UNC
a. 1.3.1937. Sign. Barton, Craig, Savage.	750.	2000.	3500.
b. 1.7.1943. Sign. Robertson, Banting, Allen.	750.	2000.	3500.
c. 1.9.1948. Sign. Taylor, Banting, Smith.	600.	1750.	3000.
d. 1.6.1951. Sign. Taylor, Donovan, Smith.	500.	1500.	2500.
s. Specimen. Various dates.	—	—	4000.
cs. Commercial (false color) specimen.	—	—	2500.

1940 Provisional Issue

#44-46 ovpt: *GOVERNMENT OF FIJI...* on Reserve Bank of New Zealand notes. W/o TDLR imprint.

44 10 Shillings
ND (1940 - old date 1.8.1934). Ovpt. on New Zealand #154.

	VG	VF	UNC
a. Issued note (one known). Rare.	—	—	—
s. Specimen.	—	—	4000.

45 1 Pound
ND (1940 - old date 1.8.1934). Ovpt. on New Zealand #155.

	VG	VF	UNC
a. W/o wmk., 1D prefix serial #.	150.	750.	1500.
b. W/o wmk., 6D prefix serial #.	125.	550.	1250.
c. Wmk. (postal stamp) Crown/A repeated. FI/O prefix serial #.	100.	400.	1000.
s. Specimen.	—	—	2000.

46 5 Pounds
ND (1940 - old date 1.8.1934). Ovpt on New Zealand #156.

	VG	VF	UNC
a. W/o wmk. 4K serial # prefix.	2250.	5500.	12,500.
b. W/o wmk. 5K serial # prefix.	2000.	4500.	10,000.
s. Specimen.	—	—	—

1942 Emergency Issues

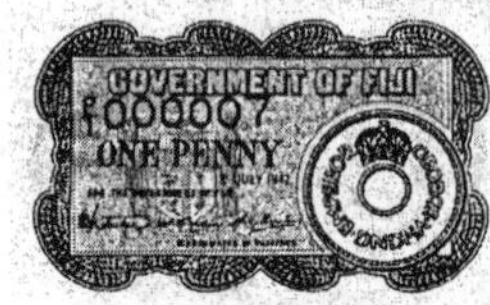

47 1 Penny
1.7.1942. Black on green unpt. Arms in unpt. at l., penny coin at lower r. Back green; penny coin at lower l.

	VG	VF	UNC
a. Issued note.	.50	2.00	9.00
s. Specimen.	—	—	100.

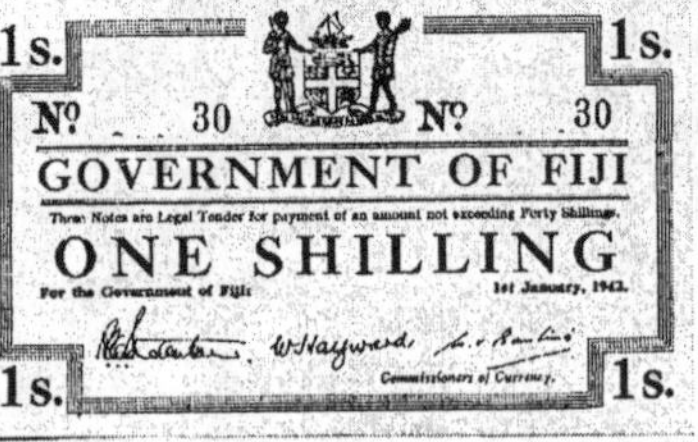

48 1 Shilling
1.1.1942. Black on gray paper. Arms at top ctr. Uniface.

	VG	VF	UNC
a. Issued note.	2.00	15.00	125.
b. Issued note w/ rampant leopard wmk.	4.00	25.00	155.
r. Remainder, w/o serial #.	—	35.00	125.
s. Specimen.	—	45.00	145.

Uncut sheets of six remainders also exist, value $950 in unc.

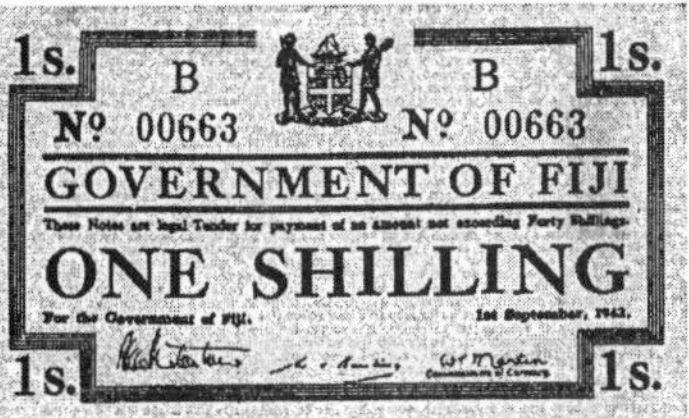

#	Denomination	VG	VF	UNC
49	**1 Shilling**			
	1.9.1942. Black on yellow unpt. words, yellow paper. Arms at top ctr.			
	a. Issued note. Block letters A, B.	2.00	25.00	165.
	s. Specimen.	—	—	185.

#	Denomination	VG	VF	UNC
50	**2 Shillings**			
	1.1.1942. Black on red unpt. like #41.			
	a. Issued note.	2.00	35.00	195.
	r. Remainder, w/o serial #.	—	40.00	140.
	s. Specimen.	—	—	145.

Jncut sheets of six notes w/o serial numbers exist. Value $950 in unc.

1954-57 ISSUE

#51-57 arms at upper ctr., portr. Qn. Elizabeth II at r. Wmk: Fijian youth's bust. Printer: BWC.

#	Denomination	VG	VF	UNC
51	**5 Shillings**			
	1957-65. Green and blue on lilac and green unpt.			
	a. 1.6.1957. Sign. Davidson, Griffiths, Marais.	10.00	75.00	350.
	b. 28.4.1961. Sign. Bevington, Griffiths, Cruickshank.	10.00	75.00	350.
	c. 1.12.1962. Sign. Ritchie, Griffiths, Cruickshank.	8.00	60.00	325.
	d. 1.9.1964. Sign. Ritchie, Griffiths, Cruickshank.	7.50	50.00	275.
	e. 1.10.1965. Sign. Ritchie, Griffiths, Cruickshank.	7.50	40.00	225.
	s. Specimen. Various dates.	—	—	450.
	cs. Commercial (false color) specimen.	—	—	350.

#	Denomination	VG	VF	UNC
52	**10 Shillings**			
	1957-65. Brown on lilac and green unpt.			
	a. 1.6.1957. Sign. Davidson, Griffiths, Marais.	17.50	100.	500.
	b. 28.4.1961. Sign. Bevington, Griffiths, Cruickshank.	17.50	120.	550.
	c. 1.12.1962. Sign. Ritchie, Griffiths, Cruickshank.	10.00	80.00	450.
	d. 1.9.1964. Sign. Ritchie, Griffiths, Cruickshank.	12.50	125.	600.
	e. 1.10.1965. Sign. Ritchie, Griffiths, Cruickshank.	10.00	95.00	600.
	s. Specimen. Various dates.	—	—	650.
	cs. Commercial (false color) specimen.	—	—	500.

#	Denomination	VG	VF	UNC
53	**1 Pound**			
	1954-67. Green on yellow and blue unpt.			
	a. 1.7.1954. Sign. Davidson, Donovan, Davis.	20.00	130.	625.
	b. 1.6.1957. Sign. Davidson, Griffiths, Marais.	25.00	145.	725.
	c. 1.9.1959. Sign. Ritchie, Griffiths, Cruickshank.	20.00	130.	625.
	d. 1.12.1961. Sign. ritchie, Griffiths, Cruickshank.	27.50	145.	725.
	e. 1.12.1962. Sign. Ritchie, Griffiths, Cruickshank.	25.00	145.	700.
	f. 20.1.1964. Sign. Ritchie, Griffiths, Cruickshank.	22.50	140.	625.
	g. 1.5.1965. Sign. Ritchie, Griffiths, Cruickshank.	20.00	130.	600.
	h. 1.12.1965. Sign. Ritchie, Griffiths, Cruickshank.	25.00	135.	575.
	i. 1.1.1967. Sign. Ritchie, Griffiths, Cruickshank.	17.50	125.	575.
	s. Specimen. Various dates.	—	—	850.
	cs. Commercial (false color) specimen.	—	—	700.

#	Denomination	VG	VF	UNC
54	**5 Pounds**			
	1954-67. Purple on lt. orange and green unpt.			
	a. 1.7.1954. Sign. Davidson, Donovan, Davis.	125.	750.	1500.
	b. 1.9.1959. Sign. Bevington, Griffiths, Marais.	125.	750.	1500.
	c. 1.10.1960. Sign. Bevington, Griffiths, Cruickshank.	95.00	750.	1500.
	d. 1.12.1962. Sign. Ritchie, Griffiths, Cruickshank.	85.00	725.	1250.
	e. 20.1.1964. Sign. Ritchie, Griffiths, Cruickshank.	85.00	700.	1100.
	f. 1.1.1967. Sign. Ritchie, Griffiths, Cruickshank.	80.00	700.	1100.
	s. Specimen. Various dates.	—	—	1000.
	cs. Commercial (false color) specimen.	—	—	850.

#	Denomination	VG	VF	UNC
55	**10 Pounds**			
	1954-64. Blue on blue, orange and green unpt.			
	a. 1.7.1954. Sign. Davidson, Donovan, Davis.	250.	1250.	2000.
	b. 1.9.1959. Sign. Bevington, Griffiths, Marais.	250.	1250.	2000.
	c. 1.10.1960. Sign. Bevington, Griffiths, Cruickshank.	180.	1100.	2000.
	d. 20.1.1964. Sign. Ritchie, Griffiths, Cruickshank.	170.	1000.	1850.
	e. 11.6.1964. Sign. Ritchie, Griffiths, Cruickshank.	160.	900.	1750.
	f. 1.5.1965. Not released. Sign. Ritchie, Griffiths, Cruickshank.	—	—	—
	s. Specimen. Various dates.	—	—	1100.
	cs. Commercial (false color) specimen.	—	—	950.
56	**20 Pounds**			
	1.1.1953. Black and purple on purple unpt.			
	a. 1.1.1953. Sign. Davidson, Donovan, Smith.	950.	1250.	4000.
	s. Specimen.	—	—	3500.
	cs. Commercial (false color) specimen.	—	—	1200.
57	**20 Pounds**			
	1.7.1954; 1.11.1958. Red on red and green unpt.			
	a. 1.7.1954. Sign. Davidson, Donovan, Davis.	750.	1250.	3000.
	b. 1.11.1958. Sign. Bevington, Griffiths, Marais.	600.	1000.	2500.
	s. Specimen.	—	—	2000.
	cs. Commercial (false color) specimen.	—	—	1000.

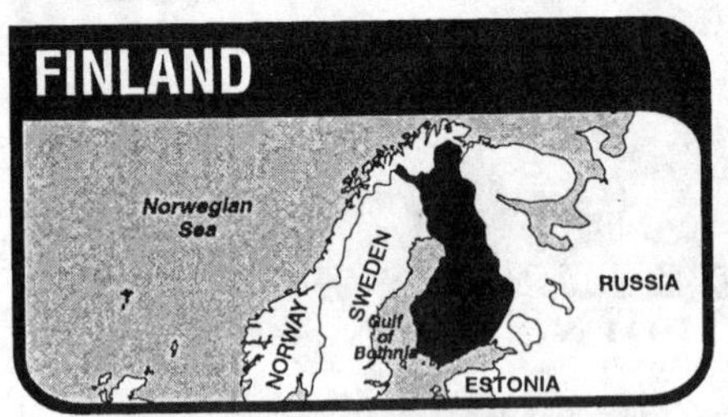

The Republic of Finland, the second most northerly state of the European continent, has an area of 130,120 sq. mi. (337,009 sq. km.) and a population of 5.21 million. Capital: Helsinki. Electrical/optical equipment, shipbuilding, metal and woodworking are the leading industries. Paper, wood pulp, plywood and telecommunication equipment are exported.

The Finns, who probably originated in the Volga region of Russia, took Finland from the Lapps late in the 7th century. They were conquered in the 12th century by Eric IX of Sweden, and brought into contact with Western Christendom. In 1809, Sweden was invaded by Alexander I of Russia, and the peace terms gave Finland to Russia. It became a grand duchy within the Russian Empire until Dec. 6, 1917, when, shortly after the Bolshevik revolution, it declared its independence. After a brief but bitter civil war between the Russian sympathizers and Finnish nationalists in which the Whites (nationalists) were victorious, a new constitution was adopted, and on Dec. 6, 1917 Finland was established as a republic. In 1939 Soviet troops invaded Finland over disputed territorial concessions which were later granted in the peace treaty of 1940. When the Germans invaded Russia, Finland also became involved and in the Armistice of 1944 lost the Petsamo area also to the USSR.

RULERS:

Gustaf III, 1771-1792, of Sweden
Gustaf IV Adolph, 1792-1809
Alexander I, 1809-1825, of Russia
Nicholas I, 1825-1855
Alexander II, 1855-1881
Alexander III, 1881-1894
Nicholas II, 1894-1917

MONETARY SYSTEM:

(With Sweden to 1809)
1 Riksdaler Specie = 48 Skilling Specie
(With Russia 1809-1917)
1 Ruble = 100 Kopeks, 1809-1860
1 Markka = 100 Penniä, 1860-1963
1 Markka = 100 Penniä
1 Markka = 100 "Old" Markkaa, 1963-2001
1 Markka = 100 Penniä, 1963-2001
1 Euro = 100 Cents, 2002

REPLACEMENT NOTES:

These were introduced in 1955. Until 1980, replacement notes have an asterisk after the serial number.

SWEDISH ADMINISTRATION

KONGL. GENERAL KRIGS COMMISSARIATET

KING'S GENERAL WAR COMMISSARIAT

1790 ISSUE

#A1-A12 w/o pictorial design. Various handwritten dates w/ printed 1790. Embossed seal w/legend: K. FINSKA G: KRIGS COMMISARIATET around crowned arms at top ctr. Printed sign. of Fahnehjelm with an additional handwritten sign. Uniface. Minor varieties exist.

		Good	Fine	XF
A1	**8 Skilling Specie** 1790.	500.	1500.	—
A2	**12 Skilling Specie** 1790.	500.	1500.	—
A3	**16 Skilling Specie** 1790.	500.	1500.	—
A4	**24 Skilling Specie** 1790.	500.	1500.	—
A5	**32 Skilling Specie** 1790.	—	—	—
A6	**1 Riksdaler Specie** 1790.	—	—	—
A7	**1 Riksdaler 8 Skilling Specie** 1790.	—	—	—
A8	**1 Riksdaler 16 Skilling Specie** 1790.	—	—	—
A9	**1 Riksdaler 24 Skilling Specie** 1790.	—	—	—
A10	**1 Riksdaler 32 Skilling Specie** 1790.	—	—	—
A11	**1 Riksdaler 40 Skilling Specie** 1790.	—	—	—
A12	**2 Riksdaler Specie** 1790.	—	—	—

RUSSIAN ADMINISTRATION

GRAND DUCHY OF FINLAND

STORFURSTENDÖMET FINLANDS WÄXEL-LÅNE-OCH DEPOSITIONS-CONTOR

ÅBO

1812 ASSIGNATES ISSUE

#A13-15 denominations in oval, w/o pictorial design. Various sign. and handwritten dates w/printed 18, w/ or w/o various wmks.

		Good	Fine	XF
A13	**20 Kopeks** 1812-18.	300.	1000.	3000.
A14	**50 Kopeks** 1812-19.	300.	850.	250
A15	**75 Kopeks** 1812-21.	250.	750.	200

STORFURSTENDÖMET FINLANDS

WÄXEL-DEPOSITIONS-OCH LÅNE-BANK

1818-21 ASSIGNATES ISSUE

		Good	Fine	X
A16	**20 Kopeks** 1818-19.	500.	1200.	350
A17	**50 Kopeks** 1819-20.	500.	1200.	35
A18	**75 Kopeks** 1821. Rare.	—	—	

HELSINGFORS

1819-22 ASSIGNATES ISSUE

		Good	Fine	X
A19	**20 Kopeks** 1820-22. W/ or w/o wmk.	500.	1200.	35
A20	**50 Kopeks** 1822. Rare.	—	—	
A21	**1 Ruble** 1819-20. 136 x 160 mm. Rare.	—	—	

Note: An example of #A21 sold in a 1992 auction for $40,000.

		Good	Fine	X
A22	**2 Rubles** 1819-20. 136 x 160 mm. Rare.	—	—	
A23	**4 Rubles** 1819-20. 160 x 136 mm. Rare.	—	—	

Note: An example of #A23 sold in a 1993 auction for $26,000.

STORFURSTENDÖMET FINLANDS

WÄXEL-DEPOSITIONS-OCH LÅNE-BANK

1822-24 ASSIGNATES ISSUE

#A24-A28 w/double headed eagle at top ctr. Various printed dates (on A27a and 28a handwritten). Unifac

		Good	Fine	
A24	**20 Kopeks** 1824-26; 1829-38; 1840.	100.	200.	7
A25	**50 Kopeks** 1824-26; 1830; 1835-37; 1839-40.	100.	200.	8

		Good	Fine	
A26	**75 Kopeks** 1824-26; 1831; 1836; 1839-40.	125.	300.	1
A27	**1 Ruble** 1822-29.			
	a. Handwritten serial #. 1822-24.	300.	750.	2
	b. Printed serial #. 1826; 1828-29.	250.	500.	1
A28	**2 Rubles** 1823-28.			
	a. Handwritten serial #. 1823-24.	350.	750.	3
	b. Printed serial #. 1827.	800.	1500.	5
	c. Printed serial #.	300.	700.	2

FINSKA BANKEN

BANK OF FINLAND

1841 RUBLE ISSUE

#A29-A32 w/double headed eagle at top ctr. Backed by silver. Various date and sign. varieties. Ru and Swedish text on face and Finnish text on back.

		Good	Fine	
A29	**3 Rubles** 1840-62. Green. 150 x 98 mm.			
	a. 1841; 1843; 1845-46; 1848; 1852-53; 1857; 1862. Rare.	—	—	
	b. 1842; 1847; 1855-56; 1859-61.	750.	1500.	3
A30	**5 Rubles** 1841-62. Blue. 167 x 100 mm.			
	a. 1841-43; 1847-48; 1851-53; 1860; 1862. Rare.	—	—	
	b. 1855-57; 1861.	1000.	2000.	4
A31	**10 Rubles** 1841-42; 1847; 1849; 1852-53; 1855-57. Red. 175 x 127 mm. Rare.	—	—	

		Good	Fine	XF
A32	**25 Rubles**			
	1841-57. Olive. 184 x 137 mm.			
	a. 1841.	1000.	2000.	3000.
	b. 1842-43.	1500.	2250.	4000.
	c. 1844; 1846-47; 1851-52; 1855-57. Rare.	—	—	—

Note: For #A31 and A32, the 1862 date was not issued.

FINLANDS BANK

SUOMEN PANKKI

1860-62 MARKKA ISSUE

Various date and sign. varieties.

		Good	Fine	XF
A32A	**1 Markka**			
	1860-61. Red-brown on lt. blue. Embossed arms at top.			
	a. 1860. W/o wmk.	250.	500.	2500.
	b. Wmk: *COUPON.*	250.	500.	2500.
	c. 1860. Wmk: Arms.	250.	500.	2500.
	d. 1861.	200.	400.	1800.
A33	**1 Markka**			
	1864; 1866. White arms.			
	a. 1864.	750.	1500.	3500.
	b. 1866.	300.	750.	2500.
A34	**3 Markkaa**			
	1860-61. Green on yellow. Embossed arms at top.			
	a. 1860. W/o wmk.	500.	1000.	3000.
	b. 1860. Wmk: *COUPON.*	500.	1000.	3000.
	c. 1860. Wmk: Arms.	500.	1000.	3000.
	d. 1861.	1500.	4000.	9000.
A34A	**3 Markkaa**			
	1864; 1866. White arms.			
	a. 1864.	1200.	3000.	7500.
	b. 1866. Rare.	—	—	—

		Good	Fine	XF
A35	**12 Markkaa**			
	1862. Green. Man w/stick and cap at l., young woman w/scarf at r. 136 x 72 mm.			
	a. W/o series. 7 digit serial #.	250.	500.	1500.
	b. Series B. 6 digit serial #.	350.	700.	2200.
	c. Series C. 6 digit serial #.	300.	600.	2000.

		Good	Fine	XF
A36	**20 Markkaa**			
	1862. Red. Crowned mantled arms consisting of crowned double headed eagle between man and woman at l. 141 x 77 mm.			
	a. W/o series.	300.	500.	1250.
	b. Series B.	400.	1000.	2500.
	c. Series C.	300.	550.	1500.
A37	**40 Markkaa**			
	1862. Yellow. Crowned mantled arms consisting of crowned double headed eagle at l., seated woman w/anchor and caduceus at r. 150 x 85 mm.	4000.	7500.	12,000.

		Good	Fine	XF
A38	**100 Markkaa**			
	1862. M/c. Young man w/stick and cap at l., young woman at r. 154 x 90 mm.			
	a. W/o series.	500.	1000.	2500.
	b. Series B.	700.	1500.	4000.
	c. Series C.	700.	1300.	3000.

1866-75 ISSUE

		Good	Fine	XF
A39	**1 Markka**			
	1866. Black arms ovpt. on white arms. Like #A33A.	200.	500.	1500.
A39A	**1 Markka**			
	1866-67. Blue-green and red-brown. Black arms.			
	a. Serial #11397001-1873000. 1866.	200.	500.	2000.
	b. 1867. Sign. R. Frenckell.	75.00	200.	750.
	c. As b. 7-digit serial # with double ring in eagle's wings.	200.	900.	—
	d. 1867. Aign. V. Von Hartmann.	50.00	150.	500.
A40	**3 Markkaa**			
	1866. Black arms ovpt. on white arms.	1000.	2500.	5000.
A40A	**3 Markkaa**			
	1866-75. Black arms.			
	a. 1866.	1000.	2500.	5000.
	b. 1867. Sign. R. Frenckell. Rare.	—	—	—
	c. 1867. Sign. V. von Hartmann.	150.	250.	750.
	d. 1869-70; 1872.	250.	500.	1500.
	e. 1873-75.	150.	250.	800.

Note: #A40Ae, 1874 comes in thick or thin paper varieties.

		Good	Fine	XF
A41	**5 Markkaa**			
	1875. Bluish-gray. Arms at l. *I SILFVER* below *FEM MARK.*			
	a. Serial #0000001-0186000.	250.	750.	1500.
	b. Wmk. slightly changed. Serial #0186001-1788000.	150.	350.	1200.
A42	**10 Markkaa**			
	1875. Red and gray. Arms at l. *I SILFVER* below *TIO MARK.*	700.	2500.	5000.

1878 ISSUE

		Good	Fine	XF
A43	**5 Markkaa**			
	1878. Bluish-gray. Like #A41, but *FINSKT MYNT* below *FEM MARK.*			
	a. Sign. handwritten. Serial #0000001-1926000.	100.	200.	750.
	b. Sign. printed. Serial #1926001-4876900.	70.00	120.	500.
A44	**10 Markkaa**			
	1878. Red and gray. Like #A42, but *I GULD* below *TIO MARK.*	500.	850.	1500.
A45	**500 Markkaa**			
	1878. Yellow and gray. Arms w/2 cherubs.			
	a. Printed in Copenhagen. Serial #000001-079000.	1000.	2000.	5000.
	b. Printed in Helsinki. Serial #079001-150400.	750.	1250.	4000.

1882-84 ISSUE

		Good	Fine	XF
A46	**10 Markkaa**			
	1882. Black and yellow. Like #A44, but slightly altered design.			
A47	**20 Markkaa**			
	1882; 1883. Black and brown. Arms at l.			
	a. 1882.	300.	750.	2500.
	b. 1883.	100.	200.	900.
A48	**100 Markkaa**			
	1882. Black and red. Arms at ctr.			
	a. Printed in Copenhagen. 3mm serial #000001-481300.	150.	500.	1350.
	b. Printed in Helsinki. 3.8mm serial #481301-683000.	175.	550.	1500.
A49	**50 Markkaa**			
	1884. Black and blue. Arms at ctr.	150.	300.	1500.

1886-94 ISSUE

		Good	Fine	XF
A50	**5 Markkaa**			
	1886. Black and blue. Arms at ctr.			
	a. Wmk. at ctr. r.	35.00	70.00	350.
	b. Wmk. at ctr.	30.00	50.00	300.
A51	**10 Markkaa**			
	1889. Dk. brown and red. Arms at ctr.	35.00	75.00	350.
A52	**20 Markkaa**			
	1894. Black and dk. brown. Arms at ctr. Wmk. at l. and r.			
	a. Dk. red. Serial # up to 0096584.	75.00	200.	750.
	b. Red-brown. Serial #123023-324770.	50.00	150.	700.
	c. Brown. Serial #403209-0981274.	40.00	100.	500.

1897-98 Issue

		Good	Fine	XF
1	**5 Markkaa**			
	1897. Blue on brown unpt. Arms at l., woman at ctr., head at r. Shield surrounded by spruce twigs on dk. background on back. Vertical format.			
	a. Serial #0000001-7092000.	10.00	75.00	250.
	b. Serial #7092001-7143000. Test paper.	—	1000.	—

		Good	Fine	XF
2	**5 Markkaa**			
	1897. Like #1, but shield surrounded by pine twigs on lt. background on back. 7 and 8 digilt serial #.	10.00	40.00	200.
3	**10 Markkaa**			
	1898. Purple on brown unpt. Woman standing at l. Back purple-brown.			
	a. Serial #0000001-4065000.	10.00	70.00	200.
	b. Serial #4065001-4114000. Test paper.	—	1000.	—
	c. Serial # 4114001-8560000.	5.00	40.00	150.
	d. Serial #8560001-8563000. Test paper.	—	400.	—

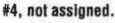

#4, not assigned.

		Good	Fine	XF
5	**20 Markkaa**			
	1898. Woman w/youth and globe.			
	a. Back green. Serial #0000001-2026000.	25.00	75.00	500.
	b. Back red. (Not issued). Serial #2026001-4196000.	15.00	50.00	350.
6	**50 Markkaa**			
	1898. Blue. Woman w/tablet at l.			
7	**100 Markkaa**			
	1898. Young farming couple at l.			
	a. Handwritten sign. to #86000.	350.	850.	1500.
	b. Lines under sign. Serial #86001-659000.	75.00	150.	800.
	c. W/o lines under sign.	40.00	100.	

		Good	Fine	XF
8	**500 Markkaa**			
	1898. Blue. Woman w/lion at l. Back brown.			
	a. Handwritten sign. to #23000.	500.	1250.	3000.
	b. Lines under sign. Serial #23001-99000.	300.	750.	2500.
	c. W/o lines under sign. Serial #99001-205000.	300.	700.	2000.

1909 First Issue

Beginning w/#9, issues are affected by WWI and many reissues of earlier dates.

#9-32 Czarist eagle at upper ctr.

		VG	VF	UNC
9	**5 Markkaa**			
	1909. Blue. Rowboat in river in black on back.			
	a. Wmk: *SPFB.*	1.50	10.00	35.00
	b. W/o wmk. 7 or 8 digit serial #.	3.00	15.00	50.00
	c. Serial # prefix A, B or C.	100.	500.	—

Note: The wmk. is found on only about half of the printings of #9a. Notes with prefix letters A, B & C are believed to be test printings.

		VG	VF	UNC
10	**10 Markkaa**			
	1909. Lilac. Stylized tree at ctr. House/w 2 cows in black on back.			
	a. Serial # 2.5 mm high.	2.00	15.00	50.00
	b. Serial # 3.5 mm high.	3.00	20.00	85.00

		VG	VF	UNC
11	**20 Markkaa**			
	1909. Orange on gray unpt. Caduceus at ctr. Stylized tree on back. Serial # varieties.			
	a. Wmk: *SPFB.*	10.00	40.00	120.
	b. W/o wmk.	10.00	40.00	120.
12	**50 Markkaa**			
	1909. Blue. Lighthouse on back.			
	a. W/o wmk.	50.00	150.	700.
	b. Wmk: *FINLANDS BANK.*	100.	500.	1500.
13	**100 Markkaa**			
	1909. Violet. Farmer plowing at l. and r. Serial # varieties.			
	a. W/o wmk.	50.00	175.	500.
	b. Wmk: *FINLANDS BANK*	100.	500.	1000.
14	**500 Markkaa**			
	1909. Orange and brown. 2 blacksmiths at anvil at ctr.	350.	1500.	3500.
15	**1000 Markkaa**			
	1909. Blue and brown. 2 men holding a caduceus at ctr.	700.	2500.	5000.

1915 Issue

		VG	VF	UNC
16	**1 Markka**			
	1915. Red. Uniface. Serial # varieties.			
	a. W/o series.	1.00	5.00	15.00
	b. Series A.	.50	2.00	7.50

1916 Issue

		VG	VF	UNC
17	**25 Penniä**			
	1916. Yellow-brown. (Not issued).	—	Unc	1000.
18	**50 Penniä**			
	1916. Gray-blue. (Not issued).	—	Unc	1000.

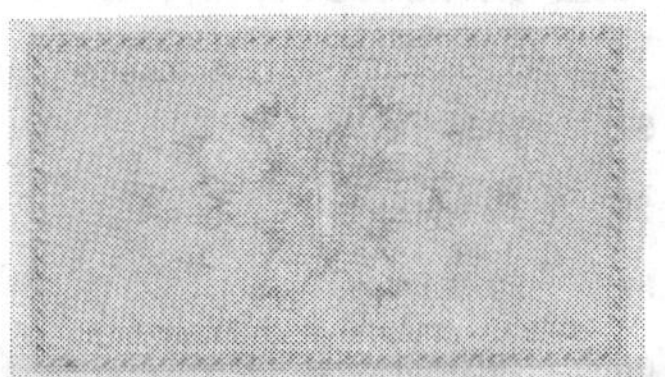

		VG	VF	UNC
9	**1 Markka** 1916. Dk. brown on lt. brown unpt. 7 and 8 digil serial #.	.25	1.50	5.00

917 SENATE ISSUE

tes printed and issued under Senate control, December 6, 1917-January 28, 1918.

		VG	VF	UNC
9A	**1 Markka** 1916. Similar to #19. Serial #18288001-20232000. Printed 6.12.1917-26.1.1918.	.25	1.50	5.00
9B	**5 Markkaa** 1909. Blue. Like #9. Serial #18573001-19397000. Printed 10.12.1917-25.1.1918.	1.00	10.00	30.00
9C	**10 Markkaa** 1909. Lilac. Similar to #10b.			
	a. 7 digit serial #9946100-9999999. Printed 20.12.1917-3.1.1918.	2.50	20.00	75.00
	b. 8 digit serial #10000000-10231000. Printed 3.1.1918-17.1.1918.	60.00	125.	250.
9D	**20 Markkaa** 1909. Similar to #11. Serial #9646001-9870000.	5.00	40.00	120.
9E	**100 Markkaa** 1909. Similar to #13. Serial #2575001-2775000.	100.	250.	750.

918 PEOPLES COMMISSARIAT ISSUE

tes printed and issued under Peoples Commissariat control, January 28, 1918-May 20, 1918.

		VG	VF	UNC
9F	**1 Markka** 1916. Like #19 but serial #20232001-20880000.	10.00	30.00	100.
9G	**1 Markka** 1916. Similar to #19F but Serial #20880001-24795000.	1.00	2.00	5.00

		VG	VF	UNC
0	**5 Markkaa** 1909 (1918). Blue. Like #19B but serial #19397001-20789000.	.50	4.00	20.00
1	**20 Markkaa** 1909 (1918). Orange-brown. Like #19D.			
	a. 7 digit serial #9874001-9999999.	4.00	30.00	100.
	b. 8 digil serial #10000000-10019001.	15.00	150.	600.
2	**100 Markkaa** 1909 (1918). Violet. Like #19E, but serial #2775001-2983000.	5.00	15.00	75.00
3	**500 Markkaa** 1909 (1918). Orange and brown. Like #14, but serial #170001-262000.	10.00	40.00	90.00

REPUBLIC OF FINLAND

FINLANDS BANK

909 DATED ISSUE (1918), LITT. A

		VG	VF	UNC
4	**5 Markkaa** 1909 (1918). Blue. Like #9.			
	a. w/o wmk.	5.00	25.00	70.00
	b. W/wmk.	5.00	25.00	70.00
5	**10 Markkaa** 1909 (1918). Lilac. Like #10.	5.00	15.00	75.00
6	**20 Markkaa** 1909 (1918). Orange-brown. Like #11.	150.	750.	1500.
27	**50 Markkaa** 1909 (1918). Blue. Like #12.	50.00	150.	500.
28	**100 Markkaa** 1909 (1918). Violet. Like #13.	500.	1500.	3500.
29	**500 Markkaa** 1909 (1918). Orange and brown. Like #14. Rare.	—	—	—

1909 DATED ISSUE (1918), *SARJA II* (SERIES II)

		VG	VF	UNC
30	**5 Markkaa** 1909 (1918). Green. Like #9.	1.00	10.00	30.00
31	**100 Markkaa** 1909 (1918). Orange and gray. Like #13.	35.00	100.	300.
32	**500 Markkaa** 1909 (1918). Gray and yellow. Like #14.	175.	850.	2000.

1918 ISSUE

#33-41 w/o Czarist eagle at upper ctr.

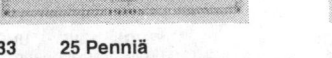

		VG	VF	UNC
33	**25 Penniä** 1918. Dk. brown on lt. brown unpt.	.50	1.50	3.00

		VG	VF	UNC
34	**50 Penniä** 1918. Dk. brown on blue unpt.	.50	1.50	3.00

		VG	VF	UNC
35	**1 Markka** 1918. Dk. brown on lt. brown unpt. Similar to #19.	.50	1.50	5.00
36	**5 Markkaa** 1918. Green. Similar to #9.	1.00	7.50	25.00
37	**10 Markkaa** 1918. Lilac. Similar to #10.	2.00	15.00	35.00

		VG	VF	UNC
38	**20 Markkaa** 1918. Blue. Similar to #11.	5.00	30.00	100.

NOTICE

Readers with unlisted dates, signature varieties, etc. are invited to submit photocopies or, high resolution (300 dpi, 100% size) scans of their notes to: Standard Catalog of World Paper Money, 700 East State St. Iola, WI 54990-0001, or E-Mail: george.cuhaj@fwpubs.com.

		VG	VF	UNC
39	**50 Markkaa** 1918. Blue. Similar to #12.	35.00	125.	300.
40	**100 Markkaa** 1918. Lt. brown on gray unpt. Similar to #13.	35.00	125.	250.
41	**1000 Markkaa** 1918. Similar to #15.	650.	2000.	3500.

1922 Dated Issue

#42-74 w/o *Litt.* Arms on back.

		VG	VF	UNC
42	**5 Markkaa** 1922. Green. Fir tree at ctr.	1.00	10.00	30.00
43	**10 Markkaa** 1922. Brown. Pine tree at ctr.	1.00	10.00	30.00
44	**20 Markkaa** 1922 (1926). Violet. Pine tree at ctr.	15.00	70.00	150.
45	**50 Markkaa** 1922 (1926). Dk. blue. Allegorical group of 6 people.	50.00	250.	500.

		VG	VF	UNC
46	**100 Markkaa** 1922. Dk. brown. Allegorical group of 6 people.	40.00	200.	500.
47	**500 Markkaa** 1922 (1924). Brown on green unpt. Allegorical group of 11 people.			
	a. W/o plate # at lower l.	150.	500.	1500.
	b. Plate # at lower l.	125.	400.	1200.
48	**1000 Markkaa** 1922 (1923). Brown. Allegorical group of 13 people.			
	a. W/o plate # at lower l.	200.	750.	1750.
	b. Plate # at lower l.	175.	700.	1350.

1922 Dated Issue, Litt. A

		VG	VF	UNC
49	**5 Markkaa** 1922 (1926). Green. Like #42.	1.00	10.00	40.00
50	**10 Markkaa** 1922 (1926). Brown. Like #43.	2.00	15.00	40.00
51	**20 Markkaa** 1922 (1927). Red. Like #44.	30.00	100.	300.
52	**50 Markkaa** 1922 (1925). Dk. blue. Like #45.	50.00	300.	700.
53	**100 Markkaa** 1922 (1923). Dk. brown. Like #46.			
	a. W/o plate # at lower l.	50.00	150.	600.
	b. Plate # at lower l.	35.00	100.	400.
54	**500 Markkaa** 1922 (1930). Brown on green unpt. Like #47.	350.	1500.	3000.
55	**1000 Markkaa** 1922 (1929). Brown. Like #48.	200.	1000.	2500.

1922 Dated Issue, Litt. B

		VG	VF	UN
56	**5 Markkaa** 1922 (1929). Green. Like #42.	3.00	20.00	75.0
57	**10 Markkaa** 1922 (1929). Brown. Like #43.	5.00	30.00	85.0
58	**20 Markkaa** 1922 (1929). Violet. Like #44.	50.00	200.	50
59	**50 Markkaa** 1922 (1929). Dk. blue. Like #45.	120.	750.	135
60	**100 Markkaa** 1922 (1929). Dk. brown. Like #46.	70.00	300.	75

1922 Dated Issue, Litt. C

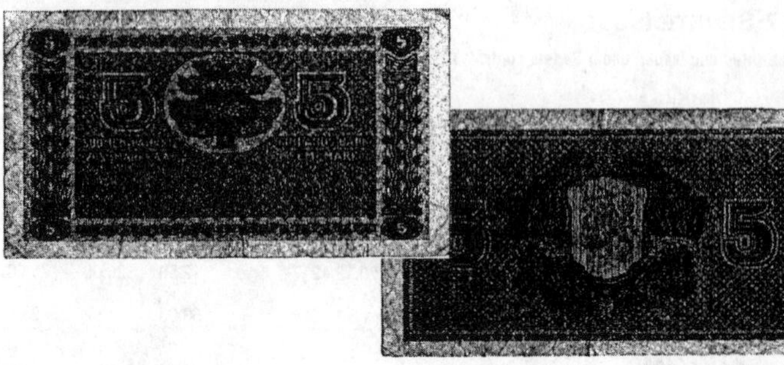

		VG	VF	UN
61	**5 Markkaa** 1922 (1930). Green. Like #42.			
	a. Issued note.	1.00	5.00	20.
	s. Specimen.	—	—	12
62	**10 Markkaa** 1922 (1930). Brown. Like #43.			
	a. Issued note.	1.00	10.00	30.0
	s. Specimen.	—	—	12
63	**20 Markkaa** 1922 (1931). Red. Like #44.			
	a. Issued note.	1.00	7.50	20.0
	s. Specimen.	—	—	15

		VG	VF	UN
64	**50 Markkaa** 1922 (1931). Dk. blue. Like #45.			
	a. Issued note.	10.00	30.00	12
	s. Specimen.	—	—	20

		VG	VF	UN
65	**100 Markkaa** 1922 (1932-45). Dk. brown. Like #46.			
	a. Issued note.	5.00	25.00	90.
	s. Specimen.	—	—	20

66	500 Markkaa	VG	VF	UNC
	1922 (1931-42). Brown on green unpt. Like #47. Serial # varieties.			
	a. Issued note.	30.00	150.	500.
	s. Specimen.	—	—	250.

67	1000 Markkaa	VG	VF	UNC
	1922 (1931-45). Brown. Like #48. Serial # varieties.			
	a. Issued note.	25.00	75.00	200.
	s. Specimen.	—	—	200.

1922 Dated Issue, Litt. D

67A	1000 Markkaa	VG	VF	UNC
	1922 (1939). Green. *Litt. D.* Like #48.	125.	750.	2000.

1939 Provisional Issue

68	5000 Markkaa	VG	VF	UNC
	1922 (1939). Brown. *Litt. A.* Blue ovpt. on #47.	2000.	7500.	12,000.

1939-41 Dated Issue

69	5 Markkaa	VG	VF	UNC
	1939 (1942-45). Green. Like #42.			
	a. Issued note.	.50	2.00	10.00
	s. Specimen.	—	—	100.

70	10 Markkaa	VG	VF	UNC
	1939 (1939-45). Brown. Like #43.			
	a. Issued note.	.50	2.00	10.00
	s. Specimen.	—	—	100.

71	20 Markkaa	VG	VF	UNC
	1939 (1939-45). Purple. Like #44.			
	a. Issued note.	1.00	3.00	10.00
	s. Specimen.	—	—	100.

72	50 Markkaa	VG	VF	UNC
	1939 (1939-45). Dk. blue. Like #45.			
	a. Issued note.	2.50	15.00	100.
	s. Specimen.	—	—	150.

73	100 Markkaa	VG	VF	UNC
	1939 (1940-45). Dk. brown. Like #46.			
	a. Issued note.	2.00	10.00	50.00
	s. Specimen.	—	—	150.
74	1000 Markkaa			
	1941 (1944-45). Brown. *Litt. E.* Like #48.	700.	2500.	5000.

		VG	VF	UNC
75	**5000 Markkaa**			
	1939 (1940). Dk. blue and violet. Snellman at l.			
	a. Denomination at ctr. and at r. w/o reddish unpt. (1940-1943).	200.	750.	1750.
	b. Denomination at ctr. and at r. w/reddish unpt. (1945).	300.	1000.	2000.
	s. Specimen.	—	—	1250.

1945 Dated Issue, Litt. A

		VG	VF	UNC
76	**5 Markkaa**			
	1945 (1946). Yellow. Fir at ctr.			
	a. Issued note.	.50	2.00	8.00
	s. Specimen.	—	—	100.

		VG	VF	UNC
77	**10 Markkaa**			
	1945. Red. Pine at ctr.			
	a. Issued note.	.50	2.00	10.00
	s. Specimen.	—	—	100.
78	**20 Markkaa**			
	1945. Blue. Pine at ctr.			
	a. Issued note.	.50	3.00	12.50
	s. Specimen.	—	—	100.
79	**50 Markkaa**			
	1945. Brown. Young farm couple on back.			
	a. Printed area on face 93 x 96mm. (A serial #).	5.00	20.00	60.00
	b. Printed area on face 88 x 92mm.	2.00	10.00	50.00
	s. Specimen.	—	—	125.
80	**100 Markkaa**			
	1945. Blue-green. Woman w/lion on back.			
	a. Issued note.	2.00	10.00	35.00
	s. Specimen.	—	—	125.

		VG	VF	UNC
81	**500 Markkaa**			
	1945. Blue. Similar to #47.			
	a. Issued note.	35.00	100.	350.
	s. Specimen.	—	—	200.

		VG	VF	UNC
82	**1000 Markkaa**			
	1945. Blue-violet. Similar to #48.			
	a. Issued note.	25.00	75.00	150.
	s. Specimen.	—	—	200.

		VG	VF	UNC
83	**5000 Markkaa**			
	1945. Dk. brown. Like #75.			
	a. One letter in serial #.	100.	300.	650.
	b. Two letters in serial #.	150.	500.	1000.
	s. Specimen.	—	—	500.

1945 Dated Issue, Litt. B

		VG	VF	UNC
84	**5 Markkaa**			
	1945 (1948). Yellow. Like #76.	1.00	5.00	15.00
85	**10 Markkaa**			
	1945 (1948). Red. Like #77.	.50	1.50	5.00

		VG	VF	UNC
86	**20 Markkaa**			
	1945 (1948). Blue. Like #78.	.50	1.50	5.00

		VG	VF	UNC
87	**50 Markkaa**			
	1945 (1948). Brown. Like #79.	1.00	7.50	20.00

		VG	VF	UN
88	**100 Markkaa**			
	1945 (1948). Blue-green. Like #80.	1.00	5.00	15.0
89	**500 Markkaa**			
	1945 (1948). Blue. Like #81.	20.00	50.00	15

		VG	VF	UNC
90	**1000 Markkaa**			
	1945 (1948). Violet. Like #82.	20.00	50.00	100.

1955 ISSUE

		VG	VF	UNC
91	**100 Markkaa**			
	1955. Brown on olive unpt. Ears of wheat at ctr.			
	a. Issued note.	1.00	3.00	12.00
	r. Replacement.	5.00	20.00	50.00
	s. Specimen.	—	—	150.
92	**500 Markkaa**			
	1955. Brown on blue unpt. Conifer branch at ctr. 2 sign. varieties.			
	a. Issued note.	30.00	90.00	150.
	r. Replacement.	35.00	170.	300.
	s. Specimen.	—	—	200.
93	**1000 Markkaa**			
	1955. Dk. green. Paasikivi at l.			
	a. Issued note.	7.00	25.00	50.00
	r. Replacement.	20.00	75.00	15.00
	s. Specimen.	—	—	100.

		VG	VF	UNC
94	**5000 Markkaa**			
	1955. Brown and lilac. K. J. Stahlberg at l.			
	a. Issued note.	35.00	100.	200.
	s. Specimen.	—	—	150.

		VG	VF	UNC
95	**10,000 Markkaa**			
	1955. Lilac. J. V. Snellman at l. ctr.			
	a. Issued note.	50.00	150.	250.
	s. Specimen.	—	—	150.

Note: #94 and 95 exist w/inverted wmk.

1956 ISSUE

		VG	VF	UNC
96	**500 Markkaa**			
	1956. Blue. Like #92. Conifer branch.			
	a. Issued note.	3.00	20.00	50.00
	r. Replacement.	50.00	200.	500.
	s. Specimen.	—	—	175.

1957 ISSUE

		VG	VF	UNC
97	**100 Markkaa**			
	1957. Dk. red on lt. brown unpt. Like #91. Ears of wheat.			
	a. Issued note.	1.00	3.00	10.00
	r. Replacement.	7.50	25.00	40.00
	s. Specimen.	—	—	200.

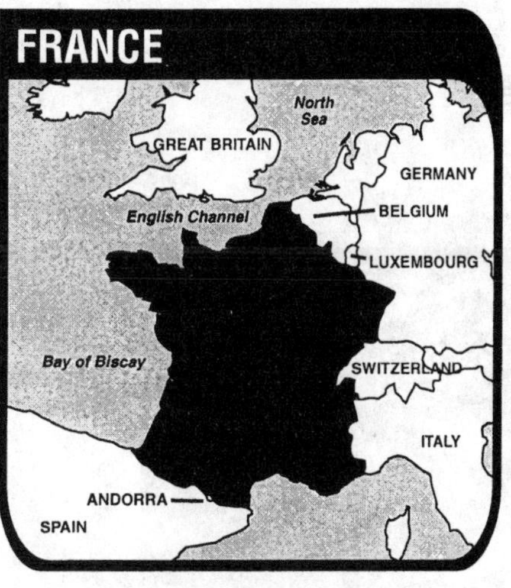

The French Republic, largest of the West European nations, has an area of 220,668 sq. mi. (547,026 sq. km.) and a population of 60 million. Capital: Paris. Agriculture, manufacturing and tourism are the most important elements of France's diversified economy. Textiles and clothing, iron and steel products, machinery and transportation equipment, agricultural products and wine are exported.

France, the Gaul of ancient times, emerged from the Renaissance as a modern centralized national state which reached its zenith during the reign of Louis XIV (1643-1715) when it became an absolute monarchy and the foremost power in Europe. Although his reign marks the golden age of French culture, the domestic abuses and extravagance of Louis XIV plunged France into a series of costly wars. This, along with a system of special privileges granted the nobility and other favored groups, weakened the monarchy, brought France to bankruptcy - and laid the way for the French Revolution of 1789-94 that shook Europe and affected the whole world.

The monarchy was abolished and the First Republic formed in 1793. The new government fell in 1799 to a coup led by Napoleon Bonaparte who, after declaring himself First Consul for life, had himself proclaimed emperor of France and king of Italy. Napoleon's military victories made him master of much of Europe, but his disastrous Russian campaign of 1812 initiated a series of defeats that led to his abdication in 1814 and exile to the island of Elba. The monarchy was briefly restored under Louis XVIII. Napoleon returned to France in March 1815, but his efforts to regain power were totally crushed at the Battle of Waterloo. He was exiled to the island of St. Helena where he died in 1821.

The monarchy under Louis XVIII was again restored in 1815, but the ultrareactionary regime of Charles X (1824-30) was overthrown by a liberal revolution and Louis Philippe of Orleans replaced him as monarch. The monarchy was ousted by the Revolution of 1848 and the Second Republic proclaimed. Louis Napoleon Bonaparte (nephew of Napoleon I) was elected president of the Second Republic. He was proclaimed emperor in 1852. As Napoleon III, he gave France two decades of prosperity under a stable, autocratic regime, but led it to defeat in the Franco-Prussian War of 1870, after which the Third Republic was established.

The Third Republic endured until 1940 and ended with the capitulation of France to the swiftly maneuvering German forces. Marshal Henri Petain formed a puppet government that sued for peace and ruled unoccupied France from Vichy. Meanwhile, General Charles de Gaulle escaped to London where he formed a wartime government in exile and the Free French army. Charles de Gaulle's provisional exile government was officially recognized by the Allies after the liberation of Paris in 1944, and de Gaulle, who had been serving as head of the provisional government, was formally elected to that position. In October 1945, the people overwhelmingly rejected a return to the prewar government, thus paving the way for the formation of the Fourth Republic.

Charles de Gaulle was unanimously elected president of the Fourth Republic, but resigned in January 1946 when leftists withdrew their support. In actual operation, the Fourth Republic was remarkably like the Third, with the National Assembly the focus of power. The later years of the Fourth Republic were marked by a burst of industrial expansion unmatched in modern French history. The growth rate, however, was marred by a nagging inflationary trend that weakened the franc and undermined the competitive posture of France's export trade. This and the Algerian conflict led to the recall of de Gaulle to power, the adoption of a new constitution vesting strong powers in the executive, and establishment in 1958 of the current Fifth Republic.

Note: Certain listings encompassing issues of various banks and regional authorities are contained in Volume 1, Specialized Issues.

RULERS:

Louis XIV, 1643-1715
Louis XV, 1715-74
Louis XVI, 1774-93
First Republic, 1793-94, L'An 2
Directory, 1795-99, L'An 4-7
Consulate, 1799-1803, L'An 8-11
Napoleon as Consul, 1799-1804
Napoleon I as Emperor, 1804-14
(First Restoration)
Louis XVIII, 1814-15
Napoleon I, 1815
(Second Restoration)
Louis XVIII, 1815-24
Charles X, 1824-30
Louis Philippe, 1830-48
Second Republic, 1848-52
Napoleon III, 1852-70

MONETARY SYSTEM:

1 Livre = 20 Sols (Sous)
1 Ecu = 6 Livres
1 Louis D'or = 4 Ecus to 1794
1 Franc = 10 Decimes = 100 Centimes, 1794-1960
1 Nouveau Franc = 100 "old" Francs, 1960-1962
1 Franc = 100 Centimes, 1962-2002
1 Euro = 100 Cents, 2002-

FRENCH DENOMINATIONS

1 Un
2 Deux
3 Trois
4 Quatre
5 Cinq
6 Six
7 Sept
8 Huit
9 Neuf
10 Dix
11 Onze
12 Douze
13 Treize
14 Quatorze
15 Quinze
16 Seize
20 Vingt
25 Vingt-Cinq
30 Trente
40 Quarante
10 Cinquante
80 Quatre-Vingts
90 Quatre-Vingt-Dix
100 Cent
125 Cent Vingt-Cinq
200 Deux Cents
250 Deux Cent Cinquante
300 Trois Cents
400 Quatre Cents
500 Cinq Cents
750 Sept Cent Cinquante
1000 Mille
2000 Deux Mille
5000 Cinq Mille
10,000 Dix Mille

KINGDOM

For the early issues values are given for the most commonly available type.

BILLETS DE MONOYE

1701-1710 ISSUE

A1 25-10,000 Livres — Good Fine XF
1701-1710.

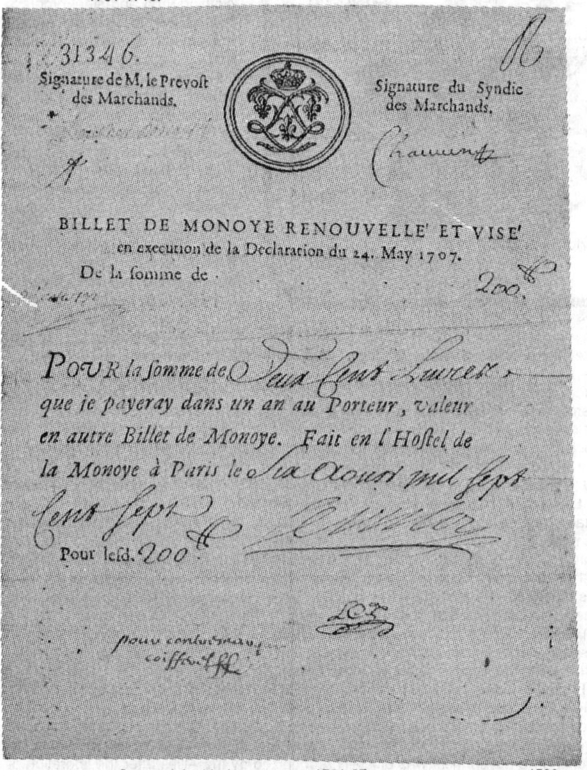

	Good	Fine	XF
a. Crowned double *L* monogram. 1701-07.	1500.	3500.	5500.

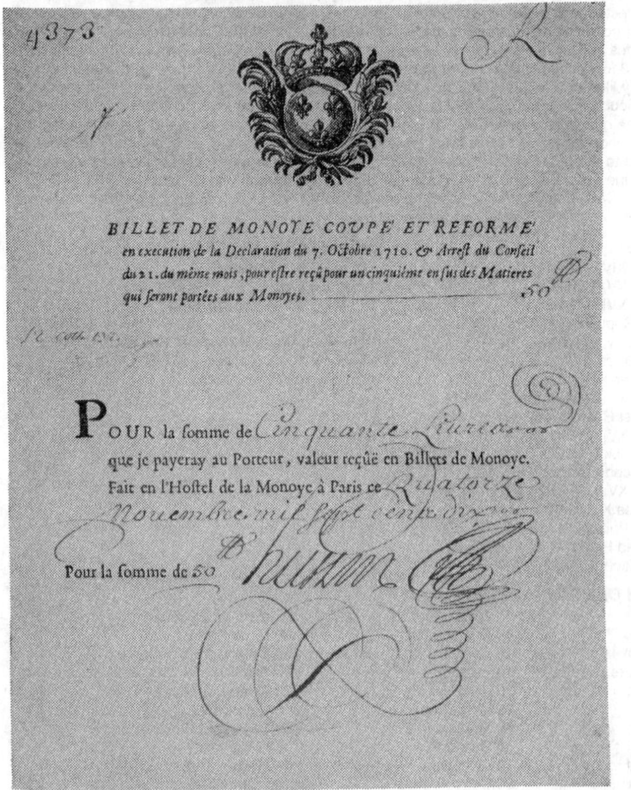

	Good	Fine	XF
b. Crowned fleur-de-lis. 1709-10.	1500.	3500.	5500.

BILLETS DE L'ESTAT

1716 ISSUE

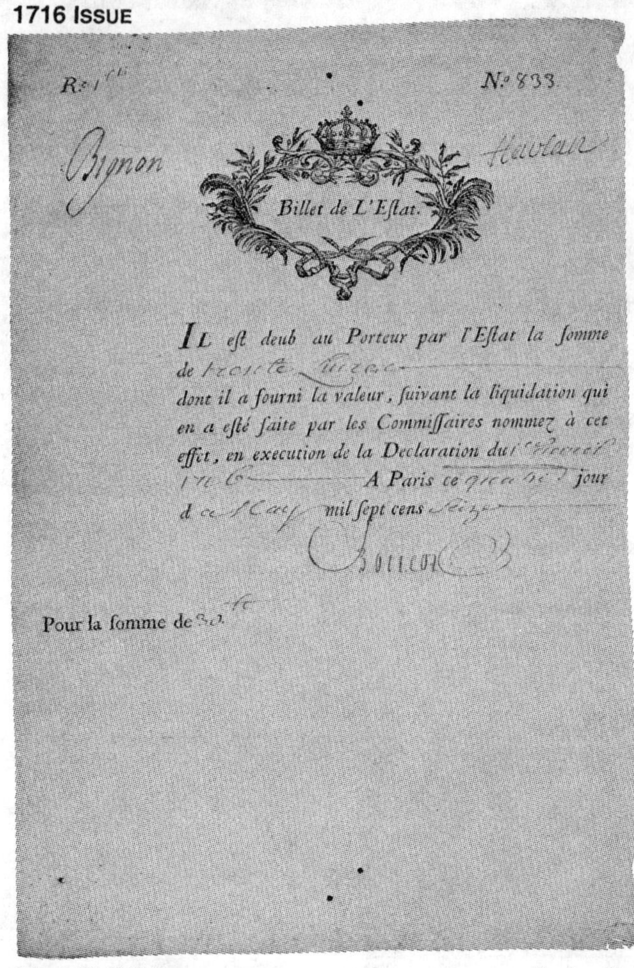

		Good	Fine	XF
A2	**30-1000 Livres** 1716.	1500.	3500.	5500.

LA BANQUE GÉNÉRALE

1716 ISSUE

		Good	Fine	XF
A3	**10 Ecus** 16.6.1716-9.11.1717.	—	—	—
A4	**40 Ecus** 13.10.1716-9.11.1717	—	—	—
A5	**100 Ecus** 16.6.1716-8.3.1718.	—	—	—
A6	**400 Ecus** 13.10.1716-8.3.1718.	—	—	—
A7	**1000 Ecus** 16.6.1716-8.3.1718.	—	—	—

1718 ISSUE

		Good	Fine	XF
A8	**10 Ecus** 8.6.1718; 30.8.1718.	—	—	—
A9	**50 Ecus** 8.6.1718; 30.8.1718; 18.10.1718.	—	—	—
A10	**500 Ecus** 8.6.1718; 30.8.1718; 18.10.1718.	—	—	—

LA BANQUE ROYALE

1719-20 ISSUE

#A12-A15 engraved ornamented monogram at l. edge.

		Good	Fine	XF
A12	**10 Livres** 1.4.1719; 25.7.1719.	300.	700.	1200.

NOTICE

Readers with unlisted dates, signature varieties, etc. are invited to submit photocopies or, high resolution (300 dpi, 100% size) scans of their notes to: Standard Catalog of World Paper Money, 700 East State St. Iola, WI 54990-0001, or E-Mail: george.cuhaj@fwpubs.com.

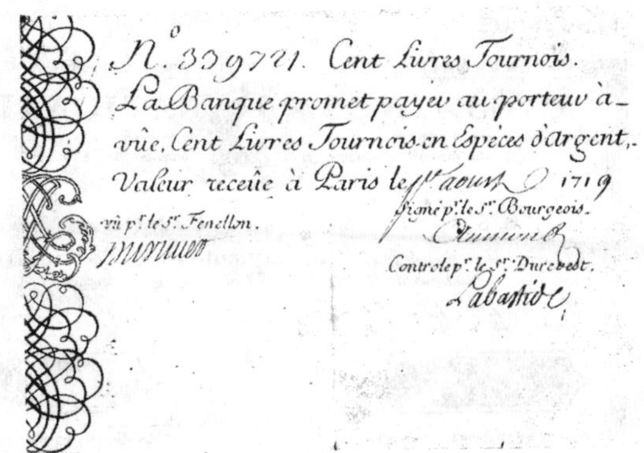

		Good	Fine	XF
A13	**100 Livres** 10.1.1719-1.1.1720.	500.	1250.	2250.
A14	**1000 Livres** 10.1.1719-1.1.1720.	500.	1250.	2250.
A15	**10,000 Livres** 1.1.1720.	—	—	—

1720 First Issue

#A16-A23 lettered l. edge.

		Good	Fine	XF
A16	**10 Livres** 1.1.1720.			
	a. W/o text: *...en Espèces d'Argent.*	250.	600.	1000.
	b. W/text: *...en Espèces d'Argent.*	65.00	175.	350.
A17	**100 Livres** 1.1.1720.			
	a. W/o text: *...en Espèces d'Argent.*	300.	700.	1200.
	b. W/text: *...en Espèces d'Argent.*	65.00	175.	350.

		Good	Fine	XF
A18	**1000 Livres** 1.1.1720.			
	a. W/o text: *...en Espèces d'Argent.*	—	—	—
	b. W/text: *...en Espèces d'Argent.*	200.	500.	900.
A19	**10,000 Livres** 1.1.1720.	—	—	—

1720 Second Issue

		Good	Fine	XF
A20	**10 Livres** 1.7.1720.			
	a. W/text: *...payer au Porteur a vue Dix livres Tournois.*	65.00	175.	350.
	b. W/text: *...payer au Porteur Dix livres a vue Tournois.*	250.	600.	1000.
	c. W/text: *...espèces* (instead of *Espèces*).	—	—	—
A21	**100 Livres** 1.7.1720.	200.	500.	900.

1720 Third Issue

		Good	Fine	XF
A22	**10 Livres** 2.9.1720.	200.	500.	900.

		Good	Fine	XF
A23	**50 Livres** 2.9.1720.	150.	350.	650.

Caisse d'Escompte

1776 Issue

#A24-A27 w/o text: *Promesse d'Assignat.*

		Good	Fine	XF
A24	**200 Livres** 1776-90. Green paper.	700.	1750.	2750.
A25	**300 Livres** 1776-90. Blue paper.	800.	2000.	3500.
A26	**600 Livres** 1776-90.	—	—	—

		Good	Fine	XF
A27	**1000 Livres** 1776-90.	250.	600.	1000.

1790 Issue

#A24A-A27A w/text: *Promesse d'Assignat.*

		Good	Fine	XF
A24A	**200 Livres** 1790-93.	—	—	—
A25A	**300 Livres** 1790-93.	—	—	—
A26A	**600 Livres** 1790-93.	—	—	—
A27A	**1000 Livres** 1790-93.	—	—	—

NOTICE

Readers with unlisted dates, signature varieties, etc. are invited to submit photocopies or, high resolution (300 dpi, 100% size) scans of their notes to: Standard Catalog of World Paper Money, 700 East State St. Iola, WI 54990-0001, or E-Mail: george.cuhaj@fwpubs.com.

ASSIGNATS

DOMAINES NATIONAUX

1789 ISSUE

#A28-A30 bust Kg. Louis XVI at upper ctr.

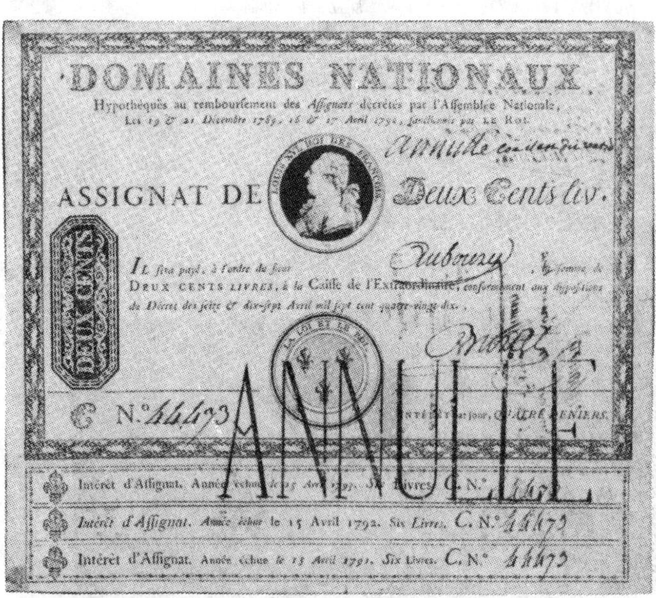

		Good	Fine	XF
A28	**200 Livres** 19&21.12.1789 and 16&17.4.1790.			
	a. Issued note complete w/3 coupons.	—	—	—
	b. Issued note w/o coupons.	350.	1250.	1750.
	c. Cancelled w/ovpt: *ANNULE*.	—	—	—
A29	**300 Livres** 19&21.12.1789 and 16&17.4.1790. Pink paper.			
	a. Issued note complete w/3 coupons.	—	—	—
	b. Issued note w/o coupons.	450.	1500.	2000.

		Good	Fine	XF
A30	**1000 Livres** 19&20.12.1789 and 16&17.4.1790. Red.			
	a. Issued note complete w/3 coupons.	—	—	—
	b. Issued note w/o coupons.	1200.	2200.	4000.

1790 INTEREST COUPONS

		Good	Fine	XF
A31	**6 Livres** 16/17.4.1790. Coupon of #A28.			
A32	**9 Livres** 16/17.4.1790. Coupon of #A29.			
	a. Single coupon. Rare.	—	—	—
	b. Sheet of 3 coupons. Rare.	—	—	—
A33	**30 Livres** 16/17.1790. Coupon of #A30.			
	a. Single coupon. Rare.	—	—	—
	b. Sheet of 3 coupons. Rare.	—	—	—

1790 ISSUE

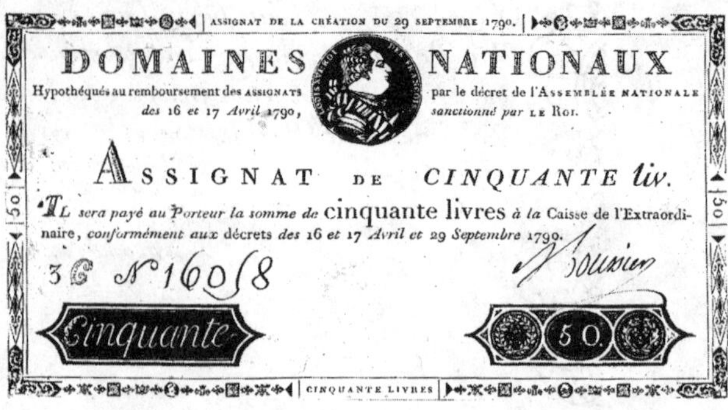

		Good	Fine	XF
A34	**50 Livres** 29.9.1790. Kg. Louis XVI at top ctr.	30.00	100.	150.
A35	**60 Livres** 29.9.1790. Kg. Louis XVI at top ctr.	40.00	120.	175.
A36	**70 Livres** 29.9.1790. Kg. Louis XVI at top ctr.	40.00	120.	175.
A37	**80 Livres** 29.9.1790. Kg. Louis XVI at top ctr.	40.00	120.	175.

		Good	Fine	XF
A38	**90 Livres** 29.9.1790. Kg. Louis XVI at top ctr.	45.00	125.	175.
A39	**100 Livres** 29.9.1790. Kg. Louis XVI at top ctr.	50.00	135.	200.

		Good	Fine	XF
A40	**500 Livres** 29.9.1790. Kg. Louis XVI at top l.	70.00	225.	350.
A41	**2000 Livres** 29.9.1790. Red. Kg. Louis XVI at top l.	1200.	2200.	4000.

1791 FIRST ISSUE

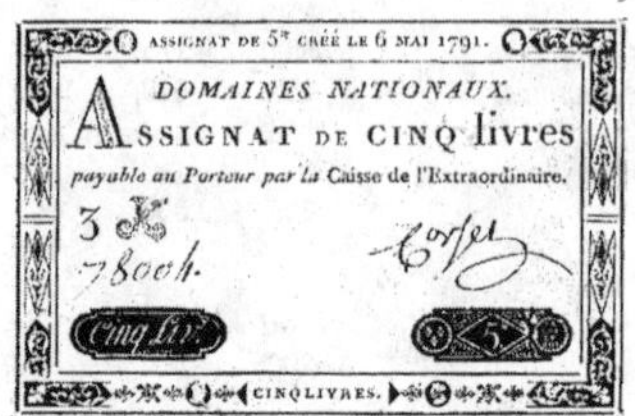

		Good	Fine	XF
A42	**5 Livres** 6.5.1791.	3.00	7.00	15.00
A43	**50 Livres** 19.6.1791. Kg. Louis XVI at top ctr.	30.00	100.	150.
A44	**60 Livres** 19.6.1791. Kg. Louis XVI at top ctr.	40.00	120.	175.

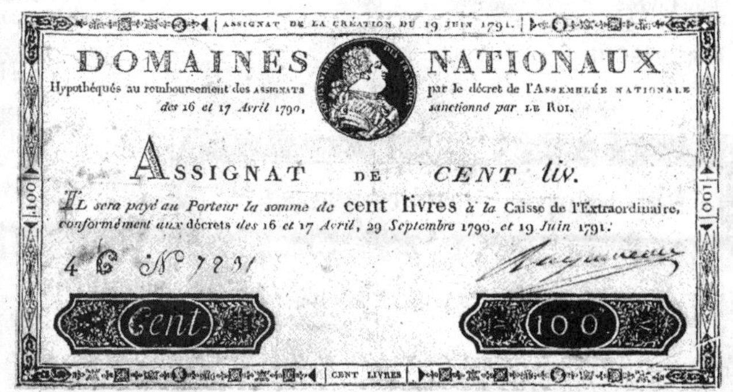

		Good	Fine	XF
A44A	**100 Livres** 19.6.1791. Kg. Louis XVI at top. ctr.	30.00	100.	150.
A46	**500 Livres** 19.6.1791. Kg. Louis XVI at top ctr.	150.	450.	600.

1791 Second Issue

		Good	Fine	XF
A47	**200 Livres** 19.6/12.9.1791. Kg. Louis XVI at top ctr.	40.00	120.	175.

		Good	Fine	XF
A48	**300 Livres** 19.6/12.9.1791. Kg. Louis XVI at top ctr.	45.00	160.	250.

1791 Third Issue

		Good	Fine	XF
A49	**5 Livres** 28.9.1791. Like #A42.	3.00	6.00	15.00
A50	**5 Livres** 1.11.1791. Like #A42.	3.00	6.00	15.00

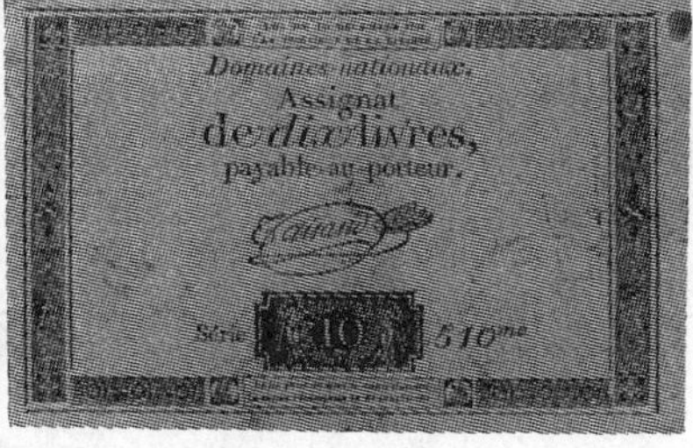

		Good	Fine	XF
A51	**10 Livres** 16.12.1791.	1.50	4.00	12.00

		Good	Fine	XF
A52	**25 Livres** 16.12.1791. Kg. Louis XVI at top r., standing figure w/Constitution at top l.	12.00	25.00	60.00

1792 First Issue

		VG	VF	UNC
A53	**10 Sous** 4.1.1792. Fasces l. and r., 2 women w/Liberty cap on pole at lower ctr.	1.00	3.00	5.00
A54	**15 Sols** 4.1.1792. 2 seated women w/Liberty cap on pole at lower ctr.	1.00	3.00	5.00
A55	**25 Sols** 4.1.1792. Eye at upper ctr., rooster at lower ctr.	1.50	4.00	7.50

		VG	VF	UNC
A56	**50 Sols** 4.1.1792. Allegorical woman at lower l. and r.	1.00	3.00	5.00
A57	**5 Livres** 30.4.1792. Like #A42.	5.00	8.00	15.00
A58	**50 Livres** 30.4.1792. Kg. Louis XVI at top ctr.	35.00	70.00	100.
A59	**200 Livres** 30.4.1792. Kg. Louis XVI at top ctr.	45.00	85.00	120.

1792 Second Issue

		VG	VF	UNC
A60	**5 Livres** 27.6.1792. Like #A42.	2.00	6.00	12.00
A61	**5 Livres** 31.7.1792. Like #A42.	2.00	6.00	12.00
A62	**50 Livres** 31.8.1792. Like #A58. Kg. Louis XVI at top ctr.	40.00	80.00	110.
A63	**200 Livres** 31.8.1792. Like #A59. Kg. Louis XVI at top ctr.	45.00	90.00	120.

1792 Third Issue

		VG	VF	UNC
A64	**10 Sous** 24.10.1792. Like #A53. Fasces l. and r., two women w/Liberty cap on pole at lower ctr.			
	a. Issued note.	1.50	4.00	7.50
	b. Error note w/text: *La loi punit...* at lower l., repeated at lower r.	50.00	200.	400.
A65	**15 Sols** 24.10.1792. Like #A54. 2 seated women w/Liberty cap on pole at lower ctr.	1.50	4.00	7.50

		VG	VF	UNC
A66	**10 Livres** 24.10.1792. Like #A51.			
	a. Wmk: Fleur-de-lis.	5.00	12.00	25.00
	b. Wmk. *RP-FR* top left. *X.*	1.50	4.00	7.50
A67	**25 Livres** 24.10.1792. Like #A52. standing figure w/Constitution at top l., Kg. Louis XVI at top r.	8.00	20.00	40.00

1793 Issue

		VG	VF	UNC
A68	**10 Sous** 23.5.1793. Like #A53. Fasces l. and r.			
	a. Wmk: *LA NATION...* Series 1/16.	3.00	7.50	15.00
	b. Wmk: *RF/Xs.*	1.50	4.00	7.50
	c. Error note w/text: *La loi puni...*at lower l., repeated at lower r.	50.00	200.	400.

		VG	VF	UNC
A69	**15 Sols** 23.5.1793. Like #A54. 2 seated women w/Liberty cap on pole at lower ctr.			
	a. Wmk: *LA NATION*... Series 1/42.	3.00	7.50	15.00
	b. Wmk: *RF/15s*.	1.50	4.00	7.50
	c. Error note w/text: *LA NATION*...at lower r., repeated at lower l.	50.00	200.	400.

		VG	VF	UNC
A70	**50 Sols** 23.5.1793. Like #A56. Allegorical women at lower l. and r.			
	a. Wmk: *LA NATION*... Series 1/36.	3.00	7.50	15.00
	b. Wmk. *RF/50s*.	1.50	3.00	4.50

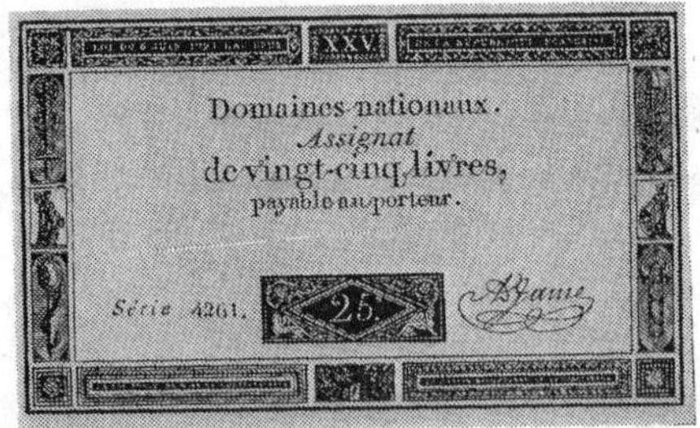

		VG	VF	UNC
A71	**25 Livres** 6.6.1793. Small standing figures at l. and r. border.	1.50	5.00	10.00

RÉPUBLIQUE FRANÇAISE

1792 ISSUE

		VG	VF	UNC
A72	**50 Livres** 14.12.1792. Seated figure w/shovel on pedestal at lower ctr.	6.00	15.00	30.00

		VG	VF	UNC
A73	**400 Livres** 21.11.1792. Eagle and Liberty cap at lower ctr., sun w/rays behind.	10.00	20.00	40.00

1793 FIRST ISSUE

		VG	VF	UNC
A74	**125 Livres** 7 Vendemiaire An II (28.9.1793).	4.00	8.00	15.00

		VG	VF	UNC
A75	**250 Livres** 7 Vendemiaire An II (28.9.1793).	5.00	12.00	25.00

1793 SECOND ISSUE

		VG	VF	UNC
A76	**5 Livres** 10 Brumaire An II (31.10.1793).	2.00	5.00	10.00

1794 ISSUE

		VG	VF	UNC
A77	**500 Livres** 20 Pluviose An II (8.2.1794).	5.00	12.00	25.00

1795 FRANC ISSUE

		Good	Fine	XF
A78	**100 Francs** 18 Nivose An III (7.1.1795).	3.00	6.00	15.00

		Good	Fine	XF
A79	**750 Francs** 18 Nivose An III (7.1.1795).	400.	1100.	1800.

		Good	Fine	XF
A80	**1000 Francs** 18 Nivose An III (7.1.1795). Red.	15.00	40.00	75.00

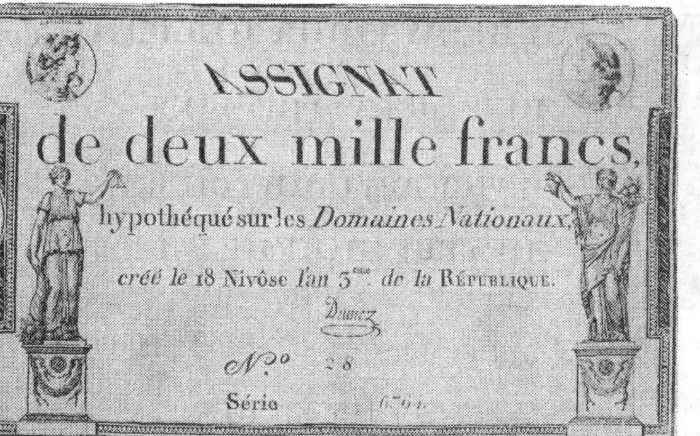

		Good	Fine	XF
A81	**2000 Francs** 18 Nivôse An III (7.1.1795).	25.00	60.00	150.

		Good	Fine	XF
A82	**10,000 Francs** 18 Nivôse An III (7.1.1795).	60.00	150.	250.

PROMESSES DE MANDATS TERRITORIAUX

1796 ISSUE

Sign. varieties.

		Good	Fine	XF
A83	**25 Francs** 28 Ventôse An IV (18.3.1796). Black and olive.			
	a. W/o *Serie.*	15.00	30.00	60.00
	b. W/*Serie.*	6.00	15.00	25.00

		Good	Fine	XF
A84	**100 Francs** 28 Ventôse An IV (18.3.1796). Red and blue-gray.			
	a. W/o *Serie.*	30.00	70.00	125.
	b. W/*Serie.*	8.00	25.00	50.00
A85	**250 Francs** 28 Ventôse An IV (18.3.1796). Olive and black.			
	a. W/o *Serie.*	25.00	70.00	125.
	b. W/*Serie.*	12.00	35.00	75.00

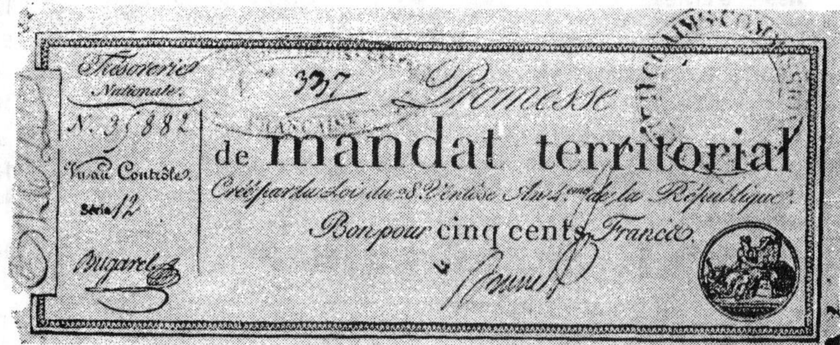

No.	Description	Good	Fine	XF
A86	**500 Francs**			
	28 Ventose An IV (18.3.1796). Gray-blue and red.			
	a. W/o *Serie.*	30.00	70.00	125.
	b. W/*Serie.*	15.00	30.00	65.00

MANDATS TERRITORIAL

1796 ISSUE

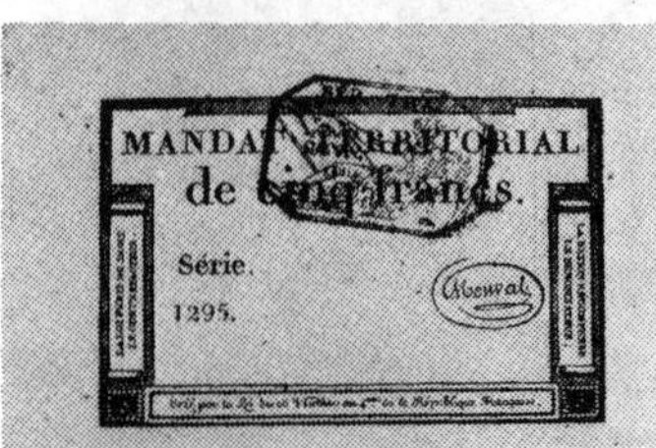

No.	Description	Good	Fine	XF
A87	**5 Francs**			
	28 Ventose An IV (18.3.1796).			
	a. W/o handstamp.	400.	800.	1300.
	b. Black handstamp: *Rep. Fra.*	50.00	100.	200.
	c. Red handstamp: *Rep. Fra.*	50.00	100.	200.

RESCRIPTIONS DE L'EMPRUNT FORCÉ

1796 ISSUE

No.	Description	Good	Fine	XF
A88	**25 Francs**	175.	400.	650.
	21 Nivôse An IV (11.1.1796).			
A89	**50 Francs**	300.	700.	1100.
	21 Nivôse An IV (11.1.1796).			

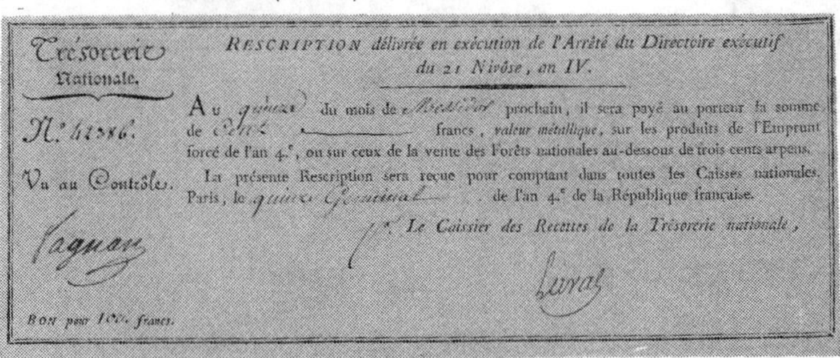

No.	Description	Good	Fine	XF
A90	**100 Francs**	175.	400.	650.
	21 Nivôse An IV (11.1.1796).			
A91	**250 Francs**	350.	750.	1200.
	21 Nivôse An IV (11.1.1796).			
A92	**500 Francs**	500.	1200.	2000.
	21 Nivôse An IV (11.1.1796).			
A93	**1000 Francs**	650.	1500.	2500.
	21 Nivôse An IV (11.1.1796).			

ARMÉE CATHOLIQUE ET ROYALE

1793 ISSUE

No.	Description	Good	Fine	XF
A94	**Sous or Livres**	—	—	—
	2.8.1793. Assignats w/handwritten notice: *Au nom du Roi bon pour...* (In the name of the king good for...)			

1793-94 BONS DE MANLEVRIER

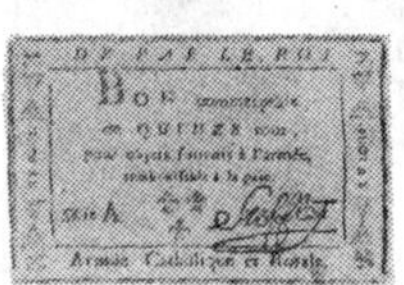

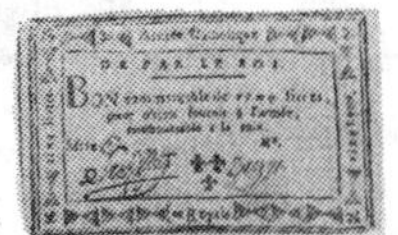

No.	Description	Good	Fine	XF
A94A	**10 Sous**	35.00	100.	250.
	ND (1794).			
A94B	**15 Sous**	35.00	100.	250.
	ND (1794).			
A95	**5 Livres**	35.00	100.	250.
	ND (Nov. 1793).			

NOTICE

Readers with unlisted dates, signature varieties, etc. are invited to submit photocopies or, high resolution (300 dpi, 100% size) scans of their notes to: Standard Catalog of World Paper Money, 700 East State St. Iola, WI 54990-0001, or E-Mail: george.cuhaj@fwpubs.com.

No.	Description	Good	Fine	XF
A96	**10 Livres**	50.00	150.	400.
	ND (Nov. 1793).			
A97	**25 Livres**	65.00	200.	500.
	ND (Nov. 1793).			
A98	**50 Livres**	75.00	225.	550.
	ND (Nov. 1793).			
A99	**100 Livres**	85.00	250.	600.
	ND (Nov. 1793).			

1794 BONS DE PASSAGE

No.	Description	Good	Fine	XF
A100	**Livres-various handwritten amt**			
	ND (1794). Deep red. Louis XVII at top ctr. Uniface.			
	a. Issued note.	750.	1500.	—
	r. Remainder w/o sign. or value filled in.	500.	1000.	—
	x. Printed *500 Livre* (counterfeit).	25.00	50.00	100.

DIRECTORATE & CONSULATE THROUGH SECOND REPUBLIC

BON AU PORTEUR (DIRECTORATE, 1795-99)

1798 ISSUE

No.	Description	Good	Fine	XF
A121	**25 Francs**			
	An VII (1798). Black.			
	a. W/o red text: *TRESIE NATL* at upper r.	75.00	150.	325.
	b. W/red text: *TRESIE NATL* at upper r.	85.00	200.	450.

BON AU PORTEUR (CONSULATE, 1799-1804)

1799 ISSUE

No.	Description	Good	Fine	XF
A131	**25 Francs**			
	(1799-1801). Black.			
	a. An VIII (1799).	75.00	150.	325.
	c. An X (1801).	75.00	150.	325.

BANQUE DE FRANCE

1800 PROVISIONAL ISSUE

No.	Description	Good	Fine	XF
1	**500 Francs**	—	—	—
	1800. Blue and red. Ovpt: *Payable a la Banque de France* on Caisse de Comptes Courants notes.			
2	**1000 Francs**	—	—	—
	1800. Black and red. Ovpt: *Payable a La Banque de France* on Caisse de Compte Courants notes. Rare.			

1800 REGULAR ISSUE

No.	Description	Good	Fine	XF
5	**500 Francs**	—	—	—
	21.6.1800-27.10.1802. Blue and red. Name as *Banque de France.* Rare.			
10	**1000 Francs**	—	—	—
	21.6.1800-28.4.1802. Black and red. Name as *Banque de France.* Rare.			

1803-06 ISSUE

No.	Description	Good	Fine	XF
15	**500 Francs**	—	—	—
	19.2.1806-29.8.1806. Allegorical figures at l. and r. Rare.			
16	**1000 Francs**	—	—	—
	14.4.1803-16.4.1812. Allegorical figures at l. and r. 4 sign. varieties. Rare.			

1810-14 Issue

#	Note	Good	Fine	XF
20	**250 Francs** 27.9.1810-2.1.1812. Green paper. W/text: *Comptoir de Lille...* Rare.	—	—	—
21	**1000 Francs** 25.4.1814-4.4.1816. Printed seal at upper l. and r. Rare.	—	—	—

1817-18 Issue

#	Note	Good	Fine	XF
25	**500 Francs** 2.1.1818-3.7.1828. Women at top ctr. and at l., Mercury at r.			
	a. Wmk: *Cinq Cents 500 Fr.* Date handwritten. 6 sign. varieties. Up to 8.8.1822. Rare.	—	—	—
	b. Wmk: *Cinq Cents Fr. Banque de France BF.* Date handwritten. 8.4.1824-22.5.1825. Rare.	—	—	—
	c. Date printed. 19.4.1827-3.7.1828. Rare.	—	—	—
26	**1000 Francs** 1817-29. Woman in chariot drawn by lions at top ctr., seated allegorical figures at l. and r.			
	a. Wmk: *Mille Francs 1000 Fr.* Rose field. 3 sign. varieties. 17.4.1817-8.4.1824. Rare.	—	—	—
	b. Wmk: Like "a", but rusty-brown field. 6 sign. varieties. 27.11.1817-13.3.1823. Rare.	—	—	—
	c. Wmk: *Mille Francs - Banque de France.* 20.1.1825-14.5.1829. Rare.	—	—	—

1829 Issue

#	Note	Good	Fine	XF
30	**500 Francs** 5.3.1829-15.9.1831. Women at top ctr. and l., Mercury at r. Top l. and r. text in circle.			
	a. Sign. title: *LE DIRECTEUR.* 2 sign. varieties. Up to 22.4.1830. Rare.	—	—	—
	b. Sign. title: *LE SECRÉTAIRE DU GOUVERNEMENT DE LA BANQUE.* 2 sign. varieties. 15.9.1831. Rare.	—	—	—
31	**1000 Francs** 26.11.1829-3.2.1831. Women in chariot drawn by lions at top ctr. Seated allegorical figures at l. and r. *Banque de France* stamped.			
	a. Sign. title: *LE DIRECTEUR.* 3 sign. varieties. 25.3.1830. Rare.	—	—	—
	b. Sign. title: *LE SECRÉTAIRE DU GOUVERNEMENT DE LA BANQUE.* Rare.	—	—	—

1831-37 Issue

#	Note	Good	Fine	XF
35	**250 Francs** 9.6.1836-13.8.1846. Green paper. Women at top ctr. and at l., Mercury at r., 2 reclining women at bottom ctr.			
	a. Sign. title: *Secrétaire du Gouvernement de la Banque.* Up to 14.10.1841. Rare.	—	—	—
	b. Sign. title: *Secrétaire Général 14.12.1843.* Rare.	—	—	—
36	**500 Francs** 1831-43. Like #30 but back printed in reverse. Women at top ctr. and l. Mercury at r. Top l. and r. text in circle.			
	a. Sign. title: *LE SECRÉTAIRE DU GOUVERNEMENT DE LA BANQUE.* 3 sign. varieties. 15.9.1831-25.11.1841. Rare.	—	—	—
	b. Sign. title: *LE SECRÉTAIRE GÉNÉRAL.* 25.6.1842-13.7.1843. Rare.	—	—	—
37	**1000 Francs** 15.9.1831-25.11.1841. Like #31, but back printed in reverse. Women in chariot drawn by lions at top ctr., seated allegorical figures at l. and r. *Bank de France* stamped. 3 sign. varieties. Rare.	—	—	—
38	**1000 Francs** 28.2.1837-17.2.1848. Like #37, but *Comptoir de ...* (name of place) stamped. Women in chariot drawn by lions at top ctr., seated allegorical figures at l. and r. Rare.	—	—	—

1842-46 Issue

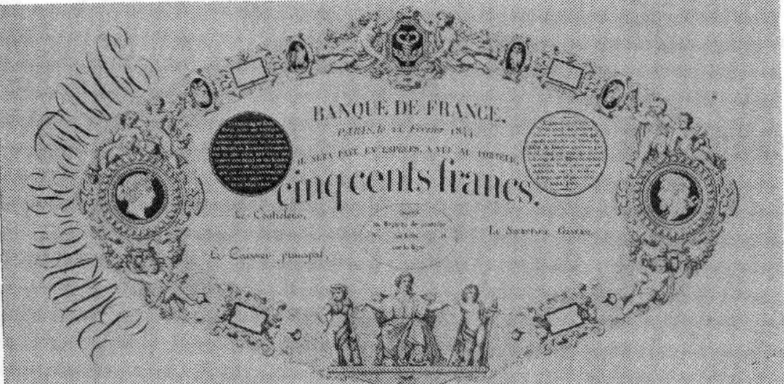

#	Note	Good	Fine	XF
40	**500 Francs** 1844-63. Woman at l., man at r., woman seated at bottom ctr. w/2 cherubs.			
	a. Wmk: *Cinq Cents Fr. Banque de France.* 22.2.1844. Rare.	—	—	—
	b. wmk: *Cinq Cents Fr. Banque de France BF.* 5.9.1844-21.10.1847. Rare.	—	—	—
	c. Wmk: *500 F. Cinq Cents Fr. Banque de France.* 6 sign. varieties. 21.4.1848-15.1.1863. Rare.	—	—	—

NOTICE

Readers with unlisted dates, signature varieties, etc. are invited to submit photocopies or, high resolution (300 dpi, 100% size) scans of their notes to: Standard Catalog of World Paper Money, 700 East State St. Iola, WI 54990-0001, or E-Mail: george.cuhaj@fwpubs.com.

#	Note	Good	Fine	XF
41	**1000 Francs** 25.6.1842-13.11.1862. 2 female allegorical figures at l., r., top ctr. and at bottom ctr.			
	a. Wmk: *Mille Francs - Banque de France.* 25.6.1842-24.10.1844. Rare.	—	—	—
	b. Wmk: *1000 Fr. Mille Francs - Banque de France.* 7 sign. varieties. From 24.10.1844. Rare.	—	—	—
	c. Name of branch bank below *Banque de France.* 12.10.1848-27.9.1849. Rare.	—	—	—
	d. Name of branch bank on counterfoil at r. 28.1.1850-23.8.1860. Rare.	—	—	—
42	**5000 Francs** 28.5.1846. Red. Women in chariot drawn by lions at top ctr. Seated allegorical figure at l. and r. 2 sign. varieties. Rare.	—	—	—

1848 Provisional Issue

#	Note	Good	Fine	XF
44	**100 Francs** 1848. Black on green unpt.			
	a. Sign. in script. 16.3.1848. Rare.	—	—	—
	b. Printed sign. Serial # at l. and r. 4.5.1848. Rare.	—	—	—
	c. Printed sign. Serial # at r., series letter at l. 15.7.1848. Rare.	—	—	—

1847-48 Regular Issues

#	Note	Good	Fine	XF
45	**100 Francs** 1848-63. Woman at top ctr., woman at l., 2 recumbent women at bottom.			
	a. Sign. black. 14.9.1848-24.1.1856. Rare.	—	—	—
	b. Sign. blue. 2 sign. varieties. 25.1.1856-8.1.1863. Rare.	—	—	—
46	**200 Francs** 10.6.1847-27.10.1864. Woman at l., Mercury at r., 2 recumbent women at bottom ctr. Oval frame. Various succursales (branches).			
	a. W/o name of branch bank below *BANQUE DE FRANCE* and w/3 sign. varieties. Rare.	—	—	—
	b. Name of branch bank below *BANQUE DE FRANCE* and w/4 sign. Rare.	—	—	—
	c. Name of branch bank in blue printing on counterfoil at r. Rare.	—	—	—
47	**200 Francs** 9.3.1848-30.3.1848. Yellowish paper. Woman in chariot drawn by lions at top ctr. Square frame. Rare.	—	—	—

1862-68 Issue

#	Note	Good	Fine	XF
50	**50 Francs** 1864-66. Blue. 2 cherubs, coat of arms at bottom ctr.			
	a. Wmk: *B-F.* 2.3.1864-6.6.1864.	2500.	4250.	9000.
	b. Wmk: Head of Mercury. 7.6.1864-8.6.1866.	2500.	4250.	9000.

#	Note	Good	Fine	XF
51	**50 Francs** 26.11.1868-16.11.1883. Blue and black. Like #50. 2 cherubs, arms at bottom ctr.			
	a. Printed serial # at upper l. and lower r. 4 sign. varieties. Paris printing.	1000.	2000.	6250.
	b. Handwritten serial # at upper l. and lower r., star at l., r., and above denomination. Clermont-Ferrand printing. 15.9.1870-27.10.1870.	—	—	—
52	**100 Francs** 1863-82. Blue. Allegorical figures of 4 women and numerous cherubs.			

#		Good	Fine	XF
52	a. Blue serial #, date on back. 8.1.1863-19.6.1866.	1800.	3500.	—
	b. Black serial #, date on face, 4 sign. varieties. 23.8.1866-13.4.1882.	700.	1500.	7000.
53	**500 Francs** 1863-87. Woman at l., man at r., woman seated at bottom ctr. w/2 cherubs. Back and face w/same imprint.			
	a. Blue serial #. 5.11.1863-2.4.1868.	2800.	6000.	—
	b. Black serial #. Sign. title: *LE CONTROLEUR*. 5 sign. varieties. 25.6.1868-19.6.1882.	2800.	6000.	—
	c. Sign. title: *LE CONTROLEUR GÉNÉRAL*. 3 sign. varieties. 20.6.1882-20.8.1887.	2250.	3800.	7000.
54	**1000 Francs** 1862-89. Blue. 2 female allegorical figures at l., r., top and bottom ctr.			
	a. Blue serial #. 4.12.1862-2.11.1866. Rare.	—	—	—
	b. Like a., but name of branch bank below *Banque de France*. Rare.	—	—	—
	c. Black serial #. Sign. title: *LE CONTROLEUR*. 20.6.1867-16.8.1882. Rare.	—	—	—
	d. Like c., but sign. title: *LE CONTROLEUR GÉNÉRAL* 4 sign. varieties. 17.8.1882-28.6.1889. Rare.	—	—	—
	e. Name of branch bank below *BANQUE DE FRANCE* and in red on counterfoil at r. Rare.	—	—	—

1870 Issue

#		Good	Fine	XF
55	**20 Francs** 23.12.1870-29.5.1873. Blue. Seated woman at lower ctr.	150.	450.	2750.

#		Good	Fine	XF
56	**25 Francs** 1870-73. Blue. Like #55. Seated woman at lower ctr.			
	a. Printed serial # at upper l. and lower r. Paris printing. 16.8.1870-17.11.1870; 10.3.1873.	1000.	2000.	5000.
	b. Handwritten serial # at upper l. and lower r., star at l., r. and above denomination (in letters). Clermont-Ferrand printing. 18.11.1870-15.9.1870.	250.	550.	3000.

Third Republic - WWII

Banque de France

Zodiac Signs

- ♒ AQUARIUS: January
- ♓ PISCES: February
- ♈ ARIES: March
- ♉ TAURUS: April
- ♊ GEMINI: May
- ♋ CANCER: June
- ♌ LEO: July
- ♍ VIRGO: August
- ♎ LIBRA: September
- ♏ SCORPIO: October
- ♐ SAGITTARIUS: November
- ♑ CAPRICORN: December

1871-74 Issue

Consecutive dates of the day of printing, thus many varieties of dates and also of sign. quoted were the first and last date of printing (not the date of issue). Listings are given by sign. combination for each note, w/values according to relative scarcity. The signs of the zodiac are used in place of the date on some notes.

#		VG	VF	UNC
60	**5 Francs** 1.12.1871-19.1.1874. Blue, denomination in black. Man standing at l., woman standing w/staff at r. 3 allegorical figures on back.	100.	400.	1000.

#		VG	VF	UNC
61	**20 Francs** 1874-1905. Blue on ochre unpt., denomination in black. Mercury seated at l., woman seated at r. Woman's head at l. and r. on back.			
	a. A. Mignot and Marsaud. 1.7.1874-7.8.1875.	200.	700.	3000.
	b. V. d'Anfreville and Giraud. 1.6.1904.	150.	600.	2000.
	c. Sign. as b. 11.1.1905.	400.	1600.	—

1882-84 Issue

#		VG	VF	UNC
62	**50 Francs** 1884-89. Blue. Women at l. and r., 2 small angels above, caduceus at each corner. Allegorical figures on back.			
	a. Sign. A. Mignot and F. Carre. 1.8.1884-23.10.1885.	1500.	3800.	—
	b. Sign. E. Bertin and F. Carre. 2.1.1886-15.2.1886.	2000.	5500.	—
	c. Sign. E. Bertin and Billotte. 18.10.1888-4.3.1889.	1600.	4000.	—
63	**100 Francs** 1882-88. Blue. 2 women seated.			
	a. Sign. A. Mignot and de Jancigny. 2.1.1882-10.1.1882.	3500.	7500.	—
	b. Sign. A. Mignot and F. Carre. 11.1.1882-31.12.1885.	1000.	3000.	—
	c. Sign. C. Bertin and F. Carre. 2.1.1886-13.1.1888.	1000.	3000.	—
	d. Sign. C. Bertin and Billotte. 16.7.1888-11.9.1888.	1900.	5000.	—

1888-89 Issue

#		VG	VF	UNC
64	**50 Francs** 1889-1927. Blue on lilac unpt. Similar to #62. Women at l. and r., 2 small angels above, caduceus at each corner. 5 women in medallions at ctr. Allegorical figures on back.			
	a. Sign. E. Bertin and Billotte. 1.5.1889-3.8.1889. Rare.	—	—	—
	b. Sign. V. d'Anfreville and Billotte. 27.2.1890-26.5.1900.	225.	500.	—

64		VG	VF	UNC
	c. Sign. V. d'Anfreville and Giraud. 2.1.1901-30.12.1905.	200.	475.	—
	d. Sign. V. d'Anfreville and E. Picard. 2.1.1906-13.7.1907.	175.	450.	—
	e. Sign. J. Laferriere and E. Picard. 16.7.1907-8.11.1919.	22.50	80.00	500.
	f. Sign. J. Laferriere and A. Aupetit. 15.11.1920-6.6.1921.	80.00	275.	—
	g. Sign. L. Platet and A. Aupetit. 1.5.1922-20.4.1925.	17.50	75.00	450.
	h. Sign. L. Platet and P. Strohl. 1.7.1926-25.3.1927.	17.50	75.00	450.

65	100 Francs	VG	VF	UNC
	1888-1909. Blue on pink unpt. Like #63 but 4 women at ctr.			
	a. Sign. C. Bertin and Billotte. 12.9.1888-31.12.1889.	400.	1050.	—
	b. Sign. V. d'Anfreville and Billotte. 2.1.1890-5.7.1900.	180.	500.	—
	c. Sign. V. d'Anfreville and Giraud. 18.7.1900-30.12.1905.	150.	400.	—
	d. Sign. V. d'Anfreville and E. Picard. 2.1.1906-12.3.1907.	150.	400.	—
	e. Sign. J. Laferriere and E. Picard. 1.8.1907-29.1.1909.	140.	375.	1200.

Note: For the 4 provisional ovpt. issues on #65b (old dates 1892-93), see French West Africa #3, Guadeloupe #15, Madagascar #34, and Tunisia #31.

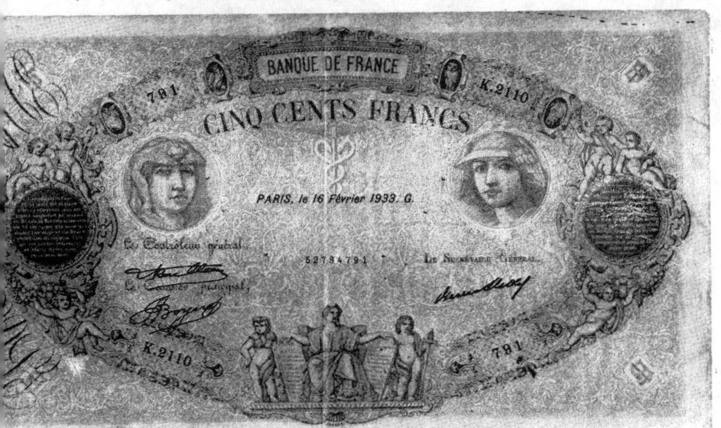

66	500 Francs	VG	VF	UNC
	1888-1937. Blue on lilac unpt. Woman at l., Mercury at r. Ornate oval border w/cherubs, animals and 3 figures at bottom. Allegorical figures on back. Sign. title: *LE CAISSIER PRINCIPAL* added.			
	a. Sign. A. Delmotte, C. Bertin and Billote. 2.11.1888-8.7.1889.	1000.	3500.	—
	b. Sign. A. Delmotte, V. d'Anfreville and Billotte. 9.1.1890-24.4.1897.	700.	1700.	—
	c. Sign. Bouchet, V. d'Anfreville and Billotte. 23.3.1899-30.6.1900.	300.	1400.	—
	d. Sign. Panhard, V. d'Anfreville and Giraud. 7.2.1901-17.4.1902.	250.	1400.	—
	e. Sign. Frachon, V. d'Anfreville and Giraud. 27.8.1903-26.12.1904.	250.	1400.	—
	f. Sign. Frachon, V. d'Anfreville and E. Picard. 22.2.1906-10.9.1906.	250.	1400.	—
	g. Sign. Frachon, J. Laferriere and E. Picard. 24.10.1907-4.10.1917.	75.00	200.	800.
	h. Sign. A. Aupetit, J. Laferriere and E. Picard. 1.4.1920-21.6.1920.	90.00	300.	—
	i. Sign. J. Emmery, J. Laferriere and A. Aupetit. 3.1.1921-9.2.1921.	100.	350.	—
	j. Sign. J. Emmery, L. Platet and A. Aupetit. 1.5.1922-11.9.1924.	50.00	180.	750.
	k. Sign. J. Emmery, L. Platet and P. Strohl. 1.7.1926-26.10.1929.	40.00	100.	500.
	l. Sign. Roulleau, L. Platet and P. Strohl. 1.4.1930-29.12.1932.	30.00	85.00	475.
	m. Sign. Roulleau, J. Boyer and P. Strohl. 12.1.1933-10.6.1937.	30.00	85.00	475.

67	1000 Francs	VG	VF	UNC
	1889-1926. Blue on lilac unpt. Mercury at l., woman in medallion at r., many allegorical figures in border. Allegorical figures on back.			
	a. Sign. A. Delmotte, C. Bertin and Billotte. 7.11.1889-29.11.1889. Rare.	—	—	—
	b. Sign. A. Delmotte, V. d'Anfreville and Billotte. 23.1.1890-14.3.1898.	600.	2200.	—
	c. Sign. Bouchet, V. d'Anfreville and Billotte. 27.10.1898-21.6.1900.	600.	2200.	—
	d. Sign. Panhard, V. d'Anfreville and Giraud. 9.4.1901-10.2.1902.	550.	2000.	—
	e. Sign. Frachon, V. d'Anfreville and Giraud. 23.10.1902-30.12.1905.	500.	1800.	—
	f. Sign. Frachon, V. d'Anfreville and E. Picard. 2.1.1906-23.5.1907.	475.	1600.	—
	g. Sign. Frachon, J. Laferriere and E. Picard. 7.5.1908-24.1.1919.	45.00	100.	650.
	h. Sign. A. Aupetit, J. Laferriere and E. Picard. 15.5.1919-27.2.1920.	45.00	100.	650.
	i. Sign. J Emmery, J. Laferriere and A. Aupetit. 15.11.1920-29.4.1921.	45.00	100.	650.
	j. Sign. J. Emmery, L. Platet and A. Aupetit. 1.5.1922-26.6.1926.	35.00	90.00	600.
	k. Sign. J. Emmery, L. Platet and P. Strohl. 1.7.1926-16.9.1926.	35.00	90.00	600.

1906-08 Issue

68	20 Francs	VG	VF	UNC
	1906-13. Blue on ochre unpt. Like #61 but denomination in blue. Mercury seated at l., women seated at r. Woman's head at l. and r. on back.			
	a. Sign. V. d'Anfreville and E. Picard. 2.1.1906-25.10.1906.	35.00	150.	850.
	b. Sign. J. Laferriere and E. Picard. 2.1.1912-12.2.1913.	30.00	110.	800.
69	**100 Francs**			
	2.1.1908-10.5.1909. M/c. Woman w/child at l. and r. Bale marked *L O M 02* at r. Blacksmith at l., woman and child at r. on back.	75.00	250.	1200.

1909-12 Issue

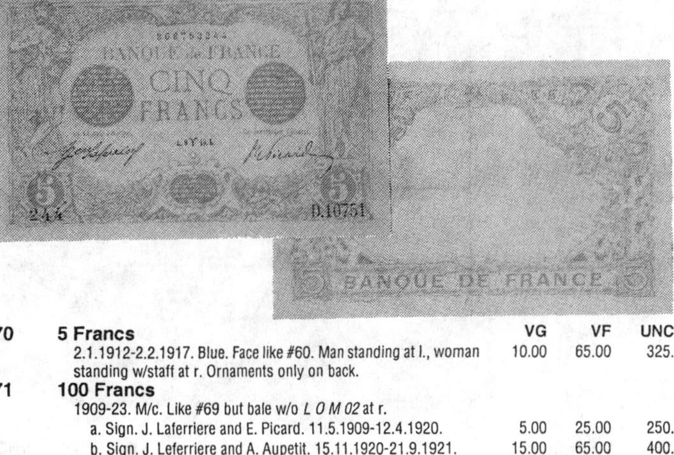

70	5 Francs	VG	VF	UNC
	2.1.1912-2.2.1917. Blue. Face like #60. Man standing at l., woman standing w/staff at r. Ornaments only on back.	10.00	65.00	325.
71	**100 Francs**			
	1909-23. M/c. Like #69 but bale w/o *L O M 02* at r.			
	a. Sign. J. Laferriere and E. Picard. 11.5.1909-12.4.1920.	5.00	25.00	250.
	b. Sign. J. Leferriere and A. Aupetit. 15.11.1920-21.9.1921.	15.00	65.00	400.
	c. Sign. L. Platet and A. Aupetit. 1.5.1922-29.11.1923.	7.50	30.00	325.

1916-18 Issue

72	5 Francs	VG	VF	UNC
	1917-33. Lilac. Woman wearing helmet at l. Dock worker and sailing ship on back. Sign. titles: *LE CAISSIER PRINCIPAL* and *LE SECRÉTAIRE GÉNÉRAL*.			
	a. Sign. J. Laferriere and E. Picard. 1.12.1917-23.1.1919.	5.00	30.00	160.
	b. Sign. J. Laferriere and A. Aupetit. 15.11.1920-11.6.1921.	15.00	75.00	240.
	c. Sign. L. Platet and A. Aupetit. 1.5.1922-21.7.1925.	2.50	20.00	90.00
	d. Sign. L. Platet and P. Strohl. 1.7.1926-29.12.1932.	2.00	17.50	80.00
	e. Sign. J. Boyer and P. Strohl. 5.1.1933-14.9.1933.	1.50	9.00	45.00

73	10 Francs	VG	VF	UNC
	1916-37. Blue. Minerva at upper l. Sitting farm woman on back. Sign. titles: *LE CAISSIER PRINCIPAL* and *LE SECRÉTAIRE GÉNÉRAL*.			
	a. Sign. J. Laferriere and E. Picard. 3.1.1916-15.11.1918.	2.50	40.00	180.
	b. Sign. J. Laferriere and A. Aupetit. 15.11.1920-6.6.1921.	7.50	90.00	450.
	c. Sign. L. Platet and A. Aupetit. 1.5.1922-26.6.1926.	1.00	20.00	100.
	d. Sign. L. Platet and P. Strohl. 1.7.1926-8.9.1932.	.50	17.50	80.00
	e. Sign. J. Boyer and P. Strohl. 17.12.1936-25.2.1937.	10.00	70.00	340.

Note: For 5 and 10 Francs similar to #72 and 73 but w/later dates, see #83 and 84.

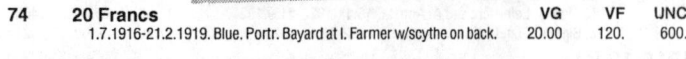

74	20 Francs	VG	VF	UNC
	1.7.1916-21.2.1919. Blue. Portr. Bayard at l. Farmer w/scythe on back.	20.00	120.	600.

75	100 Francs	Good	Fine	XF
	ND (1917). Black on m/c unpt. Standing woman at ctr. Printer: ABNC. Face proof.	—	—	2500.

76	5000 Francs	Good	Fine	XF
	2.1.1918-29.1.1918 (1938). M/c. Worker seated w/Mercury at upper l., angelic child figure w/symbols of agriculture and painting at upper r. Paris on back.	300.	950.	3600.

1923-27 Issue

77	50 Francs	VG	VF	UNC
	11.2.1927-17.7.1930. Brown, blue and m/c. 2 angels above, Mercury below. Woman and man in 2 wreaths on back. Artist's name *Luc-Olivier Merson* below frame on face and back.			
	a. 11.2.1927-13.12.1929.	35.00	110.	650.
	b. 10.7.1930-24.7.1930.	50.00	175.	1000.

78	100 Francs	VG	VF	UNC
	1923-37. M/c. Like #71, but recess in the frame for serial number expanded from 20 to 23 mm. Sign. title: *LE CAISSIER PRINCIPAL*.			
	a. Sign. L. Platet and A. Aupetit. 30.11.1923-26.6.1926.	2.00	20.00	200.
	b. Sign. L. Platet and P. Strohl. 1.7.1926-29.12.1932.	1.50	10.00	120.
	c. Sign. J. Boyer and P. Strohl. 12.1.1933-30.6.1937.	1.25	7.50	110.

79	1000 Francs	VG	VF	UNC
	1927-37. Lt. brown, blue and m/c. Ceres at l., Mercury at r., 2 small angels below. 4 different craftsmen on back. Sign. title: *LE CAISSIER PRINCIPAL*.			
	a. Sign. J. Emmery, L. Platet and P. Strohl. 11.2.1927-2.1.1930.	2.50	12.50	180.
	b. Sign. Roulleau, L. Platet and P. Strohl. 1.4.1930-29.12.1932.	2.50	12.50	180.
	c. Sign. Roulleau, J. Boyer and P. Strohl. 12.1.1933-30.6.1937.	4.00	15.00	200.

1930 Issue

80 50 Francs
1930-34. Brown, blue and m/c. Like #77 but w/o artist's name below frame. 2 angels above, Mercury below. Woman and man in 2 wreaths on back.

	VG	VF	UNC
a. Sign. L. Platet and P. Strohl. 24.7.1930-29.12.1932.	12.50	65.00	375.
b. Sign. J. Boyer and P. Strohl. 12.1.1933-16.8.1934.	12.50	65.00	375.

1934 Issue

81 50 Francs

	VG	VF	UNC
15.11.1934-30.6.1937. Brown and m/c. Ceres and Park of Versailles at l., reclining figure at r. Mercury at r. w/caduceus on back. Sign. title: *LE CAISSIER PRINCIPAL.*	4.50	27.50	160.

82 5000 Francs
1934-35. Purple and m/c. Woman w/Victory statuette and olive branch at ctr. Statuette in rotogravure on back. Sign. title: *LE CAISSIER PRINCIPAL.*

	VG	VF	UNC
a. 8.11.1934.	40.00	200.	800.
b. 16.5.1935; 11.5.1935.	32.50	165.	625.

1937-39 Issue

83 5 Francs

	VG	VF	UNC
13.7.1939-9.1.1941. Lilac. Like #72, but w/sign. titles: *LE CAISSIER GÉNÉRAL.*	.50	4.50	25.00

84 10 Francs

	VG	VF	UNC
2.2.1939-5.3.1942. Blue. Like #73, but w/sign. title: *LE CAISSIER GÉNÉRAL.*	.75	5.00	30.00

85 50 Francs
1937-40. Like #81 but w/sign. title: *LE CAISSIER GÉNÉRAL.*

	VG	VF	UNC
a. Sign. J. Boyer and R. Favre-Gilly. 5.8.1937-9.9.1937.	10.00	50.00	225.
b. Sign. P. Rousseau and R. Favre-Gilly. 4.11.1937-18.4.1940.	3.00	15.00	125.

86 100 Francs
1937-39. M/c. Like #78 but w/sign. title: *LE CAISSIER GÉNÉRAL.* Thin or thicker paper.

	VG	VF	UNC
a. Sign. J. Boyer and R. Favre-Gilly. 9.9.1937-2.12.1937.	9.00	45.00	225.
b. Sign. P. Rousseau and R. Favre-Gilly. 9.12.1937-14.9.1939.	.50	2.25	60.00

87 300 Francs

	VG	VF	UNC
ND (1938). Brown and m/c. Ceres at l. Mercury at r. on back.	50.00	180.	750.

Note: Replacement notes of #87 have *W* prefix.

88 500 Francs
1937-40. Blue on pink unpt. Like #66, but w/sign. title: *LE CAISSIER GÉNÉRAL.*

	VG	VF	UNC
a. Sign. P. Strohl, J. Boyer and R. Favre-Gilly. 5.8.1937-9.9.1937.	30.00	120.	575.
b. Sign. P. Strohl, P. Rousseau and R. Favre-Gilly. 2.12.1937-9.12.1937.	30.00	125.	600.
c. Sign. H. de Bletterie, P. Rousseau and R. Favre-Gilly. 24.3.1938-18.1.1940.	15.00	80.00	450.

89 500 Francs

	VG	VF	UNC
ND. Ovpt. on 300 Francs, Like #87. Proof.	—	—	—

90 1000 Francs
1937-40. Ochre, blue and m/c. Like #79 but w/sign. title: *LE CAISSIER GÉNÉRAL.* Thin or thicker paper.

	VG	VF	UNC
a. Sign. P. Strohl, J. Boyer and R. Favre-Gilly. 8.7.1937-26.8.1937.	17.00	55.00	250.
b. Sign. P. Strohl, P. Rousseau and R. Favre-Gilly. 4.11.1937-23.12.1937.	10.00	45.00	200.
c. Sign. H. de Bletterie, P. Rousseau and R. Favre-Gilly. 24.3.1938-25.7.1940.	2.25	12.50	100.

91 5000 Francs

	VG	VF	UNC
13.10.1938. Like #82, but w/sign. title: *LE CAISSIER GÉNÉRAL.*	65.00	350.	1000.

1939-40 Issue

		VG	VF	UNC
92	**20 Francs**			
	1939-42. Blue on m/c unpt. Allegories of Science and Labor at r. Scientist and city view w/bridge at l. on back.			
	a. 7.12.1939-3.10.1940.	3.50	18.00	200.
	b. 17.10.1940-4.12.1941.	3.00	15.00	175.
	c. 8.1.1942.	4.50	22.50	275.

		VG	VF	UNC
93	**50 Francs**			
	13.6.1940-15.5.1942. Brown, green and m/c. Jacques Coeur at l. Scene in Bourges, woman at r. on back.	.50	4.50	27.50

		VG	VF	UNC
94	**100 Francs**			
	19.5.1939-23.4.1942. Brown and m/c. Woman and child w/background of Paris. Maximilien de Béthune, Duc de Sully, looking over field scene w/farm, castle, rivers on back.	.50	4.00	21.50

		VG	VF	UNC
95	**500 Francs**			
	1940-45. Green, lilac and m/c. Pax w/wreath at l. Man and woman at r. on back.			
	a. Sign. H. de Bletterie, P. Rousseau and R. Favre-Gilly. 4.1.1940-16.1.1941.	2.50	15.00	55.00
	b. Sign. J. Belin, P. Rousseau and R. Favre-Gilly. 6.2.1941-25.2.1943.	2.50	15.00	55.00
	c. Sign. as b. 6.4.1944; 17.5.1944.	100.	250.	—
	d. Sign. as b. 8.6.1944; 15.3.1945; 19.4.1945.	—	—	—

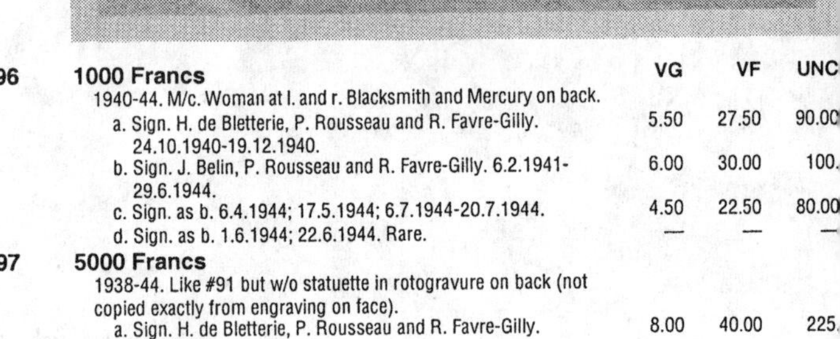

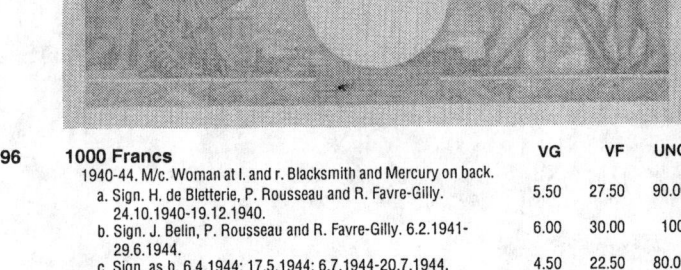

		VG	VF	UNC
96	**1000 Francs**			
	1940-44. M/c. Woman at l. and r. Blacksmith and Mercury on back.			
	a. Sign. H. de Bletterie, P. Rousseau and R. Favre-Gilly. 24.10.1940-19.12.1940.	5.50	27.50	90.00
	b. Sign. J. Belin, P. Rousseau and R. Favre-Gilly. 6.2.1941-29.6.1944.	6.00	30.00	100.
	c. Sign. as b. 6.4.1944; 17.5.1944; 6.7.1944-20.7.1944.	4.50	22.50	80.00
	d. Sign. as b. 1.6.1944; 22.6.1944. Rare.	—	—	—
97	**5000 Francs**			
	1938-44. Like #91 but w/o statuette in rotogravure on back (not copied exactly from engraving on face).			
	a. Sign. H. de Bletterie, P. Rousseau and R. Favre-Gilly. 8.12.1938-26.12.1940.	8.00	40.00	225.
	b. Sign. as a. 19.1.1939.	8.50	45.00	275
	c. Sign. J. Belin, P. Rousseau, and R. Favre-Gilly. 10.4.1941-10.12.1942.	7.50	35.00	180
	d. Sign. as c. 7.1.1943-18.3.1943.	12.50	75.00	350
	e. Sign. as c. 23.3.1944-27.4.1944.	17.50	110.	400

1941-43 Issue

		VG	VF	UNC
98	**5 Francs**			
	1943-47. Blue, green and m/c. Pyrenean shepherd at r. Woman and flowers on back.			
	a. Sign. P. Rousseau and R. Favre-Gilly. 2.6.1943-5.4.1945.	.25	1.50	12.0
	b. Sign. P. Rousseau and P. Gargam. 30.10.1947.	.50	2.50	17.5

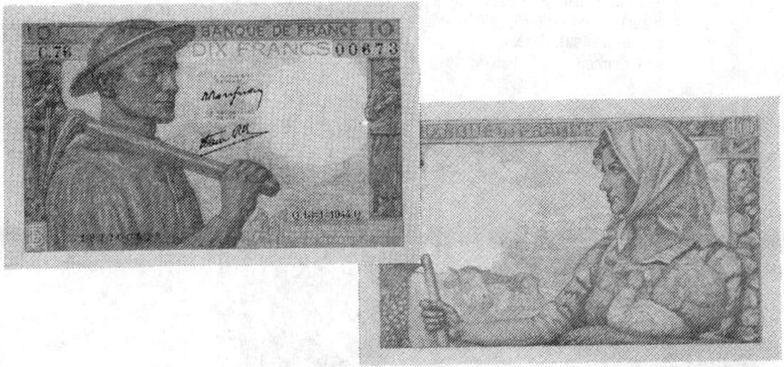

99	10 Francs	VG	VF	UNC
	1941-49. Brown and m/c. Miners at l., another at r. Cows at l., farm woman and child at r. on back.			
	a. Sign. P. Rousseau and R. Favre-Gilly. 11.9.1941.	3.00	20.00	90.00
	b. Sign as a. 9.10.1941; 19.11.1942; 14.1.1943; 19.4.1945.	1.25	6.00	22.50
	c. Sign. as a. 11.6.1942; 20.1.1944.	.40	2.25	12.00
	d. Sign. as a. 15.10.1942; 9.9.1943.	.40	2.00	9.00
	e. Sign. as a. 26.11.1942; 25.3.1943; 13.1.1944; 22.6.1944-9.1.1947.	.15	.75	5.50
	f. Sign. P. Rousseau and P. Gargam. 30.10.1947-30.6.1949.	.30	1.50	9.00

100	20 Francs	VG	VF	UNC
	1942-50. Red and m/c. Breton fisherman at r. 2 women and child at l. ctr., Breton calvary statuary at r. on back.			
	a. Sign. P. Rousseau and R. Favre-Gilly. 12.2.1942-17.5.1944.	.40	2.00	17.50
	b. Sign. as a. 5.7.1945; 9.1.1947.	.40	2.25	20.00
	c. Sign. P. Rousseau and P. Gargam. 29.1.1948-3.11.1949.	.40	2.25	20.00
	d. Sign. as c. 9.2.1950.	3.00	20.00	110.

101	100 Francs	VG	VF	UNC
	1942-44. M/c. Descartes at r. allegorical female reclining at l. Angel on back.			
	a. 15.5.1942 - 14.12.1944.	5.00	25.00	110.
	b. 7.1.1943.	25.00	100.	400.

101A	500 Francs	Good	Fine	XF
	14.1.1943-10.2.1944. Black, brown and m/c. Portr. Colbert w/globe at l., statue of Mercury at r., and early sailing ships in background. Allegorical figure at r. w/dockside scene in background on back. Wmk: Ceres. (Not issued). Rare.	—	—	—

102	1000 Francs	VG	VF	UNC
	28.5.1942-6.4.1944. Brown and m/c. Ceres seated w/Hermes at r. Mercury on back.	4.00	10.00	35.00

Note: A few notes dated 1943 and all dated 1944 were not issued.

103	5000 Francs	VG	VF	UNC
	1942-47. Brown, red and m/c. Allegory of France w/3 men (French colonies) at ctr. Same woman on back alone, but w/scenes from colonies.			
	a. Sign. J. Belin, P. Rousseau and R. Favre-Gilly. 5.3.1942-12.11.1942.	10.00	60.00	250.
	b. Sign. as a. 27.4.1944; 28.9.1944.	15.00	125.	600.
	c. Sign. as a. 18.1.1945-9.1.1947.	6.50	35.00	225.
	e. Sign. J. Belin, P. Rousseau and P. Gargam. 20.3.1947-25.9.1947.	7.50	55.00	350.

ND 1938 Provisional Issue

		Good	Fine	XF
104	**3000 Francs** ND. Green. Provisional printing. Proof.	—	—	—

WWII

Tresor Central

Government Notes

#105, 111-113 were issued in Corsica.

#105-108 English printing.

		VG	VF	UNC
105	**100 Francs** 2.10.1943. Blue on green and violet unpt. Portr. Marianne at ctr. Anchor, barrel, bale, other implements at ctr. on back.			
	a. Issued note.	15.00	60.00	180.
	s. Specimen.	—	—	400.

		VG	VF	UNC
106	**500 Francs** ND (1944). Brown. Portr. Marianne at l. 2 serial # varieties. Printer: TDLR (w/o imprint).	5.00	25.00	90.00

		VG	VF	UNC
107	**1000 Francs** ND (1944). Green. Portr. Marianne at ctr. 2 serial # varieties.	3.00	15.00	75.00

		VG	VF	UNC
108	**1000 Francs** 2.10.1943. Green. Phoenix rising. at ctr. Similar to Fr. Equatorial Africa #14. Printer: BWC (w/o imprint).			
	a. (Not issued). Rare.	—	—	—
	s. Specimen.	—	—	6500.

		VG	VF	UNC
109	**5000 Francs** ND. Blue. Portr. Marianne at r. Printer: TDLR (w/o imprint).			
	a. Issued note. Rare.	—	—	—
	s. Specimen. Rare.	—	—	—
110	**5000 Francs** 2.10.1943. Marianne w/flag and torch. Specimen. Rare.	—	—	—

1945 Provisional Issue

French printing.

		VG	VF	UNC
111	**500 Francs** ND (1945). Blue on green unpt. Ovpt: *TRESOR* on Algeria #93 (-old dates 1.10.1943-31.10.1943).	200.	1000.	—

		VG	VF	UNC
112	**1000 Francs** ND (1945). M/c. ovpt: *TRESOR* on Algeria #86 and 89.			
	a. Ovpt. on #86. Wmk: Head. (-old date 2.7.1942).	75.00	225.	800.
	b. Ovpt. on #89. Wmk: lettering: *Banque de l'Algérie* (-old dates 14.8.1942; 17.8.1942; 2.11.1942).	90.00	265.	1200.
113	**5000 Francs** 1945. Brown-violet on pink unpt. Ovpt. *TRESOR* on Algeria #90. All notes were destroyed. No examples known.	—	—	—

Allied Military Currency

1944 First Issue - Supplemental French Franc Currency

#114-121 w/text: *EMIS EN FRANCE*. Tricolor in blue, white and red on back. Printer: Forbes Lithograph Manufacturing Co., Boston (Massachusetts, U.S.A.). Replacement notes w/*X* near serial #.

		VG	VF	UNC
114	**2 Francs** 1944. Green w/black border. Torch at l. and r. in green unpt. Back blue on red unpt.			
	a. Issued note.	.25	1.00	3.00
	b. Block #2.	.25	1.00	3.00
	s. Specimen.	—	—	150.

		VG	VF	UNC
115	**5 Francs**			
	1944. Blue and black on green unpt. Like #114.			
	a. Issued note.	.25	1.00	7.50
	b. Block #2.	.25	1.00	7.50
	s. Specimen.	—	—	150.

		VG	VF	UNC
116	**10 Francs**			
	1944. Lilac and black on green unpt. Like #114.			
	a. Issued note.	.25	1.00	5.00
	s. Specimen.	—	—	160.

		VG	VF	UNC
117	**50 Francs**			
	1944. Lilac and black on green and blue unpt. Back blue on blue and red unpt.			
	a. Issued note.	2.00	7.50	50.00
	s. Specimen.	—	—	225.
118	**100 Francs**			
	1944. Dk. blue and black on green and blue unpt. Like #117.			
	a. Issued note.	1.75	6.50	45.00
	b. Block #2.	3.00	10.00	55.00
	s. Specimen.	—	—	225.

		VG	VF	UNC
119	**500 Francs**			
	1944. Brown and black on green and blue unpt. Like #117.			
	a. Issued note.	30.00	130.	675.
	s. Specimen.	—	—	400.

		VG	VF	UNC
120	**1000 Francs**			
	1944. Red and black on green and blue unpt. Like #117.			
	a. Issued note.	150.	850.	3000.
	s. Specimen.	—	—	1250.

		VG	VF	UNC
121	**5000 Francs**			
	1944. Green and black on green and blue unpt. Like #117. Specimen.	—	—	3200.

1944 Second Issue - Provisional French Franc Currency

Note: Authorized by French Committee of National Liberation.

#122-126 replacement notes w/*X* near serial #.

		VG	VF	UNC
122	**50 Francs**			
	1944. Similar to #117.			
	a. Issued note.	1.00	8.00	40.00
	b. Block #2.	1.25	9.00	45.00
	c. Block #3.	2.00	12.50	55.00
	s. Specimen perforated: *SPECIMEN.*	—	—	400.

		VG	VF	UNC
123	**100 Francs**			
	1944. Similar to #118.			
	a. Issued note.	1.00	5.00	25.00
	b. Block #2. Numbered at USA-BEP; position of small #2 at l. is at l. ctr.	1.00	5.00	25.00
	c. Blocks #3-8. Numbered at Forbes; position of larger run # at l. is nearer to l. border.	1.00	5.00	25.00
	d. Block #9.	10.00	75.00	300.
	e. Block #10.	3.00	35.00	150.
	s. Specimen.	—	—	400.
124	**500 Francs**			
	1944. Similar to #119.			
	a. Not officially issued.	1000.	3000.	—
	s. Specimen perforated: *SPECIMEN.*	—	—	1500.

		VG	VF	UNC
125	**1000 Francs**			
	1944. Similar to #120.			
	a. Issued note.	75.00	200.	550.
	b. Block #2.	75.00	200.	550.
	c. Block #3.	80.00	225.	600.
	s. Specimen w/*X.*	—	—	1000.
126	**5000 Francs**			
	1944. Similar to #121. Specimen perforated: *SPECIMEN.*	—	—	3750.

Republic

Banque de France

1945-49 Issue

For notes dated after 1945 in the old Franc currency see #98, 99, 100 and 103.

		VG	VF	UNC
126A	**10 Francs**			
	ND (1946). Blue. Mercury at l., Ceres at r. Ceres at ctr. on back. Proof.	—	—	—

127 50 Francs
1946-51. Red, blue and m/c. Leverrier at r. Neptune and date *1846* on back.

	VG	VF	UNC
a. Sign. P. Rousseau and R. Favre-Gilly. 14.3.1946-3.10.1946.	1.00	7.50	45.00
b. Sign. P. Rousseau and P. Gargam. 20.3.1947-2.3.1950.	.50	6.00	35.00
c. Sign. J. Cormier and P. Gargam. 29.6.1950-1.2.1951.	1.50	12.50	75.00
d. Sign. G. Gouin d'Ambrieres and P. Gargam. 7.6.1951.	15.00	200.	650.

Note: #59 was first issued to commemorate Leverrier's discovery of Neptune in 1846.

Hair parted on *her* l.

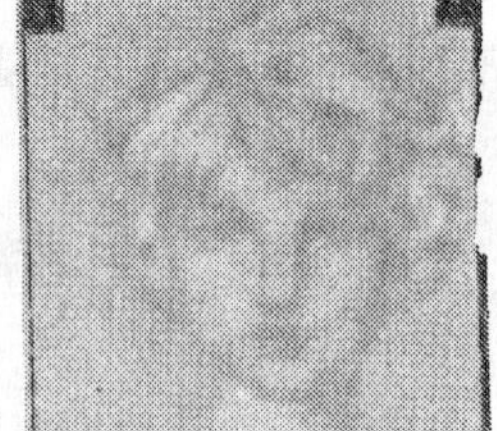
Hair parted on *her* r.

128 100 Francs
1945-54. Brown, red and m/c. Farmer w/2 oxen. Wmk: Woman w/hair parted on her l. Man, woman and children at dockside on back.

	VG	VF	UNC
a. Sign. P. Rousseau and R. Favre-Gilly. 7.11.1945-9.1.1947.	.50	5.00	27.50
b. Sign. P. Rousseau and P. Gargam. 3.4.1947-19.5.1949.	.50	5.00	27.50
c. Sign. J. Cormier and P. Gargam. 29.6.1950-16.11.1950.	1.50	15.00	70.00
d. Sign. G. Gouin d'Ambrieres and P. Gargam. 6.9.1951-1.4.1954.	.50	6.00	30.00
e. Wmk: Reversed, hair parted on her r. 2.10.1952; 6.8.1953; 1.10.1953; 7.1.1954; 4.3.1954; 1.4.1954.	8.00	50.00	225.

129 500 Francs
1945-53. Purple and m/c. Chateaubriand at ctr. w/musical instrument. Allegorical figures on back.

	VG	VF	UNC
a. Sign. J. Belin, P. Rousseau and R. Favre-Gilly. 19.7.1945-9.1.1947.	3.00	35.00	200.
b. Sign. J. Belin, P. Rousseau and P. Gargam. 13.5.1948.	10.00	125.	500.
c. Sign. J. Belin, G. Gouin d'Ambrieres and P. Gargam. 3.7.1952-2.7.1953.	3.00	37.50	210.

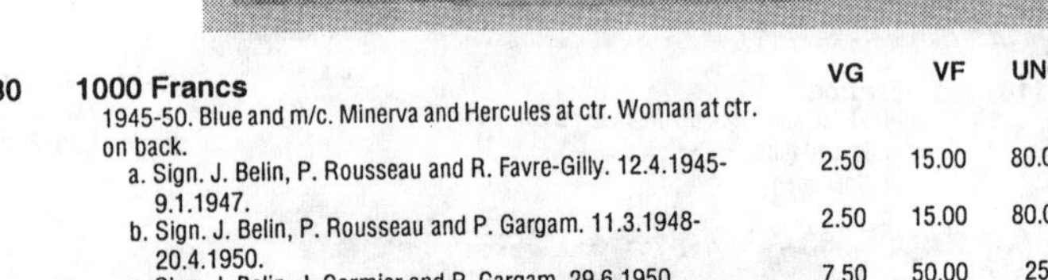

130 1000 Francs
1945-50. Blue and m/c. Minerva and Hercules at ctr. Woman at ctr. on back.

	VG	VF	UNC
a. Sign. J. Belin, P. Rousseau and R. Favre-Gilly. 12.4.1945-9.1.1947.	2.50	15.00	80.0
b. Sign. J. Belin, P. Rousseau and P. Gargam. 11.3.1948-20.4.1950.	2.50	15.00	80.0
c. Sign. J. Belin, J. Cormier and P. Gargam. 29.6.1950.	7.50	50.00	25

131 5000 Francs
1949-57. M/c. 2 allegorical figures (Sea and Countryside) at ctr. Mercury and allegorical woman on back.

	VG	VF	UN
a. Sign. J. Belin, P. Rousseau and P. Gargam. 10.3.1949-3.11.1949.	10.00	45.00	25
b. Sign. J. Belin, J. Cormier and P. Gargam. 1.2.1951-5.4.1951.	10.00	45.00	25
c. Sign. J. Belin, G. Gouin d'Ambrieres and P. Gargam. 16.8.1951-6.12.1956.	9.00	40.00	22
d. Sign. G. Gouin d'Ambrieres, R. Favre-Gilly and P. Gargam. 7.3.1957-7.11.1957.	12.50	60.00	24

132 10,000 Francs
1945-56. M/c. Young woman w/book and globe.

	VG	VF	U
a. Sign. J. Belin, P. Rousseau and R. Favre-Gilly. 27.12.1945-9.1.1947.	40.00	175.	[illegible]
b. Sign. J. Belin, P. Rousseau and P. Gargam. 3.11.1949-16.2.1950.	35.00	150.	[illegible]
c. Sign. J. Belin, J. Cormier and P. Gargam. 8.6.1950-5.4.1951.	25.00	110.	[illegible]
d. Sign. J. Belin, G. Gouin d'Ambrieres and P. Gargam. 4.5.1951-7.6.1956.	20.00	100.	[illegible]

1953-57 ISSUE

		VG	VF	UNC
133	**500 Francs** 1954-58. Blue, orange and m/c. Bldg. at l., V. Hugo at r. Hugo at l., Pantheon in Paris on back.			
	a. Sign. J. Belin, G. Gouin d'Ambrieres and P. Gargam. 7.1.1954-4.8.1955.	3.00	30.00	200.
	b. Sign. G. Gouin d'Ambrieres, R. Favre-Gilly and P. Gargam. 7.2.1957-30.10.1958.	3.50	35.00	250.

Note: #133 dated 1959 is #137 w/ovpt: 5 NF.

		VG	VF	UNC
134	**1000 Francs** 1953-57. M/c. Palais Cardinal across, Armand du Plessis, Cardinal Richelieu at r. Town gate (of Richelieu, in Indre et Loire) at r. on back.			
	a. Sign. J. Belin, G. Gouin d'Ambrieres and P. Gargam. 2.4.1953-6.12.1956.	3.00	20.00	175.
	b. Sign. G. Gouin d'Ambrieres, R. Favre-Gilly and P. Gargam. 7.3.1957-5.9.1957.	7.50	50.00	325.
135	**5000 Francs** 7.2.1957-30.10.1958. M/c. Henry IV at ctr., Paris' Pont Neuf bridge in background. Henry IV at ctr., Château de Pau at l. on back.			
	a. Sign. G. Gouin d'Ambrieres, R. Favre-Gilly, and P. Gargam. 7.2.1957-30.10.1958.			
136	**10,000 Francs** 1955-58. M/c. Arc de Triomphe at l., Napoleon Bonaparte at r. Church of the Invalides in Paris at r., Bonaparte at l. on back.			
	a. Sign. J. Belin, G. Gouin d'Ambrieres and P. Gargam. 1.12.1955-6.12.1956.	25.00	60.00	300.
	b. Sign. G. Gouin d'Ambrieres, R. Favre-Gilly, P. Gargam. 4.4.1957-30.10.1958.	20.00	50.00	275.

		VG	VF	UNC
136A	**50,000 Francs** ND (1956). M/c. Moliere at ctr. on face and back. Specimen. (Not issued).	—	—	—

1958 PROVISIONAL ISSUE

1 Nouveau Franc (NF) - 100 *old* Francs. #137-140 Ovpt: *Nouveaux Francs* (NF).

		VG	VF	UNC
137	**5 Nouveaux Francs on 500 Francs** ND (1960-old dates 1958-59). Ovpt. on #133.			
	a. 30.10.1958.	45.00	400.	1200.
	b. 12.2.1959.	35.00	200.	800.

		VG	VF	UNC
138	**ncs10 Nouveaux Francs on 1000 Fra** ND (-old date 7.3.1957). Ovpt. on #134.	30.00	175.	700.

		VG	VF	UNC
139	**50 Nouveaux Francs on 5000 Francs** ND (-old dates 1958-59). Ovpt. on #135.			
	a. 30.10.1958.	30.00	175.	700.
	b. 5.3.1959.	30.00	175.	700.

		VG	VF	UNC
140	**Francs100 Nouveaux Francs on 10,000** ND (-old date 30.10.1958). Ovpt. on #136.	45.00	200.	800.
140A	**500 Nouveaux Francs on 50,000 Francs** ND. M/c. Ovpt. on #136A.			
	a. Issued note. Rare.	—	—	—
	s. Specimen. Rare.	—	—	—

1959 ISSUE

#141-145 denomination: *NOUVEAUX FRANCS* (NF).

		VG	VF	UNC
141	**5 Nouveaux Francs** 5.3.1959-5.11.1965. Blue, orange and m/c. Like #133. Panthéon in Paris at l., Victor Hugo at r. Village at r., Victor Hugo at l. on back.			
	a. Issued note.	5.00	20.00	200.
	s. Specimen.	—	—	—

		VG	VF	UNC
142	**10 Nouveaux Francs** 5.3.1959-4.1.1963. M/c. Like #134. Palais Cardinal across, Armand du Plessis, Cardinal Richelieu at r. Town gate (of Richelieu, in Indre et Loire) at r. on back.	5.00	15.00	125.
143	**50 Nouveaux Francs** 5.3.1959-6.7.1961. M/c. Like #135. Henry IV at ctr., Paris' Pont Neuf bridge in background. Henry IV at ctr., Château de Pau at l. on back.	30.00	100.	1000.
144	**100 Nouveaux Francs** 5.3.1959-2.4.1964. M/c. Like #136. Arc de Triomphe at l., Napoléon Bonaparte at r. Church of the Invalides in Paris at r., Bonaparte at l. on back.	20.00	40.00	700.

		VG	VF	UNC
145	**500 Nouveaux Francs** 1959-66. M/c. Like #136A. Jean Baptiste Poquelin called Molière at ctr. Paris' Palais Royal in background. Theater in Versailles on back.			
	a. Sign. G. Gouin D'Ambrières, R. Tondu and P. Gargam. 2.7.1959-8.1.1965.	FV	200.	1000.
	b. Sign. H. Morant, R. Tondu and P. Gargam. 6.1.1966; 1.9.1966.	FV	200.	1000.
	s. Specimen. As b.	—	—	—

Note: #145b dated 1.9.1966 was not released for circulation, but examples with pin-hole cancelations are known.

REGIONAL

RÉGIE DES CHEMINS DE FER DES TERRITOIRES OCCUPÉS

FRANCO-BELGIAN RAILWAYS ADMINISTRATION IN OCCUPIED GERMAN TERRITORY

1923 ND ISSUE

#R1-10 steam locomotive at top ctr. Rhine landscape in unpt. at ctr. Neptune at r. on back.

		VG	VF	UNC
R1	**.05 Franc** ND (1923). Dk. blue on orange unpt., red border.	.50	2.00	8.00
R2	**.10 Franc** ND (1923). Dk. brown on lt. blue unpt., green border.	.50	2.00	8.00
R3	**.25 Franc** ND (1923). Violet on lilac unpt., gold border.	.75	2.50	10.00

		VG	VF	UNC
R4	**.50 Franc** ND (1923). Dk. green on olive unpt., gold border.	1.00	3.00	12.00
R5	**1 Franc** ND (1923). Dk. blue on gray-green unpt., gold border.	1.50	5.00	20.00

		VG	VF	UNC
R6	**5 Francs** ND (1923). Dk. blue on gray unpt., red border.	3.00	7.50	25.00
R7	**10 Francs** ND (1923). Black on gray-blue unpt.	5.00	25.00	75.00
R8	**20 Francs** ND (1923). Violet unpt.	10.00	35.00	125.
R9	**50 Francs** ND (1923). Pink unpt.			
	a. Issued note.	35.00	125.	300.
	b. Series B21. (Not issued).	25.00	100.	225.
R10	**100 Francs** ND (1923). Black on pink unpt., gold border.	50.00	175.	350.

MILITARY - WWI

TRESORERIE AUX ARMEES

ARMY TREASURY

1917 ND ISSUE

#M1-M5 woman w/child at l., soldier w/dog at r. *RF* monogram in shield at ctr. on back.

#M1-M3 French text on back: *up to the end of the second year after the armistice.*

		VG	VF	UNC
M1	**50 Centimes** ND (1917). Blue.	1.50	7.50	40.00
M2	**1 Franc** ND (1917). Lt. brown.	1.75	8.50	45.00
M3	**2 Francs** ND (1917). Lilac.	5.00	40.00	160.

1919 ND ISSUE

#M4-M5 French text on back: *up to the end of the fourth year after the armistice.*

		VG	VF	UNC
M4	**50 Centimes** ND (1919). Blue. Like #M1.	2.00	10.00	50.00
M5	**1 Franc** ND (1919). Lt. brown. Like #M2.	3.00	15.00	80.00

MILITARY - POST WWII

TRESOR FRANÇAIS

1947 ND ISSUE

#M6-M10 *TRESOR FRANÇAIS.*

		VG	VF	UNC
M6	**5 Francs** ND (1947). Brown, red and m/c. Woman at ctr. Wheat harvesting on back.			
	a. Issued note.	2.50	20.00	95.00
	s. Specimen.	—	—	400
M7	**10 Francs** ND (1947). Lt. blue and m/c. Like #M6.			
	a. Issued note.	4.50	27.50	100
	s. Specimen.	—	—	400

#M8-M10 Mercury at ctr. Reclining woman on back.

		VG	VF	UNC
M8	**50 Francs** ND (1947). Blue and m/c.	7.50	60.00	225.

		VG	VF	UNC
M9	**100 Francs** ND (1947). Brown and m/c.	7.50	55.00	200.
M10	**1000 Francs** ND (1947). Blue-green and m/c.	100.	275.	1000.

1955 ND ISSUE

#M11-M15 *TRESOR PUBLIC*.

		VG	VF	UNC
M11	**100 Francs** ND (1955). Like #M9.			
	a. Issued note.	10.00	70.00	300.
	s. Specimen.	—	—	700.
M12	**1000 Francs** ND (1955). M/c. Mercury at l. ctr.			
	a. Issued note.	100.	400.	—
	s. Specimen.	—	—	1200.

		VG	VF	UNC
M13	**5000 Francs** ND (1955). M/c. Young farm couple at ctr.			
	a. Issued note.	275.	500.	—
	s. Specimen.	—	—	1500.

1960 ND ISSUE

		VG	VF	UNC
M14	**5 Nouveaux Francs on 500 Francs** ND (1960). M/c. Mercury facing.	60.00	300.	1400.
M14A	**ncs10 Nouveaux Francs on 1000 Fra** ND (1960). M/c. Mercury at l. ctr. Ovpt. on #M12.	175.	1100.	—
M15	**50 Nouveaux Francs on 5000 Francs** ND (1960). M/c. Ovpt. on #M13.	200.	1400.	—

SUEZ CRISIS, 1956

FORCES FRANÇAISES EN MEDITERRANEE ORIENTALE

1956 ND ISSUE

#M16-M18 ovpt: *FORCES FRANÇAISES EN MEDITERRANEE ORIENTALE*.

		VG	VF	UNC
M16	**50 Francs** ND (1956). M/c. Ovpt. on #M8.	125.	700.	—
M17	**100 Francs** ND (1956). Ovpt. on #M9.	100.	600.	—
M18	**1000 Francs** ND (1956). Ovpt. on #M10.	300.	1800.	—

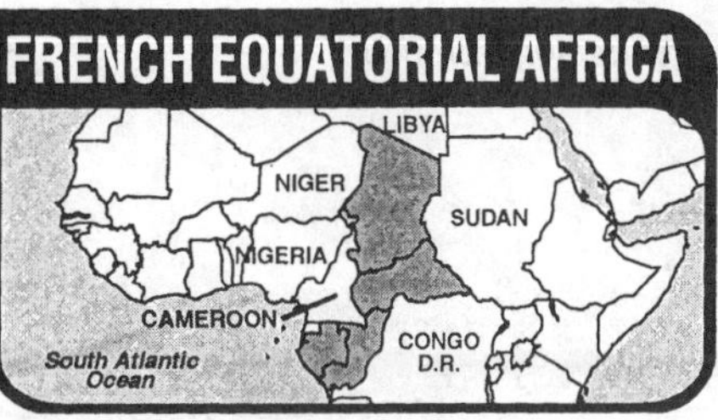

French Equatorial Africa, an area consisting of four self governing dependencies (Middle Congo, Ubangi-Shari, Chad and Gabon) in west-central Africa, has an area of 969,111 sq. mi. (2,509,987 sq. km.) and a population of 3.5 million. Capital: Brazzaville. The area, rich in natural resources, exported cotton, timber, coffee, cacoa, diamonds and gold.

Little is known of the history of these parts of Africa prior to French occupation - which began with no thought of territorial acquisition. France's initial intent was simply to establish a few supply stations along the west coast of Africa to service the warships assigned to combat the slave trade in the early part of the 19th century. French settlement began in 1839. Gabon (then Gabun) and the Middle Congo were secured between 1885 and 1891; Chad and the Ubangi-Shari between 1894 and 1897. The four colonies were joined to form French Equatorial Africa in 1910. The dependencies were changed from colonies to territories within the French Union in 1946, and all the inhabitants were made French citizens. In 1958, they voted to become autonomous republics within the new French Community, and attained full independence in 1960.

RULERS:
French

MONETARY SYSTEM:
1 Franc = 100 Centimes

FRENCH ADMINISTRATION

GOUVERNEMENT GÉNÉRAL DE L'AFRIQUE EQUATORIALE FRANÇAISE

1917 ND EMERGENCY ISSUE

		VG	VF	UNC
1	**50 Centimes** ND (1917). Green on blue unpt.			
	a. W/o wmk. 3 sign. varieties.	20.00	90.00	175.
	b. Wmk: Laurel leaves.	20.00	90.00	175.

		VG	VF	UNC
2	**1 Franc** ND (1917). Red on blue unpt.			
	a. W/o wmk. 3 sign. varieties.	25.00	100.	225.
	b. Wmk: Laurel leaves.	25.00	100.	225.

		VG	VF	UNC
3	**2 Francs** ND (1917). Blue on yellow unpt. Like #2. 2 sign. varieties.	40.00	140.	350.

1925 PROVISIONAL ISSUE

		VG	VF	UNC
3A	**25 Francs** 9.7.1925. Ovpt: *AFRIQUE EQUATORIALE FRANÇAISE* on French West Africa #7B. Rare.	—	—	—

BONS DE CAISSE

1940 EMERGENCY WWII ISSUE

		VG	VF	UNC
4	**1000 Francs** 25.10.1940; 20.12.1940. Green on yellow paper. Man rowing boat at ctr. Rare.	—	—	—

		VG	VF	UNC
4A	**1000 Francs** ND (1940). Man at ctr. Specimen. Rare.	—	—	—

		VG	VF	UNC
5	**5000 Francs** 25.10.1940. Red. Dancer at ctr. Specimen. Rare.	—	—	—

NOTICE

Readers with unlisted dates, signature varieties, etc. are invited to submit photocopies or, high resolution (300 dpi, 100% size) scans of their notes to: Standard Catalog of World Paper Money, 700 East State St. Iola, WI 54990-0001, or E-Mail: george.cuhaj@fwpubs.com.

AFRIQUE FRANÇAISE LIBRE

ND 1941 ISSUE

#6-9 flag in upper r. corner.

		VG	VF	UNC
6	**5 Francs** ND (1941). Green, brown and m/c. Man at ctr. Man weaving on back.	5.00	25.00	75.00
7	**25 Francs** ND (1941). Red, blue and m/c. Man wearing turban w/horse. Lion on back.			
	a. Issued note.	17.50	90.00	300.
	s. Specimen.	—	—	175.

		VG	VF	UNC
8	**100 Francs** ND (1941). Dk. brown, lilac and m/c. 2 women at ctr. Woman w/basket on back.	65.00	275.	—
9	**1000 Francs** ND (1941). Brown, yellow and green. French woman w/African woman and child. Printer: BWC.			
	a. Issued note.	1000.	2250.	—
	s. Specimen.	—	—	2500.

Note: For issues similar to #6-9 but w/heading: *Afrique Occidentale*, see French W. Africa #21-24.

CAISSE CENTRALE DE LA FRANCE LIBRE

ORDONNANCE DU 2 DEC. 1941

#10-14A printed in England. Printer: BWC (w/o imprint).

		VG	VF	UNC
10	**5 Francs** L.1941. Red on orange and lilac unpt. Portr. Marianne at ctr.			
	a. Issued note.	20.00	80.00	240
	s. Specimen, punched hole cancelled.	—	—	175
11	**10 Francs** L.1941. Purple on lt. brown and lt. blue unpt. Like #10.			
	a. Issued note.	22.50	125.	—
	s. Specimen, punched hole cancelled.	—	—	200

		VG	VF	UNC
12	**20 Francs** L.1941. Green on lilac and olive unpt. Like #10.			
	a. Issued note.	30.00	150.	—
	s. Specimen, punched hole cancelled.	—	—	225
13	**100 Francs** L.1941. Blue-green on gold and orange unpt. Face similar to #10. Anchor, barrel, bale and other implements on back. Like France #105.			
	a. Issued note.	45.00	200.	—
	s. Specimen, punched hole cancelled.	—	—	300

		VG	VF	UNC
14	**1000 Francs** L.1941. Dk. blue. Phoenix rising from flames. Like #19.			
	a. Issued note.	300.	1200.	—
	p. Red. Proof.	—	—	750.
	s1. Specimen, punched hole cancelled.	—	—	950.
	s2. As a. Specimen w/ovpt. and perforated: *SPÉCMEN.*	—	—	950.

		VG	VF	UNC
14A	**5000 Francs** L.1941. Violet. Marianne advancing w/torch in l. hand and flag in r. hand. Proof. Rare.	—	—	—

Note: #10, 13, 14 issues for Reunion w/special serial # ranges, see Reunion. Note: #10, 11, 12, 13, 14 issues for St. Pierre w/special serial # ranges, see St. Pierre.

CAISSE CENTRALE DE LA FRANCE D'OUTRE-MER

ORDONNANCE DU 2 FEB. 1944

#15-19 w/o imprinted name of colony. For notes w/imprinted name see Guadeloupe, French Guiana or Martinique. Printer: BWC (w/o imprint).

		VG	VF	UNC
15	**5 Francs** L.1944. Red. Portr. Marianne at ctr. Similar to #10.			
	a. Sign. A. Duval. Blue serial #.	5.00	25.00	100.
	b. Sign. A. Postel-Vinay. Blue serial #.	4.00	20.00	80.00
	c. Sign. A. Postel-Vinay. W/o serial #.	6.00	30.00	120.
	d. Black serial # w/prefix A (in plate).	7.00	35.00	140.
	e. Black serial # w/prefix B (in plate).	6.00	30.00	120.
	f. Black serial # w/prefix C (in plate).	6.00	30.00	120.
	g. Black serial # w/prefix D (in plate).	6.00	30.00	120.
16	**10 Francs** L.1944. Purple. Like #15.			
	a. Sign. A. Duval. Red Serial #.	7.50	35.00	110.
	b. Sign. A. Postel-Vinay. Red serial #.	7.50	35.00	110.
	c. Sign. A. Postel-Vinay. Black serial #.	10.00	45.00	125.
	d. Black serial # w/prefix A (in plate).	10.00	50.00	200.
	e. Black serial # w/prefix B (in plate).	10.00	55.00	220.
17	**20 Francs** L.1944. Green. Like #15.			
	a. Sign. A. Duval. Red serial #.	15.00	70.00	280.
	b. Sign. A. Postel-Vinay. Red serial #.	12.50	65.00	260.

		VG	VF	UNC
17	c. Sign. A. Postel-Vinay. Black serial #.	12.50	65.00	260.
	d. Black serial # w/prefix A (in plate).	12.50	65.00	260.
18	**100 Francs** L.1944. Green. Like #13.	40.00	125.	500.

		VG	VF	UNC
19	**1000 Francs** L.1944. Dk. blue. Phoenix rising from flames War-scared landscape at l., peaceful landscape at r., on back.			
	a. Black serial #.	450.	1000.	—
	s1. As a. Specimen ovpt: *SPÉCIMEN.*	—	—	1200.
	s2. Specimen ovpt. and perforated SPÉCIMEN. Red serial #.	—	—	1350.
20	**5000 Francs** L. 1944. Violet. Like #14A. Proof. Rare.	—	—	—

Note: #15, 16, 17, 19 issues for St. Pierre w/special serial# ranges, see St. Pierre. Note: #18, 19 issues for Reunion w/special serial # ranges, see Reunion.

1947-52 ISSUE

#20B-27 w/o imprinted name of colony. For notes w/imprinted name see French Antilles, French Guiana, Guadeloupe, Martinique, Reunion or Saint Pierre et Miquelon. Printed in France.

		VG	VF	UNC
20B	**5 Francs** ND (1947). Blue and m/c. Ship at l., Bougainville at r. Woman w/fruits on back.	2.50	12.00	45.00

		VG	VF	UNC
21	**10 Francs** ND (1947). Blue and m/c. Colbert at l. River scene on back.	3.00	15.00	55.00

		VG	VF	UNC
22	**20 Francs** ND (1947). Brown and m/c. E. Gentil at r., villagers at l. ctr. Man at l. and r. on back.	4.00	17.50	75.00

		VG	VF	UNC
23	**50 Francs** ND (1947). M/c. Belain d'Esnambuc at l., sailing ship at r. Woman at l. on back.	7.50	25.00	115.

		VG	VF	UNC
24	**100 Francs** ND (1947). M/c. La Bourdonnais at l., women at r. Woman at r., mountain scenery in background on back. 2 serial # varieties.	15.00	45.00	150.
25	**500 Francs** ND (1949). M/c. 2 girls at r.	50.00	200.	525.
26	**1000 Francs** ND (1947). M/c. 2 women (symbol of the "Union Francaise") at r. 2 serial # varieties.	45.00	165.	425.
27	**5000 Francs** ND (1952). Brown. Gen. Schoelcher at ctr. r.	95.00	350.	850.

Note: #20B, 21, 22, 23 issues for St. Pierre w/special serial # ranges, see St. Pierre.

INSTITUT D'EMISSION DE L'AFRIQUE EQUATORIALE FRANÇAISE ET DU CAMEROUN

1957 ISSUE

		VG	VF	UNC
28	**5 Francs** ND. M/c. Like #20B.	15.00	45.00	140.
29	**10 Francs** ND. M/c. Like #21.	20.00	55.00	150.
30	**20 Francs** ND. Olive-brown. Like #22.	25.00	75.00	185.

		VG	VF	UNC
31	**50 Francs** ND (1957). Green and m/c. Woman picking coffee beans at l. Men logging in river on back.	6.00	17.50	75.00
32	**100 Francs** ND (1957). Blue and m/c. Gov. Gen. Felix Eboue at ctr. Cargo ships, man on back.	10.00	30.00	110.

		VG	VF	UNC
33	**500 Francs** ND (1957). Brown and m/c. Woman in front of huts. Freight train crossing bridge at ctr. on back.	35.00	140.	400.

		VG	VF	UNC
34	**1000 Francs** ND (1957). M/c. Woman w/harvest of cocoa. Man picking cotton on back.	45.00	150.	425.

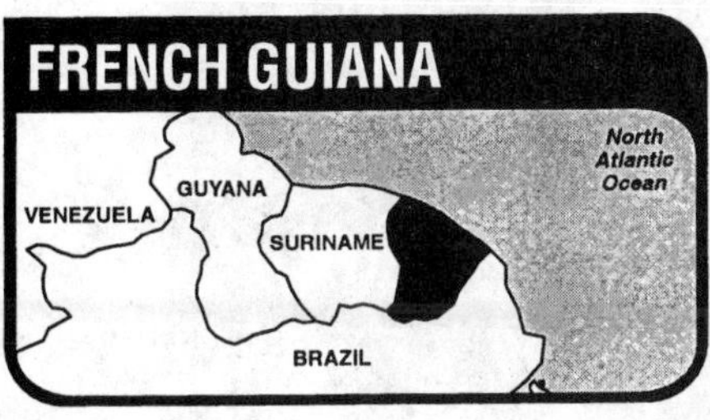

The French Overseas Department of French Guiana, located on the northeast coast of South America, bordered by Surinam and Brazil, has an area of 32,252 sq. mi. (91,000 sq. km.) and a population of 173,000. Capital: Cayenne. Placer gold mining and shrimp processing are the chief industries. Shrimp, lumber, gold, cocoa and bananas are exported.

The coast of Guiana was sighted by Columbus in 1498 and explored by Amerigo Vespucci in 1499. The French established the first successful trading stations and settlements, and placed the area under direct control of the French Crown in 1674. Portuguese and British forces occupied French Guiana for five years during the Napoleonic Wars. Devil's Island, the notorious penal colony in French Guiana where Capt. Alfred Dreyfus was imprisoned, was established in 1852 - and finally closed in 1947. When France adopted a new constitution in 1946, French Guiana voted to remain within the French Union as an overseas department.

RULERS:

French

MONETARY SYSTEM:

1 Franc = 10 Decimes = 100 Centimes to 1960
1 Nouveau (new) Franc = 100 "old" Francs, 1961-

FRENCH ADMINISTRATION

TREASURY

1795 EMERGENCY ISSUE

COLONIES. Exer. 1794. POUR LA SOMME DE 40 l.
Il sera tenu compte par le Trésor, au Porteur, de la somme de QUARANTE LIVRES.
No. 19963 A Cayenne, le 22. frimaire 1794, l'an troisième de la République française.
Vû par nous Sous-chef d'Administration chargé du détail des fonds.
Vû par nous Sous-chef d'Administration fous-contrôleur.
Vû par nous Chef d'Administration, Ordonnateur de la Guiane Française.

		Good	Fine	XF
A5	**40 Livres** 13.12.1795. Black. Uniface.	250.	500.	—

Note: #A5 is dated *22 frimare an 3 eme* which relates to the 3rd month, 3rd year of the First French Republic.

BANQUE DE LA GUYANE

1888-1922 ISSUES

Sign. varieties.

		Good	Fine	XF
1	**5 Francs** L.1901 (1922-47). Blue. Man at l., woman at r.			
	a. Sign. title: *Directeur* H. Poulet (1922).	20.00	50.00	170.
	b. Sign. title: *Directeur* P. L. Lamer (1933).	18.00	45.00	150.
	c. Sign. titles: *Directeur* C. Halleguen and *Caissier* E. Brais (1939).	15.00	35.00	125.
	d. Sign. titles: *Directeur* C. Halleguen, and *Caissier* ? (1942).	10.00	30.00	125.
	e. Sign. title: *Directeur* M. Buy (1947).	10.00	25.00	115.

		Good	Fine	XF
2	**25 Francs** ND (1910). Black and green. Back pink.	200.	725.	—
3	**100 Francs** ND. Red and blue. Back green. Rare.	—	—	—
4	**500 Francs** ND (1888-89). Red. Rare.	—	—	—

1916 EMERGENCY ISSUE

		Good	Fine	XF
5	**1 Franc** 16.12.1916 (1917-19). Blue and gray. 2 sign. varieties.	25.00	80.00	275.
6	**2 Francs** 16.12.1916 (1917-19). Red and blue. 2 sign. varieties.	30.00	90.00	350.

1933-38 ND ISSUE

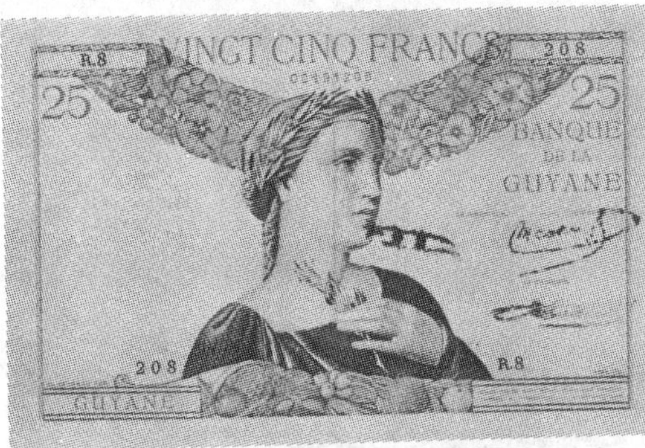

		Good	Fine	XF
7	**25 Francs** ND (1933-45). Purple and m/c. Woman w/wreath at ctr. Trees l. and r., ship in water at ctr. on back. 5 sign. varieties.	35.00	175.	500.

		Good	Fine	XF
8	**100 Francs** ND (1933-42). M/c. Woman holding staff at l. 4 sign. varieties.	110.	350.	800.
9	**500 Francs** ND (1938-40). M/c. Like #8. 2 sign. varieties.	250.	850.	—

#10 not assigned.

1942; 1945 ND WWII EMERGENCY ISSUES

#11-11A Bank name 40mm long. Border w/design element at upper and lower ctr. Bank name stamped in oval on back. Hand stamped sign. 2 sign. varieties. Local printing.

		VG	VF	UNC
11	**1 Franc** ND (1942). Red.	60.00	135.	250.
11A	**2 Francs** ND (1942). Blue-green.	70.00	150.	300.

#11B-11C local printing similar to above. Bank name 51mm long. Unbroken pattern w/o design element in upper and lower border.

		VG	VF	UNC
11B	**1 Franc** ND (1945). Red.	70.00	150.	300.
11C	**2 Francs** ND (1945). Blue-green.			
	a. Hand sign.	75.00	175.	350.
	b. Stamped sign.	70.00	150.	300.

1942 ND Issue

#12-15 various sign. varieties. printer. E. A. Wright, Philadelphia, Penn. U.S.A.

		VG	VF	UNC
12	**5 Francs** ND (1942). Black on green unpt. Justice at l.			
	r. Unsigned remainder.	—	—	2000.
	s. Specimen.	—	—	1500.

		VG	VF	UNC
13	**100 Francs** ND (1942). Black on red unpt. Map of Guiana at l. Back dk. green on brown unpt. 2 sign. varieties.			
	a. Sign. Halleguen as *LE DIRECTEUR.*	200.	650.	1500.
	b. Sign. Buy as *LE DIRECTEUR.*	240.	775.	1750.

		VG	VF	UNC
14	**500 Francs** ND (1942). Black on yellow unpt. "Flying boat" at ctr. Back dk. red on blue unpt.; caravelle *Santa Maria* at ctr. 2 sign. varieties.			
	a. Sign. Collat as *UN CENSEUR.*	1250.	2750.	—
	b. Sign. St.-Clair as *UN CENSEUR.*	1250.	2750.	—
	s. Specimen.	—	—	1150.
15	**1000 Francs** ND (1942). Green. Seated woman at l. and r. Back brown; Liberty at ctr. 3 sign varieties.	1750.	3500.	—

Caisse Centrale de la France Libre

Ordonnance du 2 Dec. 1941

#16 and 16A English printing.

		VG	VF	UNC
16	**100 Francs** L.1941. Green on orange unpt. Marianne at ctr. Anchor, barrel, bale and other implements on back. Ovpt: GUYANE.			
	a. Issued note.	110.	275.	700.
	s. Specimen.	—	—	450.

> **NOTICE**
> Readers with unlisted dates, signature varieties, etc. are invited to submit photocopies or, high resolution (300 dpi, 100% size) scans of their notes to: Standard Catalog of World Paper Money, 700 East State St. Iola, WI 54990-0001, or E-Mail: george.cuhaj@fwpubs.com.

		VG	VF	UNC
16A	**1000 Francs** L.1941. Blue. Phoenix rising from flames. Black handstamp: GUYANE FRANÇAISE twice. Handstamp: ANNULE (cancelled).	—	850.	2250.

Caisse Centrale de la France d'Outre-Mer

Ordonnance du 2 Feb. 1944

#17 and 18 ovpt. or handstamped: *GUYANE.* English printing.

		VG	VF	UNC
17	**100 Francs** L.1944. Green on orange unpt. Like #16.			
	a. Issued note.	50.00	200.	575.
	s. Specimen.	—	—	400.
18	**1000 Francs** L.1944. Blue. Phoenix rising from flames. Like #16A.			
	a. Dk. blue serial #.	750.	1650.	—
	b. Blue serial #. Ovpt: *GUYANE.* W/o wmk.	750.	1650.	—
	c. Red serial #. Hand-stamped: *GUYANE FRANÇAISE.* Wmk. paper.	850.	1750.	—
	d. As c. Cancelled w/black stamp *ANNULÉ.*	—	—	—
	s. As a. Specimen.	—	—	1250.

1947 Issue

#19-26 ovpt: GUYANE French printing. Standard designs.

		VG	VF	UNC
19	**5 Francs** ND (1947-49). M/c. Bougainville at r.			
	a. Issued note.	7.50	25.00	85.00
	s. Specimen.	—	—	90.00
20	**10 Francs** ND (1947-49). M/c. Colbert at l.			
	a. Issued note.	10.00	30.00	110
	s. Specimen.	—	—	90.00
21	**20 Francs** ND (1947-49). M/c. E. Gentil at r.			
	a. Issued note.	12.50	35.00	135
	s. Specimen.	—	—	100

		VG	VF	UNC
22	**50 Francs** ND (1947-49). M/c. B. d'Esnambuc at l., sailing ship at r.			
	a. Issued note.	25.00	75.00	285
	s. Specimen.	—	—	125

		VG	VF	UNC
23	**100 Francs** ND (1947-49). M/c. La Bourdonnais at l., women at r.			
	a. Issued note.	35.00	100.	350.
	s. Specimen.	—	—	150.
24	**500 Francs** ND (1947-49). M/c. 2 women at r.			
	a. Issued note.	75.00	250.	800.
	s. Specimen.	—	—	250.
25	**1000 Francs** ND (1947-49). M/c. 2 women at r.			
	a. Issued note.	100.	300.	900.
	s. Specimen.	—	—	275.
26	**5000 Francs** ND (1947-49). M/c. Gen. Schoelcher at ctr. r.			
	a. Issued note.	100.	450.	1100.
	s. Specimen.	—	—	325.

1960 ISSUE

		VG	VF	UNC
27	**1000 Francs** ND (1960). M/c. Fishermen. Specimen.	—	—	850.
28	**5000 Francs** ND (1960). M/c. Woman w/fruit bowl.			
	a. Issued note.	400.	750.	1850.
	s. Specimen.	—	—	500.

Note: For notes ovpt. in *Nouveaux Francs* see Volume 3.

French India consisted of five settlements in India that formerly constituted a territory of France: Pondicherry (Pondichery), Chandemagor, Karikal and Yanam on the east coast, and Mahe on the west coast. The combined settlements had an area of 197 sq. mi. (500 sq. km). Capital: Pondicherry.

French interest in the East was evident as early as the opening of the 16th century, but initial individual efforts were checked by the Portuguese. After a number of false starts, they acquired Pondicherry, 85 miles (137 Km.) south of Madras, in 1654. Chandernagor, 16 miles (26 km) north of Calcutta, was acquired in 1690-92. Mahe was acquired in 1725 and Karikai in 1739. Yanam was founded in 1750. The French enclaves were captured (by the Dutch and British) and restored several times before French possession was established, by treaties, 1914-17.

Chandernagor voted in 1949 to join India and became part of the Republic of India in 1950. Pondicherry, Karikal, Yanam and Mahe formed the Pondicherry Union Territory and joined the Republic of India in 1954.

RULERS

French to 1954

MONTETARY SYSTEM

1 Roupie = 8 Fanons = 16 Annas

FRENCH ADMINISTRATION

BANQUE DE L'INDOCHINE, PONDICHERY

DÉCRET DU 21.1.1875

#A1 and A2 various date and sign. varieties.

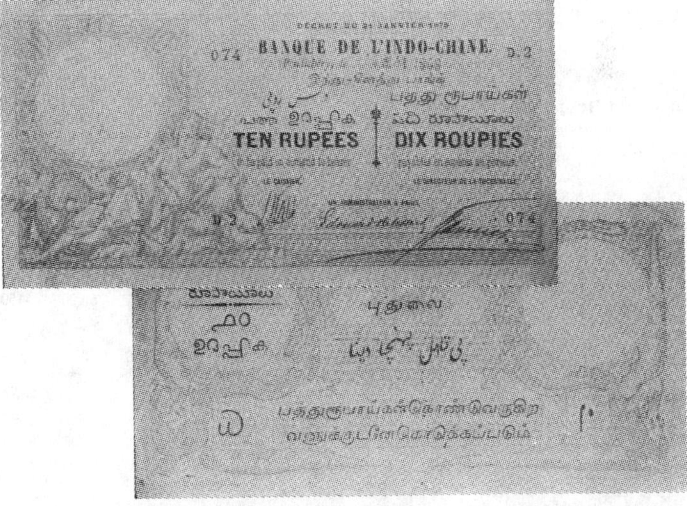

		Good	Fine	XF
A1	**10 Roupies** 1.1.1874; 3.4.1901; 24.5.1909. Blue. Neptune reclining holding trident at lower l. Multiple language texts on back.			
	a. Issued note. Rare.	—	—	—
	s. O.5.1910. Specimen. Rare.	—	—	—
A2	**50 Roupies** (1877-). Blue-gray and red-brown. Elephant columns l. and r., 2 reclining women w/ox l., tiger r. at lower border. Decree in ribbon in border at top ctr. Rare.	—	—	—

DÉCRETS DES 21.1.1875 ET 20.2.1888

		Good	Fine	XF
A3	**50 Roupies** 10.9.1898. Like #A2 but printed date. Rare.	—	—	—

Décrets des 21.1.1875, 20.2.1888 et 16.5.1900

		Good	Fine	XF
1	**50 Roupies** (1902-). Like #A3, but printed decree. W/counterfeiting clause replacing decrees in ribbon in border at top ctr.	—	—	—

Décrets des 21.1.1875, 20.2.1888, 16.5.1900 et 3.4.1901

		Good	Fine	XF
2	**10 Roupies** 3.11.1919. Like #A1 but printed date.			
	a. Issued note. Rare.	—	—	—
	b. Cancelled w/handstamp: *ANNULÉ.*	—	—	2500.
3	**50 Roupies** 17.6.1915. Like #1.			
	a. Issued note. Rare.	—	—	—
	b. Cancelled w/handstamp: *ANNULÉ.* Rare.	—	—	—

W/o Décrets

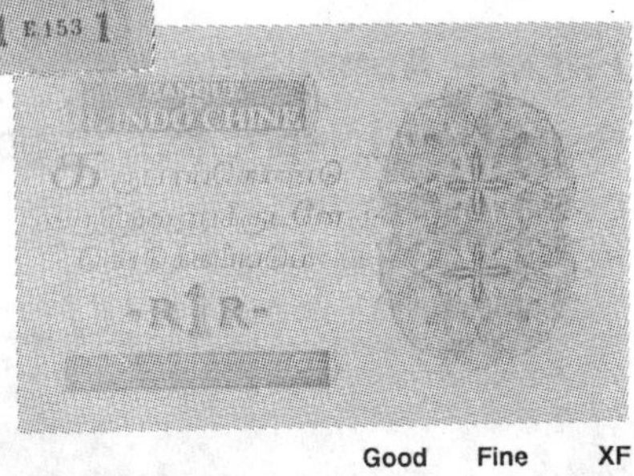

		Good	Fine	XF
4	**1 Roupie** 1919-45. Blue and brown on lt. orange unpt. Helmeted woman at l. Back orange-brown.			
	a. Sign titles: *L'ADMININSTRATEUR-DIRECTEUR* and *UN ADMINISTRATEUR.* 12.11.1919.	85.00	250.	550.
	b. Sign titles: *UN ADMINISTRATEUR* and *LE DIRECTEUR.* 2 sign varieties. 1.8.1923; 1.1.1928.	75.00	175.	350.
	c. Sign. titles: *UN ADMININSTRATEUR* and *LE DIRECTEUR GÉNÉRAL.* 5.4.1932.	70.00	150.	300.
	d. Sign. titles: *LE PRÉSIDENT* and *LE DIRECTEUR GÉNÉRAL.* 2 sign. varieties. 13.2.1936; 8.3.1938; 8.9.1945.	30.00	90.00	225.
	e. As d. Punched hole cancelled w/handstamp: *ANNULÉ.* 8.9.1945.	20.00	50.00	150.
4A	**1 Roupie** 8.9.1945. Face like #4. Back guilloche w/3 cross-shapes instead of 2.	60.00	200.	—

1936-37 ND Issue

		Good	Fine	XF
5	**5 Roupies** ND (1937). Brown and orange on m/c unpt. Women wearing helmet holding lance at l., denomination numeral *5* over wreath at upper r. Woman w/headress at l., ancient statues at r. on back.			
	a. Sign. titles: *LE PRÉSIDENT* and *LE DIRECTEUR GÉNÉRAL.* (1937).	85.00	185.	400.
	b. Sign titles: *LE PRÉSIDENT and LE DIRECTEUR GAL. ADJOINT. (1946).*	75.00	150.	350.
	c. As b. Punched hole cancelled w/handstamp: *ANNULÉ.*	45.00	90.00	200.
	s. As b. Specimen perforated *SPECIMEN.*	—	—	500.

		Good	Fine	XF
7	**50 Roupies** ND (1936). M/c. Ornamental stove at l. Portr. Dupleix on back.			
	a. Sign. Thion de la Chaume as *LE PRÉSIDENT* and Baudouin as *LE DIRECTEUR GÉNÉRAL* (1936). Rare.	—	—	—
	b. Sign. Borduge-Baudouin. (1937-40).	600.	1800.	—
	c. Sign. Minost-Laurent. (1945).	700.	1800.	—
	d. Punched hole cancelled w/handstamp: *ANNULÉ.*	350.	900.	—
	s. Specimen perforated: *SPECIMEN.*	—	—	500.

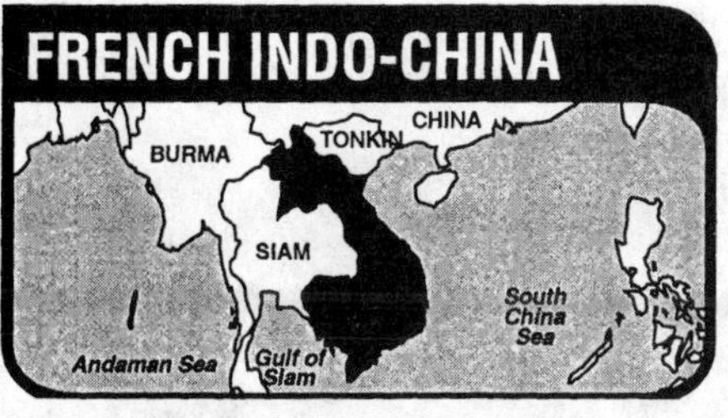

French Indo-China (l'Indo-Chine) was located on the Indo-Chinese peninsula of Southeast Asia. It was a French colonial possession from the later 19th century until 1954. A French Governor-General headed a federal-type central government and colonial administration, but reported directly to France which retained exclusive authority over foreign affairs, defense, customs, finance and public works. The colony covered 286,194 sq. mi. (741,242 sq. km.) and had a population of 24 million. It consisted of 5 protectorates: Tonkin (northern Vietnam), Annam (central Vietnam), Cochin-China (southern Vietnam), Laos and Cambodia. Principal cities were: Saigon, Hanoi, Haiphong, Pnom-Penh and Vientiane. From 1875 to 1951, the exclusive right to issue banknotes within the colony was held by the Bank of Indochina (Banque de l'Indochine). On December 31, 1951 this privilege was transferred to the Issuing Authority of the States of Cambodia, Laos and Vietnam (Institut d'Emission des Etats du Cambodge, du Laos et du Vietnam).

From the moment of their conquest, the Indochinese people resisted French rule. The degree of resistance varied, being strongest in central and northern Vietnam, but was evident throughout Indochina. There were unsuccessful attempts by Vietnamese nationals, headed by Nguyen Ai Quoc (later known as Ho Chi Minh), to gain recognition/independence at the Versailles Peace Conference following World War I.

Japan occupied French Indochina at the start of World War II, but allowed the local French (Vichy) government to remain in power until March 1945. Meanwhile, many nationalists (communist and non-communist alike) followed Ho Chi Minh's leadership in the formation of the League for Independence of Vietnam (Viet-Minh) which took an active anti-Japanese part during the war. France reoccupied the area after the Japanese surrender, and established the Associated States of Indochina, with each of the five political subdivisions having limited independence within the French Union. Disagreement over the degree of independence and the reunification of the three Vietnamese subdivisions led to armed conflict with the Viet-Minh and a protracted war (The First Indochina War). In 1949/1950, in an attempt to retain her holdings, France recognized Laos, Cambodia and Vietnam as semi-independent self governing States within the French Union, but retained financial and economic control. Fighting continued and culminated with the French military disaster at Dien Bien Phu in May 1954. The subsequent Geneva Agreement brought full independence to Laos, Cambodia and Vietnam (*temporarily* divided at the 17th parallel of latitude), and with it, an end to French rule in Indochina.

See also Vietnam, South Vietnam, Laos and Cambodia.

RULERS:

French to 1954

MONETARY SYSTEM:

1 Piastre = 1 (Mexican Silver) Dollar = 100 Cents,1875-1903
1 Piastre = 100 Cents, 1903-1951
1 Piastre = 100 Cents = 1 Riel (Cambodia), 1951-1954
1 Piastre = 100 Cents = 1 Kip (Laos)
1 Piastre = 100 Cents = 1 Dong (Vietnam)

SIGNATURE VARIETIES/TITLE COMBINATIONS BANQUE DE L'INDOCHINE, 1875–1951

No.		
1	Edwuoard Delessert, Un Administrateur a Paris. NOTE: Also handsigned by Le Cassier and Le Directeur de la Succursale.	
2	Aduoard Delessert, Un Administrateur	Stanislas Simon, Le Directeur
3	Ernest Denormandie, Un Administrateur	Stanislas Simon, Le Directeur
4	Baron Hely D'Oissel, Un Administrateur	Stanislas Simon, Le Directeur
5	Baron Hely D'Oissel, Un Administrateur	Stanislas Simon, Le Administrateur-Directeur
6	Albert de Monplanet, Un Administrateur	René Thion de la Chaume, Le Directeur
7	Stanislas Simon, Un Administrateur	René Thion de la Chaume, Le Directeur
8	René Thion de la Chaume, Le President	Paul Baudouin, Le Directeur-General
9	Macel Borduge, Le President	Paul Baudouin, Le Directeur-General
10	Paul Gannay, L'Inspecteur-General	Edmond Bruno, Le Directeur de la Succursale de Salgon
11	Emile Minost, Le President	Jean Laurent, Le Directeur-General Adjoin

FRENCH ADMINISTRATION

BANQUE DE L'INDO-CHINE

HAIPHONG

DÉCRET DU 21.1.1875

		Good	Fine	XF
1	**5 Dollars = 5 Piastres** 1876-96 (17.10.1896). Ovpt: *HAIPHONG* on #21. Rare.	600.	1500.	—
1A	**20 Dollars = 20 Piastres** (1876-92). Ovpt: *HAIPHONG* on #22. Rare.	1000.	2500.	—

DÉCRETS DES 21.1.1875 ET 20.2.1888

#2-4 handstamped city name. Date printed.

#2 w/text: *Emission autorisée 3 Aôut 1891.*

		Good	Fine	XF
2	**1 Dollar = 1 Piastre** ND (1892-99). Like #24.	400.	1200.	—
3	**20 Dollars = 20 Piastres** 1892-93 (25.4.1893; 28.4.1893.) Like #25. Rare.	800.	2000.	—
4	**100 Dollars = 100 Piastres** 1893-1907 (5.5.1893.) Like #26. Rare.	1500.	4000.	—

1897-99 ISSUE

#5 w/text: *Emission autorisée 3 Aôut 1891.*

#6 w/printed city and date.

		Good	Fine	XF
5	**1 Dollar = 1 Piastre** ND (1900-03). Like #27.	300.	800.	—
6	**5 Dollars = 5 Piastres** 1897-1900 (4.2.1897; 6.2.1897.) Like #28. Rare.	600.	1500.	—

***#7 Deleted*, see #1A and 3.**

1899-1900 ISSUE

		Good	Fine	XF
8	**5 Dollars = 5 Piastres** 19.9.1900; 20.9.1900. Red. Like #29.	400.	1000.	—
9	**20 Dollars = 20 Piastres** 12.9.1898; 13.9.1898; 14.9.1898; 15.9.1898. Red. Like #30. Rare.	600.	1500.	—
10	**100 Dollars = 100 Piastres** 17.2.1899. Red. Like #31. Rare.	1000.	2500.	—

DÉCRETS DES 21.1.1875, 20.2.1888 ET 16.5.1900

Notes in Piastres only.

		Good	Fine	XF
11	**100 Dollars = 100 Piastres** (1903). Red. Like #10. Reported not confirmed.	—	—	—

		Good	Fine	XF
12	**100 Piastres** 3.7.1903-22.3.1907. Red. Like #11. Sign. 4. Rare.	800.	2000.	—

DÉCRETS DES 21.1.1875, 20.2.1888, 16.5.1900 ET 3.4.1901

#13 w/text: ***Emission autorisée 3 Août 1891.***

		Good	Fine	XF
13	**1 Piastre** ND (1903-21). Like #34. City of issue handstamped.			
	a. Sign. 4 w/titles: *Un Administrateur* and *Le Directeur*. (1903-09).	50.00	150.	500.
	b. Sign. 5 w/titles: *Un Administrateur* and *L'Administrateur - Directeur*.(1909-21).	15.00	50.00	200.

		Good	Fine	XF
14	**5 Piastres** 9.6.1905; 10.6.1905; 1.3.1907; 2.3.1907. Red. Like #35. Sign. 4.	175.	1000.	1750.
15	**20 Piastres** 10.6.1905; 11.3.1907. Red. Like #36. Sign. 4.			
	a. Issued note.	300.	1200.	2000.
	s. Specimen. 30.2.1905.	—	—	—

1909-19 ISSUE

		Good	Fine	XF
16	**5 Piastres** 1.9.1910-29.11.1915. Green. Like #37.			
	a. Sign. 4 w/titles: *Un Administrateur* and *Le Directeur*. (1910).	100.	400.	1200.
	b. Sign. 5 w/titles: *Un Administrateur* and *L'Administrateur - Directeur*. (1910-15).	40.00	275.	900.

		Good	Fine	XF
17	**20 Piastres** 12.1.1909-6.4.1917. Green. Like #38.			
	a. Sign. 4 w/titles: *Un Administrateur* and *Le Directeur*. (1909).	200.	750.	1500.
	b. Sign. 5 w/titles: *Un Administrateur* and *L'Administrateur - Directeur* (1917).	50.00	300.	800.

		Good	Fine	XF
18	**100 Piastres** 6.5.1911-11.4.1919. Green and brown. Like #39. Sign. 5 w/titles: *Un Administrateur* and *L'Administrateur - Directeur*.	250.	800.	1500.

1920; 1925 ISSUE

#19 and 20 w/o décrets or autograph sign., w/o sign. titles: ***Le Caissier...***

		Good	Fine	XF
19	**5 Piastres** 27.5.1920. (1926-27). Green. Like #37. Sign. 5.	75.00	200.	600.

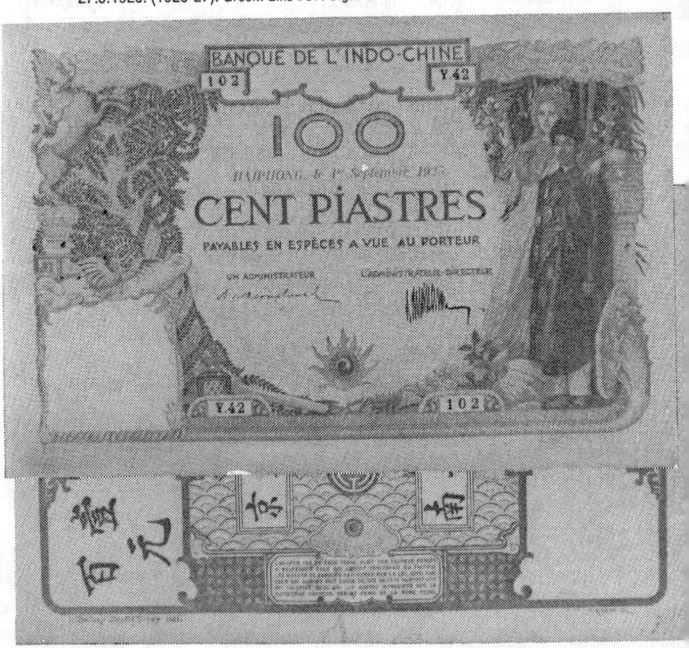

		Good	Fine	X[illegible]
20	**100 Piastres** 1.9.1925. Green and brown. Like #39. Sign. 6.	200.	600.	175[illegible]

SAIGON

DÉCRET DU 21.1.1875

#21-23 city of issue printed. Dates handwritten or handstamped.

		Good	Fine	XF
21	**5 Dollars = 5 Piastres** 1876-96 (19.7.1893; 8.2.1895; 30.1.1896). Blue. Neptune reclining holding trident at lower l. Sign. l.	750.	2500.	3500.

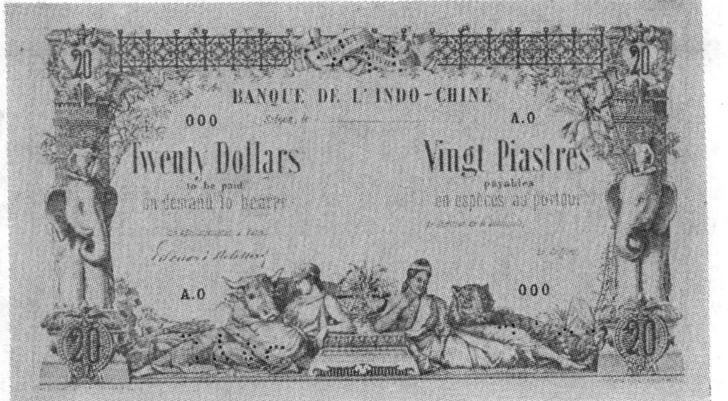

		Good	Fine	XF
22	**20 Dollars = 20 Piastres** (1876-92). Blue. Elephant columns l. and r. 2 reclining women w/ox l., tiger r. at lower border. Sign l.	750.	3000.	4500.

		Good	Fine	XF
23	**100 Dollars = 100 Piastres** (1877-93). 22.2.1879; 24.6.1890. Blue. Vasco da Gama at l., sailing ships at lower ctr., Polynesian man w/paddle by dragon boat at r. Sign l.	1000.	4000.	6000.

SAIGON

DÉCRETS DES 21.1.1875 ET 20.2.1888

#24-26 handstamped city name. Dates printed.

#24 w/text: *Emission autorisée 3 Aôut 1891.*

		Good	Fine	XF
24	**1 Dollar = 1 Piastre** ND (1892-99). Blue. Oriental woman seated below France seated holding caduceus at l. Sign 2.	200.	600.	1000.
25	**20 Dollars = 20 Piastres** 25.4.1893. Like #22. Issue date printed. Sign. 2.	500.	1500.	—
26	**100 Dollars = 100 Piastres** 2.5.1893; 5.5.1893; 9.5.1893; 12.5.1893. Like #23. Issue date printed. Sign. 2.			
	a. Issued note.	750.	2500.	—
	b. Cancelled w/handstamp: *ANNULÉ.* 2.5.1893; 9.5.1893.	750.	2500.	—

1897-1900 ISSUE

#27 w/text: *Emission autorisée 3 Aôut 1891.*

#28 printed city name and date.

		Good	Fine	XF
27	**1 Dollar = 1 Piastre** ND (1900-03). Red-brown. Like #24. Sign. 3.	250.	600.	1000.

		Good	Fine	XF
28	**5 Dollars = 5 Piastres** 9.1.1897; 23.1.1897. Like #21. Sign. 2.			
	a. Issued note.	275.	750.	1500.
	s. Specimen. 30.2.1899.	—	—	—

1900 ISSUE

		Good	Fine	XF
29	**5 Dollars = 5 Piastres** 26.9.1900; 27.9.1900; 1.10.1900; 4.10.1900; 5.10.1900. Blue. Like #28. Sign. 3.	500.	2000.	—
30	**20 Dollars = 20 Piastres** 3.9.1898; 5.9.1898; 6.9.1898; 7.9.1898. Blue. Like #22. Sign. 3.	750.	2500.	—
31	**100 Dollars = 100 Piastres** 16.2.1899. Blue. Like #23. Sign. 3.	1000.	4000.	—

DÉCRETS DES 21.1.1875, 20.2.1888 ET 16.5.1900

		Good	Fine	XF
32	**100 Dollars = 100 Piastres** 9.3.1903. Blue. Like #31. Sign. 4.	600.	2000.	—

1903 "PIASTRES" ISSUE

		Good	Fine	XF
33	**100 Piastres** 4.7.1903-20.3.1907. Blue w/black text. Like #32. Sign 4.	500.	2000.	—

DÉCRETS DES 21.1.1875, 20.2.1888, 16.5.1900 ET 3.4.1901

#34 w/text: *Emission autorisée 3 Aôut 1891.*

		Good	Fine	XF
34	**1 Piastre** ND (1903-21). Red-brown. Like #27. City of issue handstamped.			
	a. Sign. 4 w/titles: *Un Administrateur* and *Le Directeur.* (1903-09).	25.00	125.	500.
	b. Sign. 5 w/titles: *Un Administrateur* and *L'Administrateur - Directeur.* (1909-21).	10.00	50.00	150.
35	**5 Piastres** 5.6.1905; 7.6.1905; 8.6.1905; 4.3.1907; 5.3.1907; 6.3.1907. Like #29. Sign. 4.	200.	600.	1500.

		Good	Fine	XF
36	**20 Piastres** 5.6.1905; 6.6.1905; 14.3.1907; 15.3.1907; 16.3.1907. Blue. Like #22. Sign. 4.	350.	800.	1500.

1909-19 Issue

		Good	Fine	XF
37	**5 Piastres** 2.1.1909-15.11.1916. Purple. Ships in background at l., flowers at ctr. Dragon on back.			
	a. Sign. 4 w/titles: *Un Administrateur* and *Le Directeur.* (1909).	100.	300.	1000.
	b. Sign. 5 w/titles: *Un Administrateur* and *L'Administrateur - Directeur.* (1910-16).	25.00	100.	400.
38	**20 Piastres** 3.3.1913;23.5.1917. (1909). Purple. Seated woman w/sword at l., coupe at r. 2 dragons on back.			
	a. Sign. 4 w/titles: *Un Administrateur* and *Le Directeur.* (1909).	125.	300.	1250.
	b. Sign. 5 w/titles: *Un Administrateur* and *L'Administrateur - Directeur.* (1913-17).	50.00	200.	600.

		Good	Fine	XF
39	**100 Piastres** 3.5.1911-14.4.1919. Purple. Woman w/branch and wreath at r., mandarin in front. Dragon design on back. Sign 5 w/titles: *Un Administrateur* and *L'Administrateur - Directeur.*	75.00	200.	1000.

1920 Issue

#40-42 w/o décrets or autograph sign., w/o titles: *Le Caissier...*

		Good	Fine	XF
40	**5 Piastres** 5.1.1920-15.3.1920. Purple. Like #37. Sign. 5.	15.00	75.00	300.

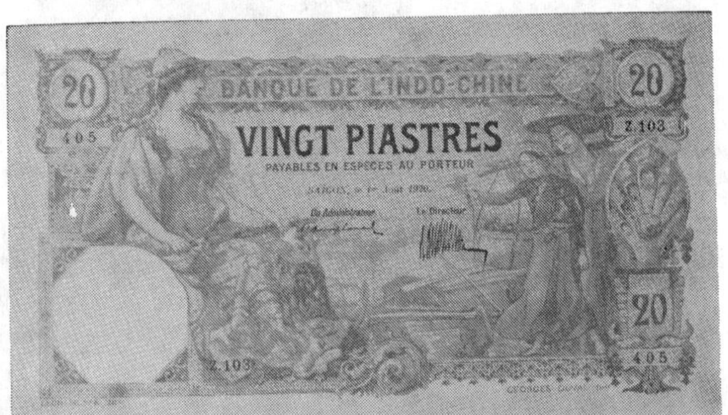

		Good	Fine	XF
41	**20 Piastres** 1.8.1920. Purple. Like #38. Sign. 6.	25.00	100.	400.

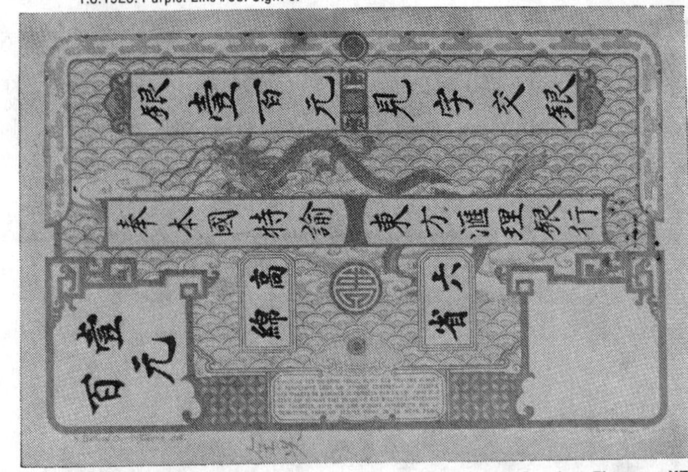

		Good	Fine	XF
42	**100 Piastres** 5.1.1920-27.1.1920. Purple. Like #39. Sign. 5.	50.00	200.	750.

Banque de l'Indo-Chine (1920s)

1920 Fractional Issue

Décret of 3.4.1901 and authorization date 6.10.1919 on back.

#43-47 printer: Chaix.

		VG	VF	UNC
43	**10 Cents** L.1919 (1920-23). Blue. Black serial #. Sign. 5.	10.00	20.00	90.00

		VG	VF	UNC
44	**10 Cents** L.1919 (1920-23). Blue like #43 but red serial #. Red Chinese and Vietnamese denomination ovpt. on back. Sign. 6.	5.00	25.00	100.

		VG	VF	UNC
45	**20 Cents** L.1919 (1920-23) Purple on gold unpt. Black serial #. Sign. 5.			
	a. Printer's name at lower r. on back.	5.00	30.00	125.
	b. W/o imprint.	4.00	20.00	90.00

		VG	VF	UNC
46	**50 Cents** L.1919 (1920-23). Red. Black serial #. Sign. 5.	5.00	35.00	150.

1921-28 ND Issue

		VG	VF	UNC
48	**1 Piastre** ND (1921-31). Brown and blue on lt. tan unpt. Helmeted woman at l. Large *$1* on back.			
	a. Sign. 6. (1921-26).	5.00	20.00	60.00
	b. Sign. 7. (1927-31).	1.00	10.00	30.00

		VG	VF	UNC
49	**5 Piastres** ND (1926-31). M/c. Woman w/wreath at r. Peacock on back.			
	a. Sign. 6. (1926).	25.00	100.	300.
	b. Sign. 7. (1927-31).	12.50	75.00	200.

		VG	VF	UNC
50	**20 Piastres** ND (1928-31). M/c. Woman w/wreath holding branch and golden sphere at ctr. Ancient statue on back. Sign. 7.	40.00	175.	800.

		VG	VF	UNC
51	**100 Piastres** ND (1925-39). M/c. Golden vessel w/dog on top at l. Bust statue of Duplex at ctr., head at r. on back			
	a. Sign. 6. (1925-26).	20.00	100.	400.
	b. Sign. 7. (1927-31).	17.50	75.00	300.
	c. Sign. 8. (1932-35).	30.00	120.	500.
	d. Sign. 9. (1936-39).	15.00	50.00	250.

BANQUE DE L'INDO-CHINE (1930S)

1932 ND ISSUE

#52-53 w/o Lao text on back.

		VG	VF	UNC
52	**1 Piastre** ND (1932). Brown, red amd m/c. Woman at r., bldg. at ctr., blue denomination numeral *1*. Man w/baskets on back. Sign. 8.	7.50	45.00	150.

53 5 Piastres
ND (1932). Brown, orange and m/c. Woman w/helmet and lance at l., denomination numeral *5* over wreath at upper r. Women w/headdress at l., ancient statues at r. on back. Sign. 8.

	VG	VF	UNC
a. Issued note.	25.00	50.00	200.
x. Contemporary counterfeit on genuine wmk. paper.	—	—	10.00

1932-39 ND Issue

#54-55 Lao text added on back.

Note: For 100 Piastres of this series, see #51c and #51d.

56 20 Piastres
ND (1936-39). Purple, blue and m/c. Helmeted woman holding wreath at ctr., Athens standing in background, maroon bank name and denomination *20*, blue *VINGT PIASTRES*. Helmeted woman holding wreath at ctr r. on back.

	VG	VF	UNC
a. Sign. 8. (1936). Specimen only.	—	—	400.
b. Sign. 9. (1936-39).	10.00	30.00	100.

57 500 Piastres
ND (from 1939). M/c. Woman and child examining globe; blue bank name and denomination numerals. 2 elephants behind woman and child on back. Sign. 9.

VG	VF	UNC
10.00	50.00	1500.

1942-45 ND Issues

#58-73 printed in French Indochina by the Imprimerie de l'Extreme Orient (I.D.E.O.) in Hanoi. Sign. 10.

58 1 Piastre
ND (1942-45). Dk. blue-black on orange unpt. Junks at l. Figure w/hands together on back.

	VG	VF	UNC
a. 7-digit serial #, 2.4mm tall.	1.00	4.00	25.00
b. 7-digit serial #, 2.0mm tall.	1.00	4.00	25.00
c. Letter and 6 digits in serial #, w/o serifs.	1.00	4.00	25.00

59 1 Piastre
ND. (1942-45) Black on blue unpt. Like #58.

	VG	VF	UNC
a. 7-digit serial #.	1.00	4.00	25.00
b. Letter and 6 digits in serial #, w/o serifs.	1.00	4.00	25.00

60 1 Piastre
ND. (1942-45) Dk. brown on purple unpt. (color shades). Like #58. 7-digit serial #.

VG	VF	UNC
.50	2.50	10.00

61 5 Piastres
ND (1942-45). Dk. green on red and m/c unpt. Back dk. brown on green unpt. Pavilion at water's edge.

VG	VF	UNC
1.00	10.00	55.00

62 5 Piastres
ND (1942-45). Like #61. Back gray and black.

	VG	VF	UNC
a. Serial # 4mm tall, w/serifs.	12.50	65.00	150.
b. Serial # 4.5mm tall, w/o serifs.	12.50	65.00	150.

63 5 Piastres
ND (1942-45). Dk. brown on pinkish brown and m/c unpt. Like #61.

VG	VF	UNC
2.00	15.00	35.00

64 5 Piastres
ND (1942-45). Violet, bright pink and m/c unpt. Like #61.

VG	VF	UNC
7.50	45.00	110.

#65-69 autograph sign. w/titles: *LE CAISSIER DE LA SUCCURSALE*.

65 20 Piastres
ND (1942-45). Blue on gray unpt. Like #71. Walled fortress at r. Seated figure on back. Letters: A-F.

VG	VF	UNC
2.00	15.00	40.00

		VG	VF	UNC
66	**100 Piastres** ND (1942-45). Lilac and orange frame and vignette. Market scenes at l. and r. Back orange and red, w/pagoda. Letters: A-G.	2.00	12.50	30.00
67	**100 Piastres** ND (1942-45). Violet frame, green and violet vignette. Like #66. Back violet. Letters: A-G.	3.00	15.00	40.00

		VG	VF	UNC
68	**500 Piastres** ND (1944-45). Blue on yellow unpt. Red value at ctr. r., 6 men on irrigation work. Back blue and m/c; dragon.	10.00	50.00	175.
69	**500 Piastres** ND (1945). Dk. green and gray. Like #68.	10.00	50.00	175.

1942-45 ND SECOND ISSUES

#70-73 printed sign. w/titles: *LE CAISSIER...*

		VG	VF	UNC
70	**20 Piastres** ND (1942-45). Green and yellow. Like #71. Letters: A-E.	2.00	15.00	30.00

		VG	VF	UNC
71	**20 Piastres** ND (1942-45). Black and gray on brown unpt. Like #65. Letters: A-L.	1.00	5.00	20.00
72	**20 Piastres** ND (1942-45). Pink and black. Like #65. Letters: A-E.	10.00	40.00	100.

		VG	VF	UNC
73	**100 Piastres** ND (1942-45). Black-green frame, orange, brown and yellow vignette. Back dk. brown. Like #66. Letters: A-Q.	2.00	12.50	30.00

1949; 1951 ND ISSUE

#74-75 printed in Japan in 1944 for issue in Indochina.

		VG	VF	UNC
74	**1 Piastre** ND (1949). Green, orange and m/c. 2 farmers w/ox. 2 women w/branches on back. Sign. 10.			
	a. Issued note.	2.50	10.00	30.00
	s. Specimen.		150.	300.

		VG	VF	UNC
75	**5 Piastres** ND. (1951) Green and m/c. Farmers working in rice fields. Temple w/Buddhists on back. Sign. 10.			
	a. Issued note w/regular serial #.	—	—	500.
	s1. Unfinished specimen, w/o signs. or serial #.	—	—	400.
	s2. Finished specimen w/2 signs. and serial # all zeros. Ovpt: *MIHON.*	—	—	800.

1945 ND ISSUE

#76-79 printed in the U.S. and England for issue in Indochina after WW II. All with Sign. 10.

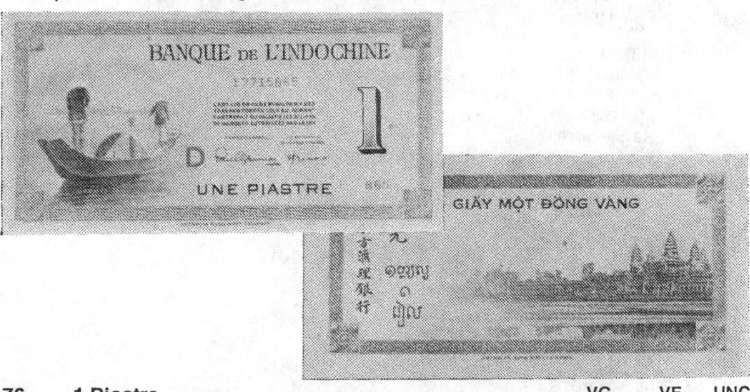

		VG	VF	UNC
76	**1 Piastre** ND (1945). Brown on lt. green unpt. 2 men w/boat. Back brown; Angkor Wat at r. Printer: ABNC.			
	a. Red letter B (Possibly not issued).	.10	.50	2.50
	b. Red letters A; C; D; E (1951).	1.00	2.00	15.00
	c. Red letter F (1951).	1.00	4.00	20.00
	s. Specimen.	—	—	100.

		VG	VF	UNC
77	**50 Piastres** ND (1945). Green. Man w/straw hat and baskets at r. Frieze from Angkor Wat on back. Printer: ABNC (w/o imprint).			
	a. Issued note.	10.00	40.00	200.
	s. Specimen.	—	—	375.

78 **100 Piastres**
ND (1945). Blue. Statues at Angkor Wat at l. 5 workers carrying baskets on back. Printer: ABNC (w/o imprint).

	VG	VF	UNC
a. Issued note.	2.00	12.50	100.
s. Specimen.	—	—	175.

1946 ND Issue

79 **100 Piastres**
ND (1946). Blue on m/c unpt. BIC bank bldg. at ctr. Back blue; 2 junks. Printer: TDLR (w/o imprint).

	VG	VF	UNC
a. Issued note.	10.00	50.00	300.
s. Specimen.	—	—	500.
x. Contemporary counterfeit, brown paper.	2.50	10.00	30.00

1947-51 ND Issue

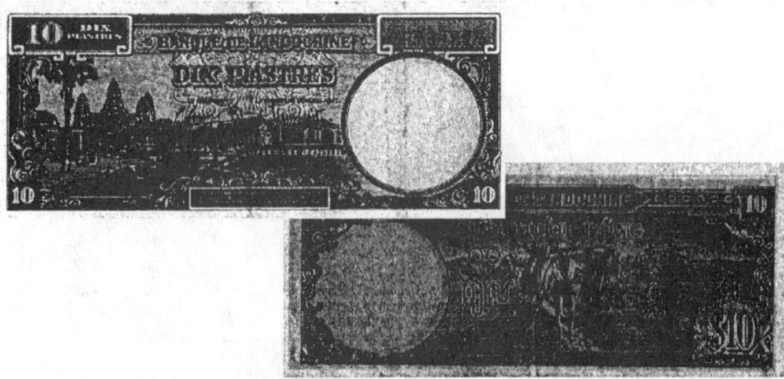

80 **10 Piastres**
ND (1947). Dk. purple on m/c unpt. Angkor Wat at l. Back red; field worker. Sign. 11. 2 Serial # varieties. Printer: TDLR (w/o imprint).

VG	VF	UNC
3.00	8.00	40.00

81 **20 Piastres**
ND (1949). M/c. Like #56, but white bank name and value *20* on red background, red *VINGT PIASTRES.* Sign. 11.

	VG	VF	UNC
a. Issued note.	5.00	30.00	125.
s. Specimen.	—	—	—

82 **100 Piastres**
ND (1947-54). M/c. Mercury at l. Man w/2 elephants at l., man at r. on back. Sign 11.

	VG	VF	UNC
a. Type I Lao text on back. (1947-49).	2.50	20.00	100.
b. Type II Lao text on back. 1949-54).	1.50	7.50	50.00
s. Specimen.	—	—	250.

83 **500 Piastres**
ND (1951). M/c. Like #57, but white bank name and value numerals on red background. Sign. 11.

	VG	VF	UNC
a. Issued note.	45.00	175.	500.
s. Specimen.	—	—	1000.

84 **1000 Piastres**
ND (printed 1951). Gray, orange and m/c. Elephant at l., water buffaloes at r. Bayon head (Angkor) at l., tree at r. on back. Wmk. Woman in Cambodian dancer's headdress. Sign. 11 w /title: *Le Directeur General.*

	VG	VF	UNC
s1. Specimen (serial # all O's).	—	—	1500.
s2. Note w/regular serial # perforated: *SPECIMEN.* Rare.	—	—	—

Note: Several known of #84s1, only 1 of #84s2. For issued note of similar design see #98, also #109.

NOTICE

Readers with unlisted dates, signature varieties, etc.
are invited to submit photocopies or,
high resolution (300 dpi, 100% size) scans of their notes to:
Standard Catalog of World Paper Money,
700 East State St. Iola, WI 54990-0001,
or E-Mail: george.cuhaj@fwpubs.com.

GOUVERNEMENT GENERAL DE L'INDOCHINE

#85-91 issued during WW II by French Indochina colonial administration. Printed by the Imprimerie de l'Extreme Orient (I.D.E.O.) in Hanoi.

SIGNATURE VARIETIES/TITLE COMBINATIONS BANQUE DE L'INDOCHINE ISSUES, 1939–43

No.	Signature	Title	Signature	Title
12	Emile Henry	Le Tresorier Payeur General	Yves Cazaux	Le Directeur des Finances
13	Louis Mayet	Le Tresorier General	Yves Cazaux	Le Directeur des Finances
14	Louis Mayet	Le Tresorier General	Jean Cousin	Le Directeur des Finances

1939 ND ISSUE

		VG	VF	UNC
85	**10 Cents**			
	ND (1939). Red-brown. Sculptures at l., dancer at r. Market scene w/elephants on back.			
	a. *Le Tresorier Payeur General* in 2 lines at lower l. Denominations in Chinese, Cambodian and Vietnamese on back. Sign. 12.	6.50	25.00	75.00
	b. Like #85a, but denomination in Lao added on back. Sign. 12.	6.50	25.00	75.00
	c. *Le Tresorier General* in 1 line at lower l. Sign. 13.	1.00	2.00	12.50
	d. Like #85c, serial # format 123456LL. Sign. 14.	.25	1.50	7.50
	e. Like #85d, but serial # format LL 123.456. Color is dk. brown.	.25	1.00	4.00

		VG	VF	UNC
86	**20 Cents**			
	ND (1939). Red-brown and green. Women w/conical hat at l., boat at ctr. on back.			
	a. Like #85a. Sign. 12.	7.00	27.50	100.
	b. *Deleted.*	—	—	—
	c. Like #85c. Sign. 13.	1.00	3.00	15.00
	d. Like #85d. Sign. 14.	1.00	3.00	15.00

		VG	VF	UNC
87	**50 Cents**			
	ND (1939). Red-brown and purple. Woman w/pole on back.			
	a. Like #85a. Sign. 12.	3.00	20.00	100.
	b. *Deleted.*	—	—	—
	c. Like #85c. Sign. 13.	2.00	7.50	20.00
	d. Like #85d. Sign. 14.	2.00	7.50	20.00
	e. Like #87d, but coffee-brown and black.	4.00	15.00	40.00

1942 ND ISSUE

#89-91, (from 1942-43) Pham-Ngoc-Khue, designer. Color shades vary. Sign. 14.

		VG	VF	UNC
88	**5 Cents**			
	ND (1942). Green on pale blue unpt.			
	a. Signs., titles and penalty clause in black. Serial # format: 123456L.	.25	2.00	6.00
	b. Green unpt. Sign., titles and penalty clause in green. Serial # format: LL123456.	.25	1.00	3.00

		VG	VF	UNC
89	**10 Cents**			
	ND (1942). Brown on tan unpt.			
	a. Serial # format: LL123.456.	.25	1.00	2.00
	b. Serial # format: 1LL234.567.	1.25	5.00	15.00

		VG	VF	UNC
90	**20 Cents**			
	ND (1942). Red-violet on pinkish unpt. Dragons and flames at ctr.	.50	1.75	4.00
91	**50 Cents**			
	ND (1942). Green on lt. green unpt. Dragons in unpt. at l. and r. w/rice underneath on back.			
	a. Serial # format: LL123.456.	.50	2.00	5.00
	b. Serial # format: 1LL234.567.	1.25	5.00	15.00

INSTITUT D'EMISSION DES ETATS DU CAMBODGE, DU LAOS ET DU VIETNAM

On 31.12.1951 the exclusive privilege of banknote issue was withdrawn from the Banque de l'Indochine and transferred to the "Issuing Authority of the (Associated) States of Cambodia, Laos and Vietnam." Institut d'Emission notes, with but one exception, distinct for each state, were legal tender in all three until 1955. They were exchangeable at par with Banque de l'Indochine notes which not only remained in circulation but continued to be issued until existing stocks, transferred to the Institut d'Emission, were exhausted. The Piastre-French Franc exchange rate, reset at 1:17 in 1946, continued unchanged until May 1953 when France unilaterally adjusted it to 1:10.

SIGNATURE VARIETIES/TITLE COMBINATIONS ON INSTITUT D'EMISSION NOTES

No.	Signature / Title	Signature / Title	
15	Gaston Cusin, Le President	M. Lacoutre, Le Caissier Central	ALL THREE STATES
16		Le Caissier General (unidentified)	ALL THREE STATES
17		Chhean Vam	CAMBODIA
18		Son Sann	CAMBODIA
19		Khun One Voravong, Un Administrateur	LAOS
20		Le Ky Huong	LAOS
21		Nghiem Van Tri, Un Administrateur	VIET-NAM

CAMBODIA, LAOS AND VIETNAM COMBINED ISSUE

1953 ND ISSUE

		VG	VF	UNC
92	**1 Piastre** ND (1953). Brown, red and m/c. Woman at r. Similar to #54, but modified legends in red. Sign. 15.	.50	4.00	15.00

CAMBODIA ISSUE

1953-54 ND ISSUES

#93-98 wmk: Elephant head. Cambodian title on back.

		VG	VF	UNC
93	**1 Piastre = 1 Riel** ND (1953). Green and blue on yellow and m/c unpt. Young Kg. Sihanouk at ctr. Back red on yellow unpt. Sign. 16.	10.00	40.00	100.

		VG	VF	UNC
94	**1 Piastre = 1 Riel** ND (1954). Blue and green. Face like #100 and 105 w/trees. Back blue and brown; royal houseboat at l. Sign. 18.	3.00	20.00	75.00

		VG	VF	UNC
95	**5 Piastres = 5 Riels** ND (1953). Green on pink and green unpt. Face like #101 and 106 w/banana trees at l., palms at r. Naga (mythical snake) head at l. on back. Sign. 18.	3.00	25.00	80.00

		VG	VF	UNC
96	**10 Piastres = 10 Riels** ND (1953). Red on blue and gold unpt. Face like #102 and 107 w/stylized sunburst at ctr. 2 dancers at l. on back.			
	a. Sign. 17.	3.00	6.00	40.00
	b. Sign. 18.	3.00	30.00	100.

		VG	VF	UNC
97	**100 Piastres = 100 Riels** ND (1954). Orange and m/c. Face like #103 and 108 w/3 women at l. representing Cambodia, Laos & Vietnam. Back brown and m/c; Temple of Angkor. Sign. 18.	5.00	30.00	150.

		VG	VF	UNC
98	**200 Piastres = 200 Riels** ND (1953). Green and brown. Face like #84 and 109. Elephant at l., 2 water buffaloes at r. Bayon head (Angkor) at l., tree at r. on back. Sign. 17.	35.00	85.00	300.

Note: For later issues see Cambodia.

LAOS ISSUE

1953-54 ND ISSUES

#99-103 wmk: Elephant head. Laotian title on back.

		VG	VF	UNC
99	**1 Piastre = 1 Kip** ND (1953). Blue-black on green, pale yellow and m/c unpt. Kg. Sisavang Vong at ctr. Back red on yellow unpt. Sign. 16.	3.00	12.50	75.00

		VG	VF	UNC
100	**1 Piastre = 1 Kip** ND (1954). Blue and green. Face like #94 and 105. Back brown and blue; pagoda w/3 roofs at l. Luang-Prabang at l. Sign. 19.	15.00	50.00	100.

		VG	VF	UNC
101	**5 Piastres = 5 Kip** ND (1953). Green on pink and green unpt. Face like #96 and 106. Stupa at That Luang at l. on back. Sign. 19.	5.00	40.00	100.

		VG	VF	UNC
102	**10 Piastres = 10 Kip** ND (1953). Red on blue and gold unpt. Face like #96 and 107. Laotian woman at l. on back. Sign. 19.	3.00	20.00	75.00
103	**100 Piastres = 100 Kip** ND (1954). M/c. Face like #97 and 108. Pagoda at Vientiane at ctr., Laotian woman w/bowl of roses at r. on back. Sign. 20.	10.00	40.00	150.

Note: For later issues see Laos.

VIETNAM ISSUE

1953-54 ND ISSUES

#104-109 wmk: Tiger head. Vietnamese title on back: VIÊN PHÁT-HÀNH.

		VG	VF	UNC
104	**1 Piastre = 1 Dong** ND (1953). Blue-black on green, pale yellow and m/c unpt. Bao Dai at ctr. Back red on yellow unpt. Sign. 16.	1.00	5.00	20.00

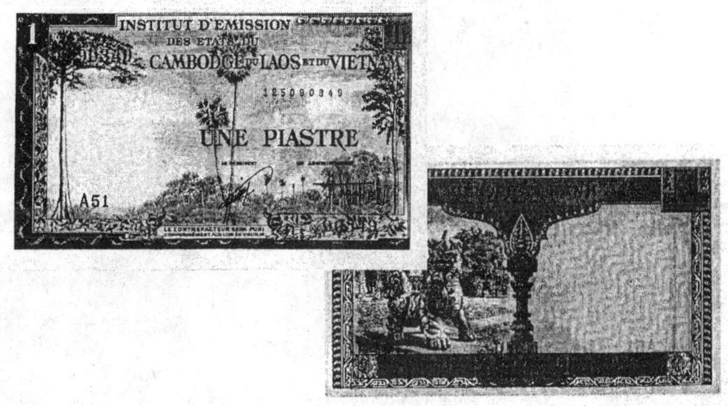

		VG	VF	UNC
105	**1 Piastre = 1 Dong** ND (1954). Blue and green. Face like #94 and 100. Back brown and blue; dragon at l. Sign. 21. Thin white or white/tan paper.	1.00	2.00	8.00

		VG	VF	UNC
106	**5 Piastres = 5 Dong** ND (1953). Green on pink and green unpt. Face like #95 and 101. Bao Dai at l. on back. Sign. 21.	1.00	4.00	20.00

		VG	VF	UNC
107	**10 Piastres = 10 Dong** ND (1953). Red on blue and gold unpt. Face like #96 and 102. Rock in the Bay of Along at l. on back. Sign. 21.	1.00	6.00	30.00

108	100 Piastres = 100 Dong	VG	VF	UNC
	ND (1954). M/c. Face like #97 and 103. Small bldg. at ctr., Bao Dai at r. on back. Sign. 21.	2.00	15.00	80.00

109	200 Piastres = 200 Dong	VG	VF	UNC
	ND (1953). Green, brown and pink. Face like #98. Bao Dai at l., pagoda at ctr. on back. Sign. 21.	6.00	40.00	200.

Note: For later issues see Viet Nam.

JAPANESE OCCUPATION, WW II

JAPANESE IMPERIAL GOVERNMENT

大日本帝國政府

Ta Jih Pen Ti Kuo Cheng Fu

1938-40 ND ISSUE

		VG	VF	UNC
M1	**50 Sen** ND (1940). Blue on yellow-green and lt. purple unpt. Dragon at l. Back blue.	50.00	125.	250.
M2	**1 Yen** ND (1940). Purple on yellow-green and brown unpt. Onagadori cockerel at l. Back purple.	150.	250.	500.
M3	**5 Yen** ND (1940). Gray-green on gray-blue and lt. purple unpt. Onagadori cockerel at l. and r. Back dk. green.	600.	1000.	2000.
M4	**10 Yen** ND (1940). Brown on lt. blue and pink unpt. Onagadori cockerel at l. and r. Block # and serial #. Back brown.	600.	1000.	2000.
M5	**100 Yen** ND (1938). Blue-green on lt. lilac unpt. Onagadori cockerel at l. and r. Specimen.	—	—	500.

Note: For 100 Yen of same design but different color printing, see China #M21.

1942 ND ISSUE

M6	1 Yen	VG	VF	UNC
	ND (ca.1942). Purple on yellow-green unpt, lithograph. Like #M2 but only 2 block #. W/o *Ro* prefix. Back purple. Specimen.	—	—	500.

M7	10 Yen	VG	VF	UNC
	ND (ca.1942). Brown on lt. blue unpt., lithograph. Like #M4 but only 2 block #. W/o *Ro* prefix. Back brown.	.50	2.50	10.00

The colony of French Oceania (now the Territory of French Polynesia), comprising 130 basalt and coral islands scattered among five archipelagoes in the South Pacific, had an area of 1,544 sq. mi. (3,999 sq. km.) and a population of about 185,000, mostly Polynesians. Capital: Papeete. The colony produced phosphates, copra and vanilla.

Tahiti of the Society Islands, the hub of French Oceania, was visited by Capt. Cook in 1769 and by Capt. Bligh in the Bounty 1788-89. The Society Islands were claimed by France in 1768, and in 1903 grouped with the Marquesas Islands, the Tuamotu Archipelago, the Gambier Islands and the Astral Islands under a single administrative head located at Papeete, Tahiti, to form the colony of French Oceania.

RULERS:
French

MONETARY SYSTEM:
1 Franc = 100 Centimes

FRENCH ADMINISTRATION

CHAMBRE DE COMMERCE DES ETABLISSEMENTS FRANÇAIS DE L'OCÉANIE

1919 FIRST ISSUE

Arrété du 29 Decembre 1919

#1-4 woman leaning on arch at l. and r. Helmeted head at l. and r. on back. Printer: Halpin Lithograph Co., San Francisco.

		Good	Fine	XF
1	**25 Centimes** L.1919. Brown.	35.00	125.	500.

		Good	Fine	XF
2	**50 Centimes** L.1919. Green.	35.00	125.	500.

		Good	Fine	XF
3	**1 Franc** L.1919. Orange. Black or red serial #.	35.00	135.	550.

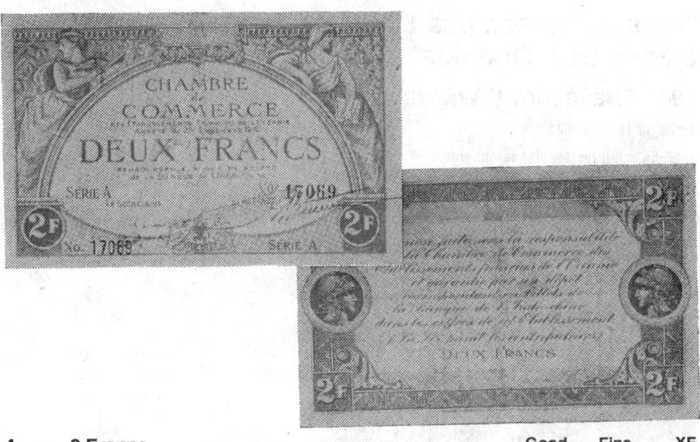

		Good	Fine	XF
4	**2 Francs** L.1919. Purple.	35.00	135.	550.

1919 SECOND ISSUE

#1A-2A, 5-6 w/o design, but same date as previous issue. Local printer.

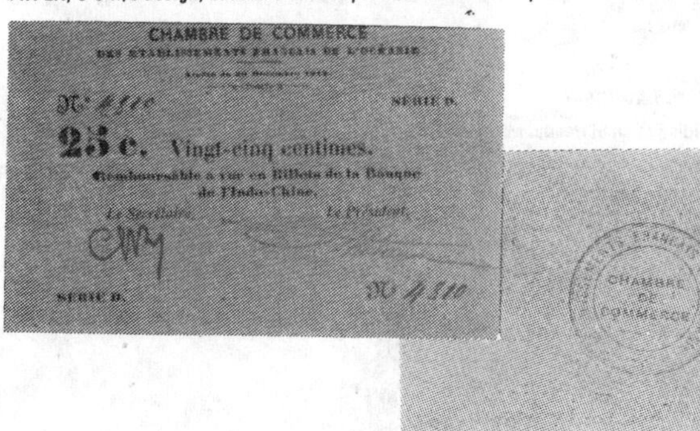

		Good	Fine	XF
4A	**25 Centimes** L.1919. Brown.	60.00	200.	550.
4B	**50 Centimes** L.1919. Blue.	60.00	200.	550.

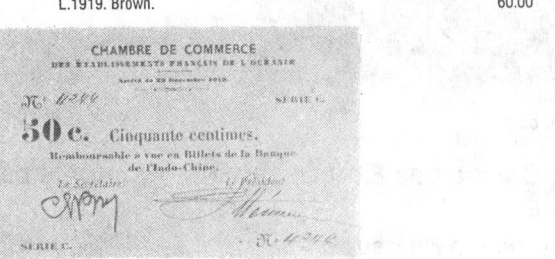

		Good	Fine	XF
5	**1 Franc** L.1919. Black. Dk. brown paper.	60.00	200.	550.
6	**2 Francs** L.1919. Black. Tan paper.	60.00	200.	550.

Bons de Caisse des Etablissements Français Libres de L'Océanie

1941 Emergency WWII Issue

Arrêté du 18 Aôut 1941

#A6A-6B small rectangular cardboards.

		VG	VF	UNC
6A	**1 Franc** D.1941. Black. Soccer player at ctr. on back. Rare.	—	—	—

		VG	VF	UNC
6B	**1 Franc** D. 1941. Black. Plow at ctr. on back. Rare.	—	—	—

		VG	VF	UNC
6C	**2 Francs** D.1941. Rare.	—	—	—

1942 Issue

Arrêté No. 300 A.G.F. du 7 Avril 1942

#7-9 upright hand holding torch of freedom behind shield of Lorraine at ctr.

		VG	VF	UNC
7	**50 Centimes** L.1942. Orange and green. 2 sign. varieties.	65.00	275.	650.
8	**1 Franc** L.1942. Green and red. 2 sign. varieties.	75.00	300.	700.

		VG	VF	UNC
9	**2 Francs** L.1942. Blue and black. 2 sign. varieties.	85.00	325.	750.

Bons de Caisse des Etablissements Français de L'Océanie

1943 Emergency WWII Issue

Arrêté No. 698 S.G. du 25 Septembre 1943

		VG	VF	UNC
10	**50 Centimes** L.1943. Orange and black. Map outline on back w/text inside.			
	a. Circular violet handstamp.	37.50	125.	300.
	b. Wreath in circular violet handstamp.	40.00	135.	350.
	c. Embossed seal.	37.50	125.	325.
11	**1 Franc** L.1943. Green and purple. Like #10.			
	a. Circular violet handstamp.	37.50	135.	325.
	b. Wreath in circular violet handstamp.	40.00	165.	400.
	c. Embossed seal.	37.50	125.	300.
12	**2 Francs** L.1943. Blue and green. Like #10.			
	a. Circular violet handstamp.	50.00	165.	375.
	b. Wreath in circular violet handstamp.	60.00	200.	500.
	c. Embossed seal.	50.00	165.	375.
	d. W/o seal.	60.00	165.	350.

		VG	VF	UNC
13	**2.50 Francs** L.1943. Black and red. Like #10.			
	a. Circular violet handstamp.	50.00	165.	375.
	b. Wreath in circular violet handstamp.	60.00	200.	500.
	c. Embossed seal.	50.00	165.	375.

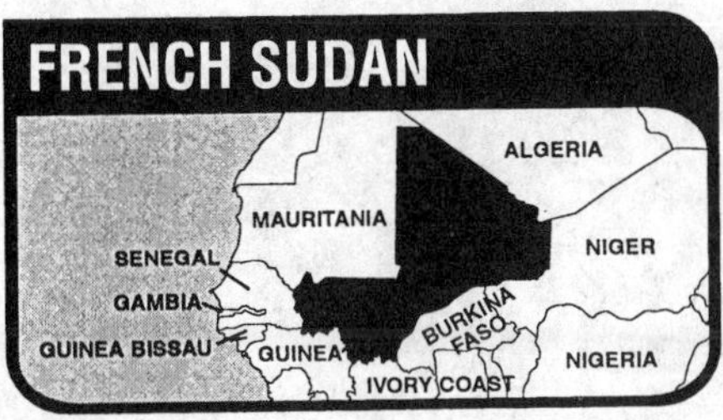

The French Sudan, a landlocked country in the interior of West Africa southwest of Algeria, has an area of 478,764 sq. mi. (1,240,000 sq. km.). Capital: Bamako. Livestock, fish, cotton and peanuts are exported.

French Sudanese are descendants of the ancient Malinke Kingdom of Mali that controlled the middle Niger from the 11th to the 17th centuries. The French penetrated the Sudan (now Mali) about 1880, and established their rule in 1898 after subduing fierce native resistance. In 1904 the are became the colony of Upper Senegal-Niger (changed to French Sudan in 1920), and became part of the French Union in 1946. In 1958 French Sudan became the Sudanese Republic with complete internal autonomy. Senegal joined with the Sudanese Republic in 1959 to form the Mali Federation which, in 1960, became a fully independent member of the French Community. Upon Senegal's subsequent withdrawal from the Federation, the Sudanese, on Sept. 22, 1960, proclaimed their nation the fully independent Republic of Mali and severed all ties with France.

RULERS:

French

MONETARY SYSTEM:

1 Franc = 100 Centimes

French Administration

Gouvernement Général de l'Afrique

Occidentale Française

Colonie du Soudan Française

1917 Emergency WWI Issue

Décret du 11.2.1917 Soudan Française

		VG	VF	UNC
A1	**0.50 Franc**			
	D.1917.			
	a. Wmk: Bees.	85.00	235.	650.
	b. Wmk: Laurel leaves.	75.00	225.	550.

Note: Denominations of 1 Franc and 2 Francs probably exist but have not been reported. For later issues see Mali in Volume 3.

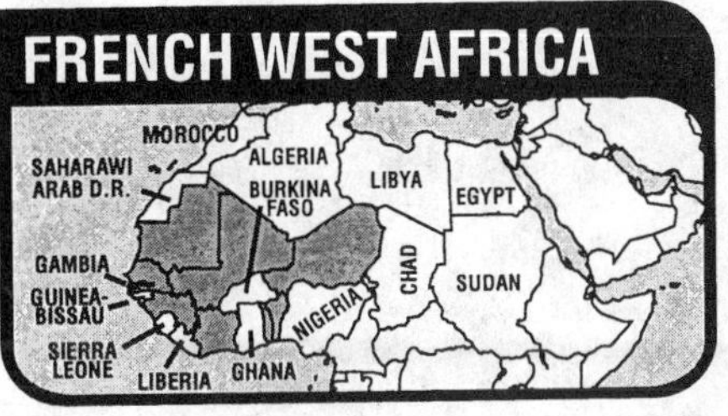

French West Africa (Afrique Occidentale Francaise), a former federation of French colonial territories on the northwest coast of Africa, has an area of 1,831,079 (4,742,495 sq. km.) and a population of about 17 million. Capital: Dakar. The constituent territories were Mauritania, Senegal, Dahomey, French Sudan, Ivory Coast, Upper Volta, Niger, French Guinea, and later on the mandated area of Togo. Peanuts, palm kernels, cacao, coffee and bananas were exported.

Prior to the mid-19th century, France, as the other European states, maintained establishments on the west coast of Africa for the purpose of trading in slaves and gum, but made no serious attempt at colonization. From 1854 onward, the coastal settlements were gradually extended into the interior until, by the opening of the 20th century, acquisition ended and organization and development began. French West Africa was formed in 1895 by grouping the several colonies under one administration (at Dakar) while retaining a large measure of autonomy to each of the constituent territories. The inhabitants of French West Africa were made French citizens in 1946. With the exception of French Guinea, all of the colonies voted in 1958 to become autonomous members of the new French Community. French Guinea voted to become the fully independent Republic of Guinea. The present-day independent states are members of the "Union Monetaire Ouest-Africaine."

Also see West African States.

MONETARY SYSTEM:

1 Franc = 100 Centimes
1 Unit = 5 Francs

French Administration

Banque de l'Afrique Occidentale

SIGNATURE TITLES:

a, c, f, h, j, l: ***Un Administrateur, Le Directeur***
b, e: ***Un Administrateur, Le Directeur, Le Caissier***
d, g, i, k: ***Le Président, L'Administrateur- Directeur***
m: ***Le Président, Le Directeur General***

CITIES OF ISSUE:

In addition to city of issue designation, the back color is the same for all denominations within a city.

A - Conakri, Conakry (French Guinea) Back: green.
B - Dakar (Senegal) Back: red (5 Francs green)
C - Duala (Cameroon) Ovpt. on Conakry or Dakar notes.
D - Grand-Bassam (Ivory Coast) Back: blue.
E - Porto Novo (Dahomey) Back: dk. brown or red.
F - St. Louis (Senegal) Back: red.

NOTE: The first issue of the bank also circulated in Equatorial Africa, Togo and Cameroon. Dakar is most frequently encountered. Notes with Lome (Togo) imprint allegedly exist but no examples have been reported.

Conakry

1903-24 Issue

		Good	Fine	XF
5A	**5 Francs**			
	1904-1919. Blue and yellow. Lion at l.; bowl, drum and other objects at r.			
	a. *CONAKRI.* Sign. titles: a. 13.1.1904; 5.2.1904.	85.00	225.	500.
	b. *CONAKRY.* Sign. titles: c. 10.7.1919.	75.00	200.	450.
9A	**50 Francs**			
	1920-24. Blue and yellow. Elephant head and tree and l. at r. *CONAKRY.* Sign. titles: h.			
	a. Sign. titles: e. 12.2.1920.	—	—	—
	b. Sign. titles: h. 12.6.1924.	100.	350.	650.
10A	**100 Francs**			
	1903-24. Red and green. Like #9A. *CONAKRY.*			
	a. Sign. titles: a. 3.1.1903.	140.	500.	—
	b. Sign. titles: e. 12.2.1920.	100.	350.	650.
	c. Sign. titles: i. 13.11.1924.	110.	375.	700.
	s. Specimen. As a.	—	—	—
13A	**500 Francs**			
	1912-24. Blue and yellow. Like #9A. *CONAKRY.*			
	a. Sign. titles: b. 12.9.1912.	350.	850.	—
	b. Sign. titles: g. 10.11.1921.	300.	750.	—
	c. Sign. titles: i. 10.4.1924.	300.	750.	—

		Good	Fine	XF
15A	**1000 Francs**			
	10.4.1924. Red and green. Like #9A. *CONAKRY.* Sign. titles: i.	375.	1000.	—

DAKAR

1892 ND PROVISIONAL ISSUE

		Good	Fine	XF
3	**100 Francs** ND (old dates 26; 30.11.1892). Blue on pink unpt. Ovpt. new heading at top and *DAKAR* at lower ctr. on unissued 1892 France 100 Francs. Rare.	—	—	—

1916-24 ISSUE

		Good	Fine	XF
5B	**5 Francs** 1916-32. Blue and yellow. Like #5A.			
	a. Sign. titles: c. 8.6.1916; 28.5.1918; 10.7.1919.	17.50	55.00	135.
	b. Sign. titles: h. 14.12.1922; 10.4.1924.	15.00	40.00	125.
	c. Sign. titles: j. 1.8.1925; 17.2.1926; 21.10.1926.	12.00	35.00	120.
	d. Sign. titles: k. 10.6.1926.	12.00	35.00	120.
	e. Sign. titles: m. 16.5.1929; 1.9.1932.	17.50	55.00	135.

		Good	Fine	XF
7B	**25 Francs** 1920-26. Gray-brown and green. Like #9A.			
	a. Sign. titles: d. 15.4.1920.	50.00	150.	425.
	b. Sign. titles: i. 9.7.1925.	30.00	125.	300.
	c. Sign. titles: k. 10.6.1926.	30.00	125.	300.
9B	**50 Francs** 1919; 1926; 1929. Blue and yellow. Like #9A.			
	a. Sign. titles: b. 11.9.1919.	50.00	150.	425.
	b. Sign. titles: k. 11.2.1926.	35.00	115.	300.
	c. Sign. titles: m. 14.3.1929.	50.00	150.	425.

		Good	Fine	XF
10B	**100 Francs** 15.4.1920. Red and green. Like #9A. Ovpt: *DAKAR* on CONAKRY. Ovpt: *SENEGAL* in large lettering across green back. Sign. titles: f.	100.	250.	550.
11B	**100 Francs** 1924; 1926. Normally printed city of issue, otherwise face like #10B.			
	a. Sign. titles: i. 13.11.1924.	50.00	150.	425.
	b. Sign. titles: k. 24.9.1926.	50.00	150.	425.

		Good	Fine	XF
12B	**500 Francs** 10.11.1921. Blue and yellow. Ovpt: *DAKAR* on CONAKRY. Ovpt: *Senegal* in lg. lettering across green back. Sign. titles: g.	300.	650.	—
13B	**500 Francs** 1919-24. Blue and yellow. Like #13A.			
	a. Sign. titles: d. 11.9.1919.	350.	850.	—
	b. Sign. titles: g. 10.11.1921.	300.	750.	—
	c. Sign. titles: i. 10.4.1924.	275.	675.	—
15B	**1000 Francs** 10.4.1924. Red and green. Like #9A. Sign. titles: i.	325.	900.	—

DUALA

1919-21 ISSUE

		Good	Fine	XF
6C	**25 Francs** 15.4.1920. Ovpt: *DUALA* on CONAKRY. Sign. titles: f.	250.	550.	—
13C	**500 Francs** 10.11.1921. Blue and yellow. Ovpt: *DUALA* on DAKAR. *DUALA* in lg. lettering across green back. Sign. titles: g.	500.	1500.	—
14C	**1000 Francs** 11.9.1919. Ovpt: *DUALA* similar to #13C. Sign. titles: d.	600.	1750.	—

GRAND-BASSAM

1904-24 ISSUES

		Good	Fine	XF
5D	**5 Francs** 1904-19. Like #5A.			
	a. Sign. titles: a. 26.2.1904; 1.3.1904.	90.00	250.	600.
	b. Sign. titles: c. 8.6.1916; 18.5.1918; 28.5.1918; 10.7.1919.	85.00	235.	475.

		Good	Fine	XF
6D	**25 Francs** 12.7.1923. Gray-brown. Like #9A. Ovpt: *GRAND-BASSAM* on *CONAKRI*. Ovpt. *COTE de IVOIRE* in lg. lettering across green back. Sign. titles: h.	265.	550.	—
7D	**25 Francs** 1920; 1923. Normally printed city of issue, otherwise like #6D.			
	a. Sign. titles: f. 12.2.1920.	180.	500.	1000.
	b. Sign. titles: i. 12.7.1923.	180.	500.	1000.
9D	**50 Francs** 1920; 1924. Like #9A.			
	a. Sign. titles: f. 12.2.1920.	275.	675.	—
	b. Sign. titles: i. 12.6.1924.	275.	675.	—
11D	**100 Francs** 1910-24. Like #11B.			
	a. Sign. titles: b. 18.8.1910; 9.3.1916.	325.	750.	—
	b. Sign. titles: e. 12.2.1920.	325.	750.	—
	c. Sign. titles: f. 15.4.1920.	325.	750.	—
	d. Sign. titles: i. 13.11.1924.	325.	750.	—
12D	**100 Francs** 15.4.1920. Ovpt: *GRAND-BASSAM* similar to #6D. sign. titles: f.	375.	750.	—
13D	**500 Francs** 15.4.1924. Like #13A. Sign. titles: f.	450.	950.	—
14D	**1000 Francs** 15.4.1924. Like #9A. Sign. titles: f.	600.	1500.	—

PORTO-NOVO

1916-24 ISSUE

		Good	Fine	XF
5E	**5 Francs** 8.6.1916; 28.5.1918; 10.7.1919. Like #5A. Sign. titles: c.	85.00	225.	500.
7E	**25 Francs** 1920; 1923. Like #7B.			
	a. Sign. titles: e. 12.2.1920.	180.	500.	950.
	b. Sign. titles: i. 12.7.1923.	180.	500.	950.
10E	**50 Francs** 1920; 1924. Like #9A.			
	a. Sign. titles: e. 12.2.1920.	300.	675.	—
	b. Sign. titles: i. 12.6.1924.	300.	675.	—
11E	**100 Francs** 1920; 1924. Like #11B.			
	a. Sign. titles: f. 15.4.1920.	325.	750.	—
	b. Sign. titles: i. 13.11.1924.	325.	750.	—
12E	**100 Francs** 9.3.1916. Like #12D. Ovpt: *PORTO NOVO* on GRAND BASSAM. Ovpt: *DAHOMEY* in lg. lettering across back. Sign. titles: b.	325.	750.	—
13E	**500 Francs** 10.4.1924. Like #13A. Sign. titles: f.	450.	1100.	—
14E	**1000 Francs** 11.9.1919. Red and green. Ovpt. *PORTO-NOVO* on DAKAR. Ovpt. *DAHOMEY* in lg. lettering across red back. Sign. titles: d.	600.	1500.	—
15E	**1000 Francs** 10.4.1924. Like #9A. Sign. titles: i.	600.	1500.	—

SAINT-LOUIS

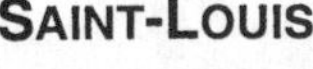

1904-17 ISSUES

		Good	Fine	XF
5F	**5 Francs** 1904; 1916. Like #5A.			
	a. Sign. titles: a. 1.2.1904.	200.	550.	—
	b. Sign. titles: c. 8.6.1916; 15.8.1918.	140.	400.	650.
7F	**25 Francs** 9.11.1917. Sign. titles: b.	250.	600.	—
9F	**50 Francs** 9.10.1905. Like #9A. Sign. titles: b.	275.	750.	—
13F	**500 Francs** 12.9.1912; 11.9.1913. Like #13A. Sign. titles: b.	500.	1150.	—
14F	**1000 Francs** 14.10.1905. Sign. titles: a.	600.	1500.	—

W/O

1919 ISSUE

		Good	Fine	XF
5G	**5 Francs** 10.7.1919. Like #5A. Sign. titles: c.	100.	275.	575.

1934-37 ISSUE

#21-27 w/o city of issue. Printed by the Banque de France (w/o imprint). Various dates and sign. varieties.

		VG	VF	UNC
21	**5 Francs** 17.7.1934-6.3.1941. Brown, green and m/c. Man at ctr. Man weaving on back. Value in dk. blue.	1.50	7.50	27.50
22	**25 Francs** 1.5.1936-9.3.1939. M/c. Young man wearing turban w/horse at l. ctr. Value in blue. Lion at r. on back.	5.00	17.50	55.00

		VG	VF	UNC
23	**100 Francs** 17.11.1936; 11.1.1940; 10.9.1941. Blue. and brown. 2 women w/fancy hairdress. Woman w/basket on back.	25.00	85.00	265.
24	**1000 Francs** 21.10.1937; 28.9.1939; 5.6.1941; 28.4.1945. M/c. French woman w/African women w/child.	150.	525.	—

Note: For issues similar to #21-24 but w/heading *Afrique Française Libre*, see French Equatorial Africa #6-9.

1941-43 ISSUES

		VG	VF	UNC
25	**5 Francs** 6.3.1941-1.10.1942. M/c. Like #21 but value in lt. blue.	1.50	8.50	30.00
26	**5 Francs** 2.3.1943. M/c. Like #25 but value, date and sign. in red.	6.00	20.00	57.50

		VG	VF	UNC
27	**25 Francs** 9.1.1942; 24.2.1942; 22.4.1942; 1.10.1942. M/c. Like #22 but value in red.	7.00	27.50	65.00

Note: For #25-27 w/*RF-FEZZAN* ovpt. see Libya.

1942-43 WWII ISSUE

#28. 30, 31 Printer: E.A. Wright. Phila. Sign. varieties.

		VG	VF	UNC
28	**5 Francs** 14.12.1942. Black on gold unpt. Woman at ctr. Back red-violet on blue unpt.			
	a. Serial #. Wide V in l. sign.	3.00	10.00	25.00
	b. As a. Narrow V in l. sign.	2.00	7.50	20.00
	c. W/o serial #.	10.00	30.00	75.00
	s1. As a. Specimen.	—	—	100.
	s2. As b. Specimen.	—	—	85.00

		VG	VF	UNC
29	**10 Francs** 2.1.1943. Violet on gold unpt. Woman at r. Algerian printing.	25.00	75.00	225.

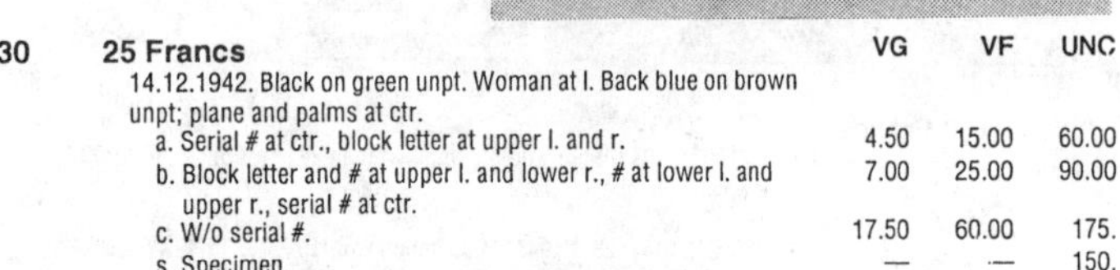

		VG	VF	UNC
30	**25 Francs** 14.12.1942. Black on green unpt. Woman at l. Back blue on brown unpt; plane and palms at ctr.			
	a. Serial # at ctr., block letter at upper l. and r.	4.50	15.00	60.00
	b. Block letter and # at upper l. and lower r., # at lower l. and upper r., serial # at ctr.	7.00	25.00	90.00
	c. W/o serial #.	17.50	60.00	175.
	s. Specimen.	—	—	150.

		VG	VF	UNC
31	**100 Francs** 14.12.1942. Black on pink unpt. Baobab tree at ctr. Back green on gold unpt; huts and palms at ctr.			
	a. Serial #.	15.00	45.00	150.
	b. W/o serial #.	30.00	90.00	200.
	s. Specimen.	—	—	175.

		VG	VF	UNC
32	**1000 Francs** 14.12.1942. Purple on lt. green and pinkish unpt. Ships and train at ctr. *BAO* in wreath on back. Printer: ABNC.	225.	675.	1200.

> **NOTICE**
> Readers with unlisted dates, signature varieties, etc. are invited to submit photocopies or, high resolution (300 dpi, 100% size) scans of their notes to: Standard Catalog of World Paper Money, 700 East State St. Iola, WI 54990-0001, or E-Mail: george.cuhaj@fwpubs.com.

AFRIQUE OCCIDENTALE FRANÇAISE

1944 ND ISSUE

		VG	VF	UNC
33	**0.50 Franc** ND (1944). Orange. Fortress at ctr. W/ or w/o security strip.	2.00	6.00	20.00

		VG	VF	UNC
34	**1 Franc** ND (1944). Dk. brown. Fisherman in boat at l., woman at r.			
	a. Lt. blue paper.	2.00	6.00	20.00
	b. Lt. brown on yellow paper.	2.00	6.00	20.00

		VG	VF	UNC
35	**2 Francs** ND (1944). Blue. Beach w/palm tree at l.	20.00	60.00	225.

BANQUE DE L'AFRIQUE OCCIDENTALE (RESUMED)

1943-48 ISSUE

#36-43 French printing (w/o imprint).

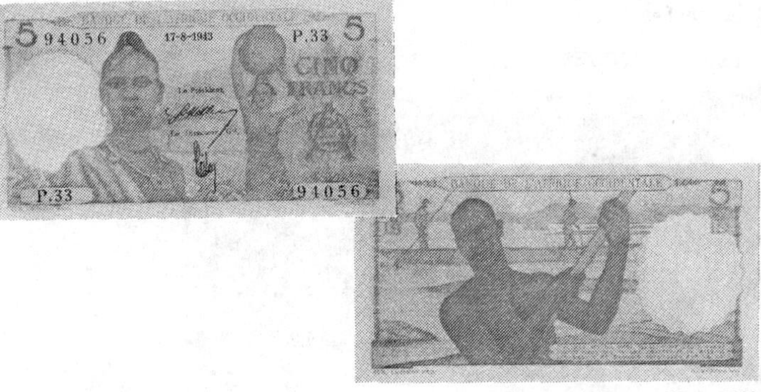

		VG	VF	UNC
36	**5 Francs** 17.8.1943 (1945)-28.10.1954. M/c. 2 women, 1 w/finery, 1 w/jug. Men poling in long boats at l. ctr. on back.	2.00	7.50	20.00

		VG	VF	UNC
37	**10 Francs** 18.1.1946-28.10.1954. M/c. 2 bow hunters at ctr. Man carring gazelle on back.	2.50	10.00	30.00

		VG	VF	UNC
38	**25 Francs** 17.8.1943(1945)-28.10.1954. M/c. Woman at ctr. Man w/bull at ctr. on back.	4.00	17.50	75.00

		VG	VF	UNC
39	**50 Francs** 27.9.1944(1945)-28.10.1954. M/c. Women at ctr., old man wearing fez at r. Man w/stalk of bananas at ctr. on back.	5.00	25.00	100.

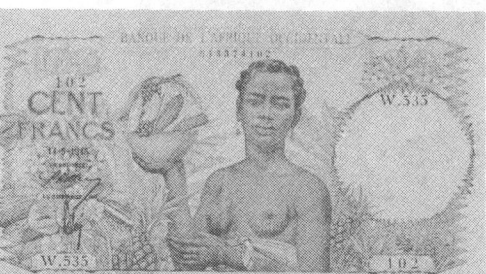

		VG	VF	UNC
40	**100 Francs** 10.5.1945-28.10.1954. M/c. Woman w/fruit bowl at ctr. Family on back.	7.50	27.50	110.

		VG	VF	UNC
41	**500 Francs** 6.2.1946-21.11.1953. M/c. Woman w/flag at ctr. Colonial soldiers on back.	35.00	175.	650.

		VG	VF	UNC
42	**1000 Francs** 16.4.1948-28.10.1954. M/c. Woman w/2 jugs at l. ctr. woman w/high headdress at ctr. on back.	60.00	185.	750.

		VG	VF	UNC
43	**5000 Francs** 10.4.1947; 15.11.1948; 27.12.1948; 22.12.1950. M/c. France w/2 local women at ctr.	150.	350.	850.

INSTITUT D'EMISSION DE L'A.O.F. ET DU TOGO

1955-56 ISSUE

		VG	VF	UNC
44	**50 Francs** 5.10.1955. M/c. Like #39.	60.00	225.	500.

		VG	VF	UNC
45	**50 Francs** ND (1956). Black and m/c. 3 women at ctr. Woman w/headdress, city in background at ctr. on back.	3.50	15.00	75.00
46	**100 Francs** 23.10.1956; 20.5.1957. M/c. Mask at l., woman w/braids at r. Woman at l. on back.	6.00	25.00	100.
47	**500 Francs** 23.10.1956. M/c. People at field work at l., mask at r.	30.00	100.	350.
48	**1000 Francs** 5.10.1955. M/c. Like #42.	125.	225.	550.

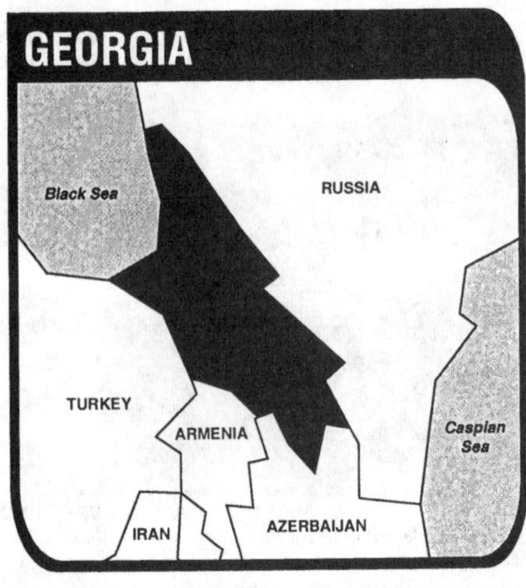

Georgia is bounded by the Black Sea to the west and by Turkey, Armenia and Azerbaijan. It occupies the western part of Transcaucasia covering an area of 26,900 sq. mi. (69,700 sq. km.), and a population of 5.42 million. Capital: Tbilisi. Hydro-electricity, minerals, forestry and agriculture are the chief industries.

The Georgian dynasty first emerged after the Macedonian victory over the Achaemenid Persian empire in the 4th century B.C. Roman "friendship" was imposed in 65 B.C. after Pompey's victory over Mithradates. The Georgians embraced Christianity in the 4th century A.D. During the next three centuries Georgia was involved in the ongoing conflicts between the Byzantine and Persian empires. The latter developed control until Georgia regained its independence in 450-503 A.D. but then it reverted to a Persian province in 533 A.D., then restored as a kingdom by the Byzantines in 562 A.D. It was established as an Arab emirate in the 8th century. Over the following centuries Turkish and Persian rivalries along with civil strife, divided the area under the two influences.

Russian interests increased and a treaty of alliance was signed on July 24, 1773 whereby Russia guaranteed Georgian independence while it acknowledged Russian suzerainty. Persia invaded again in 1795. Russia slowly took over annexing piece by piece and soon developed total domination. After the Russian Revolution, the Georgians, Armenians and Azerbaijanis formed the short- lived Transcaucasian Federal Republic on Sept. 20, 1917, which broke up into three independent republics on May 26, 1918. A Germano-Georgian treaty was signed on May 28, 1918, followed by a Turko-Georgian peace treaty on June 4. The end of WW I and the collapse of the central powers allowed free elections.

On May 20, 1920, Soviet Russia concluded a peace treaty recognizing its independence, but later invaded on Feb. 11, 1921 and a soviet republic was proclaimed. On March 12, 1922 Stalin included Georgia in a newly formed Transcaucasian Soviet Federated Socialist Republic. On Dec. 5, 1936, the T.S.F.S.R. was dissolved and Georgia became a direct member of the U.S.S.R. The collapse of the U.S.S.R. allowed full transition to independence and on April 9, 1991, the republic, as an independent state, d on its original treaty of independence of May 1918 was declared.

Independent from May 26, 1918 to March 18, 1921. Commonly r efered to in Russian as 'Gruzia' it was the last area in Tra nscaucasia to fall under Bolshevik control.

MONETARY SYSTEM:

1 Lari = 1,000,000 'old' Laris, 1995-
1 Lari = 100 Thetri to 1995

ГРУЗИНСКОИ РЕСПУБЛИКИ

GEORGIA, AUTONOMOUS REPUBLIC

TREASURY

1919 ОБЯЗАТЕЛЬСТВО КАЗНАЧЕИСТВА DEBENTURE BONDS

		VG	VF	UNC
1	**25 Rubles** 15.1.1919.	2.50	10.00	30.00

		VG	VF	UNC
2	**100 Rubles** 15.1.1919.	2.50	12.00	37.50
3	**500 Rubles** 15.1.1919.	2.50	15.00	48.00
4	**1000 Rubles** 15.1.1919.	2.50	15.00	45.00
5	**5000 Rubles** 15.1.1919.	5.00	25.00	75.00

1919-21 STATE NOTES

#6-15 St. George on horseback on back.

		VG	VF	UNC
6	**50 Kopeks** ND (1919). Blue on lt. brown unpt.	.25	1.50	4.50

		VG	VF	UNC
7	**1 Ruble** 1919. Brown on pink unpt.	.50	2.50	7.50
8	**3 Rubles** 1919. Black on green unpt.	.75	3.00	9.00

		VG	VF	UNC
9	**5 Rubles** 1919. Black on orange unpt.	.75	3.00	9.00
10	**10 Rubles** 1919. Brown on red-brown unpt.	.75	3.00	9.00
11	**50 Rubles** 1919. Violet on brown unpt. Green also in unpt. on back.	1.00	4.00	12.00

		VG	VF	UNC
12	**100 Rubles** 1919. Green. Lilac in unpt. on back.	1.00	5.00	15.00

		VG	VF	UNC
13	**500 Rubles** 1919. Black-green on red-brown unpt. Woman seated w/shield and lance at ctr.			
	a. Wmk: plaited lines.	2.50	10.00	30.0
	b. Thick or thin paper w/o wmk.	1.00	4.00	12.0
14	**1000 Rubles** 1920. Brown on blue and tan unpt.			
	a. Wmk: Plaited lines.	3.00	12.00	37.5
	b. W/o wmk.	1.50	6.00	18.0
15	**5000 Rubles** 1921. Lilac to brown. Bldg. w/flags at ctr. Margin circles around corner numerals are ringed once at each side.			
	a. Wmk: Monograms.	2.00	9.00	27.0
	b. W/o wmk.	1.00	5.00	15.0
	c. Ruled on back.	3.00	12.00	37.5

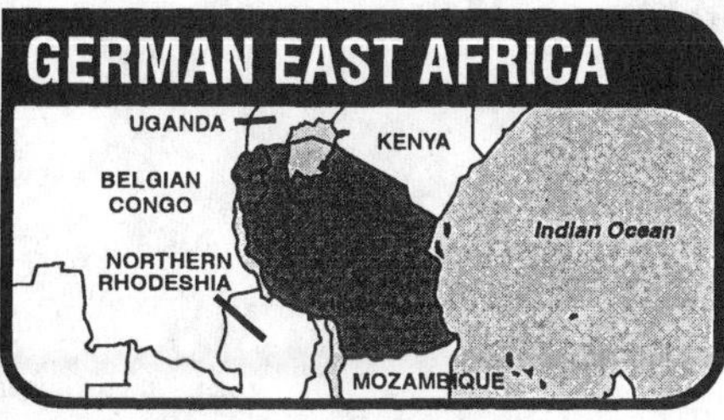

German East Africa (Tanganyika), located on the coast of east-central Africa between British East Africa (now Kenya) and Portuguese East Africa (now Mozambique) had an area of 362,284 sq. mi. (938,216 sq. km.) and a population of about 6 million. Capital: Dar es Salam. Chief products prior to German control were ivory and slaves; after German control, sisal, coffee and rubber.

The East African coast first felt the impact of foreign influence in the eighth century, when Arab traders arrived. By the 12th century, traders and immigrants from the Near East and India had built highly developed city/trading states along the coast. By 1506, Portugal claimed control along the entire coast, but made no attempt to establish a colony or to explore the interior.

Germany acquired control of the area by treaties in 1884, and established it as a protectorate administered by the German East Africa Company. In 1891, the German government assumed direct administration of the area, which was proclaimed the Colony of German East Africa in 1897.

German colonial domination of Tanganyika ended with World War I. Control of most of the territory passed to Great Britain, under a League of Nations mandate. British control was continued after World War II, under a United Nations trusteeship. Thereafter, Tanganyika moved gradually toward self-government. It became autonomous in May 1961. Full independence was achieved on Dec. 9 of the same year.

RULERS:

German, 1884-1918
British, 1918-1961

MONETARY SYSTEM:

1 Rupie = 100 Heller

GERMAN ADMINISTRATION

DEUTSCH-OSTAFRIKANISCHE BANK

1905-12 ISSUE

#1-5 printer: G&D.

		Good	Fine	XF
1	**5 Rupien** 15.6.1905. Blue on brown and m/c unpt. 2 lions at bottom ctr.	17.50	45.00	200.

		Good	Fine	XF
2	**10 Rupien** 15.6.1905. Black on red unpt. Dar es Salam Harbor at lower ctr.	30.00	75.00	275.

		Good	Fine	XF
3	**50 Rupien** 15.6.1905. Black on blue unpt. Portr. Kaiser Wilhelm II in cavalry uniform at l.			
	a. 2 serial # on face only.	60.00	150.	750.
	b. 2 serial # each on face and back.	35.00	100.	400.

		Good	Fine	XF
4	**100 Rupien** 15.6.1905. Black on green unpt. Portr. Kaiser Wilhelm II in cavalry uniform at ctr.	40.00	150.	450.

		Good	Fine	XF
5	**500 Rupien** 2.9.1912. Black on purple unpt. Portr. Kaiser Wilhelm II in admiral's uniform at l.	500.	1000.	1800.

1915-17 EMERGENCY WWI ISSUES

Many varieties of sign., serial #, wmk., eagle types and letters.

		VG	VF	UNC
6	**1 Rupie** 1.9.1915. Blue-gray paper. Letter A. No eagle.	10.00	25.00	60.00
7	**1 Rupie** 1.11.1915. Blue-gray paper. Letter A on back. W/text: *Gebucht von* below date at l.			
	a. W/bank handstamp.	12.50	20.00	50.00
	b. W/o bank handstamp.	5.00	10.00	25.00

Interims-Banknote
Die
Deutsch-Ostafrikanische Bank
zahlt bei ihren Kassen im D. O. A. Schutzgebiet dem Einlieferer dieser Banknote ohne Legitimationsprüfung
1 Eine Rupie 1
Daressalam/Tabora 1. November 1915.
Deutsch-Ostafrikanische Bank Zweigniederlassung Daressalam in Vollmacht:

		VG	VF	UNC
8	**1 Rupie** 1.11.1915. Lt. green paper. Letter B. W/o text: *Gebucht von.*	5.00	12.50	35.00
9	**1 Rupie** 1.11.1915. W/text: *Kraft besonderer Ermächtigung* below date at l. Both sign. handwritten.			
	a. Lt. green paper. Letter B.	2.50	5.00	15.00
	b. Gray-brown paper. Letters B; C.	1.00	3.00	7.00
	c. Gray-brown paper. Letter P.	50.00	80.00	180.
9A	**1 Rupie** 1.11.1915. W/text:*Kraft besonderer Ermächtigung* below date at l. Stamped sign. at r.			
	a. Gray-brown paper. Letter B, C.	5.00	10.00	25.00
	b. Gray-white paper. Letters P, Q (2 diff. types), R, S, T, U, V, Y, A2, B2, C2, D2, E2, F2.	2.50	5.00	15.00
10	**1 Rupie** 1.11.1915. W/text: *Kraft besonderer Ermächtigung* below sign. at l. Stamped sign. at r.			
	a. Gray-brown paper. Letter C.	1.00	3.00	7.00
	b. Thick olive-brown paper. Letter D.	1.00	3.00	7.00
	c. Thick gray paper. Letter D.	1.00	3.00	7.00

#		VG	VF	UNC
11	**1 Rupie**			
	1.11.1915. *Gez.: A Frühling* printed at r.			
	a. Thick gray paper. Letter E.	1.00	4.00	8.00
	b. Thin gray-white paper. Letters E; F; G.	1.00	4.00	8.00

#		VG	VF	UNC
12	**1 Rupie**			
	1.11.1915. *A. Frühling (w/o gez.)* printed at r.			
	a. W/o wmk. Letter H.	1.00	2.00	5.00
	b. W/wmk. Letter H.	1.00	2.00	5.00
	c. Wmk: Meander stripe. Letters H; P.	2.00	5.00	10.00
13	**1 Rupie**			
	1.12.1915. W/text: *Gebucht von...* below date at l. Letter H.	1.00	3.00	7.00
14	**1 Rupie**			
	1.12.1915. W/o text: *Gebucht von...* Letters H; J.	2.50	6.00	12.00
15	**1 Rupie**			
	1.12.1915. W/text: *Kraft besonderer Ermächtigung* below date at l., *gez. A. Frühling* printed at r.			
	a. Red-brown paper. Letter J.	1.00	3.00	7.00
	b. Gray-brown paper. Letters J; K (K repl & right in same positions).	1.00	3.00	7.00
	c. As b. Letters K left high, right below.	20.00	50.00	
	d. As b. Letters left high and center below.	25.00	60.00	120.

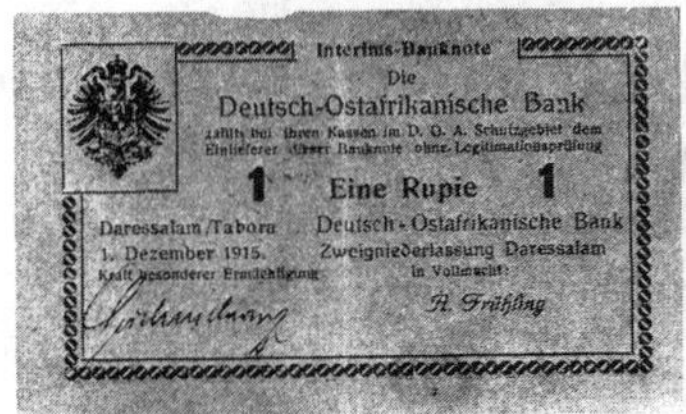

#		VG	VF	UNC
16	**1 Rupie**			
	1.12.1915. W/text: *Kraft besonderer Ermächtigung* below date at l. *A. Frühling* (w/o *gez.)* printed at r.			
	a. Gray-brown paper. Letter K (3 different positions).	1.00	3.00	7.00
	b. Dk. brown wrapping paper. Letters K; L.	1.00	3.00	7.00
17	**1 Rupie**			
	1.12.1915. W/text: *Kraft besonderer Ermächtigung* below date at l., printed sign. at r. Letter L.	2.00	4.00	8.00
18	**1 Rupie**			
	1.2.1916. W/o text: *Gebucht von* at l., eagle on face 20mm high.			
	a. Brown transparent oil paper. Letters L; M; N.	1.00	3.00	7.00
	b. Thick gray-brown paper. Letter N.	5.00	15.00	50.00
	c. Norman light-brown paper. Serie N. Rare.			
	ax. Error, w/o sign. Letter L.	10.00	20.00	40.00

#		VG	VF	UNC
19	**1 Rupie**			
	1.2.1916. W/text: *Gebucht von* at l., eagle on face 15mm high; frame at upper l. has 7 stars and at upper r. 14 stars. Black printing. Letters F2; G2; H2; J2; K2; L2; M2; N2; O2; P2; Q2; R2; S2; T2; U2; V2; W2; X2; Y2; Z2; A3; B3; C3; D3; E3; F3; G3.	1.00	2.00	5.00

#		VG	VF	UNC
20	**1 Rupie**			
	1.2.1916. W/text: *Gebucht von* at l., eagle on face 15mm high; frame at upper l. has 6 stars and at upper r. 13 stars. Black printing.			
	a. Letters: G3; H3; J3; K3; L3; M3; N3; O3; P3; Q3, (normal paper, 4 different types); R3; S3; T3; U3; V3.	1.00	2.00	4.50
	b. Square lined paper. Letter Q3 (4 different types).	2.00	5.00	10.00
	x. Error: 3 instead of N3.	4.00	8.00	—
	y. Error w/o sign. (V).	10.00	17.50	—
	z. Error w/word on back: *Kaiserl ches* w/letter "i" dropped out.	10.00	17.50	—
21	**1 Rupie**			
	1.2.1916. Like #19 but blue and blue-green printing. Letter A4.	1.00	2.00	4.00

#		VG	VF	UNC
22	**1 Rupie**			
	1.7.1917. Printed w/rubber type (so-called "bush notes"). Eagle stamp on back in different sizes.			
	a. Eagle on back 15mm high. Letters EP.	2.00	7.50	15.00
	b. Eagle on back 23mm high. Letters EP.	1.00	3.00	7.50
	c. Letters ER.	1.00	10.00	20.00
	d. Eagle on back 15mm high. Letters FP.	4.00	8.00	20.00
	e. Eagle on back 19mm high. Letters FP.	4.00	8.00	20.00
	f. Letters IP.	5.00	10.00	35.00
	ax. Error w/back inverted.	4.00	8.00	20.00
	bx. Error w/back inverted.	4.00	8.00	20.00
	by. Error: *Daressalan* on face.	1.50	4.00	8.50
	cx. Error w/back inverted.	12.50	25.00	—
	cy. Error w/letters EP on face, ER on back. Rare.	—	—	—
	dx. Error w/back inverted.	4.00	8.00	20.00
	ex. Error w/back inverted. Error w/letters Ep on face, ER on back. Rare.	4.00	8.00	20.00
23	**1 Rupie**			
	ND. #15b (J) and #18a (N) on back w/lg. violet stamp: *W* over original letter.	10.00	40.00	85.00
24	**1 Rupie**			
	ND. #10f (Q, V, Y) on back w/violet stamp: *X* over original letter, 1 serial # crossed out and 2 new serial # added.	7.50	15.00	30.00
24A	**1 Rupie**			
	ND. Violet. Handstamp: *Z* on back over original letter, 1 serial # crossed out and 2 new serial # added. The following notes are known with stamp: 10 (P, Q, R, S, T, U, V); 18 (N); 19 (N2, O2, P2, Q2, R2, A3).	10.00	20.00	45.00
25	**1 Rupie**			
	ND. Stamp: *X* as on #24 but 2 serial # crossed out and 2 new serial # added. The following notes are known: 7b (A); 8 (B); 10f (T, V, Y, A2, B2, C2, D2); 11a (E); 18a (M); 19 (X2, B3, C3).	7.50	17.50	30.00
25A	**1 Rupie**			
	ND. Violet. Handstamp: *Z* 2 serial #'s crossed out and 2 serial # added. The following notes are known with stamp: 10 (P, Q, R, T, U,V); 18 (L, M, N); 19 (F2, N2, O2, P2, R2, S2, T2, X2, Z2, A3).	7.50	17.50	30.00

#		VG	VF	UNC
26	**1 Rupie**			
	ND. Stamp: *X* as on #24 but w/o change of serial #. The following notes are known: 8 (B); 10d (P, Q, R, T, U, Y, B2, C2, E2, F2); 11b (F, G); 12a (H); 14 (J); 15a (J); 16b (K, L); 17 (L); 18a (M, N); 19 (H2, L2, O2, Q2, S2, V2, W2, Y2, A3, B3, C3, D3, E3, F3, G3); 20 (G3, H3, J3, K3, L3, M3, N3, O3, P3, Q3, R3, S3, T3, U3, V3); 21 (A4).	15.00	30.00	60.00
26A	**1 Rupie**			
	ND. Violet. Handstamp *Z* over original letter w/o change of serial #. The following notes are known with stamp: 10 (C, S, U); 11 (E, F, G); 12 (H); 14 (H); 15 (J); 16 (K); 17 (L); 18 (M, N); 19 (J2, M2, N2, R2, S2, U2).	7.50	17.50	30.00

#26B and 26C deleted, see #24A and 25A.

33984

#		VG	VF	UNC
27	**1 Rupie**			
	ND. Date (from stationery used as printing paper); 5 different dateline types exist.			
	a. Dateline on back of the following notes: 19 (F3, G3); 20 (H3, J3, K3, L3, M3, N3, O3, P3, Q3, R3, S3, T3, U3, V3).	30.00	75.00	200.
	b. Dateline on back of the following notes: 22a (EP); 22b (EP); 22c (ER); 22e (FP); 22f (IP); 26 (M3, V3).	30.00	75.00	200.
	c. Dateline on front of the following notes: 22b (EP); 22c (ER).	30.00	75.00	200.

		VG	VF	UNC
28	**1 Rupie** ND. Letterhead on back (from stationery used as printing paper), so-called "letterhead notes". 14 different types of letterheads exist on the following notes: 22a (EP); 22b (EP); 22c (ER); 22d (FP); 22e (FP); 22f (IP).	50.00	120.	250.
29	**5 Rupien** 15.8.1915. Value in letters only, both sign. handwritten. W/o series letter.	6.00	17.50	30.00
30	**5 Rupien** 15.8.1915. Like #29 but sign. at r. facsimile stamped. W/o series letter.	12.50	25.00	50.00

		VG	VF	UNC
31	**5 Rupien** 15.8.1915. Value in letters and #, both sign. handwritten. Series letters B (2 varieties); C.	6.00	17.50	30.00
32	**5 Rupien** 15.8.1915. Like #31 but sign. at r. facsimile stamped. Letter C.	5.00	10.00	25.00
33	**5 Rupien** 1.11.1915. *Daressalam/Tabora* in 2 lines. Letter D.	20.00	30.00	60.00

		VG	VF	UNC
34	**5 Rupien** 1.11.1915. *Daressalam/Tabora* in 1 line. Text: *Kraft besonderer Ermächtigung* at lower l. Sign. at l. handwritten.			
	a. Gray-green cardboard w/blue fibres. Letters D; E.	5.00	10.00	20.00
	b. Gray-green cardboard w/blue fibres (darker than #34a) and impressed jute texture. Letters D; E.	5.00	10.00	20.00
	c. Gray-green cardboard w/o blue fibres. Letter E.	5.00	10.00	20.00
	d. Dk. green cardboard w/o impressed jute texture. Letters E; F.	5.00	10.00	20.00
35	**5 Rupien** 1.11.1915. Like #34 but both sign. facsimile stamped. Letters E; F.	10.00	20.00	80.00
36	**5 Rupien** 1.2.1916. *Gebucht von* below date at l.			
	a. Stiff gray-blue cardboard. Letter F.	5.00	10.00	20.00
	b. Soft dk. blue cardboard. Letters F; G.	5.00	10.00	20.00
	c. Stiff dk. gray cardboard. Letter F.	5.00	10.00	20.00
	d. Green cardboard. Letters G; F.	5.00	10.00	20.00
	e. Green paper. Letters G; H.	5.00	10.00	20.00
	f. Letter X/F, new serial #. Dk. blue. Rare.	—	—	—

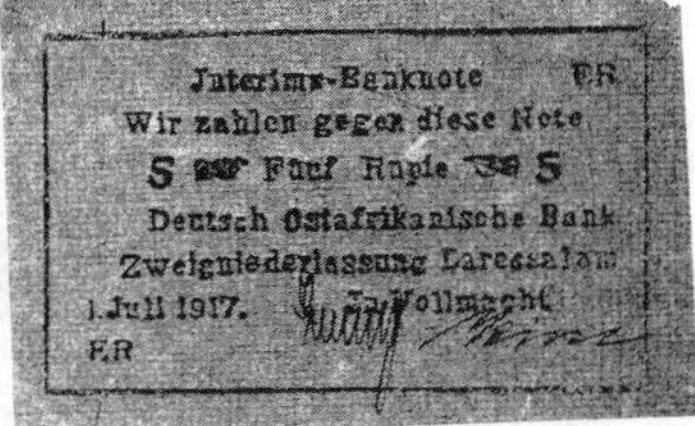

		VG	VF	UNC
37	**5 Rupien** 1.7.1917. Printed w/rubber type (so-called *bush notes*).			
	a. Value *5* 3.5mm high.	15.00	30.00	60.00
	b. Value *5* 5mm high.	12.00	22.50	45.00

#38-49 serial # and sign. varieties.

		VG	VF	UNC
38	**10 Rupien** 1.10.1915. Dk. brown cardboard.			
	a. W/o serial letter.	10.00	17.50	30.00
	b. Handwritten B.	20.00	45.00	80.00

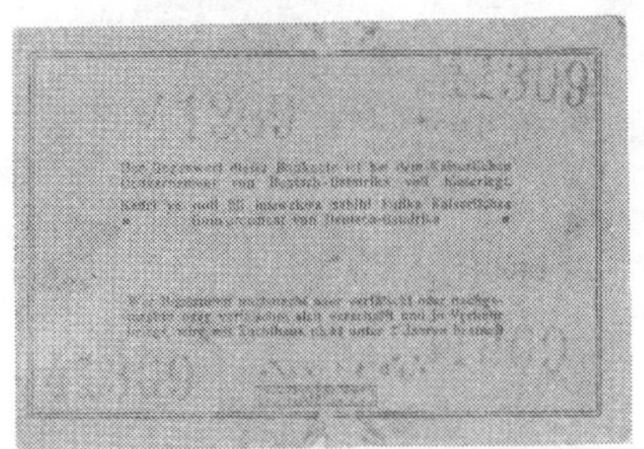

		VG	VF	UNC
39	**10 Rupien** 1.10.1915. Like #38 but w/violet stamp: *Z* on back.	12.50	25.00	60.00
40	**10 Rupien** 1.2.1916. Dk. brown cardboard. W/o letter or w/B. *DOAB* in ornamental letters on top r. and bottom l. on back.	10.00	30.00	80.00

		VG	VF	UNC
41	**10 Rupien** 1.6.1916. Yellow-brown paper. Letter B.	10.00	25.00	50.00
42	**10 Rupien** 1.6.1916. Like #41 but violet stamp: *X* over B on back.	50.00	100.	200.
43	**10 Rupien** 1.7.1917. Printed w/rubber type (so-called *bush notes*).			
	a. Value 3mm high and 4mm wide.	20.00	45.00	100.
	b. Value 5mm high and 4-5mm wide.	20.00	45.00	100.
	c. Value 5mm high and 7mm wide.	20.00	45.00	100.
44	**20 Rupien** 15.3.1915. White cardboard.			
	a. Both sign. handwritten. Serial # on face handwritten.			
	b. British forgery on thick cardboard. Serial # on face and back do not match. Rare.			

		VG	VF	UNC
45	**20 Rupien** 15.3.1915. Lilac cardboard. Both sign. handwritten. Serial # on back only.			
	a. Both sign. handwritten.	25.00	50.00	125.
	b. Left sign. handwritten, right sign. facsimile stamped.	20.00	45.00	100.

#		VG	VF	UNC
46	**50 Rupien**			
	1.10.1915.			
	a. Soft gray cardboard.	30.00	60.00	100.
	b. Stiff brown cardboard.	70.00	150.	250.

#		VG	VF	UNC
47	**50 Rupien**			
	1.10.1917. Printed w/rubber type (so-called *bush notes*).			
	a. W/sign., back printed.	200.	450.	1200.
	b. W/o sign. Back not printed. (Not issued).	75.00	150.	300.
48	**200 Rupien**			
	15.4.1915. W/o wmk.	250.	600.	1500.

#		VG	VF	UNC
49	**200 Rupien**			
	15.6.1915. Wmk: Wavy lines.	250.	600.	1500.

German New Guinea (also known as Neu Guinea or Kaiser Wilhelmsland, now part of Papua New Guinea) included the northeast corner of the island of New Guinea, the islands of the Bismarck Archipelago, Bougainville and Buka Islands, and about 600 small offshore islands. Bounded on the west coast by West Irian, to the north and east by the Pacific Ocean and to the south by Papua, it had an area of 92,159 sq. mi. (238,692 sq. km.) and, under German administration, had a population of about 250,000. Capital: Herbertshohe, later moved to Rabaul. Copra was the chief export.

Germany took formal possession of German New Guinea in 1884. It was administered by the German New Guinea Company until 1899, when control was assumed by the German imperial government. On the outbreak of World War I in 1914, Australia occupied the territory and it remained under military control until 1921, when it became an Australian mandate of the League of Nations. During World War II, between 1942 and 1945, the territory was occupied by Japan. Following the Japanese surrender, it was administered by Australia under the United Nations trusteeship system. In 1949, Papua and New Guinea were combined as one administrative unit known as Papua New Guinea, which attained internal autonomy on Dec. 1, 1973. Papua New Guinea achieved full independence on Sept. 16, 1975.

German Reichsbanknoten and Reichskassenscheine circulated until 1914.

RULERS:
German, 1884-1914

MONETARY SYSTEM:
1 Mark = 100 Pfennig

AUSTRALIAN OCCUPATION - WWI

TREASURY NOTES

1914-15 ISSUE

#1-5 w/o pictorial design, w/text: *Payable in coin at the Treasury, Rabaul.*

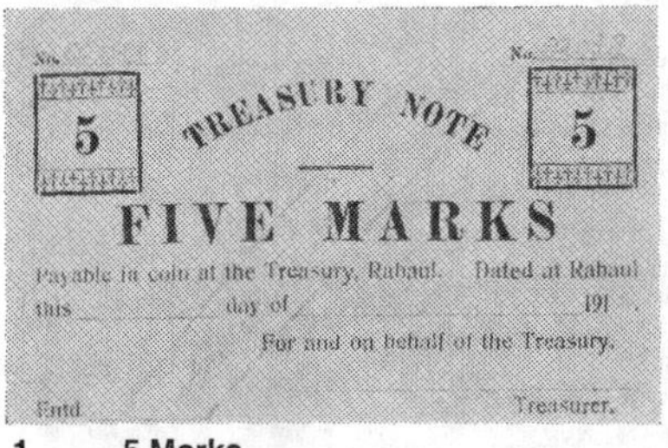

#		VG	VF	UNC
1	**5 Marks**			
	1914-15.			
	a. 14.10.1914. Rare.	—	—	—
	b. Pen *cancelled* 1.1.1915. Rare.	—	—	—

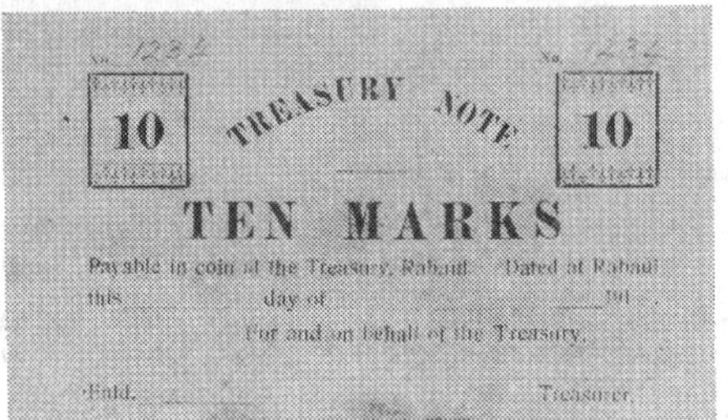

#		VG	VF	UNC
2	**10 Marks**			
	1914-15.			
	a. 14.10.1914. Rare.	—	—	—
	b. Pen *cancelled* 1.1.1915. Rare.	—	—	—
3	**20 Marks**			
	1914.			
	a. 1914. Rare.	—	—	—
	b. Pen *cancelled* 1.1.1915. Rare.	—	—	—

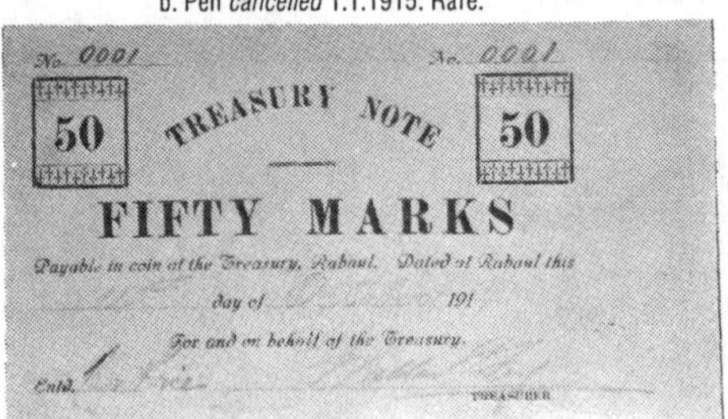

#		VG	VF	UNC
4	**50 Marks**			
	1914.			
	a. 16.10.1914	3500.	7500.	—
	b. Pen *cancelled* 1.1.1915. Rare.	—	—	—

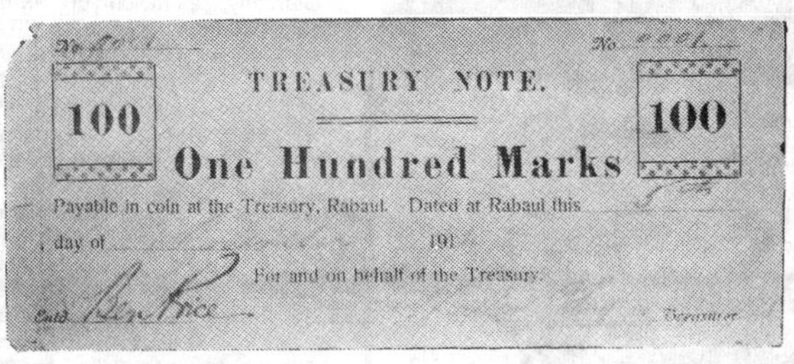

5	100 Marks	VG	VF	UNC
	5.11.1914. Rare.	—	—	—

Note: A primitive 20 Mark note printed with boot polish is also reputed to have existed which was used for paying the wages of the German Voluntary Brigade.

German South West Africa (Deutsch-Sudwestafrika) is a former German territory situated on the Atlantic coast of southern Africa. The colony had an area of 318,261 sq. mi. (824,293 sq. km.). Capital: Windhoek.

The first Europeans to land on the shores of the area were 15th-century Portuguese navigators. The interior, however, was not explored until the middle of the 18th century. Great Britain annexed the Walvis Bay area in 1878; it was incorporated into the Cape of Good Hope in 1884. The rest of the coastal area was annexed by Germany in 1885. South African forces occupied German South West Africa during World War I. South Africa received it as a League of Nations mandate on Dec. 17, 1920.

South Africa's mandate was terminated by the United Nations on Oct. 27, 1966. In June 1968 the UN General Assembly voted to rename the country Namibia. South Africa found both actions unacceptable. After many years of dispute, independence of Namibia was finally achieved on March 21, 1990. German Reichsbanknoten and Reichskassenscheine circulated until 1914.

RULERS:

German to 1914

MONETARY SYSTEM:

1 Mark = 100 Pfennig

GERMAN ADMINISTRATION

KASSENSCHEIN

1914 ISSUE

#1-5 are so-called *Seitz notes*, named after the Imperial Governor whose sign. is printed on some of the notes.

1	5 Mark	Good	Fine	XF
	8.8.1914. Green.			
	a. Issued note.	65.00	300.	600.
	b. Cancelled.	50.00	250.	450.

2	10 Mark	Good	Fine	XF
	8.8.1914. Red-brown.			
	a. Issued note.	65.00	200.	500.
	b. Cancelled.	50.00	150.	300.
3	20 Mark			
	8.8.1914. Brown-violet.			
	a. Issued note.	65.00	200.	400.
	b. Cancelled.	50.00	150.	300.
4	50 Mark			
	8.8.1914. Red.			
	a. Issued note.	90.00	275.	575.
	b. Cancelled.	65.00	200.	400.

5	100 Mark	Good	Fine	XF
	8.8.1914. Blue.			
	a. Issued note.	125.	400.	950.
	b. Cancelled.	100.	300.	700.

SWAKOPMUNDER BUCHHANDLUNG

1915-18 ND ISSUE

6	10 Pfennig	Good	Fine	XF
	ND (1916-18). Green linen. Value: *Zehn Pfg.*; w/o *NUMMER* at upper r.			
	a. 1 sign.	17.50	50.00	135.
	b. 2 sign.	12.50	35.00	100.

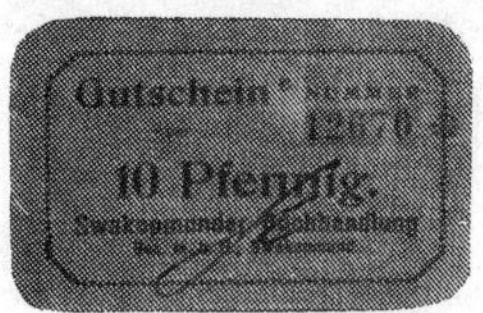

No.		Good	Fine	XF
7	**10 Pfennig** ND (1916-18). Green linen. Value: *10 Pfennig; NUMMER* at upper r. W/ or w/o letter *B*.	12.50	35.00	100.

No.		Good	Fine	XF
8	**25 Pfennig** ND (1916-18). Pale blue or white paper (cloth fabric between paper layers). Red-brown text, green value (diagonal). W/o *NUMMER* at upper r.			
	a. Rounded corners. 2 handwritten sign.	12.50	35.00	100.
	b. Square corners. 1 facsimile sign.	15.00	40.00	100.
9	**25 Pfennig** ND (1916-18). Pale blue paper (cloth fabric between paper layers). Red-brown text, black value on green unpt. *NUMMER* at upper r.	35.00	100.	250.
10	**50 Pfennig** ND (1916-18). Blue on lt. blue linen. Value: *Funfzig Pfg;* w/o *NUMMER* at upper r.			
	a. Rounded corners. 2 handwritten sign.	20.00	57.50	170.
	b. Square corners. 1 facsimile sign.	21.00	65.00	190.

No.		Good	Fine	XF
11	**50 Pfennig** ND (1916-18). Blue-green on white linen. Value: *0,50 Mark; NUMMER* at upper r. (2 varieties of *M* in <l >Mark; w/ or w/o period after *Mark*).	12.50	40.00	125.
12	**1 Mark** ND (1916-18). Yellowish cardboard. Black text on green unpt. W/o *NUMMER* at upper r. 2 sign. varieties.	12.50	40.00	125.
13	**1 Mark** ND (1916-18). Lt. green cardboard. Black and red-brown on dk. green unpt. *NUMMER* at upper l.	12.50	40.00	125.

No.		Good	Fine	XF
14	**1 Mark** ND (1916-18). Rose linen. Red-brown unpt. extending over entire note. *Ausgabe B* at upper r.	12.50	35.00	100.
15	**2 Mark** ND (1916-18). Black and salmon text. Value: *Zwei;* w/o *NUMMER* at r. 1 or 2 sign.			
	a. Rose colored cardboard w/impressed linen texture.	35.00	90.00	225.
	b. Yellowish cardboard w/impressed linen texture.	35.00	90.00	225.
16	**2 Mark** ND (1916-18). Brown. Value: *2; NUMMER* at upper r. (2 varieties of *M* in *Mark*).			
	a. Lt. gray cardboard w/impressed linen texture.	20.00	65.00	190.
	b. Lt. brown cardboard w/impressed linen texture.	30.00	90.00	225.

No.		Good	Fine	XF
17	**3 Mark** ND (1916-18). Green unpt. Lt. green cardboard w/linen texture. W/o *NUMMER* at upper r.	32.50	100.	275.
18	**3 Mark** ND (1916-18). Brown unpt. Lt. brown cardboard. *NUMMER* at upper r. (2 varieties of *M* in *Mark*).	37.50	110.	300.

Germany, a nation of north-central Europe which from 1871 to 1945 was, successively, an empire, a republic and a totalitarian state, attained its territorial peak as an empire when it comprised a 208,780 sq. mi. (540,740 sq. km.) homeland and an overseas colonial empire.

As the power of the Roman Empire waned, several warlike tribes residing in northern Germany moved south and west, invading France, Belgium, England, Italy and Spain. In 800 AD the Frankish King Charlemagne, who ruled most of present-day France and Germany, was crowned Emperor of the Holy Roman Empire. Under his successors, this empire was divided into France in the West and Germany (including the Emperor's title) in the East. Over the centuries the German part developed into a loose federation of an estimated 1,800 German States that lasted until 1806. Modern Germany was formed from the eastern part of Charlemagne's empire.

In 1815, the German States were reduced to a federation of 32, of which Prussia was the strongest. In 1871, Prussian Chancellor Otto Von Bismarck united the German States into an empire ruled by Wilhelm I, the Prussian king. The empire initiated a colonial endeavor and became one of the world's greatest powers. Germany disintegrated as a result of World War I, and was reestablished as the Weimar Republic. The humiliation of defeat, economic depression, poverty and discontent gave rise to Adolf Hitler in 1933, who reconstituted Germany as the Third Reich and after initial diplomatic and military triumphs, led it to disaster in World War II. During the postwar era, the western provinces were occupied by the Allied forces while the eastern provinces were occupied and administered by the Soviet Union. East Germany and West Germany were established in 1949.

The post-WWII division of Germany ended on Oct. 3, 1990, when the German Democratic Republic (East Germany) ceased to exist and its five constituent provinces were formally admitted to the Federal Republic of Germany. An election held on Dec. 2, 1990 chose representatives to the united federal parliament (Bundestag), which then conducted its opening session in Berlin in the old Reichstag building. The Capital remained in Bonn until 1999.

For subsequent history, see German Federal Republic and German Democratic Republic.

RULERS:

Wilhelm I, 1871-1888
Friedrich III, 1888
Wilhelm II, 1888-1918

MONETARY SYSTEM:

1 Mark = 100 Pfennig
1 Mark = 100 Pfennig to 1923
1000 Milliarden Mark = 1 Billion Mark = 1 Rentenmark = 100 Rentenpfennig, 1923-1924
1 Rentenmark = 1 Reichsmark = 100 Reichspfennig, 1924-1948
1 AMC Mark = 100 AMC Pfennig, 1945-1948
1 Million = 1,000,000
10 Millionen = 10,000,000
1 Milliarde = 1,000,000,000 (English 1 Billion)
10 Milliarden = 10,000,000,000
1 Billion = 1,000,000,000,000 (English 1 Trillion)
10 Billionen = 10,000,000,000,000

WATERMARK VARIETIES

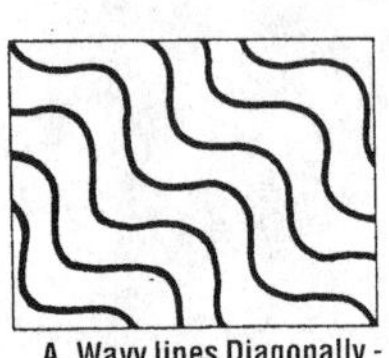
A. Wavy lines Diagonally - Congruent

B. Pattern of triangles with concave sides within circles

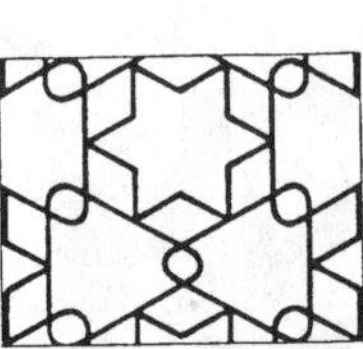
C. 6-pointed stars within rounded triangle pattern

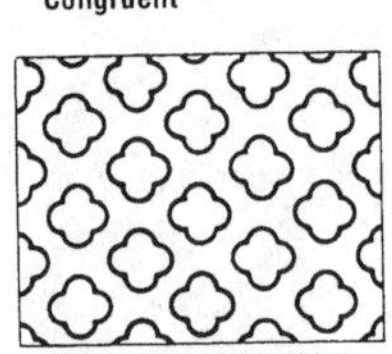
D. Small crucifera blossoms

E. G, D within 6-pointed stars and Z's

F. Greek pattern

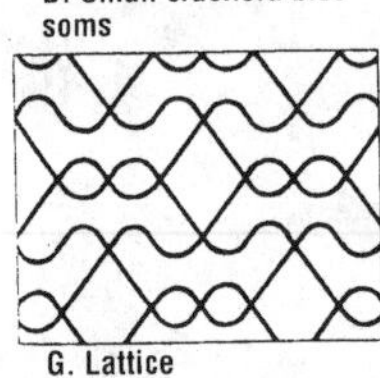
G. Lattice

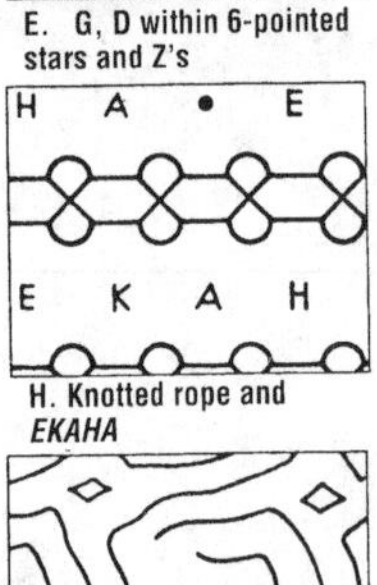

H. Knotted rope and *EKAHA*

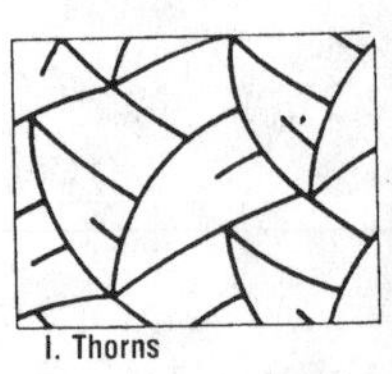
I. Thorns

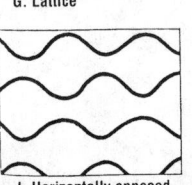

J. Horizontally opposed wavy lines

K. Diamonds in maze

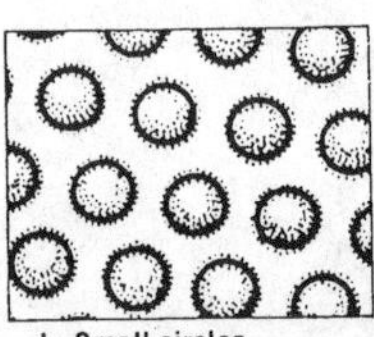
L. Small circles

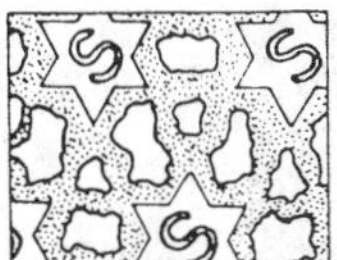

M. S in 6-pointed stars within clouds

N. Diamond pattern

O. Tuning fork H's pattern

P. HUDS-in circular pattern

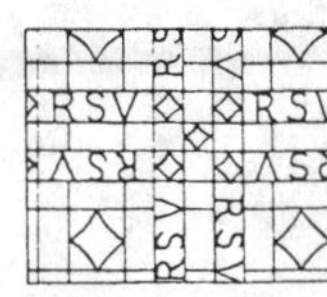

Q. RSV-Linear pattern

R. Contoured chain pattern

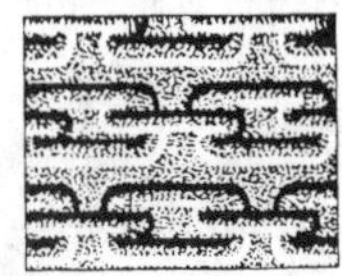

S. Straight chain pattern

NOTE: The above wmks. are from "Papiergeld-Spezialkatalog Deutschland, 1874-1980" by Pick/Rixen (published by Battenberg Verlag, Munich).

EMPIRE

REICHSKASSENSCHEINE

IMPERIAL TREASURY NOTES

1874 ISSUE

		Good	Fine	XF
1	**5 Mark** 11.7.1874. Dk. blue and gray-blue. 2 children seated at lower ctr. w/arms between them.	350.	700.	—

		Good	Fine	XF
2	**20 Mark** 11.7.1874. Green and yellow. Allegorical man wearing shirt w/arms and holding a staff w/arms at l. ctr. Rare.	—	—	—
3	**50 Mark** 11.7.1874. Dk. violet, brown and dk. green. 2 allegorical figures at ctr., arms at each corner. Rare.	—	—	—

1882 ISSUE

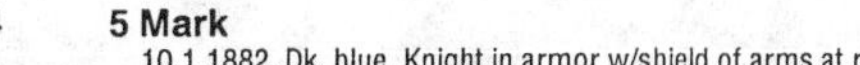

		Good	Fine	XF
4	**5 Mark** 10.1.1882. Dk. blue. Knight in armor w/shield of arms at r.	90.00	250.	1000.

		Good	Fine	XF
5	**20 Mark** 10.1.1882. Green. 2 small boys w/fruit at l. and r.	400.	1000.	4000.
6	**50 Mark** 10.1.1882. Dk. brown. Allegorical winged figure at r.	2000.	5000.	—

1899 ISSUE

		Good	Fine	XF
7	**50 Mark** 5.1.1899. Dk. green and brown-olive. Germania seated at l.	1500.	2500.	6000.

1904-06 ISSUE

		Good	Fine	XF
8	**5 Mark** 31.10.1904. Blue and blue-green. Germania w/child and dove at l. Dragon on back.			
	a. 6 digit serial #.	.50	3.50	14.00
	b. 7 digit serial #.	.50	2.00	12.00

		Good	Fine	XF
9	**10 Mark** 6.10.1906. Dk. green and olive-green. Woman standing holding palm branch at r.			
	a. 6 digit serial #.	5.00	20.00	120.
	b. 7 digit serial #.	2.50	10.00	60.00

REICHSBANKNOTE

IMPERIAL BANK NOTES

1876 ISSUE

		Good	Fine	XF
10	**100 Mark** 1.1.1876. Dk. blue and gray-blue. Arms at l., Minerva in wreath at r. Rare.	—	—	—

		Good	Fine	XF
11	**1000 Mark** 1.1.1876. Brown. Arms at l. Woman w/small angels on back. Specimen. (Not issued). Rare.	—	—	—

1883-84 ISSUE

		Good	Fine	XF
12	**100 Mark** 3.9.1883. Dk. blue on lt. blue unpt. 1 red seal. Medallic woman's head supported by 2 women on back.	200.	500.	1600.
13	**1000 Mark** 2.1.1884. Brown. 1 red seal. Allegorical figures of Navigation and Agriculture on back.	1000.	1800.	5000.

1891 FIRST ISSUE

		Good	Fine	XF
14	**1000 Mark** 1.1.1891. Brown. Like #13, but different sign. 1 red seal.	—	Rare	—

1891 SECOND ISSUE

		Good	Fine	XF
15	**100 Mark** 1.5.1891. Blue. Like #12, but different sign. 1 red seal.	200.	600.	1500.

1895 ISSUE

		Good	Fine	XF
16	**100 Mark** 1.3.1895. Blue. Like #12.			
	a. Issued note. 2 red seals.	200.	600.	1500.
	s. Specimen. 1 red seal.	—	—	—
17	**1000 Mark** 1.3.1895. Brown. Like #13. 2 red seals. Rare.	—	—	—

1896 ISSUE

		Good	Fine	XF
18	**100 Mark** 10.4.1896. Blue. Like #12. 2 red seals.	75.00	300.	1200.

		Good	Fine	XF
19	**1000 Mark** 10.4.1896. Brown. Like #17. 2 red seals.	325.	650.	1500.

1898 ISSUE

		Good	Fine	XF
20	**100 Mark** 1.7.1898. Blue. Like #16. 2 seals.			
	a. Issued note.	3.00	50.00	500.
	b. W/ovpt: *Im Ausland ungiltig, nur zahlbar bei der Staatsbenk Munchen.*	—	—	—
21	**1000 Mark** 1.7.1898. Brown. Like #17. 2 seals.	5.00	35.00	500.

1903 ISSUE

		VG	VF	UNC
22	**100 Mark** 17.4.1903. Blue. Like #16. 2 seals.	.75	35.00	200.
23	**1000 Mark** 10.10.1903. Brown. Like #17. 2 seals.	3.00	50.00	300.

1905 ISSUE

		VG	VF	UNC
24	**100 Mark** 18.12.1905. Blue. Like #16. 2 seals.			
	a. 24mm serial #.	.50	7.50	100.
	b. 29mm serial #.	.50	7.50	100.

1906 ISSUE

		VG	VF	UNC
25	**20 Mark** 10.3.1906. Blue. Eagle at upper r. Back red and blue.			
	a. 6 digit serial #.	.25	30.00	250.
	b. 7 digit serial #.	.25	30.00	250.

		VG	VF	UNC
26	**50 Mark** 10.3.1906. Green on pink unpt. Germania at upper l. and r.			
	a. 6 digit serial #.	.25	10.00	100
	b. 7 digit serial #.	.25	10.00	100
27	**1000 Mark** 26.7.1906. Brown. Like #17.	5.00	50.00	300

1907 ISSUE

		VG	VF	UNC
28	**20 Mark** 8.6.1907. Blue. Like #25.	.25	3.00	175.
29	**50 Mark** 8.6.1907. Green. Like #26b.	40.00	225.	2000.
30	**100 Mark** 8.6.1907. Blue. Like #16.	1.00	10.00	450.

1908 ISSUE

		VG	VF	UNC
31	**20 Mark** 7.2.1908. Blue. Like #25b.	.25	4.00	175.
32	**50 Mark** 7.2.1908. Green. Like #26b.	.25	2.50	250.

		VG	VF	UNC
33	**100 Mark** 7.2.1908. Dk. blue on lt. blue unpt. Red serial # and seal. Like #16.			
	a. Serial # 29mm long.	.25	.50	4.00
	b. Serial # 24mm long.	.50	12.00	350.
34	**100 Mark** 7.2.1908. Dk. blue on lt. blue unpt. Like #16 but green serial # and seal (reissue 1918-22).	.25	.50	6.00
35	**100 Mark** 7.2.1908. Blue. Mercury at l., Ceres at r. Germania seated w/shield and sword on back. Wmk: Wilhelm I and *100*. 207 x 102mm.	.50	5.00	200.
36	**1000 Mark** 7.2.1908. Brown. Like #17.	3.00	35.00	600.

1909 ISSUE

		VG	VF	UNC
37	**20 Mark** 10.9.1909. Blue. Like #25b.	.25	15.00	200.

		VG	VF	UNC
38	**100 Mark** 10.9.1909. Blue. Like #35.	.50	6.00	250.
39	**1000 Mark** 10.9.1909. Brown. Like #17.	2.00	45.00	750.

1910 ISSUE

		VG	VF	UNC
40	**20 Mark** 21.4.1910. Like #25b.			
	a. W/o wmk. 6 digit serial #.	.50	4.00	50.00
	b. W/o wmk. 7 digit serial #.	.25	1.00	30.00
	c. Wmk: *20 Mark.*	2.00	25.00	250.

		VG	VF	UNC
41	**50 Mark** 21.4.1910. Green. Like #26b.	.25	2.50	60.00

		VG	VF	UNC
42	**100 Mark** 21.4.1910. Dk. blue on lt. blue-gray unpt. Like #35.	.25	2.00	20.00
43	**100 Mark** 21.4.1910. Dk. blue on lt. blue unpt. Like #35 but green serial # and seal. (reprint 1918-22).	.25	2.00	25.00
44	**1000 Mark** 21.4.1910. Brown. Like #17. Red serial # and seal.			
	a. 6 digit serial # (until 1916).	.25	3.00	30.00
	b. 7 digit serial #.	.25	.50	2.00

		VG	VF	UNC
45	**1000 Mark** 21.4.1910. Dk. brown on tan unpt. Like #17 but green serial # and seal. (reprint 1918-22).			
	a. 6 digit serial #.	1.00	5.00	30.00
	b. 7 digit serial #.	.25	.50	2.00

1914 Issue

		VG	VF	UNC
46	**20 Mark** 19.2.1914. Like #25.			
	a. 6 digit serial #.	.50	2.00	100.
	b. 7 digit serial #.	.25	.50	10.00

1914 First Issue

		VG	VF	UNC
47	**5 Mark** 5.8.1914. Black on gray-violet unpt. Germania at l. and r. on blue back.			
	a. 6 digit serial #.	1.00	5.00	150.
	b. 7 digit serial #.	.25	5.00	45.00
	c. 8 digit serial #.	.25	5.00	45.00

		VG	VF	UNC
48	**20 Mark** 5.8.1914. Dk. brown on brown and lilac unpt. Minerva at l., Mercury at r. on brown back.			
	a. 6 digit serial #.	.25	5.00	125.
	b. 7 digit serial #.	.25	3.00	100.

		VG	VF	UNC
49	**50 Mark** 5.8.1914. Black and lilac-red on gray unpt. Germania at l. and r. on green back.			
	a. 6 digit serial #.	.25	3.00	175.
	b. 7 digit serial #.	.25	3.00	20.00

1914 Second Issue

		VG	VF	UNC
50	**1 Mark** 12.8.1914. Black on lt. green and lilac unpt. Red serial # and seal. White paper. Back green w/o unpt.	.20	.50	2.50

		VG	VF	UNC
51	**1 Mark** 12.8.1914. Black on lt. green and lilac unpt. LIke #50 but lt. brown pattern over entire note. Back w/green unpt. (Issued 1917).	.20	.50	2.50
52	**1 Mark** 12.8.1914. Like #51 but blue serial # and seal. (Issued 1920).	.20	.50	2.50

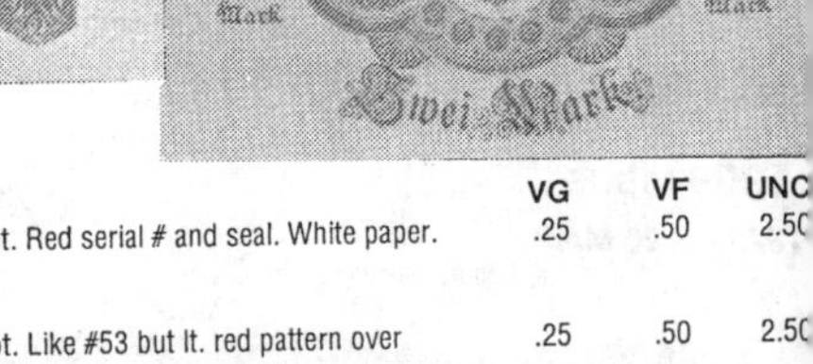

		VG	VF	UNC
53	**2 Mark** 12.8.1914. Black on red unpt. Red serial # and seal. White paper. Back red w/o unpt.	.25	.50	2.50
54	**2 Mark** 12.8.1914. Black on red unpt. Like #53 but lt. red pattern over entire note. Back w/lt. red unpt.	.25	.50	2.50
55	**2 Mark** 12.8.1914. Like #54 but blue serial # and seal.	.25	.50	2.50

1917-18 Issue

Note: Spelling of heading changed to *Darlehnskassenschein* from 1917 onwards.

		VG	VF	UNC
56	**5 Mark** 1.8.1917. Black and purplish blue. Girl at upper r. Back black on green and blue unpt.			
	a. 7 digit serial #.	.20	1.50	6.5
	b. 8 digit serial #.	.20	1.50	5.0

		VG	VF	UNC
57	**20 Mark** 20.2.1918. Dk. brown on carmine unpt. Minerva at l., Mercury at r. Back brown; man in armor at l., allegorical woman at r.	.25	2.00	12.50

1920 ISSUES (WEIMAR REPUBLIC)

		VG	VF	UNC
58	**1 Mark** 1.3.1920. Dk. brown on green and olive unpt. Back dk. green.	.10	.25	1.00

		VG	VF	UNC
59	**2 Mark** 1.3.1920. Red on lt. brown unpt. Brown serial # and seal. Back red-brown.	.10	.25	1.00
60	**2 Mark** 1.3.1920. Dk. brown on blue and lt. brown unpt. Red serial # and seal. Back darker red-brown.	.10	.25	1.00

1922 ISSUE

		VG	VF	UNC
61	**1 Mark** 15.9.1922. Dk. green on lt. green unpt.			
	a. Lt. green paper.	.10	.25	1.00
	b. Gray paper.	5.00	12.00	40.00
62	**2 Mark** 15.9.1922. Brown on pink unpt.	.10	.25	1.00

REICHSBANKNOTEN (RESUMED)

IMPERIAL BANK NOTES

1915-19 ISSUE

		VG	VF	UNC
63	**20 Mark** 4.11.1915. Dk. blue on lt. blue unpt. 2 men w/cornucopias filled w/money at upper ctr. Man and woman on back.	.25	2.00	5.00

		VG	VF	UNC
64	**50 Mark** 20.10.1918. Dk. brown on gray-violet unpt. Green guilloche at l. Dk. line margin (known as the "Mourning Note").			
	a. Wmk: J.	30.00	75.00	225.
	b. Wmk: A.	27.50	60.00	200.
	c. Wmk: B.	25.00	55.00	170.

		VG	VF	UNC
65	**50 Mark** 30.11.1918. Olive-brown on gray unpt. Broad margin, w/egg-shaped white area on back (known as the "Egg Note").	1.50	9.00	30.00

		VG	VF	UNC
66	**50 Mark** 24.6.1919. Green on lt. brown unpt. Woman at upper r. Reihe 1-4. Back blue.	.25	2.00	12.00

WEIMAR REPUBLIC

REICHSBANKNOTE

REPUBLIC TREASURY NOTES

1920 ISSUE

		VG	VF	UNC
67	**10 Mark**			
	6.2.1920. Dk. green and black on olive unpt.			
	a. Unpt. letters.	.10	.25	3.00
	b. W/o unpt. letters.	50.00	300.	700.

		VG	VF	UNC
68	**50 Mark** 23.7.1920. Dk. green and green. Woman w/flowers and fruit at r. Farmer and worker on back.	.25	.50	12.00

		VG	VF	UNC
69	**100 Mark**			
	1.11.1920. Dk. brown w/black text on blue and red unpt. "Bamberg Horseman" (in Bamberg Cathedral) at upper l. and r.			
	a. 7 digit serial #.	.15	.25	6.00
	b. 8 digit serial #.	.15	.25	4.00
	c. W/o unpt. letters. Rare..	—	—	—

1922 FIRST ISSUE

		VG	VF	UNC
70	**10,000 Mark** 19.1.1922. Blue-green on olive-green unpt. Male portr. at r. by Albrecht Durer, like #71. Eagle in rectangular ornament on back.	.75	2.50	8.00

		VG	VF	UN
71	**10,000 Mark** 19.1.1922. Blue-green on olive-green unpt. Face like #70 but monochrome below eagle on back. 210 x 124mm.	.75	2.50	8.0

		VG	VF	UN
72	**10,000 Mark** 19.1.1922. Blue-green on olive-brown unpt. Like #71, but 180 x 100mm.	.75	1.50	6.

1922 Second Issue

		VG	VF	UNC
73	**500 Mark** 27.3.1922. Dk. blue and olive-green. Portr. J. Mayer at upper r.	.50	5.00	30.00

		VG	VF	UNC
74	**500 Mark** 7.7.1922. Black. R. margin tinted. Uniface.			
	a. Red serial # (valid until 1.1.1923).	1.00	2.50	150.
	b. Green 7-digit serial # (valid until 1.4.1923).	.20	1.00	10.00
	c. Green 8-digit serial # (valid until 1.4.1923).	.20	1.00	5.00

1922 Third Issue

		VG	VF	UNC
75	**100 Mark** 4.8.1922. Black-blue. L. and r. margins tinted.	.25	2.00	10.00

		VG	VF	UNC
76	**1000 Mark** 15.9.1922. Dk. green on green and lilac unpt.			
	a. Wmk: E. White paper.	.10	.25	1.00
	b. Wmk: I. Yellow paper.	.10	.25	1.00
	c. Wmk: F. White paper.	.10	.25	1.00
	d. Wmk: D. White paper.	.10	.25	1.00
	e. Wmk: G. White paper.	.10	.25	1.00
	f. Wmk: H. White paper.	.10	.25	1.00
	g. Wmk: J. Pale green paper.	.10	.25	1.00
	h. Wmk: K. Pale green paper.	.10	.25	1.00

		VG	VF	UNC
77	**5000 Mark** 16.9.1922. Blue and brown on gray and green unpt. Portr. mintmaster Spinelli at r. by Memling.	2.00	17.50	125.
78	**5000 Mark** 19.11.1922. Dk. brown on brown unpt. Chamberlain H. Urmiller at l.	1.25	4.00	60.00

		VG	VF	UNC
79	**50,000 Mark** 19.11.1922. Black on white w/green tint at r. Portr. Burgermaster Brauweiler at upper l. by B. Bruyn, w/o unpt.	.75	2.00	8.00
80	**50,000 Mark** 19.11.1922. Dk. brown on pink and green. Like #79 but w/unpt.	.75	2.00	8.00

1922 Fourth Issue

		VG	VF	UNC
81	**5000 Mark** 2.12.1922. Brown on green and lt. brown unpt. Portr. merchant Imhof at r. by A. Durer.			
	a. Wmk: G/D in stars, E.	.10	.25	1.50
	b. Wmk: Lattice, G.	.10	.25	1.50
	c. Wmk: Thorns, I.	.10	.25	1.50
	d. Wmk: Greek pattern, F.	.10	.25	1.50
	e. Wmk: Wavy lines, J.	.25	1.00	3.00

NOTICE

Readers with unlisted dates, signature varieties, etc. are invited to submit photocopies or, high resolution (300 dpi, 100% size) scans of their notes to: Standard Catalog of World Paper Money, 700 East State St. Iola, WI 54990-0001, or E-Mail: george.cuhaj@fwpubs.com.

1922 Fifth Issue

		VG	VF	UNC
82	**1000 Mark** 15.12.1922. Black on dk. brown unpt. Portr. mintmaster J. Herz at upper l. by G. Penz. (Not issued).			
	a. Various styles of serial #, 4mm or less.	5.00	20.00	50.00
	b. Serial # 4.5mm w/single prefix letter.	—	150.	400.

Note: For #82 with ovpt: *EINE MILLIARDE*, see #113.

1923 First Issue

		VG	VF	UNC
83	**100,000 Mark** 1.2.1923. Dk. brown on lilac w/lilac tint at r. Portr. merchant Gisze at l. by H. Holbein.			
	a. W/o *T* at l. of portr.	2.00	3.50	10.00
	b. W/*T* at l. of portr. Two serial #.	2.00	6.00	20.00
	c. W/*T* at l. or portr. One serial #.	2.00	3.50	10.00

1923 Second Issue

		VG	VF	UNC
84	**10,000 Mark** 3.2.1923. Dk. blue on green and red unpt. (Not issued).			
	r. Remainder.	—	700.	1500.
	s. Specimen ovpt: *MUSTER*.	—	—	850.

		VG	VF	UNC
85	**20,000 Mark** 20.2.1923. Blue-black on pink and green unpt.			
	a. Wmk: Small circles, L. 2 serial # varieties.	.15	.50	3.00
	b. Wmk: *G/D* in stars, E.	.15	.50	3.00
	c. Wmk: Lattice, G.	.25	.50	3.00
	d. Wmk: Thorns, I.	.25	.75	5.00
	e. Wmk: Greek pattern, F.	.25	.75	5.00
	f. Wmk: Wavy lines, J.	.25	.75	5.00

		VG	VF	UNC
86	**1 Million Mark** 20.2.1923. Dk. brown on lt. brown and dk. green unpt. Uniface.			
	a. Series letters and serial # at l. and r.	.20	1.50	15.00
	b. Series letters and serial # at upper l. and upper r.	.20	1.50	15.00

1923 Third Issue

		VG	VF	UNC
87	**5000 Mark** 15.3.1923. Dk. brown on olive-brown. Chamberlain H. Urmiller. (Not issued).	—	200.	400.

Note: #87 w/ovpt: *500 MILLIARDEN*, see #124.

		VG	VF	UNC
88	**500,000 Mark** 1.5.1923. Dk. green on lilac and green unpt. Portr. man wearing Jacobite cap at l. and r.			
	a. Serial # on face and back.	4.00	10.00	20.00
	b. Serial # on face only.	4.00	10.00	20.00

		VG	VF	UNC
89	**2 Millionen Mark** 23.7.1923. Dk. brown on pink and green unpt. Merchant Gisze at l. and r. by H. Holbein.			
	a. Issued note.	4.00	9.00	25.00
	b. Error: *MULIONEN*.	100.	300.	1000.

		VG	VF	UNC
90	**5 Millionen Mark** 1.6.1923. Brown on lilac and green w/yellow tint at r. Portr. woman (Constitutional Medallion) at upper l. ctr.	7.00	20.00	75.00

1923 Fourth Issues

		VG	VF	UNC
91	**100,000 Mark** 25.7.1923. Black on green unpt. Uniface.			
	a. Wmk: *G/D* in stars, E, green paper.	.15	.50	1.25
	b. Wmk: Wavy lines, J, white paper.	.15	1.50	5.00

		VG	VF	UNC
92	**500,000 Mark** 25.7.1923. Carmine w/violet tint at r. Uniface.	.25	1.25	6.00

		VG	VF	UNC
93	**1 Million Mark** 25.7.1923. Dk. blue on lilac and lt. brown unpt. Denomination field like #85 w/new denomination ovpt. at l. on face. Printed back.	2.00	10.00	50.00

		VG	VF	UNC
94	**1 Million Mark** 25.7.1923. Black on white w/yellow tint at r. Uniface.	.20	1.00	10.00
95	**5 Millionen Mark** 25.7.1923. Black on white w/blue-green tint at l.	.20	1.00	12.50

		VG	VF	UNC
96	**10 Millionen Mark** 25.7.1923. Black and dk. green w/yellow tint at r.	.20	1.00	8.00

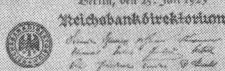

		VG	VF	UNC
97	**20 Millionen Mark** 25.7.1923. Black and lt. blue w/lilac tint at r.			
	a. 7 digit serial #.	.20	1.00	5.00
	b. 6 or 8 digit serial #.	.20	1.00	5.00

		VG	VF	UNC
98	**50 Millionen Mark** 25.7.1923. Black and lilac-brown w/lilac tint at r. Uniface.			
	a. 7 digit serial #.	.25	1.00	5.00
	b. 8 digit serial #.	.25	1.00	5.00

1923 Fifth Issues

		VG	VF	UNC
99	**50,000 Mark** 9.8.1923. Black on lt. brown unpt. Uniface.	.50	2.00	7.50

		VG	VF	UNC
100	**200,000 Mark** 9.8.1923. Black on gray unpt. Uniface.	.20	1.00	3.00

101 1 Million Mark

	VG	VF	UNC
9.8.1923. Black. White paper, w/green tint at r. Serial # at bottom. Wmk: Oak leaves. Uniface.	.20	1.00	5.00

102 1 Million Mark

9.8.1923. Black. Green unpt. panel at r. W/o serial #. Uniface.

	VG	VF	UNC
a. Wmk: *G/D* in stars, E.	.10	.50	2.00
b. Wmk: Small circles, L.	.15	.50	2.00
c. Wmk: Lattice, G.	.15	.50	2.00
d. Wmk: Wavy lines, J.	.20	1.00	5.00

103 2 Millionen Mark

	VG	VF	UNC
9.8.1923. Black. White paper, w/lilac tint at r. Serial # at bottom. Wmk: Oak leaves. Uniface.	.20	1.00	4.00

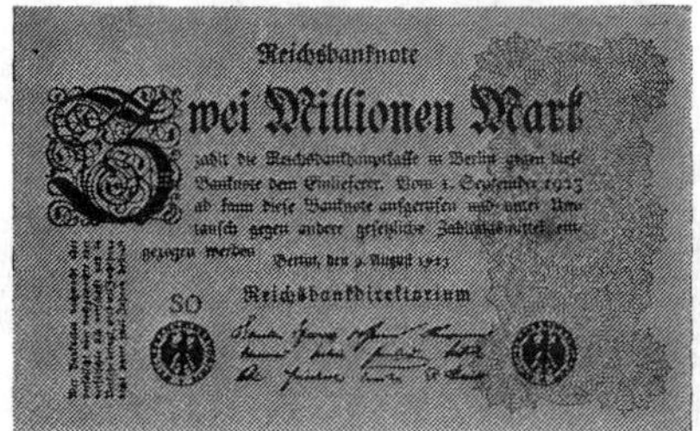

104 2 Millionen Mark

9.8.1923. Black. Lilac guilloche at r. W/o serial #. Uniface.

	VG	VF	UNC
a. Wmk: *G/D* in stars, E.	.20	.50	1.50
b. Wmk: Small circles, L.	.20	.50	1.50
c. Wmk: Lattice w/*8*, G.	.20	.50	1.50
d. Wmk: Wavy lines, J.	.20	1.00	3.00

105 5 Millionen Mark

	VG	VF	UNC
20.8.1923. Black on gray-green unpt. Pink paper. Uniface.	.50	1.50	5.00

106 10 Millionen Mark

22.8.1923. Black on pale olive-green and blue-gray unpt. Uniface.

	VG	VF	UNC
a. Wmk: *G/D* in stars, E.	.15	1.00	3.00
b. Wmk: Small circles, L.	.15	1.00	3.00
c. Wmk: Lattice w/*8*, G.	.15	1.00	3.00
d. Wmk: Wavy lines, J.	.15	1.00	3.00

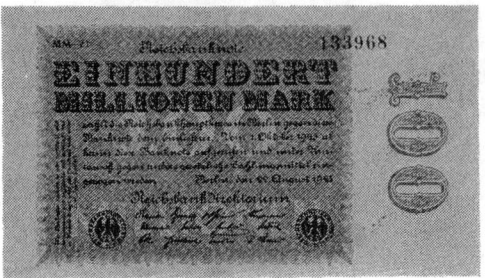

107 100 Millionen Mark

22.8.1923. Black on blue-green and olive-brown unpt. Uniface.

	VG	VF	UNC
a. Wmk: Oak leaves, gray tint at r.	.25	1.00	4.00
b. Wmk: Small crucifera blossoms, D. W/embedded fibre strips in paper on back.	.25	2.00	8.00
c. Wmk: Small crucifera blossoms, D. W/o embedded fibre strips in paper on back.	.25	1.00	4.00
d. Wmk: *G/D* in stars, E.	.25	1.00	4.00
e. Wmk: Small circles, L.	.25	1.00	4.00
f. Wmk: *S* in stars, M.	.25	1.00	4.00
g. Wmk: Lozenges, N.	.25	1.00	4.00

1923 Sixth Issue

108 20 Millionen Mark

1.9.1923. Black on olive-brown and dk. green unpt. Uniface.

	VG	VF	UNC
a. Wmk: Small circles. L.	.15	.50	3.00
b. Wmk: Lozenges, N.	.25	1.00	4.00
c. Wmk: *G/D* in stars, E.	.15	.50	3.00
d. Wmk: Wavy lines, J.	.25	.50	1.00
e. Wmk: Lattice, G.	.25	.50	1.00
f. Wmk: *S* in stars, M.	2.00	10.00	30.00

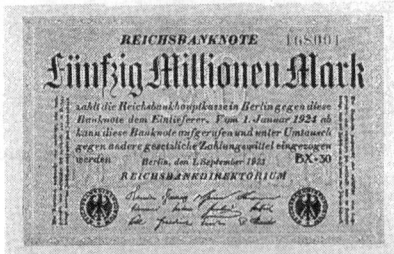

109 50 Millionen Mark

1.9.1923. Black on gray and lilac unpt. Uniface.

	VG	VF	UNC
a. Wmk: Small crucifera blossoms, gray paper. D.	.20	.50	3.00
b. Wmk: *G/D* in stars, E. White paper.	.20	.50	3.00
c. Wmk: Small circles, L. White paper.	.25	.50	3.00
d. Wmk: Lozenges, N. White paper.	.25	.50	3.00
e. Wmk: *S* in stars, M. White paper.	.25	.50	3.00
f. Wmk: Lattice, G. White paper.	.25	.50	3.00

		VG	VF	UNC
110	**500 Millionen Mark** 1.9.1923. Dk. brown on lt. brown and lilac unpt. *500* facing inwardly at r. margin. Uniface.			
	a. Wmk: Thistle leaves, lilac tint at r.	.25	1.00	5.00
	b. Wmk: Small crucifera blossoms, *500* facing inwardly at r. margin.	.25	1.00	5.00
	c. Like b, but *500* facing outwardly at r. margin, D.	50.00	200.	500.
	d. Wmk: *G/D* in stars, E.	.25	1.00	5.00
	e. Wmk: Small circles, L.	.25	1.00	5.00
	f. Wmk: *S* in stars. M.	.25	1.00	5.00
	g. Wmk: Lozenges. N.	40.00	150.	300.
	h. Wmk: Lattice. G.	.50	2.00	5.00
111	**500 Milliarden Mark** 1.9.1923. Blue, lilac and green. Vienna printing. Allegorical head at upper r. Specimen only. Rare.	—	—	—

		VG	VF	UNC
112	**1 Billion Mark** 1.9.1923. Violet and lilac. Allegorical head at r. Vienna printing. Specimen only. Rare.	—	—	—

1923 Seventh Issues

		VG	VF	UNC
113	**1 Milliarde Mark on 1000 Mark** ND (Sept. 1923 - old date 15.12.1922). Black on dk. brown. Red new denomination ovpt. on #82.			
	a. Wmk: *1000*, brown tint at r. White paper.	2.00	4.50	10.00
	b. Wmk: Small crucifera blossoms, D. Brown paper.	2.00	4.50	10.00
	c. Wmk: Small crucifera blossoms, D. White paper.	2.00	4.50	10.00
	d. Ovpt. inverted.	50.00	100.	200.
	e. Ovpt. on back only.	50.00	100.	200.
	f. Ovpt. on face only.	50.00	100.	200.

		VG	VF	UNC
114	**1 Milliarde Mark** 5.9.1923. Black on dk. green, lilac and blue. Blue-green tint at r. Uniface.	.50	3.50	15.00

		VG	VF	UNC
115	**5 Milliarden Mark** 10.9.1923. Black on olive-brown unpt. Uniface.			
	a. Wmk: Oak leaves, lilac tint at r.	2.00	5.00	20.00
	b. Wmk: Small crucifera blossoms, D.	2.00	6.00	20.00

		VG	VF	UNC
116	**10 Milliarden Mark** 15.9.1923. Black on gray-lilac and blue-green unpt. Format similar to #114. Uniface.			
	a. Wmk: Thistle leaves, yellow tint at r.	2.00	6.00	30.00
	b. Wmk: Small crucifera blossoms, D.	2.00	9.00	35.00
117	**10 Milliarden Mark** 1.10.1923. Black-green (shades) on lilac and green unpt. Format similar to #118. 160 x 105mm. Uniface.			
	a. Wmk: *G/D* in stars, E.	2.00	15.00	40.00
	b. Wmk: Small circles, L.	2.00	15.00	40.00
	c. Wmk: *S* in stars, M.	3.00	25.00	75.00
	d. Wmk: Lozenges, N.	30.00	100.	250.
	e. Wmk: Lattice, G.	3.00	25.00	75.00

		VG	VF	UNC
118	**20 Milliarden Mark** 1.10.1923. Dk. green on blue and orange unpt. Format similar to 117. 140 x 93 (90)mm. Uniface.			
	a. Wmk: *G/D* in stars. 5 or 6 digit serial #. E.	4.00	10.00	25.00
	b. Wmk: *G/D* in stars, E. Error w/*20 MILLIARDEN* on l. edge. Format 175 x 85mm.	40.00	90.00	325.
	c. Wmk: Small circles. L.	3.00	7.00	25.00
	d. Wmk: Small circles, L. W/error *20 MILLIARDEN* on l. edge.	40.00	90.00	325.
	e. Wmk: Lozenges, N.	3.00	7.00	25.00
	f. Wmk: Lattice, G.	3.00	7.00	25.00
	g. Wmk: *S* in stars, M.	3.00	7.00	25.00

		VG	VF	UNC
119	**50 Milliarden Mark** 10.10.1923. Black on orange and blue unpt. Uniface.			
	a. Wmk: Oak leaves, green tint at r.	3.50	9.00	30.00
	b. Wmk: Small crucifera blossoms, D. White paper.	3.50	9.00	30.00
	c. Wmk: Small crucifera blossoms, D. White paper. W/o serial #.	3.00	7.00	30.00
	d. Wmk: Small crucifera blossoms, D. Gray paper. W/o serial #.	3.00	7.00	30.00

		VG	VF	UNC
120	**50 Milliarden Mark** 10.10.1923. Black on orange, blue and green. Like #119b but green rectangular unpt. at r. Uniface.			
	a. Wmk: *G/D* in stars, E.	3.00	7.00	35.00
	b. Wmk: Small circles, L.	3.00	10.00	40.00
	c. Wmk: *S* in stars, M.	1.00	10.00	40.00

		VG	VF	UNC
121	**200 Milliarden Mark** 15.10.1923. Black on violet and green unpt. Uniface.			
	a. Wmk: *G/D* in stars, E.	1.50	15.00	40.00
	b. Wmk: Small circles, L.	3.00	20.00	50.00
	c. Wmk: *S* in stars, M.	4.50	20.00	50.00
	d. Wmk: Lattice, G.	15.00	40.00	100.
	e. Wmk: Lozenges. Rare..	—	—	—

1923 Eighth Issue

		VG	VF	UNC
122	**1 Milliarde Mark** 20.10.1923. Black on blue-green unpt. Uniface.	.25	.75	6.50
123	**5 Milliarden Mark** 20.10.1923. Black on violet-brown unpt. Uniface.			
	a. With serial #.	.50	2.00	15.00
	b. W/o serial #.	.25	1.00	9.00

		VG	VF	UNC
124	**500 Milliarden Mark on 5000 Mark** ND (Oct. 1923 - old date 15.3.1923). Dk. brown on olive-brown unpt. New denomination ovpt. on #87.			
	a. Ovpt. on face and back.	12.50	40.00	150.
	b. Ovpt. on back only (error).	100.	600.	1250.
	c. Ovpt. on face only (error).	100.	600.	1250.

1923 Ninth Issue

		VG	VF	UNC
125	**50 Milliarden Mark** 26.10.1923. Black on blue-green unpt. Uniface.			
	a. Gray paper.	1.50	14.00	25.00
	b. Green paper.	1.50	14.00	25.00
126	**100 Milliarden Mark** 26.10.1923. Dk. blue on white, blue tint at r. Uniface.	1.50	10.00	26.00

		VG	VF	UNC
127	**500 Milliarden Mark** 26.10.1923. Dk. brown on white. Uniface.			
	a. Wmk: Oak leaves, green tint at r.	5.00	15.00	55.00
	b. Wmk: *500M*, blue or violet tint at r.	5.00	15.00	55.00

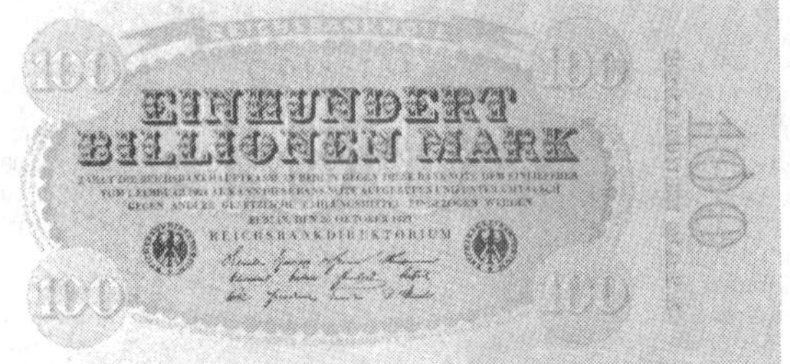

		VG	VF	UNC
128	**100 Billionen Mark** 26.10.1923. Black on lilac and gray, brown tint at r. Uniface.	250.	800.	1500.

1923 Tenth Issue

		VG	VF	UNC
129	**1 Billion Mark** 1.11.1923. Brown-violet, lilac tint at r. Uniface.	12.00	35.00	120.

		VG	VF	UNC
130	**5 Billionen Mark** 1.11.1923. Black on light blue and pink unpt. Uniface.			
	a. Wmk: Thistles, yellow tint at r.	35.00	100.	250.
	b. Wmk: Small crucifera blossoms, D.	50.00	125.	400.
131	**10 Billionen Mark** 1.11.1923. Black on green and lt. brown unpt. Uniface.			
	a. Wmk: Thistles, blue-green tint at r.	45.00	200.	500.
	b. Wmk: Small crucifera blossoms, D.	65.00	225.	600.
132	**10 Billionen Mark** 1.11.1923. Black on brown and blue-green unpt. Uniface.			
	a. Wmk: *G/D* in stars, E.	40.00	200.	600.
	b. Wmk: Small circles, L.	40.00	200.	600.

1923 Eleventh Issue

		VG	VF	UNC
133	**100 Milliarden Mark** 5.11.1923. Red-brown on olive and blue-green unpt. Uniface.	1.00	12.00	25.00

		VG	VF	UNC
134	**1 Billion Mark** 5.11.1923. Black on violet and brown unpt. Uniface.	10.00	60.00	150.

		VG	VF	UNC
135	**2 Billionen Mark** 5.11.1923. Black on green and pink unpt. Uniface.			
	a. Wmk: *G/D* in stars, E.	15.00	35.00	150.
	b. Wmk: Small circles, L.	15.00	35.00	150.
	c. Wmk: *S* in stars, M.	20.00	50.00	150.

		VG	VF	UNC
136	**5 Billionen Mark** 7.11.1923. Black on blue and pink unpt. Uniface.			
	a. Wmk: Thistles. Yellow tint at r.	80.00	350.	700.
	b. Wmk: Small crucifera blossoms, D.	70.00	300.	600.
	c. Wmk: *G/D* in stars, E.	70.00	300.	600.
	d. Wmk: Small circles, L.	70.00	300.	600.

1924 FIRST ISSUE

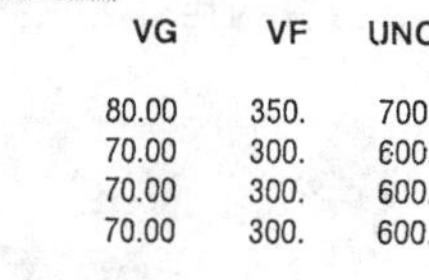

		VG	VF	UNC
137	**10 Billionen Mark** 1.2.1924. Brown on green, lilac tint at r. Uniface.	30.00	300.	600.

		VG	VF	UNC
138	**20 Billionen Mark** 5.2.1924. Blue-green and violet, lt. violet tint at r. Portr. woman at upper r. by A. Durer.	150.	450.	1000.

		VG	VF	UNC
139	**50 Billionen Mark** 10.2.1924. Brown and olive, green tint at r. Portr. Councillor J. Muffel at ctr. r. by A. Durer.	300.	900.	2500.

		VG	VF	UNC
140	**100 Billionen Mark** 15.2.1924. Red-brown and blue, lt. blue tint at r. Portr. W. Pirkheimer at r. by A. Durer.	700.	2000.	4500.

1924 SECOND ISSUE

		VG	VF	UNC
141	**5 Billionen Mark** 15.3.1924. Dk. brown on green and lilac unpt. Back green.	30.00	125.	500.

REICHSSCHULDENVERWALTUNG

IMPERIAL DEBT ADMINISTRATION

1915 EMERGENCY INTEREST COUPON ISSUE

In October 1918 all interest coupons of war loans, due on 2.1.1919 (letter q), were temporarily declared legal tender.

		VG	VF	UNC
142	**2.50 Mark** Year of loan: 1915; 1916; 1917; 1918.	15.00	40.00	75.00
143	**5.00 Mark** Year of loan: 1915; 1916; 1917; 1918.	20.00	50.00	100.

		VG	VF	UNC
144	**12.50 Mark** Year of loan: 1915; 1916; 1917; 1918.	40.00	100.	200.
145	**25.00 Mark** Year of loan: 1915; 1916; 1917; 1918.	40.00	100.	200.

		VG	VF	UNC
146	**50.00 Mark** Year of loan: 1915; 1916; 1917; 1918.	100.	200.	300.
147	**125.00 Mark** Year of loan: 1915; 1916; 1917; 1918.	200.	500.	900.

ZWISCHENSCHEINE - SCHATZANWEISUNGEN

IMPERIAL TREASURY

1923 INTERIM NOTE ISSUE

In October 1923, interim notes of the Reichsbank for Treasury certificates, partial bonds of the treasury certificates of the German Reich were declared legal tender.

		VG	VF	UNC
148	**0.42 Goldmark = 1/10 Dollar (U.S.A.)** 23.10.1923. Wmk: O.	4.00	40.00	85.00
149	**1.05 Goldmark = 1/4 Dollar (U.S.A.)** 23.10.1923. Wmk: *5*. Uniface.	10.00	60.00	100.
150	**1.05 Goldmark = 1/4 Dollar (U.S.A.)** 23.10.1923. Wmk: *50*. Capital letters on back.	8.00	60.00	100.

		VG	VF	UNC
151	**2.10 Goldmark = 1/2 Dollar (U.S.A.)** 23.10.1923. Wmk: *20 MARK*.	10.00	200.	350.

1923 PARTIAL BOND OF TREASURY CERTIFICATES ISSUES

		VG	VF	UNC
152	**0.42 Goldmark = 1/10 Dollar (U.S.A.)** 26.10.1923. Wmk: Oak and thistles.	4.00	35.00	75.00
153	**1.05 Goldmark = 1/4 Dollar (U.S.A.)** 26.10.1923. Wmk: *5*.	12.00	40.00	110.

		VG	VF	UNC
154	**1.05 Goldmark = 1/4 Dollar (U.S.A.)** 26.10.1923. Wmk: *10*.	10.00	40.00	125.
155	**1.05 Goldmark = 1/4 Dollar (U.S.A.)** 26.10.1923. Wmk: *50*.	7.50	40.00	120.
156	**2.10 Goldmark = 1/2 Dollar (U.S.A.)** 26.10.1923. Wmk: *5*.	18.00	65.00	200.

		VG	VF	UNC
157	**2.10 Goldmark = 1/2 Dollar (U.S.A.)** 26.10.1923. Wmk: *20*.	10.00	45.00	150.

1923 WHOLE TREASURY CERTIFICATES ISSUES

3 different issues each:

1. Wmk: Ornaments.
2. *Ausgefertigt*, at lower r. Wmk: Lines and *RSV*.
3. Like #2 but w/o *Ausgefertigt* at lower r.

NOTICE

Readers with unlisted dates, signature varieties, etc. are invited to submit photocopies or, high resolution (300 dpi, 100% size) scans of their notes to: Standard Catalog of World Paper Money, 700 East State St. Iola, WI 54990-0001, or E-Mail: george.cuhaj@fwpubs.com.

		VG	VF	UNC
158	**4.20 Goldmark = 1 Dollar (U.S.A.)** 25.8.1923.			
	a. Wmk: P.	30.00	150.	275.
	b. Wmk: Q.	30.00	150.	275.
159	**8.40 Goldmark = 2 Dollars (U.S.A.)** 25.8.1923.			
	a. Wmk: P.	100.	650.	1000.
	b. Wmk: Q.	100.	650.	1000.

		VG	VF	UNC
160	**21.00 Goldmark = 5 Dollars (U.S.A.)** 25.8.1923.			
	a. Wmk: P.	150.	1200.	2500.
	b. Wmk: Q.	150.	1200.	2500.

RENTENBANK - STABILIZATION BANK

1923 RENTENMARKSCHEIN ISSUE

		VG	VF	UNC
161	**1 Rentenmark** 1.11.1923. Olive.	2.00	20.00	80.00
162	**2 Rentenmark** 1.11.1923. Red and green.	7.00	45.00	250.
163	**5 Rentenmark** 1.11.1923. Blue-green and violet.	20.00	80.00	275.

		VG	VF	UNC
164	**10 Rentenmark** 1.11.1923. Lilac and green.	50.00	200.	700

		VG	VF	UNC
165	**50 Rentenmark** 1.11.1923. Brown and violet.	250.	1500.	3750.
166	**100 Rentenmark** 1.11.1923. Brown and blue-green.	120.	350.	3000.
167	**500 Rentenmark** 1.11.1923. Blue-gray and green.			
	a. Issued note. Rare..	—	—	—
	s. Specimen ovpt: *MUSTER.*	—	—	5000.

		VG	VF	UNC
168	**1000 Rentenmark** 1.11.1923. Brown and lt. green.			
	a. Issued note.	1000.	2000.	5000.
	s. Specimen ovpt: *MUSTER.*	—	—	3000.

1925-26 Issue

		VG	VF	UNC
169	**5 Rentenmark** 2.1.1926. Dk. green and olive. Portr. farm girl at upper ctr. r. 7 or 8 digit serial #.	1.00	8.50	120.

		VG	VF	UNC
170	**10 Rentenmark** 3.7.1925. Green and brown. Portr. farm woman at l.	60.00	300.	1500.

		VG	VF	UNC
171	**50 Rentenmark** 20.3.1925. Brown, green and lilac. Farmer at r.	60.00	325.	1500.

1934 Issue

		VG	VF	UNC
172	**50 Rentenmark** 6.7.1934. Dk. brown on olive. Freiherr vom Stein at r.	20.00	100.	600.

1937 Issue

#173 and 174 blind embossed seal at lower r.

		VG	VF	UNC
173	**1 Rentenmark** 30.1.1937. Olive. Yellow stripe at right. Lg. or sm. size numerals in serial #.			
	a. 7 digit serial #.	2.00	15.00	75.00
	b. 8 digit serial #.	.10	.25	4.00

		VG	VF	UNC
174	**2 Rentenmark** 30.1.1937. Brown. Yellow strip at right. Lg. or sm. size numerals in serial #.			
	a. 7 digit serial #.	2.00	15.00	50.00
	b. 8 digit serial #.	.10	.25	7.00

Deutsche Golddiskontbank

German Gold Discount Bank

This bank did not exercise its right of issuing banknotes. The notes that were printed in anticipation of release were destroyed but for only 3 specimens of each.

1924 Issue

		VG	VF	UNC
174A	**5 Pounds** 20.4.1924. Brown. Youth. Specimen. Rare.	—	—	—

		VG	VF	UNC
174B	**10 Pounds** 20.4.1924. Gray-green. Portr. youth w/wreath at upper ctr. r. Specimen. Rare.	—	—	—

Reichsbanknotes

1924 Issue

		VG	VF	UNC
175	**10 Reichsmark** 11.10.1924. Dk. green and red-lilac. Portr. merchant Dietrich Born by H. Holbein at upper ctr. r.	40.00	175.	2500.

		VG	VF	UNC
176	**20 Reichsmark** 11.10.1924. Brown and red-lilac. Portr. woman by H. Holbein at upper ctr. r.	40.00	175.	3000.

		VG	VF	UNC
177	**50 Reichsmark** 11.10.1924. Brown and dk. green. Portr. man by H. Holbein at upper ctr. r.	8.00	25.00	300.
178	**100 Reichsmark** 11.10.1924. Brown and blue-green. Portr. English Lady by H. Holbein at upper ctr. r.	8.00	25.00	300.

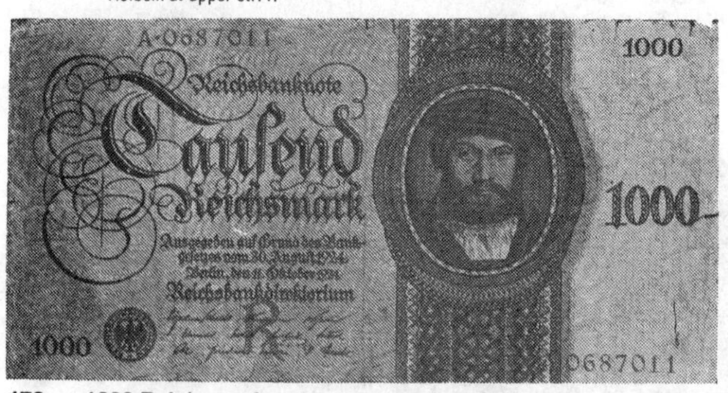

		VG	VF	UNC
179	**1000 Reichsmark** 11.10.1924. Brown and blue. Portr. Patrician Wedigh by H. Holbein at upper ctr. r.	30.00	85.00	375.

1929-36; (1945) Issue

#180-183 serial # on face and back for first variety; serial # on face only for second variety.

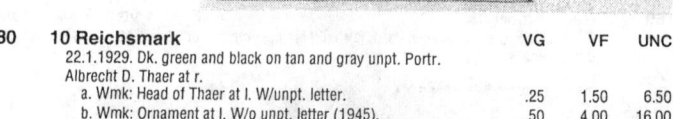

		VG	VF	UNC
180	**10 Reichsmark** 22.1.1929. Dk. green and black on tan and gray unpt. Portr. Albrecht D. Thaer at r.			
	a. Wmk: Head of Thaer at l. W/unpt. letter.	.25	1.50	6.50
	b. Wmk: Ornament at l. W/o unpt. letter (1945).	.50	4.00	16.00

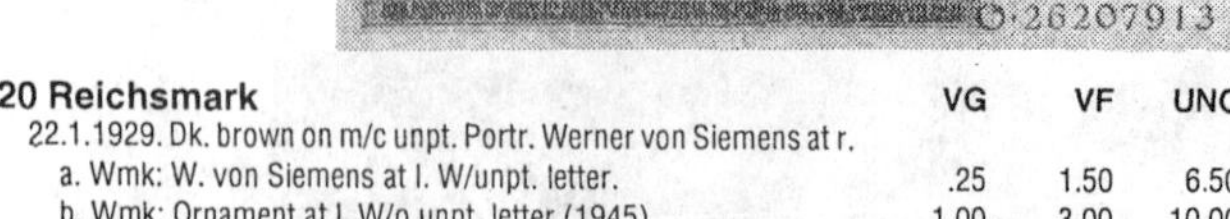

		VG	VF	UNC
181	**20 Reichsmark** 22.1.1929. Dk. brown on m/c unpt. Portr. Werner von Siemens at r.			
	a. Wmk: W. von Siemens at l. W/unpt. letter.	.25	1.50	6.50
	b. Wmk: Ornament at l. W/o unpt. letter (1945).	1.00	3.00	10.00

182	50 Reichsmark	VG	VF	UNC
	30.3.1933. Green and black on m/c unpt. Portr. David Hansemann at r. 7 or 8 digit serial #.			
	a. Wmk: David Hansemann at l. W/unpt. letter.	.25	2.00	7.50
	b. Wmk: Ornament at l. W/o unpt. letter (1945).	1.00	4.00	12.00

183	100 Reichsmark	VG	VF	UNC
	24.6.1935. Blue. Portr. Justus von Liebig at r., swastika in unpt. at ctr. 7 or 8 digit serial #.			
	a. Wmk: J. von Liebig at l. W/unpt. letter.	2.00	4.50	12.50
	b. Wmk: Ornament at l. W/o unpt. letter (1945).	4.00	9.00	17.50

184	1000 Reichsmark	VG	VF	UNC
	22.2.1936. Brown and olive. Portr. Karl-Friedrich Schinkel at r., swastika unpt. at ctr.	15.00	30.00	80.00

1939 Issue

185	20 Reichsmark	VG	VF	UNC
	16.6.1939. Brown. Portr. woman holding edelweiss at r. (Similar to Austria #101).	.50	5.00	18.00

1942 Issue

186	5 Reichsmark	VG	VF	UNC
	1.8.1942. Red-brown. Portr. young man at r. Wmk: *5* straight up at l., either frontwards or backwards.			
	a. Issued note.	.75	2.00	8.00
	b. Wmk: *5* upside down at l.	10.00	25.00	60.00

Local

Eupen-Malmedy

The territory of Eupen-Malmedy was part of the German Reich until 1919, when as a result of the Treaty of Versailles it was given to Belgium. After occupation of Belgium in WW II (1940) this territory was re-united with the Reich - therefore the circulation of German banknotes. After the entry of Allied troops the circulating German notes were hand-stamped by the returning Belgian authorities. In the territory of Eupen-Malmedy, before the entry of the Allied troops in 1944, the locally valid German banknotes, occasionally also Reich's Credit Treasury Notes, were handstamped by various municipalities, previously Belgian. The handstamped notes were legal tender until exchanged for Belgian notes. Almost all handstamped notes of this type are very scarce.

Sudetenland and Lower Silesia

1945 Kassenschein Emergency Issue

187	20 Reichsmark	VG	VF	UNC
	28.4.1945. Red-brown on tan unpt. Back brown.	.50	1.00	7.50

Reichsbank Offices in Graz, Linz and Salzburg

1945 Emergency Reissue

Photo-mechanically produced notes, following the pattern of the notes already in circulation. All notes of a particular denomination have identical serial #.

187A	5 Reichsmark	VG	VF	UNC
	ND (1945-old date 1/8/1942). Red-brown. Like #186. Portr. young man at r. Serial #G.13663932. Reported not confirmed.	—	—	—

188	10 Reichsmark	VG	VF	UNC
	ND (1945-old date 22.1.1929). Blue-green. Like #180. Portr. A. D. Thaer at r., blurred printing. Serial #D.02776733.			
	a. W/o holes.	30.00	250.	500.
	b. W/holes.	12.00	100.	250.

		VG	VF	UNC
189	**50 Reichsmark** ND (1945-old date 30.3.1933). Green. Like #182. Portr. D. Hansemann at r., blurred printing. Serial #E.06647727.			
	a. W/o holes.	20.00	150.	400.
	b. W/holes.	8.00	50.00	85.00
190	**100 Reichsmark** ND (1945-old date 24.6.1935). Blue. Like #183. Portr. J. von Liebig at r., blurred printing. Serial #T.7396475.			
	a. W/o holes.	20.00	40.00	130.
	b. W/holes.	8.00	25.00	80.00

ALLIED OCCUPATION - WWII

ALLIED MILITARY CURRENCY

The territory of Eupen-Malmedy was part of the German Reich until 1919, when as a result of the Treaty of Versailles it was given to Belgium. After occupation of Belgium in WW II (1940) this territory was re-united with the Reich - therefore the circulation of German banknotes. After the entry of Allied troops the circulating German notes were hand-stamped by the returning Belgian authorities.

1944 ISSUE

#191-198 back brown; lg. *M* at ctr.

		VG	VF	UNC
191	**1/2 Mark** 1944. Green on lt. blue unpt.			
	a. 9 digit serial # w/*F*.	.25	1.00	10.00
	b. 8 digit serial # w/dash, w/*F*.	15.00	60.00	250.
	c. 8 digit serial # w/dash, w/o *F*.	3.00	10.00	75.00

		VG	VF	UNC
192	**1 Mark** 1944. Blue on lt. blue unpt.			
	a. 9 digit serial # w/*F*.	.25	1.50	6.00
	b. 9 digit serial # w/o *F*.	.25	1.00	5.00
	c. 8 digit serial # w/dash, w/*F*.	15.00	100.	150.
	d. 8 digit serial # w/dash, w/o *F*.	.75	3.00	10.00

		VG	VF	UNC
193	**5 Mark** 1944. Lilac on lt. blue unpt.			
	a. 9 digit serial # w/*F*.	.25	1.50	5.00
	b. 9 digit serial # w/o *F*.	8.00	12.00	30.00
	c. 8 digit serial # w/dash, w/*F*.	20.00	100.	250.
	d. 8 digit serial # w/dash, w/o *F*.	1.00	3.00	20.00

		VG	VF	UNC
194	**10 Mark** 1944. Blue on lt. blue unpt.			
	a. 9 digit serial # w/*F*.	1.50	15.00	30.00
	b. 9 digit serial # w/o *F*.	10.00	22.00	40.00
	c. 8 digit serial # w/dash, w/*F*.	25.00	185.	400.
	d. 8 digit serial # w/dash, w/o *F*.	1.00	10.00	25.00

		VG	VF	UNC
195	**20 Mark** 1944. Red on lt. blue unpt.			
	a. 9 digit serial # w/*F*.	1.00	4.00	35.00
	b. 9 digit serial # w/o *F*.	2.00	5.00	40.00
	c. 8 digit serial # w/dash, w/*F*.	40.00	260.	450.
	d. 8 digit serial # w/dash, w/o *F*.	1.00	5.00	15.00

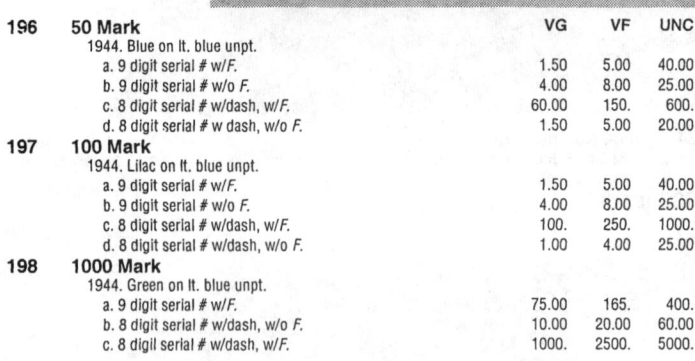

		VG	VF	UNC
196	**50 Mark** 1944. Blue on lt. blue unpt.			
	a. 9 digit serial # w/*F*.	1.50	5.00	40.00
	b. 9 digit serial # w/o *F*.	4.00	8.00	25.00
	c. 8 digit serial # w/dash, w/*F*.	60.00	150.	600.
	d. 8 digit serial # w dash, w/o *F*.	1.50	5.00	20.00
197	**100 Mark** 1944. Lilac on lt. blue unpt.			
	a. 9 digit serial # w/*F*.	1.50	5.00	40.00
	b. 9 digit serial # w/o *F*.	4.00	8.00	25.00
	c. 8 digit serial # w/dash, w/*F*.	100.	250.	1000.
	d. 8 digit serial # w/dash, w/o *F*.	1.00	4.00	25.00
198	**1000 Mark** 1944. Green on lt. blue unpt.			
	a. 9 digit serial # w/*F*.	75.00	165.	400.
	b. 8 digit serial # w/dash, w/o *F*.	10.00	20.00	60.00
	c. 8 digil serial # w/dash, w/*F*.	1000.	2500.	5000.

THIRD REICH

KONVERSIONSKASSE FÜR DEUTSCHE AUSLANDSSCHULDEN

CONVERSION FUND FOR GERMAN FOREIGN DEBTS

1933 ISSUE

		VG	VF	UNC
199	**5 Reichsmark** 28.8.1933. Black, green and brown.	10.00	20.00	35.00

		VG	VF	UNC
200	**10 Reichsmark** 28.8.1933. Black and lilac.	12.50	25.00	50.00
201	**30 Reichsmark** 28.8.1933. Black, red and brown.	30.00	100.	250.
202	**40 Reichsmark** 28.8.1933. Black, blue and brown.	50.00	150.	375.
203	**50 Reichsmark** 28.8.1933. Black, brown and blue.	30.00	60.00	200.
204	**100 Reichsmark** 28.8.1933. Black, brown and green.	30.00	60.00	200.
205	**500 Reichsmark** 28.8.1933.	—	—	—
206	**1000 Reichsmark** 28.8.1933.	—	—	—

1934 ISSUE

#207-214 ovpt. 2 red guilloches at l., the lower one containing the date 1934.

		VG	VF	UNC
207	**5 Reichsmark** 1934. Ovpt. on #199.	10.00	20.00	35.00
208	**10 Reichsmark** 1934. Ovpt. on #200.	15.00	30.00	50.00
209	**30 Reichsmark** 1934. Ovpt. on #201.	27.50	75.00	200.
210	**40 Reichsmark** 1934. Ovpt. on #202.	30.00	90.00	275.

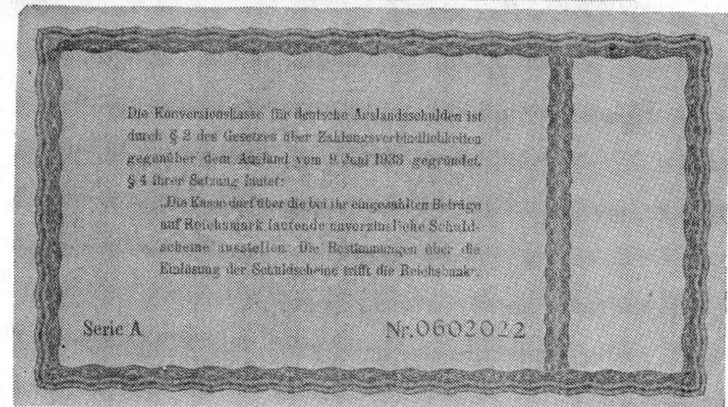

		VG	VF	UNC
211	**50 Reichsmark** 1934. Ovpt. on #203.	20.00	40.00	150.
212	**100 Reichsmark** 1934. Ovpt. on #204.	12.50	25.00	150.
213	**500 Reichsmark** 1934. Ovpt. on #205.	—	—	—
214	**1000 Reichsmark** 1934. Ovpt. on #206.	—	—	—

REGIONAL - OCCUPATION OF LITHUANIA - WWI

OSTBANK FÜR HANDEL UND GEWERBE,

DARLEHNSKASSENSCHEINE

STATE LOAN BANK CURRENCY NOTES, EASTERN BANK OF COMMERCE AND INDUSTRY, POSEN (POZNAN)

1916 ISSUE

#R120-R126 circulated in Lithuania until 1922.

		VG	VF	UNC
R120	**20 Kopeken** 17.4.1916. Blue-green.	1.50	4.00	30.00

		VG	VF	UNC
R121	**50 Kopeken** 17.4.1916. Black on red-brown and blue-green unpt.			
	a. *ASTUN GADEEM* last 2 words at bottom r. on back. Capital letters of bottom text 1.8mm tall. *AISDEWU KASES SIME* at r. w/*S* in form of *f*.	1.50	4.00	30.00
	b. As above but capital letters only. 1.2-1.4mm tall.	3.50	10.00	85.00
	c. *ASTONI GADEEM* last 2 words at bottom r. on back. Capital letter of bottom text 1.8mm tall. *AISDEWU KASES SIHME* at r.	1.50	4.00	25.00
	d. As above but capital letters only 1.2-1.4mm tall. Text poorly printed.	1.50	4.00	25.00

		VG	VF	UNC
R122	**1 Rubel** 17.4.1916. Black on blue and brown unpt.			
	a. Like #R121a.	1.50	4.00	30.00
	b. Like #R121b.	3.00	15.00	85.00
	c. Like #R121c.	1.50	4.00	25.00
	d. Like #R121d.	1.50	4.00	25.00
R123	**3 Rubel** 17.4.1916. Dk. brown on green and lilac unpt.			
	a. *AIFDEWU* w/crossed *F* (Gothic *F*).	7.00	50.00	300.
	b. *AIFDEWU* w/uncrossed *F* (Gothic *S*).	3.00	15.00	70.00
R124	**10 Rubel** 17.4.1916. Red-brown on red and green unpt.	7.00	20.00	100.

		VG	VF	UNC
R125	**25 Rubel** 17.4.1916. Dk. blue on lilac unpt.	12.00	35.00	200.

		VG	VF	UNC
R126	**100 Rubel** 17.4.1916. Blue. Woman at l., man wearing helmet at r.	12.00	60.00	200.

DARLEHNSKASSE OST

STATE LOAN BANK EAST

KOWNO (KAUNAS)

1918 ISSUE

#R127-R134 circulated in Lithuania until 1922.

		VG	VF	UNC
R127	**1/2 Mark** 4.4.1918. Black on lilac and lt. brown unpt.	1.50	4.00	20.00
R128	**1 Mark** 4.4.1918. Dk. brown on green unpt.	1.50	4.00	15.00
R129	**2 Mark** 4.4.1918. Red-brown on lilac unpt.	5.00	50.00	150.
R130	**5 Mark** 4.4.1918. Brown and blue.	2.00	10.00	30.00

		VG	VF	UNC
R131	**20 Mark** 4.4.1918. Red-brown on green and pink unpt.	4.00	15.00	60.00
R132	**50 Mark** 4.4.1918. Dk. blue on gray-violet unpt.	5.00	15.00	60.00

		VG	VF	UNC
R133	**100 Mark** 4.4.1918. Brown. Woman at l., man wearing helmet at r. Similar to #R126.	7.00	17.50	65.00

		VG	VF	UNC
R134	**1000 Mark** 4.4.1918. Green. Mercury and youth in armor at r.			
	a. 6 digit serial #, black sign.	12.00	60.00	250.
	b. 7 digit serial #, green sign.	10.00	50.00	200.

GERMAN OCCUPIED TERRITORIES - WWII

REICHSKREDITKASSEN

REICH'S CREDIT TREASURY NOTES

1940 ISSUE

#R135-R140 legal tender alongside the currency of the country in numerous occupied countries and territories during WW II.

		VG	VF	UNC
R135	**50 Reichspfennig** ND (1940-45). Green on tan unpt.	.50	2.50	15.00

		VG	VF	UNC
R136	**1 Reichsmark** ND (1940-45). Greenish black on brown and m/c unpt.			
	a. Embossed stamp. Series 1-480.	.25	1.00	2.50
	b. W/o embossed stamp. Series 481-702.	.50	4.00	15.00

		VG	VF	UNC
R137	**2 Reichsmark** ND (1940-45). Grayish brown on green and tan unpt.			
	a. Embossed stamp. 7 digit serial #.	.25	1.00	2.50
	b. W/o embossed stamp. 8 digit serial #.	.50	2.50	10.00

		VG	VF	UNC
R138	**5 Reichsmark**			
	ND (1940-45). Blue-black on brown and gray unpt. Portr. farmer at l., factory worker at r. Berlin War Memorial at ctr. on back.			
	a. Embossed stamp. 7 digit serial #.	.50	1.25	4.00
	b. W/o embossed stamp, 8 digit serial #.	.50	1.50	5.00

		VG	VF	UNC
R139	**20 Reichsmark**			
	ND (1940-45). Dk. brown on red-brown and pale olive unpt. "The Architect" by A. Durer at r. Brandenburg Gate at ctr. on back.	.75	2.00	15.00

		VG	VF	UNC
R140	**50 Reichsmark**			
	ND (1940-45). Blue-black on dull violet unpt. Portr. woman at r. Marienburg castle at ctr. on back.	1.00	3.00	20.00

Note: Immediately after the end of the war, Reichs Credit Treasury Notes were authorized in the British zone of occupation in the denominations of 5, 20 and 50 Reichsmark, provided they had been given a stamp of a Reichsbank office located in the British zone of occupation. All such notes with different stamps are scarce ($40.00 each).

MILITARY PAYMENT CERTIFICATES

ETAPPEN - INSPEKTION

BASE INSPECTORATE I, 1ST ARMY

1915 ISSUE

#M1-M4 issued in occupied French territory. All w/different dates in script, only *1915* year date printed.

		VG	VF	UNC
M1	**50 Centimes** 1915.	40.00	70.00	120.
M2	**1 Franc** 1915.	40.00	70.00	120.

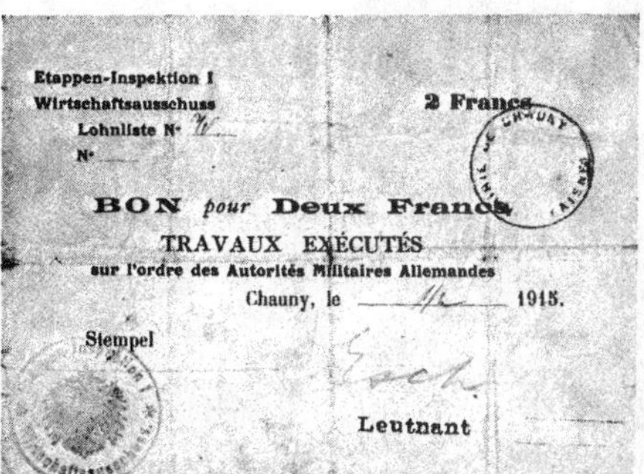
Etappen-Inspektion I
Wirtschaftsausschuss
2 Francs
Lohnliste N°
N°
BON pour Deux Francs
TRAVAUX EXÉCUTÉS
sur l'ordre des Autorités Militaires Allemandes
Chauny, le 1915.
Stempel
Leutnant

		VG	VF	UNC
M3	**2 Francs** 1915.	30.00	50.00	100.
M4	**5 Francs** 1915.	30.00	50.00	100.

ETAPPEN - KOMMANDANTUR

BASE LOCAL HEADQUARTERS

1915 ISSUE

#M5-M8 like #M1-M4. Issued in occupied French territory.

		VG	VF	UNC
M5	**50 Centimes** 1915.	40.00	70.00	120.
M6	**1 Franc** 1915.	30.00	50.00	100.
M7	**2 Francs** 1915.	30.00	50.00	100.

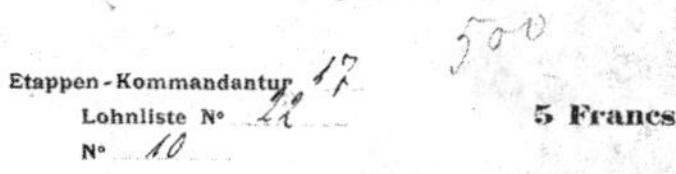
Etappen-Kommandantur 17
Lohnliste N° 22
N° 10
5 Francs

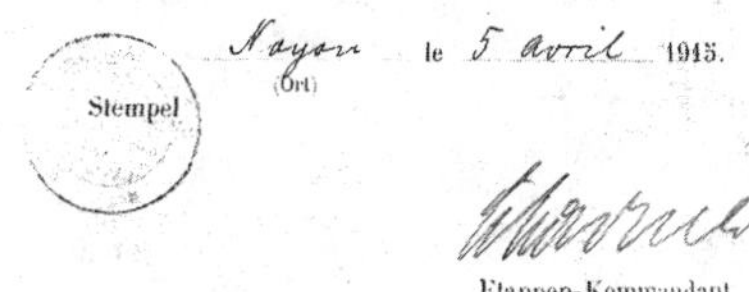
BON pour Cinq Francs
TRAVAUX EXÉCUTÉS
sur l'ordre des Autorités Militaires Allemandes
Noyon le 5 avril 1915.
(Ort)
Stempel
Etappen-Kommandant.

		VG	VF	UNC
M8	**5 Francs** 1915.	30.00	50.00	100.

ETAPPEN - INSPEKTION

BASE INSPECTORATE, 2ND ARMY

1914-15 ISSUE

#M9-M12 issued in occupied French territory, so-called "Deichmann-Bons", w/different handstamps of various French municipalities.

		VG	VF	UNC
M9	**5 Francs** 1914-15.	40.00	125.	250.
M10	**10 Francs** 1914-15.	40.00	150.	300.
M11	**20 Francs** 1914-15.	40.00	150.	300.

		VG	VF	UNC
M12	**50 Francs** 1914-15.	40.00	200.	400.
M13	**100 Francs** 1914-15.	40.00	200.	400.

#M14-M18 Deleted, see #M9-M13.

ETAPPEN - INSPEKTION (RESUMED)

BASE INSPECTORATE, 3RD ARMY

1915 ISSUE

#M19-M26 issued in occupied French territory.

		VG	VF	UNC
M19	**1 Franc** 1915.	40.00	125.	250.
M20	**2 Francs** 1915.	40.00	125.	250.
M21	**3 Francs** 1915.	40.00	125.	250.
M22	**5 Francs** 1915.	40.00	125.	250.
M23	**10 Francs** 1915.	40.00	125.	250.
M24	**25 Francs** 1915.	40.00	125.	250.
M25	**100 Francs** 1915.	40.00	150.	300.
M26	**100 Francs** 1915.	40.00	150.	300.

REICHSMARINE DES OSTSEEBEREICHES

REICH'S NAVY OF THE BALTIC SEA ZONE

KIEL

1923 ISSUE

		VG	VF	UNC
M27	**1 Milliarde Mark** 27.10.1923.	10.00	20.00	40.00

		VG	VF	UNC
M28	**5 Milliarden Mark**	7.00	15.00	40.00
M29	**20 Milliarden Mark**	7.00	15.00	40.00
M30	**50 Milliarden Mark**	7.00	15.00	40.00

BEHELFSZAHLUNGSMITTEL FÜR DIE DEUTSCHE WEHRMACHT

AUXILIARY PAYMENT CERTIFICATES, GERMAN ARMED FORCES

1940 ND ISSUE

Intended as legal tender within the services during World War II. Worth 10 times the face value if spent in military channels.

		VG	VF	UNC
M31	**1 Reichspfennig** ND (1940). Lilac-brown. Swastika at ctr. in unpt.	25.00	100.	250.

1942 ND ISSUE

#M32-M37 unpt. eagle w/small swastika in unpt. at ctr.

		VG	VF	UNC
M32	**1 Reichspfennig** ND (1942). Blue.	2.00	4.00	10.00
M33	**5 Reichspfennig** ND (1942). Red.	2.00	4.00	10.00

		VG	VF	UNC
M34	**10 Reichspfennig** ND (1942). Green.	1.00	3.00	15.00
M35	**50 Reichspfennig** ND (1942). Red-orange.	2.00	10.00	35.00
M36	**1 Reichsmark** ND (1942). Brown on orange unpt.	5.00	15.00	75.00

		VG	VF	UNC
M37	**2 Reichsmark** ND (1942). Dk. blue on lilac unpt.	15.00	75.00	250.

Note: Also see Greece #M19-M22.

VERRECHNUNGSSCHEINE FÜR DIE DEUTSCHE WEHRMACHT

CLEARING NOTES FOR GERMAN ARMED FORCES

1944 ISSUE

		VG	VF	UNC
M38	**1 Reichsmark** 15.9.1944. Green.	.50	1.00	5.00

		VG	VF	UNC
M39	**5 Reichsmark** 15.9.1944. Blue.	.75	2.50	10.00

		VG	VF	UNC
M40	**10 Reichsmark** 15.9.1944. Red.	.50	1.50	7.50

		VG	VF	UNC
M41	**50 Reichsmark** 15.9.1944. Lilac-brown.	5.00	12.50	40.00

The Federal Republic of Germany (formerly West Germany), located in north-central Europe, since 1990 with the unification of East Germany, has an area of 137,782 sq. mi. (356,854 sq. km.) and a population of 82.69 million. Capital: Berlin. The economy centers about one of the world's foremost industrial establishments. Machinery, motor vehicles, iron, steel, chemicals, yarns and fabrics are exported.

During the post-Normandy phase of World War II, Allied troops occupied the western German provinces of Schleswig-Holstein, Hamburg, Lower Saxony, Bremen, North Rhine-Westphalia, Hesse, Rhineland-Palatinate, Baden-Wurttemberg, Bavaria and Saarland. The conquered provinces were divided into American, British and French occupation zones. Five eastern German provinces were occupied and administered by the forces of the Soviet Union.

The western occupation forces restored the civil status of their zones on Sept. 21, 1949, and resumed diplomatic relations with the provinces on July 2, 1951. On May 5, 1955, nine of the ten western provinces, organized as the Federal Republic of Germany, became fully independent. The tenth province, Saarland, was restored to the republic on Jan. 1, 1957.

The post-WW II division of Germany ended on Oct. 3, 1990, when the German Democratic Republic (East Germany) ceased to exist and its five constituent provinces were formally admitted to the Federal Republic of Germany. An election Dec. 2, 1990, chose representatives to the united federal parliament (Bundestag), which then conducted its opening session in Berlin in the old Reichstag building.

MONETARY SYSTEM:

1 Deutsche Mark (DM) = 100 Pfennig, 1948-2001
1 Euro = 100 Cents, 2002-

ALLIED OCCUPATION - POST WW II

U.S. ARMY COMMAND

1948 FIRST ISSUE

#1 and 2 printer: Forbes Litho (w/o imprint).

#3 and 4 printer: Tudor Press, Boston, Mass. U.S.A. (W/o imprint).

#5-8 printer: ABNC (w/o imprint).

#1-10 were issued under military authority and w/o name of country.

#1-10, also #13-17 may come w/stamped: *B* in circle, perforated: *B* or w/both varieties on the same note. These markings were made as a temporary check on currency circulating in West Berlin.

		VG	VF	UNC
1	**1/2 Deutsche Mark**			
	1948. Green on lt. green and lt. brown unpt. Back brown and blue.			
	a. Issued note.	2.50	20.00	125.
	b. Stamped: *B* in circle.	2.50	17.50	200.
	c. Perforated: *B.*	5.00	60.00	250.
	d. Stamped and perforated: *B* on the same note.	10.00	125.	300.
	s1. As a. perforated: *SPECIMEN.*	—	—	150.
	s2. Specimen w/red ovpt: *MUSTER.*	—	—	150.
2	**1 Deutsche Mark**			
	1948. Blue on blue-green and lilac unpt. Back brown on lilac unpt.			
	a. Issued note.	2.00	20.00	100.
	b. Stamped: *B* in circle.	2.00	20.00	175.
	c. Perforated: *B.*	2.00	30.00	225.
	d. Stamped and perforated: *B* on the same note.	2.50	60.00	250.
	s1. As a. perforated: *SPECIMEN.*	—	—	125.
	s2. Specimen w/red ovpt: *MUSTER.*	—	—	125.

		VG	VF	UNC
3	**2 Deutsche Mark**			
	1948. Lilac on blue-green unpt. Allegorical woman seated at l. holding tablet. Back green on red unpt.			
	a. Issued note.	7.50	60.00	400.
	b. Stamped: *B* in circle.	7.50	100.	600.
	c. Perforated: *B.*	7.50	120.	1000.
	d. Stamped and perforated: *B* on the same note.	9.00	400.	1200.
	s1. As a. perforated: *SPECIMEN.*	—	—	250.
	s2. Specimen w/red ovpt: *MUSTER.*	—	—	200.

		VG	VF	UNC
4	**5 Deutsche Mark**			
	1948. Brown on green and gold unpt. Man seated at r. Back lilac and blue.			
	a. Issued note.	6.00	45.00	250.
	b. Stamped: *B* in circle.	7.50	50.00	375.
	c. Perforated: *B.*	7.50	50.00	600.
	d. Stamped and perforated: *B* on the same note.	7.50	50.00	700.
	s1. As a. perforated: *SPECIMEN*	—	—	175.
	s2. Specimen w/44mm red ovpt: *MUSTER.*	—	—	175.
	s3. Specimen w/54mm red ovpt: *MUSTER.*	—	—	175.
5	**10 Deutsche Mark**			
	1948. Blue on m/c unpt. Allegorical figures of 2 women and a man at ctr.			
	a. Issued note.	8.00	60.00	350.
	b. Handstamped: *B* in circle.	10.00	70.00	375.
	c. Perforated: *B.*	15.00	100.	425.
	d. Handstamped and perforated: *B* on the same note.	20.00	150.	500.
	s1. As a. perforated: *SPECIMEN.*	—	—	200.
	s2. Specimen w/red ovpt: *MUSTER.*	—	—	200.
	s3. As s2. perforated *SPECIMEN.*	—	—	200.

		VG	VF	UNC
6	**20 Deutsche Mark**			
	1948. Green on m/c unpt. 2 allegorical figures at l.			
	a. Issued note.	17.50	55.00	350.
	b. Handstamped: *B* in circle.	20.00	75.00	400.
	c. Perforated: *B.*	25.00	90.00	450.
	d. Handstamped and perforated: *B* on the same note.	30.00	150.	500.
	s1. As a. perforated *SPECIMEN.*	—	—	200.
	s2. Speciman w/red ovpt: *MUSTER.*	—	—	200.

		VG	VF	UNC
7	**50 Deutsche Mark**			
	1948. Purple on m/c unpt. Allegorical woman at ctr.			
	a. Issued note.	35.00	80.00	1000.
	b. Handstamped: *B* in circle.	40.00	90.00	1000.
	c. Perforated: *B.*	100.	250.	1250.
	d. Handstamped and perforated: *B* on the same note.	100.	350.	1500.
	s1. Specimen w/red ovpt: *MUSTER.*	—	—	200.

8 100 Deutsche Mark

1948. Red on m/c unpt. Allegorical woman w/globe at ctr.

	VG	VF	UNC
a. Issued note.	100.	750.	2000.
b. Handstamped: *B* in circle.	100.	1000.	3000.
c. Perforated: *B.*	300.	1500.	4000.
d. Handstamped and perforated: *B* on the same note.	350.	2000.	4500.
s1. As d. perforated *SPECIMEN.*	—	—	250.
s2. Specimen w/red ovpt: *MUSTER* perforated *SPECIMEN.*	—	—	250.

1948 ND Second Issue

#9-10 printer: Tudor Press, Boston, Mass. U.S.A. (w/o imprint.)

9 20 Deutsche Mark

ND (1948). Blue on blue-green and orange unpt. Medallic woman's head at l. Back red on green unpt.

	VG	VF	UNC
a. Issued note.	150.	400.	1200.
b. Handstamped: *B* in circle.	200.	500.	1400.
c. Perforated: *B.*	225.	1000.	2000.
d. Handstamped and perforated: *B* on the same note.	250.	1750.	3750.
s1. As a. perforated *SPECIMEN.*	—	—	200.
s2. Specimen w/red ovpt: *MUSTER.*	—	—	200.
s3. As s2. perforated: *SPECIMEN.*	—	—	200.

10 50 Deutsche Mark

ND (1948). Green-blue. Allegorical woman's head at ctr.

	VG	VF	UNC
a. Issued note.	1000.	1500.	4000.
b. Handstamped: *B* in circle. Rare..	—	—	—
s1. Specimen.	—	—	1000.
s2. Specimen w/red ovpt: *MUSTER.*	—	—	1000.
s3. Specimen perforated: *B.* Rare..	—	—	—

Note: #10 was in circulation for only a very few days.

Bank Deutscher Länder

1948 Issue

11 5 Pfennig

ND (1948). Green on lilac unpt. Back lilac.

	VG	VF	UNC
a. Issued note.	.75	3.00	15.00
s. Specimen w/red ovpt: *MUSTER.*	—	—	60.00

12 10 Pfennig

ND (1948). Blue on brown unpt. Back brown.

	VG	VF	UNC
a. Issued note.	.75	3.00	15.00
s. Specimen w/red ovpt: *MUSTER.*	—	—	60.00

13 5 Deutsche Mark

9.12.1948. Black on green and yellow unpt. Woman (Europa) on the bull at r. Wmk: Woman's head.

	VG	VF	UNC
a. Single series letter. Printer: TDLR (w/o imprint).	10.00	35.00	300.
b. As a. handstamped *B* in circle.	18.00	60.00	500.
c. As a. perforated *B.*	20.00	65.00	150.
d. As a. handstamped and perforated *B* on same note.	22.50	75.00	175.
e. Number w/series letter in front of serial #.	6.00	25.00	150.
f. As e. handstamped *B* in circle.	17.50	60.00	300.
g. As e. perforated *B.*	10.00	20.00	—
h. As e. handstamped and perforated *B* on same note.	15.00	30.00	75.00

13

	VG	VF	UNC
i. Number w/series letter 7A-(?). Printer: BDK (w/o imprint).	4.00	7.50	100.
s1. Series letter A w/red ovpt: *SPECIMEN* perforated *SPECIMEN.*	—	—	150.
s2. Series letter 7A w/red ovpt: *MUSTER* on face and back.	—	—	150.

#14-15 portr. as wmk. Printer: Banque de France.

14 50 Deutsche Mark

9.12.1948. Brown and black on yellow-green unpt. Merchant Hans Imhof by Albrecht Dürer at r. Imhof at l., men w/ship at r. on back.

	VG	VF	UNC
a. Issued note.	32.50	50.00	200.
b. Handstamped: *B* in circle.	40.00	100.	400.
s. Specimen w/red ovpt: *MUSTER.*	—	—	200.

15 100 Deutsche Mark

9.12.1948. Black and brown on blue unpt. Councillor Jakob Muffel by Albrecht Dürer at r. Muffel at l., old city view of Nürnberg at ctr. on back.

	VG	VF	UNC
a. Issued note.	62.50	100.	400.
b. Stamped: *B* in circle.	62.50	250.	900.
s1. Specimen w/89mm red ovpt: *MUSTER.*	—	—	200.
s2. Specimen w/99mm red ovpt: *MUSTER.*	—	—	200.

1949 Issue

#16-17 printer: ABNC (w/o imprint).

16 10 Deutsche Mark

22.8.1949. Blue. Similar to #5 but w/bank name.

	VG	VF	UNC
a. Issued note.	6.50	10.00	60.00
b. Stamped: *B* in circle.	10.00	125.	300.
s1. As a. w/red ovpt: *MUSTER.*	—	—	100.
s2. As s1. perforated *SPECIMEN.*	—	—	100.

17 20 Deutsche Mark

22.8.1949. Green. Similar to #6 but w/bank name.

	VG	VF	UNC
a. Issued note.	12.50	30.00	225.
b. Handstamped: *B* in circle.	15.00	125.	400.
s1. As a. perforated: *SPECIMEN.*	—	—	100.
s2. As s1. w/red ovpt: *MUSTER.*	—	—	100.

Federal Republic

Deutsche Bundesbank

1960 Issue

#18-24 portr. as wmk. Replacement notes: Serial # prefix *Y, Z.*
#18-22 w/ or w/o ultraviolet sensitive features.

18 5 Deutsche Mark

2.1.1960. Green on m/c unpt. Young Venetian woman by Albrecht Dürer (1505) at r. Oak sprig at l. ctr. on back.

	VG	VF	UNC
a. Issued note.	FV	FV	14.00
s. Specimen.	—	—	100.

		VG	VF	UNC
19	**10 Deutsche Mark**			
	2.1.1960. Blue on m/c unpt. Young man by Albrecht Dürer at r. Sail training ship *Gorch Fock* on back.			
	a. Issued note.	FV	12.00	50.00
	s. Specimen.	—	—	100.

		VG	VF	UNC
20	**20 Deutsche Mark**			
	2.1.1960. Black and green on m/c unpt. Elsbeth Tucher by Albrecht Dürer (1499) at r. Violin, bow and clarinet on back.			
	a. Issued note.	FV	20.00	65.00
	s. Specimen.	—	—	100.
21	**50 Deutsche Mark**			
	2.1.1960. Brown and olive-green on m/c unpt. Portrait of Hand Urmiller by Barthel Beham (about 1525) at r. Holsten-Tor gate in Lübeck on back.			
	a. Issued note.	FV	20.00	80.00
	s. Specimen.	—	—	100.

		VG	VF	UNC
22	**100 Deutsche Mark**			
	2.1.1960. Blue on m/c unpt. *Master Sebastian Münster* by Christoph Amberger (1552) at r. Eagle on back.			
	a. Issued note.	FV	75.00	190.
	s. Specimen.	—	—	150.
23	**500 Deutsche Mark**			
	2.1.1960. Brown-lilac on m/c unpt. Male portrait by Hans Maler zu Schwaz. Eltz Castle on back.			
	a. Issued note.	FV	375.	750.
	s. Specimen.	—	—	400.

		VG	VF	UNC
24	**1000 Deutsche Mark**			
	2.1.1960. Dk. brown on m/c unpt. Astronomer Johann Schöner by Lucas Cranach the Elder at r. Cathedral of Limburg on the Lahn on back.			
	a. Issued note.	FV	700.	1100.
	s. Specimen.	—	—	600.

The German Democratic Republic (East Germany), located on the great north European plain, ceased to exist in 1990. During the closing days of World War II in Europe, Soviet troops advancing into Germany from the east occupied the German provinces of Mecklenburg, Brandenburg, Saxony-Anhalt, Saxony and Thuringia. These five provinces comprised the occupation zone administered by the Soviet Union after the cessation of hostilities. The other three zones were administered by the United States, Great Britain and France. Under the Potsdam agreement, questions affecting Germany as a whole were to be settled by the commanders in chief of the occupation zones acting jointly and by unanimous decision. When Soviet intransigence rendered the quadripartite commission inoperable, the three western zones were united to form the Federal Republic of Germany, May 23, 1949. Thereupon the Soviet Union dissolved its occupation zone and established it as the Democratic Republic of Germany, Oct. 7, 1949. East and West Germany became reunited as one country on Oct. 3, 1990.

MONETARY SYSTEM:

1 Mark = 100 Pfennig

SOVIET OCCUPATION - POST WW II

TREASURY

1948 CURRENCY REFORM ISSUE

Introduction of the Deutsche Mark-Ost (East).

#1-7 adhesive validation stamps on old Rentenmark and Reichsbank notes.

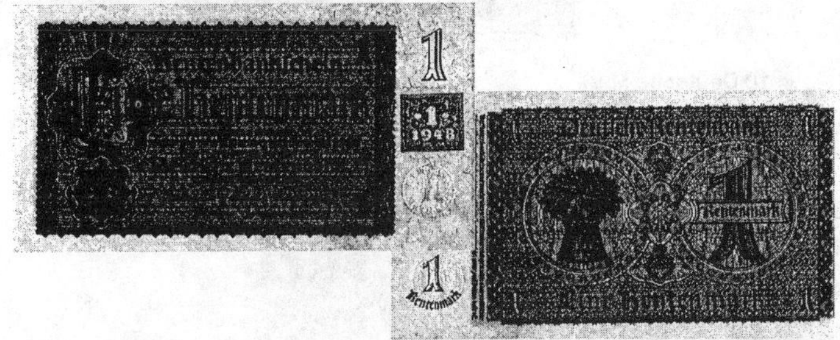

		VG	VF	UNC
1	**1 Deutsche Mark**			
	1948 (- old date 30.1.1937). Blue adhesive stamp on Germany 1 Rentenmark #173.	1.00	5.00	15.00

		VG	VF	UNC
2	**2 Deutsche Mark**			
	1948 (- old date 30.1.1937). Green adhesive stamp on Germany 2 Rentenmark #174.	1.50	7.50	20.00

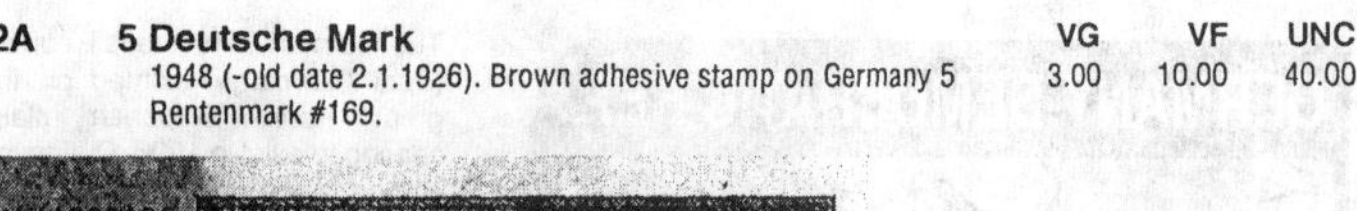

		VG	VF	UNC
2A	**5 Deutsche Mark** 1948 (-old date 2.1.1926). Brown adhesive stamp on Germany 5 Rentenmark #169.	3.00	10.00	40.00

		VG	VF	UNC
3	**5 Deutsche Mark** 1948 (- old date 1.8.1942). Brown adhesive stamp on Germany 5 Reichsmark #186.	1.50	7.50	20.00

		VG	VF	UNC
4	**10 Deutsche Mark** 1948 (- old date 22.1.1929). Lilac adhesive stamp.			
	a. On Germany 10 Reichsmark #180a.	1.50	7.50	20.00
	b. On Germany 10 Reichsmark #180b.	1.50	7.50	20.00

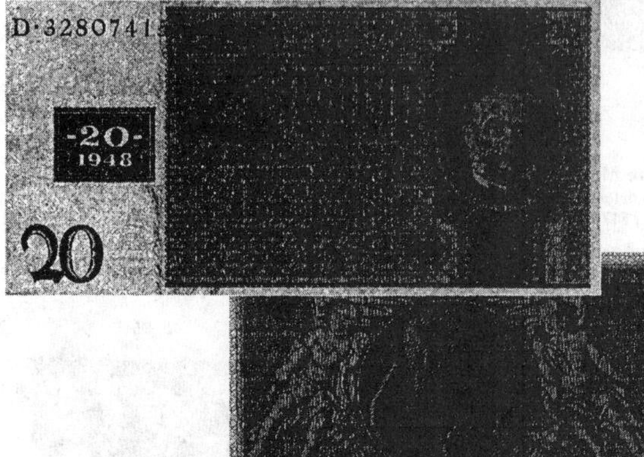

		VG	VF	UNC
5	**20 Deutsche Mark** 1948 (- old dates 1929; 1939). Brown adhesive stamp.			
	a. On Germany 20 Reichsmark #181a. (-old date 22.1.1929).	2.50	10.00	35.00
	b. On Germany 20 Reichsmark #181b. (-old date 22.1.1929).	2.50	10.00	35.00
5A	**20 Deutsche Mark** 1948 (-old date 16.6.1939). Brown adhesive stamp on Germany 20 Reichsmark #185.	3.00	10.00	40.00

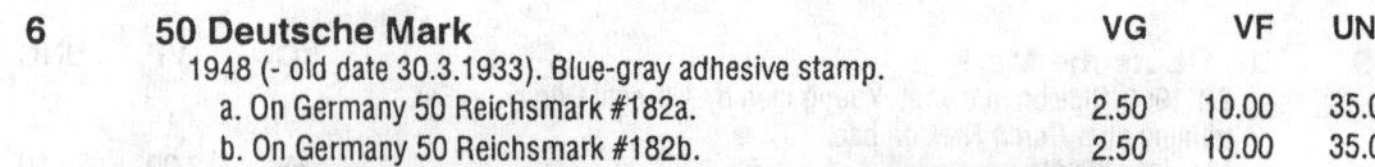

		VG	VF	UNC
6	**50 Deutsche Mark** 1948 (- old date 30.3.1933). Blue-gray adhesive stamp.			
	a. On Germany 50 Reichsmark #182a.	2.50	10.00	35.00
	b. On Germany 50 Reichsmark #182b.	2.50	10.00	35.00

		VG	VF	UNC
7	**100 Deutsche Mark** 1948 (- old date 24.6.1935). Blue-green adhesive stamp.			
	a. On Germany 100 Reichsmark #183a.	4.00	12.50	50.00
	b. On Germany 100 Reichsmark #183b.	4.00	12.50	50.00

Note: Germany #171, 172, 177 and 178 are also encountered with these adhesive stamps although they were not officially issued as such.

DEMOCRATIC REPUBLIC

DEUTSCHE NOTENBANK

1948 ISSUE

#8-16 w/o pictorial design.

#8a-13a printer: Goznak, USSR.

#8b-13b printer: East Germany.

		VG	VF	UNC
8	**50 Deutsche Pfennig** 1948. Blue on brown unpt.			
	a. 6 digit serial #.	2.50	7.50	35.00
	b. 7 digit serial #.	.50	1.75	7.50
	s. Specimen.	—	—	75.00
9	**1 Deutsche Mark** 1948. Olive-brown on olive and brown unpt.			
	a. 6 digit serial #.	2.00	6.00	30.00
	b. 7 digit serial #.	.25	1.00	5.00
	s. Specimen.	—	—	75.00

		VG	VF	UNC
10	**2 Deutsche Mark** 1948. Brown on lt. brown and green unpt.			
	a. 6 digit serial #.	2.00	6.00	30.00
	b. 7 digit serial #.	.50	1.50	6.00
	s. Specimen.	—	—	75.00
11	**5 Deutsche Mark** 1948. Dk. brown on green and lt. brown unpt.			
	a. 6 digit serial #, w/o plate #.	1.75	5.00	30.00
	b. 7 digit serial #, w/plate #.	.25	1.00	5.00
	s. Specimen.	—	—	75.00
12	**10 Deutsche Mark** 1948. Black on green and lt. brown unpt.			
	a. 6 digit serial #, w/o plate #.	2.50	7.50	50.00
	b. 7 digit serial #, w/plate #.	.50	1.75	7.50
	s. Specimen.	—	—	75.00

NOTICE

Readers with unlisted dates, signature varieties, etc. are invited to submit photocopies or, high resolution (300 dpi, 100% size) scans of their notes to: Standard Catalog of World Paper Money, 700 East State St. Iola, WI 54990-0001, or E-Mail: george.cuhaj@fwpubs.com.

13 20 Deutsche Mark
1948. Dk. brown on red-brown and green unpt.

	VG	VF	UNC
a. 6 digit serial #, w/o plate #.	2.00	6.00	30.00
b. 7 digit serial #, w/plate #.	.50	2.00	10.00
s. Specimen.	—	—	75.00

14 50 Deutsche Mark
1948. Green on brown unpt.

	VG	VF	UNC
a. W/o plate #. Single letter prefix.	1.50	5.00	50.00
b. W/plate #. Double letter prefix.	.50	1.75	7.50
s. Specimen.	—	—	75.00

15 100 Deutsche Mark
1948. Blue on green and lt. brown unpt.

	VG	VF	UNC
a. Issued note.	1.00	4.00	17.50
s. Specimen.	—	—	75.00

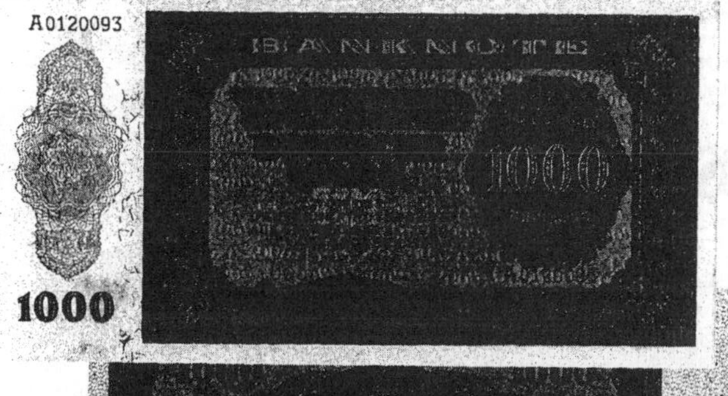

16 1000 Deutsche Mark
1948. Brown on green and lt. brown unpt.

	VG	VF	UNC
a. Issued note.	7.50	25.00	75.00
s. Specimen.	—	—	75.00

1955 ISSUE

#17-21 like previous issue.

17 5 Deutsche Mark
1955. Gray and black on brown and red-brown unpt.

	VG	VF	UNC
	1.00	4.00	10.00

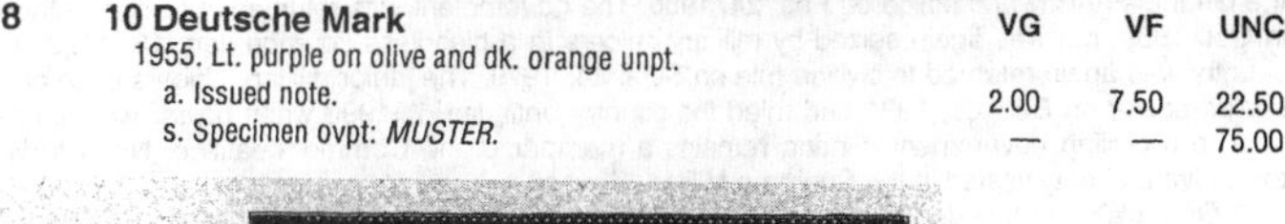

18 10 Deutsche Mark
1955. Lt. purple on olive and dk. orange unpt.

	VG	VF	UNC
a. Issued note.	2.00	7.50	22.50
s. Specimen ovpt: *MUSTER.*	—	—	75.00

19 20 Deutsche Mark
1955. Dk. blue on lt. tan and red-brown unpt. Like #13.

	VG	VF	UNC
a. Issued note.	2.00	7.50	25.00
s. Specimen ovpt: *MUSTER.*	—	—	75.00

20 50 Deutsche Mark
1955. Dk. red on orange and lt. green unpt. Like #14.

	VG	VF	UNC
a. Issued note.	3.00	10.00	40.00
s. Specimen ovpt: *MUSTER.*	—	—	75.00

21 100 Deutsche Mark
1955. Brown on lt. blue, green and pink unpt. Like #15.

	VG	VF	UNC
	6.00	20.00	70.00

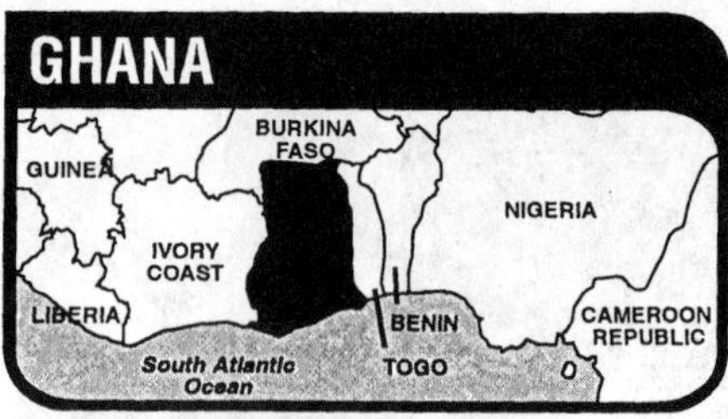

The Republic of Ghana, a member of the British Commonwealth situated on the West Coast of Africa between the Ivory Coast and Togo, has an area of 92,098 sq. mi. (238,537 sq. km.) and a population of 19.93 million, almost entirely African. Capital: Accra. Traditional exports include cocoa, coffee, timber, gold, industrial diamonds, maganese and bauxite. Additional exports include pineapples, bananas, yams, tuna, cola and salt.

Ghana was first visited by Portuguese traders in 1470, and through the 17th century was used by various European powers - England, Denmark, Holland, Germany - as a center for their slave trade. Britain achieved control of the Gold Coast in 1821, and established the colony of Gold Coast in 1874. In 1901, Britain annexed the neighboring Ashanti Kingdom; the same year a northern region known as the Northern Territories became a British protectorate. Part of the former German colony of Togoland was mandated to Britain by the League of Nations and administered as part of the Gold Coast. The state of Ghana, comprising the Gold Coast and British Togoland, obtained independence on March 6, 1957, becoming the first black African colony to do so. On July 1, 1960, Ghana adopted a republican constitution, changing from a ministerial to a presidential form of government. The government was overthrown, the constitution suspended and the National Assembly dissolved by the Ghanaian Army and police on Feb. 24, 1966. The government was returned to civilian authority in Oct. 1969, but was again seized by military officers in a bloodless coup on Jan. 13, 1972. The country was again returned to civilian rule on Sept. 24, 1979. The junior military officers once again seized power on Dec. 31, 1981 and ruled the country until Jan. 7, 1993 when power was handed over to a civilian government. Ghana remains a member of the Commonwealth of Nations, with executive authority vested in the Supreme Military Council.

Ghana's monetary denomination of "cedi" is derived from the word "sedie" meaning cowrie, a shell money commonly employed by coastal tribes.

MONETARY SYSTEM:

1 Shilling = 12 Pence
1 Pound = 20 Shillings to 1965
1 Cedi = 100 Pesewas, 1965-

REPUBLIC

BANK OF GHANA

1958-63 ISSUE

#1-3 wmk: *GHANA* in star.

		VG	VF	UNC
1	**10 Shillings** 1958-63. Green and brown on m/c unpt. Bank of Ghana bldg. in Accra at ctr. r. Star on back.			
	a. 2 sign. Printer: TDLR. 1.7.1958.	4.00	20.00	55.00
	b. W/o imprint. 1.7.1961.	2.50	12.50	35.00
	c. W/o imprint. 1.7.1962.	4.25	20.00	57.50
	d. 1 sign. 1.7.1963.	1.25	7.00	27.50
	s. As a. Specimen.	—	—	75.00

		VG	VF	UNC
2	**1 Pound** 1958-62. Red-brown and blue on m/c unpt. Bank of Ghana bldg. in Accra at ctr. Cocoa pods in 2 heaps on back.			
	a. Printer: TDLR. 1.7.1958; 1.4.1959.	3.25	10.00	30.00
	b. W/o imprint. 1.7.1961; 1.7.1962.	3.00	9.00	25.00
	s. As a. Specimen.	—	—	75.00

		VG	VF	UNC
3	**5 Pounds** 1.7.1958-1.7.1962. Purple and orange on m/c unpt. Bank of Ghana bldg. in Accra at ctr. Cargo ships, logs in water on back.			
	a. Issued note.	10.00	25.00	80.00
	s1. Specimen. 1.7.1958.	—	—	100.
	s2. Specimen. Perforated: *CANCELLED.*	—	—	200.

		VG	VF	UNC
4	**1000 Pounds** 1.7.1958. Blackish brown. Bank of Ghana bldg. in Accra at lower r. Ornate design on back.	10.00	100.	300.

Note: #4 was used in interbank transactions.

GIBRALTAR

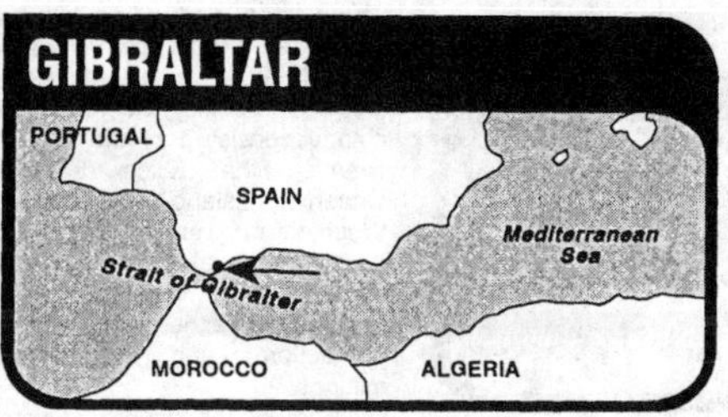

The British Colony of Gibraltar, located at the southernmost point of the Iberian Peninsula, has an area of 2.25 sq. mi. (5.8 sq. km.) and a population of 29,000. Capital (and only town): Gibraltar. Aside from its strategic importance as guardian of the western entrance to the Mediterranean Sea, Gibraltar is also a free port and a British naval .

Gibraltar, rooted in Greek mythology as one of the Pillars of Hercules, has long been a coveted stronghold. Moslems took it from Spain and fortified it in 711. Spain retook it in 1309, lost it again to the Moors in 1333, and retook it in 1462. After Barbarossa sacked Gibraltar in 1540, Spain strengthened its defenses and held it until the War of the Spanish Succession when it was captured by a combined British and Dutch force, 1704. Britain held it against the Franco-Spanish attacks of 1704-05 and through the historic "Great Siege" of 1779-83. Recently Spain has attempted to discourage British occupancy by harassment and economic devices. In 1967, Gibraltar's inhabitants voted to remain under British rule.

RULERS:

British

MONETARY SYSTEM:

1 Shilling = 12 Pence
1 Pound = 20 Shillings to 1971
1 Pound = 100 New Pence, 1971-

BRITISH ADMINISTRATION

GOVERNMENT OF GIBRALTAR

1914 EMERGENCY WW I SERIES A

#1-5 embossed stamp of the *Anglo-Egyptian Bank, Ltd., Gibraltar.*

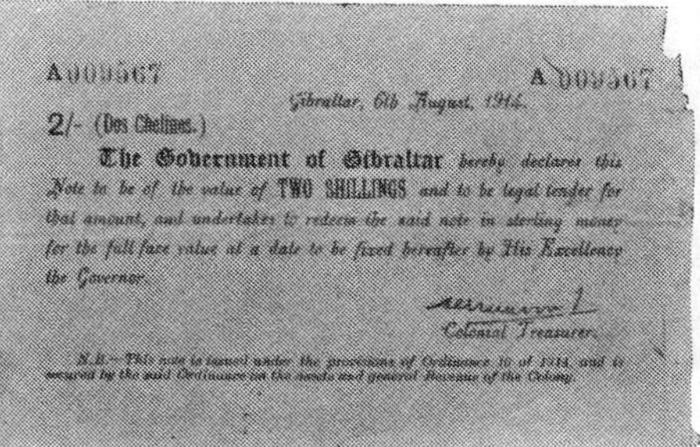

		Good	Fine	XF
1	**2 Shillings = 2 Chelines** 6.8.1914. Red.	425.	1500.	—
2	**10 Shillings = 10 Chelines** 6.8.1914. Blue.	850.	2500.	—
3	**1 Pound = 1 Libra** 6.8.1914. Black. Yellow paper.	1250.	3750.	—
4	**5 Pounds = 5 Libras** 6.8.1914. Black. Blue paper. Rare.	—	—	—
5	**50 Pounds = 50 Libras** 6.8.1914. Black. Blue paper. Rare.	—	—	—

1914 SERIES B

		Good	Fine	XF
6	**2 Shillings = 2 Chelines** 6.8.1914. Green on pink. Arms at top ctr.	100.	250.	750.

		Good	Fine	XF
7	**10 Shillings = 10 Chelines** 6.8.1914. Lilac on pink.	200.	650.	—
8	**1 Pound = 1 Libra** 6.8.1914. Blue on green.	275.	1000.	—
9	**5 Pounds = 5 Libras** 6.8.1914. Brown on green. Rare.	—	—	—
10	**50 Pounds = 50 Libras** 6.8.1914. Pink on green. Rare.	—	—	—

1927 ORDINANCE, REGULAR ISSUE

#11-13 arms at ctr. on back. Printer: W&S.

		VG	VF	UNC
11	**10 Shillings** 1.10.1927. Blue on yellow-brown unpt. Rock of Gibraltar at upper l.	30.00	125.	600.
12	**1 Pound** 1.10.1927. Green on yellow-brown unpt. Rock of Gibraltar at bottom ctr.	30.00	125.	600.
13	**5 Pounds** 1.10.1927. Brown. Rock of Gibraltar at bottom ctr.	60.00	300.	—

1934 ORDINANCE, 1938-42 ISSUE

#14-16 arms at ctr. on back. Printer: W&S.

		VG	VF	UNC
14	**10 Shillings** 1937-58. Blue on yellow-brown unpt. Like #11. Rock of Gibraltar at upper l. 2 serial # varieties and 4 sign. varieties.			
	a. Sign. title: *TREASURER.* 1.2.1937.	15.00	75.00	450.
	b. Sign. title: *FINANCIAL SECRETARY.* 1.6.1942; 1.7.1954; 3.10.1958.	5.00	25.00	200.
	c. As b. 1.7.1954. W/security thread.	5.00	25.00	200.

		VG	VF	UNC
15	**1 Pound** 1938-58. Green on yellow-brown unpt. Like #12. Rock of Gibraltar at bottom ctr. 2 serial varieties and 5 sign. varieties.			
	a. Sign. title: *TREASURER.* 1.6.1938.	25.00	100.	600.
	b. Sign. title: *FINANCIAL SECRETARY.* 1.6.1942; 1.12.1949.	5.00	25.00	200.
	c. As b. 1.7.1954; 3.10.1958.	3.00	15.00	150.
16	**5 Pounds** 1942-58. Brown. Like #13. Rock of Gilbraltar at bottom ctr. 2 serial # varieties and 4 sign. varieties.			
	a. 1.6.1942.	20.00	90.00	500.
	b. 1.12.1949.	15.00	70.00	450.
	c. 1.7.1954; 3.10.1958.	12.50	60.00	425.

1934 ORDINANCE; 1958 ISSUE

#17-19 arms at ctr. on back. Printer: TDLR.

		VG	VF	UNC
17	**10 Shillings** 3.10.1958; 1.5.1965. Blue on yellow-brown unpt. Like #11. Rock of Gilbraltar at l.	10.00	60.00	250.

		VG	VF	UNC
18	**1 Pound**			
	1958-75. Green on yellow-brown unpt. Like #12. Rock of Gibraltar at bottom ctr.			
	a. Sign. title: *FINANCIAL SECRETARY.* 3.10.1958; 1.5.1965.	4.00	15.00	90.00
	b. Sign. title: *FINANCIAL AND DEVELOPMENT SECRETARY.* 20.11.1971.	3.00	10.00	50.00
	c. 20.11.1975.	7.50	30.00	175.
	s. Specimen. As a-c.	—	—	—

		VG	VF	UNC
19	**5 Pounds**			
	1958-75. Brown. Like #13. Rock of Gibraltar at bottom ctr.			
	a. Sign. title: *FINANCIAL SECRETARY.* 3.10.1958; 1.5.1965.	25.00	100.	575.
	b. Sign. title: *FINANCIAL AND DEVELOPMENT SECRETARY.* 1.5.1965; 20.11.1971; 20.11.1975.	17.50	80.00	400.
	s. Specimen. As a-b.	—	—	—

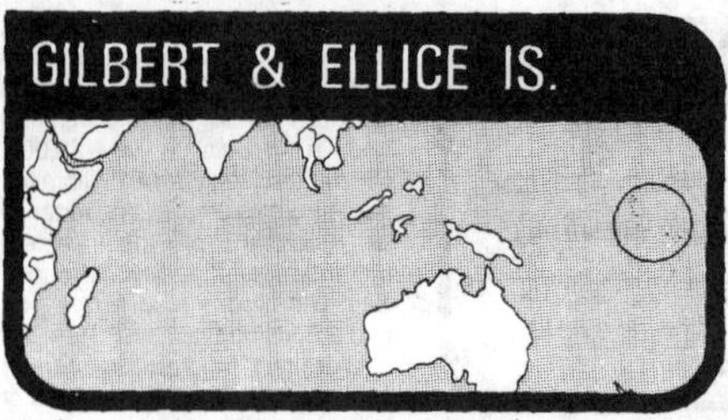

The Gilbert and Ellice Islands comprised a British colony made up of 40 atolls and islands in the western Pacific Ocean. The colony consisted of the Gilbert Islands, the Ellice Islands, Ocean Island, Fanning, Washington and Christmas Island in the Line Islands, and the Phoenix Islands. The principal industries were copra production and phosphate mining.

Early inhabitants were Melanesian but the Ellice Islands were occupied in the 16th century by the Samoans, who established the Polynesian culture there. The first Europeans to land in the islands came in 1764. James Cook visited in 1777. Britain declared a protectorate over the islands in 1892 and made it a colony in 1915. In World War II the Gilberts were occupied by the Japanese from Dec. 1941 to Nov. 1943. The colony adopted a new constitution and became self-governing in 1971. The Ellice Islands became Tuvalu in 1976 with independence in 1978. The balance of the colony became Kiribati in 1979.

Australian currency is currently used in circulation.

RULERS:

British until 1978-79

MONETARY SYSTEM:

1 Pound = 20 Shillings
1 Shilling = 12 Pence

BRITISH ADMINISTRATION

GILBERT AND ELLICE ISLANDS COLONY

1942 EMERGENCY WWII ISSUE

#1-5 made by mimeograph process. Embossed seal: *COURT OF H.B.M. HIGH COMMISSIONER FOR WESTERN PACIFIC* at l. Uniface.

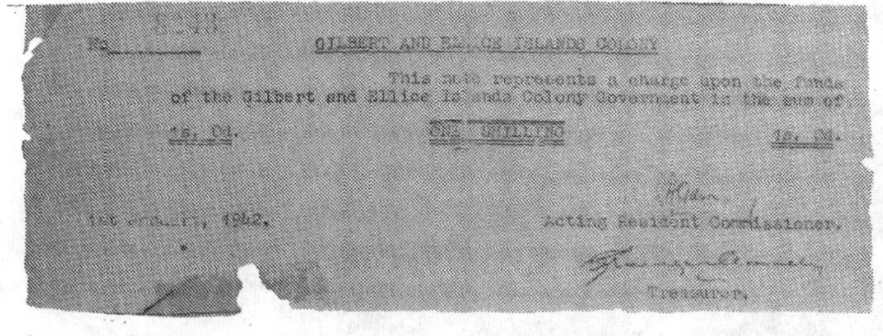

		Good	Fine	XF
1	**1 Shilling**			
	1.1.1942. White paper.	5000.	14,000.	—
2	**2 Shillings**			
	1.1.1942.	5000.	14,000.	—
4	**10 Shillings**			
	1.1.1942.	5000.	14,000.	—

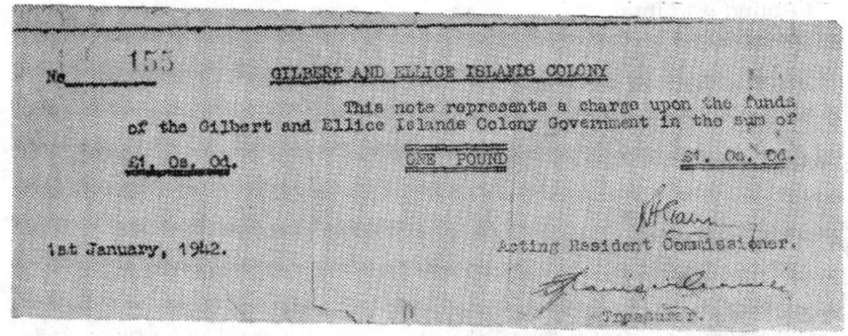

		Good	Fine	XF
5	**1 Pound**			
	1.1.1942. Pink paper.	5000.	14,000.	—

GREAT BRITAIN

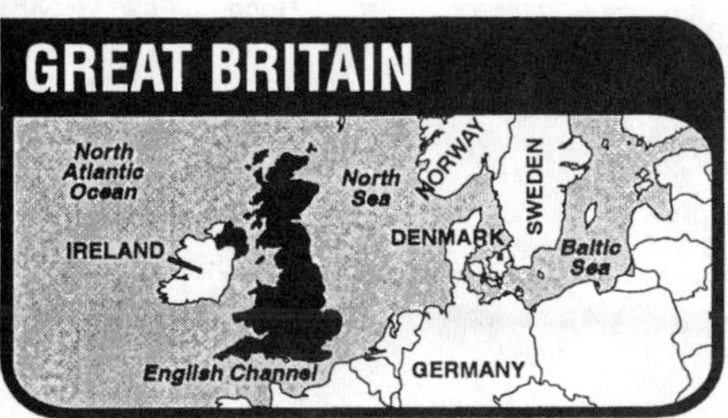

The United Kingdom of Great Britain and Northern Ireland, (including England, Scotland, Wales and Norhtern Ireland) is located off the northwest coast of the European continent, has an area of 94,227 sq. mi. (244,046 sq. km.), and a population of 59.45 million. Capital: London.

The economy is d on industrial activity, trading and financial services. Machinery, motor vehicles, chemicals and textile yarns and fabrics are exported.

After the departure of the Romans, who brought Britain into an active relationship with Europe, Britain fell prey to invaders from Scandinavia and the Low Countries who drove the original Britons into Scotland and Wales, and established a profusion of kingdoms that finally united in the 11th century under the Danish King Canute. Norman rule, following the conquest of 1066, stimulated the development of those institutions which have since distinguished British life. Henry VIII (1509-47) turned Britain from continental adventuring and faced it to the sea - a decision that made Britain a world power during the reign of Elizabeth I (1558-1603). Strengthened by the Industrial Revolution and the defeat of Napoleon, 19th century Britain turned to the remote parts of the world and established a colonial empire of such extent and prosperity that the world has never seen its like. World Wars I and II sealed the fate of the Empire and relegated Britain to a lesser role in world affairs by draining her resources and inaugurating a worldwide movement toward national self-determination in her former colonies.

By the mid-20th century, most of the former British Empire had gained independence and had evolved into the Commonwealth of Nations. This association of equal and and autonomous states, set out to agree views and special relationships with one another (appointing High Commissioners rather than Ambassadors) for mutual benefit, trade interests, etc. The Commonwealth is presently (1999) composed of 54 member nations, including the United Kingdom. All recognize the monarch as Head of the Commonwealth; 16 continue to recognize Queen Elizabeth II as Head of State. In addition to the United Kingdom, they are: Antigua & Barbuda, Australia, The Bahamas, Barbados Belize, Canada, Grenada, Paupa New Guinea, St. Christopher & Nevis, St. Lucia, St. Vincent & the Grenadines, Solomon Islands.

RULERS:

William III, 1694-1702
Anne, 1702-1714
George I, 1714-1727
George II, 1727-1760
George III, 1760-1820
George IV, 1820-1830
William IV, 1830-1837
Victoria, 1837-1901
Edward VII, 1901-1910
George V, 1910-1936
Edward VIII, 1936
George VI, 1936-1952
Elizabeth II, 1952

MONETARY SYSTEM:

1 Shilling = 12 Pence
1 Pound = 20 Shillings to 1971
1 Guinea = 21 Shillings
1 Pound = 100 (New) Pence, 1971-

BRANCH OFFICES:

Branch office notes were introduced beginning w/Henry Hase in 1826.

Birmingham (1826-1939)
Gloucester (1826-1849)
Manchester (1826-1939)
Bristol (1827-1939)
Leeds (1827-1939)
Newcastle (1828-1939)
Exeter (1827-1834)
Liverpool (1827-1939)
Swansea (1826-1859)

Note: Branch office notes are worth from twice as much or more compared with the more common "London" issues. Additional branch offices of this series includes Hull (1829-1939)Plymouth (1834-1939) Norwich (1829-1852)Portsmouth (1834-1914).

KINGDOM

BANK OF ENGLAND

Founded in 1694, the Bank of England is the greatest banking institution formed. Although torn by crisis in its infancy, today it enjoys the public's confidence in the expression *As safe as the Bank of England.*

The earliest recorded notes were all handwritten promissory notes and certificates of deposit of 1694. The first partially printed notes were introduced ca. 1696 with handwritten amounts. By 1745 all notes were printed with partial denominations of round figures in denominations of 20 Pounds through 1000 Pounds, allowing handwritten denominations of shillings to be added on.

In 1759 the word *POUNDS* was also printed on the notes.

From 1752 the Chief Cashier's handwritten name as payee is usually found and from 1782 it was used exclusively. From 1798 until 1855 it was actually printed on the notes. In 1855 notes were produced made simply payable to *bearer.* Notes were issued in denominations of 1 Pound through 1000 Pounds.

For specialized listings of Bank of England notes refer to *English Paper Money*, by Vincent Duggleby; published by Pam West, www.west-banknotes.co.uk.

1694-95 ISSUE

#25-29 handwritten, sign. of Thomas Speed.

		Good	Fine	XF
25	**5 Pounds** 1695-99. Black. a. 1695-97. W/o wmk. in paper.	—	—	—
	b. 1697-99. W/wmk. in paper. Rare.	—	—	—
26	**10 Pounds** 1694-99. Black. Rare.	—	—	—
27	**20 Pounds** 1694-99. Black. Rare.	—	—	—
28	**50 Pounds** 1694-99. Black. Rare.	—	—	—
29	**100 Pounds** 1694-99. Black. Rare.	—	—	—

1699 ISSUE

#35-39 medallion of Britannia w/spear and olive branch. Handwritten denominations. Sign. of Thomas Madocks.

		Good	Fine	XF
35	**5 Pounds** 1699-1707. Black. Rare.	—	—	—
36	**10 Pounds** 1699-1707. Black. Rare.	—	—	—
37	**20 Pounds** 1699-1707. Black. Rare.	—	—	—
38	**50 Pounds** 1699-1707. Black. Rare.	—	—	—
39	**100 Pounds** 1699-1707. Black. Rare.	—	—	—

1707 ISSUE

#40-44 medallion of Britannia within foliate border. Sign. of Thomas Madocks.

		Good	Fine	XF
40	**5 Pounds** 1707-25. Black. Rare.	—	—	—
41	**10 Pounds** 1707-25. Black. Rare.	—	—	—
42	**20 Pounds** 1707-25. Black. Rare.	—	—	—
43	**50 Pounds** 1707-25. Black. Rare.	—	—	—
44	**100 Pounds** 1707-25. Black. Rare.	—	—	—

1725 ISSUE

		Good	Fine	XF
50	**20 Pounds** 1725-39. Black. Rare.	—	—	—
51	**30 Pounds** 1725-39. Black. Rare.	—	—	—
52	**40 Pounds** 1725-39. Black. Rare.	—	—	—
53	**50 Pounds** 1725-39. Black. Rare.	—	—	—
54	**60 Pounds** 1725-39. Black. Rare.	—	—	—
55	**70 Pounds** 1725-39. Black. Rare.	—	—	—
56	**80 Pounds** 1725-39. Black. Rare.	—	—	—
57	**90 Pounds** 1725-39. Black. Rare.	—	—	—
58	**100 Pounds** 1725-39. Black. Rare.	—	—	—
59	**200 Pounds** 1725-39. Black. Rare.	—	—	—
60	**300 Pounds** 1725-39. Black. Rare.	—	—	—
61	**400 Pounds** 1725-39. Black. Rare.	—	—	—
62	**500 Pounds** 1725-39. Black. Rare.	—	—	—
63	**1000 Pounds** 1725-39. Black. Rare.	—	—	—

1739 ISSUE

#66-78 sign. of James Collier and Daniel Race.

		Good	Fine	XF
65	**20 Pounds** 1739-51. Black. Rare.	—	—	—
66	**30 Pounds** 1739-51. Black. Rare.	—	—	—
67	**40 Pounds** 1739-51. Black. Rare.	—	—	—
68	**50 Pounds** 1739-51. Black. Rare.	—	—	—
69	**60 Pounds** 1739-51. Black. Rare.	—	—	—
70	**70 Pounds** 1739-51. Black. Rare.	—	—	—
71	**80 Pounds** 1739-51. Black. Rare.	—	—	—
72	**90 Pounds** 1739-51. Black. Rare.	—	—	—
73	**100 Pounds** 1739-51. Black. Rare.	—	—	—
74	**200 Pounds** 1739-51. Black. Rare.	—	—	—
75	**300 Pounds** 1739-51. Black. Rare.	—	—	—
76	**400 Pounds** 1739-51. Black. Rare.	—	—	—
77	**500 Pounds** 1739-51. Black. Rare.	—	—	—

No.	Denomination	Good	Fine	XF
78	**1000 Pounds** 1739-51. Black. Rare.	—	—	—

1751; 1759 ISSUE

#80-95 sign. of Daniel Race and Elias Simes.

No.	Denomination	Good	Fine	XF
80	**10 Pounds** 1759. Black. Rare.	—	—	—
81	**15 Pounds** 1759. Black. Rare.	—	—	—
82	**20 Pounds** 1751-59. Black. Rare.	—	—	—
83	**30 Pounds** 1751-59. Black. Rare.	—	—	—
84	**40 Pounds** 1751-59. Black. Rare.	—	—	—
85	**50 Pounds** 1751-59. Black. Rare.	—	—	—
86	**60 Pounds** 1751-59. Black. Rare.	—	—	—
87	**70 Pounds** 1751-59. Black. Rare.	—	—	—
88	**80 Pounds** 1751-59. Black. Rare.	—	—	—
89	**90 Pounds** 1751-59. Black. Rare.	—	—	—
90	**100 Pounds** 1751-59. Black. Rare.	—	—	—
91	**200 Pounds** 1751-59. Black. Rare.	—	—	—
92	**300 Pounds** 1751-59. Black. Rare.	—	—	—
93	**400 Pounds** 1751-59. Black. Rare.	—	—	—
94	**500 Pounds** 1751-59. Black. Rare.	—	—	—
95	**1000 Pounds** 1751-59. Black. Rare.	—	—	—

1759; 1765 ISSUE

#100-116 sign. of Daniel Race.

No.	Denomination	Good	Fine	XF
100	**10 Pounds** 1759-75. Black. Rare.	—	—	—
101	**15 Pounds** 1759-75. Black. Rare.	—	—	—
102	**20 Pounds** 1759-75. Black. Rare.	—	—	—
103	**25 Pounds** 1765-75. Black. Rare.	—	—	—
104	**30 Pounds** 1759-75. Black. Rare.	—	—	—
105	**40 Pounds** 1759-75. Black. Rare.	—	—	—
106	**50 Pounds** 1759-75. Black. Rare.	—	—	—
107	**60 Pounds** 1759-75. Black. Rare.	—	—	—
108	**70 Pounds** 1759-75. Black. Rare.	—	—	—
109	**80 Pounds** 1759-75. Black. Rare.	—	—	—
110	**90 Pounds** 1759-75. Black. Rare.	—	—	—
111	**100 Pounds** 1759-75. Black. Rare.	—	—	—
112	**200 Pounds** 1759-75. Balck. Rare.	—	—	—
113	**300 Pounds** 1759-75. Black. Rare.	—	—	—
114	**400 Pounds** 1759-75. Black. Rare.	—	—	—
115	**500 Pounds** 1759-75. Black. Rare.	—	—	—
116	**100 Pounds** 1759-75. Black. Rare.	—	—	—

1775 ISSUE

#130-146 sign. of Charles Jewson.

No.	Denomination	Good	Fine	XF
130	**10 Pounds** 1775-78. Black. Rare.	—	—	—
131	**15 Pounds** 1775-78. Black. Rare.	—	—	—
132	**20 Pounds** 1775-78. Black. Rare.	—	—	—
133	**25 Pounds** 1775-78. Black. Rare.	—	—	—
134	**30 Pounds** 1775-78. Black. Rare.	—	—	—
135	**40 Pounds** 1775-78. Black. Rare.	—	—	—
136	**50 Pounds** 1775-78. Black. Rare.	—	—	—
137	**60 Pounds** 1775-78. Black. Rare.	—	—	—
138	**70 Pounds** 1775-78. Black. Rare.	—	—	—
139	**80 Pounds** 1775-78. Black. Rare.	—	—	—
140	**90 Pounds** 1775-78. Black. Rare.	—	—	—
141	**100 Pounds** 1775-78. Black. Rare.	—	—	—
142	**200 Pounds** 1775-78. Black. Rare.	—	—	—
143	**300 Pounds** 1775-78. Black. Rare.	—	—	—
144	**400 Pounds** 1775-78. Black. Rare.	—	—	—
145	**500 Pounds** 1775-78. Black. Rare.	—	—	—
146	**1000 Pounds** 1775-78. Black. Rare.	—	—	—

1778 ISSUE

#150-166 sign. of Abraham Newland.

No.	Denomination	Good	Fine	XF
150	**10 Pounds** 1778-97. Black. Rare.	—	—	—
151	**15 Pounds** 1778-1807. Black. Rare.	—	—	—
152	**20 Pounds** 1778-1807. Black. Rare.	—	—	—
153	**25 Pounds** 1778-1807. Black. Rare.	—	—	—
154	**30 Pounds** 1778-1807. Black. Rare.	—	—	—
155	**40 Pounds** 1778-1807. Black. Rare.	—	—	—
156	**50 Pounds** 1778-1807. Black. Rare.	—	—	—
157	**60 Pounds** 1778-1807. Black. Rare.	—	—	—
158	**70 Pounds** 1778-1807. Black. Rare.	—	—	—
159	**80 Pounds** 1778-1807. Black. Rare.	—	—	—
160	**90 Pounds** 1778-1807. Black. Rare.	—	—	—
161	**100 Pounds** 1778-1807. Black. Rare.	—	—	—
162	**200 Pounds** 1778-1807. Black. Rare.	—	—	—
163	**300 Pounds** 1778-1807. Black. Rare.	—	—	—
164	**400 Pounds** 1778-1807. Black. Rare.	—	—	—
165	**500 Pounds** 1778-1807. Black. Rare.	—	—	—
166	**1000 Pounds** 1778-1807. Black. Rare.	—	—	—

1793 ISSUE

No.	Denomination	Good	Fine	XF
168	**5 Pounds** 1793-1807. Black.	8000.	22,000.	—

1797 ISSUE

#170-172 handwritten date, serial # and Cashier's name.

No.	Denomination	Good	Fine	XF
170	**1 Pound** 1797. Black.	3000.	8500.	—
171	**2 Pounds** 1797. Black.	4500.	13,000.	—
172	**10 Pounds** 1797. Black. Rare.	—	—	—

1798 ISSUE

#175-177 printed Cashier's name. Smaller size.

No.	Denomination	Good	Fine	XF
175	**1 Pound** 1798-1801. Black.	2500.	6500.	—
176	**2 Pounds** 1798-1801. Black.	4000.	11,000.	—
177	**10 Pounds** 1798-1805. Black. Rare.	12,500.	37,500.	—

1801 ISSUE

#180-181 new wmk., standard size.

No.	Denomination	Good	Fine	XF
180	**1 Pound** 1801-03. Black.	1500.	4000.	—
181	**2 Pounds** 1801-03. Black.	3500.	9250.	—

1803 ISSUE

#184-185 denomination in wmk.

No.	Denomination	Good	Fine	XF
184	**1 Pound** 1803-07. Black.	1250.	3750.	—
185	**2 Pounds** 1803-05. Black.	4000.	11,000.	—

1805 ISSUE

#187-188 Bank of England head.

No.	Denomination	Good	Fine	XF
187	**2 Pounds** 1805-07. Black.	2700.	7500.	—
188	**10 Pounds** 1805-07. Black. Rare.	12,500.	37,500.	—

1807 ISSUE

#190-204 Henry Hase as Chief Cashier. Branch as London. Additional branches opened: 1826 - Gloucester, Manchester, Swansea; 1827 - Birmingham, Bristol, Exter, Leeds, Liverpool; 1828 - Newcastle.

No.	Denomination	Good	Fine	XF
190	**1 Pound** 1807-21; 1825-26. Black.			
	a. Handwritten date, w/countersignature.	2500.	6500.	—
	b. Handwritten date, w/o countersignature.	1750.	4750.	—
	c. Printed date and serial #.	800.	2500.	—
	d. As c. but dated 1821 at top and 1826 or 1826 in center (reissue).	800.	2500.	—

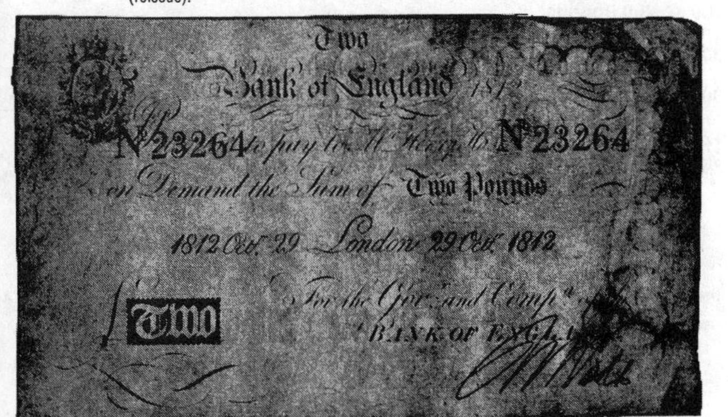

No.	Denomination	Good	Fine	XF
191	**2 Pounds** 1807-21. Black.			
	a. Handwritten date, w/countersignature.	2850.	8000.	—
	b. Handwritten date, w/o countersignature.	2650.	7500.	—
	c. Printed date and serial #.	2200.	5750.	—
192	**5 Pounds** 1807-29. Black.			
	a. Handwritten date.	4500.	13,000.	—
	b. Printed date and serial #.	4000.	11,000.	—
193	**10 Pounds** 1807-29. Black. Rare.	—	—	—
194	**15 Pounds** 1807-22. Black. Rare.	—	—	—
195	**20 Pounds** 1807-29. Black. Rare.	—	—	—
196	**25 Pounds** 1807-22. Black. Rare.	—	—	—
197	**30 Pounds** 1807-29. Black. Rare.	—	—	—
198	**40 Pounds** 1807-29. Black. Rare.	—	—	—
199	**50 Pounds** 1807-29. Black. Rare.	—	—	—
200	**100 Pounds** 1807-29. Black. Rare.	—	—	—
201	**200 Pounds** 1807-29. Black. Rare.	—	—	—
202	**300 Pounds** 1807-29. Black. Rare.	—	—	—
203	**500 Pounds** 1807-29. Black. Rare.	—	—	—
204	**1000 Pounds** 1807-29. Black. Rare.	—	—	—

1829 ISSUE

#210-220 Thomas Rippon as Chief Cashier. Branch as London. Additional Branches were opened at Hull and Norwich (1829); Portsmouth (1834). Exeter closed in 1834.

No.	Denomination	Good	Fine	XF
210	**5 Pounds** 1829-35. Black.	3750.	10,000.	—
211	**10 Pounds** 1829-35. Black.	6500.	18,000.	—
212	**20 Pounds** 1829-35. Black. Rare.	—	—	—
213	**30 Pounds** 1829-35. Black. Rare.	—	—	—
214	**40 Pounds** 1829-35. Black. Rare.	—	—	—
215	**50 Pounds** 1829-35. Black. Rare.	—	—	—
216	**100 Pounds** 1829-35. Black. Rare.	—	—	—
217	**200 Pounds** 1829-35. Black. Rare.	—	—	—
218	**300 Pounds** 1829-35. Black. Rare.	—	—	—
219	**500 Pounds** 1829-35. Black. Rare.	—	—	—
220	**1000 Pounds** 1829-35. Black. Rare.	—	—	—

1835 ISSUE

#221-231 payable to Matthew Marshall as Chief Cashier.

No.	Denomination	Good	Fine	XF
221	**5 Pounds** 1835-53. Black.	2750.	8000.	—

Note: An example of #221 dated 26.10.1849, Portsmouth Branch in VF was auctioned for $32,580 in 2003.

No.	Denomination	Good	Fine	XF
222	**10 Pounds** 1835-53. Black.	4250.	12,000.	—
223	**20 Pounds** 1835-53. Black. Rare.	—	—	—
224	**30 Pounds** 1835-52. Black. Rare.	—	—	—
225	**40 Pounds** 1835-51. Black. Rare.	—	—	—
226	**50 Pounds** 1835-53. Black. Rare.	—	—	—
227	**100 Pounds** 1835-53. Black. Rare.	—	—	—
228	**200 Pounds** 1835-53. Black. Rare.	—	—	—
229	**300 Pounds** 1835-53. Black. Rare.	—	—	—
230	**500 Pounds** 1835-53. Black. Rare.	—	—	—
231	**1000 Pounds** 1835-53. Black. Rare.	—	—	—

1853 ISSUE

#232-240 payable to Matthew Marshall as Chief Cashier. Printed sign. of Bank officials: J. Vautin, H. Bock, J. Ferraby, J. Williams and J. Luson.

No.	Denomination	Good	Fine	XF
232	**5 Pounds** 1853-55. Black.	2750.	8000.	—
233	**10 Pounds** 1853-55. Black.	4250.	12,000.	—
234	**20 Pounds** 1853-55. Black. Rare.	—	—	—
235	**50 Pounds** 1853-55. Black. Rare.	—	—	—
236	**100 Pounds** 1853-55. Black. Rare.	—	—	—
237	**200 Pounds** 1853-55. Black. Rare.	—	—	—

No.	Denomination	Good	Fine	XF
238	**300 Pounds** 1853-55. Black. Rare.	—	—	—
239	**500 Pounds** 1853-55. Black. Rare.	—	—	—
240	**1000 Pounds** 1853-55. Black. Rare.	—	—	—

1855 Issue

#241-249 "Pay to the bearer" notes, London. Modified Britannia vignette. The wmk. of Matthew Marshall's sign. was added to that of the value and bank name.

No.	Denomination	Good	Fine	XF
241	**5 Pounds** 1855.			
	a. Sign. J. Vautin.	2750.	8000.	—
	b. Sign. H. Bock.	2750.	8000.	—
	c. Sign. J. Ferraby.	2750.	8000.	—
242	**10 Pounds** 1855.			
	a. Sign. J. Vautin.	4250.	12,000.	—
	b. Sign. H. Bock.	4250.	12,000.	—
	c. Sign. J. Ferraby.	4250.	12,000.	—
243	**20 Pounds** 1855. Sign. J. Williams. Rare.	—	—	—
244	**50 Pounds** 1855. Sign. J. Williams. Rare.	—	—	—
245	**100 Pounds** 1855. Sign. J. Williams. Rare.	—	—	—
246	**200 Pounds** 1855. Sign. J. Luson. Rare.	—	—	—
247	**300 Pounds** 1855. Sign. J. Luson. Rare.	—	—	—
248	**500 Pounds** 1855. Sign. J. Luson. Rare.	—	—	—
249	**1000 Pounds** 1855. Sign. J. Luson. Rare.	—	—	—

1860 Issue

#250-258 additional branch office of this series is: Leicester (1843-1872).

No.	Denomination	Good	Fine	XF
250	**5 Pounds** 1860. Sign. W. P. Gattie. London.	2750.	8000.	—
251	**10 Pounds** 1860. Sign. W. P. Gattie. London.	4250.	12,000.	—
252	**20 Pounds** 1860. Sign. T. Kent. London. Rare.	—	—	—
253	**50 Pounds** 1860. Sign. T. Kent. London. Rare.	—	—	—
254	**100 Pounds** 1860. Sign. T. Kent. London. Rare.	—	—	—
255	**200 Pounds** 1860. Sign. C. T. Whitmell. London. Rare.	—	—	—
256	**300 Pounds** 1860. Sign. C. T. Whitmell. London. Rare.	—	—	—
257	**500 Pounds** 1860. Sign. C. T. Whitmell. London. Rare.	—	—	—
258	**1000 Pounds** 1860. Sign. C. T. Whitmell. London. Rare.	—	—	—

1864 Issue

#259-267 William Miller as Chief Cashier.

No.	Denomination	Good	Fine	XF
259	**5 Pounds** 1864-66. Sign. W. P. Gattie. London.	6000.	15,000.	—
260	**10 Pounds** 1864-66. Sign. W. P. Gattie. London. Rare.	10,000.	26,000.	—
261	**20 Pounds** 1864-66. Sign. T. Kent. London. Rare.	—	—	—
262	**50 Pounds** 1864-66. Sign. T. Kent. London. Rare.	—	—	—
263	**100 Pounds** 1864-66. Sign. T. Kent. London. Rare.	—	—	—
264	**200 Pounds** 1864-66. Sign. C. T. Whitmell. London. Rare.	—	—	—
265	**300 Pounds** 1864-66. Sign. C. T. Whitmell. London. Rare.	—	—	—
266	**500 Pounds** 1864-66. Sign. C. T. Whitmell. London. Rare.	—	—	—
267	**1000 Pounds** 1864-66. Sign. C. T. Whitmell. London. Rare.	—	—	—

1866 Issue

#268-276 sign. of George Forbes in wmk.

No.	Denomination	Good	Fine	XF
268	**5 Pounds** 1866-70. Sign. Hy Dixon. London.	3250.	9500.	—
269	**10 Pounds** 1866-70. Sign. Hy Dixon. London. Rare.	7500.	20,000.	—
270	**20 Pounds** 1866-70. Sign. T. Puzey. London. Rare.	—	—	—
271	**50 Pounds** 1866-70. Sign. T. Puzey. London. Rare.	—	—	—
272	**100 Pounds** 1866-70. Sign. T. Puzey. London. Rare.	—	—	—
273	**200 Pounds** 1866-70. Sign. W. O. Wheeler. London. Rare.	—	—	—
274	**300 Pounds** 1866-70. Sign. W. O. Wheeler. London. Rare.	—	—	—
275	**500 Pounds** 1866-70. Sign. W. O. Wheeler. London. Rare.	—	—	—
276	**1000 Pounds** 1866-70. Sign. W. O. Wheeler. London. Rare.	—	—	—

1870 Issue

#277-285 the printed sign. of the Chief Cashier appears on all the notes from 1870 onward w/title: *Chief Cashier* printed under his name.

No.	Denomination	Good	Fine	XF
277	**5 Pounds** 1870-73. London.	6250.	16,000.	—
278	**10 Pounds** 1870-73. London. Rare.	—	—	—
279	**20 Pounds** 1870-73. London. Rare.	—	—	—
280	**50 Pounds** 1870-73. London. Rare.	—	—	—
281	**100 Pounds** 1870-73. London. Rare.	—	—	—
282	**200 Pounds** 1870-73. London. Rare.	—	—	—
283	**300 Pounds** 1870-73. London. Rare.	—	—	—
284	**500 Pounds** 1870-73. London. Rare.	—	—	—
285	**1000 Pounds** 1870-73. London. Rare.	—	—	—

1873 Issue

#286-294 Frank May as Chief Cashier.

No.	Denomination	Good	Fine	XF
286	**5 Pounds** 1873-93. London.	2250.	5500.	—
287	**10 Pounds** 1873-93. London.	5250.	14,000.	—
288	**20 Pounds** 1873-93. London. Rare.	—	—	—
289	**50 Pounds** 1873-93. London. Rare.	—	—	—
290	**100 Pounds** 1873-93. London. Rare.	—	—	—
291	**200 Pounds** 1873-93. London. Rare.	—	—	—
292	**300 Pounds** 1873-93. London. Rare.	—	—	—
293	**500 Pounds** 1873-93. London. Rare.	—	—	—
294	**1000 Pounds** 1873-93. London. Rare.	—	—	—

1893 Issue

#295-302 sign. of Horace G. Bowen as Chief Cashier.

No.	Denomination	Good	Fine	XF
295	**5 Pounds** 1893-1902. London.	2250.	5500.	12,500
296	**10 Pounds** 1893-1902. London.	5000.	13,500.	—
297	**20 Pounds** 1893-1902. London. Rare.	—	—	—
298	**50 Pounds** 1893-1902. London. Rare.	—	—	—
299	**100 Pounds** 1893-1902. London. Rare.	—	—	—
300	**200 Pounds** 1893-1902. London. Rare.	—	—	—
301	**500 Pounds** 1893-1902. London. Rare.	—	—	—
302	**1000 Pounds** 1893-1902. London. Rare.	—	—	—

1902 Issue

#303-311 sign. of John G. Nairne as Chief Cashier.

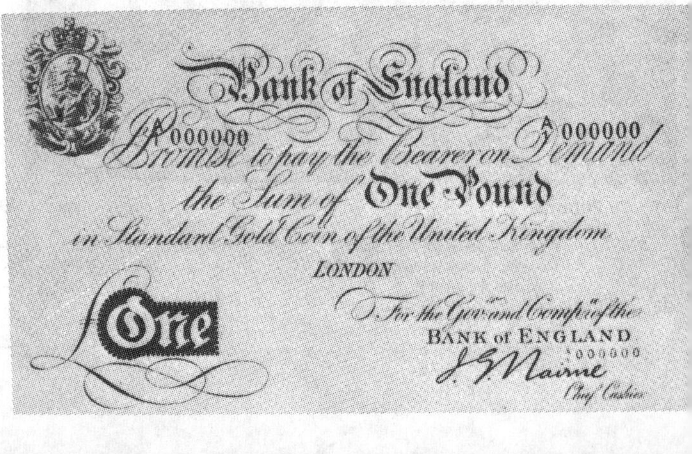

		Good	Fine	XF
303	**1 Pound**			
	ND. London. Specimen.	—	Unc	17,500.
304	**5 Pounds**			
	1902-18. London.	200.	475.	1100.
305	**10 Pounds**			
	1902-18. London.	300.	775.	1850.
306	**20 Pounds**			
	1902-18.			
	a. London.	1000.	2500.	6500.
	b. Manchester.	1250.	3000.	7750.

		Good	Fine	XF
307	**50 Pounds**			
	1902-18. London.			
	a. London. Rare..	1000.	2500.	6500.
	b. Manchester.	8500.	2150.	5500.
308	**100 Pounds**			
	1902-18.			
	a. London. Rare..	1100.	2750.	7000.
	b. Manchester.	850.	2100.	5000.
309	**200 Pounds**			
	1902-18. London. Rare.	—	—	—
310	**500 Pounds**			
	1902-18. London. Rare.	—	—	—
311	**1000 Pounds**	Good	Fine	XF
	1902-18. London. Rare.	—	—	—

1918 ISSUE

#312-319 sign. of Ernest M. Harvey as Chief Cashier.

		Good	Fine	XF
12	**5 Pounds**			
	1918-25.			
	a. London.	85.00	200.	450.
	b. Leeds.	200.	500.	1200.
	c. Liverpool.	210.	525.	1300.
	d. Manchester.	220.	535.	1350.
	e. Hull.	350.	850.	2150.

te: Branches of Birmingham, Bristol, Newcastle and Plymouth are known, but scarce.

		Good	Fine	XF
13	**10 Pounds**			
	1918-25. London.	175.	450.	1100.

		Good	Fine	XF
314	**20 Pounds**			
	1918-25. London.	550.	1400.	3700.
315	**50 Pounds**			
	1918-25. London.	575.	1450.	4000.

		Good	Fine	XF
316	**100 Pounds**			
	1918-25. London.	600.	1500.	4250.
317	**200 Pounds**			
	1918-25. London. Rare.	—	—	—
318	**500 Pounds**			
	1918-25. London. Rare.	—	—	—
319	**1000 Pounds**			
	1918-25. London. Rare.	—	—	—

1925 ISSUE

#320-327 sign of Cyril P. Mahon as Chief Cashier.

		Good	Fine	XF
320	**5 Pounds**			
	1925-29.			
	a. London.	150.	400.	950.
	b. Manchester.	235.	575.	1400.
	c. Leeds.	235.	575.	1400.
	d. Hull.	275.	750.	1750.
	e. Liverpool.	400.	1000.	2600.
	f. Birmingham.	500.	1250.	3250.
	g. Newcastle.	500.	1250.	3250.
	h. Plymouth. Rare..	1250.	3250.	8500.
	i. Bristol. Rare..	2000.	5000.	13,000.
321	**10 Pounds**			
	1925-29.			
	a. London.	235.	575.	1400.
	b. Manchester.	475.	1200.	3000.
	c. Liverpool.	475.	1200.	3000.
322	**20 Pounds**			
	1925-29. London.	575.	1450.	4000.
323	**50 Pounds**			
	1925-29. London.	550.	1400.	3750.
324	**100 Pounds**			
	1925-29. London.	800.	2000.	5000.
325	**200 Pounds**			
	1925-29. London. Rare.	—	—	—
326	**500 Pounds**			
	1925-29. London. Rare.	—	—	—

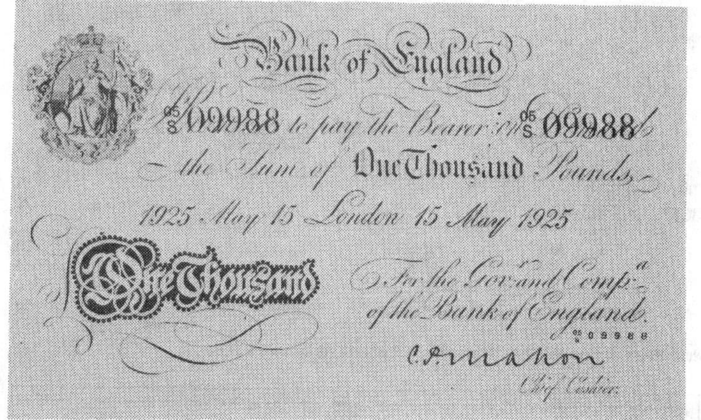

		Good	Fine	XF
327	**1000 Pounds**			
	1925-29. London. Rare.	—	—	—

1929 ISSUE

#328-334 sign. of Basil G. Catterns as Chief Cashier.

		Good	Fine	XF
328	**5 Pounds**			
	1929-34.			
	a. London.	120.	320.	785.
	b. Leeds.	165.	450.	1100.
	c. Manchester.	200.	525.	1300.

		Good	Fine	XF
328	d. Hull.	235.	575.	1400.
	e. Liverpool.	325.	800.	2000.

Note: Notes from Birmingham, Bristol, Newcastle and Plymouth are scarce.

		Good	Fine	XF
329	**10 Pounds** 1929-34.			
	a. London.	200.	500.	1200.
	b. Liverpool.	250.	650.	1650.
330	**20 Pounds** 1929-34. London.	550.	1400.	3500.

		Good	Fine	XF
331	**50 Pounds** 1929-34. London.	450.	1100.	2750.
332	**100 Pounds** 1929-34. London.	700.	1725.	4200.
333	**500 Pounds** 1929-34. London. Rare.	—	Rare	—
334	**1000 Pounds** 1929-34. London. Rare.	—	—	45,000.

1934 Issue

#335-341 Kenneth O. Peppiatt as Chief Cashier.

OPERATION BERNHARD FORGERIES

During World War II *almost perfect* forgeries of Bank of England Pound notes were produced by prisoners in a German concentration camp. The enterprise was code named "Operation Bernhard". The following occur: 5, 10, 20 and 50 Pound notes with different dates, also including branch office issues such as Leeds and Bristol. There are a number of very small but discernible differences between the Operation Bernhard counterfeits and genuine notes. For example, most counterfeits have a dull look in Britannia's eyes and less clarity on the cross at top of her crown. Average market value in XF condition $45.00-90.00.

		Good	Fine	XF
335	**5 Pounds** 1934-44.			
	a. London.	85.00	175.	425.
	b. Liverpool.	130.	350.	850.
	c. Manchester.	130.	350.	850.
	d. Leeds.	130.	350.	850.
	e. Birmingham.	250.	675.	1650.

Note: Notes from Bristol, Hull, Newcastle and Plymouth are known but scarce.

		Good	Fine	XF
336	**10 Pounds** Aug. 1934-Aug. 1943. London.	120.	275.	700.
337	**20 Pounds** Aug. 1934-Aug. 1943.			
	a. London.	400.	1000.	2400.
	b. Liverpool.	725.	1800.	4500.
338	**50 Pounds** 1934-38.			
	a. London.	300.	750.	1850.
	b. Liverpool.	500.	1300.	3150.
	c. Manchester.	585.	1500.	3600.
339	**100 Pounds** 1934-43.			
	a. 1934-43. London.	450.	1150.	2800.
	b. 1934-38. Liverpool.	425.	1100.	2300.
340	**500 Pounds** Aug. 1934-Aug. 1943. London.	2000.	5500.	13,000.

		Good	Fine	XF
341	**1000 Pounds** April 1934-Aug. 1943. London.	—	—	42,500.

1944-47 Issue

		Good	Fine	XF
342	**5 Pounds** 1944-47. Thick paper. London.	45.00	110.	275
343	**5 Pounds** 1947. Thin paper. London.	40.00	90.00	225

1949 ISSUE

		Good	Fine	XF
344	**5 Pounds** 1949-55. London.	40.00	90.00	225.

1955 ISSUE

		Good	Fine	XF
345	**5 Pounds** 1955-56. London.	40.00	90.00	225.

TREASURY NOTES

1914 ND ISSUE

#346-347 Portr. Kg. George V at l. Sign. John Bradbury. Uniface.

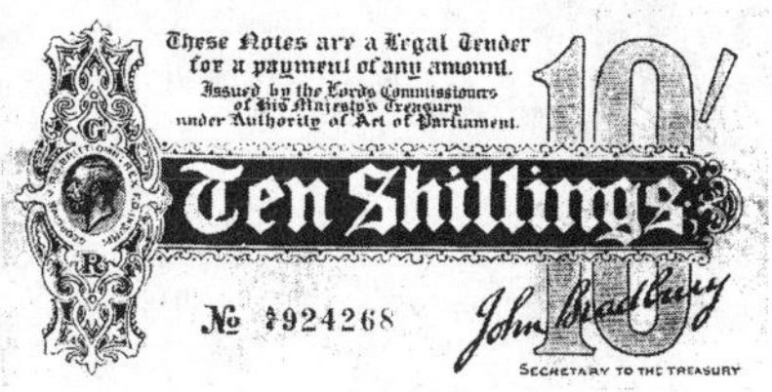

		Good	Fine	XF
346	**10 Shillings** ND (Aug. 1914). Red. 3 serial # varieties.	165.	450.	1100.
347	**1 Pound** ND (Aug. 1914). Black. 13 serial # varieties.	200.	550.	1550.

1914-15 ISSUE

#348-349 portr. Kg. George V at upper l., St. George at at upper r. Uniface. Sign. John Bradbury.

#348-359 w/title: *UNITED KINGDOM OF GREAT BRITAIN AND IRELAND*.

		Good	Fine	XF
348	**10 Shillings** ND (Jan. 1915). Red. 5 serial # varieties.			
	a. Issued note.	120.	260.	800.
	b. W/black ovpt. in Arabic: *Piastres silver 60.*	275.	700.	2750.

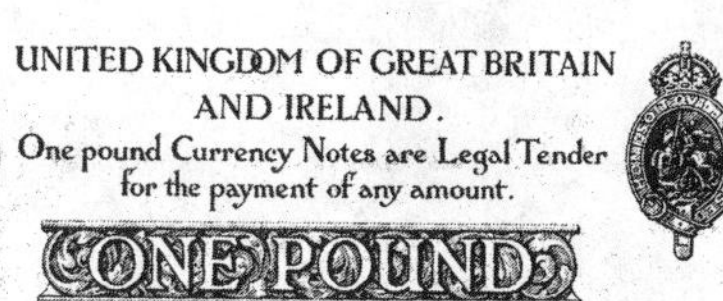

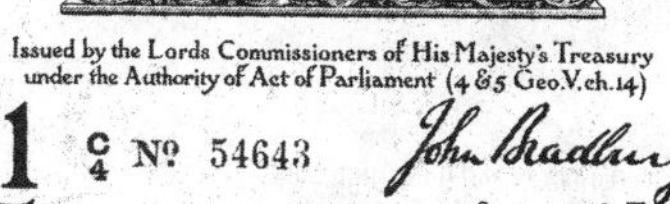

		Good	Fine	XF
49	**1 Pound** ND (23.10.1914). Black. 2 serial # varieties.			
	a. Issued note.	130.	285.	875.
	b. W/red ovpt. in Arabic: *Piastres silver 120.*	2000.	5500.	18,000.

te: #348b and 349b w/Turkish ovpt. were formerly listed as Turkey #M1 and M2. Counterfeits exist.

917-18 ND ISSUE

50-351 portr. Kg. George V at r. Sign. John Bradbury.

		Good	Fine	XF
50	**10 Shillings** ND (1918). Green. Britannia at l.			
	a. Black serial #. (Nov.)	160.	400.	1100.
	b. Red serial #. (Dec.)	125.	275.	825.

		Good	Fine	XF
351	**1 Pound** ND (Feb. 1917). Brown and green. St. George slaying dragon at l.	50.00	110.	325.

1919 ND FIRST ISSUE

		Good	Fine	XF
352	**5 Shillings** ND (1919). Red-violet and green. Portr. Kg. George V at ctr. Back gray. Sign. John Bradbury. Rare.	—	Rare	—

1919 ND SECOND ISSUE

#353-361 sign. N. K. Warren Fisher.

#353-359 w/*GREAT BRITAIN AND IRELAND* text in heading.

		Good	Fine	XF
353	**1 Shilling** ND (1919). Green and brown. Portr. Kg. George V at ctr. Coin on back. Not issued.	2500.	6000.	—

		Good	Fine	XF
354	**2 Shillings - 6 Pence** ND (1919). Olive-green and deep brown. Similar to #353.	2500.	6000.	—
355	**5 Shillings** ND (1919). Deep violet and green. Like #352.	2250.	5000.	—

Note: #353-355 were never officially released, but a few apparently found their way into circulation.

1919 ND THIRD ISSUE

		Good	Fine	XF
356	**10 Shillings** ND (Oct. 1919). Green. Like #350. 2 serial # varieties.	55.00	165.	575.
357	**1 Pound** ND (Oct. 1919). Brown and green. Like #351. Wmk: *ONE POUND* at ctr. in 1 line.	20.00	65.00	225.

1922 ND ISSUE

		Good	Fine	XF
358	**10 Shillings** ND (1922-23). Green. Like #356 but serial # w/o *No.*	45.00	140.	425.
359	**1 Pound** ND (1922-23). Brown. Like #357 but wmk: *ONE POUND* in two lines at ctr.			
	a. Letter and figure *1* over number (dot).	20.00	70.00	240.
	b. Letter and figure *1* over number (square dot).	65.00	220.	600.

1928 ND ISSUE

#360 and 361 w/title: *UNITED KINGDOM OF GREAT BRITAIN AND NORTHERN IRELAND.*

		Good	Fine	XF
360	**10 Shillings** ND (1928). Green. Britannia at l., portr. Kg. George V at r.	45.00	140.	475.
361	**1 Pound** ND (1928). Brown. St. George slaying dragon at l., portr. Kg. George V at r.			
	a. Letter and figure *1* over number (dot).	25.00	75.00	300.
	b. Letter and figure *1* over number (square dot).	65.00	220.	600.

BANK OF ENGLAND (CONTINUED)

1928-48 ND ISSUE

		VG	VF	UNC
362	**10 Shillings** ND (1928-48). Brown. Seated Britannia at l. Paper w/o security thread.			
	a. Sign. C. P. Mahon (1928-29).	40.00	130.	500.
	b. Sign. B. G. Catterns (1929-34).	25.00	75.00	200.
	c. Sign. K. O. Peppiatt (1934-39).	17.50	50.00	200.
	d. Sign. like c. Series w/L (1948).	27.50	85.00	335.

		VG	VF	UNC
363	**1 Pound** ND (1928-48). Green. Seated Britannia at upper l. Paper w/o security thread.			
	a. Sign. C. P. Mahon (1928-29).	30.00	90.00	300.
	b. Sign. B. G. Catterns (1929-34).	16.00	47.50	150.
	c. Sign. K. O. Peppiatt (1934-39).	9.00	27.50	100.
	d. Sign. like c. Series letters R-A; S-A (1948).	10.00	35.00	110.
	e. Ovpt: *Withdrawn from circulation September 18th, 1941.* on a.	275.	825.	
	f. Ovpt. as e on b.	250.	750.	—
	g. Ovpt. as e on c, w/serial prefix letters: B; C; D; E; H; J; K; L; M; N; O; R; S; T; U; W; X; Y; Z.	215.	650.	—
	h. Ovpt. as e on c, w/serial # prefix A-A; B-A; C-A; D-A; E-A; H-A; J-A; K-A.	120.	300.	925.
	i. Ovpt: *Withdrawn from circulation November 10th 1941* on c. Period on face and back. Serial E03A only.	225.	675.	1800.
	j. Ovpt. as i on c. No period on face but period on back. Serial E15A only.	140.	425.	1250.

Note: During the WW II German occupation of Guernsey, 5000 pieces of #363 were withdrawn and replaced with new small change notes. Before the notes were turned over to the occupation forces, local officials had them overprinted on face and back, quickly ending any further redeemability.

1940-41 ND EMERGENCY ISSUE

		VG	VF	UNC
364	**2 Shillings - 6 Pence** ND (1941). Black on lt. blue unpt. Sign. K. O. Peppiatt. (Not issued).	2500.	6500.	—

		VG	VF	UNC
365	**5 Shillings** ND (1941). Olive on pink unpt. Sign. K. O. Peppiatt. (Not issued).	2500.	6500.	—

		VG	VF	UNC
366	**10 Shillings** ND (1940-48). Mauve. Seated Britannia at l. Paper w/security thread. Sign. K. O. Peppiatt.	14.00	40.00	150.
367	**1 Pound** ND (1940-48). Lt. or dk. blue and pink. Seated Britannia at upper l. Paper w/security thread. Sign. K. O. Peppiatt.			
	a. Issued note.	4.00	12.50	45.00
	b. Ovpt: *Withdrawn from circulation September 18th, 1941.* Serial prefix A-D.	375.	900.	2500.
	c. Ovpt: *Withdrawn from circulation September 18th 1941.* Serial prefix C-D.	275.	750.	2000.

Note: Many shade varieties exist such as pale blue and pink, blue and deep pink or deep blue and buff. The back shade varieties range from pale blue to blue-green. Note: #367b Guernsey withdrawal, for other issues see also #363e-363g.

1948 ND ISSUE

		VG	VF	UNC
368	**10 Shillings** ND (1948-60). Brown-violet and brown on gray and pink unpt. Like #362 but paper w/security thread. Wmk: Head of Minerva.			
	a. Sign. K. O. Peppiatt. (1948-49).	12.50	35.00	140.
	b. Sign. P. S. Beale. (1949-55).	7.50	20.00	90.00
	c. Sign. L. K. O'Brien. (1955-60).	7.00	18.00	75.00

369	1 Pound	VG	VF	UNC
	ND (1948-60). Green. Like #363 but paper w/security thread.			
	a. Sign. K. O. Peppiatt. (1948-49).	8.00	22.50	80.00
	b. Sign. P. S. Beale. (1949-55).	5.00	8.00	22.50
	c. Sign. L. K. O'Brien. (1955-60).	5.00	8.00	25.00
	d. As a but w/lt. blue cross at end of *Demand* on face.	12.50	30.00	65.00

Note: #369d was most likely used to track movement of notes from Jersey and England in the immediate post-WWII era (1948-49).

#370 not assigned.

1957-61 ND ISSUE

371	5 Pounds	VG	VF	UNC
	ND (1957-67). Blue and m/c. Helmeted Britannia hd. at l., St. George and dragon at lower ctr., denomination *£5* in blue print on back. Sign. L. K. O'Brien.	17.50	55.00	130.
372	5 Pounds			
	ND (1961-63). Blue and m/c. Like #371 but denomination *£5* recessed in white on back.	17.50	60.00	140.

1960-64 ND ISSUE

373-376 portr. Qn. Elizabeth II at r.

373-375 wmk: Laureate heads in continuous vertical row at l.

373	10 Shillings	VG	VF	UNC
	ND (1960-70). Brown on m/c unpt. Britannia seated w/shield in circle at ctr. r. on back.			
	a. Sign. L. K. O'Brien. (1960-61).	1.50	4.00	15.00
	b. Sign. J. Q. Hollom. (1962-66).	1.00	3.00	12.50
	c. Sign. J. S. Fforde. (1966-70).	1.00	2.50	10.00
	s. Specimen. As a; c.	—	—	—

374	1 Pound	VG	VF	UNC
	ND (1960-77). Deep green on m/c unpt. Back similar to #373.			
	a. Sign. L. K. O'Brien. (1960-61).	2.00	4.00	12.00
	b. Sign. as a. Small letter *R* (for Research) at lower l. ctr. on back. (Notes printed on reel-fed web press.) Serial # prefixes A01N; A05N; A06N.	125.	350.	1000.
	c. Sign. J. Q. Hollom. (1962-66).	FV	4.00	10.00
	d. Sign. as c. Letter *G* at lower l. ctr. on back. (Printed on experimental German Goebel Press.)	4.00	12.50	25.00
	e. Sign. J. S. Fforde. (1966-70).	FV	4.00	9.00
	f. Sign. as e. Letter *G* at lower ctr. on back.	4.00	12.50	30.00
	g. Sign. J. B. Page. (1970-77).	FV	4.00	9.00
	s. Specimen. As a-c.	—	—	—

MILITARY

BRITISH MILITARY AUTHORITY

1943 ND ISSUE

Originally issued in 1943 for use by British troops in North Africa. One Pound notes w/ovpt: *BULGARIA, FRANCE* and *GREECE* were prepared but not issued. The remaining stock was later sent to Cyprus in 1956.

#M1-M6 lion on crown device.

M1	6 Pence	VG	VF	UNC
	ND (1943). Red-brown on green and peach unpt. Back red, green, blue and purple.	6.00	20.00	70.00

M2	1 Shilling	VG	VF	UNC
	ND (1943). Black on gray and violet unpt. Back purple on brown, green and blue unpt.	3.00	12.00	35.00

M3	2 Shillings - 6 Pence	VG	VF	UNC
	ND (1943). Green on pink unpt. Back olive green and brown on lilac and olive unpt.	4.00	17.50	40.00

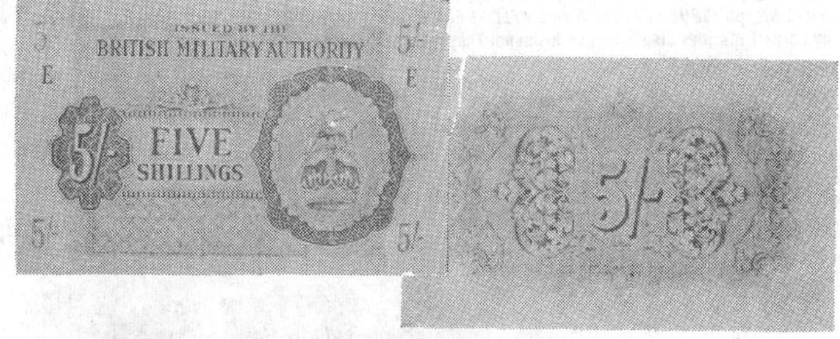

M4	5 Shillings	VG	VF	UNC
	ND (1943). Brown on blue and green unpt. Back violet on green and blue unpt.	5.00	20.00	50.00

		VG	VF	UNC
M5	**10 Shillings** ND (1943). Blue on olive and lilac unpt. Back olive brown on gray and brown unpt.	8.00	35.00	80.00

		VG	VF	UNC
M6	**1 Pound** ND (1943-45). Purple on orange and green unpt. Back orange, green and black.			
	a. Issued note w/o ovpt.	15.00	45.00	100.
	b. Ovpt: *BULGARIA*. 25 prepared.	—	—	1500.
	c. Ovpt: *FRANCE*. 50 prepared.	—	—	1000.
	d. Ovpt: *GREECE*. 25 prepared.	—	—	1500.

BRITISH ARMED FORCES

1946 ND TOKEN ISSUE

#M7-M8 text printed on paper, then laminated for issue. Printer: TDLR (w/o imprint).

		VG	VF	UNC
M7	**1/2 Penny** ND (1946). Black on dk. brown. Round printed disk of laminated paper.	4.00	10.00	25.00

		VG	VF	UNC
M8	**1 Penny** ND (1946). Black on dk. brown. Round printed disk of laminated paper.	4.00	10.00	25.00

BRITISH ARMED FORCES, SPECIAL VOUCHERS

1946 ND FIRST SERIES

Originally issued on Aug. 1, 1946 for use by British forces in occupied Germany and Austria. They were later released to British forces in occupied Japan on May 6, 1947. Some notes of the First Series are found w/ovpt: *ISSUED IN H.M. SHIPS AFLOAT FOR USE IN NAAFI CANTEENS ONLY*, which were used by Force T marines also assigned to Japan. They were part of the B.C.O.F.

#M9-M15 printer: TDLR.

		VG	VF	UNC
M9	**3 Pence** ND (1946). Lilac on orange and green unpt.			
	a. Issued note.	3.00	35.00	80.00
	b. Ovpt: ....*NAAFI CANTEENS ONLY*.	40.00	150.	300.
M10	**6 Pence** ND (1946). Brown on lilac and blue unpt.			
	a. Issued note.	3.00	20.00	60.00
	b. Ovpt:....*NAAFI CANTEENS ONLY*.	40.00	150.	300.
M11	**1 Shilling** ND (1946). Gray-blue on olive green and orange unpt.			
	a. Issued note.	6.00	35.00	90.00
	b. Ovpt:....*NAAFI CANTEENS ONLY*.	40.00	150.	300.

		VG	VF	UNC
M12	**2 Shillings - 6 Pence** ND (1946). Pale red on green and violet unpt. Back pale red and violet.			
	a. Issued note.	10.00	45.00	120.
	b. Ovpt:....*NAAFI CANTEENS ONLY*.	40.00	150.	300.
M13	**5 Shillings** ND (1946). Green on violet and orange unpt. Back green and pale red.			
	a. Issued note.	15.00	50.00	130.
	b. Ovpt:....*NAAFI CANTEENS ONLY*.	40.00	150.	300.
M14	**10 Shillings** ND (1946). Purple on orange and red-brown unpt.			
	a. Issued note.	12.00	50.00	130.
	b. Ovpt:....*NAAFI CANTEENS ONLY*.	40.00	150.	300.

		VG	VF	UNC
M15	**1 Pound** ND (1946). Blue on red and green unpt.			
	a. Issued note.	20.00	55.00	150.
	b. Ovpt:....*NAAFI CANTEENS ONLY*.	100.	250.	—

1948 ND SECOND SERIES

#M16-M23 printer: TDLR.

Note: This series was retired in 1971.

		VG	VF	UNC
M16	**3 Pence** ND (1948). Brown on lt. red and green unpt.			
	a. Paper w/metal strip. (1948).	1.00	4.00	17.50
	b. Wmk. paper. (1961).	.50	2.50	10.00

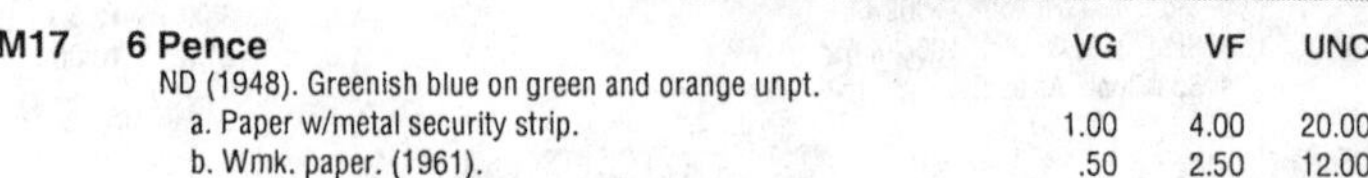

		VG	VF	UNC
M17	**6 Pence** ND (1948). Greenish blue on green and orange unpt.			
	a. Paper w/metal security strip.	1.00	4.00	20.00
	b. Wmk. paper. (1961).	.50	2.50	12.00

		VG	VF	UNC
M18	**1 Shilling** ND (1948). Red-orange on purple and green unpt.			
	a. Paper w/metal security strip. (1948).	1.00	4.50	30.00
	b. Wmk. paper. (1961).	.50	2.50	15.00
M19	**2 Shillings - 6 Pence** ND (1948). Lilac on lt. green and orange unpt.			
	a. Paper w/metal security strip.	1.25—	4.50	20.00—
	b. Wmk. paper. (1961).	1.00—	3.00	15.00—

		VG	VF	UNC
M20	**5 Shillings** ND (1948). Blue on orange and lt. red unpt.			
	a. Paper w/metal security strip. (1948).	6.00	15.00	30.00
	b. Wmk. paper, black serial #. (1961).	4.00	10.00	25.00
	c. Wmk. paper, red serial #.	4.00	10.00	25.00
	d. Cancelled remainder w/normal serial # and 2 punched holes.	—	Unc	4.00
M21	**10 Shillings** ND (1948). Green.			
	a. Paper w/metal security strip. (1948).	2.00	5.00	25.00
	b. Wmk. paper. (1961).	2.00	5.00	25.00

		VG	VF	UNC
M22	**1 Pound** ND (1948). Lilac on red and blue unpt.			
	a. Paper w/metal strip. (1948).	.50	1.50	3.00
	b. Wmk. paper.	—	—	—

		VG	VF	UNC
M23	**5 Pounds** ND (1958). Dk. blue on olive and brown unpt. Wmk. paper.	.50	1.50	4.00

1956 ND THIRD SERIES

Printed in 1948, they were not issued until 1956 for use during the Suez Canal crisis. This situation was quickly resolved, lasting only 2 months.

#M24-M29 imprint: TDLR. Printer: J. Waddington Ltd.

		VG	VF	UNC
M24	**3 Pence** ND (1956). Green, orange and pink. Back green.	60.00	150.	250.

		VG	VF	UNC
M25	**6 Pence** ND (1956). Lilac and green.	20.00	60.00	120.

		VG	VF	UNC
M26	**1 Shilling** ND (1956). Blue and pink.			
	a. W/o punch cancel holes.	10.00	35.00	100.
	b. Cancelled remainder w/2 punched holes.	—	—	4.00
	s. Specimen w/1 punched hole.	—	—	35.00

		VG	VF	UNC
M26A	**2 Shillings - 6 Pence** ND. Specimen.	—	Unc	300.
M27	**5 Shillings** ND (1956). Orange and green.	60.00	150.	250.

		VG	VF	UNC
M28	**10 Shillings** ND (1956). Red, green and orange.			
	a. W/o punch cancel holes.	4.00	20.00	80.00
	b. Cancelled remainder w/normal serial # and 2 punched holes.	—	Unc	4.00
M29	**1 Pound** ND (1956). Brown, pink and purple.	—	—	3.00

The Hellenic Republic of Greece is situated in southeastern Europe on the southern tip of the Balkan Peninsula. The republic includes many islands, the most important of which are Crete and the Ionian Islands. Greece (including islands) has an area of 50,949 sq. mi. (131,957 sq. km.) and a population of 10.6 million. Capital: Athens. Greece is still largely agricultural. Tobacco, cotton, fruit and wool are exported.

Greece, the Mother of Western civilization, attained the peak of its culture in the 5th century BC, when it contributed more to government, drama, art and architecture than any other people to this time. Greece fell under Roman domination in the 2nd and 1st centuries BC, becoming part of the Byzantine Empire until Constantinople fell to the Crusaders in 1202. With the fall of Constantinople to the Turks in 1453, Greece became part of the Ottoman Empire. Independence from Turkey was won with the revolution of 1821-27. In 1833, Greece was established as a monarchy, with sovereignty guaranteed by Britain, France and Russia. After a lengthy power struggle between the monarchist forces and democratic factions, Greece was proclaimed a republic in 1925. The monarchy was restored in 1935 and reconfirmed by a plebiscite in 1946. The Italians invaded Greece via Albania on Oct. 28, 1940 but were driven back well within the Albanian border. Germany began its invasion on April 6, 1941 and quickly overran the entire country, driving off a British Expeditionary force by the end of April. King George II and his new government went into exile. The German - Italian occupation of Greece lasted until Oct. 1944. On April 21, 1967, a military junta took control of the government and suspended the constitution. King Constantine II made an unsuccessful attempt against the junta in the fall of 1968 and consequently fled to Italy. The monarchy was formally abolished by plebiscite, Dec. 8, 1974, and Greece established as the "Hellenic Republic," the third republic in Greek history.

The island of Crete (Kreti), located 60 miles southeast of the Peloponnesus, was the center of a brilliant civilization that flourished before the advent of Greek culture. After being conquered by the Romans, Byzantines, Moslems and Venetians, Crete became part of the Turkish Empire in 1669. As a consequence of the Greek Revolution of the 1820s, it was ceded to Egypt. Egypt returned the island to the Turks in 1840, and they ceded it to Greece in 1913, after the Second Balkan War.

The Ionian Islands, situated in the Ionian Sea to the west of Greece, is the collective name for the islands of Corfu, Cephalonia, Zante, Santa Maura, Ithaca, Cthera and Paxo, with their minor dependencies. Before Britain acquired the islands, 1809-1814, they were at various times subject to the authority of Venice, France, Russia and Turkey. They remained under British control until their cession to Greece on March 29, 1864.

RULERS:

Paul I, 1947-1964
Constantine II, 1964-1973

MONETARY SYSTEM:

1 Phoenix = 100 Lepta, 1828-31
1 Drachma = 100 Lepta, 1841-2001
1 Euro = 100 Cents, 2002-

DENOMINATIONS

1 - MIA
2 - DUO
5 - PENTE
10 - DEKA
20 - EIKOSI
25 - EIKOSIPENTE
50 - PENTHKONTA
100 - EKATON
200 - DIAKOSIA
250 - DIAKOSIA PENTHKONTA
500 - PENTAKOSIAI
750 - EPTAKOSIA PENTHKONTA
1000 - CILIAI
2000 - DUO CILIADES
5000 - PENTE CILIADES
10,000 - DEKA CILIADES
20,000 - EIKOSI CILIADES
25,000 - EIKOSI PENTE CILIADES
50,000 - PENTHKONTA CILIADES
100,000 - EKATON CILIADES
500,000 - PENTAKOSIAI CILIADES
1,000,000 - EN EKATOMMURION
5,000,000 - PENTE EKATOMMURIA
10,000,000 - DEKA EKATOMMURIA
25,000,000 - EIKOSI PENTE EKATOMMURIA
50,000,000 - PENTHKONTA EKATOMMURIA
100,000,000 - EKATON EKATOMMURIA
200,000,000 - DIAKOSIA EKATOMMURIA
500,000,000 - PENTHAKONTA EKOTOMMURIA
2,000,000,000 - DUO CILIADES EKATOMMURIA
10,000,000,000 - DEKA DISEKATOMMURIA
100,000,000,000 - EKATON DISEKATOMMURIA

EKDOSIS ISSUES

Many notes can be differentiated by the designation of the Ekdosis (EK.) on the back of the notes. The issue numbers quoted here are found on the note in Greek letters in each case following " " i.e.

1	ΠΡΩΤΗ	**6**	ΕΚΤΗ	**11**	ΕΝΔΕΚΑΤΗ
2	ΔΕΥΤΕΡΑ	**7**	ΕΒΔΟΜΗ	**12**	ΔΩΔΕΚΑΤΗ
3	ΤΡΙΤΗ	**8**	ΟΓΔΟΗ	**13**	ΔΕΚΑΤΗ ΤΡΙΤΗ
4	ΤΕΤΑΡΤΗ	**9**	ΕΝΑΤΗ (ΕΝΝΑΤΗ)	**14**	ΔΕΚΑΤΗ ΤΕΤΑΡΤΗ
5	ΠΕΜΠΤΗ	**10**	ΔΕΚΑΤΗ		

GREEK ALPHABET

Α	α	Alpha	(ä)	Ι	ι	Iota	(ē)	Ρ	ρ	Rho	(r)
Β	β	Beta	(b)	Κ	κ	Kappa	(k)	Σ	σ	Sigma	(s)6
Γ	γ	Gamma	(g)	Λ	λ	Lambda	(l)	Τ	τ	Tau	(t)
Δ	δ	Delta	(d)	Μ	μ	Mu	(m)	Υ	υ	Upsilon	(o̅o̅)
Ε	ε	Epsilon	(e)	Ν	ν	Nu	(n)	Φ	φ	Phi	(f)
Ζ	ζ	Zeta	(z)	Ξ	ξ	Xi	(ks)	Χ	χ	Chi	(H)
Η	η	Eta	(ā)	Ο	ο	Omicron	(o)	Ψ	ψ	Psi	(ps)
Θ	θ	Theta	(th)	Π	π	Pi	(p)	Ω	ω	Omega	(ō)

Note: Certain listings encompassing issues circulated by various bank and regional authorities are contained in Volume 1.

INDEPENDENT GREECE

ΠΡΟΣΩΡΙΝΗ ΔΙΟΙΚΗΣΙΣ ΤΗΣ ΕΛΛΑΔΟΣ

PROVISIONAL ADMINISTRATION OF GREECE

1822 ISSUE

#1-5 bonds that circulated as currency. Issued in Corinth and Nauplion. Denominations in Gr. (Grossi = Piastres).

		Good	Fine	XF
1	**100 Grossi** 1822.	100.	500.	900.
2	**250 Grossi** 1822.	100.	500.	900.
3	**500 Grossi** 1822.	100.	500.	900.
4	**750 Grossi** 1822.	200.	800.	1500.

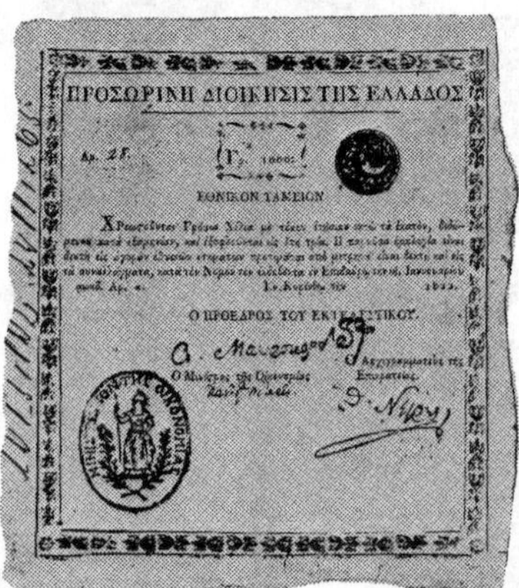

		Good	Fine	XF
5	**1000 Grossi** 1822.	300.	1000.	2000.

NOTICE

Readers with unlisted dates, signature varieties, etc. are invited to submit photocopies or, high resolution (300 dpi, 100% size) scans of their notes to: Standard Catalog of World Paper Money, 700 East State St. Iola, WI 54990-0001, or E-Mail: george.cuhaj@fwpubs.com.

NATIONAL FINANCE BANK

1831 ISSUE

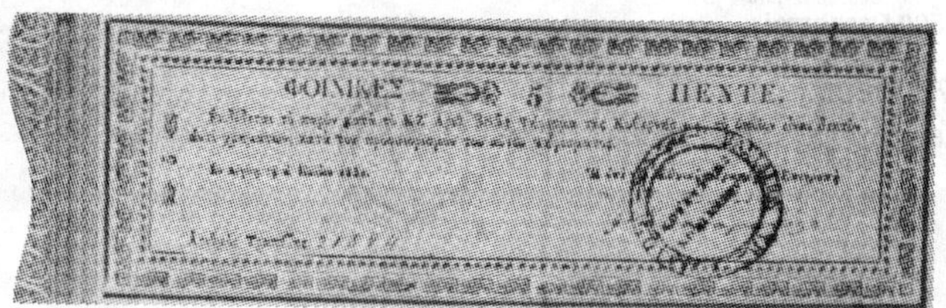

		Good	Fine	XF
6	**5 Phoenix** 30.6.1831. Red.	300.	1000.	2000.

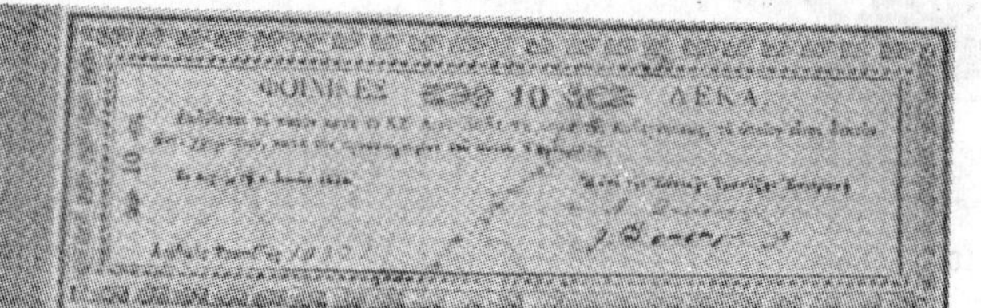

		Good	Fine	XF
7	**10 Phoenix** 30.6.1831. Red.	750.	2000.	4000.

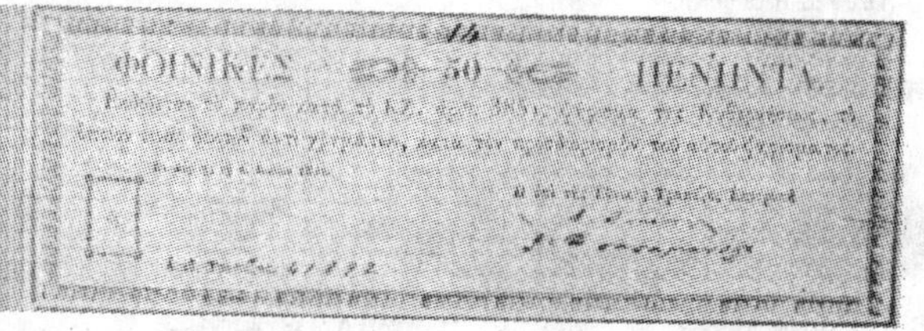

		Good	Fine	XF
8	**50 Phoenix** 30.6.1831. Lt. blue. Rare.	—	—	—

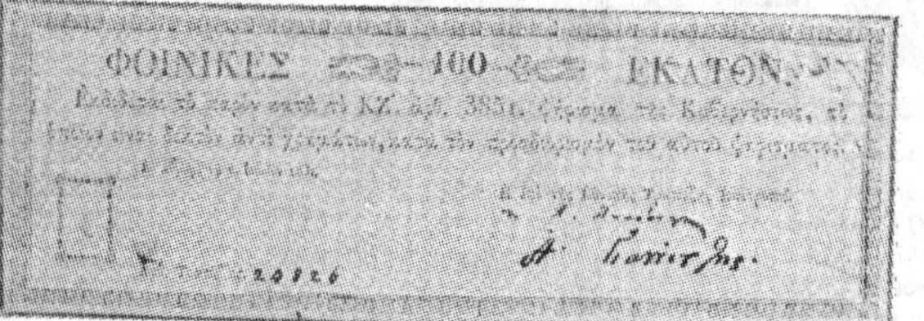

		Good	Fine	XF
	100 Phoenix 30.6.1831. Lt. blue. Rare.	—	—	—

KINGDOM

ΕΛΛΗΝΙΚΗ ΤΡΑΠΕΖΑ

BANK OF GREECE

1841 ISSUE

#10-13 uniface.

		Good	Fine	XF
	25 Drachmai 30.3.1841. Black on green paper. Arms of Kg. Othon at upper ctr. Rare.	—	—	—
	50 Drachmai 30.3.1841. Like #10. Rare.	—	—	—

		Good	Fine	XF
12	**100 Drachmai** 30.3.1841. Black on lt. brown paper. Like #10 but oval at ctr. Rare.	—	—	—
13	**500 Drachmai** 30.3.1841. Like #10. Rare.	—	—	—

ΕΘΝΙΚΗ ΤΡΑΠΕΖΑ ΤΗΣ ΕΛΛΑΔΟΣ

NATIONAL BANK OF GREECE

LAW OF 30.2.1841

#14-18 statue at l. and r. Embossed seal at r.

		Good	Fine	XF
14	**10 Drachmai** L.1841. Blue. Rare.	—	—	—
15	**25 Drachmai** L.1841. Rare.	—	—	—
16	**50 Drachmai** L.1841. Rare.	—	—	—
17	**100 Drachmai** L.1841. Rare.	—	—	—
18	**500 Drachmai** L.1841. Black. Rare.	—	—	—

1852 ISSUE

#19-21 uniface.

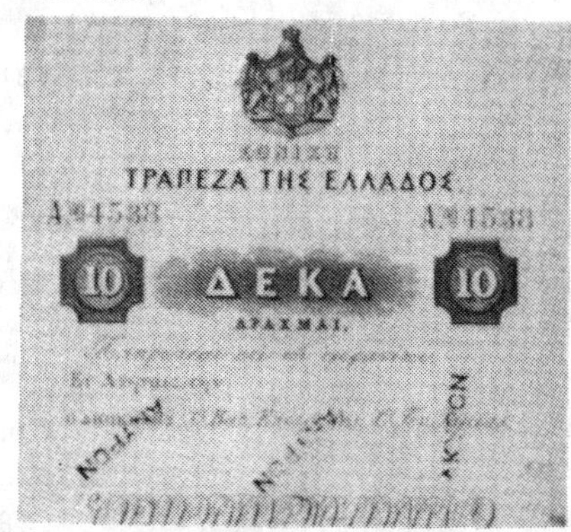

		Good	Fine	XF
19	**10 Drachmai** 1852. Arms of Kg. Othon at top ctr. Rare.	—	—	—
20	**25 Drachmai** 1852. Arms of Kg. Othon. Rare.	—	—	—

NOTICE

Readers with unlisted dates, signature varieties, etc. are invited to submit photocopies or, high resolution (300 dpi, 100% size) scans of their notes to: Standard Catalog of World Paper Money, 700 East State St. Iola, WI 54990-0001, or E-Mail: george.cuhaj@fwpubs.com.

21 **100 Drachmai** — Good — Fine — XF —
1852. Green denomination guilloches. Arms of Kg. Othon at upper l. Rare.

#22 not assigned.

1863-67 ISSUE

#23-25 portr. G. Stavros, first governor of the National Bank of Greece. Uniface. Printer: ABNC.

		Good	Fine	XF
23	**10 Drachmai** 15.7.1863; 10.3.1867. Black on red and green unpt. Arms of Kg. Othon at l., G. Stavros at top ctr., Nereid at lower r.	1500.	4000.	—

		Good	Fine	XF
24	**25 Drachmai** Black on red and green unpt. G. Stavros at upper l., 2 women at upper ctr., arms of Kg. Othon at lower r. Specimen.	—	—	5000.
25	**100 Drachmai** Black on red and green unpt. G. Stavros at upper l., woman reclining w/shield at upper ctr., arms of Kg. Othon at bottom r. Specimen.	—	—	5000.

#26 not assigned.

1867-69 ISSUE

#27-29 G. Stavros, arms of Kg. George I. Uniface. Printer: ABNC.

		Good	Fine	XF
27	**10 Drachmai** ca. 1867. Like #23 but arms of Kg. George I. Reported not confirmed.	—	—	—

		Good	Fine	XF
28	**25 Drachmai** 3.7.1867; 8.3.1868; 28.6.1868. Black, red and green. Like #24 but arms of Kg. George I.	1000.	1600.	3000.

		Good	Fine	XF
29	**100 Drachmai** 4.8.1867; 25.8.1869. Black, red and green. Like #25 but arms of Kg. George I. Rare.	—	—	—
29A	**500 Drachmai** Similar to #33. Reported not confirmed.	—	—	—

1870-78 ISSUE

#30-33 G. Stavros. 2 lg. N's on face (for New Drachmai of Latin Monetary Union). Printer: ABNC.

		Good	Fine	XF
30	**10 Drachmai** 18.8.1878-3.8.1883. Black, blue and red. Like #23 but arms of Kg. George I. Back red.	1000.	1800.	3000.
31	**25 Drachmai** 30.12.1871; 20.5.1882-12.8.1886. Black on blue and green unpt. Like #28. Back green.	400.	1000.	2000.

		Good	Fine	XF
32	**100 Drachmai** 1870-20.5.1882. Black, red and green. Like #29.	400.	1000.	2000.
33	**500 Drachmai** 1872-5.8.1886. Green and brown. Arms of Kg. George I at upper l., women at lower r. Back brown. Rare.	—	—	—

LAW OF 21.12.1885

#34 and 35 printer: BWC.

		Good	Fine	XF
34	**1 Drachma** L.1885. Black on blue yellow unpt. Portr. Hermes at lower l. Back blue; arms of Kg. George I at ctr.	20.00	65.00	175.

		Good	Fine	XF
35	**2 Drachmai** L.1885. Black on blue and yellow unpt. Portr. Hermes at l., Athena at r. Back like #34.	30.00	100.	200.

1885 ND PROVISIONAL ISSUE

		Good	Fine	XF
36	**5 Drachmai** ND (-old dates 1878-1900). L. or r. half of 10 Drachmai #30, 37, 43 and 46.	50.00	100.	300.

Note: Regarding #36, demand for the 5 Drachmai denomination was satisfied by cutting the 10 Drachmai notes in half. The practice continued apparently beyond 1910 despite the issuance of 5 Drachmai notes in 1897 as these were not enough to satisfy the demand.

1886-97 ISSUE

		Good	Fine	XF
36A	**2 Drachmai** 1.3.1886. Black on pink and green unpt. Back pink; Athena bust r. at ctr. Printer: G&D (w/o imprint). Proof.	—	—	—

#37-39 G. Stavros at l. Printer: ABNC.

		Good	Fine	XF
37	**10 Drachmai** 18.9.1889-5.8.1893. Orange and blue. Arms of Kg. George I at ctr., Hermes at r. Back red; woman and sheep.	400.	1000.	1800.
38	**25 Drachmai** 30.5.1888-12.6.1897. Black on red and green unpt. Reclining woman at ctr., arms of Kg. George I at r. Back brown; woman at ctr.	600.	1300.	2500.
39	**100 Drachmai** 25.2.1886; 6.3.1886; 18.9.1887. Like #32, but red denomination in unpt. Rare.	—	—	—

1897 ND Issue

Law of 21.12.1885

#40-42 printer: BWC.

		Good	Fine	XF
40	**1 Drachma** L.1885 (1897). Black on blue and orange unpt. Athena at l. Back similar to #34.	10.00	40.00	90.00

		Good	Fine	XF
41	**2 Drachmai** L.1885 (1897). Black on blue and orange unpt. Hermes at r. Back similar to #34.	17.50	75.00	175.

Note: For #40-41 ovpt: *1917* in red, see #301-302.

1897 Issue

		Good	Fine	XF
42	**5 Drachmai** 2.10.1897; 10.11.1897; 12.12.1897. Black on orange and purple unpt. Arms of Kg. George I at l., portr. G. Stavros at top ctr. Back blue; Athena at ctr.	50.00	150.	450.

1892; 1897 Issue

		Good	Fine	XF
43	**10 Drachmai** 14.9.1892-June 1900. Purple on tan unpt. Mercury at l., arms of Kg. George I at ctr. Printed in Vienna.	1000.	2800.	—

		Good	Fine	XF
44	**25 Drachmai** 12.8.1897-31.8.1900. Black on orange and blue unpt. Athena at l., male portr. at ctr. r., arms of Kg. George I at r. Back blue; Hermes at ctr. Printer: W&S.	900.	2000.	—

		Good	Fine	XF
45	**100 Drachmai** 12.2.1892-12.4.1893; 20.5.1899. Purple. Athena reclining on lion chair at l., arms of Kg. George I at top ctr., male portr. at r. Printed in Vienna.	1200.	3500.	—

1900; 1903 Issue

#46-48 portr. G. Stavros at l., arms of Kg. George I at r.

		Good	Fine	XF
46	**10 Drachmai** 1.6.1900; 20.6.1900; 15.7.1900. Green. Hermes at ctr. on back. Printer: BWC.	200.	600.	1400.
47	**25 Drachmai** 1.5.1903-2.9.1903. EK. 8. Black on red and blue unpt. 2 women at ctr. Child and fish at ctr. on back. Printer: ABNC.			
	a. Issued note.	75.00	350.	750.
	s. Specimen.	—	Unc	1000.
48	**100 Drachmai** 10.6.1900; 1.7.1900; 15.7.1900. Black on purple and orange unpt. Back green; Athena at ctr. Printer: BWC.	350.	1200.	2500.

1901 Issue

#49 and 50 portr. G. Stavros at l., arms of Kg. George I at r. Printer: ABNC.

		Good	Fine	XF
49	**500 Drachmai** 2.1.1901. EK. 6. Brown and green. Portr. Athena at ctr. Woman and sheep on back.			
	a. Issued note.	360.	1400.	—
	s. Specimen.	—	Unc	1500.

50	1000 Drachmai	Good	Fine	XF
	30.3.1901; 30.5.1901. Black on m/c unpt. Hermes at ctr. Woman at ctr. on back.			
	a. Issued note.	450.	1800.	—
	s. Specimen.	—	Unc	1500.

1905-10 Issue

#51-53 portr. G. Stavros at l., arms of Kg. George I at r. Sign. varieties. Printer: ABNC.

51	10 Drachmai	Good	Fine	XF
	12.3.1910-24.3.1917. Black on purple and green unpt. Hermes at ctr. on back.			
	a. Issued note.	25.00	100.	250.
	s. Specimen. Rare.	—	—	—

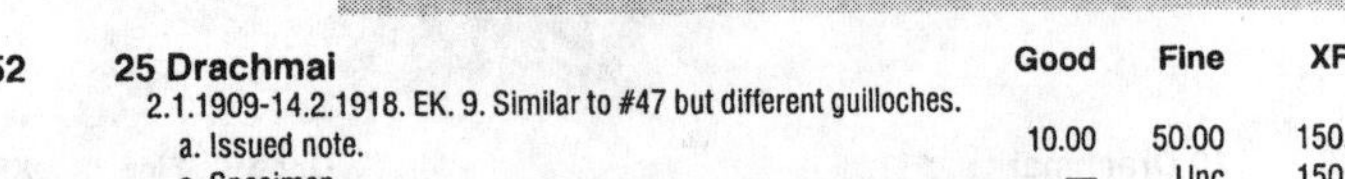

52	25 Drachmai	Good	Fine	XF
	2.1.1909-14.2.1918. EK. 9. Similar to #47 but different guilloches.			
	a. Issued note.	10.00	50.00	150.
	s. Specimen.	—	Unc	150.

53	100 Drachmai	Good	Fine	XF
	1.10.1905-12.11.1917. EK. 9. Black on purple and green unpt. Woman holding child at ctr. on back.			
	a. Issued note.	12.50	100.	250.
	s. Specimen.	—	Unc	250.

1905-17 Issue

#54-57 portr. G. Stavros at l., arms of Kg. George I at r. Printer: ABNC.

54	5 Drachmai	Good	Fine	XF
	1.10.1905-15.3.1918. EK. 2. Black on purple and green unpt. Athena at ctr. on back.			
	a. Issued note.	5.00	20.00	50.00
	s. Speicmen.	—	Unc	50.00

55	100 Drachmai	Good	Fine	XF
	10.12.1917-Sept.1918. EK. 10. Similar to #53 but different guilloches. Temple at ctr. on back.			
	a. Issued note.	50.00	250.	400.
	s. Specimen.	—	Unc	400.

56	500 Drachmai	Good	Fine	XF
	5.5.1914-20.12.1918. EK. 7. Black on m/c unpt. Similar to #49 but different guilloches. Back black, violet and m/c.			
	a. Issued note.	100.	300.	600.
	s. Specimen.	—	Unc	600.

57	1000 Drachmai	Good	Fine	XF
	15.4.1917-16.12.1918. Black on m/c unpt. Similar to #50.			
	a. Issued note.	400.	800.	2000.
	s. Speicmen.	—	Unc	2000.

Note: #57 illustrates 2 different half notes together.

1922 Emergency Issue

Law of 25.3.1922

Note: Many National Bank notes in circulation were cut in half. The l. half remained legal tender until 1927 at half face value. The r. half was considered a compulsory loan, equally valued at half face value.

		Good	Fine	XF
58	**5 Drachmai = 2 1/2 Drachmai** L.1922. EK. 2 (#54).	4.00	12.00	25.00
59	**10 Drachmai = 5 Drachmai** L.1922. EK. 8, 9 (#46, 51).	5.00	15.00	35.00

		Good	Fine	XF
60	**25 Drachmai = 12 1/2 Drachmai** L.1922. EK. 7, 8, 9 (#44, 47, 52).	7.50	20.00	40.00
61	**100 Drachmai = 50 Drachmai** L.1922. EK. 8, 9, 10 (#48, 53, 55).	7.50	20.00	45.00
62	**500 Drachmai = 250 Drachmai** L.1922. EK. 5, 6, 7 (#33, 49, 56).	30.00	90.00	150.
63	**1000 Drachmai = 500 Drachmai** L.1922. EK. 1 (#50, 57).	50.00	125.	300.

1922 *NEON* ISSUE

#64-69 portr. G.Stavros at l., ovpt: *NEON* over arms of Kg. George I at r. Issued w/ovpt. in 1922.

#64-66, 68 and 69 printer: ABNC.

		Good	Fine	XF
64	**5 Drachmai** 31.5.1918-8.1.1919 (1922). Black on red and m/c unpt. Black ovpt: *NEON*. Athena at ctr. on back.			
	a. Issued note.	6.00	30.00	60.00
	s. Specimen.	—	Unc	60.00

		Good	Fine	XF
65	**25 Drachmai** 2.5.1918-25.11.1919 (1922). Black on blue unpt. Seated figure at ctr. Red ovpt: *NEON*. 2 allegorical women on back.			
	a. Issued note.	15.00	75.00	150.
	s. Specimen.	—	Unc	150.

		Good	Fine	XF
66	**50 Drachmai** 16.9.1921-24.2.1922 (1922) Brown on green unpt. Relief from Sarcophagus at ctr. Red ovpt: *NEON*. Back blue; Alexander at ctr.			
	a. Issued note.	25.00	150.	350.
	s. Specimen.	—	Unc	350.

		Good	Fine	XF
67	**100 Drachmai** 8.2.1922; 17.2.1922. Blue on lt. green and red-orange unpt. 2 women reclining at ctr. Red ovpt: *NEON*. Back brown on lt. green and orange unpt. Temple at ctr. Printer: BWC.			
	a. Issued note.	25.00	100.	300.
	s. Specimen.	—	Unc	600.

		Good	Fine	XF
68	**500 Drachmai** 13.10.1921; 25.1.1922 (1922). Black on brown and green unpt. Woman at ctr. Red ovpt: *NEON*. Statue at l. and r., temple at ctr. on back.			
	a. Issued note.	75.00	250.	600.
	s. Specimen.	—	Unc	600.

		Good	Fine	XF
69	**1000 Drachmai** 15.6.1921-25.1.1922 (1922). Blue on m/c unpt. Woman at ctr. Red ovpt: *NEON*. Back black on red and m/c unpt. Urn at l. and r., temple at ctr.			
	a. Issued note.	100.	250.	400.
	s. Specimen.	—	Unc	500.

1923 First Issue

#70-72 portr. G. Stavros at l. Printer: BWC.

		Good	Fine	XF
70	**5 Drachmai** 24.3.1923. Green on orange unpt. Back red-brown; Alexander at ctr.			
	a. Issued note.	7.50	20.00	50.00
	s. Specimen.	—	Unc	50.00

		Good	Fine	XF
71	**25 Drachmai** 5.3.1923. Brown. Back blue; temple at ctr.			
	a. Issued note.	10.00	40.00	100.
	s. Specimen.	—	Unc	200.

		Good	Fine	XF
72	**1000 Drachmai** 5.1.1923. Blue on brown unpt. Parthenon at ctr. on back. Rare.	—	—	—

1923 Second Issue

#73-77 and 79 printer: ABNC.

		Good	Fine	XF
73	**5 Drachmai** 28.4.1923. Black on orange and green unpt. Back green and m/c; Athena at ctr.			
	a. Issued note.	6.00	25.00	80.00
	s. Specimen.	—	Unc	100.

		Good	Fine	XF
74	**25 Drachmai** 15.4.1923. Black on green and m/c unpt. Ancient coin at l. and r. on brown and purple back.			
	a. Issued note.	15.00	80.00	200.
	s. Specimen.	—	Unc	300.
75	**50 Drachmai** 12.3.1923. Black on m/c unpt. Back brown on blue unpt; Hermes at ctr.			
	a. Issued note.	100.	200.	350.
	s. Specimen.	—	Unc	500.

		Good	Fine	XF
76	**100 Drachmai** 1.3.1923. Black and m/c. Back blue and m/c; relief of Elusis at ctr.	120.	350.	850.
77	**500 Drachmai** 8.1.1923. Black on yellow and green unpt. Church at ctr. on back. Rare.	—	—	—
78	**500 Drachmai** 8.1.1923. Similar to #77. Ruins at ctr. on back. Printer: Gebr. Parcus, Munich (w/o imprint). Specimen.	—	—	400.
79	**1000 Drachmai** 4.4.1923; 14.7.1923. Black on m/c unpt. Statue at l. and r. 4 columns and view of ruins at ctr. on back. Rare.	—	—	—
	s. Specimen.	—	Unc	1500.

Republic - 1920s

ΕΘΝΙΚΗ ΤΡΑΠΕΖΑ ΤΗΣ ΕΛΛΑΔΟΣ

National Bank of Greece (continued)

1926 Emergency Issue

Law of 23.1.1926

Older National Bank 50-1000 Drachmai notes were cut w/the left-hand portion 3/4 of the width leaving the right-hand portion 1/4 in width. Later on, the large left-hand pieces were exchanged at 3/4 of original face value and at 1/4 of the 3/4 face value for debentures of compulsory loan. The smaller 1/4 right-hand pieces were also exchanged for debentures.

		Good	Fine	XF
80	**50 Drachmai** L.1926. EK. 3, 4 (#66, 75).	7.50	20.00	45.00

		Good	Fine	XF
81	**100 Drachmai** L.1926. EK. 11, 12 (#67, 76).	7.50	20.00	45.00
82	**500 Drachmai** L.1926. EK. 8, 9 (#68, 77).	20.00	75.00	150.

		Good	Fine	XF
83	**1000 Drachmai** L.1926. EK. 2, 3, 4 (#69, 72, 79).	40.00	100.	250.

Note: #83 illustrates 2 different pieces together.

1926 *NEON* ISSUE

#84-86 w/red ovpt: *NEON* in circle. Printer: BWC.

		Good	Fine	XF
84	**50 Drachmai** ND(1926-old date 6.5.1923). Purple on green and orange unpt. Portr. G. Stavros at l. Back purple; statue at ctr.	7.50	40.00	100.

		Good	Fine	XF
85	**100 Drachmai** ND(1926-old date 20.4.1923). Green. Portr. G. Stavros at ctr. Back olive; church at ctr.			
	a. Black sign. of Royal Commissioner.	15.00	70.00	200.
	b. Red sign. of Royal Commissioner.	7.50	40.00	125.

		Good	Fine	XF
86	**500 Drachmai** ND(1926-old date 12.4.1923). Brown. Portr. G. Stavros at ctr. Back brown; city at ctr.	15.00	75.00	200.

1926 THIRD ISSUE

#88 and 89 portr. G. Stavros at ctr. Printer: ABNC.

Note: #87 was issued as a provisional note of the Bank of Greece. See #94.

		Good	Fine	XF
87	**5 Drachmai** 17.12.1926. Brown on green unpt. Back brown; ancient coin at l. and r.			
	a. Issued note.	100.	300.	800.
	s. Specimen.	—	Unc	800.

		Good	Fine	XF
88	**10 Drachmai** 15.7.1926; 5.8.1926. Blue on yellow and orange unpt. Ancient coin at l. and r. on back.	10.00	50.00	160.

		Good	Fine	XF
89	**500 Drachmai** 21.11.1926. Purple on m/c unpt. Back purple; church at ctr., mythical animal at l. and r.			
	a. Black sign. of Commissioner.	15.00	80.00	200.
	b. Red sign. of Commissioner.	10.00	40.00	150.

1927 ISSUE

#90 and 91 printer: ABNC.

		Good	Fine	XF
90	**50 Drachmai** 30.4.1927; 13.5.1927; 24.5.1927. Brown on orange and green unpt. Columns at l. and r., portr. G. Stavros at ctr. Ancient coin at l. and r. on back. (Not issued).			
	a. Issued note.	20.00	50.00	175.
	s. Specimen.	—	Unc	175.

		Good	Fine	XF
91	**100 Drachmai** 25.5.1927; 6.6.1927; 14.6.1927. Green on orange and brown unpt. Portr. G. Stavros at l., ancient coin at r. Coin w/Apollo at ctr. on back. (Not issued).			
	a. Issued note.	20.00	50.00	175.
	s. Specimen.	—	Unc	175.

Note: #90-91 were issued only as provisional notes of the Bank of Greece. See #97-98.

ΤΡΑΠΕΖΑ ΤΗΣ ΕΛΛΑΔΟΣ

BANK OF GREECE

CA. 1928 FIRST PROVISIONAL ISSUE

#92 and 93 ovpt: new bank name on notes of the National Bank of Greece.

		Good	Fine	XF
92	**50 Drachmai** ND (-old date 6.5.1923). Ovpt. on #84.			
	a. Issued note.	7.50	50.00	100.
	s. Specimen.	—	Unc	300.

		Good	Fine	XF
93	**100 Drachmai** ND (-old date 20.4.1923). Ovpt. on #85.			
	a. Issued note.	7.50	50.00	100.
	s. Specimen.	—	Unc	300.

CA. 1928 SECOND PROVISIONAL ISSUE

#94-101 ovpt: new bank name on notes of the National Bank of Greece.

		Good	Fine	XF
94	**5 Drachmai**			
	ND (-old date 17.11.1926). Black ovpt. at lower r. on #87.			
	a. Issued note.	5.00	50.00	100.
	s. Specimen.	—	Unc	300.

Note: The ovpt. is often very weak and hardly discernible.

CA. 1928 THIRD PROVISIONAL ISSUE

#95-101 red ovpt. new bank name in curved line across upper ctr.

		Good	Fine	XF
95	**20 Drachmai**			
	ND (-old dates 19.10.1926; 5.11.1926. Brown on m/c unpt. G. Stavros at l. Back brown; woman at ctr.			
	a. Issued note.	25.00	80.00	250.
	s. Specimen.	—	Unc	500.
96	**25 Drachmai**			
	ND (-old date 15.4.1923). Ovpt. on #74.			
	a. Issued note.	40.00	180.	450.
	s. Specimen.	—	Unc	1000.
97	**50 Drachmai**			
	ND (-old date 30.4.1927). Ovpt. on #90.			
	a. Issued note.	10.00	30.00	100.
	s. Specimen.	—	Unc	500.
98	**100 Drachmai**			
	ND (-old date 6.6.1927). Ovpt. on #91.			
	a. Issued note.	35.00	100.	200.
	s. Specimen.	—	Unc	500.
99	**500 Drachmai**			
	ND (-old date 21.11.1926). Ovpt. on #89a or 89b.			
	a. Issued note.	25.00	100.	200.
	s. Specimen.	—	Unc	500.

		Good	Fine	XF
100	**1000 Drachmai**			
	ND (-old date 1926). Black on green and m/c unpt. Portr. G. Stavros at ctr. Back w/blue and pink unpt. Stone carving at ctr.			
	a. W/o sign. under red bar at lower r. Old date 15.10.1926.	2.50	10.00	25.00
	b. W/o sign. under red bar at lower r. Old date 4.11.1926.	2.00	7.50	10.00
	c. Red bar ovpt. over sign. at lower r.	20.00	100.	—
	s. Specimen w/o overprint.	—	Unc	500.

		Good	Fine	XF
101	**5000 Drachmai**			
	ND (-old date 5.10.1926). Brown on green unpt. Frieze at top, portr. G. Stavros at ctr. Back brown; stone carving at ctr.			
	a. Issued note.	70.00	250.	600.
	s. Specimen.	—	Unc	2000.

NOTICE

Readers with unlisted dates, signature varieties, etc. are invited to submit photocopies or, high resolution (300 dpi, 100% size) scans of their notes to: Standard Catalog of World Paper Money, 700 East State St. Iola, WI 54990-0001, or E-Mail: george.cuhaj@fwpubs.com.

1932 ISSUE

#102 and 103 printer: ABNC.

		VG	VF	UNC
102	**500 Drachmai**			
	1.10.1932. M/c. Portr. Athena at ctr. Stone carving at ctr. on back.			
	a. Issued note.	1.00	4.00	10.00
	s. Specimen.	—	—	200.

		VG	VF	UNC
103	**5000 Drachmai**			
	1.9.1932. Brown. Portr. Athena at ctr. Back green; mythical bird at ctr.			
	a. Issued note.	1.50	4.00	15.00
	s. Specimen.	—	—	200.

KINGDOM 1935-41

ΤΡΑΠΕΖΑ ΤΗΣ ΕΛΛΑΔΟΣ

BANK OF GREECE (CONTINUED)

1935 ISSUE

#104-106 printed in France.

		VG	VF	UNC
104	**50 Drachmai**			
	1.9.1935. M/c. Girl w/sheaf of wheat at l. Relief of Elusis at ctr., woman at r. on back.			
	a. Issued note.	1.50	15.00	50.00
	s. Specimen.	—	—	500.

105	100 Drachmai	VG	VF	UNC
	1.9.1935. M/c. Hermes at ctr. Woman holding basket at ctr. on back.			
	a. Issued note.	2.00	25.00	80.00
	s. Specimen.	—	—	500.

106	1000 Drachmai	VG	VF	UNC
	1.5.1935. M/c. Girl in national costume at ctr. Workman at l. and r., girl in national costume at ctr. on back.			
	a. Issued note.	2.00	40.00	100.
	s. Specimen.	—	—	1000.

1939 ISSUE

107	50 Drachmai	VG	VF	UNC
	1.1.1939. Green. Hesiod at l. Frieze at ctr. on back. Printer: TDLR (w/o imprint).			
	a. Issued note.	.50	1.50	5.00
	s. Specimen.	—	—	100.

ote: For a note similar to #107 in red-brown and dated 1941, see #168.

08	100 Drachmai	VG	VF	UNC
	1.1.1939. Green and yellow. 2 peasant women at lower l. Stone carving in country scene on back. Printer: W&S (w/o imprint). (Not issued).			
	a. Issued note.	1.00	4.50	12.50
	s. Specimen.	—	—	40.00

109	500 Drachmai	VG	VF	UNC
	1.1.1939. Purple and lilac. Portr. woman in national costume at l. Back blue-green; view of city and woman in oval. Printer: BWC (w/o imprint).			
	a. ΕΠΙ in line below Greek denomination.	1.00	2.00	12.50
	b. Error: ΕΝΙ instead of ΕΠΙ.	1.00	2.00	12.50
	s. Specimen.	—	—	100.

110	1000 Drachmai	VG	VF	UNC
	1.1.1939. Green. Woman in national costume at r. Back blue-green; Athena at l. and view of Parthenon ruins at ctr. Printer: BWC (w/o imprint).			
	a. Issued note.	1.00	2.00	10.00
	s. Specimen.	—	—	100.

1939 PROVISIONAL ISSUE

111	1000 Drachmai on 100 Drachmai	VG	VF	UNC
	1939. Ovpt. on both sides of #108.	1.00	3.00	8.00

GERMAN / ITALIAN OCCUPATION - WWII

BANK OF GREECE

1941 EMERGENCY REISSUE

Because of a shortage of notes caused by the German-Italian occupation, Greek authorities on April 25, 1941 reissued cancelled notes readied for destruction. These were in use for about a year, and were redeemed on 1.4.1942 by exchanging them for new notes. Some are hole- cancelled (probably issued in Athens), while others also bear local stamps of branches of the Bank of Greece. Clear stamps are worth considerably more. The condition of all these notes is usually very low.

112	50 Drachmai	Good	Fine	XF
	(1941). Reissue of #97, 104.	6.00	15.00	—

		Good	Fine	XF
113	**100 Drachmai** (1941). Reissue of #98, 105.	5.00	10.00	—
114	**500 Drachmai** (1941). Reissue of #102.	4.00	10.00	—
115	**1000 Drachmai** (1941). Reissue of #100a, 100b, 106.	2.50	7.50	—
115A	**5000 Drachmai** (1941). Reissue of #103. Rare.	—	—	—

1941 Inflation Issue

Serial # varieties including positioning.

		VG	VF	UNC
116	**100 Drachmai** 10.7.1941. Brown. Bird frieze at l. and r. Back brown and green; Kapnikarea Church at ctr.			
	a. Issued note.	.25	.75	3.50
	s. Specimen.	—	—	20.00

		VG	VF	UNC
117	**1000 Drachmai** 1.10.1941. Blue and brown. Coin of Alexander at l. Back green and yellow.			
	a. Title of picture on illustration.	1.00	2.50	10.00
	b. Title of picture on white background.	.50	2.00	6.00
	s. Specimen.	—	—	20.00

1942 Inflation Issue

		VG	VF	UNC
118	**1000 Drachmai** 21.8.1942. Black on blue-gray and pale orange unpt. Bust of young girl from Thasos at ctr. Statue of Lion of Amphipolis at ctr. on back.			
	a. Issued note.	.25	.50	3.00
	s. Specimen.	—	—	20.00

		VG	VF	UNC
119	**5000 Drachmai** 20.6.1942. Black on pale red, blue and m/c unpt. Factories and ships at lower l., statue of Nike of Samothrace between male workers at ctr., fisherman and shoreline at lower r. Back dk. brown on lt. blue and yellow-orange unpt.; farmers sowing and plowing w/horses at ctr.			
	a. Paper w/o wmk.	.25	1.00	4.00
	b. Wmk. paper (same paper used for Agricultural Bonds #136-144).	1.00	4.00	12.00
	s. Specimen.	—	—	20.00
120	**10,000 Drachmai** 29.12.1942. Brown. Young farm couple from Delphi at l. Treasure of the Athenians in Delphi on back.			
	a. Title of picture on illustration.	.25	.75	4.00
	b. Title of picture in lt. background.	.25	.75	4.00
	s. Specimen.	—	—	20.00

1943 Inflation Issue

		VG	VF	UNC
121	**50 Drachmai** 1.2.1943. Brown on blue unpt. Woman from Paramithia at l. Back brown; ancient coin at l. and r.			
	a. Issued note.	.25	.50	3.00
	s. Specimen.	—	—	20.00

		VG	VF	UNC
122	**5000 Drachmai** 19.7.1943. Green and brown. Frieze at l. and r., Athena at ctr. Back brown; relief at ctr.			
	a. Issued note.	.25	.50	3.00
	s. Specimen.	—	—	20.00

		VG	VF	UNC
123	**25,000 Drachmai** 12.8.1943. Black on brown and lt. blue-green unpt. Bust of Nymph Deidamia at l. Back black on olive green; ruins of Olympian Temple of Zeus at ctr.			
	a. Issued note.	.25	.50	3.00
	s. Speicmen.	—	—	20.00

1944 Inflation Issue

		VG	VF	UNC
124	**50,000 Drachmai** 14.1.1944. Blue. Athlete at ctr. Back dk. brown.			
	a. Issued note.	2.50	5.00	30.00
	s. Specimen. Rare.	—	—	—

		VG	VF	UNC
125	**100,000 Drachmai** 21.1.1944. Black on brown and lt. blue-green unpt. Ancient silver tetradrachm coin of Athens at l. and r. Ruins of the Temple of Aphaea Athena in Aegina at ctr. on back.			
	a. Serial number w/prefix letters.	.25	1.00	6.00
	b. Serial number w/suffix letters.	.25	1.00	6.00
	s. Specimen.	—	—	20.00

		VG	VF	UNC
126	**500,000 Drachmai** 20.3.1944. Black on dull violet-brown unpt. Head of Zeus at l. Back black on blue-green and pale olive green unpt; ears of wheat at ctr.			
	a. Serial #w/prefix letters.	.25	.50	2.50
	b. Serial # w/suffix letters.	.25	.50	2.50
	s. Specimen.	—	—	20.00

		VG	VF	UNC
127	**1,000,000 Drachmai** 29.6.1944. Black on blue-green and pale orange unpt. Bust of youth from Antikythera at ctr. Back black on blue and pink unpt; ruins of Temple of Poseidon in Sounion at ctr.			
	a. Serial # w/prefix letters.	.25	.50	3.00
	b. Serial # w/suffix letters.	.25	.50	3.00
	s. Specimen.	—	—	20.00

		VG	VF	UNC
128	**5,000,000 Drachmai** 20.7.1944. Brown. Arethusa on dekadrachm of Syracuse at l. Back dk. brown and gray.			
	a. Serial # w/prefix letters.	.25	.50	3.00
	b. Serial # w/suffix letters.	.25	.50	3.00
	s. Specimen.	—	—	20.00

		VG	VF	UNC
129	**10,000,000 Drachmai** 29.7.1944. Brown. Dk. brown fringe around denomination guilloche and sign.			
	a. Serial # w/prefix letters.	.25	.50	3.00
	b. Serial # w/suffix letters.	.25	.50	3.00
	s. Specimen.	—	—	20.00

		VG	VF	UNC
130	**25,000,000 Drachmai** 10.8.1944. Green. Ancient Greek coin at l. and r.			
	a. Serial # w/prefix letters.	.25	.50	2.00
	b. Serial # w/suffix letters.	.25	.50	2.00
	s. Specimen.	—	—	20.00

		VG	VF	UNC
131	**200,000,000 Drachmai** 9.9.1944. Brown and red-brown. Parthenon frieze at ctr. Back brown.			
	a. Unpt. in tightly woven pattern w/o circles.	.25	.50	2.00
	b. Unpt. interconnecting circles w/dots.	3.00	7.00	25.00
	s. Specimen.	—	—	20.00

		VG	VF	UNC
132	**500,000,000 Drachmai** 1.10.1944. Blue-green. Apollo at l. Relief at ctr. on back.			
	a. Serial # w/prefix letters.	.25	.50	2.00
	b. Serial # w/suffix letters.	.25	.50	2.00
	s. Specimen.	—	—	20.00

		VG	VF	UNC
133	**2,000,000,000 Drachmai** 11.10.1944. Black on pale lt. green unpt. Like #131. Back aqua.			
	a. Serial # w/prefix letters.	.25	.50	2.00
	b. Serial # w/suffix letters.	.25	.50	2.00
	s. Specimen.	—	—	20.00

		VG	VF	UNC
134	**10,000,000,000 Drachmai** 20.10.1944. Black and blue-black on tan unpt. Face like #128. Back dull dk. blue.			
	a. Serial # w/prefix letters.	.25	.50	2.00
	b. Serial # w/suffix letters.	.25	.50	2.00
	s. Specimen.	—	—	20.00

		VG	VF	UNC
135	**100,000,000,000,000 Drachmai** 3.11.1944. Red-brown. Nymph Deidamia at l. Ancient coin at l. and r. on back.			
	a. Issued note.	.50	1.00	4.00
	s. Specimen.	—	—	20.00

ΤΑΜΕΙΑΚΟΝ ΓΡΑΜΜΑΤΙΟΝ

AGRICULTURAL TREASURY BONDS

1942 ISSUE

		VG	VF	UNC
136	**25,000 Drachmai** 26.11.1942. Lt. orange. Back brown. Series 1.	25.00	50.00	75.00
137	**100,000 Drachmai** 27.11.1942. Dk. green. Back blue-green. Series 1.	—	—	95.00
138	**500,000 Drachmai** 27.11.1942. Brown and green Series 1.	—	—	350.

1943 FIRST ISSUE

		VG	VF	UNC
139	**25,000 Drachmai** 5.3.1943. Blue and gray. Series 2.	—	—	75.00
140	**100,000 Drachmai** 5.3.1943. Blue and red. Series 2.	—	—	95.00

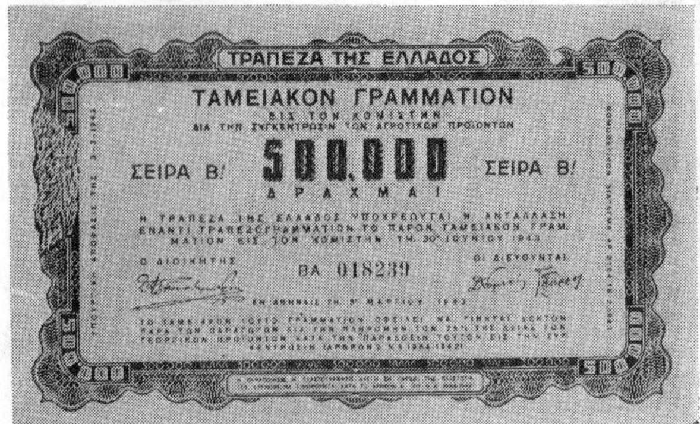

		VG	VF	UNC
141	**500,000 Drachmai** 5.3.1943. Lt. orange. Series 2.	—	—	150.

1943 SECOND ISSUE

		VG	VF	UNC
142	**25,000 Drachmai** 15.5.1943. Gray, blue and green. Series 3. (Not issued).	—	—	250.
143	**100,000 Drachmai** 15.5.1943. Green. Series 3. (Not issued).	—	—	250.
144	**500,000 Drachmai** 15.5.1943. Green and brown. Series 3. (Not issued).	—	—	250.

REGIONAL - WWII

BANK OF GREECE

ΑΓΡΙΝΙΟΥ – Αγρινιον

1944 TREASURY NOTES

#145-150 bank name in capital or small letters. Uniface.

		VG	VF	UNC
145	**100,000,000 Drachmai** Oct. 1944.	20.00	60.00	175.
146	**200,000,000 Drachmai** Oct. 1944.	25.00	75.00	225.
147	**300,000,000, Drachmai** Oct. 1944.	25.00	75.00	225.
148	**500,000,000 Drachmai** 9.10.1944. Blue text.	25.00	75.00	225.
149	**1,000,000,000 Drachmai** Oct. 1944.	25.00	75.00	225.
150	**2,000,000,000 Drachmai** 2.10.1944.			
	a. Bank name w/capital letters.	25.00	75.00	225.
	b. Bank name w/small letters.	25.00	75.00	225.

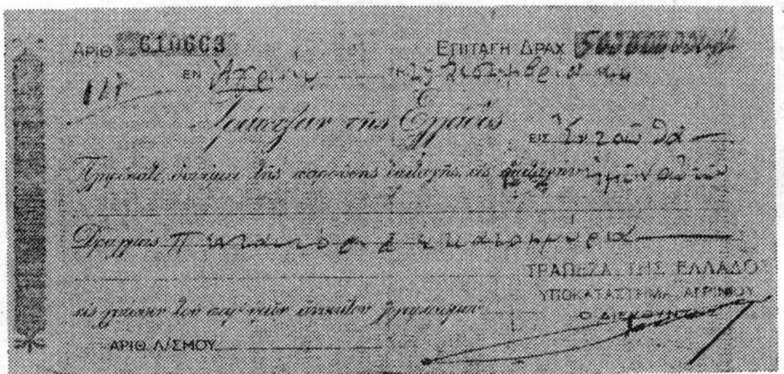

		VG	VF	UNC
150A	**Various Amounts** Sept.-Oct. 1944. Regular checks of the Agrinion branch made payable to *Ourselves* by bank manager. Amounts in millions of drachmai.	100.	175.	350.

ΚΕΦΑΛΛΗΝΙΑ – ΙΘΑΚΑ CEPHALONIA - ITHAKA

1944 TREASURY NOTES

		VG	VF	UNC
151	**50,000,000 Drachmai** 6.10.1944. Yellowish paper.	20.00	100.	200.
152	**100,000,000 Drachmai** 6.10.1944. Bluish paper.	10.00	50.00	100.

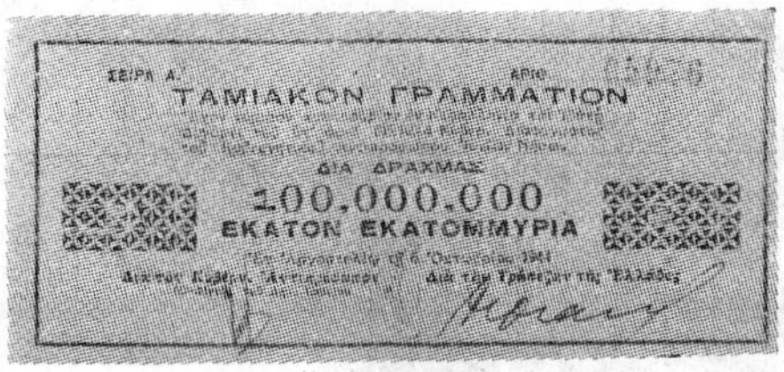

ΚΕΡΚΥΡΑ - CORFU

1944 PROVISIONAL ISSUE

Red ovpt. on Ionian Islands notes #M14, M15 and M16 for use in Corfu.

		VG	VF	UNC
153	**20 Drachmai on 50 Drachmai** 18.12.1944. Rare.	100.	—	—
154	**100 Drachmai on 100 Drachmai** 18.12.1944. Rare.	200.	—	—
155	**500 Drachmai on 1000 Drachmai** 18.12.1944. Rare.	300.	—	—

1944 TREASURY NOTE W/KERKYRA NAME

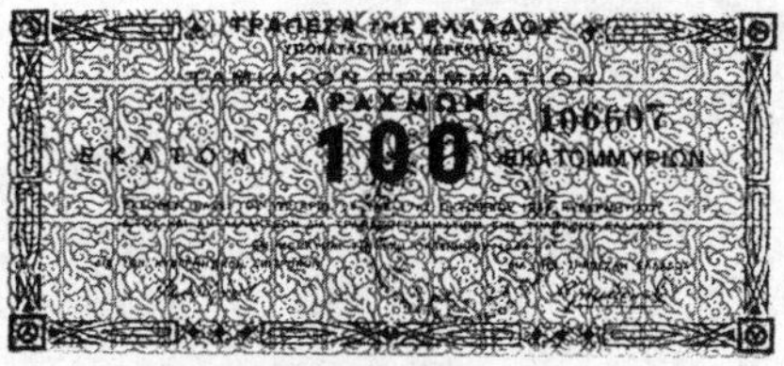

		VG	VF	UNC
156	**100,000,000 Drachmai** 17.10.1944. Green on yellow.	8.00	20.00	60.00

ΚΑΛΑΜΑΤΑ - KALAMATA

1944 FIRST ISSUE TREASURY NOTES

#157-160 uniface. Flag at l. and r.

		VG	VF	UNC
157	**25,000,000 Drachmai** 20.9.1944. Brown.	25.00	65.00	175.
158	**50,000,000 Drachmai** 20.9.1944. Violet.	15.00	40.00	125.
159	**100,000,000 Drachmai** 20.9.1944. Lt. blue.	12.00	30.00	100.
160	**500,000,000 Drachmai** 20.9.1944. Green.	25.00	65.00	175.

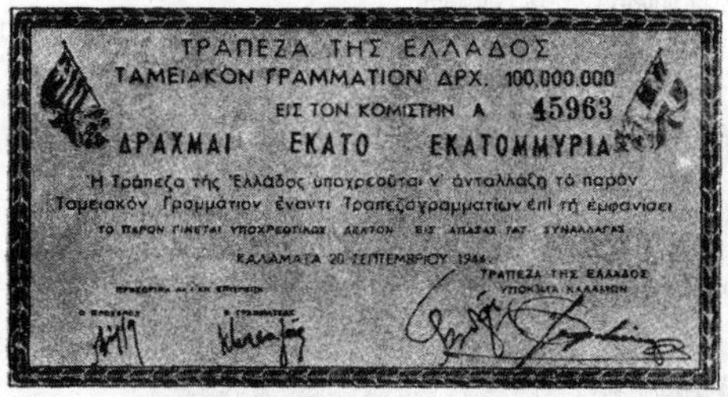

1944 SECOND ISSUE

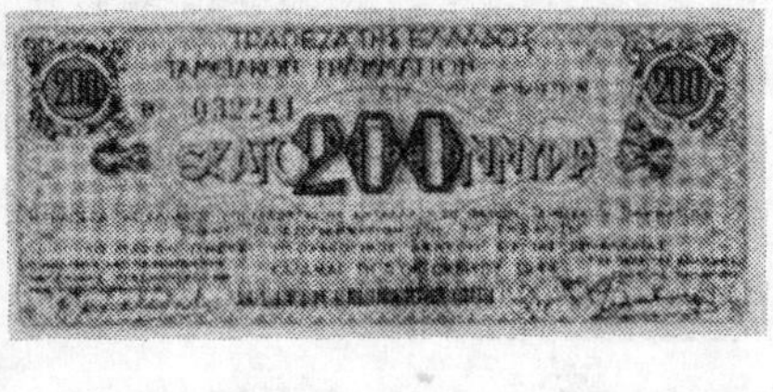

		VG	VF	UNC
161	**200,000,000 Drachmai** 5.10.1944. Orange. Back brown.			
	a. Greek handstamp on back.	12.00	30.00	100.
	b. French handstamp on back.	15.00	40.00	125.
	c. Stamp for *TRIPOLIS* branch on back.	100.	200.	325.

ΝΑΥΠΛΙΟΥ - NAUPLIA

1944 PROVISIONAL TREASURY NOTES

#162-163 ovpt. on Bank of Greece notes.

		VG	VF	UNC
162	**100,000,000 Drachmai** 19.9.1944. Red ovpt. on back of #128.	30.00	80.00	225.
163	**500,000,000 Drachmai** 19.9.1944. Black ovpt. on back of #119. Rare.	500.	—	—

ΥΠΟΚΑΤΑΣΤΗΜΑ ΠΑΤΡΩΝ - PATRAS

1944 TREASURY NOTES

#164-165 uniface.

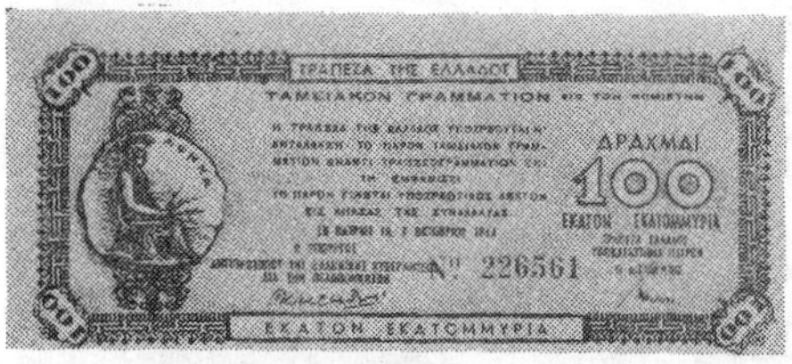

		VG	VF	UNC
164	**100,000,000 Drachmai** 7.10.1944. Brown. Ancient Greek coin at l.	6.00	15.00	50.00
165	**500,000,000 Drachmai** 7.10.1944. Blue-gray. Ancient Greek coin at ctr.	6.00	15.00	50.00

ΤΡΙΚΑΛΩΝ - TRIKALA

1944 PROVISIONAL TREASURY NOTES

#166-167 ovpt. on Bank of Greece notes.

		VG	VF	UNC
166	**10,000,000 Drachmai** 29.9.1944. Black ovpt. on back of #118.	—	—	—

Note for #166: All ovpt. on #118 are believed to be spurious.

		VG	VF	UNC
167	**200,000,000 Drachmai** 29.9.1944. Black ovpt. and red German stamping on back of #122.	100.	300.	—

Note: A 500 Million Drachmai issue from the Zakinthos branch dated Oct. 1944 is reported.

KINGDOM - POST WWII

ΤΡΑΠΕΖΑ ΤΗΣ ΕΛΛΑΔΟΣ

BANK OF GREECE

1941-44 ISSUE

		VG	VF	UNC
168	**50 Drachmai** 1.1.1941 (2.1.1945). Red-brown on lilac unpt. Like #107. Wmk: Young male head. Printer: TDLR (w/o imprint).	.50	1.00	3.50

Note: For similar note to #168 in green and dated 1939, see #107.

		VG	VF	UNC
169	**50 Drachmai** 9.11.1944. Brown on blue and gold unpt. Statue of Nike of Samothrake at l. Phoenix at ctr. on back.	3.00	7.50	30.00

1944-46 ND ISSUE

#170-176 issued 1944-46.

		VG	VF	UNC
170	**100 Drachmai** ND (1944). Blue on gold unpt. Canaris (maritime hero) at r. Goddess at ctr. on back. Printer: W&S (w/o imprint).			
	a. Issued note.	3.00	7.50	30.00
	s. Specimen.	—	—	100.

#171-176 printer: BWC (w/o imprint).

		VG	VF	UNC
171	**500 Drachmai** ND (1945). Green. Portr. Capodistrias (statesman) at l. University of Athens at bottom ctr. on back.			
	a. Issued note.	2.00	8.00	40.00
	s. Specimen.	—	—	100.

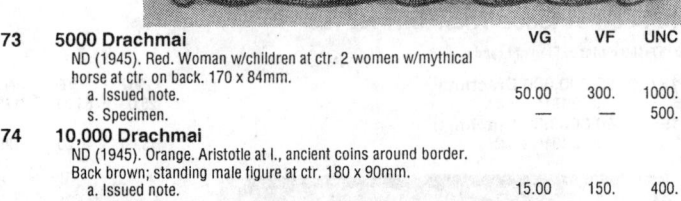

		VG	VF	UNC
172	**1000 Drachmai** ND (1944). Brown. Portr. Kolokotronis (hero of freedom) at l. Soldier at ctr. on back. 161 x 80mm.			
	a. Issued note.	3.00	8.00	50.00
	s. Specimen.	—	—	100.

		VG	VF	UNC
173	**5000 Drachmai** ND (1945). Red. Woman w/children at ctr. 2 women w/mythical horse at ctr. on back. 170 x 84mm.			
	a. Issued note.	50.00	300.	1000.
	s. Specimen.	—	—	500.
174	**10,000 Drachmai** ND (1945). Orange. Aristotle at l., ancient coins around border. Back brown; standing male figure at ctr. 180 x 90mm.			
	a. Issued note.	15.00	150.	400.
	s. Specimen.	—	—	300.

		VG	VF	UNC
175	**10,000 Drachmai** ND (1946). Blue. Like #174. 180 x 90mm.			
	a. Issued note.	20.00	200.	550.
	s. Specimen.	—	—	1000.

		VG	VF	UNC
176	**20,000 Drachmai** ND (1946). Dk. green. Athena at l., ancient coin at bottom. Medusa at upper ctr., chicken at lower ctr. on back. 180 x 90mm.			
	a. Issued note.	30.00	250.	700.
	s. Specimen.	—	—	1000.

1947 ND ISSUE

#177-179 reduced size, two signs. Issued in 1947.

		VG	VF	UNC
177	**5000 Drachmai** ND (1947). Purple on orange unpt. Like #173 but 153 x 80mm.			
	a. Issued note.	15.00	75.00	250.
	s. Specimen.	—	—	300.
178	**10,000 Drachmai** ND (1947). Orange. Like #174 but 153 x 80mm.			
	a. Issued note.	25.00	250.	750.
	s. Specimen.	—	—	1000.
179	**20,000 Drachmai** ND (1947). Dk. green. Like #176 but 153 x 80mm.			
	a. W/o security strip.	15.00	150.	500.
	b. W/security strip.	12.50	125.	400.
	s. Specimen.	—	—	1000.

1947; 1949 ISSUE

#180-183 3 signs.

		VG	VF	UNC
180	**1000 Drachmai** 1947. Brown. Like #172 but 145 x 75mm.			
	a. 9.1.1947. Wmk: Ancient warrior w/helmet.	2.00	7.00	45.00
	b. 14.11.1947. W/o wmk.	2.00	6.00	45.00
	s. Specimen.	—	—	100.

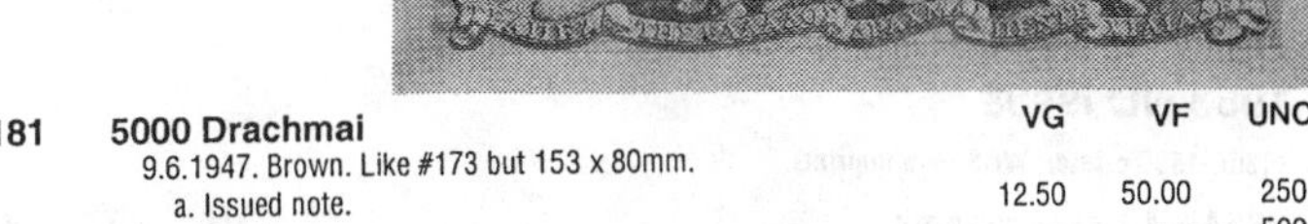

		VG	VF	UNC
181	**5000 Drachmai** 9.6.1947. Brown. Like #173 but 153 x 80mm.			
	a. Issued note.	12.50	50.00	250.
	s. Specimen.	—	—	500.

		VG	VF	UNC
182	**10,000 Drachmai** 29.12.1947. Orange. Like #174 but 150 x 79mm.			
	a. W/o printer's name at bottom on back. (Printer: BWC.)	2.00	25.00	150.
	b. Greek printer's name at bottom on back. Same numeral style as a.	5.00	60.00	350.
	c. Printer like b., but small serial # prefix letters.	3.00	25.00	175.
	s. Specimen.	—	—	500.

		VG	VF	UNC
183	**20,000 Drachmai** 29.12.1949. Blue on m/c unpt. Like #176 but 147 x 78mm.			
	a. Issued note.	4.00	35.00	215.
	s. Specimen.	—	—	500.

1950 ISSUE

		VG	VF	UNC
184	**5000 Drachmai** 28.10.1950. Brown. Portr. Solomos at l. Battle of Mesolonghi on back.			
	a. Issued note.	3.00	30.00	250.
	s. Specimen.	—	—	500.

		VG	VF	UNC
185	**50,000 Drachmai** 1.12.1950. Olive and gray. Portr. woman at l. Ruins at ctr. on back.			
	a. Issued note.	3.00	25.00	175.
	s. Specimen.	—	—	300.

1953 ND Issue

#185A-185C printer: W&S (w/o imprint).

		VG	VF	UNC
185A	**1 New Drachma** ND (1953). Dull blue on m/c unpt. Portr. Athena at r. Specimen.	—	—	—
185B	**5 New Drachmai** ND (1953). Dk. olive-brown on m/c unpt. Portr. Homer at lower r. Specimen.	—	—	—
185C	**10 New Drachmai** ND (1953). Green on m/c unpt. Portr. archaic woman at lower r. Specimen.	—	—	—

1954 Issue

#186-188 ΝΕΑ ΕΚΔΟΣΙΣ (New Issue) at r

		VG	VF	UNC
186	**10 Drachmai** 15.1.1954. Orange. Like #182.			
	a. Issued note.	50.00	400.	800.
	s. Specimen.	—	—	800.

		VG	VF	UNC
187	**20 Drachmai** 15.1.1954. Blue. Like #183.			
	a. Issued note.	50.00	400.	800.
	s. Specimen.	—	—	800.

		VG	VF	UNC
188	**50 Drachmai** 15.1.1954. Green and gray. Like #185.			
	a. Issued note.	25.00	125.	450.
	s. Specimen.	—	—	800.

1954-56 Issue

		VG	VF	UNC
189	**10 Drachmai** 1954-55. Orange. Kg. George I at l. Church at ctr. on back.			
	a. 15.5.1954.	4.00	30.00	250.
	b. 1.3.1955.	3.00	20.00	175.
	s. Specimen.	—	—	300.

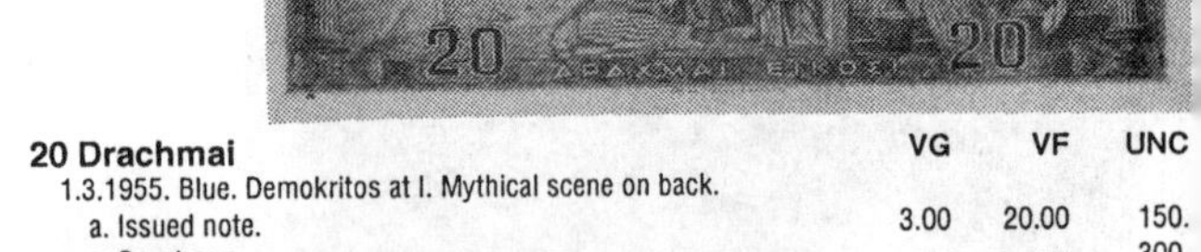

		VG	VF	UNC
190	**20 Drachmai** 1.3.1955. Blue. Demokritos at l. Mythical scene on back.			
	a. Issued note.	3.00	20.00	150.
	s. Specimen.	—	—	300.

		VG	VF	UNC
191	**50 Drachmai**			
	1.3.1955. Dk. green. Pericles at ctr. Pericles speaking on back.			
	a. Issued note.	2.00	15.00	100.
	s. Specimen.	—	—	45.00

		VG	VF	UNC
192	**100 Drachmai**			
	1954-55. Red on m/c unpt. Themistocles at l., galley at bottom r. Sailing ships on back.			
	a. 31.3.1954.	5.00	75.00	200.
	b. 1.7.1955.	2.50	25.00	100.
	s. As b. Specimen.	—	—	300.
	s1. Specimen.	—	—	300.

		VG	VF	UNC
193	**500 Drachmai**			
	8.8.1955. Green on m/c unpt. Socrates at ctr. Apostle Paul speaking to assembly on back.			
	a. Issued note.	4.00	30.00	120.
	s. Specimen.	—	—	300.

		VG	VF	UNC
194	**1000 Drachmai**			
	16.4.1956. Brown. Alexander at l., frieze at bottom. Alexander in battle on back.			
	a. Issued note.	5.00	60.00	150.
	s. Specimen.	—	—	300.

MINISTRY OF FINANCE

GREEK STATE

1917 PROVISIONAL ISSUE

#301 and 302 red ovpt: *NOMOE/991/1917*. Printer: BWC.

		VG	VF	UNC
301	**1 Drachma**			
	1917 (-old date 21.12.1885). Ovpt. on #40.	20.00	100.	200.
302	**2 Drachmai**			
	1917 (-old date 21.12.1885). Ovpt. on #41.	25.00	125.	250.

ΒΑΣΙΛΕΙΟΝ ΤΗΣ ΕΛΛΑΔΟΣ

KINGDOM OF GREECE

1917-20 ND ISSUE

#303-307 arms of Kg. George I. Printer: Aspiotis Freres.

		VG	VF	UNC
303	**50 Lepta**			
	ND (1920). Blue. Standing Athena at ctr. Back blue; ancient coin at l. and r.			
	a. Square perforations.	2.00	7.50	20.00
	b. Zig-zag perforations.	4.00	10.00	40.00

		VG	VF	UNC
304	**1 Drachma**			
	27.10.1917. Brown. Hermes seated at ctr. Back blue.			
	a. Brown on gold unpt. W/o inner line in diamond surrounding Hermes, diamond dk. brown.	2.50	10.00	30.00
	b. Darker brown w/o unpt. Inner line in diamond surrounding Hermes, diamond brown.	1.00	3.00	17.50

		VG	VF	UNC
305	**1 Drachma**			
	ND (1918). Brown. Pericles at r. Back green; medal at ctr.	3.00	15.00	50.00
306	**2 Drachmai**			
	27.10.1917. Blue and brown. Like #304. Back brown.	3.00	15.00	50.00
307	**2 Drachmai**			
	ND (1918). Black on gold unpt. Pericles at l. Back brown; ancient coin at middle l. and r.	12.00	60.00	150.

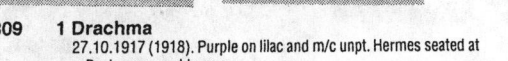

1917 (1918) ISSUE

#308-312 printer: BWC.

Note: All issues w/1917 date were released in 1918.

		VG	VF	UNC
308	**1 Drachma**			
	27.10.1917 (1918). Black on lt. green and pink unpt. Homer at ctr. Back green and lt. brown.	4.00	12.00	80.00

		VG	VF	UNC
309	**1 Drachma**			
	27.10.1917 (1918). Purple on lilac and m/c unpt. Hermes seated at r. Back green and brown.	2.00	6.00	40.00

		VG	VF	UNC
310	**2 Drachmai**			
	27.10.1917 (1918). Blue on brown and orange unpt. Zeus at l. Back green.	4.00	12.00	80.00

		VG	VF	UNC
311	**2 Drachmai** 27.10.1917 (1918). Red-brown on m/c unpt. Orpheus w/lyre at ctr. Back blue and lilac.	5.00	25.00	120.

1918 Issue

		VG	VF	UNC
312	**5 Drachmai** 14.6.1918. Green and m/c. Athena at l. Back purple and red. (Not issued).	200.	500.	1250.

ΕΛΛΑΣ

1922 ND Postage Stamp Currency Issue

		VG	VF	UNC
313	**10 Lepta** ND (1922). Brown. Hermes. Same design in reverse on back. Postage stamp of the 1911-21 issue (Michel #162, Scott #202).			
	a. Square perforations.	2.00	7.50	20.00
	b. Zig-zag perforations.	2.00	6.00	15.00

ΒΑΣΙΛΕΙΟΝ ΤΗΣ ΕΛΛΑΔΟΕ (χοντινυεδ)

1940 Issue

		VG	VF	UNC
314	**10 Drachmai** 6.4.1940. Blue on green and lt. brown unpt. Ancient coin w/Demeter at l. Back blue and brown; university at ctr.	.10	.25	2.00

		VG	VF	UNC
315	**20 Drachmai** 6.4.1940. Green on lt. lilac and orange unpt. Ancient coin w/Poseidon at l. Back purple and green; Parthenon at ctr.	.10	.25	2.00

ΕΛΛΗΝΙΚΝ ΠΟΛΙΤΕΙΑ

Greek State (resumed)

1941 Issue

#316-319 printer: Aspiotis - ELKA.

		VG	VF	UNC
316	**50 Lepta** 18.6.1941. Red and black on lt. brown unpt. Nike of Samothrake at l. Church on back.	.25	.50	2.00

		VG	VF	UNC
317	**1 Drachma** 18.6.1941. Red and blue on gray unpt. Aristotle at l. Back blue and brown; ancient coin at ctr.	.25	.50	2.00

		VG	VF	UNC
318	**2 Drachmai** 18.6.1941. Purple and black on lt. brown unpt. Ancient coin of Alexander at l. Back blue and gray; ancient coin at ctr.	.25	.50	2.00

		VG	VF	UNC
319	**5 Drachmai** 18.6.1941. Black and red on pale yellow unpt. 3 women of Knossos at ctr. Back yellow and brown; column at ctr.	.25	.50	2.00

ΒΑΣΙΛΕΙΟΝ ΤΗΣ ΕΛΛΑΔΟΣ

Kingdom of Greece (resumed)

1944; 1945 Issue

		VG	VF	UNC
320	**1 Drachma** 9.11.1944. Blue on green unpt. Back blue; Phoenix at ctr.	.25	.50	2.0

		VG	VF	UNC
321	**5 Drachmai** 15.1.1945. Brown and yellow-orange.	.25	.50	2.0
322	**10 Drachmai** 9.11.1944. Brown on green and orange unpt. Laborer at l. and r. Church at ctr. on back.	.25	.50	2.0

		VG	VF	UNC
323	**20 Drachmai** 9.11.1944. Blue on orange unpt. Zeus on ancient coin at ctr. Angel at ctr. on back.	.25	.50	2.00

1950 ISSUE

		VG	VF	UNC
324	**100 Drachmai** 1950-53. Blue on orange unpt. Constantine at ctr. Church at ctr. on back.			
	a. 10.7.1950.	.25	1.00	4.00
	b. 1.11.1953.	.25	1.25	4.50

		VG	VF	UNC
325	**500 Drachmai** 1950-53. Green on brown unpt. Byzantine coin at l. Church at ctr. on back.			
	a. 10.7.1950.	.25	1.00	4.00
	b. 1.11.1953.	.50	2.50	7.50

		VG	VF	UNC
326	**1000 Drachmai** 1950-53. Brown on orange and green unpt. Ancient coin at l. and r. Back brown and pink; stone carving of a lion at ctr.			
	a. 10.7.1950.	.25	1.50	4.50
	b. 1.11.1953.	.50	2.50	7.50

ITALIAN OCCUPATION - WWII

CASSA MEDITERRANEA DI CREDITO PER LA GRECIA

1941 ISSUE

#M1-M4 Hermes at r. on back. Circulated 1941-44.

		VG	VF	UNC
M1	**5 Drachmai** ND (1941). Green. Wheat at l.	2.00	12.50	40.00

		VG	VF	UNC
M2	**10 Drachmai** ND (1941). Red-orange. Prow of ancient ship at l.	2.00	15.00	50.00
M3	**50 Drachmai** ND (1941). Blue. Wheat at l.	2.00	15.00	65.00
M4	**100 Drachmai** ND (1941). Brown on orange unpt. Prow of ship at l.	2.50	17.50	70.00

#M5-M10 Michaelangelo's *David* at l.

		VG	VF	UNC
M5	**500 Drachmai** ND (1941). Dk. green.	5.00	30.00	175.
M6	**1000 Drachmai** ND (1941). Lt. brown.	7.00	20.00	100.
M7	**5000 Drachmai** ND (1941). Lilac.	10.00	50.00	250.

		VG	VF	UNC
M8	**10,000 Drachmai** ND (1941). Gray.	25.00	75.00	350.
M9	**20,000 Drachmai** ND (1941). Blue.	25.00	125.	450.

IONIAN ISLANDS

BIGLIETTO A CORSO LEGALE PER LE ISOLE JONIE

1941 ND ISSUE

#M11-M18 issued for the Ionian Islands.

		VG	VF	UNC
M11	**1 Drachma** ND (1941). Dk. green. Back w/tan unpt.	1.50	10.00	40.00

		VG	VF	UNC
M12	**5 Drachmai** ND (1941). Red. Alexander at l. Ancient picture at ctr. on back.	5.00	15.00	60.00
M13	**10 Drachmai** ND (1941). Green. Like #M12.	7.50	15.00	70.00
M14	**50 Drachmai** ND (1941). Brown. Old man at l.	7.50	15.00	75.00

		VG	VF	UNC
M15	**100 Drachmai** ND (1941). Blue. Like #M14.	7.50	15.00	75.00
M16	**500 Drachmai** ND (1941). Lilac on blue unpt. Caesar hd. at l. Ancient frieze of 2 horsemen on back.			
	a. Issued note.	15.00	50.00	150.
	b. Blue Imperial handstamp w/sign. at l.	100.	500.	1000.
M17	**1000 Drachmai** ND (1941). Brown. Like #M16.			
	a. Issued note.	2.50	10.00	45.00
	b. Blue Imperial handstamp w/sign. at l.	100.	500.	1000.

		VG	VF	UNC
M18	**5000 Drachmai** ND (1941). Blue on gray unpt. Like #M16. Ionian emblems and landscape at ctr. on back.			
	a. Issued note.	15.00	75.00	250.
	b. Blue Imperial handstamp w/sign. at l.	100.	500.	1000.

GERMAN OCCUPATION - WWII

GERMAN ARMED FORCES

AUXILIARY PAYMENT CERTIFICATES

#M19-M22 issued for the German Armed Forces.

German Nazi (3 varieties), Salonika-Aegean and Greek handstamps on back of Germany #M32-M35.

		VG	VF	UNC
M19	**1 Pfennig** ND. Blue. Stamped on Germany #M32.	4.00	20.00	50.00

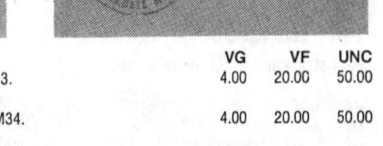

		VG	VF	UNC
M20	**5 Pfennig** ND. Red. Stamped on Germany #M33.	4.00	20.00	50.00
M21	**10 Pfennig** ND. Green. Stamped on Germany #M34.	4.00	20.00	50.00
M22	**50 Pfennig** ND. Orange. Stamped on Germany #M35.	30.00	150.	300.

GREECE

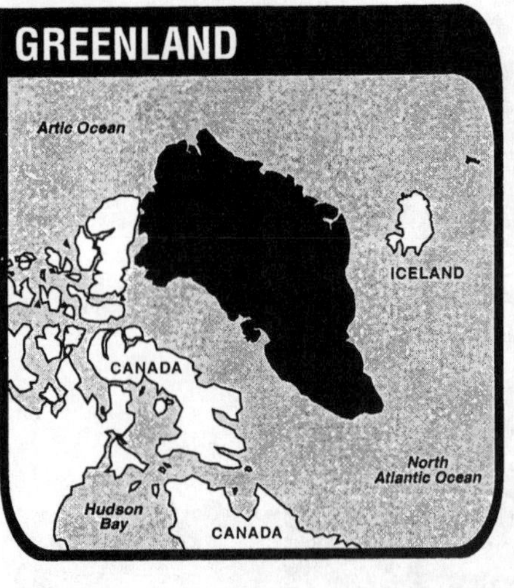

Greenland, an integral part of the Danish realm, is a huge island situated between the North Atlantic Ocean and the Polar Sea, almost entirely within the Artic Circle. It has an area of 840,000 sq. mi. (2,175,600 sq. km.) and a population of 56,087. Capital: Godthab. Greenland is the world's only source of natural cryolite, a fluoride of sodium and aluminum important in making aluminum. Fish products and minerals are exported.

Eric the Red discovered Greenland in 982 and established the first settlement in 986. Greenland was a republic until 1261, when the sovereignty of Norway was extended to the island. The original colony was abandoned about 1400 when increasing cold interfered with the breeding of cattle. Successful recolonization was undertaken by Denmark in 1721. In 1921 Denmark extended its claim to include the entire island, and made it a colony of the crown in 1924. The island's colonial status was abolished by amendment to the Danish constitution on June 5, 1953, and Greenland became an integral part of the Kingdom of Denmark. It has been an autonomous state since May 1, 1979.

RULERS:

Danish

MONETARY SYSTEM:

1 Rigsbankdaler = 96 Skilling to 1874
1 Krone = 48 Skilling
1 Krone = 100 Óre, 1874-

DANISH ADMINISTRATION

KONGEL. GRØNLANDSKE HANDEL

1803 ISSUE

#A1-A4 value text at upper r. Julianehaab District.

		Good	Fine	XF
A1	**12 Skilling** 1803.	600.	1600.	3000.

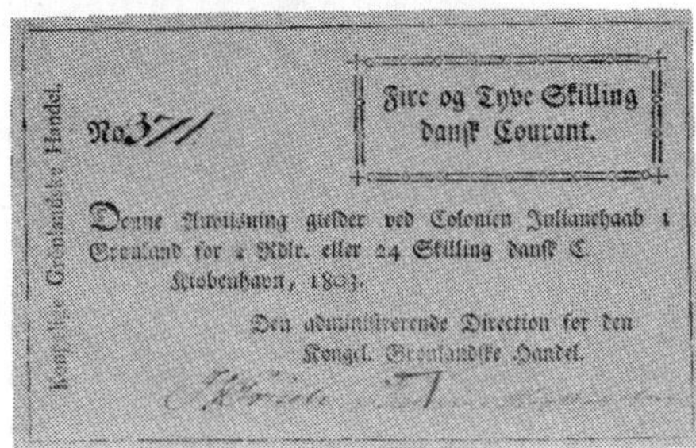

		Good	Fine	XF
A2	**24 Skilling** 1803.	600.	1800.	3500.

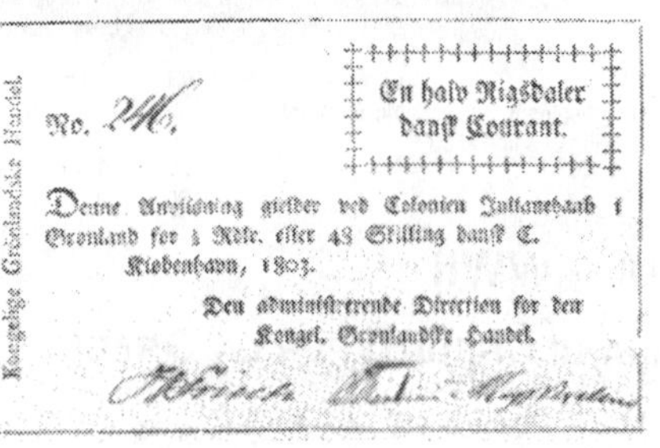

		Good	Fine	XF
A3	**1/2 Rigsdaler** 1803.	600.	1500.	3000.
A4	**1 Rigsdaler** 1803.	600.	1500.	—

Note: An 1801 issue (possibly handwritten) is reported.

HANDELSSTEDERNE I GRØNLAND

1804 ISSUE

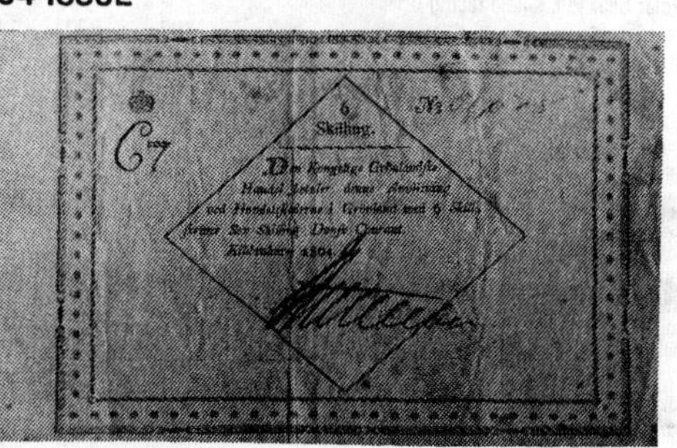

		Good	Fine	XF
A5	**6 Skilling** 1804. Text in diamond at ctr.	275.	650.	1200.
A6	**12 Skilling** 1804. Similar to #A5.	450.	900.	1400.

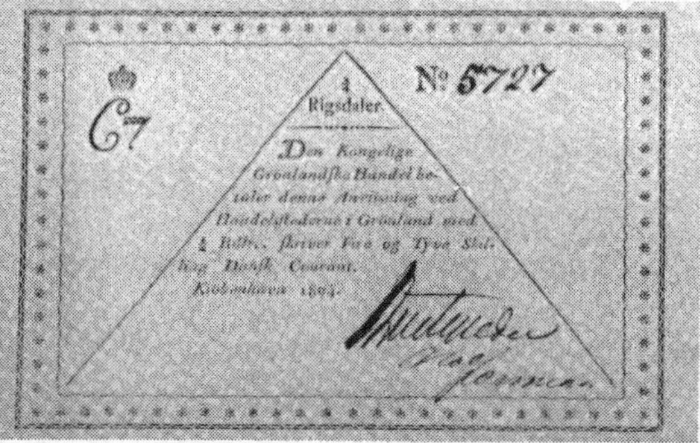

		Good	Fine	XF
A7	**1/4 Rigsdaler** 1804. Text in triangle at ctr.	450.	900.	2000.
A8	**1/2 Rigsdaler** 1804. Similar to #A7.	475.	1000.	2200.
A9	**1 Rigsdaler** 1804.	500.	1050.	2400.

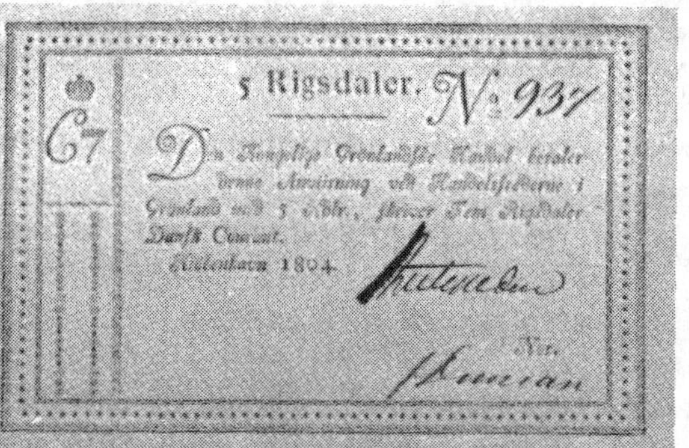

		Good	Fine	XF
A10	**5 Rigsdaler** 1804.	550.	1150.	3000.

1819 ISSUE

		Good	Fine	XF
A11	**6 Skilling** 1819.	—	—	—
A12	**12 Skilling** 1819.	—	—	—
A13	**24 Skilling** 1819.	—	—	—
A14	**1 Rigsbankdaler** 1819.	—	—	—

1841 ISSUE

		Good	Fine	XF
A19	**6 Skilling** 1841. a. Issued note. r. Remainder.	— —	— —	— —
A20	**12 Skilling** 1841.	—	—	—
A21	**24 Skilling** 1841.	—	—	—
A22	**1 Rigsbankdaler** 1841.	—	—	—

1837 ISSUE

		Good	Fine	XF
A15	**6 Skilling** 1837.	—	—	—
A16	**12 Skilling** 1837.	—	—	—
A17	**24 Skilling** 1837.	—	—	—
A18	**1 Rigsbankdaler** 1837.	—	—	—

1844 ISSUE

		Good	Fine	XF
A23	**6 Skilling** 1844.	—	—	—
A24	**12 Skilling** 1844.	—	—	—
A25	**24 Skilling** 1844.	—	—	—
A26	**1 Rigsbankdaler** 1844.	—	—	—

1848 ISSUE

		Good	Fine	XF
A27	**6 Skilling** 1848.	—	—	—
A28	**12 Skilling** 1848.	—	—	—
A29	**24 Skilling** 1848.	—	—	—
A30	**1 Rigsbankdaler** 1848.	—	—	—

1853 ISSUE

		Good	Fine	XF
A31	**6 Skilling** 1853.	—	—	—
A32	**1 Rigsbankdaler** 1853.	—	—	—

1856 ISSUE

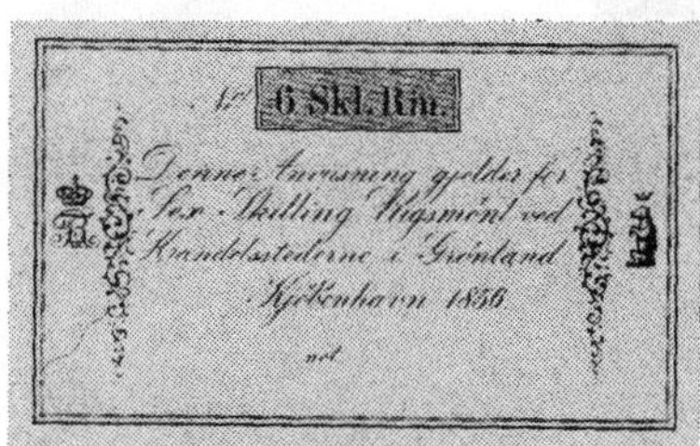

		Good	Fine	XF
A33	**6 Skilling R.M.** 1856. Red on blue paper. a. Issued note. r. Unsigned remainder.	500. —	900. Unc	2000. 350.

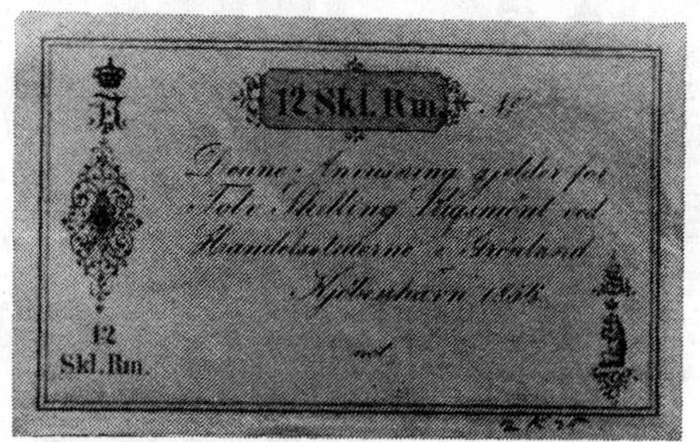

		Good	Fine	XF
A34	**12 Skilling R.M.** 1856. a. Issued note. r. Unsigned remainder.	750. —	— Unc	— 350.
A35	**24 Skilling R.M.** 1856. Red and blue. a. Issued note. r. Unsigned remainder.	850. —	2000. Unc	4500. 600.
A36	**1 Rigsbankdaler** 1856. Blue and red on blue paper. a. Issued note. r. Remainder.	1000. —	3000. Unc	— 700.

1874 ISSUE

#A37-A39 monogram at l., crowned small polar bear at r.

		Good	Fine	XF
A37	**50 Øre** 1874. Gray. a. Issued note. r. Unsigned remainder.	400. —	800. Unc	1600. 350.

		Good	Fine	XF
A38	**1 Krone**			
	1874. Blue.			
	a. Issued note.	450.	1250.	2000.
	r. Unsigned remainder.	—	Unc	450.

1875 Issue

		Good	Fine	XF
A39	**25 Øre**			
	1875. Lt. brown.			
	a. Issued note.	225.	600.	1500.
	r. Unsigned remainder.	—	Unc	400.

1883; 1887 Issue

		Good	Fine	XF
A40	**1 Krone**	400.	900.	1500.
	1883. Blue. Crowned polar bears at l. and r.			
A40A	**1 Krone**			
	1887. Like #A40.	325.	725.	1125.

		Good	Fine	XF
A41	**5 Kronen**			
	1887. Green. Polar bear at l. facing l.			
	a. Serial # handwritten.	2000.	5000.	10,000.
	b. Serial # printed.	8000.	14,000.	—
	r. Unsigned remainder.	—	Unc	550.

1888 Issue

		Good	Fine	XF
1	**50 Øre**			
	1888. Brown. Greenland seal on ice slab at ctr. Polar bear in l. shield facing r.			
	a. Serial # handwritten.	400.	900.	2600.
	b. Serial # printed.	400.	1100.	2000.

1892 Issue

		Good	Fine	XF
2	**25 Øre**			
	1892. Black. Polar bear in l. shield facing r.			
	a. Serial # handwritten.	200.	600.	2000.
	b. Serial # printed.	150.	500.	1000.

1897 Issue

		Good	Fine	XF
5	**1 Krone**			
	1897; 1905. Blue. Polar bear in l. shield facing l.			
	a. 1897.	300.	900.	1400.
	b. 1905.	125.	150.	700.

1905 Issue

		Good	Fine	XF
4	**25 Øre**			
	1905. Red. Polar bear in l. shield facing l.			
	a. Sign. Ryberg-Krenchel.	60.00	175.	500.
	b. Sign. Ryberg-Bergh.	17.50	45.00	100.
	c. As a. With star.	—	—	—

Den Kongelige Grønlandske Handel

1911 Provisional Issue

		Good	Fine	XF
6	**1 Krone**			
	1911 (-old date 1905). Blue.			
	a. Ovpt.: *Den kgl. grønlandske Handel 1911* across lower ctr. on #5.	600.	1200.	3000
	b. W/additional ovpt.: *Kolonien Holstensborg* at top.	1000.	2000.	4000

1911 Issue

#7, 8, 10: 2 wmk. varieties.

		Good	Fine	XF
7	**25 Øre**			
	1911. Red. Eider duck on rock in water at ctr.	700.	1800.	2500
8	**50 Øre**			
	1911. Brown. Greenland seal on ice at ctr.	325.	900.	1650

		Good	Fine	XF
9	**1 Krone**			
	1911. Blue. Reindeer in mountains at ctr.	400.	1250.	250
10	**5 Kroner**			
	1911. Green. Polar bear on ice at ctr. Outer edges perforated.			
	a. W/o ovpt.	500.	1250.	225
	b. W/ovpt.: *Kolonien Holstensborg* at top.	800.	2000.	-

Styrelsen af Kolonierne i Grønland

State Notes

1913 Issue

		VG	VF	UNC
11	**25 Øre**			
	ND (1913). Red. Common eider duck on rock in water at ctr.	17.50	65.00	12

		VG	VF	UNC
12	**50 Øre** ND (1913). Brown. Saddleback seal on ice at ctr.	25.00	80.00	200.

		VG	VF	UNC
13	**1 Krone** ND (1913). Blue. Reindeer in mountains at ctr.	35.00	125.	275.
14	**5 Kroner** ND (1913). Dark green on blue green unpt. Polar bear on ice at ctr. Back blue-green.	60.00	175.	300.
14A	**5 Kroner** (500 pieces made available in 1981).	—	—	150.

GRØNLANDS STYRELSE

STATE NOTES

1926-52 ISSUE

15-17 w/text: *GRØNLANDS STYRELSE* on all sides of face and around map at ctr. on back.

		VG	VF	UNC
15	**5 Kroner** ND (1926-52). Green. Polar bear on ice at ctr.			
	a. Green unpt. fine screening through border. ND (1926).	50.00	250.	900.
	b. Green unpt. of diagonal lines; white border. ND (1945)	35.00	140.	400.

		VG	VF	UNC
16	**10 Kroner** ND (1926-52). Brown. Hump-back whale at ctr.			
	a. Green unpt. fine screening through border. ND (1926).	50.00	275.	1100.
	b. Brown unpt of diagonal lines, white border. ND (1945).	45.00	200.	450.
17	**50 Kroner** ND (1926-52). Lilac. Clipper ship at ctr.			
	a. Lilac unpt fine screening through border. ND (1926).	2250.	4500.	18,000.
	b. Lilac unpt of diagonal lines; white border. ND (1945).	1250.	2250.	—

DEN KONGELIGE GRØNLANDSKE HANDEL (RESUMED)

1953 ISSUE

18-20 w/text: *DEN KONGELIGE GRÖNLANDSKE HANDEL* at l. and r. margin, across bottom, and around map at ctr. on back.

		VG	VF	UNC
18	**5 Kroner** ND (1953-67). Green. Similar to #15.			
	a. Issued note.	15.00	40.00	125.
	s. Specimen.	—	—	—

		VG	VF	UNC
19	**10 Kroner** ND (1953-67). Brown. Similar to #16.			
	a. Issued note.	15.00	60.00	250.
	s. Specimen.	—	—	—

		VG	VF	UNC
20	**50 Kroner** ND (1953-67). Lilac. Similar to #17.			
	a. Issued note.	75.00	300.	800.
	s. Specimen.	—	—	—

KREDITSEDDEL

CREDIT NOTES

1953 ISSUE

		VG	VF	UNC
21	**100 Kroner** 16.1.1953. Black, orange and blue-green. Portr. K. Rasmussen at l., dog sled, lake and hill at lower r. Back red; crown at l. ctr., map at r.			
	a. Issued note. Sign: A.W. Nielsen.	150.	500.	1500.
	b. Issued note. Sign: Hans C. Christensen.	150.	400.	800.
	s. Specimen.	—	—	600.

Note: Since 1968 only Danish currency is in circulation.

MILITARY

GRØNLANDS ADMINISTRATION

1940'S TRADE CERTIFICATES

#M1-M4 are perforated, narrow cardboard tokens w/denomination and *Grl. Adm.* Issued for American troops stationed in Greenland during World War II.

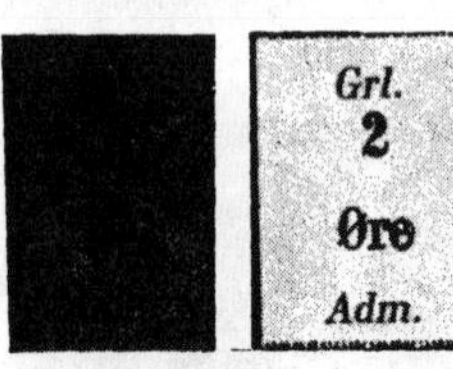

		VG	VF	UNC
M1	**1 Øre** ND. Brown cardboard.	20.00	50.00	125.
M2	**2 Øre** ND. Yellow cardboard.	20.00	50.00	125.
M3	**5 Øre** ND. Violet cardboard.	35.00	100.	300.
M4	**10 Øre** ND. White cardboard.	35.00	110.	275.

1941 ND TRADE CERTIFICATES

#M5-M7 embossed circular seal w/crown over *GRØNLANDS ADMINISTRATION* at l.

		VG	VF	UNC
M5	**1 Skilling** ND (1941). Red. Like #M6.	200.	400.	850.

		VG	VF	UNC
M6	**5 Skilling** ND (1941). Blue.	225.	450.	1000.
M7	**20 Skilling** ND (1941). Green. Like #M6.	25.00	65.00	150.

Note: A quantity of #M7 was made available during 1981-83.

1942 ND TRADE CERTIFICATES

#M8-M10 black handstamp: *GRØNLANDS ADMINISTRATION* around crown at l.

		VG	VF	UNC
M8	**1 Skilling** ND (1942). Red. Like #M10.	—	—	20.00
M9	**5 Skilling** ND (1942). Blue. Like #M10.	—	—	20.00

		VG	VF	UNC
M10	**20 Skilling** ND (1942). Green.	—	—	20.00

Note: A quantity of #M8-M10 was made available in 1981-83.

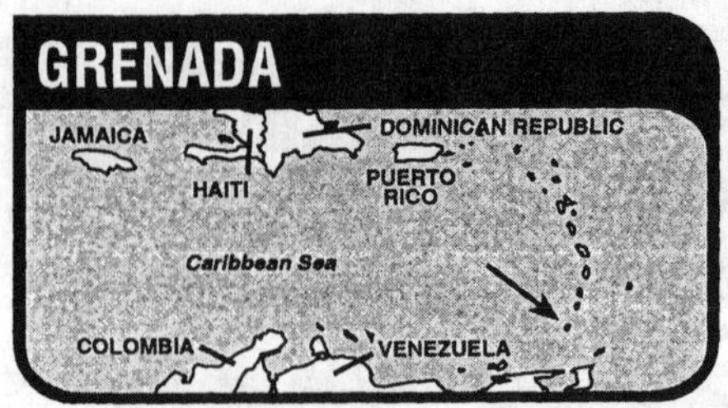

Grenada, located in th Windward islands of th Caribbean Sea 90 miles (14 km.) north of Trinidad, has (wit Carriacou and Petit Martinique an area of 133 sq. mi. (344 sc km.) and a population of 99,70C Capital: St. George's. Grenada i the smallest independent natio in the Western Hemisphere.

Columbus discovered Grenad in 1498 during his third voyage t the Americas. Spain failed t colonize the island, and in 162 granted it to the British who sol it to the French who colonized it in 1650. Grenada was captured by the British in 1763, retaken b the French in 1779, and finally ceded to the British in 1783. In 1958 Grenada joined the Federatio of the West Indies, which was dissolved in 1962. In 1967, it became an internally self-governin British associated state. Full independence was attained on Feb. 4, 1974. Grenada is a member c the Commonwealth of Nations. The prime minister is the Head of Government.

RULERS:

British

MONETARY SYSTEM:

1 Shilling = 12 Pence
1 Pound = 20 Shillings to 1970
1 Dollar = 100 Cents
1 British West Indies Dollar = 4 Shillings-2 Pence

BRITISH ADMINISTRATION

GOVERNMENT OF GRENADA

1920 ISSUE

#1-3 portr. Kg. George V at r. on face. Sailing ship at ctr. on back. Printer: TDLR.

		Good	Fine	XF
1	**2 Shillings 6 Pence** 1.7.1920. Red and olive-gray. Back olive. Rare.	—	—	—

		Good	Fine	XF
2	**5 Shillings** 1.7.1920. Blue and green. Back brown. Rare.	—	—	—
3	**10 Shillings** 1.7.1920. Blue-gray and green. Back blue. Rare.	—	—	—

Note: For earlier commercial bank issues see Volume I. For later issues see British Caribbean Territories and East Caribbean States.

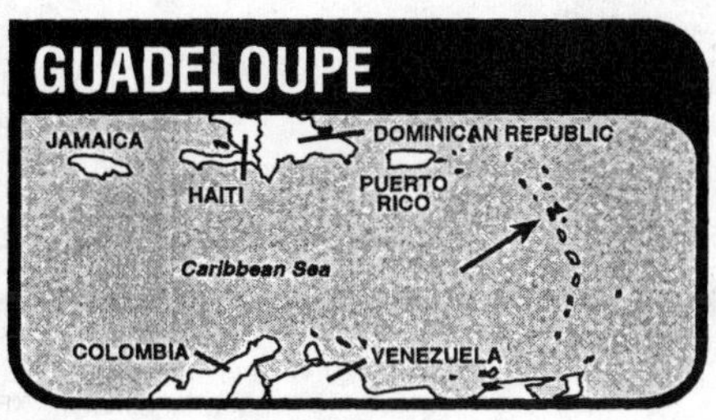

The French Overseas Department of Guadeloupe, located in the Leeward Islands of the West Indies about 300 miles (493 km.) southeast of Puerto Rico, has an area of 687 sq. mi. (1,779 sq. km.) and a population of 425,000. Actually it is two islands separated by a narrow salt water stream: volcanic Basse-Terre to the west and the flatter limestone formation of Grande-Terre to the east. Capital: Basse-Terre, on the island of that name. The principal industries are agriculture, the distillation of liquors, and tourism. Sugar, bananas and rum are exported.

Guadeloupe was discovered by Columbus in 1493 and settled in 1635 by two Frenchmen, L'Olive and Dupiessis, who took possession in the name of the French Company of the Islands of America. When repeated efforts by private companies to colonize the island failed, it was relinquished to the French crown in 1674, and established as a dependency of Martinique. The British occupied the island on two occasions, 1759-1763 and 1810-1816, before it passed permanently to France. A colony until 1946, Guadeloupe was then made an overseas territory of the French Union. In 1958 it voted to become an Overseas Department within the new French Community.

Grande-Terre, as noted in the first paragraph, is the eastern member of two-island Guadeloupe. Isle Desirade (La Desirade), located east of Grande-Terre, and Les Saintes (Iles des Saintes), located south of Basse-Terre, are dependencies of Guadeloupe.

RULERS

French

MONETARY SYSTEM

1 Franc = 100 Centimes
1 Nouveau Franc = 100 "old" Francs, 1960-

French Administration

Banque de Pret

1848 Issue

		Good	Fine	XF
A1	**5 Francs** 1848. Rare.	—	—	—
A2	**10 Francs** 1848. Rare.	—	—	—
A3	**50 Francs** 1848. Rare.	—	—	—
A4	**100 Francs** 1848. Rare.	—	—	—
A5	**500 Francs** 1848. Rare.	—	—	—
A6	**1000 Francs** 1848. Rare.	—	—	—

1851 Issue

		Good	Fine	XF
A7	**5 Francs** 13.5.1851. Rare.	—	—	—
A8	**10 Francs** 13.5.1851. Rare.	—	—	—

Guadeloupe Trésor Colonial

Bons de Caisse

Décret du 25.5.1854

		Good	Fine	XF
A12	**1 Franc** 1.6.1854. Black on lt. green paper. Uniface. Rare.	—	—	—

Décrets des 13.4.1855 et 3.3.1858

		Good	Fine	XF
A12A	**1 Franc** 6.11.1863. Red. Rare.	—	—	—

Décrets des 23.4.1855, 3.3.1858 et 2.6.1863

#A13-A15 various date and sign. varieties. Sailing ship at lower l. Border of trees, barrels, arms etc. Uniface.

		Good	Fine	XF
A13	**1 Franc** 6.3.1863; 13.11.1863; 15.11.1863. Red. Rare.	—	—	—
A14	**2 Francs** 9.12.1864. Red. Rare.	—	—	—
A15	**5 Francs** ND. (Not issued). Rare.	—	—	—

Guadeloupe et Dependances, Trésor Colonial

Décret du 18.8.1884

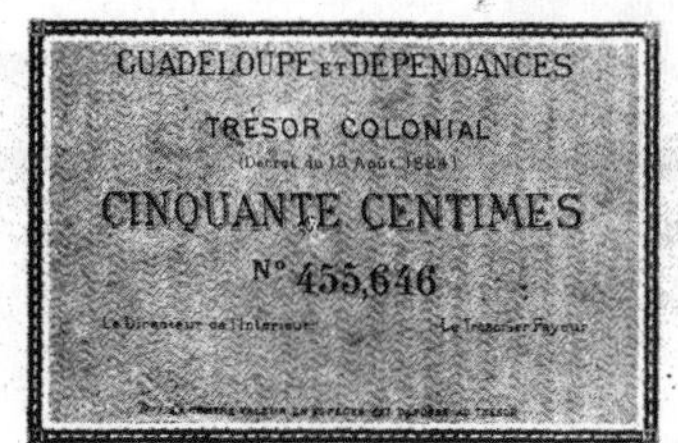

		Good	Fine	XF
1	**50 Centimes** D.1884. Brown.			
	a. Issued note.	—	—	—
	r. Unsigned remainder.	100.	400.	—
1A	**1 Franc** D.1884. Black on gray unpt. Format as #1.	—	—	—

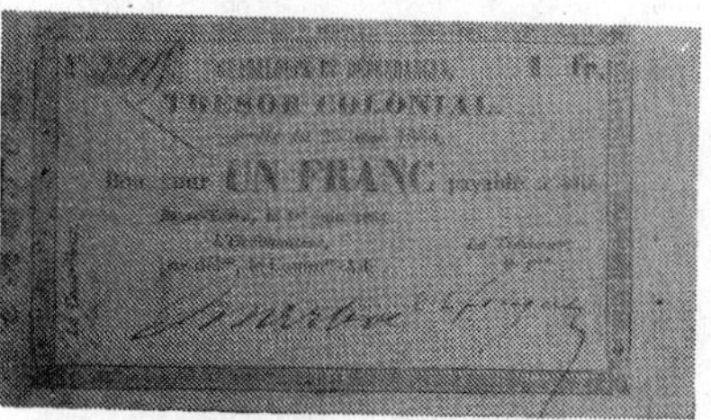

		Good	Fine	XF
2	**1 Franc** D.1884. Different format.			
	a. Issued note.	—	—	—
	r. Unsigned remainder.	150.	425.	—
3	**2 Francs** D.1884. Brown unpt. Uniface.			
	a. Issued note.	—	—	—
	r. Unsigned remainder.	175.	500.	—

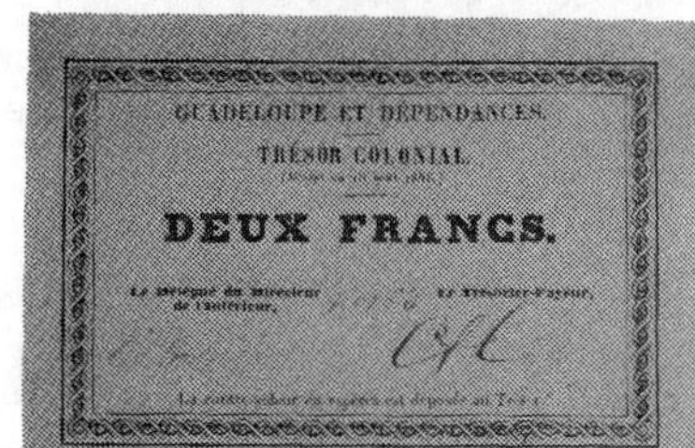

		Good	Fine	XF
3A	**2 Francs** D.1884. Black on purple paper. Uniface. Rare.	—	—	—

		Good	Fine	XF
4	**5 Francs** D.1884. Uniface. Format as #1.			
	a. Blue on green unpt.	—	—	—
	b. Black on green paper. Rare.	—	—	—
	r. Unsigned remainder.	250.	650.	—
5	**10 Francs** D.1884. Black.			
	a. Cream paper. Rare.	—	—	—
	b. Brown paper. Rare.	—	—	—

Banque de la Guadeloupe

Law of 1874

		Good	Fine	XF
6	**5 Francs** L.1874. Blue. Like #7. Rare.	—	—	—

LAW OF 1901

		Good	Fine	XF
7	**5 Francs** L.1901 (1928-45). Red. Man at l., woman at r. Law date on back.			
	a. Sign. A. Mollenthiel.	30.00	75.00	200.
	b. Sign. C. Damoiseau. (1928).	30.00	70.00	175.
	c. Sign. H. Marconnet. (1934, 1943).	15.00	40.00	130.
	d. Sign. G. Devineau. (1944).	20.00	55.00	150.
	e. Sign. A. Boudin. (1945).	10.00	30.00	120.

		Good	Fine	XF
8	**25 Francs** ND (1920-44). Black and red. Scales and cornucopias at ctr. of lower frame. 6 sign. varieties.	150.	500.	—

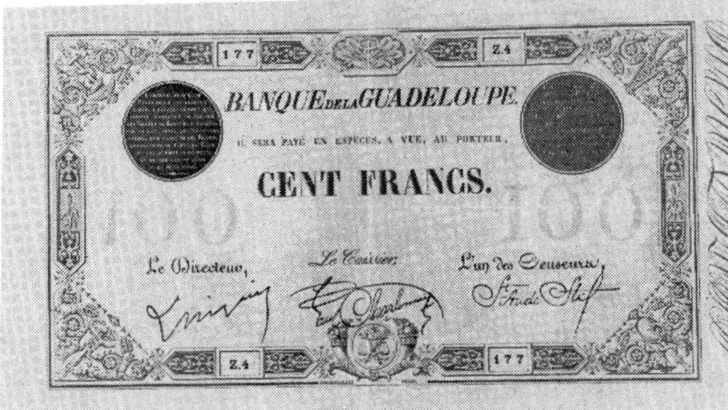

		Good	Fine	XF
9	**100 Francs** ND (1920-21; 1925). Red and blue. Like #8. 2 sign. varieties.	225.	800.	—
9A	**250 Francs** ND. Black. Like #8. Rare.	—	—	—
10	**500 Francs** ND (1887-1929). Black and red. Standing figures at l. and r. 5 sign. varieties.			
	a. Wmk: Lion and snake. *COLONIES* text. Rare.	—	—	—
	b. Wmk: Numerals of value *500*. Rare.	—	—	—

LAW OF 1901, 1920 ISSUE

		VG	VF	UNC
11	**50 Centimes** 1920. Blue on purple unpt.	35.00	200.	450.

		Good	Fine	XF
12	**1 Franc** 1920. Brown on aqua unpt.	45.00	225.	500.

		Good	Fine	XF
13	**2 Francs** 1920. Green on orange unpt.	65.00	300.	650.

		Good	Fine	XF
14	**25 Francs** ND (1934; 1944). M/c. Woman w/wreath at ctr., flowers on top, fruit on bottom. 2 sign. varieties.	40.00	150.	500.

1920 (ND) PROVISIONAL ISSUE

Ovpt: *BANQUE DE LA GUADELOUPE* on unissued Banque de France notes (old dates of 1892-93).

15	**100 Francs** ND (1920-old dates 1892-93). Violet, blue and brown. Woman seated at l. and r. Ovpt. on France #65b. Rare.	—	—	—

1934 ND ISSUE

		Good	Fine	XF
16	**100 Francs** ND (1934; 1944). M/c. Woman w/staff at l., ship in background at lower ctr. r. 2 sign. varieties.	150.	400.	1500.

		Good	Fine	XF
17	**500 Francs** ND (1934). M/c. Like #16.	250.	750.	—

#18 *Deleted.* #19 *Deleted.* See #15.

EMERGENCY BANK CHECK ISSUES

#20A-20E early bank checks (ca. 1870-1900) w/partially printed date and value.

		Good	Fine	XF
20A	**50 Centimes** ca. 1870-1900. Printed partial dates 187x, 189x, 190x. Blue-green. Rare.	—	—	—
20B	**50 Centimes** ca. 1890-1900. Printed partial dates 189x, 190x. Orange-brown. Rare.	—	—	—

		Good	Fine	XF
20C	**1 Franc** ca. 1870-1900. Printed partial dates 187x, 190x. (1902 reported). Blue. Rare.	—	—	—
20D	**2 Francs** 189x; 190x. Red. Rare.	—	—	—
20E	**5 Francs** 187x; 2.4.1890. Black and red on tan unpt. Rare.	—	—	—

1940 EMERGENCY WWII BANK CHECK ISSUE

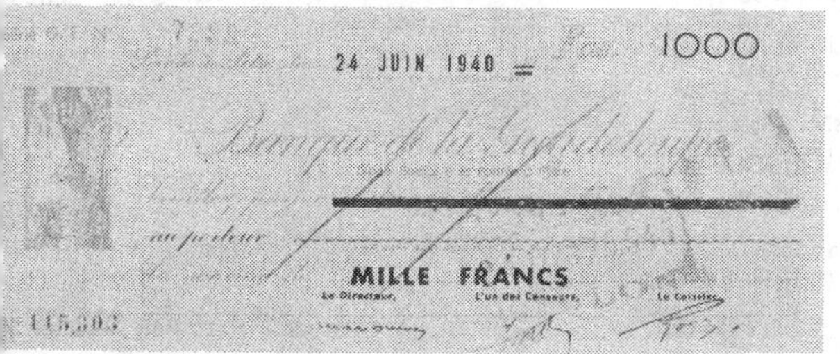

		Good	Fine	XF
20F	**1000 Francs** 24.6.1940; 27.1.1942. Purple. View of island w/2 sailing ships sideways at l. Printer: Fortin, Paris. Rare.	—	—	—

1942 ISSUE

#21-26A sign. varieties. Printer: E.A. Wright, Philadelphia, Pa., United States.

		VG	VF	UNC
21	**5 Francs** ND (1942). Black on yellow unpt. Columbus at ctr. Back red-brown.			
	a. Sign. G. Devineau w/title: *LE DIRECTEUR.*	35.00	175.	450.
	b. Sign. A. Boudin w/title: *LE DIRECTEUR.*	30.00	150.	400.
	s. Specimen.	—	—	185.

		VG	VF	UNC
22	**25 Francs** ND (1942). Black on green unpt. Map of Guadeloupe at l. Back blue; woman at ctr.			
	a. Sign. G. Devineau w/title: *LE DIRECTEUR.*	45.00	225.	550.
	b. Sign. A. Boudin w/title: *LE DIRECTEUR.*	40.00	175.	500.
	s. Specimen.	—	—	235.

		VG	VF	UNC
23	**100 Francs** ND (1942). Black on red-orange unpt. Oxcart at ctr. Back green; small sailing boat at ctr.			
	a. Sign. G. Devineau w/title: *LE DIRECTEUR.*	125.	375.	950.
	b. Sign. A. Boudin w/title: *LE DIRECTEUR.*	110.	350.	850.
	s. Specimen.	—	—	475.
24	**500 Francs** ND (1942). Black on red unpt. Sailing ship "Santa Maria" at l. Flying boat on back. 161 x 115mm.			
	a. Sign. H. Marconnet w/title: *LE DIRECTEUR.*	750.	1850.	—
	b. Sign. G. Devineau w/title: *LE DIRECTEUR.*	675.	1600.	—
	s. Specimen.	—	—	2000.

		VG	VF	UNC
25	**500 Francs** ND (1942). Face similar to #24. 150 x 85mm.			
	a. Issued note.	900.	2500.	—
	s. Specimen.	—	—	1500.

		VG	VF	UNC
26	**1000 Francs** ND (1942). Black on blue unpt. Bust of Karukera at ctr. Back orange on lt. red unpt. 178 x 117mm.			
	a. Sign. H. Marconnet w/title: *LE DIRECTEUR.*	750.	1500.	3000.
	b. Sign. G. Devineau w/title: *LE DIRECTEUR.*	675.	1350.	2250.
	s. Specimen.	—	—	1250.

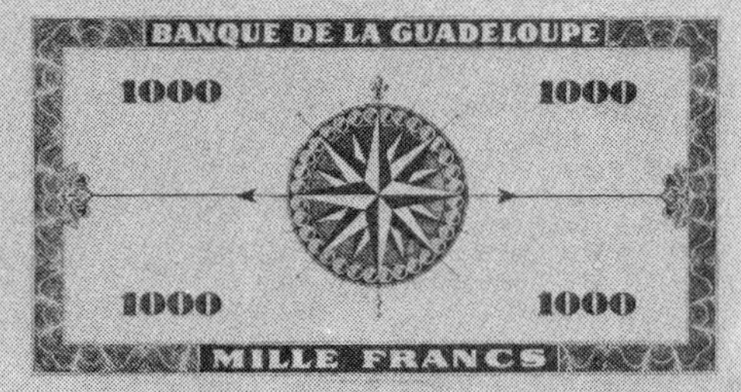

		VG	VF	UNC
26A	**1000 Francs** ND (1942). Similar to #26 but reduced size.			
	a. Issued note.	1200.	3000.	—
	s. Specimen.	—	—	1750.

CAISSE CENTRALE DE LA FRANCE D'OUTRE-MER

GUADELOUPE

1944 ISSUE

#27-30 ovpt: *GUADELOUPE*. English printing.

		VG	VF	UNC
27	**10 Francs** 2.2.1944. Purple. Marianne at ctr.			
	a. Issued note.	15.00	40.00	150.
	s. Specimen. W/regular serial #.	—	Unc	225.

		VG	VF	UNC
28	**20 Francs** 2.2.1944. Green. Marianne at ctr.			
	a. Issued note.	25.00	75.00	225.
	s. Specimen.	—	Unc	225.

		VG	VF	UNC
29	**100 Francs** 2.2.1944. Green on orange unpt. Marianne at ctr.			
	a. Issued note.	50.00	200.	650.
	s. Specimen.	—	Unc	450.

		VG	VF	UNC
30	**1000 Francs** 2.2.1944. Blue. Phoenix rising from flames. War/peace scenes on back.			
	a. W/o wmk.	400.	1400.	—
	b. Wmk: Marianne.	400.	1400.	—
	s. As a. Specimen.	—	—	1200.

1947-52 ND ISSUE

#31-40 ovpt: *GUADELOUPE*. French printing w/standard designs.

		VG	VF	UNC
31	**5 Francs** ND (1947-49). M/c. Bougainville at r.	2.50	9.00	85.00

		VG	VF	UNC
32	**10 Francs** ND (1947-49). M/c. Colbert at l., sailing ships at ctr. r.	2.50	15.00	110.
33	**20 Francs** ND (1947-1949. M/c. E. Gentil at r., 4 people w/huts at l. ctr.	3.00	20.00	140.
34	**50 Francs** ND (1947-49). M/c. B. d'Esnambuc at l., sailing ship at r.	4.00	25.00	225.

5	100 Francs	VG	VF	UNC
	ND (1947-49). M/c. La Bourdonnais at l., 2 women at r.	6.00	30.00	275.

6	500 Francs	VG	VF	UNC
	ND (1947-49). M/c. 2 women at r., sailboat at l.	25.00	200.	750.

	1000 Francs	VG	VF	UNC
	ND (1947-49). M/c. 2 women at r.			
	a. Issued note.	40.00	200.	850.
	s. Specimen.	—	—	350.
	5000 Francs			
	ND (1952). M/c. Gen. Schoelcher.			
	a. Issued note.	250.	650.	—
	s. Specimen.	—	—	325.

60 ND Issue

	1000 Francs	VG	VF	UNC
	ND (1960). M/c. Fishermen from the Antilles.			
	a. Issued note.	100.	275.	750.
	s. Specimen.	—	—	325.

40	5000 Francs	VG	VF	UNC
	ND (1960). M/c. Woman w/fruit bowl at ctr. r., palm trees at l.	200.	700.	—

1960 ND Provisional Issue

#41-44 ovpt: *GUADELOUPE* and new denomination.

41	1 Nouveau Franc on 100 Francs	VG	VF	UNC
	ND (1960). Ovpt. on #35.	10.00	55.00	400.
42	**5 Nouveaux Francs on 500 Francs**			
	ND (1960). Ovpt. on #36.	30.00	175.	750.

43	10 Nouveaux Francs on 1000 Fracs	VG	VF	UNC
	ND (1960). Ovpt. on #39.	100.	300.	950.
44	**50 Nouveaux Francs on 5000 Francs**			
	ND (1960). Ovpt. on #40.	200.	900.	—

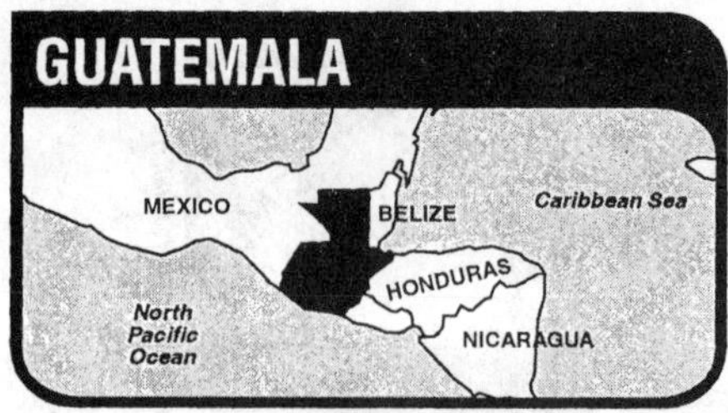

The Republic of Guatemala, the northernmost of the five Central American republics, has an area of 42,042 sq. mi. (108,889 sq. km.) and a population of 12.22 million. Capital: Guatemala City. The economy of Guatemala is heavily dependent on resources which are being developed. Coffee, cotton and bananas are exported.

Guatemala, once the site of the ancient Mayan civilization, was conquered by Pedro de Alvarado, the lieutenant of Cortes who undertook the conquest from Mexico. Skilled in strategy and cruelty, he progressed rapidly along the Pacific coastal lowlands to the highland plain of Quezaltenango where the decisive battle for Guatemala was fought. After routing the Mayan forces, he established the first capital of Guatemala in 1524.

Guatemala of the colonial period included all of Central America but Panama. Guatemala declared its independence of Spain in 1821 and was absorbed into the short-lived Mexican empire of Augustin Iturbide, 1822-23. From 1823 to 1839 Guatemala was a constituent state of the Central American Republic. Upon dissolution of the federation, Guatemala became an independent republic.

MONETARY SYSTEM:

1 Peso = 100 Centavos to 1924
1 Quetzal = 100 Centavos, 1924-

Note: Certain listings encompassing issues circulated by various bank and regional authorities are contained in Volume 1.

GOVERNMENT

TESORERÍA NACIONAL DE GUATEMALA

1881-85 ND FIRST ISSUE

#A1-A3 printer: CCBB.

		Good	Fine	XF
A1	**1 Peso** ND (ca.1881). Black on red unpt. Seated allegorical woman at lower l. and r., portr. Pres. J. Rufino Barrios at l. ctr., arms at ctr. r. Back green; Treasury seal.			
	a. Ovpt: *PAGADERO EN LA ADMINISTRACION DE COBAN* on back.	—	—	—
	b. Ovpt: *PAGADERO EN LA ADMINISTRACION DE ESQUINTLA* on back.	—	—	—
	c. Ovpt: *PAGADERO EN LA ADMINISTRACION DE MAZATENANGO* on back.	—	—	—
	d. Ovpt: *PAGADERO EN LA ADMINISTRACION DE QUEZAL TENANGO* on back.	—	—	—
A2	**5 Pesos** ND. Black. Portr. Pres. J. R. Barrios at lower l., allegorical woman at ctr., arms at lower r. Back green.	—	—	—

		Good	Fine	XF
A3	**10 Pesos** ND. Black. Portr. Pres. J. R. Barrios at upper l., arms at lower l., standing allegorical woman w/tablet inscribed: *30 DE JUNIO DE 1871.*	—	—	—

1882 ND SECOND ISSUE

#A4-A7 printer: ABNC.

		Good	Fine	XF
A4	**1 Peso** ND (ca.1882). Black on orange and olive unpt. Reclining woman w/book at l., arms at ctr., woman w/scales and cornucopia filled w/coins at r. Back green.			
	a. Black sign. W/o series, series A; B; C; E; plate A.	12.50	45.00	175.
	b. Red sign. Plate A.	20.00	60.00	225.
	s. Specimen.	—	Unc	225.

		Good	Fine	XF
A5	**5 Pesos** ND (ca.1882). Black on orange and blue unpt. Steam locomotive at l., arms at r. Black sign. Back blue. Series A; B; E.			
	a. Issued note.	45.00	175.	500.
	s. Specimen.	—	Unc	400.

		Good	Fine	XF
A6	**10 Pesos** ND (ca.1882). Black on green and red unpt. 2 cherubs at l., woman's head at ctr., arms at r. Back brown.			
	a. Red sign. Plate C.	85.00	275.	—
	b. Black sign. Series B; C; D; plate E.	85.00	275.	—
	s. Specimen.	—	Unc	600.

		Good	Fine	XF
A7	**25 Pesos** ND (ca.1888). Black on orange and yellow unpt. Arms at l., house in forest scene beneath, cherub at top ctr., allegorical woman holding wheat and sickle at ctr. r. Back orange. Specimen.			
	a. Issued note.	—	—	—
	p. Proof.	—	—	—
	s. Specimen.			

1890's Cedulas Fiscales (Fiscal Notes) Issue

#A21-A24 issued to facilitate payment of taxes.

		Good	Fine	XF
A21	**1 Peso Plata** 189x. Arms at ctr.	—	—	—
A22	**5 Pesos Plata** 189x. Reported not confirmed.	—	—	—
A23	**25 Pesos Plata** 189x. Reported not confirmed.	—	—	—
A24	**100 Pesos Plata** 189x. Reported not confirmed.	—	—	—

1902 Vales al Portador (Notes Payable to Bearer) Issue

#A31-A34 issued to pay customs duties on exportation of coffee.

		Good	Fine	XF
A31	**1 Peso** 6.8.1902. Reported not confirmed.	—	—	—
A32	**6 Pesos** 6.8.1902. Reported not confirmed.	—	—	—
A33	**100 Pesos** 6.8.1902. Reported not confirmed.	—	—	—
A34	**1000 Pesos** 6.8.1902. Arms at upper ctr.	—	—	—

Republic

Banco Central de Guatemala

Ley 7 de Julio de 1926

#6-10 w/engraved law date 7.7.1926. Printer: TDLR.

		Good	Fine	XF
	1 Quetzal 21.4.1927; 29.4.1927; 13.6.1927; 31.10.1928. Green on orange unpt. Portr. Gen J. María Orellana at l., workers loading bales w/steam crane in background. Monolith of Quirigua at ctr. on back.	158.	75.00	275.
	5 Quetzales 13.6.1927. 21.11.1927; 13.4.1928; 7.4.1934. Purple on lt. green and blue unpt. Workers by Gen. J. María Orellana at l. Town and mountains on back.	17.50	100.	400.

		Good	Fine	XF
	20 Quetzales 1927-45. Blue on yellow and green unpt. Portr. Gen. J. María Orellana at lower l., w/Mercury reclining at upper r. Palace of the Captains General on back.			
	a. W/o *Acuerdo de*. Sign. title *GERENTE* at r. 25.7.1927; 13.4.1928.	75.00	250.	650.
	b. *Acuerdo de*. Sign. title: *SUB-GERENTE* at r. 1.2.1945.	65.00	200.	500.

		Good	Fine	XF
	100 Quetzales L.1926. Dk. green on orange and yellow unpt. Portr. Gen. J. María Orellana at l. Specimen.	—	—	—

1928 Issue

#11 and 12 printer: W&S.

		Good	Fine	XF
11	**1 Quetzal** 13.4.1928; 31.10.1928; 17.3.1934. Green. Like #6.			
	a. Issued note.	15.00	50.00	200.
	s. Specimen.	—	Unc	125.

		Good	Fine	XF
12	**10 Quetzales** 24.12.1929; 11.5.1931; 21.4.1934; 21.5.1935. Red on yellow and green unpt. Portr. Gen. J. María Orellana at l. Back red; ornate bridge.			
	a. Issued note.	40.00	140.	500.
	s. Specimen.	—	Unc	400.

1933-36 Issue

#13-18 printer: W&S.
#14-18 quetzal bird at l. and r.

		Good	Fine	XF
13	**1/2 Quetzal** 1933-42. Brown on blue unpt. Banana plantation at r. Lake and mountain on back.			
	a. Sign. title: *GERENTE* at r. 26.1.1933; 2.12.1938; 19.2.1941; 21.10.1942.	2.00	10.00	40.00
	b. Sign. title: *SUB-GERENTE* at r. 21.10.1942.	2.00	12.50	45.00

		Good	Fine	XF
14	**1 Quetzal** 1934-45. Deep green on lilac and ochre unpt. Farm bldgs. and truck at l. ctr. Back like #6.			
	a. Sign. title: *GERENTE* at r. 17.3.1934-19.9.1942.	2.00	12.50	50.00
	b. Sign. title: *SUB-GERENTE* at r. 19.9.1942; 31.10.1945.	2.00	12.50	50.00

		Good	Fine	XF
15	**2 Quetzales** 1936-42. Orange on green and violet unpt. Mountains and lake at l. Back like #7.			

15		Good	Fine	XF
	a. Sign. title: *GERENTE* at r. 25.1.1936; 4.2.1942.	8.00	45.00	225.
	b. Sign. title: *SUB-GERENTE* at r. 4.2.1942.	8.00	45.00	225.

16	**5 Quetzales**	Good	Fine	XF
	1934-45. Purple on orange and green unpt. Ship at dockside at l. Quetzal on back.			
	a. Sign. title: *GERENTE* at r. 7.4.1934-8.1.1943.	10.00	50.00	225.
	b. Sign. title: *SUB-GERENTE* at r. 29.1.1945.	12.50	50.00	250.

17	**10 Quetzales**	Good	Fine	XF
	1935-45. Dk. red on green unpt. Mountains and lake at l. Back like #12.			
	a. Sign. title: *GERENTE* at r. 21.5.1935-12.6.1943.	15.00	50.00	250.
	b. Sign. title: *SUB-GERENTE* at r. 1.2.1945; 22.5.1945.	17.50	60.00	275.

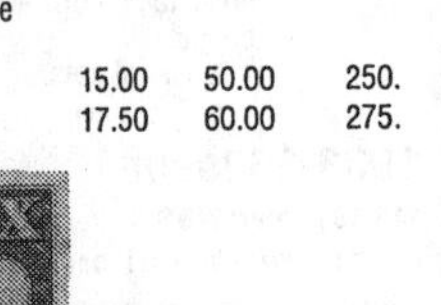

18	**20 Quetzales**	Good	Fine	XF
	1936-44. Blue on green and m/c unpt. Dock workers at l. Back like #9. Sign. title: *GERENTE* at r.			
	a. 2.5.1936.	40.00	145.	400.
	b. 14.1.1937/2.5.1936.	65.00	300.	—
	c. 4.2.1942; 3.9.1943; 3.2.1944; 9.8.1944.	40.00	145.	375.

1936 Issue

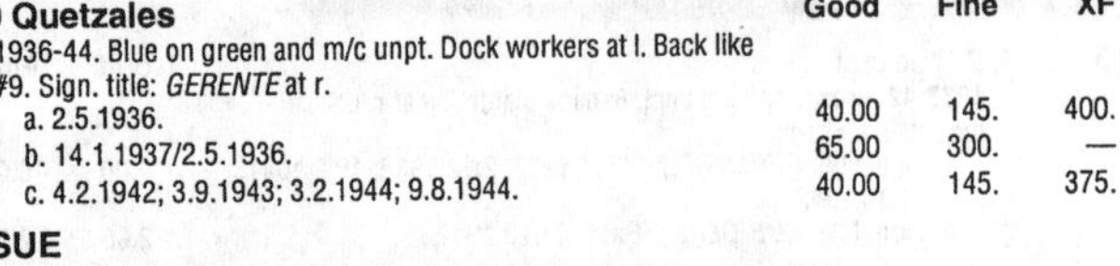

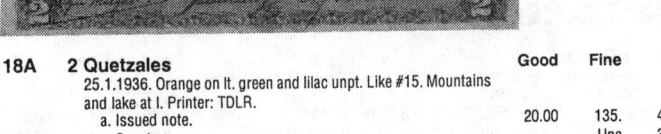

18A	**2 Quetzales**	Good	Fine	XF
	25.1.1936. Orange on lt. green and lilac unpt. Like #15. Mountains and lake at l. Printer: TDLR.			
	a. Issued note.	20.00	135.	450.
	s. Specimen.	—	Unc	350.

Banco de Guatemala

1946 Provisional Issue

#19-22 ovpt: *BANCO DE GUATEMALA* on Banco Central de Guatemala notes. Sign. title ovpt: *PRESIDENTE TRIBUNAL DE CUENTAS* at l., *PRESIDENTE DEL BANCO* at r.

19	**1/2 Quetzal**	VG	VF	UNC
	1946; 1948. Ovpt. on #13.			
	a. 12.8.1946.	2.00	10.00	50.00
	b. 10.3.1948.	15.00	85.00	225.

20	**1 Quetzal**	VG	VF	UNC
	12.8.1946. Ovpt. on #14.	4.50	15.00	65.00

21	**5 Quetzales**	VG	VF	UNC
	12.8.1946. Ovpt. on #16.	17.50	75.00	300.

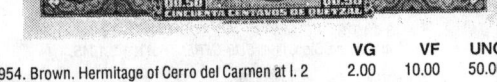

22	**20 Quetzales**	VG	VF	UNC
	12.8.1946; 28.3.1947. Ovpt. on #18.	40.00	225.	550.

1948 Issue

#23-28 Quetzal bird in flight above denomination. sign. title: *PRESIDENTE DEL...* at r. Sign. varieties. Printer: ABNC.

23	**1/2 Quetzal**	VG	VF	UNC
	15.9.1948-5.1.1954. Brown. Hermitage of Cerro del Carmen at l. 2 Guatemalans on back.	2.00	10.00	50.00

24	**1 Quetzal**	VG	VF	UNC
	1948-55. Green. Palace of the Captains General at l. Lake Atitlan on back.			
	a. Date alone at r. 15.9.1948-5.1.1954.	1.50	10.00	50.00
	b. W/*Autorizacion de.* 5.1.1955.	2.00	15.00	60.00

#	Denomination / Description	VG	VF	UNC
25	**5 Quetzales** 15.9.1948-5.1.1954. Purple. Vase (Vasija de Uaxactun) at l. Mayan-Spanish conflict on back.	17.50	50.00	150.
26	**10 Quetzales** 1948-55. Red. Round stone carving (Ara de Tikal) at l. Founding of old Guatemala on back.			
	a. Date alone at r. 15.9.1948-5.1.1954.	25.00	60.00	200.
	b. W/*Autorizacion de.* 5.1.1955.	25.00	75.00	225.
27	**20 Quetzales** 15.9.1948; 18.2.1949; 7.9.1949; 3.5.1950; 5.1.1954. Blue. Portr. R. Landivar at l. Meeting of Independence on back.	30.00	115.	300.
28	**100 Quetzales** 1948-52. Black on m/c unpt. Indio de Nahuala at l. Valley and mountain on back.			
	a. 15.9.1948; 21.5.1952.	65.00	175.	400.
	b. 3.8.1949.	100.	200.	500.

1955-56 Issue

#30-34 sign. varieties. Printer: W&S.

#	Denomination / Description	VG	VF	UNC
29	**1/2 Quetzal** 5.1.1955; 22.2.1956; 16.1.1957. Brown. Similar to #23 but bldg. at r.	1.00	10.00	50.00

#	Denomination / Description	VG	VF	UNC
30	**1 Quetzal** 5.1.1955; 22.2.1956; 16.1.1957. Green. Similar to #24 but bldg. at ctr. r.	1.00	10.00	50.00

#	Denomination / Description	VG	VF	UNC
31	**5 Quetzales** 5.1.1955; 22.2.1956; 16.1.1957. Purple. Similar to #25 but vase at r.	5.00	35.00	130.
32	**10 Quetzales** 22.2.1956; 16.1.1957; 22.1.1958. Red. Similar to #26 but round stone at r.	12.50	50.00	200.
33	**20 Quetzales** 5.1.1955-18.2.1959. Blue. Similar to #27 but R. Landivar at ctr.	25.00	100.	275.

#	Denomination / Description	VG	VF	UNC
34	**100 Quetzales** 5.1.1955; 22.2.1956; 16.1.1957; 22.1.1958. Dk. blue. Similar to #28 but Indio de Nahuala at ctr.	100.	250.	550.

1957-63 Issue

#35-50 sign. title: *JEFE DE...* at r.

#35-39 Printer: ABNC.

#	Denomination / Description	VG	VF	UNC
35	**1/2 Quetzal** 22.1.1958. Brown on m/c unpt. Like #23. Hermitage of Cerro del Carmen at l. Two Guatemalans on back.	3.00	15.00	75.00
36	**1 Quetzal** 16.1.1957; 22.1.1958. Green on m/c unpt. Like #24. Palace of the Captains General at l. Lake Atitlan on back.	3.00	10.00	50.00

#	Denomination / Description	VG	VF	UNC
37	**5 Quetzales** 22.1.1958. Purple. Like #25. Vase *Vasija de Uaxactum* at l. Mayan-Spanish battle scene on back.	8.00	35.00	125.
38	**10 Quetzales** 22.1.1958; 12.1.1962; 9.1.1963; 8.1.1964. Red. Like #26. Round stone carving *Ara de Tikal* at l. Founding of old Guatemala on back.	12.50	65.00	200.

#	Denomination / Description	VG	VF	UNC
39	**20 Quetzales** 9.1.1963; 8.1.1964; 15.1.1965. Blue. Like #27. R. Landivar at l. Meeting of Independence on back.	20.00	75.00	250.

1959-60 Issues

#40-50 sign. varieties. Printer: W&S.

#	Denomination / Description	VG	VF	UNC
40	**1/2 Quetzal** 18.2.1959. Like #29. Lighter brown shadings around value guilloche at l. Printed area 2mm smaller than #41. 6-digit serial #.	2.00	10.00	60.00

#	Denomination / Description	VG	VF	UNC
41	**1/2 Quetzal** 18.2.1959; 13.1.1960; 18.1.1961. Similar to #40 but darker brown shadings around value guilloche at l. 7-digit serial #.			
	a. Issued note.	2.00	7.50	40.00
	s. Specimen.	—	—	30.00
42	**1 Quetzal** 18.2.1959. Green palace. Like #30. Dull green back. 6-digit serial #.			
	a. Issued note.	2.00	10.00	60.00
	s. Specimen.	—	—	—
43	**1 Quetzal** 18.2.1959; 13.1.1960; 18.1.1961; 12.1.1962; 9.1.1963; 8.1.1964. Black and green. Like #42, but black palace. Back bright green. 7-digit serial #.			
	a. Issued note.	2.00	7.50	40.00
	s. Specimen.	—	—	—

#	Denomination / Description	VG	VF	UNC
44	**5 Quetzales** 18.2.1959. Like #31. Value at l. ctr. Vase in purple.	8.00	30.00	110.

		VG	VF	UNC
45	**5 Quetzales** 18.2.1959-8.1.1964. Similar to #44 but redesigned guilloche. Value at ctr and vase in brown.			
	a. Issued note.	5.00	25.00	100.
	s. Specimen.	—	—	—
46	**10 Quetzales** 18.2.1959. Like #32. Stone in red.	15.00	50.00	200.

		VG	VF	UNC
47	**10 Quetzales** 18.2.1959; 13.1.1960; 18.1.1961. Similar to #46 but redesigned guilloche. Stone in brown.			
	a. Issued note.	15.00	35.00	150.
	s. Specimen.	—	—	—

		VG	VF	UNC
48	**20 Quetzales** 13.1.1960-15.1.1965. Blue. Similar to #33, but portr. R. Landivar at r.			
	a. Issued note.	20.00	65.00	200.
	s. Specimen.	—	—	—
49	**100 Quetzales** 18.2.1959. Dk. blue. Like #34, w/*Indio de Nahuala* in blue at ctr.	115.	250.	550.

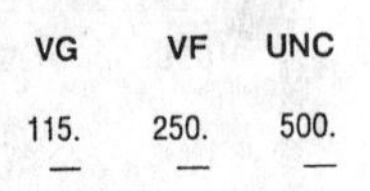

		VG	VF	UNC
50	**100 Quetzales** 13.1.1960-15.1.1965. Dk. blue. Portr. *Indio de Nahuala* in brown at r.			
	a. Issued note.	115.	250.	500.
	s. Specimen.	—	—	—

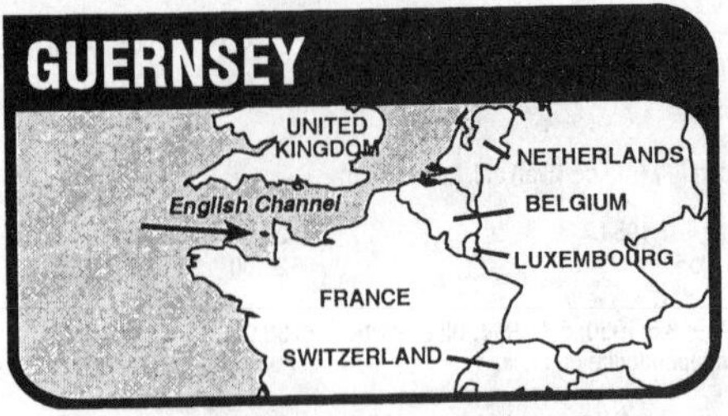

The Bailiwick of Guernsey, a British crown dependency located in the English Channel 30 miles (48 km.) west of Normandy, France, has an area of 30 sq. mi. (78 sq. km.), including the Isles of Alderney, Jethou, Herm, Brechou and Sark, and a population of 58,681. Capital: St. Peter Port. Agriculture and cattle breeding are the main occupations.

Militant monks from the Duchy of Normandy established the first permanent settlements on Guernsey prior to the Norman invasion of England, but the prevalence of prehistoric monuments suggests an earlier occupancy. The island, the only part of the Duchy of Normandy belonging to the British crown, has been a possession of Britain since the Norman Conquest of 1066. During the Anglo-French Wars, the harbors of Guernsey were employed in the building and outfitting of ships for the English privateers preying on French shipping. Guernsey is administered by its own laws and customs. Acts passed by the British Parliament are not applicable to Guernsey unless the island is specifically mentioned. During World War II, German troops occupied the island from 1940 to 1944.

United Kingdom bank notes and coinage circulate concurrently with Guernsey money as legal tender.

RULERS:

British to 1940, 1944-
German Occupation, June 1940-June 1944

MONETARY SYSTEM:

1 Penny = 8 Doubles
1 Shilling = 12 Pence
5 Shillings = 6 Francs
1 Pound = 20 Shillings to 1971
1 Pound = 100 New Pence 1971-

British Administration

States of Guernsey

1825; 1857 Government Notes

		Good	Fine	XF
A1	**1 Pound** 1827-36. Britannia standing w/shield and lion at upper l., allegorical woman standing at upper r. Lg. *ONE* in guilloche at lower l.			
	a. 21.11.1827; 15.4.1828. Rare.	—	—	—
	b. 10.7.1829; 1.12.1829; 1.10.1836. Rare.	—	—	—

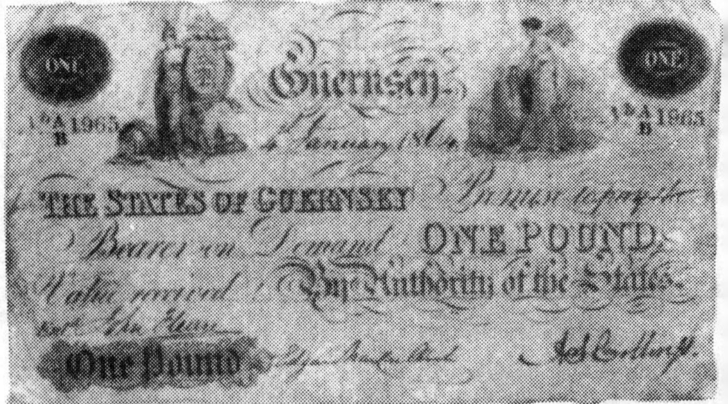

		Good	Fine	XF
A2	**1 Pound** 28.3.1857-22.5.1894. Similar to #A1, but lg. *One Pound* in guilloche at lower l. Rare.	—	—	—

1895; 1903 GOVERNMENT NOTES

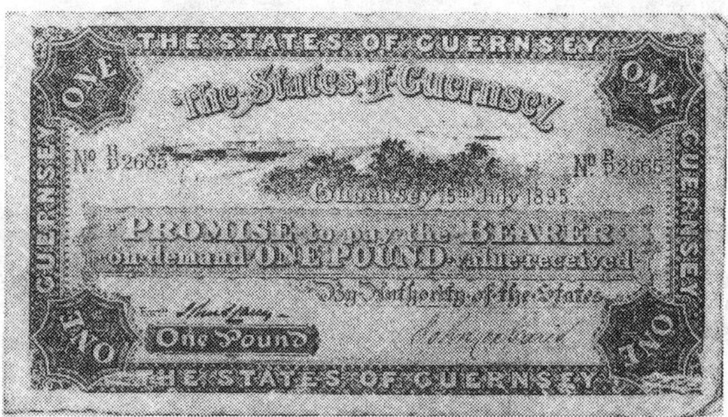

		Good	Fine	XF
1	**1 Pound** 15.7.1895. Sailing ships anchored along coastline across upper ctr. (St. Sampson's Harbor). Back green; arms medallion at ctr. in ornate pattern. Printer: PBC. Rare.	—	—	—
1A	**1 Pound** 23.3.1903. Rare.	—	—	—
2	**5 Pounds** Reported not confirmed.	—	—	—

1914 EMERGENCY WWI ISSUE

#3 and 4 denominated in British sterling and French francs. Arms at ctr. in unpt.

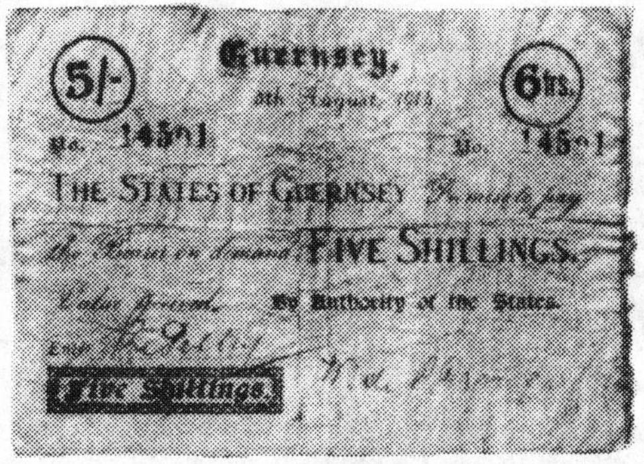

		Good	Fine	XF
3	**5 Shillings = 6 Francs** 5.8.1914. Printer: The Star, Guernsey. Rare.	—	—	—
4	**10 Shillings = 12 Francs** 7.8.1914. Printer: The Evening Press, Guernsey. Rare.	—	—	—

1914 ISSUE

#5 and 6 denominated in British sterling and French francs. Arms medallion at ctr. in guilloche on back. Printer: PBC.

		Good	Fine	XF
5	**5 Shillings = 6 Francs** 1.9.1914. Black on red unpt. Back red. Rare.	—	—	—
6	**10 Shillings = 12 Francs** 1.9.1914; 19.7.1919. Similar to #5. Rare.	—	—	—
7	**1 Pound** 3.4.1914; 1.9.1916; 1.9.1917; 1.8.1919. Like #1. Rare.	—	—	—

ote: The date 1.9.1914 for #7 is reported, not confirmed.

921 PROVISIONAL ISSUE

-9A ovpt: *BRITISH*.

		Good	Fine	XF
8	**5 Shillings = 6 Francs** ND (Apr. 1921-old date 1.9.1914). Red ovpt: *BRITISH* on #5. Rare.	—	—	—
9	**10 Shillings = 12 Francs** ND (Apr. 1921-old date 1.9.1914). Red ovpt: *BRITISH* on #6. Rare.	—	—	—

		Good	Fine	XF
9A	**1 Pound** ND (Apr. 1921-old date 1.8.1919). Red ovpt: *BRITISH* on #7. Rare.	—	—	—

1921-24 ISSUE

#10 and 11 St. Sampson's Harbor scene across upper ctr.

		Good	Fine	XF
10	**10 Shillings** 17.5.1924. Black and gray. W/o denomination in numerals at ctr.	150.	450.	—
11	**1 Pound** 1.3.1921; 9.2.1924; 17.5.1924. Black and gray on orange unpt. W/o denomination in numerals at ctr. Like #10. Rare.	—	—	—

1927 ISSUE

		Good	Fine	XF
12	**1 Pound** 6.12.1927; 12.4.1928. Black and gray on red unpt. Like #10. Denomination *£1* in unpt. at ctr.	150.	450.	1000.

1933 ISSUE

		Good	Fine	XF
13	**10 Shillings** 18.11.1933. Lt. blue and brown. Like #10. Denomination *10/-* unpt. at ctr., only 1 sign. English wording on back.	100.	400.	900.
14	**1 Pound** 3.1.1933-18.11.1933. Gray on red unpt. Like #12 but w/o *ENTD* at lower l., only 1 sign. English wording on back.	100.	400.	950.

Note: Additional dates for #10-13 may exist and need confirmation. *All* dates for #14 need confirmation.

1934 ISSUE

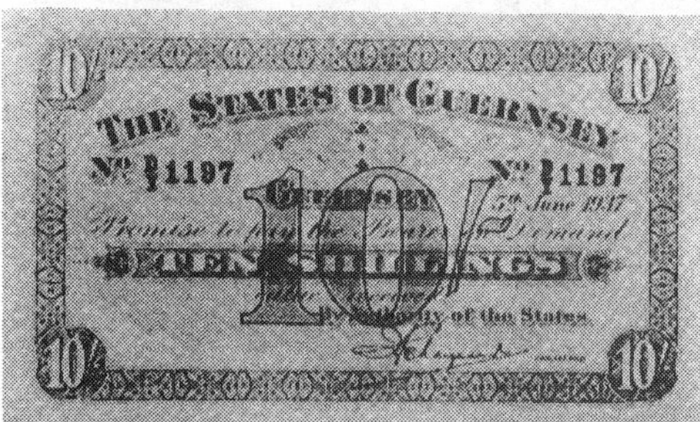

		Good	Fine	XF
15	**10 Shillings** 29.3.1934; 5.6.1937; 1.7.1939; 9.3.1940. Lt. blue and orange. Like #13. Back red; *S'BALLIVIE INSULE DEGERNEREYE* (Seal of the Island of Guernsey).	100.	500.	1250.

		Good	Fine	XF
16	**1 Pound** 1934-40. Gray. Like #14. Back blue. *S'BALLIVIE INSULE DEGERNEREYE* (Seal of the Island of Guernsey).			
	a. 29.3.1934-1.7.1939.	185.	600.	1400.
	b. 9.3.1940.	75.00	300.	750.

German Occupation - WW II

Government of Guernsey

1941 First Issue

		Good	Fine	XF
18	**2 Shillings 6 Pence** 25.3.1941. Blue on orange unpt. Back dk. blue.	35.00	100.	225.

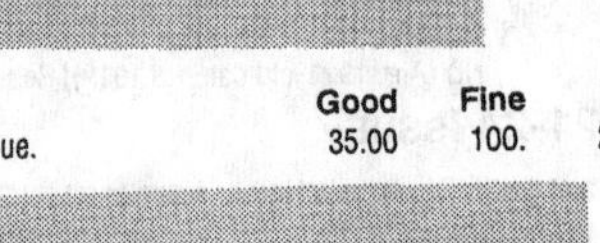

		Good	Fine	XF
19	**5 Shillings** 25.3.1941. Black on red unpt. Back red.	40.00	140.	325.

1941 Second Issue

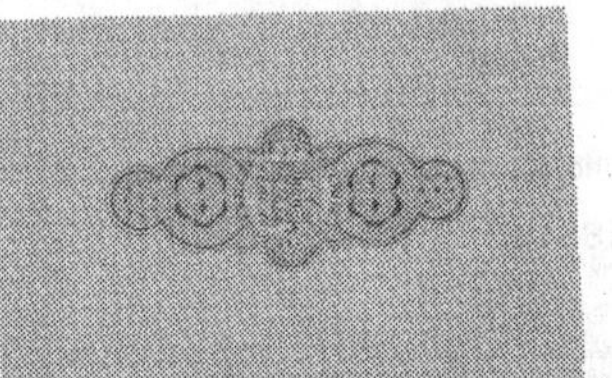

		Good	Fine	XF
20	**2 Shillings 6 Pence** 17.5.1941. Like #18.	35.00	125.	275.
21	**5 Shillings** 17.5.1941. Like #19.	50.00	150.	400.

1941 Third Issue

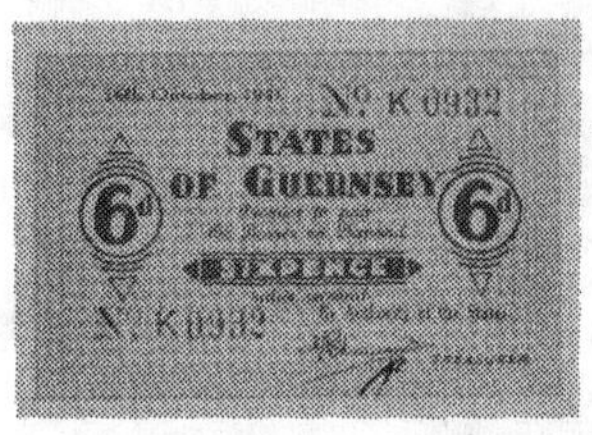

		Good	Fine	XF
22	**6 Pence** 16.10.1941. Black on lt. blue and orange unpt. Back purple.	25.00	100.	200.

		Good	Fine	XF
23	**1 Shilling 3 Pence** 16.10.1941. Black on yellow and brown unpt. Back brown.	45.00	175.	400.

1942 First Issue

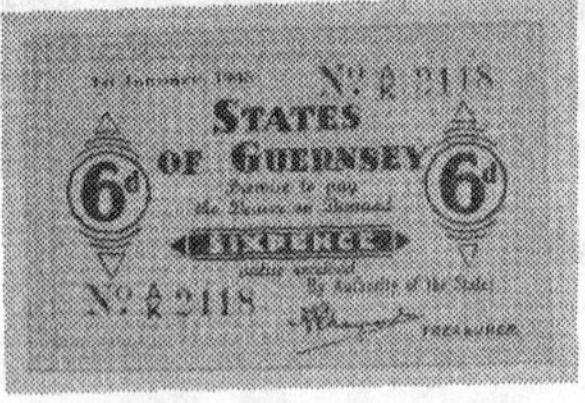

		Good	Fine	XF
24	**6 Pence** 1.1.1942. Like #22. Blue paper.	40.00	140.	325.
25	**1 Shilling on 1/3d** 1.1.1942. Orange ovpt. of new denomination. Blue paper.	15.00	80.00	175.

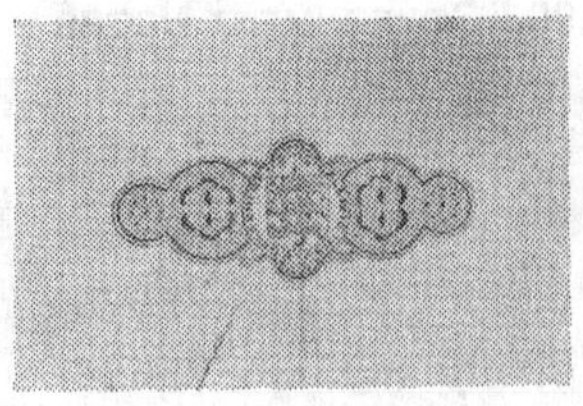

		Good	Fine	XF
25A	**2 Shillings 6 Pence** 1.1.1942. Like #18. Blue paper.	15.00	80.00	175.
25B	**5 Shillings** 1.1.1942.	25.00	100.	225.

1942 Second Issue

		Good	Fine	XF
26	**1 Shilling 3 Pence** 18.7.1942. Black on yellow unpt. Blue paper. Back gray.	20.00	90.00	200.
27	**1 Shilling on 1/3d** 18.7.1942. Orange ovpt. on #26.	25.00	100.	250.

1943 Issue

		Good	Fine	XF
28	**6 Pence** 1.1.1943. Like #22. White paper.	25.00	100.	200.
29	**1 Shilling on 1/3d** 1.1.1943. Orange ovpt. on #26.	30.00	110.	250.
30	**2 Shillings 6 Pence** 1.1.1943. Blue.	30.00	110.	250.

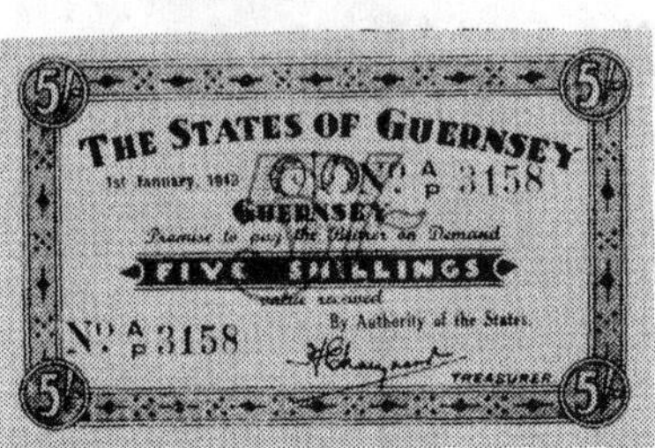

		Good	Fine	XF
31	**5 Shillings** 1.1.1943. Black on red denomination. Back red.	30.00	175.	450.
32	**10 Shillings** 1.1.1943. Blue on red denomination. Back red.	75.00	275.	700.
33	**1 Pound** 1.1.1943. Black on red unpt. Sailing ships and coastline across upper ctr. (St. Sampson's Harbor). Back blue.	80.00	300.	750

British Administration - Resumed

States of Guernsey

1945 First Issue

		Good	Fine	XF
33A	**1 Pound** 1.1.1945. Like #33.	75.00	275.	700

Note: A blue paper variety of #33A is reported but not confirmed.

		Good	Fine	XF
33B	**5 Pounds** 1.1.1945. Green on green paper. Arms at upper l. Rare.	—	—	—

Note: #33B was withdrawn shortly after its release.

1945 Second Issue

#34-37 w/text...*backed by Guernsey Notes.* Printed on blue French paper.

		VG	VF	UNC
34	**5 Shillings** 1.1.1945. Rare.	—	—	—
35	**10 Shillings** 1.1.1945. Rare.	—	—	—
36	**1 Pound** 1.1.1945. Like #33. Rare.	—	—	—
37	**5 Pounds** 1.1.1945. Rare.	—	—	—

1945 Third Issue

#38-41 w/text...*backed by British Notes.*

		VG	VF	UNC
38	**5 Shillings** 1.1.1945. Rare.	—	—	—
39	**10 Shillings** 1.1.1945. Rare.	—	—	—
40	**1 Pound** 1.1.1945. Rare.	—	—	—
41	**5 Pounds** 1.1.1945. Rare.	—	—	—

1945; 1956 Issue

#42-44 printer: PBC.

		VG	VF	UNC
42	**10 Shillings** 1945-66. Lilac on lt. green unpt. Back purple.			
	a. 1.8.1945-1.9.1957.	20.00	75.00	400.
	b. 1.7.1958-1.3.1965.	10.00	60.00	150.
	c. 1.7.1966.	5.00	35.00	85.00
	s. As c. Specimen.	—	—	—

		VG	VF	UNC
43	**1 Pound** 1945-66. Purple on green unpt. Harbor entrance across ctr. Back green.			
	a. 1.8.1945-1.3.1957.	10.00	75.00	500.
	b. 1.9.1957-1.3.1962; 1.6.1963; 1.3.1965.	8.00	50.00	250.
	c. 1.7.1966.	6.00	30.00	125.
	s. As c. Specimen.	—	—	—

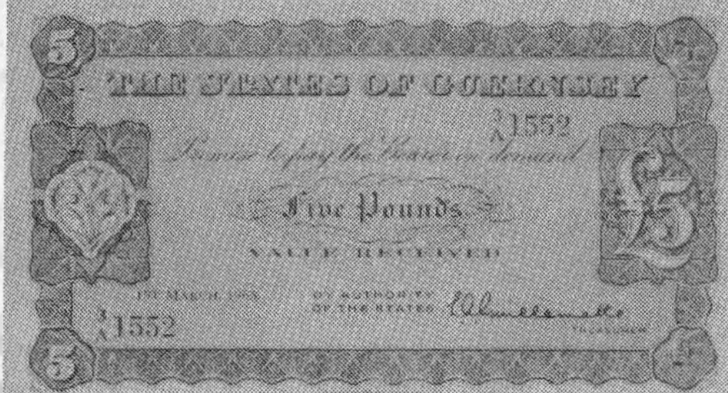

		VG	VF	UNC
44	**5 Pounds** 1.12.1956; 1.3.1965; 1.7.1966. Green and blue. Flowers at l.	60.00	325.	850.

GUINEA

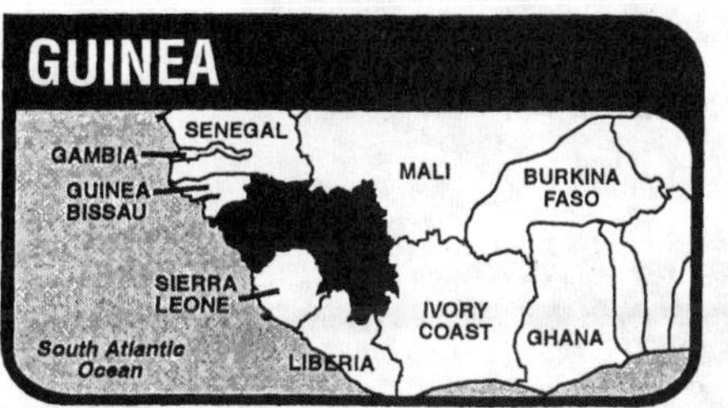

The Republic of Guinea (formerly French Guinea), situated on the Atlantic coast of Africa between Sierra Leone and Guinea-Bissau, has an area of 94,964 sq. mi. (245,957 sq. km.) and a population of 7.86 million. Capital: Conakry. Although Guinea contains one-third of the world's reserves of bauxite and significant deposits of iron ore, gold and diamonds, the economy is still dependent on agriculture. Aluminum, bananas, copra and coffee are exported.

The coast of Guinea was known to Portuguese navigators of the 15th century but was seldom visited by European traders of the 16th-18th centuries because of its dangerous coastal waters. French penetration of the area began in the mid-19th century with the entering into of protectorate treaties with several of the coastal chiefs. After a long struggle with Guinea's native leader Samory Toure, France secured the area and until 1890 administered it as a part of Senegal. In 1895 the colony (Guinee Francaise) became an autonomous part of the federation of French West Africa. The inhabitants were extended French citizenship in 1946 when the colony became an overseas territory of the French Union. Guinea became an independent republic on Oct. 2, 1958, when it declined to enter the new French Community.

RULERS:

French to 1958

MONETARY SYSTEM:

1 Franc = 100 Centimes to 1971
1 Syli = 10 Francs, 1971-1980
Franc System, 1985-

French Administration

Gouvernement Général de l'Afrique Occidentale Française

Colonie de la Guinée Française

Décret du 11.2.1917

#1

#2

		VG	VF	UNC
1	**0.50 Franc** D.1917. Dk. brown on lt. brown unpt. Reverse and obverse of 50 Centimes coin on face. Back black text.			
	a. Wmk: Bees. Imprint on back 23mm long.	30.00	100.	250.
	b. Wmk: Bees. Imprint on back 26mm long.	37.50	125.	300.
	c. Wmk: Laurel leaves.	37.50	125.	300.
	d. W/o wmk.	30.00	100.	250.
2	**1 Franc** D.1917. Blue on green unpt. Reverse and obverse of 1 Franc coin on face.			
	a. Wmk: Bees.	40.00	150.	325.
	b. Wmk: Laurel leaves.	45.00	175.	375.
	c. W/o wmk.	40.00	150.	325.

1920 Emergency Postage Stamp Issue

#3-5 adhesive postage stamps (Michel #66, 67 and 70, or Scott #54, 56 and 61) affixed to colored cardboard w/ovpt: *VALEUR D'ECHANGE* in two lines on face. Value in ornate frame at ctr. on back.

		VG	VF	UNC
3	**5 Centimes** ND (1920). Green. Orange cardboard.	85.00	200.	350.
4	**10 Centimes** ND (1920). Rose. Green cardboard.	85.00	200.	350.
5	**25 Centimes** ND (1920). Blue. Red cardboard.	100.	225.	400.

REPUBLIC

LIQUE DE GUINÉEBANQUE DE LA RÉPUBLIQUE DE GUINÉE

1958 ISSUE

#6-11 Pres. Sekou Toure at l.

		VG	VF	UNC
6	**50 Francs** 2.10.1958. Brown. Mask at ctr. on back.	8.00	50.00	225.

		VG	VF	UNC
7	**100 Francs** 2.10.1958. Lilac. Woman and child w/village on back.	15.00	50.00	250.
8	**500 Francs** 2.10.1958. Red-orange. Pineapple field on back.	30.00	150.	500.

		VG	VF	UNC
9	**1000 Francs** 2.10.1958. Blue. Small boats at shore, man at ctr. r. on back.	20.00	110.	475.

		VG	VF	UNC
10	**5000 Francs** 2.10.1958. Green. Banana harvesting on back.	75.00	350.	—

		VG	VF	UNC
11	**10,000 Francs** 2.10.1958. Dk. brown. Mining on back.	125.	475.	—

BANQUE CENTRALE DE LA RÉPUBLIQUE DE GUINÉE

1960 ISSUE

#12-15A Pres. Sekou Toure at l. Wmk: Dove.

		VG	VF	UN
15A	**5000 Francs** 1.3.1960. Purple on green and m/c unpt. Pres. Sekou Toure at l. Woman in headdress at l. huts at r. on back. (Not issued). Specimen.	—	—	40

The Republic of Haiti, occupying the western one third of the island of Hispañola in the Caribbean Sea between Puerto Rico and Cuba, has an area of 10,714 sq. mi. (27,750 sq. km.) and a population of 7.82 million. Capital: Port-au-Prince. The economy is d on agriculture, light manufacturing and tourism which is becoming increasingly important. Coffee, bauxite, sugar, essential oils and handicrafts are exported.

Columbus discovered Hispañola in 1492. Spain colonized the island, making Santo Domingo the for exploration of the Western Hemisphere. Later French buccaneers settled the western third of Hispañola which was ceded to France by Spain in 1697. Slaves brought over from Africa to work the coffee and sugar cane plantations made it one of the richest colonies of the French Empire. The Republic of Haiti was established in 1804 after the slave revolts of the 1790's.

As a republic from 1915-1934 it was occupied by the U.S. Francois Duvalier was president 1957-1981, and his son 1981-1986, when a quick succession of governments continued with U.N. and U.S. intervention through the 1990's.

MONETARY SYSTEM:

1 Gourde = 100 Centimes
1 Piastre = 300 Gourdes, 1873
5 Gourdes = 1 U.S. Dollar, 1919-89

FRENCH ADMINISTRATION

DEPARTMENT OF PORT-DU-PAIX

1790's ND ISSUE

		Good	Fine	XF
A1	**4 Escalins** ND. Arms at ctr. Uniface.	—	—	—

ST. DOMINGUE

1810s ISSUE

		Good	Fine	XF
A11	**4 Escalins** ND. Arms at ctr. Uniface.	—	—	—

REPUBLIC (FIRST)

RÉPUBLIQUE D'HAITI

BILLETS DE CAISSE

DECRET DU 8 MAI 1813

		Good	Fine	XF
31	**5 Gourdes** Reported not confirmed.	—	—	—
33	**50 Gourdes** Reported not confirmed.	—	—	—
34	**100 Gourdes** Reported not confirmed.	—	—	—

ARRETÉ DU 26 SEPTEMBRE 1826

		Good	Fine	XF
51	**1 Gourde** Reported not confirmed.	—	—	—
52	**2 Gourdes** Reported not confirmed.	—	—	—
53	**5 Gourdes** 3.10.1826. Rare.	—	—	—

LOI DU 10 AVRIL 1827

		Good	Fine	XF
54	**10 Gourdes** L.1827. Rare.	—	—	—

LOI DU 16 AVRIL 1827 - FIRST ISSUE

#1-10 lg. format w/arms at upper ctr.

		Good	Fine	XF
1	**1 Gourde** L.1827. Black or gray on large, thin white or off-white paper. Very wide margins (often trimmed). Print frame ca. 204 x 112mm.	40.00	100.	200.
2	**2 Gourdes** L.1827.			
	a. Thin paper w/o wmk.	20.00	50.00	130.
	b. Thick paper w/o wmk.	20.00	50.00	130.
	c. Thin yellow paper. Wmk: *REPUBLIQUE D'HAITI.*	20.00	50.00	130.
3	**5 Gourdes** L.1827. Rare.	—	—	—

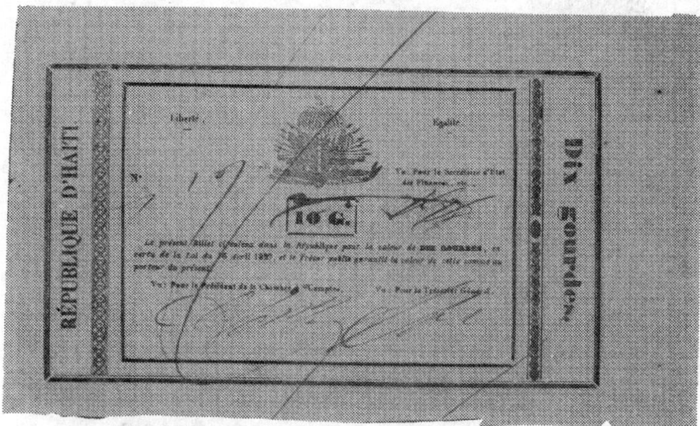

		Good	Fine	XF
4	**10 Gourdes** L.1827. Value 10 G. in ctr. box. W/o wmk.			
	a. Thin paper.	25.00	80.00	225.
	b. Thick paper.	25.00	80.00	225.

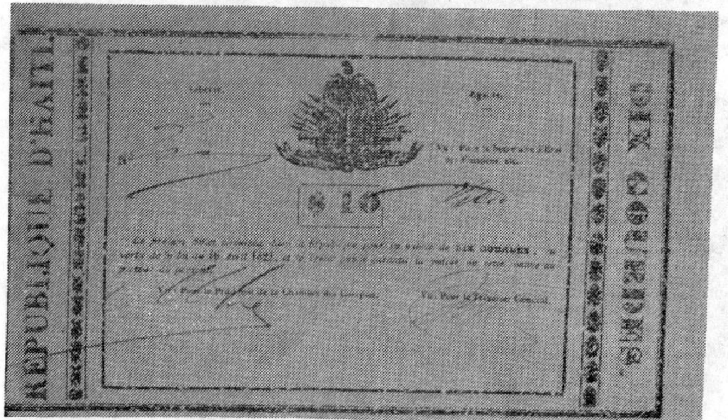

		Good	Fine	XF
5	**10 Gourdes** L.1827. Value $10 in ctr. box.			
	a. Thin paper. Wmk: *REPUBLIQUE D'HAITI.*	25.00	80.00	225.
	b. Thick paper w/o wmk.	25.00	80.00	225.
5A	**10 Gourdes** L.1827. Value 1000 in ctr. box.	—	—	—

NOTICE

Readers with unlisted dates, signature varieties, etc. are invited to submit photocopies or, high resolution (300 dpi, 100% size) scans of their notes to: Standard Catalog of World Paper Money, 700 East State St. Iola, WI 54990-0001, or E-Mail: george.cuhaj@fwpubs.com.

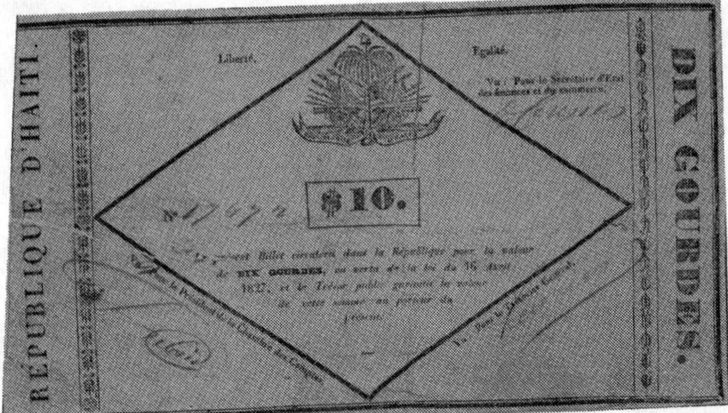

		Good	Fine	XF
6	**10 Gourdes** L.1827. Thin yellow paper. Large lozenge around ctr. Wmk. in 2 lines.	100.	250.	—

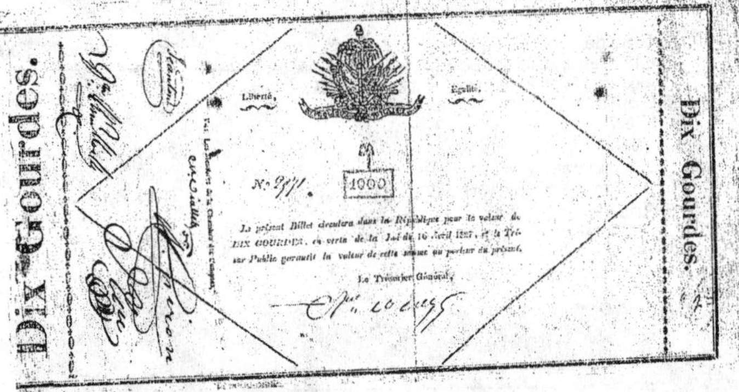

		Good	Fine	XF
6A	**10 Gourdes** L.1827. Similar to #6, but value in centimes in central box under arms. Rare.	—	—	—
7	**25 Gourdes** L.1827. Thin white paper. Numeral 2 has straight bottom.	25.00	80.00	225.

		Good	Fine	XF
8	**25 Gourdes** L.1827. Thick brown paper. Numeral 2 has curved bottom.	20.00	75.00	200.

		Good	Fine	XF
10	**100 Gourdes** L.1827. Heavy paper. Similar to #6. Wmk: Lg. oval.	30.00	100.	250.

ARRETÉ DU 31 JUILLET 1849

		Good	Fine	XF
11	**50 Centimes** L.1849. Black. Arms at upper ctr. Rare.	—	—	—

EMPIRE D'HAITI

TREASURY

LOI DU 16 AVRIL 1851

		Good	Fine	XF
15	**2 Gourdes** L.1851. Black. Arms at upper ctr. Very wide margins (often trimmed). Frame 200 x 112mm.			
	a. Yellow paper. Lg. 2-line wmk: *EMPIRE D'HAYTI* (sometimes w/crown in wmk.).	40.00	100.	25
	b. Wmk: *REPUBLIQUE D'HAYTI.*	50.00	120.	27
	c. Pale blue-green paper w/o wmk.	50.00	120.	27

RÉPUBLIQUE D'HAITI

TREASURY (1827)

LOI DU 16 AVRIL 1827 - SECOND ISSUE

#18-21 'Simple format' style. Arms at upper ctr.

		Good	Fine
18	**2 Gourdes** L.1827. Thin white paper w/o wmk. Frame about 134 x 75mm.	100.	250.
20	**10 Gourdes** L.1827. W/ or w/o printed Serie A and No.1.	100.	250.

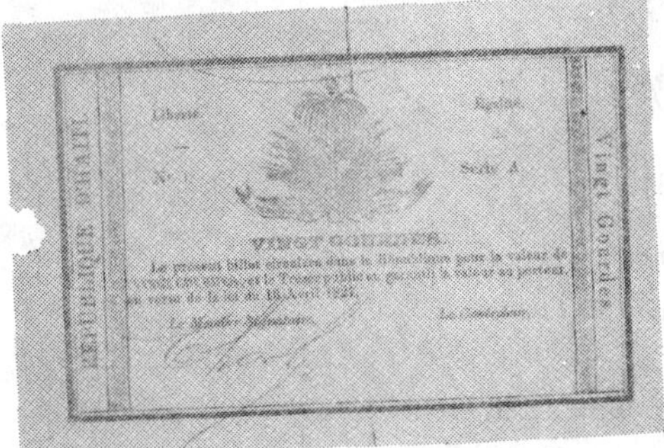

		Good	Fine
21	**20 Gourdes** L.1827. Like #20.	120.	300.

LOI DU 16 AVRIL 1827 - THIRD ISSUE

#25 'Long format' style.

		Good	Fine
25	**20 Gourdes** L.1827. Arms at upper ctr. Printed Serie A and No 1. Frame about 174 x 74mm.	120.	300.

LOI DU 16 AVRIL 1827 - FOURTH ISSUE

		Good	Fine	XF
27	**4 Gourdes** L.1827. Value 400 in box at upper ctr. W/o arms. Le Membre Signataire in italics. Rare.	—	—	—

#28-30 'Diamond frame format' style. W/o arms.

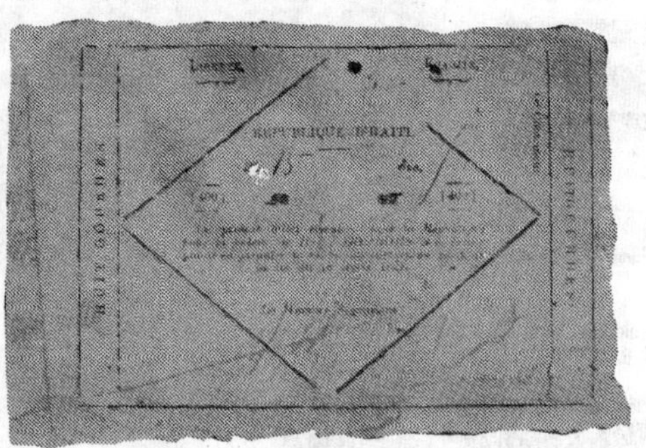

		Good	Fine	XF
28	**8 Gourdes** L.1827. Frame about 120 x 84mm.			
	a. *HUIT GOURDES* at l. reads bottom to top.	200.	400.	—
	b. *HUIT GOURDES* at l. reads top to bottom.	200.	400.	—
30	**16 Gourdes** L.1827.			
	a. "Le Membre Signataire" in standard type.	80.00	150.	—
	b. *Le Membre Signataire* in italics.	80.00	150.	—

LOI DU 16 AVRIL 1827 - FIFTH ISSUES

#33-34, 36-37 printer: CS&E.

#33-36 ornate format w/oval arms at top ctr.

		Good	Fine	XF
33	**2 Gourdes** L.1827. Black on yellow paper w/wmk. Frame ca. 94 x 61mm. Series A-D.	8.00	20.00	60.00

		Good	Fine	XF
34	**5 Gourdes** L.1827. Black on white paper. Similar to #33. Series A-D.	10.00	25.00	70.00

		Good	Fine	XF
35	**2 Gourdes** L.1827. Black on white paper w/wmk. Series D11-K12. Printer: W&S.	8.00	20.00	60.00

NOTICE

Readers with unlisted dates, signature varieties, etc. are invited to submit photocopies or, high resolution (300 dpi, 100% size) scans of their notes to: Standard Catalog of World Paper Money, 700 East State St. Iola, WI 54990-0001, or E-Mail: george.cuhaj@fwpubs.com.

		Good	Fine	XF
36	**10 Gourdes** L.1827. Black on blue paper w/wmk. Printed back. Series A-F.	10.00	25.00	70.00

		Good	Fine	XF
37	**25 Gourdes** L.1827. Black on green paper w/wmk. Series G.	15.00	50.00	110.

LOI DU 16 AVRIL 1827 - SIXTH ISSUE

#41 and 42 'Fancy format' style. Portr. Pres. Fabre-Nicolas Geffrard (1859-67). Printer: W&S.

		Good	Fine	XF
41	**1 Gourde** L.1827. Black on pink or rose paper w/fancy wmk. (rarely w/o). Portr. Pres. Geffrard at upper l. Frame about 94 x 62mm. Wide margins (sometimes trimmed).	5.00	20.00	60.00

		Good	Fine	XF
42	**2 Gourdes** L.1827. Black on white paper w/wmk. Portr. Pres. Geffrard at upper l and r. Series A1-U10.	5.00	20.00	60.00
45	**2 Gourdes** L.1827. Blue on white paper. Printer: TDLR. Specimen. Rare.	—	—	—

GOUVERNEMENT DU SUD D'HAITI

GOVERNMENT OF SOUTH HAITI

EN DATE DU 13 OCTOBRE 1868

#51-58 black. Arms at upper ctr.

		Good	Fine	XF
51	**2 Gourdes** L.1868. Series A-D.	200.	—	—
52	**4 Gourdes** L.1868. Series A; C; F; L; N; O; P.			
	a. White or off-white paper.	150.	250.	—
	b. Blue paper.	150.	250.	—

		Good	Fine	XF
54	**12 Gourdes** L.1868. Paper color varieties: orange, yellow, blue, pink, green, violet etc. W/o Series, or Series E-V.	150.	250.	—

Note: #54 is found w/many typographical varieties.

		Good	Fine	XF
55	**24 Gourdes** L.1868. Series B.	300.	—	—

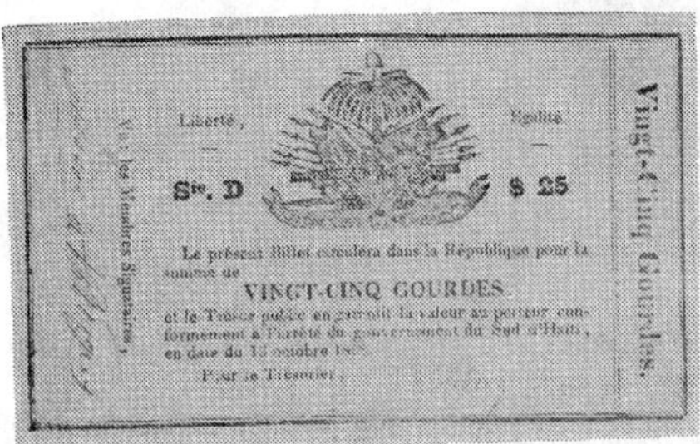

		Good	Fine	XF
56	**25 Gourdes** L.1868. Series D.	300.	—	—

		Good	Fine	XF
57	**48 Gourdes** L.1868. W/o Series.	300.	—	—
58	**100 Gourdes** L.1868. Frame ca. 196 x 72mm.	350.	—	—

Loi du 28 Octobre 1869

		Good	Fine	XF
60	**10 Piastres Fortes** L.1869. Arms at upper ctr. Thin white paper. Frame 170 x 75mm. Rare.	—	—	—

Loi du 22 Juillet 1871

#64-65 black. Arms at upper ctr.

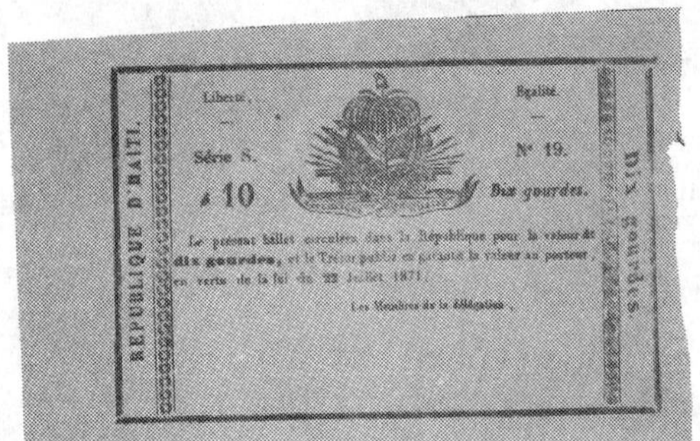

		Good	Fine	XF
64	**10 Gourdes** L.1871. Green or blue-green paper. Series E-X4.	30.00	120.	225.
65	**20 Gourdes** L.1871. White or off-white paper. Series A-Q5.	30.00	120.	225.

La Banque Nationale d'Haiti

Septre. 1875

#68-72 Pres. Michel Domingue. Issued w/o signs. (but some have had fraudulent signs. added later). Some have irregular edges from having been torn from sheets. Printer: ABNC.

		Good	Fine	XF
68	**25 Centimes** Sept.1875. Black on pink unpt. Portr. Pres. Domingue at l., arms at r. Frame 112 x 56mm. Back red.	8.00	20.00	60.00

		Good	Fine	XF
70	**1 Piastre** Sept. 1875. Black on blue and orange unpt. Portr. Pres. Domingue at l., arms at ctr., allegorical woman (Agriculture) at r. Frame 155 x 77mm. Back blue.	10.00	35.00	100.

		Good	Fine	XF
72	**5 Piastres** Sept. 1875. Black on lt. green and pink unpt. Woman ("Justice") at l., arms at ctr., portr. Pres. Domingue at r. Back orange.	12.50	50.00	125.

1880s Issue

		Good	Fine	XF
74	**5 Gourdes** ND. Blue and buff. Justice at l., arms in orange at r. Back pale blue. 136 x 79mm. Printer: Imp. Filigranique G. Richard et Cie., Paris.	1000.	—	—
74A	**10 Gourdes** ND. Rare.	—	—	—

Treasury (1883-89)

Loi du 28 Aout 1883

#75, 76 *Salomon Jeune* first issue. Printer: ABNC.

		Good	Fine	XF
75	**1 Gourde** L.1883. Black on blue unpt. Arms at upper ctr., Female portr. (Majesty No. 2) at r. Frame 177 x 77mm. Back blue. Series through A48.			
	a. Issued note.	250.	650.	—
	s. Specimen.	—	Unc	1000

76 **2 Gourdes**

L.1883. Black on pink unpt. Dog at upper l., arms at upper r. Back salmon-pink. Series through B14.

	Good	Fine	XF
a. Issued note.	300.	800.	—
s. Specimen.	—	Unc	1250.

LOI DU 6 OCTOBRE 1884

#77, 78 *Salomon Jeune* second issue. Printer: ABNC.

77 **1 Gourde**

L.1884. Black on orange and blue unpt. "Naiad" reclining at l., arms at r. Frame 170 x 74mm. Back orange. Series through C54.

	Good	Fine	XF
a. Issued note.	200.	500.	—
s. Specimen.	—	Unc	850.

78 **2 Gourdes**

L.1884. Black on green and orange unpt. "Agriculture" at l. Back green. Series through D32.

	Good	Fine	XF
a. Issued note.	300.	800.	—
s. Specimen.	—	Unc	1250.

LOI DU 3 NOVEMBRE 1887

#79, 80 *Salomon Jeune* third issue. Printer: CS&E.

79 **1 Gourde**

L.1887. Black on orange and blue unpt. Arms at upper l., Ceres reclining at r. Back red. Series through E100.

	Good	Fine	XF
a. Issued note.	200.	500.	—
s. Specimen.	—	Unc	750.

80 **2 Gourdes**

L.1887. Black on green and orange unpt. Farmers and horse at l., portr. girl at upper r., arms at lower r. Back green. Series through F50.

	Good	Fine	XF
a. Issued note.	300.	700.	—
s. Specimen.	—	Unc	1250.

DECRET ... DU 28 JUIN 1889

#83-85 issued in Port-au-Prince by Pres. Francois Denis Légitime.

		Good	Fine	XF
83	**10 Centimes** ND. Heavy gray wmk. paper. Frame 118 x 61mm.			
	a. Black print.	250.	—	—
	b. Blue print.	250.	—	—
84	**20 Centimes** ND. Green on heavy gray wmk. paper. Frame 118 x 61mm.	250.	—	—

		Good	Fine	XF
85	**1 Gourde** D.1889. Green on heavy white wmk. paper. Frame 166 x 61mm.	1000.	—	—

RÉPUBLIQUE SEPTENTRIONALE D'HAITI

1888 ND ISSUE

Govt. of Gen. Floraville Hippolyte 1888-89 in North Haiti.
#88-95 printer: HLBNC.

		Good	Fine	XF
88	**10 Centimes** ND (1888). Black on gray unpt. Arms at upper l. Back green. Series A. 82 x 42mm.	200.	400.	—

		Good	Fine	XF
89	**25 Centimes** ND (1888). Black on lt. blue unpt. Arms at r. Back blue. Series A. 110 x 62mm.	175.	350.	—

		Good	Fine	XF
90	**50 Centimes** ND (1888). Black on pale orange unpt. Arms at l. Back violet-brown. Series A. 110 x 64mm.	250.	450.	—

91 1 Gourde
ND (1888). Black on pink and green unpt. Justice and Youth at upper l., arms at r. Back green. Series A. 154 x 100mm.

	Good	Fine	XF
a. Issued note.	200.	400.	—
s. Specimen.	—	Unc	800.

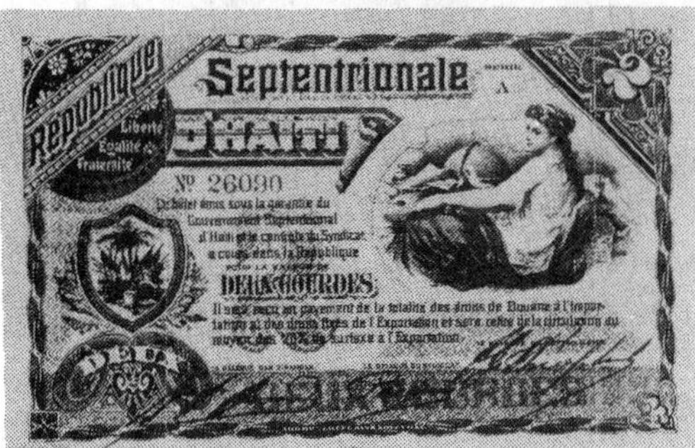

92 2 Gourdes
ND (1888). Black on orange and blue unpt. Arms at l., woman seated w/globe at r. Back red. Series A. 154 x 100mm.

	Good	Fine	XF
a. Issued note.	250.	500.	—
s. Specimen.	—	Unc	1000.

1889 ND Issue

95 1 Gourde
ND (1889). Woman at l. Serial # and 2 of 3 sign. in red. Back blue. Series T. 165 x 74mm.

Good	Fine	XF
250.	600.	—

Treasury (1892)

Loi du 29 Septembre 1892

#101 and 102 portr. J. J. Dessalines at l., arms at r. Printer: ABNC.

101 1 Gourde
L.1892. Black on yellow and blue unpt. Back red. Series B-V. 182 x 80mm.

	Good	Fine	XF
a. Issued note.	20.00	100.	300.
s. Specimen.	—	Unc	350.

102 2 Gourdes
L.1892. Black on yellow and pink unpt. Back blue. Series AB; BC-OP.

	Good	Fine	XF
a. Issued note.	25.00	150.	425.
s. Specimen.	—	Unc	400.

Treasury (1903-08)

Loi Du 10 Aout 1903 - Commemorative

#110 and 111, Centennial of Haitian Independence, 1804-1904.

#110 and 111 portr. J. J. Dessalines and date 1804 at l., arms at ctr. Portr. Nord Alexis and date 1904 at r. Printer: ABNC.

110 1 Gourde
L.1903. Black on blue-gray unpt. Back green, w/o vignette, 176 x 80mm. Series A-G.

	Good	Fine	XF
a. Issued note.	7.50	60.00	225.
s. Specimen.	—	Unc	250.

111 2 Gourdes
L.1903. Black on green-gray unpt. Back red, w/o vignette. Series AA-JJ.

	Good	Fine	XF
a. Issued note.	10.00	70.00	250.
s. Specimen.	—	Unc	300.

Loi Du 27 Fevrier 1904 - Commemorative

#120 and 121, Centennial of Haitian Independence, 1804-1904.

#120 and 121 like #110 and 111.

120 1 Gourde
L.1904. Series A-R. Like #110.

	Good	Fine	XF
a. Issued note.	6.00	40.00	200.
s. Specimen.	—	Unc	250.

121 2 Gourdes
L.1904. Series BB-OO. Like #111.

	Good	Fine	XF
a. Issued note.	7.50	60.00	225
s. Specimen.	—	Unc	300

LOI DU 14 MAI 1908

		Good	Fine	XF
125	**5 Gourdes** L.1908. Black on pink unpt. Portr. Nord Alexis at both l. and r. Back red. Series C3-19. 169 x 73mm. Printer: ABNC.			
	a. Issued note.	150.	550.	—
	s. Specimen.	—	Unc	750.

Note: It is probable that #125 was issued upon the death of Nord Alexis in 1908.

L'ARRETE DU 22 JANVIER 1915

#127-129 local print.

		Good	Fine	XF
127	**1 Gourde** L.1915. Black. Arms at ctr. Back dk. blue. Heavy manila paper. Series A; B.	10.00	40.00	100.
128	**2 Gourdes** L.1915. Like #127. Back pale red. Series AA.	25.00	100.	250.
129	**5 Gourdes** L.1915. Like #127. Back red-brown. Series AAA.			
	a. Red serial #.	10.00	50.00	150.
	b. Black serial #.	8.00	40.00	120.

BON DU TRESOR

TREASURY

LOI DU 22 DECEMBRE 1914 (ISSUED FEB. 1915)

#131 and 132 printer: ABNC.

		Good	Fine	XF
131	**1 Gourde** L.1914. Black on blue unpt. Face similar to #110. W/o ovpt. Farming scene at ctr. on green back. Series A.			
	a. Issued note.	8.00	50.00	150.
	s. Specimen.	—	Unc	400.

		Good	Fine	XF
132	**2 Gourdes** L.1914. Black on green unpt. Face similar to #110. W/o ovpt. Mining scene at ctr. on red back. Series AA-FF.			
	a. Issued note.	10.00	60.00	165.
	s. Specimen.	—	Unc	500.

1916 ND ISSUE

#134-136 local printing.

		Good	Fine	XF
134	**1 Gourde** ND (1916). Black and orange. Back brown. Series A.	150.	300.	650.
135	**1 Gourde** ND (1916). Blue and black w/red title and text. Back blue. 184 x 82mm. Series D; E; J.	125.	250.	550.

		Good	Fine	XF
136	**2 Gourdes** ND (1916). Red and black w/blue title and text. Like #135. Back red. Series K-O.	150.	275.	600.

BANQUE NATIONALE DE LA RÉPUBLIQUE D'HAITI

1916 PROVISIONAL ISSUE

#137-141 w/vertical red ovpt. lines of French text on unsigned notes of the Eighteenth Issue of République (1914). Red dates either 1916 and 1913, or 1919 and 1913. The distinguishing 1916 or 1919 date is vertical in red near the top ctr. of the note.

		Good	Fine	XF
137	**1 Gourde** L.1916. 1916 ovpt. on #131. Series A-D.	15.00	50.00	200.
138	**2 Gourdes** I>L.1916. 1916 ovpt. on #132. Series AA-II. Rare.	—	—	—

1919 PROVISIONAL ISSUE

		Good	Fine	XF
140	**1 Gourde** L.1919. 1919 ovpt. on #131. Series D-M.			
	a. Issued note.	8.00	30.00	150.
	s. Specimen.	—	Unc	120.

		Good	Fine	XF
141	**2 Gourdes** L.1919. 1919 ovpt. on #132. Series HH-RR.			
	a. Issued note.	10.00	35.00	175.
	s. Specimen.	—	Unc	140.

Convention du 2 Mai 1919 - First Issue (ca.1920-24)

#150-153 banana plant on face, coffee plant on back. Size: 163 x 87mm. Printer: ABNC.

		Good	Fine	XF
150	**1 Gourde** L.1919. Black on green and brown unpt. Plant at l. Back dk. brown. Prefix letters. A-L. 2 sign. varieties.			
	a. Issued note.	5.00	35.00	175.
	s. Specimen.	—	Unc	150.

		Good	Fine	XF
151	**2 Gourdes** L.1919. Black on green and brown unpt. Plant at r. Back blue. Prefix letters A-J. 2 sign. varieties.			
	a. Issued note.	15.00	100.	350.
	s. Specimen.	—	Unc	225.

		Good	Fine	XF
152	**5 Gourdes** L.1919. Black on red, blue and green unpt. Plant at r. ctr. Back orange. Prefix Letters A and B. 2 sign. varieties.			
	a. Issued note.	50.00	250.	750.
	s. Specimen.	—	Unc	450.
153	**10 Gourdes** L.1919. Black on green and brown unpt. Like #152. Back green. Prefix letter A.			
	a. Issued note.	125.	600.	—
	s. Specimen.	—	Unc	750.
154	**20 Gourdes** L.1919. Black on blue and m/c unpt. Similar to #152. Back orange. (Not issued). Archive example.	—	—	—

Convention du 12 Avril 1919 - Second Issue (ca.1925-32)

#160-166 third sign. title: *Pour Controle...* Arms on back. Printer: ABNC.

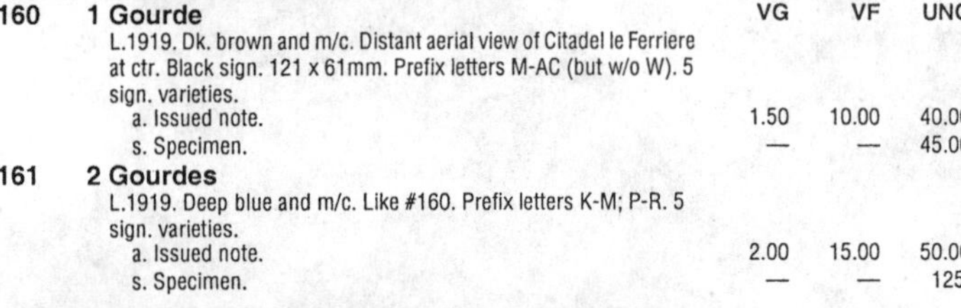

		VG	VF	UNC
160	**1 Gourde** L.1919. Dk. brown and m/c. Distant aerial view of Citadel le Ferriere at ctr. Black sign. 121 x 61mm. Prefix letters M-AC (but w/o W). 5 sign. varieties.			
	a. Issued note.	1.50	10.00	40.00
	s. Specimen.	—	—	45.00
161	**2 Gourdes** L.1919. Deep blue and m/c. Like #160. Prefix letters K-M; P-R. 5 sign. varieties.			
	a. Issued note.	2.00	15.00	50.00
	s. Specimen.	—	—	125.

		VG	VF	UNC
162	**5 Gourdes** L.1919. Orange on lt. green and m/c. unpt. Women harvesting coffee at l. Black sign. 162 x 70mm. Prefix letters C; D. 3 sign. varieties.			
	a. Issued note.	1.50	10.00	75.00
	s. Specimen.	—	—	150.
163	**10 Gourdes** L.1919. Green and m/c. Coffee plant at ctr. Prefix letter B. 2 sign. varieties.			
	a. Issued note.	5.00	30.00	100.
	s. Specimen.	—	—	175.

		VG	VF	UNC
164	**20 Gourdes** L.1919. Red-brown and m/c. Palm tree at r. Back brown. Prefix letter A.			
	a. Issued note.	200.	600.	—
	s. Specimen.	—	—	500.
165	**50 Gourdes** L.1919. Dk. olive and m/c. Cotton bolls at ctr. Prefix letter A.			
	a. Issued note.	50.00	300.	—
	s. Specimen.	—	—	400.
166	**100 Gourdes** L.1919. Purple and m/c. Field workers at l. Prefix letter A.			
	a. Issued note.	50.00	300.	—
	s. Specimen.	—	—	400.

CONVENTION DU 12 AVRIL 1919 - THIRD ISSUE (CA.1935-42)

#167 and 168 portr. Pres. Stenio Vincent at ctr. Printer: ABNC.

		VG	VF	UNC
167	**1 Gourde** L.1919. Dk. brown and m/c. Prefix letter W.			
	a. Issued note.	30.00	150.	300.
	s. Specimen.	—	—	175.
168	**2 Gourdes** L.1919. Blue and m/c. Like #167. Prefix letter N.			
	a. Issued note.	30.00	175.	375.
	s. Specimen.	—	—	250.

CONVENTION DU 12 AVRIL 1919 - FOURTH ISSUE (CA.1946-50)

#170-173 first and third sign. title each: *Un Administrateur*. Printer: ABNC.

		VG	VF	UNC
170	**1 Gourde** L.1919. Like #160, but brown sign. Prefix letters AD-AR. 4 sign. varieties.			
	a. Issued note.	1.00	4.00	25.00
	s. Specimen.	—	—	40.00
171	**2 Gourdes** L.1919. Like #161, but blue sign. Prefix letters S-Y. 4 sign. varieties.			
	a. Issued note.	1.00	5.00	30.00
	s. Specimen.	—	—	75.00
172	**5 Gourdes** L.1919. Like #162. Prefix letters D; E. 3 sign. varieties.			
	a. Orange sign. Prefix letter D.	2.00	12.50	45.00
	b. Black sign. Prefix letter E.	1.50	10.00	30.00
	s1. Like a. Specimen.	—	—	75.00
	s2. Like b. Specimen.	—	—	60.00
173	**10 Gourdes** L.1919. Like #163. Prefix letter B.			
	a. Issued note.	5.00	25.00	60.00
	s. Specimen.	—	—	80.00

CONVENTION DU 12 AVRIL 1919 - FIFTH ISSUE (CA.1950)

#174-177 printer: W&S.

		VG	VF	UNC
174	**1 Gourde** L.1919. Dk. brown and m/c. Closeup view of Citadel Rampart at ctr. Prefix letters WA-WD. 2 sign. varieties.	20.00	70.00	200.
175	**2 Gourdes** L.1919. Blue and m/c. Like #174. Prefix letters WA and WB. 2 sign. varieties.	40.00	125.	350.

		VG	VF	UNC
176	**50 Gourdes** L.1919. Dk. olive and m/c. Like #165.			
	a. Issued note.	—	—	—
	s. Specimen, w/ or w/o punched hole cancel.	—	—	200.
177	**100 Gourdes** L.1919. Brown. Like #166. Uniface specimen pair.	—	—	250.

REPUBLIC (SECOND)

BANQUE NATIONALE DE LA RÉPUBLIQUE D'HAITI

CONVENTION DU 12 AVRIL 1919

SIXTH ISSUE (CA.1951-64)

#178-184 arms at ctr. on back. First sign. title: *Le President*. Printer: ABNC.

		VG	VF	UNC
178	**1 Gourde** L.1919. Dk. brown on lt. blue and m/c unpt. Closeup view of Citadel Rampart at ctr. Prefix letters AS-BM. 5 sign. varieties.			
	a. Issued note.	.75	2.00	17.50
	s. Specimen.	—	—	35.00
179	**2 Gourdes** L.1919. Blue and m/c. Lt. green in unpt. Citadel rampart at ctr. Prefix letters Y-AF. 6 sign. varieties.			
	a. Issued note.	1.00	4.00	25.00
	s. Specimen.	—	—	60.00
180	**5 Gourdes** L.1919. Orange and m/c. Green in unpt. Woman harvesting coffee at l. Prefix letters G-M. 3 sign. varieties.			
	a. Issued note.	1.25	6.00	35.00
	s. Specimen, punch hole cancelled.	—	—	50.00

		VG	VF	UNC
181	**10 Gourdes** L.1919. Green on m/c unpt. Coffee plant at ctr. Prefix letters B-D. 2 sign. varieties.			
	a. Issued note.	3.00	12.50	55.00
	s. Specimen, punch hole cancelled.	—	—	70.00

#182 not assigned.

		VG	VF	UNC
183	**50 Gourdes** L.1919. Olive-green on m/c unpt. Cotton bolls at ctr. Specimen.	—	Unc	225.
184	**100 Gourdes** L.1919. Purple on m/c unpt. Field workers at l. Prefix letter A.			
	a. Issued note.	30.00	125.	350.
	s. Specimen, punched hole cancelled.	—	Unc	175.

Note: For similar notes but w/new guilloche patterns w/o green unpt., printer: ABNC, see Vol. 3. Note: For similar notes but printed by TDLR, see Vol. 3.

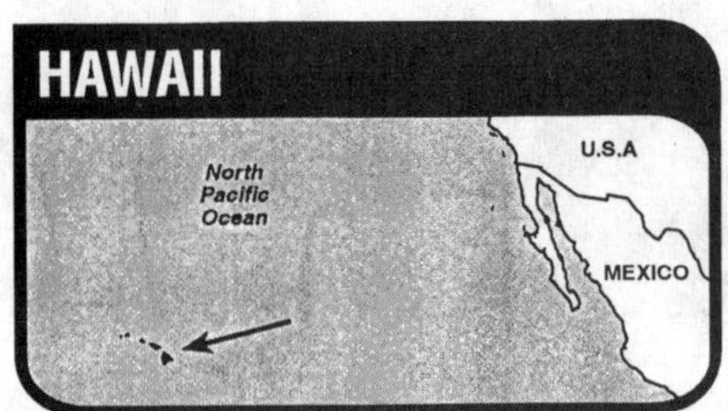

Hawaii consists of eight main islands and numerous smaller islands of coral and volcanic origin situated in the central Pacific Ocean 2,400 miles (3,862 km.) from San Francisco. The archipelago has an area of 6,471 sq. mi. (16,641 sq. km.) and a population of 1.1 million. Capital: Honolulu. The principal industries are tourism and agriculture. Cane sugar and pineapples are exported.

The islands, originally populated by Polynesians who traveled from the Society Islands, were discovered by British navigator Capt. James Cook in 1778. He named them the Sandwich Islands. King Kamehameha the Great united the islands under one kingdom (1795-1810) which endured until 1893 when Queen Liliuokalani, the gifted composer of "Aloha Oe" and other songs, was deposed and a provisional government established. This was followed by a republic which governed Hawaii until 1898 when it ceded itself to the United States. Hawaii was organized as a territory in 1900 and became the 50th state of the United States on Aug. 21, 1959.

RULERS

King Kalakaua, 1874-1891
Queen Liliuokalani, 1891-1893
Provisional Govt., 1893-1894
Republic, 1894-1898
Annexed to U.S., 1898-1900
Territory, 1900-1959

MONETARY SYSTEM

1 Dollar = 100 Cents

KINGDOM

DEPARTMENT OF FINANCE

1879 (1880) SILVER CERTIFICATE OF DEPOSIT - SERIES A

#1-5 arms at ctr. on back. Printer: ABNC.

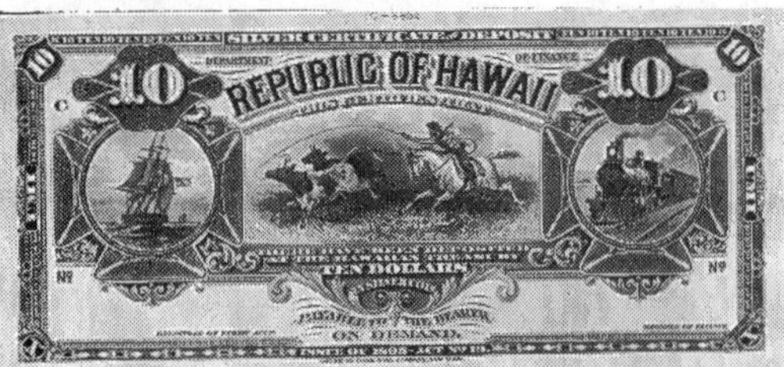

		VG	VF	UNC
1	**10 Dollars** ND (1880). Black on orange unpt. Sailing ship at l. cowboy roping steers at ctr., steam locomotive at r. Back orange.			
	a. Issued note.	—	—	—
	b. Punched or cut cancelled. Unknown in private hands.	—	—	—
	p. Proof pair, face and back.	—	—	3000.

		VG	VF	UNC
2	**20 Dollars** ND (1879). Black on brown unpt. Portr. girl w/dog at lower l., portr. woman between steam paddlewheel ship and steam passenger train at ctr., anchor at lower r. Back brown.			
	a. Issued note. Reported not confirmed.	—	—	—
	b. Punched or cut cancelled. Rare.	—	—	—
	p. Proof pair, face and back.	—	—	3500.

		VG	VF	UNC
3	**50 Dollars** ND (1879). Black on green unpt. Ram at l., allegorical woman at ctr., girl at r. Back green.			

		VG	VF	UNC
3	a. Issued note. Rare.	—	—	—
	b. Punched or cut cancelled. Unknown in private hands.	—	—	—
	p. Proof pair, face and back.	—	—	4000.

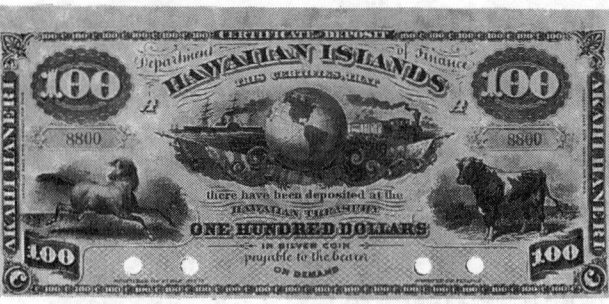

		VG	VF	UNC
4	**100 Dollars** ND (1879). Black on blue unpt. Galloping horse at lower l., globe between steam passenger train and sailing ship at ctr., cow at lower r. Back blue.			
	a. Issued note. Rare.	—	—	—
	b. Punched or cut cancelled.	—	—	7500.
	p. Proof pair, face and back.	—	—	5000.

		VG	VF	UNC
5	**500 Dollars** ND (1879). Black on orange unpt. Portr. Kg. Kalakaua I at l., steam locomotive between sailing ships at ctr., farmer carrying produce at r. Back orange. Proof pair, face and back. Rare.	—	—	—

REPUBLIC OF HAWAII

DEPARTMENT OF FINANCE

1895 (1899) GOLD CERTIFICATE OF DEPOSIT ISSUE - SERIES B

#6-10 black on gold unpt. Back gold; arms in circle at ctr. Printer: ABNC.

		VG	VF	UNC
6	**5 Dollars** 1895 (1899). Woman "Haidee" at l., bldg. and trees at ctr., steer at r.			
	a. Issued note. Rare.	—	—	—
	b. Cancelled.	—	—	6000.
	p. Proof pair, face and back.	—	—	5500.

		VG	VF	UNC
7	**10 Dollars**			
	1895 (1899). Steamship at l., sugar cane harvest at ctr., woman at r.			
	a. Issued note Reported not confirmed.	—	—	—
	b. Cancelled.	—	—	7000.
	p. Proof pair, face and back.	—	—	6000.

		VG	VF	UNC
8	**20 Dollars**			
	1895 (1899). Woman standing at l., sugar cane harvest at ctr., horse's head at r.			
	a. Issued note. Rare.	—	—	—
	b. Cancelled.	—	—	8000.
	p. Proof pair, face and back.	—	—	7000.

		VG	VF	UNC
	50 Dollars			
	1895 (1899). Woman at l., longhorns w/cowboy on horseback at ctr., tree at r.			
	a. Issued note. Reported not confirmed.	—	—	—
	b. Cancelled. Unknown in private hands.	—	—	—
	p. Proof pair, face and back.	—	—	8000.
0	**100 Dollars**			
	1895 (1899). 2 allegorical women at l., cowboys and steam passenger train at ctr., horse at r.			
	a. Issued note. Reported not confirmed.	—	—	—
	b. Cancelled.	—	—	10,000.
	p. Proof pair, face and back.	—	—	9000.

895 (1897) Silver Certificate of Deposit Issue - Series C

1-15 Black on blue unpt. Back blue; arms at ctr. Printer: ABNC.

		VG	VF	UNC
1	**5 Dollars**			
	1895 (1897). Palm tree at l., Iolani Palace at ctr., kneeling man at r.			
	a. Issued note.	4500.	8000.	—
	b. Cancelled. Reported not confirmed.	—	—	—
	p. Proof pair, face and back.	—	—	5000.
2	**10 Dollars**			
	1895 (1897). Similar to #1.			
	a. Issued note. Rare.	—	—	—
	b. Cancelled.	3500.	—	—
	p. Proof pair, face and back.	—	—	5500.
13	**20 Dollars**			
	1895 (1897). Similar to #2.			
	a. Issued note. Reported not confirmed.	—	—	—
	b. Cancelled. Unknown in private hands.	—	—	—
	p. Proof pair, face and back.	—	—	6000.
14	**50 Dollars**			
	1895 (1897). Similar to #3.			
	a. Issued note. Reported not confirmed.	—	—	—
	b. Cancelled. Unknown in private hands.	—	—	—
	p. Proof pair, face and back.	—	—	7500.
15	**100 Dollars**			
	1895 (1897). Similar to #4.			
	a. Issued note. Reported not confirmed.	—	—	—
	b. Cancelled. Unknown in private hands.	—	—	—
	p. Proof pair, face and back.	—	—	8500.

United States of America - Territorial

Issued in 1942 after the Japanese attack on Pearl Harbor. Used as a financial precaution to a possible invasion of the islands and capture of U.S. currency.

Treasury

1935 A (1942) Emergency Silver Certificate Issue

#36, ovpt: *HAWAII* on face and back of 1935 A series.

		VG	VF	UNC
36	**1 Dollar**			
	1935 A (1942). Portr. G. Washington at ctr. Brown serial # and seal at r. Back green.	12.50	30.00	120.

Federal Reserve

1934 (1942) Emergency Issue

#37-41 w/brown serial # and seal at r. Ovpt: *HAWAII* on face and back of San Francisco 1934 and 1934 A Series 'L' notes.

		VG	VF	UNC
37	**5 Dollars**			
	1934 (1942). Portr. A. Lincoln at ctr. Back green; Lincoln Memorial at ctr.	20.00	40.00	150.
38	**5 Dollars**			
	1934 A (1942). Like #37.	20.00	50.00	175.

		VG	VF	UNC
39	**10 Dollars**			
	1934 A (1942). Black. Portr. A. Hamilton at ctr. Back green; Treasury bldg. at ctr.	20.00	60.00	250.

		VG	VF	UNC
40	**20 Dollars**			
	1934 (1942). Black. Portr. A. Jackson at ctr. Back green; White House at ctr.	30.00	75.00	400.
41	**20 Dollars**			
	1934 A (1942). Like #40.	30.00	75.00	400.

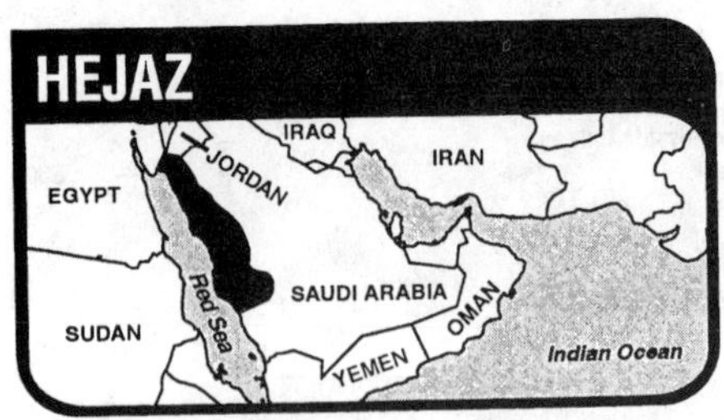

Hejaz, a province of Saudi Arabia and a former vilayet of the Ottoman Empire, occupies an 800-mile-long (1,287 km.) coastal strip between Nejd and the Red Sea. Population: 1.4 million. Hejaz contains the holy cities of Mecca and Medina. The economy is d on pilgrimage spending, light industries, limited agriculture production and the wealth generated by the oil deposits of Saudi Arabia.

The province was a Turkish dependency until freed in World War I. Husain Ibn Ali, Amir of Mecca, opposed the Turkish control and, with the aid of Lawrence of Arabia, wrested much of Hejaz from the Turks and in 1916 assumed the title of King of Hejaz. Ibn Sa'ud of Nejd conquered Hejaz in 1925, and in 1932 combined it with Nejd and other provinces under his control to form the Kingdom of Saudi Arabia.

RULERS

Husain Ibn Ali, AH1334-1373 (AD 1916-1924)
Abd Al-Aziz Ibn Sa'ud, AH1342-1373 (AD 1924-1953)

MONETARY SYSTEM

1 Pound (Riyal) = 20 Ghirsh (Piastres)

HEJAZ

ARABIAN NATIONAL BANK OF HEDJAZ

DECREE OF 23 SHAWAL AH1343 (1924)

		Good	Fine	XF
1	**1/2 Pound** D. AH1343 (1924). Red. Kaaba (or Ka'bah-Moslem shrine in Mecca). Indian coin on back. Rare.	—	—	—

#2-6 arms at ctr. on back.

		Good	Fine	XF
2	**1 Pound** D. AH1343 (1924). Green, brown and m/c. City view at ctr. Rare.	—	—	—
3	**5 Pounds** D. AH1343 (1924). Brown, gold and m/c. Ornate bldg. at upper r. Rare.	—	—	—
4	**10 Pounds** D. AH1343 (1924). Brown, blue, pink and m/c. Temple at ctr., columns at l. and r. Rare.	—	—	—

		Good	Fine	XF
5	**50 Pounds** D. AH1343 (1924). Blue, orange and m/c. Cedar tree at l., ruins at r. Rare.	—	—	—
6	**100 Pounds** D. AH1343 (1924). Brown, blue, lilac and m/c. Oasis at ctr., facing ancient winged statues at l. and r. of archway. Rare.	—	—	—

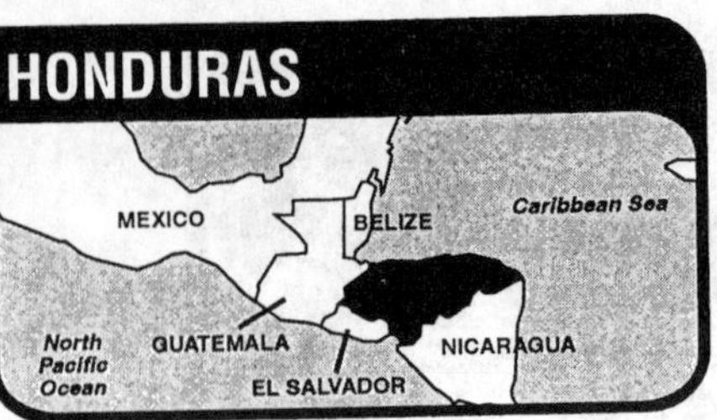

The Republic of Honduras, situated in Central America between El Salvador, Nicaragua and Guatemala, has an area of 43,277 sq. mi. (112,088 sq. km.) and a population of 6.48 million. Capital: Tegucigalpa. Tourism, agriculture, mining (gold and silver), and logging are the chief industries. Bananas, timber and coffee are exported.

Honduras, a site of the ancient Mayan Empire, was claimed for Spain by Columbus in 1502 during his last voyage to the Americas. The first settlement was made by Cristobal de Olid under orders of Hernan Cortes, then in Mexico. The area, regarded as one of the most promising sources of gold and silver in the New World, was a part of the Captaincy General of Guatemala throughout the colonial period. After declaring its independence from Spain in 1821, Honduras fell briefly to the Mexican Empire of Agustin de Iturbide, and then joined the Central American Federation (1823-39). Upon dissolution of the federation, Honduras became an independent republic.

MONETARY SYSTEM:

1 Peso = 100 Centavos, 1871-1926
1 Lempira = 100 Centavos, 1926-

Note: Certain listings encompassing issues circulated by provincial, state and commercial banking authorities are contained in Volume 1.

REPÚBLICA DE HONDURAS

VALES OF 1848

1848 ISSUE

#1-6 authorized by Decree of 9.9.1848. Black on off-white paper, large format. Uniface. Some may be found with written cancellation on back, along with punched holes.

		Good	Fine	X
1	**1 Peso** D. 1848. Wreath at ctr.	—	—	75
2	**2 Pesos** D. 1848. Like #1.	—	—	75
3	**10 Pesos** D. 1848.	—	—	100

		Good	Fine	
4	**15 Pesos** D. 1848. Like #1.	—	—	7
5	**25 Pesos** D. 1848.	—	—	12
6	**100 Pesos** D. 1848.	—	—	15

VALES OF 1863

1863 ISSUE

		Good	Fine	XF
7	**5 Pesos** D. 1863. Black on off-white paper. Arms at upper ctr., ribbon at l. and r. Punch cancelled.	—	—	1500.

VALE AL PORTADOR

BILLETE DEL TESORO

1889 ISSUE

#9-13 receipts issued by the Bogran government w/circular handstamp: *REPUBLICA DE HONDURAS* at l., embossed circular seal:...*PUBLICO*...at ctr. and w/ or w/o oval handstamp: *OFICINA GENERAL* at r.

		Good	Fine	XF
9	**5 Pesos** 1.1.1889.	—	—	—
10	**10 Pesos** 1.1.1889.	—	—	—
11	**25 Pesos** 1.1.1889.	—	—	—
12	**50 Pesos** 1.1.1889. Gray w/maroon denomination at l. and r. w/2 red handstamps.	—	—	—

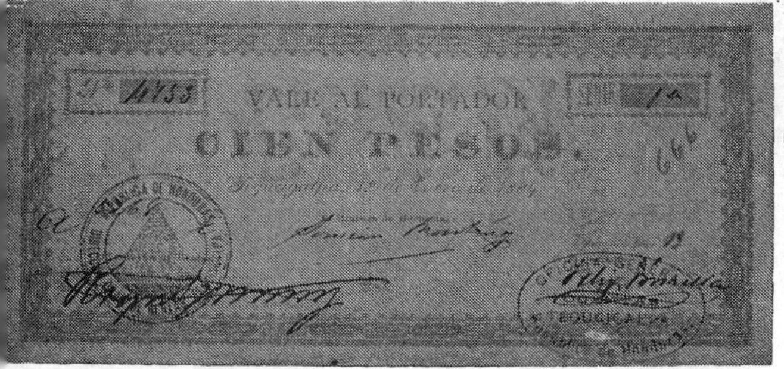

		Good	Fine	XF
13	**100 Pesos** 1.1.1889. Orange-brown w/2 handstamps.	—	—	—

BILLETE PRIVILEGIADO

1891 ISSUE

		Good	Fine	XF
14	**2 Pesos** 15.7.1891. Brown. Arms at ctr. Back black.	—	—	—

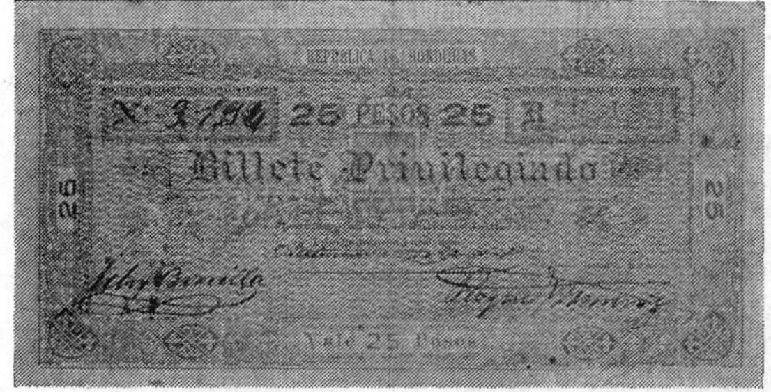

		Good	Fine	XF
15	**25 Pesos** 15.7.1891. Gray-green. Like #14. Arms at ctr. Back black.	—	—	—

VALE AL PORTADOR REISSUE

BILLETE DEL TESORO

TREASURY NOTE

1889 ISSUE

#16-20 like #9-13.

		Good	Fine	XF
16	**5 Pesos** 1889.	—	—	—
17	**10 Pesos** 1889.	—	—	—
18	**25 Pesos** 1889.	—	—	—
19	**50 Pesos** 1889.	—	—	—
20	**100 Pesos** 1889.	—	—	—

BANCO DE HONDURAS

1889 ISSUE

#22-24 various dates including authorization dates on backs and sign. varieties. Printer: ABNC.

		Good	Fine	XF
22	**5 Pesos** 1.10.1889. Black on orange and yellow unpt. Steer's head at l., arms at r. Back red. Rare.	—	—	—

		Good	Fine	XF
23	**50 Pesos** 1.10.1889. Black on brown and yellow unpt. Allegorical woman w/3 children and globe at l., arms at lower l. Indian w/bow at r. Back brown. Archive copy.	—	—	—
24	**100 Pesos** 1.10.1889. Black on orange and yellow unpt. Seated woman at l., steer's head at ctr., arms at r. Back orange. Rare.	—	—	—

1913 Issue

#25 - 27 printer: ABNC.

		Good	Fine	XF
25	**10 Pesos** 1.10.1913. Black on m/c unpt. Steer's head at l. Back red; arms at ctr. Series A. Rare.	—	—	—

		Good	Fine	XF
26	**20 Pesos** 1.10.1913. Black on m/c unpt. Steer's head at r. Back olive-green; arms at ctr. Rare.	—	—	—
27	**50 Pesos** 1.10.1913. Black on m/c unpt. Steer's head at ctr. Back green; arms at ctr. Proof.	—	—	—

1922 Issue

		Good	Fine	XF
28	**50 Centavos** 27.5.1922. M/c. Steer's head at l., church at ctr. Arms on back. Printer: W&S. Specimen, punched hole cancelled.			

		Good	Fine	XF
29	**1 Peso** 27.5.1922. Black on purple and m/c unpt. Steer's head at r. Back dk. blue; arms at ctr. New authorization date of 13.7.1925 and text ovpt. in upper margin on back. Printer: ABNC	—	—	—

1932 Issue

#34-37 Lempira at l., arms at r. Bank at ctr. on back. Printer: W&S.

		Good	Fine	XF
34	**1 Lempira** 11.2.1932. Blue on m/c unpt. Series A.	20.00	85.00	350.
35	**2 Lempiras** 11.2.1932. Green on m/c unpt. Series A.	50.00	400.	—
36	**5 Lempiras** 11.2.1932. Brown on m/c unpt. Series A.	75.00	600.	—

		Good	Fine	XF
37	**10 Lempiras** 11.2.1932. Black on lt. green and m/c unpt. Series A.	100.	850.	—

#38-41 *Deleted.*

1941 Issue

#42-44 printer: ABNC.

		Good	Fine	XF
42	**5 Lempiras**			
	5.3.1941. Brown on red unpt. Portr. Morazán at l. Steer's head on brown back. Series B.			
	a. W/o green ovpt. on back.	25.00	150.	375.
	b. Green ovpt: *Autorizada su circulacion...25.5.1948* in three lines of text and sign. on back.	200.	550.	—

		Good	Fine	XF
43	**10 Lempiras**			
	5.3.1941. Green on brown unpt. Portr. S. Soto at r. Back green; like #42. Series B.			
	a. W/o red ovpt. on back.	75.00	325.	—
	b. Red ovpt: *Autorizada su circulacion...25.5.1948* in 3 lines of text and sign. on back.	200.	550.	—

		Good	Fine	XF
44	**20 Lempiras**			
	5.3.1941. Black on olive unpt. l. Portr. Agurcia at l. Steer's head at ctr. on black back. Series A.			
	a. W/o red ovpt. on back.	90.00	650.	—
	b. Red ovpt: *Autorizada su circulacion...25.5.1948* in 3 lines of text and sign. on back.	90.00	650.	—

BANCO CENTRAL DE HONDURAS

1950-51 ISSUE

		VG	VF	UNC
45	**1 Lempira**			
	1951. Red on lt. tan unpt. Lempira at l., arms at r. Monolith on back. Red serial #. Printer: W&S.			
	a. 16.3.1951; 4.5.1951.	2.00	6.00	35.00
	b. 28.12.1951.	1.50	4.50	27.50
	s. Specimen, punched hole cancelled.	—	—	40.00

		VG	VF	UNC
46	**5 Lempiras**			
	1950-51. Dk. blue-gray on m/c unpt. Morazán at l. Arms at ctr. on back. Printer: ABNC.			
	a. 1.7.1950; 11.7.1950; 22.9.1950; 22.12.1950.	12.50	75.00	—
	b. 16.2.1951.	8.50	65.00	—
	s. Specimen, punched hole cancelled.	—	—	100.

NOTICE

Readers with unlisted dates, signature varieties, etc. are invited to submit photocopies or, high resolution (300 dpi, 100% size) scans of their notes to: Standard Catalog of World Paper Money, 700 East State St. Iola, WI 54990-0001, or E-Mail: george.cuhaj@fwpubs.com.

		VG	VF	UNC
47	**10 Lempiras**			
	25.5.1951-26.3.1954. Brown on m/c unpt. Cabañas at l. Plantation work on back. Printer: W&S.			
	a. Issued note.	25.00	125.	300.
	s. Specimen, punched hole cancelled.	—	—	135.

		VG	VF	UNC
48	**20 Lempiras**			
	25.5.1951-4.6.1954. Purple on m/c unpt. D. Herrera at l. Cattle on back. Printer: W&S.			
	a. Issued note.	20.00	75.00	300.
	s. Specimen, punched hole cancelled.	—	—	175.

		VG	VF	UNC
49	**100 Lempiras**			
	1951-73. Yellow on m/c unpt. Valle at l., arms at r. Village and bridge on back.			
	a. W/o security thread, lilac-pink unpt. Printer: W&S. 16.3.1951; 8.3.1957.	70.00	300.	1000.
	b. W/o security thread, w/fibers at r. ctr., lt. green and lt. orange unpt. Printer: W&S. 5.2.1964; 5.11.1965; 22.3.1968; 10.12.1969.	100.	300.	1250.
	c. W/security thread, yellow unpt. 13.10.1972. Reported not confirmed.	—	—	—
	d. As c. but w/o security thread. 13.10.1972; 23.3.1973.	45.00	175.	375.
	s. Specimen, punched hole cancelled.	—	—	250.

#50 not assigned.

1953-56 ISSUE

		VG	VF	UNC
51	**5 Lempiras**			
	1953-68. Gray on m/c unpt. Morazán at l., arms at r. Serial # at upper l. and upper r. Battle of Trinidad on back. Printer: ABNC.			
	a. Date horizontal. 17.3.1953; 19.3.1954; 7.5.1954.	6.00	35.00	175.
	b. As a. 22.11.1957-7.1.1966.	4.00	25.00	125.
	c. Date vertical. 15.4.1966; 29.9.1967; 22.3.1968.	3.50	17.50	70.00

		VG	VF	UNC
52	**10 Lempiras**			
	1954-69. Brown on m/c unpt. Cabañas at l., arms at r. Old bank on back. Date and sign. style varieties. Printer: TDLR.			
	a. R. sign. title: *MINISTRO DE HACIENDA...* 19.11.1954.	15.00	75.00	300.
	b. R. sign. title: *MINISTRO DE ECONOMIA...* 19.2.1960-10.1.1969.	10.00	35.00	250.

		VG	VF	UNC
53	**20 Lempiras** 1954-72. Green. D. de Herrera at l., arms at r. Waterfalls on back. Printer: TDLR.			
	a. 4.6.1954; 26.11.1954; 5.4.1957; 6.3.1959; 8.5.1959.	22.50	75.00	325.
	b. 19.2.1960; 27.4.1962; 19.4.1963; 6.3.1964.	17.50	50.00	275.
	c. 7.1.1966-18.2.1972.	15.00	45.00	250.

		VG	VF	UNC
54	**50 Lempiras** 20.1.1956. Deep blue on m/c unpt. Dr. J. Trinidad Reyes at l., arms at r. University of Honduras on back.			
	a. Issued note.	35.00	125.	450.
	s. Specimen, punched hole cancelled.	—	—	275.

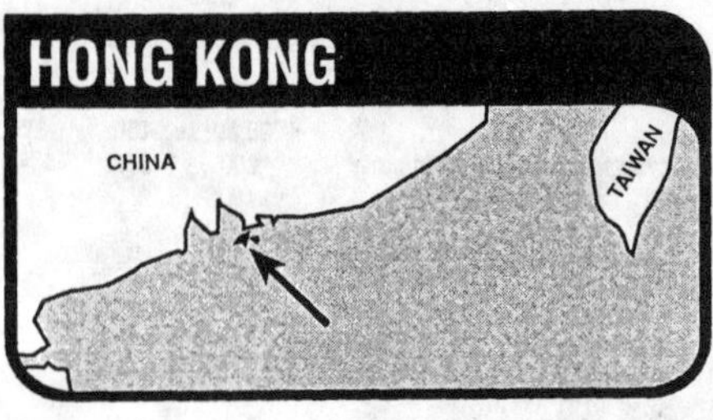

Hong Kong S.A.R., a former British Colony, is situated at the mouth of the Canton or Pearl River 90 miles (145 km.) southeast of Canton, has an area of 409 sq. mi. (1,091 sq. km.) and an estimated population of nearly 7 million. Capital: Central (formerly Victoria). The port of Hong Kong had developed as the commercial center of the Far East, a transshipment point for goods destined for China and the countries of the Pacific rim. Light manufacturing and tourism are important components of the economy.

Long a haven for fishermen-pirates and opium smugglers, the island of Hong Kong was ceded to Britain at the conclusion of the first Opium War (1839-1842). At the time, the acquisition of "a barren rock" was ridiculed by both London and English merchants operating in the Far East. The Kowloon Peninsula and Stonecutter's Island were ceded in 1860 and the so-called New Territories, comprising most of the mainland of the colony, were leased to Britain for 99 years in 1898.

When the Japanese opened hostilities in World War II, on Dec. 7, 1941, they immediately attacked Hong Kong which fell, after some bitter fighting, on Christmas Day. The colony was liberated by British troops on Aug. 30, 1945, when it was found that the population was no more than 600,000, of whom 80 percent were suffering from malnutrition. Hong Kong's economic life was dead. A brief period of military administration was followed by the formal re-establishment of civil government in May 1946. Hong Kong made a dramatic recovery and at the close of 1947 the population had reached 1,800,000. With the disintegration of the Nationalist Chinese forces and the establishment of the Central Peoples government, from 1948 to April 1950, an unprecedented influx of refugees took place, raising the population to about 2,360,000. It is currently near 7 million.

Hong Kong was returned to the Peoples Republic of China on July 1, 1997 and was made a Special Administrative Region, enjoying a high degree of autonomy and vested with executive, legislative and independent judicial power.

RULERS:
British (1842-1997)

MONETARY SYSTEM:
1 Dollar = 100 Cents

COMMERCIAL BANKS:

NOTE ON VALUATIONS: Most valuations are for issued notes. At times specimen or proof notes are listed w/valuations, but these are only cases where a regularly issued example is not known to exist.

BRITISH ADMINISTRATION

AGRA & UNITED SERVICE BANK, LIMITED

行銀理匯剌加呵

A Jai La Hui Li Yin Hang

1862 ISSUE

#5-8 Royal arms at top ctr. Printer: John Biden, London.

		Good	Fine	XF
5	**100 Dollars** ca.1862. Proof. Rare.	—	—	—
6	**200 Dollars** ca.1862. Proof. Rare.	—	—	—

		Good	Fine	XF
7	**300 Dollars** ca.1862. Proof. Rare.	—	—	—
8	**500 Dollars** ca.1862. Proof. Rare.	—	—	—

ASIATIC BANKING CORPORATION

行銀理匯特鴉西亞

Ya Hsi Ya De Hui Li Yin Hang

1800'S ISSUE

#13, 14 arms at upper ctr.

		Good	Fine	XF
11	**10 Dollars** 18xx. Specimen. Rare.	—	—	—
13	**50 Dollars** 18xx. Rare.	—	—	—

		Good	Fine	XF
14	**100 Dollars** 18xx. Specimen. Rare.	—	—	—
15	**500 Dollars** 18xx. Specimen. Rare.	—	—	—

BANK OF HINDUSTAN, CHINA & JAPAN

行銀理匯本日國中丹士度慳

Keng Tu Shi Dan Chung Kuo Jih Ben Hui Li Yin Hang

HONG KONG

1863 ISSUE

		Good	Fine	XF
20	**1000 Dollars** 18xx. Arms at upper ctr. Printer: Batho, Sprague & Co., London. Remainder. Rare.	—	—	—

CHARTERED BANK OF INDIA, AUSTRALIA & CHINA

行銀理滙國中山金新度印

Yin Tu Hsin Chin Shan Chung Kuo Hui Li Yin Hang

行銀利加麥國中山金新度印

Yin Tu Hsin Chin Shan Chung Kuo Ta Cha Yin Hang

1865 ISSUE

#21-26 arms at upper or top ctr. Printer: Batho, Sprague & Co.

		Good	Fine	XF
21	**5 Dollars** 1865-79. Gray frame. 2 handwritten sign.			
	a. 2.1.1865. Rare.	—	—	—
	b. 1.1.1874; 1.1.1879. Rare.	—	—	—
22	**10 Dollars** 18xx. Gray frame. Back red-orange. Proof. Rare.	—	—	—

Note: A forgery of #22 dated 15.1.1906 is known.

		Good	Fine	XF
23	**25 Dollars** 18xx. Blue. Back red-orange. Proof. Rare.	—	—	—
24	**50 Dollars** 18xx. Lt. blue frame. Back orange. Proof. Rare.	—	—	—

		Good	Fine	XF
25	**100 Dollars** 18xx. Red-orange. Proof. Rare.	—	—	—
26	**500 Dollars** 18xx. Gray frame. Gray *500* below arms. Back red-orange; lg. *500* in guilloche. Proof. Rare.	—	—	—

1879 ISSUE

#27-32 arms at upper ctr. Printer: WWS.

		VG	VF	UNC
27	**5 Dollars** 1.1.1879. Blue-gray frame. Back green. Proof.	—	—	17,500.
28	**10 Dollars** 1.1.1879. Brown frame. Back green. Proof.	—	—	17,500.
29	**25 Dollars** 1.1.1879. Green on red unpt. Back green. Proof.	—	—	25,000.
30	**50 Dollars** 1.1.1879. Orange on red unpt. Back dk. green. Proof.	—	—	21,000.
31	**100 Dollars** 1.1.1879. Black on red unpt. Back dk. green. Proof.	—	—	21,000.
32	**500 Dollars** 1.1.1879. Black. Back red; dragon at ctr. Proof.	—	—	25,000.

1897-1910 Issues

		Good	Fine	XF
33	**5 Dollars** 1.11.1897; 15.11.1897. Gray frame. Like #21. Sign. at r. printed. Printer: Batho, Sprague & Co.	1250.	6500.	—

		Good	Fine	XF
40	**500 Dollars** 8.9.1910; 6.10.1910; 20.10.1910; 1.7.1911. Red on olive-green and pink unpt. Arms at top ctr., lg. *500* below. Back greenish black. Rare.	—	—	—

		Good	Fine	XF
34	**5 Dollars** 1.10.1903; 1.1.1905; 19.1.1910; 1.7.1911; 1.10.1912. Blue-green frame on brown-orange unpt. Last 2 digits of year stamped on printed *190x*. Printer: WWS.	750.	4500.	10,000.
35	**10 Dollars** 190x; 19.1.1910. Brown frame on brown-orange unpt. w/purple TEN at lower ctr. Back gray. Printer: WWS.	3500.	8000.	—
36	**25 Dollars** 1.1.1897. Green. Arms at upper ctr. Back green. Printer: Batho, Sprague & Co. Rare.	—	—	—

#37-40 printer: WWS.

		Good	Fine	XF
37	**25 Dollars** 189x.; 1903. Green on purple and red unpt. Like #36. Rare.	—	—	—
38	**50 Dollars** 6.10.1910; 8.9.1910. Yellow-orange on purple and yellow unpt. Back green. Rare.	—	—	—
39	**100 Dollars** 8.9.1910. Gray on purple and pink unpt. Back green.	3000.	8000.	25,000.

1911-23 Issues

#41-46 printer: W&S.

		Good	Fine	XF
41	**5 Dollars** 1.11.1911-1.7.1922. Blue and black. Workmen at l., arms at upper ctr., river scene at r. Large blue *5* in unpt. at bottom ctr. Bldg. at ctr. on back.	400.	1500.	8500
42	**10 Dollars** 1.12.1911-1.7.1922. Black and red-violet on m/c unpt. Boats and pagoda at l., boats in cove at r. Bldg. at ctr. on back.	500.	1500.	700

43 50 Dollars

	Good	Fine	XF
1.1.1912. Black and orange-brown. *50* at upper l. and at each side of vignette. Back yellow-green; old bank bldg. at ctr.	2000.	6000.	18,000.

44 50 Dollars

	Good	Fine	XF
1.11.1923; 1.5.1924; 1.11.1929. Black and orange-brown on m/c unpt. Red *FIFTY* at each side of central vignette. Back olive-green and brown-violet; old bank bldg. at ctr.	1000.	4000.	12,000.

45 100 Dollars

	Good	Fine	XF
1.2.1912; 1.5.1924; 1.2.1926; 1.9.1927. Black and green on m/c unpt. Bridge at upper l., pavilion at upper r. Back black and red; old bank bldg. at ctr.	1500.	5000.	20,000.

46 500 Dollars

1912-26. Pale red and blue-black on m/c unpt. Boat, coastline at ctr. Back blue and black; old bank bldg. at ctr.

	Good	Fine	XF
a. 1.3.1912; 1.7.1912.	2500.	7500.	30,000.
b. 1.2.1921; 1.7.1922; 1.10.1926.	2000.	5000.	22,000.

1923-29 Issues

#47-52 printer: W&S.

47 5 Dollars

	Good	Fine	XF
1.9.1923; 1.11.1923. Blue and black. Like #41 but w/red *FIVE* at lower ctr. Back red.	500.	1400.	4500.

48 5 Dollars

	Good	Fine	XF
1.5.1924; 1.9.1927. Blue. Like #47 but Chinese character *Wu* (5) in red in either side of arms. Back brown.	450.	1200.	3750.

49 10 Dollars

	Good	Fine	XF
1.3.1923-1.11.1923. Black and violet unpt. Like #42 but w/red *TEN* at lower ctr.	550.	1400.	4750.

50 10 Dollars

	Good	Fine	XF
1.5.1924; 1.9.1927; 1.8.1929. Like #49 but w/red *TEN* between red Chinese characters *Shih* (ten) at lower ctr.	400.	1000.	3500.

51 50 Dollars

	Good	Fine	XF
1.5.1923; 1.11.1923; 1.5.1924; 1.11.1929. Black and orange-brown on m/c unpt. *50* at upper r. Back olive-green and violet.	1500.	4000.	10,000.

52 100 Dollars

	Good	Fine	XF
2.12.1929; 2.6.1930. Black and dk. blue on m/c unpt. Britannia at l. Junk and sampan at ctr. on back.	700.	2000.	5500.

1930-34 Issues

#53-59 printer: W&S.

53 5 Dollars

	Good	Fine	XF
18.8.1930; 1.9.1931. Green. Short red 30mm *5* in unpt. at ctr. Helmeted warrior's head at l.	350.	900.	2750.

		Good	Fine	XF
54	**5 Dollars** 1934-56. Like #53 but tall red 50mm *5* in unpt. at ctr.			
	a. Sign. at r. printed. 2.4.1934-20.9.1940.	100.	350.	1000.
	b. 2 sign. printed. 28.10.1941-6.12.1956.	55.00	140.	550.

		Good	Fine	XF
55	**10 Dollars** 1931-56. Black and red on green unpt. Helmeted warrior's head at l., arms at ctr. Woman harvesting rice at ctr. on back.			
	a. Sign. at r. printed. 1.7.1931.	90.00	275.	1000.
	b. 2.4.1934-20.9.1940.	80.00	250.	850.
	c. 2 sign. printed. 18.11.1941-1.9.1956.	25.00	100.	325.
56	**50 Dollars** 1.7.1931; 2.4.1934; 1.11.1934. Black and brown on m/c unpt. Helmeted warrior's head at l. Woman harvesting rice at r. on back.	350.	1000.	3500.

		Good	Fine	XF
57	**100 Dollars** 1934-56. Dk. green and dk. brown on m/c unpt. Britannia seated holding trident w/shield and lion at ctr., arms at upper r. Statue Square, Supreme Court bldg. at ctr. r. on back.			
	a. Sign. at r. printed. 1.5.1934; 2.7.1934.	400.	1250.	3500.
	b. 28.3.1936-1.11.1939.	325.	850.	2000.
	c. 2 sign. printed. 8.12.1941-1.9.1956.	150.	500.	1200.

		Good	Fine	XF
58	**500 Dollars** 1.8.1930. Dk. blue on m/c unpt. Helmeted warrior's head at lower ctr. Sampan at r. on back. Rare.	—	—	—

		Good	Fine	XF
59	**500 Dollars** 1934-52. Black and dk. brown on m/c unpt. Man at l. Boat, harbor view at ctr. r. on back.			
	a. 1.6.1934.	375.	1000.	2500
	b. 14.9.1936.	275.	800.	2000
	c. 1.11.1939.	225.	750.	1950
	d. 6.8.1947.	175.	700.	1900
	e. 1.7.1949.	—	—	—
	f. 1.8.1951; 1.11.1952.	125.	650.	1850

CHARTERED BANK

行銀打渣

Cha Ta Yin Han

1956-59 ISSUES

#62-67 wmk: Helmeted warrior's head. Printer: W&S.

		VG	VF	UNC
62	**5 Dollars** 9.4.1959. Black and dk. green on m/c unpt. Arms at lower l. Chinese junk and sampan at ctr. on back.	15.00	50.00	140
63	**10 Dollars** 6.12.1956. Black and red. Helmeted warrior's head at l. Woman harvesting rice at ctr. on back.	40.00	125.	400

		VG	VF	UNC
64	**10 Dollars** 9.4.1959. Black and red-violet on red unpt. Arms at l. Bank bldg. at ctr. on back.	12.50	30.00	90.00
65	**100 Dollars** 6.12.1956. Dk. green and brown on m/c unpt. Britannia seated holding trident w/shield and lion at ctr., arms at upper r. Statue Sqaure, Supreme Court bldg. at ctr. r. on back.	325.	900.	2000.
66	**100 Dollars** 9.4.1959. Dk. green and brown on m/c unpt. Arms at ctr. Harbor view on back.	40.00	125.	550.
67	**500 Dollars** 1.9.1957; 14.12.1959. Black and dk. brown on m/c unpt. Man at l. Boat, harbor view at ctr. r. on back.	250.	600.	1250.

CHARTERED MERCANTILE BANK OF INDIA, LONDON & CHINA

行銀理匯處三國中頓倫度印

Yin Tu Lun Dun Chung Kuo San Zhu Hui Li Yin Hang

HONG KONG

1858 ISSUE

#82-86 black. Britannia seated w/crowned shield at upper ctr. Uniface. Printer: Batho & Co.

		Good	Fine	XF
82	**5 Dollars** 18xx. Lg. blue *FIVE* in unpt. Proof.	—	—	—
83	**10 Dollars** 18xx. Lg. gray *TEN* in unpt. Proof.	—	—	—

		Good	Fine	XF
84	**25 Dollars** 18xx. Lg. red-orange *TWENTY FIVE* in unpt. Proof.	—	—	—

		Good	Fine	XF
85	**50 Dollars** 18xx. Lg. green *FIFTY* in unpt. Proof.	—	—	—

		Good	Fine	XF
86	**100 Dollars** 18xx. Lg. red-orange *ONE HUNDRED* in unpt. Proof.	—	—	—

1873-90 ISSUE

#87-91 arms at upper ctr. Printer: PBC.

		Good	Fine	XF
87	**5 Dollars** 1873-90. Red *FIVE* in unpt.			
	a. Perforated: *CANCELLED*. 8.1.1873; 1.9.1880; 1.5.1882. Rare.	—	—	—
	b. 1.12.1888; 1.9.1889; 1.1.1890. Rare.	—	—	—
88	**10 Dollars** 16.7.1883; 16.12.1887; 16.5.1889. Rare.	—	—	—
89	**25 Dollars** 1.1.1880; 1.9.1880; 1.1.1890. Proof.	—	—	25,000.

		VG	VF	UNC
90	**50 Dollars** 1.9.1888; 1.1.1890. Proof.	—	—	14,000.
91	**100 Dollars** 18xx; 1.9.1880; 1.9.1888. Proof.	—	—	14,000.

HONG KONG & SHANGHAI BANKING COMPANY, LIMITED

行銀豐滙海上港香商英

Ying Shang Hsiang K'ang Shang Hai Hui Feng Yin Hang

1865 ISSUE

#96-101 arms at upper ctr. Printer: Ashby & Co.

		VG	VF	UNC
96	**5 Dollars** 18xx. Proof.	—	—	10,000.
97	**10 Dollars** 18xx. Proof.	—	—	10,000.

		VG	VF	UNC
98	**25 Dollars** 18xx. Black. Back orange. Proof. Rare.	—	—	—
99	**50 Dollars** 16.4.1865. Rare.	—	—	—
100	**100 Dollars** 18xx. Proof.	—	—	15,000.
101	**500 Dollars** 18xx. Proof.	—	—	19,500.

HONG KONG & SHANGHAI BANKING CORPORATION

行銀理滙海上港香

Hsiang K'ang Shang Hai Hui Li Yin Hang

HONG KONG

1867-89 ISSUES

#111-135 arms at upper ctr. Bank arms at ctr. on back. Printer: Ashby & Co.

No.	Denomination	Good	Fine	XF
111	**1 Dollar** 1.10.1872-30.11.1872. Gray frame w/red-orange *$1-* Chinese character-*1$* in unpt. Back lilac.	700.	1800.	4000.
112	**1 Dollar** 1.4.1873-1.6.1874. Like #111 but w/lilac unpt.	700.	1800.	4000.
113	**1 Dollar** 30.6.1879-1.9.1879. Like #112 but w/red unpt. Back red-orange.	700.	1800.	4000.

No.	Denomination	Good	Fine	XF
114	**1 Dollar** 1.6.1884-20.9.1888. Face like #113. Back red-orange.	500.	1500.	3250.
115	**5 Dollars** 1.1.1867. Lt. green unpt. Back lt. brown. Rare.	—	—	—
116	**5 Dollars** 16.7.1877. Green unpt. 198 x 117mm. Rare.	—	—	—

No.	Denomination	Good	Fine	XF
117	**5 Dollars** 3.1.1882; 1.2.1883; 6.2.1883. Gray frame on green unpt. w/dk. blue *$5 - 5$* at l. and r. Back dk. green. Rare.	—	—	—
119	**10 Dollars** 16.7.1877. Blue and black. Back red-orange. Proof.			

No.	Denomination	Good	Fine	XF
121	**25 Dollars** 18xx; 1880; 1884. Black w/blue-black *$25-25$* at l. and r. Back lt. orange. 201 x 105mm.			
	a. 1.11.1880; 1.12.1884. Rare.	—	—	—
	p. Proof. 18xx.	—	—	—
	r. Remainder w/oval handstamp: *CANCELLED-JUL 16 1877.* 18xx. Rare.	—	—	—
122	**25 Dollars** 1.11.1889. Brown w/red *$25 - 25$* at l. and r. Arms at upper ctr. Back red-orange. Rare.	—	—	—

123, 124 not assigned.

No.	Denomination	Good	Fine	XF
125	**50 Dollars** 16.7.1877. Blue and black. Back dk. gray, 203 x 120mm. Remainder w/oval handstamp: *CANCELLED-SEP 4 1877.*	—	Unc	16,000.
127	**50 Dollars** 1.1.1884. Lt. brown. Like #125. Rare.	—	—	—
129	**100 Dollars** 16.7.1877. Blue and black. Back orange. Proof.			
131	**100 Dollars** 6.2.1885; 10.2.1888. Red. 196 x 125mm. Rare.	—	—	—
132	**100 Dollars** 31.12.1888; 2.1.1890; 1.9.1893. Red w/lg. outlined *100* in blue oval frame in unpt. Back red-orange. Rare.	—	—	—
134	**500 Dollars** 18xx. Black w/dk. blue *$500-500$* at l. and r. Back black.			
135	**500 Dollars** 16.7.1877. Blue and black. Back blue. Proof. Rare.	—	—	—

1884-96 ISSUES

#136-149 printer: BFL.

		Good	Fine	XF
136	**1 Dollar** 1889-99. Black frame on lt. blue and brown unpt. Back red-orange.			
	a. Handwritten date. 1.11.1889.	250.	1250.	4500.
	b. 2.1.1890.	200.	700.	2000.
	c. Printed dates. 18.11.1895; 2.1.1899.	150.	500.	1500.
137	**5 Dollars** 1.5.1884-1.12.1889. Gray frame on green unpt. w/red-orange *$5-5$* at l. and r. Back red-orange. Rare.	—	—	—
138	**5 Dollars** 2.1.1890-1.9.1893. Gray frame on lt. green unpt. Back red.	2000.	4000.	9000.

		Good	Fine	XF
139	**5 Dollars** 1.3.1897; 1.9.1897; 1.3.1898. Gray frame on yellow unpt. Back red-orange.	1500.	3250.	7250.
41	**10 Dollars** 26.4.1888. Lt. blue. Back orange. Rare.	—	—	—
42	**10 Dollars** 1.3.1890; 15.12.1890. Lt. green. Back lt. brown. Rare.	—	—	—

		Good	Fine	XF
43	**10 Dollars** 1.4.1893-1.3.1898. Blue-gray on pink unpt. Back brown-orange.	2000.	4500.	9000.

		Good	Fine	XF
5	**50 Dollars** 2.1.1890; 1.3.1897; 1.3.1898. Violet on red unpt. Back red-orange. Rare.	—	—	—

NOTICE

Readers with unlisted dates, signature varieties, etc. are invited to submit photocopies or, high resolution (300 dpi, 100% size) scans of their notes to: Standard Catalog of World Paper Money, 700 East State St. ola, WI 54990-0001, or E-Mail: george.cuhaj@fwpubs.com.

		Good	Fine	XF
146	**100 Dollars** 18xx. Black on brown unpt. Qn. Victoria at l., colony arms at r. Specimen. Rare.	—	—	—

		Good	Fine	XF
147	**100 Dollars** 1895-96. Red on blue unpt. arms at top ctr.			
	a. 1.1.1895. Rare.	—	—	—
	b. 1.3.1896.	1500.	4500.	15,000.

		VG	VF	UNC
149	**500 Dollars** 1896-97. Red-orange on lt. green unpt. Back red-orange w/colony arms at ctr.			
	a. Issued note. 1.3.1896. Rare.	—	—	—
	r. Remainder, perforated: *CANCELLED*. 1.3.1897.	—	—	19,000.

1900-01 ISSUE

#150-154 printer: BWC.

		Good	Fine	XF
150	**5 Dollars** 1.12.1900; 1.1.1901. Olive-green on yellow unpt. Lg. curved *FIVE* in unpt. below arms at upper ctr.	750.	2500.	6000.

		Good	Fine	XF
151	**10 Dollars** 1.12.1900; 1.1.1901; 1.7.1902. Dk. blue on red unpt. Lg. *TEN* in unpt. below arms at upper ctr. Back red.	700.	2500.	7500.

		Good	Fine	XF
152	**50 Dollars** 1.1.1901. Violet on tan unpt. Lg. *FIFTY* below arms at upper ctr. Arms at upper ctr. under arched bank name. Back red-orange; allegorical woman reclining at ctr. Specimen.	—	Unc	10,000.

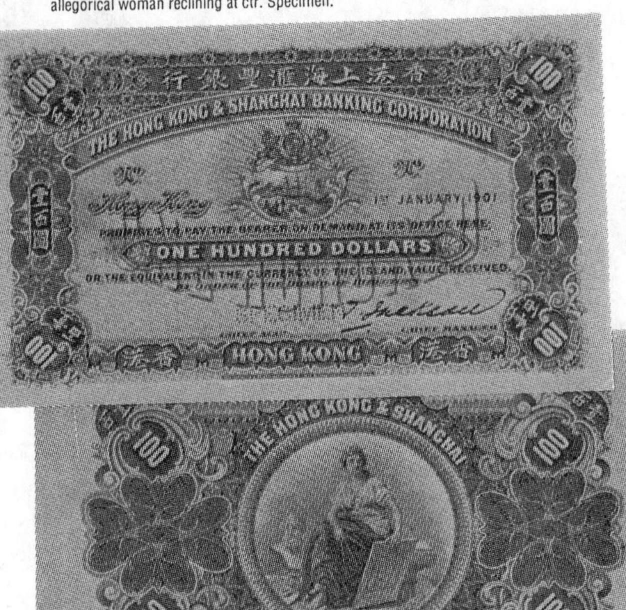

		Good	Fine	XF
153	**100 Dollars** 1.1.1901. Red on green. Lg. curved *ONE HUNDRED* in unpt. below arms at upper ctr. Allegorical woman artist seated at ctr. on back. Specimen.	—	Unc	12,500.

		Good	Fine	XF
154	**500 Dollars** 1.1.1901. Brown on blue unpt. Lg. curved *FIVE HUNDRED* in unpt. under arms at upper ctr. Back red; seated allegorical woman w/3 cherubs at ctr. Specimen.	—	Unc	15,000

NOTICE

Readers with unlisted dates, signature varieties, etc. are invited to submit photocopies or, high resolution (300 dpi, 100% size) scans of their notes to: Standard Catalog of World Paper Money, 700 East State St. Iola, WI 54990-0001, or E-Mail: george.cuhaj@fwpubs.com.

1904-05 ISSUE

#155-160 printer: BWC.

		Good	Fine	XF
155	**1 Dollar** 1904-06; 1913. Black on blue and yellow unpt. Helmeted woman at l., port scene and arms at lower r. Bank name in curved line. Back red-orange; seated allegorical woman w/lyre at ctr.			
	a. 1 printed sign. 1.1.1904; 1.5.1906.	150.	500.	1400.
	b. 2 printed sign. 1.7.1913.	50.00	200.	500.

#156-160 arms at upper ctr. similar to #150-154.

		Good	Fine	XF
156	**5 Dollars** 1.5.1904; 1.6.1905. Olive on yellow unpt. Similar to #150 but different unpt. design. Back red-orange.	650.	2000.	5250.

		Good	Fine	XF
157	**10 Dollars** 1.5.1904; 1.1.1905; 1.6.1905. Dk. blue on tan unpt. Similar to #151 but different unpt. design.	500.	2400.	6000.

158 has been moved to #162A.

		Good	Fine	XF
159	**100 Dollars** 1.5.1904; 1.1.1906. Red on m/c unpt. Similar to #153 but different unpt. design. Back brown. 198 x 127mm.	2000.	6000.	15,000.

		Good	Fine	XF
160	**500 Dollars** 1.5.1904; 1.1.1905; 1.6.1907. Brown on m/c unpt. Similar to #154 but different unpt. design. Back dk. red.	3000.	8000.	25,000.

1905-15 ISSUE

#161-165 old bank bldg. at ctr. on back. Printer: W&S.

		Good	Fine	XF
161	**5 Dollars** 1.1.1906; 1.1.1909. Olive and brown on orange unpt. Water carrier and sedan bearers at l., ship at r. Back red and black.	500.	1500.	4000.
162	**10 Dollars** 1.1.1909. Black and dk. blue on lt. blue and pink unpt. Waterfront at l., horseman and walkers at r., ships and houses in background. Back lt. red-brown and black.	500.	1500.	4000.
162A	**50 Dollars** 1905; 1909. Black, purple and dk. green on lt. green unpt. Bank shield at l., head of Greek male statue at ctr., Great Wall of China vignette at r. Back red-orange and black.			
	a. 1.1.1905.	1250.	5000.	12,000.
	b. 1.1.1909.	850.	4000.	8000.

NOTICE

Readers with unlisted dates, signature varieties, etc. are invited to submit photocopies or, high resolution (300 dpi, 100% size) scans of their notes to: Standard Catalog of World Paper Money, 700 East State St. Iola, WI 54990-0001, or E-Mail: george.cuhaj@fwpubs.com.

		Good	Fine	XF
163	**100 Dollars** 1906; 1909. Orange and black on lt. blue unpt. Bank shield at upper l., Chinese laborers w/baskets at l. and r. Back red-brown and black.			
	a. Issued note. 1.1.1909.	2000.	6000.	18,000.
	s. Specimen. 1.1.1906.	—	Unc	13,500.

		Good	Fine	XF
164	**500 Dollars** 1909; 1912. Black and brown on lt. blue unpt. Farmer w/ox at l., arms at ctr., Botanic Garden at r.			
	a. 1.1.1909.	3000.	7500.	25,000.
	b. 1.1.1912.	3000.	7500.	25,000.
165	**500 Dollars** 1.1.1915. Deep brown and black on lt. blue unpt. Like #164. Back red-violet and black.	3000.	7500.	25,000.

1912-21 ISSUE

#166-170 printer: W&S.

		Good	Fine	XF
166	**5 Dollars** 1.7.1916; 1.1.1921; 1.1.1923; 1.5.1923. Like #161 but olive and brown back.	650.	1800.	4500.

		Good	Fine	XF
167	**10 Dollars** 1.7.1913; 1.1.1921; 1.1.1923. Blue on red unpt. Like #162 but back olive-green and dk. brown.	300.	1500.	4000.

		Good	Fine	XF
168	**50 Dollars** 1.1.1921; 1.1.1923. Like #162A but back green and black.	2500.	4000.	10,000.

		Good	Fine	XF
169	**100 Dollars** 1912-23. Orange and black on lt. blue unpt. Like #163 but back olive and brown.			
	a. 1.1.1912.	2000.	7500.	35,000.
	b. 1.1.1921; 1.1.1923.	1750.	6500.	32,000.
170	**500 Dollars** 1.1.1921; 1.7.1925. Like #165, but back olive-green and olive-brown.	2000.	7500.	30,000.

Note: Bank records show that all the 1.7.1925 notes have been redeemed.

1923 ISSUE

#171-188 printer: BWC.

		VG	VF	UNC
171	**1 Dollar** 1.1.1923; 1.1.1925. Black on blue and yellow unpt. Similar to #155 but bank name in straight line. Back maroon and brown; like #155.	45.00	250.	800.

1926-27 ISSUE

		VG	VF	UNC
172	**1 Dollar** 1926-35. Blue on yellow and lt. green unpt. Helmeted woman at l. Back purple; allegorical woman w/torch at ctr.			
	a. 1.1.1926.	60.00	250.	800.
	b. 1.1.1929.	35.00	110.	400.
	c. 1.6.1935.	20.00	50.00	250.

#173-177 old bank bldg. below angel playing trumpet at ctr. on back.

		VG	VF	UNC
73	**5 Dollars** 1927-46. Dk. brown on m/c unpt. Woman seated at r. *HONGKONG* at date not divided. W/4 serial # on back.			
	a. 1 printed sign. 1.10.1927; 1.1.1929; 1.9.1930.	50.00	250.	600.
	b. 1.1.1930-1.1.1938.	30.00	150.	400.
	c. 2 printed sign. w/additional vertical serial # on face and back. 1.4.1940; 1.4.1941.	32.50	125.	375.
	d. W/o serial # on back. 1.4.1941.	7.00	20.00	180.
	e. 30.3.1946.	5.00	15.00	150.
74	**10 Dollars** 1927-30. Dk. blue on m/c unpt. Woman holding sheaf of grain at l., *HONGKONG* at date not divided. W/4 serial # on back.			
	a. 1.10.1927. Green.	75.00	250.	900.
	b. 1.1.1929; 1.1.1930.	65.00	200.	850.
	c. 1.9.1930.	100.	275.	1400.

		VG	VF	UNC
175	**50 Dollars** 1927-37. Dk. green on m/c unpt. Woman standing on winged wheel w/vines and fruit at l., arms at top ctr.			
	a. 1.10.1927.	275.	750.	2200.
	b. 1.10.1930.	250.	700.	1800.
	c. 1.1.1934.	200.	500.	1300.
	d. "Duress" note issued during Japanese occupation w/serial #B350,001 to B550,000. 1934-37.	200.	500.	1300.
176	**100 Dollars** 1927-59. Red. Woman seated w/book at l., arms at upper ctr.			
	a. 1 printed sign. 1.10.1927; 1.9.1930; 2.1.1933.	150.	500.	1750.
	b. 2.1.1934; 1.1.1936.	125.	350.	1600.
	c. 1.7.1937.	120.	300.	1500.
	d. "Duress" note issued during Japanese occupation w/serial #B485,001 to B650,000. 1934-37.	135.	350.	1600.
	e. 1.4.1941-1.3.1955.	100.	250.	800.
	f. 5.9.1956; 25.2.1958; 24.9.1958.	75.00	225.	700.
	g. 4.2.1959.	100.	300.	900.

		VG	VF	UNC
177	**500 Dollars** 1927; 1930. Dk. brown on purple and m/c unpt. Woman seated holding tablet at r. Back purple and yellow-brown.			
	a. 1.10.1927.	700.	2000.	7500.
	b. 1.7.1930.	600.	1750.	4500.
	c. "Duress" note issued during Japanese occupation w/serial #C126,001 to C300,000. 1.7.1930.	600.	1750.	4500.

1932-35 ISSUE

		VG	VF	UNC
178	**10 Dollars** 1930-48. Dk. green on m/c unpt. Like #174.			
	a. 1 printed sign. W/4 serial # on back. 1.10.1930-1.1.1938.	8.50	75.00	350.
	b. W/ additional small serial # printed vertically on face and back. 1.4.1941.	35.00	125.	400.
	c. 2 printed sign. W/o serial # on back. 1.4.1941.	6.00	25.00	300.
	d. 30.3.1946; 31.3.1947; 1.4.1948.	5.00	20.00	200.

179 500 Dollars

1935-69. Brown and blue. Arms at top ctr., Sir T. Jackson at r. Back blue; allegorical female head at l., bank bldg. at ctr.

	VG	VF	UNC
a. Handsigned. 1.6.1935-1.7.1937.	225.	1250.	3000.
b. Printed sign. 1.4.1941-1.8.1952.	175.	450.	1250.
c. 11.7.1960-1.8.1966.	150.	250.	900.
d. 31.7.1967.	150.	200.	400.
e. 11.2.1968.	FV	100.	250.
f. 27.3.1969.	FV	100.	300.

1949 Issue

179A 10 Dollars

1949-59. Dk. green on m/c unpt. Like #178 but w/*HONG KONG* at date divided.

	VG	VF	UNC
a. 1.7.1949; 31.12.1953.	12.00	30.00	150.
b. 1.7.1954-14.1.1958.	7.50	17.50	125.
c. 26.3.1958.	17.50	75.00	350.
d. 14.9.1958; 24.9.1958.	7.50	17.50	125.
e. 4.2.1959.	12.00	30.00	150.

1954 Issue

180 5 Dollars

1954-59. Brown. Like #173 but w/*HONG KONG* at date divided.

	VG	VF	UNC
a. 1.7.1954-7.8.1958.	3.50	25.00	160.
b. 4.2.1959.	9.50	35.00	180.

1959 Issue

#181-183 wmk: Helmeted warrior's head. Printer: BWC.

181 5 Dollars

1959-75. Brown on m/c unpt. Woman seated at r. New bank bldg. at ctr. on back.

	VG	VF	UNC
a. Sign. titles: *CHIEF ACCOUNTANT* and *CHIEF MANAGER.* 2.5.1959-29.6.1960.	3.00	15.00	45.00
b. 1.5.1963.	50.00	175.	750.
c. 1.5.1964-27.3.1969.	1.50	4.00	15.00
d. Sign. titles: *CHIEF ACCOUNTANT* and *GENERAL MANAGER.* 1.4.1970-18.3.1971.	1.00	3.50	12.50
e. 13.3.1972; 31.10.1972.	.75	2.00	9.00
f. Sm. serial #. 31.10.1973; 31.3.1975.	.75	1.25	7.00
s. Specimen.	—	—	—

182 10 Dollars

1959-83. Dk. green on m/c unpt. Portr. woman w/sheaf of grain at upper l., arms below. Back similar to #184.

	VG	VF	UNC
a. Sign. titles: *CHIEF ACCOUNTANT* and *CHIEF MANAGER.* 21.5.1959-1.9.1962.	5.00	15.00	45.00
b. 1.5.1963; 1.9.1963.	6.00	20.00	60.00
c. 1.5.1964; 1.9.1964.	5.00	15.00	55.00
d. 1.10.1964.	40.00	200.	800.
e. 1.2.1965; 1.8.1966; 31.7.1967.	2.00	6.00	20.00
f. 20.3.1968; 23.11.1968; 27.3.1969.	2.00	6.00	18.00
g. Sign. titles: *CHIEF ACCOUNTANT* and *GENERAL MANAGER.* 1.4.1970-31.3.1976.	1.50	3.75	10.00
h. Sign. titles: *CHIEF ACCOUNTANT* and *EXECUTIVE DIRECTOR.* 31.3.1977; 31.3.1978; 31.3.1979.	1.50	3.00	12.00
i. Sign. titles: *CHIEF ACCOUNTANT* and *GENERAL MANAGER.* 31.3.1980; 31.3.1981.	1.50	2.00	9.00
j. Sign. titles: *MANAGER* and *GENERAL MANAGER.* 31.3.1982; 31.3.1983.	1.50	2.00	9.00
s. Specimen.	—	—	—

183 100 Dollars

1959-72. Red on m/c unpt. Woman seated at l. w/open book, arms at upper ctr. Wmk: Helmeted warrior's head and denomination.

	VG	VF	UNC
a. Sign. titles: *CHIEF ACCOUNTANT* and *CHIEF MANAGER.* 12.8.1959-1.10.1964.	20.00	50.00	175.
b. 1.2.1965-27.3.1969.	20.00	35.00	125.
c. Sign. titles: *CHIEF ACCOUNTANT* and *GENERAL MANAGER.* 1.4.1970; 18.3.1971; 13.3.1972.	15.00	30.00	90.00

NOTICE

Readers with unlisted dates, signature varieties, etc. are invited to submit photocopies or, high resolution (300 dpi, 100% size) scans of their notes to: Standard Catalog of World Paper Money, 700 East State St. Iola, WI 54990-0001, or E-Mail: george.cuhaj@fwpubs.com.

MERCANTILE BANK OF INDIA, LIMITED

行銀利有 港香

Hsiang K'ang Yu Li Yin Hang

Formerly The Chartered Mercantile Bank of India, London and China. In 1912 it became the Mercantile Bank of India, Limited. In 1958 it became The Mercantile Bank Limited. Various date and sign. varieties. These listings are for notes w/*HONG KONG* as city of issue. Similar notes w/*SHANGHAI* were Chinese branch office issue.

1912 ISSUE

#235-241 printer: W&S.

#235-239 Mercury at ctr. on back.

235	**5 Dollars**	Good	Fine	XF
	1912-41. Olive on tan unpt. Boats at ctr. w/houses and towers in background. Back dk. red and black.			
	a. 2 serial # on back. 1.3.1912.	1000.	2500.	8000.
	b. As a. 1.5.1924; 1.1.1930.	750.	1750.	6000.
	c. 4 serial # on back. 1.7.1936; 1.12.1937.	675.	1500.	4000.
	d. 2 serial # on back. 29.11.1941.	600.	1300.	3500.

236	**10 Dollars**	Good	Fine	XF
	1912-41. Red-brown on lt. yellow-green unpt. Houses and mountains near water, bridge at ctr. Back green and black.			
	a. 2 serial # on back. 1.3.1912.	800.	2500.	9000.
	b. As a. 1.1.1930.	500.	1250.	6000.
	c. 4 serial # on back. 1.7.1936.	550.	1250.	6000.
	d. As c. 1.12.1937.	750.	1500.	7000.
	e. 2 serial # on back. 29.11.1941.	275.	750.	2750.

237	**25 Dollars**	Good	Fine	XF
	1.3.1912. Blue on yellow unpt. River view w/boats and houses at l.	3000.	9000.	25,000.

238	**50 Dollars**	Good	Fine	XF
	1.3.1912; 1.5.1924; 1.1.1930. Brown and black. Ships at ctr., mountains in background.	1800.	4000.	11,000.

239	**100 Dollars**	Good	Fine	XF
	1912-56. Red-violet on orange and lt. blue unpt. Houses below mountains at water's edge at ctr.			
	a. 1.3.1912.	1500.	4000.	10,000.
	b. 1.5.1924; 1.1.1930.	1200.	3000.	8000.
	c. 4 serial # on back. 1.7.1936; 1.12.1937.	1200.	3000.	8000.
	d. 2 serial # on back. 24.8.1948; 28.3.1950; 10.3.1953; 26.10.1954; 4.10.1955; 2.1.1956.	375.	950.	3750.

1935 ISSUE

240	**50 Dollars**	Good	Fine	XF
	1935-41. Dk. brown on m/c unpt. Male bust at l. and as wmk. Chinese mansion on back.			
	a. W/2 serial # on back. 1.7.1935.	450.	1500.	4250.
	b. W/4 serial # on back. 1.12.1937.	1000.	4000.	15,000.
	c. W/2 serial # on back. 29.11.1941.	750.	1750.	5750.

1948 ISSUE

		Good	Fine	XF
241	**500 Dollars** 24.8.1948. Dk. blue on yellow and lt. blue unpt. Mercury at r. Gateway on back. Handsigned. Wmk: *500.* Rare.	—	—	—

MERCANTILE BANK LIMITED

香港有利銀行

Hsiang K'ang Yu Li Yin Hang

1958-60 ISSUE

#242-243 printer: W&S.

		VG	VF	UNC
242	**100 Dollars** 1958-60. Brown-violet on orange and lt. blue unpt. Similar to #239 but w/new bank name.			
	a. 3.1.1958; 12.8.1958; 26.5.1959.	375.	1250.	3500.
	b. 20.9.1960; 6.12.1960.	325.	1150.	3000.

		VG	VF	UNC
243	**500 Dollars** 26.5.1959. Blue on yellow and lt. blue unpt. Similar to #241 w/new bank name. Printed sign. Wmk: *500.* Rare.	—	—	—

NATIONAL BANK OF CHINA LIMITED

香港中華滙理銀行

Hsiang K'ang Chung Hua Hui Li Yin Hang

HONG KONG

1892 ISSUE

#247-251 black text. Arms at upper ctr. Junks over harbor view at ctr. on back. Various dates between 1892-1911. Printer: W&S.

		Good	Fine	XF
247	**5 Dollars** 1894. Deep red on yellow and orange unpt. Back red-orange.			
	a. Issued note w/printed date. 2.5.1894.	4000.	12,000.	—
	b. Partially printed date, 2 handwritten sign. 189x. Rare.	—	—	—
	r1. Remainder w/partially printed date, printed sign. at r., punched holed and perforated: *CANCELLED.* 189x. Rare.	—	—	—
	r2. Remainder w/o sign. 189x. Rare.	—	—	—
	s. Salesman's sample punched hole cancelled, w/W&S printer's seal, ovpt: *SPECIMEN.* Rare.	—	—	—
248	**10 Dollars** 2.5.1894. Green on lt. green and yellow unpt. Remainder.	4500.	15,000.	—

		Good	Fine	XF
249	**50 Dollars** 189x. Red on yellow unpt. Back brown. Unsigned remainder punch holed and perforated: *CANCELLED.*	—	Unc	22,00
250	**100 Dollars** 189x. Purple on lilac and yellow unpt. Unsigned remainder punched holed and perforated: *CANCELLED.*	—	Unc	17,00
251	**500 Dollars** 189x. Brown on gold and yellow unpt. Back brown. Unsigned remainder punched holed and perforated: *CANCELLED.*	—	Unc	19,50

ORIENTAL BANK CORPORATION

東藩滙理銀行

Tung Fan Hui Li Yin Ha

VICTORIA, HONG KONG

1860'S ISSUE

#260, 263 and 264 royal crowned shield between lion and unicorn at upper ctr. Printer: PBC.

		Good	Fine
260	**5 Dollars** 18xx. Black. Proof handstamped: *SPECIMEN.*	—	—

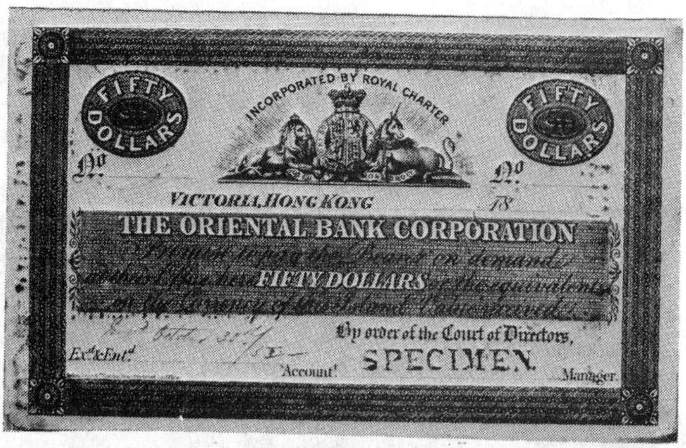

		Good	Fine	XF
263	**50 Dollars** 18xx. Black. Proof handstamped: *SPECIMEN.*	—	—	—

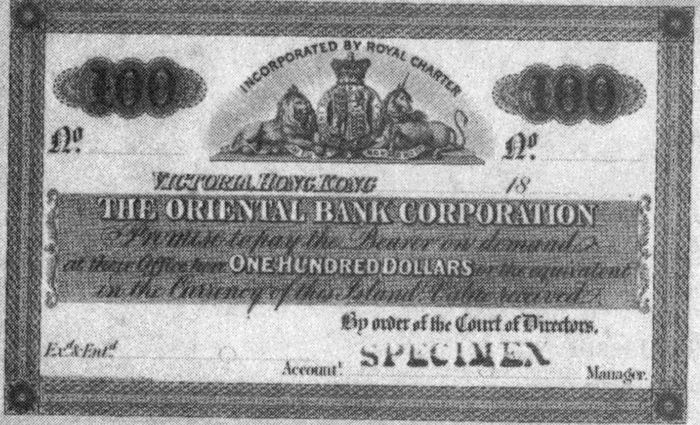

		Good	Fine	XF
264	**100 Dollars** 18xx. Black. Proof handstamped: *SPECIMEN.*	—	—	—

HONG KONG

1866 ISSUE

#267-270 crowned shield between lion and unicorn at upper ctr. Printer: PBC.

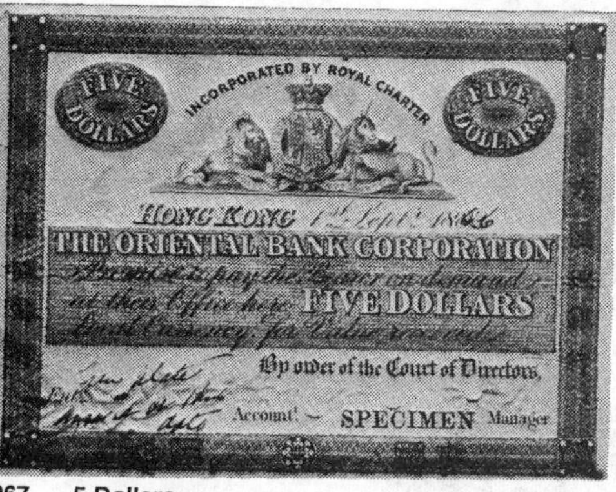

		Good	Fine	XF
267	**5 Dollars** 1866-82.			
	a. Issued note. 7.3.1866.	8500.	30,000.	—
	b. Issued note. 7.3.1879. Rare.	—	—	—
	s. Specimen. 4.9.1866; 1.9.1882. Rare.	—	—	—

		Good	Fine	XF
268	**25 Dollars** 7.5.1866; 7.5.1879/1866. Orange on yellow unpt. Rare.	—	—	—
269	**50 Dollars** 7.3.1866; 1.5.1883. Black. Proof. Rare.	—	—	—

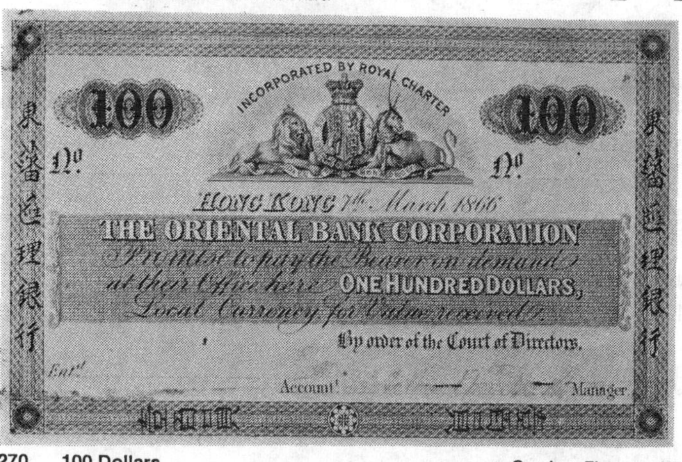

		Good	Fine	XF
270	**100 Dollars** 7.3.1866; 1.5.1883. Proof. Rare.	—	—	—

GOVERNMENT OF HONG KONG

HSIANG K'ANG CHENG FU

1935 ND ISSUE

#311-312 printer: BWC.

		VG	VF	UNC
311	**1 Dollar** ND (1935). Purple on m/c unpt. Portr. Kg. George V at r.	25.00	350.	1000.

1936 ND ISSUE

		VG	VF	UNC
312	**1 Dollar** ND (1936). Purple on m/c unpt. Portr. Kg. George VI at r.	5.00	25.00	175.

Note: For similar issues in blue, see #316; in green, see #324.

1940-41 ND ISSUES

		VG	VF	UNC
313	**1 Cent** ND (1941). Brown on ochre unpt. Back red.			
	a. W/o serial # prefix.	.25	1.50	6.00
	b. Prefix A.	.25	1.00	4.00
	c. Prefix B.	.25	.50	3.00

		VG	VF	UNC
314	**5 Cents** ND (1941). Green on pale orange unpt. Back purple.	3.00	20.00	100.
315	**10 Cents** ND (1941). Red on yellow unpt. Back blue.			
	a. W/o serial # prefix.	.50	3.00	40.00
	b. Prefix A.	.25	2.50	40.00
316	**1 Dollar** ND (1940-41). Dk. blue on m/c unpt. Portr. Kg. George VI at r. Printer: BWC.	4.00	20.00	140.

Note: For similar issue in purple see #312; in green see #324.

1941 ND EMERGENCY ISSUE

		VG	VF	UNC
317	**1 Dollar on 5 Yuan** ND (Dec. 1941 - old date 1941). Dk. blue on m/c unpt. Red ovpt. on Bank of China #93.	35.00	125.	650.

Note: #317 was in circulation for less than 2 weeks prior to the surrender of British and Hong Kong defense forces on Dec. 25, 1941.

1945 ND EMERGENCY ISSUE

#318-320 prepared by the British Military Administration to replace the "duress" notes of the Hong Kong and Shanghai Banking Corporation in circulation immediately following the Japanese surrender. (Not issued).

		VG	VF	UNC
318	**1 Dollar on 1000 Yen** ND. Red. W/ or w/o yellow unpt. Temple at l., man at r. Plate includes all legends and lineout bar.	75.00	325.	950.

		VG	VF	UNC
319	**5 Dollars on 1000 Yuan** ND (1945 - old date 1944). Blue. Ovpt. on Central Reserve Bank of China #J32.	150.	500.	1250.

		VG	VF	UNC
320	**10 Dollars on 5000 Yuan** ND (1945 - old date 1945). Gray. Ovpt. on Central Reserve Bank of China #J42.	150.	450.	1000.

Note: Other ovpt. notes have been reported, but their authenticity is doubtful.

1945-49 ND ISSUE

#321-324 portr. Kg. George VI at r.

#321-323 uniface.

		VG	VF	UNC
321	**1 Cent** ND (1945). Brown on lt. blue unpt.	.15	.30	1.00
322	**5 Cents** ND (1945). Green on lilac unpt.	.25	3.00	35.00

		VG	VF	UNC
323	**10 Cents** ND (1945). Red on grayish unpt.	.25	1.00	15.00

		VG	VF	UNC
324	**1 Dollar** 1949; 1952. Dk. green on m/c unpt. Printer: BWC.			
	a. 9.4.1949.	4.00	20.00	90.00
	b. 1.1.1952.	4.00	22.50	100.

Note: for similar issue in purple see #312; in blue see #316.

1952 ND ISSUE

		VG	VF	UNC
324A	**1 Dollar** 1952-59. Dk. green on m/c unpt. Portr. Qn. Elizabeth II at r. Printer: BWC.			
	a. 1.7.1952; 1.7.1954; 1.7.1955.	.75	3.00	30.00
	b. 1.6.1956-1.7.1959.	.25	2.00	20.00

The Hungarian Republic, located in central Europe, has an area of 35,919 sq. mi. (93,030 sq. km.) and a population of 9.81 million. Capital: Budapest. The economy is d on agriculture and a rapidly expanding industrial sector. Machinery, chemicals, iron and steel, and fruits and vegetables are exported.

The ancient kingdom of Hungary, founded by the Magyars in the 9th century, expanded its greatest power and authority in the mid-14th century. After suffering repeated Turkish invasions, Hungary accepted Habsburg rule to escape Turkish occupation, regaining independence in 1867 with the Emperor of Austria as king of a dual Austro-Hungarian Empire.

Sharing the defeat of the Central Powers in World War I, Hungary lost the greater part of its territory and population and underwent a period of drastic political revision. The short-lived republic of 1918 was followed by a chaotic interval of communist rule during 1919, and the restoration of the kingdom in 1920 with Admiral Horthy as regent of a kingdom without a king. Although a German ally in World War II, Hungary was occupied by German troops who imposed a pro-Nazi dictatorship in 1944. Soviet armies drove out the Germans in 1945 and assisted the communist minority in seizing power. A revised constitution published on Aug. 20, 1949, had established Hungary as a "People's Republic" of the Soviet type, but it is once again a republic as of Oct. 23, 1989. Entered the European Union in 2004.

RULERS:

Austrian to 1918

MONETARY SYSTEM:

1 Korona = 100 Fillér to 1926
1 Pengö = 100 Fillér to 1946
1 Milpengö = 1 Million Pengö
1 B(illió) Pengö = 1 Billion Pengö
1 Adopengö = 1 Tax Pengö
1 Forint = 100 Fillér 1946-
1 Forint = 100 Fillér 1946-
1 Forint (Florin) = 60 Krajczar

DENOMINATIONS

Egy = 1Ötven = 50
Két = Kettö = 2Száz = 100
Öt = 5Ezer = 1000
Tïz = 10Millió = Million
Húsz = 20Milliárd = 1,000 Million
Huszonöt = 25 These words used separately or in combination give denomination.

AUSTRO-HUNGARIAN EMPIRE

MAGYAR KIRÁLY KÖLCSÖNPÉNZTÁR-JEGY

ROYAL HUNGARIAN WAR LOAN BANK

1914 ISSUE

		VG	VF	UNC
1	**250 Korona** 27.9.1914. Specimen perforated: *MINTA*.	—	—	850.

		VG	VF	UNC
2	**2000 Korona** 27.9.1914. Portr. Empress Zita at r. Specimen perforated: *MINTA.*	—	—	850.

		VG	VF	UNC
3	**10,000 Korona** 27.9.1914. Specimen perforated: *MINTA.*	—	—	900.

AZ OSZTRÁK-MAGYAR BANK PÉNZTÁRJEGYE

AUSTRO-HUNGARIAN BANK

#4-9, non-interest bearing Treasury notes of Hungarian branches. Text in Hungarian, various dates (ca.1918) and place names handstamped.

KOLOZSVÁR

1918 ISSUE

		VG	VF	UNC
4	**1000 Korona** 1918.	500.	1000.	2000.
5	**5000 Korona** 1918.	500.	1000.	2000.
6	**10,000 Korona** 1918.	500.	1000.	2000.

SZATMÁR-NÉMETI

1918 ISSUE

		VG	VF	UNC
7	**1000 Korona** 29.11.1918.	550.	1100.	2200.
8	**5000 Korona** 29.11.1918.	550.	1100.	2200.
9	**10,000 Korona** 29.11.1918.	550.	1100.	2200.

1919 ISSUE

#10-16, notes printed in Budapest in 1919 w/variations from the regular notes printed in Austria. Bilingual text.

		VG	VF	UNC
10	**1 Korona** 1.12.1916. (1919). Red. Helmeted warrior's head at ctr. Woman's head at upper l. and r. on back. Like Austria #20. Series # above 7000. (Communist regime in Budapest).	2.50	5.00	12.50
11	**2 Korona** 1.3.1917 (1919). Red. Like Austria #21 but series # above 7000.			
	a. Issued note.	1.50	4.00	10.00
	x. Error: w/*Genenalsekretar.*	5.00	15.00	35.00

		VG	VF	UNC
12	**25 Korona** 27.10.1918 (1919). Blue on lt. brown unpt., uniface. Like Austria #23 but series # above 3000. 2 serial # varieties. (Soviet Republic of Bela Kun. 21.3.1919-4.8.1919).	3.00	7.50	20.00
13	**25 Korona** 27.10.1918 (1919). Blue on lt. brown unpt. Like #12 but wavy lines on back. Series #1001-1999. 3 serial # varieties.	3.00	9.00	22.50
14	**200 Korona** 27.10.1918 (1919). Green on red-brown unpt. Like Austria #24 but series A up to 2000. (People's Republic, 16.11.1918-21.3.1919).	3.00	10.00	25.00
15	**200 Korona** 27.10.1918 (1919). Green on red-brown unpt., uniface. Like #14 but series A above 2000. (Soviet Republic of Bela Kun 21.3.1919-4.8.1919).	3.00	7.50	20.00
16	**200 Korona** 27.10.1918 (1919). Green on red-brown unpt. Like #15 but wavy lines on back. Series A2101; Series B1001-B1999.	3.00	7.50	20.00

AZ OSZTRÁK-MAGYAR BANK - BUDAPESTI FÖINTEZETE

TREASURY NOTE OF THE BUDAPEST HEAD OFFICE

1918 ISSUE

		VG	VF	UNC
17	**200 Korona** 3.11.1918. Hungarian legends on face. Specimen only.	—	350.	75

1920 ND PROVISIONAL ISSUE

#18-32 ovpt: *MAGYARORSZÁG* and Hungarian coat of arms. Issued as state notes w/seal upright or turne to l. Only the 1000 and 10,000 Korona w/seal turned to r. are rare.

		VG	VF	UNC
18	**10 Korona** ND (1920 - old date 2.1.1904). Ovpt. on Austria #9.	3.00	12.00	30.0

		VG	VF	UNC
19	**10 Korona** ND (1920 - old date 2.1.1915). Ovpt. on Austria #19.	1.00	2.00	5.00

		VG	VF	UNC
20	**20 Korona** ND (1920 - old date 2.1.1913). Ovpt. on Austria #13.	1.00	2.00	5.00

		VG	VF	UNC
21	**20 Korona** ND (1920 - old date 2.1.1913). Ovpt. on Austria #14. W/*II. Auflage.* (2nd issue).	1.00	2.00	5.00
22	**25 Korona** ND (1920 - old date 27.10.1918). Ovpt. on Austria #23. Series up to 3000.	3.00	15.00	40.00

		VG	VF	UNC
23	**25 Korona** ND (1920 - old date 27.10.1918). Series above 3000.	4.00	20.00	50.00
24	**50 Korona** ND (1920 - old date 2.1.1902). Ovpt. on Austria #6.	45.00	120.	300.
25	**50 Korona** ND (1920 - old date 2.1.1914). Ovpt. on Austria #15.	1.00	2.00	5.00

		VG	VF	UNC
26	**100 Korona** ND (1920 - old date 2.1.1910). Ovpt. on Austria #11.	75.00	225.	600.
27	**100 Korona** ND (1920 - old date 2.1.1912). Ovpt. on Austria #12.	1.00	2.00	4.00

		VG	VF	UNC
28	**200 Korona** ND (1920 - old date 27.10.1918). Ovpt. on Austria #24. Series A.			
	a. Wavy lines on back.	30.00	75.00	175.
	b. W/o wavy lines on back.	30.00	75.00	175.
29	**200 Korona** ND (1920 - old date 27.10.1918). Ovpt. on Austria #24. Series B.	40.00	100.	250.
30	**200 Korona** ND (1920 - old date 27.10.1918). 6 digit serial #.	40.00	100.	250.
31	**1000 Korona** ND (1920 - old date 2.1.1902). Ovpt. on Austria #8.	1.50	4.00	10.00

		VG	VF	UNC
32	**10,000 Korona** ND (1920 - old date 2.11.1918). Ovpt. on Austria #25.	5.00	15.00	40.00

Note: #18-32 are also found with additional South Slavonian or Romanian handstamps. Notes with forged MAGYARORSZÁG ovpt. were given a black, thick-ruled cross (#18-23, 25, 27-32) w/handstamp: *Stempel wurde von ... als unecht befunden.* Note: The numerous local or military ovpt. and cancellations are beyond the scope of this catalog.

REGENCY

MAGYAR POSTATAKARÉKPÉNZTÁR

HUNGARIAN POST OFFICE SAVINGS BANK

1919 FIRST ISSUE

		VG	VF	UNC
33	**5 Korona** 1.5.1919. Specimen. (1 known).	—	—	—
34	**5 Korona** 15.5.1919. Blue on green unpt. Man sowing at r. *AZ OSZTRÁK-MAGYAR BANK BANKJEGYEIRE* on face. Back green.	1.00	2.50	7.50

		VG	VF	UNC
35	**5 Korona** 15.1919. Blue on green unpt. Like #34. *MÁS TÖRVÉNYES PENZNEMEKRE* on face. Back blue.	1.00	2.50	7.50
36	**10 Korona** 15.5.1919. Specimen.	—	—	—

		VG	VF	UNC
37	**10 Korona** 15.7.1919. Blue on green-blue unpt. Woman wearing Phrygian cap at l.	1.50	8.00	35.00

		VG	VF	UNC
38	**20 Korona** 15.7.1919. Dk. blue. Woman w/2 small children at ctr. 2 serial # varieties.			
	a. Olive unpt.	2.00	10.00	40.00
	b. Yellow unpt.	2.00	10.00	40.00

#37-38 color trials also exist.

		VG	VF	UNC
39	**100 Korona** 15.7.1919. Blue and olive. Man seated w/sword at ctr. (Not issued.) (2 known.)	—	—	—

		VG	VF	UNC
39A	**1000 Korona** 15.7.1919. Specimen.	—	—	—

1919 Second Issue

		VG	VF	UNC
40	**5 Korona** 9.8.1919. Specimen. (1 known).	—	—	—

		VG	VF	UNC
41	**10 Korona** 9.8.1919. Gray-blue on brown unpt. Similar to #37, but woman w/o cap. 3 serial # varieties.	2.00	12.50	70.00
42	**20 Korona** 9.8.1919. Dk. blue on green and pink unpt. Similar to #38, but w/o *20* at lower l. and r. Back black on lt. red unpt.	2.00	10.00	40.00

1920 Issue

		VG	VF	UNC
43	**20 Fillér** 2.10.1920. Brown. Arms at upper ctr. Back gray.	.25	1.00	3.0
44	**50 Fillér** 2.10.1920. Blue. Arms at l. Back purple.	.25	1.00	3.0

1921 Issue

		VG	VF	UNC
45	**10 Million Korona** 1.5.1921. Specimen.	—	—	—

MAGYAR NEMZETI BANK

HUNGARIAN NATIONAL BANK

1919 FIRST ISSUE

		VG	VF	UNC
46	**50 Korona** 15.3.1919. Specimen.	—	—	—
47	**1000 Korona** 15.3.1919. Specimen.	—	—	—

1919 SECOND ISSUE

		VG	VF	UNC
48	**25 Korona** 2.5.1919. Specimen. (1 known)	—	—	—

1919 THIRD ISSUE

		VG	VF	UNC
49	**2 Korona** 2.6.1919. Specimen.	—	—	—
50	**20 Korona** 2.6.1919. Specimen.	—	—	—

1919 FOURTH ISSUE

		VG	VF	UNC
51	**10 Korona** 1.8.1919. Specimen.	—	—	—
52	**100 Korona** 15.8.1919. Specimen. (2 known)	—	—	—
53	**1000 Korona** 15.8.1919. Specimen.	—	—	—

PÉNZÜGYMINISZTÉRIUM

STATE NOTES OF THE MINISTRY OF FINANCE

1920 FIRST ISSUE

		VG	VF	UNC
54	**50 Fillér** 1920. Circular, 30mm. Specimen.	—	—	—
55	**1 Korona** 1920. Circular, 35mm. Specimen.	—	—	—
56	**2 Korona** 1920. Circular, 40mm. Specimen.	—	—	—

1920 SECOND ISSUE

		VG	VF	UNC
57	**1 Korona** 1.1.1920. Blue. Woman at r. Serial # red or dk. red. Arms at r. on back.	.20	.50	2.50

		VG	VF	UNC
58	**2 Korona** 1.1.1920. Red on lt. brown unpt. Arms at l., reaping farmer at r. 2 serial # varieties.	.20	.50	2.50
59	**5 Korona** 1.1.1920. Face specimen.	—	—	—

		VG	VF	UNC
60	**10 Korona** 1.1.1920. Brown on blue-green unpt. Chain bridge, Budapest at upper ctr. Arms at r. on back. Serial # varieties.	.20	.50	2.50

		VG	VF	UNC
61	**20 Korona** 1.1.1920. Black on green and pale orange unpt. Mátyás Church in Budapest at r. Arms at upper ctr. on back. 2 serial # varieties.	.20	.50	2.50

		VG	VF	UNC
62	**50 Korona** 1.1.1920. Dk. brown on brown and tan unpt. Portr. Prince F. Rákóczi at r. Printer: OFZ.	.25	1.00	5.00

		VG	VF	UNC
63	**100 Korona** 1.1.1920. Brown on lt. brown unpt. Portr. Kg. Mátyás wearing wreath at r. 155 x 100mm. Printer: OFZ.	.25	1.00	5.00
64	**100 Korona** 1.1.1920. 119 x 70mm. Specimen perforated: *MINTA*.	—	—	—

#65-68 printer: OFZ.

		VG	VF	UNC
65	**500 Korona** 1.1.1920. Dk. green on brown-olive unpt. Portr. Prince Árpád wearing helmet at r.	.50	2.00	10.00

66	1000 Korona	VG	VF	UNC
	1.1.1920. Dk. brown on brown unpt. Portr. St. Stephan at r.			
	a. Issued note.	1.00	3.00	20.00
	s. Specimen perforated: *MINTA*.	—	—	50.00

67	5000 Korona	VG	VF	UNC
	1.1.1920. Dk. brown on green and gray unpt. "Patrona Hungariae" at r.	1.50	5.00	40.00

68	10,000 Korona	VG	VF	UNC
	1.1.1920. Dk. green and violet. "Patrona Hungariae" at r.	2.00	10.00	50.00

1922 ISSUE

69	25,000 Korona	VG	VF	UNC
	15.8.1922. Violet. "Patrona Hungariae" at r.			
	a. Paper w/o silk thread.	7.00	25.00	100.
	b. Paper w/silk thread.	15.00	50.00	150.
	s. As a. perforated: *MINTA*.	—	—	100.
70	50,000 Korona			
	15.8.1922. Proof.	—	—	—

1923 FIRST ISSUE

71	50,000 Korona	VG	VF	UNC
	1.5.1923. Red. Portr. young man at r.			
	a. Imprint: Orell Füssli.	6.00	20.00	90.00
	b. W/o imprint.	8.00	25.00	100.

72	100,000 Korona	VG	VF	UNC
	1.5.1923. Dk. blue. Portr. young man at r.			
	a. Imprint: Orell Füssli.	20.00	75.00	225.
	b. Imprint: Magyar Pénzjegynyomda Rt.	25.00	85.00	250.
	s. As a. perforated: *MINTA*.	—	—	125.

1923 SECOND ISSUE

73	100 Korona	VG	VF	UNC
	1.7.1923. Brown. Portr. Kg. Mátyáas wearing a wreath at r.			
	a. Imprint: Magyar Pénzjegynyomda Rt.	.25	1.00	3.00
	b. W/o imprint.	.25	1.00	3.00

74	500 Korona	VG	VF	UNC
	1.7.1923. Dk. green on lt. brown unpt. Portr. Prince Árpád wearing helmet at r.			
	a. Imprint: Magyar Pénzjegynyomda Rt.	.25	1.00	3.00
	b. W/o imprint.	.25	.75	2.00

		VG	VF	UNC
75	**1000 Korona** 1.7.1923. Black on brown unpt. Portr. St. Stephan at r.			
	a. Imprint: Magyar Pénzjegynyomda Rt.	.25	1.00	3.00
	b. W/o imprint.	.25	1.00	4.00

		VG	VF	UNC
76	**5000 Korona** 1.7.1923. Dk. brown on tan and lt. blue unpt. Hungáia at r.			
	a. Imprint: Magyar Pénzjegynyomda Rt.	.25	2.00	5.00
	b. W/o imprint.	.50	2.50	6.00

		VG	VF	UNC
77	**10,000 Korona** 1.7.1923. Dk. green on tan and lilac unpt. "Patrona Hungariae" at r.			
	a. Imprint: Magyar Pénzjegynyomda Rt.	1.00	2.00	7.00
	b. W/o imprint.	1.00	2.50	9.00
	c. Imprint: Orell Füssli, Zürich.	1.00	2.50	9.00

		VG	VF	UNC
78	**25,000 Korona** 1.7.1923. Violet. Portr. St. Ladislaus wearing crown at r. Printer: Orell Füssli, Zürich.	10.00	40.00	150.

		VG	VF	UNC
79	**500,000 Korona** 1.7.1923. Violet and brown. Portr. woman wearing a wreath at r.			
	a. Imprint: Magyar Pénzjegynyomda Rt.	40.00	150.	400.
	b. Imprint: Orell Füssli.	60.00	200.	500.

		VG	VF	UNC
80	**1,000,000 Korona** 4.9.1923. Blue on green unpt. Like #79.			
	a. Imprint: Magyar Pénzjegynyomda Rt.	150.	350.	750.
	b. W/o imprint.	150.	350.	750.
	c. W/o portr. and w/o serial # (half-finished printing).	—	—	500.

Note: Treasury certificates of the State Note Issuing Office (5, 10, 50 and 100 million Korona w/date 14.7.1923) are reputed to have been printed, but have not been confirmed.

1925 ND PROVISIONAL ISSUE

Monetary reform. 1 Pengo = 12,500 "old" Korona. #81-88 new denominations ovpt. on old notes.

		VG	VF	UNC
81	**8 Fillér on 1000 Korona** ND (1925 - old date 1.7.1923). Red ovpt. on #75.			
	a. Imprint: Magyar Pénzjegynyomda Rt.	5.00	12.00	45.00
	b. W/o imprint.	4.00	10.00	40.00

		VG	VF	UNC
82	**40 Fillér on 5000 Korona** ND (1925 - old date 1.7.1923). Green ovpt. on #76.			
	a. Imprint: Magyar Pénzjegynyomda Rt.	7.00	15.00	60.00
	b. W/o imprint.	6.00	12.50	55.00

		VG	VF	UNC
83	**80 Fillér on 10,000 Korona** ND (1925 - old date 1.7.1923). Red ovpt. on #77.			
	a. Imprint: Magyar Pénzjegynyomda Rt.	10.00	25.00	90.00
	b. W/o imprint.	10.00	25.00	90.00
	c. Imprint: Orell Füssli.	12.00	30.00	100.
84	**2 Pengö on 25,000 Korona** ND (1925 - old date 1.7.1923). Red ovpt. on #78.	20.00	60.00	175.
85	**4 Pengö on 50,000 Korona** ND (1925 - old date 1.5.1923). Green ovpt. on #71.			
	a. Imprint: Orell Füssli.	35.00	100.	250.
	b. W/o imprint.	35.00	100.	250.
86	**8 Pengö on 100,000 Korona** ND (1925 - old date 1.5.1923). Red ovpt. on #72.			
	a. Imprint: Orell Füssli.	75.00	175.	400.
	b. Imprint: Magyar Pénzjegynyomda Rt.	75.00	175.	400.
87	**40 Pengö on 500,000 Korona** ND (1925 - old date 1.7.1923). Red ovpt. on #79.			
	a. Imprint: Magyar Pénzjegynyomda Rt.	—	—	—
	b. W/o imprint.	—	—	—
88	**80 Pengö on 1,000,000 Korona** ND (1925 - old date 4.9.1923). Red ovpt. on #80.			
	a. Imprint: Magyar Pénzjegynyomda Rt.	—	—	—
	b. W/o imprint.	—	—	—

MAGYAR NEMZETI BANK (RESUMED)

HUNGARIAN NATIONAL BANK

1926-27 ISSUE

		VG	VF	UNC
89	**5 Pengö** 1.3.1926. Brown. Portr. Count I. Széchenyi at r. Bridge on back.			
	a. Issued note.	10.00	35.00	175.
	s. Specimen perforated: *MINTA.*	—	—	85.00

		VG	VF	UNC
90	**10 Pengö** 1.3.1926. Green on lt. tan unpt. Portr. F. Deák at r. Parliament House on back.			
	a. Issued note.	50.00	200.	600.
	s. Specimen perforated: *MINTA.*	—	—	350.

		VG	VF	UNC
91	**20 Pengö** 1.3.1926. Brown on green unpt. Portr. L. Kossuth at r.			
	a. Issued note.	100.	450.	1100.
	s. Specimen perforated: *MINTA.*	—	—	475.

		VG	VF	UNC
92	**50 Pengö** 1.3.1926. Blue. Portr. Prince F. Rákóczi at r. Horses in field w/dk. clouds above on back. It is K. Lotz painting.			
	a. Issued note.	200.	675.	1700.
	s. Specimen perforated: *MINTA.*	—	—	750.

		VG	VF	UNC
93	**100 Pengö** 1.3.1926. Brown-lilac. Portr. Kg. Mátyáas at r. Royal Palace at Budapest at ctr. on back.			
	a. Issued note.	200.	675.	1700.
	s. Specimen perforated: *MINTA.*	—	—	750.

		VG	VF	UNC
94	**1000 Pengö** 1.7.1927. Blue, green and red. Portr. Hungaria at upper r. Gyula Benczúr's painting *Baptism of Vajk* at ctr. on back.			
	a. Issued note.	400.	1000.	2700.
	s. Specimen perforated: *MINTA.*	—	—	850.

1928-30 ISSUE

		VG	VF	UNC
95	**5 Pengö** 1.8.1928. Blue. Portr. Count I. Széchenyi at r. Bridge on back.	8.00	22.50	75.00

NOTICE

Readers with unlisted dates, signature varieties, etc. are invited to submit photocopies or, high resolution (300 dpi, 100% size) scans of their notes to: Standard Catalog of World Paper Money, 700 East State St. Iola, WI 54990-0001, or E-Mail: george.cuhaj@fwpubs.com.

		VG	VF	UNC
96	**10 Pengö** 1.2.1929. Green. Portr. F. Deák at r. Parliament House on back.	3.00	10.00	40.00
97	**20 Pengö** 2.1.1930. Dk. blue. Portr. L. Kossuth at r. Hungarian National Bank bldg. on back.	.25	2.00	12.50

		VG	VF	UNC
98	**100 Pengö** 1.7.1930. Violet. Portr. Kg. Mátyáas at r. Series # w/o asterisk. Back violet and dk. blue; Royal Palace at Budapest at ctr.	.25	.75	3.00

Note: Also see #112.

1932 ISSUE

		VG	VF	UNC
99	**50 Pengö** 1.10.1932. Red-brown on green and blue unpt. Arms at upper l., portr. S. Petöfi at r. Painting. "Horse driving in Hortobá gy" on back.	.25	.75	3.00

1936 ISSUE

		VG	VF	UNC
100	**10 Pengö** 22.12.1936. Green on orange, green and purple unpt. *Patrona Hungariae* at l., girl at at r. Series # w/o asterisk. Equestrian statue of St. Stephan on back.	.25	.50	2.00

Note: Also see #113.

1938 ISSUE

		VG	VF	UNC
101	**50 Fillér** 15.1.1938. Proof.	—	—	—

		VG	VF	UNC
102	**1 Pengö** 15.1.1938. Dk. blue on brown unpt. Arms at l., portr. girl at r. Series # w/o asterisk.	1.00	2.50	8.50

Note: Also see #114.

		VG	VF	UNC
103	**2 Pengö** 15.1.1938. Specimen.	—	—	65.00

		VG	VF	UNC
104	**5 Pengö** 15.1.1938. Brown on green unpt. Girl at r.	10.00	30.00	80.00
105	**20 Pengö on 50 Fillér** 15.1.1938. Proof.	—	—	—

1939 ISSUE

		VG	VF	UNC
106	**5 Pengö** 25.10.1939. Brown on green unpt. Arms at lower l. ctr., portr. girl at r. Man w/balalaika on back.	1.00	3.00	10.00
107	**100 Pengö on 5 Pengö** 25.10.1939. Proof.	—	—	—

1940-45 ISSUE

		VG	VF	UNC
108	**2 Pengö** 15.7.1940. Green on peach unpt. Arms at l., portr. girl at r. Woman and child at ctr. on back. White or yellow paper.	1.00	3.00	10.00

109	20 Pengö	VG	VF	UNC
	15.1.1941. Blue on tan and lt. green unpt. Shepherd and sheep at lower ctr., portr. woman wearing national costume at r. Old man and young woman at ctr. on back.	.25	.50	2.00

110	50 Pengö	VG	VF	UNC
	5.4.1945. Brown on green unpt. Portr. Prince F. Rákóczi at r. Horses in field w/dk. clouds above on back.			
	a. Printed on both sides.	.25	1.00	4.00
	x. Printed on face only.	—	—	4.00

111	100 Pengö	VG	VF	UNC
	5.4.1945. Purple on lt. blue and lilac unpt. Portr. Kg. Mátyáas at r. Royal Palace at Budapest on back.			
	a. W/wmk.	.25	1.00	4.00
	b. W/o wmk.	.25	1.00	4.00

SZÁLASI GOVERNMENT IN VESZPRÉM, 1944-1945

MAGYAR NEMZETI BANK

1930-DATED ISSUE

112	100 Pengö	VG	VF	UNC
	1.7.1930. Violet. Like #98, but series # w/asterisk.	.50	2.00	6.00

1936-DATED ISSUE

113	10 Pengö	VG	VF	UNC
	22.12.1936. Green on orange, green and purple unpt. Like #100, but series # w/asterisk.	2.50	7.50	20.00

1938-DATED ISSUE

114	1 Pengö	VG	VF	UNC
	15.1.1938. Blue on brown unpt. Like #102 but series # w/asterisk.	3.00	10.00	30.00

1943 ISSUE

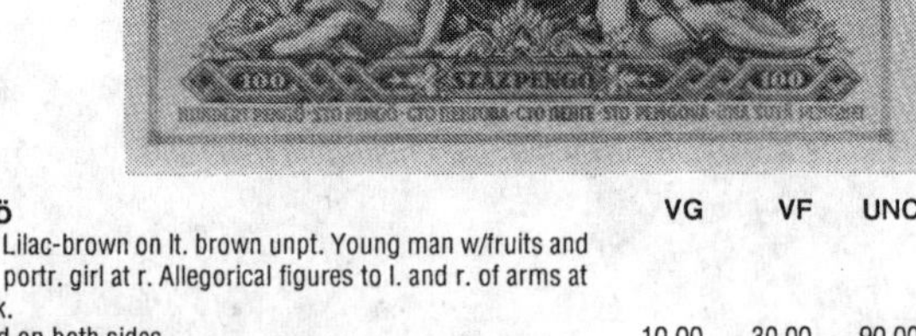

115	100 Pengö	VG	VF	UNC
	24.2.1943. Lilac-brown on lt. brown unpt. Young man w/fruits and doves at l., portr. girl at r. Allegorical figures to l. and r. of arms at ctr. on back.			
	a. Printed on both sides.	10.00	30.00	90.00
	x1. Printed on face only.	—	—	—
	x2. Printed on back only.	3.00	10.00	35.00

116	1000 Pengö	VG	VF	UNC
	24.2.1943. Brown on lilac and green unpt. Portr. *Hungaria* at r. Arms at l., city scene w/bridge at ctr., portr. *Hungaria* at r. on back.	.50	2.00	5.00

POST WWII INFLATIONARY ERA

Since Hungarian inflation notes have the denomination in word form, the numerical equivalents are shown below:

Tiz Pengo	10
Husz Pengo	20
Otven Pengo	50
Szaz Pengo	100
Otazaz Pengo	500
Ezer Pengo	1,000
Tizezer Pengo	10,000
Szazezer Pengo	100,000
Egymillo Pengo	1,000,000
Tizmillio Pengo	10,000,000
Szazmillio Pengo	100,000,000
Egymilliard Pengo	1,000,000,000
Tizezer Milpengo	10,000,000,000
Szazezer Milpengo	100,000,000,000
Egymillio Milpengo	1,000,000,000,000
Tizmillio Milpengo	10,000,000,000,000
Szazmillio Milpengo	100,000,000,000,000
Egymilliard Milpengo	1,000,000,000,000,000
Tizezer B. - Pengo	10,000,000,000,000,000
Szazezer B. - Pengo	100,000,000,000,000,000
Egymilio B. - Pengo	1,000,000,000,000,000,000
Tizmillio B. - Pengo	10,000,000,000,000,000,000
Szazmillio B. - Pengo	100,000,000,000,000,000,000
Egymilliard B. - Pengo	1,000,000,000,000,000,000,000

MAGYAR NEMZETI BANK

HUNGARIAN NATIONAL BANK

1945-46 PENGÖ ISSUE

17 500 Pengö — VG VF UNC

15.5.1945. Blue on dull lilac and orange unpt. Portr. woman wearing wreath at r. First Russian word at upper l. on back correctly spelled ПЯТЬСОТ.

	VG	VF	UNC
a. Issued note. First letter П.	.25	.75	2.00
x. Error w/ word incorrectly spelled NЯТЬСОТ.	2.00	7.50	20.00

18, 119 and 121 adhesive stamps have 2 types of letter *B* in MNB.

18 1000 Pengö — VG VF UNC

15.7.1945. Dk. green on red-brown unpt. Portr. woman wearing flowers at r. 2 serial # varieties.

	VG	VF	UNC
a. W/o adhesive stamp.	.25	.75	2.00
b. Red adhesive stamp.	.25	.75	2.50

9 10,000 Pengö — VG VF UNC

15.7.1945. Lilac-brown on green unpt. Portr. woman at r.

	VG	VF	UNC
a. W/o adhesive stamp.	.25	.50	2.00
b. Brown on lt. green adhesive stamp.	.25	.75	2.00
c. Blue adhesive stamp.	.25	.75	2.00

120 100,000 Pengö — VG VF UNC

23.10.1945. Brown on green-blue unpt. Portr. woman wearing national costume at r. Arms at ctr. on back.

	VG	VF	UNC
a. W/o adhesive stamp.	.25	.50	2.00
b. Red adhesive stamp.	.25	.50	2.00

121 100,000 Pengö

23.10.1945. Blue. Like #120.

	VG	VF	UNC
a. W/o adhesive stamp.	25.00	60.00	150.
b. Green adhesive stamp.	35.00	75.00	200.

122 1,000,000 Pengö — VG VF UNC

16.11.1945. Blue on brown and green unpt. Portr. L. Kossuth at r. Painting "At the shore of Lake Balaton" (by G. Mészöly) on back. — .25 .75 2.00

123 10,000,000 Pengö — VG VF UNC

16.11.1945. Dk. green on m/c unpt. Portr. L. Kossuth at r. Dove w/olive branch on back. — .25 .75 2.50

124 100,000,000 Pengö — VG VF UNC

18.3.1946. Brown on green unpt. Portr. woman wearing headscarf at r. Parliament House on back. — .25 .75 2.50

		VG	VF	UNC
125	**1 Milliard Pengö** 18.3.1946. Violet on lt. orange unpt. Portr. woman at r.	.25	.75	2.50

1946 Milpengö Issues

		VG	VF	UNC
126	**10,000 Milpengö** 29.4.1946. Dk. blue and red. Like #119.	.25	.75	2.50

		VG	VF	UNC
127	**100,000 Milpengö** 29.4.1946. Dk. green and red. Like #120.	.25	.75	2.50

		VG	VF	UNC
128	**1 Million Milpengö** 24.5.1946. Brown on yellow unpt. Like #122.	.25	.75	2.50

> **NOTICE**
>
> Readers with unlisted dates, signature varieties, etc. are invited to submit photocopies or, high resolution (300 dpi, 100% size) scans of their notes to: Standard Catalog of World Paper Money, 700 East State St. Iola, WI 54990-0001, or E-Mail: george.cuhaj@fwpubs.com.

		VG	VF	UNC
129	**10 Million Milpengö** 24.5.1946. Brown on blue unpt. Like #123.	.25	.75	2.50
130	**100 Million Milpengö** 3.6.1946. Green. Like #124.	.25	.75	2.50

		VG	VF	UNC
131	**1 Milliard Milpengö** 3.6.1946. Blue. Like #125.	.25	.75	2.50

1946 "B.-Pengö" Issues

#132-137 w/o serial #.

		VG	VF	UNC
132	**10,000 B.-Pengö** 3.6.1946. Brown on violet unpt. Like #126.	.25	.75	2.50
133	**100,000 B.-Pengö** 3.6.1946. Red-brown. Like #127.	.25	.75	3.00
134	**1,000,000 B.-Pengö** 3.6.1946. Dk. brown. Like #128.	.25	.75	3.00
135	**10,000,000 B.-Pengö** 3.6.1946. Purple. Like #129.	.25	.75	5.00

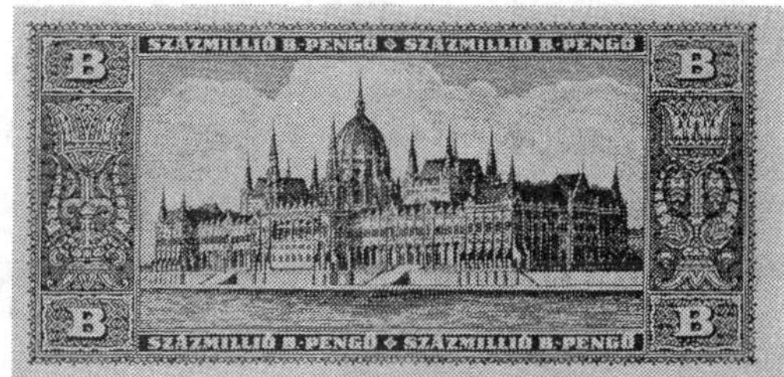

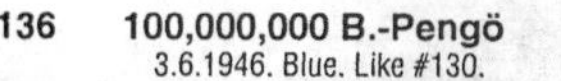

		VG	VF	UNC
136	**100,000,000 B.-Pengö** 3.6.1946. Blue. Like #130.	.50	1.50	10.00

		VG	VF	UNC
137	**1 Milliard B.-Pengö** 3.6.1946. Green. Like #131. (Not issued.)	10.00	40.00	160.

MINISTRY OF FINANCE

1946 ADÓPENGÖ (TAX PENGÖ) SYSTEM - FIRST ISSUE

#138-144 arms in unpt. at ctr. on back.

		VG	VF	UNC
138	**50,000 (Ötvenezer) Adópengö** 25.5.1946. Green.			
	a. Gray paper w/wmk. and serial #.	.50	2.00	5.00
	b. Gray paper w/wmk., w/o serial #.	.50	2.00	5.00
	c. White paper w/o wmk.,w/o serial #.	.50	2.00	5.00

		VG	VF	UNC
139	**500,000 (Ötszazezer) Adópengö** 25.5.1946. Dk. blue.			
	a. Gray paper w/wmk. and serial #.	.50	2.00	6.00
	b. White paper w/o wmk., w/o serial #.	.50	2.00	5.00
140	**1,000,000 (Egymillió) Adópengö** 25.5.1946. Red on gray unpt.			
	a. Gray paper w/wmk. and serial #.	.50	2.00	5.00
	b. Like a, but arms in unpt. on back reversed (cross at l.).	.50	3.00	7.00
	c. White paper w/o wmk., w/o serial #.	.50	2.00	5.00
141	**10,000,000 (Tizmillió) Adópengö** 25.5.1946. Blue on yellow unpt.			
	a. White paper w/o wmk., w/o serial #.	.50	2.00	6.00
	b. Like a, but arms in unpt. on back reversed (cross at l.).	2.50	7.50	20.00
	c. Gray paper w/wmk., w/o serial # but arms in unpt. on back reversed (cross at l.).	2.50	7.50	20.00

		VG	VF	UNC
142	**100,000,000 (Szazmillio) Adópengö** 25.5.1946. Gray-blue on pink unpt.			
	a. White paper w/o wmk., w/o serial #.	1.00	5.00	15.00
	b. Like a, but arms in unpt. on back at l. and r. reversed (cross at l.).	4.00	15.00	40.00
	c. Gray paper, w/o serial #.	2.00	6.00	20.00
142A	**1 Md. (Egymilliárd) Adópengö** 25.5.1946. Lilac on lt. blue unpt. (Not issued). Rare.	—	—	—

1946 ADÓPENGÖ (TAX PENGÖ) SYSTEM - SECOND ISSUE

		VG	VF	UNC
143	**10,000 (Tizezer) Adópengö** 28.5.1946. Brown.			
	a. Gray paper w/wmk. and serial #. *5.970/1946, M.E.* on back.	.50	2.00	5.00
	b. Gray paper w/wmk., w/o serial #.	.50	2.00	5.00
	c. White paper w/o wmk., w/o serial #. *5.600/1946 M.E.* on back.	4.00	12.00	40.00

		VG	VF	UNC
144	**100,000 (Egyszázezer) Adópengö** 28.5.1946. Brown-lilac on pink unpt.			
	a. Gray paper w/wmk. and serial #. *5.970/1946. M.E.* on back.	.50	2.00	5.00
	b. Gray paper w/wmk., w/o serial #. *5.970/1946. M.E.* on back.	.50	2.00	5.00
	c. Like b, but arms in unpt. on back reversed (cross at l.).	4.00	15.00	45.00
	d. Gray paper w/wmk. and serial #. *5.600/1946. M.E.* on back.	4.00	15.00	45.00
	e. White paper w/o wmk., w/o serial #. *5.600/1946. M.E.* on back.	1.00	5.00	15.00

In accordance with an ordinance by the Ministry of Finance, numerous tax-accounting letters of credit, law court fee, and deed stamps were declared legal tender.

MAGYAR POSTATAKARÉKPÉNZTÁR

HUNGARIAN POSTAL SAVINGS BANK

RESZBETETJEGY

1946 FIRST ISSUE

#145-148, regulations on back. Issued 29.6.1946.

		VG	VF	UNC
145	**10,000 (Tizezer) Adópengö** 22.4.1946. Black. *Kir.*	8.00	20.00	50.00
146	**10,000 (Tizezer) Adópengö** 22.4.1946. Black. W/o *Kir.*	5.00	15.00	45.00
147	**100,000 (Százezer) Adópengö** 22.4.1946. Red. *Kir.*	8.00	20.00	50.00
148	**100,000 (Százezer) Adópengö** 22.4.1946. Red. W/o *Kir.*	8.00	20.00	50.00

1946 SECOND ISSUE

#149-152, dated 1946 within the postal handstamp. Face w/*MASRA AT NEM RUHAZHATO* at bottom, text on back.

		VG	VF	UNC
149	**10,000 (Tizezer) Adópengö** 1946. Black on gray unpt.	2.00	5.00	15.00

		VG	VF	UNC
150	**100,000 (Százezer) Adópengö** 1946. Red on lt. red unpt.	2.00	5.00	15.00
151	**1,000,000 (Egymillió) Adópengö** 1946. Dk. blue on lt. blue unpt.	2.00	5.00	15.00
152	**10,000,000 (Tizmillió) Adópengö** 1946. Dk. green on lt. green unpt.	2.00	5.00	15.00

1946 THIRD ISSUE

#153 and 154 like #148 - but uniface, w/o text on back.

		VG	VF	UNC
153	**100,000 (Százezer) Adópengö** 1946.			
	a. W/serial #.	—	—	—
	b. W/o serial #.	3.00	10.00	30.00
154	**1,000,000 (Egymillió) Adópengö** 1946.			
	a. W/serial #.	—	—	—
	b. W/o serial #.	3.00	10.00	30.00

1946 FOURTH ISSUE

#155 and 156 like #149 - but w/o *Masra at Nem Ruhazhato* on face. Text on back.

		VG	VF	UNC
155	**10,000 (Tizezer) Adópengö** 1946.			
	a. W/serial #.	—	—	—
	b. W/o serial #.	3.00	10.00	30.00
156	**1,000,000 (Egymillió) Adópengö** 1946.			
	a. W/serial #.	—	—	—
	b. W/o serial #.	3.00	10.00	30.00

1946 FIFTH ISSUE

#157 and 158 like #149 - but uniface, w/o text on back.

		VG	VF	UNC
157	**10,000 (Tizezer) Adópengö** 1946.	2.00	8.00	20.00
158	**10,000,000 (Tizmillió) Adópengö** 1946.	2.00	8.00	20.00

Note: #149-158 exist w/postal handstamp on lower l. or w/o handstamp. Unfinished, partially printed notes exist for #157 and 158.

MAGYAR NEMZETI BANK (RESUMED)

HUNGARIAN NATIONAL BANK

1946 FORINT ISSUE

		VG	VF	UNC
159	**10 Forint** 3.6.1946. Green on lt. tan unpt. Blue denomination guilloche at r. Portr. young man w/hammer at l. Arms on back.			
	a. Issued note.	5.00	20.00	70.00
	s. Specimen perforated: *MINTA*.	—	—	50.00

		VG	VF	UNC
160	**100 Forint** 3.6.1946. Blue on green unpt. Red denomination guilloche at r. Portr. young woman w/sickle and ear of corn at at l. Hands grasping hammer and wheat on back.			
	a. Issued note.	5.00	20.00	70.00
	s. Specimen perforated: *MINTA*.	—	—	50.00

1947 ISSUE

		VG	VF	UNC
161	**10 Forint** 27.2.1947. Green and blue-black on orange and lilac unpt. Portr. S. Petőfi at r. Sign. w/titles. Painting *Birth of the Song* by J. Jankó on back.			
	a. Issued note.	5.00	30.00	70.00
	s. Specimen perforated: *MINTA*.	—	—	50.00
162	**20 Forint** 27.2.1947. Blue and green on lt. green and pink unpt. Portr. Gy. Dózsa at r. Penthathlete Csaba Hegedűs w/hammer and wheat at ctr. on back.			
	a. Issued note.	5.00	35.00	80.00
	s. Specimen perforated: *MINTA*.	—	—	50.00

		VG	VF	UNC
163	**100 Forint** 27.2.1947. Red-brown on blue and orange unpt. Arms at upper ctr., portr. L. Kossuth at r. Horse-drawn wagon scene from *Took Refuge from the Storm* by K. Lotz at ctr. on back.			
	a. Issued note.	5.00	35.00	80.00
	s. Specimen perforated: *MINTA*.	—	—	50.00

1949 ISSUE

		VG	VF	UNC
164	**10 Forint** 24.10.1949. Green and blue-black on orange and lilac unpt. Like #161 but arms w/star. Sign. w/o titles.			
	a. Issued note.	1.00	5.00	20.00
	s. Specimen perforated: *MINTA*.	—	—	50.00

		VG	VF	UNC
165	**20 Forint** 24.10.1949. Blue and green on lt. green and pink unpt. Like #162 but arms w/star. Sig n. w/o titles.			
	a. Issued note.	.50	3.50	12.50
	s. Specimen.	—	—	50.00
166	**100 Forint** 24.10.1949. Red-violet on blue and orange unpt. Like #163 but arms w/star. Sign. w/o titles.			
	a. Issued note.	1.00	5.00	15.00
	s. Specimen w/ red ovpt. and perforated: *MINTA*.	—	—	50.00

1951 ISSUE

		VG	VF	UNC
167	**50 Forint** 1.9.1951. Brown on blue and orange unpt. Portr. Prince F. Rákóczi at r. Battle of the Hungarian insurrectionists (kuruc) against pro-Austrian soldiers (tabanc) at ctr. on back.			
	a. Issued note.	1.00	5.00	15.00
	s. Specimen w/ red ovpt and perforated: *MINTA*.	—	—	50.00

PEOPLES REPUBLIC

MAGYAR NEMZETI BANK

HUNGARIAN NATIONAL BANK

1957-83 ISSUE

#168-171 The variety in the serial # occurs in 1975 when the letter and numbers are narrower and larger. #170, 172 and 173 arms of 3-bar shield w/star in grain spray.

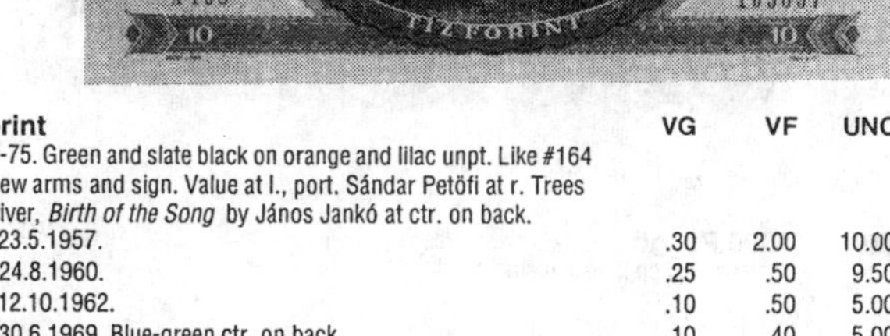

168	10 Forint	VG	VF	UNC
	1957-75. Green and slate black on orange and lilac unpt. Like #164 but new arms and sign. Value at l., port. Sándar Petőfi at r. Trees and river, *Birth of the Song* by János Jankó at ctr. on back.			
	a. 23.5.1957.	.30	2.00	10.00
	b. 24.8.1960.	.25	.50	9.50
	c. 12.10.1962.	.10	.50	5.00
	d. 30.6.1969. Blue-green ctr. on back.	.10	.40	5.00
	e. Serial # varieties. 28.10.1975.	.10	.25	7.50
	s1. As a, b, c. Specimen w/red ovpt. and perforated: *MINTA.*	—	—	45.00
	s2. As d, e. Specimen.	—	—	27.50

169	20 Forint	VG	VF	UNC
	1957-80. Blue and green on lt. green and pink unpt. Like #165 but new arms and sign. Value at l., portr. György Dózsa at r. Penthathlete Csaba Hegedüs with hammer and wheat at ctr. on back.			
	a. 23.5.1957.	.25	3.00	12.50
	b. 24.8.1960.	2.00	7.50	45.00
	c. 12.10.1962.	.20	1.50	12.50
	d. 3.9.1965.	.20	1.00	12.50
	e. 30.6.1969.	.20	.75	9.00
	f. Serial # varieties. 28.10.1975.	.15	.50	12.50
	g. 30.9.1980.	.15	.40	12.50
	s1. As a; c; d. Specimen w/red ovpt. and perforated: *MINTA.*	—	—	27.50
	s2. As b. Specimen.	—	—	35.00
	s3. As e; f; g. Specimen.	—	—	25.00

170	50 Forint	VG	VF	UNC
	1965-89. Brown on blue and orange unpt. Value at l., Like #167 but new arms and sign. portr. Prince Ferencz Rákóczi II at r. Battle of the Hungarian insurrectionists (Kuruc) against pro-Austrian soldiers (Labanc) scene at ctr. on back.			
	a. 3.9.1965.	.25	1.50	25.00
	b. 30.6.1969.	.25	1.50	20.00
	c. Serial # varieties. 28.10.1975.	1.00	2.00	12.50
	d. Serial # prefix D. 30.9.1980.	.20	.75	12.50
	e. Serial # prefix H. 30.9.1980.	1.00	2.50	15.00
	f. 10.11.1983.	.10	.50	9.00
	g. 4.11.1986.	.10	.50	27.50
	h. 10.1.1989.	.10	.50	17.50
	s1. As a. Specimen. Ovpt *MINTA.*	—	—	50.00
	s2. As b-h. Specimen.	—	—	25.00

171	100 Forint	VG	VF	UNC
	1957-89. Red-violet on blue and orange unpt. Like #166 but new arms and sign. Value at l., portr. Lajos Kossuth at r. Horse-drawn wagon from *Took Refuge from the Storm* by Károly Lotz at ctr. on back.			
	a. 23.5.1957.	1.00	3.00	15.00
	b. 24.8.1960.	2.00	4.00	15.00
	c. 12.10.1962.	1.00	3.00	12.50
	d. 24.10.1968.		FV	12.50
	e. 28.10.1975. Serial # varieties.	FV	2.00	10.00
	f. 30.9.1980.	FV	FV	10.00
	g. 30.10.1984.	FV	FV	10.00
	h. 10.1.1989.	FV	FV	9.00
	s1. As a. Specimen w/red ovpt. and perforted: *MINTA.*	—	—	65.00
	s2. As b; c. Specimen.	—	—	—
	s3. As d; e. Specimen.	—	—	35.00
	s4. As f; g. Specimen.	—	—	30.00
	s5. As h. Specimen.	—	—	30.00

RUSSIAN ARMY OCCUPATION - WWII

A VÖRÖSHADSEREG PARANCSNOKSÁGA

1944 ISSUE

M1	1 Pengö	VG	VF	UNC
	1944. Blue on lt. brown unpt. Printing size on date side 106 x 49mm.			
	a. Unpt. horizontal wavy lines.	.50	1.50	6.00
	b. Unpt. vertical wavy lines.	.50	1.50	6.00

NOTICE

Readers with unlisted dates, signature varieties, etc.
are invited to submit photocopies or,
high resolution (300 dpi, 100% size) scans of their notes to:
Standard Catalog of World Paper Money,
700 East State St. Iola, WI 54990-0001,
or E-Mail: george.cuhaj@fwpubs.com.

		VG	VF	UNC
M2	**1 Pengö**			
	1944. Blue on lt. brown unpt. Printing size on date side 118 x 54mm.			
	a. W/o serial #, w/horizontal wavy lines.	.25	.50	3.00
	b. W/o serial #, w/vertical wavy lines.	.25	.50	3.00
	c. W/serial #.	8.00	20.00	50.00

		VG	VF	UNC
M3	**2 Pengö**			
	1944. Blue on green unpt.	.25	.50	3.00

		VG	VF	UNC
M4	**5 Pengö**			
	1944. Lilac on lt. blue unpt.	.25	.50	3.00

		VG	VF	UNC
M5	**10 Pengö**			
	1944. Dk. green on lilac and green unpt.	.50	2.00	8.00

		VG	VF	UNC
M6	**20 Pengö**			
	1944. Gray on dull olive unpt.			
	a. W/o serial #.	10.00	25.00	60.00
	b. W/serial #. 2 serial # varieties.	.50	2.00	8.00

		VG	VF	UNC
M7	**50 Pengö**			
	1944. Olive on lt. brown and blue unpt. 2 serial # varieties.	.50	1.50	10.00
M8	**100 Pengö**			
	1944. Dk. brown on dull orange unpt. 2 serial # varieties.	.50	1.50	10.00

		VG	VF	UNC
M9	**1000 Pengö**			
	1944. Red on lt. blue unpt.	3.50	8.00	30.00

ICELAND

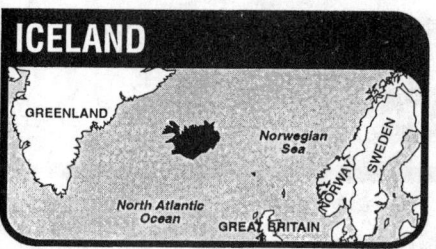

The Republic of Iceland, an island of recent volcanic origin in the North Atlantic east of Greenland and immediately south of the Arctic Circle, has an area of 39,768 sq. mi. (103,000 sq. km.) and a population of 283,000. Capital: Reykjavík. Fishing is the chief industry and accounts for more than 60 percent of the exports.

Iceland was settled by Norwegians in the 9th century and established as an independent republic in 930. The Icelandic assembly called the "Althing," also established in 930, is the oldest parliament in the world. Iceland came under Norwegian sovereignty in 1262, and passed to Denmark when Norway and Denmark were united under the Danish crown in 1384. In 1918, it was established as a virtually independent kingdom in union with Denmark. On June 17, 1944, while Denmark was still under occupation by troops of the Third Reich, Iceland was established by plebiscite as an independent republic.

RULERS:

Danish until 1873
Christian IX, 1863-1906
Frederik VIII, 1906-1912
Christian X, 1912-1944

MONETARY SYSTEM:

1 Krona = 100 Aurar, 1874-

DANISH ADMINISTRATION

COURANT BANK

1778-92 PROVISIONAL ISSUES

#A1, A2, A5, A6 and A11 reissue of early Danish State notes.

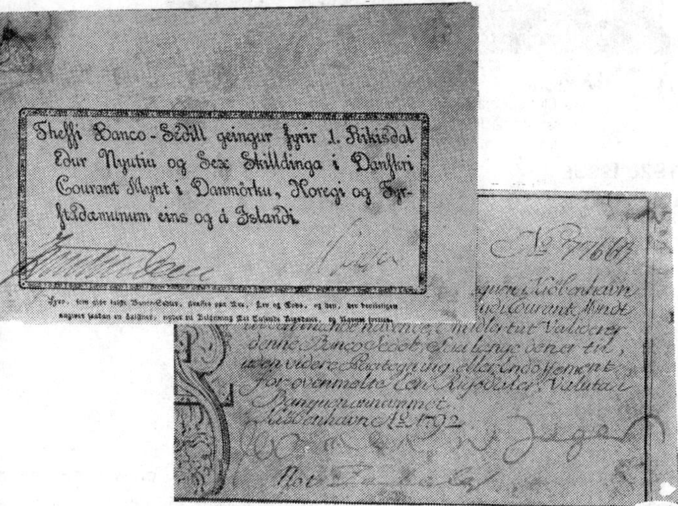

		Good	Fine	XF
A1	**1 Rigsdaler** 1777-80; 1783-84; 1788-89; 1791-92. Black. Printed on the back of Denmark #A24c.	450.	1250.	—
A2	**5 Rigsdaler** 1778-79. Black. Printed on the back of Denmark #A29a.	—	—	—

1795-1801 PROVISIONAL ISSUES

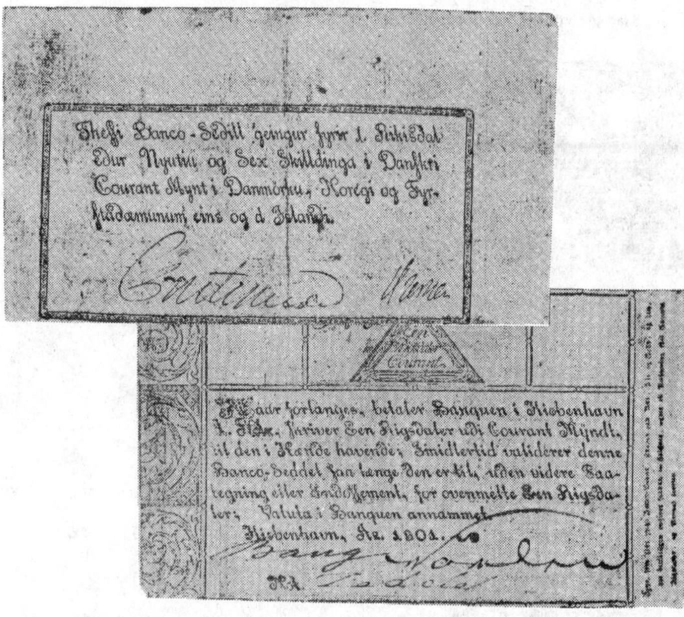

		Good	Fine	XF
A5	**1 Rigsdaler** 1792-94; 1801. Black. Printed on the back of Denmark #A28.			
	a. Issued note.	425.	1000.	—
	b. Handstamped: "A" in circle. 1792-94.	625.	1200.	—
	c. Handstamped: "B" in circle. 1794.	850.	2000.	—
	d. Handstamped: "C" in circle. 1801.	625.	1200.	—
	e. Handstamped: "D" in circle. 1801.	625.	1200.	—

Note: The stamping *A, B, C, D* was a precautionary measure during the Napoleonic War. A lot of money had been seized by the Allies against Napoleon, as Denmark was one of his supporters. All notes (dates and types) that exist with the handstamp are also found w/o the handstamp.

		Good	Fine	XF
A6	**5 Rigsdaler** 1800-01. Black on blue paper. Printed on the back of Denmark #A29b. Handstamped: "C" in circle.	—	3500.	—

RIGSBANK

1815 PROVISIONAL ISSUE

		Good	Fine	XF
A11	**1 Rigsbankdaler** 20.3.1815 (- old date 1814). printed on the back of Rigsbanken i København notes. Rare.	—	—	—

Note: For similar issues refer to Danish West Indies and Faeroe Islands listings.

LANDSSJOD ÍSLANDS

LAW OF 18.9.1885

#1-3 portr. Kg. Christian IX at l. in profile.

		Good	Fine	XF
1	**5 Krónur** L.1885. Gray-brown and black. Uniface.			
	a. Issued note.	600.	1300.	1600.
	r. Unissued remainder.	—	Unc	1000.
2	**10 Krónur** L.1885. Blue. Uniface.			
	a. Issued note.	650.	1400.	2000.
	r. Unissued remainder.	—	Unc	1000.
3	**50 Krónur** L.1885. Gray-green and lt. brown. Allegorical figure at ctr. on back.			
	a. Issued note. Rare.	—	—	—
	r. Unissued remainder. Reported not confirmed.	—	—	—

LAWS OF 18.9.1885 AND 12.1.1900 - FIRST ISSUE

#4 and 5 facing portr. Kg. Christian IX at l.

		Good	Fine	XF
4	**5 Krónur**			
	L.1885 and 1900 (1900-06). Brown and gray. Bird at ctr. on back.			
	a. Issued note.	350.	900.	—
	b. Punched hole cancelled.	—	150.	—
5	**10 Krónur**			
	L.1885 and 1900 (1900-06). Blue and brown. Allegorical figure at ctr. on back.			
	a. Issued note.	225.	475.	1000.
	b. Punched hole cancelled.	—	250.	—
6	**50 Krónur**			
	L.1885 and 1900 (1906-12). Gray-green and brown. Portr. Kg. Frederik VIII at l. Portr. Kg. Frederik VIII at l. Back Like #5.			
	a. Issued note. Rare.	—	—	—
	b. Punched hole cancelled.	—	2000.	—

LAWS OF 18.9.1885 AND 12.1.1900 - SECOND ISSUE

#7-9 portr. Kg. Christian X at l.

		Good	Fine	XF
7	**5 Krónur**			
	L.1885 and 1900 (1912). Brown and green-gray.			
	a. Issued note.	400.	1100.	—
	b. Punched hole cancelled.	—	100.	—
8	**10 Krónur**			
	L.1885 and 1900 (1912). Blue and brown.			
	a. Issued note.	400.	1100.	—
	b. Punched hole cancelled.	—	150.	—
9	**50 Krónur**			
	L.1885 and 1900 (1912). Gray-green and lt. brown.			
	a. Issued note. Rare.	—	—	—
	b. Punched hole cancelled.	—	350.	—

ÍSLANDS BANKI

1904 ISSUE

#10-14 portr. Kg. Christian IX at l.

		Good	Fine	XF
10	**5 Krónur**			
	1904. Black on red and violet unpt. Bird at l. on back.	110.	325.	1200.

		Good	Fine	XF
11	**10 Krónur**			
	1904. Black on blue and tan unpt. Bird at r. on back.	165.	450.	1500.
12	**50 Krónur**			
	1904. Black on red and violet unpt. Volcano and river at r. Back similar to #11. Rare.	—	—	—

		Good	Fine	XF
13	**100 Krónur**			
	1904. Black on blue and tan unpt. Geyser at l. Bird at ctr. on back. Rare.	—	—	—

1919 PROVISIONAL ISSUE

		Good	Fine	XF
14	**100 Krónur**			
	1919. Blue and gray. Ovpt. on back of #1.			
	a. Issued note. Rare.	—	—	—
	r. Unissued remainder.			

1920 ISSUE

#15-16 printer: G&D.

		Good	Fine	XF
15	**5 Krónur**			
	1920. Black on red and violet unpt. Geyser at l. Back red and blue.			
	a. Issued note.	250.	625.	165[illegible]
	r. Remainder (1 signature).	—	Unc	30[illegible]
16	**10 Krónur**			
	1920. Black on blue and tan unpt. Volcano and river at l. Back blue and brown.	250.	650.	170[illegible]

RIKISSJOD ÍSLANDS

LAWS OF 18.9.1885 AND 12.1.1900 (1921)

#17 and 18 printer: R. Gutenberg, Reykjavik.

		Good	Fine	XF
17	**1 Króna** L.1885 and 1900. Dk. blue. Unpt. of double-line circles. Arms on back.			
	a. Blue serial # at bottom ctr. (1921).	20.00	60.00	135.
	b. Dk. blue serial # at upper l. (1922).	15.00	40.00	100.

		Good	Fine	XF
18	**1 Króna** L.1885 and 1900. Dk. blue. Unpt. of simple circles. Arms on back.			
	a. Black serial #. (1922-23).	10.00	30.00	80.00
	b. Prefix A, circles behind red serial #. (1924-25).	15.00	40.00	100.
	c. Prefix B, w/o circles behind red serial #. (1925).	15.00	40.00	100.

#19-21 portr. Kg. Christian X at l.

		Good	Fine	XF
19	**5 Krónur** ND. Brown and green. Like #7 but w/*Fyrir Rikissjod Íslands.*	200.	500.	1300.
20	**10 Krónur** ND. Dk. green on green unpt. Like #8 but w/*Fyrir Rikissjod Íslands.*	200.	500.	1300.
21	**50 Krónur** ND. Gray-green and lt. brown. Like #9 but w/*Fyrir Rikissjod Íslands.*	850.	2450.	—

1941 Emergency WW II Issue

22 1 Króna VG VF UNC
1941 (1941-47). All on very thin paper, w/short (3.5mm) or large serial numbers (4mm). Arms on back. Printer: R. Gutenberg, Reykjavik.

22		VG	VF	UNC
	a. Dk. green on lt. green paper. 000001-200000, (1941).	5.00	20.00	70.00
	b. Green on lt. green paper. 200001-250000, (1942).	20.00	75.00	150.
	c. Brown on lt. brown paper. 250001-350000, (1942-43).	10.00	30.00	75.00
	d. Brown on white paper. 350001-500000, (1944-47).	15.00	40.00	100.
	e. Brown on white paper. 500001-636000, (1944-45).	15.00	40.00	100.
	f. Brown on white paper. 636001-1000000, (1945).	10.00	35.00	75.00
	g. Blue-green on white paper. Serial # 3.5mm tall. 000001S-216000S, (1947).	5.00	20.00	50.00
	h. Dk. blue on white paper. 216001-332000, (1944).	10.00	30.00	70.00
	i. Dk. blue on white paper. 332001-452000, (1944-45).	15.00	40.00	100.
	j. Dk. blue on white paper. 452001-576000, (1945).	5.00	20.00	50.00
	k. Dk. blue on yellow paper. 576001-760000, (1945).	5.00	20.00	50.00
	l. Blue-green on white paper. 760001-1000000, (1946).	10.00	30.00	70.00
	m. Blue-green on white paper. Serial # 4mm tall. 000001-260000, (1946-47).	10.00	25.00	60.00
	n. Blue-green on white paper. 260001-558000, (1947).	5.00	20.00	50.00
	o. Lt. blue on white paper. 558001-806000, (1947).	5.00	20.00	50.00

Note: Varieties a-f compose the first printing; g-l the second; m-o the third.

Landsbanki Íslands

Laws of 31.5.1927 and 15.4.1928

#23-26 portr. Kg. Christian X at l. Varieties in r. sign.

#23-25 mention 1928 law date; #26 shows the 1927 date.

		Good	Fine	XF
23	**5 Krónur** L.1928 (1929). Brown on green unpt. Like #19 but w/Landsbanki Íslands.	180.	300.	700.
24	**10 Krónur** L.1928 (1929). Dk. blue on lt. blue unpt. Like #20 but w/Landsbanki Íslands.	200.	350.	850.
25	**50 Krónur** L.1928 (1929). Gray-green on lt. brown unpt. Like #21 but w/Landsbanki Íslands.	300.	600.	1500.

Note: For similar notes but ND see #19-21.

		Good	Fine	XF
26	**100 Krónur** 31.5.1927. Gray-blue on gray unpt. Back like #24.	500.	1000.	2500.

Law of 15.4.1928

SIGNATURE VARIETIES

1	Jón Árnason – Magnús Sigurthsson, 1917-1945
2	Jón Árnason – Lúthvik Kaaber, 1918–1940
3	Jón Árnason – Georg Ólafsson, 1921–1941
4	Jón Árnason – Vilhjálmur Thor, 1940–1945
5	Jón Árnason – Pétur Magnússon, 1941–1944

#27-31 notes issued 1934-47. Sign. of Bank Director at l., Bank Governor at r. Printer: BWC.

		VG	VF	UNC
27	**5 Krónur** L.1928. Brown and violet on m/c unpt. Portr. J. Eriksson at l. Bldg. at r. on back.			
	a. W/o serial # prefix. Sign. 1-3.	15.00	40.00	140.
	b. Serial # prefix A. Sign. 1, 3, 4.	10.00	32.50	90.00
	c. Serial # prefix B. Sign. 1.	10.00	27.50	80.00
	s. Specimen.	—	—	235.

		VG	VF	UNC
28	**10 Krónur**			
	L.1928. Blue on m/c unpt. Portr. J. Sigurdsson at l. Waterfalls at r. on back.			
	a. W/o serial # prefix. Sign. 1-3.	12.50	35.00	135.
	b. Serial # prefix A. Sign. 1, 3, 4.	7.50	30.00	90.00
	c. Serial # prefix B. Sign. 1, 4, 5.	7.50	25.00	80.00
	s. Specimen.			225.
29	**50 Krónur**			
	L.1928. Violet. Like #27. Men w/fishing boats and freighter on back.			
	a. W/o serial # prefix. Sign. 1-3.	75.00	200.	550.
	b. Serial # prefix A. Sign. 1, 3, 4.	65.00	165.	435.
	c. Serial # prefix B. Sign. 1, 4, 5.	55.00	135.	400.
	s. Specimen.			650.
30	**100 Krónur**			
	L.1928. Red on m/c unpt. Like #28. Flock of sheep on back.			
	a. W/o serial # prefix. Sign. 3.	100.	250.	600.
	b. Serial # prefix A. Sign. 1, 3, 4.	85.00	200.	550.
	c. Serial # prefix B. Sign. 1, 4, 5.	75.00	175.	475.
	d. Serial # prefix C. Sign. 1, 4, 5.	65.00	150.	450.
	e. Serial # prefix D. Sign. 1, 4, 5.	60.00	135.	425.
	s. Specimen.			1000.
31	**500 Krónur**			
	L.1928. Green on m/c unpt. Like #28. Sign. 1, 4-5. River, rocks and mountains on back.			
	a. W/o serial # prefix. Sign. 1, 4, 5.	250.	600.	160.
	s. Specimen.			2000.

REPUBLIC

LANDSBANKI ÍSLANDS

LAW OF 15.4.1928

#32-36 issued 1948-56. Designs like #27-31. Sign. of Bank Director at l., Bank Governor at r. Printer: BWC.

SIGNATURE VARIETIES	
6	Magnús Jónsson – Magnús Sigurthsson, 1946-1947
7	Magnús Jónsson – Vilhjálmur Thor, 1955–1957
8	Magnús Jónsson – Jón Árnason, 1946–1954
9	Magnús Jónsson – Jón G. Maríasson, 1943-1957
10	Magnús Jónsson – Gunnar Vithar, 1948–1955
11	Magnús Jónsson – Pétur Benediktsson, 1956–1957

NOTICE

Readers with unlisted dates, signature varieties, etc. are invited to submit photocopies or, high resolution (300 dpi, 100% size) scans of their notes to: Standard Catalog of World Paper Money, 700 East State St. Iola, WI 54990-0001, or E-Mail: george.cuhaj@fwpubs.com.

		VG	VF	UNC
32	**5 Krónur**			
	L.1928. Green on m/c unpt. Like #27.			
	a. W/o serial # prefix. Sign. 6, 8-11.	2.00	6.00	22.50
	b. Serial # prefix C. Sign. 7, 9, 11.	2.00	5.00	20.00
	s. Specimen.	—	—	150.

		VG	VF	UNC
33	**10 Krónur**			
	L.1928. Red on m/c unpt. Like #28.			
	a. W/o serial # prefix. Sign. 6, 8-11.	2.00	6.00	22.50
	b. Serial # prefix C. Sign. 8-11.	2.00	5.00	20.00
	s. Specimen.	—	—	165.

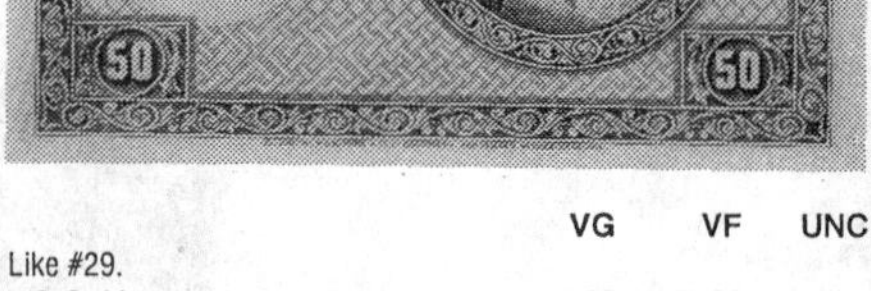

		VG	VF	UNC
34	**50 Krónur**			
	L.1928. Green on m/c unpt. Like #29.			
	a. W/o serial # prefix. Sign. 6, 8, 11.	10.00	30.00	110.
	s. Specimen.	—	—	135.

		VG	VF	UNC
35	**100 Krónur**			
	L.1928. Blue on m/c unpt. Like #30.			
	a. W/o serial # prefix. Sign. 6, 8-11.	20.00	45.00	135.
	b. Serial # prefix C. Sign. 7, 9, 11.	15.00	35.00	110.
	s. Specimen.	—	—	200.

36	500 Krónur	VG	VF	UNC
	L.1928. Brown on m/c unpt. Like #31.			
	a. W/o serial # prefix. Sign. 6, 8-11.	50.00	165.	425.
	b. Serial # prefix C. Sign. 8-10.	45.00	150.	425.
	s. Specimen.	—	—	675.

Landsbanki Íslands-Sedlabankinn

Law of 21.6.1957

#37-41 printer: BWC (w/o imprint).

7	5 Krónur	VG	VF	UNC
	L.1957. Orange-brown on m/c unpt. Viking I. Arnarson at I. Farm bldgs. on gray back.			
	a. Buff paper (first printing).	.50	2.00	5.00
	b. White paper (second printing).	.50	1.50	4.00
	s1. As a. Specimen.	—	—	125.
	s2. As b. Specimen.	—	—	150.

3	10 Krónur	VG	VF	UNC
	L.1957. Violet-brown on green and orange unpt. Portr. J. Eiriksson at I. Dock scene on green back.			
	a. Letter *O* in *REYKJAVIKURHOFN* on back w/o umlaut (error).	1.00	4.00	10.00
	b. Letter *Ö* w/umlaut on top. (corrected).	2.00	6.00	15.00
	s1. As a. Specimen.	—	—	150.
	s2. As b. Specimen.	—	—	150.

	25 Krónur	VG	VF	UNC
	L.1957. Purple on m/c unpt. Portr. M. Stephensen Logmadur at I., fjord at ctr. Fishing boats near large rock formation in water on back.			

39		VG	VF	UNC
	a. Issued note.	.75	3.00	10.00
	s. Specimen.	—	—	150.

40	100 Krónur	VG	VF	UNC
	L.1957. Blue-green on m/c unpt. Portr. T. Gunnarsson at I. Back green; herd of sheep and mountain at ctr.			
	a. Issued note.	1.00	2.50	10.00
	s. Specimen.	—	—	150.

41	1000 Krónur	VG	VF	UNC
	L.1957. Blue and green on m/c unpt. Bldg at lower ctr., portr. J. Sigurdsson at r. Rock formations on back.			
	a. Issued note.	15.00	50.00	200.
	s. Specimen.	—	—	265.

Note: For notes similar to above but dated 1961 see Volume 3.

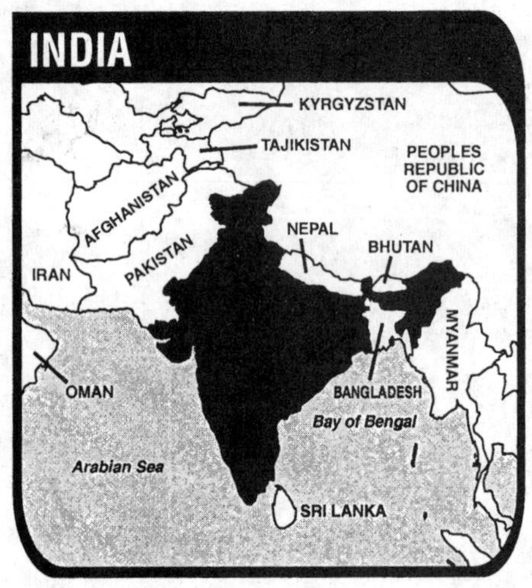

The Republic of India, a subcontinent jutting southward from the mainland of Asia, has an area of 1,266,595 sq. mi. (3,287,590 sq. km.) and a population of 1,006.8 million, second only to that of the Peoples Republic of China. Capital: New Delhi. India's economy is d on agriculture and industrial activity. Engineering goods, cotton apparel and fabrics, handicrafts, tea, iron and steel are exported.

The people of India have had a continuous civilization since about 2500 BC, when an urban culture d on commerce and trade, and to a lesser extent, agriculture, was developed by the inhabitants of the Indus River Valley. The origins of this civilization are uncertain, but it declined about 1500 B.C., when the region was conquered by the Aryans. Over the following 2,000 years, the Aryans developed a Brahmanic civilization and introduced the caste system. Several successive empires flourished in India over the following centuries, notably those of the Mauryans, Guptas and Mughals. In the 7th and 8th centuries AD, the Arabs expanded into western India, bringing with them the Islamic faith. A Muslim dynasty (the Mughal Empire) controlled virtually the entire subcontinent during the period preceding the arrival of the Europeans; an Indo-Islamic style of art and architecture evolved, of which the Taj Mahal is a splendid example.

The Portuguese were the first to arrive, off Calicut in May 1498. It was not until 1612, after Portuguese and Spanish power began to wane, that the English East India Company established its initial settlement at Surat. By the end of the century, English traders were firmly established in Bombay, Madras and Calcutta, as well as in some parts of the interior, and Britain was implementing a policy to create the civil and military institutions that would insure British dominion over the country. By 1757, following the successful conclusion of a war of colonial rivalry with France, the British were firmly established in India not only as traders, but as conquerors. During the next 60 years, the English East India Company acquired dominion over most of India by bribery and force, and ruled directly or through puppet princelings.

The Indian Mutiny (also called Sepoy Mutiny) of 1857-59, begun by Indian troops in the service of the British East India Company, revealed the intensity of the growing resentment against British domination. The widespread rebellion against British rule was unsuccessful, but resulted in the transfer of government from the company to the British crown.

Following World War I, in which India sent six million troops to fight at the side of the Allies, Indian nationalism intensified under the banner of the Indian National Congress and the leadership of Mohandas Gandhi, who called the non-violent revolt against British authority. The Government of India Act of 1935 proposed a federal status linking the British India provinces with the many princely states; in addition, provincial legislatures were to be created. The federal status was never implemented, but the legislatures were created after the election of 1937, with the National Congress winning majorities in most of the provinces.

When Britain declared war on Germany in Sept., 1939, the viceroy declared India also to be at war with a common enemy. The Congress, however, demanded independence as a condition for cooperation. Britain refused. But as the Japanese advanced into Asia, Britain offered to transfer to Indians power over all but military affairs during the war, and set forth a plan for postwar independence. Congress was willing to accept the wartime transfer of power, but both Congress and the Muslim League rejected Britain's plan for independence; Congress because it did not sufficiently safeguard Indian unity, the Muslims (who wanted a separate Muslim state) because of fears of what would happen to Muslims within a united India.

Early in 1947, Prime Minister Clement Attlee announced that Britain would leave India "by a date not later than June 1948," even though the Hindus and Muslims could not agree among themselves on a plan for self-government. The National Congress, aware that the Muslim League would revolt rather than accept an all-India government, reluctantly agreed to the formation of a separate Muslim state. The Muslim-populated provinces of the northwest frontier, Sindh and West Punjab in the west, and East Bengal in the east were separated from India to form the Muslim state of Pakistan, which became independent on August 14, 1947. India became independent on the following day. Initially, Pakistan consisted of East and West Pakistan, two areas separated by 1,000 miles of Indian territory. East Pakistan seceded from Pakistan on March 26, 1971, and with the support of India established itself as the independent Peoples Republic of Bangladesh.

The Republic of India is a member of the Commonwealth of Nations. The president is the Chief of State. The prime minister is the Head of Government.

RULERS:

British to 1047

MONETARY SYSTEM:

1 Rupee = 16 Annas to 1957
1 Rupee = 100 Naye Paise, 1957-1964
1 Rupee = 100 Paise, 1964-

Note: Staple holes and condition:

Perfect uncirculated notes are rarely encountered without having at least two tiny holes made by staples, stick pins or stitching having been done during age old accounting practices before and after a note is released to circulation. Staples were officially discontinued in 1998.

Note: Certain listings encompassing issues circulated by various commercial bank and regional authorities are contained in Volume 1.

NOTICE

Readers with unlisted dates, signature varieties, etc. are invited to submit photocopies or, high resolution (300 dpi, 100% size) scans of their notes to: Standard Catalog of World Paper Money, 700 East State St. Iola, WI 54990-0001, or E-Mail: george.cuhaj@fwpubs.com.

COLONIAL OFFICES

	Allahabad	K	Karachi
B	Bombay	L	Lahore
C	Calcutta	M	Madras
	Calicut	R	Rangoon, refer to Myanmar listings
A	Cawnpore		

DENOMINATION LANGUAGE PANELS

Bengali	Marathi
Burmese	Tamil
Gujarati	Telugu
Gujarati (var.)	Persian (Farsi)
Hindi	Urdu
Kannada	

SIGNATURE VARIETIES

Dates appearing on notes are not when the notes were printed. Dates of manufacture may be deduced from a wmk. code, i.e. A 41 06 means Vat A, week 41, year 1906. This date is sometimes one or two years later than the printed date. Signatures are left off until the notes are actually issued, sometimes many years after the notes were printed. Therefore, the dates below do not correspond exactly with the years the signers held office.

A.V.V. Aiyar, 1919	Stephen Jacob, 1886–1896
J.A. Ballard, 1861–1863	E. Jay, 1884
O.T. Barrow, 1899–1906	C.E. Jones, 1941
C.W.C. Cassog, 1913–1915	J.W. Kelly, 1935
A.F. Cox, 1891–1905	A. Kingstocke, 1913
H. Denning, 1920–1925	R. Logan, 1887–1899
C.D. Deshmukh, 1943–1947	A.C. McWatters, 1916–1922
R.W. Gillan, 1907–1913	W.H. Michael, 1906
M.M.S. Gubbay, 1913–1919	Hugh Sandeman, 1872

E.F. Harrison, 1873	I.L. Sundtrayton (?), 1872
F.C. Harrison, 1904–1905	J.B. Taylor, 1925
D. Hastings, 1901	A.C. Merell Tupps, 1872–1886
H.F. Howard, 1912–1916	J. Westland, 1882

BRITISH ADMINISTRATION

GOVERNMENT OF INDIA

1861-65 ISSUE

#A1-A1A Qn. Victoria in sprays at upper l. Two language panels. Uniface. Sign. J. A. Ballard w/title: *COMMISSIONER*.

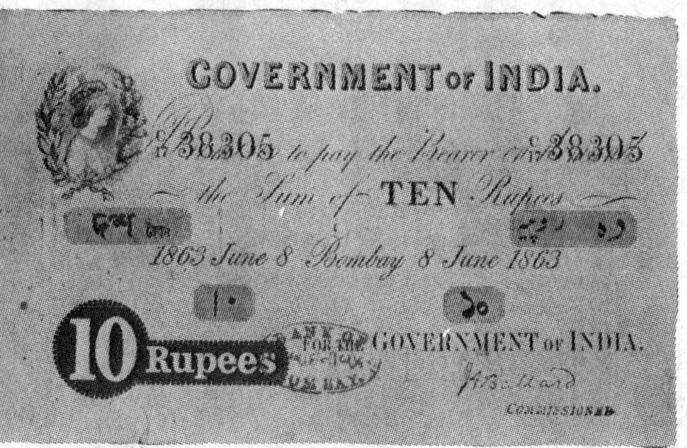

		Good	Fine	XF
A1	**10 Rupees** 6.8.1861; 9.5.1862; 7.6.1862; 8.6.1863; 14.6.1864; 6.6.1865. Rare.	—	—	—
A1A	**20 Rupees** 10.6.1864. Second sign. of S. K. Lambert (?). Rare.	—	—	—

1872-1927 ISSUE

#A2-A20 uniface Colonial types w/o portrait. Issued 1872-1927.

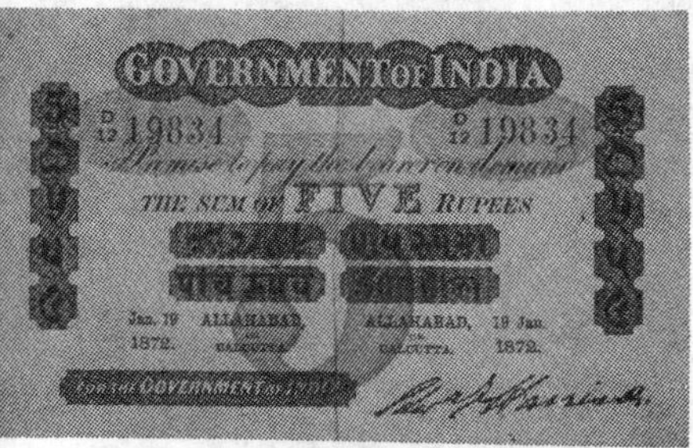

		Good	Fine	XF
A2	**5 Rupees** 1872-1901. Green unpt. 4 language panels, 2 serial #.			
	a. *ALLAHABAD* or *CALCUTTA*. Sign. Edw. A. Harrison. 19.1.1872.	150.	250.	900.
	b. *BOMBAY*. Sign. A. C. Merell Tupps. 27.5.1872; 11.11.1886.	150.	250.	900.
	c. *BOMBAY*. Sign. A. F. Cox. 7.5.1891; 5.2.1899-8.6.1899.	100.	200.	800.
	d. *BOMBAY*. Sign. O. T. Barrow. 1.11.1894-9.1.1901.	100.	200.	800.
	e. *CALCUTTA*. Sign. E. Jay. 10.5.1884.	150.	250.	850.
	f. *CALCUTTA*. Sign. Stephen Jacob. 1.10.1886; 1.6.1888.	150.	250.	850.

		Good	Fine	XF
A3	**5 Rupees** 1901-03. Green unpt. 6 language panels, 4 serial #.			
	a. *BOMBAY*. Sign. A. F. Cox. 3.3.1902-1.8.1903.	70.00	150.	350.
	b. *BOMBAY*. Sign. O. T. Barrow. 9.1.1901; 1.3.1902.	70.00	150.	350.
	c. *CALCUTTA*. Sign. A. F. Cox. 4.2.1901.	70.00	150.	350.

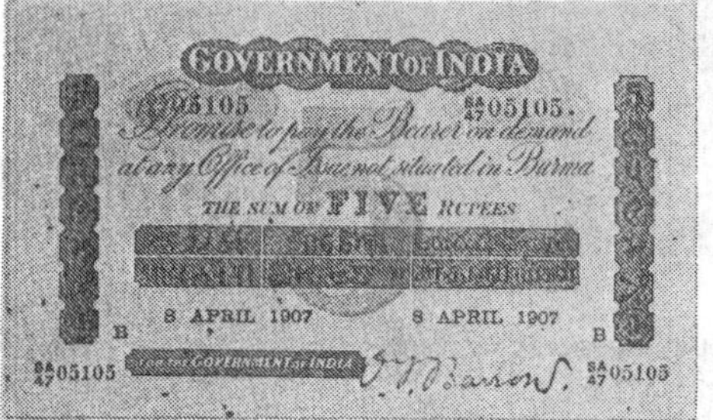

		Good	Fine	XF
A4	**5 Rupees** 1903. Black and pink. 8 language panels and 4 serial #. *at any Office of Issue not situated in Burma* added to text. Letter for city of issue.			
	a. L (Lahore). Sign. A. F. Cox. Reported not confirmed.	—	—	—
	b. B (Bombay). Sign. O. T. Barrow. 12.7.1905; 1.8.1905; 6.4.1907; 8.4.1907.	100.	200.	400.

		Good	Fine	XF
A5	**5 Rupees** 1907-15. Red-pink unpt. 8 language panels, 4 serial #. *at any Office of Issue* added to text. Letter for city of issue.			
	a. B (Bombay). Sign. H. F. Howard. 9.11.1907; 7.2.1912; 13.10.1913; 14.10.1913; 31.10.1913.	25.00	50.00	150.
	b. B (Bombay). Sign. M. M. S. Gubbay. 7.1.1914; 28.4.1914; 18.5.1914; 19.5.1914; 8.4.1915.	25.00	50.00	150.
	c. B (Bombay). Sign. R. W. Gillan. 8.2.1909; 2.10.1909.	25.00	50.00	150.
	d. C (Calcutta). Sign. R. W. Gillan. 20.5.1907; 12.10.1907.	25.00	50.00	150.
	e. C (Calcutta). Sign. M. M. S. Gubbay. 4.3.1914.	25.00	50.00	150.
	f. C (Calcutta). Sign. H. F. Howard. 23.9.1912; 25.10.1912; 30.10.1912; 31.7.1913.	25.00	50.00	150.
	g. A (Cawnpore). Sign. H. F. Howard. 2.10.1912.	25.00	50.00	150.
	h. M (Madras). Sign. M. M. S. Gubbay. 22.7.1914.	25.00	50.00	150.

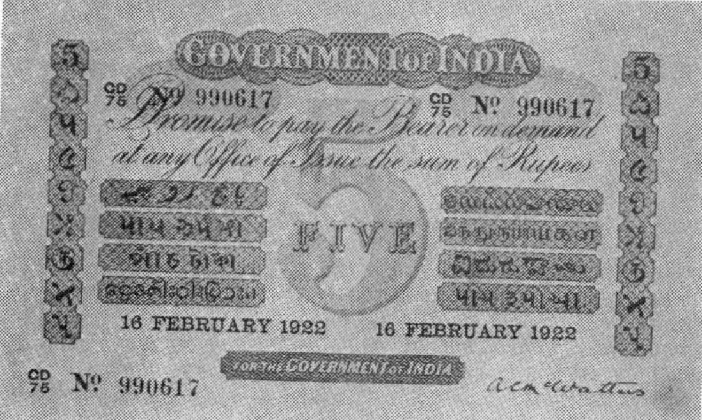

		Good	Fine	XF
A6	**5 Rupees** 1914-24. Black on pink unpt. 3 serial #. W/ or w/o letter for city of issue.			

A6	Good	Fine	XF
a. B (Bombay). Sign. M. M. S. Gubbay. 8.4.1915-8.8.1916.	20.00	40.00	100.
b. C (Calcutta). Sign. M. M. S. Gubbay. 9.1.1915-21.7.1916.	25.00	50.00	125.
c. C (Calcutta). Sign. H. F. Howard. 4.5.1916; 13.7.1916.	25.00	50.00	125.
d. A (Cawnpore). Sign. M. M. S. Gubbay. 2.2.1915; 28.12.1915.	20.00	40.00	100.
e. L (Lahore). Sign. M. M. S. Gubbay. 31.7.1916.	30.00	60.00	135.
f. M (Madras). Sign. M. M. S. Gubbay. 12.8.1914-23.10.1918.	20.00	40.00	100.
g. W/o letter. Sign. M. M. S. Gubbay. 26.10.1918-23.1.1920.	15.00	30.00	85.00
h. W/o letter. Sign. A. C. McWatters. 12.1.1922-8.2.1924.	15.00	30.00	85.00
i. W/o letter. Sign. H. Denning. 24.1.1924; 25.1.1924; 8.2.1924; 11.2.1924.	15.00	30.00	85.00

A7 10 Rupees

1872-1901. Green unpt. 4 languages on 2 panels, 2 serial #.

	Good	Fine	XF
a. *ALLAHABAD* or *CALCUTTA*. Sign. E. Jay. 24.3.1884.	100.	250.	900.
b. *BOMBAY*. Sign. R. Logan. 10.3.1887; 16.6.1899.	100.	200.	800.
c. *BOMBAY*. Sign. O. T. Barrow. 1.7.1899; 2.2.1900.	100.	200.	800.
d. *BOMBAY*. Sign. I. L. Sundtrayton. 7.5.1872. Rare.			
e. *CALCUTTA*. Sign. H. Sandeman. 1872.	100.	200.	800.
f. *CALCUTTA*. Sign. J. Westland. 15.4.1882; 10.12.1883.	100.	200.	800.
g. *CALCUTTA*. Sign. Stephen Jacob. 6.1.1893; 10.2.1893.	100.	200.	800.
h. *CALCUTTA*. Sign. A. F. Cox. 17.1.1898-14.10.1901.	100.	200.	800.
i. *LAHORE* or *CALCUTTA*. *Sign. Stephen Jacob. 25.11.1896.*Rare.	—	—	—
j. *MADRAS/Rangoon*. 1896. Reported not confirmed.	—	—	—
k. *MADRAS/L*. 1896. Rare.	—	—	—

A8 10 Rupees

1903-06. Green unpt. 4 language panels, 4 serial #. BOMBAY.

	Good	Fine	XF
a. Sign. O. T. Barrow. 14.8.1903; 19.8.1903; 1.9.1905.	60.00	125.	375.
b. Sign. F. C. Harrison. 2.9.1905; 6.9.1905; 3.10.1905; 12.10.1905.	60.00	125.	375.
c. Sign. W. H. Michael. 3.1.1906.	60.00	125.	375.

A9 10 Rupees

1903-06. Green unpt. 4 languages on 2 panels, 4 serial #. CALCUTTA.

	Good	Fine	XF
a. Sign. A. F. Cox. 10.6.1903; 5.8.1904; 20.12.1904.	60.00	125.	375.
b. Sign. O. T. Barrow. 1.11.1904-3.12.1906.	60.00	125.	375.
c. *CAWNPORE* or *CALCUTTA*. Sign. R. W. Gillan. 29.8.1906.	60.00	125.	375.

A10 10 Rupees

1910-20. Red unpt. 8 language panels, 4 serial #. *at any Office of Issue* added to text. Letter for city of issue.

	Good	Fine	XF
a. B (Bombay). Sign. R. W. Gillan. 24.8.1910; 26.8.1910; 16.11.1911.	17.50	45.00	140.
b. B (Bombay). Sign. H. F. Howard. 1914-26.4.1916; 29.5.1916.	17.50	45.00	140.
c. B (Bombay). Sign. M. M. S. Gubbay. 1916-17.2.1919.	17.50	45.00	140.
d. C (Calcutta). Sign. R. W. Gillan. 21.2.1910; 31.5.1912.	17.50	45.00	140.
e. C (Calcutta). Sign. H. F. Howard. 31.5.1912-6.4.1916.	17.50	45.00	140.
f. C (Calcutta). Sign. M. M. S. Gubbay. 3.8.1916-1919.	17.50	45.00	140.
g. A (Cawnpore). Sign. M. M. S. Gubbay. 23.12.1915-1919.	20.00	50.00	140.
h. K (Karachi). Sign. M. M. S. Gubbay. 27.2.1918.	20.00	50.00	140.
i. L (Lahore). Sign. M. M. S. Gubbay. 10.10.1917.	20.00	50.00	140.
j. M (Madras). Sign. M. M. S. Gubbay. 1914-19.	20.00	50.00	140.

A10	Good	Fine	XF
k. W/o letter. Sign. M. M. S. Gubbay. 27.2.1919-16.8.1920.	15.00	40.00	125.
l. W/o letter. Sign. A. C. McWatters. 10.2.1920.	15.00	40.00	125.

Note: For similar issues w/R (Rangoon) see Burma.

A11 20 Rupees

	Good	Fine	XF
5.7.1899; 1.1.1901. Green unpt. 4 language panels, 2 serial #. BOMBAY. Sign. O. T. Barrow.	250.	800.	—

A12 20 Rupees

1904-06. Green unpt. 4 language panels, 4 serial #. BOMBAY.

	Good	Fine	XF
a. Sign. F. C. Harrison. 11.1.1904; 12.1.1904; 17.10.1905.	200.	650.	—
b. Sign. W. H. Michael. 18.10.1905; 16.1.1906.	200.	650.	—

A13 20 Rupees

1894-1901. Green unpt. 4 languages on 2 panels, 2 serial #.

	Good	Fine	XF
a. *ALLAHABAD* or CALCUTTA. Sign. A. F. Cox. 26.6.1894; 26.2.1901. 4 serial #.	300.	875.	—
b. *LAHORE* or *CALCUTTA*. Sign. A. F. Cox. 28.8.1900.	300.	875.	—

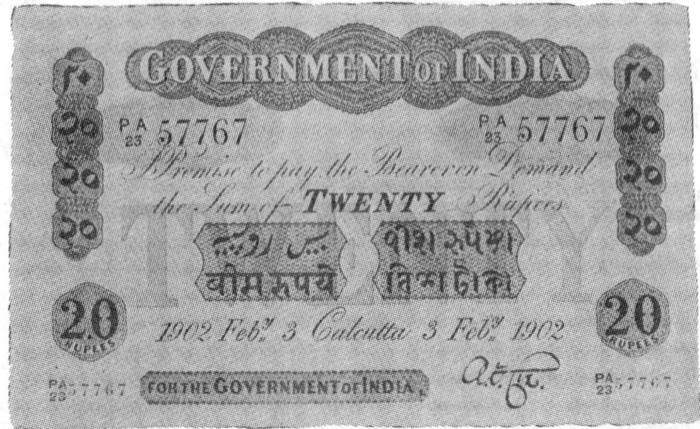

A14 20 Rupees

1902-05. Green unpt. 4 languages on 2 panels, 4 serial #.

	Good	Fine	XF
a. *CALCUTTA*. Sign. A. F. Cox. 3.2.1902.	200.	600.	—
b. *CALCUTTA*. Sign. O. T. Barrow. 10.3.1905.	200.	600.	—
c. *LAHORE* or *CALCUTTA*. Sign. A. A. Cox. 27.3.1902.	200.	600.	—
d. *LAHORE* or *CALCUTTA*. Sign. O. T. Barrow. 30.8.1905.	200.	600.	—

A14A 50 Rupees

	Good	Fine	XF
19.9.1905. Green unpt. 4 language panels, 4 serial #. *BOMBAY*. Sign. F. C. Harrison.	350.	825.	—

A15 50 Rupees

1913-22. Red unpt. 8 language panels, 4 serial #. Text: *at any Office of Issue*. Letter for city of issue.

	Good	Fine	XF
a. B (Bombay). Sign. H. F. Howard. 11.6.1913; 17.6.1913; 10.6.1920.	300.	750.	—
b. B (Bombay). Sign. A. C. McWatters. 8.2.1916.	300.	750.	—

A15		Good	Fine	XF
	c. B (Bombay). Sign. H. Denning. 8.6.1920.	300.	750.	—
	d. C (Calcutta). Sign. H. Denning. 15.1.1918; 9.3.1920; 10.3.1920; 28.10.1922.	300.	750.	—
	e. A (Cawnpore). Sign. A. C. McWatters. 29.4.1919.	300.	750.	—
	f. K (Karachi). Sign. M. M. S. Gubbay. 1.12.1913.	300.	750.	—
	g. L (Lahore). 21.3.1918. Rare.	—	—	—
	h. M (Madras). Sign. H. F. Howard. 23.6.1913. Rare.	—	—	—
	i. C (Calcutta). Sign. A. C. McWatters. 11.1.1918. Rare.	—	—	—

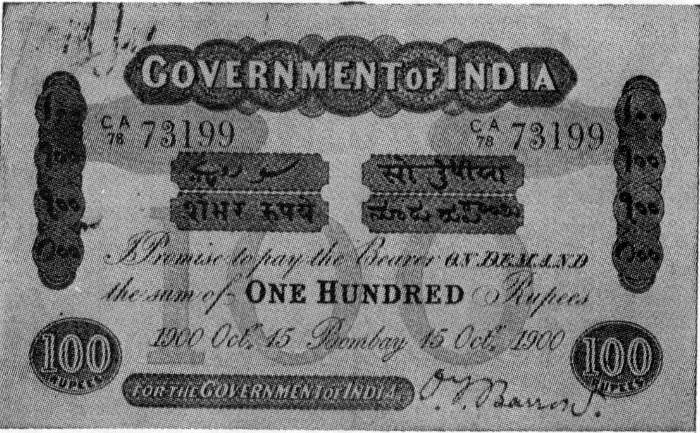

		Good	Fine	XF
A16	**100 Rupees** 1.7.1900; 15.10.1900. Green unpt. 4 language panels, 2 serial #. BOMBAY. Sign. O. T. Barrow.	150.	400.	700.
A17	**100 Rupees** 1904-27. Green unpt. 4 language panels, 4 serial #.			
	a. *BOMBAY*. Sign. H. F. Howard. 26.2.1913.	100.	200.	425.
	b. *BOMBAY*. Sign. M. M. S. Gubbay. 14.7.1914; 26.4.1916; 16.7.1916.	100.	200.	425.
	c. *BOMBAY*. Sign. A. C. McWatters. 10.6.1918-12.9.1919.	100.	200.	425.
	d. *BOMBAY*. Sign. H. Denning. 3.7.1920; 17.7.1920; 26.7.1920; 4.1.1923; 24.1.1925.	100.	200.	425.
	e. *CALCUTTA*. Sign. A. F. Cox. 22.9.1904; 23.3 1905.	100.	200.	425.
	f. *CALCUTTA*. Sign. A. C. McWatters. 31.1.1918-22.11.1925.	100.	200.	425.
	g. *CALCUTTA*. Sign. O. T. Barrow. 23.3.1905.	100.	200.	425.
	h. *CALCUTTA*. Sign. H. Denning. 27.3.1920; 30.10.1922; 31.10.1922.	100.	200.	425.
	i. *CAWNPORE*. Sign. H. Denning. 11.3.1918; 6.6.1919; 14.6.1919; 15.4.1920.	100.	200.	425.
	j. *KARACHI*. 30.12.1915.	125.	280.	525.
	k. 6.9.1913-24.5.1920.	100.	200.	425.
	l. *LAHORE*. 1901-27 (30.3.1916; 25.4.1918).	100.	200.	425.
	m. *MADRAS*. Sign. H. Denning. 3.9.1920-13.2.1925.	100.	200.	425.

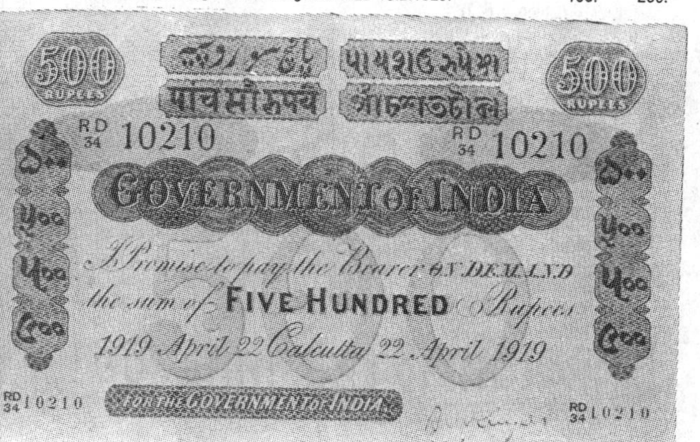

		Good	Fine	XF
A18	**500 Rupees** 1907-22. Green unpt. 4 language panels at top, 4 serial #.			
	a. *BOMBAY*. Sign. A. Kingstocke. 8.5.1913.	500.	1250.	—
	b. *BOMBAY*. Sign. C. W. C. Cassog. 9.5.1913.	500.	1250.	—
	c. *BOMBAY*. Sign. H. Denning. 10.5.1913.	500.	1250.	—
	d. *CALCUTTA*. Sign. A. V. V. Aiyar. 22.4.1919. Rare.	—	—	—
	e. *CALCUTTA*. Sign. H. Denning. 2.5.1922; 29.5.1922. Rare.	—	—	—
	f. *CAWNPORE* or *CALCUTTA*. Sign. J. W. Kelly. 26.6.1907; 27.6.1907. Rare.	—	—	—

NOTICE

Readers with unlisted dates, signature varieties, etc. are invited to submit photocopies or, high resolution (300 dpi, 100% size) scans of their notes to: Standard Catalog of World Paper Money, 700 East State St. Iola, WI 54990-0001, or E-Mail: george.cuhaj@fwpubs.com.

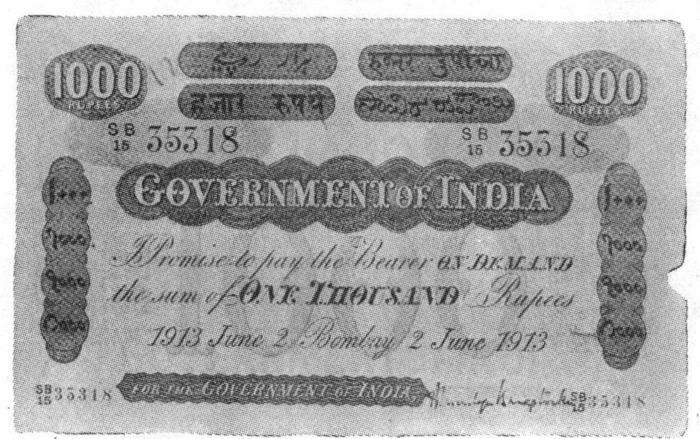

		Good	Fine	XF
A19	**1000 Rupees** 1909-27. Lt. green unpt. 4 language panels at top, 4 serial #.			
	a. *BOMBAY*. Sign. A. Kingstocke. 1909; 2.6.1913.	250.	750.	—
	b. *BOMBAY*. Sign. C. W. C. Cassog. 20.9.1915.	250.	750.	—
	c. *BOMBAY*. Sign. H. Denning. 20.9.1915; 9.8.1918; 10.8.1918; 12.8.1925; 14.8.1925; 7.7.1926.	250.	750.	—
	d. *BOMBAY*. Sign. A. V. V. Aiyar. 22.9.1919; 12.8.1925-7.7.1926.	250.	750.	—
	e. *CALCUTTA*. Sign. H. Denning. 6.4.1920; 19.8.1927; 22.8.1927.	250.	750.	—
A20	**10,000 Rupees** 22.4.1899. Green unpt. 4 languages on 1 panel, 4 serial #. *CALCUTTA*. Rare.	—	—	—

1917-30 Issue

#1-16 portr. Kg. George V.

		VG	VF	UNC
1	**1 Rupee** 1917. Black on red unpt. Coin w/Kg. George V at upper l. W/ or w/o perforation on l. border. Also isssued in booklets of 25 pcs.			
	a. Wmk: Rayed star in plain field at r. Sign. M. M. S. Gubbay.	25.00	100.	250.
	b. Wmk: Rayed star in plain field at r. Sign. A. C. McWatters.	25.00	100.	250.
	c. Wmk: Rayed star in plain field at r. Sign. H. Denning.	30.00	125.	300.
	d. Wmk: Rayed star in square at r. Smaller letters in last line (Gujarati) on back. Sign. H. Denning.	25.00	100.	250.
	e. Wmk: Rayed star in square at r. Larger letters in last line on back. Sign. A. C. McWatters.	20.00	90.00	200.
	f. Wmk: Rayed star in square at r. Larger letters in last line on back. Sign. H. Denning.	20.00	90.00	200.
	g. Wmk: Rayed star in square. Sign. M. M. S. Gubbay.	20.00	90.00	200.

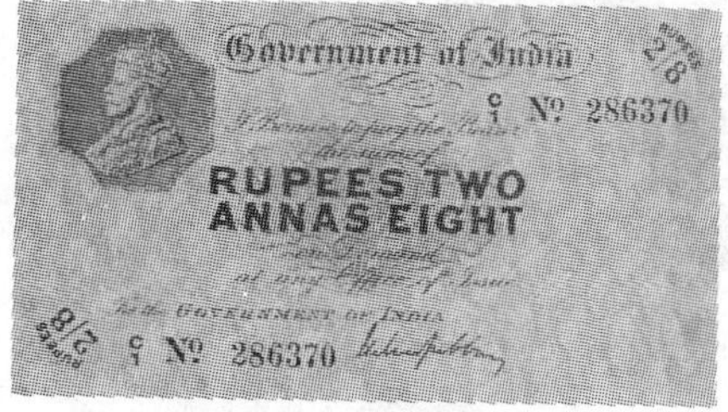

		VG	VF	UNC
2	**2 Rupees 8 Annas** ND (1917). Black on green and red-brown unpt. Kg. George V in octagon at upper l. Sign. M. M. S. Gubbay.	750.	2750.	6500.

		VG	VF	UNC
3	**5 Rupees** ND. Green on brown unpt. Oval portr. of Kg. George V at upper r. Inverted 5 at lower l. on back. Trial piece. Sign. M. M. S. Gubbay.	—	—	2500.

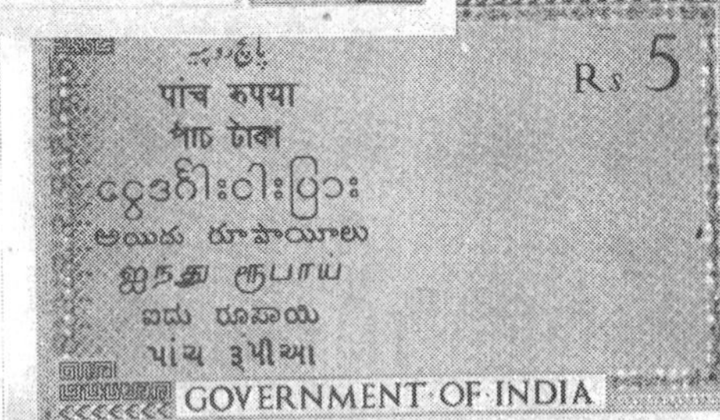

		VG	VF	UNC
4	**5 Rupees** ND. Brown-violet, green and lt. brown. Kg. George V at upper r.			
	a. Sign. H. Denning.	100.	300.	750.
	b. Sign. J. B. Taylor.	100.	300.	750.

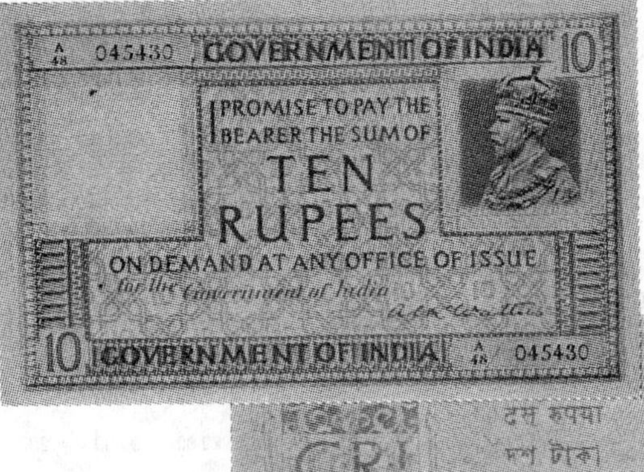

		VG	VF	UNC
5	**10 Rupees** ND. Blue and brown. Kg. George V at upper r. Serial # at upper l. and lower r.			
	a. Sign. A. C. McWatters.	100.	300.	750.
	b. Sign. H. Denning.	100.	300.	750.
6	**10 Rupees** ND. Green and brown. Similar to #5 but serial # at lower l. and upper r. Sign. H. Denning.	90.00	275.	700.

		VG	VF	UNC
7	**10 Rupees** ND. Dk. blue on gray and purple unpt. Kg. George V at r.			
	a. Sign. H. Denning.	60.00	200.	500.
	b. Sign. J. B. Taylor.	60.00	200.	500.

		VG	VF	UNC
8	**50 Rupees** ND. Coin w/Kg. George V at upper r. CAWNPORE. W/o sign. Uniface. Perforated: *SPECIMEN.*			
	a. Blue, green and brown.			3500.
	b. Brown, red and yellow.			900.
9	**50 Rupees** ND (1930). Lilac and brown. Kg. George V in oval at r.			
	a. *BOMBAY.* Sign. H. Denning.	1000.	3750.	8500.
	b. *BOMBAY.* Sign. J. B. Taylor.	1000.	3750.	8500.
	c. *CALCUTTA.* Sign. H. Denning.	1000.	3750.	8500.
	d. *CALCUTTA.* Sign. J. B. Taylor.	1000.	3750.	8500.
	e. *CAWNPORE.* Sign. J. B. Taylor.	1250.	4250.	9500.
	f. *KARACHI.* Sign. J. B. Taylor.	1250.	4250.	9500.
	g. *MADRAS.* Sign. J. B. Taylor.	1250.	4250.	9500.

Note: For similar 50 Rupees w/*RANGOON*, see Burma.

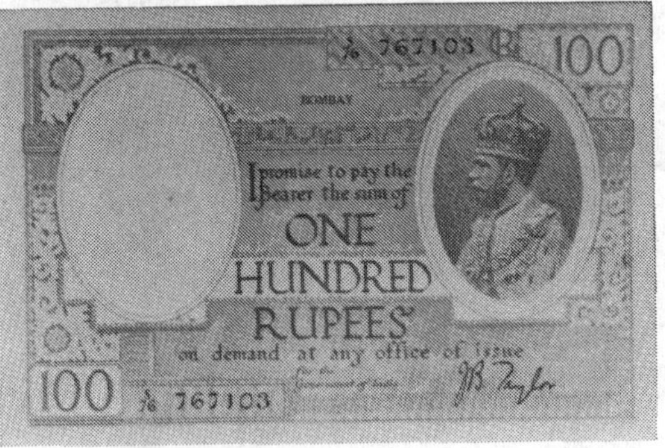

		VG	VF	UNC
10	**100 Rupees** ND. Violet and green. Oval portr. of Kg. George V at upper r.			
	a. Sm. *BOMBAY* in black. Sign. H. Denning.	450.	1250.	3000.
	b. Lg. (13mm) *BOMBAY* in green. Sign. J. B. Taylor.	450.	1250.	3000.
	c. Lg. *BOMBAY* in green, prefix letter: T. Sign. J. W. Kelly.	450.	1250.	3000
	d. Sm. *CALCUTTA* in black. Sign. H. Denning.	450.	1250.	3000
	e. Lg. or sm. *CALCUTTA* in green. Sign. H. Denning.	450.	1250.	3000.
	f. Lg. *CALCUTTA* in green. Sign. J. B. Taylor.	450.	1250.	3000.
	g. Lg. *CALCUTTA* in green, prefix letter: T. Sign. J. B. Taylor.	450.	1250.	3000.
	h. Lg. *CALCUTTA* in green, prefix letter: T. Sign. J. W. Kelly.	450.	1250.	3000
	i. Sm. *CAWNPORE* in green. Sign. H. Denning.	450.	1250.	3000
	j. Lg. *CAWNPORE* in green. Sign. J. B. Taylor.	450.	1250.	3000
	k. Lg. *CAWNPORE* in green, prefix letter: T. Sign. J. W. Kelly.	450.	1250.	3000
	l. Lg. or sm. *KARACHI* in green. Sign. H. Denning.	450.	1250.	3000
	m. Lg. *LAHORE* in green. Sign. H. Denning.	450.	1250.	3000
	n. Lg. *LAHORE* in green. Sign. J. B. Taylor.	450.	1250.	3000
	o. Lg. *LAHORE* in green, prefix letter: *T.* Sign. J. W. Kelly.	450.	1250.	3000
	p. Sm. *MADRAS* in green. Sign. H. Denning.	450.	1250.	3000
	q. Lg. *MADRAS* in green. Sign. J. B. Taylor.	450.	1250.	3000
	r. Lg. *MADRAS* in green, prefix letter: *T.* Sign. J. W. Kelly.	450.	1250.	3000

Note: For similar 100 Rupees w/*RANGOON*, see Burma. Note: Letter *T* may have been used oficially for "thinner paper" as all notes w/*T* prefix are on thinner stock.

		VG	VF	UNC
11	**500 Rupees**			
	ND (1928). Rare.	—	—	—

		VG	VF	UNC
12	**1000 Rupees**			
	ND (1928). Violet and green. Oval portr. of Kg. George V in sprays at r. Farmer plowing w/oxen at ctr. on back.			
	a. *BOMBAY*. Sign. J. B. Taylor.	1400.	4000.	—
	b. *CALCUTTA*. Sign. J. B. Taylor.	1400.	4000.	—
	c. *CALCUTTA*. Sign. J. W. Kelly.	1400.	4000.	—
	d. *LAHORE*. Sign. J. B. Taylor.	1400.	4000.	—

		VG	VF	UNC
13	**10,000 Rupees**			
	ND (1928). Green and brown. Oval portr. of Kg. George V at ctr., wmk. at l. and at r. Back blue.			
	a. *BOMBAY*. Sign. J. B. Taylor. Rare.	—	—	—
	b. *CALCUTTA*. Sign. J. B. Taylor. Rare.	—	—	—
	c. *KARACHI*. Sign. J. W. Kelly. Rare.	—	—	—

1928-35 Issue

		VG	VF	UNC
4	**1 Rupee**			
	1935. Green-blue. Coin w/Kg. George V at r. Reverse of coin w/date on back. W/ or w/o perforation on l. border. Those perforated were issued in booklets of 25 notes.			
	a. Wmk: Portr. Sign. J. W. Kelly.	10.00	40.00	100.
	b. Wmk: W/o portr. Sign. J. W. Kelly.	12.50	65.00	150.

		VG	VF	UNC
15	**5 Rupees**			
	ND (1928-1935). Brown-violet and lt. brown. Oval portr. Kg. George V at r.			
	a. Sign. J. B. Taylor.	15.00	85.00	250.
	b. Sign. J. W. Kelly.	15.00	85.00	250.

		VG	VF	UNC
16	**10 Rupees**			
	ND. Blue or dk. blue. Palm tree, lake and mountains at ctr. Elephants on back.			
	a. Sign. J. B. Taylor.	20.00	100.	325.
	b. Sign. J. W. Kelly.	20.00	100.	325.

Reserve Bank of India

1937 Issue

#17-22 Kg. George VI at r.

#17-19 w/o place names.

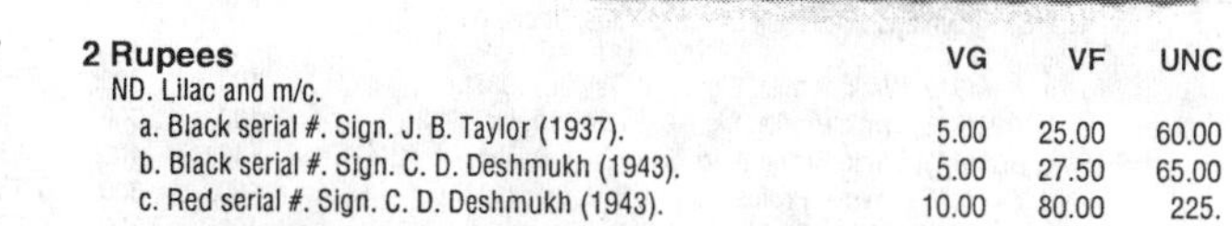

		VG	VF	UNC
17	**2 Rupees**			
	ND. Lilac and m/c.			
	a. Black serial #. Sign. J. B. Taylor (1937).	5.00	25.00	60.00
	b. Black serial #. Sign. C. D. Deshmukh (1943).	5.00	27.50	65.00
	c. Red serial #. Sign. C. D. Deshmukh (1943).	10.00	80.00	225.

18	5 Rupees	VG	VF	UNC
	ND. Brown and green. Similar to #15.			
	a. Sign. J. B. Taylor (1937).	5.00	20.00	50.00
	b. Sign. C. D. Deshmukh (1943).	5.00	20.00	50.00

19	10 Rupees	VG	VF	UNC
	ND. Blue-violet and olive. Similar to #16. Back blue; elephants at ctr.			
	a. Sign. J. B. Taylor (1937).	10.00	35.00	100.
	b. Sign. C. D. Deshmukh (1943).	10.00	35.00	100.

#20-22 w/place names.

20	100 Rupees	VG	VF	UNC
	ND. Dk. green and lilac. Back dk. green; tiger at ctr. Wmk: Kg. George VI.			
	a. *BOMBAY.* Wmk: Profile. Sign. J. B. Taylor (1937).	100.	300.	750.
	b. *BOMBAY.* Wmk: Profile. Sign. C. D. Deshmukh (1943).	100.	300.	750.
	c. *BOMBAY.* Wmk: Facing portr. Sign. C. D. Deshmukh (1943).	140.	400.	950.
	d. *CALCUTTA.* Wmk: Profile. Sign. J. B. Taylor (1937).	100.	300.	750.
	e. *CALCUTTA.* Wmk: Profile. Sign. C. D. Deshmukh (1943).	100.	300.	750.
	f. *CALCUTTA.* Wmk: Facing portr. Sign. C. D. Deshmukh (1943).	140.	400.	950.
	g. *CAWNPORE.* Wmk: Profile. Sign. J. B. Taylor (1937).	100.	300.	750.
	h. *CAWNPORE.* Wmk: Profile. Sign. C. D. Deshmukh (1943).	100.	300.	750.
	i. *KANPUR (Cawnpore).* Wmk: Facing portr. Sign. C. D. Deshmukh (1943).	200.	600.	—
	j. *DELHI.* Wmk: Profile. Sign. C. D. Deshmukh (1943).	150.	475.	1100.
	k. *KARACHI.* Wmk: Profile. Sign. C. D. Deshmukh (1943).	100.	300.	750.
	l. *LAHORE.* Wmk: Profile. Sign. J. B. Taylor (1937).	100.	300.	750.
	m. *LAHORE.* Wmk: Profile. Sign. C. D. Deshmukh (1943).	100.	300.	750.
	n. *MADRAS.* Wmk: Profile. Sign. J. B. Taylor (1937).	100.	300.	750.
	o. *MADRAS.* Wmk: Profile. Sign. C. D. Deshmukh (1943).	100.	300.	750.
	p. *MADRAS.* Wmk: Facing. Sign. C. D. Deshmukh (1943).	140.	400.	950.
	q. *KARACHI.* Wmk: Profile. Sign. J. B. Taylor.	100.	300.	750.

21	1000 Rupees	VG	VF	UNC
	ND (1937). Lilac, violet and green. Mountain scene on back. Sign. J. B. Taylor. Wmk: Kg. George VI.			
	a. *BOMBAY.*	450.	1250.	3000.
	b. *CALCUTTA.*	450.	1250.	3000.
	c. *CAWNPORE.*	450.	1250.	3000.
	d. *KARACHI.*	450.	1250.	3000.
	e. *LAHORE.*	450.	1250.	3000.
	f. *MADRAS.*	450.	1250.	3000.
22	10,000 Rupees			
	ND (1938). Rare.	—	—	—

ND 1943 ISSUE

#23-24 Kg. George VI facing at r. Sign. C. D. Deshmukh.

23	5 Rupees	VG	VF	UNC
	ND (1943). Green and m/c. antelope on back.			
	a. Black serial #.	10.00	45.00	120.
	b. Red serial #.	35.00	125.	350.

24	10 Rupees	VG	VF	UNC
	ND (1943). Purple and m/c. Dhow on back.	2.50	10.00	30.00

GOVERNMENT OF INDIA (RESUMED)

1940 ISSUE

25	1 Rupee	VG	VF	UNC
	1940. Blue-gray and m/c. Coin w/Kg. George VI at r. Coin w/date on back. Sign. C. E. Jones.			
	a. Black serial #.	1.75	6.00	20.00
	b. Red serial #.	15.00	75.00	250
	c. Black serial #, letter A.	15.00	75.00	250
	d. Green serial #, letter A.	1.50	5.00	17.50

REPUBLIC OF INDIA

	SIGNATURE VARIETIES	
	Governors, Reserve Bank of India (all except 1 Rupee notes)	
71	C. D. Deshmukh August 1943-June 1949	C.D. Deshmukh
72	B. Rama Rau July 1949-January 1957	B Rama Rau
73	K. G. Ambegaonkar January 1957-February 1957	
74	H. V. R. Iengar March 1957-February 1962	
75	P. C. Bhattacharyya March 1962-June 1967	

RESERVE BANK OF INDIA

FIRST SERIES

#27-47 Asoka column at r. Lg. letters in unpt. beneath serial #. Wmk: Asoka column.

Error singular Hindi = *RUPAYA* | **Corrected plural Hindi = *RUPAYE***

VARIETIES: #27-28, 33, 38, 42, 46, 48 and 50 have large headings in Hindi expressing value incorrectly in the singular form Rupaya.

Note: For similar notes but in different colors, please see Haj Pilgrim and Persian Gulf listings at the end of this country listing.

#		VG	VF	UNC
27	**2 Rupees** ND. Red-brown on violet and green unpt. Tiger head at l. on back. Value in English and error Hindi on face and back. Hindi numeral *2* at upper r. 8 value text lines on back. Sign. 72.	1.50	6.00	20.00
28	**2 Rupees** ND. Similar to #27 but English *2* at upper l. and r. Redesigned panels on face. 7 value text lines on back; third line 18mm long. Sign 72.	.50	2.00	5.00

#		VG	VF	UNC
29	**2 Rupees** ND. Red-brown on violet and green unpt. Like #28 but value in English and corrected Hindi on both sides. Tiger hea d at l. looking to l., third value text line on back 24mm long.			
	a. Sign. 72.	1.00	6.00	10.00
	b. Sign. 74.	.75	2.00	5.00
30	**2 Rupees** ND. Red-brown on green unpt. Face like #29. Tiger head at l. looking to r., w/13 value text lines at ctr. on back. Sign. 75.	.75	4.00	10.00

NOTICE

Readers with unlisted dates, signature varieties, etc. are invited to submit photocopies or, high resolution (300 dpi, 100% size) scans of their notes to: Standard Catalog of World Paper Money, 700 East State St. Iola, WI 54990-0001, or E-Mail: george.cuhaj@fwpubs.com.

#		VG	VF	UNC
31	**2 Rupees** ND. Olive on tan unpt. Like #30. Sign. 75.	.50	2.50	12.50

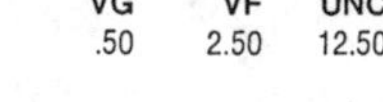

#		VG	VF	UNC
32	**5 Rupees** ND. Green on brown unpt. English value only on face, serial # at ctr. *Rs. 5* and antelope on back. Sign. 72 .	1.00	8.00	40.00
33	**5 Rupees** ND. Like #32 but value in English and error Hindi on face, serial # at r. 8 value lines on back, fourth line 21mm long. Sign. 72.	.50	2.00	5.00

#		VG	VF	UNC
34	**5 Rupees** ND. Like #33 but Hindi corrected. Fourth value text line on back 26mm long. Sign. 72.	1.00	8.00	50.00
35	**5 Rupees** ND. Green on brown unpt. Like #34 but redesigned panels at l. and r.			
	a. W/o letter. Sign. 74.	.75	4.00	15.00
	b. Letter A. Sign. 74.	.50	3.50	10.00
	c. Letter A. Sign. 75.	.75	5.00	15.00
	d. Letter B. Sign. 75.	.75	5.00	15.00

Note: For similar note but in orange, see #R2 (Persian Gulf listings).

#		VG	VF	UNC
37	**10 Rupees** ND. Purple on m/c unpt. English value only on face. *Rs. 10* at lower ctr., 1 serial #. English in both lower corners, dhow at ctr. on back.			
	a. Sign. 71.	4.00	17.50	100.
	b. Sign. 72.	3.00	10.00	25.00

		VG	VF	UNC
38	**10 Rupees** ND. Like #37 but value in English and error Hindi on face and back. 2 serial #. Third value text line on back 24mm long. Sign. 72.	.75	2.00	5.00
39	**10 Rupees** ND. Purple on m/c unpt. Like #38 but Hindi corrected. Third value text line on back 29mm long.			
	a. W/o letter. Sign. 72.	1.00	5.00	15.00
	b. W/o letter. Sign. 74.	1.00	5.00	15.00
	c. Letter A. Sign. 74.	.75	2.00	5.00

Note: For similar note but in red, see #R3 (Persian Gulf listings); in blue, see #R5 (Haj Pilgrim listings).

		VG	VF	UNC
41	**100 Rupees** ND. Blue on m/c unpt. English value only on face. Two elephants at ctr. 8 value text lines below and bank emblem at l. on back.			
	a. Dk. blue. Sign. 72.	25.00	60.00	140.
	b. Lt. blue. Sign. 72.	25.00	60.00	140.
42	**100 Rupees** ND. Purplish-blue on m/c unpt. Like #41 but value in English and error Hindi on face and back. 7 value text lines on back; third 27mm long.			
	a. Black serial #. Sign. 72.	15.00	45.00	120.
	b. Red serial #. Sign. 72.	15.00	45.00	120.

		VG	VF	UNC
43	**100 Rupees** ND. Purplish blue on m/c unpt. Like #42 but Hindi corrected. Third value text line 40mm long.			
	a. W/o letter, thin paper. Sign. 72.	15.00	45.00	120.
	b. W/o letter, thin paper. Sign. 74.	12.50	40.00	100.

Note: For similar note but in green, see #R4 (Persian Gulf listings); in red, see #R6 (Haj Pilgrim listings).

		VG	VF	UNC
44	**100 Rupees** ND. Purple and m/c. Heading in rectangle at top, serial # at upper l. and lower r. Title: *GOVERNOR* at ctr. r. Dam at ctr. w/13 value text lines at l. on back. Sign. 74.	12.50	30.00	60.00

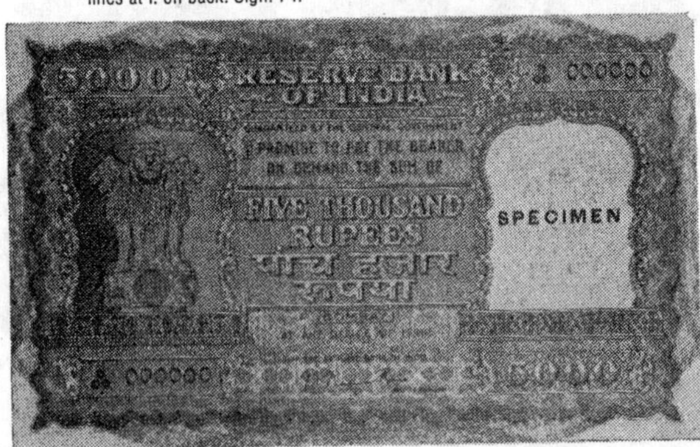

		VG	VF	UNC
48	**5000 Rupees** ND. Green, violet and brown. Asoka column at l. Value in English and error Hindi on face and back. Gateway of India on back.			
	a. *BOMBAY.* Sign. 72. Rare.	—	—	—
	b. *CALCUTTA.* Sign. 72. Rare.	—	—	—
	c. *DELHI.* Sign. 72. Rare.	—	—	—
49	**5000 Rupees** ND. Green, violet and brown. Like #48 but Hindi corrected.			
	a. *BOMBAY.* Sign. 74.	200.	375.	800
	b. *MADRAS.* Sign. 74.	200.	375.	800

		Good	Fine	XF
50	**10,000 Rupees**			
	ND. Blue, violet and brown. Asoka column at ctr. Value in English and error Hindi on face and back.			
	a. *BOMBAY.* Sign. 72.	300.	700.	1500.
	b. *CALCUTTA.* Sign. 72.	300.	700.	1500.
	s. As B. Specimen. Sign. 72.			
50A	**10,000 Rupees**			
	ND. Like #50 but Hindi corrected.			
	a. *BOMBAY.* Sign. 74.	300.	700.	1500.
	b. *MADRAS.* Sign. 74.	400.	800.	1750.
	c. *NEW DELHI.* Sign. 74.	400.	800.	1750.
	d. *BOMBAY.* Sign. 76.	400.	800.	1750.

GOVERNMENT OF INDIA

SIGNATURE VARIETIES

SECRETARIES, MINISTRY OF FINANCE (1 Rupee notes only)

K. R. K. Menon, 1944	A. K. Roy, 1957
K. G. Ambegaonkar, 1949-1951	L. K. Jha, 1957-1963
H. M. Patel, 1951-1957	

OTE: The sign. H.M. Patel is often misread as "Mehta". There was never any such individual serving as ecretary. Also, do not confuse H.M. Patel with I.G. Patel who served later.

949-51 ISSUE

		VG	VF	UNC
1	**1 Rupee**			
	ND (1949-50). Green-gray and m/c. Asoka column at r. W/o coin design on face or back.			
	a. Sign. K. R. K. Menon. (1949).	.25	2.50	8.00
	b. Sign. K. G. Ambegaonkar. (1949-50).	.25	2.50	8.00

		VG	VF	UNC
	1 Rupee			
	1951. Green-gray and m/c. Coin w/Asoka column at r. Reverse of coin dated 1951 on back. Sign. K. G. Ambegaonkar.	.25	2.00	6.50
	1 Rupee			
	ND (- old date 1951). Violet and m/c. Like #72. Sign. K. G. Ambegaonkar.	.25	2.00	6.50

		VG	VF	UNC
74	**1 Rupee**			
	ND (- old date 1951). Like #73 except different rendition of all value lines on back.			
	a. W/o letter. Sign. H. M. Patel. (1956).	.20	1.50	4.00
	b. Letter A. Sign. H. M. Patel.	.20	1.50	4.00

1957; 1963 ISSUE

		VG	VF	UNC
75	**1 Rupee**			
	1957. Violet on m/c unpt. Redesigned coin w/Asoka column at r. Coin dated 1957 and *100 Naye Paise* in Hindi, 7 value text lines on back. Wmk: Asoka column.			
	a. Letter A. Sign. H. M. Patel w/sign. title: *SECRETARY...* (1957).	.50	3.00	10.00
	b. Letter A. Sign. H. M. Patel w/sign. title: *PRINCIPAL SECRETARY...* 1957.	.25	2.00	8.00
	c. Letter B. Sign. A. K. Roy. 1957.	.50	4.00	12.50
	d. Letter B. Sign. L. K. Jha. 1957.	.75	6.00	40.00
	e. Letter C. Sign. L. K. Jha. 1957.	.25	1.25	5.00
	f. Letter D. Sign. L. K. Jha. 1957.	.25	1.25	5.00

Note: For similar note but in red, see #R1 (Persian Gulf listings).

PERSIAN GULF

Intended for circulation in areas of Oman, Bahrain, Qatar and Trucial States during 1950's and early 1960's.

"Z" prefix in serial # Known as "Gulf Rupees".

GOVERNMENT OF INDIA

ND ISSUE

		VG	VF	UNC
R1	**1 Rupee**			
	ND. Red. Like #75c. Sign. A. K. Roy; L. K. Jha or H. V. R. Iengar.	25.00	50.00	200.

RESERVE BANK OF INDIA

ND ISSUE

		VG	VF	UNC
R2	**5 Rupees**			
	ND. Orange. Like #35a. Sign. H. V. R. Iengar.	100.	200.	500.

		VG	VF	UNC
R3	**10 Rupees** ND. Red. Like #39c. Letter A. Sign. H. V. R. Iengar.	25.00	125.	350.

		VG	VF	UNC
R4	**100 Rupees** ND. Green. Like #43b. Sign. H. V. R. Iengar.	65.00	350.	1350.

Haj Pilgrim

Intended for use by Moslem pilgrims in Mecca, Saudi Arabia.

Reserve Bank of India

(ND) Issue

#R5 and R6 Asoka column at r. Letters *HA* near serial #, and *HAJ* at l. and r. of bank title at top.

		VG	VF	UNC
R5	**10 Rupees** ND. Blue. Like #39c. Sign. H. V. R. Iengar.	250.	500.	1000.
R6	**100 Rupees** ND. Red. Like #43b. Sign. H. V. R. Iengar.	500.	1000.	—

The Republic of Indonesia, the world's largest archipelago, extends for more than 3,000 miles (4,827 km.) along the equator from the mainland of southeast Asia to Australia. The 13,667 islands comprising the archipelago have a combined area of 735,268 sq. mi. (2,042,005 sq. km.) and a population of 202 million, including East Timor. Capital: Jakarta. Petroleum, timber, rubber and coffee are exported.

Had Columbus succeeded in reaching the fabled Spice Islands, he would have found advanced civilizations a millennium old, and temples still ranked among the finest examples of ancient art. During the opening centuries of the Christian era, the islands were influenced by Hindu priests and traders who spread their culture and religion. Moslem invasions began in the 13th century, fragmenting the island kingdoms into small states which were unable to resist Western colonial infiltration. Portuguese traders established posts in the 16th century, but they were soon outnumbered by the Dutch who arrived in 1602 and gradually asserted control over the islands comprising present-day Indonesia. Dutch dominance, interrupted by British incursions during the Napoleonic Wars, established the Netherlands East Indies as one of the richest colonial possessions in the world.

The Indonesian independence movement, which began between the two world wars, was encouraged by the Japanese during their 3-year occupation during World War II. Indonesia proclaimed its independence on Aug. 17, 1945, three days after the surrender of Japan, and was established on Dec. 28, 1949, after four years of Dutch military efforts to reassert control. West Irian, formerly Netherlands New Guinea, came under the administration of Indonesia on May 1, 1963.

MONETARY SYSTEM:

1 Gulden = 100 Cents to 1948

1 Gulden = 100 Cents to 1948

1 Rupiah = 100 Sen, 1945-

Republic

Republik Indonesia

1945 Issue

#1-12 Deleted. Refer to Netherlands Indies.

#13-29 many paper and printing varieties.

		VG	VF	UNC
13	**1 Sen** 17.10.1945. Green. Dagger in numeral at l.	.25	.75	2.00

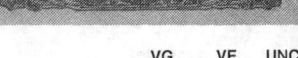

		VG	VF	UNC
14	**5 Sen** 17.10.1945. Gray-violet.	.25	.75	2.00

		VG	VF	UNC
15	**10 Sen** 17.10.1945. Brown on tan unpt.			
	a. Printing size 94 x 43mm.	.25	1.50	3.50
	b. Printing size 100 x 44mm.	.25	1.00	3.00

		VG	VF	UNC
16	**1/2 Rupiah** 17.10.1945. Green on pale peach unpt.	2.00	5.00	14.00

#17-20 Sukarno at l.

		VG	VF	UNC
17	**1 Rupiah** 17.10.1945. Gray-blue to dk. blue. Smoking volcano on blue-green back.			
	a. Serial # and letters.	.50	2.00	6.00
	b. Letters only.	.50	2.00	6.00

		VG	VF	UNC
18	**5 Rupiah** 17.10.1945. Green.	1.00	3.00	10.00

		VG	VF	UNC
19	**10 Rupiah** 17.10.1945. Blue. Volcano at r.	2.00	5.00	12.00

		VG	VF	UNC
0	**100 Rupiah** 17.10.1945. Green-blue.	7.50	20.00	60.00

947 First Issue

		VG	VF	UNC
1	**5 Rupiah** 1.1.1947. Green. Like #18.	2.00	5.00	10.00
22	**10 Rupiah** 1.1.1947. Blue. Like #19.	4.00	15.00	40.00

		VG	VF	UNC
23	**25 Rupiah** 1.1.1947. Brown. Portr. Sukarno at r., mountain scene at l. ctr.	3.00	10.00	30.00
24	**100 Rupiah** 1.1.1947. Green-blue. Like #20.			
	a. Unpt.	12.00	30.00	80.00
	b. W/o unpt.	12.00	30.00	75.00

1947 Second Issue

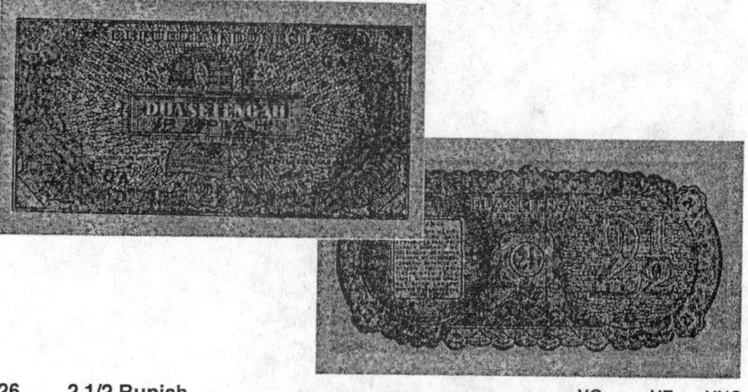

		VG	VF	UNC
25	**1/2 Rupiah** 26.7.1947. Red.	3.00	8.00	25.00

		VG	VF	UNC
26	**2 1/2 Rupiah** 26.7.1947. Brown.	3.00	12.00	30.00

Note: What purports to be #26 in red is a modern fantasy.

		VG	VF	UNC
27	**25 Rupiah** 26.7.1947. Dk. blue on green unpt. Like #23.	2.00	5.00	14.00

		VG	VF	UNC
28	**50 Rupiah** 26.7.1947. Brown on orange unpt. Portr. Sukarno at l. Workers in rubber plantation at r.	25.00	75.00	200.

		VG	VF	UNC
29	**100 Rupiah** 26.7.1947. Brown on brown-orange or pink unpt. Portr. Sukarno at l. Block letters *SDA 1* part of plate.	1.50	6.00	17.50

		VG	VF	UNC
29A	**100 Rupiah** 26.7.1947. Green and brown. Portr. Sukarno at l. Tobacco field and mountain at r.	15.00	50.00	200.

		VG	VF	UNC
30	**250 Rupiah** 26.7.1947. Brown on orange unpt. Portr. Sukarno at l. Peasant at r.			
	a. Serial # printed.	10.00	40.00	150.
	b. Serial # typed.	25.00	75.00	250.

1947 Third Issue

		VG	VF	UNC
31	**10 Sen** 1.12.1947. Dk. green on gray unpt. Back red; palms at ctr.	.25	1.00	3.00
32	**25 Sen** 1.12.1947. Brown. Like #31.	.25	1.25	3.50

1948 Issue

		VG	VF	UNC
33	**40 Rupiah** 23.8.1948. Gray and lilac. Sukarno at l., female weaver at r.	10.00	25.00	75.00

		VG	VF	UNC
33A	**75 Rupiah** 23.8.1948. Brown. Portr. Sukarno at l., 2 smiths at r.	25.00	75.00	250.
34	**100 Rupiah** 23.8.1948. Dk. brown. Like #29A.	20.00	50.00	200.

		VG	VF	UNC
35	**400 Rupiah** 23.8.1948. Dk. brown and green. Portr. Sukarno at l. Sugar plantation at r.			
	a. Serial # printed.	2.00	5.00	12.00
	b. Serial # typed.	30.00	85.00	200.

Note: Most examples of #35a in high grade are believed to be contemporary copies.

		VG	VF	UNC
35A	**600 Rupiah** 23.8.1948. Orange. Portr. Sukarno at l., ornamental *RI* at r. Uniface proof.	—	—	2000.

1949 Revaluation Issue

#35B-35G prepared in sen and rupiah baru (new cents and rupiah).

		VG	VF	UNC
35B	**10 New Cents** 17.8.1949.			
	a. Dk. blue. Red sign.	7.00	15.00	60.00
	b. Red. Black sign.	6.00	15.00	55.00

		VG	VF	UNC
35C	**1/2 New Rupiah** 17.8.1949.			
	a. Green. Red sign.	5.00	15.00	50.00
	b. Red. Black sign.	5.00	15.00	50.00
35D	**1 New Rupiah** 17.8.1949.			
	a. Purple. Red sign.	8.00	30.00	65.00
	b. Green. Reported not confirmed.	—	—	—

		VG	VF	UNC
35E	**10 New Rupiah** 17.8.1949. Portr. Sukarno at upper l.			
	a. Black on yellow unpt. Red sign.	15.00	50.00	100.
	b. Brown on yellow unpt. Black sign.	10.00	40.00	100.
35F	**25 New Rupiah** 17.8.1949. Reported not confirmed.	—	—	—
35G	**100 New Rupiah** 17.8.1949. Purple on yellow unpt. Portr. Sukarno at upper l.	20.00	60.00	150.

Note: Unfinished notes of the above series exist also.

REPUBLIK INDONESIA SERIKAT

UNITED STATES OF INDONESIA

TREASURY

1950 ISSUE

#36 and 37 printer: TDLR.

		VG	VF	UNC
36	**5 Rupiah** 1.1.1950. Orange. Portr. Sukarno at r. Paddy field and palms on back.	1.50	5.00	20.00
37	**10 Rupiah** 1.1.1950. Purple. Like #36.	2.00	7.50	22.50

Note: The Javasche Bank notes cut in half (from 5 Gulden) and those of the Republic of Indonesia originate from the currency reform of 1950. The left half of a note was valid for exchange against new notes at 50% of nominal denomination; the right half was also accepted at half its face value for a 3% government bond issue. Verification of any of these pieces in collections is needed.

REPUBLIK INDONESIA

1951 ISSUE

#38-41 printer: SBNC.

		VG	VF	UNC
38	**1 Rupiah** 1951. Blue. Beach w/palms at l., terraced field at r. Mountain on back.	.50	1.50	4.00

		VG	VF	UNC
39	**2 1/2 Rupiah** 1951. Orange. Steep coast at l., palm trees at r. Back green; arms at ctr.	.50	1.50	4.00

1953 ISSUE

		VG	VF	UNC
40	**1 Rupiah** 1953. Blue. Like #38.	.50	1.00	3.00

		VG	VF	UNC
41	**2 1/2 Rupiah** 1953. Orange. Like #39.	.50	1.75	4.00

BANK INDONESIA

1952 ISSUE

		VG	VF	UNC
42	**5 Rupiah** 1952. Gray-blue. Portr. A. Kartini at l.	.75	3.00	6.00

		VG	VF	UNC
43	**10 Rupiah**			
	1952. Brown. Statue of a goddess Prajñaparamita at l.			
	a. Printer: Joh. Enschede on face.	1.00	4.00	10.00
	b. Printer: Pertjetakan on back.	1.00	4.00	10.00

		VG	VF	UNC
44	**25 Rupiah**			
	1952. Dk. blue. Cloth designs at l. and r. Back lt. brown and green.			
	a. Printer: Joh. Enschede on face.	1.00	6.00	15.00
	b. Printer: Pertjetakan on back.	1.00	6.00	15.00

		VG	VF	UNC
45	**50 Rupiah**			
	1952. Green. Stylized trees w/bird at l. and r.	1.00	6.00	15.00

		VG	VF	UNC
46	**100 Rupiah**			
	1952. Brown. Lion at l., portr. Prince Diponegoro at r.	2.00	8.00	20.00

		VG	VF	UNC
47	**500 Rupiah**			
	1952. Orange-brown, green and brown. Frieze at ctr. r.	3.00	12.00	30.00

		VG	VF	UNC
48	**1000 Rupiah**			
	1952. Green and brown. Woman w/ornamented helmet at r.	5.00	17.50	45.0

Note: For #42-#48 w/revolutionary ovpt. see Volume 1.

1957 Issue

		VG	VF	UN
49	**5 Rupiah**			
	ND (1957). Green on pink and yellow unpt. Orangutan at l. Prambanan temple in blue on back.	.25	1.50	5.0

		VG	VF	UN
A50	**10 Rupiah**			
	ND (1957). Red-brown and m/c. Stag at upper l., longboat on back.	100.	250.	50

B50 **25 Rupiah**
ND (1957). Purple and m/c. Java rhinoceros at upper l. Back brown; Batak houses at at ctr.

VG	VF	UNC
100.	250.	600.

Note: #A50 and B50 were issued for only 3 days.

50 **50 Rupiah**
ND (1957). Maroon on green unpt. Crocodile at l. Back purple; Deli Mosque at upper l. and r.

VG	VF	UNC
2.00	7.50	25.00

51 **100 Rupiah**
ND (1957). Gray-blue on pink unpt. Squirrel at l. Back red; President's palace across ctr.

VG	VF	UNC
1.50	5.00	15.00

52 **500 Rupiah**
ND (1957). Brown. Tiger at l. Paddy terraces and buffalos on green back.

VG	VF	UNC
7.50	20.00	50.00

53 **1000 Rupiah**
ND (1957). Gray-blue. Elephant at l. Back brown; fishing.

VG	VF	UNC
7.50	20.00	50.00

54 **2500 Rupiah**
ND (1957). Green. Leguan at l. Back brown; village at lakeshore.

VG	VF	UNC
8.00	25.00	65.00

54A **5000 Rupiah**
ND. Dk. red and m/c. Wild buffalo at l. Back dk. purple; tugboat w/ship in harbor. Specimen.

VG	VF	UNC
—	—	—

1958 ISSUE

#55-63 wmk: Buffalo.

#55-62 various Indonesian houses on back.

55 **5 Rupiah**
ND (1958). Green and red-brown. Woman applying wax to cloth (batiking) at l.

VG	VF	UNC
.10	.30	.50

		VG	VF	UNC
56	**10 Rupiah** 1958. Dk. blue and m/c. Carver at l. Mask at r. on back.	.10	.30	1.00

		VG	VF	UNC
57	**25 Rupiah** 1958. Green and brown. Woman weaver at l.	.25	.75	2.00
58	**50 Rupiah** 1958. Dk. brown. Woman spinner at l.	.25	1.00	3.00

		VG	VF	UNC
59	**100 Rupiah** 1958. Red and red-brown. Worker on rubber plantation at l.	.25	.75	2.50

		VG	VF	UNC
60	**500 Rupiah** 1958. Dk. brown and red-brown. Man w/coconuts at l.	1.50	5.00	20.00

		VG	VF	UNC
61	**1000 Rupiah** 1958. Red-brown. Man making a silver plate at l. Back brown and green.	.25	1.00	2.50
62	**1000 Rupiah** 1958. Purple and green. Like #61.	.50	1.50	5.00
63	**5000 Rupiah** 1958. Dk. green and brown. Woman gathering rice at l. River and rice terraces on back.	2.00	8.00	25.00

		VG	VF	UNC
64	**5000 Rupiah** 1958. Lilac. Like #63, but printed Indonesian arms in wmk. area. Wmk: Arms at ctr. Back brown and red-brown.	2.00	5.00	10.00

1959 Issue

#65-71 wmk: Arms. Printer: TDLR.

		VG	VF	UNC
65	**5 Rupiah** 1.1.1959. Blue and yellow. Flowers at ctr. Sunbirds on back.	.10	.25	.75

		VG	VF	UNC
66	**10 Rupiah** 1.1.1959. Red-violet on m/c unpt. Flowers at ctr. Back green on pale green and ochre unpt.; Salmon-crested cockatoos.	.10	.25	1.00

		VG	VF	UNC
67	**25 Rupiah** 1.1.1959. Green on m/c unpt. Water lilies at l. Back blue; great egrets.	.25	.50	2.50

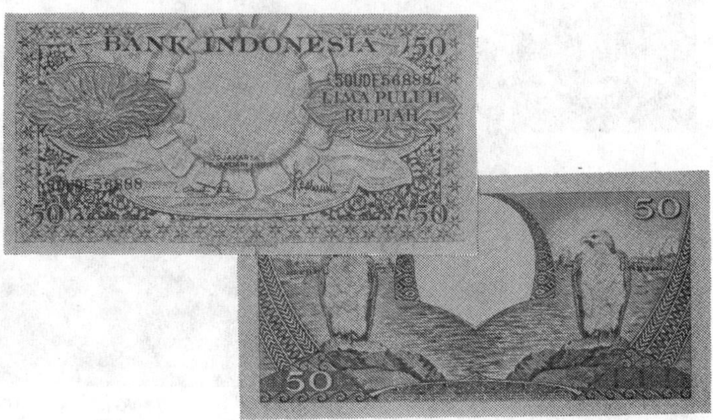

		VG	VF	UNC
68	**50 Rupiah** 1.1.1959. Dk. brown, blue and orange. Sunflower at ctr. Back purple; white-bellied fish eagle.	.25	1.00	3.50

		VG	VF	UNC
69	**100 Rupiah** 1.1.1959. Dk. brown and red on m/c unpt. Giant Rafflessia Patma flowers at ctr. Back violet on m/c unpt.; rhinoceros hornbills.	.25	1.00	3.50

		VG	VF	UNC
70	**500 Rupiah** 1.1.1959. Blue on m/c unpt. Flowers at ctr. Crested fireback on back.	3.00	8.00	20.00

		VG	VF	UNC
71	**1000 Rupiah** 1.1.1959. Black-green and lilac on m/c unpt. Flowers at ctr. Back dk. blue; Birds of Paradise.			
	a. Imprint TDLR at bottom ctr. on face.	2.00	5.00	15.00
	b. W/o imprint.	.50	1.50	5.00

Republik Indonesia (Resumed)

1954 Issue

#72-73 arms at ctr. on back.

		VG	VF	UNC
72	**1 Rupiah** 1954. Blue. Portr. Javanese girl at r.	.25	.75	2.00
73	**2 1/2 Rupiah** 1954. Red-brown. Portr. old Rotinese man at l. Back green.	.25	.75	2.00

1956 Issue

#74-75 arms at ctr. on back.

		VG	VF	UNC
74	**1 Rupiah** 1956. Blue. Like #72.	.10	.50	1.00

		VG	VF	UNC
75	**2 1/2 Rupiah** 1956. Red-brown. Like #73.	.10	.50	1.25

1960 Issue

		VG	VF	UNC
76	**1 Rupiah** 1960. Dk. green on orange unpt. Rice field workers at l. Farm produce on back.	.25	.50	1.25

		VG	VF	UNC
77	**2 1/2 Rupiah** 1960. Black, dk. blue and brown on blue-green unpt. Corn field work at l.	.25	.75	1.75

1964 ISSUE (1960 DATED)

#80 and 81 portr. Pres. Sukarno at l. Wmk: Arms at ctr.

		VG	VF	UNC
82	**5 Rupiah** 1960. Lilac. Female dancer at r. on back.			
	a. Wmk: Sukarno.	.25	1.50	5.00
	b. Wmk: Water buffalo.	.30	.60	6.00

BANK INDONESIA

1960 DATED (1964) ISSUE

#82-88 Pres. Sukarno at l. Dancers on back.

		VG	VF	UNC
83	**10 Rupiah** 1960. Green. 2 female dancers. Wmk: Sukarno.	.50	2.00	6.00

		VG	VF	UNC
84	**25 Rupiah** 1960. Green on yellow. Female dancer on back.			
	a. Printer: TDLR. Wmk: Sukarno.	1.00	4.00	10.00
	b. Printer: Pertjetakan. Wmk: Water buffalo.	1.00	4.00	10.00

		VG	VF	UNC
85	**50 Rupiah** 1960. Dk. blue. Female dancer and 2 men on back.			
	a. Printer: TDLR. Wmk: Sukarno.	2.00	8.00	20.00
	b. Printer: Pertjetakan. Wmk: Water buffalo.	1.50	4.50	12.50

		VG	VF	UNC
86	**100 Rupiah** 1960. Red-brown. Man and woman dancer on back.			
	a. Printer: Pertjetakan. Wmk: Sukarno.	2.50	10.00	22.50
	b. Wmk: Water buffalo. Reported not confirmed.	—	—	—

		VG	VF	UNC
87	**500 Rupiah** 1960. Black. Two dancers on back.			
	a. Printer: TDLR. Wmk: Sukarno.	7.50	15.00	75.00
	b. Printer: Pertjetakan. Wmk: Sukarno.	7.50	15.00	75.00
	c. Printer like b. Wmk: Water buffalo.	7.50	15.00	75.00
	d. Printer like b. Wmk: Arms.	10.00	20.00	80.00

		VG	VF	UNC
88	**1000 Rupiah** 1960. Dk. green. 2 dancers on back.			
	a. Printer: TDLR. Wmk: Sukarno.	25.00	60.00	150[illegible]
	b. Printer: Pertjetakan. Wmk: Water buffalo.	15.00	40.00	11[illegible]

The Islamic Republic of Iran, located between the Caspian Sea and the Persian Gulf in southwestern Asia, has an area of 636,296 sq. mi. (1,648,000 sq. km.) and a population of 76.43 million. Capital: Tehran. Although predominantly an agricultural state, Iran depends heavily on oil for foreign exchange. Crude oil, carpets and agricultural products are exported.

Iran (historically known as Persia) is one of the world's most ancient and resilient nations. Strategically astride the lower land gate to Asia, it has been conqueror and conquered, sovereign nation and vassal state, ever emerging from its periods of glory or travail with its culture and political individuality intact. Iran (Persia) was a powerful empire under Cyrus the Great (600-529 B.C.), its borders extending from the Indus to the Nile. It has also been conquered by the predatory empires of antique and recent times - Assyrian, Medean, Macedonian, Seljuq, Turk, Mongol - and more recently been coveted by Russia, Germany and Great Britain. Revolts against the absolute power of the Shahs resulted in the establishment of a constitutional monarchy in 1906. In 1931 the Kingdom of Persia became known as the Kingdom of Iran. In 1979, the Pahlavi monarchy was toppled and an Islamic Republic proclaimed.

RULERS:

QAJAR DYNASTY

Sultan Ahmad Shah, AH1327-44/1909-25AD

PAHLAVI DYNASTY

Reza Shah, SH1304-20/1925-41AD
Mohammad Reza Pahlavi, SH1320-58/1941-79AD

MONETARY SYSTEM:

1 Shahi = 50 Dinars
1 Kran (Qiran) = 20 Shahis
1 Toman = 10 Krans AH1241-1344, SH1304-09 (1825-1931)
1 Shahi = 5 Dinars
1 Rial 100 Dinars = 20 Shahis
1 Toman = 10 Rials SH1310- (1932-)

SIGNATURE/TITLE VARIETIES

	GENERAL DIRECTOR	MINISTER OF FINANCE
1	Mohammad Ali Bamdad	Abol Hossein Ebtehaj
2	Ahmad Razavi	Ebrahim Zand
3	Mohammad Ali Varesteh	Ebrahim Zand
4	Nezam-ed-Din Emani	Ali Asghar Nasser
5	Nasrullah Jahangir	Ali Asghar Nasser
6	Mohammad Reza Vishkai	Ebrahim Kashani

KINGDOM OF PERSIA

IMPERIAL BANK OF PERSIA

1890 FIRST ISSUE

		VG	VF	UNC
A1	**1 Toman** 25.10.1890; 24.1.1894; 1.1.1896. Portr. Shah Nasr-ed-Din at r. Back w/o lion. *BUSHIRE*. Rare.	—	—	—

1890 SECOND ISSUE

#1-10 portr. Shah Nasr-ed-Din at r., lion at ctr on back. Printer: BWC. W/ or w/o places of redemption such as Abadan, Bushire, Meshed, Shiraz, Resht, Hamadan, Isfahan, Kermanshah, Basrah, Tabriz, Teheran. Varieties exist of the government seal w/lion. Various date and sign. varieties.

#1-6 Dates in the 1890s command a premium.

		Good	Fine	XF
1	**1 Toman** 1890-1923. Black on pink and lt. green unpt. Back green.			
	a. Red serial #.	125.	250.	750.
	b. Black serial #.	100.	200.	600.

		Good	Fine	XF
2	**2 Tomans** 1890-1923. Pink and lt. green.	125.	250.	550.

		Good	Fine	XF
2A	**3 Tomans** 1890-1923. Green. Back blue.	1500.	3000.	4000.

		Good	Fine	XF
3	**5 Tomans** 1890-1923 (16.4.1912). Red-brown. Back brown. *Teheran.*	150.	325.	950.
4	**10 Tomans** 1890-1923. Black.	250.	600.	1250.
5	**20 Tomans** 1890-1923. Orange.	500.	1500.	—
6	**25 Tomans** 1890-1923. Dk. green. Rare.	—	—	—

		Good	Fine	XF
7	**50 Tomans** 1890-1923 (1.6.1918). Dk. brown. *Teheran.* Rare.	—	—	—
8	**100 Tomans** 1890-1923. Red. Rare.	—	—	—
9	**500 Tomans** 1890-1923. Blue. Specimen. Rare.	—	—	—
10	**1000 Tomans** 1890-1923 (10.9.1904). Black on lilac and green unpt. green unpt. (10.9.1904). *Teheran.* Rare.	—	—	—

Note: #9 and 10 were held in reserve at the National Treasury. A 30 Toman note has been reported.

1924 Issue

#11-17 w/ or w/o different places of redemption such as Abadan, Barfrush, Bunder-Abbas, Bushire, Dizful, Hamadan, Kazrin, Kermanshah, Meshed, Pehlevi, Shiraz, Tabriz, Muhammerah, Teheran. The redemption endorsement for Teheran was printed for the denominations of 1 to 10 Tomans #11-14; other place names and higher denominations for Teheran were hand stamped. Various date and sign. varieties.

		Good	Fine	XF
11	**1 Toman** 1924-32. Black on pink and lt. green. unpt. Portr. Muzaffar-al-Din at upper l. Printer: W&S.	50.00	150.	500.

		Good	Fine	XF
12	**2 Tomans** 1924-32. Green. Portr. Nasr-ed-Din at r. Lg. *2* at ctr. on back. Printer: BWC.	500.	1200.	1900.

		Good	Fine	XF
13	**5 Tomans** 1924-32. Lt. green and lilac. Portr. Muzaffar-al-Din at r. Lg. *5* at ctr. on back. Printer: W&S.	750.	1250.	1500.

		Good	Fine	XF
14	**10 Tomans** 1924-32. Blue. Portr. Muzaffar-al Din at r. Lg. *10* at ctr. on back. Printer: W&S.	275.	750.	2000.

#15-17 printer: BWC.

		VG	VF	UNC
15	**20 Tomans** 1924-32. Red, green and purple. Portr. Nasr-ed-Din at r. Lion at ctr. on back.	2750.	4000.	—

		Good	Fine	XF
16	**50 Tomans** 1924-32. Brown, green and lt. brown. Portr. Nasr-ed-Din at ctr. r. Lion at ctr. on back.	700.	1750.	—

		Good	Fine	XF
17	**100 Tomans** 1924-32. Dk. blue and brown. Portr. Nasr-ed-Din at r. Back red-brown and blue.	800.	2250.	—

KINGDOM OF IRAN

BANK MELLI IRAN

ND ISSUE

		VG	VF	UNC
17A	**500 Rials = 5 Pahlevis** ND. Blue. Portr. Shah at r. Palace of the 40 columns at ctr. on back. Proof ovpt: *SPECIMEN.*	—	—	—

1932 ISSUE

#18-23 portr. Shah Reza w/high cap full face. Printer: ABNC.

		VG	VF	UNC
18	**5 Rials** AH1311 (1932). Dk. green on m/c unpt. Portr. Shah Reza at l.	300.	750.	1500.

		VG	VF	UNC
19	**10 Rials** AH1311 (1932). Brown on m/c unpt. Portr. Shah Reza at r.	20.00	700.	1250.
20	**20 Rials** AH1311 (1932). Red on m/c unpt. Portr. Shah Reza at ctr.	500.	1250.	2000.

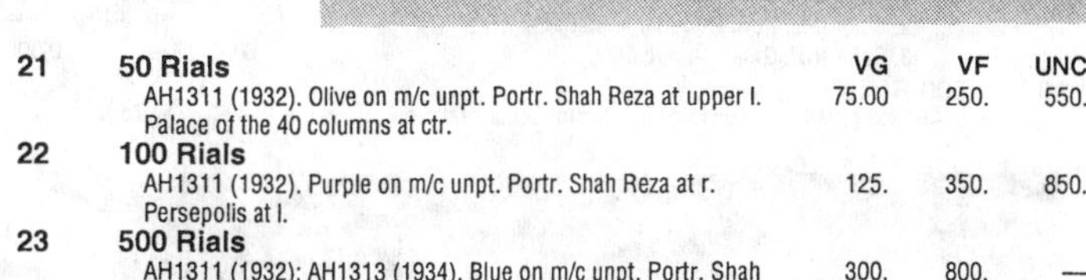

		VG	VF	UNC
21	**50 Rials** AH1311 (1932). Olive on m/c unpt. Portr. Shah Reza at upper l. Palace of the 40 columns at ctr.	75.00	250.	550.
22	**100 Rials** AH1311 (1932). Purple on m/c unpt. Portr. Shah Reza at r. Persepolis at l.	125.	350.	850.
23	**500 Rials** AH1311 (1932); AH1313 (1934). Blue on m/c unpt. Portr. Shah Reza at l. Mount Demavand at r.	300.	800.	—

1933-34 ISSUE

#24-30 portr. Shah Reza w/high cap in three-quarter face (towards l.). Various dates stamped on back. (AH1312; 1313; 1314; or ND). All except #24 and #29 have 2 sign. varieties.

		VG	VF	UNC
24	**5 Rials** ND (1933). Dk. green on m/c unpt. Portr. at l.	200.	500.	1000.
25	**10 Rials** AH1313 (1934). Brown on m/c unpt. (AH1312; 1313; 1314). Portr. at r.			
	a. Sign. in German and Farsi.	150.	400.	750.
	b. Both sign. in Farsi.	15.00	65.00	200.
26	**20 Rials** AH1313 (1934). Red on m/c unpt. (AH1312; 1313; 1314). Portr. at ctr.			
	a. Sign. in German and Farsi.	250.	750.	1500.
	b. Both sign. in Farsi.	200.	700.	1500.

		VG	VF	UNC
27	**50 Rials**			
	AH1313 (1934). Olive on m/c unpt. (AH1312; 1313; 1314). Portr. at l.			
	a. Sign. in German and Farsi.	85.00	200.	500.
	b. Both sign. in Farsi.	350.	1000.	2000.

		VG	VF	UNC
28	**100 Rials**			
	AH1313 (1934). Purple on m/c unpt. (AH1312, 1313, 1314). Portr. at r.			
	a. Sign. in German and Farsi.	135.	300.	700.
	b. Both sign. in Farsi.	125.	275.	650.
	s. Specimen. Punch hole cancelled.	—	—	3000.

		VG	VF	UNC
28A	**100 Rials**			
	ND (1935). Portr. at l. French text on back.			
	t1. Color trial. Brown on m/c unpt.	6000.		10,000.
	t2. Color trial. Purple on m/c unpt. Rare.	—	—	—
	t3. Color trial. Green on m/c unpt.	6000.		10,000.
29	**500 Rials**			
	AH1313 (1934). Blue on m/c unpt. Mount Demavarst at r. Portr. at l.	250.	750.	1750.

		VG	VF	UNC
30	**1000 Rials**			
	AH1313 (1934). Green on m/c unpt. Warrior killing fabulous creature at l. Mythical figure w/wings on back. (AH1313; 1314).			
	a. Sign. in German and Farsi.	1000.	1750.	2250.
	b. Both sign. in Farsi.	150.	450.	1500.

1936 ISSUE

		VG	VF	UNC
31	**10 Rials**			
	AH1315 (1936). Purple on m/c unpt. Portr. Shah Reza at r. French text; mountains on back.	30.00	150.	300.

1937-38 ISSUE

#32-38A portr. Shah Reza in three-quarter face towards l. w/o cap at r.; serial # in Western or Persian numerals. Various issuing stamps on back. AH1316 and 1317 dates printed on face. AH1319; 1320; 1321 dates stamped on back.

		VG	VF	UNC
32	**5 Rials**			
	AH1316 (1937). Red-brown on m/c unpt. French text; Tomb of Daniel in Susa at ctr. on back.			
	a. Red-brown ovpt. 17/5/15 (15 Mordad 1317) on back.	30.00	150.	300.
	s. W/o ovpt. on back. Specimen.			

		VG	VF	UNC
32A	**5 Rials**			
	AH1317 (1938). Red-brown on m/c unpt. Persian text on back. Similar to #32.			
	a. W/o date stamp on back.	15.00	50.00	150.
	b. Red-orange or purple date stamp 1319 on back.	30.00	75.00	300.
	c. Outlined red-brown date stamp 1319 on back.	8.00	30.00	80.00
	d. Purple date stamp 1320 on back.	15.00	60.00	200.
	e. Purple or slate blue date stamp 1321 on back.	25.00	75.00	250.

		VG	VF	UNC
33	**10 Rials**			
	AH1316 (1937). Purple on m/c unpt. Similar to #31, but modified Shah's portr. French text on back.			

33

	VG	VF	UNC
a. W/o ovpt. on back.	50.00	150.	350.
b. Purple ovpt. 17/5/15 (15 Mordad 1317) on back.	25.00	100.	350.
c. Purple date stamp 1319 on back.	50.00	150.	350.
s. Specimen. Pin hole cancelled.			

33A 10 Rials

AH1317 (1938). Purple on m/c unpt. Like #33. Persian text on back.

	VG	VF	UNC
a. W/o date stamp on back.	20.00	100.	200.
b. Violet or slate blue date stamp 1319 on back.	75.00	150.	250.
c. Blue date stamp 1320 on back.	25.00	100.	200.
d. Blue date stamp 1321 on back.	25.00	100.	225.

34 20 Rials

AH1316 (1937). Orange on m/c unpt. French text; bridges across river in valley at ctr. on back.

	VG	VF	UNC
a. W/o ovpt. on back.	125.	300.	500.
b. Orange ovpt. 17/5/15 (15 Mordad 1317) on back.	125.	300.	500.
c. Orange date stamp 1319 on back.	17.50	85.00	225.
d. Purple date stamp 1320 on back.	150.	350.	550.

34A 20 Rials

AH1317 (1938). Orange on m/c unpt. Like #34. Persian text on back.

	VG	VF	UNC
a. Western serial #.	25.00	150.	350.
b. Persian serial #, w/o date stamp.	2.00	150.	350.
c. Orange or purple date stamp 1319 on back.	8.00	35.00	130.
d. Blue (or purple) outlined date stamp on back.	2.50	15.00	110.
e. Purple date stamp 1320 on back.	50.00	175.	450.
f. Purple date stamp 1321 on back.	50.00	175.	450.

35 50 Rials

AH1316 (1937). Green on m/c unpt. Mt. Damavand at l. French text; ruins at ctr. on back.

	VG	VF	UNC
a. W/o ovpt. on back.	20.00	85.00	375.
b. Green ovpt. 17/5/15 (15 Mordad 1317) on back.	175.	500.	1000.

35A 50 Rials

AH1317 (1938). Green on m/c unpt. Like #35. Persian text on back.

	VG	VF	UNC
a. Western # on face.	75.00	250.	600.
b. Persian # on face w/o date stamp on back.	50.00	200.	550.
c. Green or red date stamp 1319 on back.	15.00	95.00	285.
d. Red outlined date stamp 1319 on back.	20.00	110.	350.
e. Red date stamp 1320 on back.	75.00	250.	650.
f. Red date stamp 1321 on back.	50.00	200.	600.

35B 100 Rials

AH1316 (1937). Shah Reza facing at r., arms at l. Fortress ruins at ctr. on back. Specimen perforated: *SPECIMEN.*

s. Dark blue and purple on m/c unpt.

t. Red on m/c unpt. Color trial.

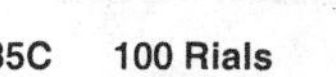

35C 100 Rials

ND (1937). Brown on m/c unpt. Reza Shah 3/4 facing, with short hair on top of head. Specimen. Punch hole cancelled.

36 100 Rials

AH1316 (1937). Lt. brown on m/c unpt. Bank Melli at ctr. French text; ship at ctr. on back.

	VG	VF	UNC
a. W/o ovpt. on back.	15.00	125.	400.
b. Brown ovpt. 17/5/15 (15 Mordad 1317) on back.	25.00	175.	525.
c. Purple date stamp 1320 on back.	30.00	150.	500.
s. Specimen.	—	—	3000.

36A 100 Rials

AH1317 (1938). Lt. brown on m/c unpt. Like #36. Persian text on back.

	VG	VF	UNC
a. Western serial #.	100.	300.	750.
b. Persian serial #. W/o date stamp on back.	100.	300.	750.
c. Brown or purple date stamp 1319 on back.	25.00	75.00	300.
d. Purple or slate gray date stamp 1320 on back.	125.	350.	800.
e. Slate gray date stamp 1321 on back.	125.	350.	800.
s. Brown on m/c unpt. Specimen. Pin hole cancelled.			

36B 500 Rials

ND (1937). Reza Shah at r. facing front. French text on back. Latin serial #. Specimen. Punch hole cancelled.

37 500 Rials

AH1317 (1938). Blue on m/c unpt. Persian text; Grave of Cyrus the Great at Pasargarde on back.

	VG	VF	UNC
a. Western serial #.	200.	750.	1250.
b. Persian serial #. W/o date stamp on back.	200.	750.	1250.
c. Blue or red date stamp 1319 on back.	35.00	125.	500.
d. Orange-red date stamp 1320 on back.	200.	800.	1500.
e. Red date stamp 1321 on back.	200.	750.	1250.

37A 1000 Rials

ND (1937). Green on m/c unpt. Reza Shah at l. French text at back. Latin serial #.

a. Issued note.

s. Specimen. Punch hole cancelled.

38	1000 Rials	VG	VF	UNC
	AH1316 (1937). Green on m/c unpt. French text; mountains at ctr. on back.			
	a. Green ovpt. 17/5/15 (145 Mordad 1317) on back.	75.00	300.	750.
	b. Red date stamp 1320 on back.	300.	1000.	2500.
	c. Red date stamp 1321 on back.	300.	1000.	2500.
	s. W/o ovpt. on back. Specimen.			

38A	1000 Rials	VG	VF	UNC
	AH1317 (1938). Green on m/c unpt. Like #38. Persian text on back.			
	a. Western serial #.	250.	1000.	2500.
	b. Persian serial #. W/o date stamp on back.	250.	1000.	2500.
	c. Date stamp 1319 on back. Rare.			
	d. Red date stamp 1320 on back.	300.	1250.	2750.
	e. Red date stamp 1321 on back.	300.	1250.	2750.

38B	10,000 Rials	VG	VF	UNC
	a. AH1316 (1937). Blue on pink, yellow and m/c unpt. Shah with short hair at ctr. and as wmk. Bldg. at l., ruins at r. 4 Western style serial #. Pillar at l., long bridge across ctr., arms at upper r., French text on back. Specimen. Rare.	—	—	—
	b. AH1316 (1937). Same as above, but Shah facing and looking forward.			30,000.

38C	10,000 Rials	VG	VF	UNC
	AH1317 (1938). Purple and yellow on m/c unpt. Reza Shah 3/4 l. at ctr. Persian serial #. Specimen.	—	—	—

Shah Mohammad Reza Pahlavi, SH1323-40/1944-61AD

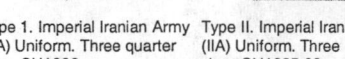

Type 1. Imperial Iranian Army (IIA) Uniform. Three quarter view. SH1323.

Type II. Imperial Iranian Army (IIA) Uniform. Three view. SH1325-29

Type III. Civilian Attire. Full face. SH1330-32.

Type IV. Imperial Iranian Army (IIA) Uniform. Full left profile. SH1333.

Type V. Imperial Iranian Army (IIA). Uniform. Full face. SH1337-40.

1944 Issue

#39-46 first portr. Shah Pahlavi in army uniform at r. Wmk: Imperial Crown. Sign. 1. Large format. Printer: Harrison (w/o imprint).

		VG	VF	UNC
39	**5 Rials** ND (1944). Reddish brown on lt. green and pink unpt. Tomb of Daniel Nabi in Susa on back.	5.00	15.00	35.00
40	**10 Rials** ND (1944). Purple on lt. orange and m/c unpt. Ornate geometric design at ctr. Caspian Seaside of Alborz Mountains on back.	7.50	25.00	75.00
41	**20 Rials** ND (1944). Orange on m/c unpt. Scene from Persepolis at ctr. Railroad tunnel and bridges on back.	25.00	100.	350.

		VG	VF	UNC
42	**50 Rials** ND (1944). Dk. green on lavender and violet unpt. Stylized cock and ornate design at ctr. Tomb of Cyrus at Pasargadae on back.	35.00	150.	500.

		VG	VF	UNC
43	**100 Rials** ND (1944). Brown and green. Bank Melli and ornate design at ctr. Steamship and dhow at Port of Enzely on back.	175.	500.	1250.

		VG	VF	UNC
44	**100 Rials** ND (1944). Purple on orange unpt. Stylized horse and ornate design at ctr. Bridge and dam at Dezful on back.	175.	500.	1250.

		VG	VF	UNC
45	**500 Rials** ND (1944). Dk. blue and purple. M/c design and winged horse at ctr. Ruins of Persepolis on back.	250.	750.	1800.
46	**1000 Rials** ND (1944). Green, orange and blue. Winged bull and floral design at ctr. Mount Damavand on back.	300.	1000.	2500.

1948-51 ISSUE

#47-53 second portr. Shah Pahlavi in army uniform at r. Wmk: Young Shah Mohammad Reza Pahlavi. Sign. 1. Small format. Printer: Harrison (w/o imprint).

		VG	VF	UNC
47	**10 Rials** ND (1948). Dk. blue on orange unpt. M/c design at ctr. Winged Saurian from Tagh-I-Bostan on back.	5.00	10.00	30.00
48	**20 Rials** ND (1948). Dk. brown, green and orange. M/c stone sculpture at ctr. Lion biting stylized bull on back.	10.00	25.00	100.

		VG	VF	UNC
49	**50 Rials** ND (1948). Green on orange and green unpt. Sun disk at ctr. 5 Persian figures from Persepolis sculpture on back.	20.00	50.00	150.

		VG	VF	UNC
50	**100 Rials** ND (1951). Red-violet on lt. green unpt. Winged lion and m/c design at ctr. Ruins of Palace of Darius at Persepolis on back.	20.00	50.00	150.

		VG	VF	UNC
51	**200 Rials** ND (1951). Dk. green and lt. yellow. Carved tray at ctr. Railroad bridge and tunnels on back.	30.00	75.00	250.
52	**500 Rials** ND (1951). Dk. blue, purple and red. Rectangular design at ctr. 4 oriental figures in orchard on back.	100.	300.	750.
53	**1000 Rials** ND (1951). Brown, red and lt. green. M/c floral design and birds at ctr. Mount Damavand on back.	150.	400.	1250.

1951 ISSUE

#54-58 third portr. Shah Pahlavi in civilian attire at r. Yellow security thread runs vertically. Printer: Harrison (w/o imprint).

#54-55, 58 Sign. 2.

		VG	VF	UNC
54	**10 Rials** SH1330 (1951). Dk. blue and m/c. Shepherd and ram at ctr., w/o wmk. Royal seal of Darius on back.	2.00	7.00	15.00
55	**20 Rials** SH1330 (1951). Dk. brown on orange and m/c unpt. Winged bull and spear bearer at ctr., w/o wmk. Ali Ghapoo in Isfahan on back.	3.00	12.00	25.00

#56-57 Sign. 3. #56-58 wmk; Young Shah Pahlavi.

		VG	VF	UNC
56	**50 Rials** SH1330 (1951). Green on lt. orange and m/c unpt. Pharaotic figure w/urn at ctr. Palace of Darius in Persepolis on back.	3.00	12.00	30.00
57	**100 Rials** SH1330 (1951). Maroon on m/c unpt. Mythical figure at ctr. Darius in royal coach on back.	5.00	20.00	50.00
58	**200 Rials** SH1330 (1951). Dk. blue, lt. blue and brown. Ruins of Persepolis at ctr. Allahverdikhan bridge in Isfahan on back. Sign. 2.	7.50	30.00	125.

1953 ISSUE

#59, 60, 62 Sign. 4. #59-62 designs like 1951 Issue.

		VG	VF	UNC
59	**10 Rials** SH1332 (1953). Dk. blue and m/c. Like #54.	2.00	7.00	15.00

		VG	VF	UNC
60	**20 Rials** SH1332 (1953). Dk. brown on orange and m/c unpt. Like #55.	3.00	12.00	25.00
61	**50 Rials** SH1332 (1953). Green on lt. orange and m/c unpt. Like #56. Sign. N. Jahangir and A. A. Nasser.	15.00	50.00	100.

		VG	VF	UNC
62	**100 Rials** SH1332 (1953). Maroon on m/c unpt. Like #57.	20.00	60.00	175.

1954 ISSUE

#64-67 fourth portr. Shah Pahlavi in army uniform at r. Yellow security thread runs vertically. Sign. 4. Printer: Harrison (w/o imprint).

		VG	VF	UNC
64	**10 Rials** SH1333 (1954). Dk. blue on orange, green and m/c unpt. Ruins of Persepolis at l., w/o wmk. Tomb of Ibn Sina in Hamadan at back.	2.00	7.00	15.00

		VG	VF	UNC
65	**20 Rials** SH1333 (1954). Dk. brown on orange and m/c unpt. Man slaying beast at l., w/o wmk. Back red-brown; Bank Melli in Tehran at ctr.	3.00	12.00	25.00

#66-67 wmk: Young Shah Pahlavi.

		VG	VF	UNC
66	**50 Rials** SH1333 (1954). Green on purple and m/c unpt. Geometric design and floral motifs at ctr., Koohrang Dam and tunnel on back.	3.00	12.00	30.00
67	**100 Rials** SH1333 (1954). Maroon on lt. green and m/c unpt. Geometric design and floral motifs at ctr. Oil refinery at Abadan on back.	5.00	20.00	50.00

1958 Issue

#68-70 fifth portr. Shah Pahlavi in army uniform at r. Wmk: Young Shah Pahlavi. Yellow security thread runs vertically. Sign. 6. Printer: Harrison (w/o imprint).

		VG	VF	UNC
68	**10 Rials** SH1337 (1958). Dk. blue on green and orange unpt. Ornate floral design at ctr. Amir Kabir Dam near Karaj on back.	1.50	5.00	12.00

		VG	VF	UNC
69	**20 Rials** SH1337 (1958). Dk. brown on lt. brown, lilac and m/c unpt. Ornate floral design at ctr. Statue of Shah and Ramsar Hotel on back.	2.50	7.50	20.00

		VG	VF	UNC
70	**200 Rials** SH1337 (1958). Blue on purple, orange and m/c unpt. Ruins of Persepolis at ctr. Mehrabad Airport in Tehran on back.	15.00	40.00	75.00

1952 Emergency Circulating Check

#70A-70C stamped date, seal at l. Uniface.

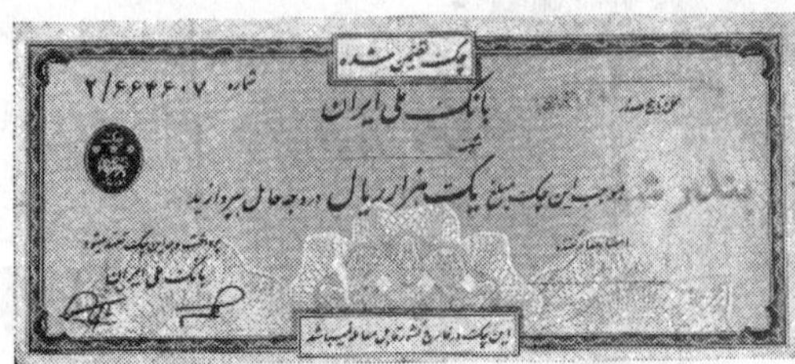

		VG	VF	UNC
70A	**1000 Rials** SH1331 (1952). Blue on gold and gray unpt. Issued at Bandar Shah.	15.00	50.00	150.
70B	**5000 Rials** SH1331 (1952). Red on lt. red and blue unpt. Specimen.			
70C	**10,000 Rials** SH1331 (1952). Dk. green on blue and lt. red unpt. Specimen.	—	—	150.

Note: For similar issues from Bank Markazi Iran, see Volume 3.

Military

German Treasury - WWI

1916-17 Issue

#M1-M2 w/red ovpt. of denomination in Persian on both sides of German Treasury notes.

		Good	Fine	XF
M1	**12 Kran 10 Shahi on 5 Mark** ND (1916-17 - old date 3.10.1904). Ovpt. on Germany #8.	1500.	3000.	5000.

		Good	Fine	XF
M2	**25 Kran on 10 Mark** ND (1916-17 - old date 6.10.1906). Ovpt. on Germany #9.	1000.	2000.	3000.

#M3-M5 w/red ovpt. on German Reichsbank notes.

		Good	Fine	XF
M3	**5 Tomans on 20 Mark** ND (1916-17 - old date 19.2.1914). Ovpt. on Germany #40.	625.	1250.	2500.

M4 **25 Tomans on 100 Mark**

ND (1916-17 - old date 21.4.1910). Ovpt. on Germany #42.

	Good	Fine	XF
a. Issued note. Rare.	—	—	—
s. Specimen perforated: *DRUCKPROBE.*	—	—	—

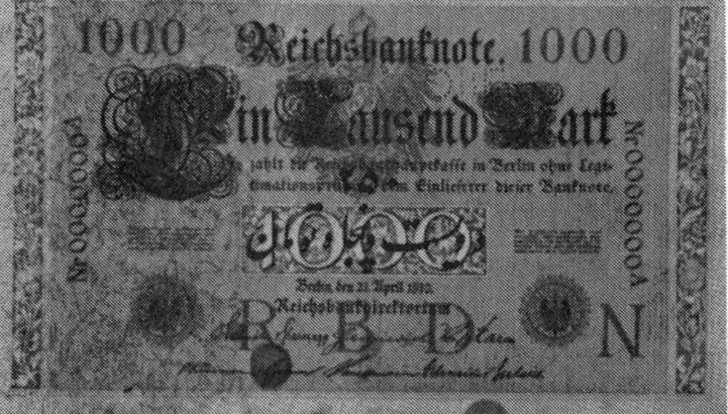

M5 **250 Tomans on 1000 Mark**

ND (1916-17 - old date 21.4.1910). Ovpt. on Germany #44.

	Good	Fine	XF
a. Issued note. Rare.	—	—	—
s. Specimen perforated: *DRUCKPROBE.*	—	—	—

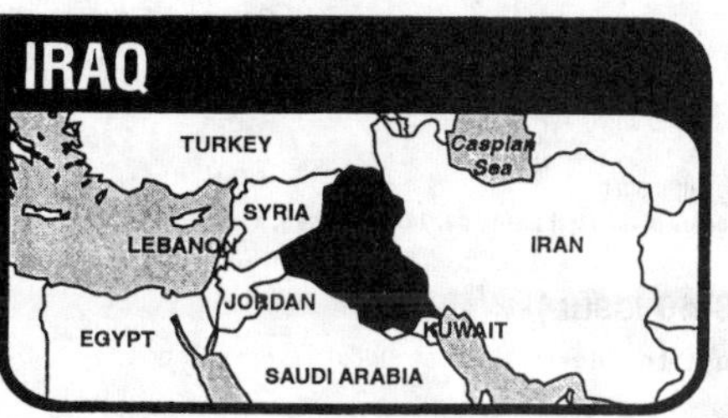

The Republic of Iraq, historically known as Mesopotamia, is located in the Near East and is bordered by Kuwait, Iran, Turkey, Syria, Jordan and Saudi Arabia. It has an area of 167,925 sq. mi. (434,924 sq. km.) and a population of 23.11 million. Capital: Baghdad. The economy of Iraq is d on agriculture and petroleum. Crude oil accounts for 94 percent of the exports before the war with Iran began in 1980.

Iraq was the site of a number of flourishing civilizations of antiquity - Sumerian, Assyrian, Babylonian, Parthian, Persian - and of the Biblical cities of Ur, Nineveh and Babylon. Desired because of its favored location which embraced the fertile alluvial plains of the Tigris and Euphrates Rivers, Mesopotamia - "land between the rivers" - was conquered by Cyrus the Great of Persia, Alexander of Macedonia and by Arabs who made the legendary city of Baghdad the capital of the ruling caliphate. Suleiman the Great conquered Mesopotamia for Turkey in 1534, and it formed part of the Ottoman Empire until 1623, and from 1638 to 1917. Great Britain, given a League of Nations mandate over the territory in 1920, recognized Iraq as a kingdom in 1922. Iraq became an independent constitutional monarchy presided over by the Hashemite family, direct descendants of the prophet Mohammed, in 1932. In 1958, the army-led revolution of July 14 overthrew the monarchy and proclaimed a republic. After several military coups, Saddam Hussein became president in 1979. In 2003 he was overthrown by a coalition of foreign forces lead by the United States.

RULERS:

Faisal I, 1921-1933
Ghazi I, 1933-1939
Faisal II, 1939-1958

MONETARY SYSTEM:

1 Dirham = 50 Fils
1 Riyal = 200 Fils
1 Dinar = 1000 Fils

KINGDOM

GOVERNMENT OF IRAQ

1931 ISSUE

#1-6 portr. Kg. Faisal I w/goatee at r. and as wmk. Printer: BWC.

		Good	Fine	XF
1	**1/4 Dinar**			
	1931-32. Green on m/c unpt. English text on back.			
	a. 1.7.1931.	50.00	135.	325.
	b. 1.8.1932.	100.	225.	—
2	**1/2 Dinar**			
	1931-32. Brown on m/c unpt.			
	a. 1.7.1931.	75.00	190.	450.
	b. 1.8.1932.	150.	400.	—

		Good	Fine	XF
3	**1 Dinar**			
	1931-32. Blue on m/c unpt.			
	a. 1.7.1931.	50.00	160.	350.
	b. 1.8.1932.	175	500	

		Good	Fine	XF
4	**5 Dinars** 1.7.1931. Brown-violet on m/c unpt.	150.	400.	1000.
5	**10 Dinars** 1.7.1931. Purple and blue on m/c unpt.	—	—	—
6	**100 Dinars** 1.7.1931. Blue and ochre on m/c unpt.	—	—	—

Note: Approval dates are known for 3 notes of the First Issue: #4, 14.9.1931; #5, 21.9.1931: #6, 2.10.1931.

LAW #44 OF 1931 (1933-40 ISSUE)

#7-12 portr. Kg. Ghazi in military uniform at r. and as wmk. Printer: BWC.

		Good	Fine	XF
7	**1/4 Dinar** L.1931. (1935). Green on m/c unpt. 5 sign. varieties.	20.00	70.00	175.
8	**1/2 Dinar** L.1931. (1935). Brown on m/c unpt. 5 sign. varieties.	40.00	125.	375.

		Good	Fine	XF
9	**1 Dinar** L.1931. (1934). Blue on m/c unpt. 5 sign. varieties.	35.00	100.	300.
10	**5 Dinars** L.1931. (1940). Brown-violet on m/c unpt. 2 sign. varieties.	100.	275.	600.

		Good	Fine	XF
11	**10 Dinars** L.1931. (1938). Purple and blue on m/c unpt. 2 sign. varieties.	150.	375.	750.

		Good	Fine	XF
12	**100 Dinars** L.1931. (1936). Blue and ochre on m/c unpt. 2 sign. varieties.	250.	700.	1500.

LAW #44 OF 1931 (1941 ISSUE)

#13-15 portr. Kg. Faisal II as a child at r. Printed in India (w/o imprint). Sign. L. M. Swan at l. Obrahim Kamal at r.

		Good	Fine	XF
13	**1/4 Dinar** L.1931. (1941). Green on brown and blue unpt.	20.00	85.00	275.
14	**1/2 Dinar** L.1931. (1941). Brown.	40.00	150.	425

		Good	Fine	XF
15	**1 Dinar** L.1931. (1941). Blue.	35.00	125.	350

LAW #44 OF 1931 (1942 ISSUE)

#16-21 portr. Kg. Faisal II as child at r. Sign. Kennet at l. Other sign. varieties. Wmk: Kg. Faisal. Printer: BWC

		Good	Fine	XF
16	**1/4 Dinar** L.1931. (1942). Green on m/c unpt. 3 sign. varieties.	9.00	30.00	12[illegible]
17	**1/2 Dinar** L.1931. (1942). Brown on m/c unpt. 2 sign. varieties.	25.00	75.00	22[illegible]

		Good	Fine	XF
18	**1 Dinar** L.1931. (1942). Blue on m/c unpt. 2 sign. varieties.	15.00	50.00	175.

		Good	Fine	XF
19	**5 Dinars** L.1931. (1942). Brown on m/c unpt. 2 sign. varieties.	40.00	100.	350.
20	**10 Dinars** L.1931. (1942). Purple and blue on m/c unpt. 2 sign. varieties.	65.00	225.	450.

		Good	Fine	XF
21	**100 Dinars** L.1931. Dk. blue and m/c.	150.	550.	1250.

Note: Approval date of Nov. 1941 is known for #19-21.

LAW #44 OF 1931 (1945 ISSUE)

#22-23 portr. young Kg. Faisal II at r. and as wmk. Printer: BWC.

		Good	Fine	XF
22	**1/4 Dinar** L. 1931. Green on m/c unpt.	15.00	65.00	285.

LAW #44 OF 1931 (1944 ISSUE)

		Good	Fine	XF
A22	**50 Fils** L.1931. Green. Portr. Kg. Faisal at l. Printer: BWC. Proof.	—	—	—

Note: #A22 was approved 6.3.1944 but apparently never issued.

LAW #44 OF 1931 (1945 ISSUE)

#22-23 portr. young Kg. Faisal II at r. and as wmk. Printer: BWC.

		Good	Fine	XF
23	**1/2 Dinar** L.1931. Brown on m/c unpt.	25.00	90.00	350.

Note: #24-26 have been deleted.

NATIONAL BANK OF IRAQ

LAW #42 OF 1947

FIRST ISSUE

#27-31 portr. young Kg. Faisal II at r. and as wmk. Printer: BWC.

		Good	Fine	XF
27	**1/4 Dinar** L.1947. (1950). Green on m/c unpt. Palm trees at ctr. on back.	5.00	20.00	65.00

		Good	Fine	XF
28	**1/2 Dinar** L.1947. (1950). Brown on m/c unpt. Ruins of the mosque and spiral minaret at Samarra on back.	10.00	35.00	125.

		Good	Fine	XF
29	**1 Dinar** L.1947. (1950). Blue on m/c unpt. Equestrian statue of Kg. Faisal I on back.	7.50	30.00	85.00

		Good	Fine	XF
30	**5 Dinars** L.1947. (1950). Red on m/c unpt. Ancient carving of Hammurabi receiving the laws on back.	30.00	85.00	250.
31	**10 Dinars** L.1947. (1950). Purple and blue on m/c unpt. Winged Assyrian ox and an Assyrian priest at ctr. on back.	35.00	125.	350.

SECOND ISSUE

#32-36 portr. young Kg. Faisal II at r. Wmk: Kg's. head as a child. Backs like previous issue. Printer: BWC.

		Good	Fine	XF
32	**1/4 Dinar** L.1947. Green on m/c unpt.	5.00	20.00	60.00
33	**1/2 Dinar** L.1947. Brown on m/c unpt.	12.00	30.00	100.
34	**1 Dinar** L.1947. Blue on m/c unpt.	10.00	25.00	80.00
35	**5 Dinars** L.1947. Red on m/c unpt.	25.00	70.00	225.

		Good	Fine	XF
36	**10 Dinars** L.1947. Purple on m/c unpt.	45 00	140.	350.

THIRD ISSUE

#37-41 portr. Kg. Faisal II as an adolescent at r. Wmk: Kg's head as a youth. Backs like previous issue. Printer: BWC.

		Good	Fine	XF
37	**1/4 Dinar** L.1947. Green on m/c unpt.	4.00	17.50	50.00
38	**1/2 Dinar** L.1947. Brown on m/c unpt.			
	a. Wmk: Large head.	10.00	27.50	95.00
	b. Wmk: Small head.	10.00	27.50	95.00

		Good	Fine	XF
39	**1 Dinar** L.1947. Blue on m/c unpt.			
	a. Wmk. lg. head.	9.00	25.00	85.00
	b. Wmk. sm. head.	9.00	25.00	85.00

		Good	Fine	XF
40	**5 Dinars** L.1947. Red on m/c unpt.			
	a. Wmk: Large head.	30.00	75.00	250
	b. Wmk: Small head.	30.00	75.00	250

	Good	Fine	XF
10 Dinars L.1947. Purple on m/c unpt.			
a. Wmk: Large head.	45.00	140.	350.
b. Wmk: Small head.	45.00	450.	350.

ENTRAL BANK OF IRAQ

AW #42 OF 1947

2-43 designs like #37-38.

	Good	Fine	XF
1/4 Dinar L.1947. Green on m/c unpt. Like #37.	3.00	12.00	40.00

	Good	Fine	XF
1/2 Dinar L.1947. Brown on m/c unpt. Like #38.	2.50	10.00	30.00

nd 45 have been deleted.

COND ISSUE

50 portr. Kg. Faisal II as a young man at r.

	Good	Fine	XF
1/4 Dinar L.1947. Green on m/c unpt.	2.00	10.00	55.00

as been deleted.

	Good	Fine	XF
1 Dinar L.1947. Blue on m/c unpt.	7.50	20.00	75.00
5 Dinars L.1947. Red on m/c unpt.	25.00	60.00	175.
10 Dinars L.1947. Purple and blue on m/c unpt.	40.00	125.	300.

PUBLIC

NTRAL BANK OF IRAQ

9 ISSUE

new Republic arms w/1958 at r. and as wmk. Sign. 10, 11, 12.

		VG	VF	UNC
51	**1/4 Dinar** ND (1959). Green on m/c unpt. Palm trees at ctr. on back.			
	a. W/o security thread. 1 sign. varieties.	1.00	5.00	15.00
	b. W/security thread. 2 sign. varieties.	1.00	5.00	5.00
	s. Specimen. Punched hole cancelled.	—	—	30.00

		VG	VF	UNC
52	**1/2 Dinar** ND (1959). Brown on m/c unpt. Ruins of the mosque and spiral minaret at Samarra on back.			
	a. W/o security thread. 1 sign. variety.	2.00	7.50	30.00
	b. W/security thread. 2 sign. varieties.	2.00	7.50	30.00
	s. Specimen. Punched hole cancelled.	—	—	30.00

		VG	VF	UNC
53	**1 Dinar** ND (1959). Blue on m/c unpt. The *Harp of Ur* at ctr. on back.			
	a. W/o security thread. 1 sign. variety.	1.50	5.00	20.00
	b. W/security thread. Blue lines over wmk. area. 2 sign. varieties.	1.50	5.00	20.00
	s. Specimen. Punched hole cancelled.	—	—	30.00

		VG	VF	UNC
54	**5 Dinars** ND (1959). Lt. purple on m/c unpt. Ancient carving of Hammurabi receiving the laws on back.			
	a. W/o security thread. 1 sign. variety.	2.50	12.50	35.00
	b. W/security thread.	2.50	12.50	35.00
	s. Specimen. Punched hole cancelled.	—	—	30.00

NOTICE

Readers with unlisted dates, signature varieties, etc. are invited to submit photocopies or, high resolution (300 dpi, 100% size) scans of their notes to: Standard Catalog of World Paper Money, 700 East State St. Iola, WI 54990-0001, or E-Mail: george.cuhaj@fwpubs.com.

55	10 Dinars	VG	VF	UNC
	ND (1959). Purple on m/c unpt. Carvings of a winged Assyrian ox and an Assyrian priest on back.			
	a. W/o security thread. 1 sign. variety.	3.00	10.00	50.00
	b. W/security thread. 2 sign. varieties.	3.00	10.00	50.00
	s. Specimen. Punched hole cancelled.	—	—	30.00

Note: Various hoards of #51-55 have appeared on the market during the past several years. Values shown are speculative for all these pieces.

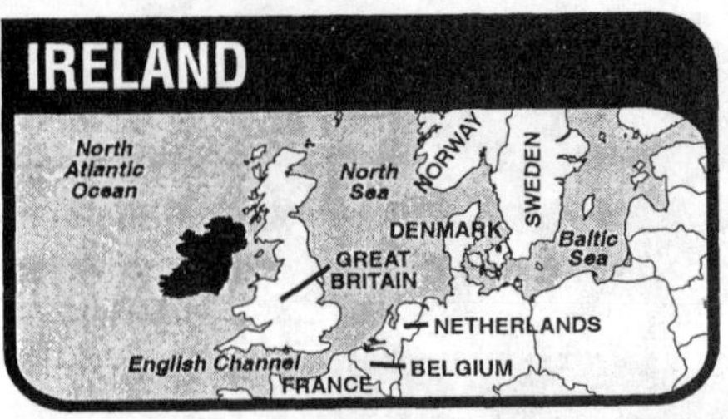

Ireland, the island located in th Atlantic Ocean west of Grea Britain, was settled by dark an swarthy Celts from Gaul abo 400 BC, but eventually the became known for their red ha and light complexions afte frequent Viking invasions. Th Celts assimilated the nativ Erainn and Picts and establishe a Gaelic civilization. After th arrival of St. Patrick in 432 AI Ireland evolved into a center Latin learning which ser missionaries to Europe ar possibly North America. In 1154, Pope Adrian IV gave all of Ireland to English King Henry II administer as a Papal fief. Because of the enactment of anti-Catholic laws and the awarding vast tracts of Irish land to Protestant absentee landowners, English control did not becom reasonably absolute until 1800 when England and Ireland became the "United Kingdom of Gre Britain and Ireland". Religious freedom was restored to the Irish in 1829, but agitation for politic autonomy continued until the Irish Free State was established as a dominion on Dec. 6, 1921 whi Northern Ireland remained within the United Kingdom.

RULERS:

British to 1921

MONETARY SYSTEM:

1 Shilling = 12 Pence
1 Pound = 20 Shillings to 1971
1 Guinea = 21 Shillings
1 Pound = 100 Pence 1971-

COMMERCIAL BANKS:

Bank of Ireland .... #A5-A4
Belfast Banking Company .... #A45-A4
Belfast Banking Company Limited .... #A50-A5
National Bank .... #A5
National Bank Limited .... #A57-A6
Northern Banking Company .... #A6
Northern Banking Compnay Limited .... #A68-A7
Provincial Bank of Ireland .... #A89-#A10
Provincial Bank of Ireland Limited .... #A106-A1
Ulster Bank Limited .... #A131-A1

BRITISH ADMINISTRATION

BANK OF IRELAND

DUBLIN

1808 ISSUE

A5	1 Pound	Good	Fine
	4.3.1808. Black. Hibernia seated w/harp at upper l.	—	—

1836 ISSUE

A10	30 Shillings	Good	Fine
	1.12.1836. Hibernia seated at upper l. and r.	—	—

		Good	Fine	XF
A10A	**50 Pounds** 7.1.1831.	—	—	—

1840 Issue

#A14-A39 Hibernia standing w/harp at l. and r., Medusa heads across top. Various date and sign. varieties.

		Good	Fine	XF
A14	**1 Pound** 3.2.1840. W/o *ONE* in protector at bottom.	175.	425.	—

1849 Issue

		Good	Fine	XF
A15	**1 Pound** 16.8.1849. *ONE* in protector at bottom.	175.	425.	—

1877 Issue

		Good	Fine	XF
20	**1 Pound** 10.3.1877; 23.8.1878. Wavy design protector at bottom. Offices of issue in 4 lines below *Dublin.*	125.	300.	—

889-91 Issue

		Good	Fine	XF
25	**1 Pound** 1891-1905. Similar to #A20 but offices of issue in 4 lines of narrower type below *Dublin.*			
	a. 16.3.1891; 30.6.1891.	100.	250.	—
	b. 20.1.1905.	100.	250.	—

		Good	Fine	XF
A26	**5 Pounds** 1889-1919. Black on green unpt.			
	a. 29.6.1889.	—	—	—
	b. 25.4.1914; 14.12.1916; 11.12.1918; 27.1.1919.	110.	275.	—

		Good	Fine	XF
A27	**10 Pounds** 1890-1917. Black on red unpt.			
	a. 10.11.1890.	—	—	—
	b. 26.9.1911; 12.2.1913; 15.12.1915; 22.9.1917; 18.12.1917.	135.	275.	—

1911-15 Issue

		Good	Fine	XF
A30	**1 Pound** 13.11.1911; 12.11.1914; 20.10.1916; 12.1.1917. Similar to #A25 but offices of issue in 5 lines of type below *Dublin.*	100.	250.	—

NOTICE

Readers with unlisted dates, signature varieties, etc.
are invited to submit photocopies or,
high resolution (300 dpi, 100% size) scans of their notes to:
Standard Catalog of World Paper Money,
700 East State St. Iola, WI 54990-0001,
or E-Mail: george.cuhaj@fwpubs.com.

		Good	Fine	XF
A30A	**3 Pounds** 10.10.1914.	—	—	—
A33	**20 Pounds** 10.11.1915.	225.	500.	—

1918 Issue

		Good	Fine	XF
A35	**1 Pound** 10.1.1918; 22.7.1918; 28.3.1919; 21.1.1920. Black on red unpt. Like #A30 but offices of issue in 8 lines of type below title: *Dublin. Chief Cashier* below sign.	55.00	120.	300.

1920 Issue

		Good	Fine	XF
A37	**1 Pound** 13.8.1920; 12.10.1921. Black on red unpt. W/o offices of issue.	50.00	85.00	200.
A38A	**5 Pounds** 1920-21. Black on green unpt.			
	a. W/title: *Chief Cashier* below sign. 10.8.1920.	85.00	200.	400.
	b. W/o title: *Chief Cashier* below sign. 12.5.1921.	85.00	200.	400.

1922-25 Issue

		Good	Fine	XF
A39	**1 Pound** 1922-27. Black on green unpt. Similar to #A37 but reduced size. "Commerce" seated w/anchor at ctr. on back.			
	a. Sign. S. Hinton. 13.6.1922; 15.6.1922.	20.00	60.00	135.
	b. Sign. J. A. Gargan. 20.1.1924; 19.3.1924; 20.1.1925; 14.4.1925; 25.8.1926; 11.2.1927.	17.50	50.00	120.

		Good	Fine	XF
A40	**5 Pounds** 24.9.1925; 17.7.1926. W/title: *Chief Cashier* below sign.	60.00	185.	350.
A41	**10 Pounds** 10.10.1925. W/title: *Dublin, Chief Cashier* below sign.	65.00	200.	450.

See also Ireland (Eire) and Northern Ireland.

Belfast Banking Company

Belfast

1874 Issue

#A45-A46 arms at l. and upper ctr. r.

		Good	Fine	XF
A45	**1 Pound** 4.12.1874.	—	—	—
A46	**5 Pounds** ND (ca.1874). Proof perforated: *CANCELLED.*	—	—	—

Belfast Banking Company Limited

1905-13 Issue

#A50-A55 various date and sign. varieties to 1922. Printer: CS&E.

		Good	Fine	XF
A50	**1 Pound** 5.1.1905.	30.00	70.00	150.

		Good	Fine	XF
A51	**5 Pounds** 3.12.1913; 7.3.1917. Brown unpt. Arms at l. and at ctr.	45.00	90.00	200.
A52	**10 Pounds** 6.7.1916.	90.00	175.	375.
A53	**20 Pounds**	—	—	—
A54	**50 Pounds**	—	—	—
A55	**100 Pounds**	—	—	—

National Bank

Dublin

1870 Issue

		Good	Fine	XF
A56	**1 Pound** 1.1.1870; 1.1.1873. Arms at upper l., Hibernia seated w/harp at upper ctr. Specimen.	—	—	—

National Bank Limited

1885-99 Issue

#A56A-A56D arms at upper l., Hibernia seated w/harp at upper ctr.

		Good	Fine	XF
A56A	**3 Pounds** 3.6.1885; 3.5.1894; 3.12.1896. Black. Face proof.	—	—	600
A56B	**5 Pounds** 5.5.1890; 5.10.1893. Black. Face proof.	—	—	600
A56C	**10 Pounds** 10.2.1890; 10.12.1891. Black. Face proof.	—	—	650
A56D	**20 Pounds** 20.7.1899; 20.5.1905. Black. Face proof.	—	—	700

Note: Proofs listed above have a significant portion of the design cut off from the bottom area.

1905-13 Issue

#A57-A63 arms at upper l., Hibernia seated w/harp at upper ctr. Various date and sign. varieties to 1928.

		Good	Fine	XF
A57	**1 Pound** 1.10.1913; 2.11.1914; 1.9.1919. W/branch offices.	65.00	140.	300.

		Good	Fine	XF
A58	**3 Pounds** 1.10.1913. Black on green unpt.	—	850.	—
A59	**10 Pounds** 11.8.1905; 10.2.1908; 10.3.1910. Lg. *TEN* at ctr.	125.	250.	500.

1920-24 Issue

#A60-A63 reduced size.

		Good	Fine	XF
A60	**1 Pound** 1.11.1924; 1.10.1925.	—	—	250.
A61	**5 Pounds** 5.6.1923; 5.10.1925. Blue on brown unpt.	—	—	350.

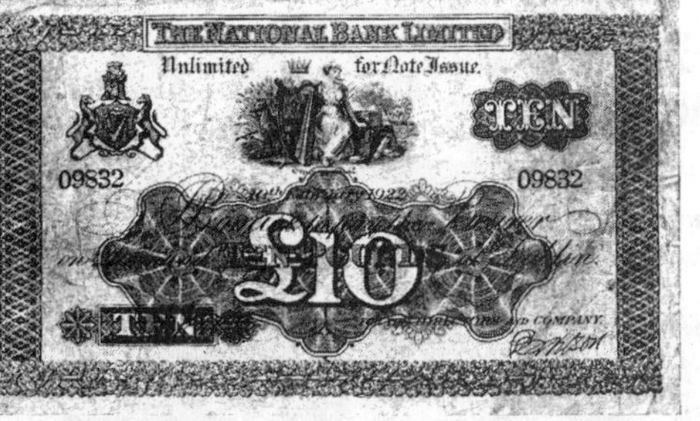

		Good	Fine	XF
A62	**10 Pounds** 10.2.1920; 10.2.1922; 10.11.1924. Green on brown unpt. *£10* at ctr.	200.	400.	750.
A63	**20 Pounds** Proof.	—	—	—

Northern Banking Company

Belfast

1850s Issue

		Good	Fine	XF
A64	**5 Pounds** 18xx (ca.1850). Sailing ship, plow and man at grindstone at upper ctr. w/branch offices in upper frame. Proof.	—	—	—

Northern Banking Company Limited

1908-21 Issue

#A68-75 sailing ship, plow and man at grindstone at upper ctr.

		Good	Fine	XF
A68	**1 Pound** 1.1.1908; 11.11.1918. Black on deep blue unpt.	—	—	—
A70	**5 Pounds** 5.10.1921. Dk. blue unpt.	—	—	—
A71	**10 Pounds** Dk. blue unpt.	—	—	—
A72	**10 Pounds** Dk. blue unpt. Similar to #A71 but w/*TEN* in guilloches at l. and r.	—	—	—
A73	**20 Pounds** 20.10.1921. Dk. blue unpt.	—	—	—
A74	**50 Pounds** Dk. blue unpt.	—	—	—
A75	**50 Pounds** Dk. blue unpt. Similar to #A74 but w/*BALLY MONEY* at lower l. and *AUGHNA CLOY. MILFORD* at lower r.	—	—	—
A76	**100 Pounds** Dk. blue unpt.	—	—	—

Provincial Bank of Ireland

1835 Issue

		Good	Fine	XF
A89	**10 Pounds** 15.6.1835. Portr. Kg. William IV at upper l., Britannia and Hibernia seated at upper ctr.	—	—	—

Galway

1843-52 Issue

		Good	Fine	XF
A90	**5 Pounds** 11.8.1843.	—	—	—
A91	**10 Pounds** 1.9.1852. Split and hand cancelled.	—	—	—

Parsontown

1852 Issue

#A92-A95 portr. Qn. Victoria at upper l., Britannia and Hibernia seated at upper ctr. Similar to previous issues.

		Good	Fine	XF
A92	**1 Pound** 1.8.1856. Split and hand cancelled.	—	—	—

Sligo

1858 Issue

		Good	Fine	XF
A93	**2 Pounds** 1.11.1858. Split and hand cancelled.	—	—	—

Wexford

1854 Issue

		Good	Fine	XF
A98	**5 Pounds** 15.9.1854.	—	—	—

Youghal

1858 Issue

		Good	Fine	XF
A99	**1 Pound** 15.7.1858. Split and hand cancelled.	—	—	—

W/o Branch

1878-81 Issue

		Good	Fine	XF
A100	**3 Pounds** 3.12.1881. Similar to previous issue but w/o branch office name in frame. Proof.	—	—	—
A102	**10 Pounds** 10.10.1878. Similar to #A100. Face proof.	—	—	—

Provincial Bank of Ireland Limited

Dublin

1874 Issue

		Good	Fine	XF
A105	**1 Pound** 1.1.1874. Black. Like #A106 but w/o *UNLIMITED FOR NOTE ISSUE* at top.	—	—	—

1885-89 Issue

		Good	Fine	XF
A106	1 Pound 1.8.1885; 1.9.1892; 1.9.1892; 1.12.1894.	—	—	—

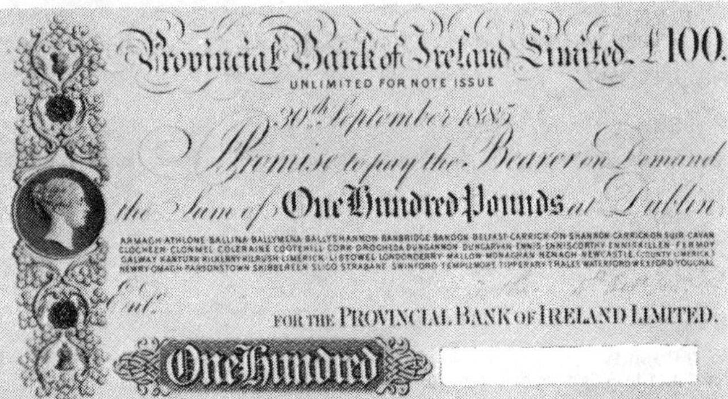

		Good	Fine	XF
A108	5 Pounds 5.3.1889.	—	—	—

		Good	Fine	XF
A110	100 Pounds 30.9.1885. Cameo portr. Qn. Victoria at l. Sign. cut out. Remainder.	—	—	—

1903-04 Issue

#A116-A124 Britannia and Hibernia seated at upper ctr. Various date and sign. varieties.

		Good	Fine	XF
A116	1 Pound 1903; 1914. Blue.			
	a. Branch office listings in 4 lines. 2.11.1903.	40.00	85.00	300.
	b. Branch office listings in 4-1/2 lines. 1.10.1914.	50.00	125.	350.

		Good	Fine	XF
A117	5 Pounds 5.2.1904. Blue.	100.	300.	600.

		Good	Fine	XF
A118	10 Pounds 1904; 1915. Blue.			
	a. 10.3.1904.	150.	400.	—
	b. 10.7.1915.	75.00	175.	—
A119	20 Pounds 20.10.1904. Blue.	250.	500.	—
A120	50 Pounds ca. 1900's.	—	—	—
A121	100 Pounds ca. 1900's.	—	—	—

1919 Issue

		Good	Fine	XF
A123	1 Pound 1.8.1919. W/branch office listings ovpt. in 5-1/2 lines.	25.00	95.00	250.

1921 Issue

		Good	Fine	XF
A124	1 Pound 1.7.1921; 1.2.1922; 1.12.1926. Green. Reduced size.	20.00	60.00	125

Ulster Bank Limited

Belfast & Dublin

1900-18 Issue

#A131-A136 sailing ship, plow and blacksmiths at upper ctr. Various date and sign. varieties. Printe CS&E (w/o imprint).

		Good	Fine	X
A131	1 Pound 1902-18. Black on blue unpt.			
	a. 1.6.1909; 1.3.1912.	40.00	100.	25
	b. 1.6.1916; 2.7.1917; 1.10.1918.	25.00	80.00	17
	p. Proof w/o unpt. Perforated: *SPECIMEN* and printer's name. 1.12.1902; 1906; 2.5.1910; 1.12.1910.	—	—	

		Good	Fine	XF
A132	**5 Pounds** 1.5.1918. Black on green unpt.	75.00	200.	450.

		Good	Fine	XF
A133	**10 Pounds** 1900-17. Black on red unpt.			
	a. 1.8.1900; 1.1.1908.	125.	300.	—
	b. 1.6.1916; 1.2.1917.	100.	250.	—
A134	**20 Pounds** 1.10.1910. Black on blue unpt.	150.	350.	—
A135	**50 Pounds** 1.11.1904. Proof w/o unpt., perforated: *SPECIMEN* and printer's name.	—	—	—

		Good	Fine	XF
A136	**100 Pounds** 1.11.1904. Proof w/o unpt., perforated: *SPECIMEN* and printer's name.	—	—	—

1920 Issue

		Good	Fine	XF
A137	**1 Pound** 1920-24. Black on blue unpt. W/o branch office listings at l. or r. Reduced size.			
	a. Issued note. 1.10.1923; 1.10.1924.	30.00	75.00	150.
	p. Proof. 1.6.1920.	—	—	—

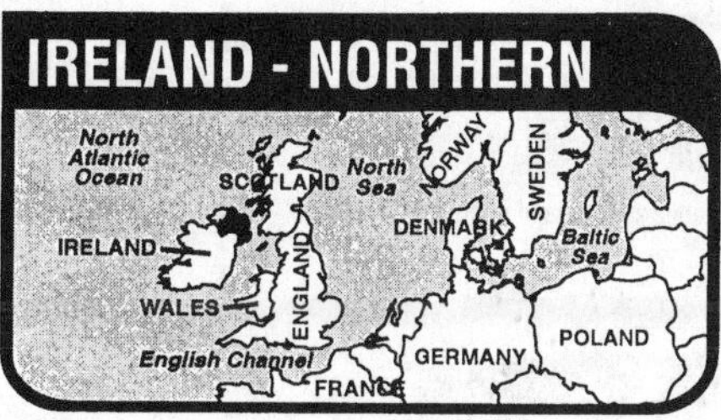

From 1800 to 1921 Ireland was an integral part of the United Kingdom. The Anglo-Irish treaty of 1921 established the Irish Free State of 26 counties within the Commonwealth of Nations and recognized the partition of Ireland. The six predominantly Protestant counties of northeast Ulster chose to remain a part of the United Kingdom with a limited self-government.

Up to 1928 banknotes issued by six of the nine joint stock commercial banks were circulating in the whole of Ireland. After the establishment of the Irish Free State, the commercial notes were issued for circulation only in Northern Ireland, with the Consolidated Banknotes being issued by the eight commercial banks operating in the Irish Free State.

RULERS:

British

MONETARY SYSTEM:

1 Shilling = 12 Pence
1 Pound = 20 Shillings to 1971
1 Pound = 100 New Pence, 1971-

British Administration

Bank of Ireland

Belfast

1929 Issue

#51-55 woman w/harp at l. and r., Medusa head across top. Bank crest on back.

		Good	Fine	XF
51	**1 Pound** 1929-36. Black on green and blue unpt.			
	a. Sign. J. H. Craig. 6.5.1929; 8.5.1929.	7.50	30.00	70.00
	b. Sign. G. W. Frazer. 3.4.1933; 9.3.1936.	5.00	20.00	60.00

#52-55 Mercury at ctr.

		Good	Fine	XF
52	**5 Pounds** 1929-58. Red and ochre.			
	a. Sign. J. H. Craig. 5.5.1929-15.5.1929.	17.50	35.00	125.
	b. Sign. G. W. Frazer. 15.8.1935-2.12.1940.	15.00	30.00	90.00
	c. Sign. H. J. Adams. 16.2.1942-20.12.1943.	12.50	17.50	70.00
	d. Sign. S. E. Skuce. 1.9.1958; 1.10.1958; 10.10.1958.	10.00	15.00	50.00

		Good	Fine	XF
53	**10 Pounds**			
	1929-43. Blue and green.			
	a. Sign. J. H. Craig. 9.5.1929; 14.5.1929.	30.00	80.00	250.
	b. Sign. H. J. Adams. 26.1.1942; 19.1.1943.	25.00	35.00	100.
54	**20 Pounds**			
	9.5.1929. Black on yellow-orange and lt. green unpt. Sign. J. H. Craig.	60.00	120.	450.

1936 ISSUE

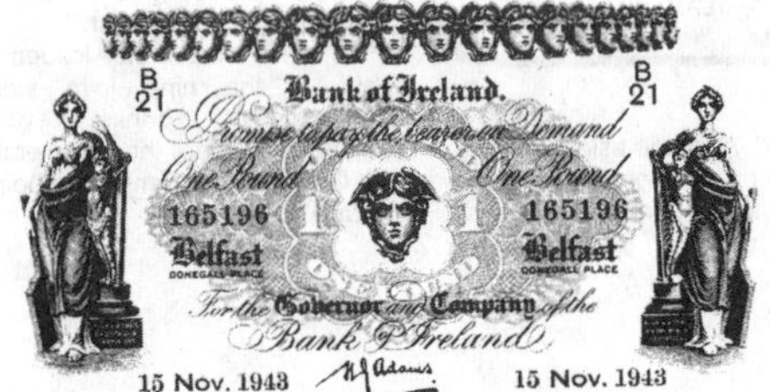

		Good	Fine	XF
55	**1 Pound**			
	1936-43. Black on gray-green and lt. blue unpt.			
	a. Sign. G. W. Frazer. 9.3.1936-1.11.1940.	3.00	7.50	50.00
	b. Sign. H. J. Adams. 23.2.1942-15.11.1943.	2.00	5.00	25.00

BELFAST BANKING COMPANY LIMITED

1922-23 ISSUE

#126-131 arms at top or upper ctr. w/payable text: . . . *at our Head Office, Belfast.*

#127-131 arms at top or upper ctr. w/payable text: . . . *at our Head Office, Belfast.*

		VG	VF	UNC
126	**1 Pound**			
	1922-40. Black on blue unpt.			
	a. Black serial #. 2.1.1922-8.11.1928.	6.00	35.00	100.
	b. Blue serial #. 9.11.1939; 10.8.1940.	3.00	12.00	50.00

		VG	VF	UNC
127	**5 Pounds**			
	1923-66. Black on red unpt.			
	a. Black serial #. 3.1.1923; 3.5.1923; 7.9.1927.	30.00	42.50	375.
	b. Red serial #. 8.3.1928-2.10.1942.	22.50	75.00	240.
	c. Red serial #. 6.1.1966.	18.00	45.00	130.

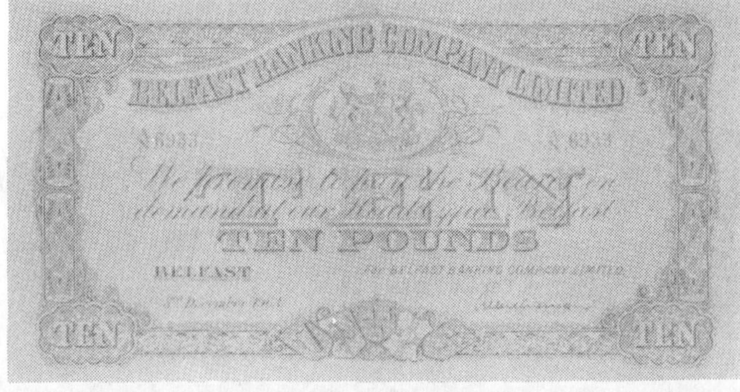

		VG	VF	UNC
128	**10 Pounds**			
	1923-65. Black on green unpt.			
	a. Black serial #. 3.1.1923.	90.00	160.	650.
	b. Green serial #. 9.1.1929-1.1.1943.	50.00	100.	300.
	c. Green serial #. 3.12.1963; 5.6.1965.	35.00	80.00	190.
129	**20 Pounds**			
	1923-65. Black on purple unpt.			
	a. Black serial #. 3.1.1923.	90.00	275.	850.
	b. Mauve serial #. 9.11.1939; 10.8.1940.	65.00	180.	425.
	c. Black serial #. 3.2.1943.	55.00	130.	350.
	d. Black serial #. 5.6.1965.	50.00	110.	275.

		VG	VF	UNC
130	**50 Pounds**			
	1923-63. Black on orange unpt.			
	a. Black serial #. 3.1.1923; 3.5.1923.	250.	475.	1100.
	b. Yellow serial #. 9.11.1939; 10.8.1940.	190.	325.	700.
	c. Black serial #. 3.2.1943.	150.	300.	650.
	d. Black serial #. 3.12.1963.	130.	275.	500.

		VG	VF	UNC
131	**100 Pounds**			
	1923-68. Black on red unpt.			
	a. 3.1.1923; 3.5.1923.	325.	800.	1400.
	b. 9.11.1939; 3.2.1943.	300.	650.	1100.
	c. 3.12.1963.	275.	500.	750.
	d. 8.5.1968.	275.	500.	700.

NATIONAL BANK LIMITED

1929 ISSUE

#151-154 arms at upper ctr.

		Good	Fine	XF
151	**1 Pound**			
	6.5.1929-1.8.1933. Black on green unpt.	12.00	25.00	75.00
152	**5 Pounds**			
	6.5.1929-1.10.1934. Blue on brown unpt.	35.00	75.00	200.
153	**10 Pounds**			
	6.5.1929; 2.10.1931; 1.8.1933. Green on brown unpt.	65.00	135.	350.
154	**20 Pounds**			
	6.5.1929. Brown on blue unpt.	125.	275.	600.

1937 ISSUE

#155-158 wmk: *THE NATIONAL BANK LIMITED* across bottom, man's head at l.

		VG	VF	UNC
155	**1 Pound** 1.2.1937; 1.9.1937; 2.10.1939. Black and green. Hibernia w/harp at ctr. Arms at l. on back.	10.00	25.00	85.00

		VG	VF	UNC
156	**5 Pounds** 1.2.1937; 1.9.1937; 2.10.1939. Blue and brown. Hibernia w/harp at lower l.	20.00	50.00	170.
157	**10 Pounds** 1.2.1937; 1.9.1937; 2.10.1939. Green and lt. brown. Hibernia w/harp at ctr.	40.00	95.00	250.
158	**20 Pounds** 1.2.1937; 2.10.1939. Brown and green. Hibernia w/harp at lower l.	75.00	200.	475.

1942 ISSUE

#159-161 wmk: *NATIONAL BANK LIMITED* at lower r. and D. O'Connell at l.

		VG	VF	UNC
159	**5 Pounds** 1.8.1942; 1.1.1949; 2.5.1949. Like #156.	17.50	37.50	125.
160	**10 Pounds** 1942-59. Like #157.			
	a. 1.8.1942; 2.5.1949.	35.00	85.00	200.
	b. 1.7.1959.	30.00	50.00	125.
161	**20 Pounds** 1942-59. Like #158.			
	a. 1.8.1942; 1.1.1949.	65.00	175.	375.
	b. 1.7.1959.	60.00	100.	250.

NORTHERN BANK LIMITED

1929 PROVISIONAL ISSUES

#171-177 new bank name ovpt. on notes of the Northern Banking Company Ltd.

		Good	Fine	XF
171	**5 Pounds** 1.9.1927. Ovpt. on #A70.	50.00	100.	200.
172	**10 Pounds** 1.3.1920. Ovpt. on #A71.	100.	200.	350.
173	**10 Pounds** 10.10.1921. Ovpt. on #A72.	100.	200.	350.
174	**20 Pounds** 20.10.1921. Ovpt. on #A73.	150.	300.	500.
175	**50 Pounds** 5.8.1914. Ovpt. on #A74.	175.	350.	600.

		Good	Fine	XF
176	**50 Pounds** 25.4.1918. Ovpt. on #A75.	175.	350.	600.

		Good	Fine	XF
177	**100 Pounds** 2.6.1919. Blue unpt. Ovpt. on #A76.	200.	400.	1000.

Note: Although certain notes are dated before 1922 they were actually issued later. See also Ireland-Republic.

1929 REGULAR ISSUE

#178; 181 sailing ship, plow and man at grindstone at upper ctr.

		VG	VF	UNC
178	**1 Pound** 1929-68. Black. Blue guilloche.			
	a. Red serial #. 6.5.1929; 1.7.1929; 1.8.1929.	22.50	65.00	160.
	b. Black prefix letters and serial #. 1.1.1940.	12.00	40.00	100.
	c. 1.10.1968.	10.00	30.00	70.00

		VG	VF	UNC
179	**5 Pounds** 6.5.1929. Black on dk. blue unpt.	25.00	90.00	200.
180	**5 Pounds** 1937-43. Black on green unpt. Imprint varieties.			
	a. Red serial #. 1.9.1937.	20.00	65.00	150.
	b. Black serial #. 1.1.1940-1.11.1943.	15.00	30.00	80.00

		VG	VF	UNC
181	**10 Pounds** 1930-68. Black on red unpt.			
	a. Red serial #. 1.1.1930-1.1.1940.	100.	225.	450.

		VG	VF	UNC
181				
	b. Black serial #. 1.8.1940; 1.9.1940.	70.00	150.	350.
	c. Red serial #. 1.1.1942-1.11.1943.	65.00	140.	300.
	d. Imprint on back below central design. 1.10.1968.		100.	180.
182	**50 Pounds** 1.1.1943. Black on dk. blue unpt. *NBC* monogram on back.	100.	200.	450.
183	**100 Pounds** 1.1.1943. Black on dk. blue unpt. *NBC* monogram on back.	200.	400.	750.

PROVINCIAL BANK OF IRELAND LIMITED

BELFAST

1929 ISSUES

#231-240 bank bldg. at upper ctr.

		VG	VF	UNC
231	**1 Pound** 1929-34. Green unpt. *ONE POUND* at lower l., *£1* at ctr. Back blue.			
	a. Sign. H. Robertson. 6.5.1929.	10.00	30.00	100.
	b. Sign. F. S. Forde. 1.2.1932; 1.4.1933; 1.6.1934.	10.00	30.00	75.00
232	**5 Pounds** 1929-36. Blue unpt. Shaded *£5* at ctr.			
	a. Sign. H. Robertson. 6.5.1929; 29.1.1931.	35.00	75.00	175.
	b. Sign. F. S. Forde. 5.5.1936.	30.00	65.00	150.

		VG	VF	UNC
233	**10 Pounds** 1929; 1934. Red-brown unpt. Similar to #238 but *£10* shaded at ctr. Back purple.			
	a. Sign. H. Robertson. 6.5.1929.	70.00	130.	325.
	b. Sign. F. S. Forde. 10.12.1934.	60.00	120.	300.

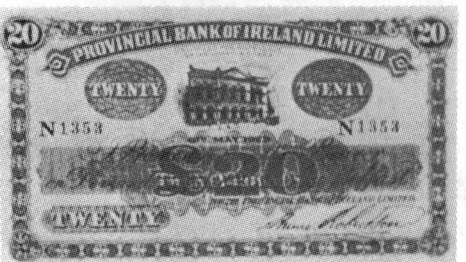

		VG	VF	UNC
234	**20 Pounds** 6.5.1929; 1.6.1929; 20.4.1943; 20.11.1944. Red-brown unpt. Similar to #238.	80.00	200.	450.

1935-38 ISSUE

		VG	VF	UNC
235	**1 Pound** 1935-46. Green unpt. Similar to #231 but *£1* outlined in white at ctr. Back green.			
	a. Sign. F. S. Forde. 1.8.1935; 2.11.1936.	12.00	30.00	80.00
	b. Sign. G. A. Kennedy. 2.11.1936-1.5.1946.	10.00	20.00	70.00

		VG	VF	UNC
236	**5 Pounds** 5.5.1938-5.4.1946. Brown unpt. Similar to #232 but *£5* outlined in white at ctr.	20.00	60.00	125
237	**10 Pounds** 10.10.1938-10.4.1946. Similar to #233 but *£10* outlined in white at ctr. Back red.	30.00	100.	225

1948; 1951 ISSUE

		VG	VF	UNC
238	**1 Pound** 1.9.1951. Green guilloche on pink unpt. Similar to #231 but *ONE* at lower l. Back green.	7.50	20.00	75.0
239	**5 Pounds** 5.1.1948-5.4.1952. Gray on brown and pink unpt. Similar to #232.	10.00	30.00	75.0
240	**10 Pounds** 10.1.1948. Green on red unpt. and green and pink mesh.			
	a. Sign. H. Robertson.	25.00	60.00	12
	b. Sign. F. S. Forde.	22.00	55.00	11
	c. Sign. G. A. Kennedy.	20.00	50.00	10

1954 ISSUE

		VG	VF	UNC
241	**1 Pound** 1.10.1954. Green. 148 x 84mm.	20.00	70.00	14
242	**5 Pounds** 5.10.1954-5.7.1961. Brown.	30.00	90.00	20

ULSTER BANK LIMITED

1929 PROVISIONAL ISSUE

		Good	Fine	X
301	**1 Pound** 6.5.1929 (- old date 1.12.1927). Sailing ship, plow and blacksmiths at upper ctr. Curved ovpt: *ISSUED IN NORTHERN IRELAND AFTER / 6th MAY, 1929.*	—	—	

NOTICE

Readers with unlisted dates, signature varieties, etc. are invited to submit photocopies or, high resolution (300 dpi, 100% size) scans of their notes to: Standard Catalog of World Paper Money, 700 East State St. Iola, WI 54990-0001, or E-Mail: george.cuhaj@fwpubs.com.

1929 REGULAR ISSUE

#306-311 sailing ship, plow and blacksmiths at upper ctr. w/curved ovpt: *NORTHERN IRELAND ISSUE*. Sign. varieties.

		Good	Fine	XF
306	**1 Pound** 1.6.1929-1.1.1934. Black on blue unpt. Hand signed. Uniface.	15.00	40.00	100.
307	**5 Pounds** 6.5.1929-1.1.1934. Black on green unpt. Like #306.	17.50	45.00	125.
308	**10 Pounds** 1.6.1929; 1.10.1930; 1.5.1933. Black on red unpt. Uniface.	40.00	110.	225.
309	**20 Pounds** 1.6.1929. Black on blue unpt. Similar to #306. Uniface.	60.00	150.	350.
310	**50 Pounds** 1.6.1929. Black on blue unpt. Similar to #306. Uniface.	150.	250.	500.
311	**100 Pounds** 1.6.1929. Black on blue unpt. Similar to #306. Uniface.	300.	500.	900.

1935-36 ISSUE

#312-314 sailing ship, plow and blacksmiths at upper ctr.

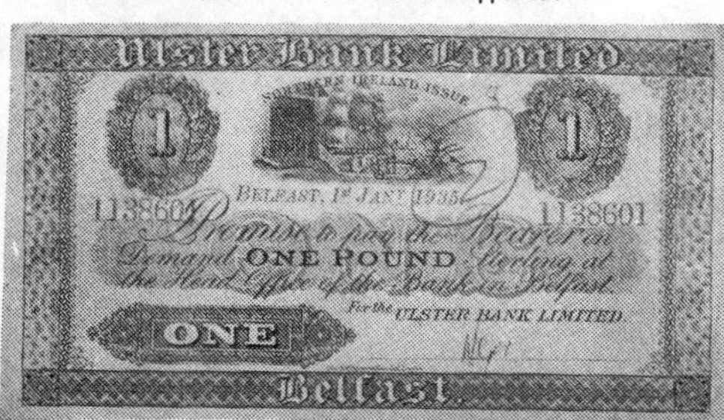

		Good	Fine	XF
312	**1 Pound** 1.1.1935-1.2.1938. Like #306 but bldg. w/o frame at ctr. on back.	12.00	35.00	100.
313	**5 Pounds** 1.1.1935; 1.1.1936; 1.10.1937. Like #307.	17.50	45.00	125.
314	**10 Pounds** 1.5.1936. Black on orange unpt. Back like #307.	35.00	80.00	185.

939-41 ISSUE

315-319 sailing ship, plow and blacksmiths at upper ctr.

		Good	Fine	XF
15	**1 Pound** 1939-56. Like #312 but bldg. within frame at ctr. on back.			
	a. Hand sign. 1.9.1939; 1.1.1940. 2 sign. varieties.	8.00	30.00	90.00
	c. Printed sign. 1.5.1956.	6.00	20.00	50.00
	p. Printed sign. Proof. 1.1.1948.	—	—	—

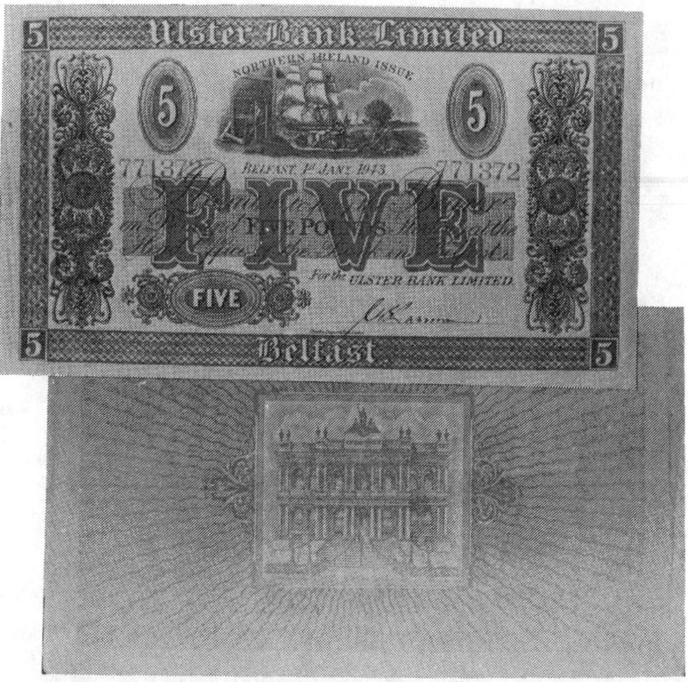

		Good	Fine	XF
316	**5 Pounds** 1939-56. Like #308.			
	a. Hand sign. 1.2.1939; 1.10.1940; 1.1.1942; 1.1.1943.	15.00	40.00	100.
	b. Printed sign. 1.5.1956.	12.50	35.00	80.00

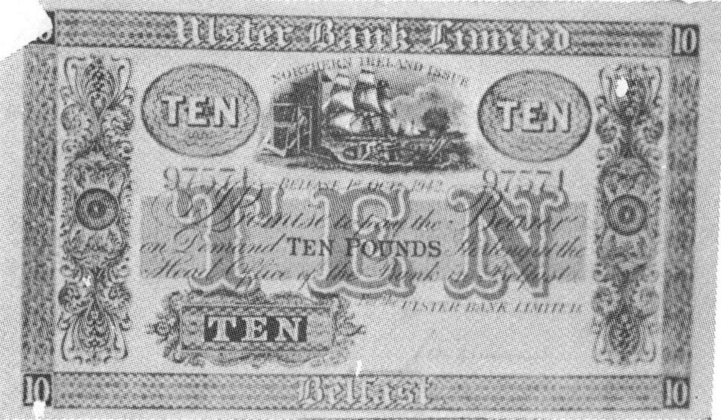

		Good	Fine	XF
317	**10 Pounds** 1.2.1939-1.1.1948. Back like #308.	25.00	65.00	150.

		Good	Fine	XF
318	**20 Pounds** 1.3.1941; 1.1.1943; 1.4.1943; 1.1.1944; 1.1.1948. Similar to #308.	55.00	125.	250.

NOTICE

Readers with unlisted dates, signature varieties, etc. are invited to submit photocopies or, high resolution (300 dpi, 100% size) scans of their notes to: Standard Catalog of World Paper Money, 700 East State St. Iola, WI 54990-0001, or E-Mail: george.cuhaj@fwpubs.com.

		Good	Fine	XF
319	**50 Pounds** 1.3.1941; 1.1.1943. Like #308.	125.	225.	600.

		Good	Fine	XF
320	**100 Pounds** 1.3.1941; 1.1.1943. Like #308.	250.	550.	1100.

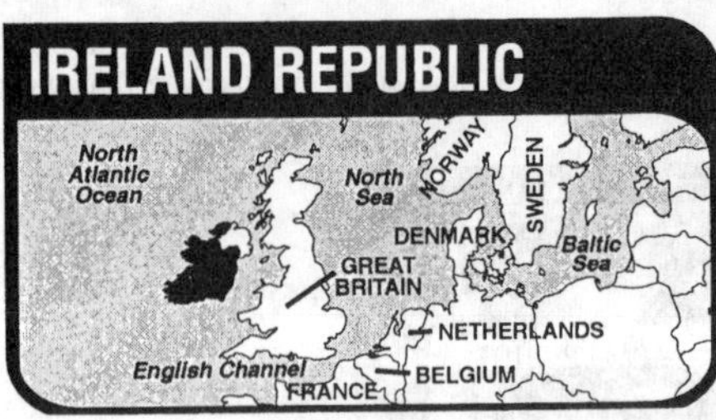

The Republic of Ireland (Éire) which occupies five-sixths of the Island of Ireland located in the Atlantic Ocean west of Great Britain, has an area of 27,135 sq. mi. (70,283 sq. km.) and a population of 3.71 million. Capital: Dublin. Agriculture and dairy farming are the principal industries. Meat, livestock, dairy products and textiles are exported.

The Irish Free State was established as a dominion on Dec. 6, 1921. Ireland withdrew from the Commonwealth and proclaimed itself a republic on April 18, 1949. The government, however, does not use the term "Republic of Ireland," which tacitly acknowledges the partitioning of the island into Ireland and Northern Ireland, but refers to the country simply as "Éire" or just "Ireland."

RULERS:

British

MONETARY SYSTEM:

1 Shilling = 12 Pence
1 Pound = 20 Shillings to 1971
1 Pound = 100 New Pence, 1971-2001
1 Euro = 100 Cents, 2002-

Printers: W&S 1928-1959, TDLR 1959-1976 (w/o imprint from either company on notes).

GOVERNMENT NOTES

All notes bilingual. 2 varieties of serial #, fractional or whole # prefixes. Each back has a different sculptured river-mask carved in the 18th century.

IRELAND

COIMISIÚN AIRGID REATHA SAORSTAT ÉIREANN

CURRENCY COMMISSION IRISH FREE STATE

1928 ISSUE

#1A-3A face portrait (head only) of Lady Hazel Lavery at l.

		Good	Fine	XF
1A	**10 Shillings** 10.9.1928-4.8.1937. Orange on purple and green unpt. River Blackwater river-mask on back.	10.00	45.00	135.

		Good	Fine	XF
2A	**1 Pound** 10.9.1928-23.12.1937. Green on orange and purple unpt. Rive Lee river-mask on back.	15.00	50.00	150.
3A	**5 Pounds** 10.9.1928-19.8.1937. Brown on orange and pink unpt. River Lagan river-mask on back.	25.00	70.00	225.

#4A-7 Lady Hazel Lavery in Irish national costume w/chin resting on her hand and leaning on an Irish harp. Lakes and mountains in background.

		Good	Fine	XF
4A	**10 Pounds** 10.9.1928-16.1.1933. Blue on green and purple unpt. River Bann river-mask on back.	60.00	125.	325.
5	**20 Pounds** 10.9.1928. Red on orange and purple unpt. River Boyne river-mask on back. Rare.	—	—	—
6	**50 Pounds** 10.9.1928. Purple on lt. brown and green unpt. River Shannon river-mask on back. Rare.	—	—	—
7	**100 Pounds** 10.9.1928-20.12.1937. Olive on lt. and dk. brown unpt. River Erne river-mask on back. Rare.	—	—	—

COIMISIÚN AIRGID REATHA ÉIRE

CURRENCY COMMISSION IRELAND

1938-39 ISSUE

		Good	Fine	XF
1B	**10 Shillings** 17.1.1938-20.12.1939. Similar to #1A.	7.50	20.00	100
2B	**1 Pound** 9.1.1939-8.12.1939. Similar to #2A.	10.00	25.00	140
3B	**5 Pounds** 5.7.1938-1.11.1939. Similar to #3A.	20.00	60.00	200
4B	**10 Pounds** 17.1.1938-14.12.1938. Similar to #4A.	40.00	100.	300

COIMISIÚN AIRGID REATHA ÉIRE

CURRENCY COMMISSION IRELAND

1940-41 ISSUE

#1C-4C identifying code letter in circle at top l. and bottom r. Such letters were to aid in keeping track of notes en route from England to Ireland.

No.	Denomination	Good	Fine	XF
1C	**10 Shillings** 30.7.1940-1.12.1941. Like #1A. Code letters: H; K; J.	3.00	10.00	90.00
2C	**1 Pound** 14.3.1941-22.9.1942. Like #2A. Code letters: T; B; P; V.	4.00	15.00	100.

No.	Denomination	Good	Fine	XF
3C	**5 Pounds** 12.9.1940-8.10.1942. Like #3B. Code letters: A; C; D.	15.00	40.00	200.
4C	**10 Pounds** 1940-42. Like #4B. Code letters: E; F.			
	a. W/o code letter. 2.7.1940.	32.50	75.00	300.
	b. W/code letters: E; F. 9.10.1941-5.10.1942.	30.00	70.00	275.

BANC CEANNAIS NA h-ÉIREANN

CENTRAL BANK OF IRELAND

1943-44 ISSUE

No.	Denomination	Good	Fine	XF
1D	**10 Shillings** 8.2.1943-28.3.1944. Similar to #1C. Code letters: L; M; R.	4.00	12.00	90.00
2D	**1 Pound** 3.2.1943-6.12.1944. Like #2C. Code letters: E-G.	6.00	17.50	100.
3D	**5 Pounds** 3.2.1943-14.7.1944. Like #3C. Code letters: M (brown); N (black); R (red).	12.50	35.00	200.
4D	**10 Pounds** 2.3.1943-11.12.1944. Like #4C. Code letters: B (purple); G (black); S (orange); W (blue).	30.00	75.00	250.
5D	**20 Pounds** 11.2.1943- 10.1.1944. Similar to #5.	100.	300.	—

CURRENCY COMMISSION

BANK OF IRELAND

1929 ISSUE

No.	Denomination	Good	Fine	XF
8	**1 Pound** 1929-39. Green on orange and purple unpt. Govt. bldg. on back.			
	a. Sign. J. Brennan and J. A. Gargon. 6.5.1929-4.10.1938.	15.00	60.00	275.
	b. Sign. J. Brennan and H. J. Johnston. 10.1.1939; 9.2.1939; 3.7.1939.	15.00	50.00	275.

No.	Denomination	Good	Fine	XF
9	**5 Pounds** 1929-39. Brown on green unpt. Bridge w/town behind on back.			
	a. Sign. J. Brennan and J. A. Gargon. 6.5.1929; 29.1.1931; 8.5.1931.	30.00	100.	350.
	b. Sign. J. Brennan and H. J. Johnston. 14.9.1939.	35.00	120.	375.
10	**10 Pounds** 6.5.1929. Blue on green and purple unpt. Entrance to ornate bldg. on back.	50.00	150.	500.
11	**20 Pounds** 10.6.1929. Deep red on pink and green unpt. Medieval castle on back.	—	—	—
12	**50 Pounds** 10.6.1929. Purple on gray and pink unpt. Mountains and valley on back.	—	—	—
13	**100 Pounds** 10.6.1929. Olive on brown unpt. Shoreline w/mountain landscape on back.	—	—	—

HIBERNIAN BANK LTD.

1929-31 ISSUE

#14-17 designs like previous issue.

No.	Denomination	Good	Fine	XF
14	**1 Pound** 1929-39. Green on orange and purple unpt.			
	a. Sign. J. Brennan and H. J. Campbell. 6.5.1929-4.5.1939.	15.00	60.00	275.
	b. Sign. J. Brennan and A. K. Hodges. 5.8.1939.	25.00	100.	300.

No.	Denomination	Good	Fine	XF
15	**5 Pounds** 1929-39. Brown on green unpt.			
	a. Sign. J. Brennan and H. J. Campbell. 6.5.1929; 15.3.1933; 4.1.1938; 5.8.1938.	25.00	150.	400.
	b. Sign. J. Brennan and A. K. Hodges. 8.5.1939.	45.00	175.	500.
16	**10 Pounds** 1931; 1939. Blue on green and purple unpt.			
	a. Sign. J. Brennan and H. J. Campbell. 5.12.1931.	55.00	250.	700.
	b. Sign. J. Brennan and A. K. Hodges. 24.7.1939.	—	—	—
17	**20 Pounds** 10.6.1929. Deep red on pink and green unpt.	—	—	—

#18 and 19 *Deleted*.

MUNSTER AND LEINSTER BANK LTD.

1929 ISSUE

#20-25 designs like previous issues.

No.	Denomination	Good	Fine	XF
20	**1 Pound** 1929-39. Green on orange and purple unpt.			
	a. Sign. J. Brennan and J. L. Gubbins. 6.5.1929-5.3.1935.	15.00	60.00	275.
	b. Sign. J. Brennan and A. E. Hosford. 7.2.1936-10.10.1939.	15.00	60.00	275.
21	**5 Pounds** 1929-39. Brown on green unpt.			
	a. Sign. J. Brennan and J. L. Gubbins. 6.5.1929; 15.3.1933.	30.00	100.	350.
	b. Sign. J. Brennan and A. E. Hosford. 7.4.1938; 9.3.1939.	30.00	100.	350.

No.	Denomination	Good	Fine	XF
22	**10 Pounds** 1929-38. Blue on green and purple unpt.			
	a. Sign. J. Brennan and J. L. Gubbins. 6.5.1929; 5.12.1931.	55.00	200.	550.
	b. Sign. J. Brennan and A. E. Hosford. 7.3.1938.	55.00	200.	550.
23	**20 Pounds** 10.6.1929. Deep red on pink and green unpt.	—	—	—
24	**50 Pounds** 10.6.1929. Purple on gray and pink unpt.	—	—	—

		Good	Fine	XF
25	**100 Pounds** 10.6.1929. Olive on brown unpt.	—	—	—

NATIONAL BANK LTD.

1929 ISSUE

#26-28 designs like previous issues.

		Good	Fine	XF
26	**1 Pound** 6.5.1929-2.9.1939. Green on orange and purple unpt.	15.00	60.00	275.

		Good	Fine	XF
27	**5 Pounds** 6.5.1929-5.1.1939. Brown on green unpt.	30.00	125.	400.
28	**10 Pounds** 6.5.1929; 2.10.1931. Blue on green and purple unpt.	55.00	250.	700.

#29-31 *Deleted.*

NORTHERN BANK LTD.

1929 ISSUE

#32-35 designs like previous issues.

		Good	Fine	XF
32	**1 Pound** 1929-31. Green on orange and purple unpt.			
	a. Sign. J. Brennan and S. W. Knox. 6.5.1929; 10.6.1929.	30.00	150.	450.
	b. Sign. J. Brennan and H. H. Stewart. 7.1.1931.	50.00	175.	475.
33	**5 Pounds** 1929-33. Brown on green unpt.			
	a. Sign. J. Brennan and S. W. Knox. 6.5.1929.	—	—	—
	b. Sign. J. Brennan and H. H. Stewart. 29.1.1931; 8.5.1931; 15.3.1933.	75.00	225.	750.
34	**10 Pounds** 6.5.1929. Blue on green and purple unpt.	125.	375.	950.
35	**20 Pounds** 10.6.1929. Deep red on pink and green unpt.	—	—	—

#36 and 37 *Deleted.*

PROVINCIAL BANK OF IRELAND LTD.

1929 ISSUE

#38-41 designs like previous issues.

		Good	Fine	XF
38	**1 Pound** 1929-39. Green on orange and purple unpt.			
	a. Sign. J. Brennan and H. Robertson. 6.5.1929; 10.6.1929.	15.00	60.00	275.
	b. Sign. J. Brennan and F. S. Forde. 7.1.1931-5.9.1936.	15.00	60.00	275.
	c. Sign. J. Brennan and G. A. Kennedy. 3.6.1937-4.11.1939.	15.00	60.00	275.

		Good	Fine	XF
39	**5 Pounds** 1929-39. Brown on green unpt.			
	a. Sign. J. Brennan and H. Robertson. 6.5.1929.	45.00	175.	500.
	b. Sign. J. Brennan and F. S. Forde. 29.1.1931; 8.5.1831.	45.00	175.	500.
	c. Sign. J. Brennan and G. A. Kennedy. 3.4.1939.	45.00	175.	500.
40	**10 Pounds** 1929; 1931. Blue on green and purple unpt.			
	a. Sign. J. Brennan and H. Robertson. 6.5.1929.	100.	300.	675.
	b. Sign. J. Brennan and F. S. Forde. 2.10.1931.	100.	300.	675.
41	**20 Pounds** 10.6.1929. Deep red on pink and green unpt.	—	—	—

#42 and 43 *Deleted.*

ROYAL BANK OF IRELAND LTD.

1929 ISSUE

#44-49 designs like previous issues.

		Good	Fine	XF
44	**1 Pound** 1929-39. Green on orange and purple unpt.			
	a. Sign. J. Brennan and G. A. Stanley. 6.5.1929; 10.6.1929.	12.50	50.00	250.
	b. Sign. J. Brennan and D. R. Mack. 7.1.1931-8.3.1939.	12.50	50.00	250.
	c. Sign. J. Brennan and J. S. Wilson. 2.5.1939; 5.6.1939; 6.9.1939.	12.50	50.00	250.
45	**5 Pounds** 1929-39. Brown on green and purple unpt.			
	a. Sign. J. Brennan and G. A. Stanley. 6.5.1929.	45.00	175.	500.
	b. Sign. J. Brennan and D. R. Mack. 29.1.1931; 8.5.1931.	45.00	175.	500.
	c. Sign. J. Brennan and J. S. Wilson. 21.9.1939.	45.00	175.	500.
46	**10 Pounds** 6.5.1929. Blue on green and purple unpt.	100.	300.	675.
47	**20 Pounds** 10.6.1929. Deep red on pink and green unpt.	—	—	—
48	**50 Pounds** 10.6.1929. Purple on gray and pink unpt.	—	—	—
49	**100 Pounds** 10.6.1929. Olive on brown unpt.	—	—	—

ULSTER BANK LTD.

1929 ISSUE

#50-55 designs like previous issues.

		Good	Fine	XF
50	**1 Pound** 1929-39. Green on orange and purple unpt.			
	a. Sign. J. Brennan and C. W. Patton. 6.5.1929-17.6.1935.	25.00	85.00	275.
	b. Sign. J. Brennan and C. W. Lester. 5.8.1937-4.12.1939.	25.00	85.00	275.
51	**5 Pounds** 1929-39. Brown on green unpt.			
	a. Sign. J. Brennan and C. W. Patton. 6.5.1929; 15.3.1933.	50.00	175.	475.
	b. Sign. J. Brennan and C. W. Lester. 3.5.1938; 7.2.1939.	50.00	175.	475.
52	**10 Pounds** 1929; 1938. Blue on green and purple unpt.			
	a. Sign. J. Brennan and C. W. Patton. 6.5.1929.	90.00	275.	625.
	b. Sign. J. Brennan and C. W. Lester. 9.8.1938.	90.00	275.	625.
53	**20 Pounds** 10.6.1929. Deep red on pink and green unpt.	—	—	—
54	**50 Pounds** 10.6.1929. Purple on gray and pink unpt.	—	—	—
55	**100 Pounds** 10.6.1929. Olive on brown unpt.	—	—	—

BANC CEANNAIS NA H-ÉIREANN

CENTRAL BANK OF IRELAND

1943-45 ISSUE

#56-62 like #1-7 of the Currency Commission, but w/*Central Bank of Ireland.* Below denomination is wording: *Payable to bearer on demand in London.*

#56-58 face portr. of Lady Hazel Lavery at l.

		VG	VF	UNC
56	**10 Shillings** 1945-59. Orange.			
	a. Deleted. See #1D.	—	—	—
	b. W/o letter ovpt. Sign. J. Brennan and J. J. McElligott. Lower sign. title w/*Runaidhe.* 15.5.1945-22.10.1952.	3.00	9.00	40.00
	c. Sign. J. J. McElligott and K. Redmond, lower sign. title w/*Runai.* 19.10.1955.	2.00	8.00	30.00
	d. Sign. J. J. McElligott and T. K. Whitaker. 28.5.1957; 11.3.1959; 1.9.1959.	1.50	5.00	30.00

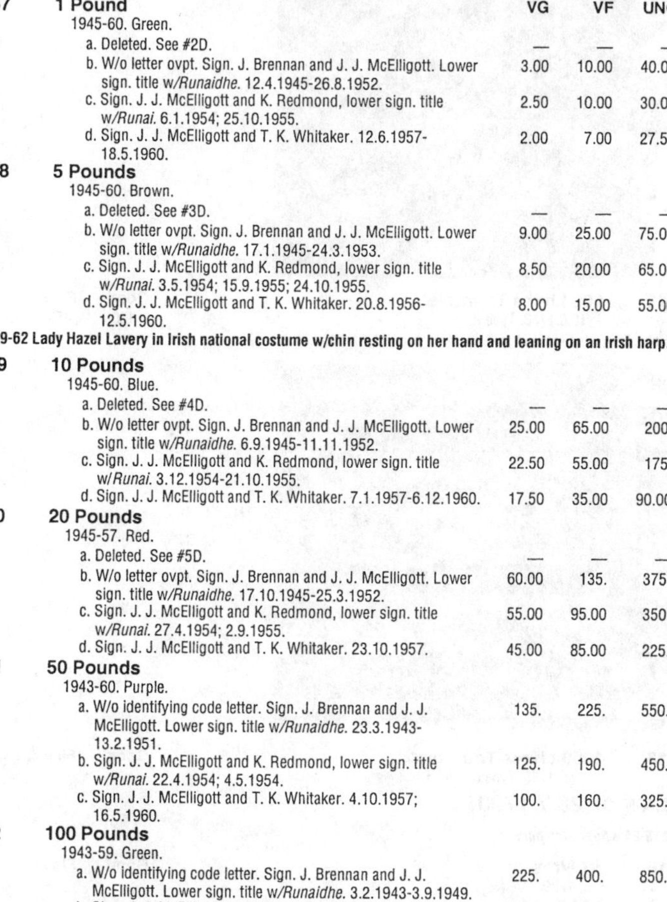

		VG	VF	UNC
57	**1 Pound** 1945-60. Green.			
	a. Deleted. See #2D.	—	—	—
	b. W/o letter ovpt. Sign. J. Brennan and J. J. McElligott. Lower sign. title w/*Runaidhe*. 12.4.1945-26.8.1952.	3.00	10.00	40.00
	c. Sign. J. J. McElligott and K. Redmond, lower sign. title w/*Runai*. 6.1.1954; 25.10.1955.	2.50	10.00	30.00
	d. Sign. J. J. McElligott and T. K. Whitaker. 12.6.1957-18.5.1960.	2.00	7.00	27.50
58	**5 Pounds** 1945-60. Brown.			
	a. Deleted. See #3D.	—	—	—
	b. W/o letter ovpt. Sign. J. Brennan and J. J. McElligott. Lower sign. title w/*Runaidhe*. 17.1.1945-24.3.1953.	9.00	25.00	75.00
	c. Sign. J. J. McElligott and K. Redmond, lower sign. title w/*Runai*. 3.5.1954; 15.9.1955; 24.10.1955.	8.50	20.00	65.00
	d. Sign. J. J. McElligott and T. K. Whitaker. 20.8.1956-12.5.1960.	8.00	15.00	55.00

#59-62 Lady Hazel Lavery in Irish national costume w/chin resting on her hand and leaning on an Irish harp.

		VG	VF	UNC
59	**10 Pounds** 1945-60. Blue.			
	a. Deleted. See #4D.	—	—	—
	b. W/o letter ovpt. Sign. J. Brennan and J. J. McElligott. Lower sign. title w/*Runaidhe*. 6.9.1945-11.11.1952.	25.00	65.00	200.
	c. Sign. J. J. McElligott and K. Redmond, lower sign. title w/*Runai*. 3.12.1954-21.10.1955.	22.50	55.00	175.
	d. Sign. J. J. McElligott and T. K. Whitaker. 7.1.1957-6.12.1960.	17.50	35.00	90.00
60	**20 Pounds** 1945-57. Red.			
	a. Deleted. See #5D.	—	—	—
	b. W/o letter ovpt. Sign. J. Brennan and J. J. McElligott. Lower sign. title w/*Runaidhe*. 17.10.1945-25.3.1952.	60.00	135.	375.
	c. Sign. J. J. McElligott and K. Redmond, lower sign. title w/*Runai*. 27.4.1954; 2.9.1955.	55.00	95.00	350.
	d. Sign. J. J. McElligott and T. K. Whitaker. 23.10.1957.	45.00	85.00	225.
61	**50 Pounds** 1943-60. Purple.			
	a. W/o identifying code letter. Sign. J. Brennan and J. J. McElligott. Lower sign. title w/*Runaidhe*. 23.3.1943-13.2.1951.	135.	225.	550.
	b. Sign. J. J. McElligott and K. Redmond, lower sign. title w/*Runai*. 22.4.1954; 4.5.1954.	125.	190.	450.
	c. Sign. J. J. McElligott and T. K. Whitaker. 4.10.1957; 16.5.1960.	100.	160.	325.
62	**100 Pounds** 1943-59. Green.			
	a. W/o identifying code letter. Sign. J. Brennan and J. J. McElligott. Lower sign. title w/*Runaidhe*. 3.2.1943-3.9.1949.	225.	400.	850.
	b. Sign. J. J. McElligott and K. Redmond, lower sign. title w/*Runai*. 21.4.1954; 1.5.1954.	200.	350.	750.
	c. Sign. J. J. McElligott and T. K. Whitaker. 14.10.1959; 11.11.1959.	200.	300.	500.

ISLES OF FRANCE AND OF BOURBON

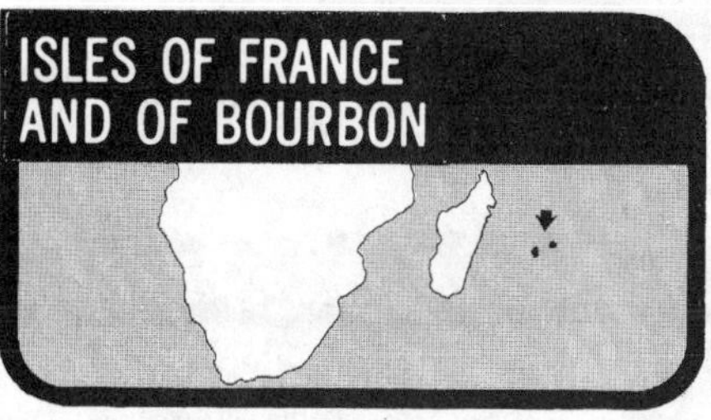

Isles of France and Bourbon (now the separate entities of Mauritius and Reunion), located in the Indian Ocean about 500 miles east of Madagascar, were at one time administered by France as a single colony, at which time they utilized a common currency issue. Ownership of Mauritius passed to Great Britain in 1810-14. Isle of Bourbon, renamed Reunion in 1793, remained a French possession and is now an overseas department.

RULERS:
French until 1810

MONETARY SYSTEM:
1 Livre = 20 Sols (Sous)

FRENCH ADMINISTRATION

ISLE DE BOURBON

1766 ISSUE

Note: Denominations of 10 and 20 Sous and 3 Livres are reported to have been issued.

		Good	Fine	XF
A1	**40 Sous Tournois** Dec. 1766. Crowned arms at top ctr. Uniface. Rare.	—	—	—

1793 ISSUE

#A3 and A5 w/text: *Papier de confiance et d'echange.*

		Good	Fine	XF
A3	**40 Sols Tournois** 11-13.4.1793.	—	—	—

		Good	Fine	XF
A5	**50 Livres Tournois** 11-13.4.1793.	—	—	—

ISLE DE LA RÉUNION

1793-94 ISSUE

#A6-A9 w/text: *Papier de confiance et d'echange.*

		Good	Fine	XF
A6	**20 Sols Tournois** 11.4.1793.	—	—	—
A7	**20 Sols Tournois** 10.5.1794.	—	—	—

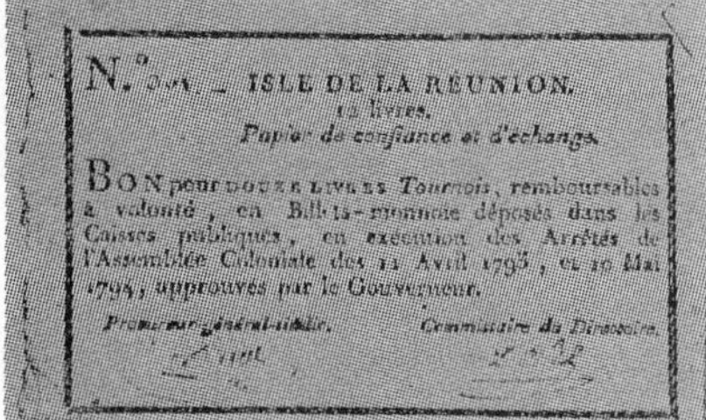

		Good	Fine	XF
A9	**12 Livres Tournois** 10.5.1794.	—	—	—

BURE DU CONSOLE

1768 ISSUE

		Good	Fine	XF
A12	**6 Livres** July 1768. Black. Uniface.	800.	2000.	—

ISLES DE FRANCE ET DE BOURBON

1768 ISSUE

		Good	Fine	XF
A15	**3 Livres Tournois** July 1768. Rare.	—	—	—
A16	**6 Livres Tournois** July 1768. Rare.	—	—	—
A17	**12 Livres Tournois** July 1768. Rare.	—	—	—

		Good	Fine	XF
A18	**24 Livres Tournois** July 1768. Rare.	—	—	—

ND Issue

#1-4 w/text: *Billet de...or Bon pour...*

Type I text: *Intendant general des Colonies*

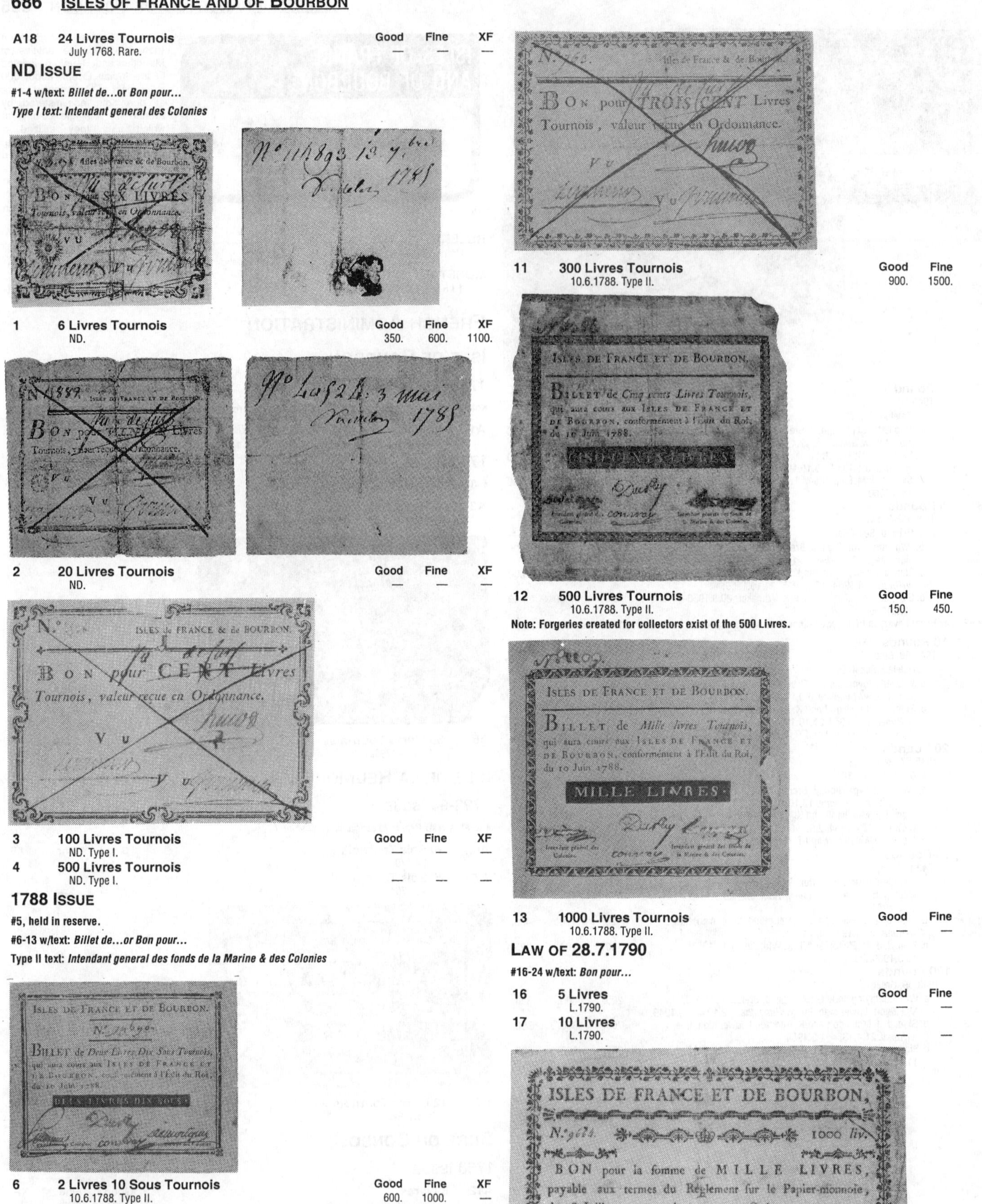

		Good	Fine	XF
1	**6 Livres Tournois** ND.	350.	600.	1100.

		Good	Fine	XF
2	**20 Livres Tournois** ND.	—	—	—

		Good	Fine	XF
3	**100 Livres Tournois** ND. Type I.	—	—	—
4	**500 Livres Tournois** ND. Type I.	—	—	—

1788 Issue

#5, held in reserve.

#6-13 w/text: *Billet de...or Bon pour...*

Type II text: *Intendant general des fonds de la Marine & des Colonies*

		Good	Fine	XF
6	**2 Livres 10 Sous Tournois** 10.6.1788. Type II.	600.	1000.	—
7	**5 Livres Tournois** 10.6.1788. Type II.	—	—	—
8	**10 Livres Tournois** 10.6.1788. Type II.	—	—	—
9	**50 Livres Tournois** 10.6.1788. Type II.	—	—	—
10	**100 Livres Tournois** 10.6.1788. Type II.	—	—	—

		Good	Fine	XF
11	**300 Livres Tournois** 10.6.1788. Type II.	900.	1500.	—

		Good	Fine	XF
12	**500 Livres Tournois** 10.6.1788. Type II.	150.	450.	—

Note: Forgeries created for collectors exist of the 500 Livres.

		Good	Fine	XF
13	**1000 Livres Tournois** 10.6.1788. Type II.	—	—	—

Law of 28.7.1790

#16-24 w/text: *Bon pour...*

		Good	Fine	XF
16	**5 Livres** L.1790.	—	—	—
17	**10 Livres** L.1790.	—	—	—

		Good	Fine	XF
22	**1000 Livres** L.1790. Wavy bar under title.			
	a. Off-white paper.	400.	800.	1600.
	b. Bluish paper. Rare.	—	—	—
	x. Error: inverted *D* in *DE BOURBON*. Rare.	—	—	—
23	**1000 Livres** L.1790. Straight bar under title.	400.	800.	1600.

		Good	Fine	XF
24	**10,000 Livres** L.1790. Rare.	—	—	—

1795-96 ISSUE

#26 and 28 w/text: *Bon pour...*

		Good	Fine	XF
26	**2 Livres 10 Sols** 1795. Black. Uniface.	—	—	—

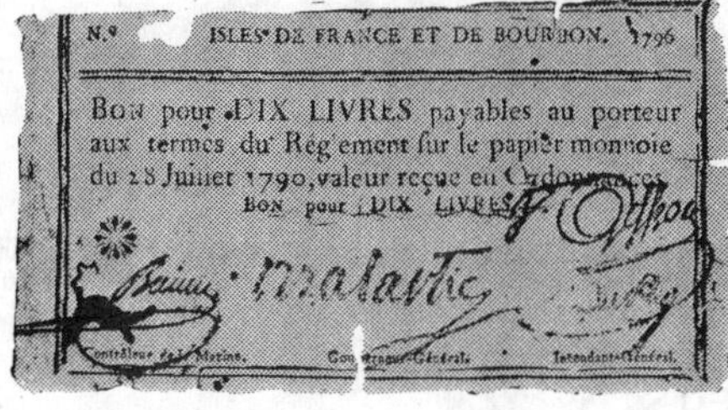

		Good	Fine	XF
28	**10 Livres** 1795-96. Black. Uniface.	—	—	—

Note: For later issues see Mauritius and Reunion.

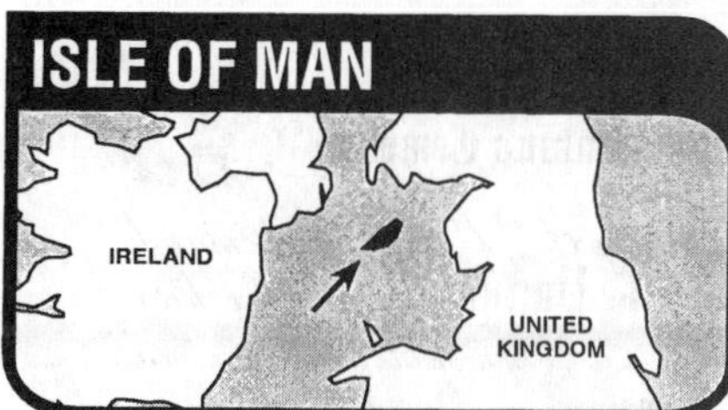

The Isle of Man, a dependency of the British Crown located in the Irish Sea equidistant from Ireland, Scotland and England, has an area of 227 sq. mi. (588 sq. km.) and a population of 71,714. Capital: Douglas. Agriculture, dairy farming, fishing and tourism are the chief industries.

The prevalence of prehistoric artifacts and monuments on the island gives evidence that its mild, almost sub-tropical climate was enjoyed by mankind before the dawn of history. Vikings came to the Isle of Man during the 9th century and remained until ejected by Scotland in 1266. The island came under the protection of the English Crown in 1288, and in 1406 was granted, in perpetuity, to the Earls of Derby. In 1736 it was inherited by the Duke of Atholl. Rights and title were purchased from the Duke of Atholl in 1765 by the British Crown; the remaining privileges of the Atholl family were transferred to the crown in 1829. The Sovereign of the United Kingdom (currently Queen Elizabeth II) holds the title Lord of Man. The Isle of Man is ruled by its own legislative council and the House of Keys, one of the oldest legislative assemblies in the world. Acts of Parliament passed in London do not affect the island unless it is specifically mentioned.

United Kingdom bank notes and coinage circulate concurrently with Isle of Man money as legal tender.

RULERS:

French until 1810

MONETARY SYSTEM:

1 Pound = 20 Shillings to 1971
1 Pound = 100 New Pence, 1971-
1 Guinea = 1 Pound 1 Shilling

BRITISH ADMINISTRATION

BARCLAYS BANK LIMITED

1924 ISSUE

		Good	Fine	XF
1	**1 Pound** 1924-60. Brown and green. Triskele in unpt. at ctr. Douglas harbor on back. Printer: W&S.			
	a. 7.6.1924-7.4.1937.	375.	750.	1500.
	b. 17.12.1937-4.12.1953.	100.	300.	600.
	c. 10.4.1954-10.3.1959.	80.00	150.	400.
	d. 30.3.1960.	100.	200.	450.

ISLE OF MAN BANKING CO. LIMITED

1865 ISSUE

#2-3, Douglas harbor at upper ctr. Triskele at ctr. on back. Printer: W. & A. K. Johnston Ltd., Edinburgh. Various date and sign. varieties.

		Good	Fine	XF
2	**1 Pound** 1865-1915. Black and brown. Vertical blue lines and border on back.	500.	1250.	—

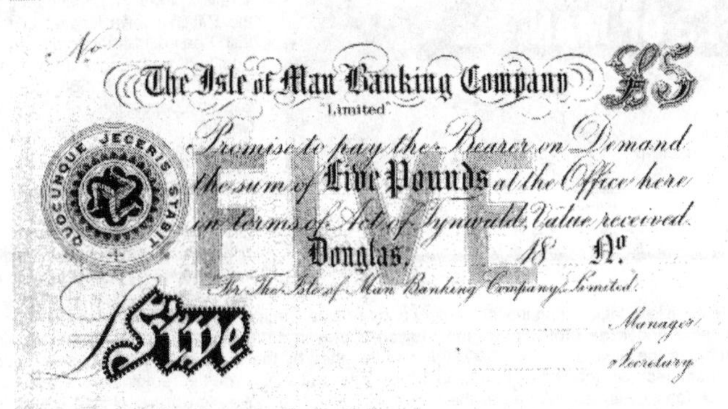

		Good	Fine	XF
3	**5 Pounds** 1894-1920. Black and blue. Seal of arms at l.			
	a. 1.11.1894; 1.1.1900; 4.12.1911; 7.8.1914; 1.3.1920.	2500.	5000.	—
	r. Unsigned remainder. ND.	—	—	—

1914 ISSUE

		Good	Fine	XF
3A	**1 Pound** 1914-26. Black and brown. Like #2 but w/o vertical blue lines or border on back.			
	a. 1.8.1914.	250.	600.	1500.
	b. 8.1.1916-1.3.1926.	150.	500.	1100.

ISLE OF MAN BANK LIMITED

1926-27 ISSUE

#4 and 5, Douglas harbor above bank title. Triskele at ctr. on back. Various date and sign. varieties.

		Good	Fine	XF
4	**1 Pound** 1.12.1926-4.9.1933. Black and pink. Printer: W. & A. K. Johnston Ltd., Edinburgh.	200.	400.	800.

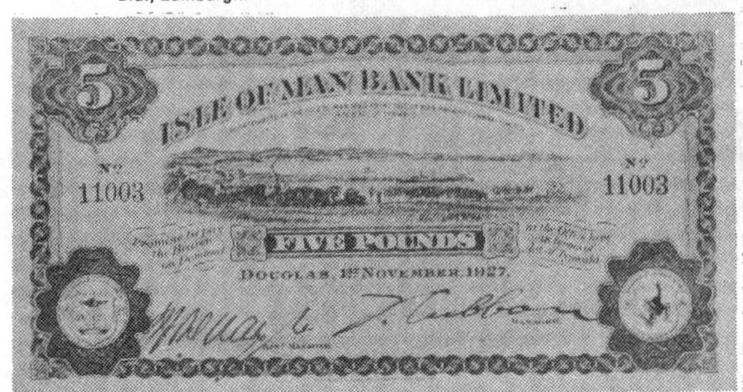

		Good	Fine	XF
5	**5 Pounds** 1.11.1927. Blue, green and pink. 2 sign. varieties. Printer: W&S.	40.00	175.	400.

1934-36 ISSUE

#6 and 6A Douglas harbor above bank title. Triskele at ctr. on back. Various date and sign. varieties. Printer: W&S.

		Good	Fine	XF
6	**1 Pound** 1934-60. Blue, brown and green.			
	a. 1.10.1934-5.5.1937.	40.00	100.	275.
	b. 4.2.1938-18.10.1952.	20.00	50.00	120.
	c. 1.12.1953; 29.11.1954. 2 sign. varieties.	40.00	90.00	175.
	d. 5.1.1956-24.10.1960.	20.00	50.00	150.
6A	**5 Pounds** 1936-60. Brown, pink and green. Like #5.			
	a. 1.12.1936.	50.00	175.	550.
	b. 3.1.1945; 7.4.1960.	150.	400.	1000.

LANCASHIRE & YORKSHIRE BANK LIMITED

MANX BANK

1904 ISSUE

#7-8, various date and sign. varieties.

		Good	Fine	XF
7	**1 Pound** 31.8.1904-30.10.1920. Slate gray. Tower of Refuge at ctr. Title: *MANX BANK / BRANCH OF THE / LANCASHIRE & YORKSHIRE BANK LIMITED*. Bank arms on back. Douglas.	275.	600.	1500.

1920 W/O BRANCH NAME ISSUE

		Good	Fine	XF
8	**1 Pound** 13.12.1920-28.12.1927. Slate gray. Bank arms at l., Tower of Refuge at r. Title: *LANCASHIRE & YORKSHIRE BANK LIMITED*. Castle Rushen at l., triskele at ctr., Laxey wheel at r. on back.	375.	850.	1750.

LLOYDS BANK LIMITED

1919-29 ISSUES

#9-13 various date and sign. varieties.

		Good	Fine	XF
9	**1 Pound** 23.4.1919-10.12.1920. Black and green.	350.	750.	1750.
10	**1 Pound** 23.3.1921-21.1.1927. Like #9 but pink unpt. *ONE POUND*.	350.	750.	1750.
11	**1 Pound** 1.8.1929-14.2.1934. Black and green on pink unpt. Text: *INCORPORATED IN ENGLAND* in 1 line.	300.	600.	1500.

1935 ISSUE

		Good	Fine	XF
12	**1 Pound** 1935-54. Like #11 but w/text: *INCORPORATED IN ENGLAND* divided. Letters of bank name w/shading on back.			
	a. 28.1.1935-27.4.1949.	175.	350.	850.
	b. 27.2.1951-26.2.1954.	100.	250.	500.

1955 ISSUE

		Good	Fine	XF
13	**1 Pound** 21.1.1955-14.3.1961. Black on green unpt. Bank arms at upper ctr. Like #12 but bank title enlarged on back.			
	a. Issued note.	90.00	180.	400.
	r. Unsigned remainder. ND.	—	—	120.

LONDON COUNTY WESTMINSTER AND PARR'S BANK LIMITED

1918 PROVISIONAL ISSUE

#14, various date and sign. varieties.

		Good	Fine	XF
14	1 Pound 28.3.1918-22.11.1918. Ovpt: *LONDON COUNTY WESTMINSTER* on #21.	500.	1000.	2400.

1919 REGULAR ISSUE

#15, various date and sign. varieties.

		Good	Fine	XF
15	1 Pound 11.10.1919; 11.1.1921; 25.11.1921. Like #14 but newly printed bank name. Printer: W&S.	500.	1000.	2400.

MANX BANK LIMITED

1882 ISSUE

#16, various date and sign. varieties.

		Good	Fine	XF
16	1 Pound 11.11.1882-30.5.1900. Black. Tower of Refuge at ctr. Printer: W&S.	500.	1000.	2000.

MARTINS BANK LIMITED

1928 PROVISIONAL ISSUE

		Good	Fine	XF
17	1 Pound 9.10.1928; 3.11.1928. Ovpt: *MARTINS BANK LIMITED* on #8.	500.	1000.	2000.

1928 ISSUE

#18-19, bank shield at l., Tower of Refuge at r. Castle Rushen at l., Albert Tower at r. on back.

		Good	Fine	XF
18	1 Pound 1929-38. Black. Bird on dk. hatched field in bank shield.			
	a. Red serial #. 2.4.1929; 1.12.1931; 31.12.1932.	150.	300.	725.
	b. Black serial #. 1.8.1934; 1.10.1938.	100.	200.	500.

1946 ISSUE

		Good	Fine	XF
19	1 Pound 1946-57. Black. Like #18 but bird on lightly stippled field in bank shield at l.			
	a. 1.3.1946.	50.00	130.	350.
	b. 1.6.1950; 1.5.1953; 1.2.1957.	20.00	50.00	200.

MERCANTILE BANK OF LANCASHIRE LIMITED

1901 ISSUE

#20, various date and sign. varieties.

		Good	Fine	XF
20	1 Pound 13.6.1901-6.9.1902. Black. Tower of Refuge at ctr. Like #16. Printer: W&S.	500.	1000.	2000.

PARR'S BANK LIMITED

1900 ISSUE

#21, various date and sign. varieties.

		Good	Fine	XF
21	1 Pound 1900-16. Gray. Crowned triskele supported by lion l., unicorn r.			
	a. Handwritten dates. 20.8.1900; 23.1.1901; 1.6.1906.	500.	1000.	2400.
	b. Printed dates. 2.4.1909-10.11.1916.	500.	1000.	2400.

WESTMINSTER BANK LIMITED

1923 PROVISIONAL ISSUE

#22, various date and sign. varieties.

		Good	Fine	XF
22	1 Pound 1923-27. Ovpt: *WESTMINSTER BANK LIMITED* on #15.			
	a. 4.7.1923; 17.12.1923; 5.2.1924.	500.	1000.	2000.
	b. 20.10.1924-4.4.1927.	500.	1000.	2000.

1929 REGULAR ISSUE

#23, various date and sign. varieties.

		Good	Fine	XF
23	1 Pound 1929-55. Black on lt. yellow unpt. Crowned triskele supported by lion l., unicorn r., at upper ctr. Printer: W&S.			
	a. 9.1.1929; 24.10.1929; 14.11.1933.	150.	300.	750.
	b. 22.1.1935-4.2.1943.	110.	225.	450.
	c. 11.2.1944-18.3.1949.	80.00	160.	400.
	d. 7.11.1950-30.3.1955.	60.00	125.	250.

1955 ISSUE

#23A, various date and sign. varieties.

		Good	Fine	XF
23A	1 Pound 1955-61. Black on lt. yellow unpt. Like #23 but w/text: *INCORPORATED IN ENGLAND* added below bank name. Printer: W&S.			
	a. 23.11.1955.	100.	200.	500.
	b. 4.4.1956-10.3.1961.	40.00	100.	225.

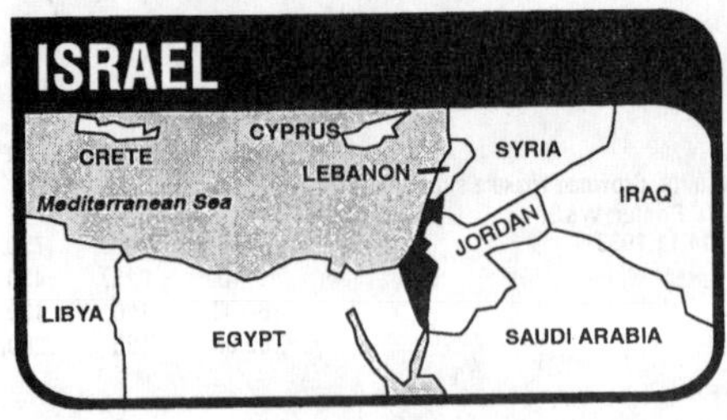

The State of Israel, at the eastern end of the Mediterranean Sea, bounded by Lebanon on the north, Syria on the northeast, Jordan on the east, and Egypt on the southwest, has an area of 7,847 sq. mi. (23,309 sq. km.) and a population of 6.08 million. Capital: Jerusalem. Diamonds, chemicals, citrus, textiles, and minerals are exported, local tourism to religious sites.

Palestine, which corresponds to Canaan of the Bible, was settled by the Philistines about the 12th century B.C. and shortly thereafter was invaded by the Jews who established the kingdoms of Israel and Judah. Because of its position as part of the land bridge connecting Asia and Africa, Palestine was invaded and conquered by nearly all of the historic empires of ancient Europe and Asia. In the 16th century it became a Turkish satrap. After falling to the British in World War I, it, together with Transjordan, was mandated to Great Britain by the League of Nations in 1922.

For more than half a century prior to the termination of the British mandate over Palestine in 1948, Zionist leaders had sought to create a Jewish homeland for Jews dispersed throughout the world. Israel was the logical location choice as it had long been the Jewish religious and cultural homeland. Also, for almost as long, Jews fleeing persecution had immigrated to Palestine. The Nazi persecutions of the 1930s and 1940s increased the Jewish relocation to Palestine and generated international support for the creation of a Jewish state, first promulgated by the Balfour Declaration of 1917 which asserted British support for the endeavor. The dream of a Jewish homeland was realized on May 14, 1948 when Palestine was proclaimed the State of Israel.

MONETARY SYSTEM:

1 Palestine Pound = 1000 Mils to 1948
1 Lira = 1000 Prutot, 1948-1960
1 Lira = 100 Agorot, 1958-1980
1 Sheqel = 10 "old" Lirot, 1980-85
1 Sheqel = 100 New Agorot, 1980-1985
1 New Sheqel = 1000 "old" Sheqalim, 1985-
1 New Sheqel = 100 Agorot, 1985-

STATE OF ISRAEL

ANGLO-PALESTINE BANK LIMITED

1948 PROVISIONAL ISSUE

Printed in the event that notes ordered might not be ready on time; destroyed in October, only a few sets preserved. #1-4 uniface.

		VG	VF	UNC
1	**500 Mils** 16.5.1948. Purple.			
	a. Issued note.	—	—	1500.
	s. Specimen.	—	—	1500.
2	**1 Palestine Pound** 16.5.1948. Green.			
	a. Issued note.	—	—	1500.
	s. Specimen.	—	—	1500.
3	**5 Palestine Pounds** 16.5.1948. Brown.			
	a. Issued note.	—	—	1500.
	s. Specimen.	—	—	1500.
4	**10 Palestine Pounds** 16.5.1948. Blue.			
	a. Issued note.	—	—	1500.
	s. Specimen.	—	—	1500.

#5 Not assigned.

		VG	VF	UNC
5	**50 Palestine Pounds** 16.5.1948. Proof examples only.	—	—	—

ISRAEL GOVERNMENT

Signature Varieties

1. Zagaggi	E. Kaplan
2. Zagaggi	L. Eshkol
3. A. Neeman	L. Eshkol

1952-53 ND FRACTIONAL NOTE ISSUES

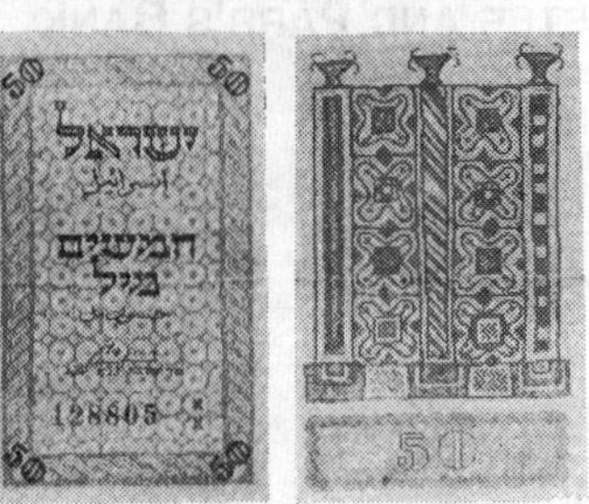

		VG	VF	UNC
6	**50 Mils** ND (printed 1948, issued 1952). Dk. red and orange. Vertical format.	30.00	75.00	300.

		VG	VF	UNC
7	**100 Mils** ND (printed 1948, issued 1952). Green. Vertical format.	30.00	75.00	300
8	**50 Pruta** ND (1952). Blue-black. Horizontal format. Sign. 1.	15.00	50.00	200

		VG	VF	UNC
9	**50 Pruta** ND (1952). Red on pink unpt. Back gray. Sign. 1.	10.00	25.00	100
10	**50 Pruta** ND (1952). Red on red or orange unpt. Back red or orange.			
	a. Sign. 1.	10.00	25.00	100
	b. Sign. 2.	10.00	25.00	100
	c. Sign. 3.	.75	3.00	7.5

		VG	VF	UNC
11	**100 Pruta** ND (1952). Green on lt. green unpt. Back gray. Sign. 1.	10.00	25.00	100
12	**100 Pruta** ND (1952). Blue on green unpt. Back green.			
	a. Sign. 1.	10.00	25.00	100
	b. Sign. 2.	10.00	25.00	100
	c. Sign. 3.	1.00	3.00	7.5
	d. Sign. 3 w/A. Neeman inverted (error).	500.	1200.	300

Note: Paper thickness varies.

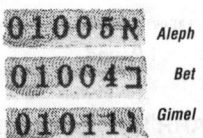

01005א *Aleph*

01004ב *Bet*

01011ג *Gimel*

		VG	VF	UNC
13	**250 Pruta** ND (1953). Dk. brown on green unpt. Back dk. green on orange unpt; Sea of Galilee w/Arbel mountain at ctr. r.			
	a. *Aleph* series w/menorah.	3.00	15.00	65.
	b. *Aleph* series w/o menorah.	2.50	12.50	45.

13

	VG	VF	UNC
c. *Bet* series w/o menorah.	2.50	10.00	35.00
d. *Gimel* series w/menorah at l.	3.00	15.00	75.00
e. *Gimel* series w/menorah at r.	3.00	15.00	75.00
f. *Aleph* series w/*250* under guilloche on face.	—	—	—

Note: *Aleph, Bet* and *Gimel* series refer to the first 3 letters of the Hebrew alphabet. The series suffix letter follows the serial #. On some series, a very faint gold-colored Menorah appears on face at upper l. or upper r. when exposed to ultra-violet lighting.

Anglo-Palestine Bank Limited

1948-51 ND Issue

#14-18 printer: ABNC (w/o imprint). Serial # varieties.

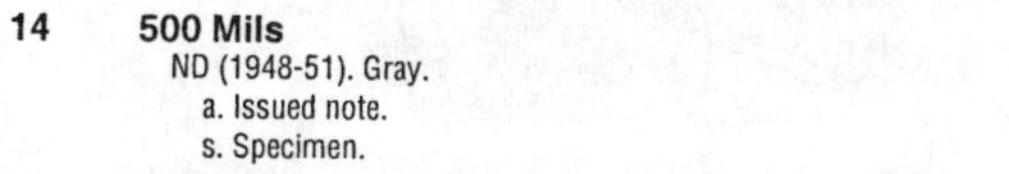

14 **500 Mils**

ND (1948-51). Gray.

	VG	VF	UNC
a. Issued note.	30.00	100.	750.
s. Specimen.	—	—	300.

15 **1 Pound**

ND (1948-51). Blue. Similar to #14.

	VG	VF	UNC
a. Issued note.	5.00	30.00	175.
s. Specimen.	—	—	300.

16 **5 Pounds**

ND (1948-51). Brown. Similar to #14.

	VG	VF	UNC
a. Issued note.	10.00	35.00	200.
s. Specimen.	—	—	300.

17 **10 Pounds**

ND (1948-51). Red. Similar to #14.

	VG	VF	UNC
a. Issued note.	15.00	60.00	300.
s. Specimen.	—	—	300.

18 **50 Pounds**

ND (1948-51). Lilac. Similar to #14.

	VG	VF	UNC
a. Issued note.	2000.	3250.	—
s. Specimen.	—	—	400.

Bank Leumi Le-Israel B.M.

1952 ND Issue

#19-23 similar to #14-18. Printer: ABNC (w/o Imprint).

19 **500 Prutah**

ND (9.6.1952). Gray-green on lt. blue unpt.

	VG	VF	UNC
a. Issued note.	8.00	75.00	550.
s. Specimen.	—	—	300.

20 **1 Pound**

ND (9.6.1952). Olive on pink unpt.

	VG	VF	UNC
a. Issued note.	4.00	15.00	55.00
s. Specimen.	—	—	300.

21 **5 Pounds**

ND (9.6.1952). Brown on yellow unpt.

	VG	VF	UNC
a. Issued note.	12.00	45.00	250.
s. Specimen.	—	—	300.

		VG	VF	UNC
22	**10 Pounds**			
	ND (9.6.1952). Gray on orange unpt.			
	a. Issued note.	15.00	75.00	375.
	s. Specimen.	—	—	300.

		VG	VF	UNC
23	**50 Pounds**			
	ND (9.6.1952). Dk. brown on lt. blue unpt.			
	a. Issued note.	200.	600.	1500.
	s. Specimen.	—	—	400.

Bank of Israel

1955 / 5715 Issue

#24-28 various geometric designs on back. Wmk: Menorah. Printer: TDLR (w/o imprint).

		VG	VF	UNC
24	**500 Pruta**			
	1955/5715. Red on green unpt. Ruin of an ancient synagogue near Bir'am at l., flowers at upper r. Modernistic design on back.			
	a. Issued note.	2.50	12.50	55.00
	s. Specimen.	—	—	150.

		VG	VF	UNC
25	**1 Lira**			
	1955/5715. Blue on m/c unpt. Landscape in Upper Galiiee across bottom, flowers at upper r.			
	a. Issued note.	3.00	15.00	65.00
	s. Specimen.	—	—	150.

		VG	VF	UNC
26	**5 Lirot**			
	1955/5715. Brown on lt. blue unpt. Negev landscape across ctr., flowers at upper r.			
	a. Issued note.	4.00	20.00	90.00
	s. Specimen.	—	—	150.

		VG	VF	UNC
27	**10 Lirot**			
	1955/5715. Dk. green on m/c unpt. Landscape in the Plain of Jezreel across ctr., flowers at upper r.			
	a. Red serial #.	5.00	17.50	55.00
	b. Black serial #.	4.00	15.00	50.00
	s. Specimen.	—	—	150.

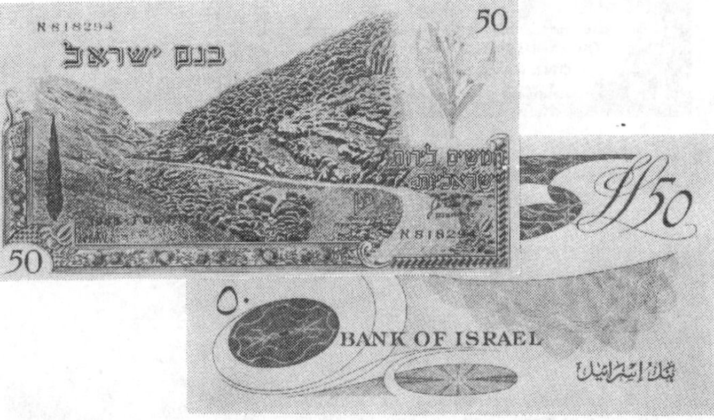

		VG	VF	UNC
28	**50 Lirot**			
	1955/5715. Dk. blue and m/c. Jerusalem Road between mountains, flowers at upper r. on face.			
	a. Black serial #.	12.50	50.00	150.
	b. Red serial #.	20.00	70.00	200.
	s. Specimen.	—	—	200.

1958-60 / 5718-20 Issue

Lira system

#29-33 wmk. as portrait.

#29, 30 and 33 printer: JEZ (w/o imprint).

29	1/2 Lira	VG	VF	UNC
	1958/5718. Green on green and peach unpt. Woman soldier w/basket full of oranges at l. Tombs of the Sanhedrin at r. on back.			
	a. Issued note.	.50	1.50	5.00
	s. Specimen.	—	—	295.

30	1 Lira	VG	VF	UNC
	1958/5718. Blue on lt. blue and peach unpt. Fisherman w/net and anchor at l. Synagogue mosaic at r. on back.			
	a. Paper w/security thread at l. Black serial #.	.50	1.25	4.00
	b. Red serial #.	.50	1.25	4.00
	c. Paper w/security thread and morse tape, brown serial #.	.50	1.00	3.00
	s. Specimen.	—	—	295.

#31 and 32 printer: TDLR (w/o imprint).

31	5 Lirot	VG	VF	UNC
	1958/5718. Brown on m/c unpt. Worker w/hammer in front of factory at l. Seal of Shema at r. on back.			
	a. Issued note.	.50	2.00	5.00
	s. Specimen.	—	—	295.

32	10 Lirot	VG	VF	UNC
	1958/5718. Lilac and purple on m/c unpt. Scientist w/microscope and test tube at l. Dead Sea scroll and vases at r. on back.			
	a. Paper w/security thread. Black serial #.	.50	2.00	10.00
	b. Paper w/security thread and morse tape. Red serial #.	.50	2.00	18.00
	c. Paper w/security thread and morse tape. Blue serial #.	.50	2.00	18.00
	d. Paper w/security thread and morse tape. Brown serial #.	.50	1.50	7.50
	s. Specimen.	—	—	295.

33	50 Lirot	VG	VF	UNC
	1960/5720. Brown and m/c. Boy and girl at l. Mosaic of menorah at r. on back.			
	a. Paper w/security thread. Black serial #.	2.00	10.00	45.00
	b. Paper w/security thread. Red serial #.	2.00	10.00	45.00
	c. Paper w/security thread and morse tape. Blue serial #.	1.50	6.00	45.00
	d. Paper w/security thread and morse tape. Green serial #.	1.50	6.00	30.00
	e. Paper w/security thread and morse tape. Brown serial #.	1.50	5.00	30.00
	s. Specimen.	—	—	400.

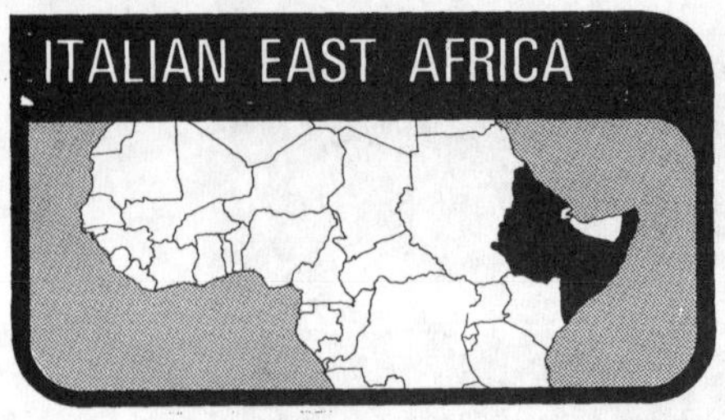

Italian East Africa was a former Italian possession made up of Eritrea (Italian colony since 1890), Ethiopia (invaded by Italy from Eritrea in 1935 and annexed in 1936) and Italian Somaliland (under Italian influence since 1889). Founded in 1936, it lasted until British-led colonial forces came into each of the areas in 1941.

ITALIAN OCCUPATION - WW II

BANCA D'ITALIA

AFRICA ORIENTALE ITALIANA

1938-39 ISSUE

Note: This issue circulated in all the Italian occupied areas and colonies in Africa.
#1-4 ovpt: *SERIE SPECIALE AFRICA ORIENTALE ITALIANA.*

		VG	VF	UNC
1	**50 Lire** 1938-39. Green on lt. green unpt. Head of Italia seal at r. Back blue-green; statue of she-wolf w/Romulus and Remus at ctr. Wmk: Man's head facing r.			
	a. 14.6.-12.9.1938.	12.50	60.00	325.
	b. 14.1.1939.	15.00	70.00	375.
2	**100 Lire** 1938-39. Blue-green on orange unpt. Reclining Roma w/shield and spear holding Victory, statue of she-wolf w/Romulus and Remus at bottom ctr. Back blue-green and brown; eagle and wreath at ctr.			
	a. 14.6.-12.9.1938.	15.00	70.00	375.
	b. 14.1.1939.	20.00	100.	600.

		VG	VF	UNC
3	**500 Lire** 1938-39. Blue and green. Peasant woman w/sheaf of grain and sickle at r. Back green and red-brown; crowned arms at l., Roma seated between allegorical male figures at ctr., fasces seal below.			
	a. 14.6.-12.9.1938.	90.00	275.	1100.
	b. 14.1.1939.	110.	350.	1500.

		VG	VF	UNC
4	**1000 Lire** 1938-39. Violet, brown and blue. 2 women (Venezia and Genova) reclining at bottom ctr. Back violet and green; allegorical woman seated between reclining male and Mercury at ctr. on back, fasces seal above.			
	a. 14.6.-12.9.1938.	75.00	260.	1050.
	b. 14.1.1939.	110.	360.	1600.

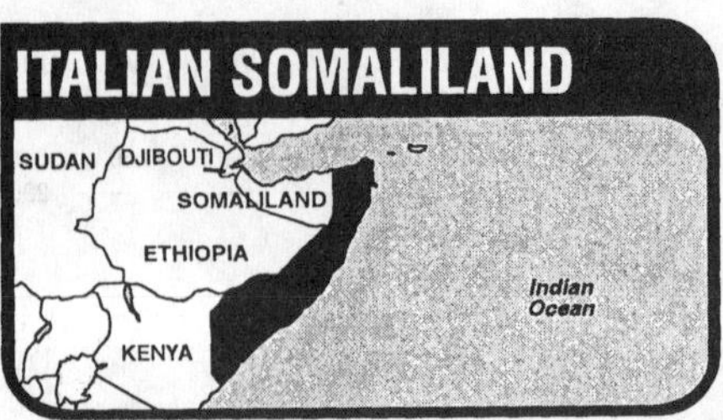

Italian Somaliland, a former Italian colony in East Africa, extended south from Ras Asir to Kenya. Area: 178,218 sq. mil. (461,585 sq. km.). Captial: Mogadisho.

In 1885, Italy obtained commercial concessions in the area from the sultan of Zanzibar,and in 1905 purchased the coast from Warshek to Brava. The Italians then extended their occupation inward. Cession of Jubaland Province by Britain in 1924, and seizure of the sultanates of Obbia and Mijertein in 1925-27 brought direct Italian administration over the whole territory. Italian dominance continued until World War II.

British troops occupied Italian Somaliland in 1941. Britain administered the colony until 1950, when it became a UN trust territory administered by Italy. On July 1, 1960, Italian Somaliland united with British Somaliland to form the independent Somali Democratic Republic.

RULERS:

Italian, 1892-1941, 1950-1960
British, 1941-1950

MONETARY SYSTEM:

1 Rupia = 100 Bese to 1925
1 Somali = 1 Lira = 100 Centesimi, 1925-1960
1 Shilling = 100 Cents, WW II British occupation

V. FILONARDI & CO.

1893 ISSUE

		VG	VF	UNC
1	**5 Rupias** 15.7.1893. Black on lt. green unpt. White 5-pointed star at ctr., embossed seal at l. Red Arabic text at l., denomination at lower r. on back.	200.	750.	1800.

BANCA D'ITALIA

SOMALIA ITALIANA

1920 BUONI DI CASSA ISSUE

		Good	Fine	XF
2	**1 Rupia** 1920-21. Black and red. Back brown.			
	a. 13.5.1920.	175.	500.	1200.
	b. 2.6.1921.	200.	700.	1500.

		Good	Fine	XF
3	**5 Rupias** 13.5.1920. Pink and brown. Back brown.	300.	1000.	3000.

		Good	Fine	XF
4	**10 Rupias** 13.5.1920. Yellowish brown and m/c. Back blue-green.	600.	1800.	5500.

#5 and #6 *Deleted*.

Cassa per la Circolazione Monetaria della Somalia

1950 Issue

		VG	VF	UNC
11	**1 Somali** 1950. Brown and yellow. Leopard at ctr.			
	a. Issued note.	125.	650.	1500.
	s. Specimen.	—	—	1250.
12	**5 Somali** 1950. Blue and yellow.			
	a. Issued note.	100.	500.	1350.
	s. Specimen.	—	—	1100.
13	**10 Somali** 1950. Green and yellow. 3 sign. varieties.			
	a. Issued note.	65.00	350.	900.
	s. Specimen.	—	—	750.

		VG	VF	UNC
14	**20 Somali** 1950. Brown and yellow. 3 sign. varieties.			
	a. Issued note.	65.00	350.	875.
	s. Specimen.	—	—	750.

		VG	VF	UNC
5	**100 Somali** 1950. Violet and lt. brown. Lion at l. 3 sign. varieties.			
	a. Issued note.	500.	1500.	3500.
	s. Specimen.	—	—	2350.

951 Issue

		VG	VF	UNC
6	**5 Somali** 1951. Brown-violet and lt. blue. Leopard at ctr. and as wmk. Like #11.	40.00	225.	600.

The Italian Republic, a 700-mile-long peninsula extending into the heart of the Mediterranean Sea, has an area of 116,304 sq. mi. (301,308 sq. km.) and a population of 57.46 million. Captal: Rome. The economy centers about agriculture, manufacturing, forestry and fishing. Machinery, textiles, clothing and motor vehicles are exported.

From the fall of Rome until modern times, "Italy" was little more than a geographical expression. Although nominally included in the Empire of Charlemagne and the Holy Roman Empire, it was in reality divided into a number of independent states and kingdoms presided over by wealthy families, soldiers of fortune or hereditary rulers. The 19th century unification movement fostered by Mazzini, Garibaldi and Cavor attained fruition in 1860-1870 with the creation of the Kingdom of Italy and the installation of Victor Emanuele, King of Italy. Benito Mussolini came to power during the post-World War I period of economic and political unrest, installed a Fascist dictatorship with a figurehead king as titular Head of State.

Mussolini entered Italy into the German-Japanese anti-Comintern pact (Tri-Partite Pact) and withdrew from the League of Nations. The war did not go well for Italy and Germany was forced to assist Italy in its failed invasion of Greece. The Allied invasion of Sicily on July 10, 1943 and bombing Rome brought the Fascist council to a no vote of confidence on July 24, 1943. Mussolini was arrested but soon escaped and set up a government in Saló. Rome fell to the Allied forces in June 1944 and the country was allowed the status of co-belligerent against Germany. The Germans held northern Italy for another year. Mussolini was eventually captured and executed by partisans. Following the defeat of the Axis powers the Italian monarchy was dissolved by plebiscite, and the Italian Republic proclaimed on June 10, 1946.

RULERS:

Umberto I, 1878-1900
Vittorio Emanuele III, 1900-1946

MONETARY SYSTEM:

1 Lira = 100 Centesimi, to 2001
1 Euro = 100 Cents, 2001-

DECREES:

There are many different dates found on the following notes of the Banca d'Italia. These include ART. DELLA LEGGE (law date) and the more important DECRETO MINISTERIALE (D. M. date). The earliest D.M. date is usually found on the back of the note while later D.M. dates are found grouped together. The actual latest date (of issue) is referred to in the following listings.

PRINTERS:

Further differentiations are made in respect to the printers w/the place name *Roma* or *L'Aquila* (1942-44).

NOTE: Certain listings encompassing issues circulated by various bank and regional authorities are contained in Volume 1.

FACE SEAL VARIETIES

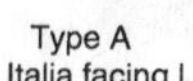

Type A
Italia facing l.

Type B
Facing head of Medusa

Type C
Winged lion of St. Mark of Venice above 3 shields of Genoa, Pisa and Amalfi

BACK SEAL VARIETIES

Type D
"Decreto Ministeriale De 30 Luglio 1896"
(17.7.1896-17.1.1930)

Type E
"Otto-Bre 1922"
w/fasces
(19.5.1926-6.8.1943)

Type F
Banco d'Italia monogram
(7.8.1943-21.3.1947)

KINGDOM

FEDERAL BIGLIETTI CONSORZIALE

LAW OF 30.4.1874

Note: All notes mention this law date, but Regal Decrees from 2.7.1875 to 3.11.1877 were the authorizing determinants.

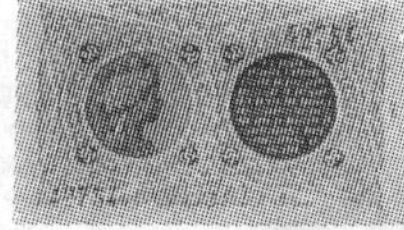

		Good	Fine	XF
1	**50 Centesimi** L. 1874. Black and blue on brown unpt. Back blue; Italia at l.	3.00	10.00	35.00

		Good	Fine	XF
2	**1 Lira** L. 1874. Black and brown on green unpt. Back brown; Italia at l.	2.00	8.00	30.00

		Good	Fine	XF
3	**2 Lire** L. 1874. Green and black on peach unpt. Italia at l. Back dk. green.	2.00	8.00	40.00

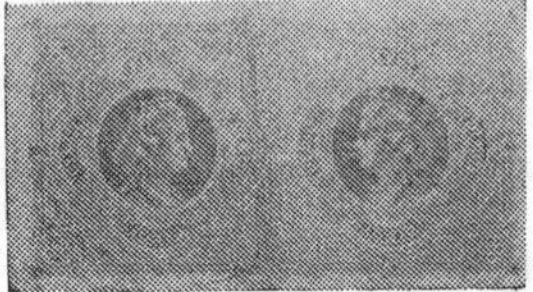

		Good	Fine	XF
4	**5 Lire** L. 1874. Brown, tan and black on lt. orange unpt. Back brown; Italia at l. and r.	2.00	8.00	30.00

		Good	Fine	XF
5	**10 Lire** L. 1874. Blue and black on brown unpt. Back blue; Italia at l. and r.	3.00	10.00	35.00
6	**20 Lire** L. 1874. Black text, blue on orange unpt. Arms at upper ctr., cherubs at lower ctr., ornamental border. Back black; crowned Italia at ctr.	60.00	180.	650.

		Good	Fine	XF
7	**100 Lire** L. 1874. Black text, blue on gold unpt. Crowned supported arms at top ctr., allegorical figures around border. Back dk. brown; crowned Italia at ctr.	50.00	160.	500.
8	**250 Lire** L. 1874. Black on brown unpt. Allegorical figures at bottom and around border. Back black on green unpt; crowned Italia at ctr.	120.	360.	1100.

		Good	Fine	XF
9	**1000 Lire** L. 1874. Black on lt. green unpt. Crowned supported arms at top ctr., allegorical women and cherubs at sides and bottom. Back black on lt. blue unpt; crowned Italia at ctr.	180.	700.	2200.

FEDERAL BIGLIETTI GIÀ CONSORZIALE

LAW OF 25.12.1881

Note: All notes mention this law date but Regal Decrees of 1881 and 1882 actually governed their issuance. Like previous issue, but different colors.

		Good	Fine	XF
10	**1 Lira** L. 1881. Black text, red on lt. tan unpt. Back red. Like #2.	3.00	10.00	50.00

		Good	Fine	XF
11	**2 Lire** L. 1881. Black text, blue on blue-gray unpt. Back blue. Like #3.	3.00	10.00	50.00
12	**5 Lire** L. 1881. Black text, lt. blue on gold unpt. Back lt. blue. Like #4.	40.00	200.	800.
13	**10 Lire** L. 1881. Black text, orange on green unpt. Back orange. Like #5.	40.00	250.	1000.
14	**20 Lire** L. 1881. Gray on blue unpt. Back gray. Like #6.	100.	400.	1500.
15	**100 Lire** L. 1881. Black and green on lt. blue unpt. Back blue and green. Like #7.	120.	600.	1800.
16	**250 Lire** L. 1881. Blue and green. Like #8. Unique.	—	—	—
17	**1000 Lire** L. 1881. Black and green. Like #9.	500.	3500.	10,000.

TREASURY BIGLIETTI DI STATO

1882-95 ISSUES

		VG	VF	UNC
18	**5 Lire** D.1882-92. Blue. Portr. Kg. Umberto I at l.			
	a. Sign. Dell'Ara and Crodara. 17.12.1882.	20.00	60.00	450.
	b. Sign. Dell'Ara and Pia. 6.8.1889.	30.00	120.	750.
	c. Sign. Dell'Ara and Righetti. 25.10.1892.	15.00	50.00	350.
19	**10 Lire** D.11.3.1883. Blue. Portr. Kg. Umberto I at l. on both sides. Sign. Dell'Ara and Crodara.	130.	500.	2200.

		VG	VF	UNC
20	**10 Lire** 1888-1925. Blue on pink unpt. Portr. Kg. Umberto I at l. Only denomination in oval at l. on back.			
	a. Sign. Dell'Ara and Crodara. 5.2.1888.	100.	200.	800.
	b. Sign. Dell'Ara and Pia. 6.8.1889.	20.00	50.00	350.

20

	VG	VF	UNC
c. Sign. Dell'Ara and Righetti. 25.10.1892.	6.00	15.00	100.
d. Sign. Dell'Ara and Altamura. 22.1.1911.	7.00	20.00	140.
e. Sign. Dell'Ara and Righetti. 23.4.1914.	6.00	12.00	90.00
f. Sign. Giu. Dell'Ara and Righetti. 11.10.1915.	6.00	12.00	90.00
g. Sign. Giu. Dell'Ara and Porena. 29.7.1918.	6.00	12.00	90.00
h. Sign. Maltese and Rossolini. 10.9.1923.	6.00	12.00	90.00
i. Sign. Maltese and Rosi Bernardini. 20.12.1925.	6.00	15.00	120.

21	25 Lire	VG	VF	UNC
	21.7.1895. Blue on pink unpt. "Italia" at l. Back green.	250.	800.	2800.

1902 ISSUE

22	25 Lire	VG	VF	UNC
	23.3.1902. Blue on orange unpt. Portr. Kg. V. Emanuele III at l. Heraldic eagle at r. on back.	2000.	4000.	12,000.

1904 ISSUE

23	5 Lire	VG	VF	UNC
	1904-25. Blue and black on pink unpt. Portr. Kg. V. Emanuele III at r.			
	a. Sign. Dell'Ara and Righetti. 19.10.1904.	2.00	6.00	60.00
	b. Sign. Dell'Ara and Altamura. 8.11.1904.	4.00	10.00	80.00
	c. Sign. Dell'Ara and Righetti. 29.3.1914.	2.00	10.00	90.00
	d. Sign. Giu. Dell'Ara and Righetti. 17.6.1915.	2.00	10.00	90.00
	e. Sign. G. Dell'Ara and Porena. 29.7.1918.	2.00	10.00	90.00
	f. Sign. Maltese and Rossolini. 10.9.1923.	2.00	10.00	90.00
	g. Sign. Maltese and Rosi Bernardini. 20.12.1925.	3.00	12.00	120.

REGNO D'ITALIA BIGLIETTO DI STATO

923 ISSUE

4	25 Lire	VG	VF	UNC
	20.8.1923. Brown. Similar to #42. Seals: Type A/E.			
	a. Sign. Maltese and Rossolini. Series 001-116.	140.	450.	2400.
	b. Sign. Maltese and Rosi Bernardini. Series 117-120.	800.	2400.	6500.

te: For similar type but headed *Banca d'Italia* and dated 1918-19, see #42.

1935 ISSUE

25	10 Lire	VG	VF	UNC
	1935; 1938-XVII; 1939-XVIII; 1944-XXII. Blue. Portr. Kg. V. Emanuele III at l. "Italia" at r. on back. Date at bottom ctr. edge. Wmk: Woman's head facing l.			
	a. Sign. Grassi, Rosi Bernardini and Collari. 18.6.1935.	1.00	2.00	40.00
	b. Sign. Grassi, Cossu and Collari. 1938.	2.00	6.00	70.00
	c. Sign. Grassi, Porena and Cossu. 1939; 1944.	1.00	2.00	35.00

1939; 1940 ISSUE

		VG	VF	UNC
26	**1 Lira** 14.11.1939. Dk. brown on lt. brown unpt. Caesar Augustus at ctr. on back.	.10	.30	3.00
27	**2 Lire** 14.11.1939. Blue-violet on pale lilac unpt. Julius Caesar on back.	.10	.30	4.00

28	5 Lire	VG	VF	UNC
	1940; 1944. Violet on brown unpt. Portr. Kg. V. Emanuele III at l. Date at bottom ctr. edge. Back blue on yellow unpt. eagle w/sword at ctr.	1.00	2.00	20.00

ITALIA - BIGLIETTO DI STATO

1944 ISSUE

29	1 Lira	VG	VF	UNC
	23.11.1944. Brown on pink unpt. "Italia" at l. Back green.			
	a. Sign. Ventura, Simoneschi and Giovinco.	.10	.25	3.00
	b. Sign. Bolaffi, Cavallaro and Giovinco.	.10	.25	3.00
	c. Sign. DiCristina, Cavallaro and Zaini.	.10	.25	5.00

30	2 Lire	VG	VF	UNC
	23.11.1944. Green on lt. orange unpt. "Italia" at l. Back orange or gold.			
	a. Sign. Ventura, Simoneschi and Giovinco.	.20	5.00	12.50
	b. Sign. Bolaffi, Cavallaro and Giovinco.	.20	.50	12.50

31 5 Lire
23.11.1944. Violet-brown. Archaic helmeted female head at l.

		VG	VF	UNC
31				
	a. Sign. Ventura, Simoneschi and Giovinco.	.10	.35	5.00
	b. Sign. Bolaffi, Simoneschi and Giovinco.	.10	.25	3.00
	c. Sign. Bolaffi, Cavallaro and Giovinco.	.10	.25	3.00

		VG	VF	UNC
32	**10 Lire** 23.11.1944. Blue. Jupiter at l. Engraved or lithographed. (The lithographed note has a blue line design in wmk. area at ctr.) 2 allegorical men on back.			
	a. Sign. Ventura, Simoneschi and Giovinco.	.10	.25	7.00
	b. Sign. Bolaffi, Simoneschi and Giovinco.	.10	.30	5.00
	c. Sign. Bolaffi, Cavallaro and Giovinco.	.10	.25	5.00

TREASURY BUONI DI CASSA

R. DECRETO 4.8.1893/DECRETO MINISTERIALE 22.2.1894

		VG	VF	UNC
33	**1 Lira** D.1893 (1893-94). Red-brown w/black text on green unpt. Portr. Kg. Umberto I at l. Back blue. Series 001-032. W/o wmk.	25.00	50.00	375.

1894 ISSUE

		VG	VF	UNC
34	**1 Lira** L.1894 (1894-98). Like #33. Series 033-119. Sign. Dell'Ara and Righetti. Wmk: Waves.	22.50	45.00	350.

		VG	VF	UNC
35	**2 Lire** D.1894 (1894-98). Dk. blue w/black text on grayish brown unpt. Portr. Kg. Umberto I at l. Back red-brown. Series 001-069.	80.00	180.	1000.

1914 ISSUE

		VG	VF	UNC
36	**1 Lira** D.1914 (1914-21). Dk. olive-brown on lt. blue unpt. Portr. Kg. V. Emanuele III at l. Back red; arms at ctr.			
	a. Sign. Dell'Ara and Righetti. Series 001-150 (1914-17).	2.00	5.00	30.00
	b. Sign. Giu. Dell'Ara and Righetti. Series 151-200.	2.00	5.00	30.00
	c. Sign. Giu. Dell'Ara and Porena. Series 200-266 (1921).	40.00	100.	400.

		VG	VF	UNC
37	**2 Lire** D.1914 (1914-22). Brown-violet on lt. red-brown unpt. Kg. V. Emanuele III at l. Back brown; arms at ctr.			
	a. Sign. Dell'Ara and Righetti. Series 001-075 (1914-17).	2.00	5.00	50.00
	b. Sign. Giu. Dell'Ara and Righetti. Series 076-100.	2.00	5.00	50.00
	c. Sign. Giu. Dell'Ara and Porena. Series 101-165 (1920-22).	2.00	5.00	50.00

BANCA D'ITALIA

BANK OF ITALY

DECRETO MINISTERIALE 30.7.1896 AND 12.9.1896

		VG	VF	UNC
38	**50 Lire** 1896-1926. Blue on green unpt. W/counterfoil, large letter *L* and woman w/3 children at l. Woman at r. on back. Seals: Type A/D.			
	a. Sign. Marchiori and Nazari. 12.9.1896; 9.2.1899.	100.	500.	1800.
	b. Sign. Stringher and Accame. 9.12.1899; 9.6.1910.	50.00	100.	750.
	c. Sign. Stringher and Sacchi. 2.1.1912-4.10.1918.	35.00	70.00	500.
	d. Sign. Canovai and Sacchi. 22.1.1919; 12.5.1919.	60.00	120.	700.
	e. Sign. Stringher and Sacchi. 15.8.1919-29.6.1926.	30.00	60.00	450.

NOTICE

Readers with unlisted dates, signature varieties, etc. are invited to submit photocopies or, high resolution (300 dpi, 100% size) scans of their notes to: Standard Catalog of World Paper Money, 700 East State St. Iola, WI 54990-0001, or E-Mail: george.cuhaj@fwpubs.com.

		VG	VF	UNC
39	**100 Lire** 1897-1926. Brown and pink. w/counterfoil, lg. *B* and woman seated w/small angels at l. Seals: Type A/D. Wmk: Head of Mercury.			
	a. Sign. Marchiori and Nazari. 30.10.1897.	120.	600.	2800.
	b. Sign. Marchiori and Accame. 9.12.1899.	150.	700.	3200.
	c. Sign. Stringher and Accame. 9.12.1899-9.6.1910.	40.00	100.	650.
	d. Sign. Stringher and Sacchi. 10.9.1911-4.10.1918.	35.00	90.00	600.
	e. Sign. Canovai and Sacchi. 22.1.1919; 12.5.1919.	60.00	140.	850.
	f. Sign. Stringher and Sacchi. 15.8.1919-8.9.1926.	35.00	90.00	600.
40	**500 Lire** 1898-1921. Dk. blue on pink-brown unpt. W/counterfoil, oval ornament w/allegorical figures. Seals: Type A/D. Wmk: Head of Roma.			
	a. Sign. Marchiori and Nazari. 25.10.1898.	1000.	2500.	7000.
	b. Sign. Marchiori and Accame. 25.10.1898-9.12.1899.	1400.	3500.	8500.
	c. Sign. Stringher and Accame. 9.12.1899-15.11.1909.	900.	2200.	6000.
	d. Sign. Stringher and Sacchi. 9.6.1910; 6.12.1918.	500.	1600.	4500.
	e. Sign. Canovai and Sacchi. 12.5.1919.	900.	2200.	5500.
	f. Sign. Stringher and Sacchi. 15.8.1919; 12.2.1921.	400.	900.	3400.
41	**1000 Lire** 1897-1920. Violet-brown and brown. W/counterfoil, lg. *M* at l. Seals: Type A/D. Wmk: Head of "Italia" at at r. and *1000* at l.			
	a. Sign. Marchiori and Nazari. 16.12.1897.	1500.	4000.	12,000.
	b. Sign. Marchiori and Accame. 2.12.1899.	1800.	5000.	14,000.
	c. Sign. Stringher and Accame. 9.12.1899; 9.6.1910.	1200.	3200.	6800.
	d. Sign. Stringher and Sacchi. 13.11.1911-1.7.1918.	400.	1200.	3000.
	e. Sign. Canavai and Sacchi. 22.1.1919.	500.	1800.	4000.
	f. Sign. Stringher and Sacchi. 15.8.1919-17.8.1920.	400.	1200.	3000.

1915-21 ISSUES

		VG	VF	UNC
42	**25 Lire** 1918-19. Deep brown on brown unpt. Medallic head of "Italia" at r., eagle w/flag above. Back blue-black on blue-gray; head of Minerva in oval at l. and as wmk. Seals: Type A/D.			
	a. Sign. Stringher and Sacchi. 24.1.1918; 1.7.1918.	100.	350.	1600
	b. Sign. Canavai and Sacchi. 22.1.1919; 12.5.1919.	100.	350.	1600

Note: For similar issue to #42 but headed *Regno d'Italia Biglietto di Stato* and dated 1923, see #24.

43 **50 Lire**

	VG	VF	UNC
1915-20. Black on orange unpt. Seated "Italia" at r. Farmer w/oxen on back. Seals: Type A/D. Wmk: Dante.			
a. Sign. Stringher and Sacchi. 15.6.1915; 4.10.1918.	100.	350.	2000.
b. Sign. Canovai and Sacchi. 22.1.1919-12.5.1919.	100.	325.	1800.
c. Sign. Stringher and Sacchi. 15.8.1919; 7.6.1920.	100.	350.	2000.

#44 Deleted, see #43.

5 **500 Lire**

	VG	VF	UNC
16.7.1919-13.4.1926. Olive-brown on violet and m/c unpt. Peasant woman w/sickle and sheaf at r. Crowned arms at l. Roma seated between allegorical male figures at ctr. Seals: Type A/D. Wmk: L. da Vinci. Sign. Stringher and Sacchi.	40.00	200.	800.

6 **1000 Lire**

	VG	VF	UNC
19.8.1921-8.8.1926. Voilet-brown and brown. W/o counterfoil. Seals: Type A/D. Wmk: Banca d'Italia at l., head of "Italia" at r. Sign. Stringher and Sacchi.	90.00	250.	1000.

926 Issue

47 **50 Lire**

	VG	VF	UNC
1926-36. Blue on green unpt. Like #38 w/counterfoil at l. Seals: Type A/D.			
a. Sign. Stringher and Sacchi. 8.9.1926-2.6.1928.	25.00	50.00	250.
b. Sign. Stringher and Cima. 15.1.1929-17.11.1930.	25.00	50.00	250.
c. Sign. Azzolini and Cima. 2.3.1931-17.3.1936.	25.00	50.00	250.

48 **100 Lire**

	VG	VF	UNC
1927-30. Brown and pink. W/counterfoil. Seals: Type A/E.			
a. Sign. Stringher and Sacchi. 12.2.1927-2.6.1928.	45.00	140.	600.
b. Sign. Stringher and Cima. 15.1.1929-17.11.1930.	45.00	140.	600.

49 **100 Lire**

	VG	VF	UNC
2.2.1926; 8.8.1926. Blue. W/o counterfoil. Seals: Type A/D. Wmk: Head of "Italia". Sign. Stringher and Sacchi.	90.00	320.	1200.

50 **100 Lire**

	VG	VF	UNC
1926-34. Blue. Seals: Type A/E. Like #49.			
a. Sign. Stringher and Sacchi. 18.11.1926; 12.2.1927; 9.4.1928.	40.00	125.	575.
b. Sign. Stringher and Cima. 12.4.1929-22.4.1930.	40.00	125.	575.
c. Sign. Azzolini and Cima. 2.3.1931-17.10.1934.	40.00	125.	575.

51 **500 Lire**

	VG	VF	UNC
1926-42. Violet and olive-brown. Seals: Type A/E. *ROMA* at end of imprint. Like #45 but back Seal: Type E.			
a. Sign. Stringher and Sacchi. 6.12.1926-21.6.1928.	35.00	80.00	550.
b. Sign. Stringher and Cima. 6.6.1929; 21.3.1930.	35.00	80.00	550.
c. Sign. Azzolini and Cima. 18.2.1932-16.10.1935.	30.00	75.00	450.
d. Sign. Azzolini and Urbini. 22.12.1937-23.3.1942.	30.00	75.00	425.

Note: For similar type but green w/ovpt: *AFRICA ORIENTALE ITALIANA* see Italian East Africa #3.

52 **1000 Lire**

	VG	VF	UNC
1926-32. Violet-brown and brown. W/o counterfoil. Seals: Type A/E.			
a. Sign. Stringher and Sacchi. 8.8.1926-21.6.1928.	60.00	140.	650.
b. Sign. Stringher and Cima. 12.4.1929; 5.12.1929; 20.10.1930.	60.00	140.	650.
c. Sign. Azzolini and Cima. 2.1.1932.	80.00	160.	900.

1930-33 Issue

54 **50 Lire**

	VG	VF	UNC
1933-40. Blue-violet and yellow brown on orange and yellow unpt. She/wolf w/Romulus and Remus on back. Seals: Type A/E. Wmk: Julius Caesar. *Roma* at end of imprint on back. 128 x 75mm.			
a. Sign. Azzolini and Cima. 11.10.1933-16.12..1936.	3.00	12.00	120.
b. Sign. Azzolini and Urbini. 30.4.1937; 19.8.1941.	3.00	12.00	100.

Note: For similar type but green w/ovpt: *AFRICA ORIENTALE ITALIANA* see Italian East Africa #1.

55 **100 Lire**

	VG	VF	UNC
1931-42. Olive and brown. Roma reclining w/spear and shield holding Victory, wolf w/twins at bottom ctr. Eagle and wreath at ctr. on back. Seals: Type A/E. Wmk: "Italia" and Dante. *ROMA* at end of imprint.			
a. Sign. Azzolini and Cima. 5.10.1931-16.12.1936.	5.00	12.50	240.
b. Sign. Azzolini and Urbini. 13.3.1937-11.6.1942.	5.00	12.50	225.

Note: For similar type but green w/ovpt: *AFRICA ORIENTALE ITALIANA* see Italian East Africa #2.

56 **1000 Lire**

1930-41. Black, blue, green, and brown. 2 women reclining at bottom ctr. (Venezia and Genova). 3 allegorical figures at ctr. on back. Seals: Type A/D. Wmk: "Italia" at l., Columbus at r. *ROMA* at end of imprint.

56		VG	VF	UNC
	a. Sign. Stringher and Cima. 7.7.1930.	35.00	120.	650.
	b. Sign. Azzolini and Cima. 28.6.1930-17.3.1936.	25.00	75.00	425.
	c. Sign. Azzolini and Urbini. 21.10.1938-13.11.1941.	25.00	75.00	425.

Note: For similar type but green w/ovpt: *AFRICA ORIENTALE ITALIANA* see Italian East Africa #4.

1941-42 Issue

57	50 Lire	VG	VF	UNC
	19.8.1941; 24.1.1942; 18.7.1942. Design like #54 but slightly reduced size. Sign. Azzolini and Urbini. 120 x 70mm.	4.00	20.00	420.

58	50 Lire	VG	VF	UNC
	28.8.1942-6.8.1943. blue-violet and yellow-brown on orange and yellow unpt. Like #54 but w/*L'AQUILA* at end of imprint. Seals: Type A/E. Sign. Azzolini and Urbini.	7.00	22.50	240.

59	100 Lire	VG	VF	UNC
	9.12.1942; 15.3.1943. Brown on yellow unpt. Seals: Type A/E. Sign. Azzolini and Urbini.	8.00	25.00	180.
60	100 Lire			
	28.8.1942-17.5.1943. Olive-green and brown. Seals: Type A/E. *L'AQUILA* at end of imprint. Sign. Azzolini and Urbini	9.00	25.00	260.

61	500 Lire	VG	VF	UNC
	21.10.1942; 18.1.1943; 17.5.1943. Olive-brown on violet and m/c unpt. Seals: Type A/E. *L'AQUILA* at end of imprint. Sign. Azzolini and Urbini.	60.00	125.	700.
62	1000 Lire			
	12.12.1942; 6.2.1943. Like #52. Seals: Type A/E. Sign. Azzolini and Urbini.	30.00	90.00	600.

63	1000 Lire	VG	VF	UNC
	28.8.1942-6.8.1943. Blue and brown. *L'AQUILA* at end of imprint. Sign. Azzolini and Urbini.	50.00	120.	750

1943 Issues

64	50 Lire	VG	VF	UN
	31.3.1943. Blue on green unpt. Like #47 but w/o counterfoil. Woman's head at r. on back. Seals: Type A/E. Sign. Azzolini and Urbini.	10.00	30.00	20
65	50 Lire			
	11.8.1943; 8.10.1943; 11.11.1944. Blue on green unpt. Like #64 but w/seals: Type A/F. Sign. Azzolini and Urbini.	10.00	30.00	22

66	50 Lire	VG	VF	UN
	23.8.1943; 8.10.1943; 1.2.1944. Blue-violet and yellow-brown. Like #58. Seals: Type A/F. Sign. Azzolini and Urbini.	15.00	35.00	22
67	100 Lire			
	1943-44. Brown on yellow unpt. Seals: Type A/F.			
	a. Sign. Azzolini and Urbini. 23.8.1943-11.11.1944.	12.50	60.00	32
	b. Sign. Introna and Urbini. 20.12.1944.	25.00	140.	55
68	100 Lire			
	23.8.1943; 8.10.1943. Olive-green and brown. Seals: Type A/F. Sign. Azzolini and Urbini.	15.00	60.00	42
69	500 Lire			
	31.3.1943. Dk. red on pink unpt. W/o counterfoil. Seals: Type A/E. Sign. Azzolini and Urbini.	35.00	80.00	55

		VG	VF	UNC
70	**500 Lire** 1943-47. Dk. red on pink unpt. Ornate border of allegorical figures. Seals: Type A/F. Wmk: Mercury.			
	a. Sign. Azzolini and Urbini. 23.8.1943-17.8.1944.	35.00	80.00	650.
	b. Sign. Introna and Urbini. 7.10.1944.	40.00	90.00	750.
	c. Sign. Azzolini and Urbini. 11.11.1944; 13.12.1945.	35.00	80.00	650.
	d. Sign. Einaudi and Urbini. 8.6.1945-19.2.1947.	35.00	80.00	650.
71	**500 Lire** 23.8.1943. Colors as #61. Seals: Type A/F. Sign. Azzolini and Urbini.	100.	250.	950.

		VG	VF	UNC
	1000 Lire 1943-47. Violet-brown and brown. Ornate border w/shield at upper ctr. Seals: Type A/F.			
	a. Sign. Azzolini and Urbini. 11.8.1943-1.8.1944; 11.11.1944.	20.00	50.00	400.
	b. Sign. Introna and Urbini. 7.10.1944; 30.11.1944.	25.00	80.00	500.
	c. Sign. Einaudi and Urbini. 8.3.1945-12.7.1947.	20.00	70.00	440.
	1000 Lire 23.8.1943; 8.10.1943. Blue and brown. Seals: Type A/F. Sign. Azzolini and Urbini.	50.00	160.	700.

INTERIM GOVERNMENT

BANCA D'ITALIA

1944 ISSUE

		VG	VF	UNC
74	**50 Lire** 10.12.1944. Green on pale orange unpt. Medallic head of "Italia" in oval at l. Seal: Type A. Wmk: *50.* Sign. Introna and Urbini.	1.00	10.00	60.00

		VG	VF	UNC
75	**100 Lire** 1944; 1946 Red on gray unpt. Medallic head of "Italia" at l. Seal: Type A. Wmk: *100.*			
	a. 10.12.1944. Sign. Introna and Urbini.	1.00	7.50	50.00
	b. 20.4.1946. Sign. Einaudi and Urbini.	1.00	7.50	50.00
76	**500 Lire** 10.12.1944. Dk. red on yellow unpt. Medallic head of "Italia" at l. (Not issued). Sign. Introna and Urbini. Rare.	—	—	—
77	**1000 Lire** 10.12.1944. Blue on blue-green unpt. Medallic head of "Italia" at l. (Not issued). Sign. Introna and Urbini. Rare.	—	—	—

REPUBLIC

BANCA D'ITALIA

BANK OF ITALY

1945 PROVISIONAL ISSUE

		VG	VF	UNC
78	**5000 Lire** 1945-47. Blue w/text: *Titolo provvisorio...* at l. and r. in head of "Italia" unpt. Seal: Type A. Wmk: Head of "Italia".			
	a. Sign. Einaudi and Urbini. 4.8.1945.	50.00	225.	900.
	b. Sign. Einaudi and Urbini. 4.1.1947-12.7.1947.	40.00	180.	700.
79	**10,000 Lire** 4.8.1945; 4.1.1947; 12.7.1947. Red-brown w/text: *Titolo provvisorio...* in head of "Italia" unpt. at l. and r. Seal: Type A. Wmk: Head of "Italia". Sign. Einaudi and Urbini.	45.00	200.	950.

1947 ISSUES

		VG	VF	UNC
80	**500 Lire** 1947-61. Purple on lt. brown unpt. "Italia" at l. Back purple on gray unpt. Seal: Type B. Wmk: Head of "Italia".			
	a. Sign. Einaudi and Urbini. 20.3.1947; 10.2.1948.	4.00	30.00	200.
	b. Sign. Carli and Ripa. 23.3.1961.	4.00	35.00	275.
81	**1000 Lire** 1947-50. Violet-brown and brown. Seals: Type B/F.			
	a. Sign. Einaudi and Urbini. 22.11.1947; 14.4.1948.	60.00	120.	850.
	b. Sign. Menichella and Urbini. 14.11.1950.	600.	1200.	3600.

		VG	VF	UNC
82	**1000 Lire** 20.3.1947. Purple and brown. "Italia" at l. Seal: Type A. Wmk: Head of "Italia". Back blue on gray unpt. Sign. Einaudi and Urbini.	5.00	35.00	275.
83	**1000 Lire** 20.3.1947. Like #82. Seal: Type B. Sign. Einaudi and Urbini.	4.00	15.00	150.
84	**5000 Lire** 17.1.1947. Green and brown. 2 women seated at lower ctr. (Venezia and Genova). Seal: Type A. Sign. Einaudi and Urbini.	250.	1200.	3500.

		VG	VF	UNC
85	**5000 Lire**			
	1947-63. Green and brown. 2 women seated at ctr. (Venezia and Genova). Woman at ctr. on back. Seals: Type A/F. Wmk: Dante at l., "Italia" at r.			
	a. Sign. Einaudi and Urbini. 17.1.1947; 27.10.1947; 23.4.1948.	50.00	175.	900.
	b. Sign. Menichella and Urbini. 10.2.1949; 5.5.1952; 7.2.1953.	45.00	125.	650.
	c. Sign. Menichella and Boggione. 27.10.1953; 4.3.1959; 12.5.1960.	45.00	125.	650.
	d. Sign. Carli and Ripa. 23.3.1961; 7.1.1963.	45.00	125.	650.

1947 Provisional Issue

		VG	VF	UNC
86	**5000 Lire**			
	1947-49. Blue. Like #78. Seal: Type B.			
	a. Sign. Einaudi and Urbini. 8.9.1947; 18.11.1947; 17.12.1947; 28.1.1948.	40.00	200.	600.
	b. Sign. Menichella and Urbini. 22.11.1949.	40.00	200.	600.
87	**10,000 Lire**			
	1947-50. Red-brown. Like #79 but w/seal: Type B.			
	a. Sign. Einaudi and Urbini. 8.9.1947; 18.11.1947; 17.12.1947; 28.1.1948.	25.00	60.00	350.
	b. Sign. Menichella and Urbini. 6.9.1949; 12.6.1950.	25.00	60.00	350.

1948 Issue

		VG	VF	UNC
88	**1000 Lire**			
	1948-61. Purple and brown. "Italia" at l. and as wmk. Back blue on gray unpt. Seal: Type B.			
	a. Sign. Einaudi and Urbini. 10.2.1948.	3.00	15.00	175.
	b. Sign. Menichella and Urbini. 11.2.1949.	4.00	30.00	275.
	c. Blue-gray. Sign. Menichella and Boggione. 15.9.1959.	3.00	15.00	175.
	d. Color like *c*. Sign. Carli and Ripa. 25.9.1961.	3.00	15.00	175.

		VG	VF	UNC
89	**10,000 Lire**			
	1948-62. Brown, orange and m/c. 2 women seated at ctr. (Venezia and Genova). Seal: Type B. Wmk: Verdi at l., Galilei at r.			
	a. Sign. Einaudi and Urbini. 8.5.1948.	35.00	90.00	600.
	b. Sign. Menichella and Urbini. 10.2.1949-7.2.1953.	35.00	75.00	550.
	c. Sign. Menichella and Boggione. 27.10.1953-12.5.1960.	35.00	75.00	550.
	d. Sign. Carli and Ripa. 23.3.1961-24.3.1962.	30.00	75.00	500.

1950 Issue

		VG	VF	UNC
90	**500 Lire**			
	14.11.1950. Dk. red on pink unpt. Seals: Type B/F. Sign. Menichella and Urbini.	800.	3500.	7500.

Repubblica Italiana - Biglietto di Stato

1951 Issue

		VG	VF	UNC
91	**50 Lire**			
	31.12.1951. Green on yellow unpt. "Italia" at l.			
	a. Sign. Bolaffi, Cavallaro and Giovinco.	1.00	6.00	55.00
	b. Sign. DiCristina, Cavallaro and Parisi.	1.50	10.00	90.00

		VG	VF	UNC
92	**100 Lire**			
	31.12.1951. Deep red, violet border on yellow unpt. "Italia" at l. Back red on yellow unpt.			
	a. Sign. Bolaffi, Cavallaro and Giovinco.	1.00	6.00	55.00
	b. Sign. DiCristina, Cavallaro and Parisi.	1.50	10.00	90.00

Military

Cassa Veneta dei Prestiti

Currency Notes

Buoni di Cassa

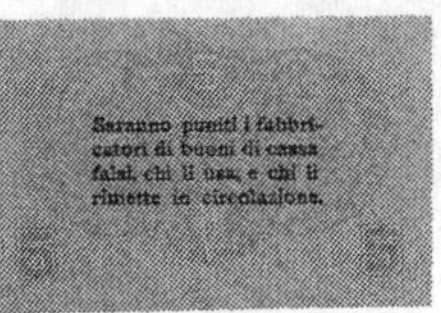

		VG	VF	UNC
M1	**5 Centesimi**			
	2.1.1918. Black on blue unpt. Serial # w/ or w/o *No.*	.50	1.00	3.00

		VG	VF	UNC
M2	**10 Centesimi**			
	2.1.1918. Black on lt. brown unpt.	.50	1.00	3.00
M3	**50 Centesimi**			
	2.1.1918. Black on red unpt.	.50	1.00	3.00

#M4-M9 "Italia" at l.

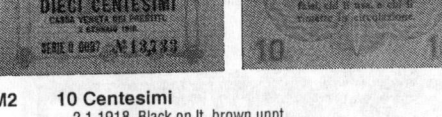

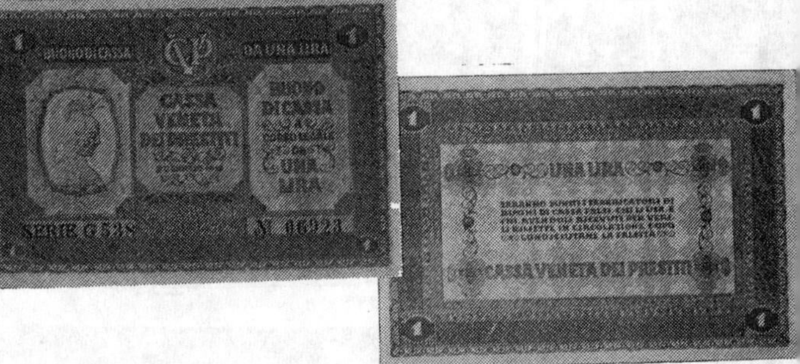

		VG	VF	UNC
M4	**1 Lira**			
	2.1.1918. Lilac. 2 serial # varieties.	1.00	2.00	4.0
M5	**2 Lire**			
	2.1.1918. Green. 3 serial # varieties.	1.00	2.50	5.0

		VG	VF	UNC
M6	**10 Lire**			
	2.1.1918. Blue. 2 serial # varieties.	1.50	5.00	10.

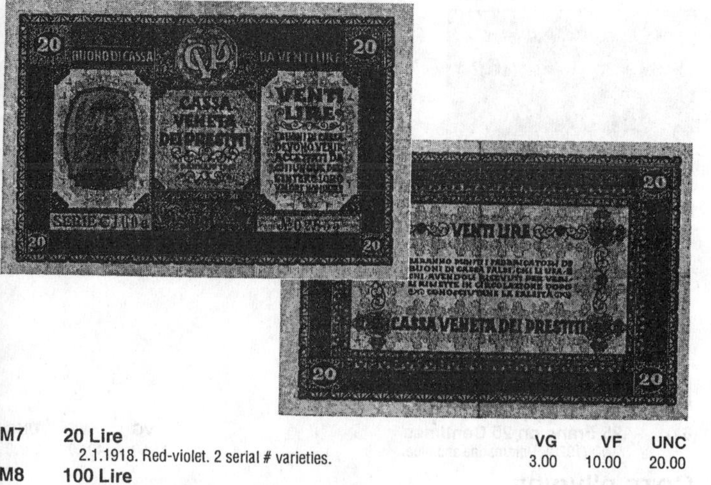

		VG	VF	UNC
M7	**20 Lire** 2.1.1918. Red-violet. 2 serial # varieties.	3.00	10.00	20.00
M8	**100 Lire** 2.1.1918. Brown and green.	15.00	50.00	100.
M9	**1000 Lire** 2.1.1918. Brown.	65.00	175.	650.

ALLIED MILITARY CURRENCY

SERIES 1943

		VG	VF	UNC
M10	**1 Lira** 1943. Blue and brown.			
	a. *F.*	.20	1.00	5.00
	b. W/o *F.*	.20	1.00	5.00
M11	**2 Lire** 1943. Violet and brown.			
	a. *F.*	.20	1.00	6.00
	b. W/o *F.*	.20	1.00	6.00
M12	**5 Lire** 1943. Green and brown.			
	a. *F.*	.30	1.25	12.50
	b. W/o *F.*	.30	2.00	15.00

		VG	VF	UNC
13	**10 Lire** 1943. Black and brown.			
	a. *F.*	1.00	7.00	50.00
	b. W/o *F.*	1.00	8.00	55.00
14	**50 Lire** 1943. Blue.			
	a. *F.*	2.00	7.50	75.00
	b. W/o *F.*	3.00	10.00	85.00
15	**100 Lire** 1943. Violet and blue.			
	a. *F.*	4.00	10.00	100.
	b. W/o *F.*	4.00	12.50	125.
16	**500 Lire** 1943. Green and blue.			
	a. *F.*	35.00	150.	600.
	b. W/o *F.*	40.00	175.	700.

		VG	VF	UNC
M17	**1000 Lire** 1943. Black and blue.			
	a. *F.*	80.00	225.	900.
	b. W/o *F.*	75.00	200.	850.

SERIES OF 1943 A

Printer: Forbes.

		VG	VF	UNC
M18	**5 Lire** 1943. A. Green and brown.			
	a. Serial # prefix/suffix A-A.	.50	1.50	7.50
	b. Serial # prefix/suffix A-B.	.50	1.50	7.50
	s. Specimen perforated: *SPECIMEN.*	—	—	140.
M19	**10 Lire** 1943 A. Black and brown.			
	a. Serial # prefix/suffix A-A.	.50	2.00	12.50
	b. Serial # prefix/suffix A-B.	.50	2.00	12.50
	s. Specimen perforated: *SPECIMEN.*	—	—	140.
M20	**50 Lire** 1943 A. Blue.			
	a. Serial # prefix/suffix A-A.	2.00	7.00	50.00
	b. Serial # prefix/suffix A-B.	2.00	7.00	50.00
	s. Specimen perforated: *SPECIMEN.*	—	—	175.

		VG	VF	UNC
M21	**100 Lire** 1943 A. Violet and blue.			
	a. Serial # prefix/suffix A-A.	2.00	7.00	50.00
	b. Serial # prefix/suffix A-B.	2.00	7.00	50.00
	c. Serial # prefix/suffix A-C.	2.00	7.00	50.00
	s. Specimen perforated: *SPECIMEN.*	—	—	150.
M22	**500 Lire** 1943 A. Green and blue.			
	a. Issued note.	25.00	75.00	500.
	s. Specimen perforated: *SPECIMEN.*	—	—	850.
M23	**1000 Lire** 1943 A. Black and blue.			
	a. Issued note.	20.00	70.00	450.
	s. Specimen perforated: *SPECIMEN.*	—	—	850.

GOVERNO DELLE ISOLE ITALIANE DELL'EGEO

DODECANESE

GOVERNMENT OF ITALIAN ISLANDS IN THE AEGEAN

1944 ISSUE

		Good	Fine	XF
M24	**50 Lire** 15.4.1944-21.4.1944. Green and brown on yellow unpt. Wolf w/Romulus and Remus at ctr., island fortress in background.	500.	1500.	3500.

		Good	Fine	XF
M25	**100 Lire** 15.4.1944-21.4.1944. Blue and brown on yellow unpt. Stag at l.	400.	1300.	3000.

CAUTION: Forgeries have recently appeared on the Italian market. They may be recognized by the bad quality printing, especially the signature and the missing yellow unpt.

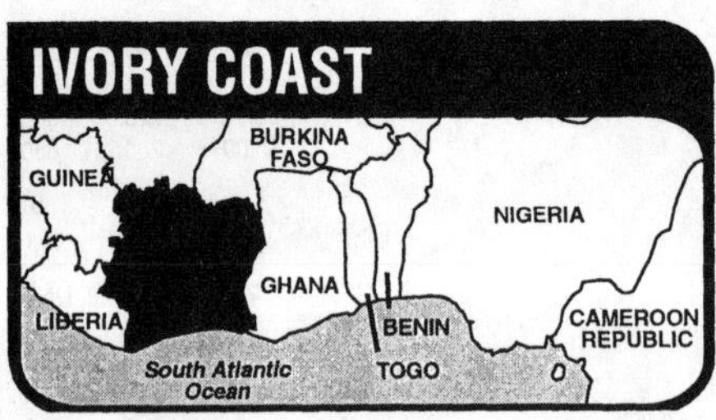

The Republic of Cote d'Ivoire (Ivory Coast), a former French overseas territory located on the south side of the African bulge between Nigeria and Ghana, has an area of 124,504 sq. mi. (322,463 sq. km.) and a population of 15.14 million. Capital: Abidjan. The predominantly agricultural economy is one of Africa's most prosperous. Coffee, tropical woods, cocoa, and bananas are exported.

The Ivory Coast was first visited by French and Portuguese navigators in the 15th century. French traders set up establishments in the 19th century, and gradually extended their influence along the coast and inland. The area was organized as a territory in 1893, and from 1904 to 1958 was a constituent unit of the Federation of French West Africa - as a Colony under the Third Republic and an Overseas Territory under the Fourth. In 1958 the Ivory Coast became an autonomous republic within the French Community. Independence was attained on Aug. 7, 1960.

Together with other West African states, the Cote d'Ivoire is a member of the "Union Monetaire Ouest-Africaine."

Also see French West Africa and West African Monetary Union.

RULERS:

French to 1960

MONETARY SYSTEM:

1 Franc = 100 Centimes

FRENCH ADMINISTRATION

GOUVERNEMENT GÉNÉRAL DE L'AFRIQUE

OCCIDENTALE FRANÇAISE (A.O.F.)

COLONIE DE LA COTE D'IVOIRE

DÉCRET DU 11.2.1917

		VG	VF	UNC
1	**.50 Franc** D.1917. Black and orange on yellow unpt. Obverse and reverse of French 50 Centimes coin. Black text on back.			
	a. Wmk: Bees.	15.00	65.00	175.
	b. Wmk: Laurel leaves.	20.00	75.00	200.
	c. W/o wmk.	10.00	55.00	165.

		VG	VF	UNC
2	**1 Franc** D.1917. Black and green on yellow unpt. Obverse and reverse of French 1 Franc coin.			
	a. Wmk: Bees.	15.00	65.00	200.
	b. Wmk: Laurel leaves.	20.00	80.00	225.
3	**2 Francs** D.1917. Red and black on lt. orange unpt. Obverse and reverse of French 2-Franc coin.			
	a. Wmk: Bees.	20.00	100.	250.
	b. Wmk: Laurel leaves.	20.00	100.	250.

1920 ND POSTAGE STAMP ISSUE

#4-6 postage stamps of the Ivory Coast (Michel #44, 45, and 48, or Scott #45, 47 and 52 w/men in boat) pasted on cardboard and w/ovpt: *Valeur d'echange* and value.

		VG	VF	UNC
4	**.05 Franc on 5 Centimes** ND (1920). Yellow-green and blue-green.	15.00	40.00	90.00

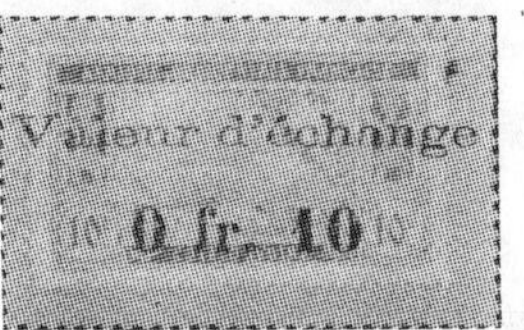

		VG	VF	UNC
5	**.10 Franc on 10 Centimes** ND (1920). Red-orange and rose.	15.00	40.00	90.00

		VG	VF	UNC
6	**.25 Franc on 25 Centimes** ND (1920). Ultramarine and blue.	15.00	40.00	90.00

COTE D'IVOIRE

1943 ND EMERGENCY WW II ISSUE

#A7-8 elephant head in unpt. at ctr.

		VG	VF	UNC
6A	**50 Centimes** ND. Dk. blue and yellow. Rare.	—	—	—

		VG	VF	UNC
7	**1 Franc** ND. Blue on yellow unpt. Rare.	—	—	—

		VG	VF	UNC
8	**2 Francs** ND. Blue on yellow unpt. Rare.	—	—	—

Note: Issues specially marked with letter *A* for Ivory Coast were made by the Banque Centrale des Etats de l'Afrique de l'Ouest. For listing see West African States.

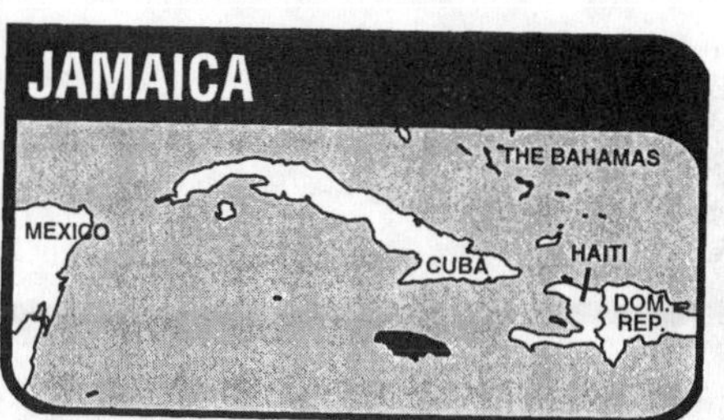

Jamaica, a member of the British Commonwealth situated in the Caribbean Sea 90 miles south of Cuba, has an area of 4,232 sq. mi. (10,991 sq. km.) and a population of 2.59 million. Capital: Kingston. The economy is founded chiefly on mining, tourism and agriculture. Alumina, bauxite, sugar, rum and molasses are exported.

Jamaica was discovered by Columbus on May 3, 1494, and settled by Spain in 1509. The island was captured in 1655 by a British naval force under the command of Admiral William Penn, and ceded to Britain by the Treaty of Madrid in 1670. For more than 150 years, the Jamaican economy of sugar, slaves and piracy was one of the most prosperous in the New World. Dissension between the property-oriented island legislature and the home government prompted Parliament to establish a crown colony government for Jamaica in 1866. From 1958 to 1961 Jamaica was a member of the West Indies Federation, withdrawing when Jamaican voters rejected the association. The colony attained independence on Aug. 6, 1962.

Jamaica is a member of the Commonwealth of Nations. Elizabeth II is the Head of State, as Queen of Jamaica.

A decimal standard currency system was adopted on Sept. 8, 1969.

RULERS:

British

MONETARY SYSTEM:

1 Shilling = 12 Pence
1 Pound = 20 Shillings to 1969
1 Dollar = 100 Cents, 1969-

Note: Certain listings encompassing issues circulated by various bank and regional authorities are contained in Volume 1.

BRITISH ADMINISTRATION

TREASURY

LAW 27/1904 AND 17/1918

#27-30 printer: TDLR.

		Good	Fine	XF
7	**2 Shillings 6 Pence** L.1904/18. Green. Portr. Kg. George V at r. Back orange; woman w/hat at ctr.	500.	1250.	2500.

		Good	Fine	XF
	5 Shillings L.1904/18. Red on green and brown unpt. Portr. Kg. George V at upper r. Back brown; sailing ship at ctr.			
	a. 1 serial #, at upper ctr.	350.	850.	2000.
	b. 2 serial #, lower l. and upper r. 2 sign. varieties.	350.	850.	2000.
	not assigned.			
	10 Shillings L.1904/18. Blue. Portr. Kg. George V at upper r. Back green; lion at ctr. 2 sign. varieties.	400.	950.	2250.

NOTICE

Readers with unlisted dates, signature varieties, etc. are invited to submit photocopies or, high resolution (300 dpi, 100% size) scans of their notes to: Standard Catalog of World Paper Money, 700 East State St. Iola, WI 54990-0001, or E-Mail: george.cuhaj@fwpubs.com.

GOVERNMENT OF JAMAICA

LAW 27/1904 AND 17/1918

#32 and 33 arms at upper l., waterfalls at ctr., Portr. Kg. George V at upper r. Printer: W&S.

#31, 34-36 *Deleted.*

		Good	Fine	XF
32	**5 Shillings** L.1904/18. Brown. River and bridge at ctr. on back.			
	a. 2 serial #. 2 sign varieties.	125.	400.	950.
	b. 1 serial #. Reported not confirmed.	—	—	—

		Good	Fine	XF
33	**10 Shillings** L.1904/18. Green.			
	a. 2 serial #. 2 sign. varieties.	350.	750.	1750.
	b. 1 serial #. Reported not confirmed.	—	—	—

1939-52 ISSUES

#37-43 portr. Kg. George VI at l. Printer: TDLR.

		VG	VF	UNC
37	**5 Shillings** 1939-58. Orange. Back m/c; w/*FIVE SHILLINGS* in 2 lines.			
	a. 2.1.1939-15.6.1950.	7.50	40.00	150.
	b. 1.3.1953-15.8.1958.	5.00	27.50	120.
38	**10 Shillings** 1939-48. Blue. Back m/c; w/*TEN SHILLINGS* in 2 lines.			
	a. 2.1.1939.	12.50	75.00	200.
	b. 1.11.1940.	10.00	40.00	140.
	c. 30.11.1942.	50.00	200.	—
	d. 2.1.1948.	12.50	75.00	200.

		VG	VF	UNC
39	**10 Shillings** 15.6.1950-17.3.1960. Purple. Back like #38.	5.00	25.00	125.
40	**1 Pound** 1.11.1940. Blue. Back m/c.			
	a. Red serial #.	40.00	150.	—
	b. Black serial #.	40.00	125.	—
41	**1 Pound** 1942-60. Green. Back like #40, w/*ONE POUND* in 2 lines.			
	a. 30.11.1942; 2.1.1948.	15.00	75.00	375.
	b. 15.6.1950-17.3.1960.	7.50	45.00	250.
42	**5 Pounds** 30.11.1942. Maroon.	250.	800.	—

		VG	VF	UNC
43	**5 Pounds** 1.8.1952; 7.4.1955; 15.8.1957; 1.9.1957. Brown. Like #42.	150.	550.	1400.

1960 Issue

#45-47 portr. Kg. George VI at l. New back design. Printer: TDLR.

		VG	VF	UNC
45	**5 Shillings** 17.3.1960; 4.7.1960. Orange. *FIVE SHILLINGS* in 1 line on back.	7.50	35.00	160.

		VG	VF	UNC
46	**10 Shillings** 4.7.1960. Purple. *TEN SHILLINGS* in 1 line on back.	9.00	45.00	200.
47	**1 Pound** 19.5.1960. Green. *ONE POUND* in 1 line on back.	12.00	65.00	250.

		VG	VF	UNC
48	**5 Pounds** 1960. Blue and m/c. Qn. Elizabeth II at l. Factory and banana tree on back.			
	a. 17.3.1960.	200.	500.	—
	b. 4.7.1960.	60.00	250.	1000.

Japan, a constitutional monarchy situated off the east coast of Asia, has an area of 145,856 sq. mi. (377,819 sq. km.) and a population of 127.13 million. Capital: Tokyo. Japan, one of the three major industrial nations of the free world, exports machinery, motor vehicles, textiles and chemicals.

Founded (so legend holds) in 660 BC by a direct descendant of the Sun Goddess, the country was first brought into contact with the west by a storm-blown Portuguese ship in 1542. European traders and missionaries proceeded to enlarge the contact until the Shogunate, sensing a military threat in the foreign presence, expelled all foreigners and severed relations with the outside world in the 17th century. (Except for one Dutch outpost in Nagasaki.) After contact was reestablished by Commodore Perry of the U.S. Navy in 1854, Japan rapidly industrialized, abolished the Shogunate and established a parliamentary form of government, and by the end of the 19th century achieved the status of a modern economic and military power. A series of wars with China and Russia, and participation with the Allies in World War I, enlarged Japan territorially but brought its interests into conflict with the Far Eastern interests of the United States and Britain, causing it to align with the Axis powers for the pursuit of World War II. After its defeat in World War II, Japan renounced military aggression as a political instrument, established democratic self-government, and quickly reasserted its position as an economic world power.

See also Burma, China (Japanese military issues, Central Reserve Bank, Federal Reserve Bank, Hua Hsing Commercial Bank, Mengchiang Bank, Chanan Bank, Chi Tung Bank and Manchukuo), Hong Kong, Indochina, Malaya, Netherlands Indies, Oceania, the Philippines, Korea and Taiwan.

RULERS:

Mutsuhito (Meiji), Years 1-45, (1868-1912) 明治

Yoshihito (Taisho), 1912-1926 大正

Hirohito (Showa), 1926-1989 昭和

Akihito (Heisei)

MONETARY SYSTEM:

NOTE: Certain listings encompassing issues circulated by various bank and regional authorities are contained in Volume 1.

MONETARY UNITS:

1 Sen = 10 Rin
1 Yen = 100 Sen

 Rin;  Sen; 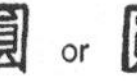 or  or  or 円 Yen

PORTRAIT VARIETIES

#1 Takeuchi Sukune

#2 Sugawara Michizane

#3 Wakeno Kiyomaro

#4 Fujiwara Kamatari

#5 Wakeno Kiyomaro

#6 Shotoku-taishi

#7 Yamato Takeru No Mikoto

CONSTITUTIONAL MONARCHY

GREAT JAPANESE GOVERNMENT - MINISTRY OF FINANCE

大日本政府大蔵省

Dai Nip-pon Sei-fu O-kura-sho

1872 ISSUE

#1-9 Meiji Tsuho-Satsu w/facing Onagadori cockerels at top and 2 facing dragons at bottom. Printer: Dondorf and Naumann, Frankfurt, Germany.

10 SEN

20 SEN

1/2 YEN

		Good	Fine	XF
1	**10 Sen** ND (1872). Black on pink unpt. Back green.	20.00	35.00	70.00
2	**20 Sen** ND (1872). Black on brown unpt. Back blue.	40.00	75.00	150.
3	**1/2 Yen** ND (1872). Black on green unpt. Back brown.	60.00	125.	250.

		Good	Fine	XF
4	**1 Yen** ND (1872). Black on brown unpt. Back blue.	50.00	100.	200.
5	**2 Yen** ND (1872). Black on blue unpt. Back brown.	200.	400.	800.

		Good	Fine	XF
6	**5 Yen** ND (1872). Black on brown unpt. Back blue.	750.	1500.	3000.
7	**10 Yen** ND (1872). Black on blue unpt. Back lilac.	450.	900.	1750.
8	**50 Yen** ND (1872). Black on lilac unpt. Back blue. Rare.	—	—	—
9	**100 Yen** ND (1872). Black on blue unpt. Back red. Rare.	—	—	—

GREAT IMPERIAL JAPANESE CIRCULATING NOTE

大日本帝國通用紙幣

Dai Nip-pon Tei-koku Tus-yo Shi-hei

1873 "PAPER CURRENCY" ISSUE

#10-14 black w/number of issuing national bank and location at lower ctr. All have black face, green and black back showing equivalent gold coin. Printer: CONB.

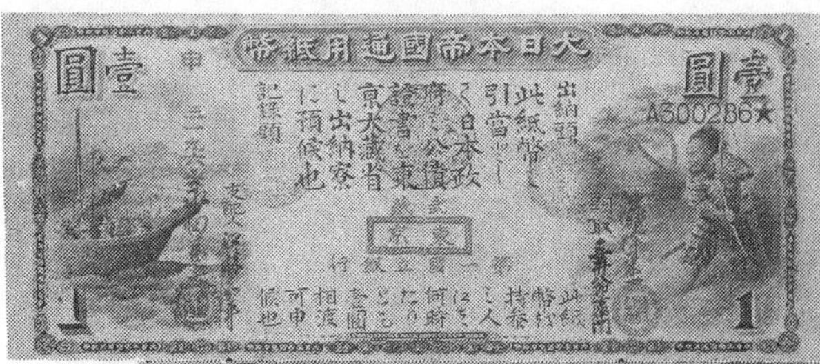

			Good	Fine	XF
10	1 Yen	ND (1873). Prow of a ship at l. Warrior w/bow and arrows at r. Gold 1 yen coin at l. and r., defeat of the Mongols in Hakata harbor at ctr. on back.	800.	1750.	3500.

			Good	Fine	XF
11	2 Yen	ND (1873). Warrior in armor at l. and r. Castle gateway on back.	1750.	3500.	—

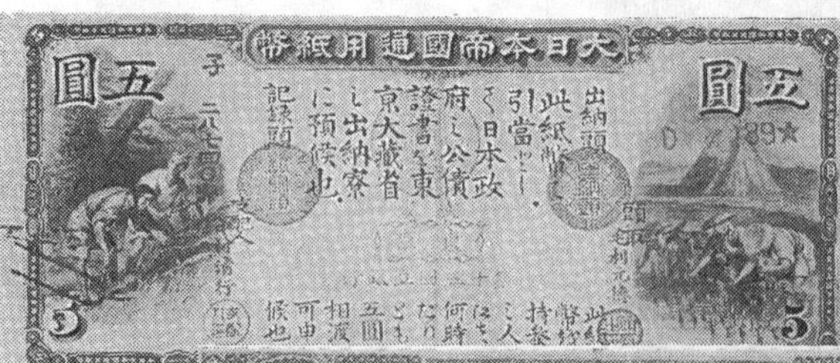

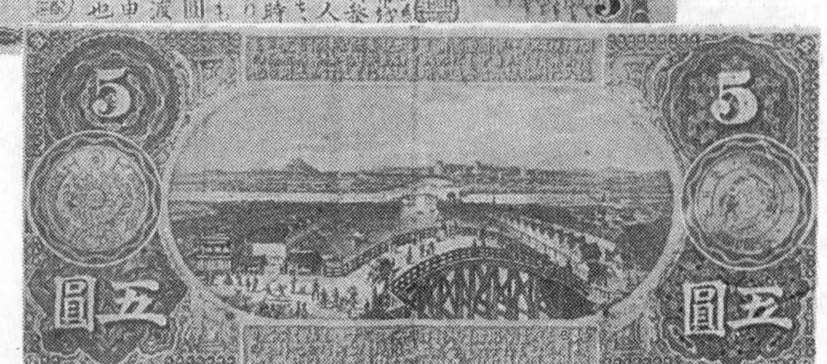

			Good	Fine	XF
12	5 Yen	ND (1873). Field work at l. and r. Nihonbashi Bridge on back.	4000.	8000.	—

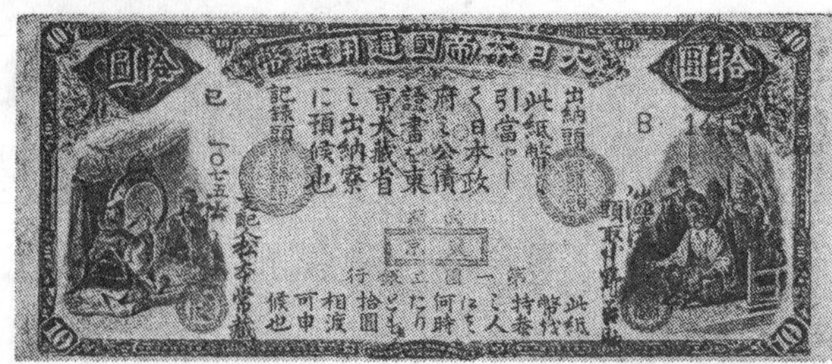

			Good	Fine	XF
13	10 Yen	ND (1873). Musicians at l. and r. Empress Jingu on horseback arriving on beach on back. Rare.	—	—	—

			Good	Fine	XF
14	20 Yen	ND (1873). Dragon at l., kneeling man at r. Warriors at beach on back. Rare.	—	—	—

GREAT IMPERIAL JAPANESE GOVERNMENT NOTE

大日本帝國政府紙幣

Dai Nip-pon Tei-koku Sei-fu Shi-hei

1881-83 "PAPER MONEY" ISSUE

			Good	Fine	XF
15	20 Sen	1881 (1882). Brown unpt. w/brown seal at r.	30.00	75.00	150.
16	50 Sen	1881 (1882). Brown unpt. w/brown seal at r.	150.	400.	850.

#17-19 brown unpt. Portr. Empress Jingu at r. Ornate denomination w/red seal on back.

			Good	Fine	XF
17	1 Yen	1878 (1881).	150.	300.	600.
18	5 Yen	1880 (1882).	800.	1500.	3000.

		Good	Fine	XF
19	**10 Yen** 1881 (1883).	1500.	3000.	6000.

GREAT IMPERIAL JAPANESE NATIONAL BANK

大日本帝國國立銀行

Dai Nip-pon Tei-koku Koku-ritsu Gin-ko

1877-78 ISSUE

#20 and 21 have only the issuing bank number on face; issue location and bank number on back.

		Good	Fine	XF
20	**1 Yen** ND (1877). Black on yellow-brown unpt. 2 sailors at r. Back dk. green w/Ebisu, god of household thrift and industry.	300.	600.	1200.
21	**5 Yen** ND (1878). Black on green unpt. 3 blacksmiths at r. Back black and green w/Ebisu.	750.	1500.	3000.

BANK OF JAPAN

日本銀行兌換券

Nip-pon Gin-ko Da Kan Gin Ken

1885-86 CONVERTIBLE SILVER NOTE ISSUE

#22-25 Daikoku (God of Fortune) sitting on rice bales.
#22, 23 and 25 w/text: *Nippon Ginko Promises to Pay the Bearer on Demand...Yen in Silver* on face.

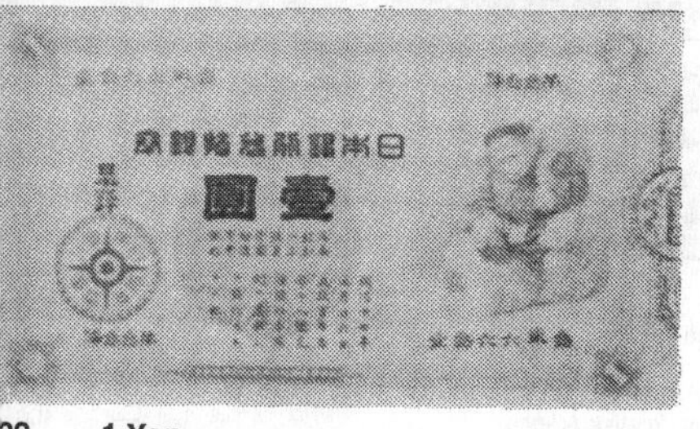

		Good	Fine	XF
22	**1 Yen** ND (1885). Blue. Daikoku at r.	125.	300.	600.
23	**5 Yen** ND (1886). Blue. Daikoku on back.	1250.	2500.	5000.
24	**10 Yen** ND (1885). Blue. Daikoku at r.	2000.	5000.	—
25	**100 Yen** ND (1885). Blue. Daikoku at r. Rare.	—	—	—

1889-91 CONVERTIBLE SILVER NOTE ISSUE

26-29 serial # in Japanese numerals.

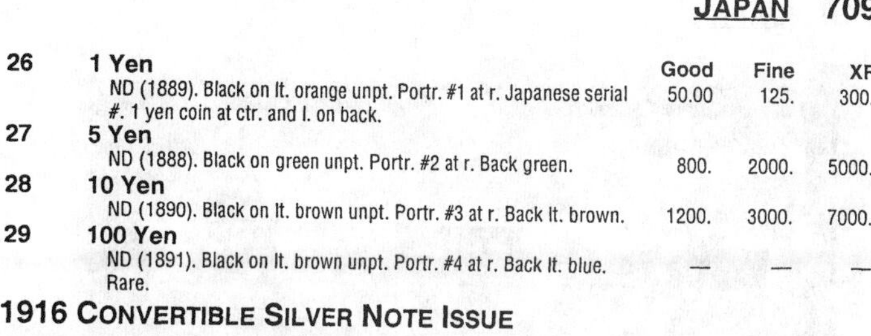

		Good	Fine	XF
26	**1 Yen** ND (1889). Black on lt. orange unpt. Portr. #1 at r. Japanese serial #. 1 yen coin at ctr. and l. on back.	50.00	125.	300.
27	**5 Yen** ND (1888). Black on green unpt. Portr. #2 at r. Back green.	800.	2000.	5000.
28	**10 Yen** ND (1890). Black on lt. brown unpt. Portr. #3 at r. Back lt. brown.	1200.	3000.	7000.
29	**100 Yen** ND (1891). Black on lt. brown unpt. Portr. #4 at r. Back lt. blue. Rare.	—	—	—

1916 CONVERTIBLE SILVER NOTE ISSUE

Issuer's name reads l. to r. or r. to l.

		Good	Fine	XF
30	**1 Yen** ND (1916). Like #26 but Western serial #.			
	a. Block # below 200.	15.00	40.00	75.00
	b. Block #200-299.	4.00	8.00	15.00
	c. Block #300 and higher.	.50	1.50	3.00
	s. As c. Vermilion ovpt: *Mi-hon.* Regular serial #.	—	Unc	100.

1899-1900 CONVERTIBLE GOLD NOTE ISSUE

		Good	Fine	XF
31	**5 Yen** 1899-1910. Black on pale green unpt. Portr. #1 at ctr. Back orange.			
	a. Japanese block character.	250.	500.	1000.
	b. Western block #.	400.	800.	1750.

		Good	Fine	XF
32	**10 Yen** 1899-1913. Black on lt. brown unpt. Goo Shrine at l., portr. #3 at r. Back green; boar at ctr.			
	a. Japanese block character.	300.	600.	1200.
	b. Western block #.	350.	750.	1500.

		Good	Fine	XF
33	**100 Yen** 1900-13. Black on lt. brown unpt. Park w/Danzan Shrine at l., portr. #4 at r. Back purple; Bank of Japan.			
	a. Japanese block character.	3500.	8000.	—
	b. Western block #.	1500.	3000.	—

1910 Convertible Gold Note Issue

		Good	Fine	XF
34	**5 Yen** ND (1910). Green on violet unpt. Portr. #2 at r. Back violet. Wmk: Daikoku.	250.	500.	1000.

1915-1917 Convertible Gold Note Issue

		Good	Fine	XF
35	**5 Yen** ND (1916). Black on lt. green unpt. Ube Shrine w/stairs at l., portr. #1 at r. Back brown.	50.00	100.	250.

		Good	Fine	XF
36	**10 Yen** ND (1915). Gray. Portr. #5 at l., Goo Shrine at r. Back green and brown.	50.00	100.	200.
37	**20 Yen** ND (1917). Black on m/c unpt. Portr. #2 at r. Back violet; Kitano Shrine.	300.	1000.	2500.

1927 Emergency Issue

		Good	Fine	XF
37A	**50 Yen** ND (1927). Guilloche at l. and r. of ctr. Uniface. Specimen. Rare.	—	—	—

		Good	Fine	XF
37B	**200 Yen** ND (1927). Greenish black w/black text. Guilloche at ctr. w/o portr. Uniface. Rare.	—	—	—

1927 ND Issue

		Good	Fine	XF
38	**200 Yen** ND (1927). Black on green unpt. Portr. *#1* at r. Back red. Specimen. Rare.	—	—	—

Note: For similar note but w/pale blue unpt., see #43A.

1930-31 ND Issue

#39-45 Japanese text w/denomination in English on back.

		VG	VF	UNC
39	**5 Yen** ND (1930). Black on green and orange unpt. Kitano Shrine at l., green guilloche at ctr., Portr. #2 at r. Back brown and olive.			
	a. Issued note.	2.00	10.00	60.00
	s1. Specimen w/ovpt. and perforated *Mi-hon.*	—	—	400.
	s2. Specimen w/sm. vermilion stamping: *Mi-hon.* Regular serial #.	—	—	75.00

		VG	VF	UNC
40	**10 Yen** ND (1930). Black on green and brown unpt. Portr. #3 at r. Back green and brown.			
	a. Issued note.	1.50	4.00	20.00
	s1. Specimen w/ovpt. and perforated: *Mi-hon.*	—	—	400.
	s2. Specimen w/sm. vermilion stamping: *Mi-hon.* Regular serial #.	—	—	75.00
	z. Face as a. Propaganda message in Japanese text on back. (4 varieties).	20.00	45.00	80.00

Note: 4 different propaganda notes w/face of #40 and different messages on back in Japanese are frequently encountered.

41	20 Yen	VG	VF	UNC
	ND (1931). Black on green unpt. Danzan Shrine at l., portr. #4 at r. Back blue and brown; another view of same shrine.			
	a. Issued note.	50.00	150.	350.
	s1. Specimen w/ovpt. and perforated: *Mi-hon.*	—	—	1200.
	s2. Specimen w/sm. vermilion stamping: *Mi-hon. SPECIMEN* on back. Regular serial #.	—	—	250.
	s3. Specimen w/blue stamping: *SPECIMEN* on face and back. Regular serial #.	—	—	200.

42	100 Yen	VG	VF	UNC
	ND (1930). Black on blue and brown unpt. Yumedono Pavilion at l., portr. #6 at r. Back green and brown; Horyuji Temple at ctr.			
	a. Issued note.	15.00	50.00	125.
	s. Specimen w/sm. vermilion stamping: *Mi-hon.* Regular serial #.	—	50.00	125.

1942 ND ISSUE

43	5 Yen	VG	VF	UNC
	ND (1942). Similar to #39 but w/o ctr. guilloche. Back red-brown and lilac.			
	a. Issued note.	2.00	5.00	25.00
	s1. Specimen w/ovpt. and perforated: *Mi-hon.*	—	—	400.
	s2. Specimen w/sm. vermilion stamping: *Mi-hon.* Regular serial #.	—	—	75.00
	s3. Specimen w/red stamping: *SPECIMEN* on face and back. Regular serial #.	—	—	75.00

1945 ND ISSUE

43A	200 Yen	Good	Fine	XF
	ND (1945). Black on pale blue unpt. Portr. #1 at r. Back red; English denomination. (Originally printed in 1927).			
	a. Issued note.	300.	700.	1500.
	s1. Specimen w/ovpt. and perforated *Mi-hon.*			
	s2. Specimen w/vermilion ovpt: *Mi-hon. Specimen* on back. Regular serial #.			
	s3. Specimen w/sm. vermilion stamping: *Mi-hon.* Regular serial #.			

44	200 Yen	VG	VF	UNC
	ND (1945). Black on gray and green unpt. Danzon Shrine at l., portr. #4 at r. Back blue; another view of same shrine.			
	a. Issued note.	75.00	200.	400.
	s1. Specimen w/ovpt. and perforated: *Mi-hon.*	—	—	1500.
	s2. Specimen w/vermilion ovpt: *Mi-hon. SPECIMEN* on back. Regular serial #.	—	—	400.
	s3. Specimen w/sm. vermilion stamping: *Mi-hon.* Regular serial #.	—	—	500.
	s4. Specimen w/blue stamping: *SPECIMEN* on face and back. Regular serial #.	—	—	500.

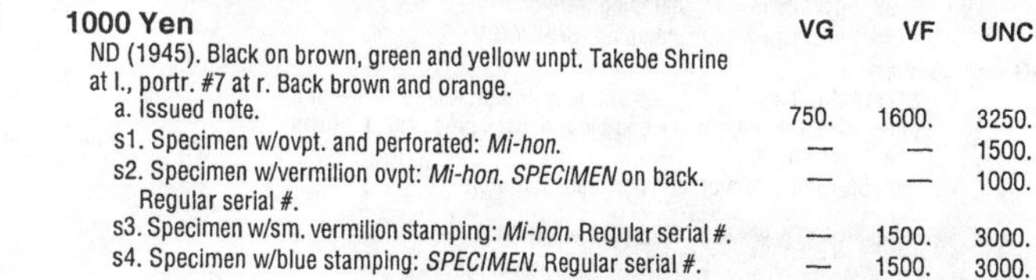

45	1000 Yen	VG	VF	UNC
	ND (1945). Black on brown, green and yellow unpt. Takebe Shrine at l., portr. #7 at r. Back brown and orange.			
	a. Issued note.	750.	1600.	3250.
	s1. Specimen w/ovpt. and perforated: *Mi-hon.*	—	—	1500.
	s2. Specimen w/vermilion ovpt: *Mi-hon. SPECIMEN* on back. Regular serial #.	—	—	1000.
	s3. Specimen w/sm. vermilion stamping: *Mi-hon.* Regular serial #.	—	1500.	3000.
	s4. Specimen w/blue stamping: *SPECIMEN.* Regular serial #.	—	1500.	3000.

GREAT IMPERIAL JAPANESE GOVERNMENT (RESUMED)

大日本帝國政府紙幣

Dai Nip-pon Tei-koku Sei-fu Shi-hei

1917 "PAPER MONEY" ISSUE

46	10 Sen	VG	VF	UNC
	1917-21. Black on orange unpt. Red seal at l., denomination numeral at r.			
	a. Taisho yr. 6.	2.50	7.50	20.00
	b. Taisho yrs. 7; 8.	1.00	4.00	10.00
	c. Taisho yrs. 9; 10.	1.00	4.00	8.00

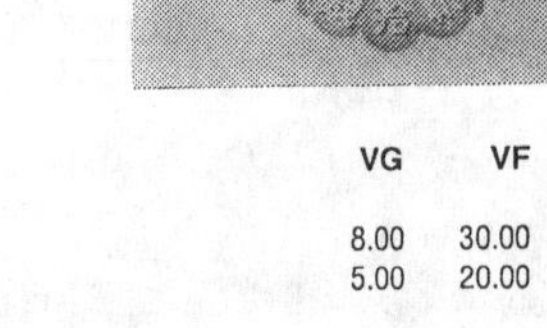

		VG	VF	UNC
47	**20 Sen**			
	1917-19. Black on green unpt. Like #48.			
	a. Taisho yr. 6.	8.00	30.00	100.
	b. Taisho yrs. 7; 8.	5.00	20.00	60.00

		VG	VF	UNC
48	**50 Sen**			
	1917-22. Black on pink unpt. Red seal at l., denomination numeral at r.			
	a. Taisho yr. 6.	7.00	25.00	100.
	b. Taisho yrs. 7; 8.	4.00	15.00	60.00
	c. Taisho yrs. 9; 10; 11.	2.00	10.00	40.00

BANK OF JAPAN (CONTINUED)

券行銀本日

Nip-pon Gin-ko Ken

1943 ND ISSUE

#49-51, Japanese text only.

		VG	VF	UNC
49	**1 Yen**			
	ND (1943). Black on lt. blue unpt. Portr. #1 at ctr., serial # and block #1-34. Ube Shrine at ctr. on back.			
	a. Issued note.	.50	3.00	10.00
	s1. Specimen w/ovpt. and perforated: *Mi-hon.*	—	—	400.
	s2. Specimen w/red ovpt. *SPECIMEN* on face and back.	—	—	700.
	s3. Specimen w/sm. stamping: *Mi-hon.*	—	—	75.00
	s4. Specimen w/blue stamping: *SPECIMEN.*	—	—	75.00
50	**5 Yen**			
	ND (1943). Black on lt. green and purple unpt. Kitano Shrine at l., portr. #2 at r. Black serial # and block #. Back green and lt. brown.			
	a. Issued note.	.75	4.00	20.00
	s. Specimen w/ovpt. and perforated: *Mi-hon.*	—	Unc	400.

		VG	VF	UNC
51	**10 Yen**			
	ND (1943-44). Black on brown and lt. blue unpt. Portr. #3 at r. Black serial # and block #. Back blue; Goo Shrine at ctr.			
	a. Wmk: *10 Yen* in Japanese characters at top ctr. (1943).	1.00	3.00	12.50
	b. Wmk: Repeating characters *NIHON* and *JU. (10). (1944).*	2.00	4.00	15.00
	s1. As a. Specimen w/ovpt. and perforated: *Mi-hon.*	—	—	400.
	s2. As a. Specimen w/blue stamping: *SPECIMEN.* Regular serial #.	—	—	75.00

1944 ND ISSUE

#52-57, Japanese text only.

		VG	VF	UNC
52	**5 Sen**			
	ND (1944). Black on yellow unpt. Equestrian statue at l.			
	a. Issued note.	.10	25.00	1.50
	s1. Specimen ovpt: *Mi-hon.* Block #1.	—	—	250.
	s2. Specimen w/sm. stamping: *Mi-hon.* Regular block #.	—	—	75.00

		VG	VF	UNC
53	**10 Sen**			
	ND (1944). Black on purple unpt. Tower monument at l.			
	a. Issued note.	.10	.50	2.00
	s1. Specimen w/ovpt:*Mi-hon.* Block #1.	—	—	250.
	s2. Specimen w/sm. stamping: *Mi-hon.* Regular block #.	—	—	75.00
54	**1 Yen**			
	ND (1944-45). Like #49. Block #.			
	a. Wmk: Fancy floral design. Block #35-47 (1944).	.50	3.00	15.00
	b. Wmk: Outline of kiri leaf. Block #48-49 (1945).	1.50	4.00	20.00
	s1. As a. Specimen w/ovpt. and perforated: *Mi-hon.*	—	—	600.
	s2. As a. Speciman w/red ovpt: *SPECIMEN.*	—	—	750.

		VG	VF	UNC
55	**5 Yen**			
	ND (1944). Like #50 but only red block #.			
	a. Issued note.	35.00	75.00	225.
	s1. Specimen w/ovpt. and perforated: *Mi-hon.*	—	—	600.
	s2. Specimen w/sm. ovpt: *Mi-hon.* Regular block #.	30.00	60.00	125.

		VG	VF	UNC
56	**10 Yen**			
	ND (1944-45). Like #51 but w/only red block #.			
	a. Wmk: Repeating characters *NIHON* and *JU. (10) (1944).*	2.00	6.00	20.00
	b. Wmk: Repeating Bank of Japan logos (circles) (1945).	3.00	8.00	25.00
	c. Wmk: Outline of Kiri leaf (1945).	4.00	10.00	35.00
	s1. As a. Specimen w/ovpt. and perforated: *Mi-hon.*	—	—	600.
	s2. As b. Specimen w/ovpt: *Mi-hon.* Regular block #.	—	—	250.

		VG	VF	UNC
57	**100 Yen** ND (1944). Black on brown unpt. of leaves. Yumedono Pavilion at l., portr. #6 at r. Back lilac; temple.			
	a. Wmk: Arabesque phoenix design at l.	5.00	20.00	60.00
	b. Wmk: Kiri leaves.	9.00	25.00	75.00
	s1. As a. Specimen w/ovpt. and perforated: *Mi-hon.*	—	—	400.
	s2. As a. Specimen w/sm. stamping: *Mi-hon.* Regular block #.	—	—	100.

GREAT IMPERIAL JAPANESE GOVERNMENT (CONT.)

1938 "PAPER MONEY" ISSUE

		VG	VF	UNC
58	**50 Sen** 1938. Black on yellow and blue unpt. Fuji and cherry blossoms. (Showa yr. 13 at l.) Back lt. green.			
	a. Issued note.	.25	.75	6.00
	s. Specimen w/sm. stamping: *Mi-hon.* Regular block #.	—	—	75.00

Note: Date shown at r. on #58 is 2598 years since foundation of Japan (old calendar year).

1942 "PAPER MONEY" ISSUE

		VG	VF	UNC
59	**50 Sen** 1942-44. Black on green and brown unpt. Yasukuni Shrine. Back green; mountain at ctr.			
	a. Showa yr. 17.	.25	1.00	8.00
	b. Showa yr. 18.	.25	.75	2.50
	c. Showa yr. 19.	.25	.75	3.50
	s1. As c. Specimen w/sm. stamping: *Mi-hon.* Regular block #.	—	—	100.
	s2. As c. Specimen w/red stamping: *SPECIMEN.* Regular block.	—	—	75.00

IMPERIAL JAPANESE GOVERNMENT

幣紙府政國帝本日

Nip-pon Tei-koku Sei-fu Shi-hei

1945 "PAPER MONEY" ISSUE

		VG	VF	UNC
60	**50 Sen** 1945. Black on lilac unpt. Like # 59. Showa yr. 20.			
	a. Issued note.	.25	.75	4.00
	s1. Specimen w/ovpt: *MI-hon.* Block #1.	—	—	250.
	s2. Specimen w/red ovpt: *SPECIMEN.* Block #22.	—	—	500.

NOTICE

Readers with unlisted dates, signature varieties, etc. are invited to submit photocopies or, high resolution (300 dpi, 100% size) scans of their notes to: Standard Catalog of World Paper Money, 700 East State St. Iola, WI 54990-0001, or E-Mail: george.cuhaj@fwpubs.com.

JAPANESE GOVERNMENT

日本政府紙幣

Nip-pon Sei-fu Shi-hei

1948 "PAPER MONEY" ISSUE

#61, issuer's name reads l. to r.

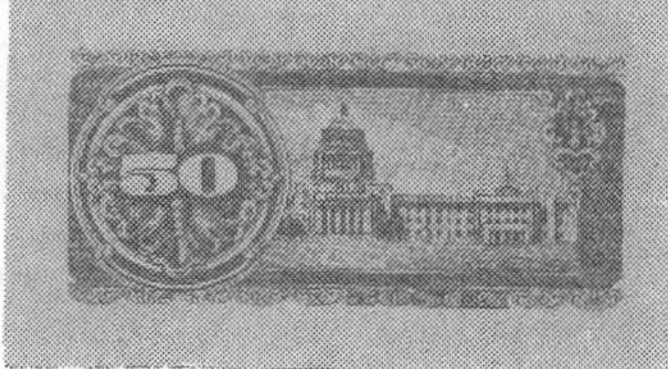

		VG	VF	UNC
61	**50 Sen** 1948. Black on lilac unpt. Portr. Itagaki Taisuke at r. Back green; Diet Bldg. at ctr.			
	a. Gray paper.	.25	.50	2.00
	b. White paper.	.25	.50	2.00

ALLIED MILITARY CURRENCY - WWII

1945-51 ND ISSUE

#62-76 black on lt. blue unpt. Back brown.

		VG	VF	UNC
62	**10 Sen** ND (1946). A in unpt.	4.00	10.00	45.00

		VG	VF	UNC
63	**10 Sen** ND (1945). B in unpt.	.50	1.50	3.50
64	**50 Sen** ND (1946). A in unpt.	3.00	7.50	40.00

		VG	VF	UNC
65	**50 Sen** ND (1945). B in unpt.	.75	2.00	4.50
66	**1 Yen** ND (1946). A in unpt.	3.00	10.00	50.00

		VG	VF	UNC
67	**1 Yen** ND. B in unpt.			
	a. Serial # prefix - suffix A-A. (1945).	.75	2.00	4.50
	b. Serial # prefix - suffix B-B. (1955).	6.00	15.00	50.00
	c. Serial # prefix - suffix C-C. (1956).	2.50	10.00	30.00
	d. Serial # prefix - suffix D-D. (1957).	2.50	10.00	30.00
68	**5 Yen** ND (1946). A in unpt.	15.00	50.00	200.

		VG	VF	UNC
69	**5 Yen** ND (1945). B in unpt.			
	a. Serial # prefix - suffix A-A.	1.00	4.00	12.00
	b. Serial # prefix - suffix B-B.	4.00	15.00	50.00
70	**10 Yen** ND (1946). A in unpt.	20.00	70.00	250.
71	**10 Yen** ND (1945). B in unpt.	1.00	4.00	15.00

		VG	VF	UNC
72	**20 Yen** ND (1946). A in unpt.	125.	300.	750.
73	**20 Yen** ND (1945). B in unpt.	4.00	15.00	50.00

		VG	VF	UNC
74	**100 Yen** ND (1946). A in unpt.	200.	450.	1000.

		VG	VF	UNC
75	**100 Yen** ND (1945). B in unpt.	4.00	15.00	50.00

ONE THOUSAND YEN note (B in unpt.)

		VG	VF	UNC
76	**1000 Yen** ND (1951). B in unpt.			
	a. Block letters A; B; C.	650.	1250.	2750.
	b. Block letters D; E.	500.	1100.	2000.

Bank of Japan (continued)

券行銀本日
Nip-pon Gin-ko Ken

1945 ND Issue

Issuer's name reads l. to r. or r. to l.

		VG	VF	UNC
77	**10 Yen** ND (1945). Black. Portr. #3 at ctr. Back brown.			
	a. Green and gray unpt. Wmk: Quatrefoil. Blocks #1-69.	25.00	75.00	175.
	b. Lilac unpt. W/o wmk. Blocks #70-165.	35.00	125.	300.
	s1. As a. Specimen w/ovpt. and perforated: *Mi-hon.*	—	—	400.
	s2. As a. Specimen w/sm. stamping: *Mi-hon.* Regular block #.	—	—	125.
78	**10 Yen** ND (1945). Black, green and lilac. Portr. #3 at r. Back green. Specimen.	—	—	—
78A	**100 Yen** ND (1945). Black on green unpt. Portr. #6 at ctr. Back dk. green.			
	a. Wmk: Quatrefoil. Shaded gray to dull gray-green to gray unpt. Block #1-43.	35.00	75.00	175.
	b. Wmk: Kiri leaves. Dull gray-green unpt. Block #44-190.	25.00	60.00	150.
	s1. As a. Specimen w/ovpt. and perforated: *Mi-hon.*	—	—	750.
	s2. As b. Specimen w/sm. stamping: *Mi-hon.* Regular block #.	—	—	125.
78B	**500 Yen** ND (1945). Black on orange unpt. Portr. #1 at ctr. Back brown. Specimen.	—	—	—
78C	**1000 Yen** ND (1945). Black and blue. similar to #45 but lithographed. Back lt. blue. Specimen.	—	—	—

1946 Provisional Issue

#79-82 March 1946 Currency Reform. Old notes from 10 to 1000 Yen were revalidated w/validation adhesive stamps (Shoshi) of corresponding values.

		VG	VF	UNC
79	**10 Yen** ND (1946). Validation adhesive stamp.			
	a. Affixed to 10 Yen #40.	7.50	10.00	25.00
	b. Affixed to 10 Yen #51.	5.00	8.00	17.50
	c. Affixed to 10 Yen #56.	10.00	20.00	30.00
	d. Affixed to 10 Yen #77.	25.00	75.00	250.

		VG	VF	UNC
80	**100 Yen** ND (1946). Validation adhesive stamp.			
	a. Affixed to 100 Yen #42.	20.00	60.00	125.
	b. Affixed to 100 Yen #57.	15.00	35.00	70.00
	c. Affixed to 100 Yen #78A.	30.00	90.00	175.
81	**200 Yen** ND (1946). Validation adhesive stamp.			
	a. Affixed to 200 Yen #43A.	—	—	—
	b. Affixed to 200 Yen #44.	—	—	—
82	**1000 Yen** ND (1946). Validation adhesive stamp affixed to 1000 Yen #45.	—	—	—

1946-51 ND ISSUE

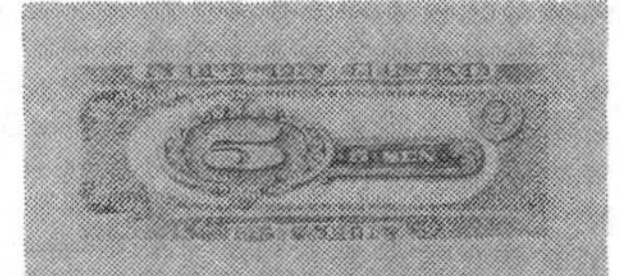

		VG	VF	UNC
83	**5 Sen** ND (1948). Black on yellow unpt. Plum blossoms at r. Back lt. brown.	.25	1.00	3.00

		VG	VF	UNC
84	**10 Sen** ND (1947). Black on blue unpt. Doves at r. Back lt. red-brown; Diet Bldg. at l.	.10	.25	1.50

		VG	VF	UNC
85	**1 Yen** ND (1946). Black on lt. brown unpt. Cockerel at lower ctr., portr. Ninomiya Sontoku at r. Back blue.			
	a. Issued note.	.10	.30	1.00
	s. Specimen w/ovpt: *Mi-hon. SPECIMEN* on back.	—	—	500.
86	**5 Yen** ND (1946). Dk. brown on green unpt. W/o vignette. Back blue.			
	a. Issued note.	.50	1.50	5.00
	s. Specimen w/ovpt: *Mi-hon. SPECIMEN* on back.	—	—	500.

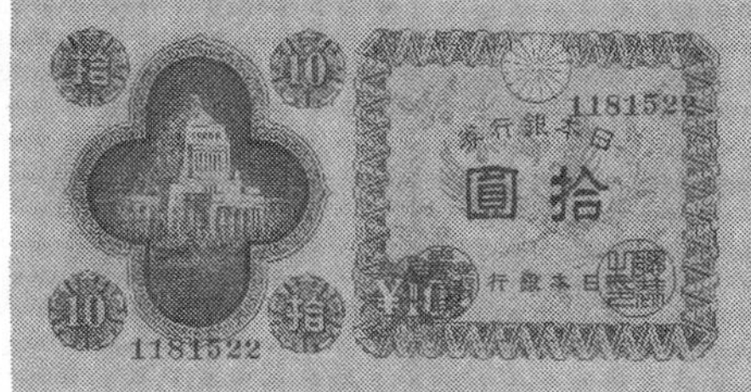

		VG	VF	UNC
87	**10 Yen** ND (1946). Black on gray-blue unpt. Diet Bldg. at l. Back green.			
	a. Issued note.	.25	1.25	4.00
	s1. Specimen w/stamping: *SPECIMEN.*	—	—	600.
	s2. Specimen w/sm. stamping: *Mi-hon.* Regular block #.	—	—	100.

		VG	VF	UNC
88	**50 Yen** ND (1951). Black on orange and olive unpt. Portr. Takahashi Korekiyo at r. Back brown; Bank of Japan at bldg. at l.	4.00	10.00	30.00

		VG	VF	UNC
89	**100 Yen** ND (1946). Like #57 but lilac unpt. of leaves. Back blue. Black control and serial #. Horyuji Temple on back.			
	a. Wmk: Kiri leaves.	2.00	5.00	12.50
	b. Wmk: Arabesque - phoenix design.	4.00	10.00	25.00
	s1. As a. Specimen w/ovpt: *SPECIMEN.*	—	—	850.
	s2. As a. Specimen w/sm. stamping: *Mi-hon.* Regular block #.	—	—	100.
89A	**1000 Yen** ND. Black on rose unpt. Similar to #45. Back green and lt. blue. Specimen. Rare.	—	—	—

1950-58 ND ISSUE

		VG	VF	UNC
90	**100 Yen** ND (1953). Brown-violet on green and m/c unpt. Portr. Itagaki Taisuke at r. 12 varieties exist. Diet Bldg. at r. on back.			
	a. Single letter serial # prefix.	4.00	12.50	40.00
	b. Double letter serial # prefix. Lt. brown paper.	.75	2.00	5.00
	c. As b., but white paper.	FV	FV	2.00
	s. As a. Specimen w/red ovpt. and perforated: *mihon.*	—	—	1500.

		VG	VF	UNC
91	**500 Yen** ND (1951). Blue on m/c unpt. Portr. Iwakura Tomomi at r. Back gray and pale green; Mt. Fuji at r.			
	a. Single letter serial # prefix.	6.00	12.50	35.00
	b. Double letter serial # prefix. Cream paper.	FV	6.00	12.50
	c. As b., but white paper.	FV	5.00	10.00
	s. As a. Specimen w/red ovpt. and perforated: *mihon.*	—	—	1500.
92	**1000 Yen** ND (1950). Black on green and m/c unpt. Portr. #6 at r. Back brown and blue; Yumedono Pavilion at l.			
	a. Single letter serial # prefix.	10.00	30.00	75.00
	b. Double letter serial # prefix.	FV	15.00	30.00
	s. As a. Specimen w/red ovpt. *mihon* punched hole cancelled.	—	—	1500.

		VG	VF	UNC
93	**5000 Yen** ND (1957). Dk. green on m/c unpt. Portr. #6 at ctr. and as wmk. Back green; Bank of Japan at ctr.			
	a. Single letter serial # prefix.	FV	50.00	65.00
	b. Double letter serial # prefix.	FV	FV	55.00

		VG	VF	UNC
94	**10,000 Yen** ND (1958). Dk. brown and dk. green on m/c unpt. Portr. #6 at r. Back brown; phoenix at l. and r. in unpt. within ornate frame. Wmk: Yumedono Pavilion.			
	a. Single letter serial # prefix.	FV	FV	125.
	b. Double letter serial # prefix.	FV	FV	100.

JAPANESE MILITARY CURRENCY

See also China, Hong Kong and occupation issues for Burma, French Indochina, Malaya, Netherlands Indies, Oceania and the Philippines.

GREAT JAPANESE GOVERNMENT - MINISTRY OF FINANCE

省蔵大府政本日大

Dai Nip-pon Sei-fu O-kura-sho

1895 SINO-JAPANESE WAR ISSUE

Issued in North China.

#MA1-M18 2 Onagadori cockerels at top and 2 dragons at bottom.

#MA1-MA5 Meiji yr. 28.

		Good	Fine	XF
MA1	**2 Mace 5 Candareens** 1895. Black on ochre unpt. Back brown. Rare.	—	—	—
MA2	**5 Mace** 1895. Black on gray-violet unpt. Back black. Rare.	—	—	—

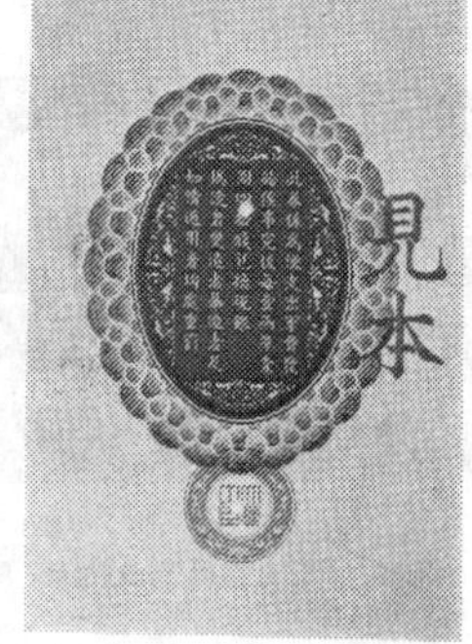

		Good	Fine	XF
MA3	**1 Tael** 1895. Black on lt. blue unpt. Back dk. blue. Rare.	—	—	—

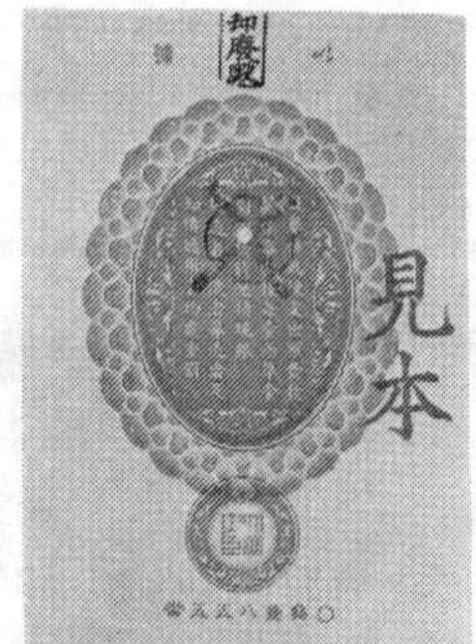

		Good	Fine	XF
MA4	**5 Taels** 1895. Black on green unpt. Back green. Rare.	—	—	—
MA5	**10 Taels** 1895. Black on ochre unpt. Back brown-orange. Rare.	—	—	—

1904 RUSSO-JAPANESE WAR ISSUE

Issued in Korea, North China and Sakhalin in Eastern Siberia. Meiji yr. 37.

10 SEN

50 SEN

		Good	Fine	XF
M1	**10 Sen** 1904. Black on lt. red-brown unpt. Back red-brown.			
	a. W/serial # at top on back.	20.00	40.00	75.00
	b. W/o serial # on back.	10.00	20.00	40.00
M2	**20 Sen** 1904. Black on green unpt. Back green.			
	a. W/serial # at top on back.	75.00	150.	300.
	b. W/o serial # on back.	40.00	75.00	150.
M3	**50 Sen** 1904. Black on lt. gray-violet unpt. Back lt. gray-violet.			
	a. W/ serial # at top on back.	75.00	150.	300.
	b. W/o serial # on back.	40.00	75.00	150.

Note: For issues w/design like #M1-M3 but having a 10-pointed star above cockerels' heads, see Korea #7-9.

		Good	Fine	XF
M4	**1 Yen** 1904. Black on ochre unpt. Back yellow-brown.			
	a. W/serial # at top on back.	125.	250.	500.
	b. W/o serial # on back.	80.00	200.	400.
M5	**5 Yen** 1904. Black on lt. blue-gray unpt. Back blue-gray.			
	a. W/serial # at top of rack.	750.	1500.	3000.
	b. W/o serial # on back.	500.	1250.	2500.
M6	**10 Yen** 1904. Black on lt. brown-violet unpt. Back brown-violet.			
	a. W/serial # at top on back.	1000.	2000.	—
	b. W/o serial # on back.	700.	1750.	—

1914 OCCUPATION OF TSINGTAO ISSUE

#M7-M12 English legends - *in silver* at l., and r. and at top on back. Taisho yr. 3 (except #M7a and M9a, Meiji Yr. 37).

		Good	Fine	XF
M7	**10 Sen** 1914. Black on red-brown unpt. Back red-brown.			
	a. Like #M1 but ovpt: *10 SEN IN SILVER* in capital letters.	300.	500.	1000.
	b. Ovpt. in small letters.	750.	1000.	2500.
M8	**20 Sen** 1914. Black on lt. green unpt. Back lt. green.	375.	950.	1250.
M9	**50 Sen** 1914. Black on lt. purple unpt. Back lt. purple.			
	a. Like #M3 but ovpt: *50 SEN IN SILVER* in capital letters.	375.	950.	1500.
	b. Ovpt. in small letters.	1200.	2000.	4000.
M10	**1 Yen** 1914. Black on yellow unpt. Back orange.	1000.	1750.	3500.

5 YEN

10 YEN

		Good	Fine	XF
M11	**5 Yen** 1914. Black on lt. blue unpt. Back blue-gray. Rare.	—	—	—
M12	**10 Yen** 1914. Black on lt. red-brown unpt. Back red-brown. Rare.	—	—	—

1918 Occupation Of Siberia Issue

#M13-M18 Russian legends at l. and r. Taisho yr. 7.

10 SEN

50 SEN

		Good	Fine	XF
M13	**10 Sen** 1918. Black on ochre unpt. Back yellow-brown.	50.00	100.	200.
M14	**20 Sen** 1918. Black on lt. green unpt. Back lt. green.	60.00	125.	250.
M15	**50 Sen** 1918. Black on tan unpt. Back brown.	75.00	350.	500.

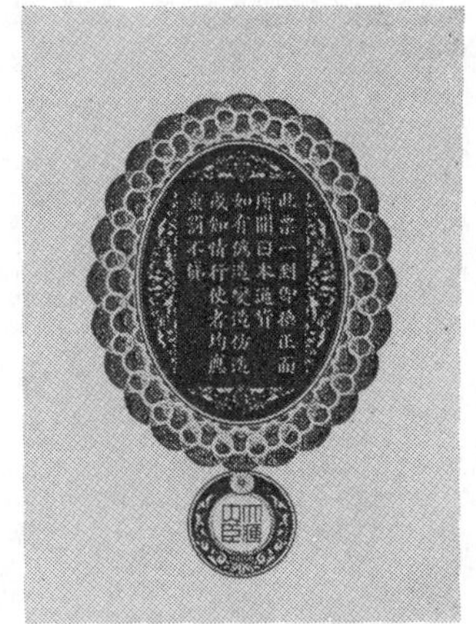

		Good	Fine	XF
M16	**1 Yen** 1918. Black on lt. blue unpt. Back dk. blue.	250.	500.	1000.
M17	**5 Yen** 1918. Black on lt. brown-violet unpt. Back brown-violet.	1100.	2250.	4500.
M18	**10 Yen** 1918. Black.			
	a. Lt. purple unpt. Back blue-violet.	1250.	2500.	5500.
	s. Lt. violet unpt. Back violet. Specimen. Rare.	—	—	—

Note: For similar notes dated Showa yr. 12 (1937), see China #M1-M5.

1940's ND Occupation Of Russian Territory Issue

#M19-M23 w/Russian text and block #.

		Good	Fine	XF
M19	**10 Kopeks** ND. Gray-green on blue unpt. Rare.	—	—	—
M20	**50 Kopeks** ND. Red-brown on pink unpt. Similar to Malaya 50 cents, #M4. Rare.	—	—	—
M21	**1 Ruble** ND. Brown on tan unpt. Similar to Malaya 1 Dollar, #M5. Rare.	—	—	—
M22	**5 Rubles** ND. Blue on plae blue unpt. Similar to Malaya 5 Dollars, #M6. Rare.	—	—	—
M23	**1 Chervonetz** ND. Dk. blue on pale blue. 2 peasant woman at r. Similar to Oceania 1£, #4. Rare.	—	—	—

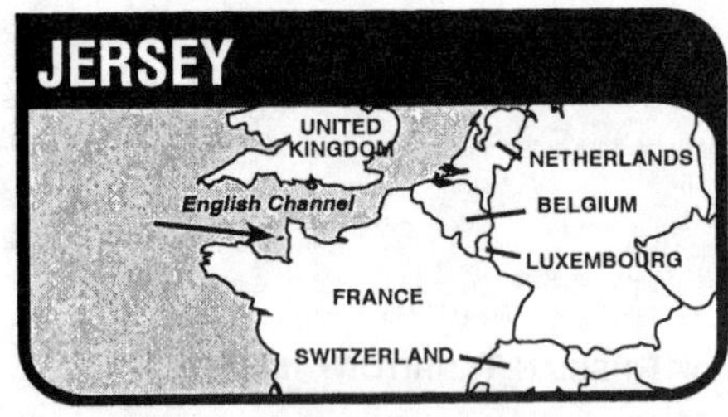

The Bailiwick of Jersey, a British Crown dependency located in the English Channel 12 miles (19 km.) west of Normandy, France, has an area of 45 sq. mi. (117 sq. km.) and a population of 90,000. Capital: St. Helier. The economy is d on agriculture and cattle breeding - the importation of cattle is prohibited to protect the purity of the island's world-famous strain of milk cows.

Jersey was occupied by Neanderthal man 100,000 years B.C., and by Iberians of 2000 B.C. who left their chamber tombs in the island's granite cliffs. Roman legions almost certainly visited the island although they left no evidence of settlement. The country folk of Jersey still speak an archaic form of Norman-French, lingering evidence of the Norman annexation of the island in 933 B.C. Jersey was annexed to England in 1206, 140 years after the Norman Conquest. The dependency is administered by its own laws and customs; laws enacted by the British Parliament do not apply to Jersey unless it is specifically mentioned. During World War II, German troops occupied the island from 1940 until 1944.

United Kingdom bank notes and coinage circulate concurrently with Jersey money as legal tender.

RULERS:

British

MONETARY SYSTEM:

1 Shilling = 12 Pence
1 Pound = 20 Shillings to 1971

NOTE: Certain listings encompassing issues circulated by various bank and regional authorities are contained in Vol. 1.

BRITISH ADMINISTRATION

STATES OF THE ISLAND OF JERSEY

1840 INTEREST BEARING NOTES

		Good	Fine	XF
A1	**5 Pounds** 1.9.1840. Black. Arms at upper ctr. *JERSEY STATES' BOND for FIVE POUNDS BRITISH.* on back. Printer: W. Adams.			
	a. Issued note. Rare.	—	—	—
	b. Pen cancelled.	20.00	40.00	80.00
	r. Remainder. 18xx.	20.00	40.00	80.00

GERMAN OCCUPATION - WWII

STATES OF JERSEY

1941 ND ISSUES

#1-6 arms at upper l.

		VG	VF	UNC
1	**6 Pence** ND (1941-42). Black on orange unpt. Back orange. Wmk: thick or thin chain.			
	a. Issued note.	20.00	55.00	140.
	b. Cancelled.	12.00	30.00	80.00
	r. Remainder. W/o serial #.	—	—	—

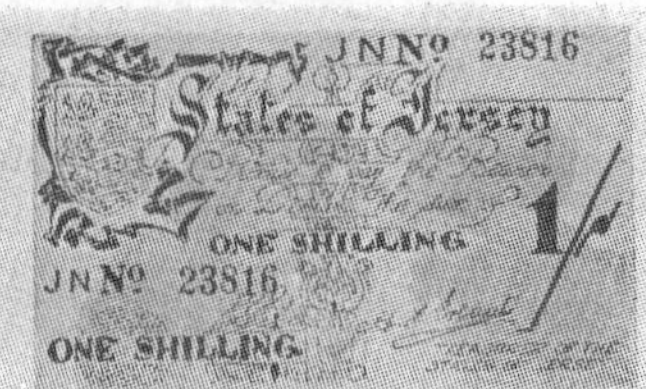

		VG	VF	UNC
2	**1 Shilling** ND (1941-42). Dk. brown on blue unpt. 2 men in unpt. Same 2 men in brown on back. Wmk: thick chain.			
	a. Issued note.	25.00	65.00	175.
	b. Cancelled.	15.00	40.00	100.
	r. Remainder. W/o serial #.	—	—	—

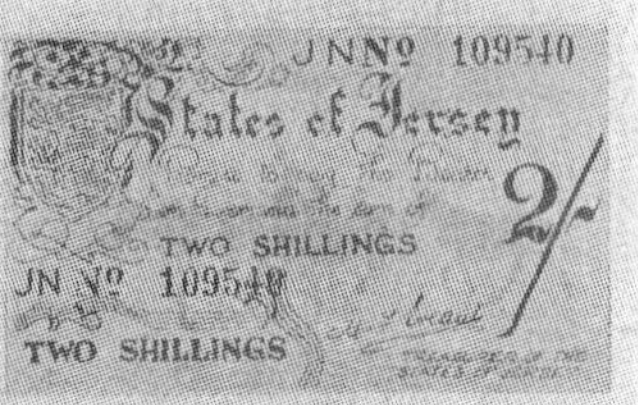

		VG	VF	UNC
3	**2 Shillings** ND (1941-42). Blue on lt. brown unpt. Horse-drawn cart in unpt. Same cart in blue on back. Wmk: thick chain.			
	a. Issued note.	40.00	100.	275.
	b. Cancelled.	25.00	60.00	150.
	r. Remainder. W/o serial #.	—	—	—

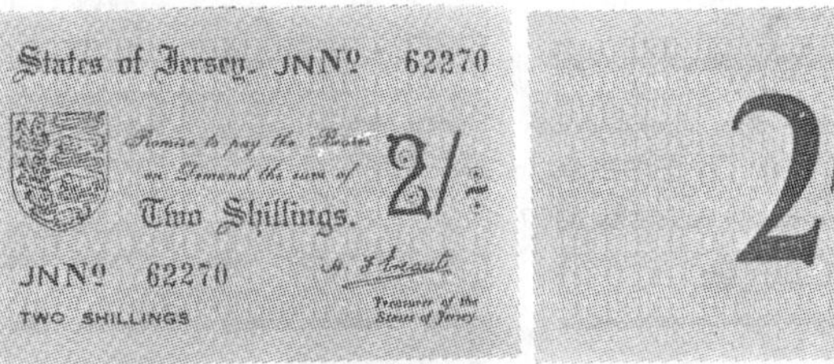

		VG	VF	UNC
4	**2 Shillings** ND (1941-42). Dk. blue-violet on pale orange unpt. W/o cart scene on back. Wmk: thick chain.			
	a. Issued note.	65.00	175.	450.
	b. Cancelled.	35.00	85.00	200.

		VG	VF	UNC
5	**10 SHILLINGS** ND (1941-42). Green. Girl w/cows on back. Wmk: thick or thin chain.			
	a. Issued note.	45.00	95.00	250.00
	b. Cancelled.	25.00	55.00	125.00
6	**1 POUND** ND (1941-42). Purple on green unpt. Face similar to #5. Back purple; men w/horse and cart gathering seaweed. Wmk: thick chain.	VG	VF	UNC
	a. Issued note.	60.00	120.00	350.00
	b. Cancelled.	36.00	72.00	180.00

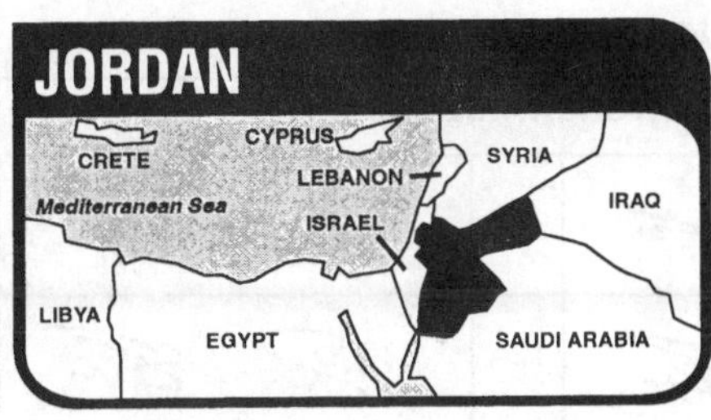

The Hashemite Kingdom of Jordan, a constitutional monarchy in southwest Asia, has an area of 37,738 sq. mi. (97,740 sq. km.) and a population of 5.46 million. Capital: Amman. Agriculture and tourism comprise Jordan's economic . Chief exports are phosphates, tomatoes and oranges.

Jordan is the Edom and Moab of the time of Moses. It became part of the Roman province of Arabia in 106 AD, was conquered by the Arabs in 633-36, and was part of the Ottoman Empire from the 16th century until World War I. At that time, the regions presently known as Jordan and Israel were mandated to Great Britain by the League of Nations as Transjordan and Palestine. In 1922 Transjordan was established as the semi-autonomous Emirate of Transjordan, ruled by the Hashemite Prince Abdullah but still nominally a part of the British mandate. The mandate over Transjordan was terminated in 1946, the country becoming the independent Hashemite Kingdom of Transjordan. The kingdom was renamed The Hashemite Kingdom of The Jordan in 1950.

RULERS:

Abdullah I, 1946-1951
Hussein I, 1952-1999
Abdullah II

MONETARY SYSTEM:

1 Dinar = 10 Dirhams
1 Dirham = 10 Piastres = 10 Qirsh
1 Piastre = 1 Qirsh = 10 Fils

SIGNATURE VARIETIES					
1			6		
2			6A		
3			7		
4			8		
5			9		

KINGDOM

THE HASHEMITE KINGDOM OF THE JORDAN

JORDAN CURRENCY BOARD FIRST ISSUE

#1-5 wmk. Kg. Abdullah. Printer: TDLR.

#2-5 Kg. Abdullah at r.

		VG	VF	UNC
1	**500 Fils**			
	L.1949. Lilac. Landscape w/irrigation system. Cows in hayfield on back.			
	a. Issued note. Sign. 1, 2.	15.00	60.00	250.
	s. Specimen perforated: *Cancelled.* Sign. 1.	—	—	200.

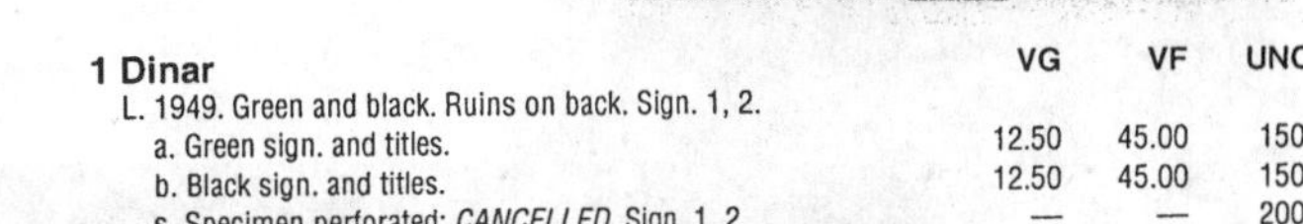

		VG	VF	UNC
2	**1 Dinar**			
	L. 1949. Green and black. Ruins on back. Sign. 1, 2.			
	a. Green sign. and titles.	12.50	45.00	150.
	b. Black sign. and titles.	12.50	45.00	150.
	s. Specimen perforated: *CANCELLED.* Sign. 1, 2.	—	—	200.

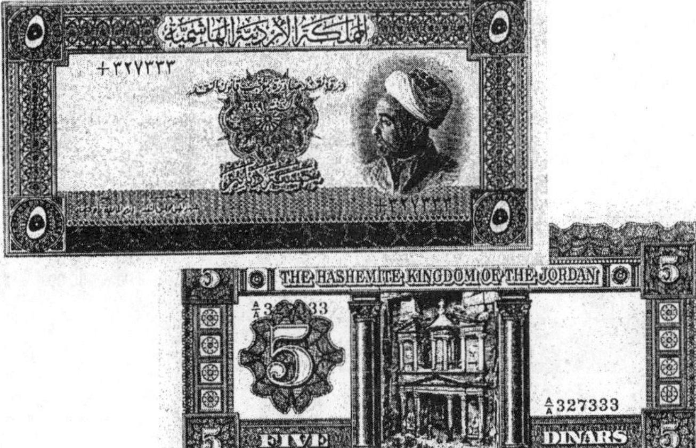

		VG	VF	UNC
3	**5 Dinars**			
	L.1949. Red and black. El Hazne, Treasury of Pharaoh at Petra at ctr. on back. Sign 1.			
	a. Issued note.	50.00	150.	350.
	s. Specimen perforated: *CANCELLED.*	—	—	350.

		VG	VF	UNC
4	**10 Dinars**			
	L.1949. Blue and black. El Hazne, Treasury of Pharaoh at Petra at ctr. on back. Sign. 1.			
	a. Issued note.	50.00	125.	300.
	s. Specimen perforated: *CANCELLED.*	—	—	350.
5	**50 Dinars**			
	L. 1949. Brown. Aqaba beach on back. Sign. 2.			
	a. Issued note. Rare.	—	—	—
	s. Specimen perforated: *CANCELLED.*	—	—	2000.

THE HASHEMITE KINGDOM OF JORDAN

JORDAN CURRENCY BOARD SECOND ISSUE

#A6-8 backs like #1-5. Wmk: Young Kg. Hussein w/o head covering. Printer: TDLR.

#6-8 Kg. Hussein at r.

		VG	VF	UNC
6	**1 Dinar** L.1949. (1952). Green and black. Back like #2.			
	a. Sign. 3; 6A.	5.00	30.00	150.
	b. Sign. 6.	7.50	50.00	200.

		VG	VF	UNC
A6	**500 Fils** L.1949. (1952) Lilac. Like #1.			
	a. Sign. 3.	7.50	50.00	200.
	b. Sign. 4; 5.	6.00	35.00	150.

		VG	VF	UNC
7	**5 Dinars** L.1949. (1952). Red and black. Back like #3.			
	a. Sign. 3; 9.	25.00	150.	375.
	b. Sign. 7.	30.00	175.	400.

		VG	VF	UNC
8	**10 Dinars** L.1949. (1952). Blue and black. Back like #4.			
	a. Sign. 3; 4.	50.00	200.	475.
	b. Sign. 5.	45.00	175.	400.

CENTRAL BANK OF JORDAN

SIGNATURE VARIETIES			
9		10	
11		12A	
12		13	
14		15	

FIRST ISSUE - LAW 1959

#9-12 Kg. Hussein at l. w/law date 1959 (in Arabic *1909*).

		VG	VF	UNC
9	**500 Fils** L.1959. Brown on m/c unpt. Jerash Forum on back. FIVE HUNDRED FILS at bottom margin on back. Sign. 10.			
	a. Issued note.	10.00	50.00	100.
	s. Specimen.	—	—	100.

		VG	VF	UNC
10	**1 Dinar** L.1959. Green on m/c unpt. Al-Aqsa Mosque "Dome of the Rock" at ctr. w/columns at r. on back. Sign. 10.			
	a. Issued note.	4.00	20.00	65.00
	s. Specimen.	—	—	100.

		VG	VF	UNC
11	**5 Dinars** L.1959. Red-brown on m/c unpt. Al-Hazne, Treasury of Pharaoh at Petra at ctr. r. on back.			
	a. Sign. 10; 11; 12.	10.00	35.00	125.
	s. Specimen. Sign. 10.	—	—	125.

		VG	VF	UNC
12	**10 Dinars** L.1959. Blue-gray on m/c unpt. Baptismal site on River Jordan on back.			
	a. Sign. 10; 11, 12.	25.00	65.00	235.
	s. Specimen. Sign. 10.	—	—	125.

SECOND ND ISSUE

#13-16 like #9-12. Kg. Hussein I at l., but w/o law date *1959* (in Arabic *1909*). Wmk: Kg. Hussein wearing turban.

		VG	VF	UNC
13	**1/2 DINAR** ND. Like #9, but w/*HALF DINAR* at bottom margin on back.			
	a. Sign. 12.	1.50	7.50	30.00
	b. Sign. 12A.	1.50	7.50	30.00
	c. Sign. 14.	1.00	3.00	12.00
14	**1 DINAR** ND. Like #10.			
	a. Sign. 13.	3.00	10.00	37.50
	b. Sign. 14.	2.00	6.00	25.00
15	**5 DINARS** ND. Like #11.			
	a. Sign. 12.	4.00	12.50	60.00
	b. Sign. 15.	3.00	10.00	35.00

		VG	VF	UNC
16	**10 DINARS** ND. Like #12.			
	a. Sign. 12; 12A.	8.50	25.00	100.00
	b. Sign. 13; 14.	8.50	25.00	125.00
	c. Sign. 15.	FV	FV	85.00

Kiau Chau (Kiao Chau, Kiaochow, Kiautscho), a former German trading enclave, including the port of Tsingtao, was located on the Shantung Peninsula of eastern China. Following the murder of two missionaries in Shantung in 1897, Germany occupied Kiaochow Bay, and during subsequent negotiations with the Chinese government obtained a 99-year lease on 177 sq. mi. of land. The enclave s established as a free port in 1899, and a customs ouse set up to collect tariffs on goods moving to and from the Chinese interior. The Japanese took siege to the port on Aug. 27, 1914 as their first action in World War I to deprive German sea marauders of their east Asian supply and refitting . Aided by British forces the siege ended on Nov. 7. Japan retained possession until 1922, when it was restored to China by the Washington Conference on China and naval armaments. It fell again to Japan in 1938, but not until the Chinese had destroyed its manufacturing facilities. Since 1949 it has been a part of the Peoples Republic of China.

RULERS:

German, 1897-1914
Japanese, 1914-1922, 1938-1945

MONETARY SYSTEM:

1 Dollar = 100 Cents

Note: *S/M #* refer to *Chinese Banknotes* by Ward D. Smith and Brian Matravers.

GERMAN ADMINISTRATION

DEUTSCH-ASIATISCHE BANK

行銀華德
Te Hua Yin Hang

For notes of the Deutsch-Asiatische Bank issued by branches *HANKOW, PEKING* or *SHANGHAI* other than *TSINGTAO*, refer to Foreign Banks in China listings, Volume 1.

TSINGTAO

1907; 1914 ISSUE

#1-7 printer: G&D.

		Good	Fine	XF
1	**1 Dollar** 1.3.1907. Blue and rose. "Germania" standing at r. w/spear. *(S/M #T101-40)*.			
	a. Wmk: 8 cornered crossflower.	750.	2000.	—
	b. Wmk: *GD*.	750.	2000.	—
2	**5 Dollars** 1907; 1914. Dk. green and violet. Like #1. *(S/M #T101-41)*.			
	a. Wmk: 8 cornered crossflower. 1.3.1907.	350.	1000.	—
	b. Wmk: *GD*. 1.3.1907.	350.	1000.	—
	c. Wmk: *GD*. 1.7.1914. (Not issued). Rare.	—	—	—

		Good	Fine	XF
3	**10 Dollars** 1907; 1914. Brown and blue. Like #1. *(S/M #T101-42)*.			
	a. Wmk: 8 cornered crossflower.	450.	1250.	—
	b. Wmk: *GD*. 1.3.1907. Reported not confirmed.	—	—	—
	c. Wmk: *GD*. 1.7.1914. (Not issued). Rare.	—	—	—
4	**25 Dollars** 1.3.1907. Green and rose. Like #1. *(S/M #T101-43)*.			
	a. Wmk: 8 cornered crossflower. Rare.	—	—	—
	b. Wmk: *GD*.	—	—	—
5	**50 Dollars** 1.3.1907. Violet and gray. Like #1. *(S/M #T101-44)*.			
	a. Wmk: 8 cornered crossflower. Rare.	—	—	—
	b. Wmk: *GD*. Reported not confirmed.	—	—	—

		Good	Fine	XF
6	**200 Dollars** 1.7.1914. Like #1. Wmk: *GD. (S/M #T101-45).*	—	—	—
7	**500 Dollars** 1.7.1914. Like #1. Wmk: *GD. (S/M #T101-46).* Rare.	—	—	—

Note: Denominations of 1, 50, 100 and 200 Dollars are reported, but not confirmed.

1914 TAEL ISSUE

#8-10 printer: G&D.

		Good	Fine	XF
8	**50 Taels** 1.7.1914. Like #1. Wmk: *GD. (S/M #T101-51).*	—	—	—
9	**100 Taels** 1.7.1914. Like #1. Wmk: *GD. (S/M #T101-52).*	—	—	—
10	**500 Taels** 1.7.1914. Like #1. *(S/M #T101-53).*	—	—	—

Note: Denominations of 1, 5, 10 and 20 Taels dated 1914 are reported, but not confirmed.

Korea,"Land of the Morning Calm" occupies a mountainous peninsula in northeast Asia bounded by Manchuria, the Yellow Sea and the Sea of Japan. According to legend the first Korean dynasty, that of the House of Tangun, ruled from 233 BC to 1122 BC. It was followed by the dynasty of Kija, a Chinese scholar, which continued until 19 BC and brought a high civilization to Korea. The first recorded period in the history of Korea, the Period of the Three Kingdoms, lasted from 57 BC to 935 AD and achieved the first political unification on the peninsula. The Kingdom of Koryo, from which Korea derives its name, was founded in 935 and continued until 1392, when it was superseded by the Yi dynasty of King Yi, Sung Kye which was to last until the Japanese annexation in 1910.

At the end of the 16th century Korea was invaded and occupied for 7 years by Japan, and from 1627 until the late 19th century it was a semi-independent tributary of China. Japan replaced China as the predominant foreign influence at the end of the Sino-Japanese War (1894-95), only to find its position threatened by Russian influence from 1896 to 1904. The Russian threat was eliminated by the Russo-Japanese War (1904-05) and in 1905 Japan established a direct protectorate over Korea. On Aug. 22, 1910, the last Korean ruler signed the treaty that annexed Korea to Japan as a government general in the Japanese Empire. Japanese suzerainty was maintained until the end of World War II.

The Potsdam conference in 1945 set the 38th parallel as the line dividing the occupation forces of the United States in the south and the Soviet Union in the north.

A contingent of the United States Army landed at Inchon to begin the acceptance of the surrender of Japanese forces in the south on Sept. 8, 1945. Unissued Japanese printed stock was released during the U.S. Army's administration for circulation in the southern sector.

RULERS:

Japanese, 1910-1945
Yi Hyong (Kojong), 1864-1897
as Kwangmu, 1897-1907
Yung Hi, 19

MONETARY SYSTEM:

1 Yang = 100 Fun
1 Whan = 5 Yang to 1902
1 Won = 100 Chon 1902-
1 Yen = 100 Sen

MONETARY UNITS:

REPLACEMENT NOTES:

#29-34, 36: notes w/first digit 9 in serial number.

KINGDOM OF KOREA

TREASURY DEPARTMENT

HOJO

1893 CONVERTIBLE NOTES

#1-3 dragons around text in circle at ctr. Printed in 1893 (30th year of King Kojong). Issuing Agency: Ta Whan Shou (Conversion Office). (Not issued).

		Good	Fine	XF
1	**5 Yang** Yr. 30 (1893). Rare.	—	—	—
2	**10 Yang** Yr. 30 (1893). Rare.	—	—	—
2A	**20 Yang** Yr. 30 (1893). Rare.	—	—	—

		Good	Fine	XF
3	**50 Yang** Yr. 30 (1893). Rare.	—	—	—

JAPANESE PROTECTORATE

DAI ICHI GINKO

FIRST NATIONAL BANK OF JAPAN

1902 ISSUE

#4-12 w/10 pronged star at top ctr.

#4-6 S. Eiichi at r.

		Good	Fine	XF
4	**1 Yen** 1902; 1904. Black on blue-green unpt. Back dk. blue.			
	a. Stars in corners on face. 1902. (Meiji yr. 35).	300.	800.	1750.
	b. Numerals in corners on face. 1904. (Meiji yr. 37).	225.	700.	1500.

		Good	Fine	XF
5	**5 Yen** 1902; 1904. Black on ochre unpt. Like #4. Back grayish blue-green.			
	a. Stars in corners on face. 1902. (Meiji yr. 35).	600.	1500.	—
	b. Numerals in corners on face. 1904. (Meiji yr. 37).	500.	1250.	4000.

		Good	Fine	XF
6	**10 Yen** 1902; 1904. Black on lt. blue unpt. Like #4. Back dark red-brown.			
	a. Stars in corners on face. 1902. (Meiji yr. 35).	700.	2000.	—
	b. Numerals in corners on face. 1904. (Meiji yr. 37).	550.	1750.	—

1904 ISSUE

		Good	Fine	XF
7	**10 Sen** 1904. (Meiji yr. 37). Red. 2 Onagadori cockerels at top w/2 dragons below.	75.00	250.	850.
8	**20 Sen** 1904. (Meiji yr. 37). Blue. Like #7.	200.	600.	1500.
9	**50 Sen** 1904. (Meiji yr. 37). Yellow. Like #7. Back purple.	250.	850.	2000.

Note: For issues similar to #7-9 but w/chrysanthemum crest above cockerels' heads see Japan - Military Issues #M1-M3.

1907 ISSUE

		Good	Fine	XF
9A	**5 Yen** 1907. Black. Peacock at l., temple at ctr. Back purple on ochre unpt. (Meiji yr. 39). Specimen ovpt: *Mi-hon*. Rare.	—	—	—

1908-09 ISSUE

		Good	Fine	XF
10	**1 Yen** 1908. (Meiji yr. 40). Blue on pink unpt. Bridge shelter at l. Back red on lt. blue unpt.	175.	600.	1250.

		Good	Fine	XF
11	**5 Yen** 1909. (Meiji yr. 41). Black on lt. orange-brown unpt. Shrine at r. Back purple w/black text on lt. green unpt. Rare.	—	—	—

		Good	Fine	XF
12	**10 Yen** 1909. (Meiji yr. 41). Green. Back brown-violet; house at r. Rare.	—	—	—

BANK OF KOREA

1909 ISSUE

#13-15 plum blossom at top ctr. Dated Yung Hi yr. 3.

		Good	Fine	XF
13	**1 Yen** 1909 (1910). Similar to #10. Back brown-orange.	100.	350.	950.
14	**5 Yen** 1909 (1911). Black on lt. violet-brown unpt. Like #11. Back blue-black on lt. green unpt.	375.	1250.	4000.
15	**10 Yen** 1909 (1911). Dk. gray-green on lilac unpt. Like #12. Back brown.	350.	850.	2750.

BANK OF CHOSEN

1911 (1914) FIRST ISSUE

#16-16A 2 printers, distinguished by serial # style. Dated Meiji yr. 44 (1911). Stylized serial # (Korean). Regular style serial # (Japanese).

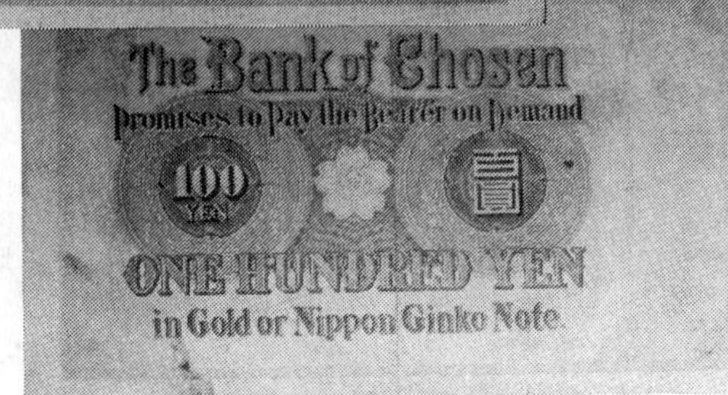

193415 | 899296

		Good	Fine	XF
16	**100 Yen** 1911 (1914). Purple on lilac and ochre unpt. God of Fortune sitting on rice bales w/sack over shoulder. Stylized serial # (Korean).	65.00	200.	1250.
16A	**100 Yen** 1911 (1914). Like #16 but blue. Regular style serial # (Japanese).	50.00	175.	1000.

1911 (1915) SECOND ISSUE

#17-19 2 printers, distinguished by serial # style. Dated Meiji yr. 44 (1911). Stylized serial # (Korean). Regular style serial # (Japanese).

		VG	VF	UNC
17	**1 Yen** 1911 (1915). Black on lt. red unpt. Man w/beard. *ONE YEN* at l.			
	a. Stylized serial # (Korean).	15.00	60.00	300.
	b. Regular style serial # (Japanese).	10.00	45.00	200.
18	**5 Yen** 1911 (1915). Brown. Man w/beard at r.			
	a. Stylized serial # (Korean).	75.00	450.	2000.
	b. Regular style serial # Japanese).	60.00	400.	1750.

		VG	VF	UNC
19	**10 Yen** 1911 (1915). Green. *TEN YEN* at l., man w/beard at r.			
	a. Stylized serial # (Korean).	60.00	400.	1600
	b. Regular style serial # (Japanese).	50.00	275.	1250

1916 ISSUE

#20-22 dated Taisho yr. 5.

		VG	VF	UNC
20	**10 Sen** 1916. Blue on pink unpt. W/o Western numerals for denomination on face. Back red.	30.00	100.	400
21	**20 Sen** 1916. Blue on orange unpt. W/o Western numerals for denomination on face.	135.	475.	1500

		VG	VF	UNC
22	**50 Sen** 1916. Blue on lt. green unpt. W/o Western numerals for denomination on face.	135.	475.	1500.

1919 ISSUE

#23-25 Russian, Japanese and English text: ***payable in Japanese currency at any of its Manchurian offices.*** **Dated Taisho yr. 8.**

		VG	VF	UNC
23	**10 Sen** 20.10.1919. Green on pink unpt. Western numerals for denomination at r. on face. Russian and English wording on pink back.			
	a. 7 character imprint (Korean).	12.50	50.00	175.
	b. 14 character imprint (Japanese).	20.00	75.00	225.

		VG	VF	UNC
24	**20 Sen** 20.10.1919. Black on yellow unpt. Western numerals for denomination at r. on face. Russian legends on back.	30.00	100.	350.
25	**50 Sen** 20.10.1919. Black on green unpt. Western numerals for denomination at r. on face. Russian legends on back.			
	a. 7 character imprint (Korean). Blocks 1-6.	20.00	125.	375.
	b. 14 character imprint (Japanese). Blocks 6-7.	30.00	175.	500.

1917 PROVISIONAL POSTAL STAMP ISSUE

		VG	VF	UNC
26	**5 Sen** 1917. Japanese 5 Sen postal adhesive stamp (type Tazawa) affixed to a special form.	200.	500.	1100.

1932-38 ND AND DATED ISSUE

		VG	VF	UNC
27	**10 Sen** 1937. Like #23 but w/o Russian wording on back. (Showa yr. 12).	12.50	50.00	200.
28	**50 Sen** 1937. Like #25 but w/o Russian legends on back. (Showa yr. 12).			
	a. Issued note.	10.00	40.00	175.
	s. Specimen w/red ovpt: *Mi-hon.*	—	—	200.

#29-32 w/o bank name in English on back.

		VG	VF	UNC
29	**1 Yen** ND (1932). Black on lt. brown unpt. Brown guilloche at l., green guilloche at ctr., man w/beard at r. Serial # and block #. 14 character imprint.			
	a. Issued note.	.25	2.00	7.50
	s1. Specimen w/red ovpt. and perforated: *Mi-hon.*	—	—	200.
	s2. Specimen w/vermilion ovpt: *Mi-hon.*	—	—	125.
	s3. Specimen w/red ovpt: *Mi-hon,* punched hole cancelled.	—	—	75.00
30	**5 Yen** ND (1935). Black on lt. brown, green and lilac unpt. Man w/beard at r. Back green; *5 YEN* at bottom. 7 character imprint.			
	a. Issued note.	8.00	25.00	200.
	s1. Specimen w/red ovpt. and perforated: *Mi-hon.*	—	—	200.
	s2. Specimen w/red ovpt: *Mi-hon,* punched hole cancelled.	—	—	100.
31	**10 Yen** ND (1932). Black. Green and olive guilloche at ctr., man w/beard at r. Back green and brown; bldg. at ctr., *10 YEN* at bottom. 14 character imprint.			
	a. Issued note.	1.00	3.00	15.00
	s. Specimen w/red ovpt. and perforated: *Mi-hon.*	—	—	200.

		VG	VF	UNC
32	**100 Yen** ND (1938). Black on pink, green and violet unpt. Man w/beard at r. *100 YEN* at bottom on back. Wmk: Plum branches. 12 character imprint.			
	a. Issued note.	5.00	15.00	80.00
	s. Specimen w/red ovpt: *Mi-hon,* punched hole cancelled.	—	—	200.

1944 ND ISSUES

		VG	VF	UNC
33	**1 Yen** ND (1944). Like #29 but block # only.			
	a. Issued note.	.50	4.50	15.00
	s1. Specimen w/red ovpt: *Mi-hon.*	—	—	150.
	s2. Specimen w/vermilion ovpt: *Mi-hon* on face and back.	—	—	100.
34	**5 Yen** ND (1944). Like #30 but w/o 5 YEN at bottom on back. Serial # and block #. 10 character imprint.			
	a. Issued note.	4.00	25.00	135.
	s1. Specimen w/red ovpt. and perforated: *Mi-hon.*	—	—	250.
	s2. Specimen w/vermilion ovpt: *Mi-hon* on face and back.	—	—	200.
	s3. Specimen w/vermilion ovpt: *Mi-yo* in frame. *Specimen* on back.	—	—	100.
35	**10 Yen** ND (1944). Black on blue unpt. Brown and green guilloche at ctr., man w/beard at r. W/o *10 YEN* at bottom on dull green back. Serial # and block #. 7 character imprint.			
	a. Issued note.	2.00	10.00	85.00
	s. Specimen w/red ovpt. and perforated: *Mi-hon.*	—	—	225.

		VG	VF	UNC
36	**10 Yen** ND (1944-45). Like #35 but block # only. 7 character imprint.			
	a. Wmk: *CHOSEN GINKO* (4 characters) at bottom, ornaments at ctr. (1944).	3.00	10.00	50.00
	b. Wmk: *CHO* character and cherry blossoms repeated. (1945).	2.00	7.50	40.00
	s1. As a. Specimen w/vermilion ovpt: *Mi-hon* on face and back.	—	—	150.
	s2. As a. Specimen w/vermilion ovpt: *Mi-hon.*	—	—	100.
	s3. As a. Specimen w/purple ovpt: *Mi-yo* in frame. *Specimen* on back.	—	—	100.
	s4. As b. Specimen w/vermilion ovpt: *Mi-hon* on face and back.	—	—	150.
37	**100 Yen** ND (1944). Black on green, blue and violet unpt. Guilloche at ctr., man w/beard at r. W/o *100 YEN* at bottom on back. Serial and block #. W/ or w/o wmk. 10 character imprint.			

		VG	VF	UNC
37				
	a. Issued note.	3.00	10.00	45.00
	s1. Specimen w/red ovpt: *Mi-hon.*	—	—	215.
	s2. Specimen w/vermilion ovpt: *Mi-hon* on face and back.	—	—	150.
	s3. Specimen w/vermilion ovpt: *Mi-hon.*	—	—	100.

1945 ND Issue

		VG	VF	UNC
38	**1 Yen** ND (1945). Black on pale green and brown unpt. Guilloche brown at l. w/o guilloche at ctr. Man w/beard at r. Block # only. Back green. Lithographed.			
	a. Issued note.	.25	2.00	7.50
	s1. Specimen w/red ovpt: *Mi-hon.* Special serial # on back.	—	—	125.
	s2. Specimen w/red ovpt: *Mi-hon* in frame.	—	—	75.00
	s3. Specimen w/vermilion ovpt: *Mi-hon* in frame on face and back.	—	—	75.00
	s4. Specimen w/vermilion ovpt: *Mi-yo* in frame. *Specimen* on back.	—	—	75.00
39	**5 Yen** ND (1945). Like #34 but block # only.			
	a. Issued note.	3.00	10.00	75.00
	s. Specimen w/vermilion ovpt: *Mi-yo* in frame. *Specimen* on back.	—	—	100.

		VG	VF	UNC
40	**10 Yen** ND (1945-46). Black on purple unpt. Gray guilloche at ctr., man w/beard at r., paulownia crest at top ctr. Block # only. Back gray to grayish purple. 7 character imprint.			
	a. Block # 1; 2 (1945).	10.00	45.00	325.
	b. Block # 3; 4 (1946).	15.00	65.00	400.
	s1. As a. Specimen w/red ovpt: *Mi-hon.* Special serial # on back.	—	—	200.
	s2. As a. Specimen w/vermilion ovpt: *Mi-yo* in frame. *Specimen* on back.	—	—	125.
	s3. As b. Specimen w/vermilion ovpt: *Mi-yo* in frame.	—	—	125.

		VG	VF	UNC
41	**100 Yen** ND (1945). Black. Face like #32 and #37 but litho. Lt. blue unpt. and guilloche at l. Paulownia crest above portr. Blocks 1 and 2 only. Back dull gray-brown; design like #37.	350.	1000.	3500.
42	**1000 Yen** ND (1945). Lt. purple. Man w/beard at r. Back gray.			
	a. Block #1. (Not issued).	—	2000.	5000.
	s. Specimen w/red ovpt: *Mi-hon.*	—	2500.	6000.

1945 ND Provisional Issue

		VG	VF	UNC
42A	**1000 Yen** ND (1945). 5 character red ovpt: *Chosen Ginko Ken* (Bank of Chosen Note) on Japan #45. (Not issued).	—	Unc	6000.

Note: #37 and 37A may have been issued by the South Korean government.

U.S. Army Administration

Issued for circulation in the southern sector.

Bank of Chosen

1946-47 Issue

		VG	VF	UNC
43	**10 Yen = 10 Won** ND (1946). Black on pale green unpt, blue-green guilloche at ctr. Man w/beard at r. 5 petaled white hibiscus flower at upper ctr. Block # only. Back gray. 12 character imprint.	.75	4.00	22.50
44	**100 Yen = 100 Won** ND (1946). Black. Olive guilloche at l. Man w/beard at r., paulownia crest at r. Block # only.	15.00	75.00	400.

		VG	VF	UNC
45	**100 Yen = 100 Won** ND (1946). Blue. Orange guilloche at ctr. 5 petaled white hibiscus flower above portr. Back brown w/orange guilloche. Color variations.	2.50	15.00	50.00

		VG	VF	UN
46	**100 Yen = 100 Won** ND (1947). Like #45. Face guilloche orange to yellow (varies). Back green w/violet guilloche. Wm varieties.			
	a. Gray paper, w/wmk.	.50	2.00	10.0
	b. White paper, w/o wmk.	.25	1.00	3.0

NOTE: For later issues see Korea/North and Korea/South.

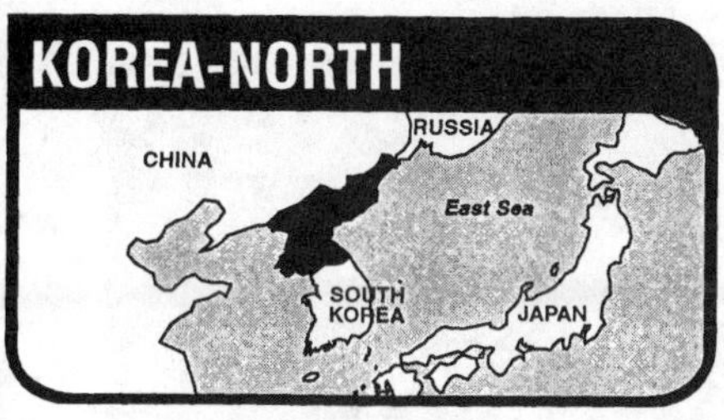

The Democratic Peoples Republic of Korea, situated in in northeastern Asia on the northern half of the Korean peninsula between the Peoples Republic of China and the Republic of Korea, has an area of 46,540 sq. mi. (120,538 sq. km.) and a population of 23.26 million. Capital: Pyongyang. The economy is d on heavy d on heavy industry and agriculture. Metals, minerals and farm produce are exported.

Japan replaced China as the predominant foreign influence in Korea in 1895 and annexed the peninsular country in 1910. Defeat in World War II brought an end to Japanese rule. U.S. troops entered Korea from the south and Soviet forces entered from the north. The Cairo conference (1943) had established that Korea should be "free and independent." The Potsdam conference (1945) set the 38th parallel as the line dividing the occupation forces of the United States and Russia. When Russia refused to permit a U.N. commission designated to supervise reunification elections to enter North Korea, an election was held in South Korea which established the Republic of Korea on Aug. 15, 1948. North Korea held an unsupervised election on Aug. 25, 1948, and on the following day proclaimed the establishment of the Democratic Peoples Republic of Korea.

MONETARY SYSTEM:
1 Won = 100 Chon

SOVIET MILITARY OCCUPATION

RUSSIAN ARMY HEADQUARTERS

1945 ISSUE

#1-4 design w/o vignettes.

		VG	VF	UNC
1	**1 Won** 1945. Green on lt. brown unpt.	10.00	50.00	125.
2	**5 Won** 1945. Brown on blue unpt.	12.50	60.00	150.
3	**10 Won** 1945. Violet on lt. green unpt.	15.00	75.00	200.

		VG	VF	UNC
4	**100 Won** 1945. Red on gray unpt.			
	a. Wmk., serial # 17mm long.	22.50	85.00	225.
	b. W/o wmk., serial # 15 mm long.	22.50	85.00	225.

NORTH KOREA CENTRAL BANK

1947 ISSUES

		VG	VF	UNC
5	**15 Chon** 1947. Brown			
	a. W/wmk.	.75	2.50	8.00
	b. W/o wmk.	.25	.50	2.50
6	**20 Chon** 1947. Green.			
	a. W/wmk.	1.00	3.00	9.00
	b. W/o wmk.	.30	.75	3.00

		VG	VF	UNC
7	**50 Chon** 1947. Blue on lt. olive unpt.			
	a. W/wmk.	.50	1.50	5.00
	b. W/o wmk.	.30	.75	3.00

#8-11 worker and farmer at l. ctr. Mountain on back.

		VG	VF	UNC
8	**1 Won** 1947. Black on orange and green unpt.			
	a. W/wmk.	.80	3.00	8.00
	b. W/o wmk.	.40	1.00	4.00
9	**5 Won** 1947. Black on blue and red unpt. 4 lines between second and third character at bottom; segmented Korean numeral at lower r. Back blue.	.75	2.00	7.50

		VG	VF	UNC
10	**5 Won** 1947. Like #9 but 8 lines between second and third character at bottom; more connected Korean numeral at lower r.			
	a. W/wmk.	1.25	3.50	12.00
	b. W/o wmk.	.80	2.00	8.00
10A	**10 Won** 1947. Black on red and green unpt.			
	a. W/wmk.	2.00	6.00	20.00
	b. W/o wmk.	1.50	3.50	10.00
11	**100 Won** 1947. Black on red, orange and lilac unpt.			
	a. W/wmk.	4.00	10.00	40.00
	b. W/o wmk.	2.00	4.00	18.00

Note: #5-11 w/o wmk. are modern reprints.

DEMOCRATIC PEOPLES REPUBLIC

KOREAN CENTRAL BANK

1959 ISSUE

#12-17 arms at l. or upper l. Wmk. paper.

		VG	VF	UNC
12	**50 Chon** 1959. Blue on m/c unpt. Arms at upper l.	.80	2.50	8.00

13 **1 Won**

	VG	VF	UNC
1959. Red-brown on m/c unpt. Fishing boat at ctr.	.60	1.75	6.00

14 **5 Won**

	VG	VF	UNC
1959. Green on m/c unpt. Lg. bldg. at ctr.	.75	2.00	7.00

15 **10 Won**

	VG	VF	UNC
1959. Red on m/c unpt. Fortress gateway at ctr. r. Woman picking fruit on back.	.80	2.25	8.00

16 **50 Won**

	VG	VF	UNC
1959. Purple on m/c unpt. Bridge and city at ctr. Woman w/wheat on back.	1.00	3.50	10.00

17 **100 Won**

	VG	VF	UNC
1959. Green on m/c unpt. Steam freight train in factory area at ctr. River w/cliffs on back.	1.50	4.50	15.00

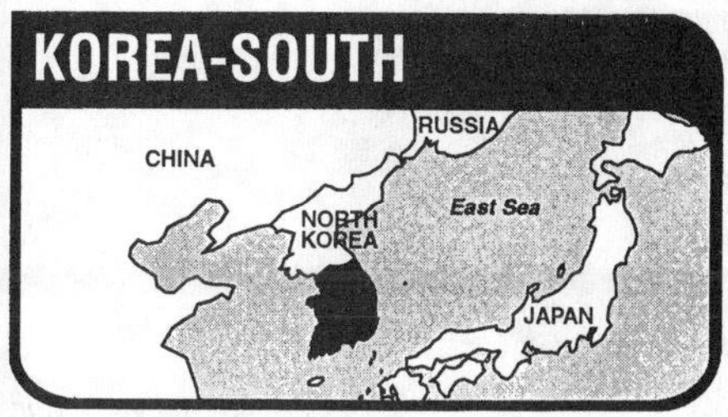

The Republic of Korea, situated in northeastern Asia on the southern half of the Korean peninsula between North Korea and the Korean Strait, has an area of 38,025 sq. mi. (98,484 sq. km.) and a population of 44.61 million. Capital: Seoul. The economy is d on agriculture and textiles. Clothing, plywood and textile products are exported.

Japan replaced China as the predominant foreign influence in Korea in 1895 and annexed the peninsular country in 1910. Defeat in World War II brought an end to Japanese rule. U.S. troops entered Korea from the south and Soviet forces entered from the north. The Cairo Conference (1943) had established that Korea should be "free and independent." The Potsdam Conference (1945) set the 38th parallel as the line dividing the occupation forces of the United States and Russia. When Russia refused to permit a U.N. commission designated to supervise reunification elections to enter North Korea, an election was held in South Korea on May 10, 1948. By its determination, the Republic of Korea was inaugurated on Aug. 15, 1948.

Note: For Bank of Chosen notes issued in South Korea under the Allied occupation during the post WWII period 1945 to 1948 refer to Korea listings.

MONETARY SYSTEM:

1 Won (Hwan) = 100 Chon
1 new Won = 10 old Hwan, 1962-

DATING:

The modern notes of Korea are dated according to the founding of the first Korean dynasty, that of the house of Tangun, in 2333 BC.

REPUBLIC

BANK OF CHOSEN

1949 ND ISSUE

		VG	VF	UNC
1	**5 Won** ND (1949). Black on orange unpt.. Archway at r. Back red-brown; bldg. at ctr.	1.50	5.00	40.00

		VG	VF	UNC
2	**10 Won** ND (1949). Black on lilac unpt. Like #1. Back black.	1.00	4.00	25.00

		VG	VF	UNC
3	**1000 Won** ND (1950). Lilac. Man w/beard at l. Back lt. blue.	.50	2.00	10.00

Note: #3 was issued unofficially by the North Korean Army in 1950 during the Korean conflict.

BANK OF KOREA

1949 ISSUE

		VG	VF	UNC
4	**5 Chon** 1949. Red. Like #6.	4.00	12.50	60.00
5	**10 Chon** 1949. Brown. Like #6.	4.00	15.00	75.00

		VG	VF	UNC
6	**50 Chon** 1949. Blue. 5-petaled blossom within circle at ctr.	2.00	7.50	50.00

1950 ISSUE

		VG	VF	UNC
7	**100 Won** ND (1950). Brown. City gate at l. Color varieties.	.50	2.00	9.00

		VG	VF	UNC
8	**1000 Won** ND (1950). Green. Portr. Syngman Rhee at l. Color varieties.	.50	2.00	12.50

1952 ISSUE

		VG	VF	UNC
9	**500 Won** 4285 (1952). Blue. Portr. Syngman Rhee at l. Back brown; pagoda at ctr.	5.00	40.00	275.

		VG	VF	UNC
10	**1000 Won** 4285 (1952); 4286 (1953). Black-green. Portr. Syngman Rhee at l. Back like #9.			
	a. Lg. date. 4285	.50	2.00	12.00
	b. Sm. date. 4286.	.50	2.50	14.00

1953 ND ISSUE

#11-12 printed in Korea from glass positives furnished by the U.S.A. BEP.

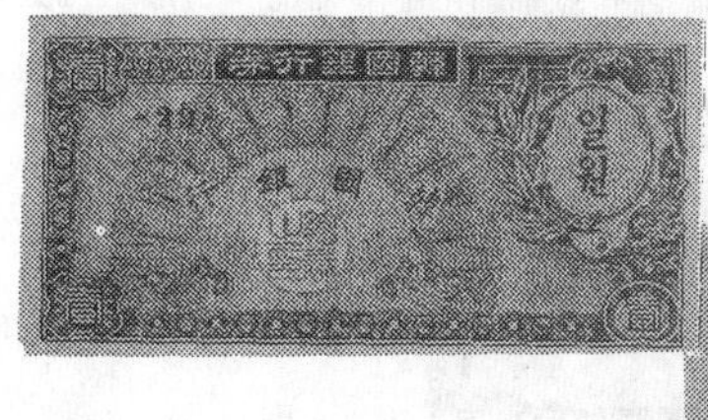

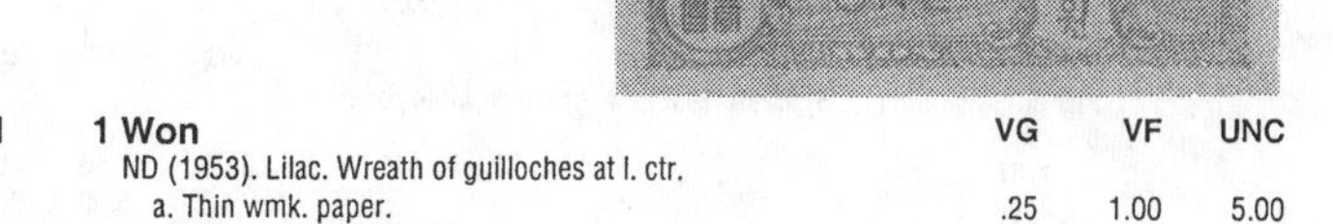

		VG	VF	UNC
11	**1 Won** ND (1953). Lilac. Wreath of guilloches at l. ctr.			
	a. Thin wmk. paper.	.25	1.00	5.00
	b. Thick paper, w/o wmk.	.50	2.50	15.00

		VG	VF	UNC
12	**5 Won** ND (1953). Red. Wreath of guilloches at l. ctr.	1.00	5.00	45.00

#13-15 medieval tortoise warship at r. Printed by Tudor Press, Boston, Mass. U.S.A. through the Bureau of Engraving and Printing. Replacement notes: Prefix D and no suffix letter.

		VG	VF	UNC
13	**10 Won** ND (1953). Blue.	2.00	15.00	100.
14	**100 Won** ND (1953). Green.	3.00	35.00	200.
15	**1000 Won** ND (1953). Brown.			
	a. Issued note.	25.00	125.	400.
	s. Specimen.	—	—	500.

1953-56 Issues

		VG	VF	UNC
16	**10 Hwan** 4286 (1953). Green-black on lt. blue unpt. on gray paper. Pagoda portal at r. Rock formations in water on purple back.	2.50	10.00	75.00

		VG	VF	UNC
17	**10 Hwan** 4286 (1953)-4291 (1958). Gray-blue on white paper. Like #16. Back purple.			
	a. 4286.	1.00	5.00	25.00
	b. 4287.	4.00	12.00	90.00
	c. 4288.	2.00	8.00	55.00
	d. 4289.	1.00	5.00	25.00
	e. 4290.	1.00	4.00	20.00
	f. 4291.	.50	2.50	12.50
18	**100 Hwan** 4286 (1953). Dk. green on yellowish paper. Portr. Syngman Rhee at l. Archway on back.	30.00	275.	950.

		VG	VF	UNC
19	**100 Hwan** 4287 (1954); 4288 (1955); 4289 (1956). Dk. green on white paper. Like #18.			
	a. 4287.	3.00	7.50	50.00
	b. 4288.	2.00	5.00	30.00
	c. 4289.	1.00	4.00	22.50

		VG	VF	UNC
20	**500 Hwan** 4289 (1956); 4290 (1957). Gray-blue on green unpt. Portr. Syngman Rhee at ctr. Back brown.	12.50	100.	500.

1957 Issue

		VG	VF	UNC
21	**100 Hwan** 4290 (1957). Gray on olive-green and brown unpt. Portr. Syngman Rhee at r. Back green.	3.00	25.00	120.

		VG	VF	UNC
22	**1000 Hwan** 4290 (1957)-4293 (1960). Purple on brown and green unpt. Portr. Syngman Rhee at r. Back black on green unpt; date at ctr.			
	a. 4290.	12.00	60.00	300.
	b. 4291.	6.00	30.00	150.
	c. 4292.	4.00	12.00	100.
	d. 4293.	4.00	12.00	100.

1958-60 Issue

		VG	VF	UNC
23	**50 Hwan** 4291 (1958). Green-blue on olive-green unpt. Archway at l. Back green; statue at ctr., medieval tortoise warship at r.	20.00	60.00	350.
24	**500 Hwan** 4291 (1958); 4292 (1959). Dk. green. Portr. Syngman Rhee at r. Back brownish purple.	7.50	40.00	350.

25	1000 Hwan	VG	VF	UNC
	4293 (1960); 4294 (1961); 1962. Black on olive unpt. Kg. Sejong the Great at r. Back blue-green and lt. brown; flaming torch at ctr.			
	a. 4293 (1960).	2.50	10.00	100.
	b. 4294 (1961).	1.50	6.00	60.00
	c. 1962.	1.75	7.00	65.00

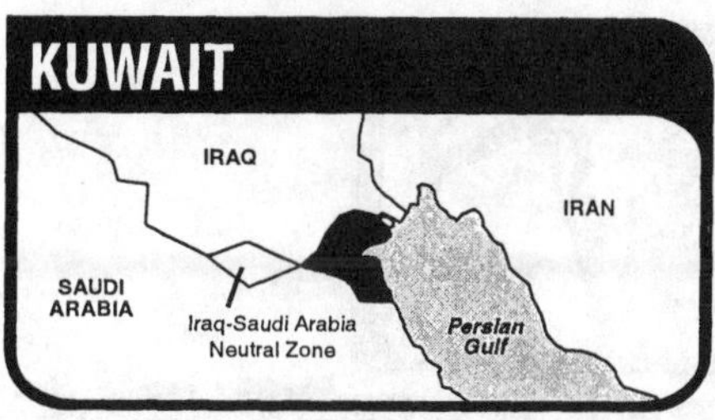

The State of Kuwait, a constitutional monarchy located on the Arabian Peninsula at the northwestern corner of the Persian Gulf, has an area of 6,880 sq. mi. (17,818 sq. km.) and a population of 1.97 million. Capital: Kuwait. Petroleum, the basis of the economy, provides 95 per cent of the exports.

The modern history of Kuwait began with the founding of the men who wandered northward from the region of the Qatar Peninsula of eastern Arabia. Fearing that the Turks would take over the sheikhdom, Shaikh Mubarak entered into an agreement with Great Britain, 1899, placing Kuwait under the protection of Britain and empowering Britain to conduct its foreign affairs. Britain terminated the protectorate on June 19, 1961, giving Kuwait its independence (by a simple exchange of notes) but agreeing to furnish military aid on request.

The Kuwait dinar, one of the world's strongest currencies, is backed 100 percent by gold and foreign exchange holdings.

On Aug. 2, 1990 Iraqi forces invaded and rapidly overran Kuwaiti forces. Annexation by Iraq was declared on Aug. 8. The Kuwaiti government established itself in exile in Saudi Arabia. The United Nations forces attacked on Feb. 24, 1991 and Kuwait City was liberated on Feb. 26. Iraq quickly withdrew remaining forces.

RULERS:

British to 1961
Abdullah, 1961-1965
Sabah Ibn Salim Al Sabah, 1965-1977
Jabir Ibn Ahmad Al Sabah, 1977-2006
Sabah Al Ahmad Al Sabah

MONETARY SYSTEM:

1 Dinar = 1000 Fils

STATE

KUWAIT CURRENCY BOARD

LAW OF 1960, 1961 ND ISSUE

#1-5 Amir Shaikh Abdullah at r. and as wmk. Sign. 1.

1	1/4 Dinar	VG	VF	UNC
	L.1960 (1961). Brown on m/c unpt. Aerial view, Port of Kuwait at ctr. on back.	4.00	15.00	45.00

		VG	VF	UNC
2	**1/2 Dinar** L.1960 (1961). Purple on m/c unpt. School at ctr. on back.	5.00	25.00	90.00
3	**1 Dinar** L.1960 (1961). Red-brown on m/c unpt. Cement plant at ctr. on back.	7.50	40.00	125.

		VG	VF	UNC
4	**5 Dinars** L.1960 (1961). Blue on m/c unpt. Street scene on back.	30.00	150.	500.

		VG	VF	UNC
5	**10 Dinars** L.1960 (1961). Green on m/c unpt. Dhow on back.	30.00	150.	475.

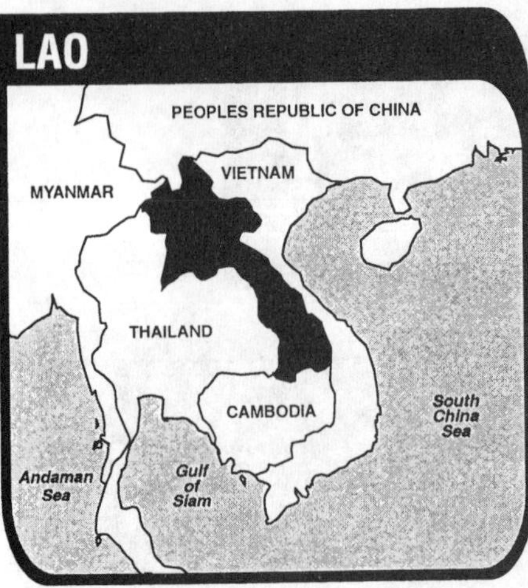

The Lao People's Democratic Republic, located on the Indo-Chinese Peninsula between the Socialist Republic of Vietnam and the Kingdom of Thailand, has an area of 91,429 sq. mi. (236,800 sq. km.) and a population of 5.69 million. Captial: Vientiane. Agriculture employs 95 percent of the people. Tin, lumber and coffee are exported.

The first United Kingdom of Laos was established in the mid-14th century by King Fa Ngum who ruled an area including present Laos, northeastern Thailand, and the southern part of China's Yunnan province from his capital at Luang Prabang. Thailand and Vietnam obtained control over much of the present Lao territory in the 18th century and remained dominant until France established a protectorate over the area in 1893 and incorporated it into the Union of Indo-China. The Independence of Laos was proclaimed in March of 1945, during the last days of the Japanese occupation of World War II. France reoccupied Laos in 1946, and established it as a constitutional monarchy within the French Union in 1949. In 1953, war erupted between the government and the Pathet Lao, a Communist movement supported by the Vietnamese Communist forces. Peace was declared in 1954 with Laos becoming fully independent in 1955 and the Pathet Lao being permitted to occupy two northern provinces. Civil war broke out again in 1960 with the United States supporting the government of the Kingdom of Laos and the North Vietnamese helping the Communist Pathet Lao, and continued, with intervals of truce and political compromise, until the formation of the Lao People's Democratic Republic on Dec. 2, 1975.

RULERS:

Sisavang Vong, 1949-1959
Savang Vatthana, 1959-1975

MONETARY SYSTEM:

1 Piastre = 100 Cents to 1955
1 Kip = 100 At, 1955-1978
1 new Kip = 100 old Kip, 1979-

FREE LAO GOVERNMENT

Government of 1945-46 established in Vientiane after the Japanese surrender.

LAO ISSARA

1945-46 ISSUE

#A3, some minor varieties exist in rendition of characters also.

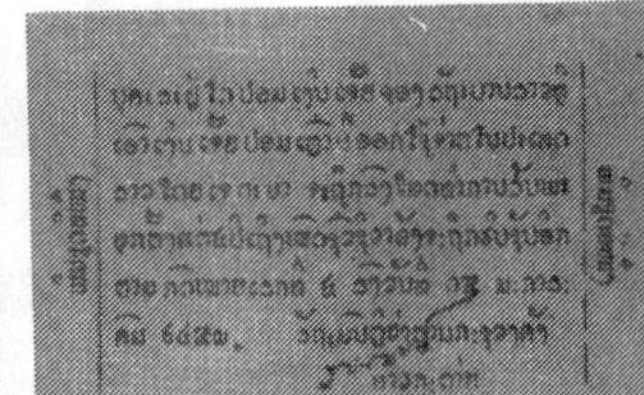

		Good	Fine	X
A1	**10 At** ND. Black. Kneeling Buddhist monk w/parasol at ctr. Series 1. Plain paper.	80.00	200.	32

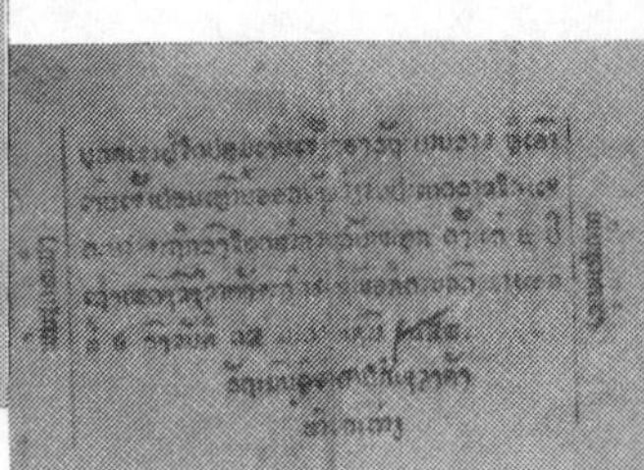

		Good	Fine	X
A2	**20 At** ND. Black. Lao temple at ctr. Series 1. Plain paper.	60.00	130.	2

		Good	Fine	XF
A3	**50 At** ND. Black. Symbol of constitution at ctr.			
	a. W/o *50* on back. Plain paper. Series 1.	5.00	20.00	40.00
	b. Sm. *50* 4mm high on back, top of 5 curved. Plain paper. Series 2-7.	5.00	20.00	40.00
	c. Sm. *50* 4mm high on back, top of 5 straight, first character on fifth line is as illustration. Vertical lined paper. Series 2; 5; 6.	5.00	20.00	40.00
	d. Like #A3c but character as illustrated is last on fourth line. Vertical lined paper. Series 10.	5.00	20.00	40.00
	e. Lg. *50* 5.5mm high on back. Last character separated from last word of third line by a space. Verical lined paper. Series 10, 13.	5.00	20.00	40.00
	f. Lg. *50* 5.5mm high on back, but w/o printer's identification line on face. Vertical lined paper. Series 9.	5.00	20.00	40.00
	g. Like #A3e but w/designer name Phong on face on a vertical line inside the lower l. Letters VS in lower corner. Series II.			
	h. Series # on face (Lao numeral) different from the # (in words) on back. Plain paper. Rare.			
	i. As b. but line 7 on back is missing : character. Series 4.	—	—	—
	j. As b. Vertical lined paper. Series 2-7.	5.00	20.00	40.00
	k. As d. Horizontal lined paper. Series 10.			
	l. As f. Horizontal lined paper. Series 9.			
	m. Like A3e. Character is part of last word of 3rd line on back. Vertical lined paper. Series 3, 12.	5.00	20.00	40.00
	n. Like #A3e. 2nd line on back divided into 3 groups of characters. Character separated from last word of 4th line on back. Vertical lined paper. Series 5, 8.	5.00	20.00	40.00
	o. Like A3e. Wrong character in 4th line on back. Vertical lined paper. Series 13.	5.00	20.00	40.00

Word for c. and d.

		Good	Fine	XF
4	**10 Kip** ND. Purple. W/or w/o pink unpt. Garuda bird at top ctr. Temple on back.			
	a. Serial # in Western numerals Sign. Khammao Vilay.	70.00	150.	350.
	b. Serial # in Lao and European characters. Sign. Katay Don Sasorith.	20.00	75.00	250.

INGDOM

ANQUE NATIONALE DU LAOS

SIGNATURE VARIETIES		
	LE GOUVERNEUR	UN CENSEUR
1		
2		
3		

57 ND ISSUE

6 Lao Tricephalic Elephant Arms at upper ctr. Sign. 1.

-3b, and 5b were printed by the Pathet Lao during the Civil War. This second issue was printed in Bulgaria on paper w/o planchettes (security dots). Serial # style is different from notes printed by SBNC.

		VG	VF	UNC
1	**1 Kip** ND (1957). Green. That Ing Hang at l. Farmer w/water buffalo on back.			
	a. Security dots. Printer: SBNC.	.25	1.00	15.00
	b. W/o security dots (second issue).	.25	1.00	4.00
	s. As a. Specimen.	—	—	100.

		VG	VF	UNC
2	**5 Kip** ND (1957). Brown on pale orange unpt. That Makmo at r. Ox cart on back.			
	a. Security dots. Printer: SBNC.	1.00	15.00	50.00
	b. W/o security dots (second issue).	.25	1.00	4.00
	s. As a. Specimen.	—	—	100.

		VG	VF	UNC
3	**10 Kip** ND (1957). Blue. Pagoda Wat Ong Teu at r. Workers in rice field on back.			
	a. Security dots. Printer: SBNC.	.50	5.00	30.00
	b. W/o security dots (second issue).	.50	1.00	5.00
	s. As a. Specimen.	—	—	100.

		VG	VF	UNC
4	**20 Kip** ND (1957). Purple. Govt. palace. Woman weaving on back. Printer: SBNC.			
	a. Issued note.	2.00	20.00	85.00
	s. Specimen.	—	—	125.

		VG	VF	UNC
5	**50 Kip** ND (1957). Red-orange. National Assembly bldg. Back orange; logger on elephant.			
	a. Security dots. Printer: SBNC.	7.50	50.00	250.
	b. W/o security dots (second issue).	1.00	2.00	6.00
	s1. As a. Specimen.	—	—	150.
	s2. As b. Specimen.	—	—	200.

		VG	VF	UNC
6	**100 Kip** ND (1957). Brown and m/c. S. Vong at l., vessels at ctr., dragons at r. Woman w/bowl of roses at r., bldg. at ctr. on back (like Fr. Indochina #103). Wmk.: Tricephalic arms. Printer: Bank of France (w/o imprint).			
	a. Issued note.	1.00	3.00	10.00
	s. Specimen. Perforated.	—	—	275.

1957 Commemorative Issue

#7, 2500th Year of Buddhist Era

		VG	VF	UNC
7	**500 Kip** Yr. 2500 (1957). Red and m/c. S. Vong at l., bldg. at ctr. Back purple on blue unpt; bldgs. Wmk.: Tricephalic elephant arms. Sign. 3.			
	a. Issued note.	5.00	60.00	125.
	s. Specimen.	—	—	200.
	s2. TDLR specimen (red oval).			200.

The Republic of Latvia, the central Baltic state in eas Europe, has an area of 24,595 sq. mi. (43,601 sq. km.) and a population of 2.4 million. Capital Riga. Livestock raising and manufacturing are the chie industries. Butter, bacon fertilizers and telephone equipment are exported.

The Latvians, of Aryan descent were nomadic tribesmen who settled along the Baltic prior t the 13th century. Lacking a central government, they were easily conquered by the German Teutonic knights, Russia, Sweden and Poland. Following the third partition of Poland by Austria, Prussia and Russia in 1795, Latvia came under Russian domination and did not experience autonomy until the Russian Revolution of 1917 provided an opportunity for freedom. The Latvian republic was established on Nov. 18, 1918. It was occupie by Soviet troops in 1939 and annexed to the Soviet Union in 1940. Following the German occupation of 1941-44, it was retaken by Russia and reestablished as a member S.S. Republic o the Soviet Union. Western countries, including the United States, did not recognize Latvia' incorporation into the Soviet Union. Latvia declared its independence from the former U.S.S.R. o Aug. 22, 1991.

MONETARY SYSTEM:

1 Rublis = 100 Kapeikas, 1919-22
1 Lats = 100 Santimu, 1923-40; 1992
1 Lats = 200 Rublu, 1993
1 Rublis = 1 Russian Ruble, 1992

Russian Administration

Rigaer Borsen-Bank

Stock Exchange Bank of Riga

1863 Issue

		Good	Fine	X
A1	**10 Kop.** 1863. Rare.	—	—	—
A2	**15 Kop.** 1863. Rare.	—	—	—
A3	**20 Kop.** 1863. Rare.	—	—	—
A4	**25 Kop.** 1863. Rare.	—	—	—

		Good	Fine	X
A5	**50 Kop.** 1863. Rare.	—	—	

Republic

Latwijas Walsts Kases Sihme

Latvian Government Currency Note

1919-20 Issue

		VG	VF	U
1	**1 Rublis** 1919. Blue and brown. Flaming ball with L and 3 stars above legend. Wmk: Wavy lines. Sign. 1 & 2. Series A.	15.00	75.00	2

1 Rublis

1919. Lt. and dk. green. Like #1.

	VG	VF	UNC
a. Wmk: Wavy lines. Sign. 3 & 4. Series B, C, D.	4.00	15.00	50.00
b. Wmk: Lt. lines. Series E, F, G, H, K.	3.00	10.00	35.00
s1. Specimen. Perforated: *PARAUGS* 10mm.	—	—	400.
s2. Specimen. Perforated: *PARAUGS* 14mm. Series F.	—	—	300.

5 Rubli

ND (1919). Lt. and dk. blue. Woman's head facing l. at ctr.

	VG	VF	UNC
a. Wmk: Wavy lines. Sign. 4 & 5. Series Aa.	25.00	75.00	200.
b. As a, but Series A, B, C.	15.00	50.00	150.
c. Wmk: Lt. lines. Sign. 5 & 4. Series D.	10.00	30.00	100.
d. As c. Sign. 3 & 4.	30.00	100.	250.
e. As d. Series E.	5.00	25.00	75.00
f. Wmk: as c. Sign. 6 & 4. Series F, G, H, K.	4.00	20.00	65.00
s. Specimen. Ovpt: *PARAUGS.* Several varieties exist.	—	—	500.

10 Rubli

1919. Red-brown and green. Sailing ship at ctr.

	VG	VF	UNC
a. Wmk: Wavy lines. Sign. 5 & 4. Series Aa, Bb.	20.00	65.00	200.
b. Wmk: Lt. lines. Sign. 5 & 4. Series Ab, Ba, Bb, Bc, Bd, Be, Bk.	15.00	50.00	150.
c. Wmk: Lt. lines. Sign. 3 & 4. Series Bb, Bd, Bg, Bh, Bl, Bm.	12.50	40.00	125.
d. As c. Series A, B.	10.00	30.00	100.
e. As d, but 2 serial #. Series C, D, E.	10.00	30.00	100.
f. As e, but sign. 6 & 4. Series F, G, H, K, L.	7.50	25.00	75.00
s. Specimen. Ovpt. or perforated: *PARAUGS.* Several varieties exist.	—	—	500.

5 **25 Rubli**

1919. Brown. 3 stylized ears of corn on back.

	VG	VF	UNC
a. Wmk: Line groups. Black serial #. Sign. 3 & 4. Rare.	—	—	—
b. As a, but blue serial #. Rare.	—	—	—
c. As a, but red serial #. Series A. Rare.	—	—	—
d. As c, but green serial #. Series B.	150.	500.	—
e. As d, but wmk: Stars & hexagons. Series C, D.	30.00	100.	300.
f. As e, but wmk: Lt. lines. Series E, F, G.	25.00	85.00	250.
g. As f, but sign. 6 & 4. Series F, G.	20.00	60.00	175.
h. As g, but 2 serial #. Series H, K, L, M, N, P, R, S.	15.00	50.00	150.
s. Specimen. Ovpt. or perforated: *PARAUGS.* Several varieties exist.	—	—	550.

6 **50 Rubli**

	VG	VF	UNC
1919. Green and gray. Wmk: Wavy lines. Sign. 5 & 4.	30.00	125.	400.

Note: Excellent Russian forgeries exist of #6.

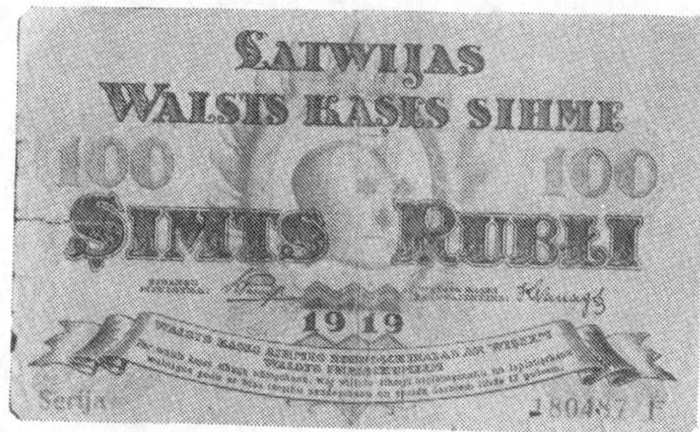

7 **100 Rubli**

1919. Brown and dk. brown. Oak tree on back. 3 legend varieties.

	VG	VF	UNC
a. Wmk: Lt. lines. Sign. 5 & 4. Series A, B, C.	30.00	100.	300.
b. As a, but sign. 3 & 4. Series C, D, E, F, G, H, K.	20.00	75.00	200.
c. As b, but sign. 6 & 4. Series K. Rare.	—	—	—
d. Sign. 6 & 4. Series L. 2 serial #.	17.50	60.00	175.
e. As c, but single serial # w/*No.* Series M.	17.50	60.00	175.
f. As c, but series N, P, R, S, T, U.	17.50	60.00	175.
g. As e. Paper w/o wmk. Series U. Rare.	—	—	—
s. Specimen. Ovpt. or perforated: *PARAUGS.* Several varieties exist.	—	—	500.

8 **500 Rubli**

1920. Lt. and dk. green. Symbols of agriculture, industry and navigation on back.

	VG	VF	UNC
a. Wmk: Lt. lines. Sign. 3 & 4. Series A-F.	75.00	250.	750.
b. As a, but sign. 6 & 4. Series G, H, K.	75.00	250.	750.
c. As b, but wmk: Interlocked wave-bands. Series L-N, P, R-W, Z.	60.00	185.	550.
s. Specimen. Ovpt. or perforated: *PARAUGS.* Several varieties exist. Rare.	—	—	—

Note: Excellent Russian forgeries exist of #8.

		VG	VF	UNC
A21	**5 Kapeikas** ND (1919). Black on lt. beige paper. (Not issued).	—	—	—

		VG	VF	UNC
A22	**10 Kapeikas** ND (1919). Black on purple unpt. Back black on red-brown unpt. (Not issued).	—	—	—

		VG	VF	UNC
A23	**50 Kapeikas** ND (1919). Black on red-violet unpt. (Not issued).	—	—	—

Latwijas Mainas Sihme

Latvian Small Exchange Note

1920 ND Issue

#9-12 face like back.

		VG	VF	UNC
9	**5 Kapeikas** ND (1920). Red.			
	a. Issued note.	1.00	3.00	10.00
	s. Specimen. Ovpt: *PARAUGS.*	—	3.00	25.00

		VG	VF	UNC
10	**10 Kapeikas** ND (1920). Blue.			
	a. Issued note.	1.00	3.00	10.00
	s. Specimen. Ovpt: *PARAUGS.*	—	—	25.00
11	**25 Kapeikas** ND (1920). Brown.			
	a. Issued note.	1.00	3.00	10.00
	s. Specimen. Ovpt: *PARAUGS.*	—	—	25.00
12	**50 Kapeikas** ND (1920). Purple.			
	a. Issued note.	1.00	3.00	10.00
	s. Specimen. Ovpt: *PARAUGS.*	—	—	25.00

Latvijas Bankas

Bank of Latvia

Naudas Zime

Money Note

Provisional Issue

Individual sign. for #13-22:

Sign. 1	President of the Bank Council	Ringold Kalnings
Sign. 2	General Director	Edgars Schwede
Sign. 3	President of the Bank Council	J. Clems
Sign. 4	General Director	K. Vanags
Sign. 5	President of the Bank Council	A. Klive

		VG	VF	UN
13	**10 Latu on 500 Rubli** ND (-old date 1920). Red ovpt. on #8b.			
	a. Issued note. Series A-E.	75.00	300.	9
	s1. Specimen. Perforated: *PARAUGS* 15mm. Face and back pair. Rare.	—	—	
	s2. As s1, but single example printed on both sides. Rare.	—	—	

1923 Issue

		VG	VF	U
14	**100 Latu** 1923. Blue. 2 seated women in national costume on back. 2 legend varieties.			
	a. Sign. 1 & 2. #A 000001-110000.	80.00	250.	
	b. Sign. 3 & 4. #A 110001-160000.	55.00	165.	
	s. Specimen. Ovpt. or perforated: *PARAUGS.* Several varieties exist. Rare.	—	—	

1924 Issue

		VG	VF
15	**20 Latu** 1924. Black on orange unpt. Lt. tan paper. Farmer sowing. Back red; arms at ctr. (Issued only briefly.)		
	a. Issued note. Rare.	—	—
	s. Specimen. Ovpt: *PARAUGS BEZ VERTIBAS* in red. Rare.	—	—

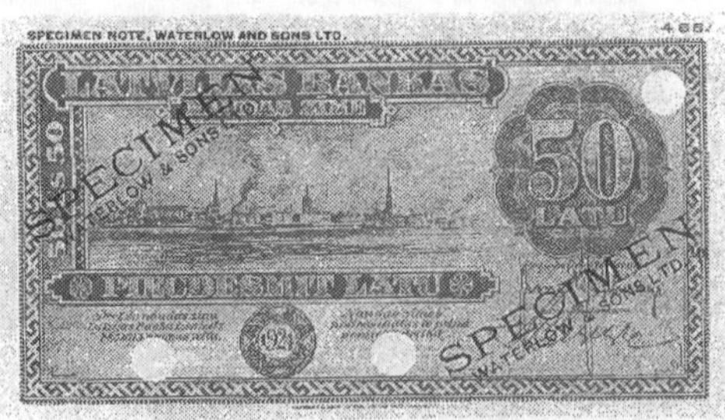

16	50 Latu	VG	VF	UNC
	1924. Brown on green unpt. River Dvina (Daugava) w/view of Riga. Arms at l. on back.			
	a. Issued note.	325.	1000.	—
	s. Specimen. Ovpt: *PARAUGS BEZ VERTIBAS* in red. Rare.	—	—	—

1925 Issue

17	20 Latu	VG	VF	UNC
	1925. Black on yellow and green unpt. Portr. Pres. J. Cakste at top ctr. Arms on back. Printer: W&S.			
	a. Issued note.	15.00	75.00	300.
	s. Specimen. Ovpt: *PARAUGS BEZ VERTIBAS* in red. Rare.	—	—	—

1928-29 Issue

18	25 Latu	VG	VF	UNC
	1928. Black on yellow unpt. K. Valdemars at top ctr., ships l. and r. Back blue; arms at ctr. Printer: W&S.			
	a. Issued note.	15.00	50.00	200.
	s. Specimen. Ovpt: *PARAUGS BEZ VERTIBAS* in red. Rare.	—	—	—

19	500 Latu	VG	VF	UNC
	1929. Blue and brown. Girl in national costume at r. Cows and sheaves on back. Printer: BWC.			
	a. Issued note.	45.00	175.	750.
	s. Specimen. Ovpt: *PARAUGS.* Several varieties exist. Rare.	—	—	—

1934 Issue

20	50 Latu	VG	VF	UNC
	1934. Blue. Prime Minister K. Ulmanis at r. Printer: TDLR.			
	a. Issued note.	5.00	15.00	50.00
	s1. Specimen. Perforated: *PARAUGS*, 9mm.	—	—	500.
	s2. Specimen. TDLR oval seal.	—	—	400.

1938-39 Issue

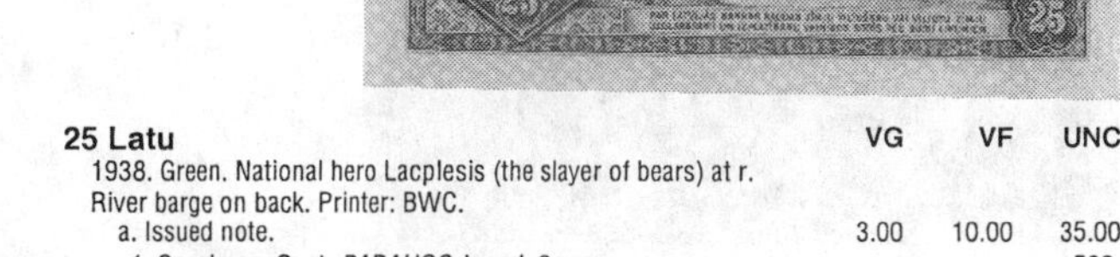

21	25 Latu	VG	VF	UNC
	1938. Green. National hero Lacplesis (the slayer of bears) at r. River barge on back. Printer: BWC.			
	a. Issued note.	3.00	10.00	35.00
	s1. Specimen. Ovpt: *PARAUGS* in red, 6mm.	—	—	500.
	s2. Specimen. BWC red seal. Rare.	—	—	—

22	100 Latu	VG	VF	UNC
	1939. Red. Farm couple w/daughter. Cargo ship dockside on back.			
	a. Issued note.	5.00	15.00	45.00
	s. Specimen. Perforated: *PARAUGS.* 10mm. and ovpt. 6mm in green.	—	—	750.

Latvijas Valsts Kases Zime

Latvian Government State Treasury Note

1925-26 Issue

Individual sign. for #23-33:

Sign. 1	Director of the Credit Dept.	A. Karklins
Sign. 2	Vice-Director	Robert Baltgailis
Sign. 3	Minister of Finance	V. Bastjanis
Sign. 4	Substitute Director of the Credit Dept.	A. Kacens
Sign. 5	Minister of Finance	R. Leepinsch
Sign. 6	Substitute Director of the Credit Dept.	J. Miezis
Sign. 7	Minister of Finance	A. Petrevics
Sign. 8	Minister of Finance	M. Skujenieks
Sign. 9	Minister of Finance	J. Blumbergs
Sign. 10	Minister of Finance	J. Annuss
Sign. 11	Substitute Director of the State Economic Department	J. Skujevics
Sign. 12	Minister of Finance	E. Rimbenieks
Sign. 13	Minister of Finance	L. Ekis
Sign. 14	Minister of Finance	A. Valdmanis
Sign. 15	Minister of Finance	J. Kaminskis
Sign. 16	Minister of Finance	K. Karlsons
Sign. 17	Director of the State Economic Dept.	V. Bastjanis

23	5 Lati	Good	Fine	XF
	1926. Brown. Symbols of commerce and navigation on back.			
	a. Issued note.	200.	500.	—
	s. Specimen. Perforated: *PARAUGS.* Two varieties exist. Rare.	—	—	—

		Good	Fine	XF
24	**10 Latu** 1925. Red-brown. Oak tree and cornfield on back. 5 sign. varieties.			
	a. Sign. 1 & 2. Series A, B.	50.00	175.	500.
	b. Sign. 3 & 4. Series C-K.	15.00	75.00	300.
	c. Sign. 5 & 6. Series K, L.	20.00	95.00	350.
	d. Sign. 7 & 6. Series M-T.	15.00	75.00	300.
	e. Sign. 8 & 6. Series T, U.	25.00	100.	400.
	s. Specimen. Perforated: *PARAUGS.* Several varieties exist. Rare.	—	—	—

1933 Issue

		VG	VF	UNC
25	**10 Latu** 1933-34. Blue-green. Seated woman in national costume on back.			
	a. Sign. 10 & 11. Series A-G. 1933.	10.00	30.00	100.
	b. As a. Series H. 1933.	20.00	65.00	200.
	c. Sign. 10 & 11. Series H, J-N, P. 1934.	15.00	50.00	150.
	d. Sign. 12 & 11. Series R-U. 1934.	12.50	40.00	125.
	e. Sign. 13 & 11. Series V, Z. 1934.	12.50	40.00	125.
	f. As e, but 2-letter series AA-AH, AJ. 1934.	12.50	40.00	125.
	s1. Specimen. Perforated: *PARAUGS*, 19mm. Face and back pair. 1933.	—	—	
	s2. As s1, but single example printed on both sides. 1933.	—	—	

1935 Issue

		Good	Fine	XF
26	**10 Latu** 1935. Deep brown and deep violet on m/c unpt. Bondage (?) monument at l. Back blue-black on lt. blue, arms at ctr. r. Specimen perforated: *PARAUGS.* Rare.	—	—	—

		Good	Fine	XF
27	**20 Latu** 1935. Deep brown on gray unpt. Lacplesis w/bear at l., arms at upper ctr. on back. Specimen perforated: *PARAUGS.* Rare.	—	—	—

#28 not assigned.

1935-37 Issue

		VG	VF	UNC
29	**10 Latu** 1937-40. Dk. brown and m/c. Fishermen and net at ctr. Back blue-black; man sowing at ctr.			
	a. Sign. 13 & 11. Series A-Z. 1937.	3.00	10.00	35.00
	b. Sign. 13 & 11. Series AA-ZZ; BA-BD. 1938.	3.00	10.00	35.00
	c. Sign. 13 & 11. Series BE-BK. 1939.	10.00	30.00	100.
	d. Sign. 14 & 11. Series BL-BZ; CA-CV. 1939.	5.00	15.00	50.00
	e. Sign. 15 & 11. Series CZ; DA-DM. 1940.	5.00	15.00	50.00
	s1. Specimen. Like a. Perforated: *PARAUGS.* 1937.	—	—	750.
	s2. Specimen. Like c. Perforated: *PARAUGS.* 1939.	—	—	750.

#31-32 not assigned.

		VG	VF	UNC
30	**20 Latu** 1935-36. Brown. Castle of Riga. Farmer at l., woman in national costume at r. on back.			
	a. Sign. 13 & 11. Series A-J. 1935.	15.00	55.00	175.
	b. Sign. 13 & 11. Series R-U. 1936.	12.50	50.00	150.
	s1. Specimen. Like a. Perforated: *PARAUGS.* 1935.	—	—	750.
	s2. Specimen. Like b. Perforated: *PARAUGS.* 1936. Rare.	—	—	—

1940 Issue

		Good	Fine	XF
33	**20 Latu** 1940. Blue. Academy of Agriculture in Jelgava.			
	a. Issued note.	35.00	200.	750.
	s. Specimen. Perforated: *PARAUGS.* W/ or w/o #. Rare.	—	—	—

Latvijas Valsts Kases Mainas Zime

Latvian Government Exchange Note

1940 Issue

Sign. 1	Minister of Finance	K. Karlsons
Sign. 2	Peoples Commissary of Finance	A. Tabaks
Sign. 3	Director of the State Economic Dept.	V. Bastjanis

Individual Sign. for #34 and 34A:

34 **5 Lati**

1940. Blue, gray and brown. Bridge across the River Guaja. Back brown; arms at ctr.

	VG	VF	UNC
a. Sign. 1 & 3. Series A-D. Sign. title at l.: *Finansu Ministrs.*	5.00	35.00	150.
b. Sign. 2 & 3. Series D. Sign. title at l.: *Finansu Tautas Komisars.*	10.00	50.00	200.
c. As b, but Series E.	65.00	200.	500.
s. Specimen. Perforated: *PARAUGS.* Several varieties exist. Rare.	—	—	—

LATVIJAS SOCIALISTISKAS PADOMJU REPUBLIKAS KASES ZIME

LATVIAN SOCIALISTIC SOVIET REPUBLIC CURRENCY NOTE

1940 ISSUE

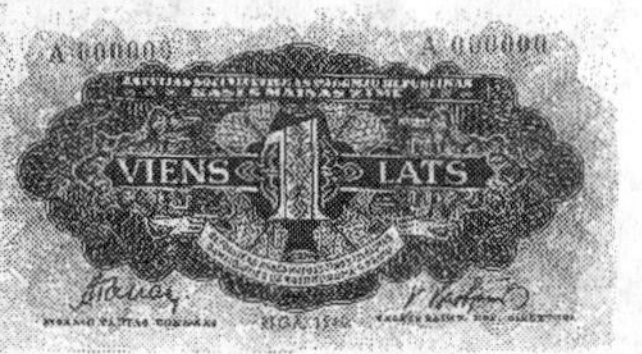

34A **1 Lats**

	VG	VF	UNC
1940. Black on gray and lt. brown unpt. Specimen only. Face and back pair. Serial #A. Rare.	—	—	—

Note: A single set of notes was ovpt. *LATVIJA 1941 1.JULIJS* possibly in anticipation of a new issue of Latvian notes in 1941. Notes thus ovpt. included 5 Lati 1940 (#34), 10 Latu 1937 (#29), 20 Latu 1935 (#27), 100 Latu 1939, 2 var. of ovpt. (#22), and 500 Latu 1929 (#19). They were never issued; instead, the German occupation forces issued Reichskreditkassen notes.

REGIONAL

RIGAS STRADNEEKU DEPUTATU PADOMES

RIGA'S WORKERS DEPUTIES' SOVIET

1919 ISSUE

#R1-R4 star, w/hammer and sickle. Wmk. paper. Circulated in all parts of Latvia.

Note: #R1-R4 also exist as unfinished notes. Unfinished sheets of #R3 and R4 w/printing on only 1 side were used in producing some Latvian postage stamps.

R1 **1 Rublis**

	VG	VF	UNC
1919. Red and brown.	.25	1.00	3.50

R2 **3 Rubli**

1919. Red, olive green and black.

	VG	VF	UNC
a. Issued note.	.50	1.50	4.00
x. Back inverted. Rare.	—	—	—

R3 **5 Rubli**

1919. Red and blue.

	VG	VF	UNC
a. Issued note.	.50	1.50	5.00
x. Back inverted. Rare.	—	—	—

R4 **10 Rubli**

	VG	VF	UNC
1919. Red, green and lilac.	.75	2.50	7.50

The Republic of Lebanon, situated on the eastern shore of the Mediterranean Sea between Syria and Israel, has an area of 4,015 sq. mi. (10,400 sq. km.) and a population of 3.29 million. Capital: Beirut. The economy is d on agriculture, trade and tourism. Fruit, other foodstuffs and textiles are exported.

Almost at the beginning of recorded history, Lebanon appeared as the well-wooded hinterland of the Phoenicians who exploited its famous forests of cedar. The mountains were a Christian refuge and a Crusader stronghold. Lebanon, the history of which is essentially the same as that of Syria, came under control of the Ottoman Turks early in the 16th century. Following the collapse of the Ottoman Empire after World War I, Lebanon, along with Syria, became a French mandate. The French drew a border around the predominantly Christian Lebanon Sanjak or administrative subdivision and on Sept. 1, 1920 proclaimed the area the State of Grand Lebanon (Etat du Grand Liban), a republic under French control. France announced the independence of Lebanon during WWII after Vichy control was deposed on Nov. 26, 1941. It became fully independent on Jan. 1, 1944, but the last British and French troops did not leave until the end of Aug. 1946.

Since the late 1950's the independent Palestinian movement caused government friction. By 1976 large-scale fighting broke out, which continued thru 1990. In April 1996, Israel staged a 17 day bombardment of the southern areas.

RULERS

French to 1943

MONETARY SYSTEM

1 Livre (Pound) = 100 Piastres

OVERPRINT VARIETIES:

OVERPRINT VARIETIES				
/ Type A	// Type B	V Type C	V Type D	◇ Type E

FRENCH ADMINISTRATION

BANQUE DE SYRIE ET DU GRAND-LIBAN

1925 ISSUE

#1-8 *GRAND-LIBAN* heading on notes similar to some Syrian issues.

		Good	Fine	XF
1	**25 Piastres** 15.4.1925. M/c. Similar to Syria #21. Water mill on back.	50.00	300.	950.
2	**50 Piastres** 15.4.1925. M/c. Similar to Syria #22.	100.	500.	—
3	**1 Livre** 15.4.1925. M/c.	200.	800.	—
4	**5 Livres** 15.4.1925. Blue, orange and m/c.	250.	1000.	—
5	**10 Livres** 15.4.1925. M/c.	—	—	—
6	**25 Livres** 15.4.1925. M/c.	—	—	—

		Good	Fine	X
7	**50 Livres** 15.4.1925. M/c. Bldgs. across ctr. on back.	—	—	—
8	**100 Livres** 15.4.1925. M/c.	—	—	—

1930 ISSUE

#8A-11 *GRAND-LIBAN* heading on notes similar to some Syrian issues.

		Good	Fine	X
8A	**1 Livre** 1.11.1930. M/c. Similar to Syria #29A.	—	—	—

		Good	Fine	X
9	**5 Livres** 1.11.1930. M/c. Similar to Syria #30. Hillside fortress on back.	250.	1250.	
10	**10 Livres** 1.11.1930. M/c. Similar to Syria #31. Ornate ruins at l. ctr. on back.	—	—	
11	**25 Livres** 1.11.1930. M/c. Similar to Syria #32.	—	—	

1935 ISSUE

		Good	Fine	X
12	**1 Livre** 1.2.1935. M/c. Similar to Syria #34. Harbor and mountain landscape across l. and ctr. panels on back.	50.00	250.	7

		Good	Fine	XF
12A	**5 Livres** 1.2.1935. M/c. Similar to Syria #36. Bldg. across ctr., *LIBAN* at upper ctr. on back.	125.	850.	—
12F	**100 Livres** 1.2.1935. Violet ovpt. Type A. Printer: BWC.	—	—	—

1939 Provisional Issue

 # A13-14 ovpt: *LIBAN 1939* on various earlier Lebanese and Syrian notes.

		Good	Fine	XF
13	**5 Livres** 1939 (- old date 1935). Ovpt. across upper ctr. on face of Syria #36. *SYRIE* at upper ctr. on back.	75.00	325.	—

		Good	Fine	XF
13A	**5 Livres** 1939 (- old date 1935). Ovpt. across lower ctr. of Lebanon #12A.	100.	450.	—
13B	**10 Livres** 1939 (- old date 1930). Ovpt. at upper ctr. on Lebanon #10.	225.	1000.	—

		Good	Fine	XF
13C	**25 Livres** 1939 (- old date 1.2.1935). M/c. Ovpt. at upper ctr. Ornamented flower pattern at l. and r. on back, bridge and bldgs. at ctr.	—	—	—
13D	**50 Livres** 1939 (- old date 1938). Ovpt. at upper ctr. on Syria #39.	—	—	—
A13	**1 Livre** 1939 (- old date 1935). Ovpt. on face of #12.			
	a. Ovpt. at upper ctr.	40.00	225.	650.
	b. Ovpt. at lower ctr.	40.00	225.	650.
14	**100 Livres** 1939 (- old date 1935). Ovpt. on Lebanon #12F.			
	a. Green ovpt. Type A.	—	—	—
	b. Orange ovpt. Type B.	—	—	—
	c. Lilac ovpt. Type C.	—	—	—

Banque de Syrie et du Liban

1939 First Issue

		Good	Fine	XF
15	**1 Livre** 1.9.1939. Blue and m/c. View of of Cyprus on back. Like #48.	17.50	110.	350.
16	**5 Livres** 1.9.1939. Type C1. Serveau. City views on back. Like #49.	45.00	325.	1100.
17	**10 Livres** 1.9.1939. Type C1. Serveau w/*Livres*, bldg. on back.	—	—	—
18	**25 Livres** 1.9.1939. Type Seb. Laurent w/*Livres*, columns on face.	—	—	—
19	**50 Livres** 1.9.1939. Type Seb. Laurent w/*Livres*. City scene at ctr.	—	—	—

#20 not assigned.

		Good	Fine	XF
21	**250 Livres** 1.9.1939. M/c. Well w/dome on face.	—	—	—

1939 Second Issue

#22-24 like #17-19 but w/*Livres Libanaises*.

25 *Deleted*. See #21.

		Good	Fine	XF
22	**10 Livres** 1.9.1939. Like #17 but w/*Livres Libanaises*.	—	—	—
23	**25 Livres** 1.9.1939. Like #18 but w/*Livres Libanaises*.	—	—	—
24	**50 Livres** 1.9.1939. Like #19 but w/*Livres Libanaises*.	—	—	—

1939 Provisional Issue

#26-27 printer: BWC.

		Good	Fine	XF
26	**1 Livre** 1.9.1939. Green on lilac unpt. Columns of Baalbek at l. Ovpt: *LIBAN*. Back red on olive unpt.; city view at ctr.			
	a. Blue ovpt. Type A.	7.50	25.00	150.
	b. Lilac ovpt. Type B.	7.50	25.00	150.
	c. Olive ovpt. Type C.	7.50	25.00	150.
	d. Pink ovpt. Type D.	7.50	25.00	150.
	e. Blue ovpt. Type E.	7.50	25.00	150.

		Good	Fine	XF
27	**5 Livres** 1.9.1939. Brown. Cedar tree at r. Ovpt: *LIBAN*.			
	a. Violet ovpt. Type A.	22.50	110.	350.
	b. Pink ovpt. Type B.	22.50	110.	350.
	c. Green ovpt. Type C.	22.50	110.	350.
	d. Blue ovpt. Type E.	22.50	110.	350.

Note: Notes w/*BEYROUTH* ovpt. on *DAMAS* are forgeries. In 1947, new Syrian notes were introduced and all former issues of Syria were cancelled whereas Lebanese notes remained valid (and were redeemable for many years afterwards); therefore, some attempts were made to "change" Syrian notes into Lebanese issues. These series, however, are different for the 2 countries and allow easy identification.

		Good	Fine	XF
28	**10 Livres** 1.9.1939. Brown-violet. Clock tower at l. Like Syria #42. Ovpt: *LIBAN*.			
	a. Pink ovpt. Type A.	50.00	250.	650.
	b. Green ovpt. Type B.	50.00	250.	650.
	c. Blue ovpt. Type C.	50.00	250.	650.
29	**25 Livres** 1.9.1939. Purple. Caravan at lower ctr. Like Syria #43. Ovpt: *LIBAN*.			
	a. Blue-gray ovpt. Type A.	75.00	375.	1000.
	b. Orange ovpt. Type C.	75.00	375.	1000.

		Good	Fine	XF
30	**50 Livres** 1.9.1939. Brown and m/c. Like Syria #44. Ovpt: *LIBAN*.			
	a. Brown ovpt. Type A.	150.	750.	—
	b. Olive ovpt. Type E.	150.	750.	—

1942 Issue

		Good	Fine	XF
31	**5 Livres** 1.8.1942. Dk. brown. Ovpt: *BEYROUTH* on Syria #46.	75.00	350.	1000.
32	**50 Livres** 1.8.1942. Dk. brown. Ovpt: *BEYROUTH* on Syria #47.	—	—	—
33	**100 Livres** 1.8.1942. Blue. Ovpt: *BEYROUTH* on Syria #48.	—	—	—

République Libanaise

Government Banknotes

1942 Issue

		VG	VF	UNC
34	**5 Piastres** 15.7.1942. Purple and green. Cedar tree at l. Back dk. blue.	1.50	10.00	35.00
35	**10 Piastres** 31.7.1942. Dk. blue on lt. green. 3 Arabs sitting near coastline on back.	2.00	15.00	45.00

#36-37 printer: BWC.

		VG	VF	UNC
36	**25 Piastres** 1.8.1942. Lilac and tan. Omayyad Mosque in Damascus at ctr. Back blue and lt. orange.	5.00	25.00	90.00

		VG	VF	UNC
37	**50 Piastres** 1.8.1942. Green and lilac. Trees at top ctr., mosque w/2 minarets at r.	10.00	30.00	100.

1944 Issue

		VG	VF	UNC
38	**5 Piastres** 15.2.1944. Purple and green. Like #34.	1.00	8.00	30.00

		VG	VF	UNC
39	**10 Piastres** 15.2.1944. Dk. blue on lt. green unpt. Like #35. Back brown.	2.00	15.00	45.00

1948 Issue

		VG	VF	UNC
40	**5 Piastres** 12.1.1948. Blue and yellow. Like #38. Back green.	1.00	3.50	25.00

		VG	VF	UNC
41	**10 Piastres** 12.1.1948. Lilac-brown on lt. blue unpt. Like #39. Back blue.	1.50	12.50	40.00

		VG	VF	UNC
42	**25 Piastres** 12.1.1948; 6.11.1950. Violet on green and orange unpt. Cedar tree at r. Lion at ctr. on back.	3.50	20.00	60.00

		VG	VF	UNC
43	**50 Piastres** 12.1.1948; 6.11.1950. Green on m/c unpt. Columns of Baalbek at ctr. Ruins on back.	10.00	30.00	100.

1950 ISSUE

		VG	VF	UNC
46	**5 Piastres** 21.11.1950. Brown on red-brown unpt. Krak des Chevaliers on back.	2.00	15.00	45.00

		VG	VF	UNC
47	**10 Piastres** 21.11.1950. Blue-violet on lilac unpt. Back blue, Palais Beit-ed-Din on back.	1.50	10.00	30.00

BANQUE DE SYRIE ET DU LIBAN

1945 ISSUE

		Good	Fine	XF
48	**1 Livre** 1.12.1945; 1.8.1950. Blue and m/c. Like #15.	17.50	100.	325.

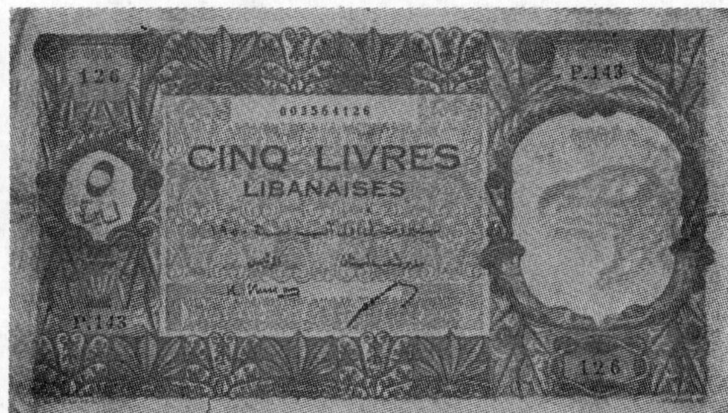

		Good	Fine	XF
49	**5 Livres** 1.12.1945; 1.8.1950. Blue, orange and m/c. Like #16.	45.00	325.	850.
50	**10 Livres** 1.12.1945; 1.8.1950. M/c. Like #17.	60.00	500.	—

		Good	Fine	XF
51	**25 Livres** 1.12.1945; 1.8.1950. M/c. Like #18.	90.00	475.	1150.

		Good	Fine	XF
52	**50 Livres** 1.12.1945; 1.8.1950. M/c. Like #19.	100.	400.	1000.

		Good	Fine	XF
53	**100 Livres** 1.12.1945. M/c. Cedar tree and mountain on back.	—	—	—

1952; 1956 ISSUE

#55-60 all dated 1st of January. Sign. varieties. Printer: TDLR.

		VG	VF	UNC
55	**1 Livre** 1.1.1952-64. Brown on m/c unpt. Crusader Castle at Saida (Sidon) at l. Columns of Baalbek on back. W/ or w/o security strip.			
	a. Issued note.	1.00	8.00	40.00
	s. Specimen. Oval TDLR stamp, punch hole cancelled.	—	—	30.00

		VG	VF	UNC
56	**5 Livres** 1.1.1952-64. Blue on m/c unpt. Courtyard of the Palais de Beit-ed-Din. Snowy mountains w/trees on back. W/ or w/o security strip.			
	a. Issued note.	3.00	35.00	140.
	s. Specimen. Oval TDLR stamp, punch hole cancelled.	—	—	40.00

		VG	VF	UNC
57	**10 Livres** 1.1.1956; 1.1.1961; 1.1.1963. Green on m/c unpt. Ruins of Temple of Bacchus temple at Baalbek. Shoreline w/city in hills on back.			
	a. Issued note.	6.00	45.00	200.
	s. Speciemen. Oval TDLR stamp, punch hole cancelled.	—	—	—

		VG	VF	UNC
58	**25 Livres** 1.1.1952; 1.1.1953. Blue-gray on m/c unpt. Harbor town. Stone arch bridge at ctr. r. on back. Wmk: Lion's head.			
	a. Issued note.	50.00	175.	750.
	s. Specimen. Oval TDLR stamp, punch hole cancelled.	—	—	120.

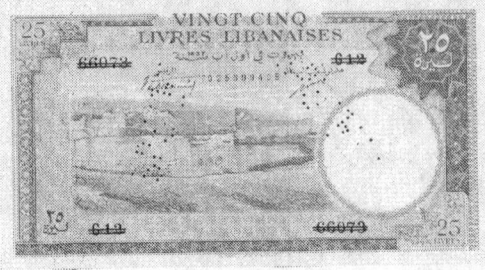

		VG	VF	UNC
59	**50 Livres** 1.1.1952; 1.1.1953; 1.1.1964. Deep brown on m/c unpt. Coast landscape. Lg. rock formations in water on back. Wmk: Lion's head.			
	a. Issued note.	45.00	165.	725.
	s. Specimen. Oval TDLR stamp, punch hole cancelled.	—	—	125.

		VG	VF	UNC
60	**100 Livres** 1.1.1952; 1.1.1953; 1.1.1958; 1.1.1963. Blue on m/c unpt. View of Beirut and harbor. Cedar tree at ctr. on back and as wmk.			
	a. Issued note.	12.50	35.00	150
	s. Specimen. Oval TDLR stamp, punch hole cancelled.	—	—	120

LEEWARD ISLANDS

Leeward Islands is a geographical name, always distinguished from the Windward Islands. In English terminology, the term "Leeward Islands" applies to the northernmost Lesser Antilles, from the Virgin Islands to Guadeloupe, sometimes including Dominica.

From 1871 to 1956, the British colonies of Antigua (with Barbuda and Redonda), St. Kitts-Nevis-Anguilla, Montserrat, and the British Virgin Islands were collectively administered as the Leeward Islands.

See separate listings for the individual colonies; also see British East Caribbean Territories.

RULERS:
British

MONETARY SYSTEM:
1 Shilling = 12 Pence
1 Pound = 20 Shillings

BRITISH ADMINISTRATION

GOVERNMENT OF THE LEEWARD ISLANDS

1921 ISSUE

#1 and 2 portr. Kg. George V at top ctr. Arms at ctr. on back. Printer: TDLR.

		Good	Fine	XF
1	**5 Shillings** 1.1.1921. Red on gray unpt. Back green. Rare.	—	—	—

		Good	Fine	XF
2	**10 Shillings** 1.1.1921. Green on blue unpt. Like #1. Back lt. brown. Rare.	—	—	—

Note: A 2 Shillings 6 Pence (2/6d) note possibly exists. For later issues see East Caribbean States.

LIBERIA

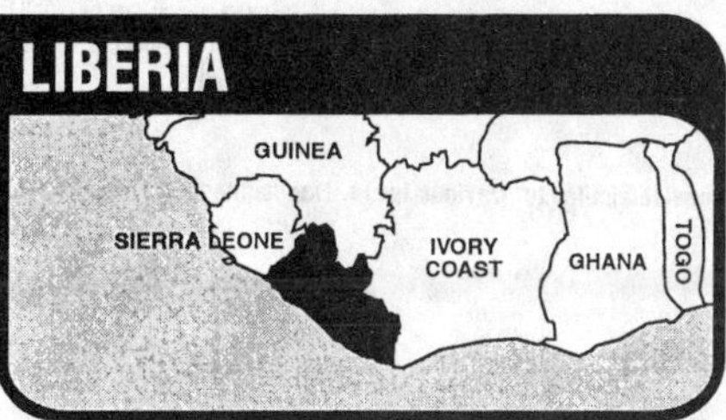

The Republic of Liberia, located on the southern side of the west African bulge between Sierra Leone and the Ivory Coast, has an area of 38,250 sq. mi. (111,369 sq. km.) and a population of 3.26 million. Capital: Monrovia. The major industries are agriculture, mining and lumbering. Iron ore, diamonds, rubber, coffee and cocoa are exported.

The Liberian coast was explored and chartered by Portuguese navigator Pedro de Cintra in 1461. For the following three centuries Portuguese traders visited the area regularly to trade for gold, slaves and pepper. The modern country of Liberia, Africa's first republic, was settled in 1822 by the American Colonization Society as a homeland for American freed slaves, with the U.S. government furnishing funds and assisting in negotiations for procurement of land from the indigenous chiefs. The various settlements united in 1839 to form the Commonwealth of Liberia, and in 1847 established the country as a republic with a constitution modeled after that of the United States.

Notes were issued from 1857 through 1880; thereafter the introduction of dollar notes of the United States took place. U.S. money was declared legal tender in Liberia in 1943, replacing British West African currencies. Not until 1989 was a distinctive Liberian currency again issued.

MONETARY SYSTEM:
1 Dollar = 100 Cents

Note: Certain listings encompassing issues circulated by various bank and regional authorities are contained in Volume 1.

REPUBLIC

TREASURY DEPARTMENT

1857-62 ISSUE

#6-9 various partly handwritten dates. Black printing; notes w/ctr. design shore w/plow and palm tree w/sailing ship in background.

TYPE I: W/text: *Pay to bearer in Gold or Silver coin;* handsigned by Secretary of the Treasury and President.

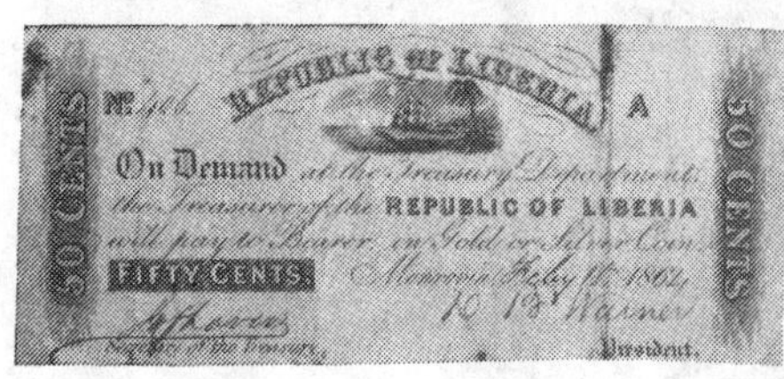

		Good	Fine	XF
6	**50 Cents** 1858-66.			
	a. 26.2.1858.	300.	750.	—
	b. *18__* in printing plate. 6.2.1862; 26.2.1862; 25.2.1863; 7.4.1863.	175.	450.	—
	c. *186_* in printing plate. 24.8.1863; 26.8.1863; 28.12.1863; 18.2.1864; 18.2.1866.	175.	450.	

		Good	Fine	XF
7	**1 Dollar** 1857-64.			
	a. 25.4.1857.	300.	800.	—
	b. *18__* in printing plate. 26.2.1862; 26.7.1862; 21.8.1862; 26.2.1863.	200.	500.	—
	c. *186_* in printing plate. 7.8.1863; 24.8.1863; 28.12.1863; 18.2.1864.	200.	500.	—

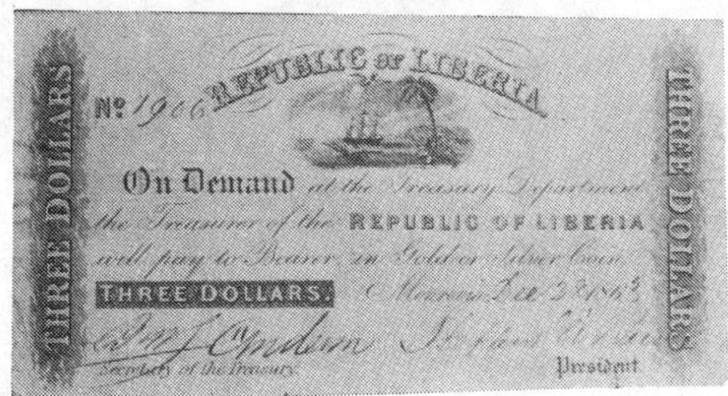

		Good	Fine	XF
8	**3 Dollars** 26.2.1862; 26.7.1862; 28.12.1863; 18.2.1864.	250.	550.	—

		Good	Fine	XF
9	**5 Dollars** 26.8.1858; 26.2.1862; 24.8.1863; 28.12.1863.	275.	600.	—

Note: Sizes in both outer dimensions and printed areas may vary by as much as 8-10mm.

1876-80 Issue

TYPE II: W/o specie payment clause, otherwise similar to previous issue. Handsigned by Treasurer and Secretary of the Treasury.

		Good	Fine	XF
10	**10 Cents** 26.8.1880.	225.	600.	—

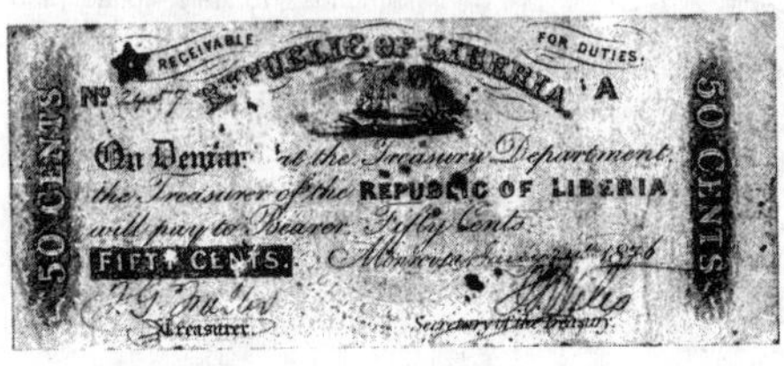

		Good	Fine	XF
11	**50 Cents** 24.1.1876. 141 x 63mm.	250.	700.	—
11A	**50 Cents** 26.8.1880. 91 x 55mm.	250.	700.	—
12	**1 Dollar** 24.1.1876; 26.8.1880.	250.	700.	—
13	**2 Dollars** 24.1.1876; 26.8.1880.	300.	750.	—

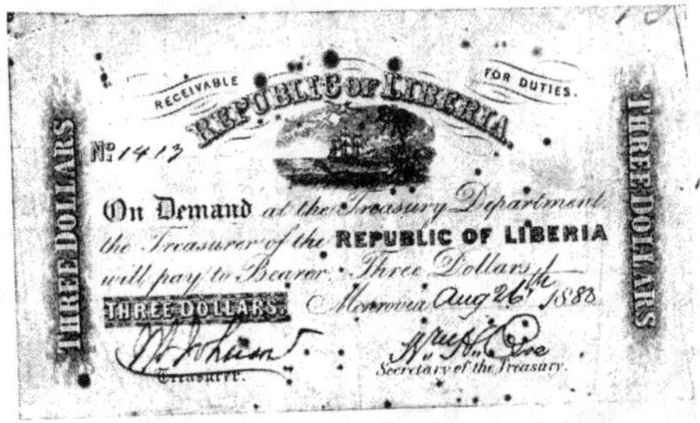

		Good	Fine	XF
14	**3 Dollars** 26.8.1880.	325.	825.	—
15	**5 Dollars** 24.1.1876; 1.3.1880; 26.8.1880.	300.	750.	—

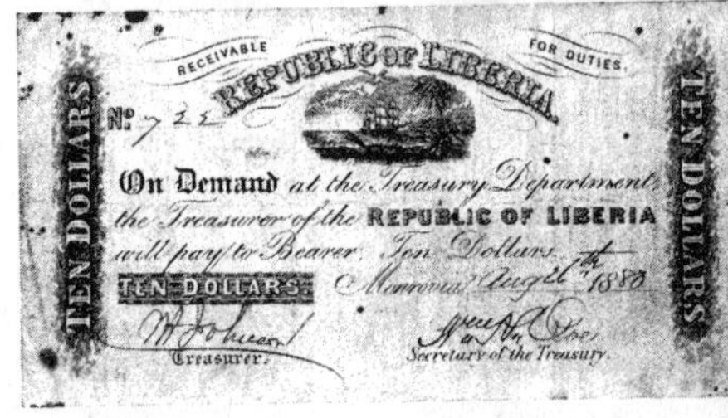

		Good	Fine	XF
16	**10 Dollars** 26.8.1880.	375.	1000.	—

Treasury Department Payment Certificates

Monrovia

1880's Issue

		Good	Fine	XF
17	**Var. Handwritten Denominations** Various handwritten dates.	50.00	125.	275.

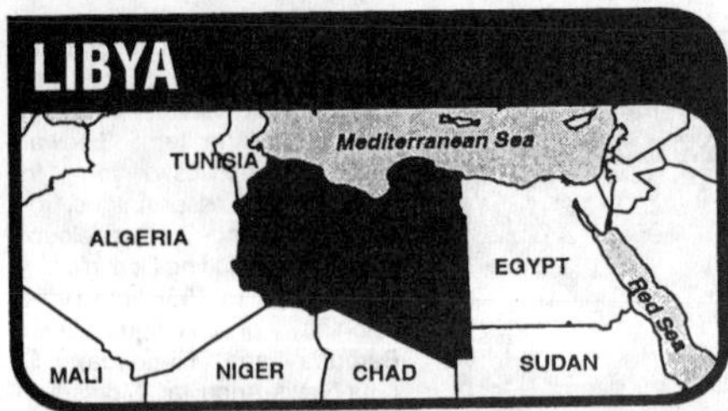

The Socialist People's Libyan Arab Jamahiriya, located on the north central coast of Africa between Tunisia and Egypt, has an area of 679,359 sq. mi. (1,759,540 sq. km.) and a population of 6.39 million. Capital: Tripoli. Crude oil, which accounts for 90 percent of the export earnings, is the mainstay of the economy.

Libya has been subjected to foreign rule throughout most of its history, various parts of it having been ruled by the Phoenicians, Carthaginians, Vandals, Byzantines, Greeks, Romans, Egyptians, and in the following centuries the Arab's language, culture and religion were adopted by the indigenous population. Libya was conquered by the Ottoman Turks in 1553, and remained under Turkish domination, becoming a Turkish vilayet in 1835, until it was conquered by Italy and made into a colony in 1911. The name "Libya", the ancient Greek name for North Africa exclusive of Egypt, was given to the colony by Italy in 1934. Libya came under Allied administration after the fall of Tripoli on Jan. 23, 1943 and was divided into zones of British and French control. On Dec. 24, 1951, in accordance with a United Nations resolution, Libya proclaimed its independence as a constitutional monarchy, thereby becoming the first country to achieve independence through the United Nations. The monarchy was overthrown by a coup d'etat on Sept. 1, 1969, and Libya was established as a republic.

RULERS:

Idris I, 1951-1969

MONETARY SYSTEM:

1 Piastre = 10 Milliemes
1 Pound = 100 Piastres = 1000 Milliemes, 1951-1971
1 Dinar = 1000 Dirhams, 1971-

United Kingdom

Note: Previously listed #1-4 are now shown as Italian East Africa.

Treasury

Law of 24.10.1951

		VG	VF	UNC
5	**5 Piastres** L.1951. Red on lt. yellow unpt. Colonnade at l., palm tree at r.	1.00	6.50	20.00

		VG	VF	UNC
6	**10 Piastres** L.1951. Green on lt. orange unpt. Ruins of gate at l., palm tree at r.	1.50	8.50	30.00

		VG	VF	UNC
7	**1/4 Pound** L.1951. Blue on lt. orange unpt. Ruins of columns at l., palm tree at r.	6.00	30.00	175

#8-11 arms at l. denomination in lg. # at r. over wmk. area.

		VG	VF	UNC
8	**1/2 Pound** L.1951. Purple on m/c unpt.	7.00	50.00	175
9	**1 Pound** L.1951. Blue on m/c unpt.	7.00	50.00	175
10	**5 Pounds** L.1951. Green on m/c unpt.	35.00	200.	—
11	**10 Pounds** L.1951. Brown on m/c unpt.	45.00	350.	—

KINGDOM

TREASURY

1952 ISSUE

#12-14 portr. Kg. Idris I at l., palm tree at r.

		VG	VF	UNC
12	**5 Piastres** 1.1.1952. Red on lt. yellow unpt.	1.50	8.50	45.00

		VG	VF	UNC
13	**10 Piastres** 1.1.1952. Green.	2.50	15.00	85.00

		VG	VF	UNC
14	**1/4 Pound** 1.1.1952. Orange.	7.50	35.00	185.

#15-18 portr. Kg. Idris at l., bush at lower ctr.

		VG	VF	UNC
15	**1/2 Pound** 1.1.1952. Purple.	8.00	40.00	150.
16	**1 Pound** 1.1.1952. Blue.	10.00	65.00	200.
17	**5 Pounds** 1.1.1952. Green.	30.00	300.	—
18	**10 Pounds** 1.1.1952. Brown.	75.00	500.	—

NATIONAL BANK OF LIBYA

LAW OF 26.4.1955

1958-59 ISSUE

#19-22 arms at l. 2 sign. varieties.

		Good	Fine	XF
19	**1/2 Pound** L.1955 (1959). Purple. Similar to #8.			
	a. Black serial #	5.00	25.00	125.
	b. Red serial #.	5.00	25.00	125.

		Good	Fine	XF
20	**1 Pound** L.1955 (1959). Blue. Similar to #9.	6.00	30.00	150.
21	**5 Pounds** L.1955 (1958). Green. Similar to #10.	25.00	150.	—
22	**10 Pounds** L.1955 (1958). Brown. Similar to #11.	40.00	200.	—

Note: For similar notes issued by the Bank of Libya, see Volume 3 listings.

BRITISH OCCUPATION - WW II

MILITARY AUTHORITY IN TRIPOLITANIA

1943 ND ISSUE

#M1-M8 lion on crown at ctr. or at r.

		VG	VF	UNC
M1	**1 Lira** ND (1943). Green.			
	a. Issued note.	1.00	8.00	40.00
	s. Specimen.	—	—	135.
M2	**2 Lire** ND (1943). Blue on green unpt.			
	a. Issued note.	5.00	40.00	120.
	s. Specimen.	—	—	150.

Note: #M2 is scarce as there was a coin of equivalent value in circulation at the time of issue.

		VG	VF	UNC
M3	**5 Lire** ND (1943). Green on red-brown unpt.			
	a. Issued note.	1.00	7.50	40.00
	s. Specimen.	—	—	150.
M4	**10 Lire** ND (1943). Lilac on green unpt.			
	a. Issued note.	4.00	15.00	65.00
	s. Specimen.	—	—	175.

		VG	VF	UNC
M5	**50 Lire** ND (1943). Brown.			
	a. Issued note.	10.00	50.00	135.
	s. Specimen.	—	—	200.
M6	**100 Lire** ND (1943). Red-orange on blue unpt.			
	a. Issued note.	15.00	60.00	185.
	s. Specimen.	—	—	200.

		VG	VF	UNC
M7	**500 Lire** ND (1943). Green on blue unpt.			
	a. Issued note.	80.00	400.	1150.
	s. Specimen.	—	—	600.
M8	**1000 Lire** ND (1943). Blue on brown unpt.			
	a. Issued note.	125.	600.	1500.
	s. Specimen.	—	—	800.

FRENCH OCCUPATION OF THE FEZZAN - WW II

REPUBLIQUE FRANCAISE

1936-38 ND ISSUE

#M9-M11 black handstamp: *R-F/FEZZAN* (in rectangle); letters in stamp 12 and 14mm high on Banque de l'Afrique Occidentale notes. Forgeries, created for collectors, exist (w/letters in stamp taller and different dates after 1940).

Note: There is a possibility that all Fezzan ovpt. notes except some of #M9 are spurious.

		VG	VF	UNC
M9	**5 Francs** ND (-old date 10.3.1938). M/c. Ovpt. on French West Africa #21.	150.	275.	—

		VG	VF	UNC
M10	**25 Francs** ND (-old date 10.3.1938). Ovpt. on French West Africa #24.	—	—	—

		VG	VF	UNC
M11	**100 Francs** ND (-old date 17.11.1936). Ovpt. on French West Africa #26.	—	—	—

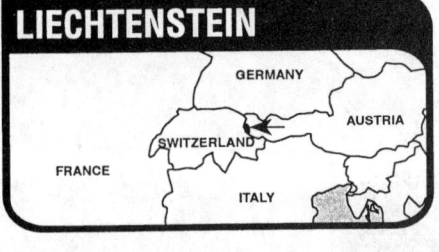

LIECHTENSTEIN

GERMANY
AUSTRIA
SWITZERLAND
FRANCE
ITALY

The Principality of Liechtenstein, located in central Europe on the east bank of the Rhine between Austria and Switzerland, has an area of 62 sq. mi. (157 sq. km.) and a population of 33,000. Capital: Vaduz. The ecomomy is d on agriculture and light manufacturing. Canned goods, textiles, ceramics and precision instruments are exported. Liechtenstein assumed its present form in 1719 when the lordships of Schellenburg and Vaduz were merged into a principality. It was a member of the Rhine Confederation from 1806 to 1815, and of the German Confederation from 1815 to 1866 when it became independent. Liechtenstein's long and close association with Austria was terminated by World War I. In 1921 it adopted the coinage of Switzerland, and two years later entered into a customs union with the Swiss, who also operate its postal and telegraph systems and represent it in international affairs. The tiny principality abolished its army in 1868 and has avoided involvement in all European wars since that time.

RULERS:

Prince John II, 1858-1929
Prince Franz I, 1929-1938
Prince Franz Josef II, 1938-1989
Prince Hans Adam II, 1989-

MONETARY SYSTEM:

1 Krone = 100 Heller to 1924
1 Frank = 100 Rappen, 1924-

PRINCIPALITY

FURSTENTUM LIECHTENSTEIN GUTSCHEINE

DUCHY OF LEICHTENSTEIN CREDIT NOTES

1920 ISSUE

		VG	VF	UNC
1	**10 Heller** ND (1920). Red and blue. Arms at l. Villa on back.	1.00	5.00	20.00

		VG	VF	UNC
2	**20 Heller** ND (1920). Red and blue. Arms at l. Castle at Vaduz on back.	1.00	5.00	20.00

		VG	VF	UNC
3	**50 Heller** ND (1920). Red and blue w/arms in unpt. at ctr. Landscape on back.	1.00	5.00	20.00

LITHUANIA

The Republic of Lithuania southernmost of the Baltic states in east Europe, has an area of 26,173 sq. mi. (65,301 sq. km.) and a population of 3.69 million. Capital: Vilnius. The economy is d on livestock raising and manufacturing. Hogs, cattle, hides and electric motors are exported.

Lithuania emerged as a grand duchy joined to Poland through the Lublin Union in 1569. In the 15th century it was a major power of central Europe, stretching from the Baltic to the Black Sea. Following the 1795 partition of Poland by Austria, Prussia and Russia, Lithuania came under Russian domination and did not regain its independence until shortly before the end of World War I when it declared itself a sovereign republic. The republic was occupied by Soviet troops in June of 1940 and annexed to the U.S.S.R. Following the German occupation of 1941-44, it was retaken by Russia and reestablished as a member republic of the Soviet Union. Western countries, including the United States, did not recognize Lithuania's incorporation into the Soviet Union.

Lithuania declared its independence March 11, 1990. Lithuania was seated in the UN General Assembly on Sept. 17, 1991; and joined the European Union on May 1, 2004.

MONETARY SYSTEM:

1 Litas = 100 Centu

REPUBLIC

LIETUVOS UKIO BANKAS

1919 ISSUE

#A1-A4 circulating checks *Sio cekio pao...*

		VG	VF	UNC
A1	**50 Ost. Markiu** ND (1919-20). Rare.	—	—	—
A2	**100 Ost. Markiu** ND (1919-20). Black and gold. Rare.	—	—	—
A3	**500 Ost. Markiu** ND (1919-20). Black. Rare.	—	—	—

		VG	VF	UNC
A4	**1000 Ost. Markiu** ND (1919-20). Green. Back m/c. Rare.	—	—	—

LIETUVOS BANKAS

BANK OF LITHUANIA

1922 SEPTEMBER ISSUE

#1-6 knight on horseback at ctr. on back. Printer: Otto Elsner, Berlin.

		VG	VF	UNC
1	**1 Centas** 10.9.1922. Blue.			
	a. Issued note.	8.00	25.00	60.00
	s1. Specimen perforated: *PAVYZDYS.*	—	—	70.00
	s2. Specimen ovpt: *Ungiltig als Banknote!...* Rare.	—	—	—

		VG	VF	UNC
2	**5 Centai** 10.9.1922. Green.			
	a. Issued note.	8.00	25.00	60.00
	s1. Specimen perforated: *PAVYZDYS.*	—	—	70.00
	s2. Specimen ovpt: *Ungiltig als Banknote!...* Rare.	—	—	—
3	**20 Centu** 10.9.1922. Red-brown.			
	a. Issued note.	12.50	40.00	125.
	s1. Specimen perforated: *PAVYZDYS.*	—	—	125.
	s2. Specimen ovpt: *Ungiltig als Banknote!...* Rare.	—	—	—
4	**50 Centu** 10.9.1922. Purple.			
	a. Issued note.	17.50	50.00	135.
	s1. Specimen perforated: *PAVYZDYS.*	—	—	135.
	s2. Specimen ovpt: *Ungiltig als Banknote!...* Rare.	—	—	—

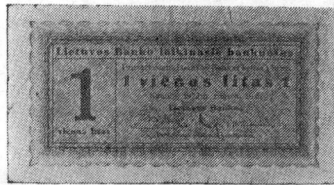

		VG	VF	UNC
5	**1 Litas** 10.9.1922. Gray.			
	a. Wmk: Strands.	30.00	100.	275.
	b. Wmk: Loop.	30.00	100.	275.
	s1. Specimen perforated: *PAVYZDYS.*	—	—	265.
	s2. Specimen ovpt: *Ungiltig als Banknote!*	—	—	265.

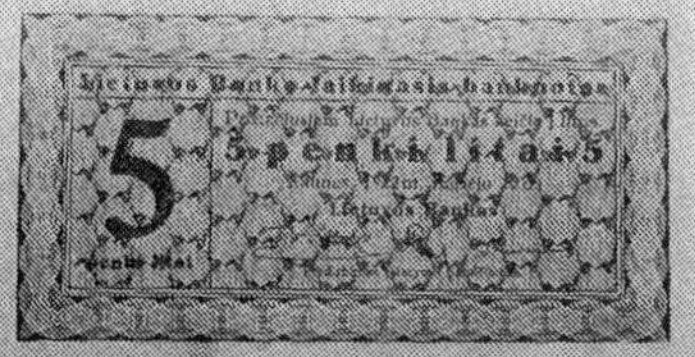

		VG	VF	UNC
6	**5 Litai** 10.9.1922. Dk. brown.			
	a. Issued note.	60.00	175.	475.
	s1. Specimen perforated: *PAVYZDYS.*	—	—	375.
	s2. Specimen ovpt: *Ungiltig als Banknote!* Rare.	—	—	—

1922 NOVEMBER ISSUE

#7-B21 printer: Andreas Haase, Prague.

		VG	VF	UNC
7	**1 Centas** 16.11.1922. Blue and burgundy-red. Back green and dk. red.			
	a. Issued note.	6.50	25.00	55.00
	s1. Specimen perforated: *PAVYZDYS.*	—	—	70.00
	s2. Specimen ovpt: *VALEUR NON VALABLE! ECHANTILLON!*	—	—	70.00
	s3. Specimen ovpt: *Pavyzdys-bevertis.*	—	—	70.00

		VG	VF	UNC
8	**2 Centu** 16.11.1922. Dk. green on gray-violet. Back lt. and dk. brown.			
	a. Issued note.	7.50	30.00	65.00
	s1. Specimen perforated: *PAVYZDYS.*	—	—	80.00
	s2. Specimen ovpt: *VALEUR NON VALABLE! ECHANTILLON!*	—	—	80.00
	s3. Specimen ovpt: *Pavyzdys-bevertis.*	—	—	80.00

		VG	VF	UNC
9	**5 Centai** 16.11.1922. Blue on green. Back brown and purple.			
	a. Issued note.	8.00	32.50	70.00
	s1. Specimen perforated: *PAVYZDYS.*	—	—	80.00
	s2. Specimen ovpt: *VALEUR NON VALABLE! ECHANTILLON!*	—	—	80.00
	s3. Specimen ovpt: *Pavyzdys-bevertis.*	—	—	80.00

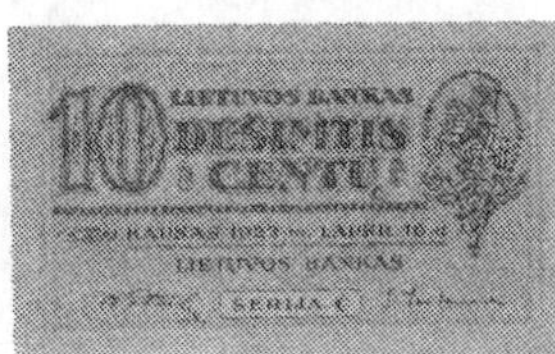

		VG	VF	UNC
10	**10 Centu**			
	16.11.1922. Red-brown on gray-violet. Back red on brown.			
	a. Issued note.	8.00	35.00	75.00
	s1. Specimen perforated: *PAVYZDYS.*	—	—	90.00
	s2. Specimen ovpt: *VALEUR NON VALABLE! ECHANTILLON!*	—	—	90.00
	s3. Specimen ovpt: *Pavyzdys-bevertis.*	—	—	90.00

		VG	VF	UNC
11	**20 Centu**			
	16.11.1922. Dk. blue on gray. Back dk. and lt. brown.			
	a. Issued note.	10.00	40.00	100.
	s1. Specimen perforated: *PAVYZDYS.*	—	—	110.
	s2. Specimen ovpt: *VALEUR NON VALABLE! ECHANTILLON!*	—	—	110.
	s3. Specimen ovpt: *Pavyzdys-bevertis.*	—	—	110.

		VG	VF	UNC
12	**50 Centu**			
	16.11.1922. Purple and green. Back dk. green and brown.			
	a. Issued note.	20.00	55.00	150.
	s1. Specimen perforated: *PAVYZDYS.*	—	—	175.
	s2. Specimen ovpt: *VALEUR NON VALABLE! ECHANTILLON!*	—	—	175.
	s3. Specimen ovpt: *Pavyzdys-bevertis.*	—	—	175.

		VG	VF	UNC
13	**1 Litas**			
	16.11.1922. Red-brown on gray. Back red and purple on tan.			
	a. Issued note.	30.00	100.	275.
	s1. Specimen perforated: *PAVYZDYS.*	—	—	225.
	s2. Specimen ovpt: *VALEUR NON VALABLE! ECHANTILLON!*	—	—	225.
	s3. Specimen ovpt: *Pavyzdys-bevertis.*	—	—	225.

		VG	VF	UNC
14	**2 Litu**			
	16.11.1922. Blue on gray. Back dk. blue and purple.			
	a. Issued note.	37.50	115.	300.
	s1. Specimen perforated: *PAVYZDYS.*	—	—	250.
	s2. Specimen ovpt: *VALEUR NON VALABLE! ECHANTILLON!*	—	—	250.
	s3. Specimen ovpt: *Pavyzdys-bevertis.*	—	—	250.

		VG	VF	UNC
15	**5 Litai**			
	16.11.1922. Purple and blue. Farmer sowing at ctr. Black Serial # at lower ctr. Back green and brown; woman at r.			
	a. Issued note.	50.00	175.	450.
	s1. Specimen perforated: *PAVYZDYS.*	—	—	400.
	s2. Specimen ovpt: *VALEUR NON VALABLE! ECHANTILLON!*	—	—	400
	s3. Specimen ovpt: *Pavyzdys-bevertis.*	—	—	400

		VG	VF	UNC
16	**5 Litai**			
	16.11.1922. Olive-green, blue and black. Similar to #15 but ornamentation on face slightly changed. Red serial # at upper r.			
	a. Issued note.	40.00	125.	350
	s1. Specimen perforated: *PAVYZDYS.*	—	—	325
	s2. Specimen ovpt: *VALEUR NON VALABLE! ECHANTILLON!*	—	—	325
	s3. Specimen ovpt: *Pavyzdys-bevertis.*	—	—	325
17	**5 Litai**			
	16.11.1922. Red-brown and dk. gray. Face like #16. Ornamentation on back is changed. Green serial #.			
	a. Issued note.	45.00	150.	450
	s1. Specimen perforated: *PAVYZDYS.*	—	—	425
	s2. Specimen ovpt: *VALEUR NON VALABLE! ECHANTILLON!*	—	—	425
	s3. Specimen ovpt: *Pavyzdys-bevertis.*	—	—	425

		VG	VF	UN
18	**10 Litu**			
	16.11.1922. Blue, purple and brown. Raftsman at r. Woman at l. and r. on back.			
	a. Issued note.	75.00	225.	50
	s1. Specimen perforated: *PAVYZDYS.*	—	—	45
	s2. Specimen ovpt: *VALEUR NON VALABLE! ECHANTILLON!*	—	—	45
	s3. Specimen ovpt: *Pavyzdys-bevertis.*	—	—	45

		VG	VF	UNC
19	**50 Litu** 16.11.1922. Dk. green and brown. City arms o Kaunas, Vilnius and Klaipeda from l. to ctr., Lithuanian Grand Duke Gediminas at r. Bldg. behind ornamented gate on back.			
	a. Issued note.	200.	600.	900.
	s1. Specimen perforated: *PAVYZDYS.*	—	—	700.
	s2. Specimen ovpt: *VALEUR NON VALABLE! ECHANTILLON!*	—	—	700.
	s3. Specimen ovpt: *Pavyzdys-bevertis.*	—	—	700.

		VG	VF	UNC
20	**100 Litu** 16.11.1922. Blue and purple. Arms at l; Vytautas the Great at r.			
	a. Issued note.	175.	450.	1000.
	s1. Specimen perforated: *PAVYZDYS.*	—	—	900.
	s2. Specimen ovpt: *VALEUR NON VALABLE! ECHANTILLON!*	—	—	900.
	s3. Specimen ovpt: *Pavyzdys-bevertis.*	—	—	900.

		VG	VF	UNC
20A	**500 Litu** 10.8.1924. Back brown; Lithuanian emblem. (Not issued). Rare.	—	—	—

		VG	VF	UNC
20B	**1000 Litu** 10.8.1924. Blue and orange. Face similar to #A21. Map at l., snakes in limbs on back. (Not issued). Rare.	—	—	—

DECEMBER 11, 1924 ISSUE

#21-25 printer: BWC.

		VG	VF	UNC
21	**500 Litu** 11.12.1924. Dk. brown. Back blue.			
	a. Issued note.	80.00	250.	800.
	s1. Specimen perforated: *PAVYZDYS.*	—	—	650.
	s2. Specimen ovpt: *PAVYZDYS.*	—	—	650.

		VG	VF	UNC
22	**1000 Litu** 11.12.1924. Green. Arms at ctr. Girl in Lithuanian national costume at l., seated youth at r. on back.			
	a. Issued note.	175.	500.	1250.
	s1. Specimen perforated: *PAVYZDYS.*	—	—	1000.
	s2. Specimen ovpt: *PAVYZDYS*	—	—	1000.

1927-28 ISSUE

		VG	VF	UNC
23	**10 Litu**			
	24.11.1927. Green. Farmers tilling the fields on back.			
	a. Issued note.	12.50	35.00	125.
	s1. Specimen perforated: *PAVYZDYS.*	—	—	100.
	s2. Specimen ovpt: *PAVYZDYS.*	—	—	100.

		VG	VF	UNC
24	**50 Litu**			
	31.3.1928. Dk. blue. Dr. Jonas Basanavicius at l. Ornate bldg. on back.			
	a. Issued note.	12.50	45.00	125.
	s1. Specimen perforated: *PAVYZDYS.*	—	—	100.
	s2. Specimen perforated. Cancelled and ovpt: *PAVYZDYS.*	—	—	100.

		VG	VF	UNC
25	**100 Litu**			
	31.3.1928. Dk. purple. Seated woman at l., boy w/staff of Mercury at r. Bldg. on back.			
	a. Issued note.	15.00	35.00	125.
	s1. Specimen perforated: *PAVYZDYS.*	—	—	125.
	s2. Specimen ovpt: *PAVYZDYS.*	—	—	125.

1929-30 Commemorative Issue

#26 and 27, 500th Anniversary Vytautas the Great. Printer: BWC.

		VG	VF	UNC
26	**5 Litai**			
	24.6.1929. Brown. Grand Duke Vytautas the Great at l. Medieval warriors on horseback on back.			
	a. Issued note.	12.50	40.00	150.
	s1. Specimen perforated: *PAVYZDYS.*	—	—	125.
	s2. Specimen ovpt: *PAVYZDYS.*	—	—	125.

		VG	VF	UNC
27	**20 Litu**			
	5.7.1930. Brown on green and blue unpt. Grand Duke Vytautas the Great at l. Vytautas Church at ctr. Cargo ship and statue on back.			
	a. Issued note.	12.50	40.00	150.
	s1. Specimen perforated: *PAVYZDYS.*	—	—	125.
	s2. Specimen ovpt: *PAVYZDYS.*	—	—	125.

1938 Commemorative Issue

#28, 20th Anniversary of Independence

Printer: BWC.

		VG	VF	UNC
28	**10 Litu**			
	16.2.1938. Green and orange. Pres. Antanas Smetona at l. Council of Lithuania on back. Specimen ovpt: *PAVYZDYS.* Printer: BWC.	—	—	3000.

Note: For notes issued by the Darlehnskasse Ost at Kaunas in 1918 w/Lithuanian language, see Germany, Occupied Territories WWI.

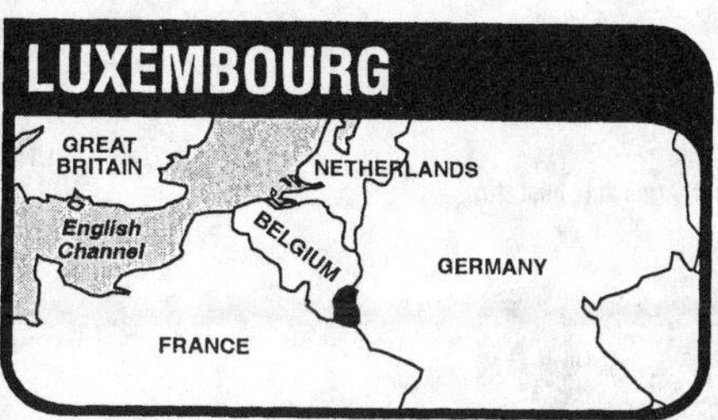

The Grand Duchy of Luxembourg is located in western Europe between Belgium, Germany and France. It has an area of 998 sq. mi. (2,586 sq. km.) and a population of 430,000. Capital: Luxembourg. The economy is d on steel - Luxembourg's per capita production of 16 tons is the highest in the world.

Founded about 963, Luxembourg was a prominent country of the Holy Roman Empire; one of its sovereigns became Holy Roman Emperor as Henry VII, 1308. After being made a duchy by Emperor Charles IV, 1534, Luxembourg passed under the domination of Burgundy, Spain, Austria and France in 1443-1815. It regained autonomy under the Treaty of Vienna, 1815, as a grand duchy in union with the Netherlands, though ostensibly a member of the German Confederation. When Belgium seceded from the Kingdom of the Netherlands, in 1830, Luxembourg was forced to cede its greater western section to Belgium. The tiny duchy left the German Confederation in 1867 when the Treaty of London recognized it as an independent state and guaranteed its perpetual neutrality. Luxembourg was occupied by Germany and liberated by American forces in both world wars.

RULERS:

William III (Netherlands), 1849-90 (represented by brother Henry)
Adolphe, 1890-1905
William IV, 1905-12
Marie Adelaide, 1912-19
Charlotte, 1919-64
Jean, 1964-

MONETARY SYSTEM:

1 Thaler = 30 Groschen
1 Mark = 100 Pfennig = 1 Franc (Franken) 25 Centimes
1 Franc = 100 Centimes, to 2001
1 Euro = 100 Cents, 2001-

GRAND DUCHY

BANQUE INTERNATIONALE A LUXEMBOURG

INTERNATIONAL BANK IN LUXEMBOURG

1856 GULDEN ISSUE

		Good	Fine	XF
A1	**5 Gulden** 1.9.1856. Proof.	—	—	—
A2	**10 Gulden** 1.9.1856. Proof.	—	—	—
A3	**25 Gulden** 1.9.1856. Proof.	—	—	—

1856 THALER ISSUE

		Good	Fine	XF
1	**10 Thaler** 1.9.1856; 30.9.1885; 15.9.1894. Black on yellow unpt. Back blue; seated woman and 3 cherubs. Rare.	—	—	—

1856 FRANC/MARK ISSUE

		Good	Fine	XF
2	**25 Francs = 20 Mark** 1.9.1856; 30.9.1886; 15.4.1894. Brown on yellow unpt. Back like #1. Rare.	—	—	—
3	**100 Francs = 80 Mark** 1.9.1856; 30.9.1886; 15.9.1894. Brown on yellow unpt. Back like #1.	—	—	—

1900 ISSUE

#4 and 5 printer: G&D.

		Good	Fine	XF
4	**20 Mark** 1.7.1900. Blue and brown on m/c unpt. Foundry worker w/factory in background at l.	500.	1200.	2750.

		Good	Fine	XF
5	**50 Mark** 1.7.1900. Green and red-brown. Miner at l., farmer at r.	650.	1750.	—

1914 WW I EMERGENCY ISSUE

#6-8 circular arms at l. on back.

		Good	Fine	XF
6	**1 Mark** 5.8.1914. Blue. Like #7.	37.50	110.	300.

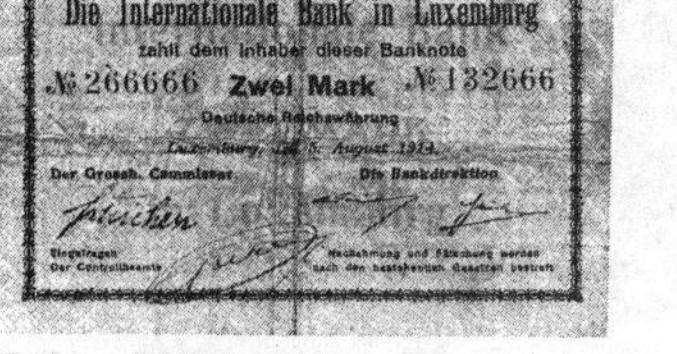

		Good	Fine	XF
7	**2 Mark** 5.8.1914. Brown.	50.00	160.	400.
8	**5 Mark** 5.8.1914. Blue text (w/o vignette). Black text on back.	100.	325.	650.

1923 ISSUE

		Good	Fine	XF
9	**100 Francs** 10.2.1923; 1.4.1930. Yellow and blue. City of Luxembourg on face. Back red and blue; Vianden Castle at r.	120.	350.	800.
10	**100 Francs** 18.12.1930. Yellow and blue. Like #9.	100.	325.	750.

1936 ISSUE

		Good	Fine	XF
11	**100 Francs** 1.8.1936; 18.12.1940. Yellow and blue. Like #9.	120.	350.	800.

1947 Issue

		VG	VF	UNC
12	**100 Francs** 15.5.1947. Brown and blue. Farm wife at l., portr. Grand Duchess Charlotte at ctr. facing l., farmer at r. 3 steelworkers on back.	12.50	85.00	475.

1956 Issue

		VG	VF	UNC
13	**100 Francs** 21.4.1956. Dk. green. Farm wife at l., portr. Grand Duchess Charlotte at ctr. facing r., farmer at r. Back similar to #12.			
	a. Issued note.	6.00	35.00	275.
	s. Specimen w/red ovpt: *SPECIMEN.*	—	—	165.

Note: For #14 and 14A see Vol. 3.

Grosshherzoglich Luxemburgische National Bank

Grand Dukal Luxembourg National Bank

1873 Thaler Issue

		Good	Fine	XF
15	**5 Thaler** 1.7.1873. Brown. Arms at l. and r.			
	a. Issued note. Rare.	—	—	—
	s. Specimen.	—	—	—
16	**10 Thaler** 1.7.1873. Gray.			
	a. Issued note. Rare.	—	—	—
	s. Specimen.	—	—	—

		Good	Fine	XF
17	**20 Thaler** 1.7.1873. Lt. brown. Arms at l., allegorical figures at r.			
	a. Issued note. Rare.	—	—	—
	s. Specimen.	—	—	—

1873 Franc Issue

		Good	Fine	XF
17A	**20 Francs** 1.7.1873. Blue on pink unpt. Rare.	—	—	—
17B	**100 Francs** 1.7.1873. Rare.	—	—	—

1876 Mark Issue

		VG	VF	UNC
18	**5 Mark** 25.3.1876. Blue on violet unpt. Arms at l., bust at r.			
	a. Issued note. Rare.	—	—	—
	s. Specimen.	—	—	1500.

		Good	Fine	XF
19	**10 Mark** 25.3.1876. Brown.			
	a. Issued note. Rare.	—	—	—
	s. Specimen.	—	—	—
20	**20 Mark** 25.3.1876. Gray-green.			
	a. Issued note. Rare.	—	—	—
	s. Specimen.	—	—	—

État du Grand-Duché de Luxembourg

Grossherzoglich Luxemburgischer Staat

Kassenscheine

Law of 28.11.1914

#21-25 sign. varieties. Printer: G&D.

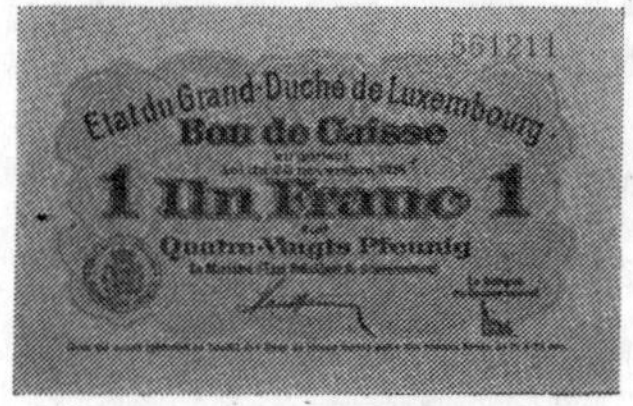

		Good	Fine	XF
21	**1 Frank = 80 Pfennig** L. 1914. Black on blue unpt.	8.50	35.00	150.

		Good	Fine	XF
22	**2 Franken = 1 Mark 60 Pfennig** L.1914. Dk. brown on orange and green unpt.	12.50	50.00	200.

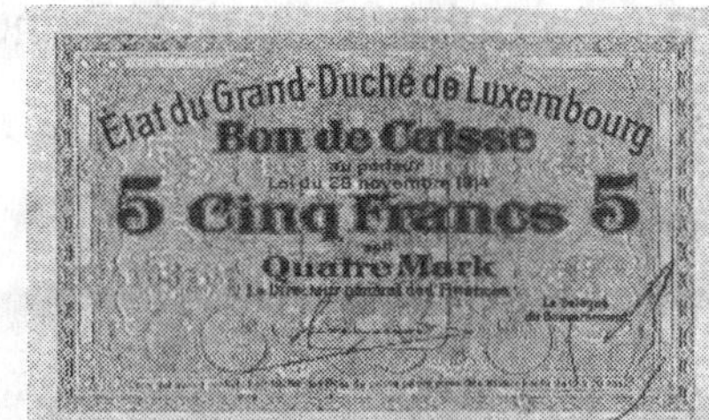

		Good	Fine	XF
23	**5 Franken = 4 Mark** L.1914. Brownish purple on lilac and green unpt. Sign. title: Le Directeur...Finances.	20.00	85.00	300.
23A	**5 Franken = 4 Mark** L.1914. Like #23 but sign. title: Le Ministre d'État, President du Gouvernement.	25.00	175.	—
24	**25 Franken = 20 Mark** L.1914. Violet and green.	65.00	150.	550.
25	**125 Franken = 100 Mark** L.1914. Lilac and green.			
	a. Issued note.	125.	375.	—
	r. Remainder.	—	Unc	300.

LAW OF 28.11.1914 AND 11.12.1918

#26-33 have Law dates 28.11.1914-11.12.1918 but were issued in 1919.

#26-30, 32 printer: G&D.

		Good	Fine	XF
26	**50 Centimes** L.1914-1918 (1919). Dk. brown on lilac unpt. Sign. varieties.	4.00	25.00	100.

		Good	Fine	XF
27	**1 Franc** L.1914-1918 (1919). Black on blue unpt. Like #21.	5.00	30.00	125.

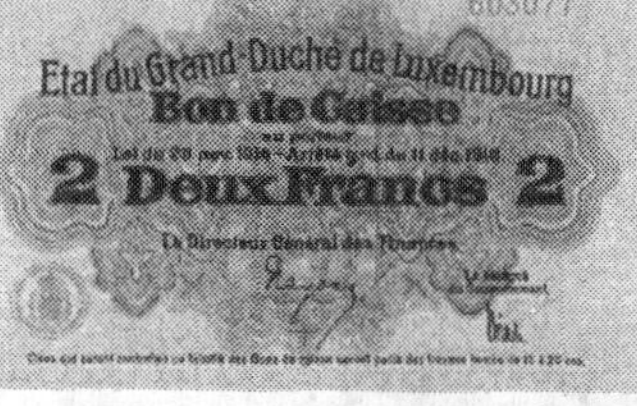

		Good	Fine	XF
28	**2 Francs** L.1914-1918 (1919). Dk. brown on orange and green unpt. Like #22.	7.50	40.00	200.

		Good	Fine	XF
29	**5 Francs** L.1914-1918 (1919). Brownish purple on lilac and green unpt. Like #23.			
	a. Red seal.	8.00	60.00	250.
	b. Dk. brown seal.	8.00	60.00	250.
	c. Black seal.	8.00	60.00	250.

		Good	Fine	XF
30	**10 Francs** L.1914-1918 (1919). Blue on blue-gray. Allegorical woman at l. and r.	325.	850.	—
31	**25 Francs** L.1914-1918 (1919). Blue-green on lt. green unpt.			
	a. W/o serial # (unfinished).	—	Unc	40.00
	b. W/serial #, blue and green.	35.00	150.	350.

		Good	Fine	XF
32	**125 Francs** L.1914-1918 (1919). Lilac and green.	100.	500.	—

		Good	Fine	XF
33	**500 Francs**			
	L.1914-1918 (1919).			
	a. W/o seal or serial # on back (unfinished).	—	Unc	50.00
	b. W/serial #, pink unpt.	150.	500.	—

1923-27 Issue

		Good	Fine	XF
34	**10 Francs** ND (1923). Blue. Farmer's wife at l., worker at r. Portr. Grand Duchess Charlotte at l. on back.	65.00	250.	750.

#35-36 printer: G&D.

		Good	Fine	XF
35	**20 Francs** L.1914-1918 (1926). Violet and green. Arms at ctr. Portr. Grand Duchess Charlotte and bldgs. on back.	55.00	250.	750.

		Good	Fine	XF
36	**100 Francs** ND (1927). Brown and green. Portr. Grand Duchess Charlotte at l. 12 coats of arms on back.	75.00	300.	850.

Grand Duché de Luxembourg

1929-39 Issue

#37-38 printer: JEZ.

		Good	Fine	XF
37	**20 Francs**			
	1.10.1929. Blue. Grape harvest. Farmer plowing on back.			
	a. Issued note.	25.00	80.00	250.
	s. Specimen w/red ovpt: *SPECIMEN.*	—	Unc	135.

		Good	Fine	XF
38	**50 Francs**			
	1.10.1932. Green-blue on tan unpt. Grand Duchess Charlotte at upper r. Palace in Luxembourg on back. Printer: JEZ.			
	a. Issued note.	20.00	70.00	225.
	s1. As a. Specimen w/red ovpt: *SPECIMEN.*	—	Unc	110.
	s2. Lilac. Specimen.	—	Unc	250.
39	**100 Francs**			
	ND (1934). Black on green, brown and m/c unpt. Portr. Grand Duchess Charlotte at l., arms at ctr. Back green; seated woman w/globe and anvil at ctr., Adolphe Bridge and city of Luxembourg behind. Printer: ABNC.			
	a. Issued note.	17.50	60.00	175.
	s. Specimen.	—	Unc	85.00

		Good	Fine	XF
40	**1000 Francs**			
	1.9.1939. (Issued 1940). Dk. brown and green. Arms in unpt. Printer: G&D.			
	a. Issued note.	250.	825.	—
	r. Remainder w/o date.	175.	425.	—
	s. Specimen.	—	Unc	1250.

GERMAN OCCUPATION - WW II

LETZEBURG

1940 ISSUE

		Good	Fine	XF
41	**10 (zeng) Frang** 20.4.1940. Brown w/pink unpt. P. Eyschen at l. Arms on back. Printer: G&D. (Not issued). Rare.	—	—	—
41A	**20 Frang** ND (ca. 1939-40). Blue and brown. Harvesting at l. and r. (Not issued). Rare.	—	—	—

ALLIED OCCUPATION - WW II

GRAND DUCHÉ DE LUXEMBOURG

LETZEBURG

1943 ISSUE

		VG	VF	UNC
42	**20 Frang** 1943. Brown on m/c unpt. Arms at l., portr. Grand Duchess Charlotte at r. Back purple; farmer w/sickle and corn. Printer: W&S.			
	a. Issued note.	.75	5.00	70.00
	s. Specimen w/red ovpt: *SPECIMEN*, punched hole cancelled.	—	—	140.

1944 ND ISSUE

		VG	VF	UNC
43	**5 Francs** ND (1944). Olive-green. Portr. Grand Duchess Charlotte at ctr. Back red; arms at ctr. Printer: ABNC.			
	a. 000000-222222. W/o serial # prefix,	.50	5.00	60.00
	b. Serial # prefix A. 222223-.	.50	3.00	45.00
	p. Proof. Uniface pair.	—	—	175.
	s. Specimen w/red ovpt: *SPECIMEN.*	—	—	125.
44	**10 Francs** ND (1944). Purple. Like #43. Back olive. Printer: ABNC.			
	a. Issued note.	.50	3.00	45.00
	p. Proof. Uniface pair.	—	—	175.
	s. Specimen w/red ovpt: *SPECIMEN.*	—	—	150.

		VG	VF	UNC
45	**50 Francs** ND (1944). Dk. green on m/c unpt. Portr. Grand Duchess Charlotte at l. and as wmk., arms at ctr . Vianden Castle at lower ctr., guilloche ovpt. covering German wording below on back. Serial # prefix A. Printer: BWC.	2.00	12.50	175.

		VG	VF	UNC
46	**50 Francs** ND (1944). Dk. green on m/c unpt. Like #45 but back w/o wording at bottom and also w/o guilloche. Serial # prefix B-D. Printer: BWC.			
	a. Issued note.	1.50	7.50	150.
	s. Specimen w/red ovpt: *SPECIMEN*, punched hole cancelled.	—	—	225.

		VG	VF	UNC
47	**100 Francs** ND (1944). Blue on m/c unpt. Back red-brown. Like #39. Printer: ABNC.			
	a. Issued note.	10.00	50.00	300.
	p. Proof. Uniface pair.	—	—	225.
	s. Specimen w/red ovpt: *SPECIMEN*, punched hole cancelled.	—	—	175.

1954-56 Issue

#48-50 wmk: Grand Duchess Charlotte.

		VG	VF	UNC
48	**10 Francs** ND (1954). Green on m/c unpt. Portr. Grand Duchess Charlotte at r. Vianden Castle at l., arms at ctr., hillside at r. on back. Sign. varieties.			
	a. Issued note.	1.50	4.50	15.00
	s. Specimen w/red ovpt: *SPECIMEN*, punched hole cancelled.	—	—	45.00

		VG	VF	UNC
49	**20 Francs** ND (1955). Blue on m/c unpt. Grand Duchess Charlotte at r. Moselle River w/village of Ehnen on back.			
	a. Issued note.	1.00	4.00	12.00
	s. Specimen w/red ovpt: *SPECIMEN*, punched hole cancelled.	—	—	50.00

		VG	VF	UNC
50	**100 Francs** 15.6.1956. Red-brown on blue and m/c unpt. Portr. Grand Duchess Charlotte with tiara at r. Differdange steelworks on back.			
	a. Issued note.	4.00	10.00	30.00
	s. Specimen w/red ovpt: *SPECIMEN*, punched hole cancelled.	—	—	80.00

MACAO

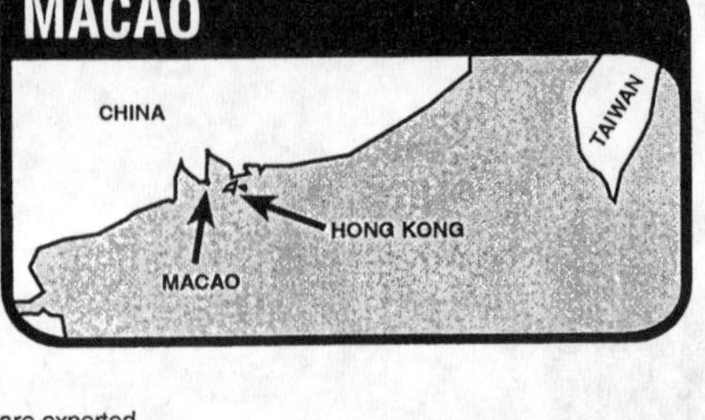

The Macau R.A.E.M., a forme Portuguese overseas provinc located in the South China Sea 3 miles (56 km.) southwest of Hon Kong, consists of the peninsul and the islands of Taipa an Coloane. It has an area of 14 sc mi. (21.45 sq. km.) and population of 415,850. Capita Macau. The economy is d o tourism, gambling, commerce an gold trading - Macau is one of th few entirely free markets for go in the world. Cement, textiles vegetable oils and metal product are exported.

Established by the Portuguese in 1557, Macau is the oldest European settlement in the Fa East. The Chinese, while agreeing to Portuguese settlement, did not recognize Portugues sovereign rights and the Portuguese remained largely under control of the Chinese until 184 when the Portuguese abolished the Chinese custom house and declared the independence of th port. The Manchu government formally recognized the Portuguese right to *perpetual occupation* c Macau in 1887. In March 1940 the Japanese army demanded recognition of the nearby "puppe government at Changshan. In Sept. 1943 they demanded installation of their "advisors" in lieu of military occupation.

Macau became a special administrative area known as Macau R.A.E.M. under The People Republic of China on December 20, 1999.

RULERS:

Portuguese from 1849-1999

MONETARY SYSTEM:

1 Dollar = 100 Cents
1 Pataca = 100 Avos

Note: Certain listings encompassing issues circulated by various bank and regional authorities are contained in Volume I.

Portuguese Administration

Banco Nacional Ultramarino

行銀理滙外海國洋西

Ta Hsi Yang Kuo Hai Wai Hui Li Yin Har

1905-07 Issue

#1-6 printer: BFL.

		Good	Fine	X
1	**1 Pataca** 1905; 1911. Brown on blue unpt. Imprint: *Lisboa... 19...*, date partially handwritten. Crowned arms at ctr. on back.			
	a. 4.9.1905.	200.	600.	200
	b. 1.8.1911.	250.	750.	
2	**5 Patacas** 4.9.1905; 4.10.1910; 4.12.1910. Blue on orange unpt. Sailing ship at upper ctr.	800.	4000.	

3 **10 Patacas**

	Good	Fine	XF
2.1.1907; 30.1.1922; 31.3.1924; 4.12.1924; 18.6.1936; 23.12.1941. Lt. red on green unpt. Crowned arms at upper l., sailing ship at upper ctr. Serrated l. edge.	800.	2500.	6500.

Note: Contemporary forgeries exist ($150.00 value in Fine).

4 **25 Patacas**

	Good	Fine	XF
2.1.1907; 22.1.1907. Black on rose unpt. Like #3. Rare.	—	—	—

5 **50 Patacas**

	Good	Fine	XF
1.1.1906. Blue on rose unpt. Sailing ship at upper ctr., lg. red *50* in unpt. at lower ctr. Rare.	—	—	—

6 **100 Patacas**

	Good	Fine	XF
1.1.1906. Dk. green on green, lt. brown and yellow unpt. Crowned arms at upper l., sailing ship at upper l. ctr., lg. *100* in unpt. at ctr. Rare.	—	—	—

1912-24 Issue

7 **1 Pataca**

	Good	Fine	XF
1.1.1912. Brown on blue unpt. Like #1 but place and date printed. Arms w/o crown at ctr. on back. Printer: BWC.	20.00	125.	750.

8 **5 Patacas**

	Good	Fine	XF
1.1.1924. Green on yellow unpt. Steamship at l., junks at r. Printer: TDLR.	250.	1000.	3500.

9 **100 Patacas**

	Good	Fine	XF
22.7.1919. Brown on m/c unpt. Arms at upper l., steamship at upper l. ctr., steamship seal at lower r. Printer: BWC. Rare.	—	—	—

1920 ND Subsidiary Note Issue

#10-12 printer: HKP.

10 **5 Avos**

	VG	VF	UNC
ND (1920). Brown on green unpt. Arms at upper l.	7.50	25.00	75.00

11 **10 Avos**

	VG	VF	UNC
ND (1920). Green on yellow unpt. Arms at upper l.	8.50	30.00	85.00

12 **50 Avos**

	VG	VF	UNC
ND (1920). Black on green unpt. Arms at top ctr. Handwritten sign. Back orange.	50.00	150.	400.

1942 ND Subsidiary Note Issue

#13-17 printer: HKP.

		VG	VF	UNC
13	**1 Avo** ND (1942). Grayish brown. Arms at upper l.	2.50	10.00	40.00
14	**5 Avos** ND (1942). Brown on green unpt. Like #10.	4.00	20.00	80.00

		VG	VF	UNC
15	**10 Avos** ND (1942). Blue on yellow unpt. Arms at upper l.	4.00	35.00	120.

Note: Also see #19.

		VG	VF	UNC
16	**20 Avos** ND (1942). Brown on green unpt.	7.50	30.00	110.
17	**50 Avos** ND (1942). Purple on green unpt. Arms at top ctr.	10.00	50.00	200.

Note: Also see #21.

Japanese Administration - WWII

Banco Nacional Ultramarino

1944 ND Subsidiary Note Issue

		VG	VF	UNC
18	**5 Avos** ND (1944). Red on green unpt. Arms at upper l.	10.00	35.00	120.

		VG	VF	UNC
19	**10 Avos** ND (1944). Blue on yellow unpt. Like #15 but 100 x 55mm.	5.00	30.00	120.
20	**20 Avos** ND (1944). Red on lt. olive unpt. Back lt. orange.	4.00	25.00	100.

		VG	VF	UNC
21	**50 Avos** ND (1944). Purple on lt. green unpt. Like #17 but w/letters A-J at l. and r. Also on thin paper. Back orange.	4.00	12.50	75.00

1944 Emergency Certificate Issue

Decreto No. 33:517

#22-27 arms at l., steamship seal at r., vertical backs. Sign. varieties. Printer: Sin Chun and Company.

		VG	VF	UNC
22	**5 Patacas** D.5.2.1944. Black-blue w/maroon guilloche. Back green.	15.00	80.00	450.

		VG	VF	UNC
23	**10 Patacas** D.5.2.1944. Brown w/maroon guilloche. Back brown.	25.00	150.	550.
24	**25 Patacas** D.5.2.1944. Brown.	200.	850.	—

		VG	VF	UNC
25	**50 Patacas** D.5.2.1944. Olive w/maroon guilloche. Back brown.	150.	600.	—

		VG	VF	UNC
26	**100 Patacas** D.5.2.1944. Red-violet w/lt. blue guilloche. Back red.	700.	2000.	—
27	**500 Patacas** D.5.2.1944. Brown on m/c unpt. Rare.	—	—	—

PORTUGUESE ADMINISTRATION - POST WWII

BANCO NACIONAL ULTRAMARINO

1945 REGULAR ISSUE

#28-34 temple at r. Steamship seal at ctr. on back. Sign. varieties. Printer: W&S.

		VG	VF	UNC
28	**1 Pataca** 16.11.1945. Blue on red and green unpt.	1.50	17.50	70.00

		VG	VF	UNC
29	**5 Patacas** 16.11.1945. Green on green and red unpt.	4.00	27.50	150.
30	**10 Patacas** 16.11.1945. Brown.	10.00	100.	350.
31	**25 Patacas** 16.11.1945. Red-orange on lt. green unpt.	150.	600.	—
32	**50 Patacas** 16.11.1945. Blue-gray.	100.	325.	—

		VG	VF	UNC
33	**100 Patacas** 16.11.1945. Violet.	400.	1600.	—
34	**500 Patacas** 16.11.1945. Brown.	1000.	5000.	—

1946-50 ISSUE

#35-38 printer: HKP.

		VG	VF	UNC
35	**5 Avos** 6.8.1946. Dk. brown on green unpt. Back green.			
	a. Issued note.	1.50	7.50	45.00
	r. Remainder w/o serial #.	—	—	15.00

		VG	VF	UNC
36	**10 Avos** 6.8.1946. Red on blue unpt. Ship and light tower at ctr. Back gray.			
	a. Issued note.	2.00	8.00	50.00
	r. Remainder w/o serial #.	—	—	15.00

		VG	VF	UNC
37	**20 Avos** 6.8.1946. Violet on gray unpt. Ruins of S. Paulo at l. Back red-brown.			
	a. Issued note.	2.00	8.00	50.00
	r. Remainder w/o serial #.	—	—	15.00

		VG	VF	UNC
38	**50 Avos** 6.8.1946. Blue on tan unpt. Junks at l., steamship seal at r. Back violet.			
	a. Issued note.	2.00	8.00	40.00
	r. Remainder w/o serial #.	—	—	15.00
39	**25 Patacas** 20.4.1948. Brown. Portr. L. de Camoes at r. *MACAU* below.	50.00	300.	750.

		VG	VF	UNC
39A	**100 Patacas** 27.11.1950. Brown on m/c unpt. Portr. Colonel J. M. Ferreira da Amabal at r. Printer: W&S. Specimen.	—	—	—

1952 FIRST ISSUE

#40-43 arms at lower ctr. on face, steamship seal at ctr. on back.

		VG	VF	UNC
40	**2 Avos** 19.1.1952. Purple. Like #42. Specimen.	—	—	200.
41	**5 Avos** 19.1.1952. Brown. Like #42. Specimen.	—	—	200.

		VG	VF	UNC
42	**10 Avos** 19.1.1952. Green on lt. brown and blue unpt.			
	r. Remainder.	—	—	40.00
	s. Specimen.	—	—	175.

Note: #42a was not officially released. A quantity of approximately 5000 notes mysteriously found its way into today's market.

		VG	VF	UNC
43	**20 Avos** 19.1.1952. Olive. Like #42. Specimen.	—	—	200.

DECRETO NO. 17154

		VG	VF	UNC
44	**100 Patacas** 19.5.1952. Brown on lt. green unpt. Portr. M. de Arriaga Brum da Silveira at r. Archway w/flag at ctr. on back. Sign. varieties. Printer: W&S.			
	a. Issued note.	50.00	200.	650.
	s. Specimen.	—	—	300.

1958 Issue

Decreto - Lei No. 39,221

#45-48 portr. L. de Camoes at r. and as wmk. Printer: BWC.

		VG	VF	UNC
45	**10 Patacas**			
	20.11.1958. Blue on m/c unpt. Sign. varieties.			
	a. Issued note.	20.00	100.	275.
	s. Specimen.	—	—	200.
46	**25 Patacas**			
	20.11.1958. Brown on m/c unpt.			
	a. Issued note.	40.00	200.	600.
	s. Specimen.	—	—	400.

		VG	VF	UNC
47	**50 Patacas**			
	20.11.1958. Dk. green on m/c unpt.			
	a. Issued note.	40.00	200.	550.
	s. Specimen.	—	—	300.

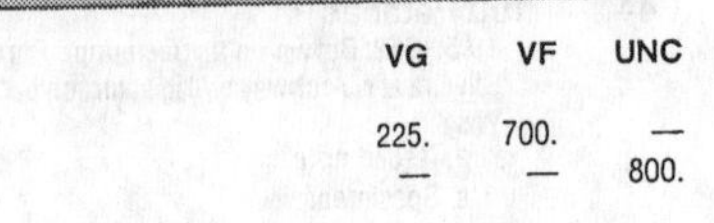

		VG	VF	UNC
48	**500 Patacas**			
	20.11.1958. Olive-brown on m/c unpt.			
	a. Issued note.	225.	700.	—
	s. Specimen.	—	—	800.

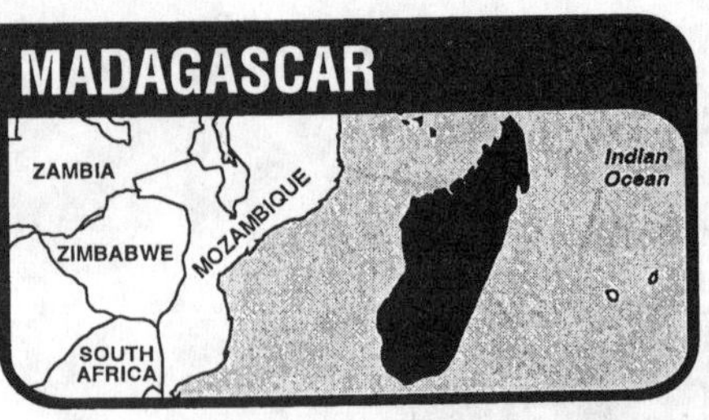

The Democratic Republic of Madagascar, an independent member of the French Community located in the Indian Ocean 250 miles (402 km.) off the southeast coast of Africa, has an area of 226,658 sq. mi. (587,041 sq. km.) and a population of 17.39 million. Capital: Antananarivo. The economy is primarily agricultural; large bauxite deposits are presently being developed. Coffee, vanilla, graphite and rice are exported.

Diago Diaz, a Portuguese navigator, sighted the island of Madagascar on Aug. 10, 1500, when his ship became separated from an India-bound fleet. Attempts at settlement by the British during the reign of Charles I and by the French during the 17th and 18th centuries were of no avail, and the island became a refuge and supply for Indian Ocean pirates. Despite considerable influence on the island, the British accepted the imposition of a French protectorate in 1886 in return for French recognition of Britain's sphere of influence in Zanzibar. Madagascar was made a French colony in 1896 after absolute control had been established by military force. Britain occupied the island after the fall of France in 1942, to prevent its seizure by the Japanese, and gave it to the Free French in 1943. On Oct. 14, 1958, following a decade of intermittent but bitter warfare, Madagascar, as the Malagasy Republic, became an autonomous state within the French Community. On June 27, 1960, it became a sovereign independent nation, though remaining nominally within the French Community. The Malagasy Republic was renamed the Democratic Republic of Madagascar in 1976.

MONETARY SYSTEM:

1 French Franc = 100 Centimes to 1945
1 CFA Franc = 1.70 French Francs, 1945-1948
1 CFA Franc = 2 French Francs, 1948-1959
1 CFA Franc = 0.02 French Franc, 1959-1961
5 Malagasy Francs (F.M.G.) = 1 Ariary, 1961-2003
1 Ariary = 5 Francs, 2003-

Republic

Gouverneur Général, Tananarive

Décret du 17.9.1914

		VG	VF	UNC
1	**5 Francs**			
	D.1914.	—	—	—
2	**10 Francs**			
	29.3.1917.	—	—	—
3	**20 Francs**			
	29.3.1917.	—	—	—

Emergency Postage Stamp Issues

Postage stamps of type "Filanzane" (Michel #77, 78, 81, 86, 88, 89, or Scott #82, 84, 91, 102, 109, 113, transportation by sedan chair) pasted on rectangular cardboard.

Type I

Type II

Type III

Type I: Gray cardboard. Dog on back; value on stamps only.

Type II: Gray cardboard. Dog on back; value in numerals at r. on back.

Type III: Gray cardboard. Dog on back; value on back in numerals at r. and in words at l., imprinted separately.

Type IV: Gray cardboard. Dog on back; value on back in numerals at r. and in words at l., printed simultaneously w/picture.

Type V: Like Type IV but cardboard of varnished stock.

Type VI: Gray cardboard. Zebu on back.

Type VII: Brown cardboard. Zebu on back.

Type VIII: Like Type VII but cardboard of varnished stock.

Type IX: Gray cardboard. Zebu on back. Value at r. in thinner numerals.

1916 Issue Type I

		VG	VF	UNC
4	**0.25 Franc**			
	ND (1916). Blue.	50.00	100.	250
5	**0.50 Franc**			
	ND (1916). Violet.	50.00	100.	250

No.	Description	VG	VF	UNC
5A	**1 Franc** ND (1916). Brown and green. Reported not confirmed.	—	—	—
6	**2 Francs** ND (1916). Blue and olive.	50.00	100.	250.

1916 Issue Type II

No.	Description	VG	VF	UNC
7	**0.10 Franc** ND (1916). Red and brown.	50.00	100.	250.

1916 Issue Type III

No.	Description	VG	VF	UNC
8	**0.05 Franc** ND (1916). Blue-green and olive.	50.00	100.	250.

1916 Issue Type IV

No.	Description	VG	VF	UNC
9	**0.05 Franc** ND (1916). Blue-green and olive.	50.00	100.	250.
10	**0.10 Franc** ND (1916). Red and brown.	50.00	100.	250.
11	**0.25 Franc** ND (1916). Blue.	50.00	100.	250.
11A	**0.50 Franc** ND (1916).	50.00	100.	250.
11B	**1 Franc** ND (1916).	50.00	100.	250.

No.	Description	VG	VF	UNC
11C	**2 Francs** ND (1916).	50.00	100.	250.

1916 Issue Type V

No.	Description	VG	VF	UNC
12	**0.05 Franc** ND (1916). Green.	50.00	100.	250.
13	**0.50 Franc** ND (1916). Violet.	50.00	100.	250.
14	**1 Franc** ND (1916). Brown and green.	50.00	100.	250.
15	**2 Francs** ND (1916). Blue and green.	50.00	100.	250.

1916 Issue Type VI

No.	Description	VG	VF	UNC
6	**0.05 Franc** ND (1916). Blue-green and olive.	50.00	100.	250.
7	**0.10 Franc** ND (1916). Red and brown.	50.00	100.	250.
8	**0.25 Franc** ND (1916). Blue.	50.00	100.	250.
9	**0.50 Franc** ND (1916). Violet.	50.00	100.	250.
0	**1 Franc** ND (1916). Brown and green.	50.00	100.	250.
1	**2 Francs** ND (1916). Blue and green.	50.00	100.	250.

916 Issue Type VII

No.	Description	VG	VF	UNC
2	**0.05 Franc** ND (1916). Blue-green and olive. Reported not confirmed.	—	—	—
3	**0.10 Franc** ND (1916). Red and brown.	50.00	100.	250.
4	**0.25 Franc** ND (1916). Blue.	50.00	100.	250.
5	**0.50 Franc** ND (1916). Violet.	50.00	100.	250.
6	**1 Franc** ND (1916). Brown and green.	50.00	100.	250.
7	**2 Francs** ND (1916). Blue and green. Reported not confirmed.	—	—	—

916 Issue Type VIII

No.	Description	VG	VF	UNC
3	**0.05 Franc** ND (1916). Blue-green and olive.	50.00	100.	250.
	0.10 Franc ND (1916). Red and green.	50.00	100.	250.
	0.25 Franc ND (1916). Blue.	50.00	100.	250.
	0.50 Franc ND (1916). Violet.	50.00	100.	250.
	1 Franc ND (1916). Brown and green.	50.00	100.	250.
	2 Francs ND (1916). Blue and green.	50.00	100.	250.

1916 Issue Type IX

No.	Description	VG	VF	UNC
33A	**0.05 Franc** ND (1916). Blue-green and olive.	60.00	125.	300.
33B	**0.10 Franc** ND (1916). Red and green.	60.00	125.	300.
33C	**0.50 Franc** ND (1916). Violet.	60.00	125.	300.
33D	**1 Franc** ND (1916). Brown and green.	60.00	125.	300.

Note: For smaller stamps w/*MADAGASCAR ET DEPENDANCES* or *MOHELI* pasted on square cardboard w/dog on back, see Comoros.

Banque de Madagascar

1926 ND Provisional Issue

No.	Description	Good	Fine	XF
34	**100 Francs** ND (1926 - old dates 3.12.1892-13.2.1893). Ovpt: *BANQUE DE MADAGASCAR* on unissued notes of the Banque de France (#65b).	150.	500.	—

1930's Issue

No.	Description	VG	VF	UNC
35	**5 Francs** ND (ca.1937). Red-brown on blue and green unpt. Goddess Juno at l. 2 sign. varieties.	2.50	17.50	60.00

No.	Description	VG	VF	UNC
36	**10 Francs** ND (ca. 1937-47). Green and blue. Woman w/fruit at r. Farmer plowing on back. 2 sign. varieties.	5.00	25.00	85.00

		VG	VF	UNC
37	**20 Francs** ND (ca. 1937-47). Yellow-brown. France and African woman w/child at r. Man at l. on back. 3 sign. varieties.	8.50	35.00	125.

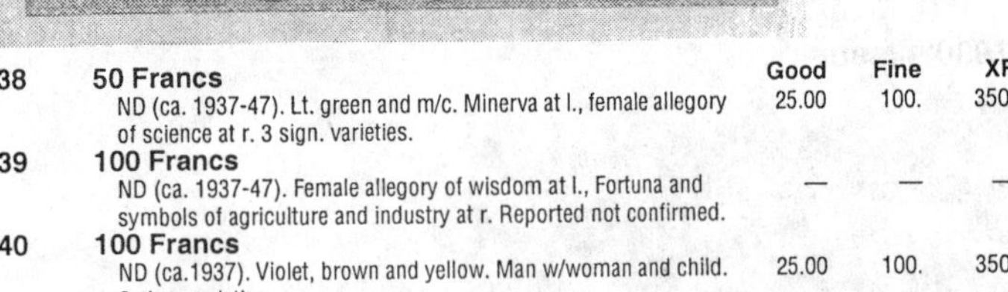

		Good	Fine	XF
38	**50 Francs** ND (ca. 1937-47). Lt. green and m/c. Minerva at l., female allegory of science at r. 3 sign. varieties.	25.00	100.	350.
39	**100 Francs** ND (ca. 1937-47). Female allegory of wisdom at l., Fortuna and symbols of agriculture and industry at r. Reported not confirmed.	—	—	—
40	**100 Francs** ND (ca.1937). Violet, brown and yellow. Man w/woman and child. 2 sign. varieties.	25.00	100.	350.

		Good	Fine	XF
41	**1000 Francs** 11.7.1933; 19.5.1945; 28.12.1948. M/c. Female allegory of the French Republic at l., African woman at r. 3 sign. varieties.	100.	400.	1200.

		Good	Fine	XF
42	**1000 Francs** ND (ca. 1937). Blue and m/c. Female allegory of industry at l., female allegory of agriculture at r.	150.	500.	1300.

1941 Emergency Issue

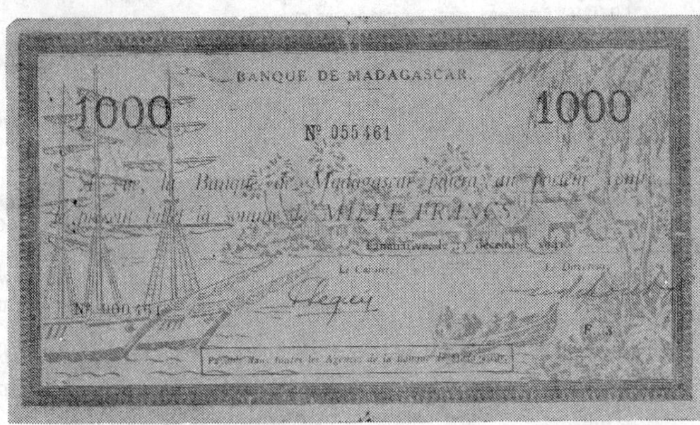

		Good	Fine	XF
43	**1000 Francs** 1941; 1946. Blue and brown. Sailing ships at l., coastal scenery.			
	a. Sign. handwritten. 15.12.1941.	1650.	—	—
	b. Sign. handwritten or stamped. 15.3.1946.	1650.	—	—

1942 Bons de Caisse

		Good	Fine	XF
44	**5000 Francs** 30.4.1942. Green. 2 oxen. Animals, woman w/fruit, and workers on back.			
	a. Issued note. Rare.	—	—	—
	s. Specimen.			

Banque de Madagascar et des Comores

1950-51 Issue

#45-49 wmk: Woman's head.

		VG	VF	UNC
45	**50 Francs** ND. Brown and m/c. Woman w/hat at r. Man at ctr. on back. 2 sign. varieties.			
	a. Sign. title: *LE CONTROLEUR GÉNÉRAL.*	2.50	22.50	75.00
	b. Sign. title: *LE DIRECTOR GÉNÉRAL ADJOINT.*	2.50	22.50	75.00

		VG	VF	UNC
46	**100 Francs** ND. M/c. Woman at r., w/palace of the qn. of Tananariva in background. Woman, boats, and animals on back.			
	a. Sign. title: *LE CONTROLEUR GÉNÉRAL.*	3.00	25.00	85.00
	b. Sign. title: *LE DIRECTEUR GÉNÉRAL ADJOINT.*	3.00	25.00	85.00

47 500 Francs

30.6.1950; 18.6.1951; 9.10.1952; 6.5.1958. M/c. Man w/fruit at ctr. Woman on back.

	VG	VF	UNC
a. Sign. title: *LE CONTROLEUR GÉNÉRAL.*	15.00	90.00	375.
b. Sign. title: *LE DIRECTEUR GÉNÉRAL ADJOINT.*	15.00	90.00	375.

48 1000 Francs

14.3.1950; 1.2.1951. M/c. Woman and man at l. ctr. Ox cart on back. 158 x 104mm.

	VG	VF	UNC
a. Sign. title: *LE CONTROLEUR GÉNÉRAL.*	30.00	175.	550.
b. Sign. title: *LE DIRECTEUR GÉNÉRAL ADJOINT.*	30.00	175.	550.

Note: For #48 dated 9.10.1952 w/provisional ovpt., see #54.

49 5000 Francs

30.6.1950; 23.11.1955. M/c. Portr. Gallieni at upper l., portr. young woman at r. Huts at l., woman w/baby at r. on back.

	VG	VF	UNC
a. Sign. title: *LE CONTROLEUR GÉNÉRAL.*	175.	450.	1000.
b. Sign. title: *LE DIRECTEUR GÉNÉRAL ADJOINT.*	175.	450.	1000.

MALAGASY

INSTITUT D'EMISSION MALGACHE

1961 ND PROVISIONAL ISSUE

#51-55 new bank name and new Ariary denominations ovpt. on previous issue of Banque de Madagascar et des Comores. Wmk: Woman's head.

51 50 Francs = 10 Ariary

ND (1961). M/c. Woman w/hat at ctr. r. Man at ctr. on back. Ovpt. on #45.

	VG	VF	UNC
a. Sign. title: *LE CONTROLEUR GENERAL.*	2.00	17.50	70.00
b. Sign. title: *LE DIRECTEUR GENERAL ADJOINT.*	2.50	20.00	75.00

52 100 Francs = 20 Ariary

	VG	VF	UNC
ND (1961). M/c. Woman at ctr. r., palace of the Qn. of Tananariva in background. Woman, boats and animals on back. Ovpt. on #46b.	3.00	30.00	110.

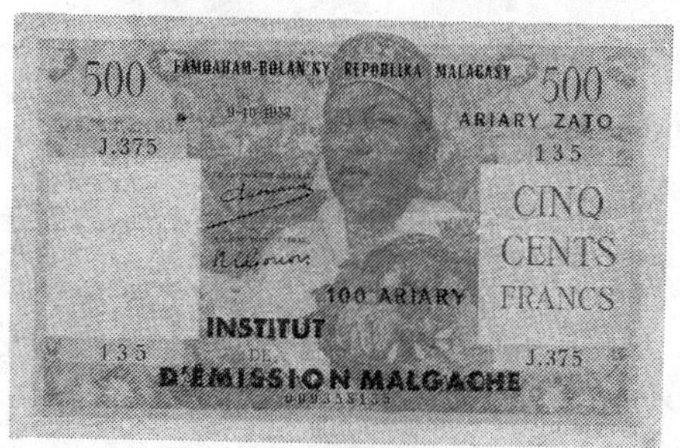

53 500 Francs = 100 Ariary

	VG	VF	UNC
ND (1961 - old date 9.10.1952). M/c. Man w/fruit at ctr. Ovpt. on #47.	15.00	90.00	400.

54 1000 Francs = 200 Ariary

	VG	VF	UNC
ND (1961 - old date 9.10.1952). M/c. Man and woman at l. ctr. Ox cart at ctr. r. on back. Ovpt. on #48.	20.00	175.	500.

55 5000 Francs = 1000 Ariary

	VG	VF	UNC
ND (1961). M/c. Gallieni at upper l., woman at r. Woman and baby on back. Ovpt. on #49.	50.00	325.	800.

Note: #53-55 some notes also have old dates of intended or original issue (1952-55).

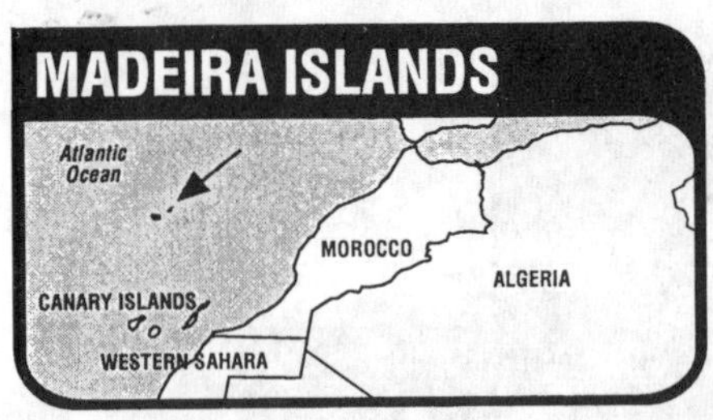

The Madeira Islands, which belong to Portugal, are located 360 miles (492 km.) off the northwest coast of Africa. They have an area of 307 sq. mi. (795 sq. km.) and a population of 267,000. The group consists of two inhabited islands named Madeira and Porto Santo and two groups of uninhabited rocks named Desertas and Selvagens. Capital: Funchal. The three staple products are wine, flowers and sugar.

Although the evidence is insufficient, it is thought that the Phoenicians visited Madeira at an early period. The Portuguese navigator Goncalvez Zarco first sighted Porto Santo in 1418, having been driven there by a storm while he was exploring the coast of West Africa. Madeira itself was discovered in 1420. The islands were uninhabited when visited by Zarco, but their colonization was immediately begun by Prince Henry the Navigator, aided by the knights of the Order of Christ. British troops occupied the islands in 1801, and again in 1807-14. Since 1976 Madeira is politically and administratively an autonomous region with a regional government and a parliament.

RULERS:

Portuguese

PORTUGUESE ADMINISTRATION

BANCO DE PORTUGAL

AGENCIA NO FUNCHAL

1875 ISSUE

		Good	Fine	XF
1	**20,000 Reis** 2.3.1875-4.3.1876. Blue. Seated figure at l. and r., arms at ctr. Oval ovpt. vertically at l. and r. Uniface. Rare.	—	—	—

1878 ISSUE

		Good	Fine	XF
2	**10,000 Reis** 5.11.1878. Brown on blue-green unpt. Arms w/2 women in oval at ctr. Back green. Rare.	—	—	—

1879 PROVISIONAL ISSUE

		Good	Fine	XF
3	**10,000 Reis** ND (1879 -old date 5.11.1878). Ovpt: *MOEDA FORTE* across bottom and at upper l. and r. on #2. Rare.	—	—	—

#4 Deleted, see #9.

1891 PROVISIONAL ISSUE

#5-11 oval ovpt. at r.

		Good	Fine	XF
5	**500 Reis** 18.7.1891. Reported not confirmed.	—	—	—
6	**1000 Reis** 18.7.1891. Reported not confirmed.	—	—	—
7	**2500 Reis** 18.7.1891. Reported not confirmed.	—	—	—
8	**5000 Reis** 18.7.1891. Reported not confirmed.	—	—	—

		Good	Fine	XF
9	**10,000 Reis** 18.7.1891. Blue oval ovpt: *DOMICILIADA NA AGENCIA DO FUNCHAL....BANCO DE PORTUGAL* at r. on #3. Punched hole cancelled: *SEM VALOR*. Rare.	—	—	—
10	**20,000 Reis** 18.7.1891. Reported not confirmed.	—	—	—
11	**50,000 Reis** 18.7.1891. Rare.	—	—	—

1892 PROVISIONAL ISSUE

		Good	Fine	XF
11A	**50 Reis** 3.2.1892 (- old date 6.8.1891). W/3-line diagonal ovpt. like #12 on Portugal #87.	400.	1000.	—

		Good	Fine	XF
12	**100 Reis** 3.2.1892 (- old date 6.8.1891). W/3 line diagonal ovpt: *Domiciliada para circular no districto do Funchal em virtude do Decreto de 3 de Fevereiro de 1892* on Portugal #89.	300.	700.	—

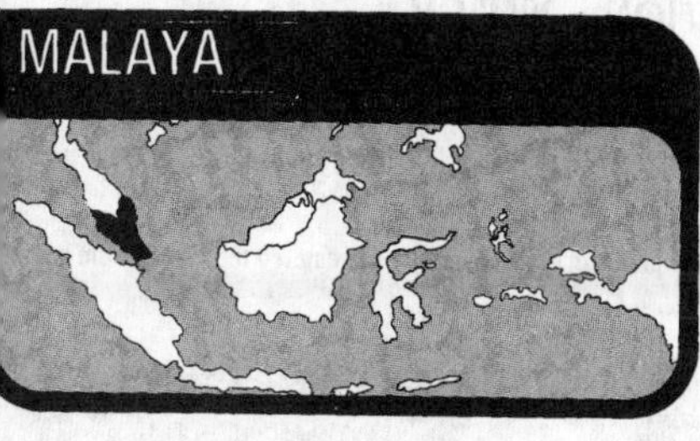

Malaya, a former member of the British Commonwealth located in the southern part of the Malay Peninsula, consisted of 11 states: the unfederated Malay states of Johore, Kedah, Kelantan, Perlis and Trengganu; the federated Malay states of Negri Sembilan, Pahang, Perak and Selangor; and former members of the Straits Settlements, Malacca and Penang. The federation had an area of about 60,000 sq. mi. (155,400 sq. km.). Capital: Kuala
umpur. It was occupied by Japan from 1941-1945. Malaya was organized February 1, 1948, was anted full independence on August 31, 1957, and became part of the Federation of Malaysia on eptember 16, 1963.

See also Straits Settlements and Malaysia.

ULERS:
British

ONETARY SYSTEM:
1 Dollar = 100 Cents

RITISH ADMINISTRATION

OARD OF COMMISSIONERS OF CURRENCY

940 FIRST ISSUE

	VG	VF	UNC
10 Dollars 1.1.1940. Violet on green unpt. Portr. Kg. George VI at r. Arms of the 11 states on back. Printer: W&S.	150.	500.	1700.

e: A shipment of 1 and 5 Dollar bills dated 1940 was captured by the Germans. The bills were not issued. Later ovprinted in 1945 by the British Military Government. See #4 and 5.

940 SECOND ISSUE

and 3 designed and printed by Survey Dept. F. M. S.

	VG	VF	UNC
10 Cents 15.8.1940. Dk. blue on lilac and brown unpt. Portr. Kg. George VI at l. Uniface.	15.00	60.00	225.
25 Cents 1.9.1940. Aqua on blue, orange and lilac unpt. Portr. Kg. George VI at r. Arms of the 11 states on back.	30.00	225.	825.

40 (1945) ISSUE

nd 5 portr. Kg. George VI at r. States' arms on back. Printer: W&S.

	VG	VF	UNC
1 Dollar 1.1.1940 (Aug. 1945). Green and m/c. Ovpt: *NOT LEGAL TENDER. SPECIMEN ONLY. NO VALUE.*			
a. Ovpt. as described.	425.	1400.	8000.
b. W/o ovpt.	500.	2500.	8800.
5 Dollars 1.1.1940 (Aug. 1945). Blue and m/c.			
a. Ovpt: *NOT LEGAL...*	3000.	7000.	1600.
b. W/o ovpt. Rare.	—	—	—

41-42 (1945) ISSUE

printer: TDLR.

portr. Kg. George VI at l.

RTRAIT VARIETIES:

TYPE 1

TYPE 2

TYPE 3

	VG	VF	UNC
1 Cent 1.7.1941 (1945). Lilac on lt. orange unpt. Uniface.	1.00	3.50	10.00

		VG	VF	UNC
7	**5 Cents** 1.7.1941 (1945). Red on lt. green unpt. Uniface.			
	a. Jawi script at lower l.: ليمسين	1.00	6.00	14.00
	b. Jawi script at lower l.: ليماسين	1.00	6.00	14.00
8	**10 Cents** 1.7.1941 (1945). Blue on pink unpt. Uniface. 3 portr. varieties.	1.00	5.00	12.00

#9 and 10 printer: W&S.

		VG	VF	UNC
9	**20 Cents** 1.7.1941 (1945). Brown on orange and green unpt. States' arms on back.			
	a. Jawi script at lower l.: سين	5.00	30.00	100.
	b. Jawi script at lower l.: سن	5.00	40.00	130.

		VG	VF	UNC
10	**50 Cents** 1.7.1941 (1945). Violet on orange and blue unpt. Similar to #7. Portr. varieties.			
	a. Jawi script at lower l.: ليما فوله	6.00	12.50	55.00
	b. Jawi script at lower l.: ليم قوله	6.00	12.50	55.00

#11-15 portr. Kg. George VI at r. States' arms on back. #11-13 printer: W&S.

		VG	VF	UNC
11	**1 Dollar** 1.7.1941 (1945). Blue on orange and m/c unpt.	9.00	25.00	100.
12	**5 Dollars** 1.7.1941 (1945). Green on gray and m/c unpt.	25.00	100.	425.

		VG	VF	UNC
13	**10 Dollars** 1.7.1941 (1945). Red and m/c.	30.00	100.	625.

#14-16 wmk: Lion's head. Printer: BWC.

		VG	VF	UNC
14	**50 Dollars** 1.1.1942 (1945). Blue.	200.	950.	3750.

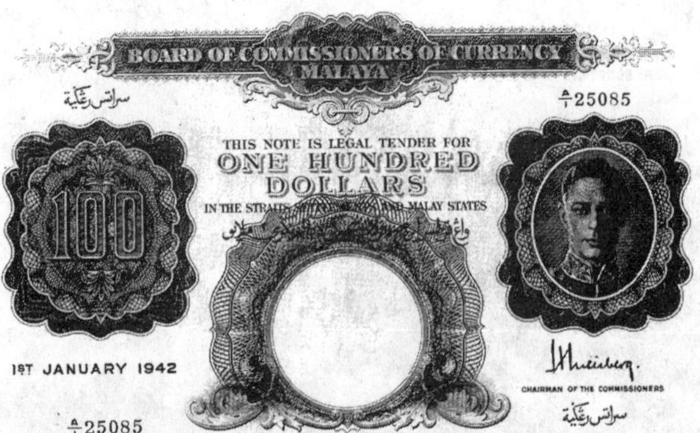

		VG	VF	UNC
15	**100 Dollars** 1.1.1942 (1945). Red and green. Like #14.	250.	1100.	4250.
16	**1000 Dollars** 1.1.1942 (1945). Violet. Rare.	—	—	—
17	**10,000 Dollars** 1.1.1942 (1945).			
	a. Issued note. Reported not confirmed.	—	—	—
	s. Specimen. Rare.	—	—	—

JAPANESE OCCUPATION - WW II

JAPANESE GOVERNMENT

1942-45 ISSUE

#M1-M10 block letters commencing w/M.

Note: Many modern *'replicas'* from paste-up plates in strange colors have entered the market from sources in Southeast Asia.

		VG	VF	UNC
M1	**1 Cent** ND (1942). Dk. blue on lt. green unpt.			
	a. 2 block letters, format: MA.	.10	2.00	4.0
	b. Fractional block letters, format: M/AA.	.05	.50	1.0
	s. As a. Specimen w/red ovpt: *Mi-hon. SPECIMEN* on back.	—	—	120

		VG	VF	UNC
M2	**5 Cents** ND (1942). Brown-violet and gray.			
	a. 2 block letters.	.10	1.00	6.0
	b. Fractional block letters.	.10	.60	1.0
	s. As a. Specimen w/red ovpt: *Mi-hon. SPECIMEN* on back.	—	—	15

		VG	VF	UNC
M3	**10 Cents** ND (1942). Green and lt. blue.			
	a. 2 block letters.	.50	2.00	8.
	b. Fractional block letters.	.10	.50	1.
	s. As a. Specimen w/red ovpt: *Mi-hon. SPECIMEN* on back.	—	—	12

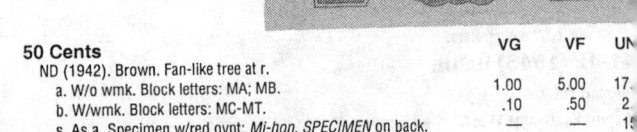

		VG	VF	UNC
M4	**50 Cents** ND (1942). Brown. Fan-like tree at r.			
	a. W/o wmk. Block letters: MA; MB.	1.00	5.00	17.
	b. W/wmk. Block letters: MC-MT.	.10	.50	2.
	s. As a. Specimen w/red ovpt: *Mi-hon. SPECIMEN* on back.	—	—	1

		VG	VF	UNC
M5	**1 Dollar** ND (1942). Dk. blue on pink unpt. Breadfruit tree at l., coconut palm at r.			

M5

	VG	VF	UNC
a. W/o wmk. Block letters: MA w/serial #.	12.50	60.00	160.
b. W/wmk. Block letters: MB-MH; MJ-MN; MR.	.25	1.00	4.00
c. W/wmk. Block letters: MI; MO; MS.	.20	.40	1.00
s. Block letters: MB. Specimen w/red ovpt: *Mi-hon. SPECIMEN* on back.	—	—	150.

M6 5 Dollars
ND (1942). Lilac on orange unpt. Coconut palm at l., paw-paw tree at r.

	VG	VF	UNC
a. Block letters: MA w/serial #.	5.00	20.00	90.00
b. Block letters MB-MJ; MO; MP.	1.00	3.00	9.00
c. Block letters MK; MR.	.20	.50	1.00
d. Woven paper.	.30	1.25	4.00
s. As b. Specimen w/red ovpt: *Mi-hon. SPECIMEN* on back.	—	—	150.

M7 10 Dollars
ND (1942-44). Blue-green on lt. yellow unpt. Trees and fruits. Back green to bluish green or lt. blue; ship on horizon.

	VG	VF	UNC
a. Block letters w/serial #.	5.00	20.00	90.00
b. Block letters: MB-MP. M w/vertical upstroke and downstroke. W/wmk.	.25	.50	1.50
c. Block letters w/o serial #. *M* w/sloping upstroke and downstroke. Paper w/silk threads, w/o wmk. MP. (1944).	.10	.25	1.00
s. As b. Specimen w/red ovpt: *Mi-hon. SPECIMEN* on back.	—	—	150.

M8 100 Dollars
ND (1944). Brown. Hut and trees on the water. Man w/buffalos in river on back.

	VG	VF	UNC
a. M w/vertical upstroke and downstroke. Wmk. paper.	.25	1.00	4.50
b. *M* w/sloping upstroke and downstroke. Paper w/silk threads, w/o wmk.	.15	.50	3.00
c. Block letters only. Wmk. woven paper.	.50	3.00	6.00
s. As a. Specimen w/red ovpt: *Mi-hon. SPECIMEN* on back.	—	—	150.
x. Purple face (probable error). Block letters MT.	2.50	10.00	35.00

M9 100 Dollars

	VG	VF	UNC
ND (1945). Brown. Workers on a rubber estate at r. Back green; houses and seashore at ctr.	5.00	10.00	25.00

M10 1000 Dollars
ND (1945). Greenish black on green unpt. Ox cart at ctr. back green; design like #M8.

	VG	VF	UNC
a. Black block letters. M w/vertical upstroke and downstroke. W/wmk.	60.00	300.	750.
b. Red block letters. *M* w/sloping upstroke and dowstroke. Paper w/silk threads, w/o wmk.	2.00	7.00	25.00
s. As a. Specimen w/red ovpt: *Mi-hon.*	—	—	900.

Note: Many new "replicas" from paste-up plates in strange colors are entering the market from Southeast Asian sources.

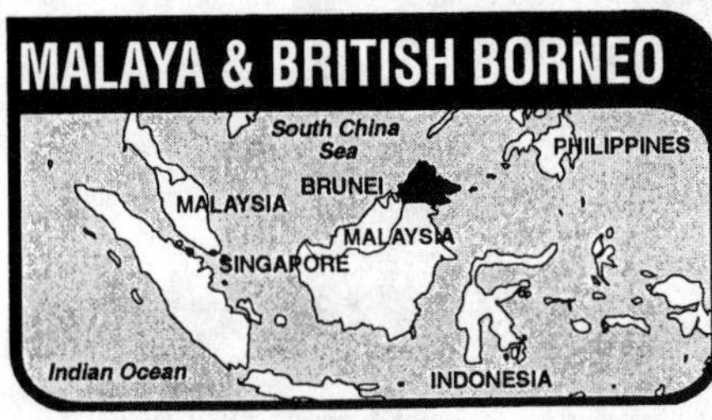

Malaya and British Borneo, a Currency Commission named the Board of Commissioners of Currency, Malaya and British North Borneo, was initiated on Jan. 1, 1952, for the purpose of providing a common currency for use in Johore, Kelantan, Kedah, Perlis, Trengganu, Negri Sembilan, Pahang, Perak, Salangor, Penang, Malacca, Singapore, North Borneo, Sarawak and Brunei.

For later issues see Brunei, Malaysia and Singapore.

RULERS:
British

MONETARY SYSTEM:
1 Dollar = 100 Cents

BRITISH ADMINISTRATION

BOARD OF COMMISSIONERS OF CURRENCY

1953 ISSUE

#1-7 Qn. Elizabeth II at r.

#1-3 arms of the 16 states on back. Wmk: Tiger's head. Printer: W&S.

#		VG	VF	UNC
1	**1 Dollar** 21.3.1953. Blue on red and m/c unpt.			
	a. Issued note.	5.00	25.00	80.00
	s. Specimen.	—	—	500.

#		VG	VF	UNC
2	**5 Dollars** 21.3.1953. Green on brown and m/c unpt.			
	a. Issued note.	17.50	90.00	360.
	s. Specimen.	—	—	1000.

#		VG	VF	UNC
3	**10 Dollars** 21.3.1953. Red on green and m/c unpt.			
	a. Issued note.	20.00	90.00	375.
	s. Specimen.	—	—	1000.

#4-7 printer: BWC.

#		VG	VF	UNC
4	**50 Dollars** 21.3.1953. Blue and green.			
	a. Back blue-gray. Block A1-A9.	100.	300.	650.
	b. Back blue. Block A10-.	100.	300.	650.
	s. Specimen.	—	—	1000.

#		VG	VF	UNC
5	**100 Dollars** 21.3.1953. Violet and brown.			
	a. Issued note.	300.	1000.	4500.
	s. Specimen.	—	—	1500.

#		VG	VF	UNC
6	**1000 Dollars** 21.3.1953. Violet on m/c unpt.			
	a. Issued note. Rare.	—	—	—
	s. Specimen.	—	—	3000.
7	**10,000 Dollars** 21.3.1953. Green on m/c unpt.			
	a. Issued note. Rare.	—	—	—
	s. Specimen.	—	Rare	—

1959-61 ISSUE

#8-9 wmk: Tiger's head.

#		VG	VF	UNC
8	**1 Dollar** 1.3.1959. Blue on m/c unpt. Sailing boat at l. Men w/boat and arms of 5 states on back. Printer: W&S.			
	a. Issued note.	6.00	25.00	150.
	s. Specimen.	—	—	—
8A	**1 Dollar** 1.3.1959. Blue on m/c unpt. Like #8. Printer: TDLR.	4.00	40.00	75.00

#		VG	VF	UNC
9	**10 DOLLARS** 1.3.1961. Red and dk. brown on m/c unpt. Farmer plowing w/ox at r. Printer: TDLR.			
	a. Sm. serial #. Series A.	20.00	60.00	200.00
	b. Lg. serial #. Series A.	20.00	60.00	250.00
	c. Lg. serial #. Series B.	20.00	75.00	250.00
	s. As a. Specimen.	—	—	150.00

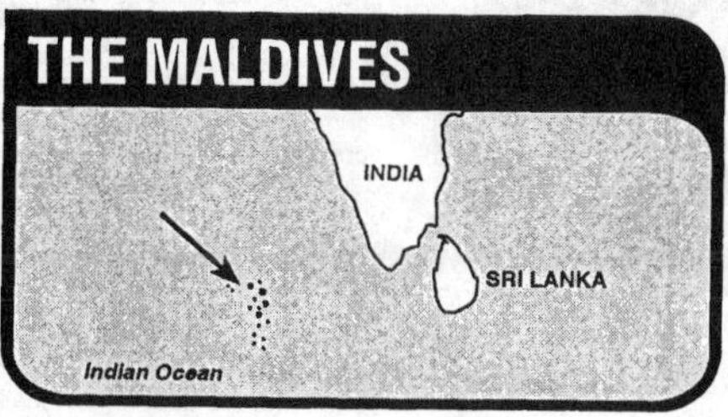

The Republic of Maldives, an archipelago of about 2,000 coral islets in the northern Indian Ocean 417 miles (671 km.) southwest of Ceylon, has an area of 115 sq. mi. (298 sq. km.) and a population of 302,000. Capital: Malé. Fishing employs 95 percent of the work force. Dried fish, copra and coir yarn are exported.

The Maldive Islands were visited by Arab traders and converted to Islam in 1153. After being harassed in the 16th and 17th centuries by Mopla pirates of the Malabar coast and Portuguese raiders, the Maldivians voluntarily placed themselves under the suzerainty of Ceylon. In 1887, the islands became an internally self-governing British protectorate and a nominal dependency of Ceylon. Traditionally a sultanate, the Maldives became a republic in 1953 but restored the sultanate in 1954. The Sultanate of the Maldive Islands attained complete internal and external autonomy within the Commonwealth on July 26, 1965, and on Nov. 11, 1968 again became a republic.

RULERS:

British to 1965

MONETARY SYSTEM:

1 Rufiyaa (Rupee) = 100 Lari

REPUBLIC

MALDIVIAN STATE, GOVERNMENT TREASURER

1947; 1960 ISSUE

		VG	VF	UNC
1	**1/2 Rupee** 14.11.1947/AH1367. Orange and m/c. Palm tree and dhow at ctr. Uniface.	30.00	100.	275.

#2-7 palm tree and dhow at l., dhow at r.

		VG	VF	UNC
2	**1 Rupee** 1947; 1960. Blue and green on m/c unpt. Bldgs. at r. on back.			
	a. 14.11.1947/AH1367.	1.50	7.50	25.00
	b. 4.6.1960/AH1379.	.30	1.00	2.50

		VG	VF	UNC
3	**2 Rupees** 1947; 1960. Brown and blue on m/c unpt. Pavilion at ctr. r. on back.			
	a. 14.11.1947/AH1367.	9.00	50.00	125.
	b. 4.6.1960/AH1379.	.50	1.50	5.00

		VG	VF	UNC
4	**5 Rupees** 1947; 1960. Violet and orange on m/c unpt. Bldg. at ctr. on back.			
	a. 14.11.1947/AH1367.	1.50	7.50	20.00
	b. 4.6.1960/AH1379.	.75	2.50	7.50

		VG	VF	UNC
5	**10 Rupees** 1947; 1960. Brown on m/c unpt. Bldg. at ctr. on back.			
	a. 14.11.1947/AH1367.	2.00	7.50	25.00
	b. 4.6.1960/AH1379.	2.50	10.00	30.00

1951; 1960; 1980 ISSUE

		VG	VF	UNC
6	**50 Rupees** 1951-80. Blue on m/c unpt. Royal Embarkation Gate at Male at ctr. on back			
	a. 1951/AH1371.	35.00	150.	400.
	b. 4.6.1960/AH1379.	4.00	20.00	60.00
	c. Litho. 1.8.1980/AH17.7.1400.	5.00	25.00	85.00
	s. As c. Specimen.	—	—	175.

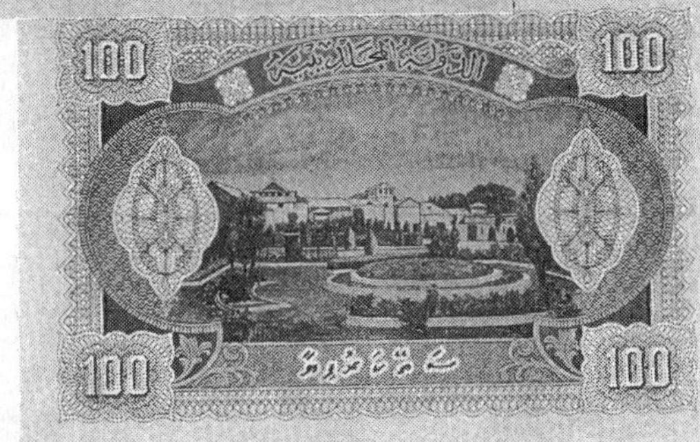

		VG	VF	UNC
7	**100 Rupees** 1951; 1960. Green on m/c unpt. Back brown, violet and m/c; park and bldg. complex at ctr.			
	a. 1951/AH1371.	45.00	175.	500.
	b. 4.6.1960/AH1379.	7.50	30.00	100.

#8 not assigned.

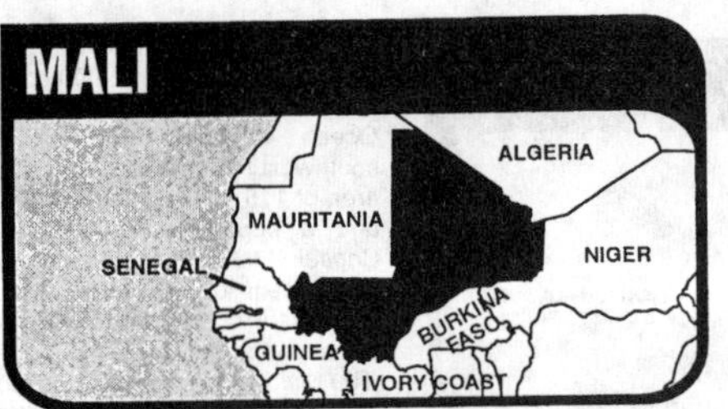

The Republic of Mali, a landlocked country in the interior of West Africa southwest of Algeria, has an area of 478,764 sq. mi. (1,240,000 sq. km.) and a population of 12.56 million. Capital: Bamako. Livestock, fish, cotton and peanuts are exported.

Malians are descendants of the ancient Malinke Kingdom of Mali that controlled the middle Niger from the 11th to the 17th centuries. The French penetrated the Sudan (now Mali) about 1880, and established their rule in 1898 after subduing fierce native resistance. In 1904 the area became the colony of Upper Senegal-Niger (changed to French Sudan in 1920), and became part of the French Union in 1946. In 1958 French Sudan became the Sudanese Republic with complete internal autonomy. Senegal joined with the Sudanese Republic in 1959 to form the Mali Federation which, in 1960, became a fully independent member of the French Community. Upon Senegal's subsequent withdrawal from the Federation, the Sudanese, on Sept. 22, 1960, proclaimed their nation the fully independent Republic of Mali and severed all ties with France.

Mali seceded from the African Financial Community in 1962, then rejoined in 1984. Issues specially marked with letter *D* for Mali were made by the Banque des Etats de l'Afrique de l'Ouest. See also French West Africa, and West African States.

MONETARY SYSTEM:

1 Franc = 100 Centimes

Republic

Banque de la République du Mali

First 1960 (1962) Issue

Note: Post-dated on Day of Independence.

#1-5 Pres. Modibo Keita at l. Sign. 1.

		VG	VF	UNC
1	**50 Francs** 22.9.1960. Purple on m/c unpt. Village on back.	10.00	35.00	125.
2	**100 Francs** 22.9.1960. Brown on yellow unpt. Cattle on back.	10.00	50.00	165.
3	**500 Francs** 22.9.1960. Red on lt. blue and orange unpt. Woman and tent on back.	60.00	400.	1000.
4	**1000 Francs** 22.9.1960. Blue on lt. green and orange unpt. Farmers w/oxen at lower r. Back blue; man and huts.	25.00	100.	500.
5	**5000 Francs** 22.9.1960. Green on m/c unpt. 2 farmers plowing w/oxen at r. Market scene and bldg. on back.	85.00	285.	—

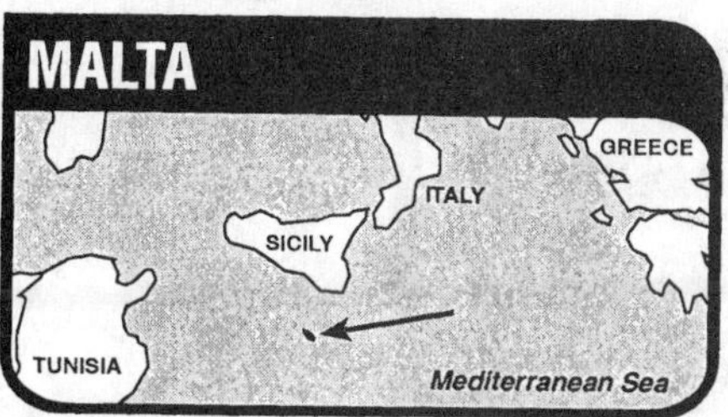

The Republic of Malta, an independent parliamentary democracy within the British Commonwealth, is situated in the Mediterranean Sea between Sicily and North Africa. With the islands of Gozo and Comino, Malta has an area of 122 sq. mi. (316 sq. km.) and a population of 379,000. Capital: Valletta. With the islands of Gozo (Ghawdex), Comino, Cominetto and Filfla, Malta has no proven mineral resources, an agriculture insufficient to its needs and a small but expanding, manufacturing facility. Clothing, textile yarns and fabrics, and knitted wear are exported.

For more than 3,500 years Malta was ruled, in succession, by Phoenicians, Carthaginians, Romans, Arabs, Normans, the Knights of Malta, France and Britain. Napoleon seized Malta by treachery in 1798. The French were ousted by a Maltese insurrection assisted by Britain, and in 1814, Malta, of its own free will, became part of the British Empire. The island was awarded the George Cross for conspicuous corrage during World War II. Malta obtained full independence in September 1964, electing to remain within the Commonwealth with Elizabeth II as Head of State as Queen of Malta.

RULERS:

British to 1974

MONETARY SYSTEM:

1 Shilling = 12 Pence
1 Pound = 20 Shillings to 1971

NOTE: Certain listings encompassing issues circulated by various bank and regional authorities are contained in Vol. 1.

British Administration

Government of Malta

1914 First Issue

#2 and 3, arms at upper ctr.

		Good	Fine	XF
2	**5 Shillings** 13.8.1914. Black on blue unpt. Like #3.	100.	350.	750.
	10 Shillings 12.8.1914. Black on red unpt. Back pink.	125.	400.	850.

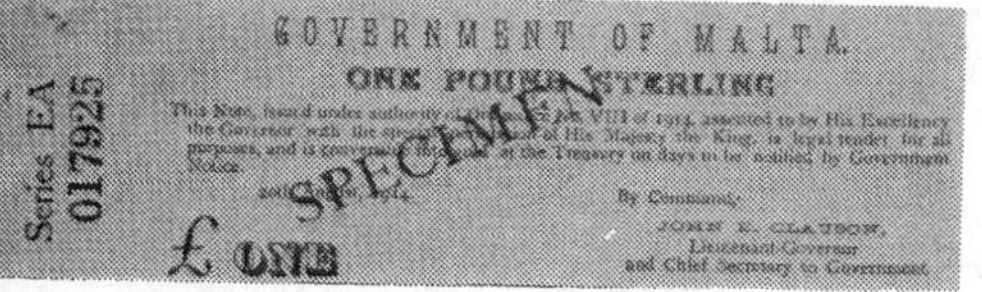

		Good	Fine	XF
	1 Pound 20.8.1914. Black.	125.	450.	850.

		Good	Fine	XF
5	**5 Pounds** 14.8.1914. Black on ornate green unpt.	185.	700.	1850.

		Good	Fine	XF
6	**10 Pounds** 14.8.1914. Black on yellow unpt. Rare.	—	—	—

1914 Second Issue

		Good	Fine	XF
7	**5 Shillings** 4.9.1914. Black on blue unpt. Like #3.	75.00	350.	750.
8	**1 Pound** 14.9.1914. Black on pink unpt. Like #4.	95.00	425.	850.

1918 Issue

#9-10 printer: TDLR.

		Good	Fine	XF
9	**2 Shillings** 20.11.1918. Green on lt. blue unpt. Portr. Kg. George V at r. Back blue. (Not issued, see #15). Rare.	—	—	—
10	**5 Shillings** 20.11.1918. Red on blue unpt. Like #9. Back green; Grand Harbour. Rare.	—	—	—

Note: From 1919-39 Malta did not issue notes of its own; Bank of England notes were in general circulation.

1939 Issue

#11-14 portr. Kg. George VI at r. Date in written style under sign. at bottom. Uniface. Printer: BWC (w/o imprint).

		VG	VF	UNC
11	**2 Shillings 6 Pence** 13.9.1939. Violet, blue and green.	12.00	60.00	275.

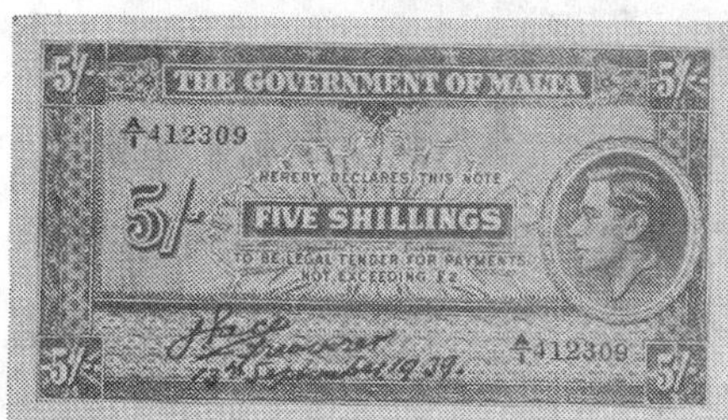

		VG	VF	UNC
12	**5 Shillings** 13.9.1939. Green and red.	10.00	37.50	285.

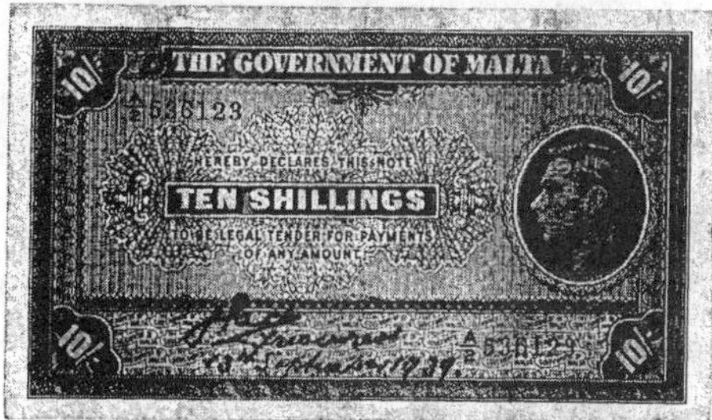

		VG	VF	UNC
13	**10 Shillings** 13.9.1939. Blue, violet and olive.	10.00	50.00	250.
14	**1 Pound** 13.9.1939. Brown and purple.	12.50	45.00	200.

1940 Provisional Issue

		VG	VF	UNC
15	**1 Shilling on 2 Shillings** ND (1940 - old date 20.11.1918). Green and lt. blue. Red ovpt. on #9.	6.00	20.00	85.00

1940-43 Issue

#16-20 w/o date. Uniface. Printer: BWC (w/o imprint).

		VG	VF	UNC
16	**1 Shilling** ND (1943). Purplish-blue and lilac. Portr. Kg. George VI at ctr.	2.00	8.00	37.50

#17-20 portr. Kg. George VI at r.

		VG	VF	UNC
17	**2 Shillings** ND (1942). Brown and green.			
	a. Sign. J. Pace. No wmk.	4.00	25.00	125.
	b. Sign. E. Cuschieri. No wmk.	3.50	20.00	100.
	c. Sign. like b. Heavier paper w/wmk: Map of Malaya.	5.00	25.00	150.

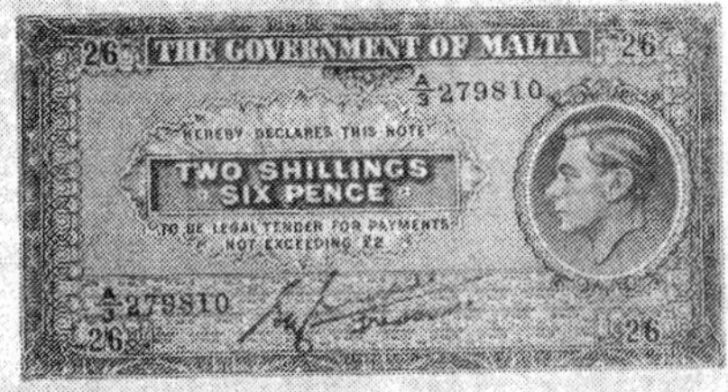

		VG	VF	UNC
18	**2 Shillings 6 Pence** ND (1940). Violet and blue.	7.00	25.00	185.
19	**10 Shillings** ND (1940). Blue, violet and olive.	4.00	12.50	50.00

		VG	VF	UNC
20	**1 Pound** ND (1940). Brown and violet.			
	a. Sign. J. Pace.	8.00	22.50	95.00
	b. Sign. E. Cuschieri w/title: *Treasurer* below sign. in script.	5.00	15.00	50.00
	c. Sign. E. Cuschieri w/title: *Treasurer* below sign. in small block letters.	6.00	20.00	70.00

Ordinance 1949 (1951 Issue)

#21-22 English George Cross at l., portr. Kg. George VI at r. Printer: TDLR.

		VG	VF	UNC
21	**10 Shillings** L.1949 (1951). Green.	5.00	30.00	200.

		VG	VF	UNC
22	**1 Pound** L.1949 (1951). Brown.			
	a. Issued note.	3.00	12.50	50.00
	s. Specimen.	—	—	50.00

Ordinance 1949 (1954 Issue)

#23-24 English George Cross at l., portr. Qn. Elizabeth II at r. Printer: TDLR.

		VG	VF	UNC
23	**10 Shillings** L.1949 (1954). Green.			
	a. Sign. E. Cuschieri (1954).	7.50	40.00	25[illegible]
	b. Sign. D. A. Shepherd.	10.00	50.00	30[illegible]
	s. As a. Specimen.	—	—	50.[illegible]

		VG	VF	UNC
24	**1 Pound** L.1949 (1954). Brown. Like #23.			
	a. Sign. E. Cuschieri (1954).	5.00	25.00	[illegible]
	b. Sign. D. A. Shepherd.	3.00	12.50	[illegible]

Note: For later issues of Qn. Elizabeth II, see Volume III.

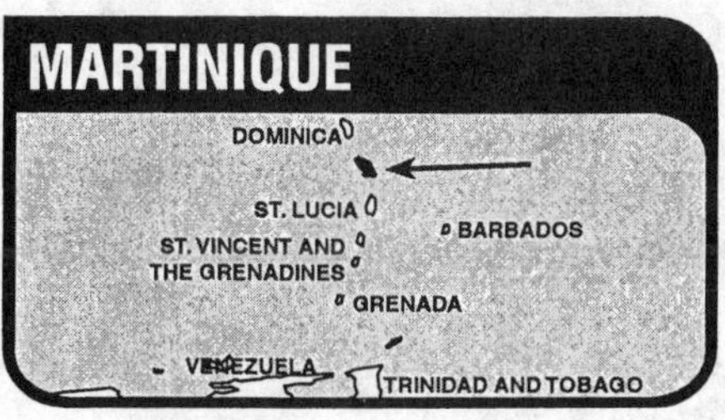

The French Overseas Department of Martinique, located in the Lesser Antilles of the West Indies between Dominica and Saint Lucia, has an area of 425 sq. mi. (1,101 sq. km.) and a population of 384,000. Capital: Fort-de-France. Agriculture and tourism are the major sources of income. Bananas, sugar and rum are exported.

Christopher Columbus discovered Martinique, probably on June 15, 1502. France took possession on June 25, 1635, and has maintained possession since that time except for three short periods of British occupation during the Napoleonic Wars. A French department since 1946, Martinique voted a reaffirmation of that status in 1958, remaining within the new French Community. Martinique was the birthplace of Napoleon's Empress Josephine, and the site of the eruption of Mt. Pelee in 1902 that claimed over 40,000 lives.

RULERS:
French

MONETARY SYSTEM:
1 Franc = 100 Centimes

FRENCH ADMINISTRATION

TRÉSOR COLONIAL

FORT DE FRANCE OFFICE

DÉCRET DU 23.4.1855

#A1 and 1 breadfruit tree, snake, shrubbery at upper l., old sailing ship at lower l., crowned arms at top ctr, palm tree, snake and shrubbery at r., various cargo along bottom border. Uniface.

		Good	Fine	XF
1A	**1 Franc** D.1855. W/text: Remboursalbe le 31 Mai 1858. a. Issued note. 27.2.1856. Rare. r. Unsigned remainder. Rare.	 — —	 — —	 — —
A1A	**5 Francs** D.1855. Rare.	—	—	—

DÉCRETS DES 23.4.1855 ET DU 3.3.1858

		Good	Fine	XF
A2	**1 Franc** D.1855 & 1858. Black. W/text: Remboursable le 31 Mai 1863. Uniface. a. Issued note. 6.2.1869. Rare. r. Unsigned remainder w/counterfoil, ND. Rare.	 — —	 — —	 — —
A2A	**2 Francs** D. 1855 & 1858. Rare.	—	—	—
A3	**5 Francs** D.1855 & 1858. Similar to #A2. Rare.	—	—	—

DÉCRET DU 18.8.1884

		Good	Fine	XF
2	**1 Franc** D.1884. Red. Border of trees and plants. 2 sign. varieties. Uniface.	600.	1250.	—

#3A-5 w/o border of trees and plants. Uniface.

		Good	Fine	XF
3	**2 Francs** D.1884. Green. Similar to #2. Rare.	—	—	—

Note: A 50 Centimes similar to above notes is reported.

		Good	Fine	XF
3A	**1 Franc** D.1884. Red. Similar to #4. Rare.	—	—	—

		Good	Fine	XF
4	**5 Francs** D.1884. Black. Thin border design, and space for serial # at ctr. Rare.	—	—	—
4A	**5 Francs** D.1884. Black on yellow-green paper. Similar to #4 but thicker border design, w/o space for serial # at ctr. Rare.	—	—	—
4B	**5 Francs** D.1884. Similar to #4A, but gray paper. Rare.	—	—	—
5	**10 Francs** D.1884. Orange paper. Similar to #4A. Rare.	—	—	—

BANQUE DE LA MARTINIQUE

1870'S PROVISIONAL ISSUE

#5A and 5B chéques w/printed value.

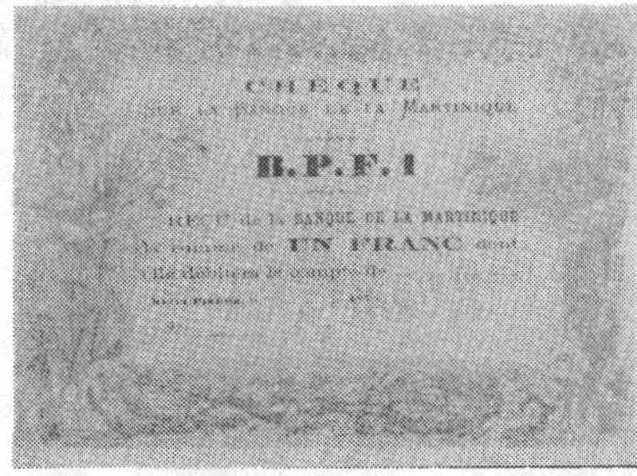

		Good	Fine	XF
5A	**1 Franc** 187x. Violet w/lt. blue text. Uniface.	15.00	50.00	115.
5B	**5 Francs** 3.11.1878. Blue w/red value. W/ or w/o sign. Like #5A. Rare.	—	—	—

LAW OF 1874

		Good	Fine	XF
5C	**5 Francs** L.1874. Blue. Similar to #6.	—	—	—

LAW OF 1901

		Good	Fine	XF
6	**5 Francs** L.1901 (1934-45). Purple. Man at l., woman at r. Law date on blue-green back. 3 sign. varieties.	12.50	50.00	175.
6A	**5 Francs** L.1901 (1903-34). Red. Like #6. Back blue-green. 5 sign. varieties.	15.00	75.00	250.

		Good	Fine	XF
7	**25 Francs** ND (1922-30). 2 sign. varieties.			
	a. Black and blue.	—	—	—
	b. Brown and blue. Back blue.	—	—	—
8	**100 Francs** ND (1905-32). Black and green. Similar to #7. Back brown. 3 sign. varieties.	—	—	—

		Good	Fine	XF
9	**500 Francs** ND (1905-22). Brown and gray. Allegorical figures on borders. Back reverse image. 4 sign. varieties. Rare.	—	—	—

1915 Issue

#10 and 11, 2 sign. varieties.

		Good	Fine	XF
10	**1 Franc** 1915. Red on blue unpt. Date in unpt. Arms at ctr. on back.	15.00	75.00	325.
11	**2 Francs** 1915. Blue. Woman's head at ctr. on back.	20.00	85.00	350.

1930-32 Issue

		Good	Fine	XF
12	**25 Francs** ND (1930-45). M/c. Woman w/wreath at ctr., floral drapery behind fruit at bottom. 3 sign. varieties.	25.00	150.	500.

		Good	Fine	XF
13	**100 Francs** ND (1932-45). M/c. Woman w/sceptre at l., ship in background at ctr. 4 sign. varieties.	100.	400.	1200.

		Good	Fine	XF
14	**500 Francs** ND (1932-45). M/c. Like #13. 4 sign. varieties.	250.	1000.	—

#15 Deleted.

1942 Emergency Issues

#16, 17 and 20 printer: EAW.

		Good	Fine	XF
16	**5 Francs** ND (1942). Black on dull red unpt. Allegorical female figure at l. Back blue; woman at ctr.			
	a. Red serial #.	25.00	90.00	275.
	b. Blue serial #.	15.00	75.00	225.

		Good	Fine	XF
16A	**5 Francs** ND (1942). Blue. Column at l., lg. *5* at r. Back like #18. Local printing.	350.	1250.	—

		Good	Fine	XF
17	**25 Francs** ND (1943-45). Black on yellow unpt. Woman seated w/fruit at r. Back green; ship and tree at ctr. 3 sign. varieties.	20.00	50.00	300.

		Good	Fine	XF
18	**25 Francs** ND (1942). Violet w/black text on rose paper. Column at l. Bank monogram at ctr. on back. Local printing.	400.	1500.	—

1942 ISSUE

#19 and 21 printer: ABNC.

		Good	Fine	XF
19	**100 Francs** ND (1942). Green on m/c unpt. Allegorical woman seated w/fruit at l. Seated allegorical woman w/child on back. 2 sign. varieties.			
	a. Issued note.	85.00	300.	900.
	s. Specimen.	—	Unc	1200.

		Good	Fine	XF
20	**1000 Francs** ND (1942). Blue. Women seated at l. and r. Back orange; woman at ctr.	650.	1500.	—
21	**1000 Francs** ND (1942). Red-brown on lt. green and m/c unpt. Allegorical man, woman and child at r. 3 sign. varieties. Allegorical figures on back.			
	a. Issued note.	650.	1500.	—
	s. Specimen.	—	Unc	3250.

CAISSE CENTRALE DE LA FRANCE LIBRE

1941 ISSUE

#22 ovpt: *MARTINIQUE*. English printing.

		Good	Fine	XF
22	**1000 Francs** L. 2.12.1941 (1944-47). Blue. Phoenix rising from flames. War/peace scenes on back.			
	a. Ovpt. below *Caisse Centrale.*	400.	1000.	3000.
	b. Ovpt. like a., cancelled w/stamp *ANNULE.*	—	—	1750.
	c. Ovpt. at top and diagonally from lower l. to upper r.	400.	1100.	3250.
	s. Specimen.	—	—	1750.

CAISSE CENTRALE DE LA FRANCE D'OUTRE-MER

LAW OF 2.2.1944

#23-25 Marianne at ctr., red ovpt: *MARTINIQUE* at l. and r. English printing.

		VG	VF	UNC
23	**10 Francs** L. 2.2.1944. Violet on red unpt.	7.50	30.00	150.
24	**20 Francs** L. 2.2.1944. Green on red unpt.	15.00	50.00	225.

NOTICE

Readers with unlisted dates, signature varieties, etc. are invited to submit photocopies or, high resolution (300 dpi, 100% size) scans of their notes to: Standard Catalog of World Paper Money, 700 East State St. Iola, WI 54990-0001, or E-Mail: george.cuhaj@fwpubs.com.

		VG	VF	UNC
25	**100 Francs** L. 2.2.1944. Green on orange unpt. Anchor, barrel, bale and other implements on back.	45.00	150.	575.
26	**1000 Francs** L. 2.2.1944. Blue. Like #22.			
	a. Issued note.	350.	850.	2500.
	s. Specimen.	—	—	1500.

1947 ND Issue

#27-36 ovpt: *MARTINIQUE*. French printing, w/usual designs.

		VG	VF	UNC
27	**5 Francs** ND (1947-49). M/c. Portr. Bougainville at r. 2 wmk. varieties.	2.50	12.50	85.00

		VG	VF	UNC
28	**10 Francs** ND (1947-49). M/c. Colbert at l. Boat at ctr. r. on back.	3.00	25.00	110.
29	**20 Francs** ND (1947-49). M/c. E. Gentil at r.	4.00	25.00	125.
30	**50 Francs** ND (1947-49). M/c. Belain d'Esnambuc at l.	7.50	40.00	225.

		VG	VF	UNC
31	**100 Francs** ND (1947-49). M/c. La Bourdonnais at l., couple at r.	15.00	75.00	275.

		VG	VF	UNC
32	**500 Francs** ND (1947-49). M/c. Two women at r., sailboat at l. Farmers w/ox-carts on back.	50.00	250.	800.

		VG	VF	UNC
33	**1000 Francs** ND (1947-49). M/c. Two women at r.	100.	275.	875.

1952 ND Issue

		VG	VF	UNC
34	**5000 Francs** ND (1952). M/c. Gen. Schoelcher.			
	a. Issued note.	225.	750.	1750.
	s. Specimen.	—	—	325.

1960 ND Issue

		VG	VF	UNC
35	**1000 Francs** ND (1960). M/c. Fishermen from Antilles. Woman w/box of produce on her head at l. ctr. on back.	75.00	200.	750.

		VG	VF	UNC
36	**5000 Francs** ND (1960). M/c. Woman holding fruit bowl at ctr. Harvesting scene on back.			
	a. Issued note.	250.	850.	—
	s. Specimen w/ovpt. and perforated: *SPECIMEN*.	—	—	600.

1960 ND Provisional Issue

#37-41 ovpt: *MARTINIQUE* and new denominations on previous "old" Franc issues.

		VG	VF	UNC
37	**1 Nouveau Franc on 100 Francs** ND (1960). M/c. Ovpt. on #31.	20.00	150.	450.

		VG	VF	UNC
38	**5 Nouveaux Francs on 500 Francs** ND (1960). M/c. Ovpt. on #32.	20.00	175.	550.

		VG	VF	UNC
39	**10 Nouveaux Francs on 1000 Francs** ND (1960). M/c. Ovpt. on #35.	40.00	250.	750.
40	**50 Nouveaux Francs on 5000 Francs** ND (1960). M/c. Ovpt. on #36.	150.	750.	—
41	**50 Nouveaux Francs on 5000 Francs** ND (1960). M/c. Ovpt. on #34. Specimen.	—	—	—

Note: For later issues see French Antilles.

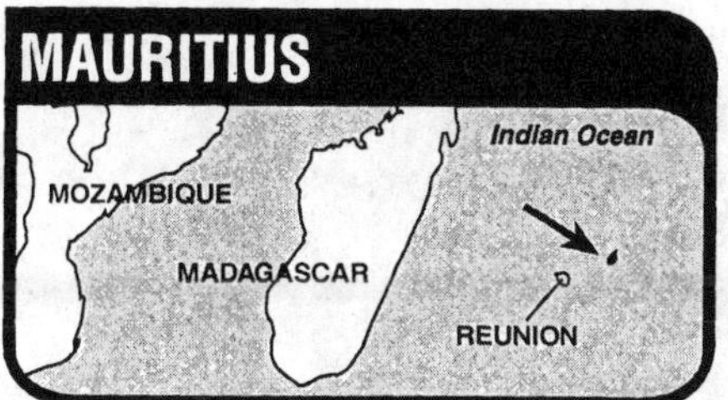

The island of Mauritius, a member of the British Commonwealth located in the Indian Ocean 500 miles (805 km.) east of Madagascar, has an area of 790 sq. mi. (2,045 sq. km.) and a population of 1.18 million. Capital: Port Louis. Sugar provides 90 percent of the export revenue.

Cartographic evidence indicates that Arabs and Malays arrived at Mauritius during the Middle Ages. Domingo Fernandez, a Portuguese navigator, visited the island in the early 16th century, but Portugal made no attempt at settlement. The Dutch took possession, and named the island, in 1598. Their colony failed to prosper and was abandoned in 1710. France claimed Mauritius in 1715 and developed a strong and prosperous colony that endured until the island was captured by the British in 1810, during the Napoleonic Wars. British possession was confirmed by the Treaty of Paris, 1814. Mauritius became independent on March 12, 1968, with Elizabeth II as Head of State as Queen of Mauritius. Mauritius became a Republic on March 12, 1992, with a President as Head of State.

RULERS:

British

MONETARY SYSTEM:

1 Shilling = 12 Pence
1 Crown = 5 Shillings
1 Pound = 4 Crowns
1 Pound = 5 Dollars to 1948
1 Rupee = 100 Cents, 1848-
1 Crown = 10 Mauritius Livres

NOTE: Certain listings encompassing issues circulated by various bank and regional authorities are contained in Volume 1.

British Administration

Special Finance Committee

1842 Emergency Issue

		Good	Fine	XF
1F	**1 Dollar** 1.9.1842. Port Louis. 5 sign. varieties.	85.00	225.	450.

Note: #1F is printed on the back of cut up and cancelled Mauritius Commercial Bank issues.

Currency Commissioners of Mauritius

1848 Issue

#8-9 arms at upper ctr. Sign. varieties.

		Good	Fine	XF
8	**5 Rupees** 5.6.1848; 1849. Currency Commissioners' seal at top ctr. Port Louis. Rare.	—	—	—
9	**10 Rupees** 1848-49. Rare.	—	—	—

Government of Mauritius

1860-66 Issue

#10-11 arms at upper ctr. Various dates and sign. Counterfoil at l.

		Good	Fine	XF
10	**5 Shillings** 1866. Rare.	—	—	—

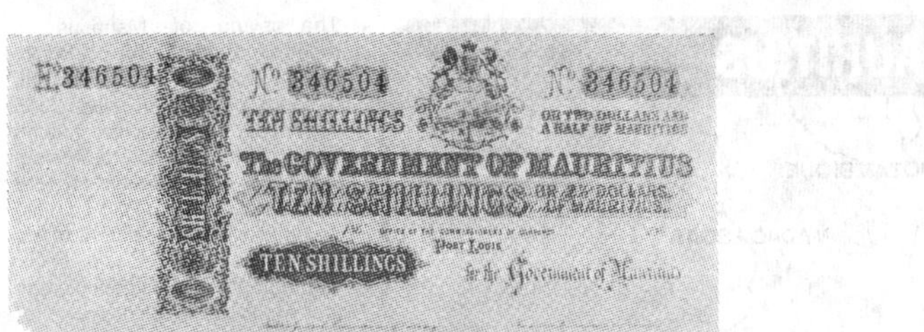

		Good	Fine	XF
11	**10 Shillings** 22.8.1860; 1866; 1.11.1867. Black and green on cream paper. Arms at top ctr. Rare.	—	—	—
12	**1 Pound** 1866. Rare.	—	—	—

		Good	Fine	XF
12A	**5 Pounds/25 Dollars** 186x. Arms at upper ctr. Specimen w/counterfoil. Rare.			

1876; 1877 Issue

#13-15 arms at top ctr. Various dates and sign. Counterfoil at l.

		Good	Fine	XF
13	**5 Rupees** 1876-1902.			
	a. 1876; 23.10.1878. Rare.	—	—	—
	b. 5.10.1896; 13.11.1900; 17.11.1902.	500.	1200.	—
14	**10 Rupees** 1.10.1877. Rare.	—	—	—

		Good	Fine	XF
15	**50 Rupees** 1.12.1876. Black. Arms at top ctr. Rare.	—	—	—

Note: Spink Mauritius collection 10-96, #15 in fine $10,600, one of two known.

1907-14 Issue

#16-18 arms at top ctr. Sign. title varieties.

		Good	Fine	XF
16	**5 Rupees** 1.10.1914-1.10.1930. Greenish brown paper.	225.	450.	1100.
17	**10 Rupees** 1.10.1914-1.10.1930. Lilac paper.	300.	800.	1750.
18	**50 Rupees** 19.10.1907; 1.1.1920. Rare.	—	—	—

1919 Issue

		Good	Fine	XF
19	**1 Rupee** 1.7.1919; 1.7.1928. Brown on green unpt. Sailing ship and mountains at r. Printer: TDLR.	100.	350.	850.

1930 Issue

#20 and 21 arms at l., portr. Kg. George V at r. Wmk: Stylized sailing ship. Printer: W&S.

		Good	Fine	XF
20	**5 Rupees** ND (1930). Blue on m/c unpt.	30.00	150.	850.

		Good	Fine	XF
21	**10 Rupees** ND (1930). Brown on m/c unpt.	100.	500.	1600.

1937 Issue

#22 and 23 portr. Kg. George VI at r. Printer: W&S.

		Good	Fine	XF
22	**5 Rupees** ND (1937). Blue on m/c unpt.	17.50	50.00	225.

		Good	Fine	XF
23	**10 Rupees** ND (1937). Brown on m/c unpt.			
	a. Portr. in brown.	40.00	150.	800.
	b. Portr. in green.	45.00	175.	850.

1940 Issue

#24-26 portr. Kg. George at r. W/o imprint.

#24 #25

		VG	VF	UNC
24	**25 Cents** ND (1940). Blue. Uniface.			
	a. Serial # at ctr. Prefix A.	25.00	100.	500.
	b. Serial # at lower l. Prefix A.	40.00	150.	600.
	c. Serial # position like b. Prefix B.	25.00	90.00	450.
	d. Like b. Prefix C.	25.00	90.00	450.
25	**50 Cents** ND (1940). Lilac. Uniface.			
	a. Serial # at ctr. Prefix A.	35.00	125.	650.
	b. Serial # at lower l. Prefix A.	50.00	175.	700.
	c. Serial # position like b. Prefix B.	25.00	120.	625.

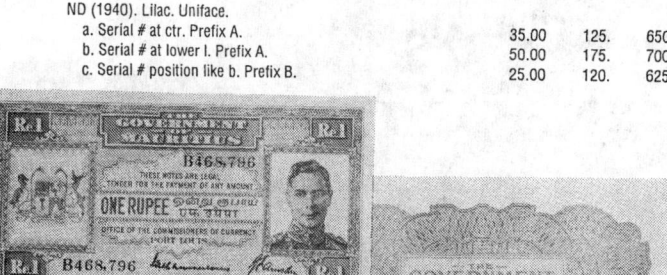

		VG	VF	UNC
26	**1 Rupee** ND (1940). Green on lilac unpt. Sign. varieties.	20.00	65.00	600.

1942 Emergency Issue

		VG	VF	UNC
26A	**1 Rupee** 27.3.1942 (-old date 1.7.1924; 1.10.1930). Printed on partial backs of 10 Rupees notes #17.	700.	1400.	—

1954 Issue

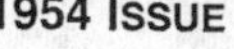

#27-29A portr. Qn. Elizabeth II at r. Sign. varieties. Wmk: Stylized sailing ship. Printer: BWC.

		VG	VF	UNC
27	**5 Rupees** ND (1954). Blue on m/c unpt. Mountain scene at lower l. Arms on back.	7.00	40.00	250.

		VG	VF	UNC
28	**10 Rupees** ND (1954). Red on m/c unpt. Mountain scene at lower ctr.	25.00	150.	650.

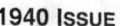

		VG	VF	UNC
29	**25 Rupees** ND (1954). Green on m/c unpt. Bldg. at lower ctr.	100.	700.	1600.

		VG	VF	UNC
29A	**1000 Rupees** ND (1954). Mauve on m/c unpt. Bldg. like #29 at lower ctr. Rare.	—	—	—

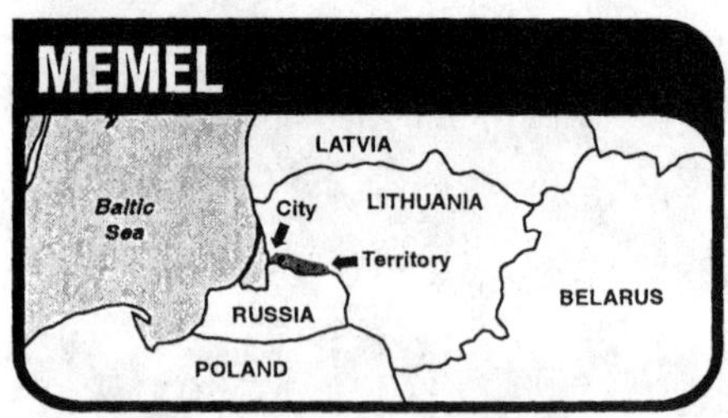

Memel is the German name for Klaipeda, a town and port of Lithuania on the Baltic Sea at the mouth of the Nemunas River. It is the of a large fishing fleet, and has major shipbuilding and repair yards.

Founded as a fort in the early 13th century, Klaipeda was seized and destroyed in 1252 by the Teutonic Knights, who built a new fortress called Memelburg. The town, later called Memel, and adjacent territory was held by the Swedes through most of the 17th century. After the Swedish occupation, the area became part of East Prussia though briefly occupied by the Russians in 1757 and 1813. During World War I, Memel was captured by the Russians again and after 1919 was administered by France under a League of Nations mandate. On Jan. 15, 1923, it was seized by the Lithuanians as their only good port and made a part of the autonomous Klaipeda territory. It was taken by Soviet forces in Jan. 1945 and made a part of the Lithuanian Soviet Socialist Republic until Lithuanian independence was achieved in 1991.

MONETARY SYSTEM:
1 Mark = 100 Pfennig

FRENCH ADMINISTRATION - POST WW I

HANDELSKAMMER DES MEMELGEBIETS

CHAMBER OF COMMERCE, TERRITORY OF MEMEL

1922 ISSUE

#1-9 authorized by the Interallied Commission.

		VG	VF	UNC
1	**1/2 Mark**			
	22.2.1922. Blue. Bay on back.	1.00	2.50	7.50

		VG	VF	UNC
2	**1 Mark**			
	22.2.1922. Brown. Spit of land on back.	1.00	3.50	8.00

		VG	VF	UNC
3	**2 Mark**			
	22.2.1922. Blue and olive-brown. Memel in 1630 on back.			
	a. Wmk: Sculptured chain.	1.00	4.00	12.00
	b. Wmk: Contoured chain.	1.00	4.00	12.00

		VG	VF	UNC
4	**5 Mark**			
	22.2.1922. Blue and yellow. Stock exchange on back.			
	a. Wmk: Sculptured chain.	2.00	5.00	15.00
	b. Wmk: Contoured chain.	2.00	5.00	15.00

		VG	VF	UNC
5	**10 Mark**			
	22.2.1922. Yellow-brown and blue. Couple, lighthouse and man on back.			
	a. Wmk: Sculptured chain.	2.00	6.00	20.00
	b. Wmk: Contoured chain.	2.00	5.00	18.00

		VG	VF	UNC
6	**20 Mark**			
	22.2.1922. Lilac and violet. Cow, farmhouse and horse on back.			
	a. Wmk: Sculptured chain.	3.00	7.50	35.00
	b. Wmk: Contoured chain.	3.00	7.50	30.00

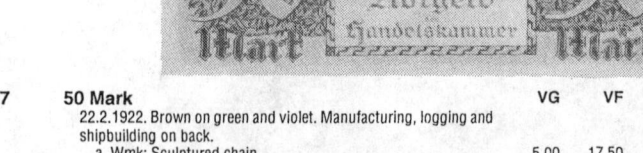

		VG	VF	UNC
7	**50 Mark**			
	22.2.1922. Brown on green and violet. Manufacturing, logging and shipbuilding on back.			
	a. Wmk: Sculptured chain.	5.00	17.50	65.00
	b. Wmk: Contoured chain.	5.00	17.50	65.00

8	75 Mark	VG	VF	UNC
	22.2.1922. Brown on blue and pink unpt. New and old sawmills on back.	7.50	20.00	65.00

9	100 Mark	VG	VF	UNC
	22.2.1922. Blue and lt. brown. General view of Memel on back.	8.00	30.00	85.00

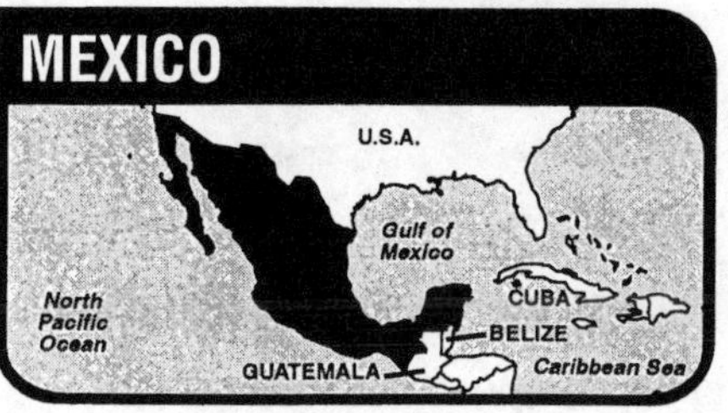

The United States of Mexico, located immediately south of the United States, has an area of 1,222,612 sq. mi. (1,967,183 sq. km.) and a population of 98.88 million. Capital: Mexico City. The economy is based on agriculture, manufacturing and mining. Cotton, sugar, coffee and shrimp are exported.

Mexico was the site of highly advanced Indian civilizations 1,500 years before conquistador Hernando Cortes conquered the wealthy Aztec empire of Montezuma, 1519-1521, and founded a Spanish colony which lasted for nearly 300 years. During the Spanish period, Mexico, then called New Spain, stretched from Guatemala to the present states of Wyoming and California, its present northern boundary having been established by the secession of Texas (1836) and the war of 1846-1848 with the United States.

Independence from Spain was declared by Father Miguel Hidalgo on Sept. 16, 1810, Mexican Independence Day, and was achieved by General Agustin de Iturbide in 1821. Iturbide became emperor in 1822 but was deposed when a republic was established a year later. For more than half a century following the birth of the republic, the political scene of Mexico was characterized by turmoil which saw two emperors (including the unfortunate Maximilian), several dictators and an average of one new government every nine months passing swiftly from obscurity to oblivion. The land, social, economic and labor reforms promulgated by the Reform Constitution of Feb. 5, 1917 established the basis for a sustained economic development and participative democracy that have made Mexico one of the most politically stable countries of modern Latin America.

EMPIRE OF ITURBIDE

EL IMPERIO MEXICANO, DISTRITO FEDERAL

1823 ISSUE

#1-3 issued by Emperor Agustin de Iturbide in 1823. All have arms in oval at upper ctr. Black on thin white paper, uniface. Most were cancelled with a 2-inch cut at bottom.

		Good	Fine	XF
1	**1 Peso**			
	1.1.1823. *(PR-DF-1).*			
	a. Issued note.	20.00	45.00	100.
	b. Cut cancelled. *PR-DF-5).*	15.00	30.00	80.00
	c. Handwritten cancellation: *Ynutilizado, Oaxaca 16.5.1825. (PR-DF-3).*	20.00	40.00	60.00
	d. Ovpt: *LEON* on face in red.	30.00	70.00	125.
2	**2 Pesos**			
	1.1.1823. *(PR-DF-6).*			
	a. Issued note.	30.00	60.00	100.
	b. Cut cancelled. *PR-DF-8).*	20.00	40.00	60.00
	c. Handwritten cancellation like #1c. *(PR-DF-7).*	20.00	45.00	75.00
3	**10 Pesos**			
	1.1.1823. *(PR-DF-11).*			
	a. Issued note.	200.	300.	400.
	b. Cut cancelled. *PR-DF-12).*	35.00	75.00	125.

REPUBLIC

LAS TESORERÍAS DE LA NACIÓN

THE TREASURY OF THE NATION

DECREE OF APRIL 11, 1823

#4-6 designs similar to Empire issue. Many are cut cancelled. Printed on backs of Papal Bulls (Lent authorizations) dated 1818 and 1819.

		Good	Fine	XF
4	**1 Peso**			
	5.5.1823. *(PR-DF-13).*			
	a. Issued note.	40.00	100.	200.
	b. Cut cancelled. *(PR-DF-15).*	20.00	50.00	100.
5	**2 Pesos**			
	5.5.1823. *(PR-DF-17).*			
	a. Issued note.	40.00	100.	200.
	b. Cut cancelled. *(PR-DF-19).*	25.00	75.00	150.

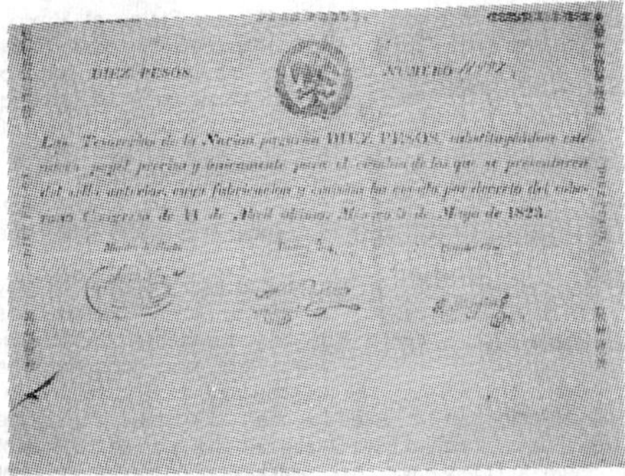

		Good	Fine	XF
6	**10 Pesos** 5.5.1823. *(PR-DF-21).*	100.	150.	275.

EMPIRE OF MAXIMILIAN

BANCO DE MÉXICO

1866 ISSUE

#7-10 prepared for Emperor Maximillian (1864-67).

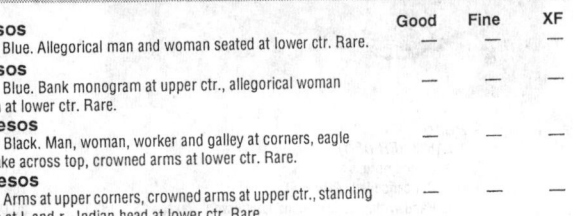

		Good	Fine	XF
7	**10 Pesos** 1866. Blue. Allegorical man and woman seated at lower ctr. Rare.	—	—	—
8	**20 Pesos** 1866. Blue. Bank monogram at upper ctr., allegorical woman w/lion at lower ctr. Rare.	—	—	—
9	**100 Pesos** 1866. Black. Man, woman, worker and galley at corners, eagle w/snake across top, crowned arms at lower ctr. Rare.	—	—	—
10	**200 Pesos** 1866. Arms at upper corners, crowned arms at upper ctr., standing figure at l. and r., Indian head at lower ctr. Rare.	—	—	—

ESTADOS UNIDOS MÉXICANOS

UNITED STATES OF MEXICO

BANCO DE LA REPÚBLICA MÉXICANA

1918 SERIES A

#11-15 Aztec calendar at ctr. on back. Printer: ABNC.

		VG	VF	UNC
11	**5 Pesos** 1918. Black. "Kalliope" seated w/globe at ctr. Back deep blue.			
	p1. Face proof.	—	—	200.
	p2. Back proof.	—	—	50.00
	s. Specimen, punched hole cancelled.	—	—	200.

		VG	VF	UNC
12	**10 Pesos** 1918. Black. Reclining female w/lion at ctr. Back deep green.			
	p1. Face proof.	—	—	200.
	p2. Back proof.	—	—	50.00
	s. Specimen, punched hole cancelled.	—	—	200.

		VG	VF	UNC
13	**20 Pesos** 1918. Black. Allegorical female standing holding model airplane next to seated seated female at r. Back deep brown.			
	p1. Face proof.	—	—	200.
	p2. Back proof.	—	—	50.00
	s. Specimen, punched hole cancelled.	—	—	200.

		VG	VF	UNC
14	**50 Pesos** 1918. Black. Allegorical male seated w/sheaf and scythe at l., Allegorical female seated w/ship and rudder at r. Back olive-brown.			
	p1. Face proof.	—	—	20
	p2. Back proof.	—	—	50.0
	s. Specimen, punched hole cancelled.	—	—	20

		VG	VF	UNC
15	**100 Pesos** 1918. Black. Cherub standing between two reclining females at ctr. Back deep red.			
	p1. Face proof.	—	—	2
	p2. Back proof.	—	—	50.
	s. Specimen, punched hole cancelled.	—	—	2

COMISIÓN MONETARIA

1920 ISSUE

#16 and 17 printer: Oficina Imp. de Hacienda.

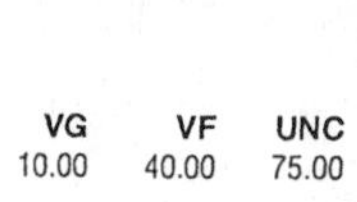

		VG	VF	UNC
16	**50 Centavos** 10.1.1920. Black on gray. Minerva at l. Back green; allegorical figures at ctr. *(PT-DF-1).*	10.00	40.00	75.00

		VG	VF	UNC
17	**1 Peso** 10.1.1920. Brown. Goddess of Plenty w/2 cherubs at ctr. Back blue; like #16. *(PT-DF-2).*	15.00	45.00	85.00

BANCO DE MÉXICO

TRIAL DESIGN

		VG	VF	UNC
9	**2 Pesos** ND (ca.1930s). Black on pale green unpt. Woman standing before Aztec calendar stone. Back black; Statue of Victory at ctr. Face and back proofs. Printer: Talleres de Impresión de Estampillas y Valores. (Not issued).	—	—	350.

925 ISSUE

21-27 lg. size notes (180 x 83mm). Sign. varieties. Statue of Victory in Mexico City at ctr. on back. Printer: ABNC.

(5 Pesos note illustration above #21)

		Good	Fine	XF
1	**5 Pesos** 1925-34; ND. Black on m/c unpt. Portr. gypsy at ctr. Back black.			
	a. 1.9.1925. Series: A.	200.	450.	750.
	b. 1.8.1931. Series: C.	10.00	35.00	120.
	c. 30.4.1932. Series: D.	10.00	35.00	120.
	d. 22.6.1932. Series: E.	10.00	35.00	120.
	e. 18.1.1933. Series: F.	10.00	35.00	120.
	f. 9.8.1933. Series: G.	5.00	20.00	75.00
	g. 7.3.1934. Series: H.	5.00	20.00	75.00
	h. ND. Series: I.	5.00	20.00	75.00

NOTICE

Readers with unlisted dates, signature varieties, etc. are invited to submit photocopies or, high resolution (300 dpi, 100% size) scans of their notes to: Standard Catalog of World Paper Money, 700 East State St. Iola, WI 54990-0001, or E-Mail: george.cuhaj@fwpubs.com.

		Good	Fine	XF
22	**10 Pesos** 1925-34; ND. Black on m/c unpt. 2 winged females supporting book. Back brown.			
	a. 1.9.1925. Series: A.	800.	2000.	—
	b. 1.8.1931. Series: C.	10.00	35.00	120.
	c. 30.4.1932. Series: D.	10.00	35.00	120.
	d. 22.6.1932. Series: E.	10.00	35.00	120.
	e. 18.1.1933. Series: F.	10.00	35.00	120.
	f. 9.8.1933. Series: G.	5.00	20.00	75.00
	g. 7.3.1934. Series: H.	5.00	20.00	75.00
	h. ND. Series: I.	5.00	20.00	75.00

		Good	Fine	XF
23	**20 Pesos** 1925-34; ND. Black on m/c unpt. Dock scene w/ship and steam locomotive. Back red.			
	a. 1.9.1925. Series: A.	800.	2000.	—
	b. 1.8.1931. Series: C.	25.00	75.00	250.
	c. 30.4.1932. Series: D.	25.00	75.00	250.
	d. 22.6.1932. Series: E.	20.00	60.00	200.
	e. 18.1.1933. Series: F.	20.00	60.00	200.
	f. 9.8.1933. Series: G.	20.00	60.00	200.
	g. 7.3.1934. Series: H.	15.00	40.00	175.
	h. ND. Series: I.	15.00	40.00	175.

		Good	Fine	XF
24	**50 Pesos** 1925-34. Black on m/c unpt. Seated female holding ship at l. Back olive-green.			
	a. 1.9.1925. Series: A.	800.	2000.	—
	b. 1.8.1931. Series: C.	80.00	130.	300.
	c. 30.4.1932. Series: D.	80.00	130.	300.
	d. 22.6.1932. Series: E.	80.00	130.	300.
	e. 18.1.1933. Series: F.	80.00	130.	300.
	f. 9.8.1933. Series: G.	75.00	120.	250.
	g. 7.3.1934. Series: H.	75.00	120.	250.

		Good	Fine	XF
25	**100 Pesos** 1925-34. Black on m/c unpt. Allegorical male seated holding ship, w/youth at ctr. Back dk. green.			
	a. 1.9.1925. Series: A.	1000.	2500.	—
	b. 1.8.1931. Series: C.	100.	200.	350.
	c. 30.4.1932. Series: D.	100.	200.	350.

25		Good	Fine	XF
	d. 22.6.1932. Series: E.	100.	200.	350.
	e. 18.1.1933. Series: F.	100.	200.	350.
	f. 9.8.1933. Series: G.	90.00	175.	300.
	g. 7.3.1934. Series: H.	90.00	175.	300.

26	500 Pesos	Good	Fine	XF
	1925-34. Black on m/c unpt. "Electricity" seated at ctr. Back blue.			
	a. 1.9.1925. Series A.	1200.	2750.	—
	b. 1.8.1931. Series C.	500.	1200.	—
	c. 30.4.1932. Series D.	500.	1200.	—
	d. 22.6.1932. Series E.	500.	1200.	—
	e. 18.1.1933. Series F.	500.	1200.	—
	f. 9.8.1933. Series G.	450.	1000.	—
	g. 7.3.1934. Series H.	450.	1000.	—

27	1000 Pesos	Good	Fine	XF
	1931-34. Black on m/c unpt. Seated female w/globe. Back orange.			
	a. 1.9.1925. Series A.	2500.	3750.	—
	b. 1.8.1931. Series C.	1500.	2500.	—
	c. 30.4.1932. Series D.	1500.	2500.	—
	d. 22.6.1932. Series E.	1500.	2500.	—
	e. 18.1.1933. Series F.	1500.	2500.	—
	f. 9.8.1933. Series G.	1200.	2250.	—
	g. 7.3.1934. Series H.	1200.	2250.	—

1936 ISSUE

#28-33 small size notes (157 x 67mm). Sign. varieties. Printer: ABNC.

28	1 Peso	VG	VF	UNC
	ND (1936); 1943. Black on m/c unpt. Aztec calendar stone at ctr. *UN* in background under sign. at l. and r. Back red; Statue of Victory at ctr.			
	a. ND. Series: A.	10.00	20.00	90.00
	b. ND. Series: B.	12.00	30.00	125.
	c. ND. Series: C.	1.00	5.00	25.00
	d. ND. Series: D-F.	1.00	5.00	20.00
	e. 14.4.1943. Series: G-K.	1.00	5.00	20.00

29	5 Pesos	VG	VF	UNC
	1.4.1936. Black on m/c unpt. Like #21 but smaller, w/text: *PAGARA CINCO PESOS...EN EFECTIVO* below portr., w/curved *SERIE* at l. and r. Large BdM seal on back. Series: J.	10.00	50.00	150.

30	10 Pesos	VG	VF	UNC
	1.4.1936. Black on m/c unpt. Like #22 but smaller. Statue of Victory at ctr. on back. Series: J.	10.00	50.00	150.

31	100 Pesos	VG	VF	UNC
	1.9.1936. Black on m/c unpt. Portr. F. I. Madero at r. Bank of Mexico at ctr., lg. seal on purple back. Series: K.			
	a. Issued note.	30.00	50.00	125.
	s. Specimen, punched hole cancelled.			225.

32	500 Pesos	VG	VF	UNC
	9.1.1936. Black on m/c unpt. Portr. J. M. Morelos y Pavon at r. Middle sign. title: *INTERVENTOR DEL GOBIERNO.* Back green; miner's palace. Printed date, lg. seal. Series K.	275.	500.	—

33	1000 Pesos	VG	VF	UNC
	9.1.1936. Black on m/c upt. Portr. Cuauhtémoc at r. Middle sign. title: *INTERVENTOR DEL GOBIERNO.* Back dk. brown; El Castillo Chichen-Itza, w/lg. seal. Printed date. Series K.	325.	600.	—

1937 ISSUE

#34-37 sign. varieties. Printer: ABNC.

34	5 Pesos	VG	VF	UNC
	1937-50. Black on m/c unpt. Like #29 but w/text: *PAGARA CINCO PESOS.... AL PORTADOR* below portr., w/*EL* and *S.A.* added to face. Back gray; *S.A.* added to *BANCO DE MEXICO* w/small BdeM seal.			
	a. 22.9.1937. Series: M.	4.00	7.50	60.00
	b. 26.6.1940. Series: N.	1.50	5.00	18.00
	c. 12.11.1941. Series: O.	1.50	5.00	18.00
	d. 25.11.1942. Series: P.	1.00	3.50	10.00
	e. 7.4.1943. Series: Q.	1.00	3.00	7.50
	f. 1.9.1943. Series: R.	1.00	3.50	10.00
	g. 17.1.1945. Series: S-Z.	1.00	3.50	10.00
	h. 14.8.1946. Series: AA-AK.	1.00	3.00	8.00
	i. 3.9.1947. Series: AL-AZ.	1.00	3.00	7.00
	j. 22.12.1948. Series: BA-BT.	1.00	3.00	7.00
	k. 23.11.1949. Series: BU-BV.	.50	2.00	6.00
	l. 26.7.1950. Series: BY-CB.	.50	2.00	5.00
	s. Specimen, punched hole cancelled.	—	—	175.

35	10 Pesos	VG	VF	UNC
	1937-42. Black on m/c unpt. Portr. E. Ruiz de Velazquez at r. Middle sign. title: *INTERVENTOR DEL GOBIERNO.* Road to Guanajuato at ctr. on back. Printed date.			
	a. 22.9.1937. Series: M.	4.00	7.50	60.00
	b. 26.6.1940. Series: N.	2.50	6.00	18.00
	c. 12.11.1941. Series: O.	1.50	5.00	15.00
	d. 25.11.1942. Series: P.	1.50	5.00	15.00
	s. Specimen, punched hole cancelled.	—	—	175.

36	20 Pesos	VG	VF	UNC
	21.4.1937. Black on m/c unpt. Portr. J. Ortiz de Dominguez at l. Middle sign. title: *INTERVENTOR DEL GOBIERNO.* Back olive-green; Federal palace courtyard at ctr., lg. seal. Printed date. Series: L.	8.00	35.00	110.

37	50 Pesos	Good	Fine	XF
	1937; 1940. Purple, green, brown and m/c. Portr. I. Zaragoza at r. View of Ixtaccihuatl-Popocatepetl and volcanoes on back.			
	a. 21.4.1937. Series: L.	150.	250.	450.
	b. 26.6.1940. Series: N.	175.	300.	600.

1940-43 ISSUE

#38-45 sign. varieties. Printer: ABNC.

38	1 Peso	VG	VF	UNC
	1943-48. Like #28 but w/o "No" above serial #. *UNO* in background under sign. at l. and r.			
	a. 7.7.1943. Series: L-Q.	.50	3.00	6.00
	b. 1.9.1943. Series: R.	3.00	10.00	45.00
	c. 17.1.1945. Series: S-Z.	.50	4.00	20.00
	d. 12.5.1948. Series: AA-AJ.	.25	2.00	6.00
39	10 Pesos			
	1943-45. Black on m/c unpt. Like #35 but *MEXICO D.F.* and printed dates higher.			
	a. 7.4.1943. Series: Q.	1.50	3.50	10.00
	b. 1.9.1943. Series: R.	1.50	5.00	20.00
	c. 17.1.1945. Series: S-Z.	1.50	4.00	15.00

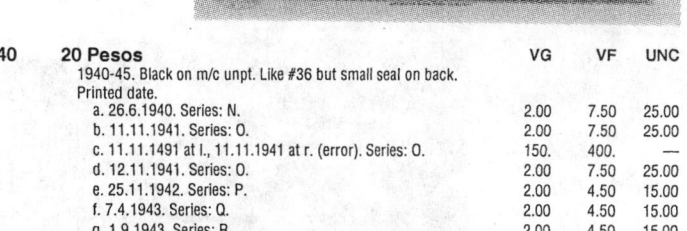

40	20 Pesos	VG	VF	UNC
	1940-45. Black on m/c unpt. Like #36 but small seal on back. Printed date.			
	a. 26.6.1940. Series: N.	2.00	7.50	25.00
	b. 11.11.1941. Series: O.	2.00	7.50	25.00
	c. 11.11.1491 at l., 11.11.1941 at r. (error). Series: O.	150.	400.	—
	d. 12.11.1941. Series: O.	2.00	7.50	25.00
	e. 25.11.1942. Series: P.	2.00	4.50	15.00
	f. 7.4.1943. Series: Q.	2.00	4.50	15.00
	g. 1.9.1943. Series: R.	2.00	4.50	15.00
	h. 17.1.1945. Series: S-Z.	2.00	4.50	15.00
	s. Specimen, punched hole cancelled.	—	—	175.

		VG	VF	UNC
41	**50 Pesos** 1941-45. Blue on m/c unpt. Portr. I. de Allende at l. Middle sign. title: *INTERVENTOR DEL GOBIERNO.* Back blue; Statue of Victory at ctr. Printed date.			
	a. 12.11.1941. Series: O; P.	5.00	30.00	125.
	b. 7.4.1943. Series Q.	3.00	10.00	60.00
	c. 25.10.1944. Series: R.	2.50	7.50	40.00
	d. 17.1.1945. Series: S-Z.	2.00	5.00	25.00
	s. Specimen, punched hole cancelled.	—	—	175.

		VG	VF	UNC
42	**100 Pesos** 1940-42. Black on m/c unpt. Like #31. Portr. F. I. Madero at r. Back purple; Bank of Mexico bldg. at ctr. Small seal.			
	a. 26.6.1940. Series: N.	35.00	60.00	140.
	b. 12.11.1941. Series: O.	35.00	60.00	140.
	c. 25.11.1942. Series: P.	35.00	60.00	140.
43	**500 Pesos** 1940-43. Black on m/c unpt. Like #32. Printed dates. Back green; miner's palace and small seal on back.			
	a. 26.6.1940. Series: N.	50.00	175.	350.
	b. 11.11.1941. Series: O.	25.00	100.	250.
	c. 25.11.1942. Series: P.	25.00	100.	250.
	d. 7.4.1943. Series: Q.	25.00	100.	250.
	e. 1.9.1943. Series: R.	25.00	100.	250.
	s. Specimen, punched hole cancelled.	—	—	225.

		VG	VF	UNC
44	**1000 Pesos** 1941-45. Black on m/c unpt. Cuauhtemoc at l. Like #33. Back dk. brown; El Castillo Chichen-itza at ctr. on back. Printed dates.			
	a. 11.11.1941. Series: O.	75.00	175.	350.
	b. 25.11.1942. Series: P.	25.00	100.	250.
	c. 7.4.1943. Series: Q.	25.00	100.	250.
	d. 20.11.1945. Series: R.	25.00	100.	250.
	s. Specimen, punched hole cancelled.	—	—	175.

		VG	VF	UNC
45	**10,000 Pesos** 1943-53. Purple on m/c unpt. Portr. M. Romero at l. Government palace on back.			
	a. 1.9.1943. Series R.	450.	850.	—
	b. 27.12.1950. Series: CS.	350.	600.	—
	c. 19.1.1953. Series: DL.	600.	900.	—
	s. Specimen, punched hole cancelled.	—	—	350.

Note: For 10,000 Pesos like #45 but dated 1978, see #72 in Volume 3.

		VG	VF	UNC
A45	**10,000 Pesos** ND (ca.1942). Purple on m/c unpt. Like #45, but sign. title: *INTERVENTOR DEL GOBIERNO* at ctr. Specimen.	—	—	—

1945-48 ISSUE

#46-52 sign. varieties. Printer: ABNC.

		VG	VF	UNC
46	**1 Peso** 1948; 1950. Like #38 but *EL* and *S.A.* added to *BANCO DE MEXICO* on face. *S.A.* added on back.			
	a. 22.12.1948. Series: BA-BJ.	.25	1.00	6.00
	b. 26.7.1950. Series: BY-CR.	.25	1.00	4.00

		VG	VF	UNC
47	**10 Pesos** 1946-50. Black on m/c unpt. Like #39 but middle sign. title: *INTERVENTOR DE LA COM. NAC. BANCARIA.* Engraved dates.			
	a. 14.8.1946. Series: AA-AJ.	1.00	3.00	9.00
	b. 3.9.1947. Series: AK-AZ.	1.00	3.00	9.00
	c. 22.12.1948. Series: BA-BJ.	1.00	3.00	9.00
	d. 23.11.1949. Series: BU.	.25	3.00	9.00
	e. 26.7.1950. Series: BY, BZ.	.25	3.00	9.00
48	**20 Pesos** 22.12.1948. Black on m/c unpt. Like #40 but middle sign. title: *INTERVENTOR DE LA COM. NAC. BANCARIA.* Engraved date. Series: BA-BE.	1.00	4.00	15.00

1945-51 ISSUE

#49-53 sign. varieties. Printer: ABNC.

		VG	VF	UNC
49	**50 Pesos** 1948-72. Blue on m/c unpt.Like #41 but middle sign. title: *INTERVENTOR DE LA COM. NAC. BANCARIA.* Engraved dates. Back blue; Independence Monument at ctr.			
	a. 22.12.1948. Black series letters. Series: BA-BD.	3.00	6.00	15.00
	b. 23.11.1949. Series: BU-BX.	3.00	6.00	15.00
	c. 26.7.1950. Series: BY-CF.	3.00	5.00	15.00
	d. 27.12.1950. Series: CS-DH.	3.00	5.00	15.00
	e. 19.1.1953. Series: DK-DV.	2.00	4.00	15.00
	f. 10.2.1954. Series: DW-EE.	2.00	4.00	15.00
	g. 8.9.1954. Series: EF-FF.	2.00	4.00	15.00
	h. 11.1.1956. Series: FK-FV.	2.00	4.00	15.00
	i. 19.6.1957. Series: FW-GP.	2.00	4.00	15.00
	j. 20.8.1958. Series: HC-HR.	2.00	4.00	15.00
	k. 18.3.1959. 2 red series letters. Series: HS-IP.	2.00	4.00	15.00
	l. 20.5.1959. Series: IQ-JN.	2.00	4.00	15.00
	m. 25.1.1961. Series: JO-LB.	1.00	3.00	8.00
	n. 8.11.1961. Series: LC-AID.	1.00	3.00	8.00

49

	VG	VF	UNC
o. 24.4.1963. Series: AIE-BAP.	1.00	3.00	6.00
p. 17.2.1965. Series: BAQ-BCD.	1.00	2.50	6.00
q. 10.5.1967. Series: BCY-BEN.	1.00	2.50	6.00
r. 19.11.1969. Series: BGK-BIC.	1.00	2.50	4.00
s. 22.7.1970. Series: BIG-BKN.	1.00	2.50	4.00
t. 27.6.1972. Series: BLI-BMG.	1.00	2.50	3.00
u. 29.12.1972. Series: BMO-BRB.	1.00	2.00	3.00
v. Specimen, punched hole cancelled.	—	—	135.

50 **100 Pesos**

17.1.1945. Brown on m/c unpt. Portr. M. Hidalgo at l., series letters above serial #. Middle sign. title: *INTERVENTOR DEL GOBIERNO.* Printed date. Back olive-green. Coin w/national coat-of-arms at ctr. Series: S-Z.

	VG	VF	UNC
a. Issued note.	5.00	15.00	70.00
s. Specimen, punched hole cancelled.	—	—	200.

1 **500 Pesos**

1948-78. Black on m/c unpt. Like #43 but w/o *No.* above serial #. Middle sign. title: *INTERVENTOR DE LA COM. NAC. BANCARIA.* Back green; Palace of Mining at ctr.

	VG	VF	UNC
a. 22.12.1948. Series: BA.	10.00	40.00	125.
b. 27.12.1950. Series: CS; CT.	4.00	12.00	30.00
c. 3.12.1951. Series: DI; DJ.	4.00	12.00	30.00
d. 19.1.1953. Series: DK-DN.	4.00	12.00	30.00
e. 31.8.1955. Series: FG-FJ.	4.00	12.00	30.00
f. 11.1.1956. Series: FK-FL.	4.00	12.00	30.00
g. 19.6.1957. Series: FW-GB.	4.00	12.00	30.00
h. 20.8.1958. Series: HC-HH.	4.00	12.00	30.00
i. 18.3.1959. Series: HS-HX.	4.00	12.00	30.00
j. 20.5.1959. Series: IQ-IV.	4.00	12.00	30.00
k. 25.1.1961. Series: JO-JT.	3.00	8.00	25.00
l. 8.11.1961. Series: LC-MP.	2.00	7.00	20.00
m. 17.2.1965. Series: BAQ-BCN.	4.00	12.00	25.00
n. 24.3.1971. Series: BKO-BKT.	2.50	5.00	12.50
o. 27.6.1972. Series: BLI-BLT.	2.50	5.00	12.50
p. 29.12.1972. Series: BNG-BNP.	2.50	5.00	12.50
q. 18.7.1973. Series: BUY-BWB.	1.50	5.00	12.50
r. 2.8.1974. Series: BXV-BZI.	1.50	3.50	10.00
s. 18.2.1977. Series: BZJ-CCK.	1.00	3.50	10.00
t. 18.1.1978. Series: CCL-CDY.	1.00	3.50	8.50

1000 Pesos

1948-77. Black on m/c unpt. Like #44 but middle sign. title: *INTERVENTOR DE LA COM. NAC. BANCARIA.* Back brown; Chichen Itza pyramid at ctr.

	VG	VF	UNC
a. 22.12.1948. Series: BA.	5.00	15.00	60.00
b. 23.11.1949. Series: BU.	5.00	15.00	60.00
c. 27.12.1950. Series: CS.	5.00	15.00	60.00
d. 3.12.1951. Series: DI; DJ.	5.00	15.00	60.00
e. 19.1.1953. Series: DK; DL.	5.00	15.00	60.00
f. 31.8.1955. Series: FG; FH.	5.00	15.00	60.00

52

	VG	VF	UNC
g. 11.1.1956. Series: FK; FL.	5.00	15.00	60.00
h. 19.6.1957. Series: FW-FZ.	5.00	15.00	60.00
i. 20.8.1958. Series: HC-HE.	5.00	15.00	60.00
j. 18.3.1959. Series: HS-HU.	5.00	15.00	60.00
k. 20.5.1959. Series: IQ-IS.	5.00	15.00	60.00
l. 25.1.1961. Series: JO-JQ.	5.00	15.00	60.00
m. 8.11.1961. Series: LC-LV.	3.00	10.00	20.00
n. 17.2.1965. Series: BAQ-BCN.	2.00	8.00	15.00
o. 24.3.1971. Series: BKO-BKT.	2.00	6.00	10.00
p. 27.6.1972. Series: BLI-BLM.	2.00	6.00	10.00
q. 29.12.1972. Series: BNG-BNK.	1.00	3.00	5.00
r. 18.7.1973. Series: BUY-BWB.	2.00	6.00	10.00
s. 2.8.1974. Series: BXV-BYY.	1.00	5.00	8.00
t. 18.2.1977. Series: BZJ-CBQ.	1.00	5.00	8.00
x. Error: *EERIE HD* rather than SERIE at left.	25.00	45.00	85.00

1950; 1951 ISSUE

#53-55 sign. varieties. Printer: ABNC.

53 **10 Pesos**

1951; 1953. Black on m/c unpt. Like #47 but w/o *No.* above serial #.

	VG	VF	UNC
a. 3.12.1951. Series: DI, DJ.	.25	2.00	5.00
b. 19.1.1953. Series: DK-DL.	.25	2.00	5.00

1950 ISSUE

#54 and 55 sign. varieties. Printer: ABNC.

54 **20 Pesos**

1950-70. Black on m/c unpt. Like #48 but w/o *No.* above serial #. Back olive-green; Federal Palace courtyard at ctr.

	VG	VF	UNC
a. 27.12.1950. Black series letters. Series: CS; CT.	1.00	3.00	15.00
b. 19.1.1953. Series: DK.	1.00	3.00	15.00
c. 10.2.1954. Red series letters. Series: DW.	1.00	2.00	10.00
d. 11.1.1956. Series: FK.	1.00	2.00	10.00
e. 10.6.1957. Series: FW.	1.00	2.00	10.00
f. 20.8.1958. Series: HC, HD.	1.00	2.00	10.00
g. 18.3.1959. Series: HS, HT.	1.00	2.00	10.00
h. 20.5.1959. Series: IQ, IR.	1.00	2.00	10.00
i. 25.1.1961. Series: JO, JP.	.50	1.50	10.00
j. 8.11.1961. Series: LC-LG.	.50	1.50	10.00
k. 24.4.1963. Series: AIE-AIH.	.50	1.50	5.00
l. 17.2.1965. Series: BAQ-BAV.	.50	1.50	5.00
m. 10.5.1967. Series: BCY-BDB.	.50	1.50	5.00
n. 27.8.1969. Series: BGA; BGB.	.50	1.50	5.00
o. 18.3.1970. Series: BID-BIF.	.50	1.50	5.00
p. 22.7.1970. Series: BIG-BIK.	.50	1.50	5.00
s. Specimen, punched hole cancelled.	—	Unc	135.

55 **100 Pesos**

1950-61. Brown on m/c unpt. Like #50 but middle sign. title: *INTERVENTOR DE LA COM. NAC. BANCARIA.* Engraved dates. Back olive-green; coin w/national seal at ctr.

	VG	VF	UNC
a. 27.12.1950. Black series letters. Series: CS-CZ.	4.00	8.00	30.00
b. 19.1.1953. Series: DK-DP.	2.00	7.00	25.00
c. 10.2.1954. Series: DW-DZ.	2.00	7.00	25.00
d. 8.9.1954. Series: EI-ET.	2.00	7.00	25.00
e. 11.1.1956. Series: FK-FV.	2.00	7.00	25.00
f. 19.6.1957. Series: FW-GH.	2.00	7.00	25.00
g. 20.8.1958. Series: HC-HR.	2.00	7.00	25.00
h. 18.3.1959. Series: HS-IH.	2.00	7.00	25.00
i. 20.5.1959. Series: IQ-JF.	2.00	7.00	25.00
j. 25.1.1961. Series: JO-KL.	2.00	7.00	25.00

1953; 1954 ISSUE

#56-58 sign. varieties. Printer: ABNC.

56 **1 Peso**

1954. Like #46 but series letters in red at lower l. and r.

	VG	VF	UNC
a. 10.2.1954. Series: DW-EF.	.25	1.00	4.00
b. 8.9.1954. Series: EI-FB.	.25	1.00	4.00

57 **5 Pesos**

1953-54. Black on m/c unpt. Like #34 but w/o *No.* above serial #, w/series letters lower.

	VG	VF	UNC
a. 19.1.1953. Series: DK-DN.	.50	2.00	5.00
b. 10.2.1954. Series: DW-DZ.	.25	1.00	4.00
c. 8.9.1954. Series: EI-EP.	.25	1.00	4.00

1954 ISSUE

		VG	VF	UNC
58	**10 Pesos**			
	1954-67. Black on m/c unpt. Portr. E. Ruiz de Velazquez at r. Like #53 but w/text: *MEXICO D.F.* above series letters. Back brown; road to Guanajuato at ctr. Printer: ABNC.			
	a. 10.2.1954. Series: DW, DX.	.50	1.50	5.00
	b. 8.9.1954. Series: EI-EN.	.50	1.50	5.00
	c. 19.6.1957. Series: FW, FX.	.50	1.50	5.00
	d. 24.7.1957. Series: GQ.	.50	1.50	5.00
	e. 20.8.1958. Series: HC-HF.	.25	1.50	6.00
	f. 18.3.1959. Series: HS-HU.	.25	1.00	5.00
	g. 20.5.1959. Series: IQ-IS.	.25	1.00	4.00
	h. 25.1.1961. Series: JO-JT.	.25	1.00	4.00
	i. 8.11.1961. Series: LC-LV.	.25	1.00	4.00
	j. 24.4.1963. Series: AIE-AIT.	.25	1.00	3.00
	k. 17.2.1965. Series: BAQ-BAX.	.25	1.00	3.00
	l. 10.5.1967. Series: BCY-BDA.	.25	1.00	3.00
	s. Specimen, punched hole cancelled.	—	Unc	150.

1957; 1961 ISSUE

#59-61 printer: ABNC.

		VG	VF	UNC
59	**1 Peso**			
	1957-70. Black on m/c unpt. Aztec calendar stone at ctr. Like #56 but w/text: *MEXICO D.F.* added above date at lower l. Back red, Independence monument at ctr.			
	a. 19.6.1957. Series: FW-GF.	.10	1.00	4.50
	b. Deleted.	—	—	—
	c. 4.12.1957. Series: GS-HB.	.10	1.00	4.50
	d. 20.8.1958. Series: HC-HL.	.10	.75	2.50
	e. 18.3.1959. Series: HS-IB.	.10	.50	2.50
	f. 20.5.1959. Series: IQ-IZ.	.10	.50	2.50
	g. 25.1.1961. Series: JO-KC.	.10	.25	2.00
	h. 8.11.1961. Series: LC; LD.	.10	.50	2.00
	i. 9.6.1965. Series: BCO-BCX.	.10	.25	2.00
	j. 10.5.1967. Series: BCY-BEB.	.10	.25	1.00
	k. 27.8.1969. Series: BGA-BGJ.	.10	.25	1.00
	l. 22.7.1970. Series: BIG-BIP.	.10	.20	1.00
	s. Specimen.	—	—	—

		VG	VF	UNC
60	**5 Pesos**			
	1957-70. Black on m/c unpt. Portr. gypsy at ctr. Like #57 but w/Text: *MEXICO D.F.* before date. Back gray; Independence Monument at ctr.			
	a. 19.6.1957. Series: FW, FX.	.25	2.00	7.00
	b. 24.7.1957. Series: GQ, GR.	.25	2.00	7.00
	c. 20.8.1958. Series: HC-HJ.	.25	1.50	6.00
	d. 18.3.1959. Series: HS-HV.	.25	1.50	6.00
	e. 20.5.1959. Series: IQ-IT.	.25	1.50	6.00
	f. 25.1.1961. Series: JO-JV.	.15	.50	4.00
	g. 8.11.1961. Series: LC-MP.	.15	.50	3.00
	h. 24.4.1963. Series: AIE-AJJ.	.15	.50	2.50
	i. 27.8.1969. Series BGJ.	.15	.50	2.50
	j. 19.11.1969. Series: BGK-BGT.	.15	.50	2.50
	k. 22.7.1970. Series: BIG-BII.	.15	.50	2.50

		VG	VF	UNC
61	**100 Pesos**			
	1961-73. Brown on m/c unpt. Like #55 but series letters below serial #.			
	a. 8.11.1961. Red series letters. Series: LE-ZZ; AAA-AEG.	2.00	5.00	12.50
	b. 24.4.1963. Series: AIK-AUG.	2.00	5.00	12.50
	c. 17.2.1965. Series: BAQ-BCD.	1.00	3.00	8.00
	d. 10.5.1967. Series: BCY-BFZ.	1.00	3.00	8.00
	e. 22.7.1970. Series: BIO-BJK.	1.00	3.00	8.00
	f. 24.3.1971. Series: BKP-BLH.	1.00	3.00	8.00
	g. 27.6.1972. Series: BLI-BNF.	1.00	3.00	8.00
	h. 29.12.1972. Series: BNG-BUX.	.50	1.50	5.00
	i. 18.7.1973. Series: BUY-BXU.	.50	1.50	5.00

The area of Moldova is bordered in the north, east, and south by the Ukraine and on the west by Romania.

The historical Romanian principality of Moldova was established in the 14th century. It fell under Turkish suzerainty in the 16th century. From 1812 to 1918, Russians occupied the eastern portion of Moldova which they named Bessarabia. In March 1918, the Bessarabian legislature voted in favor of reunification with Romania.

At the Paris Peace Conference of 1920, the union was officially recognized by several ıations, but the new Soviet government did not accept the union. In 1924, to pressure Romania, a Aoldovan Autonomous Soviet Socialist Republic (A.S.S.R.) was established within the USSR on ıe border, consisting of a strip extending east of the Dniester River. Today it is Transnistria (see country listing).

Soviet forces reoccupied the region in June 1940, and the Moldovan S.S.R. was proclaimed. Transniestria was transferred to the new republic. Ukrainian S.S.R. obtained possession of the outhern part of Bessarabia. The region was liberated by the Romanian army in 1941. The Soviets econquered the territory in 1944. A declaration of independence was adopted in June 1990 and ıe area was renamed Moldova. It became an independent republic in August 1991. In December 991, Moldova became a member of the Commonwealth of Independent States.

ΛONETARY SYSTEM:

3 Ducati = 100 Lei
100 Rubles = 1000 Cupon, 1992
1 Leu = 1000 Cupon, 1993-

REPUBLIC

BANCA NATIONALA A MOLDAVEI

1857 ISSUE

		Good	Fine	XF
A1	**3 Ducats = 100 Lei** 1.9.1857. Arms at top ctr. Printer: G&D. Rare.	—	—	—

CEMITETUL NATIONAL REVOLUTIONAR ROMAN

853 REVOLUTIONARY ISSUE

		Good	Fine	XF
A2	**10 Ducati** 1853. Eagle at top ctr. Rare.	—	—	—

ote: For later issues see Moldova in Volume 3, Modern Issues.

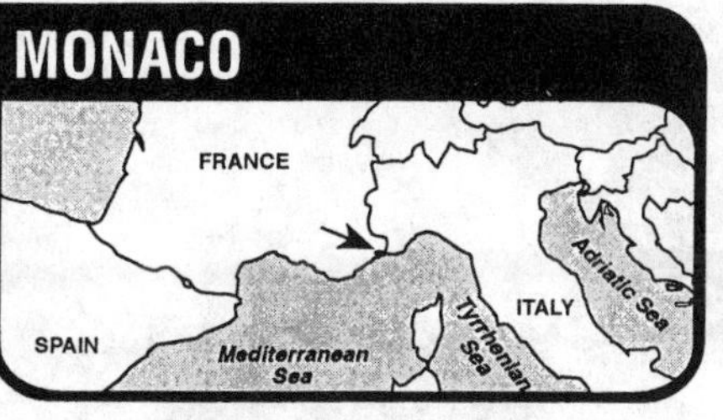

The Principality of Monaco, located on the Mediterranean coast nine miles off Nice, has an area of 0.6 sq. mi. (1.49 sq. km.) and a population of 32,000. Capital: Monaco-Ville. The economy is d on tourism and the manufacture of perfumes and liqueurs. Monaco derives most of its revenue from a tobacco monopoly, the sale of postage stamps for philatelic purpose, and the gambling tables of Monte Carlo Casino.

Monaco derived its name from "Monoikos", the Greek surname for Hercules, the mythological strong man in whose honor the Greeks erected a temple on the Monacan headland. Probably founded by the Phoenicians, Monaco has been ruled by the Genoa Grimaldi family since 1297 - Prince Rainier III, the present and 30th monarch of Monaco, is still of that line - except for a period during the French Revolution and the First Republic when it was annexed to France. Since 1865, Monaco has maintained a customs union with France which guarantees its privileged position as long as the royal male line remains intact. Under the the new constitution proclaimed on December 17, 1962, the Prince shares his power with an 18-member unicameral National Council.

RULERS:

Albert I, 1889-1922
Louis II, 1922-1949
Rainier III, 1949-

MONETARY SYSTEM:

1 Franc = 100 Centimes

PRINCIPALITY

PRINCIPAUTÉ DE MONACO

1920 EMERGENCY ISSUES

		VG	VF	UNC
1	**25 Centimes** 16.3.(20.3) 1920. (Dated 1920.) Brown. First issue.			
	a. W/o embossed arms.	10.00	40.00	150.
	b. Embossed arms in 17mm stamp.	15.00	60.00	200.
	c. Embossed arms in 22mm stamp.	10.00	40.00	150.
2	**25 Centimes** 16.3.(20.3) 1920. (Dated 1921.) Blue-violet.			
	a. W/o embossed arms.	10.00	30.00	90.00
	b. Embossed arms in 17mm stamp.	10.00	40.00	150.
	c. Embossed arms in 22mm stamp.	12.50	50.00	160.

		VG	VF	UNC
3	**50 Centimes** 16.3.(20.3) 1920. (Issued 28.4.1920.) Blue-gray. Series A-H.			
	a. Issued note.	10.00	40.00	175.
	r. Remainder w/o serial #. Series E.	—	—	60.00

		VG	VF	UNC
4	**1 Franc** 16.3.(20.3) 1920. (Issued 28.4.1920.) Brown. First issue. Lettered cartouche.			
	a. Series A.	10.00	60.00	200.
	b. Series B; C.	75.00	200.	325.

		VG	VF	UNC
5	**1 Franc** 16.3.(20.3) 1920. (Issued 28.4.1920.) Blue-gray and brown. Second issue. Plain cartouche. Series A-E.	10.00	40.00	135.

MONGOLIA

The State of Mongolia, a landlocked country in central Asia between Russia and the Peoples Republic of China, has an area of 604,247 sq. mi. (1,565,000 sq. km.) and a population of 2.74 million. Capital: Ulan Bator. Animal herds and flocks are the chief economic asset. Wool, cattle, butter, meat and hides are exported.

Mongolia (often referred to as Outer Mongolia), one of the world's oldest countries, attained its greatest power in the 13th century when Genghis Khan and his successors conquered all of China and extended their influence westward as far as Hungary and Poland. The empire dissolved in later centuries and in 1691 was brought under suzerainty of the Manchus, who had conquered China in 1644. Mongolia, with the support of Russia, proclaimed its independence from China on March 13, 1921, when the Provisional Peoples Government was established. Later, on November 26, 1924, the government proclaimed the Mongolian Peoples Republic. Opposition to the communist party developed in late 1989 and on March 12, 1990 and the new State of Mongolia was organized.

RULERS:
Chinese to 1921

MONETARY SYSTEM:
1 Tugrik (Tukhrik) = 100 Mongo

PROVISIONAL PEOPLE'S GOVERNMENT

MONGOLIAN GOVERNMENT'S TREASURE

1921 ISSUE

6% Provisionary Obligation.

#A1-A4 payable on or after November 20, 1921.

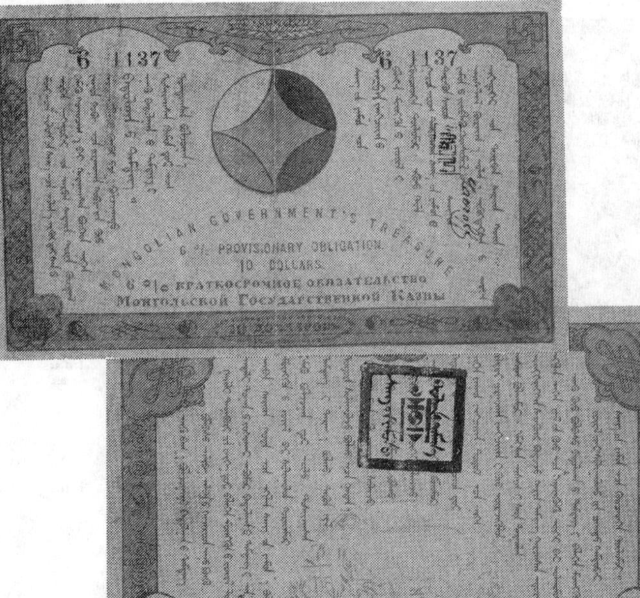

		Good	Fine	X
A1	**10 Dollars** 20.11.1921. Lt. blue w/red-brown text. White, blue, pink and yellow arms at upper ctr. Emblem at top ctr., ram at bottom ctr. on back.	450.	1500.	
A2	**25 Dollars** 21.11.1921. Red and blue. Cow at bottom ctr. on back.	450.	1600.	

		Good	Fine	XF
A3	**50 Dollars** 20.11.1921. Gold and red frame, red text. White, blue, pink and yellow arms at upper ctr. Back dk. blue frame w/red text; emblem at top ctr., horse at bottom ctr.	500.	1800.	—
A4	**100 Dollars** 20.11.1921. Yellow and red. Camel at bottom ctr. on back.	600.	2000.	—

STATE TREASURY NOTES

1924 ISSUE

#1-6 m/c. Ornamental. (Not issued).

		VG	VF	UNC
1	**50 Cents** 1924. Yellow and m/c.			
	r. Remainder.	—	—	185.
	s. Specimen perforated: ОБРАЗЕЦЪ.	—	—	450.

		VG	VF	UNC
2	**1 Dollar** 1924. Blue and m/c.			
	r. Remainder.	—	—	200.
	s. Specimen perforated: ОБРАЗЕЦЪ.	—	—	500.
3	**3 Dollars** 1924. Brown and m/c.			
	r. Remainder.	—	—	225.
	s. Specimen perforated: ОБРАЗЕЦЪ.	—	—	550.
4	**5 Dollars** 1924. Green and m/c.			
	r. Remainder.	—	—	250.
	s. Specimen perforated: ОБРАЗЕЦЪ.	—	—	600.

		VG	VF	UNC
5	**10 Dollars** 1924. Lilac and m/c.			
	r. Remainder.	—	—	275.
	s. Specimen perforated: ОБРАЗЕЦЪ.	—	—	650.
6	**25 Dollars** 1924. Blue and m/c.			
	r. Remainder.	—	—	325.
	s. Specimen perforated: ОБРАЗЕЦЪ.	—	—	750.

COMMERCIAL AND INDUSTRIAL BANK

1925 FIRST ISSUE

A7-A10 "Soembo" arms at ctr., perforated: *1.12.1925* vertically at l. Serial # prefix *A*.

		Good	Fine	XF
A7	**1 Tugrik** 1.12.1925. Yellow-brown.	15.00	60.00	200.
A8	**2 Tugrik** 1.12.1925; 8.12.1925. Green.	20.00	85.00	250.

A8 also known with perforation at l. and r.

		Good	Fine	XF
A9	**5 Tugrik** 1.12.1925. Blue and m/c. Back red.	25.00	100.	350.
A10	**10 Tugrik** 1.12.1925. Red and m/c. Back green and brown.	35.00	175.	450.

1925 SECOND ISSUE

#7-13 w/o perforated date.

		Good	Fine	XF
7	**1 Tugrik** 1925. Yellow-brown.	7.50	45.00	100.

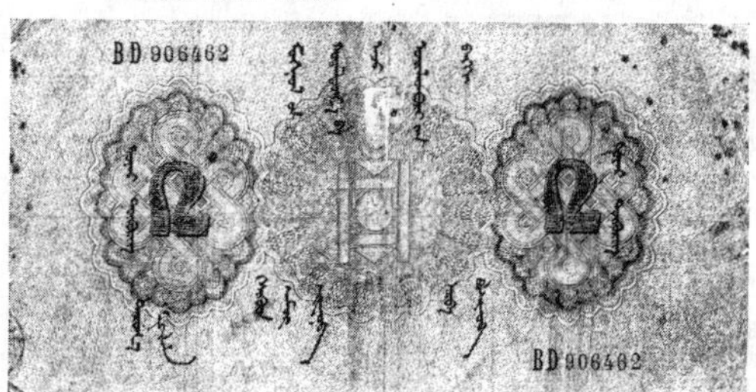

		Good	Fine	XF
8	**2 Tugrik** 1925. Green.	12.50	75.00	175.
9	**5 Tugrik** 1925. Blue and m/c. Back red-brown.	15.00	80.00	250.

		Good	Fine	XF
10	**10 Tugrik** 1925. Red and m/c. Back green and brown.	25.00	90.00	275.
11	**25 Tugrik** 1925. Brown and m/c. Back green.	30.00	125.	375.
12	**50 Tugrik** 1925. Green and m/c. Back brown.	35.00	175.	650.
13	**100 Tugrik** 1925. Blue and red.	75.00	325.	850.

MONGOLIAN PEOPLES REPUBLIC

COMMERCIAL AND INDUSTRIAL BANK

1939 ISSUE

#14-20 portr. Sukhe-Bataar at r., "Soembo" arms at l. Old Mongolian text.

		Good	Fine	XF
14	**1 Tugrik** 1939. Brown.	3.50	15.00	60.00
15	**3 Tugrik** 1939. Green.	5.00	25.00	100.

		Good	Fine	XF
16	**5 Tugrik** 1939. Blue.	7.50	35.00	125.
17	**10 Tugrik** 1939. Red.	15.00	45.00	150.

		Good	Fine	XF
18	**25 Tugrik** 1939. Gray-brown.	15.00	65.00	200.
19	**50 Tugrik** 1939. Green-brown.	35.00	80.00	275.
20	**100 Tugrik** 1939. Lt. blue.	75.00	175.	475.

1941 ISSUE

#21-27 portr. Sukhe-Bataar at r., Socialist arms at l. Old and new Mongolian (resembles Russian) text.

		Good	Fine	XF
21	**1 Tugrik** 1941. Brown.	3.00	10.00	55.00
22	**3 Tugrik** 1941. Green.	5.00	15.00	85.00
23	**5 Tugrik** 1941. Blue.	7.00	20.00	110.

		Good	Fine	XF
24	**10 Tugrik** 1941. Red.	12.00	35.00	150.
25	**25 Tugrik** 1941. Gray-brown.	15.00	55.00	185.

		Good	Fine	XF
26	**50 Tugrik** 1941. Green-brown.	40.00	75.00	250.
27	**100 Tugrik** 1941. Lt. blue.	60.00	125.	375.

УЛСЫН БАНК - STATE BANK

1955 ISSUE

#28-34 portr. Sukhe-Bataar at r., Socialist arms at l. New Mongolian text. Wmk: Symbol repeated.

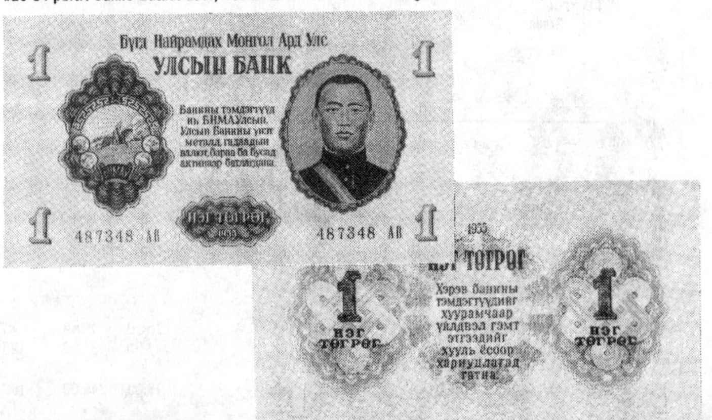

		VG	VF	UNC
28	**1 Tugrik** 1955. Black and brown on pale brown-orange and m/c unpt. Back dk. brown text on pale brown-orange and m/c unpt.	.15	.50	1.50
29	**3 Tugrik** 1955. Black on lt. green and m/c unpt. Back dk. green text on lt. green and m/c unpt.	.20	.75	2.00

		VG	VF	UNC
30	**5 Tugrik** 1955. Black on lt. blue and m/c unpt. Back blue-black text on lt. blue and m/c unpt.	.25	1.00	3.00
31	**10 Tugrik** 1955. Dp. red and red on pink and m/c unpt. Back dk. brown text on pale orange and m/c unpt.	.50	1.25	3.50

		VG	VF	UNC
32	**25 Tugrik** 1955. Black on lt. blue and m/c unpt. Back dk. brown text on tan and m/c unpt.	.50	1.50	5.00
33	**50 Tugrik** 1955. Black on lt. green and m/c unpt. Back dk. green text on lt. green and m/c unpt.	.75	2.00	7.50

		VG	VF	UNC
34	**100 Tugrik** 1955. Black on lt. blue and m/c unpt. Back black and dk. green text on lt. blue and m/c unpt.	1.00	3.00	10.00

The former independent kingdom of Montenegro, now one of the nominally autonomous federated units of Yugoslavia, was located in southeastern Europe north of Albania. As a kingdom, it had an area of 5,333 sq. mi. (13,812 sq. km.) and a population of about 250,000. The predominantly pastoral kingdom had few industries.

Montenegro became an independent state in 1355 following the breakup of the Serb empire. During the Turkish invasion of Albania and Herzegovina in the 15th century, the Montenegrins moved their capital to the remote mountain village of Cetinje where they maintained their independence through two centuries of intermittent attack, emerging as the only one of the Balkan states not subjugated by the Turks. When World War I began, Montenegro joined with Serbia and was subsequently invaded and occupied by the Austrians. Austria withdrew upon the defeat of the Central Powers, permitting the Serbians to move in and maintain the occupation. Montenegro then joined the kingdom of the Serbs, Croats and Slovenes, which later became Yugoslavia.

RULERS:

Nicholas I, 1910-1918

MONETARY SYSTEM:

1 Perper = 100 Para = 1 Austrian Crown

KINGDOM

TREASURY

1912 ISSUE

#1-6 arms at ctr.

		Good	Fine	XF
1	**1 Perper**			
	1.10.1912. Dk. blue on green paper.			
	a. Issued note.	4.00	20.00	50.00
	b. Handstamped: *CETINJE.*	15.00	50.00	—
	c. Punched hole cancelled.	2.00	7.50	20.00

		Good	Fine	XF
2	**2 Perpera**			
	1.10.1912. Lilac on reddish paper.			
	a. Issued note.	5.00	25.00	60.00
	b. Punched hole cancelled.	3.00	10.00	25.00
3	**5 Perpera**			
	1.10.1912. Dk. green on olive-green paper.			
	a. Issued note.	7.50	35.00	85.00
	b. Punched hole cancelled.	4.00	15.00	35.00

		Good	Fine	XF
4	**10 Perpera**			
	1.10.1912. Red-brown on yellowish paper.			
	a. Issued note.	30.00	100.	200.
	b. Punched hole cancelled.	15.00	45.00	90.00

		Good	Fine	XF
5	**50 Perpera**			
	1.10.1912. Blue on brown unpt. Reddish paper.			
	a. Issued note.	200.	600.	1200.
	b. Punched hole cancelled.	100.	300.	750.
6	**100 Perpera**			
	1.10.1912. Brown paper.			
	a. Issued note.	300.	800.	1600.
	b. Punched hole cancelled.	200.	500.	1000.

КРАЉЕВИНА ЦРНАГОРА

ROYAL GOVERNMENT

1914 FIRST ISSUE

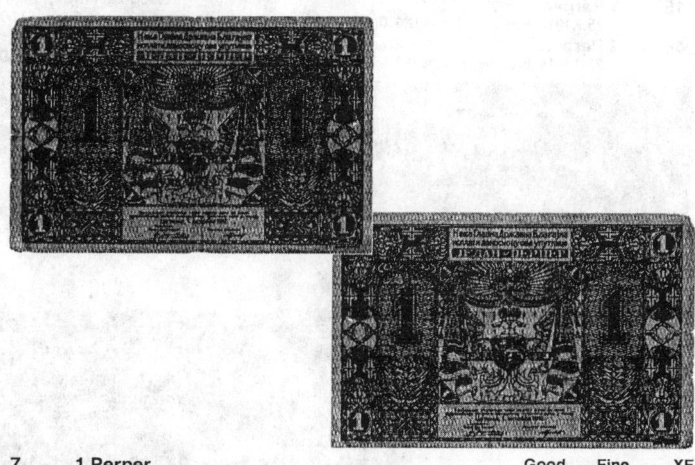

		Good	Fine	XF
7	**1 Perper**			
	25.7.1914 (-old date 1.10.1912). Red ovpt. on #1.			
	a. Issued note.	7.00	25.00	65.00
	b. W/handstamp: *CETINJE.*	10.00	35.00	—
8	**2 Perpera**			
	25.7.1914 (-old date 1.10.1912). Red ovpt. on #2.	15.00	45.00	90.00

1914 SECOND ISSUE

#9-14 arms at ctr. on both sides. All notes 155 x 107mm. Valuations for notes w/o additional handstamps. Cancelled notes worth 30% less.

		Good	Fine	XF
9	**5 Perpera**			
	25.7.1914. Blue.	2.00	10.00	35.00
10	**10 Perpera**			
	25.7.1914. Red.	2.00	12.00	40.00

		Good	Fine	XF
11	**20 Perpera** 25.7.1914. Brown.	4.00	20.00	60.00
12	**50 Perpera** 25.7.1914. Olive.	4.00	30.00	70.00
13	**100 Perpera** 25.7.1914. Lt. brown.	12.00	60.00	150.
14	**100 Perpera** 11.8.1914. Lt. brown. (Probably a trial note only).	—	—	—

1914 Third Issue

#15-21 arms at ctr. on back. Valuations for notes w/o additional handstamps. Cancelled notes worth 30% less.

		Good	Fine	XF
15	**1 Perper** 25.7.1914. Blue w/dk. brown text. Ornamental anchor at top.	1.00	3.00	12.00
16	**2 Perpera** 25.7.1914. Brown w/dk. blue text. Like #15.	1.00	4.50	17.50

		Good	Fine	XF
17	**5 Perpera** 25.7.1914. Red w/black text. Like #15.	2.00	5.00	20.00

		Good	Fine	XF
18	**10 Perpera** 25.7.1914. Blue w/dk. brown text. Arms at upper l.	2.00	5.00	20.00
19	**20 Perpera** 25.7.1914. Brown w/dk. blue text. Like #18.	4.00	10.00	35.00

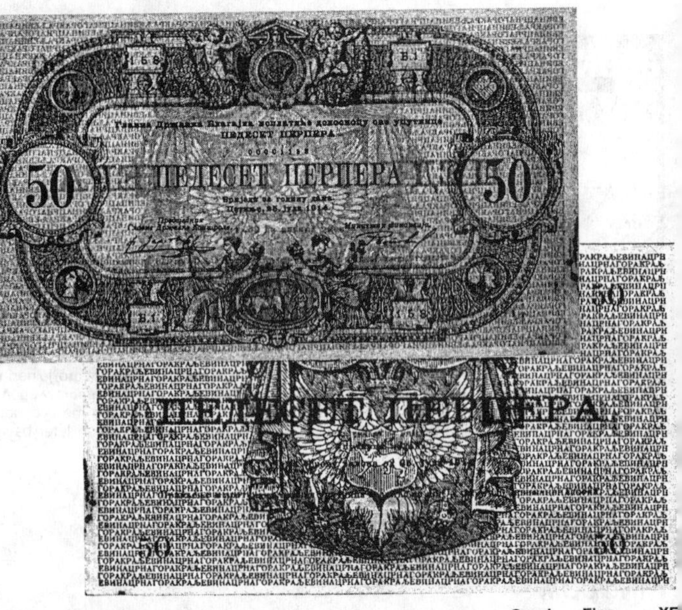

		Good	Fine	XF
20	**50 Perpera** 25.7.1914. Red w/dk. text. Like #21.	8.00	30.00	85.00

		Good	Fine	XF
21	**100 Perpera** 25.7.1914. Blue w/dk. brown text. Angels at top ctr., women seated holding cornucopias at bottom ctr.	12.50	45.00	110

Austrian Occupation - WW I

K.u.K. Militar Generalgouvernement Kreiskommando, 1916-18

Military Government District Command

Ovpt: *K.u.K. MILITAR GENERALGOUVERNEMENT IN MONTENEGRO KREISKOMMANDO* (and place name) handstamped on both sides in black, red or violet.

Cetinje Issue

1916 ND First Provisional Issue

#M1-M5 width of *CETINJE* in ovpt. 11mm.

		Good	Fine	X
M1	**5 Perpera** ND (1916-old date 25.7.1914). Ovpt. on #9.	2.00	8.00	20.C

		Good	Fine	X
M2	**10 Perpera** ND (1916-old date 25.7.1914). Ovpt. on #10.	3.00	10.00	25.

		Good	Fine	XF
M3	**20 Perpera** ND (1916-old date 25.7.1914). Ovpt. on #11.	3.00	10.00	25.00
M4	**50 Perpera** ND (1916-old date 25.7.1914). Ovpt. on #12.	3.00	10.00	25.00
M5	**100 Perpera** ND (1916-old date 25.7.1914). Ovpt. on #13.	6.00	20.00	50.00

1916 ND SECOND PROVISIONAL ISSUE

#M6-M12 width of *CETINJE* in ovpt. 11mm.

		Good	Fine	XF
M6	**1 Perper** ND (1916-old date 25.7.1914). Ovpt. on #15.	2.00	5.00	10.00

		Good	Fine	XF
M7	**2 Perpera** ND (1916-old date 25.7.1914). Ovpt. on #16.	2.00	5.00	10.00
M8	**5 Perpera** ND (1916-old date 25.7.1914). Ovpt. on #17.	2.00	5.00	10.00
M9	**10 Perpera** ND (1916-old date 25.7.1914). Ovpt. on #18.	3.00	9.00	18.00

		Good	Fine	XF
M10	**20 Perpera** ND (1916-old date 25.7.1914). Ovpt. on #19.	3.50	10.00	20.00
M11	**50 Perpera** ND (1916-old date 25.7.1914). Ovpt. on #20.	5.00	15.00	30.00
M12	**100 Perpera** ND (1916-old date 25.7.1914). Ovpt. on #21.	7.00	20.00	40.00

CETINJE ISSUE

1916 ND THIRD PROVISIONAL ISSUE

#M13-M17 width of *CETINJE* in ovpt. 16mm.

		Good	Fine	XF
M13	**5 Perpera** ND (1916-old date 25.7.1914). Ovpt. on #9.	3.50	10.00	20.00

		Good	Fine	XF
M14	**10 Perpera** ND (1916-old date 25.7.1914). Ovpt. on #10.	3.50	10.00	20.00
M15	**20 Perpera** ND (1916-old date 25.7.1914). Ovpt. on #11.	4.00	12.00	25.00

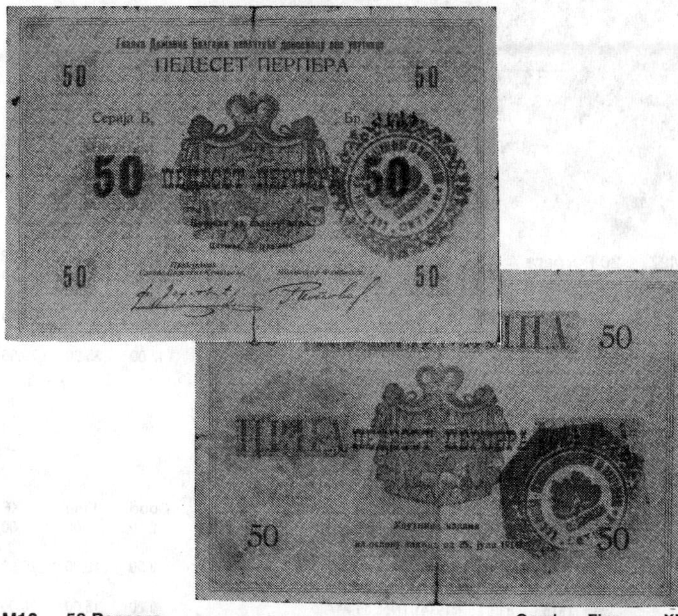

		Good	Fine	XF
M16	**50 Perpera** ND (1916-old date 25.7.1914). Ovpt. on #12.	5.00	15.00	30.00
M17	**100 Perpera** ND (1916-old date 25.7.1914). Ovpt. on #13.	7.00	20.00	40.00

1916 ND FOURTH PROVISIONAL ISSUE

#M18-M24 width of *CETINJE* in ovpt. 16mm.

		Good	Fine	XF
M18	**1 Perper** ND (1916-old date 25.7.1914). Ovpt. on #15.	2.00	5.00	10.00
M19	**2 Perpera** ND (1916-old date 25.7.1914). Ovpt. on #16.	2.00	6.00	12.00
M20	**5 Perpera** ND (1916-old date 25.7.1914). Ovpt. on #17.	3.00	9.00	18.00
M21	**10 Perpera** ND (1916-old date 25.7.1914) Ovpt. on #18.	3.50	10.00	20.00
M22	**20 Perpera** ND (1916-old date 25.7.1914). Ovpt. on #19.	4.00	12.00	25.00
M23	**50 Perpera** ND (1916-old date 25.7.1914). Ovpt. on #20.	5.00	15.00	30.00
M24	**100 Perpera** ND (1916-old date 25.7.1914). Ovpt. on #21.	7.00	20.00	40.00

Note: Examples of ovpt. notes have been observed with a narrow stamp of the place name on one side, a wide stamp of the place name on the other side.

IPEK ISSUE

1916 ND FIRST PROVISIONAL ISSUE

		Good	Fine	XF
M25	**5 Perpera** ND (1916-old date 25.7.1914). Ovpt. on #9.	3.50	10.00	20.00
M26	**10 Perpera** ND (1916-old date 25.7.1914). Ovpt. on #10.	5.00	15.00	30.00

		Good	Fine	XF
M27	20 Perpera ND (1916-old date 25.7.1914). Ovpt. on #11.	7.00	20.00	40.00
M28	50 Perpera ND (1916-old date 25.7.1914). Ovpt. on #12.	10.00	30.00	60.00
M29	100 Perpera ND (1916-old date 25.7.1914). Ovpt. on #13.	12.00	35.00	70.00

Cetinje Issue

Ipek Issue

1916 ND Second Provisional Issue

		Good	Fine	XF
M30	1 Perper ND (1916-old date 25.7.1914). Ovpt. on #15.	2.00	6.00	12.00
M31	2 Perpera ND (1916-old date 25.7.1914). Ovpt. on #16.	3.50	10.00	20.00
M32	5 Perpera ND (1916-old date 25.7.1914). Ovpt. on #17.	5.00	15.00	30.00
M33	10 Perpera ND (1916-old date 25.7.1914). Ovpt. on #18.	7.00	20.00	40.00
M34	20 Perpera ND (1916-old date 25.7.1914). Ovpt. on #19.	10.00	25.00	50.00

		Good	Fine	XF
M35	50 Perpera ND (1916-old date 25.7.1914). Ovpt. on #20.	12.00	30.00	60.00
M36	100 Perpera ND (1916-old date 25.7.1914). Ovpt. on #21.	12.50	35.00	70.00

Kolasin Issue

1916 ND First Provisional Issue

		Good	Fine	XF
M37	5 Perpera ND (1916-old date 25.7.1914). Ovpt. on #9.	4.00	12.00	25.00
M38	10 Perpera ND (1916-old date 25.7.1914). Ovpt. on #10.	5.00	15.00	30.00
M39	20 Perpera ND (1916-old date 25.7.1914). Ovpt. on #11.	10.00	25.00	50.00
M40	50 Perpera ND (1916-old date 25.7.1914). Ovpt. on #12.	12.00	30.00	60.00
M41	100 Perpera ND (1916-old date 25.7.1914). Ovpt. on #13.	25.00	75.00	150.

Kolasin Issue

1916 ND Second Provisional Issue

		Good	Fine	XF
M42	1 Perper ND (1916-old date 25.7.1914). Ovpt. on #15.	2.50	7.50	15.00
M43	2 Perpera ND (1916-old date 25.7.1914). Ovpt. on #16.	4.00	12.00	25.00
M44	5 Perpera ND (1916-old date 25.7.1914). Ovpt. on #17.	5.00	15.00	30.00
M45	10 Perpera ND (1916-old date 25.7.1914). Ovpt. on #18.	6.00	17.50	35.00
M46	20 Perpera ND (1916-old date 25.7.1914). Ovpt. on #19.	8.00	25.00	50.00
M47	50 Perpera ND (1916-old date 25.7.1914). Ovpt. on #20.	12.00	35.00	70.00

		Good	Fine	XF
M48	100 Perpera ND (1916-old date 25.7.1914). Ovpt. on #21.	20.00	60.00	120.

Niksic Issue

1916 ND First Provisional Issue

#M49-M53 width of *NIKSIC* in ovpt. 11mm.

		Good	Fine	XF
M49	5 Perpera ND (1916-old date 25.7.1914). Ovpt. on #9.	6.00	17.50	35.00
M50	10 Perpera ND (1916-old date 25.7.1914). Ovpt. on #10.	12.00	35.00	70.00
M51	20 Perpera ND (1916-old date 25.7.1914). Ovpt. on #11.	15.00	50.00	100.
M52	50 Perpera ND (1916-old date 25.7.1914). Ovpt. on #12.	20.00	60.00	120.
M53	100 Perpera ND (1916-old date 25.7.1914). Ovpt. on #13.	35.00	100.	200.

Niksic Issue

1916 ND Second Provisional Issue

#M54-M60 width of *NIKSIC* in ovpt. 11mm.

		Good	Fine	XF
M54	1 Perper ND (1916-old date 25.7.1914). Ovpt. on #15.	3.50	10.00	20.00
M55	2 Perpera ND (1916-old date 25.7.1914). Ovpt. on #16.	6.00	17.50	35.00
M56	5 Perpera ND (1916-old date 25.7.1914). Ovpt. on #17.	6.00	17.50	35.00
M57	10 Perpera ND (1916-old date 25.7.1914). Ovpt. on #18.	7.50	22.50	45.00
M58	20 Perpera ND (1916-old date 25.7.1914. Ovpt. on #19.	10.00	30.00	60.00

		Good	Fine	XF
M59	50 Perpera ND (1916-old date 25.7.1914). Ovpt. on #20.	12.50	37.50	75.00

		Good	Fine	XF
M60	100 Perpera ND (1916-old date 25.7.1914). Ovpt. on #21.	25.00	75.00	150

Niksic Issue

1916 ND Third Provisional Issue

#M61-M65 width of *NIKSIC* in ovpt. 14mm.

		Good	Fine	XF
M61	5 Perpera ND (1916-old date 25.7.1914). Ovpt. on #9.	5.00	15.00	30.0
M62	10 Perpera ND (1916-old date 25.7.1914). Ovpt. on #10.	7.50	22.50	45.0
M63	20 Perpera ND (1916-old date 25.7.1914). Ovpt. on #11.	10.00	30.00	60.0
M64	50 Perpera ND (1916-old date 25.7.1914). Ovpt. on #12.	12.50	37.50	75.0

		Good	Fine	XF
M65	**100 Perpera** ND (1916-old date 25.7.1914). Ovpt. on #13.	25.00	75.00	150.

NIKSIC ISSUE

1916 ND FOURTH PROVISIONAL ISSUE

#M66-M72 width of *NIKSIC* in ovpt. 14mm.

		Good	Fine	XF
M66	**1 Perper** ND (1916-old date 25.7.1914). Ovpt. on #15.	4.00	12.00	25.00
M67	**2 Perpera** ND (1916-old date 25.7.1914). Ovpt. on #16.	5.00	16.00	32.00
M68	**5 Perpera** ND (1916-old date 25.7.1914). Ovpt. on #17.	5.00	16.00	32.00
M69	**10 Perpera** ND (1916-old date 25.7.1914). Ovpt. on #18.	7.00	20.00	40.00
M70	**20 Perpera** ND (1916-old date 25.7.1914). Ovpt. on #19.	8.00	22.50	45.00
M71	**50 Perpera** ND (1916-old date 25.7.1914). Ovpt. on #20.	10.00	30.00	60.00
M72	**100 Perpera** ND (1916-old date 25.7.1914). Ovpt. on #21.	15.00	50.00	100.

PLEVLIE ISSUE

1916 ND FIRST PROVISIONAL ISSUE

		Good	Fine	XF
M73	**5 Perpera** ND (1916-old date 25.7.1914). Ovpt. on #9.	5.00	15.00	32.00
M74	**10 Perpera** ND (1916-old date 25.7.1914). Ovpt. on #10.	7.50	22.50	45.00

		Good	Fine	XF
M75	**20 Perpera** ND (1916-old date 25.7.1914). Ovpt. on #11.	10.00	30.00	60.00

		Good	Fine	XF
M76	**50 Perpera** ND (1916-old date 25.7.1914). Ovpt. on #12.	12.50	37.50	75.00
M77	**100 Perpera** ND (1916-old date 25.7.1914). Ovpt. on #13.	30.00	100.	200.

PLEVLIE ISSUE

1916 ND SECOND PROVISIONAL ISSUE

		Good	Fine	XF
M78	**1 Perper** ND (1916-old date 25.7.1914). Ovpt. on #15.	5.00	15.00	30.00
M79	**2 Perpera** ND (1916-old date 25.7.1914). Ovpt. on #16.	5.00	15.00	30.00
M80	**5 Perpera** ND (1916-old date 25.7.1914). Ovpt. on #17.	5.00	15.00	30.00
M81	**10 Perpera** ND (1916-old date 25.7.1914). Ovpt. on #18.	6.00	17.50	35.00
M82	**20 Perpera** ND (1916-old date 25.7.1914). Ovpt. on #19.	7.50	22.50	45.00
M83	**50 Perpera** ND (1916-old date 25.7.1914). Ovpt. on #20.	9.00	27.50	55.00
M84	**100 Perpera** ND (1916-old date 25.7.1914). Ovpt. on #21.	12.50	37.50	75.00

PODGORICA ISSUE

1916 ND FIRST PROVISIONAL ISSUE

#M85-M89 width of *Podgorica* in ovpt. 13mm.

		Good	Fine	XF
M85	**5 Perpera** ND (1916-old date 25.7.1914). Ovpt. on #9.	7.50	22.50	45.00
M86	**10 Perpera** ND (1916-old date 25.7.1914). Ovpt. on #10.	10.00	30.00	60.00
M87	**20 Perpera** ND (1916-old date 25.7.1914). Ovpt. on #11.	12.50	37.50	75.00
M88	**50 Perpera** ND (1916-old date 25.7.1914). Ovpt. on #12.	15.00	50.00	100.
M89	**100 Perpera** ND (1916-old date 25.7.1914). Ovpt. on #13.	30.00	100.	200.

PODGORICA ISSUE

1916 ND SECOND PROVISIONAL ISSUE

#M90-M96 width of *Podgorica* in ovpt. 13mm.

		Good	Fine	XF
M90	**1 Perper** ND (1916-old date 25.7.1914). Ovpt. on #15.	4.00	12.50	25.00
M91	**2 Perpera** ND (1916-old date 25.7.1914). Ovpt. on #16.	5.00	15.00	30.00
M92	**5 Perpera** ND (1916-old date 25.7.1914). Ovpt. on #17.	7.50	22.50	45.00
M93	**10 Perpera** ND (1916-old date 25.7.1914). Ovpt. on #18.	7.50	22.50	45.00
M94	**20 Perpera** ND (1916-old date 25.7.1914). Ovpt. on #19.	10.00	30.00	60.00
M95	**50 Perpera** ND (1916-old date 25.7.1914). Ovpt. on #20.	12.50	37.50	75.00
M96	**100 Perpera** ND (1916-old date 25.7.1914). Ovpt. on #21.	15.00	50.00	100.

PODGORICA ISSUE

1916 ND THIRD PROVISIONAL ISSUE

#M97-M101 width of *PODGORICA* in ovpt. 13mm.

		Good	Fine	XF
M97	**5 Perpera** ND (1916-old date 25.7.1914). Ovpt. on #9.	7.50	22.50	45.00
M98	**10 Perpera** ND (1916-old date 25.7.1914). Ovpt. on #10.	7.50	22.50	45.00

#	Denomination	Good	Fine	XF
M99	20 Perpera ND (1916-old date 25.7.1914). Ovpt. on #11.	12.50	37.50	75.00
M100	50 Perpera ND (1916-old date 25.7.1914). Ovpt. on #12.	15.00	50.00	100.
M101	100 Perpera ND (1916-old date 25.7.1914). Ovpt. on #13.	30.00	100.	200.

CETINJE ISSUE

PODGORICA ISSUE

1916 ND FOURTH PROVISIONAL ISSUE

#M102-M108 width of *PODGORICA* in ovpt. 13mm.

#	Denomination	Good	Fine	XF
M102	1 Perper ND (1916-old date 25.7.1914). Ovpt. on #15.	7.50	22.50	45.00
M103	2 Perpera ND (1916-old date 25.7.1914). Ovpt. on #16.	9.00	27.50	55.00

#	Denomination	Good	Fine	XF
M104	5 Perpera ND (1916-old date 25.7.1914). Ovpt. on #17.	12.50	37.50	75.00
M105	10 Perpera ND (1916-old date 25.7.1914). Ovpt. on #18.	15.00	50.00	100.
M106	20 Perpera ND (1916-old date 25.7.1914). Ovpt. on #19.	25.00	75.00	150.
M107	50 Perpera ND (1916-old date 25.7.1914). Ovpt. on #20.	30.00	100.	200.
M108	100 Perpera ND (1916-old date 25.7.1914). Ovpt. on #21.	35.00	125.	250.

PODGORICA ISSUE

1916 ND FIFTH PROVISIONAL ISSUE

#M109-M113 width of *PODGORICA* in ovpt. 17mm.

#	Denomination	Good	Fine	XF
M109	5 Perpera ND (1916-old date 25.7.1914). Ovpt. on #9.	6.00	17.50	35.00
M110	10 Perpera ND (1916-old date 25.7.1914). Ovpt. on #10.	7.50	22.50	45.00
M111	20 Perpera ND (1916-old date 25.7.1914). Ovpt. on #11.	10.00	30.00	60.00
M112	50 Perpera ND (1916-old date 25.7.1914). Ovpt. on #12.	7.50	22.50	45.00
M113	100 Perpera ND (1916-old date 25.7.1914). Ovpt. on #13.	12.50	37.50	75.00

1916 ND SIXTH PROVISIONAL ISSUE

#M114-M120 width of *PODGORICA* in ovpt. 17mm.

#	Denomination	Good	Fine	XF
M114	1 Perper ND (1916-old date 25.7.1914). Ovpt. on #15.	7.50	22.50	45.00
M115	2 Perpera ND (1916-old date 25.7.1914). Ovpt. on #16.	7.50	22.50	45.00
M116	5 Perpera ND (1916-old date 25.7.1914). Ovpt. on #17.	7.50	22.50	45.00
M117	10 Perpera ND (1916-old date 25.7.1914). Ovpt. on #18.	12.50	37.50	75.00
M118	20 Perpera ND (1916-old date 25.7.1914). Ovpt. on #19.	15.00	50.00	100.
M119	50 Perpera ND (1916-old date 25.7.1914). Ovpt. on #20.	20.00	60.00	125.
M120	100 Perpera ND (1916-old date 25.7.1914). Ovpt. on #21.	25.00	75.00	150.

STARI BAR ISSUE

1916 ND FIRST PROVISIONAL ISSUE

#M121-125 width of *STARI BAR* in ovpt 11mm.

#	Denomination	Good	Fine	XF
M121	5 Perpera ND (1916-old date 25.7.1914). Ovpt. on #9.	12.50	37.50	80.00
M122	10 Perpera ND (1916-old date 25.7.1914). Ovpt. on #10.	20.00	60.00	130.
M123	20 Perpera ND (1916-old date 25.7.1914). Ovpt. on #11.	20.00	60.00	130.
M124	50 Perpera ND (1916-old date 25.7.1914). Ovpt. on #12.	25.00	75.00	175.
M125	100 Perpera ND (1916-old date 25.7.1914). Ovpt. on #13.	30.00	100.	200.

STARI BAR ISSUE

1916 ND SECOND PROVISIONAL ISSUE

#M126-M132 width of *STARI BAR* in ovpt. 11mm.

#	Denomination	Good	Fine	XF
M126	1 Perper ND (1916-old date 25.7.1914). Ovpt. on #15.	15.00	50.00	120.
M127	2 Perpera ND (1916-old date 25.7.1914). Ovpt. on #16.	20.00	50.00	140.
M128	5 Perpera ND (1916-old date 25.7.1914). Ovpt. on #17.	25.00	75.00	160.
M129	10 Perpera ND (1916-old date 25.7.1914). Ovpt. on #18.	30.00	100.	200.
M130	20 Perpera ND (1916-old date 25.7.1914). Ovpt. on #19.	30.00	100.	200.
M131	50 Perpera ND (1916-old date 25.7.1914). Ovpt. on #20.	40.00	125.	275.
M132	100 Perpera ND (1916-old date 25.7.1914). Ovpt. on #21.	50.00	150.	350.

STARI BAR ISSUE

1916 ND THIRD PROVISIONAL ISSUE

#M133-M137 width of *STARI BAR* in ovpt. 16mm.

#	Denomination	Good	Fine	XF
M133	5 Perpera ND (1916-old date 25.7.1914). Ovpt. on #9.	12.50	37.50	85.00
M134	10 Perpera ND (1916-old date 25.7.1914). Ovpt. on #10.	25.00	75.00	170.
M135	20 Perpera ND (1916-old date 25.7.1914). Ovpt. on #11.	25.00	75.00	170.
M136	50 Perpera ND (1916-old date 25.7.1914). Ovpt. on #12.	40.00	125.	250.
M137	100 Perpera ND (1916-old date 25.7.1914). Ovpt. on #13.	50.00	150.	350.

STARI BAR ISSUE

1916 ND FOURTH PROVISIONAL ISSUE

#M138-M144 width of *STARI BAR* in ovpt. 16mm.

#	Denomination	Good	Fine	XF
M138	1 Perper ND (1916-old date 25.7.1914). Ovpt. on #15.	7.50	22.50	50.00
M139	2 Perpera ND (1916-old date 25.7.1914). Ovpt. on #16.	7.50	22.50	50.00
M140	5 Perpera ND (1916-old date 25.7.1914). Ovpt. on #17.	7.50	22.50	50.00
M141	10 Perpera ND (1916-old date 25.7.1914). Ovpt. on #18.	12.50	37.50	80.00
M142	20 Perpera ND (1916-old date 25.7.1914). Ovpt. on #19.	15.00	50.00	120.
M143	50 Perpera ND (1916-old date 25.7.1914). Ovpt. on #20.	20.00	60.00	125.
M144	100 Perpera ND (1916-old date 25.7.1914). Ovpt. on #21.	25.00	75.00	150.

BELGRAD ISSUE

1916 ND PROVISIONAL ISSUE

#	Denomination	Good	Fine	XF
M145	1 Perper ND (1916-old date 25.7.1914). Ovpt. on #15.	150.	450.	1000.
M146	10 Perpera ND (1916-old date 25.7.1914). Ovpt. on #18.	150.	450.	1000.

STEUER-U. ZOLLAMT KOLASIN ISSUE

1916 ND PROVISIONAL ISSUE

#	Denomination	Good	Fine	XF
M147	1 Perper ND (1916-old date 25.7.1914). Ovpt. on #1.	150.	450.	1000.

K.U.K. KREISKOMMANDO UNTERABTEILUNG

DISTRICT COMMAND SUBDIVISION

1916 ND PROVISIONAL ISSUE

		Good	Fine	XF
M147A	**1 Perper** ND (1916-old date 25.7.1914). Ovpt. w/o place name on #15.	150.	450.	1000.

K.u.K. Stationskommando

1916 Issue

M147B	**5 Perpera** ND (1616-old date 25.7.1914). Ovpt. w/o place name on #17.	—	—	—

K.u.K. Militarverwaltung

Army Administration, 1917-18

1917 Convertable Voucher Issue

		VG	VF	UNC
M148	**50 Heller1 Perper = 50 Münzperper =** 5.7.1917. Blue-green on orange unpt. Back orange w/black text on lt. green unpt.	7.00	20.00	55.00
M149	**2 Perper = 1 Münzperper = 1 Krone** 5.7.1917. Violet on green unpt. Back olive-green w/black text on lilac unpt.	7.00	25.00	70.00

		VG	VF	UNC
M150	**Para = 2 Kronen 50 Heller5 Perper = 2 Münzperper 50** 5.7.1917. Purple on green unpt. Back green w/black text on pink unpt.	10.00	30.00	80.00

		VG	VF	UNC
M151	**10 Perper = 5 Münzperper = 5 Kronen** 1.6.1917. Blue on brown unpt. Back red-brown w/black text on green unpt.	7.00	25.00	70.00

		VG	VF	UNC
M152	**20 Perper = 10 Münzperper = 10 Kronen** 20.11.1917. Red-brown on green unpt. Back green w/black text on lt. red-orange unpt.	15.00	40.00	100.

		VG	VF	UNC
M153	**25 Kronen50 Perper = 25 Münzperper =** 20.11.1917. Red-brown on green unpt. Back brown w/black text on red-brown unpt.	25.00	50.00	150.
M154	**100 Perper = 50 Münzperper = 50 Kronen** 20.11.1917. Blue on olive unpt. Back brown w/black text on blue unpt.	30.00	60.00	200.

Note: During World War II Italian ovpt. notes of Yugoslavia with *Verificato* were circulated in Montenegro. There was also an issue of *Socialniki Dinara* in 1945 (stamp money). For details of the *Verificato* notes see Yugoslavia.

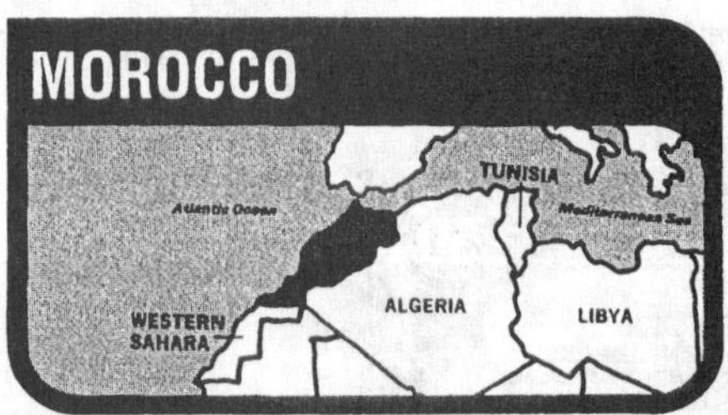

The Kingdom of Morocco, situated on the northwest corner of Africa south of Spain, has an area of 172,413 sq. mi. (712,550 sq. km.) and a population of 28.98 million. Capital: Rabat. The economy is essentially agricultural. Phosphates, fresh and preserved vegetables, canned fish and raw material are exported.

Morocco's strategic position at the gateway to western Europe has been the principal determinant of its violent, frequently unfortunate history. Time and again the fertile plain between the rugged Atlas Mountains and the sea has echoed the battle's trumpet as Phoenicians, Romans, Vandals, Visigoths, Byzantine Greeks and Islamic Arabs successively conquered and occupied the land. Modern Morocco is a remnant of an early empire formed by the Arabs at the close of the 7th century which encompassed all of northwest Africa and most of the Iberian Peninsula. During the 17th and 18th centuries, while under the control of native dynasties, it was the headquarters of the famous Sale pirates. Morocco's strategic position involved it in the competition of 19th century European powers for political influence in Africa, and resulted in the division of Morocco into French and Spanish spheres of interest which were established as protectorates in 1912. Morocco became independent on March 2, 1956, after France agreed to end its protectorate. Spain signed similar agreements on April 7 of the same year.

RULERS:

Abd Al-Aziz, AH1311-1325/1894-1908AD
Hafiz, AH1325-1330/1908-1912AD
Yusuf, AH1330-1346/1912-1927AD
Muhammad V, AH1346-1380/1927-1961AD
Hassan II, AH1380-1420 /1961-1999AD
Muhammad VI, AH1420- /1999- AD

MONETARY SYSTEM:

1 Dirham = 50 Mazunas
1 Rial = 10 Dirhams to 1921
1 Franc = 100 Centimes
1 Dirham = 100 Francs, 1921-1974
1 Dirham = 100 Centimes = 100 Santimat, 1974-
1 Riffan = 1 French Gold Franc = 10 British Pence

KINGDOM

BANQUE D'ETAT DU MAROC

STATE BANK OF MOROCCO

1910; 1917 ISSUE

#1 and 2 w/text: *PAYABLES A VUE AU PORTEUR.*

		Good	Fine	XF
1	**4 Rials = 40 Francs** 2.7.1917; 6.7.1917; 9.7.1917. Salmon, ochre and blue. Tower at ctr.	200.	600.	1750.
2	**20 Rials = 100 Francs** 31.2.1910; 15.7.1910; 18.7.1910. Violet, yellow and blue. Palm tree at ctr.	225.	650.	2000.

Note: Other denominations and issues may exist like Bons de Caisse (Issue of 1919).

PROTECTORAT DE LA FRANCE AU MAROC

1919 EMERGENCY ISSUE

		Good	Fine	XF
4	**25 Centimes** Oct. 1919. Rose cardboard. Octagonal ovpt: *MAROC 25c.*			
	a. *Octobre* in date. W/or w/o series letters.	17.50	50.00	125.
	b. OCTOBRE in date.	17.50	50.00	125.
	c. *OCTOBRE* in date.	17.50	50.00	125.
5	**50 Centimes** Oct. 1919. Orange cardboard. Octagonal ovpt: *MAROC 50c.*			
	a. *Octobre* in date. W/or w/o series letters.	17.50	50.00	125.
	b. OCTOBRE in date.	17.50	50.00	125.
	c. *OCTOBRE* in date.	17.50	50.00	125.
6	**1 Franc** Oct. 1919. Yellow cardboard. Octagonal ovpt: *MAROC 1F.*			
	a. *Octobre* in date. W/or w/o series letters.	17.50	50.00	125.
	b. OCTOBRE in date.	17.50	50.00	125.
	c. *OCTOBRE* in date.	17.50	50.00	125.

		Good	Fine	XF
7	**2 Francs** Oct. 1919. Green cardboard. Octagonal ovpt: *MAROC 2F.*			
	a. *Octobre* in date. Series A.	17.50	50.00	150.
	b. OCTOBRE in date.	17.50	50.00	150.
	c. *OCTOBRE* in date.	17.50	50.00	150.

BANQUE D'ETAT DU MAROC (RESUMED)

STATE BANK OF MOROCCO

1920-24 ISSUE

#8 and 9 w/o text: *PAYABLES A VUE...* on face. Sign. varieties. Printer: Chaix, Paris.

		Good	Fine	XF
8	**5 Francs** ND (1921). Blue and green. W/title: *BANQUE D'ETAT DU MAROC* in 1 line on back. Serial # at bottom only. 2 sign. varieties.	15.00	50.00	250.

		Good	Fine	XF
9	**5 Francs** ND (1924). Blue and green. Similar to #8 but w/title: *BANQUE D'ETAT DU MAROC* in 2 lines on back. Serial # at top and bottom. 4 sign. varieties.	10.00	35.00	150.

#10 Deleted, see 23A. #11-15 various dates and sign. varieties.

		Good	Fine	XF
11	**10 Francs** 1920-28. Blue on sepia unpt.			
	a. Serial # only at bottom. 2 sign. varieties. 4.5.1920-1.12.1923.	20.00	80.00	285.
	b. Serial # at top printed over and below ornamentation. 3 sign. varieties. 15.5.1924-1.7.1928.	15.00	70.00	250.

#12-14 w/text: *PAYABLES A VUE...*

		Good	Fine	XF
12	**20 Francs** 7.1.1920-17.4.1926. Gray, blue and sepia. Tower at ctr. Serial # at top in white fields (l. and r.) and bottom l. and r. in special blank fields. 3 sign. varieties.	25.00	100.	325.
13	**50 Francs** 13.9.1920-8.8.1928. Blue-green and lt. brown. Design style similar to #11. Serial # at l. and r. at top printed over ornamentation, and bottom l. and r. 4 sign. varieties. 170 x 98mm.	50.00	175.	500.

		Good	Fine	XF
14	**100 Francs** 15.12.1919-1.9.1926. Red. Palm tree at ctr. 3 sign. varieties. Back red w/blue text.	150.	500.	100.

		Good	Fine	XF
15	**500 Francs** 1923-48. Brown, red and m/c. View of city of Fez.			
	a. W/text: *PAYABLES A VUE AU PORTEUR.* 5 sign. varieties. 1.10.1923-29.6.1937.	150.	400.	1000.
	b. W/o text: *PAYABLES A VUE...* 3.5.1946-10.11.1948.	15.00	45.00	100.
16	**1000 Francs** 1921-50. Green, blue and ochre. View of city. 5 sign. varieties.			
	a. 1.2.1921.	75.00	175.	650.
	b. 12.6.1929-27.9.1934.	45.00	140.	575.
	c. 13.1.1937-9.2.1950.	20.00	75.00	400.

1928-29 ISSUES

		Good	Fine	XF
17	**10 Francs** 1929-42. Blue on sepia unpt. Like #11 but serial # on top in blank field.			
	a. W/text: *PAYABLES A VUE AU PORTEUR.* 2 sign. varieties. 12.6.1929; 20.5.1931.	12.00	40.00	150.
	b. W/o text: *PAYABLES A VUE..* 6.3.1941; 25.9.1942.	1.50	10.00	55.00

		Good	Fine	XF
18	**20 Francs** 1929-45. Gray-blue and sepia. Tower at ctr. Like #12 but serial # at top in special blank field.			
	a. W/text: *PAYABLES A VUE AU PORTEUR.* 2 sign. varieties. 12.6.1929; 2.12.1931.	20.00	50.00	225.
	b. W/o text: *PAYABLES A VUE...* 3 sign. varieties. 6.3.1941; 14.11.1941; 9.11.1942; 1.3.1945.	3.00	12.50	85.00
19	**50 Francs** 12.6.1929; 2.12.1931; 17.11.1932. Blue-green and lt. brown. Like #13 but serial # at top and bottom in blank field. 2 sign. varieties.	20.00	75.00	300.

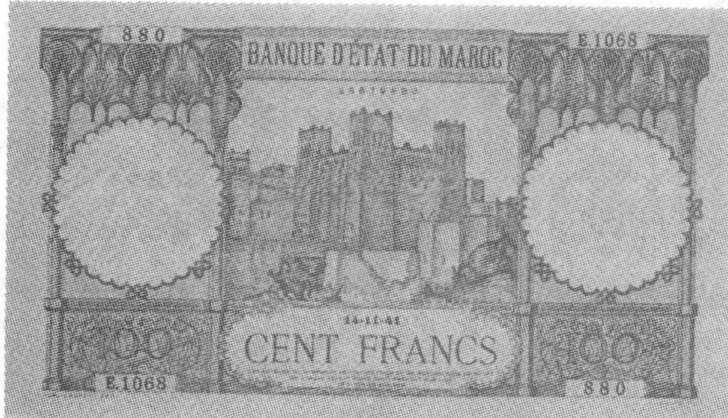

		VG	VF	UNC
20	**100 Francs** 1.7.1928-28.10.1947. M/c. Fortress (Kasbah) at ctr. 4 sign. varieties.	7.50	50.00	200.

1936; 1938 ISSUE

		VG	VF	UNC
21	**50 Francs** 23.9.1936-2.12.1949. Green, blue and sepia. Arch at ctr. 4 sign. varieties.	5.00	30.00	150.

#22 Deleted.

23 **5000 Francs**
1938-51. Brown and maroon on lt. blue and m/c unpt. Moroccan city overlooking the sea. Fortress at ctr. on back. Wmk: Lion. 3 sign. varieties.

	VG	VF	UNC
a. 28.9.1938; 14.11.1941.	90.00	350.	1000.
b. 9.11.1942.	80.00	300.	1000.
c. 21.12.1945-19.4.1951.	70.00	275.	1000.

1941 (1922) Issue

23a **5 Francs**
1922; 1941. Red, blue and sepia.

	VG	VF	UNC
a. W/text: *PAYABLES A VUE AU PORTEUR.* 1.8.1922 (issued 1941).	5.00	20.00	100.
b. W/o text: *PAYABLES A VUE...* 24.7.1941; 27.7.1941; 14.11.1941.	2.50	10.00	50.00

1943 WWII First Issue

Notes printed in Morocco or the United States during World War II.

#24-27 printer: EAW.

		VG	VF	UNC
24	**5 Francs** 1.8.1943; 1.3.1944. Blue on yellow unpt. 5-pointed star at upper ctr. on back.	1.00	3.50	15.00

		VG	VF	UNC
25	**10 Francs** 1.5.1943; 1.8.1943; 1.3.1944. Black on green unpt. 5-pointed star at ctr. Back blue on red unpt.	2.00	5.00	25.00

		VG	VF	UNC
26	**50 Francs** 1.8.1943; 1.3.1944. Black and lt. brown. Fortress at l., sailing ship at r. Back green on yellow unpt.; 5-pointed star at l. and r.	3.00	15.00	100.

		VG	VF	UNC
27	**100 Francs** 1.5.1943; 1.8.1943; 1.3.1944. M/c. Gate in city wall at ctr. 5-pointed star at l. and r. on back.	7.50	30.00	150.

#28; 32 printer: ABNC.

		VG	VF	UNC
28	**1000 Francs** 1.5.1943; 1.8.1943; 1.3.1944. Brown.	75.00	250.	800.

#29-31 Deleted.

		VG	VF	UNC
32	**5000 Francs** 1.8.1943. Green.	600.	1500.	—

1943 Second Issue

#33 and 40 printer: Imp. Réunies, Casablanca.

		VG	VF	UNC
33	**5 Francs** 14.9.1943. Blue on yellow unpt. Lg. *5* at l. Small square black area at ctr. of date.	.75	2.00	10.00

#34-38 Deleted.

		VG	VF	UNC
39	**20 Francs** ND (1943). Blue on red-brown unpt. Bldgs. on hillside at ctr.	2.00	15.00	100.
40	**50 Francs** ND (1943). Green on orange unpt. Face similar to #26. Lg. 5-pointed star at ctr. on back. 170 x 106mm.	3.00	17.50	100.

EMPIRE CHERIFIEN, PROTECTORAT DE LA RÉPUBLIQUE FRANÇAISE

1944 EMERGENCY ISSUE

#41-43 very small cardboard notes.

		VG	VF	UNC
41	**50 Centimes** 6.4.1944. Red. Fortress on back.	.75	3.00	15.00

		VG	VF	UNC
42	**1 Franc** 6.4.1944. Green. City of Fez on back.	.75	4.00	20.00

		VG	VF	UNC
43	**2 Francs** 6.4.1944. Violet-brown. House on the shore (La Menara) on back.	1.00	5.00	25.00

BANQUE D'ETAT DU MAROC - POST WW II

1948-51 ISSUES

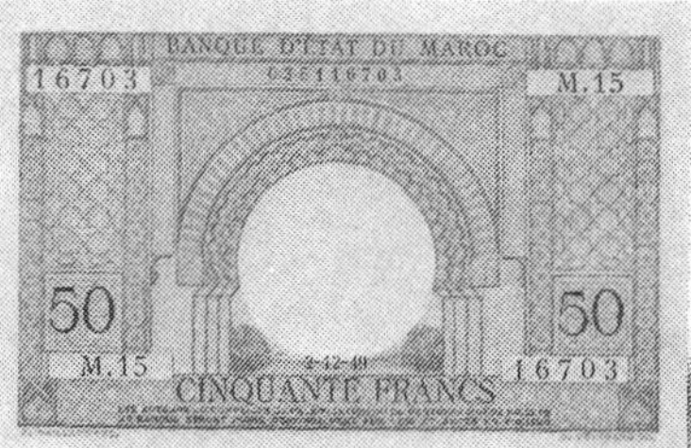

		VG	VF	UNC
44	**50 Francs** 2.12.1949. Green, blue and sepia. Like #21 but reduced size.	1.00	6.00	30.00

		VG	VF	UNC
45	**100 Francs** 10.11.1948-22.12.1952. M/c. Like #20 but reduced size.	2.50	10.00	50.00

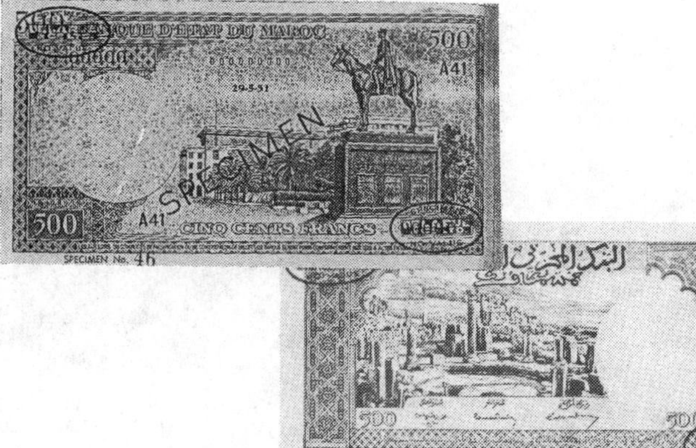

		VG	VF	UNC
45A	**500 Francs** 29.5.1951. Brown on m/c unpt. Monument in front of State Bank bldg. at ctr. r. City view on back. Wmk: Male lion's head. Printer: TDLR (w/o imprint). Specimen.	—	—	850.

		VG	VF	UNC
45B	**500 Francs** 29.5.1951. City view at ctr. r. Printer: TDLR (w/o imprint). Specimen.	—	—	850.

		VG	VF	UNC
46	**500 Francs** 18.7.1949-14.2.1958. M/c. Doorway of house w/Moroccan city in background. 2 sign. varieties.	2.50	17.50	125.

46A	**1000 Francs** 29.1.1951. Green. Bldg. at ctr. Printer: TDLR (w/o imprint). Specimen.	—	Unc	900.

		VG	VF	UNC
47	**1000 Francs** 19.4.1951-7.8.1958. M/c. Mosque, city and hills in background. 2 sign. varieties.	5.00	45.00	200.

		VG	VF	UNC
48	**5000 Francs** ND. Red-brown. Bldg. at ctr. Printer: TDLR (w/o imprint). Specimen.	—	—	1000.

		VG	VF	UNC
49	**5000 Francs** 2.4.1953; 23.7.1953; 7.8.1958. M/c. Mosque w/hills in background.	25.00	150.	475.
50	**10,000 Francs** 13.8.1953-28.4.1955. M/c. Aerial view of Casablanca.	30.00	175.	550.

1959 Provisional Dirham Issue

		VG	VF	UNC
51	**50 Dirhams on 5000 Francs** ND (-old date 23.7.1953). Ovpt. on #49.	25.00	100.	400.

		VG	VF	UNC
52	**100 Dirhams on 10,000 Francs** ND (-old dates 2.8.1954; 28.4.1955). Ovpt. on #50.	25.00	100.	400.

Regional

State Bank of the Riff

1923 Issue

Issued during the Berber uprising under Abd el-Krim, 1921-26.

		VG	VF	UNC
R1	**1 Riffan = 10 Pence** 10.10.1923. Red-orange. Horseman at l. and r. Uniface.	—	60.00	90.00
R2	**5 Riffans = 50 Pence** 10.10.1923. Lt. green. Like #R1.	—	75.00	120

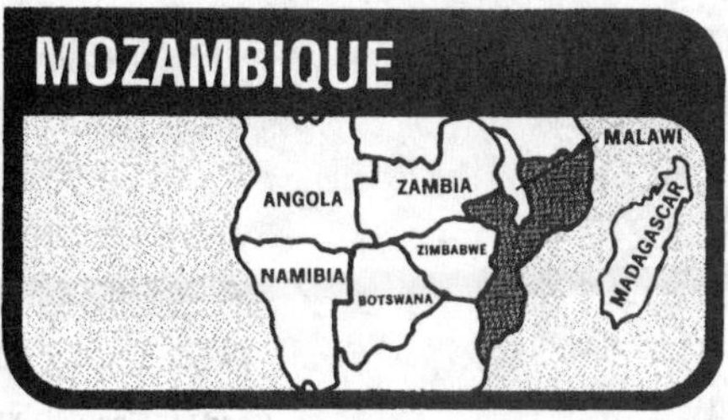

The People's Republic of Mozambique, a former overseas province of Portugal stretching for 1,430 miles (2,301 km.) along the southeast coast of Africa, has an area of 309,494 sq. mi. (783,030 sq. km.) and a population of 19.56 million. Capital: Maputo. Agriculture is the chief industry. Cashew nuts, cotton, sugar, copra and tea are exported.

Vasco da Gama explored all the coast of Mozambique in 1498 and found Arab trading posts already along the coast. Portuguese settlement dates from the establishment of the trading post of Mozambique in 1505. Within five years Portugal absorbed all the former Arab sultanates along the east African coast. The area was organized as a colony in 1907 and became an overseas province in 1952. In Sept. of 1974, after more than a decade of guerrilla warfare with the forces of the Mozambique Liberation Front, Portugal agreed to the independence of Mozambique, effective June 25, 1975. Mozambique became a member of the Commonwealth of Nations in November 1995. The President is Head of State; the Prime Minister is Head of Government.

RULERS:

Portuguese to 1975

MONETARY SYSTEM:

Pound Sterling = Libra Esterlina (pound sterling)
1 Mil Reis = 1000 Reis to 1910
1 Escudo = 100 Centavos, 1911-1975
1 Escudo = 1 Metica = 100 Centimos, 1975-

STEAMSHIP SEAL VARIETIES:

Type I LOURENÇO | Type II MARQUES LISBOA | Type III C, C, A.

C, C, A = Colonias, Commercio, Agricultura.

3 types of BANCO NACIONAL ULTRAMARINO seals are found on bank notes issued for Lourenço Marques.

Portuguese Administration

Banco Nacional Ultramarino

1877 Issue

#1-8 Lourenço Marques.

		Good	Fine	XF
1	**5000 Reis** 2.4.1877. Note of Loanda w/ovpt. for Mozambique. Rare.	—	—	—
2	**20,000 Reis** 2.4.1877. Note of Loanda w/ovpt. for Mozambique. Rare.	—	—	—

1878 Issue

		Good	Fine	XF
3	**1000 Reis** 29.1.1878.	—	—	—
4	**2000 Reis** 29.1.1878. Green. Steamship at ctr.	—	—	—
5	**2500 Reis** 29.1.1878.	—	—	—
6	**5000 Reis** 29.1.1878.	—	—	—
7	**10,000 Reis** 29.1.1878.	—	—	—
8	**20,000 Reis** 29.1.1878.	—	—	—

1884; 1897 Issues

#9-15 w/text...*Succursal em Mozambique*...

		Good	Fine	XF
9	**1000 Reis** 28.1.1884; 2.1.1897. Green.	—	—	—
10	**2000 Reis** 2.1.1897.	—	—	—
11	**2500 Reis** 2.1.1897.	—	—	—
12	**5000 Reis** 2.1.1897.	—	—	—
13	**10,000 Reis** 2.1.1897.	—	—	—
14	**20,000 Reis** 2.1.1897.	—	—	—
15	**50,000 Reis** 2.1.1897.	—	—	—

1897 Second Issue

#16-29 W/text: ...*em Lourenço Marques*...

		Good	Fine	XF
16	**1000 Reis** 2.1.1897. Standing Indian at l., ship at ctr.	—	—	—
17	**2000 Reis** 2.1.1897.	—	—	—

		Good	Fine	XF
18	**2500 Reis** 2.1.1897. Steamship at l., field at ctr., woman standing at ctr. r.	—	—	—
19	**5000 Reis** 2.1.1897.	—	—	—
20	**10,000 Reis** 2.1.1897.	—	—	—
21	**20,000 Reis** 2.1.1897.	—	—	—
22	**50,000 Reis** 2.1.1897.	—	—	—

1906 Issue

		Good	Fine	XF
23	**1000 Reis** 20.2.1906. Lt. brown. Standing Indian at l., ship at ctr. Uniface.	—	—	—
24	**2000 Reis** 20.2.1906.	—	—	—
25	**2500 Reis** 20.2.1906.	—	—	—
26	**5000 Reis** 20.2.1906. Green.	—	—	—
27	**10,000 Reis** 20.2.1906.	—	—	—
28	**20,000 Reis** 20.2.1906.	—	—	—
29	**50,000 Reis** 20.2.1906. Brown.	—	—	—

1907 Issue

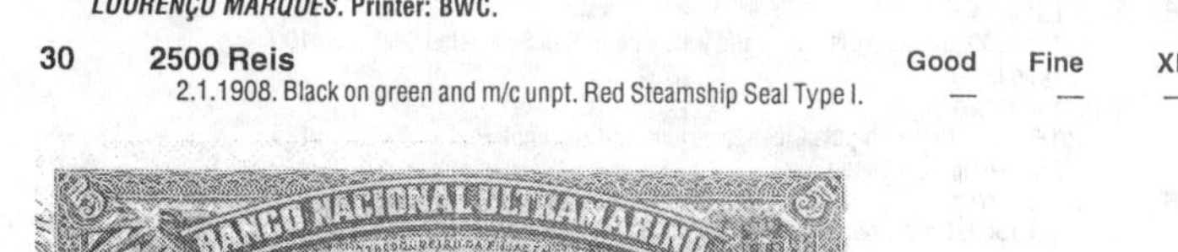

		Good	Fine	XF
29A	**10 Centavos** 1.1.1907. Red-brown. Sailing ship.	—	—	—

1908 Issue

#30-31 portr. Vasco da Gama at l., sailing ships in passage Cape of Boa Esperanca in 1498 at r. W/ovpt: *LOURENÇO MARQUES*. Printer: BWC.

		Good	Fine	XF
30	**2500 Reis** 2.1.1908. Black on green and m/c unpt. Red Steamship Seal Type I.	—	—	—

		Good	Fine	XF
31	**5000 Reis** 2.1.1908. Black on green and m/c unpt. Red Steamship Seal Type I.	—	—	—

1909 Issue

		Good	Fine	XF
32	**1000 Reis** 1.3.1909. Black on green and yellow unpt. Red Steamship Seal Type I. Printer: BWC.	50.00	150.	400.

		Good	Fine	XF
33	**1000 Reis** 1.3.1909. Black on green and yellow unpt. Steamship Seal Type III. Like #32.	35.00	125.	300.

#34-43 portr. Vasco da Gama at l., sailing ships in passage Cape of Boa Esperanca in 1498. Printer: BWC.

		Good	Fine	XF
34	**2500 Reis** 1.3.1909. Black on blue and yellow unpt. Red Steamship Seal Type I.	100.	200.	500.

		Good	Fine	XF
35	**2500 Reis** 1.3.1909. Black on blue and yellow unpt. Red Steamship Seal Type III.	100.	200.	500.
36	**5000 Reis** 1.3.1909. Black on m/c unpt. Red Steamship Seal Type I.	125.	250.	600.
37	**5000 Reis** 1.3.1909. Black on m/c unpt. Red Steamship Seal Type III.	125.	250.	600.
38	**10,000 Reis** 1.3.1909. Black on blue and yellow unpt. Red Steamship Seal Type I.	175.	350.	800.
39	**10,000 Reis** 1.3.1909. Black on blue and yellow unpt. Red Steamship Seal Type III.	175.	350.	800.

#40-43 embarkation of Vasco da Gama in 1497 at r.

		Good	Fine	XF
40	**20,000 Reis** 1.3.1909. Black on tan and pale blue unpt. Red Steamship Seal Type I.	350.	750.	1500.
41	**20,000 Reis** 1.3.1909. Black on tan and pale blue unpt. Red Steamship Seal Type III.	350.	750.	1500.
42	**50,000 Reis** 1.3.1909. Black on brown, tan and pale blue unpt. Red Steamship Seal Type I.	500.	1000.	2000.
43	**50,000 Reis** 1.3.1909. Black on brown, tan and pale blue unpt. Red Steamship Seal Type III.	500.	1000.	2000.

1909 Libra Esterlina Issue

#44-49 printer: BWC.

		Good	Fine	XF
44	**1 Libra** 1.3.1909. Black on orange and green unpt. Back brown. Red Steamship Seal Type I.	75.00	—	—
45	**1 Libra** 1.3.1909. Black on orange and green unpt. Back brown. Red Steamship Seal Type III.	50.00	—	—
46	**5 Libras** 1.3.1909. Black on pink, blue and yellow unpt. Red Steamship Seal Type I.	100.	—	—
47	**10 Libras** 1.3.1909. Black on pale green, pale blue and red unpt. Red Steamship Seal Type I.	125.	—	—
48	**20 Libras** 1.3.1909. Brown on m/c unpt. Red Steamship Seal Type I.	150.	—	—
49	**20 Libras** 1.3.1909. Brown on m/c unpt. Red Steamship Seal Type III.	150.	—	—

#50-51 deleted; see #72A-72B. #52 deleted; see #29A.

1914 First Issue

#53-55 woman seated, sailing ships in background at ctr. on back. Counterfoil at l. Printer: BWC.

		Good	Fine	XF
53	**10 Centavos** 5.11.1914. Purple on m/c unpt. Dk. green Steamship Seal Type II. Back deep blue.	2.50	15.00	60.00
54	**20 Centavos** 5.11.1914. Blue on m/c unpt. Red Steamship Seal Type II. Back purple.	4.50	25.00	85.00

		Good	Fine	XF
55	**50 Centavos** 5.11.1914. Olive green on m/c unpt. Dk. blue Steamship Seal Type II. Back brown.	5.00	25.00	85.00

1914 Second Issue

#56-58 woman seated, sailing ships in background at ctr. on back. Like #53-55 but Steamship Seal Type III. Printer: BWC.

		Good	Fine	XF
56	**10 Centavos** 5.11.1914. Purple on m/c unpt. Dk. green Steamship Seal Type III. Back deep blue.	2.00	8.00	30.00
57	**20 Centavos** 5.11.1914. Blue on m/c unpt. Red Steamship Seal Type III. Back purple.	3.00	15.00	50.00
58	**50 Centavos** 5.11.1914. Green on m/c unpt. Dk. blue Steamship Seal Type III. Back brown.	4.00	25.00	75.00

1914 Third Issue

#59-61 woman seated, sailing ships in background at ctr. on back. Like #56-58 but w/o counterfoil at l. Printer: BWC.

		Good	Fine	XF
59	**10 Centavos** 5.11.1914. Purple on m/c unpt. Steamship Seal Type III. Back deep blue.	1.00	7.50	40.00
60	**20 Centavos** 5.11.1914. Blue on m/c unpt. Red Steamship Seal Type III. Back purple.	1.50	17.50	60.00
61	**50 Centavos** 5.11.1914. Green on m/c unpt. Dk. blue Steamship Seal Type III. Back brown.	2.50	20.00	70.00

1920 Emergency Issue

#62-65 offset printed on low-grade yellowish paper in Oporto.

		Good	Fine	XF
62	**10 Centavos** 1.1.1920. Red. Sailing ship at l. and r. Back violet.	100.	250.	650.
63	**20 Centavos** 1.1.1920. Green. Allegorical figures at l. and r. Back blue.	100.	250.	650.
64	**50 Centavos** 1.1.1920. Blue. Allegorical figures at l. and r.	100.	250.	650.
65	**50 Escudos** 1.1.1920. Dk. blue on pale green unpt. Arms at upper ctr. Back brown on pale yellow-orange; palm trees at ctr.	350.	1250.	2750.

1921 Issue

#66-73 Provincia de Mozambique. Portr. F. de Oliveira Chamico at l. Seated allegorical woman and ships on back. Sign. varieties.

#66, 68-72 printer: BWC.

		Good	Fine	XF
66	**1 Escudo** 1.1.1921. Green on m/c unpt.			
	a. *Decreto.*	3.50	35.00	100.
	b. W/o *Decreto.*	3.50	35.00	100.
67	**2 1/2 Escudos** 1.1.1921. Blue on m/c unpt. Printer: TDLR.			
	a. *Decreto.*	8.50	50.00	200.
	b. W/o *Decreto.*	8.50	50.00	200.

		Good	Fine	XF
68	**5 Escudos** 1.1.1921. Brown on m/c unpt.			

		Good	Fine	XF
68	a. *Decreto.*	12.50	85.00	250.
	b. W/o *Decreto.*	12.50	85.00	250.
69	**10 Escudos** 1.1.1921. Brown-violet on m/c unpt.			
	a. *Decreto.*	17.50	125.	350.
	b. W/o *Decreto.*	17.50	125.	350.
70	**20 Escudos** 1.1.1921. Blue-green on m/c unpt.			
	a. *Decreto.*	50.00	200.	600.
	b. W/o *Decreto.*	50.00	200.	600.
71	**50 Escudos** 1.1.1921. Red-brown on m/c unpt.			
	a. *Decreto.*	125.	500.	1500.
	b. W/o *Decreto.*	125.	500.	1500.
72	**100 Escudos** 1.1.1921. Blue-green on m/c unpt.			
	a. *Decreto.*	180.	650.	2000.
	b. W/o *Decreto.*	180.	650.	2000.

1929 Provisional Issue

Decreto No. 17,154 de 26 de Julho de 1929

		Good	Fine	XF
72A	**100 Escudos on 1 Libra** ND (1929-old date 1.3.1909). Black ovpt. on #45.	150.	550.	—

		Good	Fine	XF
72B	**1000 Escudos on 20 Libras** ND (1929-old date 1.3.1909). Black ovpt. on #49.	300.	850.	—

1932 Issue

		Good	Fine	XF
73	**500 Escudos** 25.8.1932. Black on m/c unpt. Unique. Rare.	—	—	—

1937; 1938 Issue

#74-79 portr. A. Ennes at l.

#74-76 printer: BWC.

		Good	Fine	XF
74	**20 Escudos** 6.4.1937. Blue.	7.50	50.00	175.
75	**50 Escudos** 11.1.1938. Gray-olive.	12.50	75.00	275.
76	**100 Escudos** 11.1.1938. Purple.	20.00	125.	450.

1941 First Issue

		Good	Fine	XF
77	**100 Escudos** 27.3.1941. Purple.	20.00	110.	425.
78	**500 Escudos** 27.3.1941. Lilac.	35.00	175.	600.
79	**1000 Escudos** 27.3.1941. Brown.	120.	450.	1200.

1941 Emergency Second Issue

		VG	VF	UNC
80	**50 Centavos** 1.9.1941. Green on cream paper. Arms at l. Back purple; arms at ctr. Printer: Imprensa Nacional de Mocambique.	3.00	15.00	45.00

1941 Third Issue

#81-84 portr. F. de Oliveira Chamico at l., steamship seal at r. Like #66-69 but diff. sign. titles. Sign. varieties.

#81, 83-84 printer: BWC.

		VG	VF	UNC
81	**1 Escudo** 1.9.1941. Green.	3.00	17.50	65.00
82	**2 1/2 Escudos** 1.9.1941. Blue. Printer: TDLR.	6.00	40.00	150.

		VG	VF	UNC
83	**5 Escudos** 1.9.1941. Dk. brown.			
	a. Issued note.	10.00	75.00	200.
	s. Specimen, punched hole cancelled. W/o serial #.	—	Unc	175.

		VG	VF	UNC
84	**10 Escudos** 1.9.1941. Lt. brown.	12.00	90.00	250.

1941 FOURTH ISSUE

#85-88 portr. A. Ennes at l., steamship seal at r.

		VG	VF	UNC
85	**20 Escudos** 1.11.1941. Black on blue and m/c unpt. Printer: BWC.	7.50	45.00	175.

		VG	VF	UNC
86	**50 Escudos** 1.11.1941. Black on brown and m/c unpt. Printer: BWC.	10.00	60.00	225.
87	**500 Escudos** 1.11.1941. Black on lilac and m/c unpt.	40.00	175.	600.
88	**1000 Escudos** 1.11.1941. Black on brown and m/c unpt.	125.	400.	1000.

1943 ISSUE

#89-91 portr. A. Ennes at l., steamship seal at r.

#89 and 90 printer: BWC.

		VG	VF	UNC
89	**5 Escudos** 15.4.1943. Black on green and m/c unpt.	3.50	20.00	85.00
90	**10 Escudos** 15.4.1943. Black on brown-violet and m/c unpt.	7.50	30.00	125.

		VG	VF	UNC
91	**100 Escudos** 27.1.1943. Black on orange and m/c unpt.	15.00	100.	450.

1944; 1945 ISSUE

#92-99 portr. A. Ennes at l., steamship seal at r.

#92-96A printer: BWC.

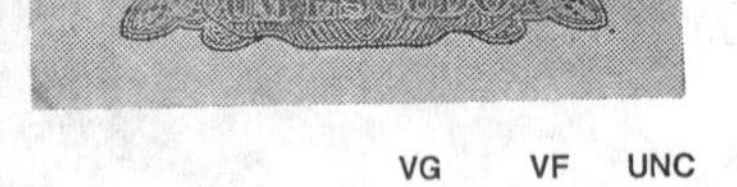

		VG	VF	UNC
92	**1 Escudo** 23.5.1944. Black on olive and m/c unpt.	1.00	8.50	35.00

		VG	VF	UNC
93	**2 1/2 Escudos** 23.5.1944. Blue.	2.00	15.00	65.00
94	**5 Escudos** 29.11.1945. Green on m/c unpt.	3.00	17.50	75.00
95	**10 Escudos** 29.11.1945. Brown on m/c unpt.	7.00	25.00	115.
96	**20 Escudos** 29.11.1945. Blue on m/c unpt.	10.00	35.00	150.
96A	**50 Escudos** 29.11.1945. Brown on m/c unpt.	10.00	50.00	200.
97	**100 Escudos** 29.11.1945. Orange on m/c unpt.	15.00	75.00	350.
98	**500 Escudos** 29.11.1945. Lilac on m/c unpt.	35.00	150.	500.
99	**1000 Escudos** 1945; 1947. Blue on m/c unpt.			
	a. 29.11.1945.	90.00	350.	850.
	b. 27.3.1947.	50.00	200.	650.

1947 ISSUE

#100 and 101 portr. A. Ennes at l., steamship seal at r.

		VG	VF	UNC
100	**100 Escudos** 27.3.1947. Orange on m/c unpt.	15.00	60.00	275.
101	**500 Escudos** 27.3.1947. Lilac on m/c unpt.	30.00	125.	450.

1950; 1953 ISSUE

#102 and 103 ornate church doorway at ctr. on back. Wmk: Arms. Printer: TDLR.

		VG	VF	UNC
102	**50 Escudos** 16.2.1950. Black on m/c unpt. Portr. E. Costa at r., w/text: *COLONIA PORTUGUESA* below bank name.	6.00	25.00	85.00

		VG	VF	UNC
103	**100 Escudos** 16.2.1950. Orange on m/c unpt. Portr. A. de Ornelas Evasconcelos at r., w/text: *COLONIA PORTUGUESA* below bank name.	10.00	40.00	125

#104 and 105 printer: BWC.

		VG	VF	UNC
104	**500 Escudos** 31.7.1953. Brown-violet on m/c unpt. Portr. C. Xavier at r.			
	a. Issued note.	15.00	50.00	15
	s. Specimen, punched hole cancelled.	—	—	75.0

		VG	VF	UNC
105	**1000 Escudos** 31.7.1953. Blue on m/c unpt. Portr. Mousinho de Albuquerque at r.			
	a. Issued note.	15.00	75.00	250.
	s. Specimen, punched hole cancelled.	—	—	100.

1958 ISSUE

#106 and 107 Similar to #102-3. Wmk: Arms. Printer: TDLR.

		VG	VF	UNC
106	**50 Escudos** 24.7.1958. Black on m/c. Like #102 but w/o text: *COLONIA PORTUGUESA* below bank name; w/o printing over wmk. at l. Back green.			
	a. Issued note.	1.00	5.00	15.00
	s. Specimen.	—	—	50.00
107	**100 Escudos** 24.7.1958. Like #103 but w/o text: *COLONIA PORTUGUESA* below bank name; w/o printing over wmk. at l.	2.50	10.00	50.00
108	**500 Escudos** 24.7.1958. Brown-violet. Portr. C. Xavier at r.	15.00	50.00	150.

REGIONAL

BANCO DA BEIRA

1919 LIBRA ISSUES

#R1-R33 values are primarily for cancelled notes. Most of those except for #R2-R4 w/o cancellations are worth at least double the valuations shown. Cancellations: *CANCELADO* in lg. letters or *PAGO 30.*(or other day) *11.1942* in small letters and #.

#R1-R9 printer: BWC.

		Good	Fine	XF
R1	**10 Centavos** 15.9.1919. Green and yellow. Back dk. brown.			
	a. Issued note.	2.00	6.00	15.00
	b. Cancelled.	2.00	6.00	15.00
R2	**20 Centavos** 15.9.1919. Green. Back black.			
	a. Issued note.	2.00	6.00	15.00
	b. Cancelled.	2.00	6.00	15.00

		Good	Fine	XF
R3	**50 Centavos** 15.9.1919. Black on orange-brown and m/c unpt. Back blue.			
	a. Lg. hand sign. at l.	3.00	8.00	17.50
	b. Sm. printed sign. at l.	2.00	6.00	15.00
	c. Cancelled.	3.00	8.00	17.50

		Good	Fine	XF
R4	**50 Centavos** 15.9.1919. Brown. *PRATA* deep blue in frame at top ctr.			
	a. Issued note.	2.00	6.00	15.00
	b. Cancelled.	2.00	6.00	15.00
R5	**1/2 Libra** 15.9.1919. Red on m/c unpt.	2.00	6.00	15.00

		Good	Fine	XF
R6	**1 Libra** 15.9.1919. Blue on m/c unpt.			
	a. Lg. hand sign. at l.	2.00	6.00	15.00
	b. Sm. printed sign. at l.	2.00	6.00	15.00
	c. Cancelled.	2.00	6.00	15.00

		Good	Fine	XF
R7	**1 Libra** 15.9.1919. Blue o m/c unpt. *OURO* in frame at bottom ctr.			
	a. Issued note.	2.00	6.00	15.00
	b. Cancelled.	2.00	6.00	15.00

		Good	Fine	XF
R8	**5 Libras** 15.9.1919. Blue on m/c unpt.			
	a. Lg. hand sign. at l.	4.00	12.00	30.00
	b. Sm. printed sign. at l.	4.00	12.00	30.00
R9	**5 Libras** 15.9.1919. Blue. *OURO* in frame at bottom ctr.	5.00	12.00	30.00
R10	**10 Libras** 15.9.1919.	15.00	50.00	175.
R11	**20 Libras** 15.9.1919.	25.00	75.00	200.

1919 Escudo Issue

		Good	Fine	XF
R11A	**1 Escudo** 15.9.1919. Brown. Back greenish gray. Printer: BWC.	5.00	12.00	30.00

1921 Issue

		Good	Fine	XF
R12	**10 Libras** 1.2.1921.	25.00	100.	225.
R13	**20 Libras** 1.2.1921.	25.00	100.	225.

Companhia de Moçambique, Beira

ND Provisional Libra Issue

#R14-R23 ovpt. new issuer name in rectangular frame. Printer: BWC.

		Good	Fine	XF
R14	**10 Centavos** ND (-old date 15.9.1919). Ovpt. on #R1.	2.00	6.00	20.00
R15	**20 Centavos** ND (-old date 15.9.1919). Ovpt. on #R2.	2.00	6.00	20.00
R16	**50 Centavos** ND (-old date 15.9.1919). Ovpt. on #R3.	2.00	6.00	20.00

		Good	Fine	XF
R17	**50 Centavos** ND (-old date 15.9.1919). Ovpt. on #R4.	2.00	6.00	20.00
R18	**1/2 Libra** ND (-old date 15.9.1919). Ovpt. on #R5.	2.00	6.00	20.00
R19	**1 Libra** ND (-old date 15.9.1919). Ovpt. on #R6.			
	a. Lg. hand sign. at l.	2.00	6.00	20.00
	b. Sm. printed sign. at l.	2.00	6.00	20.00

		Good	Fine	XF
R20	**1 Libra** ND (-old date 15.9.1919). Ovpt. on #R7.	3.00	8.00	20.00
R21	**5 Libras** ND (-old date 15.9.1919). Ovpt. on #R8.	4.00	15.00	40.00
R21A	**5 Libras** ND (-old date 15.9.1919). Ovpt. on #R9.	4.00	15.00	40.00
R22	**10 Libras** ND (-old date 1.2.1921). Ovpt. on #R12.	25.00	100.	200.
R23	**20 Libras** ND (-old date 1.2.1921). Ovpt. on #R13.	25.00	100.	200.

ND Provisional Escudo Issue

		Good	Fine	XF
R23A	**1 Escudo** ND (-old date 15.9.1919). Ovpt. on #R11A.	4.00	15.00	40.00

1930 Regular Issue

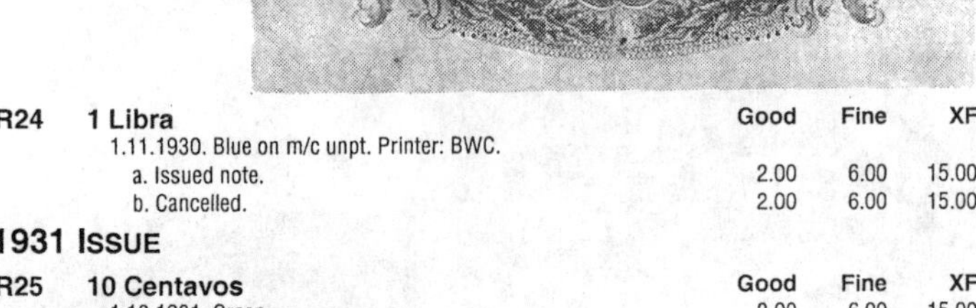

		Good	Fine	XF
R24	**1 Libra** 1.11.1930. Blue on m/c unpt. Printer: BWC.			
	a. Issued note.	2.00	6.00	15.00
	b. Cancelled.	2.00	6.00	15.00

1931 Issue

		Good	Fine	XF
R25	**10 Centavos** 1.10.1931. Green.	2.00	6.00	15.00

		Good	Fine	XF
R26	**50 Centavos** 1.10.1931. Sepia. Printer: BWC.	2.00	6.00	15.00
R27	**1/2 Libra** 1.9.1931.	2.00	6.00	15.00

1933 Issue

#R28 and R29 printer: BWC.

		Good	Fine	XF
R28	**10 Centavos** 20.10.1933. Green.	2.00	6.00	15.00

		Good	Fine	XF
R29	**20 Centavos** 25.11.1933. Blue.	2.00	6.00	12.00

1934 ISSUE

#R30-R32 printer: BWC.

		VG	VF	UNC
R30	**1/2 Libra** 15.3.1934. Red on m/c unpt. Back blue-green.			
	a. Issued note.	2.00	6.00	15.00
	s. Specimen.	—	—	35.00

		Good	Fine	XF
R31	**1 Libra** 15.3.1934. Blue.	2.00	6.00	15.00
R32	**5 Libras** 15.1.1934. Blue.	3.00	15.00	30.00

1937 ISSUE

		Good	Fine	XF
R33	**1 Escudo** 12.5.1937. Violet. Printer: BWC.	2.00	6.00	15.00

NEPAL

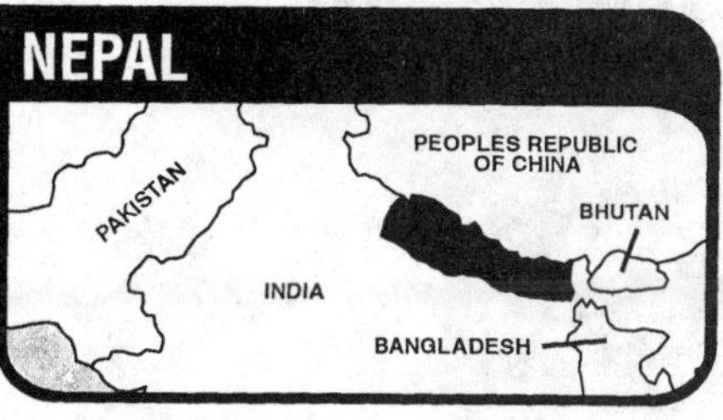

The Kingdom of Nepal, the world's only Hindu kingdom, is a landlocked country located in central Asia along the southern slopes of the Himalayan Mountains. It has an area of 56,136 sq. mi. (140,797 sq. km.) and a population of 24.35 million. Capital: Káthmandu. Nepal has substantial deposits of coal, copper, iron and cobalt but they are largely unexploited. Agriculture is the principal economic activity. Livestock, rice, timber and jute are exported.

Prithvi Narayan Shah, ruler of the principality of Gurkha, formed Nepal from a number of independent mountain states in the latter half of the 18th century. After his death a period of political instability ensued which lasted until the 1840's when the Rana family reduced the monarch to a figurehead and established itself as hereditary Prime Ministers. A popular revolution (1950-51) toppled the Rana family and reconstituted the power in the throne. In 1959 King Mahendra declared Nepal a constitutional monarchy. A new constitution promulgated in 1962 instituted a system of panchayat (village council) democracy from the village to the national levels. In 1990, following political unrest, the king's powers were reduced, and the country adopted a system of parliamentary democracy.

RULERS:

Tribhuvana Vira Vikrama Shahi Deva, 1911-1950; 1951-1955
Jnanendra Vira Vikrama Shahi Deva, 1950-1951
Mahendra Vira Vikrama Shahi Deva, 1955-1972
Birendra Bir Bikram Shahi Deva, 1972-2001
Ginendra, 2001-

MONETARY SYSTEM:

1 Mohru = 100 Paisa to 1961
1 Rupee = 100 Paisa, 1961-

HEADING VARIETIES

Type I: नेपाल सर्कार

Type II: नेपाल मरकार

NOTE: Issues in the Mohru System have reference to Rupees in English on the notes. The difference is in the Nepalese designation of the value.

For those notes in Mohru the first character at the left appears thus: म

When the Nepalese designation changes to Rupees, this character appears thus: रू

Lines where either of these appear are in the lower center on the face, or on the back. Both will never appear on the same note. All notes from the second issue of Mahendra to the present are in rupees.

SIGNATURE VARIETIES			
1	Janaph Raja	5	Laxminath Gautam
2	Bharana Raja	6	Besh Bahadur Thapa
3	Narendra Raja	7	Pradimhalal Rajbhandari
4	Himalaya Shamsher	8	Yadavnath Panta

KINGDOM

GOVERNMENT OF NEPAL

1951 ND FIRST ISSUE

		VG	VF	UNC
1	**1 Mohru** ND (1951). Blue and brown. Coin at r. w/date VS2008 (1951). Back w/coin at l., mountains at ctr. Sign. 2; 3.			
	a. Sign. 2.	1.00	2.00	6.00
	b. Sign. 3.	1.50	5.00	12.50

#2-4 portr. Kg. Tribhuvana Vira Vikrama w/plumed crown at r. Type I heading.

		VG	VF	UNC
2	**5 Mohru** ND (1951). Purple and m/c. Tiger on back. Sign. 1; 2.	3.00	15.00	50.00

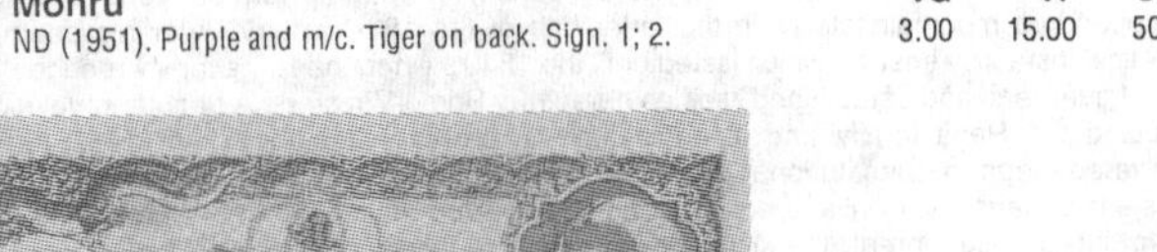

		VG	VF	UNC
3	**10 Mohru** ND (1951). Purple and m/c. Arms on back. Sign. 2.	6.00	25.00	75.00

		VG	VF	UNC
4	**100 Mohru** ND (1951). Dk. green and m/c. Rhinoceros on back.			
	a. Sign. 1.	30.00	100.	300.
	b. Sign. 2.	25.00	75.00	225.

1951 ND Second Issue

#5-7 Type II heading. Like #2-4 but sign. 3.

		VG	VF	UNC
5	**5 Mohru** ND (1951). Purple and m/c. Like #2. Sign. 3.	2.00	7.50	25.00
6	**10 Mohru** ND (1951). Purple and m/c. Like #3. Sign. 3.	3.00	10.00	40.00
7	**100 Mohru** ND (1951). Dk. green and m/c. Like #4. Sign. 3.	12.50	50.00	150.

Central Bank of Nepal

1960 ND Issue

Mohru System

		VG	VF	UNC
8	**1 Mohru** ND (1960). Violet and olive. Coin at l. w/date VS2013 (1956). Back lilac and green. Sign 4.	.50	1.50	4.00

#9-11 Port. Kg. Mahendra Vira Vikrama in civilian clothes at l.

		VG	VF	UNC
9	**5 Mohru** ND (1960). Violet and aqua. Stupa at ctr. Back violet; Himalayas. Sign. 4; 5.	.50	3.00	10.00

		VG	VF	UNC
10	**10 Mohru** ND (1960). Dk. brown and red. Temple at ctr. Back brown and gold; arms at ctr. Sign. 4; 5.	1.00	5.00	15.00

		VG	VF	UNC
11	**100 Mohru** ND (1960). Green and brown. Temple at Lalitpur at ctr. Back green; Indian rhinoceros at ctr. Sign. 4; 5.	6.00	25.00	75.00

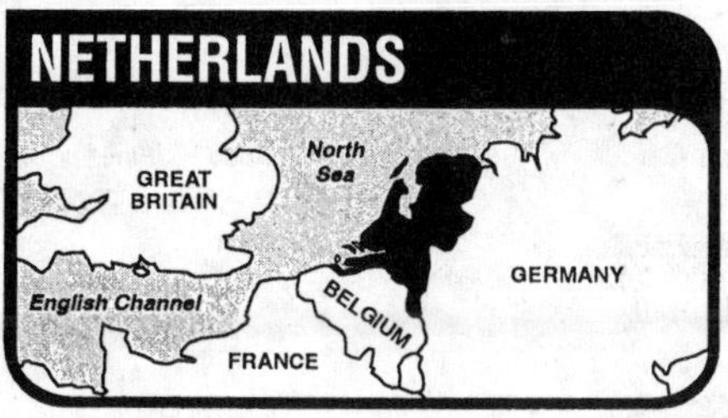

The Kingdom of the Netherlands, a country of western Europe fronting on the North Sea and bordered by Belgium and Germany, has an area of 15,770 sq. mi. (40,844 sq. km.) and a population of 15.87 million. Capital: Amsterdam, but the seat of government is at The Hague. The economy is d on dairy farming and a variety of industrial activities. Chemicals, yarns and fabrics, and meat products are exported.

After being a part of Charlemagne's empire in the 8th and 9th centuries, the Netherlands came under the control of Burgundy and the Austrian Hapsburgs, and finally were subjected to Spanish domination in the 16th century. Led by William of Orange, the Dutch revolted against Spain in 1568. The seven northern provinces formed the Union of Utrecht and declared their independence in 1581, becoming the Republic of the United Netherlands. In the following century, the "Golden Age" of Dutch history, the Netherlands became a great sea and colonial power, a patron of the arts and a refuge for the persecuted. In 1814, all the provinces of Holland and Belgium were merged into the Kingdom of the United Netherlands under William I. The Belgians withdrew in 1830 to form their own kingdom, the last substantial change in the configuration of European Netherlands. German forces invaded in 1940 and the royal family fled to England where a government in exile was formed. German High Commissioner Arthur Seyss-Inquart was placed in command until 1945 when the arrival of Allied military forces ended the occupation. Reigning since 1948, Queen Juliana abdicated in 1981. Her daughter, Beatrix, is now Queen.

RULERS:

Spanish, until 1581
William I, 1815-1840
William II, 1840-1849
William III, 1849-1890
Wilhelmina, 1890-1948
Juliana, 1948-1981
Beatrix, 1981-

MONETARY SYSTEM:

1 Gulden = 20 Stuivers
1 Gulden = 100 Cents, to 2001
1 Rijksdaalder = 2 1/2 Gulden
1 Euro = 100 Cents, 2002-

DUTCH 'RECEPIS'

GEMEENE LANDS COMPTOIREN

1794 ISSUE

		Good	Fine	XF
B5	**3 Gulden** 1.12.1794-1.1.1795. Black. Rare.	—	--	—

COMMITTF VAN FINANCIE IN 'S HAGE

FINANCE COMMITTEE IN THE HAGUE

ALKMAAR

1795 ISSUE

		Good	Fine	XF
B10	**2 1/4 Stuiver** 7.4.1795. Black. Rare.	—	—	—
B11	**4 1/2 Stuiver** 7.4.1795. Black. Rare.	—	—	—
B12	**9 Stuiver** 7.4.1795. Black. Rare.	—	—	—
B13	**11 1/4 Stuiver** 7.4.1795. Black. Rare.	—	—	—
B14	**45 Stuiver** 7.4.1795. Black. Rare.	—	—	—

DELFT

1795 ISSUE

		Good	Fine	XF
B17	**4 Stuiver & 8 Pennigen** 9.5.1795. Black. Rare.	—	—	—

DORDECHT

1795 ISSUE

		Good	Fine	XF
B20	**18 Gulden** ND (1795). Black. Rare.	—	—	—
B21	**27 Gulden** ND (1795). Black. Rare.	—	—	—
B22	**54 Gulden** ND (1795). Black. Rare.	—	—	—
B23	**90 Gulden** ND (1795). Black. Rare.	—	—	—

1795 (FEBRUARY) ISSUE

		Good	Fine	XF
B25	**2 1/2 Stuiver** 16.2.1795. Black. Rare.	—	—	—
B26	**5 Stuiver** 16.2.1795. Black. Rare.	—	—	—
B27	**24 Stuiver** 16.2.1795. Black. Rare.	—	—	—

1795 (MARCH) ISSUE

		Good	Fine	XF
B30	**10 Stuiver** 1.3.1795. Black. Rare.	—	—	—

1795 (MAY) ISSUE

		Good	Fine	XF
B32	**2 1/2 Stuiver** 1.5.1795. Black. Rare.	—	—	—

1795 BREAD EQUIVALENT ISSUE

		Good	Fine	XF
B33	**4 Stuiver = 4 Ponds Brot** ND (1796). Black.			
	a. Issued note. Rare.	—	—	—
	b. W/o serial numbers. Rare.	—	—	—

ENKUISEN

1795 ISSUE

RECEPISSE der Stad ENKHUIZEN, om in 't vervolg te verwisselen voor Lands Recepissen.
Goed voor Vier en een halve stuiv:
Enkhuizen den 15 May 1795.
In naam der Municipaliteit
4½ stuiv:
No. 900.
A. J. Kluppel.

		Good	Fine	XF
B40	**4 1/2 Stuiver** 15.5.1795. Black. Rare.	—	—	—

RECEPISSE der Stad ENKHUIZEN, om in 't vervolg te verwisselen voor Lands Recepissen.
Goed voor Ses drie quart stuiv:
Enkhuizen den 15 May 1795.
In naam der Municipaliteit
6¾ stuiv:
No. 349
A. J. Kluppel.

		Good	Fine	XF
B41	**6 3/4 Stuiver** 15.5.1795. Black. Rare.	—	—	—
B42	**22 1/2 Stuiver** 15.5.1795. Black. Rare.	—	—	—
B43	**45 Stuiver** 15.5.1795. Black. Rare.	—	—	—
B44	**90 Stuiver** 15.5.1795. Black. Rare.	—	—	—

GORINCHEM

1795 ND *VERWISFELDE ADSIGNATEN* ISSUE

Verwisselde Assignaten.
Gangbaar in Gorinchem, voor VIER en EEN HALVE stuiv:
te verwisselen in Provintiale Recepissen van wegens de Provisioneele Representanten.
4½ st. No.

		Good	Fine	XF
B47	**4 1/2 Stuiver** ND (1795). Black. Rare.	—	—	—

Verwisselde Assignaten;
Gangbaar in Gorinchem, voor ZES en DRIE QUART stuiv:
te verwisselen in Provintiale Recepissen van wegens de Provisioneele Representanten.
6¾ st. No.

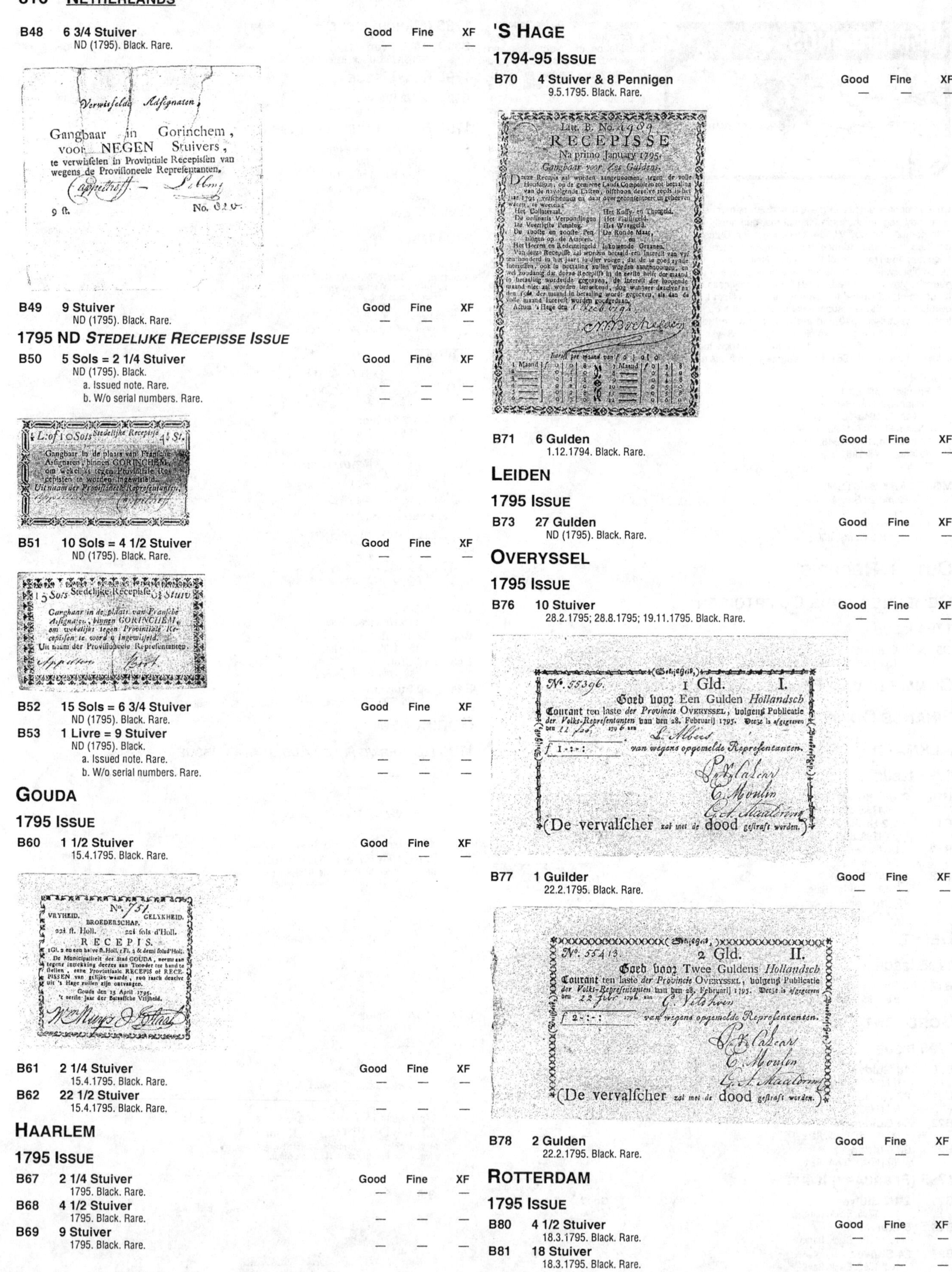

		Good	Fine	XF
B48	**6 3/4 Stuiver** ND (1795). Black. Rare.	—	—	—
B49	**9 Stuiver** ND (1795). Black. Rare.	—	—	—

1795 ND *Stedelijke Recepisse* Issue

		Good	Fine	XF
B50	**5 Sols = 2 1/4 Stuiver** ND (1795). Black.			
	a. Issued note. Rare.	—	—	—
	b. W/o serial numbers. Rare.	—	—	—
B51	**10 Sols = 4 1/2 Stuiver** ND (1795). Black. Rare.	—	—	—
B52	**15 Sols = 6 3/4 Stuiver** ND (1795). Black. Rare.	—	—	—
B53	**1 Livre = 9 Stuiver** ND (1795). Black.			
	a. Issued note. Rare.	—	—	—
	b. W/o serial numbers. Rare.	—	—	—

Gouda

1795 Issue

		Good	Fine	XF
B60	**1 1/2 Stuiver** 15.4.1795. Black. Rare.	—	—	—
B61	**2 1/4 Stuiver** 15.4.1795. Black. Rare.	—	—	—
B62	**22 1/2 Stuiver** 15.4.1795. Black. Rare.	—	—	—

Haarlem

1795 Issue

		Good	Fine	XF
B67	**2 1/4 Stuiver** 1795. Black. Rare.	—	—	—
B68	**4 1/2 Stuiver** 1795. Black. Rare.	—	—	—
B69	**9 Stuiver** 1795. Black. Rare.	—	—	—

'S Hage

1794-95 Issue

		Good	Fine	XF
B70	**4 Stuiver & 8 Pennigen** 9.5.1795. Black. Rare.	—	—	—
B71	**6 Gulden** 1.12.1794. Black. Rare.	—	—	—

Leiden

1795 Issue

		Good	Fine	XF
B73	**27 Gulden** ND (1795). Black. Rare.	—	—	—

Overyssel

1795 Issue

		Good	Fine	XF
B76	**10 Stuiver** 28.2.1795; 28.8.1795; 19.11.1795. Black. Rare.	—	—	—
B77	**1 Guilder** 22.2.1795. Black. Rare.	—	—	—
B78	**2 Gulden** 22.2.1795. Black. Rare.	—	—	—

Rotterdam

1795 Issue

		Good	Fine	XF
B80	**4 1/2 Stuiver** 18.3.1795. Black. Rare.	—	—	—
B81	**18 Stuiver** 18.3.1795. Black. Rare.	—	—	—

		Good	Fine	XF
B82	**4 Gulden & 10 Stuivers** 18.3.1795. Black. Rare.	—	—	—
B83	**9 Gulden** 18.3.1795. Black. Rare.	—	—	—

SCHIEDAM

1795 ISSUE

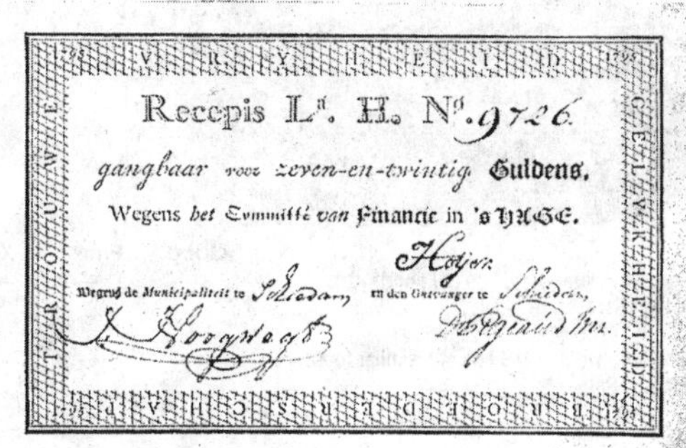

		Good	Fine	XF
B85	**27 Gulden** ND (1795). Black. Rare.	—	—	—
B86	**180 Gulden** ND (1795). Black. Rare.	—	—	—

1795 SECOND ISSUE

		Good	Fine	XF
B88	**4 1/2 Stuiver** 28.3.1795; 30.4.1795. Black. Rare.	—	—	—
B89	**9 Stuiver** 21.3.1795; 22.3.1795; 23.3.1795; 24.3.1795; 25.3.1795; 30.3.1795; 4.7.1795; 7.5.1795. Black. Rare.	—	—	—
B90	**1 Guilder & 2 Stuivers & 8 Pennnigen** 5.4.1795; 6.4.1795. Black.			
	a. Issued note. Rare.	—	—	—
	b. W/o serial numbers. Rare.	—	—	—
B91	**2 Gulden & 5 Stuivers** 29.3.1795; 4.4.1795; 6.4.1795; 8.4.1795; Black.			
	a. Issued note. Rare.	—	—	—
	b. W/o serial numbers. Rare.	—	—	—
B92	**4 Gulden & 10 Stuivers** 28.3.1795; 29.3.1795; 7.4.1795. Black.			
	a. Issued note. Rare.	—	—	—
	b. W/o serial numbers. Rare.	—	—	—
B93	**11 Gulden & 5 Stuivers** 28.3.1795; 7.4.1795. Black.			
	a. Issued note. Rare.	—	—	—
	b. W/o serial numbers. Rare.	—	—	—
B94	**22 Gulden & 10 Stuivers** 28.3.1795; 3.4.1795; 6.4.1795; 9.4.1795. Black. Rare.	—	—	—

ZEELAND

1795 ISSUE

		Good	Fine	XF
B95	**18 Duiten = 2 1/4 Stuiver** 23.3.1795. Black. *Lit: D.* Rare.	—	—	—
B96	**4 1/2 Stuiver** 23.3.1795. Black. *Lit: C.*			
	a. Issued note. Rare.	—	—	—
	b. W/o serial numbers. Rare.	—	—	—

		Good	Fine	XF
B97	**9 Stuiver** 23.3.1795. Black. *Lit: B.* Rare.	—	—	—

		Good	Fine	XF
B98	**18 Stuiver** 23.3.1795. Black. *Lit: A, AAA* or *AAAA.* Rare.	—	—	—

W/O DOMICILE

1795 ISSUE

		Good	Fine	XF
B101	**450 Gulden** ND (1795). Black. Rare.	—	—	—

KONINKRIJK - KINGDOM

DE NEDERLANDSCHE BANK

NETHERLANDS BANK

1814 ISSUE

		Good	Fine	XF
A2	**25 Gulden** 1814-38. Rose.	—	—	—
A3	**40 Gulden** 1814-38. Rose. Rare.	—	—	—
A4	**60 Gulden** 1814-38. Rose. Rare.	—	—	—
A5	**80 Gulden** 1814-25. Rose. Rare.	—	—	—
A6	**100 Gulden** 1814-38. Rose. Rare.	—	—	—
A7	**200 Gulden** 1814-38. Rose. Rare.	—	—	—
A8	**300 Gulden** 1814-38. Rose. Rare.	—	—	—
A9	**500 Gulden** 1814-38. Rose. Rare.	—	—	—
A10	**1000 Gulden** 1814-38. Rose. Earlier notes w/value written, later notes w/value printed. Rare.	—	—	—

KONINKRIJK DER NEDERLANDEN

MUNTBILJETTEN - STATE NOTES

LAW OF 18.12.1845

#A11-A15 wmk: *RIJKS MUNT.* Uniface.

		Good	Fine	XF
A11	**5 Gulden** 1.1.1846. Red. Rare.	—	—	—
A12	**10 Gulden** 1.1.1846. Brown. Rare.	—	—	—

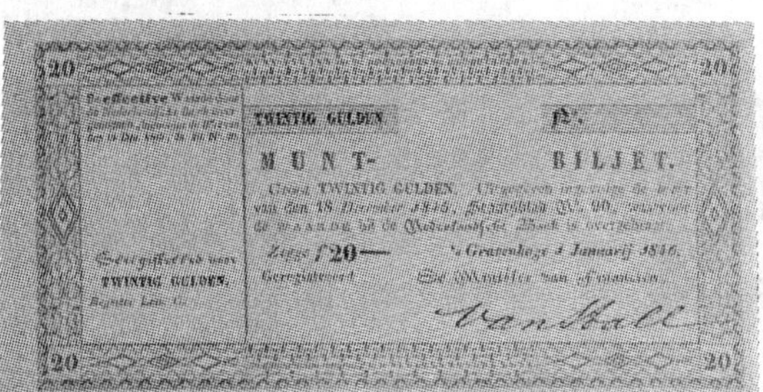

		Good	Fine	XF
A13	**20 Gulden** 1.1.1846. Green. Rare.	—	—	—

NOTICE

Readers with unlisted dates, signature varieties, etc. are invited to submit photocopies or, high resolution (300 dpi, 100% size) scans of their notes to: Standard Catalog of World Paper Money, 700 East State St. Iola, WI 54990-0001, or E-Mail: george.cuhaj@fwpubs.com.

		Good	Fine	XF
A14	**100 Gulden** 1.1.1846. Blue. Rare.	—	—	—
A15	**500 Gulden** 1.1.1846. Yellow. Rare.	—	—	—

LAW OF 17.9.1849

#A16-A18 various printed or handwritten dates in 1849.

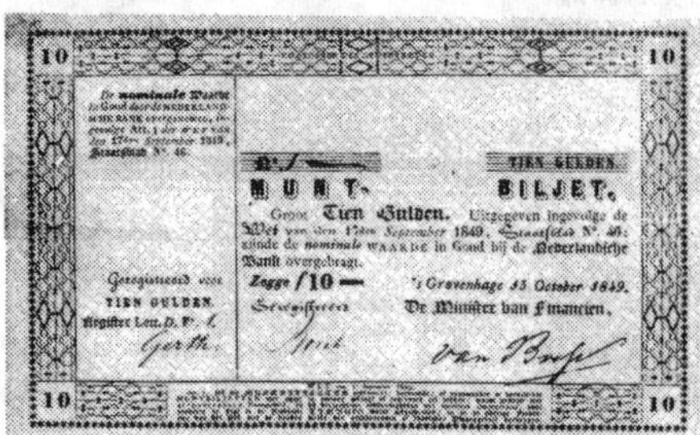

		Good	Fine	XF
A16	**10 Gulden** 15.10.1849. Blue. Rare.	—	—	—
A17	**100 Gulden** 1849. Red on gray unpt. Rare.	—	—	—
A18	**500 Gulden** 1849. Brown on blue unpt. Rare.	—	—	—
A19	**1000 Gulden** 1849. Green on red unpt. Rare.	—	—	—

1852 ISSUE

		Good	Fine	XF
A20	**10 Gulden** 1852-78. Lt. blue. Allegorical figures on borders, arms at upper ctr. Various date and sign. varieties. Rare.	—	—	—

1878 ISSUE

		Good	Fine	XF
1	**10 Gulden** 1878-94. Lt. brown. Arms at upper ctr., ornate border. Various date and sign. varieties. Rare.	—	—	—

1884-94 ISSUE

#2 and 3, various date and sign. varieties.

		Good	Fine	XF
2	**10 Gulden** 1894-98. Brown. Standing woman and lion at l., portr. Qn. Wilhelmina as child at r. Rare.	—	—	—
3	**50 Gulden** 1884-1914. Blue. Standing women and lion at l. similar to #2. Portr. Kg. William III at r. Rare.	—	—	—

1898 ISSUE

		Good	Fine	XF
3A	**10 Gulden** 1898-1914. Similar to #2 but older portr. Qn. Wilhelmina at r. Various date and sign. varieties. Rare.	—	—	—

ZILVERBONNEN - SILVER NOTES

1914 ISSUE

		Good	Fine	XF
4	**1 Gulden** 7.8.1914. Brown. Value *1* at ctr.			
	a. Issued note.	12.50	60.00	150.
	p. Proof.	—	Unc	30.00

		Good	Fine	XF
5	**2 1/2 Gulden** 7.8.1914. Blue on green unpt. Value *2.50* at ctr. Thick or thin paper.			
	a. Issued note.	50.00	150.	350.
	p. Proof.	—	Unc	50.00

		Good	Fine	XF
6	**5 Gulden** 7.8.1914. Green.			
	a. Issued note.	70.00	250.	650.
	p. Proof.	—	Unc	75.00

1915 ISSUE

		Good	Fine	XF
7	**2 1/2 Gulden** 30.3.1915. Blue. Value *2.50* at ctr. and at the 4 corners.	30.00	100.	300.

1916 Issue

		Good	Fine	XF
8	**1 Gulden** 1.5.1916. Brown. Value *1* at ctr. and at the 4 corners.	10.00	50.00	150.
9	**2 1/2 Gulden** 31.3.1916. Blue. Like #7.	30.00	100.	300.

1917 Issue

		Good	Fine	XF
10	**1 Gulden** 1.11.1917. Brown. Like #8.	10.00	50.00	150.
11	**2 1/2 Gulden** 1.8.1917. Blue. Like #7.	20.00	80.00	250.

1918 First Issue

		Good	Fine	XF
12	**2 1/2 Gulden** 1.7.1918. Blue on gray and yellow unpt. Value *2.50* at l., at ctr. and upper and lower r.	10.00	50.00	150.

1918 Second Issue

		Good	Fine	XF
13	**1 Gulden** 1.10.1918. Brown. Like #8.	10.00	50.00	150.
14	**2 1/2 Gulden** 1.10.1918. Like #12.	10.00	50.00	150.

1920 Issue

		Good	Fine	XF
15	**1 Gulden** 1.2.1920. Brown on lt. green unpt. Portr. Qn. Wilhelmina at l.	3.50	25.00	100.
16	**2 1/2 Gulden** 1.10.1920. Like #12.	5.00	30.00	125.

1922 Issues

		Good	Fine	XF
17	**2 1/2 Gulden** 1.5.1922. Like #12.			
	a. Issued note.	5.00	30.00	125.
	x. Counterfeit w/date: 1.10.1922.	5.00	30.00	125.

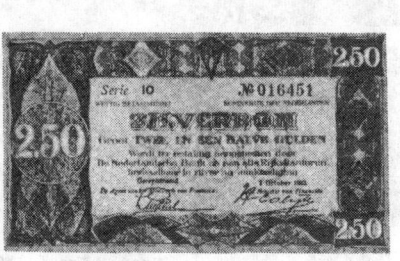

		Good	Fine	XF
18	**2 1/2 Gulden** 1.12.1922. Like #12.	5.00	30.00	125.

1923 Issue

		Good	Fine	XF
19	**2 1/2 Gulden** 1.10.1923. Face like #12. Back w/o unpt. in inner rectangle.			
	a. Issued note.	5.00	30.00	125.
	p. Proof.	—	Unc	35.00

1927 Issue

		Good	Fine	XF
20	**2 1/2 Gulden** 1.10.1927. Like #19.	4.00	25.00	100.

De Nederlandsche Bank

Netherlands Bank

1904-11 "Old Style" Issue

#21-27 various date and sign. varieties.

#21-23 arms w/caduceus and lion at top ctr.

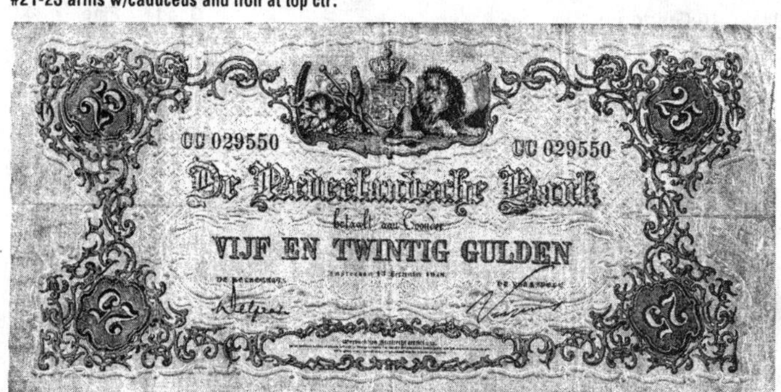

		Good	Fine	XF
21	**25 Gulden** 27.9.1904-7.12.1921. Black on orange unpt. 7 sign. varieties. Uniface.	150.	450.	1000.

		Good	Fine	XF
22	**40 Gulden** 6.6.1910; 11.7.1921; 13.9.1921; 11.12.1922. Black on green unpt. Like #21. 6 sign. varieties. Uniface.	300.	800.	2000.

		Good	Fine	XF
23	**60 Gulden** 11.8.1910-1.9.1924. Black on lilac-brown unpt. Like #21. 6 sign. varieties. Uniface.	300.	800.	2000.

#24-27 portr. Minerva at top ctr.

		Good	Fine	XF
24	**100 Gulden** 1.3.1911; 17.2.1919; 2.1.1920; 13.10.1921. Black. Back blue. 4 sign. varieties.	300.	850.	2250.
25	**200 Gulden** 18.10.1910; 2.7.1921. Black. Back orange. Like #24. 3 sign. varieties.	500.	1500.	3000.
26	**300 Gulden** 15.2.1909; 3.1.1921. Black. Back green. Like #24. 3 sign. varieties.	500.	1500.	3000.
27	**1000 Gulden** 3.10.1910; 22.5.1916. Black and blue. Back red. Like #24. 4 sign. varieties. Rare.	—	—	—

1906 "New Style" Issue

		Good	Fine	XF
34	**10 Gulden** 18.6.1906; 24.9.1913; 18.3.1914; 29.6.1916; 20.10.1920-5.2.1921. Blue. Allegorical figures of Labor at l., Welfare at r. *AMSTERDAM* and serial # on face. 4 sign varieties. Back brown and green.	175.	500.	1200.

1914 "Old Style" Issue

		Good	Fine	XF
28	**10 Gulden** 1.8.1914. Red on green unpt. W/o vignette. Back blue. Rare.	—	—	—

		Good	Fine	XF
29	**25 Gulden** 1.8.1914. Red on green unpt. Like #28. Rare.	—	—	—
30	**40 Gulden** 1.8.1914. Green on lt. green unpt. Like #28. Rare.	—	—	—

		Good	Fine	XF
31	**60 Gulden** 1.8.1914. Brown on green unpt. Like #28. Rare.	—	—	—

#32-33 portr. Minerva at top ctr.

		Good	Fine	XF
32	**100 Gulden** 1.8.1914. Black on rose unpt. Rare.	—	—	—

		Good	Fine	XF
32A	**200 Gulden** 1.8.1914. Black on orange unpt. Rare.	—	—	—

		Good	Fine	XF
32B	**300 Gulden** 1.8.1914. Black on green unpt. Rare.	—	—	—
33	**1000 Gulden** 1.8.1914. Black on blue unpt. Rare.	—	—	—

1919-23 "New Style" Issue

		Good	Fine	XF
35	**10 Gulden** 9.5.1921-16.5.1923. Like #34 but *AMSTERDAM* and serial # on back.	12.50	50.00	175

		Good	Fine	XF
36	**25 Gulden** 1921. Red. Mercury seated at l., portr. William of Orange at top ctr., galleon at r. Back red and green; bank bldg. at ctr. Sign. handwritten. Thick or thin paper.			
	a. *AMSTERDAM* in date 17mm wide; serial # prefix letters extra bold. 26.9.1921; 30.9.1921; 3.10.1921.	75.00	200.	550.
	b. *AMSTERDAM* in date 19mm wide; serial # prefix letters in 1 or 2 lines. 9.8.1921; 15.8.1921.	50.00	150.	450.

		Good	Fine	XF
37	**40 Gulden** 1.2.1923; 12.2.1923; 15.2.1923. Green. Mercury seated at l., portr. Prince Maurits at top ctr., galleon at r. bottom (riverside in Amsterdam from a painting by J.H. Maris (1537-1599).) Back green; bank bldg.	350.	750.	1850.

		Good	Fine	XF
38	**60 Gulden** 9.4.1923. Brown-violet. Mercury seated at l., Prince Frederik Hendrik at top ctr., galleon at r. bottom (riverside in Amsterdam). Back green; bank bldg.	300.	650.	1250.

#39-42 woman seated at l.

		Good	Fine	XF
39	**100 Gulden** 1922-29. Blue.			
	a. Prefix letter and serial # 4mm. W/o serial # on back. 23.1.1922; 4.2.1922.	30.00	120.	400.
	b. Prefix letter and serial # 4mm. Serial # and text on back. *Hij die biljetten...* 10.9.1924; 15.9.1924.	25.00	100.	350.
	c. Prefix letter and serial # 4mm. Serial # and text on back: *Het Namaken...* 12.3.1926.	20.00	75.00	250.
	d. Prefix letter and serial # 3mm. Serial # and text on back. *Het Namaken...* 11.2.1927; 4.12.1928; 7.12.1928; 8.12.1928; 6.9.1929.	20.00	75.00	250.

NOTICE

Readers with unlisted dates, signature varieties, etc. are invited to submit photocopies or, high resolution (300 dpi, 100% size) scans of their notes to: Standard Catalog of World Paper Money, 700 East State St. Iola, WI 54990-0001, or E-Mail: george.cuhaj@fwpubs.com.

		Good	Fine	XF
40	**200 Gulden** 1.12.1922; 3.1.1925; 8.4.1926; 18.2.1927. Red-brown.	300.	850.	2000.

		Good	Fine	XF
41	**300 Gulden** 2.12.1922; 9.4.1926; 19.2.1927. Green.	300.	850.	2000.
42	**1000 Gulden** 23.6.1919-5.3.1921. Sepia.	225.	500.	1250.

1924-29 ISSUES

		Good	Fine	XF
43	**10 Gulden** 1924-32. Dk. blue. Zeeland farmer's wife at lower ctr. Back purple and brown.			
	a. Black sign. w/text: *Het in vooraad...* on back. 29.3.1924; 10.7.1924.	4.00	15.00	50.00
	b. Black sign. w/text: *Het namaken...* Prefix letter before serial # on back. (2 types). 1.3.1924 - 8.4.1930.	3.50	12.00	45.00
	c. Blue sign. w/text: *Het namaken...* Prefix letter before serial # at lower l. and at upper r. on back. 2 sign. varieties. Vissering/Delprat or Trip/Delprat). 20.4.1930; 1.8.1930; 11.9.1930; 2.1.1931; 7.4.1931; 13.4.1934; 25.6.1934; 1.8.1931; 8.4.1932.	3.50	12.00	45.00
	d. Blue sign. w/text: *Wetboek van Strafrecht...* on back. 21.3.1932; 6.5.1932.	3.50	12.00	45.00

		Good	Fine	XF
44	**20 Gulden** 2.1.1926-25.11.1936. Black on olive unpt. Sailor at the helm at bottom ctr. r. 2 sign. varieties.	8.50	45.00	150.

		Good	Fine	XF
45	**25 Gulden** 13.7.1927-3.8.1928. Blue. Face like #36. Back blue and brown; w/o bank at ctr. Sign. handwritten.	20.00	50.00	125.
46	**25 Gulden** 15.7.1929-28.6.1930. Red face and back. Like #45. Sign. printed.	12.00	40.00	125.

		Good	Fine	XF
47	**50 Gulden** 18.4.1929-18.5.1931. Gray-blue. Helmeted Minerva at r. (Wisdom), black or blue sign.	8.00	35.00	125.

		Good	Fine	XF
48	**1000 Gulden** 1.10.1926-19.9.1938. Dk. green and violet. Like #42. Serial # over serial letter prefix unpt. on back. 3 sign. varieties.	20.00	75.00	250.

1930-33 Issue

		Good	Fine	XF
49	**10 Gulden** 1.6.1933-18.9.1939. Dk. blue. Portr. old man wearing a cap at r. by Rembrandt. Back green, brown and m/c.	1.00	6.00	30.00

		Good	Fine	XF
50	**25 Gulden** 1.6.1931-19.3.1941. Red and m/c. Portr. bank president W. C. Mees at lower r. 2 sign. varieties.	1.50	8.00	40.00

		Good	Fine	XF
51	**100 Gulden** 1930-44. Brown and m/c. Portr. women at top l. ctr. and upper r. (reflected images).			
	a. Date at ctr. on back. 4 sign. varieties. 1.10.1930; 9.3.1931; 28.11.1936; 1.12.1936.	3.00	20.00	80.00
	b. As a. 13.3.1939-28.5.1941.	2.50	12.00	60.00
	c. Date at upper l. and at lower r. on back. 12.1.1942-30.3.1944.	1.50	8.00	40.00

		Good	Fine	XF
52	**500 Gulden** 1.12.1930; 2.12.1930; 4.12.1930. Gray-blue and m/c. Portr. Stadhouder/Kg. William III at top ctr. r. Galleon in unpt.	90.00	400.	950.

1939-41 Issues

		Good	Fine	XF
53	**10 Gulden** 1.5.1940-3.1.1941. Brown and dk. green. Portr. Qn. Emma at r.	4.00	15.00	45.00

		Good	Fine	XF
54	**20 Gulden** 20.7.1939-19.3.1941. Violet and olive. Portr. Qn. Emma at r. "Men-O-War" of the 17th century at l. Schreiers Tower l. and St. Nicolaas Church r. on back. (Both in Amsterdam.)	2.00	10.00	50.00

		Good	Fine	XF
55	**20 Gulden** 19.3.1941. Ovpt: *AMSTERDAM* new date w/bar obliterating old date on #54.	40.00	125.	275.

1940; 1941 ISSUE

		Good	Fine	XF
56	**10 Gulden** 1940-42. Blue and green. Young girl at r. by P.J. Moreelse (1571-1638).			
	a. Wmk: Head of an old man. 19.7. 1940-19.3.1941.	1.00	4.00	17.50
	b. Wmk: Grapes. 10.4.1941-19.9.1942.	1.00	3.00	12.50

		Good	Fine	XF
57	**25 Gulden** 20.5.1940. Olive-brown. Young girl at r. by P.J. Moreelse. Wide margin unprinted at l. Geometric designs on back.	3.50	20.00	65.00

		Good	Fine	XF
58	**50 Gulden** 7.1.1941-6.2.1943. Dk. brown and m/c. Woman at l. and at r. by J. Steen. "Winter Landscape" by I. van Ostade on back.	4.50	20.00	50.00

1943 ISSUE

		Good	Fine	XF
59	**10 Gulden** 4.1.1943-21.4.1944. Blue, violet-blue and m/c. Man w/hat painting by Rembrandt.	.75	3.00	10.00

		Good	Fine	XF
60	**25 Gulden** 4.10.1943-13.4.1944. Red-brown. Like #57 but *DNB* in frame in l. margin.	1.50	7.50	25.00

KONINKRIJK DER NEDERLANDEN

ZILVERBONNEN - SILVER NOTES

1938 ISSUE

		VG	VF	UNC
61	**1 Gulden** 1.10.1938. Brown. Similar to #15. Arms and text in green on back.	.25	.50	5.00

		VG	VF	UNC
62	**2 1/2 Gulden** 1.10.1938. Blue. Similar to #12, but different border and w/o value at upper r.	.25	.75	7.00

1944 Issue

		VG	VF	UNC
63	**5 Gulden** 16.10.1944. Green. Large *5's* at l. and r. 3 serial # varieties.	3.00	8.00	40.00

Muntbiljetten - State Notes

1943 Issue

#64-69 portr. Qn. Wilhelmina at ctr. Back orange; arms at ctr. Printer: ABNC.

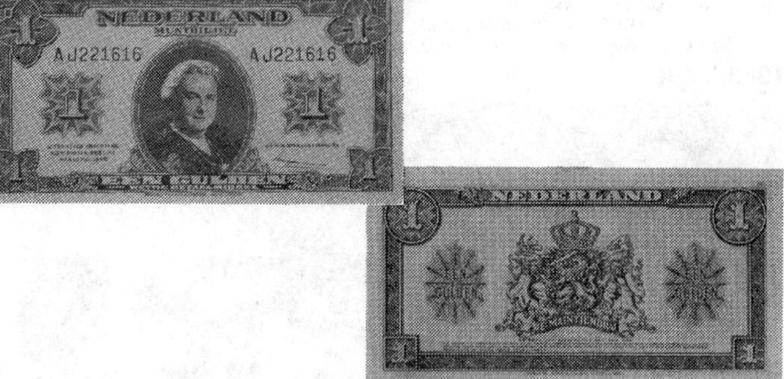

		VG	VF	UNC
64	**1 Gulden** 4.2.1943. Red.	.50	4.00	15.00

		VG	VF	UNC
65	**2 1/2 Gulden** 4.2.1943. Green.	2.00	7.50	30.00
66	**10 Gulden** 4.2.1943. Blue.	7.50	40.00	110.

		VG	VF	UNC
67	**25 Gulden** 4.2.1943. Olive.	100.	275.	550.

		VG	VF	UNC
68	**50 Gulden** 4.2.1943. Brown.	150.	375.	750.

		VG	VF	UNC
69	**100 Gulden** 4.2.1943. Black.	95.00	200.	400.

1945 Issue

#70-71 arms at ctr. on back. Printer: TDLR.

		VG	VF	UNC
70	**1 Gulden** 18.5.1945. Brown on lt. green unpt. Portr. Qn. Wilhelmina at ctr. 2 serial # varieties.	.50	3.00	15.00
71	**2 1/2 Gulden** 18.5.1945. Blue on pink unpt. Like #70. 3 serial # varieties.	.50	4.00	20.00

1949 Issue

#72-73 printer: JEZ.

		VG	VF	UNC
72	**1 Gulden** 8.8.1949. Brown on lt. green unpt. Portr. Qn. Juliana at l.	.25	1.00	8.00
73	**2 1/2 Gulden** 8.8.1949. Blue. Like #72.	.25	1.50	10.00

De Nederlandsche Bank

1945 Issue

		VG	VF	UNC
74	**10 Gulden** 7.5.1945. Blue and brown-violet. Stylized arms w/lion at bottom ctr. 2 serial # varieties.	5.00	35.00	100.

#75-76 printer: TDLR.

		VG	VF	UNC
75	**10 Gulden** 7.5.1945. Blue on m/c unpt. Portr. Kg. William I at r. Back red and olive; colliery. 2 serial # varieties.			
	a. Date at r. 1788-1843 (incorrect).	10.00	30.00	85.00
	b. Date at r. 1772-1843.	7.50	20.00	60.00

		VG	VF	UNC
76	**20 Gulden** 7.5.1945. Brown. Portr. Stadhouder/Kg. William III at r. Back green; Moerdyk bridge. 2 serial # varieties.	15.00	45.00	150.

		VG	VF	UNC
77	**25 Gulden** 7.5.1945. Maroon and tan. Young girl at r., a painting *The Girl in Blue* by J.C. Verspronk (1597-1662). 2 serial # varieties.	15.00	55.00	160.

		VG	VF	UNC
78	**50 Gulden** 7.5.1945. Brown. Prince William II as a youth at r.	25.00	80.00	200.
79	**100 Gulden** 7.5.1945. Brown. W/o vignette.	70.00	150.	350.

		VG	VF	UNC
80	**1000 Gulden** 7.5.1945. Blue-black on orange and green unpt. Portr. William the Silent at r. Back blue and gray; dike at ctr. Printer: W&S.	200.	600.	1250.

1947 ISSUE

		VG	VF	UNC
81	**25 Gulden** 19.3.1947. Red and green. Young girl wearing flowers in her hair at r.	20.00	60.00	200.
82	**100 Gulden** 9.7.1947. Brown. Woman at r. Back m/c.	30.00	100.	225.

1949 ISSUE

		VG	VF	UNC
83	**10 Gulden** 4.3.1949. Blue. Face like #75b. Landscape w/windmill (after a painting by J. I. Ruisdael) on back. Printer: TDLR.	5.00	15.00	65.00

		VG	VF	UNC
84	**25 Gulden** 1.7.1949. Brownish orange. Kg. Solomon at r. Printer: JEZ.	7.50	30.00	100.

1953; 1956 ISSUE

#85-89 printer: JEZ.

		VG	VF	UNC
85	**10 Gulden** 23.3.1953. Blue, brown and green. H. de Groot. at r.	FV	6.50	20.00

		VG	VF	UNC
86	**20 Gulden** 8.11.1955. Green and lilac. Boerhaave at r. Serpent at l. on back.	5.00	20.00	80.00
87	**25 Gulden** 10.4.1955. Red, orange and brown. C. Huygens at r.	FV	15.00	50.00

		VG	VF	UNC
88	**100 Gulden** 2.2.1953. Dk. brown. Erasmus at r. Back red-brown; stylized bird at l.	FV	75.00	200.

		VG	VF	UNC
89	**1000 Gulden** 15.7.1956. Brown and green. Rembrandt at r. Hand w/brush and palette on back.	FV	700.	1000.

Occupation of Germany, Post - WWII

Ministerie van Oorlog

ND Issues

		VG	VF	UNC
M1	**1 Gulden** ND. Brown. Like #M3.	75.00	150.	300.
M2	**5 Gulden** ND. Green. Like #M3.	100.	200.	400.

		VG	VF	UNC
M3	**25 Gulden** ND. Violet.	125.	275.	500.

NETHERLANDS ANTILLES

The Netherlands Antilles, part of the Netherlands realm, comprise two groups of islands in the West Indies: Bonaire and Curacao near the Venezuelan coast; and St. Eustatius, and the southern part of St. Martin (St. Maarten) southeast of Puerto Rico. The island group has an area of 385 sq. mi. (961 sq. km.) and a population of 210,000. Capital: Willemstad. Chief industries are the refining of crude oil, and tourism. Petroleum products and phosphates are exported.

On Dec. 15, 1954, the Netherlands Antilles were given complete domestic autonomy and granted equality within the Kingdom with Surinam and the Netherlands. The island of Aruba gained independence in 1986.

RULERS:
Dutch

MONETARY SYSTEM:
1 Gulden = 100 Cents

Dutch Administration

Nederlandse Antillen

1955 Muntbiljet Note Issue

		VG	VF	UNC
A1	**2 1/2 Gulden** 1955; 1964. Blue. Ship in dry dock at ctr. Crowned supported arms at ctr. on back. Printer: ABNC.			
	a. 1955.	7.50	35.00	200.
	b. 1964.	5.00	25.00	175.
	s. As a or b. Specimen.	—	—	240.

West-Indische Bank

1800s Issue

		Good	Fine	XF
A5	**50 Gulden** ND. (1800's) Uniface. Remainder w/o sign.	—	—	—

Netherlands Indies (now Indonesia) comprised Sumatra and adjacent islands, Java with Madura, Borneo (except for Sabah, Sarawak and Brunei), Celebes with Sangir and Talaud Islands, and the Moluccas and Lesser Sunda Islands east of Java (excepting the Portuguese half of Timor and the Portuguese enclave of Oe-Cusse). Netherlands New Guinea (now Irian Jaya) was ceded to Indonesia in 1962. The Dutch colonial holdings formed an archipelago of more than 13,667 islands spread across 3,000 miles (4,824 km.) in southeast Asia. The area is rich in oil, rubber, timber and tin.

Portuguese traders established posts in the East Indies in the 16th century, but they were soon outnumbered by the Dutch VOC (United East India Company) who arrived in 1602 and gradually established themselves as the dominant colonial power. Dutch dominance, interrupted by British incursions during the Napoleonic Wars, established the Netherlands Indies as one of the richest colonial possessions in the world.

One day after the Japanese attack on Pearl Harbor the Netherlands declared war against Japan and therefore a state of war existed between Japan and the Dutch East Indies. The main islands of the archipelago were taken by the Japanese during the first three months of 1942; on March 8, 1942 the Royal Netherlands Indies Army surrendered in Kalidjati (between Jakarta and Bandung on Java island). The Japanese placed Sumatra and former British Malaya (including Singapore) under the administration of the 25th army, Java and Madura under the 16th army and the rest of Indonesia, including Borneo and Sulawesi (Celebes), under the administration of the Japanese navy. The 1942 series was placed in circulation immediately after the conquest of Borneo. Initially the notes were printed in Japan, later they were printed locally.

From September 1944 the 1942 series was replaced by a set in the Indonesian (and Japanese) language instead of Dutch as the Japanese wanted to support the growing nationalist movement in Indonesia in this way as well.

The 100 and 1000 rupiah which are similar to Malayan notes issued in 1942 (#M8-9 and 10) are believed to have been issued in Sumatra only; the 1000 rupiah never reached normal circulation at all (see #126 and 127).

The Japanese surrendered on August 15, 1945 (effective for Java and Sumatra on September 12) and the Republic of Indonesia was proclaimed on August 17, 1945. During 1946-1949 (the first Dutch troops returned to Java March 6, 1946) the struggle for independence by the Indonesian nationalists against the Dutch caused monetary chaos (see also the Indonesia section in Volume One of this catalog) and the Japanese invasion money remained valid in both the Dutch and Indonesian nationalist-controlled areas as late as 1948 and 1949 at different rates to the Netherlands Indies gulden and the Indonesian rupiah.

RULERS:

United East India Company, 1602-1799
Batavian Republic, 1799-1806
Louis Napoleon, King of Holland, 1806-1811
British Administration, 1811-1816
Kingdom of the Netherlands, 1816-1942
Dutch to 1949

MONETARY SYSTEM:

1 Gulden = 100 Cent
1 Roepiah (1943-45) = 100 Sen

DUTCH ADMINISTRATION

GOVERNMENT - STATE NOTES

1815 CREATIE ISSUE

#1-9 issued after the Dutch regained control over their possessions in the East Indies. All have handwritten sign. and serial #'s; stamped crowned 'W' (King Willem I). Border w/musical notation and 'Nederlandsch Oostindien / India 'Olland' (both meaning Netherlands East Indies). Dated in Arabic numerals. Uniface. Wmk: Waves. Printer: JEZ.

		Good	Fine	XF
1	**1 Gulden** 1815. Black.			
	a. Issued note.	—	—	—
	r. Unsigned remainder, w/o stamp or serial #.	50.00	100.	250.
2	**5 Gulden** 1815. Brown.			
	a. Issued note.	—	—	—
	r. Unsigned remainder, w/o stamp or serial #.	50.00	100.	250.
3	**10 Gulden** 1815. Blue.			
	a. Issued note.	—	—	—
	r. Unsigned remainder, w/o stamp or serial #.	50.00	100.	250.
4	**25 Gulden** 1815. Black.			
	a. Issued note.	—	—	—
	r. Unsigned remainder, w/o stamp or serial #.	50.00	100.	250.
5	**50 Gulden** 1815. Red.			
	a. Issued note.	—	—	—
	r. Unsigned remainder, w/o stamp or serial #.	75.00	150.	350.
6	**100 Gulden** 1815. Blue.			
	a. Issued note.	—	—	—
	r. Unsigned remainder, w/o stamp or serial #.	75.00	150.	350.
7	**300 Gulden** 1815. Black.			
	a. Issued note.	—	—	—
	r. Unsigned remainder, w/o stamp or serial #.	100.	200.	500.
8	**600 Gulden** 1815. Brown.			
	a. Issued note.	—	—	—
	r. Unsigned remainder, w/o stamp or serial #.	100.	200.	500.

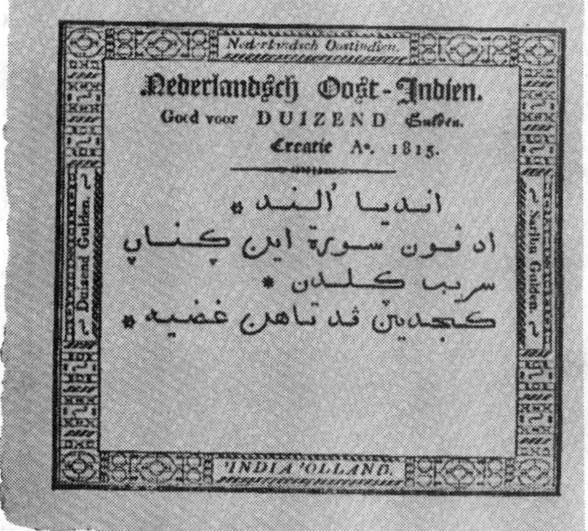

		Good	Fine	XF
9	**1000 Gulden** 1815. Blue.			
	a. Issued note.	—	—	—
	r. Unsigned remainder, w/o stamp or serial #.	100.	200.	500.

DE JAVASCHE BANK

1828 GOED VOOR ISSUE

#10-16 three handwritten sign., serial #. Value ovpt. Border w/musical notation and 'Oost-Indien' (East Indies). Wmk: *JAVASCHE BANK.* Uniface. Printer: JEZ. Authorized 30.1.1827. Issued 11.3.1828.

		Good	Fine	XF
10	**25 Gulden** 1827. Black.	—	—	—
11	**50 Gulden** 1827. Black.	—	—	—
12	**100 Gulden** 1827. Black.	—	—	—
13	**200 Gulden** 1827. Black.	—	—	—
14	**300 Gulden** 1827. Black.	—	—	—
15	**500 Gulden** 1827. Black.	—	—	—
16	**1000 Gulden** 1827. Black.	—	—	—

1832 *KOPERGELD* ISSUE

#17-24 two handwritten sign., serial # and value. Value also printed. Border w/musical notation and 'Kopergeld' (Copper money). These notes were redeemable only in copper coin. Wmk: *JAVASCHE BANK.* Uniface. Printer: JEZ. Authorized 23.8.1832. Issued Oct. 1832.

		Good	Fine	XF
17	**1 Gulden** ND. Green. W/o series letter.	—	—	—
18	**5 Gulden** ND. Black. Series A.	—	—	—
19	**10 Gulden** ND. Black. Series B.	—	—	—
20	**25 Gulden** ND. Black. Series C.	—	—	—
21	**50 Gulden** ND. Black. Series D.	—	—	—
22	**100 Gulden** ND. Blue. Series E.	—	—	—
23	**500 Gulden** ND. Red. Series F.	—	—	—
24	**1000 Gulden** ND. Red. Series G.	—	—	—

Note: #17-24 were withdrawn in Oct. 1858.

1853 GOED VOOR ISSUE

#25-32 similar to #10-16 w/date, three handwritten sign. and serial #. Value printed. Border w/musical notation and 'Neerlands-Indie' (Netherlands Indies). Wmk: *JAVASCHE BANK.* Uniface. Printer: JEZ. Issued from 1.4.1853.

		Good	Fine	XF
25	**10 Gulden** Handwritten dates from 1.4.1858. Dk. green and black, value in red.	—	—	—

		Good	Fine	XF
26	**25 Gulden** Handwritten dates from 1.4.1858. Blue, value in black.	—	—	—
27	**50 Gulden** Handwritten dates from 1.4.1858. Blue, value in black.	—	—	—
28	**100 Gulden** Handwritten dates from 1.4.1858. Red, value in black.	—	—	—
29	**200 Gulden** Handwritten dates from 1.4.1858. Red, value in black.	—	—	—
30	**300 Gulden** Handwritten dates from 1.4.1858. Red, value in black.	—	—	—
31	**500 Gulden** Handwritten dates from 1.4.1858. Red, value in black.	—	—	—
32	**1000 Gulden** Handwritten dates from 1.4.1858. Red, value in black.	—	—	—

1840s ND *Kopergeld* Issue

#33-38 similar to #18-23. Authorized 14.10.1842.
#33-38 Series N.

		Good	Fine	XF
33	**5 Gulden** ND.	—	—	—

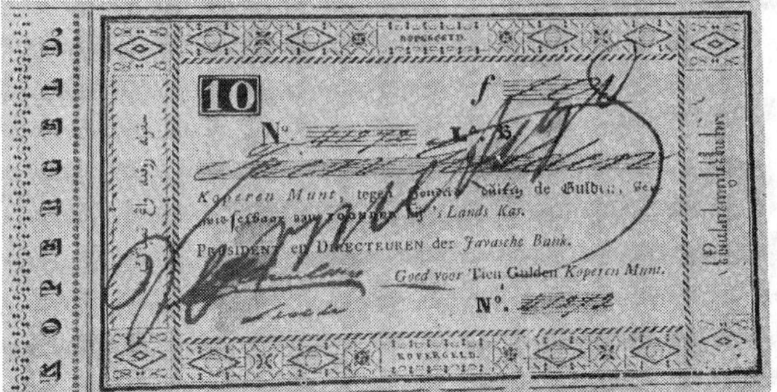

		Good	Fine	XF
34	**10 Gulden** ND.	—	—	—
35	**25 Gulden** ND.	—	—	—
36	**50 Gulden** ND.	—	—	—
37	**100 Gulden** ND.	—	—	—
38	**500 Gulden** ND.	—	—	—

Note: #33-38 were withdrawn in Oct. 1858.

Government (Resumed)

1846 Recepis Issue

#39-44 handwritten sign., date and serial #. Border w/musical notation. Wmk: Waves. *Recepis* (scrip certificate). Uniface. Printer: JEZ. Authorized 4.2.1846. Issued from 1.4.1846.

		Good	Fine	XF
39	**1 Gulden** Various handwritten dates from 1.4.1846. Black.			
	a. Issued note.	60.00	125.	275.
	r. Unsigned remainder, w/o serial #.	25.00	50.00	100.
40	**5 Gulden** Various handwritten dates from 1.4.1846. Red.			
	a. Issued note.	—	—	—
	r. Unsigned remainder, w/o serial #.	25.00	50.00	100.
41	**10 Gulden** Various handwritten dates from 1.4.1846. Green.			
	a. Issued note.	—	—	—
	r. Unsigned remainder, w/o serial #.	25.00	50.00	100.
42	**25 Gulden** Various handwritten dates from 1.4.1846. Brown.			
	a. Issued note.	—	—	—
	r. Unsigned remainder, w/o serial #.	60.00	100.	200.
43	**100 Gulden** Various handwritten dates from 1.4.1846. Blue.			
	a. Issued note.	—	—	—
	r. Unsigned remainder, w/o serial #.	60.00	100.	200.
44	**500 Gulden** Various handwritten dates from 1.4.1846. Orange.			
	a. Issued note.	—	—	—
	r. Unsigned remainder, w/o serial #.	60.00	100.	200.

Note: #39-44 were withdrawn 30.6.1861.

De Javasche Bank (Resumed)

1864 Issue

#45-51 legal text in 4 languages: Dutch, Javanese, Chinese, and Arabic on back. Watermark: #45. "Javasche Bank," #46-51 "Jav. Bank." Printer: JEZ (w/o imprint).

SIGNATURE VARIETIES, 1863-1949

	SECRETARIS	PRESIDENT	PERIOD
1	G. Hoeven	C.F.W. Wiggers van Kerchem	1863-1866
2	J.W.C. Diepenheim	C.F.W. Wiggers van Kerchem	1866-1868
3	D. Schuurman	J.W.C. Diepenheim	1868-1870
4	D.N. Versteegh	F. Alting Mees	1870-1873
5	D.N. Versteegh	N.P. van den Berg	1873-1876
6	A.A. Buyskes	N.P. van den Berg	1876-1877
7	D. Groeneveld	N.P. van den Berg	1877-1889
8	D. Groeneveld	S.B. Zeverijn	1889-1892
9	H.P.J. van den Berg	D. Groeneveld	1893-1898
10	J.F.H. de Vignon Vandevelde	J. Reijsenbach	1899-1901
11	H.J. Meertens	J.F.H. de Vignon Vandevelde	Jan.-April 1901
12	H.J. Meertens	J. Reijsenbach	1899-1902
13	A.F. van Suchtelen	J. Reijsenbach	1902-1906
14	A.F. van Suchtelen	G. Vissering	1906-1908
15	J. Gerritzen	G. Vissering	1908-1912
16	J. Gerritzen	E.A. Zeilinga Azn	1912-1913
17	K.F. van den Berg	E.A. Zeilinga Azn	1912-1920
18	L. von Hemert	E.A. Zeilinga Azn	1920-1922
19	J.F. van Rossem	E.A. Zeilinga Azn	1922-1924
20	J.F. van Rossem	L.J.A. Trip	1924-1928
21	Th. Ligthart	L.J.A. Trip	November 1925
22	K.W.J. Michielsen	L.J.A. Trip	January - June 1929
23	K.W.J. Michielsen	G.G. van Buttingha Wichers	November 1930
24	A. Praasterink	G.G. van Buttingha Wichers	1929-1937
25	J.C. van Waveren	G.G. van Buttingha Wichers	1937-1939
26	R.E. Smits	G.G. van Buttingha Wichers	1939-1942
27	World War II Occupation		
28	H. Teunissen	R.E. Smits	1947-1949
29	H. Teunissen	A. Houwink	1949-1950

		Good	Fine	XF
45	**5 Gulden** 1866-1901. Black and brown. Dutch arms at top ctr. Back brown.			
	a. 1.10.1866. Sign. 2.	230.	625.	—
	b. 5.4.1895. Sign. 9.	250.	685.	—
	s. Ovpt: *SPECIMEN.*	100.	210.	375

		Good	Fine	XF
46	**10 Gulden** 1864-90. Black. Batavia city arms w/lion at lower ctr. Back green and black.			
	a. 1.2.1864; 1.2.1866; 1.2.1872; 1.2.1876. Sign. 1; 2; 4; 5. Rare.	—	—	-
	b. 1.3.1877; 1.3.1879; 1.2.1888. Sign. 6; 7.	350.	1050.	-
	c. 1.2.1890. Sign. 8.	250.	675.	-
	s. Ovpt: *SPECIMEN.*	100.	210.	37

#	Denomination	Good	Fine	XF
47	**25 Gulden**			
	1864-90. Black. Like #46. Back blue and red.			
	a. 1.8.1864; 1.8.1866; 1.8.1872; 1.8.1876. Sign. 1; 2; 4; 5. Rare.	—	—	—
	b. 1.3.1877; 1.3.1879; 1.3.1884. Sign. 6; 7.	350.	1050.	—
	c. 1.2.1890. Sign. 8.	250.	675.	—
	s. Ovpt: *SPECIMEN.*	100.	210.	375.
48	**50 Gulden**			
	1864-73. Violet. Like #46. Back blue.			
	a. 1.9.1864. Sign. 1. Rare.	—	—	—
	b. 1.9.1866. Sign 2.	350.	1050.	—
	s. Ovpt: *SPECIMEN.*	100.	210.	375.

Note: #48a and #48b withdrawn from circulation in 1873, because of counterfeiting. (See #55). #49 to #51 portr. Jan Pieterzoon COEN at top ctr.

#	Denomination	Good	Fine	XF
49	**100 Gulden**			
	1864-90. Black. Like #51. Back green and brown.			
	a. 1.3.1864; 1.3.1866; 1.3.1872; 1.3.1873. Sign. 1; 2; 4. Rare.	—	—	—
	b. 1.3.1874; 1.3.1876; 1.3.1877; 1.3.1879. Sign. 5; 7. Rare.	—	—	—
	c. 1.2.1890. Sign. 8.	350.	1050.	—
	s. Ovpt: *SPECIMEN.*	100.	210.	375.
49A	**200 Gulden**			
	1864-90. Black. Like #51. Back blue and black.			
	a. 1.1.1864; 1.1.1866; -1873. Sign. 1; 2; 4. Rare.	—	—	—
	b. 15.1.1876; 15.1.1879; 15.1.1888. Sign. 5; 7. Rare.	—	—	—
	c. 15.1.1890. Sign. 8.	350.	1050.	—
	s. Ovpt: *SPECIMEN.*	150.	300.	500.
49B	**300 Gulden**			
	1864-88. Black. Like #51. Back violet and red.			
	a. 2.5.1864; 2.5.1866. Sign. 1; 2. Rare.	—	—	—
	s. Ovpt: *SPECIMEN.*	300.	600.	1000.
50	**500 Gulden**			
	1864-88. Black. Like #51. Back orange and brown.			
	a. 1.6.1864; 1.6.1872. Sign. 1; 4. Rare.	—	—	—
	b. 1.6.1873; -1879; -1888. Sign. 5; 7. Rare.	—	—	—
	s. Ovpt: *SPECIMEN.*	150.	300.	500.

#	Denomination	Good	Fine	XF
51	**1000 Gulden**			
	1864-90. Black. Back violet and black.			
	a. 1.7.1864; 1.7.1872. Sign. 1; 4. Rare.	—	—	—
	b. 1.7.1873; -1874; -1888. Sign. 5; 7. Rare.	—	—	—
	c. -1890. Sign. 8.	350.	1000.	—
	s. Ovpt: *SPECIMEN.*	150.	300.	500.

ND 1875 ISSUE

		VG	VF	UNC
52	**2 1/2 Gulden**			
	ND (1875). Blue on brown unpt. Landscape at l. and r., Dutch arms at bottom ctr. Javasche Bank arms at ctr., legal text in 4 languages (Dutch, Javanese, Chinese and Arabic) on back. Printer: Albrecht & Co. (Not issued).			

1876 ISSUE

#53-60 legal text (with varieties) in 4 languages: Dutch, Javanese, Chinese and Arabic on back. Wmk: "JAV. BANK." Printer: JEZ (w/o imprint on #53, #54, and #55).

#55 (50 gulden) issued 1876 to replace withdrawn notes #48.

#	Denomination	Good	Fine	XF
53	**10 Gulden**			
	1896-1924. Blue-green. Batavia city arms at top ctr. Back green.			
	a. -1896; 16.7.1897; 3.4.1913. Sign. 9; 10; 13; 14; 15; 16.	100.	250.	685.
	b. 13.5.1913-13.6.1924. Sign. 17; 18; 19.	80.00	200.	565.
	c. 17.7.1924-29.7.1924. Sign.	60.00	150.	450.
	s. Ovpt: *SPECIMEN.*	50.00	100.	200.
54	**25 Gulden**			
	1896-1921. Brown. Like #53. Back purple.			
	a. 1.6.1897-11.12.1912. Sign. 9; 10; 12; 13; 14; 15; 16.	100.	250.	686.
	b. 2.6.1913-4.2.1921. Sign. 17; 18.	80.00	200.	565.
	s. Ovpt: *SPECIMEN.*	50.00	100.	200.

#	Denomination	Good	Fine	XF
55	**50 Gulden**			
	1876-1922. Grey. Like #53. Back light brown.			
	a. 15.10.1873; 15.2.1876; 15.2.1879; 15.2.1890; 15.2.1896. Sign. 5; 7; 9. Rare.	—	—	—
	b. 1.5.1911; 17.4.1913. Sign. 16. Rare.	—	—	—
	c. 3.5.1913; 31.8.1922. Sign. 17; 18; 19.	250.	750.	—
	s. Ovpt: *SPECIMEN.*	100.	200.	375.

#56-60 Mercury at l., 3 crowned city arms (Batavia ctr., Surabaya at l., Semarang at r.) in wreaths at upper ctr., J.P. Coen w/ruffled collar at r. This banknote was reintroduced in 1911 (re#55b).

#	Denomination	Good	Fine	XF
56	**100 Gulden**			
	1896-1921. Blue-gray and deep blue-green. Back blue-gray and brown.			
	a. 1.6.1897; 18.4.1913. Sign. 9; 10; 13; 15; 16. Rare.	—	—	—
	b. 1.5.1916 - 15.6.1921. Sign. 17; 18.	200.	600.	—
	s. Ovpt: *SPECIMEN.*	75.00	150.	300.

#	Denomination / Variety	Good	Fine	XF
57	**200 Gulden**			
	1897-1921. Brown. Like #56. Back brown and violet.			
	a. 1.6.1897 - -1913. Sign. 9; 10; 14; 15; 16. Rare.	—	—	—
	b. 11.9.1916 - 21.8.1922. Sign. 17; 19.	400.	1250.	—
	s. Ovpt: *SPECIMEN.*	75.00	150.	300.
58	**300 Gulden**			
	1897-1901. Green. Like #56. Back green and brown.			
	a. 1.6.1897. Sign. 9. Rare.	—	—	—
	b. 29.1.1901 - 30.4.1901. Sign. 11. Rare.	—	—	—
	s. Ovpt: *SPECIMEN.*	150.	300.	500.
59	**500 Gulden**			
	1897-1919. Gray and brown. Like #56. Back purple and brown.			
	a. 2.6.1897 - -1913. Sign. 9; 10; 15; 16. Rare.	—	—	—
	b. 1.2.1916 - 5.7.1919. Sign. 17.	400.	1250.	—
	s. Ovpt: *SPECIMEN.*	75.00	150.	300.
60	**1000 Gulden**			
	1897-1919. Brown. Like #56. Back yellow, brown and green.			
	a. 1.6.1897 - 16.4.1912. Sign. 9; 10; 15; 16. Rare.	—	—	—
	b. 17.10.1914 - 5.7.1919. Sign. 17.	550.	1500.	—
	s. As a. Ovpt: *SPECIMEN.*	75.00	150.	300.

1901 ISSUE

#	Denomination / Variety	Good	Fine	XF
61	**5 Gulden**			
	1901-24. Blue. Portr. J.P. Coen at r. Black or red serial number (#61c). Back brown on blue unpt. Wmk: Large "J.B.", gothic style. Printer: JEZ.			
	a. 28.9.1901 - 26.4.1913. Sign. 10; 13; 14; 15; 16.	100.	300.	500.
	b. 5.6.1913 - 11.6.1920. Sign. 17.	75.00	225.	400.
	c. 18.9.1920 - 17.10-1924. Sign. 18; 19; 21.	50.00	150.	250.
	s. Ovpt: *SPECIMEN.*	50.00	100.	200.

1904-08 ISSUE

#	Denomination / Variety	Good	Fine	XF
62	**10 Gulden**			
	June 1908. Similar to #53 but 2 lg. value *10* in ctr. replace 1 value. (Not issued).	—	—	—
62A	**25 Gulden**			
	June 1908. Similar to #54 but 2 lg. value *25* in ctr. replace 1 value. (Not issued).	—	—	—
62B	**50 Gulden**			
	June 1908. Similar to #55 but 2 lg. value *50* in ctr. replace 1 value. (Not issued).	—	—	—
63	**200 Gulden**			
	June 1908. Similar to #58 but serial # panels and lg. 100 *200* replace 3 crowned city arms in wreaths at upper ctr. (Not issued).	—	—	—
63A	**200 Gulden**			
	May 1904; June 1908. Similar to #57 but serial # panels and lg. *200* replace 3 crowned city arms in wreaths at upper ctr. (Not issued).	—	—	—
64	**500 Gulden**			
	June 1908. Similar to #59 but serial # panels and lg. *500* replace 3 crowned city arms in wreaths at upper ctr. (Not issued).	—	—	—
65	**1000 Gulden**			
	May 1904. June 1908. Similar to #60 but serial # panels and lg. *1000* replace 3 crowned city arms in wreaths at upper ctr. (Not issued).	—	—	—

1919-21 ISSUE

#66-68 Javasche Bank building in Batavia at ctr. Legal text in 4 languages: Dutch, Javanese, Chinese and Arabic on back. W/o wmk. Printer: ABNC.

#	Denomination / Variety	Good	Fine	XF
66	**20 Gulden**			
	1919-21. Orange. Back orange, green and blue.			
	a. 12.8.1919 - 26.4.1920. Sign. 17.	150.	550.	1300.
	b. 6.1.1921. Sign. 18.	150.	550.	1300.
	s. Ovpt: *SPECIMEN.*	50.00	150.	350.

Note: #66 was withdrawn from circulation in 1931/33 because of counterfeiting.

#	Denomination / Variety	Good	Fine	XF
67	**30 Gulden**			
	1919-21. Blue. Back blue, green and brown.			
	a. 8.9.1919 - 21.4.1920. Sign. 17.	120.	525.	1250.
	b. 14.1.1921. Sign. 18.	120.	525.	1250.
	s. Ovpt: *SPECIMEN.*	50.00	150.	350.
68	**40 Gulden**			
	1919-21. Green. Back green, brown and blue.			
	a. 22.8.1919 - 27.4.1920. Sign. 17.	120.	525.	1250.
	b. 20.1.1921. Sign. 18.	120.	525.	1250.
	s. Ovpt: *SPECIMEN.*	50.00	150.	350.

Note: Two varieties of word *Batavia* on #68.

1925-31 ISSUE

#69-77 portr. of J.P. Coen w/ruffled collar at r. (except #69). Javasche Bank building in Batavia at ctr., legal text in 4 languages: Dutch, Javanese, Chinese and Arabic on back. Wmk: J's and B's in a honeycomb pattern. Printer: JEZ.

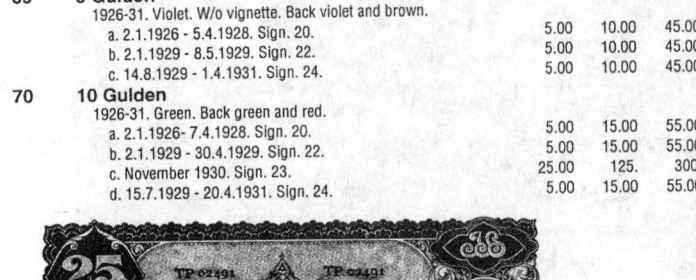

#	Denomination / Variety	Good	Fine	XF
69	**5 Gulden**			
	1926-31. Violet. W/o vignette. Back violet and brown.			
	a. 2.1.1926 - 5.4.1928. Sign. 20.	5.00	10.00	45.00
	b. 2.1.1929 - 8.5.1929. Sign. 22.	5.00	10.00	45.00
	c. 14.8.1929 - 1.4.1931. Sign. 24.	5.00	10.00	45.00
70	**10 Gulden**			
	1926-31. Green. Back green and red.			
	a. 2.1.1926- 7.4.1928. Sign. 20.	5.00	15.00	55.00
	b. 2.1.1929 - 30.4.1929. Sign. 22.	5.00	15.00	55.00
	c. November 1930. Sign. 23.	25.00	125.	300.
	d. 15.7.1929 - 20.4.1931. Sign. 24.	5.00	15.00	55.00

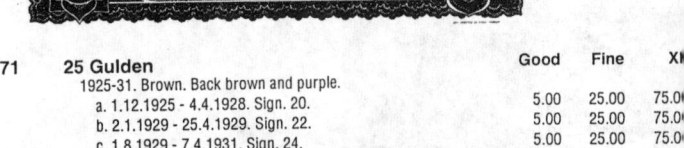

#	Denomination / Variety	Good	Fine	XF
71	**25 Gulden**			
	1925-31. Brown. Back brown and purple.			
	a. 1.12.1925 - 4.4.1928. Sign. 20.	5.00	25.00	75.0
	b. 2.1.1929 - 25.4.1929. Sign. 22.	5.00	25.00	75.0
	c. 1.8.1929 - 7.4.1931. Sign. 24.	5.00	25.00	75.0

#	Denomination / Variety	Good	Fine	XF
72	**50 Gulden**			
	1926-30. Orange. Back brown and orange.			
	a. 2.1.1926 - 14.3.1928. Sign. 20.	10.00	50.00	10
	b. 2.1.1929 - 30.4.1929. Sign. 22.	10.00	50.00	10
	c. 1.8.1929 - 31.10.1930. Sign. 24.	10.00	50.00	10

#		Good	Fine	XF
3	**100 Gulden**			
	1925-30. Black. Back light green.			
	a. 2.11.1925 - 5.11.1925. Sign. 21.	50.00	250.	600.
	b. 6.11.1925 - 10.2.1928. Sign. 20.	10.00	50.00	100.
	c. 1.11.1929 - 28.10.1930. Sign. 24.	10.00	50.00	100.
4	**200 Gulden**			
	1925-30. Red. Back red and brown.			
	a. 2.11.1925 - 4.11.1925. Sign. 21.	50.00	250.	600.
	b. 5.11.1925 - 2.7.1926. Sign. 20.	35.00	175.	500.
	c. 15.10.1930 - 20.10.1930. Sign. 24.	35.00	175.	500.
5	**300 Gulden**			
	2.1.1926 - 11.1.1926. Violet Back violet and green.	100.	350.	850.
6	**500 Gulden**			
	1926-30. Blue. Back brown and blue.			
	a. 2.1.1926 - 2.7.1926. Sign. 20.	35.00	175.	500.
	b. 15.8.1930 - 19.8.1930. Sign. 24.	35.00	175.	500.
7	**1000 Gulden**			
	1926-30. Red. Back brown and red.			
	a. 1.4.1926 - 2.7.1926. Sign. 20.	40.00	200.	550.
	b. 7.5.1930 - 8.5.1930. Sign. 24.	40.00	200.	550.

933-39 ISSUE

8-85 legal text in 4 languages: Dutch, Javanese, Chinese and Arabic on back. Printer: JEZ. (Fec: Lion Cachet).

#		Good	Fine	XF
8	**5 Gulden**			
	1934-39. Brown on lt. brown and pale green unpt. Javanese dancer at l. Back m/c. Wmk: J's and B's in a honeycomb pattern.			
	a. 23.4.1934 - 5.6.1937. Sign. 24.	3.00	10.00	30.00
	b. 4.10.1937 - 3.5.1939. Sign. 25.	3.00	10.00	30.00
	c. 3.7.1939 - 17.8.1939. Sign. 26.	3.00	10.00	30.00

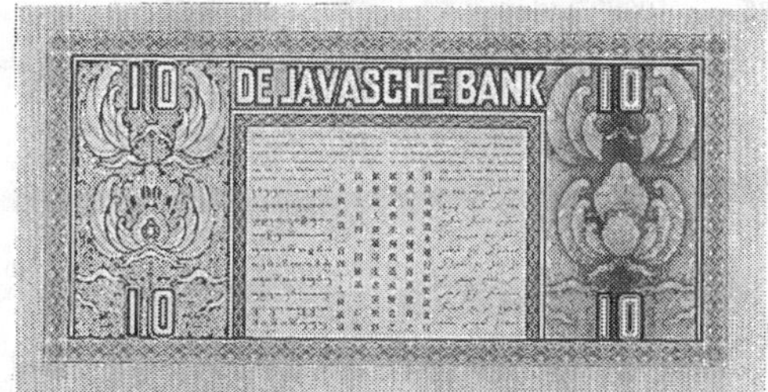

#		Good	Fine	XF
79	**10 Gulden**			
	1933-39. Dk. blue on lt. blue and pink unpt. Javanese dancers at l. and r. Back green, red and blue. Wmk: Wavy lines.			
	a. 2.10.1933 - 6.2.1934. Sign. 24.	4.00	12.50	35.00
	b. 20.9.1937 - 19.9.1938. Sign. 25.	4.00	12.50	35.00
	c. 28.7.1939 - 31.8.1939. Sign. 26.	4.00	12.50	35.00

#		Good	Fine	XF
80	**25 Gulden**			
	1934-39. Purple on m/c unpt. Javanese dancer at l. and r. Back brown on red and blue unpt. Wmk: Zigzag lines.			
	a. 14.12.1934 - 13.2.1935. Sign. 24.	5.00	15.00	60.00
	b. 17.10.1938 - 30.6.1939. Sign. 25.	5.00	15.00	60.00
	c. 1.7.1939 - 4.7.1939. Sign. 26.	10.00	30.00	120.

#81-85 wmk: Head of the Goddess of Justice and Truth.

#		Good	Fine	XF
81	**50 Gulden**			
	19.4.1938 - 14.4.1939. Black on red, green and blue unpt. Javanese dancers at l. and r. Back brown and violet. Sign. 25.	17.50	50.00	150.
82	**100 Gulden**			
	7.2.1938 - 22.4.1939. Violet and orange. Javanese dancers at l. and r. Back m/c. Sign. 25.	30.00	75.00	225.
83	**200 Gulden**			
	23.5.1938 - 24.4.1939. Green and brown. Javanese dancers at l. and r. Back m/c. Sign. 25.	200.	550.	1250.

#		VG	VF	UNC
84	**500 Gulden**			
	2.6.1938 - 27.4.1939. Green and brown. Javanese dancers at l. and r. Back m/c. Sign. 25.	175.	500.	1100.

		VG	VF	UNC
85	**1000 Gulden** 1938-39. Green. Javanese dancers at l. and r. Back m/c.			
	a. 30.5.1938 - 29.4.1939. Sign. 25.	250.	750.	1500.
	p. Proof perforated: 32.9.(19)36.	—	—	1000.
	s. Specimen w/ovpt: *SPECIMEN* perforated: 34.5.(19)68.	—	—	1000.

1942 ISSUE

		VG	VF	UNC
86	**5 Gulden** 15.1.1942. Black on lt. blue and gray unpt. Floral design at r. Back m/c; ornate tree at ctr. Printer: G. Kolff & Co., Batavia. (Not issued).	—	—	150.

1946 ISSUE

#87-96 printer: JEZ.

#87-90 wmk: Floral design.

Note: Also encountered perforated: *INGETROKKEN 2.4.47* (withdrawn).

		VG	VF	UNC
87	**5 Gulden** 1946. Violet and red. Lotus at l.	3.50	15.00	60.00
88	**5 Gulden** 1946. Green and orange. Like #87.	3.50	15.00	60.00
89	**10 Gulden** 1946. Green. Mangosteen at l.	3.50	15.00	60.00
90	**10 Gulden** 1946. Purple. Like #89.	4.00	17.50	70.00

		VG	VF	UNC
91	**25 Gulden** 1946. Green. Beach w/palms at l.	5.00	20.00	75.00
92	**25 Gulden** 1946. Red-orange. Like #91.	6.00	25.00	85.00

		VG	VF	UNC
93	**50 Gulden** 1946. Dk. blue. Sailboat at l.	10.00	35.00	125.
94	**100 Gulden** 1946. Brown. Rice fields w/mountain in background at l.	8.50	30.00	110.
95	**500 Gulden** 1946. Red. Like #94.	40.00	125.	650.

		VG	VF	UNC
96	**1000 Gulden** 1946. Gray. Like #94.	250.	550.	1250.

Note: The Javasche Bank notes cut in half (from 5 Gulden) and those of the Republic of Indonesia originate from the currency reform of 1950. The left half of a note was valid for exchange against new notes (see Indonesia #36-37) at 50% of face value; the right half was also accepted at half its face value for a 3% government bond issue.

1948 ISSUE

		VG	VF	UNC
97	**1/2 Gulden** 1948. Lilac on pale green unpt . Moon orchids at l. 2 serial # varieties.	1.00	4.00	15.0
98	**1 Gulden** 1948. Blue. Palms at l. 2 serial # varieties.	1.00	4.00	15.0
99	**2 1/2 Gulden** 1948. Red. Blossoms at l. 2 serial # varieties.	3.00	8.00	25.0

GOVERNMENT (20TH CENTURY)

1919 MUNTBILJETTEN ISSUE

#100 and 101 portr. Qn. Wilhelmina at ctr. Arms at ctr. on back. Printer: ABNC.

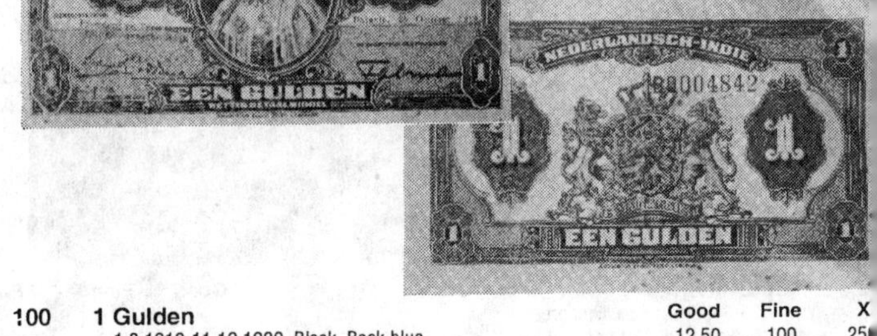

		Good	Fine	X
100	**1 Gulden** 1.8.1919-11.10.1920. Black. Back blue.	12.50	100.	25
101	**2 1/2 Gulden** 4.8.1919-28.2.1920. Dk. green. Back brown.	15.00	120.	30

Note: Earlier dates of #100-101 have sign. title ovpt. at l. Later dates have sign. title printed.

1920 MUNTBILJETTEN ISSUE

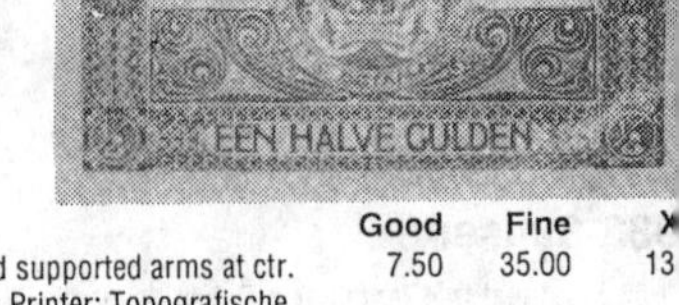

		Good	Fine	X
102	**1/2 Gulden** 14.1.1920. Black on green unpt. Crowned supported arms at ctr. Back gray-green. Plain or textured paper. Printer: Topografische Inrichting Batavia.	7.50	35.00	13

#103 and 104 printer: De Bussy, Amsterdam.

		Good	Fine	X
103	**1 Gulden** 1.1.1920. Green and blue. W/o vignette. Back blue.	7.50	35.00	13

		Good	Fine	X
104	**2 1/2 Gulden** 1.5.1920. Green, brown and violet. Similar to #103. Back brown.	12.50	50.00	17

1939 MUNTBILJETTEN ISSUE

#105-107 coin at ctr. r. Printer: G. Kolff & Co., Batavia.

		VG	VF	UNC
105	**1 Gulden**			
	1.11.1939. Brown and green. Back blue. Proof.	—	—	350.
106	**1 Gulden**			
	1.11.1939. Brown and lilac. Back brown. Proof.	—	—	350.
107	**1 Gulden**			
	1.11.1939. Blue, green and orange. Back brown. Proof.	—	—	350.

1940 Muntbiljetten Issue

#108 and 109 printer: G. Kolff & Co., Batavia.

		VG	VF	UNC
108	**1 Gulden**			
	15.6.1940. Brown, blue and m/c. Coin at ctr. r. Back brown; Borubudur Temple at ctr.			
	a. Serial # and letters.	2.00	5.00	20.00
	b. Letters only.	2.00	5.00	20.00

		VG	VF	UNC
109	**2 1/2 Gulden**			
	15.6.1940. Gray-brown. J. P. Coen at ctr. Back brown and violet; arms.	4.00	10.00	30.00

#108-109 issued 24.4.1941 because of a shortage of coin normally minted by the United States.

1943 Muntbiljetten Issue

#110-118 portr. Qn. Wilhelmina at r., crowned supported arms at l. Back green. Printer: ABNC.

		VG	VF	UNC
110	**50 Cents**			
	2.3.1943. Orange.			
	a. Issued note.	1.00	3.00	10.00
	p. Proof.	—	—	200.
	s. Specimen.	—	—	125.

		VG	VF	UNC
111	**1 Gulden**			
	2.3.1943. Black.			
	a. Issued note.	.50	2.00	10.00
	p. Proof.	—	—	200.
	s. Specimen.	—	—	125.

		VG	VF	UNC
112	**2 1/2 Gulden**			
	2.3.1943. Purple.			
	a. Issued note.	2.00	6.00	15.00
	p. Proof.	—	—	225.
	s. Specimen.	—	—	150.

#113-118 plane, soldier and warship on back.

		VG	VF	UNC
113	**5 Gulden**			
	2.3.1943. Blue.			
	a. Issued note.	1.25	4.00	10.00
	p. Proof.	—	—	225.
	s. Specimen.	—	—	150.
114	**10 Gulden**			
	2.3.1943. Red.			
	a. Issued note.	2.00	7.50	20.00
	p. Proof.	—	—	225.
	s. Specimen.	—	—	150.

		VG	VF	UNC
115	**25 Gulden**			
	2.3.1943. Brown.			
	a. Issued note.	4.00	12.50	50.00
	p. Proof.	—	—	275.
	s. Specimen.	—	—	200.
116	**50 Gulden**			
	2.3.1943. Green.			
	a. Issued note.	4.00	12.50	50.00
	p. Proof.	—	—	275.
	s. Specimen.	—	—	225.

		VG	VF	UNC
117	**100 Gulden**			
	2.3.1943. Dk. brown.			
	a. Issued note.	6.00	20.00	75.00
	p. Proof.	—	—	325.
	s. Specimen.	—	—	275.
118	**500 Gulden**			
	2.3.1943. Gray-blue.			
	a. Issued note.	200.	500.	1200.
	p. Proof.	—	—	600.
	s. Specimen.	—	—	550.

JAPANESE OCCUPATION - WWII

DE JAPANSCHE REGEERING

THE JAPANESE GOVERNMENT

1942 ND ISSUE

#119-133 plate letter *S* prefix.

#119-133 w/2 lg. Japanese characters *Mi-hon* in red and w/ or w/o *Specimen* on the back are all various types of specimens.

		VG	VF	UNC
119	**1 Cent**			
	ND (1942). Dk. green on pink unpt. Back green.			
	a. 2 block letters, format SA.	.25	.50	1.25
	b. Fractional block letters, format S/AA.	.10	.25	.75
	s. As a. Specimen w/red ovpt: *Mi-hon. SPECIMEN* on back.	—	—	100.
120	**5 Cents**			
	ND (1942). Blue on lt. tan unpt. Back blue.			
	a. Letter *S* followed by a one or two digit number, format S1 to S31.	.50	1.50	5.00
	b. 2 block letters.	.25	1.00	2.00
	c. Fractional block letters.	.20	.40	1.00
	s. As a. Specimen w/red ovpt: *Mi-hon. SPECIMEN* on back.	—	—	100.
121	**10 Cents**			
	ND (1942). Purple on pale yellow unpt. Back purple.			
	a. Letter *S* followed by number, S1 to S31.	.50	1.50	5.00
	b. 2 block letters.	7.00	20.00	75.00
	c. Fractional block letters.	.25	.50	1.00
	s. As a. Specimen w/red ovpt: *Mi-hon. SPECIMEN* on back.	—	—	100.

#122-125 w/Dutch text: *DE JAPANSCHE REGEERING BETAALT AAN TOONDER* (The Japanese Government pays to the bearer). Wmk: repeated kiri-flower, but it is sometimes not discernible. (Exceptions: #122a, block SA, and 123a.)

		VG	VF	UNC
122	**1/2 Gulden**			
	ND (1942). Blue on pale yellow and pink unpt. Fan palm at r. Back blue.			
	a. Block letters SA-SK, SM.	.50	1.50	4.00
	b. Block letters SL.	.25	.75	2.00
	s. As a. Specimen w/ovpt: *Mi-hon. SPECIMEN* on back.	—	—	100.

		VG	VF	UNC
123	**1 Gulden**			
	ND (1942). Brown on green unpt. Breadfruit tree at l., coconut palm at r. Back brown.			
	a. Block letters SA; SB, serial #, w/o wmk.	25.00	90.00	150.
	b. Block letters SB-SH; SL.	.50	1.50	4.00
	c. Block letters SI; SN.	.25	.50	1.00
	s. As a. Specimen w/ovpt: *Mi-hon. SPECIMEN* on back.	—	—	100.

		VG	VF	UNC
124	**5 Gulden**			
	ND (1942). Green on yellow and pale lilac unpt. Coconut palm at l., papaw at r. Back green.			
	a. Block letters SA; SB, serial #.	25.00	90.00	150.
	b. Block letters SB-SF.	1.00	2.50	6.00
	c. Block letters SG.	.25	1.00	2.50
	s. As a. Specimen w/ovpt: *Mi-hon. SPECIMEN* on back.	—	—	100.

		VG	VF	UNC
125	**10 Gulden**			
	ND (1942). Purple on pale green unpt. Banana tree at ctr., coconut palm at r. Back purple; ship at ctr.			
	a. Block letters SA only, serial #.	25.00	90.00	150.
	b. Block letters SB-SH; SK.	1.00	2.50	6.00
	c. Block letters SI; SL.	.25	1.00	2.50
	s. As a. Specimen w/ovpt: *Mi-hon. SPECIMEN* on back.	—	—	100.

#123-125 w/ovpt: *Republik Islam Indonesia*, see Volume 1, Indonesia #S511-S529. Other ovpts. exist, but are believed to be recent fantasies. These include black bar ovpt: *Republik Maluku Selatan R.M.S.* and *Persatuan Islam Borneo* with sign.

PEMERINTAH DAI NIPPON

THE JAPANESE GOVERNMENT

1944-45 ND ISSUE

#126 and 127 w/Indonesian text: *Pemerintah Dai Nippon* (The Japanese Government).

		VG	VF	UNC
126	**100 Roepiah**			
	ND (1944-45). Brown-violet and dk. green. Hut under trees on a shore at ctr. Back red-brown. Farmer in stream w/2 water buffalo at ctr.			
	a. Engraved face. Standard kiri-flowers wmk.	10.00	35.00	100.
	b. Lithographed face, paper w/o silk threads, block letters SO sans serif, 4mm. high. W/o wmk.	5.00	15.00	35.00
	c. Lithographed face, paper w/silk threads, block l letters SO not sans serif, 4mm. high. W/o wmk.	5.00	15.00	35.00
	r. Remainder, w/o block letters SO.	5.00	15.00	35.00
	s. As a. Specimen w/ovpt: *Mi-hon. SPECIMEN* on back.	—	—	125.

Note: Deceptive counterfeits of #126b exist.

		VG	VF	UNC
127	**1000 Roepiah**			
	ND (1945). Blue-green and purple. Pair of oxen pulling cart at ctr. Back same as #126, dk. green. Lithographed face. Standard kiri-flowers wmk.			
	a. Issued note.	75.00	200.	650.
	s. Specimen w/ovpt: *Mi-hon.*			400.

DAI NIPPON TEIKOKU SEIHU

IMPERIAL JAPANESE GOVERNMENT

1944 ND ISSUE

		VG	VF	UNC
128	**1/2 Roepiah**			
	ND (1944). Gray-black on lt. tan unpt. Stylized dragon. Back gray-black.			

128	VG	VF	UNC
a. Issued note.	1.00	2.50	7.50
s. Specimen w/red ovpt: *Mi-hon.*	—	—	100.

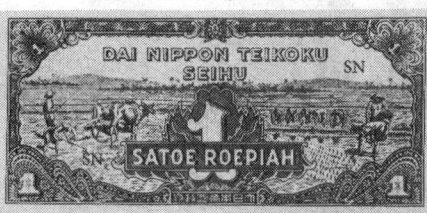

129 **1 Roepiah**	VG	VF	UNC
ND (1944). Black-green and green. Field work (rice growing). Back brown; Banyan tree and temples of Dieng Plateau.			
a. Issued note.	1.00	2.50	7.50
s. Specimen w/red ovpt: *Mi-hon.*	—	—	100.

130 **5 Roepiah**	VG	VF	UNC
ND (1944). Olive-green on lt. green unpt. Batak house at l. Back green; Batak woman (Sumatera) at ctr.			
a. Issued note.	1.00	2.50	7.50
s. Specimen w/red ovpt: *Mi-hon.*	—	—	100.

131 **10 Roepiah**	VG	VF	UNC
ND (1944). Dk. brown on lt. tan unpt. Javanese dancer at l. Back purple; stupas and statues of Buddha from Borobudur Temple at l. and r.			
a. Issued note.	1.00	2.50	7.50
p. Proof w/pale blue unpt. Rare.	—	—	—
s. Specimen w/red ovpt: *Mi-hon.*	—	—	100.

Note: Two different falsifications of #131 exist.

132 **100 Roepiah**	VG	VF	UNC
ND (1944). Dk. brown on pale green unpt. Lion statue at l., statue of Vishnu on Garuda at r. and Saruda at l. Back dk. green; Wayang puppet at ctr.			
a. Issued note.	2.50	10.00	45.00
s. Specimen w/red ovpt: *Mi-hon.*	—	—	100.

133 **100 Roepiah**			
ND (1943). Violet on yellow unpt. *DAI NIPPON* on face 59mm, *SERATOES ROEPIAH* on back 75mm. Proof. Rare.	—	—	—

Note: #119-132 are known w/o block letters, and for most of the notes, proofs also in modified designs are known. Unfinished notes, especially of the 1944 series, #128-132, some of which are uniface, are printers' leftovers which became available after the Japanese surrender of 1945. There is controversy about the legitimacy of #120, 121, 125, 128-130 and possibly others of this series w/o block letters. Very deceptive counterfeits of some notes from ##128-132 have recently been seen.

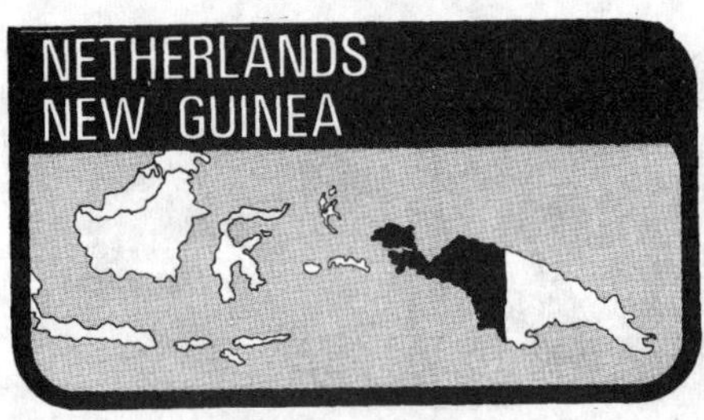

Dutch New Guinea (Irian Jaya, Irian Barat, West Irian, West New Guinea), a province of Indonesia consisting of the western half of the island of New Guinea and adjacent islands, has an area of 159,376 sq. mi. (412,781 sq. km.) and a population of 930,000. Capital: Jayapura. Many regions are but partially explored. Rubber, copra and tea are produced.

Northwest New Guinea was first visited by Dutch navigators in the 17th century. Dutch sovereignty was established and extended throughout the 18th century. In 1828, Dutch New Guinea was declared a dependency of Tidore (an island of the Moluccas conquered by the Dutch in 1654). The boundary was established by treaties with Great Britain (1884) and Germany (1885). Japanese forces occupied only the northern coastal area in 1942; they were driven out by the Allies in 1944.

The Netherlands retained sovereignty over Dutch New Guinea when independence was granted to Indonesia in 1949. It was placed under United Nations administration in 1962, and was transferred to Indonesia in 1963 with provision for the holding of a plebiscite by 1969 to decide the country's future. As a result, it became a province of Indonesia.

RULERS:

Dutch to 1963

MONETARY SYSTEM:

1 Gulden = 100 Cents to 1963

Note: Refer to Netherlands Indies for issues before and during WWII. For later issues see Irian Barat (Indonesia).

DUTCH ADMINISTRATION

NIEUW-GUINEA

1950 ISSUE

NOTE: #1-3 *Deleted.*

#4-10 portr. Qn. Juliana at l. Printer: JEZ.

		Good	Fine	XF
4	**1 Gulden** 2.1.1950. Green and orange. Back green and brown.			
	a. Issued note.	15.00	60.00	250.
	s. Specimen.	—	Unc	150.
5	**2 1/2 Gulden** 2.1.1950. Red-brown on blue unpt. Back red-brown and blue.			
	a. Issued note.	17.50	100.	375.
	b. Specimen.	—	Unc	200.

#6-10 Greater bird of paradise at r.

		Good	Fine	XF
6	**5 Gulden** 2.1.1950. Blue on tan unpt.			
	a. Issued note.	35.00	175.	450.
	s. Specimen.	—	Unc	250.

		Good	Fine	XF
7	**10 Gulden** 2.1.1950. Brown on gray unpt.			
	a. Issued note.	50.00	250.	750.
	s. Specimen.	—	Unc	400.
8	**25 Gulden** 2.1.1950. Green on brown unpt.			
	a. Issued note.	150.	750.	—
	s. Specimen.	—	Unc	650.
9	**100 Gulden** 2.1.1950. Lilac on green unpt.			
	a. Issued note.	175.	1000.	—
	s. Specimen.	—	Unc	800.

		Good	Fine	XF
10	**500 Gulden** 2.1.1950. Lt. brown on gray unpt.			
	a. Issued note.	—	—	—
	s. Specimen.	—	Unc	1200.

NEDERLANDS NIEUW-GUINEA

1954 ISSUE

#11-17 portr. Qn. Juliana at r., sicklebill at l.

		Good	Fine	XF
11	**1 Gulden** 8.12.1954. Green and brown. Back green and red.			
	a. Issued note.	10.00	30.00	175.
	s. Specimen.	—	Unc	100.

		Good	Fine	XF
12	**2 1/2 Gulden** 8.12.1954. Blue and brown. Back blue and green.			
	a. Issued note.	15.00	60.00	225.
	s. Specimen.	—	Unc	150.

		Good	Fine	XF
13	**5 Gulden** 8.12.1954. Lilac and brown.			
	a. Issued note.	17.50	100.	300.
	s. Specimen.	—	Unc	185.

		Good	Fine	XF
14	**10 Gulden** 8.12.1954. Purple and green. Crowned pigeon at l. Back purple and brown; stylized bird of paradise at ctr. r.			
	a. Issued note.	40.00	150.	500.
	s. Specimen.	—	Unc	250.
15	**25 Gulden** 8.12.1954. Brown and violet. Owl on back.			
	a. Issued note.	85.00	300.	750.
	s. Specimen.	—	Unc	275.
16	**100 Gulden** 8.12.1954. Lt. and dk. olive-brown and dk. blue. Back like #15.			
	a. Issued note.	150.	500.	—
	s. Specimen.	—	Unc	325.
17	**500 Gulden** 8.12.1954. Lilac, brown and m/c. Back like #15.			
	a. Issued note.	—	—	—
	s. Specimen.	—	Unc	400.

NOTE: Several notes of Netherlands Indies #29-33, 35 and Javasche Bank 5 Gulden are known w/lg. circular handstamp: *FINANCIEN NIEUW GUINEA GVT.* and other local ovpt. Further documentation is needed.

NEW CALEDONIA

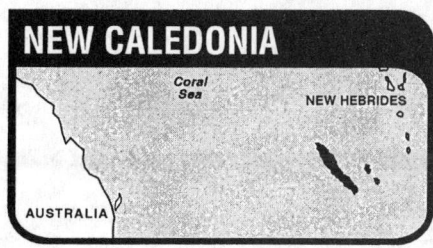

The French Overseas Territory of New Caledonia, a group of about 25 islands in the South Pacific, is situated about 750 miles (1,207 km.) east of Australia. The territory, which includes the dependencies of Ile des Pins, Loyalty Islands, Ile Huon, Isles Belep, Isles Chesterfield, and Ile Walpole, has a total land area of 6,530 sq. mi. (19,058 sq. km.) and a population of 152,000. Capital: Noumea. The islands are rich in minerals; New Caledonia has the world's largest known deposit of nickel. Nickel, nickel castings, coffee and copra are exported.

British navigator Capt. James Cook discovered New Caledonia in 1774. The French took possession in 1853, and established a penal colony on the island in 1854. The European population of the colony remained disproportionately convict until 1894. New Caledonia became an overseas territory within the French Community in 1946, and in 1958 and 1972 chose to remain affiliated with France.

RULERS:

French

MONETARY SYSTEM:

1 Franc = 100 Centimes

FRENCH ADMINISTRATION

COMPAGNIE DE LA NOUVELLE CALÉDONIE

1873-74 SUCCURSALE DE NOUMÉA ISSUE

#1-3 seal at upper l. Reversed image on back.

		Good	Fine	XF
1	**5 Francs** 1.7.1873. Black. Reported not confirmed.	—	—	—

		Good	Fine	XF
2	**5 Francs** 1.7.1874. Yellow-brown.	400.	1500.	—
3	**20 Francs** Sept. 1874. Black on green unpt.	450.	1750.	—

BANQUE DE LA NOUVELLE CALÉDONIE

1874 ISSUE

		Good	Fine	XF
4	**100 Francs** 187x. Blue. Farmer w/implements and cow at l., islander w/produce and implements at r. Remainder cancelled w/ovpt: *ANNULÉ*. Rare.	—	—	—

1875 ETABLISSEMENT DE NOUMÉA ISSUE

Décret du 14 Juillet 1874

#6-9 seal at upper l. Back reversed image.

		Good	Fine	XF
6	**5 Francs** 1875. Yellow-brown.	450.	1200.	—
7	**20 Francs** 10.4.1875. Black on green unpt.	500.	1350.	—
8	**100 Francs** 15.2.1875; 10.7.1875. Pale blue. Rare.	—	—	—
9	**500 Francs** 25.1.1875. Blue.			
	a. Issued note. Rare.	—	—	—
	r. Remainder cancelled w/ovpt: *ANNULÉ 187x*. Rare.	—	—	—

DÉCRETS DES 21.2.1875/20.2.1888

		Good	Fine	XF
10	**5 Francs** Reported not confirmed.	—	—	—
11	**20 Francs** (ca.1890). Handwritten or handstamped dates. Blue. Neptune reclining holding trident at lower l. 3 sign.	—	—	—

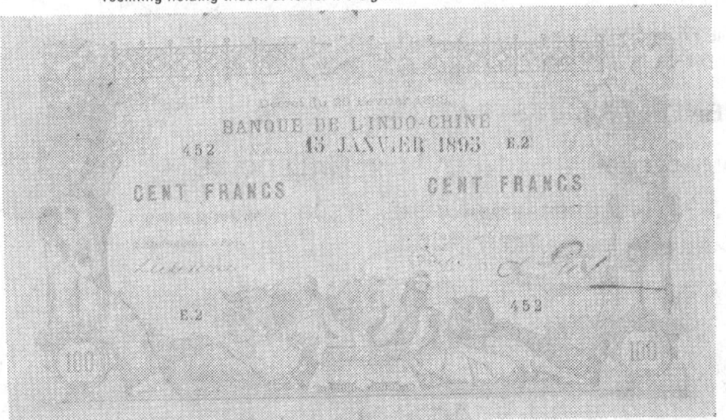

		Good	Fine	XF
12	**100 Francs** 1895; 1898. Blue and red. Elephant columns at l. and r., 2 reclining women w/ox at l., tiger r. at lower border. Back blue.			
	a. 15.1.1895; 26.10.1898.	—	—	—
	p. Proof w/o serial #, ovpt: *ANNULÉ*. 1.7.1898.	—	—	—

		Good	Fine	XF
13	**500 Francs** 1.7.1898. Blue and red. Vasco da Gama at l., sailing ships at lower ctr., Polynesian man holding paddle on "sea-dragon" boat at r.			
	a. Issued note.	—	—	—
	p. Proof w/o block or serial #, ovpt: *Annulé*.	—	—	—

BANQUE DE L'INDO-CHINE

NOUMÉA

DÉCRETS DES 21.2.1875/20.2.1888/16.5.1900

		Good	Fine	XF
14	**20 Francs** 3.3.1902. Like #11. Series X.6.	—	—	—

NOTICE

Readers with unlisted dates, signature varieties, etc. are invited to submit photocopies or, high resolution (300 dpi, 100% size) scans of their notes to: Standard Catalog of World Paper Money, 700 East State St. Iola, WI 54990-0001, or E-Mail: george.cuhaj@fwpubs.com.

DÉCRETS DES 21.2.1875/20.2.1888/16.5.1900/3.4.1901

		Good	Fine	XF
15	**5 Francs** 13.6.1916; 15.6.1916; 17.6.1916. Blue and red. Oriental woman seated below Liberty seated holding caduceus at l. Back blue.			
	a. Issued note.	250.	850.	—
	b. Cancelled w/ovpt: *Annulé*.	150.	450.	—

		Good	Fine	XF
16	**20 Francs** 1905; 1913. Blue. Like #11 and 14.			
	a. Issued note. 25.9.1913.	—	—	—
	b. Cancelled w/ovpt: *Annulé*	—	—	—
	s. Specimen 3.7.1905.	—	—	—

		Good	Fine	XF
17	**100 Francs** 3.3.1914; 10.3.1914; 11.3.1914. Blue and red. Like #12. 3 sign.	175.	450.	1000

1916-25 ISSUE (W/O DÉCRETS)

		Good	Fine	XF
18	**5 Francs** 6.6.1916; 19.6.1916. Lt. green. 2 sign.	75.00	300.	750
19	**5 Francs** 2.6.1924. Blue.	75.00	275.	600

		Good	Fine	XF
20	**20 Francs** 3.1.1921; 2.6.1924; 2.6.1925. Blue and red. Like #11. 2 sign.	150.	450.	1000
21	**100 Francs** 2.6.1925. Blue and red. Like #12.	200.	600.	1250

		Good	Fine	XF
22	**500 Francs** 3.1.1921. Blue and red. Like #13.	500.	1500.	—

1914 ND Emergency Postage Stamp Card Issues

#23-27 adhesive postal stamps affixed to cardboard w/handstamp: *TRESORIER PAYEUR DE LA NOUVELLE CÁLEDONIE* and *SECRETARIAT GENERAL* on back.

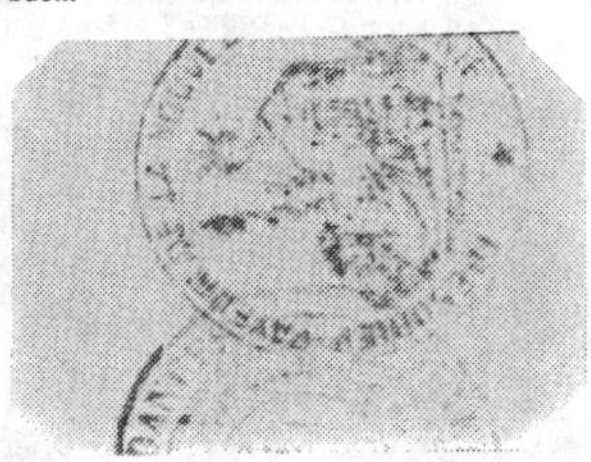

		VG	VF	UNC
23	**25 Centimes** ND (1914-23). Kanaka village on stamp. Hand stampings on back. 52 x 39mm to 61 x 40mm.	150.	300.	600.

		VG	VF	UNC
24	**50 Centimes (35 and 15 Cent.)** ND (1914-23). Kanaka village and Kagu bird on stamps.	200.	425.	700.
25	**50 Centimes** ND (1914-23). Kanaka village on stamp.	175.	350.	600.
26	**1 Franc** ND (1914-23).	175.	350.	600.
27	**2 Francs** ND (1914-23).	225.	425.	700.

1922 ND Encapsulated Postage Stamp

		VG	VF	UNC
28	**25 Centimes** ND (1922). Stamp encapsuled in aluminum w/embossing: *BANQUE DE L'INDOCHINE, NOUMÉA.*	15.00	45.00	100.
29	**50 Centimes** ND (1922). Like #28 but different stamp.	20.00	60.00	150.

Trésorerie de Nouméa

1918 First Issue

		Good	Fine	XF
30	**0.50 Franc** 14.11.1918-13.1.1919. *L'Article 139 du Code penal* in 3 lines on back.	35.00	150.	450.
31	**1 Franc** 14.11.1918-13.1.1919. Like #30.	40.00	175.	500.
32	**2 Francs** 14.11.1918-13.1.1919. Like #30.	60.00	200.	600.

1918 Second Issue

#33-35 similar to #30-32 except for arrangement of text as indicated.

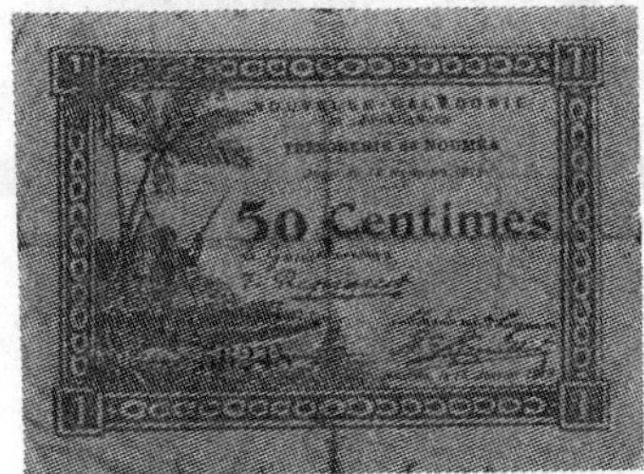

		Good	Fine	XF
33	**0.50 Franc** 14.11.1918-13.1.1919. Blue. *L'Article 139 du Code penal* in 4 lines on back.			
	a. Sm. numerals on back.	15.00	75.00	250.
	b. Lg. numerals on back.	15.00	75.00	250.
34	**1 Franc** 14.11.1918-13.1.1919. Brown. Like #33.			
	a. Sm. numerals on back.	20.00	85.00	300.
	b. Lg. numerals on back.	20.00	85.00	300.
35	**2 Francs** 14.11.1918-13.1.1919. Blue-green. Like #33.			
	a. Sm. numerals on back.	25.00	100.	350.
	b. Lg. numerals on back.	25.00	100.	350.

Banque de l'Indochine

Nouméa

1926-29 Issue

		VG	VF	UNC
36	**5 Francs** ND (ca. 1926). Brown on lt. green unpt. Woman w/helmet at lower l. Imprint: Ch. Walhain and E. Deloche.			
	a. Sign. titles: *UN ADMINISTRATEUR* and *LE DIRECTEUR.*	2.50	20.00	75.00
	b. Sign. titles: *LE PRÉSIDENT* and *LE DIRECTEUR GÉNÉRAL.*	1.00	5.00	25.00

		VG	VF	UNC
37	**20 Francs** ND (ca.1929). Lilac-brown. Woman at r. Peacock on back. Imprint: Cl. Serveau and E. Deloche.			
	a. Sign. titles: *UN ADMINISTRATEUR* and *LE DIRECTEUR.*	6.00	30.00	125.
	b. Sign. titles: *LE PRÉSIDENT* and *LE DIRECTEUR GÉNÉRAL.*	5.00	25.00	100.

		VG	VF	UNC
38	**500 Francs** 27.12.1927; 8.3.1938. Lilac-brown and olive. Woman standing at l., ships at top ctr.	100.	250.	650.

1939 ND Provisional Issue

		VG	VF	UNC
39	**100 Francs on 20 Piastres** ND (1939). M/c. Ovpt. on French Indochina #56b.	50.00	200.	600.

		Good	Fine	XF
40	**1000 Francs on 100 Piastres** ND (1939-old date 1920). Ovpt. on French Indochina #42. Rare.	—	—	—

1939 Emergency Bearer Check Issue

		Good	Fine	XF
41	**5000 Francs** 16.9.1939-16.7.1943. Black, check format. Rare.	—	—	—

1937; 1940 ND Issue

		VG	VF	UNC
42	**100 Francs** ND (1937-67). M/c. Woman w/wreath and sm. figure of Athena at ctr. Statue of Angkor at ctr. on back. Imprint: Seb. Laurent and Rita. 205 x 120mm.			
	a. Sign. titles: *UN ADMINISTRATEUR* and *LE DIRECTEUR GENERAL* (1937).	5.00	25.00	100.
	b. Sign. titles: *LE PRESIDENT* Borduge and *LE DIRECTEUR GENERAL* Baudouin (1937).	4.00	12.00	85.00
	c. Sign. titles: *LE PRESIDENT* and *L'ADMINISTRATEUR DIRECTOR GENERAL* (1953).	4.00	12.00	70.00
	d. Sign. titles: *LE PRESIDENT* and *LE VICE-PRESIDENT DIRECTEUR-GENERAL* (1957).	4.00	12.00	60.00
	e. Sign. titles: *LE PRESIDENT* de Flers and *LE DIRECTEUR GENERAL* Robert (1963).	3.00	10.00	50.00

		VG	VF	UNC
43	**1000 Francs** ND (1940-65). M/c. Market scene in background and at l., woman sitting at r. Imprint: L. Jonas and G. Beltrand.			
	a. Sign. M. Borduge w/title: *LE PRÉSIDENT* and P. Baudouin w/title: *LE DIRECTEUR GÉNÉRAL* (1940).	40.00	150.	450.
	b. Sign. titles: *LE PRÉSIDENT* and *L' ADMINISTRATEUR DIRECTEUR GÉNÉRAL.*	55.00	200.	550.
	c. Sign. titles: *LE PRÉSIDENT* and *LE VICE-PRÉSIDENT DIRECTEUR GÉNÉRAL.*	30.00	100.	350.
	d. Sign. F. de la Motte Angode Flers w/title: *LE PRÉSIDENT* and M. Robert w/title: *LE DIRECTEUR GÉNÉRAL.* (1963).	32.50	125.	400.

NOTICE

Readers with unlisted dates, signature varieties, etc. are invited to submit photocopies or, high resolution (300 dpi, 100% size) scans of their notes to: Standard Catalog of World Paper Money, 700 East State St. Iola, WI 54990-0001, or E-Mail: george.cuhaj@fwpubs.com.

1942; 1943 ND ISSUE

		VG	VF	UNC
44	**100 Francs** ND (1942). Brown. Woman wearing wreath and holding sm. figure of Athena at ctr. Statue of Angkor on back. 160 x 102mm. Australian printing.	30.00	125.	400.
45	**1000 Francs** ND (1943). Blue. Statues of Angkor at l. W/o *EMISSION* and date ovpt. Printer: ABNC (w/o imprint).	150.	350.	750.

1943 ISSUE

		VG	VF	UNC
46	**100 Francs** 1943; 1944. Brown. Like #44.			
	a. Ovpt: *EMISSION 1943.*	50.00	200.	500.
	b. Ovpt: *EMISSION 1944.*	65.00	250.	600.

		VG	VF	UNC
47	**1000 Francs** 1943; 1944. Blue. Like #45.			
	a. Ovpt: *EMISSION 1943.* Reported not confirmed.	—	—	—
	b. Ovpt: *EMISSION 1944.*	150.	375.	800.

1944 ND ISSUE

#48-49 Australian printing.

		VG	VF	UNC
48	**5 Francs** ND (1944). Dk. blue. Woman wearing wreath and holding sm. figure of Athena at ctr. Statue of Angkor at ctr. on back.	15.00	75.00	225.

		VG	VF	UNC
49	**20 Francs** ND (1944). Green. Woman at l., boat at ctr., fisherman at r. Mask on back.	8.00	25.00	90.00

1951 ND ISSUE

		VG	VF	UNC
50	**20 Francs** ND. (1951-63). M/c. Youth at l., flute player at r. Fruit bowl at l., woman at r. ctr. on back.			
	a. Sign. titles: *LE PRESIDENT* and *LE DIRECTEUR GAL.* (1951).	2.50	10.00	27.00
	b. Sign. titles: *LE PRESIDENT* and *LE VICE-PRESIDENT DIRECTEUR GÉNÉRAL.* (1954; 1958).	1.50	5.00	20.00
	c. Sign. titles: *LE PRESIDENT* and *LE DIRECTOR GÉNÉRAL.* (1963).	1.00	4.50	17.50

NOUVELLE CALÉDONIE

TRÉSORERIE DE NOUMÉA, BON DE CAISSE

ARRÊTÉ DU 9.7.1942

		VG	VF	UNC
51	**50 Centimes** 15.7.1942. Dk. green.	1.50	6.00	30.00
52	**1 Franc** 15.7.1942. Purple.	1.50	6.00	30.00

		VG	VF	UNC
53	**2 Francs** 15.7.1942. Brown.	2.50	8.00	35.00

ARRÊTÉ DU 29.1.1943

		VG	VF	UNC
54	**50 Centimes** 29.3.1943. Green.	1.50	6.00	30.00
55	**1 Franc** 29.3.1943. Blue.			
	a. Thin numerals *1* at upper l. and r.	1.50	6.00	30.00
	b. Thick numerals *1* at upper l. and r.	1.50	6.00	30.00

		VG	VF	UNC
56	**2 Francs** 29.3.1943. Brown.			
	a. Thin numerals *2* at upper l. and r.	2.50	10.00	40.00
	b. Thick numerals *2* at upper l. and r.	2.50	10.00	40.00

		VG	VF	UNC
57	**20 Francs** 30.4.1943; 1943. Red.			
	a. W/o *Deuxieme Emission* at bottom ctr. on back. 30.4.1943.	10.00	50.00	200.
	b. *Deuxieme Emission*. 1943.	10.00	50.00	200.

ARRÊTÉ DU 11.6.1943

		VG	VF	UNC
58	**5 Francs** 15.6.1943. Pale green w/lt. brown text.	1.50	6.50	40.00

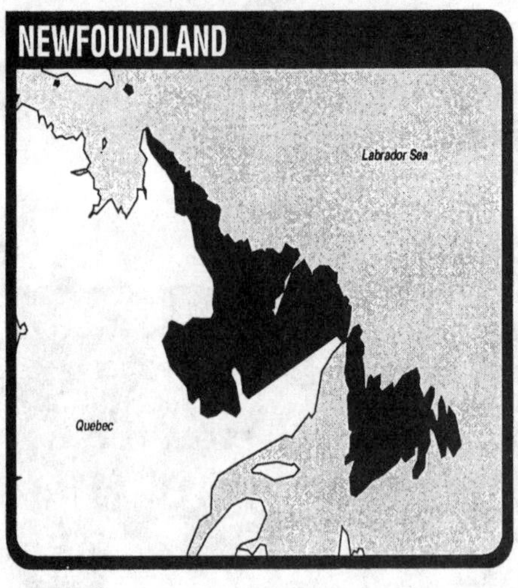

John Cabot, who visited Newfoundland in 1497, is given the title of discoverer although it is likely that Vikings visited its shore on their various trips to the west. Early settlement efforts were made by the British involving such men as Sir Humphrey Gilbert, John Guy and Sir George Calvert. There was much dispute between the French and the British for the island and its fishing rights. Awarded to England by the Treaty of Utrecht of 1713. Granted first governor in 1728. Adequate local government did not develop until the mid 1800s. Made a British colony in 1934 and became a province of Canada (along with Labrador) in 1949.

RULERS:
British

MONETARY SYSTEM:
1 Pound = 4 Dollars = 20 Shillings
1 Dollar = 100 Cents

NEWFOUNDLAND

ISLAND OF NEWFOUNDLAND

1850 TREASURY NOTE

		Good	Fine	XF
A3A	**1 Pound** 16.10.1850. Black. Sailing ship at top ctr. Uniface.			
	a. 2 sign.	90.00	300.	—
	b. 3 sign.	275.	650.	—
	r. Unsigned remainder.	35.00	100.	225.

NEWFOUNDLAND GOVERNMENT

DEPARTMENT OF PUBLIC WORKS

1901 CASH NOTE ISSUE

#A4-A8 consecutive year dates from 1901 to 1908. Printer: ABNC.

		Good	Fine	XF
A4	**40 Cents** 1901-08.	60.00	250.	800.
A5	**50 Cents** 1901-08. Like #A4.	60.00	250.	800.
A6	**80 Cents** 1901-08. Like #A4.	75.00	300.	900.

		Good	Fine	XF
A7	**1 Dollar** 1901-08.	100.	400.	900.
A8	**5 Dollars** 1901-08. Like #A7.	300.	1200.	—

1910 ISSUE

#A9-A13 view of waterfall at upper ctr. Consecutive "double" year dates 1910-11; 1911-12; 1912-13; 1913-14. Printer: Whitehead, Morris & Co., Engravers, London.

		Good	Fine	XF
A9	**25 Cents** 1910-11-1913-14. Black on maroon unpt. Back brown and gray.	20.00	120.	400.
A10	**50 Cents** 1910-11-1913-14. Black on dull red and gray-brown unpt.	25.00	150.	500.
A11	**1 Dollar** 1910-11-1913-14. Black on green, dull red and gray-brown unpt.	60.00	250.	600.
A12	**2 Dollars** 1910-11-1913-14. Black on yellow, blue-gray and gray-brown unpt.	400.	1500.	—
A13	**5 Dollars** 1910-11-1913-14. Black on blue and gray unpt.	600.	2000.	—

GOVERNMENT OF NEWFOUNDLAND

1920 TREASURY NOTE ISSUE

#A14-A15 caribou head at r., sailing ship at l., ornate seal at ctr. Anchor against rocks at r. on back. Printer: ABNC.

		VG	VF	UNC
A14	**1 Dollar** 2.1.1920. Black on blue unpt. Portr. Kg. George V at l. Back blue.			
	a. Sign. Bursell and Brownrigg.	100.	600.	1500.
	b. Sign. Hickey and Brownrigg.	75.00	450.	1150.
	c. Sign. Keating and Brownrigg.	75.00	450.	1200.
	d. Sign. Renouf and Brownrigg.	75.00	450.	1150.

		VG	VF	UNC
A15	**2 Dollars** 2.1.1920. Black on yellow brown and blue unpt. Mine workers at ctr. Back brown.			
	a. Sign. Bursell and Brownrigg.	125.	800.	2250.
	b. Sign. Hickey and Brownrigg.	80.00	700.	2000.
	c. Sign. Keating and Brownrigg.	85.00	750.	2100.
	d. Sign. Renouf and Brownrigg.	110.	600.	1850.

NEW HEBRIDES

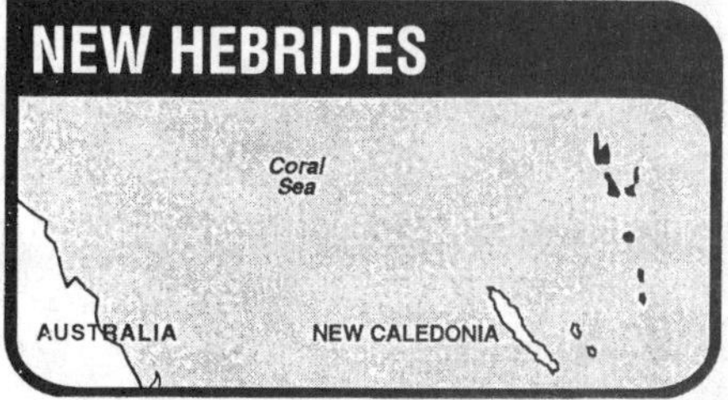

New Hebrides Condominium, a group of islands located in the South Pacific 500 miles (800 km.) west of Fiji, were under the joint sovereignty of Great Britain and France. The islands have an area of 5,700 sq. mi. (14,763 sq. km.) and a population of mainly Melanesians of mixed blood. Capital: Port-Vila. The volcanic and coral islands, while malarial and subject to frequent earthquakes, are extremely fertile, and produce copra, coffee, tropical fruits and timber for export.

The New Hebrides were discovered by Portuguese navigator Pedro de Quiros in 1606, visited by French explorer Bougainville in 1768, and named by British navigator Capt. James Cook in 1774. Ships of all nations converged on the islands to trade for sandalwood, prompting France and Britain to relinquish their individual claims and declare the islands a neutral zone in 1878. The New Hebrides were placed under the control of a mixed Anglo-French commission of naval officers during the native uprisings of 1887, and established as a condominium under the joint sovereignty of France and Great Britain in 1906.

RULERS:

British and French to 1980

MONETARY SYSTEM:

1 Franc = 100 Centimes

BRITISH AND FRENCH ADMINISTRATION

COMPTOIRS FRANÇAIS DES NOUVELLES-HÉBRIDES

1921 ISSUE

		Good	Fine	XF
A1	**25 Francs** 22.8.1921. Red and blue. Thatched house at lower l., bridge at ctr., trees at l. and r. Back; red; pottery at l. and r.	300.	750.	—

Note: A few examples of #A1 have entered the market during the past several years.

SERVICES NATIONAUX FRANÇAIS DES NOUVELLES HÉBRIDES

1943 EMERGENCY WW II ISSUE

#1-3B black on green and pink unpt. Cross of Lorraine at top ctr. above 2 palm branches.

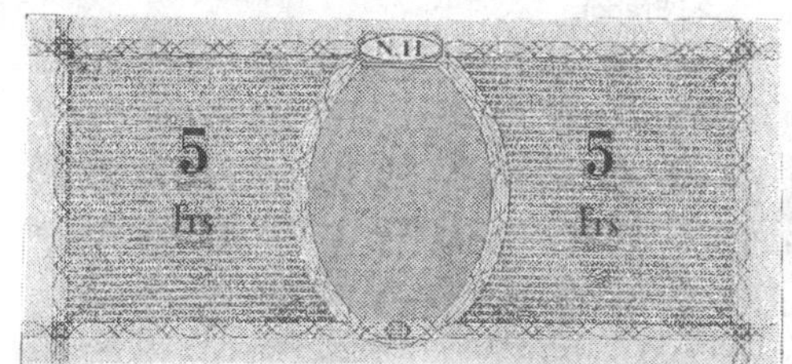

		Good	Fine	XF
1	**5 Francs** ND (1943). 2 sign. varieties.	30.00	100.	275.
2	**20 Francs** ND (1943). 2 sign. varieties.	85.00	250.	550.
3	**100 Francs** ND (1943).	250.	800.	—
3A	**500 Francs** ND (1943). Orange value and Serial #. Rare.	—	—	—
3B	**1000 Francs** ND (1943). Rare.	—	—	—

BANQUE DE L'INDOCHINE

NOUVELLES HÉBRIDES

1941-45 ND PROVISIONAL ISSUES

Ovpt. A: Red oval w/*NOUVELLES HÉBRIDES FRANCE LIBRE*, palms and Cross of Lorraine.

Ovpt. B: Red *NOUVELLES HÉBRIDES*.

		Good	Fine	XF
4	**5 Francs**			
	ND (1941). Brown and green. Ovpt. A on New Caledonia #36.			
	a. Sign. de la Chaume and Baudouin.	12.50	60.00	250.
	b. Sign. Borduge and Baudouin.	10.00	50.00	200.

		Good	Fine	XF
5	**5 Francs**			
	ND (1945). Blue. Ovpt. A on New Caledonia #48.	20.00	100.	300.

		Good	Fine	XF
6	**20 Francs**			
	ND (1941). Lilac-brown. Ovpt. A on New Caledonia #37.	25.00	100.	300.

		Good	Fine	XF
7	**20 Francs**			
	ND (1945). Green. Ovpt. A on New Caledonia #49.	30.00	125.	350.

		VG	VF	UNC
8	**20 Francs**			
	ND. (1941-45) M/c. Ovpt. B on New Caledonia #50.			
	a. Sign. titles: *LE PRÉSIDENT* and *VICE-PRÉSIDENT DIRECTEUR GÉNÉRAL.*	3.00	7.50	35.00
	b. Sign. titles: *LE PRÉSIDENT* and *LE DIRECTEUR GÉNÉRAL.*	2.00	5.00	30.00

		Good	Fine	XF
9	**100 Francs**			
	ND. (1941-45) M/c. Ovpt. A at ctr.			
	a. Ovpt. on New Caledonia #42a.	125.	350.	900.
	b. Ovpt. on New Caledonia #42b.	150.	400.	1000.

		Good	Fine	XF
10	**100 Francs**			
	ND. (1941-45). M/c. Like #9, but ovpt. B across lower ctr.			
	a. Sign. titles: *PRÉSIDENT* and *DIRECTEUR,* length of ovpt. 89mm.	10.00	60.00	150.
	b. Sign. titles: *PRÉSIDENT* and *ADMINISTRATEUR,* length of ovpt. 68mm.	12.50	75.00	175.
	c. Sign. titles: *PRÉSIDENT* and *VICE-PRÉSIDENT,* length of ovpt. 68mm.	10.00	60.00	150.
10A	**100 Francs**			
	ND (1945). Brown. Ovpt. A on New Caledonia #44.	135.	325.	600.

		Good	Fine	XF
11	**100 Francs** ND (1946-old date 1943). Brown. Ovpt. A on New Caledonia #46a.	125.	300.	550.
12	**100 Francs** ND (1947-old date 1944). Brown. Ovpt. A on New Caledonia #46b.	125.	300.	550.

		Good	Fine	XF
12A	**500 Francs** ND (-old date 8.3.1938). Lilac-brown. Ovpt. A at ctr. on New Caledonia #38. Rare.	—	—	—

		Good	Fine	XF
13	**1000 Francs** ND (1945-47 - old date 1944). Blue. Ovpt. A on New Caledonia #47b.	150.	350.	750.
14	**1000 Francs** 1944. Blue. Like #13, but ovpt. B.	125.	300.	600.

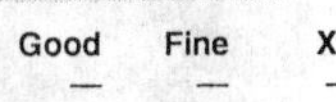

		Good	Fine	XF
14A	**1000 Francs** ND (1941). M/c. Ovpt. A on New Caledonia #43. Rare.	—	—	—

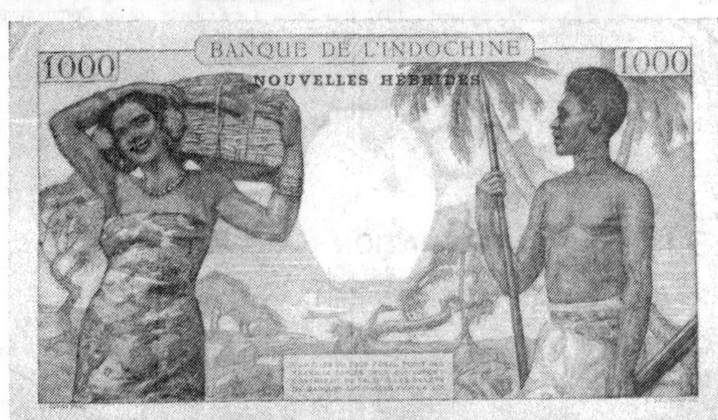

		Good	Fine	XF
15	**1000 Francs** ND. (1941-45) M/c. Like #14A but ovpt. B across bottom ctr.	35.00	90.00	275.

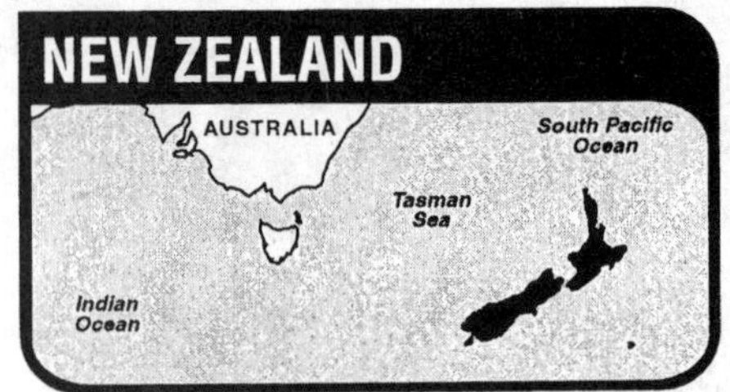

New Zealand, a parliamentary state located in the southwestern Pacific 1,250 miles (2,011 km.) east of Australia, has an area of 103,736 sq. mi. (269,056 sq. km.) and a population of 3.8 million. Capital: Wellington. Wool, meat, dairy products and some manufactured items are exported.

New Zealand was discovered and named by Dutch navigator Abel Tasman in 1642, and explored by British navigator Capt. James Cook who surveyed it in 1769 and annexed the land to Great Britain. The British government disavowed the annexation and for the next 70 years the only white settlers to arrive were adventurers attracted by the prospects of lumbering, sealing and whaling. Great Britain annexed the land in 1840 by treaty with the native chiefs and made it a dependency of New South Wales. The colony was granted self-government in 1852, a ministerial form of government in 1856, and full dominion status on Sept. 26, 1907. Full internal and external autonomy, which New Zealand had in effect possessed for many years, was formally extended in 1947. New Zealand is a member of the Commonwealth of Nations. Elizabeth II is Head of State as Queen of New Zealand.

RULERS:

British

MONETARY SYSTEM:

1 Shilling = 12 Pence
1 Pound = 20 Shillings to 1967
1 Dollar = 100 Cents, 1967-

BRITISH ADMINISTRATION

RESERVE BANK OF NEW ZEALAND

1934 ISSUE

Pound System

#154-157 kiwi at l. arms at upper ctr., portr. Maori chief at r. Milford Sound and Mitre Peak at ctr. on back. Printer: TDLR.

		VG	VF	UNC
154	**10 Shillings** 1.8.1934. Red on m/c unpt.	45.00	275.	1600.

		VG	VF	UNC
155	**1 Pound** 1.8.1934. Purple on m/c unpt.	30.00	135.	800.

		VG	VF	UNC
156	**5 Pounds** 1.8.1934. Blue on m/c unpt.	600.	265.	1600.

		VG	VF	UNC
157	**50 Pounds** 1.8.1934. Red on m/c unpt.	2500.	6000.	—

1940 ND ISSUE

#158-162 portr. Capt. J. Cook at lower r. Sign. title: *CHIEF CASHIER*. Wmk: Maori chief. Printer: TDLR.

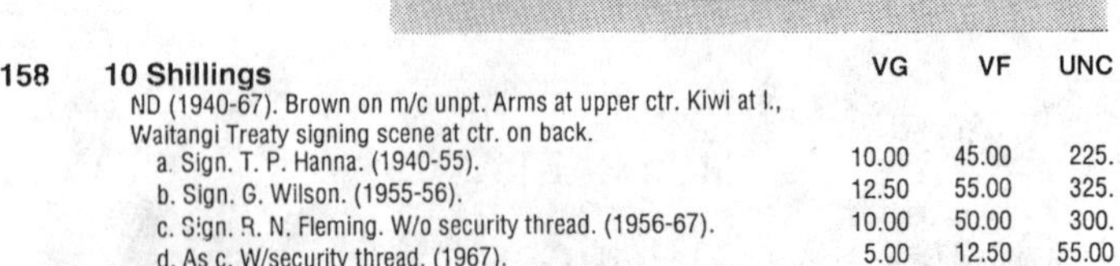

		VG	VF	UNC
158	**10 Shillings** ND (1940-67). Brown on m/c unpt. Arms at upper ctr. Kiwi at l. Waitangi Treaty signing scene at ctr. on back.			
	a. Sign. T. P. Hanna. (1940-55).	10.00	45.00	225.
	b. Sign. G. Wilson. (1955-56).	12.50	55.00	325.
	c. Sign. R. N. Fleming. W/o security thread. (1956-67).	10.00	50.00	300.
	d. As c. W/security thread. (1967).	5.00	12.50	55.00

159	1 Pound	VG	VF	UNC
	ND (1940-67). Purple on m/c unpt. Arms at upper ctr. Sailing ship on sea at l. on back.			
	a. Sign. T. P. Hanna. (1940-55).	8.00	30.00	200.
	b. Sign. G. Wilson. (1955-56).	10.00	40.00	275.
	c. Sign. R. N. Fleming. W/o security thread. (1956-67).	8.00	30.00	215.
	d. As c. W/security thread. (1967).	4.00	13.50	65.00

160	5 Pounds	VG	VF	UNC
	ND (1940-67). Blue on m/c unpt. Crowned arms at upper ctr. Lake Pukaki and Mt. Cook on back.			
	a. Sign. T. P. Hanna. (1940-55).	12.50	60.00	225.
	b. Sign. G. Wilson. (1955-56).	12.50	65.00	275.
	c. Sign. R. N. Fleming. W/o security thread. (1956-67).	12.50	40.00	275.
	d. As c. W/security thread. (1967).	12.50	30.00	120.

161	10 Pounds	VG	VF	UNC
	ND (1940-67). Green on m/c unpt. Crowned arms, sailing ship at l. Flock of sheep at l. ctr. on back.			
	a. Sign. T. P. Hanna. (1940-55).	55.00	130.	875.
	b. Sign. G. Wilson. (1955-56).	70.00	225.	1000.
	c. Sign. R. N. Fleming. (1956-67).	50.00	100.	425.
	d. As c. W/security thread. (1967).	40.00	90.00	275.

162	50 Pounds	VG	VF	UNC
	ND (1940-67). Red on m/c unpt. Crowned arms, sailing ship at l. Dairy farm and Mt. Egmont on back.			
	a. Sign. T. P. Hanna. (1940-55).	450.	1100.	5000.
	b. Sign. G. Wilson. (1955-56).	500.	1150.	5500.
	c. Sign. R. N. Fleming. (1956-67).	225.	750.	2500.

The Republic of Nicaragua, situated in Central America between Honduras and Costa Rica, has an area of 50,193 sq. mi (130,000 sq. km.) and a population of 4.69 million. Capital: Managua. Agriculture, mining (gold and silver) and hardwood logging are the principal industries. Cotton, meat, coffee, tobacco and sugar are exported.

Columbus sighted the coast of Nicaragua in 1502 during the course of his last voyage of discovery. It was first visited in 1522 by conquistadors from Panama, under command of Gonzalez Davila. After the first settlements were established in 1524 at Granada and Leon, Nicaragua was incorporated, for administrative purpose, in the Captaincy General of Guatemala, which included every Central American state but Panama. The Captaincy General declared its independence from Spain on Sept. 15, 1821. The next year Nicaragua united with the Mexican Empire of Agustin de Iturbide, then in 1823 with the Central American Republic. When the federation was dissolved, Nicaragua declared itself an independent republic in 1838.

MONETARY SYSTEM:

1 Peso = 100 Centavos to 1912
1 Córdoba = 100 Centavos, 1912-1987
1 New Córdoba = 1000 Old Córdobas, 1988-90
1 Córdoba Oro = 100 Centavos, 1990-

Note: Certain listings encompassing issues circulated by various bank and regional authorities are contained in Volume 1.

REPUBLIC

TESORERÍA GENERAL

1896 PROVISIONAL ISSUE

DECRETO 30.3.1896

Ovpt: *TESORERÍA GENERAL* on face and back of issues of Banco Agricola-Mercantil. Issued by revolutionary forces in Leon.

		Good	Fine	XF
A13	**50 Centavos** D.1896. Dk. blue ovpt. on l. or r. half of #S107. Treasury registration stamp at ctr. on back.	200.	600.	—

		Good	Fine	XF
A14	**1 Peso** 1.4.1896 (-old date 6.11.1888). Dk. green ovpt. on #S107.			
	a. Handstamp: *TESORERÍA GENERAL NICARAGUA* on back.	20.00	75.00	175.
	b. Handstamp: Tesorería General *LEON NIC* on back.	30.00	100.	200.
	c. W/o circular handstamp on back.	25.00	85.00	185.

		Good	Fine	XF
A15	**5 Pesos** 1.4.1896 (-old date 6.11.1888). Orange ovpt. on #S108.			
	a. Ovpt: Text w/circular handstamp on back.	20.00	75.00	175.
	b. Ovpt: Text w/o circular handstamp on back.	15.00	60.00	150.
	c. W/o ovpt. text or circular handstamp on back.	45.00	150.	250.

Note: For listing of #A14 and A15 w/o ovpt. see #S107 and S108 in Volume 1.

BILLETES DEL TESORO NACIONAL

DECRETO 15.9.1880

		Good	Fine	XF
A22	**1 Peso** D.1880. Series I. Black on lt. blue unpt. Seated Liberty w/shield of national arms and staff at lower l. Two dry seals. Wmk. paper. Uniface. Rare.	—	—	—

DECRETO 24.9.1881

#1-5 printer: HLBNC.

		Good	Fine	XF
1	**1 Peso** D.1881. Brown. Liberty bust at bottom ctr., arms at upper l. Series I.	250.	500.	—
2	**5 Pesos** D.1881. Series II. Like #1. Remainder w/stub.	—	—	—
3	**25 Pesos** D.1881. Series III.	—	—	—
4	**50 Pesos** D.1881. Series IV.	—	—	—
5	**100 Pesos** D.1881. Series V.	—	—	—

DECRETO 30.6.1883

		Good	Fine	XF
6	**25 Pesos** D.1883. Series III.	—	—	—
7	**50 Pesos** D.1883. Series IV.	—	—	—
8	**100 Pesos** D.1883. Series V.	—	—	—

DECRETO 20.3.1885

#9-10 printer: HLBNC.

		Good	Fine	XF
9	**20 Centavos** D.1885. Black. Arms at r. Round purple handstamp on back. Uniface. Series VII.			
	a. Issued note.	175.	450.	—
	r. Remainder w/stub.	—	—	—

		Good	Fine	XF
10	**50 Centavos** D.1885. Black on pink paper. Arms at ctr. Purple handstamps on face and back. Uniface. Series VI.			
	a. Issued note.	175.	450.	—
	r. Remainder w/stub.	—	—	—

DECRETO 10.11.1885

		Good	Fine	XF
11	**10 Centavos** D.1885. Red. Purple handstamps on face and back. Local printing. Uniface.	—	—	—
12	**10 Centavos** D.1885. Black. Arms at upper l. Purple handstamps of Secretaria de Hacienda, facsimile sign. of EL TESORERO on back. Uniface. Series VIII. Printer: HLBNC.			
	a. Issued note.	175.	450.	—
	r. Remainder w/stub.	—	—	—
12A	**50 Centavos** D. 1885. Local printing. Uniface.	—	—	—

DECRETO 20.3.1886

		Good	Fine	XF
13	**20 Centavos** D.1886. Series VII.	—	—	—
14	**50 Centavos** D.1886. Series VI.	—	—	—
15	**1 Peso** D.1886. Series I.	—	—	—

DECRETO 12.10.1894

		Good	Fine	XF
16	**5 Centavos** ND (1894). Black on blue-green unpt. W/o decreto. Back dk. green. Local printing. Series 9.	25.00	85.00	225.

#17-19 arms at upper l. Printer: Paydt, Upham & Co. S.F.

		Good	Fine	XF
17	**10 Centavos** D.1894. Dk. brown on orange and green unpt. Back brown. Series XI.			
	a. Red sign.	25.00	75.00	200.
	b. Black sign.	17.50	65.00	175.
18	**20 Centavos** D.1894. Dk. brown on brown and green unpt. Back green. Series X.			
	a. 2 sign. varieties.	30.00	100.	250.
	b. W/o sign.	—	—	—

		Good	Fine	XF
19	**50 Centavos** D.1894. Dk. brown on green and tan unpt. Back blue. Series I; 6; IX.			
	a. *Series I* at top, blue serial #. 2 sign. varieties.	35.00	110.	250.
	b. *Series 6* at top, red serial #. 3 sign. varieties.	35.00	110.	250.
	c. *Series IX* at top, red serial #. 2 sign. varieties.	35.00	125.	275.
	d. Like c., but w/o sign.	30.00	100.	200.

1894 COMMEMORATIVE ISSUE

#20-23A, 402nd Anniversary of the Discovery of America. Local printing.

		Good	Fine	XF
20	**20 Centavos** D.1894. Blue. Back black on brown unpt. w/seated Liberty at l. looking at 5 mountains and sunrise at r. Series 1. Rare.	—	—	—
21	**50 Centavos** D.1894. Black on lt. tan unpt. Similar to #20. Back black on green unpt. Rare.	—	—	—

		Good	Fine	XF
22	**1 Peso** D.1894. Black. Arms at upper ctr. Seated Liberty (Ms. Rafaela Herrera) w/arms and bales at l., seated Indian w/huts at r. on back.			
	a. Sign. title: *El Ministro General* at l. All titles in sm. lettering.	400.	950.	—
	b. Sign. title: *El Ministro de Hacienda* at l. All titles in lg. lettering.	400.	950.	—

		Good	Fine	XF
23	**5 Pesos** D. 1894. Black and red. Seated Liberty (Ms. Herrera) w/arms at l., Chief Nicarao at r. on back. Rare.	—	—	—
23A	**10 Pesos** D. 1894. Black and orange. Arms on back. Rare.	—	—	—

1894 ISSUE

		Good	Fine	XF
24	**1 Peso** D.1894. Black. Portr. S. Bolivár at ctr., arms in blue at lower r. Back dk. green; arms at ctr.			
	a. *Series No. VII.* Imprint: *Paydt Upham & Co. S.F.*	225.	500.	—
	b. *Series No. VIII.* Imprint: *Lith. Paydt Upham & Co. S.F.* 2 sign. varieties.	200.	450.	—
	r. Remainder w/o sign.	175.	425.	—

		Good	Fine	XF
25	**5 Pesos** D.1894. Black on pink and lt. blue unpt. Portr. Herrera at upper l., arms at lower r. Back green; arms at ctr. Series III.	225.	500.	—

		Good	Fine	XF
26	**10 Pesos** D.1894. Black. Red arms at ctr. Portr. Jerez at r. Back blue and inverted; arms at ctr. Imprint: Lith. Paydt, Upham & Co. S.F. Series IV.			
	a. Sign. titles: *El Ministro General* and *El Tesorero.*	400.	1000.	—
	b. Ovpt. sign. titles: *El Ministro de Hacienda* and *El Tesorero General.*	400.	1000.	—
27	**50 Pesos** D.1894. Black on green unpt. Portr. Morazán at l. Back lt. brown; arms at ctr. Series V.			
	a. Issued note.	—	—	—
	r. Unsigned remainder.	—	—	—

1900 ISSUE

#28-33 arms on back. Printer: W&S.

		Good	Fine	XF
28	**50 Centavos** 15.9.1900. Black on blue and red unpt. Woman seated at ctr. Back blue.	25.00	85.00	275.

		Good	Fine	XF
29	**1 Peso** 15.9.1900. Black on green and gold unpt. Portr. Jerez at l., cattle at r. Back brown.			
	a. Issued note.	30.00	150.	400.
	s. Specimen. Yellow and orange; back green.	—	—	—

		Good	Fine	XF
30	**5 Pesos** 15.9.1900. Black on red unpt. Portr. Zelaya at l., steam passenger train at ctr. Back brown.	100.	450.	—
31	**10 Pesos** 15.9.1900. Black and purple on gold unpt. Herrera at top ctr., farmer plowing w/oxen below. Back dull purple.	175.	600.	—
32	**25 Pesos** 15.9.1900. Black on blue-green unpt. Portr. D. F. Morazán at l., Liberty in winged chariot drawn by lions at ctr. Back pale green.	—	—	—

		Good	Fine	XF
33	**50 Pesos** 15.9.1900. Black on yellow and orange unpt. Liberty and portr. S. Bolivar at l. Back brown. Specimen.	—	—	—

1906-08 ISSUE

#34-39 printer: Waterlow Bros. & Layton, Ltd., London.

		Good	Fine	XF
34	**50 Centavos** 1.1.1906. Black on red and green unpt. Allegorical woman seated w/sword and trumpet at l. Back blue; arms at ctr.	12.50	60.00	200.

		Good	Fine	XF
35	**1 Peso** 1.1.1906. Black on red and orange unpt. 2 women and child gathering fruit at upper l., portr. woman at r. Back brown; arms at ctr.	15.00	90.00	225.

		Good	Fine	XF
36	**5 Pesos** 1.1.1908. Black on tan and purple unpt. Steam locomotive at l., portr. Zelaya at ctr. r. Back orange; arms at r.	200.	700.	—

		Good	Fine	XF
37	**10 Pesos** 1.1.1908. Red and brown. Portr. Gen. D. M. Jerez at l. Back purple; arms at r.	300.	1000.	—

		Good	Fine	XF
38	**50 Pesos** 1.1.1908. Black on yellow and green unpt. Portr. S. Bolívar at l., man w/ox-cart at ctr. Back brown; arms at r.	—	—	—

		Good	Fine	XF
39	**100 Pesos** 1.1.1908. Black on green and tan unpt. Seated woman at l., equestrian statue of Nicarao at r. Back green. Rare.	—	—	—

1909 Issue

		Good	Fine	XF
40	**50 Pesos** D.24.11.1909. Black on red unpt., blue border. Portr. J.S. Zelaya at l. Arms at ctr. on back. Local printing. Rare.	—	—	—

1910 Provisional Issue

		Good	Fine	XF
41	**5 Pesos** D.3.2.1910. Portr. Dr. J. Madriz at l. Local printing.	200.	600.	—

		Good	Fine	XF
42	**5 Pesos** D.3.3.1910. Black on blue and lt. red unpt. Arms at ctr. on back. Local printing.	200.	600.	—

1911 Issue (Dated 1910)

#43-49 portr. Columbus on face. Sign. varieties. Printer: ABNC.

		Good	Fine	XF
43	**50 Centavos** 1.1.1910. Black on green and m/c unpt. Portr. C. Columbus at r. Back dk. green. Series A.			
	a. Ctr. sign. Pres. *José Madriz.*	15.00	40.00	150.
	b. Ctr. sign. Pres. *Juan J. Estrada.*	15.00	40.00	150.
	s. Specimen.	—	Unc	175.

		Good	Fine	XF
44	**1 Peso** 1.1.1910. Black on orange-brown unpt. Portr. C. Columbus at l. Back orange. Series B.			
	a. Ctr. sign. Pres. *José Madriz.*	15.00	50.00	175.
	b. Ctr. sign. Pres. *Juan J. Estrada.*	15.00	50.00	175.
	s. Specimen.	—	Unc	175.

		Good	Fine	XF
45	**5 Pesos** 1.1.1910. Black on blue and m/c unpt. Seated woman at l., portr. C. Columbus at ctr. r. Back dk. blue. Series C.			
	a. Ctr. sign. Pres. *José Madriz.*	50.00	200.	500.
	b. Ctr. sign. Pres. *Juan J. Estrada.*	50.00	200.	500.
	s. Specimen.	—	Unc	400.

46	10 Pesos	Good	Fine	XF
	1.1.1910. Black on red and m/c unpt. Woman and child at l., portr. C. Columbus at r. Back red-brown. Series D.			
	a. Ctr. sign. Pres. *José Madriz.*	100.	400.	—
	b. Ctr. sign. Pres. *Juan J. Estrada.*	100.	400.	—
	s. Specimen.	—	Unc	450.

47	25 Pesos	Good	Fine	XF
	1.1.1910. Black on m/c unpt. Portr. C. Columbus at l., arms at ctr. Back olive; monument at ctr. Series E.			
	a. Ctr. sign. Pres. *José Madriz.*	175.	550.	—
	b. Ctr. sign. Pres. *Juan J. Estrada.*	175.	550.	
	s. Specimen.	—	Unc	600.
48	**50 Pesos**			
	1.1.1910. Black on purple and m/c unpt. Arms at ctr., portr. C. Columbus at r. Back purple; lg. bldg. at ctr. Series F.			
	a. Ctr. sign. Pres. *José Madriz.* Rare.	—	—	—
	b. Ctr. sign. Pres. *Juan J. Estrada.* Reported not confirmed.	—	—	—
	s1. Sign. as a. Specimen.			
	s2. Sign. as b. Specimen.			
49	**100 Pesos**			
	1.1.1910. Black on orange and m/c unpt. Portr. C. Columbus at l. ctr., arms at r. Back red; gateway to govt. bldg. at ctr. Series G.			
	a. Ctr. sign. Pres. *José Madriz.* Rare.	—	—	—
	b. Ctr. sign. Pres *Juan J. Estrada.* Rare.	—	—	—
	s. Specimen.			

1912 ND Provisional Issue

Ovpt: *ESTE BILLETE VALE ... CENTAVOS DE CÓRDOBA* vertically in red on face.

50	4 (Cuatro) Centavos on 50 Centavos	Good	Fine	XF
	ND (-old date 1.1.1910). Ovpt. on #43b.	35.00	120.	250.

51	8 (Ocho) Centavos on 1 Peso	Good	Fine	XF
	ND (-old date 1.1.1910). Ovpt. on #44b.	40.00	150.	300.

> **NOTICE**
> Readers with unlisted dates, signature varieties, etc. are invited to submit photocopies or, high resolution (300 dpi, 100% size) scans of their notes to: Standard Catalog of World Paper Money, 700 East State St. Iola, WI 54990-0001, or E-Mail: george.cuhaj@fwpubs.com.

Banco Nacional de Nicaragua

Ley de 20 de Marzo de 1912

#52-54 fractional notes w/o date. Arms at ctr. on back. Printer: ABNC.

52	10 Centavos	Good	Fine	XF
	L.1912. Black on green unpt. Portr. Liberty at l. Back green.			
	a. W/o prefix. Pres. sign. *Adolfo Díaz* (Oct. 1914).	8.00	25.00	75.00
	b. Prefix A. Pres. sign. as a.	8.00	25.00	75.00
	c. Prefix B. Pres. sign. *E. Chamorro* (Oct. 1918).	8.00	25.00	75.00
	d. Prefix C. Pres. sign. *Diego M. Chamorro.* (July 1922).	12.00	40.00	100.
	e. Prefix D. Pres. sign. as d.	6.00	20.00	50.00
	f. Prefix E. Pres. sign. *Emiliano Chamorro* (Sept. 1926).	6.00	20.00	50.00
	s. Specimen.	—	Unc	110.

53	25 Centavos	Good	Fine	XF
	L. 1912. Black on orange unpt. Portr. Liberty at r. Back orange.			
	a. W/o prefix. Pres. sign. *Adolfo Diaz* (Oct. 1914). Red serial #.	10.00	35.00	75.00
	b. Prefix A. Pres. sign. *E. Chamorro* (Oct. 1918). Blue serial #.	10.00	40.00	90.00
	s. Specimen.	—	Unc	110.

54	50 Centavos	Good	Fine	XF
	L. 1912. Black on blue unpt. Portr. Liberty at l. Back gray. Red serial #.			
	a. W/o prefix. Pres. sign. *Adolfo Diaz* (Oct. 1914).	12.50	40.00	100.
	b. Prefix A. Pres. sign. *E. Chamorro* (Oct. 1918).	15.00	50.00	125.
	s. Specimen.	—	Unc	125.

Note: For similar issues but w/later dates see #85-89. #55-60 portr. Córdoba at l. #55-61 larger notes. Printer: HBNC.

55	1 Córdoba	Good	Fine	XF
	L. 1912. Black on green unpt. Portr. Nicarao at lower r. Back green; arms at ctr.			
	a. W/o prefix. Pres. sign. *Adolfo Diaz* (Oct. 1914). Red serial #.	100.	300.	—
	b. Prefix A. Pres. sign. *E. Chamorro* (Oct. 1918). Blue serial #.	100.	300.	—
	c. Prefix B. Pres. Sign. *Carlos José Solózano.*	150.	500.	—
	s. Specimen. Pres. sign. *Carlos José Solózano.*	—	—	—

56	2 Córdobas	Good	Fine	XF
	L. 1912. Black on brown unpt. Portr. De la Cerda at r. Back maroon; arms at ctr.			
	a. W/o prefix. Pres. sign. *Adolfo Diaz* (Oct. 1914).	—	—	—
	b. Prefix A. Pres. sign. *E. Chamorro* (Oct. 1918).	150.	500.	—
	s. Specimen.	—	—	—

57 5 Córdobas
L. 1912. Portr. Larreynaga at r.

	Good	Fine	XF
a. Issued note.	—	—	—
s. Specimen.	—	—	—

58 10 Córdobas
L. 1912. Black on orange unpt. Portr. Chamerra at r. Back orange.

	Good	Fine	XF
a. Issued note.	—	—	—
s. Specimen.	—	—	—

59 20 Córdobas
L. 1912. Portr. Martinez at r.

	Good	Fine	XF
a. Issued note.	—	—	—
s. Specimen.	—	—	—

60 50 Córdobas
L. 1912. Portr. Estrada at r.

	Good	Fine	XF
a. Issued note.	—	—	—
s. Specimen.	—	—	—

61 100 Córdobas
L. 1912. Palm trees, Lake Managua and volcano at ctr.

	Good	Fine	XF
a. Issued note.	—	—	—
s. Specimen.	—	—	—

1927-39 Issue

#62-69, bank name in English in upper frame above Spanish name. National arms on back. Printer: ABNC.

62 1 Córdoba
1927; 1930. Green on m/c unpt. Woman at ctr. Back dk. brown.

	Good	Fine	XF
a. Minister *Guzman.* 1927 (Mar. 1927).	80.00	225.	450.
b. Minister *Lopez.* 1927 (July, 1928).	80.00	225.	450.
c. 1930 (Dec. 1929).	—	—	—
s. Specimen.	—	Unc	400.

64 2 Córdobas
1939. Green on m/c unpt. Ox-cart in front of sugar cane mill at l. Back red-orange.

	Good	Fine	XF
a. Issued note.	10.00	50.00	200.
s. Specimen.	—	Unc	160.

65 5 Córdobas
1927-39. Gray on m/c unpt. Cattle at ctr. Back brown.

	Good	Fine	XF
a. 1927.	—	—	—
b. 1938; 1939.	8.50	40.00	150.
s. Specimen.	—	Unc	200.

66 10 Córdobas
1929-39. Brown on m/c unpt. Portr. Liberty at r. Like #94. Back carmine.

	Good	Fine	XF
a. 1929.	—	—	—
b. 1938; 1939.	22.50	100.	325.
s. Specimen.	—	Unc	275.

67 20 Córdobas
1929-39. Orange on m/c unpt. Bay and port of Corinto. Back blue.

	Good	Fine	XF
a. 1929.	—	—	—
b. 1937; 1939.	60.00	300.	—
s. Specimen, punched hole cancelled.	—	Unc	275.

68 50 Córdobas
1929; 1937; 1939. Purple on m/c unpt. 2 women w/wheat laureates at l. Back orange.

	Good	Fine	XF
a. Issued note.	—	—	—
s. Specimen, punched hole cancelled.	—	Unc	550.

69 100 Córdobas
1939. Red on m/c unpt. Woman w/fruits before altar at r. Back dk. olive brown.

	Good	Fine	XF
a. Issued note.	—	—	—
s. Specimen.	—	Unc	700.

1934 ND Revalidation

The Decree of January 2, 1934, ordered all circulating notes to be exchanged against new notes w/red ovpt: *REVALIDADO.* The ovpt. was printed on notes in stock in the vaults of the B.N.N.

70 1 Córdoba

	Good	Fine	XF
ND *(D.1934).* Ovpt. on #62.	25.00	100.	300.

71 1 Córdoba

	Good	Fine	XF
ND *(D.1934).* Ovpt. on #63a.	20.00	100.	250.

72 5 Córdobas

	Good	Fine	XF
ND *(D.1934).* Ovpt. on #65a.	30.00	150.	—

		Good	Fine	XF
73	**10 Córdobas** ND *(D.1934)*. Ovpt. on #58.	100.	400.	—
74	**10 Córdobas** ND *(D.1934)*. Ovpt. on #66a.	75.00	325.	—
75	**20 Córdobas** ND *(D.1934)*. Ovpt. on #59.	—	—	—
76	**20 Córdobas** ND *(D.1934)*. Ovpt. on #67a.	—	—	—

		Good	Fine	XF
77	**50 Córdobas** ND *(D.1934)*. Ovpt. on #68.	—	—	—
78	**100 Córdobas** ND *(D.1934)*. Ovpt. on #61.	—	—	—

Note: The old notes w/o ovpt. became worthless on June 1, 1934. Later dates (1937-39) of the 2nd issue were put into circulation w/o ovpt. No 2 Cordobas notes or fractional currency notes were issued w/ovpt.

1935-38 Issue

#79-84 arms at ctr. on back. Printer: HBNC.

		Good	Fine	XF
79	**10 Centavos** 1938. Black on green unpt. Portr. Liberty at l. Back green.	4.50	30.00	100.

		Good	Fine	XF
80	**25 Centavos** 1938. Black on orange unpt. Portr. Liberty at r. Back orange.	6.00	40.00	150.

		Good	Fine	XF
81	**50 Centavos** 1938. Black on dk. blue unpt. Portr. Liberty at l. Back blue.	10.00	60.00	225.

		Good	Fine	XF
82	**1 Córdoba** 1935; 1938. Blue on peach unpt. 2 allegories people on cliff above sea at ctr. Back green.	20.00	100.	325.
83	**5 Córdobas** 1935. Black on lt. green and red unpt. Woman's head at ctr. Back brown.	35.00	175.	475.

		Good	Fine	XF
84	**10 Córdobas** 1935. Brown on purple and green unpt. Palm trees, lake and volcano at ctr. Back carmine.	70.00	350.	—

1937 ND Issue

#85 and 86 portr. Liberty. Arms at ctr. on back. Similar to #87 and 88. Printer: ABNC.

		Good	Fine	XF
85	**10 Centavos** ND (1937). Similar to #87 but w/o the 6 lines of text on face referring to Law of 1912.			
	a. Sign. title: *DIRECTOR GERENTE* at bottom.	4.00	15.00	60.00
	b. Sign. title: *GERENTE GENERAL* at bottom.	5.00	20.00	75.00
	s. Specimen.	—	Unc	100.
86	**25 Centavos** ND (1937). Similar to #88 but w/o text on face referring to Law of 1912.			
	a. Sign. title: *DIRECTOR GERENTE* at bottom.	5.00	20.00	85.00
	b. Sign. title: *GERENTE GENERAL* at bottom.	25.00	100.	250.
	s. Specimen.	—	Unc	100.

1938 Issue

#87-89 similar to previous issue. Printer: ABNC.

		Good	Fine	XF
87	**10 Centavos** 1938. Black on green unpt. Like #52.			
	a. Issued note.	3.50	15.00	50.00
	s. Specimen.	—	Unc	100.

88	25 Centavos	Good	Fine	XF
	1938. Black on orange unpt. Like #53.			
	a. Issued note.	4.50	20.00	75.00
	s. Specimen.	—	Unc	100.

89	50 Centavos	Good	Fine	XF
	1938. Black on blue unpt. Like #54.			
	a. Issued note.	6.50	30.00	100.
	s. Specimen.	—	Unc	140.

1941-45 Issue

The English bank name in upper frame has been removed. Face and back designs and colors similar to the 1927-39 issue notes except for #90 and 91. Printer: ABNC.

90	1 Córdoba	VG	VF	UNC
	1941-45. Blue on m/c unpt. Portr. Indian girl wearing feather at ctr. Back dk. olive-brown. *SERIE DE* (date) engraved and printed in blue.			
	a. 1941.	1.00	3.50	15.00
	b. 1942; 1945.	2.00	12.50	60.00
	s. Specimen.			125.
91	1 Córdoba			
	1949; 1951. Like #90 but *SERIE DE* (date) typographed and printed in red.			
	a. 1949.	2.00	12.50	75.00
	b. 1951.	1.50	7.50	50.00
	s. Specimen.			100.

92	2 Córdobas	VG	VF	UNC
	1941; 1945. Green on m/c unpt. Similar to #64.			
	a. 1941.	4.00	20.00	100.
	b. 1945.	3.00	15.00	90.00
	s. Specimen.			125.

93	5 Córdobas	VG	VF	UNC
	1942; 1945; 1951. Gray on m/c unpt. Similar to #65.			
	a. 1942.	5.00	30.00	150.
	b. 1945.	4.50	25.00	120.
	c. 1951.	4.00	20.00	100.
	s. Specimen.			100.

94	10 Córdobas	VG	VF	UNC
	1942; 1945; 1951. Brown on m/c unpt. Similar to #66.			
	a. 1942.	15.00	75.00	350.
	b. 1945.	12.50	60.00	300.
	c. 1951.	10.00	50.00	250.
	s. Specimen.			150.
95	20 Córdobas			
	1942; 1945; 1951. Orange on m/c unpt. Similar to #67.			
	a. 1942.	35.00	200.	650.
	b. 1945.	30.00	175.	600.
	c. 1951.	25.00	150.	550.
	s. Specimen.			260.
96	50 Córdobas			
	1942; 1945. Purple on m/c unpt. Similar to #68.			
	a. 1942.	75.00	300.	—
	b. 1945. 2 sign. varieties for r. h. sign.	30.00	75.00	150.
	s1. Specimen. 1942.			260.
	s2. Specimen. 1945.			175.

97	100 Córdobas	VG	VF	UNC
	1941; 1942; 1945. Red on m/c unpt. Similar to #69.			
	a. 1941; 1942.	150.	450.	—
	b. 1945. 2 sign. varieties for r. h. sign.	125.	425.	—
	s. Specimen.			275.

98	500 Córdobas	VG	VF	UNC
	1945. Black on m/c unpt. Portr. R. Dario at ctr. Back green. 2 sign. varieties for r. h. sign.			
	a. Issued note.	100.	225.	425.
	s. Specimen.	—	—	—

1953-54 Issue

#99-106, all notes except #105 and 106 come in two date varieties:

a. *SERIE DE* (date) engraved, printed in note color. 1953-58.

b. *SERIE DE* (date) typographed, printed in black. 1959-60. Printer: TDLR.

99 1 Córdoba
1953-60. Dk. blue on m/c unpt. Portr. Indian girl wearing feather at ctr. Bank on back.

	VG	VF	UNC
a. Engraved date. 1953; 1954.	2.50	12.50	60.00
b. Engraved date. 1957; 1958.	2.00	10.00	50.00
c. Typographed date. 1959; 1960.	1.50	7.50	35.00
s. Specimen.	—	—	—

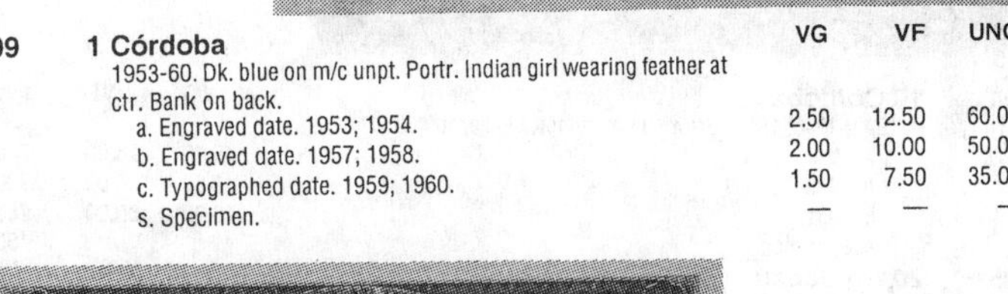

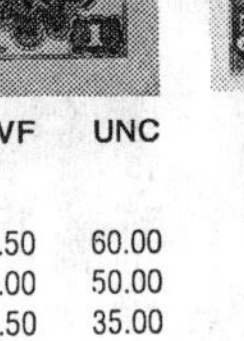

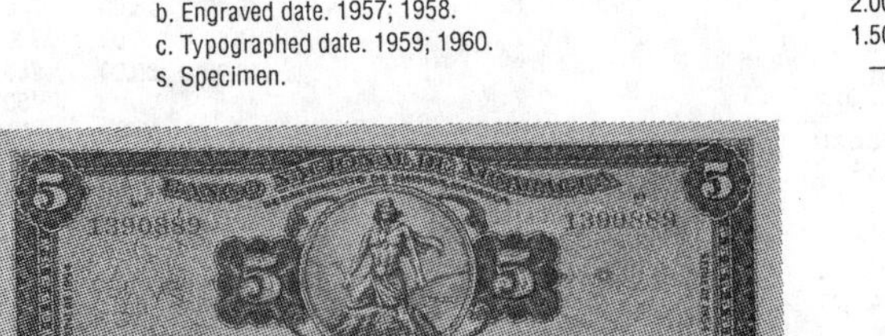

100 5 Córdobas
1953-60. Dk. green on m/c unpt. C. Nicarao at ctr. Carved statue on back at ctr., arms at r.

	VG	VF	UNC
a. Engraved date. 1953.	20.00	100.	250.
b. Engraved date. 1954; 1957; 1958.	12.50	60.00	175.
c. Typographed date. 1959; 1960.	5.00	50.00	150.
s. Specimen.	—	—	—

101 10 Córdobas
1953-60. Red on m/c unpt. Arms at l., portr. M. de Larreynaga at r. Independence meeting on back.

	VG	VF	UNC
a. Engraved date. 1953; 1954; 1957; 1958.	10.00	75.00	350.
b. Typographed date. 1959; 1960.	7.50	60.00	250.
s. Specimen.	—	—	—

102 20 Córdobas
1953-60. Orange-brown on m/c unpt. Scene w/R. Herrera at ctr. Map on back.

	VG	VF	UNC
a. Engraved date. 1953; 1954; 1957; 1958.	15.00	150.	550.
b. Typographed date. 1959; 1960.	10.00	125.	500.
s. Specimen.	—	—	—

103 50 Córdobas
1953-60. Dk. blue on m/c unpt. Portr. M. Jerez at l., Gen. T. Martinez at r. Flag on back.

	VG	VF	UNC
a. Engraved date. 1953; 1954; 1957; 1958.	40.00	200.	800.
b. Typographed date. 1959; 1960.	30.00	150.	750.
s. Specimen.	—	—	—

104 100 Córdobas
1953-60. Purple on m/c unpt. Portr. J. Dolores Estrada at r. National Palace on back.

	VG	VF	UNC
a. Engraved date. 1953; 1954; 1957; 1958.	30.00	175.	700.
b. Typographed date. 1959; 1960.	20.00	100.	600.
s. Specimen.	—	—	—

105 500 Córdobas
1953-54. Black on m/c unpt. Portr. R. Dario at ctr. Monument in Dario Park at ctr. on back.

	VG	VF	UNC
a. Engraved date. 1953; 1954.	150.	650.	—
b. Typographed date. 1959; 1960.	125.	550.	—
s. Specimen.	—	—	—

106 1000 Córdobas
1953-54. Brown on m/c unpt. Portr. Pres. Gen. A. Somoza at lower l., arms at r. Stadium on back.

	VG	VF	UNC
a. Engraved date. 1953; 1954.	175.	700.	—
b. Typographed date. 1959; 1960.	150.	600.	—
s. Specimen.	—	—	—

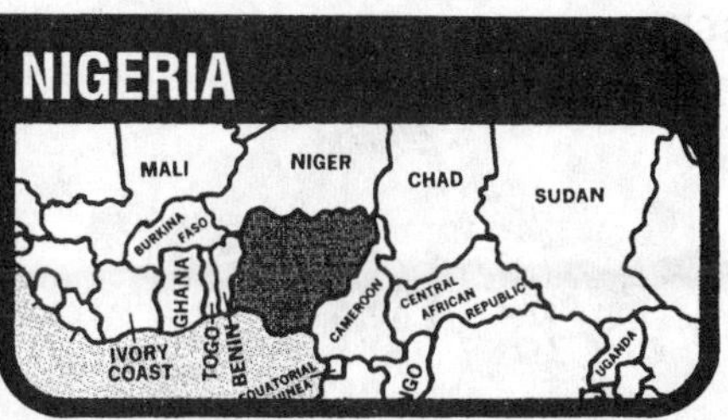

The Federal Republic of Nigeria, situated on the Atlantic coast of Africa between Benin and Cameroon, has an area of 356,667 sq. mi. (923,768 sq. km.) and a population of 128.79 million. Capital: Abuja. The economy is d on petroleum and agriculture. Crude oil, cocoa, tobacco and tin are exported.

Following the Napoleonic Wars, the British expanded their trade with the interior of Nigeria. British claims to a sphere of influence in that area were recognized by the Berlin Conference of 1885, and in the following year the Royal Niger Company was chartered. Direct British control of the territory was initiated in 1900, and in 1914 the amalgamation of northern and southern Nigeria into the Colony and Protectorate of Nigeria was effected. In 1960, following a number of territorial and constitutional changes, Nigeria was granted independence within the British Commonwealth as a federation of the northern, western and eastern regions. Nigeria altered its political relationship with Great Britain on Oct. 1, 1963, by proclaiming itself a republic. It did, however, elect to remain a member of the Commonwealth. The Supreme Commander of Armed Forces is the Head of the Federal Military Government.

On May 30, 1967, the Eastern Region of the republic - an area occupied principally by the proud and resourceful Ibo tribe - seceded from Nigeria and proclaimed itself the independent Republic of Biafra. Civil war erupted and raged for 31 months. Casualties, including civilian, were about two million, the majority succumbing to malnutrition and disease. Biafra surrendered to the federal government on January 15, 1970. After military coups in 1983 and 1985 the government was assumed by an Armed Forces Ruling Council. A transitional civilian council was formed in 1993. Nigeria was suspended from the Commonwealth in November 1995, but was re-admitted on May 29, 1999.

RULERS:

British to 1963

MONETARY SYSTEM:

1 Shilling = 12 Pence
1 Pound = 20 Shillings to 1973
1 Naira (10 Shillings) = 100 Kobo, 1973-

BRITISH ADMINISTRATION

GOVERNMENT OF NIGERIA

1918 WW I EMERGENCY ISSUE

#1-1B w/text: *issued under Ord. XXII, 1918* at upper l. and r.

		Good	Fine	XF
1	**1 Shilling** Dec. 1918. Green.	400.	1200.	2500.
1A	**10 Shillings** Dec. 1918. Red. Rare.	—	—	—

		Good	Fine	XF
1B	**20 Shillings** Dec. 1918. Black. Rare.	—	—	—

Note: This issue was printed locally to alleviate a shortage of silver coins after the end of WWI.

FEDERATION OF NIGERIA

CENTRAL BANK OF NIGERIA

1958 ISSUE

#2-5 river scene and palm trees. Printer: W&S.

		VG	VF	UNC
2	**5 Shillings** 15.9.1958. Lilac and blue-green. Back lilac; palms.			
	a. Issued note.	5.00	25.00	75.00
	s. Specimen.	—	—	—
3	**10 Shillings** 15.9.1958. Green and brown. Back green; crop sowing and man w/produce.			
	a. Issued note.	10.00	65.00	275.
	s. Specimen.	—	—	—

		VG	VF	UNC
4	**1 Pound** 15.9.1958. Red and dk. brown. Back red; harvesting coconuts.			
	a. Issued note.	1.50	6.00	35.00
	s. Specimen.	—	—	—

		VG	VF	UNC
5	**5 Pounds** 15.9.1958. Dk. green on green and purple unpt. Back purple; fruit farming at r.			
	a. Issued note.	15.00	75.00	350.
	s. Specimen.	—	—	—

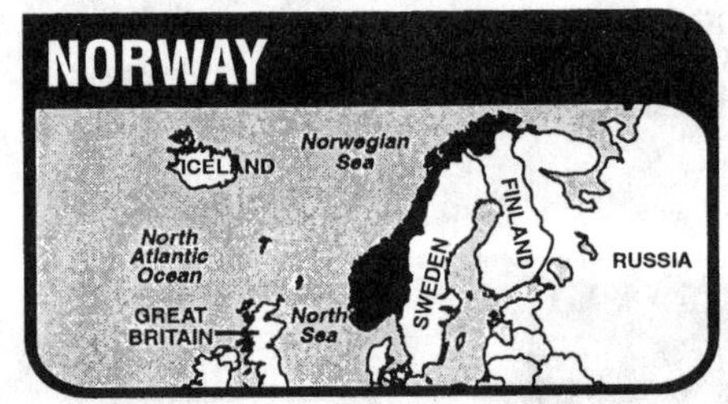

The Kingdom of Norway, a constitutional monarchy located in northwestern Europe, has an area of 150,000 sq. mi. (388,500 sq. km.) including the island territories of Spitzbergen (Svalbard) and Jan Mayen, and a population of 4.46 million. Capital: Oslo. The diversified economic of Norway includes shipping, fishing, forestry, agriculture and manufacturing. Nonferrous metals, paper and paperboard, paper pulp, iron, steel and oil are exported.

A United Norwegian kingdom was established in the 9th century, the era of the indomitable Norse Vikings who ranged far and wide, visiting the coasts of northwestern Europe, the Mediterranean, Greenland and North America. In the 13th century, the Norse kingdom was united briefly with Sweden, then passed, through the Union of Kalmar, 1397, to the rule of Denmark which was maintained until 1814. In 1814, Norway fell again under the rule of Sweden. The union lasted until 1905 when the Norwegian Parliament arranged a peaceful separation and invited a Danish prince (King Haakon VII) to occupy the throne of an independent Kingdom of Norway.

RULERS:

Christian V, 1670-1699
Frederik IV, 1699-1730
Christian VI, 1730-1746
Frederik V, 1746-1766
Christian VII, 1766-1808
Frederik VI, 1808-1814
Carl XIII, 1814-1818
Carl XIV Johan, 1818-1844
Oscar I, 1844-1859
Carl XV, 1859-1872
Oscar II, 1872-1905
Haakon VII, 1905-1957
Olav V, 1957-1991
Harald V, 1991-

MONETARY SYSTEM:

1 Speciedaler = 96 Skilling to 1816
1 Speciedaler = 120 Skilling, 1816-1873
1 Krone = 100 Øre, 1873-

REPLACEMENT NOTES:

#15, 16, 25-28, 30-33, 37-40 with 1945 or later dates, Z prefix.

KINGDOM

THOR MØHLEN NOTES

1695 ISSUE

#A1-A5 black text w/red wax seals. Uniface.

Note: All valuations for notes w/o talon (counterfoil). Notes with matching stub are worth at least a 50% premium.

		Good	Fine	XF
A1	**10 Rixdaler Croner** 1695.	575.	1200.	2500.
A2	**20 Rixdaler Croner** 1695.	600.	1200.	2750.

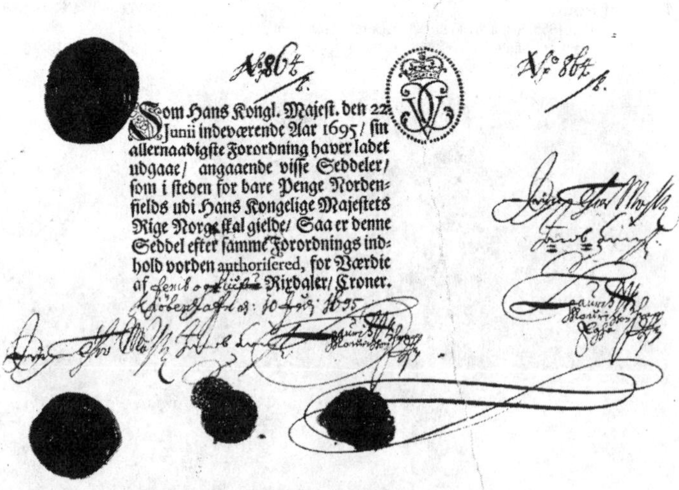

		Good	Fine	XF
A3	**25 Rixdaler Croner** 1695.	800.	1450.	2750.
A4	**50 Rixdaler Croner** 1695.	900.	1600.	3500.
A5	**100 Rixdaler Croner** 1695.	900.	1600.	3500.

A commemorative reproduction of A5 was made in 1995.

REGERINGS KOMMISSION

CHRISTIANIA

1807-10 ISSUE

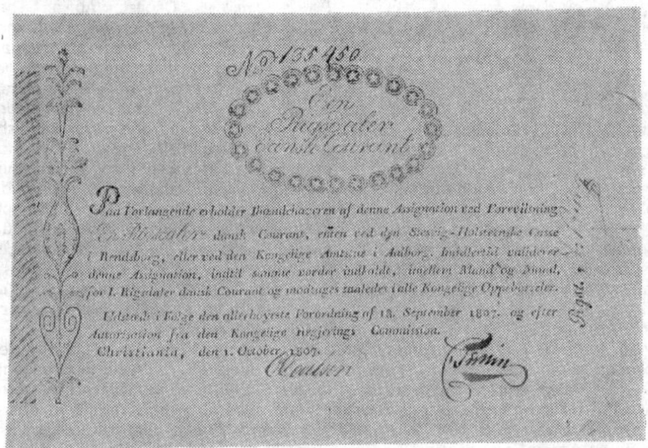

		Good	Fine	X
A6	**1 Rigsdaler** 1.10.1807.	250.	500.	110
A7	**5 Rigsdaler** 1.10.1807.	275.	600.	115

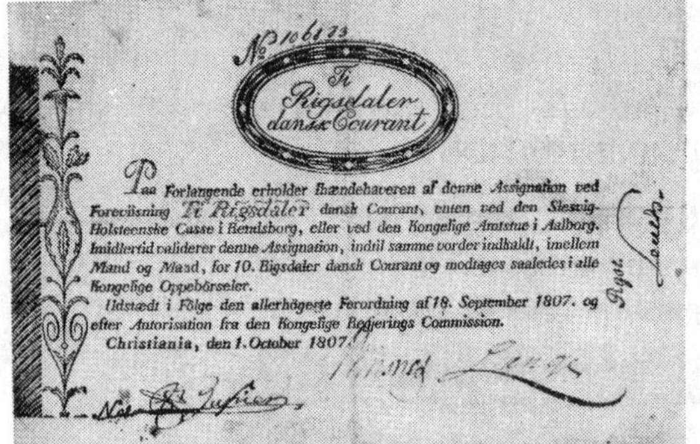

		Good	Fine	X
A8	**10 Rigsdaler** 1.10.1807.	550.	900.	-
A10	**100 Rigsdaler** 1.10.1807.	600.	1000.	-

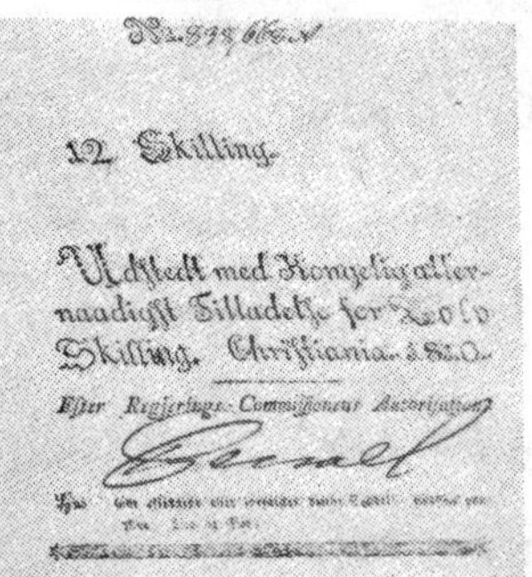

		Good	Fine	X
A11	**12 Skilling** 1810.	50.00	135.	30

Note: The 24 skilling of 1810 was printed in Copenhagen.

RIGSBANKENS NORSKE AVDELING

1813 ISSUE

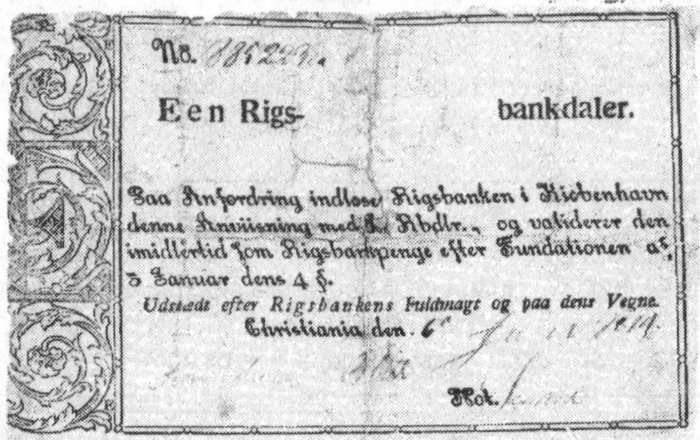

		Good	Fine	XF
A12	**1 Rigsbankdaler** 1813-14.	150.	350.	1000.
A13	**5 Rigsbankdaler** 1813-14.	200.	450.	1200.
A15	**50 Rigsbankdaler** 1813-14.	500.	1500.	—
A16	**100 Rigsbankdaler** 1813-14. Rare.	—	—	—

STATTHOLDERBEVIS (PRINSESEDLER)

1815 ISSUE

		Good	Fine	XF
A17	**1 Rigsbankdaler** 1815.	300.	800.	1500.
A18	**5 Rigsbankdaler** 1815. Rare.	—	—	—
A19	**15 Rigsbankdaler** 1815. Rare.	—	—	—
A20	**25 Rigsbankdaler** 1815. Rare.	—	—	—

		Good	Fine	XF
A21	**50 Rigsbankdaler** 1815. Rare.	—	—	—

NORGES MIDLERTIDIGE RIGSBANK

1814 FRACTIONAL NOTE ISSUE

		Good	Fine	XF
A22	**3 Rigsbank-skilling** 1814.	50.00	175.	400.

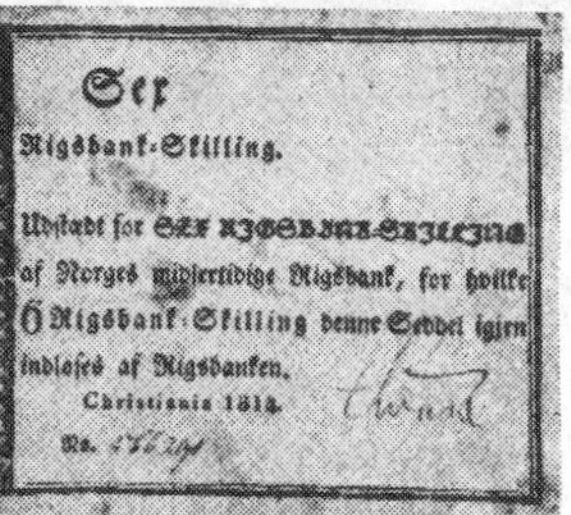

		Good	Fine	XF
A23	**6 Rigsbank-skilling** 1814.	50.00	175.	400.
A24	**8 Rigsbank-skilling** 1814.	70.00	200.	425.
A25	**16 Rigsbank-skilling** 1814.	60.00	180.	400.

		Good	Fine	XF
A26	**1/2 Rigsbankdaler-48 Skilling** 1814.	90.00	325.	700.

NORGES BANK

TRONDHJEM

1817-22 ISSUES

#A28-A34 w/handwritten serial #.

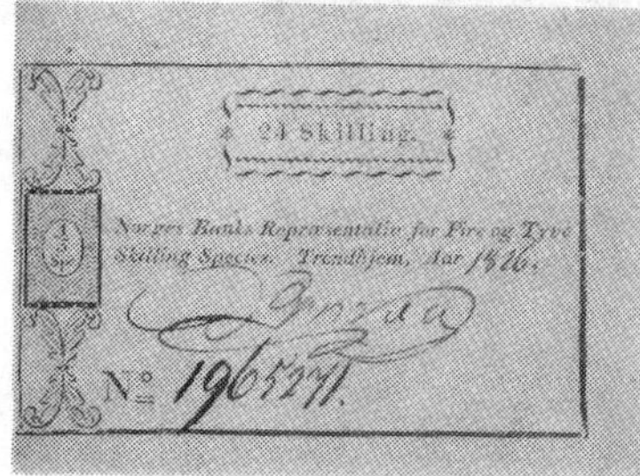

		Good	Fine	XF
A28	**24 Skilling Species** 1822-26.	350.	700.	1400.

		Good	Fine	XF
A29	**1/2 Speciedaler** 1822-30.	350.	700.	1400.

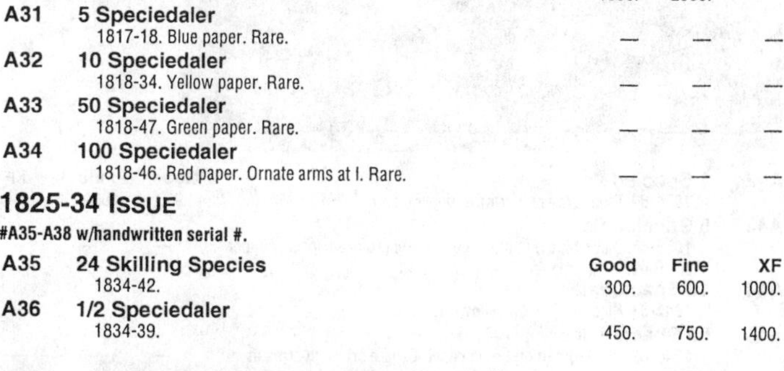

		Good	Fine	XF
A30	**1 Speciedaler** 1817-24.	1000.	2500.	—
A31	**5 Speciedaler** 1817-18. Blue paper. Rare.	—	—	—
A32	**10 Speciedaler** 1818-34. Yellow paper. Rare.	—	—	—
A33	**50 Speciedaler** 1818-47. Green paper. Rare.	—	—	—
A34	**100 Speciedaler** 1818-46. Red paper. Ornate arms at l. Rare.	—	—	—

1825-34 ISSUE

#A35-A38 w/handwritten serial #.

		Good	Fine	XF
A35	**24 Skilling Species** 1834-42.	300.	600.	1000.
A36	**1/2 Speciedaler** 1834-39.	450.	750.	1400.

		Good	Fine	XF
A37	**1 Speciedaler** 1825-43.	1000.	2400.	—

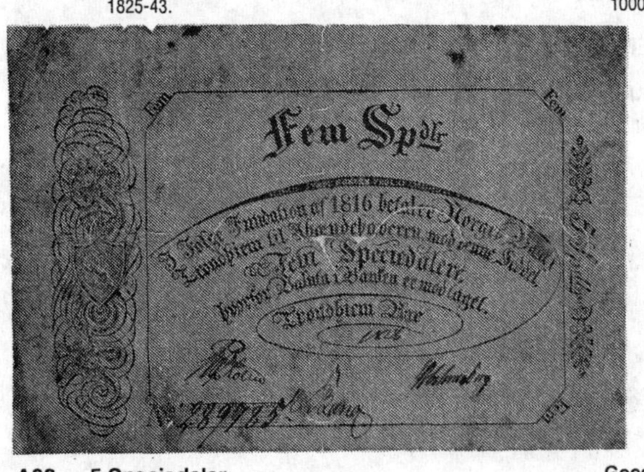

		Good	Fine	XF
A38	**5 Speciedaler** 1826-28. Blue paper.	1000.	2400.	—

1841-47 ISSUE

#A39 and A40 w/handwritten serial #.

		Good	Fine	XF
A39	**1 Speciedaler** 1845-49. Gray.	1000.	2400.	—
A40	**5 Speciedaler** 1841-54. Blue-black. Crowned arms at upper ctr. Rare.	—	—	—

1847-54 ISSUES

		Good	Fine	XF
A41	**1 Speciedaler** 1849-53. Black. Crowned arms at upper ctr.	900.	2000.	—

		Good	Fine	XF
A42	**1 Speciedaler** 1854-66. Blue. Crowned arms at upper ctr.	900.	1600.	—
A43	**5 Speciedaler** 1853-66. Black-blue on blue paper. Ornate crowned arms at upper ctr. Rare.	—	—	—
A44	**10 Speciedaler** 1847-64. Black-yellow on yellow paper. Rare.	—	—	—
A45	**50 Speciedaler** 1849-66. Black-green on green paper. Ornate crowned arms at upper ctr. Rare.	—	—	—
A46	**100 Speciedaler** 1847-65. Black and red on red paper. Rare.	—	—	—

NOTICE

Readers with unlisted dates, signature varieties, etc. are invited to submit photocopies or, high resolution (300 dpi, 100% size) scans of their notes to: Standard Catalog of World Paper Money, 700 East State St. Iola, WI 54990-0001, or E-Mail: george.cuhaj@fwpubs.com.

1865-68 ISSUE

#A47-A52 black, red and green on different colors of paper. 4 allegorical figures supporting crowned arm at upper ctr. Crowned arms at ctr. on back. Printer: Saunders, London.<PAR >

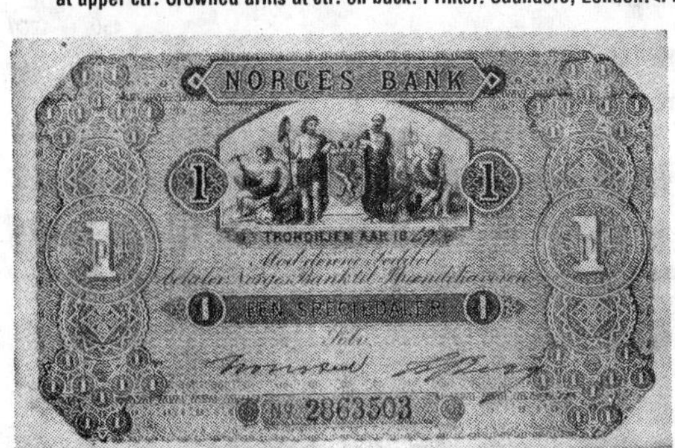

		Good	Fine	XF
A47	**1 Speciedaler** 1865-77. White paper.	600.	1100.	2500
A48	**5 Speciedaler** 1866-77. Blue paper. Rare.	—	—	—
A49	**10 Speciedaler** 1866-77. Yellow paper. Rare.	—	—	—
A50	**50 Speciedaler** 1866-77. Green paper. Rare.	—	—	—
A51	**100 Speciedaler** 1866-69. Yellowish paper. Rare.	—	—	—
A52	**100 Speciedaler** 1868-77. Red paper. Rare.	—	—	—

1877 ISSUE

#1-6 portr. Kg. Oscar II at l. or at top ctr.

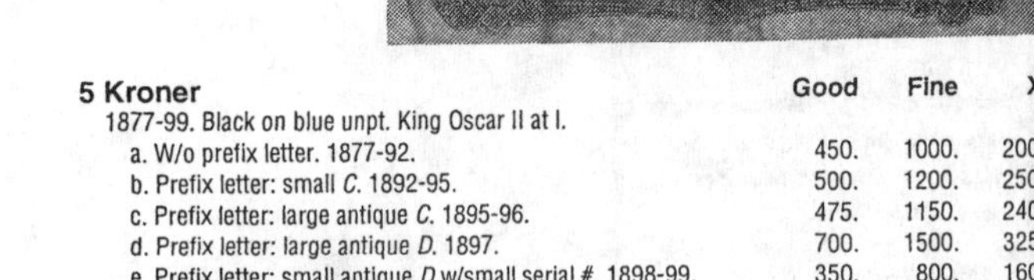

		Good	Fine	XF
1	**5 Kroner** 1877-99. Black on blue unpt. King Oscar II at l.			
	a. W/o prefix letter. 1877-92.	450.	1000.	2000
	b. Prefix letter: small *C*. 1892-95.	500.	1200.	2500
	c. Prefix letter: large antique *C*. 1895-96.	475.	1150.	240
	d. Prefix letter: large antique *D*. 1897.	700.	1500.	3250
	e. Prefix letter: small antique *D* w/small serial #. 1898-99.	350.	800.	1600

		Good	Fine	XF
2	**10 Kroner** 1877-99. Black on yellow unpt.			
	a. W/o prefix letter. Large serial #. 1877-90.	600.	1600.	—
	b. Prefix letter: small italic antique *B*. 1890-91.	600.	1600.	—
	c. Prefix letter: small italic Roman *B*. 1892-95.	600.	1600.	350
	d. Prefix letter: large italic antique *B*. 1895-97.	600.	1600.	350
	e. Prefix letter: large italic antique *C*. 1897. Unique.	—	—	—
	f. Prefix letter: small antique *C*. Small serial #. 1897-99.	400.	850.	200

	Good	Fine	XF
50 Kroner			
1877-99. Black on green unpt.	5000.	8000.	—
100 Kroner			
1877-80; 1892; 1894; 1896-98. Black on pink unpt.	9500.	14,500.	—

	Good	Fine	XF
500 Kroner			
1877-96. Black on brown unpt.			
a. Issued note.	16,500.	22,750.	—
b. Cancelled with holes.	9000.	13,000.	—

	Good	Fine	XF
1000 Kroner			
1877-98. Black on orange-brown unpt.			
a. Issued note.	20,000.	27,500.	—
b. Cancelled with holes.	12,500.	16,500.	—

NOTICE

Readers with unlisted dates, signature varieties, etc. are invited to submit photocopies or, high resolution (300 dpi, 100% size) scans of their notes to: Standard Catalog of World Paper Money, 700 East State St. Iola, WI 54990-0001, or E-Mail: george.cuhaj@fwpubs.com.

1901 Issue

#7-12 portr. Pres. Christie at l. Arms at r. on back.

Note: 150 sets of remainders ovpt: *SPECIMEN*, w/4 punch hole cancellations, were distributed by the Norges Bank in 1945, after the series was replaced.

		Good	Fine	XF
7	**5 Kroner**			
	1901-44. Dk. green. Back blue.			
	a. Sign. H. V. Hansen. 1901-16. Prefix A-E.	75.00	175.	375.
	b. Sign. S. Cederholm. 1916-34. Prefix E-N.	15.00	50.00	120.
	c. Sign. G. Meldahl Nielsen. 1935-44. Prefix N-W.	5.00	20.00	50.00
	r. As. c. Remainder ovpt: *SPECIMEN.* 1944.	—	Unc	125.
8	**10 Kroner**			
	1901-44. Purple. Portr. Adm. Tordenskjold at r. Back tan.			
	a. Sign. H. V. Hansen. 1901-16. Prefix A-F.	40.00	120.	275.
	b. Sign. S. Cederholm. 1917-34. Prefix F-T.	8.00	30.00	80.00
	c. Sign. G. Meldahl Nielsen. 1935-44. Prefix A-F.	2.00	8.00	22.50
	r. As c. Remainder ovpt: *SPECIMEN.* 1944.	—	Unc	100.

		Good	Fine	XF
9	**50 Kroner**			
	1901-45. Green. Bldg. at ctr. on back. Square format.			
	a. Sign. H. V. Hansen. 1901-12. Prefix A.	850.	2500.	—
	b. Sign. H. V. Hansen. 1913-15. Block serial #.	500.	1000.	—
	c1. Sign. S. Cederholm. 1917-28. Prefix A.	40.00	125.	400.
	c2. Sign. S. Cederholm. 1929-34. Prefix B.	30.00	90.00	220.
	d. Sign. G. Meldahl Neilsen. 1935-45. Prefix B-D.	15.00	70.00	140.
	r. As c. Remainder ovpt: *SPECIMEN.* 1945.	—	Unc	175.

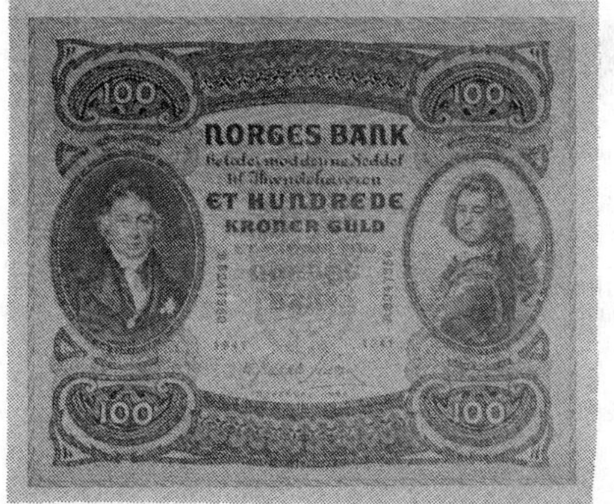

		Good	Fine	XF
10	**100 Kroner**			
	1901-45. Purple. Portr. Adm. Tordenskjold at r. Bldg. at ctr. on back. Square format.			
	a. Sign. H. V. Hansen. 1901-16. Prefix A.	275.	650.	1400.
	b. Sign. S. Cederholm. 1917-34. Prefix A; B.	17.50	75.00	150.
	c. Sign. G. Meldahl Nielsen. 1935-44. Prefix B; C.	12.50	40.00	95.00
	d. Sign. G. Meldahl Nielsen. 1945. Prefix. C.	475.	1000.	2000.
	r. As c. Remainder ovpt: *SPECIMEN*. 1945.	—	Unc	175.

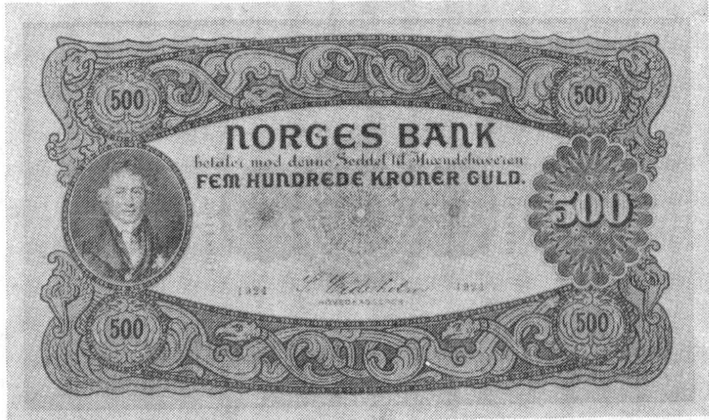

		Good	Fine	XF
11	**500 Kroner**			
	1901-44. Blue-gray. Bldg. at ctr. on back.			
	a. Sign. H. V. Hansen. 1901-16. Prefix A.	2500.	6750.	10,500.
	b. Sign. S. Cederholm. 1918-32. Prefix A.	800.	1600.	3000.
	c. Sign. G. Meldahl Nielsen. 1936-44. Prefix A.	500.	1100.	1800.
	r. As c. Remainder ovpt: *SPECIMEN*. 1944.	—	Unc	600.

		Good	Fine	XF
12	**1000 Kroner**			
	1901-43. Violet. Portr. Adm. Tordenskjold at r. Church at ctr. on back. Prefix A.			
	a. Sign. H. V. Hansen. 1901-16. Rare.	—	—	—
	b. Sign. S. Cederholm. 1917-32.	250.	700.	1200.
	c. Sign. G. Meldahl Nielsen. 1936-43.	200.	500.	875.
	r. As c. Remainder ovpt: *SPECIMEN*. 1943.	—	Unc	400.

1917-22 SKILLEMYNTSEDLER ISSUE

Small change notes.

		VG	VF	UN
13	**1 Krone**			
	1917. Black on green unpt. Back green; crowned arms at ctr. Prefix A-F; and w/o.	10.00	32.50	95.
14	**2 Kroner**			
	1918; 1922. Black on pink unpt. Like #13. Back red.			
	a. 1918.	15.00	45.00	12
	b. 1922.	25.00	75.00	17

1940 SKILLEMYNTSEDLER ISSUE

		VG	VF	UN
15	**1 Krone**			
	1940-50. Brown on green unpt. Back green.			
	a. Sign. G. Meldahl Nielsen. 1940-45. Prefix A-I.	9.00	25.00	65.
	b. Sign. E. Thorp. 1946-50. Prefix I-N.	7.50	17.50	50.
16	**2 Kroner**			
	1940-50. Brown on pink unpt. Like #15. Back red.			
	a1. Sign. G. Meldahl Nielsen. 1940-42; 1943. Prefix C. 1945; Prefix D.	10.00	25.00	60.
	a2. Sign. G. Meldahl Nielsen. 1943. Prefix B.	55.00	120.	2
	a3. Sign. G. Meldahl Nielsen. 1945. Prefix E.	80.00	150.	2
	b. Sign. E. Thorp. 1946-50. Prefix E-G.	7.50	17.50	50

1942 ISSUE

WW II Government-in-Exile

#17-24 printer: W&S.

		VG	VF	U
17	**1 Krone**			
	1942. Dk. brown on green unpt. Back green.			
	a. Prefix A.	25.00	85.00	2
	b. Prefix B.	900.	1600.	
	r. As a. Remainder w/ovpt: *SPECIMEN*, punched hole cancelled.	—	—	75
	s. Specimen w/red ovpt: *SPECIMEN*.	—	—	1

		VG	VF	U
18	**2 Kroner**			
	1942. Dk. brown on pink unpt. Back red.			
	a. Issued note.	35.00	110.	3
	r. As a. Remainder w/ovpt: *SPECIMEN*, punched hole cancelled.	—	—	75
	s. Specimen w/red ovpt: *SPECIMEN*.	—	—	1

#19b-24b w/*KRIGSSEDDEL*.

19	5 Kroner	VG	VF	UNC
	1942; 1944. Arms at l.			
	a. 1942. Dk. green and red on blue unpt. Frame brown. Back blue. (Not officially issued). Prefix A. Rare.	—	—	—
	b. 1944. Dk. brown and yellow on orange unpt. Frame green. Back brown. Prefix X; Y. (Not a replacement.)	75.00	175.	450.
	r1. As a. Remainder w/ovpt: *SPECIMEN*, punched hole cancelled.	—	—	225.
	r2. As b. Remainder w/ovpt: *SPECIMEN*, punched hole cancelled.	—	—	200.
	s1. As a. Specimen w/red ovpt: *SPECIMEN*.	—	—	400.
	s2. As b. Specimen w/red ovpt: *SPECIMEN*.	—	—	225.

20	10 Kroner	VG	VF	UNC
	1942; 1944. Arms at top ctr.			
	a. 1942. Dk. brown and lilac on blue-green and green unpt. Back orange. (Not officially issued). Prefix A. Rare.	—	—	—
	b. 1944. Brown-red on blue-green and green unpt. Back green. Prefix X; Y; Z. (Not a replacement.)	45.00	125.	350.
	r1. As a. Remainder w/ovpt: *SPECIMEN*, punched hole cancelled.	—	—	350.
	r2. As b. Remainder w/ovpt: *SPECIMEN*, punched hole cancelled.	—	—	150.
	s1. As a. Specimen w/red ovpt: *SPECIMEN*.	—	—	700.
	s2. As b. Specimen w/red ovpt: *SPECIMEN*.	—	—	200.

21	50 Kroner	VG	VF	UNC
	1942; 1944. Arms at top l. ctr.			
	a. 1942. Dk. gray on green and lilac unpt. Back green. (Not officially issued.) Prefix A. Rare.	—	—	—
	b. 1944. Dk. brown and pink on light green unpt. Back blue. Prefix X. (Not a replacement.)	500.	1100.	—
	r1. As a. Remainder w/ovpt: *SPECIMEN*, punched hole cancelled.	—	—	350.
	r2. As b. Remainder w/ovpt: *SPECIMEN*, punched hole cancelled.	—	—	350.
	s1. As a. Specimen w/red ovpt: *SPECIMEN*.	—	—	650.
	s2. As b. Specimen w/red ovpt: *SPECIMEN*.	—	—	600.

22	100 Kroner	VG	VF	UNC
	1942; 1944. Arms at top l. ctr.			
	a. 1942. Dk. purple and light blue on light brown-purple unpt. Back brown-red. (Not officially issued.) Prefix A. Rare.	—	—	—
	b. 1944. Dk. blue on red and green unpt. Back orange. Prefix X. (Not a replacement.)	800.	1500.	—
	r1. As a. Remainder w/ovpt: *SPECIMEN*, punched hole cancelled.	—	—	350.
	r2. As b. Remainder w/ovpt: *SPECIMEN*, punched hole cancelled.	—	—	600.
	s1. As a. Specimen w/red ovpt: *SPECIMEN*.	—	—	850.
	s2. As b. Specimen w/red ovpt: *SPECIMEN*.	—	—	650.

23	500 Kroner	VG	VF	UNC
	1942. Dk. blue-green and orange. Back green.			
	a. Not officially issued. Prefix A. Rare.	—	—	—
	r. Remainder w/ovpt: *SPECIMEN*, punched hole cancelled.	—	—	500.
	s. Specimen w/red ovpt: *SPECIMEN*.	—	—	850.

24	1000 Kroner	VG	VF	UNC
	1942. Brown and orange on yellow-green unpt. Back grey-brown.			
	a. Not officially issued. Prefix A. Rare.	—	—	—
	r. Remainder w/red ovpt: *SPECIMEN*, punched hole cancelled.	—	—	600.
	s. Specimen w/red ovpt: *SPECIMEN*.	—	—	900.

NORGES BANK - POST WW II

1945 ISSUE

25	5 Kroner	VG	VF	UNC
	1945-54. Blue. Arms at l.			
	a. Sign. G. Meldahl Nielsen. 1945. Prefix A; B.	8.00	35.00	90.00
	b. Sign. E. Thorp. 1946-50. Prefix B-F.	8.00	40.00	100.
	c. Sign. E. Thorp. 1951. Prefix F.	55.00	120.	270.
	d. Sign. E. Thorp. 1951-53. Prefix G-K.	8.00	40.00	90.00
	e. Sign. E. Thorp. 1954. Prefix K.	50.00	100.	240.

26	10 Kroner	VG	VF	UNC
	1945-53. Yellow-brown. Arms at l.			
	a. Sign. G. Meldahl Nielsen. 1945. Prefix A-C.	5.00	12.50	50.00
	b. Sign. G. Meldahl Nielsen. 1945. Prefix D.	10.00	30.00	100.
	c. Sign. G. Meldahl Nielsen. 1946. Prefix E.	17.50	60.00	150.

26		VG	VF	UNC
	d. Sign. E. Thorp. 1946-47. Prefix E.	20.00	60.00	180.
	e. Sign. E. Thorp. 1947. Prefix F.	6.00	25.00	125.
	f. Sign. E. Thorp. 1947. Prefix G.	12.50	55.00	140.
	g. Sign. E. Thorp. 1948. Prefix G.	10.00	30.00	110.
	h. Sign. E. Thorp. 1948. Prefix H-I.	5.00	12.50	65.00
	i. Sign. E. Thorp. 1948. Prefix J.	12.50	55.00	140.
	j. Sign. E. Thorp. 1949. Prefix J-K.	5.00	12.50	65.00
	k. Sign. E. Thorp. 1949. Prefix L.	10.00	30.00	105.
	l. Sign. E. Thorp. 1950-53. Prefix L-Y.	5.00	12.50	65.00

27	50 Kroner	VG	VF	UNC
	1945-50. Green. Arms at l.			
	a. Sign. G. Meldahl Nielsen. 1945; 1947; 1948. Prefix A.	40.00	100.	325.
	b. Sign. E. Thorp. 1947. Prefix A.	100.	270.	600.
	c. Sign. E. Thorp. 1948. Prefix A.	250.	500.	1000.
	d. Sign. E. Thorp. 1948-50. Prefix B.	70.00	190.	425.
	s. Specimen, punched hole cancelled.	—	—	1500.
28	**100 Kroner**			
	1945-49. Red. Arms at l.			
	a1. Sign. G. Meldahl Nielsen. 1945. Prefix A.	25.00	60.00	225.
	a2. Sign. G. Meldahl Nielsen. 1946. Prefix A.	50.00	140.	525.
	a3. Sign. G. Meldahl Nielsen. 1946. Prefix B.	27.50	75.00	300.
	b. Sign. E. Thorp. 1947-49. Prefix B; C.	25.00	75.00	350.
29	**1000 Kroner**			
	1945-47. Lt. brown. Similar to #12, but *GULD* (gold) blocked out at ctr. Prefix A.			
	a. Sign. G. Meldahl Nielsen. 1945-46.	350.	700.	1500.
	b. Sign. E. Thorp. 1947.	750.	1300.	2250.

1948-55 Issue

#30-33 Replacement notes: Serial # prefix *Z*. Wmk: value repeated.

30	5 Kroner	VG	VF	UNC
	1955-63. Blue on gray and m/c unpt. Portr. Fridtjof Nansen at l. Fishing scene on back.			
	a. Sign. Brofoss - Thorp. 1955-57. Prefix A-F.	10.00	20.00	75.00
	b. Sign. Brofoss - Ottesen. 1959-63. Prefix F-L.	7.50	17.50	65.00
	s. As a. Specimen.	—	150.	300.

31	10 Kroner	VG	VF	UNC
	1954-73. Yellow-brown on gray unpt. Portr. Christian Michelsen at l. Mercury w/ships on back.			
	a. Sign. Jahn - Thorp. 1954. Prefix A-D.	2.50	7.50	40.00
	b1. Sign. Brofoss - Thorp. 1954-55. Prefix D-G.	2.00	7.00	35.00
	b2. Sign. Brofoss - Thorp. 1955. Prefix H.	180.	350.	800.
	b3. Sign. Brofoss - Thorp. 1956. Prefix H-I.	2.00	7.00	35.00
	b4. Sign. Brofoss - Thorp. 1957. Prefix I.	12.50	40.00	100.
	b5. Sign. Brofoss - Thorp. 1957-58. Prefix J-M.	2.00	7.00	35.00
	b6. Sign. Brofoss - Thorp. 1958. Prefix N.	7.00	30.00	85.00
	c. Sign. Brofoss - Ottesen. 1959-65. Prefix N-E.	2.00	4.00	20.00
	d. Sign. Brofoss - Petersen. 1965-69. Prefix F-V.	FV	3.00	12.50
	e. Sign. Brofoss - Odegaard. 1970. Prefix W-Ø.	FV	2.00	10.00
	f. Sign. Wold - Odegaard. 1971-73. Prefix Á-R.	FV	1.75	7.50
	s. As a, d, f. Specimen.	—	150.	300.

#31 replacement notes: Serial # prefix *X* (1966-72) *Z* (1954-73).

32	50 Kroner	VG	VF	UNC
	1950-65. Dk. green. Portr. Bjørnstjerne Björnson at upper l. and as wmk., crowned arms at upper ctr. Harvesting on back.			
	a1. Sign. Jahn - Thorp. 1950-52. Prefix A.	15.00	55.00	200.
	a2. Sign. Jahn - Thorp. 1952. Prefix B.	60.00	120.	550.
	a3. Sign. Jan - Thorp. 1953-54. Prefix B.	15.00	55.00	200.
	b1. Sign. Brofoss - Thorp. 1954. Prefix B.	70.00	150.	650.
	b2. Sign. Brofoss - Thorp. 1955-58. Prefix B; C.	17.50	50.00	170.
	b3. Sign. Brofoss - Thorp. 1958. Prefix D.	24.00	95.00	350.
	c. Sign. Brofoss - Ottesen. 1959-65. Prefix D-F.	12.50	35.00	130.
	s. As a. 1951. Specimen.	—	—	—

33	100 Kroner	VG	VF	UNC
	1949-62. Red. Portr. Henrik Wergeland at upper l. and as wmk., crowned arms at upper ctr. Logging on back.			
	a1. Sign. Jahn - Thorp. 1949-52. Prefix A.	22.50	50.00	175.

33		VG	VF	UNC
	a2. Sign. Jahn - Thorp. 1952. Prefix C.	800.	1250.	—
	a3. Sign. Jahn - Thorp. 1953-54. Prefix C.	22.50	50.00	175.
	b. Sign. Brofoss - Thorp. 1954-58. Prefix D-G.	20.00	50.00	175.
	c. Sign. Brofoss - Ottesen. 1959-62. Prefix G-I.	20.00	40.00	140.

34	500 Kroner	VG	VF	UNC
	1948-76. Dk. green. Portr. Niels Henrik Abel at upper l. and as wmk., crowned supported arms at upper ctr. Factory workers on back. Prefix A.			
	a. Sign. Jahn - Thorp. 1948; 1951.	175.	350.	1000.
	b1. Sign. Brofoss - Thorp. 1954; 1956.	175.	350.	1000.
	b2. Sign. Brofoss - Thorp. 1958.	100.	200.	675.
	c. Sign. Brofoss - Ottesen. 1960-64.	90.00	160.	550.
	d. Sign. Brofoss - Petersen. 1966-69.	85.00	140.	400.
	e. Sign. Brofoss - Odegaard. 1970.	80.00	130.	325.
	f. Sign. Wold - Odegaard. 1971-76.	75.00	120.	275.
	s. As a. Specimen.	—	600.	850.

35	1000 Kroner	VG	VF	UNC
	1949-74. Red-brown. Portr. H. Ibsen at l. and as wmk., crowned supported arms at upper ctr. Old man and child on back. Prefix A.			
	a. Sign. Jahn - Thorp. 1949; 1951; 1953.	175.	425.	800.
	b. Sign. Brofoss - Thorp. 1955; 1958.	160.	290.	600.
	c. Sign. Brofoss - Ottesen. 1961; 1962.	150.	225.	500.
	d. Sign. Brofoss - Petersen. 1965-70.	140.	210.	400.
	e. Sign. Brofoss - Odegaard. 1971-74.	130.	200.	325.
	s. As a. Specimen.	—	600.	850.

#34 and 35 replacement notes: Serial # prefix *G*.

MILITARY - WW II

IHENDEHAVARGJELDSBREV

ARMY HIGH COMMAND

1940 ISSUE

#M1-M3 ornamental border at l. Uniface.

Note: Issued by Maj. Gen. W. Steffens in Voss w/approval of the branch of the Norges Bank.

M1	5 Kroner	VG	VF	UNC
	14.4.1940. Black.	300.	550.	700.

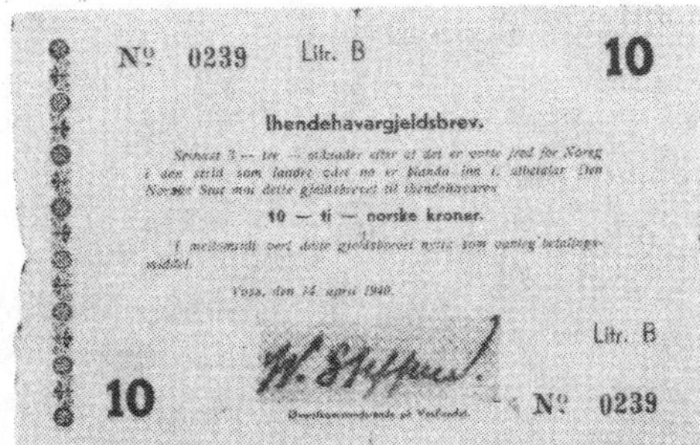

M2	10 Kroner	VG	VF	UNC
	14.4.1940. Black.	225.	400.	600.
M3	100 Kroner			
	14.4.1940. Black.	—	—	—

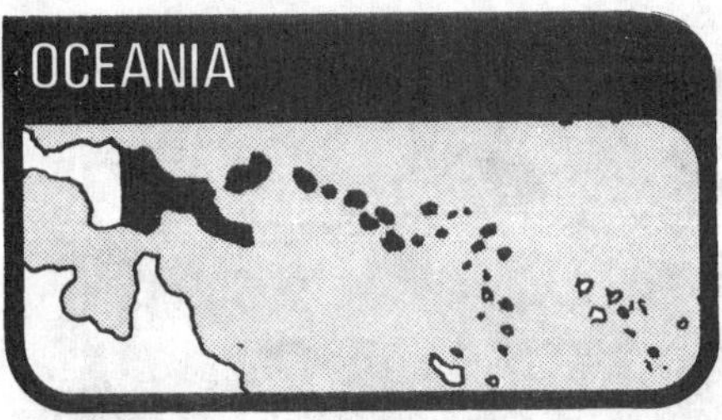

In general usage, Oceania is the collective name for the islands scattered throughout most of the Pacific Ocean. It has traditionally been divided into four parts: Australasia (Australia and New Zealand), Melenesia, Micronesia and Polynesia.

Numismatically, Oceania is the name applied to the Gilbert and Solomon Islands, New Britain, and Papua New Guinea, hence the British denominations.

See also French Oceania.

MONETARY SYSTEM:

1 Pound = 20 Shillings

JAPANESE OCCUPATION - WW II

JAPANESE GOVERNMENT

1942 ND ISSUE

#1-4 w/block letter *O* preceding another letter.

		VG	VF	UNC
1	**1/2 Shilling** ND (1942). Purple on yellow-brown unpt. Palm trees along the beach at r. Block letters: OA-OC.			
	a. Block letters spaced 42mm apart.	1.00	4.00	10.00
	b. Block letters: OA; OB spaced 50-53mm apart.	.50	2.50	6.00
	c. Block letters: OC spaced 50-53mm apart.	.25	.75	2.50
	s. Specimen w/red ovpt: *Mi-hon. Specimen* on back.	—	—	150.

Note: Block letters OC may be 42mm or 50-53mm apart.

		VG	VF	UNC
2	**1 Shilling** ND (1942). Blue on green unpt. Breadfruit tree at l., palm trees along the beach at r. Block letters: OA-OC.			
	a. Issued note.	.50	2.50	7.50
	s1. Specimen w/red ovpt: *Mi-hon. Specimen* on back.	—	—	150.
	s2. Specimen w/lg. red ovpt: *Mi-hon.*	—	—	150.
3	**10 Shillings** ND (1942). Brown. Palm trees along the beach at r. Block letters : OA.			
	a. Issued note.	3.00	15.00	75.00
	s. Specimen w/red ovpt: *Mi-hon. Specimen* on back.	—	—	200.

		VG	VF	UNC
4	**1 Pound** ND (1942). Green on lt. blue unpt. Palm trees along beach at r. Block letters : OA.			
	a. Issued note.	1.00	4.00	10.00
	s. Specimen w/red ovpt: *Mi-hon. Specimen* on back.	—	—	175.

Note: Spurious 1/4 Shilling notes exist.

AUSTRALIAN "REPLICAS"

1943 ND ISSUE

Note: Reprints of #1, 2 and 4 were reportedly made in Australia possibly in 1943 (poor printing paper w/weak wmk.), mostly w/ovpt: *REPLICA* on back.

		VG	VF	UNC
R1	**1/2 Shilling** ND (1943). Purple on yellow-brown unpt. Like #1 w/red ovpt: *REPLICA*. Block letters: OC.	12.50	35.00	100.
R2	**1 Shilling** ND (1943). Bright blue on green unpt. Like #2 w/red ovpt: *REPLICA*. Block letters: OC.	12.50	35.00	100.
R3	**1 Shilling** ND (1943). Dk. blue-gray w/o guilloche or ovpt: *REPLICA*. Block letters : OC.	12.50	35.00	100.
R4	**1 Pound** ND (1943). Green w/modified blue guilloche. Red ovpt: *REPLICA* on back. Block letters : OA.	15.00	50.00	125.
R5	**1 Pound** ND (1943). W/o ovpt: *REPLICA* on back.			
	a. Green w/modified pale blue guilloche.	12.50	35.00	100.
	b. Dk. olive-green.	15.00	50.00	—
	c. Bright green.	15.00	50.00	—

Note: More recent copies also exist.

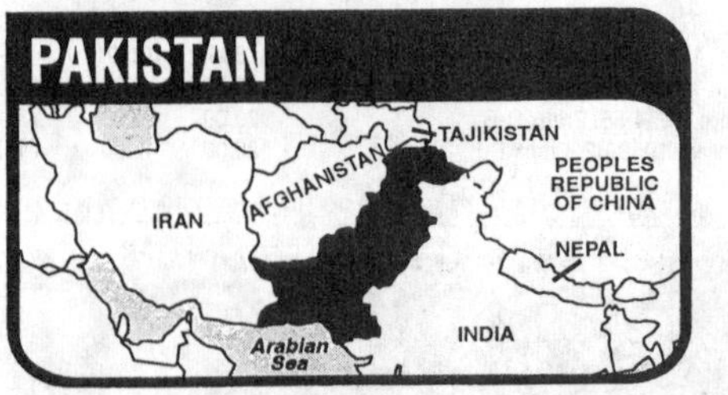

PAKISTAN

TAJIKISTAN
AFGHANISTAN
PEOPLES REPUBLIC OF CHINA
IRAN
NEPAL
INDIA
Arabian Sea

The Islamic Republic c Pakistan, located on the India subcontinent between India an Afghanistan, has an area c 310,404 sq. mi. (803,943 sq. m and a population of 156 millior Capital: Islamabad. Pakistan i mainly an agricultural land. Yarr cotton, rice and leather ar exported.

Afghan and Turkish intrusion into northern India between th 11th and 18th centuries resulte in large numbers of Indian being converted to Islam. Th idea of a separate Moslem state independent of Hindu India developed in the 1930's and wa agreed to by Britain in 1946. The Islamic majority areas of India, consisting of the separat geographic entities known as East and West Pakistan, achieved self-government as Pakistan, wi dominion status in the British Commonwealth, when the British withdrew from India on Aug. 1 1947. Pakistan became a republic in 1956. When a basic constitutional crisis initiated by th election of Dec. 1, 1970 - the first direct general election in Pakistani history - could not be resolve by the leaders of East and West Pakistan, the East Pakistanis seceded from the Islamic Republ of Pakistan (March 26, 1971) and formed the independent People's Republic of Bangladesh.

Pakistan was expelled from the Commonwealth on January 20, 1972 and re-admitted aga on October 1, 1989.

MONETARY SYSTEM:

1 Rupee = 16 Annas to 1961
1 Rupee = 100 Paisa (Pice), 1961-

REPUBLIC

GOVERNMENT OF PAKISTAN

1948 ND PROVISIONAL ISSUE

#1-3A new plates w/*GOVERNMENT OF PAKISTAN* in English and Urdu on Government and Reserve Bank India notes.

		Good	Fine	X
1	**1 Rupee** ND (1948). Gray-green. New plate like India #25c.	5.00	30.00	85.(

		Good	Fine	X
1A	**2 Rupees** ND (1948). Lilac. New plate like India #17b.	10.00	60.00	15

Note: It is now believed that the note w/red serial # and ovpt. on India 17c, formerly listed as 1Ab, is spurious

		Good	Fine	X
2	**5 Rupees** ND (1948). Green. New plate like India #23a.	15.00	85.00	22

		Good	Fine	XF
3	**10 Rupees** ND (1948). Violet. New plate like India #24.	15.00	85.00	225.
3A	**100 Rupees** ND (1948). Dk. green and lilac. New plate like India #20k.	35.00	225.	450.

1948-49 ND ISSUE

#4-10 crescent moon and star at r.

		VG	VF	UNC
4	**1 Rupee** ND (1949). Green on m/c unpt. Archway at l. ctr. on back. Wmk: Crescent moon and star.	2.00	15.00	35.00

		VG	VF	UNC
5	**5 Rupees** ND (1948). Blue on tan unpt.	5.00	25.00	90.00

		VG	VF	UNC
6	**10 Rupees** ND (1948). Orange on green unpt.	8.00	35.00	125.

		VG	VF	UNC
7	**100 Rupees** ND (1948). Green on tan unpt.	50.00	200.	600.

1951-73 ND ISSUES

		VG	VF	UNC
8	**1 Rupee** ND (1951). Blue on m/c unpt. Back violet. Archway at l. ctr. Like #4. 2 sign. varieties.	15.00	60.00	100.

		VG	VF	UNC
9	**1 Rupee** ND (1953-63). Blue on m/c unpt. Like #8 but larger size serial #. Back blue. 6 sign. varieties.	3.00	5.00	10.00

Note: The scarce sign. is Abdul Qadir, valued at $50. in Unc.

		VG	VF	UNC
9A	**1 Rupee** ND (1964). Blue on m/c unpt. Back violet. Like #8 but differnt font for serial #. 3 sign. varieties.	1.00	2.50	4.50

STATE BANK OF PAKISTAN

CITY OVERPRINT VARIETIES

ঢাকা ڈھاکہ করাচী کراچی লাহোর لاہور

Dacca Karachi Lahore

Some notes exist w/Urdu and some w/Bengali ovpt. denoting city of issue, Dacca, Karachi or Lahore. These are much scarcer than the regular issues. Sign. varieties.

1949-53 ND ISSUE

#11-14 wmk: Crescent moon and star.

		VG	VF	UNC
11	**2 Rupees** ND (1949). Brown on pink and lt. green unpt. Tower on wall encircling the tomb of Jahangir in Lahore at l. Badshahi Mosque in Lahore at l. ctr. on back. Printer BWC (w/o imprint.)	15.00	50.00	175.

		VG	VF	UNC
12	**5 Rupees** ND (1951). Purple on lt. green unpt. A jute laden boat at ctr. Khyber Pass on back. 3 sign. varieties.	.75	5.00	25.00

		VG	VF	UNC
13	**10 Rupees** ND (1951). Brown on lt. yellow unpt. Shalimar Gardens in Lahore. Tombs near Thatta on back. 4 sign. varieties.	2.00	10.00	35.00
14	**100 Rupees** ND (1953). Red-brown. Similar to #7. Wmk. area at r. on face. 2 sign. varieties.			
	a. *DACCA* in Urdu at bottom of note.	20.00	75.00	175.
	b. *KARACHI* in Urdu at bottom of note.	20.00	75.00	175.

1957-66 ND ISSUE

#15-19 Portr. Mohammed Ali Jinnah and as wmk.

		VG	VF	UNC
18	**100 Rupees** ND (1957). Green on violet and peach unpt. Mohammed Ali Jinnah at ctr. back. Badshahi Mosque in Lahore on			
	a. W/o overprint. 2 sign. varieties.	3.00	6.00	10.00
	b. Ovpt: *Dhaka.* 2 sign. varieties.	3.00	6.00	10.00
	c. Ovpt: *Karachi.* 2 sign. varieties.	3.00	6.00	10.00
	d. Ovpt: *Lahore.* 2 sign. varieties.	3.00	6.00	10.00

REGIONAL

GOVERNMENT OF PAKISTAN

1950 ND PILGRIM ISSUE

		VG	VF	UNC
R1	**100 Rupees** ND (1950). Red. Like #7 but w/ovpt: *FOR PILGRIMS FROM PAKISTAN FOR USE IN SAUDI ARABIA AND IRAQ.*	500.	1500.	—

STATE BANK OF PAKISTAN

1950 ND HAJ PILGRIM ISSUE

		VG	VF	UNC
R2	**10 Rupees** ND (1950). Green. Like #13 but w/ovpt: *FOR HAJ PILGRIMS FROM PAKISTAN FOR USE IN SAUDI ARABIA ONLY.* 3 sign. varieties.	25.00	100.	275.

Palestine, a former British mandate in southwest Asia at the eastern end of the Mediterranean Sea, had an area of 10,160 sq. mi. (26,315 sq. km.). It included Israel and that part of Jordan lying west of the Jordan River. Ancient Palestine (the territory owned in biblical times by the kingdoms of Israel and Judah) was somewhat larger, including lands east of the Jordan River.

Because of its position as part of the land bridge connecting Asia and Africa, Palestine was invaded and conquered by virtually all the historic powers of Europe and the Near East. From 1516 to 1917, it was held by the Ottoman Empire. In 1917, it was conquered by the British under Allenby and assigned as a British mandate, effective 1922. The British ruled Palestine until 1948, and succeeded in satisfying neither the Arab nor the Jewish population. The United Nations recommended the establishment of separate Jewish and Arab states in Palestine.

The British left Palestine on May 14, 1948, and the State of Israel was proclaimed. In 1950, the Kingdom of Jordan annexed the west bank of the Jordan River. This was seized by Israel during the 1967 war, bringing the entire former mandate under Israeli administration.

RULERS:
British, 1917-1948

MONETARY SYSTEM:
1 Pound = 1000 Mils Note: For issues of the Anglo-Palestine Bank Ltd., refer to Israel.

BRITISH ADMINISTRATION

PALESTINE CURRENCY BOARD

1927 ISSUE

#6-11 Citadel of Jerusalem (commonly called the Tower of David) at ctr. on back. Printer: TDLR.

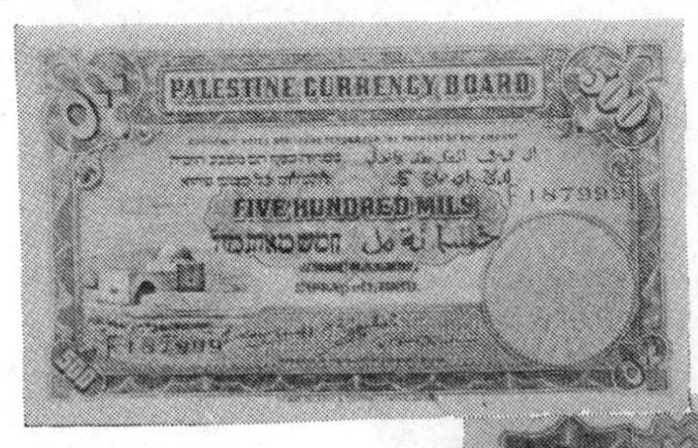

		Good	Fine	X
6	**500 Mils** 1927-45. Purple on green unpt. Rachel's tomb near Bethlehem at lower l.			
	a. 1.9.1927.	80.00	200.	50
	b. 30.9.1929.	70.00	150.	35
	c. 20.4.1939.	60.00	125.	32
	d. 15.8.1945.	70.00	150.	35

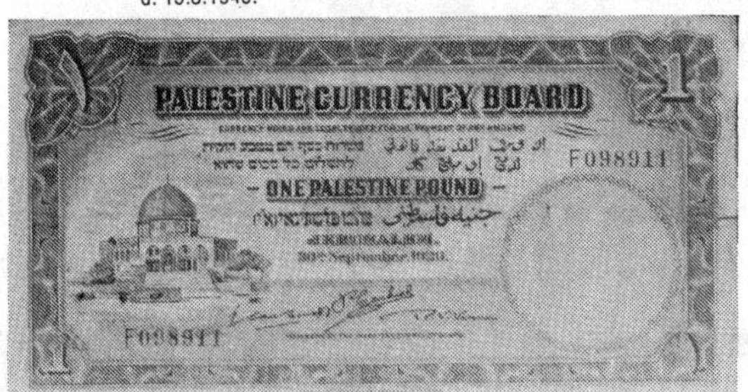

		Good	Fine	X
7	**1 Pound** 1927-44. Green and black. Dome on the Rock at l.			
	a. 1.9.1927.	85.00	250.	65
	b. 30.9.1929.	50.00	150.	42
	c. 20.4.1939.	45.00	125.	35
	d. 1.1.1944.	50.00	150.	40

		Good	Fine	XF
8	**5 Pounds**			
	1927-44. Red and black. Crusader's Tower at Ramleh at l.			
	a. 1.9.1927. Rare.	—	—	—
	b. 30.9.1929.	110.	300.	700.
	c. 20.4.1939.	100.	275.	600.
	d. 1.1.1944.	110.	285.	650.
	x. Counterfeit. 20.4.1939.	50.00	80.00	—

		Good	Fine	XF
9	**10 Pounds**			
	1927-44. Blue and black. Like #8.			
	a. 1.9.1927. Rare.	—	—	—
	b. 30.9.1929.	125.	450.	1000.
	c. 7.9.1939.	100.	350.	800.
	d. 1.1.1944.	100.	400.	900.
10	**50 Pounds**			
	1927-39. Purple and black. Like #8.			
	a. 1.9.1927. Rare.	—	—	—
	b. 30.9.1929. Rare.	—	—	—
	c. 7.9.1939. Rare.	—	—	—
11	**100 Pounds**			
	1927-42. Green and black. Like #8.			
	a. 1.9.1927. Rare.	—	—	—
	b. 30.9.1929. Rare.	—	—	—
	c. 10.9.1942. Reported not confirmed.	—	—	—

Note: According to Bank of England records, only 6 examples of #11 are outstanding. Four are known.

The Republic of Panama, a Central American country situated between Costa Rica and Colombia, has an area of 29,206 sq. mi. (77,083 sq. km.) and a population of 2.86 million. Capital: Panama City. The Panama Canal is the country's biggest asset; servicing world related transit trade and international commerce. Bananas, refined petroleum, sugar and shrimp are exported.

Panama was visited by Christopher Columbus in 1502 during his fourth voyage to the Americas. It was explored by Vasco de Balboa in 1513. Panama City, founded in 1519, was a primary trans-shipment center for treasure and supplies both to and from Spain and the Colonies. Panama declared its independence in 1821 and joined the Confederation of Greater Colombia. In 1903, after Colombia rejected a treaty enabling the United States to build the Canal across the Isthmus, Panama, with the support of the United States, proclaimed its independence from Colombia and became a sovereign republic.

Notes of the United States have normally circulated throughout Panama.

MONETARY SYSTEM:

1 Balboa = 100 Centesimos Note: Certain listings encompassing issues circulated by various bank and regional authorities are contained in Volume 1 under Colombia.

REPUBLIC OF PANAMÁ

REPÚBLICA DE PANAMÁ

1933 "SOSA" ISSUE

		Good	Fine	XF
21	**1 Balboa**			
	5.8.1933. Arms at l., Balboa standing w/sword and flag at r. (Not issued).	—	—	—
21A	**10 Balboas**			
	1933. Reported not confirmed.	—	—	—

Note: The Sosa Project was conceived by Don Martin Sosa Comptroller General of Panama in 1933.

BANCO CENTRAL DE EMISIÓN

1941 "ARIAS" ISSUE

#22-25 arms at ctr. on back. Printer: HBNC.

		Good	Fine	XF
22	**1 Balboa**			
	1941. Black on green and red unpt. Portr. Balboa at ctr. Back green.			
	a. Issued note.	275.	800.	1350.
	s. Specimen.	—	—	700.

		Good	Fine	XF
23	**5 Balboas**			
	1941. Black on blue, violet and orange unpt. Urraca at l. Back blue.			
	a. Issued note.	1000.	2750.	5000.
	s. Specimen.	—	Unc	1250.

		Good	Fine	XF
24	**10 Balboas**			
	1941. Black on violet, orange and green unpt. Old fortress at ctr. Back brown.			
	a. Issued note.	1500.	4500.	7500.
	s. Specimen.	—	Unc	2000.

		Good	Fine	XF
25	**20 Balboas** 1941. Black on orange, red and violet. Ox cart at ctr. Back orange.			
	a. Issued note.	2500.	5500.	8500.
	s. Specimen.	—	Unc	3000.

Note: After a very short circulation period #22-25 were recalled and almost all destroyed.

Papua New Guinea, an independent member of the British Commonwealth, occupies the eastern half of the island of New Guinea. It lies north of Australia near the equator and borders on West Irian. The country, which includes nearby Bismarck Archipelago, Buka and Bougainville, has an area of 176,280 sq. mi. (461,691 sq. km.) and a population of 4.81 million who are divided into more than 1,000 separate tribes speaking more than 700 mutually unintelligible languages. Capital: Port Moresby. The economy is agricultural, and exports include copra, rubber, cocoa, coffee, tea, gold and copper.

New Guinea, the world's largest island after Greenland, was discovered by Spanish navigator Jorge de Menezes, who landed on the northwest shore in 1527. European interests, attracted by exaggerated estimates of the resources of the area, resulted in the island being claimed in whole or part by Spain, the Netherlands, Great Britain and Germany.

Papua (formerly British New Guinea), situated in the southeastern part of the island of New Guinea, has an area of 90,540 sq. mi. (234,499 sq. km.) and a population of 740,000. It was temporarily annexed by Queensland in 1883 and by the British Crown in 1888. Papua came under control of the Australian Commonwealth in 1901 and became the Territory of Papua in 1906. Japan invaded New Guinea and Papua early in 1942, but Australian control was restored before the end of the year in Papua and in 1945 in New Guinea.

In 1884 Germany annexed the area known as German New Guinea (also Neu-Guinea or Kaiser Wilhelmsland) comprising the northern section of eastern New Guinea, and granted its administration and development to the New-Guinea Compagnie. Administration reverted to Germany in 1889 following the failure of the company to exercise adequate administration. While a German protectorate, German New Guinea had an area of 92,159 sq. mi. (238,692 sq. km.) and a population of about 250,000. Capital: Herbertshohe, later named Rabaul. Copra was the chief crop. Australian troops occupied German New Guinea in Aug. 1914, shortly after Great Britain declared war on Germany. It was mandated to Australia by the League of Nations in 1920 and known as the Territory of New Guinea. The territory was invaded and occupied by Japan in 1942. Following the Japanese surrender, it came under U.N. trusteeship, Dec. 13, 1946, with Australia as the administering power.

The Papua and New Guinea Act, 1949, provided for the government of Papua and New Guinea as one administrative unit. On Dec. 1, 1973, Papua New Guinea became self-governing with Australia retaining responsibility for defense and foreign affairs. Full independence was achieved on Sept. 16, 1975 and Papua New Guinea is now a member of the Commonwealth of Nations. The Queen of England is Chief of State.

RULERS:

British

MONETARY SYSTEM:

1 Kina = 100 Toea, 1975-
1 Shilling = 12 Pence
1 Crown = 5 Shillings
1 Pound = 4 Crowns

BRITISH ADMINISTRATION

BANK OF NEW SOUTH WALES

PORT MORESBY

1910 ISSUE

		Good	Fine	XF
A5	**1 Pound** 1.5.1910; 1.6.1910. Black. Allegorical woman seated, holding caduceus by sheep w/sailing ship in background at top ctr. Printer: CS&E. Rare.	—	—	—

PARAGUAY

The Republic of Paraguay, a landlocked country in the heart of South America surrounded by Argentina, Bolivia and Brazil, has an area of 157,042 sq. mi. (406,752 sq. km.) and a population of 5.5 million, 95 percent of whom are of mixed Spanish and Indian descent. Capital: Asunción. The country is predominantly agrarian, with no important mineral deposits or oil reserves. Meat, timber, oilseeds, tobacco and cotton account for 70 percent of Paraguay's export revenue.

Paraguay was first visited by Alejo Garcia, a shipwrecked Spaniard, in 1520. The interior was explored by Sebastian Cabot in 1526 and 1529, when he sailed up the Paraná and Paraguay Rivers. Asunción, which would become the center of a province embracing much of southern South America, was established by the Spanish explorer Juan de Salazar on Aug. 15, 1537. For a century and a half the history of Paraguay was largely the history of the agricultural colonies established by the Jesuits in the south and east to Christianize the Indians. In 1811, following the outbreak of the South American wars of independence, Paraguayan patriots overthrew the local Spanish authorities and proclaimed their country's independence.

MONETARY SYSTEM:

1 Peso = 100 Centavos to 1870
1 Peso = 8 Reales to 1872
1 Peso = 100 Centésimos to 1870
1 Peso = 100 Centavos (Centésimos) to 1944
1 Guaraní = 100 Céntimos, 1944-

REPÚBLICA DEL PARAGUAY

EL TESORO NACIONAL

NATIONAL TREASURY

DECRETO DE 13 DE FEBRERO DE 1856

#1-4 black seal at ctr.

		Good	Fine	XF
1	**1/2 Real** ND (1856). Black. Flowers at l. 175 x 120mm.	25.00	80.00	200.

		Good	Fine	XF
2	**4 Reales** ND (1856). Black. Burro at upper l. 155 x 105mm.	30.00	100.	225.
3	**1 Peso** ND (1856). Black. Leopard at upper l. 165 x 120mm.	20.00	50.00	125.
4	**2 Pesos** ND (1856). Black. Goat looking l. at upper l. 160 x 120mm.	20.00	50.00	125.

DECRETO DE 29 DE ABRIL DE 1859

		Good	Fine	XF
5	**1 Real** ND (1859). Black. Bottle at upper l., black seal at ctr. 170 x 110mm.	45.00	75.00	175.

DECRETO DE 17 DE MAYO DE 1859

		Good	Fine	XF
6	**1 Peso** ND (1859). Black. Leopard at upper ctr. 160 x 115mm.	—	—	—

DECRETO DE 10 DE JUNIO DE 1860

		Good	Fine	XF
7	**1/2 Real** ND (1860). Black. Flowers at upper l., arms at upper ctr. 105 x 65mm.	25.00	80.00	200.

		Good	Fine	XF
8	**1 Real** ND (1860). Black. Bottle at l., arms at upper ctr. 120 x 75mm.	20.00	50.00	125.
9	**2 Reales** ND (1860). Black. Man w/horse at upper l., arms at upper ctr. and r. 2 sign. varieties. 125 x 80mm.	7.50	17.50	50.00

		Good	Fine	XF
10	**4 Reales** ND (1860). Black. Burro (donkey) at upper l., arms at upper ctr. 2 sign. varieties. 140 x 100mm.	10.00	30.00	80.00

		Good	Fine	XF
11	**1 Peso** ND (1860). Black. Leopard at upper l., arms at upper ctr. 3 sign. varieties. 150 x 105mm.	10.00	30.00	80.00

		Good	Fine	XF
12	**2 Pesos** ND (1860). Black and pink. Goat looking r. at upper l., arms at upper ctr. 165 x 105mm.	6.00	15.00	50.00

		Good	Fine	XF
13	**3 Pesos** ND (1860). Black and lt. green. Woman, harvest and ship at upper l., arms at upper ctr. 185 x 115mm.	7.50	20.00	60.00

DECRETO DE 21 DE SETIEMBRE DE 1861

		Good	Fine	XF
14	**5 Pesos** ND (1861). Black. Steam passenger train at upper l., arms at upper ctr. 175 x 115mm.	7.50	20.00	60.00

DECRETO DE 14 DE NOVIEMBRE DE 1861

		Good	Fine	XF
15	**4 Pesos** ND (1861). Blue. Blindfolded Justice seated at upper l., oval arms at upper ctr. 180 x 115mm.	10.00	30.00	80.00

NOTICE

Readers with unlisted dates, signature varieties, etc. are invited to submit photocopies or, high resolution (300 dpi, 100% size) scans of their notes to: Standard Catalog of World Paper Money, 700 East State St. Iola, WI 54990-0001, or E-Mail: george.cuhaj@fwpubs.com.

DECRETO DE 31 DE MARZO DE 1862

#16-17 oval arms at ctr.

		Good	Fine	XF
16	**4 Pesos** ND (1862). Black. Oxen w/plow at l. 190 x 125mm.	3.00	10.00	35.00

		Good	Fine	XF
17	**5 Pesos** ND (1862). Black. Man riding w/2 burros at upper l. 180 x 120mm.	7.50	20.00	60.00

DECRETO DE 25 DE MARZO DE 1865

Issues of Mariscal Francisco Solano Lopez, the son of Carlos Antonio Lopez who took the presidency of the Republic in 1862. #18-30 black seal at upper ctr.

		Good	Fine	XF
18	**1 Real** ND (1865). Black. Man walking w/sack on stick at upper l. 140 x 90mm.	10.00	40.00	100.

		Good	Fine	XF
19	**2 Reales** ND (1865). Black. Floral design at l. 140 x 95mm.	3.50	17.50	40.00

		Good	Fine	XF
20	**4 Reales** ND (1865). Black. Ram at upper l. 145 x 95mm.	3.50	17.50	40.00

		Good	Fine	XF
21	**1 Peso** ND (1865). Blue. Ox at upper l. 155 x 105mm.	3.50	17.50	40.00

		Good	Fine	XF
22	**2 Pesos** ND (1865). Blue. Man w/horse-drawn cart at upper l. 165 x 95mm.	3.50	17.50	40.00

		Good	Fine	XF
23	**3 Pesos** ND (1865). Blue. Ship at upper l. 160 x 110mm.	3.50	17.50	40.00

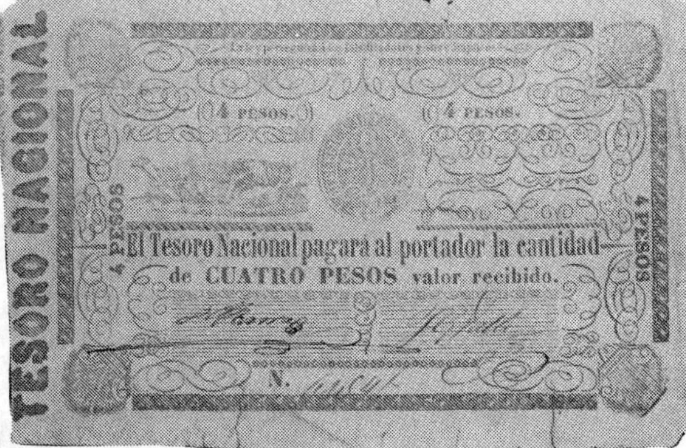

		Good	Fine	XF
24	**4 Pesos** ND (1865). Blue. Oxen w/plow at l. 190 x 115mm.	3.50	17.50	40.00

		Good	Fine	XF
25	**5 Pesos** ND (1865). Blue. Similar to #17, but w/o monogram at r. Slightly reduced size, 170 x 115mm.	3.00	15.00	35.00

		Good	Fine	XF
26	**10 Pesos** ND (1865). Blue. Woman carrying sack at l., arms at l. and r. 190 x 125mm.	3.50	17.50	40.00

1865-70 Issue

#27-30, reduced size notes. W/o signatures or just one signature.

		Good	Fine	XF
27	**3 Pesos** ND (1865-70). Black. Ship at upper l. 160 x 90mm.	7.50	25.00	75.00
28	**4 Pesos** ND (1865-70). Black. Oxen w/plow at l. 175 x 95mm.	7.50	25.00	75.00
29	**5 Pesos** ND (1865-70). Black. Similar to #25. 155 x 95mm.	15.00	40.00	100.
30	**10 Pesos** ND (1865-70). Black. Similar to #26, but w/o arms at l. and r. 200 x 95mm.	3.50	17.50	40.00

War of the Triple Alliance, 1864-70

1868 Issue

		Good	Fine	XF
31	**3 Pesos** ND (1868). Red ovpt. on #27.	3.50	12.50	35.00

		Good	Fine	XF
32	**4 Pesos** ND (1868). Red ovpt. on #28.	3.50	12.50	35.00
33	**5 Pesos** ND (1868). Red ovpt. on #29.	3.50	12.50	35.00

Note: The 3 Pesos depicting a tree at l. and arms at ctr. (formerly #A19A) has been determined to be a spurious issue.

1870 Issue

		Good	Fine	XF
34	**1 Real** 29.12.1870. Black and green. Arms at l.	—	—	—
35	**2 Reales** 29.12.1870.	—	—	—
36	**4 Reales** 29.12.1870. Black and green. Dog at l., arms at upper ctr.	—	—	—

#37-39 issued w/ or w/o 2 oval handstamps on back. The handstamps are: *MINISTERIO DE HACIENDA* and *TESORERÍA GENERAL-ASUNCIÓN* around arms.

		Good	Fine	XF
37	**50 Centésimos** 29.12.1870. Black. a. W/o 2 oval handstamps on back. Rare. b. W/2 oval handstamps on back. Rare.	 — —	 — —	 — —

		Good	Fine	XF
38	**1 Peso** 29.12.1870. Black. Bull at ctr. a. W/o 2 oval handstamps on back. Rare. b. W/2 oval handstamps on back. Rare.	 — —	 — —	 — —

		Good	Fine	XF
39	**5 Pesos** 29.12.1870. Black. Arms at ctr. a. W/o 2 oval handstamps on back. Rare. b. W/2 oval handstamps on back.	 — 	 — 	 —

#40 not assigned.

1871 Issue, La Tesoreria General

		Good	Fine	XF
41	**1/2 Real** 1871. Black. Arms at upper l., rooster at ctr. a. Issued note. r. Unsigned remainder.	 — —	 — —	 — —

		Good	Fine	XF
42	**1 Real** 15.7.1871. Black. Arms at l. 2 sign. varieties.	—	—	—
43	**2 Reales** 15.7.1871.	—	—	—

		Good	Fine	XF
44	**4 Reales** 15.7.1871. Black. Dog at l., arms at upper ctr. 2 sign. varieties.	—	—	—
45	**1 Peso** 15.7.1871.	—	—	—
46	**5 Pesos** 15.7.1871.	—	—	—
47	**10 Pesos** 15.7.1871.	—	—	—

Caja de Conversión

Law of 9.1.1874; Decree of 4.3.1874

#48-52 printer: Ludovico Sartori y Cía. Uniface.

		Good	Fine	XF
48	**10 Centavos** 15.3.1874. Black. 2 sign. varieties. Rare.	—	—	—

Note: Some examples of #48 appear w/2 oval overstamps on back.

		Good	Fine	XF
49	**20 Centavos** 15.3.1874. Brown. 2 sign varieties. Rare.	—	—	—
50	**50 Centavos** 15.3.1874. Black. Sheep at ctr. 2 sign. varieties. Rare.	—	—	—
51	**1 Peso** 15.3.1874. Orange and black. 4 sign. varieties. a. Issued note. Rare. b. W/2 oval handstamps on back (like #37b-39b). Rare.	 — —	 — —	 — —
52	**5 Pesos** 1874. 2 sign. varieties. Rare.	—	—	—

#51-59 not assigned.

Tesoro Nacional

National Treasury

Ley de 22.4.1875

#60, 61, 66 and 67 printer: Lit. San Martín-Argentina.

		Good	Fine	XF
60	**5 Centavos** L.1875. Green. Ram at upper ctr. 2 sign. varieties. Rare.	—	—	—
61	**20 Centavos** L.1875.	—	—	—

Note: Apparently #60 and 61 are part of a later series because of their signatures. #62-65 not assigned.

#		Good	Fine	XF
66	**10 Pesos** L.1875. Orange and black. Woman's head at l. and r., mountain scene at ctr.	—	—	—
67	**20 Pesos** L.1875. M/c. Boy standing at l., paddle wheel steamer at upper ctr.	—	—	—

#68-86 not assigned.

REPÚBLICA DEL PARAGUAY

LEY DE 24 DE SETIEMBRE DE 1894

#87-94 printer: G&D.

#		Good	Fine	XF
87	**50 Centavos** L.1894. Orange and black. Arms at ctr. 4 sign. varieties.	8.00	25.00	80.00
88	**1 Peso** L.1894. Black, dk. red and blue. Arms at l. Back dk. red. 3 sign. varieties.	10.00	50.00	175.
89	**5 Pesos** L.1894. Blue and orange. Arms at r. 3 sign. varieties.	15.00	80.00	225.
90	**10 Pesos** L.1894. Reported not confirmed.	—	—	—
91	**20 Pesos** L.1894. Arms at l. Rare.	—	—	—
92	**50 Pesos** L.1894. Reported not confirmed.	—	—	—
93	**100 Pesos** L.1894. Black and orange. Woman w/torch at l., arms at ctr. 2 sign. varieties. Rare.	—	—	—

#		Good	Fine	XF
94	**200 Pesos** L.1894. Lt. blue and orange unpt. Arms at l., portr. Gen. Egusquiza at top ctr. 2 sign. varieties.	150.	600.	—

LEY DE 18 DE NOVIEMBRE DE 1899

#95-157 each denomination within this range has an identical design (but some have minor variations).

#95-104 arms on back. Printer: ABNC.

#		Good	Fine	XF
95	**50 Centavos** L.1899. Black on orange unpt. Minerva wearing helmet at l. Back orange.	2.50	7.50	30.00
96	**1 Peso** L.1899. Black on green unpt. Woman wearing straw hat at ctr. Back green. 2 sign. varieties.	3.50	12.50	35.00
97	**2 Pesos** L.1899. Black on lt. brown unpt. Government palace at ctr. Back brown. 2 sign. varieties.	4.50	20.00	50.00
98	**5 Pesos** L.1899. Black on lilac, peach and blue unpt. View of city of Asunción from river. Back dk. blue.	6.00	30.00	75.00
99	**10 Pesos** L.1899. Black on green unpt. Cathedral at r. ctr. Back gray-green.	10.00	40.00	95.00
100	**20 Pesos** L.1899. Black on blue and yellow unpt. Congressional palace at ctr. Back dk. blue. 2 sign. varieties.	15.00	50.00	125.
101	**50 Pesos** L.1899. Black on yellow and brown unpt. Municipal theater at r. Back dk. brown; man's head at ctr.	20.00	75.00	175.
102	**100 Pesos** L.1899. Black on red and yellow unpt. Guaira waterfall at ctr. Back red; woman's head at ctr.	22.50	100.	225.
103	**200 Pesos** L.1899. Black on yellow and orange unpt. Mountain and farm at ctr. r. Back orange; woman's head at l.	40.00	150.	400.

#		Good	Fine	XF
104	**500 Pesos** L.1899. Black on lilac and yellow unpt. Woman w/child at l., ruins at Humaita at r. Back blue-gray.	50.00	250.	600.

LEY DE 14 DE JULIO DE 1903

#105-114 date of the law in 1 or 2 lines, arms on back. Printer: ABNC.

#		Good	Fine	XF
105	**50 Centavos** L.1903. Like #95. Back green. 4 sign. varieties.			
	a. Date in 2 lines.	2.00	5.00	20.00
	b. Date in 1 line.	2.00	5.00	20.00

#		Good	Fine	XF
106	**1 Peso** L.1903. Like #96. Date in 1 line. Back brown. 4 sign. varieties.			
	a. Serial # at upper r.	3.00	8.00	30.00
	b. Serial # at bottom ctr.	2.50	7.50	25.00

#		Good	Fine	XF
107	**2 Pesos** L.1903. Like #97. Date in 1 line. Back brown. 2 sign. varieties.			
	a. Serial # at upper r.	4.00	12.50	40.00
	b. Serial # at bottom ctr.	3.00	10.00	30.00

		Good	Fine	XF
108	5 Pesos L.1903. Like #98. Back brown. 5 sign. varieties.			
	a. Date in 2 lines.	5.00	17.50	55.00
	b. Date in 1 line.	4.00	15.00	45.00
109	10 Pesos L.1903. Like #99. Date in 1 line. Back olive. 5 sign. varieties.			
	a. Serial # at bottom l. and r.	8.00	25.00	85.00
	b. Serial # at bottom ctr.	7.00	22.50	70.00
110	20 Pesos L.1903. Like #100. 2 sign. varieties.			
	a. Date in 2 lines.	10.00	35.00	100.
	b. Date in 1 line.	12.50	37.50	110.
111	50 Pesos L.1903. Like #101. Date in 2 lines. Back brown. 5 sign. varieties.			
	a. Serial # at bottom l. and r.	17.50	50.00	125.
	b. Serial # at bottom ctr.	15.00	45.00	115.
112	100 Pesos L.1903. Like #102. Date in 1 line. Back red. 3 sign. varieties.			
	a. Serial # at upper l. and r.	20.00	65.00	160.
	b. Serial # at bottom ctr.	17.50	55.00	140.
113	200 Pesos L.1903. Like #103. Date in 1 line. Back orange. 6 sign varieties.			
	a. Serial # at lower l. and upper r.	35.00	100.	300.
	b. Serial # at bottom ctr.	30.00	90.00	225.
114	500 Pesos L.1903. Like #104. Date in 2 lines. Back blue. 5 sign. varieties.			
	a. Serial # at upper l. and lower r.	35.00	175.	375.
	b. Serial # at bottom ctr.	40.00	170.	350.

LEY DE 26 DE DICIEMBRE DE 1907

#115-124 arms on back. Printer: ABNC.

#115-120 sign. Evaristo Acosta and Juan Y. Ugarte.

		VG	VF	UNC
115	50 Centavos L.1907. Black on green unpt. Like #95. Back green.	2.00	5.00	15.00
116	1 Peso L.1907. Black on orange unpt. Like #96. Back orange.	2.50	7.50	25.00

		VG	VF	UNC
117	2 Pesos L.1907. Black on blue unpt. Like #97. Back blue.	3.00	10.00	35.00

		VG	VF	UNC
118	5 Pesos L.1907. Black on yellow and orange unpt. Like #98.	4.00	15.00	45.00
119	10 Pesos L.1907. Black on yellow and green unpt. Like #99.	6.00	17.50	50.00
120	20 Pesos L.1907. Black on yellow unpt. Like #100.	10.00	30.00	85.00

		VG	VF	UNC
121	50 Pesos L.1907. Black on rose and yellow unpt. Like #101. 2 sign. varieties.	10.00	30.00	85.00
122	100 Pesos L.1907. Black on yellow and tan unpt. Like #102. 3 sign. varieties.	12.50	30.00	100.
123	200 Pesos L.1907. Back lilac. Like #103. 6 sign. varieties.	30.00	80.00	225.
124	500 Pesos L.1907. Back orange. Like #104. 7 sign. varieties.	30.00	80.00	225.

1912 PROVISIONAL ISSUE

#125-133 w/black oval ovpt: *EMISIÓN DEL ESTADO LEY 11 DE ENERO DE 1912.*

#127, 129, 132 and 134 w/ PESOS ORO SELLADO barred out.

#126, 128 and 130 not assigned.

		Good	Fine	XF
125	2 Pesos L.1912. Ovpt. on #107.	15.00	50.00	125.
127	5 Pesos L.1912. Ovpt. on #156.	15.00	50.00	125.

		Good	Fine	XF
129	10 Pesos L.1912. Ovpt. on #157.	15.00	50.00	125.
131	50 Pesos L.1912. Ovpt. on #111.	30.00	80.00	250.

		Good	Fine	XF
132	50 Pesos L.1912. Ovpt. on #158.	25.00	75.00	225.
133	100 Pesos L.1912. Ovpt. on #112.	35.00	90.00	275.
134	100 Pesos L.1912. Ovpt. on #159.	35.00	90.00	275.
135	200 Pesos L.1912. Ovpt. on #113.	30.00	80.00	250.

		Good	Fine	XF
136	**500 Pesos** L.1912. Ovpt. on #114.	30.00	80.00	250.

LEY DE 28 DE ENERO DE 1916

#137-142 w/text: *LA OFICINA DE CAMBIOS* below serial #. Arms on back. Printer: ABNC.

		VG	VF	UNC
137	**50 Centavos** L.1916. Like #115. Back green. 4 sign. varieties.	1.50	4.00	15.00

		VG	VF	UNC
138	**1 Peso** L.1916. Like #116. Back orange. 4 sign. varieties.	2.00	5.00	20.00
139	**2 Pesos** L.1916. Like #117. Back blue. 5 sign. varieties.	2.50	7.50	30.00
140	**5 Pesos** L.1916. Like #118. Back brown. 3 sign. varieties.	3.00	10.00	40.00
141	**10 Pesos** L.1916. Like #119. Back gray. 3 sign. varieties.	10.00	45.00	110.
142	**20 Pesos** L.1916. Like #120. Back: olive. 2 sign. varieties.	20.00	60.00	175.

LEY NO. 463 DE 30 DE DICIEMBRE DE 1920

#143-148 arms on back. Printer: ABNC.

		VG	VF	UNC
143	**5 Pesos** L.1920. Like #140. 2 sign. varieties.	1.50	4.00	15.00
144	**10 Pesos** L.1920. Like #141. 2 sign. varieties.	3.00	7.50	20.00

		VG	VF	UNC
145	**50 Pesos** L.1920. Like #121. Back brown. 2 sign. varieties.	6.00	20.00	70.00

		VG	VF	UNC
146	**100 Pesos** L.1920. Like #122. Back blue. 2 sign. varieties.	10.00	35.00	100.
147	**200 Pesos** L.1920. Back orange. Like #123. Reported not confirmed.	—	—	—

NOTICE

Readers with unlisted dates, signature varieties, etc. are invited to submit photocopies or, high resolution (300 dpi, 100% size) scans of their notes to: Standard Catalog of World Paper Money, 700 East State St. Iola, WI 54990-0001, or E-Mail: george.cuhaj@fwpubs.com.

		VG	VF	UNC
148	**500 Pesos** L.1920. Back lilac. Like #124.	30.00	100.	225.

LEYES 1920 & 1923

POR OFICINA DE CAMBIO

#149-155 sign. varieties, arms on back. Printer: ABNC.

		VG	VF	UNC
149	**5 Pesos** L.1920 & 1923. Like #143. 3 sign. varieties.	1.50	6.00	20.00

		VG	VF	UNC
150	**10 Pesos** L.1920 & 1923. Like #144. 3 sign. varieties.	3.00	8.00	25.00
151	**50 Pesos** L.1920 & 1923. Like #145. Back brown. 4 sign. varieties.	5.00	15.00	40.00

		VG	VF	UNC
152	**100 Pesos** L.1920 & 1923. Like #146. Back blue. 5 sign. varieties.	8.50	30.00	75.00

		VG	VF	UNC
153	**200 Pesos** L.1920 & 1923. Back orange. Like #123. 5 sign. varieties.	17.50	75.00	175.
154	**500 Pesos** L.1920 & 1923. Back lilac. Like #148. 7 sign. varieties.	20.00	90.00	200.

155 **1000 Pesos** | VG | VF | UNC
L.1920 & 1923. Black on m/c unpt. Woman holding fasces at l. Back black; arms at ctr. 8 sign. varieties. | 30.00 | 125. | 300.

Banco de la República

Ley de 26 de diciembre de 1907

#156-159 arms at ctr. on back. Printer: W&S.

156 **5 Pesos M.N. = 1/2 Peso Oro** | VG | VF | UNC
L.1907. Black on blue unpt. Woman wearing Liberty cap at ctr. Back brown. 2 sign. varieties. | .25 | 1.00 | 5.00

157 **10 Pesos M.N. = 1 Peso Oro** | VG | VF | UNC
L.1907. Black on red unpt. Railroad station at ctr. Back green. 2 sign. varieties. | 4.00 | 10.00 | 35.00

158 **50 Pesos M.N. = 5 Pesos Oro**
L.1907. Black on green unpt. National Congress at ctr. | 30.00 | 85.00 | 200.

159 **100 Pesos M.N. = 10 Pesos Oro** | VG | VF | UNC
L.1907. Black on yellow unpt. Bldg. at ctr. Back blue. 4 sign. varieties. | 1.00 | 4.00 | 12.50

160 **1000 Pesos M.N. = 100 Pesos Oro**
L.1907. Woman w/children. Printer: P. Bouchard-Buenos Aires. | 35.00 | 130. | 300.

Ley 8.9.1920

161 **1000 Pesos** | VG | VF | UNC
L.1920. Rectangular ovpt: EL BANCO DE LA REPÚBLICA, LEY No. 432, 8 de Setiembre de 1920 on #160. | — | — | —

Ley 469, Dec. 31, 1920

162 **1000 Pesos** | VG | VF | UNC
L.1920. Rectangular ovpt. on #160. | — | — | —

Ley 30.12.1920/25.10.1923, Banco de la Republica

#163-164 printer: ABNC.

163 **5 Pesos** | VG | VF | UNC
L.1920, 1923. Like #149 but w/text: POR EL BANCO DE LA REPÚBLICA DEL PARAGUAY at bottom. 4 sign. varieties. | 3.50 | 12.50 | 35.00

164 **10 Pesos**
L.1920, 1923. Like #150 but w/text: POR EL BANCO DE LA REPÚBLICA DEL PARAGUAY at bottom. 2 sign. varieties. | 4.50 | 15.00 | 40.00

Ley No. 550 de 25 de octubre de 1923

#165-168 printer: ABNC.

165 **50 Pesos** | VG | VF | UNC
L.1923. Blue on m/c unpt. Bldg. at ctr. Back red; star at ctr. | 40.00 | 150. | 375.

166 **50 Pesos** | VG | VF | UNC
L.1923. Blue on m/c unpt. Bldg. at ctr. Back red; shield w/lion at ctr. | 2.00 | 12.50 | 40.00

167 **100 Pesos** | VG | VF | UNC
L.1923. Blue on m/c unpt. Face like #168. Back brown; star at ctr. | 50.00 | 175. | 400.

168 **100 Pesos** | VG | VF | UNC
L.1923. Olive-green on brown and m/c unpt. Bldg. at ctr. Back brown; shield w/lion at ctr. | 2.00 | 12.50 | 40.00

		VG	VF	UNC
169	**500 Pesos** L.1923. Gray-green. Portr. C. A. Lopez at upper l. ctr., cows at lower r. Printer: W&S.	15.00	40.00	100.
170	**1000 Pesos** L.1923. Like #155. Printer: ABNC.	30.00	85.00	250.

1943 ND PROVISIONAL ISSUE

Guarani System

		VG	VF	UNC
171	**s50 Centimos on 50 Pesos Fuerte** ND (1943). Red ovpt. on #165. Reported not confirmed.	—	—	—

		VG	VF	UNC
172	**s50 Centimos on 50 Pesos Fuerte** ND (1943).			
	a. Red ovpt. on #166.	15.00	60.00	175.
	b. Black ovpt. on #166. Reported not confirmed.	—	—	—
173	**1 Guarani on 100 Pesos Fuertes** ND (1943).			
	a. Red ovpt. on #168.	10.00	50.00	125.
	b. Black ovpt. on #168. Reported not confirmed.	—	—	—

		VG	VF	UNC
174	**5 Guaranies on 500 Pesos Fuertes** ND (1943). Red ovpt. on #169.	25.00	75.00	200.
175	**5 Guaranies on 500 Pesos Fuertes** ND (1943). Ovpt. on #154.	40.00	100.	225.
176	**rtes10 Guaranies on 1000 Pesos Fue** ND (1943). Ovpt. on #155.	45.00	120.	300.

BANCO DEL PARAGUAY

LEY NO. 11, 22.2.1936

		VG	VF	UNC
177	**1 Guaraní** L.1936. (Not issued). Reported not confirmed.	—	—	—

DECRETO LEY 655 DEL 5 DE OCTUBRE DE 1943

DEPARTAMENTO MONETARIO

#178-184 arms at upper r. Series A. Printer: TDLR. Sign. title: *Gerente General* at l. Sign. varieties.

		VG	VF	UNC
178	**1 Guaraní** L.1943. Green. Soldier at ctr. Back brown; bldg. at ctr. 4 sign. varieties.	.75	2.50	10.00

		VG	VF	UNC
179	**5 Guaraníes** L.1943. Blue. Gen. J. E. Diaz at ctr. Back dk. red; bldg. 2 sign. varieties.	2.00	6.00	17.50

		VG	VF	UNC
180	**10 Guaraníes** L.1943. Red. D. Carlos Antonio Lopez at ctr. Back purple; bldg. 3 sign. varieties.	3.00	8.00	25.00
181	**50 Guaraníes** L.1943. Brown. Dr. J. Gaspar Rodriguez de Francia at ctr. Back gray-brown; bldg. 3 sign. varieties.	5.00	15.00	45.00

		VG	VF	UNC
182	**100 Guaraníes** L.1943. Green. M. José F. Estigarribia at ctr. Back blue; lg. bldg. facing r. 2 sign. varieties.	8.00	30.00	70.00
183	**500 Guaraníes** L.1943. Blue. M. Francisco Solano Lopez at ctr. Back red; lg. bldg. 3 sign. varieties.	25.00	80.00	175.
184	**1000 Guaraníes** L.1943. Red-violet. Declaration of Independence on 14.4.1811 at ctr. Back orange; Presidential palace. 2 sign. varieties.	35.00	100.	250.

Note: For later issues of similar design see Banco Central, #185-191.

BANCO CENTRAL DEL PARAGUAY

DECRETO LEY NO. 18 DEL 25 DE MARZO DE 1952

#185-191 black security thread in l. half of notes. Later issues have m/c fibers in r. half of notes. Arms at r. Sign. title: *Gerente* at l., lg. or sm. size signs. Printer: TDLR.

		VG	VF	UNC
185	**1 Guaraní** L.1952. Green. Like #178. 6 sign. varieties.			
	a. 1 red serial #. Lg. or sm. sign. Series A.	.75	1.50	6.00

185		VG	VF	UNC
	b. 1 red serial #. Fibers at r. Series B.	.50	1.25	3.50
	c. 2 black serial #. Fibers at r. Serial # prefix B.	.25	.50	1.50

186 5 Guaraníes
L.1952. Blue. Like #179. 4 sign. varieties.

	VG	VF	UNC
a. 1 red serial #. Lg. or sm. sign. Series A.	.75	1.50	5.00
b. 1 red serial #. Fibers at r. Series A.	.50	1.25	3.50
c. 2 black serial #. Fibers at r. Serial # prefix A.	.25	.75	2.00

187 10 Guaraníes
L.1952. Red. Like #180. 6 sign. varieties.

	VG	VF	UNC
a. 1 black serial #. Lg. or sm. sign. Series A.	1.00	2.50	9.00
b. 1 black serial #. Fibers at r. Series A.	.75	1.50	4.00
c. 2 black serial #. Fibers at r. Serial # prefix B.	.50	1.25	3.50

188 50 Guaraníes
L.1952. Brown. Like #181. 5 sign. varieties.

	VG	VF	UNC
a. W/o fibers at r. Lg. or sm. sign.	1.00	4.00	15.00
b. Fibers at r.	1.00	4.00	10.00

189 100 Guaraníes
L.1952. Green. Face like #182. Back blue; bldg. facing l. Lg. or sm. sign. 5 sign. varieties.

	VG	VF	UNC
a. W/o fibers at r.	2.00	8.00	20.00
b. Fibers at r.	1.50	6.00	15.00

190 500 Guaraníes
L.1952. Blue. Face like #183. Back red; domed bldg. at ctr. 6 sign. varieties.

	VG	VF	UNC
a. W/o fibers at r.	30.00	75.00	150.
b. Fibers at r.	25.00	60.00	125.

191 1000 Guaraníes
L.1952. Lilac. Face like #184. Back orange; bldg. w/courtyard. 5 sign. varieties.

	VG	VF	UNC
a. W/o fibers at r.	40.00	90.00	200.
b. Fibers at r.	35.00	75.00	150.

The Republic of Perú, located on the Pacific coast of South America, has an area of 496,222 sq. mi. (1,285,216 sq. km.) and a population of 25.66 million. Capital: Lima. The diversified economy includes mining, fishing and agriculture. Fish meal, copper, sugar, zinc and iron ore are exported.

Once part of a great Inca Empire that reached from northern Ecuador to central Chile, Perú was conquered in 1531-33 by Francisco Pizarro. Desirable as the richest of the Spanish viceroyalties, it was torn by warfare between avaricious Spaniards until the arrival in 1569 of Francisco de Toledo, who initiated 2 1/2 centuries of efficient colonial rule which made Lima the most aristocratic colonial capital and the stronghold of Spain's South American possessions. José de San Martín of Argentina proclaimed Perú's independence on July 28, 1821; Simón Bolívar of Venezuela secured it in Dec. of 1824 when he defeated the last Spanish army in South America. After several futile attempts to re-establish its South American empire, Spain recognized Perú's independence in 1879.

MONETARY SYSTEM:

1 Sol = 1 Sol de Oro = 100 Centavos, 1879-1985
1 Libra = 10 Soles
1 Inti = 1000 Soles de Oro, 1986-1991
1 Nuevo Sol = 100 Centimes = 1 Million Intis, 1991-
1 Sol = 100 Centavos (10 Dineros)

REPÚBLICA DEL PERÚ

JUNTA ADMINISTRADORA

1879 ISSUE

#1-10 sign. varieties. Printer: ABNC.

		Good	Fine	XF
1	**1 Sol** 30.6.1879. Black on yellow-brown and blue unpt. Cupids at l. and r., woman w/fruit at ctr. Back brown; sailing ship at ctr.	1.50	10.00	50.00

		Good	Fine	XF
2	**2 Soles** 30.6.1879. Black on green and brown unpt. Steam passenger trains at lower l. and r., woman at fountain at lower ctr. Back red-orange. 3 serial # varieties.	1.50	10.00	60.00

		Good	Fine	XF
3	**5 Soles** 30.6.1879. Black on green and red unpt. Woman and child at l., woman w/2 children at r. Red numeral *V* at upper l. and r. in unpt. Upper line of lg. green *5* at ctr. measures 16mm across. Back brown.	2.50	12.50	60.00

		Good	Fine	XF
4	**5 Soles** 30.6.1879. Black on green and red unpt. Like #3 but w/o red *V* in unpt. Lg. green numeral *5* at ctr. measures 20.5mm across at top.	2.00	12.50	60.00

		Good	Fine	XF
5	**10 Soles** 30.6.1879. Black on brown and lt. blue unpt. Woman sitting w/staff and scales at l., woman w/wreath at ctr., arms at r. Back green; woman sitting w/llama at ctr.	3.00	30.00	100.

		Good	Fine	XF
6	**20 Soles** 30.6.1879. Black on brown unpt. Woman w/book and pen at ctr. W/o green *20* in unpt. Back blue.	2.00	12.50	60.00

		Good	Fine	XF
7	**20 Soles** 30.6.1879. Black on yellow and lt. green unpt. Like #6 but w/lg. green *20's* at lower l. and r. in unpt. Back blue.			
	a. Issued note.	2.00	12.50	60.00
	b. Cut cancelled, w/circular ovpt: *DIRECCION DEL TESORO* (arms) *LIMA JULIO 30 DE 1899* at r.	5.00	30.00	90.00

		Good	Fine	XF
8	**50 Soles** 30.6.1879. Black on blue-green unpt. Woman w/2 shields at l., woman and child at lower r. Back brown; allegorical woman and 2 children at ctr.	25.00	125.	325.

		Good	Fine	XF
9	**100 Soles** 30.6.1879. Black on red and green unpt. Young sailor at l., arms flanked by women on each side at ctr., filleted woman at r. Back red and black; horse and girl.	20.00	100.	300.

		Good	Fine	XF
10	**500 Soles** 30.6.1879. Black on yellow and gold unpt. Heraldic shield and 4 angels at ctr. Back green and black; funeral of Atahualpa.	60.00	200.	500.

1881 Arequipa Provisional Issue

		Good	Fine	XF
1A	**1 Sol** 1881 (- old date 30.6.1879). Black circular ovpt: *COMISION DE SUBSIDIOS AREQUIPA 1881* at r. on #1. (For circulation in Arequipa).	40.00	175.	—
2A	**2 Soles** 1881 (- old date 30.6.1879). Black circular ovpt: *COMISION DE SUBSIDIOS AREQUIPA 1881* at ctr. on #2.	45.00	200.	—
3A	**5 Soles** 1881 (- old date 30.6.1879). Black circular ovpt: *COMISION DE SUBSIDIOS AREQUIPA 1881* at r. on #3.	45.00	200.	—
6A	**20 Soles** 1881 (- old date 30.6.1879). Black circular ovpt: *COMISION DE SUBSIDIOS AREQUIPA 1881* at r. on #6.	60.00	275.	—
7A	**20 Soles** 1881 (-old date 30.6.1879). Black circular ovpt: *COMISION DE SUBSIDIOS AREQUIPA 1881* at r. on #7.	50.00	250.	—

1881 Provisional Issue

Inca system

#11-13 *BILLETE PROVISIONAL* w/new denomination and new date ovpt. on face and/or back of 1873 notes of the Banca de la Compania General del Peru. Printers: NBNC for face, ABNC for back.

		Good	Fine	XF
11	**1 Real de Inca on 1 Sol** 1.9.1881 (- old date 1873). Ovpt. on #S131. W/ or w/o sign.	5.00	30.00	85.00

		Good	Fine	XF
12	**5 Reales de Inca on 5 Soles** 1.9.1881 (- old date 1873). Ovpt. on #S132. W/ or w/o sign.	7.50	35.00	100.
13	**100 Centavos de Inca on 100 Soles** 1.9.1881 (- old date 1873). Ovpt. on #S134. W/ or w/o sign.	15.00	75.00	200

Note: #11-13 sometimes have an additional sign. guaranteeing the authenticity of the note. This sign. was an official endorsement.

1881 Inca Issue

#14-17 sign. titles: *SECRETARIO DE HACIENDA Y COMERCIO* and *JUNTA FISCAL* on new notes.

		Good	Fine	XI
14	**1 Inca** 1.9.1881. Blue.	25.00	125.	275

		Good	Fine	XF
15	**5 Incas** 1.9.1881. Blue. Cherub at upper l. and r., arms at top ctr. W/o ovpt.	12.50	40.00	90.00
16	**5 Incas** 1.9.1881. Blue. Ovpt: *LEGITIMO* on #15.	9.00	30.00	80.00

		Good	Fine	XF
17	**100 Incas** 1.9.1881. Blue. Seated Mercury at l., seated allegorical woman at r. W/o ovpt.	40.00	150.	350.

1881 Provisional Soles Issue

#18-20 ovpt. for Soles on Incas notes.

		Good	Fine	XF
18	**50 Soles** 1.9.1881. Blue. Oval ovpt: *VALE POR / CINCUENTA SOLES / 1881 / EMISION FISCAL* on #15.	9.00	30.00	80.00

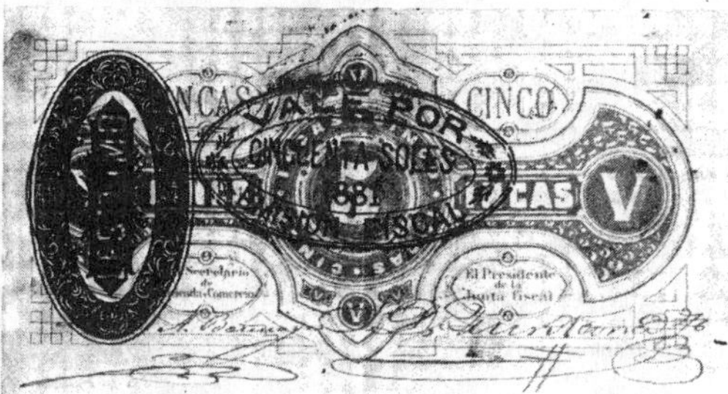

		Good	Fine	XF
19	**50 Soles** 1.9.1881. Blue. Oval ovpt: *VALE POR....* on #16.	9.00	30.00	80.00
20	**1000 Soles** 1.9.1881. Blue. Oval ovpt: *VALE POR / MIL SOLES / 1881 / EMISION FISCAL* on #17.	30.00	125.	325.

Junta de Vigilancia

1914 Cheques Circulares First Issue

Libra system

Circulating drafts issued on the following banks: Banco del Peru y Londres, Banco Italiano, Banco Internacional del Peru, Banco Popular del Peru, Banco Alemán Transatlántico, Caja de Ahorros de Lima.

#21-24 printer: T. Scheuch, Lima.

		Good	Fine	XF
21	**1/2 Libra** 3.10.1914. Black on green unpt. Worker at ctr. Back green.	25.00	90.00	250.
22	**1 Libra** 8.9.1914. Black on yellow unpt. Woman seated w/caduceus at l.	50.00	175.	400.
23	**5 Libras** 8.9.1914. Black on blue unpt. Justice seated at l.	35.00	125.	300.

		Good	Fine	XF
24	**10 Libras** 8.9.1914. Black on green unpt. Woman w/flag at l.	—	—	—

1914 Cheques Circulares Second Issue

#25-28 have issuing banks listed in 3 lines of text under top heading. Printer: ABNC.

		Good	Fine	XF
25	**1/2 Libra** 3.10.1914. Black on green unpt. Liberty at ctr. Back green.	20.00	85.00	200.
26	**1 Libra** 3.10.1914. Black on red-orange unpt. Woman seated at l. Back red-orange; drill worker at ctr.	20.00	85.00	200.
27	**5 Libras** 3.10.1914. Black on blue unpt. Child and lamb at r. Back blue; 2 allegorical women at ctr.	40.00	150.	350.

		Good	Fine	XF
28	**10 Libras** 3.10.1914. Black on m/c unpt. Rubber tree worker at l. Back orange; steam train at ctr.	—	—	—

1917 Certificado de Deposito de Oro Issue

#29 and 30 printer: Scheuch, Lima.

		Good	Fine	XF
29	**5 Centavos** 17.8.1917. Black on blue unpt. Back dk. orange; sun face at ctr.	2.00	15.00	40.00

		Good	Fine	XF
30	**50 Centavos** 17.8.1917. Dk. blue on green unpt. Liberty seated w/shield and staff at ctr. Back brown; arms at ctr.	2.50	20.00	55.00

		Good	Fine	XF
31	**1 Sol** 10.8.1917. Dk. blue. Liberty seated similar to #30. Back brown; arms at ctr. Printer: ABNC.	4.00	25.00	60.00

1918 Cheques Circulares First Issue

#32-35 printer: Fabbri.

		Good	Fine	XF
32	**1/2 Libra** 13.6.1918. Reported not confirmed.	—	—	—
33	**1 Libra** 13.6.1918. Winged woman at l. and r.	—	—	—

		Good	Fine	XF
34	**5 Libras** 13.6.1918. Black. Liberty at l., globe at r.	—	—	—
35	**10 Libras** 13.6.1918. Reported not confirmed.	—	—	—

1918 Cheques Circulares Second Issue

#36-39 have issuing banks listed in 2 lines of text under top heading. Printer: ABNC.

		Good	Fine	XF
36	**1/2 Libra** 14.9.1918. Similar to #25.	40.00	110.	250.
37	**1 Libra** 14.9.1918. Similar to #26.	40.00	110.	250.

		Good	Fine	XF
38	**5 Libras** 14.9.1918. Similar to #27.	45.00	125.	275.
39	**10 Libras** 14.9.1918. Similar to #28. Uniface proof.	—	—	—

1918 Sol Issue

		Good	Fine	XF
40	**1 Sol** 14.9.1918. Dk. blue. Like #31. Liberty seated w/shield and staff at ctr. Back brown; arms at ctr. Printer: ABNC.	4.00	15.00	40.00

Banco de Reserva del Peru

1922 Issue

#48-51 dated 1922. Printer: ABNC.

		Good	Fine	XF
48	**1/2 Libra** 12.4.1922. Similar to #36.	10.00	40.00	100.

		Good	Fine	XF
49	**1 Libra** 12.4.1922. Similar to #37.	15.00	45.00	125.

		Good	Fine	XF
50	**5 Libras** 12.4.1922. Similar to #38.	25.00	75.00	175.

		Good	Fine	XF
51	**10 Libras** 12.4.1922. Black on yellow unpt. Similar to #39.	—	—	—

1926 Issue

#52-55 like #48-51 but dated 1926. Printer: ABNC.

		Good	Fine	XF
52	**1/2 Libra** 11.8.1926. Black on green unpt. (Not issued).	—	—	—
53	**1 Libra** 11.8.1926. Black on red unpt. (Not issued).	—	—	—
54	**5 Libras** 11.8.1926. Black on blue unpt. (Not issued).	—	—	—
55	**10 Libras** 11.8.1926. Black on yellow unpt. (Not issued).	—	—	—

Banco Central de Reserva del Peru

1935 ND Provisional Issue (1922 Dated notes)

#56-59 ovpt. new bank name and new denomination ovpt. on backs of notes of the Banco de Reserva del Peru dated 1922.

		Good	Fine	XF
56	**5 Soles on 1/2 Libra** ND (- old date 12.4.1922). Ovpt. on #48.	20.00	70.00	175.
57	**10 Soles on 1 Libra** ND (- old date 12.4.1922). Ovpt. on #49.	25.00	85.00	200.

		Good	Fine	XF
58	**50 Soles on 5 Libras** ND (- old date 12.4.1922). Ovpt. on #50.	40.00	125.	300.
59	**100 Soles on 10 Libras** ND (- old date 12.4.1922). Ovpt. on #51.	50.00	175.	—

1935 ND Provisional Issue (1926 Dated notes)

#60-63 ovpt. on notes dated 1926.

		Good	Fine	XF
60	**5 Soles on 1/2 Libra** ND (- old date 11.8.1926). Ovpt. on #52.	20.00	70.00	175.

		Good	Fine	XF
1	**10 Soles on 1 Libra** ND (- old date 11.8.1926). Ovpt. on #53.	25.00	85.00	200.
2	**50 Soles on 5 Libras** ND (- old date 11.8.1926). Ovpt. on #54.	40.00	175.	300.
3	**100 Soles on 10 Libras** ND (- old date 11.8.1926). Ovpt. on #55.	50.00	175.	—

935 Issues

		VG	VF	UNC
4	**50 Centavos** 3.5.1935. Blue. Similar to #65. Back lt. brown. Printer: Fabbri, Lima. Series A-E.	4.00	15.00	50.00

		VG	VF	UNC
5	**1 Sol** 26.4.1935. Blue. Liberty seated w/shield and staff at ctr. Back brown; arms at ctr. Printer: ABNC. Series A-E.	2.00	7.50	25.00

933 Issue (Ley 7137)

6-69 printer: ABNC. Sign. title varieties; title above ctr. sign:

PRESIDENTE DEL DIRECTORIO **(to 1941)**

VICE-PRESIDENTE **(1944-45)**

PRESIDENTE **(1946-47)**

		VG	VF	UNC
	5 Soles 31.3.1933; 6.3.1936; 5.8.1938; 8.9.1939. Black on m/c unpt. Portr. Liberty at ctr. Back green; mine workers at ctr. 135 x 67mm.	3.00	8.00	25.00

		VG	VF	UNC
	10 Soles 31.3.1933; 6.3.1936; 5.8.1938; 8.9.1939. Black on m/c unpt. Seated woman holding basket w/flowers at l. Back orange; mine driller at ctr. 144 x 76mm.	3.00	10.00	30.00

		VG	VF	UNC
68	**50 Soles** 31.3.1933; 21.5.1937; 8.9.1937. Black on m/c unpt. Girl w/lamb and sheep at r. Back blue; two allegorical women at ctr. 158 x 77mm.	6.00	25.00	80.00
69	**100 Soles** 31.3.1933; 21.5.1937; 8.9.1939. Black on m/c unpt. Similar to #28. Back orange; steam train at ctr. 172 x 79mm.	25.00	75.00	200.

1941 Issue

		VG	VF	UNC
66A	**5 Soles** 26.9.1941; 26.5.1944; 17.10.1947. Like #66. 141 x 68mm.	2.00	5.00	25.00
67A	**10 Soles** 26.9.1941; 26.5.1944; 13.7.1945; 15.11.1946; 17.10.1947. Black on m/c unpt. Like #67. 152 x 77mm.	2.00	6.00	20.00
68A	**50 Soles** 26.9.1941; 26.5.1944; 13.7.1945; 15.11.1946; 17.10.1947; 28.9.1950. Black. Like #68. 165 x 78mm.	5.00	15.00	60.00

		VG	VF	UNC
69A	**100 Soles** 26.9.1941; 26.5.1944; 13.7.1945; 15.11.1946; 17.10.1947; 28.9.1950. Black. Like #69. 177 x 80mm.	12.00	50.00	120.

1946-51 Issue

#70-74 seated Liberty holding shield and staff at ctr. Arms at ctr. on back. Sign. varieties.

#70-73 printer: TDLR.

		VG	VF	UNC
70	**5 Soles** 20.3.1952; 16.9.1954. Green on plain lt. blue unpt. Serial # at upper l. and r.			
	a. Issued note.	1.00	3.00	7.00
	s. Specimen.	—	—	—

		VG	VF	UNC
71	**10 Soles** 12.7.1951-17.2.1955. Black on m/c unpt. Back orange.			
	a. Issued note.	1.00	4.00	8.00
	s. Specimen.	—	—	—
72	**50 Soles** 31.3.1949; 12.7.1951; 16.9.1954. Black on m/c unpt. Back blue.	2.00	5.00	20.00
73	**100 Soles** 31.3.1949-16.9.1954. Black on m/c unpt. Back orange.	4.00	10.00	30.00
74	**500 Soles** 4.10.1946; 10.7.1952. Brown on m/c unpt. Back deep red. Printer: W&S.	12.00	30.00	90.00

1955 Issue

		VG	VF	UNC
75	**10 Soles** 17.2.1955. Black, green-black and brown. Like #71. Printer: G&D. Proof.	—	—	100.

Ley 10535, 1956 Issue

#76-80 seated Liberty holding shield and staff at ctr. Arms at ctr. on back. Sign. varieties.

		VG	VF	UNC
76	**5 Soles** 22.3.1956; 18.3.1960. Green on patterned lt. blue unpt. Like #70. Printer: TDLR.	.50	1.50	5.00

		VG	VF	UNC
77	**10 Soles** 9.7.1956. Orange on m/c unpt. Similar to #71. Printer: G&D.	2.00	6.00	20.00

#78-80 printer: TDLR.

		VG	VF	UNC
78	**50 Soles** 22.3.1956; 24.10.1957; 13.5.1959. Dk. blue on lilac unpt. Like #72. Serial # at upper l. and r.			
	a. Issued note.	1.50	4.50	17.50
	s. Specimen.	—	—	—
79	**100 Soles** 1956-61. Black on lt. blue unpt. Like #73 but different guilloche. Back black.			
	a. *LIMA* at lower l. 22.3.1956; 24.10.1957.	4.00	12.00	30.00
	b. *LIMA* at lower r. w/date. 13.5.1959.	4.00	12.00	30.00
	c. As b. Series and serial # at lower l. and upper r. 1.2.1961.	4.00	12.00	30.00
	s. As a. Specimen.	—	—	—
80	**500 Soles** 1956-61. Brown on lt. brown and lilac unpt. Similar to #74. Back brown.			
	a. Series and serial # at upper corners. 22.3.1956; 24.10.1957.	8.00	25.00	75.00
	b. Series and serial # at lower l. and upper r. 10.12.1959; 16.6.1961.	8.00	25.00	75.00
	s. As b. Specimen.	—	—	—

1958 Issue

#81-82 printer: W&S.

		VG	VF	UNC
81	**5 Soles** 21.8.1958. Green. Like #70 but different guilloche on back.	1.00	4.00	7.50

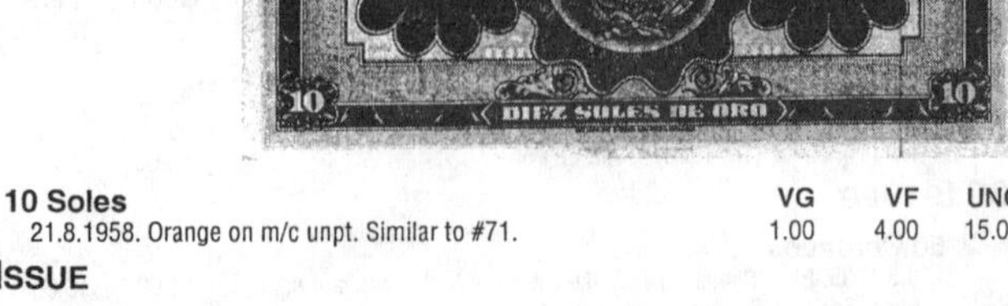

		VG	VF	UNC
82	**10 Soles** 21.8.1958. Orange on m/c unpt. Similar to #71.	1.00	4.00	15.00

1960 Issue

		VG	VF	UNC
82A	**10 Soles** 8.7.1960; 1.2.1961. Orange on m/c unpt. Liberty seated holding shield and staff at ctr. Serial # and series at lower l. and upper r. Printer: TDLR.	.75	1.50	6.00

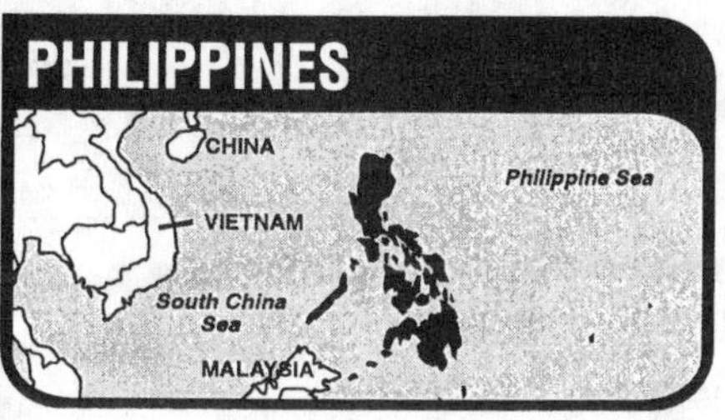

The Republic of the Philippines, an archipelago in the western Pacific 500 miles (805 km.) from the southeast coast of Asia, has an area of 115,830 sq. mi. (300,000 sq. km.) and a population of 75.04 million. Capital: Manila. The economy of the 7,000-island group is d on agriculture, forestry and fishing. Timber, coconut products, sugar and hemp are exported.

Migration to the Philippines began about 30,000 years ago when land bridges connected the islands with Borneo and Sumatra. Ferdinand Magellan claimed the islands for Spain in 1521. The first permanent settlement was established by Miguel de Legazpi at Cebu in April of 1565; Manila was established in 1572. A British expedition captured Manila and occupied the Spanish colony in Oct. of 1762, but it was returned to Spain by the treaty of Paris, 1763. Spain held the Philippines amid a growing movement of Filipino nationalism until 1898 when they were ceded to the United States at the end of the Spanish-American War. The Filipinos then fought unsuccessfully against the United States to maintain their independent Republic proclaimed by Emilio Aguinaldo. The country became a self-governing Commonwealth of the United States in 1935, and attained independence as the Republic of the Philippines on July 4, 1946. During World War II the Japanese had set up a puppet republic, but this quasi-government failed to achieve worldwide recognition. The occupation lasted from late 1941 to 1945. Ferdinand Marcos lost to Corazón Aquino in elections of 1986. Marcos then fled the country. In 1992 Fidel Ramos was elected president. He was succeeded in 1998 by Joseph E. Estrada, who was deposed in January 2001 and replaced by his vice-president Gloria Macapagal Arroyo.

RULERS:

Spanish to 1898
United States, 1898-1946

MONETARY SYSTEM:

1 Peso = 100 Centavos to 1967
1 Piso = 100 Sentimos, 1967-

SPANISH ADMINISTRATION

BANCO ESPAÑOL FILIPINO DE ISABEL 2A

1852 ISSUE

#A1-A3 crowned portr. Qn. Isabel II at top ctr. Printer: BWC.

		Good	Fine	XF
A1	**10 Pesos** 1.5.1852; 1.1.1865. Black on brown or white paper.	—	—	—
A2	**25 Pesos** 1.5.1852; 1.1.1865. Green paper. Rare.	—	—	—

		Good	Fine	XF
A3	**50 Pesos** 1.5.1852; 1.1.1865. Brown paper. Rare.	—	—	—

BANCO ESPAÑOL FILIPINO

1883 ISSUE

#A4-A6 bank arms at top ctr. Uniface.

		Good	Fine	XF
A4	**10 Pesos** 1.1.1883. Brown paper. Rare.	—	—	—
A5	**25 Pesos** 1.1.1883. Green paper. Rare.	—	—	—

		Good	Fine	XF
A6	**50 Pesos** 1.1.1883. Brown paper. Rare.	—	—	—

1896 ISSUE

#A7-A10 bank arms at upper ctr. Printed on both sides. Printer: BFL.

		Good	Fine	XF
A7	**5 Pesos** 1.6.1896. Black on brown paper.			
	a. Issued note.	1500.	3000.	—
	b. Cancelled w/handstamp: *PAGADO.*	750.	1500.	—

		Good	Fine	XF
A8	**10 Pesos** 1.6.1896. Black on yellow paper.			
	a. Issued note. Rare.	—	—	—
	b. Cancelled w/handstamp: *PAGADO.* Rare.	—	—	—
A9	**25 Pesos** 1.6.1896. Black on blue paper. Rare.	—	—	—
A10	**50 Pesos** 1.6.1896. Black on pink paper. Rare.	—	—	—

Note: For similar 1904 issue order U.S. administration see #A31-A36.

BILLETE DEL TESORO

TREASURY NOTE

1877 ISSUE

#A11-A15 uniface.

		Good	Fine	XF
A11	**1 Peso** 26.4.1877. Black. Arms at upper ctr. Rare.	—	—	—
A13	**4 Pesos** 26.4.1877. Black on orange paper. Arms at l. Rare.	—	—	—

		Good	Fine	XF
A15	**25 Pesos** 26.4.1877. Black on blue paper. Arms at upper ctr. Rare.	—	—	—

REPUBLIC

REPÚBLICA FILIPINA

LEY 26 NOVIEMBRE 1898

		VG	VF	UNC
A25	**5 Pesos** L.1898. Black on red unpt. W/serial #, w/o sign. Back black.	350.	750.	1500.

LEY 30.11.1898 AND 24.4.1899

Most notes are w/o sign. and w/o serial #.

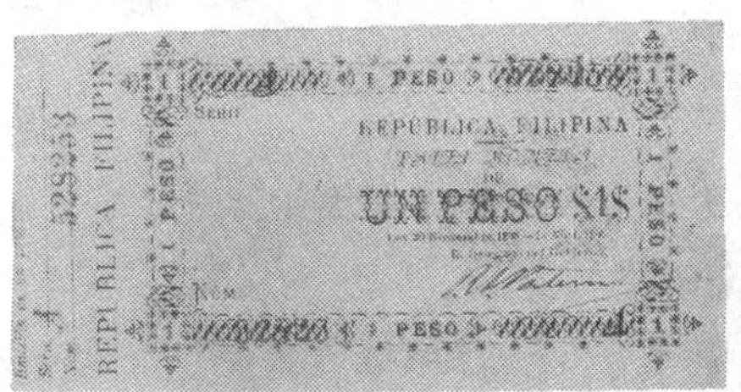

		VG	VF	UNC
A26	**1 Peso** L. 1898-99. Black.			
	a. Issued note w/sign. and serial #. Rare.	—	—	—
	r. Remainder w/o sign. or serial #.	100.	250.	500.

		VG	VF	UNC
A27	**5 Pesos** L.1898-99. Black. Similar to #A25.			
	a. Issued note w/sign. and serial #. Rare.	—	—	—
	r. Remainder w/o sign. or serial #.	125.	300.	575.

LEY 24.4.1899

		VG	VF	UNC
A28	**1 Peso** L.1899. Black. Similar to #A26.			
	a. Unissued note but w/embossed seal at l. ctr. and 3 serial #. Rare.	—	—	—
	r. Unsigned remainder w/o serial # or seal.	75.00	250.	450.

Note: 2, 10, 20, 25, 50 and 100 Peso notes were authorized but no examples are known.

UNITED STATES ADMINISTRATION

BANCO ESPAÑOL FILIPINO

1904 ISSUE

#A31-A36 bank arms at upper ctr. Denominations w/o *FUERTES*. Printer: BFL.

		Good	Fine	XF
A31	**5 Pesos** 1.1.1904. Black on pink paper. Rare.	—	—	—
A32	**10 Pesos** 1.1.1904. Black on green paper. Rare.	—	—	—

		Good	Fine	XF
A33	**25 Pesos** 1.1.1904. Black on lt. purple paper. Rare.	—	—	—
A34	**50 Pesos** 1.1.1904. Black on green paper. Rare.	—	—	—

		Good	Fine	XF
A35	**100 Pesos** 1.1.1904. Black on yellowish brown paper. Rare.	—	—	—

NOTICE

Readers with unlisted dates, signature varieties, etc. are invited to submit photocopies or, high resolution (300 dpi, 100% size) scans of their notes to: Standard Catalog of World Paper Money, 700 East State St. Iola, WI 54990-0001, or E-Mail: george.cuhaj@fwpubs.com.

		Good	Fine	XF
A36	**200 Pesos** 1.1.1904. Black on yellowish brown paper. Back m/c. Rare.	—	—	—

1908 Issue

#1-6 printer: USBEP (w/o imprint).
#1 and 2 w/1 stamped sign. (at l.) and 2 printed sign.
#4-6 w/only 2 printed sign.

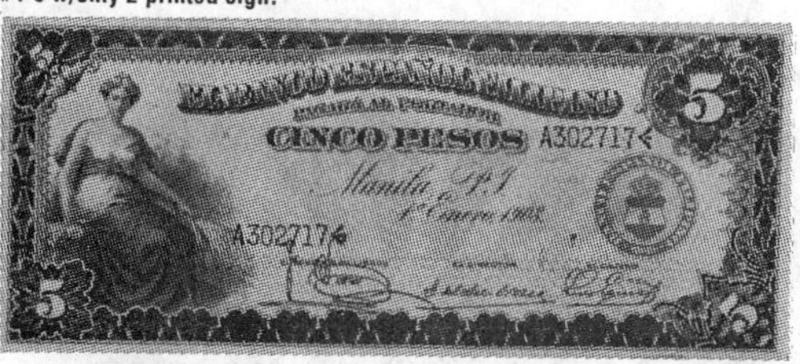

		Good	Fine	XF
1	**5 Pesos** 1.1.1908. Black on red unpt. Woman seated at l. Back red. Sign. *J. Serrano* at l.	75.00	150.	325.

		Good	Fine	XF
2	**10 Pesos** 1.1.1908. Black on brown unpt. Woman w/flowers at ctr. Back brown.			
	a. Sign. *Julian Serrano* at l. Rare.	—	—	—
	b. Sign. *J. Serrano* at l.	175.	500.	—
3	**20 Pesos** 1.1.1908. Black on lilac unpt. Woman at l. Back tan.			
	a. Sign. Julian Serrano at l. Rare.	—	—	—
	b. Sign. J. Serrano at l.	500.	1000.	—

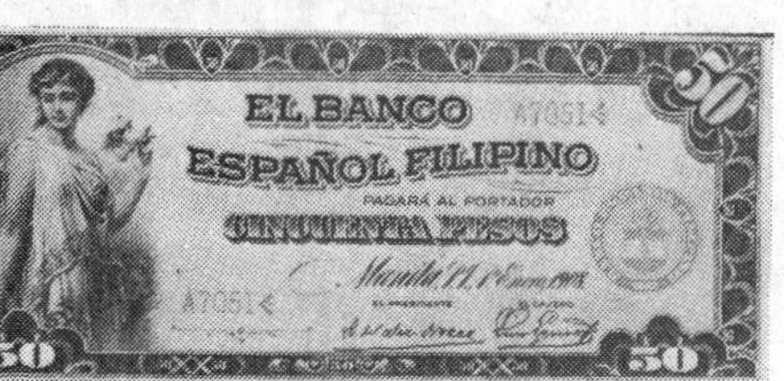

		Good	Fine	XF
4	**50 Pesos** 1.1.1908. Black on blue unpt. Woman standing w/flower at l. Back red.	250.	650.	—
5	**100 Pesos** 1.1.1908. Black on green unpt. Woman seated w/scroll and globe at l. Back olive.	350.	700.	—
6	**200 Pesos** 1.1.1908. Black on tan unpt. Justice w/scales and shield at ctr. Back orange. Rare.	—	—	—

Bank of the Philippine Islands

1912 Issue

#7-12 designs like previous issue. Printer: USBEP (w/o imprint). Replacement notes of b. varieties: Star prefix.

		Good	Fine	XF
7	**5 Pesos** 1.1.1912. Black on red unpt. Similar to #1. Back light red.			
	a. Sign. D. Garcia and Jno. S. Hord.	5.00	35.00	75.00
	b. Sign. D. Garcia and E. Sendres.	7.50	40.00	85.00
8	**10 Pesos** 1.1.1912. Black on brown unpt. Similar to #2.			
	a. Sign. D. Garcia and Jno. S. Hord.	5.00	25.00	75.00
	b. Sign. D. Garcia and E. Sendres.	5.00	25.00	75.00

		Good	Fine	XF
9	**20 Pesos** 1.1.1912. Black on lilac unpt. Similar to #3.			
	a. Sign. D. Garcia and Jno. S. Hord.	7.50	40.00	100.
	b. Sign. D. Garcia and E. Sendres.	7.50	35.00	90.00

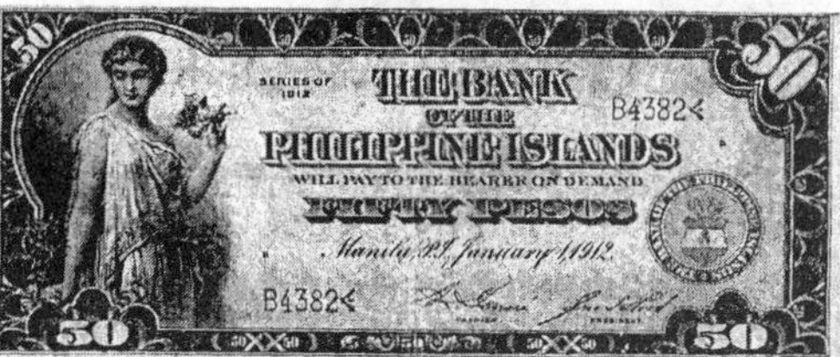

		Good	Fine	XF
10	**50 Pesos** 1.1.1912. Black on blue unpt. Similar to #4.			
	a. Sign. D. Garcia and Jno. S. Hord.	25.00	125.	300.
	b. Sign. D. Garcia and E. Sendres.	20.00	100.	250.

		Good	Fine	XF
11	**100 Pesos** 1.1.1912. Black on green unpt. Similar to #5.			
	a. Sign. D. Garcia and Jno. S. Hord.	100.	300.	550.
	b. Sign. D. Garcia and E. Sendres.	75.00	250.	500.

		Good	Fine	XF
12	**200 Pesos** 1.1.1912. Black on tan unpt. Similar to #6. Sign. D. Garcia and Jno. S. Hord.	300.	800.	—

1920 Issue

#13-15 like #7b-9b except for date and serial # prefix-suffix. Sign. D. Garcia and E. Sendres. Printer: USBEP (w/o imprint). Replacement notes: Star prefix.

		Good	Fine	XF
13	**5 Pesos** 1.1.1920. Black on red unpt. Like #7b. Back orange.	5.00	12.50	50.00

		Good	Fine	XF
14	**10 Pesos** 1.1.1920. Black on brown unpt. Like #8b.	5.00	20.00	75.00

		Good	Fine	XF
15	**20 Pesos** 1.1.1920. Black on lilac unpt. Like #9b.	5.00	30.00	85.00

1928 Issue

#16-21 designs like #7-12 but w/o unpt. Sign. D. Garcia and Fulg. Borromeo. Printer: USBEP (w/o imprint). Replacement notes: Star prefix.

		Good	Fine	XF
16	**5 Pesos** 1.1.1928. Black. Like #7. Back orange.	2.00	10.00	50.00
17	**10 Pesos** 1.1.1928. Black. Like #8.	5.00	20.00	60.00
18	**20 Pesos** 1.1.1928. Black. Like #9.	5.00	25.00	80.00

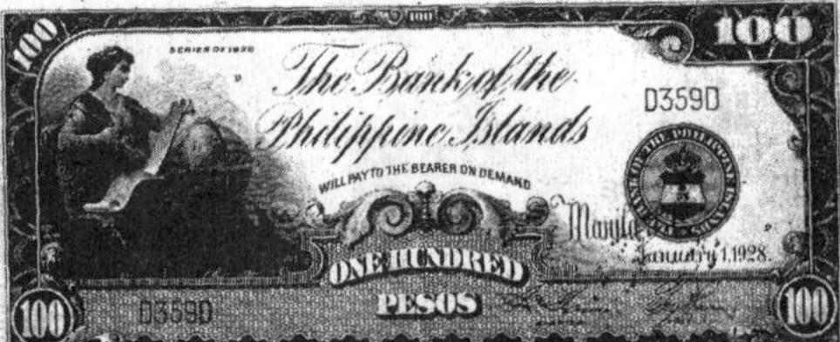

		Good	Fine	XF
19	**50 Pesos** 1.1.1928. Black. Like #10.	25.00	80.00	190.

		Good	Fine	XF
20	**100 Pesos** 1.1.1928. Black. Like #11.	60.00	200.	500.

		Good	Fine	XF
21	**200 Pesos** 1.1.1928. Black. Like #12.	175.	400.	850.

1933 Issue

#22-24 like #16-18 except for date and serial # prefix-suffix. Sign. D. Garcia and P.J. Campos. Printer: USBEP (w/o imprint). Replacement notes: Star prefix.

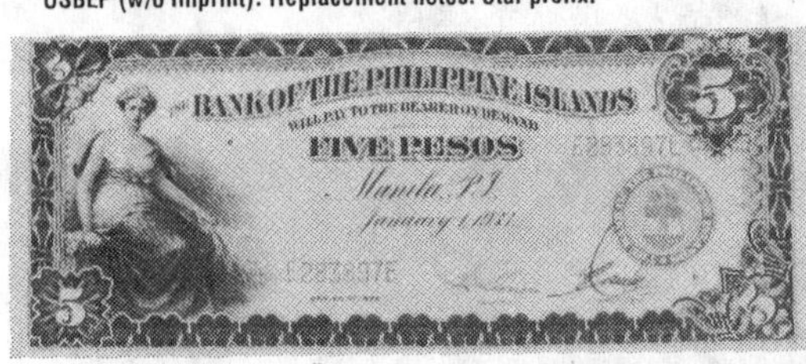

		Good	Fine	XF
22	**5 Pesos** 1.1.1933. Black. Like #16.	3.00	10.00	50.00
23	**10 Pesos** 1.1.1933. Black. Like #17.	6.00	15.00	50.00
24	**20 Pesos** 1.1.1933. Black. Like #18.	7.50	25.00	85.00

Philippine Islands

1903 Issue

#25-38 printer: USBEP (w/o imprint).

		Good	Fine	XF
25	**2 Pesos** 1903. Black on blue unpt. Portr. José Rizal at upper l. Back blue.			
	a. Sign. William H. Taft and Frank A. Branagan.	100.	300.	650.
	b. Sign. Luke E. Wright and Frank A. Branagan.	200.	600.	1000.

		Good	Fine	XF
26	**5 Pesos** 1903. Black on red unpt. Portr. Pres. William McKinley at l. Back red.			
	a. Sign. William H. Taft and Frank A. Branagan.	100.	450.	1400.
	b. Sign. Luke E. Wright and Frank A. Branagan.	200.	550.	1500.
27	**10 Pesos** 1903. Black on brown unpt. Portr. George Washington at lower ctr. Back brown.			
	a. Sign. William H. Taft and Frank A. Branagan.	175.	650.	1500.
	b. Sign. Luke E. Wright and Frank A. Branagan.	250.	1000.	2000.

		Good	Fine	XF
27A	**10 Pesos** 1903. Like #27 but black vertical text ovpt: *Subject to the provisions of the/Act of Congress approved/ June 23, 1906* on face. Sign. Henry C. Ide w/title: *Governor General* and Frank A. Branagan.	1500.	3250.	—

Note: The chief executive's title before 1905 was: *Civil Governor*.

1905 ISSUE

#28-31 issued w/ovpt. like #27A. Sign. Luke E. Wright w/title: *Governor General* and Frank A. Branagan.

		Good	Fine	XF
28	**20 Pesos** 1905. Black on yellow unpt. Mt. Mayon at ctr. Back tan. Rare.	—	—	—
29	**50 Pesos** 1905. Black on red unpt. Portr. Gen. Henry W. Lawton at l. Back red. Rare.	—	—	—
30	**100 Pesos** 1905. Black on green unpt. Portr. Ferdinand Magellan at ctr. Back olive. Rare.	—	—	—
31	**500 Pesos** 1905. Black. Portr. Miguel Lopez de Legazpi at ctr. Back purple. Rare.	—	—	—

1906 ISSUE

		Good	Fine	XF
32	**2 Pesos** 1906. Black on blue unpt. Similar to #25 but new authorization date, and payable in silver or gold.			
	a. Sign. James F. Smith and Frank A. Branagan.	60.00	150.	325.
	b. Sign. W. Cameron Forbes and J. L. Barrett.	80.00	300.	—
	c. Sign. W. Cameron Forbes and J. L. Manning.	90.00	400.	550.
	d. Sign. Francis Burton Harrison and J. L. Manning.	60.00	175.	350.
	e. Sign. like d., but w/o blue unpt. (error).	50.00	175.	—
	f. Sign. Francis Burton Harrison and A. P. Fitzsimmons.	30.00	75.00	175.
33	**500 Pesos** 1906. Black. Similar to #31.			
	a. Sign. James F. Smith and Frank A. Branagan. Rare.		30,000.	
	b. Sign. W. Cameron Forbes and J. L. Barrett. Rare.	—	—	—
	c. Sign. Francis Burton Harrison and A. P. Fitzsimmons. Rare.	—	—	—

1908 ISSUE

		Good	Fine	XF
34	**20 Pesos** 1908. Black on yellow unpt. Similar to #28.			
	a. Sign. James F. Smith and Frank A. Branagan.	100.	350.	—
	b. Sign. W. Cameron Forbes and J. L. Barrett.	125.	400.	800.
	c. Sign. W. Cameron Forbes and J. L. Manning.	125.	400.	—
	d. Sign. Francis Burton Harrison and J. L. Manning.	125.	350.	—
	e. Sign. Francis Burton Harrison and A. P. Fitzsimmons.	75.00	325.	—

1910 ISSUE

		Good	Fine	XF
35	**5 Pesos** 1910. Black on red unpt. Similar to #26.			
	a. Sign. W. Cameron Forbes and J. L. Barrett.	75.00	200.	550.
	b. Sign. W. Cameron Forbes and J. L. Manning.	75.00	200.	—
	c. Sign. Francis Burton Harrison and J. L. Manning.	75.00	200.	—
	d. Sign. Francis Burton Harrison and A. P. Fitzsimmons.	40.00	150.	400.

1912 ISSUE

		Good	Fine	XF
36	**10 Pesos** 1912. Black on brown unpt. Similar to #27.			
	a. Sign. W. Cameron Forbes and J. L. Barrett.	85.00	275.	—
	b. Sign. W. Cameron Forbes and J. L. Manning.	85.00	275.	—
	c. Sign. Francis Burton Harrison and J. L. Manning.	85.00	275.	—
	d. Sign. Francis Burton Harrison and A. P. Fitzsimmons.	40.00	175.	450.

1916 ISSUE

		Good	Fine	XF
37	**50 Pesos** 1916. Black on red unpt. Similar to #29. Rare.	—	—	—
38	**100 Pesos** 1916. Black on green unpt. Similar to #30. Rare.	—	—	—

PHILIPPINE NATIONAL BANK

1917 EMERGENCY WW I ISSUE

#39-42 American bald eagle on back. Local printing.

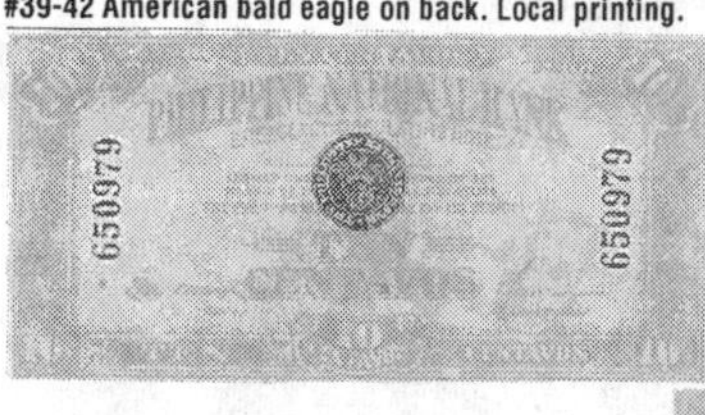

		VG	VF	UNC
39	**10 Centavos** 20.11.1917. Gold on yellow unpt. Back yellow.	—	20.00	50.00

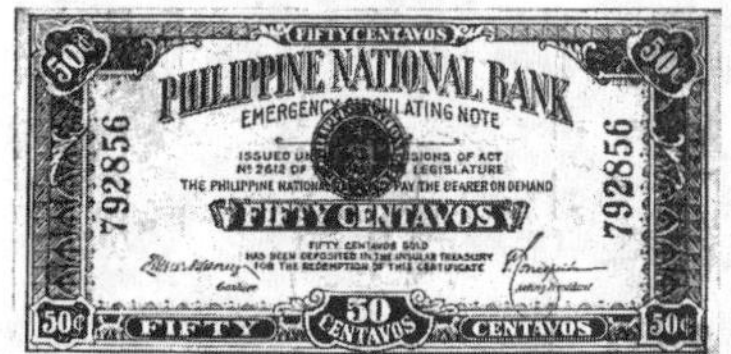

		VG	VF	UNC
40	**20 Centavos** 20.11.1917. Blue on yellow unpt. Back blue.	—	20.00	50.00
41	**50 Centavos** 22.9.1917. Black on green unpt. Back green.	5.00	25.00	65.00
42	**1 Peso** 22.9.1917. Black on red unpt. Back red.	10.00	40.00	125.

1919 ND EMERGENCY ISSUE

#43-43B new bank name, seal, sign. ovpt on Bank of the Philippine Islands notes.

		VG	VF	UNC
43	**5 Pesos** ND (1919 - old date 1912). Ovpt. on #7. Rare.	2000.	6000.	—

		VG	VF	UNC
43A	**10 Pesos** ND (1919 - old date 1912). Ovpt. on #8. Rare.	—	8000.	
43B	**20 Pesos** ND (1919 - old date 1912). Ovpt. on #9. Rare.	5500.	—	—

1916-20 Regular Issue

#44-50 printer: USBEP (w/o imprint). Replacement notes: Star prefix.

		Good	Fine	XF
44	**1 Peso** 1918. Black on orange unpt. Portr. Charles A. Conant at l. Back green.	45.00	150.	450.

		Good	Fine	XF
45	**2 Pesos** 1916. Black on blue unpt. Portr. José Rizal at l. (similar to Silver and Treasury Certificates). Back blue.	65.00	225.	400.
46	**5 Pesos** 1916. Black on red unpt. Portr. Pres. William McKinley at l. (similar to Silver and Treasury Certificates). Back red-orange.			
	a. Sign. S. Ferguson and H. Parker Willis.	125.	400.	—
	b. Sign. S. Mercado and V. Concepcion.	1.50	5.00	20.00

		Good	Fine	XF
47	**10 Pesos** 1916. Black on brown unpt. Portr. George Washington at ctr. (similar to Silver and Treasury Certificates). Back brown.			
	a. Sign. S. Ferguson and H. Parker Willis.	125.	400.	—
	b. Sign. S. Mercado and V. Concepcion.	4.00	20.00	100.

		Good	Fine	XF
48	**20 Pesos** 1919. Black on yellow unpt. Portr. Congressman William A. Jones at lower ctr. Back tan.	100.	400.	—

		Good	Fine	XF
49	**50 Pesos** 1920. Black on green unpt. Portr. Gen. Henry W. Lawton at l. Back red.	6.00	25.00	90.00

Note: #49 was never officially issued. 10,000 pieces were captured and issued during WW II by the Japanese (serial #90001-100000). The others were looted by Moros in the province of Mindanao who sold them at one-tenth of their face value. This accounts for their relative availability.

		Good	Fine	XF
50	**100 Pesos** 1920. Green on red unpt. Portr. Ferdinand Magellan at ctr. Back olive. Rare.	—	3000.	—

1921 Issue

#51-55 designs like previous issue but notes w/o unpt. Printer: USBEP (w/o imprint). Replacemnet notes: Star prefix.

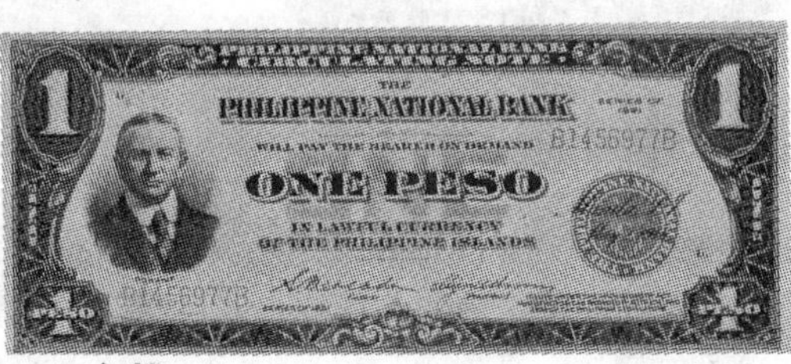

		Good	Fine	XF
51	**1 Peso** 1921. Like #44.	40.00	125.	300
52	**2 Pesos** 1921. Like #45.	50.00	150.	375

		Good	Fine	XF
53	**5 Pesos** 1921. Like #46.	1.50	4.00	15.0

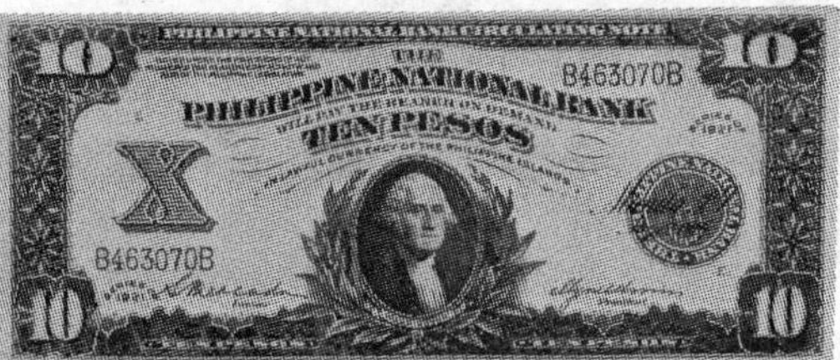

		Good	Fine	XF
54	**10 Pesos** 1921. Like #47.	5.00	25.00	75.0

		Good	Fine	XF
55	**20 Pesos** 1921. Like #48.	10.00	50.00	35[illegible]

1924 Issue

#56, replacement notes: Star prefix.

		Good	Fine	XF
56	**1 Peso** 1924. Like #51.	10.00	65.00	15[illegible]

1937 Issue

#57-59 printer: USBEP w/imprint on back. Text reads: *PHILIPPINES* instead of *PHILIPPINE ISLANDS*. Replacement notes: Star prefix.

		VG	VF	UNC
57	**5 Pesos** 1937. Similar to #53.	5.00	20.00	60.0

		VG	VF	UNC
58	**10 Pesos**			
	1937. Similar to #54.	10.00	40.00	125.
59	**20 Pesos**			
	1937. Similar to #55.	65.00	175.	600.

PHILIPPINE ISLANDS (RESUMED)

1918 ISSUE

#60-67 printer: USBEP (w/o imprint). Replacement notes: Star prefix.

No.	Denomination / Description	Good	Fine	XF
60	**1 Peso**			
	1918. Black on green unpt. Portr. A. Mabini at l. Back green.			
	a. Sign. Francis Burton Harrison and A. P. Fitzsimmons.	8.50	50.00	200.
	b. Sign. Francis Burton Harrison and V. Carmona.	10.00	75.00	250.
61	**2 Pesos**			
	1918. Black on blue unpt. Portr. J. Rizal at l. Back blue.	35.00	200.	350.
62	**5 Pesos**			
	1918. Black on lt. red unpt. Portr. Pres. Wm. McKinley at l. Back red-orange.	60.00	200.	—
63	**10 Pesos**			
	1918. Black on brown unpt. Portr. George Washington at ctr. Back brown.	200.	700.	—
63A	**20 Pesos**			
	1918. Black on yellow unpt. Mayon volcano at ctr. Ornate blue *XX* at upper l. Back tan. Sign. Francis Burton Harrison and A. P. and A. P. Fitzsimmons.	60.00	250.	550.

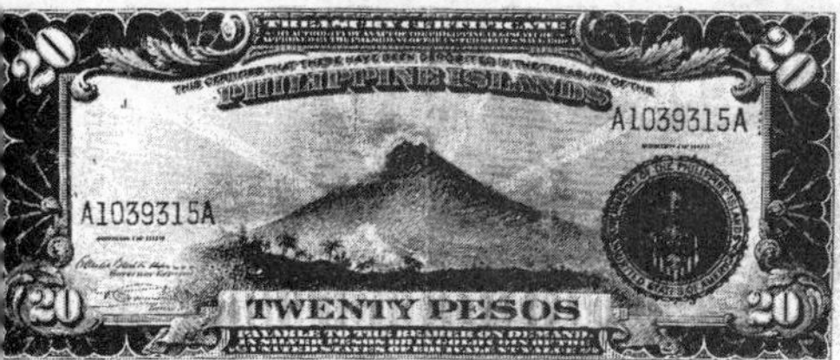

No.	Denomination / Description	Good	Fine	XF
64	**20 Pesos**			
	1918. Like #63A but w/o ornate *XX* at l. Sign. Francis Burton Harrison and V. Carmona.	60.00	225.	550.
65	**50 Pesos**			
	1918. Black on green unpt. Portr. Gen. Lawton at l. Back red.			
	a. Sign. Francis Burton Harrison and A. P. Fitzsimmons.	200.	600.	—
	b. Sign. Francis Burton Harrison and V. Carmona.	200.	600.	—

No.	Denomination / Description	Good	Fine	XF
66	**100 Pesos**			
	1918. Black on green unpt. Portr. F. Magellan at ctr. Back olive.			
	a. Sign. Francis Burton Harrison and A. P. Fitzsimmons. Rare.	—	—	—
	b. Sign. Francis Burton Harrison and V. Carmona. Rare.	—	—	—
67	**500 Pesos**			
	1918. Black on orange unpt. Portr. Legazpi at ctr. Back purple. Rare.	—	—	—

1924 ISSUE

#68-72 w/o unpt., otherwise designs like previous issue. Printer: USBEP (w/o imprint). Replacement notes: Star prefix.

No.	Denomination / Description	Good	Fine	XF
68	**1 Peso**			
	1924. Like #60.			
	a. Sign. Leonard Wood and Salv. Lagdameo w/title: *Acting Treasurer.*	8.00	50.00	150.
	b. Sign. Leonard Wood and Salv. Lagdameo w/title: *Treasurer.*	15.00	70.00	200.
	c. Sign. H. L. Stimson and Salv. Lagdameo.	7.50	40.00	140.
69	**2 Pesos**			
	1924. Like #61, but lg. denomination numeral added in red at lower l. ctr.			
	a. Sign. Leonard Wood and Salv. Lagdameo w/title: *Acting Treasurer.*	20.00	100.	250.
	b. Sign. Leonard Wood and Salv. Lagdameo w/title: *Treasurer.*	25.00	110.	260.
	c. Sign. Henry L. Stimson and Salv. Lagdameo.	10.00	75.00	175.

No.	Denomination / Description	Good	Fine	XF
70	**5 Pesos**			
	1924. Black. Like #62.	20.00	80.00	300.

No.	Denomination / Description	Good	Fine	XF
71	**10 Pesos**			
	1924. Black. Like #63.	15.00	70.00	250.

No.	Denomination / Description	Good	Fine	XF
72	**500 Pesos**			
	1924. Like #67. Blue unpt. and numeral.			
	a. Back lt. green.	1500.	5000.	—
	p. Back purple. Proof.	—	—	—

Note: Though official records indicate that the backs of #72 were printed in purple, the only issued notes seen in collections have lt. green backs. Further reports are needed.

NOTICE

Readers with unlisted dates, signature varieties, etc. are invited to submit photocopies or, high resolution (300 dpi, 100% size) scans of their notes to: Standard Catalog of World Paper Money, 700 East State St. Iola, WI 54990-0001, or E-Mail: george.cuhaj@fwpubs.com.

1929 Issue

#73-80 printer: USBEP (w/o imprint). Replacement notes: Star prefix.

Many changes were effected on US-Philippine currency with the 1929 Issue, as the United States changed from the large to small size formats. Significant design alterations were introduced as well as some color changes.

		Good	Fine	XF
73	**1 Peso** 1929. Black on orange unpt. Portr. A. Mabini at l. Similar to #60 but several minor alterations in plate. Back orange.			
	a. Sign. Dwight F. Davis and Salv. Lagdameo.	5.00	40.00	125.
	b. Sign. Theodore Roosevelt and Salv. Lagdameo.	15.00	75.00	225.
	c. Sign. Frank Murphy and Salv. Lagdameo.	3.00	15.00	800.
74	**2 Pesos** 1929. Black on blue unpt. Portr. J. Rizal at l. Similar to #61 but several minor alterations in plate. Back blue.			
	a. Sign. Theodore Roosevelt and Salv. Lagdameo.	6.00	50.00	150.
	b. Sign. Frank Murphy and Salv. Lagdameo.	3.00	15.00	80.00
75	**5 Pesos** 1929. Black on yellow unpt. Portr. Wm. McKinley at l., Adm. Dewey at r. Back yellow.	10.00	50.00	325.

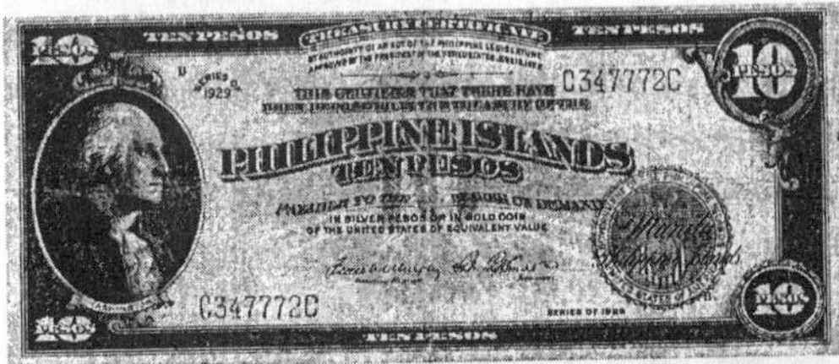

		Good	Fine	XF
76	**10 Pesos** 1929. Black on brown unpt. Portr. G. Washington at l. Back brown.	15.00	60.00	325.

		Good	Fine	XF
77	**20 Pesos** 1929. Black on yellow unpt. Mayon volcano at ctr. Similar to #64 but several minor alterations in plate. Back tan.	20.00	100.	350.
78	**50 Pesos** 1929. Black on pink unpt. Portr. Gen. Lawton at l. Back dk. red.	125.	500.	—

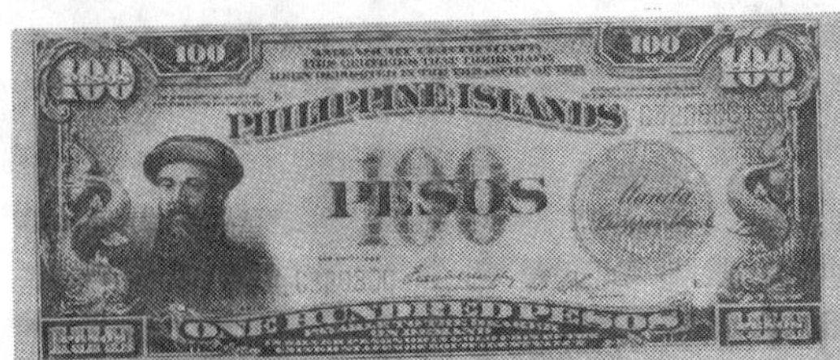

		Good	Fine	XF
79	**100 Pesos** 1929. Black on green unpt. Portr. F. Magellan at l. Back green. Rare.	—	2500.	—

		Good	Fine	XF
80	**500 Pesos** 1929. Black on orange unpt. Portr. Legazpi at l. Back purple. Rare.	—	—	—

Commonwealth

Philippines

1936 Issue

#81-88 new red Commonwealth seal. Sign. Manuel Quezon and Antonio Ramos. Title reads: *PHILIPPINES* instead of *PHILIPPINE ISLANDS*. Printer: USBEP (w/o imprint). Replacement notes: Star prefix.

		VG	VF	UNC
81	**1 Peso** 1936. Similar to #73.	1.50	4.00	25.00

		VG	VF	UNC
82	**2 Pesos** 1936. Similar to #74.	3.00	10.00	55.0
83	**5 Pesos** 1936. Similar to #75.			
	a. Regular issue. Serial # D1D to D3 244 000D.	3.00	10.00	50.0
	b. U.S.A. War Dept. issue (1944). D3 244 001D to D3 544 000D.	50.00	150.	35

		VG	VF	UN
84	**10 Pesos** 1936. Similar to #76.			
	a. Regular issue. Serial # D1D to D2 024 000D.	5.00	50.00	37
	b. U.S.A. War Dept. issue (1944). D2 024 001D to D2 174 000D.	75.00	275.	6C
85	**20 Pesos** 1936. Similar to #77.			
	a. Regular issue. D1D to D1 664 000D.	15.00	60.00	3C
	b. U.S.A. War Dept. issue (1944). D1 664 001D to D1 739 000D.	75.00	350.	15C
86	**50 Pesos** 1936. Similar to #78.	125.	300.	6C
87	**100 Pesos** 1936. Similar to #79.			
	a. Regular issue. Serial # D1D to D41 000D.	200.	500.	
	b. U.S.A. War Dept. issue (1944). D41 001D to D56 000D. Rare.	600.	—	
88	**500 Pesos** 1936. Similar to #80. Rare.	—	—	

Note: #83b, 84b, 85b and 87b were made at the request of Army Headquarters, Brisbane, Australia in 19 for use in military operations.

1941 ISSUE

#89-93 like previous issue. Sign. Manuel Quezon and A.S. de Leon. Printer: USBEP (w/o imprint). Replacement notes: Star prefix.

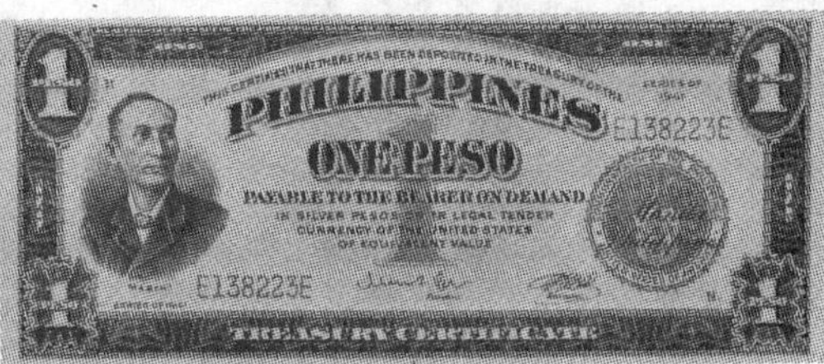

		VG	VF	UNC
89	**1 Peso**			
	1941. Like #81.			
	a. Regular issue. Serial # E1E to E6 000 000E.	1.50	3.50	12.50
	b. Processed to simulate used currency at Bureau of Standards (1943). #E6 008 001E to E6 056 000E; E6 064 001E to E6 072 000E; E6 080 001E to E6 324 000E. Total 300,000 notes.	150.	200.	—
	c. Naval Aviators' Emergency Money Packet notes (1944). E6 324 001E to E6 524 000E.	5.00	15.00	50.00
90	**2 Pesos**			
	1941. Like #82.	4.00	25.00	100.

		VG	VF	UNC
91	**5 Pesos**			
	1941. Like #83.			
	a. Regular issue. Serial #E1E to E1 188 000E.	10.00	35.00	100.
	b. Processed like #89b (1943). #E1 208 001E to E1 328 000E.	350.	—	—
	c. Packet notes like #89c (1944). #E1 328 001E to E1 348 000E.	15.00	75.00	300.

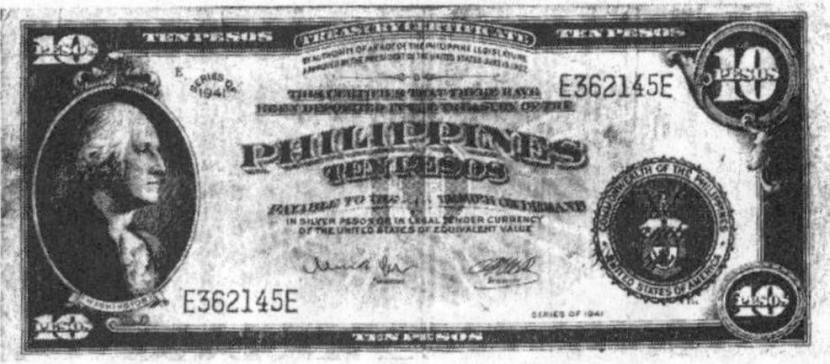

		VG	VF	UNC
92	**10 Pesos**			
	1941. Like #84.			
	a. Regular issue. Serial #E1E to E800 000E.	10.00	75.00	350.
	b. Processed like #89b (1943). E810 001E to E870 000E.	400.	—	—
	c. Packet notes like #89c (1944). #E870 001E to E890 000E.	20.00	85.00	400.
93	**20 Pesos**			
	1941. Like #85.	75.00	325.	—

Note: 50, 100 and 500 Pesos notes Series of 1941 were printed but never shipped because of the outbreak of World War II. All were destroyed in 1949, leaving extant only proof impressions and specimen sheets.

1944 ND VICTORY ISSUE

#94-101 w/text: *VICTORY Series No. 66* twice on face instead of date, blue seal. Black ovpt: *VICTORY* in lg. letters on back. Printer: USBEP (w/o imprint). Replacement notes: Star suffix.

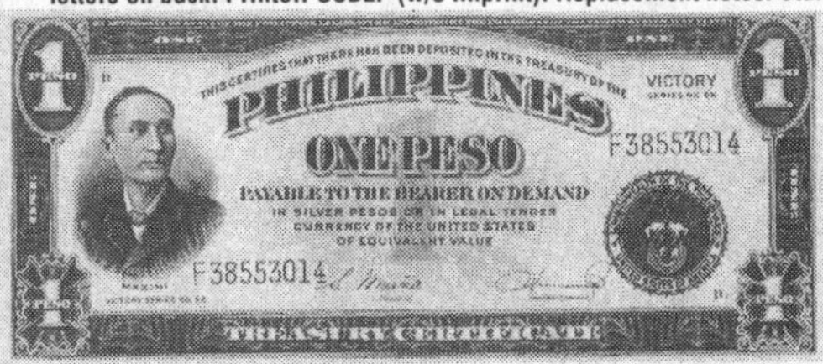

		VG	VF	UNC
94	**1 Peso**			
	ND (1944). Like #89. Sign. Sergio Osmeña and J. Hernandez.	.75	2.00	6.00

		VG	VF	UNC
95	**2 Pesos**			
	ND (1944). Like #90.			
	a. Sign. Sergio Osmeña and J. Hernandez w/title: *Auditor General.*	1.00	3.00	15.00
	b. Sign. Manuel Roxas and M. Guevara w/title: *Treasurer.*	5.00	20.00	75.00
96	**5 Pesos**			
	ND (1944). Like #91. Sign. Sergio Osmeña and J. Hernandez.	2.50	10.00	65.00
97	**10 Pesos**			
	ND (1944). Like #92. Sign. Sergio Osmeña and J. Hernandez.	5.00	20.00	125.

		VG	VF	UNC
98	**20 Pesos**			
	ND (1944). Like #93.			
	a. Sign. Sergio Osmeña and J. Hernandez w/title: *Auditor General.*	5.00	35.00	85.00
	b. Sign. Manuel Roxas and M. Guevara w/title: *Treasurer.*	20.00	75.00	300.

		VG	VF	UNC
99	**50 Pesos**			
	ND (1944). Like #86.			
	a. Sign. Sergio Osmeña and J. Hernandez w/title: *Auditor General.*	30.00	120.	400.
	b. Sign. Manuel Roxas and M. Guevara w/title: *Treasurer.*	30.00	150.	575.

		VG	VF	UNC
101	**500 Pesos**			
	ND (1944). Like #88.			
	a. Sign. Sergio Osmeña and J. Hernandez w/title: *Auditor General.*	500.	1000.	2500.
	b. Sign. Sergio Osmeña and M. Guevara w/title: *Treasurer.*	250.	850.	2000.
	c. Sign. Manuel Roxas and M. Guevara.	350.	900.	2200.

JAPANESE OCCUPATION - WWII

JAPANESE GOVERNMENT

1942 ND ISSUE

Notes w/block letter *P* preceding other letter(s).

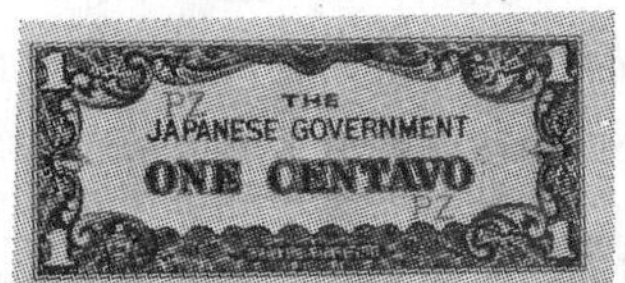

		VG	VF	UNC
102	**1 Centavo**			
	ND (1942). Black on green unpt. Back green.			
	a. 2 block letters.	.10	.20	.50
	b. Fractional block letters.	.10	.20	1.00
	s. As a. Specimen w/red ovpt: *Mi-hon. SPECIMEN* on back.	—	—	100.

		VG	VF	UNC
103	**5 Centavos**			
	ND (1942). Black on blue unpt. Back blue.			
	a. 2 block letters.	.10	.20	.50
	b. Fractional block letters.	.20	.50	2.00
	s. As a. Specimen w/red ovpt: *Mi-hon. SPECIMEN* on back.	—	—	100.

		VG	VF	UNC
104	**10 Centavos**			
	ND (1942). Black on lt. brown unpt. Back brown.			
	a. 2 block letters.	.10	.20	.50
	b. Fractional block letters.	.10	.25	1.00
	s. As a. Specimen w/red ovpt: *Mi-hon. SPECIMEN* on back.	—	—	100.

		VG	VF	UNC
105	**50 Centavos**			
	ND (1942). Black on lt. purple unpt. Plantation at r. Back purple.			
	a. Buff colored paper.	.10	.25	1.00
	b. White paper.	.10	.20	.75
	s. Specimen w/red ovpt: *Mi-hon. SPECIMEN* on back.	—	—	100.

		VG	VF	UNC
106	**1 Peso**			
	ND (1942). Black on lt. green unpt. Plantation at l. Back green.			
	a. Buff to lt. brown paper.	.50	2.00	4.25
	b. White paper.	.25	1.00	3.25
	s. Specimen w/red ovpt: *Mi-hon. SPECIMEN* on back.	—	—	100.

		VG	VF	UNC
107	**5 Pesos**			
	ND (1942). Black on lt. blue unpt. Plantation at ctr. Back orange.			
	a. Buff to lt. brown paper.	.50	1.25	3.25
	b. White paper.	.25	.75	2.75
	s. Specimen w/red ovpt: *Mi-hon. SPECIMEN* on back.	—	—	100.
107A	**5 Pesos**			
	ND (1942). Black on lt. orange unpt. Like #107b. Back gold-yellow.	.75	1.75	5.00

		VG	VF	UNC
108	**10 Pesos**			
	ND (1942). Black on blue unpt. Plantation at r. Back brown.			
	a. Buff paper.	.25	.75	1.75
	b. White paper.	.10	.25	1.00
	s. Specimen w/red ovpt: *Mi-hon. SPECIMEN* on back.	—	—	100

1943 ND Issue

#109-112 engraved face plates w/Rizal Monument at l. or r. Wmk: Banana tree.

		VG	VF	UN
109	**1 Peso**			
	ND (1943). Black on lt. green and pink unpt. Monument at l. Back blue on pink unpt.			
	a. Serial # and block #. (#1-81).	.20	.50	1.2
	b. Block # only (82-87).	1.00	2.50	7.0
	s. As a. Specimen w/red ovpt: *Mi-hon. SPECIMEN* on back.	—	—	15

		VG	VF	UN
110	**5 Pesos**			
	ND (1943). Black on green and yellow unpt. Monument at l. Back brown on gray unpt.			
	a. Issued note.	.25	.75	2.
	s. Specimen w/ovpt: *Mi-hon.*	—	—	15

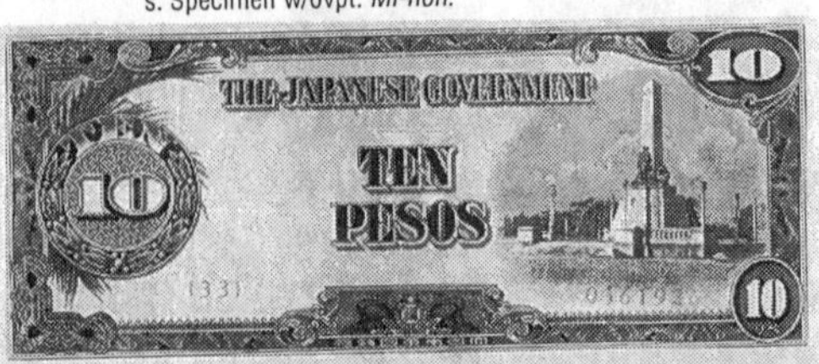

		VG	VF	UNC
111	**10 Pesos** ND (1943). Black on green unpt. Monument at r. Back green on yellow unpt.			
	a. Issued note.	.25	.75	2.00
	s. Specimen w/red ovpt: *Mi-hon.*	—	—	150.

		VG	VF	UNC
112	**100 Pesos** ND (1944). Black on lt. blue and tan unpt. Monument at r. Back purple on green unpt.			
	a. Issued note.	.25	.75	2.00
	s. Specimen w/red ovpt: *Mi-hon.*	—	—	250.

1944-45 ND Inflation Issue

		VG	VF	UNC
113	**100 Pesos** ND (1945). Black on brown on lt. green unpt. Back yellow-brown. W/o wmk. Similar to #115. Block letters PV. Rare.	—	—	—

		VG	VF	UNC
114	**500 Pesos** ND (1944). Black on purple unpt. Rizal Monument at r. Back brown. Lithographed.			
	a. Wmk: Banana tree. Buff paper. Block letters PF.	.50	1.25	5.00
	b. Wmk: Quatrefoil kiri flower. Most on white paper. Block letters PG.	.50	1.00	4.25
	s1. Specimen w/red ovpt: *Mi-hon. SPECIMEN* on back.	—	—	250.
	s2. Specimen w/ovpt: *Mi-hon.*	—	—	150.

		VG	VF	UNC
115	**1000 Pesos** ND (1945). Blue-purple. Similar to #113. Back olive. Block letters PU.			
	a. Purple on lilac unpt. (shades). Back dk. olive-green w/o offset.	.50	1.00	6.00
	b. As a., but back lt. olive-green w/o offset.	.50	1.00	5.00
	c. As a., but back w/offset from face plate.	.50	1.00	4.00
	d. As b., but back w/offset from face plate.	.50	1.00	4.00

OVERPRINT VARIETIES:

A. The Filipino organization called JAPWANCAP, Inc., (Japanese War Notes Claimants Association of the Philippines) made a very serious attempt in 1967 to obtain funds from the United States for redemption of millions of pesos in Japanese occupation currency. Notes being held by that group were marked with a number of different stampings. Most are seen on higher denomination notes, but occasionally lower values are found thus marked as well. Such marked notes have no particular value above the unmarked pieces.

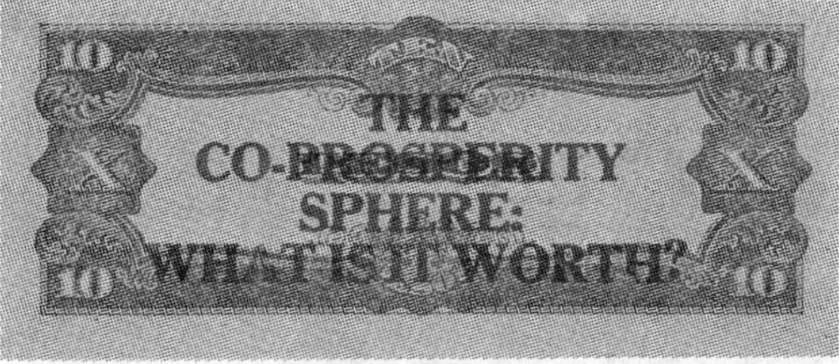

B. Various Japanese occupation notes exist with propaganda ovpt:THE CO-PROSPERITY SPHERE: WHAT IS IT WORTH?

Bangko Sentral Ng Pilipinas

1944 Issue

		VG	VF	UNC
115A	**10 Piso** L.29.2.1944. Brown on brown unpt. J. Rizal at l. (A few made in 1944 as essays; not approved for circulation). Rare.	—	—	—

		VG	VF	UNC
116	**100 Piso** L.29.2.1944. Black on pink unpt. Portr. J. Rizal at l. Back red and orange. (Printed 1944; not issued).			
	r. Remainder w/o block and serial #.	100.	250.	425.
	s1. Specimen w/single red ovpt: *MI-HON.* W/block # and serial #.	—	—	1200.
	s2. As s1. Specimen w/red ovpt: *Specimen* w/serial # all zeros.	—	—	750.
	s3. Red ovpt: *MI-HON* at l. and r. Otherwise as s1.	—	—	1200.

Republic

Central Bank of the Philippines

1949 ND Provisional Issue

#117-124 Treasury Certificates of Victory Series w/red ovpt: *CENTRAL BANK/OF THE PHILIPPINES* on back.

		VG	VF	UNC
117	**1 Peso** ND (1949). Ovpt. on #94.			
	a. Thick lettering in ovpt.	1.00	3.00	17.50
	b. Medium-thick lettering in ovpt.	1.50	4.00	20.00
	c. Thin lettering in ovpt.	1.00	3.00	17.50
118	**2 Pesos** ND (1949). Ovpt. on #95. Thick lettering in ovpt.			
	a. Sign. Sergio Osmeña and J. Hernandez.	—	1000.	—
	b. Sign. Manuel Roxas and M. Guevara.	5.00	20.00	125.
119	**5 Pesos** ND (1949). Ovpt. on #96.			
	a. Thick lettering in ovpt.	3.00	12.00	60.00
	b. Thin lettering in ovpt.	4.00	15.00	75.00

		VG	VF	UNC
120	**10 Pesos** ND (1949). Ovpt. on #97. Thick lettering in ovpt.	7.50	45.00	175.

		VG	VF	UNC
121	**20 Pesos** ND (1949). Ovpt. on #98. Thick lettering in ovpt.			

		VG	VF	UNC
121				
	a. Sign. Sergio Osmeña and J. Hernandez.	25.00	75.00	400.
	b. Sign. Manuel Roxas and M. Guevara.	25.00	75.00	400.
122	**50 Pesos** ND (1949). Ovpt. on #99. Thin lettering in ovpt.			
	a. Sign. Sergio Osmeña and J. Hernandez.	35.00	90.00	450.
	b. Sign. Manuel Roxas and M. Guevara.	35.00	90.00	450.
	c. Sign. Osmeña-Hernandez. Thick lettering in overprint.	40.00	90.00	600.
123	**100 Pesos** ND (1949). Ovpt. on #100. Thick lettering in ovpt.			
	a. Sign. Sergio Osmeña and J. Hernandez.	60.00	175.	475.
	b. Sign. Sergio Osmeña and M. Guevara.	60.00	175.	475.
	c. Sign. Manuel Roxas and M. Guevara.	50.00	125.	375.

		VG	VF	UNC
124	**500 Pesos** ND (1949). Ovpt. on #101. Thick lettering in ovpt.			
	a. Sign. Sergio Osmeña and J. Hernandez.	500.	1500.	3000.
	b. Sign. Sergio Osmeña and M. Guevara.	250.	750.	2100.
	c. Sign. Manuel Roxas and M. Guevara.	250.	750.	2100.

1949 ND "ENGLISH" ISSUES

#125, 127, and 129 sign. 1.

		VG	VF	UNC
125	**5 Centavos** ND (1949). Red on tan unpt. Back red.	.15	.50	1.75

		VG	VF	UNC
126	**5 Centavos** ND. Like #125. Sign. 2. Printer: W&S.			
	a. Issued note.	.10	.25	1.50
	p. Proof.	—	—	250.
127	**10 Centavos** ND. Brownish purple on tan unpt. Back brownish purple.			
	a. Issued note.	.25	.50	2.50
	r. Remainder w/o serial #.	—	100.	250.

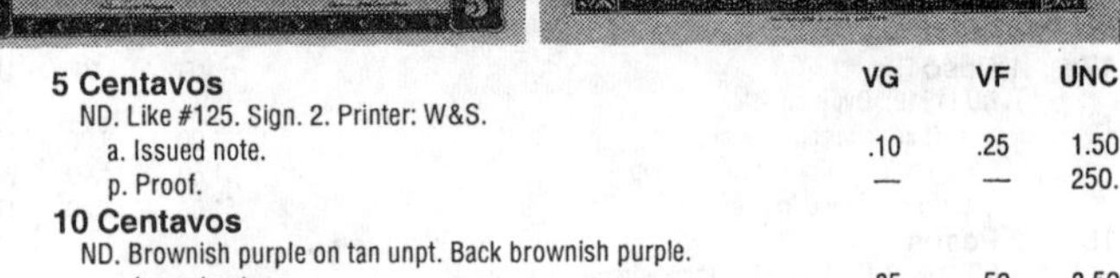

		VG	VF	UNC
128	**10 Centavos** ND. Like #127. Sign. 2. Printer: W&S.	.25	.50	1.25
129	**20 Centavos** ND. Green on lt. green unpt. Back green.			
	a. Issued note.	.25	.75	2.50
	r. Remainder w/o serial #.	—	100.	250.

#130-141 printer: TDLR.

		VG	VF	UNC
130	**20 Centavos** ND. Green on lt. green unpt. Back green.			
	a. Sign. 2.	.20	.50	2.00
	b. Sign. 3.	.20	.50	2.00

		VG	VF	UNC
131	**50 Centavos** ND. Blue on lt. blue unpt. Back blue. Sign. 2.			
	a. Issued note.	.20	.50	2.00
	p. Proof.	—	—	250.

#132-141 large Central Bank Seal Type 1 bank seal at lower r.

		VG	VF	UNC
132	**1/2 Peso** ND. Green on yellow and blue unpt. Ox-cart w/Mt. Mayon in background at ctr. Back green. Sign. 2.	.25	1.00	3.50

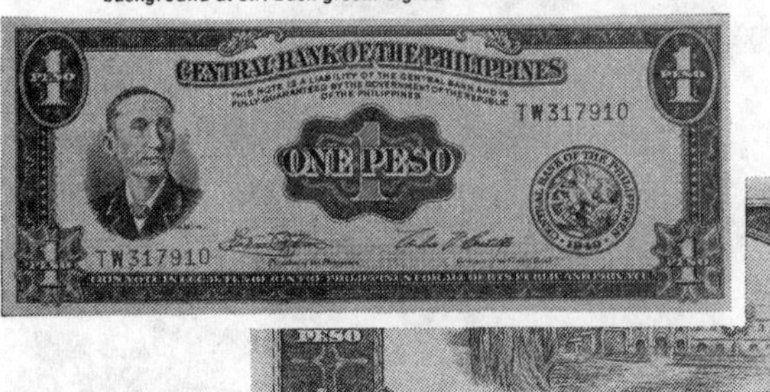

		VG	VF	UNC
133	**1 Peso** ND. Black on lt. gold and blue unpt. Portr. A. Mabini at l. Back black; Barasoain Church at ctr.			
	a. Sign. 1. *GENUINE* in very lt. tan letters just beneath top heading on face.	7.50	25.00	110.
	b. Sign. 1. W/o *GENUINE* on face.	.50	2.00	10.00
	c. Sign. 2.	.75	2.50	15.00
	d. Sign. 3.	.25	2.00	12.50
	e. Sign. 4.	.50	1.25	8.00
	f. Sign. 5.	.25	1.00	5.00
	g. Sign. 6.	.10	.50	2.50
	h. Sign. 7.	.10	1.00	3.00
	s1. Sign. as a. Specimen.	—	—	200.
	s2. Sign. as b. Specimen. (De La Rue).	—	—	200.
	s3. Sign. as c. Specimen. (De La Rue).	—	—	200.
	s4. Sign. as d. Specimen. (De La Rue).	—	—	200.
	s5. Sign. as e. Specimen. (De La Rue).	—	—	200.
	s6. Sign. as f. Specimen.	—	—	45.00
	s7. Sign. as f. Specimen. (De La Rue).	—	—	250.
	s8. Sign. as g. Specimen.	—	—	50.00
	s9. Sign. as g. Specimen. (De La Rue).	—	—	250.
	10. Sign. as h. Specimen.	—	—	30.00
	11. Sign. as h. Specimen. (De La Rue).	—	—	250.

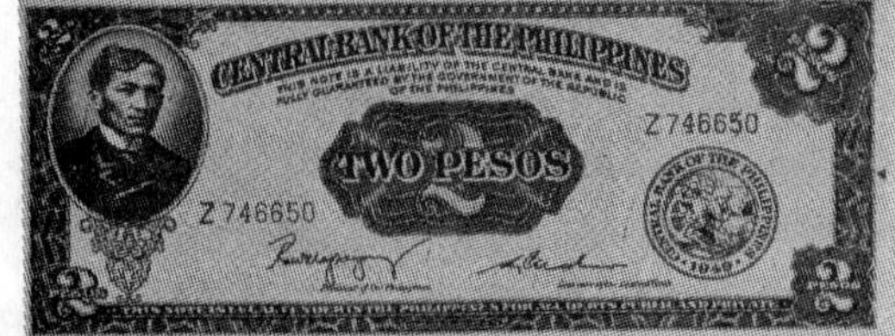

134 2 Pesos

ND. Black on blue and gold unpt. Portr. J. Rizal at l. Back blue; landing of Magellan in the Philippines.

	VG	VF	UNC
a. Sign. 1.	1.50	7.50	15.00
b. Sign. 2.	.75	2.00	5.00
c. Sign. 4.	1.00	2.50	10.00
d. Sign. 5.	.15	.50	2.00
p. Sign. as b. Proof.	—	—	125.
s1. Sign. as a. Specimen. (De La Rue) Cancelled.	—	—	250.
s2. Sign. as b. Specimen.	—	—	60.00
s3. Sign. as b. Specimen. (De La Rue).	—	—	250.
s4. Sign. as c. Specimen. (De La Rue).			250.
s5. Sign. as d. Specimen.	—	—	60.00

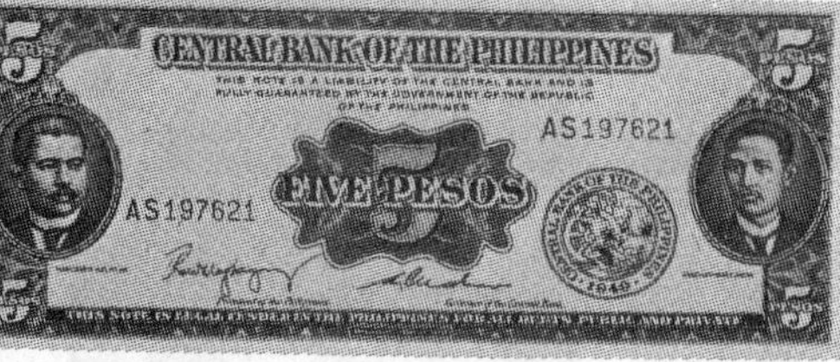

35 5 Pesos

ND. Black on yellow and gold unpt. Portr. M. H. del Pilar at l., Lopez Jaena at r. Back gold; newspaper "La Solidaridad".

	VG	VF	UNC
a. Sign. 1.	1.50	7.50	40.00
b. Sign. 2.	.75	3.50	12.50
c. Sign. 3.	.75	5.00	17.50
d. Sign. 4.	.75	3.00	10.00
e. Sign. 5.	.20	.50	3.00
f. Sign. 8.	.20	.50	2.00
p. Proof.	—	—	150.
s1. Sign. as a. Specimen. (De La Rue).	—	—	250.
s2. Sign. as b. Specimen. (De La Rue).	—	—	250.
s3. Sign. as d. Specimen. (De La Rue).	—	—	250.
s4. Sign. as e. Specimen.	—	—	65.00
s5. Sign. as e. Specimen. (De La Rue).	—	—	200.
s6. Sign. as f. Specimen.	—	—	65.00

6 10 Pesos

ND. Black on tan and lt. red unpt. Fathers Burgos, Gomez and Zamora at l. Back brown; monument.

	VG	VF	UNC
a. Sign. 1.	75.00	200.	500.
b. Sign. 2.	2.50	5.00	25.00
c. Sign. 3.	2.50	5.00	25.00
d. Sign. 4.	2.50	5.00	30.00
e. Sign. 5.	.25	.50	2.00
f. Sign. 8.	1.00	2.00	5.00
s1. Sign. as b. Specimen.	—	—	70.00
s2. Sign. as c. Specimen.	—	—	70.00
s3. Sign. as c. Specimen. (De La Rue).	—	—	250.
s4. Sign. as d. Specimen	—	—	75.00
s5. Sign. as d. Specimen. (De La Rue).	—	—	250.
s6. Sign. as e. Specimen. (De La Rue).	—	—	200.
s7. Sign. as f. Specimen.	—	—	70.00

137 20 Pesos

ND. Black on yellow unpt. Portr. A. Bonifacio at l., E. Jacinto at r. Back brownish orange; flag and monument.

	VG	VF	UNC
a. Sign. 1.	10.00	75.00	200.
b. Sign. 2.	3.00	20.00	50.00
c. Sign. 4.	3.00	10.00	20.00
d. Sign. 5.	.50	1.50	2.25
e. Sign. 8.	.25	1.00	2.50
p. Sign. as d. Proof.	—	—	150.
s1. Sign. as a. Specimen.	—	—	175.
s2. Sign. as c. Specimen. (De La Rue).	—	—	200.
s3. Sign. as d. Specimen.	—	—	125.
s4. Sign. as d. Specimen (De La Rue).	—	—	175.
s5. Sign. as e. Specimen.	—	—	70.00

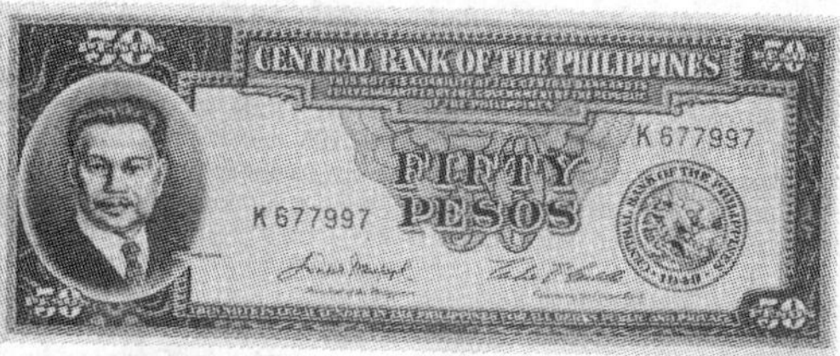

138 50 Pesos

ND. Black on pink and lt. tan unpt. Portr. A. Luna at l. Back red; scene of blood compact of Sikatuna and Legaspi.

	VG	VF	UNC
a. Sign. 1.	125.	500.	—
b. Sign. 2.	15.00	50.00	125.
c. Sign. 3.	5.00	15.00	40.00
d. Sign. 5.	.25	1.00	2.50
p. Sign. as d. Proof.	—	—	175.
s1. Sign. as a. Specimen. (De La Rue).	—	—	500.
s2. Sign. as b. Specimen. (De La Rue).	—	—	300.
s3. Sign. as d. Specimen.	—	—	75.00
s4. Sign. as d. Specimen. (De La Rue).	—	—	500.

139 100 Pesos

ND. Black on gold unpt. Portr. T. Sora at l. Back yellow; regimental flags. Sign. 1.

	VG	VF	UNC
a. Issued note.	2.00	6.00	15.00
s. Specimen.	—	—	85.00

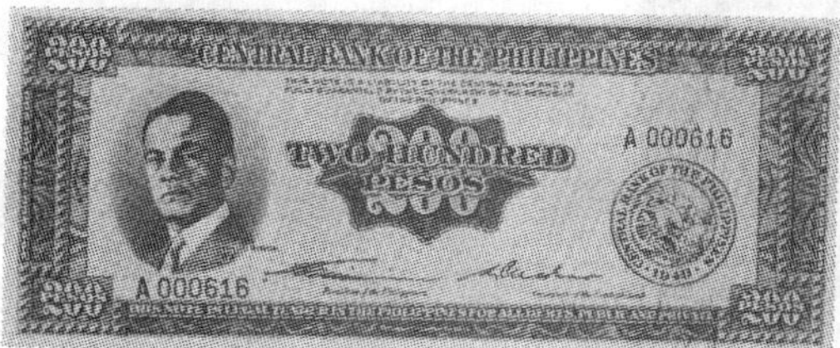

140 200 Pesos

ND. Green on pink and lt. blue unpt. Portr. Pres. Manuel Quezon at l. Back green; Legislative bldg. Sign. 1.

	VG	VF	UNC
a. Issued note.	3.00	7.50	20.00
s. Specimen (De La Rue).	—	—	350.

141 500 Pesos

ND. Black on purple and lt. tan unpt. Portr. Pres. Manuel Roxas at l. Back purple; Central Bank. Sign. 1.

	VG	VF	UNC
a. Issued note.	10.00	25.00	70.00
s. Specimen. (De La Rue).	—	—	300.

The Republic of Poland, formerly the Polish Peoples Republic, located in central Europe, has an area of 120,725 sq. mi. (312,677 sq. km.) and a population of 38.73 million. Capital: Warsaw. The economy is essentially agricultural, but industrial activity provides the products for foreign trade. Machinery, coal, coke, iron, steel and transport equipment are exported.

Poland, which began as a Slavic duchy in the 10th century and reached its peak of power between the 14th and 16th centuries, has had a turbulent history of invasion, occupation or partition by Mongols, Turkey, Hungary, Sweden, Austria, Prussia and Russia.

The first partition took place in 1772. Prussia took Polish Pomerania. Russia took part of the eastern provinces. Austria took Galicia, in which lay the fortress city of Krakow (Cracow). The second partition occurred in 1793 when Russia took another slice of the eastern provinces and Prussia took what remained of western Poland. The third partition, 1795, literally removed Poland from the map. Russia took what was left of the eastern provinces. Prussia seized most of central Poland, including Warsaw. Austria took what was left of the south. Napoleon restored to Poland much of the territory lost to Prussia and Austria, but after his defeat another partition returned the Duchy of Warsaw to Prussia, made Kracow into a tiny republic, and declared what remained to be the Kingdom of Poland under the czar and in permanent union with Russia.

Poland re-emerged as an independent state recognized by the Treaty of Versailles on June 28, 1919, and maintained its independence until 1939 when it was invaded by Germany, then partitioned between Germany and Russia. Poland's present boundaries were determined by the U.S.-British-Russian agreement of Aug. 16, 1945. The Government of National Unity was replaced when the Polish Communist-Socialist faction won a decisive victory at the polls in 1947 and established a "People's Democratic Republic" of the Soviet type. In Dec. 1989, Poland became a republic once again.

RULERS:

Stanislaw Augustus, 1764-1795
Fryderyk August I, King of Saxony, as Grand Duke, 1807-1814
Alexander I, Czar of Russia, as King, 1815-1825
Nikolaj (Mikolay) I, Czar of Russia, as King, 1825-1855

MONETARY SYSTEM:

1 Marka = 100 Fenigow to 1919
1 Zloty = 100 Groszy, 1919-

KINGDOM

BILET SKARBOWY

TREASURY NOTE

1794 FIRST ISSUE

#A1-A11 arms at upper ctr. Issued by Gen. Kosciuszko.

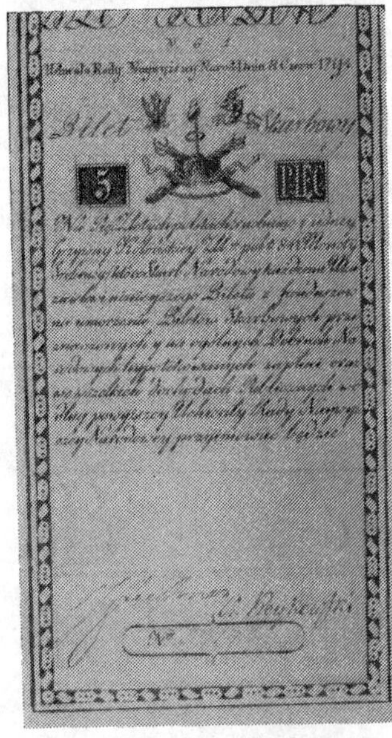

		Good	Fine	XF
A1	**5 Zlotych** 8.6.1794. Black on lt. brown paper.	7.50	20.00	50.00

NOTICE

Readers with unlisted dates, signature varieties, etc. are invited to submit photocopies or, high resolution (300 dpi, 100% size) scans of their notes to: Standard Catalog of World Paper Money, 700 East State St. Iola, WI 54990-0001, or E-Mail: george.cuhaj@fwpubs.com.

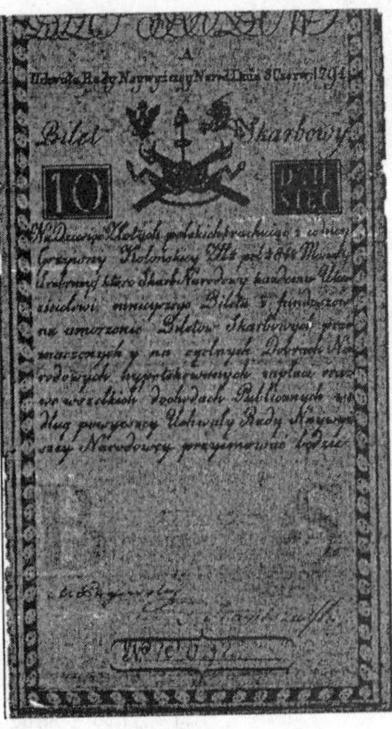
A2

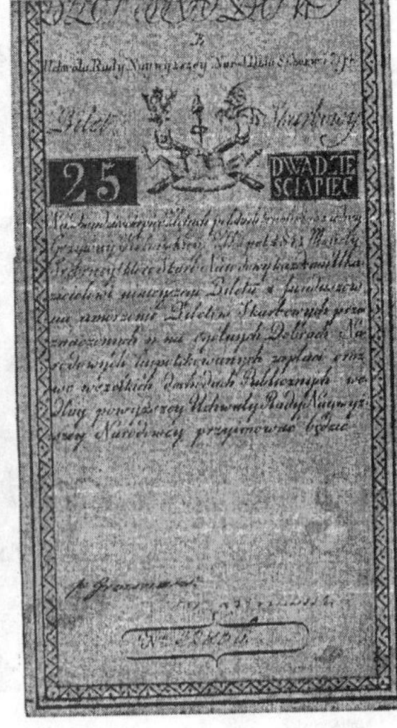
A3

		Good	Fine	XF
A2	**10 Zlotych** 8.6.1794.	12.00	25.00	55.00
A3	**25 Zlotych** 8.6.1794. White paper.	12.00	30.00	65.00
A4	**50 Zlotych** 8.6.1794. Red-brown paper.	25.00	50.00	100
A5	**100 Zlotych** 8.6.1794. Red paper.	25.00	55.00	120
A6	**500 Zlotych** 8.6.1794. Black and red on dk. pink paper.	250.	500.	1000
A7	**1000 Zlotych** 8.6.1794. Rare.	—	—	—

1794 SECOND ISSUE

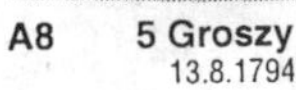

		Good	Fine	XF
A8	**5 Groszy** 13.8.1794.	6.00	15.00	35.0

		Good	Fine	XF
A9	**10 Groszy** 13.8.1794.	6.00	15.00	35.
A10	**1 Zloty** 13.8.1794.	75.00	150.	3

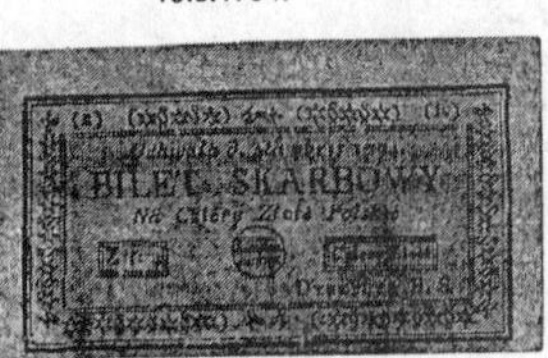

		Good	Fine	XF
A11	**4 Zlote** 4.9.1794.	5.00	10.00	25

#A8-A11 uniface w/name: *F. MALINOWSKI* on back (as illustrated) are modern reproductions.

DUCHY OF WARSAW

KASSOWY-BILLET XIESTWA WARSZAWSKIEGO

1810 STATE TREASURY NOTE

#A12-A14 arms at upper ctr. There are 9 different sign. Also exist as "Formulare" w/red stamps but w/o the printed seal. Market value: $500.00.

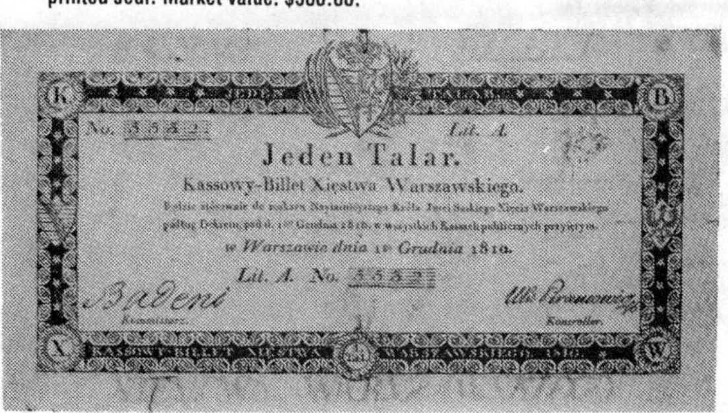

		Good	Fine	XF
A12	1 Talar 1.12.1810. Black.	40.00	100.	275.
A13	2 Talary 1.12.1810. Black.	50.00	125.	325.
A14	5 Talarow 1.12.1810. Black.	75.00	175.	450.

BILLET KASSOWY KROLESTWA POLSKIEGO

1824 ISSUE

		Good	Fine	XF
A15	5 Zlotych 1824.	75.00	175.	350.

		Good	Fine	XF
A16	10 Zlotych 1824.	150.	300.	550.
A17	50 Zlotych 1824.	—	—	—
A18	100 Zlotych 1824.	—	—	—

INSURRECTION OF 1831

ASSYGNACYA SKARBOWA

1831 ISSUE

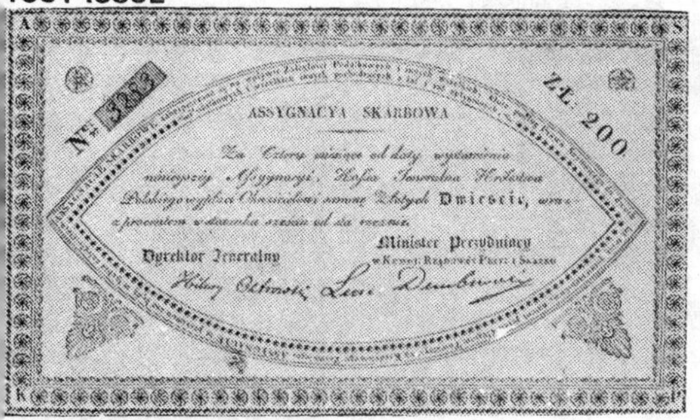

		Good	Fine	XF
A18A	200 Zlotych 1831.	—	—	500.

		Good	Fine	XF
A18B	500 Zlotych 1831. Black and blue. Ornate border w/tridents. Black text on back.	—	—	350.

RUSSIAN ADMINISTRATION

BANK POLSKI

1830 ISSUE

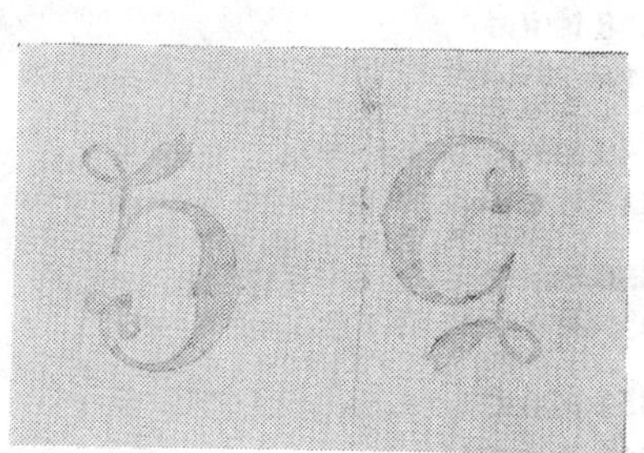

		Good	Fine	XF
A19	5 Zlotych 1.5.1830.	70.00	150.	350.
A20	50 Zlotych 1.5.1830.	200.	400.	850.

		Good	Fine	XF
A21	100 Zlotych 1.5.1830.	150.	325.	550.

1831 ISSUE

		Good	Fine	XF
A22	1 Zloty 1831.	60.00	125.	275.

1841 ISSUE

		Good	Fine	XF
A23	3 Rubel 1841.	80.00	175.	375.

1842 ISSUE

		Good	Fine	XF
A24	3 Rubel 1842.	80.00	175.	375.

1843 ISSUE

		Good	Fine	XF
A25	3 Rubel 1843.	80.00	175.	375.
A25A	10 Rubel 1843.	80.00	175.	375.

1844 ISSUE

		Good	Fine	XF
A26	10 Rubel 1844.	200.	400.	850.
A27	25 Rubel 1844.	275.	550.	1200.

1846 ISSUE

		Good	Fine	XF
A28	3 Rubel 1846.	80.00	175.	375.

1847 ISSUE

		Good	Fine	XF
A29	1 Rubel 1847.	70.00	150.	350.

		Good	Fine	XF
A30	10 Rubel 1847. Crowned imperial eagle at top ctr.	200.	400.	850.

1848 ISSUE

		Good	Fine	XF
A31	25 Rubel 1848.	275.	550.	1200.

1849 ISSUE

		Good	Fine	XF
A32	1 Rubel 1849.	70.00	150.	350.

1850 ISSUE

		Good	Fine	XF
A33	3 Rubel 1850.	80.00	175.	375.

1851 ISSUE

		Good	Fine	XF
A34	1 Rubel 1851.	70.00	150.	350.
A35	3 Rubel 1851.	80.00	175.	375.

1852 ISSUE

		Good	Fine	XF
A36	1 Rubel 1852.	70.00	150.	350.
A37	3 Rubel 1852.	80.00	175.	375.

1853 ISSUE

		Good	Fine	XF
A38	1 Rubel 1853.	70.00	150.	350.
A39	3 Rubel 1853.	80.00	175.	375.

1854 ISSUE

		Good	Fine	XF
A40	1 Rubel 1854.	70.00	150.	350.
A41	3 Rubel 1854.	80.00	175.	375.

1855 ISSUE

		Good	Fine	XF
A42	1 Rubel 1855.	70.00	150.	350.

1856 ISSUE

		Good	Fine	XF
A43	1 Rubel 1856.	70.00	150.	350.

1857 ISSUE

		Good	Fine	XF
A44	1 Rubel 1857.	100.	200.	450.

1858 ISSUE

		Good	Fine	XF
A45	1 Rubel 1858.	70.00	150.	350.
A46	3 Rubel 1858.	80.00	175.	375.

1864 ISSUE

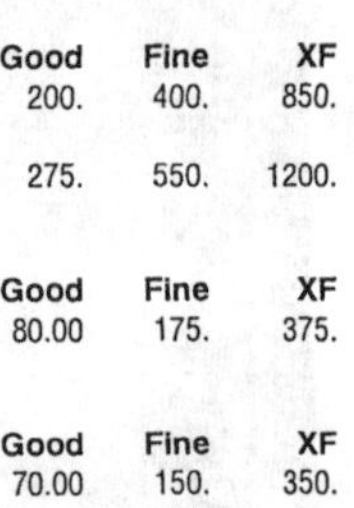

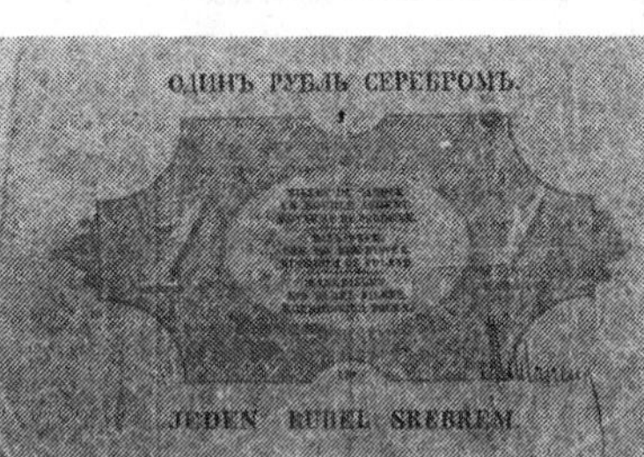

		Good	Fine	XF
A47	1 Rubel 1864. Crowned imperial eagle at ctr.	70.00	150.	350.

1865 ISSUE

		Good	Fine	XF
A48	3 Rubel 1865.	80.00	175.	375.
A49	25 Rubel 1865.	275.	550.	1200.

1866 FIRST ISSUE

		Good	Fine	XF
A50	1 Rubel 1866.	70.00	150.	350.
A51	3 Rubel 1866.	80.00	175.	375.
A52	10 Rubel 1866.	200.	400.	850.

		Good	Fine	XF
A53	25 Rubel 1866. Crowned imperial eagle at upper ctr.	275.	550.	1200.

1866 ND ISSUE

		Good	Fine	XF
A54	1 Rubel ND (1866).	—	—	—

GERMAN OCCUPATION, WW I

POLSKA KRAJOWA KASA POZYCZKOWA

POLISH STATE LOAN BANK

1916-17 FIRST ISSUE

#1-6 face red and black w/text: *Zarzad jeneral-gubernatorstwa.*

		VG	VF	UNC
1	1/2 Marki 1917. Crowned eagle at l. Back blue and olive.	.75	3.00	20.00

		VG	VF	UNC
2	**1 Marka** 1917. Crowned eagle at l. Back blue and red.	1.50	5.00	25.00

		VG	VF	UNC
3	**2 Marki** 1917. Crowned eagle at l. Back orange and green.	1.50	6.00	30.00
3A	**5 Marek** 1917. Back gray-blue and yellow (Not issued). Proof.	—	—	—
3B	**10 Marek** 1917. Back violet-brown and green (Not issued). Proof.	—	—	—

		Good	Fine	XF
4	**20 Marek** 1917. Crowned eagle at ctr. Back purple and lt. brown.	6.00	20.00	60.00

		Good	Fine	XF
5	**50 Marek** 1917. Crowned eagle at ctr. Back green and pink.	5.00	15.00	40.00
6	**100 Marek** 9.12.1916. Crowned eagle at l. Back dk. blue and orange.			
	a. 6-digit serial #.	6.00	20.00	60.00
	b. 7-digit serial #.	6.00	20.00	60.00

1916-17 Second Issue

#7-16 w/text: *Zarzad General-Gubernatorstwa.*

		VG	VF	UNC
7	**1/2 Marki** 1917. Like #1. Back blue and olive.	1.00	3.00	15.00
8	**1 Marka** 1917. Like #2. Back blue and red.	1.00	3.00	20.00

		Good	Fine	XF
9	**2 Marki** 1917. Like #3. Back orange and green.	1.00	5.00	22.50

#10-14 crowned eagle at ctr.

		Good	Fine	XF
10	**5 Marek** 1917. Red and black on green unpt. Text at l.: *...biletow Polskiej Krajowej...* Back gray-blue on yellow unpt.	2.00	8.00	30.00
11	**5 Marek** 1917. Like #10 but text at l.: *...Biletow Kasy Pozyczkowej...*	2.00	8.50	35.00

		Good	Fine	XF
12	**10 Marek** 1917. Red and black. Text at l.: *...biletow Polskiej Krajowej...* Back violet-brown on green unpt.	2.00	8.50	35.00
13	**10 Marek** 1917. Like #12 but text at l.: *...Biletow Kasy Pozyczkowej...*	15.00	45.00	120.

		Good	Fine	XF
14	**20 Marek** 1917. Like #4. Back purple and lt. brown.	8.00	20.00	60.00

		Good	Fine	XF
15	**100 Marek** 9.12.1916. Like #6. Blue and red. Facing busts of Minerva at l. and r. on back.	3.00	12.50	30.00

		Good	Fine	XF
16	**1000 Marek** 1917. Brown and red. Face like #15. Busts of Roman soldier at l. man at r. on back.	10.00	45.00	125.

REPUBLIC

POLSKA KRAJOWA KASA POZYCZKOWA

POLISH STATE LOAN BANK

1919 FIRST ISSUE

		VG	VF	UNC
17	**100 Marek** 15.2.1919. Green and gray-violet. Portr. T. Kosciuszko at l.			
	a. Wmk: Honeycombs. Brownish paper w/engraver's name at lower l. and r.	1.00	3.00	12.50
	b. Wmk: Honeycombs. Brownish paper w/o engraver's name.	1.50	5.00	15.00
	c. Indistinct wmk: (Polish eagle). White paper.	2.00	7.00	17.50

		VG	VF	UNC
18	**500 Marek** 15.1.1919. Green and red. Crowned eagle at l. Back dk. and lt. green.	12.50	50.00	250.

1919 SECOND ISSUE

		VG	VF	UNC
19	**1 Marka** 17.5.1919. Gray-violet and violet. Eagle at ctr. on back. 3 serial # varieties.	.50	3.00	10.00

		VG	VF	UNC
20	**5 Marek** 17.5.1919. Dk. green on tan paper. Small eagle at upper ctr. B. Glowacki (Pres.) at r. on back.			
	a. Engraver's name at lower l. and r. on back.	.75	3.00	12.50
	b. W/o engravers' names. 2 serial # varieties.	.75	3.00	12.50

		VG	VF	UNC
21	**20 Marek** 17.5.1919. Brown on tan paper. Crowned eagle at ctr. Back brown and green; Kosciuszko at ctr. 3 serial # varieties.	2.00	7.00	25.00

		VG	VF	UNC
22	**1000 Marek** 17.5.1919. Green and brown. Kosciuszko at l. Back brown; crowned eagle at l. ctr.			
	a. Wmk: Honeycombs. Brownish paper w/engraver's name at lower l. and r. on back. 2 serial # varieties.	1.00	3.00	10.00
	b. Wmk: Honeycombs. Brownish paper w/o engraver's name.	2.00	5.00	15.00
	c. Indistinct wmk: (crowned eagle). White paper w/engraver's name at lower l. and r. on back.	1.00	3.00	10.00
	d. Indistinct wmk: (crowned eagle). White paper w/o engravers' names. 2 serial # varieties.	1.00	3.00	10.00

1919 Third Issue

#23-31 crowned eagle on back.

		VG	VF	UNC
23	**1 Marka** 23.8.1919. Red on brown unpt. Arms at l., woman at r. 2 serial # varieties.	.25	.60	2.50

		VG	VF	UNC
24	**5 Marek** 23.8.1919. Green on brown unpt. Arms at l., portr. T. Kosciuszko at r. 2 serial # varieties.	.25	.50	2.50
25	**10 Marek** 23.8.1919. Blue-green on brown unpt. Similar to #24. 2 serial # varieties.	.25	.75	3.50

		VG	VF	UNC
26	**20 Marek** 23.8.1919. Red on brown unpt. Portr. woman at r. 2 serial # varieties.	.50	1.00	3.50

		VG	VF	UNC
27	**100 Marek** 23.8.1919. Blue on brown unpt. Portr. T. Kosciuszko at r. 2 serial # varieties.	.75	1.50	4.50
28	**500 Marek** 23.8.1919. Green on brown unpt. Portr. woman at r. 3 serial # varieties.	.75	3.00	10.00

		VG	VF	UNC
29	**1000 Marek** 23.8.1919. Purple on brown unpt. Portr. T. Kosciuszko at r. 6 serial # varieties.	.25	.75	6.00

1920 Issue

No.	Denomination	VG	VF	UNC
30	**1/2 Marki** 7.2.1920. Green on brown unpt. Portr. T. Kosciuszko at r.	.25	1.00	3.00
31	**5000 Marek** 7.2.1920. Blue on brown unpt. Portr. woman at l., Kosciuszko at r. 4 serial # varieties.	.75	3.00	20.00

1922-23 Inflation Issues

		Good	Fine	XF
32	**10,000 Marek** 11.3.1922. Greenish black on lt. tan unpt. Woman's head at l. and r. Eagle at ctr. on back.	2.00	7.50	25.00

		Good	Fine	XF
33	**50,000 Marek** 10.10.1922. Brown on lt. tan and blue unpt. Eagle at l. on back.	1.50	5.00	17.50
34	**100,000 Marek** 30.8.1923. Brown. Back blue-gray; eagle at ctr.	4.00	12.50	45.00

Note: For #34 there exists two error dates: 25.4.1922 and 25.4.1523.

		Good	Fine	XF
35	**250,000 Marek** 25.4.1923. Gray-brown on lt. bluish unpt. Eagle at ctr. on back. 2 serial # varieties.	3.00	12.50	50.00

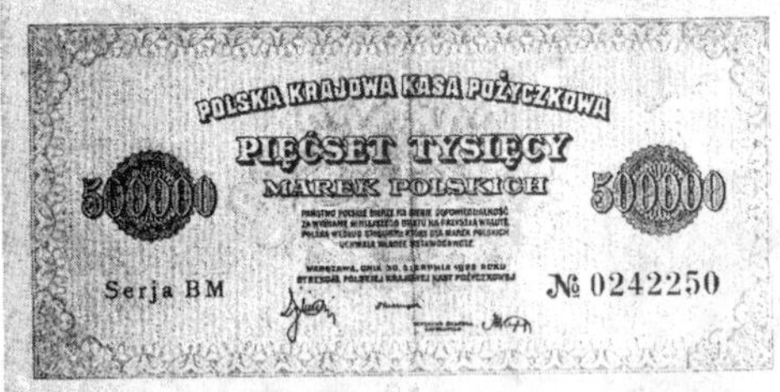

		Good	Fine	XF
36	**500,000 Marek** 30.8.1923. Gray on lt. green unpt. Eagle at ctr. on back. 5 serial # varieties.	3.00	10.00	40.00
37	**1,000,000 Marek** 30.8.1923. Olive-brown on lt. blue unpt. Town view at l. Back green; eagle at ctr. 2 serial # varieties.	5.00	20.00	75.00
38	**5,000,000 Marek** 20.11.1923. Brown on pink and blue unpt. Eagle at upper ctr. Back blue-gray; eagle at l.	10.00	50.00	150.

		Good	Fine	XF
39	**10,000,000 Marek** 20.11.1923. Green and blue on lt. tan and green unpt. Town view w/2 towers at l., crowned eagle at r. Back brown; eagle at upper l. 2 serial # varieties.	20.00	100.	225.
40	**50,000,000 Marek** 20.11.1923. Black on blue unpt. Uniface.	50.00	225.	500.

		Good	Fine	XF
41	**100,000,000 Marek** 20.11.1923. Black on pink unpt. Uniface.	75.00	250.	550.

MINISTERSTWO SKARBU

MINISTRY OF FINANCE

1924 PROVISIONAL BILET ZDAWKOWY ISSUE

		VG	VF	UNC
42	**1 Grosz** 28.4.1924. Red ovpt. w/new denomination and coin on bisected note #36.			
	a. L. half.	3.00	10.00	35.00
	b. R. half.	3.00	10.00	35.00

		VG	VF	UNC
43	**5 Groszy** 28.4.1924. Red ovpt. w/new denomination and coin on bisected note #39.			
	a. L. half.	10.00	35.00	85.00
	b. R. half.	10.00	35.00	85.00

1924-25 BILET ZDAWKOWY ISSUE

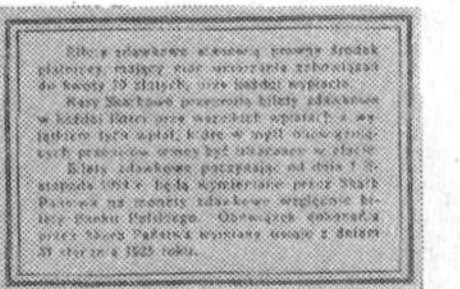

		VG	VF	UNC
44	**10 Groszy** 28.4.1924. Blue. Bldg. w/column at ctr., coin at l. and r.	1.50	7.50	30.00

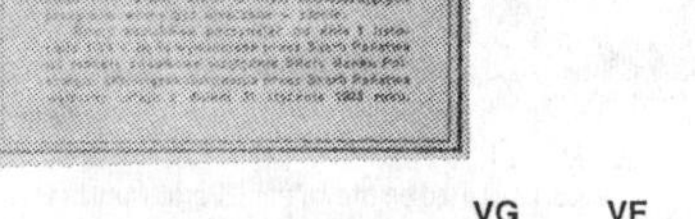

		VG	VF	UNC
45	**20 Groszy** 28.4.1924. Brown. Copernicus monument at ctr., coin at l. and r.	2.00	10.00	40.00

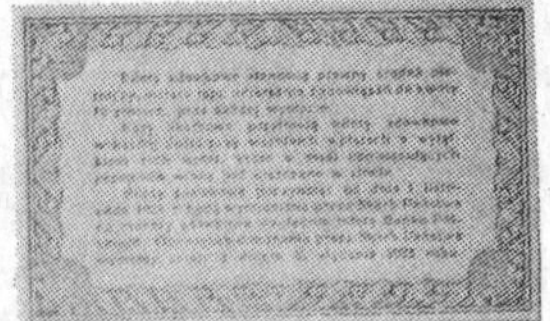

		VG	VF	UNC
46	**50 Groszy** 28.4.1924. Red. Equestrian statue of J. Poniatowski at ctr., coin at lower l. and r.	3.00	20.00	60.00

		VG	VF	UNC
47	**2 Zlote** 1.5.1925. Gray-violet on gray-green. Obverse and reverse of 2 Zlote coin.			
	a. Back right side up.	30.00	75.00	175.
	b. Misprint: back inverted.	—	—	—
48	**5 Zlotych** 1.5.1925. Green and brown. Obv. of coin at l.	40.00	150.	350.

1926 Bilet Panstwowy Issue

		VG	VF	UNC
49	**5 Zlotych** 25.10.1926. Dk. olive and brown. Woman at ctr. Worker on back.	30.00	75.00	175.

1938 Bilet Panstwowy Issue

		VG	VF	UNC
50	**1 Zloty** 1.10.1938. Gray on yellow-brown unpt. Portr. man w/crown at r.	10.00	35.00	95.00

Bank Polski

1919 (1924) Dated Issue

#51-56 2 sign. w/o titles.

		Good	Fine	XF
51	**1 Zloty** 28.2.1919 (1924). Purple on lilac unpt. Portr. T. Kosciuszko at l. Eagle at r. on back.	5.00	20.00	60.00
52	**2 Zlote** 28.2.1919 (1924). Lt. and dk. blue on lt. brown unpt. Portr. T. Kosciuszko at l.	17.50	50.00	130.

		Good	Fine	XF
53	**5 Zlotych** 28.2.1919 (1924). Brown. Portr. Prince J. Poniatowski at r. Eagle at l. on back.	25.00	75.00	200.

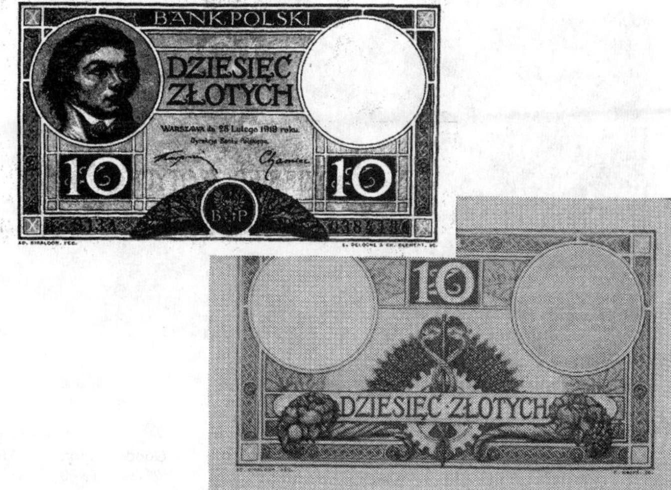

		Good	Fine	XF
54	**10 Zlotych** 28.2.1919 (1924). Purple and brown. Portr. T. Kosciuszko at upper l. and as wmk.	35.00	100.	225.
55	**20 Zlotych** 28.2.1919 (1924). M/c. Portr. Kosciuszko at l.	50.00	150.	275.
56	**50 Zlotych** 28.2.1919 (1924). Violet-brown and violet. Kosciuszko at l. Eagle at ctr. r. on back.	150.	375.	650.

#57-59 printer: W&S.

		Good	Fine	XF
57	**100 Zlotych** 28.2.1919 (1924). Blue and brown. Kosciuszko at l.	12.00	35.00	80.00

		Good	Fine	XF
58	**500 Zlotych** 28.2.1919 (1924). Purple and green. Kosciuszko at l.	2.50	7.50	20.00

		Good	Fine	XF
59	**1000 Zlotych** 28.2.1919 (1924). Brown. Kosciuszko at l.			
	a. Issued note.	100.	225.	500.
	s. Specimen.	—	—	225.

60	**5000 Zlotych** 28.2.1919 (1924). Green. Portr. T. Kosciuszko at lower l. Specimen.	—	Unc	300.

1924 ISSUE

		Good	Fine	XF
61	**5 Zlotych** 15.7.1924. Brown. Like #53.	20.00	65.00	175.
62	**10 Zlotych** 15.7.1924. Purple. Like #54.			
	a. White paper.	35.00	100.	225.
	b. Gray paper.	35.00	100.	225.

		Good	Fine	XF
63	**20 Zlotych** 15.7.1924. M/c. Like #55.			
	a. White paper.	55.00	175.	400.
	b. Gray paper.	55.00	175.	400.
64	**50 Zlotych** 28.8.1925. Green, brown and blue. Farmer's wife at l., Mercury at r. 2 bldgs. on back.	20.00	65.00	175.

1926 ISSUE

		Good	Fine	XF
65	**10 Zlotych** 20.7.1926. Brown, olive and blue. Allegorical woman at l. and r. Three standing figures on back.			
	a. Wmk: Kg. w/numbers.	25.00	75.00	200.
	b. Wmk: Kg. w/dates.	15.00	40.00	85.00
66	**20 Zlotych** 1.3.1926. Blue and olive. Like #64.	50.00	150.	300.

1928 ISSUE

#67-68 printer: Orell Füssli, Zurich (w/o imprint).

		VG	VF	UNC
67	**10 Zlotych** 2.1.1928. Dk. blue. Portr. youth at upper r.	—	500.	800.
68	**20 Zlotych** 2.1.1928. Dk. purple. Woman at r. Specimen only.	—	450.	650.

1929 ISSUE

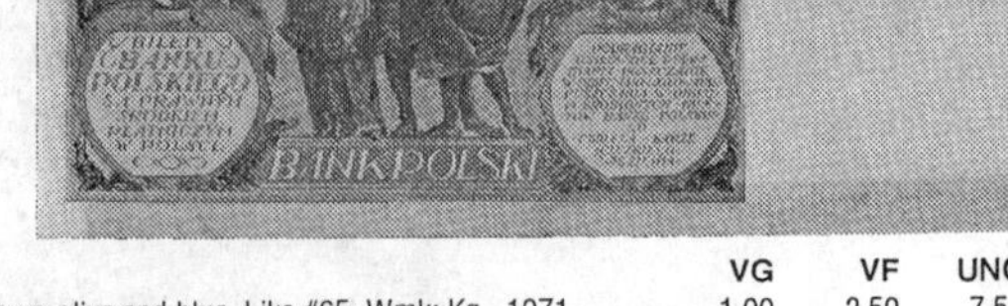

		VG	VF	UNC
69	**10 Zlotych** 20.7.1929. Brown-olive and blue. Like #65. Wmk: Kg., 10Z1.	1.00	2.50	7.50
70	**20 Zlotych** 1.9.1929. Blue and olive. Like #66.	40.00	120.	300.

		VG	VF	UNC
71	**50 Zlotych** 1.9.1929. Green, brown and blue. Like #64. Wmk: Man's head.	.50	2.00	5.00

1930-32 ISSUE

		VG	VF	UNC
72	**5 Zlotych** 2.1.1930. Blue on gray unpt. E. Plater at r. Crowned eagle at upper l. ctr. on back. Wmk: Head.	.50	2.00	5.00

		VG	VF	UNC
73	**20 Zlotych** 20.6.1931. Blue on brown and tan unpt. Portr. E. Plater at upper r. Back brown and blue; farm woman and 2 children at l. ctr. Wmk: Kg.	.50	2.00	5.00

		VG	VF	UNC
74	**100 Zlotych** 2.6.1932. Brown on gold unpt. Portr. Prince J. Poniatowski at r. Back brown, orange and m/c. Allegorical figures at l. and r., lg. tree at l. ctr.			
	a. Wmk: Qn. Jadwigi/100 Zt.	1.00	2.50	6.00
	b. Wmk: Qn. Jadwigi/100Zt, +X+.	1.00	2.50	6.00

1934 ISSUE

		VG	VF	UNC
75	**100 Zlotych** 9.11.1934. Brown. Like #74. Wmk. like #74a or b.	1.00	2.50	6.00

1936 ISSUE

		VG	VF	UNC
76	**2 Zlote** 26.2.1936. Grayish brown on yellow and lt. blue unpt. Portr. girl in Dabrowki national costume at r. Eagle at ctr. on back.			
	a. Issued note.	.50	2.00	6.00
	r. Remainder w/o serial #.	—	Unc	10.00

		VG	VF	UNC
77	**20 Zlotych** 11.11.1936. Blue on lt. peach unpt. Statue of woman w/2 children at l., E. Plater at upper r. Standing figures at l. and r., church at ctr. on back. Wmk: Girl's head.	.50	2.00	5.00
78	**50 Zlotych** 11.11.1936. Green. Standing woman at l. ctr., man at upper r. and as wmk., eagle at lower r. 5 allegorical figures on back.			
	a. Issued note.	200.	500.	1000.
	b. Back only.	20.00	50.00	125.

GOVERNMENT-IN-EXILE, WW II

BANK POLSKI

1939 FIRST ISSUE

#79-88 printed in England and the United States.

#79-81 printer: BWC.

		VG	VF	UNC
79	**1 Zloty** 15.8.1939. Purple. (Not issued).			
	r. Remainder.	—	—	275.
	s. Specimen.	—	—	150.

		VG	VF	UNC
80	**2 Zlote** 15.8.1939. Green. (Not issued).			
	r. Remainder.	—	—	275.
	s. Specimen.	—	—	150.

		VG	VF	UNC
81	**5 Zlotych** 15.8.1939. Blue. Portr. girl wearing national costume at r. (Not issued).			
	r. Remainder.	—	—	300.
	s. Specimen.	—	—	150.

#82-86 printer: TDLR.

		VG	VF	UNC
82	**10 Zlotych** 15.8.1939. Red-orange. Young woman wearing head scarf at r. (Not issued).			
	r. Remainder.	—	—	275.
	s. Specimen.	—	—	150.

		VG	VF	UNC
83	**20 Zlotych** 15.8.1939. Blue. Old woman wearing head scarf at r. (Not issued).			
	r. Remainder.	—	—	275.
	s. Specimen.	—	—	150.

		VG	VF	UNC
84	**50 Zlotych** 15.8.1939. Green. Man wearing national costume at r. (Not issued).			
	r. Remainder.	—	—	275.
	s. Specimen.	—	—	150.

		VG	VF	UNC
85	**100 Zlotych** 15.8.1939. Brown. Man w/mustache at r. (Not issued).			
	r. Remainder.	—	—	275.
	s. Specimen.	—	—	150.

		VG	VF	UNC
86	**500 Zlotych** 15.8.1939. Purple. Sailor w/pipe at r. (Not issued).			
	r. Remainder.	—	—	275.
	s. Specimen.	—	—	150.

1939 Second Issue

#87 and 88 printer: ABNC.

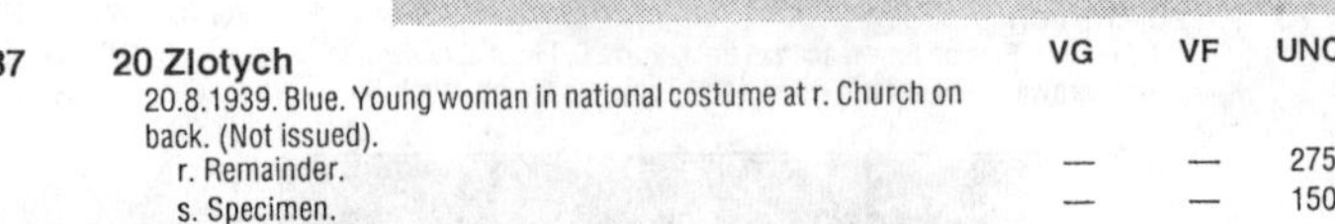

		VG	VF	UNC
87	**20 Zlotych** 20.8.1939. Blue. Young woman in national costume at r. Church on back. (Not issued).			
	r. Remainder.	—	—	275.
	s. Specimen.	—	—	150.

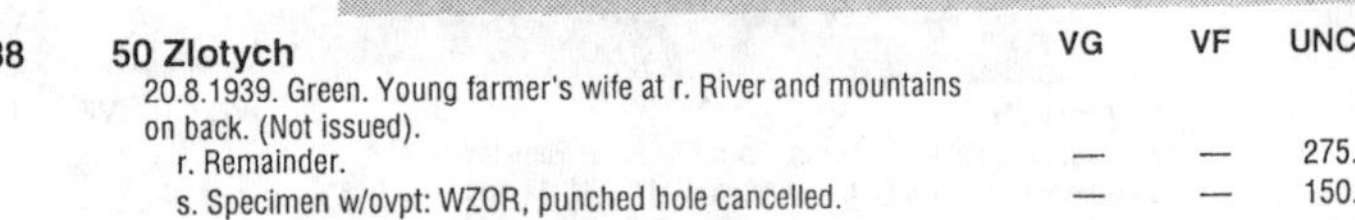

		VG	VF	UNC
88	**50 Zlotych** 20.8.1939. Green. Young farmer's wife at r. River and mountains on back. (Not issued).			
	r. Remainder.	—	—	275.
	s. Specimen w/ovpt: WZOR, punched hole cancelled.	—	—	150.

German Occupation, WW II

Generalgouvernement

1939 Provisional Issue

#89 and 90 ovpt: *Generalgouvernement für die besetzten polnischen Gebiete.*

		VG	VF	UNC
89	**100 Zlotych** ND (1939 - old date 2.6.1932). Red ovpt. on #74.	10.00	30.00	75.00
90	**100 Zlotych** ND (1939 - old date 9.9.1934). Red ovpt. on #75.	10.00	30.00	75.00

Note: #89 and #90 are frequently found with forged ovpt.

BANK EMISYJNY W POLSCE

EMISSION BANK OF POLAND

1940 ISSUE

		VG	VF	UNC
91	**1 Zloty** 1.3.1940. Gray-blue on lt. tan unpt.	.25	2.00	7.50

		VG	VF	UNC
92	**2 Zlote** 1.3.1940. Brown on blue and brown unpt. Portr. woman wearing head scarf at upper r.	.25	2.00	7.50
93	**5 Zlotych** 1.3.1940. Green-blue on tan and blue unpt. Man in cap at l., girl at r. Similar to #72.	7.50	25.00	75.00

		VG	VF	UNC
94	**10 Zlotych** 1.3.1940. Brown on tan and blue unpt. Girl in headdress on wmk. area at l., allegorical woman at l. and r. Sculpture on back.	.25	.75	3.00

		VG	VF	UNC
95	**20 Zlotych** 1.3.1940. Gray-blue on blue and red unpt. Man in cap on wmk. area at l., female statue w/2 children at l. ctr. E. Plater at r. Similar to #77.	.25	1.00	3.00
96	**50 Zlotych** 1.3.1940. Blue-green on brown unpt. Man in cap at l., woman's statue at l. ctr., young man at r. Ornate bldg. on back.	10.00	20.00	60.00

		VG	VF	UNC
97	**100 Zlotych** 1.3.1940. Brown on lt. green and orange unpt. Patrician of old Warsaw at l. Bldg. at l. on back.	.75	1.50	5.00

		VG	VF	UNC
98	**500 Zlotych** 1.3.1940. Gray-blue on olive unpt. Portr. Gorale at upper r. and as wmk. River in mountains on back.	2.50	6.00	30.00

1941 ISSUE

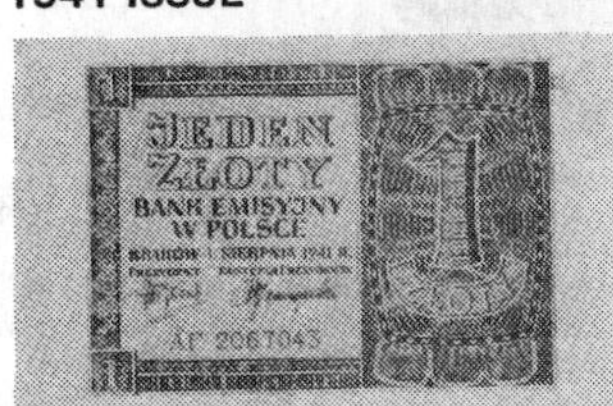

		VG	VF	UNC
99	**1 Zloty** 1.8.1941. Gray-blue. Like #91.	.25	.50	2.00

		VG	VF	UNC
100	**2 Zlote** 1.8.1941. Brown. Like #92.	.25	.75	3.00

		VG	VF	UNC
101	**5 Zlotych** 1.8.1941. Green-blue. Like #93.	.25	.50	2.50
102	**50 Zlotych** 1.8.1941. Dk. green and blue. Similar to #96. Wmk: Man in cap.	.25	.75	3.00

		VG	VF	UNC
103	**100 Zlotych** 1.8.1941. Brown and blue on lt. brown and gold unpt. Allegorical winged figure at upper ctr. Six church spires at ctr. on back. Wmk: Man w/beard.	.50	1.25	4.00

		Good	Fine	XF
103A	**1000 Zlotych** 1.8.1941. Man at r. Bldg. and Russian text on back. (Not issued).			

Note: Various notes of #91-103 also exist w/handstamps of the Warsaw Resistance Fighters of 1944, *A. K. Regula; Pierwszy zold powstancy, Sierpien 1944; Okreg Warszawski-Dowodztwo zgrup. IV* or *Braterstwo Broni Anglii Ameryki Polski Niech Zyje* (long live the Anglo-American-Polish brotherhood in arms).

POST WW II COMMITTEE OF NATIONAL LIBERATION

NARODOWY BANK POLSKI

POLISH NATIONAL BANK

1944 ISSUE

#104 (w/o misspelled word), 105, 106, 108, 110, 112, 114, 118 first printing: w/*OBOWIAZKOWYM* (spelling error). Printer: Goznak (Russia).

#107, 109, 111, 113, 115, 117, 119 second printing: w/*OBOWIAZKOWE* (corrected spelling). Printer: Polish National Bank.

#104, 105, 107, 109, 111, 113, 115, 117 and 119 reprinted w/inscription: *EMISJA PAMIATKOWA - ODBITA W 1974 r.Z ORYGINALNYCH KLISZ* across top border on face of each note.

		VG	VF	UNC
104	**50 Groszy** 1944. Reddish maroon.			
	a. Issued note.	1.00	3.00	10.00
	b. 1974 (- old date 1944). Reprint.	—	—	3.00

		VG	VF	UNC
105	**1 Zloty** 1944. Dk. green on orange unpt.			
	a. Issued note w/*OBOWIAZKOWYM*.	1.00	3.50	12.50
	b. 1974 (- old date 1944). Reprint. Serial #764560.	—	—	3.00

		VG	VF	UNC
106	**2 Zlote** 1944. Brown on lt. blue unpt. *OBOWIAZKOWYM* at bottom. 3 serial # varieties.	1.00	3.00	10.00
107	**2 Zlote** 1944. Brown on lt. blue unpt. *OBOWIAZKOWE* at bottom.			
	a. Issued note.	1.50	5.00	15.00
	b. 1974 (- old date 1944). Reprint. Serial #111111.	—	—	3.00

		VG	VF	UNC
108	**5 Zlotych** 1944. Violet-brown on green unpt. *OBOWIAZKOWYM* at bottom.	1.00	3.50	15.00

		VG	VF	UNC
109	**5 Zlotych** 1944. Violet-brown on green unpt. *OBOWIAZKOWE at bottom.*			
	a. Issued note.	1.50	5.00	15.00
	b. 1974 (- old date 1944). Reprint. Serial #518823.	—	—	3.00

		VG	VF	UNC
110	**10 Zlotych** 1944. Blue on lt. green unpt. *OBOWIAZKOWYM* at bottom.	1.00	4.00	20.00
111	**10 Zlotych** 1944. Blue on lt. green unpt. *OBOWIAZKOWE* at bottom.			

		VG	VF	UNC
111				
	a. Issued note.	1.50	5.00	25.00
	b. 1974 (- old date 1944). Reprint. Serial #823518.	—	—	3.00

		VG	VF	UNC
112	**20 Zlotych**			
	1944. Blue-black on lilac unpt. *OBOWIAZKOWYM* at bottom.	1.00	3.50	15.00

		VG	VF	UNC
113	**20 Zlotych**			
	1944. Blue-black on lilac unpt. *OBOWIAZKOWE* at bottom. 2 Serial # varieties.			
	a. Issued note.	2.50	7.50	25.00
	b. 1974 (- old date 1944). Reprint. Serial #671154.	—	—	3.00
114	**50 Zlotych**			
	1944. Blue on lilac unpt. *OBOWIAZKOWYM* at bottom.	3.00	7.50	25.00

		VG	VF	UNC
115	**50 Zlotych**			
	1944. Deep blue-violet on lilac unpt. *OBOWIAZKOWE* at bottom. 2 serial # varieties.			
	a. Issued note.	4.00	10.00	30.00
	b. 1974 (- old date 1944). Reprint. Serial #889147.	—	—	3.00
116	**100 Zlotych**			
	1944. Red on blue unpt. *OBOWIAZKOWYM* at bottom.	5.00	15.00	35.00

		VG	VF	UNC
117	**100 Zlotych**			
	1944. Red on blue unpt. *OBOWIAZKOWE* at bottom. 3 serial # varieties.			
	a. Issued note.	4.00	12.50	40.00
	b. 1974 (- old date 1944). Reprint. Serial # 778093.	—	—	3.00

		VG	VF	UNC
118	**500 Zlotych**			
	1944. Black on orange unpt. *OBOWIAZKOWYM* at bottom.	6.00	20.00	50.00
119	**500 Zlotych**			
	1944. Black on orange unpt. *OBOWIAZKOWE* at bottom. 2 serial # varieties.			
	a. Issued note.	7.50	25.00	75.00
	b. 1974 (- old date 1944). Reprint. Serial #780347.	—	—	3.00

GOVERNMENT OF NATIONAL UNITY - POST WW II

NARODOWY BANK POLSKI

POLISH NATIONAL BANK

1945 ISSUE

		VG	VF	UNC
120	**1000 Zlotych**			
	1945. Brown on tan unpt. Eagle in unpt. at ctr. 2 serial # varieties.	20.00	45.00	100.

1946 FIRST ISSUE

		VG	VF	UNC
121	**500 Zlotych** 15.1.1946. Dk. blue and green. Man holding boat at l., fisherman at r. View of old town on back.	17.50	40.00	85.00
122	**1000 Zlotych** 15.1.1946. Brown. Miner at l., worker at r. 4 serial # varieties.	15.00	35.00	70.00

1946 Second Issue

		VG	VF	UNC
123	**1 Zloty** 15.5.1946. Deep lilac.	.50	1.25	2.50

		VG	VF	UNC
124	**2 Zlote** 15.5.1946. Green on buff paper. Wmk: Stars.	.50	1.75	3.50

		VG	VF	UNC
125	**5 Zlotych** 15.5.1946. Gray-blue.	1.00	2.50	5.00
126	**10 Zlotych** 15.5.1946. Red-brown on green and gold unpt. Eagle at upper ctr.	1.00	2.50	5.00
127	**20 Zlotych** 15.5.1946. Green and brown. Eagle at upper ctr. 2 airplanes at ctr. on back.	5.00	10.00	30.00

		VG	VF	UNC
128	**50 Zlotych** 15.5.1946. Brown and purple on gold unpt. Sailing ship at l., ocean freighter at r., eagle at upper ctr. Ships and sailboat on back.	7.50	15.00	40.00
129	**100 Zlotych** 15.5.1946. Red on orange unpt. Farmer's wife at l., farmer at r. Farmer w/tractor on back.	6.00	12.50	35.00

Peoples Democratic Republic

Narodowy Bank Polski

Polish National Bank

1947 Issue

		VG	VF	UNC
130	**20 Zlotych** 15.7.1947. Green on olive unpt. Eagle at lower ctr. Tools, globe and book on back.	6.00	12.50	35.00

		VG	VF	UNC
131	**100 Zlotych** 1947; 1948. Red on lilac unpt. Farmer's wife at ctr. Horses on back.			
	a. Issued note. 15.7.1947.	8.00	17.50	45.00
	p. Proof. 1.7.1948.	—	Unc	500.

		VG	VF	UNC
132	**500 Zlotych** 15.7.1947. Blue on tan and olive unpt. Eagle at l. ctr., woman w/oar and anchor at ctr. Ships and loading dock on back.	10.00	20.00	45.00

		VG	VF	UNC
133	**1000 Zlotych** 15.7.1947. Brown and olive. Worker at ctr.	12.00	25.00	65.00

Peoples Republic

Narodowy Bank Polski

Polish National Bank

1948 Issue

		VG	VF	UNC
134	**2 Zlote** 1.7.1948. Dk. olive-green on lt. olive-green and lt. orange unpt. Eagle at r. Bldg. on back. 2 serial # varieties.	.15	.75	4.50

		VG	VF	UNC
135	**5 Zlotych** 1.7.1948. Red-brown on brown and red-brown unpt. Farmer plowing on back. 2 serial # varieties. Wmk: Woman.	5.00	15.00	75.00

		VG	VF	UNC
136	**10 Zlotych** 1.7.1948. Brown on lt. brown and lt. red unpt. Portr. man at r. Stacking hay on back. 2 serial # varieties. Wmk: Woman.	.50	1.50	7.50

		VG	VF	UNC
137	**20 Zlotych** 1.7.1948. Dk. blue on pale blue and lt. red unpt. Portr. woman wearing a head scarf at r., eagle at ctr. Ornate bldg. on back. 4 serial # varieties.	.25	1.50	7.50

		VG	VF	UNC
138	**50 Zlotych** 1.7.1948. Green on lt. green and olive unpt. Portr. sailor at r., eagle at ctr. Ships at dockside on back. 4 serial # varieties. Wmk: Woman.	.25	1.50	7.50

NOTICE

Readers with unlisted dates, signature varieties, etc. are invited to submit photocopies or, high resolution (300 dpi, 100% size) scans of their notes to: Standard Catalog of World Paper Money, 700 East State St. Iola, WI 54990-0001, or E-Mail: george.cuhaj@fwpubs.com.

		VG	VF	UNC
139	**100 Zlotych** 1.7.1948. Red on lt. red and m/c unpt. Man at r., eagle at upper ctr. Factory on back. 3 serial # varieties. Wmk: Woman.			
	a. *100* in ctr. guilloche w/fine line around edge. Buff or white paper.	.75	2.25	10.00
	b. *100* in ctr. guilloche w/o fine line around edge. Series GF.	3.00	10.00	42.50

		VG	VF	UNC
140	**500 Zlotych** 1.7.1948. Dk. brown on lt. brown and m/c unpt. Portr. coal miner at r., eagle at upper ctr. Coal miners on back. 2 serial # varieties. Wmk: Woman.	1.00	4.00	12.00

FOREIGN EXCHANGE CERTIFICATES

WAROWYPEKAO TRADING CO. (P.K.O.) / BANK POLSKA

BON TOWAROWY (TRADE VOUCHER)

1960 FIRST SERIES

#FX1-FX10 serial # prefix *A; B*.

		VG	VF	UNC
FX1	**1 Cent** 1960. Pale blue and lilac.	1.50	4.50	7.50
FX2	**5 Cents** 1960.	10.00	17.50	30.00
FX3	**10 Cents** 1960.	5.00	12.00	20.00
FX4	**50 Cents** 1960.	8.00	20.00	35.00

		VG	VF	UNC
FX5	**1 Dollar** 1960.	—	—	—
FX6	**5 Dollars** 1960.	—	—	—
FX7	**10 Dollars** 1960.	—	—	—
FX8	**20 Dollars** 1960.	50.00	—	—
FX9	**50 Dollars** 1960.	—	—	—
FX10	**100 Dollars** 1960.	—	—	—

1960 Second Series

#FX11-FX20 similar to #FX1-FX10 but w/text on modified backs. Serial # prefix *C; D*.

		VG	VF	UNC
FX11	**1 Cent** 1960.	2.50	6.00	10.00
FX12	**5 Cents** 1960.	7.50	18.00	30.00
FX13	**10 Cents** 1960.	5.00	12.00	20.00
FX14	**50 Cents** 1960.	8.00	20.00	35.00
FX15	**1 Dollar** 1960.	7.50	18.00	30.00
FX16	**5 Dollars** 1960.	12.00	30.00	—
FX17	**10 Dollars** 1960.	15.00	40.00	—
FX18	**20 Dollars** 1960.	20.00	50.00	—
FX19	**50 Dollars** 1960.	40.00	100.	—
FX20	**100 Dollars** 1960.	80.00	200.	—

Collector Series

Narodowy Bank Polski

ND (1948; 1965) Issue

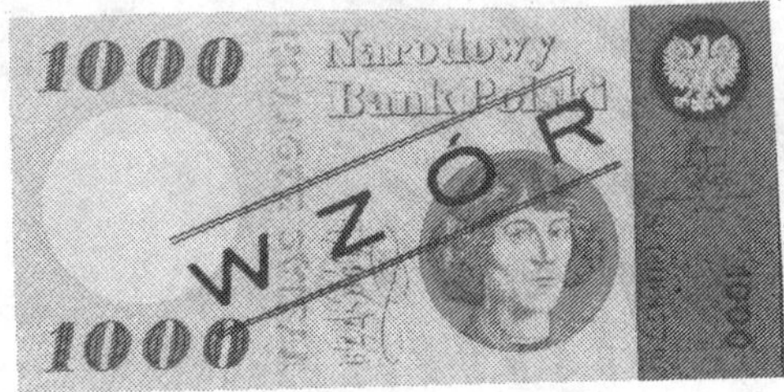

CS1	**Collector Set** Deep red ovpt: *WZOR* on 1948-dated 20, 50, 100, 500 Zlotych #137, 138, 139 and on 1965-dated 1000 Zlotych #141a. All w/normal serial #.	—	—	75.00

1974 Issue

CS3	**Collector Set** Reprints of 1944 Russian issue from 50 Groszy-500 Zlotych #104b-119b. Indicated as reprints of 1974 but w/o other ovpt. Made for the 30th anniversary of the Polish Peoples Republic.	12.50	—	20.00

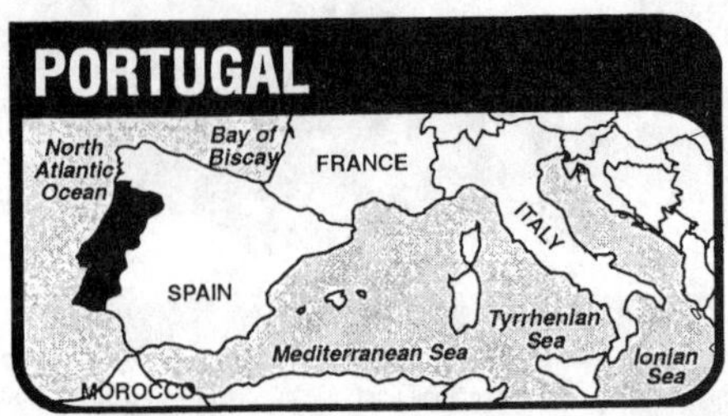

The Portuguese Republic, located in the western part of the Iberian Peninsula in southwestern Europe, has an area of 35,553 sq. mi. (91,905 sq. km.) and a population of 9.79 million. Capital: Lisbon. Portugal's economy is d on agriculture and a small but expanding industrial sector. Textiles, machinery, chemicals, wine and cork are exported.

After centuries of domination by Romans, Visigoths and Moors, Portugal emerged in the 12th century as an independent kingdom financially and philosophically prepared for the great period of exploration that would follow. Attuned to the inspiration of Prince Henry the Navigator (1394-1460), Portugal's daring explorers of the 14th and 15th centuries roamed the world's oceans from Brazil to Japan in an unprecedented burst of energy and endeavor that culminated in 1494 with Portugal laying claim to half the transoceanic world. Unfortunately for the fortunes of the tiny kingdom, the Portuguese proved to be inept colonizers. Less than a century after Portugal laid claim to half the world, English, French and Dutch trading companies had seized the lion's share of the world's colonies and commerce, and Portugal's place as an imperial power was lost forever. The monarchy was overthrown in 1910 and a republic established.

On April 25, 1974, the government of Portugal was seized by a military junta which reached agreements providing for independence for the Portuguese overseas provinces of Portuguese Guinea (Guinea-Bissau), Mozambique, Cape Verde Islands, Angola, and St. Thomas and Prince Islands (São Tomé e Príncipe).

RULERS:

Spanish, 1580-1640
Luis I, 1861-1889
Carlos I, 1889-1908
Manuel II, 1908-1910
Republic, 1910-

MONETARY SYSTEM:

1 Mil Reis = 1000 Reis to 1910
1 Escudo = 100 Centavos, 1910-2001
1 Euro = 100 Cents, 2002-

Note: Prata = Silver, Ouro = Gold.
Contracto do Sabão#S281
Contracto do Tabaco#S291-S293

Kingdom

Notes were first issued in Portugal in 1797 because of poor economic conditions brought about by the war between Spain and France. Many of these notes were officially repaired and handstamped on the back (and sometimes on the face) with various dates and endorsements a they continued to circulate. Most are found in very worn condition. Variations on the notes includ partially or fully printed year dates both in numerals and in words, also printed date altered to later date by hand.

Imperial Treasury

1797 Issue

#1 and 2 brown. Impressed royal arms at top ctr. Uniface.

		Good	Fine	XF
1	**5000 Reis** 1797. 4 allegorical vignettes in ovals across top.	—	—	—
2	**10,000 Reis** 1797. Vignettes of barrels, animal, soldiers, spinning across top in octagons.	—	—	—

1798 Issues

#3-7 brown. Impressed royal arms at top ctr. Various handwritten dates. Uniface.

		Good	Fine	XF
3	**2400 Reis** 1798. Bldg. in ornate rectangle at upper l. and r.	—	—	—
4	**2400 Reis** 1798-99. Walled cities at upper l. and r., 2 cherubs w/garlands at top ctr.	—	—	—
5	**10,000 Reis** 1798. Winged cherub approaching stylized beehive at upper l., pastoral scene w/castle behind, cherub w/dog at upper r.	—	—	—
6	**20,000 Reis** 1798-99. Cherubs at upper l. and r.	—	—	—
7	**20,000 Reis** 1798. 4 allegorical vignettes in ornate squarish frames across top; oval design at ctr.	—	—	—

1799 Issues

#8-15 brown. Impressed royal arms at top ctr. Various handwritten dates. Uniface.

		Good	Fine	XF
8	**1200 Reis** 24.4.1799. Ornate vines at l. and r. across top.	—	—	—
9	**2400 Reis** 1799. Vignettes in 2 oval frames at l. and r.	—	—	—
10	**5000 Reis** 1799. Young couples w/the males playing musical instruments at upper l. and r.	—	—	—
11	**5000 Reis** 1799. 4 vignettes of animals (goats, birds, chickens, lions) across upper l. and r.	—	—	—
12	**6400 Reis** 1799. 2 facing dogs (under the sun and under the moon) in oval frames at top ctr.	—	—	—

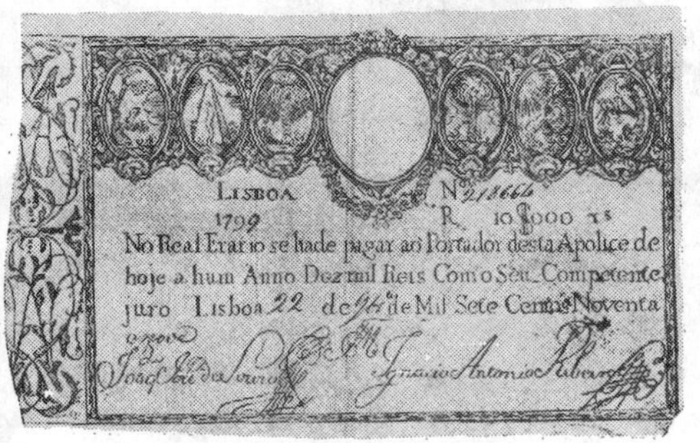

		Good	Fine	XF
13	**10,000 Reis** 1799. 6 vignettes in oval frames across top.			
	a. Date w/handwritten last numeral *9*.	—	—	—
	b. Entire date printed.	—	—	—
14	**12,800 Reis** 1799. 2 long-necked birds, oyster and pearl in ornate frames at top ctr.	—	—	—
15	**20,000 Reis** 1799. 8 vignettes in oval frames across top.	—	—	—

LAW OF 1.4.1805/1805 ISSUE

Law of 2.4.1805

#16 and 17 brown. Various handwritten dates. Uniface.

		Good	Fine	XF
16	**1200 Reis** 28.6.1805. 2 children watering a flower at top ctr.	—	—	—
17	**2400 Reis** 5.10.1805. Youthful helmeted warrior w/lion in frame at top ctr.	—	—	—

DECREE OF 31.10.1807/1807 ISSUE

#18 and 19 brown. Uniface.

		Good	Fine	XF
18	**1200 Reis** 28.11.1807. Like #16.	—	—	—
19	**2400 Reis** 5.12.1807. Like #17.	—	—	—

WAR OF THE TWO BROTHERS

IMPERIAL TREASURY

1826 REVALIDATION ISSUES

#19A-28 red crowned ovpt: *D./PEDRO IV/1826* in starburst.

		Good	Fine	XF
19A	**1200 Reis** 1826 (- old date 1805). Ovpt. on #16.	25.00	—	—

		Good	Fine	XF
20	**1200 Reis** 1826 (- old date 1807). Ovpt. on #18.	20.00	—	—
20A	**2400 Reis** 1826 (- old date 1798-99). Ovpt. on #4.	25.00	—	—

		Good	Fine	XF
21	**2400 Reis** 1826 (- old date 1805). Ovpt. on #17.	20.00	—	—
22	**2400 Reis** 1826 (- old date 1807). Ovpt. on #19.	25.00	—	—
23	**5000 Reis** 1826 (- old date 1797). Ovpt. on #1.	20.00	—	—

		Good	Fine	XF
24	**5000 Reis** 1826 (- old date 1799). Ovpt. on #10.	20.00	—	—

		Good	Fine	XF
25	**5000 Reis** 1826 (- old date 1799). Ovpt. on #11.	20.00	—	—

		Good	Fine	XF
27	**6400 Reis** 1826 (- old date 1799). Ovpt. on #12.	20.00	—	—

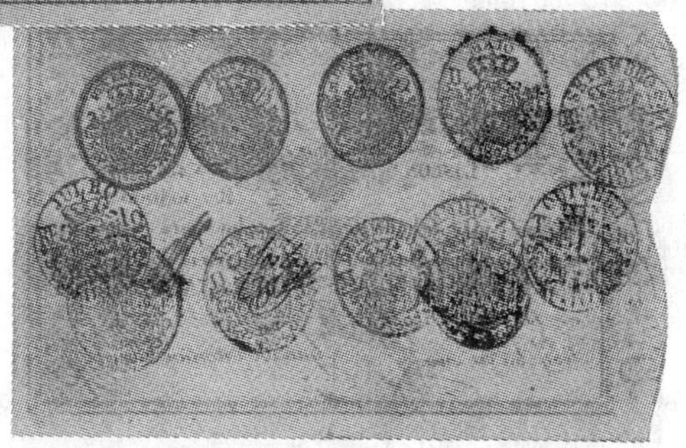

		Good	Fine	XF
28	**10,000 Reis** 1826 (- old date 1798). Ovpt. on #5.	20.00	—	—
29	**12,800 Reis** 1826 (- old date 1799). Ovpt. on #14.	35.00	—	—
30	**20,000 Reis** 1826 (- old date 1799). Ovpt. on #6.	30.00	—	—

		Good	Fine	XF
31	**20,000 Reis** 1826 (- old date 1799). Ovpt. on #15.	25.00	—	—

1828 Revalidation Issues

#32-46 red ovpt: Crowned *D./MIGUEL I/1828* in starburst.

		Good	Fine	XF
32	**1200 Reis** 1828 (- old date 1799). Ovpt. on #8.	25.00	—	—

		Good	Fine	XF
33	**1200 Reis** 1828 (- old date 1805). Ovpt. on #16.	20.00	—	—

		Good	Fine	XF
34	**2400 Reis** 1828 (- old date 1799). Ovpt. on #4.	20.00	—	—

		Good	Fine	XF
35	**2400 Reis** 1828 (- old date 1805). Ovpt. on #17.	20.00	—	—

		Good	Fine	XF
38	**2400 Reis** 1828 (- old date 1807). Ovpt. on #19.	20.00	—	—
38A	**5000 Reis** 1828 (- old date 1798). Ovpt. on #10.	25.00	—	—
38B	**5000 Reis** 1828 (- old date 1799). Ovpt. on #11.	25.00	—	—
39	**10,000 Reis** 1828 (- old date 1797). Ovpt. on #2.	25.00	—	—
40	**10,000 Reis** 1828 (- old date 1798). Ovpt. on #5.	25.00	—	—

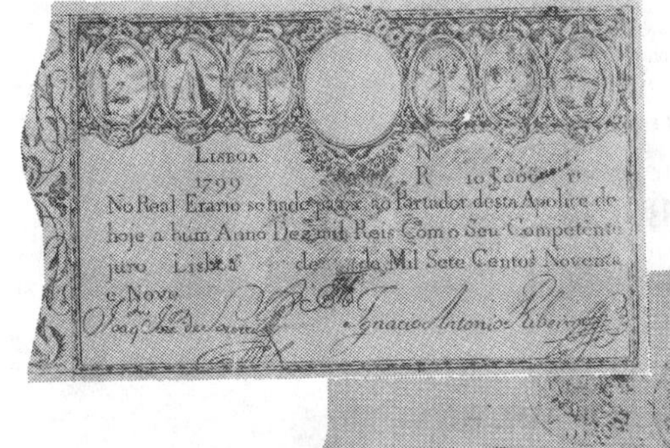

		Good	Fine	XF
41	**10,000 Reis** 1828 (- old date 1799).			
	a. Ovpt. on #13a.	25.00	—	—
	b. Ovpt. on #13b.	25.00	—	—

		Good	Fine	XF
44	**12,800 Reis** 1828 (- old date 1799). Ovpt. on #14.	30.00	—	—

		Good	Fine	XF
45	**20,000 Reis** 1828 (- old date 1799). Ovpt. on #7.	30.00	—	—

No.	Denomination	Good	Fine	XF
46	**20,000 Reis** 1828 (- old date 1799). Ovpt. on #15.	30.00	—	—
47	**20,000 Reis** 1828 (-old date 1799/98). Ovpt. on #6.	30.00	—	—

BANCO DE PORTUGAL

1847 ISSUE

No.	Denomination	Good	Fine	XF
49	**10 Mil Reis** 30.6.1847-16.6.1873 (handwritten dates). Brown. Allegorical figure in each corner. Back blue.	—	—	—
50	**20 Mil Reis** 1.5.1847-1.5.1850. Red. Allegorical figure in each corner. Back blue.	—	—	—

1854 ISSUE

No.	Denomination	Good	Fine	XF
51	**18 Mil Reis** 20.6.1854-12.4.1867 (handwritten dates). Black. Seated allegorical figure at either side of arms at upper ctr. Back blue.	—	—	—

1867 ISSUE

No.	Denomination	Good	Fine	XF
52	**20 Mil Reis** 29.10.1867; 20.12.1867. Black on yellow unpt. Ctr. design similar to #51. Figure in yellow at l. and r. Uniface.	—	—	—

1869 ISSUE

No.	Denomination	Good	Fine	XF
53	**20 Mil Reis** 4.3.1869; 25.1.1870; 22.2.1870 22.2.1870. Black on green unpt. Design like #52. Figures at l. and r. in red.	—	—	—

1871 ISSUE

No.	Denomination	Good	Fine	XF
54	**20 Mil Reis** 4.11.1871-17.8.1875. Blue. Design like #52. Figures at l. and r. in black.	—	—	—

1876 ISSUE

No.	Denomination	Good	Fine	XF
55	**10 Mil Reis** 15.5.1876-28.12.1877. Violet. Design like #49.	—	—	—
56	**20 Mil Reis** 15.5.1876. Blue. Portr. D. Luis I at ctr. Back red.	—	—	—

1877 ISSUE

No.	Denomination	Good	Fine	XF
57	**20 Mil Reis** 6.7.1877-17.12.1886. Blue-black. 3 allegorical figures w/arms at l. Back brown; arms at ctr.	—	—	—

1878 ISSUE

No.	Denomination	Good	Fine	XF
58	**10 Mil Reis** 28.1.1878-21.3.1882. Brown on pink unpt. Ctr. design like #83. Back red.	—	—	—

1879 ISSUE

No.	Denomination	Good	Fine	XF
59	**10 Mil Reis** 24.10.1879-18.10.1881. Black. Seated figure at either side of arms at ctr. Back lilac.	—	—	—

1883-86 ISSUE

No.	Denomination	Good	Fine	XF
60	**5 Mil Reis** 2.1.1883-17.4.1889 (handwritten dates). Brown on yellow unpt. Standing figure at l. and r. Arms at ctr. on back.	—	—	—
61	**20 Mil Reis** 4.1.1884-20.8.1889. Brown. Seated woman w/arms at upper ctr. Back blue.	—	—	—
62	**50 Mil Reis** 25.6.1886-26.2.1892 (handwritten dates). Black on lt. red unpt. Allegorical figure at l. and r., arms at lower ctr. Back brown.	—	—	—

1890-91 ISSUE

No.	Denomination	Good	Fine	XF
63	**200 Reis** 1.8.1891. Blue on gray unpt. Arms at l. Arms at ctr. r. on back.	—	—	—
64	**500 Reis** 12.5.1891. Black. (Not issued.)	—	—	—

No.	Denomination	Good	Fine	XF
65	**500 Reis** 1.7.1891. Lilac on tan unpt. Arms at ctr. on face and back.	30.00	100.	250.
66	**1 Mil Reis** 1.7.1891. Brown on pink unpt. Arms at upper ctr. and at ctr. on back.	—	—	—
67	**2 1/2 Mil Reis** 1.6.1891. Red on green unpt. Arms at l. Arms at ctr. on back.	—	—	—
68	**5 Mil Reis** 26.5.1890. Blue. Woman at l., arms at upper ctr.	—	—	—

No.	Denomination	Good	Fine	XF
69	**5 Mil Reis** 8.11.1890. Blue. Allegorical seated figures w/arms at upper ctr. Back pale brown.	—	—	—
70	**5 Mil Reis** 3.3.1891-15.6.1892. Blue. Mercury head at upper ctr. Back brown.	—	—	—
71	**20 Mil Reis** 8.11.1890-23.6.1898. Blue. Allegorical figures at l. and r., arms at upper ctr. Back gray on lilac unpt. Wmk: Bank name and date *29.7.87.*	—	—	—

1893-99 ISSUE

No.	Denomination	Good	Fine	XF
72	**500 Reis** 22.7.1899; 25.5.1900. Lt. brown. Woman and shield at l. Back red on blue unpt.; arms at ctr.	30.00	125.	350.

		Good	Fine	XF
73	**1 Mil Reis** 24.3.1896; 31.12.1897; 31.10.1899; 30.11.1900. Blue on pink unpt. Arms at upper l. woman w/winged cap and staff at r. Back brown; arms at ctr.	30.00	150.	450.

		Good	Fine	XF
74	**2 1/2 Mil Reis** 16.2.1893-25.5.1900. Black on violet and brown unpt. Standing woman at l. and r., arms at upper ctr. Back blue-gray; arms at ctr.	—	—	—
75	**5 Mil Reis** 16.4.1894. Pink-violet. Peace at l., arms at upper ctr. r. Vertical design at l. and r., arms at ctr. on back.	—	—	—
76	**10 Mil Reis** 1.12.1894. Aqua. Seated allegorical figure at l. and r., arms at upper ctr. Standing allegorical figure at l. and r., medallion of Lusitania at top ctr. on back.	—	—	—
77	**50 Mil Reis** 18.10.1898; 31.10.1898; 3.11.1898; 30.10.1900. Brown. Seated woman at either side of arms at lower ctr., vertical design at l. and r. Arms at ctr. on back. Wmk: Allegorical heads.	—	—	—

		Good	Fine	XF
78	**100 Mil Reis** 1.12.1894-10.3.1909. Blue. Allegorical figures at l. and r., arms at lower ctr. Back blue and gray; allegorical figure on tall pedestal at l. and r. Wmk: Allegorical heads.	350.	950.	—

1901-03 Issue, W/o Chapa; Chapa 3

Listed in accordance w/the nominal denomination and plate numbers (Ch. = Chapa = plate), which describe the different types of notes. Various date and sign. varieties.

		Good	Fine	XF
79	**2 1/2 Mil Reis** 29.9.1903; 11.3.1904; 30.8.1904; 25.8.1905. Ch. 3. Brown. Helmeted woman seated w/arms at l. Arms at r. on back.	100.	300.	800.
80	**5 Mil Reis** 20.9.1901. W/o Chapa. Blue on yellow unpt. Angel at l., 6 busts across upper border, old boats at bottom ctr. r. Back green; arms at r.	—	—	—

		Good	Fine	XF
81	**10 Mil Reis** 29.11.1902; 26.6.1903; 30.8.1904; 22.5.1908; 30.12.1909. Ch. 3. Brown on yellow unpt. Luis de Camões at l., 2 figures and globe at lower ctr., ships at r. Infante D. Henrique at upper l. on back. Wmk: A. de Albuquerque.	185.	600.	1500.
82	**20 Mil Reis** 26.2.1901. W/o *Chapa*. Blue on tan unpt. Standing figure at l. and r., arms at lower ctr. Back orange and blue.	—	—	—

1903-06 Issue, Chapa 3, 6 and 8

		Good	Fine	XF
83	**5 Mil Reis** 31.7.1903-25.8.1905; 9.7.1907. Ch. 6. Blue on brown unpt. 3 figures w/arms at ctr. Arms at ctr. on back.	80.00	200.	—
84	**20 Mil Reis** 12.10.1906. Ch. 8. Blue on gold unpt. Face similar to #82. Portr. D. Affonso Henriques at ctr., helmeted figure at l. and r. on back.	185.	600.	—
85	**50 Mil Reis** 29.1.1904-30.9.1910. Ch. 3. Blue-gray. Statues of Principe Perfetto and B. Dias at l. and r., heads of Pero de Alenquer and Diogo Cao at lower l. and r., w/anchor and ships, allegorical woman at ctr.r. Back brown; arms at l. Wmk: L. de Camoes.	275.	850.	—

Casa da Moeda

1891 Reis Issues

		VG	VF	UNC
86	**50 Reis** 6.8.1891. Green on lilac unpt. Arms at l. and r.	10.00	20.00	60.00
87	**50 Reis** 6.8.1891. Blue. Arms at upper ctr.	10.00	20.00	60.00

Note: #87 w/3-line diagonal ovpt. for Funchal district, see Madeira #11.

		VG	VF	UNC
88	**100 Reis** 6.8.1891. Brown on lt. brown unpt. Arms at l. and r. Back pale gray.	10.00	20.00	60.00

		VG	VF	UNC
89	**100 Reis** 6.8.1891. Dk. brown on lt. green unpt. Back green; arms in circle at ctr.	10.00	20.00	60.00

Note: #89 w/3-line diagonal ovpt. for Funchal district, see Madeira #12.

		VG	VF	UNC
90	**100 Reis** D.6.8.1891. Brown. Curtain, man sitting on anvil at l., figures of cherubs at r. Arms at ctr. on back. Similar to #93. p. Many proof prints in different colors each.	— 	20.00	—

Republic

Casa da Moeda

State Notes of the Mint

1917 Provisional Issues

#91 and 92 old date 6.8.1891 blocked out.

		VG	VF	UNC
91	**5 Centavos** ND (-old date 6.8.1891). Bronze and blue-green. Probably only proof print.	—	—	—
92	**5 Centavos** ND (-old date 6.8.1891). Bronze and blue. Probably only proof print.	—	—	—

Decreto de 15 de Agosto de 1917

		VG	VF	UNC
93	**10 Centavos** D.1917. Bronze and dk. brown. Curtain, man sitting on anvil. Similar to #90. Back green; arms at ctr.			
	a. Issued note.	1.50	3.50	12.50
	p. Proof prints (10 different colors) each.	—	Unc	20.00

94 **10 Centavos** VG VF UNC
D.1917. Dk. blue on lt. tan unpt. Columns at l. and r., arms at upper ctr. Paper gray and thin or yellowish and thicker. Back blue-green.

	VG	VF	UNC
a. Issued note.	1.00	3.00	10.00
p. Proof print in different colors.	—	Unc	20.00

95 **10 Centavos** VG VF UNC
D.1917. Blue on green unpt. Seated woman at l. and r., arms at lower ctr. Back blue; seated figures at ctr., arms above.

	VG	VF	UNC
a. Wmk: Ovals.	1.50	5.00	17.50
b. Wmk: Casa da Moeda.	1.00	3.50	10.00
c. W/o wmk.	1.00	3.50	10.00

96 **10 Centavos**
D.1917. Red-brown on lt. brownish gray unpt. Seated man at l. Chimney stacks, ships, bridge in background. Arms at upper r. Back lt. brown; coin at ctr. White, gray, yellow-brown or brown paper. 1.00 3.50 12.00

1918-22 ISSUES

97 **5 Centavos** VG VF UNC
5.4.1918. Blue-green on gray-violet unpt. Arms at upper ctr. Back brown. Gray and thin or yellowish and thicker paper. 1.00 3.50 10.00

98 **5 Centavos** VG VF UNC
D.5.4.1918. Red on pale orange unpt. Small child at l., bust at r., coin at ctr. below. Back aqua; arms at ctr. 1.00 3.50 10.00

Note: Some of #44 may have a faint lt. orange unpt at ctr.

99 **5 Centavos** VG VF UNC
D.5.4.1918. Dk. brown on yellow-brown unpt. Arms at upper ctr. White or yellowish paper. 1.00 3.50 10.00

100 **20 Centavos** VG VF UNC
D.4.8.1922. Dk. brown on blue unpt. Seated man at l., woman at r., arms at upper ctr. Back purplish black; allegorical figures and ship. 1.00 3.50 10.00

1925 FIRST ISSUE - DECRETOS DE 15.8.1917 AND 11.4.1925

101 **10 Centavos** VG VF UNC
D.1917 and 1925. Red-brown on gray unpt. Arms at l., woman w/torch at r. Back brown; Comercio Square in Lisbon at ctr. Printer: W&S. 1.00 3.50 10.00

1925 SECOND ISSUE - DECRETOS DE 4.8.1922 AND 11.4.1925

102 **20 Centavos** VG VF UNC
D.1922 and 1925. Brown on gray unpt. Woman at l., arms above. Back gray; Casa da Moeda at ctr. Printer: W&S. 2.00 5.00 15.00

BANCO DE PORTUGAL

1911 INTERIM ISSUE

104 **5 Mil Reis** Good Fine XF
14.11.1906; 30.12.1909; 30.3.1910 (1911). Ch. 7. Black on blue and m/c unpt. Portr. Marquez de Pombal at l. Arms at ctr., woman seated at r. on back. Wmk: Minerva. Printer: BWC. 60.00 150. —

1912-17 ND PROVISIONAL ISSUE

105 **500 Reis** Good Fine XF
ND (1917 - old dates 27.12.1904; 30.9.1910). Ch. 3. Black on green unpt. *Republica* over crowned arms at top ctr. Back brown; woman's head at l. Wmk: Mercury.

	Good	Fine	XF
a. Black ovpt: *REPUBLICA.*	3.50	15.00	60.00
b. Engraved *REPUBLICA.*	1.50	12.50	50.00

106 **1 Mil Reis** Good Fine XF
ND (1917 - old date 30.9.1910). Ch. 3. Blue. Arms at lower l. ctr., seated woman at r. W/*REPUBLICA* over crowned arms at bottom. Back red; seated woman at l. 20.00 90.00 225.

		Good	Fine	XF
107	**2 1/2 Mil Reis** ND (1916 - old dates 20.6.1909; 30.6.1909; 30.9.1910; 27.6.1919). Ch. 4. Black and green on orange unpt. Portr. A. de Albuquerque at r. Mercury at l. on back. Black ovpt: *REPUBLICA* over crowned arms at ctr. on back.	20.00	60.00	200.

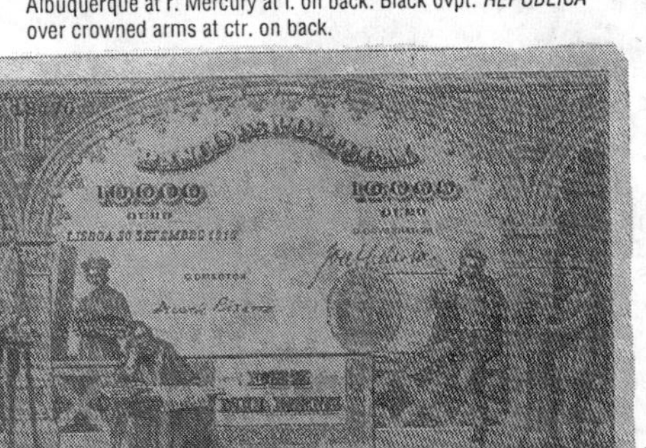

		Good	Fine	XF
108	**10 Mil Reis** ND (1917 - old dates 22.5.1908; 30.9.1910). Ch. 4. Black on tan unpt. 5 men representing sculpture, painting, reading, music and writing. Back green and pink; allegorical woman at l., helmeted woman at r. Wmk: Woman's head. Printer: BWC (w/o imprint).			
	a. Ovpt: *Republica* over crowned arms on back. 30.9.1910.	150.	375.	850.
	b. Engraved *Republica* over crowned arms on back.	150.	375.	850.
109	**20 Mil Reis** ND (1912 - old dates 30.12.1909; 30.3.1912). Ch. 9. Blue on tan unpt. Portr. Vasco da Gama in pillar at l., Luis de Camoes in pillar at r., arms at lower ctr. Back brown; ovpt: *REPUBLICA* on crowned arms at l. Wmk: D. Joao II.	150.	600.	—
110	**50 Mil Reis** ND (1917 - old date 30.9.1910). Ch. 4. Blue. Middle East kg. on throne at l., voyagers at r. Ovpt: *REPUBLICA.* on crowned arms at lower ctr. Medallion of Lusitania at r. on back. Wmk: Man w/turban.	200.	700.	—

		Good	Fine	XF
111	**100 Mil Reis** ND (1916 - old dates 22.5.1908; 10.3.1909; 30.9.1910). Green on yellow unpt. Scene of arrival of P. A. Cabral at Lisbon 8.3.1500. Back red-brown and tan; arms at upper ctr. Black ovpt: *REPUBLICA* on crowned arms at top ctr. on back.	350.	950.	—

1913-18 Regular Issue

Escudo system.

#112-115 printer: BWC (w/o imprint).

		Good	Fine	XF
112	**50 Centavos** 1918; 1920. Ch. 1. Purple and m/c. Woman w/ship in her hand at l. Back purple and green; woman w/staff and scale at ctr. Wmk: Minerva head.			
	a. Serial #. 5.7.1918.	3.50	7.50	35.00
	b. Block # and letters in 2 lines. 5.7.1918; 25.6.1920.	2.00	5.00	30.00

		Good	Fine	XF
113	**1 Escudo** 1917-20. Ch. 1. Red, violet and m/c. Woman seated holding book at l. Back brown; woman w/lyre at r. Wmk: Allegorical head.			
	a. 7.9.1917; 25.6.1920.	3.50	10.00	45.00
	b. 29.11.1918. Rare.	—	—	—

		Good	Fine	XF
114	**5 Escudos** 29.7.1913-1.2.1923. Ch. 1. Purple on lt. blue unpt. Woman seated at l. offering wreath, portr. A. Herculano at top ctr. Back brown; fortress at ctr. Wmk: Minerva head.	40.00	125.	350.

		Good	Fine	XF
115	**20 Escudos** 1915-18. Ch 1. Brown-lilac and green. Woman at l. and r., portr. A. Garrett at ctr. Back blue on lt. green unpt; arms at ctr.			
	a. Issued note. 5.1.1915-26.3.1918.	85.00	300.	500
	b. Kingdom of the North ovpt: *REINO DE PORTUGAL / 19 de Janeiro de 1919* (-old date 14.4.1915). Rare.	—	—	—

		Good	Fine	XF
116	**100 Escudos** 13.8.1918; 5.2.1920. Ch. 1. Deep blue on m/c unpt. Indians, ships (discovery of Brazil) and medallic portr. of P. Alvares Cabral at ctr. r. Back brown and m/c; 2 heads and Cabral's arrival in 1500 (similar to #111) at ctr. Wmk: Man's head.	600.	1500.	—

1919 Issue, Chapa 1 and 2

#117-118 printer: BWC (w/o imprint).

No.	Denomination	Good	Fine	XF
117	**10 Escudos** 21.10.1919; 7.7.1920. Ch. 1. Blue on yellow and brown unpt. Portr. A. de Albuquerque at l., explorer scene at bottom ctr. Back brown on yellow unpt; allegorical figures at bottom ctr., head at r. Wmk: Allegorical head.	100.	300.	650.
118	**20 Escudos** 12.8.1919-7.7.1920. Ch. 2. Blue on brown and green unpt. Portr. J. DeCastro at l. Back maroon and m/c; bldg. at ctr., arms at r. Wmk: Allegorical head.	75.00	200.	500.

1920 Issues, Chapa A, 1, 2 and 3

#119-124 printer: BWC (w/o imprint).

No.	Denomination	Good	Fine	XF
119	**2 Escudos 50 Centavos** 10.7.1920; 3.2.1922. Ch. 1. Green and m/c. Portr. D. Nuno Álvarez Pereira at r. Back blue-green and red; woman w/globe at l.	30.00	100.	225.
120	**5 Escudos** 10.7.1920-13.1.1925. Ch. 2. Violet-brown and green. Portr. J. das Regras at l. Back blue; convent at r. Wmk: Allegorical head.	30.00	100.	225.

No.	Denomination	Good	Fine	XF
121	**10 Escudos** 9.8.1920; 31.8.1926; 2.11.1927; 28.1.1928. Ch. 2. Brown on yellow-green unpt. Portr. M. de Sa da Bandeira at ctr. Back blue; arms at upper ctr.	50.00	175.	500.
122	**20 Escudos** 9.8.1920-3.2.1927. Ch. 3. Brown, green and m/c. Portr. J. Estevao Coelho de Magalhaes at l., woman seated w/arms and globe at r. Back brown; warrior's head at l. and r. Wmk: Allegorical head.	100.	350.	650.

No.	Denomination	Good	Fine	XF
123	**50 Escudos** 31.8.1920; 3.2.1927. Ch. 1. Red-brown and m/c. Portr. Passos Manoel at ctr. Statue and ornate archway on back. Wmk: Allegorical head.	175.	500.	1250.

No.	Denomination	Good	Fine	XF
124	**100 Escudos** 31.8.1920; 27.4.1922; 13.4.1926; 15.8.1927; 28.1.1928. Ch. 2. Brown. Portr. D. do Couto at l. Back maroon and brown; castle at ctr., allegorical figures at r. Wmk: Man's head.	625.	1500.	—
125	**1000 Escudos** 10.7.1920. Ch. A. Blue on m/c unpt. Portr. Duque da Terceira at upper l., arms at upper r. Back brown on yellow unpt; vertical design at l. and r. Wmk: Bank name. Rare.	—	—	—
126	**1000 Escudos** 28.7.1920. Ch. 1. Slate blue on m/c unpt. Portr. L. de Camões at r. Allegorical women at l. and r. on back. Printer: BWC (w/o imprint). Rare.	—	—	—

1922 Issues, Chapa 1 and 2

No.	Denomination	Good	Fine	XF
127	**2 Escudos 50 Centavos** 17.11.1922; 18.11.1925; 18.11.1926. Ch. 2. Blue on orange and yellow unpt. Portr. M. da Silveira at ctr. Back orange on yellow unpt., arms at ctr. Wmk: Bank name repeated. Printer: W&S (w/o imprint).	15.00	60.00	125.

No.	Denomination	Good	Fine	XF
128	**50 Escudos** 6.2.1922; 18.11.1925. Ch. 2. Blue on m/c unpt. Angel of Peace at l., cherubs at r. corners. Back brown and m/c; radiant sun at ctr., woman and lions at r. Wmk: Head. Printer: BWC (w/o imprint).	350.	750.	—
129	**500 Escudos** 4.5.1922; 8.12.1925. Ch. 1. Brown on m/c unpt. Portr. João de Deus at l., arms at upper r. Back brown and green; allegorical child w/flute at r. Wmk: Head representing the Republic. Printer: BWC (w/o imprint).	700.	1500.	—
130	**500 Escudos** 17.11.1922. Ch. 2. Purple and black on tan unpt. Portr. Vasco da Gama at l., sailing ships at r. Back purple; arms at ctr. Wmk: Bank name repeated. Printer: W&S.	300.	800.	2000.

Note: Through swindle, #130 was reprinted for Alves Reis who secured false authorization for millions of escudos to be made for his illegal use - a most famous episode.

No.	Denomination	Good	Fine	XF
131	**1000 Escudos** 27.4.1922; 13.4.1926. Ch. 2. Dk. blue and purple. Portr. A. F. Castilho at ctr., arms at r. Back purple and lilac; 2 allegorical women w/lyre and torch at ctr. Printer: BWC (w/o imprint). Rare.	—	—	—

1924-25 Issues, Chapa 3 and 4

No.	Denomination	Good	Fine	XF
132	**5 Escudos** 10.11.1924. Ch. 3. Black on orange and blue unpt. Allegorical woman and child at l., Agriculture at r. Back blue; Palacio da Bolsa in Porto at ctr. Wmk: Allegorical head. Printer: BWC (w/o imprint).	—	—	—

#133-136 wmk: bank name repeated. Printer: W&S (w/o imprint).

133 5 Escudos — Good 25.00 | Fine 80.00 | XF 200.

13.1.1925. Ch. 4. Gray on yellow-brown and lt. blue unpt. Portr. D. Alvaro Vaz d'Almada at lower ctr. Back blue; arms at ctr. 2 sign. varieties.

134 10 Escudos — Good 40.00 | Fine 125. | XF 300.

13.1.1925. Ch. 3. Black on pink unpt. Monastery in Lisbon at l., portr. E. de Queiroz at r. Back brown; arms at l.

135 20 Escudos — Good 75.00 | Fine 225. | XF 600.

13.1.1925. Ch 4. Red on yellow unpt. Portr. M. de Pombal at top ctr. *Comercio* Square below. Back red; arms at ctr.

136 50 Escudos — Good 150. | Fine 400. | XF 850.

13.1.1925. Ch. 3. Blue on lt. pink and green unpt. Portr. Vasco da Gama at l., Monastery of Mafra at ctr r. Arms at ctr. on back.

137 100 Escudos — Good — | Fine — | XF —

13.1.1925. Ch. 3. Black on salmon unpt. Portr. Mareshal Duque de Saldanha at l., monument w/city scene at ctr. r. Arms at ctr. on back. Wmk: Bank name repeated. Printer: W&S. (Not issued.)

138 500 Escudos — Good — | Fine — | XF —

13.1.1925. Ch. 3. Brown on lt. green unpt. Portr. Camillo Branco at l., city scene w/river at r. Arms at ctr. on back. Wmk: Bank name repeated. Printer: W&S. (Not issued.)

139 1000 Escudos — Good — | Fine — | XF —

13.1.1925. Ch. 3. Tan and black. Portr. Visconde de Seabra at l., cathedral at r. Arms at ctr. on back. Printer: W&S. Specimen.

1927-28 Issue, Chapa 3 and 4

#140-142 printer: BWC (w/o imprint).

140 100 Escudos — Good 75.00 | Fine 225. | XF 450.

4.4.1928; 12.8.1930. Ch. 4. Blue on green and red unpt. Portr. G. Freire at l., allegorical figures w/arms at upper ctr., pillars at lower ctr. Back red-brown; horsecart and town at ctr., bank arms at r. Wmk: Head symbolizing the Republic.

141 500 Escudos — Good 500. | Fine 1200. | XF —

4.4.1928; 19.4.1929. Ch. 4. Red-violet on m/c unpt. Castle at l., portr. D. de Palmella at r. and as wmk. Back green; bank arms at l., horse-drawn carts at lower ctr.

142 1000 Escudos — Good — | Fine — | XF —

25.11.1927. Ch. 3. Blue on lt. tan unpt. Convent at ctr., O. Martins at r. and as wmk. Back red-brown; bank arms at ctr.

NOTICE

Readers with unlisted dates, signature varieties, etc. are invited to submit photocopies or, high resolution (300 dpi, 100% size) scans of their notes to: Standard Catalog of World Paper Money, 700 East State St. Iola, WI 54990-0001, or E-Mail: george.cuhaj@fwpubs.com.

1929 Issue, Chapa 4 and 5

#143-145 printer: BWC (w/o imprint).

143 20 Escudos — Good 35.00 | Fine 100. | XF 225

17.9.1929-27.2.1940. Ch 5. Red-violet and m/c. Portr. M. d' Albuquerque at l. and as wmk., ornate bldg. at r. Back violet; Guimaraes Castle at l.

144 50 Escudos — Good 80.00 | Fine 250. | XF 450

17.9.1929; 7.3.1933. Ch. 4. Violet and m/c. Portr. B. Carneiro at l. ctr. Back blue and m/c; Coimbra University at ctr., warrior head at r. Wmk: Allegorical head of Justice.

145 1000 Escudos — Good 700. | Fine 1500. | XF —

17.9.1929. Ch. 4. Green, violet and m/c. Bridge at ctr., Gen. M. de Sa da Bandeira at r. Back brown; bank arms, woman's head and field workers. Wmk: Allegorical head.

1932 Issue, Chapa 5

		Good	Fine	XF
146	**50 Escudos** 18.11.1932. Ch. 5. Purple and m/c. D. de Saldanha at l., monument at ctr. Back blue; farmer and oxen plowing at ctr., bank arms at r. Wmk: Head. Printer: TDLR (w/o imprint).	75.00	225.	—
147	**500 Escudos** 18.11.1932; 31.8.1934. Ch. 5. Brown-violet and blue on m/c unpt. J. da Silva Carvalho at l., palace at ctr. Back green; river and wall at ctr., Liberty at r. Wmk: Homer. Printer: BWC (w/o imprint).	200.	500.	—
148	**1000 Escudos** 18.11.1932. Ch. 5. Dk. green and purple on m/c unpt. C. de Castelo-Melhor at l., National Palace at ctr., bank arms at lower r. Back brown; island castle at ctr. Wmk: Allegorical head. Printer: BWC (w/o imprint).	500.	1000.	—

1935; 1938 Issue, Chapa 5 and 6

		Good	Fine	XF
149	**50 Escudos** 3.3.1938. Ch. 6. Brown-violet and dk. blue on m/c unpt. Arms at ctr., R. Ortigao at r. Back blue-green; head at l., monastery at ctr. Wmk: Woman's head. Printer: BWC (w/o imprint).	40.00	90.00	200.

		Good	Fine	XF
150	**100 Escudos** 21.2.1935; 13.3.1941. Ch. 5. Blue-green and brown. J. Pinto Ribeiro at l., arms at upper ctr. Back dk. red; monument for 1.12.1640 (Restoration of independence) at ctr., bank arms at r. Wmk: Head of Victory from monument. Printer: BWC (w/o imprint).	40.00	90.00	225.
151	**500 Escudos** 26.4.1938. Ch. 6. Brown on green and gold unpt. Arms at lower l., Infante Don Henriques in black at r. Back green; tomb at l. ctr. Wmk: Allegorical head. Printer: W&S (w/o imprint).	75.00	200.	450.

		Good	Fine	XF
152	**1000 Escudos** 17.6.1938. Ch. 6. Green on tan and blue unpt. Arms at lower l., portr. M. de Aviz in black at r. ctr., spires at r. Back brown; monastery at ctr. Wmk: Woman's head. Printer: W&S (w/o imprint).	60.00	125.	300.

1941 Issue, Chapa 6 and 6A

153-154 printer: BWC (w/o imprint).

		Good	Fine	XF
153	**20 Escudos** 1941-59. Ch. 6. Green and purple on m/c unpt. Portr. D. Antonio Luiz de Menezes at r. Back green on m/c unpt; bank arms at ctr. Wmk: Man's head.			
	a. Sign. title at l.: *O VICE-GOVERNADOR.* 28.1.1941-25.5.1954.	8.00	15.00	30.00
	b. Sign. title at l.: *O GOVERNADOR.* 27.1.1959.	8.00	15.00	30.00

		Good	Fine	XF
154	**50 Escudos** 25.11.1941-28.6.1949. Ch. 6A. Similar to #149. Back brown-violet and green.	15.00	30.00	90.00

1942 Issue, Chapa 1 and 7

		Good	Fine	XF
155	**500 Escudos** 29.9.1942. Ch. 7. Brown-violet and green on m/c unpt. Cherubs at ctr., D. de Goes at r. Back blue; pulpit in Coimbra's Santa Cruz church at ctr. Wmk: Bank name repeated. Printer: W&S (w/o imprint).	35.00	100.	225.
156	**1000 Escudos** 29.9.1942. Ch. 7. Dk. green and blue on m/c unpt. Knight and Arab on horseback at l., portr. D. Afonso Henriques at r. and as wmk. Back brown; head at l., ornate tomb at ctr. Printer: BWC (w/o imprint).	12.00	40.00	125.
157	**5000 Escudos** 29.9.1942. Ch. 1. Purple and m/c. Allegorical children at lower l., Qn. D. Leonor at r. Allegorical figures on back. Printer: BWC (w/o imprint). Specimen.	—	—	—

1944 Issue, Chapa 8

		VG	VF	UNC
158	**500 Escudos** 28.11.1944; 11.3.1952. Ch. 8. Dk. red and black on m/c unpt. Arms at upper ctr., D. Joao IV at r. Kg. and crowd on back. Wmk: Allegorical head. Printer: BWC (w/o imprint).	20.00	40.00	100.

1947 Issue, Chapa 6

		VG	VF	UNC
159	**100 Escudos** 28.10.1947; 24.10.1950; 22.6.1954; 25.6.1957. Ch. 6. Dk. green and lilac on m/c unpt. Arms at upper ctr., P. Nunes at r. and as wmk. Back brown; fountain in arches at ctr. Printer: BWC (w/o imprint).	6.00	12.50	30.00

1953 ISSUE, CHAPA 7

		VG	VF	UNC
160	**50 Escudos** 28.4.1953; 24.6.1955. Ch. 7. Blue on m/c unpt. Arms at top ctr., F. Pereira de Mello at r. and in profile as wmk. Back olive and green; bank arms at l., statue *The Thinker* at ctr. Printer: TDLR (w/o imprint).	8.00	15.00	35.00

1956 ISSUE, CHAPA 8

		VG	VF	UNC
161	**1000 Escudos** 31.1.1956. Ch. 8. Greenish gray and violet on m/c unpt. Castle at l., arms at lower ctr., D. Filipa de Lencastre at r. Back green; Qn. in oval at l., Qn. and 2 men at ctr. Wmk: Man's head. Printer: BWC (w/o imprint).	10.00	40.00	100.

1958 ISSUE, CHAPA 9

		VG	VF	UNC
162	**500 Escudos** 27.5.1958. Ch. 9. Olive-brown on m/c unpt. D. Francisco d' Almeida at r. and as wmk. Back brown; 3 medieval men at l. Printer: BWC (w/o imprint).	35.00	100.	200.

1960; 1961 ISSUE

		VG	VF	UNC
163	**20 Escudos** 26.7.1960. Ch. 6A. Dk. green and purple on m/c unpt. Portr. Dom Antonio Luiz de Menezes at r. and as wmk. Back purple and m/c; bank seal at l. 8 sign. varieties. Printer: BWC (w/o imprint).	4.00	10.00	60.00

		VG	VF	UNC
164	**50 Escudos** 24.6.1960. Ch. 7A. Blue on m/c unpt. Arms at upper ctr., Fontes Pereira de Mello at r. and as wmk. Back dk. green and m/c; bank seal at upper l., statue *The Thinker* at l. 8 sign. varieties. Printer: TDLR (w/o imprint).	10.00	30.00	100

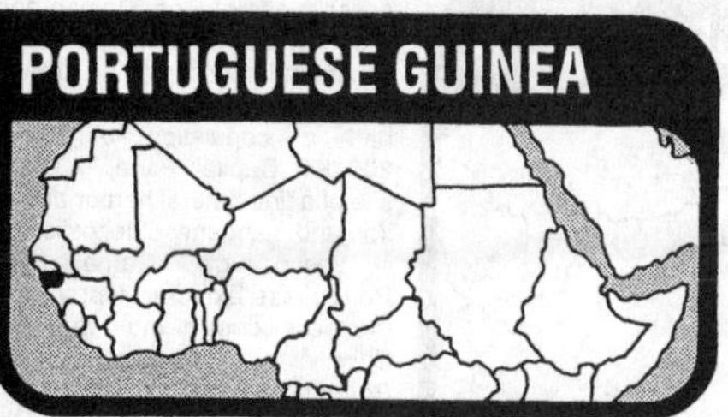

Portuguese Guinea (now Guinea-Bissau), a former Portuguese province off the west coast of Africa bounded on the north by Senegal and on the east and southeast by Guinea, had an area of 13,948 sq. mi. (36,125 sq. km.). Capital: Bissau. The province exported peanuts, timber and beeswax.

Portuguese Guinea was discovered by Portuguese navigator Nuno Tristao in 1446. Trading rights in the area were granted to Cape Verde islanders ut few prominent posts were established before 1851, and they were principally coastal nstallations. The chief export of this colony's early period was slaves for South America, a practice hat adversely affected trade with the native people and retarded subjection of the interior. Territorial disputes with France delayed final demarcation of the colony's frontiers until 1905.

The African Party for the Independence of Guinea-Bissau was founded in 1956, and several ears later began a guerrilla warfare that grew in effectiveness until 1974, when the rebels controlled nost of the colony. Portugal's costly overseas wars in her African territories resulted in a military oup in Portugal in April 1974, that appreciably brightened the prospects for freedom for Guinea-Bissau. In August, 1974, the Lisbon government signed an agreement granting independence to Portuguese Guinea effective Sept. 10, 1974. The new republic took the name of Guinea-Bissau.

RULERS:

Portuguese to 1974

MONETARY SYSTEM:

1 Mil Reis = 1000 Reis to 1910
1 Escudo = 100 Centavos, 1910-1975

STEAMSHIP SEALS:

Type I

Type II

Type III

NOTE: For later issues see Guinea-Bissau.

NOTE: Three types of *BANCO NACIONAL ULTRAMARINO* seals are found on the bank notes originally issued for Bolama.

PORTUGUESE ADMINISTRATION

BANCO NACIONAL ULTRAMARINO, GUINÉ

1909 FIRST ISSUE

#1-5B ovpt: *BOLAMA*. Printer: BWC.

#	Denomination	Good	Fine	XF
	1 Mil Reis 1.3.1909. Steamship Seal Type I at r.	100.	300.	750.
	2.5 Mil Reis 1.3.1909. Steamship Seal Type I at r.	125.	400.	850.
	5 Mil Reis 1.3.1909. Steamship Seal Type I at r.	150.	600.	1250.
	10 Mil Reis 1.3.1909. Steamship Seal Type I at r.	200.	750.	1750.
	20 Mil Reis 1.3.1909. Steamship Seal Type I at r.	250.	900.	—
B	**50 Mil Reis** 1.3.1909.	800.	2250.	—

1909 SECOND ISSUE

#1A-5A ovpt.: *BOLAMA*. Printer: BWC.

#	Denomination	Good	Fine	XF
A	**1 Mil Reis** 1.3.1909. Steamship Seal Type III at r.	100.	200.	550.
A	**2.5 Mil Reis** 1.3.1909. Steamship Seal Type III at r.	125.	325.	700.
A	**5 Mil Reis** 1.3.1909. Steamship Seal Type III at r.	150.	425.	900.
A	**10 Mil Reis** 1.3.1909. Steamship Seal Type III at r.	200.	600.	1250.
A	**20 Mil Reis** 1.3.1909. Steamship Seal Type III at r.	250.	700.	1750.

1909 PROVISIONAL ISSUE

#	Denomination	Good	Fine	XF
5F	**5 Mil Reis** 1.3.1909. Rectangular ovpt: *PAGAVEL... ces agencias de GUINÉ* on Cape Verde #6b.	—	—	—

1914 FIRST FRACTIONAL ISSUE

#6-8 ovpt: *BOLAMA*. Printer: BWC.

#	Denomination	Good	Fine	XF
6	**10 Centavos** 5.11.1914. Purple on m/c unpt. Steamship Seal Type II at bottom ctr.	25.00	100.	250.

#	Denomination	Good	Fine	XF
7	**20 Centavos** 5.11.1914. Blue on m/c unpt. Steamship Seal Type II.	25.00	100.	250.
8	**50 Centavos** 5.11.1914. Green on m/c unpt. Steamship Seal Type II.	25.00	100.	275.

1914 SECOND FRACTIONAL ISSUE

#9-11 ovpt: *BOLAMA*. Printer: BWC.

#	Denomination	Good	Fine	XF
9	**10 Centavos** 5.11.1914. Purple on m/c unpt. Like #6 but Steamship Seal Type III.	20.00	75.00	200.
10	**20 Centavos** 5.11.1914. Blue on m/c unpt. Like #7 but Steamship Seal Type III.	20.00	85.00	225.
11	**50 Centavos** 5.11.1914. Green on m/c unpt. Like #8 but Steamship Seal Type III.	20.00	85.00	225.

1921 ISSUE

#12-18 portr. Oliveira Chamico at l. Ovpt: *GUINÉ*.

#12, 14-18 printer: BWC.

#	Denomination	Good	Fine	XF
12	**1 Escudo** 1.1.1921. Green.	20.00	60.00	175.
13	**2 1/2 Escudos** 1.1.1921. Dk. blue on yellow and red-violet unpt. Printer: TDLR.	20.00	80.00	250.
14	**5 Escudos** 1.1.1921. Black.	25.00	100.	325.
15	**10 Escudos** 1.1.1921. Brown.	50.00	150.	425.
16	**20 Escudos** 1.1.1921. Dk. blue.	100.	300.	700.
17	**50 Escudos** 1.1.1921. Blue.	150.	500.	1250.
18	**100 Escudos** 1.1.1921. Brown.	200.	750.	1750.

1937 ISSUE

#21-24 J. Texeira Pinto at l. Ovpt: *GUINÉ*. Printer: BWC.

#	Denomination	Good	Fine	XF
21	**10 Escudos** 14.9.1937. Red-brown on m/c unpt.	30.00	100.	325.
22	**20 Escudos** 14.9.1937. Blue on m/c unpt.	60.00	200.	500.
23	**50 Escudos** 14.9.1937. Red on m/c unpt.	100.	300.	750.
24	**100 Escudos** 14.9.1937. Purple on m/c unpt.	125.	400.	1000.

1944 ISSUE

		VG	VF	UNC
25	**5 Escudos** 2.11.1944. Olive and m/c. J. Texeira Pinto at l., steamship seal at r. Ovpt: *GUINÉ*. Printer: BWC.	15.00	75.00	175.

1945 ISSUE

#26-32 portr. J. Texeira Pinto at l., steamship at r. Ovpt: *GUINÉ*. Printer: BWC.

		VG	VF	UNC
26	**2 1/2 Escudos** 2.1.1945. Purple and m/c.	10.00	45.00	150.
27	**5 Escudos** 16.11.1945. Green.	15.00	75.00	200.
28	**10 Escudos** 16.11.1945. Brown.	20.00	100.	300.
29	**20 Escudos** 16.11.1945. Blue.	25.00	125.	350.
30	**50 Escudos** 16.11.1945. Yellow and green.	30.00	150.	450.
31	**100 Escudos** 16.11.1945. Red.	40.00	200.	600.
32	**500 Escudos** 16.11.1945. Green.	60.00	300.	800.

1947 Issue

#33-36 J. Texeira Pinto at l., steamship seal at r. Ovpt: *GUINÉ*. Printer: BWC.

		VG	VF	UNC
33	**20 Escudos** 27.3.1947. Blue.	20.00	100.	300.
34	**50 Escudos** 27.3.1947. Red.	25.00	125.	400.
35	**100 Escudos** 27.3.1947. Purple.	30.00	150.	500.
36	**500 Escudos** 27.3.1947. Green.	50.00	250.	700.

1958 Issue

#37-39 J. Texeira Pinto at l., steamship seal at r. Ovpt: *GUINÉ*. Serial # prefix B. Printer: BWC.

		VG	VF	UNC
37	**50 Escudos** 20.11.1958. Red, green and m/c.			
	a. Issued note.	15.00	75.00	250.
	s. Specimen, punched hole cancelled.	—	—	125.
38	**100 Escudos** 20.11.1958. Purple and m/c.			
	a. Issued note.	20.00	100.	350.
	s. Specimen, punched hole cancelled.	—	—	200.

		VG	VF	UNC
39	**500 Escudos** 20.11.1958. Green and m/c.			
	a. Issued note.	40.00	175.	500.
	s. Specimen, punched hole cancelled.	—	—	275.

PORTUGUESE GUINEA

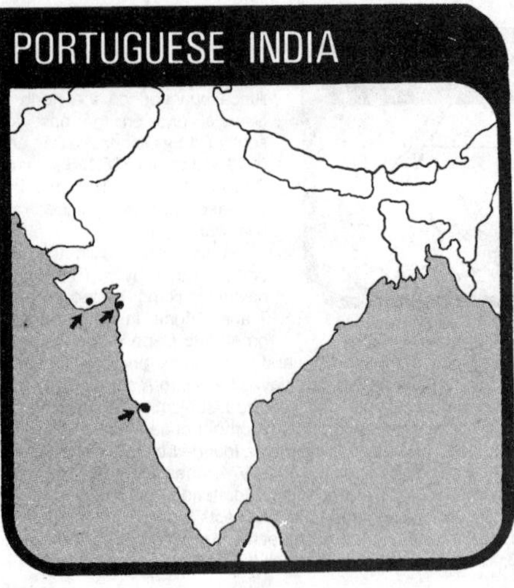

The former Portuguese possessions of Goa, Daman and Diu (now a union territory of west-central India) occupied an area of 1,441 sq. mi. (3,733 sq. km.) and had a population of about 200,000. Capital: Panaji. It is the site of a fine natural harbor and of iron and manganese deposits.

Vasco da Gama, the Portuguese explorer, first visited the west coast of India in 1498. Shortly thereafter the Portuguese arrived in strength and captured Goa (1510), Diu (1535), Daman (1559), and a number of other coastal enclaves and small islands, and for more then a century enjoyed a virtual monopoly on trade. With the arrival of powerful Dutch and English fleets in the first half of the 17th century, Portuguese power in the area declined, until virtually all that remained under Portuguese control were the enclaves of Goa (south of Bombay), Daman (due north of Bombay) and Diu (northwest of Bombay). They were invaded by India in 1961 and annexed to India in 1962.

RULERS:

Portuguese to 1961

MONETARY SYSTEM:

1 Rupia = 16 Tangas = 960 Reis to 1958
1 Escudo = 100 Centavos, 1958-1962

STEAMSHIP SEALS VARIETIES

Type I	Type II	Type III
LISBOA/C,C,A	*LISBOA*	*C, C, A*

C,C,A = Colonias, Commercio, Agricultura

NOTE: Three types of *BANCO NACIONAL ULTRAMARINO* seals are found on the bank notes issued for Nova Goa.

Portuguese Administration

Junta da Fazenda Publica

1882 Issue

#A2-A3 portr. Kg. Carlos I at upper ctr.

		Good	Fine	X
A2	**10 Rupias** 2.11.1882. Rare.	—	—	—
A3	**20 Rupias** 2.11.1882; 3.11.1882. Rare.	—	—	—

Governo Geral do Estado da India

1883 Issue

		Good	Fine	X
1	**5 Rupias** 1883.	—	—	—
2	**10 Rupias** 1883.	—	—	—
3	**20 Rupias** 1883.	—	—	—
4	**50 Rupias** 1883.	—	—	—

		Good	Fine	XF
5	**100 Rupias** 1883.	—	—	—
6	**500 Rupias** 1883.	—	—	—

1896 ISSUE

		Good	Fine	XF
7	**5 Rupias** 1.12.1896. Green and black. Portr. Kg. Carlos I at upper ctr.	—	—	—
8	**10 Rupias** 1.12.1896.	—	—	—
9	**20 Rupias** 1.12.1896.	—	—	—
10	**50 Rupias** 1.12.1896.	—	—	—

1899 ISSUE

		Good	Fine	XF
11	**5 Rupias** 15.11.1899. Brown and black. Portr. Kg. Carlos I and lg. *CINCO.* at ctr.	—	—	—
12	**10 Rupias** 15.11.1899.	—	—	—
13	**20 Rupias** 15.11.1899.	—	—	—
14	**50 Rupias** 15.11.1899.	—	—	—

BANCO NACIONAL ULTRAMARINO

NOVA GOA

1906 ISSUE

#15-18A printer: BWC.

		Good	Fine	XF
15	**5 Rupias** 1.1.1906. Blue and m/c. Allegorical woman w/trident at l. Back blue and maroon.			
	a. Steamship seal Type I (1906-18).	375.	1150.	—
	b. Steamship seal Type III (1918-21).	350.	1000.	—

#16-18A allegorical woman w/trident at ctr.

		Good	Fine	XF
16	**10 Rupias** 1.1.1906. Black and m/c. Back green and maroon.			
	a. Steamship seal Type I (1906-18).	375.	1150.	—
	b. Steamship seal Type III (1918-21).	350.	1000.	—
17	**20 Rupias** 1.1.1906. Black on lt. green unpt. Back lt. brown. Steamship seal Type I (1906-18). Rare.	—	—	—
17A	**20 Rupias** 1.1.1906. Dk. blue and m/c. Back purple and brown. Steamship seal Type III (1918-21). Rare.	—	—	—
18	**50 Rupias** 1.1.1906. Black and m/c. Back maroon and green. Steamship seal Type I (1906-18). Rare.	—	—	—
18A	**50 Rupias** 1.1.1906. Blue on m/c. Steamship seal Type III (1918-21). Rare.	—	—	—

1917 ISSUE

#19-22A printer: BWC.

#19-21A allegorical woman seated, anchor, sailing ship, sailboat in harbor at ctr.

		Good	Fine	XF
19	**4 Tangas** 1.10.1917. Red-brown and green. Back olive and maroon w/woman at ctr. Deep green steamship seal Type II.	30.00	100.	375.
19A	**4 Tangas** 1.10.1917. Violet and m/c. Like #19. Back blue and maroon. Blue steamship seal Type II.	—	—	—

		Good	Fine	XF
20	**8 Tangas** 1.10.1917. Green and red. Back green.	40.00	175.	475.
20A	**8 Tangas** 1.10.1917. Blue and m/c. Like #20. Back blue and maroon.	—	—	—
21	**1 Rupia** 1.10.1917. Brown. Back red.			
	a. Blue steamship seal Type I.	75.00	300.	750.
	b. Blue steamship seal Type II.	50.00	200.	600.
21A	**1 Rupia** 1.10.1917. Blue. Like #21. Back Maroon; woman w/caduceus seated by globe, cornucopia w/produce and anchor at ctr. on back. Brown steamship seal Type III.	50.00	200.	600.
22	**2 1/2 Rupias** 1.10.1917. Maroon and m/c. Like 22A. Back brown. Dull red steamship seal Type II.	125.	450.	1000.

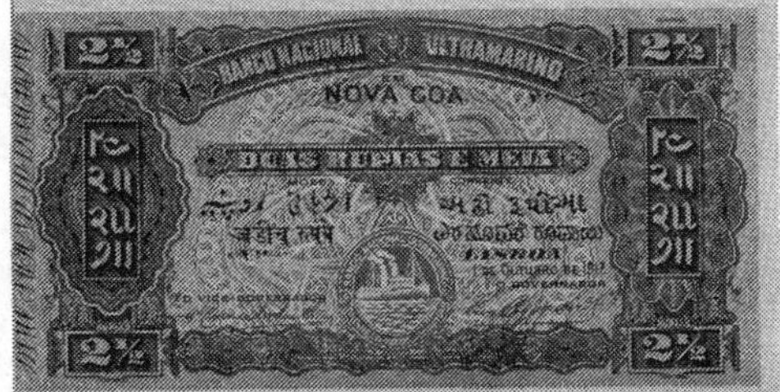

		Good	Fine	XF
22A	**2 1/2 Rupias** 1.10.1917. Red and m/c. Back green. Violet steamship seal Type III.	75.00	300.	750.

W/O DECRETO

		Good	Fine	XF
23	**1 Rupia** 1.1.1924. Blue and gold. Tiger head at ctr. Local bldg. on back.	25.00	85.00	300.
23A	**1 Rupia** 1.1.1924 (1929). Like #23.	20.00	50.00	175.

		Good	Fine	XF
24	**2 1/2 Rupias** 1.1.1924. Blue and purple. Like #23. Back purple.	150.	450.	1000.

		Good	Fine	XF
25	**5 Rupias** 1.1.1924. Green. Palace at ctr. Tiger on back.	100.	400.	850.
25A	**5 Rupias** 1.1.1924 (1929). Green. Like #25.	100.	350.	750.
26	**10 Rupias** 1.1.1924. Violet and blue. Similar to #25. Back violet.	150.	450.	1000.
26A	**10 Rupias** 1.1.1924 (1929). Like #26.			
	a. Sign. titles: *VICE GOVERNADOR* and *GOVERNADOR.*	100.	400.	850.
	b. Sign. titles: *ADMINISTRADOR* and *PRESIDENTE DO CONSELHO ADMINISTRATIVO.*	150.	450.	1000.
27	**20 Rupias** 1.1.1924. Violet and pink. Similar to #25. Back brownish violet.	200.	600.	—
28	**50 Rupias** 1.1.1924. Purple and maroon. Elephant at ctr. Back purple; sailing ship. Rare.	—	—	—

		Good	Fine	XF
29	**100 Rupias** 1.1.1924. Purple and brown. Similar to #28. Back purple. Rare.	—	—	—
30	**500 Rupias** 1.1.1924. Blue and maroon. Similar to #28. Back grayish purple. Rare.	—	—	—

DECRETO NO. 17 154 (1929)

#23-30 printer: TDLR.

1938 ISSUE

		Good	Fine	XF
31	**5 Rupias** 11.1.1938. Green on lilac unpt. Like #25 but date at upper l.	50.00	125.	300.

		Good	Fine	XF
32	**10 Rupias** 11.1.1938, Red-violet on blue unpt. Like #26 but date at upper l.	50.00	125.	300

Note: Crude reproductions of #32 are forgeries, not an emergency issue.

		Good	Fine	XF
33	**20 Rupias** 11.1.1938. Olive-brown on peach unpt. Like #27 but date at upper l.	75.00	175.	400

		Good	Fine	XF
34	**50 Rupias** 11.1.1938. Blue on brown unpt. Like #28. Rare.	—	—	—

INDIA PORTUGUESA

1945 ISSUE

#35-40 steamship seal at upper l., portr. A. de Albuquerque at r. Woman, sailing ships at ctr., arms at upper r. on back. Printer: BWC.

		Good	Fine	XF
35	**5 Rupias** 29.11.1945. Green on blue and brown unpt.	8.00	40.00	100.

		Good	Fine	XF
36	**10 Rupias** 29.11.1945. Brown and m/c.	10.00	50.00	150.

		Good	Fine	XF
37	**20 Rupias** 29.11.1945. Blue and m/c.	20.00	75.00	250.
38	**50 Rupias** 29.11.1945. Dk. red and m/c.	30.00	200.	450.

		Good	Fine	XF
39	**100 Rupias** 29.11.1945. Purple and m/c.	50.00	225.	500.

		Good	Fine	XF
40	**500 Rupias** 29.11.1945. Green and m/c.	375.	850.	—

INDIA PORTUGUESA

1959 ISSUE

#41-46 portr. A. de Albuquerque at r. Steamship seal at upper l. Early explorer, sailing ships at ctr. on back. Sign. varieties. Printer: TDLR.

		VG	VF	UNC
41	**30 Escudos** 2.1.1959. Dk. red and m/c.	5.00	20.00	60.00

		VG	VF	UNC
42	**60 Escudos** 2.1.1959. Black and m/c.	7.50	25.00	80.00

		VG	VF	UNC
43	**100 Escudos** 2.1.1959. Blue and m/c.	10.00	40.00	175.
44	**300 Escudos** 2.1.1959. Violet and m/c.	25.00	100.	250.
45	**600 Escudos** 2.1.1959. Green and m/c.	40.00	125.	375.

		VG	VF	UNC
46	**1000 Escudos** 2.1.1959. Brown and m/c.	75.00	200.	500.

PUERTO RICO

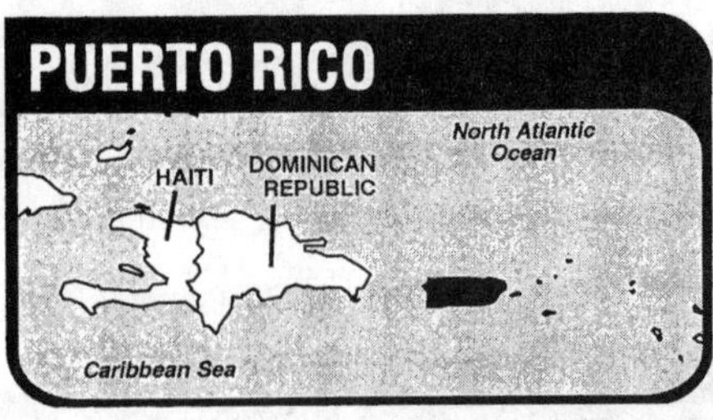

The Commonwealth of Puerto Rico, the easternmost island of the Greater Antilles in the West Indies, has an area of 3,435 sq. mi. (9,104 sq. km.) and a population of 3.3 million. Capital: San Juan. The commonwealth has its own constitution and elects its own governor. Its people are citizens of the United States, liable to the draft - but not to federal taxation. The chief industries of Puerto Rico are manufacturing, agriculture, and tourism. Manufactured goods, cement, dairy and livestock products, sugar, rum, and coffee are exported, mainly to the United States.

Puerto Rico ("Rich Port") was discovered by Columbus who landed on the island and took possession for Spain on Oct. 19, 1493 - the only time Columbus set foot on the soil of what is now a possession of the United States. The first settlement, Caparra, was established by Ponce de Leon in 1508. The early years of the colony were not promising. Considerable gold was found, but the supply was soon exhausted. Efforts to enslave the Indians caused violent reprisals. Hurricanes destroyed crops and homes. French, Dutch, and English freebooters burned the towns. Puerto Rico remained a Spanish possession until 1898, when it was ceded to the United States following the Spanish-American War. Puerto Ricans were granted a measure of self-government and U.S. citizenship in 1917. Effective July 25, 1952, a Congressional resolution elevated Puerto Rico to the status of a free commonwealth associated with the United States.

Vieque (or Crab Island), located to the east of Puerto Rico, is the largest of the Commonwealth's major offshore islands. The others are Culebra, a naval station to the east, and Mona to the west.

RULERS:

Spanish, 1493-1898 United States of America, 1898-present

MONETARY SYSTEM:

1 Peso = 5 Pesetas = 100 Centavos to 1898
1 Dollar = 100 Cents, 1898-

SPANISH ADMINISTRATION

TESORERÍA NACIONAL

1812 ISSUE

		Good	Fine	XF
1	**8 Reales** 1812. Black. Arms in circle of dots at ctr. Rare.	—	—	—

1813 ISSUE

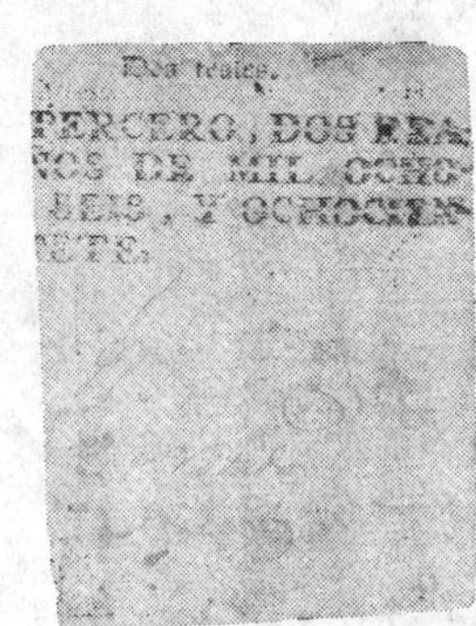

		Good	Fine	XF
2	**8 Reales** 1813. Black. Paschal lamb at ctr.			
	a. White paper.	—	—	—
	b. Blue paper. Rare.	—	—	—

DECREES OF 3.9.1811 AND 29.6.1813

Issued in 1814.

		Good	Fine	XF
3	**3 Pesos** 1814 (Roman Numerals). Black. Uniface, vertical format. Rare.	—	—	—

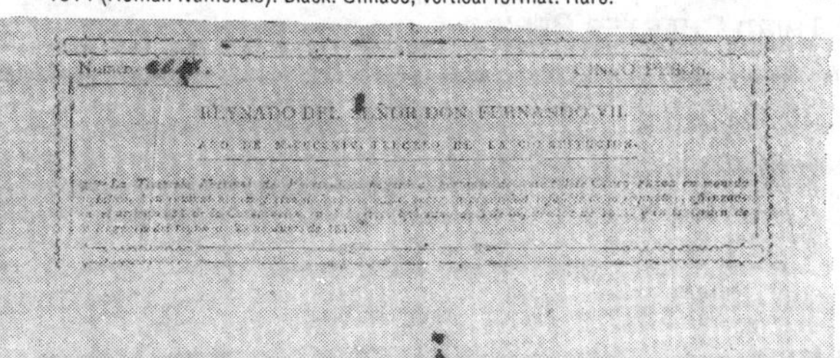

		Good	Fine	XF
4	**5 Pesos** 1814 (Roman Numerals). Black. Uniface, horizontal format. Rare.	—	—	—

1815-19 ISSUE

#5-6 uniface. Printer: Murray Draper Fairman.

		Good	Fine	XF
5	**3 Pesos** July 1815; 4.8.1815. Black. Crowned Spanish arms at upper ctr.	1500.	3000.	6000.

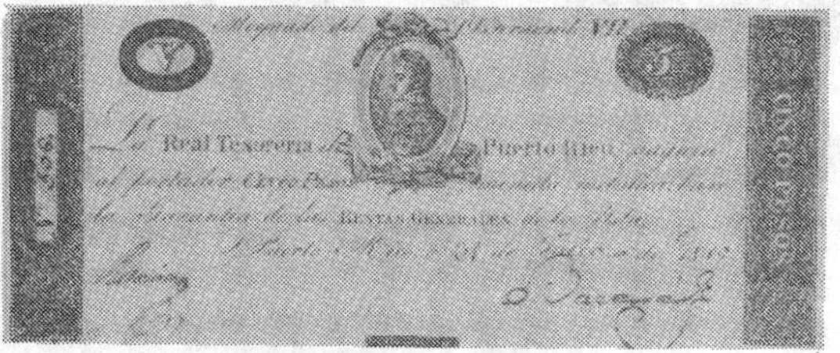

		Good	Fine	XF
6	**5 Pesos** 25.7.1819; 31.7.1819. Black. Portr. Kg. Ferdinand VII at top ctr.	1500.	3000.	6000.

MINISTERIO DE ULTRAMAR

1895 BILLETE DE CANJE

Circulating Bill

		Good	Fine	XF
7	**1 Peso** 17.8.1895. Black on yellow unpt. Portr. man at l. Back blue; crowned arms of Spain at ctr.			
	a. W/full counterfoil.	30.00	85.00	200.
	b. W/partial counterfoil.	25.00	75.00	185.
	c. W/o counterfoil.	20.00	60.00	150.

BANCO ESPAÑOL DE PUERTO RICO

SERIES A

#8-11 Paschal lamb at l. Printer: ABNC.

		Good	Fine	XF
8	**5 Pesos** ND (ca.1889). Black on green and yellow unpt. Seated child painting at r. Back green; crowned Spanish arms at l. Specimen or proof.	—	—	—

#9-13 crowned Spanish arms at ctr. on back.

		Good	Fine	XF
9	**10 Pesos** ND (ca.1889). Black on yellow and brown unpt. 2 coastwatchers at r. Back brown.			
	a. Issued note.	—	—	—
	p. Proof.	—	—	—
10	**20 Pesos** ND (ca.1889). Black on orange and yellow unpt. 3 men lifting crate at upper ctr. Back orange. Specimen or proof.	—	—	—
11	**50 Pesos** ND (ca.1889). Black on blue and yellow unpt. Columbus sighting land at ctr. r. Back blue. Proof.	—	—	—

#12-13 Paschal lamb at r. Printer: ABNC.

		Good	Fine	XF
12	**100 Pesos** ND (ca.1889). Black on yellow and brown unpt. Man w/globe and map at l., 2 allegorical women at ctr. Back brown. Proof.	—	—	—
13	**200 Pesos** ND (ca.1889). Black on orange and yellow unpt. Justice at l., seated woman w/globe at ctr. Back orange. Archive copy.	—	—	—

SERIES B

#14-19 designs like previous issue. Printer: ABNC.

		Good	Fine	XF
14	**5 Pesos** ND. Black on brown and yellow unpt. Like #8. Back brown. Archive copy.	—	—	—
15	**10 Pesos** ND. Black on yellow and blue unpt. Like #9. Back tan. Archive copy.	—	—	—
16	**20 Pesos** ND. Black on orange and blue unpt. Like #10. Back blue. Archive copy.	—	—	—
17	**50 Pesos** ND. Black on brown and yellow unpt. Like #11. Back blue. Specimen.	—	—	—
18	**100 Pesos** ND. Black on yellow and red unpt. Like #12. Back red. Archive copy.	—	—	—
19	**200 Pesos** ND. Black on green and yellow unpt. Like #13. Back green. Archive copy.	—	—	—

SERIES C

#20-25 designs like previous issue. Printer: ABNC.

		Good	Fine	XF
20	**5 Pesos** ND. Black on red and yellow unpt. Like #8. Back tan. Archive copy.	—	—	—
21	**10 Pesos** ND. Black on green and red unpt. Like #9. Back blue. Archive copy.	—	—	—
22	**20 Pesos** ND. Black on orange and brown unpt. Like #10. Back brown. Archive copy.	—	—	—
23	**50 Pesos** ND. Black on red and yellow unpt. Like #11. Back red. Specimen or proof.	—	—	—
24	**100 Pesos** ND. Black on yellow and green unpt. Like #12. Back green. Specimen or proof.	—	—	—
25	**200 Pesos** ND. Black on brown and yellow unpt. Like #13. Back brown. Specimen.	—	—	—

1894 SERIES D

#26-29 portr. Qn. mother and regent of Spain's Maria Christina. Printer: ABNC.

		Good	Fine	XF
26	**5 Pesos** 1.12.1894; 2.3.1896; 3.11.1896; 1.7.1897. Black on brown and yellow unpt. Similar to #8. Back brown.			
	a. Issued note.	—	—	—
	b. Ovpt: *MAYAGUEZ*. 1.12.1894.	—	—	—

		Good	Fine	XF
27	**10 Pesos** 1894-97. Black on blue and yellow unpt. Similar to #9. Back orange.	—	—	—
28	**20 Pesos** 1894-97. Black on blue and yellow unpt. Similar to #10. Back blue. Specimen or proof.	—	—	—

		Good	Fine	XF
29	**50 Pesos** 1894-97. Black on brown and yellow unpt. Similar to #11. Back brown. Specimen or proof.	—	—	—

#30-34 portr. Regent at r.

		Good	Fine	XF
30	**100 Pesos** 1894-97. Black on orange and yellow unpt. Similar to #12. Back orange. Specimen or proof.	—	—	—
31	**200 Pesos** 1895-97. Black on green and yellow unpt. Similar to #13. Back green. Specimen.	—	—	—

United States Administration

Banco Español de Puerto Rico

1900 Provisional Issue

		Good	Fine	XF
32	**5 Pesos** 1.5.1900. Ovpt: *MONEDA AMERICANA* on #20. Series C.	—	—	—

First National Bank of Porto Rico at San Juan

1902 Third Charter Period

#33-36 red seal at lower r.

		Good	Fine	XF
33	**10 Dollars** 1902. Black. Portr. McKinley at l. Back deep green. Rare.	—	—	—
34	**20 Dollars** 1902. Black. Portr. McCulloch at l. Back deep green. Rare.	—	—	—
35	**50 Dollars** 1902. Black. Portr. Sherman at l. Back deep green. Unique	—	—	—
36	**100 Dollars** 27.10.1902. Black. Portr. Knox at l. Back green. Unique	—	—	—

1908 Issue

#37-40 blue seal at lower r. Dates *1902, 1908* on back. Designs like #33-36.

		Good	Fine	XF
37	**10 Dollars** 27.10.1902. Black. Back green. Unique.	—	—	—
38	**20 Dollars** ca.1908. Unknown in private hands.	—	—	—
39	**50 Dollars** ca.1908. Unknown in private hands.	—	—	—
40	**100 Dollars** ca.1908. Unknown in private hands.	—	—	—

Banco de Puerto Rico

1901-04 Series E

#41-46 have "U.S. Cy." (U.S. Currency) on face, Paschal lamb at ctr. on back. Printer: ABNC.

		Good	Fine	XF
41	**5 Pesos = 5 Dollars** 1.7.1904. Black on orange unpt. Seated woman holding scale by cornucopia w/money and chest at ctr. Back orange.	1250.	3000.	—
42	**10 Pesos = 10 Dollars** ND (ca.1901-04). Black on brown and yellow unpt. Seated allegorical woman w/marine implements at ctr. Back brown. Proof.	—	—	—
43	**20 Pesos = 20 Dollars** ND (ca.1901-04). Black on blue and yellow unpt. Seated allegorical woman w/harvest at ctr. Back blue. Proof.	—	—	—
44	**50 Pesos = 50 Dollars** ND (ca.1901-04). Black on olive and yellow unpt. Train, allegorical women w/industrial implements, and sailing ships at ctr. r. Back olive. Archive copy.	—	—	—
45	**100 Pesos = 100 Dollars** ND (ca.1901-04). Black on olive and red unpt. Allegorical woman w/sacks and barrels at ctr. Back red. Proof.	—	—	—
46	**200 Pesos = 200 Dollars** ND (ca.1901-04). Black on yellow and purple unpt. Cherub at upper l. and r., allegorical woman w/plants and bird at ctr. Back purple. Proof.	—	—	—

1909 Series F

		Good	Fine	XF
47	**5 Dollars** 1.7.1909. Black. Portr. Columbus at l., red Paschal lamb seal at r. Back green; seated woman w/lamb at ctr.			
	a. Issued note.	600.	1750.	4250.
	b. Cancelled w/ovpt: *CANCELADO* w/or w/o punched holes.	400.	1000.	2000.

		Good	Fine	XF
48	**10 Dollars** 1.7.1909. Black. Ponce de Leon at l., red Paschal lamb seal at r. Back brown; Liberty at ctr.			
	a. Issued note.	1000.	2750.	—
	b. Cancelled w/punched holes.	500.	1400.	—

Note: Uniface trial designs similar to #47 and #48 but dated 1907 were in the ABNC archives.

QATAR & DUBAI

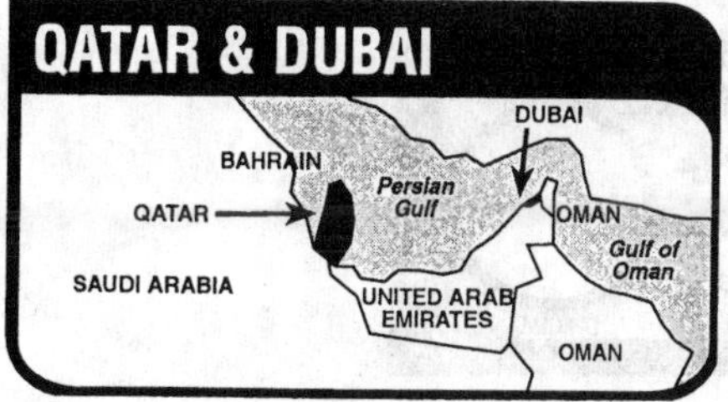

The State of Qatar, which occupies the Qatar Peninsula jutting into the Persian Gulf from eastern Saudi Arabia, has an area of 4,247 sq. mi. (11,000 sq. km.) and a population of 382,000. Capital: Doha. The traditional occupations of pearling, fishing and herding have been replaced in economics by petroleum-related industries. Crude oil, petroleum products, and tomatoes are exported.

Dubai is one of the seven sheikhdoms comprising the United Arab Emirates (formerly Trucial States) located along the southern shore of the Persian Gulf. It has a population of about 60,000. Qatar, which initiated protective treaty relations with Great Britain in 1820, achieved independence on Sept. 3, 1971, upon withdrawal of the British military presence from the Persian Gulf, and replaced its special treaty arrangement with Britain with a treaty of general friendship. Dubai attended independence on Dec. 1, 1971, upon termination of Britain's protective treaty with the trucial sheikhdoms, and on Dec. 2, 1971, entered into the union of the United Arab Emirates.

Despite the fact that the sultanate of Qatar and the sheikhdom of Dubai were merged under a monetary union, the two territories were governed independently from each other. Qatar now uses its own currency while Dubai uses the United Arab Emirates currency and coins.

MONETARY SYSTEM:

1 Riyal = 100 Dirhem

SULTANATE AND SHEIKHDOM

QATAR AND DUBAI CURRENCY BOARD

1960s ND ISSUE

#1-6 dhow, derrick and palm tree at l. Wmk: Falcon's head.

		VG	VF	UNC
1	**1 Riyal** ND. Dk. green on m/c unpt.			
	a. Issued note.	10.00	50.00	150.
	s. Specimen, punch hole cancelled.	—	—	125.

		VG	VF	UNC
2	**5 Riyals** ND. Purple on m/c unpt.			
	a. Issued note.	20.00	100.	800.
	s. Specimen, punch hole cancelled.	—	—	200.

		VG	VF	UNC
3	**10 Riyals** ND. Gray-blue on m/c unpt.			
	a. Issued note.	40.00	175.	1100.
	s. Specimen, punch hole cancelled.	—	—	300.
4	**25 Riyals** ND. Blue on m/c unpt.			
	a. Issued note.	500.	2000.	5000.
	s. Specimen, punch hole cancelled.	—	—	1500.

#		VG	VF	UNC
5	**50 Riyals** ND. Red on m/c unpt.			
	a. Issued note.	350.	1500.	4000.
	s. Specimen, punch hole cancelled.	—	—	1300.

#		VG	VF	UNC
6	**100 Riyals** ND. Olive on m/c unpt.			
	a. Issued note.	250.	1250.	3000.
	s. Specimen, punch hole cancelled.	—	—	1250.

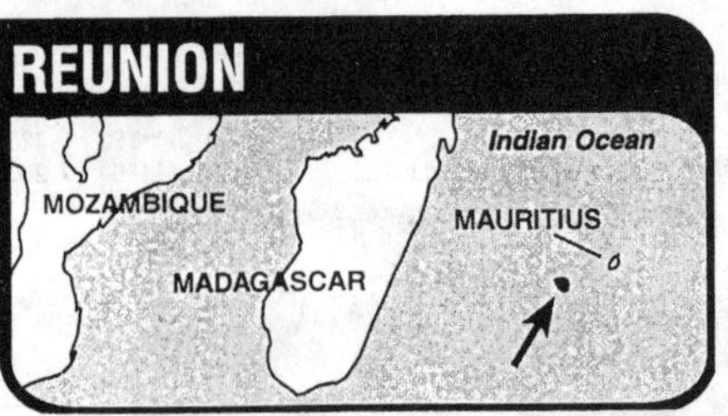

The Department of Reunion, an overseas department of France located in the Indian Ocean 400 miles (640 km.) east of Madagascar, has an area of 969 sq. mi. (2,510 sq. km.) and a population of 556,000. Capital: Saint-Denis. The island's volcanic soil is extremely fertile. Sugar, vanilla, coffee and rum are exported.

Although first visited by Portuguese navigators in the 16th century, Reunion was uninhabited when claimed for France by Capt. Goubert in 1638. It was first colonized as Isle de Bourbon by the French in 1662 as a layover station for ships rounding the Cape of Good Hope to India. It was renamed Reunion in 1793. The island remained in French possession except for the period of 1810-15, when it was occupied by the British. Reunion became an overseas department of France in 1946, and in 1958 voted to continue that status within the new French Union. Banque de France notes were introduced 1.1.1973.

RULERS:

French, 1638-1810, 1815-
British, 1810-1815

MONETARY SYSTEM:

1 Franc = 100 Centimes
1 Nouveau Franc = 50 Old Francs, 1960 Note: For earlier issues see Isles of France and of Bourbon.

FRENCH ADMINISTRATION

ILE DE LA RÉUNION - TRÉSOR COLONIAL

DECRET DU 2.5.1879 (1884 FIRST ISSUE)

#1-4 uniface.

#		Good	Fine	XF
1	**50 Centimes** 8.7.1884. Black.	150.	450.	—
2	**1 Franc** 8.7.1884. Black. Like #1. 2 plate varieties.	165.	500.	—
3	**2 Francs** 8.7.1884. Black on yellow paper.	200.	600.	—

#		Good	Fine	XF
4	**3 Francs** 4.6.1884. Black on green paper. Rare.	—	—	—

Note: Denominations of 30, 50 and 100 Francs are reported.

DECRET DU 2.5.1879 (1884 SECOND ISSUE)

#5-7 w/different appearance of text and border (similar to Guadeloupe #1).

#		Good	Fine	XF
5	**50 Centimes** 4.6 1884. Black on cream paper.	450.	—	—
6	**1 Franc** 4.6 1884. Black on dark blue paper.	500.	—	—
7	**2 Francs** 4.6. 1884. Black on gray paper.	550.	—	—

1886 ISSUE

#8-10 cherub w/pillar and cornucopia at l. and r., allegories of Agriculture and Commerce at ctr. on face. Head at l. and r., value over anchor at ctr. on back.

		Good	Fine	XF
8	**50 Centimes** 21.6.1886. Black on lt. gray paper.	150.	450.	—
9	**1 Franc** 10.3.1886. Black on pale blue or lt. green paper.	185.	550.	—

		Good	Fine	XF
10	**2 Francs** 1886. Black.	225.	675.	—

Banque de la Réunion

Law of 12.9.1873

		Good	Fine	XF
11	**5 Francs** L. 1873. Border of trees and cornucopia. Brown paper. Uniface. Rare.	—	—	—
12	**10 Francs** L.1873. Border of flowers and 3 cherubs. White paper. Uniface. Rare.	—	—	—

Law of 1874

		Good	Fine	XF
13	**5 Francs** L.1874 (1890-1912). Blue. Medallic head at l. and r. 10 sign. varieties.	200.	—	—

Law of 1901

		Good	Fine	XF
14	**5 Francs** L1901 (1912-44). Red. Like #13. Back gray. 6 sign. varieties.	20.00	60.00	150.

1874; 1875 Issue

		Good	Fine	XF
15	**25 Francs** ND (1876-1908). Blue. Flowers and fruit w/landscape in background on brown back. 3 sign. varieties.	250.	550.	1500.
16	**100 Francs** ND (1874-1917). Red. Like #15. 6 sign. varieties. Rare.	—	—	—
17	**500 Francs** ND (1875-1929). Black on cream unpt. Like #16. 5 sign. varieties. Rare.	—	—	—

1912; 1914 Issue

		Good	Fine	XF
18	**25 Francs** ND (1912-30). Blue w/black text. Like #15. Back maroon. 5 sign. varieties.	175.	500.	—
19	**100 Francs** ND (1914-29). Maroon. Like #16. Back blue. 4 sign. varieties. Rare.	—	—	—

1917 Emergency WWI Fractional Issue

		VG	VF	UNC
20	**5 Centimes** ND (1917). Black on red cardboard w/embossed seal. Uniface.	15.00	70.00	200.

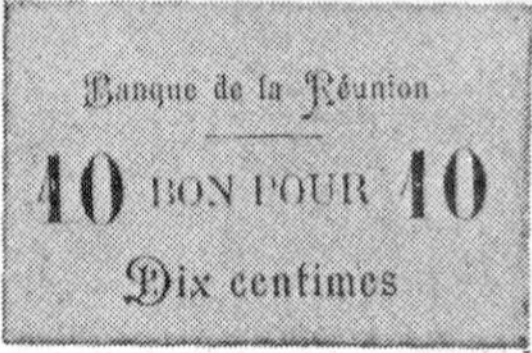

		VG	VF	UNC
21	**10 Centimes** ND (1917). Black on brown cardboard w/embossed seal. Uniface.	35.00	125.	350.

#22 not assigned.

1923-30 Issue

		Good	Fine	XF
23	**25 Francs** ND (1930-44). Purple and m/c. Woman wearing wreath at ctr., flowers and fruit in background. 4 sign. varieties.	40.00	150.	500.

		Good	Fine	XF
24	**100 Francs** ND (1926-44). M/c. Woman w/staff at l. 5 sign. varieties.	150.	400.	1000.
25	**500 Francs** ND (1923-44). M/c. Like #24. 5 sign. varieties.	225.	700.	—

1937-40 Emergency Circulating Bearer Check Issue

		Good	Fine	XF
26	**100 Francs** 29.11.1937; 8.10.1940; 5.11.1940. Apricot paper. Rare.	—	—	—
27	**500 Francs** 29.11.1937; 8.10.1940; 5.11.1940; 25.11.1940. Rare.	—	—	—
28	**1000 Francs** 29.11.1937; 8.10.1940; 5.11.1940. Rare.	—	—	—
29	**5000 Francs** 8.10.1940; 5.11.1940. Rare.	—	—	—

Note: An issue of circulating checks dated 1932 is reported in denominations of 100, 500 and 1000 Francs.

Vichy French Government

Banque de la Réunion

Arreté Local Du 8.10.1942

#30-32 Francisque (Vichy axe) at upper l. and r.

		Good	Fine	XF
30	**50 Centimes** L. 1942. Lt. purple unpt.	175.	400.	900.
31	**1 Franc** L. 1942. Lt. blue unpt.	175.	400.	900.

		Good	Fine	XF
32	**2 Francs** L. 1942. Orange unpt.	175.	400.	900.

FREE FRENCH GOVERNMENT

BANQUE DE LA RÉUNION

1942 ND ISSUE

		Good	Fine	XF
32A	**2 Francs** ND (-old date 8.10.1942). Like #35 but w/black ovpt. line on *Décret du 8 October 1942.* Both Crosses of Lorraine in black. Rare.	—	—	—

ARRETÉ LOCAL DU 12.8.1943

#33-35 Cross of Lorraine in red at upper l. and r.

		Good	Fine	XF
33	**50 Centimes** L. 1943. Lt. purple unpt.	160.	325.	725.
34	**1 Franc** L. 1943. Lt. blue unpt.	160.	325.	725.
35	**2 Francs** L. 1943. Orange unpt.	160.	325.	725.

2 Provisional Issues w/o Reunion Name

CAISSE CENTRALE DE LA FRANCE LIBRE

1943 ND PROVISIONAL ISSUE

#36-38 types of French Equatorial Africa w/special serial # ranges. Reunion not mentioned. Printer: BWC (w/o imprint).

		Good	Fine	XF
36	**5 Francs** L.1941 (ca. 1943). Type of FEA #10. Serial # AN 100 001-AN 260 000.	20.00	60.00	—
37	**100 Francs** L.1941 (1944-45). Tyype of FEA #13.			
	a. Serial # range PA 270 001 - PA 470 000. (July 1944.)	50.00	150.	—
	b. Serial # range PB 700 001 - PB 900 000. (Jan. 1945.)	70.00	150.	—
	c. Serial # range PE 590 001 - PF 090 000. (31.12.1945).	70.00	150.	—
38	**1000 Francs** L.1941 (ca. 1943). Type of FEA #14. Serial TA 030 001-TA 060 000; TA 215 001-TA 235 000; TA 255 001-TA 275 000.	400.	1000.	2000.

Note: See also St. Pierre & Miquelon #10-14.

CAISSE CENTRALE DE LA FRANCE D'OUTRE-MER

1944 ND PROVISIONAL ISSUE

#39-40 types of French Equatorial Africa w/special serial # ranges. Reunion not mentioned. Printer: BWC (w/o imprint).

		Good	Fine	XF
39	**100 Francs** L.1944. Similar to FEA #18.			
	a. Serial # PQ 200 001 - PQ 700 000.	50.00	150.	—
	b. Serial # PS 700 001 - PS 800 000.	50.00	150.	—
40	**1000 Francs** L.1944. Similar to FEA #19. Serial # TD 125 001 - TD 135 000; TD 185 001 - TD 235 000.	700.	1500.	—

Note: See also St. Pierre & Miquelon #15-18.

1947 ND ISSUE

#41-48 ovpt: *LA RÉUNION* on French Equatorial Africa Issues.

		VG	VF	UNC
41	**5 Francs** ND (1947). Blue and m/c. Ship at l., Bougainville at r. Woman w/fruit and house on back.			
	a. Issued note.	7.50	40.00	165.
	s. Specimen.	—	—	90.00
42	**10 Francs** ND (1947). Blue and m/c. Colbert at l., ships at r. River scene and plants on back.			
	a. Issued note.	7.50	50.00	185.
	s. Specimen.	—	—	100.
43	**20 Francs** ND (1947). Brown and m/c. 4 people w/huts at l. E. Gentil at r. 2 men on back.			
	a. Issued note.	10.00	60.00	200.
	s. Specimen.	—	—	110.

		VG	VF	UNC
44	**50 Francs** ND (1947). M/c. B d'Esnambuc at l., ship at r. Woman on back.			
	a. Issued note.	10.00	50.00	250.
	s. Specimen.	—	—	150.
45	**100 Francs** ND (1947). M/c. La Bourdonnais at l., 2 women at r. Woman looking at mountains on back.			
	a. Issued note.	15.00	75.00	350.
	s. Specimen.	—	—	175.
46	**500 Francs** ND (1947). M/c. Bldgs. and sailboat at l., 2 women at r. Ox-carts w/wood and plants on back.			
	a. Issued note.	40.00	125.	500.
	s. Specimen.	—	—	225.

		VG	VF	UNC
47	**1000 Francs** ND (1947). M/c. 2 women at r. Woman at r., 2 men in small boat on back.			
	a. Issued note.	50.00	150.	675.
	s. Specimen.	—	—	250.
48	**5000 Francs** ND (1947). Brown and m/c. Gen Schoelcher at ctr. r. Family on back.			
	a. Issued note.	125.	350.	1100.
	s. Specimen.	—	—	375.

INSTITUT D'EMISSION DES DÉPARTEMENTS D'OUTRE-MER

1960 ND PROVISIONAL ISSUE

#49 and 50 ovpt: *LA RÉUNION.*

		VG	VF	UNC
49	**100 Francs** ND (1960). M/c. Like #45.			
	a. Issued note.	25.00	100.	300.
	s. Specimen.	—	—	200.

		VG	VF	UNC
50	**5000 Francs** ND (1960). Brown and m/c. Like #48.			
	a. Issued note.	100.	300.	1000.
	s. Specimen.	—	—	450.

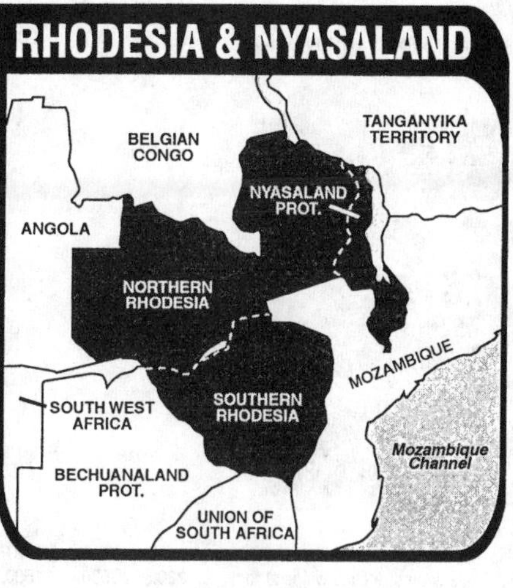

Rhodesia and Nyasaland (now the Republics of Malawi, Zambia and Zimbabwe) was located in the east-central part of southern Africa, had an area of 487,133 sq. mi. (1,261,678 sq. km.). Capital: Salisbury. The area was the habitat of paleolithic man, contains extensive evidence of earlier civilizations, notably the world-famous ruins of Zimbabwe, a gold-trading center that flourished about the 14th or 15th century AD. The Portuguese of the 16th century were the first Europeans to attempt to develop south-central Africa, but it remained for Cecil Rhodes and the British South Africa Co. to open the hinterlands. Rhodes obtained a concession for mineral rights from local chiefs in 1888 and administered his African empire (named Southern Rhodesia in 1895) through the British South Africa Co. until 1923, when the British government annexed the area after the white settlers voted for existence as a separate entity, rather than for incorporation into the Union of South Africa. From Sept. of 1953 through 1963 Southern Rhodesia was joined with the British protectorates of Northern Rhodesia and Nyasaland into a multiracial federation. When the federation was dissolved at the end of 1963, Northern Rhodesia and Nyasaland became the independent states of Zambia and Malawi.

Britain was prepared to grant independence to Southern Rhodesia but declined to do so when the politically dominant white Rhodesians refused to give assurances of representative government. On May 11, 1965, following two years of unsuccessful negotiation with the British government, Prime Minister Ian Smith issued a unilateral declaration of independence. Britain responded with economic sanctions supported by the United Nations. After further futile attempts to effect an accommodation, the Rhodesian Parliament severed all ties with Britain, and on March 2, 1970, established the Republic of Rhodesia.

On March 3, 1978, Prime Minister Ian Smith and three moderate black nationalist leaders signed an agreement providing for black majority rule. The name of the country was changed to Zimbabwe Rhodesia.

After the election of March 3, 1980, the country again changed its name to the Republic of Zimbabwe. The Federation of Rhodesia and Nyasaland (or the Central African Federation), comprising the British protectorates of Northern Rhodesia and Nyasaland and the self-governing colony of Southern Rhodesia, was located in the east-central part of southern Africa. The multiracial federation had an area of about 487,000 sq. mi. (1,261,330 sq. km.) and a population of 6.8 million. Capital: Salisbury, in Southern Rhodesia. The geographical unity of the three British possessions suggested the desirability of political and economic union as early as 1924. Despite objections by the African constituency of Northern Rhodesia and Nyasaland, who feared the dominant influence of prosperious and self governing Southern Rhodesia, the Central African Federation was established in Sept. of 1953. As feared, the Federation was effectively and profitably dominated by the European consituency of Southern Rhodesia despite the fact that the three component countries retained their basic prefederation political structure. It was dissolved at the end of 1963, largely because of the effective opposition of the Nyasaland African Congress. Northern Rhodesia and Nyasaland became independent states of Zambia and Malawi in 1964. Southern Rhodesia unilaterally declared its independence as Rhodesia the following year; this act was not recognized by the British Government.

RULERS:

British to 1963

MONETARY SYSTEM:

1 Shilling = 12 Pence
1 Pound = 20 Shillings to 1963

BRITISH ADMINISTRATION

BANK OF RHODESIA AND NYASALAND

1956 ISSUE

#20-23 portr. Qn. Elizabeth II at r. Various date and sign. varieties. Wmk: C. Rhodes. Printer: BWC.

		VG	VF	UNC
20	**10 Shillings** 1956-61. Reddish brown on m/c unpt. Fish eagle at lower l. River scene on back.			
	a. Sign. A. P. Grafftey-Smith. 3.4.1956-17.6.1960.	45.00	250.	1000.
	b. Sign. B. C. J. Richards. 30.12.1960-1.2.1961.	50.00	285.	1100.
	s. As a. Specimen punched hole cancelled. 3.4.1956.	—	—	450.
	ct. Color trial. Green on pink unpt.	—	—	850.

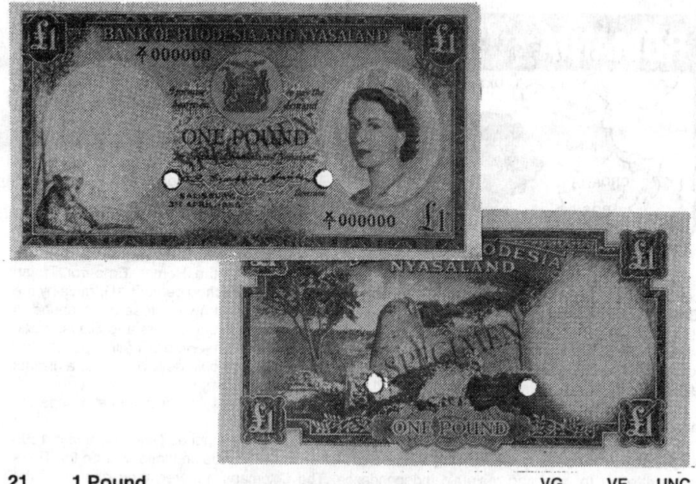

		VG	VF	UNC
21	**1 Pound** 1956-61. Green on m/c unpt. Leopard at lower l. Zimbabwe ruins at ctr. on back.			
	a. Sign. A. P. Grafftey-Smith. 3.4.1956-17.6.1960.	35.00	225.	1100.
	b. Sign. B. C. J. Richards. 23.12.1960-1.2.1961.	40.00	235.	1200.
	s. As a. Specimen punched hole cancelled. 2.5.1956.	—	—	550.
	ct. Color trial. Blue on orange unpt.	—	—	850.

		VG	VF	UNC
22	**5 Pounds** 1956-61. Blue on m/c unpt. Sable antelope at lower l. Victoria Falls on back.			
	a. Sign. A. P. Grafftey-Smith. 3.4.1956-17.6.1960.	85.00	375.	1400.
	b. Sign. B. C. J. Richards. 23.1.1961-3.2.1961.	95.00	425.	1750.
	s. As a. Specimen punched hole cancelled. 3.4.1956.	—	—	900.
	ct. Color trial. Red-brown on blue unpt.	—	—	1350.

		VG	VF	UNC
23	**10 Pounds** 1956-61. Brown on m/c unpt. Back gray-green; elephants at ctr.			
	a. Sign. A. P. Grafftey-Smith. 3.4.1956-17.6.1960.	350.	1000.	—
	b. Sign. B. C. J. Richards. 1.2.1961; 3.1.1961.	400.	1200.	—
	s. As a. Specimen punched hole cancelled. 3.4.1956.	—	—	1800.
	ct. Color trial. Green on m/c unpt.	—	—	2250.

Note: For earlier issues refer to Southern Rhodesia in Volume 2. For later issues refer to Malawi, Zambia, Rhodesia and Zimbabwe in Volume 3.

Romania, located in southeast Europe, has an area of 91,699 sq. mi. (237,500 sq. km.) and a population of 22.5 million. Capital: Bucharest. Machinery, foodstuffs, raw minerals and petroleum products are exported. The area of Romania, generally referred to as Dacia, was inhabited by Dacians or Getae, a people of Thracian stock. The kingdom of Dacia existed as early as 200 BC. After military campaigns in 105-106 AD the Roman Emperor Trajan conquered Dacia and converted it into a Roman province. During the third century AD, raids by the Goths became such a menace that the Roman legions were withdrawn across the Danube in 271AD. Successive waves of invaders, including Goths, Huns, Gepidae, Avars and Slavs, made the country a battleground although the Romanized population preserved a Latin speech and identity. Through gradual assimilation of the Slavonic tribes, these people developed into a distinct ethnic group called Wallachians (Valachs or Vlachs).

With defeat in 1526, Hungary came under Turkish rule. Transylvania became a separate principality under the protection of the Sultan (1541).

At the close of the sixteenth century, the three principalities were united (Transylvania in 1599 and Moldavia in 1600) by Prince Mihai Viteazul of Wallachia, who made continual war on the Turks in an attempt to gain and maintain independence. The Ottomans restored their control of the principalities after Michael's death. The last Turkish vassal was eliminated in 1699 and Austria obtained the possession of Transylvania by the Treaty of Karlowitz. Under Hapsburg's administration, the region was made into a grand principality in 1765.

Because of the decline of Turkish power during the eighteenth century, the Austrian and later Russian influence became preeminent in the area.

After 1821 Romanian rulers were reestablished. The principalities, although remaining under Sultan control, were more autonomous. In 1829, the Turkish monopoly of commerce was abolished. Important institutional reforms were adopted.

The results of the European insurrectionist movements of 1848 saw the Moldovaian and Wallachian provisional revolutionary governments put down by Russo-Turkish military intervention. In 1867, Transylvania was incorporated under Hungarian administration. The question of the union of Wallachia and Moldavia was resolved in 1859. The two assemblies elected a single prince, Alexandru Ioan Cuza, establishing the fruition of Romania. Prince Cuza was deposed in 1866. A provisional government then elected Prince Karl of Hohenzollern-Sigmaringen, who as Carol I was vested as hereditary prince. A rapid modernization of the country was perceived. Romania was successful in a war against Turkey (1877-78) and proclaimed itself to be independent. The Congress of Berlin (1878) recognized this fact. In 1881, Carol I became king. In 1888, Romania became a constitutional monarchy with a bicameral legislature.

A new constitution was adopted in 1923. During this time the government struggled with domestic problems, agrarian reform and economic reconstruction.

The government was reorganized along Fascist lines between September 14, 1940 - January 23, 1941. A military dictatorship followed. Marshal Ion Antonescu installed himself as chief of state. When the Germans invaded the Soviet Union, Romania also became involved in recovering the regions of Bessarabia and northern Bukovina annexed by Stalin in 1940.

On August 23, 1944, King Mihai I proclaimed an armistice with the Allied Forces. The Romanian army drove out the Germans and Hungarians in northern Transylvania, but the country was subsequently occupied by the Soviet army. That monarchy was abolished on December 30, 1947, and Romania became a "People's Republic" d on the Soviet regime. With the accession of N. Ceausescu to power, Romania began to exercise a considerable degree of independence, refusing to participate in the 1968 invasion of Czechoslovakia. In 1965, it was proclaimed a "Socialist Republic". After 1977, an oppressed and impoverished domestic scene worsened.

On December 17, 1989, an anti-Communist revolt began in Timisoara. On December 22, 1989 the Communist government was overthrown by organized freedom fighters in Bucharest. Ceausescu and his wife were arrested and later executed. The new government has established a republic.

RULERS:

Carol I (as Prince), 1866-81 (as King) 1881-1914
Ferdinand I, 1914-1927
Mihai I, 1927-1930
Carol II, 1930-1940
Mihai I, 1940-1947

MONETARY SYSTEM: 10,000 "old" Lei = 1 "new" Leu, 1.7.2005

1 Leu = 100 Bani

DATING

as found on certain issues

19	- VII	- 31	- 34
Century	Month	Day	Year

KINGDOM

BILET HYPOTHECAR

STATE NOTES OF THE PRINCIPALITY

1877 ISSUE

#1-4 Wmk: Trajan.

		Good	Fine	XF
1	**5 Lei** 12.6.1877. Blue. 2 allegorical women at lower ctr., children at l. and r. Arms at lower ctr. on back.	135.	380.	1200.

		Good	Fine	XF
2	**10 Lei** 12.6.1877. Blue. Similar to #1. Eagle w/outstretched wings at top ctr.	220.	530.	1600.
3	**20 Lei** 12.6.1877. Blue. 2 men and a woman at l., river and bridge scene at lower ctr., arms at r. 2 farm wives w/poles at r. on back.	250.	800.	—

		Good	Fine	XF
4	**50 Lei** 12.6.1877. Blue. Similar to #3. Eagle added as on #2.	300.	850.	—

#5 and 6 wmk: Minerva and Trajan.

		Good	Fine	XF
5	**100 Lei** 12.6.1877. Blue. Woman w/children at lower ctr. Allegorical figures, arms and eagle at ctr. on back.	320.	900.	—

		Good	Fine	XF
6	**500 Lei** 12.6.1877. Blue. 2 women and girl at l., arms at lower ctr., 3 women w/boy at r. Standing figure at l. and r., bust at ctr. on back.	330.	1000.	—

BANCA NATIONALA A ROMANIEI

1880 PROVISIONAL ISSUE

#7-12 ovpt. of new bank name on Bilet Hypothecar notes dated 12.8.1877.

		Good	Fine	XF
7	**5 Lei** 9.9.1880 (-old date 12.6.1877). Ovpt. on #1. (Not Issued).	—	—	—
8	**10 Lei** 9.9.1880 (-old date 12.6.1877). Ovpt. on #2.	—	—	—

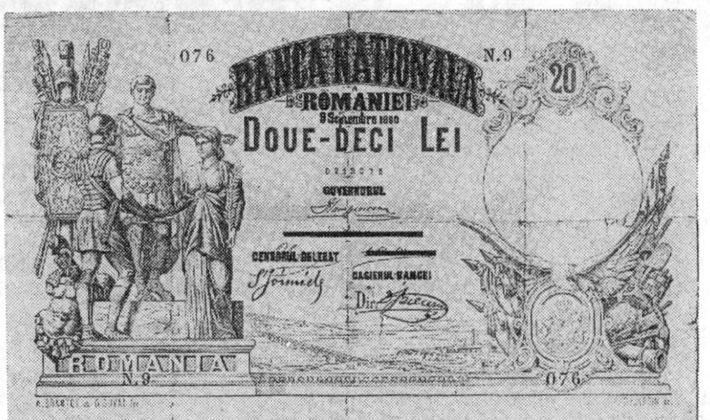

		Good	Fine	XF
9	**20 Lei** 9.9.1880 (-old date 12.6.1877). Ovpt. on #3.	—	—	—
10	**50 Lei** 9.9.1880 (-old date 12.6.1877). Ovpt. on #4.			
	a. Issued note.	—	—	—
	b. Cancelled note hand-stamped and perforated: *ANULAT*.	—	—	—
11	**100 Lei** 9.9.1880 (-old date 12.6.1877). Ovpt. on #5.			
	a. Issued note.	—	—	—
	b. Cancelled note hand-stamped and perforated: *ANULAT*.	—	—	—
12	**500 Lei** 9.9.1880 (-old date 12.6.1877). Ovpt. on #6.	—	—	—

1881 ISSUE

		Good	Fine	XF
13	**20 Lei** 19.1.1881-31.8.1895. Blue. 2 boys at ctr., boy at r. w/staff of Mercury. 7 sign. varieties.	—		

		VG	VF	UNC
14	**100 Lei** 28.2.1881-11.11.1907. Blue. 2 little children at upper l. and r.; eagle at top ctr. 9 sign. varieties.	25.00	100.	220.
15	**1000 Lei** 1881-1906. Blue. Woman w/sickle at l., woman w/oar at r. Round medallion w/bust of Trajan at upper ctr. on back. Sign. varieties.			
	a. 28.2.1881-1.6.1895. Rare.	—	—	—
	b. 19.9.1902-23.3.1906.	160.	375.	—

1896 ISSUE

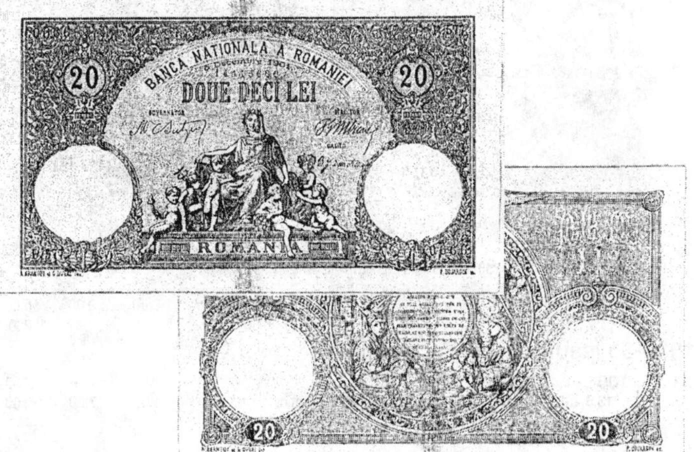

		VG	VF	UNC
16	**20 Lei** 14.3.1896-28.8.1908. Blue. Woman w/6 children at ctr. 3 sign. varieties.	45.00	120.	320.

1909-16 ISSUE

		VG	VF	UNC
17	**1 Leu** 12.3.1915; 27.3.1916. Violet-blue on pale pink unpt. (Unpt. usually barely visible; notes thus appear to be blue). Columns at l., woman at r. 3 signs. Wolf w/Romulus and Remus on back.	1.50	4.00	12.00

		VG	VF	UNC
18	**2 Lei** 12.3.1915. Violet-blue on pink unpt. (see #17). Woman at l., eagle w/cross in its mouth at r. Soldier w/sword at l., soldier w/bugle at r. on back. 3 sign., 2 sign. varieties.	2.00	5.00	15.00

		VG	VF	UNC
19	**5 Lei** 31.7.1914-22.11.1928. Violet. Farmer's wife w/distaff at l., arms at r. Woman and child picking apples at ctr. on back. Value numerals in violet. Wmk: Heads of Trajan and Minerva. 3 sign., w/6 sign. varieties.			
	a. Issued note.	2.50	8.50	22.50
	s. Specimen. 25.3.1920.	—	—	35.00

		VG	VF	UNC
20	**20 Lei** 26.2.1909-31.1.1929. Blue-violet. Girl w/fruit at l., boy w/oar at r. Flying eagle w/cross and arms flying over river on back. Wmk: Minerva and Trajan. 12 sign. varieties.	3.00	12.50	42.50

		VG	VF	UNC
21	**100 Lei** 14.1.1910-31.1.1929. Violet-blue. Woman seated wearing national costume at l. Wmk: head of Trajan and Minerva. 9 sign. varieties.	6.00	18.00	52.50

		VG	VF	UNC
22	**500 Lei** 11.2.1916-12.2.1920. Violet-blue. Woman w/boy at l., farmer's wife seated at r. 2 farm wives on back. 9 sign. varieties.			
	a. Issued note.	10.00	30.00	100.
	s. As a. specimen.	—	Unc	200.
23	**1000 Lei** 20.5.1910-22.10.1931. Woman w/sickle at l., woman w/oar at r. Similar to #15 but round medallion blank on back.			
	a. Issued note.	80.00	160.	320.
	s. Specimen. 31.1.1929.	—	—	—

1917 Issue

		VG	VF	UNC
24	**5 Lei** 16.2.1917. Violet-brown. Like #19. Numerals of value on back in yellow. Wmk: Lt. and dk. half-spheres.			
	a. 133 x 79mm.	2.00	6.00	25.00
	b. 139 x 87mm.	2.50	7.00	26.00
25	**100 Lei** 16.2.1917. Violet. Like #21. Wmk: Lt. and dk. half-spheres.			
	a. Issued note.	10.00	30.00	75.00
	s. Specimen w/o date, sign. or serial #.	—	—	35.00

1920 Issue

		VG	VF	UNC
26	**1 Leu** 17.7.1920. Violet-blue on lt. pink unpt. Like #17 but larger date on back. Columns at l., woman at r. Wolf w/Romulus and Remus on back.			
	a. Issued note.	1.00	3.50	12.50
	s. Specimen w/o sign., series or serial #.	—	Unc	25.00

		VG	VF	UNC
27	**2 Lei** 17.7.1920. Blue-black on pale pink unpt. Like #18 but larger date on back. Woman at l. Eagle w/cross in its mouth at r. Soldier w/sword at l., soldier w/bugle at r. on gray back.			
	a. Issued note.	2.00	6.00	15.00
	s. As a. w/red ovpt: *SPECIMEN.*	—	—	30.00

1924 Issue

		VG	VF	UNC
28	**500 Lei** 12.6.1924. M/c. Farmer's wife w/distaff at l., woman w/infant at r. 3 sign. varaieties.	10.00	30.00	80.00

1925-29 Issue

		VG	VF	UNC
29	**5 Lei** 19.9.1929. Violet. Like #19. Farmer's wife w/distaff at l., arms at r. Woman and child picking apples at ctr. on back. Wmk: Heads of Trajan and Minerva. 2. sign.	1.00	3.50	15.00

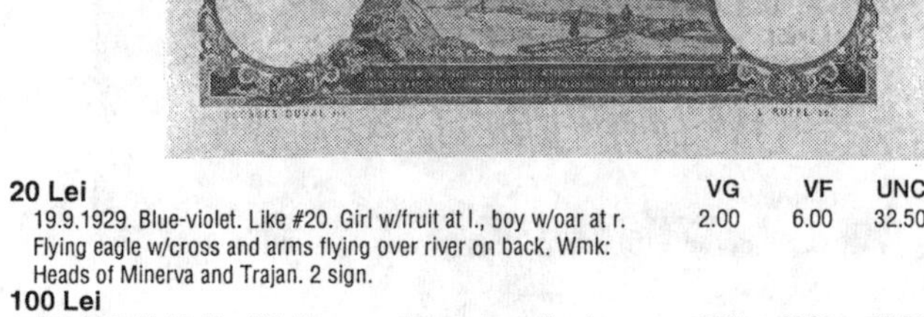

		VG	VF	UNC
30	**20 Lei** 19.9.1929. Blue-violet. Like #20. Girl w/fruit at l., boy w/oar at r. Flying eagle w/cross and arms flying over river on back. Wmk: Heads of Minerva and Trajan. 2 sign.	2.00	6.00	32.50
31	**100 Lei** 19.9.1929. Violet. Like #21. Woman seated wearing national costume at l. Wmk: Heads of Trajan and Minerva. 2 sign.	6.00	25.00	75.00

		VG	VF	UNC
32	**500 Lei** 1.10.1925-27.1.1938. M/c. Like #28. Farmer's wife w/distaff at l. woman w/infant at r. 2 signs., 6 sign. varieties.			
	a. Issued note.	7.50	20.00	55.00
	s. Specimen.			250.

1930-33 Issue

		VG	VF	UNC
33	**100 Lei** 13.5.1930-13.5.1932. Olive-brown. Like #31. Woman seated wearing national costume at l. Wmk: Heads of Trajan and Minerva. 3 sign. varieties.	5.00	17.50	50.00

		Good	Fine	XF
34	**1000 Lei** 15.6.1933. Blue and m/c. Woman at lower l., man at lower r. Mercury at l. and r. on back.	100.	200.	450.
35	**5000 Lei** 31.3.1931. Dk. blue. Danube landscape at lower l., arms at ctr. Portr. Kg. Carol II at r. Medieval scene on back. Printer: BWC. (See #48 for ovpt. type.)			
	a. Issued note. Rare.	—	—	—
	s. Specimen.			

Note: #35 was reportedly in circulation only a few months (March 1 to Dec. 1, 1932).

1934 ISSUE

		VG	VF	UNC
36	**500 Lei** 31.7.1934. Dk. green on m/c unpt. Portr. Kg. Carol II at l. Villa w/trees on back. Printer: BWC.			
	a. Issued note.	6.00	20.00	60.00
	s. Specimen w/o sign., series or serial #.	—	—	65.00

		VG	VF	UNC
37	**1000 Lei** 15.3.1934. Brown and m/c. Portr. Kg. Carol II at l. Complex design w/2 women and child at r. on back.			
	a. Issued note.	80.00	175.	400.
	s. Specimen.	—	—	220.

1936-39 ISSUES

		VG	VF	UNC
38	**1 Leu** 28.10.1937; 21.12.1938. Lilac-brown. Columns at l. woman at r. Similar to #26, but date on face. 2 signs., 2 sign. varieties.			
	a. Issued note.	1.50	6.00	20.00
	s. Specimen w/o sign., series or serial #. 28.10.1937.	—	—	30.00
39	**2 Lei** 1937-40. Lilac-brown. Similar to #27. Woman at l., eagle w/cross in its mouth at r. Soldier w/sword at l., soldier w/bugle at r. on back. 2 sign., 2 sign. varieties.			
	a. Lilac-brown. 28.10.1937; 21.12.1938.	2.00	7.00	35.00
	b. Deep purple on red unpt. 1.11.1940.	15.00	40.00	100.
	s. As a. w/red ovpt: *SPECIMEN*. 21.12.1938.	—	—	40.00

		VG	VF	UNC
40	**5 Lei** 21.12.1938. Like #19 and #24. Farmer's wife w/distaff at l., arms at r. Woman and child picking apples at ctr. on back. Wmk: *BNR*. Specimen.			
	a. Issued note.	30.00	70.00	240.
	s. Specimen.			150.

		VG	VF	UNC
41	**20 Lei** 28.4.1939. Green. Like #30. Girl w/fruit at l., boy w/oar at r. Flying eagle w/cross and arms ~~over river on back~~. Denomination stated *DOUA ZECI LEI*. Wmk: *BNR*. Specimen.	32.00	75.00	280.

		VG	VF	UNC
42	**500 Lei** 30.4.1936; 26.5.1939; 1.11.1940. Gray-blue on m/c unpt. Similar to #36.			
	a. Issued note.	2.50	6.00	25.00
	s. Specimen. 30.4.1936.	—	—	65.00

		VG	VF	UNC
43	**500 Lei** 30.1.1936; 26.5.1939; 1.9.1940. Gray. Like #42, but vignette ovpt. of 2 farm wives at l. on back.			
	a. Issued note.	6.00	15.00	40.00
	s. Specimen.	8.00	20.00	80.00
44	**1000 Lei** 25.6.1936. Brown and green. 2 farm wives w/3 children each at l. and r. 2 farm wives at l. and one w/ladder at r. on back. Wmk. Kg. Carol II w/wreath.			
	a. Issued note.	2.50	8.00	30.00
	s. Specimen.	—	—	55.00

		VG	VF	UNC
45	**1000 Lei** 25.6.1936. Brown and green. Like #44, but w/vignette ovpt: 2 farm wives.			
	a. Issued note.	35.00	80.00	175.
	s. Specimen.			150.

		VG	VF	UNC
46	**1000 Lei** 19.12.1938-1.11.1940. Brown and green. Like #44, but wmk: Kg. Carol II w/o wreath.	1.00	4.00	12.50
47	**1000 Lei** 21.12.1938; 28.4.1939; 1.11.1940. Brown and green. Like #46, but w/vignette ovpt: 2 farm wives.	35.00	85.00	180.

1940 Commemorative Issue

		VG	VF	UNC
48	**5000 Lei** 6.9.1940 (-old date 31.3.1931). Dk. blue. Like #35 but crowned *MI* monogram in cross design on wmk. area at upper l., Danube landscape below, arms at ctr. Portr. Kg. Carol II at r. *6 SEPTEMVRIE 1940* text in plate over Kg. Carol. Medieval scene on back. Printer: BWC.			
	a. Issued note.	25.00	65.00	130.
	s. Specimen. Pin holed cancelled with ovpt.	—	—	450.

Note: #48 is purported to commemorate the coronation of Kg. Michael I.

1940 Issue

		VG	VF	UNC
49	**100 Lei** 19.2.1940. Dk. brown. Like #31. Wmk: Heads of Trajan and Minerva.	5.00	20.00	60.00

		VG	VF	UNC
50	**100 Lei** 19.2.1940; 1.11.1940. Dk. brown. Like #49. Wmk: *BNR*. 2 sign. varieties.			
	a. Issued note.	4.00	18.00	50.00
	s. Specimen.	—	—	65.00

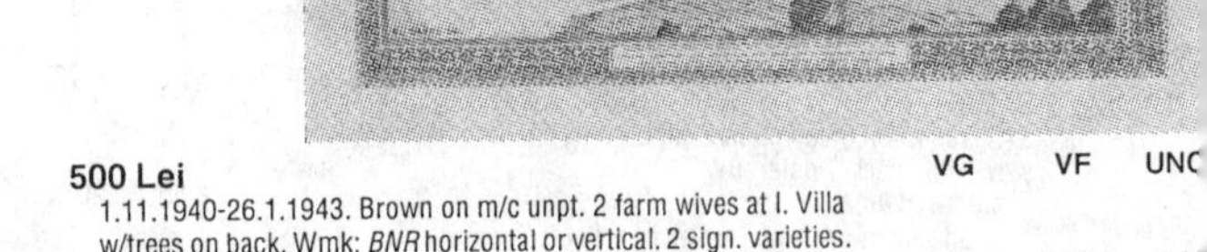

		VG	VF	UNC
51	**500 Lei** 1.11.1940-26.1.1943. Brown on m/c unpt. 2 farm wives at l. Villa w/trees on back. Wmk: *BNR* horizontal or vertical. 2 sign. varieties.			
	a. Issued note.	1.00	3.00	9.0
	s. Specimen. 20.4.1942.	—	—	30.0

1941 Issue

		VG	VF	UNC
52	**1000 Lei** 10.9.1941-20.3.1945. Blue and green on pink unpt. Similar to #45, but wmk: Head of Trajan. Value *UNA MIE LEI* at lower ctr. 3 sign. varieties.	.75	2.00	7.

		VG	VF	UNC
53	**2000 Lei**			
	18.11.1941; 10.10.1944. Brown, violet and yellow. Farm wife w/distaff at l., woman w/infant at r. 2 farm wives at l., oil refinery at r. on back. Wmk: Head of Trajan. 2 sign. varieties.			
	a. Issued note.	.75	4.00	16.00
	s. Specimen.			40.00

1943 Issue

		VG	VF	UNC
54	**2000 Lei**			
	23.3.1943-20.3.1945. Brown, violet and yellow. Like #53. Wmk: *BNR* in shield. 2 sign. varieties.			
	a. Issued note.	.50	3.00	12.50
	s. Specimen. 23.3.1943.	—	—	25.00

		VG	VF	UNC
55	**5000 Lei**			
	28.9.1943; 2.5.1944; 22.8.1944. Lt. blue on m/c unpt. 2 male heads of Trajan and Decebal at upper l., arms at ctr. Man and oxen looking towards city on back. Wmk: Portr. of Trajan. 2 sign. varieties.	1.00	3.00	8.00

1944 Issue

		VG	VF	UNC
56	**5000 Lei**			
	10.10.1944-20.12.1945. Lt. blue. Like #55. Wmk: *BNR* horizontal or vertical. 2 sign. varieties.			
	a. Issued note.	.50	1.50	6.00
	s. Specimen. 10.10.1944.	—	—	25.00

1945 Issue

		VG	VF	UNC
57	**10,000 Lei**			
	18.5.1945; 20.12.1945; 28.5.1946. Brown and red. Similar to #44. Arms at ctr. 2 sign. varieties.			
	a. Issued note.	.50	2.00	8.00
	s. Specimen. 18.5.1945.	—	—	32.50

		VG	VF	UNC
58	**100,000 Lei**			
	7.8.1945-8.5.1947. Green and gray. Woman w/boy at l., farm wife at r. 2 farm wives on back. Wmk: *BNR*.			
	a. Issued note.	.50	1.50	6.00
	s. Specimen. 7.8.1945.	—	—	22.50

1947 Issue

		VG	VF	UNC
59	**100,000 Lei**			
	25.1.1947. Lilac, brown and m/c. Trajan and Decebal at ctr. 2 farmers at l., arms at ctr. 2 women and child at r. on back.			
	a. Issued note.	.75	3.00	12.00
	s. Specimen.	—	—	50.00
60	**1,000,000 Lei**			
	16.4.1947. Blue-green and gray-brown on lt. tan and blue unpt. Like #59.			
	a. Issued note.	3.00	6.00	18.00
	s. Specimen.	—	—	55.00

		VG	VF	UNC
61	**5,000,000 Lei**			
	25.6.1947. Olive and brown on m/c unpt. Women and children at l. and r., wolf w/Romulus and Remus at ctr. 2 farm wives at l. and r. on back.			
	a. White wmk. paper.	10.00	25.00	50.00
	b. Ruled paper.	5.00	15.00	42.50
	s. Specimen.	—	—	60.00

1947 First Issue

#62-64 issued after 1947 currency reform.

		VG	VF	UNC
62	**100 Lei**			
	25.6.1947. Dk. brown on lt. brown unpt. 3 men w/torch, ears of corn and hammer at r.	2.00	6.00	16.00

		VG	VF	UNC
63	**500 Lei**			
	25.6.1947. Brown. Woman at cttr. Farmer and wheat on back.			
	a. Issued note.	8.00	17.50	40.00
	s. Specimen.	—	—	32.50
64	**1000 Lei**			
	25.6.1947. Blue on m/c unpt. T. Vladimirescu at ctr. Arms at ctr. on back.			
	a. Issued note.	10.00	25.00	60.00
	s. Specimen.	—	—	80.00

1947 Second Issue

		VG	VF	UNC
65	**100 Lei**			
	27.8.1947. Brown. Like #62. Rev: Romanian Kingdom King Mihai I.	1.00	4.00	15.00
66	**1000 Lei**			
	30.9.1947. Blue. Like #64.	8.00	25.00	60.00

1947 Third Issue

		VG	VF	UNC
67	**100 Lei**			
	5.12.1947. Brown. Like #62.			
	a. Issued note.	1.00	5.00	20.00
	s. Specimen.	—	—	20.00
68	**1000 Lei**			
	5.12.1947. Blue. Like #64. Rev: Romanian Kingdom King Mihai I.	7.00	22.50	50.00

Ministerul Finantelor

Ministry of Finance

1917 Emergency WW I Issue

#69-71 Kg. Ferdinand I at ctr. Crowned supported arms on back. Small rectangular notes.

#69 #70 #71

		VG	VF	UNC
69	**10 Bani**			
	1917. Dk. green on olive ovpt.	.75	2.50	6.00
70	**25 Bani**			
	1917. Dk. brown on ochre ovpt.	1.00	3.00	10.00

		VG	VF	UNC
71	**50 Bani**			
	1917. Dk. blue on lt. brown on peach unpt.	1.00	4.00	15.00

1920 ND ISSUE

#72-75 portr. Kg. Ferdinand I over crowned supported arms at ctr. *MF* monograms at l. and r. Printer: ABNC. (Not issued.)

		VG	VF	UNC
72	**10 Lei** ND (ca.1920). Brown on red unpt. Back green.			
	p. Proof. Black. Punched hole cancelled.	—	—	250.
	s. Specimen.	—	—	700.
73	**50 Lei** ND (ca.1920). Blue on red unpt. Back purple.			
	p. Proof. Black. Punched hole cancelled.	—	—	—
	s. Specimen.	—	—	900.

		VG	VF	UNC
74	**200 Lei** ND (ca.1920). Brown on red unpt. Back orange.			
	p. Proof. Punched hole cancelled.	—	—	—
	s. Specimen.	—	—	1100.

		VG	VF	UNC
5	**2000 Lei** ND (ca.1920). Green on red unpt. back dk. brown.			
	p. Proof. Punched hole cancelled.	—	—	—
	s. Specimen.	—	—	1300.

ote: Several examples of pieces from the 1920 ND printing are known in "issued" form.

945; 1947 ND ISSUE

New Leu = 20,000 Old Lei

		VG	VF	UNC
6	**20 Lei** 1945. Brown on lt. brown unpt. Portr. Kg. Michael at ctr.	.25	.75	3.00
7	**20 Lei** ND (1947). Dk. brown on green unpt. Trajan and Decebal at at upper l. Woman sitting on woodpile on back. Wmk: *M. F.* Sign. title: *DIRECTORUL GENERAL AL BUGETULUI.* 2 sign. varieties.	.50	3.00	15.00

		VG	VF	UNC
78	**100 Lei** 1945. Blue on lt. blue unpt. Like #76.	.25	.75	2.50

REPUBLICA POPULARA ROMANA

MINISTERUL FINANTELOR

MINISTRY OF FINANCE

1948 ND ISSUE

		VG	VF	UNC
79	**20 Lei** ND (1948). Brown and green. Like #77. Wmk: *RPR.*	1.00	4.00	16.00

		VG	VF	UNC
80	**20 Lei** ND (1948). Dk. brown on green unpt. Like #79. Lower sign. title: *DIRECTORUL BUGETULUI.*	1.00	4.00	18.00

1952 ISSUE

		VG	VF	UNC
81	**1 Leu** 1952. Brown on lt. orange unpt. Arms at ctr. on back.			
	a. Red series and serial #.	.50	1.50	5.00
	b. Blue series and serial #.	.25	.75	2.00
	s. As b. Specimen.	—	—	15.00

		VG	VF	UNC
82	**3 Lei**			
	1952. Violet-brown on greenish gray unpt. Arms at ctr. on back.			
	a. Red series and serial #.	.75	2.00	8.00
	b. Blue series and serial #.	.50	1.25	3.00
	s. As b. Specimen.	—	—	15.00

		VG	VF	UNC
83	**5 Lei**			
	1952. Blue on lt. brown and lt. orange unpt. Girl at l., arms at upper r. Dam construction on back.			
	a. Red series and serial #.	.75	3.00	10.00
	b. Blue series and serial #.	.50	1.50	3.50
	s. As b. Specimen.	—	—	15.00

		VG	VF	UNC
84	**20 Lei**			
	15.6.1950. Dk. green on gray unpt. Girl's head at r. Arms at ctr. on back.			
	a. Issued note.	.50	2.00	6.00
	s. Specimen.	—	—	32.50

BANCA NATIONALA A ROMANIEI

ROMANIAN NATIONAL BANK

1948 ISSUE

		VG	VF	UNC
85	**1000 Lei**			
	18.6.1948. Blue. Like #64.			
	a. Issued note.	2.00	5.00	24.00
	s. Specimen.	—	—	75.00

BANCA REPUBLICII POPULARE ROMANE - BANCA DE STAT

1949-52 ISSUE

		VG	VF	UNC
86	**500 Lei**			
	15.10.1949. Brown. 3 men at l. ctr.			
	a. Issued note.	4.00	14.00	40.00
	s. Specimen. In blue and brown.	—	—	60.00

		VG	VF	UNC
87	**1000 Lei**			
	20.9.1950. Blue and m/c. Balcescu at l. River and mountains on back.	3.00	8.50	32.50

1952 ISSUE

1 New Leu = 20 Old Lei

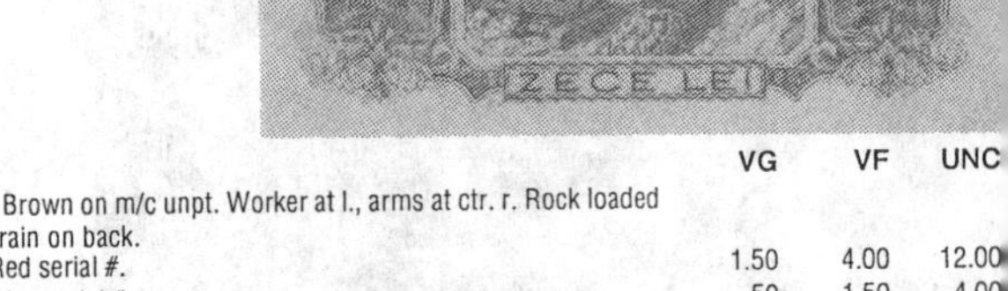

		VG	VF	UNC
88	**10 Lei**			
	1952. Brown on m/c unpt. Worker at l., arms at ctr. r. Rock loaded onto train on back.			
	a. Red serial #.	1.50	4.00	12.00
	b. Blue serial #.	.50	1.50	4.00
	s. As b. Specimen. Schmal and big letters.	—	—	16.00

		VG	VF	UNC
89	**25 Lei**			
	1952. Brown on violet unpt. T. Vladimirescu at l. Wheat harvesting on back.			
	a. Red serial #.	1.50	5.00	17.5
	b. Blue serial #.	.50	1.50	4.0
	s. As b. Specimen.	—	—	20.0

90	100 Lei	VG	VF	UNC
	1952. Blue on lt. blue unpt. N. Balcescu at l., arms at ctr. r. Lg. bldgs. on back.			
	a. Red serial #.	3.00	10.00	25.00
	b. Blue serial #.	1.50	4.00	12.50
	s. As b. Specimen.	—	—	30.00

GERMAN OCCUPATION - WW I

BANCA GENERALA ROMANA

1917 ISSUE

#M1-M8 often found w/numerous different handstamps of military units and Romanian authorities. Such notes are generally well worn. Printed in Germany.

M1	25 Bani	VG	VF	UNC
	ND (1917). Olive-brown. Mercury at r.	.50	2.00	8.00

M2	50 Bani	VG	VF	UNC
	ND (1917). Pale blue-gray. Woman at upper l.	.50	2.50	12.50

M3	1 Leu	VG	VF	UNC
	ND (1917). Black text on green unpt. Mercury at l., laureate woman's head at r.	.50	3.00	15.00

M4	2 Lei	VG	VF	UNC
	ND (1917). Black text on pale red unpt. Woman at l., Mercury at r.	.50	4.00	17.50

M5	5 Lei	VG	VF	UNC
	ND (1917). Black text on lilac unpt. Woman at l. and at r. Back blue-gray.	1.00	5.00	22.50
M6	20 Lei			
	ND (1917). Black text on brown unpt. Woman at l., Mercury at r. on back.	2.00	8.00	35.00
M7	100 Lei			
	ND (1917). Black text on olive and blue unpt. Mercury at l., woman at r. on back.	6.00	17.50	75.00
M8	1000 Lei			
	ND (1917). Brown and m/c. Back like #M7.	12.00	32.50	95.00

RUSSIAN OCCUPATION - WW II

COMANDAMENTUL ARMATEI ROSSII

1944 ISSUE

#M9 *Deleted.*

M10	5 Lei	VG	VF	UNC
	1944. Blue.	15.00	30.00	100.

M11	10 Lei	VG	VF	UNC
	1944. Brown.	15.00	40.00	120.
M12	20 Lei			
	1944. Blue.	25.00	60.00	150.
M13	100 Lei			
	1944. Brown-olive.	50.00	100.	225.

		VG	VF	UNC
M14	500 Lei 1944. Brown on blue unpt.	60.00	125.	275.
M15	1000 Lei 1944.	75.00	150.	350.

		VG	VF	UNC
M16	5000 Lei 1944. Rare.	—	—	—

Romanian Occupation of U.S.S.R. - WW II

On 22 June 1941, Romania declared war on the U.S.S.R. and Romanian troops fought alongside the Germans up to Stalingrad. A Romanian occupation area between the Dniestr and Bug Rivers called Transnistria was established in October 1941, and was used mainly as a dumping ground for Jews deported from Romania. Its center was the port of Odessa. A special issue of notes for use in Transnistria was made by the Romanian government. In 1944, the Russians recaptured Transnis

Institutul de Finantare Externa (Infinex)

1941-44 Bon de Credit Issue

Note: This issue bears unusual denominations because of the exchange rate set by Germany, as follows:

6 Lei = 10 Reichspfennig or 1 Ruble/Karbowanez (Ukrainian German Issue).
1200 Lei = 20 Reichsmark or 200 Rubles/Karbowanez.

		Good	Fine	XF
M17	1 Leu ND (1941-44). Gray.	100.	300.	700.
M18	6 Lei ND (1941-44). Gray-blue.	100.	300.	700.

		Good	Fine	XF
M19	24 Lei ND (1941-44). Brown.	100.	300.	750.

		Good	Fine	XF
M20	120 Lei ND (1941-44). Blue. Sunflower at r.	125.	375.	800.

		Good	Fine	XF
M21	600 Lei ND (1941-44). Gray on brown-violet unpt. Cross at ctr.	125.	375.	850.

		Good	Fine	XF
M22	1200 Lei ND (1941-44). Gray on tan unpt. Grapes at ctr. Boat on river at ctr. on back.	100.	350.	700.

Regional

Treasury

1919 First Provisional Issue

Romania Timbru Special **handstamp on the Austrian (for Bukovina) or Hungarian (for Siebenbérgen and Banat) side of Austro-Hungarian bank notes. All issued in 1919.**

#R1-R11 handstamp on Austrian side (Bukovina). Also frequently encountered w/additional Hungarian or Yugoslav handstamps (usually of military units).

		Good	Fine	XF
R1	10 Kronen ND (1919 - old date 2.1.1904). Handstamp on Austria #9.	6.00	15.00	30.00
R2	10 Kronen ND (1919 - old date 2.1.1915). Handstamp on Austria #19.	4.00	10.00	20.00
R3	20 Kronen ND (1919 - old date 2.1.1907). Handstamp on Austria #10.	60.00	150.	300.
R4	20 Kronen ND (1919 - old date 2.1.1913). Handstamp on Austria #13.	6.00	15.00	30.00
R5	20 Kronen ND (1919 - old date 2.1.1913). Handstamp on Austria #14.	2.00	5.00	10.00
R6	50 Kronen ND (1919 - old date 2.1.1902). Handstamp on Austria #6.	60.00	150.	300.

		Good	Fine	XF
R7	50 Kronen ND (1919 - old date 2.1.1914). Handstamp on Austria #15.	4.00	10.00	20.00
R8	100 Kronen ND (1919 - old date 2.1.1910). Handstamp on Austria #11.	60.00	150.	300

		Good	Fine	XF
R9	100 Kronen ND (1919 - old date 2.1.1912). Handstamp on Austria #12.	2.00	5.00	10.0
R10	1000 Kronen ND (1919 - old date 2.1.1902). Handstamp on Austria #8.	4.00	10.00	20.0
R11	10,000 Kronen ND (1919 - old date 2.11.1918). Handstamp on Austria #25.	10.00	25.00	50.0

1919 Second Provisional Issue

#R12-R22 handstamp on Hungarian side (Siebenbérgen and Banat). Also frequently encountered w/additional Hungarian or Yugoslav handstamps (usually of military units).

		Good	Fine	XF
R12	**10 Korona** ND (1919 - old date 2.1.1904). Handstamp on Austria #9.	6.00	15.00	30.00
R13	**10 Korona** ND (1919 - old date 2.1.1915). Handstamp on Austria #19.	4.00	10.00	20.00
R14	**20 Korona** ND (1919 - old date 2.1.1907). Handstamp on Austria #10.	60.00	150.	300.

		Good	Fine	XF
R15	**20 Korona** ND (1919 - old date 2.1.1913). Handstamp on Austria #13.	6.00	15.00	30.00
R16	**20 Korona** ND (1919 - old date 2.1.1913). Handstamp on Austria #14.	2.00	5.00	10.00

		Good	Fine	XF
R17	**50 Korona** ND (1919 - old date 2.1.1902). Handstamp on Austria #6.	60.00	150.	300.
R18	**50 Korona** ND (1919 - old date 2.1.1914). Handstamp on Austria #15.	4.00	10.00	20.00
R19	**100 Korona** ND (1919 - old date 2.1.1910). Handstamp on Austria #11.	60.00	150.	300.
R20	**100 Korona** ND (1919 - old date 2.1.1912). Handstamp on Austria #12.	2.00	5.00	10.00
R21	**1000 Korona** ND (1919 - old date 2.1.1902). Handstamp on Austria #8.	4.00	10.00	20.00
R22	**10,000 Korona** ND (1919 - old date 2.11.1918). Handstamp on Austria #25.	10.00	25.00	50.00

RUSSIA

Russia, (formerly the central power of the Union of Soviet Socialist Republics and now of the Commonwealth of Independent States) occupying the northern part of Asia and the far eastern part of Europe, has an area of 8,649,538 sq. mi. (17,075,450 sq. km.) and a population of 146.2 million. Capital: Moscow. Exports include machinery, iron and steel, oil, timber and nonferrous metals.

The first Russian dynasty was founded in Novgorod by the Viking, Rurik in 862 AD. Under Yaroslav the Wise (1019-54) the subsequent Kievan state (Kyiv's Rus') became one of the great commercial and cultural centers of Europe before falling to the Mongols in the 13th century, who ruled Russia until late in the 15th century when Ivan III threw off the Mongol yoke. The Russian Empire was enlarged and solidified during the reigns of Ivan the Terrible, Peter the Great and Catherine the Great, and by 1881 extended to the Pacific and into Central Asia.

Assignats, the first government paper money of the Russian Empire, were introduced in 1769, and gave way to State Credit Notes in 1843. Russia was put on the gold standard in 1897 and reformed its currency at that time.

All pre-1898 notes were destroyed as they were turned in to the Treasury, accounting for their uniform scarcity today.

The last Russian Czar, Nicholas II (1894-1917), was deposed by the provisional government under Prince Lvov and later Alexander Kerensky during the military defeat in World War I. This government rapidly lost ground to the Bolshevik wing of the Socialist Democratic Labor Party. During the Russian Civil War (1917-1922) many regional governments, national states and armies in the field were formed which issued their own paper money (see Vol. I).

After the victory of the Red armies, many of these areas became federal republics of the Russian Socialist Federal Soviet Republic (RSfSR), or autonomous soviet republics which united on Dec. 30, 1922, to form the Union of Soviet Socialist Republics (SSSR). Beginning with the downfall of the communist government in Poland (1989), other European countries occupied since WW II began democratic elections that spread into Russia itself, leaving the remaining states united in a newly founded Commonwealth of Independent States (C.I.S.). The USSR Supreme Soviet voted a formal end to the treaty of union signed in 1922 and dissolved itself.

RULERS:

Catherine II (the Great), 1762-1796
Paul I, 1796-1801
Alexander I, 1801-1825
Nicholas I, 1825-1855
Alexander II, 1855-1881
Alexander III, 1881-1894
Nicholas II, 1894-1917

MONETARY SYSTEM:

1 Ruble = 100 Kopeks, until 1997
1 Chervonetz = 10 Gold Rubles
1 Ruble = 1000 "old" Rubles

Note: Certain listings encompassing issues circulated by various bank and regional authorities are contained in Volume 1.

CYRILLIC ALPHABET

А	а	А	а	A
Б	б	Б	б	B
В	в	В	в	V
Г	г	Г	г	G
Д	д	Д	д	D
Е	е	Е	е	ye
Ё	ё	Ё	ё	yo
Ж	ж	Ж	ж	zh
З	з	З	з	Z
И	и	И	и	I
Й	й	Й	й	J
К	к	К	к	K
Л	л	Л	л	L
М	м	М	м	M
Н	н	Н	н	N
О	о	О	о	O
П	п	П	п	P
Р	р	Р	р	R

С	с	С	с	S
Т	т	Т	т	T
У	у	У	у	U
Ф	ф	Ф	ф	F
Х	х	Х	х	Kh
Ц	ц	Ц	ц	C
Ч	ч	Ч	ч	ch
Ш	ш	Ш	ш	sh
Щ	щ	Щ	щ	shch
Ъ*)	ъ*)	—	ъ	'
Ы	ы	—	ы	
Ь**)	ь**)	—	ь	'
Э		Э		E
Ю	ю	Ю	ю	yu
Я	я	Я	я	ya
I	і	I	і	I
Ѣ	ѣ	Ѣ	ѣ	ye

*) "hard", and **) "soft" signs; both soundless. I and Ѣ were dropped in 1918.

(Some other areas whose notes are listed in this volume had local currencies.)

ISSUE IDENTIFICATION CHART

ISSUE IDENTIFICATION CHART

CZARIST EMPIRE, 1769-1917

DATE	ISSUER	CAT.#
1769-1843	ГОСУДАРСТВЕННОЙ АССИГНАЦІИ	A1-A24
1840	ГОСУДАРСТВЕННЫЙ КОММЕРЧЕСКІЙ БАНКЪ	A25-A30
1841	КРЕДИТНЫЙ БИЛЕТЪ СОХРАННЫХЪКАЗЕНЪ И ГОСУДАРСТВЕННАГО БАНКА	A31-32
1843-1895	ГОСУДАРСТВЕННЫЙ КРЕДИТНЫЙ БИЛЕТЪ	A33-A64
1876-1895	ГОСУДАРСТВЕННЫЙ БАНКЪ: ДЕПОЗИТНАЯ МЕТАЛЛИЧЕСКАЯКВИТАНЦІЯ	A65-A83
1895	БИЛЕТЪ ГОСУААРСТВЕННАГО КАЗНАУЕЙСТВА	A84
1898-1915	ГОСУДАРСТВЕННЫЙ КРЕДИТНЫЙБИЛЕТЪ	1-15
1915	Postage Stamp Currency	16-23
1915	Treasury Small Change Notes	24-31
1915-1917	5% КРАТКОСРОЧНОЕ ОБЯЗАТЕЛЬСТВОГСУДАР. (СТВЕННАГО) КАЗНАЧЕЙСТВА	31A-31X

PROVISIONAL GOVERNMENT, 1917-1918

1917	Postage Stamp Currency	32-34
1917	ОСУДАРСТВЕННЫЙ КРЕДИТНЫЙ БИЛЕТЪ	35-37
1917	5% ОБЛИГАЦІЯ ЗАЕМЪ СВОБОДЫ	37A-37
1917	КАЗНАЧЕЙСКІЙ ЗНАКЪ	38-39
1918-1919	ГОСУДАРСТВЕННЫЙ КРЕДИТНЫЙ БИЛЕТЪ	39A-42
1917	ГОСУДАРСТВЕННЫЙ КРЕДИТНЫЙ БИЛЕТ	43-47

RUSSIAN SOCIALIST FEDERATED SOVIET REPUBLIC, 1918-1924

1918	БИЛЕТЬ ГОСУДАРСТВЕННАГО КАЗНАЧЕЙСТВА	48-60
1918	РАСЧЕТНЫЙ ЗНАК	81-85
1918	ГОСУДАРСТВЕННЫЙ КРЕДИТНЫЙ БИЛЕТЪ	86-97
1919-1921	РАСЧЕТНЫЙ ЗНАК	98-117
1921	ОбЯЗАТЕЛЬСТВО РОССИЙСКОЙ СОЦИАЛИСТИЧЕСКОЙ ФЕДЕРАТИВНОЙ СОВЕТСКОЙРЕСПУБЛИКИ	120-125
1922	ГОСУДАРСТВЕННЫЙ ДЕНЕЖНЫЙ ЗНАК	126-138
1922-1923	БАНКОВЫЙ БИЛЕТ	139-145A
1922-1923	ГОСУДАРСТВЕННЫЙ ДЕНЕЖНЫЙ ЗНАК	146-171A
1923	ПЛАТЕЖНОЕ ОБЯЗАТЕЛЬСТВО НКФР. С.Ф.С.Р	172-175
1923-1924	ТРАНСПОРТНЫЙСЕРТИФИКАТ	176-180

UNION OF SOVIET SOCIALIST REPUBLICS, 1924-91

1924-1925	ГОСУДАРСТВЕННЫЙ ДЕНЕЖНЫЙ ЗНАК	181-183, 186-190
1924-1926	ПЛАТЕЖНОЕ ОБЯЗАТЕЛЬСТВО НКФС.С.С.Р.	184-185A
1928	НАРОДНОГО КОМИССАРІАТА ФИНАНСОВ СОЮЗА С.С.Р.	185B-185E
1924	Small Change Notes	191-196
1924-1957	БИЛЕТ ГОСУДАРСТВЕННОГО БАНКАС.С.С.Р.	196A-205, 225-232
1928-1957	ГОСУДАРСТВЕННЫЙ КАЗНАЧЕЙСКИЙ БИЛЕТ	206-221

MONETARY UNITS

KOPEK	КОПЕЙКА
KOPEKS	КОПЕЙКИ, КОПЕЕКЪ
RUBLE	РУБЛЬ
RUBLES	РУБЛЯ or РУБЛЕЙ
CHERVONETZ	ЧЕРВОНЕЦ
CHERVONTSA	ЧЕРВОНЦА
CHERVONTSEV	ЧЕРВОНЦЕВ

DENOMINATIONS

1	ОДИН, ОДИНЪ or ОДНА
2	ДВА or ДВЕ
3	ТРИ
5	ПЯТЬ
10	ДЕСЯТЬ
20	ДВАДЦАТЬ
25	ДВАДЦАТЬ ПЯТЬ
30	ТРИДЦАТЬ
40	СОРОК or СОРОКЪ
50	ПЯТЬДЕСЯТ or ПЯТЬДЕСЯТЪ
60	ШЕСТЬДЕСЯТ or ЩЕСТЬДЕСЯТЬ
100	СТО
250	ДВЬСТИ ПЯТЪДЕСЯТЪ or ДВЕСТИ ПЯТЪДЕСЯТ
500	ПЯТЬСОТ or ПЯТЬСОТЪ
1,000	ТЫСЯЧА
5,000	ПЯТЬ ТЫСЯЧ or ТЫСЯЧЪ
10,000	ДЕСЯТЬ ТЫСЯЧ or ТЫСЯЧЪ
15,000	ПЯТНАДЦАТЬ ТЫСЯЧ or ТЫСЯЧЬ
25,000	ДВАДЦАТЬ ПЯТЬ ТЫСЯЧ
50,000	ПЯТЬ ДЕСЯТ ТЫСЯЧ or ПЯТЬДЕСЯТЬ ТЫСЯЧЪ
100,000	СТО ТЫСЯЧ or ТЫСЯЧЪ
250,000	ДВЬСТИ ПЯТЬДЕСЯТ ТЫСЯЧ
500,000	ПЯТЬСОТЪ ТЫСЯЧ
1,000,000	ОДИН МИЛЛИОН or МИЛЛИОНЪ
5,000,000	ПЯТЬ МИЛЛИОНОВ

IMPERIAL RUSSIA

ГОСУДАРСТВЕННОЙ АССИГНАЦІИ

STATE ASSIGNATS

1769 ISSUE

Size: 190 x 250mm. Wmk: Words on perimeter.

		Good	Fine	XF
A1	**25 Rubles** 1769-73. 1 serial # at ctr. above *ASSIGNAT*. Rare.	—	—	—
A2	**50 Rubles** 1769-73. 1 serial # at ctr. above *ASSIGNAT*. Rare.	—	—	—
A3	**75 Rubles** 1769-72. 1 serial # at ctr. above *ASSIGNAT*. Rare.	—	—	—
A4	**100 Rubles** 1769-73. 1 serial # at ctr above *ASSIGNAT*. Rare.	—	—	—

1774 ISSUE

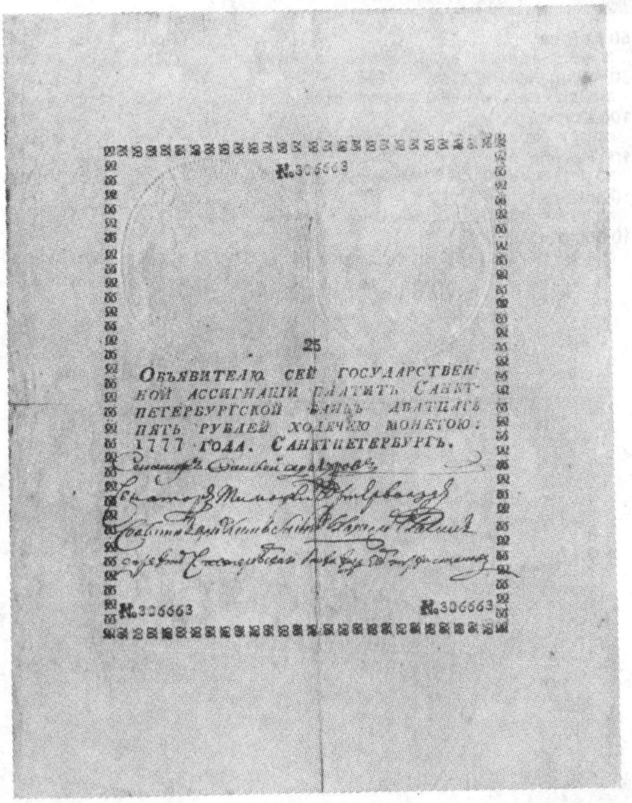

		Good	Fine	XF
A5	**25 Rubles** 1774-84. 3 serial #: at ctr., at lower l. and lower r. Rare.	—	—	
A6	**50 Rubles** 1774-84. 3 serial #: at ctr., at lower l. and lower r. Rare.	—	—	
A7	**100 Rubles** 1774-84. 3 serial #: at ctr., at lower l. and lower r. Rare.	—	—	

1785-87 ISSUE

#A8-A12 are 130 x 170 mm.; text w/o frame, various year dates, 2 handwritten sign. on face and 1 handwritten sign. on back. Many sign. varieties. Also Napoleonic forgeries w/2 or 3 printed sign. exist and some of these have printing errors in 1 or 2 words.

Correct:
ГОСУДАРСТВЕННОЙ ХОДЯЧЕЮ
Error:
ГОСУЛАРСТВЕННОЙ ХОЛЯЧЕЮ

Note: Some forged notes have Cyrillic Ë (L) instead of Ä (D) in text.

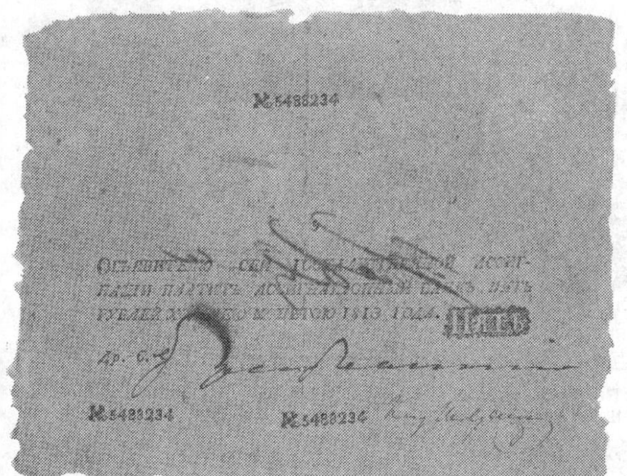

		Good	Fine	XF
A8	**5 Rubles** 1787-1818. Gray to bluish paper.			
	a. 1787-1802.	800.	—	—
	b. 1803-1818.	300.	750.	—

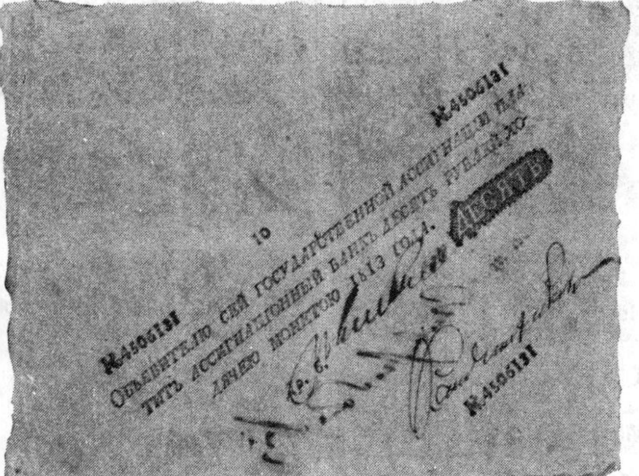

		Good	Fine	XF
A9	**10 Rubles** 1787-1817. Pink paper.			
	a. 1787-1801.	1000.	2000.	—
	b. 1803-1817.	400.	800.	—

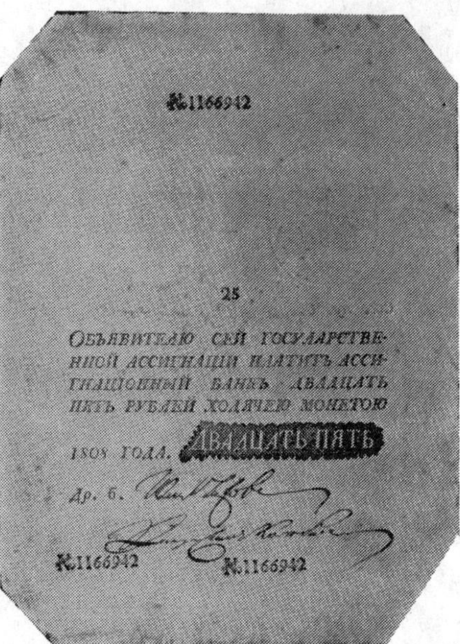

		Good	Fine	XF
A10	**25 Rubles** 1785-1818. White paper. Issued w/clipped corners.			
	a. 1785-1802. Rare.	—	—	—
	b. 1803-1818. Rare.	—	—	—
	x. 1803-1811. Napoleonic forgery.	100.	300.	650.

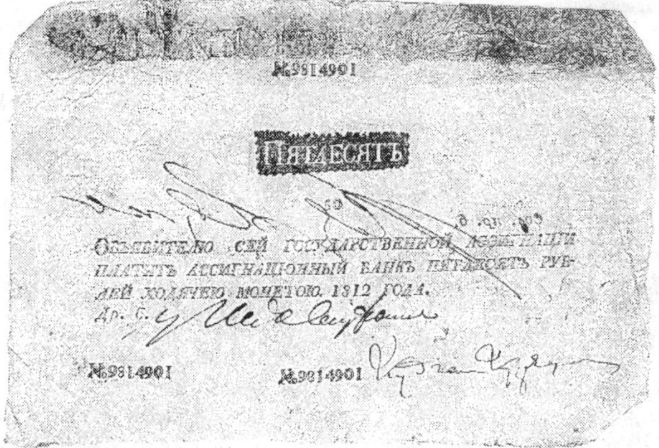

		Good	Fine	XF
A11	**50 Rubles** 1785-1818. White paper.			
	a. 1785-1802. Rare.	—	—	—
	b. 1803-1818. Rare.	—	—	—
	x. 1805-08. Napoleonic forgery.	300.	950.	2500.
A12	**100 Rubles** 1785-1818. White paper.			
	a. 1785-1801. Rare.	—	—	—
	b. 1803-1818. Rare.	—	—	—

1802 ISSUE

#A13-A16 black on white paper.

		Good	Fine	XF
A13	**5 Rubles** 1802. Specimen only. 115 x 115mm. Rare.	—	—	—
A14	**10 Rubles** 1802-03. Specimen only. 175 x 115mm. Rare.	—	—	—
A15	**25 Rubles** 1802. Specimen only. 185 x 185mm. Rare.	—	—	—
A16	**100 Rubles** 1802. Specimen only. 185 x 185mm. Rare.	—	—	—

1818-43 ISSUES

#A17-A24 crowned double headed eagle w/shield; different year dates; first sign. (director) Hovanskii (printed), second sign. (cashier, handwritten). Many varieties.

		Good	Fine	XF
A17	**5 Rubles** 1819-43. Blue paper.	200.	550.	—
A18	**10 Rubles** 1819-43. Pink paper.	300.	650.	—
A19	**20 Rubles** 1822. Green paper. Specimen. Rare.	—	—	—
A20	**20 Rubles** 1822. Reddish paper. Specimen.	—	—	—

		Good	Fine	XF
A21	**25 Rubles** 1818-43. White paper.	450.	900.	—

		Good	Fine	XF
A22	**50 Rubles** 1818-43. Yellowish paper.	2000.	—	—

		Good	Fine	X
A23	**100 Rubles** 1819-43. White paper. Rare.	—	—	

		Good	Fine	X
A24	**200 Rubles** 1819-43. Gray paper. Rare.	—	—	

ГОСУДАРСТВЕННЫЙ КОММЕРЧЕСКІЙ БАНКЪ

STATE COMMERCIAL BANK

1840-41 ISSUE

#A25-A30 first sign. printed, second and third sign. handwritten. Many sign. varieties.

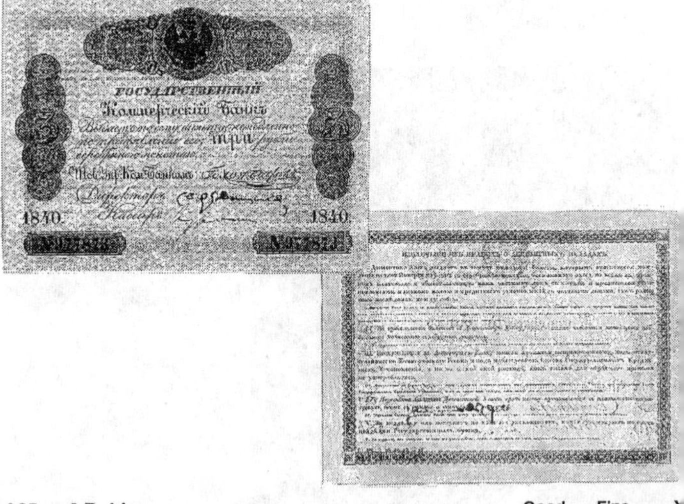

		Good	Fine	X
A25	**3 Rubles** 1840. Green.	1000.	2000.	
A26	**5 Rubles** 1840. Blue.	1500.	3000.	

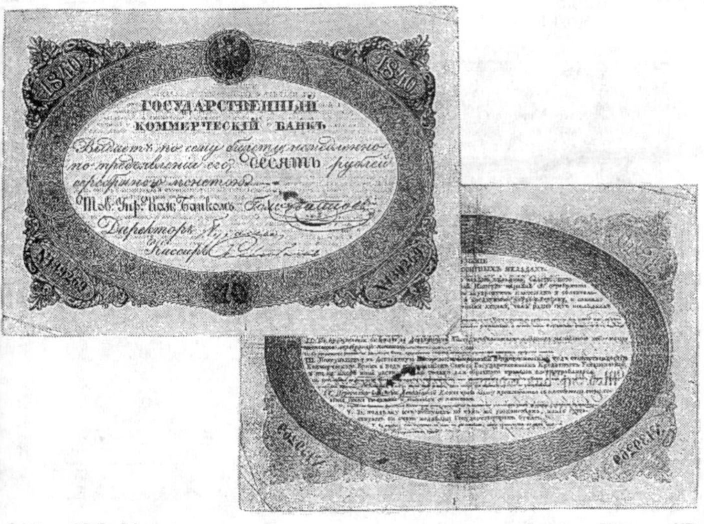

		Good	Fine	XF
A27	**10 Rubles** 1840. Pink. Rare.	—	—	—
A28	**25 Rubles** 1840. Black. Rare.	—	—	—

		Good	Fine	XF
A29	**50 Rubles** 1840. Brown. Rare.	—	—	—
A30	**100 Rubles** 1841. M/c. Rare.	—	—	—

КРЕДИТНЫЙ БИЛЕТЪ СОХРАННЫХЪ

КАЗЕНЪ И ГОСУДАРСТВЕННЫХЪ ЗАЕМНАГО БАНКА

CUSTODY TREASURY AND STATE LOAN BANK CREDIT NOTES

1841 ISSUE

		Good	Fine	XF
A31	**50 Rubles** 1841. Dk green, light seal. Yellowish paper. Rare.	—	—	—

		Good	Fine	XF
A32	**50 Rubles** 1841. Lt. green, black seal. Yellowish paper. Rare.	—	—	—

ГОСУДАРСТВЕННЫЙ КРЕДИТНЫЙ БИЛЕТЪ

STATE CREDIT NOTES

1843-56 ISSUE

#A33-A40 crowned double headed eagle in shield within sprays or ornate frame at top ctr. Different year dates on face. First sign. printed (until 1851 Halchinskii); handwritten (1854 Jurev, 1855-1860 Rostovchev, 1861-1865 Lamanskii), second and third sign. handwritten varieties. From 1851 all sign. were printed.

		Good	Fine	XF
A33	**1 Ruble** 1843-65. Brown on yellow.			
	a. 1843-64.	125.	300.	600.
	b. 1865.	100.	225.	450.

		Good	Fine	XF
A34	**3 Rubles** 1843-65. Green on lt. green.	175.	400.	—
A35	**5 Rubles** 1843-65. Blue on lt. blue.	325.	700.	—
A36	**10 Rubles** 1843-65. Red on pink unpt.	750.	2000.	—

		Good	Fine	XF
A37	**15 Rubles** 1856. M/c. Specimen. Rare.	—	—	—

		Good	Fine	XF
A38	**25 Rubles** 1843-65. Violet on lilac unpt.	1000.	2000.	—
A39	**50 Rubles** 1843-65. Black on gray unpt. Rare.	—	—	—
A40	**100 Rubles** 1843-65. Brown-violet on brown. Rare.	—	—	—

1866 ISSUE

#A41-A47 crowned double-headed eagle above monogram of Czar Alexander II at l. Different year dates on back; first sign: Lamanskii (1866 as vice-director, 1870-1880 as director). Many varieties of the second sign.

		Good	Fine	XF
A41	**1 Ruble** 1866-80. Black on lt. brown unpt.	60.00	125.	250.

		Good	Fine	XF
A42	**3 Rubles** 1866-80. Black on lt. green unpt.	125.	350.	—

		Good	Fine	XF
A43	**5 Rubles** 1866-80. Black on lt. blue unpt. Portr. D. Ivanovich Donskoi at ctr. on back.	200.	450.	—
A44	**10 Rubles** 1866-80. Black on red unpt. M. Feodorovich at ctr. on back.	350.	750.	—
A45	**25 Rubles** 1866-76. Black on lilac unpt. A. Mikhailovich at ctr. on back.	750.	1500.	—

		Good	Fine	XF
A45A	**25 Rubles** 1876; 1884; 1886. Black. Arms at upper l. Uniface. Wmk: Czar Alexey Mikhailovich, wavy line and letters Г.К.Б. Rare.	—	—	—

		Good	Fine	XF
A46	**50 Rubles** 1866. Black on gray unpt. Portr. Peter the Great at ctr. on back. Rare.	—	—	—
A47	**100 Rubles** 1872-80. Black on yellow unpt. Catherine the Great at ctr. on back. Rare.	—	—	—

882-86 ISSUE

A48-A53 design like #A41-A47 but w/monogram of Czar Alexander III. Different year dates on back. First sign. Cimsen (until 1886), Zhukovskii (1889-1892), Pleske (1894-1896); second sign. varieties.

		Good	Fine	XF
A48	**1 Ruble** 1882; 1884; 1886. Black on lt. brown unpt.	50.00	100.	250.
A49	**3 Rubles** 1882; 1884; 1886. Black on lt. green unpt.	150.	350.	700.

		Good	Fine	XF
50	**5 Rubles** 1882; 1884; 1886. Black on lt. blue unpt.	200.	450.	—
51	**10 Rubles** 1882; 1884; 1886. Black on red unpt.	350.	750.	—
52	**25 Rubles** 1884; 1886. Black. Like #A45A. Rare.	—	—	—

		Good	Fine	XF
53	**100 Rubles** 1882-94. Black on yellow unpt. Rare.	—	—	—

1887-94 ISSUE

#A54-A60 new type of notes w/monogram of Czar Alexander III. Different year dates; first sign. Cimsen (1887), Zhukovskii (1889-1892), E. Pleske (1894). Many varieties of second sign.

		Good	Fine	XF
A54	**1 Ruble** 1887-94. Black on lt. brown unpt. Crowned arms at l., monogram at r. Back brown.	175.	350.	—
A55	**3 Rubles** 1887-94. Black on lt. green unpt. Crowned arms at l. Back green.	150.	450.	900.

		Good	Fine	XF
A56	**5 Rubles** 1887-94. Black on lt. blue unpt. Back blue.	300.	700.	1500.
A57	**10 Rubles** 1887-92. Black on red unpt. Back red.	300.	700.	1500.

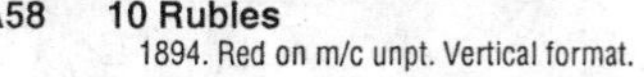

		Good	Fine	XF
A58	**10 Rubles** 1894. Red on m/c unpt. Vertical format.	175.	400.	—

		Good	Fine	XF
A59	**25 Rubles** 1887. Back violet.	—	—	—

Note: Only 1 example of #A59 is known uncancelled.

		Good	Fine	XF
A60	**25 Rubles** 1890. Blue. Back m/c. Specimen only. Rare.	—	—	—
A60A	**25 Rubles** 1892. Lilac.			
	a. Sign. Pleske.	600.	1300.	—
	b. Sign. Zhukovsky. Rare.	—	—	—

1895 Issue

#A61-A64 monogram of Nicholas II at l. Sign. E. Pleske. Second sign. varies.

		Good	Fine	XF
A61	**1 Ruble** 1895. Like #A54.	40.00	100.	250.
A62	**3 Rubles** 1895. Similar to #A55.	200.	400.	—
A63	**5 Rubles** 1895. Blue and m/c. Like #3.	150.	350.	—
A64	**100 Rubles** 1895, 1896. Like #A53. Rare.	—	—	—

Note: For #A64 1895 date is not confirmed.

ГОСУДАРСТВЕННЫЙ БАНКЪ ДЕПОЗИТНАЯ МЕТАЛЛИЧЕСКАЯ КВИТАНЦІЯ

State Bank Metal Deposit Receipts

1876 Issue

		Good	Fine	XF
A65	**50 Rubles = 10 Half Imperials** 1876. Specimen, perforated: *ОБРАЗЕЦЪ*. Rare.	—	—	—
A66	**100 Rubles = 10 Imperials** 1876. Specimen. Rare.	—	—	—

1886 Issue

		Good	Fine	XF
A67	**50 Rubles** 1886. Specimen, ovpt: *ОБРАЗЕЦЪ*. Rare.	—	—	—
A68	**100 Rubles** 1886. Specimen. Rare.	—	—	—
A69	**500 Rubles** 1886. Specimen. Rare.	—	—	—
A70	**1000 Rubles** 1886. Specimen. Rare.	—	—	—

1895 Issue

		Good	Fine	XF
A71	**5 Rubles** 1895. Specimen, perforated: *ОБРАЗЕЦЪ*.	—	—	1000.
A72	**10 Rubles** 1895. Specimen.	—	—	700.
A73	**25 Rubles** 1895. Specimen.	—	—	1000
A74	**50 Rubles** 1895. Specimen.	—	—	1000.
A75	**100 Rubles** 1895. Specimen.	—	—	1000

		Good	Fine	XF
A76	**500 Rubles** 1895. Specimen.	—	—	1000
A77	**1000 Rubles** 1895. Specimen.	—	—	1000

1896 Issue

		Good	Fine	XF
A78	**5 Rubles** 1896. Specimen, perforated: *ОБРАЗЕЦЪ*. Rare.	—	—	—
A79	**10 Rubles** 1896. Specimen. Rare.	—	—	—
A80	**30 Rubles** 1896. Specimen. Rare.	—	—	—
A81	**100 Rubles** 1896. Specimen. Rare.	—	—	—
A82	**500 Rubles** 1896. Specimen. Rare.	—	—	—
A83	**1000 Rubles** 1896. Specimen. Rare.	—	—	—

БИЛЕТЪ ГОЧУДАРСТВЕНАГО КАЗНАЧЕЙСТВА

State Treasury Note

1895 Issue

		Good	Fine	XF
A84	**50 Rubles** 1895. Specimen only. Rare.	—	—	

NOTICE

Readers with unlisted dates, signature varieties, etc. are invited to submit photocopies or, high resolution (300 dpi, 100% size) scans of their notes to: Standard Catalog of World Paper Money, 700 East State St. Iola, WI 54990-0001, or E-Mail: george.cuhaj@fwpubs.com.

ГОСУДАРСТВЕННЫЙ КРЕДИТНЫЙ БИЛЕТЪ

STATE CREDIT NOTES

1898 ISSUE

These notes can be dated according to the sign. of the State Bank Director: E. Pleske (1898-1903); S. Timashev (1903-09); A. Konshin (1909-12); I. Shipov (1912-17).

SIGNATURE VARIETIES	
E. Pleske, to 1903	S. Timashev, 1903-1909
A. Konshin, 1909-1912	I. Shipov, 1912-1917

1 Ruble	VG	VF	UNC
1898. Blue on red-brown unpt. Like #A54. Russian eagle at l., monogram at r. Full serial #. Back red-brown.			
a. Sign. Pleske.	4.00	20.00	75.00
b. Sign. Timashev.	3.00	15.00	50.00
c. Sign. Konshin.	15.00	75.00	250.
d. Sign. Shipov.	.50	2.00	4.00
s. Specimen. Sign. Pleske.	—	—	350.

e: For 1 Ruble 1898 w/series # (2 letters HA or HB and 1, 2 or 3 numerals) instead of serial #, see #15.

3 Rubles	Good	Fine	XF
1898. Blue on brown unpt. Like #A55. Russian eagle at l. Back green.			
a. Sign. Pleske.	20.00	100.	300.
b. Sign. Timashev.	15.00	75.00	200.
s1. Specimen. Sign. Pleske.			
s2. Specimen. Sign. Timashev.			

#		Good	Fine	XF
3	**5 Rubles**			
	1898. Blue on m/c. Like #A63. Allegory of Russia seated holding shield and sword. Portr. at each corner on back. Wmk: value within diamond, repeated.			
	a. Sign. Pleske.	12.50	40.00	200.
	b. Sign. Timashev.	10.00	30.00	150.
	s. Specimen.	—	Unc	500.
4	**10 Rubles**			
	1898. Red on m/c. Like #A58. Allegory of Russia seated holding shield and laurel branch. Wmk: value in diamond, repeated.			
	a. Sign. Pleske.	20.00	85.00	300.
	b. Sign. Timashev.	15.00	60.00	250.
	s. Specimen. W/o sign.	—	Unc	500.

#		Good	Fine	XF
5	**100 Rubles**			
	1898. Black on tan unpt. Portr. Catherine II at l. Back blue on green and lilac unpt. Wmk: value.			
	a. Sign. Pleske.	20.00	85.00	350.
	b. Sign. Timashev.	20.00	60.00	250.
	c. Sign. Konshin.	10.00	35.00	200.
	s. Specimen. Sign. Pleske.	—	Unc	600.
6	**500 Rubles**			
	1898. Black, green, red and blue. Peter I at l. Wmk: value.			
	a. Sign. Pleske.	40.00	125.	500.
	b. Sign. Timashev.	20.00	85.00	350.
	c. Sign. Konshin.	15.00	65.00	250.
	s. Specimen. W/o sign.	—	Unc	750.

1899 ISSUE

		Good	Fine	XF
7	**25 Rubles** 1899. Lilac. Like #A60. Allegory of Russia standing w/shield, 2 seated children at l. Back blue and maroon; 6 heads at r. Wmk: value.			
	a. Sign. Pleske.	22.50	75.00	350.
	b. Sign. Timashev.	20.00	70.00	250.
	s. Specimen. W/o sign.	—	Unc	650.

		Good	Fine	XF
8	**50 Rubles** 1899. Black. Portr. Nicholas I at l. Back green and m/c.			
	a. Sign. Pleske.	50.00	200.	800.
	b. Sign. Timashev.	30.00	125.	450.
	c. Sign. Konshin.	5.00	10.00	50.00
	d. Sign. Shipov.	2.50	6.00	30.00
	s. Specimen. W/o sign.	—	Unc	450.

1905-12 Issue

#9-14 wmk: value.

		VG	VF	UNC
9	**3 Rubles** 1905. Black on green and m/c.			
	a. Sign. Timashev.	5.00	25.00	100.
	b. Sign. Konshin.	.50	2.50	15.00
	c. Sign. Shipov.	.25	.50	1.50
	s. Specimen.	—	—	200.

		VG	VF	UNC
10	**5 Rubles** 1909. Blue-black on blue and m/c unpt. Eagle at top ctr. Vertical format. Back dk. gray on blue and m/c unpt. Full serial #.			
	a. Sign. Konshin.	.50	2.50	12.50
	b. Sign. Shipov.	.20	.50	1.50
	s. Specimen. Sign. Konshin.	—	—	200

Note: For 5 Rubles 1909 w/series # (2 letters and 3 numerals) instead of serial #, see #35.

		VG	VF	UN
11	**10 Rubles** 1909. Deep olive-green on green and red unpt. Imperial eagle at top ctr., produce at l. and r. Vertical format.			
	a. Sign. Timashev.	5.00	25.00	10
	b. Sign. Konshin.	1.00	4.00	17.
	c. Sign. Shipov.	.20	.50	2.
	s. Specimen. Sign. Timashev.	—	—	25

		VG	VF	UN
12	**25 Rubles** 1909. Black on red and blue unpt. Back black on red and green unpt; Alexander III at r.			
	a. Sign. Konshin.	.75	2.50	15
	b. Sign. Shipov.	.50	1.50	4
	s. Specimen. Sign. Konshin.	—	—	3

		VG	VF	UNC
13	**100 Rubles** 1910. Dk. brown on lt. brown and m/c unpt. Allegorical man w/sword, Catherine II at l. on back. 258 x 121mm.			
	a. Sign. Konshin.	2.00	10.00	25.00
	b. Sign. Shipov.	.75	2.50	10.00
	s. Specimen. Sign. Konshin.	—	—	350.

		VG	VF	UNC
14	**500 Rubles** 1912. Black on green and m/c unpt. Peter I at l. on back. 272 x 126mm.			
	a. Sign. Konshin.	2.50	10.00	40.00
	b. Sign. Shipov.	1.50	4.00	15.00
	s. Specimen. Sign. Konshin.	—	—	400.

1915 ISSUE

		VG	VF	UNC
15	**1 Ruble** ND (1915 -old date 1898). Blue on brown unpt. Like #1 but control # instead of serial #. 13 sign. varieties. Top sign. Shipov. Prefix letters HA001-127.	.25	1.00	4.00

Note: Some of the Shipov notes were later printed by the Provisional Government and also by the Soviet Government. They will have higher prefix letter-number combinations. They are also lighter in color than those originally printed during the Czarist period.

СБВЕРНАЯ РОССІЯ

POSTAGE STAMP CURRENCY ISSUE

1915 ND ISSUE

Romanov Tercentenary stamps of 1913 printed on thin card stock; legend and eagle on back. The 1 and 2 Kopek pieces usually carry a denomination ovpt. also. Portraits: #16-17 Peter I, #18-19 Alexander II, #20 Alexander III, #21 Nicholas II, #22 Nicholas I, #23 Alexander I.

		VG	VF	UNC
16	**1 Kopek** ND (1915). Brown-orange. Ovpt: *1* on face. (Scott #112).	1.00	2.00	5.00
17	**1 Kopek** ND (1916-17). Brown-orange. #16 w/o *1* ovpt. (Scott #114).	7.50	30.00	100.
18	**2 Kopeks** ND (1915). Green. Ovpt: *2* on face. (Scott #113).	1.00	2.00	5.00
19	**2 Kopeks** ND (1915). Green. #18 w/o *2* ovpt., (Scott #115).	7.50	30.00	100.

		VG	VF	UNC
20	**3 Kopeks** ND (1915). Red. (Scott #116).	.50	1.00	3.00

		VG	VF	UNC
21	**10 Kopeks** ND (1915). Blue. (Scott #105).	.25	.75	2.50
22	**15 Kopeks** ND (1915). Brown. (Scott #106).	.25	.75	2.50
23	**20 Kopeks** ND (1915). Green. (Scott #107).	.25	.75	2.50

Note: #21-23 also exist imperforate; these are scarcer than perforated pieces. Beware of perforated examples which have been trimmed into imperforates. For postage stamp currency issue w/o eagle on back, refer to #32-34.

TREASURY SMALL CHANGE NOTES

1915 ND ISSUE

#24-31 arms at upper ctr. on face; at ctr. on back.

		VG	VF	UNC
24	**1 Kopek** ND (1915). Black on brown-orange unpt.			
	a. Issued note.	.25	1.00	3.00
	s. Specimen.	—	—	150.
25	**2 Kopeks** ND (1915). Black on lt. brown unpt.			
	a. Issued note.	.25	1.00	3.00
	s. Specimen.	—	—	150.
26	**3 Kopeks** ND (1915). Green on lt. green unpt.			
	a. Issued note.	.25	1.00	3.00
	s. Specimen.	—	—	150.
27	**5 Kopeks** ND (1915). Black on lt. blue unpt.			
	a. Issued note.	.25	1.00	3.00
	s. Specimen.	—	—	150.
28	**10 Kopeks** ND (1915). Blue on red-orange unpt. (Not issued).	15.00	40.00	150.

		VG	VF	UNC
29	**15 Kopeks** ND (1915). Red-brown on yellow unpt. (Not issued).	15.00	40.00	150.
30	**20 Kopeks** ND (1915). Green on lilac unpt. (Not issued).	15.00	40.00	150.

		VG	VF	UNC
31	**50 Kopeks** ND (1915). Blue on gold or yellow unpt.			
	a. Issued note.	.25	1.00	3.50
	s. Specimen.	—	Unc	200.

5% КРАТКОСРОЧНОЕ ОБЯЗАТЕЛЪСТВО ГОСУДАР. (СТВЕННАГО)КАЗНАЧЕЙСТВА

STATE TREASURY 5% SHORT-TERM OBLIGATIONS

1915 ISSUE

#31A-31E arms at ctr. on face.

		VG	VF	UNC
31A	**5000 Rubles** 15.8.1915. M/c. Specimen only. Rare.	—	—	—
31B	**10,000 Rubles** 1.8.1915. M/c. Specimen only. Rare.	—	—	—
31C	**25,000 Rubles** 20.7.1915. M/c. Specimen only. Rare.	—	—	—
31D	**50,000 Rubles** 20.6.1915. M/c. Specimen only. Rare.	—	—	—
31E	**100,000 Rubles** 15.8.1915. M/c. Specimen only. Rare.	—	—	—

1916-17 (1918) ISSUE

Note: For similar issues w/crownless eagle, see Volume 1 - Siberia, #S821-S825 and S831-S870.

		Good	Fine	XF
31F	**1000 Rubles** 1916 (1918). Lilac-brown. (12 month).	4.00	15.00	75.00
31G	**1000 Rubles** 1917 (1918). Lilac-brown. (9 month).	4.00	15.00	75.00

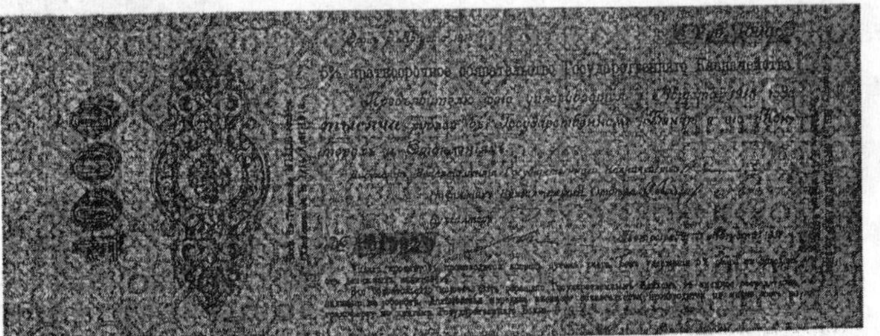

		Good	Fine	XF
31H	**1000 Rubles** 1917 (1918). Red-violet on brown and orange unpt. (12 month).	3.00	10.00	40.00
31I	**5000 Rubles** 1916-17 (1918). Orange. (12 month).	8.00	30.00	100.
31J	**5000 Rubles** 1.5.1917. (12 month).	8.00	30.00	100.
31K	**10,000 Rubles** 1.10.1915. (9 month). Specimen.	—	—	750.
31L	**10,000 Rubles** 1916 (1918). Red. (12 month).	10.00	40.00	150.
31M	**10,000 Rubles** 1916 (1918). Red. (9 month).	15.00	45.00	200.
31N	**10,000 Rubles** 1917 (1918). Red. (12 month).	10.00	40.00	150.
31O	**25,000 Rubles** 1916 (1918). (12 month).	20.00	75.00	300.
31P	**25,000 Rubles** 1917-18 (1918). (9 month).	30.00	100.	400.
31Q	**25,000 Rubles** 1917 (1918). (12 month).	25.00	75.00	300.
31R	**50,000 Rubles** 1916-17 (1918). (12 month).	40.00	150.	500.
31S	**50,000 Rubles** 1917 (1918). (9 month).	50.00	200.	600.
31T	**100,000 Rubles** 1916-17 (1918). (12 month).	70.00	225.	750.
31U	**100,000 Rubles** 1.4.1917. (12 month).	70.00	225.	750.
31V	**500,000 Rubles** 1916-17 (1918). (12 month). Rare.	—	—	—
31W	**500,000 Rubles** 1917 (1918). (9 month). Rare.	—	—	—

		Good	Fine	XF
31X	**1,000,000 Rubles** 1916-17 (1918). (12 month). Rare.	—	—	—

Note: Part of the above Issue was used by the Soviet government.

ВРЕМЕННОН ПРАВИТЕЛЬСТВО

PROVISIONAL GOVERNMENT

ВРЕМЕННОЕ ПРАВИТЕЛЬСТВО

POSTAGE STAMP CURRENCY

1917 ND ISSUE

		VG	VF	UNC
32	**1 Kopek** ND (1917). Brown-orange. Like #16-17 but w/o eagle on back. (Scott #139).			
	a. Ovpt: *1* on face.	.50	1.50	4.00
	b. W/o ovpt. on face. Rare.	—	—	—
33	**2 Kopeks** ND (1917). Green. Like #18-19 but w/o eagle on back. (Scott #140). Ovpt: *2* on face.	.50	1.50	4.00

		VG	VF	UNC
34	**3 Kopeks** ND (1917). Red. Like #20 but w/o eagle on back. (Scott #141).	.50	1.50	4.00

ГОСУДАРСТВЕННЫЙ КРЕДИТНЫЙ БИЛЕТЪ

GOVERNMENT CREDIT NOTES

1917 ISSUE

		VG	VF	UNC
35	**5 Rubles** ND (1917-old date 1909). Blue and m/c. Like #10 but series # (2 letters and 3 numerals) in place of serial #. 13 sign. varieties.			
	a. Issued note. Series УА001- УА043.	.25	1.00	3.0
	x. Error. Series letters АУ above and УА below.	50.00	150.	450

Note: #35 w/series УА044-200 and УБ401-510 is a Soviet Government issue.

		VG	VF	UN
36	**250 Rubles** (4.9.) 1917. Black on lilac unpt. Back dk. brown on lt. green and m/c unpt. Swastika in unpt. at ctr. 13 sign. varieties.	.50	1.50	7.5

Note: #36 with series # AA001-018 is a Provisional Government issue; Series AA019-100, АБ101-200, АВ201-300 and АГ301-376 are Soviet Government issues.

		VG	VF	UNC
37	**1000 Rubles**			
	(9.3.) 1917. Dk. brown on green unpt. Swastika in unpt. on face. Back blue on lt. brown and m/c unpt; Duma bldg. at ctr. 5 sign. varieties.	1.00	3.00	12.50

Note: #37 with series ААЦАЗ is a Provisional Government issue; Series АИЦАОъ Бъ В, ГЦГЯ are Soviet Government issues.

5% ОБЛИГАЦІЯ ЗАЕМЪ СВОБОДЫ

5% FREEDOM LOANS DEBENTURE BONDS

1917 ISSUE

		VG	VF	UNC
37A	**20 Rubles**			
	12 (27) 3.1917. Black on yellow unpt. W/coupons.	3.00	10.00	40.00
37B	**40 Rubles**			
	12 (27) 3.1917. Black. W/coupons.	4.00	20.00	75.00
37C	**50 Rubles**			
	12 (27) 3.1917. Black on green unpt. W/coupons.	4.00	20.00	75.00

		VG	VF	UNC
37D	**100 Rubles**			
	12 (27) 3.1917. Black on brown unpt. W/coupons.	4.00	20.00	75.00
37E	**500 Rubles**			
	12 (27) 3.1917. Black on blue unpt. W/coupons.	4.00	20.00	75.00
37F	**1000 Rubles**			
	12 (27) 3.1917. Black on rose unpt. 200 x 155mm. W/coupons.	7.50	30.00	100.
37G	**5000 Rubles**			
	12 (27) 3.1917. Black. W/coupons.			
	a. Issued note.	15.00	50.00	150.
	b. Specimen.	—	—	500.
37H	**10,000 Rubles**			
	W/coupons. 12 (27) 3.1917. Black.	30.00	100.	350.
37I	**25,000 Rubles**			
	12 (27) 3.1917. Black. W/coupons.	50.00	175.	500.

Note: Values for #37A-37I are for pieces w/coupons. Those w/o coupons are worth 50% less. The Soviet government used these 5% Freedom Loans in denominations of 20, 40, 50, and 100 Rubles w/o coupons as money.

КАЗНАЧЕЙСКIЙ ЗНАКЪ

TREASURY NOTES

1917 ND ISSUE

#38 and 39 so-called "Kerenki," they are frequently also called "Kerensky rubles." They were printed with plates adapted from consular revenue stamps. Eagle at upper ctr.

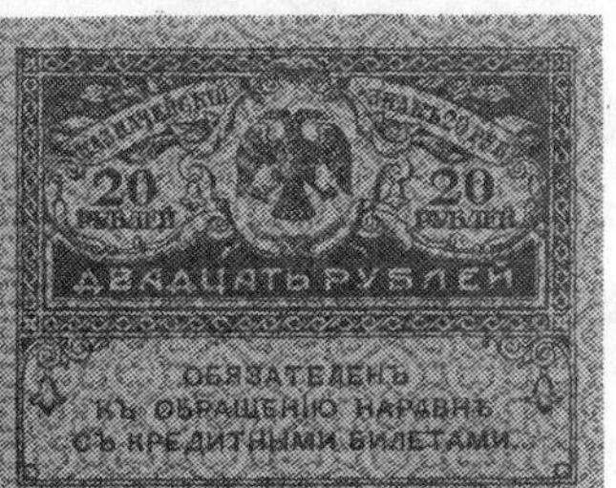

		VG	VF	UNC
38	**20 Rubles**			
	ND (4.9.1917). Brown on red-brown unpt.	.25	.50	1.25
39	**40 Rubles**			
	ND (4.9.1917). Red on green unpt.	.25	.50	1.25

Note: #38 and 39 may also appear in sheets up to 100 subjects.

ГОСУДАРСТВЕННЫЙ КРЕДИТНЫЙ БЕЛЕТ

GOVERNMENT CREDIT NOTES

1918; 1919 ISSUE

		VG	VF	UNC
39A	**25 Rubles**			
	1918. Black on blue and m/c unpt. Allegorical female at ctr. Back blue-gray.			
	a. Sign.	2.50	7.50	25.00
	b. W/o sign.	2.00	7.00	20.00
	s. Specimen w/ or w/o sign.	—	—	150.

		VG	VF	UNC
39B	**50 Rubles**			
	1919. Black on orange and m/c unpt. 2 allegorical figures at r.			
	p. Proof. Rare.	—	—	—
	s. Specimen. Rare.	—	—	—

		VG	VF	UNC
40	**100 Rubles**			
	1918. Black on brown and m/c unpt. Agriculture seated at ctr. Back brown.			
	a. Sign.	4.00	12.50	45.00
	b. W/o sign.	3.00	10.00	35.00
	s. Specimen.	—	—	150.

		VG	VF	UNC
40A	**250 Rubles**			
	1919. Black on green, blue and m/c unpt. Winged cherub and seated woman w/torch and globe at r.			
	p. Proof. Rare.	—	—	—
	s. Specimen. Rare.	—	—	—

		VG	VF	UNC
41	**500 Rubles**			
	1919. Black on brown and m/c unpt. Seated woman w/2 cherubs at ctr.			
	p. Proof. Rare.	—	—	—
	s. Specimen. Rare.	—	—	—

		VG	VF	UNC
42	**1000 Rubles**			
	1919. Black on lilac, green and m/c unpt. Seated woman w/globe at l.			
	p. Proof. Rare.	—	—	—
	s. Specimen. Rare.	—	—	—

Note: For #39A and 40 issued by other authorities during the Civil War, see Volume 1, #S1196-S1197, S1213-S1214 and S1248-S1249.

1917 Issue

		VG	VF	UNC
43	**25 Rubles**			
	ND (1917). Green. Back lt. brown. W/o sign.	75.00	200.	450.

		VG	VF	UNC
44	**50 Rubles**			
	ND (1917). Brown. Back green. W/o sign.	50.00	150.	350.
45	**100 Rubles**			
	ND (1917). Yellowish brown. Back yellow-green. W/o sign. (Not issued). Rare.	—	—	—

#46 *Deleted.*

		VG	VF	UNC
47	**500 Rubles**			
	ND (1917). Brown. Back blue-gray. W/o sign. Govt. check. Proof. (Soviet government). Rare.	—	—	—

R.S.F.S.R.-Russian Socialist Federated Soviet Republic

БИЛЕТЪ ГОСУДАРСТВЕННАГО КАЗНАЧЕЙСТВА

State Treasury Notes

1908-1916 (1918) Issues

Р.С.Ф.С. Р.

РОССИЙСКИЙ СОЦИАЛИСТИЧЕСКИХ ФЕДЕРАТИВНОЙ

СОВЕТСКИХ РЕСПУБЛИК

		VG	VF	UNC
48	**25 Rubles**			
	1915 (1918). Green on violet unpt.	1.50	6.00	20.00
49	**50 Rubles**			
	1908 (1918). Brown on green unpt.	17.50	60.00	200.
50	**50 Rubles**			
	1912 (1918). Brown on green unpt.	8.00	25.00	75.00
51	**50 Rubles**			
	1913 (1918). Brown on green unpt.	8.00	25.00	75.00

		VG	VF	UNC
52	**50 Rubles**			
	1914 (1918). Brown on green unpt.	1.50	4.50	15.00
53	**50 Rubles**			
	1915 (1918). Brown on green unpt.	1.00	4.00	12.50
54	**100 Rubles**			
	1908 (1918). Black on pink unpt.	20.00	60.00	250.
55	**100 Rubles**			
	1912 (1918). Black on pink unpt.	10.00	35.00	100.
56	**100 Rubles**			
	1913 (1918). Black on pink unpt.	10.00	35.00	100.
57	**100 Rubles**			
	1914 (1918). Black on pink unpt.	4.00	10.00	40.00
58	**100 Rubles**			
	1915 (1918). Black on pink unpt.	4.00	10.00	40.00
59	**500 Rubles**			
	1915 (1918). Black on blue unpt.	5.00	15.00	60.00
60	**500 Rubles**			
	1916 (1918). Black on lt. blue unpt.	6.00	20.00	75.00

#61-80 not assigned.

РАСЧЕТНЫЙ ЗНАК

Currency Notes

1919 ND Issue

#81-83 arms at ctr.

		VG	VF	UNC
81	**1 Ruble**			
	ND (1919). Brown. Back m/c.	.25	.75	2.50
82	**2 Rubles**			
	ND (1919). Dk. brown. Back m/c.	.25	1.00	3.00
83	**3 Rubles**			
	ND (1919). Green. Back m/c. Wmk: Lozenges.	.25	1.00	3.00

1921 ND ISSUE

#84-85 arms at ctr.

		VG	VF	UNC
84	**3 Rubles**			
	ND (1921). Green.			
	a. Wmk: Spades.	.50	1.50	4.00
	b. Wmk: Stars.	.50	2.50	10.00
85	**5 Rubles**			
	ND (1921). Dk. blue.			
	a. Wmk: Lozenges.	.50	1.50	5.00
	b. Wmk: Spades.	1.00	4.00	10.00
	c. Wmk: Stars.	1.00	4.00	10.00
	d. W/o wmk.	.50	1.50	5.00

ГОСУДАРСТВЕННЫЙ КРЕДИТНЫЙ БИЛЕТЪ

STATE TREASURY NOTES

1918 ISSUE

#86-97 double-headed eagle at ctr. on back. Wmk: value.

#86-93, 96, 97 w/10 sign. varieties.

#94-95 w/11 sign. varieties.

		VG	VF	UNC
86	**1 Ruble**			
	1918. Brown on tan unpt.			
	a. Issued note.	.50	1.25	3.50
	x. Error: Russian letter *P* missing at r. on back.	30.00	100.	250.
87	**3 Rubles**			
	1918. Green on lt. green unpt.	.50	1.25	3.50
88	**5 Rubles**			
	1918. Blue-black on lt. blue unpt.	.50	1.50	5.00
89	**10 Rubles**			
	1918. Red-brown on lt. red unpt. Back dk. brown on red-brown unpt.	.50	1.50	5.00

		VG	VF	UNC
0	**25 Rubles**			
	1918. Red-brown on lt. brown unpt. Back dull purple on brown unpt.	.50	1.75	6.00
1	**50 Rubles**			
	1918. Dk. brown on lt. brown unpt.	.50	1.75	6.00

		VG	VF	UNC
92	**100 Rubles**			
	1918. Brown on lt. red unpt.	.50	1.75	6.50
93	**250 Rubles**			
	1918. Green on lt. green unpt.	.50	2.00	7.00
94	**500 Rubles**			
	1918. Dk. olive-green on pale olive-green unpt. Back black on brown and pale olive-green unpt.			
	a. Horizontal wmk.	1.00	3.00	7.50
	b. Vertical wmk.	1.00	5.00	15.00

		VG	VF	UNC
95	**1000 Rubles**			
	1918. Brown on tan unpt.			
	a. Horizontal wmk.	1.50	3.50	10.00
	b. Vertical wmk.	2.00	7.50	22.50
	x. Error. Back top to top w/back inverted.	50.00	125.	300.
96	**5000 Rubles**			
	1918. Black on blue unpt. Swastika in unpt. Back brown on blue unpt.			
	a. Horizontal wmk.	1.75	5.00	15.00
	b. Vertical wmk.	3.00	10.00	45.00
97	**10,000 Rubles**			
	1918. Dk. brown on brown and red unpt. Swastika in unpt.			
	a. Horizontal wmk.	2.00	5.00	15.00
	b. Vertical wmk.	3.00	10.00	45.00

РАСЧЕТНЫЙ ЗНАК

CURRENCY NOTES

1919-20 (ND) ISSUE

#98-100 wmk: stars. Because of the multi-language text, these notes are sometimes called "Babylonians".

		VG	VF	UNC
98	**15 Rubles**			
	ND (1919). Brown on lt. brown unpt. Back m/c; arms at ctr. 8 sign. varieties.	.50	1.25	4.00
99	**30 Rubles**			
	ND (1919). Brown on green unpt. Arms at ctr. on back.			
	a. Issued note.	.50	1.50	5.00
	x. Error. Back inverted.	60.00	150.	350.
100	**60 Rubles**			
	ND (1919). Blue-black on gray unpt. Arms at ctr. on back.	.50	1.50	5.00

#101-106 w/10 sign. varieties. Text in 7 languages, says: "Workers of the World, Unite!"

		VG	VF	UNC
101	**100 Rubles** 1919 (1920). Dk. brown or black on lt. brown unpt. Arms at upper l. on back.			
	a. Horizontal wmk: *100.*	.50	1.25	3.00
	b. Vertical wmk: *100.*	.50	1.50	4.00
102	**250 Rubles** 1919 (1920). Black on red-brown unpt. Back like #101.			
	a. Wmk: *250.*	.50	1.25	3.00
	b. Wmk: Stars.	.50	2.50	7.50
103	**500 Rubles** 1919 (1920). Black on olive unpt. Back like #101.			
	a. Wmk: *500.*	.50	2.00	5.00
	b. Wmk: Stars.	1.00	3.00	10.00

		VG	VF	UNC
104	**1000 Rubles** 1919 (1920). Black on green unpt. Back like #101.			
	a. Wmk: *1000.*	.50	1.50	4.00
	b. Wmk: Sm. stars.	.50	2.50	7.50
	c. Wmk: Lg. stars.	.50	2.50	7.50
	d. Wmk: Lozenges.	1.00	5.00	15.00
	e. Vertical wmk: *1000.*	.50	2.50	7.50

		VG	VF	UNC
105	**5000 Rubles** 1919 (1920). Blue on yellow and m/c unpt. Arms at ctr. on back.			
	a. Wmk: Broad waves.	1.00	3.00	10.00
	b. Wmk: Narrow waves.	2.00	7.50	25.00
	c. Wmk: Stars.	3.00	15.00	50.00
106	**10,000 Rubles** 1919 (1920). Red on purple and m/c unpt. Back like #105.			
	a. Wmk: Broad waves.	1.00	3.50	12.50
	b. Wmk: Narrow waves.	2.00	6.00	25.00
	c. Wmk: Stars.	5.00	25.00	75.00

1921 ISSUE

		VG	VF	UNC
106A	**50 Kopeks** ND (1921). Specimen only. Rare.	—	—	—

		VG	VF	UNC
107	**50 Rubles** ND (1921). Brown. Arms at ctr.			
	a. Wmk: Lozenges.	.50	2.00	6.00
	b. Wmk: Lg. stars.	.25	1.75	5.00
	c. Wmk: Sm. stars.	.50	2.00	6.00
	d. W/o wmk.	.50	2.00	6.00
108	**100 Rubles** 1921. Yellow. Arms at r.	1.50	2.50	8.00
109	**100 Rubles** 1921. Orange. Like #108.	.50	2.25	6.00
110	**250 Rubles** 1921. Green. Arms at l.			
	a. Wmk: *250.*	.50	2.50	7.00
	b. Wmk: Stars.	.50	2.50	8.00

		VG	VF	UNC
111	**500 Rubles** 1921. Blue. Arms at ctr.			
	a. Wmk: *500.*	.50	1.50	6.00
	b. Wmk: Stars.	.50	1.25	6.00
	c. Wmk: Lozenges.	.50	1.50	6.00
112	**1000 Rubles** 1921. Red. Arms at l.			
	a. Wmk: *1000.*	.50	1.25	5.00
	b. Wmk: Sm. stars.	.50	1.25	5.00
	c. Wmk: Lg. stars.	.50	2.50	7.50
	d. Wmk: Lozenges.	.50	1.25	5.00

Note: #107-112 may be found in various uncut forms, i.e., block of 4, vertical or horizontal pair, etc. #113-117 w/10 sign. varieties.

		VG	VF	UNC
113	**5000 Rubles** 1921. Blue on brown unpt. Arms at upper ctr. on back.			
	a. Issued note.	.50	2.50	7.50
	x. Error. Misprint: *PROLETAPIER* instead of *PROLETARIER* at upper l. on back.	1.00	3.00	10.00
114	**10,000 Rubles** 1921. Dk. red on lt. red unpt. Arms at ctr. on back.	1.00	4.00	12.50

		VG	VF	UNC
115	**25,000 Rubles** 1921. Red brown.			
	a. Wmk: Lg. stars.	.50	2.50	10.00
	b. Wmk: Sm. stars.	5.00	20.00	75.00

		VG	VF	UNC
116	**50,000 Rubles** 1921. Blue-green. Arms at lower ctr.			
	a. Wmk: Lg. stars.	.50	2.50	10.00
	b. Wmk: Sm. stars.	6.00	25.00	100.
	c. Wmk: Crosses.	15.00	60.00	250.
	d. Wmk: Carpet design. Rare.	—	—	—

		VG	VF	UNC
117	**100,000 Rubles** 1921. Red. Arms at l. ctr.			
	a. Wmk: lg. stars.	.50	2.50	10.00
	b. Wmk: Crosses.	20.00	60.00	250.

#118-119 *Deleted.*

ОБЯЗАТЕЛЬСТВО РОССИЙСКОЙ СОЦИАЛИСТИЧЕСКОЙ ФЕДЕРАТИВНОЙ СОВЕТСКОЙ РЕСПУБЛИКИ

TREASURY SHORT-TERM CERTIFICATES

1921 ISSUE

1 New Ruble = 10,000 Old Rubles.

		VG	VF	UNC
120	**1,000,000 Rubles** 1921. Black on yellowish paper.	10.00	40.00	150.
121	**5,000,000 Rubles** 1921. Black on bluish paper.	20.00	80.00	250.
122	**10,000,000 Rubles** 1921. Black on bluish paper.	15.00	70.00	200.

1922 ISSUE

		VG	VF	UNC
123	**5000 Rubles** 1922.	10.00	40.00	150.
124	**10,000 Rubles** 1922. Black on gray-blue paper.	15.00	70.00	200.

		VG	VF	UNC
125	**25,000 Rubles** 1922. Specimen.			
	s1. Specimen. White paper.	50.00	200.	650.
	s2. Specimen. Brown paper. 1 example known. Rare.	—	—	—

ГОСУДАРСТВЕННЫЙ ДЕНЕЖНЫЙ ЗНАК

STATE CURRENCY NOTES

1922 ISSUE

		VG	VF	UNC
126	**50 Kopeks** 1922. Proof. Rare.	—	—	—

#127-130 arms at upper l.

		VG	VF	UNC
127	**1 Ruble** 1922. Brownish orange. 9 sign. varieties.	.50	2.00	6.00

#128-138 each w/10 sign. varieties.

		VG	VF	UNC
128	**3 Rubles** 1922. Green.	.50	2.00	6.00
129	**5 Rubles** 1922. Blue.	.50	2.50	8.00
130	**10 Rubles** 1922. Red.	.50	2.50	8.00

		VG	VF	UNC
131	**25 Rubles** 1922. Brown-lilac on yellow and blue unpt.	1.00	3.00	10.00
132	**50 Rubles** 1922. Blue on pink unpt.	1.00	3.50	12.50
133	**100 Rubles** 1922. Red on blue unpt.	1.50	5.00	15.00
134	**250 Rubles** 1922. Dk. green on blue and orange unpt.	4.00	12.50	45.00
135	**500 Rubles** 1922. Dk. blue on lt. brown unpt.	2.00	5.00	20.00

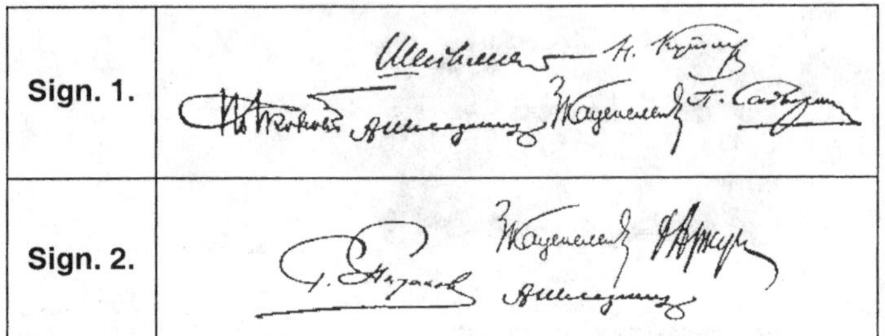

		VG	VF	UNC
136	**1000 Rubles** 1922. Brown on red, blue and green unpt.	4.00	12.50	35.00
137	**5000 Rubles** 1922. Black. Back green and pink.	12.50	35.00	100.
138	**10,000 Rubles** 1922. Red. Back red and green.	20.00	60.00	175.

БАНКОВЫЙ БИЛЕТ

STATE BANK NOTES

Sign. 1.	
Sign. 2.	

1922 ISSUE

#139-145 m/c guilloche at l.

		VG	VF	UNC
139	**1 Chervonetz** 1922.			
	a. Sign. 1.	30.00	100.	200.
	b. Sign. 2.	60.00	200.	400.

#140 Deleted.

		VG	VF	UNC
141	**3 Chervontsa** 1922. Rare.	—	—	—
142	**5 Chervontsev** 1922. Rare.	—	—	—

		VG	VF	UNC
143	**10 Chervontsev** 1922.	50.00	150.	400.
144	**25 Chervontsev** 1922. Rare.	—	—	—

1923 ISSUE

145A	**1/2 Chervonetz** 1923. Brown text. Specimen. Rare.	—	—	—

ГОСУДАРСТВЕННІЙ ДЕНЕЖНЫЙ ЗНАК

STATE CURRENCY NOTES

1922 ISSUE

#146-151 "Promissory note" type. Arms at upper ctr.

		VG	VF	UNC
146	**1 Ruble** 1922. Brown on gold unpt.	.50	2.50	7.50

		VG	VF	UNC
147	**3 Rubles** 1922. Green.	.50	2.50	8.00

		VG	VF	UNC
148	**5 Rubles** 1922. Blue.	.50	2.50	8.00
149	**10 Rubles** 1922. Red.	.50	2.50	8.00
150	**25 Rubles** 1922. Purple.	1.00	3.00	12.50

		VG	VF	UNC
151	**50 Rubles** 1922. Brown on green unpt.	1.50	4.50	17.50

1923 ISSUE

#151A-155 "coin notes" w/o promissory designation. Image of coin shown.

		VG	VF	UNC
151A	**5 Kopeks** 1923. Proof. Rare.	—	—	—
152	**10 Kopeks** 1923. Proof. Rare.	—	—	—
153	**15 Kopeks** 1923. Proof. Rare.	—	—	—
154	**20 Kopeks** 1923. Proof. Rare.	—	—	—

		VG	VF	UNC
155	**50 Kopeks** 1923. Blue.	1.50	4.00	15.00

Note: #155 may be found in various uncut forms, i.e. block of 4, strip of 2, etc.

1923 First Issue

1 "New" Ruble = 1,000,000 "Old" Rubles.

#156-162 text on back in 7 lines. Wmk: tile pattern.

		VG	VF	UNC
156	**1 Ruble** 1923. Brown. 3 sign. varieties.	.50	2.00	6.00

#157-162 each w/10 sign. varieties.

		VG	VF	UNC
157	**5 Rubles** 1923. Green.	.50	2.00	6.00
158	**10 Rubles** 1923. Dk. purple. Back brown.	.50	2.00	6.00
159	**25 Rubles** 1923. Blue.	.50	2.00	6.00
160	**50 Rubles** 1923. Olive.	.50	2.00	6.00
161	**100 Rubles** 1923. Purple and m/c.	1.00	4.00	12.50

		VG	VF	UNC
162	**250 Rubles** 1923. Dk. blue.	1.50	5.00	17.50

1923 Second Issue

#163-171 text on back in 8 lines.

		VG	VF	UNC
163	**1 Ruble** 1923. Brown. 3 sign. varieties.	.50	1.50	5.00

#164-171 each w/10 sign. varieties.

		VG	VF	UNC
164	**5 Rubles** 1923. Green.	.50	1.50	5.00
165	**10 Rubles** 1923. Black on gray unpt. Back brown.			
	a. Wmk: Lozenges.	.50	1.50	5.00
	b. Wmk: Stars.	1.00	3.00	8.00
166	**25 Rubles** 1923. Blue.			
	a. Wmk: Lozenges.	.50	1.50	5.00
	b. Wmk: Stars.	1.00	3.00	8.00
167	**50 Rubles** 1923. Brown.			
	a. Wmk: Lozenges.	1.00	3.00	8.00
	b. Wmk: Stars.	1.50	4.00	12.50

#168-171 arms at ctr. in unpt.

		VG	VF	UNC
168	**100 Rubles** 1923. Purple on m/c unpt.			
	a. Wmk: Lozenges.	2.00	6.50	20.00
	b. Wmk: Stars.	1.50	5.00	15.00
169	**500 Rubles** 1923. Dk. brown on m/c unpt.	2.50	7.50	25.00
170	**1000 Rubles** 1923. Red on m/c unpt.	4.00	12.50	40.00
171	**5000 Rubles** 1923. Green on m/c unpt.	6.00	20.00	60.00

		VG	VF	UNC
171A	**10,000 Rubles** 1923. Red on lt. brown paper. 6-pointed star at upper ctr. Wmk: Lozenges. (Not issued). Rare.	—	—	—

ПЛАТЕЖНОЕ ОБЯЗАТЕЛЬСТВОН.К.Ф.Р.С.Ф.С.Р.

N.K.F. PAYMENT OBLIGATIONS OF THE R.S.F.S.R.

1923 (1924) ISSUE

		VG	VF	UNC
172	**100 Gold Rubles** 1923 (1924). Specimen, perforated: *ОБРАЗЕЦ*. Rare.	—	—	—

		VG	VF	UNC
173	**250 Gold Rubles** 1923 (1924). Specimen.	—	500.	1000.
174	**500 Gold Rubles** 1923 (1924). Specimen.	—	500.	1000.
175	**1000 Gold Rubles** 1923 (1924). Specimen.	—	500.	1000.

ТРАНСПОРТНЫЙ СЕРТИФИКАТ

TRANSPORT CERTIFICATES

1923-24 ISSUE

		VG	VF	UNC
176	**3 Gold Rubles** 1.3.1924. Front view steam locomotive at ctr., axe and anchor at upper r. Specimen only. Rare.	—	—	—

Note: Deceptive counterfeits of #176 are occasionally encountered.

No.	Denomination	Good	Fine	XF
177	**5 Gold Rubles** 1923. Series 1-5.	100.	300.	950.
178	**5 Gold Rubles** 1923. Series 6-10.	100.	300.	950.

No.	Denomination	Good	Fine	XF
179	**5 Gold Rubles** 1923. Series 11-15. Like #178 but change in text on back.	100.	300.	950.
180	**5 Gold Rubles** 1923. Series 16-24. Like #179 but repeated change in text on back.	100.	300.	950.

С.С.С.Р.
СОЮЗСОВЕТСКИХ СОЦИАЛИС ТИЧЕСКИХ РЕСЛУБЛИК

U.S.S.R. - UNION OF SOVIET SOCIALIST REPUBLICS

ГОСУДАРСТВЕННЫЙ ДЕНЕЖНЫЙ ЗНАК

STATE CURRENCY NOTES

1923 (1924) ISSUE

#181-183 Arms at upper l.

		VG	VF	UNC
181	**10,000 Rubles** 1923 (1924). Lilac on green unpt. View of Kremlin. 10 sign. varieties.	15.00	60.00	200.

		VG	VF	UNC
182	**15,000 Rubles** 1923 (1924). Brown. Man at ctr. 10 sign. varieties.	20.00	75.00	250

		VG	VF	UNC
183	**25,000 Rubles** 1923 (1924). Dk. blue and green on lilac unpt. Soldier at ctr. 4 sign. varieties.	25.00	85.00	300.

ПЛАТЕЖНОЕ ОБЯЗАТЕЛЬСТВО Н.К.Ф.С.С.С.Р.

N.K.F. PAYMENT OBLIGATIONS OF THE U.S.S.R.

1924-26 ISSUE

		VG	VF	UNC
184	**100 Gold Rubles** 1924-28. Specimen only, perforated: *ОБРАЗЕЦ*. Rare.	—	—	—

		VG	VF	UNC
184A	**250 Gold Rubles** 1924-28. Specimen only. Rare.	—	—	—
185	**500 Gold Rubles** 1924-28. Specimen only. Rare.	—	—	—
185A	**1000 Gold Rubles** 1926-28. Specimen only. Rare.	—	—	—

НАРОДНОГО КОМИССАРІАТА ФИНАНСОВ СОЮЗА С.С.Р.КРАТКОСРОЧНОЕ ПЛАТЕЖНОЕ ОБЯЗАТЕЛЬСТВО

N.F.K. SHORT-TERM PAYMENT OBLIGATIONS OF THE U.S.S.R.

1928 ISSUE

		VG	VF	UNC
185B	**100 Gold Rubles** 1928-29. W/coupons. Specimen only. Rare.	—	—	—
185C	**250 Gold Rubles** 1928-29. W/coupons. Specimen only. Rare.	—	—	—
185D	**500 Gold Rubles** 1928-29. W/coupons. Specimen only. Rare.	—	—	—
185E	**1000 Gold Rubles** Specimen only. 1928-29. W/coupons. Rare.	—	—	—

NOTICE

Readers with unlisted dates, signature varieties, etc. are invited to submit photocopies or, high resolution (300 dpi, 100% size) scans of their notes to: Standard Catalog of World Paper Money, 700 East State St. Iola, WI 54990-0001, or E-Mail: george.cuhaj@fwpubs.com.

ГОСУДАРСТВЕННЫЙ ДЕНЕЖНЫЙ ЗНАК

STATE CURRENCY NOTES

1924 ISSUE

#186-188 w/5 sign. varieties.

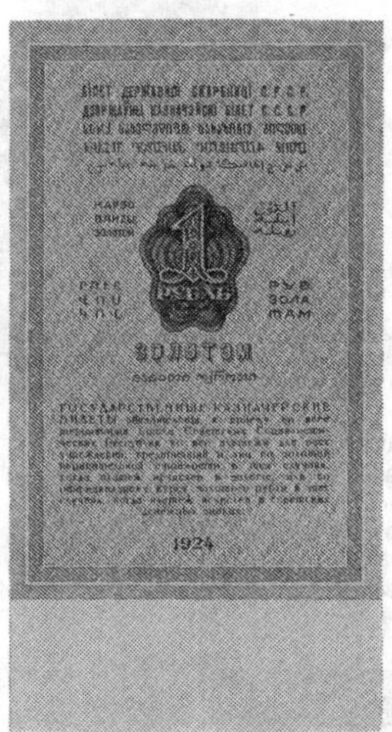

		VG	VF	UNC
186	**1 Gold Ruble** 1924. Blue on lt. brown and m/c unpt. Arms at upper ctr. Vertical format, w/and w/o series *СЕРИЯ*.	10.00	30.00	125.

		VG	VF	UNC
187	**3 Gold Rubles** 1924. Green. 2 reclining men at lower ctr.	100.	400.	950.

		VG	VF	UNC
188	**5 Gold Rubles** 1924. Blue. Tractor plowing at lower ctr.	100.	400.	950.

1925 ISSUE

#189-190 each w/10 sign. varieties. Arms at upper ctr.

		VG	VF	UNC
189	**3 Rubles** 1925. Dk. green.	2.50	10.00	35.00

		VG	VF	UNC
190	**5 Rubles** 1925. Dk. blue. Worker at l.	5.00	17.50	60.00

SMALL CHANGE NOTES

1924 ISSUE

#191-195 arms at upper ctr.

		VG	VF	UNC
191	**1 Kopek** 1924. Lt. brown.	1.50	5.00	17.50
192	**2 Kopeks** 1924. Brown.	1.50	5.00	20.00
193	**3 Kopeks** 1924. Green.	1.50	5.00	20.00
194	**5 Kopeks** 1924. Blue.	1.50	5.00	20.00

		VG	VF	UNC
195	**20 Kopeks** 1924. Brown on rose unpt. Specimen.	150.	400.	950.

		VG	VF	UNC
196	**50 Kopeks** 1924. Blue on brown unpt. Arms at upper l.	5.00	20.00	75.00

БИЛЕТ ГОСТДАРСТВЕННОГО БАНКА С.С.С.Р.

1924 ISSUE

		VG	VF	UNC
196A	**1 Chervonetz** 1924 (date in wmk.). Specimen only. Rare.	—	—	—

NOTICE

Readers with unlisted dates, signature varieties, etc. are invited to submit photocopies or, high resolution (300 dpi, 100% size) scans of their notes to: Standard Catalog of World Paper Money, 700 East State St. Iola, WI 54990-0001, or E-Mail: george.cuhaj@fwpubs.com.

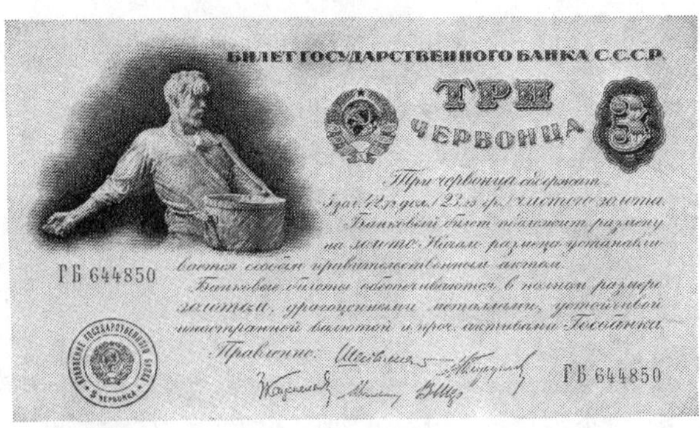

197 3 Chervontsa
1924 (date in wmk.). Black. Uniface. Farmer sowing at l., arms at upper ctr.

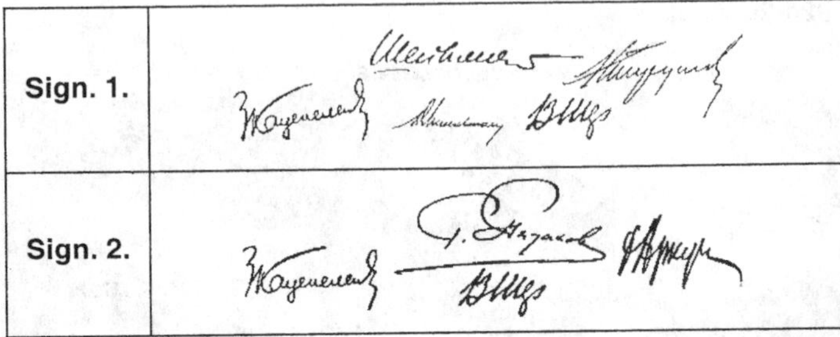

	VG	VF	UNC
a. Sign. 1.	50.00	150.	300.
b. Sign. 2.	150.	600.	1200.

		VG	VF	UNC
197A	**5 Chervontsev** 1924 (date in wmk.). Specimen only. Rare.	—	—	—

1926; 1928 ISSUE

		VG	VF	UNC
198	**1 Chervonetz** 1926. Dk. blue. Arms at upper l.			

Sign. 1.	
Sign. 2.	
Sign. 3.	
Sign. 4.	

	VG	VF	UNC
a. Sign. 1.	8.00	25.00	100.
b. Sign. 2.	8.00	25.00	100.
c. Sign. 3.	8.00	25.00	100.
d. Sign. 4.	8.00	25.00	100.

		VG	VF	UNC
199	**2 Chervontsa** 1928. Green. Arms at upper ctr.			

Sign. 1.	
Sign. 2.	
Sign. 3.	
Sign. 4.	

	VG	VF	UNC
a. Sign. 1.	15.00	50.00	150.
b. Sign. 2.	15.00	50.00	150.
c. Sign. 3.	15.00	50.00	150.
d. Sign. 4.	60.00	150.	300.

		VG	VF	UNC
200	**5 Chervontsev** 1928. Dk. blue. Uniface. Arms at upper l.			

Sign. 1.	
Sign. 2.	
Sign. 3.	
Sign. 4.	

	VG	VF	UNC
a. Sign. 1.	100.	350.	950.
b. Sign. 2.	75.00	250.	750.
c. Sign. 3.	75.00	250.	750.
d. Sign. 4.	75.00	250.	750.

1932 ISSUE

		VG	VF	UNC
201	**3 Chervontsa** 1932. Green. Arms at upper ctr.	5.00	20.00	75.00

1937 ISSUE

#202-205 arms at upper l. ctr., portr. V. Lenin at r.

		VG	VF	UNC
202	**1 Chervonetz** 1937. Black. Back black on blue and m/c unpt.	.75	3.00	15.00
203	**3 Chervontsa** 1937. Red. Back brown on m/c unpt.	.75	3.00	15.00

		VG	VF	UNC
204	**5 Chervontsev** Back black on m/c unpt. 1937. Dk. olive-green.	1.00	5.00	20.00
205	**10 Chervontsev** 1937. Black. Back dk. blue.	1.50	6.00	30.00

Note: It is reported that #202-205 were issued for the 20th Anniversary of the October 1917 Revolution.

ГОСУДАРСТВЕННЫЙ КАЗНАЧЕЙСКИЙ БИЛЕТ

STATE TREASURY NOTE

1928 ISSUE

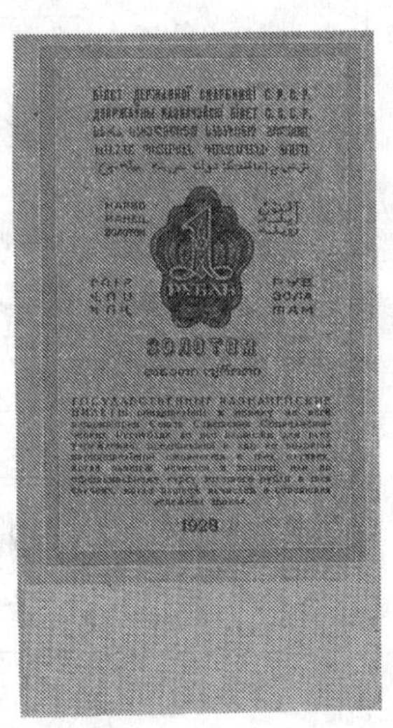

		VG	VF	UNC
206	**1 Gold Ruble** 1928. Blue on lt. brown and m/c unpt. Like #186. 5 sign. varieties. W/ or w/o series *СЕРИЯ*.	3.50	15.00	60.00

1934 ISSUE

#207-212 arms at upper ctr.

		VG	VF	UNC
207	**1 Gold Ruble** 1934. Dk. blue on peach paper. Back brown on m/c unpt. W/sign.	1.50	5.00	20.00

		VG	VF	UNC
208	**1 Gold Ruble** 1934. Dk. blue. Like #207. W/o sign.	.50	2.00	7.50
209	**3 Gold Rubles** 1934. Green. W/sign.	1.50	5.00	20.00

		VG	VF	UNC
210	**3 Gold Rubles** 1934. Green. Like #209. W/o sign.	1.00	4.00	12.50
211	**5 Gold Rubles** 1934. Gray-blue on lt. blue. W/sign.	2.50	7.50	27.50
212	**5 Gold Rubles** 1934. Gray-blue on lt. blue. Like #211. W/o sign.	1.00	4.00	17.50

1938 ISSUE

#213-215 arms at upper l.

		VG	VF	UNC
213	**1 Ruble** 1938. Brown on gold unpt. Miner at r.	.50	1.50	5.00

		VG	VF	UNC
214	**3 Rubles** 1938. Dk. green. Soldiers at l.	.50	1.75	6.00

		VG	VF	UNC
215	**5 Rubles** 1938. Dk. blue. Aviator at r.	.50	1.75	6.00

1947 ISSUE

Type I: 16 scrolls of denominations on wreath around arms (8 at l., 7 at r., 1 at ctr.).

Type II: 15 scrolls of denominations on wreath around arms (7 at l., 7 at r., 1 at ctr.).

		VG	VF	UNC
216	**1 Ruble** 1947. Blue-black on pale orange unpt. Back m/c. Type I.	.25	1.25	5.00
217	**1 Ruble** 1947 (1957). Type II.	.25	1.00	4.00
218	**3 Rubles** 1947. Dk. green on lt. green and lilac unpt. Type I.	.25	2.00	7.50
219	**3 Rubles** 1947 (1957). Type II.	.25	1.50	5.00

		VG	VF	UNC
220	**5 Rubles** 1947. Black on blue and lt. orange unpt. Back blue and m/c. Type I.	.50	4.00	12.50
221	**5 Rubles** 1947 (1957). Type II.	.25	1.75	6.00

БИЛЕТ ГОСУДАРСТВЕННОГО БАНКА С.С.С.Р.

STATE BANK NOTE U.S.S.R.

1947 ISSUE

		VG	VF	UNC
225	**10 Rubles** 1947. Black on blue and m/c unpt. Type I. V. Lenin at l. on back.	1.00	6.00	20.00
226	**10 Rubles** 1947 (1957). Type II.	.50	3.00	12.50

		VG	VF	UNC
227	**25 Rubles** 1947. Blue on green and m/c unpt. Type I. Back black on blue and green unpt. V. Lenin at l. Similar to #225.	1.50	7.50	25.00
228	**25 Rubles** 1947 (1957). Type II.	1.00	3.50	17.50
229	**50 Rubles** 1947. Blue on yellow-green and m/c unpt. Type I. Back black on m/c unpt. Similar to #225.	2.50	8.50	32.50
230	**50 Rubles** 1947 (1957) Type II.	1.50	6.50	22.50
231	**100 Rubles** 1947. Black on m/c unpt. Type I. V. Lenin at l. Back black on ochre and lilac unpt.; view of Kremlin.	3.00	12.50	40.00
232	**100 Rubles** 1947 (1957). Type II.	2.00	8.50	25.00

FOREIGN EXCHANGE CERTIFICATES

TORGSIN

1932 HARD CURRENCY NOTES

		Good	Fine	XF
FX1	**1 Kopek** 1932. M/c.			
	a. Ornamental underprint.	75.00	200.	400.
	b. Rectangular underprint.	75.00	200.	400.
FX2	**3 Kopek** 1932. M/c.			
	a. Ornamental underprint. Rare.	—	—	—
	b. Rectangular underprint. Rare.	—	—	—
FX3	**5 Kopek** 1932.			
	a. Ornamental underprint. Rare.	—	—	—
	b. Rectangular underprint. Rare.	—	—	—
	s. As b. *SPECIMEN*. Rare.	—	—	—
FX4	**10 Kopek** 1932.			
	a. Ornamental underprint. Rare.	—	—	—
	b. Rectangular underprint. Rare.	—	—	—
	s. As b. *SPECIMEN*. Rare.	—	—	—
FX5	**15 Kopek** 1932.			
	a. Ornamental underprint. Rare.	—	—	—
	b. Rectangular underprint. Rare.	—	—	—
FX6	**20 Kopek** 1932.			
	a. Ornamental underprint. Rare.	—	—	—
	b. Rectangular underprint. Rare.	—	—	—
	s. As b. *SPECIMEN*. Rare.	—	—	—
FX7	**50 Kopek** 1932.			
	a. Ornamental underprint. Rare.	—	—	—
	b. Rectangular underprint. Rare.	—	—	—
	s. As b. *SPECIMEN*. Rare.	—	—	—
FX8	**1 Ruble** 1932.			
	a. Ornamental underprint. Rare.	—	—	—
	b. Rectangular underprint. Rare.	—	—	—
	s. As b. *SPECIMEN*. Rare.	—	—	—
FX9	**3 Ruble** 1932. Ornamental underprint. *SPECIMEN* only. Rare.	—	—	—
FX10	**5 Ruble** 1932. Ornamental underprint. *SPECIMEN* only. Rare.	—	—	—
FX11	**10 Ruble** 1932. Ornamental underprint. *SPECIMEN* only. Rare.	—	—	—
FX12	**25 Ruble** 1932. Ornamental underprint. *SPECIMEN* only. Rare.	—	—	—

1932 SOVIET TRADING FLEET "SOVTORGFLEET"

FX13	**1 Ruble** ND (1932). Rare.	—	—	—
FX14	**3 Ruble** ND (1932). Rare.	—	—	—

Rwanda-Burundi, a Belgian League of Nations mandate and United Nations trust territory comprising the provinces of Rwanda and Burundi of the former colony of German East Africa, was located in central Africa between the present Republic of the Congo, Uganda and mainland Tanzania. The mandate-trust territory had an area of 20,916 sq. mi. (54,272 sq. km.).

For specific statistics and history of Rwanda and Burundi see individual entries.

When Rwanda and Burundi were formed into a mandate for administration by Belgium, their names were changed to Ruanda and Urundi and they were organized as an integral part of the Belgian Congo, during which time they used a common banknote issue with the Belgian Congo. After the Belgian Congo acquired independence as the Republic of the Congo, the provinces of Ruanda and Urundi reverted to their former names of Rwanda and Burundi and issued notes with both names on them. In 1962, both Rwanda and Burundi became separate independent states.

Also see Belgian Congo, Burundi and Rwanda.

MONETARY SYSTEM:

1 Franc = 100 Centimes

MANDATE - TRUST TERRITORY

BANQUE D'EMISSION DU RWANDA ET DU BURUNDI

1960 ISSUE

#1-7 various date and sign. varieties.

		VG	VF	UNC
1	**5 Francs**			
	1960-63. Lt. brown on green unpt. Impala at l.			
	a. 15.9.1960; 15.5.1961.	12.50	50.00	200.
	b. 15.4.1963.	15.00	60.00	250.

		Good	Fine	XF
2	**10 Francs** 15.9.1960; 5.10.1960. Dull gray on pale blue and pale orange unpt. Hippopotamus at l. Printer: TDLR.	15.00	65.00	225.

		Good	Fine	XF
3	**20 Francs** 15.9.1960; 5.10.1960. Green on tan and pink unpt. Crocodile at r. Printer: TDLR.	20.00	85.00	325.

		Good	Fine	X
4	**50 Francs** 15.9.1960; 1.10.1960. Red on m/c unpt. Lioness at ctr. r.	20.00	75.00	30[illegible]

		Good	Fine	X
5	**100 Francs** 15.9.1960; 1.10.1960; 31.7.1962. Blue on lt. green and tan unpt. Zebu at l.	15.00	60.00	17[illegible]

		Good	Fine	X
6	**500 Francs** 15.9.1960; 15.5.1961; 15.9.1961. Lilac-brown on m/c unpt. Black Rhinoceros at ctr. r.	185.	800.	160[illegible]

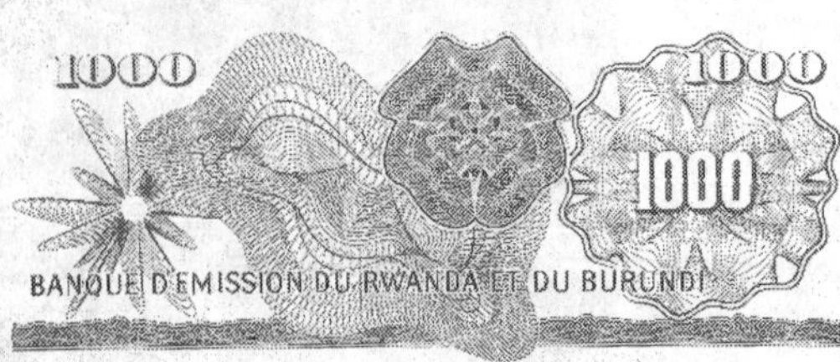

		Good	Fine	X
7	**1000 Francs**			
	15.9.1960; 15.5.1961; 31.7.1962. Green on m/c unpt. Zebra at r.			
	a. Issued note.	165.	700.	14[illegible]
	ct. Color trial in purple on m/c unpt.	—	Unc	15[illegible]

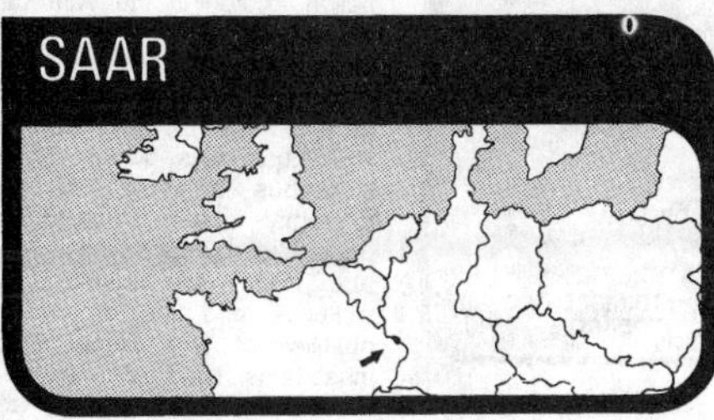

Saar (Sarre, Saarland), the smallest of the ten states of West Germany, is bounded by France to the south and by Luxembourg to the west. It has an area of 991 sq. mi. (2,568 sq. km.) and a population of 1.2 million. Capital: Saarbrucken. Principal products are iron and steel, chemicals, glass and coal.

The area of the Saar became part of France in 1766, but was divided between Prussia and Bavaria by the Treaty of Paris, 1815. The Treaty of Versailles, 1919, made the Saar an autonomous territory of the League of Nations, while assigning the coal mines to France. It was returned to Germany, by plebiscite, in 1935. France reoccupied the Saar in 1945. In 1946 it was assigned to the French occupation zone, and was united economically to France in 1947. Following a plebiscite, the Saar became a state of West Germany in 1957.

The Saar mark had no actual fractional divisions produced.

MONETARY SYSTEM:

1 Franc = 100 Centimes to 1930
1 Mark = 100 Pfennig, 1930-1957

AUTONOMOUS TERRITORY

MINES DOMANIALES DE LA SARRE, ETAT FRANÇAIS

1919 ND ISSUE

		VG	VF	UNC
1	**50 Centimes** ND (1919). Blue-gray w/brown text. Portr. woman at l.	12.50	32.50	85.00

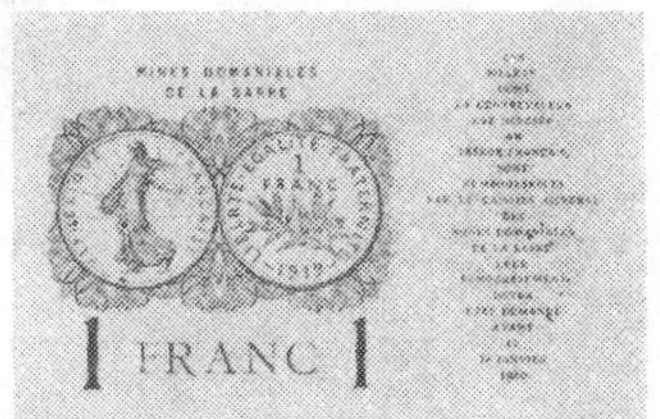

		VG	VF	UNC
2	**1 Franc** ND (1919). Red-brown on gold unpt. Portr. woman at r. Obverse and reverse of 1-franc coin dated 1919 at l. ctr. on back.	15.00	40.00	90.00

Note: #1 and #2 circulated from 1919 until 1.1.1930.

SARRE

TREASURY

1947 ISSUE

#6-8 wmk: Head at l. and r.

		VG	VF	UNC
3	**1 Mark** 1947. Blue and brown. Bearded classic man at ctr. Woman w/fruit on back.	15.00	40.00	90.00
4	**2 Mark** 1947. Lilac and brown on yellow unpt. Like #3.	80.00	225.	450.
5	**5 Mark** 1947. Pink and violet on lt. blue and orange unpt. Like #3.	30.00	90.00	300.

		VG	VF	UNC
6	**10 Mark** 1947. Green, red and m/c. woman at ctr. Man and horse on back.	50.00	175.	400.
7	**50 Mark** 1947. Green, yellow and m/c. Like #6.	300.	850.	—
8	**100 Mark** 1947. Yellow-brown, blue-green and m/c. Like #6. Rare.	—	—	—

SAINT HELENA

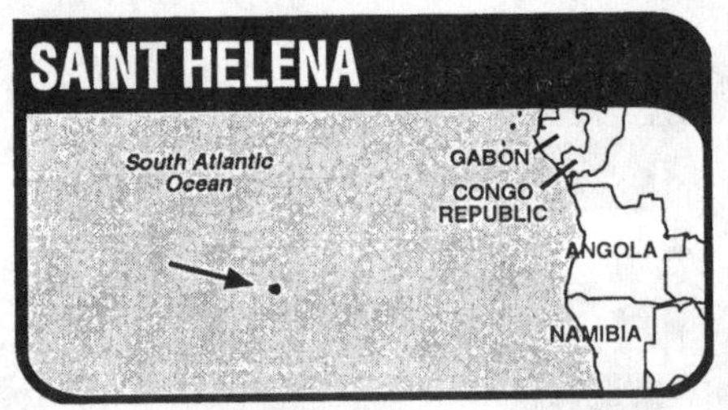

The Colony of St. Helena, a British colony located about 1,150 miles (1,850 km.) from the west coast of Africa, has an area of 47 sq. mi. (122 sq. km.) and a population of 5,700. Capital: Jamestown. Flax, lace and rope are produced for export. Ascension and Tristan da Cunha are dependencies of St. Helena.

The island was discovered and named by the Portuguese navigator João da Nova Castella in 1502. The Portuguese imported livestock, fruit trees and vegetables but established no permanent settlement. The Dutch occupied the island temporarily, 1645-1651. The original European settlement was founded by representatives of the British East India Company sent to annex the island after the departure of the Dutch. The Dutch returned and captured St. Helena from the British on New Year's Day, 1673, but were in turn ejected by a British force under Sir Richard Munden. Thereafter St. Helena was the undisputed possession of Great Britain. The island served as the place of exile for Napoleon, several Zulu chiefs, and and an ex-Sultan of Zanzibar.

St. Helena banknotes are also used on the islands of Assencion and Tristan de Cunia.

RULERS:
British

MONETARY SYSTEM:
1 Pound = 20 Shillings to 1971
1 Pound = 100 New Pence, 1971-

BRITISH ADMINISTRATION

GOVERNOR AND COUNCIL OF THE ISLAND OF ST. HELENA

1722 ISSUE

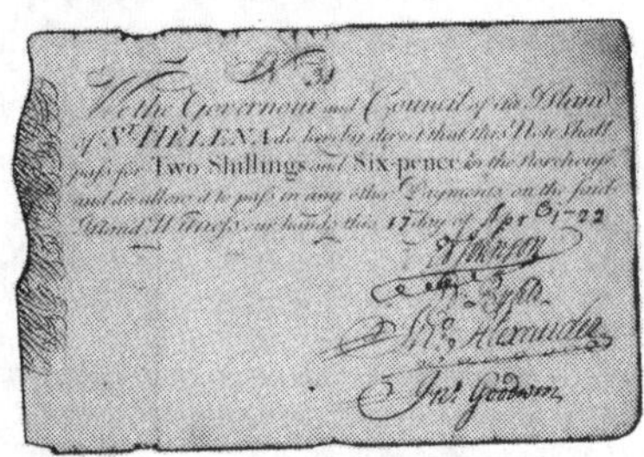

		Good	Fine	XF
1	**2 Shillings 6 Pence** 17.4.1722. Black. Uniface. Rare.	—	—	—

Note: #1 brought over $8,500. at auction in Oct. 1989 (Phillips London, Lot #315).

ST. HELENA CURRENCY BOARD

1917 ISSUE

		Good	Fine	XF
2	**5 Shillings** ca. 1917. Rare.	—	—	—
3	**20 Shillings** ca. 1917. Rare.	—	—	—
4	**40 Shillings** ca. 1917. Rare.	—	—	—

SAINT LUCIA

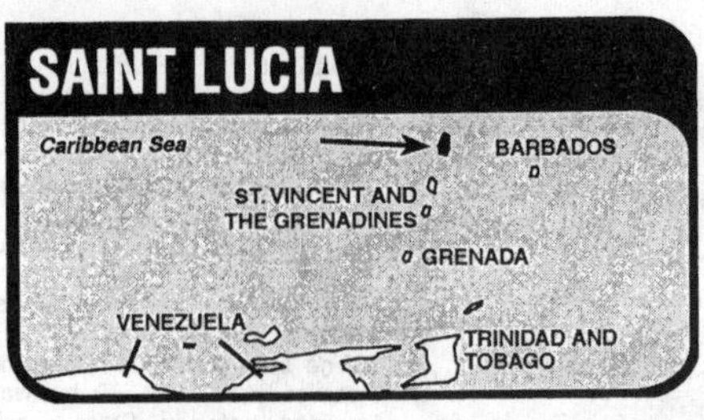

Saint Lucia, an independent island nation located in the Windward Islands of the West Indies between St. Vincent and Martinique, has an area of 238 sq. mi. (616 sq. km). Capital: Castries.

St. Lucia was discovered by Columbus in 1502. The first attempts at settlements undertaken by the British in 1605 and 1638 were frustrated by sickness and the determined hostility of the fierce Carib inhabitants. The French settled it in 1650 and made a treaty with the indigenous population. Until 1814, when the island became a definite British possession, it was the scene of a continuous conflict between the British and French which saw the island change loyalty on at least 14 occasions.

RULERS:
British

MONETARY SYSTEM:
1 Pound = 20 Shillings until 1948
1 Dollar = 100 Cents, 1949-
1 Pound = 20 Shillings
1 Dollar = 100 Cents

NOTE: For later issues refer to East Caribbean States/British East Caribbean Territories.

BRITISH ADMINISTRATION

GOVERNMENT

1920 ISSUE

#1 and 2 printer: TDLR.

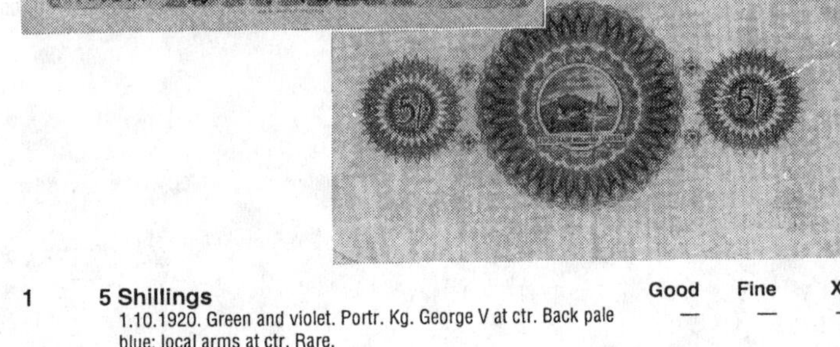

		Good	Fine	XF
1	**5 Shillings** 1.10.1920. Green and violet. Portr. Kg. George V at ctr. Back pale blue; local arms at ctr. Rare.	—	—	—
2	**10 Shillings** 1.10.1920. Reported not confirmed.	—	—	—

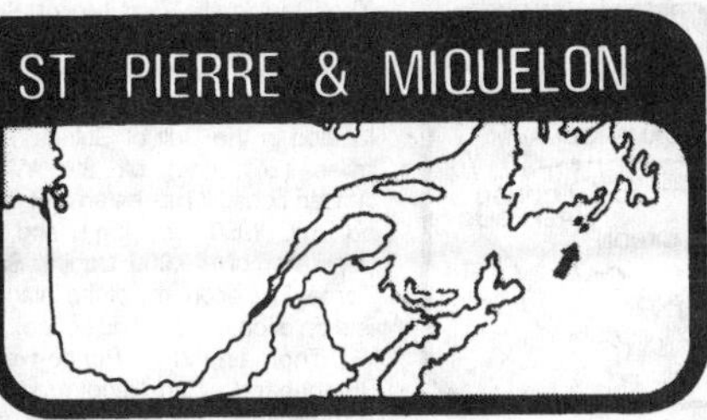

The Territorial Collectivity of St. Pierre and Miquelon, a French overseas territory located 10 miles (16 km.) off the south coast of Newfoundland, has an area of 93 sq. mi. (242 sq. km.) and a population of about 6,000. Capital: St. Pierre. The economy of the barren archipelago is d on cod fishing and fur farming Fish and fish products, and mink and silver fox pelts are exported.

The islands, occupied by the French in 1604, were captured by the British in 1702 and held ntil 1763 when they were returned to the possession of France and employed as a fishing station. hey passed between France and England on six more occasions between 1778 and 1814 when ney were awarded permanently to France by the Treaty of Paris. The rugged, soil-poor granite slands, which will support only evergreen shrubs, are all that remain to France of her extensive olonies in North America. In 1958 St. Pierre and Miquelon voted in favor of the new constitution of e Fifth Republic of France, thereby choosing to remain within the French Community.

Notes of the Banque de France circulated 1937-1942; afterwards notes of the Caisse Centrale de la France Libre and the Caisse Centrale de la France d'Outre-Mer were in use.

ULERS:
French

ONETARY SYSTEM:
1 Franc = 100 Centimes
5 Francs 40 Centimes = 1 Canada Dollar
1 Nouveau Franc = 100 "old" Francs, 1960-

FRENCH ADMINISTRATION

BANQUE DES ISLES SAINT-PIERRE ET MIQUELON

SAINT-PIERRE

897 ISSUE

		Good	Fine	XF
	27 Francs 1.4.1897. Blue. Sailing ship at l., woman seated at upper ctr., fish at r.			
	a. Not cancelled. Rare.	—	—	—
	b. Hand cancelled. Rare.	—	—	—

AINT-PIERRE & MIQUELON

890-95 ISSUE

		Good	Fine	XF
	27 Francs 1895. Blue. Woman seated, sailing ship at l., fish, woman seated at r. on back. 2 sign. varieties. Hand cancelled, handstamped: *ANNULÉ*. Rare.	—	—	—

		Good	Fine	XF
	54 Francs 1890-95. Blue. Like #2. Hand cancelled, handstamped: *ANNULÉ*. Rare.	—	—	—

CHAMBRE DE COMMERCE

1920 ISSUE

		Good	Fine	XF
4	**0.05 Franc** 15.5.1920.	—	—	—
5	**0.10 Franc** 15.5. 1920.	—	—	—
6	**0.25 Franc** 15.5.1920. (1st and 2nd issue).	50.00	200.	500.
7	**0.50 Franc** 15.5.1920.	300.	800.	—
8	**1 Franc** 15.5.1920.	—	—	—
9	**2 Francs** 15.5.1920.	—	—	—

2 Provisional WW II Issues w/o St. Pierre Name

CAISSE CENTRALE DE LA FRANCE LIBRE

ORDONNANCE DU 2.12.1941

#10-14 types of French Equatorial Africa w/special serial # ranges. Printer: BWC (w/o imprint).

		Good	Fine	XF
10	**5 Francs** L.1941 (1943). Type of F.E.A. #10. Serial # AA 000 001-AA 030 000 (20.1.1943).	20.00	60.00	—
11	**10 Francs** L.1941 (1943). Type of F.E.A. #11.			
	a. Serial # FA 000 001-FA 015 000 (20.1.1943).	25.00	75.00	—
	b. Serial # 2 520 001-2 533 120.	25.00	75.00	
12	**20 Francs** L.1941 (ca. 1943). Type of F.E.A. #12. Serial # LA 000 001-LA 030 000.	30.00	95.00	—
13	**100 Francs** L.1941. (1943).Type of F.E.A. #13. Serial # PA 000 001-PA 070 000 (July 1943).	70.00	150.	—
14	**1000 Francs** 1941. (1943). Type of F.E.A. #14.			
	a. Serial # TA 000 001-TA 030 000 (July 1943).	400.	1000.	—
	b. Serial # TA 275 001-TA 295 000 (Oct. 1944).	400.	1000.	—

Note: See also Reunion #36-38.

CAISSE CENTRALE DE LA FRANCE D'OUTRE-MER

SAINT-PIERRE-ET-MIQUELON

ORDONNANCE DU 2.2.1944

#15-18 types of French Equatorial Africa w/special serial # ranges. Printer: BWC (w/o imprint).

		Good	Fine	XF
15	**5 Francs** L.1944 (1945). Type of F.E.A. #15. Serial # AM 000 001-AM 020 000 (3.10.1945).	20.00	60.00	—
16	**10 Francs** L.1944 (1946). Type of F.E.A. #16. Serial # 2 520 001-2 533 120 (4.2.1946).	25.00	75.00	—
17	**20 Francs** L.1944 (1945-46). Type of F.E.A. #17.			
	a. Serial # 2 509 001-2 509 279 (22.1.1945).	30.00	95.00	—
	b. Serial # 2 510 001-2 531 200 (4.2.1946).	30.00	95.00	—
18	**1000 Francs** L.1944 (1945-46). Type of F.E.A. #19.			
	a. Serial # TD 021 001-TD 046 000 (5.9.1945).	400.	1000.	—
	b. Serial # TD 235 001-TD 255 000 (17.6.1946).	400.	1000.	—

Note: See also Reunion #39-40.

1947 ND ISSUE W/O ST. PIERRE NAME

#19-21 types of French Equatorial Africa post WW II Issue.

		Good	Fine	XF
19	**10 Francs** ND (1947). Type of FEA #21, also St. Pierre #23.			
	a. Serial # 2 520 001-2 550 00 Printer: Desfosses, Paris.	5.00	15.00	45.00
	b. Serial # 19 100 001-19 200 000. Printer: Banque de France.	5.00	15.00	45.00
20	**20 Francs** ND (1947). Type of FEA #22, also St. Pierre #24. Serial # 2 509 001-2 509 279; 2 510 001-2 531 200.	7.50	25.00	65.00
21	**50 Francs** ND (1947). Type of FEA #23, also St. Pierre # 25. Serial # 8 600 001-8 700 000.	10.00	35.00	95.00

1950 ND ISSUE

#22-29 ovpt: *SAINT-PIERRE-ET-MIQUELON.*

		VG	VF	UNC
22	**5 Francs** ND (1950-60). Blue and m/c. Ship at l., Bougainville at r. Woman w/fruit and house on back.	3.50	10.00	35.00

		VG	VF	UNC
23	**10 Francs** ND (1950-60). Blue and m/c. Colbert at l., ships at r. River scene and plants on back.	4.00	17.50	55.00

		VG	VF	UNC
24	**20 Francs** ND (1950-60). Brown and m/c. 4 people w/huts at l., E. Gentil at r. 2 men on back.	7.50	22.50	75.00

		VG	VF	UNC
25	**50 Francs** ND (1950-60). M/c. B. d'Esnambuc at l., ship at r. Woman on back.	25.00	100.	300.
26	**100 Francs** ND (1950-60). M/c. La Bourdonnais at l., 2 women at r. Woman looking at mountains on back.	30.00	125.	385.
27	**500 Francs** ND (1950-60). M/c. Bldgs. and sailboat at l., 2 women at r. Ox-carts w/wood and plants on back.	75.00	250.	775.

		VG	VF	UNC
28	**1000 Francs** ND (1950-60). M/c. 2 women at r. Woman at r, 2 men in small boat on back.	75.00	300.	850.
29	**5000 Francs** ND (1950-60). M/c. Gen. Schoelcher at r. ctr. Family on back.	120.	500.	—

SAINT THOMAS & PRINCE

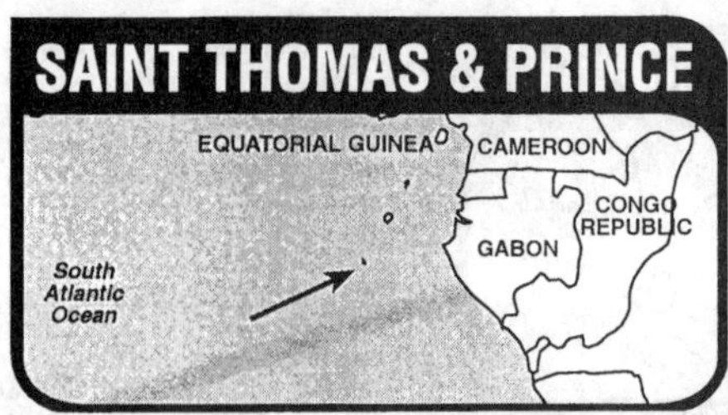

The Democratic Republic of Sã Tomé and Príncipe (formerly th Portuguese overseas province o St. Thomas and Prince Islands) located in the Gulf of Guinea 15 miles (241 km.) off the We African coast. It has an area of 37 sq. mi. (960 sq. km.) and population of 149,000. Capital: Sã Tomé. The economy of the island is d on cocoa, copra and coffee.

St. Thomas and St. Prince we uninhabited when discovered b Portuguese navigators Joao d Santarem and Pedro de Escob in 1470. After the failure of their initial settlement, 1485, the Portuguese successfully colonized S Thomas with a colony of prisoners and exiled Jews, 1493. An initial prosperity d on the sugar trac gave way to a time of misfortune, 1567-1709, that saw the colony attacked and occupied plundered by the French and Dutch; ravaged by the slave revolt of 1595; and finally rendere destitute by the transfer of the world sugar trade to Brazil. In the late 1800s, the colony turned fro the production of sugar to cocoa, the basis of its present prosperity.

The islands were designated a Portuguese overseas province in 1951. On April 25, 1974, th government of Portugal was seized by a military junta which reached agreements providing fo independence for the Portuguese overseas provinces of Portuguese Guinea (Guinea-Bissau Mozambique, Cape Verde Islands, Angola, and St. Thomas and Prince Islands. The Democrat Republic of São Tomé and Príncipe was declared on July 12, 1975.

RULERS:

Portuguese to 1975

MONETARY SYSTEM:

1 Mil Reis = 1000 Reis to 1914
1 Escudo = 100 Centavos, 1911-1976
1 Dobra = 100 Centimos, 1977-

Type I
S. THOMÉ

Type II
LISBOA

Type III
C,C,A

C,C,A = Colonias, Commercio, Agricultura

PORTUGUESE ADMINISTRATION

BANCO NACIONAL ULTRAMARINO

AGENCIA EM. S. THOMÉ

1897 ISSUE

#1-6 different dates handwritten.

		Good	Fine	X
1	**1000 Reis** 2.1.1897. Green. Man w/bow and arrow below arms at l., steamship at upper ctr. Rare.	—	—	—
2	**2000 Reis** ND (1897). Reported not confirmed.	—	—	—
3	**2500 Reis** Gray-blue. Steamship at l., landscape at ctr. Rare.	—	—	—
4	**5000 Reis** Violet. Woman at l., steamship at ctr. Rare.	—	—	—

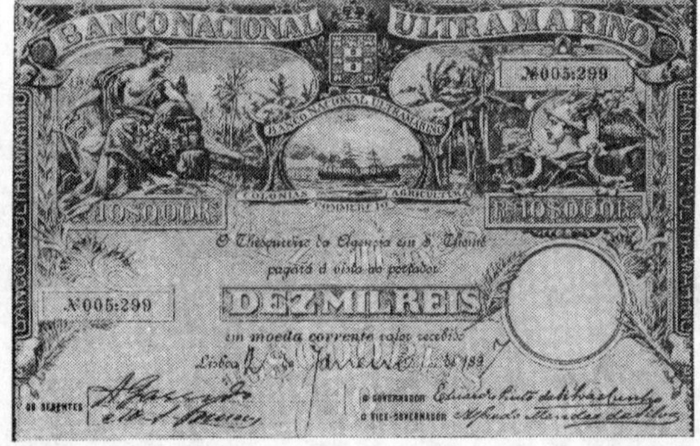

		Good	Fine	XF
5	**10,000 Reis** 2.1.1897. Brown w/black text on yellow unpt. Seated woman (allegory) at upper l., steamship at upper ctr., bust of Mercury at r. Rare.	—	—	—

		Good	Fine	XF
6	**20,000 Reis** 2.1.1897. Blue-green on yellow unpt. Brown text. Arms at top l., steamship at upper ctr. Rare.	—	—	—

S. THOMÉ

1909 ISSUE

#7-12 ovpt: *S. THOMÉ*. Printer: BWC.

		Good	Fine	XF
7	**1000 Reis** 1.3.1909. Black on green and yellow unpt.			
	a. Steamship seal Type I.	125.	350.	850.
	b. Steamship seal Type III.	125.	300.	750.

#8-12 portr. Vasco da Gama at l.

		Good	Fine	XF
8	**2500 Reis** 1.3.1909. Black on m/c unpt.			
	a. Steamship seal Type I.	175.	550.	1250.
	b. Steamship seal Type III.	175.	485.	900.
9	**5 Mil Reis** 1.3.1909. Black on m/c unpt.			
	a. Steamship seal Type I.	225.	650.	1500.
	b. Steamship seal Type III.	225.	550.	1150.

		Good	Fine	XF
10	**10 Mil Reis** 1.3.1909. Black on m/c unpt.			
	a. Steamship seal Type I.	275.	800.	1750.
	b. Steamship seal Type III.	275.	700.	1350.
11	**20 Mil Reis** 1.3.1909. Black on m/c unpt.			
	a. Steamship seal Type I.	350.	950.	2500.
	b. Steamship seal Type III.	350.	950.	2200.
12	**50 Mil Reis** 1.3.1909. Black and green on m/c unpt.			
	a. Steamship seal Type I.	1000.	2500.	—
	b. Steamship seal Type III.	1000.	2250.	—

1914 FIRST ISSUE

#13-18 ovpt: *S. TOMÉ* in black (scarcer), or *S. THOMÉ* in green. Printer: BWC.

		Good	Fine	XF
13	**10 Centavos** 5.11.1914. Purple on m/c unpt. Steamship seal Type II.	15.00	75.00	200.
14	**20 Centavos** 5.11.1914. Dk. blue on m/c unpt. Steamship seal Type II.	20.00	100.	300.
15	**50 Centavos** 5.11.1914. Dk. green m/c unpt. Steamship seal Type II.	40.00	125.	350.

1914 SECOND ISSUE

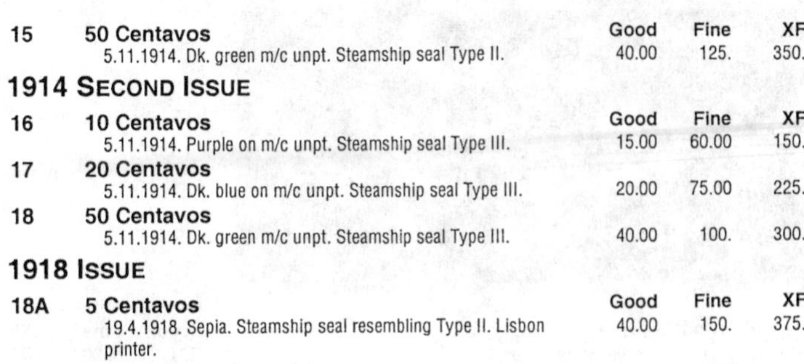

		Good	Fine	XF
16	**10 Centavos** 5.11.1914. Purple on m/c unpt. Steamship seal Type III.	15.00	60.00	150.
17	**20 Centavos** 5.11.1914. Dk. blue on m/c unpt. Steamship seal Type III.	20.00	75.00	225.
18	**50 Centavos** 5.11.1914. Dk. green m/c unpt. Steamship seal Type III.	40.00	100.	300.

1918 ISSUE

		Good	Fine	XF
18A	**5 Centavos** 19.4.1918. Sepia. Steamship seal resembling Type II. Lisbon printer.	40.00	150.	375.

S. TOMÉ E PRÍNCIPE

1921 ISSUE

#19-25 portr. F. de Oliveira Chamico at l. Ovpt: *S. TOMÉ E PRÍNCIPE*. Sign. varieties.

#19, 21-25 printer: BWC.

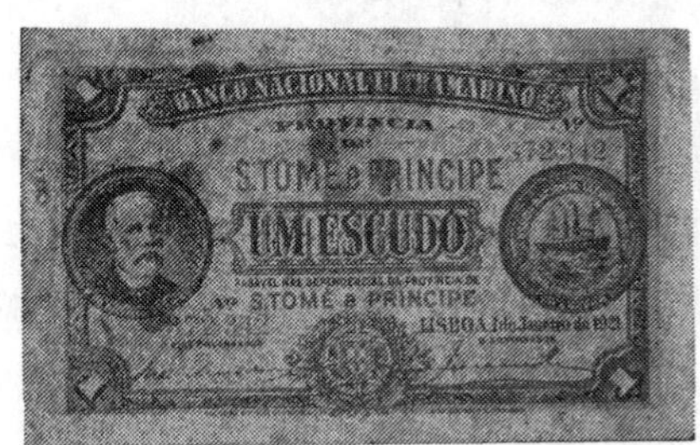

		Good	Fine	XF
19	**1 Escudo** 1.1.1921. Green.	15.00	75.00	225.
20	**2 1/2 Escudos** 1.1.1921. Blue. Printer: TDLR.	25.00	100.	300.
21	**5 Escudos** 1.1.1921.	35.00	150.	500.
22	**10 Escudos** 1.1.1921.	45.00	225.	650.
23	**20 Escudos** 1.1.1921.	95.00	300.	900.
24	**50 Escudos** 1.1.1921.	160.	500.	1250.
25	**100 Escudos** 1.1.1921.	250.	800.	—

1935 ISSUE

#26-28 portr. F. de Oliveira Chamico at l., arms at bottom ctr., steamship seal at r. Printer: BWC.

		Good	Fine	XF
26	**5 Escudos** 26.6.1935.	40.00	150.	450.
27	**10 Escudos** 26.6.1935.	50.00	200.	600.
28	**20 Escudos** 26.6.1935.	65.00	250.	700.

1944 ISSUE

#29-31 similar to previous issue.

		Good	Fine	XF
29	**20 Escudos** 21.3.1944.	70.00	275.	750.
30	**50 Escudos** 21.3.1944.	100.	350.	1000.
31	**100 Escudos** 21.3.1944.	250.	750.	—

1946 ISSUE

#32-34 steamship seal at l., arms at upper ctr., D. Afonso V at r. Printer: BWC.

		Good	Fine	XF
32	**20 Escudos** 12.8.1946. Brown on m/c unpt.	8.00	40.00	125.
33	**50 Escudos** 12.8.1946. Brown-violet on m/c unpt.	12.00	50.00	150.

		Good	Fine	XF
34	**100 Escudos** 12.8.1946. Purple on m/c unpt.	20.00	75.00	300.

1947 Circulating Bearer Check Issue

#35A-35C Steamship seal at l. Uniface.

		Good	Fine	XF
35A	**100 Escudos** 10.2.1947; 24.2.1947; 29.4.1947; 2.5.1947. Red on pink unpt.	40.00	150.	350.

		Good	Fine	XF
35B	**500 Escudos** 27.3.1947; 28.3.1947. Violet. Rectangular handstamp: *NULO* (null).	160.	500.	—

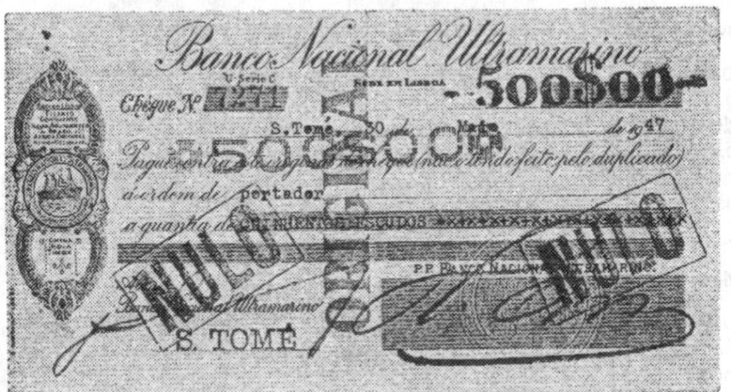

		Good	Fine	XF
35C	**500 Escudos** 30.5.1947. Red on pink unpt. Rectangular ovpt: *NULO* (null). Rare.	—	—	—

1956-64 Issue

#36-39 bank seal at l., Portuguese arms at lower ctr., D. Afonso V at lower r. Printer: BWC.

		VG	VF	UNC
36	**20 Escudos** 20.11.1958. Brown on m/c unpt.			
	a. Issued note.	2.00	5.00	12.50
	s. Specimen.	—	—	50.00
	ct. Color trial. Green on m/c unpt.	—	—	240.

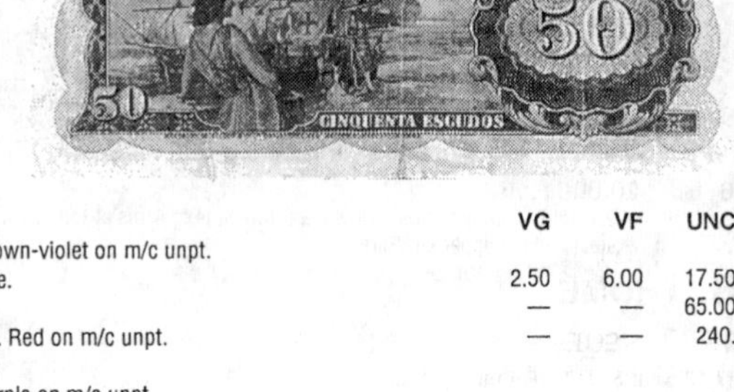

		VG	VF	UNC
37	**50 Escudos** 20.11.1958. Brown-violet on m/c unpt.			
	a. Issued note.	2.50	6.00	17.50
	s. Specimen.	—	—	65.00
	ct. Color trial. Red on m/c unpt.	—	—	240.
38	**100 Escudos** 20.11.1958. Purple on m/c unpt.			
	a. Issued note.	3.00	10.00	35.00
	s. Specimen.	—	—	—
	ct. Color trial. Brown on m/c unpt.	—	—	240.
39	**500 Escudos** 18.4.1956. Blue on m/c unpt. Portuguese arms at lower r.			
	a. Issued note.	35.00	125.	300.
	s. Specimen.	—	—	—
	ct. Color trial. Purple on m/c unpt.	—	—	375.

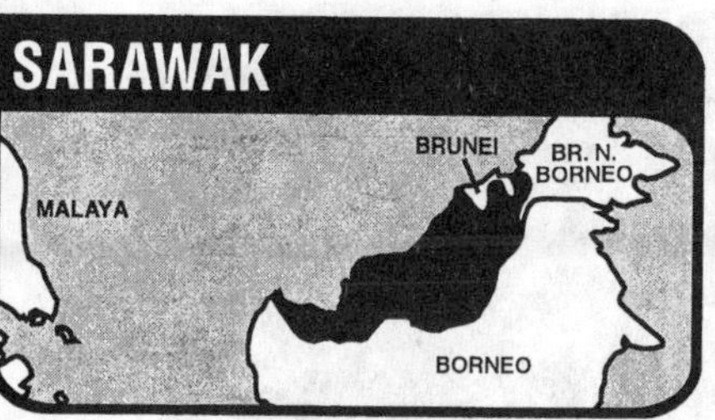

Sarawak, which with Sabah forms the eastern sector (East Malaysia) of the Federation of Malaysia, is situated on northwestern Borneo bounded by Brunei and Sabah state on the north and Kalimantan (Indonesian Borneo) on the east and south. It has an area of 48,050 sq. mi. (131,582 sq. km.) and a population of 980,000. Capital: Kuching. Coconuts, rice, rubber and oil are exported.

Sarawak became the southern province of the sultanate of runei upon the decline of the Majapahit empire of Java in the 15th century. In 1839, James rooke, an English adventurer, visited the territory and assisted the sultan in suppressing a revolt. s a reward, the sultan installed Brooke as the sultan of Sarawak (1841), then consisting of 7,000 q. mi. (18,130 sq. km.) in the southern part of Brunei. It was subsequently enlarged through urchase and annexation. Sarawak was recognized as a separate state by the United States 850) and Great Britain (1864), and voluntarily became a British protectorate in 1888.

The Brooke family continued to rule Sarawak until World War II, when (1941) Sir Charles yner Brooke, the third "White Raja", enacted a constitution designed to establish democratic self-overnment. Japan occupied the country during 1941-1945. In 1946 the territory was ceded to reat Britain and constituted as a crown colony. It achieved self-government and joined Malaysia 1963.

ULERS:

James Brooke, Rajah, 1841-1868
Charles J. Brooke, Rajah, 1868-1917
Charles V. Brooke, Rajah, 1917-1946
British, 1946-1963

ONETARY SYSTEM:

1 Dollar = 100 Cents

ULTANATE

ARAWAK GOVERNMENT TREASURY

858-59 ISSUE

1-A5 handstamped and dated seal of Office of Registry at lower r. Sign. C. A. Crymble. Uniface.

		Good	Fine	XF
1	**5 Cents** 3.9.1858. Black. Rare.	—	—	—
2	**10 Cents** 6.7.1858. Black. Rare.	—	—	—

		Good	Fine	XF
A	**10 Cents** 9.3.1858. Black. Handwritten denomination.	—	—	—

e: Some believe #A2A to be a contemporary counterfeit.

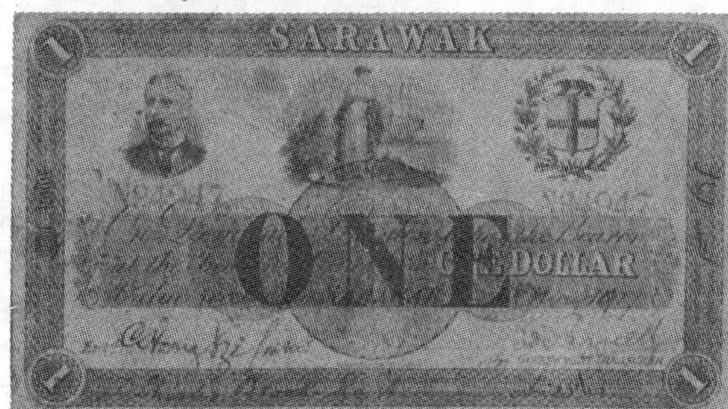

		Good	Fine	XF
	20 Cents 7.5.1859. Black. Rare.	—	—	—
	25 Cents 9.3.1858. Black. Rare.	—	—	—

		Good	Fine	XF
A5	**50 Cents** 4.4.1858. Black. Rare.	—	—	—

1862 ND ISSUE

#1 and 1A handstamped oval seal of Sarawak Gov't Treasury. Uniface.

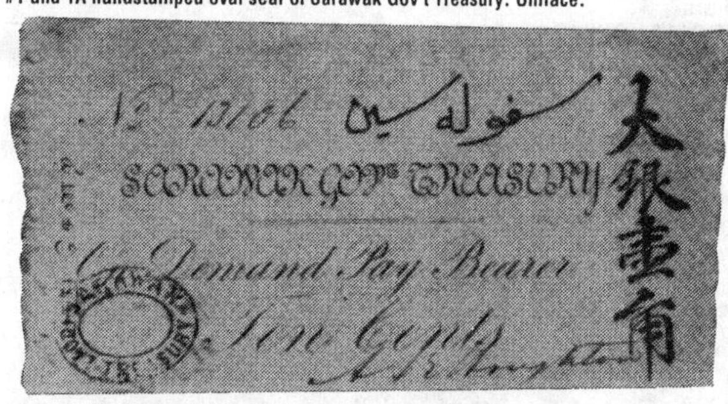

		Good	Fine	XF
1	**10 Cents** ND (1862-63). Black. Sign. H. E. Houghton. Rare.	—	—	—

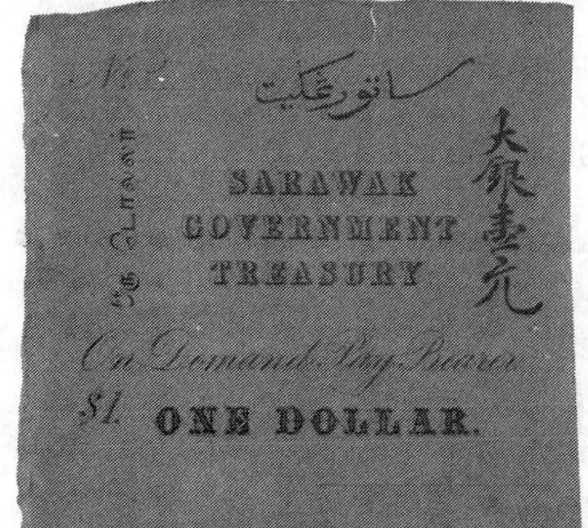

		Good	Fine	XF
1A	**1 Dollar** ND (1862-63). Black.			
	a. Issued note. Rare.	—	—	—
	r. Unsigned remainder. Rare.	—	—	—

GOVERNMENT OF SARAWAK

1880-1900 ISSUE

#2-6 C. Johnson Brooke at upper l., standing Baroness Burdett Coutte at upper ctr., arms at upper r. Various date and sign. varieties. Printer: PBC.

		Good	Fine	XF
2	**1 Dollar** 1.6.1894-1.5.1917. Black on green unpt. Uniface. Rare.	—	—	—
3	**5 Dollars** 1.9.1880-27.10.1903. Black on blue unpt. Rare.	—	—	—

		Good	Fine	XF
4	**10 Dollars** 1.9.1880-7.10.1903. Black on red unpt. Rare.	—	—	—
5	**25 Dollars** 19.7.1900-7.10.1903. Black on violet unpt. Rare.	—	—	—
6	**50 Dollars** 19.7.1900-31.8.1903. Black on yellow unpt. Rare.	—	—	—

SARAWAK GOVERNMENT TREASURY (RESUMED)

1919 ISSUE

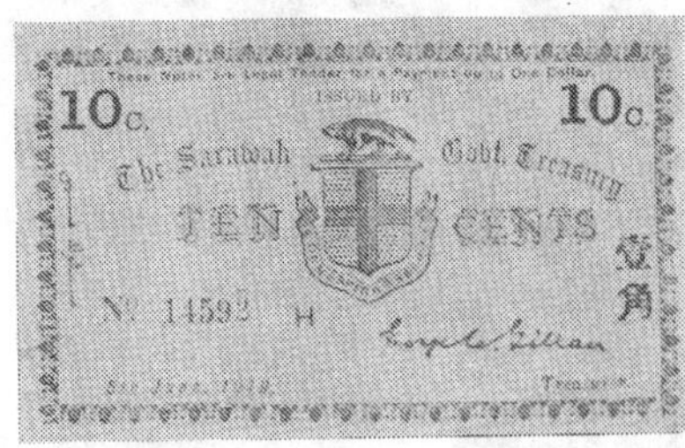

		Good	Fine	XF
7	**10 Cents** 5.6.1919. Black. Arms at ctr. Several printing varieties.	300.	800.	2000.
8	**25 Cents** 1.7.1919. Red.	650.	1600.	3500.

GOVERNMENT OF SARAWAK (RESUMED)

1918-21 ISSUE

#9-13 C. Vyner Brooke at upper l., standing Baroness Burdett Coutte at upper ctr., arms at upper r. Printer: PBC.

		Good	Fine	XF
9	**1 Dollar** 1.7.1919. Black on green unpt. Like #2.	600.	1600.	7200.

		Good	Fine	XF
10	**5 Dollars** 5.6.1918-1922. Black on blue unpt. Like #3.	1100.	3000.	—

NOTICE

Readers with unlisted dates, signature varieties, etc.
are invited to submit photocopies or,
high resolution (300 dpi, 100% size) scans of their notes to:
Standard Catalog of World Paper Money,
700 East State St. Iola, WI 54990-0001,
or E-Mail: george.cuhaj@fwpubs.com.

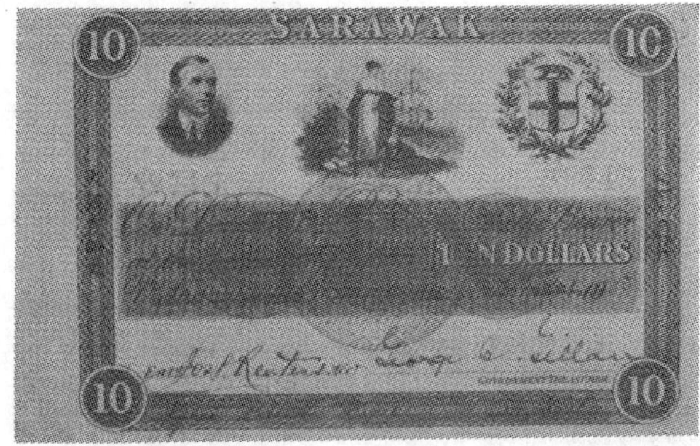

		Good	Fine	XF
11	**10 Dollars** 5.6.1918-1922. Black on red unpt. Like #4.	1500.	3800.	–
12	**25 Dollars** 18.5.1921. Black on violet unpt. Like #5. Rare.	—	—	–
13	**50 Dollars** 18.5.1921. Black on yellow unpt. Like #6. Rare.	—	—	–

1929 ISSUE

#14-19 palm trees at l. Printer: BWC.

#14-16 C. Vyner Brooke at r.

		Good	Fine	XF
14	**1 Dollar** 1.7.1929. Purple and m/c.	70.00	190.	40

		Good	Fine	XF
15	**5 Dollars** 1.7.1929. Brown and m/c. Arms at lower l.	100.	300.	6

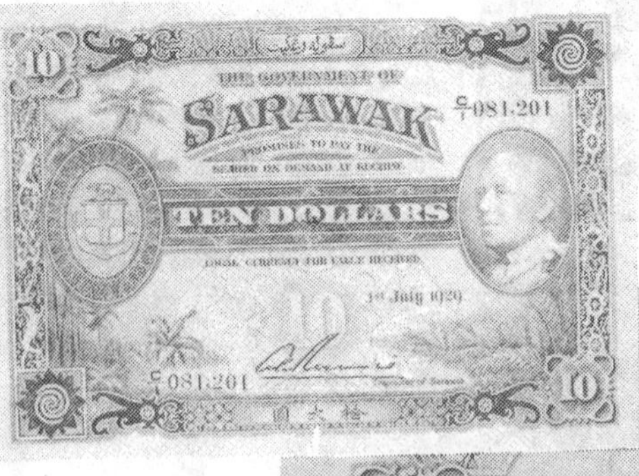

		Good	Fine	XF
16	**10 Dollars** 1.7.1929. Red and m/c. Arms at l.	250.	375.	1

#17-19 C. Vyner Brooke above arms at ctr.

		Good	Fine	XF
17	**25 Dollars** 1.7.1929. Blue and m/c. Govt. bldg. on back.	1000.	2300.	7000.
18	**50 Dollars** 1.7.1929. Green and m/c. Rare.	—	—	—
19	**100 Dollars** 1.7.1929. Purple and m/c. Rare.	—	—	—

ote: A VG example of #19 brought $7150. in a 1989 Spink-Taisei Sale held in Singapore.

1935-38 ISSUE

20-22 like previous issue. Printer: BWC.

		Good	Fine	XF
0	**1 Dollar** 1.1.1935. Green and m/c. Like #14.	40.00	85.00	350.

		Good	Fine	XF
1	**5 Dollars** 1.1.1938. Brown and m/c. Like #15. Sign. title: *Financial Secretary.*	55.00	190.	700.
2	**10 Dollars** 1.6.1937. Red and m/c. Like #16.	110.	330.	1000.

940 ISSUE

		Good	Fine	XF
3	**1 Dollar** 1.1.1940. Green and m/c. Like #14.	40.00	110.	380.

		Good	Fine	XF
4	**10 Dollars** 1.1.1940. Red and m/c. Like #16.	100.	310.	950.

1940 EMERGENCY FRACTIONAL ISSUE

		VG	VF	UNC
25	**10 Cents** 1.8.1940. Red on orange and blue-green unpt. Arms at upper l., C. Vyner Brooke at r. Uniface. Wmk: SDM monogram and map of Malay. Printer: Survey Dept. Fed. Malay States, Kuala Lumpur.			
	a. Series A.	30.00	80.00	420.
	b. Series B.	20.00	70.00	380.
	c. Series C.	20.00	70.00	380.

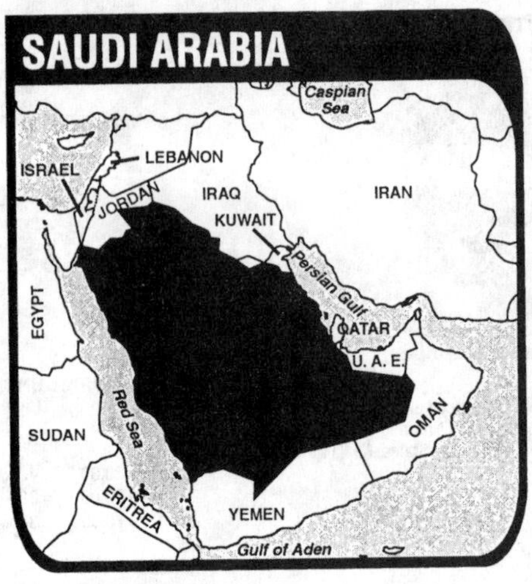

The Kingdom of Saudi Arabia, an independent and absolute hereditary monarchy comprising the former sultanate of Nejd, the old kingdom of Hejaz, Asir and El Hasa, occupies four-fifths of the Arabian peninsula. The kingdom has an area of 830,000 sq. mi. (2,149,690 sq. km.) and a population of 21.66 million. Capital: Riyadh. The economy is d on oil, which provides 85 percent of Saudi Arabia's revenue.

Mohammed united the Arabs in the 7th century and his followers founded a great empire with its capital at Medina. The Turks established nominal rule over much of Arabia in the 16th and 17th centuries, and in the 18th century divided it into principalities.

The Kingdom of Saudi Arabia was created by King Ibn-Saud (1882-1953), a descendant of earlier Wahabi rulers of the Arabian peninsula. In 1901 he seized Riyadh, capital of the Sultanate of Nejd, and in 1905 established himself as Sultan. In 1913 he captured the Turkish province of Hasa; took the Hejaz in 1925 and by 1926 most of Asir. In 1932 he combined Nejd and Hejaz into the single kingdom of Saudi Arabia. Asir was incorporated into the kingdom a year later.

One of the principal cities, Mecca, is the Holy center of Islam and is the scene of an annual Pilgrimage from the entire Moslem world.

RULERS:

Abd Al-Aziz Ibn Sa'ud, AH1334-1373/1926-1953AD
Sa'ud Ibn Abdul Aziz, AH1373-1383/1953-1964AD
Faisal, AH1383-1395/1964-1975AD
Khaled, AH1395-1402/1975-1982AD
Fahd, AH1402-/1982AD-

MONETARY SYSTEM:

1 Riyal = 20 Ghirsh

REPLACEMENT NOTES:

#1-4, serial number starting with an Arabic zero.

KINGDOM

SAUDI ARABIAN MONETARY AGENCY

1953 HAJ PILGRIM RECEIPT ISSUE

		VG	VF	UNC
1	**10 Riyals** AH1372 (1953). Green and m/c. Palm tree above crossed swords at ctr. Printer: TDLR.	100.	350.	950.

1954; 1956 HAJ PILGRIM RECEIPT ISSUE

		VG	VF	UNC
2	**1 Riyal** AH1375 (1956). Red and m/c. Entrance to the Royal Palace in Jedda at ctr. Back brown.	5.00	25.00	100.
3	**5 Riyals** AH1373 (1954). Blue and m/c. Dhow in Jedda harbor at ctr. Back like face of #1.	12.50	45.00	275.

		VG	VF	UNC
4	**10 Riyals** AH1373 (1954). Dk. green and m/c. 2 dhows in Jedda Harbor at ctr. Palm tree w/crossed swords at l. and r. on back.	10.00	40.00	250.

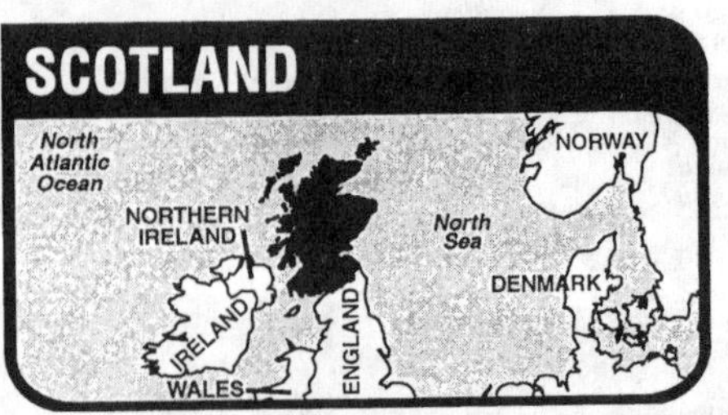

Scotland, a part of the Unite Kingdom of Great Britain an Northern Ireland, consists of th northern part of the island c Great Britain. It has an area c 30,414 sq. mi. (78,772 sq. km.) Capital: Edinburgh. Principa industries are agriculture, fishing manufacturing and ship-building.

In the 5th century, Scotlan consisted of four kingdoms; tha of the Picts, the Scots Strathclyde, and Northumbria The Scottish kingdom was unite by Malcolm II (1005-34), but i ruler was forced to payo homage to the English crown in 1174. Scotland won independence unde Robert Bruce at Bannockburn in 1314 and was ruled by the house of Stuart from 1371 to 168 The personal union of the kingdoms of England and Scotland was achieved in 1603 by th accession of King James VI of Scotland as James I of England. Scotland was united with Englan by Parliamentary act in 1707.

RULERS:

British

MONETARY SYSTEM:

1 Shilling = 12 Pence
1 Guinea = 21 Shillings
1 Pound Sterling = 12 Pounds Scots
1 Pound = 20 Shillings to 1971

BRITISH ADMINISTRATION

BANK OF SCOTLAND

1695 ISSUE

#1-5 w/o vignette or emblem. Embossed w/bank seal.

		Good	Fine
1	**5 Pounds** 1695. Black.	—	—
2	**10 Pounds** 1695. Black.	—	—
3	**20 Pounds** 1695. Black.	—	—
4	**50 Pounds** 1695. Black.	—	—
5	**100 Pounds** 1695. Black.	—	—

1704 ISSUE

		Good	Fine
6	**20 Shillings** 1704. Black.	—	—
7	**12 Pounds Scots** 1704. Black.	—	—

1716 ISSUE

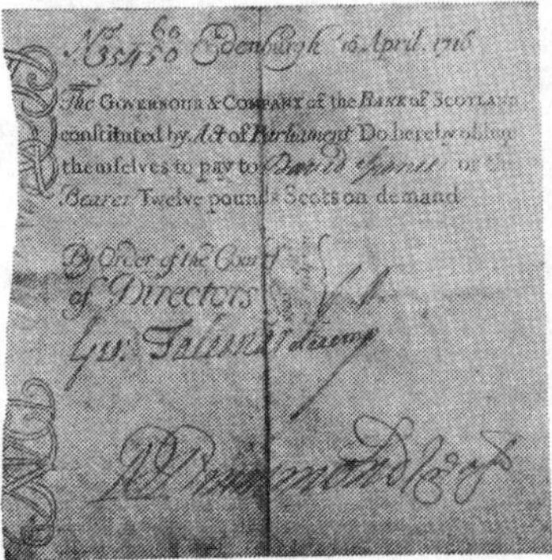

		Good	Fine
8	**12 Pounds Scots** 16.4.1716. Black. *Edenburgh* in heading.	—	—

1723 ISSUE

#	Denomination	Good	Fine	XF
9	**12 Pounds Scots** 24.6.1723. Black. *Edenburgh* in heading.	—	—	—

1730 Issue

#	Denomination	Good	Fine	XF
10	**5 Pounds** 1730. Black. Text w/option clause concerning redemption.	—	—	—

1731 Issue

#	Denomination	Good	Fine	XF
11	**12 Pounds Scots** 4.2.1731. Black. Similar to #9. *Edinr.* in heading.	—	—	—

1732 Issue

#	Denomination	Good	Fine	XF
12	**12 Pounds Scots** 12.12.1732; 25.3.1741; 2.6.1748. Black. Handwritten date. Text w/option clause.	—	—	—

1750 Issue

#	Denomination	Good	Fine	XF
13	**1 Pound** (1750). Black.			
	a. Option clause w/text: *By Order of the Directors.*	—	—	—
	b. Legend in italic type except for *Directors* (Gothic script).	—	—	—
14	**5 Pounds** 1.9.1751. Black. Vertical panel at l. of interwoven letters.	—	—	—
15	**10 Pounds** (1750). Black. Similar to #14.	—	—	—
16	**20 Pounds** (1750). Black. Similar to #14.	—	—	—
17	**50 Pounds** (1750). Black. Similar to #14.	—	—	—
18	**100 Pounds** (1750). Black. Similar to #14.	—	—	—

1760 Issue

#	Denomination	Good	Fine	XF
19	**10 Shillings = 6 Pounds Scots** 15.5.1760. Black. No option clause. Proof.	—	—	—
20	**5 Pounds** (1760). Black. Text w/option clause.	—	—	—
21	**10 Pounds** (1760). W/text: *for value received.* No option clause.	—	—	—
22	**10 Pounds** (1760). Text w/option clause.	—	—	—
23	**20 Pounds** (1760). Black. Similar to #21.	—	—	—
24	**20 Pounds** (1760). Black. Similar to #22.	—	—	—
25	**50 Pounds** (1760). Black. Text w/option clause.	—	—	—
26	**100 Pounds** (1760). Black. Similar to #18.	—	—	—

1765 Issue

Notes from this date and later do not carry the option clause. Title: *Governor* spelled w/o letter *u*.

#	Denomination	Good	Fine	XF
27	**1 Pound** 1.8.1765. Black.	—	—	—
28	**5 Pounds** (1765). Black. Similar to #27.	—	—	—
29	**10 Pounds** (1765). Black. Similar to #27.	—	—	—
30	**20 Pounds** (1765). Black. Similar to #27.	—	—	—
31	**50 Pounds** (1765). Black. Similar to #27.	—	—	—
32	**100 Pounds** (1765). Black. Similar to #27.	—	—	—

1768 Issue

#	Denomination	Good	Fine	XF
33	**1 Guinea** 2.5.1768. Black. Value in words across top.	—	—	—

1774 Issue

#	Denomination	Good	Fine	XF
34	**1 Guinea** 2.2.1774. Black and blue. Similar to #33.	—	—	—

1780 Issue

#35-39 improved plates w/design used until 1810.

#	Denomination	Good	Fine	XF
35	**1 Pound** (1780). Black. Plates G; H; K. Letters *ND* at upper l.	500.	1500.	—
36	**1 Guinea** 1.3.1780; 11.10.1808. Black. Plates B-G; plates H-S w/serial # prefix *No.G* at upper l.	500.	1500.	—
37	**5 Pounds** (1780). Black.	—	—	—
38	**10 Pounds** (1780). Black.	—	—	—
39	**20 Pounds** (1780). Black.	—	—	—

1810 Issue

#	Denomination	Good	Fine	XF
40	**1 Pound** (1810). Black. Seated Scotia w/thistle in oval at top ctr., crown above, bank arms at l.			
	a. Engraved by W. & D. Lizars.	450.	1350.	—
	b. Engraved by W. H. Lizars.	450.	1350.	—
41	**1 Guinea** (1810). Black. Similar to #40.			
	a. Engraved by W. & D. Lizars. Plate G.	400.	1250.	—
	b. Engraved by John Menzies. Plate D.	400.	1250.	—
42	**2 Pounds** (1810). Black. Bank arms at upper ctr.	—	—	—
43	**2 Guineas** (1810). Black. Similar to #42.	—	—	—

#44-46 w/o vignette or emblem.

#	Denomination	Good	Fine	XF
44	**5 Pounds** (1810). Black. Engraved by H. Ashby, London.	—	—	—
45	**10 Pounds** (1810). Black.	—	—	—
46	**20 Pounds** (1810). Black.	—	—	—

1825 Issue

#	Denomination	Good	Fine	XF
47	**1 Guinea** (1825). Allegorical woman at l. and r., bank arms at upper ctr. Plate A.	400.	1200.	—

#	Denomination	Good	Fine	XF
48	**5 Pounds** (1825). Similar to #47.	—	—	—

1825 Steel Engraved Issue

Plates for #51-54 were engraved by Perkins Bacon & Petch (later Perkins & Bacon, then Perkins Bacon & Co.). Crowned Scotia at l., bank arms at upper ctr.

#	Denomination	Good	Fine	XF
51	**1 Pound** (1825).			
	a. Imprint: P. B. & P.	400.	1100.	—
	b. Imprint: P. & B (1833).	400.	1100.	—
	c. Imprint: P. B. C.	400.	1100.	—
52	**10 Pounds** (1825).			
	a. Imprint: P. B. & P.	—	—	—
	b. Imprint: P. & B (1833).			
	c. Imprint: P. B. C.			
53	**20 Pounds** (1825).			

	Good	Fine	XF
a. Imprint: P. B. & P.	—	—	—
b. Imprint: P. & B (1833).			
c. Imprint: P. B. C.			

		Good	Fine	XF
54	**100 Pounds** (1825).			
	a. Imprint: P. B. & P.	—	—	—
	b. Imprint: P. & B (1833).			
	c. Imprint: P. B. C.			

1850 Issue

		Good	Fine	XF
55	**5 Pounds** (1850). Printer: W. H. Lizars.			
	a. W/o text above vignette. Proof.	—	—	—
	b. W/text: *Pursuant to Act 16 & 17 Victoria Cap. 63* above vignette. Proof.	—	—	—

1851 Issue

#56-60 notes payable to bearer, not to a named official. Printer: PBC.

		Good	Fine	XF
56	**1 Pound** (1851). Black.	350.	1000.	—
57	**5 Pounds** (1851). Black.	500.	1500.	—
58	**10 Pounds** (1851). Black.	1100.	3500.	—
59	**20 Pounds** (1851). Black.	—	—	—
60	**100 Pounds** (1851). Black.	—	—	—

1860 Issue

#65-69 obverse and reverse of the Great Seal of Scotland on l. panel. Lg. denomination wording protector added to design, in red except for #69. Printer: PBC.

		Good	Fine	XF
65	**1 Pound** (1860); 15.5.1878; 10.3.1881. Black and red.	400.	1000.	—
66	**5 Pounds** (1860). Black and red.	500.	1500.	—
67	**10 Pounds** (1860). Black and red.	—	—	—
68	**20 Pounds** (1860). Black and red.	—	—	—
69	**100 Pounds** (1860). Black and green.	—	—	—

1885 Issue

#76-80 brown, yellow and blue-gray. Bank arms at upper ctr. flanked by value. Panel at l. is similar to previous issue but has Scottish arms w/date 1695 between sides of Seal. Lithographed by George Waterston & Sons, Edinburgh.

		Good	Fine	XF
76	**1 Pound** 22.4.1885.	350.	1100.	—
77	**5 Pounds** ND (1885).	500.	1500.	—
78	**10 Pounds** ND (1885).	—	—	—
79	**20 Pounds** ND (1885).	—	—	—
80	**100 Pounds** ND (1885).	—	—	—

1889-90 Issue

#81-110 various imprints as follows:

Imprint Varieties

Type A: G. Waterston & Sons Edin. (1885-1917).
Type B: G. Waterston & Sons Ld. (1917-1964).
Type C: G. Waterston & Sons Ltd. (1965-1967).
Type D: Waterston (1968-1969) - on back.

Note: The registered number of the wmk. appearing as an imprint on 5-100 Pound notes was omitted in 1960

		Good	Fine	XF
81	**1 Pound** 10.11.1889-10.10.1927. Yellow-brown and gray-blue. Medallion of Goddess of Fortune below arms at r. ctr. Uniface.			
	a. Sign. J. F. Stormonth Darling (to 1893).	300.	1250.	2000
	b. Sign. D. McNeill (to 1910).	250.	800.	1250
	c. Sign. P. Macdonald (to 1920).	75.00	275.	700
	d. Sign. A. Rose (to 1927).	65.00	250.	650

		Good	Fine	XF
82	**5 Pounds** 1889-1932. Like #81.			
	a. Sign. J. F. Stormonth Darling. 24.5.1889-20.2.1893.	600.	1800.	3000.
	b. Sign. D. McNeill. 5.5.1894-6.9.1910.	300.	700.	1250.
	c. Sign. P. Macdonald. 15.9.1911-3.6.1919.	140.	300.	850.
	d. Sign. A. Rose. 7.10.1920-28.7.1931.	125.	275.	800.
83	**10 Pounds** 1890-1929. Like #81.			
	a. Sign. J. F. Stormonth Darling. 20.8.1839-23.12.1890.	—	—	—
	b. Sign. D. McNeill. 16.10.1894-30.9.1909.	450.	1000.	1800.
	c. Sign. P. Macdonald. 30.11.1912-5.11.1919.	375.	800.	1600.
	d. Sign. A. Rose. 15.8.1921-9.3.1929.	325.	750.	1500.
84	**20 Pounds** 1890-1932. Like #81.			
	a. Sign. J. F. Stormonth Darling. 9.7.1890-30.1.1893.	—	—	—
	b. Sign. D. McNeill. 26.5.1894-2.3.1910.	400.	900.	1750.
	c. Sign. P. Macdonald. 26.10.1911-8.10.1919.	375.	800.	1600.
	d. Sign. A. Rose. 11.10.1920-25.9.1930.	325.	750.	1500.
85	**100 Pounds** 1889-1930. Like #81.			
	a. Sign. J. F. Stormonth Darling. 27.8.1889-10.2.1893.	—	—	—
	b. Sign. D. McNeill. 12.7.1894-9.12.1910.	—	—	—
	c. Sign. P. Macdonald. 11.12.1911-17.4.1919.	—	—	—
	d. Sign. A. Rose. 7.7.1920-6.6.1930.	—	—	—

1929-35 Issue

		VG	VF	UNC
86	**1 Pound** 22.1.1929-17.7.1933. Yellow-brown and gray-blue. Reduced size. Bank bldg. on back. Sign. Lord Elphinstone and G. J. Scott.	40.00	125.	300.
87	**5 Pounds** 7.1.1932-25.3.1933. Like #86. Sign. Lord Elphinstone and G. J. Scott.	75.00	300.	600.

#88 Deleted.

		VG	VF	UNC
89	**20 Pounds** 21.6.1932; 2.12.1932. Like #86. Sign. Lord Elphinstone and G. J. Scott.	150.	600.	1350.
90	**100 Pounds** 28.5.1932; 2.11.1932. Like #86. Sign. Lord Elphinstone and G. J. Scott.	400.	1000.	2200.

1935; 1938 Issue

		VG	VF	UNC
91	**1 Pound** 1937-43. Yellow-brown, dk. brown and gray-blue. Like #86 but arms of the bank at l.			
	a. Sign. Lord Elphinstone and A. W. M. Beveridge. 15.1.1935-15.9.1937.	15.00	80.00	225.
	b. Sign. Lord Elphinstone and J. Macfarlane. 5.1.1939-7.5.1941.	15.00	75.00	200.
	c. Sign. Lord Elphinstone and J. B. Crawford. 2.6.1942; 16.10.1943.	15.00	75.00	225.
	s. As c. Specimen.	—	—	175.

		VG	VF	UNC
92	**5 Pounds** 1935-44. Like #86 but thistle motif at l.			
	a. Sign. Lord Elphinstone and A. W. M. Beveridge. 17.1.1935-17.3.1938.	60.00	225.	600.
	b. Sign. Lord Elphinstone and J. Macfarlane. Black value panels. 24.4.1939-16.10.1941.	60.00	225.	600.
	c. Sign. Lord Elphinstone and J. B. Crawford. 5.6.1942-26.9.1944.	50.00	210.	550.
	s. As c. Specimen.	—	—	175.
93	**10 Pounds** 1938-63. Scottish arms in panel at l., medallion of Goddess of fortune below arms at r. Bank bldg. on back.			
	a. Sign. Lord Elphinstone and A. W. M. Beveridge. 24.1.1935; 28.6.1938.	250.	900.	2000.
	b. Sign. Lord Elphinstone and J. B. Crawford. 16.7.1942; 15.10.1942.	225.	800.	1800.
	c. Sign. Lord Bilsland and Sir Wm. Watson. 26.9.1963; 27.9.1963.	175.	500.	1350.
94	**20 Pounds** 1935-65. Like #93.			
	a. Sign. Lord Elphinstone and A. W. M. Beveridge. 11.1.1935-22.7.1938.	100.	350.	1000.
	b. Sign. Lord Elphinstone and J. Macfarlane. 16.5.1939; 12.7.1939.	100.	400.	1100.
	c. Sign. Lord Elphinstone and J. B. Crawford. 5.6.1942-11.8.1952.	75.00	300.	800.
	d. Sign. Lord Elphinstone and Sir Wm. Watson. 5.12.1952; 14.4.1953.	100.	375.	1000.
	e. Sign. Sir J. Craig and Sir Wm. Watson. 6.4.1955-12.6.1956	60.00	250.	750.
	f. Sign. Lord Bilsland and Sir Wm. Watson. 21.3.1958-3.10.1963.	60.00	250.	700.

		VG	VF	UNC
95	**100 Pounds** 1935-62. Like #93.			
	a. Sign. Lord Elphinstone and A. W. M. Beveridge. 8.1.1935-12.8.1937.	450.	1450.	3200.
	b. Sign. Lord Elphinstone and J. Macfarlane. 2.4.1940; 15.7.1940.	400.	1200.	2650.
	c. Sign. Lord Elphinestone and J. B. Crawford. 10.6.1942; 14.12.1951.	350.	1000.	2400.
	d. Sign. John Craig and Sir Wm. Watson. 14.9.1956-3.12.1956.	350.	950.	2200.
	e. Sign. Lord Bilsland and Sir Wm. Watson. 24.3.1959-30.11.1962.	350.	900.	2100.

1945 Issue

		VG	VF	UNC
96	**1 Pound** 1945-53. Yellow and gray. Medallion at ctr. w/o arms at l. Arms on back.			
	a. Back brown. Sign. Lord Elphinstone and J. B. Crawford. 4.1.1945-6.2.1945.	20.00	60.00	240.
	b. Back lt. brown. Sign. Lord Elphinstone and J. B. Crawford. 6.2.1945-19.11.1952.	12.50	30.00	90.00
	c. Sign. Lord Elphinstone and Sir Wm. Watson. 4.9.1953; 16.10.1953; 9.11.1953.	12.50	30.00	75.00
	s. As c. Specimen.	—	—	100.

		VG	VF	UNC
97	**5 Pounds** 1945-48. Gray and lt. brown. Arms on back. Sign. Lord Elphinstone and J. B. Crawford.			
	a. Back dk. brown. 3.1.1945; 15.1.1945; 1.2.1945; 2.3.1945.	50.00	125.	350.
	b. Back lt. brown. 16.3.1945-10.1.1948.	30.00	80.00	200.

1950 Issue

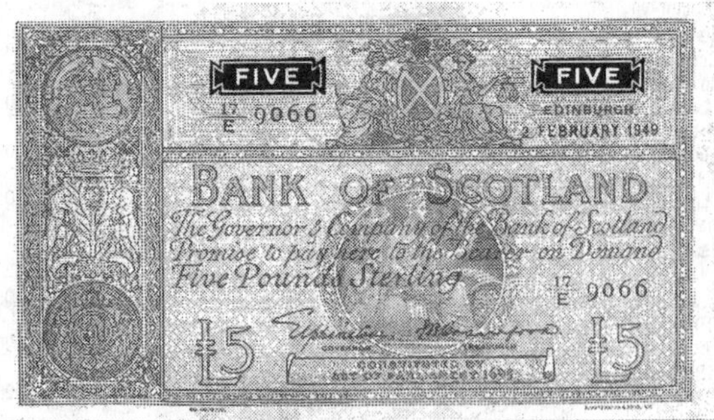

		VG	VF	UNC
98	**5 Pounds** 1948-52. Like #97, but reduced size.			
	a. Denomination panels in black. Sign. Lord Elphinstone and J. B. Crawford. 16.11.1948-21.11.1952.	20.00	60.00	150.
	b. Gray-brown medallion. Sign. Lord Elphinstone and Sir Wm. Watson. 10.12.1952-4.12.1953.	20.00	60.00	150.

1955 Issue

		VG	VF	UNC
99	**5 Pounds** 1955. Denomination panels in black, medallion in blue. Like #98.			
	a. Sign. Lord Elphinstone and Sir Wm. Watson. 1.3.1955; 2.3.1955; 3.3.1955.	25.00	65.00	175.
	b. Sign. Sir J. Craig and Sir Wm. Watson. 6.4.1955-3.9.1955.	20.00	60.00	150.

1955-56 Issue

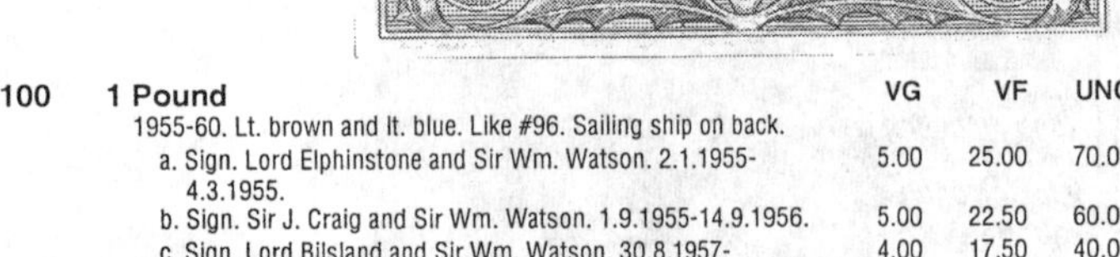

		VG	VF	UNC
100	**1 Pound** 1955-60. Lt. brown and lt. blue. Like #96. Sailing ship on back.			
	a. Sign. Lord Elphinstone and Sir Wm. Watson. 2.1.1955-4.3.1955.	5.00	25.00	70.00
	b. Sign. Sir J. Craig and Sir Wm. Watson. 1.9.1955-14.9.1956.	5.00	22.50	60.00
	c. Sign. Lord Bilsland and Sir Wm. Watson. 30.8.1957-30.11.1960.	4.00	17.50	40.00

		VG	VF	UNC
101	**5 Pounds** 1956-60. Blue and lt. brown. Like #97. Arms and ship on back. Numeral of value below in 2 lines.			
	a. Sign. Sir J. Craig and Sir Wm. Watson. 9.4.1956-14.4.1956.	15.00	50.00	120.
	b. Sign. Lord Bilsland and Sir Wm. Watson. 1.5.1957-24.5.1960.	12.00	40.00	100.

British Linen Bank

1906; 1907 Issue

#146-150 blue w/lg. red: *B.L.B.* protector. Facing view of seated Britannia in emblem at l.

		Good	Fine	XF
146	**1 Pound** 15.1.1907; 16.12.1907; 2.11.1908; 15.7.1910; 11.8.1911; 29.10.1912; 17.9.1913.	200.	550.	1200.
147	**5 Pounds** 4.1.1907-12.9.1915.	300.	1000.	2000.
148	**10 Pounds** 30.1.1907.	450.	1200.	2500.
149	**20 Pounds** 2.1.1907-18.11.1912.	300.	1000.	2000.
150	**100 Pounds** 11.2.1907; 2.4.1908; 15.5.1912. Rare.	—	—	—

1914; 1916 Issue

#151-155 side view of seated Britannia in emblem at l., arms at upper r. Back blue.

		Good	Fine	XF
151	**1 Pound** 1914-25. Similar to #146 with red sunburst overlay.			
	a. 23.9.1914-5.11.1918.	60.00	225.	600.
	b. 19.8.1919-31.7.1924.	60.00	225.	600.
	c. 15.10.1925.	60.00	225.	600.

		Good	Fine	XF
152	**5 Pounds** 1.2.1916-3.8.1933. Similar to #147 with red sunburst overlay.	120.	350.	800.
153	**10 Pounds** 15.2.1916; 9.2.1920; 15.3.1920. Similar to #148 with red sunburst overlay.	400.	1000.	1800.

		Good	Fine	XF
154	**20 Pounds** 3.5.1916. Similar to #149 with red sunburst overlay.	150.	500.	1000.
155	**100 Pounds** 7.1.1916; 12.12.1916; 15.1.1918; 1.3.1918; 18.7.1933. Similar to #150 with red sunburst overlay.	400.	1000.	2000.

1926 Issue

		Good	Fine	XF
156	**1 Pound** 1.5.1926-2.8.1934. Blue and red. Similar to #151 but reduced size and only 1 sign.	20.00	70.00	150.

1935 Issue

#157-160 bank arms at upper ctr. Britannia at l. vertical. Sign. title and serial # varieties. Printer: W&S.

		Good	Fine	XF
157	**1 Pound** 1935-60. Similar to #156.			
	a. 18.1.1935; 4.7.1937; 10.8.1937; 8.11.1938; 2.8.1939; 13.11.1939.	17.50	50.00	125.
	b. 7.3.1940-5.4.1944.	12.50	40.00	90.00
	c. 4.1.1946-5.8.1950.	10.00	30.00	70.00
	d. 4.6.1951-12.5.1959.	6.00	20.00	50.00
	e. 15.4.1960.	7.50	30.00	70.00
158	**5 Pounds** 1935-43. Similar to #152.			
	a. Printed sign. of *GENERAL MANAGER* and handsigned on behalf of *ACCOUNTANT*. 16.9.1935-12.1.1943.	60.00	175.	400.
	b. Printed sign. of *ACCOUNTANT & CASHIER* and *GENERAL MANAGER*. 11.2.1943-28.1.1944.	40.00	125.	300.

		Good	Fine	XF
159	**20 Pounds** 1939-57. Similar to #154.			
	a. As #158a. 6.8.1935-24.2.1945.	85.00	200.	550.
	b. Printed sign. of *GENERAL MANAGER* (only). 2.9.1946-11.12.1957.	60.00	160.	400.
160	**100 Pounds** 1935-60. Similar to #155.			
	a. As #159a. 4.2.1942; 3.3.1943.	350.	800.	—
	b. As #159b. 6.4.1951; 5.8.1954; 27.11.1957.	300.	700.	—

1944 Issue

		Good	Fine	XF
161	**5 Pounds** 1944-59. Blue and red. Similar to #158 but reduced size and some minor plate changes.			
	a. Printed sign. of *GENERAL MANAGER* and *ACCOUNTANT & CASHIER*. 25.6.1944-3.11.1944.	25.00	120.	250.
	b. Printed sign. of *GENERAL MANAGER* (only). 10.9.1946-4.8.1959.	20.00	60.00	150.

Clydesdale Banking Company

1838 Issue

#171-175 black arms of Glasgow in circle at upper ctr., vertical floral pattern in panel at l. Uniface. Printer: W. & A. K. Johnston, Edinburgh.

		Good	Fine	XF
171	**1 Pound** (1838).	650.	2000.	—
172	**5 Pounds** (1838).	900.	2500.	—
173	**10 Pounds** (1838).	—	—	—
174	**20 Pounds** (1838).	—	—	—
175	**100 Pounds** (1838).	—	—	—

1858 Issue

New design with Arms of Glasgow top center and vignettes lower right and left. Red line overlay with Clydesdale Bank in white in large letters. Printer: Hugh Wilson.

		VG	VF	UNC
175A	**1 Pound** 16.4.1858-20.4.1863.	600.	1600.	

1864 Issue

#176-179 similar to previous issue w/red ovpt: *CLYDESDALE BANK* and value.

		Good	Fine	XF
176	**1 Pound** 16.11.1864.	550.	1600.	—
177	**5 Pounds** (1864). Imprint: Hugh Wilson.	750.	2200.	—
178	**20 Pounds** (1864). Imprint: W. & A. K. Johnston.	1000.	2600.	—
179	**100 Pounds** (1864); 16.9.1868. Ovpt: *CLYDESDALE BANKING COMPANY.*	—	—	—

1870 ISSUE

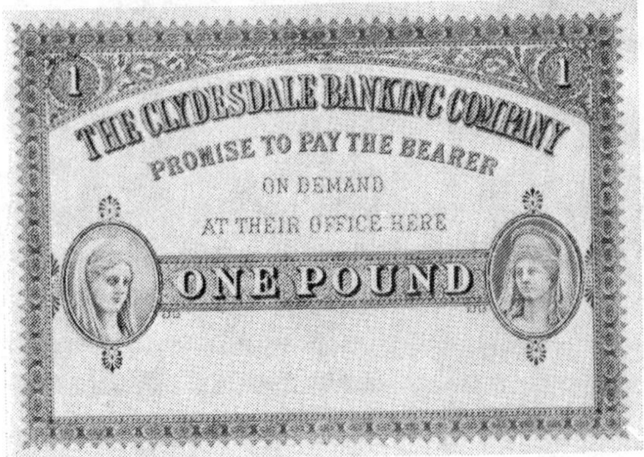

		Good	Fine	XF
180	**1 Pound** 28.2.1872; 4.3.1874; 9.2.1876. Green and purple. Woman at l. and r. Printer: TDLR.			
	a. Issued note.	450.	120.	—
	s. Specimen.	350.	650.	—

CLYDESDALE BANK LTD.

1882 ISSUE

		VG	VF	UNC
181	**1 Pound** 1882-1921. Red. 3 allegorical women around Glasgow seal at top ctr., 2 at l., 1 at r. Uniface.			
	a. W/o serial # prefix letter. 4.7.1882-30.10.1912.	200.	600.	1500.
	b. W/serial # prefix letter. 8.10.1913-7.1.1920.	120.	300.	1000.
	c. Printed sign. of Accountant; Handsigned sign. of Joint General Manager. 9.2.1921.	250.	600.	1500.
182	**5 Pounds** 4.7.1882-9.2.1921. Like #181.	250.	600.	1500.
183	**20 Pounds** 4.7.1882-9.6.1920. Like #181.	450.	1400.	3000.
184	**100 Pounds** 16.1.1884-5.8.1914. Like #181. Unknown	—	—	—

1922 ISSUE

		VG	VF	UNC
185	**1 Pound** 4.1.1922-27.10.1926. Similar to #181, but w/rays in unpt.	150.	350.	1000.

1922-47 ISSUE

		VG	VF	UNC
186	**5 Pounds** 15.2.1922-10.7.1946. Blue and red. Ornate design around seal w/tree and *LET GLASGOW FLOURISH.*	125.	350.	800.
187	**20 Pounds** 15.2.1922-4.6.1947. Like #186.	175.	450.	1250

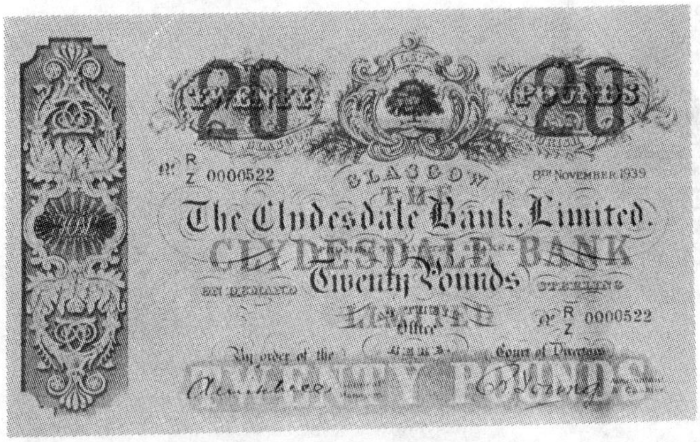

		VG	VF	UNC
188	**100 Pounds** 15.2.1922-26.3.1947. Similar to #187.	700.	1750.	300

1927 ISSUE

		VG	VF	UNC
189	**1 Pound** 1927-49. Blue and orange. Allegorical figures at lower l. and r. (Industry and Agriculture). Serial # varieties.			
	a. 3.1.1927-7.10.1931.	40.00	110.	300.
	b. 2.3.1932-5.11.1941.	30.00	80.00	175.
	c. 25.2.1942-24.10.1945.	30.00	80.00	175.
	d. 1.5.1946.	40.00	120.	325.
	e. 20.11.1946-3.9.1947.	30.00	80.00	175.
	f. 7.4.1948-14.12.1949.	30.00	70.00	150.

1948 ISSUE

		VG	VF	UNC
190	**5 Pounds** 3.3.1948; 12.1.1949. Lt. blue unpt. Like #186.	150.	500.	1000.

CLYDESDALE AND NORTH OF SCOTLAND BANK LTD.

1950-51 ISSUE

		VG	VF	UNC
191	**1 Pound** 1950-60. Blue, red and orange. Ships at dockside at l., landscape (sheaves) at r. River scene w/trees on back.			
	a. 1.11.1950-1.11.1956.	10.00	45.00	150.
	b. 1.5.1958-1.11.1960.	10.00	40.00	125.
	s. As a. Specimen.	—	—	200.

		VG	VF	UNC
192	**5 Pounds** 2.5.1951-1.3.1960. Purple. King's College at Aberdeen at lower l., Glasgow Cathedral at lower r.			
	a. Sign. J. J. Campbell.	25.00	80.00	250.
	b. Sign. R. D. Fairbairn.	25.00	85.00	250.

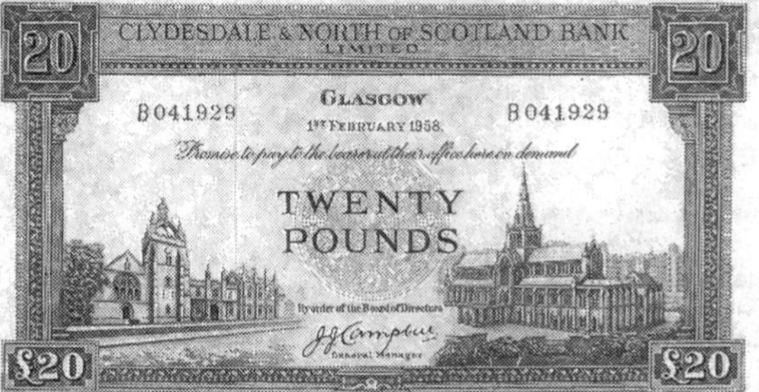

		VG	VF	UNC
193	**20 Pounds** 2.5.1951-1.8.1962. Green on m/c unpt. Like #192. 180 x 97mm.			
	a. Sign. J. J. Campbell.	45.00	90.00	350.
	b. Sign. R. D. Fairbairn.	45.00	90.00	350.
194	**100 Pounds** 2.5.1951. Blue. Like #192. 180 x 97mm. Sign. J. J. Campbell.	400.	850.	1750.

1961 ISSUE

#195 and 196 arms at r.

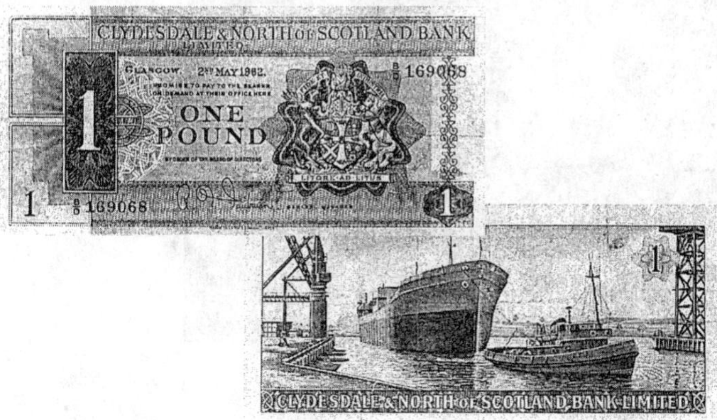

		VG	VF	UNC
195	**1 Pound** 1.3.1961; 2.5.1962; 1.2.1963. Green on m/c unpt. Ship and tug at ctr. on back.			
	a. Issued note.	6.50	35.00	100.
	s. Specimen.	—	—	160.

		VG	VF	UNC
196	**5 Pounds** 20.9.1961; 1.6.1962; 1.2.1963. Dk. blue on m/c unpt. King's College at Aberdeen on back.	17.50	60.00	175.

NATIONAL BANK OF SCOTLAND

1825 ISSUE

#230-230E black. Royal arms w/St. Andrew and cross at upper ctr. Printer: Perkins & Bacon. Uniface.

		Good	Fine	XF
230	**1 Pound** 11.10.1825.	—	—	—
230A	**1 Guinea** (ca.1825).	—	—	—
230B	**5 Pounds** (ca.1825).	—	—	—
230C	**10 Pounds** (ca.1825).	—	—	—
230D	**20 Pounds** (ca.1825).	—	—	—
230E	**100 Pounds** (ca.1825).	—	—	—

1831 ISSUE

#231-235 plates modified to include text: *INCORPORATED BY ROYAL CHARTER* under royal arms at ctr. Text: *UNDER ACT 16 & 17 VICT. CAP. 68* in top border.

		Good	Fine	XF
231	**1 Pound** (ca.1831).	—	—	—
232	**5 Pounds** (ca.1831).	—	—	—
233	**10 Pounds** (ca.1831).	—	—	—
234	**20 Pounds** (ca.1831).	—	—	—
235	**100 Pounds** (ca.1831).	—	—	—

1862 Issue

#236-239 black w/red lithographed protector across face. Uniface. Date and serial # printed.

		Good	Fine	XF
236	1 Pound 11.11.1862; 11.11.1864.	300.	550.	—
237	5 Pounds (ca.1862).	350.	800.	—

		Good	Fine	XF
238	20 Pounds (ca.1862).	—	—	—
239	100 Pounds (ca.1862).	—	—	—

National Bank of Scotland Limited

1881-82 Issue

With the asssumption of limited liability by the bank in 1882, new plates were made adding the word: *LIMITED* to bank title. Caption under the portrait in one line. Most details remain similar to previous issue.

		Good	Fine	XF
240	1 Pound (ca.1881-89). Black w/maroon protector.			
	a. Red serial #. 1.11.1881.	450.	1200.	—
	b. 11.11.1886.	350.	1000.	—
	c. Black serial # (ca.1889).	300.	500.	—
241	5 Pounds (ca.1882).	600.	1400.	—
242	20 Pounds (ca.1882).	700.	1700.	—
243	100 Pounds (ca.1882).	—	—	—

1893; 1895 Issue

#244-247 sign. titles: *Manager* and *Accountant*. Caption under the portrait in two lines.

		Good	Fine	XF
244	1 Pound 2.1.1893; 1.1.1898; 1.1.1903; 2.1.1905; 1.1.1907. Blue, yellow and red. Marquess of Lothian at l., arms at upper ctr.	225.	600.	1400.
245	5 Pounds 1893-1907. Blue, yellow and red. Like #244. Rare.	—	—	—
246	20 Pounds 1893-1907. Blue, yellow, red and pink. Like #244. Rare.	—	—	—
247	100 Pounds 1893-1907. Blue, yellow, red and pink. Like #244. Rare.	—	—	—

1908-14 Issue

#248-251 sign. titles: *General Manager* and *Accountant*.

		Good	Fine	XF
248	1 Pound 1908-24. Blue on yellow and brown. Like #244. 167 x 126mm.			
	a. Printed sign. of *GENERAL MANAGER* and handsigned on behalf of *ACCOUNTANT*. 15.5.1908-15.5.1919.	70.00	225.	450.
	b. As a. but w/printed sign. of *ACCOUNTANT*. 11.11.1919-15.5.1924.	60.00	200.	400.
249	5 Pounds 1909-20. Blue, yellow and red. Like #245.			
	a. Handsigned on behalf of *GENERAL MANAGER* and *ACCOUNTANT*. 15.5.1909-15.5.1918.	125.	275.	650.
	b. Printed sign. of *GENERAL MANAGER* and handsigned on behalf of *ACCOUNTANT*. 11.11.1919; 8.7.1920.	125.	300.	700.
250	20 Pounds 15.5.1908; 1.8.1914; 8.7.1920. Blue, yellow, red and pink. Like #246.	400.	1000.	2200.
251	100 Pounds 1908-24. Blue, yellow, red and pink. Like #247.	600.	1100.	2500.

1925-28 Issue

#252-255 sign. titles: *Cashier* and *Accountant*.

		Good	Fine	XF
252	1 Pound 1.3.1925; 15.5.1925; 2.1.1926; 1.7.1926. Like #248.	45.00	150.	400.
253	5 Pounds 1.7.1927; 2.7.1928; 11.11.1930; 11.11.1932. Like #249.	135.	350.	800.
254	20 Pounds 1.3.1928; 2.1.1930; 11.11.1932. Like #250.	200.	675.	1350.
255	100 Pounds 16.5.1935. Like #251.	500.	1200.	2500.

1927 Issue

		VG	VF	UNC
256	1 Pound 2.11.1927-2.2.1931. Black, red and yellow. Bldgs. at l. and r., royal arms at upper ctr. Reduced size. Printer: W&S.	25.00	70.00	225.

1931 Issue

		VG	VF	UNC
257	1 Pound 2.2.1931; 11.11.1932; 11.11.1933. Black, yellow and red. Like #256. Imprint: W. & A. K. Johnston.	17.50	45.00	125.

1934-36 Issue

		VG	VF	UNC
258	**1 Pound** 1934-59. Black, yellow and red. Similar to #256 but bank arms at upper ctr.			
	a. Imprint: W. & A. K. Johnston Ltd. 12.11.1934-1.5.1942.	10.00	30.00	75.00
	b. 15.3.1943-2.1.1953.	8.00	25.00	60.00
	c. Imprint: W. & A. K. Johnston & G. W. Bacon Ltd. 1.6.1953-2.5.1959.	7.00	20.00	50.00

#259-261 printer: W&S.

		VG	VF	UNC
259	**5 Pounds** 1936-56. Blue, red and yellow. Similar to #245.			
	a. Sign. vertical alignment w/printed sign. of *CASHIER* and handsigned on behalf of *ACCOUNTANT.* 1.7.1936.	40.00	150.	400.
	b. As a. but w/printed sign. of *ACCOUNTANT* and *CASHIER.* 1.8.1939; 1.7.1940; 1.3.1941.	35.00	125.	350.
	c. As a. but w/printed sign. of *CHIEF ACCOUNTANT* and *CASHIER.* 6.7.1942.	35.00	125.	350.
	d. Sign. horizontal alignment w/printed sign. of *GENERAL MANAGER* and *CASHIER.* 11.1.1943-31.12.1956.	30.00	75.00	225.
260	**20 Pounds** 1935-56. Blue, yellow, red and pink.			
	a. Sign. vertical alignment w/printed sign. of *CASHIER* and handsigned on behalf of *ACCOUNTANT.* 16.5.1935; 1.7.1936; 1.8.1939; 1.4.1941.	125.	350.	900.
	b. As a. but w/printed sign. of *CHIEF ACCOUNTANT* and handsigned on behalf of *CASHIER.* 8.12.1941; 6.7.1942.	125.	350.	900.
	c. Sign. horizontal alignment w/printed sign. of *GENERAL MANAGER* and *CASHIER.* 11.1.1943-31.12.1956.	90.00	275.	550.
261	**100 Pounds** 1943-52. Blue, yellow, red and pink.			
	a. Sign. vertical alignment. Reported, not confirmed.	—	—	—
	b. Sign. horizontal alignment. 11.1.1943-1.3.1952.	400.	800.	1500.

1957 Issue

#262-264 arms at lower l. on face. Forth Railway bridge on back. Printer: W&S.

		VG	VF	UNC
262	**5 Pounds** 1.11.1957. Green and m/c.	30.00	90.00	250.

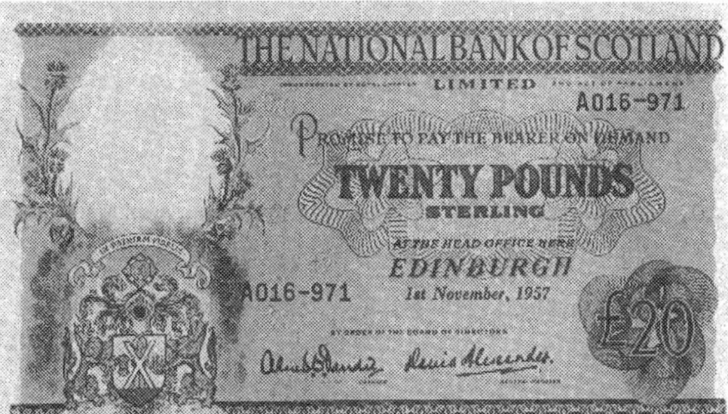

		VG	VF	UNC
263	**20 Pounds** 1.11.1957. Red and m/c.	70.00	175.	500.
264	**100 Pounds** 1.11.1957. Blue and m/c.	250.	600.	1200.

National Commercial Bank of Scotland Limited

1959 Issue

		VG	VF	UNC
265	**1 Pound** 16.9.1959. Blue on m/c unpt. Forth Railway bridge at l. ctr. Arms on back.	6.00	20.00	50.00

#266-268 arms at ctr. r. Forth Railway bridge on back.

		VG	VF	UNC
266	**5 Pounds** 16.9.1959. Green on m/c unpt.	15.00	45.00	125.

		VG	VF	UNC
267	**20 Pounds** 16.9.1959. Red on m/c unpt.	55.00	125.	300.

#		VG	VF	UNC
268	**100 Pounds** 16.9.1959. Purple on m/c unpt.	350.	600.	1000.

Royal Bank of Scotland

1727 Issue

#276-279 oval portr. Kg. George II at upper l. All notes embossed w/bank seal.

Most notes of this bank from 1727-1854 are printed in black. Uniface.

#		Good	Fine	XF
276	**20 Shillings** 8.12.1727.	—	—	—
277	**10 Pounds** (1727).	—	—	—
278	**50 Pounds** (1727).	—	—	—
279	**100 Pounds** (1727).	—	—	—

Note: No examples of #277-279 are presently known to exist.

1742 Issue

#		Good	Fine	XF
280	**20 Shillings = 12 Pounds Scots** 6.4.1742. More ornate style, otherwise similar to #276.	—	—	—

1750 Issue

#		Good	Fine	XF
281	**20 Shillings = 12 Pounds Scots** 9.2.1750. Kg. George II in profile. Printed date.	—	—	—

1758 Issue

#		Good	Fine	XF
282	**1 Guinea** (1758). Portr. as before, but different text.	1250.	3500.	—

1762 Issue

#283-286 w/text of option clause referring to redemption of the note. Design includes portr. Kg. George III at upper l. Printed date.

#		Good	Fine	XF
283	**1 Pound** 5.4.1762.	—	—	—
284	**10 Pounds** 5.4.1762.	—	—	—
285	**20 Pounds** 5.4.1762.	—	—	—
286	**100 Pounds** 5.4.1762.	—	—	—

1777 Issue

#		Good	Fine	XF
287	**1 Guinea** 1.9.1777. Head of Kg. George III in red at upper l., panel w/denomination in words at upper r. in blue. Body of note in black.	1000.	3000.	—

1785 Issue

#288-291 portr. Kg. George III. Other details of design not known.

#		Good	Fine	XF
288	**5 Pounds** (1785).	—	—	—
289	**10 Pounds** (1785).	—	—	—
290	**20 Pounds** (1785).	—	—	—
291	**100 Pounds** (1785).	—	—	—

1792 Issue

#		Good	Fine	XF
292	**20 Shillings** 9.2.1792. Kg. George III in profile at upper l. Red serial #.	500.	1500.	—
292A	**1 Guinea** 1.9.1792.	800.	2000.	—

1797 Issue

#		Good	Fine	XF
293	**5 Shillings** 3.4.1797. Panel of thistles and crown at l. Printed date.	500.	1500.	—

1799 Issue

#		Good	Fine	XF
294	**1 Guinea** 2.12.1799. Coinage head of Kg. George III.	600.	1600.	—

1801 Issue

#		Good	Fine	XF
295	**1 Pound** 25.3.1801. Royal Regalia design.	500.	1500.	—

1807 Issue

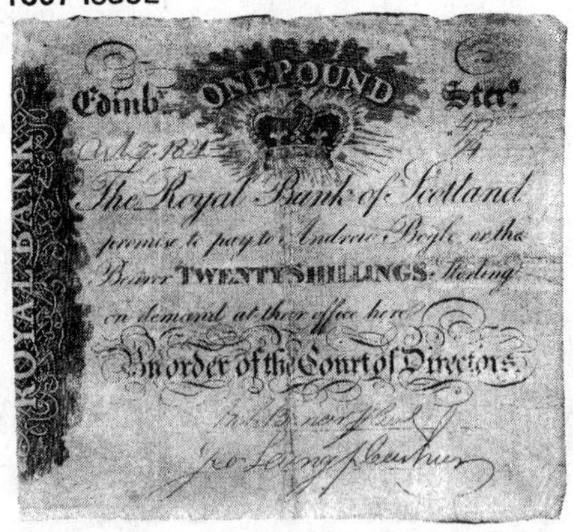

#		Good	Fine	XF
296	**20 Shillings** (1807). Modified Regalia design showing only the Crown. Hand dated and numbered.	500.	1400.	—

1813 Issue

#		Good	Fine	XF
297	**1 Guinea** (1813); 3.3.182x. Coinage head of Kg. George III. Hand dated and numbered.	500.	1400.	—

1826 Issue

#		Good	Fine	XF
298	**20 Shillings** 4.11.1826; 5.4.1827; 6.5.1831; 9.5.1832. Portr. Kg. George IV flanked by elaborate engraving and engine work of circular and oval panels. Printed back w/elaborate geometric design. Hand dated and numbered. Printer: W. H. Lizars.	400.	1100.	—
299	**1 Guinea** (1826). Reclining woman w/lion, also some geometric panels. Back w/elaborate panel design.	450.	1200.	—

1830 Issue

#300-303 portr. Kg. George II and value design. Hand dated and numbered.

#		Good	Fine	XF
300	**5 Pounds** (1830).	550.	1500.	—
301	**10 Pounds** (1830).	700.	2000.	—
302	**20 Pounds** (1830).	—	—	—
303	**100 Pounds** (1830).	—	—	—

1832 Issue

#		Good	Fine	XF
304	**20 Shillings** (1832); 1.11.1841; 1.11.1848. Standing Britannia and standing figure of Plenty at l. and r., portr. Kg. George I w/unicorn and lion at upper ctr. Hand dated and numbered. Printer: W. H. Lizars.	400.	1100.	—

1853 Issue

#		Good	Fine	XF
305	**1 Pound** (1853). Similar to #304.	400.	1100.	—

1854 Issue

#305A-309 plates altered to include text: *PURSUANT TO ACT OF PARLIAMENT* at top of notes. Hand dat and numbered.

#		Good	Fine	XF
305A	**1 Pound** 1.10.1855.	400.	1000.	—
306	**5 Pounds** (1854); 2.11.1857.	450.	1400.	—
307	**10 Pounds** (1854).	700.	1800.	—
308	**20 Pounds** (1854).	600.	1600.	
309	**100 Pounds** (1854).	—	—	

1860 Issue

#		Good	Fine	XF
310	**1 Pound** (1860). Blue w/red letters: *R B S* on face. Printed date and serial #.	350.	1100.	

1861 Issue

#311-314 Royal arms w/figures of value in black, red denomination wording, and red overlay on lege panel. Hand dated, printed serial #. Printer: W. & A. K. Johnston.

#		Good	Fine	XF
311	**5 Pounds** (1861).	700.	1500.	
312	**10 Pounds** (1861).	1000.	2000.	
313	**20 Pounds** (1861).	800.	1800.	
314	**100 Pounds** (1861).	—	—	

1865 Issue

#		Good	Fine	XF
315	**1 Pound** 1.5.1865. Similar to #310 but added text at top: *PURSUANT TO ACT OF PARLIAMENT*. Printer: W. & A. K. Johnston.	500.	1100.	

1875; 1887 ISSUE

		Good	Fine	XF
316	**1 Pound** 1875-1926. Blue and red. Allegorical figures at lower l. and lower r. Uniface.			
	a. Sign: W. Turnbull. 1875-78.	325.	1100.	—
	b. Sign: F. A. Mackay. 1878-87.	300.	1000.	—
	c. Sign: W. Templeton. 1887-1908.	135.	500.	1000.
	d. Sign: D. S. Lunan. 5.5.1908-24.3.1920.	50.00	300.	600.
	e. Sign: D. Speed. Yellow unpt., red serial letters. 14.5.1920-14.5.1926.	40.00	250.	500.

		Good	Fine	XF
317	**5 Pounds** 1875-1951. Blue and red-brown (earlier), orange-brown (later). Uniface.			
	a. Sign. titles: *Accountant* and *Cashier*. Imprint: W. & A. K. Johnston. 1875-1918.	200.	500.	1200.
	b. Imprint: W. & A. K. Johnston Limited. 1918-42.	80.00	275.	600.
	c. As b. Sign. titles: *Cashier & General Manager* and *Chief Accountant*. 1.7.1942-16.10.1950.	50.00	160.	350.

		Good	Fine	XF
318	**10 Pounds** 1887-1940. Blue and red. Uniface.			
	a. Plate C. 1887-1918.	650.	2000.	—
	b. Plate D. Yellow unpt. The blue is much darker than plate C. 1918-40.	200.	600.	—

		Good	Fine	XF
319	**20 Pounds** 1877-1969. Blue and brown. Uniface.			
	a. Plate C. 1877-1911.	350.	850.	2500.
	b. Plate D. Yellow unpt. Imprint: W. & A. K. Johnston 1931-47.	100.	400.	1000.
	c. Plates E; F; G; H. Unpt. w/o red. Imprint: W. & A. K. Johnston & G. W. Bacon Ltd. Both sign. printed 1947-66.	90.00	275.	600.
320	**100 Pounds** 1877-1969. Blue and red. Uniface.			
	a. Plate C. 1877-1918.	1000.	2750.	—
	b. Plates D; E. Yellow unpt. 1918-60.	350.	750.	2200.
	c. Plates F; G. Imprint: W. & A. K. Johnston & G. W. Bacon Ltd. Both sign. printed. 1960-66.	300.	700.	2000.

1927 ISSUE

		VG	VF	UNC
321	**1 Pound** 2.2.1927-24.12.1936. Blue with a brownish red unpt. Bank bldgs. at l. and r. on back. Imprint: W. & A. K. Johnston.	30.00	100.	250.

1937 ISSUE

		VG	VF	UNC
322	**1 Pound** 1937-55. Dk. blue on yellow and brown unpt.			
	a. Sign. *Chief Accountant*, David Speed. Imprint: W. & A. K. Johnston Ltd. 2.1.1937-1.7.1942.	12.50	40.00	150.
	b. Yellow unpt. Sign. *Chief Accountant*, Thomas Brown. 1.3.1943-1.7.1951.	10.00	35.00	125.
	c. Sign. w/title: *Chief Accountant* J. D. Dick. 16.7.1951-1.11.1952.	9.00	30.00	90.00
	d. Imprint: W. & A. K. Johnston & G. W. Bacon Ltd. 1.4.1953-3.1.1955.	6.00	20.00	60.00

1952 Issue

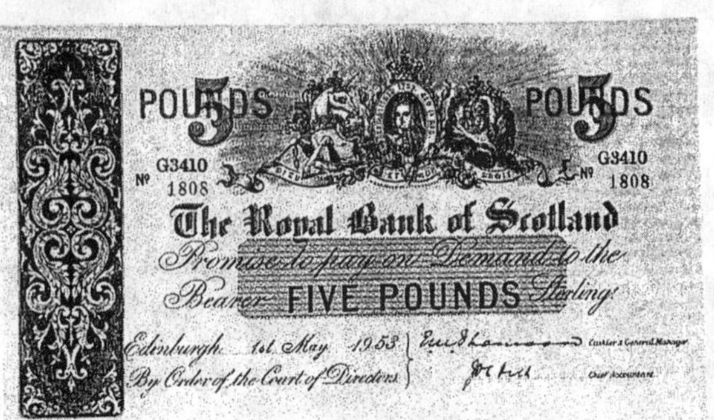

		VG	VF	UNC
323	**5 Pounds** 1952-63. Blue and red on yellow unpt. Uniface. Like #317 but reduced size.			
	a. 2 sign. Imprint: W. & A.K. Johnston Ltd. 2.1.1952-1.7.1953.	30.00	85.00	250.
	b. 3 sign. Imprint: W. & A. K. Johnston & G. W. Bacon Ltd. 1.7.1953-1.2.1954.	35.00	150.	325.
	c. 2 sign. Imprint: W. & A. K. Johnston & G. W. Bacon. 1.4.1955-3.1.1963.	25.00	60.00	175.

1955 Issue

		VG	VF	UNC
324	**1 Pound** 1955-64. Dk. blue on yellow and brown unpt. Sign. W. R. Ballantyne w/title: *General Manager.* 152 x 85mm.			
	a. W/o engraver's name on back. 1.4.1955-1.11.1955.	7.00	18.00	75.00
	b. W/engraver's name W. H. Egan upside down and in very small letters below the r. hand bank bldg. on back. 1.2.1956-1.7.1964.	6.00	15.00	60.00
	s. As a. Specimen.	—	—	—

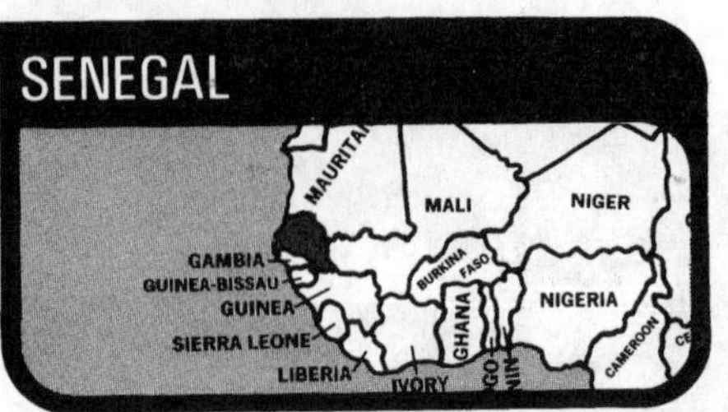

The Republic of Senegal, located on the bulge of West Africa between Mauritania and Guinea-Bissau, has an area of 75,750 sq. mi. (196,190 sq. km.) and a population of 9.49 million. Capital: Dakar. The economy is primarily agricultural. Peanuts and products, phosphates, and canned fish are exported.

An abundance of megalithic remains indicates that Senegal was inhabited in prehistoric times. The Portuguese had some trading stations on the banks of the Senegal River in the 15th century. French commercial establishments date from the 17th century. The French gradually acquired control over the interior regions, which were administered as a protectorate until 1920, and as a colony thereafter. After the 1958 French constitutional referendum, Senegal became a member of the French Community with virtual autonomy. In 1959 Senegal and the French Soudan merged to form the Mali Federation, which became fully independent on June 20, 1960. (April 4, the date the transfer of power agreement was signed with France, is celebrated as Senegal's independence day.) The Federation broke up on Aug. 20, 1960, when Senegal seceded and proclaimed the Republic of Senegal. Soudan became the Republic of Mali a month later.

Senegal became a member of the "Union Monetaire Ouest-Africaine" in 1963.

Also see French West Africa, Upper Senegal-Niger, West African States.

RULERS:
French to 1960

MONETARY SYSTEM:
1 Franc = 100 Centimes

French Administration

Banque du Sénégal

1853 Issue

		Good	Fine	XF
A1	**5 Francs** L.1874. Blue. Similar to French Colonial issues under law of 1901. Medallic head at l. and r. on face, at ctr. on back. Back black. Unsigned remainder.			
A2	**25 Francs** 1853-1901.			
A3	**100 Francs** 1853-1901.			
A4	**500 Francs** 1853-1901.			

Gouvernement General de l'A.O.F.

Colonie du Sénégal

Decret du 11 Fevrier 1917

#1-3 reverse of coin at l., obverse at r. on face.

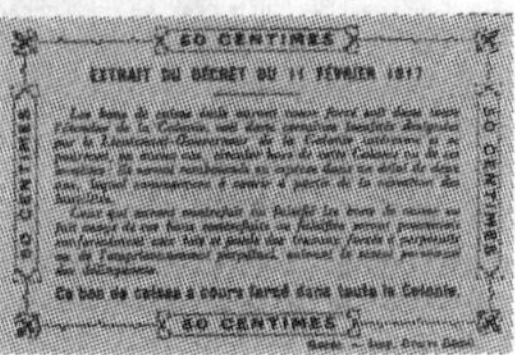

		VG	VF	UNC
1	**0.50 Franc** L.1917. Blue on green unpt.			
	a. Wmk: Bees. Imprint on back w/*gen'al.*	30.00	85.00	250
	b. Wmk: Bees. Imprint on back w/*Gen'al.*	35.00	90.00	285
	c. W/o wmk. 2 sign. varieties.	37.50	100.	325

		VG	VF	UNC
2	**1 Franc** L.1917. Red on salmon unpt.			
	a. Wmk: Bees. Imprint on back w/*gen'al.*	40.00	125.	350.
	b. Wmk: Bees. Imprint on back w/*Gen'al.*	37.50	100.	300.
	c. W/o wmk. 2 sign. varieties.	30.00	80.00	225.

		VG	VF	UNC
3	**2 Francs** L.1917. Orange on yellow unpt.			
	a. Wmk: Bees. Imprint on back w/*gen'al.*	30.00	85.00	385.
	b. Wmk: Bees. Imprint on back w/*Gen'al.*	35.00	90.00	360.
	c. W/o wmk. 2 sign. varieties.	37.50	100.	360.

SERBIA

Serbia, a former inland Balkan kingdom (now a federated republic with Montenegro) has an area of 34,116 sq. mi. (88,361 sq. km.) Capital: Belgrade.

Serbia emerged as a separate kingdom in the 12th century and attained its greatest expansion and political influence in the mid-14th century. After the Battle of Kosovo, 1389, Serbia became a vassal principality of Turkey and remained under Turkish suzerainty until it was re-established as an independent kingdom by the 1887 Treaty of Berlin. Following World War I, which was in part caused by the assassination of Austrian Archduke Francis Ferdinand by a Serbian nationalist, Serbia joined with the Croats and Slovenes to form the new kingdom of the South Slavs with Petar I of Serbia as king. The name of the kingdom was later changed to Yugoslavia. Invaded by Germany during World War II, Serbia emerged as a constituent republic of the Socialist Federal Republic of Yugoslavia.

With the breakup of Yugoslavia, a Federation of Serbia and Montenegro was formed, with each state using independent currencies.

RULERS:

Milan, Obrenovich IV, as Prince, 1868-1882
Aleksander I, 1889-1902
Petar I, 1903-1918

MONETARY SYSTEM:

1 Dinar ДИНАР = 100 Para ПАРА
Gold Dinar = Dinar Zlatu = ДИНАР ЗЛАТУ
Silver Dinar = Dinar Srebru = ДИНАР СРЕБРУ

Note: For additional issues refer to Bosnia-Herzegovina and Croatia-Knin in Volume 3, Modern Issues.

KINGDOM

STATE NOTES

1876 ISSUE

#1-6 man between cherubs at top ctr.

		Good	Fine	XF
1	**1 Dinar** 1.7.1876. Blue on yellow unpt. Portr. Prince Milan Obrenovich. Uniface.	35.00	150.	450.
2	**5 Dinara** 1.7.1876. Blue on yellow unpt. Woman standing at l., soldier standing w/rifle at r.	60.00	250.	600.

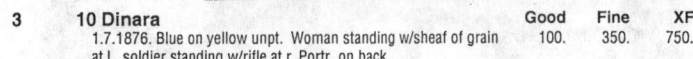

		Good	Fine	XF
3	**10 Dinara** 1.7.1876. Blue on yellow unpt. Woman standing w/sheaf of grain at l., soldier standing w/rifle at r. Portr. on back.	100.	350.	750.

		Good	Fine	XF
4	**50 Dinara** 1.7.1876. Blue on yellow unpt. Woman seated at l., soldier seated w/rifle at r.	225.	650.	—
5	**100 Dinara** 1.7.1876. Blue on yellow unpt. Woman standing w/sheaf of grain at l., soldier standing w/rifle at r.	500.	1500.	—

ПРИВИЛЕГОВАНА НАРОДНА БАНКА КРАЉЕВИНЕ СРБИЈЕ

CHARTERED NATIONAL BANK OF THE KINGDOM OF SERBIA

1884; 1885 ISSUE

		Good	Fine	XF
6	**10 Dinara** 1.11.1885. Blue on yellow unpt. Woman standing at l., soldier standing w/rifle at r.	750.	2000.	—

		Good	Fine	XF
7	**50 Dinara (zlatu)** 1885; 1886. Dk. olive. Woman standing w/children at l., woman standing w/sword and shield at r.			
	a. 1.2.1885. Rare.	—	—	—
	b. W/o sign. 1.3.1886. Rare.	—	—	—
8	**100 Dinara (zlatu)** 1884. Dk. olive. Woman seated w/tablet and sword at r.			
	a. 2.7.1884. Rare.	—	—	—
	b. 2 sign. varieties. 1.9.1884. Rare.	—	—	—
	c. W/o date or sign. Rare.	—	—	—

1887 ISSUE

		Good	Fine	XF
9	**10 Dinara (srebru)** 14.1.1887. Blue. Woman standing w/sword and shield at l., children and child 'Mercury' at r.	40.00	175.	375.

1893 ISSUE

		Good	Fine	XF
10	**10 Dinara (srebru)** 2.1.1893. Blue on brown unpt. Woman seated w/musical instrument and child at l.			
	a. W/o lozenge printing.	20.00	50.00	100.
	b. Lozenge printing.	20.00	50.00	100.
	c. Punched hole cancelled: ANNULÉ.	15.00	30.00	75.00

NOTICE

Readers with unlisted dates, signature varieties, etc. are invited to submit photocopies or, high resolution (300 dpi, 100% size) scans of their notes to: Standard Catalog of World Paper Money, 700 East State St. Iola, WI 54990-0001, or E-Mail: george.cuhaj@fwpubs.com.

1905 ISSUE

		Good	Fine	XF
11	**20 Dinara (zlatu)** 5.1.1905. Blue on brown unpt. Woman standing w/sword, shield and child at l., young woman standing at r.			
	a. W/o yellow lozenge printing.	120.	275.	600.
	b. Yellow lozenge printing.	150.	350.	750.

		Good	Fine	XF
12	**100 Dinara (srebru)** 5.1.1905. Blue on brown unpt. Woman seated w/sword at r., coastline in background. Wmk: Woman's head.			
	a. W/o yellow lozenge printing.	12.50	40.00	100.
	b. Yellow lozenge printing.	25.00	85.00	175.
	c. W/o yellow lozenge printing; thinner paper w/lighter printing.	12.50	40.00	100.

1914 EMERGENCY WW I ISSUE

		Good	Fine	XF
13	**50 Dinara (srebru)** 1.8.1914. Dk. violet. Soldier w/rifle at l., farm girl at r. Arms at l. on back.	500.	1000.	2250.

1916 ISSUE

		Good	Fine	XF
14	**5 Dinara (srebru)** 1916-18. Blue. Helmeted man at l. and as wmk. Arms and fruit on back.			
	a. 11.10.1916-31.12.1917.	7.50	35.00	85.00
	b. 1.1.1918-18.9.1918. Rare.	—	—	—

1915 EMERGENCY POSTAGE STAMP CURRENCY ISSUE

Of an already completed series of postage stamps (Michel #130. #131 I-V or Scott's #132-138), all have Kg. Peter I w/military staff in the field. Only the denominations 5 and 10 Para could be used for postal purposes because of the war. The other denominations circulated as emergency money. The stamps are perforated; however, imperforate unfinished remainders also exist.

		Good	Fine	XF
15	**5 Para** ND (1915). Lt. green.	—	Unc	15.00

16	**10 Para** ND (1915). Vermilion.	—	Unc	25.00
17	**15 Para** ND (1915). Black-gray.	—	Unc	35.00
17A	**15 Para** ND (1915). Dk. blue. Misprint.	—	Unc	165.
18	**20 Para** ND (1915). Brown.	—	Unc	15.00
19	**25 Para** ND (1915). Dk. blue.	—	Unc	45.00
20	**30 Para** ND (1915). Lt. olive.	—	Unc	50.00
21	**50 Para** ND (1915). Red-brown.	—	Unc	80.00

Note: The 10, 15, 20, 40 and 50 Para stamps affixed to cardboard (type of Michel Catalog Serbia #99) w/Kg. Peter I and printed legend and denomination on back were locally issued emergency money (for Osijek, Prima Frankova tiskara).

GERMAN OCCUPATION - WW II

СРПСКА НАРОДНА БАНКА

SERBIAN NATIONAL BANK

1941 PROVISIONAL ISSUE

		VG	VF	UNC
22	**10 Dinara** 1.5.1941. Green on tan unpt. Arms at l. Back like Yugoslavia #35 but w/black new bank name and text ovpt. Wmk: Old man in uniform.	1.50	5.00	12.50
23	**100 Dinara** 1.5.1941. Purple and yellow. Ovpt. on Yugoslavia #27.	1.00	2.00	5.00

		VG	VF	UNC
24	**1000 Dinara on 500 Dinara** 1.5.1941. Brown and m/c. 3 seated women at ctr. 3 women and cherub on back.	2.00	7.50	20.00

Note: #24 w/o ovpt. is reported, not confirmed.

1941 ISSUE

		VG	VF	UNC
25	**20 Dinara** 1.5.1941. Brown on tan and lt. brown unpt. Portr. V. Karadzic at l. Arms at r. on back. Wmk: Old man in uniform.	1.50	4.00	10.00

		VG	VF	UNC
26	**50 Dinara** 1.8.1941. Brown and m/c. Portr. woman at l. Man playing old stringed instrument at ctr., arms at r. on back. Wmk: Boy w/cap.	2.00	6.00	15.00

		VG	VF	UNC
27	**500 Dinara** 1.11.1941. Brown and m/c. Woman in national costume at ctr. Man w/bldg. materials on back.			
	a. Wmk: Kg. Aleksander I.	.50	1.50	4.00
	b. Wmk: Woman's head.	.50	1.25	3.00

1942 ISSUE

		VG	VF	UNC
28	**20 Dinara** 1.5.1942. Blue. Like #25. (Not issued).	—	100.	250.

		VG	VF	UNC
29	**50 Dinara** 1.5.1942. Brown on lt. brown unpt. Portr. Kg. Petar at l. Arms at l. on back.	1.00	3.50	8.00

		VG	VF	UNC
30	**100 Dinara** 1.5.1942. Brown and m/c. Shepherd-boy seated playing flute, flock of sheep at l. (Not issued).	—	125.	350.

		VG	VF	UNC
31	**500 Dinara** 1.5.1942. Brown and m/c. Arms at upper l., farmer seeding at r. Farmer harvesting wheat on back. Wmk: Kg. Aleksander I.	.50	1.50	6.00

		VG	VF	UNC
32	**1000 Dinara** 1.5.1942. Brown and m/c. Blacksmith at l., woman wearing costume at r. Farm wife at l., farmer at r. on back.			
	a. Wmk: Kg. Petar.	1.00	3.00	10.00
	b. Wmk: Woman's head.	1.00	3.00	10.00

1943 ISSUE

		VG	VF	UNC
33	**100 Dinara** 1.1.1943. Brown and blue on lt. brown and tan unpt. St. Sava at l. Man w/ox-cart at ctr. r. on back. Wmk: Woman's head.	2.00	5.00	12.50

MILITARY

AUSTRIAN MILITARY TERRITORIAL GOVERNMENT

BELGRAD

1917 ISSUE

		Good	Fine	XF
M1	**10 Dinara** 1917.	25.00	50.00	80.00
M2	**100 Dinara** 1917.	25.00	50.00	80.00

BELGRAD-LAND

1917 ISSUE

		Good	Fine	XF
M3	**10 Dinara** 1917.	35.00	60.00	90.00
M4	**100 Dinara** 1917.	35.00	60.00	90.00

CACAK

1917 ISSUE

		Good	Fine	XF
M5	**10 Dinara** 1917.	35.00	60.00	90.00
M6	**100 Dinara** 1917.	35.00	60.00	90.00

Gornji Milanovac

1917 Issue

		Good	Fine	XF
M7	**10 Dinara** 1917.	125.	150.	200.
M8	**100 Dinara** 1917.	125.	150.	200.

Kragujevac

1917 Issue

		Good	Fine	XF
M9	**10 Dinara** 1917.	25.00	50.00	90.00
M10	**100 Dinara** 1917.	25.00	50.00	90.00

Krusevac

1917 Issue

		Good	Fine	XF
M11	**10 Dinara** 1917.	35.00	60.00	90.00
M12	**100 Dinara** 1917.	35.00	60.00	90.00

Mitrovica

1917 Issue

		Good	Fine	XF
M13	**10 Dinara** 1917.	125.	150.	200.
M14	**100 Dinara** 1917.	125.	150.	200.

Sabac

1917 Issue

		Good	Fine	XF
M15	**10 Dinara** 1917.	40.00	70.00	100.
M16	**100 Dinara** 1917.	40.00	70.00	100.

Semendria

1917 Issue

		Good	Fine	XF
M17	**10 Dinara** 1917.	45.00	75.00	105.
M18	**100 Dinara** 1917.	45.00	75.00	105.

Smederevo

1917 Issue

		Good	Fine	XF
M19	**10 Dinara** 1917.	30.00	50.00	80.00
M20	**100 Dinara** 1917.	30.00	50.00	80.00

Uzice

1917 Issue

		Good	Fine	XF
M21	**10 Dinara** 1917.	45.00	75.00	120.
M22	**100 Dinara** 1917.	45.00	75.00	120.

Valjevo

1917 Issue

		Good	Fine	XF
M23	**10 Dinara** 1917.	60.00	80.00	120.
M24	**100 Dinara** 1917.	60.00	80.00	120.

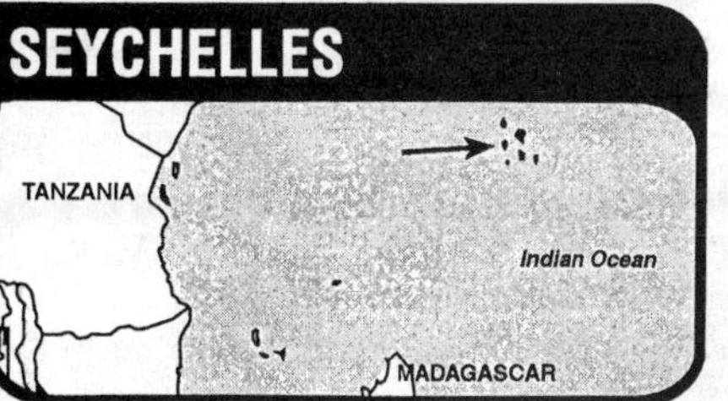

The Republic of Seychelles, an archipelago of 85 granite and coral islands situated in the Indian Ocean 600 miles (965 km.) northeast of Madagascar, has an area of 156 sq. mi. (455 sq. km.) and a population of 82,400. Among these islands are the Aldabra Islands, the Farquhar Group, and Ile Desroches, which the United Kingdom ceded to the Seychelles upon its independence. Capital: Victoria, on Mahe. The economy is d on fishing, a plantation system of agriculture and tourism. Copra, cinnamon and vanilla are exported.

Although the Seychelles are marked on Portuguese charts of the early 16th century, the first recorded visit to the islands, by an English ship, occurred in 1609. The Seychelles were annexed to France by Captain Lazare Picault in 1743 and permanently settled in 1768, with the intention of establishing spice plantations to compete with the Dutch monopoly of the spice trade. British troops seized the islands in 1810, during the Napoleonic Wars; they were formally ceded to Britain by the Treaty of Paris, 1814. The Seychelles were a dependency of Mauritius until Aug. 31, 1903, when they became a separate British Crown Colony. The colony was granted limited internal self-government in 1970, and attained independence on June 28, 1976, becoming Britain's last African possession to do so. Seychelles is a member of the Commonwealth of Nations. The president is the Head of State and of Government.

RULERS:
British to 1976

MONETARY SYSTEM:
1 Rupee = 100 Cents

British Administration

Government of Seychelles

1914 Emergency WW I Issue

#A1-A4 uniface.

		Good	Fine	XF
A1	**50 Cents** 11.8.1914. Black.	300.	650.	1400.
A2	**1 Rupee** 11.8.1914. Black.	350.	750.	1750.

		Good	Fine	XF
A3	**5 Rupees** 11.8.1914. Black.	950.	1850.	4000.
A4	**10 Rupees** 11.8.1914. Black. Like #A3.	1200.	3000.	—

1919 Emergency Issue

#A5 and A6 uniface.

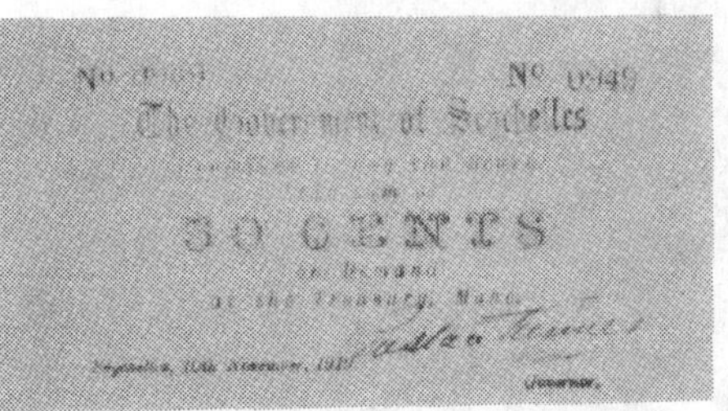

		Good	Fine	XF
A5	**50 Cents** 10.11.1919. Black.	450.	1300.	—
A6	**1 Rupee** 10.9.1919. Black. Cream paper.	—	—	—

1918-28 Issue

#1-5 portr. Kg. George V in profile at r. Various date and sign. varieties. Uniface. Printer: TDLR.

		Good	Fine	XF
1	**50 Cents**			
	1919-34; ND. Grayish green and violet.			
	a. 1.7.1919.	125.	550.	1500.
	b. 1.7.1924.	100.	500.	1500.
	c. 6.11.1928.	100.	500.	1500.
	d. 5.10.1934.	85.00	500.	1250.
	e. ND (1936).	45.00	450.	1200.

		Good	Fine	XF
2	**1 Rupee**			
	1918-34; ND. Gray and red. Like #1.			
	a. 1918.	150.	500.	1500.
	b. 1.7.1919.	150.	500.	1350.
	c. 1.7.1924.	85.00	350.	1200.
	d. 6.11.1928.	85.00	300.	1200.
	e. 5.10.1934.	50.00	225.	1000.
	f. ND (1936).	35.00	175.	900.

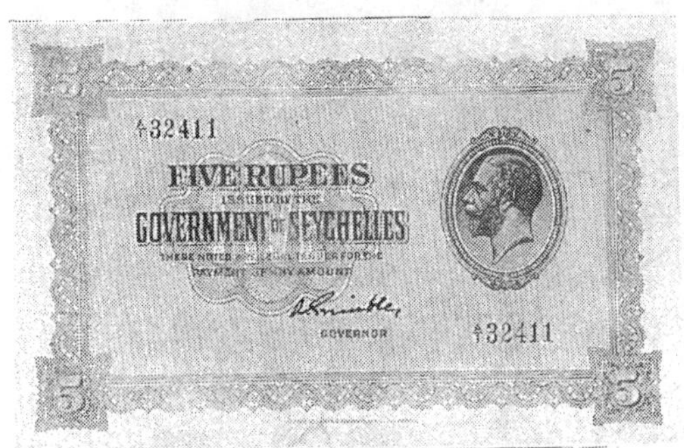

		Good	Fine	XF
3	**5 Rupees**			
	1928; 1934; ND. Lilac-brown and green.			
	a. 6.11.1928.	85.00	275.	850.
	b. 5.10.1934.	60.00	200.	750.
	c. ND (1936).	40.00	180.	550.

		Good	Fine	XF
4	**10 Rupees**			
	1928; ND. Green and red. Like #3.			
	a. 6.11.1928.	250.	700.	1750.
	b. ND (1936).	90.00	300.	1000.

		Good	Fine	XF
5	**50 Rupees**			
	1928; ND. Brown and blue.			
	a. 6.11.1928.	300.	700.	1700.
	b. ND (1936).	200.	550.	1750.

1942 Emergency WW II Issue

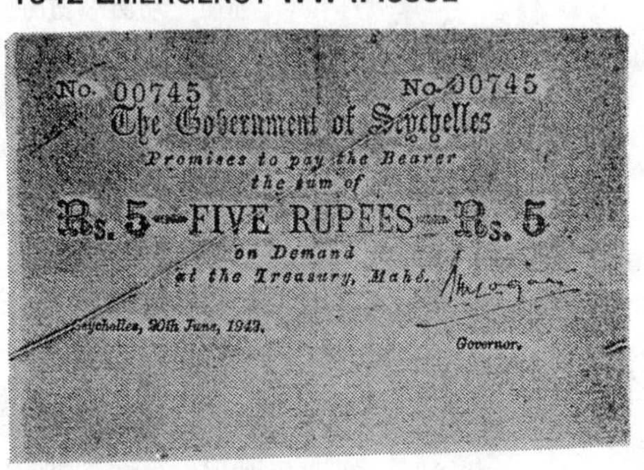

		VG	VF	UNC
5A	**5 Rupees**			
	20.6.1942. Black. Uniface.	1250.	3000.	—

1942; 1943 Issue

#6-10 portr. Kg. George VI at l. Various date and sign. varieties. Uniface. Printer: TDLR.

		VG	VF	UNC
6	**50 Cents**			
	1943-51. Grayish green and violet. Facing portr. at l.			
	a. 7.7.1943.	35.00	175.	600.
	b. Sign. title: *GOVERNOR.* 6.1.1951.	50.00	250.	750.
	c. Sign. title: *OFFICER ADMINISTERING THE GOVERNMENT.* 6.1.1951.	30.00	165.	585.

		VG	VF	UNC
7	**1 Rupee**			
	1943-51. Gray and red. Like #6.			
	a. 3.5.1943; 7.7.1943.	40.00	225.	650.
	b. Sign. title: *GOVERNOR.* 6.1.1951.	45.00	275.	750.
	c. Sign. title: *OFFICER ADMINISTERING THE GOVERNMENT.* 6.1.1951.	30.00	165.	585.

NOTICE

Readers with unlisted dates, signature varieties, etc. are invited to submit photocopies or, high resolution (300 dpi, 100% size) scans of their notes to: Standard Catalog of World Paper Money, 700 East State St. Iola, WI 54990-0001, or E-Mail: george.cuhaj@fwpubs.com.

#		VG	VF	UNC
8	**5 Rupees** 7.4.1942. Lilac-brown and green. Profile portr. at l.	25.00	100.	200.
9	**10 Rupees** 7.4.1942. Green and red. Like #8.	35.00	150.	485.
10	**50 Rupees** 7.4.1942. Lt. brown. Like #8.	85.00	350.	1200.

1954 ISSUE

#11-13 portr. Qn. Elizabeth II in profile at r. #12 and 13 portr. Qn. Elizabeth II in profile at r. Denominations on back. Various date and sign. varieties. Printer: TDLR.

#		VG	VF	UNC
11	**5 Rupees** 1954; 1960. Lilac and green.			
	a. 1.8.1954.	12.50	60.00	275.
	b. 1.8.1960.	7.50	50.00	265.

#		VG	VF	UNC
12	**10 Rupees** 1954-67. Green and red. Like #11.			
	a. 1.8.1954.	12.50	85.00	850.
	b. 1.8.1960.	10.00	80.00	800.
	c. 1.5.1963.	10.00	75.00	750.
	d. 1.1.1967.	7.50	70.00	675.

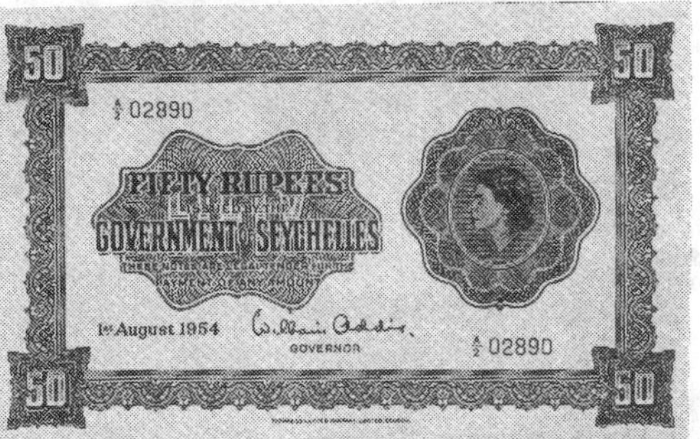

#		VG	VF	UNC
13	**50 Rupees** 1954-67. Black. Like #11.			
	a. 1.8.1954.	30.00	200.	2000.
	b. 1.8.1960.	27.50	175.	1750.
	c. 1.5.1963.	25.00	150.	1700.
	d. 1.1.1967.	25.00	150.	1600.

The Republic of Sierra Leone, a British Commonwealth nation located in western Africa between Guinea and Liberia, has an area of 27,699 sq. mi. (71,740 sq. km.) and a population of 4.87 million. Capital: Freetown. The economy is predominantly agricultural but mining contributes significantly to export revenues. Diamonds, iron ore, palm kernels, cocoa and coffee are exported.

The coast of Sierra Leone was first visited by Portuguese and British slavers in the 15th and 16th centuries. The first settlement at Freetown was established in 1787 as a refuge for freed slaves within the British Empire, runaway slaves from the United States and blacks discharged from the British armed forces. The first settlers were virtually wiped out by tribal attacks and disease. The colony was re-established under the auspices of the Sierra Leone Company and transferred to the British Crown in 1907. The interior region was secured and established as a protectorate in 1896. Sierra Leone became independent within the Commonwealth on April 27, 1961, and adopted a republican constitution ten years later. It is a member of the Commonwealth of Nations. The president is Chief of State and Head of Government.

RULERS:

British to 1971

MONETARY SYSTEM:

1 Leone = 100 Cents
1 Pound = 20 Shillings

BRITISH INFLUENCE

SIERRA LEONE

18XX ISSUE

#		VG	VF	UNC
A1	**1 Pound** 18xx. Black on white or green paper. Uniface. *CHARLES HEDDLE* across ctr.	—	—	5000.

Slovakia as a republic has an area of 18,923 sq. mi. (49,011 sq. km.) and a population of 5.37 million. Capital: Bratislava. Textiles, steel, and wood products are exported.

Slovakia was settled by Slavic Slovaks in the 6th or 7th century and was incorporated into Greater Moravia in the 9th century. After the Moravian state was destroyed early in the 10th century, Slovakia was conquered by the Magyars and remained a land of the Hungarian crown until 1918, when it joined the Czechs in forming Czechoslovakia. In 1938, the Slovaks declared themselves an autonomous state within a federal Czecho-Slovak state. After the German occupation, Slovakia became nominally independent under the protection of Germany, March 16, 1939. Father Jozef Tiso was appointed President. Slovakia was liberated from German control in Oct. 1944, but in May 1945 ceased to be an independent Slovak state. In 1968 it became a constituent state of Czechoslovakia as Slovak Socialist Republic. In January 1991 the Czech and Slovak Federal Republic was formed, and after June 1992 elections, it was decided to split the federation into the Czech Republic and Slovakia on 1 January, 1993.

MONETARY SYSTEM:

1 Korun = 100 Haleru to 1939
1 Korun = 100 Halierov, 1939-1945
1 Korun = 100 Halierov

REPUBLIC

SLOVENSKA REPUBLIKA

REPUBLIC OF SLOVAKIA

1939 ND PROVISIONAL ISSUE

#1-3 ovpt: *SLOVENSKY STAT* in guilloche on Czechoslovak National Bank notes.

		VG	VF	UNC
1	**100 Korun**			
	ND (June 1939 - old date 10.1.1931). Green. Red ovpt. on Czechoslovakia #23.			
	a. Issued note.	15.00	75.00	325.
	s. As a. perforated: *SPECIMEN.*	3.00	12.00	75.00

		VG	VF	UNC
2	**500 Korun**			
	ND (April 1939 - old date 2.5.1929). Red. Blue ovpt. on Czechoslovakia #24.			
	a. Issued note.	35.00	100.	400
	s. As a. perforated: *SPECIMEN.*	2.00	8.00	30.00
3	**1000 Korun**			
	ND (April 1939 - old date 25.5.1934). Green and blue. Lilac ovpt. on Czechoslovakia #26.			
	a. Issued note.	100.	250.	750
	s. As a. perforated: *SPECIMEN.*	7.50	30.00	100

1939 ISSUE

		VG	VF	UNC
4	**10 Korun**			
	15.9.1939. Blue and brown on lt. orange unpt. Arms at upper l., portr. A. Hlinka at r. Back green and brown; portr. girl at l.			
	a. Issued note.	2.00	10.00	32.5
	p. Print proofs uniface A or R.	—	Unc	500
	s. As a. perforated: *SPECIMEN.*	.30	1.50	4.0

		VG	VF	UNC
5	**20 Korun**			
	1939. Brown on orange and blue unpt. Similar to #4. Back brown and blue; shrine at ctr.			
	a. Darker paper.	5.00	25.00	75.0
	b. Whiter paper.	3.00	15.00	50.0
	p. Print proof uniface R.	—	Unc	50
	s. Perforated: *SPECIMEN.*	.30	1.50	5.0

1942-43 ISSUE

		VG	VF	UNC
6	**10 Korun**			
	20.7.1943. Blue and purple on brown-olive unpt. Arms at l., portr. L. Stur at r. Back maroon and brown; objects on table at r.			
	a. Issued note.	.50	1.50	10.0
	s. As a. perforated: *SPECIMEN.*	.25	.75	4.0

7	20 Korun	VG	VF	UNC
	11.9.1942. Brown on blue and pinkish unpt. Arms at l., eagle at ctr. Portr. J. Holly at r. Food implements on back.			
	a. Issued note.	.50	2.00	10.00
	s. As a. perforated: *SPECIMEN*.	.25	.75	4.00

1945 ND ISSUE

8	5 Korun	VG	VF	UNC
	ND (1945). Lilac-brown on lt. blue unpt. Arms at l., portr. girl at ctr. Back blue on tan unpt.			
	a. Issued note.	.50	1.50	10.00
	s. As a. perforated: *SPECIMEN*.	.25	.75	4.00

SLOVENSKA NÁRODNÁ BANKA

SLOVAK NATIONAL BANK

1940-44 ISSUE

Note: For listings of #10, 11, 12 and 13 w/adhesive revalidation stamps affixed, see Czechoslovakia #51-54.

9	50 Korun	VG	VF	UNC
	15.10.1940. Violet and lilac on lt. blue unpt. 2 girls in Slovak national costume at l., arms at ctr. Back brown; castle at ctr. Wmk: Woman. W/o *II EMISIA* on back. Printer: G&D.			
	a. Issued note.	1.00	3.50	15.00
	s. As a. perforated: *SPECIMEN*.	.35	1.00	4.00
9A	50 Korun			
	15.10.1940. Like #11 but *II EMISIA* in margin on back. (Not issued).	—	—	—

10	100 Korun	VG	VF	UNC
	7.10.1940. Dk. blue on m/c unpt. Portr. Prince Pribina at r. Back green on m/c unpt.; woman w/shield and arms at l. Wmk: Woman. W/o *II EMISIA* on back.			
	a. Issued note.	1.00	5.00	15.00
	s. As a. perforated: *SPECIMEN*.	.25	1.00	3.00

11	100 Korun	VG	VF	UNC
	7.10.1940. Like #10 but *II EMISIA* in margin at l. on back. Wmk: Pattern in paper.			
	a. Issued note.	1.00	5.00	15.00
	s. As a. perforated: *SPECIMEN*.	.25	1.00	3.00

12	500 Korun	VG	VF	UNC
	12.7.1941. Dk. green. Arms w/2 doves at upper ctr., portr. young man in national costume at r. Back olive; bowl of fruit, pitcher and mountains at ctr.			
	a. Issued note.	4.00	12.50	35.00
	s. As a. perforated: *SPECIMEN*.	.50	1.50	4.00

13	1000 Korun	VG	VF	UNC
	25.11.1940. Brown on m/c unpt. Arms at l. ctr., Kg. Svatopluk and his 3 sons at r. Arms on back.			
	a. Issued note.	5.00	15.00	60.00
	s. As a. perforated: *SPECIMEN*.	.50	2.00	10.00

14	5000 Korun	VG	VF	UNC
	18.12.1944. Brown on green and tan unpt. Portr. Prince K. Mojmir at r. Arms at l. on back. Wmk: Woman's head.			
	a. Issued note.	5.00	15.00	60.00
	s. As a. perforated: *SPECIMEN*.	.50	3.00	15.00

The Republic of Slovenia is bounded in the north by Austria, northeast by Hungary, southeast by Croatia and to the west by Italy. It has an area of 5,246 sq. mi. (20,251 sq. km.) and a population of 1.99 million. Capital: Ljubljana. The economy is d on electricity, minerals, forestry, agriculture and fishing. Small industries are being developed during privatization.

The Roman Province of Pannonia (Croatia-Slavonia) was conquered by the Ostrogoths and later recovered by Justinian in 535. In 568 it was conquered by the Avars who were overthrown by the Croats around 640. After changing relations with the Franks, Byzantium, Venice, Moravia and a short-lived Bulgar State, it eventually came under Magyar conquerors led by King Koloman in 1102 who was crowned King of Croatia and Dalmatia at Belgrad. Croatia was an autonomous kingdom under the Holy Crown of St. Stephen for the next eight centuries, becoming a fortress against any further invasion by the Turks. By 1699 all Croatia-Slavonia was recovered from the Turks and was settled by many Serbian refugees from Turkey. Napoleon's rise to power created an "Illyrian" state of east Adriatic territories which Austria had acquired from Venice. All were restored by 1822. The Hungarian Revolution in 1848 developed a federalist policy dissolving any legal bond with Hungary but the Austrians remained in control. From 1868 to 1914 increased political activity developed which broke out in riots in 1883. The Croatian constitution was temporarily suspended by Hungary and a royal commissioner, Count Khuen-Hédervàry, was appointed. His 20 years of rule were very humiliating for Croatia. From 1903 onwards a national feeling developed leading to quarrels with Hungary in 1907 which resulted in Cuvaj being appointed as a dictator by Hungary in 1912. The church lost its autonomy and revolutionary movements followed. The dictatorship was abolished in 1913 with somewhat of a truce with Budapest when WW I broke out. This resulted in the union of the Yugoslav Provinces on Dec. 1, 1918. The lands originally settled by Slovenes in the 6th century were steadily encroached upon by Germans. Slovenia developed as part of Austro-Hungarian Empire after the defeat of the latter in World War I it became part of the Kingdom of the Serbs, Croats and Slovenes (Yugoslavia) established on December 1, 1918. A legal opposition group, the Slovene League of Social Democrats, was formed in Jan. 1989. In Oct. 1989 the Slovene Assembly voted a constitutional amendment giving it the right to secede from Yugoslavia. On July 2, 1990 the Assembly adopted a 'declaration of sovereignty' and in Sept. proclaimed its control over the territorial defense force on its soil. A referendum on Dec. 23 resulted in a majority vote for independence, which was formally declared on Dec. 26. In Feb. 1991 parliament ruled that henceforth Slovenian law took precedence over federal. On June 25, Slovenia declared independence, but agreed to suspend this for 3 months at peace talks sponsored by the EC. The moratorium having expired, Slovenia (and Croatia) declared their complete independence of the Yugoslav federation on Oct. 8, 1991.

MONETARY SYSTEM:

1 (Tolar) = 1 Yugoslavian Dinar
1 Tolar = 100 Stotinas

REPLACEMENT NOTES:

#11-19, ZA prefix.

German Occupation - WWII

Hranilnica Ljubljanske Pokrajine/Sparkasse der Provinz Laibach

Savings Bank of the Province of Ljubliana (Laibach)

1944 Issue

#R1-R9 issued during German occupation. Text in Slovene on one side, German on the other.

		VG	VF	UNC
R1	**1/2 Lira** 28.11.1944. Dk. green. Child in national costume at l. on face and back.	1.50	4.00	10.00
R2	**1 Lira**	1.00	3.50	10.00
R3	**2 Lire** 28.11.1944. Brown. Woman w/child at l. on face and back.	2.00	6.00	15.00
R4	**5 Lire** 28.11.1944. Brown-red. Man in national costume at r. on face and back. Series A.	2.00	6.00	15.00
R5	**10 Lire** 28.11.1944. Bluish purple. Woman wearing national costume hat at l. on face and back. Series D.	2.00	6.00	15.00
R6	**50 Lire** 14.9.1944. Red on gold unpt. Farmer's wife at l. on face, at r. on back.	5.00	20.00	55.00
R7	**100 Lire** 14.9.1944. Blue on gold unpt. Farmer w/scythe at l. on face at r. on back.	10.00	30.00	80.00
R8	**500 Lire** 14.9.1944. Blue on green and gray unpt. Man in national costume at l. on face at r. on back.	12.00	40.00	100.
R9	**1000 Lire** 14.9.1944. Deep purple on pale blue unpt. Woman wearing natinal costume hat at l. on face, at r. on back. Series A; B; D.	15.00	60.00	140.

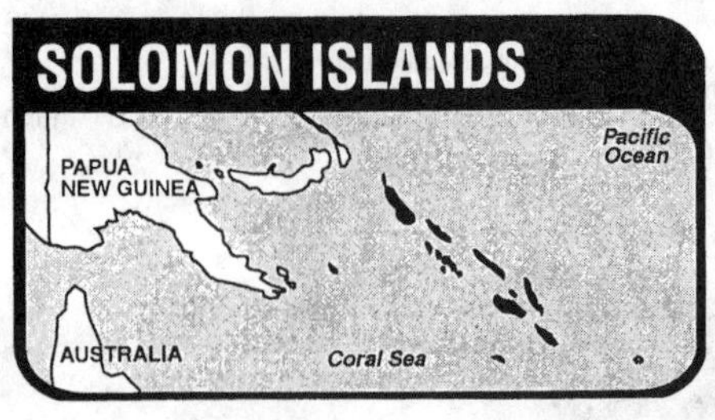

The Solomon Islands, located in the Southwest Pacific east of Papua New Guinea, has an area of 10,983 sq. mi. (28,450 sq. km.) and an estimated population of 444,000. Capital: Honiara. The most important islands of the Solomon chain are Guadalcanal (scene of some of the fiercest fighting of World War II), Malaitia, New Georgia, Florida, Vella Lavella, Choiseul, Rendova, San Cristobal, the Lord Howe group, the Santa Cruz islands, and the Duff group. Copra is the only important cash crop but it is hoped that timber will become an economic factor.

The Solomon Islands were discovered by Spanish navigator Alvaro de Mendana in 1567, and in 1569 he made an unsuccessful attempt to colonize them. European knowledge of the group would not be completed until the end of the 18th century. Germany declared a protectorate over the northern Solomons in 1885. The British protectorate over the southern Solomons was established in 1893. In 1899 Germany transferred its claim to all Solomon Islands except Buka and Bougainville to Great Britain in exchange for recognition of German claims in western Samoa. Australia occupied the two German held islands in 1914, and administered them after 1920.

The Japanese invaded the Solomons during 1942-43, but were driven out by an American counteroffensive after a series of bloody clashes.

Following World War II the islands returned to the status of a British protectorate. In 1976 the protectorate was abolished and the Solomons became a self-governing dependency. Full independence was achieved on July 7, 1978. Solomon Islands is a member of the Commonwealth of Nations. Elizabeth II is Head of State as Queen of the Solomon Islands.

RULERS:

British

MONETARY SYSTEM:

1 Shilling = 12 Pence
1 Pound = 20 Shillings to 1966
1 Dollar = 100 Cents, 1966-

British Administration

Government of the British Solomon Islands

1916 Issue

#1-4 arms at top ctr. Various date and sign. varieties.

		Good	Fine	XF
1	**5 Shillings** 18.12.1916; 27.7.1921; 2.1.1926. Green on brown unpt.	1000.	2500.	—
2	**10 Shillings** 1916-32. Red.			
	a. 18.12.1916; 27.7.1921; 2.1.1926.	1200.	2750.	—
	b. 30.6.1932. (Not issued). Rare.	—	—	—
3	**1 Pound** 18.12.1916; 2.1.1926; 30.6.1932. Blue.	1250.	3000.	—
4	**5 Pounds** 18.12.1916. Rare.	—	—	—

The Republic of South Africa, located at the southern tip of Africa, has an area, including the enclave of Walvis Bay, of 472,359 sq. mi. (1,221,040 sq. km.) and a population of 46.26 million. Capital: Administrative, Pretoria; Legislative, Cape Town; Judicial, Bloemfontein. Manufacturing, mining and agriculture are the principal industries. Exports include wool, diamonds, gold and metallic ores.

Portuguese navigator Bartholomeu Diaz became the first European to sight the region of South Africa when he rounded the Cape of Good Hope in 1488, but throughout the 16th century the only white men to come ashore were the survivors of ships wrecked while attempting the stormy Cape passage. The first permanent settlement was established by Jan van Riebeeck of the Dutch East India Company in 1652. In subsequent decades additional Dutch, Germans and Huguenot refugees from France settled in the Cape area to form the Afrikaner segment of today's population.

Great Britain captured the Cape colony in 1795, and again in 1806, receiving permanent title in 1814. To escape British political rule and cultural dominance, many Afrikaner farmers (Boers) migrated northward (the Great Trek) beginning in 1836, and established the independent Boer republics of the Transvaal (the South African Republic, Zuid-Afrikaansche Republiek) in 1852, and the Orange Free State in 1854. British political intrigues against the two republics, coupled with the discovery of diamonds and gold in the Boer-settled regions, led to the bitter Boer Wars (1880-1881, 1899-1902) and the incorporation of the Boer republics into the British Empire.

On May 31, 1910, the two former Boer republics (Transvaal and Orange Free State) were joined with the British colonies of Cape of Good Hope and Natal to form the Union of South Africa, a dominion of the British Empire. In 1934 the Union achieved status as a sovereign state within the British Empire. Political integration of the various colonies did not still the conflict between the Afrikaners and the English-speaking groups, which continued to have a significant impact on political developments. A resurgence of Afrikaner nationalism in the 1940s and 1950s led to a referendum in the white community authorizing the relinquishment of dominion status and the establishment of a republic. The decision took effect on May 31, 1961. The Republic of South Africa withdrew from the British Commonwealth in Oct., 1961. The apartheid era ended on April 27, 1994 with the first democratic election for all people of South Africa. Nelson Mandela was inaugurated as president on May 10, 1994. South Africa was readmitted to the Commonwealth of Nations.

South African currency carries inscriptions in both Afrikaans and English.

RULERS:

British to 1961

MONETARY SYSTEM:

1 Shilling = 12 Pence
1 Shilling = 12 Pence
1 Pound = 20 Shillings to 1961
1 Pound = 20 Shillings to 1961
1 Rand = 100 Cents (= 10 Shillings), 1961-

BRITISH ADMINISTRATION

EAST INDIA COMPANY

1808 ISSUE

#1-17 vertical format. Value and 1808 date around seated Britannia. Early notes entirely handwritten w/an embossed stamp.

		Good	Fine	XF
1	**1 Rix Dollar** 1808.	—	—	—
2	**2 Rix Dollar** 1808.	—	—	—
3	**3 Rix Dollar** 1808.	—	—	—
4	**4 Rix Dollar** 1808.	—	—	—
5	**5 Rix Dollar** 1808.	—	—	—
5A	**8 Rix Dollar** 1808.	—	—	—
6	**10 Rix Dollar** 1808.	—	—	—
6A	**12 Rix Dollar** 1808.	—	—	—
6B	**15 Rix Dollar** 1808.	—	—	—
7	**20 Rix Dollar** 1808.	—	—	—
8	**25 Rix Dollar** 1808.	—	—	—
9	**30 Rix Dollar** 1808.	—	—	—
10	**40 Rix Dollar** 1808.	—	—	—
11	**50 Rix Dollar** 1808.	—	—	—
11A	**60 Rix Dollar** 1808.	—	—	—
12	**75 Rix Dollar** 1808.	—	—	—
13	**100 Rix Dollar** 1808.	—	—	—
14	**250 Rix Dollar** 1808.	—	—	—
15	**300 Rix Dollar** 1808.	—	—	—
16	**400 Rix Dollar** 1808.	—	—	—
17	**500 Rix Dollar** 1808.	—	—	—

GOVERNMENT

1830'S ISSUE

		Good	Fine	XF
22	**1 Pound** 28.3.1835. Black. Value lower l. and r. Hand stamped: *CANCELLED* and *WITHDRAWN FROM CIRCULATION.*	—	—	—
23	**20 Pounds** 4.3.1834. Black. Value lower l. and r. Hand stamped: *CANCELLED* and *WITHDRAWN FROM CIRCULATION.*	—	—	—

EAST INDIA COMPANY

1810-31 ISSUE

#18-21 w/1808 date around seated Britannia. Type set.

		Good	Fine	XF
18	**2 Rix Dollar** 17.5.1816; 21.3.1821; 22.3.1825.	—	—	—
19	**10 Rix Dollar** 5.2.1810.	—	—	—
20	**20 Rix Dollar** 14.2.1823.	—	—	—
21	**100 Rix Dollar** 11.8.1831.	—	—	—

Z.A.R. - ZUID-AFRIKAANSCHE REPUBLIEK

TREASURY

PRETORIA

FIRST ISSUE, 1865

		Good	Fine	XF
24	**5 Rix Dollar** 16.9.1865. Black. Value top l. and lower r.	435.	740.	1650.
25	**10 Rix Dollar** (1865).	500.	800.	1800.

SECOND ISSUE, 1866

		Good	Fine	XF
26	**2 Shillings - 6 Pence** (1866).	—	—	—
27	**5 Shillings** (1866).	400.	565.	1500.
28	**1 Pound** (1866).	440.	650.	1700.

THIRD ISSUE, 1867

		Good	Fine	XF
29	**2 Shillings - 6 Pence** (1867).	340.	520.	1300.
30	**5 Shillings** 17.1.1867. Like #26.	400.	565.	1500.

		Good	Fine	XF
31	**1 Pound** 2.7.1868. Arms at ctr.	435.	650.	1700.
32	**5 Pounds** (1867).	480.	700.	1800.

Fourth Issue, 1868-70

#33-38 printed by C. Moll.

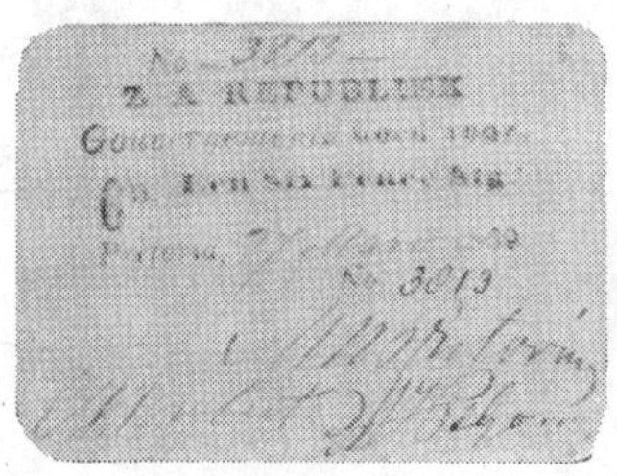

		Good	Fine	XF
33	**6 Pence** 27.3.1869.	270.	600.	1000.
34	**1 Shilling** (1868).	260.	650.	1200.
35	**2 Shillings - 6 Pence** (1868).	300.	700.	1500.
36	**5 Shillings** (1868).	340.	750.	1600.
37	**1 Pound** (1868).	380.	850.	1700.
38	**5 Pounds** (1868).	420.	900.	2000.

Fifth Issue, 1871-72

#39-42 printed by William Brown & Co.

		Good	Fine	XF
39	**1 Pond** 12.1871; 14.1.1872; 25.1.1872. Black on green paper. Arms w/flags at upper ctr., serial # at upper l. and r., 1£ immediately below.	150.	400.	975.
40	**5 Pond** ca. 1871.	400.	800.	1450.
41	**10 Pond** ca. 1871.	450.	900.	1600.
42	**20 Pond** (1871).	500.	1000.	1800.

1872 Issue (Good Fors)

		Good	Fine	XF
43	**6 Pence** 13.4.1872. Black. Serial # at top l. and r.	300.	600.	1000.
44	**1 Shilling** 7.3.1872.	325.	650.	1100.
45	**2 Shillings - 6 Pence** 1872.	350.	700.	1150.
46	**5 Shillings** 19.1.1872.	400.	750.	1400.
47	**10 Shillings** 187x.	425.	850.	1500.

De Nationale Bank der Zuid Afrikaansche Republiek Beperkt

1891-1926 Issue

#36-41 portr. Pres. Paul Kruger at l., arms at top ctr. r. Printer: CS&F. Wmk: Denomination.

		Good	Fine	X
48	**1 Pond** 1892-93. Black on blue unpt. Back blue.			
	a. Issued note.	400.	725.	125
	s. Pin hole cancelled: *SPECIMEN*, counterfoil at l.	—	Unc	100

NOTE: Practically all issued examples of #36a consist of two halves pasted together. Apparently they wer cut in half for shipment or cancellation.

		Good	Fine	X
49	**5 Pond** 189x. Black on lt. red unpt. Back lt. red.			
	a. Issued note.	450.	850.	145
	s. Specimen. Pin hole cancelled.	—	Unc	110
50	**10 Pond** 189x. Black on green unpt. Back green. Pin hole cancelled: *SPECIMEN.*			
	a. Issued note.	525.	975.	165
	s. Specimen.	—	Unc	120
51	**20 Pond** 189x. Black on lt. red unpt. Back lt. red. Pin hole cancelled: *SPECIMEN.*			
	a. Issued note.	650.	1200.	20
	s. Specimen.	—	Unc	15

		Good	Fine	
52	**50 Pond** 189x. Black on purple unpt. Back purple. Pin hole cancelled: *SPECIMEN.*			
	a. Issued note.	775.	1400.	25
	s. Specimen.	—	Unc	20
53	**100 Pond** 189x. Black on lt. brown unpt. Back lt. brown. Pin hole cancelled: *SPECIMEN.*			
	a. Issued note.	1300.	2400.	40
	s. Specimen.	—	Unc	30

ANGLO-BOER WAR

ZUID-AFRIKAANSCHE REPUBLIEK

GOUVERNEMENTS NOOT - GOVERNMENT NOTES

1900 ISSUE

Wartime Interest Bearing Notes

#42-47 greenish gray, arms at l., large embossed seal of the Republiek at l. Law text on back.

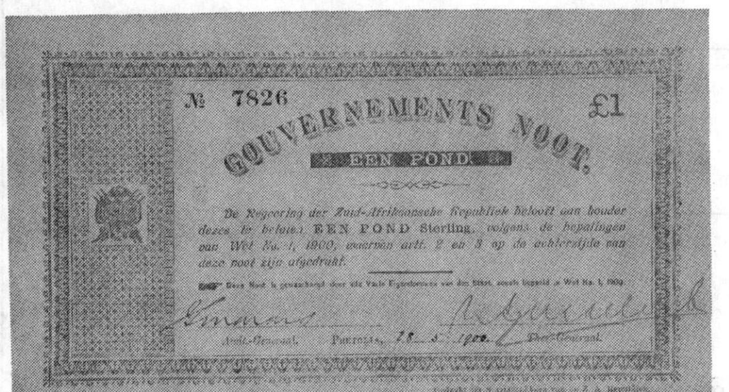

		Good	Fine	XF
54	**1 Pound**			
	28.5.1900.			
	a. Ornamental border at l. w/spikes pointing upwards. Rosette design under denomination. W/o *No.* by serial #.	10.00	25.00	70.00
	b. Ornamental border at l. w/stars and crosses. Less ornate design under denomination.	7.50	20.00	60.00
	c. Border and design like a. W/o *No.* by serial #.	7.00	17.50	55.00
55	**5 Pounds**			
	28.5.1900.			
	a. Ornamental border at l. w/spikes pointing upwards. Rosette design under denomination. W/*No.* by serial #.	12.00	40.00	120.
	b. Ornamental border at l. w/stars and crosses. Less ornate design under denomination.	15.00	45.00	140.
	c. Border and design like a. W/o *No.* by serial #.	13.00	42.00	125.
56	**10 Pounds**			
	28.5.1900.			
	a. Ornamental border at l. w/spikes pointing upward. Rosette design under denomination. W/*No.* by serial #.	20.00	55.00	180.
	b. Border and design like a. W/o *No.* by serial #.	25.00	60.00	200.

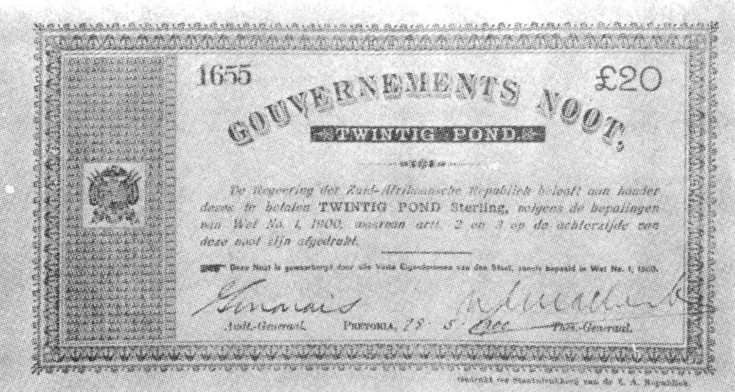

		Good	Fine	XF
57	**20 Pounds**			
	28.5.1900.			
	a. Ornamental border at l. w/spikes pointing upwards. Rosette design under denomination. W/*No.* by serial #.	25.00	80.00	225.
	b. Border and design like a. W/o *No.* by serial #.	30.00	85.00	250.
58	**50 Pounds**			
	28.5.1900. W/o *No.* by serial #.	25.00	150.	450.
59	**100 Pounds**			
	28.5.1900. W/o *No.* by serial #.	40.00	200.	500.

PIETERSBURG

1901 GOUVERNEMENTS NOOT

#48-53 arms at l., black print w/o large embossed seal.

		Good	Fine	XF
60	**1 Pound**			
	1901.			
	a. 1.2.1901.	12.50	30.00	100.
	b. 1.3.1901.	20.00	50.00	120.
	c. 1.4.1901.	10.00	25.00	90.00
61	**5 Pounds**			
	1901.			
	a. 1.2.1901.	22.50	50.00	135.
	b. 1.3.1901.	25.00	60.00	175.
	c. 1.4.1901.	20.00	45.00	125.

		Good	Fine	XF
62	**10 Pounds**			
	1.4.1901.			
	a. 1.3.1901.	35.00	75.00	250.
	b. 1.4.1901.	25.00	60.00	225.
63	**20 Pounds**			
	1.4.1901.	50.00	125.	325.
64	**50 Pounds**			
	1.4.1901.	135.	300.	650.

		Good	Fine	XF
65	**100 Pounds**			
	1.4.1901.	200.	450.	1000.

TE VELDE (IN THE FIELD)

1902 GOUVERNEMENTS NOOT

#54-56 black. Cruder arms at l.

		Good	Fine	XF
66	**1 Pound**			
	1.5.1902.	60.00	135.	300.
67	**10 Pounds**			
	1902.			
	a. 1.3.1902.	45.00	110.	250.
	b. 1.4.1902.	60.00	135.	380.
	c. 1.5.1902.	40.00	105.	245.
68	**20 Pounds**			
	1902.			
	a. 1.3.1902.	145.	250.	700.
	b. 1.4.1902.	90.00	200.	500.
	c. 1.5.1902.	60.00	135.	400.

NOTE: Cancelled notes w/oval handstamp: **CENTRAL JUDICIAL COMMISSION*/TRANSVAAL/31 JAN 1907* are known for some of the above issues; these are much scarcer than uncancelled examples.

UNION OF SOUTH AFRICA

After the Union came into being (1910), only six note issuing banks remained. The South African Reserve Bank was established in 1921 and received the exclusive note issuing privilege.

TREASURY

PRETORIA

1920 GOLD CERTIFICATE ISSUE

Issued in 1920 and circulated for only a short period. All notes have one side in English and the other in Afrikaans.

#69-73 arms at upper ctr. Wmk: *UNION/OF/SOUTH AFRICA* in wavy frame. Market values are for punched hole cancelled notes.

		VG	VF	UNC
69	**1 Pound**			
	L. 1920. Black.			
	a. Issued note - cancelled.	60.00	150.	350.
	s. Specimen.	—	—	1000.
70	**5 Pounds**			
	L. 1920. Black.			
	a. Issued note - cancelled.	65.00	170.	400.
	s. Specimen.	—	—	1000.

		VG	VF	UNC
71	**100 Pounds**			
	L. 1920. Black.			
	a. Issued note - cancelled.	90.00	300.	650.
	s. Specimen.	—	—	1000.
72	**1000 Pounds**			
	L. 1920. Black.			
	a. Issued note - cancelled.	115.	450.	900.
	s. Specimen.	—	—	1000.

		VG	VF	UNC
73	**10,000 Pounds**			
	L. 1920. Black.			
	a. Issued note - cancelled.	125.	500.	950.
	s. Specimen.	—	—	1000.

NOTICE
Readers with unlisted dates, signature varieties, etc. are invited to submit photocopies or, high resolution (300 dpi, 100% size) scans of their notes to: Standard Catalog of World Paper Money, 700 East State St. Iola, WI 54990-0001, or E-Mail: george.cuhaj@fwpubs.com.

SOUTH AFRICAN RESERVE BANK

	Governor	Term of Office
1	W.H. Clegg	17.12.1920-31.12.1931
2	Dr. J. Postmus	1.1.1932-30.6.1945
3	Dr. M.H. de Kock	1.7.1945-30.6.1962

1921-26 ISSUES

#74-78 sign. W. H. Clegg.

		VG	VF	UNC
74	**10 Shillings** 30.11.1921-31.1.1922. Blue. Wmk: Mercury head l. Back green and purple. Sign. W.H. Clegg. Printer: BWC.	180.	600.	1500.

#75-78 sailing ship at l. Wmk: van Riebeek portrait #1. Printer: St. Lukes Printing Works.

		VG	VF	UNC
75	**1 Pound** 17.9.1921-5.7.1922. Black on red unpt. Sailing ship on back. Sign. W.H. Clegg.	55.00	250.	700.
76	**5 Pounds** 27.9.1921-6.7.1922. Green and brown. Sign. W.H. Clegg.	85.00	325.	1000.
77	**20 Pounds** 29.9.1921. Blue. Sign. W.H. Clegg.	200.	800.	2800.
78	**100 Pounds** 30.9.1921. Red-brown. Sign. W.H. Clegg.	1100.	3500.	7000.

1925-28 ISSUES

		VG	VF	UNC
79	**10 Shillings** 20.9.1926-15.12.1926. Dk. brown on pink and pale green unpt. Wmk: Sailing ship and portr. J. van Riebeeck. Sign. W.H. Clegg.	135.	375.	1100.
80	**1 Pound** 1.9.1925-4.4.1928. Dk. brown. Sailing ship at l. Sign. W.H. Clegg.	75.00	300.	900.
81	**5 Pounds** 7.4.1926. Dk. green and brown. New type. Wmk: van Riebeeck only. Sign. W.H. Clegg.	150.	500.	1350.

1928-47 ISSUES

		VG	VF	UNC
82	**10 Shillings**			
	1928-47. Like #79 but English and Afrikaans text. Wmk: Sailing ship and portr. J. van Riebeeck.			
	a. Sign. W. H. Clegg. 1.9.1928-9.9.1931.	95.00	250.	700.
	b. Sign. W. H. Clegg. Date ovpt: 17.11.1931/2.4.1932. Prefixed E/12.	155.	425.	1100.
	c. Sign. W. H. Clegg. 17.11.1931. Prefix E/12.	300.	775.	2100.
	d. Sign. J. Postmus. 12.9.1932-4.4.1945.	15.00	50.00	155.
	e. Sign. Dr. M H. de Kock. 5.9.1945-14.11.1947.	15.00	40.00	140.
83	**1 Pound** 1.9.1928. Dk. brown. Like #80 but altered design on back. English and Dutch text. Sign. W.H. Clegg.	80.00	375.	1100.

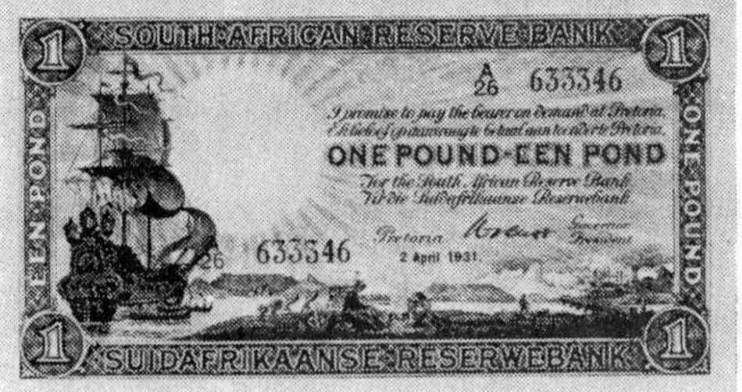

No.	Description	VG	VF	UNC
84	**1 Pound**			
	1928-49. Dk. brown. Like #83 but English and Afrikaans text.			
	a. Sign. W. M. Clegg. Dutch microprinted background. 3.12.1928-30.11.1929.	50.00	150.	450.
	b. Sign. W.H. Clegg. Afrikaans microprinted background. 30.4.1930-30.11.1931.	40.00	110.	350.
	c. Sign. Dr. J. Postmus. 5.9.1932-30.4.1938.	6.50	20.00	90.00
	d. Sign. Dr. J. Postmus. Paper w/metal thread (only series A78). 19.9.1938.	70.00	250.	900.
	e. Sign. Dr. J. Postmus. 20.9.1938-22.11.1944.	6.00	18.00	80.00
	f. Sign. Dr. M. H. de Kock. 5.9.1945-14.11.1947.	5.00	17.00	75.00
35	**5 Pounds**			
	2.4.1928. Like #82 but altered design on back. English and Dutch text. Sign. Dr. J. Postmus.	125.	350.	1100.
36	**5 Pounds**			
	1929-47. Like #85 but English and Afrikaans text.			
	a. Sign. W. H. Clegg. 2.9.1929-17.4.1931.	50.00	165.	450.
	b. Sign. J. Postmus. 1.9.1933-4.4.1944.	15.00	50.00	140.
	c. Sign. Dr. M. H. de Kock. 6.4.1946-12.11.1947.	15.00	60.00	175.

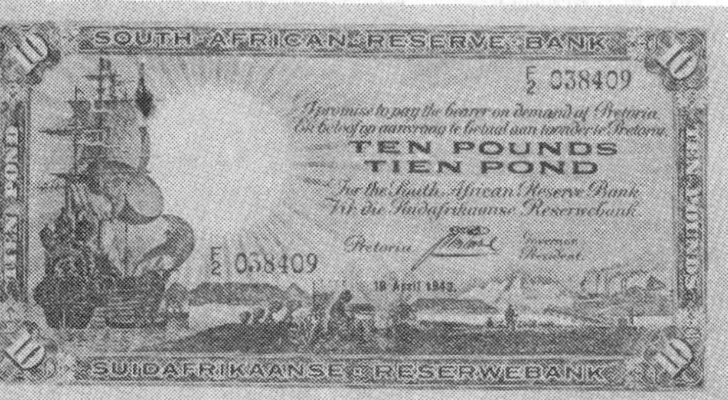

No.	Description	VG	VF	UNC
7	**10 Pounds**			
	14.4.1943; 19.4.1943. Brown. Sailing ship at l. Sign. Dr. J. Postmus.	27.50	65.00	200.
8	**20 Pounds**			
	1928; 1943. Blue. New type.			
	a. Sign. W. H. Clegg. 3.9.1928.	175.	650.	2300.
	b. Sign. Dr. J. Postmus. 4.9.1943.	120.	500.	1500.
9	**100 Pounds**			
	1928; 1933. Brown. New type.			
	a. Sign. W. H. Clegg. 4.9.1928.	900.	3000.	6000.
	b. Sign. Dr. J. Postmus. 8.9.1933.	550.	2400.	4250.

948-59 ISSUES

No.	Description	VG	VF	UNC
0	**10 Shillings**			
	1948-59. Brown. Portr. Jan van Riebeeck at l., first lines of bank name and value in English. Sign. Dr. M. H. de Kock.			
	a. Date w/name of month. 10.4.1948-21.4.1949.	8.50	30.00	95.00
	b. Date w/name of month. Melamine treated paper. 1.4.1950-30.11.1951.	13.00	35.00	85.00
	c. Date w/month by #. 1.12.1951-18.2.1959.	4.50	20.00	75.00
	10 Shillings			
	1948-59. Like #90 but first line of bank name and value in Afrikaans. Sign. Dr. M. H. de Kock.			
	a. Date w/name of month. 10.4.1948-21.4.1949.	8.50	30.00	95.00
	b. Date w/name of month, thick paper. Series A21. 22.4.1949.	105.	280.	740.
	c. Date w/name of month. Melamine treated paper. 1.4.1950-30.11.1951.	13.00	35.00	85.00
	d. Date w/month by #. 1.2.1951-18.2.1959.	4.50	20.00	75.00

No.	Description	VG	VF	UNC
	1 Pound			
	1948-59. Blue. Portr. Jan van Riebeeck at l.; first line of bank name and value in English. Sign. Dr. M. H. de Kock.			
	a. Date w/name of month. 1.9.1949-9.4.1949.	4.50	18.00	65.00
	b. Date w/name of month. 16.4.1949-3.11.1949.	8.00	23.00	75.00
	c. Date w/name of month. Melamine treated paper. 1.4.1950-30.11.1951.	5.00	15.00	50.00
	d. Date w/month by #. 1.12.1951-26.6.1959.	3.00	10.00	45.00
	1 Pound			
	1948-59. Like #92 but first line of bank name and value in Afrikaans. Sign. Dr. M. H. de Kock.			
	a. Date w/name of month. 1.9.1949-9.4.1949.	4.50	18.00	65.00
	b. Date w/name of month. Thick paper. Series B28. 12.4.1949.	100.	265.	700.
	c. Date w/name of month. 16.4.1949-3.11.1949.	8.00	23.00	75.00
	d. Date w/name of month. Melamine treated paper. 1.4.1950-30.11.1951.	5.00	15.00	50.00
	e. Date w/month by #. 1.12.1951-26.6.1959.	3.00	10.00	45.00

No.	Description	VG	VF	UNC
94	**5 Pounds**			
	1.11.1948-13.4.1949. Light green. Portr. Jan van Riebeeck at l., first line of bank name and value in English. 163 x 90mm. Sign. Dr. M. H. de Kock.	10.00	35.00	130.
95	**5 Pounds**			
	1.11.1948-13.4.1949. Light green. Like #94 but first line of bank name and value in Afrikaans. 163 x 90mm. Sign. Dr. M. H. de Kock.	12.50	36.00	115.
96	**5 Pounds**			
	1950-59. Dk. green. Like #94; first line of bank name and value in English. 171 x 97mm. Sign. Dr. M. H. de Kock.			
	a. Date w/name of month. 3.4.1950-22.4.1952.	8.00	25.00	80.00
	b. Date w/month by #. 2.1.1953-31.1.1953.	5.00	18.00	65.00
	c. Date w/month by #. Melamine treated paper. 8.2.1954-18.6.1959.	4.00	14.00	50.00
97	**5 Pounds**			
	1950-59. Dk green. Like #96 but first line of bank name and value in Afrikaans. 171 x 97mm. Sign. Dr. M. H. de Kock.			
	a. Date w/name of month. 3.4.1950-22.4.1952.	8.00	25.00	80.00
	b. Date w/month by #. 2.1.1953-31.1.1953.	5.00	18.00	65.00
	c. Date w/month by #. Melamine treated paper. 8.2.1954-18.6.1959.	4.00	14.00	50.00
98	**10 Pounds**			
	18.12.1952-19.11.1958. Brown-violet. Portr. Jan van Riebeeck at l. First line of bank name and value in English. Sign. Dr. M. H. de Kock.	15.00	50.00	175.
99	**10 Pounds**			
	18.12.1952-19.11.1958. Brown-violet. Like #98 but first line of bank name and value in Afrikaans. Sign. Dr. M. H. de Kock.	15.00	50.00	175.

No.	Description	VG	VF	UNC
100	**100 Pounds**			
	29.1.1952. Blue and m/c. Portr. Jan van Riebeeck at l., sailing ship at r. First line of bank name and value in English. Sign. Dr. M. H. de Kock.			
	a. Date w/month by #. 29.1.1952.	175.	775.	2000.
	b. Perforated: *CANCELLED.*	150.	500.	1500.
101	**100 Pounds**			
	29.1.1952. Blue and m/c. Like #100 but first line of bank name and value in Afrikaans. Sign. Dr. M. H. de Kock.			
	a. Date w/month by #. 29.1.1952.	175.	775.	2000.
	b. Perforated: *CANCELLED.*	150.	500.	1500.

Note: For issues similar to #98-101 but in Rand values, see Volume 3, Modern Issues.

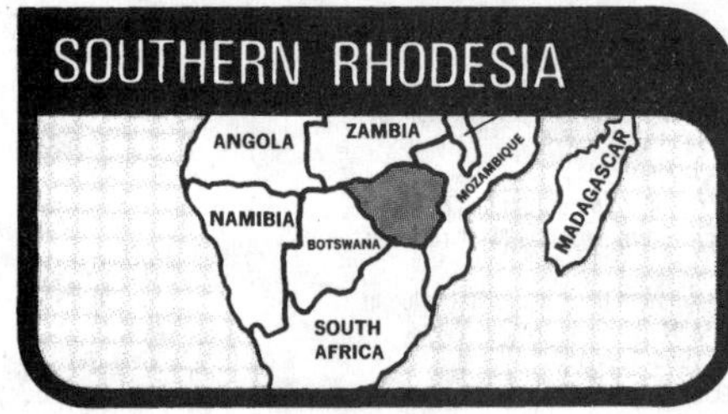

Southern Rhodesia (now Zimbabwe), located in the east-central part of southern Africa, has an area of 150,804 sq. mi. (390,580 sq. km.) and a population of 10.1 million. Capital: Salisbury. The economy is d on agriculture and mining. Tobacco, sugar, asbestos, copper and chrome ore and coal are exported.

The Rhodesian area, the habitat of paleolithic man, contains extensive evidence of earlier civilizations, notably the world-famous ruins of Zimbabwe, a gold-trading center that flourished about the 14th or 15th century AD. The Portuguese of the 16th century were the first Europeans to attempt to develop south-central Africa, but it remained for Cecil Rhodes and the British South Africa Co. to open the hinterlands. Rhodes obtained a concession for mineral rights from local chiefs in 1888 and administered his African empire (named Southern Rhodesia in 1895) through the British South Africa Co. until 1923, when the British government annexed the area after the white settlers voted for existence as a separate entity, rather than for incorporation into the Union of South Africa. From September of 1953 through 1963 Southern Rhodesia was joined with the British protectorates of Northern Rhodesia and Nyasaland into a multiracial federation. When the federation was dissolved at the end of 1963, Northern Rhodesia and Nyasaland became the independent states of Zambia and Malawi.

Britain was prepared to grant independence to Southern Rhodesia but declined to do so when the politically dominant white Rhodesians refused to give assurances of representative government. On May 11, 1965, following two years of unsuccessful negotiation with the British government, Prime Minister Ian Smith issued a unilateral declaration of independence. Britain responded with economic sanctions supported by the United Nations. After further futile attempts to effect an accommodation, the Rhodesian Parliament severed all ties with Britain, and on March 2, 1970, established the Republic of Rhodesia.

On March 3, 1978, Prime Minister Ian Smith and three moderate black nationalist leaders signed an agreement providing for black majority rule. The name of the country was changed to Zimbabwe Rhodesia.

After the election of March 3, 1980, the country changed its name again and became the Republic of Zimbabwe.

Also see Rhodesia, Rhodesia and Nyasaland, and Zimbabwe.

RULERS:

British to 1970

MONETARY SYSTEM:

1 Shilling = 12 Pence
1 Pound = 20 Shillings to 1970

BRITISH ADMINISTRATION

SOUTHERN RHODESIA CURRENCY BOARD

	Chairman Signature
1	A.W. Bessle
2	E.T. Fox
3	A.H. Strachan
4	Gordon Munro
5	Sir A.P. Grafftey-Smith

1939-52 ISSUES

#8-11 portr. Kg. George VI at r. Various date and sign. varieties. Printer: BWC.

8	**5 Shillings**	VG	VF	UNC
	1943; 1945; 1948. Purple.			
	a. Sign. A. W. Bessle. 89 x 57mm. 1.1.1943.	35.00	150.	600.
	b. Sign. E. T. Fox. 114 x 70mm. 1.2.1945; 1.10.1945; 1.1.1948.	30.00	110.	375.

9	**10 Shillings**	VG	VF	UNC
	1939-51. Brown and m/c. Sable at l., Victoria Falls at ctr. on back.			
	a. Sign. A. W. Bessle. Small prefix letters. 15.12.1939; 1.7.1942.	55.00	175.	650.
	b. Sign. A. W. Bessle. Intermediate prefix letters. 1.3.1944.	65.00	225.	700.
	c. Sign. E. T. Fox. Intermediate prefix letters. 1.2.1945; 15.3.1946; 15.1.1947.	55.00	200.	625.
	d. Sign. E. T. Fox. Large prefix letters. 1.1.1948.	65.00	200.	600.
	e. Sign. A. H. Strachan. 10.1.1950.	50.00	150.	450.
	f. Sign. Gordon Munro. 1.9.1950; 1.9.1951.	60.00	185.	550.

10	**1 Pound**			
	1939-51. Green and m/c. Sable at l., Zimbabwe ruins at ctr. on back.			
	a. Sign. A. W. Bessle. Small prefix letters. 15.12.1939; 1.7.1942.	60.00	175.	525.
	b. Sign. A. W. Bessle. Intermediate prefix letters. 1.3.1944.	60.00	185.	550.
	c. Sign. E. T. Fox. Intermediate prefix letters. 1.2.1945; 1.10.1945; 15.1.1947.	55.00	160.	475.
	d. Sign. E. T. Fox. Large prefix letters. 1.1.1948.	60.00	175.	525.
	e. Sign. A. H. Strachan. 10.1.1950.	60.00	175.	525.
	f. Sign. Gordon Munro. 1.9.1950; 1.9.1951.	45.00	135.	400.

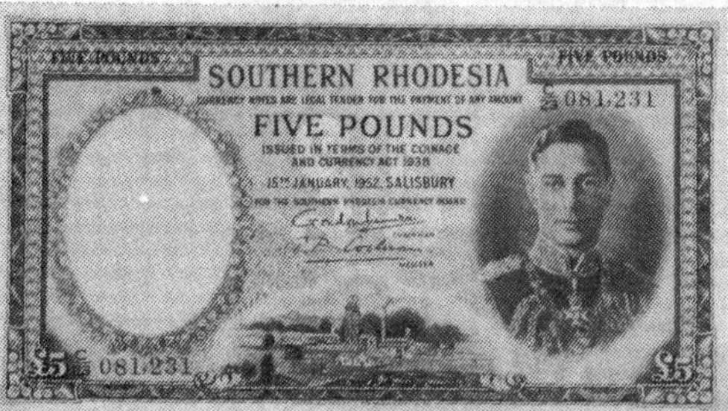

11	**5 Pounds**	VG	VF	UNC
	1939-52. Blue, brown and m/c. Factory at lower ctr. Sable at l., Victoria Falls at ctr. on back.			
	a. Sign. A. W. Bessle. W/o white *£5* in unpt. on face. 15.12.1939; 1.7.1942.	100.	300.	900.
	b. Sign. A. W. Bessle. White *£5* in unpt. on face. 1.3.1944; 1.2.1945.	75.00	225.	700.
	c. Sign. E. T. Fox. Intermediate prefix letters. 1.10.1945; 15.3.1946; 15.1.1947; 1.11.1947.	100.	300.	900.
	d. Sign. E. T. Fox. Large prefix letters. 1.1.1948.	100.	325.	950.
	e. Sign. A. H. Strachan. 10.1.1950.	100.	300.	950.
	f. Sign. Gordon Munro. 1.9.1950; 1.9.1951.	100.	275.	850.
	g. Sign. Gordon Munro. Sign. title: *CHAIRMAN* above *MEMBER.* 15.2.1952.	100.	300.	900.

1952-54 ISSUE

#12-15 portr. Qn. Elizabeth II at r. *SOUTHERN RHODESIA CURRENCY BOARD* in text. Chairman sign. 5. Printer: BWC.

12	**10 Shillings**	VG	VF	UNC
	1952-53. Brown and m/c. Back like #9; sable at l., Victoria Falls at ctr.			
	a. 1.12.1952.	65.00	220.	950.
	b. 3.1.1953.	60.00	200.	600.

		VG	VF	UNC
13	**1 Pound** 1952-54. Green and m/c. Back like #10; sable at l., Zimbabwe ruins at ctr.			
	a. 1.12.1952.	60.00	200.	575.
	b. 3.1.1953.	55.00	175.	550.
	c. 10.3.1954.	50.00	150.	500.
14	**5 Pounds** 1953-54. Blue and m/c. Back like #11; sable at l., Victoria Falls at ctr.			
	a. 1.1.1953.	150.	475.	—
	b. 15.4.1953. Reported not confirmed.	—	—	—
	c. 10.3.1954.	135.	450.	—
15	**10 Pounds** 15.4.1953; 10.3.1954. Brown and m/c.			
	a. 15.4.1953.	600.	1800.	—
	b. 10.3.1954.	700.	2000.	—

CENTRAL AFRICA CURRENCY BOARD

1955 ISSUE

#16-19 Qn. Elizabeth II at r. *CENTRAL AFRICA CURRENCY BOARD* in text. Chairman sign. 5. Printer: BWC.

		VG	VF	UNC
16	**10 Shillings** 10.9.1955. Brown and m/c. Like #12.	40.00	225.	575.
17	**1 Pound** 10.9.1955. Green and m/c. Like #13.	30.00	180.	550.
18	**5 Pounds** 10.9.1955. Blue and m/c. Like #14.	100.	550.	1300.
19	**10 Pounds** 10.9.1955. Brown and m/c. Like #15. Reported not confirmed.	—	—	—

Southwest Africa (now the Republic of Namibia), the former German territory of German Southwest Africa, is situated on the Atlantic coast of southern Africa, bounded on the north by Angola, on the east by Botswana, and on the south by South Africa. It has an area of 318,261 sq. mi. (824,290 sq. km.) and a population of 1.4 million. Capital: Windhoek. Diamonds, copper, lead, zinc and cattle are exported.

South Africa undertook the administration of Southwest Africa under the terms of a League of Nations mandate on Dec. 17, 1920. When the League of Nations was dissolved in 1946, its supervisory authority for Southwest Africa was inherited by the United Nations. In 1946 the UN denied South Africa's request to annex Southwest Africa. South Africa responded by refusing to place the territory under a UN trusteeship. In 1950 the International Court of Justice ruled that South Africa could not unilaterally modify the international status of South West Africa. A 1966 UN resolution declaring the mandate terminated was rejected by South Africa, and the status of the area remained in dispute. In June 1968 the UN General Assembly voted to rename the country Namibia. It became a republic in March 1990.

Notes of the three emission banks circulated until 1963 and were then replaced by notes of the Republic of South Africa.

Also see German Southwest Africa and Namibia.

MONETARY SYSTEM:
1 Shilling = 12 Pence
1 Pound = 20 Shillings to 1961

SOUTH AFRICAN ADMINISTRATION

BARCLAYS BANK (DOMINION, COLONIAL AND OVERSEAS)

1931 ISSUE

#1-3 *DOMINION, COLONIAL AND OVERSEAS* in title. Sheep at l. Bank arms at ctr. on back. Printer: W&S.

		Good	Fine	XF
1	**10 Shillings** 1931-54. Red on m/c unpt.			
	a. 1.6.1931.	175.	375.	750.
	b. 1.5.1943; 1.4.1949.	65.00	125.	350.
	c. 2.1.1951; 31.7.1954	50.00	100.	300.
	d. Punched hole cancelled. 31.7.1954.	20.00	50.00	—

		Good	Fine	XF
2	**1 Pound** 1931-54. Dk. blue on green m/c unpt.			
	a. 1.6.1931.	225.	550.	—
	b. 1.10.1938; 1.11.1939.	110.	250.	600.
	c. 1.11.1943; 1.4.1949.	65.00	125.	400.
	d. 2.1.1951; 29.11.1952; 31.1.1954.	40.00	100.	300.
3	**5 Pounds** 1931-54. Dk. green on red and m/c unpt.			
	a. 1.6.1931.	275.	650.	—
	b. 1.7.1944; 1.4.1949.	165.	350.	850.
	c. 2.1.1951; 31.1.1954.	125.	300.	700.
	d. Punched hole and perforated: *CANCELLED*. 1.4.1949.	75.00	150.	—

BARCLAYS BANK D.C.O.

1954 ISSUE

#4-6 shortened bank title ending *D.C.O.* 3 sheep at l. Bank arms at lower ctr. on back. Printer: W&S.

		Good	Fine	XF
4	**10 Shillings**			
	1954-58. Red on m/c unpt.			
	a. Date in red w/*No.* before serial #. 30.11.1954; 1.9.1956.	40.00	125.	350.
	b. Date in black, w/o *No.* before serial #. 29.11.1958.	35.00	100.	325.
5	**1 Pound**			
	1954-58. Dk. blue on green and m/c unpt.			
	a. Date in blue w/o *No.* before serial #. 30.11.1954; 1.9.1956.	45.00	150.	400.
	b. Date in black, w/o *No.* before serial #. 29.11.1958.	40.00	125.	350.
	c. Punched hole cancelled. 29.11.1958.	20.00	50.00	—

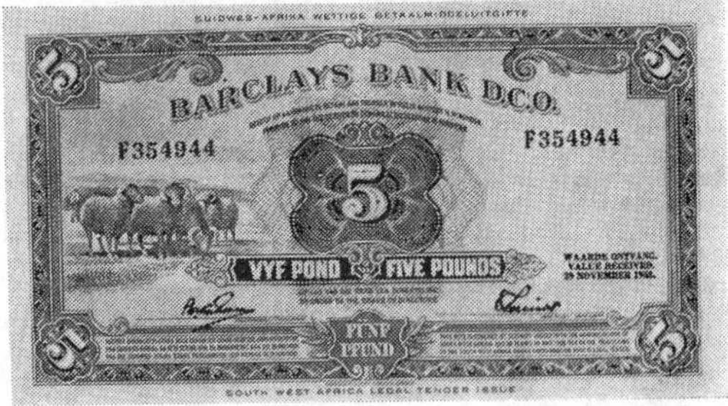

		Good	Fine	XF
6	**5 Pounds**			
	1954-58. Dk. green on red and m/c unpt.			
	a. Date in green w/*No.* before serial #. 30.11.1954; 1.9.1956.	110.	250.	550.
	b. Date in black, w/o *No.* before serial #. 29.11.1958.	100.	200.	450.
	c. Punched hole cancelled. 30.11.1954.	50.00	100.	—

STANDARD BANK OF SOUTH AFRICA LIMITED

1931 ISSUE

#7-9 waterfalls at r. Kudu, mountains at l. ctr. on back. Various date and sign. varieties. Sign. in color. Windhoek. Printer: W&S.

		Good	Fine	XF
7	**10 Shillings**			
	1931-53. Green on m/c unpt. *TEN-TIEN SHILLINGS* at ctr.			
	a. 31.10.1931; 17.4.1936.	175.	375.	750.
	b. 2.4.1940; 31.3.1942; 22.4.1943.	65.00	125.	350.
	c. 9.2.1945-4.10.1954.	50.00	100.	300.

#8 and 9 sheep under tree at l.

		Good	Fine	XF
8	**1 Pound**			
	1931-54. Orange on green and m/c unpt.			
	a. 31.10.1931.	225.	550.	—
	b. 11.1.1938; 2.4.1940; 2.5.1941; 31.3.1942; 1.10.1943; 5.8.1947; 9.8.1948.	65.00	150.	375.
	c. 6.2.1950-4.10.1954.	50.00	100.	300.
	d. Punched hole cancelled. 9.8.1948; 6.2.1950; 25.6.1951.	20.00	50.00	—
9	**5 Pounds**			
	1931-53. Carmine on green and m/c unpt.			
	a. 31.10.1931.	275.	650.	—
	b. 1933-9.2.1945.	175.	375.	875.
	c. 6.2.1950; 25.6.1951; 21.9.1953.	125.	300.	625.
	d. Punched hole cancelled. 6.2.1950.	60.00	150.	—

STANDARD BANK OF SOUTH AFRICA LIMITED

1954; 1955 ISSUE

#10-12 like #7-9. Various date and sign. varieties. Sign in black.

		Good	Fine	XF
10	**10 Shillings**			
	4.10.1954; 16.9.1955; 31.1.1958; 15.6.1959. Green on m/c unpt. Similar to #7, but value: *TEN SHILLINGS/TIEN SJIELINGS* at ctr.	50.00	100.	275.

		Good	Fine	XF
11	**1 Pound**			
	16.9.1955-15.6.1959. Orange on green and m/c unpt. Like #8.	65.00	125.	350.

		Good	Fine	XF
12	**5 Pounds**			
	1954-58. Carmine and green on m/c unpt. Kudu on back. Like #9.			
	a. 4.10.1954; 16.9.1955.	120.	250.	600.
	b. 1.9.1957; 1.5.1958; 20.11.1958.	110.	225.	550.

VOLKSKAS LIMITED

1949 ISSUE

#13-15 various date and sign. varieties. Printer: W&S.

		Good	Fine	XF
13	**10 Shillings**			
	1949-58. Blue on green and tan unpt. Scattered bldgs. w/mountains in background.			
	a. 1.6.1949; 4.6.1952.	90.00	200.	475
	b. 1.9.1958.	60.00	125.	375

		Good	Fine	XF
14	**1 Pound**			
	1949-58. Brown. Village scene at l. ctr.			
	a. 1.6.1949; 17.4.1951; 4.6.1952.	100.	225.	625
	b. 1.9.1958.	75.00	150.	425
15	**5 Pounds**			
	1949-59. Brown. Waterfall at l. Gemsbok on back.			
	a. 1.6.1949; 4.6.1952.	200.	450.	975
	b. 1.9.1958; 1.9.1959.	140.	400.	775

The Spanish State, forming the greater part of the Iberian Peninsula of southwest Europe, has an area of 194,884 sq. mi. (504,750 sq. km.) and a population of 40.5 million including the Balearic and the Canary Islands. Capital: Madrid. The economy is d on agriculture, industry and tourism. Machinery, fruit, vegetables and chemicals are exported.

It is not known when man first came to the Iberian Peninsula - the Altamira caves off the Cantabrian coast approximately 50 miles west of Santander were fashioned in Paleolithic times. Spain was a battleground for centuries before it became a united nation, fought for by Phoenicians, Carthaginians, Greeks, Celts, Romans, Vandals, Visigoths and Moors. Ferdinand and Isabella destroyed the last Moorish stronghold in 1492, freeing the national energy and resources for the era of discovery and colonization that would make Spain the most powerful country in Europe during the 16th century. After the destruction of the Spanish Armada, 1588, Spain never again played a major role in European politics. Napoleonic France ruled Spain between 1808 and 1814. The monarchy was restored in 1814 and continued, interrupted by the short-lived republic of 1873-74, until the exile of Alfonso XIII in 1931, when the Second Republic was established. A bloody civil war ensued in 1936, and Francisco Franco established himself as ruler of fascist Spain after his forces, aided by the Italians and especially the Germans, defeated the Republican forces.

The monarchy was reconstituted in 1947 under the regency of General Francisco Franco, the king designate to be crowned after Franco's death. Franco died on Nov. 30, 1975. Two days after his passing, Juan Carlos de Borbón, the grandson of Alfonso XIII, was proclaimed King of Spain.

RULERS:

Fernando VII, 1808-1833
Isabel II, 1833-1868
Amadeo I, 1871-1873
Regency, 1874
Alfonso XII, 1875-1885
Alfonso XIII, 1886-1931
2nd Republic and Civil War, 1932-1936
Francisco Franco, regent, 1937-1975
Juan Carlos I, 1975-

MONETARY SYSTEM:

1 Peseta = 100 Centimos 1874-2001
1 Euro = 100 Cents, 2002-

REPLACEMENT NOTES:

#150 and later, *9A, 9B, 9C* type prefix.

FIRST REPUBLIC, 1873-74

BANCO DE ESPAÑA

1874 ISSUE

		Good	Fine	XF
1	**25 Pesetas** 1.7.1874. Gray and cream. Bearers at l. and r. of ctr. Rare.	—	—	—

		Good	Fine	XF
2	**50 Pesetas** 1.7.1874. Black and chestnut. D. Martinez at l. Rare.	—	—	—

		Good	Fine	XF
3	**100 Pesetas** 1.7.1874. Ochre and black. Juan de Herrera at l., El Escorial Monastery at ctr. Rare.	—	—	—

		Good	Fine	XF
4	**500 Pesetas** 1.7.1874. Black and cream. Woman seated at l., Francisco de Goya at r. Rare.	—	—	—
5	**1000 Pesetas** 1.7.1874. Black and cream. Minerva at l., Alonso Cana at r. Rare.	—	—	—

KINGDOM

BANCO DE ESPAÑA

1875 ISSUE

#6-10 printer: Sanders (w/o imprint).

		Good	Fine	XF
6	**25 Pesetas** 1.1.1875. Black on lilac unpt. Woman at l.	850.	2000.	—

		Good	Fine	XF
7	**50 Pesetas** 1.1.1875. Gray, green and salmon. Women leaning against arms at top ctr., woman at bottom ctr., children at upper l. and r., lions at lower l. and r. Rare.	—	—	—

		Good	Fine	XF
8	**100 Pesetas** 1.1.1875. Gray, green and orange. Woman by castle at l., woman at r. Rare.	—	—	—

#		Good	Fine	XF
9	**500 Pesetas** 1.1.1875. Gray and blue. Women at l. and r. Rare.	—	—	—

#		Good	Fine	XF
10	**1000 Pesetas** 1.1.1875. Gray and brown. Woman w/shield and spear at l., woman at r. Rare.	—	—	—

1876 Issue

#11-13 Lope de Vega at l. Printer: ABNC.

#		Good	Fine	XF
11	**100 Pesetas** 1.7.1876. Black on m/c unpt. Woman w/children at ctr., woman seated at r. Back dk. brown; ship at l. and r., allegorical woman at ctr.	1250.	3000.	—
12	**500 Pesetas** 1.7.1876. Black on m/c unpt. Woman reclining w/children at top ctr., woman at lower r. Back red-brown; steam train at ctr.	1200.	2500.	—

#		Good	Fine	XF
13	**1000 Pesetas** 1.7.1876. Black on m/c unpt. Spaniard w/Indian maiden at ctr., Liberty at lower r. Back brown; allegorical women at l. and r., two allegorical women at ctr.	2000.	4000.	—

1878 Issue

#		Good	Fine	XF
14	**50 Pesetas** 1.1.1878. Gray and black. Pedro Calderón de la Barca at r.	1000.	2000.	—

#		Good	Fine	XF
15	**100 Pesetas** 1.1.1878. Ochre and gray. Garcilaso de la Vega at l., woman w/laureate at r.	1300.	3000.	—

#16 not assigned.

#		Good	Fine	XF
17	**250 Pesetas** 1.1.1878. Orange and gray. F. de Herrera at l.	1400.	4000.	—
18	**500 Pesetas** 1.1.1878. Cream and gray-black. P. de Cespedes at l., woman w/helmet at r.	1600.	4250.	—
19	**1000 Pesetas** 1.1.1878. Green and black. Miguel de Cervantes at l., rider on donkey at ctr.	2200.	5000.	—

1880 Issue

#		Good	Fine	XF
20	**50 Pesetas** 1.4.1880. Rose and gray-green. Count de Campomanes at l.	1200.	2000.	

#		Good	Fine
21	**100 Pesetas** 1.4.1880. Green and orange. Francisco de Quevedo at l., woman w/laureate at r.	1400.	2600.

22 500 Pesetas — Good 1400. Fine 2800. XF —
1.4.1880. Chestnut and ochre. Claudio Coello at l.

23 1000 Pesetas — Good 2200. Fine 4300. XF —
1.4.1880. Green and black. Bartolomé Murillo at l.

1884 First Issue

#24-28 printer: ABNC.

24 25 Pesetas — Good 250. Fine 450. XF 800.
1.1.1884. Red and black. Woman w/2 children at ctr. Back orange; arms at ctr.

#25-27 portr. Juan Alvarez de Mendizábal at r.

25 50 Pesetas — Good 200. Fine 500. XF 900.
1.1.1884. Black on green unpt. Woman seated by globe at l. Back green; woman and eagle at ctr.

26 100 Pesetas — Good 275. Fine 550. XF 950.
1.1.1884. Black on orange unpt. Cherubs at ctr. Back orange.

27 500 Pesetas — Good 800. Fine 1500. XF 3000.
1.1.1884. Black on ochre unpt. Woman w/sword at l., cherub at ctr. Back ochre; arms at ctr.

28 1000 Pesetas — Good 1250. Fine 2500. XF 4500.
1.1.1884. Black on orange unpt. Woman bearer at l., Portr. Mendizábal at ctr., woman standing at r. Back brown; dog and safe at ctr.

1884 Second Issue

29 25 Pesetas — Good 375. Fine 750. XF 1200.
1.7.1884. Ochre and black. Portr. R. de Santillan at ctr.

30 50 Pesetas — Good 350. Fine 600. XF 1100.
1.7.1884. Black on tan unpt. Portr. Bartolomé Murillo at ctr. Back

31 100 Pesetas — Good 250. Fine 500. XF 1000.
1.7.1884. Black on lt. tan unpt. Portr. A. Mon at top ctr. Back green; old locomotive at ctr.

32 500 Pesetas — Good 1250. Fine 2500. XF 3600.
1.7.1884. Black, chestnut and green. Girl w/dog at l., portr. Count de Floridablanca at r.

33 1000 Pesetas — Good 1600. Fine 3250. XF 5000.
1.7.1884. Green and black. Portr. Marqués de la Ensenada at l., women at r., one holding sheaf and sickle.

1886 Issue

		Good	Fine	XF
34	**25 Pesetas** 1.10.1886. Black on pale gold unpt. Francisco de Goya at ctr. Back red.	150.	500.	900.

		Good	Fine	XF
35	**50 Pesetas** 1.10.1886. Chestnut. Woman w/child at l., Francisco de Goya at r.	350.	700.	1250.
36	**100 Pesetas** 1.10.1886. Chestnut. Man standing at l., Francisco de Goya at r.	225.	550.	1300.
37	**500 Pesetas** 1.10.1886. Ochre and black. Francisco de Goya at l., woman seated at r.	700.	1600.	4000.

		Good	Fine	XF
38	**1000 Pesetas** 1.10.1886. Yellow and black. Woman seated w/harp at l. Francisco de Goya seated behind table at r.	1250.	2500.	6000.

1889 Issue

#39-41 back designs different from previous issue.

		Good	Fine	XF
39	**25 Pesetas** 1.6.1889. Black on gold unpt. Similar to #34. Back brown; Creso at ctr.	175.	350.	700.
40	**50 Pesetas** 1.6.1889. Black on yellow unpt. Similar to #35. Back green; 2 cherubs.	300.	550.	900.
41	**100 Pesetas** 1.6.1889. Black on yellow unpt. Similar to #36. Back brown; woman and cherub at ctr.	125.	250.	600.

1893 Issue

#42-44 portr. Jovellanos at l.

		Good	Fine	XF
42	**25 Pesetas** 24.7.1893. Blue and yellow. Medallion at ctr., standing figure at r. on back.	125.	225.	525.
43	**50 Pesetas** 24.7.1893. Black on yellow unpt. Seated woman at r. w/sword across lap. Back green; cherubs and winged head at ctr.	200.	350.	625.

		Good	Fine	XF
44	**100 Pesetas** 24.7.1893. Blue on pale yellow unpt. Back brown; heads at l. and r.	150.	350.	625.

1895 Issue

		Good	Fine	XF
45	**1000 Pesetas** 1.5.1895. Black on lt. tan unpt. El Conde Francisco de Cabarrus at l. w/child leaning on frame. Back brown; Kg. Carlos III and lion.	175.	375.	800.

1898 Issue

		VG	VF	UNC
46	**5 Pesetas** 1898. Qn. Isabel la Católica at l. Back proof. (Not issued).			

		Good	Fine	XF
47	**50 Pesetas** 2.1.1898. Black and yellow. Gaspar Melchior Jovellanos at l., helmeted woman at r.	150.	300.	600.
48	**100 Pesetas** 24.6.1898. Blue and yellow. Gaspar Melchior Jovellanos at l.	90.00	200.	500.

1899 Issue

		Good	Fine	XF
49	**25 Pesetas** 17.5.1899. Blue on pale green unpt. Francisco de Quevedo at l. Back brown; head at ctr., Mercury at r.	90.00	200.	500.
50	**50 Pesetas** 25.11.1899. Black on pale green unpt. Francisco de Quevedo at l., statue of man at r. Back green; woman reclining at l., man at r.	130.	300.	550.

1900 Issue

		Good	Fine	XF
51	**100 Pesetas** 1.5.1900. Blue on lt. green unpt. Francisco de Quevedo at l., medallic portr. at r. Back brown; cherubs and Athena.			
	a. Issued note.	130.	275.	600
	s. Specimen.	—	Unc	300

NOTICE

Readers with unlisted dates, signature varieties, etc. are invited to submit photocopies or, high resolution (300 dpi, 100% size) scans of their notes to: Standard Catalog of World Paper Money, 700 East State St. Iola, WI 54990-0001, or E-Mail: george.cuhaj@fwpubs.com.

1902-03 ISSUE

52	50 Pesetas	Good	Fine	XF
	30.11.1902. Black and yellow. Diego Velázquez at l.	150.	450.	1000.

53	100 Pesetas	Good	Fine	XF
	1903; 1905. Gray. Man standing w/spade in hand at l., small child on knees w/arm uplifting palm branch at r.			
	a. Issued note. 1.7.1903.	600.	1500.	3000.
	s1. As a. Specimen.	—	Unc	600.
	s2. Specimen. 21.8.1905.	—	—	—

54	500 Pesetas	Good	Fine	XF
	1.10.1903. Grayish-blue. Man and arms spread as if in flight at top ctr.			
	a. Issued note.	1500.	2750.	4000.
	b. Half finished print w/o unpt. Punched hole cancelled.	—	Unc	250.

904-05 ISSUE

		VG	VF	UNC
5	25 Pesetas	VG	VF	UNC
	1.1.1904. Blue-green. Standing figures at l. and r. (Not issued).			1300.
6	50 Pesetas			
	19.3.1905. Ochre, green and gray. José Echegaray at l.	175.	375.	1000.

ROVISIONAL REPUBLIC VALIDATION, 1931

rtain issues following have a round embossed validation applied by the Republic in 1931. This validation consists of crowned Spanish arms with 2 laurel branches at ctr., legend around: *GOBIERNO PROVISIONAL DE LA REPÚBLICA 14 ABRIL 1931*. Notes of 25, 50 and 100 Pesetas had it applied to the upper l. corner, and those of 500 and 1000 Pesetas to the upper r. corner. The embossing is not easily discernible.

1906 ISSUE

#57-59 printer: BWC.

57	25 Pesetas	Good	Fine	XF
	24.9.1906. Black and blue. Woman seated at l.			
	a. Issued note.	17.50	55.00	100.
	b. Round embossed Republic validation at upper l. corner 1931.	25.00	75.00	160.
	s. Specimen.	—	—	—

58	50 Pesetas	Good	Fine	XF
	24.9.1906. Gray-violet and green. Woman standing w/caduceus by globe at ctr.			
	a. Issued note.	20.00	60.00	120.
	b. Round embossed Republic validation at upper l. corner 1931.	25.00	70.00	150.
	s. Specimen.	—	—	—
59	100 Pesetas			
	30.6.1906. Black and blue. Women seated at l. and r.			
	a. Issued note.	22.50	65.00	160.
	b. Round embossed Republic validation at upper l. corner 1931.	55.00	130.	300.
	s. Specimen.	—	—	—

Note: #59 is also reported with oval handstamp similar to #80.

1907 FIRST ISSUE

60	500 Pesetas	Good	Fine	XF
	28.1.1907. Black on green and violet unpt. Women reclining at l. and r. leaning against medallic portr. of king at ctr. Back green; arms at ctr. Printer: BWC.			
	a. Issued note.	225.	500.	1000.
	s. Specimen.	—	—	—
61	1000 Pesetas			
	10.5.1907. Black on blue unpt. Mercury w/globe on shoulder at l., shield w/castle at lower l., shield w/rampant lion at lower r. Back brown; woman w/sword and lion at ctr.			
	a. Issued note.	225.	500.	1000.
	s. Specimen.	—	—	—

1907 Second Issue

#62-66 printer: BWC.

		Good	Fine	XF
62	**25 Pesetas** 15.7.1907. Black on dk. pink and green unpt. Woman reclining at ctr. Alhambra de Granada on back.			
	a. Issued note.	20.00	65.00	140.
	b. Round embossed Republic validation at upper l. corner 1931.	35.00	75.00	175.
	s. Specimen.	—	—	—

		Good	Fine	XF
63	**50 Pesetas** 15.7.1907. Black on yellow, red and blue unpt. Woman standing at l. and r. Cathedral of Burgos on back.			
	a. Issued note.	20.00	60.00	130.
	b. Round embossed Republic validation at upper l. corner 1931.	35.00	75.00	175.
	s. Specimen.	—	—	—
64	**100 Pesetas** 15.7.1907. Green, red, yellow and black. Woman seated at l., medallic male portr. at ctr. Cathedral of Seville on back.			
	a. Issued note.	15.00	45.00	100.
	b. Round embossed Republic validation at upper l. corner 1931.	35.00	75.00	175.
	s. Specimen.	—	—	—

		Good	Fine	XF
65	**500 Pesetas** 15.7.1907. Red, green and black. Woman standing at l., cherubs at lower r. Alcázar de Segovia on back.			
	a. Issued note.	100.	250.	500.
	b. Round embossed Republic validation at upper r. corner 1931.	75.00	185.	375.
	s. Specimen.	—	—	—
66	**1000 Pesetas** 15.7.1907. Black on ochre and red unpt. Woman seated on throne by medallic female portr. at ctr. Palacio Real de Madrid on back.			
	a. Issued note.	110.	300.	625.
	b. Round embossed Republic validation at upper r. corner 1931.	110.	260.	550.
	s. Specimen.	—	—	—

1908 Issue

		Good	Fine	XF
67	**25 Pesetas** 1.12.1908. Manuel José Quintana at l.			
	p1. Color trial of face.	—	—	—
	p2. Color trial of back (several colors known).	—	—	—

		Good	Fine	XF
68	**100 Pesetas** 1.12.1908. Blue. Conjoined portraits of Kg. Fernando and Qn. Isabel at l. (Not issued).			

1914; 1915 Issue

68A	**5 Pesetas** 1914. Fernando VI at l. (Not issued).	—	Unc	300

68B	**1000 Pesetas** 23.5.1915. Conjoined portraits of Alfonso XIII and Victoria Eugenia at l. (Not issued).	—	Unc	30

925 ISSUE

100 Pesetas

1.7.1925. Dk. blue and green on m/c unpt. Felipe II at l. and as wmk. Monastery of El Escorial at lower ctr. Retreat of Felipe II on blue and orange back. Printer: BWC.

	VG	VF	UNC
a. Serial # w/o series letter, Series A-C, and Series D to 2,000,000.	20.00	30.00	60.00
b. Round embossed Republic validation at upper l. corner 1931.	30.00	30.00	75.00
c. Serial # D2,000,001 through Series F, Republic issue (1936).	3.00	10.00	25.00
s. Specimen.	—	—	—

'e: 5 million Series G notes were printed but not released.

A **500 Pesetas**

23.1.1925. Cardinal Cisneros at l. (Not issued).

VG	VF	UNC
—	—	2500.

1000 Pesetas

1.7.1925. Chestnut, red and violet. Kg. Carlos I at r., gorgon head at top ctr. Alcázar de Toledo on back. Printer: BWC.

	VG	VF	UNC
a. Serial # to 3,646,000.	35.00	70.00	160.
b. Round embossed Republic validation at upper r. corner 1931.	40.00	80.00	180.
c. Serial # 3,646,001 to 5,000,000, Republic issue (1936).	17.50	45.00	100.
s. Specimen.	—	—	—

26; 1927 ISSUE

-73 printer: BWC.

25 Pesetas

12.10.1926. Blue and violet on m/c unpt. St. Xavier at l. St. Xavier baptizing Indians on red-brown back. Wmk: Qn.

	VG	VF	UNC
a. Issued note.	10.00	30.00	85.00
b. Round embossed Republic validation at upper l. corner 1931.	25.00	95.00	—
s. Specimen.	—	—	—

72 **50 Pesetas**

17.5.1927. Purple and violet on orange and yellow unpt. Kg. Alfonso XIII at l., fortified city at lower ctr. Founding of Buenos Aires on blue back. Wmk: Qn.

	VG	VF	UNC
a. Issued note.	40.00	100.	250.
b. Round embossed Republic validation at upper l. corner 1931.	50.00	180.	—
s. Specimen.	—	—	—

Note: #72 was validated by the Republic with oval handstamp (see #80).

73 **500 Pesetas**

24.7.1927. Blue and brown on orange and green unpt. Lions Court at Alhambra at ctr., Isabel la Católica at r. Arms on red and purple back.

	VG	VF	UNC
a. Serial # to 1,602,000.	50.00	150.	350.
b. Round embossed Republic validation at upper r. corner 1931.	50.00	150.	—
c. Serial # 1,602,001 to 2,000,000, Republic issue (1936).	15.00	40.00	120.

1928 ISSUE

Circulation of 1928-dated notes: part of the issue of 25 and 50 Pesetas was released before July 18, 1936, the date at which recognition by the Nationalist government of further issues was cut off. None of the 100, 500 or 1000 Pesetas were released before that date; therefore, they are all considered as issues of the Republic only.

#74-78 printer: BWC.

74 **25 Pesetas**

15.8.1928. Blue and brown on m/c unpt. Monument at ctr., Pedro Calderón de la Barca at r. Religious comedy scene on lilac back. Wmk: Woman.

	VG	VF	UNC
a. Serial # w/o series letter, also Series A through 7,780,000.	15.00	40.00	120.
b. Serial # A7,780,001 through Series E, Republic issue.	2.50	8.50	20.00
s. Specimen.	—	—	—

75 **50 Pesetas**

15.8.1928. Violet and black on pale blue and dull orange unpt. Prado Museum in Madrid at lower l. and ctr., Diego Velázquez at r. Painting "La rendición de Breda" by Velázquez on back. Wmk: Woman.

	VG	VF	UNC
a. Serial # w/o series letter, also Series A through 8,640,000.	5.00	12.50	35.00
b. Serial # A8,640,001 through Series E, Republic issue.	1.50	5.00	12.00
s. Specimen.	—	—	—

76 100 Pesetas

15.8.1928. Purple and black on m/c unpt. Miguel de Cervantes at l. and as wmk., monument at ctr. Painting of Don Quijote by Pidal on back.

	VG	VF	UNC
a. Issued note.	2.50	8.50	20.00
s. Specimen.	—	—	—

Note: Position of Cervantes' head in relation to border on #76 varies considerably.

77 500 Pesetas

15.8.1928. Purple and green on m/c unpt. Cathedral of Toledo at lower l., Cardinal Cisneros above. Picture by Casanova showing liberation of captives on back.

	VG	VF	UNC
a. Issued note.	8.00	35.00	80.00
s. Specimen.	—	—	—

78 1000 Pesetas

15.8.1928. Blue and purple on m/c unpt. Cathedral of Seville at lower l., San Fernando at r. Painting of King receiving communion (by A. Ferrant) on red-brown back.

	VG	VF	UNC
a. Issued note.	8.00	30.00	70.00
s. Specimen.	—	—	—

REPUBLIC

BANCO DE ESPAÑA

1931 PROVISIONAL ISSUE

Aside from the embossed notes (see #57b, 58b, 59b, 61b, 62b, 63b, 64b, 65b, 66b, 69b, 70b, 71b, 72b, 73b), the Provisional Government had at first authorized the overstamping of the 50 Pesetas (#72, with portr. of Alfonso XIII) with a purple oval handstamp consisting of arms at ctr. and legend *REPÚBLICA ESPAÑOLA* around. An earlier 50 Pesetas issue (#59) and other older notes are also reported with this handstamp.

80 50 Pesetas

	VG	VF	UNC
ND (1931 -old date 17.5.1927) . Republican handstamp over portr. at l. on #72.	20.00	50.00	150.

1931 ISSUE

#81-85 printer: BWC.

81 25 Pesetas

	VG	VF	UNC
25.4.1931. Green and brown on m/c unpt. Vicente López at r. Back brown; López's painting *Music.* Wmk: Woman in Phrygian cap.	4.00	12.50	30.00

82 50 Pesetas

	VG	VF	UNC
25.4.1931. Blue, lilac and violet. E. Rosales at l. Rosales' painting *The Death of Lucretia* on back. Wmk: Woman.	4.00	12.50	30.0

83 100 Pesetas

	VG	VF	UN
25.4.1931. Purple and black on blue, tan and m/c unpt. Gonzalo Fernández de Córdoba at l. Back green; painting by Casado del Alisal. Wmk: Helmeted man.	4.00	12.50	30.(

84 500 Pesetas

	VG	VF	UN
25.4.1931. Chestnut and blue on m/c unpt. Juan Sebastián de Elcano at l. Elias Salaverria's painting *Disembarkation* on back. Wmk: Kg.	12.00	50.00	1

84A 1000 Pesetas

25.4.1931. Green. J. Zorrilla at upper l. Zorrilla reading his poems at gathering on back. (Not issued).

	VG	VF	U
a. Unissued note.	—	—	1
s. Specimen.	—	—	

1935 (1936) SILVER CERTIFICATES

#85 and 86 printer: BWC.

		VG	VF	UNC
85	**5 Pesetas** 1935 (1936). Green and violet. Woman at l.			
	a. Issued note.	.60	2.00	9.00
	s. Specimen.	—	—	—

		VG	VF	UNC
86	**10 Pesetas** 1935 (1936). Red-brown and blue. Woman at r.			
	a. Issued note.	1.25	4.00	12.00
	s. Specimen.	—	—	—

1935; 1936 (1938) REGULAR ISSUE

#87-89 printer: TDLR.

		VG	VF	UNC
87	**25 Pesetas** 31.8.1936 (1938). Blue, chestnut and purple. Joaquín Sorolla at l., church steeple at r. ctr. Back purple; picture by Sorolla.			
	a. Issued note.	30.00	80.00	175.
	b. Series A.	90.00	200.	900.

		VG	VF	UNC
88	**50 Pesetas** 22.7.1935. Purple and black on m/c unpt. Santiago Ramón y Cajal at r. and as wmk., woman on column supports at l. and r. Monument on blue back.	4.00	12.00	30.00

		VG	VF	UNC
89	**500 Pesetas** 7.1.1935. Chestnut, green and Hernán Cortez at l., his palace in Mexico at lower r. ctr. Back red and purple; painting of Cortez burning his ships.	60.00	125.	500.

1938 ISSUES

#90-92 not issued.

		VG	VF	UNC
90	**100 Pesetas** 11.3.1938. Barcelona. Carving of Dame of Elche at l., boat at ctr. Roadway w/palms on back. Printer: TDLR. (Not issued).	—	—	3000.
91	**100 Pesetas** 15.8.1938. Gray. Barcelona. W/o vignettes. Spanish printing.	—	—	—

		VG	VF	UNC
92	**5000 Pesetas** 11.6.1938. Barcelona. M. Fortuny at r. Fortuny's picture "La Vicaria" on back. Printer: BWC. (Not issued).	—	—	4500.

MINISTERIO DE HACIENDA

MINISTRY OF FINANCE

1937-38 ISSUE

		VG	VF	UNC
93	**50 Centimos** 1937. Blue on pink unpt. Woman at ctr. Back green.	1.50	4.50	12.50
94	**1 Peseta** 1937. Brown and green. Nike of Samothrace at l. Back purple and gold, w/La Cibeles Fountain in Madrid.	1.75	5.00	15.00

		VG	VF	UNC
95	**2 Pesetas** 1938. Blue, brown and green. Woman at ctr. Back gray and purple, w/Toledo Bridge in Madrid.	1.75	5.00	15.00

POSTAGE STAMP/DISK ISSUES

1938 CORREOS "NUMERAL" SERIES

#96-96E postage stamps w/large numerals; w/o portr.
#96-96N arms on face.

		VG	VF	UNC
96	**5 Centimos** ND (1938). Brown.	1.25	4.00	10.00

		VG	VF	UNC
96A	**10 Centimos** ND (1938). Green.	1.25	4.00	10.00
96B	**15 Centimos** ND (1938). Gray.	1.25	4.00	10.00
96C	**20 Centimos** ND (1938). Violet.	1.25	4.00	10.00

		VG	VF	UNC
96D	**25 Centimos** ND (1938). Brown-violet.	1.25	4.00	10.00
96E	**30 Centimos** ND (1938). Rose.	1.25	4.00	10.00

1938 Correos "Portrait" Series

#96F-96N postage stamps w/portr.

		VG	VF	UNC
96F	**5 Centimos** ND (1938). Dk. brown.	1.25	4.00	10.00
96G	**10 Centimos** ND (1938).	1.25	4.00	10.00
96H	**15 Centimos** ND (1938).	1.25	4.00	10.00
96I	**25 Centimos** ND (1938). Red-violet.	1.25	4.00	10.00
96J	**30 Centimos** ND (1938).	1.25	4.00	10.00
96K	**40 Centimos** ND (1938).	1.25	4.00	10.00
96L	**45 Centimos** ND (1938). Red.	1.25	4.00	10.00
96M	**50 Centimos** ND (1938).	1.25	4.00	10.00
96N	**60 Centimos** ND (1938).	1.25	4.00	10.00

1938 Especial Movil (Revenue) Series

#96O-96T revenue stamps w/o portraits; w/large crowned arms between pillars (Type I) or sprays (Type II).

		VG	VF	UNC
96O	**5 Centimos** ND (1938). Blue. Type I.	1.25	4.00	10.00
96P	**10 Centimos** ND (1938). Brown. Type I.	1.25	4.00	10.00
96Q	**15 Centimos** ND (1938). Gray-green. Type I.	1.25	4.00	10.00
96R	**15 Centimos** ND (1938). Red. Type II.	1.25	4.00	10.00
96S	**30 Centimos** ND (1938).	1.25	4.00	10.00
96T	**50 Centimos** ND (1938). Red. Type I.	1.25	4.00	10.00

NOTICE

Readers with unlisted dates, signature varieties, etc. are invited to submit photocopies or, high resolution (300 dpi, 100% size) scans of their notes to: Standard Catalog of World Paper Money, 700 East State St. Iola, WI 54990-0001, or E-Mail: george.cuhaj@fwpubs.com.

Regency

Banco de España

1936 Issue

		VG	VF	UNC
97	**5 Pesetas** 21.11.1936. Brown on blue-green unpt. Arms at r.			
	a. Issued note.	125.	350.	1000.
	s. Specimen.	—	—	—

		VG	VF	UNC
98	**10 Pesetas** 21.11.1936. Blue and orange. Arms at r.			
	a. Issued note.	125.	350.	1000.
	s. Specimen.	—	—	—

#99-103 printer G&D (w/o imprint).

		VG	VF	UNC
99	**25 Pesetas** 21.11.1936. Blue on olive unpt. Head on back.			
	a. Issued note.	15.00	60.00	150.
	s. Specimen.	—	—	—

		VG	VF	UNC
100	**50 Pesetas** 21.11.1936. Brown on green unpt. Head at l. and r. on back.			
	a. Issued note.	50.00	175.	450.
	s. Specimen.	—	—	—
101	**100 Pesetas** 21.11.1936. Green on lt. green and orange unpt. Cathedral of Burgos on back.			
	a. Issued note.	14.00	50.00	135.
	s. Specimen.	—	—	—

		VG	VF	UNC
102	**500 Pesetas**			
	21.11.1936. Dk. blue. Bldg. and viaduct on back.			
	a. Issued note.	125.	350.	1000.
	s. Specimen.	—	—	—
103	**1000 Pesetas**			
	21.11.1936. Green. Old bridge and bldg. on back.			
	a. Issued note.	125.	350.	1000.
	s. Specimen.	—	—	—

1937 ISSUE

#104 and 105 printer: Coen, Milano.

		VG	VF	UNC
104	**1 Peseta**			
	12.10.1937. Lilac on blue unpt. Arms at l. Back purple on brown unpt.			
	a. Issued note.	17.50	55.00	140.
	s. Specimen.	—	—	—
105	**2 Pesetas**			
	12.10.1937. Dk. green on lt. orange and lt. lilac unpt. Gothic church in Burgos at l. Back bluish black.			
	a. Issued note.	25.00	70.00	200.
	s. Specimen.	—	—	—

		VG	VF	UNC
106	**5 Pesetas**			
	18.7.1937. Brown on tan unpt. Woman holding caduceus at r. Series A-C. Back orange; arms at ctr. Imprint: Lit. M. Portabella Zaragoza.			
	a. Issued note.	35.00	90.00	250.
	s. Specimen.	—	—	—

#106A-106E printed by an Italian firm. (Not issued.)

		VG	VF	UNC
106A	**25 Pesetas**			
	18.7.1937. Columbus at l. Columbus at the "New World" on back.	—	800.	—

		VG	VF	UNC
106B	**50 Pesetas**			
	18.7.1937.	—	800.	—

		VG	VF	UNC
106C	**100 Pesetas**			
	18.7.1937. Gen. Castaños at r. Battle of Bailén on back.	—	800.	—
106D	**500 Pesetas**			
	18.7.1937.	—	800.	—
106E	**1000 Pesetas**			
	18.7.1937. Carlos V at ctr. Battle scene on back.	—	1000.	—

1938 ISSUE

#107-109 printer: Coen, Milano.

		VG	VF	UNC
107	**1 Peseta**			
	28.2.1938. Brown on green unpt. Arms at l. Back purple.			
	a. Issued note.	6.00	20.00	70.00
	s. Specimen.	—	—	—

		VG	VF	UNC
108	**1 Peseta**			
	30.4.1938. Brown on green unpt. Like #107.			
	a. Issued note.	6.00	17.50	65.00
	s. Specimen.	—	—	—

		VG	VF	UNC
109	**2 Pesetas**			
	30.4.1938. Dk. green on orange and lilac unpt. Like #105.			
	a. Issued note.	8.00	27.50	95.00
	s. Specimen.	—	—	—

#110-115 arms unpt. Printer: G&D.

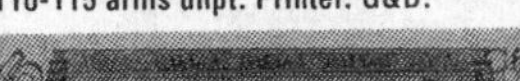

		VG	VF	UNC
110	**5 Pesetas**			
	10.8.1938. Green and red on lt. brown unpt.			
	a. Issued note.	9.00	32.50	110.
	s. Specimen.	—	—	—
111	**25 Pesetas**			
	20.5.1938. Green and pink. Church in Seville on back.			
	a. Issued note.	40.00	140.	375.
	s. Specimen.	—	—	—
112	**50 Pesetas**			
	20.5.1938. Red-brown and green. Castle at Olite on back.			
	a. Issued note.	35.00	130.	350.
	s. Specimen.	—	—	—
113	**100 Pesetas**			
	20.5.1938. Lilac-brown and orange. House of Cordón on back.			
	a. Issued note.	35.00	130.	325.
	s. Specimen.	—	—	—
114	**500 Pesetas**			
	20.5.1938. Yellow-green and lilac. Cathedral on back.			
	a. Issued note.	175.	700.	2000.
	s. Specimen.	—	—	—

		VG	VF	UNC
115	**1000 Pesetas**			
	20.5.1938. Blue and red. Historic picture on back.			
	a. Issued note.	225.	800.	2500.
	s. Specimen.	—	—	—

1940 First Issue

#116-120 printer: Calcografía & Cartevalori, Milano, Italia.

		VG	VF	UNC
116	**25 Pesetas** 9.1.1940 (1943). Gray-blue on lt. brown unpt. Juan de Herrera at l., Patio de Evangelistas at r. Arms at l. on back.			
	a. Issued note.	35.00	100.	450.
	s. Specimen.	—	—	—
117	**50 Pesetas** 9.1.1940 (1943). Green on blue and orange unpt. Menendez Pelayo at l. Back lt. blue-gray; arms at ctr.			
	a. Issued note.	14.00	45.00	210.
	s. Specimen.	—	—	—

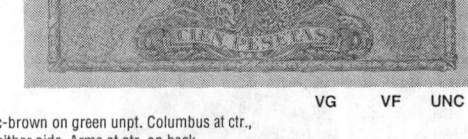

		VG	VF	UNC
118	**100 Pesetas** 9.1.1940 (1943). Lilac-brown on green unpt. Columbus at ctr., allegorical woman at either side. Arms at ctr. on back			
	a. Issued note.	14.00	47.50	225.
	s. Specimen.	—	—	—

		VG	VF	UNC
119	**500 Pesetas** 9.1.1940 (1945). Dk. green. John of Austria at r. Battle of Lepanto w/old ships on back.			
	a. Issued note.	150.	375.	1000.
	s. Specimen.	—	—	—

		VG	VF	UNC
120	**1000 Pesetas** 9.1.1940. Issue of 12.11.1943. Gray and brown. Bartolomé Murillo at ctr. Back maroon and brown; Murillo painting "Children Counting Money."			
	a. Issued note.	225.	600.	1500.
	s. Specimen.	—	—	—

1940 Second Issue

		VG	VF	UNC
121	**1 Peseta** 1.6.1940. Blue and orange. Hernán Cortez on horseback at r. Back brown; arms at ctr. Imprint: Graficas Reunidas S. A., Madrid.			
	a. Issued note.	12.50	60.00	165.
	s. Specimen.	—	—	—

		VG	VF	UNC
122	**1 Peseta** 4.9.1940. Black on gold and blue unpt. Sailing ship Santa Maria at ctr. Back dk. green on purple unpt. Imprint: Rieusset S.A. Barcelona.			
	a. Issued note.	10.00	35.00	120.
	s. Specimen.	—	—	—
123	**5 Pesetas** 4.9.1940. Dk. brown and blue-green on orange and green unpt. Arms at l., palace of Segovia at r. Back blue and green. Printer: G&D.			
	a. Issued note.	12.00	55.00	150.
	s. Specimen.	—	—	—

		VG	VF	UNC
124	**500 Pesetas** 21.10.1940. Issue of Feb. 1947. Black on lt. green, gold and pink unpt. Conde de Orgaz (Death Scene) by El Greco at r. Back gray on gold unpt.; view of Toledo at ctr.			
	a. Issued note.	150.	375.	1000.
	s. Specimen.	—	—	—
125	**1000 Pesetas** 21.10.1940. Lilac and violet. Portr. helmeted Kg. Carlos I at l. Arms of Kg. Carlos I on back.			
	a. Issued note.	160.	400.	1200.
	s. Specimen.	—	—	—

1943 Issue

#126 and 127 printer: FNMT.

126 **1 Peseta**	VG	VF	UNC
21.5.1943. Dk. brown on m/c unpt. Kg. Fernando el católico at l. Columbus landing on back.			
a. Issued note.	2.50	12.00	37.50
s. Specimen.	—	—	—

127 **5 Pesetas**	VG	VF	UNC
13.2.1943. Black on m/c unpt. Qn. Isabel la Católica at l. Columbus w/his men at ctr. on back.			
a. Issued note.	10.00	40.00	140.
s. Specimen.	—	—	—

1945 ISSUE

#128 and 129 printer: FNMT.

128 **1 Peseta**	VG	VF	UNC
15.6.1945. Brown on m/c unpt. Qn. Isabel la Católica at l. Man w/old map on back.			
a. Issued note.	2.50	12.00	35.00
s. Specimen.	—	—	—

129 **5 Pesetas**	VG	VF	UNC
15.6.1945. Black and green on m/c unpt. Qn. Isabel la Católica and Columbus at l. Spaniards fighting Moors on back. W/o series, and Series A-M.			
a. Issued note.	3.50	17.50	50.00
s. Specimen.	—	—	—

1946 ISSUE

#130-133 printer: FNMT.

130 **25 Pesetas**	VG	VF	UNC
19.2.1946 (1948). Purple and black on m/c unpt. Florez Estrada at l. View of Pola de Somiedo on back. Wmk: Greek man's head.			
a. Issued note.	6.00	25.00	90.00
s. Specimen.	—	—	—

131 **100 Pesetas**	VG	VF	UNC
19.2.1946 (1949). Brown on lilac unpt. Francisco de Goya at r. and as wmk. "The Sun Shade" by Goya on back. Series A-B.			
a. Issued note.	8.00	30.00	110.
s. Specimen.	—	—	—

132 **500 Pesetas**	VG	VF	UNC
19.2.1946 (1949). Blue on m/c unpt. Francisco de Vitoria at r. and as wmk. University of Salamanca on back.			
a. Issued note.	175.	450.	1200.
s. Specimen.	—	—	—

133 **1000 Pesetas**	VG	VF	UNC
19.2.1946 (1948). Green and brown. J. Luis Vives at r. and as wmk. Cloister at college in Valencia on back.			
a. Issued note.	175.	450.	1200.
s. Specimen.	—	—	—

1947 ISSUE

134 **5 Pesetas**	VG	VF	UNC
12.4.1947. Brown-lilac on lt. green and lt. orange unpt. Seneca at r. Back blue-black. Printre: FNMT.			
a. Issued note.	7.50	27.50	100.
s. Specimen.	—	—	—

1948 ISSUE

#135-137 printer: FNMT.

135 **1 Peseta**	VG	VF	UNC
19.6.1948. Brown on m/c unpt. Dame of Elche at r. Orange plant on back.			
a. Issued note.	1.00	5.00	15.00
s. Specimen.	—	—	—

136 **5 Pesetas**	VG	VF	UNC
5.3.1948. Dk. green on lilac unpt. Juan Sebastián Elcano at l. Wmk: Man's head.			
a. Issued note.	2.50	12.50	40.00
s. Specimen.	—	—	—

137 **100 Pesetas**	VG	VF	UNC
2.5.1948 (1950). Brown. F. Bayeu at l. Goya's "El Cacharrero" on back. Wmk: Goya.			
a. Issued note.	10.00	40.00	160.
s. Specimen.	—	—	—

1949 (1951) Issue

#		VG	VF	UNC
138	**1000 Pesetas** 4.11.1949 (1951). Black and green. Ramón de Santillan at r. Goya's "El Bebedor" on back. Wmk: Goya. Printer: FNMT.			
	a. Issued note.	45.00	165.	500.
	s. Specimen.	—	—	—

1951 Issue

139-143 printer: FNMT.

#		VG	VF	UNC
139	**1 Peseta** 19.11.1951. Brown on m/c unpt. Don Quijote at r. Shields and lance on back.			
	a. Issued note.	.75	3.50	12.50
	s. Specimen.	—	—	—

#		VG	VF	UNC
140	**5 Pesetas** 16.8.1951. Dk. green and black on olive and orange unpt. Jaime Balmes at l. and as wmk. Old bldg. on back.			
	a. Issued note.	1.00	4.50	15.00
	s. Specimen.	—	—	—

#		VG	VF	UNC
141	**50 Pesetas** 31.12.1951 (1956). Lilac-red on m/c unpt. Santiago Rusiñol at r. and as wmk. Rusiñol's *Jardines de Aranjuez on back.*			
	a. Issued note.	8.00	35.00	150.
	s. Specimen.	—	—	1500.

#		VG	VF	UNC
142	**500 Pesetas** 15.11.1951 (1952). Dk. blue. Mariano Benlliure at l. Sculpture by Benlliure on back.			
	a. Issued note.	20.00	65.00	275.
	s. Specimen.	—	—	1650.
143	**1000 Pesetas** 31.12.1951 (1953). Green. Joaquín Sorolla at ctr. Sorolla's painting *La fiesta del naranjo* on back.			
	a. Issued note.	20.00	65.00	275.
	s. Specimen.	—	—	1750.

1953 Issue

#144 and 145 printer: FNMT.

#		VG	VF	UNC
144	**1 Peseta** 22.7.1953. Brown and black on m/c unpt. Marqués de Santa Cruz at r. Old sailing ship on back.			
	a. Issued note.	.40	2.00	7.50
	s. Specimen.	—	—	900.

#		VG	VF	UNC
145	**100 Pesetas** 7.4.1953 (1955). Brown on m/c unpt. Juan Romero de Torres at ctr. Painting by Torres on back. Wmk: Woman's head.			
	a. Issued note.	1.00	4.00	15.00
	s. Specimen.	—	—	1200.

1954 Issue

#146-148 printer: FNMT.

#		VG	VF	UNC
146	**5 Pesetas** 22.7.1954. Green on lt. lilac unpt. Kg. Alfonso X at r. and as wmk. Library and museum bldg. in Madrid on back.			
	a. Issued note.	1.75	4.50	16.00
	s. Specimen.	—	—	1000.
147	**25 Pesetas** 22.7.1954. Purple on orange and m/c unpt. Isaac Albeniz at l. and as wmk. Patio scene of the Lion's Court of Alhambra on back.			
	a. Issued note.	1.75	7.50	20.00
	s. Specimen.	—	—	1150.

		VG	VF	UNC
148	**500 Pesetas**			
	22.7.1954 (1958). Blue on m/c unpt. Ignacio Zuloaga at ctr. and as wmk. Painting by Zuloaga *Vista de Toledo on back.*			
	a. Issued note.	6.00	20.00	95.00
	s. Specimen.	—	—	1750.

1957 (1958) ISSUE

		VG	VF	UNC
149	**1000 Pesetas**			
	29.11.1957 (1958). Green. *Reyes Católicos* at ctr. Arms on back. Printer: FNMT.			
	a. Issued note.	15.00	45.00	135.
	s. Specimen.	—	—	2000.

Straits Settlements is a former British crown colony on the south and west coast of Malay Peninsula consisting of Malacca, Penang, Singapore, Labuan (Borneo), Cocos Island and Christmas Island. Cocos Island, Christmas Island and Labuan were placed under control of the Governor of Straits Settlements in 1886.

The colony was united under one government as a presidency of India in 1826, was incorporated under Bengal in 1830, and was removed from control of the Indian government and placed under direct British control in 1867. Japanese forces occupied the colony in 1941-45.

RULERS:

British

MONETARY SYSTEM:

1 Dollar = 100 Cents

BRITISH ADMINISTRATION

GOVERNMENT OF THE STRAITS SETTLEMENTS

1898-1906 ISSUE

#1-4B arms at upper ctr. Various dates and sign. varieties. Printer: TDLR.

		Good	Fine	XF
1	**1 Dollar**			
	1906-24. Black. Tiger at ctr. on back.			
	a. Lt. pink paper. 2 sign. varieties. 1.9.1906.	270.	600.	2100.
	b. Dk. red paper. Unpt. like #1A. 4 sign. varieties. 1.9.1906; 8.6.1909; 17.3.1911.	270.	600.	2100.
	c. Paper and unpt. like b. 2.1.1914-4.3.1915; 10.7.1916; 29.6.1921; 5.9.1924.	90.00	200.	750.

		Good	Fine	XF
1A	**1 Dollar**			
	1.8.1906. Like #1a but unpt. shows numeral *1* at l. and ctr. r.	270.	600.	2100.
2	**5 Dollars**			
	1.9.1898; 1.3.1900. Black on lt. purple unpt. Tiger at ctr. on back. 195 x 120mm.	1100.	2700.	—

		Good	Fine	XF
3	**5 Dollars**			
	1.2.1901; 8.6.1909; 17.3.1911; 2.1.1914; 4.3.1915; 10.7.1916; 20.6.1921; 5.9.1924. Black and purple on lt. yellow paper. Similar to #2 but changes in frame ornaments on face and back. 119 x 75mm. 6 sign. varieties.	500.	1400.	4300.

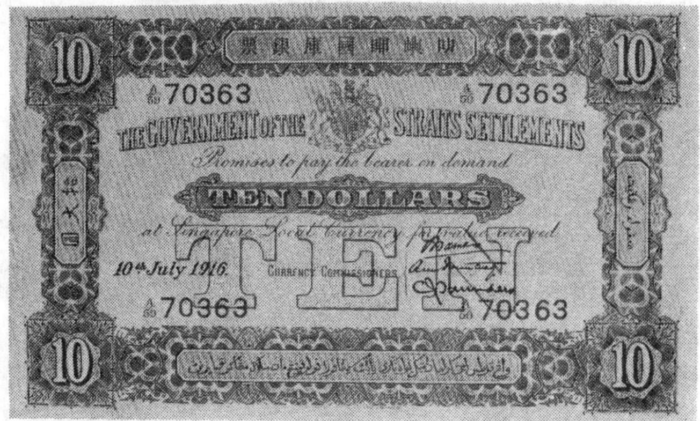

		Good	Fine	XF
4	**10 Dollars** 1898-1924. Blue on lt. purple unpt. Tiger on back. 7 sign. varieties.			
	a. 1.9.1898; 1.3.1900; 1.2.1901; 8.6.1909; 17.3.1911. Rare.	—	—	—
	b. 2.1.1914; 4.3.1915; 10.7.1916; 20.6.1921; 5.9.1924.	800.	2300.	—

		Good	Fine	XF
4A	**50 Dollars** 1.2.1901. Green on lt. purple unpt. Rare.	—	—	—
4B	**100 Dollars** 1.2.1901. Red on lt. purple unpt. Rare.	—	—	—

Note: At Singapore, in the Spink-Taisei Sale of February, 1989, #4A, $50 dated 1901 brought $7,150 in Fine condition; #4B, $100 dated 1901 brought $17,600 in VG-F condition.

		Good	Fine	XF
4C	**100 Dollars** 1.2.1901. Red on dk. olive unpt. *HUNDRED* on back. Rare.	—	—	—

1916 ISSUE

#A5 and 5 portr. Kg. George V above tiger at ctr. Uniface. Printer: TDLR.

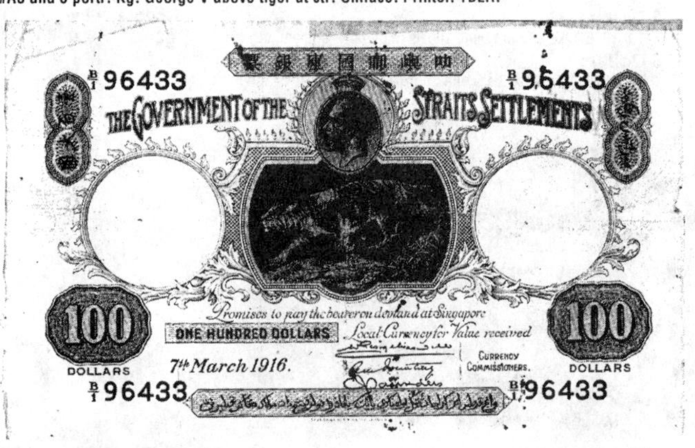

		Good	Fine	XF
5	**100 Dollars** 7.3.1916; 1.6.1920. Dk. red on olive unpt. Rare.	—	—	—

Note: For later dates see #12-13.

		Good	Fine	XF
A5	**50 Dollars** 7.3.1916. Dk. blue on gray-violet unpt. Rare.	—	—	—

Note: The authenticity of #A5 dated 1.6.1920 has not been determined.

1917 ISSUE

		Good	Fine	XF
6	**10 Cents** 1917-20. Green on yellow unpt. Arms at upper ctr. 2 sign. varieties. Date in red seal on back, day at l. of crown, month at r., year at bottom. Printer: Survey Dept. F.M.S.			
	a. Sign. H. Marriot, w/title: *Ag. Treasurer.* W/*No.* before serial #. 1.7.1917-1.10.1917.	30.00	80.00	530.
	b. As a. but w/o *No.* before serial #. 1.11.1917-1.9.1918.	30.00	80.00	530.
	c. Sign. A.M. Pountney w/title: *Treasurer.* 2.1.1919-10.6.1920.	12.50	50.00	340.

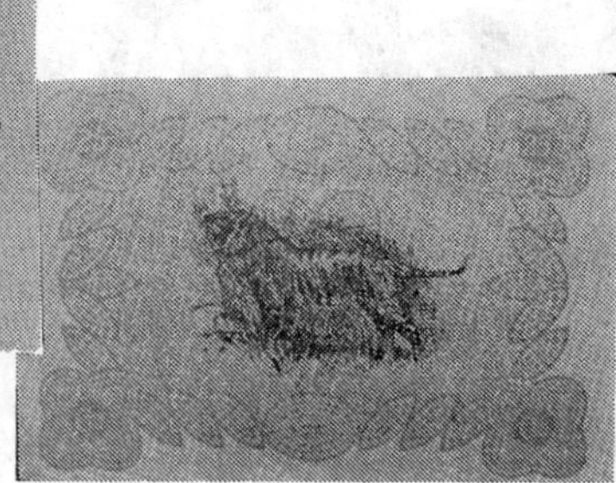

		Good	Fine	XF
7	**25 Cents** ND (1917). Black on yellow-orange unpt. Arms at top ctr. Tiger at ctr. on back. Printer: Survey Dept. F.M.S.	200.	600.	1500.

1919 ISSUE

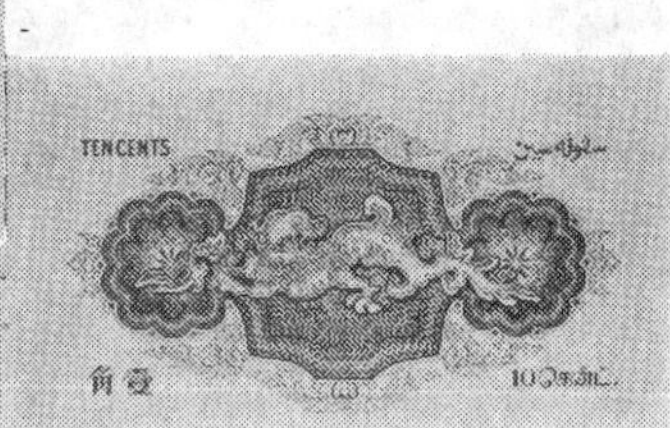

		Good	Fine	XF
8	**10 Cents** 14.10.1919. Red and green on gray-brown unpt. Arms at top ctr. Back green; dragon at ctr. Printer: TDLR.			
	a. Sign. title: *Ag. Treasurer.*	20.00	50.00	420.
	b. Sign. title: *Treasurer.*	10.00	20.00	150.

1925; 1930 ISSUE

#9-15 printer: TDLR.

		Good	Fine	XF
9	**1 Dollar** 1925-30. Red on gray-violet unpt. Palm trees at l., palm trees and huts at r. Beach w/palms at ctr. on back. 4 sign. varieties (red or black).			
	a. Red date in plate. 1.1.1925; 1.9.1927; 1.1.1929.	50.00	95.00	480.
	b. Black ovpt. date. 1.1.1930.	15.00	70.00	225.

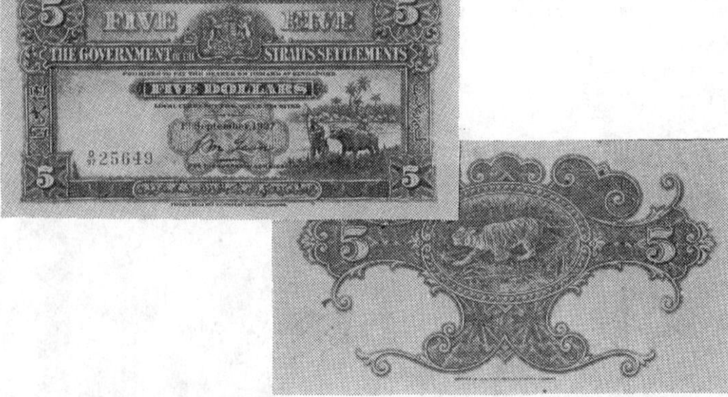

		Good	Fine	XF
10	**5 Dollars**			
	1925-30. Green. Farmer w/water buffalo ridden by child at r. Tiger in ornate cartouche at upper ctr. on back. 4 sign. varieties (red or black).			
	a. Green date in plate. 1.1.1925; 1.9.1927; 1.1.1929.	200.	500.	1750.
	b. Black ovpt. date 1.1.1930.	200.	500.	1750.

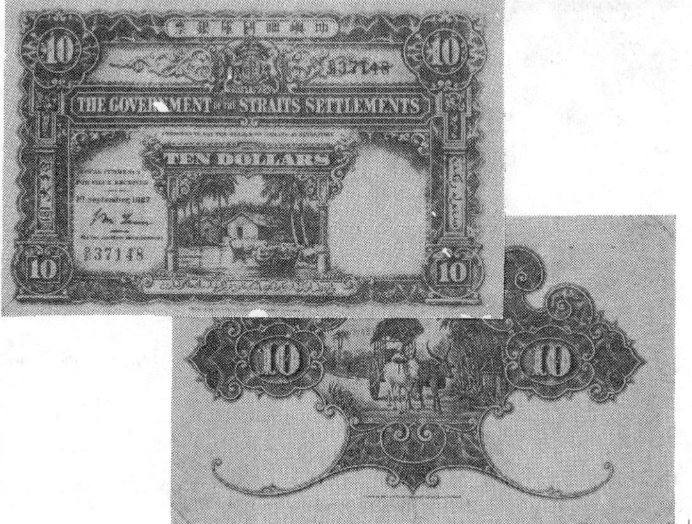

		Good	Fine	XF
11	**10 Dollars**			
	1925-30. Purple. Palm trees and huts w/fishing boats at ctr. Animal cart in ornate cartouche on back. 4 sign. varieties (red or black).			
	a. Purple date in plate. 1.1.1925; 1.9.1927; 1.1.1929.	400.	750.	3000.
	b. Black ovpt. date 1.1.1930.	400.	750.	3000.

		Good	Fine	XF
12	**50 Dollars**			
	1925; 1927. Like #A5.			
	a. 24.9.1925.	1300.	3200.	—
	b. 1.11.1927. Rare.	—	—	—

		Good	Fine	XF
13	**100 Dollars**			
	24.9.1925; 1.11.1927. Like #5.	1300.	3100.	—
14	**1000 Dollars**			
	1.10.1930. Like #5. Rare.	—	—	—
15	**10,000 Dollars**			
	1.9.1919; 24.9.1925; 1.10.1930; 8.12.1933. Like #5. Specimen. Rare.	—	—	—

Note: #15 was used only in interbank transactions.

1931 ISSUE

#16-18 portr. Kg. George V at r. Tiger at ctr., woman's head at l. on back. Printer: BWC.

		Good	Fine	XF
16	**1 Dollar**			
	1931-35. Dk. blue.			
	a. 1.1.1931-1.1.1934.	60.00	125.	550.
	b. 1.1.1935.	20.00	30.00	185.

		Good	Fine	XF
17	**5 Dollars**			
	1931-35. Violet.			
	a. 1.1.1931-1.1.1934.	100.	300.	900.
	b. 1.1.1935.	55.00	260.	800.

		Good	Fine	XF
18	**10 Dollars**			
	1931-35. Green.			
	a. 1.1.1931-1.1.1934.	110.	300.	900.
	b. 1.1.1935.	60.00	125.	750.

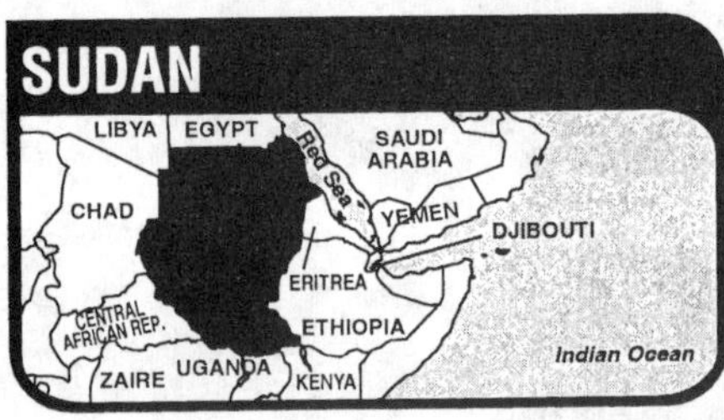

The Democratic Republic of the Sudan, located in northeast Africa on the Red Sea between Egypt and Ethiopia, has an area of 967,500 sq. mi. (2,505,810 sq. km.) and a population of 29.82 million. Capital: Khartoum. Agriculture and livestock raising are the chief occupations. Cotton, gum arabic and peanuts are exported.

The Sudan, site of the powerful Nubian kingdom of Roman times, was a collection of small independent states from the 14th century until 1820-22 when it was conquered and united by Mohammed Ali, Pasha of Egypt. Egyptian forces were driven from the area during the Mahdist revolt, 1881-98, but the Sudan was retaken by Anglo-Egyptian expeditions, 1896-98, and established as an Anglo-Egyptian condominium in 1899. Britain supplied the administrative apparatus and personnel, but the appearance of joint Anglo-Egyptian administration was continued until Jan. 9, 1954, when the first Sudanese self-government parliament was inaugurated.

The Sudan achieved independence on Jan. 1, 1956 with the consent of the British and Egyptian governments. On June 30, 1989 Gen. Omar Hassan Ahmad al-Bashir overthrew the civilian government in a military coup. The rebel guerrilla PLA forces are active in the south. Notes of Egypt were in use before 1956.

RULERS:

British, 1899-1954
Italian, 1940

MONETARY SYSTEM:

1 Ghirsh (Piastre) = 10 Millim (Milliemes)
1 Sudanese Pound = 100 Piastres to 1992
1 Dinar = 10 Old Sudanese Pounds, 1992

REPUBLIC

SUDAN GOVERNMENT - TREASURY

1955 ISSUE

#A1-A5 arms (desert camel soldier) at ctr. r. on back. Printer: W&S. (Not issued.)

		VG	VF	UNC
A1	**25 Piastres** 6.7.1955. Red on pale green and pale orange unpt. Soldiers in formation at l. Specimen, punched hole cancelled.	—	—	—

		VG	VF	UNC
A2	**50 Piastres** 6.7.1955. Green on ochre and dull violet unpt. Elephants at l. Specimen, punched hole cancelled.	—	—	800.
A3	**1 Pound** ND (1955). Blue on yellow and m/c unpt. Dam at l. Specimen, punched hole cancelled.	—	—	—

		VG	VF	UNC
A4	**5 Pounds** 6.7.1955. Dk. brown on m/c unpt. Dhow at l. Specimen, punched hole cancelled.	—	—	—

		VG	VF	UNC
A5	**10 Pounds** ND (1955). Black on m/c unpt. Bldg. at l. Specimen, punched hole cancelled.	—	—	2000.

SUDAN CURRENCY BOARD

1956 ISSUE

#1A-5 Arabic dates at lower r. Arms (desert camel soldier) at ctr. r. on back.

		VG	VF	UNC
1A	**25 Piastres** 15.9.1956. Red on pale green and pale orange unpt. Soldiers in formation at l. 3rd line of text 31mm long.	5.00	20.00	150.

		VG	VF	UNC
1B	**25 Piastres** 15.9.1956. Red on pale green and pale orange unpt. Like #1A but 3rd line of text 45mm long.			
	a. Issued note.	10.00	35.00	75.00
	s. Specimen.	—	—	175.
2A	**50 Piastres** 15.9.1956. Green on ochre and dull violet unpt. Elephants at l. 3rd line of text 31mm long.	20.00	100.	500.

		VG	VF	UNC
2B	**50 Piastres** 15.9.1956. Green on ochre and dull violet unpt. Like #2A but 3rd line of text 45mm long.			
	a. Issued note.	20.00	125.	600.
	s. Specimen.	—	—	450.

		VG	VF	UNC
3	**1 Pound** 15.9.1956. Blue on yellow and m/c unpt. Dam at l.	15.00	75.00	325.
4	**5 Pounds** 15.9.1956. Dk. brown on m/c unpt. Dhow at l.	30.00	125.	950.

		VG	VF	UNC
5	**10 Pounds** 15.9.1956. Black on m/c unpt. Bldg. at l.	45.00	225.	1200.

ITALIAN OCCUPATION - WWII

CASSA MEDITERRANEA DI CREDITO PER IL SUDAN

1940 ISSUE

#M1-M8 prepared for the Italian occupation of Sudan during World War II. Specimen.

		VG	VF	UNC
M1	**5 Piastres** ND (1940). Blue and lilac. Apollo at r. Wheat motif on back. Serial # on back. Rare.	—	—	—

		VG	VF	UNC
M2	**10 Piastres** ND (1940). Orange. Apollo at r. Rare.	—	—	—
M3	**50 Piastres** ND (1940). Blue-green. Emperor Augustus at l. Rare.	—	—	—
M4	**1 Lira** ND (1940). Green. Emperor Augustus at l. Rare.	—	—	—
M5	**5 Lire** ND (1940). Brown and yellow. Emperor Augustus at l. Rare.	—	—	—
M6	**10 Lire** ND (1940). Lilac. Emperor Augustus at l. Rare.	—	—	—
M7	**50 Lire** ND. (1940). Green and gray. Michelangelo's *David* at l. Rare.	—	—	—

		VG	VF	UNC
M8	**100 Lire** ND (1940). Blue. Michelangelo's *David* at l. Rare.	—	—	—

Note: Only one specimen set is known. For similar notes with *PER L'EGITTO* see Egypt.

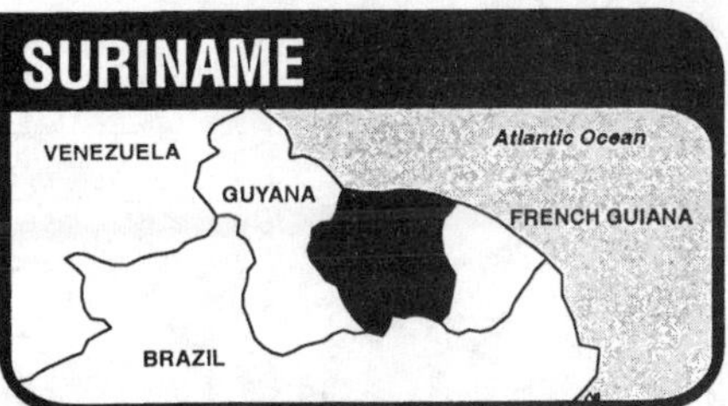

The Republic of Surinam, formerly known as Dutch Guiana, located on the north central coast of South America between Guyana and French Guiana, has an area of 63,037 sq. mi. (163,270 sq. km.) and a population of 452,000. Capital: Paramaribo. The country is rich in minerals and forests, and self-sufficient in rice, the staple food crop. The mining, processing and exporting of bauxite is the principal economic activity.

Lieutenants of Amerigo Vespucci sighted the Guiana coast in 1499. Spanish explorers of the 16th century, disappointed at finding no gold, departed leaving the area to be settled by the British in 1652. The colony prospered and the Netherlands acquired it in 1667 in exchange for the Dutch rights in Nieuw Nederland (state of New York). During the European wars of the 18th and 19th centuries, which were fought in part in the New World, Surinam was occupied by the British from 1799-1814. Surinam became an autonomous part of the Kingdom of the Netherlands on Dec. 15, 1954. Full independence was achieved on Nov. 25, 1975.

RULERS:

Dutch to 1975

MONETARY SYSTEM:

1 Gulden = 1 Florin = 100 Cents, to 2004
1 Dollar = 1000 "old" Gulden, 2004-

DUTCH ADMINISTRATION

Card Money of Surinam 1761-1826

The initial issue of card money for the Dutch colony of Surinam took place in 1761. The pieces were round in shape (38mm) and initially were backed by Bills of Exchange. Later issues did not have this backing. A rectangular shape followed shortly using plain cardboard as well as playing cards. Handwritten numbers and signatures were also applied to each piece.

Various issues took place sporadically as the need arose; they were especially prevalent during the years from 1770 to the 1820s. Card money was finally terminated with the emission of 1826. Currency issues by the official bank began shortly thereafter. All issues of card money for Surinam are considered to be extremely rare; about 25 known, nearly all of which are believed to be unique at this time.

ALGEMENE NEDERLANDSCHE MAATSCHAPPIJ / SOCIÉTÉ GÉNÉRALE POUR FAVORISER L'INDUSTRIE NATIONALE

(GENERAL NETHERLANDS SOCIETY)

1826 ISSUE

#1-9 w/border of musical note forms by J.M. Fleischman. All black, uniface, w/orange ovpt: *SURINAME*. Printer: JEZ (w/o imprint).

		Good	Fine	XF
1	**1/2 Gulden** 1.10.1826. Rare.	—	—	—
2	**1 Gulden** 1.10.1826. Rare.	—	—	—
3	**2 Gulden** 1.10.1826. Rare.	—	—	—

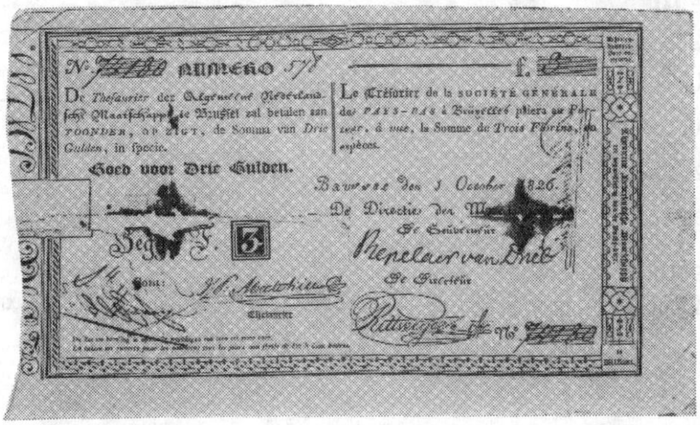

		Good	Fine	XF
4	**3 Gulden** 1.10.1826. Rare.	—	—	—

#	Denomination	Good	Fine	XF
5	**5 Gulden** 1.10.1826. Rare.	—	—	—
6	**10 Gulden** 1.10.1826. Rare.	—	—	—
7	**25 Gulden** 1.10.1826. Rare.	—	—	—
8	**50 Gulden** 1.10.1826. Rare.	—	—	—
9	**100 Gulden** 1.10.1826. Rare.	—	—	—

WEST-INDISCHE BANK

1829 ISSUE

#10-24 black, uniface. All w/Fleischman music border, printed wmk. on #16-24. Sign. varieties. Printer: JEZ (w/o imprint).

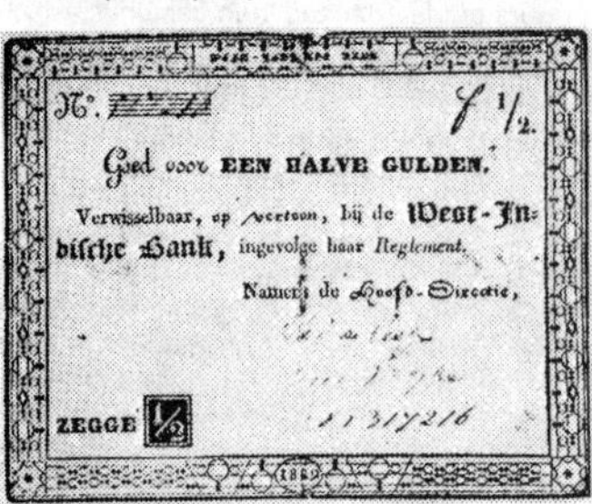

#	Denomination	Good	Fine	XF
10	**1/2 Gulden** 1829. Rare.	—	—	—
11	**1 Gulden** 1829. Rare.	—	—	—
12	**2 Gulden** 1829. Rare.	—	—	—
13	**3 Gulden** 1829. Rare.	—	—	—
14	**5 Gulden** 1829. Rare.	—	—	—
15	**10 Gulden** 1829. Rare.	—	—	—
16	**25 Gulden** 1829. Rare.	—	—	—
17	**50 Gulden** 1829. Rare.	—	—	—
18	**100 Gulden** 1829. Rare.	—	—	—
19	**150 Gulden** 1829. (Not issued). Rare.	—	—	—
20	**200 Gulden** 1829. (Not issued). Rare.	—	—	—
22	**250 Gulden** 1829. Rare.	—	—	—
23	**500 Gulden** 1829. Rare.	—	—	—
24	**1000 Gulden** 1829. Rare.	—	—	—

1837 ISSUE

#25-28 w/Fleischman music border. Uniface. Sign. varieties. Printer: JEZ (w/o imprint).

#	Denomination	Good	Fine	XF
25	**10 Centen** 1837. Brown. Square. Rare.	—	—	—
26	**15 Centen** 1837. Red. Rectangular. Rare.	—	—	—
27	**25 Centen** 1837. Black. Hexagonal. Rare.	—	—	—
28	**50 Centen** 1837. Blue. Rectangular. (Not issued). Rare.	—	—	—

1840 ISSUE

#	Denomination	Good	Fine	XF
29	**1 Gulden** 1840. Brown. Fleischman music border, uniface, octagonal, printed wmk., thick paper. Sign. varieties. Printer: JEZ (w/o imprint). Rare.	—	—	—

1844 ISSUE

#30-33 w/Fleischman music border. Uniface, real wmk., thin paper. Sign. varieties. Printer: JEZ (w/o imprint).

#	Denomination	Good	Fine	XF
30	**10 Centen** 1844.			
	a. Issued note. Rare.	—	—	—
	r. Unsigned remainder w/o serial #. Rare.	—	—	—
31	**15 Centen** 1844.			
	a. Issued note. Rare.	—	—	—
	r. Unsigned remainder w/o serial #. Rare.	—	—	—
32	**25 Centen** 1844.			
	a. Issued note. Rare.	—	—	—
	r. Unsigned remainder w/o serial #. Rare.	—	—	—
33	**50 Centen** 1844.			
	a. Issued note. Rare.	—	—	—
	r. Unsigned remainder w/o serial #. Rare.	—	—	—

SCHATKIST-BILJET DER KOLONIE SURINAME

TREASURY NOTE FOR THE COLONY OF SURINAM

1847 ISSUE

#	Denomination	Good	Fine	XF
34	**100 Gulden** 6.2.1847. Printer: JEZ (w/o imprint). Rare.	—	—	—

1848 ISSUE

#35-44 uniface, with ovpt. *SCHATKIST-BILLET K.B.6 6.February 1847). Sign. varieties. Printer: JEZ (w/o imprint).*

#	Denomination	Good	Fine	XF
35	**10 Centen** 6.2.1847 (- old date 1844). Ovpt. on #30. Rare.	—	—	—
36	**15 Centen** 6.2.1847 (- old date 1844). Ovpt. on #31. Rare.	—	—	—
37	**25 Centen** 6.2.1847 (- old date 1844). Ovpt. on #32. Rare.	—	—	—
38	**50 Centen** 6.2.1847 (- old date 1844). Ovpt. on #33. Rare.	—	—	—
39	**1 Gulden** 6.2.1847 (- old date 1840). Ovpt. on #29. Rare.	—	—	—
40	**2 Gulden** 6.2.1847 (- old date 1829). Ovpt. on #12. Rare.	—	—	—
41	**3 Gulden** 6.2.1847 (- old date 1829). Ovpt. on #13. Rare.	—	—	—
42	**5 Gulden** 6.2.1847 (- old date 1829). Ovpt. on #14. Rare.	—	—	—
43	**10 Gulden** 6.2.1847 (- old date 1829). Ovpt. on #15. Rare.	—	—	—
44	**25 Gulden** 6.2.1847 (- old date 1829). Ovpt. on #16. Rare.	—	—	—

DE SURINAAMSCHE BANK

1865 ISSUE

#45-51 uniface, allegorical border w/scrollwork, printed date. Sign. titles: *DIRECTEUR-SECRETARIS* and *DIRECTEUR-PRESIDENT*. 212 x 114mm, wmk. *SURINAAMSCHE BANK*. Sign. varieties. Printer: JEZ (w/o imprint).

#	Denomination	Good	Fine	XF
45	**10 Gulden** 1.7.1865. Black on red-brown unpt.			
	a. Issued note. Rare.	—	—	—
	r. Unsigned remainder, not dated. Rare.	—	—	—
46	**25 Gulden** 1.7.1865. Black on orange unpt.			
	a. Issued note. Rare.	—	—	—
	r. Unsigned remainder, not dated. Rare.	—	—	—
47	**50 Gulden** 1.7.1865. Black on blue unpt.			
	a. Issued note. Rare.	—	—	—
	r. Unsigned remainder, not dated. Rare.	—	—	—
48	**100 Gulden** 1.7.1865. Brown on blue unpt.			
	a. Issued note. Rare.	—	—	—
	r. Unsigned remainder, not dated. Rare.	—	—	—

		Good	Fine	XF
49	**200 Gulden** 1.7.1865. Brown on green unpt.			
	a. Issued note. Rare.	—	—	—
	r. Unsigned remainder, not dated. Rare.	—	—	—
50	**300 Gulden** 1.7.1865. Brown on lt. brown unpt.			
	a. Issued note. Rare.	—	—	—
	r. Unsigned remainder, not dated. Rare.	—	—	—
51	**1000 Gulden** 1.7.1865. Brown on red unpt.			
	a. Issued note. Rare.	—	—	—
	r. Unsigned remainder, not dated. Rare.	—	—	—

1869 ISSUE

		Good	Fine	XF
52	**5 Gulden** 1.10.1869. Black on red unpt. Uniface, scrollwork border, sign. varieties, wmk: *Surinaamsche Bank.* Sign. title: *Directeur-Secretaris.* Printer: JEZ (w/o imprint).			
	a. Issued note. Rare.	—	—	—
	p. Proof. Rare.	—	—	—

1880; 1886 ISSUE

#53-59 similar to 1865 issue. Various printed dates; titles: *Directeur* and *Directeur-President*, wmk: *Surinaamsche Bank.* Printer: JEZ (w/o imprint).

		Good	Fine	XF
53	**10 Gulden** 1886-1906. Black on red-brown unpt.			
	a. 1.7.1886. Rare.	—	—	—
	b. 1.7.1894. Rare.	—	—	—
	c. 15.2.1904. Rare.	—	—	—
	d. 1.11.1906. Rare.	—	—	—
54	**25 Gulden** 1886-1904. Black on orange unpt.			
	a. 1.7.1886. Rare.	—	—	—
	b. 1.2.1890. Rare.	—	—	—
	c. 1.7.1894. Rare.	—	—	—
	d. 15.2.1904. Rare.	—	—	—
55	**50 Gulden** 1880-1904. Black on blue unpt.			
	a. 1.7.1880. Rare.	—	—	—
	b. 1.7.1884. Rare.	—	—	—
	c. 1.7.1886. Rare.	—	—	—
	d. 1.2.1890. Rare.	—	—	—
	e. 1.7.1894. Rare.	—	—	—
	f. 1.7.1901. Rare.	—	—	—
	g. 1903 (- old date 1.7.1901). Rare.	—	—	—
	h. 15.2.1904. Rare.	—	—	—
56	**100 Gulden** 1880-1904. Brown on blue unpt.			
	a. 1.7.1880. Rare.	—	—	—
	b. 1.1.1882. Rare.	—	—	—
	c. 1.1.1884. Rare.	—	—	—
	d. 1.7.1886. Rare.	—	—	—
	e. 1.1.1894. Rare.	—	—	—
	f. 15.2.1904. Rare.	—	—	—
57	**200 Gulden** 1880-1904. Brown on green unpt.			
	a. 1.7.1880. Rare.	—	—	—
	b. 1.1.1882. Rare.	—	—	—
	c. 1.1.1884. Rare.	—	—	—
	d. 1.7.1886. Rare.	—	—	—
	e. 1.7.1894. Rare.	—	—	—
	f. 15.2.1904. Rare.	—	—	—
58	**300 Gulden** 1880-1904. Brown on lt. brown unpt.			
	a. 1.7.1880. Rare.	—	—	—
	b. 1.1.1882. Rare.	—	—	—
	c. 1.1.1884. Rare.	—	—	—
	d. 1.7.1886. Rare.	—	—	—
	e. 1.1.1894. Rare.	—	—	—
	f. 15.2.1904. Rare.	—	—	—
59	**1000 Gulden** 1880-1904. Brown on blue unpt.			
	a. 1.7.1880. Rare.	—	—	—
	b. 1.7.1883. Rare.	—	—	—
	c. 1.7.1886. Rare.	—	—	—
	d. 1.2.1890. Rare.	—	—	—
	e. 1.7.1894. Rare.	—	—	—
	f. 15.2.1904. Rare.	—	—	—

1906 ISSUE

		Good	Fine	XF
60	**5 Gulden** 1.9.1906. As #52 but printed date, title change to *Directeur* and *Directeur-President.* Printer: JEZ (w/o imprint). Rare.	—	—	—

1909-11 ISSUE

#61-66 as 1880 issue. Uniface, printed dates, slightly larger size (222 x 114mm), different color schemes to 1880 issue, wmk: *Surinaamsche Bank.* Printer: JEZ (w/o imprint).

		Good	Fine	XF
61	**10 Gulden** 1.9.1910. Pink on lt. gray unpt. Rare.	—	—	—
62	**25 Gulden** 1.9.1909; 1.12.1911. Green on brown unpt. Rare.	—	—	—
63	**100 Gulden** 1.12.1911. Brown on gray-blue unpt. Rare.	—	—	—
64	**200 Gulden** 1.9.1909. Brown-pink on pink unpt. Rare.	—	—	—
65	**300 Gulden** 1.9.1910. Purple on brown-yellow unpt. Rare.	—	—	—
66	**1000 Gulden** 1.9.1910. Purple on green unpt. Rare.	—	—	—

1911 ISSUE

		Good	Fine	XF
67	**5 Gulden** 1.11.1911. Black on lt. red unpt. As #60. Uniface, stamped date, wmk: *Surinaamsche Bank.* Printer: JEZ (w/o imprint). Rare.	—	—	—

1913 ISSUE

#68-70 uniface, dates no longer pre-printed, wmk: *Surinaamsche Bank.* Printer: JEZ (w/o imprint).

		Good	Fine	XF
68	**10 Gulden** 1.8.1915; 1.11.1919. Pink on lt. grey unpt. Similar to #61. Rare.	—	—	—
69	**25 Gulden** Ca. 1913. Green on brown unpt. Similar to #62. Rare.	—	—	—
70	**50 Gulden** Ca. 1913. Blue on gray-brown unpt. Rare.	—	—	—

1919 ISSUE

#71-73 first double-sided design, stamped dates and serial #, wmk: *Surinaamsche Bank.* Printer: JEZ (w/o imprint).

		Good	Fine	XF
71	**5 Gulden** 1919-33. Black on lt. pink paper.			
	a. 1.11.1919. Sign. titles: *Directeur* and *Directeur-President.* Rare.	—	—	—
	b. 20.12.1928; 1.3.1931. Sign. titles: *Directeur* and *Directeur-Voorzitter.* Rare.	—	—	—
	c. 1.4.1933. Penal Code change to Section 215. Rare.	—	—	—
72	**10 Gulden** Ca. 1919. Ca.1919Deep pink on gray unpt. Rare.	—	—	—
73	**50 Gulden** Ca. 1919. Blue on brown-gray unpt. Rare.	—	—	—

1920-21 ISSUE

#74-77 oval vignettes in corners depicting various aspects of the local economy. Serial # four times on face, sign. titles large, wmk: *Surinaamsche Bank.* Printer: JEZ (w/o imprint).

		Good	Fine	XF
74	**10 Gulden** 1920-25. Red.			
	a. Issued note. 1.8.1920; 1.3.1923; 1.9.1925.	400.	1500.	2500.
	s. Specimen.	—	—	—
75	**25 Gulden** 1.8.1920; 1.3.1923. Green.	400.	2000.	—
76	**50 Gulden** 1.1.1921. Blue. Rare.	—	—	—
77	**100 Gulden** 1.8.1920; 1.3.1923. Brown. Rare.	—	—	—

1925 ISSUE

#78-84 similar to #74-77. Serial # 3 times on back, sign. titles small. Various printed dates, wmk: *Surinaamsche Bank.* Printer: JEZ (w/o imprint).

		Good	Fine	XF
78	**10 Gulden** 1925-40. Rare.	—	—	—

		Good	Fine	XF
79	**25 Gulden** 1925-41. Rare.	—	—	—
80	**50 Gulden** 1925-40. Rare.	—	—	—
81	**100 Gulden** 1925-48. Rare.	—	—	—
82	**200 Gulden** 1925-48. Rare.	—	—	—

		Good	Fine	XF
83	**300 Gulden** 1925-48. Rare.	—	—	—
84	**1000 Gulden** 1925-48. Rare.	—	—	—

1935 Issue

		Good	Fine	XF
85	**5 Gulden** 1.10.1935; 3.6.1936; 15.12.1939; 28.5.1940; 1.6.1940. Blue on lt. green unpt. Arms at l., native girl wearing kotomisi head scarf at r., stamped dates, printed sign. Printer: JEZ.	175.	325.	800.

1940 ND Provisional Issue

Red ovpt. on face and back of half of #85.

		Good	Fine	XF
86	**2 1/2 Gulden** ND (1940).			
	a. Right half. Rare.	—	—	—
	b. Left half. Rare.	—	—	—

1940-42 Issue

#87-90 printer: ABNC.

		Good	Fine	XF
87	**2 1/2 Gulden** 1940-42. Lilac-red on brown unpt. Woman reclining w/branch at ctr. Arms at top ctr. on back.			
	a. Stamped date and sign. on face. 1.10.1940; 7.4.1941; 1.9.1941.	30.00	75.00	325.
	b. Printed date and sign. on back. 1.1.1942.	15.00	50.00	225.
	p. Proof.	—	Unc	250.
	s. Specimen.	—	Unc	225.

#88-91 Govt. palace at ctr., printed dates.

		Good	Fine	XF
88	**5 Gulden** 1.9.1942. Blue on m/c unpt. Arms at lower ctr. on back.			
	a. Issued note.	60.00	175.	450.
	p. Proof.	—	Unc	350.
	s. Specimen.	—	Unc	325.

		Good	Fine	XF
89	**10 Gulden** 1.9.1941; 1.6.1942. Orange on m/c unpt.			
	a. Issued note.	100.	600.	1250.
	p. Proof.	—	Unc	650.
	s. Specimen.	—	Unc	600.

		Good	Fine	XF
90	**25 Gulden** 1.2.1942; 1.12.1948. Green on m/c unpt.			
	a. 1.2.1942.	150.	750.	1600.
	b. 1.12.1948.	120.	600.	1250.
	p. Proof.	—	Unc	750.
	s. Specimen.	—	Unc	700.

		Good	Fine	XF
91	**100 Gulden** 1.9.1941; 1.4.1943; 1.4.1948. Purple on m/c unpt.			
	a. Issued note.	350.	1250.	—
	p. Proof.	—	Unc	850.
	s. Specimen.	—	Unc	800.

1951 ISSUE

#92-94 printer: De Bussy, Amsterdam.

		VG	VF	UNC
92	**10 Gulden** 1.8.1951. Green. Hut and trees at r.			
	a. Issued note. Rare.	—	—	—
	p. Proof.	—	—	600.
	r. Remainder, punch cancelled.	—	—	500.

		VG	VF	UNC
93	**25 Gulden** 1.8.1951. Bldg. w/flag at lower r.			
	a. Issued note. Rare.	—	—	—
	p. Proof.	—	—	600.
	r. Remainder, punch cancelled.	—	—	550.

		VG	VF	UNC
94	**100 Gulden** 1.8.1951. Violet and lilac. Arms w/Indian as shield supporter (Justitia, Pietas, Fides) at r.			
	a. Issued note. Rare.	—	—	—
	p. Proof.	—	—	650.
	r. Remainder, punch cancelled.	—	—	600.

ZILVERBONNEN

1918 ISSUE

#95-97 various date and sign. varieties.
#95-100 printer: JEZ (w/o imprint).

		Good	Fine	XF
95	**1/2 Gulden** 1918. Brown. Uniface.			
	a. 12.4.1918.	500.	900.	1400.
	b. 28.11.1918.	600.	1000.	1500.

		Good	Fine	XF
96	**1 Gulden** 1918-19. Brown. Like #95.			
	a. 12.4.1918.	600.	1000.	1500.
	b. 16.6.1919.	800.	1300.	1800.
97	**2 1/2 Gulden** 12.4.1918. Red-brown on lt. brown unpt. Like #95.			
	a. Issued note.	900.	1400.	1900.
	r. Unsigned remainder.	—	Unc	1200.

1920 FIRST ISSUE

		Good	Fine	XF
98	**1/2 Gulden** 2.2.1920. Brown. Like #95.	650.	1100.	1600.
99	**1 Gulden** 2.2.1920. Brown. Like #96.	600.	1000.	1500.
100	**2 1/2 Gulden** 2.2.1920. Like #97.	800.	1300.	1800.

1920 SECOND ISSUE

		Good	Fine	XF
101	**50 Cent** 1.8.1920. Blue, olive and m/c. Similar to #16.	450.	700.	1150.
102	**1 Gulden** 1.8.1920. Green, orange and m/c. Similar to #16.	550.	800.	1250.

		Good	Fine	XF
103	**2 1/2 Gulden** 1.8.1920. Brown on green unpt. Back green.	900.	1400.	2000.

1940 ISSUE

#104 and 105 printer: ABNC.

		Good	Fine	XF
104	**50 Cent** 1940-42. Orange. Helmeted woman at l.			
	a. 1 serial #. 26.6.1940; 5.7.1940; 27.9.1940; 5.10.1940; 30.10.1940.	7.50	40.00	200.
	b. As a. 1.7.1941.	7.50	40.00	200.
	c. 2 serial #. 30.4.1942.	5.00	30.00	150.
	p. Proof.	—	Unc	250.
	s. Specimen.	—	Unc	350.

		Good	Fine	XF
105	**1 Gulden** 1940-47. Gray-blue. Like #104.			
	a. 1 serial #. 26.6.1940; 5.7.1940; 19.9.1940; 5.10.1940; 30.10.1940.	8.50	45.00	200.
	b. As a. 1.7.1941.	8.50	45.00	200.
	c. 2 serial #. 30.4.1942.	5.00	40.00	175.
	d. 1.7.1947.	12.50	75.00	300.
	p. Proof.	—	Unc	250.
	s. Specimen.	—	Unc	350.

1949-55 ISSUES

#106-110 bust of Mercury at l. Printer: JEZ.

		VG	VF	UNC
106	**1 Gulden** 1.7.1949. Green, dk. brown and blue. Back brown and violet.	40.00	100.	350.
107	**1 Gulden** 1.3.1951. Like #106, but back brown and green.	40.00	100.	350.

NOTICE

Readers with unlisted dates, signature varieties, etc. are invited to submit photocopies or, high resolution (300 dpi, 100% size) scans of their notes to: Standard Catalog of World Paper Money, 700 East State St. Iola, WI 54990-0001, or E-Mail: george.cuhaj@fwpubs.com.

		VG	VF	UNC
108	**1 Gulden** 1954-60. Blue and brown.			
	a. Sign. title: *De Landsminister van Financien* at l. 1.7.1954.	25.00	60.00	130.
	b. Sign. title: *De Minister van Financien* at l. 1.5.1956; 1.4.1960.	20.00	55.00	125.
109	**2 1/2 Gulden** 1.7.1950. Red-brown on yellow-green unpt. 3 lines of text at lower ctr. r. Back red-violet and purple.	20.00	100.	300.

		VG	VF	UNC
110	**2 1/2 Gulden** 1.7.1955. Red-brown. 4 lines of text at lower ctr. r. Back red and brown.	20.00	100.	300.

Centrale Bank van Suriname

1957 Issue

#111-115 arms on back. Wmk: Toucan's head. Printer: JEZ.

		VG	VF	UNC
111	**5 Gulden** 2.1.1957. Blue on m/c unpt. Woman w/fruit basket at r.			
	a. Issued note.	25.00	60.00	200.
	s. Specimen.	—	—	150.
112	**10 Gulden** 2.1.1957. Orange on m/c unpt. Like #111.			
	a. Issued note.	40.00	100.	300.
	s. Specimen.	—	—	250.
113	**25 Gulden** 2.1.1957. Green on m/c unpt. Girl and fruit at r.			
	a. Issued note.	100.	225.	500.
	s. Specimen.	—	—	450.
114	**100 Gulden** 2.1.1957. Purple on m/c unpt. Like #113.			
	a. Issued note.	125.	275.	700.
	s. Specimen.	—	—	600.
115	**1000 Gulden** 2.1.1957. Olive green on m/c unpt. Like #113.			
	a. Issued note.	200.	400.	1200.
	s. Specimen.	—	—	900.

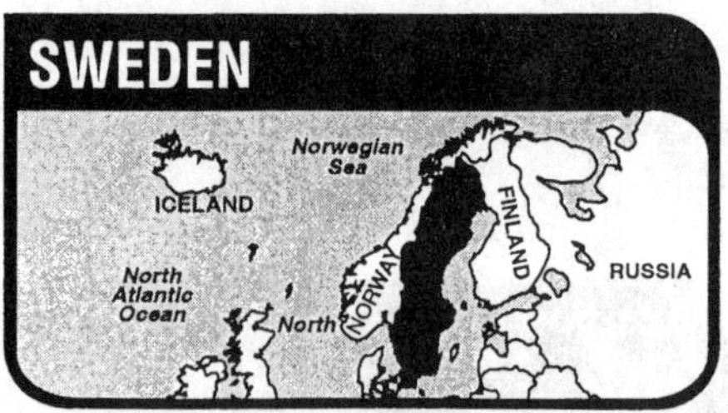

The Kingdom of Sweden, a limited constitutional monarchy located in northern Europe between Norway and Finland, has an area of 173,732 sq. mi. (449,964 sq. km.) and a population of 8.9 million. Capital: Stockholm. Mining, lumbering and a specialized machine industry dominate the economy. Machinery, paper, iron and steel, motor vehicles and wood pulp are exported.

Sweden was founded as a Christian stronghold by Olaf Skottkonung late in the 10th century. After conquering Finland late in the 13th century, Sweden, together with Norway, came under the rule of Denmark, 1397-1523, in an association known as the Union of Kalmar. Modern Sweden had its beginning in 1523 when Gustavus Vasa drove the Danes out of Sweden and was himself chosen king. Under Gustavus Adolphus II and Carl XII, Sweden was one of the great powers of 17th century Europe - until Carl invaded Russia, 1708, and was defeated at the Battle of Pultowa in June 1709. Early in the 18th century, a coalition of Russia, Poland and Denmark took away Sweden's Baltic empire and in 1809 Sweden was forced to cede Finland to Russia. Norway was ceded to Sweden by the Treaty of Kiel in January 1814. The Norwegians resisted for a time but later signed the Act of Union at the Convention of Moss in August 1814. The Union was dissolved in 1905 and Norway became independent.

A new constitution took effect on Jan. 1, 1975, restricts the function of king to a ceremonial role.

RULERS:

Carl XI, 1660-1697
Carl XII, 1697-1718
Ulrica Eleonora, 1719-1720
Fredric I, 1720-1751
Adolf Fredric, 1751-1771
Gustaf III, 1771-1792
Gustaf IV Adolf, 1792-1809
Carl XIII, 1809-1818
Carl XIV John, 1818-1844
Oscar I, 1844-1859
Carl XV, 1859-1872
Oscar II, 1872-1907
Gustaf V, 1907-1950
Gustaf VI Adolf, 1950-1973
Carl XVI Gustaf, 1973-

MONETARY SYSTEM:

1 Daler Smt. = 32 Öre Smt. (= 3 Daler Kmt.), 1665
1 Riksdaler = 48 Skilling (= 18 Daler Kmt.), 1777
1 Riksdaler = 1 1/2 Riksdaler Riksgäld, 1803
1 Riksdaler Specie = 2 2/3 Riksdaler Banco = 4 Riksdaler Riksgäld, 1834
1 Riksdaler Riksmynt = 100 Öre (= 1/4 Riksdaler Specie = 1 Riksdaler Riksgäld), 1855
1 Krona = 100 Öre (= 1 Riksdaler Riksmynt), 1873
1 Krona = 100 Öre

MONETARY ABBREVIATIONS

DALER SMT. = Daler Silvermynt
DALER KMT. = Daler Kopparmynt
KOP. SK. = Kopparschillingar
RKD. = Riksdaler
RKD. SP. = Riksdaler Specie
RKD. BC. = Riksdaler Banco
RKD. RMT. = Riksdaler Riksmynt
RKD. RGD. = Riksdaler Riksgäld
SK. = Schillingar
SK. Kop. = Kopparschillingar
SK. SP = Skillingar Specie
SK. BC. = Skillingar Banco
Kr. = Krona (Kronor)

Kingdom

Stockholms Banco

1661 Ducat Issue

		Good	Fine	XF
A1	**Various Handwritten Values** 1661.	—	—	—

1661 Riksdaler Specie Issue

#A2-A45 handwritten denominations.

		Good	Fine	XF
A2	**50 Riksdaler Specie** 1661-62.	—	—	—
A3	**100 Riksdaler Specie** 1661-62.	—	—	—
A4	**200 Riksdaler Specie** 1661-62.	—	—	—
A5	**300 Riksdaler Specie** 1661-62.	—	—	—
A6	**400 Riksdaler Specie** 1661-62.	—	—	—
A7	**500 Riksdaler Specie** 1661-62.	—	—	—
A8	**600 Riksdaler Specie** 1661-62.	—	—	—
A9	**700 Riksdaler Specie** 1661-62.	—	—	—
A10	**800 Riksdaler Specie** 1661-62.	—	—	—
A11	**900 Riksdaler Specie** 1661-62.	—	—	—
A12	**1000 Riksdaler Specie** 1661-62.	—	—	—

1661 Daler Silvermynt Issue

		Good	Fine	XF
A13	**50 Daler Silvermynt** 1661.	—	—	—

		Good	Fine	XF
A14	100 Daler Silvermynt 1661.	—	—	—
A15	200 Daler Silvermynt 1661.	—	—	—
A16	300 Daler Silvermynt 1661.	—	—	—
A17	400 Daler Silvermynt 1661.	—	—	—
A18	500 Daler Silvermynt 1661.	—	—	—
A19	600 Daler Silvermynt 1661.	—	—	—
A20	700 Daler Silvermynt 1661.	—	—	—
A21	800 Daler Silvermynt 1661.	—	—	—
A22	900 Daler Silvermynt 1661.	—	—	—
A23	1000 Daler Silvermynt 1661.	—	—	—

1661 Daler Kopparmynt Issue

Kreditiv-Sedlar (Credit Notes)

		Good	Fine	XF
A24	12 1/2 Daler Kopparmynt 1661.	—	—	—
A25	25 Daler Kopparmynt 1661.	—	—	—
A26	50 Daler Kopparmynt 1661.	—	—	—
A27	100 Daler Kopparmynt 1661.	—	—	—
A28	150 Daler Kopparmynt 1661.	—	—	—
A29	200 Daler Kopparmynt 1661.	—	—	—
A30	250 Daler Kopparmynt 1661.	—	—	—
A31	300 Daler Kopparmynt 1661.	—	—	—
A32	350 Daler Kopparmynt 1661.	—	—	—
A33	400 Daler Kopparmynt 1661.	—	—	—
A34	450 Daler Kopparmynt 1661.	—	—	—
A35	500 Daler Kopparmynt 1661.	—	—	—
A36	550 Daler Kopparmynt 1661.	—	—	—
A37	600 Daler Kopparmynt 1661.	—	—	—
A38	650 Daler Kopparmynt 1661.	—	—	—
A39	700 Daler Kopparmynt 1661.	—	—	—
A40	750 Daler Kopparmynt 1661.	—	—	—
A41	800 Daler Kopparmynt 1661.	—	—	—
A42	850 Daler Kopparmynt 1661.	—	—	—
A43	900 Daler Kopparmynt 1661.	—	—	—
A44	950 Daler Kopparmynt 1661.	—	—	—
A45	1000 Daler Kopparmynt 1661.	—	—	—

1662 Daler Kopparmynt Issue

#A46-A56 printed denominations.

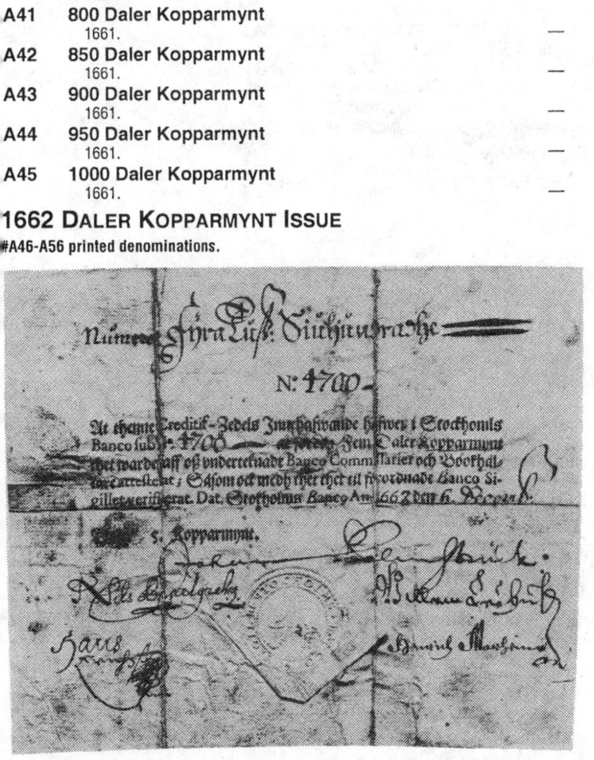

		Good	Fine	XF
A46	5 Daler Kopparmynt 1662-64.	—	—	—
A47	10 Daler Kopparmynt 1662-64.	—	—	—
A48	12 1/2 Daler Kopparmynt 1662-64.	—	—	—
A49	25 Daler Kopparmynt 1662-64.	—	—	—
A50	50 Daler Kopparmynt 1662-64.	—	—	—
A51	100 Daler Kopparmynt 1662-64.	—	—	—
A52	200 Daler Kopparmynt 1662-64.	—	—	—
A53	300 Daler Kopparmynt 1662-64.	—	—	—
A54	400 Daler Kopparmynt 1662-64.	—	—	—
A55	500 Daler Kopparmynt 1662-64.	—	—	—
A56	1000 Daler Kopparmynt 1662-64.	—	—	—

1666 Daler Silvermynt Issue

#A57-A60 printed denominations.

		Good	Fine	XF
A57	10 Daler Silvermynt 1666.	3000.	7000.	20,000.
A58	25 Daler Silvermynt 1666.	4000.	9000.	25,000.
A59	50 Daler Silvermynt 1666.	4000.	9000.	25,000.

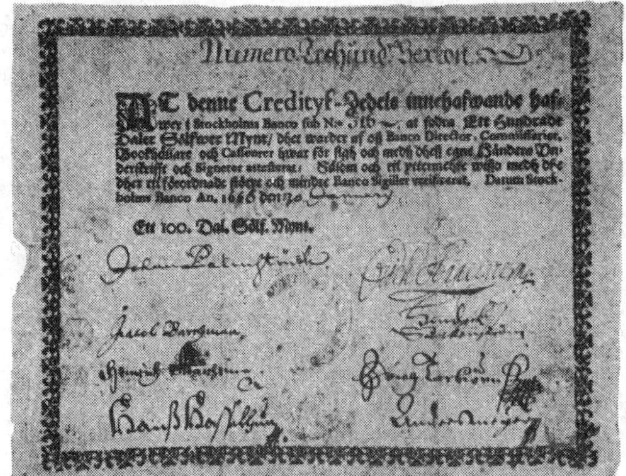

		Good	Fine	XF
A60	100 Daler Silvermynt 1666.	3000.	7000.	20,000.

1667 Transport (Transfer) Issue

		Good	Fine	XF
A61	100 Daler Silvermynt 1667. Copper money. (Negotiable only w/endorsement.)	—	—	—

NOTICE

Readers with unlisted dates, signature varieties, etc. are invited to submit photocopies or, high resolution (300 dpi, 100% size) scans of their notes to: Standard Catalog of World Paper Money, 700 East State St. Iola, WI 54990-0001, or E-Mail: george.cuhaj@fwpubs.com.

Contribution Office and Purchasing Commission

1716 Daler Silvermynt Issue

		Good	Fine	XF
A62	**25 Daler Silvermynt** 1716. Completely handwritten. a. 6 sign.	40.00	120.	320.

1717 Issue

		Good	Fine	XF
A63	**5 Daler Silvermynt** 1717. a. 3 sign.	20.00	60.00	160.
	r. Unsigned remainder.	10.00	30.00	80.00

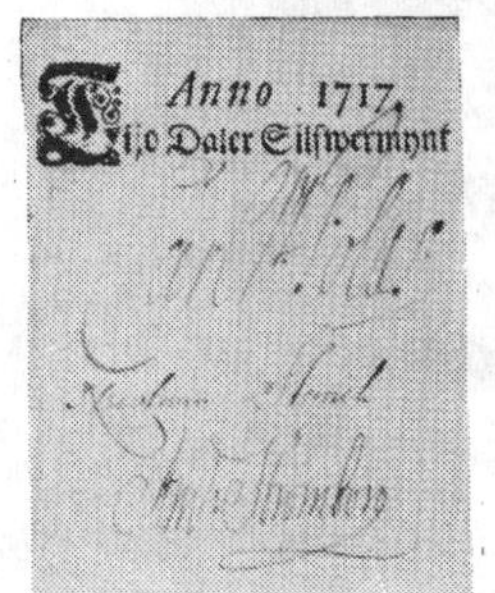

		Good	Fine	XF
A64	**10 Daler Silvermynt** 1717. a. 3 sign.	20.00	60.00	170.
	r. Unsigned remainder.	10.00	30.00	80.00

Assurance Notes

1719 Issue

		Good	Fine	XF
A65	**2 Öre** 1719-29. Handwritten dates. Exchangeable for emergency coins.	—	—	—
A66	**2 Öre** 1719-29. Handwritten dates. Exchangeable for paper money.	—	—	—
A67	**14 Öre** 1719-29. Handwritten dates. Exchangeable for emergency coins and notes.	125.	400.	—
A68	**14 Öre** 1719-29. Printed dates. Redeemable for taxes. Rare.	—	—	—
A69	**14 Öre** 1719-29. Printed dates. Rare.	—	—	—

Kongl. May: tz Ständers Wexel-Banco

1701-19 Issue

		Good	Fine	XF
A70	**Various Handwritten Values** 1702-19. Rare.	—	—	—
A71	**200 Daler Silvermynt** 1701. Handwritten. 1 known. Rare.	—	—	—

Riksens Ständers Wexel-Banco

1719 Issue

		Good	Fine	XF
A72	**Various Handwritten Values** 1719-28. 1 known. Rare.	—	—	—

1729 Issue

		Good	Fine	XF
A73	**Various Handwritten Values** 1729-31. 1 known. Rare.	—	—	—

1732 Issue

		Good	Fine	XF
A74	**Various Handwritten Values** 1732-47. Comprised of 4 pages. Rare.	—	—	—

1743-45 Issue

		Good	Fine	XF
A75	**6 Daler Kopparmynt** 1745-47. Banco Sigill seal at upper l. Rare.	—	—	—
A76	**9 Daler Kopparmynt** 1745-47. Like #A75. Rare.	—	—	—
A77	**12 Daler Kopparmynt** 1745-47. Like #A75. Rare.	—	—	—
A78	**24 Daler Kopparmynt** 1743-47. Comprised of 4 pages. Rare.	—	—	—
A79	**36 Daler Kopparmynt** 1743-47. Comprised of 4 pages. Rare.	—	—	—

1748 Issue

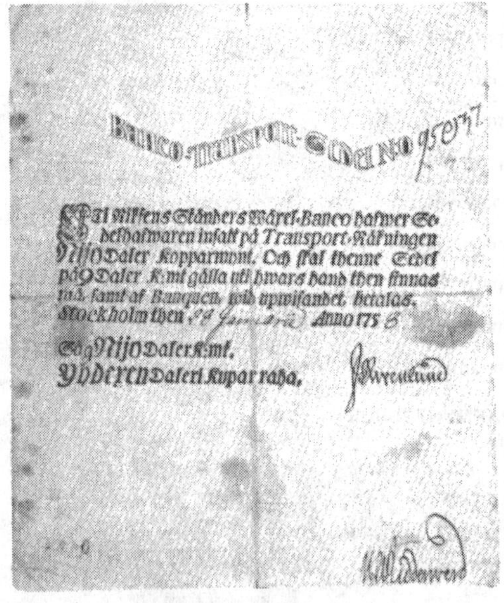

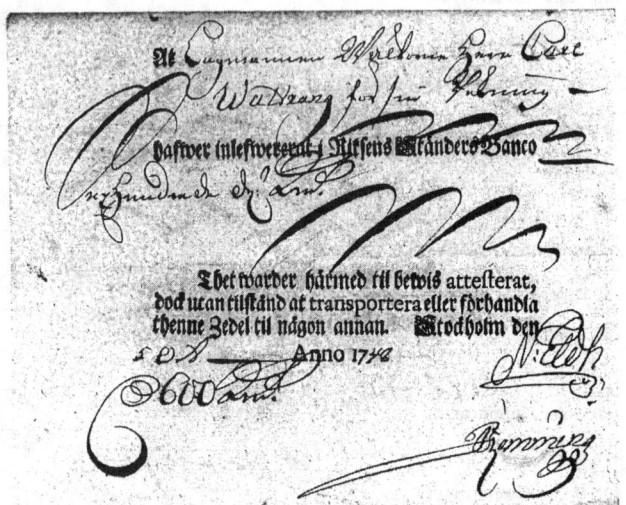

		Good	Fine	XF
A80	**Various Handwritten Values** 1748-60. Comprised of 4 pages. Rare.	—	—	—
A81	**6 Daler Kopparmynt** 1748-61. *BANCO TRANSPORT SEDEL* in uneven line.	100.	350.	—
A82	**9 Daler Kopparmynt** 1748-61. Like #A81.	100.	400.	—
A83	**12 Daler Kopparmynt** 1748-54. Like #A81.	100.	450.	—
A84	**24 Daler Kopparmynt** 1748-58. Like #A81. Comprised of 4 pages.	750.	2500.	—
A85	**36 Daler Kopparmynt** 1748-58. Like #A81. Comprised of 4 pages.	750.	2500.	—

1759-60 Issue

		Good	Fine	XF
A86	**Various Handwritten Values** 1759-76. Comprised of 4 pages. Rare.	—	—	—

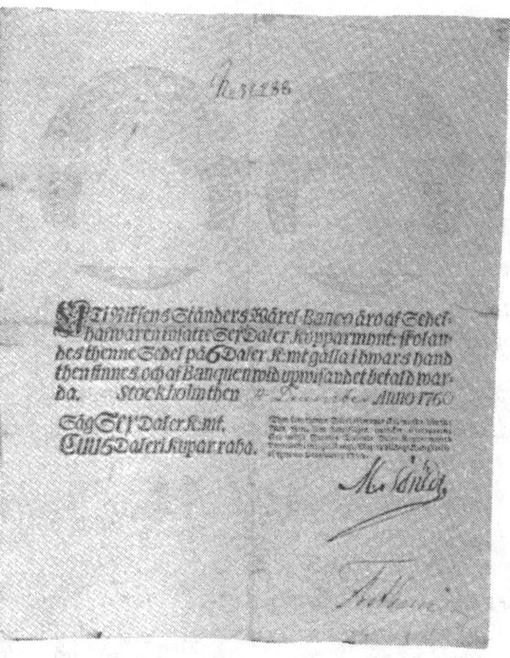

		Good	Fine	XF
A87	**6 Daler Kopparmynt** 1759-76. Embossed seals at top.	60.00	160.	650.
A88	**9 Daler Kopparmynt** 1759-76. Like #A87.	70.00	180.	700.

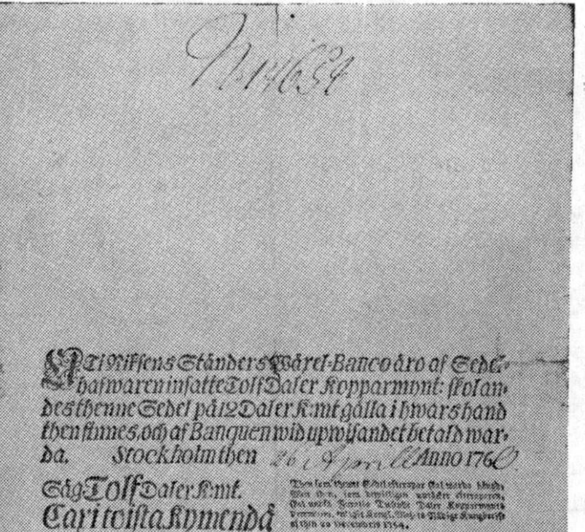

		Good	Fine	XF
A89	**12 Daler Kopparmynt** 1760-76. Like #A87.	75.00	200.	800.

1777 Transport (Transfer) Issue

		Good	Fine	XF
A90	**Various Handwritten Values** 1777-1836. Comprised of 4 pages.	—	—	—
A91	**2 Riksdaler Specie** 1777-1812. Comprised of 4 pages.			
	a. 1777-86. Embossed seal on both sheets. Rare.	—	—	—
	b. 1787-1806; 1812. Embossed seal removed from second sheet. Rare.	—	—	—
	c. 1807-1811. Printed value above obligation.	125.	350.	1400.

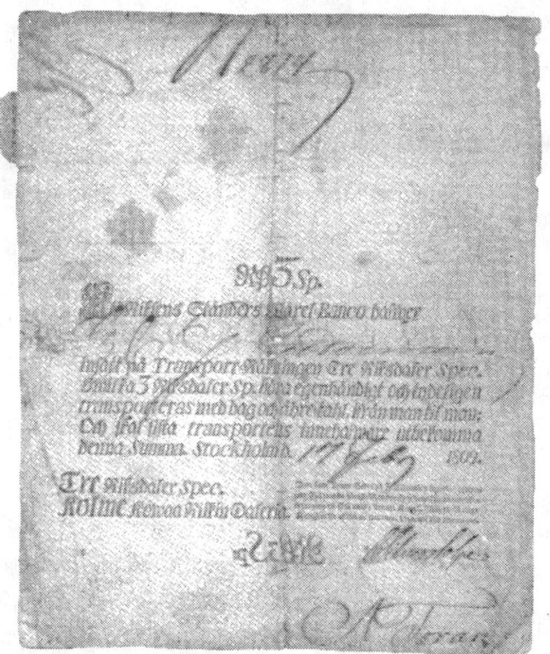

		Good	Fine	XF
A92	**3 Riksdaler Specie** 1777-1812. Like #A91. Comprised of 4 pages.			
	a. 1777-86. Embossed seal on both sheets. Rare.	—	—	—
	b. 1787-1805. Embossed seal removed from second sheet. Rare.	—	—	—
	c. 1806-12. Printed value above obligation.	100.	300.	1200.

1802 Issue

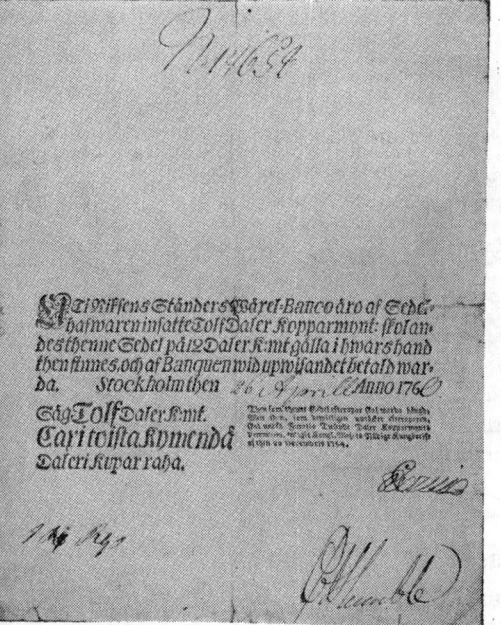

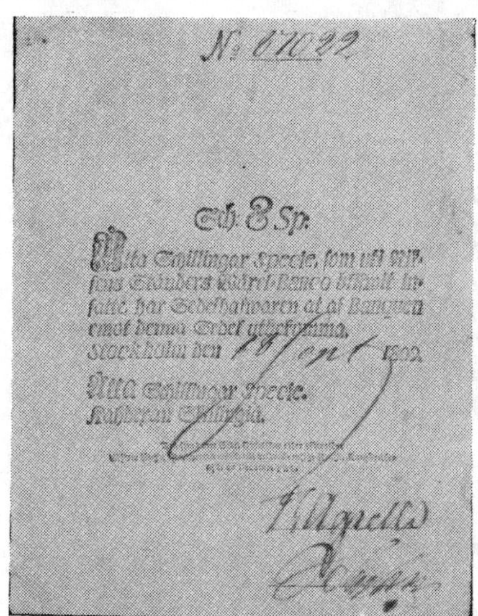

		Good	Fine	XF
A93	**8 Schillingar Specie** 1802-34. Like #A91. Printed value above obligation.			
	a. 1802-18.	50.00	100.	325.
	b. Change in punishment clause. 1819-30.	50.00	100.	325.
	c. Punishment clause in frame. 1831-34.	50.00	100.	275.
A94	**12 Schillingar Specie** 1802-34. Like #A93.			
	a. 1802-18.	50.00	150.	475.
	b. Change in punishment clause. 1819-34.	50.00	150.	400.
A95	**16 Schillingar Specie** 1802-34. Like #A91.			
	a. 1802; 1806; 1808-09; 1811-12; 1815-18.	75.00	175.	525.
	b. 1803-05; 1807; 1810; 1813-14. Rare.	—	—	—
	c. Change in punishment clause. 1819; 1823; 1825. Rare.	—	—	—
	d. Change in punishment clause. 1820-22; 1824; 1826-30.	75.00	175.	475.
	e. Horizontal format. 1831-34.	75.00	175.	500.

NOTICE

Readers with unlisted dates, signature varieties, etc. are invited to submit photocopies or, high resolution (300 dpi, 100% size) scans of their notes to: Standard Catalog of World Paper Money, 700 East State St. Iola, WI 54990-0001, or E-Mail: george.cuhaj@fwpubs.com.

1803 Issue

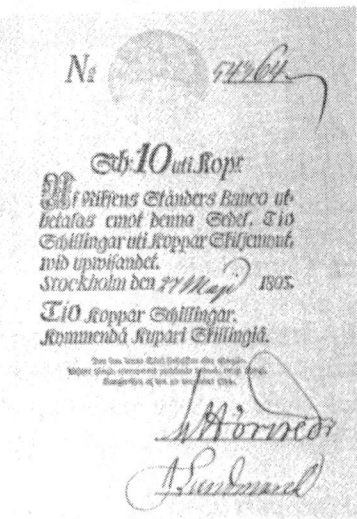

		Good	Fine	XF
A96	**10 Koppar Schillingar** 1803-04. Embossed seal at top ctr.	50.00	100.	175.

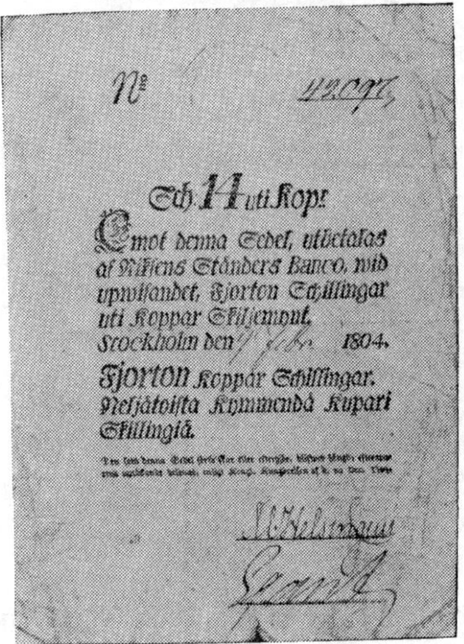

		Good	Fine	XF
A97	**14 Koppar Schillingar** 1803-04. Like #A96.	50.00	100.	175.

1812 Issue

		Good	Fine	XF
A98	**2 Riksdaler Specie** 1812-34. Like #A91. Comprised of 2 pages.			
	a. 1812-13; 1815.	70.00	200.	800.
	b. 1814; 1816-18. Rare.	—	—	—
	c. Change in punishment clause. 1819-22; 1828; 1831; 1834. Rare.	—	—	—
	d. Change in punishment clause. 1823-27; 1829-30; 1832-33.	80.00	250.	1000.
A99	**3 Riksdaler Specie** 1812-36. Like #A92. Horizontal format. Printed valyue at lower l. Comprised of 2 pages.			
	a. 1812-18. Rare.	—	—	—
	b. Change in punishment clause. 1819-23; 1825-30; 1832; 1835-36. Rare.	—	—	—
	c. Change in punishment clause. 1824; 1831; 1833-34.	70.00	200.	800.

1834 Issue

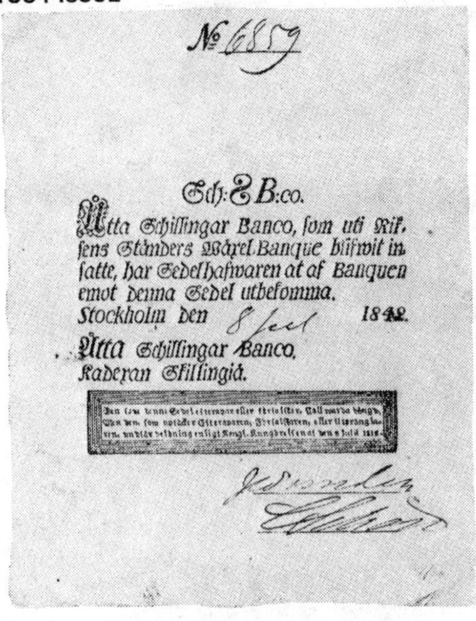

		Good	Fine	XF
A100	**8 Schillingar Banco** 1834-49. Like #A93.			
	a. Contoured letters in wmk. 1834-36.	50.00	100.	200
	b. Different wmk. 1836-49.	50.00	100.	200
A101	**12 Schillingar Banco** 1834-49. Like #A100.			
	a. Contoured letters in wmk. 1834-36.	50.00	100.	200
	b. Different wmk. 1836-49.	50.00	100.	200

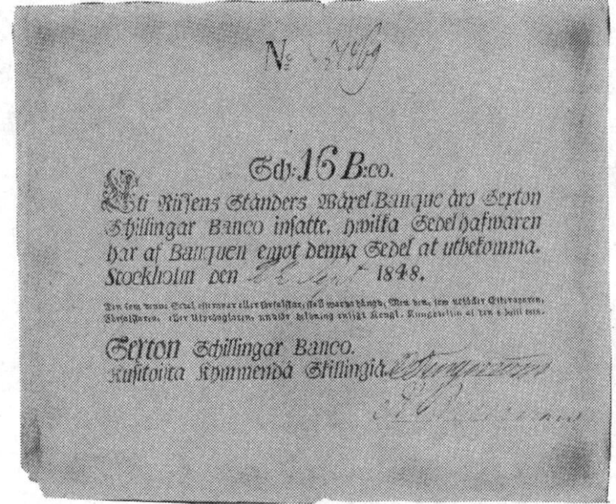

		Good	Fine	X
A102	**16 Schillingar Banco** 1834-49. Like #A99c. Horizontal format.			
	a. Contoured letters in wmk. 1834-36.	50.00	100.	30
	b. Different wmk. 1836-49.	50.00	100.	20

#A103 deleted, see #A94.

A104	**2 Riksdaler Banco** 1834-36.	100.	225.	90
A105	**3 Riksdaler Banco** 1834-36.	75.00	225.	90

RIKSENS STÄNDERS RIKSGALDS CONTOIR

1790 ISSUE

		Good	Fine	XF
A106	**Various Handwritten Values** 1790-92. Comprised of 4 pages.	—	—	—

1791 ISSUE

		Good	Fine	XF
A107	**12 Schillingar** 1791-92.	70.00	200.	800.

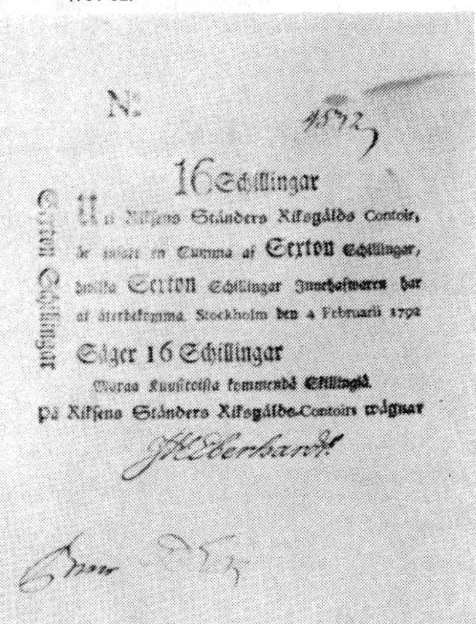

		Good	Fine	XF
A108	**16 Schillingar** 1791-92.	80.00	225.	900.
A109	**24 Schillingar** 1791-92.	90.00	250.	1000.
A110	**1 Riksdaler Specie** 1791-92.	—	—	—
A111	**2 Riksdaler Specie** 1791-92.	—	—	—
A112	**5 Riksdaler Specie** 1791-92.	—	—	—

1792; 1793 ISSUE

		Good	Fine	XF
A113	**Various Handwritten Values** 1793-1816. Comprised of 4 pages.	—	—	—
A114	**12 Schillingar** 1792-1805.			
	a. 1792-94. Uniface.	50.00	100.	325.
	b. 1795-1805. Value on back.	50.00	100.	250.
A115	**16 Schillingar** 1792-1834.			
	a. 1792-94. Uniface.	50.00	150.	625.
	b. 1795-1818. Value on back.	50.00	120.	425.
	c. 1819-34. Punishment clause change.	50.00	100.	400.
A116	**24 Schillingar** 1792-1804.			
	a. 1792-94. Uniface.	60.00	175.	675.
	b. 1795-1804. Value on back.	50.00	150.	575.

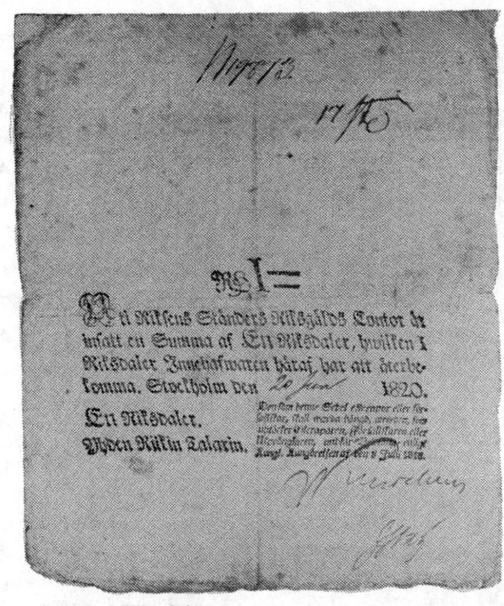

		Good	Fine	XF
A117	**1 Riksdaler** 1792-1834.			
	a. 1792-94. Uniface.	50.00	175.	650.
	b. 1795-1818. Value on back.	50.00	90.00	350.
	c. 1819-34. Punishment clause change.	50.00	90.00	350.
A118	**2 Riksdaler** 1792-1818.			
	a. 1792-94.	50.00	150.	650.
	b. 1795-1818. Value on back.	50.00	125.	500.
	c. 1819-34. Horizontal format. Punishment clause change.	50.00	100.	400.

1816 ISSUE

		Good	Fine	XF
A119	**10 Riksdaler** 1816-34.	—	—	—
A120	**50 Riksdaler** 1816-34.	—	—	—
A121	**100 Riksdaler** 1816-34.	—	—	—

SVERIGES RIKES STÄNDERS BANK

1830 ISSUE

		Good	Fine	XF
A122	**10 Riksdaler** 1830. (Not issued)			

NOTICE

Readers with unlisted dates, signature varieties, etc.
are invited to submit photocopies or,
high resolution (300 dpi, 100% size) scans of their notes to:
Standard Catalog of World Paper Money,
700 East State St. Iola, WI 54990-0001,
or E-Mail: george.cuhaj@fwpubs.com.

1835-36 ISSUE

		Good	Fine	XF
A123	**32 Skillingar Banco** 1836-58. Black on yellow paper. Lion lying in front of of crowned arms at top ctr.			
	a. Handwritten serial #. 1836.	75.00	150.	450.
	b. Handwritten serial #. 1839. Rare.	—	—	—
	c. Printed serial #. 1840-58.	37.50	75.00	300.

		Good	Fine	XF
A124	**2 Riksdaler Banco** 1836-57. Black on lt. blue paper. Like #A123.			
	a. Handwritten serial #. 1836.	80.00	250.	1000.
	b. Printed serial #. 1840; 1845; 1849; 1851; 1853; 1855; 1857.	50.00	100.	200.
	c. Printed serial #. 1848.	50.00	150.	400.
A125	**6 2/3 Riksdaler Banco** 1835-56. Black on green paper. Like #A123.			
	a. Handwritten serial #. 1835.	200.	600.	2400.
	b. Printed serial #. 1841; 1850; 1852; 1854; 1856.	70.00	200.	800.
	c. Printed serial #. 1848-49. Rare.	—	—	—

		Good	Fine	XF
A126	**10 Riksdaler Banco** 1836-57. Black on yellow paper. Like #A125.			
	a. Handwritten serial #. 28.1.1836.	300.	750.	3000.
	b. Printed serial #. 1841; 1852; 1854-55; 1857.	100.	300.	1200.
	c. Printed serial #. 1848; 1850. Rare.	—	—	—
A127	**16 2/3 Riksdaler Banco** 1836-55. Black on lt. red paper. Like #A125.			
	a. Handwritten serial #. 28.1.1836. Rare.	—	—	—
	b. Printed serial #. 1844; 1852; 1855.	400.	1200.	4000.
	c. Printed serial #. 1847; 1850. Rare.	—	—	—
A128	**33 1/3 Riksdaler Banco** 1836-57. Black on lt. blue paper. Like #A125.			
	a. Handwritten serial #. 28.1.1836. Rare.	—	—	—
	b. Printed serial #. 1840-52; 1857. Rare.	—	—	—
	c. Printed serial #. 1854; 1856.	650.	2500.	5500.
A129	**100 Riksdaler Banco** 1836-54. Black on lt. yellow paper. Svea seated below radiant crown at top ctr.			
	a. Handwritten serial #. 1836. Rare.	—	—	—
	b. Printed serial #. 1843-54. Rare.	—	—	—
A130	**500 Riksdaler Banco** 1836-54. Blue on lt. blue paper. Like #A129.			
	a. Handwritten serial #. 1836. Rare.	—	—	—
	b. Printed serial #. 1840-54. Rare.	—	—	—

1858-59 ISSUE

		Good	Fine	XF
A131	**1 Riksdaler** 1859-65. Green. Crowned and supported arms at top ctr. *EN* in ctr. rectangle.	20.00	75.00	200.
A132	**5 Riksdaler** 1858-67. Red. Like #A131.			
	a. 1858; 1863.	100.	300.	1100.
	b. Frame patterned. 1863; 1867.	70.00	250.	1000.
A133	**10 Riksdaler** 1859; 1866, 1870. Green. Like #A131.	100.	350.	1200.
A134	**50 Riksdaler** 1859; 1861; 1865. Red. Like #A131. Rare.	—	—	—
A135	**100 Riksdaler** 1859; 1864. Green. Like #A131. Rare.	—	—	—
A136	**500 Riksdaler** 3.1.1859. Red. Like #A131. Rare.	—	—	—
A137	**1000 Riksdaler** 3.1.1859. Yellow. Like #A131. Rare.	—	—	—

1865 ISSUE

		Good	Fine	XF
A138	**1 Riksdaler** 1865-69. Green on green unpt. Like #A131 but *EN* in oval at ctr.	15.00	60.00	150.

SVERIGES RIKSBANK

1869-70 ISSUE

		Good	Fine	XF
A139	**1 Riksdaler** 1869-73. Black on green unpt. Like #A138, but w/different wmk.			
	a. 2 handwritten sign. 1869-72.	15.00	60.00	150.
	b. L. sign. printed. 1872-73.	15.00	60.00	150.
	c. 2 sign. printed. 1873.	15.00	60.00	150.
A140	**5 Riksdaler** 1870-73. Black on red unpt. Like #A132.			
	a. 2 serial #. 1870-72.	75.00	225.	900.
	b. L. sign. printed. 1872-73.	60.00	175.	700.
A141	**10 Riksdaler** 1870-73. Black on green unpt. Like #A133.			
	a. 2 serial #. 1870-73.	75.00	250.	1000.
	b. L. sign. printed. 1873.	75.00	250.	1000.
A142	**50 Riksdaler** 3.1.1870. Black on red unpt. Like #A134. Rare.	—	—	—
A143	**100 Riksdaler** 1870; 1872. Black on green unpt. Like #A135. Rare.	—	—	—
A144	**500 Riksdaler** 1870. Black on red unpt. Like #A136. Rare.	—	—	—
A145	**1000 Riksdaler** 1870. Black on yellow. Like #A137. Rare.	—	—	—

1874 ISSUE

#1-6 consecutive year dates. Sign. varieties.

		VG	VF	UNC
1	**1 Krona** 1874-75. Black on green unpt. Crowned and supported arms at top ctr. 134 x 74mm.			
	a. 1874.	7.00	30.00	150.
	b. 1875.	5.00	20.00	90.00
2	**5 Kronor** 1874-78. Red on red. Like #1. 134 x 74mm.			
	a. 1874.	45.00	205.	860.
	b. 1875.	60.00	235.	940.
	c. 1876.	40.00	195.	860.
	d. 1877.	55.00	210.	880.
	e. 1878.	60.00	235.	970.

No.	Description	VG	VF	UNC
3	**10 Kronor** 1874-79. Green and black. Crowned and supported arms at top ctr. ca. 148 x 134mm			
	a. 1874.	50.00	220.	940.
	b. 1875.	65.00	270.	1060.
	c. 1876.	60.00	235.	1000.
	d. 1877.	65.00	270.	1120.
	e. 1878.	50.00	210.	905.
	f. 1879.	90.00	360.	1530.
4	**50 Kronor** 1874; 1876-79. Red and black. Crowned and supported arms over value. ca. 148 x 134mm. Rare.	—	—	—
5	**100 Kronor** 1874-79. Green and black. Crowned and supported arms over value. ca. 223 x 134mm. Rare.	—	—	—
6	**1000 Kronor** 1874-93. Yellow and black. Like #5. ca. 223 x 134mm. Rare.	—	—	—

1879-81 Issues

No.	Description	VG	VF	UNC
7	**5 Kronor** 1879. Like #8. Back blue. 121 x 70mm. Sign. at r. handwritten.	150.	470.	1590.

No.	Description	VG	VF	UNC
8	**5 Kronor** 1879-88. Black on brown design. Arms at upper ctr. back green; crowned shield at top ctr. Sign at r. handwritten.			
	a. 1879.	55.00	295.	1000.
	b. 1880.	40.00	235.	765.
	c. 1881.	40.00	210.	680.
	d. 1882.	40.00	235.	765.
	e. 1883.	40.00	235.	765.
	f. 1884.	45.00	300.	1000.
	g. 1885.	40.00	235.	765.
	h. 1886.	35.00	180.	620.
	i. 1887.	30.00	120.	445.
	j. 1888.	35.00	165.	555.

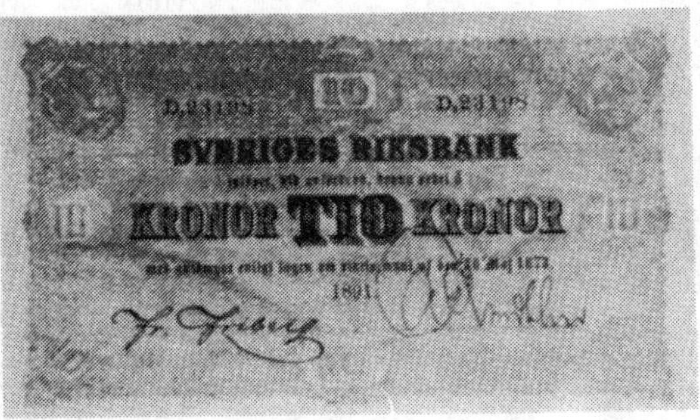

No.	Description	VG	VF	UNC
9	**10 Kronor** 1879-91. Black and blue. Crowned arms in upper corners, value at ctr. ca. 121 x 70mm.			
	a. 1879.	100.	410.	1765.
	b. 1881.	100.	410.	1180.
	c. 1882.	100.	410.	1180.
	d. 1883.	120.	470.	1650.
	e. 1884.	120.	470.	1470.
	f. 1885.	90.00	360.	1235.
	g. 1886.	90.00	360.	1235.
	h. 1887.	90.00	350.	1235.
	i. 1888.	80.00	325.	1235.
	j. 1889.	75.00	295.	1100.
	k. 1890.	75.00	295.	1095.
	l. 1891.	65.00	260.	980.
10	**50 Kronor** 1880-84; 1886; 1888-96. Maroon and black. Crowned arms over value. ca. 140 x 121mm. Rare.	—	—	—
11	**100 Kronor** 1880-96. Blue and black. Crowned arms in upper corners. Handwritten sign. ca. 140 x 121mm. Rare.	—	—	—
12	**1000 Kronor** 1881. Blue and black. Crowned arms at top ctr. 210 x 121mm. Rare.	—	—	—

1888-96 Issue

No.	Description	VG	VF	UNC
13	**5 Kronor** 1888-90. Like #8. Back green. 2 sign. printed.			
	a. 1888.	35.00	165.	325.
	b. 1889.	25.00	100.	555.
	c. 1890.	20.00	80.00	390.
14	**5 Kronor** 1890-98. Black on beige paper. Red and green guilloche. Svea seated at r. Gustav Vasa on back.			
	a. 1890.	40.00	480.	750.
	b. 1891.	40.00	210.	825.
	c. 1892.	35.00	150.	620.
	d. 1893.	40.00	210.	825.
	e. 1894.	40.00	190.	765.
	f. 1895.	30.00	150.	620.
	g. 1896.	35.00	155.	650.
	h. 1897.	30.00	130.	560.
	i. 1898.	30.00	150.	620.

No.	Description	VG	VF	UNC
15	**10 Kronor** 1892-97. Black on gray paper. Red and blue guilloche. Like #14. Svea seated at r. Portr. Gustav Vasa on back.			
	a. 1892.	40.00	180.	765.
	b. 1893.	45.00	190.	820.
	c. 1894.	40.00	155.	710.
	d. 1895.	45.00	190.	820.
	e. 1896.	45.00	190.	820.
	f. 1897.	35.00	150.	625.
16	**50 Kronor** 1896-97. Black. Red and green guilloche. Svea seated at lower r. Gustav Vasa on back.			
	a. 1896.	235.	825.	—
	b. 1897.	205.	800.	—
17	**100 Kronor** 1896-98. Like #11. L. sign. printed. Rare.	—	—	—
18	**1000 Kronor** 1894-97. Bluish paper w/red imbedded fibers. Svea seated. Gustav Vasa on back. Rare.	—	—	—

1898; 1899 Issue

No.	Description	VG	VF	UNC
19	**5 Kronor** 1899-1905. Like #14 but letter at lower l. and r. on back.			
	a. 1899.	30.00	120.	500.
	b. 1900.	35.00	130.	590.
	c. 1901.	35.00	130.	560.
	d. 1902.	30.00	120.	500.
	e. 1903.	35.00	165.	710.
	f. 1904.	35.00	150.	590.
	g. 1905.	25.00	95.00	415.
20	**10 Kronor** 1898-1905. Like #15 but letter at l. and r. on back.			
	a. 1898.	30.00	140.	590.
	b. 1899.	30.00	140.	590.
	c. 1900.	45.00	190.	825.
	d. 1901.	30.00	130.	530.
	e. 1902.	30.00	130.	560.
	f. 1903.	25.00	105.	470.

#	Description	VG	VF	UNC
20	g. 1904.	30.00	110.	500.
	h. 1905.	25.00	105.	470.

21 50 Kronor
1898-1903. Like #16 but one big letter at lower l. and r. on back.

	VG	VF	UNC
a. 1898.	250.	855.	—
b. 1899.	180.	735.	—
c. 1900.	180.	735.	—
d. 1901.	165.	710.	—
e. 1902.	145.	650.	—
f. 1903.	145.	650.	—

22 100 Kronor
1898-1903. Red and blue. Svea seated at lower r. Gustav Vasa on back.

	VG	VF	UNC
a. 1898. Rare.	—	—	—
b. 1900.			
c. 1901.	180.	650.	—
d. 1902-03.			

23 1000 Kronor
1898-1905. Like #18. 1 letter at lower l. and r. on back. Rare. — — —

1903 Issue

24 50 Kronor
1903-06. Like #21 but printed sign.

	VG	VF	UNC
a. 1903.	145.	650.	—
b. 1904.	145.	590.	—
c. 1905-06.	130.	530.	—

25 100 Kronor
1903-06. Like #22. Both sign. printed.

	VG	VF	UNC
a. 1903.	180.	650.	—
b. 1904.	145.	530.	—
c. 1905-06.	120.	470.	—

1906-09 Issue

26 5 Kronor
1906-17. Like #19 but green guilloche.

	VG	VF	UNC
a. 1906.	20.00	90.00	365.
b. 1907.	20.00	75.00	330.
c. 1908.	20.00	75.00	300.
d. 1909.	20.00	80.00	310.
e. 1910.	20.00	75.00	300.
f. 1911.	20.00	75.00	300.
g. 1912.	20.00	80.00	325.
h. 1913.	20.00	70.00	270.
i. 1914.	15.00	55.00	235.
j. 1915.	50.00	190.	700.
k. 1916.	10.00	50.00	210.
l. 1917.	10.00	50.00	190.

27 10 Kronor
1906-17. Like #20 but green guilloche.

	VG	VF	UNC
a. 1906.	30.00	120.	470.
b. 1907.	25.00	95.00	385.
c. 1908.	20.00	80.00	335.
d. 1909.	20.00	80.00	335.
e. 1910.	20.00	80.00	320.
f. 1911.	25.00	90.00	360.
g. 1912.	20.00	70.00	295.
h. 1913.	20.00	75.00	320.
i. 1914.	20.00	70.00	295.
j. 1915.	20.00	75.00	325.
k. 1916.	15.00	55.00	225.
l. 1917.	10.00	40.00	180.

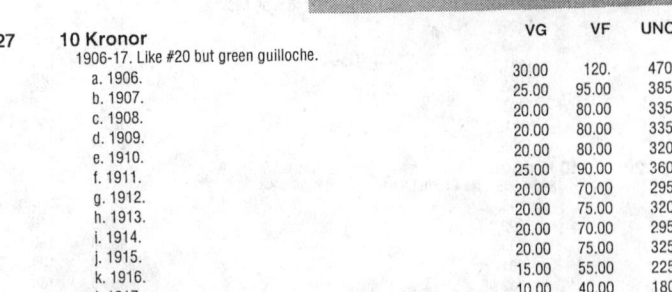

28 50 Kronor
1907-17. Like #24 but yellow unpt. added.

	VG	VF	UNC
a. 1907.	120.	505.	—
b. 1908.	120.	505.	—
c. 1909.	105.	460.	—
d. 1911.	105.	435.	—
e. 1912.	95.00	410.	—
f. 1913.	95.00	410.	—
g. 1914.	95.00	410.	—
h. 1915.	90.00	365.	—
i. 1916.	70.00	280.	—
j. 1917.	75.00	280.	—

29 100 Kronor
1907-17. Like #25. Yellow added to unpt.

	VG	VF	UNC
a. 1907.	105.	425.	—
b. 1908.	105.	425.	—
c. 1909.	105.	425.	—
d. 1910.	95.00	360.	—
e. 1911.	95.00	360.	—
f. 1912.	95.00	360.	—
g. 1913.	80.00	330.	—
h. 1914.	80.00	330.	—
i. 1915.	80.00	330.	—
j. 1916.	80.00	310.	—
k. 1917.	70.00	260.	—

30 1000 Kronor
1907. Like #23. Maroon added to unpt. Rare. — — —

31 1000 Kronor
1909; 1913; 1916; 1917. Like #30. Paper color changes to reddish w/blue imbedded fibers. Rare. — — —

1914; 1918 Issue

32 1 Krona
1914-40. Black on green unpt. Like #1. 121 x 70mm.

	VG	VF	UNC
a. 1914.	1.75	12.00	35.0
b. 1915.	3.00	15.00	50.0
c. 1916.	3.50	20.00	55.0
d. 1917.	3.50	20.00	55.0
e. 1918.	1.75	15.00	45.0
f. 1919.	2.50	15.00	50.0
g. 1920.	1.75	15.00	45.0
h. 1921.	1.75	15.00	45.0
i. 1924; 1938-39. Rare.			
j. 1940. Green paper. Small serial number w/o letter Wmk Mercury. Rare.	—	—	—
s. Specimen. 1939. W/o sign and serial number. Rare.	—	—	[illegible]
x. Error: legend missing, *lagen om rikets mynt av de.* 1920.	180.	415.	[illegible]

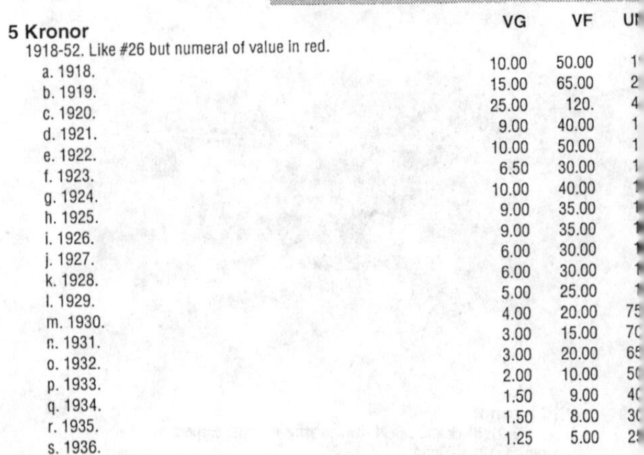

33 5 Kronor
1918-52. Like #26 but numeral of value in red.

	VG	VF	UNC
a. 1918.	10.00	50.00	[illegible]
b. 1919.	15.00	65.00	[illegible]
c. 1920.	25.00	120.	[illegible]
d. 1921.	9.00	40.00	[illegible]
e. 1922.	10.00	50.00	[illegible]
f. 1923.	6.50	30.00	[illegible]
g. 1924.	10.00	40.00	[illegible]
h. 1925.	9.00	35.00	[illegible]
i. 1926.	9.00	35.00	[illegible]
j. 1927.	6.00	30.00	[illegible]
k. 1928.	6.00	30.00	[illegible]
l. 1929.	5.00	25.00	[illegible]
m. 1930.	4.00	20.00	[illegible]
n. 1931.	3.00	15.00	[illegible]
o. 1932.	3.00	20.00	[illegible]
p. 1933.	2.00	10.00	[illegible]
q. 1934.	1.50	9.00	[illegible]
r. 1935.	1.50	8.00	[illegible]
s. 1936.	1.25	5.00	[illegible]

	VG	VF	UNC
t. 1937.	1.25	5.00	25.00
u. 1938.	.50	5.00	20.00
v. 1939.	.50	4.00	20.00
w. 1940.	.50	3.00	15.00
x. 1941.	.50	2.50	10.00
y. 1942.	.50	2.00	9.00
z. 1943.	.50	2.00	7.00
aa. 1944.	.50	2.00	9.00
ab. 1945.	.50	2.00	10.00
ac. 1946.	.50	2.00	9.00
ad. 1947.	.50	2.00	6.00
ae. 1948.	.50	2.00	6.00
af. 1949.	.50	2.00	6.00
ag. 1950.	.50	2.00	15.00
ah. 1951.	.50	2.00	6.00
ai. 1952.	.50	1.50	5.00

10 Kronor

1918-40. Like #27 but numeral of value in red.

	VG	VF	UNC
a. 1918.	15.00	60.00	225.
b. 1919.	20.00	65.00	285.
c. 1920.	15.00	60.00	230.
d. 1921.	15.00	50.00	205.
e. 1922.	15.00	35.00	150.
f. 1923.	6.00	30.00	130.
g. 1924.	5.00	30.00	155.
h. 1925.	4.00	25.00	140.
i. 1926.	3.00	20.00	120.
j. 1927.	2.00	15.00	105.
k. 1928.	1.75	10.00	95.00
l. 1929.	1.75	10.00	70.00
m. 1930.	1.75	8.00	50.00
n. 1931.	3.00	7.00	40.00
o. 1932.	3.00	5.00	30.00
p. 1933.	1.75	6.00	30.00
q. 1934.	1.50	5.00	30.00
r. 1935.	1.50	5.00	30.00
s. 1936.	1.25	5.00	30.00
t. 1937.	1.25	5.00	20.00
u. 1938.	—	Unc	15.00
v. 1939.	—	Unc	15.00
w. 1940.	—	Unc	15.00

50 Kronor

1918-53. Like #28 but numeral of value in red.

	VG	VF	UNC
a. 1918.	45.00	190.	—
b. 1919.	50.00	210.	—
c. 1920.	25.00	130.	—
d. 1921.	25.00	100.	—
e. 1922.	25.00	130.	—
f. 1923.	20.00	90.00	—
g. 1924.	20.00	90.00	—
h. 1925.	20.00	90.00	—
i. 1926.	20.00	90.00	—
j. 1927.	15.00	75.00	—
k. 1928.	15.00	75.00	—
l. 1929.	15.00	75.00	—
m. 1930.	10.00	70.00	235.
n. 1931.	10.00	70.00	235.
o. 1932.	15.00	75.00	260.
p. 1933.	15.00	75.00	260.
q. 1934.	10.00	60.00	200.
r. 1935.	10.00	60.00	200.
s. 1936.	10.00	60.00	200.
t. 1937.	10.00	50.00	165.
u. 1938.	9.00	50.00	140.
v. 1939.	8.00	40.00	110.
w. 1940.	7.00	35.00	105.
x. 1941.	—	Unc	105.
y. 1943.	—	Unc	105.
z. 1944.	—	Unc	90.00
aa. 1946.	10.00	35.00	105.
ab. 1947.	10.00	30.00	90.00
ac. 1948.	—	Unc	90.00
ad. 1949.	10.00	50.00	120.
ae. 1950.	—	Unc	65.00
af. 1953.	—	Unc	50.00

100 Kronor

1918-54. Like #29 but numeral of value in red.

	VG	VF	UNC
a. 1918.	40.00	200.	—
b. 1919.	40.00	200.	—
c. 1920.	30.00	135.	—
d. 1921.	25.00	120.	—
e. 1922.	30.00	175.	—
f. 1923.	30.00	120.	—
g. 1924.	25.00	100.	—
h. 1925.	25.00	100.	—
i. 1926.	25.00	100.	—
j. 1927.	20.00	90.00	—
k. 1928.	20.00	90.00	—
l. 1929.	20.00	90.00	—
m. 1930.	—	70.00	260.
n. 1931.	—	70.00	280.
o. 1932.	—	70.00	260.
p. 1933.	—	70.00	260.

36	VG	VF	UNC
q. 1934.	—	60.00	200.
r. 1935.	—	60.00	200.
s. 1936.	—	50.00	175.
t. 1937.	—	50.00	175.
u. 1938.	—	50.00	175.
v. 1939.	—	50.00	175.
w. 1940.	—	40.00	150.
x. 1941.	—	40.00	150.
y. 1942.	—	40.00	155.
z. 1943.	—	40.00	130.
aa. 1945.	—	40.00	130.
ab. 1946.	—	40.00	130.
ac. 1947.	—	35.00	110.
ad. 1948.	—	30.00	95.00
ae. 1949.	—	35.00	110.
af. 1950.	FV	20.00	70.00
ag. 1951.	FV	17.50	65.00
ah. 1952.	FV	17.50	65.00
ai. 1953.	FV	17.50	55.00
aj. 1954.	FV	17.50	55.00

37 1000 Kronor

1918-30. Like #31. Numeral of value in red.

	VG	VF	UNC
a. 1918.	265.	765.	—
b. 1919.	250.	735.	—
c. 1920.	265.	765.	—
d. 1921.	220.	650.	—
e. 1922.	220.	650.	—
f. 1926.	190.	500.	—
g. 1929.	165.	470.	—
h. 1930.	205.	530.	—

1932 Issue

38 1000 Kronor

1932-50. Like #37. 2 printed sign.

	VG	VF	UNC
a. 1932.	160.	380.	—
b. 1936.	150.	325.	—
c. 1938.	135.	260.	—
d. 1939.	130.	225.	—
e. 1950.	120.	210.	—

1939 Issue

39 10,000 Kronor	VG	VF	UNC
1939. Black and blue. Arms at ctr. Uniface. Wmk: Mercury head and wavy lines. Rare.	—	—	—

1940 Issue

40 10 Kronor

1940-52. Gray-blue on m/c unpt. Gustav Vasa at l. and as wmk., red dates and serial #. Arms on back.

	VG	VF	UNC
a. 1940.	25.00	100.	425.
b. 1941.	2.50	10.00	30.00
c. 1942.	1.00	5.00	20.00
d. 1943.	1.00	3.00	20.00

40		VG	VF	UNC
	e. 1944.	1.00	3.00	10.00
	f. 1945.	1.00	3.00	10.00
	g. 1946.	2.00	8.00	20.00
	h. 1947.	1.00	3.00	9.00
	i. 1948.	1.00	2.00	6.00
	j. 1949.	1.00	2.00	6.50
	k. 1950.	1.00	2.00	6.00
	l. 1951.	1.00	2.00	6.00
	m. 1952.	1.00	2.00	4.75

1948 Commemorative Issue

#41, 90th Birthday of Kg. Gustaf V.

41	5 Kronor	VG	VF	UNC
	1948. Olive on m/c unpt. Portr. Kg. Gustaf V at l., monogram at r. Back brown; arms.			
	a. W/o package.	1.25	5.00	20.00
	b. W/original package. Transparent with red printing.	—	Unc	45.00

Note: #41 was sold at twice normal face value, in special packaging.

1952-55 Issue

#42-43 replacement notes: Serial # suffix star.

42	5 Kronor	VG	VF	UNC
	1954-61. Dk. brown on red and blue unpt. Beige paper w/ red safety fibers. Portr. Kg. Gustaf VI Adolf at r. ctr. and as wmk. Svea standing w/shield at l. ctr. on back.			
	a. 1954.	.75	2.00	5.00
	b. 1955.	.75	2.00	5.00
	c. 1956.	.75	2.00	5.00
	d. 1959.	.75	2.00	7.50
	e. 1960.	.75	2.00	5.50
	f. 1961.	.75	2.00	4.00
	r1. Replacement, w/star. 1956.	2.00	20.00	100.
	r2. Replacement, w/star. 1959.	2.00	15.00	75.00
	r3. Replacement, w/star. 1960. Rare.	—	—	—
	r4. Replacement, w/star. 1961	2.00	15.00	75.00

43	10 Kronor	VG	VF	UNC
	1953-62. Gray-blue on m/c unpt. Like #40. Portr. Kg. Gustav Vasa at l. and as wmk. Arms at ctr. on back. Blue date and serial #.			

43		VG	VF	UN
	a. 1953.	FV	1.50	5.
	b. 1954.	FV	1.50	5.
	c. 1955.	FV	1.50	5
	d. 1956.	FV	1.50	5.
	e. 1957.	FV	1.50	5.
	f. 1958.	FV	1.50	5
	g. 1959.	FV	1.50	5.
	h. 1960.	FV	2.00	10
	i. 1962.	FV	2.00	6
	r1. Replacement, w/star. 1956.	2.00	30.00	1.
	r2. Replacement, w/star. 1957.	2.00	20.00	70
	r3. Replacement, w/star. 1958.	2.00	15.00	70
	r4. Replacement, w/star. 1959.	2.00	15.00	75.
	r5. Replacement, w/star. 1960.	2.00	25.00	1
	r6. Replacement, w/star. 1962.	2.00	20.00	70

44	50 Kronor	VG	VF	UN
	1955-58. Like #35. 2 small letters on back.			
	a. 1955.	FV	15.00	50
	b. 1956.	FV	15.00	50.
	c. 1957.	FV	20.00	60
	d. 1958.	FV	15.00	50
	r1. Remainder, w/star. 1956.	15.00	45.00	2
	r2. Remainder, w/star. 1957.	10.00	30.00	1
	r3. Remainder, w/star. 1958.	7.50	25.00	1

45	100 Kronor	VG	VF	UN
	1955-59. Like #36. 2 small letters on back.			
	a. 1955.	FV	17.50	55
	b. 1956.	FV	17.50	55
	c. 1957.	FV	17.50	35
	d. 1958.	FV	17.50	50
	e. 1959.	FV	17.50	35
	r1. Remainder, w/star. 1956.	20.00	40.00	1
	r2. Remainder, w/star. 1957.	17.50	30.00	1
	r3. Remainder, w/star. 1958.	15.00	30.00	1

46	1000 Kronor	VG	VF	U
	1952-73. Brown and m/c. Svea standing. Kg. Gustaf V on back and as wmk.			
	a. Blue and red safety fibers. 1952.	FV	110.	5
	b. 1957.	FV	110.	5
	c. 1962.	FV	100.	4
	d. 1965.	FV	100.	4
	e. W/security thread. 1971.	FV	90.00	4
	f. 1973.	FV	90.00	3

1958; 1959 Issue

#47 and 48 seated Svea at lower r. Kg. Gustaf Vasa at ctr. on back. Replacement notes: Serial # star suffix.

		VG	VF	UNC
47	**50 Kronor**			
	1959-62. Second sign. at l. Sm. date and serial #.			
	a. 1959.	FV	12.50	35.00
	b. 1960.	FV	12.50	35.00
	c. 1961.	FV	25.00	75.00
	d. 1962.	FV	12.50	30.00
	r1. Replacement, w/star. 1959.	12.50	20.00	120.
	r2. Replacement, w/star. 1960.	12.50	20.00	100.
	r3. Replacement, w/star. 1961.	12.50	20.00	100.
	r4. Replacement, w/star. 1962.	FV	15.00	70.00
48	**100 Kronor**			
	1959-63. Second sign. at l. Sm. date and serial #.			
	a. 1959.	FV	15.00	45.00
	b. 1960.	FV	15.00	45.00
	c. 1961.	FV	15.00	40.00
	d. 1962.	FV	15.00	35.00
	e. 1963.	FV	15.00	35.00
	r1. Remainder, w/star. 1959.	15.00	25.00	120.
	r2. Remainder, w/star. 1960.	15.00	20.00	100.
	r3. Remainder, w/star. 1961.	15.00	20.00	90.00
	r4. Remainder, w/star. 1962.	15.00	20.00	90.00
	r5. Remainder, w/star. 1963.	10.00	15.00	100.

		VG	VF	UNC
49	**10,000 Kronor**			
	1958. Green and m/c. King Gustaf VI Adolf at r. and as wmk. Svea standing w/shield at crt. on back.	1200.	1750.	3000.

SWITZERLAND

The Swiss Confederation, located in central Europe north of Italy and south of Germany, has an area of 15,941 sq. mi. (41,290 sq. km.) and a population of 7.41 million. Capital: Berne. The economy centers about a well developed manufacturing industry, however the most important economic factor is services (banks and insurance).

Switzerland, the habitat of lake dwellers in prehistoric times, was peopled by the Celtic Helvetians when Julius Caesar made it a part of the Roman Empire in 58 BC. After the decline of Rome, Switzerland was invaded by Teutonic tribes who established small temporal holdings which, in the Middle Ages, became a federation of fiefs of the Holy Roman Empire. As a nation, Switzerland originated in 1291 when the districts of Nidwalden, Schwyz and Uri united to defeat Austria and attain independence as the Swiss Confederation. After acquiring new cantons in the 14th century, Switzerland was made independent from the Holy Roman Empire by the 1648 Treaty of Westphalia. The revolutionary armies of Napoleonic France occupied Switzerland and set up the Helvetian Republic, 1798-1803. After the fall of Napoleon, the Congress of Vienna, 1815, recognized the independence of Switzerland and guaranteed its neutrality. The Swiss Constitutions of 1848, 1874, and 1999 established a union modeled upon that of the United States.

MONETARY SYSTEM:

1 Franc (Franken) = 10 Batzen = 100 Centimes (Rappen)
Plural: Francs, Franchi or Franken

The banknotes of the SNB bore three signatures until the 5th Series (1956/57 to 1980):

(1) President of the Bank Council (Präsident des Bankrates, Président du Conseil)

2) A member of the Board of Directors (Mitglid des Direktoriums, membre de la direction générale)

(3) Chief Cashier (Hauptkassier)

In the Board of Directors of the Swiss National Bank there are three members: The president of the National Bank and Chairman of Department I, the Vice-president and chairman of Department II and the Chairman of Department III. So, there are always three possible signature combinations with a single date

The Presidents of the Bank Council Der Präsident des Bankrates Le Président du Conseil	
Johann-Daniel Hirter 1906-23	[signature]
Dr. Paul Usteri 1923-27	[signature]
Dr. h. c. Alfred Sarasin 1927-35	[signature]
Dr. Gustav Schaller 1935-39 (Schaller[1])	[signature]
(Schaller[2])	[signature]
Prof. Dr. Gottlieb Bachmann 1939-47	[signature]
Dr. Alfred Müller 1947-59	[signature]
Dr. Brenno Galli 1959-78	[signature]

The Chief Cashiers Der Hauptkassier Le caissier principal	
A. Chevallier 1907-13	[signature]
K. Bornhauser 1913-36	[signature]
Erich Blumer 1936-54	[signature]
Otto Kunz 1954-66	[signature]
Rudolf Aebersold 1966-1981	[signature]

The Members of the Board of Directors Ein Mitglied des Direktoriums Un membre de la direction générale	
Heinrich Kundert 1907-15	
Rodolphe de Haller 1907-20	
August Burckhardt 1907-24	
Dr. Adolf Jöhr 1915-18	
Prof. Dr. Gottlieb Bachmann 1918-39	
Charles Schnyder von Wartensee 1920-37 (Schnyder[1])	
(Schnyder[2])	

Ernst Weber 1925-47	
Dr. h. c. Paul Rossy 1937-55	
Fritz Schnorf 1939-42	
Dr. h. c. Alfred Hirs 1942-54	
Prof. Dr. Paul Keller 1947-56	
Dr. Walter Schwegler 1954-66	
Dr. Riccardo Motta 1955-66	
Dr. Max Iklé 1956-68	

CONFEDERATION

SCHWEIZERISCHE NATIONALBANK

1907 ISSUE

#1-4 standing allegorical woman at l., cherub at lower r. Redeemable until 30.6.1945.

Note: Similar to previous Concordat note issues but w/new issuer name and a white cross in red guilloche in unpt. at upper r. For Concordat issues see Vol. 1.

#		Good	Fine	XF
1	**50 Franken** 1.2.1907. Dk. green on orange unpt.	700.	1400.	2000.

#		Good	Fine	XF
2	**100 Franken** 1.2.1907. Dk. blue on lt. blue unpt.	900.	2000.	3250.
3	**500 Franken** 1.2.1907. Green on lt. green unpt.	6000.	—	—
4	**1000 Franken** 1.2.1907. Blue on purple unpt. Rare.	—	—	—

1910-20 ISSUE

#5-8 printer: W&S.

#		Good	Fine	XF
5	**50 Franken** 1910-20. Green on orange unpt. Portr. of woman at lower l. F. Hodler's *Woodcutter* on back.			
	a. 1.1.1910.	100.	250.	550.
	b. 1.1.1914.	100.	225.	550.
	c. 1.1.1917. Series B48.	60.00	170.	375.
	d. 1.8.1920.	50.00	140.	300.
	s. Specimen. 1.1.1910.	—	—	—

#		Good	Fine	XF
6	**100 Franken** 1910-20. Dk. blue on orange unpt. Woman at l. F. Hodler's *Scyther* on back.			
	a. 1.1.1910.	100.	300.	450
	b. 1.1.1914.	90.00	180.	400
	c. 1.1.1917.	70.00	150.	375
	d. 1.8.1920.	65.00	125.	350
	s. Specimen. 1.1.1910.	—	—	—
7	**500 Franken** 1910-17. Dark red on yellow unpt. Woman from Appenzell at l. Back brown; E. Burnand's *Embroidering Appenzell Women.*			
	a. 1.1.1910. Rare.	—	—	—
	b. 1.1.1914. Rare.	—	—	—
	c. 1.1.1917.	350.	600.	1200
	s. Specimen. 1.1.1910.	—	—	—

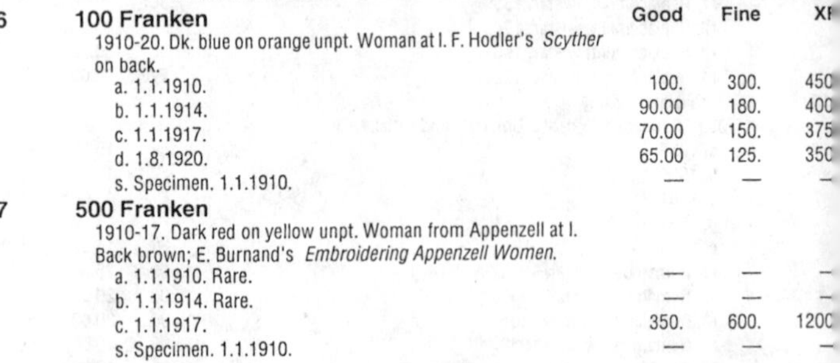

1000 Franken

1910-17. Violet on orange unpt. Portr. woman at lower l. Back black on orange unpt.; E. Burnand's *Foundry*.

	Good	Fine	XF
a. 1.1.1910. Rare.	—	—	—
b. 1.1.1914. Rare.	—	—	—
c. 1.1.1917.	500.	900.	1750.
s. Specimen, punched hole cancelled. 1.1.1910.	—	—	—

918 ISSUES

)-10 printer: OFZ.

100 Franken

1.1.1918. Blue on brown unpt. William Tell at l., Tell's Chapel at Lake Vierwaldstätten at r. Letters *T.W.* at lower l., *R.K.* at lower r. Mount Jungfrau on back.

	Good	Fine	XF
a. Issued note.	500.	1000.	1800.
s. Specimen, punched hole cancelled.	—	—	—

te: #9 was redeemable until 30.6.1945.

100 Franken

1.1.1918. Blue and brown. Similar to #9 but modified portr. of Tell. Letters *Ekn. R. K.* in the l. medallion at lower r. (Not issued).

Good	Fine	XF
—	—	—

11-14 ISSUE

5 Franken

1913-53. Red, blue and black on olive-green unpt. William Tell monument in Altdorf at l. Rutli Mountain in l. background. Back olive-green.

11	Good	Fine	XF
a. 1.8.1913.	150.	500.	2000.
b. 1.8.1914.	45.00	100.	300.
c. 1.1.1916.	45.00	100.	325.
d. 1.1.1919.	45.00	100.	325.
e. 1.1.1921.	15.00	30.00	75.00
f. 1.7.1922.	30.00	60.00	130.
g. 2.12.1926.	12.50	25.00	60.00
h. 25.9.1936.	9.00	20.00	50.00
i. 17.5.1939.	7.00	12.50	47.50
j. 4.12.1942.	4.00	7.50	35.00
k. 16.11.1944.	4.00	7.50	40.00
l. 31.8.1946.	4.00	7.50	40.00
m. 16.10.1947.	4.00	7.50	40.00
n. 20.1.1949.	4.00	7.50	40.00
o. 22.2.1951.	3.50	7.00	32.50
p. 28.3.1952.	3.50	7.00	32.50
q. 15.1.1953 (not issued).	—	—	—
r. 22.10.1953 (not issued).	—	—	—
s. As h. Specimen.	—	—	—

12 **20 Franken**

1911-22. Blue-gray, lt. and dk. brown. Woman's head *Vreneli* at l. Printer: OFZ.

	Good	Fine	XF
a. 1.12.1911.	250.	400.	750.
b. 1.9.1915.	175.	350.	700.
c. 1.1.1916.	90.00	180.	450.
d. 1.1.1918.	90.00	180.	450.
e. 1.1.1920.	75.00	160.	400.
f. 1.9.1920.	75.00	160.	400.
g. 1.1.1922.	75.00	160.	425.

13 **40 Franken**

1.9.1914. Violet-green on lt. green unpt. Arnold Winkelried at l. (Not issued).

Good	Fine	XF
—	—	—

EIDGENÖSSISCHE STAATSKASSE

LA CAISSE FÉDÉRALE (FRENCH)

LA CASSA FÉDÉRALE (ITALIAN)

FEDERAL TREASURY

1914 ISSUES

#14-22 arms at top ctr.

Note: Same design issued in either German, Italian or French.

14 **5 Franken**

10.8.1914. Blue. Portr. Libertas at l., Arnold Winkelreid at r. German text.

Good	Fine	XF
300.	750.	1400.

		Good	Fine	XF
15	**5 Francs** 10.8.1914. Blue. Like #14 but French text.	400.	900.	2000.

		Good	Fine	XF
16	**5 Franchi** 10.8.1914. Blue. Like #14 but Italian text.	1000.	2000.	3750.

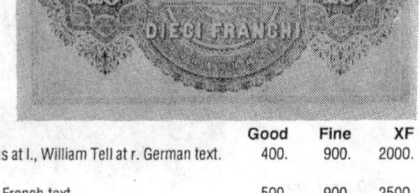

		Good	Fine	XF
17	**10 Franken** 10.8.1914. Blue. Portr. Libertas at l., William Tell at r. German text.	400.	900.	2000.
18	**10 Francs** 10.8.1914. Blue. Like #17 but French text.	500.	900.	2500.
19	**10 Franchi** 10.8.1914. Blue. Like #17 but Italian text.	1250.	2500.	4000.
20	**20 Franken** 10.8.1914. Blue. Portr. Libertas at l., Arnold Winkelreid at r. German text.	950.	1800.	3750.

		Good	Fine	XF
21	**20 Francs** 10.8.1914. Blue. Like #20 but French text.	1200.	2000.	3800.
22	**20 Franchi** 10.8.1914. Blue. Like #20 but Italian text.	2000.	3000.	4500.

Darlehenskasse der Schweizerischen Eidgenossenschaft

State Loan Bank of the Swiss Federation

1914 Issue

#23-24 printer: OFZ.

		VG	VF	UNC
23	**25 Franken** 9.9.1914. Olive-green and gray on yellow-brown unpt. 2 serial # varieties.	450.	775.	1700.
23A	**100 Franken** 9.9.1914. Green and gray on yellow-brown unpt. (Not issued.)	—	—	—
24	**100 Franken** 9.9.1914. Green and gray on yellow-brown unpt. (Not issued.)	—	—	—

1915 Issue

#25-26 printer: OFZ.

		VG	VF	UNC
25	**1 Frank** 27.4.1915. Dk. blue on orange-yellow unpt. (Not issued.)	—	—	—
26	**2 Franken** 27.4.1915. Red-brown on orange-yellow unpt. (Not issued.)	—	—	—

Schweizerische Nationalbank (Resumed)

Swiss National Bank

Gesetz vom 7.4.1921 (Law of 7.4.1921)

1922; 1923 Issue

		VG	VF	UNC
27	**20 Franken** 1.7.1922. Blue, green and brown. Like #11. Printer: OFZ.			
	a. Issued note.	100.	250.	700.
	s. Specimen.	—	—	1250.

#28-30 printer: W&S.

		VG	VF	UNC
28	**100 Franken** 1.1.1923. Blue. Like #6.	55.00	130.	400.
29	**500 Franken** 1.1.1923. Red. Like #7.	350.	650.	1250.
30	**1000 Franken** 1.1.1923. Violet. Like #8.	425.	800.	1500.

1921-28 Issue

#31-37 *GESETZGEBUNG ÜBER DIE SCHWEIZERISCHE NATIONALBANK* (Legislation governing the Swiss National Bank). Sign. varieties.

31 **10 Franken**

	VG	VF	UNC
1.4.1921. Red-brown on yellow unpt. Portr. woman in Neuchatel costume at lower l. Printer: W&S. (Not issued).	—	—	—

32 **20 Franken**

	VG	VF	UNC
16.5.1923. Dk. blue on yellow unpt. Portr. woman in Fribourg costume at l. Printer: OFZ. (Not issued.)	—	—	—

33 **20 Franken**

1.5.1923-18.4.1929. Blue, green and brown. Like #11. Printer: OFZ.

	VG	VF	UNC
a. 1.5.1923.	75.00	150.	600.
b. 1.7.1926.	75.00	150.	600.
c. 21.10.1926.	75.00	150.	600.
d. 24.3.1927.	75.00	150.	600.
e. 29.9.1927.	75.00	150.	600.
f. 1.11.1928.	75.00	150.	600.
g. 19.2.1929.	75.00	150.	600.
h. 18.4.1929.	75.00	150.	600.

34 **50 Franken**

1924-55. Green. Like #5.

	VG	VF	UNC
a. 1.4.1924.	45.00	150.	400.
b. 30.9.1926.	47.50	160.	450.
c. 23.11.1927.	47.50	160.	425.
d. 25.9.1929.	47.50	160.	400.
e. 16.9.1930.	47.50	160.	400.
f. 21.7.1931.	47.50	160.	400.
g. 27.8.1937.	42.50	130.	350.
h. 31.8.1938.	42.50	130.	350.
i. 17.3.1939.	42.50	130.	350.
j. 3.8.1939.	42.50	130.	350.
k. 15.2.1940.	42.50	130.	350.
l. 12.12.1941.	37.50	115.	300.
m. 1.10.1942.	37.50	115.	300.
n. 7.5.1943.	37.50	115.	300.
o. 16.10.1947.	35.00	100.	275.
p. 20.1.1949.	35.00	100.	275.
q. 29.10.1955.	50.00	140.	400.

35 **100 Franken**

1924-49. Dk. blue. Like #6.

	VG	VF	UNC
a. 1.4.1924.	37.50	90.00	400.
b. 16.9.1926.	30.00	80.00	375.
c. 30.3.1927.	27.50	75.00	350.
d. 23.11.1927.	27.50	75.00	350.
e. 4.10.1928.	27.50	75.00	350.
f. 16.9.1930.	25.00	65.00	325.
g. 21.7.1931.	25.00	65.00	325.
h. 19.7.1934.	25.00	65.00	325.
i. 27.8.1937.	25.00	65.00	325.
j. 31.8.1938.	25.00	65.00	325.
k. 17.3.1939.	25.00	65.00	325.
l. 3.8.1939.	25.00	65.00	325.
m. 15.2.1940.	25.00	65.00	325.
n. 1.10.1942.	25.00	65.00	325.
o. 7.5.1943.	24.00	60.00	250.
p. 7.10.1943.	24.00	60.00	250.
q. 2.12.1943.	24.00	60.00	250.
r. 23.3.1944.	24.00	60.00	250.
s. 15.3.1945.	24.00	60.00	250.
t. 31.8.1946.	22.50	55.00	200.
u. 16.10.1947.	22.50	55.00	200.
v. 20.1.1949.	22.50	55.00	200.

		VG	VF	UNC
36	**500 Franken** 1928-49. Dk. red and lilac. Like #7.			
	a. 4.10.1928.	350.	800.	1500.
	b. 16.6.1931.	300.	675.	1400.
	c. 7.9.1939.	275.	625.	1300.
	d. 4.12.1942.	250.	575.	1250.
	e. 31.8.1946.	225.	575.	1250.
	f. 16.10.1947.	225.	575.	1250.
	g. 20.1.1949. (Not issued.)	—	—	—
37	**1000 Franken** 1927-55. Violet and orange. Like #8.			
	a. 23.11.1927.	400.	900.	2250.
	b. 16.9.1930.	375.	850.	2000.
	c. 16.6.1931.	350.	675.	1800.
	d. 10.12.1931.	350.	675.	1800.
	e. 7.9.1939.	325.	625.	1700.
	f. 4.12.1942.	325.	625.	1700.
	g. 11.11.1943.	325.	625.	1700.
	h. 16.10.1947.	325.	625.	1700.
	i. 29.4.1955.	350.	675.	2500.

1929-50 Issue

		VG	VF	UNC
38	**20 Franken** 1925-26. Dk. blue on red and red and lt. blue unpt. Portr. Johann Heinrich Pestalozzi at upper r. Cross at ctr. on back. (Not issued.)			
	a. 1.1.1925. Specimen.	—	—	—
	b. 1.1.1926. Specimen.	—	—	—

		VG	VF	UNC
39	**20 Franken** 1929-52. Dk. blue on red unpt. Portr. Johann Heinrich Pestalozzi at upper r. Cross at ctr. on back. Printer: OFZ.			
	a. 21.6.1929.	22.50	70.00	300.
	b. 16.9.1930.	20.00	65.00	250.
	c. 21.7.1931.	20.00	65.00	250.
	d. 22.6.1933.	20.00	65.00	250.
	e. 11.4.1935.	20.00	65.00	250.
	f. 27.8.1937.	20.00	65.00	250.
	g. 10.3.1938.	17.50	55.00	200.
	h. 31.8.1938.	17.50	55.00	200.
	i. 17.3.1939.	17.50	55.00	200.
	j. 26.8.1939.	17.50	55.00	200.
	k. 15.8.1940.	17.50	55.00	200.
	l. 4.12.1942.	17.50	55.00	200.
	m. 23.3.1944.	17.50	55.00	200.
	n. 16.11.1944.	17.50	55.00	200.
	o. 31.8.1946.	15.00	40.00	180.
	p. 16.10.1947.	15.00	40.00	180.
	q. 21.1.1949.	15.00	40.00	180.
	r. 9.3.1950.	15.00	40.00	180.
	s. 22.2.1951.	15.00	40.00	180.
	t. 28.3.1952.	15.00	40.00	180.
	u. Specimen. 21.6.1929.	—	—	350.

1938 Issue

		VG	VF	UNC
40	**1 Frank** 27.5.1938. Dk. blue. (Not issued.)			
	a. Note w/serial #.	—	—	—
	s. Specimen.	—	—	—
41	**2 Franken** 27.5.1938. Red-brown. (Not issued.)			
	a. Note w/serial #.	—	—	—
	s. Specimen.	—	—	—

1941-50 Reserve Issue

		VG	VF	UNC
42	**50 Franken** 15.3.1946. Green on red and yellow unpt. Girl's head at r. Peasant w/bull on back. (Not issued).	—	—	—
43	**100 Franken** 4.12.1942. Blue on m/c unpt. *100* at l., Haslital's woman's head at r. Ornate designs on back. (Not issued.)			
	a. 1.8.1941.	—	—	—
	b. 4.12.1942.	—	—	—
	c. 21.10.1943.	—	—	—
	d. 15.3.1945.	—	—	—

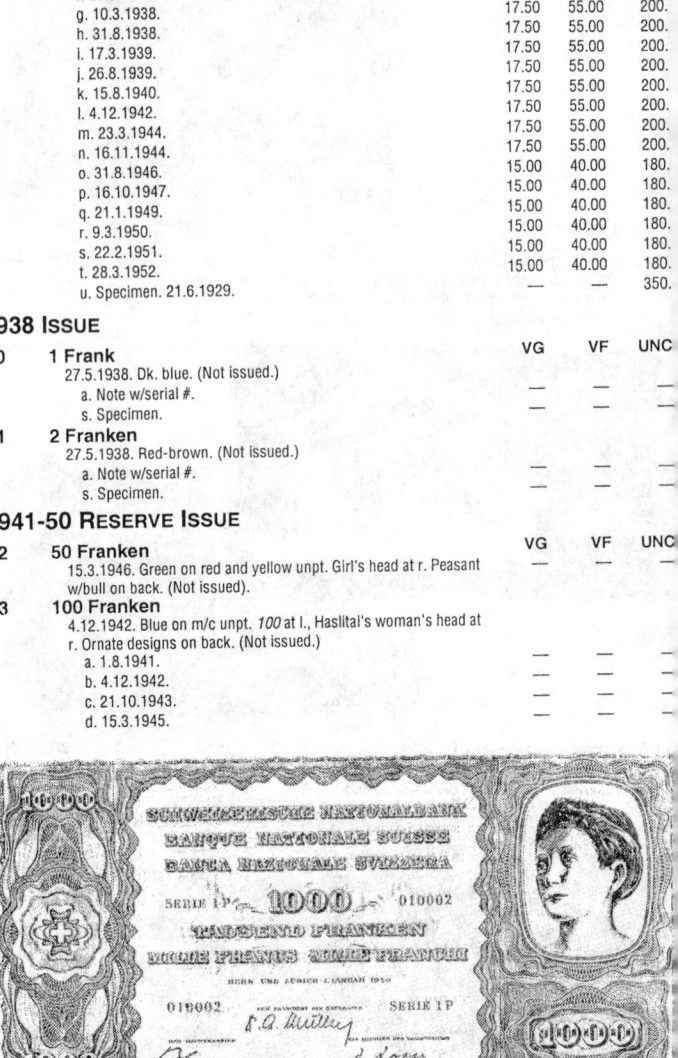

		VG	VF	UNC
44	**1000 Franken** 1.1.1950. Black, blue and violet on m/c unpt. Girl's head at r. Turbine and mountains on back. (Not issued.)	—	—	—

NOTICE

Readers with unlisted dates, signature varieties, etc. are invited to submit photocopies or, high resolution (300 dpi, 100% size) scans of their notes to: Standard Catalog of World Paper Money, 700 East State St. Iola, WI 54990-0001, or E-Mail: george.cuhaj@fwpubs.com.

SIGNATURE VARIETIES

	President, Bank Council	Director	Cashier
34	Dr. Alfred Müller 1947-59	Dr. Walter Schwegler 1954-66	Otto Kunz 1954-66
35	Dr. Alfred Müller	Dr. Paul Rossy 1937-55	Otto Kunz 1954-66
36	Dr. Alfred Müller	Dr. Paul Keller 1947-56	Otto Kunz
37	Dr. Alfred Müller	Dr. Riccardo Motta 1955-66	Otto Kunz
38	Dr. Alfred Müller	Dr. Max Iklé 1956-68	Otto Kunz
39	Dr. Brenno Galli	Dr. Walter Schweghler	Otto Kunz 1954-66
40	Dr. Brenno Galli	Dr. Riccardo Motta 1955-66	Otto Kunz
41	Dr. Brenno Galli	Dr. Max Iklé	Otto Kunz
42	Dr. Brenno Galli 1959-78	Dr. Edwin Stopper 1966-74	Rudolf Aebersold 1954-66
43	Dr. Brenno Galli	Alexandre Hay 1966-75	Rudolf Aebersold
44	Dr. Brenno Galli	Dr. Max Iklé	Rudolf Aebersold
45	Dr. Brenno Galli	Dr. Fritz Leutwiler 1968-84	Rudolf Aebersold
46	Dr. Brenno Galli	Dr. Leo Schurman 1974-80	Rudolf Aebersold
47	Dr. Brenno Galli	Dr. Pierre Languetin 1976-88	Rudolf Aebersold

NOTE: From #180 onward w/o the Chief Cashier's signature.

1954-61 ISSUE

#45-46 printer: OFZ.

Note: Sign. varieties listed after date.

		VG	VF	UNC
45	**10 Franken** 1955-77. Purple on red-brown unpt. Gottfried Keller at r. Carnation flower at l. ctr. on back. Printer: OFZ.			
	a. 25.8.1955. (34, 36, 37).	6.50	15.00	50.00
	b. 20.10.1955. (34, 36, 37).	6.50	15.00	50.00
	b2. 29.11.1956 (34, 37, 38).			
	b2. 29.11.1956 (34, 37, 38).			
	c. 29.11.1956. (34, 37, 38).	6.50	15.00	45.00

		VG	VF	UNC
46	**20 Franken** 1954-76. Blue on m/c unpt. Gen. Guillaume-Henri Dufour at r. Silver thistle at l. ctr. on back. Printer: OFZ.			
	a. 1.7.1954 (34, 35, 36).	14.00	25.00	90.00
	b. 7.7.1955 (34, 36, 37).	14.00	25.00	90.00
	c. 20.10.1955 (34, 36, 37).	14.00	25.00	90.00
	d. 5.7.1956 (34, 37, 38).	14.00	25.00	90.00
	e. 4.10.1957 (34, 37, 38).	15.00	30.00	110.
	f. 18.12.1958 (34, 37, 38).	25.00	45.00	145.
	g. 23.12.1959 (39, 40, 41).	3.00	8.00	35.00
	h. 22.12.1960 (39, 40, 41).	3.00	8.00	37.50
	i. 26.10.1961 (39, 40, 41).	3.00	8.00	27.50
	j. 28.3.1963 (39, 40, 41).	3.00	8.00	26.00
	k. 2.4.1964 (39, 40, 41).	3.00	8.00	26.00
	l. 21.1.1965 (39, 40, 41).	3.00	8.00	26.00
	m. 23.12.1965 (39, 40, 41).	3.00	8.00	26.00
	n. 1.1.1967 (42, 43, 44).	3.00	10.00	32.50
	o. 30.6.1967 (42, 43, 44).	2.75	8.00	28.00
	p. 15.5.1968 (42, 43, 45).	2.75	8.00	28.00
	q. 15.1.1969 (42, 43, 45).	2.75	8.00	28.00
	r. 5.1.1970 (42, 43, 45).	2.75	8.00	28.00
	s. 10.2.1971 (42, 43, 45).	2.75	8.00	28.00
	s1. As a. Specimen.	—	—	50.00
	t. 24.1.1972 (42, 43, 45).	2.75	8.00	28.00
	u. 7.3.1973 (42, 43, 45).	2.75	8.00	28.00
	v. 7.2.1974 (42, 43, 45).	2.75	8.00	28.00
	w. 9.4.1976 (45, 46, 47).	2.50	7.50	25.00

47 50 Franken

1955-58. Green and red-brown on yellow-green unpt. Girl at upper r. Apple harvesting scene on back (symbolizing fertility). Printer: W&S.

	VG	VF	UNC
a. 7.7.1955 (34, 36, 37).	25.00	42.50	200.
b. 4.10.1957 (34, 37, 38).	20.00	37.50	125.
c. 18.12.1958 (34, 37, 38).	150.	300.	750.

48 50 Franken

1961-74. Green and red on m/c unpt. Like #47.

	VG	VF	UNC
a. 4.5.1961 (39, 40, 41).	25.00	60.00	200.
b. 21.12.1961 (39, 40,41).	12.50	30.00	75.00
c. 28.3.1963 (39, 40, 41).	30.00	85.00	220.
d. 2.4.1964 (39, 40, 41).	35.00	90.00	225.
e. 21.1.1965 (39, 40, 41).	12.50	30.00	80.00
f. 23.12.1965 (39, 40, 41).	12.50	30.00	80.00
g. 30.6.1967 (42, 43, 44).	12.50	30.00	80.00
h. 15.5.1968 (42, 43, 45).	12.50	30.00	80.00
i. 15.1.1969 (42, 43, 45).	12.50	30.00	75.00
j. 5.1.1970 (42, 43, 45).	12.50	30.00	75.00
k. 10.2.1971 (42, 43, 45).	12.50	30.00	75.00
l. 24.1.1972 (42, 43, 45).	12.50	30.00	75.00
m. 7.3.1973 (42, 43, 45).	12.50	30.00	75.00
n. 7.2.1974 (42, 43, 45).	12.50	30.00	75.00
s. As a. Specimen.	—	—	50.00

49 100 Franken

1956-73. Dk. blue and brown-olive on m/c unpt. Boy's head at upper r w/lamb. St. Martin cutting his cape (to share) at ctr. r. on back. Printer: TDLR.

	VG	VF	UNC
a. 25.10.1956 (34, 37, 38).	30.00	57.50	200.
b. 4.10.1957 (34, 37, 38).	30.00	55.00	170.
c. 18.12.1958 (34, 37, 38).	32.50	60.00	320.
d. 21.12.1961 (39, 40, 41);	15.00	30.00	135.
e. 28.3.1963 (39, 40, 41).	15.00	30.00	135.
f. 2.4.1964 (39, 40, 41).	15.00	30.00	135.
g. 21.1.1965 (39, 40, 41).	15.00	32.50	135.
h. 23.12.1965 (39, 40, 41).	16.00	35.00	180.
i. 1.1.1967 (42, 43, 44).	16.00	35.00	170.
j. 30.6.1967 (42, 43, 44).	14.00	27.50	125.
k. 15.1.1969 (42, 43, 45).	14.00	25.00	125.
l. 5.1.1970 (42, 43, 45).	16.00	35.00	130.
m. 10.2.1971 (42, 43, 45).	12.00	25.00	120.
n. 24.1.1972 (42, 43, 45).	12.00	25.00	120.
o. 7.3.1973 (42, 43, 45).	12.00	25.00	120.
s. As a. Specimen.	—	—	100.

50 500 Franken

1957-58. Red-brown and olive on m/c unpt. Woman looking in mirror at r. Elders w/4 girls bathing at ctr. r. on back (Fountain of Youth). Printer: W&S.

	VG	VF	UNC
a. 31.1.1957 (34, 37, 38).	250.	400.	900.
b. 4.10.1957 (34, 37, 38).	200.	350.	800.
c. 18.12.1958 (34, 37, 38).	300.	500.	1000.

51 500 Franken

1961-74. Brown-orange and olive on m/c unpt. Like #50.

	VG	VF	UNC
a. 21.12.1961 (39, 40, 41).	150.	275.	750.
b. 28.3.1963 (39, 40, 41).	130.	240.	740.
c. 2.4.1964 (39, 40, 41).	140.	250.	740.
d. 21.1.1965 (39, 40, 41).	140.	250.	740.
e. 1.1.1967 (42, 43, 44).	140.	250.	700.
f. 15.5.1968 (42, 43, 45).	140.	250.	700.
g. 15.1.1969 (42, 43, 45).	140.	250.	700.
h. 5.1.1970 (42, 43, 45).	110.	235.	680.
i. 10.2.1971 (42, 43, 45).	110.	235.	680.
j. 24.1.1972 (42, 43, 45).	110.	235.	680.
k. 7.3.1973 (42, 43, 45).	100.	230.	670.
l. 7.2.1974 (42, 43, 45).	90.00	200.	650.
s. As a. Specimen.	—	—	500.

52 1000 Franken

1954-74. Red-violet and turquoise on green and lt. violet unpt. Female head at upper r. allegorical scene *Dance Macabre* on back. Printer: TDLR.

	VG	VF	UNC
a. 30.9.1954 (34, 35, 36).	250.	500.	1900
b. 4.10.1957 (34, 37, 38).	225.	425.	1650.
c. 18.12.1958 (34, 37, 38).	325.	650.	2000.
d. 22.12.1960 (39, 40, 41).	175.	350.	1550
e. 21.12.1961 (39, 40, 41).	175.	350.	1550
f. 28.3.1963 (39, 40, 41).	175.	350.	1400.
g. 21.1.1965 (39, 40, 41).	175.	350.	1300
h. 1.1.1967 (42, 43, 44).	175.	350.	1300
i. 5.1.1970 (42, 43, 45).	175.	350.	1300.
j. 10.2.1971 (42, 43, 45).	175.	350.	1175.
k. 24.1.1972 (42, 43, 45).	150.	300.	1175
l. 1.10.1973 (42, 43, 45).	140.	280.	1175
m. 7.2.1974 (42, 43, 45).	125.	260.	1150
s. As a. Specimen.	—	—	1200

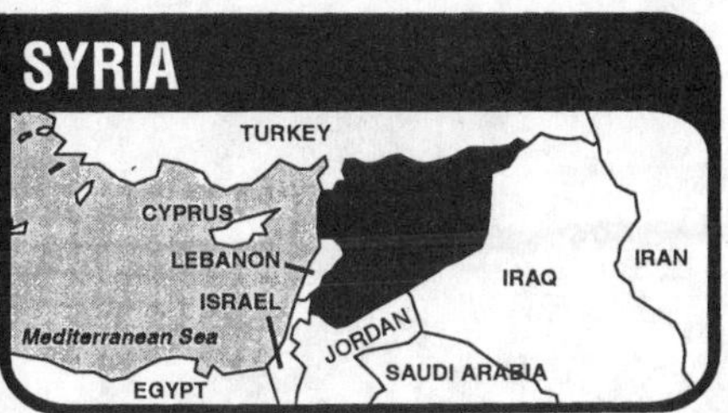

The Syrian Arab Republic, located in the Near East at the eastern end of the Mediterranean Sea, has an area of 71,498 sq. mi. (185,180 sq. km.) and a population of 16.13 million. Capital: Damascus. Agriculture and animal breeding are the chief industries. Cotton, crude oil and livestock are exported.

Ancient Syria, a land bridge connecting Europe, Africa and Asia, has spent much of its history in thrall to the conqueror's whim. Its subjection by Egypt about 1500 BC was followed by successive conquests by the Hebrews, Phoenicians, Babylonians, Assyrians, Persians, Macedonians, Romans, Byzantines and finally, in 636 AD, by the Moslems. The Arabs made Damascus, one of the oldest continuously inhabited cities of the world, the trade center and capital of an empire stretching from India to Spain. In 1517, following the total destruction of Damascus by the Mongols of Tamerlane, Syria fell to the Ottoman Turks and remained a Turkish province until World War I. The League of Nations gave France a mandate to the Levant states of Syria and Lebanon in 1920. In 1930, following a series of uprisings, France recognized Syria as an independent republic, but still subject to the mandate. Lebanon became fully independent on Nov. 22, 1943, and Syria on Jan. 1, 1944.

On Feb. 1, 1958, Egypt and Syria formed the United Arab Republic. Yemen joined on March 8 in an association known as the United Arab States. Syria withdrew from the United Arab Republic on Sept. 29, 1961, and on Dec. 26 Egypt dissolved its ties with Yemen in the United Arab States. Between 1961 and 1970 five coups brought in Lieut. Gen. Hafez el Assad as Prime Minister and in 1973 a new constitution was approved.

RULERS:

French, 1920-1944

MONETARY SYSTEM:

1 Pound (Livre) = 100 Piastres

FRENCH ADMINISTRATION

BANQUE DE SYRIE

1919 ISSUE

#1-19 printer: BWC.

		Good	Fine	XF
1	**5 Piastres** 1.8.1919. Dk. green on m/c unpt. Ruins of Baalbek at lower ctr. Back blue and lilac w/lion's head at ctr.			
	a. Sign. title: *LE SECRETAIRE GENERAL.*	5.00	35.00	100.
	b. Sign title: *LE ADMINISTRATEUR DELEGUE.*	5.00	40.00	125.

		Good	Fine	XF
2	**25 Piastres** 1.8.1919. Dk. blue and m/c. Omayyad Mosque in Damascus at ctr.	12.50	60.00	200.

		Good	Fine	XF
3	**50 Piastres** 1.8.1919. Purple and m/c. Damascus at upper ctr.	22.50	100.	325.

		Good	Fine	XF
4	**100 Piastres** 1.8.1919. Brown and m/c. Pillars of Baalbek at l. Back blue and m/c. city scene at ctr.	40.00	175.	600.

		Good	Fine	XF
5	**500 Piastres** 1.8.1919. Dk. purple and m/c. Cedar tree at r. City view at ctr. on back.	70.00	400.	1000.

1920 FIRST ISSUE

		VG	VF	UNC
6	**1 Piastre** 1.1.1920. Blue on lt. green and lt. orange unpt. Back brown and red-brown; ruins of Baalbek at ctr.	4.00	15.00	45.00
7	**10 Livres** 1.1.1920. Lt. brown. Tower of Great Serai of Beyrouth at l.			
	a. Issued note.	—	—	—
	s. Specimen.	—	—	250.
8	**25 Livres** 1.1.1920. Green. Arab cemetery at l., caravan by city gate at r.			
	a. Issued note.	—	—	—
	s. Specimen.	—	—	325.
9	**50 Livres** 1.1.1920. Blue. Road at l.			
	a. Issued note.	—	—	—
	s. Specimen.	—	—	400.

		VG	VF	UNC
10	**100 Livres** 1.1.1920. Gray.			
	a. Issued note.	—	—	—
	s. Specimen.	—	—	550.

1920 SECOND ISSUE

		Good	Fine	XF
11	**5 Piastres** 1.7.1920. Dk. green and m/c. Like #1.	5.00	35.00	100.

		Good	Fine	XF
12	**10 Piastres** 1.7.1920. Dk. blue and m/c. Shepherds gathered around a campfire, goats in background.	7.50	50.00	200.

		Good	Fine	XF
13	**25 Piastres** 1.7.1920. Dk. blue. Bldg. w/Omayyad Mosque in Damascus at lower ctr.	15.00	75.00	300.
14	**50 Piastres** 1.7.1920. Purple.	30.00	150.	450.
15	**100 Piastres** 1.7.1920. Brown. Pillars of Baalbek.	75.00	250.	650.

		Good	Fine	XF
16	**500 Piastres** 1.7.1920. Dk. purple. Like #5. Back blue. Rare.	—	—	—
17	**10 Livres** 1.7.1920. Lt. brown. Tower of the Great Serai of Beyrouth.	—	—	—
18	**25 Livres** 1.7.1920. Green. Arab cemetery at l., caravan near city gate at r.	—	—	—
19	**100 Livres** 1.7.1920. Green. Bank of Beyrouth at upper ctr.	—	—	—

BANQUE DE SYRIE ET DU GRAND-LIBAN

1925 FIRST ISSUE

		Good	Fine	XF
21	**25 Piastres** 15.4.1925. Mill on back.	35.00	150.	450.
22	**50 Piastres** 15.4.1925. Type Cl. Serveau. W/o ovpt: *SYRIE.*	40.00	200.	550.
23	**50 Piastres** 15.4.1925. Like #22, w/ovpt: *SYRIE.*	—	—	—
24	**100 Piastres** 15.4.1925.	—	—	—

1925 SECOND ISSUE

		Good	Fine	XF
25	**5 Livres** 15.4.1925.	—	—	—
26	**10 Livres** 15.4.1925.	—	—	—
27	**25 Livres** 15.4.1925.	—	—	—
28	**50 Livres** 15.4.1925.	—	—	—
29	**100 Livres** 15.4.1925. M/c. City scene on back; ornate vase at l. and r. 238 x 132mm.	—	—	—

1930 ISSUE

		Good	Fine	XF
29A	**1 Livre** 1.11.1930. M/c. Harbor and mountainous landscape on back.	30.00	100.	300.
30	**5 Livres** 1.11.1930. M/c.	35.00	125.	500.
31	**10 Livres** 1.11.1930. M/c. Ornate ruins on back.	40.00	250.	—
32	**25 Livres** 1.11.1930. M/c.	—	—	—
33	**100 Livres** 1.11.1930. M/c.	—	—	—

1935 ISSUE

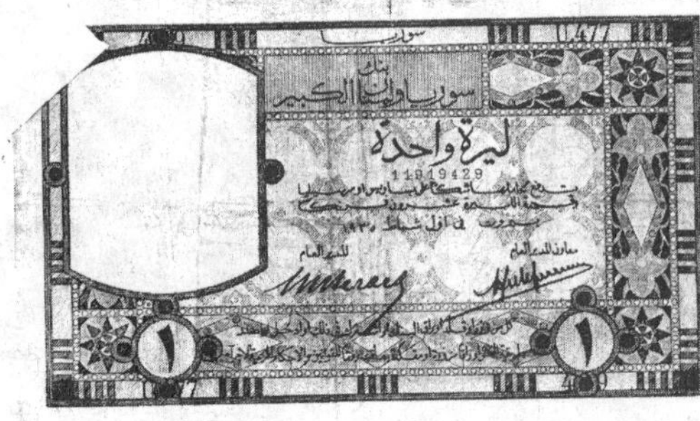

		VG	VF	UNC
34	**1 Livre** 1.2.1935. Brown and m/c. Like #29A. Harbor and mountain landscape on back.	10.00	50.00	300.

#35 not assigned.

		VG	VF	UNC
36	**5 Livres** 1.2.1935. M/c. Azam Palace at ctr. on back.	25.00	150.	600

38	100 Livres	VG	VF	UNC
	1.2.1935. Similar to #19. Ovpt: *SYRIE*. Printer: BWC.			
	a. W/o line ovpt.	—	—	—
	b. Orange ovpt. Type B.	—	—	—
	c. Lilac ovpt. Type C.	—	—	—
	d. Green ovpt. Type A.	—	—	—

1938 Issue

39	50 Livres	VG	VF	UNC
	1.1.1938. Type Cl. Serveau.	125.	500.	—

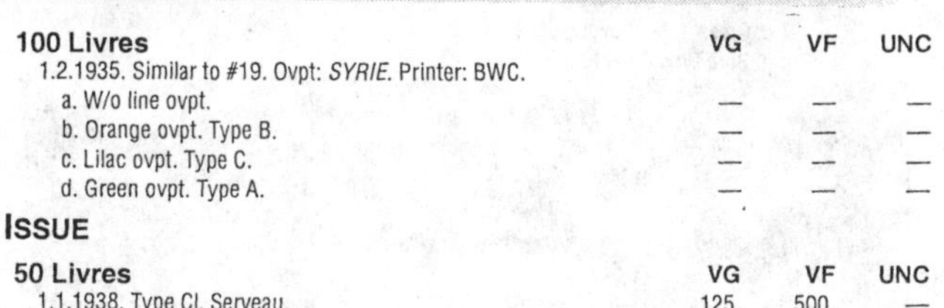

Type A Type B Type C Type D Type E

1939 Provisional Issues

#39A-39F ovpt: *SYRIE 1939*.

39A	1 Livre	Good	Fine	XF
	1939 (- old date 1.2.1935). Ovpt. on #34.	8.00	50.00	225.

39B	5 Livres	Good	Fine	XF
	1939 (- old date 1.2.1935). Ovpt. on #36.			
	a. W/ovpt: *SYRIE 1939* below central Arabic text.	20.00	100.	350.
	b. W/ovpt: *SYRIE 1939* above central Arabic text.	20.00	100.	350.

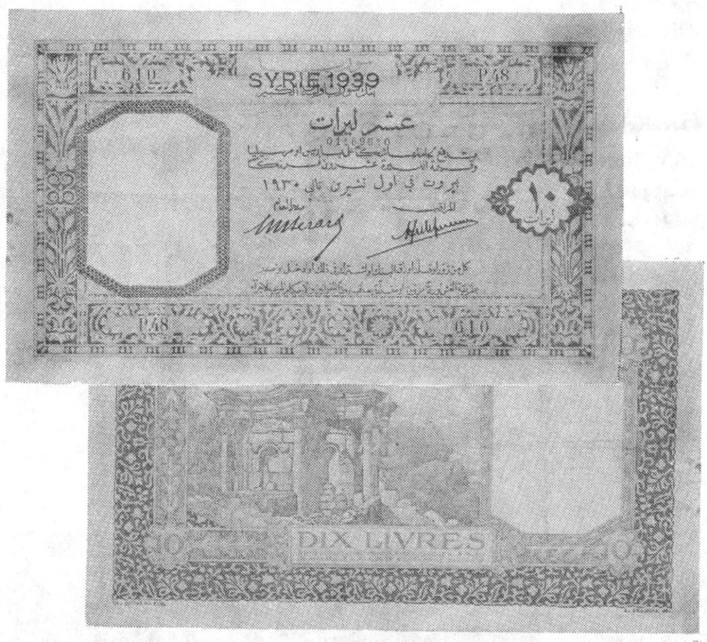

39C	10 Livres	Good	Fine	XF
	1939 (- old date 1.11.1930). Ovpt. on #31.	200.	800.	—
39D	100 Livres			
	1939 (- old date 1.11.1930). Ovpt. on #33.	150.	750.	—

39E	100 Livres	Good	Fine	XF
	1939 (- old date 1.2.1935).			
	a. Ovpt. on #38a.	120.	400.	—
	b. Ovpt. on #38b.	120.	400.	—
	c. Ovpt. on #38c.	120.	400.	—
	d. Ovpt. on #38d.	120.	400.	—

		Good	Fine	XF
39F	**100 Livres**			
	1939 (- old date 1.2.1935).			
	a. Ovpt. on Lebanon #14a.	120.	400.	—
	c. Ovpt. on Lebanon #14c.	175.	600.	—

BANQUE DE SYRIE ET DU LIBAN

1939 ISSUE

#40-45 printer: BWC.

#40-44 ovpt: *SYRIE*.

		VG	VF	UNC
40	**1 Livre**			
	1.9.1939. Green and m/c. Pillars of Baalbek at l. Back red on m/c unpt.; city view at ctr.			
	a. W/o line ovpt.	10.00	45.00	125.
	b. Violet Type A ovpt.	10.00	45.00	125.
	c. Lilac-colored Type B ovpt.	10.00	45.00	125.
	d. Green Type C ovpt.	10.00	45.00	125.
	e. Red Type D ovpt.	10.00	45.00	125.
	f. Blue Type E ovpt.	10.00	45.00	125.

		VG	VF	UNC
41	**5 Livres**			
	1.9.1939. Brown and m/c. Cedar at r. Landscape w/bldgs. in oval at ctr. on back.			
	a. W/o line ovpt.	17.50	65.00	275.
	b. Violet Type A ovpt.	17.50	65.00	275.
	c. Pink or green Type B ovpt.	17.50	65.00	275.
	d. Green Type C ovpt.	17.50	65.00	275.
	e. Blue Type E ovpt.	17.50	65.00	275.

		Good	Fine	XF
42	**10 Livres**			
	1.9.1939. Brown-violet and m/c. Clock tower at l.			
	a. W/o ovpt.	10.00	50.00	175.
	b. Green Type A ovpt.	10.00	50.00	175.
	c. Green Type B ovpt.	10.00	50.00	175.
	d. Blue Type C ovpt.	10.00	50.00	175.

		Good	Fine	XF
43	**25 Livres**			
	1.9.1939. Brown-lilac and m/c. Caravan at ctr. Back olive and m/c; ruins at ctr.			
	a. Lilac Type A ovpt.	12.50	75.00	30[illegible]
	b. Red Type C ovpt.	12.50	75.00	30[illegible]
	c. Green Type D ovpt.	12.50	75.00	30[illegible]
	d. W/o ovpt.	12.50	75.00	30[illegible]

		Good	Fine	XF
44	**50 Livres**			
	1.9.1939. Brown, blue and m/c. Street scene at l. Ovpt: *SYRIE* and green Type E.	35.00	150.	5[illegible]
45	**100 Livres**			
	1939. Green and yellow. W/o *SYRIE* ovpt.			
	a. Green type A ovpt.	30.00	120.	4[illegible]
	b. Orange type B ovpt.	30.00	120.	4[illegible]
	c. Pink type C ovpt.	30.00	120.	4[illegible]

1942 Bon de Caisse Issue

		Good	Fine	XF
46	**5 Livres** 1.8.1942. Dk. green on yellow paper. Back blue. Imprint: R. Soriano I.C. Beyrouth.	75.00	325.	650.

#47 and 48 printer: Government Printer, Palestine.

47	**50 Livres** 1.8.1942. Green.	125.	550.	—
48	**100 Livres** 1.8.1942. Blue on green and yellow unpt. Back green.	200.	600.	—

Republic

Republique Syrienne

1942 First Issue

#49-50 printer: Survey of Egypt.

		VG	VF	UNC
49	**5 Piastres** 15.7.1942. Green on lt. lilac unpt. Back purple; Citadel of Aleppo at ctr.	1.50	7.50	35.00
50	**10 Piastres** 31.7.1942. Brown on yellow unpt. Mosque w/2 minarets. Back red-brown.	2.50	12.50	60.00

#51-52 printer: BWC.

		VG	VF	UNC
51	**25 Piastres** 1.8.1942. Red and m/c. Similar to #2.	5.00	30.00	100.
52	**50 Piastres** 1.8.1942. Blue and m/c. Similar to #3.	7.50	50.00	150.

1942 Second Issue

#53-54 printer; Survey of Egypt.

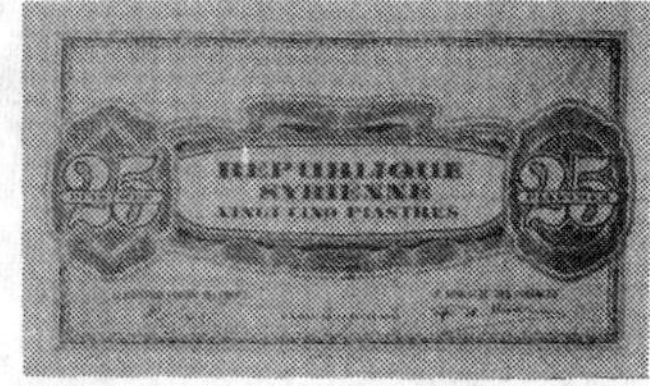

		VG	VF	UNC
53	**25 Piastres** 31.8.1942. Dk. brown on gold unpt. Mosque of Si Kabib of Homs. Back maroon.	5.00	25.00	85.00

		VG	VF	UNC
54	**50 Piastres** 31.8.1942. Blue on green unpt. Pillars. Back brown.	7.50	30.00	125.

1944 Issue

#55 and 56 printer: Moharrem Press; Alexandrie.

		VG	VF	UNC
55	**5 Piastres** 15.2.1944. Green on lt. green unpt. Similar to #49. Back blue.	1.50	5.00	30.00

		VG	VF	UNC
56	**10 Piastres** 15.2.1944. Brown on gold unpt. Similar to #50. Back maroon.	2.50	10.00	60.00

ca.1945 ND Provisional Issue

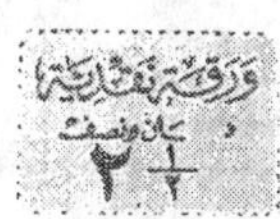

		VG	VF	UNC
56A	**2 1/2 Piastres** ND. Green tax adhesive stamp affixed to cardboard w/red text on back.	25.00	75.00	200.
56B	**5 Piastres** ND. Blue tax adhesive stamp affixed to cardboard w/red text on back.	25.00	75.00	200.

Banque de Syrie et du Liban

1947 Issue

		VG	VF	UNC
57	**1 Livre** 1.4.1947. Brown and m/c. Similar to #34.	5.00	40.00	150.
58	**10 Livres** 1.4.1947. M/c. Roman temple ruins. Type Cl. Serveau.	30.00	125.	500.

#59-61 w/green ovpt: State arms and *Ministry of Finance* in Arabic.

		VG	VF	UNC
59	**25 Livres** 1.4.1947. M/c. Arms at ctr. Citadel on back. Type Cl. Serveau.	50.00	300.	800.

		VG	VF	UNC
60	**50 Livres** 1.4.1947. M/c. Oriental house on back. Type Cl. Serveau.	75.00	425.	1000.

		VG	VF	UNC
61	**100 Livres** 1.4.1947. M/c. View of Damascus. Type Laurent.	125.	550.	—

1948 Issue

		VG	VF	UNC
62	**5 Livres** 15.12.1948. M/c. Similar to #36.	12.50	55.00	350.

1949 Issue

		VG	VF	UNC
63	**1 Livre** 1.7.1949. M/c. Like #57.	5.00	40.00	150.

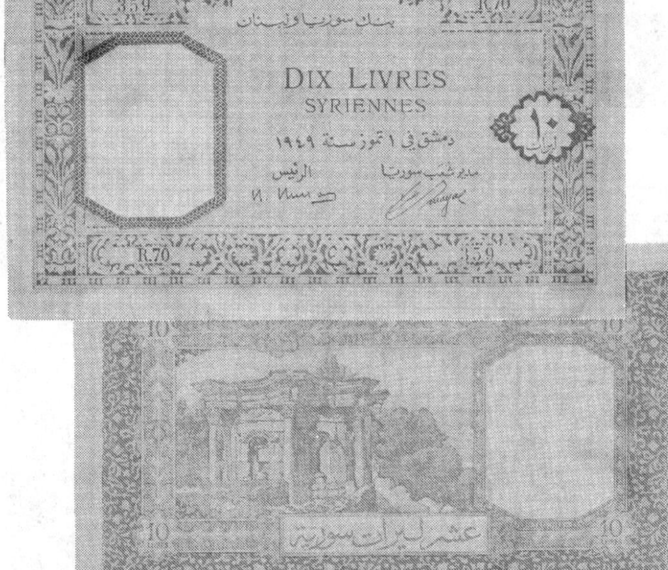

		VG	VF	UNC
64	**10 Livres** 1.7.1949. M/c. Like #58.	30.00	125.	550.

#65-67 w/green ovpt: State arms and *Ministry of Finance* in Arabic.

65	**25 Livres** 1.7.1949. M/c. Similar to #59.	50.00	200.	750.

		VG	VF	UNC
66	**50 Livres** 1.7.1949. M/c. Like #60, but w/ovpt. like #65.	150.	500.	—

		VG	VF	UNC
67	**100 Livres** 1.7.1949. M/c. Like #61, but w/ovpt. like #65.	175.	550.	—

1949 Bons de Caisse Provisional Issue

		VG	VF	UNC
68	**250 Livres** 1.7.1949. Form filled out in handwriting.	—	—	—
69	**500 Livres** 1.7.1949. Form filled out in handwriting.	—	—	—

1950 Regular Issue

		VG	VF	UNC
70	**25 Livres** 15.8.1950. M/c. Like #65.	25.00	125.	500.
71	**50 Livres** 15.8.1950. M/c. Like #66.	40.00	175.	700.
72	**100 Livres** 15.8.1950. M/c. Like #67.	100.	500.	—

Institut d'Emission de Syrie

1950's First Issue

#73-78 arms at r., *Premiere Emission.* Wmk: Horse's head.

		VG	VF	UNC
73	**1 Livre** ND. Dk. brown on m/c unpt. Inner yard of Omayyad Mosque in Damascus.	7.50	35.00	100.

		VG	VF	UNC
74	**5 Livres** ND. Orange-brown on m/c unpt. Citadel of Aleppo on back.	15.00	55.00	250.

		VG	VF	UNC
75	**10 Livres** ND. Blue-green on m/c unpt. Tekkiye Suleimanie in Damascus on back.	25.00	150.	400.

		VG	VF	UNC
76	**25 Livres** ND. Red on m/c unpt. Ruins of Palmyra on back.	40.00	250.	600.
77	**50 Livres** ND. Green on m/c ovpt. Inner yard of Azem Palace in Damascus on back.	90.00	400.	850.

		VG	VF	UNC
78	**100 Livres** ND. Blue on m/c unpt.	185.	500.	—

1955 Second Issue

#78A and 78B arms at r. *Deuxieme Emission.*

		VG	VF	UNC
78A	**10 Livres** 1955. Blue green on m/c unpt. Like #75.	20.00	90.00	350.

		VG	VF	UNC
78B	**25 Livres** 1955. Red on m/c unpt. Like #76.	45.00	225.	700.

Banque Centrale de Syrie

Central Bank of Syria

1957-58 Issue

#79-85 bank name is French on back.

		VG	VF	UNC
79	**1 Livre** 1957. Brown on m/c unpt. Similar to #73.	7.50	35.00	100.
80	**5 Livres** 1957. Brown on m/c unpt. Similar to #74.	17.50	65.00	300.

#81 Deleted.

		VG	VF	UNC
82	**10 Livres** 1957. Blue-green on m/c unpt. Similar to #75.	25.00	170.	450.
83	**25 Livres** 1957. Red on m/c unpt. Similar to #76.	40.00	250.	600.

		VG	VF	UNC
84	**50 Livres** 1957; 1958. Green on m/c unpt. Similar to #77.	60.00	275.	650.
85	**100 Livres** 1958. Blue on m/c unpt. Similar to #78.	80.00	350.	850.

1958 Issue

#86-92 bank name in English on back. Wmk: Arabian horse's head.

#86-88 printer: The Pakistan Security Printing Corporation Ltd., Karachi (w/o imprint).

		VG	VF	UNC
86	**1 Pound** 1958/AH1377. Brown on m/c unpt. Worker at r. Water wheel of Hama on back.			
	a. Issued note.	1.50	3.00	25.00
	s. Specimen.	—	—	25.00
87	**5 Pounds** 1958/AH1377. Green on m/c unpt. Face similar to #86. Citadel of Aleppo on back.			
	a. Issued note.	5.00	15.00	85.00
	s. Specimen.	—	—	45.00

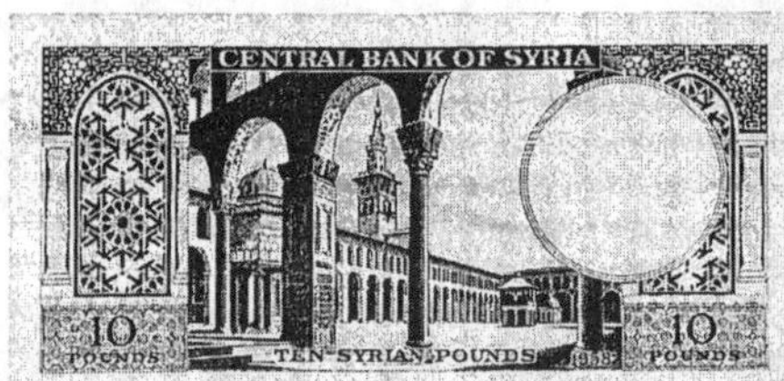

		VG	VF	UNC
88	**10 Pounds** 1958/AH1377. Purple on m/c unpt. Face similar to #86. Courtyard of Omayad Mosque on back.			
	a. Issued note.	7.50	22.50	125.
	s. Specimen.	—	—	90.00

#89-92 printer: JEZ.

		VG	VF	UNC
89	**25 Pounds** 1958/AH1377. Blue on m/c unpt. Girl w/basket at r. Interior view of Azem Palace in Damascus on back.			
	a. Issued note.	8.00	30.00	120.
	s. Specimen.	—	—	150.
90	**50 Pounds** 1958/AH1377. Red and brown on m/c unpt. Face similar to #89. Mosque of Sultan Selim on back.			
	a. Issued note.	8.00	30.00	120.
	s. Specimen.	—	—	175.
91	**100 Pounds** 1958;1962. Olive-green on m/c unpt. Face similar to #89. Old ruins of Palmyra on back.			
	a. 1958.	15.00	65.00	225.
	b. 1962.	12.50	50.00	200.
	s. Specimen.	—	—	200.

		VG	VF	UNC
92	**500 Pounds** 1958/AH1377. Brown and purple on m/c unpt. Motifs from ruins of Kingdom of Ugarit, head at r. Ancient religious wheel and cuneiform clay tablet on back.			
	a. Issued note.	35.00	150.	400.
	s. Specimen.	—	—	400.

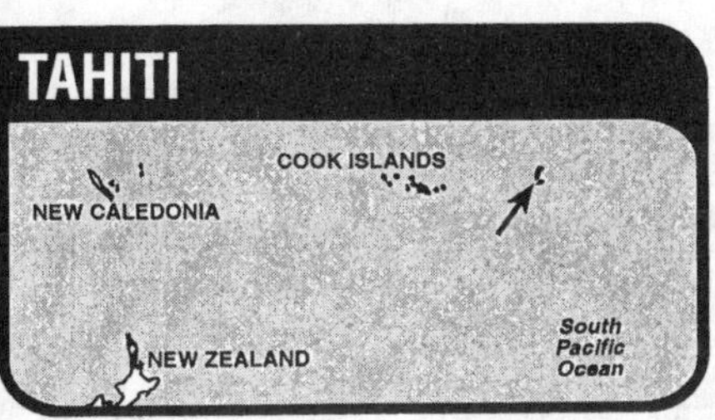

Tahiti, the largest island of the central South Pacific French overseas territory of French Polynesia, has an area of 402 sq. mi. (1,042 sq. km.) and a population of 79,024. Papeete on the northwest coast is the capital and administrative center of French Polynesia. Copra, sugar cane, vanilla and coffee are exported. Tourism is an important industry.

Capt. Samuel Wallis of the British Navy discovered Tahiti in 1768 and named it King George III Island. Louis-Antoine de Bougainville arrived the following year and claimed it for France. Subsequent English visits were by James Cook in 1769 and William Bligh in the HMS "Bounty" in 1788.

Members of the Protestant London Missionary Society established the first European settlement in 1797, and with the aid of the local Pomare family gained control of the entire island and established a "missionary kingdom" with a scriptural code of law. Nevertheless, Tahiti was subsequently declared a French protectorate (1842) and a colony (1880), and since 1958 is part of the overseas territory of French Polynesia.

RULERS:

French

MONETARY SYSTEM:

1 Franc = 100 Centimes

FRENCH ADMINISTRATION

BANQUE DE L'INDOCHINE

PAPEETE

DÉCRETS DES 21.1.1875 - 20.2.1888 - 16.5.1900 - 3.4.1901

		Good	Fine	XF
1	**5 Francs** 14.3.1914. Red. Seated oriental woman below seated Liberty holding caduceus at l. 2 sign.			
	a. Ovpt: *PAPEETE (TAHITI)* in red below decrees at ctr. r. 14.3.1914.	125.	500.	1250.
	b. Ovpt: *PAPEETE (TAHITI)* in black. 14.3.1914.	125.	500.	1250.

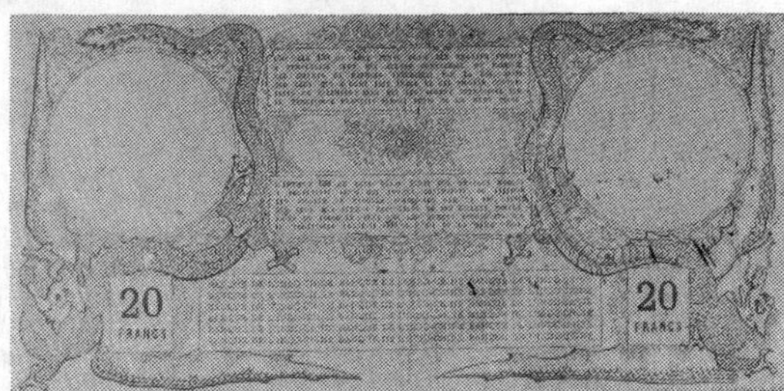

		Good	Fine	XF
2	**20 Francs** 20.3.1914. Blue-green w/black text. Neptune reclining holding trident at lower l. 3 sign.	175.	750.	—
3	**100 Francs** 1.9.1910; 10.3.1914; 12.3.1914. Elephant columns l. and r., 2 reclining women w/ox l., tiger r., at lower border. 3 sign. Rare.	—	—	—

1920 ISSUE (W/O DECRETS)

		Good	Fine	XF
4	**5 Francs** 2.1.1920; 1.8.1923. Red. Like #1, but 3 sign.	100.	300.	1000.
5	**20 Francs** 1.5.1920. Green w/black text. Like #2.	175.	750.	—

		Good	Fine	XF
6	**100 Francs** 2.1.1920. Brown. Like #3 but 2 sign.			
	a. Hand sign.	100.	350.	—
	b. Printed sign.	75.00	250.	600.

BANQUE ANDRÉ KRAJEWSKI

1920 ND ISSUE

#7-10 seated woman holding branch and frame around denomination at lower l. Printer: A. Carlisle and Co., S.F.

		Good	Fine	XF
7	**25 Centimes** ND (1920). Brown.	75.00	400.	1000.
8	**50 Centimes** ND (1920). Green.	100.	500.	1200.

		Good	Fine	XF
9	**1 Franc** ND (1920). Red.	120.	600.	1500.
10	**2 Francs** ND (1920). Orange and red.	120.	600.	1500.

BANQUE DE L'INDOCHINE (RESUMED)

1923-28 ISSUE

#11-13 sign. varieties.

		Good	Fine	XF
11	**5 Francs**			
	ND (1927). Brown. Helmeted woman at lower l.			
	a. Sign. titles: *Un Administrateur* and *Le Directeur.*	8.00	30.00	100.
	b. Sign. R. Thion de la Chaume and P. Baudouin w/titles: *Le Président* and *Le Directeur Général.*	5.00	15.00	75.00
	c. Sign. M. Borduge and P. Baudouin w/titles as b.	3.00	10.00	40.00

		Good	Fine	XF
12	**20 Francs**			
	ND (1928). Brown, lilac and red. Woman at r. Peacock on back.			
	a. Sign. titles: *Le Directeur* and *Le Administrateur.*	20.00	75.00	200.
	b. Sign. R. Thion de la Chaume and P. Baudouin w/titles: *Le Président* and *Le Directeur Général.*	15.00	50.00	125.
	c. Sign. M. Borduge and P. Baudouin w/titles as b.	7.50	25.00	75.00
	d. Sign. titles like b., but w/ovpt: *BANQUE DE L'INDOCHINE/SUCCURSALE DE PAPEETE.*	15.00	60.00	150.
	e. Sign. as c, ovpt. as d.	15.00	60.00	150.

		Good	Fine	XF
13	**500 Francs**			
	1923; 1938. Dk. purple. Standing woman at l., ships at top ctr.			
	a. Sign. titles: *LE DIRECTEUR* and *UN ADMINISTRATEUR.* 1.4.1923.	125.	400.	1000.
	b. Sign. titles: *LE PRÉSIDENT* and *LE DIRECTEUR GÉNÉRAL.* 8.3.1938.	125.	400.	1000.

> **NOTICE**
> Readers with unlisted dates, signature varieties, etc. are invited to submit photocopies or, high resolution (300 dpi, 100% size) scans of their notes to: Standard Catalog of World Paper Money, 700 East State St. Iola, WI 54990-0001, or E-Mail: george.cuhaj@fwpubs.com.

1939-40 ND ISSUE

		Good	Fine	XF
14	**100 Francs**			
	ND (1939-65). Brown and m/c. Woman wearing wreath and holding sm. figure of Athena at ctr. Angkor statue on back.			
	a. Sign. M. Borduge and P. Baudouin w/titles: *LE PRÉSIDENT* and *LE ADMINISTRATEUR DIRECTEUR GÉNÉRAL.*	6.00	20.00	70.00
	b. Sign. titles: *LE PRÉSIDENT* and *LE ADMINISTRATEUR DIRECTEUR GÉNÉRAL.*	5.00	17.50	60.00
	c. Sign. titles: *LE PRÉSIDENT* and *LE VICE-PRÉSIDENT DIRECTEUR GÉNÉRAL.*	4.00	15.00	40.00
	d. Sign. titles: *LE PRÉSIDENT* and *LE DIRECTEUR GÉNÉRAL.*	3.00	12.50	30.00
15	**1000 Francs**			
	ND (1940-57). M/c. Market scene at l. and in background, seated woman at r.			
	a. Sign. M. Borduge and P. Baudouin w/titles: *LE PRÉSIDENT* and *LE VICE-PRÉSIDENT DIRECTEUR GÉNÉRAL.*	30.00	125.	400
	b. Sign. titles: *LE PRÉSIDENT* and *LE VICE-PRÉSIDENT DIRECTEUR GÉNÉRAL.*	25.00	100.	300
	c. Sign. F.M.A. de Flers and M. Robert w/titles like a.	15.00	50.00	250

1940 ND PROVISIONAL ISSUE

		Good	Fine	XF
16	**100 Francs on 20 Francs**			
	ND (ca.1940). Black ovpt: *CENT FRANCS* and 2 sign. vertically at l. ctr., also ovpt: *CENT* across upper ctr. and *100* at lower ctr. on #12c.			
	a. Issued note. Rare.	—	—	—
	b. Punch cancelled, handstamped: *ANNULÉ.* Rare.	—	—	—
16A	**100 Francs**	Good	Fine	XF
	ND. Brown and m/c. Like #14 but Noumea issue w/red ovpt: *PAPEETE* at lower r. on face, at lower ctr. on back.	40.00	150.	375

1943 ND PROVISIONAL ISSUE

		Good	Fine	XF
17	**100 Francs on 50 Piastres**			
	ND (1943). Green. Man w/straw hat and baskets at r. Ovpt. on unfinished 50 Piastres, French Indo-China #77. Printed sign. Printer: ABNC (w/o imprint).			
	a. Text: *DE SAIGON* in r. sign. title not lined out.	50.00	150.	45
	b. Text: *DE SAIGON* in r. sign. title lined out.	35.00	125.	35
	s. Specimen, handstamped: *ANNULÉ.*	—	Unc	27

		Good	Fine	XF
18	**1000 Francs on 100 Piastres** ND (1943). Blue. Angkor statues at l. Ovpt. on unfinished 100 Piastres French Indo-China #78. Printer: ABNC (w/o imprint).			
	a. Handwritten sign. at r.	125.	400.	900.
	b. Both sign. printed.	120.	350.	750.

1944 ND Issue

#19-20 Australian printing.

		Good	Fine	XF
19	**5 Francs** ND (1944). Blue. Woman wearing wreath and holding sm. figure of Athena at ctr. Angkor statue on back. 2 sign. varieties.			
	a. Issued note.	25.00	125.	350.
	s. Specimen.	—	Unc	200.

		Good	Fine	XF
20	**20 Francs** ND (1944). Brown. Woman at l., sailboat at ctr., fisherman at r. Stylized mask on back.			
	a. Issued note.	35.00	150.	450.
	s. Specimen.	—	Unc	250.

1951 ND Issue

		VG	VF	UNC
21	**20 Francs** ND (1951-63). M/c. Youth at l., flute player at r. Fruit at l., woman at r. on back. Wmk: Man w/hat.			
	a. Sign. titles: *LE PRÉSIDENT* and *LE DIRECTEUR GAL.* (1951).	3.50	10.00	35.00
	b. Sign. titles: *LE PRÉSIDENT* and *LE VICE-PRÉSIDENT DIRECTEUR GÉNÉRAL* (1954-1958).	1.50	6.00	20.00
	c. Sign. titles: *LE PRÉSIDENT* and *LE DIRECTEUR GÉNÉRAL.* (1963).	1.50	5.00	15.00

1954 Provisional Issue

		Good	Fine	XF
22	**1000 Francs on 100 Piastres** 1954. Blue. Similar to #18. Ovpt. elements on back as well as on face.	110.	325.	750.

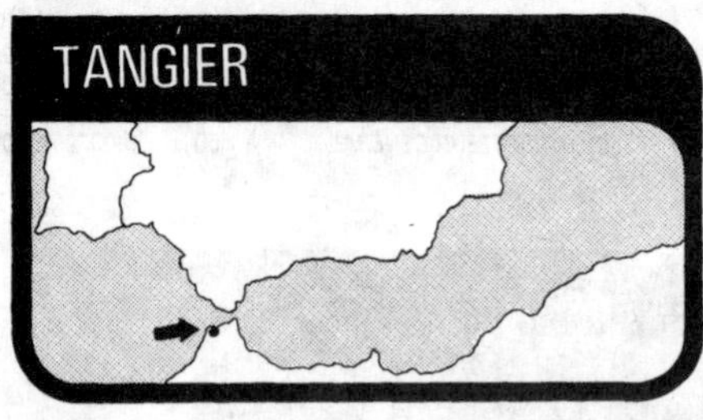

Tangier (Tangiers) is a port and city of the province of the same name in northern Morocco, at the west end of the Strait of Gibraltar, 17 miles (27 km.) from the southern tip of Spain. Tangier province has an area of 141 sq. mi. (365 sq. km.) and a population of 240,000. The town has a population of 190,000. Fishing and a textile industry supplement Tangier's role as a tourist center.

Tangier began as a 15th century BC Phoenician trading post, later becoming a Carthaginian and then a Roman settlement called Tingis. After five centuries of Roman rule, it was captured successively by the Vandals, Byzantines and Arabs. It was occupied by Islamic dynasties from about 682 to 1471, and by the Portuguese and Spanish until 1662, when sovereignty was transferred to the crown. It was returned to Morocco in 1684 and was the diplomatic capital of Morocco during the 19th century. In 1923 it became an international zone governed by representatives from Great Britain, France, Spain, Portugal, Italy, Belgium, The Netherlands, Sweden, and later, the United States. It remained an international zone except for a period of Spanish occupation during World War II and then again until 1956, when it became a part of the Kingdom of morocco.

RULERS:

French, 1912-1923
International Zone, 1923-1940, 1945-1956
Spanish, 1940-1945
Morocco, 1956-

Spanish Occupation - WWII

Servicios Municipales

1941 Emergency Issue

		Good	Fine	XF
1	**0.25 Francos** Aug. 1941; March 1942; Oct. 1942. Blue.	550.	1350.	—
2	**0.50 Francos** Aug. 1941; March 1942; Oct. 1942. Brown.	500.	1250.	—

		Good	Fine	XF
3	**1 Franco** Aug. 1941; March 1942; Oct. 1942. Violet.	550.	1350.	—
4	**2 Francos** (ca. 1941-42). Orange.	650.	1500.	—

The Tannu-Tuva Peoples Republic (Tuva), an autonomous part of the former Union of Soviet Socialist Republics located in central Asia on the northwest border of Outer Mongolia, has an area of 64,000 sq. mi. (165,760 sq. km.) and a population of about 175,000. Capital: Kyzyl. The economy is d on herding, forestry and mining. As Urianghi, Tuva was part of Outer Mongolia of the Chinese Empire when Czarist Russia, after fomenting a separatist movement, extended its protection to the mountainous country in 1914. Tuva declared its independence as the Tannu-Tuva People's Republic in 1921 under the auspices of the Tuva People's Revolutionary Party. In 1926, following Russia's successful mediation of the resultant Tuvinian-Mongolian territorial dispute, Tannu-Tuva and Outer Mongolia formally recognized each other's independence. The Tannu-Tuva People's Republic became an autonomous region of the U.S.S.R. on Oct. 13, 1944.

Russian notes circulated between 1925-1933.

MONETARY SYSTEM:

1 Lan = 1 Aksha (Ruble) = 100 Kopejek (Kopeks)

People's Republic

Treasury

1924 ND Provisional Issue

#1-4 ovpt. lines of script and a square stamp w/script on Russian Imperial notes. Most of these are spurious.

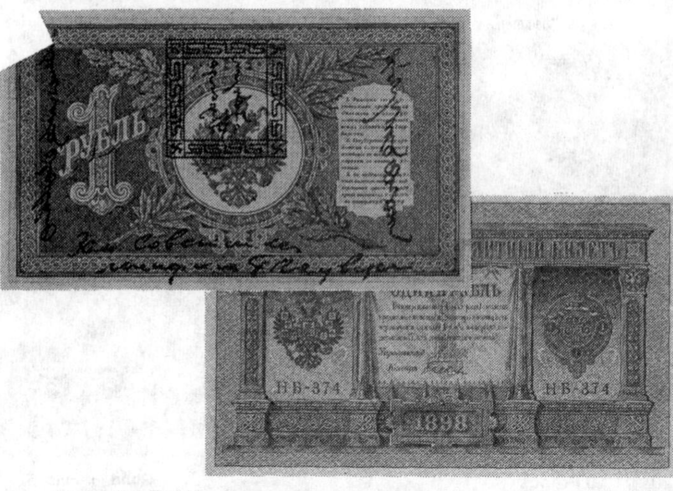

		VG	VF	UNC
1	**1 Lan on 1 Ruble** ND (1924 - old date 1898). Blue on brown unpt. Ovpt. on Russia #1.	4.00	7.50	12.50

		VG	VF	UNC
2	**3 Lan on 3 Rubles** ND (1924 - old date 1905). Green and pink. Ovpt. on Russia #9.	4.00	7.50	12.50

		VG	VF	UNC
3	**5 Lan on 5 Rubles** ND (1924 - old date 1909). Blue. Ovpt. on Russia #10.	4.00	7.50	12.50

		VG	VF	UNC
4	**10 Lan on 10 Rubles** ND (1925 - old date 1909). Red and green. Ovpt. on Russia #11.	4.00	7.50	12.50

1933 ND Provisional Issue

#5-9 vignette ovpt. on Union of Soviet Socialist Republics notes.

		VG	VF	UNC
5	**3 Rubles** ND (1933 - old date 1925). Ovpt. on Russia #189.	—	—	—
6	**5 Rubles** ND (1933 - old date 1925). Ovpt. on Russia #190.	—	—	—
7	**1 Chervonetz** ND (1933 - old date 1926). Ovpt. on Russia #198.	—	—	—
8	**2 Chervonetza** ND (1933 - old date 1926). Ovpt. on Russia #199.	—	—	—
9	**1 Gold Ruble** ND (1933 - old date 1928). Ovpt. on Russia - U.S.S.R. #206.	—	—	—

Tannu Tuva Republic

1935 Issue

#10-14 arms at upper ctr.

		Good	Fine	XF
10	**1 Aksha** 1935. Green and m/c.	300.	850.	1750.
11	**3 Aksha** 1935. M/c.	300.	850.	1750.
12	**5 Aksha** 1935. Red and m/c.	300.	850.	1750.

		VG	VF	UNC
13	**10 Aksha** 1935. Red and m/c. Rare.	—	—	—
14	**25 Aksha** 1935. Brown and m/c. Rare.	—	—	—

1940 Issue

#15-19 farmer plowing w/2 horses at ctr.

		Good	Fine	XF
15	**1 Aksha** 1940. Brown on orange and green unpt.	200.	500.	—
16	**3 Aksha** 1940. Green.	200.	500.	—
17	**5 Aksha** 1940. Blue.	200.	500.	—
18	**10 Aksha** 1940. Red.	250.	550.	—
19	**25 Aksha** 1940. Brown-violet.	250.	550.	—

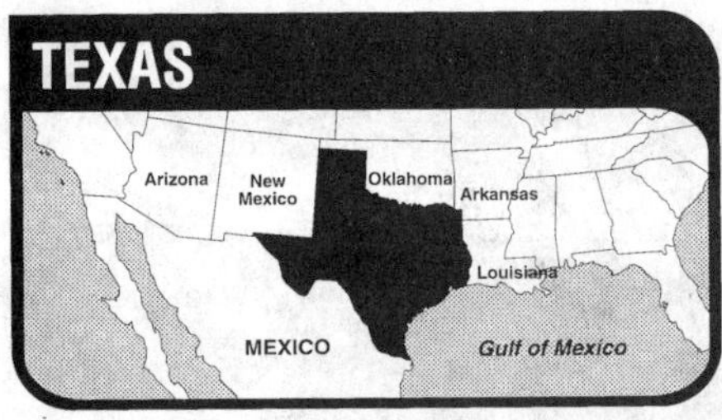

INDEPENDENT REPUBLIC

The governments and note issuing experiences fall into three well defined periods: (1) Republic of Texas, 1836-45; (2) post-Republic period as a member of the United States, 1846-60; and (3) Confederate Texas, 1861-65. This volume includes only those issues made under the Republic, 1836-45.

Within this short amount of time, Texas issued notes under the flag of Mexico, her own Republic, the United States and the Confederacy. With the exception of the pre-Republic period, notes of

TREASURER OF THE REPUBLIC

1836-45 AUDITED DRAFTS ISSUE

Issued by the Treasurer at Austin, Galveston, Houston, San Felipe de Austin, Velasco and Washington-on-the-Brazos. Drafts were in various amounts. Many varieties in plate and sign.

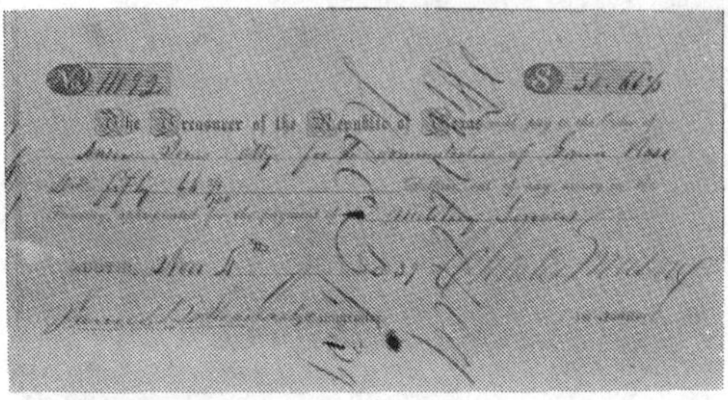

		Good	Fine	XF
1	**Various Amounts** 1836-45 Austin.	25.00	40.00	70.00
2	**Various Amounts** 1836-45. Galveston.	250.	375.	550.
3	**Various Amounts** 1836-45. Houston.	20.00	35.00	65.00
4	**Various Amounts** 1836-45. San Felipe de Austin.	200.	375.	675.
5	**Various Amounts** 1836-45. Velasco.	60.00	120.	240.
6	**Various Amounts** 1836-45. Washington-on-Brazos.	25.00	45.00	75.00

REPUBLIC

TREASURER OF THE REPUBLIC

1837-38 FIRST STAR NOTES ISSUE

Issued at Houston, 10% interest-bearing notes. Typeset, many plate varieties.

#7-12 w/lg. star at upper ctr. on face, and printed dates 1837 and 1838.

		Good	Fine	XF
7	**5 Dollars** 1837-38.			
	a. Issued note.	275.	500.	900.
	b. *Dollars* misspelled *Dollras.*	350.	550.	1000.
8	**10 Dollars** 1837-38.	225.	375.	600.

		Good	Fine	XF
9	**20 Dollars** 1837-38.			
	a. Issued note.	225.	375.	600.
	b. *Dollars* misspelled *Dollras.*	275.	450.	700.

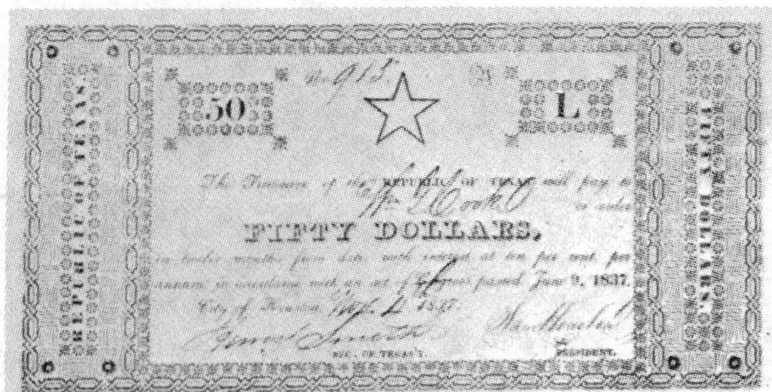

		Good	Fine	XF
10	**50 Dollars** 1837-38.	175.	400.	600.
11	**100 Dollars** 1837-38.	175.	400.	600.
12	**500 Dollars** 1837-38.	700.	2000.	3250.

Note: Pieces w/Sam Houston's name, though signed by a secretary, are worth 25% more.

ACT OF CONGRESS, DEC. 14, 1837; 1838 SECOND ISSUE

Issued at Houston. Change notes of lower denominations.

#13-15 steamboat in oval at l. Handwritten dates of 1838. Printer: Niles Print, Houston - Childs, Clark & Co., N. Orleans.

		Good	Fine	XF
13	**1 Dollar** 1838. Black. Man reclining at upper ctr., man's portr. at lower r.	200.	500.	900.
14	**2 Dollars** 1838. Black. Liberty w/eagle and shield at upper ctr.	200.	450.	750.

		Good	Fine	XF
15	**3 Dollars** 1838. Black. Similar to #13.	200.	400.	700.

ACT OF CONGRESS, JUNE 9, 1837; 1838 THIRD ISSUE

Government of Texas heading.

#16-21 black. Printer: Draper, Toppan, Longacre & Co., Phila. & N.Y.

		Good	Fine	XF
16	**1 Dollar** 1838-39. Standing Liberty w/shield and spear at l., seated Minerva w/lion at upper ctr.	175.	375.	1250.

		Good	Fine	XF
17	**3 Dollars** 1838-39. Seated Commerce w/shield w/lone star at upper ctr.	175.	350.	875.

		Good	Fine	XF
18	**5 Dollars** 1838-39. Standing Commerce at l., Indian brave hunting buffalo at ctr.	115.	225.	500

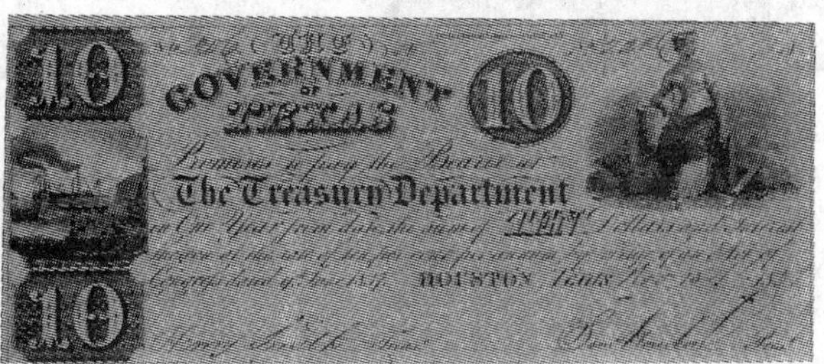

		Good	Fine	XF
19	**10 Dollars** 1838-39. Steamboat at l., seated Industry at upper r.	55.00	125.	200.

		Good	Fine	XF
20	**20 Dollars** 1838-39. Standing Liberty at l., seated Minerva at upper r.	55.00	125.	200.
21	**50 Dollars** 1838-39. Sailor w/flag seated at l., seated Justice at dockside at ctr.	55.00	125.	195.

Note: Pieces w/Sam Houston's name, though signed by a secretary, are worth approximately 25% more.

1839-41 Fourth Issue

Notes hand dated in 1839, 1840 and 1841.

#22-24 black. W/heading: *The Republic Of Texas.* Backs red-orange; lg. star at ctr. Printer: Endicott & Clark, New Orleans.

		Good	Fine	XF
22	**1 Dollar** 1839-41. Indian brave w/bow at l., seated Congress at upper ctr. r.	40.00	100.	185.

		Good	Fine	XF
23	**2 Dollars** 1839-41. Deer at l., cowboy roping steer at upper ctr. r.	65.00	140.	250.

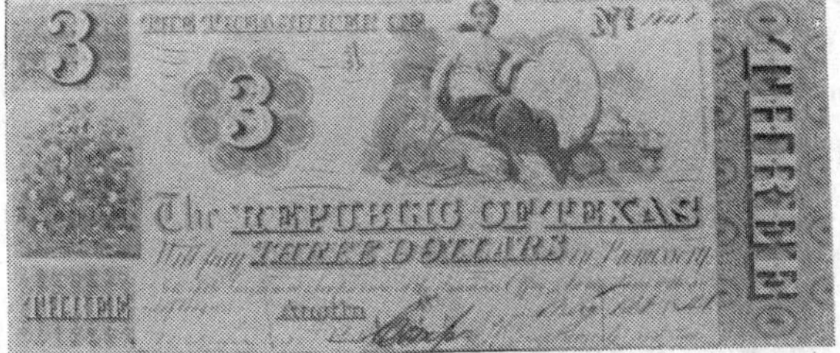

		Good	Fine	XF
24	**3 Dollars** 1839-41. Seated Ceres holding shield w/lone star at upper ctr. r.	75.00	175.	300.
25	**5 Dollars** 1839-41. Seated Indian brave at upper ctr.	65.00	150.	275.

		Good	Fine	XF
26	**10 Dollars** 1839-41. Hercules at upper l., woman's portr. at upper ctr., sailing ship at r.	40.00	125.	200.

		Good	Fine	XF
27	**20 Dollars** 1839-41. Indian brave aiming bow at upper l., standing maiden and seated Indian brave w/lone star at upper ctr. r., Minerva at lower r.	40.00	125.	200.

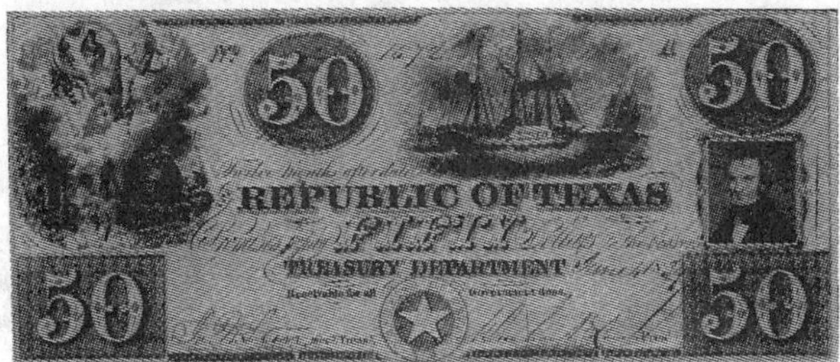

		Good	Fine	XF
28	**50 Dollars** 1839-41. Nude maiden at upper l., steam sailing ship at upper ctr. r., man's portr. at r.	45.00	125.	200.

		Good	Fine	XF
29	**100 Dollars** 1839-41. Steam passenger train at l., seated Minerva and Mercury in flight at upper ctr., sailboat at r.	85.00	150.	350.

		Good	Fine	XF
30	**500 Dollars** 1839-41. Seated Commerce and Industry at l. upper ctr., seated Liberty w/eagle at r.	400.	875.	1500.

1842-45 Exchequer Notes, Fifth Issue

Authorized January 29, 1842, issued 1842-45. Hand dated.

#31-37 and #39-41 printer: Rawdon, Wright, Hatch & Edson, New Orleans.

		Good	Fine	XF
31	**12 1/2 Cents** 1842-45. Black. Steam passenger train at l., man plowing w/horses while another man sows grain at upper ctr., woman at r. Rare.	—	—	—

		Good	Fine	XF
32	**25 Cents** 1842-45. Black. Steam passenger train at l., seated Liverty w/shield at top ctr., woman w/shield of grain at r. Rare.	—	—	—
33	**50 Cents** 1842-45. Black. Man plowing w/horses at top ctr. Rare.	—	—	—
34	**75 Cents** 1842-45. (5.5.1843). Rare.	—	—	—

		Good	Fine	XF
35	**1 Dollar** 1842-45. Black. Ceres w/cotton bale at upper ctr., steamship at r. Rare.	—	—	—
36	**2 Dollars** 1842-45. Reported not confirmed.	—	—	—
37	**3 Dollars** 1842-45. Reported not confirmed.	—	—	—
38	**5 Dollars** 1842-45. Black. Sailing ship at l., sailor at ctr. Printer: S. Whiting. Rare.	—	—	—

Note: Authenticity of #38 is questioned.

		Good	Fine	XF
39	**10 Dollars** 1842-45. Reported not confirmed.	—	—	—
40	**20 Dollars** 1842-45. Reported not confirmed.	—	—	—
41	**50 Dollars** 1842-45. Reported not confirmed.	—	—	—
42	**100 Dollars** 1842-45. Reported not confirmed.	—	—	—

Note: #36-37 and 39-42 were printed but none are known in collections at this time.

CONSOLIDATED FUND OF TEXAS

1837-40 INTEREST BEARING ISSUES

Interest-bearing issues from 1837-40. Printed date: *Sept. 1, 1837*.

		Good	Fine	XF
43	**100 Dollars** 1837-40.	30.00	65.00	125.

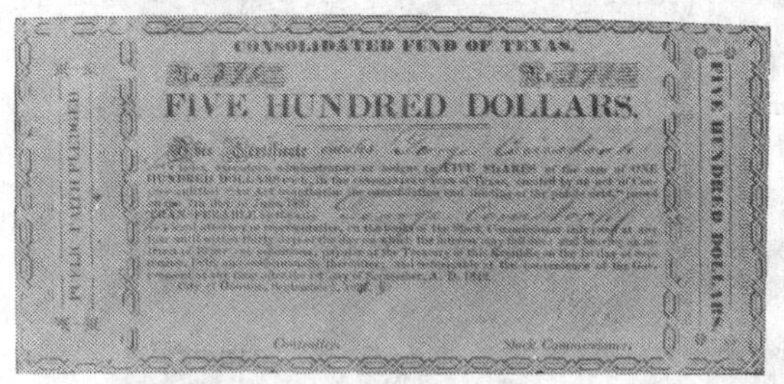

		Good	Fine	XF
44	**500 Dollars** 1837-40.	60.00	150.	250.
45	**1000 Dollars** 1837-40.	75.00	175.	275.
46	**5000 Dollars** 1837-40.	1250.	2500.	4000.
47	**10,000 Dollars** 1837-40.	—	—	8000.

1840 ISSUE

		Good	Fine	XF
48	**100 Dollars** Printed date 1840. Issued at Austin.	75.00	150.	250.

1841 NAVAL SCRIP ISSUE

Printed date: April, 1841.

		Good	Fine	XF
49	**25 Dollars** 1841. Several varieties.	25.00	50.00	90.00
50	**50 Dollars** 1841.	30.00	70.00	150.

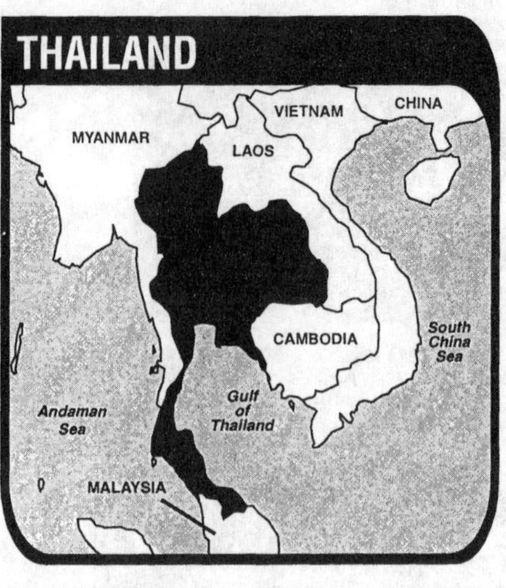

The Kingdom of Thailand, a constitutional monarchy located in the center of mainland southeast Asia between Burma and Lao, has an area of 198,457 sq. mi. (514,000 sq. km.) and a population of 60.49 million. Capital: Bangkok. The economy is d on agriculture and mining. Rubber, rice, teakwood, tin and tungsten are exported.

The history of Thailand, the only country in south and southeast Asia that was never colonized by an European power, dates from the 6th century AD when tribes of the Thai stock migrated into the area from the Asiatic continent, a process that accelerated with the Mongol invasion of China in the 13th century. After 400 years of sporadic warfare with the neighboring Burmese, King Taksin won the last battle in 1767. He founded a new capital, Dhonburi, on the west bank of Chao Praya River. King Rama I moved the capital to Bangkok in 1782.

The Thai were introduced to the Western world by the Portuguese, who were followed by the Dutch, British and French. Rama III of the present ruling dynasty negotiated a treaty of friendship and commerce with Britain in 1826, and in 1896 the independence of the kingdom was guaranteed by an Anglo-French accord. The absolute monarchy was changed into a constitutional monarchy in 1932. This was maintained when the name of the country was changed to Thailand in 1939.

In 1909 Siam ceded to Great Britain its suzerain rights over the dependencies of Kedah, Kelantan, Trengganu and Perlis, Malay states situated in southern Siam just north of British Malaya. This eliminated any British jurisdiction in Siam proper.

On December 8, 1941, after five hours of fighting, Thailand agreed to permit Japanese troops passage through the country to invade northern British Malaya. This eventually led to increased Japanese intervention and finally occupation of the country. On January 25, 1942, Thailand declared war on Great Britain and the United States. A free Thai guerrilla movement was soon organized to counteract the Japanese. In July 1943, Japan transferred the four northern Malay States back to Thailand. These were returned to Great Britain after peace treaties were signed in 1946.

RULERS:

Rama IV (Phra Chom Klao Mongkut), 1851-1868
Rama V (Phra Maha Chulalongkorn), 1868-1910
Rama VI (Vajiravudh), 1910-1925
Rama VII (Prajadhipok), 1925-1935
Rama VIII (Ananda Mahidol), 1935-1946
Rama IX (Bhumiphol Adulyadej), 1946-

MONETARY SYSTEM:

1 Baht (Tical) = 100 Satang
1 Tamlung = 4 Baht, 1853

REPLACEMENT NOTES:

#63-67, notes w/o suffix letter.

KINGDOM OF SIAM

GRAND TREASURY

1853 ISSUE

#A1-A4 represent the first paper currency issued in Siam. Size: 140 x 102mm.

		VG	VF	UNC
A1	**3 Tamlungs = 12 Ticals** 1853. Rare.	—	—	—
A2	**4 Tamlungs = 16 Ticals** 1853. Rare.	—	—	—
A3	**6 Tamlungs = 24 Ticals** 1853. Rare.	—	—	—

		VG	VF	UNC
A4	**10 Tamlungs = 40 Ticals** 1853. Rare.	—	—	—

NOTICE

Readers with unlisted dates, signature varieties, etc. are invited to submit photocopies or, high resolution (300 dpi, 100% size) scans of their notes to: Standard Catalog of World Paper Money, 700 East State St. Iola, WI 54990-0001, or E-Mail: george.cuhaj@fwpubs.com.

1850's Second Issue

Bluish paper. Size: 87 x 62mm.

A5

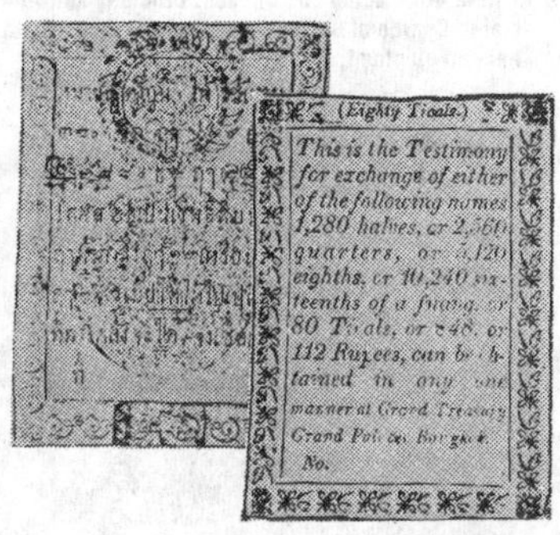

A6

		VG	VF	UNC
A5	**20 Ticals** ND. Rare.	—	—	—
A6	**80 Ticals** ND. Rare.	—	—	—

850's Third Issue

luish paper. Size: 87 x 50mm.

A7
1/8 TICAL

A8
1/4 TICAL

A9
3/8 TICAL

		Good	Fine	XF
7	**1/8 Tical** ND (1851-68).	800.	1350.	3000.
8	**1/4 Tical** ND (1851-68).	700.	1100.	3000.
9	**3/8 Tical** ND (1851-68).	1600.	3000.	5000.
10	**1/2 Tical** ND (1851-68). Reported not confirmed.	—	—	—
11	**1 Tical** ND (1851-68). Reported not confirmed.	—	—	—

850's Fourth Issue

ick cream unwmk. paper. Size: 108 x 85mm.

		Good	Fine	XF
12	**3 Tamlungs = 12 Ticals** ND. Reported not confirmed.	—	—	—
13	**4 Tamlings** ND. Reported not confirmed.	—	—	—
14	**5 Tamlungs = 20 Ticals** ND. Reported not confirmed.	—	—	—
15	**7 Tamlungs** ND. Reported not confirmed.	—	—	—
16	**8 Tamlungs** ND. Reported not confirmed.	—	—	—
17	**10 Tamlungs = 40 Ticals** ND. Reported not confirmed.	—	—	—
18	**12 Tamlungs** ND. Reported not confirmed.	—	—	—
19	**15 Tamlungs** ND. Reported not confirmed.	—	—	—
20	**1 Chang = 80 Ticals** ND. Reported not confirmed.	—	—	—
21	**1 Chang = 5 Tamlungs = 100 Ticals** ND. Reported not confirmed.	—	—	—

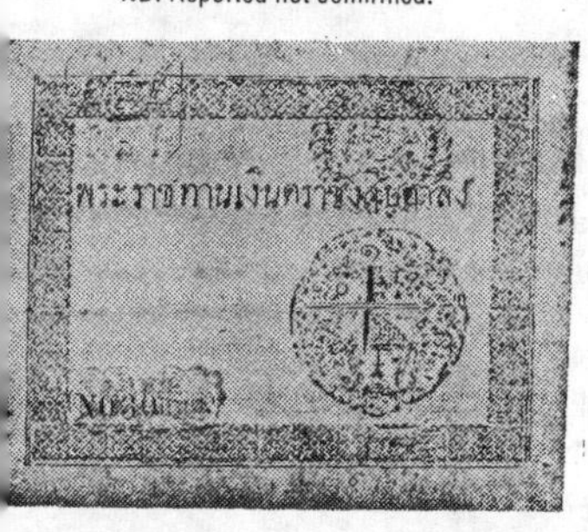

		Good	Fine	XF
A22	**cals1 Chang = 10 Tamlungs = 120 Ti** ND. Rare.	—	—	—

Royal Siamese Treasury

1874 Issue

		Good	Fine	XF
A23	**1 Att = 1/64 Tical** 1874. Black. Blind embossed w/lg. circular seal and smaller rectangle seal. Size: 147 x 93mm. Rare.	—	—	—

1892 ND Issue

#1-8 Royal arms at upper ctr. Printer: G&D. (Not issued).

		Good	Fine	XF
1	**1 Tical** ND (1892). Green on blue and lt. red unpt. Back gray-blue. Rare.	—	—	—
2	**5 Ticals** ND (1892). Pink on green unpt. Back brown.	—	—	—
3	**10 Ticals** ND (1892). Maroon and m/c.	—	—	—

		Good	Fine	XF
4	**40 Ticals** ND (1892). Red-orange and m/c. Rare.	—	—	—

		Good	Fine	XF
5	**80 Ticals** ND (1892). Blue-green and m/c. Rare.	—	—	—
6	**100 Ticals** ND (1892). Blue, tan and m/c.	—	—	—

NOTICE

Readers with unlisted dates, signature varieties, etc. are invited to submit photocopies or, high resolution (300 dpi, 100% size) scans of their notes to: Standard Catalog of World Paper Money, 700 East State St. Iola, WI 54990-0001, or E-Mail: george.cuhaj@fwpubs.com.

		Good	Fine	XF
7	**400 Ticals** ND (1892).			
	a. Purple, green and m/c. Rare.	—	—	—
	b. Green on m/c unpt. Back green-gray; arms at ctr.	—	—	—
	c. Orange on m/c unpt. Back orange on blue and m/c unpt.; arms at ctr.	—	—	—
8	**800 Ticals** ND (1892). Brown, blue-green and m/c. 8 arms duplication at ctr. on back.	—	—	—

GOVERNMENT OF SIAM

SIGNATURE VARIETIES

	Chief Of The Banknote Department เจ้าพนักงาน	Minister Of Finance เสนาบดีกระทรวงพระคลัง
1		
2		
3		
4		
5		
6		
7		
8		
9		
Minister of Finance (to 1928)	เสนาบดีกระทรวงพระคลัง	
10		
11		
Minister of Finance (from 1928)	รัฐมนตรีว่าการกระทรวงการคลัง	
12		*
13		*
14		*
15		*
16		*

1902 ISSUE, SERIES 1

#9-13 state arms at top ctr. Uniface. Officially known as "Series One." Sign. of Finance Minister at r. Official in Charge of Banknotes at l. Notes dated (date ranges for varieties in parentheses). Main wmk: 3 headed elephant. Printer: TDLR.

		Good	Fine	XF
9	**5 Ticals** 1902-25. Gray on green unpt.			
	a. Serial # at top only, green unpt. (1902-05). Sign: 1; 2.	500.	1500.	3000
	b. Serial # at top only, green unpt. (1902-05). Sign: 3.	500.	1500.	3000
	c. Serial # at top only, purple-gray on tan unpt. (1905-11). Sign: 3; 5.	400.	1200.	2400
	d. Serial # at top and bottom, purple-gray on tan unpt. (1911-25). Sign. 5; 6; 8; 9.	250.	700.	1800

		Good	Fine	XF
10	**10 Ticals** 1902-24. Brown on yellow unpt.			
	a. Serial # at top only, tan unpt. (1902-06). Sign. 1; 2.	500.	1500.	3000
	b. Serial # at top only, green unpt. (1906-13). Sign. 3; 4; 5.	200.	900.	2500
	c. Serial # at top and bottom, green unpt. (1913-24). Sign. 4; 5; 6; 8 9.	225.	950.	2400
	p. Brown. Proof. 1.1.1903.	—	—	—
11	**20 Ticals** 1902-25. Green on pale pink unpt.			
	a. Serial # at top only, yellow unpt. (1902-06). Sign 1; 2.	400.	1800.	3500
	b. Serial # at top only, yellow unpt. (1902-06). Sign: 2.	400.	1800.	3500
	c. Serial # at top only, lt. green unpt. (1906-10). Sign. 4; 5.	300.	1100.	3000
	d. Serial # at top and bottom, lt. green unpt. (1910-25). Sign. 5; 6; 8; 9.	300.	1000.	2900
	p. Green. Proof. 1.4.1902.	—	—	—

		Good	Fine	XF
12	**100 Ticals** 1902-25. Purple on pale brown unpt.			
	a. Serial # at top only, brown on yellow unpt. (1902-08). Sign. 1; 2; 3.	450.	1400.	3000.
	b. Serial # at top only, violet on brown unpt. (1908-10). Sign. 2; 3; 4; 5.	400.	1300.	2750.
	c. Serial # at top and bottom, violet on brown unpt. (1910-25). Sign. 5; 6; 8; 9.	350.	1200.	2500.
	p. Purple. Proof. 1.4.1902.	—	—	—
13	**1000 Ticals** 1.4.1902-25. Red on pale red unpt.			
	a. Serial # at top only, lt. brown unpt. (1902-09). Sign. 1; 2.	500.	1500.	6000.
	b. Serial # at top only, brown unpt. (1909-12). Sign. 5.	400.	1200.	5000.
	c. Serial # at top and bottom, brown unpt. (1912-25). Sign. 6; 8; 9.	300.	1000.	4000.
	p. Proof. 1.4.1902.	—	—	—

NOTICE

Readers with unlisted dates, signature varieties, etc.
are invited to submit photocopies or,
high resolution (300 dpi, 100% size) scans of their notes to:
Standard Catalog of World Paper Money,
700 East State St. Iola, WI 54990-0001,
or E-Mail: george.cuhaj@fwpubs.com.

1918 ISSUE

		Good	Fine	XF
14	**1 Tical** 1918-25. (15.7.1918; 5.7.1921 verified.) Black on gray or gray-brown unpt. Sign. 6; 8; 9.	100.	200.	400.

1918 ND PROVISIONAL ISSUE

		Good	Fine	XF
15	**50 Ticals** ND (1918). Ovpt. on #14. Sign. 7.			
	a. W/o embossed stamp. Rare.	—	—	—
	b. Embossed stamp of 3-headed elephant on back. Rare.	—	—	—

1925 ISSUE, SERIES 2

Dates and single sign. of Finance Minister on bottom ctr., mythological winged Garuda bird at upper l., 3-headed elephant at lower r. Common vignette at ctr. shows ceremonial parade of first plowing on back. Officially described as "Series Two."

TEXT VARIETIES (in second line on face):

Type I

สัญญาจะจ่ายสินให้แก่ผู้นำธนบัตรนี้มาขึ้นเป็นสินตราสยาม

"Contract to pay in Siamese Currency to anyone who presents this note".

Type II

ธนบัตรเป็นเงินที่ชำระหนี้ได้ตามกฎหมาย

"Banknote is legal tender for any debt".

#16-21 ceremonial procession on back. Printer: TDLR.

		Good	Fine	XF
16	**1 Baht** 1925-33. Blue on yellow unpt.			
	a. Type I text. 1.4.1925-20.4.1928. Sign. 10.	2.00	10.00	25.00
	b. Type II text. 8.9.1928-11.6.1933. Sign. 10; 11; 12; 13.	2.00	10.00	25.00

		Good	Fine	XF
17	**5 Baht** 1925-32. Purple on green unpt.			
	a. Type I text. 1.4.1925-15.2.1928. Sign. 10.	25.00	100.	250.
	b. Type II text. 29.6.1929-1.2.1932. Sign. 10; 11.	17.50	75.00	200.

		Good	Fine	XF
18	**10 Baht** 1925-34. Red-brown on pink unpt.			
	a. Type I text. 29.6.1925-15.11.1926. Sign. 10.	15.00	75.00	200.
	b. Type II text. 15.5.1929-21.3.1934. Sign. 10; 11; 12; 13.	12.00	50.00	300.

		Good	Fine	XF
19	**20 Baht** 1925-33. Green on gray unpt.			
	a. Type I text. 15.4.1925; 29.7.1925; 15.8.1925; 15.11.1926; 15.7.1927; 15.5.1928. Sign. 10.	40.00	150.	350.
	b. Type II text. 29.5.1928-1.1.1933. Sign. 10; 11; 13.	40.00	150.	350.

		Good	Fine	XF
20	**100 Baht** 1925-38. Blue on green unpt.			
	a. Type I text. 1.4.1925-1.11.1927. Sign. 10.	25.00	100.	300.
	b. Type II text. 11.9.1928-16.9.1938. Sign. 14; 15; 16.	20.00	75.00	250.
21	**1000 Baht** 1925-38. Red-brown on yellow unpt.			
	a. Type I text. 1.4.1925-1.11.1927. Sign. 10; 11.	200.	400.	1000.
	b. Type II text. 1.10.1930-11.9.1938. Sign. 11; 15.	200.	400.	1000.

1934-35 ISSUE, SERIES 3

Single sign. of Finance Minister at bottom ctr. Winged mythological figure (Garuda) at top ctr. and 3-headed elephant at lower r. corner. Temple and pagoda on an island on back. Officially described as "Series Three".

#22-25 portr. Rama VII facing at l. Printer: TDLR.

		VG	VF	UNC
22	**1 Baht** 1.4.1934-25.2.1935. Dk. blue on lt. yellow-green and pale orange unpt. Royal barge at ctr. Sign. 13; 14.	2.00	7.50	40.00

		VG	VF	UNC
23	**5 Baht** 29.5.1934-18.2.1935. Purple on yellow and orange unpt. Emerald Buddha Temple complex at ctr. Sign. 13; 14.	20.00	50.00	200.
24	**10 Baht** 1.2.1934-1.3.1935. Brown on pink unpt. River and mountains at ctr. Sign. 13; 14.	15.00	30.00	160.

		VG	VF	UNC
25	**20 Baht** 15.1.1935; 25.1.1935; 8.2.1935; 18.2.1935; 25.2.1935. Green on pale blue and tan unpt. River, village and pagoda at ctr. Sign. 14.	10.00	40.00	275.

Note: #22-25 come with 2 variations in the Finance Minister title line at bottom center of face.

1935-36 Issue

#26-29 portr. King Rama VIII as a boy 3/4 face at l. Back design like previous issue.

		VG	VF	UNC
26	**1 Baht** 18.4.1935-11.9.1938. Blue. Similar to #22. Sign. 14; 15.	2.00	10.00	50.00
27	**5 Baht** 29.4.1935-15.5.1937. Purple. Similar to #23. Sign. 14; 15.	7.50	20.00	80.00

		VG	VF	UNC
28	**10 Baht** 29.5.1935-1.10.1936. Brown. Similar to #24. Sign. 14; 15.	10.00	35.00	170.
29	**20 Baht** 1.4.1936-1.7.1936. Green. Similar to #25. Sign. 15.	15.00	40.00	200.

1939 ND Issue, Series 4A

Officially described as "Series Four (Thomas)" (notes printed in England by Thomas De La Rue) to differentiate from similar, but cruder, notes printed later by the Thai Map Department. W/o dates. Kg. Rama VIII as a boy 3/4 face at l. and 3-headed elephant at lower r. M/c guilloche unpt. at ctr. Single sign. of Finance Minister at bottom ctr. Royal Throne Hall on back.

Note: In 1939 the name *SIAM* was changed to *THAILAND*. By decree of 7.3.1939 this change was made in the main heading at top on faces of all notes as shown below:

HEADING VARIETIES รัฐบาลสยาม รัฐบาลไทย

TYPE I:TYPE II:

GOVERNMENT OF SIAMGOVERNMENT OF THAILAND

		VG	VF	UNC
30	**1 Baht** ND (from 1938). Blue. Phra Samut Chedi Temple and pagoda at ctr. Type I heading. Sign. 15, 16.	2.00	10.00	40.00

		VG	VF	UNC
31	**1 Baht** ND (from 1939). Blue. Like #30. Type II heading.			
	a. Serial # at l. w/European characters, Thai at r. Sign. 16.	2.00	7.50	30.00
	b. Both serial # w/European characters. Sign. 23 (from 1946).	2.00	7.50	30.00
32	**5 Baht** ND (from 1939). Purple. Entrance to Phra Pathom Chedi at ctr. Type I heading. Sign. 16.	15.00	80.00	300.
33	**5 Baht** ND (from 1939). Purple. Like #32 but Type II heading. Sign. 16.	80.00	100.	500.

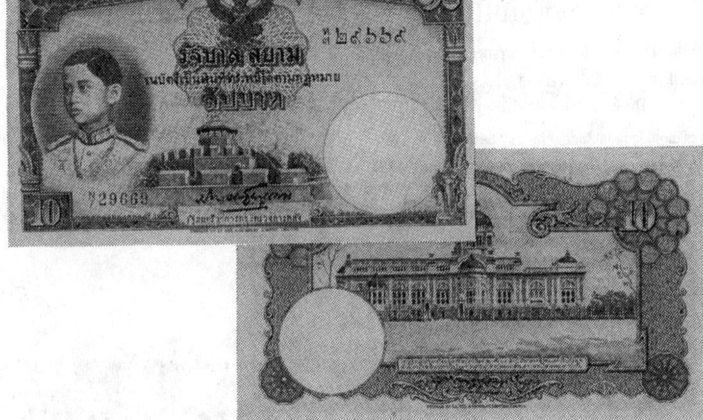

		VG	VF	UNC
34	**10 Baht** ND (from 1939). Brown. Mahagal Fortress at ctr. Type I heading. Sign. 16.	10.00	40.00	200.
35	**10 Baht** ND (from 1939). Brown. Like #34 but Type II heading.			
	a. Sign. 16; 23 (from 1939).	10.00	35.00	180.
36	**20 Baht** ND (from 1939). Green. Throne Halls at ctr. Type I heading. Sign. 16.	10.00	40.00	200.

Note: 20 Baht note w/Type II heading does not exist.

		VG	VF	UNC
37	**1000 Baht** ND (from 1939). Red-brown. Temple of the Dawn at ctr. Type I heading. Sign. 16.	100.	400.	1500.
38	**1000 Baht** ND (from 1939). Red-brown. Like #37 but w/Type II heading. Sign. 16.	100.	400.	1500.

JAPANESE INTERVENTION - WW II

GOVERNMENT OF THAILAND

1942-44 ND ISSUE, SERIES 4B

Officially described as "Series Four (Map)". Printed by Royal Thai Army Map Department, w/imprint in the bottom margin face and back. Similar to their counterparts in Series Four (Thomas), but of inferior quality. Single sign. of Minister of Finance at bottom ctr. Top legend is changed from:

To:

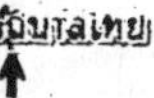

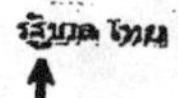

Sign. var. chart 17-24

SIGNATURE VARIETIES		
	Chief Of The Banknote department	**Minister Of Finance**
17		
	Director General Of The Treasury Department อธิบดีกรมคลัง	**Minister Of Finance** รัฐมนตรีว่าการกระทรวงการคลัง
18		
Minister Of Finance รัฐมนตรีว่าการกระทรวงการคลัง		
19		
20		
21		
22		
23		
24		

		VG	VF	UNC
39	**1 Baht**			
	ND (from 1942). Blue. Similar to #31. Wmk: Constitution on tray on pedestal.			
	a. R. serial # in Thai. Sign. 17.	2.00	15.00	45.00
	b. Both serial # in European numbers. Sign. 17; 19; 20.	2.00	12.50	40.00
40	**10 Baht**			
	ND (from 1943). Brown. Similar to #35.			
	a. Wmk: Constitution. Sign. 17.	5.00	25.00	150.
	b. Wmk: Constitution. Sign. 20.	5.00	25.00	125.
	c. Sign. 21 (probably counterfeit; # and sign. fraudulently applied to genuine note; not issued).	—	—	—
	d. Wmk: Wavy lines w/constitution printed in window. Sign. 21 (from 1945).	5.00	25.00	125.
	e. Wmk: Like d. Sign. 24.	5.00	40.00	150.
	f. Sign. 20 (like c, probably counterfeit; not issued).	—	—	—

		VG	VF	UNC
41	**20 Baht**			
	ND (from 1943). Green. Like #36. Unpt. orange and green on face. Wmk: Constitution. Sign. 17; 19; 20.	3.00	35.00	150.
42	**100 Baht**			
	ND (1944). Blue. Temple, w/walkway flanked by 2 mythological statues, at ctr. Pink and green unpt. design on face. Wmk: Constitution. Silk threads. Sign. 19; 20.	8.00	50.00	300.

1942-45 ND ISSUES, SERIES 5

Printed in Japan by Mitsui Trading Company. Officially described as "Series Five". Portr. Kg. Rama VIII full face at r. Single sign. of Finance Minister at bottom ctr. Walled temple and pagoda complex on river bank (Royal Palace) on back.

		VG	VF	UNC
43	**50 Satang**			
	ND (1942). Green on pink unpt. design. Wmk. paper. Sign. 17; 20.			
	a. Issued note.	1.00	4.00	10.00
	r. Remainder w/o sign. or block #.	—	—	150.
	s1. Specimen w/ovpt: *Mi-hon.*	—	—	—
	s2. Specimen w/ovpt: *Specimen.*	—	—	—

#44-53 wmk: Constitution on tray on pedestal.

		VG	VF	UNC
44	**1 Baht**			
	ND (1942; 1944). Brown on pink unpt. at ctr. Entrance to Wat Phumintr, flanked by mythological snakes at l.			
	a. 3 serial #, lower l. in Thai. Sign. 17.	5.00	20.00	50.00
	b. 3 serial # all w/European numerals. Sign. 17.	3.00	15.00	40.00
	c. 2 serial # (lower l. deleted). Sign. 17; 19; 20.	3.00	15.00	40.00
	r. Remainder w/o sign. or serial #.	—	—	150.
	s1. Specimen w/ovpt: *Mi-hon.*	—	—	—
	s2. Specimen w/ovpt: *Specimen.*	—	—	—
45	**5 Baht**			
	ND (1942; 1944). Green on green unpt. Marble Temple at l.			
	a. 3 serial #, lower l. in Thai. Sign. 17.	15.00	40.00	200.
	b. 3 serial #, all w/European numbers. Sign. 17.	15.00	30.00	200.
	c. 2 serial # (lower l. deleted). Sign. 17; 19; 20.	15.00	20.00	200.
	d. W/o sign.	—	—	150.
	s. Specimen w/ovpt: *Specimen.*	—	—	—

		VG	VF	UNC
46	**5 Baht**			
	ND (1945). Green. Like #45. 2 serial #. Back purple, w/constitution printed in purple on window.			
	a. Sign. 20.	20.00	50.00	250.
	b. W/o sign. Reported not confirmed.			
47	**10 Baht**			
	ND (from 1942). Purple on pink and lt. blue unpt. Part of wall and gateway to Wat Chetupon at l. Back purple.			
	a. 3 serial #, lower l. in Thai. Sign. 17.	20.00	50.00	250.
	b. 3 serial #, all w/European numbers. Sign. 17.	20.00	50.00	250.
	c. 2 serial # (lower l. deleted). Sign. 17; 20.	20.00	50.00	250.
	s. Specimen w/ovpt: *Specimen.*	—	—	—

		VG	VF	UNC
48	**10 Baht** ND (1945). Purple. Like #47c, but back lt. green. Sign. 20.	25.00	60.00	350.
49	**20 Baht** ND (from 1942). Blue on brown unpt. Throne Hall at l. Back blue.			
	a. 3 serial #. Upper r. and l. w/European letters and numerals, lower l. in Thai. Sign. 17.	5.00	20.00	100.
	b. 3 serial #, all w/European numbers. Upper l. and r. have Western letter in control prefix, lower has Thai letter prefix. Sign. 17.	5.00	20.00	100.
	c. 3 serial #, all w/European numbers. Upper r. and lower have Thai letter in control prefix (P/31-P/33 only). Sign. 17.	10.00	25.00	125.
	d. 2 serial # (lower l. deleted). Western control letter in upper l., Thai control letter in upper r. Sign. 17; 19; 20.	5.00	20.00	100.
	s. Specimen w/ovpt: *Specimen*.	—	—	—
50	**20 Baht** ND (1945). Like #49d, but back lt. brown.			
	a. Sign. 20.	5.00	25.00	85.00
	b. W/o sign. Reported not confirmed.			
51	**100 Baht** ND (1943). Red on blue and olive unpt. Temple of the Dawn at l. Back red. Sign. 17.			
	a. Issued note.	30.00	150.	400.
	r. Remainder w/o sign. or serial #.	—	—	375.
	s1. Specimen w/ovpt: *Mi-hon.*	—	—	—
	s2. Specimen w/ovpt: *Specimen.*	—	—	—

		VG	VF	UNC
52	**100 Baht** ND (1945). Red. Like #51 but back blue.			
	a. Sign. 20.	20.00	80.00	250.
	b. W/o sign.	15.00	50.00	200.
	s1. Specimen w/ovpt: *Mi-hon.*	—	—	—
	s2. Specimen w/ovpt: *Specimen.*	—	—	—

		VG	VF	UNC
53	**1000 Baht** ND (1944). Olive on pink and blue unpt. The Chakri and Dusit Maha Prasad Throne Halls at l. Back olive. Silk threads. Sign. 17.			
	a. Issued note.	200.	600.	2000.
	s1. Specimen w/ovpt: *Mi-hon.*	—	—	—
	s2. Specimen w/ovpt: *Specimen.*	—	—	—

1945 ND First Issue, Series 6

Portr. Kg. Rama VIII as a boy at l., single sign. of Finance Minister at bottom ctr. Royal Throne Hall on back. Officially described as "Series Six". Printed by Army Map Department (w/imprint) and Navy Hydrological Department (w/o imprint).

		VG	VF	UNC
53A	**20 Baht** ND (1945). Green. Like #41 but unpt. design pink. W/imprint. Sign. 20.			
	a. Wmk: Constitution on tray on pedestal, silk threads.	15.00	50.00	150.
	b. Wmk: Wavy lines. Silk threads throughout; tan constitution ovpt. in circle. W/imprint. Sign. 20; 21.	15.00	60.00	150.
	c. Wmk: Like b. W/o imprint. Sign. 21.	15.00	60.00	150.

		VG	VF	UNC
53B	**100 Baht** ND (1945). Blue. Like #42 but unpt. design mostly purple.			
	a. Wmk: Constitution. Silk threads throughout. W/imprint. Reported not confirmed.	—	—	—
	b. Wmk: Like a. W/o imprint. Sign. 20.	15.00	60.00	200.
	c. Wmk: Wavy lines. Silk threads, purple constitution ovpt. in circle. W/imprint. Sign. 20; 21.	15.00	60.00	175.
	d. Wmk: Like c. W/o imprint. Sign. 20; 21.	15.00	50.00	150.

1945 ND Second Issue, Series 7

Portr. Kg. Rama VIII full face at l., single sign. of Finance Minister at bottom ctr. Royal Throne Hall on back. Officially described as "Series Seven". Crudely printed by private printers contracted by the Bank of Thailand.

		VG	VF	UNC
54	**1 Baht** ND (1945). Blue on lt. pink unpt. Similar to #30.			
	a. Wmk: Multiple wavy lines. Sign. 20; 21.	2.00	8.00	25.00
	b. W/o wmk. Sign. 21.	2.00	8.00	25.00
55	**5 Baht** ND (1945). Purple and lt. green. Similar to #32. Lt. green constitution ovpt. in circle. Wmk: Wavy lines. Red serial #. 135 x 76mm. Sign. 20.	—	—	—
55A	**5 Baht** ND (1945). Like #55 but black serial #. 115 x 65mm. Sign. 20; 21.	10.00	25.00	100.
56	**10 Baht** ND (1945). Dk. brown. Similar to #34.			
	a. Wmk: Constitution. Sign. 20.	15.00	40.00	150.
	b. Wmk: Multiple wavy lines. Brown constitution ovpt. in circle. Sign. 20.	15.00	40.00	150.

		VG	VF	UNC
57	**50 Baht** ND (1945). Pale red on green unpt. Marble Temple at ctr.			
	a. W/o wmk. Sign. 20.	20.00	70.00	200.
	b. Wmk: Multiple wavy lines. Sign. 20; 21.	20.00	70.00	200.

KINGDOM

GOVERNMENT OF THAILAND

SIGNATURE VARIETIES

	Minister Of Finance รัฐมนตรีว่าการกระทรวงการคลัง	Governor Of The Bank Of Thailand ผู้ว่าการธนาคารแห่งประเทศไทย
25		
26		
	Minister Of Finance รัฐมนตรีว่าการกระทรวงการคลัง	
27		
28		
29		
30		
31		
32		
33		
34		
35		
36		
37		
38		
39		
40		
41		
42		
43	**	
	**signed as Undersecretary/Deputy Finance Minister	
44		

NOTICE

Readers with unlisted dates, signature varieties, etc. are invited to submit photocopies or, high resolution (300 dpi, 100% size) scans of their notes to: Standard Catalog of World Paper Money, 700 East State St. Iola, WI 54990-0001, or E-Mail: george.cuhaj@fwpubs.com.

1942-44 ND ISSUE

Different types of wartime notes, some of which were issued after the war but before supplies of new notes could be obtained for normal use. A "hodgepodge" having no common characteristics, this series, officially described as "Series Special", was printed in part in Thailand, in part in other countries.

		VG	VF	UNC
58	**1 Baht** ND (1942). Blue on red unpt. Portr. Kg. Rama VIII 3/4 face at l. Constitution on tray on pedestal embossed in oval at r. Sign. 18. Wmk.: Vertical white stripe 8mm. wide at l. ctr.			
	a. Red to orange flower in unpt. at ctr.	15.00	50.00	200.
	b. Yellow flower in unpt. at ctr. (Counterfeit).	—	—	—
59	**10 Baht** ND. Like #62 but w/o ovpt. or sign. (Not issued).	—	—	—

		VG	VF	UNC
60	**1000 Baht** ND (1943). Deep red and yellow. Portr. Kg. Rama VIII tilted to r. of vertical at r. Phrang Sam Yod (3 ornate towers) at l. Wmk: Constitution. Sign. 18.	150.	600.	2000.
61	**1000 Baht** ND (1944). Like #60, but deep brown and yellow. Sign. 18.	150.	600.	2000.

1945; 1946 ND PROVISIONAL ISSUE

		VG	VF	UNC
62	**50 Satang on 10 Baht** ND (1946). Dk. purple on gray unpt. Portal at l., Portr. Kg. Rama VIII full face at r. Royal palace on river bank on back. New value ovpt. in 3 corners on face, twice on back on #59. Sign. 22.	4.00	8.00	20.00

		VG	VF	UNC
62A	**1 Baht** ND (1946). Blue on pale olive unpt. ONE BAHT at ctr. 3-line black ovpt on face. English printing. Sign. 23.			
	a. 2nd line of ovpt. complete (29 characters).	2.00	8.00	20.00
	b. 12th character of 2nd line missing.	2.00	8.00	20.00

		VG	VF	UNC
62B	**50 Baht on 1 Dollar**			
	ND (1945). Purple and greenish yellow. Ovpt. on #R1.			
	a. Red *50* in white circle on face on back. Sign. 17; 20.	50.00	100.	400.
	b. Red *50* in white circle on face only. Sign. 20.	50.00	100.	400.
	c. W/o red *50* or obliterative ovpts. on face or back. Black denomination in words ovpt. on face. Sign. 17; 19; 20.	60.00	150.	425.

Note: #62B was originally intended for use in the northern Malay States, thus the value of 1 Dollar.

1946 ND ISSUE, SERIES 8

Printed in the U.S. by Tudor Press, Boston. This is a regular (not "Liberation") issue, officially described as "Series Eight". Portr. Kg. Rama VIII full face at l. Unpt. road w/monuments and pagoda. All have brown back, w/constitution on ceremonial vessel at ctr. Replacement notes identified by absence of letter at end of serial #. Wmk: *MILITARY AUTHORITY* repeated.

		VG	VF	UNC
63	**1 Baht**	.25	1.00	5.00
	ND (1946). Green and blue. Sign. 22.			

		VG	VF	UNC
64	**5 Baht**	1.00	5.00	25.00
	ND (1946). Dk. and lt. blue. Sign. 22.			

		VG	VF	UNC
65	**10 Baht**			
	ND (1946). Brown on blue.			
	a. Black sign. ovpt. at r. Sign. 25.	2.00	15.00	50.00
	b. 2 black sign. ovpt. Sign. 26.	2.00	15.00	50.00

		VG	VF	UNC
66	**20 Baht**			
	ND (1946). Dk. and lt. blue.			
	a. Black sign. ovpt. at r. Sign. 25.	10.00	40.00	120
	b. 2 black sign. ovpt. Sign. 26.	10.00	40.00	120

		VG	VF	UNC
67	**100 Baht**			
	ND (1946). Brown on lt. blue. Black sign. 25 (unconfirmed); 26; 28 ovpt.	20.00	80.00	200

1948 ND ISSUE, SERIES 9

W/o dates. Printed in England by TDLR and officially described as "Series Nine". With exception of #68, a have portr. Kg. Rama IX full face at l., sign. of Finance Minister at l. and Governor of the Bank Thailand at r., wmk. in circular window at r. Royal Throne Hall on back.

		VG	VF	UNC
68	**50 Satang**	1.00	2.00	8.0
	ND (1948). Green on pink unpt. Constitution on tray on pedestal in unpt. Phra Samut Chedi on back. Sign. 27.			

#69-73 portr. Kg. in uniform w/o collar insignia. Wmk: Constitution on tray on pedestal. Blue and red sec rity threads. Printer: TDLR.

		VG	VF	UNC
69	**1 Baht**			
	ND (1948). Blue on m/c unpt. Similar to #30.			
	a. Red serial #. Sign. 28; 30; 31; 32; 33; 34.	1.00	4.00	10.
	b. Black serial #. Sign. 28; 31; 32.	1.00	2.00	6.

		VG	VF	UNC
70	**5 Baht**			
	ND (1948). Purple on m/c unpt. Similar to #32.			
	a. Red serial #. Sign. 28.	10.00	30.00	1
	b. Black serial #. Sign. 28; 30; 31.	1.00	4.00	12.
71	**10 Baht**			
	ND (1948). Brown on m/c unpt. Similar to #34.			
	a. Red serial #. Sign. 28; 29; 32.	20.00	50.00	13
	b. Black serial #. Sign. 28; 30; 31; 32.	3.00	7.50	35.

72	20 Baht	VG	VF	UNC
	ND (1948). Green on m/c unpt. Similar to #36.			
	a. Red serial #. Sign. 28; 29; 30; 31.	30.00	80.00	150.
	b. Black serial #. Sign. 28; 30; 31; 32.	5.00	15.00	50.00
73	100 Baht			
	ND (1948). Red on m/c unpt. Similar to #37. Black serial # only. Sign. 28; 31; 32; 33; 34.	5.00	25.00	75.00

1953-56 ND ISSUE

74-78 slightly modified portr. Kg. in Field Marshal's uniform w/collar insignia and 3 decorations. Black serial #. Printer: TDLR.

mall letters in 2-line text on back. 

arge letters in 2-line text on back.

4	1 Baht	VG	VF	UNC
	ND (1955). Blue on m/c unpt. Like #69.			
	a. Wmk: Constitution. Red and blue security threads. Sign. 34.	.20	1.00	4.00
	b. Wmk: Constitution. Metal security strip. Sign. 34; 35 (lg. size).	.20	1.00	3.50
	c. Wmk: Kg. profile. Sm. letters in 2-line text on back. Sign. 35.	.10	.75	3.00
	d. Wmk: Kg. profile. Larger letters in 2-line text on back. Sign. 36; 37; 38; 39; 40; 4l.	.10	.75	2.50
	s. As a; d. Specimen.	—	—	250.

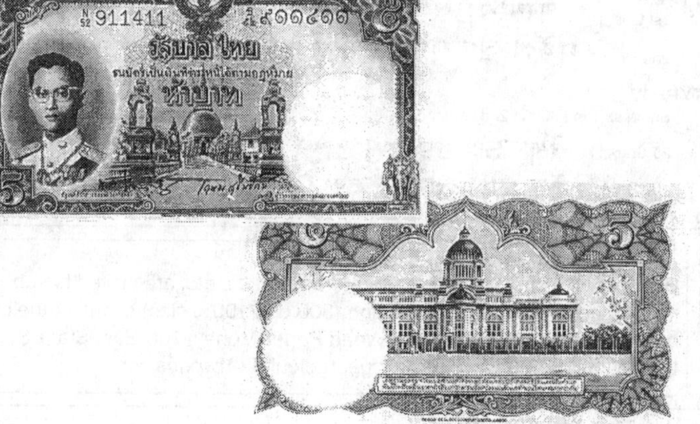

	5 Baht	VG	VF	UNC
	ND (1956). Purple on m/c unpt. Like #70.			

75		VG	VF	UNC
	a. Wmk: Constitution. Red and blue security threads. Sign. 34.	5.00	15.00	50.00
	b. Wmk: Constitution. Metal security strip. Sign. 34; 35 (lg. size).	.50	2.50	10.00
	c. Wmk: Kg. profile. Sm. letters in 2-line text on back. Sign. 35; 36.	.50	2.00	5.00
	d. Wmk: Kg. profile. Larger letters in 2-line text on back. Sign. 38; 39; 40; 41.	.50	1.50	4.50
	s. As a. Specimen.	—	—	250.

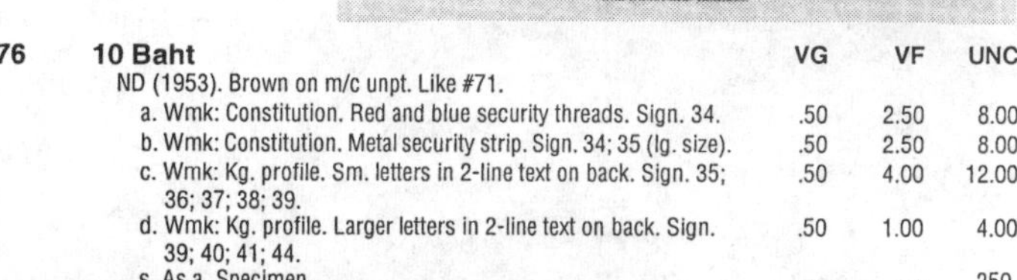

76	10 Baht	VG	VF	UNC
	ND (1953). Brown on m/c unpt. Like #71.			
	a. Wmk: Constitution. Red and blue security threads. Sign. 34.	.50	2.50	8.00
	b. Wmk: Constitution. Metal security strip. Sign. 34; 35 (lg. size).	.50	2.50	8.00
	c. Wmk: Kg. profile. Sm. letters in 2-line text on back. Sign. 35; 36; 37; 38; 39.	.50	4.00	12.00
	d. Wmk: Kg. profile. Larger letters in 2-line text on back. Sign. 39; 40; 41; 44.	.50	1.00	4.00
	s. As a. Specimen.	—	—	250.

77	20 Baht	VG	VF	UNC
	ND (1953). Olive-green on m/c unpt. Like #72.			
	a. Wmk: Constitution. Red and blue security threads. Sign. 34.	2.50	4.00	12.00
	b. Wmk: Constitution. Metal security strip. Sign. 34; 35 (lg. size).	2.50	4.00	12.50
	c. Wmk: Kg. profile. Sm. letters in 2-line text on back. Sign. 35; 37; 38.	6.00	10.00	30.00
	d. Wmk: Kg. profile. Larger letters in 2-line text on back. Sign. 38; 39; 40; 41; 44.	.50	2.00	6.00
	s. As a. Specimen.	—	—	250.
78	100 Baht			
	ND (1955). Red on m/c unpt. Like #73.			
	a. Wmk: Constitution. Red and blue security threads. Sign. 34.	8.00	20.00	60.00
	b. Wmk: Constitution. Metal security strip. Sign. 34; 35; 37; 38.	4.00	12.50	25.00
	c. Wmk: Kg. profile. Sm. letters in 2-line text on back. Sign. 38.	2.00	10.00	35.00
	d. Wmk: Kg. profile. Larger letters in 2-line text on back. Sign. 38-41.	2.00	6.00	10.00
	s. As a; c. Specimen.	—	—	250.

NOTICE

Readers with unlisted dates, signature varieties, etc. are invited to submit photocopies or, high resolution (300 dpi, 100% size) scans of their notes to: Standard Catalog of World Paper Money, 700 East State St. Iola, WI 54990-0001, or E-Mail: george.cuhaj@fwpubs.com.

REGIONAL - WW II

#R1 was issued in the northern Malay States of Kedah, Kelantan, Perlis and Trengganu which were ceded to Thailand by Japan during WW II. They were later ovpt: 50 Baht and issued for general circulation; see #62B.

TREASURY

1943 PROVISIONAL ISSUE

		VG	VF	UNC
R1	**1 Dollar** ND (1943). Purple and green. Vertical line of Chinese inscription at l., Malay at r. Throne Hall on back.			
	a. Issued note.	—	—	—
	r. Unsigned remainder.	—	100.	350.

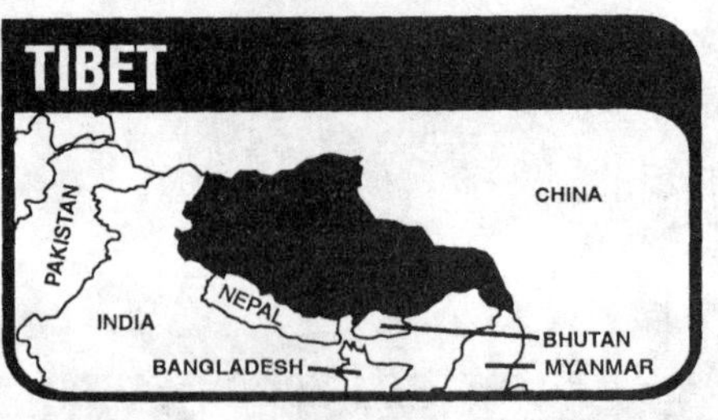

Tibet, an autonomous region o[f] China located in central Asi[a] between the Himalayan an[d] Kunlun Mountains, has an are[a] of 471,660 sq. mi. (1,221,599 s[q.] km.) and a population of 1. million. Capital: Lhasa. Th[e] economy is d on agriculture an[d] livestock raising. Wool, livestock salt and hides are exported.

Lamaism, a form of Buddhism developed in Tibet in the 8th century. From that time until th[e] 1900s, the country remaine[d] isolated from the outside world ruled from the 17th century by the Dalai Lama. The British in India achieved some influence in th[e] early 20th century, and encouraged Tibet to declare its independence from China in 1913. Th[e] communist revolution in China marked a new era in Tibetan history. Chinese Communist troop[s] invaded Tibet in Oct., 1950. After a token resistance, Tibet signed an agreement with China i[n] which China recognized the spiritual and temporal leadership of the Dalai Lama, and Tibe[t] recognized the suzerainty of China. In 1959, a nationwide revolt triggered by Communist-initiate[d] land reform broke out. The revolt was ruthlessly crushed. The Dalai Lama fled to India, and o[n] Sept. 1, 1965, the Chinese made Tibet an autonomous region of China.

NOTE: Chinese notes in Tibetan script or w/Tibetan ovpt. were not intended for circulation i[n] Tibet, but for use in bordering Chinese Provinces having a Tibetan speaking population. Refer t[o] China #209b, 214b, 217b, 219d and 220c in this volume. Also #S1739 and S1740 (Sikan[g] Provincial Bank) in Volume 1.

MONETARY SYSTEM:

7.5 Srang = 50 Tam (Tangka)

DENOMINATONS VALUES

Tam (Tangka):	ཏམ་	Five:	ལྔ་	Twenty-five:	ཉེར་ལྔ་
Srang:	སྲང་	Ten:	བཅུ་	Twenty-five:	ཉི་ཤུ་རྩ་ལྔ་
		Fifteen:	བཅོ་ལྔ་	Fifty:	ལྔ་བཅུ་
		100:	༡༠༠	Hundred:	བརྒྱ་ཐམ་པ་

DATING

Tibetan notes simply give the number of solar years which have elapsed sinc[e] the legendary founding of the government in 255 AD, which is year 1 on this reckoning. Thus, Tibetan era dates are converted to AD dates merely by addin[g] 254 to the former. Some of the later Tibetan notes give only the "rab byung" cy[-] cle (without the year) in which issued. Thus a note of the 16th cycle would impl[y] issuance any time during the 60-year period 1927-86AD.

TYPES I & II

1st Line: ༄།གངས་ལྗོངས་བདེ་རྒྱལ་ཁབ་ཆེན་པོ་འི་ ཕྱུགས་ཟུང་ཆ

2nd Line: སྲིད་དབུ་བརྙེས་ཀྱི་ལོ་

Decades: 165X ་ཆིག་སྟོང་དྲུག་བརྒྱ་ལྔ་བཅུ་ང་

166X . . . . ་དྲུག་ཅུ་རེ་ (Units see below)

167X . . . . ་བདུན་ཅུ་དོན་

168X . . . . ་བརྒྱད་ཅུ་གྱ་

169X . . . . ་དགུ་བཅུ་གོ་

Units (to be added to above):

1. གཅིག་ 4. བཞི་ 7. བདུན
2. གཉིས་ 5. ལྔ་ 8. བརྒྱད
3. གསུམ་ 6. དྲུག་ 9. དགུ

3rd Line: ༄།ཕུན་ཚོགས་སྡེ་བཞི་འི་དཔལ་མངའ་ཡན་བདེ་འི་སྐྱེ་ནར་

4th Line: ཆོས་སྲིད་གཉིས་ལྡན་གྱི་རབ་བྱུང་ [cycle] འི་ལོག་དང

15th: ་བཅོ་ལྔ་པ་

16th: ་བཅོ་དྲུག་པ་

TYPE III

1st Line: ༄།གནམ་བསྐོས་དགའ་ལྡན་ཕོ་བྲང་ཕྱོགས་ལས་རྣམ་རྒྱལ།

2nd Line: ༄།ཆོས་སྲིད་གཉིས་ལྡན་གྱི་རབ་བྱུང་བཅུ་དྲུག་པ་འི་ལོག་ད

TYPE IV

Same as Type III, but 2nd line ends:

25 Srang: ་ཤོག་དངུལ་སྲང་ཉི་ཤུ་རྩ་ལྔ།

100 Srang: ་ཤོག་དངུལ་སྲང་བརྒྱ་ཐམ་པ།

NOTICE

Readers with unlisted dates, signature varieties, etc. are invited to submit photocopies or, high resolution (300 dpi, 100% size) scans of their notes to: Standard Catalog of World Paper Money, 700 East State St. Iola, WI 54990-0001, or E-Mail: george.cuhaj@fwpubs.com.

AUTONOMOUS

GOVERNMENT OF TIBET

1658-59 (1912-13) ISSUE

#1-7A many varieties in size, printing and color.

		Good	Fine	XF
1	**5 Tam** 1658 (1912). Green. Lion and flowers. 4 lines of text. Back lt. green. 180 x 100mm.	150.	750.	—
1A	**5 Tam** 1658 (1912). Blue. Like #1. Back blue.	175.	750.	—

		Good	Fine	XF
	10 Tam 1658-59 (1912-13). Red. Lion at ctr. 4 lines of text. 175 x 95mm.	200.	800.	—

		Good	Fine	XF
	15 Tam 1659 (1913). Purple. Lion w/platter of fruit at ctr. 4 lines of text. 185 x 100mm.	175.	750.	—
	25 Tam 1659 (1913). Yellow. Lion. 4 lines of text. Mountains and elephant on back. 180 x 95mm.	175.	750.	—

		Good	Fine	XF
5	**50 Tam** 1659 (1913). Blue. 2 lions at ctr. 4 lines of text. Seated figure on back. 185 x 100mm.	150.	700.	—
6	**50 Tam** 1659 (1913). Purple. Like #5 except for color.	150.	650.	—

1672-77 (1926-31) ISSUE

		Good	Fine	XF
7	**50 Tam** 1672-87 (1926-41). Blue and red on yellow unpt. 2 lions at ctr. Back red and blue; lion, dragon, tiger and stylized creature. 201 x 118mm.			
	a. Short serial # frame. 1672 (Cycle 15); 1673-77 (Cycle 16).	25.00	125.	350.
	b. Long serial # frame. 1673-87 (Cycle 16).	25.00	125.	350.
7A	**50 Tam** 1677 (1931). Like #7, but additional red circular seal over the serial # at upper r.	35.00	150.	375.

1685-90 (1939-43) ISSUE

#8-12 many varieties in size, printing and color. These notes were made by pasting together 3 sheets, the middle one having a 2-line security legend printed on it.

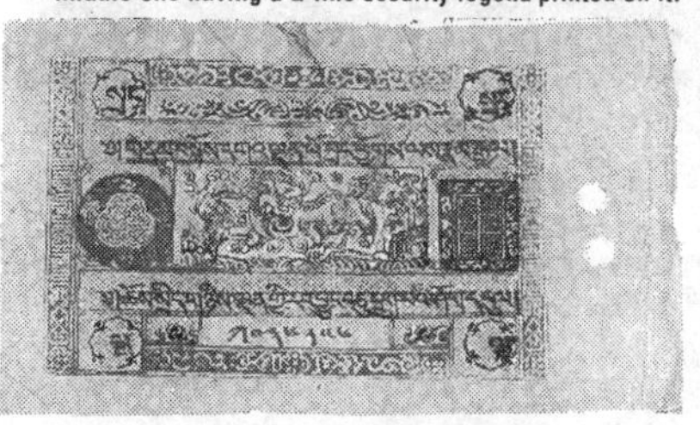

8	5 Srang	Good	Fine	XF
	ND (1942-46). Blue and red on yellow unpt. Lion at ctr. 2 lines of text. Back red and lt. blue; fountain between dragons. 121 x 73mm.	10.00	25.00	65.00

9	10 Srang	Good	Fine	XF
	1687-94 (1941-48). Blue on pink unpt. 2 lions at ctr. 4 lines of text. Dragons and lions on back. 180 x 112mm.	5.00	17.50	45.00

10	25 Srang	Good	Fine	XF
	ND (1941-48). Orange on yellow unpt. 2 lions at ctr. 2 lines of text. Back orange and blue; people, bldgs., elephant and rider. 183 x 110mm.			
	a. Lg. text 83mm long (1941-47).	5.00	15.00	40.00
	b. Sm. text 75mm long (1948).	5.00	15.00	40.00

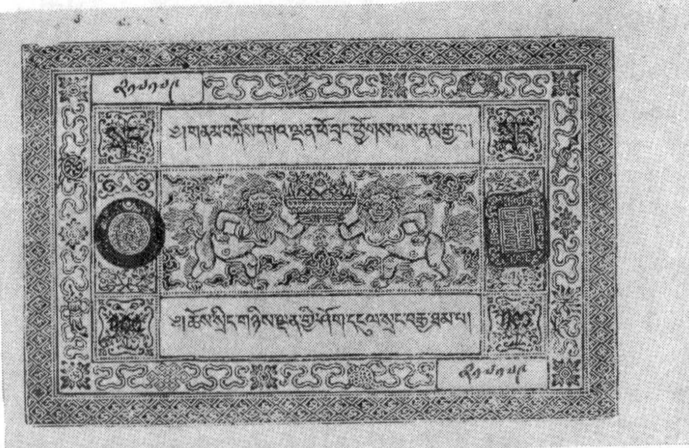

11	100 Srang	Good	Fine	XF
	ND (1942-59). Orange on yellow unpt. 2 lions w/fruit bowl at ctr. 2 lines of text. Round seal at l. Back orange, green, red and black; seated figure. 215 x 138mm			
	a. Lg. text 93-94mm long.	1.50	5.00	15.00
	b. Sm. text 85-87mm long.	1.50	5.00	15.00
	c. Center sheet w/security legend inverted.	—	—	—
	d. Inverted seal.	20.00	40.00	100.

Note: Direct reading of security text is accomplished when the face is held up to a light source.

12	100 Tam Srang			
	ND (1939-40). Like #11, but w/octagonal seal at l.	25.00	50.00	150.

Note: Chinese notes in Tibetan script or w/Tibetan ovpt. were not intended for circulation in Tibet, but for use in bordering Chinese provinces having a Tibetan speaking population. Refer to China #216e, 217d, 218f, and 220c in this volume. Also #S1739-S1741 (Sikang Provincial Bank) in Volume 1.

TIMOR

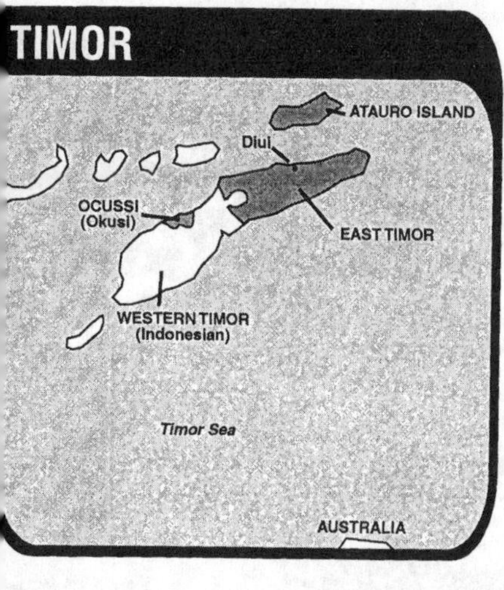

Timor, is an island between the Savu and Timor Seas, has an area, including the former colony of Portuguese Timor, of 11,883 sq. mi. (30,775 sq. km.) and a population of 1.5 million. Western Timor is administered as part of Nusa Tenggara Timur (East Nusa Tenggara) province. Capital: Kupang. The eastern half of the island, the former Portuguese colony, forms a single province, Timor Timur (East Timor). Originally the Portuguese colony also included the area around Ocussi-Ambeno and the small island of Atauro (Pulau Kambing) located north of Dili. Capital: Dili. Timor exports sandalwood, coffee, tea, hides, rubber and copra.

Portuguese traders reached Timor about 1520, and moved to the north and east when the Dutch established themselves in Kupang, a sheltered bay at the southwestern tip, in 1613. Treaties effective in 1860 and 14 established the boundaries between the two colonies. Japan occupied the entire island ring World War II. The former Dutch colony in the western part of the island became part of donesia in 1950.

At the end of Nov., 1975, the Portuguese Province of Timor attained independence as the ople's Democratic Republic of East Timur. In Dec., 1975 or early in 1976 the government of the ople's Democratic Republic was seized by a guerilla faction sympathetic to the Indonesian ritorial claim to East Timur which ousted the constitutional government and replaced it with the ovisional Government of East Timur. On July 17, 1976, the Provisional Government enacted a which dissolved the free republic and made East Timur the 24th province of Indonesia.

In 1999 a revolution suceeded, and it is once again an independent country. Note: For later ues see Indonesia.

ONETARY SYSTEM:

1 Pataca = 100 Avos to 1958
1 Escudo = 100 Centavos, 1958-1975

te: In March 1912, before any notes were made especially for Timor, certain issues from Macao were clared legal tender there. The following list shows exact details:

1 PATACA 1905.	Serial #	83,751 to 84,000	87,251 to 90,750
		84,251 to 84,500	91,001 to 92,000
		84,571 to 85,750	93,001 to 93,500
		86,001 to 86,500	94,001 to 97,000
10 PATACAS 1907.	Serial #	87,001 to 93,000	93,001 to 95,500
25 PATACAS 1907.	Serial #	47,501 to 50,000	

ORTUGUESE ADMINISTRATION

ANCO NACIONAL ULTRAMARINO

10 ISSUE

arms on back. Sign. varieties. Printer: BWC.

	Good	Fine	XF
1 Pataca 1.1.1910. Purple and lt. green.	90.00	250.	700.
5 Patacas 1.1.1910. Brown and yellow.	250.	550.	1500.
10 Patacas 1.1.1910. Dk. blue and green.	300.	750.	2000.
20 Patacas 1.1.1910. Green and gray.	400.	1000.	2500.

20 PROVISIONAL ISSUE

	Good	Fine	XF
25 Patacas 2.1.1920. Ovpt: *PAGAVEL EM DILLY TIMOR* at bottom border on Macao #4. Rare.	—	—	—

1933 ND PROVISIONAL ISSUE

		Good	Fine	XF
6	**5 Patacas** ND (1933 - old date 1.1.1924). Green on yellow unpt. Ovpt. *Pagaveis em TIMOR* at r. on Macao #8.	200.	600.	1500.

1940; 1943 ND PROVISIONAL WW II ISSUE

		Good	Fine	XF
7	**5 Avos** ND (1940). Brown. Ovpt: *PAGAVEL EM TIMOR* on Macao #10.	50.00	175.	600.

		Good	Fine	XF
8	**10 Avos** ND (1940). Green. Ovpt: *PAGAVEL EM TIMOR* on Macao #11.	150.	400.	1000.

		Good	Fine	XF
9	**50 Avos** ND (1943) Purple. Ovpt: *PAGAVEL EM TIMOR* on Macao #17.	125.	400.	950.

1945 ND Provisional Issue

#10-11B Ovpt: *PAGAVEL EM TIMOR* on older Macao notes.

		Good	Fine	XF
10	**5 Patacas** ND (1945 - old date 1.1.1924). Green on yellow unpt. Ovpt. on Macao #8.	300.	1000.	—

		Good	Fine	XF
11	**25 Patacas** ND (1945 - old date 1.1.1907). Black on rose unpt. Ovpt. on Macao #4. Rare.	—	—	—
11A	**100 Patacas** ND (1945 - old date 1.1.1906). Green on yellow unpt. Ovpt. on Macao #6. Rare.	—	—	—
11B	**100 Patacas** ND (1945 - old date 22.7.1919). Brown on m/c unpt. Ovpt. on Macao #9. Rare.	—	—	—

1940 Issue

#12-14 printer: BWC.

		VG	VF	UNC
12	**5 Avos** 19.7.1940. Red on m/c unpt. Steamship seal at upper l.	15.00	60.00	150.
13	**10 Avos** 19.7.1940. Green on m/c unpt. Like #12.	20.00	85.00	225.
14	**50 Avos** 19.7.1940. Purple. Steamship seal at ctr.	25.00	150.	350.

1945 First Issue

		VG	VF	UNC
15	**1 Pataca** 8.3.1945. Black on pink unpt. Steamship seal at l. Back brown; arms at ctr. Printer: Litografia Nacional.	30.00	175.	400.

1945 Second Issue

#16-20 huts at l., arms at r. Printer: W&S.

		VG	VF	UNC
16	**1 Pataca** 16.11.1945. Green.	12.50	50.00	125.

		VG	VF	UNC
17	**5 Patacas** 16.11.1945. Brown.	15.00	75.00	200.
18	**10 Patacas** 16.11.1945. Red.			
	a. Issued note.	20.00	100.	300.
	s. Specimen.	—	—	400.
19	**20 Patacas** 16.11.1945. Blue.	25.00	200.	500.
20	**25 Patacas** 16.11.1945. Lilac.	30.00	250.	750.

1948 Issue

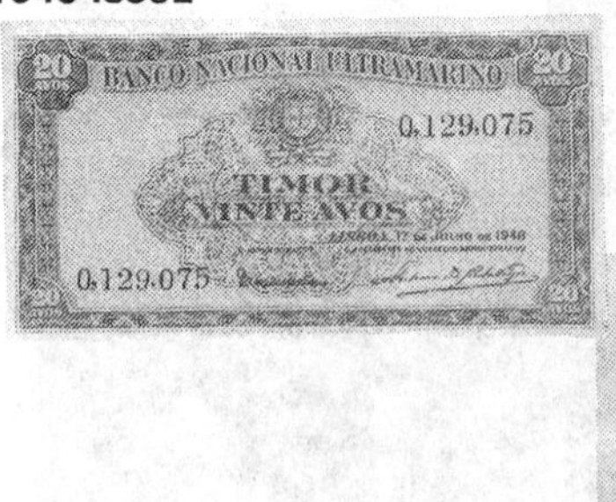

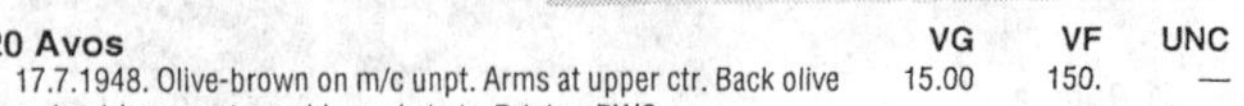

		VG	VF	UNC
21	**20 Avos** 17.7.1948. Olive-brown on m/c unpt. Arms at upper ctr. Back olive and red-brown; steamship seal at ctr. Printer: BWC.	15.00	150.	—

DECRETO LEI NO. 39221; 1959 ISSUE

#22-25 portr. J. Celestino da Silva at r. Bank ship seal at l., crowned arms at ctr. on back. Printer: BWC.

		VG	VF	UNC
22	**30 Escudos** 2.1.1959. Blue on m/c unpt. 2 sign. varieties.			
	a. Issued note.	4.00	25.00	135.
	s. Specimen.	—	—	100.
23	**60 Escudos** 2.1.1959. Red on m/c unpt.			
	a. Issued note.	5.00	25.00	170.
	s. Specimen.	—	—	135.
24	**100 Escudos** 2.1.1959. Brown on m/c unpt.			
	a. Issued note.	7.50	37.50	225.
	s. Specimen.	—	—	175.
25	**500 Escudos** 2.1.1959. Dk. brown and black on m/c unpt.			
	a. Issued note.	40.00	170.	475.
	s. Specimen.	—	—	375.

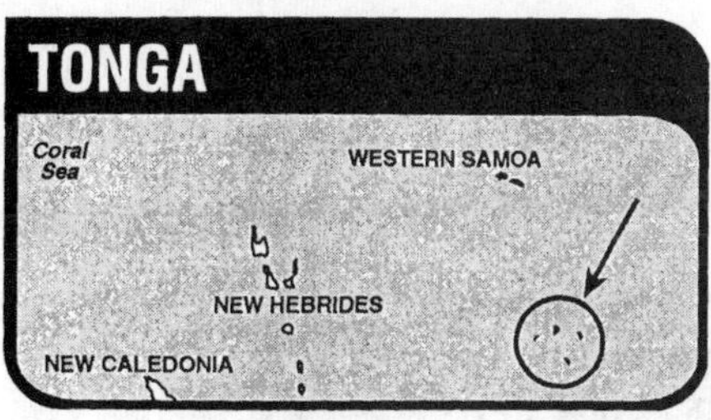

The Kingdom of Tonga (or Friendly Islands), a member of the British Commonwealth, is an archipelago situated in the southern Pacific Ocean south of Western Samoa and east of Fiji comprising 150 islands. Tonga has an area of 270 sq. mi. (748 sq. km.) and a population of 110,000. Capital: Nuku'alofa. Primarily agricultural, the kingdom exports bananas and copra.

Dutch navigators Willem Schouten and Jacob Lemaire were the first Europeans to visit Tonga in 1616. They were followed by the noted Dutch explorer Abel Tasman who visited the Tongatapu group in 1643. No further European contact was made until 1773 when British navigator Capt. James Cook arrived and, impressed by the peaceful deportment of the natives, named the islands the Friendly Islands. Within a few years of Cook's visit, Tonga was embroiled in a civil war that lasted until the great chief Taufa'ahau, who reigned as George Tupou I (1845-93), was converted to Christianity and brought unity and peace to the islands. Tonga became a self-governing protectorate of Great Britain in 1900 and a fully independent state on June 4, 1970. The monarchy is a member of the Commonwealth of Nations. The monarch is Chief of State and Head of Government.

RULERS:

Queen Salote III, 1918-1965
King Taufa'ahau IV, 1967-

MONETARY SYSTEM:

1 Shilling = 12 Pence
1 Pound = 20 Shillings to 1967
1 Pa'anga = 100 Seniti, 1967-

KINGDOM

GOVERNMENT OF TONGA

1921-33 TREASURY NOTE ISSUE

#1-4 palms at l. and r., arms at ctr., *STERLING* at r. Various date and sign. varieties. Printer: TDLR.

		Good	Fine	XF
1	**4 Shillings** 26.6.1933; 8.7.1935; 25.11.1935	—	—	—
2	**10 Shillings** 28.6.1933. Rare.	—	—	—
3	**1 Pound** 28.6.1933. Rare.	—	—	—
4	**5 Pounds** 1.1.1921. Rare.	—	—	—

1936-39 ISSUE

#5-8 palms at l. and r., arms at ctr., ovpt. of several lines or solid block over *STERLING* at r. Various date and sign. varieties. Printer: TDLR.

		Good	Fine	XF
5	**4 Shillings** 1935-41. Brown. *FOUR SHILLINGS* at l.			
	a. 8.7.1935.	—	—	—
	b. 16.12.1936-1.12.1941.	40.00	125.	450.
6	**10 Shillings** 10.12.1936; 21.4.1937; 4.5.1937; 24.1.1938; 19.5.1939. Green. *TEN SHILLINGS* at l.	65.00	250.	750.

		Good	Fine	XF
7	**1 Pound** 10.12.1936; 22.1.1937; 21.4.1937; 4.5.1937; 19.5.1939. Red. *ONE POUND* at l.	125.	350.	1000.
8	**5 Pounds** 19.5.1939. Dk. blue. *FIVE POUNDS* at l. Rare.	—	—	—

1939-42 ISSUE

#9-12 w/denomination spelled out on both sides of arms at ctr. Printer: TDLR.

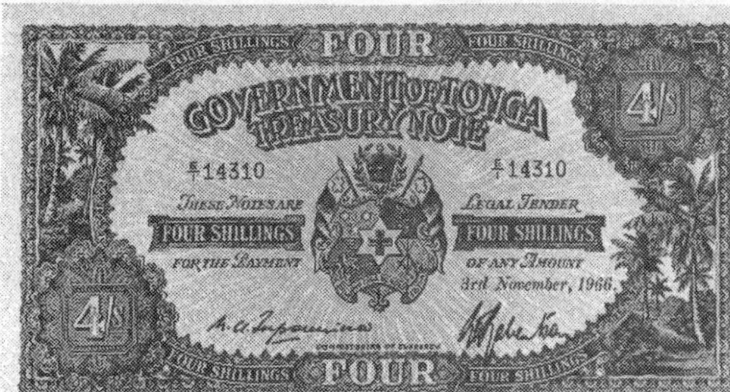

		VG	VF	UNC
9	**4 Shillings**			
	1941-66. Brown on m/c unpt. *FOUR SHILLINGS* at l. and r.			
	a. 1.12.1941-8.9.1947. 3 sign.	20.00	100.	400.
	b. 7.2.1949; 15.2.1951; 20.7.1951; 6.9.1954.	20.00	100.	350.
	c. 19.9.1955-30.11.1959.	7.50	25.00	100.
	d. 24.10.1960-27.9.1966.	7.00	25.00	75.00
	e. 3.11.1966. 2 sign.	5.00	20.00	50.00

		VG	VF	UNC
10	**10 Shillings**			
	1939-66. Green on m/c unpt. *TEN SHILLINGS* at l. and r.			
	a. 3.5.1940; 17.10.1941-28.11.1944. 3 sign.	35.00	225.	—
	b. 9.7.1949-1955.	30.00	150.	400.
	c. 2.5.1956; 22.7.1957; 10.12.1958; 13.10.1959.	7.50	35.00	250.
	d. 24.10.1960; 28.11.1962; 29.7.1964; 22.6.1965.	7.00	30.00	100.
	e. 3.11.1966. 2 sign.	5.00	22.50	65.00

		VG	VF	UNC
11	**1 Pound**			
	1940-66. Red on m/c unpt. *ONE POUND* at l. and r.			
	a. 3.5.1940-7.11.1944. 3 sign.	40.00	250.	—
	b. 15.6.1951; 11.9.1951; 19.9.1955.	30.00	175.	450.
	c. 2.5.1956; 10.12.1958; 30.11.1959; 12.12.1961.	20.00	70.00	300.
	d. 28.11.1962; 30.10.1964; 2.11.1965; 3.11.1966.	8.00	40.00	110.
	e. 2.12.1966. 2 sign.	4.00	15.00	70.00
12	**5 Pounds**			
	1942-66. Dk. blue on m/c unpt. *FIVE POUNDS* at l. and r.			
	a. 11.3.1942-1945. 3 sign.	550.	1750.	—
	b. 15.6.1951; 5.7.1955; 11.9.1956; 26.6.1958.	300.	1250.	—
	c. 30.11.1959; 2.11.1965.	175.	500.	1000.
	d. 2.12.1966. 2 sign.	15.00	60.00	110.

TRANSNISTRIA

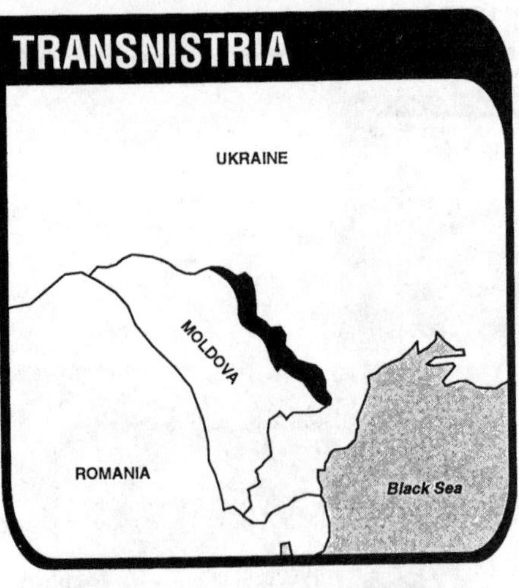

The Transnistria Moldavia Republic was formed in 199(even before the separation c Moldavia from Russia. It has a area of 11,544 sq. mi. (29,90 sq. km). and a population (700,000. Capital: Tiraspol.

The area was conquered fror the Turks in the last half of th 18th Century, and in 1792 th capital city of Tiraspol wa founded. After 1812, the are called Bessarabia (prese Moldova and part of the Ukrain became part of the Russia Empire. During the Russia Revolution, in 1918, the are was taken by Romanian troop and in 1924 the Moldavia Autonomous SSR was forme on the left bank of the Dniest River. A Romanian occupatic area between the Dniester ar Bug Rivers called *Transnistr* was established in Octob 1941. Its center was the port Odessa. A special issue of not for use in Transnistria was ma by the Romanian government. In 1944 the Russians recaptured Transnistria.

Once the Moldavian SSR declared independence in August 1991. Transnistria did not wa to be a part of Moldavia. In 1992, Moldova tried to solve the issue militarily.

Transnistria has a president, parliament, army and police forces, but as yet is lacki international recognition.

1 Ruble = 1,000 old Rubles (August 1994) 1 Ruble = 1,000,000 old Rubles (January 2001)

ROMANIAN OCCUPATION (OF U.S.S.R.) - WW II

INSTITUTUL DE FINANTARE EXTERNA (INFINEX)

1941 ND BON DE CREDIT ISSUE

Note: This issue bears unusual denominations because of the exchange rate set by Germany, as follows

6 Lei = 10 Reichspfennig or 1 Ruble/Karbowanez (Ukrainian German Issue).

1200 Lei = 20 Reichsmark or 200 Rubles/Karbowanez.

		Good	Fine	X
M1	**1 Leu** ND (1941-44). Gray.	100.	300.	6(
M2	**6 Lei** ND (1941-44). Gray-blue.	100.	300.	6
M3	**24 Lei** ND (1941-44). Brown.	100.	300.	6(
M4	**120 Lei** ND (1941-44). Blue. Sunflower at r.	125.	375.	7
M5	**600 Lei** ND (1941-44). Gray on brown-violet unpt. Cross at ctr.	125.	375.	7
M6	**1200 Lei** ND (1941-44). Gray on tan unpt. Grapes at ctr. Boat on river at ctr. on back.	225.	675.	13

TRINIDAD & TOBAGO

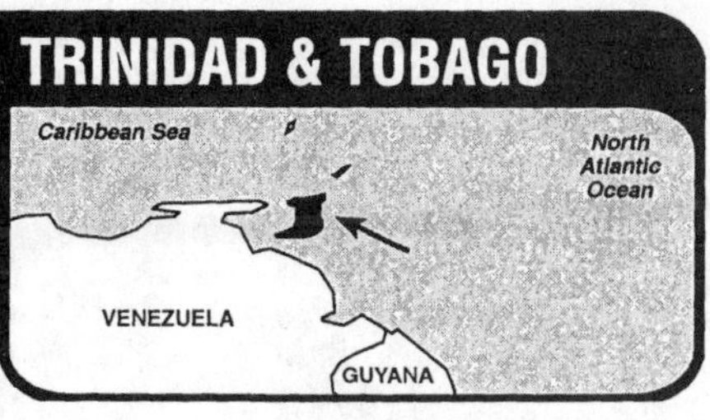

The Republic of Trinidad and Tobago, a member of the British Commonwealth situated 7 miles (11 km.) off the coast of Venezuela, has an area of 1,981 sq. mi. (5,130 sq. km.) and a population of 1.34 million. Capital: Port-of-Spain. The Island of Trinidad contains the world's largest natural asphalt bog. Birds of Paradise live on little Tobago, the only place outside of their native New Guinea where they can be found in a wild state. Petroleum and petroleum products are the mainstay of the economy. Petroleum products, crude oil and sugar are exported.

Trinidad and Tobago were discovered by Columbus in 1498. Trinidad remained under Spanish rule from the time of its settlement in 1592 until its capture by the British in 1797. It was ceded to the British in 1802. Tobago was occupied at various times by the French, Dutch and British before being ceded to Britain in 1814. Trinidad and Tobago were merged into a single colony in 1888. The colony was part of the Federation of the West Indies until Aug. 31, 1962, when it became an independent member of the Commonwealth of Nations. A new constitution establishing a republican form of government was adopted on Aug. 1, 1976. The president is Chief of State. The prime minister is Head of Government.

Notes of the British Caribbean Territories circulated between 1950-1964.

RULERS:

British to 1976

MONETARY SYSTEM:

1 Dollar = 100 Cents
5 Dollars = 1 Pound 10 Pence

BRITISH ADMINISTRATION

GOVERNMENT OF TRINIDAD AND TOBAGO

1905 ISSUE

#1-2A mountain w/sailing ship on back. Various date and sign. varieties. Printer: TDLR.

		Good	Fine	XF
1	**1 Dollar** 1905-26. Blue. Landing of Columbus at l., arms at top ctr.			
	a. Black vignette at l. 1.4.1905.	200.	400.	1200.
	b. Blue vignette. 1.4.1905.	125.	300.	950.
	c. 1.1.1924; 1.3.1926.	75.00	250.	800.

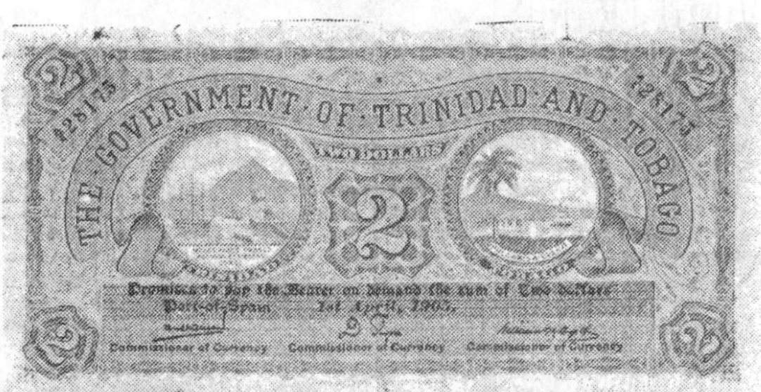

		Good	Fine	XF
2	**2 Dollars** 1.4.1905. Sailing ship in harbor at l., palm tree w/sailing ship in background at r., vignettes in circles.			
	a. Red.	200.	700.	2500.
	b. Green and red. Rare.	—	—	—

1929 ISSUE

		Good	Fine	XF
3	**1 Dollar** 1.1.1929; 1.1.1932. Blue. Landing of Columbus at l., tree at r.	75.00	250.	700.

		Good	Fine	XF
4	**2 Dollars** 1.1.1929. Red. Sailing ship in harbor at l., palm tree w/sailing ship in background at r. 178 x 89mm.	150.	350.	1250.

1934; 1935 ISSUE

#5-7 like #4 but reduced size, 150 x 82mm. Printer: TDLR.

		Good	Fine	XF
5	**1 Dollar** 1935-49. Dk. blue on m/c unpt.			
	a. 1.9.1935.	10.00	25.00	125.
	b. 2.1.1939.	1.00	5.00	35.00
	c. 1.5.1942; 1.1.1943.	1.00	5.00	35.00
	d. 1.7.1948.	1.50	6.00	50.00
	e. 1.7.1949.	1.50	6.00	65.00
6	**2 Dollars** 1934-39. Bright red on blue and m/c unpt.			
	a. 1.5.1934; 1.9.1935.	25.00	75.00	450.
	b. 2.1.1939.	7.50	35.00	250.

		Good	Fine	XF
7	**5 Dollars** 1935-42. Purple on m/c unpt.			
	a. 1.9.1935.	50.00	175.	475.
	b. 2.1.1939; 1.5.1942.	15.00	65.00	250.

1939-42 ISSUE

#8-10 like previous issue.

		Good	Fine	XF
8	**2 Dollars** 1.5.1942; 1.1.1943; 1.7.1949. Dk. red on green and m/c unpt.	7.50	40.00	265.
9	**10 Dollars** 1939; 1942. Red-brown on m/c unpt.			
	a. 2.1.1939.	100.	400.	—
	b. 1.5.1942.	75.00	275.	650.
10	**20 Dollars** 1.5.1942; 1.1.1943. Green on m/c unpt.	450.	1000.	—

1943 ISSUE

		Good	Fine	XF
11	**20 Dollars** 1.1.1943. Purple on m/c unpt. Like #10.	500.	1500.	—

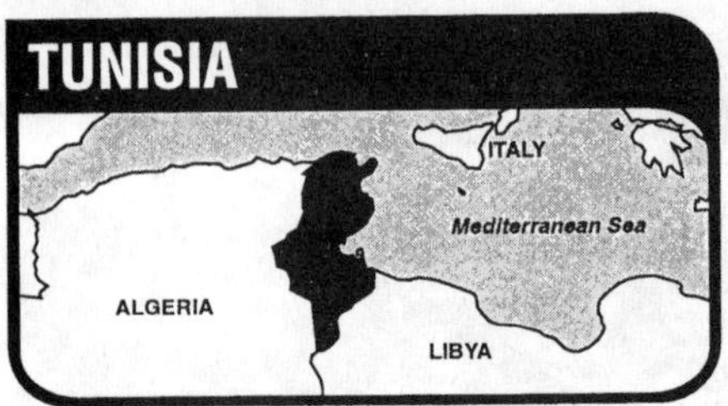

The Republic of Tunisia, located on the northern coast of Africa between Algeria and Libya, has an area of 63,170 sq. mi. (163,610 sq. km.) and a population of 9.84 million. Capital: Tunis. Agriculture is the backbone of the economy. Crude oil, phosphates, olive oil, and wine are exported.

Tunisia, settled by the Phoenicians in the 12th century BC, was the center of the seafaring Carthaginian empire. After the total destruction of Carthage, Tunisia became part of Rome's African province. It remained a part of the Roman Empire (except for the 439-533 interval Vandal conquest) until taken by the Arabs, 648, who administered it until the Turkish invasion of 1570. Under Turkish control, the public revenue was heavily dependent upon the piracy of Mediterranean shipping, an endeavor that wasn't abandoned until 1819 when a coalition of powers threatened appropriate reprisal. Deprived of its major source of income, Tunisia underwent a financial regression that ended in bankruptcy, enabling France to establish a protectorate over the country in 1881. National agitation and guerrilla fighting forced France to grant Tunisia internal autonomy in 1955 and to recognize Tunisian independence on March 20, 1956. Tunisia abolished the monarchy and established a republic on July 25, 1957.

In 1975 the constitution was changed to make Bourguiba president for life. A two party system was started in 1981, but in the 1986 elections, all but the *Frout Nationals* boycotted. Bourguiba was ousted in 1987. His successor, Zine el Abidine Ben Ali introduced some democratic reforms, but a struggle with Islamic Fundamentalists lead to sporadic violence for some time.

RULERS:

French, 1881-1956

MONETARY SYSTEM:

1 Franc = 100 Centimes to 1960
1 Dinar = 1000 Millimes, 1960-

Ottoman Administration

Dar el-Mal

State Bank

1846 Issue

		Good	Fine	XF
A2	**50 Riyals** AH1263/1846. Ornate knotted border. W/o wmk. (Discounted at 4%). Rare.	—	—	—

French Administration

Banque de l'Algérie

1903-08 Issue

#1-5 black ovpt: *TUNISIE* on notes of Algeria.

		Good	Fine	XF
1	**5 Francs** 1903-14.5.1925. Blue. Mercury at l., peasant at r. Ovpt. on Algeria #13.	15.00	70.00	275.

		Good	Fine	XF
2	**20 Francs** 1908-42. Blue. Mercury at l., Hercules at r. Ovpt. on Algeria #72.			
	a. 7.1.1908; 15.4.1908; 29.4.1908.	35.00	150.	400.
	b. 22.2.1939-28.9.1942.	12.50	50.00	175.
3	**50 Francs** 2.3.1908. Blue. Cherubs at l. and r., woman at lower ctr. Ovpt. on Algeria #73.	65.00	250.	700.

		Good	Fine	XF
4	**100 Francs** 6.2.1908; 11.2.1908; 8.11.1911. Blue. Boy standing w/oar and hammer at l., boy standing w/shovel and sickle at r. Ovpt. on Algeria #74.	70.00	300.	900.

		Good	Fine	XF
5	**500 Francs** 1904; 1909; 1924. Blue. Fortuna at l., Mercury at r., 2 boys sitting at bottom. Ovpt. on Algeria #75.			
	a. 9.5.1904; 4.1.1909. Rare.	—	—	—
	b. 3.1.1924-16.4.1924.	60.00	150.	500.

1914; 1918 Issue

#6 and 7 black ovpt: *TUNISIE* on notes of Algeria.

		Good	Fine	XF
6	**20 Francs** 1914-41. Purple on lt. blue unpt. Girl at r. 165 x 105mm. Ovpt. on Algeria #78.			
	a. 3.8.1914.	3.00	20.00	75.00
	b. 26.2.1929-2.12.1941.	1.00	7.50	35.00

		Good	Fine	XF
7	**1000 Francs**			
	1918-24. Blue. Woman sitting w/oar at l., blacksmith at r., 2 boys sitting w/lion at bottom. Ovpt. on Algeria #76.			
	a. 5.11.1918.	165.	400.	1000.
	b. 5.3.1923; 14.1.1924; 15.1.1924; 18.1.1924; 16.4.1924; 25.4.1924; 26.4.1924.	150.	350.	850.

1921-26 ISSUE

#8-11 black ovpt: *TUNISIE* on notes of Algeria.

		Good	Fine	XF
8	**5 Francs**			
	1925-41. Red-brown and violet. Girl wearing kerchief at r. 128 x 88mm. Ovpt. on Algeria #77.			
	a. 15.7.1925-28.2.1933.	1.00	7.50	30.00
	b. 2.3.1939-31.5.1941. Serial # varieties.	.75	2.00	10.00
	c. 24.5.1941. W/o serial #.	.25	1.50	7.50

Note: #8b w/1941 dates w/serial #.

9	**50 Francs**			
	18.1.1924-2.4.1937. Green. Mosque w/tower at r., city of Algiers at ctr. background. Ovpt. on Algeria #80.	7.50	50.00	125.

		Good	Fine	XF
10	**100 Francs**			
	1921-39. Blue and violet. 2 boys at l., Arab w/camel at r. Ovpt. on Algeria #81.			
	a. 11.3.1921; 25.7.1921; 18.8.1924; 17.4.1928.	12.50	50.00	175.
	b. 16.1.1933; 21.8.1933.	8.00	35.00	100.
	c. 14.3.1936-1939.	7.50	25.00	75.00
11	**1000 Francs**			
	1926-39. Brown-violet. Woman w/sword and child at l., Algerian woman w/child at r. Ovpt. on Algeria #83.			
	a. Ovpt. at l. 19.7.1926. 12.11.1926.	50.00	300.	850.
	b. Ovpt. at r. 8.2.1938; 14.2.1938; 19.4.1938; 3.8.1939; 23.9.1939; 10.10.1938; 8.8.1939.	40.00	250.	600.

NOTICE

Readers with unlisted dates, signature varieties, etc. are invited to submit photocopies or, high resolution (300 dpi, 100% size) scans of their notes to: Standard Catalog of World Paper Money, 700 East State St. Iola, WI 54990-0001, or E-Mail: george.cuhaj@fwpubs.com.

1938-39 ISSUE

#12-14 black ovpt: *TUNISIE* on notes of Algeria.

		Good	Fine	XF
12	**50 Francs**			
	1939-45. M/c. Veiled woman w/man wearing red fez at r. Ovpt. on Algeria #84.			
	a. Wmk: Head. 3.1.1939-28.5.1942; 1.5.1945.	3.00	15.00	60.00
	b. Wmk: Lettering. 6.7.1942; 27.8.1942; 1.3.1945.	1.50	12.50	40.00

		Good	Fine	XF
13	**100 Francs**			
	1939-42. M/c. Algerian w/turban at l. Ovpt. on Algeria #85.			
	a. Wmk: Head. 26.9.1939-5.1.1942.	2.00	10.00	50.00
	b. Wmk: Lettering. 27.4.1942; 6.6.1942; 26.9.1942; 2.11.1942.	3.00	15.00	60.00

		Good	Fine	XF
14	**500 Francs**			
	30.9.1938; 26.7.1939; 3.1.1942-4.2.1942. Blue-violet and m/c. Girl at l., woman w/torch and youth at r. Ovpt. on Algeria #82.	30.00	100.	400.

1941-45 Issues

#15-28 black ovpt: *TUNISIE* on notes of Algeria.

		Good	Fine	XF
15	**5 Francs** 8.2.1944; 8.3.1944. Red-brown and violet. Similar to #8 but 97 x 59mm. Sign. titles: *L' Inspecteur Gal.* and *Caissier Pal.* Ovpt. on Algeria #92.	.25	2.00	12.50
16	**5 Francs** 2.10.1944. Red-brown and violet. Like #15 but sign. titles: *Le Secretaire Gal.* and *Caissier Pal.*	1.00	5.00	22.50

		Good	Fine	XF
17	**20 Francs** 9.1.1943-10.2.1944. Similar to #6, but 122 x 90mm. Sign titles: *L'INSPECTEUR GÉNÉRAL* and *CAISSIER PRINCIPAL*. Ovpt. on Algeria #94.	.75	5.00	20.00
18	**20 Francs** 2.2.1945; 3.4.1945; 7.5.1945. Purple. Like #17 but sign. titles: *CAISSIER PRINCIPAL* and *LE SECRETAIRE GÉNÉRAL*.	1.00	7.00	25.00
19	**500 Francs** 15.3.1943; 18.5.1943; 20.5.1943; 16.7.1943; 3.2.1944. Blue and green. 2 boys at l., Arab w/camel at r. Ovpt. on Algeria #93.	30.00	150.	350.

		Good	Fine	XF
20	**1000 Francs** 1941-42. M/c. Horses at ctr., French farm family at r. French text on back. Ovpt. on Algeria #86.			
	a. Wmk: Woman's head. 18.3.1941; 24.6.1941; 23.8.1941; 3.9.1941; 4.9.1941; 9.9.1941; 19.9.1941; 29.12.1941; 2.1.1942; 14.2.1942.	30.00	75.00	250.
	b. Wmk: Lettering. 2.11.1942; 3.11.1942.	37.50	100.	300.
21	**5000 Francs** 1942. Red-orange. Young Algerian woman at l., woman w/torch and shield at r. Ovpt. on Algeria #90.	65.00	300.	750.

1946-49 Issue

		Good	Fine	XF
22	**20 Francs** 4.6.1948; 7.6.1948. Green and brown. Ornamental design. Like Algeria #103 w/title: *BANQUE DE L'ALGÉRIE/ TUNISIE*.	2.00	15.00	50.00

		Good	Fine	XF
23	**50 Francs** 3.2.1949. Blue and rose. Ornamental design w/title: *BANQUE DE L'ALGÉRIE & DE LA TUNISIE*.	12.00	60.00	150.

		Good	Fine	XF
24	**100 Francs** 5.11.1946-18.2.1948. Blue, yellow and brown. Hermes at r., Roman gate in background. Ancient mosaic w/boat and 3 people on back. Title: *BANQUE DE L'ALGÉRIE/ TUNISIE* at top. Wmk: Woman's head.	12.00	60.00	200.
25	**500 Francs** 30.1.1947; 16.1.1947. 16.5.1947. Green on yellow and m/c unpt. Winged Victory w/Roman ruins in background. 3 allegorical men on back. W/titles: *BANQUE DE L'ALGÉRIE/TUNISIE*.	15.00	100.	325.
26	**1000 Francs** 4.9.1946; 5.9.1946. M/c. Similar to #20 but w/title: *BANQUE DE L'ALGÉRIE / TUNISIE* on face. Arabic text on back.	35.00	150.	350.

		Good	Fine	XF
27	**5000 Francs** 1946. M/c. P. Apollo at l. Like Algeria #109 but w/*TUNISIE* in front of engraver's name at lower r. Arabic text on back different from #21.	40.00	200.	425.

1950 ISSUE

		Good	Fine	XF
28	**500 Francs** 31.1.1950-17.3.1950; 11.2.1952-30.7.1952; 1.12.1954. Green on yellow and m/c unpt. Similar to #25 but w/title: *BANQUE DE L'ALGÉRIE ET DE LA TUNISIE.*	15.00	100.	300.

		Good	Fine	XF
29	**1000 Francs** 1950-57. Dk. brown on blue unpt. Ruins of Roman temples at l., standing figure at ctr. r. W/title: *BANQUE DE L'ALGÉRIE ET DE LA TUNISIE.* Neptune w/trident, horses and allegorical figures at ctr. on back. Wmk: Woman's head.			
	a. 17.2.1950-26.12.1950.	20.00	100.	300.
	b. 20.3.1957.	20.00	100.	300.

		Good	Fine	XF
30	**5000 Francs** 9.1.1950-7.5.1952. Violet. Roman ruins at l., Roman Emperor Vespasian at r. W/title: *BANQUE DE L'ALGÉRIE ET DE LA TUNISIE.*			
	a.	30.00	150.	500.

GERMAN OCCUPATION - WW II

BANQUE DE L'ALGERIE

1942 PROVISIONAL ISSUE

Ovpt: *BANQUE DE L'ALGÉRIE* and new denomination on unissued 100 Francs note of the Banque de France (#65b, old dates May to August 1892). Issued during the German occupation between Dec. 1942-May 1943.

		Good	Fine	XF
31	**1000 Francs on 100 Francs** ND (1942-43). Violet, blue and brown. Woman seated at l. and r.	8.00	35.00	100.

REGENCE DE TUNIS

TREASURY ISSUE

1918 FIRST ISSUE

#32-53 exchangeable w/notes of the Banque de l'Algérie. Several different heading and frame styles used. Arms stamped at ctr. on back.

		VG	VF	UNC
32	**50 Centimes** 16.2.1918. Green.			
	a. Monogram at ctr. on back. Engraver and printer on both sides.	6.00	20.00	85.00
	b. Monogram at ctr. on back. Engraver and printer on face only.	6.00	20.00	85.00
	c. W/o monogram on back. Engraver and printer on face only.	6.00	20.00	85.00
33	**1 Franc** 16.2.1918. Red.			
	a. Wmk: *1896.*	7.50	25.00	100.
	b. Wmk: *1910.*	7.50	25.00	100.
34	**2 Francs** 16.2.1918. Brown.	8.00	40.00	125.

1918 SECOND ISSUE

		VG	VF	UNC
35	**50 Centimes** 27.4.1918. Green.	6.00	20.00	85.00

		VG	VF	UNC
36	**1 Franc** 27.4.1918. Red.			
	a. Wmk: *1912.*	6.00	20.00	85.00
	b. Wmk: *1913.*	6.00	20.00	85.00
	c. Wmk: *1916.*	6.00	20.00	85.00
	d. Wmk: *1917.*	6.00	20.00	85.00
	e. Wmk: *1918.*	6.00	20.00	85.00
37	**2 Francs** 27.4.1918. Brown.			
	a. Wmk: *1896.* Printer: PICARD.	8.00	40.00	125.
	b. Wmk: *1910.* Printer: PICARD.	8.00	40.00	125.
	c. Printer: YVORRA-BARLIER-CLAVE.	6.00	20.00	85.00
38	**2 Francs** 14.8.1918. Brown.	8.00	40.00	125.

1918 Third Issue

		VG	VF	UNC
39	**50 Centimes** 30.9.1918. Green.	7.50	25.00	100.
40	**1 Franc** 30.9.1918. Red.	7.50	25.00	100.
41	**2 Francs** 30.9.1918. Brown.	7.50	25.00	100.

1918 Fourth Issue

		VG	VF	UNC
42	**50 Centimes** 4.11.1918. Green.	7.50	25.00	100.

		VG	VF	UNC
43	**1 Franc** 4.11.1918. Red.	7.50	25.00	100.
44	**2 Francs** 4.11.1918. Brown.	7.50	25.00	100.

1919 Issue

		VG	VF	UNC
45	**50 Centimes** 17.3.1919. Green.			
	a. Printer: YVORRA-BARLIER-CLAVE.	6.00	20.00	85.00
	b. Printer: YVORRA-BARLIER.	6.00	20.00	85.00
46	**1 Franc** 17.3.1919. Red.			
	a. Printer: YVORRA-BARLIER-CLAVE.	6.00	20.00	85.00
	b. Printer: YVORRA-BARLIER.	6.00	20.00	85.00

		VG	VF	UNC
47	**2 Francs** 17.3.1919. Brown.			
	a. Printer: YVORRA-BARLIER-CLAVE.	7.50	25.00	100.
	b. Printer: YVORRA-BARLIER.	7.50	25.00	100.

1920 Issue

		VG	VF	UNC
48	**50 Centimes** 3.3.1920. Green. 3 sign. varieties.	6.00	20.00	85.00

		VG	VF	UNC
49	**1 Franc** 3.3.1920. Red. 3 sign. varieties.	6.00	20.00	85.00

		VG	VF	UNC
50	**2 Francs** 3.3.1920. Brown. 3 sign. varieties.	7.50	25.00	100.

1921 Issue

		VG	VF	UNC
51	**50 Centimes** 25.1.1921. Green.	7.50	25.00	100.

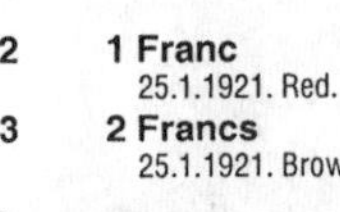

		VG	VF	UNC
52	**1 Franc** 25.1.1921. Red.	7.50	25.00	100.
53	**2 Francs** 25.1.1921. Brown.	8.00	40.00	125.

Direction des Finances - Treasury

1943 Issue

#54-56 veiled woman carrying a water jug at l., mountain at ctr., palm tree at r. Archway on back.

		VG	VF	UNC
54	**50 Centimes** 15.7.1943. Brown-violet.	2.00	6.00	20.00
55	**1 Franc** 15.7.1943. Green and brown.	2.00	6.00	20.00
56	**2 Francs** 15.7.1943. Brown-violet and blue.	2.50	7.50	25.00

Republic

Banque Centrale de Tunisie

Ca.1958 ND Issue

#57-59 wmk: Arms.

#57 and 58 portr. Habib Bourguiba at l.

		VG	VF	UNC
57	**1/2 Dinar** ND. Purple on m/c unpt. Mosque at r. Ruins at l., arms at r. on back.	4.00	35.00	150.

		VG	VF	UNC
58	**1 Dinar** ND. Green on m/c unpt. Peasant and farm machine at r. Dam on back.	4.00	37.50	175.
59	**5 Dinars** ND. Brown on m/c unpt. Habib Bourguiba at r., bridge at l., Arabic numerals *5* and serial #. Archways on back.	4.00	37.50	175.

1960; 1962 Issue

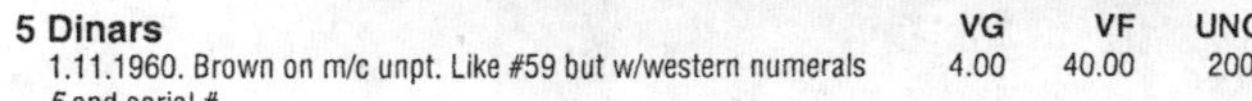

		VG	VF	UNC
60	**5 Dinars** 1.11.1960. Brown on m/c unpt. Like #59 but w/western numerals *5* and serial #.	4.00	40.00	200.

The Republic of Turkey, a parliamentary democracy of the Near East located partially in Europe and partially in Asia between the Black and the Mediterranean seas, has an area of 301,382 sq. mi. (780,580 sq. km.) and a population of 65.73 million. Capital: Ankara. Turkey exports cotton, hazelnuts and tobacco, and enjoys a virtual monopoly in meerschaum.

The Ottoman Turks, a tribe from Central Asia, first appeared in the early 13th century, and by the 17th century had established the Ottoman Empire which stretched from the Persian Gulf to the southern frontier of Poland, and from the Caspian Sea to the Algerian plateau. The defeat of the Turkish navy by the Holy League in 1571, and of the Turkish forces besieging Vienna in 1683, began the steady decline of the Ottoman Empire which, accelerated by the rise of nationalism, contracted its European border, and by the end of World War I deprived it of its Arab lands. The present Turkish boundaries were largely fixed by the Treaty of Lausanne in 1923. The sultanate and caliphate, the political and spiritual ruling institutions of the old empire, were separated and the sultanate abolished in 1922 by Mustafa Kemal Atatürk. On Oct. 29, 1923, Turkey formally became a republic and Atatürk was selected as the first president.

RULERS:

Abdul Mejid, AH1255-1277/1839-1861AD

Abdul Aziz, AH1277-1293/1861-1876AD

Murad V, AH1293/1876AD

Abdul Hamid II, AH1293-1327/1876-1909AD

Muhammad V, AH1327-1336/1909-1918AD

Muhammad VI, AH1336-1341/1918-1923AD

Republic, AH1341-/1923-AD

MONETARY SYSTEM:

1 Kurush (Gurush, Piastre) = 40 Para
1 Lira (Livre, Pound) = 100 Piastres

FINANCE MINISTER SEAL VARIETIES, 1858-1878

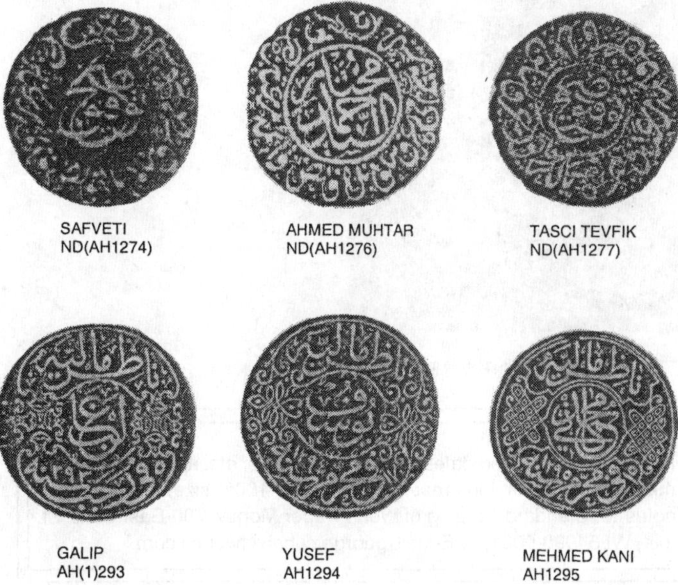

SAFVETI ND(AH1274) — AHMED MUHTAR ND(AH1276) — TASCI TEVFIK ND(AH1277)

GALIP AH(1)293 — YUSEF AH1294 — MEHMED KANI AH1295

OTTOMAN EMPIRE

Note: Early notes circulated in Constantinople, Western Anatolia and Cyprus.

TREASURY

1840 FIRST "KAIME" ISSUE, SERIES 1

Handwritten 12 1/2% Interest Bearing Notes

		Good	Fine	XF
1	**500 Kurush** AH1256 (1840).	—	—	—

1840 SECOND "KAIME" ISSUE, SERIES 2

#2-4 reduced size. Seal of Saib Pasha on back.

		Good	Fine	XF
2	**50 Kurush** AH1256 (1840). Rare.	—	—	—
3	**100 Kurush** AH1256 (1840). Rare.	—	—	—
4	**250 Kurush** AH1256 (1840). Rare.	—	—	—

1840 THIRD "KAIME" ISSUE, SERIES 3

#5-7 like previous issue.

		Good	Fine	XF
5	**500 Kurush** AH1256 (1840). Rare.	—	—	—
6	**1000 Kurush** AH1256 (1840). Rare.	—	—	—
7	**2000 Kurush** AH1256 (1840). Rare.	—	—	—

1842 "KAIME" ISSUE

Printed 12 1/2% Interest Bearing Notes w/handwritten serial # and values w/seal of Safveti.

Note: The year dates indicated are determined by the term of office of the Finance Minister's seal.

		Good	Fine	XF
8	**50 Kurush** AH1257 (1841). Black. Yellow paper. 104 x 160mm. Rare.	—	—	—

		Good	Fine	XF
9	**100 Kurush** AH1257 (1841). Black. Blue paper. 105 x 165mm. Rare.	—	—	—

NOTICE

Readers with unlisted dates, signature varieties, etc. are invited to submit photocopies or, high resolution (300 dpi, 100% size) scans of their notes to: Standard Catalog of World Paper Money, 700 East State St. Iola, WI 54990-0001, or E-Mail: george.cuhaj@fwpubs.com.

1843 FIRST "KAIME" ISSUE

10% Interest Bearing Note

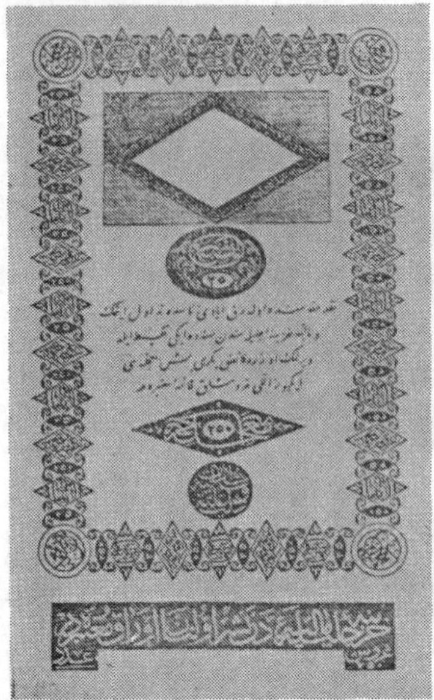

		Good	Fine	XF
10	**250 Kurush** AH1259 (1843). Black. Cream paper. 104 x 160mm. Rare.	—	—	—

1843 SECOND "KAIME" ISSUE, SERIES A

6% Interest Bearing Notes w/handwritten serial # w/seal of Hüsnü.

		Good	Fine	XF
11	**50 Kurush** AH1259 (1843). 98 x 152mm. Rare.	—	—	—
12	**100 Kurush** AH1259 (1843). 132 x 195mm. Rare.	—	—	—

1843 THIRD "KAIME" ISSUE, SERIES B

6% Interest Bearing Notes w/seal of Safveti.

		Good	Fine	XF
13	**50 Kurush** AH1259-62 (1843-46). Rare.	—	—	—
14	**100 Kurush** AH1259-62 (1843-46). Rare.	—	—	—

1848 "KAIME" ISSUE, SERIES C

6% Interest Bearing Notes w/seal of Safveti.

		Good	Fine	XF
15	**500 Kurush** AH1264-65 (1848-49). 185 x 110mm. Rare.	—	—	—
16	**1000 Kurush** AH1264-65 (1848-49). Blue. Cream paper. Rare.	—	—	—

1852 "KAIME" ISSUE

6% Interest Bearing Notes w/seal of Halid.

		Good	Fine	XF
17	**250 Kurush** AH(1)268 (1852). 178 x 117mm. Rare.	—	—	—
18	**500 Kurush** AH1268 (1852). 185 x 125mm. Rare.	—	—	—

		Good	Fine	XF
19	**1000 Kurush** AH(1)268 (1852). Brown. Yellow paper. 185 x 125mm. Rare.	—	—	—
20	**5000 Kurush** AH(1)268 (1852). Rare.	—	—	—

1851-52 ND "KAIME" ISSUE

#21 and 22 w/octagonal control seal and seal of Nafiz, A. Muhtar or Safveti.

		Good	Fine	XF
21	**10 Kurush** ND (1852).	100.	250.	600.

		Good	Fine	XF
22	**20 Kurush** ND (1852). 94 x 151mm.	100.	250.	600.

1853; 1854 ND "KAIME" ISSUE

#23 and #24 w/seal of Safveti, A. Muhtar or Tevfik.

		Good	Fine	XF
23	**10 Kurush** ND (1853-54). Black on yellow and lt. green unpt. 68 x 105mm.	70.00	175.	450.

		Good	Fine	XF
24	**20 Kurush** ND (1854). Black on yellow and lt. green unpt. 89 x 130mm.	70.00	175.	450.

1855-57 ND "KAIME" ISSUE

#25 and 26 issued for the Ordu Kaimesi (Army Corps) w/seals of Savfeti, Sefik or A. Muhtar, and "Orduyu Humayun".

		Good	Fine	XF
25	**10 Kurush** ND (1854). Black on lt. green unpt. Rare.	—	—	—

		Good	Fine	XF
26	**20 Kurush** ND (1855-57). Black on lt. green unpt.	70.00	175.	450.

1858 ISSUE, SERIES E

Engraved plates exist for notes #27-31 w/the date AH1273, but no notes have been seen w/seal of Hasib (hexagonal shaped).

		Good	Fine	XF
27	**100 Kurush** AH1274 (1858). 170 x 102mm.	—	—	—
28	**250 Kurush** AH1274 (1858). 173 x 103mm.	—	—	—
29	**500 Kurush** AH1274 (1858). 179 x 107mm.	—	—	—

		Good	Fine	XF
30	**1000 Kurush** AH1274 (1858). 184 x 110mm on yellow paper, blue unpt.	—	—	—
31	**5000 Kurush** AH1274 (1858). 185 x 110mm.	—	—	—

1858-61 Issue

32	**20 Kurush** AH1273 (1858-61). Brown. 176 x 126mm. 6 lines of text above AH1273 and seal of Savfeti on back. Rare.	—	—	—

1861 First "Kaime" Issue

#33-35A w/6 lines of text above AH1277 and seal of Tevfik on back.

		Good	Fine	XF
33	**10 Kurush** AH1277 (1861). Blue unpt. 122 x 173mm.	100.	225.	550.
34	**20 Kurush** AH1277 (1861). Yellow unpt. 126 x 176mm.	100.	225.	550.
35	**50 Kurush** AH1277 (1861). Red-brown on rose unpt. 133 x 184mm.	125.	250.	600.
35A	**100 Kurush** AH1277 (1861). Blue unpt.	—	—	—

1861 Second "Kaime" Issue

#36-38 like #34-35A but w/5 lines of text above AH1277 within wreath, and seal of Tevfik on back.

		Good	Fine	XF
36	**20 Kurush** AH1277. Black on gold unpt.	5.00	15.00	45.00

		Good	Fine	XF
37	**50 Kurush** AH1277. Red-brown.	7.50	20.00	50.00
38	**100 Kurush** AH1277. Yellow unpt. 133 x 185mm.	12.50	35.00	75.00

1861 Third "Kaime" Issue

#39 w/toughra of Abdul Aziz w/o flower at r. 6 lines of of text over AH date 1277 within wreath and w/seal of Tevfik on back.

		Good	Fine	XF
39	**50 Kurush** AH1277. Red-brown w/rose unpt.	75.00	175.	500.

1861 Fourth "Kaime" Issue

#40 and #41 w/toughra of Abdul Aziz w/o flower at r. 5 lines of new text above AH date 1277 on back.

		Good	Fine	XF
40	**50 Kurush** AH1277. Red-brown.	50.00	125.	350.

		Good	Fine	XF
41	**100 Kurush** AH1277. Gray unpt. 185 x 133mm.	20.00	60.00	175.

Note: Most notes of AH1277 are w/o handwritten serial # at l. and r. bottom in oval gaps on face.

Banque Imperiale Ottomane

1876 First "Kaime" Issue

#42-45 w/toughra of Murad V.

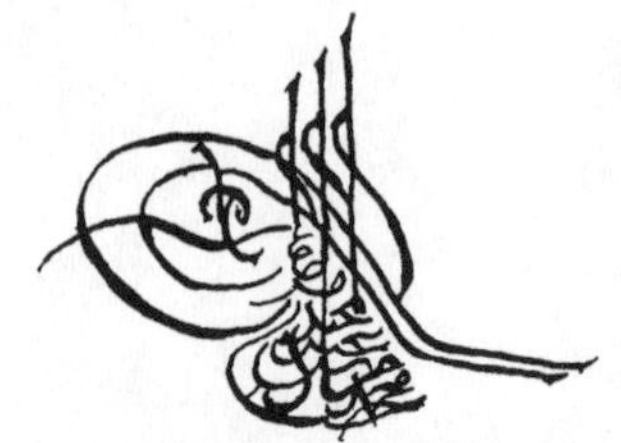

		Good	Fine	XF
42	**10 Kurush** AH1293 (1876). Lilac on lt. green unpt. W/round AH1293 handstamp. Oblong 1876 handstamp on back.	10.00	25.00	75.00

#	Denomination	Good	Fine	XF
43	**20 Kurush** AH1293 (1876). Brown-lilac on yellow unpt. W/round AH1293 handstamp. Oblong 1876 handstamp on back.	10.00	25.00	75.00
44	**50 Kurush** AH1293 (1876). Brown-lilac on yellow unpt. Vertical format. W/round AH1293 handstamp. Oval 1876 handstamp on back.	15.00	32.50	100.
45	**100 Kurush** AH1293 (1876). Brown-lilac on gray unpt. W/round AH1293 handstamp. Oblong 1876 handstamp on back.	10.00	25.00	75.00

Note: #42-45 usually occur on paper w/o wmk. Occasionally they are found on wmk. or handmade (laid) paper. Seal of Galip on back.

1876 SECOND "KAIME" ISSUE

#46-51 w/toughra of Abdul Hamid II. Seal of Galip on back.

#	Denomination	Good	Fine	XF
46	**1 Kurush** AH1293-95 (1876-78). Gray to gray-blue. Perforated edges.			
	a. W/round AH1293 handstamp, box 1876 handstamp on back.	10.00	30.00	80.00
	b. W/round AH1293 handstamp, box 1877 handstamp on back.	3.50	10.00	40.00
	c. W/15mm round AH1294 handstamp, straight line 1877 handstamp on back.	2.00	6.00	20.00
	d. W/18mm round AH1295 handstamp, straight line 1877 handstamp on back.	3.00	8.00	30.00

#47

#49

#	Denomination	Good	Fine	XF
47	**5 Kurush** AH1293-95 (1876-78). Red-brown.			
	a. W/round AH1293 handstamp, box 1876 handstamp on back.	7.50	25.00	75.00
	b. W/round AH1293 handstamp, box 1877 handstamp on back. W/o wmk.	6.00	15.00	50.00
	c. W/round AH1294 handstamp, box 1877 handstamp on back.	6.00	15.00	50.00
	d. W/round AH1295 handstamp, box 1877 handstamp on back.	7.50	25.00	75.00
48	**10 Kurush** AH1293-95 (1876-78). Lilac on lt. green.			
	a. W/round AH1293 handstamp, box 1876 or 1877 handstamp on back.	6.00	20.00	60.00
	b. W/round AH1294 handstamp, box 1877 handstamp on back.	6.00	15.00	50.00
	c. W/round AH1295 handstamp, box 1877 handstamp on back.	7.50	25.00	75.00
49	**20 Kurush** AH1293-95 (1876-78). Brown-lilac and yellow.			
	a. W/round AH1293 handstamp, box 1876 or 1877 handstamp on back.	7.50	25.00	75.00
	b. W/round AH1294 handstamp, box 1877 handstamp on back.	6.00	15.00	50.00
	c. W/round AH1295 handstamp, box 1877 handstamp on back.	7.50	25.00	75.00
50	**50 Kurush** AH1293-95 (1876-78). Brown-lilac on yellow unpt. Vertical format.			
	a. W/round AH1293 handstamp, box 1876 or 1877 handstamp on back.	7.50	25.00	75.00
	b. W/round AH1294 handstamp, box 1877 handstamp on back.	6.00	15.00	50.00
	c. W/round AH1295 handstamp, box 1877 handstamp on back.	7.50	25.00	75.00
51	**100 Kurush** AH1293-95 (1876-78). Brown-lilac on gray unpt. Vertical format.			
	a. W/round AH1293 handstamp, oval 1877 handstamp on back.	6.00	20.00	60.00
	b. W/round AH1294 handstamp, oval 1877 handstamp on back.	6.00	15.00	50.00
	c. W/round AH1295 handstamp, oval 1877 handstamp on back.	12.50	40.00	125.

1877 "KAIME" ISSUE

#	Denomination	Good	Fine	XF
52	**50 Kurush** AH1294-95 (1877-78). Black on lt. blue unpt. Horizontal format.			
	a. W/round AH1294 handstamp, box 1877 handstamp on back.	15.00	50.00	160.
	b. W/round AH1295 handstamp, box 1877 handstamp on back.	10.00	40.00	125.

#	Denomination	Good	Fine	XF
53	**100 Kurush** AH1294-95 (1877-78). Black on orange-brown unpt. Horizontal format.			
	a. W/round AH1294 handstamp, box 1877 handstamp on back.	10.00	30.00	75.00
	b. W/round AH1295 handstamp, box 1877 handstamp on back.	12.00	35.00	85.00

Note: Prior to World War I and until 1933, the Banque Imperiale Ottomane issued notes that were not legal tender in the real sense of the word, since they were traded like stocks and shares at a rate in excess of their nominal values of 1, 5, 50, and 100 Pounds.

LAW OF 15 DECEMBER AH1279 (1863)

#	Denomination	Good	Fine	XF
54	**200 Piastres** L.1279. Black, brown and green. Reimbursable in Constantinople.	350.	800.	—

#	Denomination	Good	Fine	XF
55	**200 Piastres** L.1279. Reimbursable in Smyrna. 4 sign. and 2 seals.	200.	600.	—
56	**200 Piastres** L.1279. Similar to #54 but w/text: Remboursable seulement en 10 Medjidies d'Argent (payable only in 10 Medjidies in silver) at upper l. Rare.	—	—	—
57	**2 Medjidies D'or** L.1279. Green and brown on blue-gray unpt.			
	a. Issued note.	300.	700.	—
	b. Handstamped *ANNULÉ*.	—	—	—
	c. Pin hole cancelled *PAYE*.	—	—	—
58	**5 Medjidies D'or** L.1279. Black and blue.			
	a. Issued note. Rare.	—	—	—
	b. Handstamped *ANNULÉ*.	—	—	—
	c. Pin hole cancelled *PAYE*.	—	—	—

LAW OF 20 DECEMBER AH1290 (1874)

#	Denomination	Good	Fine	XF
59	**1 Livre** L.1290 (1873). Denomination in 4 languages. Tan on brown and blue unpt. 2 sign. varieties.			
	a. Issued note. Rare.	—	—	—
	b. Handstamped *ANNULÉ*.	—	—	—

NOTICE

Readers with unlisted dates, signature varieties, etc. are invited to submit photocopies or, high resolution (300 dpi, 100% size) scans of their notes to: Standard Catalog of World Paper Money, 700 East State St. Iola, WI 54990-0001, or E-Mail: george.cuhaj@fwpubs.com.

LAW OF DECEMBER AH1299 (1882)

		Good	Fine	XF
60	**5 Livres** L.1299 (1882). Black and blue on orange and green unpt. Toughra of Abdul Hamid at top ctr.			
	a. Issued note.	350.	800.	—
	s. Specimen.	—	Unc	300.

NOTE: Values shown for #54-60 are for cancelled notes, usually stamped: *ANNULE*. Issued and uncancelled notes are very rare.

1909 ND ISSUE

		Good	Fine	XF
61	**100 Livres** ND (AH1327/1909). Green.	—	—	—

1908 ISSUE

#62 and 63 w/toughra of Abdul Hamid II. Printer: W&S.

		Good	Fine	XF
62	**5 Livres** AH1326 (1908). Blue. Back brown. Specimen.	—	Unc	150.
63	**100 Livres** AH1326 (1908). Green. Specimen.	—	Unc	300.

LAW OF 1 JANUARY AH1326 (1909)

#64-66 w/toughra of Muhammad V. Printer: W&S.

		Good	Fine	XF
64	**5 Livres** AH1326 (1909). Gray blue on lt. green, brown and lt. red unpt. Back brown. 2 sign. varieties.			
	a. Issued note.	50.00	200.	500.
	s. Specimen.			
65	**50 Livres** AH1326 (1909). Brown on red, orange and yellow unpt.			
	a. Issued note. Rare.	—	—	—
	s. Specimen.			
66	**100 Livres** AH1326 (1909). Green.			
	a. Issued note. Rare.	—	—	—
	s. Specimen.			

LAW OF JULY AH1332 (1914)

		Good	Fine	XF
67	**1 Livre** July AH1332 (1914). Blue. Specimen.	—	—	—

LAW OF AUGUST AH1332 (1914)

		Good	Fine	XF
68	**1 Livre** Aug. AH1332 (1914). Brown on lt. green and lt. red unpt. Back gray-green.			
	a. Issued note.	10.00	25.00	85.00
	r. Remainder.	—	Unc	45.00

DETTE PUBLIQUE OTTOMANE

STATE NOTES OF THE MINISTRY OF FINANCE

LAW OF 30 MARCH AH1331 (1915-16)

#69 and 70 printer: G&D.

		VG	VF	UNC
69	**1 Livre** L.1331. Black on blue frame. Pink, green and brown unpt.	5.00	20.00	75.00
70	**5 Livres** L.1331. Red-brown and m/c., black text.	30.00	100.	250.

LAW OF 18 OCTOBER AH1331 (1915-16)

		VG	VF	UNC
71	**1/4 Livre** L.1331. Dk. brown on green unpt., brown text.	5.00	20.00	75.00
72	**1/2 Livre** L.1331. Black on pink unpt., black text.	8.00	30.00	85.00
73	**1 Livre** L.1331. Dk. green on brown and m/c unpt.	7.00	25.00	75.00

		VG	VF	UNC
74	**5 Livres** L.1331. Black on blue frame. Pink, blue and brown unpt. Printer: G&D.	25.00	90.00	225.

LAW OF 16 DECEMBER AH1331 (1915-16)

#75-78 new denomination ovpt. on halved notes of earlier issue.

		Good	Fine	XF
75	**1/2 Livre** L.1331. Ovpt. on l. or r. half of #69. Rare.	—	—	—
76	**1/2 Livre** L.1331. Ovpt. on l. or r. half of #73. Rare.	—	—	—
77	**2 1/2 Livres** L.1331. Ovpt. on l. or r. half of #70. (Not issued). Rare.	—	—	—
78	**2 1/2 Livres** L.1331. Ovpt. on l. or r. half of #74. (Not issued). Rare.	—	—	—

LAW OF 22 DECEMBER AH1331 (1912)

		VG	VF	UNC
79	**5 Piastres** L.1331. Black on brown unpt.	2.00	5.00	15.00

		VG	VF	UNC
80	**20 Piastres** L.1331. Black on purple unpt.	2.50	7.50	25.00
81	**1/4 Livre** L.1331. Dk. brown on green unpt.	4.00	15.00	50.00

		VG	VF	UNC
82	**1/2 Livre** L.1331. Black on pink unpt.	5.00	17.50	55.00
83	**1 Livre** L.1331. Black, brown frame on blue, green and pink unpt.	3.00	10.00	35.00
84	**1 Livre** L.1331. Black, brown frame on pale green and pink unpt.	3.00	10.00	35.00

LAW OF 23 MAY AH1332 (1916-17)

		VG	VF	UNC
85	**1 Piastre** L.1332. Green w/black text. River w/palms and caravan at l. on back.	1.00	2.00	6.00

		VG	VF	UNC
86	**2 1/2 Piastres** L.1332. Pink w/black text. The Dardanelles at l. on back.	1.00	2.00	6.00

LAW OF 6 AUGUST AH1332 (1916-17)

		VG	VF	UNC
87	**5 Piastres** L.1332. Black text on olive unpt. White paper. Uniface. Wmk. varieties.	1.00	4.00	12.00
88	**20 Piastres** L.1332. Black text on orange unpt. Purple paper. Uniface.	2.00	6.00	20.00
89	**1/2 Livre** L.1332. Pink unpt., black text. Brownish paper.	5.00	12.50	37.50
90	**1 Livre** L.1332. Black. Green frame on blue-green and pink unpt.			
	a. Wmk: Hook pattern.	3.00	8.00	35.00
	b. Wmk: Sm. cruciferae.	4.00	12.00	45.00
91	**5 Livres** L.1332. Blue frame on m/c unpt.	30.00	75.00	210.
92	**10 Livres** L.1332. Black text on lt. blue unpt. Brown frame.	40.00	125.	350.

		Good	Fine	XF
93	**50 Livres** L.1332. Lt. blue and yellow-brown.			
	a. Wmk: Hook pattern.	150.	500.	—
	b. Wmk: Squared stars.	150.	500.	—
94	**500 Livres** L.1332. Rare.	—	—	—
95	**50,000 Livres** L.1332. Blue on pink unpt.			
	a. Issued note. Rare.	—	—	—
	s. Specimen.			

Note: #95 was a deposit note made w/the Imperial Ottoman Bank to cover the issue of #85 and #86.

LAW OF 4 FEBRUARY AH1332 (1916-17)

		VG	VF	UNC
96	**5 Piastres** L.1332. Green unpt., black text. Bluish paper. Uniface.	1.00	5.00	15.00
97	**20 Piastres** L.1332. Brown unpt., black text. Brownish paper. Uniface.	2.00	7.50	20.00
98	**1/2 Livre** L.1332. Red unpt., black text. Violet paper. Uniface.	3.00	12.50	45.00
99	**1 Livre** L.1332. Black on brown frame. Violet, pink and green unpt.	VG	VF	UNC
	a. Wmk: Fork pattern.	3.00	8.00	35.00
	b. Wmk: Sm. cruciferae.	3.00	8.00	35.00

		Good	Fine	XF
100	**2 1/2 Livres** L.1332. Orange and green.	25.00	80.00	275.
101	**10 Livres** L.1332. Gray-brown on lt. gray unpt.	40.00	200.	450.
102	**25 Livres** L.1332. Maroon and gray on lt. blue unpt. Back brown.	75.00	300.	650.
103	**100 Livres** L.1332. Brown on lt. blue unpt.	175.	450.	—

NOTICE

Readers with unlisted dates, signature varieties, etc. are invited to submit photocopies or, high resolution (300 dpi, 100% size) scans of their notes to: Standard Catalog of World Paper Money, 700 East State St. Iola, WI 54990-0001, or E-Mail: george.cuhaj@fwpubs.com.

LAW OF 28 MARCH AH1333 (1917)

#		Good	Fine	XF
104	**5 Livres** L.1333. Red-blue frame. Green and m/c unpt.	25.00	60.00	180.
105	**25 Livres** L.1333. Red. Brown frame. Lt. blue unpt.	60.00	220.	550.
106	**100 Livres** L.1333. Brown and red on lt. blue unpt. Back brown; black text.	175.	450.	1100.
107	**1000 Livres** L.1333. Black on brown, green, red and lt. blue unpt. Rare.	—	—	—

LAW OF 28 MARCH AH1334 (1918) FIRST ISSUE

#107A and 107B w/toughra of Muhammad V.

#		Good	Fine	XF
107A	**100 Livres** L.1334. Rare.	—	—	—
107B	**500 Livres** L.1334. Rare.	—	—	—
107C	**1000 Livres** L.1334. Rare.	—	—	—

LAW OF 28 MARCH AH1334 (1918) SECOND ISSUE

#108-115 toughra of Muhammad VI.

#		Good	Fine	XF
108	**2 1/2 Livres** L.1334. Orange and blue-green, w/black text. Similar to #110.			
	a. Stamp: *2 eme emission.*	40.00	125.	300.
	b. Stamp: *3 eme emission.*	25.00	75.00	200.
	c. Stamp: *5 eme emission.*	12.00	50.00	125.
109	**5 Livres** L.1334. Brown frame. Similar to #110.			
	a. Stamp: *2 eme emission.*	40.00	125.	300.
	b. Stamp: *6 eme emission.*	20.00	40.00	125.

#		Good	Fine	XF
110	**10 Livres** L.1334. Brown frame, black text. Lt. blue unpt.			
	a. 1st emission (no stamping).	40.00	125.	350.
	b. *2 eme emission* stamping.	50.00	150.	500.
	c. *3 eme emission* stamping.	60.00	150.	450.
	d. *4 eme emission* stamping.	30.00	100.	300.
	e. *5 eme emission* stamping.	30.00	100.	300.
	x. *2 eme emission.* Thought to be a British military counterfeit paper w/o wmk. Small "10s" in denomination in l. border on back facing out instead of in. (illustrated).	10.00	25.00	60.00
111	**25 Livres** L.1334.	70.00	300.	650.
112	**50 Livres** L.1334. Lt. gray on blue unpt. Back yellow.	150.	400.	800.
113	**100 Livres** L.1334. Dk. brown on yellow unpt. Back blue.	200.	500.	—
114	**500 Livres** L.1334. Blue on lt. blue. Rare.	—	—	—
115	**1000 Livres** L.1334. Brown and dk. blue. Rare.	—	—	—

POSTAGE STAMP MONEY

1917 ISSUE

#116-118 non-issued adhesive postage stamps (#116 and #117) and adhesive revenue stamp (#118) affixed to colored cardboard.

#		VG	VF	UNC
116	**5 Para** ND (1917). Carmine on yellow or pink cardboard. Gun emplacement.	1.00	3.00	9.00
117	**10 Para** ND (1917). Green on blue, green, yellow or pink cardboard. Hagia Sophia Mosque.	1.00	3.00	9.00
118	**10 Para** ND (1917). Green and pink on blue, yellow or pink cardboard. Camel. Arabic ovpt: *10 Para.*	2.00	6.00	15.00

REPUBLIC

STATE NOTES OF THE MINISTRY OF FINANCE

1926 ISSUE

#119-125 Arabic legend and *Law #701 of 30 KANUNUEVVEL (AH)1341* (January 12, 1926) at ctr. Wmk: Ataturk. Printer: TDLR.

#		VG	VF	UNC
119	**1 Livre** L.1341 (1926). Green. Farmer w/2 oxen. Bldg. on back.			
	a. Issued note.	10.00	40.00	150.
	s. Specimen.	—	—	100.
120	**5 Livres** L.1341 (1926). Blue. Bounding wolf at ctr., bldgs. at r. Bridge and city view on back.			
	a. Issued note.	30.00	150.	600.
	s. Specimen.			

		Good	Fine	XF
121	**10 Livres** L.1341 (1926). Purple. Bounding wolf at r. Rock mountain w/bridge on back.			
	a. Issued note.	65.00	250.	800.
	s. Specimen.	—	Unc	500.

#122-125 portr. Kemal Ataturk at r.

		Good	Fine	XF
122	**50 Livres** L.1341 (1926). Brown. Town view w/mountains on back.			
	a. Issued note.	175.	600.	—
	s. Specimen.	—	Unc	1000.
123	**100 Livres** L.1341 (1926). Green. Ankara new town on back.			
	a. Issued note. Rare.	—	—	—
	s. Specimen.	—	Unc	1250.

		Good	Fine	XF
124	**500 Livres** L.1341 (1926). Red-brown on blue and gold unpt. Mosque at l. Town view on back.			
	a. Issued note. Rare.	—	—	—
	s. Specimen.	—	Unc	1500.

		Good	Fine	XF
125	**1000 Livres** L.1341 (1926). Dk. blue. Railroad through mountain pass on back.			
	a. Issued note. Rare.	—	—	—
	s. Specimen.	—	Unc	1750.

TÜRKIYE CÜMHURIYET MERKEZ BANKASI

CENTRAL BANK OF TURKEY

LAW OF 11 HAZIRAN 1930; SECOND ISSUE (1937-39)

#126-132 portr. Pres K. Ataturk at r. and as wmk. Printer: TDLR.

		VG	VF	UNC
126	**2 1/2 Lira** L.1930 (25.4.1939). Green. Monument of the Square of the Nation on back.	7.50	35.00	125.
127	**5 Lira** L.1930 (15.10.1937). Dk. blue. Back green, Monument of Security in Ankara.	15.00	50.00	200.
128	**10 Lira** L.1930 (16.5.1938). Red-brown. Citadel of Ankara on back.	30.00	125.	300.
129	**50 Lira** L.1930 (1.4.1938). Purple. Angora sheep and farmhouse on back.	50.00	200.	500.
130	**100 Lira** L.1930 (1.3.1938). Dk. brown. The Dardanelles on back.	500.	1250.	—
131	**500 Lira** L.1930 (15.6.1939). Olive. Rumeli-Hissar Palace on back. Rare.	—	—	—
132	**1000 Lira** L.1930 (15.6.1939). Dk. blue. Monument of Security in Ankara on back. Rare.	—	—	—

LAW OF 11 HAZIRAN 1930; INTERIM ISSUE (1942-44)

#133, 135-139 portr. Pres. I. Inonu at r. and as wmk.

		VG	VF	UNC
133	**50 Kurus** L.1930. Dk. brown on lilac. Bank on back. Printer: BWC. (Not issued).	1.50	5.00	15.00

Note: #133 was on a ship bombed by the Germans while at Piraeus Harbor near the beginning of WW II. Subsequent retrieval by Greek citizens caused the Turkish government to cancel the issue and arrange for another instead. #134 was the result. All available examples of #133 were rescued from the sea; therefore, practically all show signs of water damage.

		VG	VF	UNC
134	**50 Kurus** L.1930 (26.6.1944). Brown and green. Portr. Pres. Inonu at ctr. Bank on back. No wmk. Printer: Reichsdruckerei.	7.50	50.00	125.

		VG	VF	UNC
135	**1 Lira** L.1930 (25.4.1942). Lilac. The Bosporus Strait on back. Printer: BWC.	5.00	17.50	75.00

#136-139 printer: TDLR.

136	**50 Lira** L.1930. Purple. Back like #129 (Not issued).	—	—	—

#137 Deleted, see #130.

		VG	VF	UNC
138	**500 Lira** L.1930 (18.11.1940). Dk. green. Rumeli-Hissar Palace on back.	250.	850.	—
139	**1000 Lira** L.1930 (18.11.1940). Blue. Monument of Security on back.	375.	1150.	—

LAW OF 11 HAZIRAN 1930; THIRD ISSUE (1942-47)

		VG	VF	UNC
140	**2 1/2 Lira** L.1930 (27.3.1947). Dk. brown on lilac unpt. Portr. Pres. Inonu at r. and as wmk. Bank on back. Printer: BWC.	5.00	35.00	100.

#141-146 w/o wmk.

		VG	VF	UNC
141	**10 Lira** L.1930 (15.1.1942). Brown and red-brown. Portr. Pres. Inonu at l. 3 peasant women on back. Printer: Reichsdruckerei.	10.00	75.00	200.

#142, 143, 145 and 146 printer: ABNC.

		VG	VF	UNC
142	**50 Lira** L.1930 (25.4.1942). Purple on m/c unpt. Portr. Pres. Inonu w/long tie at r. Goats on back.			
	a. Issued note.	50.00	150.	400.
	s. Specimen.	—	—	375.
142A	**50 Lira** L.1930. Purple on m/c unpt. Similar to #142 but Pres. Inonu w/white bowtie.	50.00	150.	400.
143	**50 Lira** L.1930 (17.2.1947). Slate blue on m/c unpt. Like #142. Portr. Pres. Inonu w/white bowtie at r.			
	a. Issued note.	50.00	150.	400.
	s. Specimen.	—	—	375.

		VG	VF	UNC
144	**100 Lira** L.1930 (15.8.1942). Dk. and lt. brown. Portr. Pres. Inonu at l. Girl w/grapes on back. Printer: Reichsdruckerei.			
	a. Imprint: *REICHSDRUCKEREI* at bottom margin on face.	20.00	75.00	250.
	b. W/o imprint at bottom.	25.00	100.	300.
	c. Semi-finished note w/imprint.	20.00	75.00	250.
145	**500 Lira** L.1930 (24.4.1946). Dk. olive on m/c unpt. Portr. Pres. Inonu at ctr. Factory workers at machines on back.			
	a. Issued note.	150.	500.	1200.
	s. Specimen.	—	Unc	750.
146	**1000 Lira** L.1930 (24.4.1946). Blue on m/c unpt. Portr. Pres. Inonu at r. Military buglers on back.			
	a. Issued note.	—	—	—
	s. Specimen.	—	—	1200.

LAW 11 HAZIRAN 1930; FOURTH ISSUE (1947-48)

#147-149 printer: ABNC.

		VG	VF	UNC
147	**10 Lira** L.1930 (7.2.1947). Red on m/c unpt. Portr. Pres. Inonu w/tie at r. Fountain of Ahmed III on back.			
	a. Issued note.	25.00	125.	325.
	s. Specimen.	—	—	225.
148	**10 Lira** L.1930 (15.9.1948). Brown on m/c unpt. Pres. Inonu w/bow tie at r. Similar to #147.			
	a. Issued note.	20.00	100.	300.
	s. Specimen.	—	—	240.

		VG	VF	UNC
149	**100 Lira** L.1930 (18.7.1947). Green on m/c unpt. Portr. Pres. Inonu at ctr. Rumeli-Hissar Fortress on back.			
	a. Issued note.	50.00	225.	600.
	s. Specimen.	—	—	450.

LAW 11 HAZIRAN 1930; FIFTH ISSUE (1951-60)

#150-172 portr. Pres. K. Ataturk at r. Earlier issues printed by TDLR and BWC. Later issues by Devlet Banknot Matbassi, Ankara (w/o imprint). Sign. varieties.

All notes have Ataturk wmk. from #150 on.

#150-153 printer: TDLR.

		VG	VF	UNC
150	**2 1/2 Lira** L.1930 (15.7.1952). Lilac on m/c unpt. Central bank on back.			
	a. Issued note.	2.00	12.50	75.00
	s. Specimen.	—	—	—
151	**2 1/2 Lira** L.1930 (3.1.1955). Lilac. Like #150 but back brown.			
	a. Issued note.	1.50	10.00	60.00
	s. Specimen.	—	—	—
152	**2 1/2 Lira** L.1930 (1.7.1957). Lilac. Like #150 but back red.			
	a. Issued note.	1.50	10.00	60.00
	s. Specimen.	—	—	—

		VG	VF	UNC
153	**2 1/2 Lira**			
	L.1930 (15.2.1960). Lilac. Like #150 but back lt. green.			
	a. Issued note.	1.50	10.00	60.00
	s. Specimen.	—	—	—

		VG	VF	UNC
154	**5 Lira**			
	L.1930 (10.11.1952). Blue on m/c unpt. Back blue; 3 peasant women w/baskets of hazelnuts at ctr. Series A-D. Printer: BWC.			
	a. Issued note.	2.00	10.00	60.00
	s. Specimen.	—	—	—
155	**5 Lira**			
	L.1930 (8.6.1959). Like #154, but back green. Series E.			
	a. Issued note.	2.00	12.50	75.00
	s. Specimen.	—	—	—
156	**10 Lira**			
	L.1930. Green face and back. River and bridge on back. Series A-J. Printer: TDLR.			
	a. Issued note.	5.00	30.00	100.
	s. Specimen.	—	—	—

		VG	VF	UNC
157	**10 Lira**			
	L.1930 (2.6.1952). Green. Like #156. Back brownish-red. Series K-U. Printer: TDLR.			
	a. Issued note.	1.50	10.00	60.00
	s. Specimen.	—	—	—
158	**10 Lira**			
	L.1930 (24.3.1958). Green face. Like #159 but lt. blue and red on face. Back brown. Series V; Y. Printer: TDLR.			
	a. Issued note.	1.50	10.00	60.00
	s. Specimen.	—	—	—
159	**10 Lira**			
	L.1930. Green face and back. Similar to #157 but different guilloche on face. Series Z1-Z36. W/o imprint.			
	a. Issued note.	1.50	10.00	60.00
	s. Specimen.	—	—	—
160	**10 Lira**			
	L.1930 (26.10.1953). Green. Like #159 but back red. Series Z37-.			
	a. Issued note.	5.00	30.00	100.
	s. Specimen.	—	—	—
161	**10 Lira**			
	L.1930 (25.4.1960). Green. Like #160 but back green. Different sign. Series A; B. W/o imprint.	1.50	7.50	50.00

162-165, 167, 168 and 170-172 printer: BWC.

		VG	VF	UNC
162	**50 Lira**			
	L.1930 (1.12.1951). Brown on m/c unpt. Back brown; statue of soldier holding rifle at l. ctr.			
	a. Issued note.	5.00	30.00	100.
	s. Specimen.	—	—	—
163	**50 Lira**			
	L.1930 (2.2.1953). Brown on m/c unpt. Like #162 but back orange.			
	a. Issued note.	6.00	40.00	125.
	s. Specimen.	—	—	—
164	**50 Lira**			
	L.1930 (15.10.1956). Brown on m/c unpt. Like #162 but back red.			
	a. Issued note.	6.00	40.00	125.
	s. Specimen.	—	40.00	125.
165	**50 Lira**			
	L.1930 (1.10.1957). Brown on unpt. Like #162 but back blue-gray.			
	a. Issued note.	5.00	30.00	100.
	s. Specimen.	—	—	—
166	**50 Lira**			
	L.1930 (15.2.1960). Purple on m/c unpt. Similar to #162 but different style of numbers. Reddish guilloche at ctr. W/o imprint.	7.50	35.00	115.
167	**100 Lira**			
	L.1930 (10.10.1952). Olive on m/c unpt. Park w/bridge in Ankara on back, Ankara fortress behind.			
	a. Issued note.	12.50	60.00	200.
	s. Specimen.	—	—	—

		VG	VF	UNC
168	**100 Lira**			
	L.1930 (2.7.1956). Like #167 but back lt. blue. SERI H, I and J.			
	a. Issued note.	12.50	60.00	200.
	s. Specimen.	—	—	—
169	**100 Lira**			
	L.1930. Olive on m/c unpt. Similar to #167 but w/o imprint, and w/o SERI in front of number. Different sign. Series K-P.			
	a. Issued note.	10.00	50.00	150.
	s. Specimen.	—	—	—
170	**500 Lira**			
	L.1930 (15.4.1953). Red-brown and m/c. Byzantine hippodrome w/mosque in Istanbul on back.			
	a. Issued note.	40.00	250.	850.
	s. Specimen.	—	—	—
171	**500 Lira**			
	L.1930 (16.2.1959). Brown and m/c. Like #170, but w/o SERI in front of number. Different sign.			
	a. Issued note.	40.00	250.	850.
	s. Specimen.	—	—	—
172	**1000 Lira**			
	L.1930 (15.4.1953). Purple. Bosporus and fortress on back.			
	a. Issued note.	45.00	300.	1000.
	s. Specimen.	—	—	—

TÜRKIYE CÜMHURIYET MERKEZ BANKASI

CENTRAL BANK OF TURKEY

LAW 11 HAZIRAN 1930; 1961-65 ND ISSUE

#173-178 portr. Pres. K. Atatürk at r. and as wmk. Printer: DBM-A (w/o imprint).

		VG	VF	UNC
174	**5 Lira**			
	L.1930 (4.1.1965). Blue-green. Back blue-gray, like #173.			
	a. Issued note.	2.00	6.00	45.00
	s. Specimen.	—	—	200.

		VG	VF	UNC
175	**50 Lira** L.1930 (1.6.1964). Brown on m/c unpt. 3 sign. Soldier holding rifle figure from the Victory statue at Ulus Square in Ankara at ctr. on back.			
	a. Issued note.	5.00	20.00	75.00
	s. Specimen.	—	—	250.
176	**100 Lira** L.1930 (15.3.1962). Olive on orange and m/c guilloche. Youth Park w/bridge in Ankara on back.	VG	VF	UNC
	a. Issued note.	12.50	50.00	125.
	s. Specimen.	—	—	350.

		VG	VF	UNC
177	**100 Lira** L.1930 (1.10.1964). Like #176, but guilloche blue, lilac and m/c. Different sign.			
	a. Issued note.	8.50	35.00	100.
	s. Specimen.	—	—	350.

		VG	VF	UNC
178	**500 Lira** L.1930 (1.12.1962). Purple and brown on m/c unpt. Sultan Ahmet Mosque, the Obelisc and the Hippodrome in Istanbul on back.			
	a. Issued note.	50.00	150.	400.
	s. Specimen.	—	—	500.

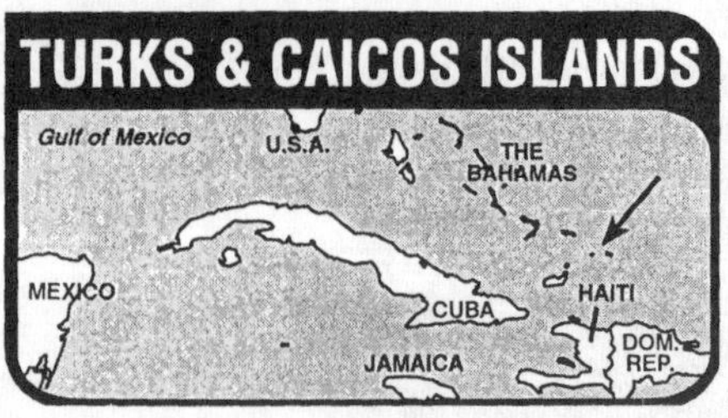

The Colony of the Turks and Caicos Islands, a British colony situated in the West Indies at the eastern end of the Bahama Islands, has an area of 166 sq. mi. (430 sq. km.) and a population of *10,000. Capital: Cockburn Town on Grand Turk. The principal industry of the colony is the production of salt, which is gathered by raking. Salt, crayfish and conch shells are exported.

The Turks and Caicos Islands were discovered by Juan Ponce de Leon in 1512, but were not settled until 1678 when Bermudians arrived to rake salt from the salt ponds. The British settlers were driven from the island by the Spanish in 1710, during the long War of the Spanish Succession. They returned and throughout the remaining years of the war repulsed repeated attacks by France and Spain. In 1799 the islands were granted representation in the Bahamian assembly, but in 1848, on petition of the inhabitants, they were made a separate colony under Jamaica. They were annexed by Jamaica in 1873 and remained a dependency until 1959 when they became a unit territory of the Federation of the West Indies. When the Federation was dissolved in 1962, the Turks and Caicos Islands became a separate Crown Colony with its economy d on the USA dollar which is currently in circulation.

RULERS:
British

MONETARY SYSTEM:
1 Shilling = 12 Pence
1 Pound = 20 Shillings to 1971
1 Dollar (USA) = 100 Cents

British Administration

Government of the Turks and Caicos Islands

1903-28 Issue

#1-4 arms at top ctr. Various date and sign. varieties. Printer: TDLR.

		Good	Fine	XF
1	**5 Shillings** 10.1.1928. Black and blue on yellow unpt. Back blue; arms at ctr.	1250.	5000.	—

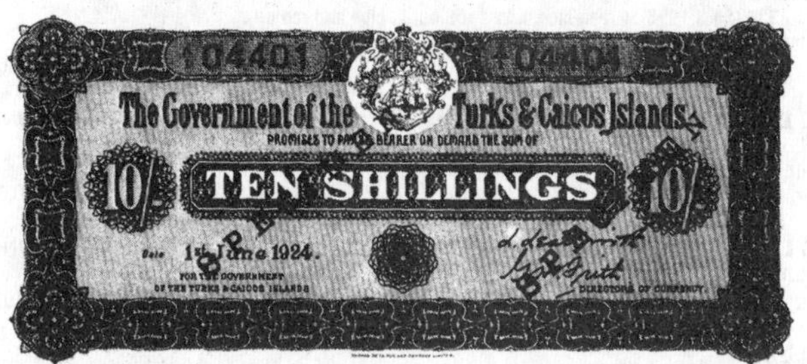

		Good	Fine	XF
2	**10 Shillings** 1.6.1924. Dk. brown.	1750.	6000.	—

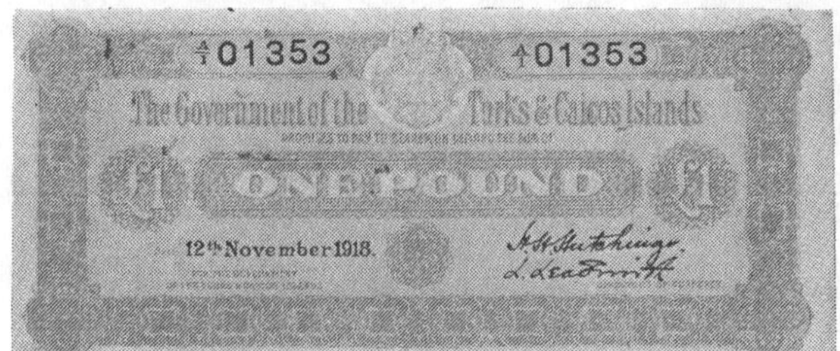

		Good	Fine	XF
3	**1 Pound** 1903; 1918. Red on blue-green unpt.			
	a. 2.12.1903. Hand dated and handsigned. Rare.	—	—	—
	b. 12.11.1918. Rare.	—	—	—
4	**1 Pound** 12.11.1928. Red and pink on yellow unpt. Uniface. Rare.	—	—	—

Ukraine is bordered by Russia to the east, Russia and Belarus to the north, Poland, Slovakia and Hungary to the west, Romania and Moldova to the southwest and in the south by the Black Sea and the Sea of Azov. It has an area of 233,088 sq. mi. (603,700 sq. km.) and a population of 50.8 million. Capital: Kyiv (Kiev). Coal, grain, vegetables and heavy industrial machinery are major exports.

The territory of Ukraine has been inhabited for over 30,000 years. As the result of its location, Ukraine has served as the gateway to Europe for millennia and its early history has been recorded by Arabic, Greek, Roman, as well as Ukrainian historians.

Ukraine, which was known as Rus' until the sixteenth century (and from which the name Russia was derived in the 17th century), became the major political and cultural center of Eastern Europe in the 9th century. The Rus' Kingdom, under a dynasty of Varangian origin, because of its position on the intersection of the north-south Scandinavia to Byzantium and the east-west Orient to Europe trade routes, became a focal point of world trade. At its apex Rus' stretched from the Baltic to the Black Sea and from the upper Volga River in the east, almost to the Vistula River in the west. In 988 the Rus' adopted Christianity from Byzantium. The Mongol invasion in 1240 brought an end to the might of the Rus' Kingdom.

In the seventeenth century, after almost four hundred years of Mongol, Lithuanian, Polish, and Turkish domination, the Cossack State regained Ukrainian independence. The Hetman State lasted until the mid-eighteenth century and was followed by a period of foreign rule: Eastern Ukraine was controlled by Russia; Western Ukraine came under relatively benign Austro-Hungarian rule.

With the disintegration of the Russian and Austro-Hungarian Empires in 1917 and 1918, Eastern Ukraine declared its full independence on January 22, 1918 and Western Ukraine followed suit on November 1 of that year. On January 22, 1919 both parts united into one state that had to defend itself on three fronts: from the "Red" Bolsheviks and their puppet Ukrainian Soviet Republic formed in Kharkiv, from the "White" czarist Russian forces, and from Poland. Ukraine lost the war. In 1920, Eastern Ukraine was occupied by the Bolsheviks and in 1922 was incorporated into the Soviet Union. There followed a brief resurgence of Ukrainian language and culture until it was suppressed in 1928. Western Ukraine was partitioned between Poland, Romania, Hungary and Czechoslovakia.

During the period of independence 1917-1920, Ukraine issued its own currency in Karbovanets denominations under the Central Rada of social-democrats (#1-11) and in Hryvnia denominations during the monarchy of Hetman Pavlo Skoropadsky (#12-19 and #29-34). During WW II German occupation forces issued Karbowanez currency.

On August 24, 1991 Ukraine once again declared its independence. On December 5, 1991 the Ukrainian Parliament abrogated the 1922 treaty which incorporated Ukraine into the Soviet Union.

During the changeover from the Ruble currency of the Soviet Union to the Karbovanets of Ukraine, as a transition measure and to restrict unlicensed export of scarce goods, coupon cards (202 x 82mm), similar to ration cards, were issued in various denominations. They were valid for one month and were given to employees in amounts equal to their pay. Each card contained multiples of 1, 3, 5, 10, 25 and sometimes 50 Karbovanets valued coupons, to be cut apart. They were supposed to be used for purchases together with ruble notes. In January 1992 Ukraine began issuing individual coupons in Karbovanets denominations from 1 krb to 100 krb (printed in France and dated 1991). They were replaced by the Hryvnia.

Ukraine is a charter member of the United Nations.

RULERS:

Polish, 1569-1654
Polish and Russian, 1654-1671
Polish, Ottoman and Russian, 1672-1684
Russian, 1685-1794
Austrian (Western Ukraine), 1774-1918
Russian, 1793-1917

MONETARY SYSTEM:

1 Karbovanets (Karbovantsiv) КАРБОВАНЕЦЬ, КАРБОВАНЦІВ = 2 Hryven ГРИВЕНЬ
1917-1920 = 200 Shahiv ШАГІВ
1 Karvovanets (Karbovantsiv) КАРБОВАНЕЦЬ, КАРБОВАНЦІВ = 1 Russian Ruble, 1991-96
1 Hryvnia (Hryvni, Hryven) ГРИВНЯ (ГРИВНІ, ГРИВЕНЬ) = 100,000 Karbovantsiv, 1996-

AUTONOMOUS REPUBLIC

УКРАЇНСЬКА НАРОДНЯ РЕСПУБЛІКА

UKRAINIAN NATIONAL REPUBLIC

CENTRAL RADA

1917 ISSUE

#		Good	Fine	XF
1	**100 Karbovantsiv** 1917. Brown, orange and yellow. Inscription on back in Polish, Russian and Yiddish.			
	a. Printing same way up on both sides. Rare.	—	—	—
	b. Back inverted.	20.00	60.00	150.

ЗНАК ДЕРЖАВНОЇ СКАРБНИЦІ

STATE TREASURY NOTES

1918 (ND) ISSUE

#		VG	VF	UNC
2	**25 Karbovantsiv** ND (1918). Green. Man standing w/spade at l., woman w/sheafs at r. W/o serial # prefix letters (issued in Kiev).			
	a. W/text: КРЕДИТОВИМ.	10.00	20.00	50.00
	b. W/text: КРЕДІТОВИМ.	20.00	50.00	125.

#		VG	VF	UNC
3	**25 Karbovantsiv** ND (1918). Green. Like #2 but serial # prefix letters: *AO* (issued in Odessa).	25.00	75.00	200.
4	**50 Karbovantsiv** ND (1918). Green. Type of #2 (issued in Kiev).			
	a. W/text: КРЕДИТОВИМ.	7.50	20.00	50.00
	b. W/text: КРЕДИТОВИМИ.	5.00	12.50	25.00
5	**50 Karbovantsiv** ND (1918). Green. Like #4 but serial # prefix letters: *AKI* or *AKII* (issued in Kiev).			
	a. Issued note.	2.00	6.00	12.50
	x. Error, w/back only in red. (AKII).	10.00	20.00	50.00

#		VG	VF	UNC
6	**50 Karbovantsiv** ND (1918). Green. Like #4 but w/serial # prefix letters: *AO* (issued in Odessa).			
	a. Serial # to 209.	1.00	3.00	7.50
	b. Serial # from 210 (issued by Gen. Denikin and labeled as false by the Ukrainian Government).	1.00	3.00	7.50

Postage Stamp Currency

1918; 1919 ND Emergency Issue

#7-11 postage stamp designs, Michel catalogue #1-5 or Scott #67-71, printed on ungummed cardboard w/trident arms over black text within single line or double line border.

		VG	VF	UNC
7	**10 Shahiv** ND (1918). Yellow-brown. Arms.	1.00	3.00	7.00
8	**20 Shahiv** ND (1918). Dk. brown. Peasant.	1.00	3.00	7.50
9	**30 Shahiv** ND (1918). Head of Ceres.			
	a. Ultramarine.	1.50	3.00	7.50
	b. Gray-violet.	2.00	7.50	15.00

		VG	VF	UNC
10	**40 Shahiv** ND (1918). Green. Trident arms.			
	a. Perforated.	1.00	3.00	7.50
	b. Imperforate.	17.50	30.00	70.00
10A	**5 Karbowanez** ND (1919). Ovpt.: Soviet arms in wreath on back of #10.	—	—	—
11	**50 Shahiv** ND (1918). Red. Wreath around value *50*.			
	a. Perforated.	1.00	2.50	6.00
	b. Imperforate.	20.00	40.00	75.00

3.6% БІЛЕТ ДЕРЖАВНОЇ СКАРБНИЦІ

Bond Certificates, 3.6%

1918 Issue

#12-15 bond certificates w/interest coupons.

		Good	Fine	XF
12	**50 Hryven** 1918. Green and brown.	5.00	15.00	40.00

		Good	Fine	XF
13	**100 Hryven** 1918. Brown on green and red.	3.00	15.00	40.00
14	**200 Hryven** 1918. Blue.	3.00	10.00	25.00
15	**1000 Hryven** 1918. Brown on yellow-brown.	3.00	15.00	40.00

Note: Bonds complete w/six coupons are worth triple the market value indicated.

NOTICE

Readers with unlisted dates, signature varieties, etc. are invited to submit photocopies or, high resolution (300 dpi, 100% size) scans of their notes to: Standard Catalog of World Paper Money, 700 East State St. Iola, WI 54990-0001, or E-Mail: george.cuhaj@fwpubs.com.

Interest Coupons

1918 Issue

		Good	Fine	XF
16	**90 Shahiv** 1918. Black on pale green unpt. Back red on pale green unpt.	.50	1.00	2.50
17	**1 Hryven 80 Shahiv** 1918. Red-brown.	.50	1.00	2.50

		Good	Fine	XF
18	**3 Hryven 60 Shahiv** 1918. Black on lt. blue and gray unpt. Back pale red on lt. blue unpt.	.50	1.00	2.50

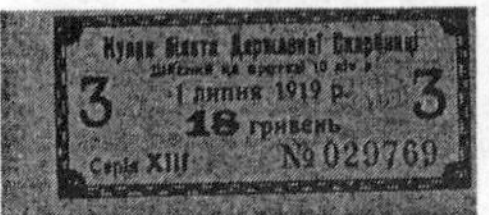

		Good	Fine	XF
19	**18 Hryven** 1918. Yellow-brown.	.50	1.00	2.50

ДЕРЛАВНИЙ КРЕДИТОВИЙ БІЛЕТ

State Credit Notes

1918 Issue

		VG	VF	UNC
20	**2 Hryven** 1918. Green. Arms at r.			
	a. Yellowish background. Serial # prefix letter: *A*.	1.50	3.50	10.00
	b. Brown background. Serial # prefix letter: Б.	2.00	6.50	15.00

		VG	VF	UNC
21	**10 Hryven** 1918. Red-brown. Arms at upper ctr.			
	a. Serial # prefix letter: *A*.	1.00	3.00	10.00
	b. Serial # prefix letter: Б,	2.00	7.50	17.50
	c. Serial # prefix letter: В.	—	—	—

2	100 Hryven	VG	VF	UNC
	1918. Blue-violet. Farmer's wife at l., worker at r., arms at ctr.			
	a. Blue background. Serial # prefix letter: *A*.	4.00	10.00	25.00
	b. Gray-violet unpt. Serial # prefix letter: Б **(not issued).**	—	150.	350.

500 Hryven	VG	VF	UNC
1918. Green and orange. Ceres head at upper ctr., arms at l. and r.	4.00	10.00	25.00

24	1000 Hryven	VG	VF	UNC
	1918. Blue on orange and yellow unpt.	4.00	15.00	40.00

25	2000 Hryven	VG	VF	UNC
	1918. Red on blue unpt. Arms in unpt at ctr. on back.	8.00	30.00	60.00

1920 Issue

#26-28 Austrian printing.

		VG	VF	UNC
26	**50 Hryven** 1920. Black and blue. Allegorical figures at l. and r., arms at upper ctr. Portr. of Petro Loroshenko in cartouche at l., arms above. Proof. Rare.	—	—	—
27	**50 Hryven** 1920. Brown. Proof. Rare.	—	—	—
28	**1000 Hryven** 1920. Gray and orange. Proof. Rare.	—	—	—

Note: It is reported that only 2 sets of #26-28 exist.

5% КР. ОБЯЗАТ. ГОСУД. КАЗНАЧ.

Russian State Debenture Bonds, 5%

1918 ND Issue

#29-34 exist w/different stamps of the State Bank branches. Validated October - December 1918.

		Good	Fine	XF
29	**1000 Rubles** ND (1918). Red-brown on gray.	6.00	15.00	25.00
30	**5000 Rubles** ND (1918).	9.00	17.50	35.00
31	**10,000 Rubles** ND (1918).	10.00	22.50	40.00
32	**25,000 Rubles** ND (1918).	10.00	25.00	50.00
33	**50,000 Rubles** ND (1918).	15.00	35.00	75.00
34	**500,000 Rubles** ND (1918).	—	—	—

ЗНАК ДЕРЖАВНОЇ СКАРБНИЦІ

State Treasury Notes

1918 ND Issue

		VG	VF	UNC
35	**1000 Karbovantsiv** ND (1918). Deep brown and m/c on tan unpt. Black sign. Back brown; trident arms at top ctr. between 2 standing allegorical women supporting frame w/value.			
	a. Wmk: Wavy lines.	3.00	12.50	25.00
	b. Zigzag lines of varnish printed on paper.	2.00	10.00	20.00

Semen Petlyura Directorate

1918-19 Issue

NOTE: #S293 was issued under the Ukrainian Socialist Soviet Republic and is not considered to be a truly independent issue. It is similar to #36 but is w/o serial #, only a block #.

		VG	VF	UNC
36	**10 Karbovantsiv** ND (1919). Brown or red-brown on gray paper. Wmk: Spades. 3 serial # varieties. See also #S293 (Russia-Vol. I).	4.00	15.00	40.00

Note: #S293 was issued under the Ukrainian Socialist Soviet Republic and is not considered to be a truly independent issue. It is similar to #36 but has no serial #, only a block #.

		VG	VF	UNC
37	**25 Karbovantsiv** 1919. Violet-brown. Arms and Cossack at upper ctr. Back brown; conjoined heads facing r. at ctr. w/ or w/o serial #.	4.00	12.50	40.00
38	**100 Karbovantsiv** 1918. Brown and gray-green. Small wreath w/Cossack at upper ctr.			
	a. Wmk: Stars. 2 serial # varieties.	3.00	7.50	17.50
	b. Wmk: Spades. 2 serial # varieties.	4.00	12.50	40.00

		VG	VF	UNC
39	**250 Karbovantsiv** 1918. Brown and gray on olive unpt. Arms at ctr. on face at l. on back.			
	a. Lg. letters; serial # prefix: АА, АБ, АГ.	4.00	12.50	40.00
	b. Sm. letters; serial # prefix: АБ, АВ, АГ.	4.00	12.50	40.00

#		VG	VF	UNC
40	**1000 Karbovantsiv** ND (1918). Brown-violet and m/c on tan unpt. Brown-violet sign. Like #35. Back brown-violet.			
	a. Wmk: Wavy lines.	4.00	12.50	40.00
	b. Wmk: Linked stars.	3.00	17.50	50.00

NOTE: Violet color appears only on #40a. #40b differs from #35a or b only by wmk.

РОЗМІННИЙ ЗНАК ДЕРЖАВНОЇ СКАРБНИЦІ

STATE NOTES

1920 ND ISSUE

#		VG	VF	UNC
41	**5 Hryven** ND (1920). Black on gray unpt. Arms in square design at l. on back.			
	a. Issued note.	3.00	12.50	30.00
	x. Error: ГИБЕНЬ. (w/o P).	35.00	100.	250.

GERMAN OCCUPATION - WW II

ЭМИССИОННЫЙ БАНК

EMISSION BANK

KIEV

1941 ISSUE

#42-48 were printed by the German government for use in occupied areas during WW II, but the Germans rejected the idea of Russian language on occupation notes and instead issued the Ukrainian occupation notes of the Zentralnotenbank type. Proofs perforated: *DRUCKPROBE*.

Note: Technically #42-48 were not intended as occupation notes for Ukraine. Instead, they were for possible issue in an area the Germans call "Ostland" which was to be administered from Kiev.

#		VG	VF	UNC
42	**1 Ruble** 1941. Brown. Lt. brown and green unpt.			
	a. Regular serial #.	—	—	—
	p. Proof.	—	—	1000.
43	**3 Rubles** 1941. Violet and green unpt. Proof.	—	—	1000.
44	**5 Rubles** 1941. Violet and green unpt. Proof.	—	—	1000.
45	**1 Chervonets** 1941. Blue, lt. blue and green unpt.			
	a. Regular serial #.	—	—	—
	p. Proof.	—	—	1000.

#		VG	VF	UNC
46	**3 Chervontsa** 1941. Green and violet unpt. Proof.	—	—	1000.
47	**5 Chervontsiv** 1941. Brown. Green and violet unpt.			
	a. Regular serial #.	500.	1500.	4000.
	p. Proof.	—	—	1000.
48	**10 Chervontsiv** 1941. Brown. Green and brown unpt. Proof.	—	—	1000.

ZENTRALNOTENBANK UKRAINE

UKRAINIAN CENTRAL BANK

1942 ISSUE

#		VG	VF	UNC
49	**1 Karbowanez** 10.3.1942. Olive.	1.50	5.00	15.00

#		VG	VF	UNC
50	**2 Karbowanez** 10.3.1942. Young boy wearing fur cap at r. (Not issued).	—	200.	800.

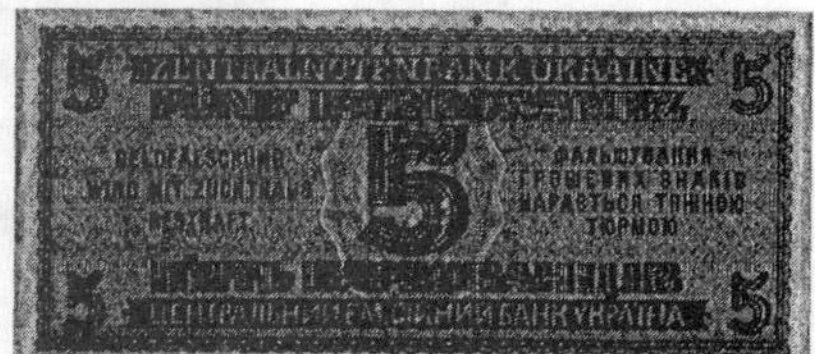

#		VG	VF	UNC
51	**5 Karbowanez** 10.3.1942. Brown-violet. Portr. young girl at r.	1.00	4.00	15.00

#		VG	VF	UNC
52	**10 Karbowanez** 10.3.1942. Red-brown. Farmer's wife at r.	1.00	5.00	20.00

		VG	VF	UNC
53	**20 Karbowanez** 10.3.1942. Gray-brown. Industrial worker at r.	1.50	7.50	35.00

		VG	VF	UNC
54	**50 Karbowanez** 10.3.1942. Green and brown. Miner at r.	3.00	20.00	55.00

		VG	VF	UNC
55	**100 Karbowanez** 10.3.1942. Blue. Portr. seaman at r.	7.50	30.00	100.

		VG	VF	UN
56	**200 Karbowanez** 10.3.1942. Olive. Peasant woman at r.	10.00	40.00	12

		VG	VF	UN
57	**500 Karbowanez** 10.3.1942. Violet. Portr. chemist at r.	20.00	60.00	15

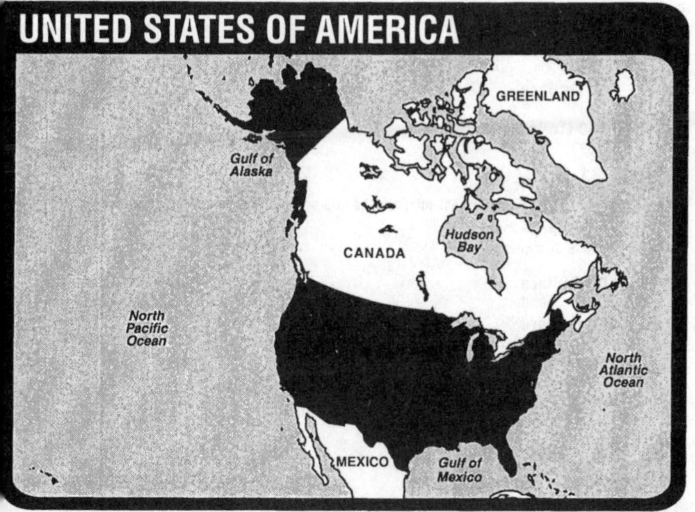

The area of the North American continent currently controlled by the United States of America ʼas originally inhabited by numerous groups of Indian tribes. Some of these groups settled in articular areas, creating permanent settlements, while others were nomadic, traveling great istances and living off the land.

English explorers John and Sebastian Cabot reached Nova Scotia in what is today Canada in 497; in 1534 the French gained a foothold with the explorations of Jacques Cartier. In 1541 the panish explorer Coronado traversed the south central portion of the country in what was to become e states of New Mexico, Texas, Nebraska and Oklahoma. In 1542 another Spaniard, Juan Cabrillo avigated north from Mexico along the Pacific coastline to California. The Spanish set up the first ermanent settlement of Europeans in North America at St. Augustine, Florida in 1565. In 1607 the nglish settled in Jamestown, Virginia, and in 1620 at Plymouth, Massachusetts. This was followed osely by Dutch settlements in Albany and New York in 1624, and in 1638 the Swedes arrived in elaware. From their foothold in Canada, French explorers pushed inland through the Great Lakes. ean Nicolet explored what was to become Wisconsin in 1634, and in 1673 explorers Marquette and oliet reached Iowa. In the 1650s the Dutch won the Swedish lands, and in 1664 the English gained ontrol of the Dutch lands, thus giving the English control all along the Atlantic Coast. The resulting irteen British colonies; New Hampshire, Vermont, Massachusetts, Rhode Island, Connecticut, New ork, Pennsylvania, Delaware, Maryland, Virginia, North Carolina, South Carolina and Georgia ormed the nucleus of what would become the United States of America.

From this point on tensions grew between the English, who could not expand westward from eir settlements along the Atlantic Coast, and the French who had settled inland into the Ohio river alley. This dispute ended in 1763 after a war with the French loosing control of lands east of the ississippi river. Manufacturing, textiles and other industry was developing at this time, and by 1775 bout one-seventh of the world's production of raw iron came from the colonies. From 1771-1783 the ar for American Independence was fought by the colonists against the English, and settled by the eace of Paris in 1783. Americans gained control of lands south of the St. Lawrence and Great akes, and east of the Mississippi, with the exception of Florida which would remain under Spanish ontrol until 1821. At the close of the war, the population was about 3 million, many of whom lived on elf-sufficient family farms. Fishing, lumbering and the production of grains for export were becoming ajor economic endeavors. The newly independent states formed a loose confederation, but in 1787 pproved the Constitution of the United States which is the framework for the goverment today. In 789 it's first president, George Washington was elected, and the capitol was set up in New York ity. In 1800 the capitol was moved to a planned city, Washington, D.C. where it remains.

Westward expansion was an inevitability as population grew. French territory west of the ississippi, stretching to the northern Pacific was purchased in 1804 under the presidency of homas Jefferson, who then sent out Lewis and Clark on expedition of discovery. Spain granted dependence to Mexico in 1821, which included lands which would become the states of alifornia, New Mexico, Arizona and Texas. From 1836-1845 Texas was an independent republic, ot joining the United States until 1845. Upon losing a war with the United States, Mexico ceded alifornia (including most of Arizonia and New Mexico) to the United States in 1848. Gold was scovered in California that year, and western migration took off on overland wagon trains or ound-the-horn sail and steam ships. Hawaii came under U.S. protection in 1851. As the country eveloped in the 19th century, the northern states increased in commerce and industry while the outhern states developed a vast agricultural through the use of slave labor. Northern political and ocial threats to slavery lead twelve southern states to secede from the Union in 1860 forming the onfederate States of America. The ensuing Civil War lasted until 1865, at which time slavery was olished and the States reunited.

In 1867 Alaska was purchased from Russia. The transcontinental railroad was completed in 869. The central region of the country west of the Mississippi River and east of the Rocky Mountains as the last to be developed, beginning after the Civil War, with the establishment of cattle ranches d farms. Between 1870 and 1891 the nomadic Native American population clashed with settlers d federal troops. By 1891 the Native Americans were confined to reservations.

At the close of the 19th century the United States embarked on a colonial mission of its own, th advances into Cuba, Puerto Rico, Panama, Nicaragua and the Philippines. This resulted in e Spanish-American War which was quickly decided, ending Spanish colonial dominance, and gnaling the rise of the United States as a world power. Slow to enter both World Wars of the 20th ntury, it was a major contributor to the conclusion of both, making it one of the major nations of e 20th century. As the Spanish Milled Dollar achieved widespread acceptance throughout the nerican colonial period, it was a natural choice on which to a national coinage system. The anish Milled Dollar had already been accorded legal tender status in several colonies, notably assachusetts, Connecticut and Virginia and the others used it. Each colony had its own shilling change for a Spanish Milled Dollar ranging from 6 to 32 1/2 shillings. When the Continental ongress issued its first paper money to finance the revolution, the notes themselves promised to y their face value in *Spanish milled dollars or the Value thereof in Gold or Silver.* The first quasi-icial American coinage, the 1776 Continental *Dollar,* while not thus denominated, was struck in e size of the Spanish Milled Dollar.

While the denomination of *One Dollar* may have been a natural choice for a national onetary system, the problem of making change for that dollar was not. In 1782, Robert Morris, perintendent of Finance, proposed a coinage system d on a unit of 1/1440th part of a dollar ich, he argued, would reconcile the different *official* values of the Spanish Milled Dollar in all the ates. A year later, he submitted a series of copper and silver pattern coinage to Congress d on e basic unit of a quarter-grain of silver. The patterns are known to collectors today as the Nova nstellatio coinage. Other leading financiers saw the traditional division of the Spanish Milled Dollar into *eight reales,* or *bits* as they were familiarly known, as too unwieldy. Gouverneur Morris, assistant financier of the government then operating under the Articles of Confederation, proposed the simple solution of a decimal coinage ratio. With the support of Thomas Jefferson, who remarked, "The most easy ratio of multiplication and division is that of ten," and George Washington, who called it, "indispensably necessary," the decimal coinage proposal won out over more complicated plans. The dollar-decimal system was adopted on July 6, 1785, creating a silver dollar, with fractional coins, also in silver, in denominations of half (50¢), quarter (25¢), tenth (10¢) and twentieth (5¢) parts of a dollar, and copper pieces in denominations of 1/100th (1¢) and 1/200th (1/2¢) of a dollar.

Continental Currency: A total of 11 separate issues of paper currency were authorized by the Continental Congress to finance the war for American independence. The first issue was dated May 10, 1775, the date of the first session of the Continental Congress; the final issue was by Resolution of Jan. 14, 1779. In all, according to early American currency expert Eric P. Newman, a total of $241,552,780 worth of Continental Currency was issued.

Backed only by faith in the success of the Revolution, there was according to a Resolution of Congress a 40-to-1 devaluation by 1780, and in the end the bills were only redeemable at 1/100th of face value in interest-bearing bonds.

MONETARY SYSTEM:

1 Dollar = 100 Cents

REPLACEMENT NOTES:

All issues since about 1916 have a star either before or after the serial number, depending on type of note.

All government notes of the United States, since issue of the Demand Notes of 1861, are still valid as legal tender. The different types of currency are treated in a number of specialized catalogs such as the following:

Friedberg, Robert; *Paper Money of the United States.*

Hickman, John and Oakes, Dean; *Standard Catalog of National Bank Notes.*

Krause, Chester L. and Lemke, Robert F.; *Standard Catalog of United States Paper Money.*

Detailed information, as given in these catalogs, is not repeated here. The following listing is limited to the individual types and their principal varieties.

REPUBLIC

TREASURY

ACT OF 30.6.1812

War of 1812

5 2/5% interest bearing notes.

		XF	AU
1	**100 Dollars** 1812. Eagle on branch at upper r.	8000.	17,250.
2	**1000 Dollars** 1812. Eagle on branch at upper l.	21,750.	—

ACT OF 25.2.1813

5 2/5% interest bearing notes.

		XF	AU
3	**100 Dollars** 1813.	—	—

ACT OF 4.3.1814

5 2/5% interest bearing notes.

		XF	AU
4	**20 Dollars** 1814.	—	—
5	**50 Dollars** 1814.	—	—

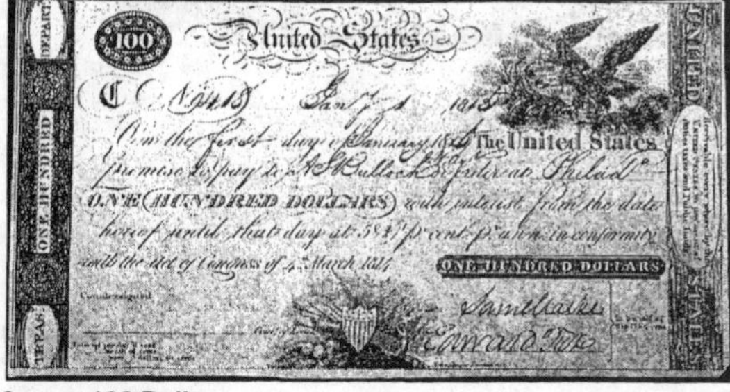

		XF	AU
6	**100 Dollars** 1814.	30,000.	—

ACT OF 26.12.1814

5 2/5% interest bearing notes.

		XF	AU
7	**20 Dollars** 1814. Eagle on shield at upper l. Printer: MDF. Rare.	12,650.	—

		XF	AU
8	**50 Dollars** 1814.	—	—
9	**100 Dollars** 1814. Eagle on branch at upper r. Printer: MDF. Rare.	22,450.	—

ACT OF 24.2.1815

Called "Small Treasury Notes". $3 to $50 notes without interest. $100 notes 5 2/5% interest bearing notes. This issue actually circulated as currency although not legal tender for all debts.

		XF	AU
10	**3 Dollars** 1815. U.S shield at upper ctr. Printer: MDF.	—	8250.
11	**5 Dollars** 1815. Eagle on branch at upper r. Printer: MDF.	—	3750.
12	**10 Dollars** 1815. Eagle on branch at upper l. Text in frame at r. Printer: MDF.	5000.	—
13	**10 Dollars** 1815. Similar to #12 but *TEN DOLLARS* in frame at r.	5250.	7000.
14	**20 Dollars** 1815. Eagle at upper l. Printer: MDF.	—	3750.
15	**50 Dollars** 1815. Eagle on branch at upper r. Printer: MDF.	—	3750.

		XF	AU
16	**100 Dollars** 1815. Eagle at upper r., shield at lower ctr. Printer: MDF.	8250.	—

ACT OF 12.10.1837

Panic of 1837

1 year notes issued at four different rates of interest - 1 mill, 2%, 5% or 6%, the rate written in ink at time of issue. The 1-mill rate, which was nominal, was used on notes intended to circulate as currency.

		XF	AU
17	**50 Dollars** 1837. Specimen.	8000.	—

		XF	AU
18	**100 Dollars** 1837. Specimen.	6100.	—
19	**500 Dollars** 1837. Specimen.	—	—
20	**1000 Dollars** 1837. Specimen.	—	—

ACT OF 21.5.1838

1 year notes at 6% interest.

		XF	AU
21	**50 Dollars** 1838.	—	—
22	**100 Dollars** 1838.	—	—
23	**500 Dollars** 1838.	—	—
24	**1000 Dollars** 1838.	—	—

ACT OF 2.3.1839

1 year notes at 2% or 6% interest.

		XF	AU
25	**50 Dollars** 1839.	—	—
26	**100 Dollars** 1839.	—	—
27	**500 Dollars** 1839.	—	—
28	**1000 Dollars** 1839.	—	—

ACT OF 31.3.1840

1 year notes at 2%, 5%, 5 2/5% or 6% interest, the rate being written in at time of issuance.

		XF	AU
29	**50 Dollars** 1840. Specimen.	—	—
30	**100 Dollars** 1840. Specimen.	—	—
31	**500 Dollars** 1840. Specimen.	—	—
32	**1000 Dollars** 1840. Specimen.	—	—
33	**10,000 Dollars** 1840. Specimen.	—	—

ACT OF 31.1.1842

1 year notes at 2% or 6% interest.

		XF	AU
34	**50 Dollars** 1842. Specimen.	—	—
35	**100 Dollars** 1842. Specimen.	—	—
36	**500 Dollars** 1842. Specimen.	—	—
37	**1000 Dollars** 1842. Specimen.	—	—

ACT OF 31.8.1842

1 year notes at 2% or 6% interest.

		XF	AU
38	**50 Dollars** 1842. Mercury at l., allegorical women at upper ctr., woman at r. Printer: RW&H. Specimen.	—	—
39	**100 Dollars** 1842. Specimen.	—	—
40	**500 Dollars** 1842. Specimen.	—	—
41	**1000 Dollars** 1842. Specimen.	—	—

ACT OF 3.3.1843

1 year notes at 1 mill or 4% interest.

		XF	AU
42	**50 Dollars** 1843. Woman at l., eagle at upper ctr., woman at r. Printer: RW&H.	—	—

Note: In 1887 there were only $83,425 outstanding in all Treasury Notes issued under acts prior to 1846.

ACT OF 22.7.1846

Mexican War

1 year notes at 1 mill or 5 2/5% interest.

		XF	AU
43	**50 Dollars** 1846. Specimen.	2500.	550
44	**100 Dollars** 1846. Specimen.	—	—
45	**500 Dollars** 1846. Specimen.	—	—
46	**1000 Dollars** 1846. Specimen.	—	—

.CT OF 28.1.1847

day or 1 or 2 year notes at 5 2/5% or 6% interest. Some notes were reissued.

		XF	AU
	50 Dollars 1847. Specimen.	4500.	8000.
	100 Dollars 1847. Specimen.	—	6000.
	500 Dollars 1847. Specimen.	—	5500.
	1000 Dollars 1847. Specimen.	—	8500.
	5000 Dollars 1847. Girl at l., eagle at upper ctr., woman at r. 2-year notes. Printer: RWH&E. Specimen.	—	—

		XF	AU
	5000 Dollars 1847. Allegorical woman w/sickle at l., eagle on branch and cameo of George Washington at upper ctr., Helmeted woman w/spear and shield at r. Printer: TCC. Specimen.	—	22,000.

:T OF 23.12.1857

ic of 1857

ear notes at 3 to 6% interest.

		XF	AU
	100 Dollars 1857. Printer: TCC.	—	5500.
	500 Dollars 1857.	—	—
	1000 Dollars 1857.	—	12,750.

ACT OF 17.12.1860

1 year notes at 6% to 12% interest.

		XF	AU
56	**50 Dollars** 1860.	—	—
57	**100 Dollars** 1860.	—	—
58	**500 Dollars** 1860.	—	—
59	**1000 Dollars** 1860.	—	21,000.

ACT OF 2.3.1861

1 or 2 year notes at 6% interest.

		XF	AU
60	**50 Dollars** 1861. Black and orange. Portr. Andrew Jackson at l., Liberty seated at ctr., portr. Daniel Webster at r. Back Blue. Printer: NBNC.	—	16,250.

		XF	AU
61	**100 Dollars** 1861. Black and orange. Seated Liberty at upper l., eagle at upper ctr. Back green.	—	30,000.
62	**500 Dollars** 1861. Black and green. Portr. George Washington at lower l., allegorical female at upper ctr., eagle at lower r. Back brown. 60-day note. Printers: ABNC and RWH&E. Specimen.	—	—

		XF	AU
63	**500 Dollars** 1861. Young man at lower l., portr. Gen. Winfield Scott at upper ctr., farmer at lower r. 2-year note.	—	25,000.
64	**1000 Dollars** 1861. Black and green. Portr. G. Washington at l., Liberty at ctr., Treasury bldg. at r. Back red-brown.	—	30,000.
65	**5000 Dollars** 1861.	—	—

FRACTIONAL CURRENCY

1862 (FIRST) ISSUE - POSTAGE CURRENCY

		FINE	XF	CU
97	**5 Cents** 17.7.1862. Brown. Facsimile 5 Cent stamp w/Jefferson at ctr. Perforated edges; ABNC monogram on back.	22.50	45.00	225.

		FINE	XF	CU
98	**10 Cents** 17.7.1862. Green. Facsimile 10 Cent stamp w/Washington at ctr. Perforated edges; ABNC monogram on back.	25.00	45.00	195.

		FINE	XF	CU
99	**25 Cents** 17.7.1862. Brown. 5 facsimile 5 Cent stamps w/Jefferson. Perforated edges; ABNC monogram on back.	30.00	75.00	325.

		FINE	XF	CU
100	**50 Cents** 17.7.1862. Green. 5 facsimile 10 Cent stamps w/Washington. 12 perforated edges; ABNC monogram on back.	55.00	100.	395.

1863 (SECOND) ISSUE - FRACTIONAL CURRENCY

Many varieties. Back w or w/o ovpt. *1863* and letters; paper w or w/o fibers.

#101-104 oval bronze ovpt. on face around Washington at ctr. and bronze numerals in outline on back.

		FINE	XF	CU
101	**5 Cents** 3.3.1863. W/o ovpt. on back.	17.50	30.00	85.00

		FINE	XF	CU
102	**10 Cents** 3.3.1863. W/o ovpt. on back.	20.00	35.00	85.00

		FINE	XF	CU
103	**25 Cents** 3.3.1863. W/o ovpt. on back.	20.00	75.00	150.

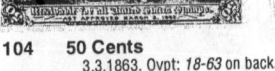

		FINE	XF	CU
104	**50 Cents** 3.3.1863. Ovpt: *18-63* on back.	35.00	75.00	325.

1863 (THIRD) ISSUE

		FINE	XF	CU
105	**3 Cents** 3.3.1863. Portr. Washington at ctr. Portr. w/lt. background.	35.00	50.00	95.00

		FINE	XF	CU
106	**5 Cents** 3.3.1863. Portr. Clark at ctr. Back red. W/o *a* on face.	22.50	75.00	200
107	**5 Cents** 3.3.1863. Like #106 but back green. W/o *a* on face.	20.00	45.00	100

		FINE	XF	CU
108	**10 Cents** 3.3.1863. Portr. Washington at ctr.; bronze *10* in each corner. Back red. Sm. sign: Colby-Spinner.	25.00	45.00	175

Note: Through an oversight, the word *CENTS* does not appear on #108.

		FINE	XF	CU
109	**25 Cents** 3.3.1863. Portr. Fessenden at ctr. Back red.	22.50	55.00	22

		FINE	XF	CU
110	**50 Cents** 3.3.1863. Portr. Spinner at ctr. Back red. Sm. sign: Colby-Spinner. Ovpt: *A-2-6-5* and multiple *50s* on back.	60.00	100.	3
111	**50 Cents** 3.3.1863. Like #110 but back green. Issued note.	60.00	110.	2
112	**50 Cents** 3.3.1863. Face like #111. Portr. Spinner. Redesigned green back. *50* at ctr. Issued note.	60.00	100.	3

		FINE	XF
113	**50 Cents** 3.3.1863. Allegorical figure of seated Justice holding scales at ctr. Back red. Sm. sign.	55.00	125.
114	**50 Cents** 3.3.1863. Face like #113. Back green. Issued note.	45.00	75.00

863 (FOURTH) ISSUE

any varieties of paper, of color and size of seal. Backs green.

		FINE	XF	CU
15	**10 Cents** 3.3.1863. Liberty at l. 40mm red seal. Wmk. paper w/pink silk fibres.	25.00	35.00	95.00

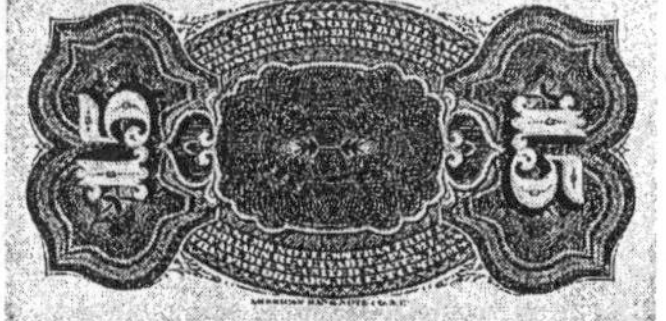

		FINE	XF	CU
16	**15 Cents** 3.3.1863. Columbia at l. 40mm red seal. Wmk. paper w/pink silk fibres.	75.00	95.00	150.

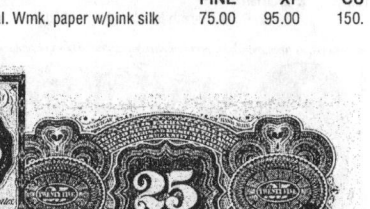

		FINE	XF	CU
18	**25 Cents** 3.3.1863. Portr. Washington at l. 40mm red seal. Wmk. paper w/pink silk fibres.	25.00	50.00	100.

		FINE	XF	CU
19	**50 Cents** 3.3.1863. Portr. Lincoln at r. Wmk. paper w/silk fibres.	100.	200.	450.

		FINE	XF	CU
20	**50 Cents** 3.3.1863. Portr. E.M. Stanton at l.	45.00	75.00	225.

		FINE	XF	CU
21	**50 Cents** 3.3.1863. Portr. Dexter at l.	35.00	55.00	125.

1874-75 (FIFTH) ISSUE

Paper varieties. Values are for most common types of each denomination.

		FINE	XF	CU
122	**10 Cents** 3.3.1863; 30.6.1864. Portr. W. Meredith at l. Green seal w/long key.	25.00	50.00	100.

		FINE	XF	CU
123	**25 Cents** 3.3.1863; 30.6.1864. Portr. R. Walker at l. Red seal w/long key.	20.00	25.00	50.00

		FINE	XF	CU
124	**50 Cents** 3.3.1863; 30.6.1864. Portr. Crawford at l.	25.00	50.00	100.

DEMAND NOTES

SERIES OF 1861

#125-127 w/o seal. Printer: ABNC.

		VG	FINE	VF
125	**5 Dollars** 10.8.1861. Statue of Columbia at l., Portr. Alexander Hamilton at r.			
	a. Payable at New York.	2000.	2750.	5800.
	b. Payable at Philadelphia.	2750.	3300.	11,750.
	c. Payable at Boston.	2300.	3000.	6400.
	d. Payable at Cincinnati. Rare.	—	—	—
	e. Payable at St. Louis.	—	—	—

126	10 Dollars	VG	FINE	VF
	10.8.1861. Portr. Abraham Lincoln at l., allegorical woman (Art) at r.			
	a. Payable at New York.	3400.	4750.	20,000.
	b. Payable at Philadelphia.	1775.	3750.	19,000.
	c. Payable at Boston.	3250.	7750.	22,000.
	d. Payable at Cincinnati.		Rare	
	e. Payable at St. Louis.		Rare	

127	20 Dollars	VG	VF	UNC
	10.8.1861. Liberty w/sword and shield at ctr.			
	a. Payable at New York.	8750.	—	—
	b. Payable at Philadelphia.	8750.	—	—
	c. Payable at Boston.	21,000.	—	—
	d. Payable at Cincinnati. Rare.	—	—	—

Note: Few Demand Notes of 1861 are known in better than VG condition.

UNITED STATES NOTES

LEGAL TENDER NOTES

1862 SERIES

128	1 Dollar	FINE	XF	CU
	1862. Portr. Salmon P. Chase at l.	500.	850.	2750.

129	2 Dollars	FINE	XF	CU
	1862. Portr. Alexander Hamilton at l. ctr.	800.	2000.	4750.

130	5 Dollars	FINE	XF	CU
	1862. Statue of Columbia at l.; Portr. Alexander Hamilton at r. Like #125 but w/o *On Demand* and w/seal.			
	a. First Obligation on back.	475.	1250.	3000.
	b. Second Obligation on back.	525.	1450.	3000.

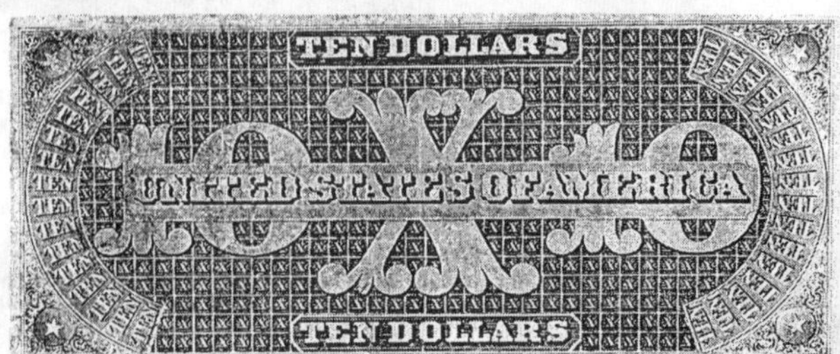

131	10 Dollars	FINE	XF	CU
	1862. Portr. Abraham Lincoln at l., allegorical woman (Art) at r. Like #126 but w/o *On Demand* and w/seal.			
	a. First Obligation on back.	1400.	2500.	9750.
	b. Second Obligation on back.	1300.	2850.	9750.

		FINE	XF	CU
132	**20 Dollars** 1862. Liberty w/sword and shield at ctr. Like #123 but w/o *On Demand* and w/seal.			
	a. First Obligation on back.	2250.	6750.	17,500.
	b. Second Obligation on back.	2250.	6750.	17,500.

		FINE	XF	CU
133	**50 Dollars** 1862. Portr. Alexander Hamilton at l. ctr.			
	a. First Obligation on back.	23,000.	58,000.	—
	b. Second Obligation on back.	12,500.	57,500.	—

		FINE	XF	CU
34	**100 Dollars** 1862. Heraldic eagle at l.			
	a. First Obligation on back.	30,000.	50,000.	75,000.
	b. Second Obligation on back.	—	—	75,000.

		VG	VF	UNC
35	**500 Dollars** 1862. Portr. Albert Gallatin at ctr.			
	a. First Obligation on back. Rare.	—	—	—
	b. Second Obligation on back. Rare.	—	—	—

		VG	VF	UNC
136	**1000 Dollars** 1862. Portr. Robert Morris at ctr.			
	a. First Obligation on back. Rare.	—	—	—
	b. Second Obligation on back. Rare.	—	—	—

1863 SERIES

		FINE	XF	CU
137	**5 Dollars** 1863. Like #130b.	575.	1500.	3000.
138	**10 Dollars** 1863. Like #131b.	1250.	3950.	9000.

		FINE	XF	CU
139	**20 Dollars** 1863. Like #132b.	2250.	6750.	11,500.
140	**50 Dollars** 1863. Like #133b.	12,500.	57,500.	—
141	**100 Dollars** 1863. Like #134b.	—	—	125,000.
142	**500 Dollars** 1863. Like #135b. Rare.	—	Rare	—
143	**1000 Dollars** 1863. Like #136b. Rare.	650,000.	—	—

1869 SERIES

		FINE	XF	CU
144	**1 Dollar** 1869. Columbus sighting land at l., Portr. George Washington at ctr. *1-ONE-DOLLAR* at ctr. on back.	500.	1500.	3000.

		FINE	XF	CU
145	**2 Dollars** 1869. Portr. Thomas Jefferson at upper l. Capitol at ctr. *2* at ctr. on back.	800.	2000.	5750.

		FINE	XF	CU
146	**5 Dollars** 1869. Portr. Andrew Jackson at lower l., pioneer family at ctr. *5* at ctr. on back.	600.	1200.	3900.

		FINE	XF	CU
147	**10 Dollars** 1869. Portr. Daniel Webster at lower l., presentation of Indian Princess at lower r. Text at ctr. on back.	750.	1500.	4400.

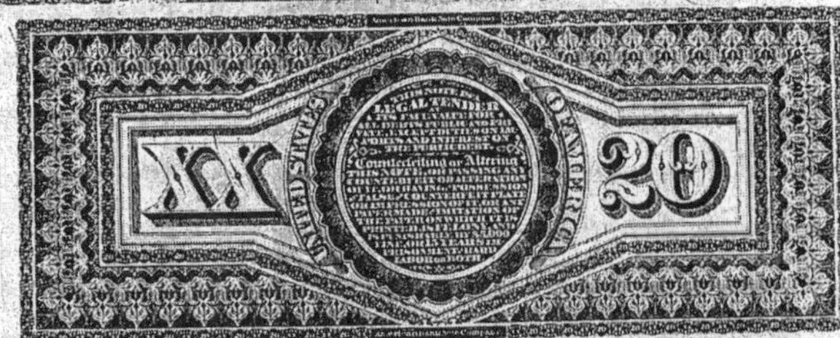

		FINE	XF	CU
148	**20 Dollars** 1869. Portr. Alexander Hamilton at l., Victory w/sword and shield at r. Text at ctr. on back.	2100.	5000.	20,000.

NOTICE

Readers with unlisted dates, signature varieties, etc. are invited to submit photocopies or, high resolution (300 dpi, 100% size) scans of their notes to: Standard Catalog of World Paper Money, 700 East State St. Iola, WI 54990-0001, or E-Mail: george.cuhaj@fwpubs.com.

		FINE	XF	CU
149	**50 Dollars** 1869. Woman holding statue of Mercury at l., portr. Henry Clay at lower r.	15,000.	65,000.	150,000.

		FINE	XF	CU
150	**100 Dollars** 1869. Portr. Abraham Lincoln at upper l., allegorical woman (Architecture) w/child at r. Text at ctr. on back.	10,000.	27,500.	—
151	**500 Dollars** 1869. Woman w/scales at l., Portr.John Quincy Adams at r. Rare.	—	—	—
152	**1000 Dollars** 1869. Portr. Columbus at l., portr. Clinton at ctr. Rare.	—	—	—

1874 SERIES

		FINE	XF	CU
153	**1 Dollar** 1874. Portr. Columbus sighting land at upper l., portr. George Washington at ctr. *UNITED STATES OF AMERICA* at ctr. on back.	250.	900.	190
154	**2 Dollars** 1874. Portr. Thomas Jefferson at l., Capitol at ctr. *2* at ctr. and *2*s in all corners on back.	550.	1450.	340

		VG	VF	UNC
155	**50 Dollars** 1874. Portr. Benjamin Franklin at upper l., Columbia at r.	15,000.	35,000.	82,500.
156	**500 Dollars** 1874. Woman standing at l., Portr. Maj. Gen. Joseph K. Mansfield at r. Rare.	—	—	—

1875 SERIES

No.	Denomination	FINE	XF	CU
157	**1 Dollar** 1875. Like #153. 2 sign. varieties.			
	a. W/o series.	265.	600.	1500.
	b. Series A.	1000.	2200.	1500.
	c. Series B.	1250.	2950.	1500.
	d. Series C.	1250.	2000.	1500.
	e. Series D.	1150.	4000.	1500.
	f. Series E.	1875.	7500.	1500.

No.	Denomination	FINE	XF	CU
158	**2 Dollars** 1875. Like #154. 2 sign. varieties.			
	a. W/o series.	500.	1000.	2250.
	b. Series A.	1000.	2400.	2250.
	c. Series B.	850.	2400.	2250.

No.	Denomination	FINE	XF	CU
159	**5 Dollars** 1875. Portr. Andrew Jackson at l., pioneer family at ctr. Ornamental design at ctr. on back. 2 sign. varieties.			
	a. W/o series.	600.	1325.	3350.
	b. Series A.	840.	1775.	3350.
	c. Series B.	350.	660.	3350.
160	**10 Dollars** 1875. Portr. Daniel Webster at l., presentation of Indian Princess at r. Ornamental design at ctr. w/text at r. on back.			
	a. W/o series.	20,000.	34,500.	—
	b. Series A.	2750.	7500.	—
161	**20 Dollars** 1875. Portr. Alexander Hamilton at upper l., Victory w/sword and shield at r. Ornamental design at ctr. w/text at l. on back.	1300.	2750.	5000.
162	**50 Dollars** 1875. Like #155. Rare.	—	Rare	—
163	**100 Dollars** 1875. Portr. Lincoln at l., woman w/child at r. Ornamental design at ctr. on back. 2 sign. varieties.	11,500.	30,000.	65,000.
164	**500 Dollars** 1875. Like #156. 2 sign. varieties. Rare.	—	Rare	—

1878 SERIES

No.	Denomination	FINE	XF	CU
165	**1 Dollar** 1878. Like #153.	225.	500.	1300.
166	**2 Dollars** 1878. Like #154. 2 sign. varieties.	400.	800.	1500.
167	**5 Dollars** 1878. Like #159.	350.	800.	2000.
		VG	VF	UNC
168	**10 Dollars** 1878. Like #160.	1000.	—	6500.

No.	Denomination	FINE	XF	CU
169	**20 Dollars** 1878. Like #161.	1100.	2500.	3750.
170	**50 Dollars** 1878. Like #155.	5000.	15,000.	42,500.
171	**100 Dollars** 1878. Like #163.	10,000.	27,500.	—

No.	Denomination	FINE	XF	CU
172	**500 Dollars** 1878. Like #156. Rare.	—	Rare	—
173	**1000 Dollars** 1878. Portr. Columbus at l., portr. Dewitt Clinton at ctr. Text at l. on back. Rare.	—	Rare	—
174	**5000 Dollars** 1878. Portr. James Madison at l. (All notes have been redeemed).	—	—	—
175	**10,000 Dollars** 1878. Portr. Andrew Jackson at l. (All notes have been redeemed).	—	—	—

1880 SERIES

176	1 Dollar	FINE	XF	CU
	1880. Like #153.			
	a. Seal at r.; red serial #; 3 sign. varieties.	200.	400.	1200.
	b. Red or brown seal at r.; blue serial #; 2 sign. varieties.	600.	1900.	1200.
	c. Seal at l.; blue serial #; 2 sign. varieties.	200.	400.	1200.

177	2 Dollars	FINE	XF	CU
	1880. Like #154.			
	a. Red serial #; 3 sign. varieties.	250.	600.	1450.
	b. Blue serial #; sm. or lg. red or brown seal; 3 sign. varieties.	350.	750.	1450.

178	5 Dollars	FINE	XF	CU
	1880. Like #159.			
	a. Red serial #. 3 sign. varieties.	450.	875.	1900.
	b. Blue serial #. 4 varieties of seals; 8 sign. varieties.	550.	1450.	1900.

179	10 Dollars	FINE	XF	CU
	1880. Like #160.			
	a. Red serial #. 3 sign. varieties.	550.	1300.	2900.
	b. Blue serial #. 4 varieties of seals; 8 sign. varieties.	550.	1400.	2900.

180	20 Dollars	FINE	XF	CU
	1880. Like #161.			
	a. Blue serial #. 4 varieties of seals; 12 sign. varieties.	2000.	4750.	9500.
	b. Red serial #. 2 sign. varieties.	565.	1250.	9500.

181	50 Dollars	FINE	XF	CU
	1880. Like #155. 4 varieties of seals; 8 sign. varieties.	4500.	9000.	22,500.

		FINE	XF	CU
182	**100 Dollars** 1880. Like #163. 4 varieties of seals; 9 sign. varieties.	9000.	30,000.	75,000.
183	**500 Dollars** 1880. Like #156. 4 varieties of seals; 10 sign. varieties. Rare.	—	Rare	—
184	**1000 Dollars** 1880. Like #173. 4 varieties of seals; 11 sign. varieties. Rare.	—	Rare	—

1901 SERIES

		FINE	XF	CU
185	**10 Dollars** 1901. Portr. Meriweather Lewis at l., bison at ctr., portr. William Clark at r. 9 sign. varieties.	900.	2900.	4750.

1907 SERIES

		FINE	XF	CU
186	**5 Dollars** 1907. Like #159. 10 sign. varieties.	200.	350.	800.

1917 SERIES

		FINE	XF	CU
87	**1 Dollar** 1917. Like #153.	110.	225.	450.

		FINE	XF	CU
88	**2 Dollars** 1917. Like #154. 4 sign. varieties.	190.	325.	500.

1923 SERIES

		FINE	XF	CU
189	**1 Dollar** 1923. Portr. George Washington at ctr.	135.	240.	775.

		FINE	XF	CU
190	**10 Dollars** 1923. Portr. Andrew Jackson at ctr.	1200.	3500.	9000.

GOLD CERTIFICATES

SERIES OF 1863

NOTE: Certain notes with listings incorporated in previous editions, encompassing various names of the actual bank of issue with national banks and national gold banks #191-244, 390-394A have been deleted from this section. The highly specialized *Standard Catalog of National Bank Notes* 1249 pages ©1990 released by Krause Publications is considered to be the ultimate reference for this colorful and rather extensive series of the chartered banks.

		FINE	XF	CU
245	**20 Dollars** 3.3.1863. Eagle w/shield at l. Rare.	—	Rare	—

		FINE	XF	CU
246	**100 Dollars** 3.3.1863. Eagle w/shield at l. Rare.	—	Rare	—
247	**100 Dollars** 3.3.1863. Portr. Thomas H. Benton. Countersigned and dated or 1872 or 1872 by hand. Rare.	—	Rare	—
248	**500 Dollars** 3.3.1863. Eagle w/shield at l. Rare.	—	Rare	—
249	**500 Dollars** 3.3.1863. Portr. Lincoln. Countersigned and dated 1870 or 1872 by hand. Rare.	—	Rare	—
250	**1000 Dollars** 3.3.1863. Eagle w/shield at l. Rare.	—	Rare	—
251	**1000 Dollars** 3.3.1863. Portr. Alexander Hamilton. Countersigned and dated 1870 or 1872 by hand. Rare.	—	Rare	—
252	**5000 Dollars** 3.3.1863. Eagle w/shield at l. Rare.	—	Rare	—
253	**5000 Dollars** 3.3.1863. Portr. James Madison. Countersigned and dated 1870 or 1871 by hand. Rare.	—	Rare	—
254	**10,000 Dollars** 3.3.1863. Eagle w/shield at l. Rare.	—	Rare	—
255	**10,000 Dollars** 3.3.1863. Portr. Andrew Jackson. Countersigned and dated 1870 or 1871 by hand. Rare.	—	Rare	—

SERIES OF 1875

		VG	VF	UNC
256	**100 Dollars** 1875. Portr. Thomas H. Benton at l. Rare.	—	Rare	—
257	**500 Dollars** 1875. Portr. Abraham Lincoln.	—	Rare	—
258	**1000 Dollars** 1875. Portr. Alexander Hamilton. Rare.	—	Rare	—

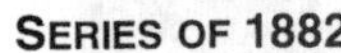

SERIES OF 1882

		FINE	XF	CU
259	**20 Dollars** 1882. Portr. James A. Garfield at r.			
	a. Countersigned sign.	3500.	8500.	14,750.
	b. W/o countersigned sign. 3 seal varieties; 4 sign. varieties.	700.	2250.	14,750.

		FINE	XF	CU
260	**50 Dollars** 1882. Portr. Silas Wright at l.			
	a. Countersigned sign.	20,000.	39,000.	—
	b. W/o countersigned sign. 4 seal varieties; 9 sign. varieties.	1750.	5000.	—

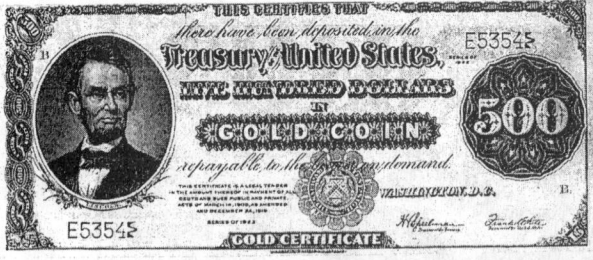

		FINE	XF	CU
261	**100 Dollars** 1882. Portr. Thomas H. Benton at l. (different than #256).			
	a. Countersigned sign.	—	Rare	—
	b. W/o countersigned sign. 4 seal varieties; 14 sign. varieties.	1150.	8000.	—

		FINE	XF	CU
262	**500 Dollars** 1882. Portr. Abraham Lincoln at l.	20,000.	—	—

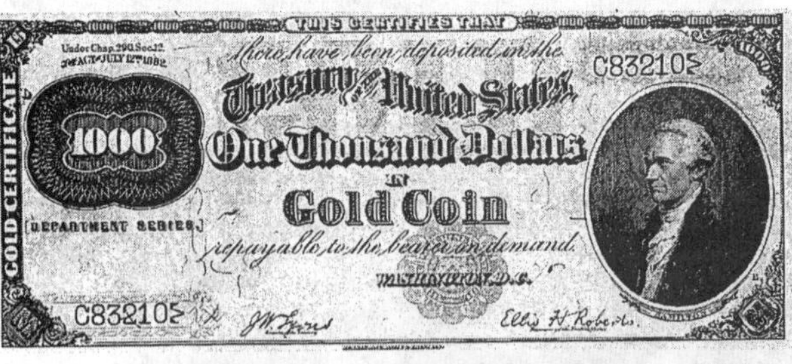

		FINE	XF	CU
263	**1000 Dollars** 1882. Portr. Alexander Hamilton at r.	97,750.	230,000.	—
		VG	VF	UNC
264	**5000 Dollars** 1882. Portr. James Madison at l. Rare.	—	—	—
265	**10,000 Dollars** 1882. Portr. Andrew Jackson at l. Rare.	—	—	—

SERIES OF 1888

		VG	VF	UNC
266	**5000 Dollars** 1888. Like #264. Rare.	—	—	—
267	**10,000 Dollars** 1888. Like #265. Rare.	—	—	—

SERIES OF 1900

		FINE	XF	CU
268	**10,000 Dollars** 28.9.1916; 22.11.1916; 6.1.1917; 9.5.1917. Like #265. Uniface.			
	a. Issued note. Rare.	—	Rare	—
	b. Redeemed w/cancelling perforations.	1750.	3750.	—

Note: During a fire at a treasury storage area in 1935 a number of cancelled examples of #268 were thrown into the street and picked up by passers-by.

SERIES OF 1905

		FINE	XF	CU
269	**20 Dollars** 1905. Portr. George Washington at ctr. Red seal. 2 sign. varieties.	1250.	6000.	9000.

SERIES OF 1906

		FINE	XF	CU
270	**20 Dollars** 1906. Like #269 but gold seal. 6 sign. varieties.	300.	600.	1750.

SERIES OF 1907

		FINE	XF	CU
271	**10 Dollars** 1907. Portr. Michael Hillegas at ctr. 6 sign. varieties.	250.	575.	1900.

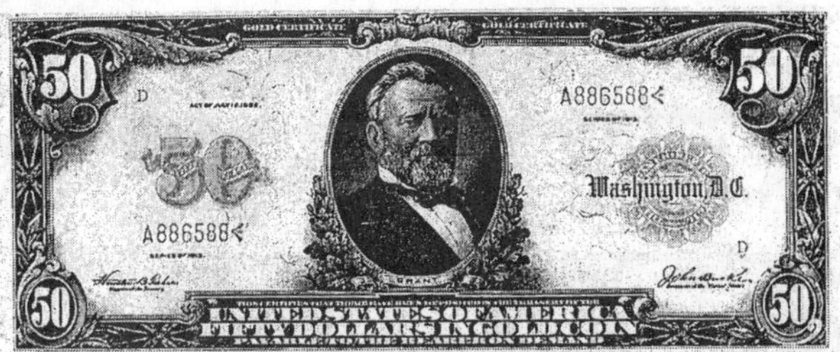

		FINE	XF	CU
272	**1000 Dollars** 1907. Portr. Alexander Hamilton at ctr.	—	—	—

SERIES OF 1913

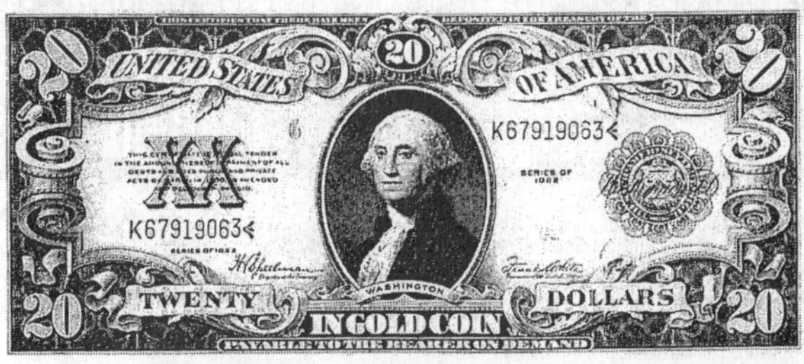

		FINE	XF	CU
273	**50 Dollars** 1913. Portr. Ulysses S. Grant at ctr. 2 sign. varieties.	600.	2500.	7500.

SERIES OF 1922

		VG	VF	UNC
274	**10 Dollars** 1922. Like #271.	250.	—	1800.

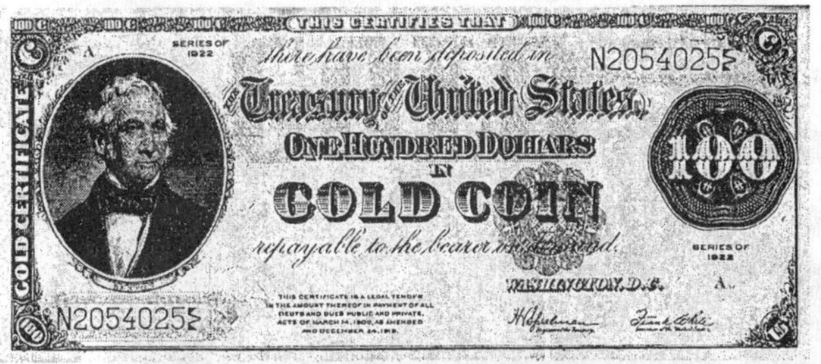

		VG	VF	UNC
275	**20 Dollars** 1922. Like #269.	300.	—	1750.
276	**50 Dollars** 1922. Like #273.	700.	—	7500.

		VG	VF	UNC
277	**100 Dollars** 1922. Like #261.	—	—	—
278	**500 Dollars** 1922. Like #262.	—	—	—
279	**1000 Dollars** 1922. Like #272.	—	—	—

INTEREST BEARING NOTES

ACT OF 17.3.1861

		VG	VF	UNC
280	**50 Dollars** 1861. Eagle at ctr. (7-3/10% interest for 3 years. 5 coupons).	—	—	—

		VG	VF	UNC
281	**100 Dollars** 1861. Portr. Gen. Winfield Scott at ctr. (7-3/10% interest for 3 years. 5 coupons). Unknown in private hands.	—	—	—
282	**500 Dollars** 1861. Portr. George Washington. (7-3/10% interest for 3 years. 5 coupons). Unknown in private hands.	—	—	—

		VG	VF	UNC
283	**1000 Dollars** 1861. Portr. Salmon P. Chase at ctr. (7-3/10% interest for 3 years. 5 coupons). Unknown in private hands.	—	—	—
284	**5000 Dollars** 1861. Justice w/sword and scales at l., Indian woman w/shield and eagle at ctr. (7-3/10% interest for 3 years. 5 coupons). Unknown in private hands.	—	—	—

ACT OF 3.3.1863

		Good	Fine	XF
285	**10 Dollars** 15.3.1864. Portr. Salmon P. Chase at lower l., eagle at ctr., allegorical woman at r. (5% interest for 1 year).	3000.	8000.	19,000.

		Good	Fine	XF
286	**20 Dollars** 5.4.1864. Liberty at l., mortar at bottom ctr., portr. Abraham Lincoln at r. (5% interest for 1 year).	4000.	15,000.	45,000.

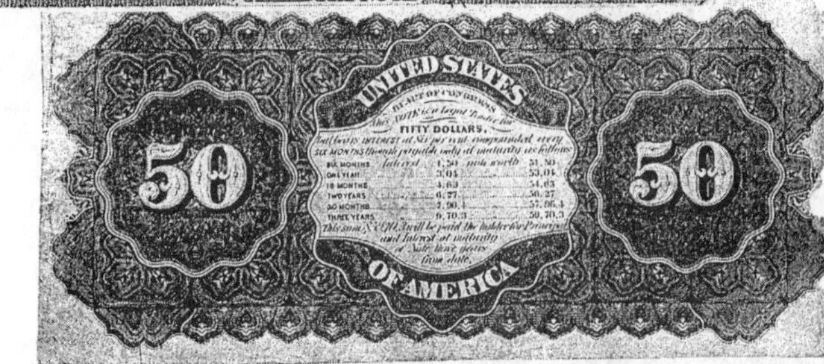

		Good	Fine	XF
287	**50 Dollars** 1863. Allegorical woman at l., portr. Alexander Hamilton at lower r. (5% interest for 1 year).	7500.	2200.	92,000.
288	**50 Dollars** 1863. Justice seated with scales and shield at ctr., allegorical woman at lower l. and r. (5% interest for 2 years).	12,500.	30,000.	65,000.

		VG	VF	UNC
289	**100 Dollars** 1864. Portr. George Washington holding scroll at ctr. (5% interest for 1 year).	—	—	—

		Good	Fine	XF
290	**100 Dollars** 14.4.1864. 2 allegorical men (Science and Industry) seated at l., bldg. at upper ctr., coastal battery at lower r. (5% interest for 2 years).	20,000.	45,000.	97,750.

		VG	VF	UNC
291	**500 Dollars** 1864. Ship "New Ironsides". (5% interest for 1 year). Unknown in private hands.	—	—	—
292	**500 Dollars** 1864. Liberty and eagle. (5% interest for 2 years). Unknown in private hands.	—	—	—
293	**1000 Dollars** 1864. Liberty and Justice. (5% interest for 1 year). Unknown in private hands.	—	—	—

		VG	VF	UNC
294	**1000 Dollars** 1864. Ships "Guerriere" and "Constitution". (5% interest for 2 years). Unknown in private hands.	—	—	—
295	**5000 Dollars** 1864. Allegorical woman. (5% interest for 1 year). Unknown in private hands.	—	—	—

ACT OF 30.6.1864

		Good	Fine	XF
296	**50 Dollars** 1864. Eagle at ctr. (7-3/10% interest for 3 years. 5 coupons).	25,000.	30,000.	65,000.

ACT OF 3.3.1865

		Good	Fine	XF
297	**50 Dollars** 15.7.1865. Eagle l. looking r. at ctr. (7-3/10% interest for 3 years. 5 coupons).	15,000.	42,000.	80,000.

298	**100 Dollars** 1865. Portr. Gen. Winfield Scott at ctr.(7-3/10% interest for 3 years. 5 coupons).	—	—	210,000.
		VG	**VF**	**UNC**
299	**500 Dollars** 1865. (7-3/10% interest for 3 years. 5 coupons). Unknown in private hands.	—	—	—
300	**1000 Dollars** 1865. Justice sitting w/scales and shield at ctr. (7-3/10% interest for 3 years. 5 coupons). Unknown in private hands.	—	—	—

COMPOUND INTEREST TREASURY NOTES

ACT OF 3.3.1863 / 30.6.1864

#301-306 ovpt: ***COMPOUND INTEREST TREASURY NOTE.***

		Good	Fine	XF
301	**10 Dollars** 10.6.1864-15.12.1864. Like #285.	300.	600.	12,500.

		Good	Fine	XF
302	**20 Dollars** 14.7.1864-16.10.1865. Like #286.	5000.	7750.	25,000.

		Good	Fine	XF
303	**50 Dollars** 10.6.1864-1.9.1865. Like #287.	16,000.	30,000.	60,000.

304	**100 Dollars** 10.6.1864-1.9.1865. Like #289. Rare.	17,500.	34,000.	—
		VG	**VF**	**UNC**
305	**500 Dollars** 10.6.1864-1.10.1865. Like #291. Unknown in private hands.	—	—	—
306	**1000 Dollars** 15.7.1864-15.9.1865. Like #293. Unknown in private hands.	—	—	—

REFUNDING CERTIFICATES

ACT OF 26.2.1879

		VG	VF	UNC
307	**10 Dollars** 1.4.1879. Portr. benjamin Franklin at upper l. *Payable to order* (4% interest).	—	—	—
308	**10 Dollars** 1.4.1879. Like #307 but *Payable to bearer* (4% interest).	1400.	2250.	5000.

Silver Certificates

1878 Series

		FINE	XF	CU
309	**10 Dollars** 1878. Portr. Robert Morris at l. Rare.	—	13,000.	16,000.

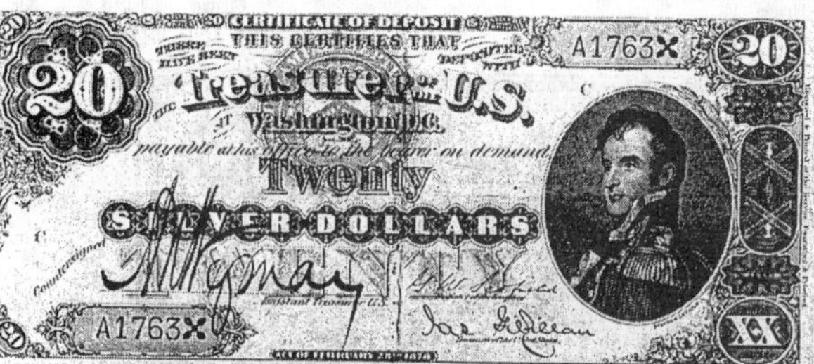

		VG	VF	UNC
310	**20 Dollars** 1878. Portr. Stephen Decatur at r. Rare.	18,000.	—	—

		VG	VF	UNC
311	**50 Dollars** 1878. *50* at upper l., vertical *Fifty* below it. Portr. Edward Everett at r. Rare.	20,000.	—	—

		VG	VF	UNC
312	**100 Dollars** 1878. Portr. James Monroe at l., *100* at lower r. Rare.	—	—	—
313	**500 Dollars** 1878. Portr. Charles Sumner at r. Rare.	—	—	—
314	**1000 Dollars** 1878. Portr. William L. Marcy at l. Rare.	—	—	—

1880 Series

		FINE	XF	CU
315	**10 Dollars** 1880. Portr. Robert Morris at l.			
	a. Countersigned sign.	5000.	10,000.	23,000.
	b. W/o countersigned sign. 2 seal varieties; 3 sign. varieties.	1750.	5250.	23,000.

Note: 1878 and 1880 countersigned notes are normally available only in circulated grades.

		FINE	XF	CU
316	**20 Dollars** 1880. Portr. Stephen Decatur at r.			
	a. Countersigned sign.	3500.	7500.	20,000.
	b. W/o countersigned sign. 2 seal varieties; 3 sign. varieties.	3750.	16,500.	20,000.

Note: 1878 and 1880 countersigned notes are normally available only in circulated grades.

		FINE	XF	CU
317	**50 Dollars** 1880. Like #311 but w/o countersigned sign. 3 seal varieties; 5 sign. varieties.	20,000.	55,000.	—

		FINE	XF	CU
318	**100 Dollars** 1880. Like #312. 3 seal varieties; 3 sign. varieties.	16,000.	45,000.	—

		FINE	XF	CU
319	**500 Dollars** 1880. Portr. Charles Sumner at r. 3 sign. varieties. Rare.	100,000.	300,000.	420,000.
320	**1000 Dollars** 1880. Portr. William L. Marcy at l. 3 sign. varieties. Rare.	250,000.	580,000.	—

1886 SERIES

		FINE	XF	CU
321	**1 Dollar** 1886. Portr. Martha Washington at l. 4 seal varieties; 4 sign. varieties.	300.	875.	2200.

		FINE	XF	CU
322	**2 Dollars** 1886. Portr. Gen. Winfield Scott Hancock at l. 2 seal varieties; 3 sign. varieties.	675.	2000.	4000.

		FINE	XF	CU
323	**5 Dollars** 1886. Portr. Ulysses S. Grant at r. Illustration of 5 silver dollars on back. 4 seal varieties; 4 sign. varieties.	1000.	4500.	7500.

		FINE	XF	CU
324	**10 Dollars** 1886. Portr. Thomas A. Hendricks at ctr. *UNITED STATES* w/text below at ctr. on back. 3 seal varieties; 4 sign. varieties.	1250.	4500.	9000.

		FINE	XF	CU
325	**20 Dollars** 1886. Portr. Daniel Manning at ctr. *20* in 4 corners on back. 3 seal varieties; 3 sign. varieties.	4000.	10,000.	35,000.

1891 SERIES

		FINE	XF	CU
326	**1 Dollar** 1891. Like #321 but different back. 2 sign. varieties.	375.	775.	2200.

		FINE	XF	CU
327	**2 Dollars** 1891. Portr. William Windom at ctr. 2 sign. varieties.	575.	2000.	4700.

		FINE	XF	CU
328	**5 Dollars** 1891. Portr. Ulysses S. Grant at r. Like #323 but w/o illustration on back. 2 sign. varieties.	750.	2000.	5000.

		FINE	XF	CU
329	**10 Dollars** 1891. Portr. Thomas A. Hendricks at ctr. *UNITED STATES* at ctr. on back. Red seal. 4 sign. varieties.	750.	1500.	4250.

		FINE	XF	CU
330	**20 Dollars** 1891. Portr. Daniel Manning at ctr. Different back w/ *XX* at upper l. and lower r. Red seal. 4 sign. varieties.	1500.	3750.	8000.
331	**20 Dollars** 1891. Like #330 but blue seal and lg. blue *XX* at l. 2 sign. varieties.	1500.	3750.	8000.

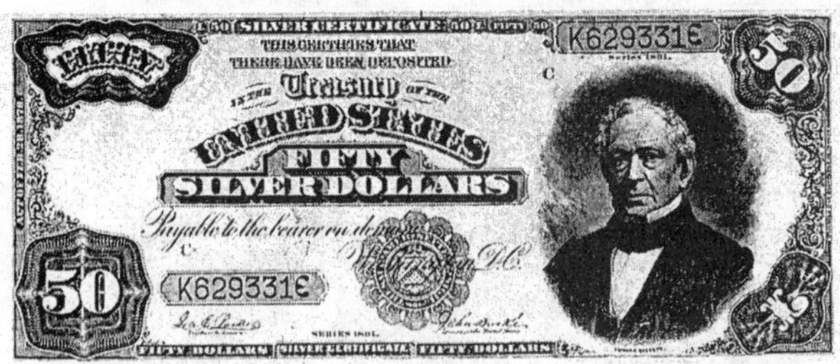

		FINE	XF	CU
332	**50 Dollars** 1891. Like #311 but *FIFTY* at upper l. Red seal.	4500.	6000.	14,000.
332A	**50 Dollars** 1891. Like #332 but blue seal.	2500.	3750.	11,000.

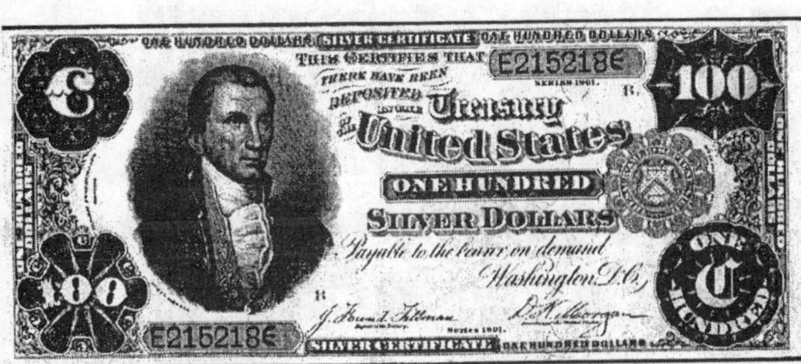

		FINE	XF	CU
333	**100 Dollars** 1891. Portr. James Monroe at l. ctr., *ONE HUNDRED* around *C* at lower r. 2 sign. varieties.	8000.	30,000.	—

		FINE	XF	CU
334	**1000 Dollars** 1891. Woman w/shield and sword at l., portr. William L. Marcy at r. Rare.	—	Rare	—

1896 SERIES

Educational Series

		FINE	XF	CU
335	**1 Dollar** 1896. "History instructing youth" at l. Border design w/names of famous Americans in wreaths. Portr. Martha and George Washington on back. 2 sign. varieties.	400.	1500.	3750.

		FINE	XF	CU
336	**2 Dollars** 1896. "Science presenting Steam and Electricity to Commerce and Manufacture." Portr. Robert Fulton and Samuel Morse on back. 2 sign. varieties.	850.	3000.	5500.

		FINE	XF	CU
337	**5 Dollars** 1896. Allegorical figures "America" at ctr. Portr. Ulysses S. Grant and Gen. Philip H. Sheridan on back. 3 sign. varieties.	1200.	4500.	9500.

1899 SERIES

		FINE	XF	CU
338	**1 Dollar** 1899. Eagle w/flag over portr. of Abraham Lincoln at l. and portr. of Ulysses S. Grant at ctr. r.			
	a. *Series of 1899* above r. serial #.	150.	350.	750.
	b. *Series of 1899* below r. serial #. 3 sign. varieties.	150.	350.	750.
	c. *Series of 1899* vertical at r. 7 sign. varieties.	110.	275.	750.

NOTICE

Readers with unlisted dates, signature varieties, etc. are invited to submit photocopies or, high resolution (300 dpi, 100% size) scans of their notes to: Standard Catalog of World Paper Money, 700 East State St. Iola, WI 54990-0001, or E-Mail: george.cuhaj@fwpubs.com.

		FINE	XF	CU
339	**2 Dollars** 1899. Portr. George Washington between allegorical figures of Commerce and Agriculture at ctr. 10 sign. varieties.	275.	550.	1500.

		FINE	XF	CU
340	**5 Dollars** 1899. Portr. Tatoka-Inyanka of the Hunkpapa Sioux w/feather headdress at ctr. 11 sign. varieties.	650.	1700.	3750.

1908 SERIES

		FINE	XF	CU
341	**10 Dollars** 1908. Like #329 but blue seal. Lg. blue *X* at l. 3 sign. varieties.	800.	1850.	5250.

1923 SERIES

		FINE	XF	CU
342	**1 Dollar** 1923. Portr. George Washington at ctr. 3 sign. varieties.	50.00	90.00	150.

		FINE	XF	CU
343	**5 Dollars** 1923. Portr. Abraham Lincoln at ctr. in circle.	900.	2750.	4500.

TREASURY OR COIN NOTES

SERIES OF 1890

		FINE	XF	CU
344	**1 Dollar** 1890. Portr. Edwin M. Stanton at upper l. ctr. Lg. *ONE* at ctr. on back. 2 seal varieties; 2 sign. varieties.	675.	3500.	9000.

		FINE	XF	CU
345	**2 Dollars** 1890. Portr. Gen. James B. McPherson at r. Lg. *TWO* at ctr. on back. 2 seal varieties; 2 sign. varieties.	1100.	4250.	12,500.

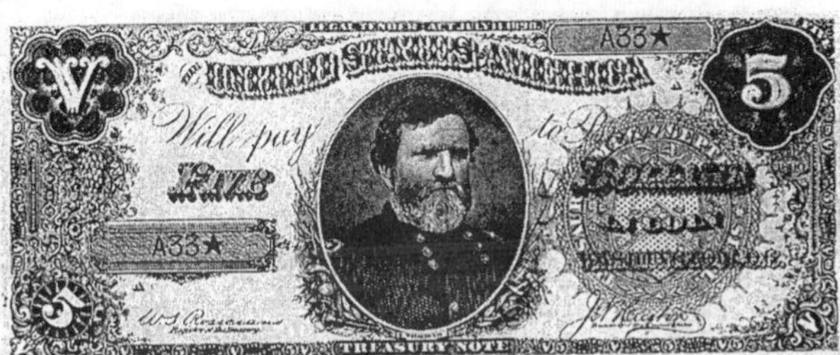

346 **5 Dollars**
1890. Portr. Gen. George H. Thomas at ctr. Lg. *FIVE* at ctr. on back. 2 varieties of seals; 2 sign. varieties.

FINE	XF	CU
750.	2250.	5000.

347 **10 Dollars**
1890. Portr. Gen. Philip Sheridan at ctr. Lg. *TEN* at ctr. on back. 2 seal varieties; 2 sign. varieties.

Fine	XF	CU
1200.	4500.	7750.

348 **20 Dollars**
1890. Portr. John Marshall at l. Lg. *TWENTY* at ctr. on back. 2 seal varieties; 2 sign. varieties.

FINE	XF	CU
4000.	8000.	17,500.

349 **100 Dollars**
1890. Portr. Commodore David G. Farragut at r. Lg. *100* at ctr. on back.

FINE	XF	CU
60,000.	18,000.	356,000.

350 **1000 Dollars**
1890. Portr. Gen. George G. Meade at l. Lg. *1000* at ctr. on back. 2 seal varieties; 2 sign. varieties. Rare.

FINE	XF	CU
—	1,095,000.	—

SERIES OF 1891

351 **1 Dollar**
1891. Portr. Edwin M. Stanton at l. Text at ctr. below sm. *ONE* on back. 3 sign. varieties.

FINE	XF	CU
350.	375.	1400.

		FINE	XF	CU
352	**2 Dollars** 1891. Portr. Gen. James B. McPherson at r. Ornament at ctr. on back. 3 sign. varieties.	525.	1600.	2900.

		FINE	XF	CU
353	**5 Dollars** 1891. Portr. Gen. George Thomas at ctr. Ornament w/*Five Dollars* inside at ctr. on back. 4 sign. varieties.	550.	1250.	3250.

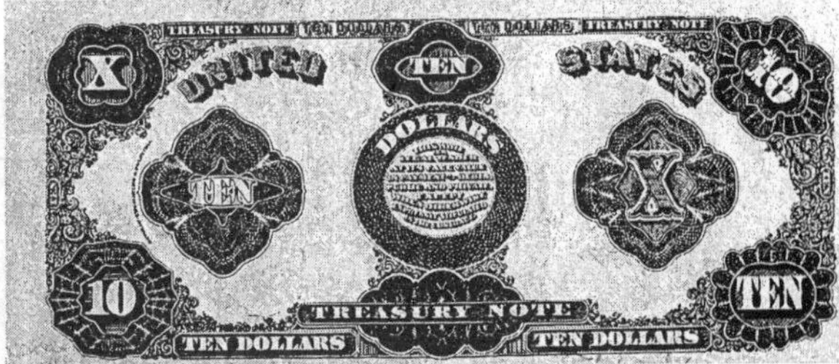

		FINE	XF	CU
354	**10 Dollars** 1891. Portr. Gen. Philip Sheridan at ctr. Text at ctr. on back. 3 sign. varieties.	900.	2000.	45,000.

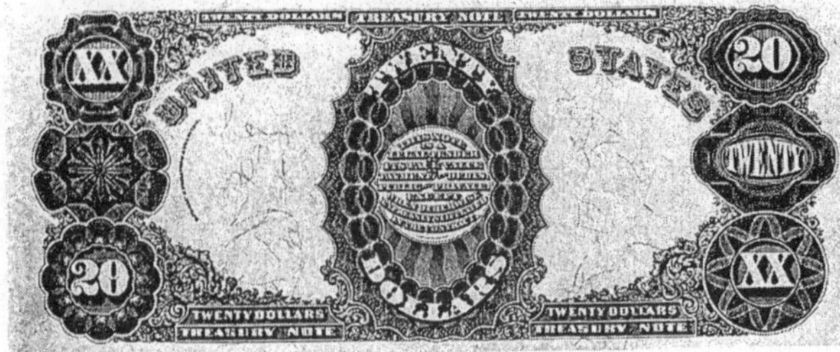

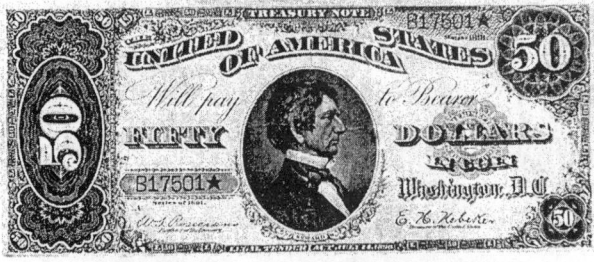

		FINE	XF	CU
355	**20 Dollars** 1891. Portr. John Marshall at l. Text at ctr. on back. 2 sign. varieties.	4750.	8000.	15,000

		FINE	XF	CU
356	**50 Dollars** 1891. Portr. William H. Seward at ctr.	50,000.	125,000.	300,000

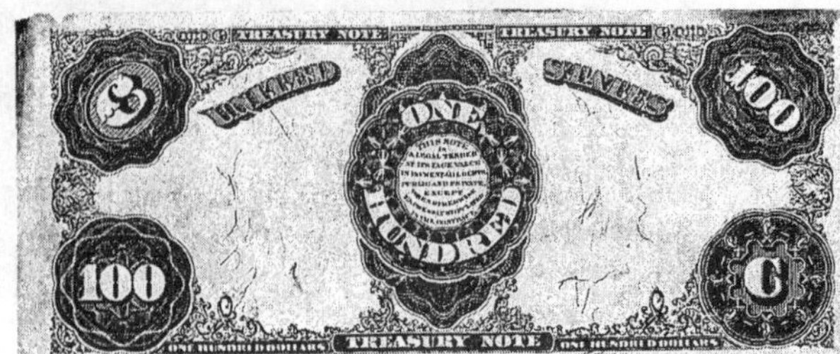

		FINE	XF	CU
357	**100 Dollars** 1891. Portr. Commodore David G. Farragut at r. Text at ctr. on back.	60,000.	140,000.	—
358	**1000 Dollars** 1891. Portr. Gen. George G. Meade at l. Text at ctr. on back. 2 sign. varieties. Rare.	—	Rare	—

FEDERAL RESERVE NOTES

1914 SERIES

		FINE	XF	CU
359	5 Dollars			
	1914. Portr. Abraham Lincoln at ctr.			
	a. Red seal.	525.	1100.	2275.
	b. Blue seal. 4 sign. varieties.	85.00	165.	2275.

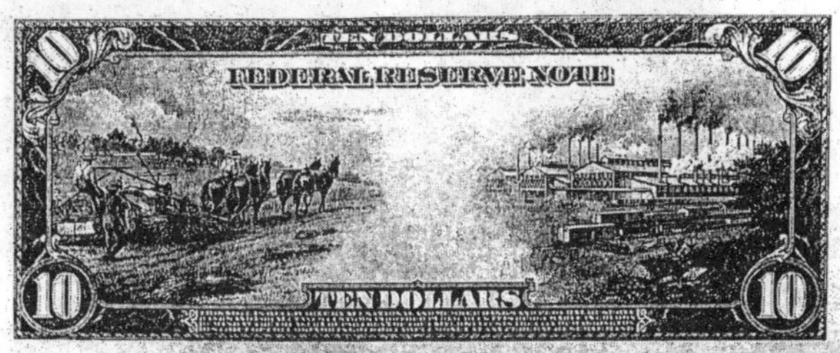

		FINE	XF	CU
360	10 Dollars			
	1914. Portr. Andrew Jackson at ctr.			
	a. Red seal.	750.	1500.	4000.
	b. Blue seal. 4 sign. varieties.	100.	225.	4000.

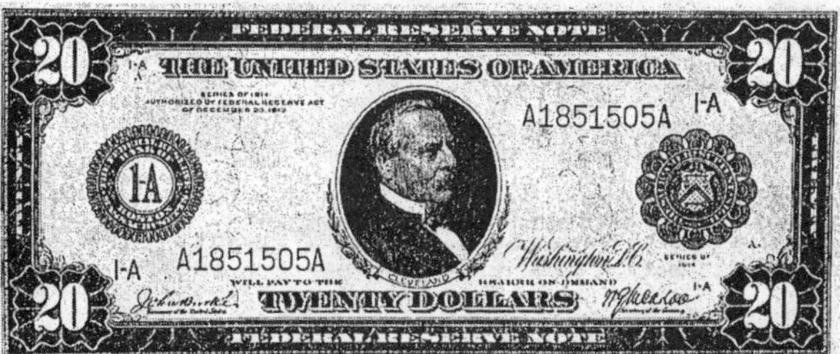

		FINE	XF	CU
361	20 Dollars			
	1914. Portr. Grover Cleveland at ctr.			
	a. Red seal.	725.	4400.	6800.
	b. Blue seal. 4 sign. varieties.	225.	400.	6800.

		FINE	XF	CU
362	50 Dollars			
	1914. Portr. Ulysses S. Grant at ctr.			
	a. Red seal.	2750.	4500.	9000.
	b. Blue seal. 4 sign. varieties.	450.	900.	9000.

		FINE	XF	CU
363	100 Dollars			
	1914. Portr. Benjamin Franklin at ctr.			
	a. Red seal.	1750.	3750.	9000.
	b. Blue seal. 4 sign. varieties.	650.	1000.	9000.

1918 SERIES

		FINE	XF	CU
364	500 Dollars			
	1918. Portr. John Marshall at ctr.	10,000.	22,500.	49,000.

		FINE	XF	CU
365	**1000 Dollars** 1918. Portr. Alexander Hamilton at ctr.	14,000.	20,000.	30,000.
366	**5000 Dollars** 1918. Portr. James Madison at ctr. Rare.	—	Rare	—

		FINE	XF	CU
367	**10,000 Dollars** 1918. Portr. Salmon P. Chase at ctr. Rare.	—	Rare	—

NATIONAL CURRENCY

FEDERAL RESERVE BANK NOTES

SERIES OF 1915

		FINE	XF	CU
368	**5 Dollars** 1915. Portr. Abraham Lincoln at l. (only: F; G; J; K; L).	250.	500.	1300.
369	**10 Dollars** 1915. Portr. Andrew Jackson at l. (only: F; G; J; K).	1300.	2750.	5000.
370	**20 Dollars** 1915. Portr. Grover Cleveland at l. (only: F; G; J; K).	2000.	3500.	7500.

SERIES OF 1918

		FINE	XF	CU
371	**1 Dollar** 1918. Portr. George Washington at l. Eagle and flag at ctr. on back.	110.	275.	550.

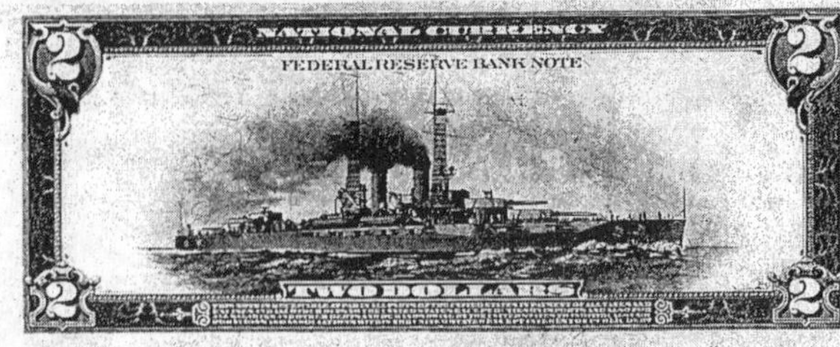

		FINE	XF	CU
372	**2 Dollars** 1918. Portr. Thomas Jefferson at l. Battleship at ctr. on back.	525.	1000.	2000.

		FINE	XF	CU
373	**5 Dollars** 1918. Portr. Abraham Lincoln at l. (all except E).	400.	850.	1600.

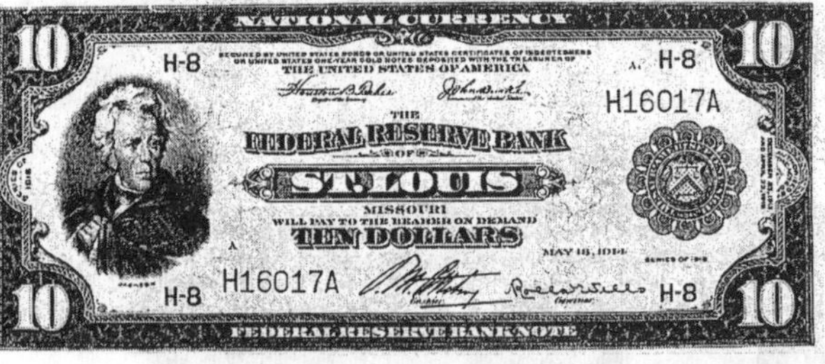

		FINE	XF	CU
374	**10 Dollars** 1918. Portr. Andrew Jackson at l. (only: B; F; G; H).	1250.	2750.	5000.

No.	Denomination	FINE	XF	CU
375	**20 Dollars**			
	1918. Portr. Grover Cleveland at l. (only: F; H).	2275.	3750.	8000.

No.	Denomination	FINE	XF	CU
376	**50 Dollars**			
	1918. Portr. Ulysses S. Grant at l. (only: H).	5000.	10,000.	17,500.

United States Notes - Small Size

Series of 1928

No.	Denomination	FINE	XF	CU
377	**1 Dollar**			
	1928.	75.00	150.	375.
378	**2 Dollars**			
	1928.	10.00	20.00	125.
	a. 1928A.	40.00	100.	125.
	b. 1928B.	80.00	300.	125.
	c. 1928C.	20.00	30.00	125.
	d. 1928D.	10.00	35.00	125.
	e. 1928E.	15.00	25.00	125.
	f. 1928F.	15.00	25.00	125.
	g. 1928G.	7.50	10.00	125.

No.	Denomination	FINE	XF	CU
379	**5 Dollars**			
	1928.	10.00	20.00	100.
	a. 1928A.	15.00	50.00	100.
	b. 1928B.	15.00	30.00	100.
	c. 1928C.	12.50	25.00	100.
	d. 1928D.	35.00	75.00	100.
	e. 1928E.	10.00	25.00	100.
	f. 1928F.	10.00	25.00	100.

Series of 1953

No.	Denomination	FINE	XF	CU
380	**2 Dollars**			
	1953.	3.50	10.00	30.00
	a. 1953A.	3.50	7.50	30.00
	b. 1953B.	3.50	7.50	30.00
	c. 1953C.	3.50	7.50	30.00

No.	Denomination	FINE	XF	CU
381	**5 Dollars**			
	1953.	10.00	15.00	50.00
	a. 1953A.	7.50	15.00	50.00
	b. 1953B.	7.50	15.00	50.00
	c. 1953C.	7.50	25.00	50.00

NATIONAL CURRENCY

FEDERAL RESERVE BANK NOTES

SERIES OF 1929

		FINE	XF	CU
395	**5 Dollars** 1929. (A-D; F-L).	20.00	50.00	200.

		FINE	XF	CU
396	**10 Dollars** 1929. (A-L).	20.00	65.00	250.
397	**20 Dollars** 1929. (A-L).	30.00	100.	275.
398	**50 Dollars** 1929. (B; D; G; I-L).	70.00	115.	300.

		FINE	XF	CU
399	**100 Dollars** 1929. (B; D-E; G; I-K).	125.	175.	275.

GOLD CERTIFICATES - SMALL SIZE

SERIES OF 1928

		FINE	XF	CU
400	**10 Dollars** 1928.	125.	250.	500.
	a. 1928A. (Not issued).	—	—	500.

		FINE	XF	CU
401	**20 Dollars** 1928.	125.	250.	875.
	a. 1928A. (Not issued).	—	—	—
402	**50 Dollars** 1928.			
403	**100 Dollars** 1928. 1928A. (Not issued).	625.	1250.	3000
404	**500 Dollars** 1928.	5750.	10,000.	37,500.
405	**1000 Dollars** 1928.	6000.	12,500.	35,000
406	**5000 Dollars** 1928.	—	Rare	—
407	**10,000 Dollars** 1928. Rare.	—	—	—

SERIES OF 1934

Issued for internal use within the Federal Reserve System. None were released for circulation.

		FINE	XF	CU
408	**100 Dollars** 1934. Portr. Franklin.	—	—	—
409	**1000 Dollars** 1934. Portr. Cleveland.	—	—	—
410	**10,000 Dollars** 1934. Portr. Chase.	—	—	—
411	**100,000 Dollars** 1934. Portr. Wilson.	—	—	—

SILVER CERTIFICATES - SMALL SIZE

SERIES OF 1928

		FINE	XF	CU
412	**1 Dollar** Lg. *ONE* across ctr. on back. 1928.	15.00	35.00	70.0
	a. 1928A.	15.00	25.00	70.0
	b. 1928B.	15.00	35.00	70.0
	c. 1928C.	175.	350.	70.0
	d. 1928D.	100.	200.	70.0
	e. 1928E.	500.	1000.	70.0

SERIES OF 1933

		FINE	XF	CU
413	**10 Dollars**			
	1933. Payable in silver coin.			
	a. 1933A. (No example known in collectors' hands).	5000.	8000.	20,000.

SERIES OF 1934

		FINE	XF	CU
414	**1 Dollar**			
	1934.	75.00	150.	325.
414A	**5 Dollars**			
	1934.	7.50	12.50	65.00
	a. 1934A.	7.50	15.00	65.00
	b. 1934B.	8.00	10.00	65.00
	c. 1934C.	10.00	15.00	65.00
	d. 1934D.	6.50	15.00	65.00
414AY	**5 Dollars**			
	1934A. Yellow seal. (Issued for military use in North Africa.)	50.00	150.	250.
415	**10 Dollars**			
	1934.	30.00	75.00	150.
	a. 1934A.	35.00	50.00	150.
	b. 1934B.	250.	750.	150.
	c. 1934C.	20.00	60.00	150.
	d. 1934D.	35.00	45.00	150.

SERIES OF 1935

		VG	VF	UNC
416	**1 Dollar**			
	1935.	75.00	150.	325.
	a. 1935A.	2.50	5.00	17.50
	b. 1935B.	2.50	5.00	20.00
	c. 1935C.	2.00	4.00	17.50

		FINE	XF	CU
416AR	**1 Dollar**			
	1935A. Experimental issue w/red *R* at lower r.	75.00	130.	475.
416AS	**1 Dollar**			
	1935A. Experimental issue w/red *S* at lower r.	75.00	150.	425.

		FINE	XF	CU
416AY	**1 Dollar**			
	1935A. Yellow seal. (Issued for military use in North Africa).	45.00	65.00	240.
416D1	**1 Dollar**			
	1935D. Type I, wide margin.	2.50	5.00	20.00

		FINE	XF	CU
416D2	**1 Dollar**			
	Type II, narrow design. 1935D.	2.50	5.00	15.00
	e. 1935E.	2.50	4.00	15.00
	f. 1935F.	2.50	4.00	15.00
416NM	**1 Dollar**			
	1935G. W/o motto.	2.00	5.00	15.00
416WM	**1 Dollar**			
	Motto: *In God We Trust* added on back. 1935G.	2.00	7.00	60.00
	h. 1935H.	2.00	5.00	60.00

SERIES OF 1953

		FINE	XF	CU
417	**5 Dollars**			
	1953.	7.50	12.50	40.00
	a. 1953A.	7.50	15.00	40.00
	b. 1953B.	7.50	15.00	40.00
418	**10 Dollars**			
	1953.	30.00	65.00	275.
	a. 1953B.	70.00	125.	275.
	b. 1953A.	25.00	75.00	275.

SERIES OF 1957

		FINE	XF	CU
419	**1 Dollar**			
	1957.	2.00	3.50	10.00
	a. 1957A.	2.00	3.50	10.00
	b. 1957B.	2.00	3.50	10.00

NOTE: For a full listing of all notes w/ovpt: *HAWAII* see Hawaii, #36-41.

FEDERAL RESERVE NOTES - SMALL SIZE

1928 SERIES

		FINE	XF	CU
420	**5 Dollars**			
	1928. (A-L).	20.00	35.00	150.
	a. 1928A. (A-L).	10.00	25.00	150.
	b. 1928B. (A-L).	10.00	25.00	150.
	c. 1928C. (D, F, L).	400.	2500.	150.
	d. 1928D. (F).	1700.	3500.	150.

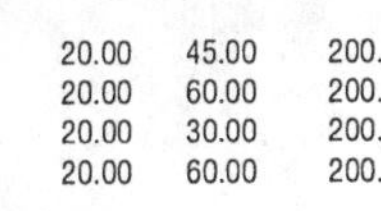

421	**10 Dollars**			
	1928. (A-L).	20.00	45.00	200.
	a. 1928A. (A-L).	20.00	60.00	200.
	b. 1928B. (A-L).	20.00	30.00	200.
	c. 1928C. (B, D, E, G).	20.00	60.00	200.

		FINE	XF	CU
422	**20 Dollars**			
	1928. (A-L).	30.00	75.00	250.
	a. 1928A. (A-H; J-K).	30.00	75.00	250.
	b. 1928B. (A-L).	30.00	50.00	250.
	c. 1928C. (G; L).	345.	800.	250.

		FINE	XF	CU
423	**50 Dollars**			
	1928. (A-L)	70.00	125.	600.
	a. 1928A. (A-L).	70.00	90.00	600.

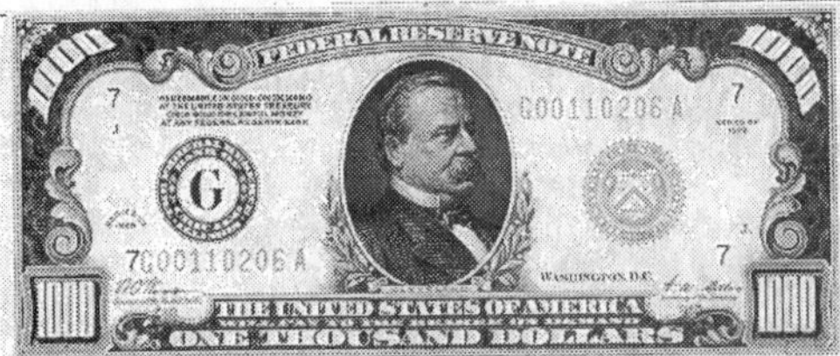

		FINE	XF	CU
424	**100 Dollars**			
	1928. (A-L).	125.	225.	750.
	a. 1928A. (A-L).	125.	175.	750.
425	**500 Dollars**			
	1928. (A-L).	750.	1000.	3000.

		FINE	XF	CU
426	**1000 Dollars**			
	1928. (A-L).	1500.	2500.	5000.

		FINE	XF	CU
427	**5000 Dollars**			
	1928. (A-B; D-G; J-L).	20,000.	40,000.	70,000.
428	**10,000 Dollars**			
	1928. (A-B; D-L).	45,000.	90,000.	150,000.

1934 Series

		FINE	XF	CU
429D	**5 Dollars**			
	Dk. green seal. (A-L). 1934.	10.00	20.00	80.00
	a. 1934A. (A-H; L).	10.00	20.00	80.00
	b. 1934B. (A-J; L).	10.00	20.00	80.00
	c. 1934C. (A-L).	10.00	20.00	80.00
	d. 1934D. (A-L).	10.00	20.00	80.00
429L	**5 Dollars**			
	1934. Lt. green seal.	—	Unc	20.00
430D	**10 Dollars**			
	Dk. green seal. (A-L). 1934.	15.00	18.00	60.00
	a. 1934A. (A-L).	12.00	15.00	60.00
	b. 1934B. (A-L).	15.00	25.00	60.00
	c. 1934C. (A-L).	12.00	15.00	60.00
	d. 1934D. (A-L).	12.00	15.00	60.00
430L	**10 Dollars**			
	1934. Lt. green seal.	—	Unc	27.50
431D	**20 Dollars**			
	Dk. green seal. (A-L). 1934.	25.00	40.00	60.00
	a. 1934A. (A-L).	25.00	30.00	60.00
	b. 1934B. (A-L).	25.00	35.00	60.00
	c. 1934C. (A-L).	25.00	35.00	60.00
	d. 1934D. (A-L).	25.00	30.00	60.00
431L	**20 Dollars**			
	1934. Lt. green seal.	—	Unc	40.00

		FINE	XF	CU
432D	**50 Dollars**			
	Dk. green seal. (A-L). 1934.	55.00	60.00	200.
	a. 1934A. (A-B; D-L).	60.00	100.	200.
	b. 1934B. (C-L).	60.00	125.	200.
	c. 1934C. (A-K).	60.00	110.	200.
	d. 1934D. (A-C; E-G; K).	85.00	200.	200.
432L	**50 Dollars**			
	1934. Lt. green seal.	—	Unc	100.

		FINE	XF	CU
433D	**100 Dollars**			
	Dk. green seal. (A-L). 1934.	125.	145.	300.
	a. 1934A. (A-L).	125.	180.	300.
	b. 1934B. (A; C-K).	150.	225.	300.
	c. 1934C. (A-D; F-L).	150.	175.	300.
	d. 1934D. (B-C; F-H, K).	175.	350.	300.
433L	**100 Dollars**			
	1934. Lt. green seal.	—	Unc	175.

		FINE	XF	CU
434	**500 Dollars**			
	1934. (A-L).	600.	850.	1500.
	a. 1934A. (B-E; G-L).	750.	1250.	1500.
	b. 1934B. (F).	—	—	1500.
	c. 1934C. (A-B).	—	—	1500.

		FINE	XF	CU
435	**1000 Dollars**			
	1934. (A-L).	1500.	2000.	3000.
	a. 1934A. (A-J; L).	1500.	2000.	3000.
	b. 1934C. (A-B).			3000.

		FINE	XF	CU
436	**5000 Dollars**			
	1934. (A-H; J-L).	15,000.	35,000.	55,000.
	a. 1934A. (H).	—	—	55,000.
	b. 1934B. (A-B).	—	—	55,000.

		FINE	XF	CU
437	**10,000 Dollars**			
	1934. (A-H; J-L).	45,000.	60,000.	75,000.
	a. 1934A. (G).	—	—	75,000.
	b. 1934B. (B).	—	—	75,000.

1950 SERIES

		FINE	XF	CU
438	**5 Dollars**			
	1950. (A-L).	7.50	12.00	50.00
	a. 1950A. (A-L).	7.50	12.00	50.00
	b. 1950B. (A-L).	7.50	12.00	50.00
	c. 1950C. (A-L).	7.50	10.00	50.00
	d. 1950D. (A-L).	7.50	10.00	50.00
	e. 1950E. (B; G; L).	7.50	15.00	50.00
439	**10 Dollars**			
	1950. (A-L).	12.50	20.00	80.00
	a. 1950A. (A-L).	12.50	30.00	80.00
	b. 1950B. (A-L).	12.50	20.00	80.00
	c. 1950C. (A-L).	12.50	25.00	80.00
	d. 1950D. (A-H; J-L).	12.50	25.00	80.00
	e. 1950E. (B; G; L).	90.00	160.	80.00
440	**20 Dollars**			
	1950. (A-L).	25.00	35.00	70.00
	a. 1950A. (A-L).	25.00	30.00	70.00
	b. 1950B. (A-L).	25.00	30.00	70.00
	c. 1950C. (A-L).	25.00	35.00	70.00
	d. 1950D. (A-L).	25.00	35.00	70.00
	e. 1950E. (B; G; L).	25.00	50.00	70.00

		FINE	XF	CU
441	**50 Dollars**			
	1950. (A-L).	75.00	125.	250.
	a. 1950A. (A-H; J-L).	75.00	100.	250.
	b. 1950B. (A-E; G-H; J-L).	60.00	80.00	250.
	c. 1950C. (A-E; G-L).	60.00	80.00	250.
	d. 1950D. (A-L).	60.00	100.	250.
	e. 1950E. (B; G; L).	175.	375.	250.
442	**100 Dollars**			
	1950. (A-L).	125.	200.	450.
	a. 1950A. (A-L).	110.	125.	450.
	b. 1950B. (A-L).	125.	185.	450.
	c. 1950C. (A-L).	FV	300.	450.
	d. 1950D. (A-L).	110.	125.	450.
	e. 1950E. (B; G; L).	150.	300.	450.

MILITARY PAYMENT CERTIFICATES

SERIES 461

16.9.1946 to 10.3.1947.

#M1-M7 blue unpt., w/o pictorial designs.

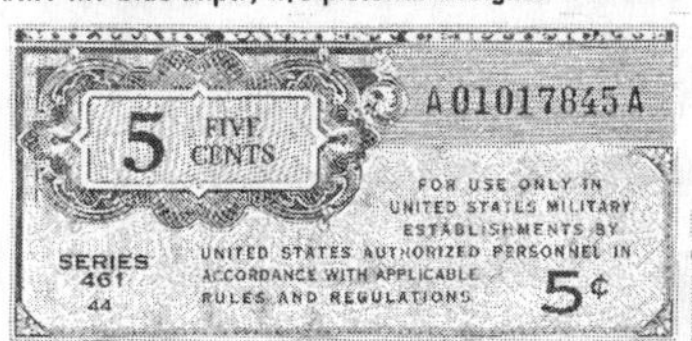

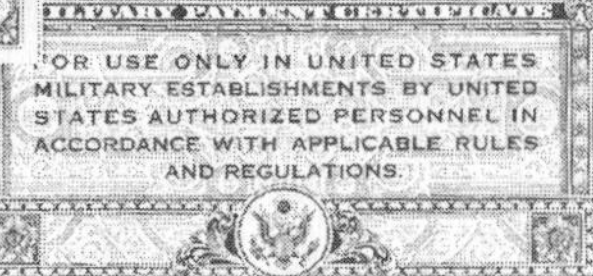

		FINE	XF	CU
M1	**5 Cents** ND (1946). Seal of the United States at lower ctr. on back.	4.00	20.00	65.00

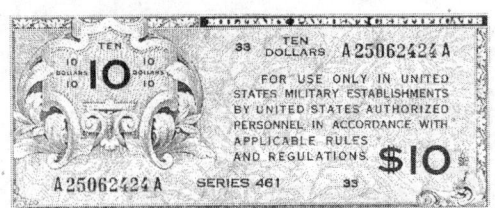

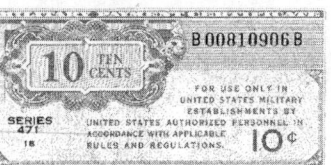

		FINE	XF	CU
M2	**10 Cents** ND (1946). Like #M1.	4.00	20.00	65.00
M3	**25 Cents** ND (1946). Like #M1.	13.00	95.00	250.
M4	**50 Cents** ND (1946). Like #M1.	14.00	70.00	250.
M5	**1 Dollar** ND (1946).	6.00	30.00	185.

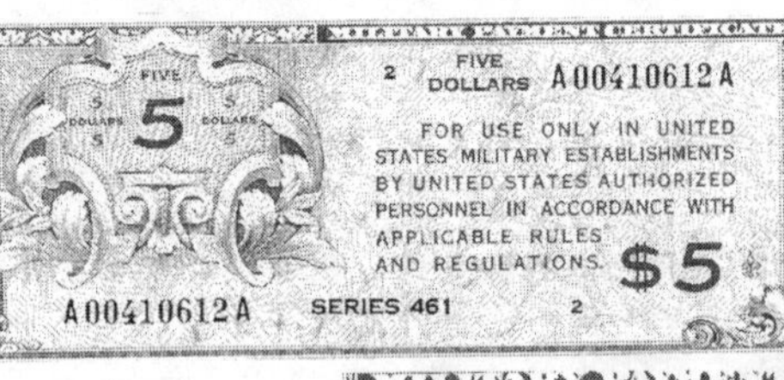

		FINE	XF	CU
M6	**5 Dollars** ND (1946). Like #M7.	32.50	125.	325.
M7	**10 Dollars** ND (1946).	25.00	75.00	300.

SERIES 471

10.3.1947 to 22.3.1948.

#M8-M14 red and blue. Design like Series 461.

		FINE	XF	CU
M8	**5 Cents** ND (1947).	7.50	30.00	90.00
M9	**10 Cents** ND (1947).	6.00	30.00	90.00

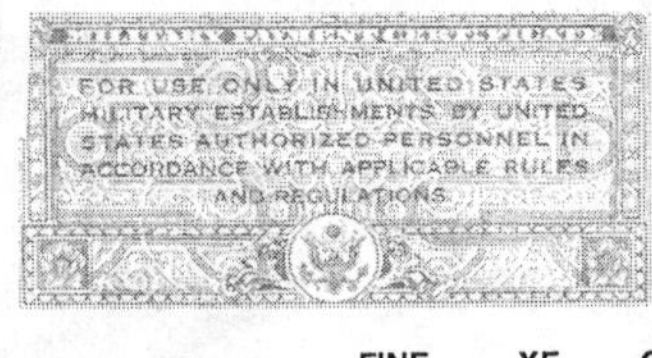

		FINE	XF	CU
M10	**25 Cents** ND (1947).	15.00	75.00	300
M11	**50 Cents** ND (1947).	20.00	110.	325

		FINE	XF	CU
M12	**1 Dollar** ND (1947).	15.00	85.00	275.

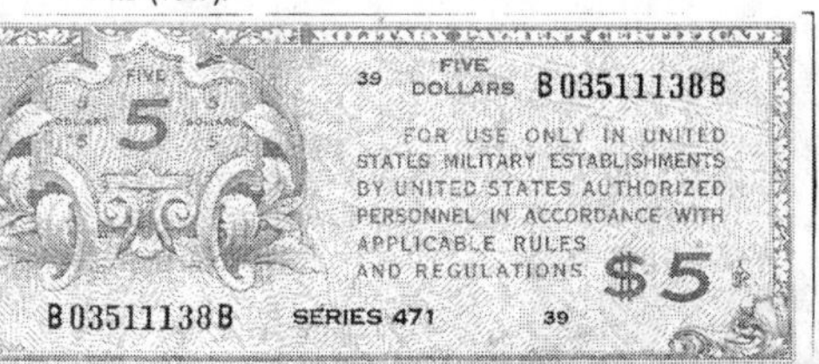

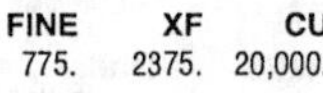

		FINE	XF	CU
M13	**5 Dollars** ND (1947).	775.	2375.	20,000.

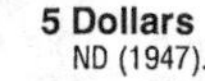

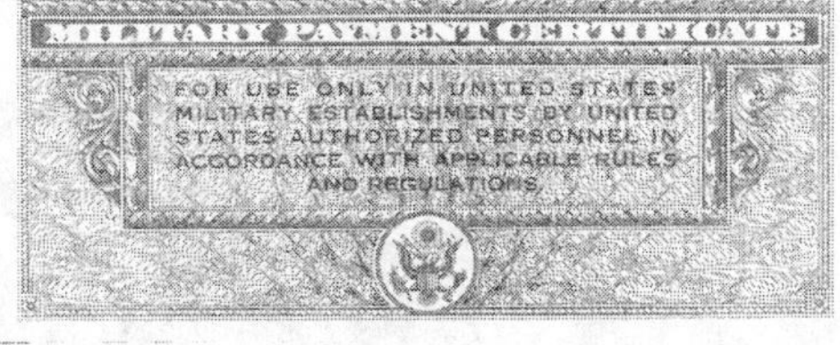

		FINE	XF	CU
M14	**10 Dollars** ND (1947).	200.	600.	2400.

SERIES 472

2.3.1948 to 20.6.1951.

M15-M21 blue unpt. and seal of the United States at ctr. Same seal at ctr. on back.

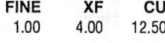

		FINE	XF	CU
M15	**5 Cents** ND (1948).	1.00	4.00	12.50

		FINE	XF	CU
M16	**10 Cents** ND (1948). Like #M15.	2.25	18.00	70.00

		FINE	XF	CU
M17	**25 Cents** ND (1948). Like #M15.	8.00	65.00	225.

		FINE	XF	CU
M18	**50 Cents** ND (1948). Like #M15.	10.00	75.00	275.

		FINE	XF	CU
M19	**1 Dollar** ND (1948).	12.00	85.00	250.

M20 5 Dollars
ND (1948).

FINE	XF	CU
125.	900.	2750.

M21 10 Dollars
ND (1948). Like #M20.

FINE	XF	CU
50.00	275.	2000.

SERIES 481

20.6.1951 to 25.5.1954.

#M22-M28 lt. blue and brown unpt.

M22 5 Cents
ND (1951). Seated woman w/compasses and sphere at l. Seal of the United States at ctr. on back.

FINE	XF	CU
2.00	9.00	27.50

M23 10 Cents
ND (1951). Like #M22.

FINE	XF	CU
2.50	15.00	35.00

M24 25 Cents
ND (1951). Like #M22.

FINE	XF	CU
10.00	25.00	60.00

M25 50 Cents
ND (1951). Like #M22.

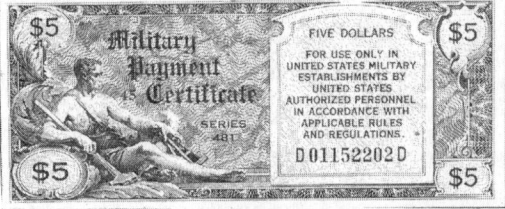

FINE	XF	CU
10.00	55.00	27

M26 1 Dollar
ND (1951). Women at upper l. and r.

FINE	XF	CU
20.00	95.00	29

NOTE: #M26 exists w/position # at r. or l.; the l. variety is worth 10 percent more.

M27 5 Dollars
ND (1951). Reclining youth w/sledge hammer at l.

FINE	XF	CU
80.00	550.	300

M28 10 Dollars
ND (1951). Like #M27.

FINE	XF	CU
35.00	300.	17

SERIES 521

25.5.1954 to 27.5.1958.

		FINE	XF	CU
M29	**5 Cents** ND (1954). Blue on green and yellow unpt. Woman w/helmet at l. Woman at ctr. on back.	2.00	9.00	30.00
M30	**10 Cents** ND (1954). Lilac on green and blue unpt. Like #M29.	3.00	12.50	32.50
M31	**25 Cents** ND (1954). Brown on green unpt. Like #M29.	8.00	27.50	85.00

		FINE	XF	CU
M32	**50 Cents** ND (1954). Green on lilac and blue unpt. Like #M29.	10.00	75.00	150.

		FINE	XF	CU
M33	**1 Dollar** ND (1954). Brown. Woman w/Liberty Cap at l. Woman at ctr. on back.	9.50	50.00	175.

		FINE	XF	CU
M34	**5 Dollars** ND (1954). Blue. Woman w/flower basket at ctr. Woman at ctr. on back.	300.	1300.	3000.

		FINE	XF	CU
M35	**10 Dollars** ND (1954). Brown-violet. Woman w/wreath at r.	100.	650.	1800.

SERIES 541

.5.1958 to 26.5.1961.

		FINE	XF	CU
M36	**5 Cents** ND (1958). Violet on green and yellow-green unpt. Woman w/wreath at l. Woman at ctr. on back.	1.50	6.00	17.50

		FINE	XF	CU
M37	**10 Cents** ND (1958). Green on orange unpt. Like #M36.	5.00	20.00	50.00
M38	**25 Cents** ND (1958). Blue on lilac unpt. Like #M36.	9.00	30.00	80.00

		FINE	XF	CU
M39	**50 Cents** ND (1958). Brown on green and yellow unpt. Like #M36.	30.00	100.	325.

		FINE	XF	CU
M40	**1 Dollar** ND (1958). Blue. Woman w/cap at ctr. Woman w/fasces and jug at ctr. on back.	30.00	100.	400.

		FINE	XF	CU
M41	**5 Dollars** ND (1958). Lilac. Woman w/wreath at l. Woman at ctr. on back.	1250.	3750.	15,000.

		FINE	XF	CU
M42	**10 Dollars** ND (1958). Brown. Woman at ctr. on face and back.	300.	1500.	3500.

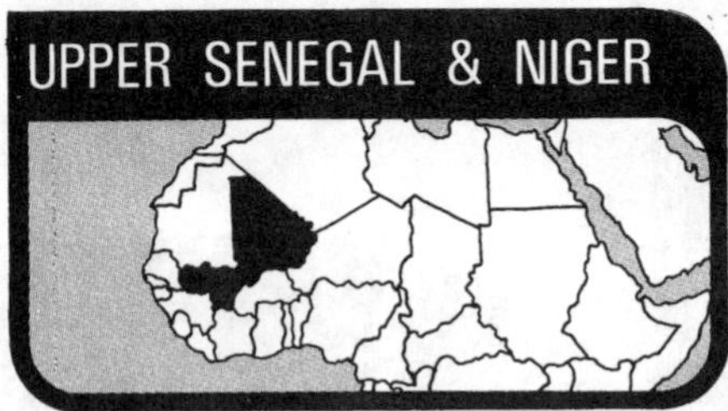

Once a part of the ancient Malinke Kingdom that controlled the area from the 11th to the 17th centuries. The upper course of the Senegal River runs through the western part of the area. The middle course of the Niger River has 1,000 miles of navigable waters within these boundaries. Legendary Tombouctou (Timbuktu) is a port on the Niger in the center of the country.

French dominance in the area occurred in the 1890s. The territories of Senegambia and Niger were formed into the colony of Upper Senegal and Niger in 1904. Following World War I the name of the area was changed to French Sudan.

RULERS:

French to 1960

MONETARY SYSTEM:

1 Franc = 100 Centimes

French Administration

Gouvernement Général de l'Afrique Occidentale Française (A.O.F.)

Haut-Senegal-Niger

Law of 11.2.1917

		VG	VF	UNC
1	**0.50 Franc** L.1917. Dk. brown on lt. brown. Reverse of 50 Centimes coin at l., obverse at r. a. Issued note	400.	1000.	2250.
2	**1 Franc** L.1917. Reported not confirmed.	—	—	—
3	**2 Francs** L.1917. Reported not confirmed.	—	—	—

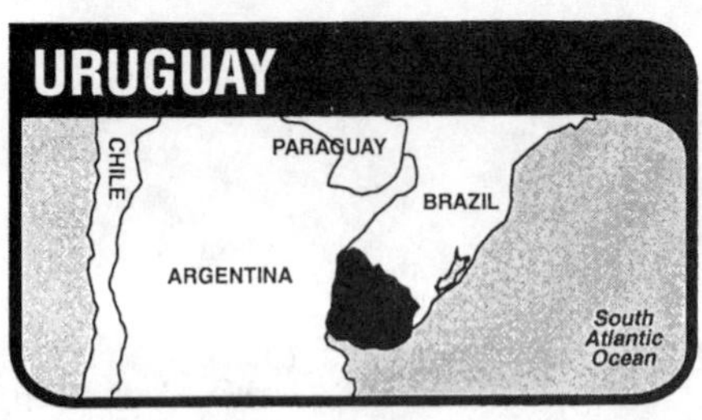

The Oriental Republic of Uruguay (so called because of its location on the east bank of the Uruguay River) is situated on the Atlantic coast of South America between Argentina and Brazil. This most advanced of South American countries has an area of 68,536 sq. mi. (176,220 sq. km.) and a population of 3.27 million. Capital: Montevideo. Uruguay's chief economic asset is its rich, rolling grassy plains. Meat, wool, hides and skins are exported.

Uruguay was discovered in 1516 by Juan Diaz de Solis, a Spaniard, but settled by the Portuguese who founded Colonia in 1680. Spain contested Portuguese possession and, after a long struggle, gained control of the country in 1778. During the general South American struggle for independence, Uruguay's first attempt was led by gaucho soldier José Gervasio Artigas leading the Banda Oriental which was quelled by Spanish and Portuguese forces in 1811. The armistice was soon broken and Argentine forces from Buenos Aires cast off the Spanish bond in the Plata region in 1814, only to be reconquered by the Portuguese from Brazil in the struggle of 1816-20. Revolt flared anew in 1825 and independence was reasserted in 1828 with the help of Argentina. The Uruguayan Republic was established in 1830.

In 1919, a new constitution established a plural executive, but this was abolished in 1933. A presidential government existed from 1933 to 1951 at which time a collective form of leadership was formed through 1966. Strikes and riots in the 1960's brought the military to power until 1985 when Julio Maria Sanguinetti established a government of national unity.

MONETARY SYSTEM:

1 Patacón = 960 Reis
1 Peso = 8 Reales to 1860
1 Peso = 100 Centésimos
1 Doblon = 10 Pesos, 1860-1875
1 Peso = 100 Centésimos, 1860-1975
1 Nuevo Peso = 1000 Old Pesos, 1975-1993
1 Peso Uruguayo = 1000 Nuevos Pesos, 1993-

Note: Certain listings encompassing issues circulated by various bank and regional authorities are contained in Volume 1.

Republic

Poliza de Deuda Publica

Public Debt Drafts

Ley de 29 April 1835

#A13-A17 black. National symbols of hill, scale, horse and bull in 4 corners, Montevideo Bay between cargo at l. and r. along bottom. Dated between 3-14.8.1835.

		Good	Fine	XF
A13	**400 Pesos** Aug. 1835.	—	40.00	100.

		Good	Fine	XF
A14	**500 Pesos** Aug. 1835. a. Handwritten denomination.	—	—	—
	b. Printed denomination.	—	—	—
A16	**2000 Pesos** Aug. 1835.	—	—	—
A17	**5000 Pesos** Aug. 1835.	—	—	—

Banco Nacional

Ley de 23 de Junio de 1862

#A87-A98 printer: W&S. Sign. varieties.

Branch Ovpt.

#A87-A98 issues were ovpt. or perforated for the branches of:

Artigas	Florida	Rosario
Canelones	Maldonado	Salto
Carmelo	Minas	San José
Cerro Largo	Paysandú	Soriano
Colonia	Rio Negro	Tacuarembo
Durazno	Rivera	Treinta y Tres
Flores	Rocha	

37 10 Centésimos

25.8.1887. Black on lt. blue unpt. Arms at l., cattle stampede at ctr. Back blue; seated woman at ctr.

	Good	Fine	XF
a. Issued note w/o branch office perforation or ovpt.	4.00	15.00	40.00
b. Cancelled w/perforation: *PAGADO 25.8.96.*	3.00	12.50	30.00
c. Issued or cancelled w/branch office perforation or ovpt.	5.00	20.00	60.00

8 20 Centésimos

25.8.1887. Black on pink unpt. Mercury seated at l., arms at r. Back green.

	Good	Fine	XF
a. Issued note w/o branch office perforation or ovpt.	4.00	15.00	40.00
b. Cancelled w/perforation: *PAGADO 25.8.96.*	3.00	12.50	30.00
c. Issued or cancelled w/branch office perforation or ovpt.	5.00	20.00	60.00

9 50 Centésimos

25.8.1887. Black on yellow unpt. Arms at l., laureate woman's head at ctr. Back brown.

	Good	Fine	XF
a. Issued note w/o branch office perforation or ovpt.	5.00	20.00	50.00
b. Cancelled w/perforation: *PAGADO 25.8.96.*	4.00	15.00	40.00
c. Issued or cancelled w/branch office perforation or ovpt.	5.00	20.00	60.00

0 1 Peso

25.8.1887. Black on green and orange unpt. Arms at l., village at ctr. Back orange; seated woman at ctr.

	Good	Fine	XF
a. Issued note w/o branch office perforation or ovpt.	8.00	25.00	65.00
b. Cancelled w/perforation: *PAGADO 25.8.96.*	6.00	20.00	60.00
c. Issued or cancelled w/branch office perforation or ovpt.	10.00	30.00	80.00

2 Pesos

25.8.1887. Black on rose and pastel blue unpt. Arms at upper l., bank at upper ctr. Back blue; woman at ctr.

	Good	Fine	XF
a. Issued note.	8.00	25.00	65.00
b. Cancelled w/perforation: *PAGADO 25.8.96.*	6.00	20.00	60.00
c. Issued or cancelled w/branch office perforation or ovpt.	10.00	30.00	80.00

A92 5 Pesos

25.8.1887. Black on gold and brown unpt. Arms at upper l., man at ctr. Back brown; bldgs. and street scene at ctr.

	Good	Fine	XF
a. Issued note w/o branch office perforation or ovpt.	10.00	30.00	80.00
b. Cancelled w/perforation: *PAGADO 25.8.96.*	6.00	20.00	60.00
c. Issued or cancelled w/branch office perforation or ovpt.	15.00	50.00	100.

A93 10 Pesos

25.8.1887. Black on green and orange unpt. Arms at l., allegorical woman holding torch at r. Back orange.

	Good	Fine	XF
a. Issued note w/o branch office perforation or ovpt.	15.00	50.00	100.
b. Cancelled w/perforation: *PAGADO 25.8.96.*	10.00	30.00	80.00
c. Issued or cancelled w/branch office perforation or ovpt.	17.50	55.00	120.

A94 20 Pesos

25.8.1887. Black on yellow and tan unpt. Man at l., arms at top l. ctr., bldg. at lower r. Back dk. blue; Liberty head at ctr.

	Good	Fine	XF
a. Issued note w/o branch office perforation or ovpt.	15.00	50.00	100.
b. Cancelled w/perforation: *PAGADO 25.8.96.*	10.00	30.00	80.00
c. Issued or cancelled w/branch office perforation or ovpt.	20.00	60.00	150.

A95 50 Pesos

25.8.1887. Black on orange and green unpt. Man at l., church at ctr., arms at r. Back dk. orange; sheep at ctr.

	Good	Fine	XF
a. Issued note w/o branch office perforation or ovpt.	20.00	60.00	150.
b. Cancelled w/perforation: *PAGADO 25.8.96.*	10.00	30.00	80.00
c. Issued or cancelled w/branch office perforation or ovpt.	30.00	85.00	200.

A96 100 Pesos

25.8.1887. Black on green and pink unpt. Man at l., arms and cherubs at ctr., train at r. Back brown; woman at ctr.

	Good	Fine	XF
a. Issued note.	40.00	100.	250.
b. Cancelled w/perforation: *PAGADO 25.8.96.*	15.00	50.00	100.

A97 200 Pesos

25.8.1887. Black on green and gold unpt. Arms at l., portr. at ctr., bldg. at r. Back green; street scene.

	Good	Fine	XF
a. Issued note.	75.00	200.	500.
b. Cancelled w/perforation: *PAGADO 25.8.96.*	50.00	150.	300.

A98 500 Pesos

25.8.1887. Black on pink unpt. Man at l., arms and cherubs at ctr., map at r. Back brown; group of men w/flag.

	Good	Fine	XF
a. Issued note.	—	—	—
b. Cancelled w/perforation: *PAGADO 25.8.96.*	100.	200.	400.

República Oriental del Uruguay

Comisión de Extinción de Billetes

1875 Issue

#A99-A107 w/ovpt: *Comisión de Extinción de Billetes* in rectangular frame on notes of La República Oriental del Uruguay. Printer: ABNC.

		Good	Fine	XF
A99	**20 Centésimos** 27.3.1875. Black on brown unpt. Raphael's Angel at ctr. Uniface.	20.00	60.00	150.

		Good	Fine	XF
A100	**50 Centésimos** 27.3.1875. Black on green unpt. Eagle at l., cows at upper ctr. Uniface.	25.00	75.00	200.

		Good	Fine	XF
A101	**1 Peso** 27.3.1875. Black on pink unpt. Standing Columbia at l., sailor and anchor at ctr. Back reddish purple.	50.00	150.	325.

		Good	Fine	XF
A102	**2 Pesos** 27.3.1875. Black on brown unpt. Ostrich at lower l., horses at top ctr.; woman at lower r. Back brown.	75.00	275.	—

		Good	Fine	XF
A103	**5 Pesos** 27.3.1875. Black on brown unpt. Arms at l., cow and calf at ctr., allegory of agriculture at r. Back brown.	—	—	—

		Good	Fine	X
A104	**10 Pesos** 27.3.1875. Black on red-brown unpt. Arms at l., cattle at ctr., shepherd w/sheep at r. Back red-brown; steam locomotive at ctr.	—	—	

		Good	Fine	X
A105	**20 Pesos** 27.3.1875. Black on orange unpt. Allegory of commerce at l., farm workers at ctr., arms at r. Steer's head at ctr. on orange back.	—	—	

		Good	Fine
A106	**50 Pesos** 27.3.1875. Black on red-orange unpt. "Columbia" at l., 3 farmers w/reaper at ctr., arms at r. Allegorical figures at ctr., ships at l. and r. on back.	—	—
A107	**100 Pesos** 27.3.1875.	—	—

Junta de Crédito Público

Ley 4.5.1870

#A108-A115 printer: BWC.

		Good	Fine	
A108	**20 Centésimos** L.1870. Black on orange unpt. on yellow paper. Stallion at l. Uniface.	5.00	25.00	60

		Good	Fine	
A109	**50 Centésimos** L.1870. Black on brown unpt. Cow at l., arms at upper ctr. r. Uniface.			
	a. Purple paper.	10.00	35.00	85
	b. White paper.	10.00	35.00	85

NOTICE

Readers with unlisted dates, signature varieties, etc. are invited to submit photocopies or, high resolution (300 dpi, 100% size) scans of thei notes to: Standard Catalog of World Paper Money, 700 East State St Iola, WI 54990-0001, or E-Mail: george.cuhaj@fwpubs.com.

		Good	Fine	XF
A110	**1 Peso** L.1870. Black on dk. green unpt. on green paper. Winged Mercury seated at l. Uniface.			
	a. Dk. green paper.	20.00	60.00	150.
	b. Lt. green paper.	20.00	60.00	150.

		Good	Fine	XF
A111	**5 Pesos** L.1870. Blue. Ewe at l., arms at upper ctr. r. Uniface.	35.00	75.00	250.
A112	**10 Pesos** L.1870. Black and brown on orange paper. Woman standing w/sword and shield at l., arms at upper ctr. r. Uniface.	35.00	75.00	250.
A113	**20 Pesos** L.1870. Brown on blue paper. Woman w/sheaf of wheat at l., arms at upper ctr. r. Uniface.	40.00	100.	300.
A114	**50 Pesos** L.1870. Green on brown paper. Justice at l.	—	—	—
A115	**100 Pesos** L.1870. Blue on yellow paper. Woman w/horn of plenty.	—	—	—

EMISION NACIONAL

LEY 25.1.1875

		Good	Fine	XF
A116	**20 Centésimos** 1.2.1875. Black on pink paper. Liberty standing at l. Uniface. Imprint: Lit. Pena.	10.00	35.00	—

		Good	Fine	XF
A117	**50 Centésimos** 1.2.1875. Black on blue unpt. Head of cow at l., arms at upper ctr. Uniface. Imprint: Litografia A. Godel.	15.00	45.00	—

#A118-A119 imprint: Lit. Hequet y Cohas.

		Good	Fine	XF
A118	**1 Peso** 1.2.1875. Black on brown unpt. Seated man at l., arms at ctr. r.	20.00	60.00	—

		Good	Fine	XF
A118A	**2 Pesos** 1.2.1875. Black on orange unpt., green paper. Horse's head at l., arms at ctr. Uniface.	—	—	—

		Good	Fine	XF
A119	**5 Pesos** 1.2.1875. Black on green unpt. Boy holding *5* at l.	10.00	25.00	50.00

CAUTELA (RESERVE)

DECRETO 26 ABRIL 1875

		Good	Fine	XF
A119E	**100 Pesos** 26.4.1875. Black on orange unpt. 2 women resting. Imprint: Litog. A. Godel, Montevideo.	—	—	—

CAUTELA (RESERVE)

LEY 23.6.1875

#A119K and A119N printer: Lit. A. Godel, Montevideo.

		Good	Fine	XF
A119K	**5 Pesos** 1.9.1875. Black on blue unpt. Boy plowing at l., arms at ctr. r. Back brown.	—	—	—
A119N	**50 Pesos** 1.10.1875. Black. Gaucho playing guitar w/girl at upper l., gaucho w/sheep at lower l.	—	—	—

VALE DE TESORERÍA

1855 ISSUE

		Good	Fine	XF
A120	**2 Reales** 12.7.1855.	50.00	100.	—
A121	**4 Reales** 12.7.1855.	50.00	100.	—
A122	**1 Peso** 12.7.1855.	60.00	125.	—
A123	**5 Pesos** 12.7.1855. 117 x 83mm.	75.00	150.	—

		Good	Fine	XF
A124	**10 Pesos** 12.7.1855. Arms at upper ctr.	—	—	—

		Good	Fine	XF
A125	**25 Pesos** 12.7.1855.	—	—	—
A126	**50 Pesos** 12.7.1855.	—	—	—
A127	**100 Pesos** 12.7.1855.	—	—	—

VALES DEL TESORO

TREASURY NOTES

LEY DE 13 DE JULIO 1886

#A127A and A127C imprint: Litografia Artistica - A. Godel - Montevideo.

		Good	Fine	XF
A127A	**1 Peso** 11.8.1886. Arms above seated woman w/sheaves of grain at l.	—	—	—

		Good	Fine	XF
A127C	**10 Pesos** 11.8.1886. Brown and black on ochre unpt. Minstrel, woman and dog in circle at l., reclining women and shield at upper ctr., vaquero and cows in circle at r. Back peach and blue.	—	—	—

REPÚBLICA (ORIENTAL) DEL URUGUAY

1868 EMERGENCY POSTAL SCRIP ISSUES

Uruguay suffered from a chronic shortage of small change during the 1860's. The apparent success of the U.S. Postage Currency issue of 1862 during the Civil War (U.S. #97-100) prompted the government of Uruguay to do much the same thing in 1868.

#A128-A132 exact copies of single current postage stamps at ctr., wide margins around. All uniface w/circular handstamp in purple or black w/issuing office and date.

#A128

#A129

		Good	Fine	XF
A128	**1 Centésimo** 1868. Black.	150.	450.	—
A129	**5 Centecimos** 1868. Blue.	200.	600.	—
A129A	**5 Centecimos** 1868. Green on pink paper.	—	—	—
A130	**10 Centécimos** 1868. Blue.	250.	750.	—
A131	**15 Centécimos** 1868. Orange on yellow paper.	300.	900.	—
A132	**20 Centécimos** 1868. Red on green paper.	300.	900.	—

BANCO DE LA REPÚBLICA ORIENTAL DEL URUGUAY

1896 PROVISIONAL ISSUE

		Good	Fine	XF
1	**20 Centésimos** L.4.8.1896. J. G. Artigas at l. Printer: CSABB. (Not issued).	—	—	—
1A	**10 Pesos** 1.10.1896. Green. Liberty head w/helmet at upper l., cherub w/shield at r. Imprint: CSABB. Rare.	—	—	—

Note: Most examples of #1A encountered are counterfeit.

		Good	Fine	XF
1B	**100 Pesos** 1.10.1896. (No examples known.)	—	—	—

1896 ISSUE

#1C eight arms on back. Printer: G&D.

		Good	Fine	XF
1C	**10 Centésimos** 24.8.1896. Brown on blue unpt. Cow's head at l. (Not issued).	—	—	—
1D	**20 Centésimos** 24.8.1896. Dk. blue on pink unpt. Helmeted man at l. (Not issued).	—	—	—

		Good	Fine	XF
2	**50 Centésimos** 24.8.1896. Black on orange and green unpt. 2 men harvesting w/horses at lower l. Arms at ctr. on back.			
	a. Imprint: G&D.	10.00	35.00	85.00
	b. Double imprint: Jacobo Peuser Buenos Aires; G&D.	15.00	40.00	100.
	c. Dk. red ovpt: *Rosario* at upper r.	—	—	—

		Good	Fine	XF
3	**1 Peso** 24.8.1896. Black on lilac and orange unpt. Portr. woman at ctr.			
	a. Imprint: G&D.	15.00	40.00	100.
	b. Double imprint: Jacobo Peuser Buenos Aires; G&D.	20.00	50.00	115.
	c. *MINAS* ovpt. on b.	—	—	—
	d. *SALTO* ovpt. on b.	—	—	—
4	**5 Pesos** 24.8.1896. Black on pink and lilac unpt. Man at l., arms at r.	50.00	125.	300.
5	**10 Pesos** 24.8.1896. Black on lt. blue and orange unpt. Sailor at l., woman and arms at r. Ships and train on back.	90.00	200.	500.

		Good	Fine	XF
5A	**10 Pesos** 24.8.1896. Pres. Idiarte Borda at l. Proof. (Not issued).	—	—	—
6	**50 Pesos** 24.8.1896. Blue and orange. Women at l. and r.	—	—	—
7	**100 Pesos** 24.8.1896. Black on lilac and blue unpt. Man at l., woman w/sword at r.	—	—	—

NOTICE

Readers with unlisted dates, signature varieties, etc. are invited to submit photocopies or, high resolution (300 dpi, 100% size) scans of their notes to: Standard Catalog of World Paper Money, 700 East State St. Iola, WI 54990-0001, or E-Mail: george.cuhaj@fwpubs.com.

		Good	Fine	XF
8	**500 Pesos** 24.8.1896. Portr. man above arms between allegorical man and woman at ctr.	—	—	—

Note: For similar design issue but dated 1934, see #20-26.

1899 ISSUE

		Good	Fine	XF
8A	**10 Pesos** 1.7.1899. Black on pink and orange unpt. Woman leaning on column at l., arms at r. Back black on yellow and lilac unpt. Seated figure at ctr. Printer: BWC.			
	a. W/o branch ovpt. Rare.	—	—	—
	b. Branch ovpt: *FLORIDA* at ctr. Rare.	—	—	—
	c. Branch ovpt: *SALTO*. Rare.	—	—	—
	d. Branch ovpt: *SORIANO*. Rare.	—	—	—
	x. Counterfeit.	20.00	40.00	—

Note: Most examples of #8A encountered are counterfeit.

LAW OF 4.8.1896 (1914 ISSUE)

#9-11 portr. Artigas at ctr. w/engraved date: *Septiembre de 1914*. Sign. title varieties. Printer: W&S.

		Good	Fine	XF
9	**1 Peso** Sept. 1914. Additional ovpt. dates 1924-35. Black on blue unpt. Back brown; arms at ctr. Issued 1915-36.			
	a. Series V-VIII. No added date. 3 sign.	3.00	8.00	35.00
	b. Series VIII-XI. Added date (diff. positions). 3 or 2 sign. 9.8.1924-14.11.1935.	2.50	6.00	30.00
	c. Series XI. Slightly modified portr., crosshatches on jacket.	2.00	5.00	25.00
	d. Series XI. No added date, and 2 sign.	2.00	5.00	25.00

		Good	Fine	XF
10	**5 Pesos** Sept. 1914. Additional ovpt. dates 1925-34. Brown on lt. red and lt. green unpt. Back green; arms at ctr. Issued 1915-34.			
	a. W/o ovpt. or additional dates.	5.00	20.00	75.00
	b. 2 ovpt. on face: *CONVERTIBLE EN EMISION MAYOR. . .20 Feb. 1919* and *CONVERTIBLE EN PLATA.*	35.00	85.00	225.
	c. Like b. but only the first ovpt. on face.	30.00	75.00	200.
	d. Ovpt: *Certificado Metalico-Plata/Ley de 14 de Enero de 1916.* Issued 1927-28. W/ or w/o added dates.	15.00	50.00	100.
	e. Added date (diff. positions). 4.8.1925-16.1.1934.	5.00	15.00	50.00

		Good	Fine	XF
11	**10 Pesos** Sept. 1914. Additional ovpt. dates 1925-35. Black on pale orange and pale green unpt. Back orange; arms at ctr. Issued 1915-35.			
	a. W/o additional ovpt. dates.	20.00	50.00	125.
	b. Added date (diff. positions). 7.1.1925-19.3.1935.	20.00	50.00	125.

#12 and 13 portr. J. G. Artigas at l. Arms on back. Printer: W&S.

		Good	Fine	XF
12	**100 Pesos** Sept. 1914. Black on brown unpt. Issued 1915-32.			
	a. W/o additional ovpt. date. 3 sign.	40.00	100.	250.
	b. Like a., but 2 sign.	40.00	100.	250.
	c. Additional ovpt. date 4.1.1932; 23.6.1932; 14.10.1935.	40.00	100.	250.

		Good	Fine	XF
13	**500 Pesos** Sept. 1914. Black on green unpt.			
	a. W/o additional ovpt. date.	—	—	—
	b. Additional ovpt. date 6.12.1924.	100.	225.	500.

1918 Provisional Issue

		Good	Fine	XF
14	**20 Centésimos on 1 Peso** Jan. 1918. Black on brown unpt. Portr. J. G. Artigas at l. 4 corners cut off, and black ovpt. lines w/new denomination on face and back. Red or black serial # (3 serial # varieties). Printer: C de M, Buenos Aires.	12.50	40.00	100.
15	**1 Peso** Jan. 1918. #14 w/o ovpt. (Not issued).	—	—	—

1918 Issue

		Good	Fine	XF
16	**100 Pesos** Jan. 1918. Purple on brown-orange unpt. Portr. J. G. Artigas at l. Similar to #14.			
	a. Issued note.	—	—	—
	x. Counterfeit.	250.	500.	—
16A	**500 Pesos** Jan. 1918. Black on green unpt. Similar to #16.	—	—	—

Note: Genuine examples of #16 have a true wmk. Counterfeits are made by putting 2 separate pieces of paper together with wmk. simulated by a drawing in between.

1930 Commemorative Issue

#17-19 Centennial of Uruguay 1830-1930. French printing. Wmk: Artigas.

		Good	Fine	XF
17	**1 Peso** 18.7.1930. M/c. Woman w/helmet at ctr. Indians at l. and r., arms at upper ctr., sailboat at r. ctr. on back.			
	a. Issued note.	40.00	150.	350.
	p. Proof w/o wmk. Uniface face.	—	Unc	500.

		Good	Fine	XF
18	**5 Pesos** 18.7.1930. M/c. Woman at ctr. Horseback riders and arms on back.	200.	900.	—
19	**10 Pesos** 18.7.1930. M/c. Woman at l. Arms and 4 allegorical women on back.	250.	1250.	—

Ley 4 Agosto de 1896 (1931-34 Issue)

#20-26 reissued. Redesigned arms. Sign. and title varieties. Printer: G&D.

		VG	VF	UNC
20	**50 Centésimos** 18.10.1934. Similar to #2.			
	a. 3 sign. Additional ovpt. dates 30.4.1935-22.9.1935.	4.00	20.00	75.00
	b. 2 sign. W/o additional ovpt. date.	4.00	20.00	75.00

		VG	VF	UNC
21	**1 Peso** 9.8.1934. Similar to #3.	8.00	30.00	90.00

		VG	VF	UNC
22	**5 Pesos** 9.8.1934. Similar to #4.	20.00	75.00	250.
23	**10 Pesos** 9.8.1934. Similar to #5.	25.00	100.	300.
26	**500 Pesos** 25.8.1931. Similar to #8.	—	—	—

Note: For similar design issues but dated 1896, see #2-8. Notes #20-23 and 9 w/2 sign. were issued under Law of 14.8.1935. #21-23 appear to exist w/2 sign. only.

DEPARTAMENTO DE EMISIÓN

LEY DE 14 DE AGOSTO DE 1935

#27-33 many sign., sign. title varieties and ovpt. Series A. Wmk: Artigas. Printer: TDLR.

Sign. titles in plate:

2 sign., *EL PRESIDENTE* and *EL DELEGADO DEL GOBIERNO*.

3 sign., *EL PRESIDENTE* or *EL VICE PRESIDENTE, EL SECRETARIO* or *SECRETARIO GENERAL*, and *GERENTE GENERAL*.

		VG	VF	UNC
27	**50 Centésimos** L.1935. Brown on orange and green unpt. Arms at ctr., man w/helmet at lower r. Back green; sailing ships. All notes have 2 sign. titles in plate.			
	a. 2 sign.	1.50	5.00	17.50
	b. 3 sign ovpt.	1.50	5.00	17.50

		VG	VF	UNC
28	**1 Peso** L.1935. Orange-brown on green unpt. Indian w/spear at l., arms at ctr. r. Back blue; conquistadores fighting against Indians.			
	a. 2 sign.	2.00	10.00	30.00
	b. 2 sign. titles in plate. 2 or 3 sign. ovpt.	2.00	10.00	30.00
	c. W/o sign. titles in plate. 3 sign. ovpt.	2.00	10.00	30.00
	d. 3 sign. titles in plate. 3 sign. ovpt.	2.00	10.00	30.00

		VG	VF	UNC
29	**5 Pesos** L.1935. Green on m/c unpt. Arms at upper l., old gaucho at lower r. Back red-brown; wagon drawn by oxen.			
	a. 2 sign. titles in plate. 2 or 3 sign. ovpt.	6.00	25.00	60.00
	b. W/o sign. titles in plate. 3 sign. ovpt.	6.00	25.00	60.00

		VG	VF	UNC
30	**10 Pesos** L.1935. Deep blue on m/c unpt. Warrior wearing helmet at l., arms at upper r. Back purple; group of men w/flag.			
	a. 2 sign. titles in plate. 2 or 3 sign. ovpt.	10.00	30.00	75.00
	b. W/o sign. titles in plate. 3 sign. ovpt.	10.00	30.00	75.00
31	**100 Pesos** L.1935. Orange-brown and violet on m/c unpt. "Constitution" at l. Back orange-brown; crowd of people in town square.			
	a. 2 sign. titles in plate. 2 or 3 sign. ovpt.	12.00	40.00	100.
	b. W/o sign. titles in plate. 3 sign. ovpt.	12.00	40.00	100.

		VG	VF	UNC
32	**500 Pesos** L.1935. Violet and blue. "Industry" at l. Back brown; group of people w/symbols of agriculture.			
	a. 2 sign. titles in plate. 2 or 3 sign. ovpt.	30.00	70.00	225.
	b. 3 sign. titles in plate. 3 sign. ovpt.	30.00	70.00	225.
33	**1000 Pesos** L.1935. Green. J. G. Artigas at r. Back blue and brown; horsemen.			
	a. 2 sign. titles in plate. 2 or 3 sign. ovpt.	100.	200.	—
	b. 3 sign. titles in plate. 3 sign. ovpt.	100.	200.	—

LEY DE 2 DE ENERO DE 1939, 1939-66 ISSUE

#35-41 w/a great many variations in sign. and sign. titles. No printed sign. titles are in plates. All notes have 2 or 3 sign. Printer: TDLR.

		VG	VF	UNC
34	**50 Centesimos** L.1939. Green on lt. tan and brown unpt. Portr. J. G. Artigas at ctr. Arms at ctr. on back. Imprint: Casa de Moneda de Chile. Series A-T.	.25	.50	2.75

		VG	VF	UNC
35	**1 Peso** L.1939. Brown on m/c unpt. Portr. J. G. Artigas at ctr., arms at upper l. Sailing ships on back.			
	a. Paper w/fibers. Series A; B.	.25	1.25	4.00
	b. Paper w/security thread. Series C.	.25	1.00	3.50
	c. Series D.	.25	.50	2.00

		VG	VF	UNC
36	**5 Pesos** L.1939. Blue on m/c unpt. J. G. Artigas at r., arms at upper l. Conquistadors fighting against Indians on back.			
	a. Paper w/fibers. Series A; B.	.50	2.50	7.00
	b. Paper w/security thread. Series C.	.50	1.00	3.50

		VG	VF	UNC
37	**10 Pesos** L.1939. Purple on m/c unpt. J. G. Artigas at ctr., arms at upper l. Farmer w/3-team ox-cart on back.			
	a. Paper w/fibers. Series A.	1.00	4.00	10.00
	b. As a. Series B.	.50	3.00	7.50
	c. Paper w/security thread. Series C.	.25	1.50	6.00
	d. Series D.	.25	1.00	3.00

#38-41 wmk: J. G. Artigas.

		VG	VF	UNC
38	**50 Pesos** L.1939. Blue and brown on m/c unpt. Warrior wearing helmet at r., arms at upper l. Group of people w/flag on back.			
	a. Paper w/fibers. Series A; B.	.50	3.00	9.00
	b. Paper w/security thread. Series C.	.25	1.50	5.00

		VG	VF	UNC
39	**100 Pesos** L.1939. Red and brown on m/c unpt. "Constitution" at r., arms at ctr. People in town square on back.			
	a. Paper w/fibers. Series A; B.	2.00	6.00	20.00
	b. Paper w/security thread. Series C.	.50	3.00	8.00
	c. Series D.	.50	2.00	6.00
40	**500 Pesos** L.1939. Green and blue on m/c unpt. "Industry" at r., arms at upper l. People w/symbols of agriculture on back.			
	a. Paper w/fibers. Series A; B.	3.00	10.00	30.00
	b. Paper w/security thread. Series C.	1.00	4.00	10.00
	c. Series D.	.50	2.00	7.00

		VG	VF	UNC
41	**1000 Pesos** L.1939. Purple and black on m/c unpt. J. G. Artigas at r., arms at upper l. Man on horseback at ctr. on back.			
	a. Paper w/fibers. Series A; B.	10.00	25.00	80.00
	b. Paper w/security thread. Series C.	3.00	10.00	30.00
	c. Series D.	2.00	5.00	15.00

BANCO CENTRAL DEL URUGUAY

1967 ND PROVISIONAL ISSUE

#42-45 Banco Central was organized in 1967 and used notes of previous issuing authority w/Banco Central sign. title ovpt. Series D. Printer: TDLR.

Office Titles:

1-Gerente General, Secretario General, Presidente
2-Co-Gerente General, Secretario General, Presidente
3-p.Gerente General, Secretario General, Presidente
4-Gerente General, Secretario General, Vicepresidente
5-Gerente General, Secretario General, 2o Vicepresidente
6-p.Gerente General, Secretario General, Vicepresidente
7-Secretario General, Presidente

		VG	VF	UNC
42	**10 Pesos** *L.1939* (1967). Purple on m/c unpt. J. G. Artigas at lower ctr., arms at upper l. Farmer w/3-team ox-cart on back. Like #37. Sign. title: 1.			
	a. Bank name below title: *Banco Central de la República.*	1.00	3.00	10.00
	b. Bank name below title: *Banco Central del Uruguay.*.	50	2.50	7.50

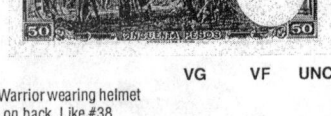

		VG	VF	UNC
42A	**50 Pesos** L.1939 (1967). Blue and brown on m/c unpt. Warrior wearing helmet at r., arms at upper l. Group of people w/flag on back. Like #38.			
	a. Bank name below all 3 sign. Sign. title: 1.	1.00	3.00	7.50
	b. Bank name below 2 sign. at r. Sign. title: 3.	1.00	3.00	10.00

		VG	VF	UNC
43	**100 Pesos** *L.1939* (1967). Red and brown. "Constitution" at r., arms at ctr. People in town square on back. Like #39.			
	a. Bank name below 3 sign. *Banco Central del Uruguay*. Sign. title: 1, 3; *PRESIDENTE* at r.	1.50	3.50	12.00
	b. Bank name below 2 sign. at l.: *Banco Central del Uruguay*. Sign. title: 4; 6 *VICE PRESIDENTE* at r.	1.00	3.50	12.00
	c. Bank name below 2 sign. at r. Sign. title: 3.	1.50	3.50	12.00

		VG	VF	UNC
44	**500 PESOS** *L.1939.* Green and blue. "Industry" at r., arms at upper l. People w/symbols of agriculture on back. Like #40.			
	a. Sign. Like #42a.	1.50	6.00	17.50
	b. Sign. like #42b.	1.50	6.00	17.50

		VG	VF	UNC
45	**1000 PESOS** *L.1939.* Purple and black on pale yellow unpt. Jose Gervasio Artigas at r., arms at upper l. Man on horseback at ctr. on back. Like #41. Sign. l ike #42a.	4.00	8.00	25.00

UZBEKISTAN

The Republic of Uzbekistan (formerly the Uzbek S.S.R.), is bordered on the north by Kazakhstan, to the east by Kirghizia and Tajikistan, on the south by Afghanistan and on the west by Turkmenistan. The republic is comprised of the regions of Andizhan, Bukhara, Dzhizak, Ferghana, Kashkadar, Khorezm (Khiva), Namangan, Navoi, Samarkand, Surkhan-Darya, Syr-Darya, Tashkent and the Karakalpak Autonomous Republic. It has an area of 172,741 sq. mi. (447,400 sq. km.) and a population of 23.5 million. Capital: Tashkent. Crude oil, natural gas, coal, copper and gold deposits make up the chief resources, while intensive farming, come with artificial irrigation, provides an abundance of cotton.

The khanate of Khokand was suppressed and on March 3, 1876, became the Fergana province. On the eve of WW I Khiva and Bukhara were enclaves within a Russian Turkestan divided into five provinces or *oblasti.* The czarist government did not attempt to Russify the indigenous Turkic or Tajik populations, preferring to keep them backward and illiterate. The revolution of March 1917 created a confused situation in the area. In Tashkent there was a Turkestan committee of the provisional government; a Communist-controlled council of workers', soldiers' and peasants' deputies; also a Moslem Turkic movement, Shuro-i-Islamiya, and a Young-Turkestan or Jaddidi (Renovation) party. The last-named party claimed full political autonomy for Turkestan and the abolition of the emirate of Bukhara and the khanate of Khiva. After the Communist *coup d'état* Petrograd, the council of people's commissars on Nov. 24 (Dec. 7), 1917, published an appeal to "all toiling Moslems in Russia and in the east" proclaiming their right to build their national life "freely and unhindered." In response, the Moslem and Jaddidi organizations in Dec. 1917 convoked a national congress in Khokand which appointed a provisional government headed by Mustafa Chokayev (or Chokaigolu; 1890-1941) and resolved to elect a constituent assembly to decide whether Turkestan should remain within a Russian federal state or proclaim its independence. In the spring of 1919 a Red army group defeated Kolchak and in September its commander, M.V. Frunze, arrived in Tashkent with V.V. Kuibyshev as political commissar. The Communists were still much too weak in Turkestan to proclaim the country part of Soviet Russia. Faizullah Khojayev organized a Young Bukhara movement, which on Sept. 14, 1920, proclaimed the dethronement of Emir Mir Alim. Bukhara was then made a S.S.R. In 1920 the Tashkent Communist government declared war on Junaid, who took to flight, and Khiva became another S.S.R. In Oct. 1921 Enver Pasha, the former leader of the Young Turks, appeared in Bukhara and assumed command of the Basmachi movement. In Aug. 1922 he was forced to retreat into Tajikistan and died on Aug. 4, in a battle near Baljuvan. Khiva concluded a treaty of alliance with the Russian S.F.S.R. in Sept. 1920, and Bukhara followed suit in March 1921. Theoretically, a Turkestan Autonomous Soviet Socialist Republic had existed since May 1, 1918; in 1920 this "Turkrepublic," as it was called, was proclaimed part of the R.S.F.S.R. On Sept. 18, 1924, the Uzbek and Turkmen peoples were authorized to form S.S.R.'s of their own, and the Kazakhs, Kirghiz and Tajiks to form autonomous S.S.R.'s. On Oct. 27, 1924, the Uzbek and Turkmen S.S.R. were officially constituted and the former was formally accepted on Jan. 15, 1925, as a member of the U.S.S.R. Tajikistan was an autonomous soviet republic within Uzbekistan until Dec. 5, 1929, when it became a S.S.R. On Dec. 5, 1936, Uzbekistan was territorially increased by incorporating into it the Kara-Kalpak A.S.S.R., which had belonged to Kazakhstan until 1930 and afterward had come under direct control of the R.S.F.S.R.

On June 20, 1990 the Uzbek Supreme Soviet adopted a declaration of sovereignty, and in Aug. 1991, following an unsuccessful coup, it declared itself independent as the 'Republic of Uzbekistan', which was confirmed by referendum in December. That same month Uzbekistan became a member of the CIS.

Monetary System:

1 ТЕНЬГА (Tenga) = 20 КОПЬЕКЪ (Kopeks)
5 ТЕНЬГОВЪ (Tengov) = 1 РЧБПЙ (Ruble)

BUKHARA, EMIRATE

RULER: Emir Sayyid Abdul Akhad Bahadu

TREASURY

1918 FIRST ISSUE

All notes in Persian script, w/only the denomination in Russian. Many printing, color and paper varieties.
Sign. seals for #1-10:

		Good	Fine	XF
1	**20 Tengas** AH1337 (1918). M/c.			
	a. Issued note.	80.00	165.	—
	x. Misprint: back inverted on back.	100.	200.	—

NOTICE

Readers with unlisted dates, signature varieties, etc. are invited to submit photocopies or, high resolution (300 dpi, 100% size) scans of their notes to: Standard Catalog of World Paper Money, 700 East State St. Iola, WI 54990-0001, or E-Mail: george.cuhaj@fwpubs.com.

Type I   Type II

		Good	Fine	XF
2	**60 Tengas** AH1337 (1918). M/c on white or yellowish paper.			
	a. Seals Type I.	100.	175.	—
	b. Seals Type II.	70.00	125.	—
3	**100 Tengas** AH1337 (1918). M/c on white or yellowish paper.	25.00	65.00	—
4	**200 Tengas** AH1337 (1918). M/c on white or yellowish paper.	25.00	65.00	—

		Good	Fine	XF
5	**300 Tengas** AH1337 (1918). M/c.			
	a. Brownish paper.	50.00	100.	—
	b. White paper. Green date on face.	120.	225.	—
	c. White paper. Red date on face.	20.00	50.00	—
6	**500 Tengas** AH1337 (1918). M/c on white or yellowish paper, thin or thick.	30.00	75.00	—

		Good	Fine	XF
7	**1000 Tengas** AH1337 (1918). White or yellowish paper.	40.00	100.	—
8	**2000 Tengas** AH1337 (1918). M/c.	50.00	110.	—
9	**3000 Tengas** AH1337 (1918). M/c.	50.00	110.	—

		Good	Fine	XF
10	**5000 Tengas** AH1337 (1918). M/c on white or yellowish paper.			
	a. Dates 4 times.	40.00	100.	—
	b. Like a., but inverted on back.	100.	200.	—
	c. Dates twice.	65.00	135.	—

1918 Second Issue

Sign. seals for #11-18:

		Good	Fine	XF
11	**100 Tengas** AH1337 (1918). M/c.	25.00	50.00	—
12	**200 Tengas** AH1337 (1918). M/c.	40.00	85.00	—
13	**300 Tengas** AH1337 (1918). M/c.	25.00	50.00	—
14	**500 Tengas** AH1337 (1918). M/c.	25.00	50.00	—
15	**1000 Tengas** AH1337 (1918). M/c.	25.00	50.00	—
16	**2000 Tengas** AH1337 (1918). M/c.	25.00	50.00	—

		Good	Fine	XF
17	**3000 Tengas** AH1337 (1918). M/c.			
	a. Turquoise frame.	25.00	50.00	—
	b. Brown frame.	30.00	75.00	—

		Good	Fine	XF
18	**5000 Tengas** AH1337 (1918). Back green and brown.			
	a. Lt. green.	12.00	25.00	65.00
	b. Dk. green.	12.00	25.00	65.00
	c. Blue, on brownish paper.	10.00	20.00	50.00

1919 Issue

Sign. seal like #11-18 and #19-24.

		Good	Fine	XF
19	**50 Tengas** AH1338 (1919). M/c.	10.00	20.00	50.00

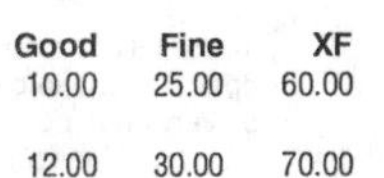

		Good	Fine	XF
20	**100 Tengas** AH1338 (1919). Olive.	10.00	25.00	60.00
21	**200 Tengas** AH1338 (1919). Dk. green.	12.00	30.00	70.00

		Good	Fine	XF
22	**500 Tengas** AH1338 (1919). Blue, red, brown and green (color variations).	15.00	35.00	85.00

		Good	Fine	XF
23	**1000 Tengas** AH1338 (1919). M/c.	15.00	30.00	85.00

		Good	Fine	XF
24	**10,000 Tengas** AH1338 (1919). M/c. 3 sign. varieties. 267 x 125mm.	17.50	40.00	100.

KHOREZM (KHIVA), KHANATE

RULER: Sayid Abdullah Khan

TREASURY

1918 ISSUE

Many varieties, especially in color, paper and printing.

		Good	Fine	XF
25	**200 Tengas** AH1337 (1918).			
	a. ТИНЬГОВЪ to be read from bottom to top. Crescent at ctr. or top at r. on back.	200.	300.	—
	b. ТИНЬГОВ to be read from top to bottom.	160.	250.	—
	c. ТИНЬГОВЪ to be read from top to bottom.	160.	250.	—
	d. ИНЬВО.	160.	250.	—
26	**250 Tengas** AH1337 (1918).			
	a. Russian wording at upper r.	160.	250.	—
	b. W/o Russian wording.	180.	275.	—
27	**500 Tengas** AH1337 (1918).			
	a. Text in the corners in ornaments.	120.	200.	—
	b. Text in squares, also Russian wording inverted.	100.	175.	—
	c. Text wording in the corners in circles.	100.	175.	—
28	**1000 Tengas** AH1337 (1918).			
	a. Text in the circle on 3 lines, also wording inverted.	120.	200.	—
	b. Text in the circle of 4 lines.	120.	200.	—
29	**2500 Tengas** AH1337 (1918).			
	a. 2 leaves below on back, also w/o *500* on back.	115.	185.	—
	b. Bush below on back, also wording inverted.	200.	300.	—

1918 PAPER ISSUE

		Good	Fine	XF
30	**50 Tengas = 10 Rubles** AH1337 (1918). 6 different wmk., and w/o wmk.	80.00	145.	225.

1918 FIRST SILK ISSUE

		Good	Fine	XF
31	**500 Tengas = 100 Rubles** AH1337 (1919).	35.00	100.	200.
32	**1000 Tengas = 200 Rubles** AH1337 (1919).	35.00	120.	225.
33	**2500 Tengas = 500 Rubles** AH1337 (1919).	60.00	200.	325.
34	**200 Tengas = 40 Rubles** AH1337 (1919).	50.00	160.	300.
36	**500 Tengas = 100 Rubles** AH1338 (1919). Red-brown on yellow. Different printing errors in the denomination.	35.00	115.	215.
37	**1000 Tengas = 200 Rubles** AH1338 (1919).	45.00	140.	250.
38	**2500 Tengas = 500 Rubles** AH1338 (1919).	50.00	160.	300.

1919 SILK ISSUE

Silk Notes in Ruble Currency

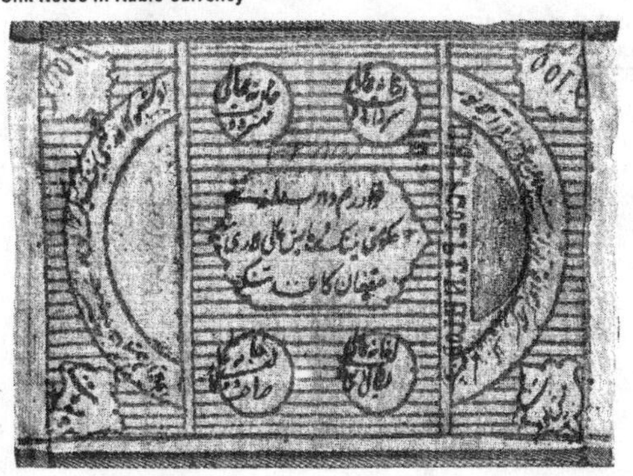

		Good	Fine	XF
39	**100 Rubles** AH1338 (1919).	30.00	80.00	160.

		Good	Fine	XF
40	**250 Rubles** AH1338 (1919). Red-brown on lt. green.	30.00	80.00	160.

1920 Paper Issue

Paper Notes in Ruble Currency

		Good	Fine	XF
41	**50 Rubles** AH1338 (1920). Blue and red.	25.00	65.00	120.
42	**100 Rubles** AH1338 (1920).	35.00	85.00	170.

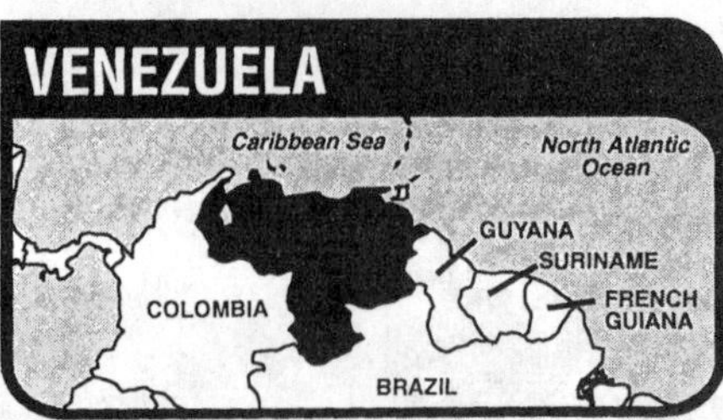

The Republic of Venezuela, located on the northern coast of South America between Colombia and Guyana, has an area of 352,145 sq. mi. (912,050 sq. km.) and a population of 24.17 million. Capital: Caracas. Petroleum and mining provide 90 percent of Venezuela's exports although they employ less than 2 percent of the work force. Coffee, grown on 60,000 plantations, is the chief crop.

Columbus discovered Venezuela on his third voyage in 1498. Initial exploration did not reveal Venezuela to be a land of great wealth. An active pearl trade operated on the off-shore islands and slavers raided the interior in search of Indians to be sold into slavery, but no significant mainland settlements were made before 1567 when Caracas was founded. Venezuela, the home of Bolívar, was among the first South American colonies to revolt against Spain in 1810. Independence was attained in 1821 but not recognized by Spain until 1845. Together with Ecuador, Panama and Colombia, Venezuela was part of "Gran Colombia" until 1830 when it became a sovereign and independent state.

MONETARY SYSTEM:

1 Bolívar = 100 Centimos, 1879-
Estado de Guayana, 1878-79#S332-S354

Note: Certain listings encompassing issues circulated by various bank and regional authorities are contained in Volume 1.

Estados Unidos de Venezuela
United States of Venezuela

Treasury

Law of 27.8.1811 First Issue

#2-4A w/1 seal. Sign. varieties. Black on heavy white paper. Uniface.

		Good	Fine	XF
2	**2 Reales** L.1811. Rare.	—	—	—

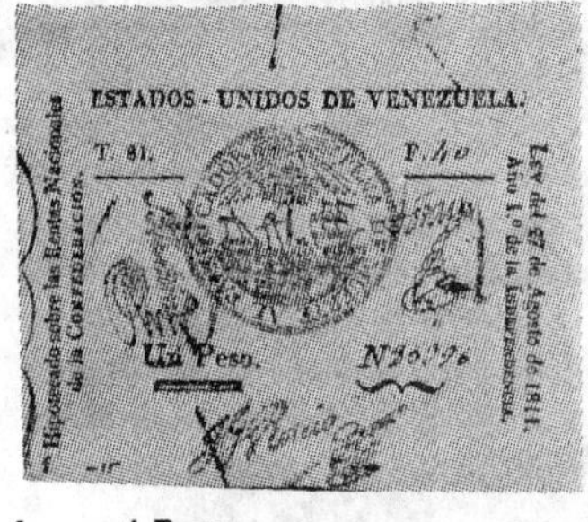

		Good	Fine	XF
4	**1 Peso** L.1811. Un Peso at l. below center design.	400.	1000.	—

Law of 27.8.1811 Second Issue

		Good	Fine	XF
4A	**1 Peso** L.1811. Un Peso at l. ctr. and not below design.	400.	1000.	—

#5-8 w/2 seals. Sign. varieties. Black on heavy white paper. Uniface.

		Good	Fine	XF
5	**2 Pesos** L.1811. Rare.	—	—	—

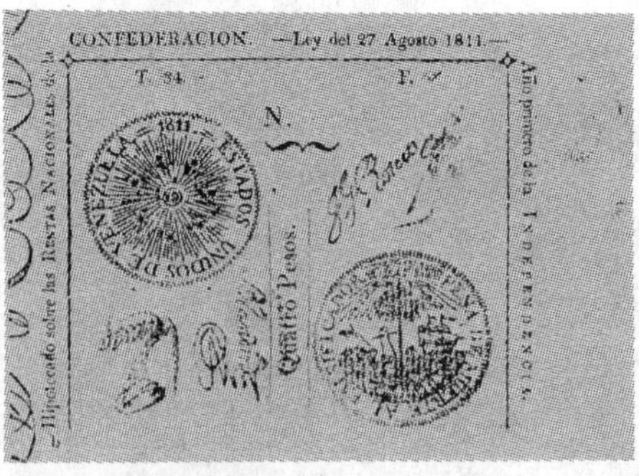

		Good	Fine	XF
6	**4 Pesos** L.1811.	1500.	4000.	—

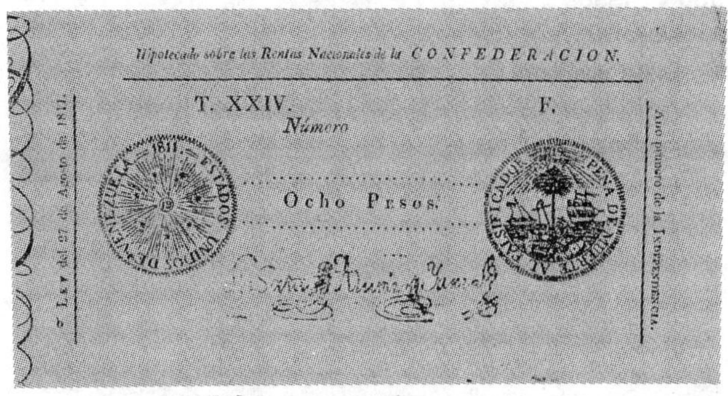

No.	Denomination	Good	Fine	XF
7	**8 Pesos** L.1811.	6500.	—	—
8	**16 Pesos** L.1811. Reported not confirmed.	—	—	—

BILLETE DE TESORERÍA

1849 ISSUE

No.	Denomination	Good	Fine	XF
9	**5 Pesos** 19.1.1849. Black. Seated Liberty at l., arms at ctr., sailing ship at r.	—	—	—

No.	Denomination	Good	Fine	XF
10	**10 Pesos** 1.10.1849. Black. Arms at upper ctr.	—	—	—

REPUBLIC

REPÚBLICA DE VENEZUELA

DECREE OF 20.10.1859

#11-27 generally similar to #25.

No.	Denomination	Good	Fine	XF
11	**5 Pesos** Black.	—	—	—
12	**10 Pesos** Black.	—	—	—
13	**50 Pesos** Black.	—	—	—
14	**100 Pesos** Black.	—	—	—
15	**500 Pesos** Black.	—	—	—
16	**1000 Pesos** Black.	—	—	—

DECREE OF 17.7.1860

No.	Denomination	Good	Fine	XF
17	**5 Pesos** Black.	—	—	—
18	**10 Pesos** Black.	—	—	—
19	**50 Pesos** Black.	—	—	—

DECREE OF 2.8.1860

No.	Denomination	Good	Fine	XF
20	**5 Pesos** 20.11.1860; 26.11.1860. Black.	—	—	—
21	**10 Pesos** 27.11.1860. Black.	—	—	—
22	**20 Pesos** Black.	—	—	—
23	**100 Pesos** Black.	—	—	—

DECREE OF 2.8.1860 AND RESOLUTION OF 18.9.1860

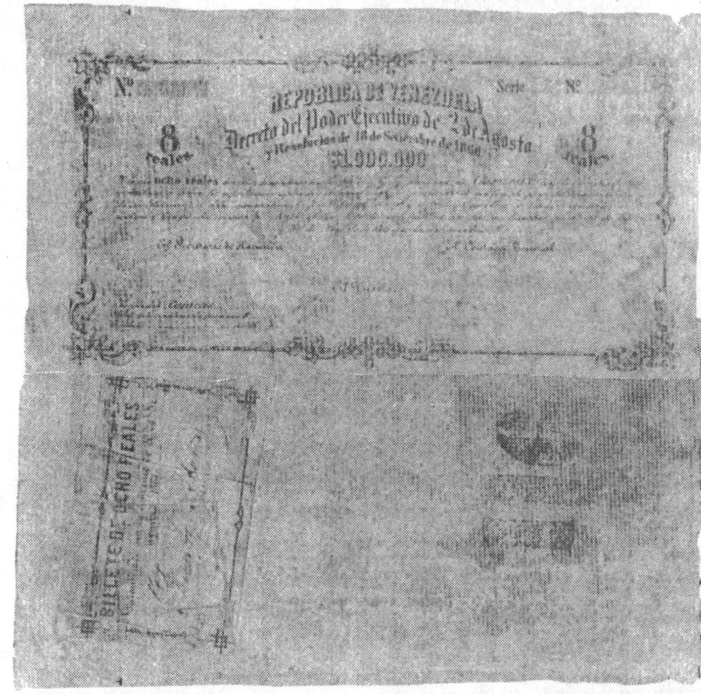

No.	Denomination	Good	Fine	XF
24	**8 Reales** 30.8.1860. Black.	—	—	—

DECREE OF 15.1.1861

		Good	Fine	XF
25	**8 Reales** D.1861. Black. Guarantee text on back.	—	—	—
26	**20 Pesos** Black.	—	—	—
27	**100 Pesos** Black.	—	—	—

BANCO CENTRAL DE VENEZUELA

1940-45 ISSUES

#31-37 Simon Bolivar on front. Arms on back. Printer: ABNC. (Series I, W not used).

		VG	VF	UNC
31	**10 Bolívares** 19.7.1945-11.3.1960. Purple on m/c unpt. Portr. Simon Bolívar at l., Antonio Jose de Sucre at r. Arms at r. on back.			
	a. 19.7.1945-17.5.1951.	5.00	40.00	125.
	b. 31.7.1952. Serial # prefix F-G.	15.00	50.00	100.
	c. 23.7.1953-17.4.1958.	5.00	30.00	60.00
	d. 18.6.1959-11.3.1960.	5.00	20.00	45.00
	s. As a. Specimen. W/o sign. Punched hole cancelled.	—	—	175.
32	**20 Bolívares** 15.2.1941-18.6.1959. Dk. green on m/c unpt. Portr. Simon Bolívar at r. Arms at l. on back.			
	a. 15.2.1941-17.1.1952.	15.00	60.00	125.
	b. 21.8.1952. Serial # prefix G-H.	20.00	50.00	100.
	c. 23.7.1953-18.6.1959.	5.00	30.00	75.00
	s. As a. Specimen. W/o sign. Punched hole cancelled.	—	—	75.00
33	**50 Bolívares** 12.12.1940-11.3.1960. Black on m/c unpt. Portr. Simon Bolívar at l. Back orange; arms at r.			
	a. 12.12.1940-17.1.1952.	25.00	100.	250.
	b. 23.7.1953. Serial # prefix C.	25.00	125.	225.
	c. 22.4.1954-11.3.1960.	15.00	65.00	125.
	s. As a. Specimen. W/o sign. Punched hole cancelled.	—	—	125.
34	**100 Bolívares** 11.12.1940-3.7.1962. Brown on m/c unpt. Portr. Simon Bolívar at ctr. Arms at ctr. on back.			
	a. 11.12.1940-30.10.1952.	30.00	125.	300.
	b. 23.7.1953. Serial # prefix D.	35.00	150.	300.
	c. 22.4.1954-29.5.1958.	20.00	75.00	175.
	d. 24.9.1959-3.7.1962.	15.00	50.00	150.
	s. As a. Specimen. W/o sign. Punched hole cancelled.	—	—	175.
35	**500 Bolívares** 10.12.1940-21.12.1940. Blue on m/c unpt. Portr. Simon Bolívar at r. Arms at l. on back.	250.	1000.	—
36	**500 Bolívares** 21.1.1943-29.11.1946. Red on m/c unpt. Like #35.	250.	1000.	—

1947 ISSUE

		VG	VF	UNC
37	**500 Bolívares** 1947-71. Orange on m/c unpt. Like #35.			
	a. 14.8.1947-21.8.1952.	75.00	250.	—
	b. 23.7.1953-29.5.1958.	30.00	125.	300.
	c. 11.3.1960-17.8.1971.	17.50	80.00	200.
	s. As b. Specimen. W/o sign. Punched hole cancelled.	—	—	135.

1952-53 ISSUE

#38-41 cruder and differently engraved portr. of Simon Bolívar and Antonio Jose de Sucre. Monument at ctr. on back. Printer: TDLR.

		VG	VF	UNC
38	**10 Bolívares** 31.7.1952. Purple on m/c unpt. Similar to #31. Arms at r. on back. Series E, F. 7 digit serial #.	30.00	125.	350.
39	**20 Bolívares** 21.8.1952. Similar to #43. Arms at l. on back. Series G. 7 digit serial #.	35.00	175.	450.
40	**50 Bolívares** 26.2.1953; 23.7.1953. Simon Bolívar at l., *CINCUENTA BOLÍVARES* at r. Arms at r. on back. Series C. 7 digit serial #.	50.00	135.	450.
41	**100 Bolívares** 23.7.1953. Portr. Simon Bolívar at r. Arms at l. on back. Series C, D. 7 digit serial #.	25.00	125.	425.

NOTICE

Readers with unlisted dates, signature varieties, etc. are invited to submit photocopies or, high resolution (300 dpi, 100% size) scans of their notes to: Standard Catalog of World Paper Money, 700 East State St. Iola, WI 54990-0001, or E-Mail: george.cuhaj@fwpubs.com.

1960-61 ISSUE

#42-44 printer: TDLR.

		VG	VF	UNC
43	**20 Bolívares** 1960-66. Dk. green on m/c unpt. Face similar to #32. Portr. Simon Bolívar at r., bank name in 1 line. Arms at l., monument at ctr. on back. 7 digit serial #.			
	a. 11.3.1960. Serial # prefix *U-X.*	4.00	20.00	50.00
	b. 6.6.1961. Serial # prefix *X-Z.*	4.00	15.00	40.00
	c. 7.5.1963. Serial # prefix *A-B.*	4.00		40.00
	d. 2.6.1964. Serial # prefix *C-D.*	4.00	15.00	40.00
	e. 10.5.1966. Serial # preifx *E-G.*	4.00	15.00	40.00
	s1. Specimen w/red ovpt: *SPECIMEN.* Paper w/colored planchettes. Serial # prefix *X.*	—	—	15.00
	s2. Specimen w/red ovpt: *ESPECIMEN SIN VALOR.* Paper w/security thread. Punched hole cancelled.	—	—	15.00
	s3. Specimen w/black ovpt: *SPECIMEN.* Serial # prefix *U.*	—	—	15.00

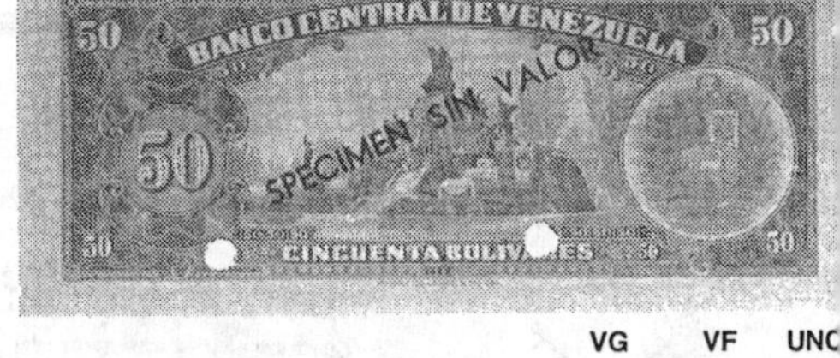

		VG	VF	UNC
44	**50 Bolívares** 6.6.1961; 7.5.1963. Black on m/c unpt. Modified portr. of Simon Bolívar at l., value *CINCUENTA BOLIVARES* at r. Back orange; monument at ctr., arms at r. on back. 7 digit serial #. Serial # prefix *H-J; J-K.*			
	a. Issued note.	8.00	50.00	125
	s. Specimen w/red ovpt: *SPECIMEN SIN VALOR.* Punched hole cancelled.	—	—	17.50

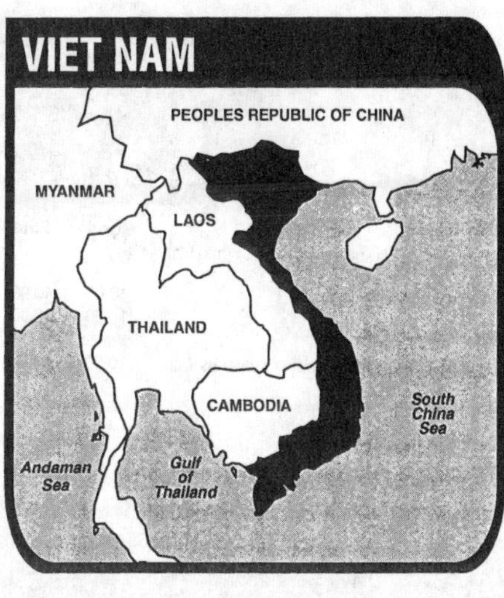

The Socialist Republic of Viet Nam, located in Southeast Asia west of the South China Sea, has an area of 127,300 sq. mi. (329,560 sq. km.) and a population of 80.55 million. Capital: Hanoi. Agricultural products, saltwater fish, shellfish, coal, mineral ores and electronic products are exported.

The Viet Namese originated in North China, from where they were driven southward by the Han Chinese. They settled in the Red River Delta in northern Viet Nam. By 208 BC, much of present-day southern China and northern Viet Nam was incorporated into the independent kingdom of Nam Viet. China annexed Nam Viet in 111 BC and ruled it until 939, when independence was reestablished. The new state then expanded until it included much of Cambodia and southern Viet Nam. Viet Nam was reconquered by the Chinese in 1407; and although they were driven out, the country was divided into two, not to be reunited until 1802.

During the latter half of the 19th century, the French gradually overran Viet Nam. Cochin-China, fell to the French in 1862-67. In 1884, France established protectorates over Annam, the central region of Viet Nam and Tonkin in the north. Cambodia, Cochin-China, Annam and Tonkin were incorporated into the Indo-Chinese Union in 1887.

At the start of World War II, many nationalists, communist and non-communist alike, fled to China and joined the League for the Independence of Viet Nam ("Viet Minh") to free Viet Nam from French rule. The Japanese occupied Viet Nam during World War II. As the end of the war drew near, the Vichy French administration and granted Viet Nam independence under a government headed by Bao Dai, emperor of Annam. The Bao Dai government collapsed at the end of the war, and on September 2, 1945, the Viet Minh proclaimed the existence of an independent Viet Nam consisting of Cochin-China, Annam and Tonkin, and set up a provisional Communist government of the Democratic Republic of Viet Nam. France recognized the new government as a free state, but later reneged and in 1949 reinstalled Bao Dai as ruler of Viet Nam and extended the regime within the French Union. The first Indochina War, against the state that raged on to the disastrous defeat of the French by the Viet Minh on May 7, 1954.

An agreement of July 21, 1954, provided for a temporary division of Viet Nam at the 17th parallel of latitude, with the Democratic Republic of Viet Nam (North Viet Nam) to the north, and the Republic of Viet Nam (South Viet Nam) to the south. In October 1955, South Viet Nam held a referendum and authorized the establishment of a republic. This Republic of Viet Nam was proclaimed on October 26, 1955, and was recognized immediately by the Western powers.

The Democratic Republic of Viet Nam, working through Viet Cong guerrillas, instigated subversion in South Viet Nam which led to the second Indochina War. This war, from the viewpoint of the North was merely a continuation of the first (anti-French) war, which came to a brief halt in 1973 but did not end until April 30, 1975 when South Viet Nam surrendered. The National Liberation Front for South Viet Nam, the political arm of the Viet Cong, assumed governmental power in the south. On July 2, 1976, North and South Viet Nam were united as the Socialist Republic of Viet Nam with Hanoi as the capital.

MONETARY SYSTEM:

1 Hao = 10 Xu
1 Dông = 100 Xu
1 Dông = 100 "Old" Dong, 1951
1 New Dong = 500 Old Dong, 1975-76

Replacement Notes:

#5-7, 11-14, star instead of series prefix of letter and number.
Note: HCM = Ho Chi Minh

VIET-NAM DAN-CU CHONG-HOA

GIAY BAC VIET NAM

VIETNAMESE BANKNOTE

1946 ND ISSUES

		Good	Fine	XF
1	**1 Dông** ND (1946). Olive. Like #9. Wmk: Oval w/*Vietnam.*	10.00	50.00	300.
2	**5 Dông** ND (1946). Crude printing of #10. Wmk: Star within circle.	5.00	20.00	50.00

		Good	Fine	XF
3	**5 Dông** ND (1946). Brown and green. Worker at l., factory in background. HCM at l. on back.			
	a. Wmk: *VNDCCH.*	5.00	20.00	75.00
	b. Wmk: Oval w/*Vietnam.*	5.00	20.00	75.00
4	**5 Dông** ND (1946). Brown and gold. Like #3 but larger note. W/o wmk.	6.50	20.00	75.00

		Good	Fine	XF
5	**20 Dông** ND (1946). Brown and olive. Flag behind HCM at l. (25mm high). Farmer w/buffalo at l., female porter w/child at r. on back. 148 x 76mm.	15.00	50.00	125.

		Good	Fine	XF
6	**20 Dông** ND (1946). Brown and olive. Like #5. HCM in oval frame (36mm high). 170 x 88mm.	15.00	50.00	125.

		Good	Fine	XF
7	**20 Dông** ND (1946). Brown and yellow. Like #5 but HCM in frame (50mm high). 170 x 88mm.	15.00	50.00	125.

		Good	Fine	XF
8	**100 Dông** ND (1946). Green and olive. Large note like #12 but HCM portr. different and smaller (57mm high).			
	a. W/o wmk.	15.00	70.00	175.
	b. Wmk: Oval w/*Vietnam.*	15.00	70.00	175.
	c. Wmk: *VNDCCH.*	15.00	70.00	175.

1947 ND ISSUE

		Good	Fine	XF
9	**1 Dông** ND (1947). Lt. to dk. blue. HCM at ctr. Denomination numerals *1* in corners contain sm. circles. 2 workers in field w/unpt. of alternating x's and squares on back. White on brown paper.			
	a. W/o wmk.	5.00	15.00	40.00
	b. Wmk: *VDCCH* horizontal and vertical.	5.00	15.00	40.00
	c. Wmk: Oval w/*Vietnam*.	2.50	7.50	15.00
	d. Wmk: Circle w/star.	3.00	10.00	30.00

		Good	Fine	XF
10	**5 Dông** ND (1947) Color varies from Red to dk. brown. HCM at top. Woman w/boy below on back. Vertical format.			
	a. W/o wmk.	2.50	7.50	15.00
	b. Sign. and sign. titles in clear unpt. area. Wmk: *VDCCH*.	2.50	7.50	15.00
	c. As b but wmk: Oval w/ *Vietnam*.	2.50	7.50	15.00
	d. Sign. and sign. titles within wavy unpt. design. Wmk: *VDCCH*.	10.00	25.00	100.
	e. As d but wmk: Oval w/ *VIETNAM*.	10.00	25.00	100.
	f. As b. but wmk: circle with star within star.	—	—	—
10A	**5 Dông** 1947. Red-brown. Like #10 but year at lower l., KIEU THU II (second issue) at lower r. on back.			
	a. W/o wmk.	10.00	20.00	100.
	b. Wmk: *VDCCH*.	10.00	20.00	100.
	c. Wmk: Oval w/*Vietnam*.	10.00	20.00	100.
10B	**5 Dông** ND. Blue. Field workers at l., HCM at r. Back red-brown; workers gathering straw at back. W/o wmk.	10.00	75.00	—

		Good	Fine	XF
11	**50 Dông** ND (1947). Blue and brown. Portr. HCM at ctr. Worker and buffalo at ctr. on back. (Shade varieties).			
	a. W/o wmk.	7.00	20.00	60.00
	b. Wmk: *VDCCH*.	7.00	20.00	60.00
	c. Wmk: Oval w/ *Vietnam*.	7.00	20.00	60.00
12	**100 Dông** ND (1947). Blue and brown. Woman w/child at l. HCM (64mm high) at ctr., 3 workers at r. Agricultural workers w/buffalo on back. 207 x 102mm. Similar to #8.			
	a. W/o wmk.	25.00	75.00	175.
	b. Wmk: Oval w/Vietnam.	25.00	75.00	175.

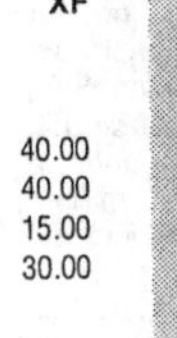

1948 ND Issue

		Good	Fine	XF
13	**20 Xu** ND (1948). Red-brown. HCM at r. Soldier and woman on back.			
	a. 5 sm. (1mm tall) stars at l. on back.	10.00	40.00	100.
	b. 5 lg. (2mm tall) stars at l. on back. Wmk: Star w/*VN* in circle.	10.00	40.00	100.

		Good	Fine	XF
14	**50 Xu** ND (1948). Green. HCM at r. 2 people standing on back. Wmk: Star w/*VN* in circle.			
	a. Blue serial #.	10.00	40.00	100.
	b. Red serial #.	10.00	40.00	100.
15	**1 Dông** ND (1948). Dk. blue. Similar to #1 and 9 but corner numerals *1* on face w/o sm. circles. Back unpt. sun rays.	20.00	40.00	125

		Good	Fine	XF
16	**1 Dông** ND (1948). Dk. blue. 2 women laborers in rice field at l., HCM at r. 5 armed women on back (Nam Bo).	1.00	3.00	10.0
17	**5 Dông** ND (1948). Green to gray. 2 men at ctr., water buffalo at r. Back brown; HCM in circle at l., man w/rifle at ctr. r. (Nam Bo).			
	a. Issued note.	1.00	3.00	10.0
	s. Uniface specimen (pair).	—	Unc	80

Note: #16 and 17 exist in a great many color and shade varieties, such as brown face w/red back, green face w/brown back, blue-green face w/orange back, black face w/purple back, etc.

		Good	Fine	XF
18	**5 Dông** ND (1948). Green. Face similar to #36. Back red-brown; 2 peasants at l. and at r.			
	a. Issued note.	7.50	20.00	50.0
	s. Uniface specimen (face).	—	Unc	25
19	**5 Dông** ND (1948). Dk. blue. HCM at r., peasants at l. Back red-brown; 2 peasants stacking grain sheaves at ctr. W/o wmk.	7.50	20.00	50.0

		Good	Fine	
20	**10 Dông** ND (1948). Red-brown. Back green to black-green; soldier and worker at ctr., HCM at r. Blurred printing.			
	a. W/o wmk.	3.00	10.00	30.
	b. Wmk: *VDCCH*.	3.00	10.00	30.
	c. Wmk: Oval w/*Vietnam*.	3.00	10.00	30.
	d. Wmk: Circle w/star.	3.00	10.00	30.
	e. Wmk: *VND*.	3.00	10.00	30.

#21 Deleted.

		Good	Fine	
22	**10 Dông** ND (1948). Red-brown on green unpt. Like #20 but clear printing (Tonkin).			
	a. W/o wmk.	5.00	20.00	60
	b. Wmk: *VDCCH*.	5.00	20.00	60
	c. Wmk: Oval w/*Vietnam*.	5.00	20.00	60
	d. Wmk: Circle w/star.	5.00	20.00	60
23	**10 Dông** ND (1948). Red-brown on green unpt. Like #20 w/red 4-line ovpt. on back (Trung-Bo).	7.50	20.00	75

		Good	Fine	XF
24	**20 Dông** ND (1948). Various shades of blue. HCM at l., type indicator text at lower r. Back red-brown; woman seated w/fruit at l., 2 blacksmiths at ctr. 145 x 67mm.			
	a. W/o wmk.	7.50	20.00	60.00
	b. Wmk: Circle w/star.	7.50	20.00	60.00
	x. Counterfeit.	—	—	—
25	**20 Dông** ND (1948). Blue. Like #24 but w/o type indicator text. Blurred printing.			
	a. W/imprint at lower r. Wmk: Circle and star. VN in star.	3.00	15.00	40.00
	b. W/o imprint. W/o wmk.	3.00	15.00	40.00

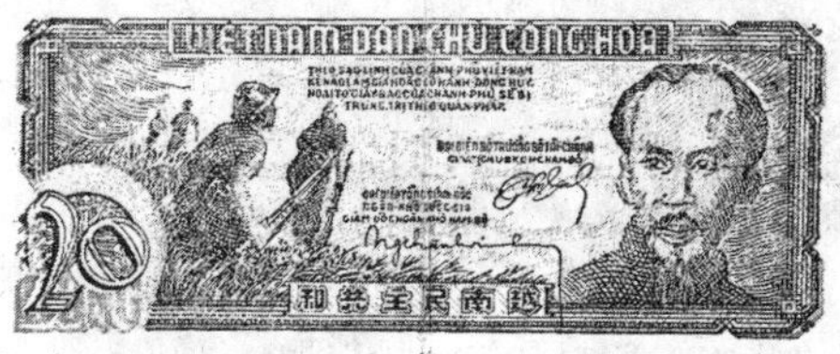

		Good	Fine	XF
26	**20 Dông** ND (1948). Brown and olive. Soldiers at l., HCM at r. Back purple-black; farmers at work. 148 x 63mm (Nam-Bo). Light and dark paper varieties.	7.50	30.00	80.00

		Good	Fine	XF
27	**50 Dông** ND (1948-49). Dk. green. Portr. HCM at l. Back dk. green on red-brown unpt; woman, 2 children and 2 men at ctr. (Clear and blurred printing varieties, also serial # sizes.)			
	a. W/o wmk.	2.00	10.00	30.00
	b. Wmk: Circle and star w/o writing.	2.00	10.00	30.00
	c. Wmk: Circle and star, *VN* within.	2.00	7.50	20.00
	d. Wmk: Circle and star, *//*.	2.00	7.50	20.00
	e. Black handstamp for Cholon.	2.00	7.50	20.00
	f. Counterfeit.	—	—	—
28	**100 Dông** ND (1948). Violet or brown on pink, orange or brown unpt. woman w/child and sm. flag at l., HCM at ctr., 3 workers at r. 2 seated women at l., soldier at ctr., agricultural worker at r. on back. 177 x 87mm. (Pink and brown shade varieties.)			
	a. W/o wmk.	3.00	10.00	30.00
	b. Wmk: Circle w/star w/VN in circle.	3.00	10.00	30.00
	c. Wmk: Oval w/*Vietnam*.	3.00	10.00	30.00
	x. Counterfeit.	5.00	20.00	—

1949 ISSUE

		Good	Fine	XF
29	**100 Dông** 1949. Green. HCM at r. Back brown; 2 soldiers at l. 160 x 66mm. Wmk: Circle and star. VN in star.	7.50	30.00	100.
30	**100 Dông** 1949. Like #29 but face and back blue.			
	a. Black serial #.	7.50	30.00	100.
	b. Red serial #.	7.50	30.00	100.

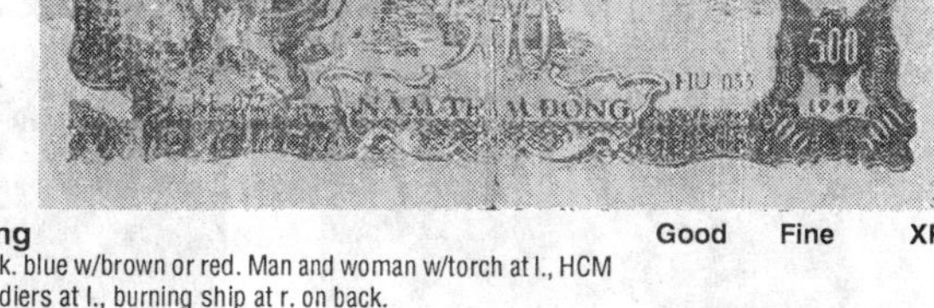

		Good	Fine	XF
31	**500 Dông** 1949. Dk. blue w/brown or red. Man and woman w/torch at l., HCM at r. Soldiers at l., burning ship at r. on back.			
	a. W/o wmk.	4.00	20.00	50.00
	b. Wmk: Circle w/star.	4.00	20.00	50.00
	s. Specimen.	—	Unc	250.

1950 ND ISSUE

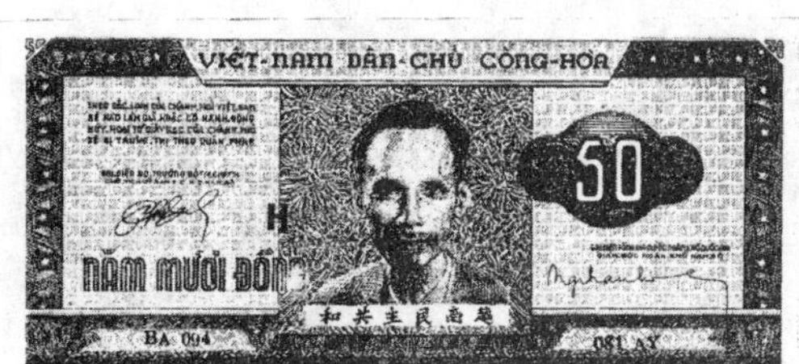

		Good	Fine	XF
32	**50 Dông** ND (1950). Black-green and yellow. HCM at ctr. Soldier w/flag at ctr. on back (Nam-Bo).	5.00	20.00	50.00

		Good	Fine	XF
33	**100 Dông** ND (1950). Blue and green. Agricultural scene at l., HCM at ctr., war scene at r. Back brown; star, worker and soldier at ctr. 170 x 98mm (Nam-Bo).	7.50	40.00	100.

		Good	Fine	XF
34	**200 Dông** 1950. Lilac-brown and dk. green. Shooting soldiers at l. and ctr., HCM at r. Soldier and 2 field workers on back. Color varieties. Clear and blurred printing varieties.			
	a. W/o wmk.	3.00	15.00	40.00
	b. Wmk: Circle w/star.	10.00	20.00	90.00

1951 ND ISSUE

		Good	Fine	XF
35	**100 Dông** ND (1951). Brown and green. HCM at l. overseeing lg. gathering. Back dk. brown and tan; 6 working women (Nam-Bo).	10.00	30.00	75.00

1952 ND ISSUE

		Good	Fine	XF
36	**5 Dông** ND (1952). Green. HCM at ctr. Back orange; 2 farmers planting at l. ctr.	75.00	150.	300.

		Good	Fine	XF
37	**10 Dông** ND (1952). Red-brown or orange-brown and lt. green. 3 laborers at l., HCM at r. Soldiers and truck on back (Nam-Bo). White or brown paper. Orange and brown shade varieties.			
	a. Wmk: Capital letters.	5.00	15.00	50.00
	b. W/o wmk.	2.00	7.50	20.00

		Good	Fine	XF
38	**20 Dông** ND (1952). Dk. brown and olive. Laborers at l. and r., HCM at ctr. Workers in factory on back (Nam-Bo). W/o wmk.	75.00	150.	350.

		Good	Fine	XF
39	**50 Dông** ND (1952). Violet on lt. or dk. yellow unpt. HCM at ctr. Back dull red; worker and woman at ctr. (Nam-Bo).	5.00	15.00	40.00
40	**100 Dông** ND (1952). Violet on lt. brown-violet unpt. HCM at l. Back lilac; harvesting scene. Wmk: Circle w/star.			
	a. *KIEU III* at lower r. W/o wmk.	50.00	125.	250.
	b. KIEV III at lower r. Wmk: circle w/star w/VNDCCH.	40.00	100.	225.
	c. Wmk: Star w/*VN* in circle.	40.00	100.	225.

		Good	Fine	XF
40A	**100 Dông** ND (ca.1953). Purple. 5 people at ctr. Back red; tropical plants. (Nam-Bo).	3.00	9.00	20.00

1953 ND ISSUE

		Good	Fine	XF
41	**20 Dông** ND (1953). Black. HCM at ctr. Light and dark paper varieties.			
	a. Brown back.	30.00	100.	200.
	b. Brown and green back. Wmk: circle w/star.	40.00	125.	250.

		Good	Fine	XF
42	**50 Dông** ND (1953). Brown and lt. green. HCM at l., rice harvesting at r. Back brown and purple; group of 10 people (Nam-Bo).	5.00	20.00	60.00

TIN PHIEU

CREDIT NOTE

1946-50 ISSUE

Issued for Trung Bo (1947-1951), w/*TIN PHIEU* indicated prominently.

		Good	Fine	XF
43	**1 Dông** ND (1946). HCM at ctr. Man w/2 water buffalos on back.			
	a. Black.	10.00	25.00	60.00
	b. Purple-brown.	10.00	25.00	60.00
	c. Brown.	10.00	25.00	60.00
44	**1 Dông** ND. Wine red. Like #43 but portr. and frame different. Back green.	10.00	25.00	60.00
45	**1 Dông** ND (1946). Lt. blue or olive. HCM at ctr. Farmer plowing w/2 oxen at l. ctr. on back. W/o wmk.	15.00	35.00	75.00

		Good	Fine	XF
46	**5 Dông** ND (1949-50). HCM at ctr. in oval wreath. Numeral *5* on back.			
	a. Lilac-brown to brown.	10.00	30.00	60.00
	b. Blue-green.	10.00	30.00	60.00
	c. Olive.	10.00	30.00	60.00
	d. Gray.	10.00	30.00	60.00
	e. Blue.	10.00	30.00	60.00
47	**5 Dông** ND (1949-50). Like #46 but portr. w/o frame. Thick and thin paper varieties for a, b and c.			
	a. Brownish orange. Green back. W/o wmk.	10.00	30.00	60.00
	b. as a. Wmk: Circle w/star.	10.00	30.00	60.00
	c. Blue. W/o wmk.	10.00	30.00	60.00
	d. Olive. Wmk: Circle w/star.	10.00	30.00	60.00

		Good	Fine	XF
48	**20 Dông** ND (1948). Orange. *TIN PHIEU* and *HAI MUOI DONG* at ctr. Back green; work scenes at l. bottom and r., crude portr. of HCM in wreath at ctr. 133 x 77mm. Light and dark paper varieties.			
	a. W/o wmk.	10.00	30.00	80.00
	b. Wmk: Circle w/star.	10.00	30.00	80.00

		Good	Fine	XF
49	**20 Dông** ND (1948). Like #48 but face and back brown on yellow unpt.			
	a. W/o wmk.	10.00	40.00	90.00
	b. Wmk: Circle w/star.	10.00	40.00	90.00

		Good	Fine	XF
50	**50 Dông** ND (1949-50). HCM in circle at lower ctr. Work scenes at l., r. and bottom. No unpt. on face. Men in sailboat on back. Brown or white paper.			
	a. Face violet-brown, back blue. W/o wmk.	10.00	40.00	90.00
	b. Face orange, back gray-green. W/o wmk.	10.00	40.00	90.00
	c. Face and back gray. W/o wmk.	10.00	40.00	90.00
	d. Violet.	10.00	40.00	90.00
	e. Brown. Back gray-green. W/o wmk. White paper.	10.00	40.00	90.00
	f. as e, Wmk: circle w/star. Brown paper.	10.00	40.00	90.00
	g. W/round handstamp and black sign. on back for Binh-Thuan Province. No wmk.	10.00	40.00	90.00
	h. W/red circular handstamp on back for Cuc-Nam Province.	10.00	40.00	90.00
51	**50 Dông** ND (1949-50). Brown and green. Like #50 but unpt. at ctr. on face.			
	a. White paper w/o wmk.	10.00	40.00	90.00
	b. Brown paper, Wmk: Circle w/star.	10.00	40.00	90.00

		Good	Fine	XF
52	**50 Dông** 1951. Dk. brown. HCM at r. Back olive; soldier, worker and farmer at ctr.			
	a. W/o wmk.	20.00	50.00	125.
	b. Wmk: Circle w/star.	20.00	50.00	125.
53	**100 Dông** ND (1950-51). Red or brown. HCM at l. Back green-gray; 2 workers and soldier.			
	a. W/o wmk.	5.00	20.00	50.00
	b. Wmk: Circle w/star.	5.00	20.00	50.00

		Good	Fine	XF
54	**100 Dông** ND (1950-51). Blue and brown. Agricultural worker w/buffalo at l., portr. HCM at r. Back pink to red-brown; star at ctr., 2 workers in front. 169 x 99mm. Many color, paper and wmk. varieties.			
	a. W/o wmk. Thin paper.	7.50	25.00	75.00
	b. Wmk: Circle w/star. Thick paper.	7.50	25.00	75.00

		Good	Fine	XF
55	**100 Dông** ND (1950-51). Green and gray. Back gray-brown; soldier, woman and children at ctr., HCM at r. 171 x 84mm.			
	a. W/o wmk. Thin paper.	30.00	50.00	150.
	b. Wmk: Circle w/star.	30.00	50.00	150.

		Good	Fine	XF
56	**100 Dông** ND (1950-51). Brownish red. HCM at r. Back blue-green and lt. brown; 2 soldiers at ctr.			
	a. W/o wmk. Thin paper.	30.00	75.00	150.
	b. Wmk: Circle w/star. Thick paper.	30.00	75.00	150.
57	**500 Dông** ND (1950-51). Gray-blue. 2 workers at ctr., HCM at r. Back green; landscape and 3 people. Wmk: Star in circle.	5.00	20.00	50.00

		Good	Fine	XF
58	**1000 Dông** ND (1950-51). Red to brown. HCM at r. Soldiers and porters on back. Wmk: Star in circle.	5.00	15.00	50.00

NGAN HANG QUOC GIA VIET NAM

NATIONAL BANK OF VIET NAM

1951-53 ISSUE

1 "New" Dong = 100 "Old" Dong

In 1952 all previously issued notes were withdrawn and demonetized. Notes in "new" Dong values, issue dated 1951 and later, were printed in Czechoslovakia and remained in circulation until 1958. Thus they were the last wartime notes issued uring the fighting against the French, and they became the official currency of the post-1954 independent Democratic Republic of Viet Nam (North Vietnam). All notes w/HCM.

#59-66 printer: CPF-Shanghai (w/o imprint).

		Good	Fine	XF
59	**10 Dông** ND. Violet-brown. HCM at l. Farmers w/water buffalos on back.	10.00	30.00	60.00

Note: For #59 ovpt. as 1 XU see #67.

		Good	Fine	XF
60	**20 Dông** 1951. Portr. HCM at l. Soldier and ships on back.			
	a. Purple.	2.00	7.50	20.00
	b. Olive.	50.00	30.00	100.
	s1. As a. Specimen.	—	—	250.
	s2. As b. Specimen.	—	—	250.

		Good	Fine	XF
61	**50 Dông** 1951. Portr. HCM at r. Harvest work on back.			
	a. Green.	2.00	12.50	40.00
	b. Brown.	2.00	20.00	50.00
	s1. As a. Specimen.	—	—	200.
	s2. As b. Specimen.	—	—	200.

		VG	VF	UNC
62	**100 Dông** 1951. HCM at r. Bomb factory on back.			
	a. Green.	2.00	12.50	40.00
	b. Blue.	5.00	20.00	50.00
	s. As a. Specimen.	—	—	200.

		VG	VF	UNC
63	**200 Dông** 1951. Portr. HCM at l., soldiers under training at ctr. Human convoy on back.			
	a. Reddish brown.	20.00	60.00	200.
	b. Green.	50.00	150.	400.
	s1. As a. Specimen.	—	—	500.
	s2. As b. Specimen.	—	—	500.

		VG	VF	UNC
64	**500 Dông** 1951. Green. HCM at l., soldiers at a gun at r. Workers tilling field on back.			
	a. Issued note.	7.50	20.00	40.00
	s. Specimen.	—	—	200.

		VG	VF	UNC
65	**1000 Dông** 1951. Brown-orange. Portr. HCM at l., soldiers advancing at ctr. Soldier, worker and farmer on back.			
	a. Issued note.	3.00	10.00	30.00
	s. Specimen.	—	—	200.
	x. Counterfeit.	—	5.00	20.00

		VG	VF	UNC
66	**5000 Dông** 1953. Blue. HCM at l. Anti-aircraft artillery emplacements on back.			
	a. Issued note.	10.00	40.00	125.
	s. Specimen.	—	—	600.

DEMOCRATIC REPUBLIC

NGÂN HÀNG QUÔC GIA VIÊT NAM

NATIONAL BANK OF VIET NAM

1958 ND PROVISIONAL ISSUE

		VG	VF	UNC
67	**1 Xu on 10 Dông** ND (1958). Ovpt. new denomination on #59 face and back.	—	500.	—

1958 ISSUE

#68-72 printer: CPF-Shanghai (w/o imprint).

		VG	VF	UNC
68	**1 Hao** 1958. Red on green unpt. Arms at ctr. Train on back.			
	a. Issued note.	.50	1.50	5.00
	b. Ovpt: *Cai Luu Hanoi Cua...* for circulation in Haiphong.	—	—	—
	c. W/control handstamp: *DA THU.* Reported not confirmed.	—	—	—
	s. Specimen.	—	—	15.00
69	**2 Hao** 1958. Green on tan unpt. Arms at ctr. Grazing animals near Coffer dam on back.			
	a. Issued note.	1.00	2.00	5.00
	b. W/control handstamp: *DA THU.*	1.00	2.00	5.00
	s. Specimen.	—	—	25.00

		VG	VF	UNC
70	**5 Hao** 1958. Brown on lt. green unpt. Arms at ctr. 4 women in spinning mill on back.			
	a. Issued note.	1.25	3.00	10.00
	b. W/control handstamp: *DA THU.* Reported not confirmed.	—	—	—
	s. Specimen.	—	—	25.00

		VG	VF	UNC
71	**1 Dông** 1958. Brown on lt. green unpt. Arms at l., monument w/tower and flag at ctr. Work in rice paddies on back.			
	a. Issued note.	1.00	3.00	10.00
	b. W/control handstamp: *DA THU.*	1.50	4.00	15.00
	s. Specimen.	—	—	25.00
	x. US lithograph counterfeit w/propaganda message at l. 6 varieties: w/o code, Code 50, Code 4540 (2 text var.) Code 4543 (2 text var.).	1.00	5.00	20.00

		VG	VF	UNC
72	**2 Dông** 1958. Blue on green unpt. Arms at l., 4 people w/flag at ctr. r. Boats and mountains on back. Wmk: White shaded star.			
	a. Issued note.	1.00	4.00	15.00
	b. W/control handstamp: *DA THU.*	2.00	6.00	20.00
	s. Specimen.	—	—	25.00
	x. US lithograph counterfeit w/propaganda message at r. Code 4541.	1.00	5.00	25.00

		VG	VF	UNC
73	**5 Dông** 1958. Brown on blue unpt. Arms at l., tractor at ctr., HCM at r. Road construction work on back.			
	a. Issued note.	2.00	7.50	20.00
	b. W/control handstamp: *DA THU.*	2.00	7.50	20.00
	s. Specimen.	—	—	30.00
	x. US lithograph counterfeit w/propaganda message at r. Code 4542.	2.00	7.50	25.00

		VG	VF	UNC
74	**10 Dông** 1958. Red on blue and green unpt. Arms at ctr., HCM at r. Factory on back.			
	a. Issued note.	2.00	7.50	25.00
	b. W/control handstamp: *DA THU.*	3.00	8.00	30.00
	s. Specimen.	—	—	35.00

Regional

Phieu Tiep Te

1949-50 ND Emergency Issues

Issued by the various local (provincial and lower) administrations.

		Good	Fine	XF
R1	**5 Cac** ND (1949-50). Dk. blue. Farmers and oxen at l. ctr. Metal working on back.	15.00	30.00	60.00
R2	**5 Cac** ND (1949-50). Red-brown. HCM at ctr. in oval wreath of corn. Soldier at l., seated man at r. on back (Soc-Trang).	25.00	50.00	100.

		Good	Fine	XF
R3	**1 Dông** ND (1949-50). Blue on brown. HCM at ctr. in oval formed of Laurel wreath. Soldier at l., star at r. on back (Soc-Trang).	20.00	40.00	100.

		Good	Fine	XF
R4	**1 Dông** ND (1949-50). Red and yellow. Man and woman. 5 soldiers on back (Thu Dau Mot).			
	a. Back w/text: *TINH-THU-DAU-MOT.*	20.00	50.00	100.
	b. Back w/text: *TINH THUDAUMOT.*	20.00	50.00	100.
	c. Back w/o either style of above legend.	20.00	50.00	100.

		Good	Fine	XF
R5	**1 Dông** ND (1949-50). Red. 5 stars at l. and r. Woman carrying load on shoulder on back (Tay Ninh).	25.00	75.00	150.
R6	**1 Dông** ND (1949-50). Blue. HCM in rectangular frame. Man carrying load on head at l., man holding spear at r. on back (Soc Trang).	20.00	50.00	100.

		Good	Fine	XF
R7	**2 Dông** ND (1949-50). Dlk. red. HCM at l. Lg. *2* at l., *HAI DONG* at r. on back.	20.00	50.00	100.

		Good	Fine	XF
R8	**2 Dông** ND (1949-50). Brown. Mountains at r. Back green; man digging at l., blacksmith at r. (Ha Tien).	30.00	100.	175.
R10	**2 Dông** 23.12.1949. Blue. Soldiers at l. attacking burning village at r. Woman w/baskets on back (Can Tho).			
	a. Back w/text: *Tat Ca De.*	30.00	100.	175.
	b. Back w/text: *Chuan Bi De.*	30.00	100.	175.

		Good	Fine	XF
R10A	**5 Dông** ND. HCM in spray at l.	20.00	50.00	125.

		Good	Fine	XF
R10B	**5 Dông** ND. Tower at ctr. Farmers and laborers on back.			
	a. W/o printer imprint.	20.00	40.00	75.00
	b. W/printer imprint at lower left on both sides.	20.00	40.00	75.00

Fantasy

1949; 1950 Dated "Issues"

A series of very clever fantasy notes appeared on the market a number of years ago. These are easily identified as the serial # printed on each note were all done with the same font of type. Listed below are 4 examples.

R(6A)	**1 Dông** 1949(1983). HCM at l. (Modern fantasy).	—	—	—

R(9) **1 Dông**
23.12.1949. Lt. brown. Woman at ctr. Star, swords and helmet on back (Can Tho). (Modern Fantasy). — — —

R(10C) **10 Dông**
9.5.1949. (Modern fantasy). — — —

R(10D) **10 Dông**
1950. Value *10* in spray at l. Laborers on back. (Modern fantasy). — — —

ND Issue

R(10E) **5 Dông**
ND. Star at ctr., fighters at sides. 3 workers at l. on back (Thu Bien).

	Good	Fine	XF
a. Red. Imprint on back at lower l. corner.	15.00	30.00	75.00
b. Orange. W/imprint.	18.00	35.00	85.00

Viet-Minh Administrative Committees

1945 ND Provisional Issues

Beginning in 1945, various Viet-Minh administrative committees (provincial, city, village and military) handstamped notes of the Banque de l'Indochine and Nam Bo. These overstamps were intended to control the use of French issued notes within the Viet-Minh liberated zones. Nam Bo notes were overstamped to assure the people who were unfamiliar with them that these newly Democratic Republic notes were authentic. These overstamps appear on numerous French Indochina issues, particularly #48, 54, 55, 66, 67 and 73. They also appear on many Nam Bo issues, particularly #17 and 50. The overstamps are found in red, black and purple ink; some are handsigned by a local Viet-Minh official, and others are either stamp signed or not signed. The Following

R11 **1 Piastre**
ND. Red circular handstamp: *BIEN HOA* on French Indochina #54c. Good 5.00, Fine 15.00, XF —

		Good	Fine	XF
R11A	**1 Piastre** ND. Red rectangular handstamp: *LONG CHAU TIEN* on French Indochina #54e for Long Xuyen, Chau Doc and Tien Giang provinces.	5.00	15.00	—
R11B	**1 Piastre** ND. Lg. circular handstamp: *THU BIEN* on French Indochina #48b. 2 sm. handstamps w/star in ctr. on back.	5.00	15.00	—
R11C	**1 Piastre** ND. Lg. circular handstamp: *CHAO DOC* on French Indochina #105.	5.00	15.00	—
R12	**5 Piastres** ND. Red circular and rectangular handstamps: *BEN TRE* on French Indochina #55.	5.00	15.00	—
R13	**5 Piastres** ND. Red circular handstamp: *CHO LON* on French Indochina #49.	5.00	15.00	—
R14	**5 Piastres** ND. Red circular handstamp: *CHO LON* on French Indochina #55.	5.00	15.00	—
R15	**10 Piastres** ND. Black circular handstamps: *LONG PHUOC* on French Indochina #80.	5.00	15.00	—
R16	**20 Piastres** ND. Red circular handstamp: *CHO LON* on French Indochina #81.	5.00	15.00	—
R17	**100 Piastres** ND. Red circular handstamp: *RACH-GIA*.			
	a. On French Indochina #66.	5.00	15.00	—
	b. On French Indochina #67.	5.00	15.00	—
	c. On French Indochina #73.	5.00	15.00	—
R18	**100 Piastres** ND. Red rectangular handstamp: *LONG CHAU HA* on French Indochina #66.	5.00	15.00	—

Note: No doubt virtually all of the Banque de l'Indochine notes in circulation at the time were overstamped by various Viet-Minh agencies. Only reported complete notes are listed above. Many more must exist.

		Good	Fine	XF
R19	**100 Piastres** ND. Red circular handstamp: *BEN-TRE* on French Indochina #66.	5.00	15.00	—

Tra Vinh Province

1951 Provisional Issue

		Good	Fine	XF
R31	**100 Dông** 18.3.1951. Control ticket added w/red-violet handstamp: *TRA VINH* on #28.	150.	300.	—

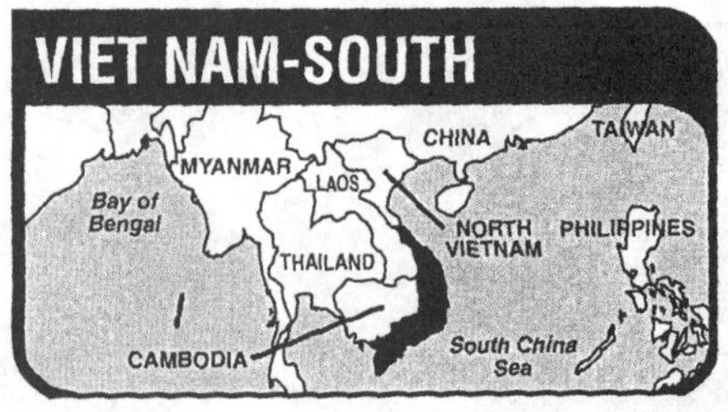

South Viet Nam (the former Republic of Viet Nam), located in Southeast Asia, bounded by North Viet Nam on the north, Laos and Cambodia on the west, and the South China Sea on the east and south, had an area of 66,280 sq. mi. (171,665 sq. km.) and a population of 20 million. Capital: Saigon. The economy of the area is predominantly agricultural.

South Viet Nam, the direct successor to the French-dominated regime (also known as the State of Viet Nam), was created after the first Indochina War (between the French and the Viet-Minh) by the Geneva agreement of 1954 which divided Viet Nam at the 17th parallel of latitude. Elections which would have reunified North and South Viet Nam in 1956 never took place, and the North continued the war for unification of Viet Nam under the the Democratic Republic of (North) Viet Nam. The Republic of Viet Nam surrendered unconditionally on April 30, 1975. There followed a short period of coexistence of the two Viet Namese states, but the South was governed by the North through the Peoples Revolutionary Government (PRG). On July 2, 1976, South and North Viet Nam joined to form the Socialist Republic of Viet Nam.

Also see Viet Nam.

MONETARY SYSTEM

1 Dông = 100 Xu

VIET NAM - SOUTH

NGÂN-HÀNG QUÔ'C-GIA VIÊT-NAM

NATIONAL BANK OF VIET NAM

1955; 1956 ND FIRST ISSUE

#1-4 wmk: Tiger's head.

		VG	VF	UNC
1	**1 Dông** ND (1956). Green on lilac unpt. Temple at r. Bldg. at l. on back.			
	a. Issued note.	.25	1.00	4.00
	s. Specimen.	—	—	125.
2	**5 Dông** ND (1955). Green on gold and lilac unpt. Bird at ctr. Farmer w/water buffalo on back.			
	a. Issued note.	.50	1.50	7.50
	s. Specimen.	—	—	150.

		VG	VF	UNC
3	**10 Dông** ND (1955). Deep red on blue and gray unpt. Fish at ctr. Coastal area w/boats on back.			
	a. Issued note.	.50	3.00	12.00
	s. Specimen.	—	—	200.

		VG	VF	UNC
4	**20 Dông** ND (1956). Green and m/c. Huts and boats at l., banana plants at r. Farmers and water buffalos on back.			
	a. Issued note.	2.00	12.50	50.00
	s. Specimen.	—	—	400.

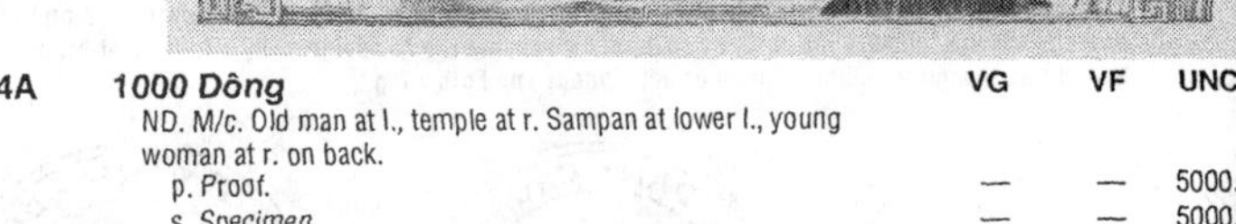

		VG	VF	UNC
4A	***1000 Dông*** ND. M/c. Old man at l., temple at r. Sampan at lower l., young woman at r. on back.			
	p. Proof.	—	—	5000.
	s. Specimen.	—	—	5000.

1955-58 ND SECOND ISSUE

		VG	VF	UNC
7	**50 Dông** ND (1956). Purple. Boy w/water buffalo at l. Sifting grain on back. Printer: SBNC.			
	a. Issued note.	3.00	12.00	75.00
	p. Uniface proof. Face and back.	—	—	—
	s. Specimen.	—	—	150.

		VG	VF	UNC
8	**100 Dông** ND (1955). Gray. Farmer on tractor at ctr. Stylized peacock on green back. Printer: ABNC (w/o imprint).			
	a. Issued note.	3.00	12.50	50.00
	p. Uniface proof mounted on card stock. Face and back.	—	—	325.
	s. Specimen.			

		VG	VF	UNC
9	**200 Dông** ND (1958). Purple on green unpt. Bank at r. Fishing boats on back. Printer: ABNC (w/o imprint).			
	a. Issued note.	5.00	17.50	80.00
	p. Uniface Proof mounted on card stock. Face and back.	—	—	—
	s. Specimen.	—	—	300.

		VG	VF	UNC
10	**500 Dông** ND (1955). Blue. Pagoda at ctr. Back orange. Printer: ABNC (w/o imprint).			
	a. Issued note.	25.00	125.	500.
	p. Uniface proof mounted on card stock. Face and back.	—	—	—
	s1. Specimen w/ovpt: *GIAY MAU*, punched hole cancelled.	—	—	750.
	s2. Specimen w/ovpt: *SPECIMEN*.	—	—	750.

1955 ND Third Issue

#11-14 printer: SBNC.

		VG	VF	UNC
11	**1 Dông** ND (1955). Gray. Woman farm worker threshing grain at l. Rice paddy worker on back.			
	a. Issued note.	.25	2.00	8.00
	s. Specimen.	—	—	175.

		VG	VF	UNC
12	**2 Dông** ND (1955). Purplish blue. Boat at r. River scene on back.			
	a. Issued note.	.25	1.25	5.00
	p. Uniface proof. Face and back.	—	—	175.
	s. Specimen.	—	—	175.

		VG	VF	UNC
13	**5 Dông** ND (1955). Dull red on peach unpt. Farmer w/water buffalo at l. River scene w/house on back.			
	a. Issued note.	.25	1.25	5.00
	p. Uniface proof. Face and back.	—	—	—
	s. Specimen.	—	—	175.
	x. Counterfeit. Propaganda on back.	—	—	25.00

		VG	VF	UNC
14	**200 Dông** ND (1955). Green. Soldier at l. Girl w/sheaves in field on back.			
	a. Issued note.	20.00	100.	400.
	s. Specimen w/ovpt: *GIAY MAU*, punched hole cancelled.	—	—	500.
14A	**200 Dông** ND. Green. Similar to #14, but engraved. (Not issued.)			
	s1. Specimen.	—	—	800.
	s2. Specimen. Uniface pair in various colors.	—	—	1000.

Note: A number of trial pieces for #14A in various colors are verified.

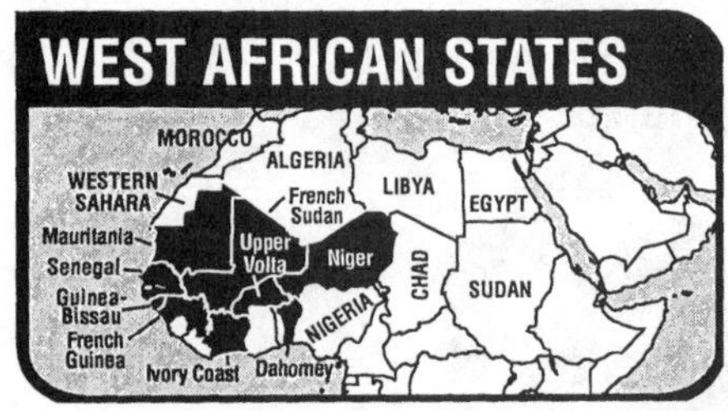

The West African States, a former federation of eight French colonial territories on the northwest coast of Africa, had an area of 1,813,079 sq. mi. (4,742,495 sq. km.) and a population of about 60 million. Capital: Dakar. The constituent territories were Mauritania, Senegal, Dahomey, French Sudan, Ivory Coast, Upper Volta, Niger and French Guinea.

The members of the federation were overseas territories within the French Union until Sept. of 1958 when all but French Guinea approved the constitution of the Fifth French Republic, thereby electing to become autonomous members of the new French Community. French Guinea voted to become the fully independent Republic of Guinea. The other seven attained independence in 1960. The French West Africa territories were provided with a common currency, a practice which was continued as the monetary union of the West African States which provides a common currency to the autonomous republics of Dahomey (now Benin), Mali, Senegal, Upper Volta (now Burkina Faso) Ivory Coast, Togo, Niger, and Guinea-Bissau.

MONETARY SYSTEM:

1 Franc = 100 Centimes

SIGNATURE VARIETIES

	Le Presidént	Le Directeur Général	Date
1			various dates - 1959 20.3.1961
2			

BANQUE CENTRALE DES ETATS DE L'AFRIQUE DE L'OUEST

GENERAL ISSUES W/O CODE LETTER

1958; 1959 ND ISSUE

#1-5 w/o code letters to signify member countries.

		VG	VF	UNC
1	**50 Francs** ND (1958). Dk. brown, blue and m/c. 3 women at ctr. Woman w/headress at ctr. on back. Sign. 1.	10.00	40.00	110.

Note: #1 was not issued w/code letters.

		VG	VF	UNC
2	**100 Francs** 1959; ND. Dk. brown, orange and m/c. Mask at l., woman at r. Woman at l., carving at lower ctr. on back. Wmk: Women's head.			
	a. Sign. 1. 23.4.1959.	10.00	40.00	90.00
	b. Sign. 5. ND.	3.00	10.00	20.00
3	**500 Francs** 15.4.1959. Brown, green and m/c. Men doing field work at l., mask carving at r. Woman at l., farmer on tractor at r. on back. Wmk: Woman's head. Sign. 1.	30.00	70.00	150.
4	**1000 Francs** 17.9.1959. Brown, blue and m/c. Man and woman at ctr. Man w/rope suspension bridge in background and pineapples on back. Wmk: Man's head. Sign. 1.	20.00	50.00	125.
5	**5000 Francs** 15.4.1959. Blue, brown and m/c. Bearded man at l., bldg. at ctr. Woman, corn grinders and huts on back. Sign. 1.	20.00	130.	—

Note: All other issues for West African States will be found in Volume 3.

A FOR COTE D'IVOIRE (IVORY COAST)

1959-65; ND ISSUE

		VG	VF	UNC
102A	**500 Francs** 1959-64; ND. Brown, green and m/c. Field workers at l., mask carving at r. Woman at l., farmer on tractor at r. on back. Wmk: Woman's head.			
	a. Engraved. Sign. 1. 15.4.1959.	25.00	55.00	150.
	b. Sign. 1. 20.3.1961.	12.00	35.00	90.00
	c. Sign. 2. 20.3.1961.	12.00	35.00	90.00
	d. Sign. 3. 2.12.1964.	25.00	55.00	150.
	e. Sign. 5. ND.	12.00	35.00	90.00
	f. Sign. 6. ND.	10.00	30.00	75.00
	g. Litho. Sign. 6. ND.	13.00	40.00	100.
	h. Sign. 7. ND.	12.00	35.00	90.00
	i. Sign. 8. ND.	20.00	50.00	120.
	j. Sign. 9. ND.	8.00	25.00	60.00
	k. Sign. 10. ND.	5.00	15.00	45.00
	l. Sign. 11. ND.	5.00	15.00	40.00
	m. Sign. 12. ND.	7.50	25.00	90.00
103A	**1000 Francs** 1959-65; ND. Brown, blue and m/c. Man and woman at ctr. Man w/rope suspension bridge in background and pineapples on back. Wmk: Man's head.			
	a. Engraved. Sign. 1. 17.9.1959.	50.00	150.	—
	b. Sign. 1. 20.3.1961.	15.00	45.00	110.
	c. Sign. 2. 20.3.1961.	15.00	45.00	110.
	d. Sign. 4. 2.3.1965.	30.00	80.00	—
	e. Sign. 5. ND.	8.00	25.00	60.00
	f. Sign. 6. ND.	8.00	25.00	60.00
	g. Litho. Sign. 6. ND.	8.00	25.00	60.00
	h. Sign. 7. ND.	10.00	30.00	70.00
	i. Sign. 8. ND.	12.00	40.00	90.00
	j. Sign. 9. ND.	8.00	25.00	60.00
	k. Sign. 10. ND.	5.00	15.00	40.00
	l. Sign. 11. ND.	5.00	15.00	35.00
	m. Sign. 12. ND.	5.00	15.00	35.00
	n. Sign. 13. ND.	5.00	15.00	35.00

D FOR MALI

1959-61; ND ISSUE

		Good	Fine	XF
402D	**500 Francs** 1959; 1961. Like #102A.			
	a. Sign. I. 15.4.1959.	100.	300.	—
	b. Sign. I. 20.3.1961.	—	—	—
403D	**1000 Francs** 1959; 1961. Like #103A.			
	a. Sign. I. 17.9.1959.	85.00	250.	500.
	b. Sign. I. 20.3.1961.	85.00	250.	500.

E FOR MAURITANIA

1959-64; ND ISSUE

		Good	Fine	XF
502E	**500 Francs** 1959-64; ND. Like #102A.			
	a. Engraved. Sign. 1. 15.4.1959.	55.00	120.	400.
	b. Sign. 1. 20.3.1961.	45.00	100.	350.
	c. Sign. 2. 20.3.1961.	45.00	100.	350.
	e. Sign. 4. 2.3.1965.	45.00	100.	350.
	f. Sign. 5. ND.	45.00	100.	350.
	g. Sign. 6. ND.	45.00	100.	350.
	h. Litho. Sign. 6. ND.	45.00	100.	350.
	i. Sign. 7. ND.	45.00	100.	350.

H FOR NIGER

1959-65; ND ISSUE

		VG	VF	UNC
602H	**500 Francs** 1959-65; ND. Like #102A.			
	a. Engraved. Sign. 1. 15.4.1959.	50.00	125.	—
	c. Sign. 2. 20.3.1961.	50.00	125.	—
	d. Sign. 3. 2.12.1964.	25.00	75.00	175.
	e. Sign. 4. 2.3.1965.	25.00	75.00	175.
	f. Sign. 5. ND.	45.00	100.	—
	g. Sign. 6. ND.	10.00	30.00	100.
	h. Litho. Sign. 6. ND.	10.00	30.00	100.
	i. Sign. 7. ND.	20.00	65.00	150.
	j. Sign. 8. ND.	10.00	30.00	100.
	k. Sign. 9. ND.	8.00	25.00	80.00
	l. Sign. 10. ND.	75.00	—	—
	m. Sign. 11. ND.	5.00	15.00	55.00

603H	1000 Francs	VG	VF	UNC
	1959-65; ND. Like #103A.			
	a. Sign. 1. 17.9.1959.	—	—	—
	b. Sign. 1. 20.3.1961.	30.00	65.00	175.
	c. Sign. 2. 20.3.1961.	75.00	—	—
	e. Sign. 4. 2.3.1965.	30.00	65.00	175.
	f. Sign. 5. ND.	30.00	65.00	175.
	g. Sign. 6. ND.	10.00	35.00	90.00
	h. Litho. Sign. 6. ND.	20.00	45.00	125.
	i. Sign. 7. ND.	10.00	35.00	100.
	j. Sign. 8. ND.	30.00	65.00	—
	k. Sign. 9. ND	8.00	30.00	70.00
	l. Sign. 10. ND.	5.00	15.00	50.00
	m. Sign. 11. ND.	5.00	15.00	45.00
	n. Sign. 12. ND.	5.00	15.00	50.00
	o. Sign. 13. ND.	5.00	20.00	60.00

K for Senegal

1959-65; ND Issue

702K	500 Francs	VG	VF	UNC
	1959-65; ND. Like #102A.			
	a. Engraved. Sign. 1. 15.4.1959.	25.00	55.00	150.
	b. Sign. 1. 20.3.1961.	15.00	45.00	120.
	c. Sign. 2. 20.3.1961.	15.00	45.00	120.
	d. Sign. 3. 2.12.1964.	15.00	45.00	120.
	e. Sign. 4. 2.3.1965.	12.00	40.00	100.
	f. Sign. 5. ND.	18.00	50.00	130.
	g. Sign. 6. ND.	8.00	25.00	75.00
	h. Litho. Sign. 6. ND.	8.00	25.00	75.00
	i. Sign. 7. ND.	12.00	40.00	100.
	j. Sign. 8. ND.	12.00	40.00	100.
	k. Sign. 9. ND.	5.00	20.00	60.00
	l. Sign. 10. ND.	4.00	15.00	50.00
	m. Sign. 11. ND.	4.00	12.00	40.00
	n. Sign. 12. ND.	4.00	15.00	45.00

703K	1000 Francs	VG	VF	UNC
	1959-65; ND. Like #103A.			
	a. Engraved. Sign. 1. 17.9.1959.	20.00	60.00	150.
	b. Sign. 1. 20.3.1961.	20.00	60.00	150.
	c. Sign. 2. 20.3.1961.	12.00	45.00	110.
	e. Sign. 4. 2.3.1965.	12.00	45.00	110.
	f. Sign. 5. ND.	35.00	90.00	—
	g. Sign. 6. ND.	35.00	90.00	—
	h. Litho. Sign. 6. ND.	5.00	15.00	50.00
	i. Sign. 7. ND.	8.00	20.00	60.00
	j. Sign. 8. ND.	8.00	20.00	60.00
	k. Sign. 9. ND.	5.00	15.00	50.00
	l. Sign. 10. ND.	4.00	12.00	40.00
	m. Sign. 11. ND.	4.00	10.00	35.00
	n. Sign. 12. ND.	4.00	12.00	40.00
	o. Sign. 13. ND.	4.00	12.00	40.00

T for Togo

1959-65; ND Issue

802T	500 Francs	VG	VF	UNC
	1959-61; ND. Like #102A.			
	a. Engraved. Sign. 1. 15.4.1959.	25.00	55.00	150.
	b. Sign. 1. 20.3.1961.	35.00	100.	—
	c. Sign. 2. 20.3.1961.	35.00	100.	—
	f. Sign. 5. ND.	25.00	55.00	150.
	g. Sign. 6. ND.	8.00	25.00	75.00
	i. Litho. Sign. 7. ND.	20.00	50.00	130.
	j. Sign. 8. ND.	20.00	50.00	130.
	k. Sign. 9. ND.	5.00	20.00	60.00
	l. Sign. 10. ND.	10.00	30.00	90.00
	m. Sign. 11. ND.	1.00	5.00	30.00

803T	1000 Francs	VG	VF	UNC
	1959-65; ND. Like #103A.			
	a. Engraved. Sign. 1. 17.9.1959.	75.00	—	—
	b. Sign. 1. 20.3.1961.	20.00	60.00	150.
	c. Sign. 2. 20.3.1961.	35.00	90.00	—
	e. Sign. 4. 2.3.1965.	20.00	60.00	140.
	f. Sign. 5. ND.	20.00	60.00	150.
	g. Sign. 6. ND.	10.00	30.00	70.00
	h. Litho. Sign. 6. ND.	25.00	70.00	—
	i. Sign. 7. ND.	10.00	30.00	70.00
	j. Sign. 8. ND.	35.00	90.00	—
	k. Sign. 9. ND.	5.00	20.00	50.00
	l. Sign. 10. ND.	5.00	15.00	40.00
	m. Sign. 11. ND.	4.00	10.00	35.00
	n. Sign. 12. ND.	5.00	15.00	40.00
	o. Sign. 13. ND.	5.00	15.00	40.00

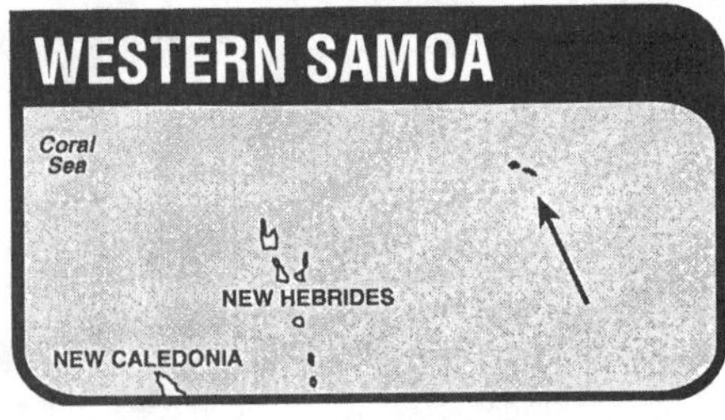

The Independent State of Western Samoa (formerly German Samoa), located in the Pacific Ocean 1,600 miles (2,574 km.) northeast of New Zealand, has an area of 1,097 sq. mi. (2,860 sq. km.) and a population of 157,000. Capital: Apia. The economy is d on agriculture, fishing and tourism. Copra, cocoa and bananas are exported.

The Samoan group of islands was discovered by Dutch navigator Jacob Roggeveen in 1772. Great Britain, the United States and Germany established consular representation at Apia in 1847, 1853 and 1861 respectively. The conflicting interests of the three powers produced the Berlin agreement of 1889 which declared Samoa neutral and had the effect of establishing a tripartite protectorate over the islands. A further agreement, 1899, recognized the rights of the United States in those islands east of 171 deg. west longitude (American Samoa) and of Germany in the other islands (Western Samoa). New Zealand occupied Western Samoa at the start of World War I and administered it as a League of Nations mandate and U.N. trusteeship until Jan. 1, 1962, when it became an independent state.

Western Samoa is a member of the Commonwealth of Nations. The Chief Executive is Chief of State. The prime minister is the Head of Government. The present Head of State, Malietoa Tanumafili II, holds his position for life. Future Heads of State will be elected by the Legislature Assembly for five-year terms.

RULERS:

British, 1914-1962
Malietoa Tanumafili II, 1962-

MONETARY SYSTEM:

1 Shilling = 12 Pence
1 Pound = 20 Shillings to 1967
1 Tala = 100 Sene, 1967-

NEW ZEALAND OCCUPATION - WW I

GOVERNMENT OF SAMOA

1920 ND PROVISIONAL ISSUE

#1-2 ovpt: *GOVERNMENT OF SAMOA/CURRENCY NOTE* on Bank of New Zealand notes until 1921.

		Good	Fine	XF
1	**10 Shillings** (1920 -old date 1917). M/c. Red ovpt. on face only on New Zealand #S223. Apia. Rare.	—	—	—
2	**1 Pound** ND (1920). Ovpt. on New Zealand #S225. Rare.	—	—	—

NEW ZEALAND ADMINISTRATION

TERRITORY OF WESTERN SAMOA

1920-22 TREASURY NOTE ISSUE

By Authority of New Zealand Government

#7-9 various date and sign. varieties. Printer: BWC.

Note: Some of these notes may appear to be ND, probably through error or washed out, faded or worn off hand-stamped dates.

		Good	Fine	XF
7	**10 Shillings** 1922-59. Black on brown and green unpt. Palm trees along beach at ctr.			
	a. 3.3.1922.	—	—	—
	b. Sign. title: *MINISTER OF EXTERNAL AFFAIRS FOR NEW ZEALAND* at l. 13.4.1938-21.11.1949.	50.00	175.	500.
	c. Sign. title: *MINISTER OF ISLAND TERRITORIES FOR NEW ZEALAND* at l. 24.5.1951-27.5.1958; 29.10.1959.	75.00	250.	700.
	d. Sign. title: *HIGH COMMISSIONER* at l. 20.3.1957-22.12.1959.	35.00	150.	500.

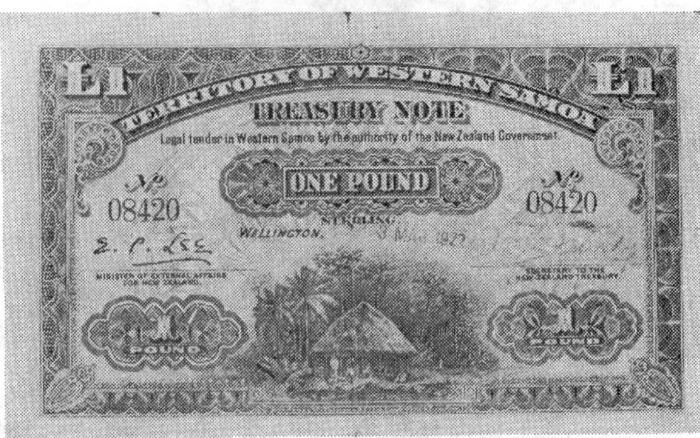

		Good	Fine	XF
8	**1 Pound** 1922-47. Purple on m/c unpt. Hut, palm trees at ctr. *STERLING* directly appears close beneath spelled out denomination at ctr.			
	a. 3.3.1922. Rare.	—	—	—
	b. Sign. title: *MINISTER OF EXTERNAL AFFAIRS FOR NEW ZEALAND* at l. 12.1.1937-12.1.1947.	65.00	200.	550.
8A	**1 Pound** 1948-61. Purple on m/c unpt. Like #8 but *STERLING* omitted from ctr.			
	a. Sign. title: *MINISTER OF ISLAND TERRITORIES FOR NEW ZEALAND* at l. 6.8.1948-7.8.1958.	100.	400.	1250.
	b. Sign. title: *HIGH COMMISSIONER* at l. 20.4.1959; 10.12.1959; 1.5.1961.	65.00	225.	1000.
9	**5 Pounds** 1920-44. Purple on m/c unpt. Boat at lower ctr. *STERLING* directly appears close beneath spelled out denomination at ctr.			
	a. (1920's). Rare.	—	—	—
	b. Sign. title: *MINISTER OF EXTERNAL AFFAIRS FOR NEW ZEALAND* at l. 3.11.1942.	1000.	3500.	—
9A	**5 Pounds** 1956-59. Purple on m/c unpt. Like #9 but *STERLING* omitted from ctr.			
	a. Sign. title *MINISTER FOR ISLAND TERRITORIES FOR NEW ZEALAND* at l. 11.4.1956. Reported not confirmed.	—	—	—
	b. Sign. title: *HIGH COMMISSIONER* at l. 30.1.1958. Rare.	—	—	—
	c. Sign. title as above. 13.10.1958; 10.12.1959.	450.	1500.	3500

BANK OF WESTERN SAMOA

1960-61 PROVISIONAL ISSUE

#10-12 red ovpt: *Bank of Western Samoa, Legal Tender in Western Samoa by virtue of the Bank of Western Samoa Ordinance 1959* on older notes. Various date and sign. varieties.

		VG	VF	UNC
10	**10 Shillings** 1960-61; ND. Ovpt. on #7.			
	a. Sign. title: *HIGH COMMISSIONER* blocked out at lower l., w/*MINISTER OF FINANCE* below. 8.12.1960; 1.5.1961.	35.00	150.	550
	b. ND. Sign. title: *MINISTER OF FINANCE* in plate w/o ovpt., at lower l.	35.00	150.	550

		VG	VF	UNC
11	**1 Pound**			
	1960-61. Ovpt. on #8.			
	a. Sign. title: *HIGH COMMISSIONER* blocked out at lower l., w/*MINISTER OF FINANCE* below. 8.11.1960; 1.5.1961.	65.00	300.	1150.
	b. Sign. title: *MINISTER OF FINANCE* in plate w/o ovpt., at lower l. 1.5.1961.	65.00	275.	1100.
12	**5 Pounds**			
	1.5.1961. Ovpt. on #9A.	500.	1750.	4500.

The Federal Republic of Yugoslavia is a Balkan country located on the east shore of the Adriatic Sea bordering Bosnia-Herzegovina and Croatia to the west, Hungary and Romania to the north, Bulgaria to the east, and Albania and Macedonia to the south. It has an area of 39,449 sq. mi. (102,173 sq. km.) and a population of 10.5 million. Capital: Belgrade. The chief industries are agriculture, mining, manufacturing and tourism. Machinery, nonferrous metals, meat and fabrics are exported.

The first South-Slavian State - Yugoslavia - was proclaimed on Dec. 1, 1918, after the union of the Kingdom of Serbia, Montenegro and the South Slav territories of Austria-Hungary; it then changed its official name from the Kingdom of the Serbs, Croats, and Slovenes to the Kingdom of Yugoslavia on Oct. 3, 1929. The Royal government of Yugoslavia attempted to remain neutral in World War II but, yielding to German pressure, aligned itself with the Axis powers in March of 1941; a few days later it was overthrown by a military-led coup and its neutrality reasserted. The Nazis occupied the country on April 17, and throughout the remaining years were resisted by a number of guerrilla armies, notably that of Marshal Josip Broz known as Tito. After the defeat of the Axis powers, a leftist coalition headed by Tito abolished the monarchy and, on Jan. 31, 1946, established a "People's Republic". Tito's rival General Draza Mihajlovic, who led the Chetniks against the Germans and Tito's forces, was arrested on March 13, 1946 and executed the following day after having been convicted by a partisan court.

The Federal Republic of Yugoslavia was composed of six autonomous republics: Serbia, Croatia, Slovenia, Bosnia-Herzegovina, Macedonia and Montenegro with two autonomous provinces within Serbia: Kosovo-Metohija and Vojvodina. The collapse of the Socialist Federal Republic of Yugoslavia during 1991-92 has resulted in the autonomous republics of Croatia, Slovenia, Bosnia-Herzegovina and Macedonia declaring their respective independence.

The Federal Republic of Yugoslavia was proclaimed in 1992; it consists of the former Republics of Serbia and Montenegro.

RULERS:

Peter I, 1918-1921
Alexander I, 1921-1934
Peter II, 1934-1945

MONETARY SYSTEM:

1 Dinar = 100 Para
1 Dinar = 100 *Old* Dinara, 1965
1 Dinar = 10,000 *Old* Dinara, 1990-91
1 Dinar = 10 *Old* Dinara, 1992
1 Dinar = 1 Million *Old* Dinara, 1.10.1993
1 Dinar = 1 Milliard *Old* Dinara, 1.1.1994
1 Novi Dinar = 1 German Mark = 12,000,000 Dinara, 1.24.94

WATERMARK VARIETIES

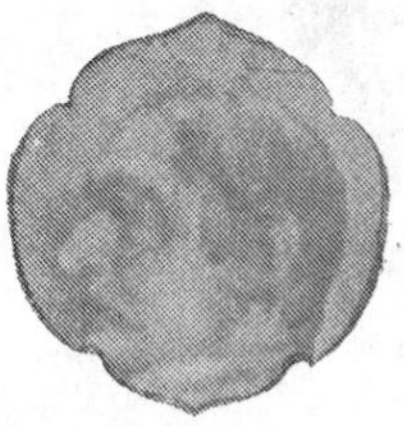
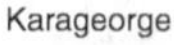

Karageorge

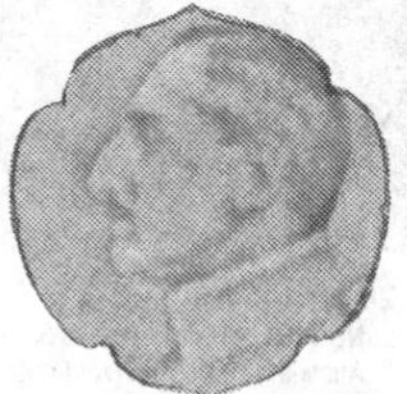

Alexander I

КРАЉЕВСТВО СРБА ХРВАТА И СЛОВЕНАЦА

Kingdom of Serbs, Croats and Slovenes

МИНИСТАРСТВО ФИНАНСИЈА

Ministry of Finance

Adhesive stamps affixed to old notes of the Austro-Hungarian Bank (including some already ovpt. in previous issue).

NOTE: Numerous local and government ovpt. (usually w/handstamp indicating redemption to Yugoslav currency) exist on notes of the Austro-Hungarian Bank and Serbian ovpt. on Bulgarian notes. As part of this second revalidation, special adhesive stamps were affixed to the notes. Wording on the 10, 20, and 50 Kronen stamps is tri-lingual (Serbian, Croatian, and Slovene), thus there is for lower denominations only one kind of stamp. Adhesive stamps affixed to 100 and 1000 Kronen notes have wording in only one language, Serbian (Cyrillic), Croatian or Slovene. Thus there are 3 different adhesive stamps for higher denominations.

Slovenian text: KRALJESTVO • SRBOV • HRVATOV • SLOVENCEV

Croatian text: KRALJEVSTVO • SRBA • HRVATA • SLOVENACA

1919 First Provisional Issues

Black round ovpt. of inscription and eagle on old notes of the Austro-Hungarian Bank.

		Good	Fine	XF
1	**10 Kronen** ND (1919 - old date 2.1.1915). Ovpt. on Austria #19.	8.00	20.00	65.00
2	**20 Kronen** ND (1919 - old date 2.1.1913). Ovpt. on Austria #13.	40.00	100.	200.
3	**50 Kronen** ND (1919 - old date 2.1.1914). Ovpt. on Austria #15.	10.00	25.00	50.00

		Good	Fine	XF
4	**100 Kronen** ND (1919 - old date 2.1.1912). Ovpt. on Austria #12.	8.00	20.00	50.00
5	**1000 Kronen** ND (1919 - old date 2.1.1902). Ovpt. on Austria #8.	17.50	50.00	100.

1919 Second Provisional Issues

#6-10B descriptions refer only to the adhesive stamps affixed.

		Good	Fine	XF
6	**10 Kronen** ND (1919). Orange. Text in 3 languages; woman facing l.			
	a. Adhesive stamp affixed to Austria #9 (-old date 2.1.1904).	3.00	8.00	20.00
	b. Adhesive stamp affixed to Austria #19 (-old date 2.1.1915).	2.00	6.00	15.00

		Good	Fine	XF
7	**20 Kronen** ND (1919). Lilac. Text in 3 languages; woman facing l. affixed to Austria #13 or #14 (-old date 2.1.1913).	2.00	6.00	15.00
8	**50 Kronen** ND (1919). Green. Text in 3 languages; woman facing l.			
	a. Adhesive stamp affixed to Austria #6 (-old date 2.1.1902).	8.00	20.00	50.00
	b. Adhesive stamp affixed to Austria #15 (-old date 2.1.1914).	3.00	10.00	25.00

		Good	Fine	XF
9	**100 Kronen** ND (1919-old date 2.1.1912). Brown. Text in Serbian (Cyrillic letters). Adhesive stamp affixed to Austria #12.	4.00	12.00	30.00
9A	**100 Kronen** ND (1919-old date 2.1.1912). Brown. Text in Croatian. Adhesive stamp affixed to Austria #12.	3.00	10.00	25.00
9B	**100 Kronen** ND (1919-old date 2.1.1912). Text in Slovenian. Adhesive stamp affixed to Austria #12.	4.00	12.00	30.00

Note: On #9, 9A and 9B the stamp is either perforated or straight edged.

		Good	Fine	XF
10	**1000 Kronen** ND (1919-old date 2.1.1902). Blue, brown and orange. Text in Serbian (Cyrillic letters). Adhesive stamp affixed to Austria #8.	5.00	15.00	35.00

		Good	Fine	XF
10A	**1000 Kronen** ND (1919-old date 2.1.1902). Lt. blue, brown and orange. Text in Croatian. Adhesive stamp affixed to Austria #8.	4.00	12.00	30.00

		Good	Fine	XF
10B	**1000 Kronen** ND (1919-old date 2.1.1902). Dk. blue, brown and orange. Text in Slovenian. Adhesive stamp affixed to Austria #8.	4.00	12.00	30.00

1919 Dinar Issue

		VG	VF	UNC
11	**1/2 Dinara** 1.2.1919. Brown and aqua on pink unpt. Arms at ctr. Back green and tan.	1.00	5.00	12.50
12	**1 Dinar** ND (1919). Orange-brown on lt. tan unpt. Helmeted man at l.	2.00	7.50	20.00
12A	**5 Dinara** ND (1919). Lilac and brown on lt. blue unpt. Like #16 but w/o ovpt.	25.00	60.00	—

1921 ISSUE

		VG	VF	UNC
13	**25 Para = 1/4 Dinar** 21.3.1921. Blue on olive unpt. Girl at l. and r., bldg. at ctr. Back brown; church at l., equestrian statue at r.	1.00	5.00	15.00

1919 KRONE PROVISIONAL ISSUE

#14-20 ovpt. in Kronen-currency (Kpyha-Kruna-Kron). Color varieties of ovpt.

		VG	VF	UNC
14	**2 Kronen on 1/2 Dinara** ND (-old date 1.2.1919). Red ovpt. on #11.			
	a. *KPYHE* (correct form).	2.00	8.00	22.50
	x. *KYPHE* (error). Rare.	—	—	—

		VG	VF	UNC
15	**4 Kronen on 1 Dinar** ND (1919). Red ovpt. (always w/error *KYPHE*) on #12.	2.00	8.00	22.50

		VG	VF	UNC
16	**20 Kronen on 5 Dinara** ND (1919). Lilac and brown on lt. blue unpt. Helmeted man at l. Caduceus w/wreath on back. Ovpt. on #12A.			
	a. *KPYHA* (correct form).	2.00	15.00	45.00
	x. *KYPHA* (error).	20.00	60.00	120.

		VG	VF	UNC
17	**40 Kronen on 10 Dinara** 1.2.1919. Blue w/black text. Blacksmith standing at l. Fruit baskets upper l. and r. on back.	5.00	25.00	75.00

		VG	VF	UNC
18	**80 Kronen on 20 Dinara** 1.2.1919. Olive. Farmers plowing w/oxen. Back blue on red unpt.; wheat in field.	6.00	40.00	100.

		VG	VF	UNC
19	**400 Kronen on 100 Dinara** ND (1919). Lilac. Children at lower l. and r.	60.00	150.	500.
20	**4000 Kronen on 1000 Dinara** ND (1919). Gray-violet. 3 allegorical figures at l. and r. Figures in ornamented circle at ctr., allegorical heads at l. and r. on back. Wmk: Helmeted man. Rare.	—	—	—

НАРОДНА БАНКА КРАЉЕВИНЕ СРБА ХРВАТА И СЛОВЕНАЦА

NATIONAL BANK, KINGDOM OF SERBS, CROATS AND SLOVENES

1920 ISSUES

		VG	VF	UNC
21	**10 Dinara** 1.11.1920. Blue on m/c unpt. "Progress" (man w/wheel) at l. Rocks and mountains on back. Printer: ABNC.			
	a. Issued note.	7.50	50.00	200.
	s. Specimen.	—	100.	200.

		VG	VF	UNC
22	**100 Dinara** 30.11.1920. Purple on yellow unpt. Boats in water at ctr., seated woman w/sword at r. Violet and m/c back; sailboats at ctr., man w/fruit leaning on shield w/arms at r. Wmk: Karageorge.	15.00	75.00	300.
23	**1000 Dinara** 30.11.1920. Brown and m/c. St. George slaying dragon at l., church at ctr. r. 5 city and farm scenes on back.			
	a. Issued note. Rare.	—	—	—
	x1. Counterfeit w/o wmk. or serial # and on thicker paper.	10.00	20.00	50.00
	x2. Counterfeit w/serial # and printed wmk.	15.00	30.00	65.00

		VG	VF	UNC
24	**1000 Dinara** 30.11.1920. Brown and m/c. Like #23 but blue ovpt. of male head (Karageorge) and inscription for Kingdom of Yugoslavia; colored rosette printing extending vertically through ctr.	100.	200.	550.

Note: Deceptive counterfeits of #24 are reported to exist. Genuine examples have a wmk.

1926 Issue

		VG	VF	UNC
25	**10 Dinara** 26.5.1926. Red-orange, blue and m/c. Woman at r. Arms at l. on back. Wmk: Woman's head. French printing.	10.00	50.00	175.

КРАЉЕВИНЕ ЈУГОСЛАВИЈЕ

Kingdom of Yugoslavia

НАРОДНА БАНКА

National Bank

1929 Issue

		VG	VF	UNC
26	**10 Dinara** 1.12.1929. Red-orange, blue and m/c. Similar to #25.	20.00	80.00	250.

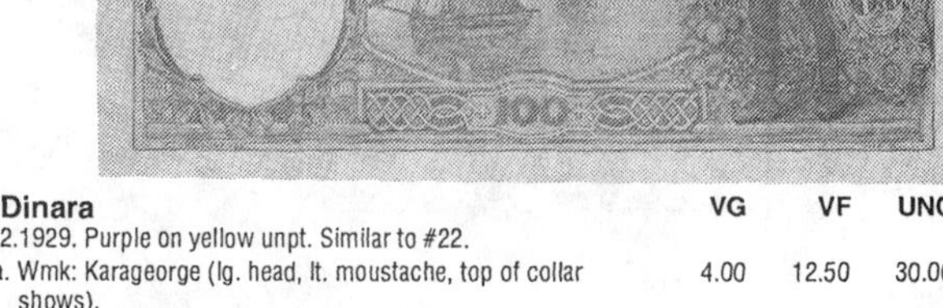

		VG	VF	UNC
27	**100 Dinara** 1.12.1929. Purple on yellow unpt. Similar to #22.			
	a. Wmk: Karageorge (lg. head, lt. moustache, top of collar shows).	4.00	12.50	30.00
	b. Wmk: Alexander I (smaller head w/dk. moustache, full collar shows).	.25	1.00	4.00

NOTE: #27 was ovpt. for use in Serbia during WW II (see Serbia #23).

1931 Issue

		VG	VF	UNC
28	**50 Dinara** 1.12.1931. Brown and m/c. Portr. Kg. Alexander I at l. Equestrian statue on back (issued in 1941 only as a Serbian note).	1.00	3.00	12.50

29	1000 Dinara	VG	VF	UNC
	1.12.1931. Blue-gray and brown. Qn. Marie at l., bird at r. Standing women at l. and r. on back.	2.00	8.00	20.00

1934-36 Issue

30	20 Dinara	VG	VF	UNC
	6.9.1936. Brown on blue and m/c unpt. Kg. Peter II at ctr. Woman w/wreath at l. on back (issued in 1941 only as a Serbian note).	.50	2.00	8.50

31	100 Dinara	VG	VF	UNC
	15.7.1934. Blue and m/c. Woman seated w/boy at r. ctr. Shield w/arms and 2 seated women on back. (Not issued).	10.00	25.00	75.00

32	500 Dinara	VG	VF	UNC
	6.9.1935. Green on lt. blue and pink unpt. Peter II at l. Women seated w/sheaves of wheat on back.	3.00	10.00	30.00

33	1000 Dinara	VG	VF	UNC
	6.9.1935. M/c. Group of 6 people w/3 horses and lion. (Not issued).	20.00	100.	300.

34	10,000 Dinara	VG	VF	UNC
	6.9.1936. Brown on m/c unpt. Kg. Peter II at l. (Not issued).	150.	400.	1000.

1939 Issue

		VG	VF	UNC
35	**10 Dinara** 22.9.1939. Green. Kg. Peter II at l., bridge at ctr. Woman in national costume at r. on back. Wmk: Older man in uniform.	2.00	8.00	20.00

1943 Issue

Kingdom in exile during WW II

#35A-35F portr. Kg. Peter II at ctr. English printing. (Not issued).

		VG	VF	UNC
35A	**5 Dinara** ND (1943). Dk. green. Goats on hillside on back.			
	a. Regular serial #.	125.	400.	—
	s. Specimen.	—	—	350.

		VG	VF	UNC
35B	**10 Dinara** ND (1943). Red and green. Landscape on back.			
	a. Regular serial #.	125.	400.	—
	s. Specimen.	—	—	350.

		VG	VF	UNC
35C	**25 Dinara** ND (1943). Blue and yellow. Monument on back.			
	a. Regular serial #.	125.	400.	—
	s. Specimen.	—	—	400.
35D	**100 Dinara** Sept. 1943. Green. Factory on back.			
	a. Regular serial #.	125.	400.	—
	s. Specimen.	—	—	350.

		VG	VF	UNC
35E	**500 Dinara** Sept. 1943. Brown and green. Factory on back.			
	a. Regular serial #.	150.	500.	—
	s. Specimen.	—	—	500
35F	**1000 Dinara** Sept. 1943. Black and green. Mountains and lake on back.			
	a. Regular serial #.	150.	500.	—
	s. Specimen.	—	—	500

Demokratska Federativna Jugoslavija

Democratic Federation of Yugoslavia

1944 Issue

#48-55 soldier w/rifle at r. Arms w/date *29.X1.1943* at l. on back.

		VG	VF	UNC
48	**1 Dinar** 1944. Olive-brown.			
	a. Thin paper.	.25	.50	1.00
	b. Thick paper, w/o security thread.	.25	.50	1.50
	c. Thin vertical security thread.	.25	.75	3.00
	d. Thin horizontal security thread.	.25	.75	3.00

		VG	VF	UNC
49	**5 Dinara** 1944. Blue. W/ or w/o security thread.			
	a. Thick paper.	.25	.50	2.00
	b. Thin vertical security thread.	.25	1.00	4.00

		VG	VF	UNC
50	**10 Dinara** 1944. Black on orange unpt.			
	a. Paper w/small fibres.	.25	.75	3.00
	b. Thin vertical security thread.	.50	2.00	7.00
	c. Thick paper, bright orange unpt.	.50	3.00	10.00

		VG	VF	UNC
51	**20 Dinara** 1944. Orange on lt. tan unpt.			
	a. Ornamented paper, baroque style serial #.	.25	1,50	5.00
	b. Paper as a, typewriter style serial #.	1.00	4,00	12.00
	c. Paper w/small fibres.	.25	2,00	6.00
	d. Thin vertical security thread.	.50	2.50	7.50
52	**50 Dinara** ND (1944). Violet on gray unpt.			
	a. Sm. size numerals in serial # (Russian print).	2.50	8.50	35.00
	b. Lg. size numerals in serial # (Yugoslavian print).	4.00	15.00	45.00
53	**100 Dinara** ND (1944). Dk. green on gray and lilac unpt.			

		VG	VF	UNC
53				
	a. Like #52a.	1.50	5.00	25.00
	b. Like #52b.	2.00	6.00	30.00
54	**500 Dinara**			
	1944. Brown on orange and lt. green unpt.			
	a. Like #52a.	6.00	40.00	160.
	b. Like #52b.	7.50	55.00	210.

		VG	VF	UNC
55	**1000 Dinara**			
	1944. Dk. green on blue and tan unpt.			
	a. Like #52a.	7.50	25.00	70.00
	b. Like #52b.	4.00	15.00	50.00

FEDERATIVNE NARODNE REPUBLIKE JUGOSLAVIJE

NARODNA BANKA - NATIONAL BANK

1946 ISSUE

		VG	VF	UNC
64	**50 Dinara**			
	1.5.1946. Brown on m/c unpt. Miner at l. Arms at l., woodchopper at ctr. on back.			
	a. 1st issue: 8-digit serial #.	.25	1.50	4.00
	b. 2nd issue: 9-digit serial #.	.25	1.50	4.00

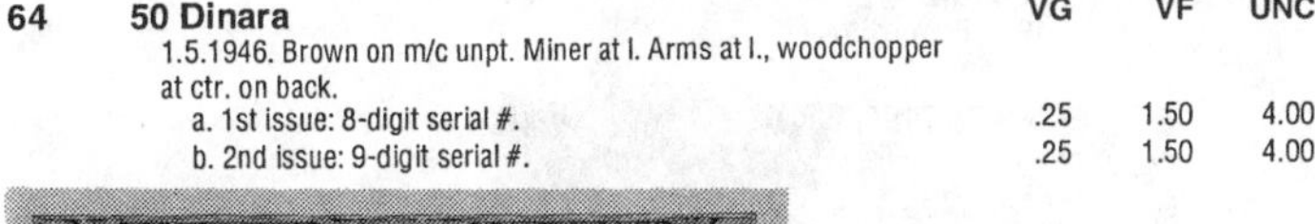

		VG	VF	UNC
65	**100 Dinara**			
	1.5.1946. Brown on gold unpt. Blacksmith at l., arms at upper ctr., farmer at r. Fisherman on back.			
	a. W/o security thread, sm. numerals in serial #.	.25	1.00	3.00
	b. Horizontal thin security thread, lg. numerals in serial #.	.25	1.00	3.00
	c. Like a., but error in Cyrillic: ЈУГОСААВИЈА **(2 letter As) instead of ЛА (L and A) at lower l.**	4.00	10.00	20.00

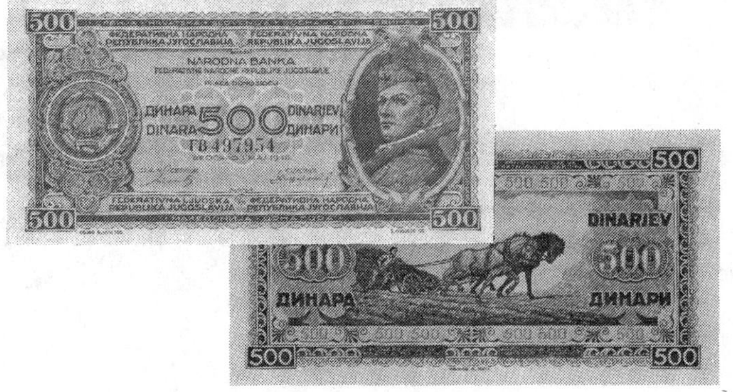

		VG	VF	UNC
66	**500 Dinara**			
	1.5.1946. Brown on m/c unpt. Arms at l., soldier w/rifle at r. Farmers plowing w/horses on back.			
	a. W/o security thread.	.25	1.00	5.00
	b. W/security thread.	.25	1.00	5.00

		VG	VF	UNC
67	**1000 Dinara**			
	1.5.1946. Brown on m/c unpt. Arms at l., woman w/ears of corn at r. Waterfalls at l., standing woman w/sword at r. on back.			
	a. W/o security thread.	.50	2.50	7.50
	b. W/horizontal security thread.	.50	2.50	7.50
	c. W/vertical security thread.	.50	3.00	10.00

1949-51 ISSUE

#67I-67N (Not issued).

		VG	VF	UNC
67I	**10 Dinara**			
	1951. Brown.	—	—	300.

		VG	VF	UNC
67J	**20 Dinara**			
	1951. Dk. blue. 2 serial # varieties.	—	—	325.

		VG	VF	UNC
67K	**50 Dinara**			
	1.5.1950. Green. Partisan fighters at l. Women w/sheaves in field on back.	—	600.	900.

67L	100 Dinara	VG	VF	UNC
	1.5.1949. Blue and yellow. Similar to #68.	—	800.	1200.

67M	1000 Dinara	VG	VF	UNC
	1.5.1949. Green. Farm workers at l. and r. Stonemasons at l., steel workers at r. on back. 2 serial # varieties.	—	500.	800.

67N	5000 Dinara	VG	VF	UNC
	1.11.1950. Blue and yellow. Cargo ship at dockside at l. Steel workers at ctr. r. on back.	—	700.	1350.

1950 Issue

#67P-67Y arms at l. on back. (Not issued.)

67P	1 Dinar	VG	VF	UNC
	1950. Blue.			
	a. Note w/o serial #.	—	—	120.
	s. Specimen.	—	—	120.

67Q	2 Dinara	VG	VF	UNC
	1950. Red.			
	a. Note w/o serial #.	—	—	120.
	s. Specimen.	—	—	120.
67R	5 Dinara			
	1950. Dk. brown.			
	a. Note w/o serial #.	—	—	50.00
	s. Specimen.	—	—	120.

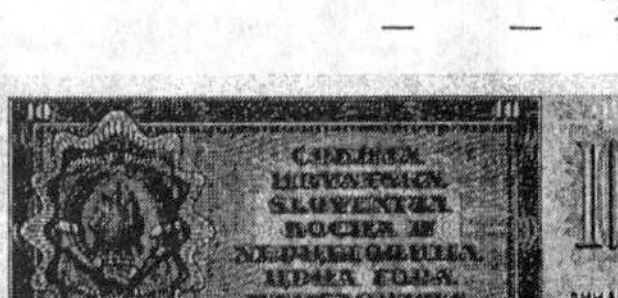

67S	10 Dinara	VG	VF	UNC
	1950. Green. Portr. of young soldier at r.			
	a. Note w/o serial #.	—	—	60.00
	s. Specimen.	—	—	120.

67T	20 Dinara	VG	VF	UNC
	1950. Brown. Boy at r.	—	100.	200.

67U	50 Dinara	VG	VF	UNC
	1950. Green. Farm woman w/sickle at r.	—	125.	225.

67V	100 Dinara	VG	VF	UNC
	1950. Blue. Man w/hammer over shoulder at r.	—	125.	250.

		VG	VF	UNC
67W	**500 Dinara** 1950. Dk. blue. Soldier at r.	—	350.	450.
67X	**1000 Dinara** 1950. Brown. Worker and woman at r.	—	700.	1750.

		VG	VF	UNC
67Y	**5000 Dinara** 1950. Green. 3 workers at r.	—	675.	1500.

1953 ISSUE

		VG	VF	UNC
68	**100 Dinara** 1.5.1953. Brown and black on m/c unpt. 4 workers at steam locomotive wheels, arms at upper r. Farmers harvesting wheat on back.	5.00	25.00	85.00

1955 ISSUE

		VG	VF	UNC
69	**100 Dinara** 1.5.1955. Red on m/c unpt. Woman wearing national costume at l. Back m/c; view of Dubrovnik.	.10	.50	2.00

		VG	VF	UNC
70	**500 Dinara** 1.5.1955. Dk. green on m/c unpt. Farm woman w/sickle at l. 2 farm combines cutting wheat on back.	.25	1.00	5.00

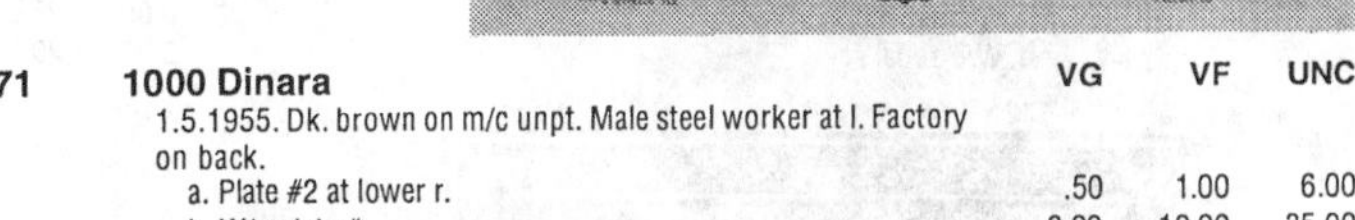

		VG	VF	UNC
71	**1000 Dinara** 1.5.1955. Dk. brown on m/c unpt. Male steel worker at l. Factory on back.			
	a. Plate #2 at lower r.	.50	1.00	6.00
	b. W/o plate #.	2.00	10.00	35.00

		VG	VF	UNC
72	**5000 Dinara** 1.5.1955. Blue-black on m/c unpt. Relief of Mestrovic at l. Parliament bldg. in Belgrade at ctr. on back.			
	a. Plate #2 at lower r.	7.50	25.00	65.00
	b. W/o plate #.	10.00	30.00	100.

REGIONAL

GOSPODARSKA BANKA ZA ISTRU, RIJEKU I SLOVENSKO PRIMORJE

STATE BANK FOR ISTRIA, FIUME AND SLOVENE COASTAL AREA

1945 ISSUE

#R1-R8 sailboat on back.

		VG	VF	UNC
R1	**1 Lira** 1945. Brown. Female soldier at l. on back.	2.00	5.00	40.00

		VG	VF	UNC
R2	**5 Lire** 1945. Green.	2.00	5.00	15.00
R3	**10 Lire** 1945. Brown on green unpt.	2.00	5.00	15.00

		VG	VF	UNC
R4	**20 Lire** 1945. Purple on lt. green unpt.			
	a. W/serial #.	2.00	5.00	20.00
	b. W/o serial #.	3.00	7.50	30.00
R5	**50 Lire** 1945. Red-brown.			
	a. Red serial #.	3.00	7.50	30.00
	b. Black serial #.	15.00	50.00	175.
	c. W/o serial #.	20.00	60.00	225.
R6	**100 Lire** 1945. Brown and blue.			
	a. W/serial #.	5.00	25.00	75.00
	b. W/o serial #.	3.00	20.00	60.00

		VG	VF	UNC
R7	**500 Lire** 1945. Gray on green unpt. Back brown on green unpt.	12.00	30.00	90.00
R8	**1000 Lire** 1945. Purple and lt. brown. Farmer plowing w/ox on back.	8.00	25.00	75.00

NOTICE

Readers with unlisted dates, signature varieties, etc. are invited to submit photocopies or, high resolution (300 dpi, 100% size) scans of their notes to: Standard Catalog of World Paper Money, 700 East State St. Iola, WI 54990-0001, or E-Mail: george.cuhaj@fwpubs.com.

HUNGARIAN OCCUPATION OF BACKA - WW II

HUNGARIAN ARMED FORCES

1941 ISSUE

		VG	VF	UNC
R9A	**1000 Dinara** ND (1941). Revalidation adhesive stamp affixed to #29.	—	—	—

ITALIAN OCCUPATION OF MONTENEGRO - WW II

ITALIAN ARMED FORCES

1941 ISSUE

#R10-R15 *VERIFICATO* handstamp on Yugoslav notes.

		Good	Fine	XF
R10	**10 Dinara** ND (1941 - old date 22.9.1939). Handstamp on #35.	1.00	4.50	15.00

		Good	Fine	XF
R11	**20 Dinara** ND (1941 - old date 6.9.1936). Handstamp on #33.	1.00	4.50	15.00

		Good	Fine	XF
R12	**50 Dinara** ND (1941 - old date 1.12.1931). Handstamp on #28.	1.00	3.50	12.50

		Good	Fine	XF
R13	**100 Dinara** ND (1941 - old date 1.12.1929). Handstamp on #27.			
	a. Wmk: Karageorge.	2.00	8.00	20.00
	b. Wmk: Alexander.	.50	2.00	6.00
R13A	**100 Dinara** ND (1941 - old date 30.11.1920). Handstamp on #22 in error. Rare.	—	—	—
R14	**500 Dinara** ND (1941 - old date 3.9.1935). Handstamp on #31.	10.00	20.00	50.00

		Good	Fine	XF
R15	**1000 Dinara** ND (1941 - old date 1.12.1931). Handstamp on #29.	10.00	20.00	50.00

GERMAN OCCUPATION - WWII

HRANILNICA LJUBLJANSKE POKRAJINE

SPARKASSE DER PROVINZ LAIBACH

1944 ISSUE

#R16-R24 issued during German occupation. Text in Slovene on one side, German on the other.

		VG	VF	UNC
R16	**50 Cent. = 1/2 (Lira)** 28.11.1944. Dk. green. Child in national costume at l. on face and back.	2.00	7.50	20.00
R17	**1 Lira** 28.11.1944. Dk. brown. Tower w/dragon at r. on face and back.	1.50	6.00	17.50
R18	**2 Liri** 28.11.1944. Brown. Woman w/child at l. on face and back.	2.50	10.00	25.00

		VG	VF	UNC
R19	**5 Lir** 28.11.1944. Brown-red. Man in national costume at r. on face and back. Series A.	2.50	10.00	25.00

		VG	VF	UNC
R20	**10 Lir** 28.11.1944. Bluish-purple. Woman wearing national costume hat at l. on face and back. Series D.	2.50	10.00	25.00
R21	**50 Lir** 14.9.1944. Red on gold unpt. Farmer's wife at l. on face, at r. on back.	2.50	12.50	30.00
R22	**100 Lir** 14.9.1944. Blue on gold unpt. Farmer w/scythe at l. on face, at r. on back.	4.00	15.00	45.00

		VG	VF	UNC
R23	**500 Lir** 14.9.1944. Blue on green and gray unpt. Man in national costume at l. on face, at r. on back.	5.00	25.00	70.00

		VG	VF	UNC
R24	**1000 Lir** 14.9.1944. Brown on tan unpt. Woman wearing national costume hat at l. on face, at r. on back.	10.00	50.00	125.

The British protectorate of Zanzibar and adjacent small islands, located in the Indian Ocean 22 miles (35 km.) off the coast of Tanganyika, comprised a portion of British East Africa. Zanzibar was also the name of a sultanate which included the Zanzibar and Kenya protectorates. Zanzibar has an area of 637 sq. mi. (1,651 sq. km.). Chief city: Zanzibar. The islands are noted for their cloves of which Zanzibar is the world's foremost producer.

Zanzibar came under Portuguese control in 1503, was conquered by the Omani Arabs in 1698, became independent of Oman in 1860, and (with Pemba) came under British control in 1890. Britain granted the protectorate self-government in 1961, and independence within the British Commonwealth on Dec. 19, 1963. On April 26, 1964, Tanganyika and Zanzibar (with Pemba) united to form the United Republic of Tanganyika and Zanzibar. The name of the country, which remained within the British Commonwealth, was changed to Tanzania on Oct. 29, 1964.

RULERS:

British to 1963

MONETARY SYSTEM:

1 Rupee = 100 Cents

British Administration

Zanzibar Government

1908-20 Issue

#1-7 dhow at lower l., group of 8 fruit pickers at lower r.

		Good	Fine	XF
1	**1 Rupee** 1.9.1920. Lt. blue on green and brown. Uniface. Printer: TDLR.	1000.	2000.	—

#2-4, 6 printer: W&S. Sign. titles: *Financial Member of Council* and *Treasurer* 1908; *Chief Secretary* and *Treasurer* 1916-28.

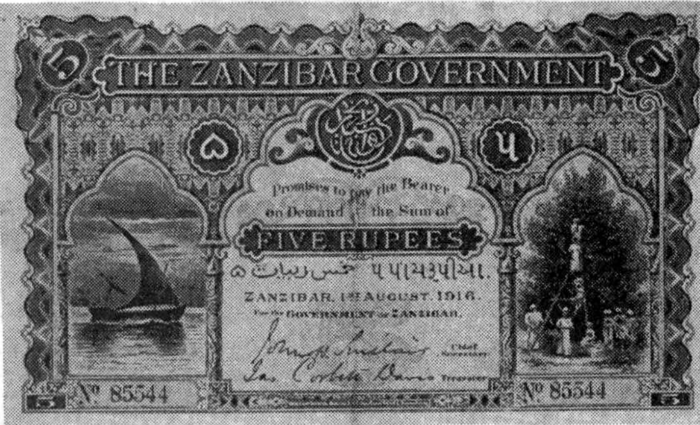

		Good	Fine	XF
2	**5 Rupees** 1.1.1908; 1.8.1916; 1.2.1928. Black on orange and green unpt. Uniface.	1250.	3000.	—

		Good	Fine	XF
3	**10 Rupees** 1.1.1908; 1.8.1916; 1.9.1916; 1.2.1928. Red. Rare.	—	—	—

		Good	Fine	XF
4	**20 Rupees** 1.1.1908; 1.8.1916; 1.2.1928. Lilac. Uniface.			
	a. Issued note. Rare.	—	—	—
	s. Specimen. Rare.	—	—	—
5	**50 Rupees** 1.1.1908; 1.8.1916. Rare.	—	—	—

		Good	Fine	XF
6	**100 Rupees** 1.1.1908; 1.8.1916. Dk. blue and red-brown. Rare.	—	—	—

Note: Spink 10-96 100 Rupees #6 F-VF dated 1.8.1916 realized $7,360.

		Good	Fine	XF
7	**500 Rupees** 1.9.1920. Rare.	—	—	—

Note: From 1936 notes of the East African Currency Board were in general use until notes of Tanzania were issued in 1966.

Collecting Paper Money

by Albert Pick
Translated by E. Sheridan

"To kill a person needs no knife . . .
a piece of paper that is written
. . . or printed on suffices."

With this observation the Chinese, as the inventors of paper, wished to emphasize the great need for responsibility in dealing with this material.

There is hardly any application of paper qualified to such a degree as paper money in providing that it is within man's power to have it be a benefit or a curse to mankind. On the one hand, lack of credit and a shortage of legal tender have been overcome by issues of paper money to serve trade and industry commensurate with economic development; yet on the other hand, the immense increase in the volume of paper money in inflationary periods has been the cause of economic and personal catastrophes. The many issues of paper money retaining their full value were mostly destroyed after redemption and have largely faded from the memory of man. The paper money originating during times of inflation and then becoming worthless has outlived the period, since it was no longer redeemable, and it acts as a constant reminder of the period of monetary devaluation.

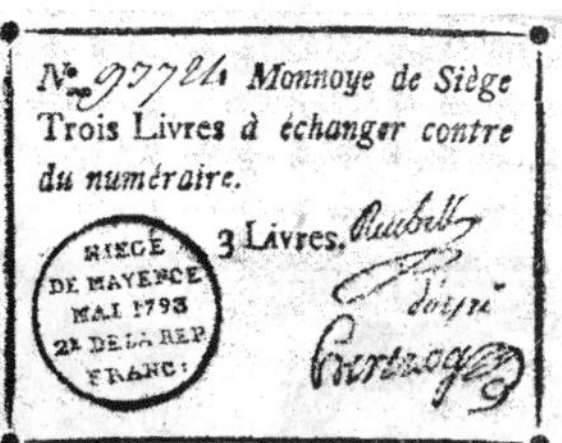

France, 3 Livres, siege note, Mainz 1793

Germany, 2 Groschen, siege note of Kolberg, 1807

Thus, paper money is considered by many people around the world as legal tender with an inglorious tradition. As negatively as periods of inflation influence the opinion of a superficial observer of the history of paper money, these relics of a monetary devaluation have positively influenced the collecting of paper money.

Italy, 500 Lire

Frequently, the hope of a later redemption may have contributed toward placing the old notes in safekeeping. Later on, attempts were made to complete the series of notes and in this manner the first collections may have originated; perhaps even as early as the time of the French Revolution, when in addition to the French assignats and the "mandats Territoriaux," the regional issues of "Billets de confiance" were in circulation. In the United States, too, there was a very early opportunity to collect paper money as the Colonial and Continental bills, notes of the Confederate States and the numerous notes, rich in design, of the many 19th century banks became worthless as a circulating medium.

Italy 1000 Lire, Banca d'Italia

In our own time, an ever increasing number of persons come into contact with foreign currencies through international travel – and even war. A particularly pleasing note is retained as a souvenir and not infrequently becomes the cornerstone of a bank note collection. Here, it is a feature of the bank note that because of its relatively large surface (compared with a coin or postage stamp) it offers space for many motifs and frequently impresses the viewer with the quality of its printing on high-grade paper. The catalogs published in recent years provide the necessary reference tools for building a collection, and thus it is small wonder that the number of paper money collectors is steadily on the increase.

Germany, 2 Mark, Emergency money note of Bielschowitz, 1914

Germany, Emergency money note of Bremen, 1922

Particularly for the novice collectors not yet fully acquainted with the collecting sphere, hints are given regarding the different types of paper money, various avenues of collecting, historical backgrounds and the possibilities for building a specialized collection.

Government Paper Money

—Bank Notes—

Emergency Money

For some would-be collectors, the lack of knowledge and the means for easy orientation in a hobby causes a decline in interest and often ends in a short-lived participation. Conversely, an interested person can become a real collector if he is aided in acquainting himself with his new hobby and in finding the right way to develop a meaningful collection.

The collector of paper money should know from the start which items belong to his collecting sphere and what paper money represents.

In contrast to coins, which in the past represented money of intrinsic value guaranteed by virtue of the material in which they were struck, paper money is money of no intrinsic value; it is printed paper without material value.

Today, in common hobby parlance, we categorize as paper money all forms of money made of paper or printed on a paper-like material. Only a few decades ago, the term paper money, as applied to government issues, stood in contrast to other monetary forms of paper such as bank notes. Whereas the government paper money had to be considered general legal tender because the government was obliged to accept the notes at face value

France, 5000 Francs, Banque de France, 1944

New Zealand, 2 Dollars with bird

Indonesia, 100 Rupiah with flowers, 1959

Seychelles, 10 Rupees with sea turtles

in payments to itself, in the case of the bank note, the issuing bank promises to redeem it at any time at its face value for legal tender. Still, in former times as well as today, it was difficult to recognize what was government paper money and what was bank notes.

There are many examples in the history of paper money of the adoption of bank notes by the government. Especially in times of distress, if the government had overtaxed a bank for its purposes, the bank's notes were declared government paper money (e.g. Spain, 1794, the notes of the Banco de San Carlos, and Austria, 1866). The opposite situation was less frequent; i.e., a bank adopting government paper money and making it into bank notes, yet there are also examples of this (Oldenburg, 1869). In our time, however, the difference between government paper money and the bank note is generally no longer discernible. This often involves differences contingent only on tradition or the organization of the government or banking authority which are of no consideration when using the notes as legal tender.

Differentiating between government paper money and the bank note remains for the paper money collector a purely theoretical consideration. In practice, few collectors exclude one or the other from their collecting except in rare instances.

In addition to the government paper money and the bank note, there is also a third kind of paper money, the emergency money. This form of substitute currency was issued to overcome a shortage or lack of government legal tender (for example, in times of distress, as a substitute for coins which have disappeared from circulation). Sometimes issued by authority of the official government or other competent authorizing body, but also frequently issued without such authority, these emergency issues may have been officially prohibited or tacitly tolerated, and accepted on a par with the legal tender issues they replaced, if only in a small district. Among the best known of such issues are the "notgeld," a familiar expression even to non-German speaking collectors for the emergency paper money issues of Austria and Germany circa 1914-1923. In fact, the term is being increasingly applied to many other emergency issues as well.

General Collection - Specialized Collection

A bank note collection does not always develop in a straight line dir tion. The interest in paper money is in many cases of a general nature a thus the individual collects everything he encounters. The general collecti thus formed often does not please the collector as his interest matures. may then select those collecting spheres that interest him most and w either dispose of all other notes not fitting those spheres or add to his coll tion only those notes which fit into his newly specialized collection. T sooner he can decide the limits of his collecting interests, the sooner he c concentrate on building his collection.

Thematic Collection

The creation of general paper money collections will increasing become a matter only for the museums. The majority of private collect can occupy themselves only with specialized spheres for financial reaso or lack of time, and even within these spheres the rare pieces may rema generally unobtainable for them. Thus, collectors are increasingly turni their attention to the aesthetic qualities of paper money. The idea of th matic collecting is becoming quite strong. The underlying causes for this a not only the financial considerations and the inability to acquire the rar pieces, but also in the pleasure obtained from the beauty of individual not

Over the last decade a number of countries have stimulated interest collecting bank notes by designs with definite motifs. Thus, indigeno birds are depicted on the different values of the Reserve Bank of N Zealand. In the Seychelles and a number of African states, notes show ill trations of animals. Representations of flowers are present on the Isra notes of 1955 and the 1959 Indonesian currency. According to his choice subject, the taste of the collector is not always adequate for building a c lection which will find general recognition. With more ambitious them he is obliged to acquire some basic knowledge about the topic he has ch sen. The wealth of motifs is inexhaustible, so that possibilities offer the selves even for very special themes.

Varieties

Even in the consideration of varieties, opinions of collectors differ. C collector is content to acquire one note of each basic type, and will ign minor differences; another is interested in watermark varieties, vari dates of issue, serial numbers, sheet marks, signatures, printers, color vari ies and other differences within a type. It is by no means easy for a collec to determine what he will include along these lines and what he will lea out. The differences of material value in the one collecting sphere, a which frequently occur in varying combinations, can be of no consequer for another collecting sphere. A few examples will show that general gui lines, applying to all areas of paper money collecting, are impossible.

In the case of German Reichsbank notes from 1883-1914, the few da varieties which delimit the different issues are included by almost all coll tors. On the other hand, all date varieties are not even considered by most specialized collectors of Belgian notes since the notes bear the date the day of printing. In this instance collectors are usually satisfied with note of each year. In areas such as Scottish, Italian and Romanian not there are also numerous date varieties and collectors who specialize in the On United States paper money there are only year dates, sometimes lowed by a letter suffix. This year date, as a rule, changes only when type of note changes; while the letter following the year date moves forw by one if the signature change.

Example: $1 Silver Certificate
1928-D, signature Julian/Woodin
1928-E, Julian/Morgenthau
1934, Julian/Morgenthau

The notes dated 1928 have the Treasury seal on the left, those with 19 on the right. On U.S. notes the year date hardly permits the date of issue be determined, a better clue being taken from the suffix letter, or better s the signatures.

Signature varieties are practically unknown for some countries, such with German Reichsbank notes. Other countries, however, change note s natures with any change in officials (France, Belgium, Great Britain, seve South American countries and others). Since these changes in signature also important in determining the date of issue (such as with modern Bri notes which carry no date), these different signatures are of interest to collectors. A change of signature in notes issued at the same time already known on assignats of the 18th century. It is still found today w notes of the Scandinavian countries and Switzerland, where a signat

China 1 Kuan, Ming Dynasty, 14th century

Netherlands, 20 Stuiver cardboard coin of the City of Leyden, 1574

Sweden, 10 Daler silver, Stockholms Banco, 1666, one of the oldest European banknotes

often does not change over lengthy periods (such as that of the bank president). Only the specialized collectors will deal with these changing signatures and they, too, must content themselves with the lower values.

Since variations in serial numbers, printers and colors do not occur too often in paper money, they are often included in a collection. Such things as prefix and suffix letters with serial numbers and sheet marks or plate numbers, on the other hand, may interest only specialized collectors, and then only when the bank note material is correspondingly plentiful.

History of Paper Money

In the 13th century, the famous Venetian, Marco Polo, undertook a journey to China. His records of this journey contain the first Western reports regarding the production and the use of paper money, a currency still incomprehensible for European conditions of that time, due to its lack of intrinsic worth. His contemporaries did not give credence to Marco Polo's report. Only much later were his accounts actually verified in the form of Chinese notes of the 14th century (Ming Dynasty) produced in the same manner. Today, such bluish-tinted notes are found in many of the larger collections, and it is now known that they were not the oldest notes, but stood at the end of a development which began already in the 7th century A.D. The Chinese, who called paper money "flying money" because of its light weight and ability to circulate over a wide area, had a well organized bank note clearing system as early as the 10th century.

Along with the first bank notes, the first counterfeiters also made their appearance. Numerous files still in existence provide information regarding the fight waged by the Chinese against these forgers.

The first European paper money is of much more recent origin. It was emergency money issued in 1483 by the Spaniards during the siege by the Moors. Since up to the present day not a single one of these notes has been discovered, it may be assumed that they were all destroyed after their redemption. In contrast to this, the cardboard coins produced in 1574 by the beleaguered citizens of Leyden are preserved in various denominations. The cities of Leyden and Middelburg were lacking silver for the striking of coins during the siege by the Spaniards, so they took as a material the covers of Catholic parish registers. The cardboard coins may indeed be described as the oldest preserved European money consisting of paper, but on the other hand, they are not true paper money.

Only 300 years after Marco Polo's account of Chinese paper money, the Stockholms Banco in Sweden issued the first European bank notes for circulation. The cause for the issuing of these notes was the devaluation of the copper plate money introduced in 1644. In the search for a legal tender for a transition period, Johann Palmstruch suggested the issue of so-called "Kreditivsedlar." In 1661 the first notes were issued made out in Riksdaler specie and Daler silver. It is assumed that this involved forms where the denomination and currency were inserted in handwriting. More is known about the second issue which occurred in 1662-1664. In this instance the denomination was imprinted. In 1666 the third, considerably augmented, issue was ordered. Of these notes for 10, 25, 50 and 100 Daler silver, approximately 60 specimens have been preserved.

At this time, the so-called Goldsmith Notes were already known in England. The transactions of the English goldsmiths also included brokerage and money changing. When King Charles I demanded a part of the ready money for himself, deposited by merchants in the Tower or in the office of the Chief Cashier of the government, the merchants went in search of new depositories and discovered these in the vaults of the goldsmiths. With this deposited money, the goldsmiths began speculating and were thus also able to pay interest. Withdrawal periods were laid down for deposits yielding interest, those not yielding interest being repaid on demand. The goldsmiths thus became bankers, issuing notes in respect to the deposits which, as required, were made out to the bearer without an indication of name. For the purpose of facilitating the redemption of parts of the deposited money, possibly for third parties, the notes were even issued in smaller denominations in round sums, and these notes can be considered forerunners of bank notes.

The desire for an independent credit institution was strengthened when some goldsmiths went bankrupt on the king's refusal to discharge some debts which fell due. In 1694 the Bank of England was founded, and its first notes were similar to the notes of the goldsmiths. Acts of Parliament strengthened the special position of the Bank, and merchants increasingly came to realize that support of the Bank provided them backing in time of crisis; thus the Bank of England succeeded in obtaining a firm foundation.

In Scotland, one year later than in England, a central bank, the Bank of Scotland, was also founded. In Norway, then a Danish province, the issue of

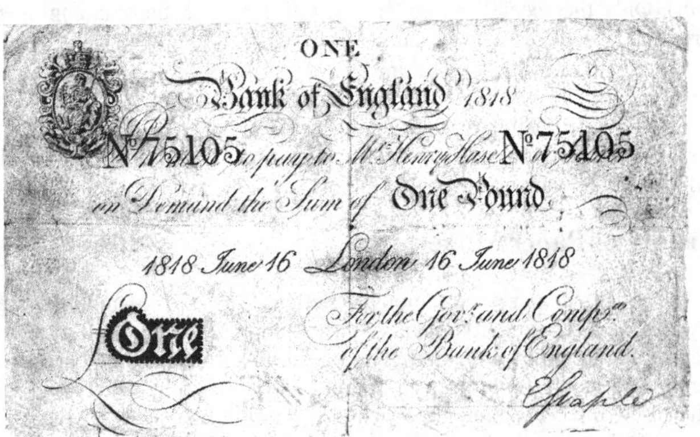

Great Britain, 1 Pound, Bank of England, 1818

Denmark, 1 Mark, 1713

non-interest bearing notes occurred in the same year on the initiative of the merchant Thor Mohlen. In Denmark itself, King Frederick IV had paper money produced 18 years later, in 1713, during the Nordic Wars.

The poor financial position of France forced King Louis XIV to carry out a "reformation" of the coins in circulation. In 1703 he ordered coins to be withdrawn, overstamped, and then reissued at a higher rate. Receipts were issued for the withdrawn coins and this so-called coin scrip was declared legal tender.

The continued indebtedness of the government persisted even after the king's death, and it was therefore not astonishing that the Scotsman John Law's ideas for the restoration of the government finances were gladly seized upon. Law wished to increase circulation of money by issuing bank notes and promoting credit. In 1716 he received permission for founding the Banque Generale which issued "Ecus" (Taler) in the form of notes. In 1718 the bank was taken over by the government. With the notes later made out to "Livres Tournois" and the shares of the two colonial companies "Compagnie des Indes" and "Compagnie D'Occident," Law indulged in a dangerous financial and stock exchange scheme which resulted in 1720 in a tremendous catastrophe. The bank was closed and Law had to leave France, abandoning his assets.

This was not to remain the only French experiment with paper money in the 18th century. France's ever-unfavorable financial position deteriorated still further through the revolution. The receding revenues of the government faced increased demands in the face of burgeoning expenditures. In accordance with a plan worked out by Tallyrand, the first assignats were issued in 1790, for which confiscated Church property was to serve as security. Notes of the first issue bore interest, while the later issues did not.

For relieving the shortage of small change, many towns and municipalities issued so-called "Billets de confiance," of which a few thousand types were in circulation. The government, too, was not printing assignats in small denominations. Simultaneously the issues of higher value were continually being increased.

The Royal Assignats were substituted at the inception of the Republic by new issues which were themselves superceded in 1795, upon the introduction of the metric system, by assignats of Franc currency. On January 1, 1796, over 27 million Livres in assignats were in circulation, the value of which merely amounted to one-half of one percent of the face value.

For the purpose of restoring confidence in the currency, it was decided abolish the assignats and to issue a new type of paper money, the "Mand Territoriaux." At a conversion ratio of 30 to 1, "Promesses des Mandats T ritoriaux" were initially issued for the assignats to be converted. The actu mandats were later issued only in small quantities. Even this new kind paper money was unable to put a brake on inflation, though. Within a f weeks the value of the mandats dropped by 95 percent. By November, 17 all notes were declared worthless.

After the disappearance of the assignats and mandats, a number of no issuing banks originated. Their notes, however, circulated only in sm quantities. Out of one of these banks, the "Caisse des Comptes Courant the Bank of France was founded in 1800, due mainly to the influence Napoleon.

In other European countries, too, attempts were made in the 18th centu to eliminate the financial difficulties of the government by issuing pa money. In Russia, the Assignation Bank was established in 1768. Its pa money was widely accepted. However, when the government began cir lating ever increasing quantities of notes during the second war against Turks (1787-1792), confidence waned and the notes lost value. Since t time Russia has continued to issue government paper money in an unint rupted sequence.

The Austrian Wars of Succession and the battles under Maria There with Frederick the Great had encumbered the Austrian government heav with debts. At that time, attention was turned to the issue of paper mon The "Banco del Giro," founded in 1703, was originally supposed to is obligations for circulation, but confidence in this bank was found wanti so the plan was quickly abandoned. Only when administration of the ba was transferred to the city of Vienna and the name changed to "Wie Stadt-Banco" did the mistrust disappear.

In 1759 the first provisional paper money issue came about. It was sup ceded by the true government paper money in 1762. Initially these not termed "Bancozettel" (Bank Scrip), were popular, but when governm indebtedness continually rose because of wars, and various new issues ever-greater quantities became necessary, the notes lost value. The war w

Poland, 10 Groszy, 1974

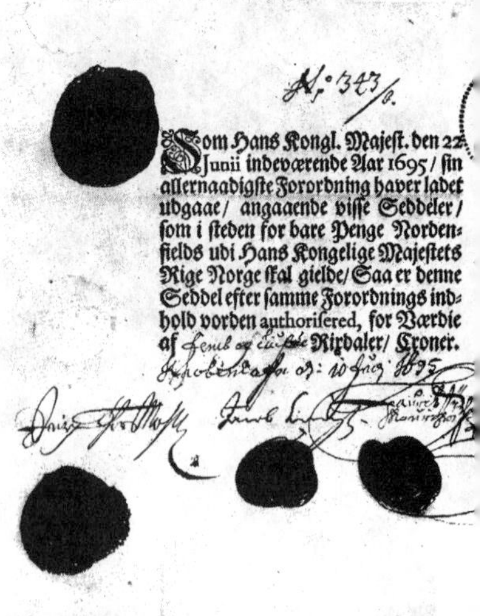

Norway, 25 Rixdaler, Thor Mohlen, 1

N.° 329771. Cent Livres Tournois.
La Banque promet payer au porteur à vüe, Cent Livres Tournois en Espèces d'argent, Valeur receüe à Paris le 1er aoust 1719

France, 1000 Livres, Banque Royale (of the time of John Law), 1719

France produced the peak of indebtedness and the government found itself incapable of continuing to redeem the notes. Only a monetary reform could prevent national bankruptcy. Thus, it was decided in 1811 to issue "Redemption Notes," which could be converted at the ratio of 1:5 for the old Banco scrip.

Soon the value of these new notes also dropped and they were followed in 1813 by another kind of paper money, the "Anticipation Notes" (anticipatory of future taxes). The end of the Napoleonic Wars gave rise to a new hope for a peaceful economic development and a stable currency. In 1816 the "Austrian National Scrip Bank" was established to create legal tender of stable value with its notes.

The first German money of paper material was the issue of the previously mentioned cardboard coins in the Dutch towns of Leyden and Middelburg in 1574. Whereas these were emergency money, the "Banco Scrip" issued in 1705 by the Elector Johann Wilhelm can be considered the first real paper money in Germany. The Elector had founded the "Banco di gyro d'affrancatione," whose notes were in fact made out to individual names, but were transferable.

In Ansbach-Bayreuth the "Hochfurstlich Brandenburgische Muntz-Banco" made out so-called "Banco-Billets" (Bank Scrip) by the middle of the 18th century. However, in exactly the same manner as the interest-bearing bank notes of the "Hochfurstlich Brandenburg-Anspach-Bayreuthische Hof-Banco," founded in 1780, they remained of little importance in the way of a legal tender.

The fear of monetary devaluation by the introduction of paper money was too deeply rooted in Germany. Until the end of the 18th century and partly until the middle of the 19th century such issues were planned but decisions postponed.

USA, 20 Dollars, Georgia, Bank of Commerce, 1857

Germany, 1 Taler, Saxony, 1855

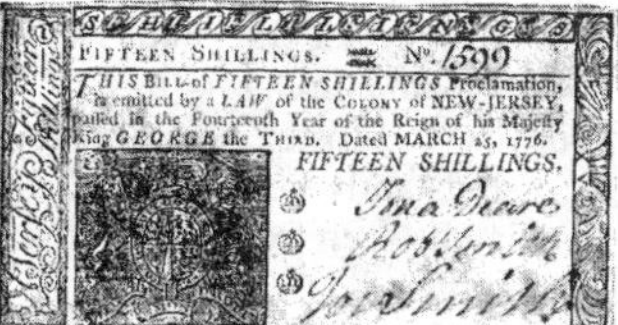

USA, 15 Shillings, New Jersey, 1776

Germany, 5 Thaler, Prussia, 1806

In Prussia the first notes were issued by the "Konigliche Giro-und Lehnbank" founded in 1765. The notes, in denominations of Pound-Banco, however, remained of little importance in circulation. Only those notes issued from 1820 onwards gained any importance. The bank name was changed to "Preussische Bank" in 1847, from which the Reichsbank originated in 1876.

Of greater importance at the beginning of the 19th century was the Prussian government paper money, the "Tresorscheine" (bank-safe notes).

In Bavaria, attempts were made at the end of the 18th and the beginning of the 19th century to create an issue of government paper money by issuing diverse monetary substitutes. Government indebtedness was therefore not less than in countries with paper money issues.

It was the time of peace following the Napoleonic Wars that brought a slow financial recovery. But the lack of credit and shortage of legal tender, due to the favorable development of trade, was not eliminated until 1835, when the Bayerische Hypotheken-und Wechselbank was founded. This institution in subsequent years issued notes of 10 and 100 Gulden and remained the only Bavarian central bank until the foundation of the German Reich.

At the beginning of the 19th century, paper money remained unpopular in Germany. A change occurred after 1848, when some German states felt the need to produce their own paper money to protect themselves against notes of smaller states whose issue quantities far exceeded the circulation requirements of their own areas. The larger states could then prohibit the circulation of these notes within their boundaries. The decisive step on the way toward centralization of banks in Germany occurred in 1875 with the new Bank Act and the foundation of the Reichsbank. The last four banks retained their issuing rights up to 1935.

In Italy the banking system developed earlier than in all other European countries. Deposit receipts and promissory notes made out by the banks existing as early as the Middle Ages, such as the "Casa di St. Giorgio," in Genoa, the "Banco di Sant' Ambrogio" in Milan and the "Banco di Rialto" in Venice, were transferable with an endorsement. These notes can be considered forerunners of modern bank notes. Real bank notes, however, were first issued in the middle of the 18th century in the Kingdom of Sardinia. Subsequently came the notes of the "Sacro Monte della Pieta di Roma" and those of the "Banco di Santo Spirito di Roma."

In Poland, issues of paper money first appeared during the 18th century. Rebels under the leadership of Kosciuszko issued various kinds of notes in 1794. With the crushing of the rebellion, paper money issues also ceased. Only in the Duchy of Warsaw, created by Napoleon (personal union with the Kingdom of Saxony), did paper money circulate again, so-called currency notes resembling Saxon currency tickets in their design.

It might be expected that paper money became known in America much later than in Europe. But exactly like in Europe, North America became acquainted with money of no intrinsic value in the 1600s.

The inadequate supply of coins in Canada under French colonial administration led to a chronic lack of legal tender. In order to at least ensure the soldiers' pay, the Canadians resorted to self-help and utilized quartered playing cards, to which the treasurer's seal and signatures of the Governor and Administrator were added, as paper currency. In 1685 the first money of this nature was circulated. It was the intention to withdraw these emer-

Italy, 7 Scudi, Banco di Santo Spirito di Roma, 1786

N° 62365

Pour 52. Loüis d'Argent.

Nous foussignez Directeurs de la Compagnie des Indes, payerons Solidairement en un an de ce jour à M ou ordre, la Somme de Cinquante-deux Loüis d'Argent du poids & titre de ce jour, valeur reçûë comptant d

Fait à Paris en l'Hôtel de ladite Compagnie le vingt neuf Novembre mil fept cens vingt.

Pour lefd. 52 Louis d'argent

France, 52 Louis d' Argent, Compagnie des Indies, Banque Royale (of the time of John Law), 1720

France, 5 Sous, Billet de confiance, St. Gaudens, 1972

France, 4000 Livres, Assignat, 1792

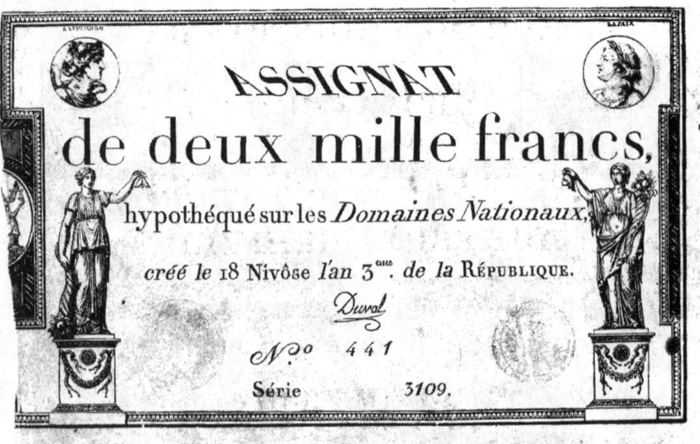

France, 2000 Francs, Assignat, 1794

N° 456823

Dix livres Tournois.

Divifion

La Banque promet payer au Porteur à vüe Dix livres Tournois en Efpeces d'Argent, valeur reçeüe. A Paris le premier Juillet mil fept cens vingt.

Vû p.r le S.r Fenellon. *Giraudeau.*

Signé p.r le S.r Bourgeois. *Delanauze.*

Controllé p.r le S.r Durevest. *Granet.*

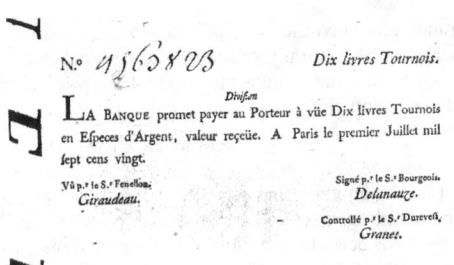

France, 10 Livres (of the time of John Law), 172

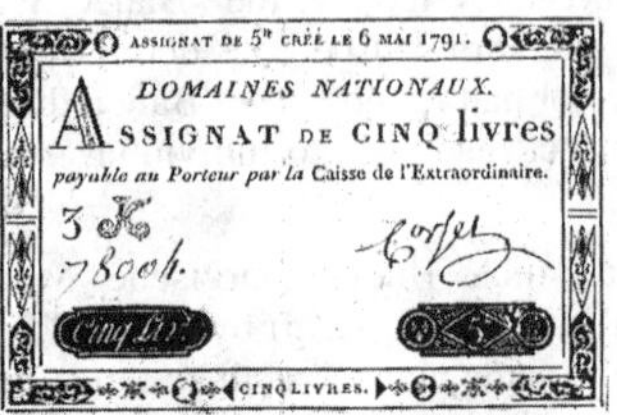

France, 5 Livres, Royal Assignat, 1791

France, 3 Livres, Billet de Confiance, Marseille, 179

gency items of legal tender immediately after adequate coin supplie arrived, but this did not happen. Further issues which included half or whol cards followed, gaining circulation throughout the whole of the colony. Th money remained valid until 1718/19 when the governor had it withdraw from circulation and prohibited further issues.

In 1729, new issues of this strange money were recorded and from the on circulated in ever increasing quantities. When the British took over th Canadian territories in 1759, more than 14 million Livres of such notes wer in circulation. Because the French government refused to redeem the note the value of playing card money dropped considerably until an agreeme was finally reached for its redemption.

In 1690, the Colony of Massachusetts lacked the necessary metallic cu rency to pay its soldiers returning from Canada and this led to the produc tion of the Colonial Bills of Credit. A few years later other colonies, such a Connecticut, New Hampshire, New Jersey, New York, Pennsylvani Rhode Island and South Carolina followed with similar issues. It wa believed that an increase in the paper money would foster general prospe ity, thus great quantities of new notes were constantly being created. Ber jamin Franklin was also of this opinion, as may be seen from his treatise " Modeste Inquiry Into the Nature and Necessity of a Paper Money." A attempts by the British government to bring the devaluation of paper mone to an end at the beginning of the 18th century failed, and thus, America wi its Colonial bills encountered the same experience France had with its Joh Law notes: they became completely worthless.

After the battle of Lexington in 1775, a new attempt was made to issu paper money in the form of Continental bills issued by order of the Cont nental Congress. After being in circulation for just a year, the notes ha already lost some of their value. By 1777, ten dollars in Continental bil was worth only one silver dollar. In 1780, one silver dollar fetched 75 of th Continental currency. By 1781, the ratio was 1000 to 1. George Washingto at the time observed in a letter that a wagon full of notes was just sufficie for purchasing a wagon full of provisions.

Liberal laws in the 19th century allowed an almost incalculable numbe of private note-issuing banks to form, many of which circulated worthles sometimes fraudulent note issues. So-called "wildcat banks" establishe their offices in such remote areas - where there were more wildcats tha people - as to make redemption of their notes virtually impossible. In th New England states, by contrast, the introduction of severe penalties again swindlers and the rise of an effective clearing house system allowed a solid banking system to develop.

Due to the Civil War, the currency confusion which existed in time of peace was further compounded, particularly as the Confederate States of America and its constituent states began issuing notes which quickly became worthless. However, it was also during the Civil War that the first United States government paper money originated, the beginning of an unbroken string of notes which remain legal tender to this day.

The American bills of the last century, rich in design and well printed, are popular with collectors today, abroad as well as in the U.S.

In most of the civilized world the development towards centralizing the bank note system took place during the second half of the 19th century or in the first decades of the 20th century. Central banks were established which ousted the private or local banks issuing notes, or at least considerably limited their influence on circulating paper money issues.

Until a few years ago, paper money could be described as the most modern form of currency, but we are today on the threshold of a new development. The system of payment by check, some two decades ago common only in business, is increasingly gaining in importance. The use of checks in the private sector has today become a matter of course. Just beyond is the use of the credit card and other electronic fund transfers which may someday create a moneyless society. The development of money from the precoin era to the days of coin as the dominant legal tender to the paper money which ousted the coin is again about to begin a new era.

Collecting Early Note Issues

Within the scope of a general collection, a collector attempting to acquire notes from the beginnings of the history of paper money will soon discover that he will hardly be in a position, due to the lack of available and affordable material, to form a review of the early history of paper money with the individual specimens he has purchased.

The oldest bank note obtainable is the Chinese Ming note. This note is indeed rare, but it is still feasible today to acquire it. The Leyden cardboard coins, too, considered to be the earliest European form of money made of paper, are still obtainable. Considerably more difficult, if not impossible, is the situation regarding the Swedish notes of the 17th century, the early Bank of England notes, the Norwegian Thor Mohlen notes and the French coin scrip. These notes are all firmly entrenched in museums and other major collections. The few specimens occasionally placed on the market fetch very high prices. Only a modicum of good fortune, along with strong financial standing, can assist in building a collection of these early notes.

It looks a little more favorable for the collector with regard to John Law notes. Of the 1720 issues (January and July), the 10 Livres note is still procurable. More difficult, though, is the 100 Livres note. The 50 and 1000 Livres of 1720 and the notes of 1719 are offered only rarely and at high prices.

French assignats and mandats of 1792-1794 are still relatively easy to obtain today, and with a great deal of endurance and collector's skill, it is possible to assemble a specialized collection.

Of the "Billets de Confiance" orginating from the same period, notes of the different local authorities and towns, there are several thousands. These notes may indeed represent the oldest group of emergency money notes. With a lot of patience a collector may gather a small collection of some 100 notes of this description during the course of several years, if he is able to build on a collection bought from French collectors.

Austria, 10 gulden (form), 1762

1 Fun

2 Fun

Japan, Hansatsu (clan or local notes)

Apart from those already mentioned, not many European notes remain from the 18th century which are within the reach of the collector.

In Poland the treasury notes in denominations of 5 and 10 Groszy, 4, 5, 10 and 25 Zloty, issued in 1794 during the Kosciuszko uprising, are obtainable. The other denominations, 1, 50 and 100 Zloty, are rare, with the 500 and 1000 Zloty practically unobtainable. The Taler notes of the Duchy of Warsaw, reminiscent of Saxony currency tickets, are also still procurable. Danish notes of 1792 until the beginning of the 19th century belong to the already expensive class of old notes from that country still on the market. Equally, Swedish and Norwegian notes of the 18th century are still obtainable. The same applies to the latter as to the Danish notes, being highly popular in Scandinavia and therefore achieving correspondingly high prices.

The old Russian notes appearing in private collections generally originate from the beginning of the 19th century. Older notes are very rare and are found only as singles in key collections.

American Colonial and Continental bills issued at the end of the 18th century can be purchased without difficulty, even though prices for such notes rose considerably in the U.S. during the 1976 Bicentennial celebration.

Among older non-European notes, mention should be made of the Japanese "Hansatsu" or "Shisatsu." These narrow, bookmark-like and thematically rich notes were issued by the many different Daimios (territorial

Austria, 10 Kreuzer,
Emergency money note,
Marienthal (Bohemia), 1848

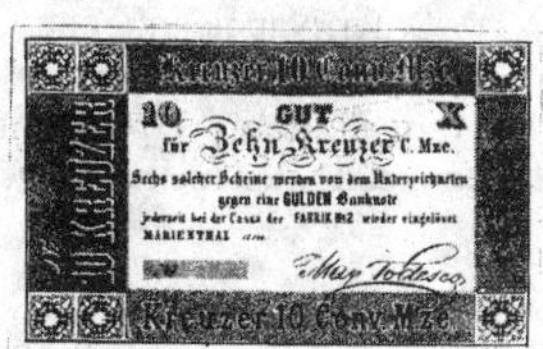

Italy, 50 Lire, Torino, 1765

Portugal, 10 Milreis, 1799

rulers) and impress the Western collector as exotic. There are many thousands of these notes available relatively cheaply. They are hard to attribute, but perhaps a Japanese collector or dealer can help.

Of the first Austrian issues through 1796, none of the original notes are offered. The low denominations of the 1800 and 1806 issues, on the other hand, are still plentiful and inexpensive today. Among the numerous other Austrian issues of the 19th century there are partly decorative notes available at a favorable price.

Among collectors of national German notes, the number of whom is rising steadily, many are now attempting to obtain German notes issued before 1871. Such old German notes, including issues of private banks in Mark currency up to 1914, can be acquired in only a few pieces. The systematic building of this type of collection is no longer feasible today.

The difficulty in procuring bank notes from the beginnings of paper money history may stimulate collectors to acquire at least some singles which are then given prominent display as very noteworthy showpieces, independently of the building of the rest of the collection.

Counterfeiters

The battle against counterfeiters pervades the entire history of paper money. The Chinese occupied themselves with protection against counterfeits by enforcing strict regulations. Forgers were given the death penalty, and the informer received a reward along with the property of the criminal. The essential aids in the battle against counterfeiting were, and remain, the finesse in printing techniques and paper manufacture, in connection with which the watermark and, during the last century, the printing of the guilloches, play a special part.

The recognition of old notes as counterfeits generally requires great experience on the part of the collector. The lack of means of comparison renders recognition difficult and frequently such notes are in a collection for many years before they are recognized. This discovery is not as painful for a paper money collector as it would be for collectors of other objects, since the value of a contemporary counterfeit bank note is little less than the original in many cases. With common notes, the counterfeit may well be worth more than the original.

Collectors of paper money differentiate between counterfeiting and alteration. A counterfeit note is false in all its parts; whereas an altered note originated from a genuine note. If, for example, an overprint has been added later, or the denomination was raised on a genuine note, then it is termed an alteration.

Most counterfeiters fail because of special types of processing machines which are not available for their use in imitating genuine production methods. Even professional qualifications and artistic abilities will not suffice for coping with the sophisticated security techniques employed by prominent bank note printers, especially with modern paper money.

If, however, such counterfeits were carried out at the instigation of the government or official authorities, then the possibility existed for achieving so-called "perfect" counterfeits. The two best-known examples in this respect are found in the last century and during World War II.

After Napoleon's entry into Vienna, he ordered the printing blocks for the Austrian Banco Scrip to be imitated, and notes, distinguishable from originals only by paper tint, to be printed in Paris. Despite the ban pronounced after his marriage to Princess Marie Louise on issuing the notes, such counterfeits did enter circulation. Russian ruble notes, too, were forg on Napoleon's instructions.

With the greatest bank note forgery of all time, known under the code "Operation Bernhard," the press, radio and television have repeatedly oc pied themselves with the postwar period, particularly since such counter notes were subsequently discovered in Lake Toplitz, Austria. Books h also been written on this subject. The German Security Service prepa counterfeit Bank of England notes during World War II after careful pre ratory work in laboratories hidden in concentration camps. The fin machinery and specifically produced watermarked paper were used experts and inmates of the camps. These notes, circulated via neutral eign countries (the payment to the spy "Cicero" became known especial were so identical to the genuine notes that the Bank of England was co pelled to withdraw the subject issue from circulation.

There are also notes which were imitated to the detriment of collect After the issuing of the first notgeld notes in 1914, the number of notg collectors began increasingly steadily during subsequent years. The h demand for these first issues prompted some local authorities and ot issuing offices to produce reprints of these sometimes primitively prin notes. In contrast to the rare originals, these reprints are generally consic ably cheaper.

The numerous fancy issues of notgeld, intended for the collector in period 1920-1922, also belong here.

Particularly easy is the counterfeiting of overprinting on notes. stamp "Fezzan," on the 5-Franc note of the Banque de l'Afrique Occid tale, is an example of such a forgery and can be differentiated only with ficulty from the original stamp.

Falsification of a Russian 25 Ru note of 1807 (by Napoleon's A

Germany, Alteration to 100 Mark of a genuine 20 Mark note, issued by Allied Military administration authority

Brazil, Alteration of a genuine 10 Milreis note to 100 M

Germany, Falsification of an English 50 Pound note (World War II)

SECURITY DEVICES

ASCENDING SIZE SERIAL NUMBER - A serial number with each digit slightly increasing in height and width. Both horizontal and vertical formats have been used. Czech Republic and Slovakia are among the countries where this may be found.

BAR CODE AND NUMERALS - Used mainly by banks for checks. Some countries have used these on banknotes. Scotland has a bar code, and Canada has used it with serial numbers. Sometimes magnetic.

COLORED FIBERS - Fibers usually red, blue or green, that are added either into the pulp mix to be randomly flowed onto the paper as it is made, or distributed onto the drying paper in particular areas of the page forming 'bars' of colored fibers, quite visible to the naked eye.

EMBEDDED SECURITY THREAD - A high strength thread, sometimes magnetic, embedded into the paper at the beginning of the drying stage. Looks to the eye as a solid dark strip within the paper.

FACE-BACK OPTICAL REGISTRATION DESIGN (TRANSPARENT REGISTER) - A design technique where half of an image in a framed area is printed on the face, and the other half is printed on the back, in exact register, so when held to a light, the two half images form one full image.

FOIL IMPRINTS - Shaped metal foil applied to the printed note, usually with an adhesive. Sometimes the foil is embossed with an image.

HOLOGRAM - Shiny application to the note containing an image that changes in design and color depending upon the viewing angle.

INVISIBLE PRINTING - Designs printed with inks detectable only when viewed under bright sunlight or ultraviolet light. Sometimes used to replace the more expensive watermark on low value notes.

LATENT IMPRESSIONS -Portions of the note containing sculptured engraving, making some legends or designs visible only when held to the light at certain angles.

KINEGRAM(r) - Similar to a foil imprint, the design and color changes at different viewing angles.

METALLIC INK - An ink with very fine granules of metal, thus giving the ink a metallic sheen.

MICRO PRINTING - Very small letters added to an intaglio printing plate, sometimes as single lines, or in multiple repeating lines forming a larger block in the underprint design. Intaglio printing keeps the design sharp and clear, but if the note is counterfeit the microprinted area usually becomes muddy and unclear.

OPTICAL VARIABLE DEVICE (OVD) - A foil that displays a three-dimensional image when viewed under proper lighting conditions. Similar to foil imprints.

OPTICALLY VARIABLE INK - An ink when printed in a special pattern changes shades when viewed and then tilted slightly.

PLANCHETTES - Tiny multicolored discs of paper embedded into the pulp mix or randomly sprinkled throughout the paper as it is drying.

RAISED MARKS - A type of braille design in notes, enabling blind people to identify note values.

SEGMENTED SECURITY THREAD -A continuous security thread, usually wide and with lettering, that is added into the paper during the drying process. Once added, a special tool is used to scrape the wet paper off only above the thread, and usually in a particular pattern, thus exposing alternate areas of the embedded thread.

UV-ULTRAVIOLET (FLOURESCENT) - When viewed in a darkened area, and exposed to a special low or high frequency UV light, a design, value, or paper fibers will glow.

WATERMARK - Extensively used as a security measure, the watermark is created by a raised design on a drying cylinder applied towards the end of the paper manufacturing process. The raised design causes a thin area in the paper which when held to the light reveals an image. This image can be words, design, or a portrait. Recent developments have made graduations available. Thus, rather than a light/dark watermark, a gradual light to dark fade can be achieved.

Notes

Notes

Notes